BRADFORD'S CROSSWORD SOLVER'S DICTIONARY

BRADFORD'S CROSSWORD SOLVER'S DICTIONARY

HarperCollins Publishers
Westerhill Road
Bishopbriggs
Glasgow
G64 2QT
Great Britain

Eighth Edition (paperback) 2010

Reprint 10 9 8 7 6 5 4 3 2 1 0

First edition published by
Longman; second, third and fourth
editions published by Peter Collin
Publishing Ltd

ISBN 978-0-00-736257-8

www.collinslanguage.com

A catalogue record for this book is
available from the British Library

Technical support and typesetting
by Thomas Callan

Printed in Italy by
LEGO Spa, Lavis (Trento)

Contents

Author's Preface

You can mince, spread, and eat them. They can be ugly, plain, or fair; first or last; good or bad; kept, exchanged, or broken; careful or careless; harsh, hard, or soft; empty or profound; bitter or sweet; kind, comforting, loving, or angry; casual or serious. You can mark, give, or take them. They can be learned, wise, or thoughtless; private, quick, and brief; brave and bandy; and, above all, **CROSS**.

I love them all and am fascinated with them, and never at a loss for them, though they may sometimes fail me. I am delighted to pass them on, in this 8th edition, and hope they will serve you right!

Anne R. Bradford 2009

Solving Crossword Clues

Crossword puzzles tend to be basically 'quick' or 'cryptic'. A 'quick' crossword usually relies on a one- or two-word clue which is a simple definition of the answer required. Many words have different meanings, so that the clue 'ball' could equally well lead to the answer 'sphere', 'orb', or 'dance'. The way to solve 'quick' crosswords is to press on until probable answers begin to interlink, which is a good sign that you are on the right track.

'Cryptic' crosswords are another matter. Here the clue usually consists of a basic definition, given at either the beginning or end of the clue, together with one or more definitions of parts of the answer. Here are some examples taken from all-time favourites recorded over the years:

1. *'Tradesman who bursts into tears'* (**Stationer**)

   Tradesman is a definition of stationer. *Bursts* is cleverly used as an indication of an anagram, which *into tears* is of stationer.

2. *'Sunday school tune'* (**Strain**)

   Here *Sunday* is used to define its abbreviation S, *school* is a synonym for train, and put together they give strain, which is a synonym of *tune*.

3. *'Result for everyone when head gets at bottom'* (**Ache**)
   (used as a 'down' clue)

   This is what is known as an '& lit' clue, meaning that the setter has hit on a happy composition which could literally be true. *Everyone* here is a synonym for each, move the *head* (first letter) of the word to the *bottom*, and the answer is revealed, the whole clue being the definition of the answer in this case.

4. *'Tin out East'* (**Sen**)

   In this example, *tin*, implying 'money', requires its chemical symbol Sn to go *out*(side) *East*, or its abbreviation, E, the whole clue being a definition of a currency (sen) used in the East.

5. *'Information given to communist in return for sex'* (**Gender**)

   Information can be defined as gen; *communist* is almost always red,
   in return indicates 'reversed', leading to gen-der, a synonym for *sex*.

6. *'Row about no enclosure of this with sardines'* (**Tin-opener**)

   Row is a synonym for tier, *about* indicates 'surrounding', *no enclosure*
   can be no pen, leading to ti-no pen-er, and another '& lit' clue.

7. *'Cake-sandwiches-meat, at Uncle Sam's party'* (**Clambake**)

   Meat here is lamb, *sandwiches* is used as a verb, so we have C-lamb-ake,
   which is a kind of party in America. *Uncle Sam* or US is often used to
   indicate America.

8. *'Initially passionate meeting of boy and girl could result in it'* (**Pregnancy**)

   Initially is usually a sign of a first letter, in this case 'p' for *passionate* +
   Reg (a *boy*) and Nancy (a *girl*), and another clever '& lit'.

With 'cryptic' clues the solver needs to try to analyse the parts to see
what he or she is looking for – which word or words can be the straight
definition, and which refer to the parts or hint at anagrams or other
subterfuges. Whilst it would be unrealistic to claim total infallibility,
practice has shown that in most crosswords some 90% of the answers are
to be found in this work.

Anne R. Bradford

How to use the Dictionary

This dictionary is the result of over fifty years' analysis of some 300,000 crossword clues, ranging from plain 'quick' crosswords requiring only synonyms to the different level of cryptic puzzles. Therefore the words listed at each entry may be connected to the keyword in various ways, such as:

- a straightforward synonym

- a commonly-associated adjective

- an associated or proper noun

- a pun or other devious play on words

Keywords are listed alphabetically; in cases where the heading consists of more than one word, the first of these words is taken to be the keyword, and in cases where the end of a word is bracketed, the material up to the opening bracket is taken to be the keyword. Keywords marked with the symbol ▸ refer the user to other entries where additional information may be found. Keywords marked with the symbol ▹ give leads to anagrams and other ploys used by crossword setters. If the keywords found in the clue do not lead directly to the required answer, the solver should look under words given as cross-references to other entries. These are indicated by the symbol →, with the cross-referenced word shown in capitals.

Some additional entries have been divided into two parts – a general entry similar to the standard entries which appear elsewhere, and a panel entry which contains a list of more specific or encyclopedic material. So, for example, the entry 'Artist(ic)' includes not only a list of general words connected with 'Artist' or 'Artistic' in some way, such as 'Bohemian', 'Cubist', 'Fine' and 'Virtuoso', but also a panel with the heading 'Artists' containing a list of the names of specific artists, such as 'Bellini', 'Constable', and 'Rembrandt'. For added help, the words in these panels are arranged by length, with all three-letter words grouped together in alphabetical order, then all four-letter words, then all five-letter words, and so on.

The Crossword Club

If you are interested in crosswords, you might like to consider joining the Crossword Club. Membership is open to all who enjoy tackling challenging crosswords and who appreciate the finer points of clue-writing and grid-construction. The Club's magazine, Crossword, contains two prize puzzles each month. A sample issue and full details are available on request.

The Crossword Club
Coombe Farm
Awbridge
Romsey, Hants.
SO51 0HN
UK

email: bh@thecrosswordclub.co.uk
website address: www.thecrosswordclub.co.uk

About the Author

Anne Bradford's love of words began to make itself evident even in her schooldays, when, as Head Girl of her school, she instituted a novel punishment – instead of making rulebreakers write lines, she had them write out pages from a dictionary, on the grounds that this was a more useful exercise. Little did she know this was soon to be her own daily routine!

In time, crosswords became a magnificent obsession for Anne. All lovers of crosswords can understand the irresistible lure of solving them, but Anne's interest went much deeper than most people's, and when she stopped work in 1957 to have her first child, she found herself starting to note down answers to particularly tricky clues as an aid to memory, in case she should come across them again in another puzzle. It was from this simple beginning that this crossword dictionary evolved.

Over the space of 25 years, Anne continued to build on her collection of solutions, analysing every crossword clue as she solved it and adding it to her steadily growing bank of entries. This unique body of material eventually reached such proportions that she had the idea of offering it to her fellow crossword-solvers as a reference book, and since then, the book has gone from strength to strength, providing valuable help to countless cruciverbalists over a number of editions.

Anne Bradford continues to devote time each day to solving crosswords, averaging some 20 a week – both quick and cryptic – and still avidly collects new solutions for her *Crossword Solver's Dictionary* at a rate of around 150 a week, compiling each solution by hand (without the use of a computer!). This latest edition therefore includes much new material, gleaned by a true crossword lover who not only solves crosswords but, as an active member of the Crossword Club, can offer the user an insight into the mind of a cunning crossword compiler.

Aa

A, An Ack, Adult, Ae, Alpha, Angstrom, Are, Argon, D, Ein, Her, If, L, One, Per, They

A1 Tiptop

AA Milne

Aardvark Ant-bear, Ant-eater, Earth-hog, Ground-hog

Aaron's Rod Hagtaper

Aba, Abba Patriarch

Abacus Counter, Soroban

Abaft Astern, Sternson

Abalone Ormer, Paua, Perlemoen

Abandon(ed), Abandonment Abdicate, Abnegate, Abort, Adrift, Aguna(h), Amoral, Apostasy, Back down, Cade, Cancel, Castaway, Corrupt, Decommission, Defect, Derelict, → **DESERT**, Desuetude, Discard, Disown, Dissolute, Ditch, Drop, Dump, Elan, Evacuate, Expose, Flagrant, Forhoo(ie), Forhow, Forlend, Forsake, Gomorra, Immoral, Jack(-in), Jettison, Jilt, Leave, Loose, Louche, Maroon, Old, Orgiastic, Profligate, Quit, Rakish, Rat, Relinquish, Renounce, Reprobate, Scrap, Shed, Sink, Strand, Vacate, Waive, Wanton, Wild, Yield

Abase Degrade, Demean, Embrute, Disgrace, Grovel, → **HUMBLE**, Kowtow, Lessen

Abash Daunt, Discountenance, Mortify

▷ **Abate** *may indicate* a contention

Abate(ment) Allay, Appal, Decrescent, Deduction, Defervescence, Diminish, Let up, Lyse, Lysis, Moderate, Reduce, Remit, → **SUBSIDE**

Abattoir Knackery, Slaughterhouse

Abbey Abbacy, Ampleforth, Bath, Buckfast, Cloister, Downside, Fonthill, Fountains, Glastonbury, Györ, Je(r)vaulx, Medmenham, Melrose, Minster, Nightmare, Northanger, Priory, Rievaulx, Tintern, Westminster, Whitby, Woburn

Abbot Aelfric, Archimandrite, Brother, Eutyches, Friar

Abbreviate, Abbreviation Abridge, Ampersand, Compendium, Condense, Curtail, → **SHORTEN**, Sigla

ABC Absey

Abdicate, Abdication Cede, Demission, Disclaim, Disown, Resign

Abdomen Belly, C(o)eliac, Epigastrium, Gaster, Hypochondrium, Opisthosoma, Paunch, Pleon, → **STOMACH**, Tummy, Venter

Abduct(ed), Abduction Asport, Enlèvement, Kidnap, Rapt, Ravish, Shanghai, Steal

Aberdeen Granite City

Aberrant, Aberration Abnormal, Aye-aye, Chromatic, Deviant, Idolon, Perverse, Spherical

Abet(tor) Aid, Back, Candle-holder, Second

Abeyance, Abeyant Dormant, Shelved, Sleeping, Store

Abhor(rent) → **DETEST**, Execrable, → **HATE**, Loathe, Odious, Shun

Abide Adhere, Dwell, Inhere, → **LAST**, Lie, Live, Observe, Remain, Stand, Tarry

Abigail Maid, Masham

Ability Aptitude, Calibre, Capacity, Cocum, → **COMPETENCE**, Efficacy, ESP, Facility, Faculty, Ingine, Initiative, Instinct, Lights, Potential, Power, Prowess, Savey, Savoir-faire, Savv(e)y, Skill, Talent

Abject Base, Craven, Grovel, Humble, Servile, Slave

Abjure Eschew, Forswear, Recant, Renege, Reny

Ablaze Afire, Aglow, Ardent

Able Ablins, Accomplished, → **ADEPT**, Aiblins, Apt, Capable, → **COMPETENT**, Fere, Fit, Literate, Proficient, Seaman, Yibbles

Abnormal(ity) Anomalous, Aplasia, Atypical, Autism, → **DEVIANT**, Dysfunction, Ectopic, Erratic, Etypical, Freakish, Hare-lip, Malocclusion, Odd, Peloria, Phenecopy, Preternatural, → **QUEER**, Sport, Teras, Trisome, Unnatural, Varus

Aboard On

Abode Domicile, Dwelling, Habitat, → **HOME**, In(n), Lain, Libken, Limbo, Midgard, Remain, Seat

Abolish, Abolition(ist) Abrogate, Annihilate, Annul, Axe, → **BAN**, D, Delete, Destroy, Eradicate, Erase, Extirpate, John Brown, Nullify, Repeal, Rescind, Wilberforce

Abomasum Read

Abominable, Abominate, Abomination Bane, Cursed, → **HATE**, Nefandous, Nefast, Revolting, Snowman, Vile, Yeti

Aboriginal, Aborigine Adivasi, Ainu, Aranda, Autochthon, Binghi, Black-fellow, Boong, Buck, Bushmen, Carib, Evolué, Fringe-dweller, Gin, Gurindji, Indigenous, Jacky(-Jacky), Kamilaroi, Kipper, Koori, Lubra, Maori, Mary, Motu, Myall, Pintubi, Pitjant(jat)jara, Pre-Dravidian, Sakai, San, Sican, Siwash, Truganini, Vedda(h), Warlpiri, Yupik

Abort(ion), Abortive Apiol, Back-street, Cancel, Contagious, Ecbolic, Miscarry, Induced, Misbirth, Moon-calf, Slip, Sooterkin, Spontaneous, Teras, Termination

Abound(ing) Bristle, Copious, Enorm, Flush, Overflow, Rife, Swarm, Teem

About A, Almost, Anent, Around, C, Ca, Circa, Circiter, Concerning, Encompass, Environs, Going, Near, Of, On, Over, Re, Regarding, Soon at

▷ **About** *may indicate* one word around another

Above Abune, Aforementioned, Aloft, Over, Overhead, Overtop, Owre, Sopra, Superior, Supra-, Suspicion, Upon

Abracadabra Cantrip, Heypass

Abrade, Abrasive Carbanado, Carborundum®, Chafe, Emery, Erode, File, Garnet paper, → **GRATE**, Rub, Sand, Scrape, Scrat, Scuff

Abraham Father of the Faithful, Lincoln, Patriarch, Urite

Abreast Alongside, Au courant, Au fait, Beside, Level, Up

Abridge(ment) Audley, Compress, Condense, Cut, Digest, Dock, Edit, Epitome, Pot, Shorten, Trim

Abroad Afield, Away, Distant, Elsewhere, Forth, Offshore, Out, Overseas

▷ **Abroad** *may indicate* an anagram

Abrogate Abolish, Repeal, Replace

▷ **Abrupt** *may indicate* a shortened word

Abrupt(ly) Bold, Brusque, Curt, Gruff, Offhand, Premorse, Prerupt, Short, Staccato, Terse

Abscess Gumboil, Impost(h)ume, Ulcer, Warble

Abscond Absquatulate, Decamp, Desert, Elope, Flee, Jump ship, Leg-bail, Levant, Skase, Welch

Abseil(ing) Dulfer, Rappel, Roping-down

Absence, Absent(ee), Absent-minded(ness) A, Abs, Abstracted, Away, Distant,

Distracted, Distrait, Dreamy, Exeat, Exile, Hookey, Malingerer, Missing, Mitch, Sabbatical, Scatty, Skip, Truant, Vacuity, Void, Wanting, Wool-gathering

Absinthe Wormwood

Absolute(ly) Bang, Complete, Dead, Deep-dyed, Downright, Fairly, Implicit, Ipso facto, Just, Meer, Mere, Mondo, Nominative, Plenary, Outright, Plumb, Quite, Real, Sheer, Simply, Thorough, Total, Truly, Unadulterated, Unconditional, Unmitigated, Unqualified, Utter, Veritable, Very

Absolve, Absolution Acquit, Assoil, Assoilzie, Clear, Exculpate, Excuse, Pardon, Shrive

Absorb(ed), Absorbent, Absorbing, Absorption Assimilate, Autism, Blot, Consume, Desiccant, Devour, Digest, Dope, Drink, → **ENGROSS**, Enrapt, Imbibe, Ingest, Inhaust, Intent, Merge(r), Occlude, Occupy, Osmosis, Permeable, Porous, Preoccupation, Preoccupied, Rapt, Sorbefacient, Spongy, Subsume, Unputdownable

Absquatulate Skedaddle

Abstain(er), Abstemious, Abstinence, Abstinent Band of Hope, Celibacy, Chastity, Continent, Desist, Eschew, Forbear, Forgo, Maigre, Nazarite, Nephalism, Pioneer, Rechab(ite), Refrain, Resist, Sober, Teetotaller, Temperate, TT

Abstract(ed), Abstraction Abrege, Abridge, Academic, Appropriate, Brief, Deduct, Digest, Discrete, Distrait, Epitome, Essence, Inconscient, Metaphysical, Musing, Notional, Précis, Preoccupied, Prepossessed, Prescind, Remove, Resumé, Reverie, Stable, Steal, Subduct, Summary, Syllabus, Tachism

Abstruse Arcane, Deep, Esoteric, Impenetrable, Obscure, Recondite

Absurd(ity) Alician, Apagoge, Fantastic, Farcical, Folly, Inept, Irrational, Laputan, Ludicrous, Madness, Nonsense, Paradox, Preposterous, Ridiculous, Silly, Solecism, Stupid, Toshy, Whim-wham

Abundance, Abundant A-gogo, Ample, Aplenty, Bounty, Copious, Corn in Egypt, Cornucopia, Cosmic, Excess, Flood, Flush, Fouth, Fowth, Fruitful, Galore, Lashings, Lavish, Mickle, Mine, Mint, Muckle, Natural, Oodles, Oodlins, Opulent, Over, Plenitude, Plenteous, → **PLENTIFUL**, Plenty, Pleroma, Plethora, Plurisie, Profusion, Prolific, Relative, Replete, Rich, Rife, Rock and manger, Routh, Rowth, Sonce, Sonse, Store, Stouth and routh, Surfeit, Tallents, Teeming, Tons, Uberous

Abuse, Abusive Assail, Becall, Billingsgate, Blackguard, Chemical, Cruelty, Flak, Fustilarian, Fustil(l)irian, Hail, Ill-treat, Insult, Invective, Jobbery, Limehouse, Malpractice, Maltreat, Miscall, → **MISTREAT**, Misuse, Mofo, Mud, Obloquy, Opprobrium, Philippic, Rail, Rampallian, Rate, Rayle, Revile, Ritual, Satanic, Satire, Scarab(ee), Scurrilous, Serve, Sexual, Slang, Slate, Sledging, Snash, Solvent, Strap, Substance, Thersitical, Tirade, Verbal, Vilify, Violate, Vituperation

Abut Adjoin, Border, Touch

Abysm(al), Abyss Avernus, Barathrum, Barranca, Chasm, Deep, Gulf, Swallet, Tartarean, Tartarus

AC Current, Erk

Acacia Bablah, Boree, Brigalow, Eumong, Eumung, Gidgee, Gidjee, Koa, Mimosa, Mulga, Myall, Sallee, Shittim, Wattle

Academic(ian) A, Acca, Acker, Della-Cruscan, Don, Erudite, Fellow, Hypothetic(al), Immortals, Literati, Master, Pedantic, PRA, Prof(essor), RA, Reader, Rector

Academy, Academic Athenaeum, Dollar, Donnish, French, Loretto, Lyceum, Military, Naval, RA, Royal, St Cyr, Sandhurst, School, Seminary, Studious, The Shop, West Point

Acanthus Blankursine, Ruellia

Accelerate, Acceleration, Accelerator Antedate, Betatron, Bevatron, Collider,

Cosmotron, Cyclotron, Festinate, G, Gal, Grav, Gun, Hasten, Increase, Linac, Linear, Rev, Signatron, Speed, Stringendo, Synchrotron

Accent(ed), Accentuate Acute, Beat, Breve, Brogue, Bur(r), Circumflex, Cut-glass, Doric, Drawl, Enclitic, Enhance, Gammat, Grave, Hacek, Intonation, Kelvinside, Long, Macron, Marcato, Martelé, Mockney, Morningside, Mummerset, Nasal, Orthotone, Oxford, Oxytone, Paroxytone, Perispomenon, Pitch, Primary, Proparoxytone, Rhythm, Secondary, Stress, Tittle, Tone, Tonic, Twang

Accentor Dunnock

Accept(able), Acceptance, Accepted A, Accede, Admit, Adopt, Agree, Allow, Approbate, Bar, Believe, Buy, Can-do, Common, Consent, Cool, Cosher, Decent, Done, Embrace, Grant, Idee recue, Kosher, Meet, Obey, On, Pocket, Putative, Resipiscence, Satisfactory, Settle, Stand, Suppose, Swallow, Take, Tolerate, U, Valid, Wear, Widespread

Access(ible) Avenue, Blue-jacking, Card, Come-at-able, Conditional, Credit, Direct, Door, Entrée, → **ENTRY**, Fit, Get-at-able, Hack, Ingo, Key, Log in, Log on, Passe-partout, Password, Phreaking, Random, Recourse, Remote, Sequential, Spasm, Wayleave

Accessory, Accessories Abettor, Addition, Aide, Ally, Ancillary, Appendage, Appurtenance, Attribute, Bandanna, Bells and whistles, Cribellum, Cuff-links, Findings, Fitment, Staffage, Trappings, Trimming

Accident(al) Adventitious, Arbitrary, Bechance, Blowdown, Blunder, Calamity, → **CHANCE**, Circumstance, Contingency, Contretemps, Crash, Criticality, Dent, Disaster, Fall, Fluke, Fortuitous, Hap, Hit and run, Inadvertent, Meltdown, Mischance, Mishap, Note, Promiscuous, Rear-ender, Shunt, Smash, Smash-up, Spill, Stramash, Unmeant, Wreck

Accidie Acedia, Sloth, Torpor

Acclaim Accolade, Applaud, Brava, Bravo, Cheer, Eclat, Fame, Fanfare, Hail, Kudos, Ovation, Praise, Salute

Accolade Award, Brace, Dubbing, Honour, Palm, Token, Tribute

Accommodate, Accommodation Adapt, Almshouse, B and B, Bedsit, Berth, Billet, Board, Botel, Bunkhouse, Camp, Chalet, Compromise, Crashpad, Digs, Flotel, Gaff, Gite, Grace and favour, Homestay, Hostel, Hotel, House, Lend, Loan, Lodge, Lodgement, Minshuku, Motel, → **OBLIGE**, Parador, Pension, Quarters, Rapprochement, Recurve, Room, Sheltered, Single-end, Sorehon, Stabling, Stateroom, Steerage, Storage, Tent, Wharepuni, Xenodochium

▷ **Accommodating** *may indicate* one word inside another

Accompany(ing), Accompanied (by), Accompaniment, Accompanist Accessory, Alberti, And, Attend, Backing, Chaperone, Chum, Concomitant, Consort, Continuo, Descant, → **ESCORT**, Fixings, Harmonise, Herewith, Obbligato, Obligate, Obligato, Repetiteur, Soundtrack, Trimmings, Vamp

Accomplice Abettor, Aide, → **ALLY**, Collaborator, Confederate, Federarie, Federary, Partner, Shill, Stale, Swagsman

Accomplish(ed), Accomplishment Able, → **ACHIEVE**, Arch, Attain, Clever, Complete, Consummate, Done, Effect, Galant, Master, Over, Perform, Polished, Prowess, Realise, Ripe, Savant, Success, Tour de force

Accord, According(ly), According to After, Agree, Ala, Allow, As per, Attune, Chime, Consensus, Congree, Give, Grant, Harmony, Jibe, Meech Lake, Meet, So, Sort, Thus

According to nature SN

Accordion Bandoneary, Button, Concertina, Flutina, Piano, Squeeze-box

Accost Abord, Approach, Greet, Hail, Importune, Molest, Solicit, Tackle

Account(s) AC, Anecdote, Appropriation, Audit, Battels, Behalf, Bill, Budget, Cause, Charge, Checking, Chequing, Chronicle, Control, Current, Deposit, Discretionary, Drawing, Enarration, Expense, Explain, Exposition, ISA, Joint, Lawin, Ledger, Log, Long, Memoir, Narration, Nominal, Nostro, Numbered, Procès-verbal, Real, Reason, Recital, Regest, Register, → **REPORT**, Repute, Resumé, Sake, Short, Suspense, Swindlesheet, Tab, Tale, Thesis, Trust, Version, Vostro

Accountable Responsible

Accountant Auditor, Bean counter, Bookkeeper, CA, Cost, Forensic, Hyde, Liquidator, Reckoner, Vestry-clerk

Accredit Attribute

Accrue Earn, Grow

Accumulate, Accumulation Accrue, Adsorb, Aggregate, → **AMASS**, Augment, Backlog, Build, Collect, Gather, Hoard, Lodg(e)ment, Pile, Pool, Rack up, Run up, Stockpile, Uplay

Accuracy, Accurate(ly) Bang-on, Cocker, → **CORRECT**, Dead-on, Exact, Fair, Fidelity, Griff, Minute, Precise, Right, Spot-on, True, Unerring, Veracious, Word-perfect

Accursed Argued, Blest, Blist, Damned, Sacred

Accusation, Accuse(d) Allege, Arraign, Asperse, Attaint, Bill, Blame, Calumny, Censure, Challenge, Charge, Criminate, Denounce, Dite, Gravamen, Impeach, Incriminate, Indictment, Information, Name, Panel, Plaint, Suspect, Tax, Threap, Threep, Traduce, Wight, Wite, Wyte

Accustom(ed) Acquaint, Attune, Enure, General, Habituate, Harden, Inure, Teach, Wont, Woon

Ace(s) Basto, Blackjack, Crabs, Dinger, → **EXPERT**, Jot, Master, Mega, Mournival, One, Quatorze, Smashing, Spadille, Spadill(i)o, Spot, Tib, Virtuoso, Wonderful

Acerbate Intensify

Acetylene Ethyne

Ache, Aching Aitch, Die, Long, Mulligrubs, Nag, Otalgia, Pain, Sore, Stitch, Stound, Stownd, Work, Yearn, Yen

Achieve(ment) Accomplish, Acquisition, Attain, Come, Compass, Cum laude, → **EFFECT**, Exploit, Feat, Fulfil, Gain, Hatchment, Masterpiece, Realise, Res gestae, Satisfice, Satisfy, Stroke, Succeed, Threepeat, Triumph, Trock, Troke, Truck

Acid(ity) Acrimony, Corrosive, Drop, EPA, Etchant, Hydroxy, Reaction, Ribosomal, Ribozyme, Sharp, Solvent, Sour, Tart, Vinegar, Vitriol

---

ACIDS

2 letters:	Pyro	Iodic	Capric
PH	Uric	L-dopa	Cholic
	Wood	Lewis	Citric
3 letters:		Malic	Cyanic
DNA	5 letters:	Mucic	Domoic
HCL	Algin	Oleic	Erucic
LSD	Amide	Orcin	Formic
Oxo	Amino	Osmic	Gallic
RNA	Auric	Trona	Lactic
	Boric		Lauric
4 letters:	Caro's	6 letters:	Leucin
Acyl	Fatty	Adipic	Lipoic
Dopa	Folic	Bromic	Lysine

6 letters – cont:
Maleic
Marine
Niacin
Nitric
Oxalic
Oxygen
Pectic
Phenol
Picric
Quinic
Serine
Sialic
Sorbic
Tannic
Tiglic
Toluic
Valine

7 letters:
Abietic
Acrylic
Alanine
Alginic
Benzoic
Butyric
Caproic
Cerotic
Chloric
Chromic
Creatin
Cystine
Ellagic
Eugenic
Ferulic
Folacin
Fumaric
Fusidic
Glycine
Guanine
Leucine
Malonic
Meconic
Melanic
Muramic
Nitrous
Nucleic
Orcinol
Peracid
Plumbic
Proline

Prussic
Pteroic
Pyruvic
Racemic
Sebacic
Selenic
Silicic
Stannic
Stearic
Suberic
Terebic
Titanic
Valeric
Vanadic
Xanthic
Xylonic

8 letters:
Abscisic
Adenylic
Arginine
Ascorbic
Aspartic
Butanoic
Caprylic
Carbamic
Carbolic
Carbonic
Chlorous
Cinnamic
Creatine
Cresylic
Crotonic
Cyclamic
Cysteine
Decanoic
Ethanoic
Fulminic
Glutamic
Glyceric
Glycolic
Guanylic
Hippuric
Iopanoic
Itaconic
Linoleic
Lysergic
Manganic
Margaric
Molybdic
Muriatic

Myristic
Nonanoic
Palmitic
Periodic
Phthalic
Retinoic
Rhodanic
Succinic
Sulfonic
Tantalic
Tartaric
Telluric
Tungstic
Tyrosine
Uridylic
Valproic

9 letters:
Aqua-regia
Cevitamic
Citydylic
Dichromic
Histidine
Hydrazoic
Hydriodic
Isocyanic
Linolenic
Methanoic
Nalidixic
Nicotinic
Ornithine
Panthenic
Pentanoic
Polybasic
Propanoic
Propenoic
Saccharic
Salicylic
Sassolite
Selenious
Sulphonic
Sulphuric
Tellurous
Threonine

10 letters:
Aquafortis
Asparagine
Barbituric
Carboxylic
Citrulline

Dithionous
Dodecanoic
Glucoronic
Glutamatic
Glutaminic
Hyaluronic
Isoleucine
Margaritic
Methionine
Neuraminic
Orthoboric
Pelargonic
Perchloric
Phosphonic
Phosphoric
Proprionic
Pyrogallic
Ricinoleic
Thiocyanic
Thymidylic
Trans-fatty
Tryptophan

11 letters:
Arachidonic
Butanedioic
Decanedioic
Ethanedioic
Ferricyanic
Ferrocyanic
Gibberellic
Hydnocarpic
Hydrobromic
Hydrocyanic
Hyponitrous
Methacrylic
Octanedioic
Pantothenic
Permanganic
Phosphorous
Ribonucleic
Sarcolactic
Taurocholic
Tryptophane

12 letters:
Dicraboxylic
Hydrochloric
Hydrofluoric
Hypochlorous
Indoleacetic

Orthosilicic	Terephthalic	Prostaglandin	**15 letters:**
Persulphuric		Pyrosulphuric	Orthophosphoric
Phenylalanin	**13 letters:**	Thiosulphuric	Pteroylglutamic
Polyadenalic	Galactosamine		
Propanedioic	Heptadecanoic	**14 letters:**	**16 letters:**
Prostacyclin	Indolebutyric	Metaphosphoric	Deoxyribonucleic
Pyroligneous	Phenylalanine	Pyrophosphoric	

Acknowledge(ment) Accept, Admit, Allow, Answer, Avow, Con, Confess, Credit, Grant, Greet, Mea culpa, Nod, Own, Receipt, Recognise, Resipiscence, Respect, Righto, Roger, Salute, Ta, Touché, Wilco, Yo

Acme Apex, Apogee, Climax, Comble, Crest, Peak, Summit, Top, Zenith

Acolyte Nethinim, Novice, Server, Thurifer

Acorn(s), Acorn-shell Balanus, Glans, Mast, Rac(c)ahout, Valonia

Acoustic(s) Harmonics, Phenocamptics, Phonics, Sonics

Acquaint(ance), Acquainted Advise, Cognisant, Enlighten, Familiar, → INFORM, Knowledge, Nodding, Notify, Tell, Versed

Acquiesce(nce), Acquiescent Accept, Bow, Conform, Resigned, Righto, Roger, Wilco, Yield

Acquire, Acquisition Acquest, Cop, Earn, Ern, Gain, → GET, Glom, Irredentist, Land, Learn, Obtain, Procure, Purchase, Steal, Take-over, Target, Usucap(t)ion

Acquit(tal) Assoil, Cleanse, Clear, Exonerate, Free, Loose, Loste, Pardon, Vindicate

Acre(s) A, Area, Bigha, Hide, Rival, Rood

Acrid, Acrimony Bitter(ness), Empyreuma, Pungent, Rough, Sour, Surly

Acrobat(s), Acrobatics Equilibrist, Gymnast, Hot dog, Jerry-come-tumble, Ropedancer, Speeler, Splits, Trampoline, Trick cyclist, Tumbler, Wing-walker

Acropolis Citadel, Parthenon

Across A, Ac, Athwart, Betwixt, Opposite, Over, Through

Act(ing), Action, Acts A, Actus reus, Affirmative, Antic, Assist, Assumpsit, Auto, Barnstorm, Barrier, Behave, Bit, Business, Camp, Campaign, Capillary, Case, Caster, Cause, Charade, Class, Come, Conduct, Consolation, Coup, Daff, Deal, Declaratory, → DEED, Delaying, Deputise, Detinue, Dido, Direct, Do, DORA, Double, Enabling, Enclosure, Epitasis, Excitement, Exert, Exploit, Factory, Feat, Feign, Forth-putting, Function, Furthcoming, Habeas corpus, Histrionic, Homestead, Identic, Impersonate, Improbation, Incident, Industrial, Juristic, Lance-jack, Law, Litigate, Lock-out, Locutionary, Masterstroke, Measure, Method, Movement, Mum, Mutiny, Navigation, Overt, Partypiece, Pas, Perform(ance), Perlocutionary, Personate, Play, Positive, Pp, Practice, Pretence, Private, Procedure, Process, Public, Qua, Qui tam, Quiver, Reflex, Reform bill, Replevin, Represent, Riot, Rising, Roleplay, Routine, Sasine, Scenery, Secondary, Septennial, Serve, Showdown, Shtick, Sick-out, Simulate, Speech, Stamp, Stanislavski, Statute, Steps, Suit, Synergy, Terminer, Test, Theatricise, Thellusson, Thing, Transitory, Treat, Trover, Truck, Turn, Twig, Uniformity, Union, Vicegerent, War, Windlass

Actinium Ac

Actinon An

Activate Arm, Engage, Goad, Spark, Spur, Stur, Styre, Trigger

Active, Activist, Activity A, Agile, Alert, At, Athletic, Brisk, Busy, Cadre, Deedy, DIY, Do(ing), Dynamited, Dynamo, Ecowarrior, Effectual, Energetic, Energic, Erupting, Exercise, Extra-curricular, Floruit, Fluster, Game, Go-go, Goings-on, Hum, Hyper, Leish, Licht, Live, Mobile, Motile, Nimble, Nippy, Ongo, On the go, Op, Operant, Optical, Play, Rambunctious, Residual, Shenanigan, Sideline,

Sprightly, Springe, Spry, Sthenic, Stir, Surge, Third house, Vacuum, Voice, Wick, Wimble, Working, Ya(u)ld

Actor(s), Actor-like Agent, Alleyn, Artist, Ashe, Barnstormer, Benson, Betterton, Bit player, Burbage, Cast, Character, Company, Diseur, Donat, Equity, Gable, Garrick, Gielgud, Guiser, Ham, Hamfatter, Heavy, Histrio(n), Impersonator, Jay, Juve(nile), Kean, Keaton, Luvvie, MacReady, Mime, Mummer, Olivier, O'Toole, Performer, Player, Playfair, Protagonist, RADA, Roscian, Roscius, Savoyard, Scofield, Sim, Spear-carrier, Stager, Strolling, Super, Thespian, Tragedian, Tree, Tritagonist, Trouper, Understudy, Utility man, Wolfit

Actress Bankhead, Buffa, Duse, Garbo, Ingenue, Loren, Pierrette, Siddons, Soubrette, Swanson, Terry, West

Actual(ity), Actually De facto, Entelechy, Literal, Live, Material, Real, Real-life, Tangible, True, Very

Acumen Insight, Sense

Acupressure Jin shin do, Shiatsu

Acupuncture Stylostixis

Acute Astute, Dire, Fitché, Incisive, → **INTENSE**, Keen, Quick-witted, Sharp

▶ **Ad** *see* **ADVERT(ISE)**

Adage Aphorism, Gnome, Maxim, Motto, Paroemia, Proverb, Saw, Saying, Truism

Adam Bede, Delved, Jailer

Adamant Firm, Inexorable, Insistent, Obdurate, Rigid, Unbending

Adapt(er), Adaptable, Adaptation, Adaptor Bushing, Ecad, Flexible, Naturalise, Persona, Pliant, Reorient, Refashion, Resilient, Tailor, Timeserver, Transform, Versatile

Add(ed), Addendum, Adder Accrue, Adscititious, Annex, → **APPENDIX**, Attach, Cast, Coopt, Death, Dub, Ech(e), Eik, Eke, Elaborate, Embroider, Enhance, Fortify, Insert, Lace, Puff, Reckon, Retrofit, Score, Spike, Sum, Summate, Tack on, Top up, Tot(e), Total, Viper

Addict(ion), Addicted, Addictive Abuser, Acidhead, Base head, Blunthead, Buff, Chocoholic, Couch potato, Dependency, Devotee, Dope-fiend, Etheromaniac, Fan, Fiend, Freak, Glue-sniffing, Hophead, Hound, Hype, Jones, Joypopper, Junkie, Lover, Mainliner, Mania, Need, Opiate, Opioid, Opium, Pillhead, Pillpopper, Pothead, Shithead, Shopaholic, Slave, Snowbird, Space-cadet, Speedfreak, Sybaritism, User, Vinolent, Wino

Addison Spectator

Addition(al), Additive Accession, Addend, Additive, Adscititious, Adulterant, Advene, Also, And, Annexure, Antiknock, (As an) in, Bolt-on, Braata, Carrageenan, Carrag(h)anin, Codicil, Corollary, Eik, Eke, Encore, Epithesis, Etc, Extender, Extension, → **EXTRA**, Extramural, Footnote, → **IN ADDITION**, Increment, Makeweight, Monkey, New, Odd, On, On top, Other, Padding, Paragog(u)e, Parergon, Plus, PS, Rider, Ripieno, Spare, Suffect, Suffix, Supplementary, Surcharge, Thereto, Top-up, Verandah

Address, Address system Accommodation, Accost, Adroit, Allocution, Apostrophe, Apostrophise, Appellation, Art, → **ATLAS**, Ave, Bub, Buster, Call, Compellation, Dedication, Delivery, Den, Diatribe, Direction, Discourse, Election, Epilogue, Epirrhema, Esquire, Gettysburg, Gospodin, Hail, Home, Homily, Inaugural, IP, Lala, Lecture, Mac, Mester, Mister, Mush, Mynheer, Nkosi, Ode, Orate, Parabasis, Pastoral, Poste-restante, Prelection, Rig, Salute, Sermon, Sir(ree), Speech, Squire, Stance, Tact, Tannoy®, → **TITLE**, Towkay, Tuan, URL, Valedictory, Wambenger, Web, Wus, Y'all, You-all

Adduce Cite

Adelphic Adam

Adept Able, Adroit, Buff, Dab, Deacon, Don, → **EXPERT**, Fit, Handy, Mahatma

Adequate Condign, Does, Due, Egal, Equal, Ere-now, Passable, Proper, → **SUFFICIENT**, Tolerable, Valid

Adhere(nt), Adherence, Adhesive Allegiance, Ally, Araldite®, Blutack®, Bond, Burr, Child, Cling, Conform, Cow Gum®, Dextrin, Disciple, Emplastic, Epoxy, Fidelity, Follower, Glue, Goldsize, Guebre, Gum, Hot-melt, Impact, Jain(a), Loyalist, Mucilage, Nomism, Partisan, Resin, Sectator, Servitor, Stand pat, Sticker, Supporter, Synechia, Votary, Waterglass

Adjacent, Adjoining Bordering, Conterminous, Contiguous, Handy, Nigh

Adjective Adnoun, Epithet, Gerundive

Adjourn(ment) Abeyance, Defer, Delay, → **POSTPONE**, Prorogate, Recess, Rise, Suspend

Adjudicate, Adjudicator Arbiter, Judge, Jury, Referee, Try, Umpire

Adjunct Addition, Aid, Ancillary, Rider

▷ **Adjust** *may indicate* an anagram

Adjust(able), Adjustment, Adjuster Accommodate, Adapt, Attune, Coapt, Dress, Ease, Fine-tune, Fit, Focus, Gang, Gauge, Gerrymander, J'adoube, Modify, Modulate, Orientate, Prepare, Primp, Redo, Reduce, Regulate, Reorientate, Reset, Retrofit, Scantle, Scotopia, Sliding, Suit, Temper, Toe-in, Tram, Trim, True, Tune, Tweak, Vernier

Adjutant Aide, Argala, Officer, Stork

Adler Irene

Ad-lib Ex tempore, Improvise, Wing it

Administer, Administration, Administrator Adhibit, Anele, Apply, Arrondissement, Bairiki, Bureaucrat, Control, Corridors of power, → **DIRECT**, Dispence, Dispense, Executive, Intendant, Intinction, → **MANAGE**, Raj, MBA, Regime, Registrar, Run, Secretariat, Soke, Steward, Sysop

Admirable, Admiration, Admire(d), Admirer Clinker, Clipper, Conquest, Crichton, Esteem, Estimable, → **EXCELLENT**, Flame, Fureur, Gaze, Ho, Iconise, Idolater, Laudable, Partisan, Regard, Ripping, Splendid, Toast, Stotter, Tribute, Venerate, Wonder, Wow

Admiral Adm, AF, Anson, Beatty, Beaufort, Benbow, Blake, Bligh, Boscawen, Butterfly, Byng, Byrd, Capitan, Drake, Effingham, Fisher, Hood, Hornblower, Howard, Jellicoe, Keyes, Marrowfat, Mountbatten, Navarch, Nelson, Old Grog, Raeder, Red, Rodney, Spee, Sturdee, Togo, Vanessa, Van Nieman, Van Tromp, White

Admission, Admit(ting), Admittance Accept, Access, Agree, Allow, Avow, Cognovit, Concede, → **CONFESS**, Enter, Entrée, Entry, Estoppel, Grant, Give, Induct, Ingress, Initiate, Intromit, Ordain, Ordination, Owe, Own, Recognise, Shrift, Take, Tho(ugh), Yield

Admonish, Admonition Caution, Chide, Lecture, Moralise, Pi-jaw, Rebuke, Reprimand, → **SCOLD**, Tip, Warn

Ado Bother, Bustle, Fuss, Lather

Adolescent Developer, Grower, Halflin, Immature, Juvenile, Neanic, Teenager, Tweenager, Veal, Youth

Adonais Keats

Adonis Pheasant's Eye

Adopt(ed) Accept, Affect, Affiliate, Assume, Dalt, Embrace, Espouse, Father, Foster, Mother

Adoration, Adore(r), Adoring Doat, Dote, Goo-goo, Homage, Idolise, Latria, Love,

Pooja(h), Puja, Revere, Venerate, Worship, Zoolater

Adorn(ed), Adornment Aplustre, Attrap, Banderol, Bedeck, Bedight, Bejewel, Caparison, Clinquant, Deck, Dight, Drape, Embellish, Emblaze, Emblazon, Embroider, Enchase, Equip, Festoon, Flourish, Furnish, Garnish, Grace, Graste, Ornament, Riband, Story, Tattoo, Tatu, Tinsel, Trappings

Adrenaline Epinephrin(e)

Adroit Adept, Clever, Dextrous, Expert, Neat, Skilful

Adulate, Adulation Flatter(y), Praise, → **WORSHIP**

Adullam Cave

Adult Amadoda, Consenting, Grown-up, Imago, Man, Mature, Upgrown, X

Adulterant, Adulterate Cut, Debase, Impurify, Lime, Load, Mix, Multum, → **POLLUTE**, Sophisticate, Weaken

Adulterer, Adultery Avoutery, Cuckold, Fornication, Francesca, Lenocinium, Two-timer

Advance(d) A, Abord, Accelerate, Anabasis, Ante, Approach, Ascend, Assert, Better(ment), Charge, Develop, Evolué, Extreme, Far, Fast-forward, Fore, Forge, Forward, Further, Gain, Get on, Grubstake, Haut(e), Hi-tec(h), Impress, Imprest, Incede, Late, Lend, → **LOAN**, March, Mortgage, On(ward), Overture, Pass, Piaffe, Posit, Postulate, Precocious, Prefer, Prest, Process, Progress, → **PROMOTE**, Propose, Propound, Retainer, Ripe, Rise, Scoop, Sub, Submit, Tiptoe, Upfront, Voorskot

Advantage(ous) Accrual, Aid, → **ASSET**, Avail, Batten, Benefit, Bisque, Boot, Edge, Emolument, Expedient, Exploit, Favour, Fruit, Gain, Grouter, Handicap, Handle, Head-start, Help, Interess, Interest, Lever(age), Mess of pottage, Nonmonetary, Obvention, Odds, One-up, Oneupmanship, Oyster, Pecuniary, Percentage, Plus, Privilege, Prize, Pro, Pull, Purchase, Salutary, Stead, Serviceable, Start, Strength, Toe-hold, Upper-hand, Upside, Use, Van, Whiphand, Whipsaw

Advent(ist) Coming, Shaker

Adventure(r), Adventuress, Adventurous Argonaut, Assay, Aunter, Bandeirante, Buccaneer, Casanova, Conquistador, Dareful, Daring, Emprise, Enterprise, Escapade, → **EXPLOIT**, Filibuster, Gest, Lark, Mata Hari, Mercenary, Merchant, Picaresque, Picaro, Picaroon, Risk, Routier, Rutter, Swashbuckler, Vamp, Voyage

Adversary Antagonist, Cope(s)mate, Enemy, Foe

Adverse, Adversity Calamity, Cross, Down, Downside, Harrow, Misery, Reversal, Setback, Unfavourable, Untoward, Woe

Advert(ise), Advertisement, Advertising Above the line, Ad, Air, Allude, Attack, Banner, Bark, Bill, Blipvert, Circular, Classified, Coign(e), Coin, Commercial, Copy, Display, Dodger, Earpiece, Flier, Flyer, Flyposting, Flysheet, Hard sell, Hype, Infomercial, Jingle, Madison Avenue, Mailshot, Market, Niche, Noise, → **NOTICE**, Out, Packshot, Parade, Personnel, Placard, Playbill, Plug, → **POSTER**, Promo, Promote, Promulgate, Prospectus, Puff, Quoin, Refer, Semisolus, Skyscraper, Sky-write, Splash, Spot, Stunt, Subliminal, Teaser, Tele-, Throwaway, Tout, Trailer, Trawl, Want(s) (ad)

Advice Conseil, Counsel, → **GUIDANCE**, Guideline, Information, Invoice, Opinion, Read, Recommendation, Reed, Re(e)de

Advise(d), Adviser, Advisable Acquaint, Avise(ment), CAB, Cabal, Camarilla, Consultant, Counsel, Egeria, Enlighten, Expedient, Genro, Induna, Inform, Instruct, Mentor, Oracle, Peritus, Politic, Prudent, Ralph, → **RECOMMEND**, Starets, Staretz, Tutor, Urge, Wise

Advocate(d) Agent, Argue, Attorney, Back, Counsel, Devil's, Endorse, Exponent, Gospel, Intercede, Lawyer, Move, Paraclete, Peat, Peddle, Pleader, Pragmatist, Preach, Proponent, Silk, Syndic, Urge

Aerial Aeolian, Aery, Antenna, Beam, Clover, Clover leaf, Communal, Dipole, Directional, Dish, Ethereal, Ferrite-rod, Folded dipole, Frame, Ground-plane, Long-wire, Loop, Minidish, Parabolic, Rhombic, Satellite dish, Slot, Yagi

Aerobatics Stunt

Aerobics Pilates, Step

Aerodrome → AIRPORT, Rotor-station

Aerofoil Spoiler, Trimtab

▶ **Aeroplane** *see* AIRCRAFT

Aerosol Atomiser, Mace®

Aesir Loki

Aesthete, Aesthetic Arty, Beautiful, Essene, Tasteful

Affable Amiable, Avuncular, Benign, Cordial, Gracious, Hearty, Suave, Urbane

Affair(s) Amour, Business, Concern, Current, Effeir, Effere, Event, External, Fight, Fling, Foreign, Go, Indaba, Internal, Intrigue, Matter, Pash, Pi(d)geon, Pidgin, Ploy, Relationship, Res, Romance, Shebang, Subject, Thing

Affect(ed), Affectation, Affection(ate), Affecting Air, Airtsy-mairtsy, Alter, Arty, Breast, Camp, Chi-chi, Concern, Cordial, Crachach, Crazy, Endearment, Euphuism, Foppery, Frappant, Grip, Heartstrings, Hit, Impress, Ladida, Lovey-dovey, Mimmick, Minauderie, Mincing, Minnick, Minnock, Mouth-made, Phoney, → POSE, Poseur, Precieuse, Preciosity, Pretence, Prick-me-dainty, Smitten, Spoilt, Stag(e)y, Storge, Susceptible, Sway, Sympathetic, Tender, Topophilia, Touched, Touchy-feely, Twee, Unction, Unnatural, Upend, Warm, Yah

Affiliate, Affiliation Adopt, Associate, Merge, Unite

Affinity Bro, Kin(ship), Penchant, Rapport, Tie

Affirm(ative), Affirmation Assert, Attest, Maintain, Positive, Predicate, Profess, Protestation, Uh-huh, → VERIFY, Yebo

Affix(ed) Append, Ascribe, → ATTACH, Connect, Fasten, On

Afflict(ed), Affliction Aggrieve, Ail, Asthma, Cross, Cup, Curse, Dead leg, Disease, Furnace, Harass, Hurt, Lacerate, Lumbago, Molest, Nosology, Palsy, Persecute, Pester, Plague, Scourge, Smit, Sore, → SORROW, Stricken, Teen, Tene, Tic, Tribulation, → TROUBLE, Try, Unweal, Visitation, Woe

Affluence, Affluent Abundance, Dinky, Ease, Fortune, Grey panther, Inflow, Opulence, Wealth

Afford Allow, Bear, Give, Manage, Offer, Provide, Spare, Yield

Affray Brawl, Fight, Mêlée, Scuffle, Skirmish

Affront Assault, Defy, Facer, → INSULT, → OFFEND, Outrage, Scandal, Slight, Slur

Afghan(istan) Bactria, Dard, Hound, Kaf(f)ir, Pakhto, Pakhtu, Pashto, Pashtu, Pathan, Pushto(o), Pushtu, Taliban

Afloat Aboard, Abroach, Adrift, Natant

Afoot Astir, Up

Aforesaid Above, Same

Afraid Adrad, Alarmed, Chicken, Fearful, Funk, Rad, Regretful, Scared, Timorous, Windy, Yellow

Africa(n) Abyssinian, Adamawa, Akan, Algerian, Amakwerekwere, Angolan, Ashanti, Baganda, Bambara, Bantu, Barbary, Barotse, Basotho, Basuto, Bechuana, Beento, Bemba, Beninese, Berber, Biafran, Bintu, Black, Boer, Botswana, Bushman, Caffre, Cairene, Carthaginian, Chewa, Chichewa, Ciskei, Congo(l)ese, Cushitic, Damara, Dark continent, Dinka, Duala, Dyula, Efik, Eritrean, Ethiopian, Eve, Fang, Fantee, Fanti, Fingo, Flytaal, Fula(h), Gabonese, Galla, Gambian, Ganda, Gazankulu, Grikwa, Griqua, Guinean, Gullah, Hamite, Hausa, Herero, Hottentot, Hutu, Ibibio, Ibo, Igbo, Impi, Kabyle, Kaffer, Kaf(f)ir, Kenyan, Khoikhoi, Kikuyu,

Kongo, Lango, Lesotho, Liberian, Libyan, Lowveld, Lozi, Luba, Luo, Maghreb, Maghrib, Malawi, Malian, Malinke, Mande, Mandingo, Masai, Mashona, Matabele, Mende, Moor, Moroccan, Mossi, Mozambican, Mswahili, Munt(u), Mzee, Nama, Nama(qua), Namibian, Negrillo, → **NEGRO**, Ngoni, Nguni, Nilot(e), Nubian, Nuer, Numidian, Nyanja, Oromo, Ovambo, Pedi, Pied noir, Pondo, Rastafarian, Rhodesian, Rwandan, Sahelian, San, Senegalese, Shilluk, Shluh, Shona, Somali, Songhai, Sotho, Soweto, Sudanese, Susu, Swahili, Swazi, Tanzanian, Temne, Tiv, Togolese, Tonga, Transkei, Transvaal, Tshi, Tsonga, Tswana, Tuareg, Tutsi, Twi, Ugandan, Venda, Voltaic, Waswahili, Watu(t)si, Wolof, X(h)osa, Yoruban, Zairean, Zulu

Afrikaan(s), Afrikaner Cape Dutch, Crunchie, Hairyback, Mynheer, Taal, Volk, Voortrekker

After(wards) About, A la, At, Behind, Beyond, Eft, Epi-, → **LATER**, On, Once, Past, Post hoc, Rear, Since, Sine, Subsequent, Syne

Afterbirth Secundines, Sooterkin

Afterimage Photogene

▷ **After injury** *may indicate* an anagram

Afterlife The Great Beyond

Aftermath Consequence, Fall out, Legacy, Mow(ing), Rawing, Rawn, Rowan, Rowen, Rowing, Sequel(a)

Afternoon A, Arvo, PM, Postmeridian, Undern

Afterpiece, Afterthought Addendum, Codicil, Epimetheus, Exode, Footnote, Note, PS, Supplement

Aftertaste T(w)ang

Again Afresh, Agen, Ancora, Anew, Back, Bis, De novo, Ditto, Do, Eft, Eftsoons, Encore, Iterum, More, Moreover, O(v)er, Re-, Recurrence, Reprise, Than, Then

Against A, Anti, Beside, Con, Counter, For, Gainsayer, Into, Nigh, On, One-to-one, Opposing, To, V, Versus

Agape Feast, Hiant, Ringent, Yawning

Agate Chalcedonyx, Moss, Murr(h)a, Onyx, Ruin

Agave Century plant, Henequen, Lily, Maenad, Maguey

Age(d), Ages, Aging Absolute, Achievement, Ae, Aeon, Aet, Alcheringa, Anno domini, Antique, Archaise, Atomic, Augustan, Azilian, Bronze, Calpa, Century, Chellean, Coon's, Copper, Cycle, Dark, Date, Day, Distress, Doddery, Eld, Elizabethan, Eon, Epact, Epoch(a), Era, Eternity, Generation, Gerontic, Golden, Grey, Heroic, Hoar, Hore, Ice, Information, Iron, Jazz, Jurassic, Kaliyuga, Kalpa, La Tene, Lias, Magdalenian, Maglemosian, Mature, Mental, Mesolithic, Middle, Millennium, Neolithic, New, New Stone, Of, Old, Oligocene, Paleolithic, Passé, Periclean, Period, Phanerozoic, Progeria, Radiometric, Reindeer, S(a)eculum, Saros, Senescence, Senility, Silver, Solera, Space, Stone, Third, Villanovan, Yellow, Yonks, Yug(a)

Agency, Agent Agitator, Alkylating, Ambassador, Antistatic, Art, Autolysin, Bailiff, Bargaining, Barm, Bicarb(onate), Bond, Broker, BSI, Bureau, Catalyst, Cat's paw, Cause, Chelating, Child support, Commis, Commission, Complexone, Comprador(e), Confidential, Consul, Consular, Counter, Countryside, Crown, Customs, Dating, Defoaming, Del credere, Developing, Disclosing, Distributor, Doer, Double, Emissary, Environment, Envoy, Enzyme, Escort, Estate, Exciseman, Executant, Executor, Factor, Fed, Finger, Flack, Forwarding, Free, Galactagogue, G-man, Go-between, Good offices, Hand, Hirudin, House, Implement, Indian, Influence, Institorial, Instrument, Intermediary, Itar Tass, Kinase, Law, Leavening, Legate, Literary, Magic bullet, Man, Masking, Means, Medium, Mercantile,

Mitogen, Mole, Moral, Mutagen, Narc, Narco, Nerve, Ninja, Nucleating, OO, Operation, -or, Orange, Order paper, Oxidizing, Parliamentaire, Parliamentary, Patent, Pathogen, Peace corps, Penetration, Pinkerton, Press, Procurator, Proxy, Realtor, Reducing, Rep(resentative), Resident, Reuters, Riot, Road, Runner, Salesman, Secret (service), Setter, Shipping, SIS, Sleeper, Solvent, Soman, Spook, Spy, Stock, Surfactant, Syndic, Tass, Teratogen, Third party, Ticket, Tiger team, Training, Travel, UNESCO, Vakeel, Vakil, Virino, Voice, Welfare, Wetting, Wire service

Agenda Business, Hidden, Order paper, Programme, Remit, Schedule

Aggie Agnes, Ines, Nessa, Nesta

Aggravate Annoy, Exasperate, Inflame, Irk, Needle, Nettle, Provoke, Try, Vex

Aggregate, Aggregation Ballast, Congeries, Detritus, Etaerio, Granulite, Gravel, Manifold, Number, Omnium, Ore, Ped, Sum, Total

Aggression, Aggressive, Aggressor Arsey, Attack, Bare-knuckle, Bellicose, Belligerent, Biffo, Bullish, Butch, Defiant, Enemy, Feisty, Foe, Gungho, Hard-hitting, Hawk, Invader, In-your-face, Laddish, Lairy, Macho, Militant, On-setter, Pushing, Rambo, Rampant, Road rage, Shirty, Truculent, Wild

Agile Acrobatic, Deft, Lissom(e), Nifty, Nimble, Quick, Spry, Supple, Swank, Twinkletoes, Wiry

▷ **Agitate** *may indicate* an anagram

Agitate(d), Agitation, Agitator Acathisia, Activist, Ado, Agitprop, Akathisia, Betoss, Boil, Bolshie, Bother, Chartist, Churn, Commotion, Commove, Convulse, Demagogue, Discompose, Distraught, → **DISTURB**, Doodah, Ebullient, Emotion, Euoi, Euouae, Evovae, Excite, Extremist, Fan, Fantad, Fanteeg, Fantigue, Fantod, Ferment, Firebrand, Flap, Flurry, Fluster, Flutter, Fraught, Frenzy, Fuss, Fusspot, Goad, Heat, Hectic, Impatience, Jabble, Khilafat, Lather, Militant, Overwrought, Panicky, Pedetic, Perturb, Poss, Pother, Rattle, Restless, Rouse, Ruffle, Seethed, Shake, Sod, Stir(-up), Swivet, Tailspin, Taking, Tempest, Tew, Thermal, Tizzy, Toss, Tremor, Trepidation, Trouble, Turmoil, Tweak, Twitchy, Unrest, Upset, Welter, Whisk, Wrought up, Ytost

Agley Awry, Unevenly

Aglow Alight, Tipsy

▶ **Agnes** *see* **AGGIE**

Agnostic Laodicean

Ago Lang syne, → **SINCE**

Agog Astir, Athirst, Eager, Keen, Pop-eyed

Agonise, Agony Ache, Anguish, Brood, Dread, Ecstasy, Heartache, → **PAIN**, Throe(s), Torment, Torture

Agree(ing), Agreed, Agreement Accede, Accept, Accord, Acquiescence, Agt, Allow, Amen, Analog(ue), Analogy, Apply, As one, Assent, Assort, Atone, Ausgleich, Aye, Bilateral, Bipartite, Bond, Camp David, Cartel, Champerty, Charterparty, Chime, Closing, Coincide, Collective, Comart, Community, Compact, Comply, Comport, Concert, Concord(at), Concur, Conform, Congree, Congruent, Consension, Consensus, → **CONSENT**, Consonant, Contract, Contrahent, Convention, Correspond, Cotton, Covenant, Covin, Covyne, Cushty, Dayton Accords, Deal, Deffo, Deign, Done, Entente, Equate, Escrow, Fadge, Finalise, Gatt, Gentleman's, Handfast, Harmony, Homologous, Indenture, Jibe, Knock-for-knock, League, Like-minded, Mercosur, Munich, National, Net Book, Nod, Nudum pactum, Okay, Pact, Pair, Placet, Plant, Plea bargaining, Prenuptial, Procedural, Productivity, Rabat(te), Repo, Repurchase, Right(o), Right on, Roger, Sanction, Schengen, Service, Settlement, Side, Sort(ance), Specialty, Sponsion, Square,

Standstill, Substantive, Suit, Sweetheart, Sympathy, Synchronise, Synesis, Syntony, Tally, Technology, Threshold, Trade, Treaty, Uh-huh, Union, Unison, Unspoken, Wilco, Wukkas, Yalta, Yea, Yea-say, Yes

Agreeable Amene, Harmonious, Pleasant, Sapid, Sweet, Well-disposed, Willing, Winsome

Agriculture, Agricultural(ist) Arval, Farming, Geoponic, Georgic, Inari, Permaculture, Slash and burn, Smallholding, Tull

Aground Ashore, Beached, Sew, Stranded

Ague Dumb

▷ **Ague(ish)** *may indicate* an anagram

Ah Ach, Ay

Ahead Anterior, Before, Foreship, Forward, Frontwards, In store, Onward, Precocious, Up

Aiblins Perhap, Perhaps, Yibbles

Aid(s), Aide Accessory, Adjutant, Artificial, Assist, Decca, → **DEPUTY**, First, Foreign, Galloper, Gift, Grant, Hearing, Help, Key, Legal, Lend-lease, Life-saver, Monitor, Optophone, Orthosis, PA, Realia, Relief, Serve, Sex, Sherpa, Subsidy, Subvention, Succour, Support, Teaching, Visual, Yeoman('s) service, Zimmer®

AIDS Slim

Ail(ment) Affect, Afflict(ion), Complaint, Croup, Disease, Malady, Misorder, Narks, Occupational, Pink-eye, Pip, Sickness

Aim Approach, Aspire, Bead, Bend, End, Ettle, Eye, Goal, Hub, Intent, Level, Mark, Mint, Mission, Object, Peg, Plan, Plank, Point, Point blank, Purpose, Quest, Reason, Sake, Seek, Sight(s), Target, Tee, Telos, Train, View, Visie, Vizy, Vizzie, Zero-in

Aimless Adrift, Drifting, Erratic, Haphazard, Random, Unmotivated

Air(s), Airer, Airy Aerate, Aerial, Aero, Affectation, Allure, Ambiance, Ambience, Aquarius, Arietta, Atmosphere, Attitude, Aura, Bearing, Breath, Calypso, Canzona, Canzone, Cavatina, Compressed, Dead, Demaine, Descant, Ditty, Draught, Dry, Emphysema, Ether(eal), Expose, Fan, Filmy, Front, Gemini, Heat-island, Heaven, Horse, Inflate, Libra, Lift, Light, Liquid, Look, Lullaby, Madrigal, Manner, Melody, Microburst, Mien, Night, Nitre, Oat, Open, Ozone, Parade, Periptery, Pneumatic, Radio, Screen, Scuba, Serenade, Serenata, Serene, Shanty, Side, Sky, Slipstream, Solo, Song, Strain, Swank, Thin, Trigon, → **TUNE**, Vent, Ventilate, Vital, Wake, Wind

Airborne Ab

Air-conditioning Plenum system

Aircraft, Airship Aerodyne, Aerostat, Angels, AST, Auster, Autoflare, Autogiro, Autogyro, Aviette, Avion, Biplane, Blimp, Brabazon, Bronco, Camel, Canard, Canberra, Chaser, Chopper, Coleopter, Comet, Concorde, Convertiplane, Corsair, Crate, Cropduster, Cyclogiro, Delta-wing, Dirigible, Dive-bomber, Doodlebug, Drone, Eagle, F, Ferret, Fixed-wing, Flivver, Flying fortress, Flying wing, Fokker, Freedom-fighter, Freighter, Galaxy, Glider, Gotha, Gyrodyne, Gyroplane, Hang-glider, Harrier, Hawkeeze, Heinkel, Helicopter, Hercules, Hunter, Hurricane, Interceptor, Intruder, Jet star, Jumbo, Jump-jet, Kite, Lancaster, Liberator, Lifting-body, Lysander, Messerschmitt, Microjet, Microlight, Microlite, MIG, Mirage, Monoplane, Mosquito, Moth, Multiplane, Nightfighter, Nightfinder, Nimrod, Oerlikon, Orion, Ornithopter, Orthopter, Parasol, Penguin, Phantom, → **PLANE**, Provider, Prowler, Pusher, Ramjet, Rigid, Rotaplane, Runabout, Scramjet, Semi-rigid, Skiplane, Skyhawk, Sopwith, Sopwith Camel, Spitfire, SST, Starfighter, Starlifter, Stealth bomber, STOL, Stratocruiser, Stratotanker, Stuka,

Super Sabre, Sweptwing, Swing-wing, Tankbuster, Taube, Taxiplane, Thunderbolt, Thunderchief, Tomcat, Tornado, Towplane, Tracker, Trident, Tri-jet, Triplane, Tube, Turbofan, Turbo-jet, Turbo-prop, Turboramjet, Variable geometry, Vigilante, Viking, Viscount, Vomit comet, Voodoo, VTOL, Wild weasel, Zeppelin

Aircraftsman, Airman AC, Aeronaut, Co-pilot, Erk, Fokker, Kiwi, LAC, Observer, RAF

Aircraftswoman Penguin, Pinguin

▶ **Airfield** *see* AIRPORT

Air force Luftwaffe

Airless Stuffy

Airlift Thermal

Airline, Airway Aeroflot, Anthem, BAC, BEA, Duct, El Al, JAL, Larynx, Lot, Lyric, Purple, Qantas, SAS, S(ch)norkel, TWA, Vent, Weasand(-pipe), Windpipe

▶ **Airman** *see* AIRCRAFTSMAN, FLIER

Airport Drome, Entebbe, Faro, Gander, Gatwick, Heliport, Idlewild, Kennedy, La Guardia, Landing strip, Lod, Luton, Lydda, Lympne, Orly, Prestwick, Runway, Shannon, Stansted, Stolport, Terminal, Vertiport, Wick

Air-raid Blitz, Mission

Air-tight Hermetic, Indisputable, Sealed

Aisle Gangway

Aitch Ache, Aspirate, H

Ajax Loo

Aka Alias

Akin Alike, Cognate, Congener, Kindred, Sib

Alabaster Oriental

Alarm(ing) Agitation, Alert, Arouse, Bell, Bleep, Caution, Concern, Dismay, Eek, False, Fire, Fricht, Fright, Ghast, Hairy, Larum, Panic, Perturb, Rock, Rouse, Siren, Smoke, Startle, Tirrit, Tocsin, Warn, Yike(s)

Alas Ah, Alack, Ay, Eheu, Ha, Haro, Harrow, Io, Lackadaisy, Lackaday, O, Oh, Ohone, O me, Ou, Sadly, Waesucks, Waly, Well-a-day, Wellanear, Wel(l)away, Woe

Alaskan AK, Sourdough, Yupik

Alb Sticharion

Alban Berg

Albanian Arna(o)ut

Albatross Alcatras, Golf, Gooney(-bird), Millstone, Omen, Onus, Quaker-bird, Wandering

Albeit Tho(ugh)

Albert Chain, Chevalier, Consort, Hall, Herring, Slang

Album Autograph, Looseleaf, Photo, Record, Stamp

Albumen, Albumin Chalaza, Glair, Leucosin, Mucin, Myogen, Protein, Ricin, Serum, Treadle, Treddle, White

Alchemic, Alchemist, Alchemy Adept, Arch-chimic, Brimstone, Faust(us), Hermetic(s), Multiplier, Orpiment, Paracelsus, Quicksilver, Sal ammoniac, Sorcery, Spagyric, Spagyrist, Witchcraft

Alcides Hercules

Alcohol(ic) Absolute, Acrolein, Aldehyde, Amyl, Bibulous, Booze, Borneol, Catechol, Cetyl, Chaptalise, Cholesterol, Choline, Citronellol, Cresol, Denatured, Diol, Dipsomaniac, Drinker, Ethal, Ethanol, Ethyl, Farnesol, Feni, Fenny, Firewater, Fusel-oil, Geraniol, Glycerin(e), Grain, Grog, Gut-rot, Hard, Hard stuff, Inebriate, Inositol, Isopropyl, Jakey, Jungle juice, Lauryl, Linalool, Lush, Mahua, Mahwa,

Malt, Mannite, Mannitol, Mercaptan, Mescal, Mescalin(e), Methanol, Meths, Methyl, Mow(r)a, Nerol, Phytol, Plonko, Propyl, Pyroligneous, Rotgut, Rubbing, Rubby, Scrumpy, Secondary, Snake juice, Sorbitol, Sphingosine, Spirits, Spirits of wine, Spirituous, Sterol, Taplash, Terpineol, Tincture, Tocopherol, Triol, Wash, Wino, Witblits, Wood, Xylitol

Alcove Apse, Bay, Bole, Carrel(l), Dinette, Inglenook, Lunette, Niche, Nook, Recess, Tokonoma

Alcyonarian Sea-feather

Aldehyde Acrolein, Aldol, Vanillin

Alder Fothergilla

Alderman Bail(l)ie, CA

Alderney CI, Cow

Ale, Alehouse Audit, Barleybree, Barley-broo, Barley-broth, Barley wine, Beer, Brown, Bummock, CAMRA, Church, Feast, Four, Heather, Humming, Humpty-dumpty, Lamb's wool, Light, Mild, Morocco, Nappy, Nog, Nogg, October, Pale, Plain, Porter, Purl, Real, Small, Stout, Swats, Tiddleywink, Tipper, White, Whitsun, Wort, Yard, Yill, Yorkshire stingo

Alert Agog, Amber, Arrect, Astir, Attentive, Aware, Conscious, Gleg, Gogo, Intelligent, Open-eyed, Qui vive, Red, Scramble, Sharp, Sprack, Sprag, Stand-to, Tentie, Up and coming, Vigilant, Volable, Wary, Watchful, Wide-awake, Yellow

Alewife Barkeeper, Gaspereau

Alexander, Alexandrine Alex, Arius, Macedonian, Pope, Sandy, Sasha, Sawn(e)y, Selkirk, Senarius

Alfalfa Lucern(e), Luzern

Alfred Dreyfus, Garnet, Jingle

Alfresco Barbecue, Plein-air

Alga(e) Anabaena, Blanketweed, Chlorella, Conferva, Desmid, Diatom, Dulse, Heterocontae, Isokont, Jelly, Nostoc, Periphyton, Phycology, Pleuston, Pond scum, Prokaryon, Protococcus, Red, Seaweed, Spirogyra, Star-jelly, Stonewort, Ulothrix, Ulotrichales, Valonia, Volvox, Witches' butter, Zooxanthella

Algebra Boolean, Linear, Quadratics

Algerian Kabyle, Nimidian

Algonquin Innu

Alias Aka, Byname, Epithet, Moni(c)ker, Nick(name), Pen-name, Pseudonym

Alibi Excuse, Watertight

Alien(ate), Alienation A-effect, Amortise, Devest, Disaffect, Ecstasy, Erotic, Estrange, ET, Exotic, External, Foreign, Forinsecal, Fremd, Hostile, Martian, Metic, Outlandish, Outsider, Philistine, Repugnant, Strange(r)

Alight Alowe, Availe, Detrain, Disembark, Dismount, In, Lambent, Land, Lit, Perch, Pitch, Rest, Settle

Align Arrange, Associate, Collimate, Dress, Juxtapose, Marshal, Orient, Straighten

▶ **Alike** *see* LIKE

Alimentary Oesophagus, Pharynx

Aliquot Submultiple

Alive Alert, Animated, Breathing, Extant, Quick

Alkali(ne), Alkaloid Antacid, Apomorphine, Atropine, Base, Bebeerine, Berberine, Betaine, Borax, Brucine, Caffein(e), Capsaicin, Chaconine, Choline, Cinchon(id)ine, Codeine, Colchicine, Corydaline, Curarine, Emetin(e), Ephedrine, Ergotamine, Gelsemin(in)e, Guanidine, Harmalin(e), Harmin(e), Hydrastine, Hyoscine, Hyoscyamine, Ibogaine, Kali, Lixivium, Lobeline, Lye, Mescalin, Narceen, Narceine, Nicotine, Papaverine, Physostigmine, Pilocarpin(e), Piperine,

Potash, Potass, Quinine, Reserpine, Rhoeadine, Scopaline, Scopolamine, Soda, Solanine, Sparteine, Thebaine, Theine, Theobromine, Theophylline, Totaquine, Tropine, Veratridine, Veratrin(e), Vinblastine, Vinca, Vincristine, Volatile, Yohimbine

Alkane Hexane

All A, → ENTIRE, Entity, Finis, Omni, Pan, Quite, Sum, → TOTAL, Toto, Tutti, Whole

Allah Bismillah, God

All at once Holus-bolus, Per saltum, Suddenly

Allay Alleviate, Calm, Disarm, Lessen, Quieten, Soothe

Allegation, Allege(d) Accuse, Assert, Aver, Claim, Mud, Obtend, Plead, Purport, Represent, Smear, So-called

Allegiance Faith, Foy, Loyalty, Tribalism

Allegory, Allegorical Apologue, Fable, Mystic, Myth, Parable

Allergy Atopy, Aversion, Bagassosis, Hay fever, Hives

Alleviate Allay, Alleg(g)e, Calm, Mitigate, Mollify, Palliate, → RELIEVE, Temper

Alley Aisle, Blind, Bonce, Bowling, Corridor, Ennog, Ginnel, Lane, Laura, Marble, Passage, Rope-walk, Silicon, Tin Pan, Twitten, Vennel, Walk, Wynd

Alliance Agnation, Axis, Bloc, Cartel, Coalition, Combine, Compact, Confederation, Dreibund, Dual, Federacy, → LEAGUE, Marriage, NATO, Quadruple, Syndicate, Triple, Union

Alligator Al(l)igarta, Avocado, Caiman, Cayman

Alliteration Cynghanedd, Head-rhyme

Allocate, Allocation Allot, Apportion(ment), Assign, Designate, Distribute, Earmark, Placement, Priorate, Ration, Share, Zone

Allot(ment), Allow(ance), Allowed, Allowing Admit, Affect, Alimony, Allocation, Although, Aret(t), Assign, Attendance, Award, Batta, Beteem(e), Brook, Budget, Cap, Charter, Cloff, Confess, Cor(r)ody, Diet, Discount, Dole, Draft, Enable, Entitle, Excuse, Expenses, Feod, Field, Fya, Give, Grant, House-bote, Husbandage, Indulge, Jobseekers', Latitude, Legit(imate), Let, Licit, Luit(en), Machining, Mag, Mobility, Okay, Palimony, Parcel, Pension, Percentage, → PERMIT, Personal, Pittance, Plot, Portion, Privy purse, Quarterage, Quota, Ratio, Ration, Rebate, Rood, Salt-money, Sanction, Separation, Sequel, Share(-out), Shrinkage, Sizings, Stint, Stipend, Subsistence, Suffer, Table money, Tare, Tax, Teene, Though, Tolerance, Tolerate, Tret, Viaticum, Weighting, Yield

Allotment-holder Cleruch

▶ **Allow** *see* ALLOT

Alloy Albata, Alnico®, Amalgam, Babbitt, Bell-metal, Billon, Brass, Britannia metal, Bronze, Cermet, Chrome(l), Compound, Constantan, Cupronickel, Duralumin®, Dutch leaf, Electron, Electrum, Eutectoid, Ferrochrome, Gunmetal, Invar®, Iridosmine, Kamacite, Latten, Magnalium, Magnox, Manganin®, Marmem, Mischmetal, Mix, Monel®, Nichrome®, Nickel-silver, Nicrosilal, Nimonic, Nitinol, Occamy, Oreide, Orichalc, Ormolu, Oroide, Osmiridium, Paktong, Pewter, Pinchbeck, Platinoid, Porous, Potin, Pot metal, Prince's metal, Shakudo, Shibuichi, Similor, Solder, Speculum, Spelter, Steel, Stellite®, Tambac, Terne, Tombac, Tombak, Tutenag, Zircal(l)oy, Zircoloy

▷ **Alloy** *may indicate* an anagram

Allright A1, Assuredly, Fit, Hale, Hunky(-dory), Jake, OK, Safe, Tickety-boo, Well

All-round Overhead, Versatile

All-seeing Panoptic

Allspice Jamaica pepper, Pimiento

All the same Nath(e)less, Nevertheless

Allude, Allusion Hint, Imply, Innuendo, Mention, Refer, Reference, Suggest

Allure, Alluring Agaçant(e), Charm, Circe, Decoy, Delilah, Entice, Femme fatale, Glam, Glamour, Inviting, It, Magnet(ic), SA, Seduce, Seductive, Tempt, Trap, Trepan, Vamp

Alluvium Carse

Ally, Allied Accomplice, Agnate, Aide, Alley, Alliance, Backer, Belamy, Cognate, Colleague, Dual, Foederatus, German(e), Holy, Marble, Marmoreal, Partner, Plonker, Related, Taw, Unholy

Almanac Calendar, Clog, Ephemeris, Nautical, Nostradamus, Whitaker's, Wisden, Zadkiel

Almighty Creator, Deity, Dollar, God, Jehovah, Omnipotent

Almond Amygdal, Burnt, Emulsion, Jordan, Marchpane, Marzipan, Orgeat, Praline, Ratafia, Sugared, Valencia

Almost Anear, Anigh, Close on, Most, Near, Nigh(ly), Practically, Ripe, Une(a)th, Virtually, Well-nigh, Welly

Alms Awmous, Charity, Dole, Handout, Zakat

Aloe Agave, Pita

Alone Hat, Jack, Lee-lane, Onely, Pat, Secco, Separate, Single, Singly, Sola, Solo, Solus, Tod, Unaccompanied, Unaided, Unattended, Unholpen

Along, Alongside Abeam, Aboard, Abreast, Apposed, Beside, By, Parallel

Aloof Abeigh, Apart, Asocial, Chilly, Cool, Detached, Distant, Hou inch, Indrawn, Mugwump, Offish, Remote, Reserved, Reticent, Skeigh, Snooty, Stand-offish, Toffee-nosed, Unapproachable

Alpaca Paco

Alphabet ABC, Absey, Augmented Roman, Black-out, Brahmi, Braille, Chalcidian, Christcross, Cyrillic, Deaf, Devanagari, Estrang(h)elo, Futhark, Futhorc, Futhork, Glagol, Glagolitic, Glossic, Grantha, Hangul, Horn-book, International, IPA, ITA, Kana, Kanji, Katakana, Kufic, Latin, Manual, Nagari, Og(h)am, Pangram, Phonetic, Pinyin, Romaji, Roman, Runic, Signary, Slavonic, Syllabary

Alpine, Alps Australian, Bernese, Cottian, Dinaric, Gentian, Graian, Julian, Laburnum, Lepontine, Maritime, Matterhorn, Ortles, Pennine, Rhaetian, Rock plant, Savoy, Southern, Transylvanian, Tyrol, Western

Also Add, And, Eke, Item, Likewise, Moreover, Plus, Too, Und

Altar, Altar-cloth, Altarpiece Butsudan, Diptych, Dossal, Dossel, High, Polyptych, Retable, Shrine, Tabula, Triptych

Alter, Alteration Adapt, Adjust, Bushel, Change, Changeover, Chop and change, Cook, Convert, Correct, Customise, Distort, Evolve, Falsify, Lib, Material, Modify, Modulate, Munge, Mutate, Recast, Revise, Transient, Transpose, Up-end, Variance, → **VARY**

▷ **Alter(native)** *may indicate* an anagram

Altercation Barney, Brawl, Fracas, Row, Words, Wrangle

Alternate, Alternating, Alternation, Alternative Boustrophedon, Bypass, Exchange, Instead, Metagenesis, → **OPTION**, Ossia, Other, Rotate, Second string, Solidus, Staggered, Systaltic, Tertian, Variant, Vicissitude

▷ **Alternately** *may indicate* every other letter

Althaea Mallow, Malva

Although Admitting, Albe(e), All-be, But, Even, Howsoever, Howsomever, Whereas, While

Altitude Elevation, Height, Meridian, Pressure, Rated

Alto Countertenor

Altogether Algate(s), All-to-one, Completely, Entirely, Holus-bolus, Idea, In all,

Lock, stock and barrel, Nude, Nudity, Purely, Slick, Tout, Uncut, Wholly

▷ **Altogether** *may indicate* words to be joined

Altruistic Heroic, Humane, Philanthropic, Selfless, Unselfish

Alum Potash

Aluminium, Alumino-silicate Al, Allanite, Bauxite, Euclase, Gibbsite, Sillimanite, Stilbite, Tinfoil

Alumnus Graduate, OB

Always Algate(s), Ay(e), Constant, E'er, Eternal, Ever(more), Forever, I, Immer, Semper, Sempre, Still

Amalgamate Coalesce, Consolidate, Fuse, Merge, Unite

Amalthea Cornucopia

Amarylli(d)s Leocojum, Lily, Polianthes

Amass Accumulate, Assemble, Collect, Gather, Heap, Hoard, Pile, Upheap

Amateur(s) A, AA, Armchair, Beginner, Corinthian, Dabbler, Dilettante, DIY, Enthusiast, Ham, Inexpert, L, Laic, Lay, Neophyte, Novice, Prosumer, Sunday painter, Tiro, Tyro

Amatory Eros, Erotic, Fervent

Amaze(d), Amazement, Amazing Astonish, Astound, Awe, Awhape, Bewilder, Cor, Criv(v)ens, Dumbfound, Far out, Flabbergast, Gee-whiz, Gobsmack, Goodnow, Grace, Incredible, Jesus wept, Magical, Monumental, O, Open-eyed, Open-mouthed, Perplex, Poleaxe, Pop-eyed, Prodigious, Stagger, Strewth, Stupefaction, Stupendous, Thunderstruck, Unreal, Wow

Amazon(ian) Ant, ATS, Brimstone, Britannia, Dragon, Hippolyta, Hoyden, Jivaro, Orellana, Penthesilea, Shield-maid, Shield-may, Thalestris, Tupi, Virago

Ambassador At-large, Diplomat, Elchee, Elchi, Eltchi, Envoy, Extraordinary, HE, Internuncio, Leaguer, Ledger, Legate, Leidger, Leiger, Lieger, Minister, Nuncio, Plenipo, Plenipotentiary, Pronuncio

Amber Colophony, Electric, Lammer, Ligure, Resin, Retinite, Succinum

Ambience Aura, Milieu, Setting

Ambiguous, Ambiguity Amphibology, Cryptic, Delphic, Double, Double entendre, Enigmatic, Epicene, Equivocal, Gnomic, Loophole, Oracular, Weasel words

Ambit Scope

Ambition, Ambitious Adventurer, Aim, Arrivisme, Aspiring, Careerism, Drive, Emulate, Go-ahead, Goal, Go-getter, Grail, High-flier, Keen, Office-hunter, Purpose, Pushy, Rome-runner, Thrusting

Amble Meander, Mosey, Pace, Poddle, Saunter, Single-foot, Stroll

Ambrose Emrys

Ambrosia(l) Amreeta, Amrita, Beebread, Fragrant, Odorant, Ragweed, Savoury

Ambulance, Ambulanceman Badger, Blood-wagon, Field, Meat wagon, Pannier, Paramedic, Van, Yellow-flag, Zambu(c)k

Ambulatory Stoa

Ambush(ed) Ambuscade, Belay, Bushwhack, Emboscata, Embusque, Forestall, Latitant, Lurch, Perdu(e), Trap, Watch, Waylay

Amelia Bloomer

Ameliorate Amend, Ease, Improve, Remedy

Amen Ammon, Approval, Inshallah, Verify

Amenable Putty

▷ **Amend** *may indicate* an anagram

Amend(ment) Alter, Change, Correct, Expiate, Expurgate, Fifth, Protocol, Redress, Reform, Repair, Restore, → **REVISE**, Satisfy

Ament Catkin, Idiot

America(n) A, Algonki(a)n, Algonqu(i)an, Am, Angeleno, Basket Maker, Caddo, Cajun, Carib, Chicano, Chickasaw, Chinook, Copperskin, Digger, Doughface, Down-easter, Federalist, Flathead, Fox, Gringo, Guyanese, Huron, Interior, Joe, Jonathan, Latino, Miskito, Mistec, Mixtec, Mound Builder, Native, New World, Norteno, Olmec, Paisano, Salish, Stateside, Statesman, Statist, Tar-heel, Tico, Tupi, Uncle Sam, US(A), WASP, Yankee, Yanqui

Americium Am

Amethyst Oriental

Amiable Friendly, Genial, Gentle, Inquiline, Mungo, Sweet, Warm

Amid(st) Among, Atween, Between, Inter, Twixt

Amide Asparagine

Amine Putrescine, Spermine

Amino-acid Dopa, Tyrosine, Valine

Amiss Awry, Ill, Up, Wrong

Ammonia(c) Amide, Amine, Choline, Ethylamine, Hartshorn, Imide, Oshac

Ammonite Serpent-stone

Ammunition Ammo, Bandoleer, Bandolier, Buckshot, Bullets, Chain-shot, Dum-dum, Grape(shot), Grenade, Round, Shot, Slug, Tracer

Amnesia Anterograde, Fugal, Fugue, Lethe, Retrograde

Amnesty Oblivion, Pardon

Amoeba Melboean

Amok Rampaging

Among Amid(st), In, Inter al, Within

Amorous(ly) Casanova, Erotic, Fervent, Lustful, Nutty, Smickly, Spoony, Warm

Amorphous Formless, Shapeless, Vague

Amount Come, Dose, Element, Figure, Handful, Lashings, Levy, Lot, Nip, Number, Ocean, Offset, Outage, Pot(s), Premium, Price, Quantity, Quantum, Shedload, Span, Stint, Sum, Throughput, Volume, Whale, Wheel

Amour Affair(e), Intrigue, Love

Ampersand Tironian sign

Amphetamine Benny, Benzedrine, Speed

Amphibian, Amphibious Amb(l)ystoma, Amtrack, Anura, Axolotl, Batrachian, Caecilia, Caecilian, Desman, Eft, Frog, Guana, Hassar, Labyrinthodont, Mermaid, Mudpuppy, Newt, Olm, Proteus, Rana, Salamander, Salientia, Seal, Siren, Tadpole, Toad, Tree frog, Urodela(n), Urodele, Weasel

Amphipod Sand-screw, Shrimp

Amphitheatre Bowl, Circus Maximus, Coliseum, Colosseum, Ring, Stage

Ample, Amplitude Bellyful, Copious, Enough, Generous, Good, Large, Opulent, Profuse, Rich, Roomy, Round, Sawtooth, Spacious, Uberous, Voluminous

Amplifier, Amplify Booster, Double, Eke, Enlarge, Hailer, Laser, Loud hailer, Maser, Megaphone, Push-pull, Solion, Tannoy®, Transistor, Treble

Amputate Sever, Transfix

Amulet Abraxas, Charm, Churinga, Fetish, Greegree, Grigri, Grisgris, Haemon, Pentacle, Periapt, Phylactery, Sea-bean, Talisman, Tiki, Toadstone, Token

Amuse(ment), Amusing(ly) Caution, Cottabus, Disport, Diversion, Divert, Divertimento, Divertissement, Drole, Droll, Game, Gas, Giocoso, Glee, Hoot, Jocular, Killing, Levity, Light, Occupy, Pleasure, Popjoy, Priceless, Regale, Rich, Scream, Slay, Solace, → **SPORT**, Tickle, Titillate, Wacky

Amy Johnson, Robsart

▶ **An** *see* **A**

Ana(s) Story, Teal

Anabaptist Abecedarian, Dipper, Dopper, Hutterite, Knipperdolling
Anableps Four-eyes
Anachronism Archaism, Solecism
Anaconda Water boa
Anacreon Te(i)an
Anaemia, Anaemic Aplastic, Cooley's, Diamond-Blackfan, Fanconi's, Favism, Haemolytic, Megaloblastic, Miner's, Pernicious, Sallow, Sickle-cell, Thalassaemia
Anaesthetic, Anaesthetise(d), Anaesthetist Analgesic, Apgar, Avertin®, Basal, Benzocaine, Bupivacaine, Caudal, Chloralose, Chloroform, Cocaine, Endotracheal, Epidural, Ether, Eucain(e), Freeze, Gas, General, Halothane, Hibernation, Infiltrate, Intravenous, Jabber, Ketamine, Lidocaine, Lignocaine, Local, Metopryl, Morphia, Novocaine, Number, Opium, Orthocaine, Pentothal, Phenacaine, Procaine, Rhigolene, Special K, Spinal, Stovaine, Topical, Trike, Twilight sleep, Under, Urethan(e)
Anagram Jumble
Anal, Anus Poepol, Proctal, Ring, Tewel
Analgesic Aspirin, Bute, Codeine, Diclofenac, Disprin, Fentanyl, Ketamine, Menthol, Meperidine, Methadone, Morphia, Moxa, Opium, Painkiller, Paracetamol, Pethidine, Phencyclidine, Quina, Salicin(e), Sedative
Analogous, Analogy Akin, Corresponding, Like, Parallel, Similar
Analyse(r), Analysis Alligate, Anagoge, Anatomy, Assess, Blot, Breakdown, Combinatorial, Conformational, Construe, Diagnosis, Discourse, Dissect, Emic, Eudiometer, Examine, Explication, Factor, Force-field, Fourier, Gap, Gravimetric, Harmonic, Input-output, Job, Kicksorter, Lexical, Linguistic, Logical, Miscue, Numerical, Parse, Pollen, Process, Psych out, Qualitative, Quant, Quantitive, Quantitative, Risk, Rundown, Sabermetrics, Scan(sion), Semantics, Sift, Spectral, Spectroscopic, Spectrum, Swot, Systems, Test, Transactional, Unpick, Volumetric
▷ **Analysis** *may indicate* an anagram
Analyst Alienist, Investment, Jung, Lay, Psychiatrist, Quant(ative), Shrink, Trick cyclist
Anarchist, Anarchy Black Bloc(k), Black Hand, Bolshevist, Chaos, Kropotkin, Nihilism, Provo, Rebel, Revolutionary, Trotskyite
Anathema Ban, Curse, Execration, Oath, Warling
Anatole, Anatolian France, Hittite, Turk
Anatomy, Anatomist Bones, De Graaf, Framework, Henle, Herophilus, Histology, Malpighi, Morbid, Pacini, Prosector, Puccini, Schneider, Spiegel, Worm
Ancestor, Ancestral, Ancestry Adam, Avital, Dawnman, Descent, Extraction, For(e)bear, Forefather, Gastraea, Humanoid, Lin(e)age, Parent, Parentage, Pedigree, Predecessor, Primogenitor, Proband, Profectitious, Progenitor, Propositus, Roots, Sire, Tipuna, Tree, Tupina
Anchor(age) Atrip, Berth, Bower, Cell, Deadman, Drag, Drift, Drogue, Eremite, Grapnel, Hawse, Hermit, Kedge, Kedger, Killick, Killock, Laura, Moor, Mud-hook, Mushroom, Nail, Ride, Roads(tead), Rode, Root, Scapa Flow, Sea, Sheet, Spithead, Stock, Stream, Toehold, Waist, Weather
Anchorite Recluse
Anchovy Fish, Pear
Ancient Antediluvian, Archaic, Auld-warld, Bygone, Early, Gonfanoner, Historic, Hoary, Iago, Immemorial, Lights, Neolithic, Ogygian, → **OLD(ER)**, Old-world, Primeval, Primitive, Pristine, Ur, Veteran
Ancient city Carthage, Ur

Ancillary Adjunct, Secondary, Subservient

And Als(o), Ampassy, Ampersand, Amperzand, Ampussyand, Besides, Et, Furthermore, Item, 'n', Plus, Tironian sign, Und

Andalusite Macle

Andiron Chenet, Dog, Firedog

Andrew(es) Aguecheek, Lancelot, Merry

Androgynous Epicene

Android Automaton, Golem, Robot

Anecdote(s) Ana, Exemplum, Story, Tale, Yarn

Anemometer Wind-sleeve, Windsock

Anemone Actinia, Pasque-flower, Windflower

Anew De integro, De novo

Angel(s) Abdiel, Adramelech, Apollyon, Archangel, Ariel, Arioch, Asmadai, Azrael, Backer, Banker, Beelzebub, Belial, Benefactor, Cake, Cherub, Clare, Destroying, Deva, Dominion, Dust, Eblis, Fallen, Falls, Fuzzy-wuzzy, Gabriel, Guardian, Heavenly host, Hierarchy, Host, Iblis, Investor, Israfel, Ithuriel, Lucifer, Michael, Nurse, Power, Principality, Raphael, Recording, Rimmon, St, Seraph, Spirit, Throne, Uriel, Uzziel, Virtue, Watcher, Zadkiel, Zephiel

Angela Brazil

Angelica Archangel

Angel's wings Begonia

Anger, Angry → **ANNOY**, Bate, Bile, Black, Bristle, Choler(ic), Conniption, Cross, Dander, Displeased, Dudgeon, Enrage, Exasperation, Face, Fuff, Fury, Gram, Heat, Het up, Horn-mad, Huff, Incense, Inflame, Infuriate, Iracund, Irascible, Ire, Kippage, Livid, Mad, Monkey, Moody, Nettle, Pique, Provoke, Radge, Rage, Rampant, Ratty, Renfierst, Rile, Roil, Rouse, Sore, Spleen, Steam, Stroppy, Tamping, Tantrum, Tarnation, Teen(e), Temper, Tene, Tooshie, Vex, Vies, Warm, Waspish, Waxy, Wound up, Wrath, Wroth, Yond

Angina Sternalgia, Vincent's

Angle(d), Angler, Angular, Angles, Angling Acute, Argument, Aspect, Attitude, Axil, Azimuthal, Canthus, Cast, Catch, Chiliagon, Coign, Complementary, Conjugate, Contrapposto, Corner, Cos, Critical, Diedral, Diedre, Dihedral, Elbow, Elevation, Ell, Exterior, Facial, Fish, Fish-hook, Fork, Geometry, Gonion, Hade, Hip, Hour, Hyzer, In, Incidence, Interior, L, Laggen, Laggin, Loft, Mitre, Mung, Negative, Oblique, Obtuse, Parallax, Pediculate, Perigon, Peterman, Piend, Piscator, Pitch, Pitch-cone, Plane, Polyhedral, Position, Positive, Quoin, Radian, Rake, Re-entrant, Reflex, Right, Rod(s)man, Rodster, Round, Salient, Sally, Saltchucker, Sine, Sinical, Slip, Solid, Spherical, Stalling, Steeve, Steradian, Straight, Supplementary, Sweepback, The gentle craft, Trotline, Vertical, Viewpoint, Visual, Walton, Waltonian, Washin, Weather, Wide-gab

Anglesey Mona

Anglican(s) CE-men, Conformist, Episcopal

Anglo-Catholic High-church, Spire

Anglo-Indian Qui-hi, Qui-hye, Topi-wallah

Angora Goat, Mohair, Rabbit

Angostura Cusparia bark

Angst Dread

Anguish(ed) Agony, Distress, Gip, Grief, Gyp, Hag-ridden, Heartache, Misery, → **PAIN**, Pang, Sorrow, Throes, → **TORMENT**, Torture, Woe

Angus Aberdeen

Animal(s) Acrita, Anoa, Armadillo, Atoc, Bag, Bandog, Barbastel, Beast, Bestial,

Brute, Cariacou, Carnal, Chalicothere, Cleanskin, Coati, Creature, Criollo, Critter, Ethology, Fauna, Felis, Feral, Gerbil, Herd, Ichneumon, Jacchus, Jerboa, Kinkajou, Klipdas, Mammal, Marmoset, Marmot, Menagerie, Moose, Noctule, Oribi, Pack, Parazoon, Pet, Political, Protozoa, Pudu, Quagga, Rac(c)oon, Rhesus, Sensual, Sloth, Stud, Symphile, Tarsier, Teledu, Urson, Waler, Xenurus, Yale, Yapock, Zerda, Zoo

Animal-catcher Utricularia

Animate(d), Animation Activate, Actuate, Arouse, Biophor, Cartoon, Ensoul, Excite, Fire, Hortatory, Hot, Inspire, Lit, Live, Morph, Mosso, Perky, Pixil(l)ation, Rouse, Spiritoso, Spritely, Suspended, Toon, Verve, Vivacity, Vivify

Animosity Enmity, Friction, Hostility, Ill-will, Malice, Pique, Rancour

Ankle Coot, Cuit, Cute, Hock, Hucklebone, Knee, Malleolus, Talus

Ankle(t), Ankle covering Cootikin, Cuitikin, Cutikin, Gaiter, Jess

Anna, Anne, Annie Boleyn, Hathaway, Laurie, Oakley, Page, Pavlova, Pice, Sewell, Sister

Annal(s) Acta, Archives, Chronicles, Register

Annatto Roucou

Annex(e) Acquire, Add, Affiliate, Attach, Codicil, Extension, Leab-to, Subjoin

Annihilate Destroy, Erase, Exterminate, Obliterate, Slay

Anniversary Birthday, Feast, Jubilee, Obit, Triennial, Wedding, Yahrzeit

Annotate, Annotator Comment, Interpret, Note, Postil, Scholiast

Announce(r), Announcement Banns, Bellman, Biil(ing), Blazon, Bulletin, Communiqué, Declare, Decree, Disclose, Divulgate, Flash, Gazette, Herald, Hermes, Inform, Intimate, Meld, Name and shame, Newsflash, Noise, Post, Preconise, Proclaim, Profess, Promulgate, Pronunciamente, Publish, Release, → **REPORT**, Rescript, Speaker(ine), State, Toastmaster, Town crier, Trumpet

Annoy(ance), Annoyed, Annoying Aggravate, Aggrieve, Anger, Antagonise, Badger, Bane, Blight, Bother, Bug, Bugbear, Chagrin, Choleric, Contrary, Cross, Deuce(d), Disturb, Doggone, Doh, Drat, Fash, Fleabite, Frab, Fumed, Gall, Gatvol, Hack off, Hang, Harass, Hatter, Hector, Hip, Hoots, Huff, Hump, Humph, Incense, Irk, → **IRRITATE**, Mickey-taking, Miff, Mischief, Molest, Moryah, Nag, Nark, Nettle, Niggle, Noisome, Noy(ance), Peeve, Pesky, Pester, Pipsqueak, Pique, Plague, Provoke, Rankle, Rats, Ratty, Resentful, Ride, Rile, Roil, Rub, Shirty, Tiresome, Tracasserie, Try, Vex, Wazzock

Annual, Annuity Book, Consolidated, Contingent, Deferred, Etesian, → **FLOWER**, Half-hardy, Hardy, Immediate, Life, Pension, Perpetuity, Rente, Tontine, Yearbook, Yearly

Annul(ment) Abolish, Abrogate, Cashier, Cassation, Dissolution, Invalidate, Irritate, Negate, Recision, Repeal, Rescind, Reversal, Revoke, Vacatur, Vacuate, → **VOID**

Annular Toric

Anodyne Balm, Narcotic, Paregoric, Sedative

Anoint(ing) Anele, Cerate, Chris(o)m, Embrocate, Grease, Hallow, Nard, Smear

Anomaly Eccentric, Gravity, Magnetic, Mean, True

▷ **Anomaly** *may indicate an anagram*

Anon Again, Anew, Later, Soon

Anonymous Adespota, Anon, A.N.Other, Faceless, Grey, Impersonal, Somebody, Unnamed, Valentine

Anorak Nerd, Wonk

Another Extra

Answer(ing), Answer(s) Account, Acknowledge, Amoebaean, Ans, Antiphon,

Because, Comeback, Crib (sheet), Defence, Dusty, Echo, Key, Lemon, Light, No, Oracle, Rebuttal, Rebutter, Rein, Rejoin(der), Repartee, Reply, Rescript, Respond, Response, Responsum, Retort, Return, Riposte, Serve, Sol, Solution, Solve, Verdict, Yes

Ant(s), Anthill Amazon, Army, Bull(dog), Carpenter, Colony, Driver, Dulosis, Emmet, Ergataner, Ergates, Ergatogyne, Ergatomorph, Fire, Formic, Formicary, Leafcutter, Legionary, Myrmecoid, Myrmidon, Nasute, Neuter, Pharaoh, Pismire, Sauba, Slave, Soldier, Termite, Thief, Umbrella, Velvet, White, Wood

Antacid Limewater, Magnesia, Peptic

Antagonist(ic), Antagonise Adverse, Estrange, Hostile, Oppugnant, Peare, Peer

Antarctica Adelie Land, Byrd Land, Graham Land, Wilkes Land

Ant-bear Tamanoir

Ante Bet, Punt, Stake

Ant-eater Aardvark, Banded, Echidna, Edental, Giant, Manis, Numbat, Pangolin, Scaly, S(e)ladang, Spiny, Tamandu, Tamandua, Tapir

Antelope Addax, Antilope, Blackbuck, Blaubok, Blesbok, Bloubok, Bluebuck, Bongo, Bontebok, Bubal(is), Bushbuck, Cabric, Chamois, Chikara, Chiru, Dikdik, Duiker, Duyker, Dzeren, Eland, Elk, Gazelle, Gemsbok, Gerenuk, Gnu, Goa, Goral, Grysbok, Harnessed, Hartbees, Hartebeest, Impala, Inyala, Kaama, Kid, Klipspringer, Kob, Kongoni, Koodoo, Kudu, Lechwe, Madoqua, Marshbuck, Mhorr, Mohr, Nagor, Nilgai, Nilgau, Nyala, Nylghau, Oribi, Oryx, Ourebi, Ox, Pale-buck, Pallah, Prongbuck, Pronghorn, Pronk, Puku, Pygarg, Reebok, Reedbuck, Rhebok, Sable, Saiga, Sasin, Sassaby, Serow, Sitatunga, Situtunga, Springbok, Steenbok, Steinbock, Stemback, Stembok, Suni, Takin, Thar, Topi, Tragelaph, Tsessebe, Waterbuck, Wildebeest

Antenna Aerial, Dipole, Dish, Feeler, Horn, Sensillum, TVRO

Anterior Anticous, Earlier, Front, Prior

Anthelmintic Worm

Anthem Chant, Die Stem, Hymn, Introit, Isodica, Marseillaise, Motet(t), National, Offertory, Psalm, Red Flag, Responsory, Song, Star Spangled Banner, Stem, Theme, Tract, Troparion

Anthology Album, Ana, Chrestomathy, Digest, Divan, Florilegium, Garland, Pick, Spicilege

Anthony Absolute, Adverse, Runt, Trollope

Anthracite Blind-coal

Anthrax Sang, Splenic fever, Woolsorter's disease

Anthropo(i)d Peripatus, Sivapithecus

Anthropologist Heyerdahl, Mead

Anti Against, Agin, Con, Hostile

Anti-abortion Right to life

Anti-aircraft AA

Anti-bacterial, Antibiotic Actinomycin, Allicin, Amoxicillin, Ampicillin, Aureomycin®, Avoparcin, Bacitracin, Bacteriostat, Cecropin, Cephalosporin, Cipro®, Ciprofloxacin, Cloxacillin, Colistin, Cortisone, Co-trimoxazole, Cycloserine, Doxorubicin, Doxycycline, Drug, Erythromycin, Gentamicin, Gramicidin, Griseofulvin, Interferon, Interleukin, Kanamycin, Lincomycin, Macrolide, Magainin, Methicillin, Mitomycin, Neomycin, Nystatin, Opsonin, Oxacillin, Oxytetracycline, Penicillin, Polymixin, Quinolone, Rifampicin, Rifamycin, Spectinomycin, Streptomycin, Streptothricin, Terramycin®, Tetracycline, Tyrocidine, Tyrothricin, Vancomycin, Virginiamycin, Wide-spectrum

Antibody Agglutinin, Alemtuzumab, Amboceptor, Antitoxin, Blocker, Catuximab,

H(a)emolysin, Hybroid, Isoagglutinin, Lysin, Monoclonal, Opsonin, Precipitin, Reagin, Retuximab, Trastuzumab

Antic(s) Caper, Dido, Frolic, Gambado, Hay, Prank, Shenanigan, Stunt

Anti-carlist Queenite

Anticipate, Anticipation Antedate, Augur, Await, Drool, → EXPECT, Forecast, Foresee, Foresight, Forestall, Foretaste, Forethought, Hope, Intuition, Preparation, Prevenancy, Prolepsis, Prospect, Second-guess, Type

Anticlimax Bathos, Damp squib, Deflation, Letdown

Anticline Upwrap

Anticlockwise Dextrorse, Laevorotatory, Widdershins, Withershins

Anticoagulant C(o)umarin, Heparin, Hirudin, Prostacyclin, Warfarin

Anticommunist Bircher, John, McCarthyism

Anticyclone High

Antidote Adder's wort, Alexipharmic, Angelica, Antivenin, Arrowroot, Bezoar, Contrayerva, Cure, Dimercaprol, Emetic, Guaco, Interleukin, Mithridate, Nostrum, Orvietan, Remedy, Ribavirin, Senega, Theriac(a), (Venice-)Treacle

Anti-freeze Glycerol, Lagging

Antigen Agglutinogen, Hapten(e)

Antihistamine Dimenhydrinate, Quercetin

Anti-imperialist Guelf, Guelph

Antimacassar Tidy

Antimonopoly Trust buster

Antimony Kohl, Sb, Speiss, Stibium, Tartar emetic

Antioxidant Lycopene

Anti-parliamentarian Poujadist

Antipasto Caponata

Antipathy Allergy, Aversion, Detest, → DISLIKE, Enmity, Intolerance, Repugnance

Anti-perfectionist Cobden

Antiphon The Reproaches

Antipodean Abo, Antarctic, Antichthon, Enzed, Underworld

Antipope Novatian(us)

Anti-protectionist Cobden

Antiquated, Antique, Antiquarian Ancient, Archaic, A(u)stringer, Bibelot, Curio, Dryasdust, Egyptian, FAS, Fog(e)y, Fogram(ite), Fossil, Old-fangled, Ostreger, Relic

Anti-reformer Obscurant

Anti-revolutionary Vendean, White

Anti-Roman Ghibel(l)ine

Anti-royalist Puritan, Whig

Anti-Semitic Pamyat

Antiseptic Acriflavine, Carbolic, Cassareep, Creosote, Cresol, Disinfectant, Eupad, Eusol, Formaldehyde, Formalin, Formol, Germicide, Guaiacol, Iodine, Lister, Lysol®, Merbromin, Phenol, Sterile, Tar, Thymol, Tutty

Anti-slavery Free-soil, Wilberforce

Anti-smoker ASH, Misocapnic

Antisocial Hoodie, Hostile, Ishmaelitish, Loner, Misanthropic, Oik, Psychopath

Antithesis Contrary, Converse, Opposite

Anti-three Noetian

Antitoxin Antibody, Antivenin, Guaco, Serum, Vaccine

Anti-union Secesher

Antivitamin Pyrithiamine

Antler(s) Bosset, Crown, Horn, Palm, Rights, Staghorn, Surroyal, Tine

Ant-proof Bilian

▸ **Anus** *see* **ANAL**

Anvil Bick-iron, Block, Incus, Stiddie, Stithy

Anxiety, Anxious Angst, Brood, Care(ful), Cark, Concern, Disquiet, Dysthymia, Edgy, Fanteeg, Fantigue, Fantod, Fear, Fraught, Grave, Heebie-jeebies, Hung-up, Hypochondria, Impatient, Inquietude, Itching, Jimjams, Jumpy, Keen, Nerviness, Reck, Restless, Scruple, Separation, Solicitous, Stewing, Stress, Suspense, Sweat, Tension, Toey, Trepidation, Twitchy, Unease, Unquiet, Upset, Uptight, White-knuckle, Worriment

Any Arrow, Ary, Some

Anybody, Anyone Everyman, One, Whoso, You

Anyhow, Anyway Anyroad(s), However, Leastways, Regardless

Anything Aught, Diddly-squat, Ought, Owt, Whatnot

▹ **Anyway** *may indicate* an anagram

Apache Arizona, AZ

Apart Aloof, Aside, Asunder, Atwain, Beside, Separate

Apartheid Racism, Verkrampte

Apartment Atrium, Ben, Condominium, Digs, Duplex, Efficiency, Flat, Insula, Mansion, Pad, Paradise, Penthouse, Pied-a-terre, Quarters, Room, Simplex, Solitude, Suite, Tenement, Unit, Walk-up

Apathetic, Apathy Accidie, Acedia, Incurious, Indifferent, Languid, Lethargic, Listless, Lobotomized, Lukewarm, Pococurante, Stoical, Torpid, Unenthusiastic

Ape(-like), Apeman Anthropoid, Barbary, Big-foot, Bonobo, Catarrhine, Copy, Dryopithecine, Gelada, Gibbon, Gorilla, → **IMITATE**, Magot, Mimic, → **MONKEY**, Orang, Paranthropus, Parrot, Pithecoid, Pongo, → **PRIMATE**, Proconsul, Sacred, Simian, Simulate, Yowie

Aperient Cascara, Laxative, Senna

Aperitif → **DRINK**, Pernod®

Aperture Balistraria, Chink, Fenestella, Hole, Keyhole, Opening, Orifice, Osculum, Peephole, Pinhole, Porta, Relative, Spiracle, Swallow, Window

Apex Acme, Culmen, Gonion, Keystone, Knoll, Knowe, Solar, Summit, Vortex

Aphid Ant-cow, Phylloxera

Aphorism Adage, Epigram, Gnome, Pensée, Proverb, Sutra

Aphrodisiac, Aphrodite Cytherean, Erotic, Idalian, Paphian, Philter, Philtre, Spanish fly, Urania, Yohimbine

Aplomb Assurance, Cool, Equanimity, Poise, Sangfroid, Serenity

Apocryphal Spurious, Tobit

Apograph Roneo®

Apollo Belvedere, Pythian, Sun

Apologetic, Apology Ashamed, Excuse, Justifier, Mockery, Oops, Pardon, Scuse, Sir-reverence

Apostate Citer, → **HERETIC**, Pervert, Rat, Recreant, Renegade, Runagate, Turncoat

Apostle, Apostolic Cuthbert, → **DISCIPLE**, Evangelist, Johannine, Jude, Matthew, Pauline, Spoon, Thad(d)eus, Twelve

Apostrophe, Apostrophise Elision, O(h), Soliloquy, Tuism

Apothecary Chemist, Dispenser, Druggist, LSA, Pharmacist, Pottinger

Apothegm Dictum, Maxim, Motto

Appal(ling) Abysmal, Affear(e), Aghast, Dire, Dismay, Egregious, Frighten, Horrify, Piacular, Shock, Tragic

▹ **Appallingly** *may indicate* an anagram

Apparatus Absorptiometer, Alembic, Alkalimeter, Appliance, Aqualung, Aspirator,

Autoclave, Breeches buoy, Bridgerama, Caisson, Calorimeter, Chemostat, Churn,
Clinostat, Codec, Coherer, Colorimeter, Commutator, Condenser, Converter,
Convertor, Cosmotron, Critical, Cryostat, Davis, Decoy, Defibrillator, Desiccator,
→ **DEVICE**, Digester, Ebullioscope, Effusiometer, Egg, Electrograph, Electrophorus,
Electroscope, Elutriator, Enlarger, Eprouvette, Equipment, Eudiometer, Exciter,
Fixings, Gadget, Gasogene, Gazogene, Generator, Giant('s) stride, Golgi, Graith,
Gyroscope, Heater, Heliograph, Helioscope, Hemocytometer, Hodoscope,
Holophote, Horse, Hydrophone, Hygrostat, Incubator, Inhalator, Injector,
Inspirator, Installation, Instrument, Iron lung, Jacquard, Kipp's, Kymograph,
Langmuir-trough, Lease-rod, Life-preserver, Loom, Masora(h), Microreader,
Mimeograph, Mine-detector, Multi-gym, Nephoscope, Nitrometer, Oscillator,
Oscillograph, Oxygenator, Pasteuriser, Percolator, Phonometer, Photophone,
Photostat®, Phytotron, Plate-warmer, Plethysmograph, Plumber's snake,
Potometer, Projector, Proto®, Pulmotor®, Radiator, Radiosonde, Rattletrap,
Rectifier, Replenisher, Resistor, Respirator, Respirometer, Resuscitator, Retort,
Rotisserie, Rounce, Scintiscanner, Scrubber, Scuba, Seeder, Semaphore, Set,
Skimmer, Slide rest, Smoker, Snorkel, Snowbox, Soundboard, Sphygmograph,
Spirophore, Starter, Stellarator, Steriliser, Still, Substage, Switchgear, Tackle,
Tackling, Talk-you-down, Telecine, Teleprinter, Teleseme, Tellurian, Thermopile,
Tokamak, Transformer, Transmitter, Tribometer, Tromp(e), Tuner, Ventouse,
Wheatstone's bridge, Whip-and-derry, ZETA

Apparel Attire, Besee, → **COSTUME**, Garb, Raiment, Wardrobe, Wardrop

▷ **Apparent** *may indicate* a hidden word

Apparent(ly) Ap, Clear, Detectable, Manifest, Ostensible, Outward, Overt, Plain,
Prima facie, Seeming, Semblance, Visible

Apparition Dream, Eidolon, Fetch, Ghost, → **ILLUSION**, Phantom, Shade, Spectre,
Vision, Visitant, Wraith

Appeal(ing) Ad, Beg, Cachet, Catchpenny, Charisma, Charm, Cri de coeur, Cry,
Entreat, Entreaty, Epirrhema, Eye-catching, Fetching, Howzat, Invocation, It,
Miserere, O, Oomph, Plead, SA, Screeve, Sex(iness), Solicit, SOS, Suit

Appear(ance) Advent, Air, Apport, Arise, Arrival, Aspect, Broo, Brow, Burst, Cast,
Colour, Compear, Debut, Effeir, Effere, Emerge, Enter, Exterior, Eye, Facade,
Facies, Far(r)and, Farrant, Fa(s)cia, Feature, Format, Garb, Guise, Habitus, Hue,
Image, Kithe, Kythe, Looks, Loom, Manifestation, → **MANNER**, Mien, Occur,
Ostensibly, Ostent, Outward, Person, Phase, Phenomenon, Physiognomy,
Presence, Prosopon, Represent, Rig, Rise, Seem, Semblance, Show, Species,
Spring, Superficies, Theophany, View, Visitation, Wraith

Appease(ment) Allay, Alleviate, Calm, Conciliation, Danegeld, Mitigate,
→ **MOLLIFY**, Munichism, Pacify, Placate, Propitiate, Satisfy, Soothe, Sop

Append(age) Adjunct, Affix, Aglet, Allantois, Annex, Antennule, Aril, Arista,
Cercus, Chelicera, Codpiece, Ctene, Fang, Flagellum, Hanger-on, Lobe, Lug,
Palp(us), Paraglossa, Parapodium, Pedipalp, Pendicle, Postfix, Stipel, Stipule,
Suffix, Swimmeret, Tail, Tailpiece, Tentacle, Ugly, Uropod, Uvula

Appendix Addendum, Apocrypha, Codicil, Grumbling, Label, Pendant, Pendent,
Rider, Schedule, Vermiform

Appetite, Appetitive, Appetise(r), Appetize(r) Amuse-bouche, Amuse-gueule,
Antepast, Antipasto, Aperitif, Appestat, Bhagee, Bhajee, Bulimia, Bulimy, Canapé,
Concupiscence, Concupy, Crudités, Desire, Dim-sum, Entremes(se), Entremets,
Flesh, Hunger, Limosis, Malacia, Meze, Mezze, Nacho, Orectic, Orexis, Passion,
Pica, Polyphagia, Relish, Tapa(s), Titillate, Twist, Ventripotent, Yerd-hunger,
Yird-hunger

Applaud, Applause Acclaim, Bravo, → **CHEER**, Clap, Claque, Eclat, Encore, Extol, Hum, Kentish fire, Olé, Ovation, Praise, Root, Ruff, Tribute

Apple Adam's, Alligator, Bad, Baldwin, Balsam, Biffin, Blenheim orange, Braeburn, Bramley, Cashew, Charlotte, Codlin(g), Cooker, Costard, Crab, Custard, Dead Sea, Discord, Eater, Granny Smith, Greening, Jenneting, John, Jonathan, Kangaroo, Leather-coat, Love, Mammee, May, McIntosh (red), Medlar, Nonpareil, Oak, Pacific Rose, Pearmain, Pippin, Pomace, Pome(roy), Pom(e)water, Pomroy, Potato, Punic, Pupil, Pyrus, Quarantine, Quarenden, Quar(r)ender, Quarrington, Queening, Quodlin, Redstreak, Reinette, Rennet, Ribston(e), Ripstone, Rotten, Royal gala, Ruddock, Russet, Seek-no-further, Snow, Sops-in-wine, Sorb, Sturmer, Sturmer (Pippin), Sugar, Sweeting, Thorn, Toffee, Windfall, Winesap

Apple juice Malic

Apple-picker Atalanta

Applicant Ordinand, Postulant

Application, Applicable, Apply, Appliance(s) Address, Adhibit, Appeal, Appose, Assiduity, Barrage, Blender, Devote, Diligence, Dressing, Exercise, Foment, Give, Implement, Inlay, Juicer, Lay, Liquidiser, Lotion, Mixer, Ointment, Opodeldoc, Pertinent, Petition, Plaster, Poultice, Put, Request, Resort, Respirator, Rub, Sinapism, Stupe, Talon, Toggle, Truss, → **USE**, Vice, White goods

Appliqué Hawaiian

Appoint(ee), Appointment Advowson, Assign, Berth, Date, Delegate, Depute, Designate, Dew, Due, Executor, Induction, Installation, Make, Name, → **NOMINATE**, Nominee, Office, Ordain, Position, Post, Posting, Rendezvous, Room, Set, Tryst

▷ **Appointed** *may indicate* an anagram

Apportion(ment) Allocate, Allot, Mete, Parcel, Ration, Share, Weigh

Apposite Apt, Cogent, Germane, Pat, Pertinent, Relevant, Suitable

Appraise, Appraisal Analyse, → **EVALUATE**, Gauge, Guesstimate, Judge, Once-over, Tape, → **VALUE**, Vet

Appreciate, Appreciation Acknowledgement, Cherish, Clap, Dig, Endear, Esteem, Gratefulness, Increase, Phwoar, Prize, Realise, Recognise, Regard, Relish, Rise, Sense, Stock, Taste, Thank you, Treasure, → **VALUE**

Apprehend, Apprehension Afears, Alarm, Arrest, → **CATCH**, Collar, Fear, Grasp, Insight, Intuit, Perceive, Quailing, See, Suspense, Take, Toey, Trepidation, Uh-oh, Unease, Uptake

Apprehensive Jumpy, Nervous, Uneasy

Apprentice(ship) Article, Commis, Cub, Devil, Garzone, Improver, Indent(ure), Jockey, L, Learner, Lehrjahre, Novice, Noviciate, Novitiate, Printer's devil, Pupillage, Snob, Tiro, Trainee, Turnover, Tyro(ne)

Approach(ing), Approachable Abord, Access, Accost, Advance, Affable, Anear, Appropinquate, Appulse, Avenue, Close, Coast, Come, Converge, Cost(e), Draw nigh, Drive, Driveway, Fairway, Feeler, Gate, Imminent, Line, Near, Nie, Overture, Pitch, Procedure, Road, Run-in, Run-up, Stealth, Towards, Verge, Warm

Appropriate(ly) Abduct, Abstract, Annex, Apposite, Apt, Aright, Asport, Assign, Bag, Borrow, Collar, Commandeer, Commensurate, Confiscate, Convenient, Due, Embezzle, Expedient, Fit, Germane, Good, Happy, Hijack, Hog, Impound, Jump, Just, Meet, Nick, Pertinent, Pilfer, Plagiarise, Pocket, Pre-empt, Proper, Purloin, Right, Seise, Seize, Sequester, Sink, Snaffle, Steal, Suit, Swipe, Take, Timely, Trouser, Usurp

Approval, Approve(d), Approbation Accolade, Adopt, Allow, Amen, Applaud, Attaboy, Aye, Blessing, Bravo, Brownie points, Change, → **COUNTENANCE**, Credit,

Cushty, Dig, Endorse, Favour, Hear hear, Homologate, Hubba-hubba, Imprimatur, Initial, Kitemark, Know, Laud, Nod, Okay, Olé, Orthodox, Plaudit, Rah, Ratify, Right-on, Rubber-stamp, Sanction, Stotter, Thumbs-up, Tick, Tribute, Yay, Yes, Zindabad

Approximate(ly), Approximation Almost, Ballpark, Circa, Close, Coarse, Estimate, Guess, Imprecise, Near, Roughly

Apricot Mebos

April, April fool Apr, Huntiegowk, Hunt-the-gowk

Apron Airside, Barm-cloth, Bib, Blacktop, Brat, Bunt, Canvas, Dick(e)y, Ephod, Fig-leaf, Gremial, Ice, Napron, Pinafore, Pinner, Pinny, Placket, Stage, Tablier, Tier, Waist

Apse Concha, Exedra, Niche, Recess, Tribune

Apt(ly) Apposite, Appropriate, Apropos, Ben trovato, Capable, Evincive, Fit, Gleg, Happy, Liable, Pat, Prone, Suitable, Tends

Aptitude Ability, Bent, Faculty, Flair, Gift, Knack, Skill, Talent, Tendency, Viability

Aqua(tic) Euglena, Flustra, Lentic, Lotic, Regia, Zizania

Aqualung Rebreather, Scuba

Aquamarine Madagascar

Aqueduct Canal, Channel, Conduit, Hadrome, Xylem

Arab(ian), Arabia, Arabic Abdul, Adeni, Algorism, Ali, Baathist, Bahraini, Bahrein, Bedouin, Druse, Druz(e), Effendi, Fedayee(n), Gamin, Geber, Hashemite, Hassaniya, Himyarite, Horse, Iraqi, Jawi, Lawrence, Moor, Mudlark, Nabat(a)ean, Nas(s)eem, Nes(h)ki, Omani, Omar, PLO, Qatari, Rag(head), Saba, Sab(a)ean, Saracen, Saudi, Semitic, Sheikh, Street, Syrian, UAR, Urchin, Yemen

Arabis Cress

Arachnid Mite, Podogona, Ricinulei, → **SPIDER**

Arbitrary Despotic, Haphazard, Peculiar, Random, Wanton

Arbitrate, Arbitration, Arbitrator, Arbiter ACAS, Censor, Daysman, Judge, Negotiator, Ombudsman, Pendulum, Prud'homme, Ref(eree), Umpire

Arboreal, Arbour Bower, Dendroid, Pergola, Trellis

Arc Azimuth, Bow, Carbon, → **CURVE**, Flashover, Fogbow, Halo, Hance, Haunch, Island, Limb, Mercury, Octant, Quadrant, Rainbow, Reflex, Seadog, Trajectory, White rainbow

Arcade Amusement, Burlington, Cloister, Gallery, Loggia, Mall, Penny, Triforium

Arcadia(n) Idyllic, Nemoral, Sylvan

Arcane Esoteric, Mystic, Obscure, Occult, Orphism, Recherché, Rune, Secret

Arch(ed), Arching Acute, Admiralty, Alveolar, Arblaster, Arcade, Arcature, Archivolt, Arcuate, Camber, Chief, Coom, Counterfort, Crafty, Cross-rib, Crown-green, Ctesiphon, → **CUNNING**, Curve, Discharging, Elfin, Embow, Espiegle, Fallen, Flying buttress, Fog-bow, Fornicate, Fornix, Gill, Gothic, Hance, Haunch, Hog, Horseshoe, Instep, Intrados, Inverted, Keel, Keystone, Lancet, Leery, Lierne, Limb-girdle, Marble, Neural, Norman, Ogee, Ogive, Opistholomos, Order, Parthian, Pectoral, Pelvic, Pointed, Portal, Proscenium, Recessed, Relieving, Roach, Roguish, Roman, Safety, Saucy, Segmental, Shouldered, Skew, Sly, Soffit, Span, Squinch, Stilted, Trajan, Triumphal, Vault, Zygoma

Archaeological, Archaeologist Carter, Dater, Dig, Evans, Industrial, Layard, Leakey, Mycenae, Petrie, Pothunter, Sutton Hoo, Wheeler, Woolley

Archangel Azrael, Gabriel, Israfeel, Israfel, Israfil, Jerahmeel, Michael, Raguel, Raphael, Sariel, Satan, Uriel, Yellow

Arch-binder Voussoir

Archbishop Anselm, Augustine, Cosmo, Cranmer, Davidson, Dunstan, Ebor,

Elector, Hatto, Lanfranc, Lang, Langton, Laud, Metropolitan, Morton, Primate, Temple, Trench, Tutu, Whitgift

Archdeacon Rev, Ven

Archduke Trio

Archer(y) Acestes, Bow-boy, → **BOWMAN**, Cupid, Eros, Hood, Petticoat, Philoctetes, Sagittary, Tell, Toxophilite

Archetype Avatar, Form, Model, Pattern

Archibald, Archie, Archy Ack-ack, Cockroach, Oerlikon, Rice, Roach

Archilochian Epode

Archimandrite Eutyches

Archimedes Screw

Archipelago Alexander, Antarctic, Azores, Bismarck, Camaguey, Dhivehi, East Indian, Fiji, Franz Josef Land, Gulag, Japan, Kerguelen, Malay, Maldives, Marquesas, Mergui, Novaya Zemlya, Palmer, Paumotu, St Pierre and Miquelon, Severnaya Zemlya, Spitsbergen, Sulu, Svalbard, Tierra del Fuego, Tonga, Tuamoto, West Indies

Architect(ure), Architectural Arcology, Baroque, Bauhaus, Bricolage, Brutalism, Byzantine, Churrigueresque, Community, Composite, Computer, Corinthian, Creator, Data-flow, Decorated, Decorated style, Designer, Domestic, Doric, Early English, Elizabethan, Entablature, Federation, Flamboyant, Georgian, Gothic, Greek Revival, Ionic, Italian, Jacobean, Landscape, Listed, Lombard, Mission, Moderne, Moorish, Moresque, Mudejar, Naval, Neoclassical, Neo-gothic, Norman, Palladian, Pelasgian, Perpendicular, Planner, Plateresque, Prostyle, Queen Anne, Romanesque, Saracenic, Saxon, Spandrel, Spandril, Tectonic, Tudor, Tudorbethan, Tuscan, Vitruvian

---

ARCHITECTS

4 letters:	Utzon	Lutyens	**10 letters:**
Adam	Wyatt	Venturi	Inigo Jones
Kent		Vignola	Mackintosh
Loos	**6 letters:**		Trophonius
Nash	Casson	**8 letters:**	Van der Rohe
Shaw	Foster	Bramante	
Webb	Nissen	Palladio	**11 letters:**
Wood	Repton	Piranesi	Abercrombie
Wren	Spence	Saarinen	Butterfield
	Street	Vanbrugh	Le Corbusier
5 letters:	Wright		
Gaudi		**9 letters:**	**12 letters:**
Inigo	**7 letters:**	Hawksmoor	Brunelleschi
Nervi	Behrens	Macquarie	
Pugin	Bernini	Vitruvius	**14 letters:**
Scott	Columbo		Vitruvius Pollo
Soane	Gropius		

Architrave Epistyle, Platband

Archive(s) Backfile, Morgue, Muniment, PRO, Records, Register

Archon Draco

Arch-villain Ringleader

Arctic Estotiland, Frigid, Hyperborean, In(n)uit, Inupiat, Polar, Tundra

Ardent, Ardour Aflame, Aglow, Boil, Broiling, Burning, Fervent, Fervid, Fiery, Fire, Flagrant, Heat, Het, → **HOT**, Hot-brained, In, Mettled, Mettlesome, Passion(ate), Perfervid, Rage, Spiritous, Vehement, Warm-blooded, Zealous, Zeloso

Arduous Laborious, Uphill

Are A, Exist, 're

Area Acre, Aleolar, Apron, Arctogaea, Are, Assisted, Bailiwick, Belt, Bovate, Broca's, Built-up, Carucate, Catchment, Centare, Centiare, Centre, Conurbation, Courtyard, Craton, Curtilage, Dec(i)are, Dedans, Depressed, Dessiatine, Development, Disaster, District, Docklands, Domain, Downtown, Endemic, Eruv, Extent, Farthingland, Forecourt, Gau, Goal, Grey, Growth, Heartland, Hectare, Henge, Hide, Hinterland, Husbandland, Imperium, Input, Karst, Landmass, Lathe, Latitude, Lek, Locality, Lodg(e)ment, Manor, Metroplex, Milieu, Mofussil, Morgen, Mush, Neogaea, No-go, No-man's-land, Notogaea, Orb, Oxgang, Oxgate, Oxland, Parish, Patch, Penalty, Place, Pleasance, Plot, Precinct, Province, Purlieu, Quad, Quadrat, Quarter, Range, Redevelopment, Refugium, → **REGION**, Renosterveld, Reserve, Rest, Restricted, Retrochoir, Rood, Rule, Sector, Service, Shire, Site, Slurb, Special, Staging, Sterling, Subtopia, Support, Surface, Target, Technical, Terrain, Territory, Theatre, Tie, Tract, Tundra, Tye, Urban, Ure, White, Work station, Yard, Zone

Arena Battleground, Circus, Cockpit, Dohyo, Field, Lists, Maidan, Olympia, → **RING**, Rink, Snowdome, Stadium, Tiltyard, Velodrome, Venue

Argal Ergo

Argent Ag, Silver

Argentina RA

Argon Ar

Argonaut Acastus, Jason, Lynceus, Meleager, Nautilus, Paper-sailor

Argot Flash, Idiom, Jargon, Lingo, Scamto, Shelta

Argue, Argument(ative) Altercation, Antistrophon, Argie-bargie, Argle-bargle, Argy-bargy, Bandy, Beef, Blue, Brush, Cangle, Case, Casuism, Choplogic, Conflict, Contend, Contest, Contra, Cosmological, Debate, Deprecate, Diallage, Difference, Dilemma, Ding-dong, Dispute, Dissent, Elenchus, Elenctic, Enthymeme, Eristic, Exchange, Expostulate, Forensic, Free-for-all, Generalisation, Hysteron proteron, Logic, Logomachy, Moot, Ob and soller, Object, Ontological, Paralogism, Patter, Pettifog, Plead, Polemic, Polylemma, Premiss, Propound, Quarrel, Quibble, Quodlibet, Rammy, Ratiocinate, → **REASON**, Remonstrate, Row, Run-in, Sophism, Sophistry, Sorites, Spar, Stickle, Straw man, Stroppy, Summation, Syllogism, Teleological, Theme, Thetic, Third man, Tiff, Transcendental, Trilemma, Wrangle, Yike

Argyle Argathelian, Gravy-boat, Sock

Aria Ballad, Cabaletta, Cantata, Melody, Song

Arid Dry, Parched

Ariel Pen

Arise Appear, Be, Develop, Emanate, Emerge, Upgo, Wax

Aristocracy, Aristocrat(ic) Blood, Boyar, Buckeen, Classy, Debrett, Duc, Elite, Eupatrid, Gentle, Gentry, Grandee, High-hat, Junker, Nob, Noble, Optimate, Passage, Patrician, Thane, Toff, Tony, U-men, Upper-crust, Well-born

Aristotle Peripatetic, Stagirite, Stagyrite

Arithmetic(ian) Algorism, Algorith, Arsmetrick, Cocker, Euclid, Logistic, Modular, Sums

Ark(wright) Chest, Noah

Arly Thicket

▷ **Arm** *may indicate* an army regiment, etc.

Arm(ed), Arms Akimbo, Arsenal, Bearing, Brachial, Branch, Bundooks, Canting, Cove, Crest, Cross bow, Embattle, Equip, Escutcheon, Estoc, Fin, Firth, Frith, Gnomon, Halbert, Hatchment, Heel, Heraldic, Inlet, Jib, Krupp, Limb, Loch, Long, Member, Olecranon, Pick-up, Quillon, Radius, Rail, Ramous, Rocker, Rotor, SAA, Secular, Shield, Shotgun, Side, Small, Smooth-bore, Spiral, Tappet, Tentacle, Timer, Tone, Tooled-up, Transept, Tremolo, Ulnar, → **WEAPON**, Whip

Armada Spanish

Armadillo Dasypod, Dasypus, Fairy, Giant, Pangolin, Peba, Pichiciago, Tatou(ay), Xenurus

Armature Keeper, Shuttle

Armenian Haikh, Yezedi

Armistice Still-stand, Truce

Armless Inermous

Armour(ed) Ailette, Armature, Armet, Barbette, Beaver, Besagew, Bevor, Brasset, Breastplate, Brigandine, Buckler, Byrnie, Camail, Cannon, Casspir, Cataphract, Chaffron, Chain, Chamfrain, Chamfron, Character, Chausses, Corium, Cors(e) let, Couter, Cuirass, Cuish, Cuisse, Culet, Curat, Curiet, Cush, Defence, Fauld, Garniture, Gear, Genouillère, Gere, Gorget, Greave, Habergeon, Hauberk, Hoplology, Jack, Jambeau, Jazerant, Jesserant, Lamboys, Loricate, Mail, Male, Mentonnière, Nasal, Nosepiece, Palette, Panoply, Panzer, Pauldron, Petta, Placcat, Placket, Plastron, Plate, Poitrel, Poleyn, Pouldron, Rerebrace, Sabaton, Scale, Secret, → **SHIELD**, Solleret, Spaudler, Splint, Stand, Tace, Tank, Taslet, Tasse(t), Thorax, Tonlet, Tuille, Vambrace, Vantbrass, Ventail, Visor, Voider, Weed

Armpit Axilla, Oxter

Armstrong Louis, Satchmo

Army Arrière-ban, BEF, Blue Ribbon, Church, Colours, Confederate, Crowd, Federal, Field, Fyrd, Golden (Horde), Horde, Host, IRA, Junior Service, Land, Landwehr, Lashkar, Legion, Line, Military, Militia, Mobile Command, Multitude, New Model, Para-military, Red, SA, Sabaoth, Salvation, SAS, Sena, Service, Soldiers, Standing, Swarm, TA, Territorial, Thin red line, Volunteer, War, Wehrmacht

▷ **Army** *may indicate* having arms

Aroma(tic) Allspice, Aniseed, Aryl, Balmy, Coriander, Fenugreek, Fragrant, Nose, Odorous, Pomander, Spicy, Stilbene, Vanillin, Wintergreen

Around About, Ambient, Circa, Near, Peri-, Skirt, Tour

▷ **Around** *may indicate* one word around another

Arouse, Arousal Alarm, → **EXCITE**, Fan, Fire, Incite, Inflame, Must(h), Needle, Provoke, Stimulate, Stole, Suscitate, Touch up, Urolagnia, Waken, Whet

▷ **Arrange** *may indicate* an anagram

Arrange(r), Arrangement Adjust, Array, Attune, Ausgleich, Bandobast, Bank, Bundobust, Concert, Concinnity, Configuration, Design, Display, Dispose, Do, Edit, Engineer, Finger, Fix, Foreordain, Format, Formation, Formwork, Grade, Ikebana, Layout, Marshal, Modus vivendi, Neaten, Orchestrate, Orchestration, Ordain, → **ORDER**, Ordnance, Organise, Pack, Pattern, Perm, Permutation, Plan, Position, Prepare, Prepense, Quincunx, Redactor, Regulate, Run, Rustle up, Schedule, Schema, Scheme, Score, Set, Settle, Sort, Spacing, Stack, Stage-manage, Stereoisomerism, Stow, Straighten, Style, System, Tabulate, Tactic, Taxis, Tidy, Transcribe, Vertical

Arras Tapestry

Array(ed) Attire, Bedight, Deck, Herse, Logic, Marshal, Muster, Panoply, Phased, Seismic

Arrear(s) Aft, Ahint, Backlog, Behind, Debt, Owing

Arrest(ed), Arresting Abort, Alguacil, Alguazil, Ament, Apprehend, Attach, Attract, Blin, Book, Bust, Caption, Capture, Cardiac, Catch, Check, Citizen's, Collar, Detain, False, Furthcoming, Hold, House, Knock, Lag, Lift, Lightning, Nab, Nail, Nick, Nip, Nobble, Pinch, Pull, Restrain, Retard, Riveting, Round-up, Run-in, Salient, Sease, Seize, Snaffle, Stasis, Stop, Sus(s)

Arris Groin

Arrival, Arrive, Arriving Accede, Advent, Attain, Come, Entrance, Get, Happen, Hit, Inbound, Influx, Johnny-come-lately, Land, Latecomer, Natal, Nativity, Newcomer, Pitch up, Reach, Roll up, Show, Strike

Arrogance, Arrogant Assumption, Bold, Bravado, Bumptious, Cavalier, Cocksure, Cocky, Contemptuous, Disdain, Dogmatic, Effrontery, Haughty, Haut(eur), High, High and mighty, High-handed, High-hat, Hogen-mogen, Hoity-toity, Hubris, Imperious, Jumped up, Lordly, Morgue, Overweening, Presumption, Pretentious, Proud, Proud-stomached, Side, Snobbish, Stuck-up, Surquedry, Surquedy, Toploftical, Topping, Turkeycock, Uppish, Uppity, Upstart

Arrogate Appropriate, Assume, Claim, Impute, Usurp

Arrow, Arrow-head Acestes, Any, Ary, Blunt, Bolt, Broad(head), Cloth-yard shaft, Dart, Dogbolt, Filter, Flechette, Flight, Missile, Pheon, Pointer, Quarrel, Reed, Sagittate, Shaft, Sheaf, Straight

Arrowroot Kuzu, Maranta, Pia

Arsenal Ammo, Armo(u)ry, Depot, Fire-arms, Magazine, Side, Toulon

Arsenate, Arsenic(al), Arsenide As, Erythrite, Realgar, Resalgar, Rosaker, Salvarsan, Scorodite, Skutterudite, Smaltite, Speiss, Zarnich

Arson(ist) Firebug, Pyromania

▷ **Art** *may indicate* an -est ending

Art(s), Arty, Art movement, Art school, Art style Abstract, Alla prima, Applied, Ars, Arte Povera, Bauhaus, Bloomsbury, Bonsai, Britart, Brut, Chiaroscuro, Clair-obscure, Clare-obscure, Clip, Cobra, Collage, Commercial, Conceptual, Constructivism, Contrapposto, Craft, Cubism, Culture vulture, Cunning, Curious, Dada, Daedal(e), Deco, Decorative, Dedal, De Stijl, Die Brucke, Diptych, Divisionism, Earth, Ekphrasis, Environmental, Es, Expressionism, Fauvism, Feat, Fine, Finesse, Flemish, Folk, Fugue, Futurism, Genre, Graphic, Guile, Impressionist, Jugendstil, Kakemono, Kano, Ka pai, Kinetic, Kirigami, Kitsch, Knack, Lacquerware, Liberal, Mandorla, Mannerism, Martial, Masterwork, Mehindi, Minimal, Modern(e), Montage, Motivated, Music, Mystery, Nabis, Nazarene, Neoclassical, Neo-impressionism, New Wave, Noli-me-tangere, Norwich, Nouveau, Optical, Origami, Orphic Cubism, Orphism, Outsider, Pastiche, Performance, Performing, Perigordian, Plastic, Pointillism, Pop, Postimpressionism, Postmodern, Practical, Pre-Raphaelite, Primitive, Psychedelic, Public, Purism, Quadratura, Quadrivium, Relievo, Sienese, → SKILL, Social realism, Still-life, Suprematism, Surrealism, Synchronism, Tachism(e), Tatum, Tenebrism, Toreutics, Trecento, Triptych, Trivium, Trompe l'oeil, Trouvé, Tsutsumu, Useful, Verism, Virtu, Visual, Vorticism

▷ **Artefact** *may indicate* an anagram

Artefact(s) Neolith, Palaeolith, Tartanalia, Tartanry, Xoanon

Artemis Selene

Artemus Ward

Artery Aorta, Brachial, Carotid, Coronary, Duct, Femoral, Frontal, Iliac, Innominate, M_1, Maxillary, Phrenic, Pulmonary, Radial, Route, Spermatic, Temporal

Artful Cute, Dodger, Foxy, Ingenious, Quirky, Shifty, Sly, Subtle, Wily, Tactician

Arthropod Limulus, Peripatus, Prototracheata, Tardigrade, Trilobite, Water-bear

Artichoke Cardoon, Jerusalem

Article(s) A, An, Apprentice, Clause, Column, Commodity, Cutting, Definite, Feature, Feuilleton, Five, Gadget, Indefinite, Indenture, Item, Leader, Leading, Op-ed, Paper, Piece, Pot-boiler, Shipping, Sidebar, Specify, The, Thing, Thinkpiece, Thirty-nine, Treatise, Ware

Articulation, Articulate(d) Clear, Coherent, Coudé, Diarthrosis, Distinct, Eloquent, Enounce, Express, Fluent, Fortis, Gimmal, Gomphosis, Hinged, Intonate, Jointed, Jymold, Lenis, Limbed, Lisp, Pretty-spoken, Pronounce, Schindylesis, Tipping, Trapezial, Utter, Vertebrae, Voice

Artifice(r), Artificial Bogus, Chouse, Contrived, Davenport-trick, Dodge, Ersatz, Factitious, Finesse, Guile, Hoax, In vitro, Logodaedaly, Man-made, Mannered, Opificer, Postiche, Pretence, Prosthetic, Pseudo, Reach, Ruse, Sell, Set, Sham, Spurious, Stratagem, → **STRATEGY**, Synthetic, Theatric, → **TRICK**, Unnatural, Wile, Wright

Artificial respiration Kiss of life, Schafer's method

Artillery Battery, Cannon, Field, Fougade, Fougasse, Guns, Mortar, Ordnance, Pyroballogy, RA, Rafale, Ramose, Ramus, Train

Artiodactyl Camel, Chevrotain, Deerlet

Artisan Craftsman, Decorator, Joiner, Journeyman, Mechanic, Peon, Pioneer, Pioner, Pyoner, Shipwright, Workman

Artist(e), Artistic Animator, Blaue Reiter, Bohemian, Cartoonist, Colourist, Cubist, Dadaist, Daedal(e), Deccie, Decorator, Die Brucke, Etcher, Fauve, Fine, Foley, Gentle, Gilder, Graffiti, ICA, Impressionist, Landscapist, Left Bank, Limner, Linear, Maestro, Master, Mime, Miniaturist, → **MUSICIAN**, Nabis, Nazarene, Oeuvre, Orphism, → **PAINTER**, Pavement, Paysagist, Perspectivist, Piss, Plein-airist, Pre-Raphaelite, Primitive, Quick-change, RA, Romantic, Screever, → **SCULPTOR**, Sideman, Sien(n)ese, Tachisme, Tap dancer, Touch, Trapeze, Trecentist, Virtuose, Virtuoso

ARTISTS

3 letters:	Phiz	Leech	*6 letters:*
Arp		Léger	Boudin
Cox	*5 letters:*	Lippi	Braque
Rap	Aiken	Lotto	Brucke
	Appel	Lowry	Calder
4 letters:	Bacon	Makar	Callot
Cuyp	Bakst	Manet	Claude
Dadd	Bosch	Monet	Clouet
Dali	Corot	Munch	Derain
Doré	Crome	Orpen	D'Orsay
Dufy	Degas	Redon	Escher
Emin	Dulac	Riley	Fuseli
Etty	Dürer	Rodin	Gilles
Goya	Ensor	Seago	Giotto
Hals	Ernst	Steen	Greuze
John	Gelée	Steer	Guardi
Klee	Hirst	Tatum	Haydon
Lely	Hoare	Watts	Ingres
Miró	Hooch		Knight
Opie	Klimt		Le Nain

Millet	El Greco	Watteau	Gericault
Moreau	Epstein	Zeuxian	Giorgione
Renoir	Gauguin	Zoffany	Grunewald
Ribera	Hobbema		Hiroshige
Rivera	Hockney	**8 letters:**	Kandinsky
Romney	Hogarth	Barbizon	Le Lorrain
Rothko	Hokusai	Bronzino	Rembrandt
Rubens	Holbein	Daubigny	Velasquez
Sendak	Hoppner	Eastlake	
Seurat	Kneller	Kirchner	**10 letters:**
Signac	Lepicie	Landseer	Alma-Tadema
Sisley	Matisse	Leonardo	Botticelli
Stubbs	Millais	Magritte	Burne-Jones
Tissot	Morisot	Mantegna	Guillaumin
Titian	Morland	Masaccio	Madox Brown
Turner	Murillo	Mondrian	Modigliani
Warhol	Nattier	Nevinson	Rowlandson
Zeuxis	Picasso	Perugino	Signorelli
	Pissaro	Piranesi	Sutherland
7 letters:	Poussin	Reynolds	Tintoretto
Apelles	Prudhon	Rousseau	Van der Goes
Audubon	Raeburn	Topolski	Waterhouse
Bellini	Raphael	Veronese	
Bernini	Rouault	Whistler	**12 letters:**
Bonnard	Sargent		Gainsborough
Boucher	Sickert	**9 letters:**	Lichtenstein
Cézanne	Spencer	Beardsley	Michelangelo
Chagall	Tiepolo	Bonington	Winterhalter
Chardin	Uccello	Canaletto	
Cimabue	Utamaro	Carpaccio	**14 letters:**
Collier	Utrillo	Constable	Jackson Pollock
Courbet	Van Dyke	Correggio	
Cranach	Van Eyck	Delacroix	**15 letters:**
Da Vinci	Van Gogh	Donatello	Hieronymus Bosch
Duchamp	Vermeer	Fragonard	Toulouse-Lautrec

Artless Candid, Homespun, Ingenuous, Innocent, Naive, Open, Seely, Simple

Art nouveau Jugendstil

Arturo Toscanini

Arum Acorus, Green-dragon, Lily, Taro

As Aesir, Als, Arsenic, Coin, Eg, Forasmuch, Kame, Qua, Ridge, 's, Since, So, Thus, Ut, While

As above US, Ut supra

Asafoetida Hing

As before Anew, Ditto, Do, Stet

Asbestos Amiant(h)us, Amosite, Chrysolite, Crocidolite, Earthflax, Fireproof, Rockwood

Ascend(ant), Ascent, Ascension Anabasis, Climb, Dominant, Escalate, Gradient, Lift, Pull, Ramp, Right, Rise, Sclim, Sklim, Slope, Up, Upgang, Uphill, Uprise, Zoom

Ascertain Determine, Discover, → **ESTABLISH**, Prove

Ascetic Agapetae, Anchor(et), Anchorite, Ancress, Ashramite, Austere, Dervish,

Diogenes, Encratite, Eremital, Essene, Fakir, Faquir, Gymnosophist, Hermit, Jain(ite), Monk, Nazarite, Nazirite, Nun's flesh, Sad(d)hu, Simeon Stylites, Stylite, Sufic, Therapeutae, Yogi(n)

Ascidian Chordate, Urochordate

Asclepiad Stapelia

Ascribe Assign, → **ATTRIBUTE**, Blame, Imply, Impute

Asdic Sonar

As far as Quoad

As good as Equal, Tantamount

Ash(es), Ashy Aesc, Aizle, Bone, Breeze, Cinders, Cinereal, Clinker(s), Easle, Embers, Fly, Fraxinas, Kali, Lahar, Pallor, Pearl, Pozz(u)olana, Prickly, Rowan, Ruins, Soda, Sorb, Spodo-, Tephra, Urn, Varec, Volcanic, Wednesday, Weeping, White, Witchen, Yg(g)drasil(l)

Ashamed Abashed, Embarrassed, Hangdog, Mortified, Repentant, Shent

Ashore Aland, Beached, Grounded, Stranded

Ash-pan Backet

Asia(n), Asiatic Afghan, Altaic, Armenian, Azari, Balinese, Bangladeshi, Bengali, Cambodian, Cantonese, Desi, E, Evenki, Ewenki, Gook, Hun, Hyksos, Indian, Indonesian, Jordanian, Karen(ni), Kashmir, Kirghiz, Korean, Kurd, Kyrgyz, Lao, Malay, Medea, Media, Mongol, Naga, Negrito, Nepalese, Phrygian, Pushtu, Samo(y)ed, Shan, Siamese, Sindi, Sogdian, Tamil, Tartar, Tibetan, Tocharian, Tokharian, Turanian, Turk(o)man, Vietnamese

Asia Minor Anatolia, Ionic

Aside Apart, By, Despite, Private, Separate, Shelved, Sotto voce

Asinine Crass, Dull, Idiotic, Puerile, Stupid

Ask Bed, Beg, Beseech, Bid, Cadge, Charge, Demand, Desire, Enquire, Entreat, Evet, Implore, Intreat, Invite, Lobby, Newt, Petition, Pray, Prithee, Pump, Quiz, Request, Require, Rogation, Seek, Solicit, Speer, Speir, Touch

Askance Asconce, Askew, Oblique, Sideways

Askew Agee, Aglee, Agley, Ajee, Aslant, Awry, Crooked, Skivie

Asleep Dormant, Dove, Inactive, Napping

As needed Ad hoc

As often as Toties quoties

Asparagus Asperge, Sparrow-grass, Spear, Sprew, Sprue

Aspect Angle, Bearing, Brow, Face, Facet, Facies, Feature, Look, Mien, Nature, Outlook, Perfective, Perspective, Sextile, Side, → **VIEW**, Visage, Vista

Aspersion, Asperse Calumny, Defame, Innuendo, Libel, Slander, Slur, Smear

Asphalt Bitumen, Blacktop, Gilsonite®, Jew's pitch, Pitch, Pitch Lake, Uinta(h)ite

Aspirant, Aspirate, Aspiration, Aspire Ambition, Breath, Buckeen, Challenger, Desire, Dream, Endeavour, Ettle, Goal, H, Hope(ful), Pretend, Pursue, Rough, Spiritus, Wannabe(e), Would be, Yearn

Ass Buridan's, Burnell, Burro, Cardophagus, Chigetai, Clot, Couscous, Cuddie, Dick(e)y, Donkey, Dziggetai, Funnel, Golden, Hemione, Hemionus, Hinny, Jack, Jenny, Jerusalem pony, Kiang, K(o)ulan, Kourbash, Kourmiss, Kouskous, Kumiss, Kurbash, Kyang, Liripipe, Liripoop, Moke, Neddy, Nitwit, Onager, Quagga, Sesterce, Simp, → **STUPID PERSON**

Assail(ant) Afflict, Assault, Attack, Batter, Bego, Belabour, Bepelt, Beset, Bombard, Harry, Impugn, Onsetter, Oppugn, Pillory, Ply, Revile

Assassin(ate), Assassination Booth, Brave, Bravo, Brutus, Casca, Cassius, Character, Cut-throat, Frag, Gunman, Highbinder, Hitman, Killer, Ninja, Sword, Sworder, Thuggee, Tyrannicide

Assault ABH, Assail, Assay, Attack, Battery, Bombard, GBH, Hamesucken, Head-butt, Indecent, Invasion, Maul, Molest, Mug, Push, → **RAID**, Scalade, Stoor, Storm, Stour, Stowre

Assay Cupel, Examine, Proof, Test, Wet

Assemble(d), Assembly Agora, Audience, Ball, Bottom-hole, Bundestag, Chapter, Chatuaqua, Cho(u)ltry, Church, Co, Collation, → **COLLECTION**, Comitia, Company, Conclave, Concourse, Congeries, Congregate, Congress, Consistory, Constituent, Convene, Conventicle, Convention, Convocation, Convoke, Corroboree, Cortes, Council, Court, Curia, Dail Eireann, Dewain, Diet, Divan, Donnybrook, Ecclesia, Eisteddfod, Erect, Feis(anna), Fit, Folkmoot, Folkmote, Force, Forgather, Fuel, Gather(ing), Gemot(e), General, Gorsedd, Group, Headstock, Hoi polloi, House, Jirga, Kgotla, Knesset, Landtag, Legislative, Lekgotla, Levee, Loya jirga, Majlis, Make, Mass, Meet, → **MEETING**, Mejlis, Moot, Muster, National, Oireachtas, Panegyry, Panoply, Parishad, Parliament, Patron, Pattern, Plenum, Pnyx, Powwow, Prefabrication, Presence, Primary, Quorum, Rally, Rallying-point, Rechate, Recheate, Reichstag, Relie, Repair, Resort, Riksdag, Roll up, Sanghat, Sanhedrin, Sanhedron, Sejm, Senate, Senedd, Skupshtina, Sobranje, Soc, Society, Stort(h)ing, Synagogue, Synedrion, Synod, T(h)ing, Tribunal, Troop, Turn out, Unlawful, Vidhan Sabha, Volksraad, Wapens(c)haw, Wapins(c)haw, Wappens(c)haw, Wardmote, Weapon-s(c)haw, Witan, Witenagemot, Zemstvo

Assent Accede, Acquiesce, Agree, Amen, Aye, Comply, Concur, Jokol, Nod, Placet, Royal, Sanction, Viceregal, Yea, Yield

Assert(ing), Assertion, Assertive Affirm, Allege, Bumptious, Constate, Contend, → **DECLARE**, Forceful, Ipse-dixit, → **MAINTAIN**, Pose, Predicate, Proclaim, Pronounce, Protest, Rumour, Swear (blind), Thetical

Assess(ment) Affeer, Appraise, Audition, Cense, Critique, Eleven-plus, Estimate, Evaluate, Formative, Gauge, Guesstimate, → **JUDGE**, Levy, Means test, Measure, Perspective, Rating, Referee, Risk, Scot and lot, Size up, Special, Stent, Stocktake, Summative, Tax, Value, Weigh

Asset(s) Advantage, Capital, Chargeable, Chattel, Current, Fixed, Floating, Goodwill, Intangible, Inventory, Liquid, Net, Plant, Property, Resource, Talent, Virtue, Wasting

Assiduous Attentive, Busy, Constant, Diligent, Studious, Thorough

Assign(ation), Assignment Allocate, → **ALLOT**, Apply, Appoint, Aret, Ascribe, Attribute, Award, Date, Dedicate, Duty, Entrust, Errand, Fix, Give, Grant, Impute, Point, Quota, Refer, Transfer, Tryst

Assimilate(d) Absorb, Blend, Digest, Esculent, Fuse, Imbibe, Incorporate, Merge, Osmose

Assist(ance), Assistant Acolyte, Adjunct, Adviser, Aid(e), Aide-de-camp, Ally, Alms, Attaché, Au pair, Best boy, Busboy, Cad, Chainman, Collaborate, Counterhand, Counter-jumper, Dresser, Ex parte, Facilitate, Factotum, Famulus, Feldschar, Felds(c)her, Gofer, → **HAND**, Handlanger, Help, Henchman, Legal aid, Matross, Mentor, National, Nipper, Offsider, Omnibus, Proproctor, Public, Reinforce, Relief, Second, Server, Servitor, Shill, Sidekick, Sidesman, Smallboy, Social, Stead, Subsidiary, Subsidy, Suffragan, Supernumerary, → **SUPPORT**, Usher

Assize Botley, Circuit, Court, Maiden, Oyer

Associate(d), Association Accomplice, Affiliate, Alliance, Amphictyony, Ass, Attach, Bedfellow, Brotherhood, Cartel, Chapel, Chum, Clang, Club, Cohort, Combine, Comecon, Community, Compeer, Complice, Comrade, Concomitant, Confrère, → **CONNECT**, Consort(ium), Co-partner, Correlate, Crony, Enclisis, Fellow, Fraternise, Free, Gesellschaft, Goose club, Guild, Hobnob, Housing,

Inquiline, Intime, Join, Kabele, Kebele, League, Liaison, Lloyds, Mell, Member, Mess, Mix, Moshav, Oddfellows, Pal, Parent teacher, Partner, Phoresy, Press, Probus, Professional, Relate, Residents', Ring, Round Table, Samit(h)i, Sangh(at), Sidekick, Sodality, Stablemate, Staff, Symbiosis, Syndicate, Synonymous, Tenant's, Toc H, Toenadering, Trade, UN(A), Union, Verein, Weiner Werkstatte, Whiteboy, Word, Yoke-mate

Assort(ed), Assortment Paraphernalia, Pick-'n'-mix, Various

▷ **Assorted** *may indicate* an anagram

Assuage Allay, Appease, Beet, Calm, Ease, Mease, Mitigate, Mollify, Slake, Soften, Soothe

As such Qua

Assume, Assuming, Assumption Adopt, Affect, Arrogate, Attire, Axiom, Believe, Don, Donné(e), Feign, Hypothesis, Lemma, Occam's Razor, Posit, Postulate, Preconception, Premise, Premiss, Presuppose, Pretentious, Principle, Putative, Saltus, Say, Suppose, Surmise, Take

▷ **Assumption** *may indicate* 'attire'

Assure(d), Assurance Aplomb, Aver, Avouch, Belief, Calm, → **CERTAIN**, Comfort, Confidence, Confirm, Earnest, Gall, Guarantee, Life, Pledge, Poise, Self-confidence, Warranty

Assuredly Indeed, Perdie, Verily, Yea

Astatine At

Astern Abaft, Apoop, Rear

Asteroid Ceres, Eros, Eros 433, Hermes, Hygiea, Juno, Pallas, Phaethon, Pholus, Planetoid, Star, Starfish, Trojan, Vesta

Astir Afoot, Agate, Agog

Astonish(ed), Astonishing, Astonishment, Astound Abash, Admiraunce, Amaze, Banjax, Bewilder, Confound, Corker, Crikey, Daze, Donnert, Dum(b)found, Dumbstruck, Eye-popping, Flabbergast, Gobsmack, Heavens, Mind-boggling, Open-eyed, Open-mouthed, Phew, Pop-eyed, Prodigious, Rouse, Singular, Stagger, Startle, Stun, Stupefaction, Stupefy, Stupendous, Surprise, Thunderstruck, Wide-eyed, Wow

Astray Abord, Amiss, Errant, Lost, Will, Wull

Astride Athwart, En cavalier, Spanning, Straddle-back

Astringent Acerbic, Alum, Catechu, Dhak, Gambi(e)r, Harsh, Kino, Krameria, Myrobalan, Obstruent, Puckery, Rhatany, Sept-foil, Severe, Sour, Styptic, Tormentil, Witch-hazel

Astrologer, Astrology, Astrological Archgenethliac, Chaldean, Culpeper, Faust, Figure-caster, Genethliac, Judicial, Lilly, Midheaven, Moore, Nostradamus, Soothsayer, Starmonger, Zadkiel

Astronaut Cosmonaut, Gagarin, Glenn, Lunarnaut, Spaceman, Spacer, Talkonaut

Astronomer, Astronomy, Astronomical Almagest, Aristarchus, Barnard, Bessel, Bradley, Brahe, Callipic, Cassini, Celsius, Coal sack, Copernicus, Eddington, Encke, Eratosthenes, Eudoxus, Flamsteed, Galileo, Gamma-ray, Hale, Halley, Herschel, Hertzsprung, Hewish, Hipparchus, Hoyle, Hubble, Huggins, Infra red, Jeans, Kepler, Lagrange, Laplace, Leverrier, Lockyer, Lovell, Meton, Neutrino, Omar Khayyam, Oort, Physical, Planetology, Ptolemy, Radar, Radio, Reber, Rees, Roche, Roemer, Russell, Ryle, Schwarzschild, Selenography, Selenology, Seyfert, Sosigenes, Stargazer, Star read, Telescopy, Tycho Brahe, Ultraviolet, Urania, Uranic, Uranography, X-ray, Zwicky

Astrophel Penthia

Astrophysicist Seifert

Astute Acute, Canny, Crafty, Cunning, Downy, Perspicacious, Shrewd, Subtle, Wide, Wily

As usual Solito

As well Additionally, Also, Both, Even, Forby, Too

Asylum Bedlam, Bin, Bughouse, Frithsoken, Funny-farm, Girth, Grith, Haven, Institution, Loony bin, Lunatic, Madhouse, Magdalene, Nuthouse, Political, Rathouse, Refuge, Retreat, Sanctuary, Shelter, Snake-pit

Asymmetric(al) Contrapposto, Lopsided, Skew

At Astatine, In, Kip, To, Up-bye

Atahualpa Inca

At all Ava, Ever, Oughtlings

At all events Algate

Atavistic Reversion, Throw-back

Atheist Doubter, Godless, Infidel, Sceptic

Athenian, Athene Attic, Cleruch, Pallas, Pericles, Solon, Timon

Athlete, Athletic(s) Agile, Agonist, Blue, Coe, Discobolus, Field, Gymnast, Hurdler, Jock, Leish, Miler, Milo, Nurmi, Olympian, Pacemaker, Quarter-miler, Runner, Sexual, Sportsman, Sprinter, Track, Track and field

Athodyd Ram-jet

Athwart Across, Awry, Oblique, Traverse

Atlantic Millpond, Pond

Atlas Dialect, Linguistic, Maps, Range, Silk

▷ **At last** *may indicate* a cobbler

Atmosphere Aeropause, Afterdamp, Air, Ambience, Aura, Chemosphere, Elements, Epedaphic, Ether, F-layer, Geocorona, Ionosphere, Lid, Magnetosphere, Mesophere, Meteorology, Miasma, Ozone, Standard, Thermosphere, Tropopause, Troposphere, Upper, Vibe(s), Vibrations

At most Al piu

Atoll Bikini, Eniwetok, Kwajalein, Male, Motu, Tarawa

Atom(ic), Atoms, Atomism Boson, Electron, Excimer, Free, Gram, Ion, Iota, Isobare, Isotone, Isotope, Labelled, Ligand, Logical, Molecule, Monad, Monovalent, Muonic, Nematic, Nuclide, Odoriphore, Particle, Pile, Primeval, Radionuclide, Recoil, Sellafield, Side-chain, Species, Steric, Stripped, Substituent, Tagged, Windscale, Xylyl

Atomiser Airbrush, Nebuliser

At once Directly, Ek dum, Holus-bolus, Immediate, Instanter, Presto, Statim, Straight away, Swith, Tight, Tit(e), Titely, Tout de suite, Tyte

Atone(ment) Aby(e), Acceptilation, Appease, Assoil, Expiate, Penance, Redeem, Redemption, Yom Kippur

Atop Upon

▷ **At random** *may indicate* an anagram

Atrocious, Atrocity Abominable, Brutal, Diabolical, Flagitious, Heinous, Horrible, Monstrous, Outrage, Piacular, Vile

Atrophy Degeneration, Marasmus, Sudeck's, Sweeny, Wasting

▷ **At sea** *may indicate* an anagram

Attach(ed), Attachment Accessory, Accrete, Adhesion, Adhibition, Adnate, Adnation, Adscript, Affix, Allonge, Annexe, Bolt, Bro, Byssus, Cleat, Covermount, Curtlilage, Devotement, Devotion, Distrain, Dobby, Feller, Garnish, Glom, Glue, → JOIN, Netsuke, Obconic, Piggyback, Pin, Reticle, Sew, Snell, Stick, Tie, Weld

Attack(ing), Attacker Access, Affect, Airstrike, Alert, Anti, Apoplexy, Asperse, Assail, Assault, At, Banzai, Batten, Bego, Belabour, Beset, Bestorm, Blitz(krieg),

Bodrag(ing), Bombard, Bordraging, Bout, Broadside, Bushwhack, Camisade, Camisado, Campaign, Cannonade, Charge, Clobber, Club, Counteroffensive, Coup de main, Denounce, Descent, Diatribe, Feint, Fit, Flèche, Foray, Gas, Get, Handbag, Hatchet job, Headbutt, Heart, Iconoclast, Ictus, Impingement, Impugn, Incursion, Inroad, Invade, Inveigh, Knee, Lampoon, Lash out, Lese-majesty, Let fly, Maraud, Molest, Mug, Offence, Offensive, Onding, Onfall, Onrush, Onset, Onslaught, Oppugn, Panic, Pillage, Polemic, Pounce, Predacious, Pre-emptive, Push, Quart(e), Raid, Rally, Rough, Sail, Sandbag, Savage, Seizure, Sic(k), Siege, Skitch, Slam, Snipe, Sortie, Storm, Strafe, Straff, Strike, Swoop, Thrust, Tilt, Vilify, Vituperate, Wage, Warison, Wolf-pack, Zap

Attain(ment) Accomplish, Arrive, Earn, Fruition, Get, Land, Reach

Attempt Attentat, Bash, Bid, Burl, Crack, Debut, Effort, Egma, Endeavour, Essay, Go, Mint, Nisus, Seek, Shot, Show, Shy, Stab, Strive, → **TRY**, Venture, Whack, Whirl

Attend(ance), Attendant Accompany, Aide, Apple-squire, Await, Batman, Bearer, Be at, Behold, Bulldog, Caddy, Cavass, Chaperone, Chasseur, Checker, Corybant, Courtier, Cuadrilla, Cupbearer, Custrel, Doula, Entourage, Equerry, Escort, Esquire, Famulus, Footman, Gate, Gillie, Hand-maiden, Harken, Hear, → **HEED**, Hello, Holla, Iras, Kavass, Led captain, → **LISTEN**, Loblolly-boy, Maenad, Marshal, Mute, Note, Orderly, Outrider, Outrunner, Page, Panisc, Panisk, Paranymph, People, Pew-opener, Presence, Pursuivant, Respect, Roll-up, S(a)ice, Satellite, Second, Server, Sowar, Steward, Syce, Trainbearer, Trolleydolly, Turn-out, Up at, Valet, Varlet, Visit, Wait, Watch, Whiffler, Zambuck

Attention, Attentive Achtung, Alert, Assiduity, Court, Coverage, Dutiful, Ear, Gallant, Gaum, Gorm, Hark, Heed, Interest, Mind, Note, Notice, Observant, Present, Ps(s)t, Punctilious, Qui vive, → **REGARD**, Selective, Solicitous, Spellbound, Spotlight, Tenty, Thought

Attenuate, Attenuation Lessen, Neper, Rarefy, Thin, Weaken

Attest Affirm, Certify, Depose, Guarantee, Notarise, Swear, → **WITNESS**

Attic Bee-bird, Cockloft, Garret, Greek, Koine, Loft, Mansard, Muse, Salt, Sky parlour, Solar, Soler, Sollar, Soller, Tallat, Tallet, Tallot

Attila Etzel, Hun

Attire Accoutre, Adorn, Apparel, Clobber, Clothe, Clothing, → **DRESS**, Garb, Habit

Attitude Air, Aspect, Behaviour, Demeanour, Light, → **MANNER**, Mindset, Nimby, Outlook, Pose, Posture, Propositional, Sense, Song, Stance, Tone, Uppity, Viewpoint

Attorney Advocate, Counsellor, DA, District, Lawyer, Private, Proctor, Prosecutor, Public

Attract(ion), Attractive(ness), Attractor Attrahent, Bait, Barrie, Beauté du diable, Becoming, Bedworthy, Bewitch, Bonny, Bootylicious, Catchy, Charisma, → **CHARM**, Cheesecake, Clou, Comely, Crowd puller, Cute, Cynosure, Dinky, Dipolar, Dish(y), Draught, → **DRAW**, Dreamboat, Duende, Engaging, Entice, Epigamic, Eye candy, Eye-catching, Eyeful, Fanciable, Fascinate, Feature, Fetching, Fox(y), Goodly, Gravity, Great, Groovy, Heartthrob, Himbo, Hot, Hot stuff, Hot(ty), Hunky, Inducement, Inviting, It, Loadstone, Lodestone, Looker, Lovable, Lovely, Lure, Luscious, Magnes, Magnet(ism), Mecca, Mediagenic, Meretricious, Nubile, Personable, Photogenic, Picturesque, Pretty, Pull, Sematic, Sexpot, Shagtastic, Sideshow, Sightly, Slick, Smasher, Snazzy, Soote, Speciosity, Spunk, Stotter, Striking, Studmuffin, Stunner, Taking, Taky, Tasteful, Tempt, Theme-park, Toothsome, Weber, Winning, Winsome, Zaftig, Zoftig

Attribute, Attribution Accredit, Allot, Ap(p)anage, Ascribe, Asset, By, Credit, Gift, Impute, Lay, Metonym, Owe, Proprium, Quality, Refer, Resource, Shtick, Strength

Attune Accord, Adapt, Temper

Atypical Aberrant, Anomalous

Aubergine Brinjal, Brown jolly, Egg-plant, Mad-apple

Aubrey Beardsley

Auburn Abram, Chestnut, Copper, Titian, Vill(age)

Auction(eer) Barter, Bridge, Cant, Dutch, Hammer, Knock out, Outcry, Outro(o)per, Roup, Sale, Subhastation, Tattersall, Trade sale, Vendue, Warrant sale

Audacious, Audacity Bald-headed, Bold, Brash, Cheek, Chutspah, Cool, Der-doing, Devil-may-care, Effrontery, Face, Hardihood, Indiscreet, Insolence, Intrepid, Neck, Nerve, Rash, Sauce

Audience, Auditorium Assembly, Court, Durbar, Gate, Hearing, House, Interview, Pit, Sphendone, Theatre, Tribunal

Audiovisual AV

Audit(or) Accountant, Check, Ear, Environmental, Examine, Green, Inspect, Listener, Medical, Position

Audition Cattle-call, Hearing, Screen-test

Auditory Acoustic, Oral

Audrey Hoyden

Auger Miser

Augment(ed) Boost, Eche, Eke, Ich, Increase, Supplement, Swell, Tritone

Augury → DIVINATION, Ornithoscopy

August Awe-inspiring, Grand, Imperial, Imposing, Lammas, Majestic, Noble, Royal, Solemn, Stately, Stern

Augustine, Augustus Austin, Hippo, John

Auk Guillemot, Ice-bird, Puffin, Roch, Rotch(e)

Aunt(ie) Agony, Augusta, Beeb, Giddy, Maiden, Naunt, Sainted, Tia

Aura Aroma, Emanation, Halo, Mystique, Nimbus, Odour, Vibe(s), Vibrations

Aureole Coronary, Halo, Nimbus

Auricle Ear, Otic

Aurora Australis, Borealis, Eos, Leigh, Matutinal, Merry dancers, Northern lights, Southern

Auspice(s) Aegis, Patronage

Auster S-wind

Austere, Austerity Ascetic, Astringent, Bleak, Dantean, Dervish, Hard, → HARSH, Moral, Plain, Rigour, Severe, Spartan, Stern, Stoic, Stoor, Strict, Vaudois, Waldensian

Austin Friar

Australia(n) Alf, Antichthone, Antipodean, Aussie, Balt, Banana-bender, Bananalander, Billjim, Bodgie, Canecutter, Cobber, Coon, Currency, Current, Darwinian, Digger, Gin, Godzone, Gumsucker, Gurindji, Jackie, Jacky, Koori, Larrikin, Lucky Country, Murree, Murri, Myall, Norm, Ocker, Ossie, Oz, Pintupi, Roy, Sandgroper, Strine, Wallaby, Yarra-yabbies

Austrian Cisleithan, Tyrolean

Authentic(ate) Certify, Des(h)i, Echt, Genuine, Honest, Notarise, Official, Real, Sign, Simon-pure, Test, True, Validate

▷ **Author** *may refer to* author of puzzle

Author(ess) Anarch, Auctorial, Inventor, Me, Parent, Scenarist, Volumist, Wordsmith, → WRITER

Authorise(d), Authorisation Accredit, Clearance, Countersign, Delegate, Empower, Enable, Exequatur, Imprimatur, Legal, Legit, → LICENCE, Official, OK, Passport, → PERMIT, Plenipotentiary, Retainer, Sanction, Sign, Stamp, Warrant

Authority, Authoritarian, Authoritative Canon, Charter, Circar, Cocker,

Commission, Commune, Crisp, Definitive, Domineering, Dominion, Establishment, Ex cathedra, Expert, Fascist, Free hand, Gravitas, Hegemony, Inquirendo, Jackboot, Leadership, Licence, Local, Magisterial, Mandate, Mantle, Mastery, Name, Oracle, Permit, PLA, Potency, → **POWER**, Prefect, Prestige, Pundit, Regime, Remit, Right, Rod, Say-so, Sceptre, Sircar, Sirkar, Source, Supremacy, Unitary, Warrant

Autobiography Memoir

Autochthonous Aboriginal

Autocrat(ic) Absolute, Caesar, Cham, Despot, Khan, Neronian, Tenno, Tsar, Tyrant

Autograph Signature

Autolycus Scrapman

Automatic, Automaton Android, Aut, Browning, Deskill, Instinctive, Knee-jerk, Machine, Mechanical, Pistol, Quarter-boy, Quarter-jack, Reflex, Robot, RUR, Zombi

Auto-pilot George

Autopsy Necropsy

Auto-suggestion Coueism

Autumn(al) Fall, Filemot, Leaf-fall, Libra, Philamot

Auxiliary Adjunct, Adjuvant, Adminicle, Aide, Ancillary, Be, Feldsher, Foederatus, Have, Helper, Ido, Modal, Subsidiary

Avail(able) Benefit, Dow, Eligible, Going, Handy, Off-the-shelf, On call, On hand, On tap, Open, Out, Pickings, → **READY**, Serve, To hand, Use, Utilise

Avalanche Bergfall, Deluge, Landfall, Landslide, Landslip, Lauwine, Slide, Slip, Snowdrop

Avant-garde Modernistic, Spearhead, Ultramodern

Avarice, Avaricious Cupidity, Gimmes, Golddigger, Greed, Money-grubbing, Pleonexia, Shylock, Sordid

Avatar Epiphany, Incarnation, Rama

Avaunt Away, Go

Avenge(r) Eriny(e)s, Eumenides, Goel, Kuraitcha, Nightrider, Punish, Redress, Requite, → **REVENGE**, Steed, Wreak

Avenue Alley, Approach, Arcade, Boulevard, Channel, Corso, Cradle-walk, Hall, Madison, Mall, Midway, Passage, Vista, Way, Xyst(us)

Aver Affirm, Assert, Asseverate, Depose, Swear, Vouch

Average Adjustment, Av, Batting, Dow Jones, Mean, Mediocre, Middle-brow, Middling, Moderate, Moving, Norm, Par, Particular, Run, Run-of-the-mill, Soso, Standard, Weighted

Averse, Aversion, Avert Against, Antipathy, Apositia, Disgust, Dislike, Distaste, Hatred, Horror, Opposed, Pet, Phengephobia, Phobic, Photophobia, Risk, Scunner, Sit(i)ophobia, Stave off

Avert Avoid, → **DEFLECT**, Forfend, Parry, Ward

Aviary Volary, Volery

Aviator Airman, Alcock, Bleriot, Brown, Byrd, De Havilland, Earhart, Flier, Hinkler, Icarus, Johnson, Lindbergh, Pilot, Red Baron, Richthofen

Avid Agog, → **EAGER**, Greedy, Keen

Avifauna Ornis

Avignon Pont

Avocado Aguacate, Guac(h)amole, Pear

Avocet Scooper

Avoid(er), Avoidance Abstain, Ba(u)lk, Boycott, Bypass, Cop-out, Cut, Dodge, Duck, Elude, Escape, Eschew, Evade, Evitate, Evite, Fly, Forbear, Gallio, Hedge, Miss, Obviate, Parry, Prevaricate, Scutage, Secede, Shelve, Shun, Sidestep, Skirt,

Spare, Spurn, Waive

Avoirdupois Size, Weight

Avow(ed) Acknowledged, Affirm, Declare, Own, Swear

Await Abide, Bide, Expect, Tarry

Awake(ning) Aware, Conscious, Conversion, Fly, Rouse, Vigilant

Award Academy, Accolade, Acquisitive, Addeem, Addoom, Allot, Alpha, Arbitrament, Aret(t), Bafta, Bar, Bestow, Bursary, Cap, Charter Mark, Clasp, Clio, Compensation, Crown, Degree, Emmy, Exhibition, Genie, Golden Raspberry, Golden Starfish, Grammy, Grant, Honours, Juno, Logie, Lourie, Medal, Meed, Mete, MOBO, Oscar, Padma Shri, Palatinate, Palme d'Or, Premium, Present(ation), Prix Goncourt, → **PRIZE**, Queen's, Razzie, Rosette, Scholarship, Tony, Trophy, Vir Chakra, Yuko

Aware(ness) Alert, Aware, Coconscious, C(o)enesthesis, Cognisant, Conscious, Conversant, ESP, Est, Hep, Hip, Informed, Knowing, Liminal, Mindshare, Onto, Panaesthesia, Prajna, Presentiment, Samadhi, Scienter, Sensible, Sensile, Sensitive, Sentience, Streetwise, Switched on, Vigilant, Weet, Wit, Wot

Away Abaxial, Absent, Afield, Apage, Avaunt, By, For-, Fro(m), Go, Hence, Off, Out, Past

▷ **Away** *may indicate* a word to be omitted

Awe(d) D(o)ulia, Dread, Fear, Intimidate, Loch, Overcome, Popeyed, Regard, Respect, Reverent, Scare, Solemn, Wonderment

Awe-inspiring Numinous

Awful(ly) Alas, Deare, Dere, Dire, Fearful, Horrendous, O so, Piacular, Rotten, Terrible

▷ **Awfully** *may indicate* an anagram

Awkward Angular, Blate, Bolshy, Bumpkin, Clumsy, Complicated, Corner, Crabby, Cubbish, Cumbersome, Cussed, Dub, Embarrassing, Farouche, Fiddly, Fix, Gangly, Gauche, Gawky, Handless, Howdy-do, Inconvenient, Inept, Kittle-cattle, Lanky, Loutish, Lurdan(e), Lurden, Maladdress, Mauther, Mawr, Naff, Nasty, Nonconformist, Ornery, Perverse, Refractory, Slummock, So-and-so, Spot, Sticky, Stiff, Stroppy, Stumblebum, Swainish, Uneasy, Ungainly, Unwieldy, Wry

Awl(-shaped) Brog, Els(h)in, Nail, Stob, Subulate

Awn(ing) Barb, Beard, Canopy, Ear, Shade, Shamiana(h), Velarium

Awry Agley, Amiss, Askent, Askew, Cam, Haywire, Kam(me), Pear-shaped, Wonky

Axe(s) Abolish, Adz(e), Bardiche, Bill, Celt, Chop(per), Cleaver, Curtal, Eatche, Gisarme, Gurlet, Halberd, Halbert, Hatchet, Holing, Ice, Jeddart staff, Jethart-staff, Labrys, Lochaber, Mattock, Palstaff, Palstave, Partisan, Piolet, Retrench, Sax, Scrub, Slate, Sparth(e), Sperthe, Spontoon, Stone, Thunderbolt, Tomahawk, Twibill, X, Y, Z

Axeman Bassist, Guitarist

Axe-shaped Securiform

Axiom Adage, Motto, Peano's, Proverb, Saw, Saying

Axis Alliance, Anorthic, Anticous, Axle, Caulome, Chital, Cob, Columella, Deer, Epaxial, Henge, Hinge, Major, Minor, Modiolus, Myelon, Neutral, Optic, Pivot, Polar, Precess, Principal, Rachis, Radical, Spindle, Sympodium, Visual, X, Y, Z, Zone

Axle, Axle-shoulder Arbor, Axis, Driving, Fulcrum, Hurter, Journal, Live, Mandrel, Mandril, Pivot, Spindle, Stub

Ay I, Indeed

Aye Always, Eer, Ever, Yea, Yes

Ayesha She

Azo-dye Para-red

Aztec Nahuatl

Bb

B Bachelor, Black, Book, Born, Boron, Bowled, Bravo, Flipside

Babble(r) Blather, Brook, Chatter, Gibber, Haver, Lallation, Lurry, Prate, Prattle, Runnel, Tonguester, Twattle, Waffle, Witter

Babel Charivari, Confusion, Din, Dovercourt, Medley

Baboon Ape, Bobbejaan, Chacma, Cynocephalus, Dog-ape, Drill, Gelada, Hamadryas, Mandrill, Sphinx

Baby Bairn, Band-Aid®, Blue, Bub, Bunting, Changeling, Coddle, Designer, Duck, Grand, Infant, Jelly, Litter, Neonate, Nursling, Pamper, Papoose, Plunket, Preverbal, Rhesus, Sis, Small, Sook, Suckling, Tar, Test tube, Thalidomide, Tot, War, Wean

Babylonian Mandaean, Semiramis, Sumerian

Bacchanalian, Bacchus Ivied, Upsee, Ups(e)y

Bacchantes Maenads

Bachelor BA, Bach, Benedict, Budge, Celibate, En garçon, Knight, Pantagamy, Parti, Seal, Single, Stag, Wifeless

Bacillus Comma, Germ, Klebs-Loffler, Micrococcus, Tubercle, Virus

Back(ing), Back out, Back up, Backward Abet, Accompany, Addorse, Again, Ago, Anticlockwise, Antimacassar, Arear, Arrear, Arrière, Assist, Baccare, Backare, Bankroll, Buckram, Champion, Chorus, Consent, Cry off, Culet, Defender, Dorsal, Dorse, Dorsum, Dos, Ebb, Empatron, Encourage, Endorse, Fakie, Finance, Frae, Fro, Full, Fund, Gaff, Half, Help, Hind, Historic, Incremental, La-la, Late, Notaeum, Notal, Notum, On, Patronise, Pendu, Poop, Pronotum, Punt, Rear(most), Retral, Retro(grade), Retrogress, Retrorse, Retrospective, Return, Rev, Reverse, Ridge, Root, Running, Shy, Spinal, Sponsor, Stern, Sternboard, Sternway, → **SUPPORT**, Sweeper, Tail, Telson, Tergum, Third, Thrae, Three-quarter, Tonneau, Ulu, Uphold, Verso, Vie, Vo, Wager, Watteau

▷ **Back(ing)** *may indicate* a word spelt backwards

Back and forth Boustrophedon

Backbiter, Backbiting Catty, Defame, Detract, Libel, Molar, Slander

Backbone Atlas, Chine, Grit, Guts, Mettle, Spina, Spine

Backchat Lip, Mouth, Sass

Backcloth Cyclorama

Backer Angel, Benefactor, Patron, Punter, Seconder, Sponsor

Backfire Boomerang

Backgammon Acey-deucy, Blot, Lurch, Tick-tack, Trick-track, Tric-trac, Verquere

Background Antecedence, Chromakey, Cyclorama, Field, Fond, History, Horizon, Microwave, Muzak, Natural, Setting, Ulterior

Backhander Bribe, Payola, Reverso, Sweetener

Backroom Boffin, Boy, Moor

Backslide(r), Backsliding Apostate, Lapse, Regress, Relapse, Revert

Backwash Rift

Backwater Bogan, Ebb, Logan, Retreat, Slough, Wake
Backwoods Boondocks, Boonies, Hinterland
Backyard Court, Patio
Bacon Bard, Canadian, Collar, Danish, Essayist, Flitch, Francis, Gammon, Lardo(o)
  n, Pancetta, Pig, Pork, Rasher, Roger, Spec(k), Streaky, Verulam
Bacteria, Bacterium Acidophilus, Actinomycete, Aerobe, Amphitricha, Bacilli,
  Bacteriological, Baregine, Botulinum, → **BUG**, Campylobacter, Chlamydia, Clostridia,
  Cocci, Coliform, Culture, Detritivore, Diplococcus, Escherichia, Foul-brood,
  → **GERM**, Gonococcus, Gram-negative, Gram-positive, Hib, Intestinal flora,
  Klebsiella, Legionella, Listeria, Lysogen, Meningococcus, Microbe, Micrococcus,
  Microphyte, Mother, MRSA, Mycoplasma, Nitrous, Nostoc, Packet, Pasteurella,
  Pathogen, Pneumococcus, Probiotic, Prokaryote, Proteus, Pseudomonas,
  Pus, Ray-fungus, Rhizobium, Rickettsia, Salmonella, Schizomycete, Septic,
  Serotype, Serum, Shigella, Spirilla, Spirochaete, Spore, Staph, Staphylococcus,
  Strep(tococcus), Streptobacillus, Streptomyces, Sulphur, Superbug, Thermophil(e),
  Treponemata, Vibrio, Vincent's angina, Vinegar-plant, Yersinia, Zoogloea
Bad, Badness Abysmal, Addled, Chronic, Crook, Defective, Diabolic, Dud, Duff,
  Dystopia, Egregious, Execrable, Faulty, God-awful, Half-pie, Heinous, Ill, Immoral,
  Inferior, Injurious, Lither, Lulu, Mal, Naughty, Nefandous, Nefarious, Nice, Off,
  Ominous, Oncus, Onkus, Parlous, Piacular, Poor, Rancid, Rank, Ropy, Scampish,
  Scoundrel, Sinful, Spoiled, Turpitude, Undesirable, Unspeakable, Useless, Wack,
  Wick, → **WICKED**
▷ **Bad(ly)** *may indicate* an anagram
Badge Brassard, Brooch, Button, Chevron, Cockade, Cockleshell, Comm, Cordon,
  Crest, Emblem, Ensign, Epaulet, Episemon, Fáinne, Film, Flash, Garter, Gorget, ID,
  Insigne, Insignia, Kikumon, Mark, Mon, Numerals, Pilgrim's sign, Pin, Rosette,
  Scallop, Scallop-shell, Shield, Shouldermark, → **SIGN**, Symbol, Tiger, Token,
  Vernicle, Vine branch, Vine-rod, Wings
Badger → **ANNOY**, Bait, Bedevil, Beset, Brock, Browbeat, Bug, Bullyrag, Cete,
  Dassi(e), Ferret, Gray, Grey, → **HARASS**, Hassle, Heckle, Hog, Honey, Hound, Nag,
  Pester, Plague, Provoke, Ratel, Ride, Roil, Sand, Sow, Stinking, Teledu, Wisconsin
Bad habit Cacoethes, Vice
Badinage Banter, Chaff, Raillery
Bad luck Ambs-ace, Ames-ace, Deuce-ace, Hard cheese, Hard lines, Hoodoo, Jinx,
  Jonah, Shame, Voodoo
Bad-tempered Carnaptious, Curmudgeon, Curnaptious, Curst, Grouchy, Grum(py),
  Irritable, Marabunta, Moody, Nowty, Patch, Scratchy, Shirty, Splenetic, Stroppy
Bad woman Harridan, Loose, Mort
Baffle(d), Baffling Anan, Balk, Bemuse, Bewilder, Confound, Confuse, Elude,
  Evade, Floor, Flummox, Foil, Fox, Get, Hush-kit, Mate, Muse, Mystify, Nark,
  Nonplus, Perplex, Pose, Puzzle, Stump, Throw, Thwart
Bag(gage), Bags Acquire, Air, Alforja, Allantois, Amaut, Amowt, Ascus, Ballonet,
  Besom, Bladder, Blue, Body, Bounty, Bulse, Bum, Buoyancy, Caba(s), Caecum,
  Callet, Capture, Carpet, Carrier, Carryall, Case, Cecum, Clutch, Cly, Cod,
  Colostomy, Cool, Corduroy, Crone, Crumenal, Cyst, Daypack, Dilli, Dilly, Dime,
  Diplomatic, Ditty, Doggy, Dorothy, Douche, Duffel, Dunnage, → **EFFECTS**, Emery,
  Excess, Fanny pack, Flannels, Flotation, Follicle, Galligaskins, Game, → **GEAR**,
  Gladstone, Goody, Grab, Grip, Gripsack, Grow, Holdall, Ice, Impedimenta, Jelly,
  Jiffy®, Kill, Knapsack, Ladies' companion, Lavender, Lithocyst, Marsupium,
  Materiel, Meal-poke, Minx, Mixed, Money, Monkey, Moon, Mummy, Musette,
  Musk, Muzzle, Mystery, Nap, Necessaire, Net, Nunny, Organiser, Overnight,

Overnighter, Oxford, Packsack, Pantaloons, Plastic, Plus fours, Pochette, Pock(et), Pocketbook, Pockmanky, Pockmantie, Poke, Politzer's, Poly(thene), Port(manteau), Portmantle, Portmantua, Post, Pot, Pouch, Pounce, Pudding, Punch, Purse, Rake, Red, Reticule, Ridicule, Rucksack, Sabretache, Sac(cule), Sachet, Sack, Saddle, Sag, Satchel, Scent, School, Scrip, Scrotum, Sea, Shopper, Sick, Slattern, Sleeping, Sponge, Sporran, Stacks, Strossers, Sugar, Survival, Tea, Tote, → **TRAP**, Trews, Trollop, Trouse(r), Tucker (box), Udder, Unmentionables, Utricle, Valise, Vanity, Viaticals, Waist, Wallet, Water, Weekend, Win, Woolpack, Work, Wrap, Wrapping, Ziplock

Bagatelle Bauble, Fico, Trifle, Trinket

Bagpipe Biniou, Chorus, Cornemuse, Drone, Gaita, Musette, Pibroch, Piffero, Skirl, Sourdeline, Uillean, Zampogna

Bahama(s), Bahamian BS, Conch

Bail(er), Bailment Bond, Ladle, Mainpernor, Mainprise, Mutuum, Replevin, Replevy, Scoop

Bailey Bridge, Castle wall, Ward

Bailiff Adam, Bandog, Beagle, Bum, Factor, Foud, Grieve, Huissier, Hundreder, Hundredor, Land-agent, Nuthook, Philistine, Reeve, Shoulder-clapper, Shoulder-knot, Steward, Tipstaff, Water

Bairn Baby, → **CHILD**, Infant, Wean

Bait Badger, Berley, Brandling, Burley, Capelin, Chum, Dap, Decoy, Entice, Gentle, Gudgeon, Harass, Hellgram(m)ite, Incentive, Lobworm, Lug(worm), Lure, Mawk, → **RAG**, Ragworm, Sledge, Teagle, Tease, Tempt, Toll

Bake(r), Baked, Baking Alaska, Batch, Baxter, Coctile, → **COOK**, Fire, Kiln-dry, Pieman, Roast, Scorch, Shir(r)

Baker's daughter Own

Baker Street Irregular

Balance(d) Account, Beam, Compensation, Counterpoise, Countervail, Counterweight, Equate, Equilibrium, Equipoise, Equiponderate, Even, Fixed, Funambulate, Gyroscope, Gyrostat, Horn, Hydrostatic, Invisible, Isostasy, Launce, Libra, Librate, Meet, Otolith, Peise, Perch, Peyse, Poise, → **REMAINDER**, Remnant, Residual, Rest, Running, Scale, Sea-legs, Spring, Stand, Steelyard, Symmetry, Torsion, → **TOTAL**, Trial, Trim, Tron(e), Unicycle, Visible

Balcony Circle, Gallery, Loggia, Mirador, Moucharaby, Pew, Porch, Quarter-gallery, Sundeck, Tarras, Terrace, Veranda(h)

Bald, Baldness Alopecia, Apterium, Awnless, Barren, Calvities, Coot, Crude, Egghead, Fox-evil, Glabrous, Hairless, Madarosis, Open, Peelgarlic, Pilgarlic(k), Pollard, Psilosis, Slaphead, Smoothpate, Stark, Tonsured

Balderdash Drivel, Flapdoodle, Nonsense, Rot

Baldmoney Emeu, Meu, Spignel

Bale Bl, Bundle, Evil, Lave, Pack, Sero(o)n, Truss

Baleful Evil, Malefic, Malignant

▶ **Balk** see **BAULK**

Balkan Albanian, Bosnian, Bulgarian, Macedon, Rumanian, Serb, Vlach

Ball(s) Aelopile, Aelopyle, Aeolipile, Aeolipyle, Agglomerate, Alley, Ally, Ammo, Aniseed, Apple, Beach, Bead, Beamer, Birthing, Bobble, Boll, Bolus, Bosey, Bosie, Bouncer, Break, Buckshot, Buzzer, Caltrap, Caltrop, Camphor, Cap, Cherry, Chin, Chinaman, Chopper, Clew, Clue, Condular, Condyle, Cotill(i)on, Cramp, Creeper, Croquette, Crystal, Cue, Curve, Daisy-cutter, → **DANCE**, Delivery, Dink, Dodge, Dollydrop, Doosra, Dot, Dribbler, Eight, Ensphere, Eolipile, Eolipyle, Eolopile, Eolopyle, Falafel, Felafel, Full-pitch, Full-toss, Fungo, Gazunder, → **GLOBE**,

Glomerate, Gobstopper, Googly, Gool(e)ys, Goolies, Grub, Grubhunter, Gutta, Gutter, Hank, Hop, Hummer, Hunt, Inswinger, Ivory, Jinglet, Jump, Knob, Knur(r), Leather, Leg-break, Leg-cutter, Lob, Long-hop, Marble, Masked, Masque(rade), Matzo, Medicine, Minié, Mirror, Moth, Nur(r), O, Object, Off-break, Off-cutter, Off-spin, Orb, Outswinger, Over, Overarm, Pakora, Parrel truck, Pea, Pellet, Pill, Poi, Pomander, Pompom, Pompon, Prom, Puck, Punch, Quenelle, Rabbit, Rissole, Root, Round, Rover, Rundle, Seamer, Shooter, Shot, Sliotar, Sneak, Sphere, Spinner, Stress, Strike, Swinger, Swiss, Taw, Testes, Thenar, Three, Tice, Time, Track(er), Witches, Wood, Yorker, Zorb®

Ballad Bab, Bothy, Broadside, Bush, Calypso, Carol, Fanzone, Folk-song, Forebitter, Lay, Lillibullero, Lilliburlero, Mento, Singsong, → SONG, Torch-song

Ballast Kentledge, Makeweight, Stabiliser, Trim, Weight

Ball-boy Dry-bob

Ballerina Coryphee, Dancer, Pavlova, Prima

Ballet, Ballet movement, Ballet-system Assemblé, Balancé, Ballon, Battement, Bharat Natyam, Bolshoi, Brisé, Cambré, Chainé, Changement, Checkmate, Daphnis and Chloe, Développé, Don Pasquale, Écarté, Echappé, Enchainement, Entrechat, Firebird, Fouette, Giselle, Jeté, Kirov, Laban, Labanotation, Leg business, Pas de basque, Pas de bourrée, Pas de chat, Petit battement, Pirouette, Plastique, Plie, Pointe, Pointer, Port de bras, Relevé, Saut, Swan Lake

Ballet-interlude Divertimento

Ballistic Wildfire

Balloon(ist) Aeronaut, Aerostat, Airship, Bag, Barrage, Billow, Blimp, Bloat, Dirigible, Dumont, Enlarge, Fumetto, Hot air, Lead, Montgolfier, Pilot, Rawinsonde, Sonde, Trial, Weather, Zeppelin

Ballot Butterfly, Election, → POLL, Referendum, Second, Suffrage, Ticket, Vote

Ballot-box Urn

Ballpoint Bic®, Biro®

Balm(y) Anetic, Arnica, Balsam, Calamint, Fragrant, Garjan, Gilead, Gurjun, Lemon, Lenitive, Lotion, → MILD, Mirbane, Myrbane, Nard, Oil, Opobalsam, Ottar, Redolent, Remedy, Soothe, Spikenard, Tiger, Tolu, Unguent

Balmoral Bonnet, Cap, Castle

Baloney Bunk, Hooey, Nonsense

Balsam Canada, Copaiba, Copaiva, Friar's, Nard, Noli-me-tangere, Peruvian, Resin, Spikenard, Tamanu, Tolu(ic), Touch-me-not, Tous-les-mois, Turpentine

Balt Esth, Lett

Baltic Estonian, Lettic

Bamboo Cane, Kendo, Split cane, Tabasheer, Whangee

Bamboozle(d) Cheat, Dupe, Flummox, Hoodwink, Mystify, Nose-led, Perplex, Trick

Ban Abolish, Accurse, Anathema, Black(ing), Censor, Debar, D-notice, Embargo, Estop, Excommunicate, Forbid, For(e)say, For(e)speak, Gag, Gate, Green, Moratorium, No, Outlaw, Prohibit, Proscribe, Suppress, Taboo, Tabu, Test, Veto

Banal Corny, Dreary, Flat, Hackneyed, Jejune, Mundane, Platitudinous, → TRITE, Trivial

Banana(s) Abaca, Hand, → MAD, Matoke, Musa, Plantain, Scitamineae, Split, Strelitzia, Top

Band(s) Absorption, Alice, Ambulacrum, Anadem, Anklet, Armlet, Barrulet, Belt, Border, Braid, Brake, Brass, Brassard, Brassart, Caravan, CB, Channel, Chinstrap, Chromosome, Cingulum, Circlet, Citizens', Clarain, Closet, Cohort, Collar, Collet, Combo, Company, Conduction, Corslet, Coterie, Crape, Crew, Deely boppers, Elastic, ELO, Endorse, Energy, Enomoty, Facia, Falling, Fascia, Fasciole, Ferret,

Ferrule, Fess, Filament, Fillet, Fraternity, Frequency, Frieze, Frog, Frontlet, Galloon, Gamelan, → **GANG**, Garage, Garland, Garter, Gasket, Gaskin, Geneva, German, Gird, Girth, Guard, → **HOOP**, Hope, Iron, Jazz, Jug, Kitchen, Label, Laticlave, Lytta, Maniple, Mariachi, Massed, Military, Mourning, Myrmidon, Noise, One-man, Orchestra, Orchestrina, Pack, Parral, Parrel, Parsal, Parsel, Pass, Patte, Pipe, Plinth, Property, Purfle, Puttee, Retinaculum, Rib, Ribbon, Rigwiddie, Rigwoodie, Rim, Ring, Robbers, Round, Rubber, Rymme, Sash, Scarf, Screed, Scrunchie, Scrunchy, Sect, Shadow, Shallal, Shash, Sheet, Shoe, Snood, Steel, Strake, Strap, Stratum, String, Stripe, Succinctory, Swath(e), Sweat, Tambu-bambu, Tape, Tendon, Thoroughbrace, Throat-latch, Tie, Tippet, Torques, Tourniquet, Train, Tribute, Troop, Troupe, Tumpline, Turm, Tyre, Unite, Valence, Vinculum, Virl, Vitrain, Vitta, Wanty, Wedding, Weed, Weeper, Welt, Wings, With(e), Wristlet, Zona, Zone, Zonule

Bandage Bind, Blindfold, Capeline, Dressing, Fillet, Ligature, Lint, Living, Pledget, Roller, Scapular, Sling, Spica, Suspensor, Swaddle, Swathe, T, Tape, Truss, Tubigrip®, Wadding

Bandicoot Bilby, Pig-rat

Bandit Apache, Bravo, Brigand, Desperado, Fruit-machine, Gunslinger, Klepht, Moss-trooper, Outlaw, Pirate, Rapparee, → **ROBBER**, Squeegee, Turpin

Bandsman, Band-leader Alexander, Bugler, Conductor, Maestro, Miller, Wait

Bandstand Kiosk, Stage

Bandy Bow, Exchange, Revie, Toss, Vie

Bane Curse, Evil, Harm, Poison

Bang(er) Amorce, Andouillette, Beat, Big, Cap, Chipolata, Clap, Cracker, Crock, Explode, Firecracker, Flivver, Fringe, Haircut, Heap, Implode, Jalopy, Maroon, Pep(p)eroni, Rattletrap, Report, Sausage, Sizzler, Slam, Sonic, Thrill, TNT, Wurst

Bangle Anklet, Armlet, Bracelet, Kara

Banish(ment) Ban, Deport, Depose, Exile, Expatriate, Expel, Extradition, Forsay, Maroon, Ostracise, → **OUTLAW**, Relegate, Rusticate

Banjo Ukulele

Bank(ing), Bank on An(n)icut, Asar, Backs, Bar, Bay, Bet, Bk, Blood, Bluff, Bottle, Brae, Brim, Bund, Camber, Cay, Central, Chesil, Clearing, Cloud, Commercial, Cooperative, Data, Depend, Deposit, Dogger, Down, Drawee, Dune, Dyke, Earthwork, Escarp, Fog, Gene, Giro, Glacis, Gradient, Gradin(e), Hack, Hele, Hill, Home, Incline, Jodrell, Land, Left, Lender, Levee, Link, Lombard Street, Memory, Merchant, Mound, Nap, National, Needle, Nore, Overslaugh, Oyster, Parapet, Penny, Piggy, Pot, Private, Rake, Ramp, Rampart, Reef, → **RELY**, Reserve, Retail, Rivage, Riverside, Rodham, Row, Sandbar, Savings, Seed, Shallow, Shelf, Side, Slope, Soil, Sperm, Staithe, State, Sunk, Telephone, Terrace, Terreplein, Tier, Trust, Vault, West, World

Banker Agent, Cert, Financial, Fugger, Gnome, Lombard, Medici, → **RIVER**, Rothschild, Shroff, Teller

▷ **Banker** *may indicate* a river

Banknote(s) Flimsy, Greenback, Snuff-paper

▷ **Bankrupt** *may indicate* 'red' around another word

Bankrupt(cy) Break, Broke, Bung, Bust, Cadaver, Carey Street, Chapter-eleven, Crash, Debtor, Deplete, Duck, Dyvour, Fail, Fold, Insolvent, Lame duck, Notour, Penniless, Receivership, Ruin, Rump, Scat, Sequestration, Skatt, Smash

Bank system Giro

Bann(s) Out-ask

Banner Banderol(e), Bandrol, Bannerol, Blue Blanket, → **FLAG**, Gumphion, Labarum, Oriflamme, Sign, Streamer

Banquet Beanfeast, Dine, Feast, Junket, Nosh-up, Spread
Banquette Firestep
Bant Diet, Reduce
Bantam Dandy-cock, Dandy-hen
Banter Backchat, Badinage, Borak, Chaff, Dicacity, Dieter, Jest, → **JOKE**, Persiflage, Picong, Rag, → **RAILLERY**, Rally, Ribaldry, Roast, Rot, Tease
Bantu Bosotho, Gazankulu, Herero, Lebowa, Qwaqwa, Shangaan, Sotho, Transkei, Tutsi, X(h)osa
Bap Bread, Roll, Tommy
Baptise(d), Baptism, Baptist Affusion, Amrit, Christen, Clinical, Conditional, Dip, Dipper, Dopper, Dunker, Hypothetical, Illuminati, Immersion, John, Mersion, Private, Sabbatarian, Sprinkle, Tinker
Bar(s) Address, Angle-iron, Anti-roll, Astragal, Asymmetric, Axletree, Bail, Ban, Barrelhouse, Baulk, Beam, Bierkeller, Bilboes, Billet, Bistro, Blackball, Blacklist, Block(ade), Bloom, Bolt, Boom, Bottega, Brasserie, Buffet, Bull, Bumper, But, Buvette, Café(-chantant), Café-concert, → **CAGE**, Cake, Came, Cantina, Capo, Capstan, Channel, Clip joint, Cocktail, Coffee, Colour, Counter, Cramp(on), Cross(head), Crow, Crush, Currency, Dive, Doggery, Double, Double-tree, Draw, Drift, Dumbbell, Efficiency, Espresso, Estop(pel), Except, Exclude, Fen, Fid, Flinders, Fonda, Forbid, Foreclose, Forestall, Fret, Gad, Gastropub, Gemel, Glazing, Grate, Grid, Grog-shop, Gunshop, Hame, Handrail, Handspike, Heck, → **HINDRANCE**, Horizontal, Hound, Hyphen, Impediment, Ingoes, Ingot, Ingowes, Inn, Inner, Judder, Juice, Karaoke, Keeper, Kickstand, Knuckleduster, Latch, Let, Lever, Limbo, Line, Local, Lounge, Macron, Mandrel, Mandril, Measure, Menu, Merchant, Milk, Mousing, Muesli, Mullion, Nail, Nanaimo, Navigation, Nineteenth hole, No-go, Norman, Obstacle, Onely, Orgue, Outer, Overslaugh, Oxygen, Parallel, Perch, Pile, Pinch, Pole, Posada, Prescription, Private, Prohibit, Pub, Public, Putlog, Rabble, Rack, Rail, Ramrod, Rance, Randle-balk, Randle-perch, Randle-tree, Raw, Reach, Restrict, Rib, Risp, Rod, Roll, Roo, Rung, Saddle, Salad, Saloon, Sans, Save, Saving, Scroll, Semantron, Shaft, Shanty, Shet, Shut, Singles, Skewer, Slice, Slot, Snack, Snug, Spacer, Spar, Speakeasy, Sperre, Spina, Spit, Splinter, Sprag, Stancher, Stanchion, Status, Stave, Sternson, Stick, Stirre, Stretcher, Stripe, Strut, Sway, Swee, T, Tael, Tap(-room), Tapas, Taphouse, Task, Tavern(a), Temple, Tiki, Title, Toll, Tombolo, Tommy, Tool, Torsion, Tow, Trace, Trangle, Transom, Trapeze, Triblet, Trundle, Type, Vinculum, Wall, Ward, Wet, Whisker, Window, Wine, Wire, Wrecking, Z, Zed, Zygon
Barabbas Robber
Barb(ed) Bur(r), Fluke, Harl, Herl, → **HOOK**, Jag(g), Jibe, Pheon, Prickle, Ramus, Tang, Thorn, Vexillum
Barbados, Barbadian Bajan, Bim(m)
Barbara Allen, Major
Barbarian, Barbaric Boor, Crude, Fifteen, Foreigner, Goth, Heathen, Hottentot, Hun, Inhuman, Lowbrow, Outlandish, Philistine, Rude, Savage, Tartar, Tatar(ic)
Barbary Ape, Roan
Barbecue Braai(vleis), Chargrill, Cook-out, Flame-grill, Grill, Hangi, Hibachi, Roast, Spit
Barbel Beard
Barber Epilate, Figaro, Scrape(r), Shaver, Strap, Todd, Tonsor, Trimmer
Barbiturate Goofball
Bard(ic) Ariosto, Gorsedd, Griot, Heine, Meat, Minstrel, Muse, Ossian, Scald, Scop, Skald, Taliesin

Bare, Bare-headed Adamic, Aphyllous, Bald, Barren, Blank, Bodkin, Cere, Décolleté, Denude, Hush, Lewd, Marginal, Moon, → **NAKED**, Open, Plain, Scablands, Scant, Sear, Stark, Timber line, Topless, Uncase, Uncover, Unveil

Barefoot Discalced, Unshod

Barely At a pinch, At a stretch, Hand-to-mouth, Hardly, Just, Merely, Scarcely, Scrimp

Bargain(ing) Bargoon, Barter, Braata, Chaffer, Champerty, → **CHEAP**, Collective, Compact, Contract, Coup, Deal, Dicker, Distributive, Effort, Find, Go, Haggle, Higgle, Horse-trade, Huckster, Indent, Integrative, Negotiate, Option, → **PACT**, Plea, Productivity, Scoop, Snip, Steal, Supersaver, Time, Trade, Trock, Troke, Truck, Wanworth, Wheeler-dealing

Barge Birlinn, Bucentaur, Budgero(w), Butty, Elbow, Gabbard, Gabbart, Galley-foist, Hopper, Intrude, Jostle, Keel, Lighter, Nudge, Obtrude, Pra(a)m, Ram, Scow, → **SHIP**, Trow, Wherry

▷ **Barge** *may indicate* an anagram

Bargee, Bargeman Hobbler, Keeler, Keelman, Legger, Lighterman, Ram, Trow

Barium Ba, Witherite

Bark Angostura, Ayelp, Azedarach, Bass, Bast, Bay, Bowwow, Calisaya, Cambium, Canella, Caribbee, Cascara, Cascara sagrada, Cascarilla, Cassia, China, Cinchona, Cinnamon, Cork, Cortex, Cusparia, Honduras, Jamaica, Jesuits', Kina, Kinakina, Latration, Liber, Mezereum, Myrica, Parchment, Peel, Pereira, Peruvian, Phloem, Quebracho, Quest, Quill, Quillai, Quina, Quinquina, Red, Rind, Sagrada, Salian, Sassafras, Scrape, Scurf, Shag, → **SHIP**, Skin, Slippery elm, Tan, Tap(p)a, Totaquine, Waff, Waugh, Winter's, Woof, Wow, Yaff, → **YAP**, Yellow, Yelp, Yip

Bar-keep(er), Barmaid, Barman, Bartender Advocate, Ale-wife, Barista, Bencher, Curate, Hebe, Luckie, Lucky, Tapster, Underskinker

Barley (water) Awn, Bear, Bere, Bigg, Hordeum, Malt, Orgeat, Pearl, Pot, Scotch, Truce, Tsamba

Barm(y) Yeast

Barmecide, Barmecidal Imaginary

Barn Bank, Byre, Cowshed, Dutch, Farm, Grange, Mow, Perchery, Skipper, Tithe

Barnaby Rudge

Barnacle Acorn, Cirriped(e), Cypris, Goose(neck), Limpet

Barometer Aneroid, Glass, Orometer, Statoscope, Sympiesometer, Torricellian tube, Weatherglass

Baron B, Corvo, Drug, Munchausen, Noble, Thyssen, Tycoon

Baronet Bart

Baronne Dudevant Sand

Baroque Fancy, Gothic, Ornate, Rococo

▷ **Baroque** *may indicate* an anagram

Barrack(s), Barracking Asteism, Boo, Cantonment, Casern(e), Cat-call, Garrison, Heckle, Irony, Jeer, Quarters

Barrage Balloon, Fusillade, Heat, Salvo

Barred Banned, Edh, Trabeculated

Barrel Bl, Butt, Cade, Capstan, Cascabel, Cask, Clavie, Cylinder, Drum, Hogshead, Keg, Kibble, Morris-tube, Oildrum, Organ, Pièce, Pork, Run(d)let, Tan-vat, Thrall, Tierce, Tun, Vat, Water, Wood

Barrel-organ Apollonicum, Hurdy-gurdy, Street piano

Barren Addle, Arid, Badlands, Blind, Blunt, Clear, Dry, Eild, → **EMPTY**, Farrow, Hardscrabble, Hirstie, Jejune, Sterile, Unbearing, Waste, Wasteland, Wilderness, Yeld, Yell

Barrier Bail, Barrage, Barricade, Bayle, Block, Breakwater, Cauld, Checkrail, Cheval de frise, Chicane, Cordon (sanitaire), Crash, Crush, → **DAM**, Defence, Drawgate, Dyke, Fence, Fraise, Gate, Heat, Hedge, Hurdle, Mach, Obstruct, Pain, Paling, Potential, Rail(-fence), Rampart, Restraint, Revetment, Roadblock, Rope, Screen, Skreen, Sonic, Sound, Spina, Stockade, Thermal, Tollgate, Trade, Transsonic, Turnpike, Turnstile, → **WALL**

Barrister Advocate, Attorney, Counsel, Devil, Lawyer, Revising, Rumpole, Sergeant (at law), Serjeant(-at-law), Silk, Templar, Utter

Barrow Dolly, Handcart, Henge, How, Hurley, Kurgan, Molehill, Mound, Pushcart, Tram, Trolley, Truck, Tumulus

Barrow-boy Coster, Trader

Bar-tail Scamel, Staniel, Stannel

Barter Chaffer, Chop, Coup, Dicker, → **EXCHANGE**, Haggle, Hawk, Niffer, Permutate, Sco(u)rse, Swap, → **TRADE**, Traffic, Truck

Basalt Diabase, Melaphyre, Tachylite, Tephrite, Toadstone, Trap(pean), Traprock, Wacke

Base Adenine, Air, Alkali, Bed, Beggarly, Billon, Bottom, Caitiff, Camp, Choline, Codon, Cytosine, Degenerate, Degraded, Dog, Down, E, Erinite, → **ESTABLISH**, First, Floor, Fond, Foot, Foothold, Footstall, Found, Foundation, Fundus, Guanine, Harlot, Histamine, Hydroxide, Ignoble, Ignominious, Indamine, Infamous, Iniquitous, Install, Knowledge, Leuco, Lewis, → **LOW**, → **MEAN**, Nefarious, Nook, Oasis®, Parasaniline, Partite, Patten, Platform, Plinth, Podium, Premise, Ptomaine, Purin(e), Pyrimidine, Pyrrolidine, Raca, Radix, Rascally, Ratty, Rests, Ribald, Root, Rosaniline, Rude, Schiff, Servile, Shameful, Shand, Sheeny, Socle, Soda, Spaceport, Staddle, → **STAND**, Station, Substrate, Ten, Thymine, Torus, Triacid, Turpitude, Unworthy, Uracil, Vile

Baseball Apple, Nine, Twi-night

Baseless Idle, Unfounded, Ungrounded

Base-line Datum

Basement Bargain, Below stairs

Bash Belt, Bonk, Clout, Go, Hit, Rave, Shot, Slog, Strike, Swat, Swipe

Bashful Awed, Blate, Coy, Modest, Retiring, Shamefast, Sheep-faced, Sheepish, → **SHY**

Basic(s), Basically, Basis ABC, Abcee, Alkaline, Aquamanale, Aquamanile, Crude, Elemental, → **ESSENTIAL**, Fiducial, Fond, Fundamental, Ground(work), Gut, In essence, Integral, Intrinsic, Logic, Meat and potatoes, Nitty-gritty, No-frills, No-nonsense, One-horse, Pou sto, Presumption, Primordial, Principle, Radical, Rudimentary, Spit-and-sawdust, Staple, Substance, Substratum, Underlying, Uracil

Basilica St Peter's

Basilisk Cannon, Lizard

Basin Aquamanale, Aquamanile, Artesian, Aspergillum, Aspersorium, Benitier, Bidet, Bowl, Canning, Catch, Catchment, Cirque, Corrie, Cwm, Dish, Dock, Doline, Donets, Drainage, Foxe, Geosyncline, Great, Impluvium, Kuzbass, Kuznetsk, Lavabo, Laver, Minas, Monteith, Ocean, Okavango, Pan, Park, Piscina, Playa, Porringer, Pudding, Reservoir, River, Scapa Flow, Sink, Slop, Stoop, Stoup, Sugar, Tank, Tarim, Tidal, Washhand

Bask Apricate, Revel, Sun, Sunbathe, → **WALLOW**

Basket, Basket-work Baalam, Bass, Bassinet, Bread, Buck, Cabas, Calathus, Canephorus, Car, Cesta, Chip, Cob, Coop, Corbeil(le), Corbicula, Corf, Creel, Cresset, Dosser, Fan, Flasket, Flax kit, Frail, Gabian, Goal, Hamper, Hask, Junket,

Kago, Kajawah, Kipe, Kit, Kite, Leap, Litter, Maund, Mocock, Mocuck, Moses, Murlain, Murlan, Murlin, Osiery, Pannier, Ped, Petara, Pitara(h), Plate, Pollen, Pottle, Punnet, Rip, Round file, Scull, Scuttle, Seed-lip, Skep, Skull, Trolley, Trout, Trug, Van, Wagger-pagger(-bagger), Waste(-paper), Wattlework, Whisket, Wicker(-work), Will(e), Wisket, Work

Basketball Tip-off

Basket-bearer Canephor(a), Canephore, Canephorus

Basket-maker Alfa, Cane, Halfa, Wicker

Basque Biscayan, Euskarian

Bass Alberti, Ale, Alfie, B, Black, Continuo, Deep, Double, El-a-mi, Figured, Fish, Ground, Largemouth, Low, Ostinato, Serran, Smallmouth, String, Thorough, Walking

Bassoon Fagotto

Bast Liber

Bastard, Bastard-wing Alula, Base, By-blow, Filius nullius, Git, Haram(za) da, Illegitimate, Mamzer, Momzer, Mongrel, Sassaby, Side-slip, Slink, Spuriae, Spurious, Whoreson

▷ **Bastard** *may indicate* an anagram

Baste Enlard, Sew, Stitch, Tack

Bastion Citadel, Lunette, Moineau

Bat(sman), Bat's wing, Batter, Batting, Batty Aliped, Ames, Assail, Barbastelle, Baton, Belfry, Blink, Chiroptera, Close, Club, Cosh, Crackers, Crease, Cudgel, Dad, Die Fledermaus, Eyelid, False vampire, Flittermouse, Flying fox, Fruit, Fungo, Grace, Hammerhead, Hatter, Haywire, Hit, Hobbs, Hook, Horseshoe, In, Ink mouse, Insectivorous, Kalong, Knock, Language, Lara, Leisler, Man, Mastiff, Maul, May, Mormops, Mouse-eared, Myopic, Nictate, Nictitate, Night, Nightwatchman, Noctilio, Nora, Nurdle, Opener, Paddle, Patagium, Pinch-hit, Pipistrel(le), Poke, Pummel, Racket, Racquet, Ram, Rearmouse, Reremice, Reremouse, Roussette, Ruin, Sauch, Saugh, Scotch hand, Serotine, Sledge, Spectre, Stick, Stonewall, Straight, Striker, Swat, Switch hitter, Trap-stick, Trunnion, Vampire, Vespertilionid, Viv, Whacky, Willow, Wood

Batch Bake, Bunch, Clutch

Bath(room) Aerotone, Aeson's, Bagnio, Bain-marie, Balneotherapy, Banya, Bed, Bidet, Blanket, Blood, Bubble, Caldarium, Cor, Dip, En suite, Epha, Foam, Hammam, Hip, Hummaum, Hummum, Jacuzzi®, Laver, Mik vah, Mud, Mustard, Oil, Piscina, Plunge, Salt, Sauna, Shower, Sitz, Slipper, Soak, Spa, Sponge, Steam, Stew, Stop, Tepidarium, Therm, Tub, Turkish, Tye, Vapour, Whirlpool, Wife

Bathe, Bathing Balneal, Balneation, Balneology, Balneotherapy, Bay(e), Beath, Bogey, Bogie, Dip, Dook, Douk, Embay, Foment, Immerse, Lave, Lip, Skinny-dip, Souse, Splash, Stupe, → **SWIM**, Tub, → **WASH**

Batman Valet

Baton Mace, Rod, Sceptre, Staff, Truncheon

Batrachian Frog, Toad

▷ **Bats, Batting** *may indicate* an anagram

Battalion Bn, Corps, Troop

Batten Dropper, Fasten, Tie

Batter(ed) Bombard, Bruise, Buffet, Decrepit, Pound

Battery Accumulator, Artillery, Button-cell, Drycell, Field, Galvanic, Heliac, Henhouse, Li(thium)-ion, Masked, Nicad, Penlight, Pra(a)m, Primary, Solar, Storage, Troop, Voltaic, Waffle, Water

Battle(s), Battleground Action, Affair, Ben, Clash, Cockpit, Combat, → **CONFLICT**, Encounter, Engagement, Field, → **FIGHT**, Fray, Front, Hosting, Joust, Maiden, Pitched, Royal, Running, Sarah, Sciamachy, Skiamachy, Spurs, Stoor, Stour, Stowre, Theatre, Wage, → **WAR**, Wargame

BATTLES

3 letters:
Kut
Ulm

4 letters:
Alma
Chad
Ivry
Jena
Laon
Lodi
Loos
Mons
Nile
Zama

5 letters:
Accra
Alamo
Allia
Arcot
Arras
Boyne
Bulge
Crecy
Ipsus
Issus
Lewes
Lissa
Marne
Mylae
Nancy
Parma
Pavia
Pydna
Sedan
Somme
Tours
Valmy
Ypres

6 letters:
Actium
Arbela

Arcola
Argyle
Arnhem
Barnet
Camlan
Cannae
Cressy
Crimea
Imphal
Lutzen
Maldon
Midway
Mohacs
Mycale
Naseby
Sadowa
Senlac
Shiloh
Tobruk
Towton
Varese
Verdun
Vigrid
Wagram
Wipers

7 letters:
Aboukir
Alamein
Almanza
Argonne
Bautzen
Beaches
Britain
Bull Run
Cambrai
Carrhae
Chalons
Colenso
Coronel
Corunna
Deorham
Dunkirk
Evesham

Flodden
Flowers
Glencoe
Iwo Jima
Jericho
Jutland
Kossovo
Legnano
Lepanto
Leuctra
Magenta
Marengo
Nations
Newbury
Nineveh
Okinawa
Orleans
Panipat
Picardy
Plassey
Plataea
Poltava
Pultowa
Salamis
Sempach
Tolouse
Vimelro
Vitoria
Warburg

8 letters:
Antietam
Ardennes
Ayacucho
Blenheim
Borodino
Bosworth
Chioggia
Clontarf
Culloden
Custozza
Edgehill
Erzurium
Flanders

Fontenay
Hastings
Hydaspes
Inkerman
Jemappes
Kulikova
Le Cateau
Lechfeld
Manassas
Marathon
Mehawand
Metaurus
Montreal
Naumachy
Navarino
Omdurman
Palo Alto
Philippi
Poitiers
Ragnarok
Rossbach
Saratoga
Solomons
Spion Kop
St Albans
Syracuse
Talavera
Waterloo
Yorktown

9 letters:
Agincourt
Balaclava
Caporetto
Castilion
Chaeronea
El Alamein
Gallipoli
Ladysmith
Moerkirch
Nicopolis
Otterburn
Oudenarde
Pharsalus

9 letters – cont:
Princeton
Ramillies
Sedgemoor
Solferino
St Vincent
Theomachy
The Saints
Trafalgar
Vercellae
Wandewash
Worcester

10 letters:
Adrianople
Armageddon
Austerlitz
Beneventum
Bennington
Brunanburh

Bunker Hill
Camperdown
Ferhbellin
Gettysburg
Lundy's Lane
Malplaquet
Mount Badon
Petersburg
Quatre Bras
River Plate
Shipka Pass
Stalingrad
Steenkerke
Tannenberg
Tewkesbury

11 letters:
Aegospotami
Aljubarotta
Armentières

Aubers Ridge
Bannockburn
Belleau Wood
Bismarck Sea
Chattanooga
Hohenlinden
Marston Moor
Philiphaugh
Prestonpans
Thermopylae
Wounded Knee

12 letters:
Flodden Field
Mons Graupius
Monte Cassino
Roncesvalles

13 letters:
Alcazar-Quivir

Bosworth Field
Little Bighorn
Neuve-Chapelle
Neville's Cross
Passchendaele
Spanish Armada

14 letters:
Castlebar Races
Stamford Bridge

15 letters:
Missionary Ridge
Plains of Abraham
Teutoberger Wald

16 letters:
Las Navas de Tolosa

Battle-axe Amazon, Bill, Gorgon, Halberd, Ogress, Sparth(e), Termagant, Termagent, Turmagant, Turmagent
Battlement Barmkin, Crenellate, Merlon, Rampart
Battle-order Phalanx
Battleship Carrier, Destroyer, Dreadnought, Gunboat, Man-o'-war, Pocket, Potemkin
Bauble Bagatelle, Gaud, Gewgaw, Trifle
Bauhaus Gropius
Baulk Demur, Gib, Hen, Impede, Jib, Reest, Reist, Shy, Thwart
Bavardage Fadaise
Bawd(y) Hare, Raunchy, Sculdudd(e)ry, Skulduddery
Bawl Bellow, Gollar, Howl, Weep
Bay Ab(o)ukir, Aere, Arm, Baffin, Bantry, Bark, Bell, Bengal, Bight, Biscay, Bonny, Botany, Broken, Byron, Cape Cod, Cardigan, Chesapeake, Cienfuegos, Cleveland, Colwyn, Corpus Christi, Cove, Covelet, Creek, Daphne, Delagoa, Delaware, Discovery, Dublin, Dundalk, Dvina, False, Famagusta, Fleet, Frobisher, Fundy, Galway, Gdansk, Georgian, Gibraltar, Glace, Golden, Great Australian Bight, Green, Guanabara, Guantanamo, Gulf, Hangzhou, Harbour, Hawke's, Herne, Horse, → **HOWL**, Hudson, Inhambane, Inlet, Ise, James, Jervis, Jiazhou, Kavalla, Kuskokwim, Laura, Laurel, Layby, Loading, Lobito, Loblolly, Lutzow-Holm, MA, Magdalena, Manila, Massachusetts, Montego, Morton, Narragansett, New York, Niche, Oleander, Omaha, Oriel, Passamaquoddy, Pegasus, Pigs, Plenty, Plymouth, Port Phillip, Poverty, Recess, Red, Roan, St Austell, St Michel, San Pedro, Scene, San Francisco, Santiago, Setubal, Shark, Sick, Sligo, Suvla, Swansea, Table, Tampa, Tasman, Thunder, Tor, Toyama, Tralee, Trincomalee, Ungava, Vae, Vigo, Vlore, Voe, Vyborg, Waff, Walfish, Walvis, Wash, Whitley, Wick, Yowl
Bayonet Jab, Skewer, Stab, Sword
Bazaar Alcaiceria, Emporium, Fair, Fete, Market, Pantechnicon, Sale, Sook, Souk
BBC Auntie
Be Exist, Live, Occur
Beach Bondi, Chesil, Coast, Daytona, Ground, Hard, Lido, Littoral, Machair, Miami,

Omaha, Palm, Plage, Raised, Sand, Seaside, Shingle, Shore, Storm, Strand, Waikiki

Beachcomber Arenaria

Beachwear Thong

Beacon Belisha, Fanal, Landing, Lightship, Need-fire, Pharos, Racon, Radar, Radio, Robot, Signal

Bead(s), Beaded Adderstone, Aggri, Aggry, Astragal, Baily's, Ballotini, Bauble, Blob, Bugle, Cabling, Chaplet, Crab's-eyes, Crab-stones, Dewdrop, Drop, Droplet, Gadroon, Gaud, Job's tears, Kumbaloi, Mala, Moniliform, Nurl, Ojime, Passament, Passement, Paternoster, Poppet, Poppit, Prayer, Rosary, Sabha, Se(a)wan, Spacer, St Cuthbert's, Subha, Sweat, Tear, Wampum(peag), Worry

Beadle Apparitor, Bederal, Bedral, Bumble, Herald, Paritor, Shammes, Verger

Beagle Spy

Beak AMA, Bailie, Bill, Cad, Cere, Coronoid, Egg-tooth, Gar, JP, Kip(p), Magistrate, Master, Metagnathous, Mittimus, Nasute, Neb, Nose, Pecker, Prow, Ram, Rostellum, Rostrum, Shovel

Beaker Bell, Cup, Goblet

Beakless Erostrate

Beak-shaped Coracoid

Beam(ing) Arbor, Balance, Bar, Ba(u)lk, Binder, Boom, Bowstring, Box, Breastsummer, Bressummer, Broadcast, Bum(p)kin, Cantilever, Carline, Carling, Cathead, Collar, Crossbar, Crosshead, Crosspiece, Deck, Effulge, Electron, Girder, Grin, Hammer, Hatch, Herisson, Holophote, I, Irradiate, Joist, Ke(e)lson, Landing, Laser, Lentel, Lintel, Manteltree, Molecular, Needle, Outrigger, Particle, Pencil, Principal, Purlin, Putlock, Putlog, Radio, → **RAFTER**, → **RAY**, Rayon, Refulgent, Rident, Ridgepole, Rood, Roof-tree, Sandwich, Scale, Scantling, Searchlight, Shaft, Shine, Shore, Sleeper, Smile, Soffit, Solive, Spar, Stanchion, Stemson, Sternpost, Straining, Streamer, Stringer, Stringpiece, Summer, Support, Tailing, Tie, Timber, Trabeate, Trabecula, Transom, Trave, Trimmer, Truss, Universal, Viga, Walking, Weigh-bauk, Yard, Yardarm

Beamish Galumphing, Nephew

Bean Abrus, Adsuki, Aduki, Adzuki, Arabica, Asparagus pea, Baked, Berry, Black, Black-eye, Borlotti, Broad, Bush, Butter, Cacao, Calabar, Castor, Cluster, Cocoa, Coffee, Cow-pea, Dwarf, Edamame, Fabaceous, Fava, Flageolet, French, Frijol(e), Garbanzo, Goa, Gram, Green, Haricot, Harmala, Head, Horse, Jack, Jelly, Jequirity, Jumping, Kachang putch, Kidney, Lablab, Lentil, Lima, Locust, Molucca, Moong, Moth, Mung, Nelumbo, Nib, Noddle, Ordeal, Pichurim, Pinto, Pulse, Runner, St Ignatius's, Scarlet, Scarlet runner, Shell, Silverskin, Snap, Snuffbox, Soy(a), String, Sugar, Sword, Tonga, Tonka, Tonquin, Urd, Wax, Winged, Yard-long

Beanfeast → **PARTY**, Spree, Wayzgoose

Bear(er), Bear lover Abide, Abrooke, Andean, Arctic, Arctophile, Baloo, Balu, Beer, Bigg, Breed, Brook, Brown, Bruin, Brunt, → **CARRY**, Cave, Churl, Cinnamon, Coati-mondi, Coati-mundi, Cub, Demean, Dree, Ean, → **ENDURE**, Engender, Exert, Fur-seal, Gest(e), Gonfalonier, Great, Grizzly, Hack, Ham(m)al, Harbinger, Have, Hod, Hold, Honey, Humf, Hump(h), Jampani, Keb, Kinkajou, Koala, Kodiak, Koolah, Lioncel(le), Lionel, Lug, Mother, Nandi, Nanook, Owe, Paddington, Panda, Polar, Pooh, Rac(c)oon, Roller, Rupert, Russia, Sackerson, Seller, Shoulder, Sit, Sloth, Spectacled, Stand, Stay, Stomach, → **SUFFER**, Sun, Sunbear, Sustain, Targeteer, Teddy, Teem, Thole, Throw, Tolerate, Tote, Transport, Undergo, Upstay, Ursine, Water, Whelp, White, Wield, Withstand, Woolly, Yield

Bearberry Manzanita, Uva-ursi

Beard(ed) Aaron, Alfalfa, Anchor, Arista, Assyrian, Aureole, Awn, Balaclava, Barb,

Barbiche, Beaver, Belgrave, Cadiz, Cathedral, Charley, Charlie, Confront, Defy, Ducktail, Face, Five o'clock shadow, Forked, Fungus, Goatee, Hair(ie), Hairy, Hear(ie), Imperial, Jewish, Kesh, Lincolnesque, Mephistopheles, Newgate frill, Newgate fringe, Old Dutch, Olympian, Outface, Peak, Pencil, Raleigh, Rivet, Roman T, Screw, Shenandoah, Spade, Stibble, Stiletto, Stubble, Swallowtail, Tackle, Tile, Trojan, Tuft, Uncle Sam, Vandyke, Whiskerando, Whiskery, Ziff

Beardless Callow, Clean, Tahr, Tehr

▷ **Bearhug** *may indicate* Teddy or similar around a word

▷ **Bearing** *may indicate* compass points

Bearing(s) Air, Allure, Amenaunce, Armorial, Aspect, Azimuth, Babbitt, Ball, Behaviour, Bush, Carriage, Deportment, Direction, E, Endurance, Gait, Gest, Gudgeon, Hatchment, Haviour, Heading, → **HERALDIC**, Hugger-mugger, Lioncel(le), Lionel, Manner, Martlet, Mascle, Middy, Mien, N, Needle, Nor, Pall, Pheon, Port, Presence, Reference, Relevant, Roller, S, Subordinary, Teeming, Tenue, Thrust, W, Yielding

Beast(ly) → **ANIMAL**, Arna, Behemoth, Brute, Caliban, Caribou, Chimera, → **CREATURE**, Dieb, Dragon, Dzeren, Gargoyle, Gayal, Genet, Godzilla, Grampus, Hippogriff, Hodog, Hog, Hy(a)ena, Hydra, Jumart, Kinkajou, Lion, Mammoth, Marmot, Mastodon, Mhorr, Monoceros, Ogre, Oliphant, Opinicus, Oryx, Panda, Potto, Quagga, Rac(c)oon, Rhytina, Rother, Rumptifusel, Sassaby, Steer, Sumpter, Swinish, Tarand, Teg, Theroid, Triceratops, Triton, Wart-hog, Whangam, Yahoo, Yak, Yale, Zizel

Beat(ing), Beaten, Beater Anoint, Arsis, Athrob, Bandy, Bang, Baste, Bastinado, Batter, Battue, Belabour, Belt, Bepat, Best, Blatter, Bless, Bo Diddley, Bubble, Cadence, Cane, Cat, Chastise, Clobber, Club, Clump, Cob, Conquer, Cream, Cudgel, Cuff, Curry, Debel, → **DEFEAT**, Ding, Donder, Dress, Drub, Duff up, Excel, Fatigue, Faze, Feague, Feeze, Fibbed, Firk, Flagellate, Flail, Flam, Float, Flog, Floor, Flush, Fly, Fustigate, Hipster, Hollow, Horsewhip, Ictus, Inteneration, Jole, Joll, Joule, Jowl, Knock, Knubble, Lace, Laidie, Laidy, Lambast(e), Larrup, Lash, Lather, Latin, Laveer, Lay, Lick, Lilt, Lounder, Mall, Malleate, Mersey, Mullah, Muller, Nubble, Onceover, Outclass, Outdo, Outflank, Outstrip, Paik, Palpitate, Pandy, Paradiddle, Pash, Paste, Pip, Ploat, Pommel, Pound, Prat, Pug, Pulsate, Pulsatile, Pulse, Pulsedge, Pummel, Pun, Quop, Raddle, Ram, Ratten, Resolve, Retreat, Rhythm, Ribroast, Rope's end, Round, Rowstow, Ruff(le), Scourge, Scutch, Slat, Smight, Smite, Soak, Sock, Sort, Strap, Strap-oil, Strike, Swinge, Swingle, Systole, Taber, Tabor, Tabrere, Tachycardia, Tact, Tala, Tan, Tattoo, Thesis, Thrash, Thresh, Throb, Thud, Thump, Thwack, Tick, Time, Tired, Top, Torture, Tricrotic, Trounce, Tuck, Tund, Verberate, Vibrate, Wallop, Wappend, Weary, Welt, Wham, Whip, Whisk, Whitewash, Wraught, Ybet, Yerk, Yirk

▷ **Beaten-up** *may indicate* an anagram

Beat it Skedaddle, Vamo(o)se

Beatitude Macarism

Beau Admirer, Blade, Brummel, Cat, Damoiseau, Dandy, Flame, Geste, Lair, Lover, Masher, Nash, Spark, Tibbs

Beaufort Scale, Windscale

Beaut(y) Advantage, Bathing, Belle, Bellibone, Bombshell, Camberwell, Charmer, Colleen, Comeliness, Corker, Dish, Doll, Glory, Houri, Hyperion, Kanta, Lana, Monism, Picture, Pride, Pulchritude, Purler, Sheen, Smasher, Stunner

Beautiful, Beautify Angelic, Astrid, Bonny, Bright, Embellish, Enhance, Exquisite, Fair, Fine, Gorgeous, Junoesque, Ornament, Pink, Radiant, Scenic, Smicker, Specious, To kalon

Beauty spot Patch, Tempe, Tika

Beaver Beard, Castor, Eager, Grind, Mountain, Oregon, Rodent, Sewellel

Because (of) As, Forasmuch, Forwhy, Hence, In, Inasmuch, Sens, Since

Beckon Gesture, Nod, Summons, Waft, Wave

Become, Becoming Apt, Besort, Decent, Decorous, Enter, Fall, Fit, Flatter, Get, Go, Grow, Happen, Occur, Seemly, Suit, Wax, Worth

Bed(s), Bedding, Bedstead Air, Allotment, Amenity, Apple-pie, Arroyo, Bacteria, Base, Bassinet, → **BEDCOVER**, Berth, Bottom, Bottomset, Box, Bundle, Bunk, Caliche, Camp, Carrycot, Channel, Charpoy, Cill, Cot(t), Couch(ette), Counterpane, Couvade, Coverlet, Cradle, Crib, Cross, Cul(t)ch, Day, Divan, Doona, Doss, Duvet, Erf, False, Feather, Filter, Fluidized, Flying, Form, Four-poster, Futon, Gault, Greensand, Hammock, Inlay, Kago, Kang, Kip, Knot, Knot garden, Layer, Lazy, Lilo®, Litter, Marriage, Mat, Matrix, Mattress, Murphy, Naked, Nap, Nest, Nookie, Oyster, Pad, Paillasse, Pallet, Palliasse, Pan, Parterre, Passage, Patch, Pavement, Pay, Pig, Plank, Plant, Plot, Procrustean, Puff, Quilt, Retire, River, Rollaway, Roost, Rota, Sack, Scalp, Settle, Shakedown, Sill, Sitter, Sleep, Sofa, Standing, Stratum, Stretcher, Sun, Tanning, T(h)alweg, Test, The downy, Thill, Trough, Truckle, Trundle, Twin, Wadi, Wady, Ware, Water, Wealden, Wedding

Bedaub Cake, Deck, Smear

Bed-bug B, B flat, Chinch, Flea, Louse, Vermin

Bedchamber, Bedroom Boudoir, Bower, Chamber, Cubicle, Dorm(itory), Dormer, Dorter, Ruelle, Ward

Bedcover Palampore, Palempore, Puff

Bedeck Adonise, Adorn, Array, Festoon

▷ **Bedevilled** *may indicate* an anagram

Bedjacket Nightingale

Bedlam Chaos, Furore, Madness, Nuthouse, Tumult, Uproar

Bed-rest Dutch-wife

Bedwetting Enuresis

Bee Athenia, Bike, Bumble, Carpenter, Cuckoo, Deborah, Debra, Deseret, Dog, Drone, Drumbledor, Dumbledore, Group, Hiver, Honey, Humble, Husking, Killer, King, Lapidary, Leaf-cutter, Mason, Melissa, Mining, Nurse, Queen, Quilting, Raising, Solitary, Spell, Spell-down, Spelling, Swarm, Worker, Working

Beech Antarctic, Copper, Fagus, Hornbeam, Mast, Taw(h)ai, Tree

Bee-eater Merops, Rainbow-bird

Beef(y) Baron, Bleat, Brawny, Bresaola, Bull(y), Bullock, Carpaccio, Charqui, Chateaubriand, Chuck, Clod, Complain, Corned, Filet mignon, Flank, Groan, Grouse, Hough, Jerk, Kobe, Liebig, Mart, Mice, Moan, Mousepiece, Muscle, Neat, Ox, Pastrami, Peeve, Plate, Porterhouse, Rother, Salt-junk, Sauerbraten, Sey, Shin, Silverside, Sirloin, Stolid, Stroganoff, Topside, Tournedos, Tranche, Undercut, Vaccine, Wellington

Beefeater Billman, Exon, Gin, Oxpecker, Warder, Yeoman

Bee-glue Propolis

Beehive Alveary, Apiary, Ball, Dioptric, Gum, Skep

Beelzebub Devil

Beer Ale, Alegar, Amber fluid, Amber liquid, Bantu, Barley sandwich, Bitter, Black, Bock, Chaser, Coldie, Draught, Drink, Dry, Entire, Export, Gill, Ginger, Granny, Grog, Guest, Heavy, Herb, Home-brew, Kaffir, Keg, Kvass, Lager, Lambic, Lite, Lush, Malt, March, Middy, Mild, Mum, Near, Nog, October, Pils(e)ner, Pint, Pony, Porter, Real, Real ale, Rice, Root, Saki, Scoobs, Sherbet, Skeechan, Small, Spruce,

Stingo, Stout, Stubby, Suds, Swankie, Swanky, Swats, Swipes, Switchel, Table, Taplash, Tinnie, Tipper, Tshwala, Tube, Wallop, Wheat, Zythum

Beer garden Brasserie

Bee's nest Bink

Beet Blite, Chard, Fat-hen, Goosefoot, Mangel(wurzel), Seakale, Silver, Spinach, Sugar

Beethoven WoO

Beetle Ambrosia, Anobiid, Argos tortoise, Asiatic, Bacon, Bark, Batler, Bee, Blister, Bloody-nosed, Boll weevil, Bombardier, Bruchid, Bug, Bum-clock, Buprestidae, Buprestus, Burying, Bustle, Buzzard-clock, Cabinet, Cadelle, Cane, Cantharis, Carabid, Cardinal, Carpet, Carrion, Chafer, Christmas, Churchyard, Cicindela, Click, Clock, Cockchafer, Cockroach, Coleoptera, Coleopterous, Colorado, Coprophagan, Curculio, Darkling, Deathwatch, Dermestid, Devil's coach-horse, Diamond, Diving, Dor(r), Dor-fly, Dumbledore, Dung, Dyticus, Dytiscus, Elater, Elytron, Elytrum, Firefly, Flea, Furniture, Glow-worm, Gold(smith), Goliath, Gregor, Ground, Hammer, Hangover, Hercules, Hop-flea, Hornbug, Huhu, Humbuzz, Impend, Japanese, Jewel, June, Khapra, Ladybird, Ladybug, Lamellicorn, Larder, Leaf, Leather, Longhorn, Longicorn, Mall(et), Maul, May-bug, Meloid, Minotaur, Museum, Musk, Oakpruner, Oil, Overhang, Pill, Pinchbuck, Pine, Pine-chafer, Potato, Project, Protrude, Race(-bug), Rhinoceros, Rhynchophora, Roach, Rosechafer, Rove, Sacred, Saw palmetto, Scamper, Scarab(ee), Scavenger, Scolytus, Scurry, Sexton, Shard, Skelter, Sledge(-hammer), Snapping, Snout, Soldier, Spanish fly, Spider, Spring, Squirr, Stag, Tenebrio, Tiger, Toktokkie, Tortoise, Tumble-bug, Tumble-dung, Turnip-flea, Typographer, Vedalia, VW, Water, Weevil, Whirligig, Wireworm, Woodborer, Wood-engraver

Beetle-crushers Cops

Befall Happen, Occur

Before(hand) A, Advance, Already, Ante, Avant, By, Coram, Earlier, Early, Ere, Erst(while), → **FORMER**, Or, Parava(u)nt, Pre, Previously, Prior, Pro, Sooner, Till, To, Until, Van, Zeroth

Before food Ac

Befriend Assist, Cotton, Fraternise, Support

Befuddle(ment) Bemuse, Dwaal, Inebriate, Stupefy

Beg(gar), Beggarly, Begging Abr(ah)am-man, Ask, Badgeman, Beseech, Besognio, Bey, Bezonian, Blighter, Blue-gown, Cadge, Calendar, Clapper-dudgeon, Crave, → **ENTREAT**, Exoration, Flagitate, Fleech, Gaberlunzie, Gangrel, Hallan-shaker, Implore, Impoverish, Irus, Jarkman, Lackall, Lazar(us), Lazzarone, Limitary, Lumpenproletariat, Maund, Mendicant, Montem, Mooch, Mouch, Mump, Niggardly, Obtest, Palliard, Panhandle, Pauper, Penelophon, Penniless, → **PLEAD**, Pled, Pray, Prig, Prog, Ptochocracy, Rag, Randie, Randy, Ruffler, Ruin(ate), Sadhu, Schnorr(er), Screeve, Scrounge, Shool(e), Skelder, Skell, Solicit, Sue, Supplicate, Thig(ger), Toe-rag, Touch, Undo, Uprightman, Whipjack

Beget Gender, Kind

Beggar rule Ptochocracy

Begging bowl Clackdish, Clapdish

Begin(ner), Beginning Ab ovo, Alpha, Alphabetarian, Author, B, Babyhood, Black, Cause, Che(e)chako, Clapdash, Commence, Daw, Dawn, Deb, Debut, Embryo, Enter, Exordium, Fall-to, Fledgling, Found, Fountainhead, Genesis, Germ, Go, Greenhorn, Inaugural, Inception, Inchoate, Incipient, Incipit, Initial, Initiate, Intro, Johnny-raw, L, Launch, Lead, Learn, Learner, Logos, Nascent, Neophyte, → **NOVICE**, Oncome, Onset, Ope(n), Ord, → **ORIGIN**, Outbreak, Pose, Prelim(inary),

Presidium, Primer, Rookie, Seed, Set, → **START**, Startup, Strike up, Takeoff, Tenderfoot, Tiro, To-fall, Tyro(ne), Yearn

Begone Aroint, Aroynt, Avaunt, Scram, Shoo, Vamo(o)se

Begonia Elephant's-ear(s)

Begorrah Bedad, Musha

Begrudge Envy, Resent

Beguile(r) Bewitch, Charm, Coax, Distract, Divert, Enchant, Ensnare, Entice, Flatter, Gull, Intrigue, Jack-a-lantern, Tice, Trick, Wile

Behalf Ex parte, For, Part, Sake

Behave, Behaviour, Behaving Accepted, Acquired, Act, Appeasement, Attitude, Conduct, Consummatory, Convenance, Decorum, Demean, Deportment, Do, Epimeletic, Etepimeletic, Ethics, Ethology, Form, Goings-on, Guise, Horme, → **MANNER**, Meme, Nature, Netiquette, Noblesse oblige, Obey, Orientation, Praxeology, Quit, React, Response, Satisficing, Strong meat, Tribalism, Unreasonable

Behead Decapitate, Decollate, Guillotine

Behind(hand) Abaft, Aft(er), Ahind, Ahint, Apoop, Arear, Arere, Arrear, Arse, Astern, Backside, Beneath, Bottom, Bum, Buttocks, Croup, Derrière, Fud, Late, Overdue, Post, Prat, → **REAR**, Slow, Tushie

Behold(en) Affine, Ecce, Eye, Grateful, Here's, Indebted, La, Lo, Look, Observe, See, View, Voilà

Beige Buff, Greige, Neutral, Suede, Tan

Being Cratur, Creature, Critter, Ens, Entia, Entity, Esse, Essence, Existence, Human, Man, Metaphysics, Mode, Nature, Omneity, Ontology, → **PERSON**, Saul, Soul, Subsistent, Substance, Supreme, Ubiety, Wight

Bejabers Arrah

Belch Boak, Boke, Brash, Burp, Emit, Eruct, Erupt, Rift, Spew, Toby, Yex

Belcher Foulard, Handkerchief, Hanky, Toby

Beldam(e) Crone, Hag, Harridan, Scold

Belfry Campanile, Tower

Belgian Flemish, Walloon

Belief, Believe, Believed, Believer, Believing Accredit, Adam and Eve, Anata, Ativism, Bigot, Buy, Capernaite, Catechism, Christian, Conviction, Creationism, Credence, Credit, Creed, Cult, Culture, Deem, Deist, Di(o)physite, Doctrine, Doxastic, Doxy, Dukkha, Dyophysite, Faith, Formulism, Gnostic, Guess, Heresy, Heterodoxy, Hold, Holist, Idea, Ideology, Islam, Ism, Latitudinarian, Ludism, Manichaeism, Meme, Messianist, Methink, Mysticism, Notion, → **OPINION**, Orthopraxy, Ovist, Pacifism, Pantheism, Persuasion, Physicism, Pluralism, Postmillenarian, Presumption, Religion, Reputed, Revelationist, Seeing, S(h)aivism, Shema, Solfidian, Superstition, Suspect, Swallow, Tenet, Test, Tetratheism, Thanatism, Theist, Theosophy, Think, Threap, Threep, Traducianism, Transcendentalism, Trinitarian, Triphysite, Trow, Trust, Ubiquitarianism, Umma(h), Unitarian, Universalism, Wear, Ween, Wis(t)

Belittle Cheapen, Cry down, Decry, Depreciate, Derogate, Detract, Diminish, Discredit, Disparage, Downgrade, Humble, Pooh-pooh, Slight

Bell(s) Acton, Agogo, Angelus, Ben, Big Ben, Bob, Bow, Bronte, Cachecope, Canterbury, Carillon, Chime, Chinese pavilion, Crotal, Curfew, Currer, Daisy, Diving, Division, Ellis, Gong, Grandsire, Jar, Liberty, Low, Lutine, Market, Mass, Minute, Mort, Muffin, Pancake, Passing, Pavilion, Peal, Peter, Pinger, Pudding, Ring, Roar, Sacring, Sanctus, Shark, Sleigh, Tailor, Tantony, Tenor, Tent, Tintinnabulum, Tocsin, Toll, Tom, Triple, Tubular, Vair, Vaire, Verry, Vesper

Bell-bird Arapunga, Campanero

Belle Beauty, Starr, Toast, Venus

Bell-founder Belleter

Bellicose, Belligerent Chippy, Combatant, Gung-ho, Hostile, Jingoist, Martial, Militant, Truculent, Warmonger

Bellow(s) Buller, Holla, Holler, Moo, Rant, Rave, Roar, Rout, Saul, Thunder, Troat, Tromp(e), Trumpet, Windbag

Bell-ringer, Bell-ringing Bob, Campanology, Changes, Clapper, Course, Grandsire, Handstroke, Hunting, Maximus, Quasimodo, Rope, Sally, Tocsin, Toller

Belly Abdomen, Alvine, Bag, Beer, Beer-gut, Boep, Bunt, Calipee, Celiac, Coeliac, Gut, Kite, Kyte, Pod, → **STOMACH**, Swell, Tum(my), Venter, Wame, Weamb, Wem(b), Womb

Belong, Belonging(s) Apply, Appurtenant, Chattels, Effects, Incident, Inhere, Intrinsic, Our, Paraphernalia, Pertain, → **PROPERTY**, Relate, Things, Traps

Beloved Acushla, Alder-lief, Amy, Boyfriend, David, Dear, Doy, Esme, Inamorata, Joy, Lief, Morna, Pet, Popular, Precious

Below Beneath, Inf(erior), Infra, Nether, Sub, Subjacent, Under, Unneath

Belt(ed) Baldric(k), Band, Bandoleer, Bandolier, Baudric(k), Bible, Black, Cartridge, Chastity, Cholera, Clitellum, Clobber, Clock, Commuter, Conveyor, Copper, Cotton, Crios, Demolition, Equator, Fan, Flog, Fold and thrust, Galvanic, Garter, Gird(le), Girt, Great, Green, Hip, Hydraulic, Inertial, Judoka, Kuiper, Lap, Larrup, Life, Lonsdale, Mitre, Money, Muesli, Orion's, Orogenic, Polt, Pound, Radiation, Roller, Roll-on, Rust, Safety, Sam Browne, Sanitary, Sash, Seat, Speed, Stockbroker, Storm, Strap, Stratosphere, Sun, Surcingle, Suspender, Swipe, Sword, Taiga, Tawse, Tear, Thump, Tore, Tract, Van Allen, Wampum, Wanty, Webbing, Wing, Zodiac, Zone, Zoster

Belt up Sh

Belvedere Gazebo, Mirador

Bemoan → **LAMENT**, Mourn, Sigh, Wail

Bemuse Infatuate, Stonn(e), Stun, Stupefy, Throw

Ben Battle, Hur, Jonson, Mountain, Nevis, Spence

Bench Banc, Banker, Bink, Bleachers, Counter, Court, Cross, Exedra, Form, Front, King's, Knifeboard, Magistrates, Optical, Pew, Queen's, Rout seat, Rusbank, → **SEAT**, Settle, Siege, Stillage, Thoft, Thwart, Treasury, Trestle, Widow's

Benchmark Criteria, Yardstick

Bend(er), Bending, Bends Angle, Arc, Arch, Articular, Becket, Bight, Binge, Bow, Buck(le), Bust, Camber, Carrick, Chicane, Circumflect, Corner, Crank(le), Cringe, → **CROOK**, Curl, Curve, Diffraction, Dog-leg, Double up, Elbow, Engouled, Epinasty, Es(s), Expansion, Falcate, Fawn, Flex(ural), Flexion, Flexure, Fold, Geller, Geniculate, Genu, Genuflect, Grecian, Hairpin, Hinge, Hook, Horseshoe, Hunch, Incline, Inflect, Kink, Knee(cap), Kneel, Knot, Kowtow, Meander, Mould, Nutant, Ox-bow, Pitch, Plash, Plié, Ply, Recline, Reflex, Retorsion, Retortion, Retroflex, Riband, S, Scarp, Sheet, Souse, Spree, Spring, Stave, Stoop, Swan-neck, Trend, Twist, U, Ups(e)y, Uri, Wale, Warp, → **YIELD**, Z

▷ **Bendy** *may indicate* an anagram

Beneath Below, Sub, Under, Unworthy

Benedict(ine) Black Monk, Cluniac, Cluny, Dom, Eggs, Maurist, Olivetan, OSB, Tironensian, Tyronensian

Benediction Blessing, God-speed

Benefactor Angel, Backer, Barmecide, Carnegie, Donor, Maecenas, → **PATRON**, Philanthropist, Promoter

Beneficial, Beneficiary, Benefit, Benefice Advantage, → **AID**, Alms, Ameliorate, Asset, Avail, Behalf, Behoof, Behove, Bespeak, Bonus, Boon, Boot, Charity, Collature, Commendam, Commensal, Devisee, Disablement, Dole, Donee, Endorsee, Enure, FIS, Fringe, Housing, Incapacity, Incumbent, Inheritor, Injury, Inure, Invalidity, Legal aid, Living, Manna, Maternity, Ménage, Neckverse, Pay, Perk, Perquisite, Plus, Portioner, Postulate, Prebend, Profit, Sake, Salutary, Sanative, Sickness, Sinecure, Spin-off, Stipend, Supplementary, Symbiotic, Trickle down, Unemployment, Use, Usufruct, Wholesome, Wonderful, Workfare

Benevolence, Benevolent Charitable, Clement, Dobbie, Dobby, Humanitarian, Kind, Liberal, Nis(se), Pecksniffian, Philanthropy, Sprite

Benighted Ignorant

Benign Affable, Altruistic, Gracious, Innocuous, Kindly, Trinal

Benin DY

Benito Duce, Mussolini

Benjamin Franklin

Bennett Alan, Phil

Bent Akimbo, Bowed, Brae, Coudé, Courb, Crooked, Curb, Determined, Dorsiflex, Falcate, Fiorin, Flair, Geniculate, Habit, Heath, Inclination, Ingenium, Intent, Inverted, Leant, Out, Peccant, Penchant, Ply, Predisposition, Reclinate, Redtop, Round-shouldered, Scoliotic, Stooped, Talent, Taste, Twisted

▷ **Bent** *may indicate* an anagram

Bent grass Fiorin, Redtop

Bentham Utilitarian

Benzine Kinone, Phene, Toluene, Toluol

Bequeath, Bequest Bestow, Chantr(e)y, Demise, Endow, Heirloom, → **LEAVE**, Legacy, Mortification, Pass down, Pittance, Transmit, Will

Berate(d) Censure, Chide, Jaw, Reproach, Scold, Shent, Slate, Vilify

Berber Almoravide, Kabyle, Moor, Rif(i), Riff, Shluh, Tuareg

Bereave(d), Bereavement Deprive, Loss, Mourning, Orb, Sorrow, Strip, Widow

Beret Green

Berg Alban, Floe

Bermuda Shorts

Bernard Levin, Shaw

Bernini Baroque

Berry Acai, Allspice, Bacca, Blackcurrant, Cubeb, Fruit, Goosegog, Haw, Konini, Miracle, Pepo, Peppercorn, Persian, Pigeon, Pimento, Poke, Pottage, Rhein, Rhine, Sal(l)al, Salmonberry, Slae, Sloe, Sop, Tomatillo

Berserk Amok, Ape-shit, Baresark, Frenzy, Gungho, Rage

Berth Anchorage, Bunk, Cabin, Couchette, Dock, Moor, Seat, Space

Beryl Aquamarine, Emerald, Heliodor, Morganite, Silica

Beryllium Be

Beseech Beg, Crave, Entreat, Implore, Invoke, Obsecrate

Beset Amidst, Assail, Assiege, Badger, Bego, Environ, Harry, Perplex, Scabrid, Siege

Beside(s) Adjacent, Alone, And, At, Au reste, Else, Forby(e), Further(more), Moreover, Next, On, To, Withal, Yet

▷ **Besiege** *may indicate* one word around another

Besiege(d) Beset, Best(ed), Blockade, Gherao, Girt, Invest, Obsess, Plague, Poliorcetic, Surround

Besmirch(ed) Bloody, Bludie, Smear, Soil, Sully

Besom Cow, Kow

Besot(ted) Dotard, Infatuate, Intoxicate, Lovesick, Stupefy

Bespangle Adorn, Gem

Bespeak, Bespoken Address, Bee, Beta, Engage, Hint

Best A1, Ace, All-time, Aristocrat, Beat, Cat's whiskers, Choice, Conquer, Cream, Creme, Damnedest, Deluxe, Elite, Eximious, Finest, Flagship, Flower, Foremost, Greatest, Ideal, Nicest, Optima, Outdo, Outwit, Overcome, Peak, Peerless, Pick, Pièce de résistance, Pink, Plum, Purler, Quintessence, Ream, Sunday, Super, The, The tops, Tiptop, Top, Topper, Transcend, Vanquish, Wale

Bestiality Zoophalia

Bestiary Physiologus

Best man Paranymph

Bestow(al) Accord, Bequeath, Confer, Donate, Endow, → **GIVE**, Impart, Investiture, Present

Bestride Cross

Bet(ting), Betting System A cheval, Ante, Antepost, Back, Banco, Chance, Daily double, Double, Each way, Flutter, Gaff, Gamble, Go, Hedge, Impone, Lay, Long shot, Martingale, Mise, Note, Pari-mutuel, Parlay, Perfecta, Pip, Place, Pot, Punt, Quadrella, Quinella, Ring, Risk, Roll up, Saver, Set, Spec, Sport, Spread, Stake, Superfecta, Tattersalls, Tatts, Totalisator, Totalise, Tote, Treble, Treble chance, Triella, Trifecta, → **WAGER**, Win, Yankee

Betel Catechu, Paan, Pan, Pawn, Siri(h)

Betimes Anon, Early, Soon

Betise Solecism

Betray(al), Betrayer Abandon, Abuse, Belewe, Bewray, Cornuto, Desert, Disclose, Divulge, Dob, Dobbin, Double-cross, Gethsemane, Giveaway, Grass, Judas, Proditor, Renegade, Renege, Rumble, Sell, Sellout, Shop, Sing, Sinon, Stab, Traditor, Traitor, Treachery, Treason, Turncoat

Betroth(ed), Betrothal Assure, Engage, Ensure, Espouse, Fiancé(e), Handfasting, Pledge, Promise, Subarr(h)ation

Better Abler, Amend, Apter, Bigger, Buck, Cap, Convalescent, Fairer, Finer, Gambler, Gamester, Imponent, Improve, Meliorate, Mend, Outdo, Outpoint, Outshine, Outsmart, Outstrip, Outwit, Preponderate, Punter, Race-goer, Reform, Superior, Surpass, Throw, Top, Turfite, Worst

Between Amid, Bet, Betwixt, Inter, Interjacent, Linking, Mesne, Twixt

Bevel Angle, Cant, Oblique, Slope, Splay

Beverage Ale, Cocoa, Coffee, Cordial, Cup, → **DRINK**, Hydromel, Nectar, Tea

Bevy Flock, Group, Herd, Host

Beware Cave, Fore, Heed, Look out, Mind, Mistrust, Pas op

Bewilder(ed), Bewildering, Bewilderment Amaze, At sea, Baffle, Buffalo, Confuse, Consternation, Daze, Flummox, Mate, Maze, Mind-boggling, Mystify, Obfuscate, Perplex, Stun, Taivert, Wander, Will, Wull

Bewitch(ed), Bewitching Charm, Delight, Elf-shot, Enchant, Ensorcell, Glam(orous), Hex, Hoodoo, Jinx, Obeah, Obiah, Strike

Beyond Above, Ayont, Besides, Farther, Outwith, Over, Past, Thule, Trans, Ulterior, Ultra

Bias(ed) Angle, Aslant, Bent, Chauvinism, Discriminatory, Grid, Imbalance, Loaded, One-sided, Partial, Parti pris, Partisan, Penchant, Preconception, Predilection, → **PREJUDICE**, Prepossess, Set, Sexism, Skew, Slope, Spin, Tendency, Unjust, Warp

Bib, Bibulous Apron, Beery, Feeder, Pout, Tope, Tucker

Bibelot Objet d'art

Bible Adulterous, Alcoran, Alkoran, Antilegomena, Apocrypha, ASV, Authority, AV, Avesta, Bamberg, Book, Breeches, Bug, Coverdale, Cranmer, Cromwell, Douai,

Douay, Family, Ferrara, Fool, Forgotten sins, Gemara, Geneva, Gideon, Good book, Goose, Gospel, Gutenberg, Haggada, Hagiographa, Halacha, Heptateuch, Hexapla, Hexateuch, Holy, Idle, Isagogic, Itala, Italic, King James (version), Leda, Matthew Parker, Mazarin(e), Midrash, Missal, Murderer, New English, NT, Omasum, Ostrog, OT, Pentateuch, Peshito, Peshitta, Peshitto, Polyglot, Psalter, Revised Version, RSV, RV, Scriptures, Septuagint, Stomach, Talmud, Tanach, Tantra, Targum, Taverner, Taverners, Thirty-six-line, Treacle, Tyndale, Unrighteous, Vinegar, Vulgate, Whig, Wicked, Wife-hater, Wyclif(fe), Zurich

Biblical scholar Rechabite, USPG, Wycliffe

Bibliophagist, Bibliophile Bookworm

Bicarb Saleratus

Bicker Argue, Bowl, Brawl, Coggie, Dispute, Tiff, Wrangle

Bicycle, Bike(r) Bambi, Bee, Bone-shaker, Chopper, Coaster, Crog(gy), Dandy-horse, Dirt, Draisene, Draisine, Exercise, Fixed-wheel, Hobby, Hobbyhorse, Mixte, Moped, Mount, Mountain, Multicycle, Ordinary, Pedal, Penny-farthing, Quad, Raleigh®, Recumbent, Roadster, Rocker, Safety, Scooter, Spin, Stationary, Tandem, Trail, Tree, Velocipede

Bid(der), Bidding (system) Acol, Apply, Blackwood, Call, Canape, Command, Contract, Cue, Declare, Double, Forcing, Gone, Hostile, Invite, Jump, Misère, Nod, NT, → **OFFER**, Order, Pass, Pre-empt, Proposal, Psychic, Puffer, Redouble, Rescue, Shut-out, Summon, Take-out, Take-over, Tell, Tender, Vied, White bonnet

Biddy Crone, Gammer, Hen

Biennial Trieteric

Bier Hearse, Litter

Big Altruistic, Beamy, Bulky, Bumper, Burly, Cob, Enormous, Fat, Ginormous, Gross, → **LARGE**, Loud, Mansize, Massive, Mighty, Obese, Skookum, Slockdoliger, Slockdologer, Soc(k)dologer, Sogdolager, Sogdoliger, Stonker, Strapping, Substantial, Swopper, Thumping, Tidy, Vast, Whacker, Whopper

Bigamy, Bigamist, Bigamous Bluebeard, Diandrous

Bighead Ego

Bight Canterbury, Great Australian, Heligoland

Bigot(ed) Chauvinist, Dogmatist, Fanatic, Hide-bound, Intolerant, Narrow-minded, Racialist, Racist, Sexist, Wowser, Zealot

Bigshot, Bigwig Cheese, Law lord, Nib, Nob, Oner, Oneyer, Oneyre, Swell, Titan, → **VIP**

Bijou Doll-like

▶ **Bike** *see* **BICYCLE**

Bikini Atoll, Tanga

Bile, Bilious(ness) Cholaemia, Choler, Gall, Icteric, Melancholy, Scholaemia, Venom, Yellow

Bilge Leak, Pump, Rhubarb, Rot, Waste

Bilingual Diglot

Bilk Default

Bill(ed), Billy Ac(c), Accommodation, Accompt, Account, Act, Ad, Addition, Appropriation, Barnacle, Beak, Becke, Budd, Buffalo, Can, Caress, Carte, Chit(ty), Cody, Coo, Coronoid, Cross(-bencher), Demand, Dixy, Docket, Double, Due, Egg-tooth, Exactment, Fin, Finance, Foreign, Gates, Goat, Hybrid, Inland, Invoice, Kaiser, → **LAW**, Lawin(g), Legislation, Liam, Liar, List, Measure, Menu, Neb, Ness, Nib, → **NOTE**, Notice, Paper, Petition, Platypus, Pork barrel, Portland, Poster, Private, Programme, Pruning, Public, Puffing, Reckoning, Reform, Remanet, Rhamphotheca, Rostral, Rostrum, Score, Short, Shot, Show, Sickle, Silly, Sparth(e),

Sperthe, Spoon, Sticker, Tab, Tenner, Tomium, Trade, Treasury, True, Twin, Victualling, Watch, Willy

Billet Berth, Casern, Cess, Chit, Coupon, Note, Quarter

Billet doux Capon, Valentine

Billiards, Billiards player, Billiards stroke Bar, Cannon-game, Cueist, Jenny, Lagging, Long jenny, Massé, Pocket, Pool, Potter, Pyramids, Short jenny, Snooker, String, Whitechapel

Billion Gillion, Milliard, Tera

Bill of sale Bs

Billow Roil, Roller, Rule, Surge, Swell, Wave

▶ **Billy** *see* **BILL**

Bin Bing, Box, Chilly, Container, Crib, Dump, Hell, Litter, Loony, Receptacle, Sin, Snake-pit, Stall, Wagger-pagger, Wheelie, Wheely

Binary ASCII, Semidetached

Bind(er), Binding Adherent, Adhesive, Akedah, Alligate, Apprentice, Astrict, Astringent, Bale, Bandage, Bandeau, Bandster, Bias, Bibliopegist, Brail, Burst, Calf, Cerlox®, Cement, Chain, Cinch, Circuit, Clamp, Colligate, Complain, Cord, Cummerbund, Deligation, Drag, Edge, Embale, Enchain, Engage, Enslave, Enwind, → **FASTEN**, Fetter, Galloon, Gird, Girdle, Grolier, Half-leather, Hay-wire, Hold, Incumbent, Indenture, Iron, Keckle, Lash(er), Law-calf, Leash, Ligament, Ligature, Mail, Marl, Morocco, Muslin, Obi, Obligate, Oblige, Oop, Organdie, Oup, Parpen, Paste grain, Perfect, Pinion, Raffia, Restrict, Ring, → **ROPE**, Roxburghe, Seize, Sheaf, Spiral, Strap, Stringent, Stygian, Swathe, Syndesis, Tape, Tether, Thirl, Thong, Three-quarter, Tie, Tree-calf, Truss, Twine, Unsewn, Valid, Whip, Withe, Yapp, Yerk, Yoke

Bindweed Bearbine, Convolvulus, With(y)wind

Bing Crosby, Go, Heap

Binge Bat, Beano, Bend(er), Blind, Carouse, → **DRINK**, Drinking-bout, Party, Riot, Soak, Souse, Splore, Spree, Toot, Tout

Bingo Beano, Housey-housey, Keno, Lotto, Tombola

Binocular(s) Glasses, Jumelle, OO, Stereoscope

Biochemical, Biochemist(ry) Ames, DNA, Proteomics

Biographer, Biography Boswell, CV, Hagiography, History, Life, Memoir, Plutarch, Potted, Prosopography, Suetonius, Vita

Biology, Biologist Algology, Cladistics, Genetics, Mendel, Molecular, Morphology, Phenetics, Photodynamics, Somatology, Stoechiology, Stoich(e)iology, Taxonomy, Teratology, Transgenics, Weismann

Bioscope Kinema

Birch Birk, Cane, Cow, Flog, Hazel, Kow, Larch, Larrup, Reis, Rice, Rod, Silver, Swish, Twig, Weeping, Whip, White, Withe

▷ **Bird** *may indicate* a prison sentence

Bird(s) Al(l)erion, Altricial, Aves, Avian, Bertram, Brood, Damsel, Doll, Early, Flier, Fowl, Gal, → **GIRL**, Grip, Hen, Jail, Left, Limicoline, Nestling, Ornis, Ornithology, Pecker, Pen, Perching, Poultry, Praecoces, Prison, Quod, Raptor, Roaster, Sentence, Sis, Skirt, Skua, Time, Visitant

BIRDS

2 letters:	3 letters:	Boo	Fum
Ka	Ani	Cob	Jay
Oi	Auk	Emu	Kae

Kea
Maw
Mew
Moa
Nun
Owl
Pea
Pie
Ree
Roc
Ruc
Tit
Tui

4 letters:
Barb
Chat
Cirl
Cobb
Coly
Coot
Crax
Crow
Dodo
Dove
→ DUCK
Emeu
Erne
Eyas
Fung
Gled
Gnow
Guan
Guga
Gull
Hawk
Hern
Huia
Huma
Ibis
Iynx
Jynx
Kagu
Kaka
Kite
Kiwi
Knot
Koel
Kora
Lark
Loom

Loon
Lory
Mina
Monk
Myna
Nene
Otis
Pavo
Pawn
Pern
Piet
Pink
Pown
Pyot
Rail
Rhea
Roch
Rook
Ruff
Ruru
Rype
Shag
Smee
Sora
Swan
Taha
Tara
Teal
Tern
Tick
Tody
Tuli
Weka
Wren
Xema
Yale
Yite

5 letters:
Agami
Ardea
Ariel
Bennu
Booby
Bosun
Cahow
Capon
Colin
Colly
Crake
Crane

Diver
Egret
Finch
Fleet
Galah
Glede
Goose
Goura
Grebe
Heron
Hobby
Homer
Isaac
Junco
Kawau
Kight
Liver
Lowan
Macaw
Madge
Manch
Mavis
Merle
Mimus
Mohua
Monal
Murre
Mynah
Nandu
Nelly
Noddy
Ousel
Ox-eye
Peggy
Pekan
Pewit
Picus
Pilot
Piper
Pipit
Pitta
Poaka
Poker
Potoo
Prion
Quail
Quest
Quist
Raven
Reeve
Robin

Rotch
Ryper
Saker
Satin
Scape
Scart
Scaup
Scops
Scray
Scrub
Serin
Shama
Sitta
Skart
Snipe
Solan
Soree
Spink
Sprug
Squab
Stare
Stilt
Stint
Stork
Swift
Sylph
Terek
Tewit
Topaz
Twite
Umber
Umbre
Urubu
Veery
Vireo
Wader
Whaup
Widow
Wonga
Yaffa

6 letters:
Aquila
Avocet
Avoset
Bantam
Barbet
Bishop
Bittor
Bittur
Bonxie

6 letters – cont:
Boubou
Brolga
Bulbul
Canary
Chough
Chukar
Condor
Corbie
Coucal
Cuckoo
Curlew
Cushat
Darter
Dikkop
Dipper
Drongo
Duiker
Dunlin
Duyker
Elanet
Evejar
Falcon
Fulmar
Gambet
Gander
Gannet
Garuda
Gentle
Gentoo
Go-away
Godwit
Gooney
Goslet
Grakle
Grouse
Hagden
Hagdon
Haglet
Hermit
Hoopoe
Houdan
Jabiru
Jacana
Jaeger
Jubjub
Kakapo
Kotare
Kotuku
Lanner
Leipoa

Linnet
Lintie
Loerie
Loriot
Lourie
Lungie
Magpie
Martin
Matata
Menura
Merlin
Merops
Missel
Mistle
Monaul
Mopoke
Mossie
Motmot
Musket
Mutton
Nandoo
Oriole
Oscine
Osprey
Oxbird
Parrot
Parson
Pavone
Peahen
Peeper
Peewee
Peewit
Pernis
Petrel
Phoebe
Pigeon
Piopio
Plover
Pouter
Progne
Puffin
Pukeko
Pullet
Queest
Quelea
Quoist
Redcap
Reeler
Roller
Rotche
Scamel

Scarth
Scaury
Scoter
Scraye
Sea-cob
Sea-mew
Seapie
Shrike
Simara
Simorg
Simurg
Siskin
Skarth
Smeath
Soland
Sorage
Strich
Sultan
Sylvia
Tailor
Takahe
Tarcel
Tassel
Tewhit
Thrush
Tom-tit
Toucan
Towhee
Trogon
Turaco
Turbit
Turkey
Tyrant
Tystie
Verdin
Walker
Waxeye
Weaver
Whidah
Whydah
Willet
Woosel
Yaffle
Ynambu
Yucker
Zoozoo

7 letters:
Amokura
Anhinga
Antbird

Apteryx
Axebird
Babbler
Bécasse
Bee-kite
Bittern
Bittour
Bluecap
Blue-eye
Blue jay
Bluetit
Boobook
Bullbat
Bunting
Buphaga
Bush-tit
Bustard
Buzzard
Cacique
Cariama
Cheeper
Chewink
Chicken
Coal-tit
Cole-tit
Colibri
Corella
Cotinga
Courlan
Courser
Cow-bird
Creeper
Crombec
Cropper
Diamond
Dinorus
Dottrel
Dovekie
Dunnock
Emu-wren
Fantail
Fern-owl
Figbird
Finfoot
Flicker
Frigate
Gleerie
Gobbler
Goburra
Gorcrow
Goshawk

Grackle
Grallae
Hacklet
Hadedah
Hagbolt
Hagdown
Halcyon
Harrier
Hemipod
Hoatzin
Humming
Ice-bird
Jacamar
Jackdaw
Kahawai
Kamichi
Kestrel
Killdee
Kinglet
Koekoea
Lapwing
Leghorn
Limpkin
Manakin
Maribou
Martlet
Mesites
Minivet
Mudlark
Oilbird
Ortolan
Oscines
Ostrich
Oven-tit
Pandion
Peacock
Peafowl
Pelican
Penguin
Phoenix
Pickmaw
Piculet
Pinnock
Pintado
Pintail
Pochard
Pockard
Poe-bird
Poy-bird
Quetzal
Rainbow

Rasores
Ratitae
Redpoll
Redwing
Regulus
Rooster
Rosella
Rotchie
Ruddock
Sakeret
Sawbill
Scooper
Scourie
Seagull
Sea-lark
Sea-mell
Simurgh
Sirgang
Sitella
Skimmer
Skylark
Snow-cap
Spadger
Sparrow
Squacco
Staniel
Stinker
Sturnus
Sunbird
Swallow
Tanager
Tanagra
Tarrock
Tattler
Teacher
Teuchat
Tiercel
Tinamou
Titanis
Titlark
Titling
Tokahea
Totanus
Touraco
Tumbler
Tweeter
Vulture
Vulturn
Wagtail
Warbler
Waxbill

Waxwing
Whooper
Widgeon
Wimbrel
Witwall
Woosell
Wren-tit
Wrybill
Wryneck
Yang-win

8 letters:

Aasvogel
Accentor
Adjutant
Aigrette
Alcatras
Altrices
Amadavat
Aquiline
Araponga
Arapunga
Arenaria
Avadavat
Barnacle
Bee-eater
Bellbird
Blackcap
Bluebird
Blue-wing
Boatbill
Boattail
Bobolink
Bob-white
Buln-buln
Caracara
Cardinal
Cargoose
Cheewink
Chirn-owl
Cockatoo
Cockerel
Coquette
Curassow
Dabchick
Didapper
Dip-chick
Dobchick
Dotterel
Estridge
Fauvette

Fernbird
Fish-hawk
Flamingo
Gambetta
Gang-gang
Garefowl
Garganey
Gnatwren
Greenlet
Grosbeak
Guacharo
Hackbolt
Hangbird
Hangnest
Hawfinch
Hazelhen
Hemipode
Hernshaw
Hickymal
Hoactzin
Hornbill
Killdeer
Kingbird
Kiskadee
Landrail
Lanneret
Laverock
Longspur
Lorikeet
Lyrebird
Magotpie
Man-of-war
Marsh-tit
Megapode
Mire-drum
Miromiro
Morepork
Murrelet
Nightjar
Notornis
Nuthatch
Ovenbird
Oxpecker
Paradise
Parakeet
Peetweet
Percolin
Petchary
Phaethon
Pheasant
Philomel

8 letters – cont:
Pihoihoi
Podargus
Poorwill
Prunella
Puffbird
Quarrian
Quarrion
Rainbird
Rallidae
Redshank
Redstart
Reedling
Reed-wren
Rice-bird
Ringtail
Riroriro
Rocketer
Sandpeep
Scolopar
Screamer
Sea-eagle
Shake-bag
Shelduck
Shoebill
Silktail
Sittella
Skua-gull
Snowbird
Snowy owl
Stanniel
Starling
Struthio
Surfbird
Swiftlet
Tantalus
Tapacolo
Tapaculo
Teru-tero
Thrasher
Thresher
Throstle
Ticklace
Titmouse
Tom-noddy
Toucanet
Tragopan
Trembler
Troopial
Troupial
Tubenose

Umbrella
Umbrette
Water-hen
Wheatear
Whimbrel
Whinchat
Whipbird
Whitecap
White-eye
Wildfowl
Wirebird
Woodchat
Woodcock
Woodlark
Woodwale
Wood wren
Xanthura
Yoldring

9 letters:
Accipiter
Aepyornis
Albatross
Aylesbury
Baldicoot
Baltimore
Beccaccia
Beccafico
Beefeater
Bergander
Blackbird
Blackhead
Blackpoll
Blood bird
Bower-bird
Brambling
Broadbill
Bullfinch
Campanero
Cassowary
Chaffinch
Chatterer
Chickadee
Coachwhip
Cockatiel
Cormorant
Corncrake
Crocodile
Cross-bill
Currawong
Dove prion

Dowitcher
Eider duck
Estreldid
Fieldfare
Fig-pecker
Fire-crest
Fledgling
Francolin
Friarbird
Frogmouth
Gallinule
Gerfalcon
Gier-eagle
Goldcrest
Goldfinch
Goosander
Grassquit
Grenadier
Guillemot
Hammerkop
Happy Jack
Helldiver
Heronshaw
Hornywink
Icteridae
Impundulu
Jack-snipe
Kittiwake
Lintwhite
Mallemuck
Merganser
Mistletoe
Mollymawk
Mousebird
Night-hawk
Nutjobber
Nutpecker
Olive-back
Organ-bird
Ossifraga
Ossifrage
Paddy bird
Pardalote
Partridge
Peaseweep
Peregrine
Phalarope
Pictarnie
Pine finch
Porphyrio
Ptarmigan

Razorbill
Riflebird
Rosy-finch
Sabrewing
Salangane
Sandpiper
Sapsucker
Satinbird
Scansores
Sea-turtle
Secretary
Sedge-wren
Seedeater
Sheldrake
Shoveller
Silver eye
Skunk-bird
Solitaire
Spoonbill
Standgale
Stonechat
Stormbird
Storm-cock
Sugarbird
Swart-back
Sword-bill
Talegalla
Thickhead
Thick-knee
Thornbill
Trochilus
Trumpeter
Turnstone
Volucrine
Water cock
Water-rail
Wind-hover
Woodshock
Woodspite
Xanthoura

10 letters:
Aberdevine
Bearded tit
Bluebreast
Bluethroat
Brain-fever
Bubbly-jock
Budgerigar
Butter-bump
Chiff-chaff

Crested tit
Demoiselle
Dickcissel
Didunculus
Dive-dapper
Dollarbird
Dung-hunter
Ember-goose
Eyas-musket
Fallow-chat
Fly-catcher
Four o'clock
Fringillid
Goatsucker
Gobemouche
Grassfinch
Greenfinch
Greenshank
Hen-harrier
Herald-duck
Honey-eater
Honey guide
Kingfisher
Kookaburra
Locust-bird
Mallee fowl
Marsh-robin
Meadowlark
Night-churr
Noisy miner
Nutcracker
Peckerwood
Pettichaps
Pettychaps
Pick-cheese
Pratincole
Quaker-bird
Racket-tail
Rafter-bird
Rain-plover
Ramphastos
Regent-bird
Rhinoceros
Roadrunner
Ruby-throat
Saddleback
Saddlebill
Sanderling

Sandgrouse
Sea swallow
Shearwater
Sheathbill
Sicklebill
Silverbill
Snowy egret
Spatchcock
Stone-snipe
Tanagridae
Tropicbird
Turtledove
Wattlebird
Weasel coot
Weaver bird
Whisky-jack
Whisky-john
Wonga-wonga
Woodpecker
Woodpigeon
Wood shrike
Wood thrush
Yaffingale
Yellowbird
Yellowhead
Yellowlegs
Yellowyite

11 letters:
Apostlebird
Bokmakierie
Bristlebird
Butcherbird
Canada goose
Cape sparrow
Cooper's hawk
Fallow-finch
Fringilline
Gnatcatcher
Golden eagle
Grallatores
Happy-family
Honey-sucker
House martin
Humming-bird
Ichthyornis
Java sparrow
Leatherhead

Mockingbird
Moss-bluiter
Moss-cheeper
Nightingale
Pied wagtail
Plantcutter
Purple finch
Pyrrhuloxia
Reed-warbler
Scissorbill
Scissortail
Snowbunting
Sparrow-hawk
Stilt-plover
Stone-curlew
Storm petrel
Stymphalian
Thunderbird
Tree-creeper
Wall creeper
Water-thrush
Weaver-finch
Whitethroat
Wishtonwish
Woodcreeper
Woodswallow
Woodwarbler
Yellow-ammer

12 letters:
Bronze-pigeon
Drongo-cuckoo
Drongo-shrike
Flowerpecker
Hedge-warbler
Honey creeper
Missel-thrush
Mosquito-hawk
Peppershrike
Ring-dotterel
Sage-thrasher
Sedge-warbler
Serpent-eater
Standard-wing
Stonechatter
Stormy petrel
Tangle-picker
Throstle-cock

Water-wagtail
Whippoorwill
Willy wagtail
Yellow-hammer
Yellow-yowley

13 letters:
Archaeopteryx
Babblingbrook
Bermuda petrel
Cetti's warbler
Chaparral cock
Cock-of-the-rock
Mocking thrush
Oyster-catcher
Pipiwharauroa
Plantain-eater
Willow-wagtail
Willow warbler
Wilson's petrel

14 letters:
Manx shearwater
Tawny frogmouth
Woodchat shrike

15 letters:
Chipping sparrow
Montagu's harrier

16 letters:
Tyrant flycatcher
White-fronted tern

17 letters:
Pectoral sandpiper
Spotted flycatcher

18 letters:
Paradise flycatcher

20 letters:
Mother Carey's
chickens

Bird-catcher Avicularia, Fowler, Papageno
Bird-like Hirundine, Sturnine

Bird's nest(ing) Caliology, Monotropa, Soup
Bird-watcher Augur, Twitcher
Birkenhead F.E.Smith
Birmingham Brum(magem)
Birth Burden, Congenital, Delivery, Drop, Extraction, Genesis, Geniture, Happy event, Jataka, Lineage, Multiple, Nativity, Natural, Origin, Parage, Parity, Parturition, Virgin
Birthday Anniversary, Genethliac
Birthmark Blemish, Mole, Mother-spot, Naevus, Port wine stain, Stigmata, Strawberry
Birthright Heritage, Mess, Patrimony
Birthwort Aristolochia
Biscuit Abernethy, Bath-oliver, Biscotto, Bourbon, Brandysnap, Brown George, Butterbake, Captain's, Charcoal, Cookie, Cracker, Cracknel, Crispbread, Dandyfunk, Digestive, Dog, Dunderfunk, Fairing, Flapjack, Florentine, Fly cemetery, Fortune cookie, Four-by-two, Garibaldi, Ginger nut, Gingersnap, Hardtack, Kiss, Langue de chat, Lavash, Lebkuchen, Macaroon, Marie, Mattress, Matza(h), Matzo(h), Nut, Oatcake, Oliver, Osborne, Parkin, Perkin, Petit four, Petticoat tail, Pig's ear, Pilot, Poppadom, Poppadum, Pretzel, Ratafia, Rice, Rusk, Rye-roll, Sea, Ship's, Shortbread, Snap, Soda, Sweetmeal, Tack, Tan, Tararua, Tea, Wafer, Water, Wine, Zwieback
Bisexual AC/DC, Freemartin, Switch-hitter
Bishop(ric) Aaronic, Abba, Aberdeen, Aidan, Ambrose, Apollinaris, Bench, Berkeley, Bp, Cambrensis, Cantuar, Chad, Chorepiscopal, Coadjutor, Coverdale, Cranmer, Diocesan, Dunelm, Ebor, Ely, Eparch, Episcopate, Eusebian, Exarch, Exon, Golias, Hatto, Henson, Jansen, Latimer, Lord, Magpie, Metropolitan, Missionary, Norvic, Odo, Ordainer, Patriarch, Peter, Petriburg, Piece, Polycarp, Pontiff, Prelate, Priest, Primate, Primus, Proudie, Ridley, Roffen, RR, Sarum, Sleeve, Sodor and Man, Suffragan, The purple, Titular, Tulchan, Weaver, Weed, Winton, Wrexham
Bismarck Otto
Bismuth Bi
Bison Bonas(s)us, Buffalo, Ox, Wisent
Bit Ate, Baud, Cantle(t), Centre, Chad, Cheesecake, Chip, Coin, Crumb, Curb, Curn, Degree, Drib, Excerpt, Flibbert, Fraction, Gag, Haet, Hate, Ion, Jaw, Jot, Mite, Modicum, Morsel, Mote, Mu, Nit, Ort, Ounce, Pelham, Peni, Penny, → **PIECE**, Port, Rap, Rare, Ratherish, Scintilla, Scrap, Section, Shaving, Shiver, Shred, Smidgen, Smidgeon, Smidgin, Snaffle, Snatch, Snippet, Some, Soupcon, Spale, Speck, Splinter, Spot, Spudding, Suspicion, Tad, Tait, Tate, Threepenny, Trace, Unce, Vestige, What, Whit
Bite(r), Biting, Bitten Astringent, Canapé, Caustic, Chelicera, Chew, Eat, Engouled, Erose, Etch, Gnash, Gnat, Hickey, Hickie, Incisor, Knap, Masticate, Midge, Molar, Mordacious, Mordant, Morsel, Morsure, Nibble, Nip(py), Occlude, Peck, Pium, Premorse, Rabid, Sarcastic, Sharp, Shrewd, Snack, Snap, Sound, Spammie, Tart
Bitter(ness) Absinth, Acerb, Acid, Acrid, Acrimonious, Ale, Aloe, Angostura, Bile, Cassareep, Caustic, Eager, Edge, Ers, Fell, Gall, Keen, Keg, Marah, Maror, Myrrh, Pique, Rancorous, Rankle, Resentful, Sarcastic, Sardonic, Snell, Sore, Spleen, Tannin, Tart(aric), Venom, Verjuice, Virulent, Vitriolic, Wersh, Wormwood, Wry
Bittern Boomer, Bull-of the-bog, Butterbump, Heron, Mossbluiter, Sedge, Siege
Bittersweet Dulcamara, Poignant, Staff-tree
Bitumen Albertite, Asphalt, Blacktop, Elaterite, Gilsonite®, Maltha, Mineral tar, Pissasphalt, Pitch, Tar, Tarseal, Uintaite

Bivalve Clam, Cockle, Lamellibranch, Mollusc, Muscle, Mussel, Oyster, Pelecypod, Piddock, Razorshell, Scallop, Tuatua, Whelk

Bivouac Camp

Bizarre Antic, Curious, Eccentric, Exotic, Fantastic, Far-out, Freaky, Gonzo, Grotesque, Odd, Off-the-wall, Outlandish, Outré, Pythonesque, Queer, Strange, Surreal, Weird

▷ **Bizarre** *may indicate* an anagram

Blab Babble, Gossip, Prate, Squeal

Black(en), Blackness Amadoda, Atramental, B, Ban, BB, Bess, → **BLACK-OUT**, Blae, Boong, Cape Coloured, Carbon, Char, Charcoal, Cilla, Coal, Coloured, Coon, Cypress, Darkie, Darky, Death, Debar, Denigrate, Dinge, Dwale, Ebon(y), Ethiop, Fuzzy-wuzzy, Geechee, Gladwellise, Graphite, Grime, Heben, Hole, Ink(y), Ivory, Japan, Jeat, Jet, Jim Crow, Kohl, Lepidomelane, Malign, Market, Melanic, Melano, Moke, Moor, Muntu, Myall, Negritude, Negro, Niello, Niger, Nigrescent, Nigritude, Obscure, Outage, Oxford, Piceous, Pitch, Platinum, Pongo, Prince, Pudding, Puke, Quashee, Quashie, Raven, Sable, Sambo, Scab, School, Sericon, Sheep, Slae, Sloe, Snowball, Sodium, Solvent, Sombre, Soot, Sooterkin, Spade, Spook, Stygian, Swart(y), Swarth(y), Tar, Uncle Tom, Weeds

Black art Necromancy, Nigromancy

Blackball Ban, Exclude, Pill, Pip, Reject

Blackberry Acini, Bramble, Mooch, Mouch

Blackbird Collybird, Crow, Jackdaw, Ousel, Raven, Woosel

Blackcurrant Quinsy-berry

Black eye(d) Half-mourning, Keeker, Mouse, Shiner, Susan

Blackguard Leg, Nithing, Raff, Revile, Rotter, Scoundrel, Sweep

Blackhead Comedo

Black hole Collapsar

Blackjack Billie, Billy, Cosh, Flag, Sphalerite, Tankard, Truncheon, Vingt(-et)-un

Blackleg Fink, Rat, Scab, Snob

Black-letter Gothic

Black magic Goety

Blackmail(er) Bleed, Chantage, Chout, Exact, Extort, Greenmail, Honey-trap, Ransom, Shakedown, Strike, Vampire

Black-out ARP, Eclipse, Faint, Obliterate, Obscure, Swoon

Black Sea Pontic, Pontus Euxinus

Black sheep Neer-do-well, Reprobate

Blacksmith Brontes, Burn-the-wind, Farrier, Forger, Harmonious, Plater, Shoer, Vulcan

Blackthorn Sloe

Bladder(wort) Air, Balloon, Blister, Cholecyst, Cyst, Gall, Hydatid, Isinglass, Popweed, Sac, Sound, Swim, Urinary, Utricle, Varec(h), Vesica, Vesicle

Blade(s) Acrospire, Bilbo, Brand, Brown Bill, Cleaver, Co(u)lter, Cutlass, Dandy, Espada, Faible, Foible, Forte, Gleave, Gouge, Guillotine, Hydrofoil, Knife, Lance, Lawnmower, Leaf, Man, Mouldboard, Oar, Omoplate, Paddle, Palmetto, Peel, Propeller, Rachilla, Rapier, Razor, Rip, Rotor, Scimitar, Scull, Scythe, Skate, Spade-, Spatula, Spatule, Spear, Spoon, Stiletto, Stock, Strigil, Sweep, → **SWORD**, Symitar, Toledo, Turbine, Vane, Vorpal, Wash, Web

Blair Eric, Lionel, Tony

Blame(worthy) Accuse, Censure, Condemn, Confound, Decry, Dirdam, Dirdum, Dispraise, Fault, Guilt, Inculpate, Odium, Rap, Reprehensible, Reproach, Reprove, Stick, Thank, Twit, Wight, Wite, Wyte

Blameless Innocent, Irreproachable, Lily-white, Unimpeachable
Blanch Bleach, Etiolate, Scaud, Whiten
Blancmange Carrageen, Flummery, Mould, Shape, Timbale
Bland Anodyne, Glop, Mild, Pigling, Sleek, Smooth, Spammy, Suave, Tame, Tasteless, Unctuous
Blandish(ment) Agremens, Agrement, Cajole, → **COAX**, Flatter, Treacle, Wheedle
Blank Burr, Cartridge, Empty, Erase, Flan, Ignore, Lacuna, Mistigris, Planchet, Shot, Space, Tabula rasa, → **VACANT**
Blanket Afghan, Bluey, Chilkat, Counterpane, Cover, Electric, Fire, General, Hudson's Bay, Kaross, Mackinaw, Manta, Obscure, Overall, Poncho, Quilt, Rug, Saddle, Sarape, Security, Serape, Shabrack, Smog, Space, Stroud, Wagga, Wet, Whittle
Blare Horn, Trumpet
Blarney Cajolery, Flattery, Nonsense, Sawder, Taffy
Blasé Worldly
Blaspheme, Blasphemous Abuse, → **CURSE**, Defame, Profanity, Revile
Blast(ed), Blasting Blight, Blore, Blow, Bombard, Dang, Darn, Dee, Drat, Dynamite, Explode, Fanfare, Flaming, Flurry, Fo(e)hn, Gale, Grit, Gust, Noser, Oath, Parp, Pryse, Rats, Ruddy, Scarth, Scath(e), Sere, Shot, Sideration, Skarth, Stormer, Tantara, Toot, Tromp(e), Trump(et), Volley
Blatant Flagrant, Hard-core, Noticeable, Open, Strident, Unashamed, Vulgar
Blather Baloney, Gabble, Gibber
Blaze(r) Beacon, Bonfire, Burn, Cannel, Conflagration, Firestorm, → **FLAME**, Flare, Glare, Jacket, Low(e), Lunt, Palatinate, Race, Ratch, Sati, Star, Sun, Tead(e)
Bleach Agene, Blanch, Chemic, Chloride, Decolorate, Etiolate, Frost, Janola®, Keir, Kier, Peroxide, Whiten, Whitster
Bleak Ablet, Bare, Barren, Blay, Bley, Cheerless, Dour, Dreary, Dreich, Gaunt, Raw, Soulless, Wintry
Bleary Blurred, Smudged
Bleat Baa, Blat, Bluster, Maa
Bleed(er), Bleeding Breakthrough, Cup, Ecchymosis, Epistaxis, Extort, Extravasate, Fleam, Haemorrhage, Leech, Menorrhagia, Menorrh(o)ea, Metrorrhagia, Milk, Purpura, Rhinorrhagia, Root-pressure
Bleep Earcon, Pager
Blefuscudian Big-endian, Little-endian
Blemish Birthmark, Blot, Blotch, Blur, Botch, Defect, Flaw, Mackle, Mark, Milium, Mote, Naevus, Scar, Smirch, Spot, Stain, Sully, Taint, Tash, Vice, Wart, Wen
Blench Flinch, Recoil, Wince
▷ **Blend** *may indicate* an anagram
Blend(ing) Amalgam, Coalesce, Commix, Contemper, Contrapuntal, Counterpoint, Electrum, Fuse, Go, Harmonize, Hydrate, Interfuse, Interlace, Liquidise, Meld, Melt, → **MERGE**, Mingle, Mix, Osmose, Portmanteau, Scumble, Sfumato, Synalepha
Blenny Eel-pout, Gunnel, Shanny
Bless(ing), Blessed(ness) Amen, Approval, Asset, Beatitude, Benedicite, Benediction, Benison, Benitier, Bensh, Bismillah, Boon, Brachah, Brocho, Charmed, Consecrate, Cup, Damosel, Darshan, Elysium, Ethereal, Felicity, Gesundheit, Godsend, Grace, Gwyneth, Holy (dam), Kiddush, Luck, Macarise, Mercy, Mixed, Sain, Saint, Sanctify, Sanctity, Sheva Brachoth, Sheva Brochos, Sneeze, Toronto, Urbi et orbi, Xenium
Bless me Lawk(s)

Blight Afflict, Ague, American, Apple, Bespot, Blast, Destroy, Early, Eyesore, Fire, Late, Planning, Potato, Rot, → **RUIN**, Rust, Sandy, Shadow, Viticide, Waldersterben, Wither

Blighter Cuss, Perisher, Varment, Varmint

Blimey Coo, Cor, Crimini, O'Riley, Strewth

Blimp Airship, Colonel

Blind(ness), Blind spot Amaurosis, Amblyopia, Artifice, Austrian, Bedazzle, Beesome, Bisson, Blend, Blotto, Carousal, Cecity, Chi(c)k, Cog, Concealed, Dazzle, Drop serene, Eyeless, Feint, Festoon, Flash, Gravel, Hemeralopia, Homer, Hood, Jalousie, Legless, Meropia, Mole, Night, Nyctalopia, Onchocerciasis, Persian, Persiennes, Pew, Prestriction, Rash, River, Roller, Roman, Scotoma, Seel, Shade, Shutter, Sightless, Snow, Stimie, Stimy, Stymie, Sun, Teichopsia, Typhlology, Venetian, Visually challenged, Window, Word, Yblent

Blindfish Amblyopsis

Blindfold Bandage, Hoodwink, Muffle, Seal, Wimple

Blindworm Anguis

Blink, Blinker(s), Blinkered, Blinking Bat, Blepharism, Blinders, Bluff, Broken, Eye-flap, Flash, Haw, Idiot, Insular, Nictate, Owl-eyed, Owly, Twink, Wapper, Water, Wink

Bliss(ful) Beatitude, Bouyan, Composer, Delight, → **ECSTASY**, Eden, Elysium, Happy, Idyll, Ignorance, Married, Millenium, Nirvana, Paradise, Rapture, Sion, Tir-na-nog, Valhalla, Walhalla, Wedded

Blister(ed), Blistering Blab, Blain, Bleb, Bubble, Bullate, Cantharidine, Cold sore, Epispastic, Fever, Herpes, Overgall, Pemphigus, Phlyct(a)ena, Scorching, Tetter, Vesicant, Vesicle, Visicate, Water

Blitz Attack, Bombard, Onslaught, Raid

Blizzard Buran, Gale, Snowstorm, Whiteout

Bloat(er) Buckling, Puff, Strout, Swell, Tumefy, Two-eyed steak, Yarmouth

Blob Bead, Bioblast, Dollop, Drop, Globule, O, Pick, Spot, Tear

Bloc Alliance, Cabal, Cartel, Party

Block(er), Blockage, Blocked, Blocking Altar, Anvil, Ashlar, Atresia, → **BAR**, Barber's, Barricade, Barrier, Battle-axe, Brake, Breeze, Brick, Briquet(te), Building, Bung, Bunt, Catasta, Cavity, Chinese, Choke, Chunk, Cinder, Cleat, Clint, Clog, Clot, Cloy, Compass, Congest, Constipated, Cut-off, Cyclopean, Cylinder, Dado, → **DAM**, Dead-eye, Debar, Delete, Dentel, Dentil, Die, Dit, Domino, Electrotint, Embolism, Emphractic, Encompass, Erratic, Euphroe, Fiddle, Fipple, Frog, Gypsum, Hack-log, Heart, High-rise, Hunk, Ice, Ileus, Impasse, Impede, Impost, Ingot, Input, Insula, Interclude, Interrupt, Investment, Jam, Licence, Lifestyle, Line, Lingot, Lodgment, Log-jam, Lump, Mental, Ministroke, Mitre, Monkey, Mounting, Mutule, Nerve, Nifedipine, Nog, Notepad, Oasis®, Obstacle, → **OBSTRUCT**, Occlude, Office, Opossum, Oppilate, Pad, Page, Parry, Perched, Pile-cap, Pile-up, Pillow, Planer, Plinth, Plummer, Power, Pre-empt, Prevent, Process, Psychological, Quad, Ram, Saddle, Scotch, Seal, Sett, Siege, Snatch, Stalemate, Stap, Starting, Stenosis, Stimie, Stimy, Stone, Stonewall, Stop, Stumbling, Stymie, Sun, Swage, Tamp, Tetrapod, Thwart, Tint, Tower, Tranche, Trig, Triglyph, Truck, Uphroe, Upping-stock, Vibropac®, Wig, Wood(cut), Wrest, Writer's, Zinco, Zugzwang

Blockbuster Epic

Blockhead Jolterhead, Mome, Nitwit, Noodle, Pig sconce, Stupid

Blockhouse Igloo

Bloke Beggar, Chap, Cove, Fellow, Gent, Man, Oik

Blond(e) Ash, Cendré, Fair, Flaxen, Goldilocks, Peroxide, Platinised, Platinum, Strawberry, Tallent, Tow-haired, Towhead

Blood(y), Blood letting A, Ancestry, B, Bad, Bally, Blue, Blut, Claret, Clot, Cold, Cruor, Cup, Ecchymosis, Ensanguine, Epigons, Factor, First, Full, → **GORE**, Haemal, Haemorrhage, Ichor, Internecine, Introduce, Kin, Kinship, Knut, Menses, Microcyte, New, Nut, O, Opsonin, Parentage, Penny dreadful, Persue, Pigeon's, Plasma, Platelet, Plurry, Properdin, Pup, Race, Rare, Red, Rh negative, Rh positive, Ruby, Sang, Schistosoma, Serum, Show, Stroma, Toff, Venisection, Welter, Whole, Young

Blood disease, Blood disorder, Blood-poisoning Haematuria, Hypinosis, Isch(a)emia, Leukemia, Lipaemia, Oligaemia, Purpura, Pyaemia, Sapraemia, Septicemia, Spanaemia, Thalassemia, Thrombocytopenia, Toxaemia, Uraemia

Bloodhound Lime, Lyam, Rach(e), Ratch, Sleuth, Spartan

Bloodless Anaemic, Isch(a)emic, Wan, White

Blood-letter Leech, Phlebotomist, Sangrado

Blood money Eric

▶ **Blood-poisoning** *see* **BLOOD DISEASE**

Blood-pressure Hypertension, Hypotension

Bloodshot Red-eyed

Blood-sport Hunting, Shooting, Venery

Blood-sucker Asp, Bed bug, Dracula, Flea, Gnat, Ked, Leech, Louse, Mosquito, Parasite, Reduviid, Sponger, Tick, Vampire(-bat)

Bloom(er), Blooming Anthesis, Bally, Blossom, Blow, Blush, Boner, Cobalt, Dew, Effloresce, Error, Film, Florence, Florescent, Flowery, Flush, Gaffe, Glaucous, Heyday, Knickers, Loaf, Miscalculation, Nickel, Out, Peach, Pruina, Rationals, Reh, Remontant, Rosy, Ruddy, Thrive, Underwear

▷ **Bloomer** *may indicate* a flower

Blossom Blow, Burgeon, Catkin, Festoon, Flourish, Flower, May, Orange, Pip

Blot Atomy, Blob, Cartel, Delete, Disgrace, Dry, Eyesore, Obscure, Smear, Smudge, Southern, Splodge, Splotch

Blotch(y) Blemish, Giraffe, Monk, Mottle(d), Spot, Stain

Blotto Legless

Blouse Choli, Garibaldi, Gimp, Guimpe, Kerbaya, Middy, Pneumonia, Sailor, Shirtwaist, Smock, Tunic, Waist(er), Windjammer

Blow(er) Appel, Bang, Bash, Bat, Bellows, Biff, Billow, Blip, Bloom, Box, Brag, Breeze, Buckhorse, Buffet, Bump, Burst, Calamity, Clap, Clat, Claut, Clip, Clout, Clump, Conk, Coup, Cuff, Dad, Daud, Dawd, Dev(v)el, Dinnyhayser, Dint, Dod, Douse, Dowse, Estramacon, Etesian, Exsufflate, Facer, Fan, Fillip, Fisticuffs, Gale, Grampus, Gust, Hammer, Hander, Haymaker, Hit, Hook, Ictus, Impact, Insufflate, Karate, Kibosh, Knuckle sandwich, KO, Lame, Lander, Left-hander, Lick, Lounder, Muff, Muzzler, Neck-herring, Northerly, Noser, Oner, One-two, Paddywhack, Paik, Pash, Peise, Phone, Piledriver, Plague, Plug, Plump(er), Polt, Pow, Puff, Punch, Purler, Raft, Rats, Rattler, Rib-roaster, Roundhouse, Sas(s)arara, Scat, Settler, Short, Sideswipe, Side-winder, Sis(s)erary, Skiff, Skite, Skyte, Slat, Slog, Slug, Snell, Snot, Sock, Sockdolager, Sockdologer, Southwester, Spanking, Spat, Spout, Squall, Squander, Squelcher, Stripe, Stroke, Strooke, Stunning, Sufflate, Supercharger, Swash, Swat, Swinger, Telephone, Thump, Thwack, Tingler, Tootle, Trump(et), Tuck, Undercut, Upper-cut, Waft, Wallop, Wap, Waste, Welt, Whammy, Whample, Whang, Whap, Wheeze, Wherret, Whiffle, Whirret, Whistle, → **WIND**, Winder, Wipe, Wuther

Blown-up Elated, Enlarged, Exploded

Blow-out Binge, Bloat, Exhale, Feast, Feed, Flat, Fulminate, Lava, Nosh-up, Snuff, Spiracle, → **SPREAD**

Blowpipe Hod, Peashooter, Sarbacane, Sumpit(an)

Blub(ber) Cry, Fat, Snotter, Sob, Speck, → **WEEP**, Whimper

Bludge Sinecure

Bludgeon Bulldoze, Bully, Club, Cosh, Cudgel, Sap

▷ **Blue** *may indicate* an anagram

Blue(s) Abattu, Accablé, Adult, Anil, Aqua, Aquamarine, Azure, Azurn, Beard, Berlin, Bice, Bleuâtre, Blow, Bottle, Butterfly, C, Caesious, Cafard, Cambridge, Cantab, Celeste, Cerulean, City, Clair de lune, Classic, Cobalt, Coomassie, Copenhagen, Cornflower, Country, Coventry, Cyan, Danish, Danube, Dejected, Dirty, Disconsolate, Doldrums, → **DOWN**, Duck-egg, Eatanswill, Eggshell, Electric, Facetiae, Firmament, Fritter, Gentian, Germander, Glaucous, Glum, Hauyne, Heliotrope, Hump, Indecent, Indigo, Indol(e), Iron, Isatin(e), Lapis lazuli, Lavender, Lewd, Lionel, Low, Mazarine, Methylene, Midnight, Monastral®, Mope, Morose, Murder, Nattier, Naughty, Navy, Nile, Obscene, Ocean, Off-colour, Oxford, Peacock, Periwinkle, Perse, Petrol, Phycocyan, Porn, Powder, Prussian, Rabbi, Ribald, Riband, Right, Ripe, Robin's egg, Royal, Sad, Sapphire, Saxe, Saxon(y), Scurrilous, → **SEA**, Shocking, Sky, Slate, Smalt(o), Smutty, Sordid, Spirit, Splurge, Squander, Stafford, Steel, Stocking, Teal, Thenard's, Tony, Tory, Trist, True, Trypan, Turnbull's, Turquoise, Ultramarine, Unhappy, Urban, Verditer, Washing, Watchet, Wedgwood®, Welkin, Woad, Zaffer, Zaffre

Bluebell Blawort, Blewart, Campanula, Harebell

Bluebottle Blawort, Blewart, Blowfly, Blowie, Brommer, Brummer, Cop, Cornflower, Fly, Policeman

▶ **Blue-legged** *see* **BLUESTOCKING**

Blueprint Cyanotype, Design, Draft, Drawing, Plan, Recipe

Bluestocking, Blue-legged Basbleu, Carter, Erudite, Femme savante, Hamburg(h), Mrs Montagu, Précieuse, Sheba

Bluff(ing) Blunt, Cle(e)ve, Cliff, Clift, Crag, Double, Fake, Flannel, Four-flush, Frank, Hal, Headland, Height, Hoodwink, Kidology, Pose, Precipice, Steep, Trick

Blunder(er), Blundering Barry (Crocker), Betise, Bévue, Bish, Bloomer, Blooper, Boob, Break, Bull, Bumble, Clanger, Clinker, Cock-up, Err, Fault, Faux pas, Floater, Flub, Fluff, Gaff(e), Goof, Howler, Inexactitude, Irish, Josser, Malapropism, → **MISTAKE**, Muddle, Mumpsimus, Ricket, Slip, Solecism, Stumble, Trip

Blunt(ed), Bluntly Abrupt, Alleviate, Bald, Bate, Bayt, Brash, Brusque, Candid, Deaden, Disedge, Downright, Dull, Forthright, Frank, Hebetate, Mole, Morned, Obtund, Obtuse, Outspoken, Pointblank, Rebate, Retund, Retuse, Roundly, Snub, Straight-out, Stubby

Blur(red), Blurring, Blurry Cloud, Confuse, Fog, Fuzz, Halation, Mackle, Macule, Muzzy, Pixilation, → **SMUDGE**, Stump, Tortillon, Unfocussed

Blurb Ad, Puff

Blush(ing) Colour, Cramoisy, Crimson, Erubescent, Erythema, Incarnadine, Mantle, → **REDDEN**, Rouge, Rubescent, Ruby, Rufescent, Rutilant

Bluster(ing), Blusterer, Blustery Arrogance, Bellow, Blore, Brag, Fanfaronade, Hector, Huff-cap, Rage, Rant, Rodomontade, Roister, Sabre-rattler, Squash, Swagger, Vapour, Windbag, Wuthering

Boar Barrow, Calydonian, Erymanthian, Hog, Pentheus, Sanglier, Sounder, Tusker, Wild

▷ **Board** *may refer to* chess or draughts

Board(s), Boarding Abat-voix, Admiralty, Aquaplane, Baffle, Banker, Barge, Bd,

Beaver, Billet, Bristol, Bulletin, Catchment, Centre, Cheese, Chevron, Circuit, Collegium, Committee, Contignation, Counter, Cribbage, Dagger, Dam, Dart, Daughter, Deal, Directors, Diving, Draft, Draining, Drawing, Embark, Embus, Emery, Enter, Entrain, Expansion, Fare, Farm out, Fascia, Featheredge, Fibro, Fibrolite®, Flannelgraph, Full, Gib(raltar), Groaning, Gunwale, Gutter, Hack, Half, Half-royal, Hawk, Hoarding, Idiot, Instrument, Insulating, Ironing, Kip, Lag, Lap, Leader, Ledger, Lee, Lodge, Magnetic, Malibu, Masonite®, Match, Message, Mill, Monkey, Mortar, Moulding, Notch, Notice, Otter, Ouija, Palette, Pallet, Panel, Paper, Parochial, Particle, Patch, Pedal, Peg(board), Pension, Planch(ette), Plank, Plug, Ply(wood), Punch, Quango, Ribbon-strip, Roof, Running, Sandwich, Sarking, Scale, Scaleboard, School, Score, Screen, Sheathing, Shelf, Shifting, Shingle, Shooting, Side-table, Sign, Skim, Skirting, Sleeve, Snow, Sounding, Splasher, Spring, Stage, Strickle, Stringboard, Supervisory, Surf, Switch, → **TABLE**, Telegraph, Thatch, Theatre, Trencher, Verge, Wainscot, Wobble, Wokka, Wood chip

Boarder Interne, Pensioner, PG, Roomer

Boarding house Digs, Kip, Lodgings, Pension

Boast(er), Boastful, Boasting Big-note, Blew, Blow, Blowhard, Bluster, Bobadil, Bounce, Brag, Braggadocio, Breeze, Bull, Cock-a-hoop, Crake, Crow, Fanfaronade, Gas, Gascon(nade), Glory, Hot air, Jact(it)ation, Line, Loudmouth, Ostent(atious), Prate, Rodomontade, Scaramouch, Self-glorious, Show-off, Skite, Spread-eagle, Swagger, Swank, Tall, Thrasonic, Vainglory, Vapour, Vaunt, Yelp

Boat Advice, Ark, Barge, Bark, Bawley, Billyboy, Black skipjack, Canal, Cat, Clinker-built, Coaster, Cock, Codder, Corvette, Cott, Cruiser, Curragh, Cutter, Double scull, Dragon, Eight, Faltboat, Ferry, Flagship, Flatboat, Fly(ing), Foldboat, Fore-and-after, Four, Foyboat, Funny, Galley, Gal(l)iot, Gallivat, Goldie, Gravy, Gulet, Hatch, Hooker, Hydroplane, Isis, Jolly, Keel, Kit, Lapstrake, Lap streak, Launch, Liberty, Long, Lymphad, Mackinaw, Monkey, Monohull, Mosquito, Motor, Narrow, Outrigger, Paddle steamer, Pair-oar, Pedalo, Pleasure, Pont, Privateer, PT, Pucan, Puffer, Pulwar, Q, Revenue cutter, Sailer, Sauce, Scooter, Sculler, Sea Dog®, Shallop, She, → **SHIP**, Sidewheeler, Skiff, Slogger, Smack, Stake, Sternwheeler, Swing, Tangle-netter, Tanker, Tender, Tilt, Torpid, Trek-ox, Trow, Vaporetto, Vedette, → **VESSEL**, Vidette, Wager, Waist, Weekender, Whaleback, Whaleboat, Wherry, Whiff

Boater → **HAT**, Punter, Straw

Boatman Bargee, Charon, Cockswain, Coxswain, George, Gondolier, Harris, Hoveller, Phaon, Voyageur, Waterman, Wet-bob

Boat population Tank(i)a

Boat-shaped Carina, Scaphoid

Boatswain Bosun, Serang, Smee

Bob Acres, Beck, Curtsey, Deaner, Dip, Dock, Dop, Duck, Dylan, Float, Hod, Hog, Jerk, Major, Maximus, Minor, Page-boy, Peal, Plain, Plumb, Plummet, Popple, Rob, Royal, S, Shingle, Skeleton, Skip, Sled(ge), Sleigh

Bobbin Quill, Reel, Shuttle, Spindle, Spool

Bobble Pompom

Bobby Bluebottle, Busy, Copper, Flatfoot, Patrolman, Peeler, Pig, → **POLICEMAN**

Bobby-dazzler Dinger, Stunner

Bock Stein

Bode Augur

Bodice Basque, Bolero, Bustier, Chemise, Chemisette, Choli, Corsage, Gilet, Halter, Jirkinet, Liberty, Plastron, Polonie, Polony, Spencer, Tucker, Watteau

Bodkin Eyeleteer, Needle, Poniard, Stilet(to)

Body, Bodies, Bodily Administration, Amount, Anatomic, Astral, Barr, Board, Bouk, Buik, Buke, Bulk, Cadaver, Cadre, Carcase, Carcass, Carnal, Caucas, Centrosome, Chapel, Chapter, Chassis, Chondriosome, Ciliary, Clay, Coachwork, Coccolite, Cohort, Column, Comet, Committee, Contingent, Cormus, Corpora, Corpor(e)al, Corps, Corpse, Corpus, Corse, Cytode, Detail, Earth, Elaiosome, Flesh, Food, Frame, Fuselage, Gazo(o)n, Golgi, Goner, Grey, → **GROUP**, Heavenly, Hull, Immune, Incarnate, Inclusion, Kenning, Ketone, Lewy, Lich, Lifting, Like, Lithites, Malpighian, → **MASS**, Militia, Mitochondrion, Moit, Mote, Mummy, Nacelle, Nucleole, Nucleolus, Olivary, Orb, Order, Pack, Personal, Phalanx, Pineal, Plant, Platelet, Platoon, Polar, Politic, Posse, Purview, Quango, Relic(t), Remains, Review, Ruck, Satellite, Senate, Shaft, Solid, Soma, Soredium, Sound-box, Soyle, Spinar, Spore, Squadron, Square, Staff, Statoblast, Stiff, Syndicate, Tagma, Testis, Thallus, Torse, Torso, Trunk, Turm, Ulema, Uvula, Vitreous, Wolffian, X

▷ **Body** *may indicate* an anagram

Body builder Expander, He-man, Steroid

Bodyguard Amulet, → **ESCORT**, Gentleman-at-arms, House-carl, Minder, Praetorian, Protector, Retinue, Schutzstaffel, → **SHIELD**, SS, Triggerman, Varangian, Yeomen

Body segment Arthromere, Genome, Metamere

Boer Afrikaner, Kruger, Van der Merwe

Boffin Brain

Bog(e)y Boggart, Bug(aboo), Bugbear, Chimera, Colonel, Eagle, Gremlin, Mumbo jumbo, Nis(se), Par, Poker, Rawhead, Scarer, Siege, Spectre, Troll

Bog(gy) Allen, Blanket, Can, Carr, Clabber, Fen, Gents, Glaur, Hag, Lair, Latrine, Letch, Loo, Machair, Marish, Marsh, Merse, Mire, Moory, Morass, Moss(-flow), Mud, Muskeg, Peat, Petary, Quag, Raised, Serbonian, Slack, Slade, Slough, Spew, Spouty, Stodge, Sump, Vlei, Washroom, WC, Yarfa, Yarpha

Boggle Astonish, Bungle, Demur, Hesitate, Perplex, Shy

Bog-trotter Tory

Bogus Assumed, Counterfeit, Fake, False, Histrionic, Phoney, → **SHAM**, Snide, Snobbish, Spoof, Spurious

Bohemian Arty, Beatnik, Boho, Calixtin(e), Demi-monde, Gypsy, Hippy, Hussite, Mimi, Offbeat, Taborite, Trustafarian

Boil(er), Boiled, Boiling (point) Angry, Anthrax, Blain, Botch, Brew, Bubble, C, Carbuncle, Coction, Cook, Copper, Cree, Dartre, Decoct, Ebullient, Foam, Furuncle, Gathering, Hen, Herpes, Kettle, Leep, Ligroin, Pimple, Pinswell, Poach, Poule, Rage, Reflux, Samovar, Seethe, Set pot, Simmer, Sod, Sore, Steam, Stew, Stye, Tea-kettle, Water tube

Boisterous Gilp(e)y, Goustrous, Gusty, Hoo, Knockabout, Noisy, Rambunctious, Randy, Riotous, Rollicking, Rorty, Rough, Stormy, Strepitoso, Termagant, Turbulent, Wild

Bold(ly), Boldness Assumptive, Audacious, Brash, Brass, Bravado, Bravery, Bravura, Brazen, Brussen, Caleb, Crust, Daredevil, Defiant, Derring-do, Diastaltic, Familiar, Free, Gallus, Hard-edge, Hardihood, Heroics, High-spirited, Impudent, Intrepid, Malapert, Mature, Outspoken, Parrhesia, Pert, Plucky, Presumptive, Rash, Risoluto, Sassy, Temerity, Unshrinking

Bole Niche, Stem, Trunk

Bolivar Liberator

Bollard Cone, Kevel

Bolshevik, Bolshie Agitator, Communist, Maximalist, Rebel, Soviet

Bolster Cushion, Dutch wife, Pillow, → **PROP**

Bolt Arrow, Captive, Carriage, Coach, Cuphead, Dash, Dead, Eat, Elope, Expansion,

Explosive, Fish, Flee, Gobble, Gollop, Gorge, Gulp, Latch, Levant, Levin, Lightning, Lock, Machine, Missile, Panic, Pig, Pintle, Ragbolt, Rivet, Roll, Scoff, Slot, Snib, Sperre, Stud, Tap, Through, Thunder, Toggle, U, Wing, Wolf, Wring

Bolus Ball

Bomb(ed), Bomber, Bombing Atom, Attack, B, Blast, Blitz, Blockbuster, Borer, Bunkerbuster, Buzz, Candle, Car, Carpet, Cluster, Cobalt, Daisycutter, Depth charge, Deterrent, Dirty, Doodlebug, Drogue, Egg, Fission, Flop, Flying, Fragmentation, Fusion, Glide, Greek fire, Grenade, H, Harris, Homicide, Hydrogen, Lancaster, Land-mine, Letter, Liberator, Loft, Logic, Mail, Megaton, Millennium, Mills, Minnie, Mint, Molotov cocktail, Mortar, Nail, Napalm, Necklace, Neutron, Nuclear, Nuke, Packet, Parcel, Petar, Petard, Petrol, Pineapple, Pipe, Plaster, Plastic, Prang, Precision, Radium, Ransom, Robot, Sex, Shell, Skip, Smart, Smoke, Sneak-raid, Stealth, Stick, Stink, Stratofortress, Stuka, Suicide, Tactical, Terrorist, Thermonuclear, Time, Torpedo, Turkey, V1, Volcanic, Vulcan, Walleye

Bombard(ment) Attack, Battery, Blitz, Cannonade, Drum-fire, Mortar, Pelt, Shell, Stone, Stonk, Strafe, Straff

Bombardon Tuba

Bombast(ic) Ampullosity, Euphuism, Fustian, Grandiloquent, Grandiose, Hot air, Magniloquence, Orotund, Pomp, Rant, Swol(le)n, Timid, Tumid, Turgent

Bombay Nasik

Bombay duck Bum(m)alo

▶ **Bomber** *see* **BOMB**

Bona fide Echt, Genuine

Bonanza Luck, Windfall

Bonaparte Boney, → **NAPOLEON**, Plon-plon

Bond(s), Bondage, Bonding, Bondsman Adhesive, Affinity, Afrikander, Agent, Assignat, Baby, Bail, Bearer, Cedula, Cement, Chain, Chemical, Compact, Connect, Consols, Coordinate, Copula, Corporate, Covalent, Covenant, Daimyo, Dative, Debenture, Deep-discount, Double, Duty, Electrovalent, English, Ernie, Escrow, Esne, Fetter, Fleming, Flemish, Geasa, Gilt, Granny, Heart, Herringbone, Hydrogen, Hyphen, Income, Investment, Ionic, James, Junk, Knot, Liaise, Ligament, Link(age), Long, Manacle, Managed, Metallic, Mortar, Municipal, Nexus, Noose, Obligation, Pair, Peptide, Performance, → **PLEDGE**, Post-obit, Premium, Property, Rapport, Recognisance, Relationship, Revenue, Running, Samurai, Security, Semipolar, Serf, Servitude, Shackle, Shogun, Single, Singlet, Slave, Solder, Stacked, Starr, Superglue, Surety, Thete, Thral(l)dom, Three-per-cent, → **TIE**, Treasury, Triple, Trivalent, Tusking, Valence, Valency, Vassal, Vinculum, Yearling, Yoke, Zebra

Bone(s), Bony Acromion, Anableps, Angular, Apatite, Astragalus, Atlas, Axis, Baculum, Busk, Calcaneus, Caluarium, Cannon, Capitate, Capitellum, Carina, Carpel, Carpus, Cartilage, Catacomb, Centrum, Chine, Chordate, Clavicle, Cly, Coccyx, Coffin, Columella, Concha, Condyle, Coracoid, Coral, Costa, Coxa, Crane, Cranium, Cuboid, Cuneiform, Cuttlefish, Dentary, Diaphysis, Dib, Dice, Diploe, Dolos, Endosteal, Ethmoid, Femur, Fetter, Fibula, Fillet, Frontal, Funny, Ganoid, Gaunt, Hamate, Haunch, Hause-bane, Horn, Humerus, Hyoid, Ilium, Incus, Innominate, Interclavicle, Involucrum, Ischium, Ivory, Jugal, Kneecap, Knuckle, Lacrimal, Lamella, Luez, Lunate, Luz, Malar, Malleolus, Malleus, Mandible, Manubrium, Marrow, Mastoid, Maxilla, Medulla, Membrane, Metacarpal, Metatarsal, Napier's, Nasal, Navicular, Occipital, Olecranon, Omoplate, Orthopaedics, Os, Ossicle, Osteo-, Palatine, Parasphenoid, Parietal, Patella, Pecten, Pectoral, Pedal, Pelvis, Pen, Percoid, Perone, Petrous, Phalanx, Pisiform, Ploughshare, Premaxilla, Pterygoid, Pubis, Pygostyle, Quadrate, Rachial, Rack,

Radialia, Radius, Relic, Rib, Rump-post, Sacrum, Scaphoid, Scapula, Sclere, Sepium, Sequestrum, Sesamoid, Share, Skeleton, Skull, Spade, Sphenoid, Splint, Splinter, Spur, Squamosal, Stapes, → **STEAL**, Sternebra, Sternum, Stifle, Stirrup, Suboperculum, T, Talus, Tarsus, Temporal, Tibia, Tibiotarsus, Tot, Trapezium, Triquetral, Trochanter, Trochlea, True-rib, Tympanic, Ulna, Vertebrae, Vomer, Whirl, Wish, Wormian, Zygomatic

Bone-head Capitellum, Capitulum

Bonehouse Ossuary

Boneshaker Dandy-horse, Draisene, Draisine

Bonfire Bale-fire, Beltane, Blaze, Chumping, Clavie, Feu de joie, Pyre

Boniface Inn-keeper, Landlord, Taverner

Bonne-bouche Cate

Bonnet Balmoral, Bongrace, Cap, Cornette, Cowl, Easter, Glengarry, Hood, Hummel, Hummle, Kiss-me(-quick), Mobcap, Mutch, Poke, Scotch, Sun, Toorie, Tourie, War

Bonny Blithe, Gay, Merry, Sonsy, Weelfar'd

Bonsai Saikei

Bonus Bisque, Bounty, Braata, Bye, Christmas box, Danger money, Dividend, Escalator, Extra, Hand-out, Lagniappe, No-claim, → **PREMIUM**, Reversionary, Reward, Scrip, Spin-off, Windfall

Boo Explode

Boob Gaffe, Nork, Simpleton, Stumer

Booby Dunce, Hick, Patch, Patchcocke, Patchoke, → **STUPID**

Boojum Snark

Book(s), Bookish, Bookwork Academic, Album, Antilegomena, Antiphonary, Appointment, Audio, B, Backlist, Bedside, Bestiary, Bestseller, Black, Block, Blockbuster, Blotter, Blue, Cash, Chrestomathy, Classic, Closed, Coffee-table, Diary, Digest, Directory, Diurnal, Ench(e)iridion, Engage, Enter, Erudite, Exercise, Facetiae, Folio, Fortune, Good, Gradual, Gradus, Guide, Hardback, Hymnal, Imprint, Issue, Lectionary, Ledger, Lib, Liber, Literary, Livraison, Manual, Memorandum, Missal, Monograph, Muster, Octavo, Octodecimo, Office, Open, Order, Page-turner, Paperback, Pass, Pedantic, Phrase, Pica, Plug, Polyglot, Potboiler, Pseudepigrapha, Publication, Puzzle prize, Quair, Quarto, Quire, → **RESERVE**, Road, Script, Sealed, Sext, Sexto, Sextodecimo, Sixmo, Sixteenmo, Sketch, Softback, Spelling, Spine-chiller, Statute, Studious, Study, Style, Swatch, Symbolical, Table, Tablet, Talking, Te igitur, Text(ual), Thirty-twomo, Thriller, Title, Titule, Tome, Trade, Transfer, Twelvemo, Twenty-fourmo, Unputdownable, Visiting, Visitor's, Vol(ume), Waste, White, Work, Year

BOOKS

2 letters:	Jud	4 letters:	Macc
NT	Lam	Acts	Mark
OT	Log	Amos	Mook
	Rag	Edda	Obad
3 letters:	Red	Ezek	Veda
Dan	Rom	Ezra	
Eph	Sir	Joel	5 letters:
Gal	Sus	John	Atlas
Hab		Jude	Bible
Hag		Luke	Chron

5 letters – cont:
Hosea
James
Kells
Kings
Manga
Micah
Nahum
Pop-up
Snobs
Sutra
To-bit

6 letters:
Aeneid
Baruch
Caxton
Course
Daniel
Eccles
Esdras
Esther
Exeter
Exodus
Haggai
Herbal
I Ching
Isaiah
Jashar
Jasher
Joshua
Judges
Prayer
Primer
Prompt
Psalms

Ration
Reader
Romans
Scroll
Tanach

7 letters:
Chumash
Cookery
Ezekiel
Genesis
Grolier
Malachi
Martyrs
Matthew
Numbers
Obadiah
Octapla
Omnibus
Orarium
Ordinal
Psalter
Susanna
Timothy

8 letters:
Breviary
Clarissa
Domesday
Doomsday
Georgics
Grimoire
Habakkuk
Haggadah
Haggadoh
Hermetic

Libretto
Megillah
Ordinary
Philemon
Porteous
Portesse
Prophets
Proverbs
Triodion
Vercelli
Vesperal

9 letters:
Apocrypha
Ephesians
Formulary
Galatians
Gazetteer
Kama Sutra
Leviticus
Maccabees
Portolano
Reference
Remainder
Satyricon
Sibylline
Sybilline
Telephone
Tripitaka
Vade-mecum
Zephadiah

10 letters:
Apocalypse
Chronicles
Compendium

Cyclopedia
Dictionary
Heptameron
Heptateuch
Hitopadesa
Incunabula
Passionary
Persuasion
Teratology

11 letters:
Commonplace
Concordance
Corinthians
Deuteronomy
Evangeliary
Hagiographa
Nomenclator
Philippians
Revelations

12 letters:
Bodice-ripper
Ecclesiastes
Encyclopedia
Lamentations
Panchatantra
Paralipomena
Processional
Responsorial
Twelve Tables

13 letters:
Penny dreadful
Pharmacopoeia
Thessalonians

Bookbinder, Bookbinding Fanfare, Grolier, Mutton-thumper, Organdie
Book-case Credenza, Press, Satchel
Bookie(s), Bookmaker Binder, John, Layer, Librettist, Luke, Mark, Matthew, Printer, Ringman, To-bit, Turf accountant
Booking Reservation
Bookkeeper, Bookkeeping Clerk, Double entry, Librarian, Posting, Recorder, Satchel, Single-entry
Booklet B, Brochure, Folder, Inlay
Book-like Solander
Book-lover Incunabulist
Bookmark Flag, Tassel
Book-scorpion Chelifer
Bookseller Bibliopole, Colporteur, Conger, Sibyl, Stallman
Bookworm Sap, Scholar

Boom(ing) Baby, Beam, Boost, Bowsprit, Bump, Fishpole, Increase, Jib, Orotund, Prosper, Resound, Roar, Sonic, Spar, Supersonic, Swinging, Thrive, Torpedo, Wishbone

Boomer Bittern, Bull-of the-bog, Butter-bump, Kangaroo, Mire-drum

Boomerang Backfire, Kiley, Kyley, Kylie, Recoil, Ricochet, Throwstick, Woomera

Boon Bene, Benefit, Blessing, Bounty, Cumshaw, Gift, Godsend, Mills, Mitzvah, Prayer, Windfall

Boor(ish) Borel, Bosthoon, Chuffy, Churl, Clodhopper, Crass, Goth, Grobian, Hog, Ill-bred, Jack, Keelie, Kern(e), Kernish, Kill-courtesy, Lob, Lout, Lumpen, Lumpkin, Ocker, Peasant, Philistine, Pleb, Trog, Uncouth, Yahoo, Yob, Yokel

Boost(er) Adrenalin, Afterburner, Bolster, Ego, Encourage, Fillip, Help, Hoist, Impetus, Increase, Injection, Lift, Promote, Raise, Rap, Reheat, Reinforce, Reinvigorate, Spike, Steal, Step up, Supercharge, Tonic, Wrap

Boot(s) Addition, Adelaide, Ankle-jack, Avail, Balmoral, Beetle-crushers, Benefit, Blucher, Bottine, Bovver, Brogan, Brogue, Buskin, Cerne, Chukka, Cockers, Cold, Combat, Concern, Cothurn(us), Cowboy, Cracowe, Crowboot, Denver, Derby, Desert, Dismiss, Field, Finn(e)sko, Finsko, Fire, Football, Galage, Galosh, Gambado, Go-go, Granny, Gum, Heave-ho, Hessian, High shoe, Hip, Jack, Jemima, Jodhpur, Kamik, Kletterschuh, Lace-up, Larrigan, Last, Mitten, Moon, Muchie, Muc(k)luc(k), Mukluk, Pac, Para, Profit, Riding, Rock, Russian, Sabot, → SACK, Seven league, → SHOE, Skivvy, Surgical, Thigh, Toe, Tonneau, Tops, Trunk, Ugh, Vibram®, Vibs, Wader, Warm, Weller, Wellie, Wellington, Welly

Booth Assassin, Crame, Kiosk, Polling, Stall, Stand, Telephone, Voting

Bootlegger Cooper, Coper, Runner

Bootless Futile, Idle, Unprofitable, Vain

Booty Creach, Creagh, Haul, Loot, Prey, Prize, Spoil(s), Spolia optima, Swag

Booze(r) → DRINK, Inn, Liquor, Pub, Spree, Tipple

Bora Rite, Wind

Borage Bugloss, Comfrey, Gromwell, Myosote

Borax Tincal

Bordeaux Claret

Border(s), Borderland, Borderline Abut, Adjoin, Apron, Bed, Bind, Bound, Boundary, Braid, Checkpoint, Coast, Cot(t)ise, Dado, Dentelle, → EDGE, Engrail, Fimbria, Frieze, Fringe, Frontier, Furbelow, Guilloche, Head-rig, Hedgerow, Hem, Herbaceous, Impale, Kerb, Lambrequin, Limb, Limbate, Limbo, Limen, Limes, Limit, Limitrophe, Lip, List, March, Marchland, → MARGIN, Mat, Mattoid, Meith, Mete, Mount, Neighbour, Orle, Pand, Pelmet, Penumbra, Perimeter, Purfle, Purlieu, Rand, Rim, Rio Grande, Roadside, Roon, Royne, Rubicon, Rund, Rymme, Scottish, Screed, Selvage, Selvedge, Side, Skirt, Skirting, Strand, Strip, Surround, Swage, The Marches, Trench, Tressure, Valance, Valence, → VERGE

▷ **Borders** *may indicate* first and last letters

Bore(d), Boredom, Borer, Boring Aiguille, Airshaft, Anobium, Anorak, Apathy, Aspergillum, Aspergillus, Aspersoir, Auger, Awl, Beetle, Bind, Bit, Broach, Brog, Bromide, Calibre, Cataclysm, Chokebore, Deadly, Drag, → DRILL, Dry, Dusty, Dweeb, Eagre, Eat, Eger, Elshin, Elsin, Endured, Ennui, Ennuye, Fag, Foozle, Gim(b)let, Gouge, Gribble, Grind, Had, Heigh-ho, Ho-hum, Irk, Jack, Jumper, Land, Listless, Longicorn, Longueur, Miser, Mole, Nerd, Noyance, Nudni(c)k, Nuisance, Nyaff, Operose, Pain, Pall, Penetrate, Perforate, Pest, Pholas, Pierce, Pill, Platitude, Probe, Prosaic, Prosy, Punch, Ream(ingbit), Rime, Saddo, Sat, Schmoe, Scolytus, Screw, Severn, Shothole, Snooze, Snore, Sondage, Spleen, Spod, Spudding-un, Sting, Stob, Stupid, Tediosity, Tedious, Tedisome, Tedium, Tedy, Terebra, Teredo,

Termes, Termite, Thirl, Tire, Trepan, Trocar, Tunnel, Turn-off, Vapid, → **WEARY**, Well, Wimble, Windbag, Wonk, Woodworm, Workaday, Worldweary, Xylophaga, Yawn

Borgia Cesare, Lucretia

Boric Sassolin, Sassolite

Born B, Free, Great, Nascent, Nat(us), Né(e)

Borneo Kalimantan

Boron B

Borough Borgo, Close, Pocket, Port, Quarter, Rotten, Township, Wick

Borrow(ed), Borrowing Adopt, Appropriate, Cadge, Copy, Derivative, Eclectic, George, Hum, Leverage, Scunge, Stooze, Straunge, → **TAKE**, Touch

Bosh Humbug, Nonsense, Rot

Bosom Abraham's, Breast, Bristols, Close, Gremial, Inarm, Intimate, Poitrine

Boson Gauge, Squark

Boss(ed), Bossy Big White Chief, Blooper, Burr, Cacique, Cow, Director, Dominate, Domineer, Gadroon, Governor, Headman, Honcho, Hump, Inian, Inion, Jewel, Knob, Knop, Knot, Leader, Maestro, → **MANAGER**, Massa, → **MISTAKE**, Mistress, Netsuke, Noop, Nose-led, Omphalos, Oubaas, Overlord, Overseer, Owner, Pannikin, Pellet, Protuberance, Ruler, Run, Sherang, Straw, Stud, Superintendent, Supremo, Taskmaster, Umbo(nate)

Boston Hub

Bot Oestrus

Botany, Botanist Banks, Bryology, Candolle, Carpology, Cockayne, Dendrologist, Frees, Garden, Godet, Graminology, Herbist, Jungermann, Linnaeus, Marchant, Mendel, Phytogenesis, Phytology, Pteridology, Tradescant, Weigel

Botch(ed) Bungle, Clamper, Cock-up, Flub, Fudge, Mismanage, Pig's ear, Spoil, Tink

Both Together, Two

Bother(some) Ado, Aggro, Brush, Care, Deave, Deeve, Disturb, Drat, Fash, Fluster, Fuss, Get, Hassle, Hector, Incommode, Irk, Irritate, Moither, Nark, Nuisance, Palaver, Perturb, Pesky, Pest(er), Pickle, Reke, Todo, → **TROUBLE**

▷ **Bottle(d)** *may indicate* an anagram or a hidden word

Bottle(s) Ampul(la), Bacbuc, Balthasar, Balthazar, Belshazzar, Borachio, Bundle, Carafe, Carboy, Case, Chapine, Cock, Cork, Costrel, Courage, Cruet, Cruse, Cucurbital, Cutter, Dead-man, Decanter, Demijohn, Fearlessness, Feeding, Fiasco, Filette, Flacket, Flacon, Flagon, Flask, Glass can, Goatskin, Gourd, Guts, Half-jack, Hen, Imperial, Jeroboam, Junk, Klein, Lachrymal, Lagena, Magnetic, Magnum, Marie-Jeanne, Matrass, Medicine, Melchior, Methuselah, Mettle, Mickey, Middy, Nansen, Nebuchadnezzar, → **NERVE**, Nursing, Phial, Pig, Pilgrim, Pitcher, Pooter, Pycnometer, Rehoboam, Resource, Retort, Salmanaser, Salmanazar, Scent, Screwtop, Siphon, Smelling, Split, Squeeze, Squeezy, Stubby, Sucking, Tear, Tube, Twenty-sixer, Vial, Vinaigret(te), Wad, Water, Water bouget, Weighing, Winchester, Wine, Woulfe

Bottom Anus, Aris, Arse, Ass, Base, Batty, Beauty, Bed, Benthos, Bilge, Booty, Breech, Bum, Butt, Buttocks, Croup(e), Croupon, Demersal, Derrière, Doup, Dowp, End, Fanny, Floor, Foot, Foundation, Fud, Fundus, Haunches, Hunkers, Hurdies, Keel(son), Kick, Lumbar, Nadir, Nates, Planning, Podex, Posterior, Pottle-deep, Prat, Pyramus, Quark, Rear, Rock, Root, Rump, Seat, Ship, Sill, Sole, Staddle, Tail, Tush, Weaver

Bottom drawer Glory box

Bottomless Subjacent

Botulism Limberneck
Boudoir Bower, Room
Bouffant Pouf
Bough Branch, Limb
Bought Coft
Boulder Erratic, Gibber, Niggerhead, Rock, → **STONE**
Boule Senate
Bounce(r), Bouncing, Bouncy Bang, Blague, Bound, Caper, Dandle, Dap, Dead-cat, Doorman, Dop, Dud, Eject, Evict, Fib, Jounce, Keepy-uppy, Kite, Lie, Lilt, Muscleman, Resilient, Ricochet, Spiccato, Spring, Stot, Tale, Tamp, Valve, Verve, Vitality, Yorker, Yump
▷ **Bouncing** *may indicate* an anagram
Bound(er), Boundary Adipose, Apprenticed, Articled, Bad, Barrier, Beholden, Border, Bourn(e), Bubalis, Cad, Cavort, Certain, Circumference, Curvet, Decreed, Demarcation, Demarkation, Divide, Dool, Dule, Duty, End, Engirt, Entrechat, Erub, Eruv, Event horizon, Exciton, Fence, Four, Frape, Frontier, Galumph, Gambado, Gambol, Girt, Harestane, Hedge, Heel, Held, Hoarstone, Hops, Hourstone, Ibex, Interface, Izard, Jump, Kangaroo, K/T, → **LEAP**, Limes, Limit, Linch, Lollop, Lope, March-stone, Meare, Meer, Meith, Mere, Merestone, Mete, Moho, Muscle, Obliged, Ourebi, Outward, Pale, Parameter, Perimeter, Periphery, Plate, Prance, Precinct, Prometheus, Purlieu, Quickset, Redound, Ring-fence, Roller, Roo, Roped, Rubicon, Scoup, Scowp, Serf, Side, Sideline, Six(er), Skelp, Skip, Spang, Spring, Sten(d), Stoit, Stylolite, Terminator, T(h)alweg, Tied, Touchline, Upstart, Vault, Verge, Wallaby
▷ **Bounds** *may indicate* outside letters
Bounty, Bountiful Aid, Bligh, Boon, Christian, Generosity, → **GIFT**, Goodness, Grant, Head money, Honorarium, Largess(e), Lavish, Queen Anne's, Queen's
Bouquet Aroma, Attar, Aura, Compliment, Corsage, Fragrancy, Garni, Nose, Nosegay, Perfume, Plaudit, Posy, Scent, Spiritual, Spray
Bourbon Alfonso
Bourgeois(ie) Biedermeier, Common, Middle class, Pleb(eian), Pooter(ish)
Bout Bender, Bust, Contest, Dose, Go, Jag, Match, Spell, Spree, Turn, Venery, Venewe, Venue
Boutique Shop
Bovine Stolid
Bow(ing), Bower, Bowman Alcove, Arbour, Arc, Arch, → **ARCHER**, Arco, Arson, Bandy, Beck, Bend, Boudoir, Butterfly, Clara, Congé(e), Crescent, Crook, Cupid, → **CURVE**, Defer, Dicky, Drail, Droop, Duck, Echelles, Eros, Eugh, Eyes, Fiddle(r), Fiddlestick, Foredeck, Halse, Hawse, Honour, Jook, Jouk, Kneel, Kotow, Laval(l)ière, Lean, Londoner, Long, Loof, Lout, Lowt, Luff, Martellato, Moulinet, Namaste, Nameste, Nod, Nutate, Obeisance, Obtemper, Paganini, Pergola, Prore, Quarrel, Reverence, Salaam, Seamer, Shelter, Slope, Sound, Spiccato, Stick, → **SUBMIT**, Tie, Torrent, Yew, Yield
Bowdler(ize) Edit(or), Water
Bowels Entrails, Guts, Innards, Viscera
▷ **Bower** *may indicate* using a bow
Bowl(ing), Bowler, Bowl over, Bowls B, Basin, Begging, Bicker, Bocce, Bocci(a), Boccie, Bodyline, Bool, Bosey, Bouncer, Cage-cup, Calabash, Candlepins, Cap, Carpet, Caup, Chalice, Cheese, Chinaman, Christie, Christy, Cog(g)ie, Concave, Coolamon, Crater, Cup, Deliver, Derby, → **DISH**, Dismiss, Dome, Doosra, Drake, Dumbfound, Dust, Ecuelle, End, Finger, Fivepin, Goblet, Goldfish, Googly, Grub, Hog, Hoop, Jack, Jeroboam, Jorum, Kegler, Krater, Lavabo, Laver, Leg-spin,

Lightweight, Lob, Locke, Mazer, Monteith, Night, Offbreak, Off-cutter, Old, Over-arm, Overpitch, Pace, Pan, Pétanque, Piggin, Pitch, Porringer, Pot-hat, Pottinger, Punch, Raku, Rice, Rink, Roll, Roundarm, Seam(er), Skip, Skittle(s), Spare, Speed, Spinner, Spofforth, Stadium, Stagger, Stummel, Sucrier, Super, Ten-pin, Tom, Underarm, Underhand, Underwood, Voce, Wassail, Wood, York(er)

Box(ing) Baignoire, Ballot, Bandbox, Bareknuckle, Bento, Bijou, Bimble, Binnacle, Black, Blow, Blue, Bonk, Booth, Buist, Bunk, Bush, Caddy, Call, Camera, Canister, Case, Cash, Casket, Cassolette, Chest, Chinese, Christmas, Ciborium, Clog, Coach, Coffer, Coffin, Coffret, Coin, Confessional, Cool, Crate, Cuff, Dabba, Deed, Dialog(ue), Dispatch, Ditty, Dog, Drawer, Encase, Enclose, Etui, → **FIGHT**, File, Fist, Fund, Fuse, Fuzz, Glory, Glove, Go-kart, Grass, Hat, Hay, Hedge, Honesty, Horse, Humidor, Hutch, Ice, Idiot, Inherce, Inro, Inter, Jewel, Journal, Junction, Jury, Keister, Kick, Kiosk, Kite, Knevell, Knowledge, Ladle, Letter, Light, Live, Locker, Lodge, Loge, Loose, Lug, Lunch, Match, Message, Mill, Mitre, Mocock, Mocuck, Money, Musical, Nest(ing), Noble art, Noble science, Omnibus, Orgone, Package, Packing, Paint, Pandora's, Papeterie, Patch, Pattress, Peepshow, Peg, Penalty, Petara, Pew, Phylactery, Pill, Pillar, Pitara, Pix, Poor, Post, Pounce(t), Powder, Press, Prompt, Protector, Puff, Pugilism, Pyxis, Register, Resonance, Ring, Rope-a-dope, Royal, Saggar(d), Sagger, Sand, Savate, Scent, Scrap, Seggar, Sentry, Set-top, Shadow, Shoe, Shooting, Side, Signal, Skinner, Skip(pet), Slipcase, Smudge, Sneeshin-mull, Sneeze, Soap, Solander, Sound, Sound body, → **SPAR**, Spice, Spit, Spring, Squawk, Squeeze, Strong, Stuffing, Swell, Tabernacle, Tee, Tefillin, Telephone, Telly, Thai, Tick, Tin, Tinder, Tool, Touch, Trunk, Tube, Tuck, TV, Urn, Vanity, Vasculum, Vinaigrette, Voice, Weather, Window, Wine, Witness, Yakhdan

Boxer Ali, Amycus, Babyweight, Bantamweight, Bruiser, Bruno, Canine, Carnera, Carpentier, Carthorse, Chinaman, Cooper, Crater, Cruiserweight, Dog, Eryx, Farr, Featherweight, Flyweight, Ham, Heavyweight, Lightweight, McCoy, Middleweight, Mosquito-weight, Pandora, Pollux, Pug, Pugil(ist), Rebellion, Rocky, Shadow, Southpaw, Strawweight, Welterweight, Wilde

Boxing-glove Hurlbat, Muffle, Whirlbat, Whorlbat

▷ **Boy** *may indicate* an abbreviated name

Boy(s) Amoretto, Anchor, Apprentice, Ball, Bevin, Blue-eyed, Bovver, Bub(by), Cabin, Callant, Catamite, Champagne, Chiel(d), → **CHILD**, Chokra, Chummy, Cub, Cupid, Dandiprat, Errant, Galopin, Garçon, Gorsoon, Gossoon, Green Mountain, Groom, Grummet, Ha, Hansel, Jack, Kid, Klonkie, Knave, Knave-bairn, Kwedien, Lackbeard, → **LAD**, Loblolly, Loon(ie), Minstrel, Nibs, Nipper, Office, Page, Poster, Pot, Prentice, Principal, Putto, Rent, Roaring, Rude, Shaver, Ship's, Son, Spalpeen, Sprig, Stripling, Tad, Tar, Ted(dy), Tiger, Toy, Urchin, Whipping, Wide, → **YOUTH**

Boycott Avoid, Ban, Bat, Black, Blacklist, Exclude, Geoff(rey), Hartal, Isolate, Ostracise, Shun, Swadeshi

Boyfriend Beau, Date, Fella, Fellow, Steady

Boyle Juno

Bp Bishop, DD, RR

Brace(s), Bracing Accolade, Couple, Crosstree, Fortify, Gallace, Gallows, Gallus(es), Gird, Hound, Invigorate, Ozone, Pair, Pr, Rear-arch, Rere-arch, Sea air, Skeg, Spider, Splint, Steady, Stiffener, Strut, → **SUPPORT**, Suspenders, Tauten, Thorough, Tone, Tonic, Two

Bracelet Armil(la), Armlet, Bangle, Cuff, Darbies, Handcuff, Identity, Manacle, Manilla

Brachiopod Ecardines, Lamp-shell, Spirifer

Bracken Brake, Fern, Pteridium, Tara

Bracket Ancon, Angle-iron, Bibb, Brace, Cantilever, Console, Corbel, Couple, Cripple, Lance rest, Misericord(e), Modillion, Mutule, Parenthesis, Potence, Pylon, Rigger, Round, Sconce, Square, Straddle, Strata, → **STRUT**, Trivet, Truss

Bract Glume(lla), Hypsophyll, Involucel, Involucre, Job's tears, Leaf, Lemma, Palea, Palet, Phyllary, Spathe

Brad Nail, Pin, Rivet, Sprig

Brag(gart), Bragging Basilisco, Birkie, Bluster, Boast, Bobadil, Boister, Braggadocio, Bull, Cockalorum, Crow, Falstaff, Fanfaronade, Gab, Gascon, Hot-air, Loudmouth, Parolles, Puckfist, Puff, Rodomontader, Skite, Slam, Swagger, Thrason, Thrasonic, Tongue-doubtie, Tongue-doughty, Vainglorious, Vapour, Vaunt

Brahma(n) San(n)yasi(n)

Braid A(i)glet, Aiguillette, Fishbone, French, Frog, Galloon, Lacet, Plait, Plat, Rickrack, Ricrac, Scrambled eggs, Seaming-lace, Sennet, Sennit, Sinnet, Soutache, Tress, Trim, Twist, Weave

Braille (system) Moon

Brain(box), Brains, Brainstorm, Brainy, Brain disease, Brain-power Amygdala, Appestat, Bean, Boffin, Bright, Cerebellum, Cerebrum, Cortex, Crane, Cranium, Diencephalon, Dura mater, Encephalon, Epencephalon, Fornix, Genius, Gyrus, Harn(s), Head, Headpiece, Hippocampus, Hydrocephalus, Hypothalamus, Inspiration, Insula, Intelligence, IQ, Kuru, Left, Limbic, Loaf, Lobe, Mastermind, Mater, Medulla, Medulla oblongata, Metencephalon, Mind, Noddle, Noesis, Nous, Peduncle, Pericranium, Pia mater, Pons, Pontile, Prosencephalon, Rhinencephalon, Rhombencephalon, Ringleader, Sconce, Sense, Sensorium, Striatum, Subcortex, Sulcus, Tapagnosia, Tectum, Telencephalon, Thalamencephalon, Thalamus, Upper stor(e)y, Vermis, Vortex, Wetware

▷ **Brain(s)** *may indicate* an anagram

Brainless Anencephaly, Bimbo, Stupid, Thick

Brainwash(ing) Indoctrinate, Menticide, Propaganda

Brake, Braking ABS, Adiantum, Aerodynamic, Air, Anchors, Antilock, Bracken, Centrifugal, Curb, Disc, Dive, Drag, Drum, Estate car, Fern, Fly, Foot, Grove, Hand, Hub, Hydraulic, Nemoral, Overrun, Ratchet, Rein, Shoe, Shooting, → **SLOW**, Spinney, Sprag, Tara, Thicket, Vacuum, Westinghouse

Bramble, Brambly Batology, Blackberry, Boysenberry, Brier, Cloudberry, Rubus, Thorn, Wait-a-bit, Youngberry

Bran Cereal, Chesil, Chisel, Oats, Pollard

Branch(ed), Branches, Branching, Branch office Affiliate, Antler, Arm, BO, Bough, Cladode, Cow, Dendron, Dept, Diversify, Diverticulum, Divide, Filiate, Fork, Grain, Jump, Kow, Lateral, Leaf-trace, Limb, Lobe, Loop, Lye, Lylum, Offshoot, Olive, Patulous, Phylloclade, Raguly, Ramate, Ramulus, Reis, Rice, Shroud, Special, Spray(ey), Sprig, Spur, Tributary, Turning, Turn-off, Twig, Wattle, Yard

Branch-rib Lierne

Brand Broadsword, Buist, Burn, Cauterise, Chop, Class, Dealer, Denounce, Earmark, Ember, Excalibur, Falchion, Faulchin, Faulchion, Flambeau, Home, Idiograph, Inust, Iron, Label, Line, → **MARK**, Marque, Name, Own, Power, Sear, Sere, Stigma, Sweard, Sword, Torch, Wipe

Brandish Bless, Flaunt, Flourish, Hurtle, Waffle, Wampish, Wave

Brandy Aguardiente, Applejack, Apricot, Aqua vitae, Armagnac, Bingo, Calvados, Cape smoke, Cherry bounce, Cognac, Cold without, Dop, Eau de vie, Fine, Fine champagne, Framboise, Grappa, Kirsch, Mampoer, Marc, Mirabelle, Mobbie,

Mobby, Nantes, Nantz, Napoleon, Palinka, Peach, Quetsch, Slivovic(a), Slivovitz, Smoke

Bras Arms

Brash Cocky, Flashy, Impudent, Jack-the-lad, Jumped-up, Pushy, Rain, Rash

Brass(y), Brassware Alpha-beta, Benares, Brazen, Cheek, Club, Corinthian, Cornet, Dinanderie, Face, Front, Harsh, High, Horn, Horse, Latten, Lip, Loot, Lota(h), Loud, Matrix, → **MONEY**, Moola(h), Oof, Oricalche, Orichalc, Pyrites, Sass, Snash, Sopranino, Talus, Top, Trombone, White, Wood

Brassard Armlet

Brass hat Brig

Brassica Brussels (sprout), → **CABBAGE**, Colza, Turnip

Brassière Gay deceiver

Brat Bairn, Bra(t)chet, Enfant terrible, Gait(t), Gamin, Geit, Get, Git, Gyte, Imp, Lad, Terror, Urchin

Braun Eva

Bravado, Brave(ry) Amerind, Apache, Bold, Conan, Corragio, Courage, Creek, Dare, → **DEFY**, Doughty, Dress, Face, Fearless, Gallant, Game, Gamy, Gutsy, Hardy, Heroism, Indian, Injun, Intrepid, Lion, Lion-hearted, Manful, Manly, → **MEXICAN**, Nannup, → **NORTH AMERICAN**, Plucky, Prow(ess), Russian roulette, Sannup, Skookum, → **SOUTH AMERICAN**, Spunk, Stout, Uncas, Valiant, Valour, Wight, Yeoman

Bravo Acclaim, B, Bandit, Bully, Desperado, Euge, Murderer, Olé, Shabash, Spadassin, Villain

Brawl(er) Affray, Bagarre, Bicker, Brabble, Donnybrook, Dust, Dust-up, Fight, Flite, Flyte, Fracas, Fratch, Fray, Melee, Prawl, Rammy, Roarer, Roughhouse, Row, Scold, Scuffle, Set-to, Shindig, Stoush, Tar, Wrangle

Brawn Beef, Burliness, Headcheese, He-man, Might, Muscle, Power, Rillettes, Sinew

Bray Cry, Heehaw, Stamp, Vicar, Whinny

Brazen Blatant, Bold, Brassy, Flagrant, Impudent, Shameless, Unabashed

Brazier Brasero, Fire, Hibachi, Mangal, Scaldino

Brazil(ian) Caboclo, Carioca, Cream-nut, Para, Yanomami, Yanomamo

Breach Assault, Break, Chasm, Cleft, Gap(e), Great schism, Infraction, Redan, Rupture, Saltus, Schism, Solecism, Solution, Trespass, Violate

Bread, Bread crumbs Afrikomen, Azym(e), Bagel, Baguette, Bannock, Bap, Barmbrack, Barm cake, Batch, Baton, Brewis, Brioche, Brownie, Bun, Cash, Chal(l)ah, Chametz, Chapati, Cheat, Ciabatta, Cob, Coburg, Compone, Corn, Corsned, Croissant, Crostini, Croute, Crouton, Crumpet, Crust, Currency, Damper, Dibs, Dika, Doorstep, Elephant's-foot, Eulogia, Fancy, Flatbread, Focaccia, Fougasse, French, Funds, Garlic, Gluten, Graham, Granary, Grissini, Guarana, Hallah, Hametz, Hometz, Horse, Host, Indian, Injera, Jannock, Johnny-cake, Kaffir, Lavash, Laver, Leavened, Loaf, Long tin, Manchet, Maori, Milk loaf, Milk-sop, → **MONEY**, Monkey, Na(a)n, Pain, Panada, Panary, Pane, Paneity, Paratha, Pay, Petit pain, Pikelet, Pit(t)a, Pone, Poori, Poppadom, Poultice, Prozymite, Pumpernickel, Puree, Puri, Raspings, Ravel, Roll, Rooty, Roti, Round, Rusk, Rye, Sally Lunn, Schnecken, Shewbread, Shive, Simnel, Sippet, Smor(re)brod, Soda, Soft-tommy, Sop, Sourdough, Staff of life, Standard, Stollen, Stottie, Sugar, Sweet, Tartine, Tea, Tommy, Tortoise-plant, Twist, Wastel, Wrap, Zakuski, Zwieback

Breadfruit Ja(c)k

Breadwinner Earner, Pa

Break, Break-down, Break down, Break-in, Break-up, Break up, Broken

Adjourn, Analyse, Apn(o)ea, Aposiopesis, Bait, Breach, Breather, Caesura, Caesure, Cantle, Career, Cark, Cesure, Chinaman, Chip, Cleave, Coffee, Comb, Comma, Commercial, Comminute, Compost, Compurgatory, Conk, Crack, Crock, Crumble, Deave, Debacle, Deeve, Demob, Destroy, Diffract, Disband, Disintegrate, Disperse, Disrupt, Erupt, Exeat, Fast, Fault, Four, → **FRACTURE**, Fragment, Fritter, Frush, Gaffe, Give, Greenstick, Half-term, Half-time, Harm, Hernia, Hiatus, Holiday, Infringe, Interim, Interlude, Intermission, Interrupt, → **INTERVAL**, Irrupt, Kark, Knap, Knickpoint, Lacuna, Lapse, Layover, Leave, Lysis, Moratorium, Nickpoint, Nooner, Outage, Parse, Part, Pause, Phreak, Playtime, Poach, Polarise, Price, Reave, Recess, Recrudescent, Relief, Rend, Resorption, Respite, Rest, Rift, Ruin, Rupture, Saltus, Schism(a), Secede, Service, Shatter, Shiver, Smash, Smokeho, Smoko, Snap, Split, Stave, Stop, Stop-over, Stove, Sunder, Take five, Take ten, Tame, Tea-ho, Tear, Time-out, Torn, Transgress, Truce, Twist, Vacation, Violate
Breakable Brittle, Delicate, Fissile, Frail, Friable
Breakdown Analyse, Autolysis, Cataclasm, Collapse, Conk, Crack-up, Glitch, Glycolosis, Glycolysis, Histolysis, Hydrolysis, Lyse, Lysis, Nervous, Ruin
Breaker Billow, Circuit, Comber, Ice, Roller, Smasher, Surf
Breakfast B, Brunch, Chota-hazri, Continental, Deskfast, Disjune, English, Kipper, Petit déjeuner, Power, Wedding
Breakneck Headlong
Breakwater Groyne, Jetty, Mole, Pier, Tetrapod
Bream Fish, Porgy, Sar(gus), Sea, Silver, Tai, White
Breast(s), Breastbone, Breastwork Bazuma, Blob, Bosom, Brave, Brisket, Bristols, Bust, Chimney, Clean, Counter, Diddy, Duddy, Dug, Falsies, Garbonza, Gazunga, Heart-spoon, Jubbies, Jugs, Knockers, Norg, Nork, Pigeon, Rampart, Redan, Sangar, Stem, Sternum, Sungar, Supreme, Tit, Xiphisternum
Breastplate Armour, Byrnie, Curat, Curiet, Pectoral, Plastron, Rational, Rest, Shield, Thorax, Xiphiplastron
Breath(e), Breathing, Breather Aerobe, Air-sac, Apneusis, Aqualung, Aspirate, Bated, Branchia, Buteyko method, Caesural, Cheyne-Stokes, Circular, Cypress-knee, Eupnoea, Exhalation, Expiration, Flatus, Gasp, Gill, H, Halitosis, Hauriant, Haurient, Hobday, Hypernoea, Hyperventilation, Hypopnoea, Inhale, Inspiration, Knee, Lung, Nares, Nostril, Orthopnoea, Oxygenator, Pant, Plosion, Pneuma, Prana, Pulmo, Rale, Respire, Respite, Rest, Rhonchus, Rough, Scuba, Smooth, Snore, Snorkel, Snortmast, Snotter, Snuffle, Spiracle, Spirit, Spiritus, Stertor, Stridor, Tachypnoea, Vent, Wheeze, Whiff, Whift, Whisper, Whist, Wind, Windpipe
Breathless(ness) Anhelation, Apnoea, Asthma, Dyspnoea, Emphysema, Orthopnoea, Puffed-out, Tachypnoea, Wheezing
Breathtaking Amazing, Asphyxia
Breech(es) Bible, Buckskin, Chaps, Flog, Galligaskins, Hose, Jodhpurs, Kneecords, Knickerbockers, Pantaloons, Petticoat, Plushes, Riding, Smallclothes, Smalls, Trews, Trouse(rs), Trunk hose, Trusses
Breed(er), Breeding(-place) Bear, Beget, Cleck, Endogamous, Engender, Engend(r)ure, Eugenics, Fancier, Fast, Generation, Gentilesse, Gentility, Gentrice, Hetero, Hotbed, In-and-in, Lineage, → **MANNERS**, Origin, Panmixia, Procreate, Propagate, Pullulate, Race, Raise, Rear, Savoir vivre, Seminary, Sire, Species, Stirpiculture, Stock, Strain, Stud, Telegony, Thremmatology, Tribe, Voltinism
Breeze, Breezy Air, Breath, Brisk, Cakewalk, Catspaw, Chipper, Doctor, Draught, Fresh, Gentle, Gust, Land, Light, Mackerel, Moderate, Pushover, Sea, Slant, Sniffler, Snifter, Strong, Tiff, Zephyr

Brethren Bohemian, Close, Darbyite, Elder, Exclusive, Herrnhuter, Ignorantine, Kin, Open, Plymouth, Trinity

Breton Armoric, Brezonek

Breve Minim, Note, O

Breviary Portesse, Portous

▶ **Brevity** *see* **BRIEF**

Brew(ery), Brewer, Brewing Ale, Billycan, Brose, Browst, Bummock, → **CONCOCT**, Contrive, Dictionary, Distillery, Elixir, Ferment, Infusion, Liquor, Malt, Percolate, Perk, Potion, Steep, Witches', Yeast, Yill, Zymurgy

Briar Bramble, Canker, Lawyer

Bribe(ry) Backhander, Barratry, Barretry, Bonus, Boodle, Bung, Carrot, Dash, Embracery, Get at, Graft, Grease, Hamper, Hush-money, Insult, Kickback, Lubricate, Oil, Palm, Palm-grease, Palm-oil, Payola, Schmear, Slush, Soap, Sop, Square, Straightener, Suborn, Sweeten(er), Tamper, Tempt, Tenderloin, Vail, Vales

Bric-a-brac Bibelot, Curio, Rattle-trap, Smytrie, Tatt, Virtu

Brick(s), Brickwork Adobe, Air, Bat, Bath, Bonder, Bondstone, Boob, Breeze, Bristol, Bullnose, Bur(r), Clanger, Clinker, Closer, Course, Dutch clinker, Fletton, Gaffe, Gault, Gold, Hard stocks, Header, Ingot, Klinker, Lateritious, Lego®, Malm, Nog(ging), Opus latericium, Red, Rubber, Soldier, Spawn, Sport, Stalwart, Stretcher, Terra-cotta, Testaceous, Tile, Trojan, Trump

Brickbat Missile

Bricklayer Churchill

Bride(s) Bartered, Danaides, Ellen, Hen, Spouse, War, Wife, Ximena

Bridesmaid Paranymph

Bridge(head), Bridge player Acol, Air, Al Sirat, Aqueduct, Auction, Australian, Avignon, Bailey, Balance, Barre, Bascule, Ba(u)lk, Bestride, Bifrost, Biritch, Board, Bridle-chord, Brig, Brooklyn, Cable-stayed, Cantilever, Capo, Capodastro, Capotasto, Catwalk, Chevalet, Chicago, Chicane, Clapper, Clifton, Contract, Counterpoise, Cross, Cut-throat, Deck, Declarer, Drawbridge, Duplicate, Flying, Flyover, Foot, Four-deal, Gangplank, Gangway, Gantry, Girder, Golden Gate, Hog's back, Humber, Humpback, Humpbacked, Ice, Irish, Jigger, Land, Lattice, Leaf, Lifting, Ligger, Link, London, Menai, Millau, Millennium, Nasion, Overpass, Pivot, Plafond, Ponceau, Pons, Ponticello, Pontifice, Pont levis, Pontoon, Raft, Rainbow, Rialto, Rubber, Sighs, Sinvat, Skew, Snow, → **SPAN**, Spanner, Stamford, Straddle, Suspension, Swing, Tay, Temper, Tête-de-pont, Through, Transporter, Traversing, Trestle, Truss, Turn, Vertical lift, Viaduct, Vint, Waterloo, Weigh, Wheatstone, Wire

Bridge pair EW, NS, SN, WE

Bridge protector Ice-apron

Bridge system Acol

Bridle Bit, Branks, Bridoon, Bristle, Browband, Crownpiece, Curb, Double, Hackamore, Halter, Headstall, Musrol, Noseband, Rein, Scold's

Bridle path Orbit, Track

Brief(s), Briefing, Briefly, Brevity Acquaint, Attorney, Awhile, Barristerial, Bluette, Brachyology, Breviate, Cape, Compact, → **CONCISE**, Conspectus, Crisp, Curt, Dossier, Fill in, Fleeting, Instruct, King's, Laconic, Lawyer, Nearly, Pants, Papal, Pennorth, Pithy, Prime, Scant, → **SHORT(EN)**, Short-term, Short-winded, Sitrep, Sparse, Succinct, Summing, Tanga, Terse, Transient, Undies, Update, Watching

Brig Br, Hermaphrodite, Jail, Nancy Bell, → **SHIP**, Snow

Brigade Boys', Corps, Fire, Fur, Girls', Green-ink, International, Naval, Red, Troop

Brigand Bandit, Bandolero, Cateran, Haidu(c)k, Heiduc, Heyduck, Klepht, Pillager, Pirate, → **ROBBER**, Rob Roy, Trailbaston

Bright, Brightness Afterglow, Alert, Ashine, Bertha, Brainbox, Brainy, Breezy, Brilliant, Brisk, Cheery, Chiarezza, Cla(i)re, Clara, Clear, Clever, Cuthbert, Danio, Effulgent, Eileen, Elaine, Ellie, Facula, Fair, Floodlit, Florid, Garish, Gay, Glad, Glow, Helen, Hono(u)r, Hubert, Light, Lit, Loud, Lucid, Luculent, Lustre, Net(t), Nit, Nitid, Radiant, Roarie, Ro(a)ry, Rorie, Rosy, Scintillating, Sematic, Sharp, Sheeny, Sheer, Shere, Skyre, Smart, Spark(y), Stilb, Sunlit, Sunny, Vive, Vivid, White, Zara

Bright spot Facula

Brilliant, Brilliance Ace, Aine, Blaze, Brainy, Bravura, Def, Effulgent, Eurian, Flashy, Galaxy, Gay, Gemmy, Gifted, Glitter, Glossy, High flyer, Humdinger, Inspired, Lambent, Leam, Lucent, Lustre, Mega-, Meteoric, Nitid, Pear, → **RADIANT**, Refulgent, Resplendent, Shiny, Spangle, Splendour, Star, Virtuoso, → **VIVID**, Water

Brim Edge, Lip, Rim, Ugly

Brimstone Hellfire, S, Sulphur

Brindisi Skolion, Toast

Brindled Piebald, Tabby, Tawny

Brine Muriatic, Ozone, Pickle, Saline, Salt

Bring Afferent, Bear, Carry, Cause, Conduct, Convey, Earn, Evoke, Fet, Fetch, Foist, Hatch, Induce, Land, Precipitate, Produce, Wreak

Bring up Breed, Educate, Exhume, Foster, Nurture, Raise, → **REAR**

Brink → **EDGE**, Lip, Rim, Shore, → **VERGE**

Brio Elan

Brisk(ly), Briskness Active, Alacrity, Alert, Allegro, Breezy, Busy, Chipper, Con moto, Crank, Crisp, Crouse, Fresh, Gaillard, Galliard, Jaunty, Kedge, Kedgy, Kidge, Lively, Nippy, Peart, Perk, Pert, Rattling, Roaring, Scherzo, Sharp, Smart, Snappy, Spanking, Spirited, Sprightly, Vivace, Yare, Zippy

Bristle, Bristling, Bristly Aciculum, Arista, Awn, Barb, Bewhiskered, Birse, Bridle, Campodeiform, Chaeta, Flurry, Fraught, Frenulum, Glochidium, Gooseflesh, Hackles, Hair, Hérissé, Hispid, Horrent, Horripilation, Nereid, Polychaete, Seta, Setose, Striga, Strigose, Stubble, Styloid, Vibraculum, Villus, Whisker

Bristle-tail Campodea

Brit Silt

Brit(ish), Briton(s) All-red, Anglo, Herring, Iceni, Insular, Isles, Kipper, Limey, Pict, Pom, Rooinek, Saxon, Silurian, UK

Britain Alban(y), Albion, GB, Old Dart

Britannia, Britannia metal Tutania

Brittany Armorica

Brittle Bruckle, Crackly, Crimp, Crisp, Delicate, Edgy, → **FRAGILE**, Frush, Hot-short, Redsear, Red-share, Red-shire, Redshort, Shivery, Spall, Spalt

▷ **Brittle** *may indicate* an anagram

Broach Approach, Open, Raise, Spit, Suggest, Tap, Widen

Broad(ly) Cheesy, Crumpet, Dame, Doll, Doxy, Drab, Eclectic, General, Generic, Hippy, Largo, Latitudinous, Loose, Outspoken, Ovate, Pro, Roomy, Spatulate, Tart, Thick, Tolerant, Wide, Woman

Broad-beaked Latirostrate

Broadcast(er), Broadcasting Ad(vertise), Air, Announce, Beam, Breaker, Broadband, CB, Disperse, Disseminate, Downlink, Emission, Ham, IBA, Monophonic, Multicast, Narrowband, Network, Newscast, OB, On, Outside, Pirate,

Programme, Promulgate, Put out, Radiate, Radio, Relay, RTE, Run, Satellite,
→ **SCATTER**, Scattershot, Screen(ed), SECAM, Seed, Simulcast, Sky, Sow, Sperse,
Spread, Sprinkle, Stereophonic, Transmission, Veejay, Ventilate, Wavelength,
Wireless

Broad-nosed Platyrrhine

Broadside Barrage, Criticism, Salvo, Tire

Broadway Boulevard, Esplanade, Great White Way, Motorway

Brocade Arrasene, Baldachin, Baldaquin, Baudekin, Bawdkin, Kincob, Zari

Brochure Leaflet, Pamphlet, Programme, Tract

Brogue Accent, → **SHOE**

Broke(n) Bankrupt, Bust(ed), Duff, Evans, Fritz, Impoverished, Insolvent, Kaput, On
the rocks, Puckeroo, Shattered, Skint, Stony, Stove, Strapped

▷ **Broken** *may indicate* an anagram

Broken off Prerupt

Broker Agent, Banian, Banyan, Go-between, Government, Jobber, Mediator,
→ **MERCHANT**, Power, Shadchan, Uncle

Bromide Halide, Haloid, Truism

Bromine Br

Bronchitis, Bronchitic Chesty, Husk

Bronte(s) Bell, Cyclops

Brontosaurus Apatosaurus

Bronze, Bronze age Aeneous, Aluminium, Bell, Bras(s), Brown, Corinthian,
Eugubine, Gunmetal, Hallstatt(ian), Helladic, Kamakura, Manganese, Minoan,
Mycenean, Ormolu, Phosphor, Schillerspar, Sextans, Talos, Tan, Third, Torso

Brooch Breastpin, Cameo, Clasp, Fibula, Luckenbooth, Ouch, Owche, Pin, Preen,
Prop, Spang, Sunburst

Brood(y) Clecking, Clock, Clucky, Clutch, Cogitate, Cour, Cover, Covey, Eye, Eyrie,
Hatch, Hover, Incubate, Introspect, Kindle, Litter, Meditate, Mill, Mope, Mull, Nest,
Nid, Perch, Pet, → **PONDER**, Repine, Roost, Sit, Sulk, Team

Brook Abide, Babbling, Becher's, Beck, Branch, Burn, Countenance, Creek, Endure,
Ghyll, Gill, Kerith, Kill, Pirl, Purl, Rill(et), River, Rivulet, Runlet, Runnel, Springlet,
Stand, Stomach, Stream, Suffer, Thole, Tolerate

Broom Besom, Brush, Butcher's, Cow, Cytisus, Genista, Gorse, Greenweed,
Knee-holly, Kow, New, Orobranche, Retama, Spart, Sweeper, Whisk

Brose Atholl, Pease

Broth Bouillon, Bree, Brew(is), Cullis, Dashi, Kail, Kale, Muslin-kale, Pot liquor,
Pottage, Ramen, Scotch, Skilly, → **SOUP**, Stock

Brothel Bagnio, Bawdy-house, Bordel(lo), Cathouse, Corinth, Crib, Den,
Flash-house, Honkytonk, Hothouse, Kip, Knocking shop, Leaping-house,
Red-light, Seraglio, Sporting house, Stew, Vaulting-house

Brother(hood) Ally, Bhai, Billie, Billy, Blood, Boet, Brethren, Bro, Bud, Comrade,
Félibre, Fellow, Fra, Freemason, Lay, → **MONK**, Moose, Plymouth, Pre-Raphaelite,
Sib(ling), Theatine, Trappist, Worker

Brow Crest, Forehead, Glabella, Ridge, Sinciput, Superciliary, Tump-line

Browbeat Badger, Bully, Butt, Cow, Hector, Nut

Brown(ed) Abram, Adust, Amber, Apricate, Auburn, Au gratin, Bay, Biscuit,
Bisque, Bister, Bistre, Bole, Br, Braise, Brindle, Bronzed, Brunette, Bruno, Burnet,
Burnt umber, Camel, Capability, Caramel, Caromel, Chamois, Cinnamon, Cook,
Coromandel, Drab, Dun, Duncan, Fallow, Filemot, Fulvous, Fusc(ous), Grill, Hazel,
Infuscate, Ivor, John, Khaki, Liver, March, Meadow, Mocha, Mousy, Mulatto,
Mushroom, Nut, Ochre, Olive, Oxblood, Philamot, Rufous, Rugbeian, Russet, Rust,

Sallow, Scorch, Seal, Sepia, Sienna, Snuff, Soare, Sore, Sorrel, Spadiceous, Tan, Tawny, Tenné, Terracotta, Testaceous, Toast, Tom, Umber, Vandyke, Wallflower, Walnut, Wholemeal, Windsor

Browne Sam

Brownie Dobbie, Dobby, Dobie, Goblin, Hob, Kobold, Leprechaun, Nis(se), Rosebud, Sprite

Browse(r) Graze, Mouch, Netscape®, Pasture, Read, Scan, Stall-read, Surf

Bruce Robert

Bruise Clour, Contund, Contuse, Crush, Damage, Ding, Ecchymosis, Frush, Golp(e), Hurt, Intuse, Livedo, Lividity, Mark, Mouse, Pound, Purpure, Rainbow, Shiner, Ston(n), Stun, Surbate, Vibex

Brummagem Tatty

Brunette Dark, Latin

Brush (off), Brushwood Bavin, Bottle, Brake, Broom, Carbon, Chaparral, Clash, Clothes, Dandy, Dismiss, Dust, Encounter, Fan, Filbert, Filecard, Firth, Fitch, Frith, Grainer, Hag, Hagg, Hair-pencil, Hog, Kiss, Liner, Lip, Loofah, Mop, Paint, Pallet, Pig, Pope's head, Putois, Rebuff, Rice, Rigger, Sable, Scrap, Scrub, Scuff, Shaving, Skim, Striper, Thicket, Touch, Undergrowth, Whisk, Wire

Brusque Abrupt, Blunt, Brief, Curt, Downright, Offhand, Pithy, Short

Brussels Carpet, Lace

Brutal, Brute Animal, Barbaric, Beast, Bête, Caesar, Caliban, Cruel, Down and dirty, Hun, Iguanodon, Inhuman, Nazi, Nero, Ostrogoth, Pitiless, Quagga, Rambo, Rottweiler, Roughshod, Ruffian, Thresher-whale, Yahoo

Brutus Wig

Bryophyte Moss, Tree-moss

Bubble(s), Bubbly Air-bell, Air-lock, Barmy, Bead(ed), Bell, Bleb, Blister, Boil, Buller, Cavitate, Champagne, Cissing, Ebullition, Effervesce, Embolus, Enthuse, Espumoso, Foam, → **FROTH**, Gassy, Globule, Gurgle, Head, Magnetic, Mantle, Mississippi, Moet, Popple, Rale, Reputation, Roundel, Rowndell, Seed, Seethe, Simmer, Soap, South Sea, Vesicle, Widow

Bubble and squeak Colcannon

Buccaneer Corsair, Dampier, Drake, Freebooter, Morgan, Picaroon, Pirate

Buck (up) Bongo, Brace, Cheer, Dandy, Deer, Dollar, Elate, Encheer, Hart, Jerk, Leash, Male, Ourebi, Pitch, Pricket, Ram, Rusa, Sore, Sorel(l), Sorrel, Spade, Spay(a)d, → **STAG**, Staggard, Stud, Water, Wheel

Buckaroo Cowboy, Cowpoke

Bucket(s) Bail, Bale, Clamshell, Ice, Jacob's ladder, Kibble, Ladle, Noria, Pail, Piggin, Rust, Scuttle, Situla, Slop, Stoop(e), Stope, Stoup, Tub

Buckeye Ohio

Buckle-beggar Patrico

Buckle Artois, Clasp, Contort, Crumple, Deform, Dent, Fasten, Warp

▷ **Buckle** *may indicate* an anagram

Buckler Ancile, Rondache, → **SHIELD**, Targe

▷ **Bucks** *may indicate* an anagram

Buckshee Free

Buckthorn Cascara, Rhineberry, Wahoo

Buckwheat Brank, Sarrasin, Sarrazin

Bucolic Aeglogue, Eglogue, Idyllic, Pastoral, Rural, Rustic

Bud(ding), Buddy Botoné, Bottony, Bulbil, Burgeon, Cacotopia, Clove, Cobber, Deb, Eye, Gem(ma), Germinate, Hibernaculum, Holly, Knop, Knosp, Knot, Nascent, Pal, Scion, Serial, Shoot, Sprout, Statoblast, Taste, Turion

Buddha, Buddhism, Buddhist Abhidhamma, Ahimsa, Amitabha, Anata, Anatta, Anicca, Arhat, Asoka, Bardo, Bodhisattva, Dalai Lama, Dukkha, Esoteric, Foism, Gautama, Hinayana, Jain, Jataka, Jodo, Kagyu, Mahatma, Mahayana, Maitreya, Maya, Nichiren, Pali, Pitaka, Pure Land, Rinzai, Ryobu, Sakya-muni, Sangha, Shinto, Siddhartha Gautama, Sila, Soka Gakkai, Soto, Sutra, Tantric, Theravada, Tripitaka, Triratna, Vajrayana, Zen(o)

Budge Jee, Move, Stir, Submit

Budgerigar Shell parrakeet, Shell parrot

Budget Allocation, Allot, Estimate, Operating, Plan, Programme, Rudder, Save, Shoestring

Buff Altogether, Beige, Birthday suit, Blind man's, Eatanswill, Fan, Fawn, Nankeen, Natural, Nude, Nut, Polish, → **RUB**, Streak

Buffalo African, Anoa, Arna, Asiatic, Bison, Bonasus, Bugle, Cap, Cape, Carabao, Ox, Perplex, Takin, Tamarao, Tamarau, Timarau, Water, Zamouse

Buffer Bootblack, Cofferdam, Cutwater, Fender, Sleek-stone

Buffet Bang, Blow, Box, Carvery, Counter, Cuff, Finger-food, Fork luncheon, Fork-supper, Hit, Lam, Maltreat, Meal, Perpendicular, Shove, Sideboard, Smorgasborg, Strike, Strook(e)

Buffoon(ery) Antic, Clown, Droll, Goliard, Harlequin, Horseplay, Iniquity, Jack pudding, Jester, Mime(r), Mome, Mountebank, Mummer, Nutter, Pantagruel, Pantaloon(ery), Pickle-herring, Pierrot, Punchinello, Scaramouch, Scogan, Scoggin, Scurrile, Slouch, Tomfool, Vice, Wag, Zany

Bug(s) Ambush, Annoy, Anoplura, Antagonise, Arthropod, Assassin, Bacteria, Bedevil, Beetle, Berry, Bishop's mitre, Bunny, Cabbage, Capsid, Chinch, Cimex, Coccidae, Cockchafer, Corixid, Creepy-crawly, Croton, Damsel, Debris, Dictograph®, Eavesdrop, E-coli, Error, Germ, Get at, Ground, Harlequin, Hassle, Hemiptera, → **INSECT**, Jitter, June, Kissing, Lace, Lightning, Listeria, Maori, May, Mealy, Micrococcus, Mike, Millennium, Mite, Nettle, Pill, Reduviid, Rhododendron, Rile, Shield, Skeeter, Sow, Squash, Tap, Vex, Water-measurer, Wheel, Wiretap

Bugbear Anathema, Bête noire, Bogey, Bogle, Bogy, Eten, Ettin, Poker, Rawhead

Buggy Beach, Car, Cart, Inside-car, Pushchair, Shay, Tipcart, Trap

Bughouse Fleapit, Loco

Bugle, Bugle call Boots and saddles, Chamade, Clarion, Cornet, Flugelhorn, Hallali, Kent, Last post, Ox, Reveille, Taps, → **TRUMPET**, Urus

Build, Building(s), Building site, Build-up Accrue, Aggrade, Anabolism, Ar(a)eostyle, Assemble, Barn, Bhavan, Big, Bricks and mortar, Capitol, Chapterhouse, Cob, Colosseum, Commons, Construction, Containment, Corncrib, Cot, → **CREATE**, Cruck, Curia, Develop, Dipteros, Dome, Drystone, Duplex, Ectomorph, Edifice, Edify, Endomorph, Erect, Exchange, Fabric, Gatehouse, Heapstead, High-rise, Hut, Infill, Insula, Kaaba, Ken, Linhay, Listed, Low-rise, Lyceum, Mesomorph, Minaret, Monopteron, Mould, Observatory, Odeon, Odeum, Outhouse, Palazzo, Pataka, Pavilion, Pentastyle, Phalanstery, Phalanx, Pile, Portakabin®, Premises, Prytaneum, Quonset®, Raise, Ribbon, Rotunda, Skyscraper, Stance, Statehouse, Structure, Suspension, Synthesis, System, Tectonic, Telecottage, Temple, Tenement, Tholos, Tower, Tower block, Town hall, Triplex®, Whata

Builder Bob, Brick, Cheops, Constructor, Engineer, Entrepreneur, Mason, Millwright, Spiderman, Stonemason, Waller

▷ **Building** *may indicate* an anagram

Built-up Urban

Bulb Camas(h), Camass, Chive, Cive, Corm, Flash, Globe, Lamp, Light, Olfactory,

Pearl, Rupert's drop, Scallion, Set, Shallot, Squill

Bulge, Bulging Astrut, Bag, Bias, Biconvex, Bug, Bulbous, Bunchy, Cockle, Entasis, Expand, Exsert, Inion, Prolate, Protrude, Protuberant, Relievo, Rotund, Shoulder, Strout, Strut, → **SWELL**, Tumid

Bulk(y) Aggregate, Ample, Big, Body, Bouk, Corpulent, Density, Extent, Gross, Hull, Immensity, Lofty, Massive, Preponderance, Roughage, Scalar, → **SIZE**, Stout, Vol(ume), Voluminous, Weight

Bull(s), Bullock, Bully Anoa, Apis, Bakha, Beef, Blarney, Bludgeon, Bluster, Bouncer, Bovine, Brag, Brave, Browbeat, Buchis, Bucko, Centre, Cuttle, Despot, Dragoon, Drawcansir, Encierro, Englishman, Eretrian, Fancyman, Farnese, Flashman, Flatter, Gold, Gosh, Hapi, Harass, Hawcubite, Haze(r), Hector, Hibernicism, Hogwash, Hoodlum, Huff, Intimidate, Investor, Iricism, Irish(ism), John, Killcow, Lambast, Maltreat, Menace, Merwer, Mick(e)(y), Mistake, Mithraism, Mohock, Nandi, Neat, Pamplona, Papal, Pennalism, Piker, Pistol, Placet, Poler, Railroad, Rhodian, Roarer, Rot, Ruffian, Sitting, Souteneur, Stag, Stale, Strong-arm, Swash-buckler, Taurine, Taurus, Toitoi, Tommy-rot, Tosh, Trash, Tripe, Twaddle, Tyran(ne), Tyrannise, Tyrant, Unigenitus, Victimise, Winged, Zo(bo)

Bulldog Marshal, Tenacious

Bulldoze(r) Angledozer, Coerce, Earthmover, Leveller, Overturn

Bullet Ammo, Balata, Ball, Baton round, Biscayan, Blank, Dumdum, Fusillade, Lead towel, Magic, Minié, Minié ball, Missile, Pellet, Percussio, Plastic, Round, Rubber, Shot, Slug, Soft-nosed, Tracer

Bulletin All points, Memo, Message, Newscast, Newsletter, Report, Summary

Bull-fight(er), Bull-fighting Banderillero, Banderillo, Corrida, Cuadrilla, Encierro, Escamillo, Matador, Picador, Rejoneador, Tauromachy, Toreador, Torero

Bull-head Cottoid, Father-lasher, Pogge, Sea-poacher

Bull-rider Europa

Bull-roarer Rhombos, Tu(r)ndun

Bull's eye Carton, God, Humbug, Target

Bullshit BS

▶ **Bully** *see* **BULL**

Bulrush Pandanaceous, Raupo, Reed, Reed-mace, Tule

Bulwark Bastion, Defence, Rampart, Resistor

Bum Ass, Beg, Deadbeat, Prat, Scrounge, Sponge, Thumb, Tramp, Vagabond

Bumble Beadle, Bedel(l)

▷ **Bumble** *may indicate* an anagram

Bumboat woman Buttercup

Bumf Spam

Bump(er), Bumps Big, Blow, Bradyseism, Bucket, Clour, Collide, Dunch, Encephalocele, Fender, Hillock, Immense, Inian, Inion, Joll, Jo(u)le, Jowl, Keltie, Kelty, Knar, Knock, Mamilla, Mogul, Organ, Overrider®, Phrenology, Reveille, Rouse, Speed, Thump

Bumph Loo-roll

Bumpkin Bucolic, Bushwhacker, Clodhopper, Hawbuck, Hayseed, Hick, Jock, Lout, Oaf, Put(t), Rube, Rustic, Yokel, Zany

Bumptious Arrogant, Brash, Randie, Randy, Uppity

Bun Barmbrack, Bath, Black, Chelsea, Chignon, Chou, Currant, Devonshire split, Hot-cross, Huffkin, Mosbolletjie, Roll, Teacake, Toorie, Wad

Bunch Acinus, Anthology, Bob, Botryoid, Bouquet, Byndle, Cluster, Fascicle, Finial, Flock, → **GROUP**, Hand, Handful, Ilk, Lot, Lump, Nosegay, Panicle, Raceme, Spray, Staphyline, Tassel, Tee, Truss, Tuft

Bundle Axoneme, Bale, Bavin, Bluey, Bottle, Byssus, Desmoid, Dorlach, Drum, Fag(g)ot, Fascicle, Fascine, Fibre, Fibrovascular, Kemple, Knitch, Lemniscus, Matilda, → **PACK(AGE)**, Parcel, Sack, Sheaf, Shiralee, Shock, Shook, Stela, Stook, Swag, Tie, Top, Trousseau, Truss, Vascular, Wad, Wadge, Wap

Bung Cork, Dook, Obturate, Plug, Stopgap, Stopper

Bungalow Dak

Bungle(r), Bungled, Bungling Blunder, Blunk, Bodge, Boob, Boss shot, Botch, Bumble, Bummle, Dub, Duff, Fluff, Foozle, Foul, Foul up, Goof, Gum up, Maladroit, Mash, Mess, Mis(h)guggle, Muddle, Muff, Mull, Prat, Screw, Spoil

Bunk(er), Bunkum Abscond, Absquatulate, Balderdash, Baloney, Berth, Blah, Bolt, Casemate, Claptrap, Clio, Entrap, Guy, Hazard, History, Hokum, Hooey, Humbug, Malarky, Nonsense, Rot, Sandtrap, Scuttle, Stokehold, Tosh, Trap, Tripe

Bunter Billy, Owl

Bunthorne Aesthete, Poet

Bunting Bird, Cirl, Flag, Fringilline, Ortolan, Pennant, Snow, Streamer, Yellow-hammer, Yowley

Buoy (up) Bell, Breeches, Can, Dan, Daymark, Dolphin, Float, Life, Marker, Nun, Raft, Reassure, Ring, Seamark, Sonar, Sonobuoy, Spar, Sustain, Wreck

Buoyant Afloat, Blithe, Floaty, Resilient

Burble Blat, Gibber

Burden Albatross, Beare, Bob, Cargo, Cark, Chant, Chorus, Cross, Cumber, Deadweight, Drone, Droore, Encumber, Encumbrance, Fa-la, Fardel, Folderol, Fraught, Freight, Gist, Handicap, Hum, Lade, → **LOAD**, Lumber, Millstone, Monkey, Oercome, Onus, Oppress, Put-upon, Refrain, Rumbelow, Saddle, Servitude, Shanty, Substance, Tax, Tenor, Torch, Trouble, Weight, White man's, Woe, Yoke

Burdensome Irksome, Onerous, Oppressive, Weighty

Burdock Clote(-bar), Clothur, Cockle-bar, Gobo, Hardoke, Weed

Bureau Agency, Agitprop, Breakfront, Cominform, Davenport, Desk, Interpol, Kominform, Marriage, → **OFFICE**, Volunteer

Bureaucracy, Bureaucrat(ic) Bean-counter, CS, Impersonal, Jack-in-office, Mandarin, Red tape, Tapist, Wallah

Burgeon(ing) Asprout, Blossom, Bud, Grow, Sprout

Burgess, Burgher Citizen, Freeman

Burgh Burrowstown, Parliamentary, Police, Royal

Burglar(y), Burgle Aggravated, Area-sneak, Cat, Crack(sman), House-breaker, Intruder, Peterman, Picklock, Raffles, Robber, Screw, Thief, Yegg

Burgundy Macon, Vin

Burial(place) Catacomb, Charnel, Committal, Crypt, Cubiculum, Darga, Funeral, God's acre, Golgotha, Grave, Interment, Kurgan, Lair, Last rites, Sepulchre, Sepulture, Tomb, Tumulus, Vault, Zoothapsis

Burin Graver

Burlesque Caricatura, Caricature, Comedy, Farce, Heroicomical, Hudibrastic(s), Hurlo-thrumbo, Lampoon, Macaronic, Parody, Satire, Skimmington, Skit, Spoof, Travesty

Burlington RA

Burly Bluff, Stout, Strapping

Burmese Karen(ni), Mon(-Khmer), Naga, Shan

Burn(er), Burning, Burnt Adust, Afire, Alow(e), Ardent, Argand, Arson, Ash, Auto-da-fé, Bake, Bats-wing, Beck, Bishop, Blaze, Blister, Blowtorch, Brand, Bren(ne), Brent, Brook, Bunsen, Causalgia, Caustic, Cauterise, Char, Chark, Chinese, Cinder, Clavie, Coal, Coke, Combust, Conflagration, Cremate, Crozzled,

Crucial, Deflagrate, Destruct, Eilding, Ember, Emboil, Empyreuma, Fervid, Fircone, → **FIRE**, Fishtail, Flagrant, Flare, Flash, Fresh(et), Gleed, Gut, Holocaust, Ignite, In, Incendiary, Incense, Incinerate, Inure, Inust(ion), Itch, Kill, Lean, Live, Lunt, Offering, On, Oxidise, Oxyacetylene, Pilot, Plo(a)t, Powder, Pyric, Pyromania, Rill, Sati, Scald, Scaud, Scorch, Scouther, Scowder, Scowther, Sear, Sienna, Sike, Singe, Sizzle, Smart, Smoulder, Suttee, Swale, Third-degree, Thurible, Torch, Umber, Urent, Ustion, Ustulation, Weeke, Welsbach, Wick

Burp Belch

Burr(ing) Brei, Brey, Clote, Croup, Dialect, Knob, Rhotacism

Burrow(er), Burrowing Dig, Earth, Fossorial, Gopher, Groundhog, Hole, How, Howk, Mole, Nuzzle, Root, Sett, Terricole, Tunnel, Viscacha, Warren, Wombat, Worm

Bursar(y) Camerlengo, Camerlingo, Coffers, Grant, Purser, Scholarship, Tertiary, Treasurer

Bursitis Beat

Burst(ing) Blowout, Brast, Break, Dehisce, Disrupt, Dissilient, Ebullient, Erumpent, Erupt, → **EXPLODE**, Flare-up, Fly, Gust, Implode, Pop, Salvo, Sforzato, Shatter, Spasm, Spirt, Split, Sprint, Spurt, Stave, Tetterous

Bury Cover, Eard, Earth, Embowel, Engrave, Enhearse, Graff, Graft, Imbed, Inearth, Inhearse, Inherce, Inhume, Inter, Inurn, Landfill, Repress, Sepulture, Sink, Ye(a)rd, Yird

Bus Aero, Bandwagon, Car, Charabanc, Coach, Crew, Double-decker, Greyhound, Hondey, Hopper, ISA, Jitney, Mammy-wagon, Purdah, Rattletrap, Single-decker, Tramcar, Trolley, Walking

Bus conductor Cad, Clippy

Bush(es), Bush-man, Bushy Bitou, Bramble, Brier, Bullace, Busket, Calico, Clump, Cotton, Dumose, Firethorn, Hawthorn, Hedge, Hibiscus, Ivy-tod, Kapok, Kiekie, Mallee, Matagouri, Mulberry, Outback, Poinsettia, Poly-poly, President, Prostanthera, Sallee, San, Scrog, Shepherd, Shrub, Sloe, Sugar, Thicket, Tire, Tod(de), Tumatakuru

Bush-baby Durukuli, Galago, Nagapie, Night-ape

Bushel Ardeb, Bu, Co(o)mb, Cor, Ephah, Fou, Homer, Peck, Weight, Wey

Bushwalker Hoon

Business Affair, Agency, Biz, Bricks and clicks, Brokerage, Bus, Cartel, Cerne, Chaebol(s), Co, Commerce, Company, Concern, Conglomerate, Craft, Duty, Enterprise, Ergon, Establishment, Exchange, Fasti, Firm, Funny, Game, Gear, Hong, Industry, Lifestyle, Line, Métier, Monkey, Office, Palaver, Pi(d)geon, Pidgin, Practice, Professional, Racket, Shebang, Shop, Show, To-do, Trade, Traffic, Transaction, Tread, Turnover, Unincorporated, Vocation, Zaibatsu, Zaikai

Businessman Babbitt, Capitalist, City, Dealer, Entrepreneur, Financier, Realtor, Taipan, Trader, Tycoon

Busk(er) Bodice, Corset, Entertainer, German-band

Buskin(s) Brod(e)kin, Cothurn(us), Shoe

Buss Kiss, Osculate, Smack

Bussu Troelie, Troely, Troolie

Bustard Bird, Otis, Turkey

Bust Beano, Boob, Brast, Break, Chest, Dollarless, Falsies, Figurehead, Herm(a), Insolvent, Mamma, Rupture, Sculp, Shatter(ed), Spree, Statue, Term(inus), To-tear, To-torne, Ups(e)y

▷ **Bust** *may indicate* an anagram

Buster Keaton

Bustle Ado, Beetle, Do, Dress-improver, Flap, Fuss, Pad, Scurry, → **STIR**, Swarm, Tournure, Whew

Busy Active, At (it), Deedy, → **DETECTIVE**, Dick, Doing, Eident, Employ, Engaged, Ergate, Eye, Goer, Hectic, Hive, Humming, Manic, Occupied, Operose, Ornate, Prodnose, Stir, Stirabout, Tec, Throng, Worksome

Busybody Bustler, Meddler, Noser, Pragmatic, Snooper, Trout, Yenta

But Aber, Algates, Bar, Except, However, Keg, Merely, Nay, Only, Save, Sed, Simply, Tun, Without

Butch He-man, Macho

Butcher(s), Butchery Cumberland, Decko, Dekko, Eyeful, Flesher, Gander, Ice, Kill, Killcow, Look, Looksee, Massacre, Ovicide, Sever, Shambles, Shochet, Shufti, Slaughter, Slay, Slink

Butler Bedivere, Bread-chipper, Jeeves, Khansama(h), Major-domo, RAB, Rhett, Samuel, Servant, Sewer, Sommelier, Steward

Butt (in) Aris, Arse, Ass, Barrel, Bumper, Bunt, Clara, Dimp, Dout, Dowt, Dunch, Enter, Geck, Glasgow kiss, Goat, Header, Horn, Jesting-stock, Laughing-stock, Mark, Nut, Outspeckle, Pantaloon, Pipe, Push, Ram, Roach, Scapegoat, Snipe, Stompie, → **STOOGE**, Straight man, Stump, Target, Tun, Ups

Butter Adulation, Apple, Billy, Brandy, Butyric, Cacao, Cocoa, Coconut, Drawn, Flatter, Galam, Garcinia, Ghee, Ghi, Goa, Goat, Illipi, Illupi, Kokum, Mahua, Mahwa, Maitre d'hotel, Mow(r)a, Nut, Nutter, Palm, Pat, Peanut, Print, Ram, Rum, Scrape, Shea, Spread, Vegetable

▷ **Butter** *may indicate* a goat or such

Buttercup Bumboat woman, Crow-foot, Crow-toe, Goldilocks, Ranunculus, Reate, Thalictrum

Butterfingers Muff

Butterfish Nine-eyes

Butterfly Apollo, Argus, Birdwing, Blue, Brimstone, Brown, Cabbage white, Camberwell beauty, Cardinal, Chequered skipper, Cleopatra, Clouded yellow, Comma, Common blue, Copper, Dilettante, Eclosion, Elfin, Emperor, Fritillary, Gate-keeper, Grayling, Hair-streak, Heath, Hesperid, Imaginal, Kallima, Large copper, Large white, Leaf, Lycaena, Marbled-white, Meadow brown, Metalmark, Milk-weed, Monarch, Morpho, Mountain ringlet, Mourning-cloak, Nerves, Nymphalid, Nymphean, Orange-tip, Owl, Painted lady, Papilionidae, Peacock, Pieris, Psyche, Purple emperor, Red admiral, Rhopalocera, Ringlet, Satyr(idae), Satyrinae, Scotch argus, Silverspot, Skipper, Small white, Speckled wood, Stamper, Stroke, Sulphur, Swallow-tail, Thecla, Thistle, Tiger swallowtail, Tortoiseshell, Two-tailed pasha, Vanessa, Wall brown, White admiral

Buttermilk Bland, Lassi

Butternut Souari

Butter-tree Mahua, Mahwa, Mow(r)a

Buttocks Aristotle, Arse, Ass, Bahookie, Booty, Bottom, Can, Cheeks, Coit, Derrière, Doup, Duff, Fanny, Fundament, Gluteus maximus, Heinie, Hinder-end, Hinderlan(d)s, Hurdies, Jacksie, Jacksy, Keester, Keister, Mooning, Nache, Nates, Posterior, Prat, Quoit, Seat, Tush

Button(s) Barrel, Bellboy, Fastener, Frog, Hot, Knob, Mescal, Mute, Netsuke, Olivet, Page(boy), Panic, Pause, Pearl, Press, Push, Snooze, Stud, Switch, Toggle, Toolbar

Buttonhole Accost, Boutonniere, Detain, Doorstep, Eye, Flower

Buttress Brace, Counterfort, Flying, Hanging, Pier, Prop, Stay, Support, Tambour

Butty Chum, Oppo

Buxom Bonnie, Busty, Plump, Sonsy, Well-endowed, Wench

Buy(ing), Buyer Believe, Bribe, Coemption, Coff, Corner, Customer, Emption, Engross, Impulse, Monopsonist, Oligopsony, Panic, Purchase, Redeem, Regrate, Shop, Shout, Spend, Take, Trade, Treat, Vendee

▷ **Buyer** *may indicate* money

Buzz(er) Bee, Birr, Bombilate, Bombinate, Button, Fly, Hum, Rumour, Scram, Whirr, Whisper, Zed, Zing, Zoom

Buzzard Bee-kite, Bird, Buteo, Hawk, Honey, Pern, Puttock, Turkey, Vulture

By Alongside, At, Gin, Gone, In, Near, Neighbouring, Nigh, Of, On, Past, Per, Through, With, X

Bye Extra

Bye-bye Adieu, Farewell, Tata

By far Out and away

Bygone B.C., Dead, Departed, Past, Yore

By Jove Egad

Bypass Avoid, Beltway, Circuit, Coronary, → **DETOUR**, Evade, Ignore, Omit, Shunt, Skirt

By-product Epiphenomenon, Spill-over, Spin-off

Byre Cowshed, Manger, Stable, Trough

By so much The

Byte Nybble

By the way Apropos, Incidentally, Ob(iter)

Byway Alley, Lane, Path

Byword Ayword, Nayword, Phrase, Proverb, Slogan

Byzantine Catapan, Comnenus, Complicated, Exarch, Intricate, Intrince, Theme

Cc

C Around, Caught, Celsius, Cent, Centigrade, Charlie, Conservative, San
Cab Boneshaker, Crawler, Drosky, Fiacre, Four-wheeler, Growler, Gurney, Hackney, Hansom, Mini, Noddy, Taxi, Vettura
Cab(b)alistic Abraxis, Mystic, Notarikon, Occult
Cabal(ler) Arlington, Ashley, Buckingham, Clifford, Clique, Conspiracy, Coterie, Faction, Junto, Lauderdale, Party, Plot
Cabaret Burlesque, Floorshow
Cabbage(-head), Cabbage soup Bok choy, Black, Borecole, Brassica, Castock, Cauliflower, Cavalo nero, Chinese, Choucroute, Cole, Collard, Crout, Custock, Drumhead, Gobi, Kerguelen, Kohlrabi, Kraut, Loaf, Loave, Mibuna, Mizuna, Pak-choi, Pamphrey, Pe-tsai, Sauerkraut, Savoy, Shchi, Shtchi, Skunk, St Patrick's, Thieve, Turnip, Wild, Wort
Caber Fir, Janker, Log, Sting
Cabin Berth, Bibby, Bothy, Box, Cabana, Caboose, Camboose, Coach, Cottage, Crannog, Crib, Cuddy, Den, Gondola, Hovel, Hut, Izba, Lodge, Loghouse, Long-house, Pod, Pressure, Room, Roundhouse, Saloon, Shanty, Stateroom, Trunk
Cabin-boy Grummet
Cabinet Armoire, Bahut, Cabale, Case, Cellaret, Chiffonier, Chill, Closet, Commode, Console, Cupboard, Display, Filing, Kitchen, Ministry, Official family, Repository, Secretaire, Shadow, Shrinal, Unit, Vitrine
Cabinet maker Banting, Chippendale, Ebeniste, Hepplewhite, Joiner, PM
Cable(way), Cable-car Chain, Coax(ial), Extension, Flex, Halser, Hawser, Jumper, Jump leads, Junk, Landline, Lead, Lead-in, Lifeline, Null-modern, Oil-filled, Outhaul, Outhauler, Rope, Shroud, Slatch, Snake, Téléférique, → **TELEGRAM**, Telegraph, Telepherique, Telpher(age), Topping lift, Trunking, Wire, Yoke
Cache Deposit, Hidlin(g)s, → **HOARD**, Inter, Stash, Store, Treasure
Cachet Prestige
Cackle Cluck, Gaggle, Gas, Haw, Snicker, Titter
Cacography Scrawl
Cacophony Babel, Caterwaul, Charivari, Discord, Jangle
Cactus, Cactus-like Alhagi, Barel, Cereus, Cholla, Christmas, Dildo, Easter, Echino-, Hedgehog, Jointed, Jojoba, Maguey, Mescal, Mistletoe, Nopal, Ocotillo, Opuntia, Organ-pipe, Peyote, Pitahaya, Prickly pear, Retama, Saguaro, Schlumbergera, Stapelia, Star, Strawberry, Torch-thistle, Tuna, Xerophytic
Cad Base, Boor, Bounder, Churl, Cocoa, Heel, Oik, Rascal, Rotter, Skunk, Varlet
Cadaver(ous) Body, Corpse, Deathly, Ghastly, Goner, Haggard, Stiff
Caddy Porter, Tea, Teapoy
Cadence Authentic, Beat, Close, Euouae, Evovae, Fa-do, Flow, Lilt, Meter, Perfect, Plagal, Rhythm
Cadenza Fireworks

Cadet(s) Junior, OTC, Plebe, Recruit, Rookie, Scion, Snooker, Space, Syen, Trainee, Younger

Cadge(r) Bludge, Bot, Bum, Impose, Mutch, Ponce, → **SCROUNGE**, Sponge

Cadmium Cd

Caesar Despot, Nero

Caesium Cs

Café, Cafeteria Automat, Bistro, Brasserie, Buvette, Canteen, Commissary, Cybercafe, Diner, Dinette, Donko, Eatery, Estaminet, Filtré, Greasy spoon, Hashhouse, Internet, Juke joint, Netcafé, Noshery, Pizzeria, Pull-in, Snackbar, Tearoom, Tea-shop, Transport, Truckstop

Cage Bar, Battery, Box, Cavie, Confine, Coop, Corf, Dray, Drey, Enmew, Faraday, Fold, Frame, Grate, Hutch, Keavie, Mew, Mortsafe, Pen, → **PRISON**, Safety, Squirrel, Trave

Cahoots Hugger-mugger

Cairn Barp, Clearance, Dog, Horned, Man, Mound, Raise

Caisson Bends

Caitiff Meanie

Cajole(ry) Beflum, Beguile, Blandish, Blarney, Carn(e)y, → **COAX**, Cuittle, Humbug, Inveigle, Jolly, Persuade, Wheedle, Whilly, Wiles

Cake Agnus dei, Angel, Baba, Babka, Baklava, Banbury, Bannock, Bara brith, Barm(brack), Battenberg, Bhaji, Biffin, Birthday, Brioche, Brownie, Buckwheat, Bun, Carcake, Cattle, Chapat(t)i, Chillada, Chupati, Chupattie, Chupatty, Clapbread, Clot, Coburg, Cookie, Corn dodger, Cotton, Croquante, Croquette, Cruller, Crumpet, Currant, Dainty, Devil's food, Drizzle, Dundee, Eccles, Eclair, Fancy, Farl(e), Filter, Fish, Flapjack, Frangipane, Frangipani, Fritter, Galette, Genoa, Gingerbread, Girdle, → **HARDEN**, Hockey, Hoe, Idli, Jannock, Johnny, Jumbal, Jumbles, Koeksister, Kruller, Kuchen, Kueh, Lady's finger, Lamington, Lardy, Latke, Layer, Linseed, Macaroon, Madeira, Madeleine, Maid of honour, Marble, Meringue, Millefeuille, Mooncake, Mud, Muffin, Napoleon, Nut, Oatmeal, Oil, Pan, Panettone, Paratha, Parkin, Parliament, Pastry, Pat, Patty, Pavlova, Pepper, Petit four, Pikelet, → **PLASTER**, Pomfret, Pone, Pontefract, Poori, Popover, Pound, Profiterole, Puff, Puftaloon(a), Puri, Queencake, Ratafia, Ready-mix, Religieuse, Rice, Rock, Rosti, Roti, Rout, Rum baba, Rusk, Sachertorte, Saffron, Sally Lunn, Salt, Sandwich, Savarin, Scone, Seed, Set, Simnel, Singing-hinny, Slab, Slapjack, Soul, Spawn, Spice, Sponge, Stollen, Stottie, Sushi, Swiss roll, Tablet, Tansy, Tea(bread), Tipsy, Torte, Tortilla, Twelfth, Upside down, Vetkoek, Wad, Wafer, Waffle, Wedding, Wonder, Yeast, Yule log

▷ **Cake** *may indicate* an anagram

Cake-shaped Placentiform

Cakestand Curate

Cakewalk Doddle

Calaboose Jail, Loghouse

Calamitous, Calamity Blow, Catastrophe, Dire, → **DISASTER**, Distress, Fatal, Ill, Jane, Ruth, Storm, Tragic, Unlucky, Visitation, Woe

Calcareous Ganoin, Lithite

Calcium Ca, Colemanite, Dogger, Dripstone, Otolith, Quicklime, Scawtite, Whewellite, Wollastonite

Calculate(d), Calculation, Calculator Abacus, Actuary, Comptometer, Compute(r), Cost, Design, Estimate, Extrapolate, Four-function, Log, Napier's bones, Number-crunch, Prorate, Quip(p)u, Rate, → **RECKON**, Slide-rule, Sofar, Soroban, Tactical, Tell

Calculus Cholelith, Differential, Functional, Infinitesimal, Integral, Lambda, Lith, Lithiasis, Predicate, Propositional, Science, Sentential, Sialolith, Stone, Tartar, Urolith

Caledonian Kanak

Calendar Advent, Agenda, Almanac, Chinese, Diary, Dies fasti, Fasti, Gregorian, Hebrew, Intercalary, Jewish, Journal, Julian, Luach, Lunisolar, Menology, Newgate, New Style, Ordo, Perpetual, Revolutionary, Roman, Sothic

Calender(ing) Dervish, Mangle, Swissing

Calf Ass, Bobby, Box, Cf, Deacon, Divinity, Dogie, Dogy, Fatted, Freemartin, Golden, Law, Leg, Maverick, Mottled, Poddy, Sleeper, Slink, Smooth, Stirk, Sural, Tollie, Tolly, Tree, Veal, Vitular

Caliban Moon-calf

Calibrate, Calibre Bore, Capacity, Graduate, Mark, → **QUALITY**, Text

California(n) Fresno, Golden State

Californium Cf

Caliph Abbasid(e), Omar, Vathek

Call(ed), Calling, Call on, Call up Adhan, Appeal, Arraign, Art, Awaken, Azan, Banco, Bawl, Beck, Behote, Bevy, Bid, Boots and saddles, Bugle, Business, Buzz, Career, Chamade, Cite, Claim, Clang, Clarion, Cleep, Clepe, Close, Cold, Conference, Conscript, Convene, Convoke, Cooee, Cry, Curtain, Dial, Drift, Dub, Effectual, Evoke, First post, Game, Go, Hail, Hallali, Haro, Heads, Heave-ho, Hech, Hete, Hey, Hight, Ho, Hot(e), Howzat, Huddup, Hurra(h), Invocation, Job, Junk, Last (post), Line, Local, Look in, Margin, Métier, Misère, Mobilise, Mot, Name, Nap, Need, Nemn, Nempt, Nominate, No trumps, Olé, Page, Peter, Phone, Photo, Pop in, Post, Proo, Pruh, Pursuit, Rechate, Recheat, Retreat, Reveille, Ring, Roll, Rort, Rouse, Route, Sa-sa, See, Sennet, → **SHOUT**, Shut-out, Slam, Slander, Slogan, Soho, Sola, SOS, STD, Style, Subpoena, Summon(s), Tails, Tantivy, Taps, Telephone, Term, Toho, Toll, Trumpet, Trunk, Tweet, Visit, Vocation, Waken, Wake-up, Whoa-ho-ho, Wo ha ho, Yell, Yo, Yodel, Yodle, Yo-ho(-ho), Yoicks, Yoo-hoo

Calla(s) Aroid, Lily, Maria

Caller Fresh, Guest, Herring, Inspector, Muezzin, Rep, Traveller, → **VISITOR**

Calligraphy Grass style, Kakemono

Callipers Odd legs

Callisthenics T'ai chi (ch'uan)

Callosity, Call(o)us Bunion, Cold, Corn, Hard, Horny, Obtuse, Ringbone, Seg, Thylose, Tough, Tylosis, Unfeeling

Callow Crude, Green, Immature, Jejune

Calm Abate, Alegge, Aleye, Allay, Allege, Appease, Ataraxy, Composed, Cool, Dead-wind, Dispassionate, Doldrums, Easy, Easy-osy, Eevn, Equable, Equanimity, Even, Eye, Flat, Glassy, Halcyon, Loun(d), Lown(d), Lull, Mellow, Mild, Milden, Millpond, Nonchalant, Pacify, Patient, Peaceable, Peaceful, Philosophical, Phlegmatic, Placate, Placid, Quell, Quiet, Relax(ed), Repose, Restful, Restrained, Self-possessed, Seraphic, Serena, Serene, Settle, Simmer down, Sleek, → **SOOTHE**, Sopite, Steady, Still, Stilly, Subside, Tranquil(lise), Unturbid, Windless

Calorie Gram, Kilogram

Calumniate, Calumny Aspersion, Backbite, Defame, Libel, Malign, Sclaunder, Slander, Slur

Calvary Golgotha

Calvin(ist), Calvinism Accusative, Coolidge, Genevan, Hopkins, Huguenot, Infralapsarian, Perseverance of saints, Predestination, Sublapsarian, Supralapsarian

Calydonian Boar
Calypso Ogygia, Siren, Soca, Sokah, → **SONG**
Cam Cog, Dwell, River, Snail, Tappet
Camaraderie Fellowship, Rapport, Team spirit
Camber Hog, Slope
Cambium Phellogen
Cambodian Khmer (Rouge), Montagnard
Cambria(n) Menevian, Wales
Cambridge Cantab, Squat, Uni
Came Arrived
Camel, Camel train Aeroplane, Arabian, Artiodactyla, Bactrian, Caisson, Colt, Dromedary, Kafila, Llama, Oont, Sopwith, Tulu
Cameo Anaglyph, Camaieu, Carving
Camera, Camera man All-round, Box, Brownie®, Camcorder, Candid, Chambers, Cine, Compact, Digicam, Digital, Disc, Dolly, Electron, Flash, Gamma, Gatso®, Grip(s), Iconoscope, Image orthicon, Instant, Kodak®, Lucida, Miniature, Minicam, Movie, Nannycam, Obscura, Orthicon, Palmcorder, Panoramic, Pantoscope, Periphery, Phone-cam, Pinhole, Polaroid®, Process, Programmed, Projectionist, Reflex, Retina, Schmidt, SLR, Somascope, Speed, Spycam, Steadicam®, Stop-frame, Subminiature, Video, Vidicon, Viewfinder, Webcam
Camouflage Conceal, → **DISGUISE**, Mark, Maskirovka, War-dress
▷ **Camouflaged** *may indicate* an anagram
Camp(er) Affectation, Aldershot, Auschwitz, Banal, Base, Belsen, Bivouac, Boma, Boot, Buchenwald, Caerleon, Cantonment, Castral, Colditz, Concentration, Dachau, David, Death, Depot, D(o)uar, Dumdum, Epicene, Faction, Fat, Flaunt, Gulag, Happy, Health, High, Holiday, L(a)ager, Labour, Laer, Lashkar, Leaguer, Low, Manyat(t)a, Motor, Oflag, Outlie, Peace, Prison, Side, Siwash, Stagey, Stalag, Stative, Swagman, Tent, Theatrical, Transit, Treblinka, Valley Forge, Work, Zare(e)ba, Zariba, Zereba, Zeriba
Campaign(er) Activist, Barnstorm, Battle, Blitz, Blitzkrieg, Canvass, Crusade, Doorknock, Drive, Enterprise, Field, Jihad, Lobby, Mission, Offensive, Pankhurst, Promotion, Roadshow, Run, Satyagraha, Smear, Stint, Strategist, The stump, Tree-hugger, Venture, Veteran, War, Warray, Warrey, Whispering, Whistle-stop, Witchhunt
Campanula Rampion
Campeador Chief, Cid
Camp-follower Lascar, Leaguer-lady, Leaguer-lass, Sutler
Camphor Carvacrol, Menthol
Campion Knap-bottle, Lychnis, Ragged robin, Silene
▷ **Camptown** *may indicate* de-
Can(s) Able, Aerosol, Billy, Bog, Capable, Churn, Cooler, Dow, Gaol, Garbage, Gents, Headphones, Is able, Jerry, Jug, Karsy, Kazi, Loo, May, Nick, Pail, Pitcher, Pot, Preserve, → **PRISON**, Privy, Six-pack, Stir, Tank, Tin, Trash, Tube, Watering
Canada, Canadian Abenaki, Acadian, Bella Bella, Bella Coola, Beothuk, Bois-brûlé, Canuck, Comox, Dene, Dogrib, Hare, Heiltsuk, Herring choker, Inuit, Johnny Canuck, Joual, Maliseet, Manitoban, Metis, Montagnais, Naskapi, Nuxalk, Péquiste, Quebeccer, Quebecker, Québecois, Salishan, Salteaux, Saulteaux, Slavey, Stoney, Tsimshian, Ungava, Yukon
Canal Alimentary, Ampul, Anal, Birth, Caledonian, Channel, Conduit, Corinth, Cruiseway, Da Yunhe, Duct, Duodenum, Ea, Enteron, Erie, Foss(e), Gota, Grand (Trunk), Grande Terre, Grand Union, Groove, Gut, Haversian, Houston Ship, Kiel,

Klong, Labyrinth, Lode, Manchester Ship, Meatus, Midi, Mittelland, Moscow, Navigation, New York State Barge, Oesophagus, Panama, Pharynx, Pipe, Pound, Regent's, Resin, Rhine-Herne, Ring, Root, Sault Sainte Marie, Scala, Schlemm's, Semi-circular, Ship, Shipway, Soo, Spinal, Stone, Suez, Suo, Urethra, Vagina, Waterway, Welland, Zanja

Canal-boat Barge, Fly-boat, Gondola, Vaporetto

Canapé Cate, Snack, Titbit

Canary Bird, Grass, Roller, Serin, Singer, Yellow

Cancel(led) Abrogate, Adeem, Annul, Counteract, Countermand, Cross, Delete, Destroy, Erase, Kill, Negate, Nullify, Obliterate, Override, Rained off, Red line, Remit, Repeal, Rescind, Retract, Retreat, Revoke, Scrub, Undo, Unmake, Void, Wipe, Write off

Cancer(ian), Cancerous Big C, Carcinoma, Crab, Curse, Hepatoma, Kaposi's sarcoma, Leukaemia, Lymphoma, Moon child, Oat-cell, Oncogenic, Tropic, Tumour, Wolf

Candela Cd

▶ **Candelabra** *see* CANDLESTICK

Candid, Candour Albedo, Blunt, Camera, Forthright, Franchise, Frank, Honesty, Open, Outspoken, Plain(-spoken), Round, Upfront

Candida Fungus

Candidate(s) Agrege, Applicant, Aspirant, Contestant, Entrant, Field, Literate, Nomenklatura, Nominee, Office-seeker, Ordinand, Postulant, Running mate, Slate, Spoiler, Stalking horse, Testee

Candied, Candy Angelica, Caramel, Cotton, Eryngo, Eye, Glace, Maple, Rock, Snow, Succade, Sucket, Sugar, → SWEET

Candle(stick), Candelabra Amandine, Bougie, Chanukiah, C(i)erge, Corpse, Dip, Fetch, Girandole, Hanukiah, International, Jesse, Lampadary, Light, Long-sixes, Menorah, Mould, New, Padella, Paschal, Pricket, Roman, Rushlight, Sconce, Serge, Shammash, Shammes, Shortsix, Slut, Sperm, Standard, Tace, Tallow, Tallow-dip, Taper, Tea-light, Torchère, Tricerion, Vigil light, Wax, Waxlight

Candlefish Eulachon, Oolakon, Oulachon, Oulakon, Ulic(h)an, Ulic(h)on, Ulikon

▶ **Candy** *see* CANDIED

Cane Arrow, Baculine, Bamboo, Baste, Beat, Birk, Crabstick, Dari, Dhurra, Doura, Dur(r)a, Ferula, Ferule, Goor, Gur, Jambee, Malacca, Narthex, Penang-lawyer, Pointer, Raspberry, Rat(t)an, Rod, Split, Stick, Sugar, Swagger-stick, Swish, Switch, Swordstick, Tan, Tickler, Vare, Wand, Whangee, Wicker(-work)

Canine Biter, C, Dhole, Dog, Eye-tooth

Canker Corrosion, Curse, Lesion, Ulcer

Cannabis Benj, Bhang, Bifter, Blow, Boneset, Durban poison, Ganja, Ganny, Grass, Hash, Hemp, Henry, Louie, Number, Pot, Skunk, Wacky baccy, Zol

Cannibal Anthropophagus, Heathen, Long pig, Man-eater, Ogre, Thyestean, Wendigo

Cannon Amusette, Barrage, Basilisk, Bombard, Breechloader, Carom, Carronade, Chaser, Collide, Criterion, Culverin, Drake, Drop, Falcon, Gun, Howitzer, Kiss, Long-tom, Loose, Monkey, Mons Meg, Nursery, Oerlikon, Saker, Stern-chaser, Water, Zamboorak, Zomboruk, Zumbooru(c)k

Cannot Canna, Cant, Downa(e), Downay

Canny Careful, Frugal, Prudent, Scot, Shrewd, Slee, Sly, Thrifty, Wice, Wily, Wise

Canoe(ist) Bidarka, Bidarkee, Canader, Canadian, Dugout, Faltboat, Kayak, Log, Mokoro, Monoxylon, Montaria, Oomiack, Paddler, Peterborough, Piragua, Pirogue, Rob Roy, Surf, Waka, Woodskin

Canon(ise) Austin, Besaint, Brocard, Camera, Cancrizens, Chapter, Chasuble, Code, Crab, Decree, Honorary, Infinite, Isidorian, → **LAW**, Line, Mathurin(e), Minor, Nocturn, Norbertine, Nursery, Pitaka, Polyphony, Prebendary, Precept, Premonstrant, Premonstratensian, Regular, Residential, Retrograde, Rota, Round, Rule, Secular, Square, Squier, Squire, Standard, Tenet, Unity, Vice-dean, White

Canopy Awning, Baldachin, Baldaquin, Chuppah, Ciborium, Clamshell, Dais, Gore, He(a)rse, Huppah, Majesty, Marquee, Marquise, Pavilion, Shamiana(h), State, Tabernacle, Tent, Tester, Veranda(h)

Cant Argot, Bevel, Doublespeak, Heel, Incline, Jargon, Mummery, Patois, Patter, Rogue's Latin, Shelta, Slang, Slope, Snivel, Snuffle, Tip

Cantankerous Cussed, Fire-eater, Ornery, Querulous, Testy, Tetchy

Cantata Kinderspiel, Motet, Tobacco

Canteen Chuck-wagon, Dry, Mess, Munga, Naafi, Wet

Canter Amble, Hypocrite, Jog, Lope, Run, Tit(t)up, Tripple

Canticle Benedictus, Nunc dimittis

Canto Air, Fit(te), Fitt, Fytte, Melody, Verse

Canton(ese) Aargau, Appenzell, Basle, District, Eyalet, Fribourg, Glarus, Graubunden, Jura, Lucerne, Neuchatel, Quarter, St Gall, Schaffhausen, Schwyz, Solothurn, Tanka, Thurgau, Ticino, Unterwalden, Uri, Valais, Vaud, Zug, Zurich

Cantor Haz(z)an

Cantred Commot(e)

Canvas Awning, Binca®, Burlap, Dra(b)bler, Fly-sheet, Lug-sail, Mainsail, Marquee, Oil-cloth, Paint, Raven's-duck, Reef, → **SAIL**, Staysail, Stuns(ai)l, Tent, Trysail, Wigan, Woolpack

Canvass(er), Canvassing Agent, Doorstep, Drum, Mainstreeting, Poll, Solicit

▷ **Canvasser** *may indicate* a painter or a camper

Canyon Box, Canada, Defile, Grand, Grand Coulee, Nal(l)a, Nallah, Submarine

Cap(ped) Abacot, Amorce, Balaclava, Balmoral, Barret, Baseball, Bathing, Bellhop, Bendigo, Ber(r)et, Biggin, Biretta, Black, Blakey, Blue, Blue-bonnet, Bonnet-rouge, Bycoket, Call, Calotte, Calpac(k), Calyptrate, Capeline, Caul, Chaco, Chape, Chapeau, Chaperon, Chapka, Chechia, Cheese-cutter, Cloth, Cockernony, Coif, College, Coonskin, Cope, Cornet, Cowl, Cradle, Crest, → **CROWN**, Czapka, Davy Crockett, Deerstalker, Dunce's, Dutch, Fatigue, Ferrule, Filler, Flat, Fool's, Forage, Gandhi, Garrison, Gimme, Glengarry, Gorblim(e)y, Grannie, Granny, → **HAT**, Havelock, Hummel bonnet, Hunting, Iceberg, International, Jockey, Juliet, Kalpak, Kepi, Kilmarnock (cowl), Kippa, Kippoth, Kipput, Kiss-me(-quick), Knee, Legal, Liberty, Lid, Maintenance, Mob, Monmouth, Monteer, Montero, Mor(r)ion, Mortar-board, Muffin, Mutch, Newsboy, Night, Old wife, Outdo, Pagri, Patellar, Percussion, Perplex, Phrygian, Pile, Pileus, Pinner, Polar, Puggaree, Quoif, Root, Schapska, Shako, Skullcap, Square, Squirrel-tail, Statute, Stocking, Summit, → **SURPASS**, Taj, Tam(-o'-shanter), Thimble, Thinking, Thrum, Toe, Toorie, Top, Toque, Toy, Trenchard, Trencher, Truck, Tuque, Turk's, Watch, Wishing, Yarmulka, Yarmulke, Zuchetto

Capable, Capability Able, Brown, Capacity, Competent, Deft, Effectual, Efficient, Firepower, Qualified, Skilled, Susceptible, Up to, Viable

Capacitance, Capacity Ability, Aptitude, C, Cab, Carrying, Competence, Content, Co(o)mb, Cor, Cubic, Endowment, Function, Gift, Legal, Limit, Log, Potency, Potential, Power, Qua, Rated, Receipt, Scope, Size, Skinful, Tankage, Thermal, Tonnage, Valence, Vital, Volume

Caparison Robe, Trap(pings)

Cape(s) Agulhas, Almuce, Athlete, Blanc(o), Bon, Burnouse, Byron, C, Calimere

Point, Canaveral, Canso, Cardinal, Chelyuskin, Cloak, Cod, Comorin, Delgado, Dezhnev, Domino, Dungeness, East(ern), Fairweather, Faldetta, Fanion, Fanon, Farewell, Fear, Fichu, Finisterre, Flattery, Gallinas Point, Good Hope, Guardafui, Harp, Hatteras, Head(land), Helles, Hoe, Hogh, Hook of Holland, Horn, Inverness, Kennedy, Leeuwin, Lindesnes, Lizard, Manteel, Mant(e)let, Mantilla, Mantle, Mantua, Matapan, May, Miseno, Mo(z)zetta, Muleta, Naze, Ness, Nordkyn, North, Northern, Ortegal, Palatine, Parry, Pelerine, Peninsula, Point, Poncho, Promontory, Race, Ras, Ray, Reinga, Roca, Ruana, Runaway, Sable, St Vincent, Sandy, Scaw, Skagen, Skaw, Sontag, Southwest, Talma, Tippet, Trafalgar, Ushant, Verde, Waterproof, Western, Wrath, York

Cape of Good Hope Stellenbosch

Caper(ing) Antic, Bean, Boer, Capparis, Capriole, Cavort, Dance, Dido, Flisk, Frisk, Frolic, Gambado, Gambol, Harmala, Harmalin(e), Harmel, Harmin(e), Prance, Prank, Saltant, Sault, Scoup, Scowp, Skip, Tit(t)up

Capet Marie Antoinette

Cape Town SA

Capital(s) A1, Assets, Block, Boodle, Bravo, Bully, Cap, Chapiter, Chaptrel, Circulating, Doric, Equity, Euge, Excellent, Fixed, Flight, Float, Floating, Fonds, Great, Helix, Human, Initial, Ionic, Lethal, Lulu, Metropolis, Principal, Refugee, Risk, Rustic, Seat, Seed, Share, Social, Splendid, Sport, Stellar, Stock, Super, Topping, UC, Upper case, Venture, Working

---

CAPITALS

3 letters:	Chur	Rome	Braga
Fes	Cluj	San'a	Cairo
Fez	Cork	Sian	Cuzco
Gap	Dili	Sion	Cuzev
Jos	Doha	Susa	Dacca
Ray	Faro	Suva	Dakar
Rio	Graz	Vila	Delhi
Ude	Homs	Xian	Dhaka
Ufa	Hums		Dijon
Zug	Ipoh	*5 letters:*	Dilli
	Jolo	Aarau	Dover
4 letters:	Kiel	Abiya	Dutse
Aden	Kiev	Abuja	Emisa
Agra	Kobe	Adana	Enugu
Albi	Laon	Agana	Goias
Apia	Laos	Aijal	Gotha
Auch	Leon	Akure	Guaco
Baki	Lima	Amman	Hanoi
Baku	Lomé	Aosta	Harar
Bari	Male	Arlon	Hefei
Bern	Metz	Assen	Hofei
Bida	Nara	Batum	Hsian
Boac	Nuuk	Belém	Ikeja
Bonn	Oslo	Berne	Jammu
Brno	Pegu	Bisho	Jinan
Caen	Pune	Boise	Kabul
Cali	Riga	Bourg	Kandy

Karor
Kazan
Kizyl
Konia
Konya
Korov
Kyoto
Lagos
Lassa
Laval
Le Puy
Lhasa
Liege
Lille
Lyons
Macao
Melun
Meroe
Minsk
Monza
Namur
Nancy
Natal
Nimes
Nukus
Oskub
Palma
Paris
Parma
Patna
Pella
Perth
Petra
Pinsk
Poona
Praha
Praia
Quito
Rabat
Rouen
Salem
Sanaa
Scone
Seoul
Simla
Sofia
Stans
Sucré
Tepic
Tokyo
Trier

Tunis
Turin
Uxmal
Vadso
Vaduz
Yanan
Yenan
Zomba

6 letters:
Abakan
Albany
Almaty
Andros
Ankara
Annecy
Anyang
Asmara
Astana
Athens
Austin
Bagdad
Baguio
Bamako
Bangui
Banjui
Bassau
Bastia
Batumi
Bauchi
Beirut
Berlin
Bhopal
Bogota
Bruges
Brunei
Cahors
Canton
Colima
Colmar
Cracow
Darwin
Denver
Dessau
Dispur
Dodoma
Dublin
Edessa
Erfurt
Fuchou
Geneva

Giyani
Gondar
Habana
Harare
Havana
Helena
Hobart
Hohhot
Ibadan
Ilorin
Imphal
Jaipur
Jalapa
Johore
Kaduna
Kaunas
Kigali
Kohima
Kuwait
Lahore
Lisbon
Loanda
Lokoja
London
Luanda
Lusaka
Macapá
Maceió
Madrid
Maikop
Majuro
Malabo
Manama
Manaus
Manila
Maputo
Marsan
Maseru
Mekele
Merano
Merida
Moroni
Moscow
Munich
Murcia
Muscat
Nagpur
Nassau
Nevers
Niamey
Nouméa

Ottawa
Oviedo
Owerri
Palmas
Panaji
Panjim
Peking
Pierre
Prague
Puebla
Punaka
Quebec
Ranchi
Recife
Regina
Rennes
Riyadh
Roseau
Ryazan
Saigon
Sardes
Sardis
Sarnen
Sendai
Skopje
Sokoto
Sparta
St Gall
St Paul
Taipei
Tallin
Tarawa
Tarbes
Tarsus
Tehran
Tetuan
Thebes
Thimbu
Tirana
Tobruk
Toledo
Toluca
Topeka
Ulundi
Umtata
Vesoul
Vienna
Warsaw
Xining
Yangon
Yaunde

6 letters – cont:
Zagreb
Zurich
Zwolle

7 letters:
Abidjan
Ajaccio
Alençon
Algiers
Altdorf
Antioch
Atlanta
Augusta
Auxerre
Baghdad
Bangkok
Barnaul
Begawan
Beijing
Belfast
Belfort
Bien Hoa
Bijapur
Bikaner
Bishkek
Bobigny
Bologna
Calabar
Caracas
Cardiff
Cayenne
Cetinje
Coblenz
Coimbra
Colombo
Conakry
Concord
Cordoba
Cuttack
Douglas
Durango
Foochow
Funchal
Gangtok
Goiania
Guiyang
Haarlem
Halifax
Hanover
Hassett

Herisau
Honiara
Huhehot
Iqaluit
Isfahan
Izhevsk
Jackson
Jakarta
Kaesong
Kaifeng
Kampala
Karachi
Kashmir
Kharkov
Khartum
Koblenz
Konakri
Kuching
Kunming
Lanchow
Lansing
Lanzhou
Lashkar
Liestal
Limoges
Lincoln
Louvain
Lucerne
Lucknow
Madison
Malacca
Managua
Masbate
Mathura
Mbabane
Memphis
Messene
Morelia
Munster
Nairobi
Nalchik
Nanjing
Nanking
Nicosia
Nineveh
Novi Sad
Olomouc
Oshogbo
Pachuca
Palermo
Palikit

Papeete
Phoenix
Pishpek
Plovdiv
Potenza
Potsdam
Punakha
Quimper
Raleigh
Rangoon
San José
San Juan
Santa Fe
Sao Tomé
Sapporo
Saransk
Stanley
St John's
Taiyuan
Tallinn
Tangier
Tbilisi
Teheran
Tel Aviv
Thimphu
Tiemcen
Toronto
Trenton
Trieste
Tripoli
Umuahia
Urumshi
Valetta
Vilnius
Vilnyus
Xanthus
Yaounde
Yerevan

8 letters:
Abeokuta
Abu Dhabi
Adelaide
Agartala
Ashgabet
Asuncion
Auckland
Bar-le-Duc
Belgrade
Belmopan
Beyrouth

Boa Vista
Brasilia
Brisbane
Brussels
Budapest
Cagliari
Calcutta
Campeche
Canberra
Cape Town
Castries
Chambéry
Chaumont
Cheyenne
Chisinau
Coahuila
Columbia
Columbus
Culiacan
Curitiba
Damascus
Dehra Dun
Djibouti
Dushanbe
Ecbatana
Edmonton
Eraklion
Florence
Freetown
Fribourg
Funafuti
Gaborone
Godthaab
Golconda
Hannover
Hargeisa
Hartford
Helsinki
Honolulu
Istanbul
Jayapura
Kandahar
Katmandu
Khartoum
Kilkenny
Kinshasa
Kirkwall
Kishinev
Lausanne
Liaoyand
Lilongwe

Luneburg
Mandalay
Mechelen
Mexicali
Monrovia
Monterey
Nanchang
Nanching
Nanterre
Narbonne
Ndjamena
Pamplona
Pergamum
Peshawar
Pnom-Penh
Port Said
Port-Vila
Pretoria
Pristina
Roskilde
Saltillo
Salvador
Salzburg
Santiago
Sao Paulo
Sarajevo
Seremban
Shah Alam
Shanghai
Shenyang
Shillong
Silvassa
Srinigar
St Helier
Tashkent
The Hague
Thonburi
Torshavn
Toulouse
Usumbura
Valletta
Victoria
Vladimir
Warangai
Windhoek
Winnipeg
Yinchuan

9 letters:
Amsterdam
Annapolis

Ashkhabad
Ayutthaya
Banda Aceh
Bandar Ser
Bangalore
Benin City
Birobijan
Bucharest
Bujumbura
Cartagena
Changchun
Changshar
Chengchow
Cherkessk
Chihuahua
Darmstadt
Des Moines
Edinburgh
Fongafale
Fortaleza
Frankfort
Grand Turk
Heraklion
Hyderabad
Innsbruck
Islamabad
Jalalabad
Jerusalem
Karlsruhe
Kathmandu
Kingstown
Knoxville
Kuch Bihar
Leningrad
Ljubljana
Magdeburg
Maiduguri
Marrakesh
Melbourne
Mogadishu
Montauban
Monterrey
Nashville
Nelspriut
Nuku'alofa
Perigueux
Perpignan
Phnom Penh
Podgorica
Polokwane
Port Blair

Port Louis
Porto Novo
Port Royal
Putrajaya
Pyongyang
Reykjavik
Rio Branco
Samarkand
San Merino
Singapore
Solothurn
St George's
Stockholm
Stuttgart
Thorshavn
Trebizond
Ulan Bator
Vientiane
Zhengzhou

10 letters:
Addis Ababa
Basse-terre
Baton Rouge
Bellinzona
Birobidzan
Bratislava
Bridgetown
Campobosso
Carson City
Chandigarh
Charleston
Cooch Behar
Copenhagen
Eisenstadt
Frauenfeld
Georgetown
Harrisburg
Heidelberg
Hermosillo
Joao Pessoa
Klagenfurt
Kragujevac
Launceston
Leeuwarden
Libreville
Little Rock
Maastricht
Mexico City
Middelburg
Mogadiscio

Montevideo
Montgomery
Montpelier
Nouakchott
Panama City
Paramaribo
Persepolis
Podgoritsa
Porto Velho
Providence
Rawalpindi
Sacramento
Trivandrum
Tskhinvali
Valladolid
Washington
Wellington
Whitehorse
Willemstad
Winchester
Yashkar-Ola

11 letters:
Bhubaneswar
Brazzaville
Buenos Aires
Campo Grande
Charlestown
Dares Salaam
Fredericton
Gandhinagar
Guadalajara
Hermoupolis
Johore Bahru
Kuala Lumpur
Montbeliard
Nakhichevan
Ouagadougou
Pandemonium
Pondicherry
Port Moresby
Porto Alegre
Port of Spain
Rio Gallegas
Saarbrucken
San Salvador
Springfield
St Peter Port
Tallahassee
Tegucigalpa
Thohoyandou

11 letters – cont:
Ulaanbaatar
Vatican City
Vladikavkaz
Yellowknife

12 letters:
Antananarivo
Anuradhapura
Bloemfontein
Chilpancingo
Fort-de-France
Indianapolis
Johannesburg
Kota Kinabalu

Mont-de-Marsan
Muzzafarabad
Pandaemonium
Petrozavodsk
Port-au-Prince
Port Harcourt
Rio de Janeiro
Salt Lake City
Santo Domingo
Schaffhausen
Schoemansdal
Seringapatam
Tenochtitlan
Villahermosa
Williamsburg

Yamoussoukro

13 letters:
Belo Horizonte
Charlottetown
Florianopolis
Funafuti Atoll
Guatemala City
Hertogenbosch
Jefferson City
Yaren District

14 letters:
Andorra la Vella
Constantinople

Kuala Trengganu
Oaxaca de Juarez
Puerto Princesa
's Hertogenbosch

15 letters:
Chalons-sur-Marne
Charlotte Amalie
Clermont-Ferrand

16 letters:
Pietermaritzburg
Trixtia Gutiérrez

Capitalise Carpe diem
Capitalist Bloated, Financier, Moneyer, Sloane
▷ **Capitalist** *may indicate* a citizen of a capital
Capitulate Acquiesce, Comply, → **SURRENDER**
Capless Bare
▷ **Capless** *may indicate* first letter missing
Capone Al, Scarface
▷ **Capriccioso** *may indicate* an anagram
Caprice, Capricious Arbitrary, Boutade, Capernoitie, Cap(p)ernoity, Conceit,
　Desultory, Erratic, Fancy, Fickle, Fitful, Freak, Humoresk, Humoresque, Irony,
　Megrim, Migraine, Mood, Perverse, Quirk, Vagary, Wayward, Whim(sy)
Capsize Crank, Overbalance, Purl, Tip, Turn turtle, Upset, Whemmle, Whomble
▷ **Capsized** *may indicate* a word upside down
Capstan Sprocket, Windlass
Capsule Amp(o)ule, Boll, Bowman's, Cachet, Habitat, Internal, Nidamentum,
　Ootheca, Orbiter, Ovisac, Pill, Pyxidium, Space, Spacecraft, Spansule,
　Spermatophore, Suppository, Time, Urn
Captain Ahab, Bligh, Bobadil, Bones, Bossyboots, Brassbound, Capt, Channel, Chief,
　Cid, Commander, Condottiere, Cook, Copper, Cuttle, Flint, Group, Hornblower,
　Kettle, Kidd, Leader, Macheath, Master, Nemo, Oates, Old man, Owner, Patron,
　Patroon, Post, Privateer, Protospatharius, Skip(per), Standish, Subah(dar), Subedar,
　Swing, Trierarch
Caption Cutline, Heading, Headline, Inscription, Masthead, Roller, Sub-title, Title
Captious Critical, Peevish
Captivate(d), Captivating Beguile, Bewitch, Charm, Enamour, Enthrall, Epris(e),
　Take, Winsome
Captive, Captivity Bonds, Duress, POW, Prisoner, Slave
Capture Abduct, Annex, Bag, Catch, Collar, Cop, Data, Electron, Enchain, Enthral(l),
　Grab, Land, Motion, Nail, Net, Prize, Rush, Seize, Snabble, Snaffle, Snare, → **TAKE**
Capuchin Cebus, Monkey, Sajou
Car Alvis, Astra, Audi, Austin, Auto, Banger, Beetle, Berlin, Biza, BL, Bluebird,
　Bomb, Boneshaker, Brake, Bubble, Buffet, Bugatti, Buick, Bumper, Bus, Cab(riolet),
　Cadillac, Catafalco, Catafalque, Chariot, Chorrie, Classic, Clunker, Coach, Company,
　Concept, Convertible, Cortina, Coupé, Courtesy, Crate, Daimler, Diner, Dodgem®,
　Drag(ster), Drophead, Dunger, Elf, Estate, E-type, Fastback, Fiat, Flivver, Ford,

Formula, Freight, Friday, Gas guzzler, Ghost, Gondola, Griddle, GT, Gyrocar, Hardtop, Hatchback, Heap, Hearse, Hillman, Horseless carriage, Hot hatch, Hot-rod, Irish, Jaguar, Jalop(p)y, Jamjar, Jammy, Jam sandwich, Jaunting, Jim Crow, Kart, Kit, Knockabout, Lada, Lagonda, Lancia, Landaulet, Landrover, Lift-back, Limo, Limousine, Merc(edes), MG, Mini, Model T, Morgan, Morris, Motor, Muscle, Nacelle, Notchback, Observation, Opel, Pace, Palace, Panda, Parlo(u)r, Patrol, Popemobile, Production, Prowl, Pullman, Racer, Ragtop, Railroad, Rattletrap, Restaurant, Roadster, Roller, Rolls (Royce), Rover, RR, Runabout, Runaround, Rust bucket, Saloon, Scout, Sedan, Service, Shooting-brake, Skoda, Sleeper, Sleeping, Soft-top, Speedster, Sports, Squad, Station wagon, Steam, Stock, Stretch-limo, Subcompact, Sunbeam, Supermini, SUV, Tank, Telepherique, Telpher, Three-wheeler, Tin Lizzie, Tonneau, Tourer, Tram, Triumph, Trolley, Tumble, Turbo, Two-seater, Vehicle, Veteran, Vintage, Voiture, VW, Wheeler, Wheels

Caramel Brûlé

Carat Point

Caravan(ner) Caf(f)ila, Convoy, Fleet, Kafila, Motor home, Safari, Trailer, Trailer trash, Winnebago®

Caravanserai Choltry, Choutry, Inn, Khan

Caraway Aj(o)wan, Carvy, Seed

Car-back Boot, Dick(e)y, Tonneau

Carbamide Urea

Carbide Silicon

Carbine Gun, Escopette, Musket

Carbohydrate Agar, Agarose, Callose, Carrageenan, Cellulose, Chitin, Dextran, Disaccharide, Glycogen, Heptose, Hexose, Inulin, Ketose, Laminarin, Mannan, Mucilage, Pectin, Pectose, Pentosan(e), Pentose, Polysaccharide, Saccharide, Sorbitol, Starch, Sucrose, Sugar

Carbolic Orcin

Carbon(ate) Activated, Ankerite, Austenite, Buckminsterfullerene, Buckyball, C, Charcoal, Coke, Dialogite, Diamond, Drice, Dry ice, Flame, Flimsy, Fullerene, Gas black, Graphite, Lampblack, Martensite, Natron, Petroleum coke, Scawtite, Soot, Spode, Spodium, Urao, Witherite, Zaratite

Carbon deficiency Acapnia

Carboy Demijohn

Carbuncle Anthrax, Ruby

Carcase, Carcass Body, Cadaver, Carrion, Corpse, Cutter, Krang, Kreng, Morkin, Mor(t)ling

Card(s), Cardboard, Carding Ace, Affinity, Amex®, Arcana, Baccarat, Basto, Bill, Birthday, Bower, Business, Calling, Canasta, Cartes, Cash, Caution, Charge, Cheque, Chicane, Cigarette, Club, Comb, Communion, Community, Compass, Court(esy), Credit, Cue, Curse of Scotland, Dance, Debit, Deck, Deuce, Devil's (picture) books, Diamond, Doffer, Donor, Drawing, Ecarté, Eccentric, Euchre, Expansion, Face, False, Flash, Flaught, Flush, Fourchette, → **GAME**, Gold, Goulash, Graphics, Green, Guide, Hand, Hard, Health, Heart, Hole, Honour, ID, Identification, Identity, Idiot, Intelligent, Jack, Jambone, Jamboree, Joker, Kanban, Key, King, Knowing, Laser, Leading, Letter, Loo, Loyalty, Magnetic, Manille, Master, Matador, Maximum, Meishi, Meld, Memory, Mise, Mistigris, Mogul, Mournival, Natural, Notelet, Oddity, Ombre, Pack, Past, Pasteboard, Payment, PC, Phone, Picture, Placard, Place, Plastic, Playing, Postal, Proximity, Punch(ed), Quatorze, Quatre, Queen, Queer, Quiz, Race, Rail, Ration, Red, Rippler, Rove, Royal marriage, Score, Scraperboard, Scratch, Screwball, Scribble, Shade, Show, SIM,

Singleton, Smart, Soda, Solo, Sound, Spade, Spadille, Squeezer, Stiffener, Store, Strawboard, Sure, Swab, Swipe, Swish, Switch, Swob, Swot, Talon, Tarok, Tarot, Tease(r), Tenace, Test, Thaumatrope, Ticket, Tiddy, Time, Top-up, Tose, Toze, Trading, Trey, Trump, Two-spot, Union, Valentine, Visa, Visiting, Wag, Warrant, Weirdie, Whitechapel, Wild, Yellow, Zener

Cardigan Ballet-wrap, Jacket, Wam(m)us, Wampus, Woolly

Cardinal Apostolic vicar, Camerlingo, Chief, College, Eight, Eminence, Eminent, Grosbeak, Hat, HE, Hume, Legate, Manning, Mazarin, Medici, Newman, Number, Pivotal, Polar, Prefect, Prelate, Radical, Red, Red-hat, Richelieu, Sacred college, Seven, Sin, Spellman, Ten, Virtue, Vital, Wolsey, Ximenes

Card-player Dealer, Pone

Care(r), Caring Attention, Burden, Cark, Caution, Cerne, Cherish, Community, → **CONCERN**, Cosset, Doula, Grief, Heed, Intensive, Kaugh, Keep, Kiaugh, Maternal, Mind, Pains, Palliative, Parabolanus, Primary, Providence, Reck(e), Reke, Residential, Respite, Retch, Shared, Solicitude, → **TEND**, Tenty, Worry

Careen(ing) Parliament-heel

Career Course, Hurtle, Life, Line, Run, Rush, Speed, Start, Tear, Vocation

▷ **Career** *may indicate* an anagram

Carefree → **CARELESS(LY)**, Dozy, Happy-go-lucky, Irresponsible, → **NEGLIGENT**, Oops, Perfunctory, Rollicking, Thoughtless

Careful(ly) Canny, Chary, Discreet, Gentle, Hooly, Leery, Meticulous, Mindful, Painstaking, Penny-pinching, Penny-wise, Pernickety, Provident, Prudent, Scrimp, Studious, Tentie, Tenty, Thorough, Vigilant, Ware, Wary

Careless(ly) Anyhow, Casual, Cheery, Debonair, Easy, Free-minded, Gallio, Improvident, Imprudent, Inadvertent, Insouciance, Irresponsible, Lax, Lighthearted, Négligé, → **NEGLIGENT**, Nonchalant, Oops, Oversight, Perfunctory, Raffish, Rash, Remiss, Resigned, Riley, Rollicking, Slam-bang, Slapdash, Slaphappy, Slipshod, Sloppy, Sloven(ly), Slubber, Taupie, Tawpie, Thoughtless, Unguarded, Unmindful, Untenty, Unwary

▷ **Carelessly** *may indicate* an anagram

Caress Bill, Coy, Embrace, Feel, Fondle, Kiss, Lallygag, Lollygag, Noursle, Nursle, Pet, Straik, Stroke, Touch

Caretaker Concierge, Curator, Custodian, Dvornik, Granthi, Guardian, Interim, Janitor, Nightwatchman, Sexton, Shammash, Shammes, Superintendent, Verger, Warden

Careworn Haggard, Lined, Tired, Weary

Cargo Boatload, Bulk, Burden, Fraught, Freight, Lading, Last, → **LOAD**, Payload, Shipload, Shipment

Caribbean Belonger, Puerto Rican, Soca, Sokah, Taino, WI

Caribou Tuktoo, Tuktu

Caricature, Caricaturist Ape, Beerbohm, Burlesque, Caran d'Ache, Cartoon, Cruikshank, Doyle, Farce, Gillray, Rowlandson, Scarfe, Skit, Spy, Tenniel, Toon, Travesty

Carlin Pug

Carmelite Barefoot, White (Friar)

Carmen AA, BL, Chai, RAC

Carnage Bloodshed, Butchery, Massacre, Slaughter

Carnal Bestial, Lewd, Outward, Sensual, Sexual, Worldly

Carnation Clove pink, Dianthus, Gillyflower, Malmaison, Picotee, Pink

Carnival Fair, Fasching, Festival, Fete, Mas, Moomba, Revelry

Carnivore, Carnivorous Cacomistle, Cacomixl, Coati, Creodont, Ermelin,

Fo(u)ssa, Genet, Glutton, Grison, Meerkat, Otter, Ratel, Stoat, Suricate, Viverridae, Wolverine, Zoophagan

Carob Algarroba, Locust, St John's bread

Carol(ler) Noel, Sing, Song, Wait, Wassail, Yodel

Carousal, Carouse Bend, Birl(e), Bouse, Bride-ale, Compotation, Drink, Mallemaroking, Mollie, Orge, Orgy, → **REVEL**, Roist, Screed, Spree, Upsee, Upsey, Upsy, Wassail

Carp(er) Beef, Cavil, Censure, Complain, Crab, Critic, Crucian, Crusian, Gibel, Goldfish, Id(e), Koi, Kvetch, Mirror, Mome, Nag, Nibble, Nitpick, Roach, Roundfish, Scold, Twitch, Whine, Yerk, Yirk

Carpenter Beveller, Bush, Cabinet-maker, Carfindo, Chips, Fitter, Joiner, Joseph, Menuisier, Quince, Tenoner, Woodworker, Wright

▷ **Carpenter** *may indicate* an anagram

Carpet(ing) Aubusson, Axminster, Beetle, Berate, Bessarabian, Body, Broadloom, Brussels, Castigate, Chide, Dhurrie, Drugget, Durrie, Dutch, Kali, Kelim, Khilim, Kidderminster, Kilim, Kirman, Lecture, Lino, Magic, Mat, Moquette, Persian, Rate, Red, Reprimand, Reproach, Rug, Runner, Shagpile, Shark, Shiraz, Stair, Turkey, Wall-to-wall, What for, Wig, Wilton

Carrageen Sea-moss

Carriage Air, Ar(a)ba, Aroba, Bandy, Barouche, Bearing, Berlin(e), Bier, Brake, Brit(sch)ka, Britska, Britzka, Brougham, Buckboard, Buggy, Cab, Calash, Calèche, Car, Cariole, Caroche, Carriole, Carryall, Cartage, Chaise, Charabanc, Charet, Chariot, Chassis, Chay, Clarence, Coach, Coch, Composite, Conveyance, Coupé, Curricle, Demeanour, Dennet, Deportment, Désobligeante, Diner, Dormeuse, Dormitory-car, Dos-a-dos, Do-si-do, Drag, Dros(h)ky, Ekka, Equipage, Fiacre, Fly, Four-in-hand, Gait, Gig, Gladstone, Go-cart, Growler, Gun, Haulage, Herdic, Horseless, Howdah, Hurley-hacket, Job, Landau(let), Landing, Limber, Mien, Non-smoker, Norimon, Observation-car, Phaeton, Pick-a-back, Pochaise, Pochay, Poise, Port(age), Portance, Postchaise, Posture, Poyse, Pram, Pullman, Purdah, Railcar, Railway, Randem, Rath(a), Remise, Rickshaw, Rig, Rockaway, Shay, Sled, Sleeper, Smoker, Sociable, Spider, Spider phaeton, Stanhope, Sulky, Surrey, Tarantas(s), Taxi, T-cart, Tender, Tenue, Tilbury, Tim-whiskey, Tonga, Trail, Trap, Van, Vetture, Victoria, Voiture, Wagonette, Waterage, Whirligig, Whisk(e)y

Carrier Aircraft, Airline, Arm, Baldric, Barkis, Barrow, Bomb-ketch, Bulk, Caddy, Cadge, Camel, Coaster, Common, Conveyor, Donkey, Escort, Fomes, Fomites, Frog, Grid, Hamper, Haversack, Hod, Janker, Jill, Majority, Minority, Nosebag, Noyade, Obo, Packhorse, Personnel, Pigeon, Porter, Rucksack, Satchel, Schistosoma, Semantide, Sling, Straddle, Stretcher, → **TRAY**, Vector, Wave

Carrion Cadaver, Carcase, Carcass, Flesh, Ket, Stapelia

Carrots Seseli, Titian

Carry(ing), Carry over Asport, Bear, Chair, Convey, Enlevé, Escort, Ferry, Frogmarch, Hawk, Hent, Humf, Hump, Humph, Kurvey, Land, Move, Pack, Pickaback, Port, Reappropriate, Stock, Sustain, Tide over, Tote, → **TRANSPORT**, Trant, Wage, With, Yank

Carry on Continue, Create, Wage

Carry out Execute, Mastermind, Pursue

Cart(er) Bandy, Barrow, Bogey, Buck, Cape, Car(r)iole, Chapel, Dandy, Democrat, Democrat wagon, Dog, Dolly, Dray, Egyptologist, Float, Furphy, Gambo, Gill, Golf, Governess, Gurney, Hackery, Jag, Jill, Lead, Mail, Night, Pie, Pram, Rickshaw, Scot, Scotch, Shandry, T, Tax(ed), Telega, Trolley, Tumbrel, Tumbril, Village, Wag(g)on, Wain, Whitechapel

Cartel Duopoly, Ring, Syndicate

Carthaginian Punic

Carthorse Aver, Shire

Carthusian Bruno

Cartilage Antitragus, Arytenoid, Chondral, Chondrin, Chondrus, Cricoid, Darwin's tubercle, Disc, Ensiform, Epiglottis, Gristle, Hyaline, Lytta, Meniscus, Semilunar, Tendron, Thyroid, Tragus, Worm, Xiphoid

Cartload Fother, Seam

Cartographer Cabot, Chartist, Kremer, Mercator, OS, Speed

Carton Box, Case, Crate, Sydney, Tub

Cartoon(ist) Animated, Bairnsfather, Caricature, Comic, Comic strip, Disney, Drawn, Emmet, Fougasse, Fumetto, Garland, Goldberg, Leech, Low, Manga, Mel, Partridge, Popeye, Robinson, Short, Shrek, Spy, Strip, Superman, Tenniel, Thurber, Tidy, Tintin, Trog

Cartridge Ball, Blank, Bullet, Cartouche, Cassette, Crystal, Doppie, Live, Magazine, Magnetic, QIC, Rim-free, Shell, Spent

Cart-track Rut

Cartwheel Handspring

Caruncle Aril, Carnosity

Carve(d), Carver, Carving Abated, Alcimedon, Armchair, Bas relief, Camaieu, Cameo, Chisel, Cilery, Crocket, Cut, Dismember, Doone, Enchase, Engrave, Entail, Entayle, Fiddlehead, Gibbons, Glyptic, Hew, Incise, Inscribe, Insculp, Intaglio, Knotwork, Netsuke, Nick, Petroglyph, Scrimshaw, Sculp(t), Slice, Tondo, Trophy, Truncheon, Tympanum, Whakairo, Whittle

Caryatid Column, Telamon

Casanova Heartbreaker, Leman, Womaniser

Cascade Cataract, Fall, Lin(n), Stream, Waterfall

Cascara Amarga, Buckthorn, Honduras bark, Rhamnus, Sagrada, Wahoo

Case(s), Casing Abessive, Ablative, Accusative, Action, Adessive, Allative, Altered, Appeal, Aril, Ascus, Assumpsit, Attaché, Basket, Beer, Bere, Bittacle, Blimp, Box, Brief, Bundwall, Burse, C, Ca, Cabinet, Calyx, Canister, Canterbury, Capsule, Cartouch(e), Cartridge, Cask, Cause celebre, Cellaret, Chase, Chitin, Chrysalis, Cocoon, Coffin, Comitative, Compact, Crate, Croustade, Crust, Cyst, Dative, Declension, Detinue, Dispatch, Dossier, Dressing, Elative, Elytron, Enallage, Ensheath, Ergative, Essive, Etui, Etwee, Example, Flan, Flapjack, Flask, Frame, Genitive, Grip, Hanaper, Hard, Hatbox, Hold-all, Housewife, Hull, Humidor, Husk, Illative, Imperial, → **IN CASE**, Index, Indusium, Inessive, Instance, Kalamdan, Keister, Locative, Locket, Lorica, Manche, Matter, Mermaid's purse, Mezuzah, Music, Nacelle, Nominative, Non-suit, Nutshell, Objective, Oblique, Ochrea, Ocrea, Outpatient, Packing, Pair, Papeterie, Patient, Pencil, Penner, Phylactery, Plight, Plummer-block, Pod, Port, Portfolio, Possessive, Prima facie, Puparium, Quiver, Recce, Reconnoitre, Sabretache, Sad, Scabbard, Sheath(e), Shell, Situation, Six-pack, Sleeve, Sporran, Stead, Sted, Subjective, Suit, Tantalus, Tea-chest, Telium, Test, Theca, Tichborne, Trial, Trunk, Valise, Vasculum, Vitrine, Vocative, Volva, Walise, Walking, Wallet, Wardian, Wing, Worst, Writing

Case-harden Nitrode

Casein Curd

Casement Frame, Roger, Sash, Window

Cash Blunt, Bonus, Bounty, Change, Coin, Dosh, Dot, Float, Hard, Idle money, Imprest, Lolly, → **MONEY**, Needful, Ochre, Oscar, Pence, Petty, Ready, Realise,

Redeem, Rhino, Spondulicks, Spot, Stumpy, Tender, Tin, Wampum, Wherewithal

Cashier, Cash machine Annul, ATM, Break, Depose, Disbar, Dismiss, Oust, Teller, Treasurer

Cashmere Circassienne

Casino Monte Carlo

Cask(et) Armet, Barrel, Barrico, Bas(i)net, Box, Breaker, Butt, Cade, Casque, Cassette, Drum, Firkin, Galeate, Harness, Heaume, Hogshead, Keg, Leaguer, Octave, Pin, Pipe, Puncheon, Pyxis, Run(d)let, Salade, Sallet, Sarcophagus, Scuttlebutt, Shook, Shrine, Solera, Tierce, Tun, Wine

Cask-stand Stillion

Cassava Manioc, Tapioca, Yucca

Casserole Diable, Osso bucco, Pot, Salmi, Terrine, Tzimmes

Cassette Cartridge, Tape, Video

Cassia Cleanser, Senna

Cassio Lieutenant

Cassiterite Needle-tin, Tinstone

Cassock Gown, Soutane, Subucula

▷ **Cast** *may indicate* an anagram or a piece of a word missing

Cast (down, off, out), Casting Abattu, Actors, Add, Angle, Appearance, Bung, Cire perdue, Death mask, Die, Discard, Ecdysis, Ectype, Eject, Emit, Endocranial, Exorcise, Exuviae, Exuvial, Fling, Found, Fusil, Grate, Hawk, Heave, Hob, Hue, Hurl, Impression, Ingo(w)es, Keb, Look, Lose, Mew, Molt, Moulage, Mould, Pick, Plaster(stone), Plastisol®, Players, Print, Put, Reject, Shed, Shoot, Sling, Slive, Slough, Spoil, Stookie, Tailstock, → **THROW**, Toss, Tot, Warp, Wax, Ytost

Castanet Crotal(um), Knackers

Castaway Adrift, Crusoe, Gunn, Left, Outcast, Selkirk, Stranded, Weft

▷ **Cast by** *may indicate* surrounded by

Caste Brahmin, Burakumin, Class, Dalit, Group, Harijan, Hova, Kshatriya, Rajpoot, Rajpout, Rajput, Rank, Scheduled, Sect, Sudra, Untouchable, Vaisya, Varna

Caster Truckle

Castigate Berate, Chastise, Criticise, Denounce, Keelhaul, Lash, Punish, Rate

Cast-iron Spiegeleisen

Castle(d) Bouncy, Broch, C, Casbah, Chateau, Citadel, Fastness, Fort, Kasba(h), Maiden, Man, Mot(t)e, Move, Rook, Sand, Schloss, Stronghold, Villa

CASTLES

4 letters:	Glamis	Canossa	*8 letters:*
Trim	Howard	Chillon	Balmoral
	Ludlow	Colditz	Bamburgh
5 letters:	Raglan	Culzean	Bastille
Blois	Wemyss	Despair	Berkeley
Conwy		Harlech	Carbonek
Corfe	*7 letters:*	Lincoln	Chepstow
Hever	Adamant	Otranto	Crotchet
Leeds	Amboise	Skipton	Doubting
Spain	Arundel	Warwick	Egremont
	Belvoir	Windsor	Elephant
6 letters:	Braemar		Elsinore
Forfar	Calzean		Inverary

8 letters – cont:	Urquhart	10 letters:	12 letters:
Kronberg	Wartburg	Caerphilly	Fotheringhay
Malperdy		Kenilworth	Herstmonceux
Pembroke	9 letters:	Pontefract	Sissinghurst
Perilous	Dangerous		
Rackrent	Dunsinane	11 letters:	13 letters:
Richmond	Edinburgh	Carisbrooke	Carrickfergus
Stirling	Lancaster	Chateauroux	
Stokesay	Rochester	Eilean Donan	14 letters:
Stormont	Sherborne	Gormenghast	Motte and bailey
Tintagel	Trausnitz		

Castor Muffineer

Castor-oil Ricinus

Castrate(d), Castrato Alter, Cut, Doctor, Emasculate, Eunuch, Evirate, Farinelli, Geld, Glib, Lib, Manzuoli, Moreschi, Mutilate, Neuter, Senesino, Spado, Spay, Swig

Castro Fidel

Casual(ly) Accidental, Adventitious, Airy, Blasé, Chance, Chav(ette), Flippant, Grass, Haphazard, Idle, Incidental, Informal, Jaunty, Lackadaisical, Nonchalant, Odd(ment), Offhand, Off-the-cuff, Orra, Overly, Passing, Promiscuous, Random, Scratch, Slaphappy, Sporadic, Stray, Temp, Throwaway

Casualty Caduac, Chance-medley, → VICTIM

Casuist Jesuit

Cat Ailuro-, Catamount, Clowder, Dandy, Domestic, Fat, Felid, Feline, Flog, Gossip, Hipster, Jazzer, Kit, Lair, Lash, Mewer, Mog, Mouser, Native, Neuter, Nib, Oriental, Painter, Palm, Pardal, Practical, Puss, Sacred, Scourge, Serval, Sick, Singed, Spew, Spue, Swinger, Top, Vomit

CATS

3 letters:	Hodge	Margay	Maltese
Gib	Korat	Musang	Nandine
Gus	Manul	Ocelot	Pallas's
Rex	Ounce	Ocicat	Panther
Tom	Quoll	Somali	Persian
	Rasse	Sphynx	Pharaoh
4 letters:	Rumpy	Tibert	Polecat
Eyra	Tabby	Tybalt	Ragdoll
Lion	Tiger	Weasel	Siamese
Lynx	Tigon	Zibeth	Tiffany
Manx	Zibet		Tigress
Musk		7 letters:	Viverra
Pard	6 letters:	Burmese	
Puma	Angora	Caracal	8 letters:
	Birman	Cheetah	Balinese
5 letters:	Bobcat	Dasyure	Baudrons
Alley	Cougar	Foumart	Cacomixl
Civet	Foussa	Genette	Cheshire
Felix	Jaguar	Leopard	Devon Rex
Fossa	La Perm	Linsang	Kilkenny
Genet	Malkin	Lioncel	Long-hair

Mountain	Maine Coon	Selkirk Rex	Turkish Angora
Munchkin	Marmalade	Turkish Van	
Ringtail	Mehitabel		*14 letters:*
Snowshoe	Niebelung	*11 letters:*	Asian Shorthair
Tiffanie	Sealpoint	Colourpoint	Australian Mist
	Shorthair	Egyptian Mau	Siberian Forest
9 letters:	Tobermory	Havana Brown	
Asparagus	Tonkinese	Russian Blue	*15 letters:*
Binturong		Tongkingese	Norwegian Forest
Bluepoint	*10 letters:*		
Chantilly	Abyssinian	*12 letters:*	*16 letters:*
Chartreux	Cacomistle	American Curl	American Wirehair
Delundung	Cornish Rex	Scottish Fold	
Grimalkin	Jaguarondi		*19 letters:*
Himalayan	Jaguarundi	*13 letters:*	Californian
Lioncelle	Ring-tailed	Tortoise-shell	Spangled

Catacomb Cemetery, Crypt, Hypogeum, Vault

Catalepsy Catatony, Trance

Catalogue(r) Categorise, Cattle dog, Dewey, Dictionary, Durchkomponi(e)rt, Index, Inventory, K(ochel), List, Litany, Magalog, MARC, Messier, Ragman, Ragment, Raisonné, Record, Register, Specialogue, Star, Subject, Table, Tabulate, Thematic, Union

Catalyst Accelerator, Agent, Chemical, Erepsin, Influence, Kryptonite, Stereospecific, Unicase, Ziegler

Catamite Gunsel, Ingle, Pathic

Catapult Ballista, Ging, Launch, Mangon(el), Perrier, Petrary, Propel, Scorpion, Shanghai, Sling, Slingshot, Stone-bow, Tormentum, Trebuchet, Wye, Y

Cataract Cascade, Film, Overfall, Pearl, Pearl-eye, Torrent, Waterfall, Web and pin

Catarrh Coryza, Rheum

Catastrophe, Catastrophic Apocalypse, Calamity, → **DISASTER**, Doom, Epitasis, Fiasco, Meltdown, Ruinous

Catatonia Stupor

Cat-call Boo, Jeer, Mew, Miaow, Miaul, Razz, Wawl, Whistle, Wrawl

Catch(y), Caught Air, Apprehend, Attract, Bag, Benet, Bone, C, Capture, Chape, Clasp, Cog, Collar, Contract, Cop, Corner, Cotton on, Ct, Deprehend, Detent, Dolly, Engage, Enmesh, Ensnare, Entoil, Entrap, Fang, Field, Fumble, Gaper, Get, Glee(some), Grasp, Had, Hank, Haud, Haul, Hear, Hitch, Hold, Hook, Inmesh, Keddah, Keight, Kep(pit), Kheda, Kill, Land, Lapse, Lasso, Latch, Lime, Lock, Morse, Nab, Nail, Net, Nick, Nim, Nobble, Noose, Overhear, Overhent, Overtake, Parti, Pawl, Rap, Release, Rope, Round, Rub, Safety, Sean, Sear, See(n), Seize, → **SNAG**, Snap, Snare, Snib, Snig, → **SONG**, Surprise, Swindle, Tack, Taen, Take, Tane, Tickle, Trammel, Trap, Trawl, Trick, Tripwire, Troll, Twenty two, Twig, Understand, Wrestle

Catchword Motto, Shibboleth, Slogan, Tag

Catechism Carritch, Shorter, Test

Categorise, Category → **CLASS**, Etic, Genre, Genus, Label, Order, Pigeonhole, Range, Stereotype, Taxon, Triage

Cater(er) Acatour, Cellarer, Feed, Manciple, → **PROVIDE**, Purveyor, Serve, Steward, Supply, Victualler, Vivandière

Caterpillar Army worm, Aweto, Boll worm, Cabbageworm, Cotton-worm, Cutworm,

Eruciform, Geometer, Gooseberry, Hop-dog, Hornworm, Inchworm, Larva, Looper, Osmeterium, Palmer, Tent, Webworm, Woolly-bear

Catfish Hassar, Woof

Cathartic Turbeth

Cathedral Amiens, Basilica, Birmingham, Burgos, Chartres, Chester, → **CHURCH**, Cologne, Cortona, Dome, Duomo, Durham, Ely, Evreux, Gloucester, Guildford, Hereford, Hertford, Huesca, Kirkwall, Lateran, Lichfield, Lincoln, Lugo, Minster, Mullingar, Notre Dame, Rheims, Ripon, Rochester, St Albans, St Davids, St Paul's, Salisbury, Santiago de Compostela, Sens, Teruel, Up(p)sala, Viseu, Wakefield, Wells, Westminster, Winchester, Worcester, York

Catherine Braganza, Parr

Catherine-wheel Girandole

Cathode Electrode, Filament, Ray

Catholic Assumptionist, Broad, Christian Socialism, Defenders, Doolan, Eclectic, Ecumenical, Fenian, General, German, Irvingism, Jebusite, Latin, Lazarist, Left-footer, Liberal, Marian, Old, Opus Dei, Ostiary, Papalist, Papaprelatist, Papist, Passionist, Recusant, Redemptionist, Roman, Salesian, Spike, Taig, Te(a)gue, Teigue, Theatine, Thomist, Tike, Tory, Tridentine, Tyke, Universal, Ursuline, Waldenses, Wide

Catkin Amentum, Chat, Lamb's tail, Pussy-willow, Salicaceous

Cat-lover Ailurophile

Catmint Nep, Nepeta

Cato Porcian, Uticensis

Cats-eye Chatoyant, Cymophane

Catsmeat Lights

Catspaw Pawn, Tool

Cat's tail Reed-mace, Typha

Cat's whiskers Vibrissa

Cattle(pen) Aberdeen Angus, Africander, Ankole, Aver, Ayrshire, Beefalo, Belgian Blue, Bestial, Black, Brahman, British White, Buffalo, Carabao, Charbray, Charolais, Chillingham, Dexter, Drove, Durham, Fee, Friesian, Friesland, Galloway, Gaur, Gayal, Guernsey, Gyal, Heard, Herd, Hereford, Highland, Holstein (Friesian), Illawarra, Jersey, Kerry, Kine, Kouprey, Kraal, Ky(e), Kyloe, Lairage, Limousin, Lincoln, Longhorn, Luing, Neat, Nout, Nowt, Owsen, Oxen, Piemontese, Rabble, Redpoll, Rother, Santa Gertrudis, Shorthorn, Simment(h)al, Soum, South Devon, Sowm, Steer, Stock, Store, Stot, Sussex, Tamarao, Tamarau, Teeswater, Welsh Black

Cattle disease Actinobacillosis, Actinomycosis, Anthrax, Black water, Dry-bible, Footrot, Gallsickness, Heart-water, Hoove, Johne's, Listeriosis, Lumpy jaw, Mange, Mastitis, Milk lameness, Moorill, New Forest, Quarter-ill, Red-water, Rinderpest, Scours, Scrapie, Texas fever, Wire-heel, Woody-tongue

Cattle food Fodder, Poonac, Silage

Cattleman Cowboy, Herder, Maverick, Rancher, Ringer, Stock-rider

Catty Kin, Spiteful

Caucasian Aryan, Azabaijani, Azeri, Cherkess, European, Georgian, Iberian, Kabardian, Melanochroi, Paleface, Semite, Shemite, White, Yezdi, Yezidee, Zezidee

Caucus Assembly, Cell, Gathering, Race

▶ **Caught** see **CATCH**

Caul Baby-hood, Kell, Membrane, Sillyhow

Cauldron Kettle, Pot

Cauliflower Curd, Ear, Floret, Gobi

Caulk Fill, Pay, Pitch, Snooze
Causation, Cause(d), Causes Aetiology, Agent, Bandwagon, Beget, Breed, Bring, Célèbre, Common, Compel, Create, Crusade, Determinant, Due, Effect, Efficient, Encheason, Engender, Expedite, Factor, Final, First, Flag-day, Formal, Gar(re), Generate, Ideal, Induce, Lead, Lost, Make, Material, Motive, Movement, Natural, → **OCCASION**, Parent, Probable, Provoke, Proximate, Reason, Root, Sake, Secondary, Show, Source, Teleology, Topic, Ultimate, Wreak
Causeway Giant's, Tombolo
Caustic Acid, Acrimonious, Alkaline, Burning, Common, Erodent, Escharotic, Lime, Lunar, Moxa, Pungent, Sarcastic, Scathing, Seare, Soda, Tart, Vitriol, Waspish, Withering
Cauterise, Cauterisation Brand, Burn, Disinfect, Inustion, Moxibustion, Sear
Caution, Cautious (person) Achitophel, Admonish, Ahithophel, Alert, Amber, Awarn, Beware, Cagey, Card, Care, Cave, Caveat, Chary, Circumspect, Credence, Cure, Defensive, Deliberate, Discretion, Fabian, Gingerly, Guard(ed), Heedful, Leery, Prudent, Rum, Scream, Skite, Tentative, Timorous, Vigilant, Ware, → **WARN**, Wary, Yellow card
Cavalcade Pageant, Parade, Procession, Sowarree, Sowarry
Cavalier Brusque, Cicisbeo, Devil-may-care, Gallant, Lively, Malignant, Offhand, Peart, Rider, Royalist
Cavalry(man) Blues, Car(a)bineer, Car(a)binier, Cornet, Cossack, Dragoon, Equites, Heavies, Horse, Horse Guards, Household, Hussar, Ironsides, Knights, Lancers, Life Guards, Light-horse, Plunger, Ressaldar, Risaldar, Rough-rider, Rutter, Sabres, Silladar, Spahee, Spahi, Uhlan, Yeomanry
Cave(rn), Caves, Cave-dwelling, Cave in Acherusia, Aladdin's, Alert, Altamira, Antar, Antre, Beware, Bone, Capitulate, Cellar, Collapse, Corycian, Den, Domdaniel, Erebus, Fingal's, Fore, Grot(to), Hollow, Jenolan, Lascaux, Look-out, Lupercal, Mammoth, Nix, Pot-hole, Proteus, Sepulchre, Snow, Spel(a)ean, Speleology, Spelunker, Speos, Tassili, Trophonian, Vault, Waitomo, Ware, Weem, Wookey Hole
Cave-dweller Troglodyte
Caveman Adullam, Aladdin, Fingal, Neanderthal, Primitive, Troglodyte, Troll
Caviare Beluga, Osietra, Roe, Sevruga, Sturgeon
Cavil Carp, Haggle, Quibble
Cavity Acetabulum, Amygdale, Amygdule, Androclinium, Archenteron, Atrial, Body, Camera, Camouflet, Celom, Chamber, Clinandrium, Coelenteron, Coelom(e), Conceptacle, Concha, Countermark, Crater, Crypt, Dent, Domatium, Druse, Enteron, Follicle, Foss, Gap, Geode, Glenoid, Hold, Hole, Lacuna, Locule, Mediastinum, Mialoritic, Orbita, Orifice, Pelvis, Pocket, Pulp, Resonant, Segmentation, Sinus, Stomod(a)eum, Tear, Thunderegg, Tympanum, Vacuole, Vein, Ventricle, Vesicle, Vitta, Vomica, Vug, Vugg, Vugh, Well
Cavort(ing) Jag
Cavy Agouti, Capybara, Hograt, Paca
Cayman Islands Tax haven
Cease(fire) Abate, Blin, Cut, Desist, Devall, Die, Disappear, Halt, Ho, Intermit, Lin, Lose, Pass, Refrain, Remit, Sessa, → **STOP**, Truce
Ceaseless Eternal, Incessant
Cecil Rhodes
Cedar(wood) Arolla, Atlas, Barbados, Cryptomeria, Deodar, Incense, Jamaica, Japanese, Toon
Cede Grant, Yield

Ceiling Absolute, Barrel, Coffered, Cove, Cupola, Dome, Glass, Lacunar, Laquearia, Limit, Plafond, Roof, Service, Soffit, Stained glass

Celebrate(d), Celebration, Celebrity Ale, Beanfeast, Besung, Big name, Bigwig, Binge, Brat-packer, Carnival, Cel, Chant, Commemorate, Distinguished, Do, Emblazon, Encaenia, Epithalamion, Epithalamium, Fame, Feast, Fest, Festivity, Fete, Fiesta, First-footing, Gala, Gaudeamus, Gaudy, Glitterati, Glorify, Grog-up, Harvest home, Hold, Holiday, Honour, Jamboree, Jol, Jollifications, Jollities, Jubilee, Keep, Large it, Laud, Legend, Lion, Loosing, Lowsening, Maffick, Mardi Gras, Mass, Mawlid al-Nabi, Megastar, Monstre sacre, Name, Noted, Nuptials, Observe, Occasion, Orgy, Panathenaea, Party, Pinata, Praise, Randan, Rave-up, Record, Rejoice, Renown, Repute, Revel, Rite, Roister, Sangeet, Saturnalia, Sex symbol, Shindig, Sing, Spree, Star, Storied, Sung, Superstar, Treat, Triumph, Wassail, Wet, Whoopee

Celerity Dispatch, Haste, Speed, Velocity

Celery Alexanders, Smallage, Stick

Celestial Chinese, Divine, Ethereal, Heavenly, Supernal, Uranic

Celibate, Celibacy Bachelor, Chaste, Paterin(e), Rappist, Rappite, Shakers, Single, Spinster

Cell(s), Cellular Battery, Black hole, Bullpen, Cadre, Chamber, Chapel, Condemned, Crypt, Cubicle, Death, Dungeon, Group, Laura, Lock up, Padded, Peter, → **PRISON**, Safety, Strip, Tank, Unit

---

CELLS

1 letter:	Basal	Cytoid	Gravity
T	Canal	Diaxon	Helper T
	Clark	Gamete	Initial
3 letters:	Cyton	Goblet	Lithite
Dry	Flame	Hadley	Myotome
Egg	Giant	Killer	Myotube
Pec	Gland	Morula	Neurite
Sex	Guard	Mother	Neurone
Wet	Islet	Neuron	Neutron
	Linin	Oocyte	Plastid
4 letters:	Lymph	Plasma	Primary
Axon	Nerve	Sensor	Purinje
Comb	Nicad	Sickle	Schwann
Cone	Solar	Somite	Sertoli
Cyte	Sperm	Target	Somatic
Fuel	Spore	Thread	Spireme
Germ	Stone	Zygote	Sporule
Hair	Swarm		Storage
HeLa	Water	*7 letters:*	Tapetum
Mast	White	Bimorph	Vesicle
Oxum	X-body	Cadmium	Voltaic
Soma		Cambium	
Stem	*6 letters:*	Cathode	*8 letters:*
Zeta	Button	Daniell	Akaryote
	Censor	Energid	Auxocyte
5 letters:	Collar	Euploid	Basidium
Ascus	Cybrid	Gemmule	Basophil

Blasteme
Blastula
Congenic
Cytology
Daughter
Defensin
Ectomere
Endoderm
Endosarc
Ependyma
Epiblast
Eukaryon
Galvanic
Gonidium
Gonocyte
Hapteron
Hemocyte
Meiocyte
Meristem
Monocyte
Myoblast
Neoblast
Palisade
Parietal
Platelet
Purkinje
Receptor
Retinula
Schizont
Selenium
Seredium
Squamous
Standard
Sweatbox
Symplast
Synergid
Tracheid
Unipolar
Zoosperm
Zoospore

9 letters:
Adipocyte

Antipodal
Astrocyte
Athrocyte
Auxospore
Basophile
Coenocyte
Companion
Corpuscle
Desmosome
Ectoplasm
Embryo-sac
Fibrocyte
Haemocyte
Hybridoma
Idioblast
Internode
Iridocyte
Karyology
Laticifer
Leclanché
Leucocyte
Leukocyte
Merozoite
Microcyte
Micromere
Myelocyte
Myofibril
Organelle
Periplasm
Periplast
Phagocyte
Phellogen
Proembryo
Secondary
Spermatid
Sporocyte
Suspensor
Syncytium
Synkaryon
Thymocyte
Trabecula
Tracheide

10 letters:
Ameloblast
Archespore
Blastoderm
Blastomere
Centrosome
Choanocyte
Chromaffin
Chromosome
Cnidoblast
Eosinophil
Epithelium
Fibroblast
Gametocyte
Histiocyte
Leucoblast
Leukoblast
Lymphocyte
Macrophage
Melanocyte
Mesenchyme
Myeloblast
Neuroblast
Neutrophil
Normoblast
Osteoblast
Osteoclast
Perikaryon
Phelloderm
Protoplast
Spermatium
Spherocyte
Suppressor
Totipotent
White-blood

11 letters:
Aplanospore
Arthrospore
Calyptrogen
Endothelium
Erythrocyte
Granulocyte

Interneuron
Kinetoplast
Lymphoblast
Megaloblast
Melanoblast
Microgamete
Microvillus
Motor neuron
Odontoblast
Poikilocyte
Propoceptor
Schistocyte
Spheroplast
Suppressor T
Trophoblast

12 letters:
Aplanogamete
Chondroblast
Electrolytic
Erythroblast
Gametrangium
Haematoblast
Interstitial
Paraphysisis
Photovoltaic
Reticulocyte
Spermatocyte
Spermatozoid
Spermatozoon
Spongioblast

13 letters:
Chromatophore
Mitochondroin
Photoelectric
Photoreceptor

14 letters:
Spermatogonium
Weston standard

Cellar Basement, Bodega, Coalhole, Dunny, Hypogeum, Ratskeller, Storm, Vault, Vaut, Wine

Cell division Amitosis

Cellist, Cello Casals, Du Pré, Hermit, Prisoner, Tortelier

Celluloid, Cellulose Acetate, Cel, Viscose, Xylonite

Celt(ic) Belgic, Breton, Brython, Cornish, Druid, Gadhel, Gael, Goidel, Helvetii, Kelt, La Tène, P, Q, Taffy, Welsh

Cement Araldite®, Asbestos, Blast-furnace, Compo, Concrete, Fix, Flaunch, Glue, Grout, Gunite, High-alumina, Hydraulic, Lute, Maltha, Mastic, Mastich, Mortar, Paste, Pointing, Porcelain, Portland, Putty, Rice-glue, Roman, Rubber, Slurry, → **STICK**, Trass, Water

Cemetery Aceldama, Arenarium, Arlington, Boneyard, Boot Hill, Campo santo, Catacomb, Churchyard, God's Acre, Golgotha, Graveyard, Musall, Necropolis, Père Lachaise, Potter's field, Saqqara, Urnfield

Censer Cassolette, Navicula, Thurible

Censor(ious), Censorship, Censure Accuse, Admonition, AD notice, Airbrush, Animadvert, Appeach, Ban, Banner, Berate, Blame, Blue-pencil, Bowdler, Braid, Cato, Comstockery, → **CONDEMN**, Critical, Criticise, Damn, Dang, Decry, Dispraise, Edit, Excommunicate, Excoriate, Expurgate, Gag, Obloquy, Opprobrium, Rap, Repress, Reprimand, Reproach, Reprobate, Reprove, Satirise, Scold, Scrub, Slam, Slate, Stricture, Suppress, Tax, Tear into, Tirade, Traduce, Wig

Census, Census taker Count, Numerator, Poll

Cent Bean, Coin, Ct, Penny, Red

Centaur Ch(e)iron, Horseman, Nessus, Sagittary, Therianthropic

Centenary, Centennial Anniversary, Colorado

Centipede Chilopoda, Earwig, Pauropod, Polypod, Scolopendra, Scutiger

Central, Centre Active, Amid, Assessment, Attendance, Axis, Broca's, Bunt, Call, Cardinal, Chakra, Civic, Community, Contact, Core, Cost, Day, Daycare, Dead, Detention, Detoxification, Deuteron, Deuton, Downtown, Drop-in, Epergne, Eye, Field, Focus, Foyer, Frontal, Garden, Health, Heart, Heritage, Hotbed, Hothouse, Hub, Incident, Inmost, Internal, Interpretive, Juvenile, Juvie, Kernel, Kingpin, Law, Leisure, Lincoln, Live, Main, Mecca, Median, Medulla, Mid(st), Mission, Music, Nave, Nerve, Nucleus, Omphalus, Pompidou, Profit, Property, Reception, Rehabilitation, Remand, Respiratory, Shopping, Social Education, Storm, Teachers', Trauma, Visitor, Waist, Weather

Central heating Cen, CH

▷ **Centre** *may indicate* middle letters

Centrepiece Epergne

Century Age, C, Era, Magdeburg, Period, Siècle, Ton

Cephalopod Ammonite, Calamary, Cuttle, Loligo, Nautilus, Octopus, Sepia, Squid

Ceramic(s) Agateware, Arcanist, China, Earthen, Ferrite, Porcelain, Pottery, Sialon, Syalon®, Tiles

Cereal Amelcorn, Barley, Blé, Bran, Buckwheat, Bulgar, Bulg(h)ur, Cassava, Corn, Cornflakes, Couscous, Emmer, Farina, Gnocchi, Grain, Granola, Groats, Hominy, Maize, Mandioc(a), Mandiocca, Mani(h)oc, Manihot, Mealie, Millet, Muesli, Oats, Paddy, Popcorn, Rye(corn), Sago, Samp, Sarassin, Seed, Semolina, Sorghum, Spelt, Tapioca, Tef(f), Triticale, Triticum, Wheat, Zea

Cerebrate, Cerebration Pore, Thought

Ceremonial, Ceremony Aarti, Amrit, Baptism, Barmitzvah, Chado, Chanoyu, Commemoration, Common Riding, Coronation, Doseh, Durbar, Encaenia, Enthronement, Etiquette, Eucharist, Flypast, Form(al), Formality, Gongyo, Habdalah, Havdalah, Havdoloh, Heraldry, Investiture, Koto(w), Matsuri, Maundy, Mummery, Observance, Occasion, Ordination, Pageantry, Parade, Pomp, Powwow, Protocol, Rite, Rite of passage, Ritual, Sacrament, Sado, Seder, Service, State, Tea, Topping-out, Trooping (the Colour), Unveiling, Usage

Cerium Ce

Cert(ain), Certainty Absolute, Actual, Assured, Banker, Bound, Cast-iron, Cinch, Cocksure, Confident, Convinced, Decided, Definite, Doubtless, Exact, Fact, Fate,

Indubitable, Inevitable, Infallible, Keen, Monte, Moral, Nap, Needly, One, Positive, Poz, Precise, Racing, Shoo-in, Siccar, Sicker, Snip, Some, → **SURE**, Sure-fire, Truth, Yes

Certainly Agreed, Ay, Certes, Fegs, Forsooth, Indeed, Iwis, Jokol, OK, Oke, Pardi(e), Pardy, Perdie, Siccar, Sicker, → **SURE**, Truly, Verily, Yea, Yes, Yokul, Ywis

Certificate, Certified, Certify Affirm, Assure, Attest, Bene decessit, Birth, Bond, Chit, Cocket, Confirm, Credential, Death, Debenture, Depose, Diploma, Docket, Document, End-user, Enseal, Gold, Guarantee, Landscrip, Licence, Lines, Medical, MOT, Notarise, Paper, Patent, Proven, Savings, School, Scrip, Scripophily, Security, Share, Stamp note, Stock, Sworn, Talon, Testamur, Testimonial, Treasury, U, Unruly, Voucher, Warrant

Cesspit Bog, Dungmere, Jawhole, Sinkhole, Slurry

Cetacean Dolphin, Porpoise, Whale

Cete(acean) Badger

Ceylon(ese) Serendip, Vedda(h)

Chafe(r), Chafing Chunter, Fray, Fret, Gall, Harass, Intertrigo, Irritate, Pan, → **RUB**, Seethe, Worry

Chaff(y) Badinage, Banter, Bran, Chip, Cornhusk, Dross, Have on, Hay, Husk, Rag, Raillery, Rally, Ramentum, Refuse, Roast, Rot, Tease, Twit

Chaffer(ing) Bandy, Bargain, Haggle, Higgle, Hucksterage, Traffic

Chaffinch Wheatbird, Whitewing

Chagrin Annoyance, Envy, Mortify, Spite, Vexation

Chain(s), Chained Acre's-breadth, Albert, Anklet, Band, Bicycle, Bind, Bond, Bracelet, Branched, Bucket, Cable, Catena, Chatelaine, Choke, Cistron, Closed, Cordillera, Cyclic, Daisy, Decca, Dixie, Drive, Duplex, Dynasty, Engineer's, Esses, Fanfarona, Fetter, Fob, Food, Furlong, Gleipnir, Golden, Grand, Gunter's, Gyve, Heavy, Human, Learner's, Lockaway, Markov, Mayor, Micella(r), Micelle, → **MOUNTAIN**, Noria, Open, Pennine, Pitch, Range, Rockies, Rode, Roller, Safety, Seal, → **SERIES**, Shackle, Side, Slang, Snigging, Snow, Span, Sprocket, Straight, String, Strobila, Supply, Surveyor's, Suspensor, Team, Tug, Voluntary, Watch

Chain-gang Coffle

Chair Balloon-back, Basket, Bath, Bench, Bentwood, Berbice, Bergère, Birthing, Bosun's, Butterfly, Camp, Cane, Captain's, Carver, Club, Cromwellian, Curule, Deck, Dining, Director's, Easy, Elbow, Electric, Emeritus, Estate, Fauteuil, Fiddle-back, Folding, Frithstool, Garden, Gestatorial, Guérite, High, Jampan, Jampanee, Jampani, Ladder-back, Lounger, Love-seat, Lug, Merlin, Morris, Musical, Nursing, Personal, Pew, Preside, Recliner, Rocker, Rush-bottomed, → **SEAT**, Sedan, Steamer, Stool, Straight, Sugan, Swivel, Throne, Wainscot, Wheel, Windsor, Wing

Chair-back Ladder, Splat

Chairman Convener, Emeritus, Humph, Landammann, Mao, MC, Pr(a)eses, Prof, Prolocutor, Sheraton, Speaker

Chalaza Albumen, Treadle, Treddle

Chalcedony Enhydros

Chaldean Babylonian, Ur

Chalet Cabana, Cot, Skio

Chalice Poisoned

Chalk(y) Black, Calcareous, Cauk, Cawk, Crayon, Credit, Cretaceous, Dentin, French, Senonian, Soapstone, Spanish, Steatite, Tailor's, White(n), Whit(en)ing

Challenge(r), Challenging Acock, Assay, Call, Cartel, Champion, Charge, Confront, Contest, Dare, Defy, Gage, Gauntlet, Glove, Hazard, Hen(ner), Iconoclasm, Impugn,

Insubordinate, Oppugn, Provoke, Query, Question, Recuse, Sconce, Shuttle, Tackle, Taker, Tall order, Tank, Threat, Vie, Wero, Whynot

Chamber(s) Airlock, Anteroom, Atrium, Auricle, Bladder, Bubble, Camarilla, Camera, Casemate, Cavern, Cavitation, Cavity, Cell(a), Chanty, Close-stool, Cloud, Cofferdam, Combustion, Cubicle, Decompression, Dene-hole, Dolmen, Echo, Float, Fogou, Fumatorium, Fume, Gas, Gazunder, Gilded, Hall, Horrors, Hyperbaric, Hypogea, Inspection, Ionization, Jerry, Jordan, Kiva, Lavatory, Lethal, Locule, Lok Sabha, Lower, Magma, Manhole, Mattamore, Mesoscaphe, Plenum, Po(t), Presence, Priest('s)-hole, Privy, Reaction, Resonance-box, Roum, Second, Serdab, Silo, Spark, Star, Stateroom, Steam-chest, Swell-box, Synod, Thalamus, Undercroft, Upper, Utricle, Vault, Ventricle, Wilson cloud, Zeta

Chamberlain Camerlengo, Camerlingo, Censor

Chameleon Adaptor, American, Anole, Ethiopian, Floating voter, Lizard, Tarand

Chamfer Bevel, Groove

Chamois Ibex, Izard, Shammy

Champ Bite, Chafe, Chew, Chomp, Eat, Gnash, Gnaw, Hero, Mash, Morsure, Munch

Champagne Boy, Bubbly, Charlie, Fizz, Gigglewater, Pop, Sillery, Simkin, Simpkin, Stillery, Troyes, Widow

Champion(s) Ace, Adopt, Ali, Apostle, Back, Belt, Campeador, Cid, Cock, Crusader, Cupholder, Defend, Don Quixote, Doucepere, Douzeper, Dymoke, Enoch, Espouse, Gladiator, Gun, Harry, → **HERO**, Horse, Kemp, Kemper(yman), King, Knight, Maintain, Matchless, Messiah, Messias, Neil, Paladin, Palmerin, Peerless, Perseus, Promachos, Proponent, Protagonist, Roland, St Anthony, St David, St Denis, St George, St James, St Patrick, Seven, Spiffing, Spokesman, Star, Support, Tribune, Upholder, Victor, Wardog, → **WINNER**, World-beater, Yokozuna

Championship Five Nations, Open, Seven, Six Nations, Super Bowl, Title, Tri-nations

Chance (upon), Chancy Accident, Aleatory, Aunter, Bet, Break, Buckley's, Cast, Casual, Cavel, Coincidence, Contingent, Dice, Earthly, Even, Fat, → **FATE**, Fighting, First refusal, Fluke, Fortuitous, Fortuity, Fortune, → **GAMBLE**, Game, Hap, Happenstance, Hobnob, Iffy, Kevel, Light, Loaves and fishes, Look-in, Lot, → **LOTTERY**, Luck, Main, Meet, Mercy, Occasion, Occur, Odds, Odds-on, Opening, Opportunity, Outside, Peradventure, Posse, Potluck, Prayer, Probability, Prospect, Random, Rise, Risk, Run into, Russian roulette, Serendipity, Slant, Snip, Spec, Sporting, Stake, Stochastic, Sweep, Toss-up, Treble, Turn, Tychism, Ventre, Venture, Wager, Wild card

Chancel Adytum, Bema, Nave

Chancellor Adolf, Bismarck, Dollfuss, Kohl, Logothete, Minister, More, Schmidt, Vicar-general, Wolsey

Chancery Court, Hanaper

Chandelier Candlestick, Corona, Drop, Electrolier, Gasolier, Girandole, Lustre, Pendant

Chandler Acater, Acatour, Raymond

Chaney Lon

Change(able), Changes, Changing About-face, Adapt, Adjust, Agio, Aleatoric, → **ALTER**, Amendment, Attorn, Backtrack, Barter, Become, Bob-major, Capricious, Cash, Catalysis, Chameleon, Channel-hop, Chop, Chump, Cline, Commute, Convert, Coppers, Cut, Denature, Departure, Development, Dichrony, Dissolve, Edit, Enallage, Esterify, Eustatic, Evolve, Exchange, Fickle, Find, Flighty, Float, Fluctuate, Flux, Grandsire, Guard, Gybe, Inflect, Innovate, Instead, Kembla, Killcrop, Labile, Loose, Make-over, Menopause, Metabolic, Metabolise,

Metamorphose, Metamorphosis, Metathesise, Mew, Mobile, Modify, Morph, Mutable, Mutalis mutandis, Mutanda, Mutation, Ontogeny, Parallax, Peal, Pejoration, Peripet(e)ia, Permute, Port, Prisere, Prophase, Protean, Quantum leap, Quarter, Rat, Realise, Recant, Rectify, Redo, Reform, Refraction, Regime, Rejig, Reshuffle, Resipiscence, Rest, Reverse, Revise, Revolutionise, Rework, Sandhi, Scourse, Sd, Sea, Seesaw, Sere, Sex, Shake-out, Shake-up, Shift, Silver, Small, Sublimation, Substitute, Swap, Swing, Switch, Tempolabile, Tolsel, Tolsey, Tolzey, Transfer, Transfiguration, Transform, Transition, Transmogrify, Transmute, Transpose, Transubstantial, Triple, Turn, Uncertain, Upheaval, U-turn, Vagary, Variant, Variation, Vary, Veer, Versatile, Vicissitude, Volatile, Volte-face, Wankle, Washers, Waver, Weathercock, Wheel, Wow

▷ **Change(d)** *may indicate* an anagram

Changeling Auf, Killcrop, Oaf, Turncoat

Channel Access, Aflaj, Aqueduct, Artery, Beagle, Bed, Billabong, Binaural, Bristol, Canal, Canaliculus, Chimb, Chime, Chine, Chute, Conduit, Culvert, Cut, Cutting, Datagram, Distribution, Ditch, Drain, Duct, Dyke, Ea, English, Estuary, Euripus, Fairway, Falaj, Feeder, Floodway, Flume, Foss, Funnel, Furrow, Gat, Gate, Geo, Gio, Glyph, Grough, Gully, Gut, Gutter, Head-race, Ingate, Katabothron, Katavothron, Khor, Kill, Kos, Kyle, Lake, La Manche, Lane, Latch, Leat, Leet, Limber, Major, Meatus, Medium, Minch, Moat, Mozambique, Multiplex, Narrows, North, Offtake, Penstock, Pentland Firth, Pescadores, Pipeline, Qanat, Race, Raceway, Rebate, Rigol(l), Rigolets, Rivulet, Run, St George's, Sea-gate, Seaway, Sewer, Shunt, Sinus, Sky, Sloot, Sluice, Sluit, Sny(e), Solent, Solway Firth, Sound, Sow, Spillway, Sprue, Strait, Suez, Sure, Swash, Tailrace, Tideway, Tracheole, Trough, Ureter, Vallecula, Vein, Wasteweir, Watercourse, Waterspout, Wireway, Yucatan

Chant Anthem, Antiphon, Canticle, Cantillate, Cantus, Chaunt, Daimoku, Decantate, Euouae, Evovae, Gregorian, Haka, Harambee, Hymn, Intone, Introit, Mantra(m), Motet, Pennillion-singing, Plainsong, Proper, Psalm, Sing, Slogan, Te Deum, The Reproaches, Yell

Chantilly Cream, Lace

Chaos, Chaotic Abyss, Anarchy, Confusion, Disorder, Fitna, Fractal, Goat fuck, Hun-tun, Jumble, Maelstrom, Mess, Mixter-maxter, Muss, Shambles, Shambolic, Snafu, Tohu bohu, Turmoil

▷ **Chaotic** *may indicate* an anagram

Chap(s) Beezer, Bloke, Bo, Bod, Bor, Cat, Chafe, Cheek, Chilblain, Chop, Cleft, Cod, Codger, Cove, Crack, Customer, Dog, Fella, Fellow, Flews, Genal, Gent, Gink, Guy, Hack, Joll, Jowl, Kibe, Lad, → **MAN**, Mouth, Mum, Ocker, Rent, Rime, Spray, Spreathe, Spreaze, Spreethe, Spreeze, Wang

Chapel Bethel, Bethesda, Beulah, Cha(u)ntry, Chevet, Ebenezer, Feretory, Galilee, Lady, Oratory, Parabema, Proprietary, Prothesis, Sacellum, Sistine

Chaperon(e) Beard, Cap, Duenna, Escort, Gooseberry, Griffin, Griffon, Gryphon, Muffin

Chaplain(cy) CF, Ordinary, Padre, Priest, Scarf, Skypilot, Slope

Chaplet Anadem, Coronet, Fillet, Garland, Wreath

▷ **Chaps** *may indicate* an anagram

Chapter Accidents, C, Canon, Cap, Capitular, Ch, Chap, Cr, Division, Episode, Lodge, Phase, Section, Social, Sura(h), Verse

Char(woman) Adust, Burn, Cleaner, Coal, Daily, Duster, Mop(p), Mrs Mop(p), Rosie Lee, Scorch, Sear, Singe, Smoulder, Toast, Togue, Torgoch

Charabanc Bus, Chara, Coach

Character(s) Aesc, Alphabet, Ampersand, Ampussyand, Atmosphere, Aura,

Backslash, Brand, Calibre, Case, Cipher, Clef, Cliff, Climate, Coloration, Complexion, Contour, Credit, Delimiter, Deuteragonist, Devanagari, Digamma, Digit, Dramatis personae, Emoticon, Ess, Essence, Eta, Ethos, → **FEATURE**, Fish, Fist, Form, Grain, Graphics, Grass, Grit, Hair, Hieroglyphic, Homophone, Hue, Ideogram, Ideograph, Italic, Kanji, Kern, Kind, La(m)bda, Letter, Logogram, Make-up, Mark, Mu, Nagari, → **NATURE**, Non-person, Nu, Ogam, Ogham, Pahlavi, Pantaloon, Part, Pehlevi, Person(a), Personage, → **PERSONALITY**, Phonogram, Physiognomy, Pi, Polyphone, Protagonist, Psi, Raisonneur, Reference, Reference-mark, Repute, Rho, Role, Rune, Runic, Sampi, San, Self, Sigma, Sirvente, Slash, Sonancy, Sort, Space, Sphenogram, Stamp, Subscript, Superhero, Superscript(ion), Swung dash, Syllabary, Symbol, Tab, Testimonial, Ton(e), Trait, Uncial, Unit, Vav, Vee, Waw, Wen, Wild card, Wyn(n), Yogh, Zeta

Characterise(d), Characterism, Characteristic(s) Acquired, Attribute, Aura, Cast, Colour, Distinctive, Earmark, Ethos, Facies, Feature, Hair, Hallmark, Has, Headmark, Idiomatic, Idiosyncrasy, Jizz, Lineament, Mien, Nature, Notate, Peculiar, Persona, Phenotype, Point, Property, Quality, Signature, Stigma, Strangeness, Streak, Style, → **TRAIT**, Transfer, Typical, Vein, Way

Characterless Anon, Inane, Wet

Charade Enigma, Pretence, Riddle

Charcoal Activated, Carbon, Coke, Fusain, Sugar

Charge(s), Charged, Charger Access, Accusal, Accuse, Aerate, Agist, Allege, Annulet, Arraign, Ascribe, Assault, Baton, Bear, Behest, Blame, Brassage, Brush, Buckshot, Bum rap, Burden, Care, Carrying, Cathexis, Commission, Community, Complaint, Congestion, Cost, Count, Cover, Criminate, Damage, Debit, Delate, Delf, Delph, Demurrage, Depth, Depute, Directive, Dittay, Dockage, Due, Duty, Dynamise, Electric, Electron, Entrust, Entry, Exit, Expense, Fare, Fee, Fill, Fixed, Flag fall, Fleur-de-lis, Floating, Flock, Freight, Fullage, Fuse, Fusil, Fuze, Gazump, Giron, Gravamen, Gyron, → **HERALDIC**, Hot, Hypothec, Impeach, Impute, Indict, Inescutcheon, Inform, Instinct, Ion, Isoelectric, Last, Lien, Lioncel(le), Lionel, Live, Load, Mandate, Mine, Mount, Nuclear, Objure, Obtest, Onrush, Onslaught, Onus, Ordinary, Orle, Overhead, Pastoral, Pervade, Pew-rent, Plaint, Positive, Premium, Prime, Prix fixe, Q, Quayage, Rack-rent, Rap, Rate, Red-dog, Rent, Report, Reprise, Reverse, Roundel, Run, → **RUSH**, Saddle, Service, Specific, Stampede, Steed, Storm, Supplement, Tariff, Tax, Tear, Terms, Tilt, Toll, → **TRAY**, Tressure, Trickle, Trust, Tutorage, Upfill, Vaire, Vairy, Verdoy, Vigorish, Ward, Warhead, Wharfage

Chariot(eer) Auriga, Automedon, Biga, Cart, Charet, Curricle, Hur, Phaethon, Quadriga, Rath(a), Vimana, Wagon, Wain

Charisma Oomph, Personality

Charitable, Charity Alms, Alms-deed, Awmous, Benign, Breadline, Caritas, Cause, Chugger, Dole, Dorcas, Eleemosynary, Good works, Kiwanis, Largesse, Leniency, Liberal, Lion, Love, Mercy, Oddfellow, Openhanded, Oxfam, Pelican, Zakat

Charivari Rough music, Uproar

Charlatan Cheat, Crocus, Empiric, Escroc, Faker, Imposter, Katerfelto, Mountebank, Poseur, Quack(salver), Saltimbanco

Charlemagne Carlovingian

Charles, Charley, Charlie Beard, Car, Champagne, Chan, Chaplin, Checkpoint, Elia, Lamb, Mug, (Old) Rowley, Pretender, Rug-gown, Sap, Schmoe, Tail-end, Watchman

Charles de Gaulle Airport

Charlock Runch

Charlotte Bronte, Russe, Yonge

Charm(er), Charmed, Charming Abracadabra, Abrasax, Abraxas, Agacerie, Allure, Amulet, Appeal, Aroma, Attraction, Beguile, Bewitch, Captivate, Charisma, Chocolate box, Circe, Comether, Cramp-bone, Cute, Cutie, Delectable, Emerods, Enamour, Enchant, Engaging, → **ENTRANCE**, Fascinate, Fay, Fetish, Grace, Greegree, Gri(s)gris, Hand of glory, Houri, Incantation, Juju, Magnetic, Mascot, Mojo, Nice, Obeah, Obi(a), Periapt, Phylactery, Porte-bonheur, Pretty, Prince, Quaint, Quark, Ravish, Siren, Smoothie, Spellbind, Suave, Sweetness, Taking, Talisman, Tefillah, Telesm, Tephillah, Tiki, Trinket, Unction, Voodoo, Winning, Winsome

▷ **Charming** *may indicate* an anagram

Chart(ed), Charting Abac, Alignment, Bar, Breakeven, Card, Control, Diagram, Eye, Flip, Flow, Gantt, Graph, Histogram, Horoscope, Hydrography, Isogram, Isopleth, List, Magna Carta, → **MAP**, Mappemond, Movement, Nomogram, Organisation, Pie, Plane, Plot, Portolano, Ringelmann, Run, Social, Sociogram, Table, Test, Timetable, Waggoner, Weather, Z

Charta, Charter Atlantic, Book, Citizen's, Covenant, Hire, Lease, Let, Novodamus, Rent, Social (Chapter), Tenants', Time, Voyage

Chary Cagey, Careful, Cautious, Frugal, Shy, Wary

Charybdis Maelstrom, Whirlpool

Chase(r), Chasing Cannock, Chace, Chevy, Chivy, Ciseleur, Ciselure, Course, Cranbome, Decorate, Drink, Game, Harass, Hound, → **HUNT**, Jumper, Oxo, Pursuit, Race, Scorse, Sic(k), Steeple, Sue, Suit, Wild-goose

Chasm Abyss, Crevasse, Fissure, Gap, Gorge, Gulf, Schism, Yawn

Chaste, Chastity Aggie, Agnes, Attic, Celibate, Classic, Clean, Continent, Fatima, Florimell, Ines, Innocent, Modesty, Nessa, → **PURE**, Vestal, Virginal, Virtue

Chasten, Chastise(d), Chastisement Beat, Correct, Discipline, Disple, Lash, Punish, Rib-roast, Rollicking, Scold, Scourge, Shame-faced, Spank, Strap, Whip

Chat, Chatter(box) Babble, Bavardage, Bird, Blab(ber), Blether, Campanero, Causerie, Chelp, Chinwag, Clack, Clishmaclaver, Confab(ulate), Converse, Cosher, Coze, Crack, Dialogue, Froth, Gab(ble), Gas, Gibble-gabble, Gossip, Gup, Hobnob, Jabber, Jargon, Jaw, Kilfud, Liaise, Madge, Mag(pie), Natter, Patter, Pie, Pourparler, Prate, Prattle, Rabbit, Rabble, Rap, Rattle, Scuttlebutt, Shmoose, Shoot the breeze, Stone, Talk, Talkee-talkee, Tattle, Tongue-work, Twattle, Waffle, Whin, Windbag, Witter, Wongi, Yacketyyak, Yad(d)a-yad(d)a-yad(d)a, Yak, Yap, Yarn, Yatter, Yellow-breasted, Yoking

Chateau Castle, Cru, Malmaison, Schloss

Chateaubriand René

Chattel Asset, Chose, Deodand

Chaucer(ian) Dan, OE

Chauffeur Cabby, Coachy, Driver, Sice, Syce

Chauvinist Alf, Bigot, Jingo, MCP, Partisan, Patriot, Sexist

Cheap A bon marché, Bargain, Base, Catchpenny, Cheesy, Chintzy, Cut-price, Downmarket, Gimcrack, Giveaway, Ignoble, Knockdown, Low, Off-peak, Poor, Sacrifice, Shoddy, Steerage, Stingy, Tatty, Tawdry, Ticky-tacky, Tinhorn, Tinpot, Tinselly, Trivial, Tuppenny, Two-bit, Twopenny, Twopenny-halfpenny, Undear, Vile

▷ **Cheap** *may indicate* a d- or p- start to a word

Cheapside Bow

Cheat(ers), Cheating Bam, Bamboozle, Beguile, Bilk, Bite(r), Bob, Bonnet, Bubble, Bucket, Bullock, Bunce, Burn, Cardsharp(er), Charlatan, Chiaus, Chicane(ry), Chisel, Chouse, Clip, Cod, Cog(ger), Colt, Con, Cony-catcher, Cozen, Crib,

Cross, Cross-bite(r), Cuckold, Cully, Defraud, Delude, Diddle, Dingo, Dish, Do, Doublecross, Duckshove, Dupe, Escroc, Faitor, Fiddle, Finagle, Fix, Flam, Flanker, Fleece, Fob, Foister, Fox, Fraud, Gaff, Gip, Glasses, Gull-catcher, Gum, Gyp, Hoax, Hocus, Hoodwink, Hornswoggle, Horse, Intake, Jockey, Leg, Magsman, Mulct, Mump, Nick, Pasteboard, Picaro(on), Poop, Queer, Rib, Rig, Rogue, Rook, Rush, Scam, Screw, Screw over, Shaft, Sharper, Short-change, Slur, Smouch, Snap, Stack, Stiff, Sting, Swindle, Thimble-rigging, Trepan, Trick(ster), Trim, Two-time, Welch, Welsh, Wheedle

Check Arrest, Audit, Bauk, Ba(u)lk, Bill, Bridle, Collate, Compesce, Confirm, Control, Count, Cramp, Cross-index, Curb, Dam, Damp, Detain, Detent, Discovered, Dogs-tooth, Examine, Foil, Frustrate, Halt, Hamper, Hobble, Houndstooth, Inhibit, Inspect, Jerk, Jerque, Let, Limit, Mate, Monitor, Observe, Overhaul, Parity, Perpetual, Prevent, Rain, Reality, Rebuff, Rebuke, Rein, Repress, Reprime, Repulse, Reread, → **RESTRAIN**, Revoke, Saccade, Screen, Service, Setback, Shepherd's, Shorten, Sit-upon, Sneap, Sneb, Snib, Snub, Sound, Spot, → **STEM**, Stent, Stint, Stocktake, Stop, Stunt, Suppress, Tab, Tally, Tartan, Tattersall, Test, Thwart, Tick, Trash, Verify, Vet

Checkers Chinese, Piece

Check-out Till

Cheddar Cheese, Gorge

Cheek(y) Alforja, Audacity, Brass-neck, Buccal, Chap, Chollers, Chutzpah, Cool, Crust, Flippant, Fresh, Gall, Gena(l), Gobby, Gum, Hard-faced, Hussy, Impertinent, Impudent, Joll, Jowl, Lip, Malapert, Malar, Masseter, Neck, Nerve, Noma, Pert, Presumption, Quean, Sass, Sauce, Sideburns, Wang, Yankie, Zygoma

Cheep Chirp, Chirrup, Peep

Cheer(s), Cheerful(ness), Cheering Acclaim, Agrin, Applaud, Banzai, Barrack, Blithe, Bonnie, Bravo, Bright, Bronx, Bubbly, Buck, Buoy, Cadgy, Canty, Carefree, Cherry, Chin-chin, Chipper, Chirpy, Chirrupy, → **COMFORT**, Crouse, Debonair, Drink, Ease, Elate, Elevate, Enliven, Exhilarate, Exuberant, Festive, Genial, Gladden, Happy-go-lucky, Hearten, Hilarity, Holiday, Hooch, Hoorah, Hurra(h), Huzzah, Insouciance, Jocund, Jovial, Kia-ora, L'allegro, Light-hearted, Lightsome, Lively, Meal, Olé, Ovate, Peart, Perky, Please, Praise, Prosit, Rah, Riant, Rivo, Root, Rumbustious, Shout, Sko(a)l, Slainte, Sonsie, Sunny, Ta, Tata, Thanks, Three, Tiger, Tiggerish, Toodle-oo, Up, Upbeat, Warm, Winsome, Yell

Cheerless Bleak, Dismal, Drab, Drear, Gloomy, Glum, Wint(e)ry

Cheese, Cheesy American, Amsterdam, Appenzell, Asiago, Bel Paese, Blue, Blue vein, Boc(c)oncini, Boursin, Brie, Caboc, Caerphilly, Cambazola, Camembert, Cantal, Casein, Caseous, Cheddar, Cheshire, Chessel, Chèvre, Colby, Cottage, Coulommiers, Cream, Crowdie, Curd, Damson, Danish blue, Derby, Dolcelatte, Double Gloucester, Dunlop, Edam, Dutch, Emmental(er), Emmenthal(er), Ermite, Esrom, Ewe, Fet(a), Fontina, Fromage frais, Fynbo, Gloucester, Goat, Gorgonzola, Gouda, Grana Padano, Grand Panjandrum, Green, Gruyère, Halloumi, Hard, Havarti, Huntsman, Ilchester, Islay, Jarlsberg®, Junket, Kebbock, Kebbuck, Kenno, Killarney, Lancashire, Leicester, Lemon, Limburg(er), Lymeswold®, Macaroni, Manchego, Mascarpone, Mousetrap, Mozzarella, Mu(e)nster, Mycella, Neufchatel, Numero uno, Oka, Orkney, Paneer, Parmesan, Pecorino, Pont l'Eveque, Port Salut, Pot, Provolone, Quark, Raclette, Rarebit, Reblochon, Red Leicester, Rennet, Ricotta, Romano, Roquefort, Sage Derby, Samso, Sapsago, Skyr, Stilton®, Stone, Stracchino, Swiss, Taleggio, Tilsit, Tofu, Truckle, Vacherin, VIP, Wensleydale, Whey

Cheesecake Pin-up, Talmouse

Cheese-scoop Pale

Chef Commis, Escoffier

Chekhov Anton

Chemical Acanthin, Acid, Acrolein, Adrenalin®, Agent Orange, Alar, Aldehyde, Alkali, Allomone, Alum, Amide, Anabolic, Barilla, Bradykinin, Bute, Camphene, Camphor, Carbide, Carnallite, Caseose, Catalyst, Cephalin, Cerebroside, Depside, Developer, Dopamine, Encephalin, Enkephalin(e), Enol, Ethanal, Fixer, Fluoride, Formyl, Freon, Fungicide, Gamone, Gibbsite, Glutamine, Glycol, Halon, Harmin, Heavy, Hecogenin, Heptane, Hexylene, Hexylresorcinol, Histamine, Hormone, Hypo, ICI, Imine, Imipramine, Indican, Interleukin, Larvicide, Lewisite, Massicot, Morphactin, Naioxone, Napalm, Natron, Neurotransmitter, Nitre, Nonylphenol, Oestrogen, Olefin, Olein, Oxide, Oxysalt, Paraben, Pentane, Pentene, Pentyl, Peptide, Periclase, Phenol, Phenyl, Pheromone, Potash, Potassa, Psoralen, Ptomaine, Reagent, Resorcin, Resorcinol, Restrainer, Serotonin, Soman, Soup, Stearate, Strontia, Styrene, Sulphide, Terpene, Thio-salt, Toluol, Toner, Trimer, Weedicide, Weedkiller

Chemise Cymar, Sark, Serk, Shift, Shirt, Simar(re), Smock, Symar

Chemist(ry) Adams, Alchemy, Alchymy, Analyst, Apothecary, Bunsen, Butenandt, Cavendish, Charles, Chemurgy, Cleve, Curie, Dalton, Davy, Debye, Dewar, Dispenser, Druggist, Drugstore, Faraday, FCS, Gahn, Hevesy, Iatrochemistry, Inorganic, Lavoisier, Le Chatelier, Leclanché, Liebig, LSA, Macadam, MPS, Nernst, Newlands, Nobel, Nuclear, Organic, Paracelsus, Pasteur, Pharmacist, Physical, Pothecary, Pottingar, Proust, Prout, Redwood, RIC, Sabatier, Sanger, Schiff, Seger, Spageric, Spagiric, Spagyric, Spicer, Stinks, Stoechiometry, Stoich(e)iometry, Technical, Urey, Von Babo, Welsbach, Zymurgy

Cheops Khufu

Cheque Blank, Bouncer, Giro, Gregory, Open, Rubber, Stumer, Tab, Traveller's

Chequer Dice

Cherish(ed) Dear, Dote, Enshrine, Entertain, Esteem, Foment, Foster, Harbour, Inshrine, Nestle, Nurse, Pamper, Pet, Precious, Treasure

Cheroot Cigar, Manil(l)a

Cherry (tree) Amarelle, Amazon, Ball, Barbados, Bigaroon, Bigarreau, Bird, Blackheart, Bladder, Cerise, Choke, Cornelian, Gean, Ground, Heart, Jerusalem, Kearton, Kermes, Kermesite, Malpighia, Marasca, Maraschino, May-duke, Maz(z)ard, Merry, Morel(lo), Prunus, Red, Sweet, Whiteheart

Cherry-pie Heliotrope

Cherub Angel, Putto, Seraph

Chervil Cow-parsley

Chess (move), Chess player, Chess term Black, Blindfold, Endgame, Euwe, Fianchetto, FIDE, Hexagonal, J'adoube, Karpov, Kasparov, Lightning, Miranda, Patzer, Plank, Rapid transit, Shogi, Speed, White, Zugzwang, Zwischenzug

Chessman Bishop, Black, Castle, Cheque, Horse, King, Knight, Pawn, Pin, Queen, Rook, White

Chest(y) Ark, Bahut, Bosom, Box, Breast, Buist, Bunker, Bureau, Bust, Caisson, Cap-case, Case, Cassone, Chapel, Charter, Chiffonier, Coffer, Coffin, Coffret, Commode, Community, Cub, Dresser, Girnel, Hope, Inro, Kist, Larnax, Locker, Lowboy, Meal-ark, Medicine, Ottoman, Pectoral, Pereion, Pigeon, Pleural, Ribcage, Safe, Scrine, Scryne, Sea, Shrine, Slop, Steam, Sternum, Tallboy, Tea, Thorax, Toolbox, Treasure, Trunk, Wangan, Wangun, Wanigan, War, Wind

Chester Deva

Chestnut Auburn, Badious, Ch, Chincapin, Chinese, Chinkapin, Chinquapin, Cliché,

Conker, Dwarf, Favel(l), Hoary, Horse, Marron, Marron glacé, Moreton Bay, Roan, Russet, Saligot, Soare, Sorrel, Spanish, Sweet, Water

Chest protector → ARMOUR, Bib

Chevalier Bayard, Knight, Pretender

Chevron Dancette, Stripe

Chew(ing) Bite, Champ, Chaw, Crunch, Cud, Eat, Fletcherism, Gnaw, Gum, Manducate, Masticate, Maul, Meditate, Moop, Mou(p), Munch, Ruminate, Siri(h), Spearmint

Chewink Ground-robin

Chiastolite Macle

Chic Dapper, Debonair, Elegant, Heroin, In, Kick, Modish, Posh, Radical, Smart, Soigné, Stylish, Swish, Tonish, Trim

Chicago Windy City

Chicane(ry) Artifice, Deception, Fraud, Wile

Chichester Yachtsman

Chichi Precious

Chick(en) Australorp, Battery, Biddy, Boiler, Broiler, Capon, Cheeper, Chittagong, Chuckie, Clutch, Cochin, Coronation, Coward, Cowherd, Eirack, Gutless, Hen, Howtowdie, Kiev, Layer, Marengo, Minorca, Mother Carey's, Niderling, Pavid, Poltroon, Poot, Pope's nose, Poult, Pout, Prairie, Precocial, Pullus, Quitter, Roaster, Spatchcock, Spring, Squab, Supreme, Timorous, Unheroic, Windy, Wyandotte, Yellow

Chickenfeed Maize, Peanuts

Chickenpox Varicella

Chickpea Chana, Garbanzo

Chickweed Snow-in-summer

Chicory Endive, Radiccio, Succory, Witloof

Chide Admonish, Berate, Dress, Objurgate, Rate, Rebuke, Reprove, Row, Scold, Tick off, Twit, Upbraid

Chief(tain) Arch, Ardrigh, Ariki, Boss, Caboceer, Cacique, Calif, Caliph, Capital, Capitan, Capitayn, Capo, Caradoc, Cazique, Ch, Chagan, Dat(t)o, DG, Dominant, Duke, Emir, Finn (MacCool), First, Foremost, Geronimo, Grand, Haggis, → HEAD, Hereward, Jarl, Kaid, Keystone, King, Leader, → MAIN, Mass, Mocuddum, Mokaddam, Mugwump, Muqaddam, Nawab, Nizam, Nkosi, Oba, Overlord, Paramount, Pendragon, Premier, Primal, Prime, Principal, Quanah, Raja(h), Rajpramukh, Rangatira, Rangatiratanga, Ratoo, Ratu, Sachem, Sagamore, Sarpanch, Sudder, Supreme, Tanist, Tank, Top

Chiffonier Cabinet, Commode

Chilblain Kibe

Child(ren), Childhood, Childish Aerie, Alannah, Ankle biter, Babe, Baby, Bach(ch) a, Badger, Bairn, Bambino, Bantling, Boy, Brat, Brood, Butter-print, Ch, Changeling, Cherub, Chick, Chickabiddy, Chit, Collop, Cub, Dream, Duddie weans, Elfin, Eyas, Feral, Foster, Foundling, Gait, Gangrel, Ge(i)t, Girl, Gyte, Heir, Hellion, Hurcheon, Imp, Infancy, Infant, Inner, Issue, It, Jailbait, Jejune, Juvenile, Kid, Kiddie(wink), Kiddy, Kinder, Lad, Latchkey, Limb, Litter, Littlie, Littling, Love, Mamzer, Mardy, Minion, Minor, Mite, Munchkin, Naive, Nipper, Nursling, Offspring, Pantywaist, Papoose, Piccaninny, Pickin, Problem, Progeny, Puerile, Puss, Putto, Ragamuffin, Rip, Romper, Rug rat, Scion, Second, Seed, Small fry, Smout, Smowt, Sprog, Street arab, Subteen, Tacker, Ted, Teeny-bopper, Tike, Toddle(r), Tot(tie), Totty, Trot, Tweenager, Tweenie, Tyke, Urchin, Waif, Wean, Weanel, Weanling, Weeny-bopper, Whelp, Young, Younker, Youth

Childbearing, Childbirth Couvade, Dystocia, Intrapartum, Lamaze, Obstetrics, Parity, Puerperal, Tocology, Tokology

Child-killer Herod

Childless Atocous, Atokous, Barren, Nullipara, Sp

Chill(er), Chilly Bleak, Cauldrife, → **COLD**, Frappé, Freeze, Freon®, Frigid, Frosty, Gelid, Ice, Iciness, Mimi, Oorie, Ourie, Owrie, Parky, Raw, Refrigerate, Rigor, Scare

Chilli Bird's eye, Cayenne, → **PEPPER**, Pimentón

Chime(s) Bell, Clam, Cymar, Jingle, Peal, Semantron, Tink, → **TOLL**, Wind

Chimera Graft

Chimney (pot), Chimney corner Can, Cow(l), Femerall, Flare stack, Flue, Funnel, Lamp, Lug, Lum, Smokestack, Stack, Stalk, Steeplejack, Tallboy, Tunnel

Chimp(anzee) Ape, Bonobo, Jocko, Pygmy

Chin, Chinwag Chitchat, Double, Genial, Hill-man, Jaw, Jowl, Mentum

China(man), Chinese Ami, Amoy, Boxer, Bud(dy), Cameoware, Cantonese, Cathay, Celestial, Ch, Chelsea, Chink(y), Chow, Coalport, Cochin, Cock, Communist, Confucius, Crackle, Crockery, Delft, Derby, Dresden, Eggshell, Etrurian, Flowery land, Friend, Fukien, Google, Googly, Goss, Hakka, Han, Hizen, Hmong, Imari, Ironstone, Kanji, Kaolin, Kuo-yu, Limoges, Macanese, Manchu, Manchurian, Mandarin, Mangi, Maoist, Mate, Meissen, Middle kingdom, Min, Ming, Minton, National, Oppo, Pal, Pareoean, Pekingese, Pe-tsai, Pinyin, Porcelain, → **POTTERY**, Putonghua, Queensware, Red, Rockingham, Royal Worcester, Semiporcelain, Seric, Sèvres, Shanghai, Sinaean, Sinic, Sino-, Spode®, Sun Yat-sen, Tai-ping, Taoist, Teng, Tocharian, Tungus, Uigur, Wal(l)y, Ware, Wedgwood®, Whiteware, Willow pattern, Willowware, Worcester, Wu, Yellow peril

Chine Chink, Chynd, Ridge

Chink Chinaman, Chop, Cleft, Clink, Cloff, Crack, Cranny, Crevice, Gap, Rent, Rift, Rima, Sinic, Window

Chintz Kalamkari

▷ **Chip** *may indicate* an anagram

Chip(s) Blitter, Blue, Bo(a)st, Carpenter, Counter, Cut, Deep-fried, EPROM, EROM, Fish, Flake, Fragment, Game, Hack, Knap, Log, Nacho(s), Neural, Nick, Pin, Potato, Shaving, Silicon, Spale, Spall, Span, Teraflop, Tortilla, Transputer, Virus

Chipmunk Gopher, Hackee, Suslik, Zizel

Chippendale Chinese

Chipper Jaunty, Spry, Wedge

Chiron Centaur

Chiropody Podiatry

Chiropractic McTimoney

Chirp(y), Chirrup Cheep, Cherup, Chirm, Chirr, Cicada, Peep, Pip, Pipe, Pitter, Stridulate, Trill, Tweet, Twitter

Chisel(ler), Chisel-like Bam, Boaster, Bolster, Bur, Burin, Carve, Cheat, Clip, Drove, Firmer, Gad, → **GOUGE**, Half-round, Mason, Paring, Scalpriform, Scauper, Scorper, Sculpt, Slick, Socket, Sting

Chit Docket, Girl, Memo, Note, Voucher

Chivalry, Chivalrous Brave, Bushido, Courtly, Gallant, Grandisonian, Quixotic

Chivvy Badger, Harass, Pursue

Chloride, Chlorine Calomel

Chlorophyll Leaf-green

Chock Trig

Chocolate Aero, Brown, Cacao, Carob, Cocoa, Dragee, Ganache, Milk, Neapolitan, Noisette, Pinole, Plain, Theobroma, Truffle, Vegelate, Vermicelli

Choice, Choose, Choosy, Chosen Adopt, Anthology, Appoint, Aryan, Cherry-pick, Cull, Dainty, Decide, Druthers, Eclectic, Elect, Elite, Esnecy, Fine, Fork, Free will, Hercules, Hobson's, Leet, Leve, Lief, List, Multiple, Opt, Option, Or, Ossian, Peach, Peculiar, → **PICK**, Picking, Plum(p), Precious, Predilect, Prefer, Proairesis, Rare, Recherché, → **SELECT**, Superb, Try(e), Via media, Volition, Wale

Choiceless Beggar

Choir, Choral, Chorister, Chorus Antiphony, Antistrophe, Anvil, Apse, Burden, Choragus, Choregus, Chorister, Dawn, Decani, Faburden, Fauxbourdon, Group, Hallelujah, Harmony, Hymeneal, Motet, Ninth, Parabasis, Precentor, Quirister, → **REFRAIN**, Ritual, Schola cantorum, Singing, Stop, Strophe, Treble, Triad, → **UNISON**

Choir-master Choragus, Choregus, Precentor

Choke(r) Block, Clog, Gag, Garotte, Glut, Silence, Smoor, Smore, Smother, Stap, Stifle, Stop, Strangle(hold), Strangulate, → **THROTTLE**, Warp

Choky Can, Prison

Choler Yellow bile

Cholera British, Hog

Cholesterol Spinacene, Squalene

Choliamb Scazon

▶ **Choose** *see* **CHOICE**

Chop, Chops, Chopper(s), Choppy Adze, Ax(e), Cakehole, Celt, Charge, Cheek, Chump, Cleave, Côtelette, Cuff, Cutlet, Dice, Fell(er), Flew, Hack, Hash, Helicopter, Hew, Ivory, Karate, Lop, Mince, Mouth, Rotaplane, Rough, Standing, Suey, Teeth, To-rend, Underhand, Wang

Chopin Pantoufle, Shoe

Chopstick(s) Waribashi

Chord(s) Altered, Arpeggio, Barré, Broken, Common, Diameter, Eleventh, Harmony, Intonator, Latus rectum, Neapolitan sixth, Nerve, Ninth, Picardy third, Riff, Seventh, Sixth, Submediant, Thirteenth, Triad, Vocal

Chore Darg, Duty, Fag, Task

Chorea Sydenham's

Choreographer Arranger, Ashton, Balanchine, Cecchetti, Cranko, Fokine, Laban, Massine

Chorus Antistrophe, Dawn, Ninth, Stop, Strophe

Chosen Korea

Chough Chewet

Chowder Bouillabaisse, Skink, Soup

Christ Ecce homo, Lamb of God, Messiah, Pantocrator, Paschal Lamb, Prince of Peace, Saviour, The Good Shepherd, The Redeemer, X, Xt

Christen(ing) Baptise, Launch, Name-day

Christian(ity) Abcee, Abecedarian, Absey, Adventist, Albigenses, Anabaptist, Beghard, Believer, Cathar(ist), Charismatic, Colossian, Coptic, Dior, Donatist, D(o)ukhobor, Ebionite, Fletcher, Galilean, Giaour, Gilbertine, Gnostic, Godsquad, Goy, Heteroousian, Holy roller, Homo(i)ousian, Hutterite, Jehovah's Witness, Lutheran, Maronite, Marrano, Melchite, Melkite, Methodist, Monarchian, Monophysite, Moral, Mozarab, Muscular, Mutineer, Nazarene, Nestorian, Phalange, Pilgrim, Presbyterian, Protestant, Quaker, Quartodeciman, RC, Sabotier, Scientist, SCM, Shambe, Solifidian, Traditor, Uniat(e), Unitarian, Valdenses, Waldensian, Wesleyan, Xian, Zwinglian

Christian Scientist Eddy

Christmas(time) Beetle, Box, Cactus, Card, Carol, C(h)rimbo, Chrissie, Day, Dec,

Island, Nativity, Noel, Nowel(l), Pudding, Stocking, Xm(as), Yuletide

Christopher Kit, Robin, Sly, Wren

Chromatin Karyotin

Chromium Cr

Chromosome Aneuploid, Autosome, Centromere, Cistron, Euchromatin, Genome, Haploid, Homologous, Id(ant), Karyotype, Lampbrush, Operon, Philadelphia, Ploid(y), Polytene, Prophage, Satellite, Telomere, Trisomy, X, Y

Chronicle(r) Anglo-Saxon, Annal, Brut, Calendar, Diary, Froissart, Hall, History, Holinshed, Logographer, Moblog, Paralipomena, Parian, Paris, → **RECORD**, Register, Stow

Chrysalis Nymph, Pupa

Chrysanthemum Corn-marigold, Feverfew, Korean

Chrysolite Olivine, Peridot

Chub Cheven, Chevin, Fish

Chubby Butterball, Plump

Chuck (out) Berry, Buzz, Chook(ie), Discard, Eject, Food, Four-jaw, Grub, Independent-jaw, Pat, Pitch, Scroll, Shy, Sling, Three-jaw, Toss, Turf

Chuckle Chortle, Giggle, Gurgle

Chukka Polo

Chum(my) Ally, Boet, Buddy, Cobber, Cock, Companion, Comrade, Crony, Mate, Pal, Playmate, Sociable, Sodality

Chump Fool, Mug(gins), Noddle, Sap, → **STUPID PERSON**

Chunk(y) Boxy, Chubby, Gob, Piece, Slab, Squat, Wad

Church Abbey, Armenian, Auld Licht, Autocephalous, Basilica, Bethel, Bethesda, Broad, Brood, Byzantine, → **CATHEDRAL**, CE, Ch, Chapel, Chevet, Clergy, Collegiate, Congregational, Coptic, Delubrum, Easter (Orthodox), Eastern, EC, Ecumenical, Episcopal, Episcopalian, Established, Faith, Fold, Free, Greek, High, House, Institutional, Kirk, Lateran, Latin, Low, Lutheran, Maronite, Melchite, Methodist, Minster, Moonie, Moravian, Mormon, Mother, National, New, New Jerusalem, Old Light, Oratory, Orthodox, Parish, Peculiar, Pentecostal, Preaching-house, Prebendal, Presbyterian, Ratana, RC, Reformed, Relief, Rome, Russian Orthodox, Schism house, Schism shop, Secession, Shrine, Smyrna, Station, Stave, Steeple, Steeplehouse, Temple, Titular, Triumphant, Unification, Unitarian, United Free, United Reformed, Visible, Wee Free, Western, Wool

Churchgoer, Churchman, Churchwarden Antiburgher, Azymite, Baptist, Barnabite, Believer, Cameronian, Classis, Clay, Cleric, Clerk, Congregation, Deacon, Dom, Dopper, Elder, Evangelist, Hatto, Ignorantine, Incumbent, Invisible, Knox, Lector, Lutheran, Marrowman, Methodist, Militant, Moderator, Moonie, Mormon, MU, Newman, Oncer, Parson, PE, Pew-opener, Pipe, Pontiff, Prebendary, Precentor, Predicant, Predikant, Prelate, Presbyterian, Priest, Protestant, Puritan, Racovian, Rector, Romanist, Ruridecanal, Sacristan, Sidesman, Sim, Simeonite, Socinian, Spike, Subdeacon, Subchanter, Succentor, Swedenborgian, Tantivy, Triumphant, Ubiquitarian, Unitarian, Verger, Visible, Wesleyan, Worshipper, Wren

Church house Deanery, Manse, Parsonage, Presbytery, Rectory, Vicarage

Churchill Tank, Winston

Churchyard God's acre

Churl(ish) Attercop, Boor, Crabby, Curmudgeonly, Cynical, Ethercap, Ettercap, Gruff, Ill-natured, Nabal, Peasant, Rustic, Serf, Surly

Churn Bubble, Kirn, Seethe, Sicken

Chute Flume, Runway

CIC Shogun, Sirdar

Cicada Greengrocer, Locust, Periodical, Tettix

Cicatrix Scar

Cicely Myrrh, Sweet

Cicero Cic, Orator, Tully

Cid Campeador, Chief, Hero

Cider Drink, Hard, Perry, Scrumpy, Sweet

Ci-devant Ex

Cigar(ette), Cigarette cards Beedi(e), Bidi, Bifter, Bumper, Burn, Camberwell
carrot, Cancer stick, Caporal, Cartophily, Cheroot, Cigarillo, Claro, Coffin
nail, Conch, Concha, Corona, Dog-end, Doob, Durry, Fag, Filter-tip, Gasper,
Giggle(-stick), Havana, Joint, Locofoco, Long-nine, Loosies, Maduro, Manilla,
Number, Panatella, Paper-cigar, Perfecto, Puritano, Reefer, Regalia, Roach,
Roll-up, Segar, Smoke, Snout, Splif(f), Stogie, Stog(e)y, Stompie, Tab, Twist, Weed,
Whiff, Woodbine, Zol

Cinch Belt, Certainty, Duck soup, Easy, Girth, Stroll

Cinchona Kina, Quina

Cinder(s) Ash, Breeze, Clinker, Dander, Embers, Slag

Cinderella Drudge, Stepdaughter

Cinema(s) Art house, Big screen, Biograph, Bioscope, Circuit, Drive-in, Films,
Fleapit, Flicks, Grindhouse, IMAX®, Megaplex, Movies, Multiplex, Multiscreen,
Mutoscope, New Wave, Nickelodeon, Nouvelle Vague, Odeon, Pictures, Plaza,
Scope, Theatre, Tivoli

Cinnabar Vermilion

Cinnamon, Cinnamon stone Canella, Cassia(bark), Essonite, Hessonite, Saigon,
Spice

Cipher Chi-rho, Code, Cryptogram, Enigma, Nihil, Nobody, → **NOTHING**, Number,
O, Steganogram, Zero

Circle Almacantar, Almucantar, Annulet, Antarctic, Arctic, Circassian, Co, Colure,
Company, Compass, Corn, Corolla, Coterie, Cromlech, Crop, Cycloid, Cyclolith,
Dip, Disc, Dress, Druidical, Eccentric, Ecliptic, Embail, Enclose, Engird, Epicyclic,
Equant, Equator, Equinoctial, Euler's, Family, Fraternity, Full, Galactic, Girdle,
Gloriole, Great, Gyre, Halo, Henge, Hoop, Horizon, Hour, Hut, Inner, Inorb,
Lap, Longitude, Loop, Magic, Malebolge, Mandala, Meridian, Mohr's, Mural,
Nimbus, O, Orb, Orbit, Parhelic, Parquet, Parterre, Penannular, Peristalith, Pitch,
Polar, Quality, Red-line, Rigol, → **RING**, Rondure, Rotate, Roundlet, Seahenge,
Sentencing, Set, Setting, Small, Sphere, Stemme, Stone, Stonehenge, Striking,
Surround, Tinchel, Traffic, Transit, Tropic, Turning, Umbel, Upper, Vertical,
Vicious, Vienna, Virtuous, Volt, Wheel

Circuit(ous) Ambit, AND, Autodyne, Bridge, Bypass, Chipset, Closed, Comparator,
Daughterboard, Diocese, Discriminator, Dolby®, Equivalent, Eyre, Gate, Gyrator,
Half-adder, IC, Integrated, Interface, Lap, Limiter, Live, Logic, Loop, Microchip,
Microprocessor, Motherboard, NAND, NOR, NOT, Open, OR, Perimeter, Phantom,
Phase, Printed, Quadripole, Reactance, Ring, Round, Scaler, Series, Short,
Smoothing, Squelch, Stage, Three-phase, Tour, Windlass, XOR

Circuit-breaker Fuse

Circular Annular, Court, Flysheet, Folder, Leaflet, Mailshot, Orby, Round, Spiral,
Unending, Wheely

Circulate, Circulation Astir, Bloodstream, Cyclosis, Disseminate, Flow, Gross,
Gyre, Issue, Mingle, Mix, Orbit, Pass, Publish, Report, Revolve, Rotate, Scope, Send
round, Spread, Stir, Troll, Utter

▷ **Circulating** *may indicate* an anagram

Circumcise(r), Circumcision Bris, Brith, Brit milah, Infibulate, Milah, Mohel, Pharaonic, Sandek

Circumference Boundary, Girth, Perimeter, Size

Circumflex Perispomenon

Circumlocution Bafflegab, Periphrasis, Tautology

Circumnavigation Periplus

Circumscribe(d) Define, Demarcate, Enclose, Eruv, Restrain

Circumspect Chary, Guarded, Prudential, Wary

Circumstance(s), Circumstantial Case, Detail, Event, Fact, Formal, → **INCIDENT**, Mitigating, Precise, Shebang, Situation, Stede

Circumvent Bypass, Dish, Evade, Outflank, Outwit, Usurp

Circus, Circus boy Arena, Big top, Eros, Flea, Flying, Harrier, Hippodrome, Marquee, Maximus, Media, Monty Python, Ring, Sanger, Slang, Three-ring

Cissy Nelly

Cistercian Trappist

Cistern Feed-head, Flush-box, Sump, Tank, Tub, Vat

Citadel Acropolis, Alhambra, Castle, Fort(ress), Keep, Kremlin, Sea-girt

Citation, Cite Adduce, Allegation, Instance, Mention, Name, Quote, Recall, Reference, Repeat, Sist, Summon

Citizen(s), Citizenship Burgess, Burgher, Civism, Cleruch, Denizen, Dicast, Ephebe, Franchise, Freeman, Jus sanguinis, Jus soli, Kane, National, Oppidan, Patrial, People, Proletarian, Propr(a)etor, Quirites, Resident, Roman, Second-class, Senior, Snob, Subject, Trainband, Trierarch, Venireman, Vigilante, Voter

Citroen DS

Citron, Citrous Bergamot

Citrus Acid, Calamondin, Cedrate, Lemon, Lime, Mandarin, Min(n)eola, Orange, Pomelo, Tangerine, Ugli

City Agra, Astrakhan, Athens, Atlantis, Babylon, Burgh, Cardboard, Carthage, Cosmopolis, Ctesiphon, Dodge, EC, Empire, Eternal, Forbidden, Free, Garden, Gath, Heavenly, Hilversum, Holy, Imperial, Inner, LA, Leonine, Medina, Megalopolis, Metropolis, Micropolis, Mother, Municipal, Mycenae, Ninevah, NY, Persepolis, Petra, Pompeii, Rhodes, Salem, Smoke, Sparta, Square mile, Tech, Teheran, The Big Smoke, Town, Ur, Vatican, Weltstadt, Wen

Civet Binturong, Cat, Fo(u)ssa, Genet(te), Herpestes, Linsang, Musang, Nandine, Palm, Paradoxine, Paradoxure, Rasse, Suricate, Toddy-cat, Viverra, Zibet

Civil(ian), Civilisation, Civilised, Civility Amenity, Amicable, Christian, Cit, Citizen, Civ(vy), Comity, Courtesy, Culture, Fertile crescent, Humane, Indus Valley, Kultur, Maya, Mufti, Municipal, Nok, Non-combatant, Polite, Politesse, Push-button, Secular, Temporal, Urbane

Civil Service CS

Clad(ding) Sarking, Weatherboard

Clag(gy) Stickjaw

Claim(s) Appeal, Arrogate, Assert, Asseverate, Bag, Challenge, Charge, Crave, Darraign(e), Darrain(e), Darrayn, Demand, Deraign, Droit, Encumbrance, Exact, Haro, Harrow, Lien, List, Maintain, Nochel, Plea, Pose, Posit, Postulate, Pretence, Pretend, Profess, Pulture, Purport, Puture, Rank, Revendicate, Right, Set-off, Small, Sue, Title

Claimant Irredentist, Petitioner, Pot-waller, Pretender, Prospector, Tichborne, Usurper

Clairvoyance, Clairvoyancy, Clairvoyant ESP, Fey, Insight, Lucidity,

Psiphenomena, Psychic, Taisch, Taish, Tel(a)esthesia, Telegnosis

Clam Bivalve, Chowder, Cohog, Geoduck, Giant, Gweduc, Hardshell, Littleneck, Mollusc, Mya, Quahang, Quahog, Round, Soft-shell, Steamer, Tridacna, Venus

Clamant Vociferous

Clamber Climb, Crawl, Scramble, Spra(i)ckle, Sprauchle

Clammy Algid, Damp, Dank, Moist, Sticky, Sweaty

Clamour(ing), Clamorous Blatant, Brouhaha, Din, Forensis strepitus, Hubbub, Hue, Outcry, Racket, Raird, Reird, Rout, Shout, Strepitant, Uproar, Utis, Vociferate

Clamp Beartrap, Clinch, Coupler, Denver boot, Fasten, Grip, Holdfast, Jumar, Pinchcock, Potato-pit, Serrefine, Stirrup, Tread, Vice, Wheel

Clan(sman) Cameron, Clique, Gens, Gentile, Group, Horde, Kiltie, Kindred, Name, Ngati, Phratry, Phyle, Sect, Sept, Society, Stewart, Stuart, Tribe

Clandestine Covert, Furtive, Secret, Underhand

Clang(er), Clanging, Clank Bell, Belleter, Boob, Boo-boo, Clash, Gong, Jangle, Plangent, Ring

Clap(per), Clapping Applaud, Blow, Castanet, Chop, Crotal, Dose, Jinglet, Peal, Plaudite, Stroke hands, Thunder, Tonant

Claptrap Bilge, Blab, Bombast, Bunkum, Eyewash, Hokum, Rot, Tripe

Claque(ur) Fans, Hat, Laudator, Sycophant

Clara Bow, Butt

Claret Blood, Loll-shraub, Loll-shrob, Vin

Clarify, Clarified, Clarifier Clear, Despumate, Dilucidate, Explain, Explicate, Fine, Finings, Ghee, Purge, Refine, Render, Simplify, Tease out

Clarinet Chalumeau, Reed

Clarion Brassy, Clear, Trumpet

Clary Orval, Sage

Clash(ing) Bang, Clangour, Clank, Claver, Coincide, Collide, Conflict, Dissonant, Friction, Gossip, → **IMPACT**, Incident, Irreconcilable, Jar, Loud, Missuit, Riot, Shock, Showdown, Strike, Swash

Clasp(ing) Adpress, Agraffe, Amplexus, Barrette, Brooch, Button, Catch, Chape, Clip, Embrace, Fibula, Grasp, Hasp, Hesp, Hook, Hug, Inarm, Interdigitate, Link, Morse, Ochreate, Ouch, Slide, Tach(e), Tie, Unite

Class(ification), Classify, Classified, Classy Acorn, Arrange, Assort, Bourgeois(ie), Bracket, Brand, Breed, Business, Cabin, Canaille, Caste, → **CATEGORY**, Chattering, Cheder, Cl, Clan, Clerisy, Clinic, Club, Composite, Course, Criminal, Dalit, Dewey, Digest, Division, Economy, Estate, Evening, Faction, First, Form, Genera, Gentry, Genus, → **GRADE**, Group, Harvard, Haryan, Heder, Hubble, Ilk, Keep-fit, Kohanga reo, League, Lesson, Life, Linn(a)ean, List, Lower, Mammal, Master, Meritocracy, Middle, Night, Number, Nursery, Order, Phenetics, Phylum, Pigeon-hole, Pleb(eian), Proper, Race, Range, Rank, Rate, Rating, Raypoot, Raypout, Reception, Remove, Salariat, Second, Secret, Seminar, Shell, Siege, Social, Sort(ation), Spectral, Steerage, Stratum, Stream, Syntax, Taxonomy, Teach-in, Third, Tony, Tourist, Tribe, Tutorial, → **TYPE**, U, Universal, Upper, Varna, Water, Working, World, Year

Classic(al), Classics, Classicist Ageless, Ancient, Basic, Derby, Elzevir, Grecian, Greek, Humane, Leger, Literature, Pliny, Purist, Roman, Standard, Traditional, Vintage

Clatch Blunk, Smear, Spoil

Clatter Bicker, Charivari, Clack, Din, Noise, Rattle

Clause Adjunct, Apodosis, Article, Basket, Complement, Condition, Conscience, Coordinate, Dependent, Disability, Endorsement, Escalator, Escape, Exclusion,

Exemption, Filioque, Four, Golden parachute, Grandfather, Independent, Main, Member, Noun, Object, Omnibus, Option, Poison-pill, Predicator, Principal, Protasis, Proviso, Reddendum, Reported, Reservation, Rider, Salvo, Saving, Sentence, Subject, Subordinate, Sunset, Tenendum, Testatum, Testing, Warrandice

Claw Chela, Claut, Crab, Dewclaw, Edate, Falcula, Grapple, Griff(e), Hook, Insessorial, Nail, Nipper, Pounce, Scrab, Scramb, Sere, Talent, → **TALON**, Tear, Telson, Tokay, Unguis

Clay Allophane, Argil, Argillite, Barbotine, B(e)auxite, Bentonite, Blaes, Blaise, Blaize, Bole, Boulder, Calm, Cam, Caum, Ceramic, Charoset(h), China, Cimolite, Cloam, Clunch, Cob, Cornish, Earth, Engobe, Fango, Figuline, Fire, Fuller's earth, Gault, Glei, Gley, Gumbotil, Hardpan, Haroset(h), Illite, Kaolin, Kokowai, Laterite, Lithomarge, Loam, London, Lute, Malm, Marl, Meerschaum, Mire, Mortal, Mud, Oxford, Papa, Pipeclay, Pipestone, Pise, Plastic, Plastilina, Porcelain, Potter's, Pottery, Puddle, Pug, Saggar(d), Sagger, Scroddle(d), Seggar, Sepiolite, Slip, Slurry, Smectite, Terra sigillata, Thill, Till(ite), Tumphy, Varve, Warrant, Warren, Wax

Clean(er), Cleaning, Cleanse Absterge, Bathbrick, Besom, Blanco, Bleach, Blue flag, Bream, Broom, Careen, Catharise, Catharsis, Char(e), Chaste, Clear, Daily, Debride, Decontaminate, Dentifrice, Depurate, Deterge(nt), Dhobi, Dialysis, Dicht, Do, Douche, Dredge, Dust(er), Dyson®, Eluant, Emunge, Enema, Erase, Ethnic, Evacuant, Evacuate, Expurgate, Fay, Fettle, Fey, Floss, Flush, Full, Grave, Groom, Gut, Heels, Hoover®, House-trained, Hygienic, Immaculate, Innocent, Launder, Lave, Linish, Lustrum, Lye, Mouthwash, Mrs Mop(p), Mundify, Net, Overhaul, Porge, Pull-through, Pumice, Pure, Purgative, Purge, Ramrod, Rebite, Rub, Rump, Sandblast, Sanitize, Scaffie, Scavenge, Scour, Scrub, Shampoo, Shot-blast, Snow-white, Soap, Soogee, Soogie, Soojey, Sponge, Spotless, Squeaky, Squeegee, Sterile, Sujee, Swab, Sweep, Tidy, Toothpick, Ultrasonic, Uproot, Vac(uum), Valet, → **WASH**, Whistle, Wipe

Clear(ance), Cleared, Clearly Absolve, Acquit, Aloof, Apparent, Assart, Bell, Berth, Bold, Bore, Brighten, Bus, Categorical, Clarify, Crystal, Decode, Definite, Delouse, Demist, Diaphanous, Dispel, Distinct, Downright, Earn, Eidetic, Evacuate, Evident, Exculpate, Exonerate, Explicit, Fair, Five-by-five, Gain, Headroom, Hyaline, Intelligible, Iron, Laund, Leap, Legible, Limpid, Lucid, Luculent, Manifest, Mop, Neat, Negotiate, Net(t), → **NOT CLEAR**, Observable, Obvious, Ope(n), Overleap, Palpable, Patent, Pellucid, Perspicuous, Plain, Play, Pratique, Predy, Pure, Purge, Quit, Rack, Realise, Remble, Rid, Ripple, Serene, Sheer, Shere, Slum, Stark, Sweep, Thro(ugh), Thwaite, Transire, Translucent, Transparent, Unblock, Unclog, Uncork(ed), Unequivocal, Unstop, Vault, Vivid, Void, Well, Windage, Wipe

Clearing Assart, Glade, Opening, Shire, Slash

Cleat Bitt, Wedge

Cleave, Cleavage, Cleft Adhere, Bisulcate, Builder's bottom, Builder's bum, Chimney, Chine, Chink, Cling, Cloff, Cohere, Cut, Divide, Division, Divorce(ment), Fissure, Gap, Ghaut, Goose-grass, Grike, Gryke, Harelip, Pharynx, Rift, Riva, Scissure, Severance, Slack, Slaty, Space, Spathose, Split, Sulcus

Clef Soprano, Treble

Clematis Montana, Old man's beard, Traveller's joy, Virgin's-bower

Clemenceau Tiger

Clemency, Clement Ahimsa, Grace, Lenience, Lenity, Mercy, Mildness, Quarter, Temperate

Cleopatra Needle

Clergy(man), Cleric(al) Abbé, Canon, Cantor, Cardinal, Chancellor, Chaplain, Cleric, Clerk, Cloth, Curate, Curé, Deacon, Dean, Ecclesiast(ic), God-botherer,

Goliard, Incumbent, Josser, Levite, Ministerial, Ministry, Minor canon, Non-juror, Non-usager, Notarial, Paperwork, Parson, Pastor, Pontifex, Pontiff, Preacher, Prebendary, Precentor, Prelate, Presbyter, Presenter, Priest, Primate, Prior, Proctor, Rabbi, Rector, Red-hat, Reverend, Rome-runner, Scribal, Secretarial, Secular, Shaveling, Shepherd, Sky pilot, Slope, Spin-text, Spirituality, Squarson, Subdeacon, Theologian, Vartabed, Vicar

Clergy-hater Misoclere

Clerk(s) Actuary, Articled, Baboo, Babu, Basoche, Circar, Cleric, Cratchit, Cursitor, Enumerator, Filing, Heep, Lay, Limb, Notary, Paper-pusher, Parish, Pen-driver, Penman, Penpusher, Petty Bag, Poster, Prot(h)onotary, Protocolist, Recorder, Salaryman, Scribe, Secretariat, Shipping, Sircar, Sirkar, St Nicholas's, Tally, Town, Vestry, Vicar, Writer

Clever(ness) Able, Adroit, Astute, Brainy, Bright, Canny, Cool, Cute, Daedal(e), Deep-browed, Deft, Genius, Gleg, Hable, Ingenious, Intellectual, Jackeen, Know-all, Natty, Nimblewit, Resourceful, Sage(ness), Shrewd, Skilful, Smart(y), Smarty-pants, Souple, Subtle

Clevis Becket

Cliché Banality, Boilerplate, Commonplace, Corn, Journalese, Platitude, Saying, Tag

Click(er), Clicking Castanet, Catch, Forge, Implosive, Pawl, Rale, Ratch(et), Snick, Succeed, Tchick, Ticktack

Client Account, Customer, Fat, Gonk, John, Patron, Thin, Trick

Cliff(s) Beachy Head, Bluff, Cleve, Corniche, Crag, Craig, Escarp, Palisade(s), Precipice, Sca(u)r

Cliffhanger Samphire, Serial, Thriller

Climate Ambience, Atmosphere, Attitude, Continental, Mood, Sun, Temperament, Temperature, Weather

Climax Apex, Apogee, Catastasis, Come, Crescendo, Crest, Crisis, Culminate, Edaphic, End, Head, Height, Heyday, Moment of truth, Orgasm, Payoff, Top, Zenith

Climb(er), Climbing Aid, Alpinist, Aralia, Aristolochia, Artificial, Ascend, Bignonian, Breast, Briony, Bryony, Clamber, Clematis, Clusia, Cowage, Cowhage, Cowitch, Crampon, Creeper, Cubeb, Cucumber, Dodder, Heart-pea, Hedera, Ivy, Jamming, Kie-kie, Kudzu, Lawyer, Layback, Liana, Liane, → **MOUNT**, Munro-bagger, Pareira, Parvenu, Pea, Peg, Prusik, Rat(t)an, Rise, Root, Rope, Scale, Scan, Scandent, Scansores, Sclim, Scramble, Shin, Shinny, Sklim, Smilax, Social, Speel, Steeplejack, Sty(e), Swarm, Timbo, Tuft-hunter, Udo, Up(hill), Uprun, Vine, Wistaria, With(y)wind, Woodbine, Zoom

Clinch Attach, Carriwitchet, Determine, Ensure, Fix, Quibble, Rivet, Secure, Settle

Cling(er), Clinging Adhere, Bur(r), Cherish, Cleave, Embrace, Hold, Hug, Ring, Tendril

Clinic Abortuary, Antenatal, Dental, Dispensary, Hospital, Hospitium, Mayo, Well-woman

Clink Gingle, Jail, Jingle, Lock up, Prison, Stir, Ting, Tinkle

Clinker Ash, Slag

Clint Limestone

Clip(ped), Clipper, Clipping Alberta, Banana, Barrette, Bicycle, Brash, Bulldog, Butterfly, Cartridge, Chelsea, Clasp, Crocodile, Crop-ear, Crutch, Curt, Curtail, Cut, Cutty Sark, Dag, Dock, Dod, Excerpt, Film, Fleece, Jubilee, Jumar, Krab, Lop, Money, Nail, Outtake, Pace, Paper, Pare, Peg, Prerupt, Prune, Roach, Scissel, Secateur, Shear, Ship, Shore, Shorn, Snip, Spring, Staccato, Tie, Tie-tack, Tinsnips, Toe, Tonsure, Topiarist, Trim

Clippy Cad, Conductor

Clique Cabal, Clan, Club, Coterie, Faction, Four Hundred, Gang, Junta, Ring, Set

Clive Arcot

Cloak(room), Cloaks Aba, Abaya, Abba, Abolla, Amice, Anonymity, Bathroom, Buffalo-robe, Burnous, Capa, Cape, Capote, Caracalla, Cardinal, Cassock, Chasuble, Chimer(e), Chlamydes, Chlamys, Chuddah, Chuddar, Cocoon, Conceal, Cope, Cover, Disguise, Dissemble, Djellaba(h), Domino, Gabardine, Gaberdine, Gal(l)abea(h), Gal(l)abi(y)a(h), Gal(l)abi(y)eh, Gentlemen, Gents, Grego, Hall-robe, Heal, Hele, Himation, Hood, Inverness, Jelab, Jellaba, Joseph, Kaross, Korowai, Manta, Manteau, Manteel, Mant(e)let, Mantle, → **MASK**, Mourning, Mousquetaire, Mozetta, Opera, Paenula, Paletot, Pallium, Paludamentum, Pelisse, Pilch, Poncho, Powder-room, Rail, Revestry, Rocklay, Rokelay, Roquelaure, Sagum, Sarafan, Scapular, → **SCREEN**, Shroud, Swathe, Talma, Toga, Vestiary, Vestry, Visite

Clobber Anoint, Apparel, Do, Dress, Garb, Habiliments, Lam, Tack

Clock Alarm, Ammonia, Analogue, Astronomical, Atomic, Beetle, Big Ben, Biological, Blowball, Body, Bracket, Bundy, Caesium, Carriage, Cartel, Clepsydra, Cuckoo, Dandelion, Digital, Doomsday, Dutch, Floral, Grandfather, Grandmother, Hit, Knock, Long case, Meter, Paenula, Parliament, Quartz, Repeater, Sandglass, Settler's, Solarium, Speaking, Speedo, Strike, Sundial, Taximeter, Tell-tale, Time(r), Turret, Wag at the wa', Water

Clockmaker Fromanteel, Graham, Harrison, Knibb, Mudge, Tompion

Clockwise Deasil, Deasiul, Deasoil, Deiseal, Deisheal

Clockwork Precision, Regular

Clod Clumsy, Divot, Glebe, Lump, Mool, Mould, Mug, Put(t), Scraw, Sod, Stupid, Turf

Clog Accloy, Ball, Block, Clam, Crowd, Dance, Fur, Galosh, Golosh, Hamper, Jam, Lump, Mire, Obstruct, Overshoe, Patten, Sabot

Cloisonné Shippo

Cloister Arcade, Confine, Cortile, Immure, Monastery, Mure, Refuge, Seclude

Clone, Cloning Ramet, Replicant, Reproduce, Therapeutic

Cloots Worricow

Close(d), Closing, Closure Agree, Airless, Alongside, Anigh, Atresia, Block, Boon, By, Cadence, Clammy, Clap, Clench, Collapse, Compact, Complete, Concentration, Cone off, Court, Dear, Debar, Dense, → **END**, Epilogue, Ewest, Eye to eye, Finale, Forby, Gare, Grapple, Handy, Hard, Hard by, Hot, Humid, Imminent, Inbye, Infibulate, Intent, Intimate, Local, Lock, Lucken, Marginal, Mean, Miserly, Muggy, Mure, Narre, Narrow, Near, Nearhand, Neist, Next, Nie, Niggardly, Nigh, Nip and tuck, Obturate, Occlude, Occlusion, Oppressive, Parochial, Penny-pinching, Placket, Precinct, Reserved, Reticent, Seal, Secret, Serre, Serried, Serry, Shet, Shut(ter), Shutdown, Silly, Slam, Snug, Stap, Sticky, Stifling, Stuffy, Sultry, Tailgate, Temenos, Tight, Uproll, Wafer, Wane, Warm, Yard

Close-cropped Crewcut, Not-pated

Close-fitting Skintight, Slinky, Tight

Closet Cabinet, Confine, Cubicle, Cupboard, Dooket, Earth, Locker, Safe, Wardrobe, WC, Zeta

Close-up Detail, Fill, Shut, Stop, Zoom

Closing-time Eleven, End

Clot(ting) Agglutinate, Ass, Clag, Clump, Coagulate, Congeal, Crassamentum, Cruor, Curdle, Dag, Duffer, Embolism, Embolus, Gel, Globule, Gob, Gout, Grume, Incrassate, Incrust, Jell, Lapper, Lopper, → **LUMP**, Mass, Prothrombin, Splatch, Stupid, Thicken, Thrombosis, Thrombus

Clotbuster Heparin

Cloth Aba, Abaya, Abba, Antependium, Bribe, Carmelite, Clergy, Cloot, Clout, Communion, Dishrag, Duster, → **FABRIC**, → **FELT**, Frocking, Frontal, Gremial, G-string, Interfacing, Jharan, Loin, Lungi, Manta, → **MATERIAL**, Mercery, Meshing, Nap, Napery, Napje, Nappie, Neckerchief, Needlework, Netting, Pack, Painted, Pall, Pane, Pilch, Priesthood, Pull-through, Purificator, Puttee, Putty, Rag, Raiment, Roll, Roon, Runner, Sashing, Scarlet, Serviette, Sheet, Sheeting, Shoddy, Stripe, Stuff, Stupe, Sudarium, Supper, Sweatband, T, Tapestry, Tea, → **TEXTILE**, Throw, Tissue, Toilet, Vernicle, Veronica, Washrag, Whole

---

CLOTH

1 letter:	Sulu	Monk's	*6 letters:*
J®	Wire	Mummy	Aertex®
	Wool	Mungo	Alpaca
3 letters:		Ninon	Angora
Abb	*5 letters:*	Nylon	Armure
Lap®	Atlas	Orlon®	Barège
Rep	Baize	Panel	Beaver
Say	Beige	Panne	Bouclé
Web	Binca	Paper	Broche
	Budge	Perse	Burlap
4 letters:	Chino	Pilot	Burnet
Aida	Crape	Piqué	Burrel
Amis	Crash	Plaid	Byssus
Baft	Crepe	Plush	Caddis
Bark	Denim	Poult	Calico
Ciré	Dobby	Print	Camlet
Doek	Drill	Rayon	Camlot
Drab	Duroy	Satin	Canvas
Duck	Fanon	Scrim	Chintz
Fent	Foulé	Serge	Cilice
Flax	Frisé	Slops	Cloqué
Gair	Gauze	Surah	Coburg
Haik	Gazar	Surat	Coutil
Harn	Grass	Surge	Covert
Hyke	Gunny	Tabby	Crepon
Ikat	Haick	Tamin	Cubica
Kelt	Honan	Tammy	Cyprus
Knit	Jaspe	Terry	Dacron®
Lamé	Kanga	Tibet	Damask
Lawn	Kente	Toile	Dévoré
Leno	Khadi	Towel	Dimity
Line	Khaki	Tulle	Domett
Mull	Kikoi	Tweed	Dossal
Nude	Linen	Tweel	Dossel
Pina	Llama	Twill	Dowlas
Puke	Loden	Union	Dralon®
Repp	Lurex®	Voile	Drapet
Rund	Lycra®	Wigan	Duffel
Shag	Moiré		Duffle
Slop	Mongo		Dupion

Durrie
Etamin
Faille
Fannel
Frieze
Gloria
Greige
Gurrah
Haique
Harden
Herden
Hodden
Hoddin
Humhum
Hurden
Jersey
Kersey
Khanga
Kincob
Lampas
Madras
Medley
Melton
Merino
Mohair
Mongoe
Moreen
Muleta
Muslin
Mutton
Nankin
Nettle
Oxford
Pongee
Rateen
Ratine
Russel
Samite
Satara
Sateen
Saxony
Sendal
Shalli
Sherpa
Sindon
Soneri
Stroud
Tactel®
Tamine
Tartan
Tencel®

Thibet
Tricot
Velour
Velure
Velvet
Vicuna
Wadmal
Wincey
Winsey

7 letters:
Abattre
Acrylic
Alamode
Alepine
Baracan
Batiste
Bolting
Brocade
Cabbage
Cambric
Camelot
Challie
Challis
Cheviot
Chiffon
Crombie
Cypress
Delaine
Dhurrie
Doeskin
Dorneck
Dornick
Drabbet
Drapery
Droguet
Drugget
Duvetyn
Etamine
Faconné
Fannell
Fishnet
Flannel
Foulard
Fustian
Galatea
Genappe
Gingham
Gore-tex®
Grogram
Hessian

Holland
Hopsack
Jaconet
Jamdani
Khaddar
Kitenge
Lockram
Mockado
Nankeen
Oil-silk
Oilskin
Organza
Orleans
Ottoman
Paisley
Percale
Printer
Rabanna
Raploch
Raschel
Ratteen
Rattine
Ripstop
Sacking
Sagathy
Schappe
Silesia
Sinamay
Spandex®
Stammel
Supplex®
Tabaret
Tabinet
Taffeta
Tiffany
Tussore
Viyella®
Wadmaal
Webbing
Woolsey
Worsted
Zanella

8 letters:
Aircraft
Algerine
American
Armozeen
Armozine
Arresine
Bagheera

Barathea
Barracan
Bayadere
Bearskin
Bobbinet
Boulting
Brocatel
Cameline
Casement
Cashmere
Casimere
Celanese
Chambray
Chamelot
Chenille
Ciclaton
Corduroy
Corporal
Coteline
Coutille
Cretonne
Drabette
Duchesse
Dungaree
Duvetine
Duvetyne
Eolienne
Florence
Gambroon
Gossamer
Homespun
Jacquard
Jeanette
Lava-lava
Lustring
Mackinaw
Mantling
Marcella
Marocain
Mazarine
Moleskin
Moquette
Nainsook
Organdie
Osnaburg
Pashmina
Plaiding
Pleather
Prunella
Rodevore
Sarcenet

8 letters – cont:
Sarsenet
Sealskin
Shabrack
Shalloon
Shantung
Sicilian
Suedette
Swanskin
Tabbinet
Tarlatan
Toilinet
Velveret
Whipcord
Wild silk
Zibeline

9 letters:
Aeroplane
Alcantara
Balzarine
Bengaline
Bombasine
Calamanco
Cassimere
Cerecloth
Charmeuse®
Ciclatoun
Corporale
Cottonade
Courtelle®
Crepoline
Crimplene®
Crinoline
Evenweave
Fabrikoid®

Farandine
Filoselle
Folk-weave
Gaberdine
Georgette
Grenadine
Grosgrain
Haircloth
Horsehair
Indiennes
Interlock
Kalamkiri
Levantine
Longcloth
Mandilion
Mandylion
Marseille
Matelassé
Messaline
Moygashel
Nitro-silk
Open-weave
Organzine
Overcheck
Paramatta
Penistone
Percaline
Persienne
Pinstripe
Polyester
Ravenduck
Sailcloth
Satin jean
Sharkskin
Silkalene
Silkaline

Stockinet
Strouding
Swansdown
Tarpaulin
Tricotine
Veloutine
Velveteen
Wire gauze
Worcester
Zibelline

10 letters:
Balbriggan
Baldachino
Book muslin
Broadcloth
Brocatelle
Candlewick
Farrandine
Fearnought
Ferrandine
Florentine
Geotextile
Kerseymere
Lutestring
Matellasse
Mousseline
Needlecord
Parramatta
Polycotton
Ravensduck
Russel-cord
Seersucker
Shabracque
Shiveshive
Sicilienne

Taftaffety
Tattersall
Toilinette
Tuftaffeta
Winceyette

11 letters:
Abercrombie
Bedford cord
Canton crepe
Cheesecloth
Cloth of gold
Dotted Swiss
Drap-de-berry
Dreadnought
Hammercloth
Kendal green
Marquisette
Nun's veiling
Sempiternum
Stockinette
Stretch knit
Swiss muslin

12 letters:
Brilliantine
Cavalry twill
Crepe de chine
Elephant cord
Leather-cloth

13 letters:
Gros de Londres
Linsey-woolsey

Cloth-designing Batik
Clothe(s), Clothing, Clothed Accoutrements, Apparel, Array, Attire, Baggies, Besee, Bib and tucker, Cape, Casuals, Chasuble, Choli, Cits, Clad, Clericals, Clobber, Coat, Combinations, Confection, Coordinates, Costume, Cour, Cover, Croptop, Cruisewear, Deck, Dicht, Diffusion line, Dight, Don, Drag, → **DRESS**, Duds, Emboss, Endue, Fig leaf, Finery, Frippery, Garb, Garments, Gear, Gere, Get-up, Glad rags, Grave, Gymslip, Habit, Haute couture, Hejab, Innerwear, Judogi, Jumps, Kimono, Layette, Leathers, Lederhosen, Long-togs, Matumba, Mocker, Muff, Outfit, Pannicle, Plain, Playsuit, Raggery, Rag trade, Raiment, Rami, Rigout, Robes, Samfoo, Samfu, Schmutter, Scrubs, Scungies, Shirtwaister, Shmatte, Shroud, Slops, Sunday best, Swaddling, Swathe, Swothling, Tackle, Things, Togs, Tracksuit, Trappings, Trews, Trousseau, Tweeds, Two-piece, Vernicle, Vestiary, Vestiture, Vestment, Wardrobe, Watteau, Weeds, Widow's weeds, Workwear, Yclad, Ycled, Y-fronts

Clothes basket, Clothes horse Airer, Petara, Winterhedge

Cloud(ing), Clouded, Cloudiness, Cloudy Altocumulus, Altostratus, Banner, Benight, C, Cataract, Cirrocumulus, Cirrostratus, Cirrus, Coalsack, Coma, Contrail, Crab Nebula, Cumulonimbus, Cumulus, Dim, Dull, Emission nebula, Fog, Fractocumulus, Fractostratus, Funnel, Goat's hair, Haze, Horsehead Nebula, Infuscate, Magellanic, Mammatus, Mare's tail, Milky, Mist, Molecular, Mushroom, Nacreous, Nephele, Nephelometer, Nepho-, Nimbostratus, Nimbus, Nubecula, Nubilous, Nuée ardente, Obnubilation, Obscure, Octa, Okta, Oort, Overcast, Pall, Pother, Protostar, Rack, Roily, Stain, Storm, Stratocumulus, Strat(o)us, Thunder(head), Turbid, Virga, War, Water-dog, Weft, Woolpack, Zero-zero

Cloudberry Mountain bramble

Cloudless Serene

Clough Dale, Gorge, Ravine

Clout Belt, Cloth, Hit, Influence, Lap(pie), Lapje, Power, Pull, Raddle

Clove Chive, Eugenia, Rose-apple, Split

Clover Alfalfa, Alsike, Berseem, Calvary, Cinque, Cow-grass, Four-leaf, Hare's foot, Hop, Hop-trefoil, Japan, Ladino, Lespedeza, Medic(k), Melilot, Owl's, Pin, Rabbit-foot, Red, Serradella, Serradilla, Shamrock, Souple, Sucklers, Suckling, Sweet, Trefoil, Trilobe, Truelove, White

Clown(ish) Airhead, Antic, Antick, August(e), Boor, Bor(r)el, Buffoon, Carl, Chough, Chuff, Clout-shoe, Coco, → **COMEDIAN**, Comic, Costard, Daff, Feste, Froth, Girner, Gobbo, Goon, Gracioso, Grimaldi, Harlequin, Hob, Idiot, Jack-pudding, Jester, Joey, Joker, Joskin, Leno, Merry Andrew, Mountebank, Nedda, Nervo, Patch(c) ocke, Peasant, Pickle-herring, Pierrot, Put, Rustic, Slouch, Thalian, Touchstone, Trinculo, Wag, Zany

Cloy(ing) Choke, Clog, Glut, Pall, Satiate, Surfeit, Sweet

Club(s), Club-like Adelphi, Airn, Alloa, Almack's, Alpeen, Apex, Army and Navy, Arsenal, Artel, Association, Athen(a)eum, Baffy, Band(y), Basto, Bat, Bath, Beefsteak, Blackjack, Blaster, Bludgeon, Boodles, Bourdon, Brassie, Breakfast, Brook's, Bulger, C, Caman, Card, Carlton, Caterpillar, Cavalry, Chartered, Chigiriki, Clavate, Cleek, Clip-joint, Combine, Compassion, Conservative, Constitutional, Cordeliers, Cosh, Cotton, Country, Crockford's, Cudgel, Devonshire, Disco(theque), Driver, Driving iron, Drones, Fan, Farm team, Fascio, Feuillant, Fleshpot, Fustigate, Garrick, Glee, Golf, Guards, Guild, Hampden, Health, Hell-fire, Hercules', Hetairia, Honky-tonk, Indian, Investment, Iron, Jacobin, Jigger, Job, Jockey, Junior Carlton, Kennel, Kierie, Kiri, Kitcat, Kiwanis, Knobkerrie, Landsdowne, Lathi, Laughter, League, Leander, Lions, Lofter, Luncheon, Mace, Mallet, Mashie, Maul, Mell, Mere, Meri, Mess, Midiron, Monday, National Liberal, Niblick, Night(stick), Nightspot, Nitery, Nulla(-nulla), Oddfellows, Paris, Patu, Pitching wedge, Polt, Pregnant, Priest, Provident, Pudding, Putter, Putting-cleek, Quarterstaff, RAC, R & A, Reform, Ring, Rota, Rotarian, Rotary, Round Table, Sand wedge, Savage, Savile, Shillelagh, Slate, Society, Soroptimist, Sorosis, Spoon, Spot, Spurs, Strike, Strip, Supper, Texas wedge, Thatched House, Tong, Travellers, Trefoil, Truncheon, Trunnion, Union, United Services, Variety, Waddy, Warehouse, Wedge, White's, Wood, Yacht, Youth

Club-foot Kyllosis, Po(u)lt-foot, Talipes, Varus

Clubman Member

Club-rush Deer-hair, Scirpus, Sedge

Cluck Chirrup, Dent

Clue Across, Anagram, Ball, Charade, Clavis, Dabs, Down, → **HINT**, Inkling, Key, Lead, Light, Rebus, Scent, Scooby(doo), Signpost, Thread, Tip

Clueless Ignorant

Clump Cluster, Finial, Knot, Mass, Mot(te), Patch, Plump, Tread, Tuft, Tump, Tussock

▷ **Clumsily** *may indicate* an anagram

Clumsy Artless, Awkward, Bauchle, Bungling, Butterfingers, Cack-handed, Calf, Chuckle, Clatch, Clodhopper, Cumbersome, Dub, Dutch, Galoot, Gauche, Gimp, Ham(-fisted), Heavy-handed, Horse-godmother, Hulk, Inapt, Inelegant, Inept, Inexpert, Klutz, Lob, Loutish, Lubbard, Lubber, Lumbering, Lummox, Lumpish, Maladdress, Maladroit, Mauther, Mawr, Mawther, Messy, Mor, Nerd, Nurd, Oafish, Off-ox, Palooka, Plonking, Rough, S(c)hlemiel, Schlemihl, Spastic, Spaz(zy), Squab, Stot, Swab, Swob, Taupie, Tawpie, Two-fisted, Unco, Ungain, Unskilful, Unsubtle, Unwieldy

Cluster Acervate, Ament, Assemble, Asterism, Bunch, Clump, Collection, Concentre, Constellate, Conurbation, Corymb, Cyme, Gather, Gear, Globular, Glomeration, Knot, Oakleaf, Packet, Plump, Raceme, Sheaf, Sorus, Strap, Thyrse, Tone, Truss, Tuffe, Tuft, Umbel, Verticillaster

Clutch(es) Battery, Brood, Chickens, Clasp, Cling, Eggs, Friction, Glaum, Grab, → **GRASP**, Gripe, Nest, Net, Seize, Sitting, Squeeze

Clutter Confusion, Litter, Mess, Rummage

Coach Battlebus, Berlin, Bogie, Bus, Car, Carriage, Chara, Clerestory, Crammer, Diligence, Dilly, Double-decker, Drag, Edifier, Fiacre, Fly, Four-in-hand, Gig, Griddle car, Hackney, Handler, Landau(let), Life, Microbus, Mourning, Phaeton, Post chaise, Pullman, Railcar, Rattler, Repetiteur, Saloon, Shay, Sleeper, Slip, Sobriety, Stage, Surrey, Tally(-ho), Teach(er), Thoroughbrace, Train(er), Tutor, Voiture

Coach-horse Rove-beetle

Coachman Automedon, Bunene, Coachy, Dragsman, Jarvey, Jehu, John

Coagulant, Coagulate, Coagulation Cautery, Clot, Congeal, Curds, Jell, Rennet, Run, Runnet, Set, Solidify, Thicken

Coal Anthracite, Bituminous, Black diamonds, Block, Brown, Burgee, Cannel, Char, Cherry, Clinker, Coking, Coom, Crow, Culm, Day, Dice, Edge, Eldin, Ember, Fusain, Gas, Gathering, Hard, Jud, Knob, Lignite, Maceral, Mineral, Nut, Open-cast, Paper, Parrot, Pea, Purse, Sapropelite, Score, Sea, Slack, Soft, Splint, Steam, Stone, Vitrain, Wallsend, White, Wood

Coalesce(nce) Amalgamate, Concrete, Fuse, Merge, Sintery, Synaloepha, Unite

Coalfish Saith

Coalition Alliance, Bloc, Janata, Merger, Rainbow, Tie

Coal-tar Cresol, Indene

Coal-tub Corf, Dan, Scuttle

Coarse(ness) Base, Bawdy, Blowzy, Bran, Broad, Common, Crude, Dowlas, Earthy, Fisherman, Foul, Gneissose, Grained, Grobian, Gross, Grossièreté, Haggery, Ham, Illbred, Indelicate, Low-bred, Plebeian, Rabelaisian, Rank, Rappee, Raunchy, Ribald, Rough, Rudas, Rude, Russet, Sackcloth, Schlub, Semple, Slob, Sotadic, Unrefined, Vulgar

Coast(al) Barbary, Beach, Bight, Caird, Causeway, Coromandel, Costa, Drift, Freewheel, Glide, Gold, Hard, Ivory, Littoral, Longshore, Malabar, Maritime, Murman(sk), Orarian, Riviera, Scrieve, Seaboard, Seafront, Seashore, Seaside, → **SHORE**, Slave, Sledge, Strand, Toboggan, Trucial

Coaster Beermat, Drog(h)er, Mat, Roller, Ship

Coastguard CG, Gobby

Coastline Watermark

Coast-road Corniche
Coat(ed), Coating Abaya, Ab(b)a, Achkan, Acton, Admiral, Afghan, Anarak,
  Anodise, Anorak, Balmacaan, Barathea, Basan, Bathrobe, Belton, Benjamin,
  Blazer, Bloomed, Box, British warm, Buff, Buff-jerkin, Calcimine, Car, Chesterfield,
  Cladding, Claw-hammer, Clearcole, Cloak, Clutch, Cocoon, Coolie, Cover,
  Covert, Creosote, Crust(a), Cutaway, Dip, Doggett's, Drape, Dress, Duffel, Duster,
  Electroplate, Enamel, Encrust, Envelope, Ermelin, Ermine, Exine, Extine,
  Fearnought, Film, Fleece, Frock, Fur, Gabardine, Galvanise, Gambeson, Ganoin,
  Glaze, Grego, Ground, Ha(c)queton, Hair, Happi, Impasto, Integument, Inverness,
  Iridise, Jack(et), Jemmy, Jerkin, Jodhpuri, Joseph, Jump, Jupon, Lacquer, Lammie,
  Lammy, Lanugo, Layer, Laying, Limewash, Loden, Lounge, Mac, Mackinaw,
  Matinee, Metallise, Morning, Newmarket, → **OVERCOAT**, Paint, Paper, Paletot,
  Palla, Parka, Parkee, Passivate, Patinate, Pebbledash, Pelage, Pelisse, Perfuse,
  Peridium, Petersham, Plate, Polo, Pos(h)teen, Primer, Primine, Prince Albert,
  Raglan, Redingote, Resin, Resist, Riding, Roquelaure, Sack, Salband, Saque, Sclera,
  Sclerotic, Scratch, Seal, Sheepskin, Shellac, Sherardise, Sherwani, Silver, Skinwork,
  Spencer, Sports, Stadium, Surtout, Swagger, Swallowtail(ed), Tabard, Taglioni,
  Tail, Tar, Teflon, Tent, Top, Trench, Truss, Trusty, Tunic, Tuxedo, Ulster(ette),
  Underseal, Veneer, Verdigris, Warm, Wash, Whitewash, Windjammer, Wool,
  Wrap-rascal, Zamarra, Zamarro, Zinc
Coat of arms Crest, Hatchment
Coat-tail Flap
Coax Blandish, Blarney, Cajole, Carn(e)y, Cuittle, Entice, Flatter, Lure, Persuade,
  Wheedle, Whillywha(w)
Cob Hazel(nut), Horse
Cobalt Co, Zaffer, Zaffre
Cobble(s), Cobbled, Cobbler(s), Cobblestone Bunkum, Claptrap, Clicker, Coggle,
  Cosier, Cozier, Mend, Patch, Pie, Rot, Snob, Soutar, Souter, Sowter, Stone, Sutor,
  Twaddle, Vamp
Cobra King
Cobweb(by) Arachnoid, Araneous, Gossamer, Snare, Trap
Cocaine Basuco, C, Charlie, Coke, Crystal, Freebase, Moonrock, Nose candy,
  Number, Ready-wash, Snow
Coccid Wax-insect
Cochlear Scala
Cock(y) Alectryon, Ball, Capon, Chanticleer, Chaparral, Erect, Escape, Fighting, Flip,
  Fowl, France, Fugie, Half, Hay, Heath, Jack-the-lad, Jaunty, Midden, Penis, Perk,
  Roadrunner, Robin, Rooster, Shake-bag, Snook, Strut, Sunshine, Swaggering, Tap,
  Tilt, Turkey, Vain, Valve, Vane
Cock-a-hoop Crowing, Elated
Cockatoo Bird, Corella, Galah, Leadbeater's, Major Mitchell, Parrot
Cockboat Cog
Cockchafer Humbuzz, Maybug
Cock crow Skreigh of the day
Cocker Blenheim, Cuiter, Spaniel
Cockeyed Agee, Askew, Skewwhiff
Cockfight(ing) By(e), Main
Cockle Bulge, Crease, Wrinkle
▷ **Cockle(s)** *may indicate* an anagram
Cockney 'Arriet, 'Arry, Bow, Eastender, Londoner, Londonese
▷ **Cockney** *may indicate* a missing h

Cockpit Greenhouse, Office, Well
Cockroach Archy, Beetle, Black beetle, Croton bug, German, Oriental, Orthoptera
▶ **Cockscomb** *see* **COXCOMB**
Cocktail Alexander, Aperitif, Atomic, Bellini, Between the sheets, Black Russian, Bloody Mary, Brandy Alexander, Buck's fizz, Bumbo, Bullshot, Calpirinha, Champagne cocktail, Cobbler, Cold duck, Crusta, Daiquiri, → **DRINK**, Egg-flip, Fruit, Fustian, Gibson, Gimlet, Grasshopper, Harvey Wallbanger, Highball, → **HORSE**, Horse's neck, Julep, Mai-Tai, Manhattan, Margarita, Martini®, Melange, Mix, Molotov, Moscow mule, Old-fashioned, Piña colada, Pink lady, Planter's punch, Prawn, Punch, Rickey, Rusty nail, Sangaree, Sangria, Sazerac®, Screwdriver, Sherry cobbler, Side-car, Singapore sling, Slammer, Snakebite, Snowball, Spritzer, Stengah, Stinger, Swizzle, Tequila sunrise, Tom Collins, Twist, White-lady, White russian
Cocoa Criollo, Nib(s)
Coconut Coco-de-mer, Coir, Copra, Head, Madafu, Poonac, Toddy-palm
Cocoon Dupion, Mother, Pod, Swathe, Trehala
Cod Bag, Cape, Coalfish, Fish, Gade, Gadus, Haberdine, Keeling, Kid, Lob, Man, Morrhua, Murray, Red, Saith, Saltfish, Stockfish, Tease, Torsk, Tusk, Whiting
Coda End(ing), Epilogue, Rondo, Tail
Coddle Cosset, Molly, Nancy, Pamper, Pet, Poach
Code, Coding, Codification Access, Alphanumeric, Amalfitan, Area, Bar, Barred, Binary, Brevity, Bushido, Canon, Character, Cipher, City, Civil, Clarendon, Codex, Colour, Computing, Condition, Cookie, Country, Cryptogram, Cryptograph, Dialling, Disciplinary, Dogma, Dress, DX, EBCDIC, Enigma, Error, Escape, Ethics, Fuero, Genetic, Gray, Green Cross, Hammurabic, Highway, Hollerith, Iddy-umpty, Justinian, MAC, Machine, Morse, Napoleon(ic), National, Object, Omerta, Opcode, Penal, PGP, Pindaric, Postal, Price, Reflective binary, Rulebook, Scytale, Sharia, Shulchan Aruch, Signal, Sort, Source, STD, Talmud, Time, Twelve Tables, Zip
Code-breaker, Code-breaking Bletchley Park, Malpractitioner
Codger Buffer, Fellow
Codicil Addition, Label, PS, Rider, Supp(lement)
Codon Initiator
Coefficient Absorption, Correlation, Differential, Diffusion, Distribution, Modulus, Partition, Pearson's correlation, Permeability, Saturation, Spearman's rank-order, Transmission, Young modulus
Coelacanth Latimeria
Coerce, Coercion Big stick, Bully, Compel, Dragoon, Duress, Gherao, Pressure, Railroad, Restrain, Threaten
Coffee, Coffee beans, Coffee pot Americano, Arabica, Brazil, Cafetiere, Cappuccino, Decaff, Demi-tasse, Espresso, Expresso, Filter, Frappuccino, Gaelic, Gloria, Granules, Instant, Irish, Java, Latte, Macchiato, Mocha, Peaberry, Percolator, Robusta, Rye, Skinny latte, Tan, Triage, Turkish
Coffee-house Lloyd's
Coffer Ark, Box, Casket, Cassone, Chest, Lacunar, Locker
Coffin Bier, Box, Casket, Hearse, Kist, Larnax, Sarcophagus, Shell, Wooden kimono, Wooden overcoat
Cog(ged) Contrate, Mitre-wheel, Nog, Pinion, Tooth
Cogent Compelling, Forceful, Good, Sound, Telling
Cogitate Deliberate, Mull, Muse, Ponder
Cognate Paronym
Cohabit Bed, Indwell, Share

Co-heir Parcener
Cohere(nt) Agglutinate, Clear, Cleave, Cling, Logical, Stick
Cohort Colleague, Crony, Soldier
Coif Calotte, Cap, Hood
Coiffure Hairdo, Pompadour, Tête
Coil(s), Coiled Armature, Bight, Bought, Choke, Choking, Circinate, Clew, Clue, Convolute(d), Convolve, Curl, Current, Fake, Fank, Flemish, Furl, Hank, Helix, Ignition, Induction, Loading, Mortal, Moving, Primary, Resistance, Rouleau, Scorpioid, Solenoid, Spark, Spiral, Spiraster, Spire, Tesla, Tickler, Toroid, Twine, Twirl, → **WIND**, Wound, Wreath, Writhe, Yoke
Coin Base, Bean, Bit, Broad(piece), Cash, Change, Coign(e), Contomiate, Copper, Create, Doctor, Dosh, Double-header, Dump(s), Fiddler's money, Fiver, Han(d)sel, Imperial, Invent, Lucky piece, Lwei, Make, Mill, Mint, → **MONEY**, Neoterise, Numismatic, Nummary, Piece, Plate, Pocket-piece, Proof, Shiner, Slip, Specie, Stamp, Sterling, Strike, Subsidiary, Sum, Tenner, Thin'un, Token, Touchpiece, Unity

COINS

1 letter:	Mna	Inti	Reis
D	Moy	Jack	Rial
	Ore	Jane	Riel
2 letters:	Pul	Jiao	Rock
As	Pya	Kina	Ryal
DM	Red	Kobo	Sene
Kr	Sen	Kuna	Sent
Rd	Sol	Kyat	Slog
Xu	Som	Lari	Tael
	Sou	Lion	Taka
3 letters:	Won	Lipa	Tala
Avo	Yen	Lira	Tein
Ban	Zuz	Loti	Toea
Bar		Luma	Tray
Bob	4 letters:	Maik	Trey
Cob	Anna	Mark	Vatu
Dam	Baht	Merk	Yuan
Ecu	Bani	Mina	Zack
Fen	Birr	Mite	
Fil	Buck	Mule	5 letters:
Fin	Cedi	Obol	Agora
Flu	Cent	Para	Angel
Hao	Chon	Paul	Asper
Jun	Dibs	Peag	Aurar
Kip	Dime	Peni	Baiza
Lat	Doit	Peso	Bekah
Lei	Dong	Pice	Belga
Lek	Dram	Pula	Bodle
Leu	Duro	Puli	Brown
Lev	Euro	Punt	Butat
Lew	Fiat	Rand	Butut
Mil	Fils	Real	Chiao

5 letters – cont:

Colon	Pengo	Danace	Satang
Conto	Penie	Deaner	Sceatt
Crore	Penni	Décime	Seniti
Cross	Penny	Denier	Sequin
Crown	Plack	Derham	Shekel
Daric	Pound	Dirham	Sickle
Dibbs	Razoo	Dirhem	Siglos
Dinar	Rider	Dodkin	Somoni
Diram	Royal	Dollar	Stater
Dobra	Ruble	Double	Stiver
Ducat	Rupee	Drachm	Stotin
Eagle	Sceat	Ekuele	Talent
Eyrir	Scudo	Escudo	Tanner
Franc	Scute	Filler	Tester
Fugio	Semis	Florin	Teston
Gazet	Sente	Forint	Thaler
Gerah	Shand	Gilder	Tickey
Gopik	Smelt	Gourde	Toonie
Groat	Soldo	Guinea	Tugrik
Grosz	Souon	Gulden	Turner
Haler	Sucre	Halala	Vellon
Khoum	Sycee	Heller	Wakiki
Krona	Tenge	Hryvna	
Krone	Thebe	Jitney	**7 letters:**
Kroon	Tical	Kobang	Afghani
Kurus	Ticky	Koruna	Austral
Laari	Tiyin	Kroner	Bolivar
Laree	Tolar	Kroona	Cardecu
Leone	Toman	Kruger	Carolus
Liard	Tyiyn	Kwacha	Centavo
Litai	Unite	Kwanza	Chetrum
Litas	Zaire	Lepton	Cordoba
Livre	Zimbi	Likuta	Crusado
Louis	Zloty	Loonie	Drachma
Lyart		Makuta	Ekpwele
Maile	**6 letters:**	Mancus	Guarani
Manat	Agorol	Markka	Guilder
Maneh	Ariary	Mawpus	Hryvnya
Mohur	Aureus	Mongoe	Jacobus
Mongo	Balboa	Pa'anga	Joannes
Mopus	Bawbee	Paduan	Kopiyka
Naira	Bender	Pagoda	Kreuzer
Nakfa	Bezant	Pataca	Lemoira
Ngwee	Boddle	Pennia	Lisente
Noble	Byzant	Peseta	Metical
Obang	Canary	Pesewa	Millime
Oscar	Centas	Qintar	Milreis
Paisa	Colone	Rappen	Moidore
Paolo	Copeck	Rouble	Ostmark
Pence	Couter	Rupiah	Ouguiya
	Dalasi	Santum	Patrick

Piastre
Piefort
Pistole
Pollard
Quarter
Quetzal
Ringgit
Ruddock
Rufiyaa
Sextans
Solidus
Spanker
Tambala
Testoon
Testril
Thick'un
Thrimsa
Thrymsa
Tughrik
Unicorn
Xerafin

8 letters:
Brockage
Cardecue
Cruzeiro
Denarius
Doubloon

Ducatoon
Emalengi
Farthing
Groschen
Johannes
Kreutzer
Llangeni
Louis d'or
Maravedi
Millieme
Napoleon
Ngultrum
Picayune
Pistolet
Planchet
Portague
Portigue
Quadrans
Rigmarie
Semuncia
Sesterce
Shilling
Skilling
Solidare
Spur-rial
Spur-ryal
Stotinka
Twopence

Xeraphin
Zecchino

9 letters:
Boliviano
Britannia
Centesimo
Dandiprat
Dandyprat
Didrachma
Dupondius
Fourpence
Half-eagle
Half-tiger
Luckpenny
Maple leaf
Ninepence
Pistareen
Rennminbi
Rix-dollar
Rose noble
Schilling
Sou marque
Sovereign
Spur-royal
Yellowboy
Zwanziger

10 letters:
Chervonets
Krugerrand
Portcullis
Reichsmark
Siege-piece

11 letters:
Bonnet-piece
Deutschmark
Double eagle
Sword-dollar
Tetradrachm

12 letters:
Antoninianus
Iraimbilanja

13 letters:
Half-sovereign
Rennminbi yuan

14 letters:
Three-farthings

18 letters:
Maria Theresa
dollar

Coinage Currency, Invention, Nonce-word
Coincide(nt), Coincidence Accident, Chance, Consilience, Conterminous, Fit,
   Fluke, Homotaxis, Overlap, Rabat(to), Simultaneous, Synastry, Synchronise, Tally
Coke Chark, Coal, Cocaine, Kola
Col Pass, Poort, Saddle
Cold(-blooded) Ague, Algid, Aloof, Apathetic, Arctic, Austere, Biting, Bitter, Bleak,
   Blue, Brr(r), C, Catarrh, Cauld(rife), Charity, Chill(y), Colubrine, Common, Coryza,
   Dead, Ectotherm, Emotionless, Frappé, Frem(d), Fremit, Frigid, Frost(y), Gelid,
   Glacial, Hiemal, Icy, Impersonal, Jeel, Nippy, Nirlit, Parky, Passionless, Perishing,
   Piercing, Poikilotherm(ic), Polar, Psychro-, Remote, Rheumy, Rigor, Rume, Snap,
   Snell, Sniffles, Sour, Standoffish, Starving, Streamer, Subzero, Taters, Unmoved,
   Weed, Wintry
Cold sore Herpes, Shiver
Coldstream Borderer, Guard
Cole Colza, King, Nat, Porter
Colic Batts, Bots, Botts, Gripe, Lead, Painter's, Sand, Upset, Zinc
Collaborate, Collaborator, Collaboration Assist, Combine, → **COOPERATE**,
   Keiretsu, Quisling, Synergy, Vichy, Vichyite, Vichysoiss(e)
Collage Cut up, Paste up
Collapse, Collapsing Apoplexy, Breakdown, Buckle, Cave, Conk, Crash, Crumble,
   Crumple, Debacle, Downfall, Fail(ure), Fall, Flake out, Fold, Founder, Give,
   Implode, Inburst, Landslide, Meltdown, Phut, Purler, Rack, Rickety, Rot, Ruin,

Scat(ter), Sink, Slump, Stroke, Subside, Sunstroke, Swoon, Telescope, Tumble, Wilt, Wrack, Zonk

▷ **Collapsing** *may indicate* an anagram

Collar(ed) Arrest, Astrakhan, Bermuda, Bertha, Berthe, Bib, Bishop, Blue, Brecham, Buster, Butterfly, Button-down, Buttonhole, Capture, Carcanet, Chevesaile, Choke(r), Clerical, Collet, Dog, Esses, Eton, Falling-band, Flea, Gorget, Grandad, Hame, Head(stall), Holderbat, Horse, Jabot, Jampot, Karenni, Mandarin, Moran, Mousquetaire, Nab, Nail, Neckband, Necklet, Ox-bow, Peter Pan, Piccadell, Piccadillo, Piccadilly, Pikadell, Pink, Polo, Puritan, Rabaline, Rabato, Rebater, Rebato, Revers, Rollneck, Roman, Ruff, Sailor, Seize, Shawl, Steel, Storm, Tackle, Tappet, Tie-neck, Torque, Turndown, Turtleneck, Vandyke, Whisk, White, Wing, Yoke

Collation Comparison, Meal, Repast

Colleague(s) Ally, Associate, Bedfellow, Confrère, Mate, Mentor, Oppo, Partner, Team, Workmate

Collect(ion), Collected, Collective(ly), Collectivism, Collector Accrue, Agglomerate, Aggregate, Album, Alms, Amass, Amildar, Ana, Anthology, Arcana, Assemble, Aumil, Bank, Bow, Budget, Bunch, Bundle, Burrell, Caboodle, Calm, Cap, Cete, Clan, Clowder, Compendium, Compile, Congeries, Conglomerate, Covey, Cull, Dossier, Dustman, Earn, Egger, Exaltation, Exordial, Fest, (Fest)schrift, Fetch, Florilegium, Gaggle, Garbo, Garner, Gather, Get, Gilbert, Glean, Glossary, Grice, Heap, Herd, Hive, Idant, In all, Jingbang, Job lot, Kit, Kitty, Levy, Library, Loan, Magpie, Meal, Meet, Meinie, Mein(e)y, Menagerie, Menyie, Miscellany, Mish-mash, Montem, Munro-bagger, Murmuration, Museum, Muster, Nide, Offertory, Omnibus, Omnium-gatherum, Pack, Paddling, Pile, Plate, Pod, Post, Prayer, Quest, Raft, Raise, Rammle, Recheat, Rhapsody, Rouleau, Scramble, Sedge, Self-possessed, Serene, Set, Shoe, Siege, Skein, Smytrie, Sord, Sottisier, Sounder, Spring, Stand, Tahsildar, Team, Toolkit, Troop, Unkindness, Ujamaa, Uplift, Watch, Wernher, Whipround, Wisp

▷ **Collection** *may indicate* an anagram

Collection-box Brod, Ladle, Rammle

Collectorate Taluk

College(s) Academy, All Souls, Alma mater, Ampleforth, Balliol, Brasenose, Business, C, Caius, Campus, CAT, Cheltenham, Clare, Classical, Coed, Commercial, Community, Corpus, Cow, Cranwell, Downing, Dulwich, Electoral, Emmanuel, Eton, Exeter, Foundation, Freshwater, Girton, Grande école, Hall, Heralds', Jail, Junior, Keble, King's, Lancing, Linacre, Lincoln, LSE, Lycée, Lyceum, Madras(s) a(h), Madressah, Magdalen(e), Marlborough, Medrese, Medresseh, Merton, Newnham, Nuffield, Open, Oriel, Pembroke, Poly, Polytechnic, Pontifical, Protonotariat, Queen's, Ruskin, Sacred, St Johns, Saliens, Sandhurst, Selwyn, Seminary, Sixth-form, Somerville, Sorbonne, Staff, Tech(nical), Technikon, Tertiary, Theologate, Training, Trinity, Tug, UMIST, Up, Village, Wadham, Winchester, Yeshiva(h)

Collide, Collision Afoul, Barge, Bird-strike, Bump, Cannon, Carom(bole), Clash, Dash, Elastic, Fender-bender, Foul, Head-on, Hurtle, Impact, Inelastic, Into, Kiss, Meet, Pile-up, Prang, Rencounter, Smash-up, Strike, Thwack

Collie Bearded, Border, Dog, Kelpie, Kelpy, Rough, Sheepdog

Collier Geordie, Hoastman, Miner, Necklace, Patience, Ship

Colloid Aerogel, Gel, Lyophil(e), Sol

Collude, Collusive Abet, Cahoots, Conspire, Deceive

Colon Aspinwall, C(a)ecum, Sigmoid, Spastic, Transverse

Colonel Blimp, Bogey, Chinstrap, Col, Everard, Goldstick, Newcome, Nissen, Pride

Colonial(ist), Colonist Ant, Antenatal, Bee, Boer, Creole, Emigré, Goan, Oecist, Oikist, Overseas, Phoenician, Pioneer, Planter, Polyp(e), Settler, Sicel(iot), Sikel(ian), Sikeliot, Stuyvesant, Swarm, Territorial, Voter, Wasp

Colonnade Eustyle, File, Gallery, Peristyle, Porch, Portico, Stoa

Colony Aden, Burkina Faso, Cape, Charter, Cleruchy, Crown, Dependency, Gibraltar, Halicarnassian, Hive, Hongkong, Kaffraria, Nudist, Penal, Plymouth, Presidio, Proprietary, Rookery, Settlement, Swarm, Termitarium, Warren, Zambia, Zimbabwe

Colophony Rosin

Colossal → ENORMOUS, Epochal, Gigantic, Huge, Vast

Colosseum Amphitheatre

Colour(ed), Colouring, Colours Achromatic, Bedye, Blee, Blush, C, Cap, Chromatic, Chrome, Complementary, Complexion, Crayon, Criant, Cross, Distort, Dye, False, Film, Flag, Florid, Flying, Gouache, Haem, → HUE, Imbue, Ink, Irised, Kalamkari, Leer, Local, Lutein, Metif, Nankeen, Orpiment, Palette, Pantone®, Pastel, Pied, Pigment, Pochoir, Polychrome, Primary, Prism, Prismatic, Process, Queen's, Raddle, Reddle, Regimental, Rinse, Riot, Ruddle, Secondary, Sematic, Shade, Shot, Solid, Spectrum, Startle, Tertiary, Tie-dye, Tinctorial, Tinc(ture), Tinge, Tint, Tone, Uvea, Wash

COLOURS

2 letters:	Roan	Rouge	Apricot
Or	Rose	Sepia	Arnotto
	Ruby	Taupe	Caramel
3 letters:	Sand	Tenné	Crimson
Bay	Teal	Tenny	Emerald
Dun	Vert	Umber	Filemot
Jet	Woad		Gamboge
Red		**6 letters:**	Magenta
Tan	**5 letters:**	Anatta	Oatmeal
	Beige	Anatto	Old gold
4 letters:	Camel	Auburn	Old rose
Anil	Chica	Bisque	Saffron
Bice	Coral	Bister	Scarlet
Blue	Cream	Bistre	Umbrage
Buff	Eosin	Cerise	
Cyan	Flame	Day-Glo®	**8 letters:**
Ecru	Green	Isabel	Alizarin
Fawn	Gules	Maroon	Burgundy
Gold	Ivory	Orange	Cardinal
Grey	Khaki	Reseda	Chestnut
Jade	Lemon	Roucou	Cinnamon
Lake	Lilac	Sienna	Eau de nil
Lime	Lovat	Titian	Lavender
Navy	Mauve	Tusser	Off-white
Pink	Ochre		Pea-green
Plum	Olive	**7 letters:**	Philamot
Puce	Peach	Annatta	Philomot
Puke	Pearl	Annatto	

9 letters:	Solferino	French navy	**12 letters:**
Alizarine	Turquoise	Tartrazine	Cappagh-brown
Anthocyan	Vermilion	Vermillion	Dragon's blood
Carnation			
Chocolate	**10 letters:**	**11 letters:**	
Royal blue	Aquamarine	Ultramarine	

Colour blindness Daltonism, Deuteranopia, Dichrom(at)ism, Monochromatic, Protanomaly, Protanopia, Protanopic, Tritanopia

▷ **Coloured** *may indicate* an anagram

Colourful Abloom, Brave, Flamboyant, Flowery, Iridescent, Kaleidoscope, Opalescent, Splashy, Vivid

Colourless Albino, Bleak, Drab, Dull, Faded, Hyalite, Pallid, Pallor, Wan, White

Colour-spot Gutta

Colt C, Cade, Foal, Gun, Hogget, Sta(i)g, Teenager, Two-year-old

Columbine Aquilegia

Column(s), Column foot Agony, Anta, Atlantes, Clustered, Commentary, Control, Corinthian, Correspondence, Cylinder, Decastyle, Diastyle, Doric, Editorial, Eustyle, Fifth, File, Flying, Fractionating, Geological, Gossip, Hypostyle, Impost, Lat, Lonelyhearts, Monolith, Nelson's, Newel, Obelisk, Pericycle, Peripteral, Peristyle, Persian, Personal, Pilaster, → **PILLAR**, Pilotis, Prostyle, Pycnostyle, Rouleau, Row, Short, Spina, Spinal, Spine, Stalactite, Stalagmite, Steering, Stylobate, Systyle, Tabulate, Telamone, Third, Tige, Tore, Torus, Trajan's, Vertebral

Columnist Advertiser, Agony aunt, Caryatid, Newsman, Stylite, Telamon, Writer

Coma(tose) Apoplexy, Crown, Sedated, Sleep, Torpor, Trance

Comb(er), Combed, Combing Afro, Alveolate, Beehive, Breaker, Card, Copple, Crest, Curry, Dredge, Fine-tooth, Hackle, Heckle, Hot, Kaim, Kame, Kangha, Kemb, Noils, Pecten, Pectinal, Rake, Red(d), Ripple(r), Rose, Scribble, Search, Side, Small tooth, Smooth, Tease(l), Toaze, Tooth, Tose, Toze, Trawl, Tuft, Wave

Combat(ant), Combative Argument, Batteilant, → **BATTLE**, Competitor, Conflict, Contest, Dispute, Duel, → **FIGHT**, Gladiator, Joust, Judicial, Jujitsu, Just, Karate, Kendo, Krav mega, List, Mêlée, Militant, Oppose, Paintball, Protagonist, Spear-running, Unarmed, Vet(eran), War

Combination, Combine(d), Combining Accrete, Alligate, Ally, Amalgam, Associate, Axis, Bloc, Cartel, Cleave, Clique, Coalesce, Coalition, Composite, Concoction, Conflated, Conglomerate, Consolidate, Consortium, Coordinate, Crasis, Fuse, Group, Harvester, Incorporate, Integration, Interfile, Join, Junta, Kartell, League, Meld, Merge(r), Mingle, Mixture, Motor cycle, Perm(utation), Piece, Pool, Quill, Ring, Solvate, Splice, Syncretize, Synthesis, Terrace, Trivalent, Trona, Unite, Valency, Wed, Zaibatsu

Comb-like Ctenoid, Pecten

Combustible, Combustion Air-gas, Ardent, Fiery, Inflammable, Phlogistic, Phlogiston, Spontaneous, Wildfire

▷ **Combustible** *may indicate* an anagram

Come, Coming (back), Coming out Accrue, Advent, Anear, Anon, Appear, Approach, Ar(r), Arise, Arrive, Attend, Debouch, Derive, Emerge, Future, Happen, Iceman, Issue, Millenarian, Orgasm, Parousia, Pass, Pop, Respond, Second, Via

Come again Eh

Comeback Boomerang, Bounce, Echo, Homer, Quip, Rally, Rearise, Rebound, Recovery, Repartee, Reply, Retort, Retour, Return, Reversion, Riposte

Come by Obtain

Comedian Benny, Buffoon, Chaplin, → CLOWN, Comic, Durante, Emery, Gagman, Goon, Groucho, Hope, Joe Miller, Joker, Jokesmith, Karno, Keaton, Leno, Punster, Quipster, Robey, Scream, Screwball, Stand-up, Starr, Tate, Tati, Tummler, Wag, Wise, Yell

Comedo Blackhead

Comedown Avale, Bathetic, Bathos, Crash landing, Disappointment, Drop, Letdown, Shower

Comedy Alternative, Black, Blackadder, Com, Custard-pie, Drama, Ealing, Errors, Farce, High, Humour, Improv(ised), Keystone, Knockabout, Lazzo, Low, Millamant, Musical, Romcom, Situation, Slapstick, Stand-up, Thalia, Travesty

Comely, Comeliness Beseen, Bonny, Fair, Goodly, Graceful, Jolly, Likely, Looks, Pleasing, Pretty, Proper

Comestible(s) Cate, Eats, Fare

Comet Chiron, Geminid, Halley's, Kohoutek, Meteor, Oort cloud, Reindeer, Shoemaker-Levy 9, Vomet, Xiphias

Come through Weather

Come to Cost, Wake(n)

Comfort(able), Comforter, Comforting, Comfy Amenity, Analeptic, Armchair, Balm, Bein, Bildad, Calm, Canny, Cheer, Cherish, Clover, Cold, Consolation, Console, Convenience, Cose, Cosh, Cosy, Couthie, Couthy, Creature, Crumb, Cushy, Dummy, Dutch, Ease, Easy, Eliphaz, Featherbed, Gemutlich, Heeled, Homely, Job's, Mumsy, Noah, Plum, Plushy, Reassure, Relaxed, Relief, Relieve, Rosewater, Rug, Scarf, Sinecure, Snug, Solace, Soothe, Succour, There, Tosh, Trig, Warm, Wealthy, Well, Well-to-do, Zophar

Comic(al) Beano, Buff, Buffo(on), Bumpkin, Buster, Chaplin, Clown, → COMEDIAN, Dandy, Droll, Eagle, Facetious, Fields, → FUNNY, Gagster, Hardy, Horror, Jester, Knock-about, Laurel, Leno, Mag, Manga, Quizzical, Rich, Robey, Strip, Tati, Trial, Wag, Zany

Comma Inverted, Oxford

Command(eer), Commanding, Commandment(s) Behest, Bid, Categorical imperative, Charge, Coerce, Control, Decalogue, Direct, Direction, Dominate, Domineer, Easy, Edict, Fiat, Fiaunt, Fighter, Firman, Haw, Hest, High, Imperious, Impress, Injunction, Instruction, Jussive, Mandate, Maritime, Mastery, Mitzvah, Mobile, → ORDER, Precept, Press, Query language, Requisition, Rule, Seize, Ukase, Warn, Warrant, Will, Wish, Writ

Commander Admiral, Ag(h)a, Ameer, Barleycorn, Bey, Bloke, Blucher, Boss, Brennus, Brig, Caliph, Centurion, Cid, Decurion, Dreyfus, Emir, Emperor, Encomendero, Field cornet, Generalissimo, Hetman, Hipparch, Imperator, Killadar, Leader, Manager, Marshal, Master, Meer, Mir, Moore, Officer, Overlord, Pendragon, Polemarch, Pr(a)efect, Raglan, Seraskier, Shogun, Sirdar, Taxiarch, Trierarch, Turcopolier, Vaivode, Voivode, Waivode, Warlord, Wing

Commando Chindit(s), Fedayee(n), Green Beret, Raider, Ranger, SAS

Commemorate, Commemoration Encaenia, Epitaph, Eulogy, Keep, Memorial, Month's mind, Monument, Plaque, Remember, Year's mind

Commence Begin, Initiate, Open, Start

Commend(ation) Belaud, Bestow, Cite, Encomium, Entrust, Laud, Mooi, Panegyric, → PRAISE, Roose, Tribute

Commensal Epizoon, Messmate

Commensurate Adequate, Enough, Equivalent, Relevant

Comment(ary), Commentator Analyst, Animadvert, Annotate, Apercu, Comm, Coryphaeus, Coverage, Critic, Critique, Descant, Discuss, Editorial, Essay, Exegete,

Explain, Exposition, Expound, Fair, Footnote, Gemara, Gloss(ographer), Glosser, Hakam, Kibitz, Margin, Marginalia, Midrashim, Note, Obiter dictum, Observation, Par, Platitude, Play-by-play, Postil, Remark, Running, Scholiast, Scholion, Scholium, Sidenote, Voice-over, Zohar

Commerce, Commercial Ad, Adland, Barter, Cabotage, Jingle, Marketable, Mercantile, Mercenary, Merchant, Retail, Shoppy, Simony, Trade, Traffic, Wholesale

Commercial traveller Drummer, Rep

Commiserate, Commiseration Compassion, Pity, Sympathise

Commissar People's, Political

Commission(er), Commissioned Agio, Audit, Authorise, Boundary, Brevet, Brokage, Brokerage, Charge, Charity, Competition, Contango, Countryside, Delegation, Depute, ECE, Employ, Engage, Envoy, Errand, European, Factor, Gosplan, High, Husbandage, Job, Kickback, Law, Magistrate, Mandate, Office(r), Official, Ombudsman, Order, Percentage, Perpetration, Place, Poundage, Price, Rake-off, Resident, Roskill, Roving, Royal, Shroffage, Task, Task force, Trust, Wreck

Commit(tal), Committed, Commitment Aret(t), Consign, Contract, Decision, Dedication, Delegate, Devotion, Devout, Do, Engage, Entrust, Enure, Impeachment, Paid up, Perpetrate, Pledge, Position, Rubicon

Committee ACRE, Audit, Board, Body, Commission, Commune, Council, Delegacy, Group, Hanging, Joint, Junta, Politburo, Presidium, Propaganda, Review body, Riding, Samiti, School, Select, Standing, Steering, Syndicate, Table, Vigilance, Watch, Works

Commode, Commodious Ample, Closestool, Roomy, Spacious

Commodities, Commodity Article, Futures, Gapeseed, Item, Physicals, Soft, Staple, Ware

Common(ly), Commoner, Commons Alike, As per usual, Average, Cad, Conventional, Diet, Dirt, Doctor's, Ealing, Eatables, Enclosure, Endemic, Epicene, Everyday, Familiar, Fare, Folk, General, Green, Greenham, House, Law, Lay, Low, Lower House, Mark, Mere, MP, Mutual, Naff, Non-U, Normal, People, Pleb, Plebe(i)an, Prevalent, Prole, Public, Related, Rife, Roturier, Ryfe, Scran, Sense, Shared, Stock, Stray, The mob, Tie, Tiers d'état, Trite, Tritical, Tuft, Tye, Use, → USUAL, Vile, Vul(gar), Vulgo, Vulgus, Widespread, Wimbledon

Commonplace Adversarian, Banal, Copybook, Everyday, Hackneyed, Homely, Humdrum, Idée reçue, Mot, Ordinary, Philistine, Plain, Platitude, Prosaic, Quotidian, Trite, Workaday

Commonsense Gumption, Nous, Savoir-faire, Smeddum, Wit

Commonwealth Protectorate, Puerto Rico, Res publica

Commotion Babel, Bluster, Bustle, Carfuffle, Clangour, Clatter, Curfuffle, Dirdam, Dirdum, Do, Dust, Ferment, Flap, Flurry, Fraise, Fuss, Hell, Hoo-ha(h), Hurly-burly, Hurry, Pother, Pudder, Racket, Romage, Rort, Ruckus, Ruction, Rumpus, Shemozzle, Shindig, Shindy, Shivaree, Steery, Stir, Stirabout, Storm, Stushie, Tirrivee, Tirrivie, To-do, Toss, Tumult, Turmoil, Upheaval, Uproar, Whirl, Wroth

Communal, Commune Agapemone, Collective, Com, Meditate, Mir, Paris, Phalanstery, Public, Talk, Township

Communicate, Communication Ampex, Anastomosis, Announce, Baud, Bluetooth, Boyau, Cable, Cellnet, Channelling, Citizen's band, Conversation, Convey, Cybernetic, E-mail, Expansive, Impart, Infobahn, Inform, Infrastructure, Intelpost, Intelsat, Internet, Lifeline, Message, Nonverbal, Note, Oracy, Paralanguage, Prestel®, Proxemics, Put across, Reach, Revelation, Road,

Semiotics, Signal, Tannoy®, Telepathy, Teletex, Telex, Telstar, Tieline, Transmit, Utraquist, Viewdata

Communion Creed, Fellowship, Host, Housel, Intinction, Lord's Supper, Species, Viaticum

Communiqué Announcement, Statement

Communism, Communist Apparat(chik), Aspheterism, Bolshevist, Brook Farm, Com, Comecon, Cominform, Comintern, Commo, Comsomol, Deviationist, Engels, Essene, Fourier, Fraction, Khmer Rouge, Komsomol, Leninite, Maoist, Marxist, Nomenklatura, Perfectionist, Pinko, Politburo, Populist, Red, Revisionism, Soviet, Spartacist, Stalinism, Tanky, Titoist, Trot, Vietcong, Vietminh

Communities, Community Agapemone, Alterne, Ashram, Association, Biome, Body, Brook Farm, Brotherhood, Clachan, Climax, Closed, Coenobitism, Coenobium, Colonia, Colony, Consocies, District, EC, Ecosystem, EEC, Enclave, European, Faith, Frat(e)ry, Gated, Global, Hamlet, Kahal, Kibbutz, Mesarch, Mir, Neighbourhood, Pantosocracy, People, Phalanx, Phyle, Preceptory, Public, Pueblo, Republic, Seral, Sere, Settlement, Shtetl, Sisterhood, Sociation, Society, Speech, Street, Toon, Town, Tribe, Ujamaa, Umma, Village, Virtual, Volost, Zupa

Commute(r) Change, Convert, Reduce, Straphanger, Travel

Como Lake, Perry

Compact Agreement, Cement, Concise, Conglobe, Covenant, Covin, Coyne, Dense, Entente, Fast, Firm, Flapjack, Hard, Knit, League, Match, Neat, Pledge, Powder, Solid, Tamp, Terse, Tight, Treaty, Well-knit

Companion(able) Achates, Arm candy, Associate, Attender, Barnacle, Bedfellow, Bonhomie, Brolga, Bud(dy), Butty, CH, China, Comate, Compeer, Compotator, Comrade, Consort, Contubernal, Crony, Cupman, Duenna, Ephesian, Escort, Feare, Felibre, → **FELLOW**, Fere, Franion, Furked, Handbook, Helpmate, Mate, Native, Pal, Pard, Pheer(e), Playmate, Pot, Sidekick, Skaines mate, Stable, Thane, Thegn, Trojan, Vade-mecum, Walker

Company, Companies Actors, Artel, Ass, Assembly, Band, Bank, Battalion, Bevy, → **BUSINESS**, Bv, Cahoot, Cartel, Cast, Cavalcade, Chartered, CIA, Circle, City, Close, Club, Co, Conger, Consort, Cordwainers, Core, Corporation, Corps, Coy, Crew, Crowd, Decury, Dotcom, East India, Enterprise, Entourage, Faction, Finance, Fire, → **FIRM**, Flock, Free, Gang, Garrison, Ging, Guild, Haberdashers, Heap, Holding, Hudson's Bay, ICI, Inc, Indie, In-house, Intercourse, Investment, Jingbang, Joint-stock, Limited, Listed, Livery, Management, Maniple, Muster, Order, Organisation, Parent, Plc, Pride, Private, Public, Public limited, Push, Quoted, Rep(ertory), Room, SA, Sedge, Set, Set out, Shell, Siege, Sort, SpA, Stationers', Stock, Subsidiary, Syndicate, Table, Team, Thiasus, Touring, Troop, Troupe, Trust, Twa, Two(some), Visitor, White, Yfere

Compare(d), Comparison Analogy, Balance, Beside, Bracket, Collate, Confront, Contrast, Correspond, Cp, Equate, Liken, Match, Odious, Parallel, Relation, Simile, Weigh

Compartment Ballonet, Bay, Booth, Box, Carriage, Casemate, Cell, Chamber, Cockpit, Cofferdam, Cubbyhole, Cubicle, Dog box, Glove, Locellate, Locker, Loculament, Loculus, Panel, Partition, Pigeonhole, Pocket, Pod, Room, Room(ette), Severy, Smoker, Stall, Till, Trunk, Watertight

Compass Ambit, Area, Beam, Binnacle, Bounds, Bow, Dividers, Extent, Gamut, Goniometer, Gyro, Gyromagnetic, Gyroscope, Infold, Magnetic, Mariner's, Needle, Orbit, Pelorus, Pencil, Perimeter, Prismatic, Radio, → **RANGE**, Reach, Rhumb, Room, Scale, Sweep, Tessitura, Trammel, Width

Compassion(ate) Aroha, Bleed(ing), Clemency, Commiseration, Empathy,

Goodwill, Heart, Humane, Kuan Yin, Kwan Yin, Mercy, Pity, Remorse, Samaritan, Sympathy, Ubuntu

Compatible Consistent, Fit, Harmonious

Compatriot National

Compel(ling), Compelled, Compulsion, Compulsive, Compulsory Addiction, Coact, Coerce, Cogent, Command, Constrain, Dragoon, Duress, Enforce, Extort, Fain, → **FORCE**, Force majeure, Gar, Make, Mandatory, Obligate, Oblige, Pathological, Steamroller, Strongarm, Tyrannise, Urge

Compendium Breviate

Compensate, Compensation Amend(s), Balance, Boot, Bote, Comp, Counterbalance, Counterpoise, Damages, Demurrage, Guerdon, Indemnity, Offset, Payment, Recoup, Redeem, Redress, Reparation, Reprisal, Requital, Restitution, Restore, Retaliation, Salvage, Satisfaction, Solatium, Wergild, X-factor

Compère Emcee, Host, MC, Presenter

Compete Contend, Emulate, Enter, Match, Outvie, Play, Rival, Vie

Competence, Competent Ability, Able, Adequate, Can, Capacity, Dab, Dow, Efficient, Fit, Proficient, Responsible, Sui juris, Worthy

Competition, Competitive, Competitor Agonist, Backmarker, Battle, Bee, Biathlon, Buckjumping, Candidate, Checks and balances, Comper, Concours, Contention, Contest, Cook off, Cup, Drive, Entrant, Event, Field, Finals, Freestyle, Gamesman, Grand prix, Gymkhana, Head-to-head, Heptathlon, Imperfect, Judoka, Jump off, Karateka, Keen, Knockout, Match, Match-play, Monopolistic, Olympiad, Open, Opponent, Outsider, Pairs, Panellist, Pentathlon, Perfect, Player, Pools, Premiership, Pro-am, Puissance, Race, Rally, Regatta, Repechage, Rival(ise), Rodeo, Runner-up, Show-jumping, Slam, Stableford, Starter, Super G, Tenson, Test, Tiger, Tournament, Tourney, Trial, Triallist, Wap(p)enshaw, Wild card

Compile(r), Compilation Anthology, Arrange, Collect, Cross, Doxographer, Edit, Prepare, Segue, Synthesis, Zadkiel

Complacent Babbitt, Fatuous, Joco, Pleasant, Self-satisfied, Smug

Complain(t), Complainer Adenoids, Affection, Affliction, Alas, Alastrim, Alopecia, Anaemia, Angashore, Angina, Arthritis, Asthma, Barrack, Beef, Bellyache, Bitch, Bleat, BSE, Carp, Cavil, Charge, Chorea, Colic, Crab, Cramp, Criticise, Diatribe, Disorder, Dropsy, Epidemic, Ergot, Exanthema, Girn, Gout, Gravamen, Gripe, Groan, Grouch, Grouse, Growl, Grudge, Grumble, Grutch, Harangue, Hives, Hone, Hypochondria, Ileitis, → **ILLNESS**, Jeremiad, Kvetch, Lupus, Malady, Mange, Mean(e), Mein, Mene, Moan, Morphew, Mumps, Murmur, Nag, Natter, Neuralgia, Ologoan, Pertussis, Plica, Poor-mouth, Protest, Pule, Pyelitis, Querimony, Rail, Remonstrate, Repine, Report, Rickets, Sapego, Sciatica, Scold, Sigh, Silicosis, Squawk, Staggers, Thrush, Tic, Tinea, Upset, Wheenge, Whimper, Whine, Whinge, Yammer, Yawp

Complaisant Agreeable, Flexible, Suave, Supple

Complement(ary) Alexin, Amount, Balance, Finish, Freebie, Gang, Lot, Reciprocate

▷ **Complement** *may indicate* a hidden word

Complete(ly), Completion Absolute, Accomplish, Achieve, All, Arrant, Attain, Clean, Congenital, Consummate, Crown, Do, End, Entire, Finalise, Finish, Flat, Follow through, Fruition, Fulfil, Full, Full-blown, Hollow, Incept, Integral, In toto, Neck and crop, One, Ouroboros, Out, Out and out, Perfect, Plenary, Pure, Quite, Ready, Root and branch, Rounded, Self-contained, Sew-up, Sheer, Spang, Sum, Teetotal, Thorough, Total, Unanimous, Unbroken, Uncensored, Uncut, Unequivocal, Unmitigated, Utter, Whole (hog), Wrap

Complex(ity) Abstruse, Advanced, Arcane, Castration, Compound, Difficult,

Electra, Golgi, Hard, Heath Robinson, Immune, Inferiority, Intricate, Intrince, Involute, Knot, Manifold, MHC, Military-industrial, Mixed, Multinucleate, Nest, Network, Obsession, Oedipus, Paranoid, Persecution, Phaedra, Plexiform, Superiority, Syndrome, System, Tangle, Web

Complexion Aspect, Blee, Hue, Leer, Permatan, Temper, Tint, View

Compliance, Compliant, Comply Agree, Amenable, Assent, Conform, Deference, Docile, Follow, Hand-in-glove, Obey, Observe, Obtemper, Sequacious, Surrender, Wilco, Yield

Complicate(d), Complication Bewilder, Complex, Deep, Elaborate, Embroil, Implex, Intricate, Involution, Involve, Inweave, Node, Nodus, Perplex, Ramification, Rigmarole, Sequela, Snarl, Tangle, Tirlie-wirlie

▷ **Complicated** *may indicate* an anagram

Compliment(s) Backhanded, Baisemain, Bouquet, Congratulate, Devoirs, Douceur, Encomium, Flatter, Flummery, Greetings, Praise, Soap, Trade-last, Tribute

Component(s) Base, Coherer, Constituent, Contact, CRT, Daisy-wheel, Element, Factor, Formant, Guidance, Hygristor, Impedor, Inductor, Ingredient, Longeron, Member, Module, → **PART**, Partial, Pre-amp, Profile, Reactance, Resistor, Subunit, Tensor

Compose(d), Composure Aplomb, Arrange, Calm, Choreograph, Consist, Cool, → **CREATE**, Equanimity, Even, Face, Improvise, Indite, Level-headed, Lull, Notate, Orchestrate, Placid, Poise, Produce, Reconcile, Sangfroid, Sedate, Serenity, Settle, Soothe, Tranquil, Unruffled, Write

Composer Contrapunt(al)ist, Hymnist, Inditer, Inventor, Maker, Melodist, Minimalist, Musician, → **POET**, Serialist, Six, Songsmith, Songwriter, Symphonist, Triadist, Tunesmith, Writer

---

COMPOSERS

3 letters:	Wolf	Gluck	Verdi
Bax		Grieg	Watts
	5 letters:	Harty	Weber
4 letters:	Auber	Haydn	Weill
Adam	Auric	Henze	Zappa
Arne	Balfe	Holst	
Bach	Berio	Ibert	*6 letters:*
Berg	Bizet	Lasso	Alfven
Blow	Bliss	Lehar	Arnold
Brel	Bloch	Liszt	Azione
Bull	Boito	Loewe	Barber
Byrd	Boyce	Lully	Bartók
Cage	Brian	Nyman	Bennet
Dima	Bruch	Parry	Berlin
Graf	Crumb	Prout	Boulez
Ives	D'Indy	Ravel	Brahms
Kern	Dukas	Reger	Bridge
Lalo	Elgar	Rossi	Burney
Monk	Falla	Satie	Busoni
Nono	Fauré	Sousa	Chopin
Orff	Field	Spohr	Coates
Peri	Finzi	Suppe	Delius
Raff	Glass	Tosti	Duparc

6 letters – cont:
Dvořák
Flotow
Franck
German
Glière
Glinka
Gounod
Handel
Hummel
Joplin
Kodaly
Lassus
Ligeti
Mahler
Mingus
Morley
Mozart
Ogolon
Pierne
Rameau
Rubbra
Schutz
Tallis
Varese
Wagner
Walton
Webern

7 letters:
Albeniz
Alberti
Allegri
Amadeus
Bantock
Bellini
Berlioz
Berners
Borodin
Britten
Brubeck
Christy
Copland
Corelli
Debussy

De Falla
Delibes
Dohnany
Dowland
Gibbons
Ireland
Janácek
Lambert
Mancini
Martinu
Menotti
Milhaud
Nielsen
Novello
Ormandy
Poulenc
Puccini
Purcell
Purnell
Quilter
Rodgers
Rodrigo
Romberg
Rossini
Roussel
Salieri
Smetana
Stainer
Strauss
Tartini
Tippett
Vivaldi
Warlock
Xenakis
Youmans

8 letters:
Alaleona
Albinoni
Boughton
Bruckner
Chabrier
Chausson
Couperin
Gabrieli

Gershwin
Gesualdo
Glazunov
Grainger
Granados
Honegger
Kreutzer
Marcello
Mascagni
Massenet
Messager
Messiaen
Paganini
Respighi
Schubert
Schumann
Scriabin
Sessions
Sibelius
Sondheim
Sullivan
Taverner
Telemann
Vangelis

9 letters:
Bacharach
Balakirev
Beethoven
Bernstein
Boulanger
Broughton
Buxtehude
Chaminade
Cherubini
Donizetti
Dunstable
Hindemith
Meyerbeer
Offenbach
Pachelbel
Pergolesi
Prokofiev
Scarlatti
Schnittke

Zemlinsky

10 letters:
Birtwistle
Boccherini
Carmichael
Cole Porter
Monteverdi
Mussorgsky
Palestrina
Ponchielli
Rawsthorne
Saint-Saëns
Schoenberg
Stravinsky
Villa-Lobos
Williamson

11 letters:
Charpentier
Frescobaldi
Humperdinck
Leoncavallo
Mendelssohn
Stockhausen
Tchaikovsky
Wolf Ferrari

12 letters:
Khachaturian
Rachmaninoff
Shostakovich

13 letters:
Havergal Brian
Maxwell Davies

14 letters:
Rimsky-Korsakov

15 letters:
Vaughan Williams

▷ **Composing** *may indicate* an anagram
Composite Aster, Costmary, Foalfoot, Gerbera, Groundsel, Hawkweed, Hybrid,
   Integral, Metal, Motley, Opinicus, Rag(weed), Sphinx, Synthesized, Thistle
Composition, Compositor Albumblatt, Aleatory, Azione, Bagatelle, Beaumontage,
   Beaumontague, Canon, Capriccio, Caprice, Cob, Concerto, Concertstuck, Creation,

Dite, Essay, Etude, Exaration, Fantasia, Inditement, Ingredient, Line, Literature, Loam, Met, Montage, Morceau, Nonet(te), Nonetto, Opus, Oratorio, Part-writing, Pastiche, Piece, Pieta, Poem, Polyphony, Polyrhythm, Port, Printer, Quartette, Raga, Repoussage, Rhapsody, Round, Setting, Ship, Sing, Smoot, Smout, Sonata, Sonatina, Structure, Study, Suite, Symphony, Synthesis, Terracotta, Texture, Toccata, Treatise, Trio, Typesetter, Verismo, Voluntary, Work

Compost Dressing, Fertilizer, Humus, Vraic, Zoo doo

Compound, Compound stop Addition, Admixture, Amalgam, Anti-inflammatory, Anti-knock, Bahuvrihi, Blend, → **CAMP**, Composite, Constitute, Coordination, Cpd, Cutting, Derivative, Ethiops, Mix, Mixture, Multiply, Racemate, Rooting, Tatpurusha, Type

COMPOUNDS

3 letters:
Azo
Hex
TBT

4 letters:
Alum
Clay
Deet
EDTA
Enol
Haem
Heme
TEPP
Urea

5 letters:
Algin
Allyl
Aloin
Amide
Amino
Azide
Azine
Azole
Caria
Diazo
Diene
Dimer
Diode
Erbia
Ester
Furan
Halon
Imide
Imine
Lipid

Nitro
Olein
Oxide
Oxime
Potin
Pyran
Salol
Sarin
Soman
Tabun
Thiol
Trona
Vinyl

6 letters:
Acetal
Alkane
Alkene
Alkyne
Ammine
Arsine
Baryta
Borane
Calque
Cetane
Chrome
Cresol
Diquat
Epimer
Fluate
Glycol
Halide
Haloid
Hexene
Isatin
Isomer
Ketone

Kinone
Lithia
Niello
Octane
Phenol
Pinene
Potash
Purine
Pyrone
Retene
Silane
Speiss
Tannin
Tartar
Tetryl
Thymol
Triene
Trimer
Uranyl

7 letters:
Acetone
Acridin
Aglycon
Ammonia
Argyrol®
Aspirin
Barilla
Bauxite
Benzene
Betaine
Borazon
Bromide
Caliche
Calomel
Camphor
Carbide

Cellose
Chelate
Choline
Cinerin
Creatin
Cumarin
Cyanide
Diamine
Diazine
Diazole
Dioxide
Dvandva
Epoxide
Erinite
Ethanol
Eugenol
Fenuron
Ferrite
Flavone
Hormone
Hydrate
Hydride
Indican
Indoxyl
Lactate
Lactone
Menthol
Metamer
Monomer
Niobite
Nitride
Nitrile
Nitrite
Oxazine
Oxonium
Pentane
Peptide

7 letters – cont:
Peptone
Polyene
Polymer
Prodrug
Protein
Quassia
Quinoid
Quinone
Realgar
Skatole
Steroid
Sulfide
Syncarp
Taurine
Terpene
Toluene
Tritide
Urethan
Uridine
Wolfram
Zymogen

8 letters:
Acridine
Aglycone
Aldehyde
Alizarin
Arginine
Asbestos
Astatide
Butyrate
Caffeine
Carbaryl
Catenane
Cephalin
Ceramide
Chloride
Chromene
Coenzyme
Coumarin
Creatine
Cyanogen
Datolite
Dieldrin
Dopamine
Ethoxide
Farnesol
Fluoride
Furfuran
Glycogen

Hydroxyl
Indoform
Isologue
Ketoxime
Lecithin
Luteolin
Massicot
Melamine
Monoxide
Oligomer
Pentosan
Peroxide
Phthalin
Piperine
Ptomaine
Purpurin
Pyrazole
Rock-alum
Rotenone
Selenate
Silicide
Siloxane
Sodamide
Stilbene
Sulphide
Sulphone
Tautomer
Tetroxid
Thiazide
Thiazine
Thiazole
Thiophen
Thiotepa
Thiourea
Titanate
Tolidine
Triazine
Triazole
Trilling
Trioxide
Tyramine
Urethane
Xanthate
Xanthine
Zirconia

9 letters:
Aflatoxin
Alicyclic
Aliphatic
Anhydride

Biguanide
Carbazole
Carnitine
Celloidin
Cellulose
Cementite
Cetrimide
Chromogen
Copolymer
Cortisone
Deuteride
Dibromide
Dipeptide
Disulfram
Endorshin
Ferrocene
Flavanone
Fool's gold
Fulleride
Glycoside
Greek fire
Guanosine
Haematein
Histamine
Hydantoin
Hydrazide
Hydroxide
Imidazole
Impsonite
Ionophore
Jasmonate
Limestone
Menadione
Mepacrine
Merbromin
Methoxide
Monoamine
Organotin
Pentoxide
Phenazine
Phenoxide
Pheromone
Phosphide
Piperonal
Polyamine
Porphyrin
Qinghaosu
Quercetus
Quinoline
Saltpetre
Salvarsan

Sapogenin
Serotonin
Sidenafil
Telluride
Tetroxide
Thiophene
Veratrine

10 letters:
Adrenaline
Amphoteric
Argyrodite
Azobenzene
Bradykinin
Cellosolve®
Cytochroma
Dichloride
Dimethoate
Disulphide
Enkephalin
Ethambutol
Halocarbon
Indophenon
Isocyanate
Lumisterol
Mercaptide
Nitrazepam
Nucleoside
Nucleotide
Phenformin
Phenocaine
Picrotoxin
Piperazine
Piperidine
Propionate
Putrescine
Pyrethroid
Pyrimidine
Sildenafil
Sulphonium
Thimerosal
Tocopherol

11 letters:
Acetanilide
Amphetamine
Coprosterol
Dimercaprol
Electrolyte
Fluorescein
Galantamina

Ghitathione
Hydrocarbon
Neostigmine
Nitrosamine
Resveratrol
Sesquioxide
Sphingosine
Tributyltin

12 letters:
Arsphenamine
Carbohydrate
Formaldehyde
Haematoxylin

Hydroquinone
Mifepristone
Permanganate
Phenanthrine
Polyurethane
Sulphonamide
Testosterone
Thiosinamine
Triglyceride
Trimethadine

13 letters:
Catecholamine
Cycloheximide

Diphenylamine
Isoproterenol
Mercurochrome
Metronidazole
Nitroglycerin
Nortriptyline
Phenothiazine
Physostigmine
Sulphonylurea
Trinucleotide

14 letters:
Cyanocobalamin
Oxyhaemoglobin

Phenolphthalin
Polycarboxylic
Polyunsaturate
Sulphonmethane
Trohalomethane

15 letters:
Perfluorocarbon
Succinylcholine

17 letters:
Pentachlorophenol

▷ **Compound(ed)** *may indicate* an anagram

Comprehend, Comprehensive All-in, Catch-all, Catholic, Compass, Compendious, Contain, Exhaustive, Fathom, Follow, Full-scale, General, Global, Grand, Grasp, Include, Indepth, Ken, Large, Omnibus, Panoramic, Perceive, School, Sweeping, Thoroughgoing, Tumble, → **UNDERSTAND**, Wide

Compress(ed), Compression, Compressor Astrict, Astringe, Axial-flow, Bale, Coarctate, Contract, Pack, Pump, Shoehorn, Solidify, Squeeze, Stupe, Thlipsis, Turbocharger

Comprise Contain, Embody, Embrace, Include

Compromise, Compromising Avoision, Brule, Commit, Concession, Endanger, Give and take, Golden mean, Happy medium, Honeytrap, Involve, Middleground, Modus vivendi, Negotiate, Settlement, Time-server, Trade off, Via media

▶ **Compulsion** *see* **COMPEL**

Compunction Hesitation, Regret, Remorse, Scruple, Sorrow

Compute(r) Analog(ue), Apple (Mac)®, Desknote, Desktop, Digital, Eniac, Fifth generation, Front-end, Host, Laptop, Mainframe, Micro, Multiuser, Network, Notebook, Number-cruncher, Palmtop, PC, Personal, Proxy server, Reckon, TALISMAN, Turing machine

Computer hardware, Computer memory Busbar, Chip, Dataglove®, DRAM, EAROM, EPROM, Floptical, IDE, Modem, Neurochip, Pentium®, Platform, Plug'n'play, Processor, PROM, RAM, ROM, Router, Tower, Track(er)ball

Computer language ADA, ALGOL, APL, ASCII, Assembly, AWK, Basic, C, COBOL, COL, Computerese, CORAL, Fortran, High-level, ICL, Java®, Java script®, LISP, LOGO, OCCAM, PASCAL, Perl, PROLOG, Python, Scratchpad, Scripting, Small-talk, SNOBOL, SQL, Visual Basic, Weblish

Computer network, Computer systems Arpa, ARPANET, BIOS, Cambridge ring, ERNIE, Ethernet, Evernet, Executive, Extranet, Fileserver, Freenet, HOLMES, Hypermedia, Internet, Intranet, JANET, LAN, Linux, MARC, MIDI, Neural, Peer-to-peer, Stand-alone, Tally, TAURUS, Telnet, Token ring, Unix, Usenet, WAN, Web, Wide-area, WIMP

Computer programs, Computer software Abandonware, Acrobat, ActiveX, Agent, Antivirus, Applet, Application, Assembler, Autotune, Bloatware, Bootstrap, Bot, Browse, CADMAT, Cancelbot, Careware, Case, Casemix, Chatbot, Checksum, Client, Closed-loop, Columbus, Courseware, Crippleware, CU See Me, Datel®, Debugger, Demo, Device-driver, Diagnostic, Dictionary, Emacs, Est, E-wallet, Extreme, Facemail, Firewall, Firmware, Flash, Formatter, Freeware, Groupware,

HAL, Hard card, Heuristic, Hypermedia, ITunes®, Linker, Loader, Macro, Malware, Middleware, Mmorpg, Module, Neural net, Object, OCR, Parser, Payware, Plug-in, Relocator, RISC, Rootkit, Screensaver, Servlet, Shareware, Shell, Shovelware, Spellchecker, Spider, Spyware, Stiffware, Systems, Translator, Trialware, Utility, Vaccine, Vaporware, Warez, Web browser, Webcast, Web crawler, Windows®, Word processor, Worm

Computer terms Address bus, Alert box, Algorism, Authoring, Autosave, Backslash, Bank-switching, Bitmap, Blog(ging), Blogroll, Bookmark, Boot, Boot-virus, Bot army, Breakpoint, Broadband, Calculate, Calculus, Cascade, Chatroom, Clickstream, Client-server, Clipboard, Coder, Conf, Core(dump), Counter, Cuspy, Cybercafe, Cyber(netics), Cyberslacking, Defrag(ment), Dial-up, DIF, Domain name, Dotcom, Earcon, Enqueue, Estimate, FAT, Figure, Flash ROM, GIGO, Gopher, Half-adder, Hashing, High-end, Hybrid, Hypertext, Inbox, Inputter, Integrator, Interface, IT, Kludge, Linear, Logic, Mail merge, Measure, Meatspace, Moblog, Morphing, Motherboard, Mouseover, Mouse potato, Mung, Network, Neural, Non-volatile, Numlock, Nybble, Object, On-line, Outbox, Package, Packet sniffer, Pageview, Patch, Path name, Peer-to-peer, Pel, Permalink, Pharming, Phishing, Pixel, Platform, Podcast, Podcatcher, Poke, Pop-up, Pseudocode, Pseudorandom, Public-key, Pushdown, Reader farm, README file, Read-out, Realtime, Reboot, Reckoner, Report program, Rogue dialler, Rootserver, Screensaver, Screen turtle, Search engine, Serial port, Server, Shell, Shovelware, Smart, Smurfing, Soft return, Source, Spigot, Spim, Splog, Spreadsheet, Sprite, String, Style sheet, Subroutine, Superserver, Systems, Tape streamer, Thick client, Thin client, Time slice, Toggle, Token ring, Turtle graphics, Unicode, Username, Utility program, Vaccine, Vlog, Vodcast, Voice response, Voxel, Webbie, WebBoard, Webfarm, Wideband, Wiki, WIMAX, Wordwrap, WORM, Wysiwyg, Yottabyte, Zettabyte

Computer user(s) Alpha geek, Anorak, Brain, Browser, Cast(er), Chiphead, Cyberpunk, Cybersurfer, Digerati, Hacker, Liveware, Luser, Mouse potato, Nerd, Nethead, Netizen, Nettie, Onliner, Otaku, Pumpking, Surfer, Tiger team, Troll, White hat

Comrade Achates, Ally, Buddy, Bully-rook, Butty, China, Fellow, Frater, Friend, Kamerad, Mate, Oliver, Pal, Pard, Roland, Tovarich, Tovaris(c)h

Con(man) Against, Anti, Bunco, Diddle, Dupe, Fleece, Hornswoggle, Inveigle, Jacob, Lag, Learn, Peruse, Pretence, Read, Scam, Scan, Steer, Sucker, Swindle, Tweedler

Concave Dished, Invexed

Conceal(ed), Concealment Blanket, Blind, Closet, Clothe, Cover, Curtain, Disguise, Dissemble, Doggo, Drown, Feal, Harbour, Heal, Heel, Hele, → **HIDE**, Latent, Misprision, Occult, Palm, Perdu(e), Recondite, Screen, Scriene, Secrete, Shroud, Sleeve, Smother, Snow job, Stash, Subreption, Ulterior, Whitewash, Wrap

Concede, Concession Acknowledge, Admit, Allow, Budge, Carta, Charter, Compromise, Confess, Favour, Forfeit, Franchise, Grant, Munich, Ou, Ow, Owe, Own, Privilege, Ship, Sop, Synchoresis, Yield

Conceit(ed) Bumptious, Caprice, Carriwitchet, Cat-witted, Concetto, Crank, Crotchet, Device, Dicty, Egoist, Egomania, Fancy, Fastuous, Figjam, Flory, Fop, Fume, Hauteur, Idea, Mugwump, Notion, Podsnappery, Prig, Princock, Princox, Puppyism, Quiblin, Self-assumption, Side, Snotty, Stuck-up, Swellhead, Toffee-nose, Vain(glory), Wind

Conceive, Conceivable Beget, Create, Credible, Imagine, Possible, Surmise

Concentrate(d), Concentration Aim, Application, Attend, Bunch, Cathexis, Centre, Collect, Condense, Dephlegmate, Distil, Elliptical, Essence, Extract, Focalise, Focus,

Geographical, Intense, Kurtosis, Listen, Major, Mantra, Mass, Molality, Molarity, Navel-gazing, Potted, Reduce, Rivet, Samadhi, Titrate, Titre, Undivided

Concept(ion) Alethic, Brain, Hent, Ideal, Ideation, Image, Immaculate, Myth, Notion, Onomascology, Sortal, Stereotype

Concern(ed), Concerning About, Affair, After, Ail, Altruism, Anent, As to, Bother, Business, Care, Cerne, Company, Disturb, Firm, Going, Heed, House, In re, Intéressé, Interest, Into, Lookout, → **MATTER**, Mell, Misease, Over, Part, Pidgin, Pigeon, Re, Reck, Regard, Reke, Respect, Retch, Solicitude, Touch, Trouble, Versant, Worry

▷ **Concerned** *may indicate* an anagram

Concert (place) Agreement, Ballad, Benefit, Chamber, Charivari, Cooperation, Device, Dutch, Gig, Hootanannie, Hootananny, Hootenanny, Hootnannie, Hootnanny, Odeon, Odeum, Pop, Prom(enade), Recital, Singsong, Smoker, Smoking, Subscription, Symphony, The Proms, Together, Unison, Unity, Wit

Concertina Bandoneon, Pleat, Squeezebox, Squiffer

Concerto Brandenburg, Emperor, Grosso

▶ **Concession** *see* **CONCEDE**

Conch Shell, Strombus

Conchie CO

Conciliate, Conciliator Allay, Calm, Disarm, Dove, Ease, Mollify, Placate, Reconcile

Concise Compact, Curt, Encapsulated, Laconic, Short, Succinct, Terse, Tight

Conclave Assembly, Caucus, Confab, Meeting

Conclude(d), Conclusion, Conclusive Achieve, A fortiori, Afterword, Amen, Binding, Button-up, Cease, Clinch, Close, Cogent, Complete, Consectary, Convincing, Dead, Decide, Deduce, → **END**, End-all, Envoi, Estoppel, Explicit, Final, Finding, Fine, Finis, → **FINISH**, Foregone, Gather, Illation, Infer, Lastly, Limit, Non sequitur, Omega, Over, Peroration, Point, Postlude, Punchline, Reason, Resolve, Settle, Showdown, Summary, Terminate, Upshot, Uptie

Concoct(ion) Brew, Compound, Creation, Plan, Trump (up)

Concord Concent, Consonance, Harmony, Peace, Plane, Sympathy, Treaty, Unity

Concorde SST

Concourse Assembly, Confluence, Esplanade, Throng

Concrete, Concretion Actual, Aggregate, Beton, Bezoar, Breeze, Cake, Calculus, Caprolite, Clot, Dogger, Gunite, Hard, Laitance, Lean, Mass, Minkstone, No-fines, Pile-cap, Positive, Prestressed, Reify, Reinforced, Siporex, Solid, Tangible, Tremie, Vacuum

Concubine Apple-squire, Campaspe, Harem, Hetaria, Madam, Mistress, Odalisk, Sultana

Concur Accord, Agree, Coincide, Comply, → **CONSENT**, Gree

Concurrent(ly) Meantime

Concuss(ion) Clash, Shock, Stun

Condemn(ation) Abominate, Accuse, Blame, Blast, Cast, Censor, Censure, Convict, Damn, Decry, Denounce, Deprecate, Doom, Judge, Kest, Obelise, Proscribe, Revile, Sentence, Theta, Upbraid

Condense(d), Condenser Abbe, Abbreviate, Abridge, Brief, Capacitator, Compress, Contract, Distil, Encapsulate, Epitomise, Jet, Liebig, Précis, Rectifier, Reduce, Shorten, Shrink, Summarise, Surface, Vernier, Vinificator

Condescend(ing) Deign, Patronise, Stoop, Superior, Vouchsafe

Condiment Caraway, Catsup, Cayenne, Chutney, Cum(m)in, Flavour, Horse radish, Kava, Ketchup, Mustard, Pepper, Relish, Salt, Sambal, Sambol, Sauce, Spice, Tracklement, Turmeric, Vinegar, Zedoary

Condition(al), Conditioning Autism, Case, Cense, Circ(s), Circumstance, Classical, Congenital, Connote, Contingent, Disomy, Dropsy, Experimental, Fettle, Finite, Going, Hammertoe, Hood, Hunk, If, → **IN GOOD CONDITION**, Kelter, Kernicterus, Kilter, Latah, Necessary, Nick, Order, Pass, Pavlovian, Plight, Pliskie, Ply, Point, Position, Predicament, Premise, Premiss, Prepare, Prerequisite, Presupposition, Protasis, Proviso, Provisory, Repair, Reservation, Reserve, Rider, Ropes, Sine qua non, Sis, Spina bifida, Standing, State, Sted, Stipulation, String, Sufficient, Term, Tid, Tox(a)emia, Trim, Trisomy, Unless, Vir(a)emia, White finger

Condom(s) Blob, Cap, Franger, French letter, Gumboot, Johnny, Letter, Prophylactic, Rubber, Rubber goods, Safe, Scumbag, Sheath

Condone Absolve, Excuse, Forgive, Overlook

Conduct(or), Conductress Accompany, Administer, Anode, Arm, Arrester, Barbirolli, Bearing, Beecham, Behaviour, Bulow, Bus-bar, Cad, Chobdar, Clippie, Coil, Comport, Demean(our), Deportment, Direct, Disorderly, Drive, Editor, Electrode, Escort, Feedthrough, Fetch, Goings-on, Haitink, Hallé, Ignitron, Karajan, Kempe, Klemperer, Lark, Lead, Liber, Lightning, Maestro, Mantovani, Mho, Microchip, Nerve, N-type, Officiate, Ormandy, Outer, Parts, Photodiode, → **PILOT**, Previn, Probe, Prosecute, Protocol, Psychagogue, Psychopomp, P-type, Rattle, Safe, Sargent, Scudaller, Scudler, Shunt, Skudler, Solicit, Solti, Stokowski, Tao, Thermal, Thermistor, Toscanini, Transact, → **USHER**, Varactor, Varistor, Wave guide, Wire, Wood, Zener diode

▷ **Conducting** *may indicate* an '-ic' ending

Conduit Aqueduct, Canal, Carrier, Duct, Main, Penstock, Pipe, Tube, Utilidor, Wireway

Cone(s), Conical, Cone-shaped Alluvial, Cappie, Circular, Conoidal, Egmont, Ellipse, Female, Fir, Fusion, Monticule, Moxa, Nose, Pastille, Peeoy, Pineal, Pingo, Pioy(e), Pottle, Puy, Pyramid, Pyrometric, Retinal, Seger, Spire, Storm, Strobilus, Taper, Tee, Traffic, Volcanic, Wind, Windsock

Coney Daman, Doe, Hyrax

Confection(er), Confectionery Bonbon, Candy, Candyfloss, Caramel, Chocolate, Concoction, Conserve, Countline, Halva, Ice, Kiss, Marzipan, Meringue, Noisette, Nougat, Quiddery, Rock, Sweet, Sweetmeat, Tablet

Confederal, Confederacy, Confederate, Confederation Accessory, Alliance, Ally, Association, Body, Bund, Bunkosteerer, Cover, Creek, F(o)edarie, Gueux, Illinois, League, Partner, Senegambia, Union

Confer(ence) Bestow, Bretton Woods, Cf, Collogue, Colloqium, Colloquy, Congress, Council, Diet, Do, Dub, Fest, Forum, Grant, Huddle, Hui, Imparlance, Imperial, Indaba, Intercommune, Lambeth, Meeting, Munich, Negotiate, News, Palaver, Parley, Pawaw, Pear, Potsdam, Pourparler, Powwow, Press, Pugwash, Quadrant, Seminar, Settle, Summit, Symposium, Synod, → **TALK**, Teach-in, Video, Vouchsafe, Yalta

Confess(ion), Confessor Acknowledge, Admit, Agnise, Avowal, Concede, Confiteor, Declare, Disclose, Edward, Own, Peccavi, Recant, Shrift, Shriver, Sing, Tetrapolitan, Verbal, Whittle

Confide(nce), Confident(ial), Confidant Aplomb, Aside, Assertive, Assured, Authoritative, Bedpost, Belief, Bottle, Can do, Certitude, Cocksure, Cocky, Cred, Crouse, Entre nous, Entrust, Extravert, Extrovert, Faith, Favourite, Fearless, Feisty, Gatepost, Hardy, Hope, Hubris, Hush-hush, Intimate, Morale, Nerve, Pack, Private, Privy, Sanguine, Secret, Secure, Self-assured, Self-possessed, Sub rosa, Sure, Sure-footed, Tell, Together, Trust, Unbosom, Under the rose, Vaulting

Confine(d), Confines, Confinement Ambit, Bail, Bale, Cage, CB, Chain, Constrain, Contain, Coop, Cramp, Crib, Detain, Emmew, Encase, Enclose, Endemic, Enmew, Ensheath, Gaol, Gate, Gender-moon, House arrest, Immanacle, Immew, Immure, Impound, → **IMPRISON**, Incage, Incarcerate, Incommunicado, Inertial, Inhoop, Intern, Limit, Local, Mail, March, Mew, Mure, Narrow, Pen, Pent, Pinion, Poky, Restrict, Rule 43, Rules, Section, Solitary, Tether, Thirl, Trammel

Confirm(ed), Confirmation Addict, Ascertain, Assure, Attest, Bear, Certify, Chris(o)m, Christen, Chronic, Clinch, Corroborate, Dyed-in-the-wool, Endorse, Homologate, Obsign, OK, Qualify, Ratify, Reassure, Sacrament, Sanction, Seal, Strengthen, Ten-four, Tie, Validate, Vouch

Confiscate, Confiscation Attainder, Deprive, Dispossess, Distrain, Escheat, Garnishee, Impound, Infangenethef, Raupatu, Seize, Sequestrate

Conflagration Blaze, Holocaust, Inferno, Wildfire

Conflict(ing) Agon, Armageddon, At odds, Battle, Boilover, Camp, Casus belli, Clash, Close, Contend, Contravene, Controversy, Disharmony, Diverge, Encounter, Feud, Fray, Inconsistent, Internecine, Jar, Lists, Mêlée, Muss, Off-key, Oppose, Psychomachia, Rift, Scrape, Strife, → **STRUGGLE**, Tergiversate, War

Conform(ist), Conformity Accord, Adjust, Comply, Conservative, Consistence, Correspond, Normalise, Obey, Observe, Procrustean, Propriety, Quadrate, Standardize, Stereotype(d), Suit, Trimmer, Yield

▷ **Confound** *may indicate* an anagram

Confound(ed) Abash, Amaze, Astound, Awhape, Baffle, Bewilder, Blamed, Blasted, Blest, Blinking, Bumbaze, Contradict, Darn, Dismay, Drat, Dumbfound, Elude, Floor, Jigger, Mate, Murrain, Nonplus, Perishing, Perplex, Rabbit, Spif(f)licate, Stump, Throw

Confrère Ally

Confront(ation) Appose, Beard, Breast, Brush, Eyeball, Face, Face down, Head-to-head, Incident, Loggerheads, Mau-Mau, Meet, Militance, Nose, Oppose, Outface, Showdown, Tackle, Toe-to-toe

Confuse(d), Confusedly, Confusion Addle, Anarchy, Astonishment, At sea, Babel, Baffle, Bazodee, Bedevil, Befog, Befuddle, Bemuse, Bewilder, Blur, Bobby-die, Burble, Bustle, Chaos, Cloud, Clutter, Complicate, Consternation, Debacle, Desorienté, Didder, Discombobulate, Disconcert, Disorient, Distract, Dither, Dizzy, Dudder, Dust, Dwaal, Egarement, Embrangle, Embroglio, Embroil, Farrago, Flap, Flat spin, Flummox, Flurry, Fluster, Fog, Fox, Fubar, Fuddle, Gaggle, Galley-west, Garble, Hash, Havoc, Hazy, Helter-skelter, Hirdy-girdy, Hubble-bubble, Huddle, Hugger-mugger, Hurly-burly, Hurry-scurry, Hurry-skurry, Imbrangle, Imbroglio, Inchoate, → **IN CONFUSION**, Indistinct, Litter, Lost, Lurry, Maelstrom, Maffled, Mayhem, Maze, Melange, Melee, Mess, Mingle, Mish-mash, Misorder, Mither, Mixter-maxter, Mixtie-maxtie, Mix-up, Mizzle, Mizzy maze, Moider, Moither, Moonstruck, Morass, → **MUDDLE**, Mudge, Muss(e), Muzzy, Obfuscate, Overset, Pellmell, Perplex, Pi(e), Pose, Ravel, Razzle-dazzle, Razzmatazz, Rout, Rummage, S(c)hemozzle, Scramble, Skimble-skamble, Snafu, Spin, Stump, Stupefy, Surprise, Swivet, Synchysis, Tangle, Throw, Tizzy, Topsy-turvy, Turbulence, Turmoil, Tzimmes, Welter, Whemmle, Whomble, Whummle, Woolly, Woozy

▷ **Confuse(d)** *may indicate* an anagram

Confute Confound, Contradict, Deny, Disprove, Infringe, Redargue, Refel

Congeal Coagulate, Freeze, Gel, Gunge, Set, Solidify

Congenial Agreeable, Amiable, Compatible, Connate, Couthie, Couthy, Happy, Kindred, Simpatico, Sympathique

Congenital Connate, Inborn, Innate, Inveterate

Congest(ed), Congestion Coryza, Cram, Crowd, Engorge, Impact, Jam, Logjam, Nasal, Turgid

Conglomerate, Conglomeration Aggregate, Banket, Chaebois, Chaebol, Empire, Gather, Heap, Mass

Congo(u) Shaba, Tea

Congratulate, Congratulation Applaud, Felicitate, Laud, Mazeltov, Preen, Salute

Congregate, Congregation(alist) Assembly, Barnabite, Body, Brownist, Class, Community, Conclave, Ecclesia, Flock, Fold, Gathering, Host, Laity, Oratory, Propaganda, Synagogue

Congress(man) ANC, Assembly, Capitol, Conclave, Continental, Council, Eisteddfod, Intercourse, Legislature, Pan-Africanist, Rally, Senator, Solon, Synod, Vienna

Conifer(ous) Araucaria, Cedar, Cypress, Cyrus, Evergreen, Larch, Macrocarpa, Picea, Pine, Retinispora, Spruce, Taiga, Taxus, Thuja, Yew

Conject(ure) Fancy, Goldbach's, Guess, Guesswork, Speculate, Surmise, Theory, View

Conjoin Alligate, Ally, Connect, Knit

Conjugate, Conjugation Couple, Hermitian, Join, Nuptial, Synopsis, Typto, Zygosis

Conjunction Alligation, Ampersand, And, Combination, Consort, Coordinating, Inferior, Nor, Polysyndeton, Subordinating, Superior, Synod, Syzygy, Together, Union, Unition, Unless

Conjure(r), Conjuror Angekkok, Charm, Contrive, Heypass, Heypresto, Hocus-pocus, Illusionist, Imagine, Invoke, Mage, Magic, Mystery-man, Palmer, Prestidigitator, Prestigiator, Thaumaturgus

Conk Nose

Connect(ed), Connection, Connector About, Accolade, Adaptor, Affiliate, Affinity, Agnate, Anastomosis, And, Associate, Attach, Band, Bind, Bridge, Bridle, Cable, Clientele, Coherent, Colligate, Conjugate, Couple, Cross-link, Delta, Dovetail, Downlink, Drawbar, Earth, Fishplate, Fistula, Hook-up, → **IN CONNECTION WITH**, Interlink, Interlock, Interrelation, Join, Jumper, Kinship, Liaison, Lifeline, Link, Linkup, Marry, Merge, Mesh, Network, Nexus, On, Online, Patch, Pons, Raphe, Rapport, Relate, Relative, Respect, Sentence, Shuttle, Splice, S-R, Synapse, Syntenosis, Syssarcosis, Tendon, Through, Tie, Tie-in, Union, Y, Yoke, Zygon

Connecticut Ct

Connive, Connivance Abet, Cahoots, Collude, Condone, Conspire, Lenocinium, Plot

Connoisseur Aesthete, Cognoscente, Epicure, Expert, Fancier, Gourmet, Judge, Maven, Mavin, Oenophil

Connotate, Connotation Imply, Infer, Intent, Meaning

Conquer(or), Conquering, Conquest Alexander, Beat, Conquistador, Cortes, Crush, Debel, Genghis Khan, Hereward, → **MASTER**, Moor, Norman, Ostrogoth, Overcome, Overpower, Overrun, Pizarro, Saladin, Subjugate, Tame, Tamerlane, Vanquish, Victor, Vincent

Conquistador Cortes, Cortez

Conscience, Conscientious Casuistic, Duteous, Heart, Inwit, Morals, Painstaking, Pang, Remorse, Scruple(s), Scrupulous, Sense, Superego, Syneidesis, Synteresis, Thorough, Twinge

Conscious(ness) Awake, Aware, Black, Chit, Deliberate, Limen, Mindful, On to, Persona, Sensible, Sentient, Witting

Conscript(ion) Blood-tax, Choco, Commandeer, Draft(ee), Impress, Inductee,

Landsturm, Levy, Nasho, → **RECRUIT**, Register

Consecrate(d), Consecration Bless, Enoch, Hallow, Noint, Oint, Sacring, Sanctify, Venerate

Consecutive Sequential, Successive

Consensus Agreement, Harmony, Unanimity

Consent Accord, Acquiesce, Affo(o)rd, Agree, Approbate, Comply, Concur, Grant, Informed, Permit, Ratify, Submit, Una voce, Volens, Yes-but, Yield

Consequence, Consequent(ial), Consequently Aftermath, Consectaneous, Corollary, Effect, End, Implication, Importance, Issue, Karma, Knock-on, Logical, Moment, Outcome, Out-turn, Ramification, Repercussion, → **RESULT**, Sequel, Thence, Threat, Thus, Upshot

Conservative Blimpish, Blue, C, Cautious, Diehard, Disraeli, Fabian, Hard-hat, Hidebound, Hunker, Neanderthal, Old guard, Old-line, Preppy, Progressive, Rearguard, Redneck, Right(-wing), Safe, Square, Thrifty, Tory, True blue, Unionist, Verkramp, Verkrampte, Young Fogey

Conservatory Hothouse, Lean-to, Orangery, Solarium

Conserve, Conservation(ist) Can, Comfiture, Husband(ry), Jam, Jelly, Maintain, Maintenance, Noah, NT, Protect, Save

Consider(able), Considerate, Consideration Animadvert, Attention, Avizandum, By-end, Case, Cerebrate, Chew over, Cogitate, Contemplate, Count, Courtesy, Debate, Deem, Deliberate, Entertain, Envisage, Factor, Fair, Feel, Forethought, Gay, Gey, Heed, Importance, Inasmuch, Judge, Many, Materially, Measure, Meditate, Muse, Pay, Perpend, Poise, Ponder, Premeditate, Pretty, Rate, Reck, Reckon, Reflect, Regard, Respect, Scruple, See, Sensitive, Several, Shortlist, Solicitous, Song, Speculate, Steem, Study, Substantial, Think, Tidy, Vast, View, Ween, Weigh

Consign(ment) Allot, Award, Batch, Bequeath, Delegate, Deliver, Drop shipment, Entrust, Lading, Ship, Shipment, Transfer

Consist(ent), Consistency Agree, Coherent, Comprise, Enduring, Even, Liaison, Rely, Sound, Steady, Texture

Consolation, Console Ancon, Appease, Balm, Cheer, Comfort, Games, Play, Reassure, Relief, Solace, Sop, Station

Consolidate Coalesce, Combine, Compact, Gel, Merge, Pun, Unify

Consommé Julienne, Soup

Consonant(s) Affricate, Agma, Agreeing, Cacuminal, Cerebral, Explosive, Fortis, Fricative, Harmonious, Implosive, Labial, Lateral, Lenis, Media, Mouillé, Plosive, Sonorant, Spirant, Surd, Tenuis, Velar

Consort Ally, Associate, Maik, Mate, Moop, Moup, Partner, Spouse

Consortium Coalition, Combine, Ring

Conspicuous Arresting, Blatant, Clear, Eminent, Glaring, Kenspeck(le), Landmark, Light, Manifest, Patent, Salient, Shining, Showy, Signal, Striking

Conspiracy, Conspirator, Conspire, Conspiring Brutus, Cabal, Casca, Cassius, Catiline, Cato St, Champerty, Cinna, Collaborate, Colleague, Collogue, Collude, Complot, Connive, Covin, Covyne, Guy, Highbinder, In cahoots, Intrigue, Oates, Omerta, → **PLOT**, Ring, Scheme

Constable Beck, Catchpole, Cop, Dogberry, Dull, Elbow, Harman(-beck), Headborough, High, Hog, John, Lord High, Officer, Painter, Petty, Pointsman, → **POLICEMAN**, Posse, Special, Thirdborough, Tipstaff, Uniformed, Verges

Constancy, Constant Abiding, Boltzmann, C, Changeless, Chronic, Coefficient, Cosmic, Cosmological, Devotion, Dielectric, Diffusion, Dilys, Dirac, Eccentricity, Eternal, Faith, Firm, Fixed, Fundamental, G, Gas, Gravitational, H, Honesty, Hubble's, K, Lambert, Leal(ty), Logical, Loyal, Magnetic, Nonstop, Often,

Parameter, → **PERPETUAL**, Pi, Planck's, Pole star, Regular, Resolute, Sad, Solar, Staunch, Steadfast, Steady, Time, True, Unfailing, Uniform, Usual

Constellation Andromeda, Antlia, Apus, Aquarius, Aquila, Ara, Argo, Aries, Auriga, Bootes, Caelum, Camelopardalis, Camelopardus, Canes Venatici, Canis Major, Canis Minor, Carina, Cassiopeia, Centaurus, Cepheus, Cetus, Cham(a)eleon, Circinus, Columba, Coma Berenices, Coma Cluster, Corvus, Crater, Cygnus, Cynosure, Delphinus, Delta, Dolphin, Dorado, Draco, Equuleus, Eridanus, Fornax, Galaxy, Gemini, Great Bear, Gru(i)s, Hercules, Horologium, Hydra, Hydrus, Indus, Lacerta, Leo, Leo Minor, Lepus, Libra, Little Bear, Little Dipper, Lupus, Lynx, Lyra, Mensa, Monoceros, Musca, Norma, Octans, Ophiuchus, Orion, Pavo, Pegasus, Perseus, Phoenix, Pictor, Piscis Austrinus, → **PLANET**, Puppis, Pyxis, Reticulum, Sagitta, Sagittarius, Scorpius, Sculptor, Scutum, Serpens, Sextans, Southern Cross, Spica, → **STAR**, Telescopium, The Rule, Triangulum (Australe), Tucana, Twins, Unicorn, Vela, Virgin, Virgo, Volans, Vulpecula, Wag(g)oner, Whale, Zodiacal

Consternation Alarm, Dismay, Doodah, Fear, Horror

Constipate(d), Constipation Astrict, Bind, Block, Costive, Mawbound, Stegnotic, Stenosis

Constituency, Constituent Borough, Component, Element, Immediate, Part, Principle, Seat, Ultimate, Voter

▷ **Constituents** *may indicate* an anagram

Constitute, Constitution(al) Appoint, Charter, Clarendon, Compose, Comprise, Congenital, Creature, Establishment, Form, Fuero, Health, Physique, Policy, Polity, Seat, State, Synthesis, Upmake, Walk

Constrain(ed), Constraint Bind, Bondage, Boundary, Coerce, Confine, Coop, Curb, Duress(e), Force, Hard, Oblige, Pressure, Repress, Stenosis, Taboo, Trammel

Constrict(ed), Constriction Bottleneck, Choke, Coarctate, Contract, Cramp, Hour-glass, Impede, Limit, Narrow, Phimosis, Squeeze, Stegnosis, Stenosis, Strangle, Strangulate, Thlipsis, Tighten, Venturi

Construct(ion), Constructor, Constructive Build, Compile, Engineer, Erect, Fabricate, Facture, Fashion, Form, Frame, Idolum, Make, Manufacture, Partners, Seabee, Stressed-skin, Tectonic, Weave

Construe Deduce, Explain, Expound, Infer

Consul Ambassador, Attaché, Horse, Lucullus, Praetor

Consult(ant), Consultation Avisement, Confer, Deliberate, Discuss, Emparl, Imparl, Joint, Peritus, See, Sexpert, Shark watcher, Surgery, Vide

Consume(r), Consumption, Consumptive Bolt, Burn, Caterpillar®, Conspicuous, Decay, Devour, Diner, Eat, Engross, Exhaust, Expend, Feed, Glutton, Hectic, Mainline, Scoff, Spend, Swallow, TB, Use, Waste, Wear

Consummate, Consummation Achieve, Crown, Keystone, Seal

Contact Abut, Adpress, Contingence, Eye, Fax, Hook-up, Lens, Liaise, Liaison, Meet, Outreach, Radio, Reach, Shoe, Taction, → **TOUCH**, Touchy-feely, Wiper

Contagious, Contagion Infection, Noxious, Poison, Taint, Variola, Viral

Contain(er) Amphora, Ampulla, Aquafer, Aquifer, Barrel, Basket, Bass, Beaker, Bidon, Billy(-can), Bin, Boat, Bottle, Box, Buddle, Butter-boat, Cachepot, Can, Canakin, Canikin, Canister, Cannikin, Cantharus, Capsule, Carafe, Carboy, Carry, Carton, Case, Cask, Cassette, Chase, Chest, Churn, Coffer, Comprise, Coolamon, Crate, Crater, Crucible, Cup, Cupel, Cuvette, Decanter, Dracone, Dredger, Enclose, Encompass, Enseam, Esky®, Feretory, Flagon, Flask, Flat, Gabion, Gourd, Growler, → **HOLD**, House, Igloo, Include, Incubator, Intray, Jar, Jeroboam, Jerrican, Jerrycan, Jug, Keg, Kirbeh, Leaguer, Lekythos, Melting-pot, Monkey, Monstrance, Mould, Olpe, Out-tray, Pail, Pinata, Piscina, Pitcher, Pithos, Pod, Pottle, Punnet, Pyxis,

Reliquary, Repository, Restrain, Sac(k), Saggar, Scyphus, Shaker, Situla, Skin, Skip, Snaptin, Spittoon, Stamnos, Stillage, Tank, Tantalus, Terrarium, Tinaja, Trough, Tub, Tun, Tupperware®, Urn, Valise, Vase, Vessel, Vinaigrette, Wardian case, Wineskin, Woolpack, Workbag

Contaminate(d), Contamination Adulterate, Corrupt, Defile, Denature, Flyblown, Impure, Infect, Mysophobia, Pollute, Soil, Stain, Tarnish

Contemplate, Contemplation Consider, Ecce, Envisage, Hesychasm, Meditate, Muse, Ponder, Reflect, Retrospection, Rue, Samadhi, Spell, Study, Think, Watch

Contemporary AD, Coetaneous, Current, Equal, Fellow, Modern, Modish, Present, Verism

Contempt(ible), Contemptuous Abject, Ageism, Aha, Arsehole, Bah, BEF, Cheap, Contumely, Crud, Crumb, Crummy, Cullion, Cynical, Derision, Despisal, Diddy, Dismissive, Dis(s), Disparaging, Disrespect, Dusty, Dog-bolt, Fico, Fig, Figo, Git, Hangdog, Ignominious, Insect, Jive-ass, Low, Mean, Measly, Misprision, Och, Odious, Paltry, Pelting, Phooey, Pish, Poof, Poxy, Pshaw, Ratfink, Rats, Razoo, Scabby, Scarab, Schlub, Scofflaw, → **SCORN**, Scumbag, Scurvy, Sdeign, Sexism, Shabby, Shitface, Shithead, Slimeball, Sneer, Sneeze, Sniffy, Snook, Snooty, Snot, Snotty, Soldier, Sorry, Sprat, Squirt, Squit, Supercilious, Toad, Toerag, Tossy, Vilipend, Weed, Whipster, Wretched

Contend(er) Argue, Candidate, Claim, Clash, Compete, Cope, Debate, Dispute, Fight, Grapple, Oppose, Rival, Stickle, → **STRIVE**, Struggle, Submit, → **VIE**, Wrestle

Content Apaid, Apay, Appay, Blissful, Happy, Inside, Please, Satisfy, Volume

▷ **Content** *may indicate* a hidden word

Contention, Contentious Argument, Bellicose, Cantankerous, Case, Combat, Competitive, Logomachy, Perverse, Polemical, Rivalry, Strife, Struggle, Sturt

Contest(ant) Agon, Battle, Beauty, Beetle drive, Biathlon, Bout, Catchweight, Challenge, Championship, Combat, Competition, Concours, Darraign, Decathlon, Defend, Deraign, Dogfight, Duathlon, Duel(lo), Entrant, Eurovision, Event, Examinee, Finalist, Free-for-all, Fronde, Handicap, Heptathlon, Kemp, Kriegspiel, Lampadephoria, Match, Matchplay, Olympiad, Pancratium, Par, Paralympics, Pentathlon, Pingle, Play-off, Prizer, Race, Rival, Roadeo, Rodeo, Scrap, Set-to, Skirmish, Slam, Slugfest, Strife, Struggle, Tenson, Tetrathlon, Tournament, Triathlon, Tug-of-war, Vie, War, With

Context Intentional, Opaque, Transparent

Continent(al) Abstinent, Asia, Atlantis, Austere, Chaste, Dark, Epeirogeny, Euro, European, Gallic, Gondwanaland, Laurasia, Lemuria, Mainland, Moderate, Pang(a)ea, Shelf, Teetotal, Temperate, Walloon

Contingency, Contingent Accident, Arm, Casual, Chance, Conditional, Dependent, Event, Fluke, Group, Prospect

Continual(ly), Continuous Adjoining, Away, Chronic, Connected, Eer, Endlong, Eternal, Eterne, Ever, Forever, Frequent, Incessant, Non-stop, On(going), Unbroken, Unceasing

Continue, Continuation, Continuing, Continuity Abye, Duration, Dure, During, Enduring, Enjamb(e)ment, Follow-on, Go on, Hold, Keep, Last, Link, Ongoing, Onward, Persevere, Persist, Proceed, Prolong, Remain, Resume, Sequence, Stand, Subsist, Survive, Sustain, Synaphe(i)a, Tenor

▷ **Continuously** *may indicate* previous words to be linked

Contort(ion) Deform, Gnarl, Jib, Twist, Warp, Wreathe, Wry

Contour Curve, Graph, Isallobar, Isobase, Isocheim, Isochime, Isogeothermal, Line, Profile, Silhouette, Streamline, Tournure

Contraband Hot, Illicit, Prohibited, Smuggled

Contraception, Contraceptive Billings method, Cap, Coil, Condom, Depo-Provera®, Diaphragm, Dutch cap, Etonogestrol, IU(C)D, Legonorgestrel, Lippes loop, Loop, Minipill, Oral, Pessary, Pill, Precautions, Prophylactic, Rubber(s), Sheath, Vimule®

Contract(ion), Contractor Abbreviate, Abridge, Affreightment, Agreement, Appalto, Astringency, Bargain, Biceps, Bottomry, Braxton-Hicks, Bridge, Builder, Catch, Champerty, Charter, Clonus, Condense, Consensual, Constringe, Contrahent, Convulsion, Covenant, Cramp, Crasis, Curtail, Debt, Develop, Diastalsis, Dupuytren's, Dwindle, Engage, Entrepreneur, Escrow, Fitzgerald-Lorentz, Flex, Forward, Gainsay, Gooseflesh, Guarantee, Hand-promise, Hire, Incur, Indenture, Jerk, Ketubah, Knit, Lease, Lessen, Levator, Lorentz-Fitzgerald, Make, Mandate, Miosis, Myosis, Narrow, Obligee, Outsource, Party, Peristalsis, Privilege, Promise, Pucker, Purse, Restriction, Risus (sardonicus), Service, Shrink, Shrivel, Sign, Slam, Social, Spasm, Specialty, Squinch, Steelbow, Stenosis, Stipulation, Straddle, Supplier, Sweetheart, Synaloepha, Syngraph, Systole, Telescope, Tetanise, Tetanus, Tic, Tighten, Time bargain, Tittle, Tonicity, Tontine, Treaty, Triceps, Trigger-finger, Trismus cynicus, Wrinkle, Yellow-dog, Z

Contradict(ion), Contradictory Ambivalent, Antilogy, Antinomy, Belie, Bull, Contrary, Counter, Dementi, Deny, Disaffirm, Disprove, Dissent, → **GAINSAY**, Negate, Oxymoron, Paradox, Sot, Stultify, Sublate, Threap, Threep, Traverse

Contraption Contrivance, Scorpion

Contrapuntal Fugue

Contrarily, Contrary Adverse, A rebours, Arsy-versy, But, Captious, Converse, Counter, Counterfleury, Crosscurrent, Cross-grained, Cross-purpose, Froward, Hostile, Inverse, Mary, Opposite, Oppugnant, Ornery, Perverse, Rebuttal, Retrograde, Wayward, Withershins

Contrast Chiaroscuro, Clash, Colour, Compare, Differ, Foil, Relief

Contravene Infringe, Oppose, Thwart, Violate

Contribute, Contribution Abet, Add, Assist, Chip in, Conduce, Donate, Dub, Furnish, Go, Help, Input, Kick in, Mite, Offering, Share, Sub, Subscribe, Whack, Widow's mite

▷ **Contributing to** *may indicate* a hidden word

Contrite, Contrition Penance, Penitent, Remorse, Repentant, Rue, → **SORRY**

Contrivance, Contrive(r), Contrived Art, Artificial, Chicaner, Contraption, Cook, Deckle, Deus ex machina, Device, Devise, Dodge, Engine, Engineer, Finesse, Frame, Gadget, Gimmick, Gin, Hatch, Hokey, Intrigue, Invention, Machinate, Manage, Manoeuvre, Page, Plan, Plot, Procure, Rest, Rowlock, Scheme, Secure, Stage, Trump, Wangle, Weave

Control(ler), Controllable Ada, Appestat, Autopilot, Big Brother, Birth, Boss, Boundary layer, Bridle, Cabotage, Chair, Check, Chokehold, Christmas tree, Contain, Corner, Corset, Curb, Cybernetics, Damage, Descendeur, Dirigible, Dirigism(e), Dominate, Dominion, Driving seat, Dynamic, Elevon, Etatiste, Fast-forward, Fader, Fet(ch), Finger, Flood, Fly-by-wire, Gain, Gar, George, Gerent, Govern, Ground, Gubernation, Harness, Hae, Have, Heck, Helm, Influence, Influx, Joystick, Keypad, Knee-swell, Lead, Lever, Line, → **MANAGE**, Martinet, Mastery, Moderate, Mouse, Nipple, Noise, Numerical, Operate, Override, Pilot, Placebo, Police, Population, Possess, Power, Preside, Price, Process, Puppeteer, Quality, Radio, Referee, Regulate, Regulo®, Rein, Remote, Rent, Repress, Restrain, Restrict, Rheostat, Ride, Ripple, Rule, Run, School, Servo, Slide(r), Snail, Solion, Steady, Steer, Stop, Stranglehold, Stringent, Subdue, Subject, Subjugate, Supervise,

Suzerain, Svengali, Sway, Switch, Takeover, Tame, Thermostat, Throttle, Tie, Tiller, Tone, Traction, Umpire, Valve, Weld, Wield, Zapper

Controversial, Controversy Argument, Contention, Debate, Dispute, Emotive, Eristic(al), Furore, Hot potato, Polemic(al), Tendentious, Troll

Conundrum Acrostic, Egma, Enigma, Puzzle, Riddle, Teaser

Convalesce(nt), Convalescence Anastatic, Mend, Rally, Recover, Recuperate, Rest-cure

▸ **Convene** *see* CONVOKE

Convenience, Convenient Behoof, Commode, Easy, Eft, Ethe, Expedient, Facility, Gain, Gents, Handsome, → HANDY, Hend, Lav, Leisure, Near, Opportune, Pat, Privy, Public, Suitable, Toilet, Use, Well

Convent Abbatial, Cloister, Fratry, Friary, House, → MONASTERY, Motherhouse, Nunnery, Port-royal, Priory, Retreat

Convention(al) Academic, Accepted, Babbitt, Blackwood, Bourgeois, Caucus, Code, Conclave, Conformity, → CUSTOMARY, Diet, Done, Formal, Geneva, Habitude, Iconic, Lame, Lingua franca, Mainstream, Meeting, Middlebrow, Middle-of-the-road, More, National, Nomic, Orthodox, Ossified, Pompier, Proper, Propriety, Readymade, Schengen, Staid, Starchy, Stereotyped, Stock, Straight, Synod, Uptight, Usage, Warsaw

Converge(nce) Approach, Focus, Inrush, Meet, Toe-in

Conversation(alist), Converse, Conversant Abreast, Antithesis, Board, Buck, Cackle, Causerie, Chat, Chitchat, Colloquy, Commune, Confab, Convo, Crack, Crosstalk, Deipnosophist, Dialogue, Discourse, Eutrapelia, Eutrapely, Hobnob, Interlocution, Jaw-jaw, Natter, Opposite, Palaver, Parley, Persiflage, Rap, Rhubarb, Shop, Shoptalk, Socialise, → TALK, Transpose, Trialogue, Wongi, Word

Conversion, Converter, Convert(ible) Adapt, Alter, Assimilate, Azotobacter, Bessemer, Cabriolet, Cash, Catalytic, Catechumen, Change, Commute, Cyanise, Damascene, Diagenesis, Disciple, Encash, Etherify, Evangelize, Exchange, Expropriate, Fixation, Gummosis, Hodja, Kho(d)ja, Landau, L-D, Liquid, Marrano, Metanoia, Neophyte, Noviciate, Novitiate, Persuade, Prill, Proselyte, Put, Ragtop, Realise, Rebirth, Reclamation, Recycle, Revamp, Sheik(h), Soft-top, Souper, Tablet, Taw, Torque, Transduce, Transform, Transmute, Try

▷ **Conversion, Converted** *may indicate* an anagram

Convex(ity) Arched, Bowed, Camber, Curved, Entasis, Extrados, Gibbous, Lenticle, Nowy

Convey(ance) Assign, BS, Carousel, Carriage, Carry, Cart, Charter, Coach, Conduct, Cycle, Deed, Deliver, Eloi(g)n, Enfeoffment, Esloyne, Exeme, Giggit, Grant, Guide, Lease, Litter, Lorry, Mailcar(t), Pirogue, Pneumatic, Re-lease, Sac, Screw, Soc, Tip, Title deed, Tote, Tram, Transfer, Transit, Transmit, Transport, Vehicle

Convict(ion) Attaint, Belief, Botany Bay, Bushranger, Canary, Certitude, Cockatoo, Cogence, Crawler, Credo, Creed, Criminal, Demon, Dogma, Emancipist, Faith, Felon, Forçat, Government man, Lag, Magwitch, Old chum, → PERSUASION, Plerophory, Record, Ring, Trusty, Vehemence, Yardbird

Convince(d), Convincing Assure, Cogent, Doubtless, Luculent, Persuade, Plausible, Satisfy, Sold, Sure

Convivial(ity) Boon, Bowl, Festive, Gay, Genial, Jovial, Social

Convoke(r) Assemble, Call, Chairman, Convene, Summon

Convolute(d), Convolution Coiled, Gyrus, Helical, Intricate, Spiral, Tortuous, Twisty, Whorl, Writhen

Convolvulus Bindweed, Dodder

Convoy Caravan, Column, Conduct, Escort, Fur brigade, Pilot, Train, Wagon-train

Convulse, Convulsion(s), Convulsive Agitate, Clonic, Clonus, Commotion, Disturb, DT, Eclampsia, → **FIT**, Galvanic, Paroxysm, Spasm, Throe, Tic

▷ **Cook** *may indicate* an anagram

Cook(s), Cooker(y), Cooking Aga®, Babbler, Babbling brook, Bake, Balti, Beeton, Benghazi, Bhindi, Bouche, Braise, Broil, Cacciatore, Calabash, Captain, Charbroil, Chargrill, Chef, Coction, Coddle, Concoct, Cordon bleu, Creole, Cuisine, Cuisinier, Deep-fry, Delia, Devil, Do, Doctor, Dumple, Easy over, Edit, En papillote, Escoffier, Explorer, Fake, Falsify, Fiddle, Fireless, Flambé, Forge, Fricassee, Fry, Fudge, Fusion, Gastronomy, Gratinate, Greasy, Griddle, Grill, Haute cuisine, Haybox, Hibachi, Jackaroo, Kiln, Lyonnaise, Marengo, Marinière, Meunière, Microwave, Mount, Nouvelle cuisine, Poach, Prepare, Pressure, Provencale, Ribroast, Rig, Ring, Roast, Roger, Sauté, Silver, Sous-chef, Spit, Steam, Stew, Stir-fry, Stove, Tandoori, Tikka, Tire, Toast

Cool(er), Coolant, Cooling, Coolness Aloof, Aplomb, Calm, Can, Chill, Collected, Composed, Cryogen, Cryostat, Defervescence, Desert, Dignified, Dispassionate, Distant, Esky®, Fan, Frappé, Fridge, Frigid, Frosty, Gaol, Goglet, Hip, Ice(box), Jail, Jug, Keel, La Nina, Lubricating oil, Maraging, Nervy, Nonchalant, Offish, Phlegm, Poise, Prison, Quad, Quod, Reefer, Refresh, Regenerative, Reserved, Sangfroid, Serene, Skeigh, Splat, Stir, Sweat, Temperate, Thou(sand), Trendy, Unruffled, Wint(e)ry

Coop Cage, Cavie, Confine, Gaol, Hutch, Mew, Pen, Rip

Cooper Gary, Henry, Tubman

Cooperate, Cooperation, Cooperative Ally, Bipartisan, Collaborate, Combine, Conspire, Contribute, Coop, Credit union, Give and take, Liaise, Pitch in, Play, Synergy, Teamwork, Together, Worker's

Coordinate(s), Coordinated, Coordination Abscissa, Abscisse, Agile, Arrange, Cartesian, Ensemble, Harmony, Nabla, Orchestrate, Ordonnance, Peer, Polar, Right ascension, Spherical, Synergy, Teamwork, Tight, Twistor, Waypoint, X, Y, Z

Coot Stupid, Sultan

Cop(s) Bag, Bull, Catch, Copper, Dick, Keystone, Peeler, Peon, → **POLICEMAN**, Silent

Copal Dammar, Resin

Cope Chlamys, Deal, Face, Handle, Make do, → **MANAGE**, Mantle, Meet, Negotiate, Pallium, Poncho

Coping (stone) Balustrade, Capstone, Skew

Copious Abundant, Affluent, Ample, Fecund, Fluent, Fruitful, Fulsome, Plentiful, Profuse

Copper As, Atacamite, Blister, Bluebottle, Bobby, Bornite, Busy, Cash, Cent, Chessylite, → **COIN**, Cu, D, Dam, Double, Erinite, Flatfoot, Lawman, Lota(h), Malachite, Mountain-blue, Ormolu, Peacock, Pence, Penny, Pfennig, Pie, Pig, Plack, Policeman, Red, Rosser, Rozzer, S, Sen(s), Slop, Special, Traybit, Venus, Verdet, Washer, Washtub, Wire bar

Coppice, Copse Thicket, Underwood

Copulate Boff, Intercourse, Line, Mate, Roger, Serve, Tread, Tup

Copy(ing), Copier, Copyist, Copywriter Adman, Aemule, Ape, Apograph, Association, Autotype, Calk, Calque, Camera-ready, Carbon, Clerk, Clone, Counterpart, Crib, Cyclostyle, Diazo, Ditto, Download, Dyeline, Echo, Echopraxia, Ectype, Edition, Eidograph, Electro, Emulate, Engross, Estreat, Example, Facsimile, Fair, Fax, Flimsy, Forge, Hard, Hectograph, → **IMITATE**, Issue, Jellygraph, Knocking, Manifold, Manuscript, Match, Me-tooer, Microdot, Milline, Mimeograph®, Mimic, Mirror, MS, Offprint, Ozalid, Pantograph, Parrot, Photostat®, Plagiarism, Polygraph, Read-out, Repeat, Replica, Repro, Reproduce,

Review, Rip, Roneo®, Scribe, Script, Scrivener, Sedulous, Show, Simulate, Skim, Soft, Spit, Stat, Stencil, Stuff, Tall, Telautograph®, Telefax, Tenor, Tenure, Trace, Transcribe, Transume, Transumpt, Vidimus, Xerox®

Copyright C, Landgrab

Coquette Agacerie, Flirt, Rosina, Tease, Vamp

Cor Bath, Crumbs, Ephah, Homer

Coracle Currach, Curragh

Coral (reef) Alcyonaria, Aldabra, Atoll, Brain, Cup, Deadmen's fingers, Gorgonia(n), Laccadives, Madrepore, Millepore, Organ-pipe, Pink, Precious, Red, Reef, Sea fan, Sea ginger, Sea-pen, Sea whip, Seed, Staghorn, Stony, Zoothome

Cord, Cord-like Aiguillette, Band, Bedford, Bind, Boondoggle, Cat-gut, Chenille, Communication, Creance, Cybernaculum, Drawstring, Elephant, Flex, Fourragère, Funicle, Gasket, Heddle, Lace, Laniard, Lanyard, Ligature, Line, Moreen, Myelon, Nerve, Net, Ocnus, Picture, Piping, Quipo, Quipu, Rep(s), Restiform, Rip, Rope, Sash, Sennit, Service, Shroudline, Sinnet, Spermatic, Spinal, → **STRING**, Tendon, Tie, Tieback, Torsade, Twine, Twitch, Umbilical, Vocal, Wick

Cordial Anise(ed), Anisette, Benedictine, Cassis, Drink, Elderflower, Gracious, Grenadine, Hearty, Hippocras, Kind, Neighbourly, Oporice, Orangeade, Persico(t), Pleasant, Ratafia, Rosa-solis, Roso(g)lio, Shrub, Tar-water, Warm

Cordon Band, Beltcourse, Picket, Ring, Sanitaire, Surround

Corduroy Rep(p)

Cordyline Ti-tree

Core Barysphere, Calandria, Campana, Centre, Chog, Essence, Filament, Hard, Heart, Hub, Kernel, Magnetic, Nife, Nitty-gritty, Plerome, Quintessence, Runt, Slug

Co-religionist Brother

Coriander Cilantro

Corinthian(s) Casuals, Caulis, Epistolaters

Cork(ed), Corker Balsa, Bouché, Bung, Float(er), Humdinger, Mountain, Oner, Periderm, Phellem, Phellogen, Plug, Seal, Shive, Stopper, Suber(ate)

Corkscrew Bore, Opening, Spiral

Cormorant Duiker, Duyker, Scart(h), Shag, Skart(h)

Corn(y) Bajr(a), Banal, Blé, Cereal, Cob, Dolly, Durra, Emmer, Epha, Flint, Gait, Graddan, Grain, Green, Grist, Guinea, Icker, Indian, Kaffir, Kanga pirau, Mabela, Maize, Mealie, Muid, Negro, Nubbin, Pickle, Pinole, Posho, Rabi, Rye, Seed, Shock, Stitch, Straw, Sugar, Sweet, Tail ends, Thrave, Trite, Zea

Corncrake Landrail

Cornel Dogberry, Tree

Corner Amen, Angle, Bend, Canthus, Cantle, Canton, Chamfer, Cranny, Dangerous, Diêdre, Elbow, Entrap, Hog, Hole, Hospital, Long, Lug, Monopoly, NE, Niche, Nook, NW, Penalty, Predicament, Quoin, SE, Short, Speakers', Spot, SW, Tack, Tight, Trap, Tree, Vertex

Cornerstone Coi(g)n, Encoignure, Skew-corbel, Skew-put, Skew-table

Cornet Cone, Cornopean, Field, Horn

Cornice Surbase

Cornish(man) Cousin Jack

Cornstalks Strammel, Straw, Strummel, Stubble

Cornucopia Amalthea, Horn

Cornwall SW

Corollary Conclusion, Dogma, Porism, Rider, Theory, Truism

Corona Aureole, Cigar, Larmier, Nimbus, Wreath

Coronation Enthronement

Coroner Procurator fiscal

Corporal Bardolph, Bodily, Bombardier, Brig(adier), Lance-pesade, Lance-prisade, Lance-prisado, Lance-speisade, Master, Naik, NCO, Nym, Pall, Physical, Trim

Corporation Belly, Body, Closed, Commune, Company, Conglomerate, Guild, Kite, Kyte, Paunch, Pot, Public, Public service, Stomach, Swag-belly, Tum, Wame, Wem

Corps Body, C, Crew, Diplomatic, Peace, RAC, REME, Unit

Corpse(s) Blob, Body, Cadaver, Carcass, Carrion, Dust, Goner, Like, Mort, Quarry, Relic, Remains, Stiff, Zombi(e)

Corpulence, Corpulent Adipose, Fat, Fleshy, Gross, Obese, Poddy, Stout, Thickset, Tubby

Corpuscle Cell, Erythrocyte, Malpighian, Meissner's, Microcyte, Neutrophil, Pacinian, Phagocyte, Porkilocyte

Correct(ive), Correcting, Correctly, Correctness, Correction, Corrector About east, Accurate, Alexander, Align, Amend, Aright, Blue-pencil, Bodkin, Castigate, Chasten, Chastise, Check, Cheese, Decorous, Diorthortic, Emend, Epanorthosis, Ethical, Exact, Fair, Fix, Grammatical, Legit, Mend, Politically, Preterition, Probity, Proofread, Proper, Propriety, Punctilious, Punish, Purism, Rebuke, Rectify, Rectitude, Redress, Remedial, Reprove, Revise, Right(en), Scold, Spinning-house, Spot-on, Sumpsimus, Tickety-boo, Trew, True, Twink, U

▷ **Corrected** *may indicate* an anagram

Correspond(ence), Correspondent, Corresponding Accord, Agree, Analogy, Assonance, Coincident, Communicate, Congruence, Counterpart, Cynghanedd, Epistolist, Equate, Equivalence, Eye-rhyme, Fit, Foreign, Hate mail, Homolog(ue), Identical, Isomorph, Lobby, Match, On all fours, One to one, Par, Parallel, Parity, Relate, Snail mail, Symmetry, Tally, Veridical, War, Write

Corridor Air, Aisle, Berlin, Entry, Gallery, Greenway, Lobby, Passage, Penthouse, Polish, Re-entry

Corroborate Confirm, Support, Verify

Corrode(d), Corrosion, Corrosive Acid, Acid rain, Brinelling, Burn, Canker, Decay, Eat, Erode, Etch, Fret, Gnaw, Hydrazine, Mordant, → **ROT**, Rubiginous, Rust, Waste

Corrugate Gimp

Corrupt(er), Corrupting, Corruption Abuse, Adulterate, Bastardise, Bent, Bobol, Bribable, Canker, Cesspit, Debase, Debauch, Debosh, Decadent, Defile, Degenerate, Depravity, Dissolute, Dry rot, Emancipate, Embrace(o)r, Embrasor, Empoison, Enseam, Etch, Evil, Fester, Gangrene, Graft(er), Immoral, Impaired, Impure, Infect, Inquinate, Jobbery, Leprosy, Malversation, Nefarious, Obelus, Payola, Perverse, Poison, Pollute, Power, Putrefaction, Putrid, Rakery, Ret(t), Rigged, Rot, Scrofulous, Seduce, Sepsis, Septic, Sleaze, Sodom, Sophisticate, Spoil, Suborn, Tammany, Twist, Venal, Vice, Vitiate

Corsage Buttonhole, Pompadour, Posy, Spray

Corsair Barbary, Picaroon, Pirate, Privateer, Robber, Rover

Corset, Corslet Belt, Bodice, Busk, Girdle, Lorica, Roll-on, Stays, Thorax, Waspie

Corsican Napoleon

Cortege Parade, Retinue, Train

Cortex Cerebral, Renal

Cortisone Hecogenin

Corundum Emery, Sapphire

Corvo Rolfe

Corybant Roisterer

Cosh Sap

Cosmetic Beautifier, Blusher, Bronzer, Chapstick, Conditioner, Eye-black, Eyeliner,

Eye-shadow, Face-pack, Foundation, Fucus, Highlighter, Kohl, Lightener, Liner, Lip gloss, Lip liner, Lipstick, Lotion, Maquillage, Mascara, Moisturizer, Mousse, Mudpack, Paint, Panstick, Pearl-powder, Pearl-white, Powder, Reface, Rouge, Talcum, Toner

▶ **Cosmic** *see* **COSMOS**

Cosmonaut Gagarin, Spaceman, Tereshkova

Cosmopolitan International, Urban

Cosmos, Cosmic Globe, Heaven, Infinite, Mundane, Nature, Universe, World

Cossack Ataman, Hetman, Kazak(h), Mazeppa, Russian, Tartar, Zaporogian

Cosset Caress, Coddle, Fondle, Nanny, Pamper

Cost(s), Costly Be, Bomb, Carriage, Charge, Current, Damage, Direct, Earth, Escuage, Estimate, Exes, → **EXPENSE**, Factor, Fetched, Fixed, Hire, Historic(al), Indirect, Loss, Marginal, Opportunity, Outlay, Overhead, Precious, Price, Prime, Quotation, Rate, Rent, Running, Sacrifice, Storage, Sumptuous, Toll, Unit, Upkeep, Usurious, Variable

Costa Rica(n) Tico

Costermonger Barrow-boy, Kerb-merchant, Pearly

Costume(s) Apparel, Attire, Camagnole, Cossie, Dress, Ensemble, Get-up, Gi(e), Guise, Judogi, Livery, Maillot, Motley, Nebris, Polonaise, Rig, Ruana, Surcoat, Tanga, Togs, Trollopee, Tutu, Uniform, Wardrobe, Wear

Cosy Cosh, Gemutlich, Intime, Snug

Cot Moses basket

Coterie Cell, Cenacle, Circle, Clan, Clique, Club, Ring, Set, Society

Cottage(r) Bach, Batch, Bordar, Bothie, Bothy, Bower, Box, Bungalow, Cabin, Cape Cod, Chalet, Cot, Crib, Dacha, Home-croft, Hut, Lodge, Mailer

Cotton Absorbent, Agree, AL, Alabama, Balbriggan, Batiste, Batting, Bengal, Calico, Candlewick, Ceiba, Chambray, Chino, Chintz, Collodion, Coutil(le), Cretonne, Denim, Dho(o)ti, Dimity, Ducks, Fustian, Galatea, Gossypine, Gossypium, Humhum, Ihram, Jaconet, Lavender, Lawn, Lea, Lille, Lint, Lisle, Longcloth, Manchester, Marcella, Muslin, Nainsook, Nankeen, Nankin, Osnaburg, Pongee, Sea-island, Seersucker, Silesia, Stranded, Surat, T-cloth, Thread, Twig, Upland, Velveteen

Cotton soil Regar, Regur

Cotyledon Seed-leaf

Couch Bed, Casting, Davenport, Daybed, → **DIVAN**, Express, Grass, Lurk, Palanquin, Palkee, Palki, Quick, Recamier, Sedan, Settee, Sofa, Studio, Triclinium, Vis-à-vis, Winnipeg, Word

Coué Auto-suggestion

Cougar Cat, Painter, Puma

Cough(ing) Bark, Chin, Croup, Expectorate, Hack, Harrumph, Hawk, Hem, Hoast, Hooping, Kink, Pertussis, Phthisis, Rale, Tisick, Tussis, Ugh, Whooping

Could Couth

Council (meeting), Councillor, Counsel(lor) Achitophel, Admonish, Admonitor, Advice, Advocate, Ahithophel, Alderman, Alfred, Amphictryon, Anziani, Aread, A(r)re(e)de, Assembly, Attorney, Aulic, Aunt, Ayuntamiento, Board, Body, Boule, Bundesrat, Burgess, Cabinet, Casemate, Committee, Consistory, Corporation, County, Cr, Decurion, Dergue, Devil, Dietine, Divan, Douma, Duma, Ecofin, Ecumenical, Egeria, Europe, European, Executive, Exhort, General, Great, Greenbag, Hebdomadal, Indaba, Induna, Industrial, Info, Islands, Jirga, Junta, Kabele, Kebele, King's, Kite, Landst(h)ing, Lateran, Leader, Legislative, Loan, Majlis, Mentor, Nestor, Nicaean, Nicene, Panchayat, Paraclete, Parish, Powwow,

Press, Privy, Provincial, Queen's, Rede, Regional, Reichsrat, Robber, Runanga, Samaritan, Sanhedrim, Sanhedrin, Security, Senate, Shoora, Shura, Sobranje, Sobranye, Soviet, States, Syndicate, Synedrion, Synod, Thing, Town, Tradeboard, Trades, Trent, Tridentine, Trullan, Vatican, Volost, Wages, Whitley, Witan, Witenagemot, Works, Zemstvo, Zila, Zila parishad, Zillah

Count(ed), Counter, Counting Abacus, Add, Algoriam, Anti, Balance, Bar, Basie, Blood, Buck, Buffet, Calculate, Calorie, Cavour, Census, Check, Chip, Compute, Coost, → **COUNTERBALANCE**, Crystal, Desk, Disc, Dracula, Dump, Earl, Enumerate, Fish, Geiger, Geiger-Muller, Graf(in), Grave, Itemise, Jet(t)on, Landgrave, Margrave, Marker, Matter, Merel(l), Meril, Milton work, Nobleman, Number, Numerate, Obviate, Olivia, Oppose, Palatine, Palsgrave, Paris, Pollen, Presume, Proportional, Rebut, → **RECKON**, Refute, Rejoinder, Rely, Retaliate, Retort, Rhinegrave, Scaler, Scintillation, Score, Sperm, Squail, Statistician, Stop, Sum, Table, Tally, Tell, Tiddlewink, Ugolino, Weigh, Zeppelin

Countenance Approve, Brow, Endorse, Face, Favour, Mug, Sanction, Support, Visage

Counteract(ing) Ant-, Antidote, Cancel, Correct, Frustrate, Neutralise, Offset, Talion

Counterbalance Bascule, Offset, Undo, Weigh

Counter-charge Recrimination

Counterclockwise L(a)evorotatory

Counterfeit(er) Bastard, Belie, Bogus, Boodle, Brum, Coiner, Doctor, Duffer, Dummy, Fain, Fantasm, Fayne, Flash, Forge, Imitant, Paperhanger, Phantasm, Phoney, Pinchbeck, Postiche, Pseudo, Queer, Rap, Schlenter, Sham, Shan(d), Simular, Simulate, Skim, Slang, Slip, Smasher, Snide, Spurious, Stumer

Counterfoil Stub

Counterglow Gegenschein

Counter-irritant Seton

Countermand Abrogate, Annul, Cancel, Override, Rescind, Retract, Revoke

Counterpart Copy, Double, Obverse, Oppo, Parallel, Shadow, Similar, Spit(ting), Tally, Twin

Counterpoint Contrapuntal, Descant

Countersign Endorse, Password

Counterthrust Riposte

Counties, County Co, Comital, Comitatus, District, Metropolitan, Palatine, Parish, Seat, Shire, Six

---

COUNTIES

2 letters:	Down	Devon	Notts
NI	Fife	Dyfed	Omagh
Sy	Kent	Essex	Perth
	Mayo	Flint	Powys
3 letters:	Ross	Gwent	Sligo
Ely		Herts	Wilts
Som	**5 letters:**	Hunts	Worcs
	Angus	Kerry	
4 letters:	Cavan	Laois	**6 letters:**
Avon	Clare	Louth	Antrim
Beds	Clwyd	Meath	Armagh
Cork	Derry	Moray	Barset

Carlow
Dorset
Dublin
Durham
Galway
Offaly
Surrey
Sussex
Tyrone

7 letters:
Cumbria
Donegal
Gwynedd
Kildare
Leitrim
Norfolk
Rutland
Suffolk
Torfaen
Wexford
Wicklow

8 letters:
Cheshire
Cornwall
Finnmark
Kesteven
Kilkenny
Limerick
Longford
Lothians
Monaghan

Somerset

9 letters:
Berkshire
Buteshire
Caithness
Champagne
Cleveland
Fermanagh
Hampshire
Loamshire
Roscommon
The Mearns
Tipperary
Waterford
Westmeath
Yorkshire

10 letters:
Banffshire
Ceredigion
Derbyshire
Devonshire
Humberside
Lancashire
Merseyside
Midlothian
Nairnshire
Perthshire
Shropshire
Sutherland
West Sussex

11 letters:
Breconshire
East Lothian
Lanarkshire
Londonderry
Oxfordshire
Radnorshire
Tyne and Wear
West Lothian

12 letters:
Berwickshire
Denbighshire
Kinrossshire
Lincolnshire
Mid-Glamorgan
Peeblesshire
Renfrewshire
Selkirkshire
Warwickshire
West Midlands
Westmoreland
Wigtownshire

13 letters:
Dumfriesshire
Herefordshire
Monmouthshire
Pembrokeshire
Roxburghshire
Staffordshire
Stirlingshire
West Glamorgan

West Yorkshire

14 letters:
Brecknockshire
Dumbartonshire
Glamorganshire
Invernessshire
Leicestershire
Merionithshire
Northumberland
North Yorkshire
South Glamorgan
South Yorkshire

15 letters:
Caernarvonshire
Carmarthenshire
Gloucestershire
Kincardineshire
Montgomeryshire
Neath Port Talbot
Ross and Cromarty
Vale of Glamorgan

16 letters:
Clackmannanshire
Northamptonshire

17 letters:
Kircudbrightshire

Countless Infinite, Innumerable, Myriad, Umpteen, Unending, Untold
Country(side), Countrified Annam, Bangladesh, Bolivia, Boondocks, Bucolic, Champaign, Clime, Colchis, Edom, Enchorial, Farmland, Fatherland, Greenwood, High, Jordan, Karoo, Karroo, → **LAND**, Lea, Lee, Low, Mongolia, Motherland, Nation, Parish, Paysage, People, Province, Realm, Region, Republic, Rural, Rustic, Satellite, Scenery, Soil, State, Sultanate, The sticks, Thrace, Tundra, Tweedy, Venezuela, Weald, Wold, Yemen
Country girl Amaryllis
Country house Hall, Manor, Quinta
Countryman Arcadian, Bacon, Boor, Culchie, Hick, Hillbilly, Hodge, National, Native, Peasant, Ruralist, Un, Yokel
Coup Blow, Deal, KO, Move, Putsch, Scoop, Stroke, Treason
Coup d'etat Putsch
Coupé Cabriolet, Landaulet
Couple(r), Coupling Acoustic, Ally, Attach, Band, Brace, Bracket, Connect, Direct, Duet, Duo, Dyad, Fishplate, Flange, Galvanic, Gemini, Geminy, Hitch, Interlock, Item, → **JOIN**, Marrow, Marry, Mate, Meng(e), Ment, Ming, Octave, Pair, Pr, Relate,

Shackle, Tenace, Tie, Tirasse, Turnbuckle, Tway, Union, Universal, Voltaic, Wed, Yoke

Couple of ducks Spectacles

Couplet Distich, Heroic, Riding-rhyme

Coupon(s) Ration, Ticket, Voucher

Courage(ous) Balls, Ballsy, Bottle, Bravado, Bravery, Bulldog, Cojones, Dutch, Fortitude, Gallantry, Game, Gimp, Grit, Gumption, Guts, Hardihood, Heart, Heroism, Lion-heart, Macho, Manful, Mettle, Moral, Moxie, Nerve, Pluck, Prowess, Rum, Spirit, Spunk, Stalwart, Steel, Stomach, Valiant, Valour, Wight

Courgette Zucchini

Courier Estafette, Fed-EX, Guide, Harbinger, Herald, → **MESSENGER**, Postillion, Postman

Course(s) Access, Afters, Aim, Aintree, Antipasto, Appetiser, Arroyo, Ascot, Assault, Atlantic, Back straight, Barge, Bearing, Beat, Belt, Canal, Career, Chantilly, Chase, Circuit, Civics, Collision, Consommé, Conversion, Correspondence, Crash, Current, Curriculum, Cursus, Daltonism, Damp(-proof), Dessert, Diadrom, Dish, Dromic, Easting, Entrée, Epsom, Fish, Food, Foundation, Going, Golf, Goodwood, Greats, Heat, Induction, Isodomon, Lacing, Lane, Lap, Layer, Leat, Leet, Line, Lingfield, Links, Longchamp, Magnetic, Main, Meal, Meat, Mess, Newbury, Newmarket, Nine-hole, Northing, Nulla, → **OF COURSE**, Orbit, Orthodromic, Period, Policy, PPE, Practicum, Procedure, Process, Programme, Progress, Pursue, Quadrivium, Race, Raik, Ravioli, Refresher, Regimen, Rhumb, Ride, Ring, Rink, Road, Rota, Route, Routine, Run, Rut, Sandown, Sandwich, Semester, Seminar, Series, Slalom, Sorbet, Soup, Southing, Stadium, Starter, Stearage, Steerage, Step(s), Stratum, Streak, Stream, Stretch, Stretching, String, Syllabus, Tack, Tanride, Tenor, Track, Trade, Trend, Troon, Vector, Via media, Water table, Way, Wearing, Wentworth, Westing

Court(ship), Courtier Address, Admiralty, Ad(vantage), Appellate, Arbitration, Arches, Areopagus, Atrium, Attention, Audience, Audiencia, Aula, Banc, Bar, Basecourt, Bench, Beth Din, Bishop's, Boondock, Caerleon, Camelot, Canoodle, Caravanserai, Cassation, Centre, Chancery, Chase, Clay, Cloister-garth, Commercial, Commissary, Commission, Conscience, Conservancy, Consistory, County, Criminal, Crown, CS, Ct, Curia, Curia Regis, Curtilage, Cutcher(r)y, Date, Dedans, Deuce, Dicastery, Diplock, District, Divisional, Doctor's Commons, Domestic, Duchy, Durbar, Dusty Feet, En tout cas, Evora, Eyre, Faculties, Federal, Fehm(gericht), Fehmgerichte, Fiars, Forensic, Forest, Forum, Fronton, Galleria, Garth, Go steady, Grass, Guildenstern, Halimot(e), Hampton, Hard, High, High Commission, Hof, Holy See, Hustings, Hypaethron, Inferior, Innyard, Intermediate, Invite, Jack, Judicatory, Justice, Juvenile, Kachahri, Kacheri, Kangaroo, Keys, King, King's Bench, Kirk Session, Knave, Law, Leet, Lobby, Lyon, Magistrate's, Majlis, Marshalsea, Mash, Moot, Old Bailey, Open, Osric, Parvis, Patio, Peristyle, Petty Sessions, Philander, Piepowder, Police, Porte, Praetorium, Prerogative, Presbytery, Prize, Probate, Provincial, Provost, Quad, Quarter Sessions, Queen, Queen's Bench, Racket, Request, Retinue, Romance, Rosenkrantz, Royal, St James's, Sanhedrim, Sanhedrin, See, Service, Session, Sheriff, Shire-moot, Spoon, Stannary, Star Chamber, Sudder, Sue, Superior, Supreme, Swanimote, Sweetheart, Synod, Thane, Thegn, Traffic, Trial, Tribunal, Vehm, Vehmgericht(e), Vestibulum, Walk out, Ward, Wardmote, Wench, Woo, World, Wow, Yard, Youth

Courteous, Courtesy Affable, Agrement, Bow, Chivalry, Civil, Comity, Devoir, Etiquette, Fair, Genteel, Gentilesse, Gentility, Gracious, Hend, Polite, Politesse, Refined, Urbanity, Well-mannered

Courtesan Anonyma, Aspasia, Bianca, Bona-roba, Delilah, Demi-monde, Demi-rep, Geisha, Hetaera, Lais, Lampadion, Lorette, Madam, Phryne, Plover, Pornocracy, Prostitute, Stallion, Thais

Courtly Chivalrous, Cringing, Dignified, Flattering, Refined

Court-martial Drumhead

Courtyard Area, Close, Cortile, Enceinte, Garth, Marae, Patio, Quad

Cousin(s) Bette, Cater, Country, Coz, Cross, First, German, Kin, Kissing, Parallel, Robin, Second, Skater

Couthy Bien, Nice

Couturier Dior, Dressmaker

Cove Abraham's, Arm, Bay, Bight, Buffer, Creek, Cure, Gink, Grot, Guy, Hithe, Hythe, Inlet, Lulworth, Nook

Covenant(er) Abrahamic, Alliance, Appurtenant, Bond, Contract, Hillmen, Pledge, Restrictive, Warranty, Whiggamore

Coventry Isolation

Cover(ed), Covering Adventitia, Air, A l'abri, Amnion, Antependium, Antimacassar, Apron, Aril, Attire, Awning, Barb, Bard(s), Bark, Bedspread, Bestrew, Bind, Blanket, Bodice, Brood, Bubblewrap, Bury, Cache-sex, Camouflage, Canopy, Cap, Caparison, Cape, Capsule, Casing, Casque, Catch-all, Caul, Ceil, Ciborium, Cladding, Clapboard, Cleithral, Clithral, Coat, Cocoon, Coleorhiza, Conceal, Cope, Copyright, Cosy, Counterpane, Cour, Covert, Cowl, Crust, Curtain, Deadlight, Debruised, Deck, Deputise, Dividend, Dome, Drape(t), Dripstone, Duchesse, Dust-sheet, Duvet, Eiderdown, Encase, Endue, Enguard, Enlace, Ensheathe, Enshroud, Envelop(e), Enwrap, Exoderm(is), Exoskeleton, Extra, Eyelid, Face, Falx, Fanfare, Felting, Fielder, Figleaf, Fingerstall, First-day, Flashing, Flown, Fother, Front, Gaiter, Gambado, Glove, Gobo, Grolier, Ground, Groundsheet, Hap, Harl, Hat, Hatch, Havelock, Heal, Heel, Hejab, Hele, Hell, Helmet, Hijab, Hood, Housing, Hubcap, Immerse, Incase, Include, Indument, Indusium, Inmask, Insulate, Insurance, Insure, Jacket, Lag, Lambrequin, Lay, Leap, Leep, Legging, Legwarmer, Lid, Ligger, Liner, Loose, Manche, Mantle, Mask, Metal, Mort-cloth, Mount, Muffle, Mulch, Notum, Numnah, Obscure, OC, Occlude, On, Operculum, Orillion, Orlop, Overlap, Overlay, Overnet, Pad, Palampore, Palempore, Pall, Pand, Parcel, Pasties, Patch, Pebbledash, Pelmet, Periderm, Perigone, Pillow sham, Plaster, Plate, Pleura, Point, Pseudonym, Pullover, Quilt, Radome, Regolith, Robe, Roof, Roughcast, Rug, Sally, Screen, Serviette, Setting, Sheath, Sheet, Shell, Shelter, Shield, Shower, Shrink-wrap, Shroud, Shuck, Skin, Smokescreen, Solleret, Span, Spat, Splashback, Stand-by, Stifle, Stomacher, Superimpose, Swathe, Tampian, Tampion, Tapadera, Tapis, Tarpaulin, Teacosy, Tectorial, Tegmen, Tegument, Tent, Test(a), Tester, Thatch, Thimble, Thumbstall, Tick(ing), Tidy, Tile, Tilt, Tonneau, Top, Trapper, Trench, Trip, Turtleback, Twill, Twilt, Umbrella, Up, Upholster, Valance, Veale, Veil, Vele, Veneer, Ventail, Vert, Vesperal, Vest, Visor, Volva, Wainscot, Warrant, Waterdeck, Whelm, Whitewash, Wrap, Wrappage, Wrapper, Yapp, Yashmak

Covert(ly) Clandestine, Copse, Privy, → **SECRET**, Shy, Sidelong, Sub rosa, Surreptitious, Tectrix, Ulterior

Covet(ed), Covetous Avaricious, Crave, Desiderata, Desire, Eager, Envy, Greedy, Hanker, Yearn

Cow Adaw, Alderney, Amate, Appal, Awe, Ayrshire, Boss(y), Bovine, Brahmin, Browbeat, Cash, Charolais, Colly, Crummy, Danton, Daunt, Dexter, Dsomo, Dun, Galloway, Gally, Goujal, Guernsey, Hawkey, Hawkie, Heifer, Hereford, Intimidate, Jersey, Kouprey, Kyloe, Lea(h), Mart, Milch, Mog(gie), Moggy, Mooly, Muley, Mulley,

Neat, Overawe, Redpoll, Red Sindhi, Rother(-beast), Sacred, Santa Gertrudis, Scare, Simmental, Slattern, Springing, Steer, Stirk, Subact, Subjugate, Teeswater, Threaten, Unnerve, Vaccine, Zebu, Z(h)o

Coward(ice), Cowardly Bessus, Cat, Chicken, Cocoa, Craven, Cuthbert, Dastard, Dingo, Dunghill, Fraidy-cat, Fugie, Funk, Gutless, Hen, Hilding, Jessie, Lily-livered, Meacock, Milk-livered, Nesh, Niddering, Nidderling, Nidering, Niderling, Niding, Nithing, Noel, Panty-waist, Poltroon, Pusillanimous, Recreant, Scaramouch, Scaredy cat, Sganarelle, Slag, Sook, Squib, Viliaco, Viliago, Villagio, Villiago, Weak-spirited, White feather, Yellow, Yellow-belly

Cowboy, Cowgirl Broncobuster, Buckaroo, Cowpoke, Cowpuncher, Gaucho, Inexpert, Io, Jerrybuilder, Leger, Llanero, Puncher, Ranchero, Ritter, Roper, Shoddy, Vaquero, Waddie, Waddy, Wrangler

Cow-catcher Fender, Reata

Cower Croodle, Crouch, Fawn, Quail, Ruck, Skulk, Wince

Cowl Bonnet, Capuchin, Granny, Hood, Kilmarnock

Cowpat Dung, Tath

Cowpox Vaccinia

Cowshed, Cowstall Byre, Crib, Shippen, Shippon, Stable, Stall, Staw

Cowslip Culver-key, Herb Peter, Pa(i)gle

Cox Helmsman, Steerer

Coxcomb Aril, Caruncle, Copple, Crest, Dandy, Dude, Fop, Jackanapes, Popinjay, Yellow-rattle

Coy Arch, Coquettish, Demure, Laithfu', Mim, Nice, Shamefast, → **SHY**, Skeigh, Skittish

Coyote SD

CPRS Think tank

▷ **Crab** *may indicate* an anagram

Crab(by), Crablike Apple, Attercop, Blue swimmer, Boston, Calling, Cancer, Cancroid, Cantankerous, Capernoity, Cock, Coconut, Daddy, Decapoda, Diogenes, Dog, Ethercap, Ettercap, Fiddler, Ghost, Grouch, Hard-shell, Hermit, Horseman, Horseshoe, King, Land, Limulus, Mantis, Mitten, Mud, Nebula, Ochidore, Oyster, Pagurian, Partan, Pea, Perverse, Podite, Roast, Robber, Rock, Sand, Saucepan-fish, Scrawl, Sentinel, Sidle, Soft-shell, Soldier, Spectre, Spider, Velvet, Velvet-fiddler, Woolly-hand, Xiphosura, Zoea

Crab-apple Scrog-bush, Scrog-buss

Crab-eater Urva

Crabs-eye Abrus

Crack(ed), Cracker(s), Cracking Ad-lib, Admirable, Bananas, Beaut, Biscuit, Bonbon, Break, Cat, Catalytic, Chap, Chasm, Chat, Chink, Chip, Chop, Clap, Cleave, Cleft, Cloff, Confab, Cranny, Craquelure, Craqueture, Craze, Cream, Crepitate, Crevasse, Crevice, Crispbread, Dawn, Decipher, Decode, Doom, Dunt, Elite, Expert, Fab, Fatiscent, Fent, Firework, First-rate, Fisgig, Fissure, Fizgig, Flaw, Flip-flop, Fracture, Go, Graham, Grike, Gryke, Gully, Hairline, Hit, Jibe, Joint, Knacker, Leak, Liar, Little-endian, Matzo, Moulin, Oner, Peterman, Pleasantry, Pore, Praise, Prawn, Quarter, Quip, Rap, Report, Rhagades, Rictus, Rift, Rille, Rima, Rime, Rimous, Rive, Rock, Saltine, Sand, Seam, Shake, Snap, Soda, Solve, Split, Squib, Sulcus, Toe, Top, Try, Waterloo, Wind shake, Yegg

Crackerjack Ace, Nailer, Trump

Crackle, Crackling Craze, Crepitation, Crepitus, Crinkle, Decrepitate, Fizz, Glaze, Rale, Skin, Static

Crackpot Nutter

Cracksman Burglar, Peterman, Raffles

Cradle Bassinet, Berceau, Book rest, Cat's, Cot, Crib, Cunabula, Hammock, Knife, Nestle, Newton's, Rocker

▷ **Craft** *may indicate* an anagram

Craft(y) Arch, Art, Aviette, Barbola, Boat, Canal boat, Cautel, Cunning, Disingenuous, Finesse, Fly, Guile, Hydroplane, Ice-breaker, Insidious, Kontiki, Landing, Loopy, Machiavellian, Mister, Mystery, Oomiack, Reynard, Saic, Shallop, Ship, Shuttle, → **SKILL**, Slee, Sleeveen, Slim, Slippy, Sly, Slyboots, State, Subdolous, Subtil(e), Subtle, Suttle, Trade, Triphibian, Umiak, Underhand, Versute, → **VESSEL**, Wile, Workmanship

Craftsman AB, Artificer, Artisan, Artist, Chippy, Coppersmith, Cutler, Ebonist, Fabergé, Finisher, Gondolier, Guild, Hand, Joiner, Journeyman, Mason, Mechanic, Morris, Opificer, Tinsmith, Wainwright, Wright

Crag(gy) Coralline, Eyrie, Height, Heuch, Heugh, Krantz, Noup, Rock

Cram(mer) Bag, Candle-waster, Cluster, Craig, Fill, Gag, Gavage, Neck, Pang, Prime, Revise, Rugged, Scar(p), Shoehorn, Spur, Stap, Stodge, Stow, Swat, Tuck

Cramp(ed) Agraffe, Charleyhorse, Claudication, Confine, Constrict, Crick, Hamper, Hamstring, Incommodious, Musician's, Myalgia, Pinch, Poky, Potbound, Restrict, Rigor, Sardines, Scrivener's palsy, Squeeze, Stunt, Tetany, Writer's

Crane, Crane-driver Australian, Brolga, Cherry picker, Container, Davit, Deck, Demoiselle, Derrick, Dogman, Dragline, Gantry, Gooseneck, Grabbing, Herd, Heron, Hooper, Ichabod, Jenny, Jib, Jigger, Kenworthy, Luffing-jib, Native companion, Numidian, Rail, Sarus, Sedge, Seriema, Shears, Sheer, Siege, Stork, Stretch, Tower, Tulip, Whooper, Whooping, Winch

Crane-fly Daddy-long-legs, Leatherjacket, Tipulidae

Cranium Harnpan

Crank(y) Bell, Eccentric, Grouch, Handle, Lever, Mot, Perverse, Whim, Wince, Winch, Wind

Crap Feculence

Crash Bingle, Collapse, Disk, Ditch, Dush, Fail, Fall, Fragor, Frush, Intrude, Linen, Nosedive, Pile up, Prang, Rack, Ram, Rote, Shunt, Slam, Smash, South Sea Bubble, Thunderclap, Topple, Wrap

▷ **Crashes** *may indicate* an anagram

Crass Coarse, Crude, Rough, Rude

Crate Biplane, Box, Case, Ceroon, Crib, Hamper, Jalopy, Sero(o)n, Soapbox, Tube

Crater Alphonsus, Aniakchak, Aristarchus, Aristotle, Askja, Autolycus, Bail(l)y, Blowhole, Caldera, Cavity, Cissing, Clavius, Copernicus, Fra Mauro, Grimaldi, Hipparchus, Hole, Hollow, Kepler, Kilauea, Maar, Meteor, Newton, Pit, Plato, Ptolemaeus, Pythagoras, Schickard, Sinus iridium, Theophilus, Tycho

Cravat Ascot, Neckatee, Neck-cloth, Oerlay, Overlay, Scarf, Soubise, Steenkirk, Steinkirk, Tie

Crave, Craving Appetent, Appetite, Aspire, Beg, Beseech, Covet, Desire, Entreat, Gasp, Greed, Hanker, Hunger, Itch, Libido, Long, Lust, Malacia, Methomania, Munchies, Opsomania, Orexis, Pica, Polyphagia, Sitomania, The munchies, Thirst, Yearn, Yen

Craven Abject, Coward, Dastard, Hen, Recreant

Crawl(er) All fours, Aswarm, Australian, Back, Clamber, Creep, Cringe, Drag, Front, Grovel, Inchworm, Isopod, Jenkins, Lag, Lickspittle, Pub, Reptile, Scramble, Scrome, Side, Skulk, Slither, Snail, Swim, Sycophant, Tantony, Trail, Trudge(o)n, Yes-man

Crayfish Astacology, Gilgie, Jilgie, Marron, Yabbie, Yabby

Crayon Chalk, Colour, Conté®, Pastel, Pencil, Sauce

Craze(d), Crazy Absurd, Ape, Apeshit, Barmy, Bats, Batty, Berserk, Bonkers, Break, Cornflake, Crack(ers), Crackpot, Cult, Daffy, Dement, Derange, Dingbats, Dippy, Distraught, Doiled, Doilt, Doolally, Doolally tap, Dottle, Dotty, Fad, Flaky, Flaw, Folie, Frantic, Furious, Furore, Furshlugginer, Gaga, Geld, Gonzo, Gyte, Haywire, Headbanger, Insane, Loco, Loony, Loopy, Lunatic, Madden, Maenad(ic), Mania, Manic, Mattoid, Melomania, Meshug(g)a, Moonstruck, Nuts, Out to lunch, Porangi, Potty, Psycho(path), Rage, Rave, Round the bend, Round the twist, Scatty, Screwball, Skivie, Slatey, Stunt, Typomania, Unhinge, Wacko, Wacky, Wet, W(h) acky, Whim, Wowf, Zany

▷ **Crazy** *may indicate* an anagram

Creak(y) Cry, Grate, Grind, Rheumatic, Scraich, Scraigh, Scroop, Seam, Squeak

Cream(y) Barrier, Bavarian, Best, Chantilly, Cherry-pick, Cleansing, Clotted, Cold, Cornish, Crème fraîche, Devonshire, Double, Elite, Foundation, Frangipane, Glacier, Heavy, Ivory, Jollop, Lanolin, Liniment, Lotion, Mousse, Off-white, Ointment, Opal, Paragon, Pastry, Pick, Ream, Rich, Salad, Salve, Sillabub, Single, Skim, Smitane, Sour, Sun(screen), Syllabub, Vanishing, Whipped, Whipping

Crease Bowling, Crumple, → **FOLD**, Goal, Lirk, Pitch, Pleat, Popping, Return, Ridge, Ruck(le), Ruga, Rugose, Wreathe, Wrinkle

Create, Creation, Creative Arty, Brainstorm, Build, Cause, Coin, Compose, Continuous, Devise, Dreamtime, Engender, Establish, Fabricate, Forgetive, Form, Found, Generate, Genesis, Godhead, Hexa(h)emeron, Ideate, Imaginative, → **INVENT**, Kittle, Knit, Omnific, Oratorio, Originate, Produce, Shape, Synthesis, Universe

Creator Ahura Mazda, Author, Demiurge, Demiurgus, God, Inventor, Maker, Ormazd, Ormuzd

Creature Animal, Ankole, Basilisk, Beast, Being, Bigfoot, Chevrotain, Cratur, Critter, Crittur, Man, Moner(on), Nekton, Saprobe, Sasquatch, Sphinx, Whiskey, Wight

Credence, Credential(s) Certificate, Document, Papers, Qualifications, Shelf, Testimonial

Credibility Street

Credible, Credit(s), Creditor Ascribe, Attribute, Belief, Billboard, Brownie points, Byline, Carbon, Catholic, Crawl, Esteem, Extended, Family, Honour, HP, Kite, Kudos, LC, Lender, Mense, On the nod, Post-war, Probable, Reliable, Renown, Repute, Revolving, Shylock, Social, Strap, Street, Tally, Tax, Tick, Title, Trust, Weight, Youth

Credulous Charlie, Gobe-mouches, Gullible, Naive, Simple, Trusting

Creed Apostle's, Athanasian, Belief, Doctrine, Faith, Ism, Nicene, Ophism, Outworn, Persuasion, Sect, Tenet

Creek Antietam, Bay, Breaches, Cooper, Cove, Crick, Dawson, Estuary, Fleet, Geo, Gio, Goe, Indian, Inlet, Kill, Pow, Slough, Vae, Voe, Wick

Creel Basket, Hask, Scull, Skull

Creep(er), Creeping, Creeps Ai, Ampelopsis, Arbutus, Aseismic, Boston ivy, Cleavers, Crawl, Function, Grew, Grovel, Grue, Heebie-jeebies, Heeby-jeebies, Herpetic, Honey, Inch, Insect, Ivy, Mission, Nerd, Nuthatch, Pussyfoot, Repent, Reptant, Sarmentous, Sidle, Sittine, Skulk, Slink, Snake, Sneak(sby), Sobole(s), Soil, Steal, Toad, Tropaeolum, Truckle, Vinca, Vine, Virginia, Wickthing, Willies

Creeping Jenny Moneywort

Cremate, Cremation, Crematorium Burn, Char, Cinerarium, Ghat, Ghaut, Incinerate, Pyre, Sati, Suttee, Ustrinium

Creole Gullah, Haitian, Kriol, Papiamento, Tok Pisin

Crepe Blini, Blintz(e), Canton, Pancake

Crescent Barchan(e), Bark(h)an, Fertile, Growing, Lune(tte), Lunulate, Lunule, Meniscus, Moon, Red, Sickle, Waxing

Cress Cardamine, Garden, Hoary, Isatis, Pepperwort, Swine's, Thale, Wart, Water, Yellow

Crest(ed) Acme, Chine, Cimier, Cockscomb, Comb, Copple, Crista, Height, Kirimon, Knap, Mon, Peak, Pileate, Pinnacle, Plume, Ridge, Summit, Tappit, Tee, → **TOP**, Tufty

Cretaceous Chalky, Senonian, The Chalk

Cretan Candiot(e), Minoan, Teucer

Crevasse Bergschrund, Chasm, Gorge, Rimaye

Crevice Chine, Cranny, Fissure, Interstice, Ravine, Vallecula

Crew Boasted, Company, Complement, Core, Deckhand, Eight, Equipage, Four, Ground, Lot, Manners, Men, Oars, Prize, Sailors, Salts, Seamen, Ship men, Team, Teme, Torpid

Crew-cut Not(t)

Crib Cheat, Cot, Cowhouse, Cratch, Filch, Horse, → **KEY**, Manger, Pony, Purloin, Putz, Shack, Stall, Steal, Trot

Crick Cramp, Kink, Spasm

Cricket(er) Balm, Bat, Bosanquet, Botham, Bowler, Bradman, CC, Cicada, Dry-bob, French, Grade, Grasshopper, Grig, Hopper, Jerusalem, Katydid, Keeper, Knott, Leg, Long-leg, Long-off, Long-on, Longstop, March, May, Mid-on, Mole, Muggleton, Nightwatchman, Opener, Overs, Packer, Point, Pyjama, Shield, Single-wicket, Slip, Sobers, Stool, Stridulate, Tate, Test, Tettix, Tip and run, Vigoro, Warner, Wart-biter, Windball, Windies, Wisden, XI(gent)

Crier Bellman, Herald, Muezzin, Niobe, Outrooper

Crime Attentat, Barratry, Bias, Caper, Chantage, Chaud-mellé, Computer, Corpus delicti, Ecocide, Fact, Felony, Fraud, GBH, Graft, Hate, Heist, Iniquity, Inside job, Insider trading, Malefaction, Mayhem, Misdeed, Misdemeanour, → **OFFENCE**, Organised, Ovicide, Peccadillo, Perjury, Pilferage, Ram raid, Rap, Rape, Rebellion, → **SIN**, Theft, Tort, Transgression, Treason, Victimless, Villa(i)ny, War, White-collar, Wrong

Crimea Balaclava

Criminal Arsonist, Bandit, Bent, Bushranger, Chain gang, Chummy, Con, Cosa Nostra, Counterfeiter, Crack-rope, → **CROOK**, Culpable, Culprit, Delinquent, Escroc, Fagin, Felon, Flagitious, Forensic, Gangster, Goombah, Hard men, Heavy, Heinous, Highbinder, Hitman, Hood(lum), Jailbird, Ladrone, Lag, Larcener, Lifer, Looter, Lowlife, Maf(f)ia, Malefactor, Maleficent, Malfeasant, Mens rea, Mob(ster), Molester, Ndrangheta, Nefarious, Nefast, Offender, Outlaw, Perp(etrator), Peterman, Racketeer, Receiver, Recidivist, Reprehensible, Rustler, Sinner, Snakehead, Thug, Triad, Triggerman, Underworld, Villain, Wicked, Wire, Yakuza, Yardie, Yegg

▷ **Criminal** *may indicate* an anagram

Criminologist Lombroso

Crimp Pleat, Quill

Crimson Carmine, Incarnadine, Modena, Red, Scarlet

Cringe, Cringing Cower, Creep, Crouch, Cultural, Fawn, Grovel, Shrink, Sneaksby, Truckle

Crinkle, Crinkly Rugate, Rugose

Crinoline Farthingale, Hoop

Cripple(d) Damage, Debilitate, Disable, Game, Hamstring, Handicap, Injure,

→ **LAME**, Lameter, Lamiter, Maim, Paralyse, Polio, Scotch, Spoil

Crisis Acme, Crunch, Drama, Emergency, Exigency, Fastigium, Fit, Flap, Head, Identity, Make or break, Midlife, Panic, Pass, Quarterlife, Shake-out, Solution, Test, Turn

Crisp(ness) Brisk, Clear, Crimp, Crunchy, Fire-edge, Fresh, Potato, Sharp, Short, Succinct, Terse

Crispin Sutor(ial)

Criss-cross Alternate, Fret, Interchange, Vein

Criteria, Criterion Benchmark, Gauge, Koch's postulates, Measure, Precedent, Proof, Rayleigh, Rule, Shibboleth, → **STANDARD**, Test, Touchstone

Critic(al), Criticise, Criticism Acute, Agate, Animadversion, Archer, Aristarch, Armchair, Arnold, Attack, Badmouth, Bagehot, Barrack, Bellettrist, Berate, Bird, Blame, Boileau, Boo, Bucket, Captious, Carp, Castigate, Cavil, Censor(ious), → **CENSURE**, Climacteric, Clobber, Comment, Condemn, Connoisseur, Crab, Criticaster, → **CRUCIAL**, Crunch, Dangle, Decisive, Denigrate, Denounce, Deprecate, Desperate, Diatribe, Do down, Dutch uncle, Earful, Etain, Exacting, Excoriate, Fastidious, Fateful, Feuilleton, Flak, Flay, Fulminous, Gosse, Harrumph, Higher, Important, Impugn, Inge, Inveigh, Judge, Judgemental, Knife-edge, Knock(er), Lash, Leavis, Life and death, Literary, Lower, Masora(h), Mas(s)orete, Mordacious, Nag, Nasute, Nibble, Nice, Niggle, Nitpicker, Overseer, Pan, Pater, Peck, Puff, Pundit, Quibble, Rap, Rebuke, Reprehend, Review(er), Rip, Roast, Ruskin, Scalp, Scarify, Scathe, Scorn, Second guess, Serious, Severe, Shaw, Sideswipe, Slag, Slam, Slashing, Slate, Sneer, Snipe, Spray, Stick, Stricture, Strop, Tense, Textual, Thersitic, Threap, Touch and go, Ultracrepidate, Upbraid, Urgent, Vet, Vitriol, Vituperation, Watershed, Zoilism

Croak Creak, Crow, Die, Grumble, Gutturalise

Croatia(n) Cravates, Glagolitic, HR, Serb

Crochet Lace, Weave

Crock Chorrie, Crate, Jar, Mug, Pig, Pitcher, Pot, Potshard, Potshare, Potsherd, Stean(e)

Crockery Ceramics, China, Dishes, Earthenware, Oddment, Service, Sunbeam, Ware

▷ **Crocks** *may indicate* an anagram

Crocodile Cayman, File, Flat dog, Garial, Gavial, Gharial, Gotcha lizard, Line, Mud gecko, Mugger, River-dragon, Saltie, Saltwater, Sebek, Teleosaur(ian)

Crocus Autumn, Meadow saffron, Naked lady, Prairie, Saffron

Croesus Lydia

Croft Bareland, Pightle

Cromwell Antimonarchist, Ironside, Lord Protector, Noll, Oliver, Protector, Richard, Roundhead

Crone(s) Beldam(e), Ewe, Graeae, Hag, Mawkin, Ribibe, Rudas, Sibyl, Sybil, Trot, Trout, → **WITCH**

Crony Anile, Chum, Intimate, Mate, Pal, Sidekick

Crook(ed), Crookedness Adunc, Ajee, Aslant, Asymmetric, Awry, Bad, Bend, Bow, Cam, Camsheugh, Camsho(ch), Cock-eyed, Criminal, Cromb, Crome, Crosier, Crummack, Crummock, Crump, Curve, Dishonest, Elbow, Fraud, Heister, Hook, Indirect, Kam(me), Kebbie, Lituus, Malpractitioner, Obliquity, Operator, Shank, Sheep-hook, Shyster, Sick, Skew(whiff), Slick(er), Squint, Staff, Swindler, Thraward, Thrawart, Thrawn, Twister, Wonky, Yeggman

▷ **Crooked** *may indicate* an anagram

Croon(er), Crooning Bing, Como, Lament, Lull, Monody, Murmur, Sing

Crop(s), Cropped, Cropping Basset, Browse, Cash, Catch, Clip, Cover, Craw, Cut, Distress, Dock, Emblements, Energy, Epilate, Eton, Foison, Forage, Harvest, Hog, Ingluvies, Kharif, Ladino, Lop, Milo, Not(t), Plant, Poll, Produce, Rabi, Riding, Rod, Root, Shingle, Silage, Standing, Stow, Strip, Subsistence, Succession, Top, Truncate, White

Cropper Downfall, Header, Purler

Croquet (term) Peel, Rover, Wire

Croquette Kromesky, Quenelle, Rissole

▷ **Cross** *may indicate* an anagram

Cross(ing), Crossbred Angry, Ankh, Ansate, Archiepiscopal, Banbury, Basta(a)rd, Baster, Beefalo, Bestride, Bois-brule, Boton(n)e, Brent, Bridge, Buddhist, Burden, Calvary, Cantankerous, Canterbury, Capital, Capuchin, Cattalo, Celtic, Channel, Chi, Chiasm(a), Choleric, Cleche, Clover-leaf, Compital, Constantine, Crosslet, Crosswalk, Crotchety, Crucifix, Crux, Cut, Decussate, Demi-wolf, Dihybrid, Double, Dso(mo), Dzobo, Eleanor, Encolpion, Faun, Fiery, Fitché, Fleury, Foil, Footbridge, Ford, Frabbit, Fractious, Frampold, Franzy, Funnel, Fylfot, Geneva, George, Grade, Greek, Holy rood, Humette, Hybrid, Ill, Imp, Indignant, Interbreed, Intersect, Intervein, Iona, Iracund, Irascible, Irate, Irked, Iron, Jerusalem, Jomo, Jumart, Kiss, Krest, Ladino, Latin, Level, Liger, Lorraine, Lurcher, Maltese, Mameluco, Market, Mermaid, Military, Misfortune, Mix, Moline, Mongrel, Mule, Narky, Nattery, Node, Norman, Northern, Nuisance, Oblique, Obverse, Ordinary, Orthodox, Overpass, Overthwart, Papal, Patonce, Patriarchal, Pattée, Pectoral, Pedestrian, Pelican, Plumcot, Plus, Pommé, Potence, Potent, Preaching, Puffin, Quadrate, Railway, Ratty, Reciprocal, Red, Roman, Rood, Rose, Rosy, Rouen, Rouge, Rubicon, Ruthwell, Sain, St Andrew's, St Anthony's, St George's, St Patrick's, St Peter's, Saltier, Saltire, Sambo, Satyr, Shirty, Sign, Snappy, Southern, Splenetic, Strid, Svastika, Swastika, T, Tangelo, Tau, Tayberry, Ten, Testy, Thraw, Thwart, Tiglon, Tigon, Times, Toucan, Transit, Transom, Transverse, Traverse, Tree, Unknown, Urdé, Vexed, Vext, Victoria, → **VOTE**, Weeping, Whippet, Wholphin, Wry, X, Yakow, Zambo, Zebra(ss), Zebrinny, Zebroid, Zebrula, Zebrule, Zedonk, Z(h)o, Zobu

▶ **Cross-bar** *see* **CROSSPIECE**

▶ **Crossbeam** *see* **CROSSPIECE**

Cross-bearer Crucifer

Cross-bill Metagnathous

Cross-bones Marrowbones

Cross-bow Arbalest, Bal(l)ista

Cross-country Langlauf, Overland

Cross-dressing En travesti, Eonism

Cross-examine Grill, Interrogate, Question, Targe

Cross-eyed Skelly(-eyed), Squint

Crossfertilisation Allogamy, Heterosis, Hybrid vigour, Xenogamy

Cross-grained Ill-haired, Mashlam, Mashlim, Mas(h)lin, Mashlock, Mashlum, Stubborn

Crosspiece, Cross-bar, Cross-beam, Cross-timber Bar, Cancelli, Fingerground, Footrail, Inter-tie, Lierne, Phillipsite, Putlock, Putlog, Quillon, Serif, Seriph, Stempel, Stemple, Stretcher, Stull, Swingle-tree, Toggle, Transom, Trave, Whiffle-tree, Whipple-tree, Yoke

Crossroads Carfax, Carfox, Carrefour, Compital, Soap

Crossword Cryptic, Grid, Puzzle, Quickie

Crotchet(y) Eccentric, Fad, Fancy, Grouch, Kink, Quarter-note, Toy

Crouch Bend, Cringe, Falcade, Fancy, Lordosis, Ruck, Set, Squat, Squinch

Croup Angina, Cough, Kink, Rump

Crow Boast, Brag, Carrion, Chewet, Chough, Corbie, Corvus, Crake, Currawong, Daw, Flute-bird, Gab, Gorcrow, Hooded, Hoodie, Huia, Jackdaw, Jim(my), Murder, Piping, Raven, Rook, Saddleback, Scald, Skite, Squawk, Swagger, Vaunt

Crowbar Gavelock, James, Jemmy, Lever

Crowd(ed) Abound, Army, Bike, Boodle, Bumper, Bunch, Byke, Caboodle, Clutter, Concourse, Congest(ed), Cram, Crush, Crwth, Dedans, Doughnut, Drove, Fill, Flock, Galere, Gang, Gate, Gathering, Herd, Horde, → **HOST**, Huddle, Hustle, Jam, Jam-packed, Lot, Many, Meinie, Mein(e)y, Menyie, Mob, Mong, Multitude, Ochlo-, Pack, Pang, Populace, Press, Rabble, Raft, Ram, Ratpack, Ring, Ruck, Scrooge, Scrouge, Scrowdge, Scrum, Serr(é), Shoal, Shove, Slew, Slue, Squash, Squeeze, Stuff, Swarm, Swell, Three, Throng, Trinity, Varletry

Crowfoot Gilcup, Reate

Crown Acme, Bays, Bull, Camp, Cantle, Cap, Capernoity, Cidaris, Civic, Coma, Corona, Cr, Diadem, Ecu, Engarland, Enthrone, Fillet, Garland, Gloria, Haku, Head, Headdress, Instal, Iron, Ivy, Krantz, Laurel, Monarch, Mural, Naval, Nole, Noll, Noul(e), Nowl, Olive, Optical, Ore, Ovation, Pate, Peak, Pschent, Sconce, Stephen's, Taj, Thick'un, Tiara, → **TOP**, Triple, Triumphal, Trophy, Vallary, Vertex

Crucial Acute, Critical, Essential, Key, Pivotal, Quintessential, Vital, Watershed

Crucible Cruset, Melting-pot, Vessel

Crucifix(ion), Crucify Calvary, Cross, Golgotha, Mortify, Rood, Torment, Torture

Crude(ness) Bald, Brash, Brute, Coarse, Earthy, Halfbaked, Immature, Incondite, No tech, Primitive, Raunch, Raw, Rough, Rough and ready, Rough-hewn, Rough-wrought, Tutty, Uncouth, Vulgar, Yahoo

▷ **Cruel** *may indicate* an anagram

Cruel(ty) Barbarous, Bloody, Brutal, Dastardly, De Sade, Draconian, Fell, Fiendish, Flinty, Hard, Heartless, Immane, Inhumane, Machiavellian, Mental, Neronic, Pitiless, Raw, Remorseless, Sadistic, Stern, Tiger, Tormentor, Vicious

Cruet Ampulla, Condiments, Decanter

Cruise(r) Booze, Busk, Cabin, Nuke, Orientation, Prowl, Rove, Sail, Sashay, Ship, Tom, Travel, Trip, Voyager

Crumb(le), Crumbly, Crumbs Coo, Decay, Disintegrate, Ee, Fragment, Friable, Golly, Law, Leavings, Moulder, Mull, Murl, Nesh, Nirl, Ort, Panko, Particle, Ped, Raspings, Rot, Rotter

Crumpet Dish, Girl, Muffin, Nooky, Pash, Pikelet

Crumple Collapse, Crunkle, Crush, Raffle, Scrunch, Wrinkle

Crunch(y) Abdominal, Chew, Craunch, Crisp, Gnash, Graunch, Grind, Munch, Occlude, Scranch

Crusade(r) Baldwin, Campaign, Cause, Pilgrim, Tancred, Templar

Crush(ed), Crusher, Crushing Acis, Anaconda, Annihilate, Beetle, Bow, Breakback, Champ, Comminute, Conquer, Contuse, Cranch, Crunch, Defeat, Destroy, Graunch, Grind, Hug, Jam, Knapper, Levigate, Mangle, Mash, Mill, Molar, Mortify, Oppress, Overcome, Overwhelm, Pash, Policeman, Pound, Press, Pulp, Pulverise, Quash, Quell, Ruin, Schwarmerei, Scotch, Scrum, Scrumple, Smash, Squabash, Squash, Squeeze, Squelch, Squish, Stamp, Stave, Steam-roll, Stove, Suppress, Telescope, Trample, Tread

Crust(y) Argol, Beeswing, Cake, Coating, Coffin, Continental, Cover, Crabby, Craton, Fur, Gratin, Heel, Horst, Kissing, Kraton, Lithosphere, Oceanic, Orogen, Osteocolla, Pie, Reh, Rind, Rine, Sal, Salband, Scab, Shell, Sial, Sima, Sinter, Sordes, Surly, Tartar, Teachie, Terrane, Tetchy, Upper, Wine-stone

Crustacea(n) Amphipod, Barnacle, Brachyuran, Branchiopoda, Camaron, Cirriped,

Cirripede, Cirripid, Cladoceran, Copepod, Crab, Crayfish, Cumacean, Cyclops, Cyprid, Cypris, Daphnia, Decapod(a), Entomostraca, Euphausia, Fishlouse, Foot-jaw, Gribble, Isopod, Krill, Langoustine, Lobster, Macrura, Malacostracan, Marine borer, Maron, Nauplius, Ostracoda, Pagurian, Phyllopod, Prawn, Red seed, Rhizocephalan, Sand-hopper, Sand-skipper, Scampi, Scampo, Schizopod, Sea slater, Shellfish, Shrimp, Slater, Squilla, Stomatopod, Woodlouse, Yabbie, Yabby

Crutch Morton's, Potent

Crux Essence, Nub

Cry(ing) Aha, Alalagmus, Alew, Banzai, Bark, Battle, Bawl, Bay, Bell, Bemoan, Bill, Blat, Bleat, Bleb, Blub(ber), Boo, Boohoo, Boom, Bray, Bump, Caramba, Caw, Cheer, Chevy, Chirm, Chivy, Clang, Crake, Croak, Crow, Dire, Euoi, Eureka, Evoe, Exclaim, Fall, Field-holler, Gardyloo, Gathering, Geronimo, Gowl, Greet, Halloo, Harambee, Haro, Harrow, Havoc, Heigh, Hemitrope, Herald, Hinny, Hoicks, Holler, Honk, Hoo, Hoop, Hosanna, Hout(s)-tout(s), Howl, Humph, Io, Kaw, Low, Mewl, Miaou, Miau(l), Miserere, Mourn, Night-shriek, Nix, O(c)hone, Oi, Olé, Ow, Pugh, Rabbito(h), Rallying, Rivo, Sab, Scape, Scream, Screech, Sell, Sese(y), Sessa, → **SHOUT**, Shriek, Slogan, Snivel, Snotter, Sob, Soho, Sola, Squall, Squawk, Street, Sursum corda, Tally-ho, Tantivy, Umph, Vagitus, View-halloo, Vivat, Vociferate, Wail, War, War whoop, Watchword, Waterworks, Waul, Wawl, Weep, Westward ho, Whee(ple), Whimper, Whine, Whinny, Whoa, Whoop, Winge, Wolf, Yammer, Yelp, Yicker, Yikker, Yip, Yippee, Yodel, Yo-heave-ho, Yo-ho-ho, Yoick, Yoop, Yowl

Crypt(ic) Catacomb, Cavern, Chamber, Crowde, Encoded, Enigmatic, Favissa, Grotto, Hidden, Obscure, Occult, Secret, Sepulchre, Short, Steganographic, Tomb, Unclear, Undercroft, Vault

Cryptaesthesia ESP

Cryptogam Acotyledon, Acrogen, Fern(-ally), Moss, Pteridophyte

Cryptographer, Cryptography Decoder, Public-key, Ventris

Crystal(s), Crystal-gazer, Crystalline, Crystallise Allotriomorphic, Axinite, Baccara(t), Beryl, Candy, Citrine, Clathrate, Clear, Cleveite, Copperas, Coumarin, Cumarin, Dendrite, Druse, Effloresce, Elaterin, Enantiomorph, Epitaxy, Erionite, Form, Fuchsin(e), Geode, Glass, Hemihedron, Hemimorphic, Hemitrope, Ice-stone, Ideal, Imazadole, Jarosite, Lase, Lead, Liquid, Lithium, Love-arrow, Macle, Macro-axis, Melamine, Mixed, Needle, Nicol, Orthogonal, Orthorhombic, Pellucid, Penninite, Pericline, Phenocryst, Piezo, Piezoelectric, Pinacoid, Pinakoid, Prism, Pseudomorph, Purin(e), Quartz, R(h)aphide, R(h)aphis, Rhinestone, Rock, Rotenone, Rubicelle, Scryer, Shoot, Skatole, Skryer, Smectic, Snowflake, Sorbitol, Spar, Spherulite, Spicule, Table, Tolan(e), Trichite, Trilling, Twin(ned), Wafer, Watch-glass, Xanthene, Xenocryst, Yag

Cub(s) Baby, Kit, Lionet, Novice, Pup, Six, Whelp, Wolf

Cube, Cubic, Cubist Bath, Braque, Cu, Die, Magic, Necker, Nosean, Quadrate, Rubik's®, Serac, Smalto, Snub, Solid, Stere, Stock, Tesseract

Cubicle Alcove, Booth, Carrel(l), Stall

Cuckold Actaeon, Cornute, Graft, Homer, Lenocinium, Vulcan's badge, Wittol

Cuckoo Ament, Ani, April fool, Bird, Brain-fever bird, Chaparral cock, Gouk, Gowk, Inquiline, Insane, Koekoea, Koel, → **MAD**, Mental, Piet-my-vrou, Stupid

▷ **Cuckoo** *may indicate* an anagram

Cuckoopint Arum

Cucumber Bitter-apple, Choko, Colocynth, Coloquintida, Dill, Elaterium, Gherkin, Pickle, Sea-slug, Squirting, Trepang, Wolly

Cuddle Canoodle, Caress, Clinch, Embrace, Fondle, Hug, Nooky, Smooch, Smuggle, Snog, Snuggle

Cudgel Alpeen, Ballow, Bludgeon, Brain, Club, Cosh, Drub, Fustigate, Oaken towel, Plant, Rack, Rung, Shillelagh, Souple, Stick, Swipple, Tan, Towel, Truncheon

Cue Billiard, Cannonade, Catchword, Feed, Feed-line, Half-butt, Hint, Mace, → **PROMPT**, Reminder, Rod, Sign, Signal, Wink

Cuff Box, Buffet, Clout, French, Gauntlet, Iron, Muffettee, Rotator, Storm, Strike, Swat

Cuirass Armour, Corselet, Lorica

Cuisine Bourgeoise, Cookery, Food, Lean, Menu, Minceur, Nouvelle

Cul-de-sac Blind, Dead-end, Impasse, Loke

Cull Gather, Pick, Select, Thin, Weed

Culminate, Culmination Apogean, Apogee, Climax, Conclusion, Crest, End, Head, Orgasm

Culpable Blameworthy, Guilty

Cult Aum Shinrikyo, Cabiri, Candomble, Cargo, Creed, Fertility, Macumba, New Age, Personality, Rastafarian, Sect, Shango, Shinto, Snake, Voodoo, Wicca, Worship

Cultivate(d), Cultivation, Cultivator Agronomy, Arty, Civilise, Developed, Dig, Dress, Ear, Ere, Farm, Garden, Genteel, Grow, Hoe, Hydroponics, Improve, Labour, Polytunnel, Pursue, Raise, Reclaim, Refine, Sative, Sophisticated, Tame, Tasteful, Till, Tilth, Wainage, Woo, Work

Culture(d), Cultural Acheulean, Acheulian, Agar, Art(y), Aurignacian, Azilian, Bel esprit, Brahmin, Canteen, Capsian, Civil(isation), Clactonian, Club, Compensation, Corporate, Dependency, Enterprise, Ethnic, Experiment, Explant, Fine arts, Gel, Gravettian, Grecian, Halafian, Hallstatt, Hip-hop, Humanism, Intelligentsia, Kultur(kreis), La Tène, Learning, Levallois, Madelenian, Magdalenian, Maglemosean, Maglemosian, Meristem, Minoan, Monolayer, Mousterian, Organisational, Perigordian, Polish, Polite, Pure, Refinement, Solutrean, Sophisticated, Starter, Strepyan, Suspension, Tardenoisian, Tissue, Villanovan, Water

Cumbersome Clumsy, Heavy, Lumbering, → **UNWIELDY**

Cunctator Dilatory

Cuneiform Wedge(d)

Cunning Arch, Art, Artifice, Astute, Cautel, Craft(y), Deceit, Deep, Devious, Down, Finesse, Foxy, Guile, Insidious, Leery, Machiavellian, Quaint, Skill, Slee(kit), Sleight, Slim, Sly(boots), Smart, Sneaky, Stratagem, Subtle, Vulpine, Wile, Wily

▷ **Cup** *may indicate* a bra size

Cup(s), Cupped Aecidium, America's, Beaker, Bledisloe, Calcutta, Calix, Calyculus, Cantharus, Chalice, Claret, Communion, Cotyle, Cruse, Cupule, Cyathus, Cylix, Davis, Demitasse, Deoch-an-doruis, Deuch-an-doris, Dish, Doch-an-dorach, Dop, Egg, European, FA, Fairs, Final, Fingan, Finjan, Fruit, Gemma, Glenoid, Goblet, Grace, Grease, Gripe's egg, Hanap, Horn, Kylix, Loving, Melbourne, Merry, Monstrance, Moustache, Mug, Noggin, Nut, Pannikin, Parting, Planchet, Plate, Poley, Posset, Pot, Procoelous, Quaff, Quaich, Quaigh, Rhyton, Rider, Ryder, Sangrado, Scyphus, Sippy, Stem, Stirrup, Tantalus, Tass(ie), Tastevin, Tazza, Tea-dish, Tig, Tot, → **TROPHY**, Tyg, UEFA, Volva, Waterloo, World

Cup-bearer Ganymede, Hebe

Cupboard Airing, Almery, Almirah, Armoire, A(u)mbry, Beauf(f)et, Cabinet, Chiffonier, Chiff(o)robe, Closet, Coolgardie safe, Court, Credenza, Dresser, Fume, Livery, Locker, Meat-safe, Press, Walk-in

Cup-holder Hanaper, Hebe, Plinth, Saucer, Zarf, Zurf

Cupid Amoretto, Amorino, Archer, Blind, Bow-boy, Cherub, Dan, Eros, Love, Putto

Cupola Belfry, Dome, Tholos

Cup-shaped Poculiform

Cur Dog, Messan, Mongrel, Mutt, Pi-dog, Scab, Scoundrel, Whelp, Wretch, Yap

Curare, Curari Ourali, Poison, Wourali

Curassow Crax

Curate Barman, Minister, Nathaniel, Padré, Perpetual, Priest

Curator Aquarist

Curb Bit, Brake, Bridle, Check, Clamp, Coaming, Dam, Edge, Puteal, Rein, Restrain, Rim, Snub, Well

Curd(s) Bean, Cheese, Junket, Lapper(ed)-milk, Lemon, Skyr, Tofu

Curdle Clot, Congeal, Earn, Erne, Lopper, Posset, Ren, Rennet, Run, Set, Sour, → TURN, Whig, Yearn

▷ **Cure** *may indicate* an anagram

Cure(d), Curative Ameliorate, Amend, Antidote, Antirachitic, Bloater, Cold turkey, Dry-salt, Dun, Euphrasy, Faith, Fix, Flue, Ginseng, Heal, Heal-all, Hobday, Hydropathy, Jadeite, Jerk, Kipper, Laetrile, Magic bullet, Medicinal, Nature, Nostrum, Panacea, Park-leaves, Prairie oyster, → PRESERVE, Reast, Recover, Recower, Reest, Re(i)st, Relief, Remede, Remedy, Restore, Salt, Salve, Save, Serum, Smoke, Smoke-dry, Snakeroot, Tan, → TREATMENT, Tutsan, Water

Curfew Bell, Gate, Prohibit, Proscribe

Curie Ci

Curio, Curiosity, Curious Agog, Bibelot, Freak, Inquisitive, Into, Interesting, Meddlesome, Nos(e)y, Objet d'art, Objet de vertu, Odd, Peculiar, Prurience, Rarity, Rum, → STRANGE, Wondering

▷ **Curious(ly)** *may indicate* an anagram

Curium Cm

Curl(s), Curler, Curling, Curly Ailes de pigeon, Bev, Bonspiel, Cirrus, Coil, Crimp, Crimple, Crinkle, Crisp, Crocket, Dildo, Earlock, Favourite, Frisette, Friz(z), Frizzle, Heart-breaker, Hog, Inwick, Kiss, Leaf, Loop, Love-lock, Outwick, Perm, Pin, Quiff, Repenter, Ringlet, Roll, Roulette, Scroll, Shaving, Spiral, Spit, Tong, Tress, Trunk, Twiddle, → TWIST, Ulotrichous, Undée, Wave, Wind

Curlew Bird, Whaup, Whimbrel

Curmudgeon Boor, Churl, Grouch, Route, Runt

Currant Berry, Flowering, Raisin, Rizard, Rizzar(t), Rizzer

Currency Cash, Circulation, → COIN, Coinage, Decimal, Euro, Finance, Fractional, Jiao, Kip, Koruna, Managed, Monetary, → MONEY, Prevalence, Reserve, Soft

▷ **Currency** *may indicate* a river

Current Abroad, AC, Actual, Alternating, Amp(ere), Amperage, California, Canary, Contemporaneous, Cromwell, Dark, DC, Direct, Draught, Drift, Dynamo, Ebbtide, Eddy, Electric, El Nino, Emission, Equatorial, Euripus, Existent, Flow, Foucault, Galvanic(al), Going, Gyre, Headstream, Humboldt, Hummock, I, Immediate, Inst, Intermittent, Japan, Kuroshio, Labrador, Maelstrom, Millrace, Modern, Newsy, North Atlantic, Now, Ongoing, Output, Peru, Present, Present day, Prevalent, Pulsating, Race, Rapid, Rife, Rip, Roost, Running, Stream, Thames, Thermal, Thermionic, Tide, Tideway, Topical, Torrent, Turbidity, Underset, Undertow, Updraught

Curriculum Core, Cursal, National, Programme

Curry Bhuna, Brush, Comb, Cuittle, Dhansak, Fawn, Groom, Ingratiate, Korma, Madras, Skater, Spice, Tan, Tandoori, Turmeric, Vindaloo

Curse Abuse, Anathema, Badmouth, Ban, Bane, Beshrew, → BLASPHEME, Blast, Chide, Dam(me), Damn, Dee, Drat, Ecod, Egad, Evil, Excommunicate, Execrate, Heck, Hex, Hoodoo, Imprecate, Jinx, Malediction, Malgre, Malison, Maranatha,

Mau(l)gré, Mockers, Moz(z), Mozzle, Nine (of diamonds), Oath, Paterson's, Pize, Plague, Rant, Rats, Scourge, 'Snails, Spell, Swear, Upbraid, Vengeance, Weary, Winze, Wo(e)

Cursive Estrang(h)elo, Run

Cursor Mouse, Turtle

Cursorily, Cursory Casual, Hasty, Lax, Obiter, Passing, Perfunctory, Sketchy, Speedy, Superficial

Curt Abrupt, Blunt, Crusty, Laconic, Offhand, Short, Snappy

Curtail(ment) Abate, Apocope, Crop, Cut, Reduce, Shorten

Curtain(s), Curtain raiser, Curtain-rod Air, Arras, Backdrop, Bamboo, Café, Canopy, Casement, Caudle, Cloth, Cyclorama, Death, Demise, Drape, Drop, Dropcloth, Dropscene, Fatal, Hanging, Iron, Lever de rideau, Louvre, Net, Pall, Portière, Purdah, Rag, Safety, Scene, Screen, Scrim, Shower, Tab, Tableau, Tormentor, Tringle, Upholstery, Vail, Valance, Veil, Vitrage, Window

Curtsey Bob, Bow, Dip, Dop, Honour

Curve(d), Curvaceous, Curvature, Curving, Curvy Adiabatic, Aduncate, Anticlastic, Apophyge, Arc, Arch, Archivolt, Assurgent, Axoid, Bend, Bezier, Bight, Bow, Brachistochrone, Camber, Cardioid, Catacaustic, Catenary, Caustic, Characteristic, Chordee, Cissoid, Conchoid, Contrapposto, Crescent, Cycloid, Demand, Diacaustic, Dogleg, Entasis, Epicycloid, Epinastic, Epitrochoid, Ess, Evolute, Exponential, Extrados, Felloe, Felly, Folium, French, Gaussian, Geodesic, Gooseneck, Growth, Hance, Harmonogram, Helix, Hodograph, Hollow-back, Hook, Hyperbola, Hypocycloid, Inswing, Intrados, Invected, Isochor, J, Jordan, Kyphosis, Laffer, Learning, Lemniscate, Limacon, Linkage, Liquidus, Lissajous figure, Lituus, Lordosis, Loxodrome, Normal, Nowy, Ogee, Parabola, Phillips, Pothook, Pott's disease, Pulvinate, Reclinate, Record, Rhumb, RIAA, Roach, Rondure, Rotundate, Scoliosis, Sheer, Sigmoid flexure, Sinuate, Sinusoid, Slice, Spiral, Spiric, Strophoid, Supply, Survival, Swayback, Synclastic, Tautochrone, Tie, Tractrix, Trajectory, Trisectrix, Trochoid, Tumble-home, Twist, Undulose, U-turn, Volute, Witch (of Agnesi)

Cushion(s) Air, Allege, Bank, Beanbag, Bolster, Buffer, Bustle, Frog, Ham, Hassock, Kneeler, → **PAD**, Pillow, Pin, Pouf(fe), Pulvillus, Scatter, Soften, Squab, Upholster, Whoopee

Cusp Horn, Spinode, Tine

Custard (apple) Crème caramel, Flam(m), Flan, Flaune, Flawn, Flummery, Pastry, Pa(w)paw, Zabaglione

Custodial, Custodian, Custody Care, Claviger, Curator, Guard, Hold, Incarceration, Janitor, Keeping, Protective, Sacrist, Steward, Trust, Ward, Wardship

Custom(ised), Customs (officer), Customs house, Customary Agriology, Chophouse, Coast-waiters, Cocket, Consuetude, Conventional, Couvade, Dedicated, De règle, Dhamma, Dharma, Douane, Exciseman, Familiar, Fashion, Folklore, → **HABIT**, Land-waiter, Lore, Manner, Montem, Mores, Nomic, Octroi, Ordinary, Practice, Praxis, Protocol, Relic, Rite, Routine, Rule, Sororate, Spanish, Sunna, Tax, Thew, Tidesman, Tide-waiter, Tikanga, Time-honoured, Tradition, Unwritten, Usance, Used, Usual, Won, Wont, Woon, Zollverein

Customer Client, Cove, Patron, Prospect, Purchaser, Shillaber, Shopper, Smooth, Stiff, Trade, Trick, Ugly

▷ **Cut** *may indicate* an anagram

Cut(ter), Cutdown, Cutting Abate, Abbreviate, Abjoint, Ablate, Abridge, Abscission, Abscond, Acute, Adeem, Adze, Aftermath, Ali Baba, Amputate,

Apocope, Axe, Bang, Bisect, Bit, Bite, Bowdlerise, Boycott, Brilliant, Broach,
Caesarean, Caique, Canal, Cantle, Caper, Carver, Castrate, Caustic, Censor, Chap,
Cheese, Chisel, Chopper, Chynd, Circumscribe, Cleaver, Clinker-built, Clip, Colter,
Commission, Concise, Coppice, Coulter, Coupé, Crew, Crop, Cruel, Cube, Culebra,
Curtail, Deadhead, Decrease, Dedekind, Dicer, Die, Director's, Discide, Disengage,
Dismember, Dissect, Division, Divorce, Dock, Dod, Edge, Edit, Emarginate,
Embankment, Engraver, Entail, Entayle, Epistolary, Epitomise, Escalope, Eschew,
Estrepe, Etch, Excalibur, Excide, Excise, Exscind, Exsect, Exude, Fashion, Fell, Filet
mignon, Fillet, Flench, Flense, Flinch, Form, Framp, Froe, Frow, Gaillard, Garb,
Gash, Go-down, Grater, Graven, Gride, Gryde, Hack, Handsaw, Hew(er), Ignore,
Incision, Incisor, Indent, Insult, Intersect, Jigsaw, Joint, Junk, Kerf, Kern, Kirn,
Lacerate, Lance, Leat, Lesion, Lin, Lop, Math, Medaillon, Medallion, Microtome,
Milling, Minimise, Mohel, Mortice, Mortise, Mower, Nache, Nick, Not, Notch,
Nott, Occlude, Omit, Open, Operate, Osteotome, Oxyacetylene, Padsaw, Pare, Pink,
Plant, Pliers, Ploughshare, Poll, Pollard, Pone, Power, Precisive, Press, Proin,
Quota, Race, Rake off, Rase, Razee, Razor, Reap, Rebate, Reduction, Re-enter,
Resect, Retrench, Revenue, Ring, Ripsaw, Roach, Rose, Rout, Saddle, Sarcastic,
Sarky, Saw-tooth, Saw(n), Scaloppine, Scarf, Scathing, Scion, Scission, Scissor,
Score, Scrap, Sculpt, Scye, Scythe, Secant, Secateurs, Sect, Section, Sever, Sey,
Share(out), Shaver, Shears, Shingle, Ship, Shive, Shorn, Short, Shred, Shun, Sickle,
Side, Sirloin, Skin, Skip, Slane, Slash, Slice(r), Slip, Slit, Sloop, Sned, Snee, Snib,
Snick, Snip, Snub, Spade, Speedy, Spin, Spud, Steak, Stencil, Stereotomy, Stir,
Stramac, Stramazon, Strimmer®, Style, Surgeon, Swath(e), Tailor(ess), Tap, Tart,
Tenderloin, Tenotomy, Tomial, Tomium, Tonsure, Tooth, Topside, Transect, Trash,
Trench, Trenchant, Trepan, Trim, Truant, Truncate, Urchin, Vivisection, Whang,
Whittle, Winey
▷ **Cutback** *may indicate* a reversed word
  Cute Ankle, Perspicacious, Pert, Pretty, Taking
  Cuticle Epidermis, Eponychium, Periplast, Pleuron, Skin
  Cut in Interpose, Interrupt
  Cutlass Machete, Sword
  Cutlery Canteen, Eating irons, Flatware, Fork, Knife, Service, Setting, Silver, Spoon,
    Spork, Sunbeam, Tableware, Trifid
  Cutlet Schnitzel
  Cut off Elide, Enisle, Estrange, Inisle, Insulate, Intercept, → **ISOLATE**, Lop, Prune
  Cut-throat Razor, Ruinous
  Cuttlebone, Cuttlefish Octopus, Pen, Polyp(e)s, Polypus, Sea-sleeve, Sepia,
    Sepiost(aire), Sepium, Squid
  CV Biodata
  Cyanide Acrylonitrile, Nitrile, Potassium, Prussiate
  Cycad Coontie, Coonty
  Cyclamen Sow-bread
  Cycle, Cyclist, Cycling Anicca, Arthurian, Bike, Biorhythm, Business, Cal(l)ippic,
    Calvin, Carbon, Carnot, Cell, Circadian, Citric acid, Closed, Daisy, Diesel, Eon,
    Era, Fairy, Four-stroke, Freewheel, Frequency, Geological, Gigahertz, Heterogony,
    Hydrologic, Indiction, Keirin, Ko, Krebs, Life, Light-year, Lunar, Lytic, Madison,
    Metonic, Moped, Natural, Nitrogen, Oestrus, Orb, Otto, Pedal, Peloton, Period,
    Product life, Rankine, Repulp, Revolution, Ride, Roadster, Rock, Rota, Round,
    Samsara, Saros, Scorch, Series, Sheng, Solar, Song, Sonnet, Sothic, Spin, Sunspot,
    TCA, Trade, Trick, Trike, Turn, UCI, Urea, Vicious, Water, Wheeler, Wheelman,
    Wu

Dd

D Daughter, Delta, Died, Edh, Eth, Penny

Dab(s) Bit, Daub, Fish, Flounder, Lemon, Pat, Print, Ringer, Smear, Smooth, Spot, Stupe, Whorl

Dabble(r) Amateur, Clatch, Dally, Dilettante, Plouter, Plowter, Potter, Smatter, Splash, Stipple, Trifle

Dachshund Teckel

Dactyl Anapaest

Dad(dy) Blow, Dev(v)el, Father, Generator, Hit, Male, Pa(pa), Pater, Polt, Pop, Slam, Sugar, Thump

Daddy-longlegs Crane-fly, Jennyspinner, Leather-jacket, Spinning-jenny, Tipula

Daffodil Asphodel, Jonquil, Lent-lily, Narcissus

Daft Absurd, Crazy, Potty, Ridiculous, Silly, Simple, Stupid

Dag Jag, Pierce, Pistol, Prick, Stab, Tag, Wool

Dagga Cape, Red, True

Dagger(s) An(e)lace, Ataghan, Baselard, Bayonet, Bodkin, Crease, Creese, Da(h), Diesis, Dirk, Double, Dudgeon, Han(d)jar, Hanger, Jambiya(h), Katar, Khanjar, Kindjahl, Kirpan, Kreese, Kris, Lath, Misericord(e), Obelisk, Obelus, Poi(g) nado, Poniard, Pugio, Puncheon, Pusser's, Quillon, Rondel, Sgian-dubh, Skean, Skene(-occle), Spanish, Stiletto, Swordbreaker, Whiniard, Whinyard, W(h)inger, Yatag(h)an

Dahlia Cosmea

Daily Adays, Char, Circadian, Cleaner, Diurnal, Domestic, Guardian, Help, Journal, Mail, Mirror, Mrs Mopp, Paper, Per diem, Quotidian, Rag, Regular, Scotsman, Sun, Tabloid

Dainty, Daintiness Cate(s), Cute, Delicacy, Elegant, Elfin, Entremesse, Entremets, Exquisite, Genty, Junket, Lickerish, Liquorish, Mignon(ne), Minikin, → **MORSEL**, Neat, Nice, Particular, Petite, Precious, Prettyism, Pussy, Sunket, Twee

Dairy Creamery, Days' house, Loan, Parlour

Dairymaid, Dairyman Cowfeeder, Dey, Patience

Dais Estate, Machan, Platform, Podium, Pulpit, Rostrum, Stage, Tribune

Daisy African, Barberton, Bell, Felicia, Gerbera, Gowan, Groundsel, Hen and chickens, Livingstone, Marguerite, Marigold, Michaelmas, Moon, Ox-eye, Ragweed, Shasta, Transvaal, Vegetable sheep

Dale(s) Dell, Dene, Dingle, Glen, Nidder, Ribbles, Swale, Vale, Valley, Wensley, Wharfe, Yorkshire

Dally Coquet(te), Dawdle, Finger, Flirt, Play, Spoon, Sport, Tick and toy, Toy, Trifle, Wait

Dam An(n)icut, Arch, Aswan, Aswan High, Bar, Barrage, Barrier, Block, Boulder, Bund, Cabora Bassa, Cauld, Check, Dental, Gravity, Hoover, Kariba, Kielder, Ma, Mangla, Mater, Obstacle, Obstruct, Pen, Sennar, Stank, → **STEM**, Sudd, Tank, Three Gorges, Turkey nest, Volta River, Weir, Yangtze

Damage(d), Damages, Damaging Accidental, Appair, Bane, Banjax, Bruise, Buckle, Charge, Chip, Collateral, Contuse, Cost, Cripple, Dent, Desecrate, Detriment, Devastate, Devastavit, Distress, Estrepe, Exemplary, Fault, Flea-bite, Foobar, Fubar, Fuck up, Harm, Havoc, Hedonic, Hit, Hole, Hurt, Impair, Injury, Insidious, Loss, Mar, Mayhem, Moth-eaten, Mutilate, Nobble, Opgefok, Pair(e), Prang, Price, Punitive, Ratten, Ravage, Retree, Sabotage, Scaith, Scath(e), Scotch, Scratch, Skaith, Smirch, Solatium, → **SPOIL**, Tangle, Tear, Tigger, Toll, Value, Vandalise, Violate, Wear and tear, Wing, Wound, Wreak, Wreck, Write off

▷ **Damage(d)** *may indicate* an anagram

Dambuster Ondatra

Dame Crone, Dowager, Edna, Gammer, Lady, Matron, Nature, Naunt, Partlet, Peacherino, Sis, Title(d), Trot, Woman

Damn(ation), Damned Accurst, Attack, Blame, Blast, Condemn, Curse, Cuss, D, Darn, Dee, Execrate, Faust, Heck, Hell, Hoot, Jigger, Malgre, Perdition, Predoom, Sink, Swear, Tarnal, Tarnation, Tinker's, Very

Damp(en), Damping, Dampness Aslake, Black, Blight, Check, Clam(my), Dank, Dewy, Fousty, Fusty, Humid, Mesarch, Moch, Moist, Muggy, Raw, Rheumy, Rising, Roric, Soggy, Sordo, Sultry, Unaired, Viscous, → **WET**, White

Damper Barrier, Check, Dashpot, Killjoy, Mute, Register-plate, Sordino, Sourdine

Damsel Girl, Lass, Maiden, Wench

Damson Plumdamas

Dan Box, Cupid, Leno, Olivetan, Scuttle, Tribe

Dance(r), Dancing Astaire, Baladin(e), Ballabile, Ballant, Ballerina, Ballroom, Bayadère, Bob, Body-popping, Caper, Chorus-girl, Comprimario, Contredanse, Corybant, Coryphee, Dervish, Diaghilev, Dinner, Dolin, Exotic, Figurant, Figure, Fooling, Foot, Foot-it, Gandy, Gigolo, Groove, Hetaera, Hetaira, Hoofer, Kick-up, Knees-up, Leap, Maenad, Majorette, Modern, Nautch-girl, Night, Nijinsky, Nod, Nureyev, Oberek, Old-time, Partner, Pavlova, Petipa, Pierette, Prom(enade), Raver, Reindeer, Ring, Ronggeng, Rug-cutting, St Vitus, Salome, Saltatorious, Skipper, Spring, Step, Strut, Table, Tea, Terpsichore, Thé dansant, Tread, Trip(pant), Whirl

DANCES

3 letters:	*4 letters:*	Juba	Spin
Bop	Alma	Juke	Spot
Fan	Ball	Kolo	Stag
Gig	Barn	Line	Taxi
Hay	Bull	Lion	Wire
Hey	Clog	Loup	
Hop	Dump	Mosh	*5 letters:*
Ice	Fado	Nach	Bamba
Jig	Folk	Pogo	B and S
Lap	Frug	Polo	Belly
Pas	Giga	Punk	Bogle
Poi	Go-go	Rain	Brawl
Sun	Haka	Reel	Break
Tap	Hora	Rope	Carol
Toe	Hula	Sand	Ceroc®
War	Jive	Shag	Conga
	Jota	Slam	Disco

Fling
Furry
Galop
Ghost
Gigue
Glide
Gopak
Horah
Limbo
Loure
Mambo
Mooch
Natch
Paspy
Pavan
Paven
Pavin
Polka
Ragga
Robot
Round
Rueda
Rumba
Salsa
Samba
Shake
Skank
Skirt
Snake
Stomp
Sword
Tango
Torch
Truck
Twist
Valse
Vogue
Volta
Waltz

6 letters:
Almain
Apache
Ballet
Bolero
Boogie
Boston
Branle
Bubble
Canary
Can-can

Cha-cha
Fading
Floral
German
Hustle
Jump-up
Kathak
Lavolt
Maxixe
Minuet
Morris
Pavane
Redowa
Shimmy
Smooch
Square
Trophe
Valeta
Veleta
Waggle

7 letters:
Bambuca
Beguine
Bourrée
Bransle
Brantle
Cantico
Capuera
Carioca
Coranto
Cossack
Country
Courant
Csardas
Farruca
Forlana
Foxtrot
Furlana
Gavotte
Halling
Hoe-down
Lambada
Lancers
Landler
Lavolta
Macabre
Mazurka
Measure
Moresco
Morisco

Morrice
Moshing
Musette
One-step
Pericon
Planxty
Polacca
Pyrrhic
Ridotto
Ringlet
Romaika
Roundel
Roundle
Routine
Sardana
Sashaya
Shuffle
Tanagra
Tordion
Toyi-toy
Trenise
Two-step
Ziganka

8 letters:
Alegrias
Boogaloo
Bunnyhop
Bunnyhug
Cachucha
Cakewalk
Canticoy
Capoeira
Chaconne
Cotillon
Courante
Egg-dance
Excuse-me
Fandango
Flamenco
Flip-flop
Galliard
Habanera
Hay-de-guy
Haymaker
Hey-de-guy
Heythrop
Hoolican
Hornpipe
Hula-hula

Irish jig
Joncanoe
Junkanoo
Kantikoy
Kapa haka
Kazachok
Kazatzka
Krumping
Lindy hop
Macarena
Marinera
Matachin
Matelote
Medicine
Merengue
Murciana
Orchesis
Rigadoon
Robotics
Saraband
Snowball
Soft-shoe
Taglioni
Trucking
Vogueing

9 letters:
Allemande
Bergamask
Bergomask
Bossanova
Caballero
Cha-cha-cha
Chipaneca
Cotillion
Ecossaise
Eightsome
Farandole
Formation
Gallopade
Hoolachan
Jitterbug
Kathakali
Malaguena
Pas de deux
Paso doble
Passepied
Paul Jones
Polonaise
Poussette
Quadrille

9 letters – cont:
Quickstep
Ring-shout
Roundelay
Siciliana
Siciliano
Sink-a-pace
Tambourin
Tripudium
Variation
Zapateado

10 letters:
Antimasque
Breakdance
Carmagnole
Charleston
Cinderella
Cinque-pace
Corroboree

Gay Gordon's
Hay-de-guise
Hay-de-guyes
Hey-de-guise
Hey-de-guyes
Hokey-cokey
Passamezzo
Petronella
Saltarello
Seguidilla
Sicilienne
Sinke-a-pace
Strathspey
Tarantella
Tripudiate
Turkey trot
Tyrolienne
Walk-around

11 letters:
Antistrophe
Black bottom
Buck and wing
Cracovienne
Eurhythmics
Lambeth walk
Palais glide
Passacaglia
Pastourelle
Progressive
Schottische
Shimmy-shake
Varsovienne

12 letters:
Bharat Natyam
Labanotation
Passemeasure
Passy-measure

Virginia reel

13 letters:
Highland fling
Virginian reel

14 letters:
Divertissement
Jack-in-the-green

15 letters:
Soft shoe shuffle

16 letters:
Circassian circle

18 letters:
Sir Roger de
   Coverley

Dance hall Disco, Juke-joint, Palais

Dance movement Arabesque, Balancé, Battement, Batterie, Benesh, Brisé, Chassé, Dos-à-dos, Dosido, Entrechat, Fishtail, Fouetté, Glissade, Jeté, Lassu, Pantalon, Pas de basque, Pas de chat, Pas seul, Pigeonwing, Pirouette, Plastique, Plié, Poule, Poussette, Routine, Sauté, Step, Twinkle

Dance tune Toy

▷ **Dancing** *may indicate* an anagram

Dancing party Ball, Ridotto

Dandelion Hawkbit, Kok-saghyz, Piss-a-bed, Scorzonera, Taraxacum

Dander Anger, Gee, Passion, Saunter, Temper

Dandle Dance, Doodle, Fondle, Pet

Dandruff Furfur, Scurf

Dandy Adonis, Beau, Blood, Boulevardier, Buck(een), Cat, Coxcomb, Dapper, → **DUDE**, Exquisite, Fantastico, Fop, Gem, Jay, Jessamy, Johnny, Kiddy, Knut, Lair, Macaroni, Masher, Modist, Monarcho, Muscadin, Nash, Nut, Posh, Puss -gentleman, Roy, Smart, Spark, Spiff, Swell, Ted, Toff, U, Yankee-doodle

Dandy-horse Draisene, Draisine

Dane(s) Clemence, Dansker, Ogier, Ostmen

Danger(ous) Apperil, Breakneck, Chancy, Crisis, Dic(e)y, Dire, Dodgy, Emprise, Fear, Hairy, Hazard, Hearie, High-risk, Hot, Insecure, Jeopardy, Lethal, Menace, Mine, Minefield, Nettle, Nocuous, Objective, Parlous, Periculous, → **PERIL**, Pitfall, Plight, Precarious, Quicksand, Risk, Rock, Serious, Severe, Snag, Snare, Tight, Tight spot, Trap, Wonchancy

Dangle A(i)glet, Aiguillette, Critic, Flourish, Hang, Loll, Swing

Daniel Dan, Defoe, Deronda, Lion-tamer, Portia, Quilp

Dank Clammy, Damp, Humid, Moist, Wet, Wormy

Daphne Agalloch, Agila, Eaglewood, Lace-bark, Laura, Laurel, Mezereon

Dapper Dressy, Natty, Neat, Smart, Spiff, Sprauncy, Spruce, Sprush, Spry, → **TRIM**

Darbies Cuffs, Irons, Snaps

Dare, Dare-devil, Daring Adventure, Audacious, Bold, Brave, Bravura,

Challenge, Courage, Dan, Da(u)nton, Defy, Durst, Emprise, Face, Gallant, Gallus, Groundbreaking, Hardihood, Hazard, Hen, Intrepid, Moxie, Neck, Prowess, Racy, Stuntman, Swashbuckler, Taunt, Venture

Dark(en), Darkie, Darkness Aphelia, Aphotic, Apophis, Black, Blind, Byronic, Cimmerian, Cloud, Colly, Crepuscular, Depth, Dim, Dingy, Dirk(e), Dusky, Eclipse, Egyptian, Erebus, Evil, Gloom, Glum, Inky, Inumbrate, Jet, Kieran, Low-key, Mare, Maria, Melanous, Mulatto, Murk(y), Negro, Night, Obfuscate, Obnubilation, Obscure, Obsidian, Ominous, Ousel, Pall, Phaeic, Pitch-black, Pit-mirk, Rooky, Sable, Sad, Secret, Shades, Shady, Shuttered, Sinister, Solein, Sombre, Sooty, Sphacelate, Stygian, Sullen, Swarthy, Tar, Tenebr(i)ous, Tenebrose, Unfair, Unlit, Wog, Woosel, Yellowboy, Yellowgirl

Darling Acushla, Alannah, Asthore, Beloved, Charlie, Cher, Chéri(e), Chick-a-biddy, Chick-a-diddle, Chuck-a-diddle, Dear, Dilling, Do(a)ting-piece, Duck(s), Favourite, Grace, Honey, Idol, Jarta, Jo(e), Lal, Love, Luv, Mavourneen, Mavournin, Minikin, Minion, Oarswoman, Own, Peat, Pet, Poppet, Precious, Sugar, Sweetheart, Sweeting, Yarta, Yarto

Darn Begorra, Blow, Doggone, Hang, Mend, Repair, Sew

Dart(s), Darter Abaris, Arrow, Banderilla, Beetle, Dace, Dash, Deadener, Dodge, Fleat, Fléchette, Flirt, Flit, Harpoon, Javelin, Launch, Leap, Lunger, Pheon, Scoot, Shanghai, Skrim, Speck, Spiculum, Sprint, Strike, Thrust, Wheech

Dash(ing), Dashed Backhander, Bally, Blade, Blight, Blow, Bribe, Buck, Charge, Collide, Cut, Dad, Dah, Damn, Dapper, Dart(le), Daud, Dawd, Debonair, Ding, Dod, Elan, Em, En, Fa(s)cia, Flair, Fly, Go-ahead, Hang, Hurl, → **HURRY**, Hustle, Hyphen, Impetuous, Jabble, Jaw, Jigger, Lace, Line, Minus, Modicum, Morse, Natty, Nip, Panache, Pebble, Race, Raffish, Rakish, Ramp, Rash, Rule, Run, Rush, Sally, Scamp(er), Scapa, Scarper, Scart, Scoot, Scrattle, Scurry, Scuttle, Shatter, Showy, Skitter, Soupçon, Souse, Spang, Speed, Splash, Splatter, Sprint, Strack, Streak, Stroke, → **STYLE**, Swung, Throw, Touch, Viretot

Dashboard Fascia

Dashwood Hell-fire club

Dastard(ly) Base, Coward, Craven, Nid(d)erling, Poltroon

Data(base), Datum Archie, Cyberspace, Donne(e), Evidence, Facts, Fiche, File, Floating-point, Garbage, Gen, HOLMES, Info, Input, IT, Material, Matrix, Newlyn, News, Ordnance, Read-out, Soft copy, Table, Triple

Date(d), Dates, Dating AD, Age, AH, Almanac, Appointment, Blind, Boyfriend, Calendar, Carbon, Carbon-14, Computer, Court, Deadline, Engagement, Epoch, Equinox, Era, Escort, Exergue, Expiry, Fission-track, Fixture, Gig, Girlfriend, Ides, Julian, Meet, Outmoded, → **OUT OF DATE**, Passé, Past, Radioactive, Radio-carbon, Radiometric, Rubidium-strontium, See, System, → **TRYST**, Ult(imo), Uranium-lead, Value

Daub Begrime, Blob, Dab, Gaum, Mess, Moil, Noint, Plaister, Plaster, → **SMEAR**, Smudge, Splodge, Teer, Wattle

Daughter (in law) Child, D, Elect, Girl, Jephthah's, Niece, Offspring, Skevington's

Daunt Adaw, Amate, Awe, Deter, Dishearten, Intimidate, Overawe, Quail, Stun, Stupefy, Subdue

Dauphin Delphin

David Dai, Psalmist

Davit Crane, Derrick, Hoist

Davy Crockett, Jones

Daw Bird, Magpie, Margery

Dawdle(r) Dally, Draggle, Drawl, Idle, Lag(gard), → **LOITER**, Potter, Shirk, Slowcoach, Tarry, Troke, Truck

Dawn(ing) Aurora, Cockcrow, Daw, Daybreak, Daylight, Day-peep, Dayspring, Enlightenment, Eoan, Eos, False, French, Light, Morrow, Occur, Prime, Roxane, Sparrowfart, Spring, Start, Sunrise, Ushas

Day(s) Account, Ahemeral, All Fools', All Hallows', All Saints', All Souls', Anniversary, Annunciation, Anzac, April Fool's, Armistice, Ascension, Australia, Bad hair, Baker, Banian, Banyan, Barnaby, Bastille, Borrowing, Box, Boxing, Broad, Calendar, Calends, Calpa, Canada, Canicular, Childermas, Civil, Columbus, Commonwealth, Contango, Continental, Continuation, D, Daft, Date, Decoration, Degree, Der Tag, Dismal, Distaff, Dog, Dominion, Double, Dressed, Duvet, Early, Ember, Empire, Epact, Fast, Fasti, Father's, Feast, Ferial, Field, Fiesta, Flag, Fri, Gang, Gaudy, Groundhog, Guy Fawkes', Halcyon, High, Hogmanay, Holy, Holy Innocents', Holy-rood, Hundred, Ides, Inauguration, Independence, Intercalary, Judgment, Juridical, Kalends, Kalpa, Labo(u)r, Lady, Laetare, Lammas, Last, Law(ful), Lay, Leap, Mardi, Market, May, Memorial, Michaelmas, Midsummer, Mon, Morrow, Mother's, Muck-up, Mufti, Mumping, Name, Ne'erday, New Year's, Nones, Nychthemeron, Oak-apple, Octave, Open, Orangeman's, Pancake, Paper, Pay, Poppy, Post, Pound, Present, Press(ed), Primrose, Pulvering, Quarter, Rag, Rainy, Red-letter, Remembrance, Rent, Rest, Robin, Rock, Rogation, Rood(-mas), Rosh Chodesh, Sabbath, Saint's, St Swithin's, St Thomas's, St Valentine's, Salad, Sansculotterie, Sat, Scambling, Settling, Sexagesima, Shick-shack, Show, Sidereal, Snow, Solar, Solstice, Speech, Sports, Station, Sun, Supply, Tag, Term, Thanksgiving, Thurs, Ticket, Time, Transfer, Trial, Triduum, Tues, Twelfth, Utas, Valentine's, Varnishing, VE, Veterans', Victoria, Visiting, VJ, Waitangi, Wed, Wedding, Working

Daybreak Cockcrow, Cockleert

Daydream(er), Daydreaming Brown study, Castle(s) in the air, Dwam, Dwaum, Fancy, Imagine, Muse, Reverie, Rêveur, Walter Mitty, Woolgathering

Daylight Artificial, Dawn, Space, Sun

Daze(d) Amaze, Bemuse, Confuse, Dwaal, Gally, Muddle, Muzzy, Petrify, Punch drunk, Reeling, Spaced out, → **STUN**, Stupefy, Stupor, Trance

Dazzle(d), Dazzling Bewilder, Blend, Blind, Eclipse, Foudroyant, Glare, Meteoric, Outshine, Radiance, Resplendent, Splendour, Yblent

Deacon Cleric, Doctor, Minister, Permanent

Deactivate Unarm

Dead(en) Abrupt, Accurate, Alamort, Asgard, Asleep, Blunt, Brown bread, Bung, Cert, Cold, Complete, D, Deceased, Defunct, Doggo, Expired, Extinct, Gone(r), Inert, Infarct, Late, Lifeless, Morkin, Muffle, Mute, Napoo, Niflheim, Numb, Obsolete, Obtund, Ringer, She'ol, Slain, Smother, Stillborn, True, Under hatches, Utter, Waned

Dead end, Deadlock Blind alley, Cut-off, Dilemma, Impasse, Logjam, Stalemate, Stand-off, Sticking-point, Stoppage

Dead-leaf colour Filemot, Philamot, Philomot

Deadline Date, Epitaph, Limit

Deadly Baleful, Dull, Fell, Funest, Internecine, → **LETHAL**, Malign, Mortal, Mortific, Pestilent, Thanatoid, Unerring, Venomous

Deadly nightshade Belladonna, Dwale

Deadpan Expressionless

Dead reckoning Dr

Dead tree Rampick, Rampike

Deaf(en), Deafening, Deafness Adder, Asonia, Deave, Deeve, Dunny, Heedless, Paracusis, Presbyac(o)usis, Presbyc(o)usis, Surd(ity)

Deal(er), Dealership, Dealing(s), Deal with Address, Agent, Agreement, Allot(ment), Arb, Arbitrageur, Bargain, Breadhead, Brinjarry, Broker, Business, Cambist, Candyman, Chandler, Chapman, Clocker, Commerce, Connection, Cope, Coup, Cover, Croupier, Dispense, Distributor, Do, Dole, East, Eggler, Exchange, Fir, Franchise, Fripper, Front-running, Goulash, Hand(le), Help, Inflict, Insider, Interbroker, Jiggery-pokery, Jobber, Lashing, Lay on, Lay out, Lot, Manage, Mercer, Merchant, Mickle, Middleman, Monger, Mort, Negotiate, New, North, Operator, Package, Pine, Plain, Port, Productivity, Pusher, Raft, Raw, Red, Sale, Serve, Side, Sight, Slanger, Sort, South, Spicer, Square, Stockist, Stockjobber, Takeover, Tape, Timber, Totter, Tout(er), → **TRADE**, Traffic, Traffick, Transaction, Treat, Truck, West, Wheeler, White, Wholesaler, Wield, Woolstapler, Yardie

Dean Acheson, Arabin, Colet, Decani, Doyen, Forest, Head, Inge, Nellie, Provost, RD, Rural, Rusk, Slade, Spooner, Swift, Vale, Vicar-forane, V rev

Dear(er), Dearest, Dear me Ay, Bach, Beloved, Cara, Caro, Cher(e), Cherie, Chou, Chuckie, Darling, Duck(s), Expensive, High, Honey(bun), Lamb, Leve, Lief, Lieve, Loor, Love, Machree, Mouse, My, Pet, Pigsney, Pigsnie, Pigsny, Steep, Sugar, Sweet, Sweetie, Sweeting, Toots(ie), Up

Dearth Famine, Lack, Paucity, Scantity, Scarcity, → **SHORTAGE**

Deaspiration Psilosis

Death(ly) Abraham's bosom, Auto-da-fe, Bane, Bargaist, Barg(h)est, Biolysis, Black, Cataplexis, Charnel, Clinical, Commorientes, Cot, Curtains, Cypress, Demise, Departure, Dormition, End, Eschatology, Euthanasia, Exit, Extinction, Fatality, Funeral, Fusillation, Gangrene, Grim Reaper, Hallal, Heat, Infarction, Jordan, Karoshi, King of Terrors, Lead colic, Lethee, Leveller, Living, Loss, Mors, Napoo, Necrosis, Nemesis, Night, Obit, Quietus, Reaper, Sati, Sergeant, SIDS, Small-back, Strae, Sudden, Suttee, Terminal, Thanatism, Thanatology, Thanatopsis, Thanatos

Death-flood Styx

Deathless(ness) Athanasy, Eternal, Eterne, Immortal, Struldberg, Timeless, Undying

Debacle Cataclysm, Collapse, Disaster, Fiasco

Debag Dack

Debar Deny, Exclude, Forbid, → **PREVENT**, Prohibit

Debase(d) Adulterate, Allay, Bemean, Cheapen, Corrupt, Demean, Depreciate, Dialectician, Dirty, Grotesque, Hedge, Lower, Pervert, Traduce, Vitiate

Debate Adjournment, Argue, Combat, Contention, Contest, Deliberate, Dialectic, Discept, Discourse, Discuss(ion), → **DISPUTE**, Flyte, Forensics, Full-dress, Moot, Paving, Polemics, Powwow, Reason, Teach-in, Warsle, Wrangle, Wrestle

Debauch(ed), Debauchee, Debauchery Corrupt, Decadent, Defile, Degenerate, Dissipate, Dissolute, Heliogabalus, Libertine, Licence, Orgy, Profligate, Raddled, Rake-hell, Riot, Roist, Roué, Royst, Seduce, Spree, Stuprate, Wet, Whore

Debenture Bond, Security

Debilitate(d), Debility Asthenia, Atonic, Cachexia, Feeble, Languid, Weak

Debit Charge, Debt, Direct

Debonair Cavalier, Gay, Gracious, Jaunty

Debrief Wash up, Wind up

Debris Bahada, Bajada, Detritus, Eluvium, Moraine, Moslings, Pyroclastics, Refuse, → **RUBBLE**, Ruins, Shrapnel, Tel, Tephra, Waste, Wreckage

▷ **Debris** *may indicate* an anagram

Debt(or) Abbey-laird, Alsatia, Arrears, Arrestee, Bonded, Dr, Due, Floating, Funded,

Insolvent, IOU, Liability, Moratoria, National, Obligation, Oxygen, Poultice, Public, Queer Street, Score, Subordinated, Tie, Unfunded

Debt-collector Bailiff, Forfaiter, Remembrancer

Debut Launch, Opening, Outset, Presentation

Debutante Bud, Deb

Decade Rosary, Ten

Decadence, Decadent Babylonian, Decaying, Degeneration, Dissolute, Effete, Fin-de-siècle, Libertine

Decamp Abscond, Absquatulate, Bolt, Bunk, Depart, Flee, Guy, Levant, Mizzle, Slide, Slope, Vamoose

Decant Pour, Unload

Decapitate, Decapitation Aphesis, → **BEHEAD**, Guillotine

▷ **Decapitated** *may indicate* first letter removed

Decay(ed), Decaying Alpha, Appair, Beta, Biodegrade, Blet, Canker, Caries, Caseation, Consenescence, Crumble, Decadent, Declension, Decline, Decompose, Decrepit, Dieback, Disintegrate, Dissolution, Doat, Doddard, Doddered, Dote, Dricksie, Druxy, Dry rot, Fail, F(o)etid, Forfair, Gangrene, Heart-rot, Impair, Moulder, Pair(e), Perish, Plaque, Putrefy, Radioactive, Ret, Rot, Rust, Saprogenic, Sap-rot, Seedy, Sepsis, Spoil, Tabes, Thoron, Time-worn, Wet-rot

Decease(d) Death, Decedent, Demise, Die, Stiff

Deceit(ful), Deceive(r) Abuse, Artifice, Bamboozle, Barrat, Befool, Bitten, Blind, Bluff, Braide, → **CHEAT**, Chicane, Chouse, Con, Cozen, Cuckold, Defraud, Deke (out), Delude, Diddle, Dissemble, Do brown, Double-cross, Double-tongued, Dupe, Duplicity, False(r), Fastie, Fast-talk, Fiddle, Fineer, Flam, Fool, Four-flusher, Fox, Fraud, Gag, Gerrymander, Gloze, Guile, Gull, Hoax, Hoodwink, Hornswoggle, Humbug, Hype, Hypocritical, Illusion, Imposition, Inveigle, Invention, Jacob, Jiggery-pokery, Kid, Liar, Malengine, Mamaguy, Mata Hari, Mendacious, Mislead, Mislippen, Perfidy, Phenakism, Poop, Poupe, Pretence, Prevaricate, Punic, Rig, Ruse, Sell, Sham, Sinon, Sleekit, Snow job, Spruce, Stratagem, Subreption, Swindle, Swizzle, Tregetour, Trick, Trump, Two-faced, Two-time, Weasel, Wile

Decency, Decent Chaste, Decorum, Fitting, Godly, Healsome, Honest, Kind, Mensch, Modest, Moral, Passable, Seemly, Sporting, Wholesome, Wise-like

Decentralise Disperse

Deception, Deceptive Abusion, Artifice, Bluff, Catchpenny, Catchy, Cheat, Chicanery, Codology, → **DECEIT**, Disguise, Dupe, Duplicity, Elusive, Eyewash, Fallacious, False, Fineer, Flam, Fraud, Fubbery, Gag, Gammon, Guile, Gullery, Have-on, Hocus-pocus, Hokey-pokey, Hum, Hunt-the-gowks, Hype, Ignes-fatui, Ignis-fatuus, Illusion, Insidious, Kidology, Lie, Moodies, Phantasmal, Runaround, Ruse, Sell, Sleight, Smoke and mirrors, Specious, Sting, The moodies, Thimblerig, → **TRICK**, Trompe l'oeil, Two-timing, Underhand

Decide(r), Decided, Decisive Addeem, Adjudge, Agree, A(r)re(e)de, Ballot, Barrage, Bottom-line, Cast, Climactic, Clinch, Clincher, Conclude, Conclusive, Critical, Crux, → **DECISION**, Deem, Definite, Determine, Distinct, Engrenage, Fatal, Final, Firm, Fix, Foregone, Jump-off, Mediate, Opt, Parti, Pivotal, Predestination, Pronounced, Rescript, → **RESOLVE**, Result, Rule, Run-off, See, Settle, Split, Sudden death, Sure, Tiebreaker, Try

Decimal Mantissa, Recurring, Repeating, Terminating

Decimate Destroy, Lessen, Weaken

▷ **Decipher(ed)** *may indicate* an 'o' removed

Decipher(ing) Cryptanalysis, Decode, Decrypt, Descramble, Discover, Interpret

Decision Arbitrium, Arrêt, Crossroads, Crunch, Crux, Decree, Engrenage, Fatwa,

Fetwa, Firman, Judg(e)ment, Parti, Placit(um), Referendum, Resolution, Resolve, Responsa, Ruling, Sentence, Sudden death, Verdict

Deck Adorn, Angled, Array, Attrap, Bejewel, Boat, Canted, Cards, Clad, Daiker, Daub, Decorate, Dizen, Embellish, Equip, Flight, Focsle, Forecastle, Garland, Hang, Helideck, Hurricane, Lower, Main, Mess, Monkey poop, Orlop, Ornament, Pack, Pedestrian, Platform, Poop, Prim, Promenade, Quarter, Saloon, Spar, Sun, Tape, Upper, Void, Well

Declare, Declaration, Declaim, Decree Absolute, Affidavit, Affirm, Air, Allege, Announce, Annunciate, Aread, A(r)e(e)de, Assert, Asseverate, Aver, Avow, Balfour, Bann(s), Bayyan, Breda, Dictum, Diktat, Doom, Edict, Elocute, Enact, Fatwa(h), Fiat, Firman, Go, Grace, Harangue, Hatti-sherif, Independence, Indiction, Indulgence, Insist, Interlocutory, Irade, Law, Mandate, Manifesto, Mecklenburg, Meld, Motu proprio, Mou(th), Nisi, Noncupate, Novel(la), Nullity, Nuncupate, Orate, Ordain, Order, Ordinance, Parlando, Pontificate, Predicate, Present, Proclaim, Profess, Promulgate, Pronounce, Protest, Psephism, Publish, Rant, Recite, Rescript, Resolve, Restatement, Rights, Rule, Ruling, Saw, SC, Sed, Senatus consultum, Senecan, Shahada, Signify, Speak, Spout, State, Statutory, Testament-dative, Testify, Testimony, UDI, Ukase, Ultimatum, Unilateral, Vie, Voice, Vouch, Will, Word

▷ **Declaring** *may indicate* a word beginning 'Im'

Decline, Declination, Declining Age, Ail, Atrophy, Catabasis, Comedown, Decadent, Degeneration, Degringoler, Deny, Descend, Deteriorate, Devall, Die, Diminish, Dip, Dissent, Downhill, Downtrend, Downturn, Droop, Dwindle, Ebb, Fade, Fall, Flag, Forbear, Magnetic, Paracme, Peter, Quail, Recede, Recession, Reflow, Refuse, Retrogression, Rot, Ruin, Rust, Sag, Senile, Set, Sink, Slide, Slump, Slumpflation, Stoop, Twilight, Wane, Welke, → **WILT**, Withdraw, Wither

Decoct(ion) Apozem, Cook, Devise, Ptisan, Tisane

Decode(d) En clair

Decolleté Low, Neckline

Decompose, Decomposition Biodegradable, Crumble, Decay, Degrade, Disintegrate, Electrolysis, Fermentation, Hydrolysis, Mor, Pyrolysis, Rot, Wither

Decompression Bends

Decor Background, Scenery

Decorate(d), Decoration, Decorative Adorn, Angelica, Aogai, Arpillera, Attrap, Award, Bargeboard, Baroque, Bauble, Beaux-arts, Bedizen, Bells and whistles, Biedermeier, Bordure, Braid, Brattishing, Braze, Breastpin, Brooch, Cartouche, Centrepiece, Chambranle, Champlevé, Chinoiserie, Christingle, Cinquefoil, Cloissoné, Coffer, Cresting, Crocket, Croix de guerre, Cul-de-lampe, Daiker, Decoupage, Dentelle, Diamante, Doodad, Dragée, Dragging, Emblazon, Emboss, Embrave, Engrail, Enrich, Epergne, Etch, Fancy, Festoon, Filigree, Finery, Finial, Fleuret(te), Fleuron, Floriated, Flushwork, Fluting, Fob, Fourragère, Frieze, Frill, Frog, Frost, Furbish, Gammadion, Garniture, Gaud, Gild, Glitter, Goffer, Gradino, Grecque key, Grotesque, Guilloche, Historiated, Ice, Illuminate, Impearl, Inlay, Intarsia, Intarsio, Interior, Knotwork, Leglet, Linen-fold, Linen-scroll, Marquetry, MC, Medal(lion), Mola, Motif, Moulding, Oath, OBE, Order, → **ORNAMENT**, Ornate, Orphrey, Overglaze, Ovolo, Paint, Paper, Parament, Pâté-sur-pâté, Photomural, Pinata, Pipe, Pokerwork, Polychromy, Pompom, Prettify, Prink, Purfle, Purple heart, Quilling, Rag-rolling, Rangoli, Repoussé, Ribbon, Rich, Rosemaling, Ruche, Scallop, Schwarzlot, Scrimshander, Scrimshaw, Serif, Set-off, Sgraffito, Skeuomorph, Soutache, Spangle, Staffage, Stomacher, Storiated, Strapwork, Studwork, Tailpiece, Tattoo, TD, Titivate, Tool, Topiary, Trim, Veneer, Vergeboard, Wallpaper, Well-dressing, Wirework

Decorous, Decorum Becoming, Demure, Etiquette, Fitness, Parliamentary, Prim, → **PROPER**, Propriety, Sedate, Seemlihe(a)d, → **SEEMLY**, Staid

Decoy Allure, Bait, Bonnet, Button, Call-bird, Coach, Crimp, Entice, Lure, Piper, Roper, Ruse, Shill, Stale, Stalking-horse, Stall, Stool-pigeon, Tame cheater, Tice, Tole, Toll, Trap, Trepan

Decrease Decrew, Diminish, Dwindle, Iron, Lessen, Press, Ramp down, Reduce, Rollback, Slim, Step-down, Subside, Wane, Wanze

▶ **Decree** *see* **DECLAIM**

Decrepit Dilapidated, Doddery, Failing, Feeble, Frail, Moth-eaten, Spavined, Time-worn, Tumbledown, Warby, Weak

Decry Condemn, Crab, Denounce, Derogate, Detract, Downgrade

Dedicate(d), Dedication Corban, Determination, Devote, Dinah, Endoss, Hallow, Inscribe, Oblate, Pious, Sacred, Single-minded, Votive

Deduce, Deduction, Deductive A priori, Assume, Conclude, Consectary, Corollary, Derive, Discount, Dockage, Gather, Illation, Infer(ence), Natural, Obvert, Off-reckoning, Reason, Rebate, Recoup, Reprise, Stoppage, Surmise, Syllogism

Deed(s) Achievement, Act(ion), Atweel, Backbond, Back letter, Charta, Charter, Defeasance, Derring-do, Disposition, Escrol(l), Escrow, Exploit, Fact(um), Feat, Indeed, Indenture, Manoeuvre, Mitzvah, Muniments, Premises, Settlement, Specialty, Starr, → **TITLE**, Trust

Deem Consider, Judge, Opine, Ordain, Proclaim, Repute, Think

Deep(en), Deeply Abstruse, Bass(o), Brine, Briny, Enhance, Excavate, Grum, Gulf, Hadal, Intense, Low, Mindanao, Mysterious, → **OCEAN**, Profound, Re-enter, Rich, Sea, Sonorous, Throaty, Upsee, Ups(e)y

Deep-rooted Inveterate

Deer(-like) Axis, Bambi, Barasing(h)a, Barking, Blacktail, Brocket, Buck, Cariacou, Caribou, Carjacou, Cervine, Chevrotain, Chital, Doe, Elaphine, Elk, Fallow, Gazelle, Hart, Hog, Jumping, Moose, Mouse, Mule, Muntjac, Muntjak, Musk, Père David's, Pricket, Pudu, Pygarg, Red, Rein, Roe, Rusa, Sambar, Sambur, Selenodont, Sika, Sorel(l), Spade, Spay(d), Spayad, Spitter, Spottie, Stag(gard), Tragule, Ungulate, Virginia, Wapiti, Water, White-tailed

Deer-hunter Tinchel

Deface Disfigure, Spoil

▷ **Defaced** *may indicate* first letter missing

Defame, Defamatory, Defamation Abase, Bad mouth, Blacken, Calumny, Cloud, Denigrate, Detract, Dishonour, Impugn, Libel, Malign, Mud, Mudslinging, Obloquy, Sclaunder, Scurrilous, Slander, Smear, Stigmatise, Traduce, Vilify

Default(er) Absentee, Bilk, Dando, Delinquent, Flit, Levant, Neglect, Omission, Waddle, Welsh

Defeat(ed), Defeatist Beat, Best, Caning, Capot, Codille, Conquer, Counteract, Debel, Defeasance, Demolish, Discomfit, Dish, Ditch, Donkey-lick, Fatalist, Floor, Foil, Foyle, Hammer, Hiding, Kippered, Laipse, Lick, Loss, Lurch, Marmelize, Master, Mate, Moral, Negative, Out, Outclass, Outdo, Outgun, Outplay, Outvote, Outwit, → **OVERCOME**, Overmarch, Overpower, Overreach, Overthrow, Overwhelm, Pip, Plaster, Pulverise, Quitter, Reverse, Rout, Rubicon, Scupper, Set, Shellacking, Sisera, Skunk, Squabash, Stump, Tank, Thrash, Thwart, Tonk, Trounce, Undo, Vanquish, War, Waterloo, Whap, Whip, Whitewash, Whop, Whup, Wipe-out, Worst

Defecate, Defecation Encopresis, Horse, Mute, Poop, Scumber, Shit, Skummer, Tenesmus

Defect(ion), Defective, Defector Abandon, Amateur, Apostasy, Bug, Coma,

Crack, Crawling, Deficient, Desert, Failing, Faulty, Flaw, → **FORSAKE**, Frenkel, Halt, Hamartia, Hiatus, Kink, Low, Manky, Mass, Mote, Natural, Paralexia, Point, Psellism, Rachischisis, Renegade, Renegate, Ridgel, Ridgil, Rig, Rogue, Runagate, Schottky, Shortcoming, Spina bifida, Stammer, Terrace, Treason, Trick, Want, Wanting, Weakness, Wreath

Defence, Defend(er), Defensible, Defensive Abat(t)is, Alexander, Alibi, Antibody, Antidote, Antihistamine, Apologia, Back, Back four, Bailey, Barbican, Barmkin, Barricade, Bastion, Battery, Battlement, Berm, Bestride, Bridgehead, Bulwark, Calt(h)rop, Catenaccio, CD, Champion, Chapparal, Civil, Curtain, Demibastion, Ditch, Embrasure, Estacade, Goalie, Hedgehog, Herisson, Hold, J(i)u-jitsu, Justify, Kaim, Keeper, Laager, Laer, Last-ditch, Libero, Linebacker, Maginot-minded, Maintain, Martello tower, MIDAS, Moat, Motte and bailey, Muniment, Outwork, Palisade, Parapet, Pentagon, Perceptual, Propugnation, Protect, Rampart, Redan, Redoubt, Refute, Resist, Ringwall, → **SHELTER**, Shield, Stonewall, Strategic, Support, Sweeper, Tenable, Tenail(le), Testudo, Tower, Trench, Trou-de-loup, Uphold, Vallation, Vallum, Vindicate, Wall, Warran(t), Zonal

Defenceless Helpless, Inerm, Naked, Sitting duck, Vulnerable

Defendant Accused, Apologist, Respondent, Richard Roe

Defer(ence), Deferential, Deferring Bow, Complaisance, Delay, Dutiful, Homage, Moratory, Morigerous, Obeisant, Pace, Polite, Postpone, Procrastinate, Protocol, Respect, Roll over, Shelve, Submit, Suspend, Waive, Yield

Defiance, Defiant, Defy Acock, Bite the thumb, Bold, Brave, Cock a snook, Contumacy, Dare, Daring, Disregard, Do or die, Flaunt, Outbrave, Outdare, Rebellion, Recusant, Resist, Scab, Stubborn, Titanism, Truculent, Unruly, Yahboo

Deficiency, Deficient Absence, Acapnia, Anaemia, Anoxia, Beriberi, Defect, Failing, Hypinosis, Inadequate, Incomplete, Kwashiorkor, Lack, Osteomalacia, Scant, Scarcity, SCID, Shortage, Shortfall, Spanaemia, Want

▷ **Deficient** *may indicate* an anagram

Deficit Anaplerotic, Arrears, Defective, Ischemia, Loss, Poor, Shortfall

Defile(ment) Abuse, Array, Barranca, Barranco, Besmear, Col, Conspurcation, Desecrate, Dishonour, Donga, Enseam, → **FOUL**, Gate, Gorge, Gully, Inquinate, Inseem, Kloof, Moil, Pass, Pollute, Poort, Ravine, Ray, Roncesvalles, Smear, Spoil, → **SULLY**

Define(d), Definition, Definitive Clear-cut, Decide, Demarcate, Determine, Diorism, Distinct, Explain, Fix, Limit, Parameter, Set, Specific, Tangible, Term

Definite(ly) Classic, Clear, Deffo, Emphatic, Firm, Hard, Indeed, Pos, Positive, Precise, Specific, Sure, Yes

Deflate Burst, Collapse, Flatten, Lower, Prick, Puncture

Deflect(or), Deflection Avert, Bend, Detour, Diverge, Divert, Glance, Holophote, Otter, Paravane, Refract, Snick, Swerve, Throw, Trochotron, Veer, Windage

Deform(ed), Deformity Anamorphosis, Blemish, Contracture, Crooked, Disfigure, Distort, Gammy, Hammer-toe, Harelip, Misborn, Miscreated, Misfeature, Mishapt, Mooncalf, Mutilate, Phocomelia, Phocomely, Polt-foot, Saddle-nose, Stenosed, Talipes, Valgus, Varus, Warp

▷ **Deformed** *may indicate* an anagram

Defraud Bilk, Cheat, Cozen, Gull, Gyp, Lurch, Mulct, Shoulder, Sting, Swindle, Trick

Defray Bear, Cover, Meet

Defrost Thaw

Deft Adept, Agile, Dab, Dexterous, Elegant, Handy, Nimble

Defunct Deceased, Extinct, Obsolete

▶ **Defy** *see* **DEFIANCE**

Degenerate, Degeneration, Degenerative Acorn-shell, Ascidian, Atrophy, Backslide, Balanus, Base, Cirrhipedea, Cirrhipedia, Cirrhopod(a), Cirripedea, Cirripedia, Decadent, Deprave, Descend, Deteriorate, Eburnation, Effete, Fatty, Kaliyuga, Necrobiosis, Pejorate, Pervert, Rakehell, Relapse, Retrogress, Salp, Stentosis, Tunicate

Degrade, Degradation Abase, Cheapen, Culvertage, Debase, Demission, Demote, Depose, Diminish, Disennoble, Embase, Humble, Imbase, Imbrute, Lessen, Lower, → SHAME, Waterloo

Degree(s) Aegrotat, As, Attila (the Hun), Azimuthal, BA, Baccalaureate, BCom, BD, B es S, C, Class, D, Desmond (Tutu), Doctoral, Double first, Douglas (Hurd), Engler, Extent, External, F, First, Forbidden, Foundation, Geoff (Hurst), German, Gradation, Grade, Grece, Gree(s), Greece, Gre(e)se, Grice, Griece, Grize, → IN A HIGH DEGREE, Incidence, K, Lambeth, Latitude, Letters, Level, Levitical, Licentiate, Longitude, MA, Measure, Mediant, Nth, Nuance, Order, Ordinary, Pass, Peg, PhD, Pin, Poll, Rate, Reaumur, Remove, Second, Stage, Status, Step, Submediant, Subtonic, Supertonic, Third, Trevor (Nunn), Water

Dehiscence Suture

Dehydrate(d) Exsiccate, Thirsty

Deification, Deify Apotheosis

Deign Condescend, Stoop

Deity Avatar, Cabiri, Demogorgon, Divine, Faun, → GOD, → GODDESS, Idolise, Immortalise, Krishna, Numen, Pan, Satyr, Zombi(e)

Deject(ed), Dejection Abase, Abattu, Alamort, Amort, Blue, Chap-fallen, Crab, Crestfallen, Despondent, Dismay, Dispirited, Down, Downcast, Gloomy, Hangdog, Humble, Low, Melancholy, Spiritless, Wae

Delaware DE(L)

Delay(ed) Adjourn(ment), Ambage, Avizandum, Behindhand, Check, Cunctator, Defer, Demurrage, Detention, Fabian, Filibuster, For(e)slow, Forsloe, Frist, Hangfire, Hesitate, Hinder, Hitch, Hold up, Hysteresis, Impede, Laches, Lag, Late, Laten, Let, Linger, Loiter, Mora(torium), Obstruct, Pause, Procrastinate, Prolong, Prorogue, Remanet, Reprieve, Respite, Retard, Rollover, Setback, Slippage, Sloth, Slow, → STALL, Stand-over, Stay, Stonewall, Suspend, Temporise, Wait

Delectable Delicious, Luscious, Tasty

Delegate, Delegation Agent, Amphictyon, Apostolic, Appoint, Assign, Commissary, Decentralise, Depute, Devolution, Mission, Nuncio, Offload, Representative, Secondary, Transfer, Vicarial, Walking

Delete Adeem, Cancel, Cut, Erase, Excise, Expunge, Purge, Rase, Scratch, Scrub, Strike, Twink out

Deliberate(ly), Deliberation Adagio, Consider, Debate, Intentional, Meditate, Moderate, Muse, Overt, Ponder, Prepensely, Ruminate, Studied, Thought, Voulu, Weigh, Witting

Delicacy, Delicate Airy-fairy, Beccafico, Blini, Canape, Cate, Caviare, Dainty, Difficult, Discreet, Dorty, Ectomorph, Eggshell, Elfin, Ethereal, Fastidious, Filigree, Fine, Finespun, Finesse, Flimsy, Fragile, → FRAIL, Friand, Gentle, Goody, Gossamer, Guga, Hothouse, Inconie, Incony, Kickshaw, Kidglove, Lac(e)y, Ladylike, Light, Lobster, Morbidezza, Nesh, Nicety, Niminy-piminy, Ortolan, Oyster, Pastel, Reedy, Roe, Sensitive, Soft, Subtle(ty), Sunket, Sweetmeat, Taste, Tender, Tenuous, Ticklish, Tidbit, Titbit, Trotter, Truffle, Wispy

Delicious Ambrosia, Delectable, Exquisite, Fragrant, Goloptious, Goluptious, Gorgeous, Lekker, Lip-smacking, Mor(e)ish, Mouthwatering, Scrummy, Scrumptious, Tasty, Toothsome, Yummo, Yummy, Yum-yum

▷ **Delight** *may indicate* 'darken'
  Delight(ed), Delightful Bewitch, Bliss, Charm, Chuff, Delice, Dreamy, Edna, Elated, Elysian, Enamour, Enjoyable, Enrapture, Exuberant, Felicity, Fetching, Frabjous, Gas, Glad, Glee, Gratify, Honey, Joy, Nice, Overjoy, Over the moon, Please, Pleasure, Precious, → **RAPTURE**, Regale, Revel, Scrummy, Super, Sweet, Taking, Tickle, Turkish, Whacko, Whee, Whoopee, Wizard, Yippee, Yum-yum
  Delineate Draft, Sketch, Trace
  Delinquent Bodgie, Criminal, Halbstarker, Juvenile, Negligent, Offender, Ted
  Delirious, Delirium Deranged, DT, Fever, Frenetic, Frenzy, Insanity, Mania, Phrenetic, Phrenitis, Spaced out, Spazz, Wild
  Deliver(ance), Delivered, Deliverer, Delivery(man) Accouchement, Bailment, Ball, Birth, Born, Bowl, Breech, Caesarean, Consign, Convey, Courier, Deal, Doosra, Drop, Elocution, Escape, Express, Extradition, Give, Googly, Jail, Lead, Liberate, Lob, Mail drop, Orate, Over, Pronounce, Receipt, Recorded, Redeem, Release, Relieve, Render, Rendition, → **RESCUE**, Rid, Round(sman), Salvation, Save, Say, Seamer, Sell, Shipment, Speak, Special, Tice, Transfer, Underarm, Underhand, Utter, Wide, Yorker
  Dell Dale, Dargle, Dene, Dimble, Dingle, Dingl(e)y, Glen, Valley
  Delphic Pythian
  Delphinium Larkspur
  Delta Camargue, D, Del, Flood-plain, Kronecker, Nabla, Nile, Oil Rivers, Triangle
  Delude, Delusion Bilk, Cheat, Deceive, Fallacy, Fool, Hoax, Megalomania, → **MISLEAD**, Paranoia, Schizothymia, Trick, Zoanthropy
  Deluge Avalanche, Flood, Ogygian, Saturate, Submerge, → **SWAMP**
  De luxe Extra, Plush, Special
  Delve Burrow, Dig, Excavate, Exhume, Explore, Probe, Search
  Demagogue Agitator, Fanariot, Leader, Mobsman, Phanariot, Speaker, Tribune
  Demand(ing) Appetite, Ball-buster, Call, Claim, Cry, Derived, Dun, Exact, Excess, Exigent, Fastidious, Final, Hest, → **INSIST**, Mandate, Market, Need, Order, Postulate, Pressure, Request, Requisition, Rigorous, Rush, Sale, Severe, Stern, Stipulate, Stringent, Summon, Ultimatum, Want
  Demean(ing) Belittle, Comport, Debase, Degrade, Humble, Infra dig, Lower, Maltreat
  Demeanour Air, Bearing, Conduct, Expression, Front, Gravitas, Mien, Port, Presence
  Dement(ed) Crazy, Hysterical, Insane, Mad, Wacko
  Demi-god Aitu, Daemon, Garuda, Hero
  Demi-mondaine Cocotte, → **LOOSE WOMAN**, Prostitute
  Demise Death, Decease, Finish
  Demo March, Parade, Protest, Rally, Sit-in
  Democracy, Democrat, Democratic D, Hunker, Industrial, Liberal, Locofoco, Menshevik, Montagnard, People's, Popular, Republic, Sansculotte, Social, Tammany
  Demoiselle Crane, Damselfish
  Demolish, Demolition Bulldoze, Devastate, Devour, Dismantle, Floor, KO, Level, Rack, → **RAZE**, Smash, Tear down, Wreck
▶ **Demon** *see* **DEVIL**
  Demoness Lilith
  Demonstrate, Demonstration, Demonstrator Agitate, Barrack, Dharma, Display, Endeictic, Evénement, Evince, Explain, Hunger march, Maffick, Manifest, March, Morcha, Ostensive, Peterloo, Portray, Protest, Prove, Provo, Send-off, → **SHOW**, Sit-in, Touchy-feely, Verify, Vigil

Demoralise, Demoralisation Bewilder, Corrupt, Depths, Destroy, Shatter, Unman, Weaken

Demote, Demotion Comedown, Degrade, Disbench, Disrate, Embace, Embase, Reduce, Relegate, Stellenbosch

Demotic Enchorial

Demur Hesitate, Jib, Object

Demure Coy, Mim, Modest, Prenzie, Primsie, Sedate, Shy

Den Dive, Domdaniel, Earth, Hell, Hide-away, Holt, Home, Lair, Lie, Lodge, Opium, Room, Shebeen, Spieler, Study, Sty, Wurley

Denial, Deny, Denier Abnegate, Antinomian, Aspheterism, Bar, Contradict, Controvert, Démenti, Disavow, Disenfranchise, Disown, Forswear, → **GAINSAY**, Nay, Negate, Nick, Nihilism, Protest, Refuse, Refute, Renague, Renay, Reneg(e), Renegue, Reney, Renig, Renounce, Reny, Repudiate, Sublate, Traverse, Withhold

Denigrate Besmirch, Blacken, Defame, Tar

Denim Jeans

Denizen Diehard, Inhabitant, Resident

Denomination Category, Cult, Sect, Variety

Denote Import, Indicate, Mean, Signify

Denouement Anagnorisis, Catastrophe, Climax, Coda, Exposure, Outcome, Showdown

Denounce, Denunciation Ban, Commination, Condemn, Criticise, Decry, Delate, Diatribe, Fulminate, Hatchet job, Hereticate, Proclaim, Proscribe, Shop, Stigmatise, Thunder, Upbraid

Denry Card

Dense, Density Buoyant, Charge, Compact, Critical, Current, D, Double, Firm, Flux, Intense, Neutral, Opaque, Optical, Packing, Reflection, Relative, Single, Solid, Spissitude, Tesla, Thick, Transmission, Vapour, Woofy

Dent(ed) Batter, Concave, Dancette, Depress, Dimple, Dinge, Dint, Nock, V

Dental (problem), Dentist(ry) DDS, Entodontics, Extractor, Kindhart, LDS, Malocclusion, Odontic, Paedodontics, Periodontic, Toothy

Dentures Biteplate, Bridge, Bridgework, False teeth, Plate, Prosthodontia, Store teeth, Wallies

▶ **Deny** *see* **DENIAL**

Deodorant Anti-perspirant, Cachou, Roll-on

Deoxidise Outgas, Reduce

Depart(ed), Departing, Departure Abscond, Absquatulate, Bunk, D, Dead, Decession, Defunct, Die, Digress, Divergence, Egress, Exception, Exit, Exodus, Flight, → **GO**, Leave, Lucky, Outbound, Rack off, Remue, Send-off, Vacate, Vade, Vamoose, Walkout

Department Achaea, Ain, Aisne, Allier, Alpes de Provence, Alpes-Maritimes, Angers, Arcadia, Ardeche, Ardennes, Argo, Argolis, Ariege, Arrondissement, Arta, Attica, Aube, Aude, Aveyron, Bas-Rhin, Belfort, Bell-chamber, Beziers, Bouches-du-Rhône, Branch, Bureau, Calvados, Cantal, Charente, Charente-Maritime, Cher, Cleansing, Commissariat, Corrèze, Cote d'Or, Cotes d'Armor, Cotes du Nord, Creuse, DEFRA, Deme, Deuxième Bureau, Deux-Sevres, Division, Dordogne, Doubs, Drôme, El(e)ia, Essonne, Eure, Eure-et-Loir, Extramural, Faculty, Finistere, Fire, FO, Gard, Gers, Gironde, Greencloth, Guadeloupe, Gulag, Hanaper, Haute-Garonne, Haute-Loire, Haute-Marne, Haute-Normandie, Hautes-Alpes, Haute-Saône, Haute Savoie, Hautes-Pyrenees, Haute-Vienne, Haut-Rhin, Hauts-de-Seine, Helpdesk, Herault, Home, Ille-et-Vilaine, Indre, Indre-et-Loire, Isere, Jura, Landes, Loire, Loiret, Loir-et-Cher,

Lot, Lot-et-Garonne, Lozere, Maine-et-Loire, Manche, Marne, Mayenne, Meurthe-et-Moselle, Meuse, Ministry, Morbihan, Moselle, Nièvre, Nome, Nomos, Nord, Office, Oise, Ordnance, Orne, Pas-de-Calais, Province, Puy de Dôme, Pyrénées(-Atlantique), Pyrénées-Orientales, Region, Rehabilitation, Rhône, Sanjak, Saône-et-Loire, Sarthe, Savoie, Secretariat(e), Section, Seine-et-Marne, Seine Maritime, Seine St Denis, Somme, Sphere, State, Tarn(-et-Garonne), Treasury, Tuscany, Val de Marne, Val d'Oise, Var, Vaucluse, Vendée, Vienne, Voiotia, War, Wardrobe, Yonne, Yvelines

Depend(ant), Dependence, Dependency, Dependent Addicted, Child, Client, Colony, Conditional, Contingent, Count, Dangle, E, Fief, Habit, Hang, Hinge, Icicle, Lean, Lippen, Minion, Pensioner, Relier, Rely, Retainer, Ross, Sponge, Stalactite, Statistical, Subject, Subordinate, Trust, Turn on, Vassal

Dependable Reliable, Reliant, Secure, Sheet-anchor, Solid, Sound, Staunch, Sure, → **TRUSTWORTHY**

Depict Delineate, Display, Draw, Limn, Paint, Portray, Present, Represent

Depilate, Depilation, Depilatory Electrolysis, Grain, Rusma, Slate

Deplete Diminish, Drain, Exhaust, Reduce

Deplorable, Deplore Base, Bemoan, Chronic, Complain, Deprecate, Dolorous, Grieve, Lament, Mourn, Piteous, Regret, Rue, Shocking

Deploy(ment) Extend, Herse, Unfold, Use

▷ **Deploy(ment)** *may indicate* an anagram

Depopulate Deracinate

Deport(ation), Deportment Address, Air, Banish, → **BEARING**, Carriage, Demeanour, Mien, Renvoi, Renvoy, Repatriation

Depose, Deposition Affirm, Banish, Dethrone, Displace, Dispossess, Overthrow, Pieta, Testify

Deposit(s), Depository Aeolian, Alluvial, Alluvium, Aquifer, Arcus, Argol, Arles, Atheroma, Bank, Bathybius, Bergmehl, Calc-sinter, Calc-tuff, Caliche, Cave-earth, Coral, Crag, Delta, Depone, Diatomite, Diluvium, Drift, Evaporite, Fan, File, Firn, Fort Knox, Fur, Glacial, Gyttja, Illuvium, Kieselguhr, Land, Laterite, Lay, Lay-by, Laydown, Limescale, Lodge(ment), Loess, Löss, Measure, Moraine, Natron, Outwatch, Park, Pay dirt, Placer, Plank, Plaque, Precipitate, Put, Repose, Residuum, Saburra, Salamander, Sandbank, Saprolite, Saturn's tree, Scale, → **SEDIMENT**, Silt, Sinter, Sludge, Stockwork, Storeroom, Stratum, Surety, Tartar, Terramara, Terramare, Till, Time, Tophus, Tripoli, Turbidite

Depot Barracoon, Base, Camp, Depository, Etape, Station, Terminus, Treasure-city, Warehouse

Deprav(ed), Depravity Bestial, Cachexia, Cachexy, Caligulism, → **CORRUPT**, Dissolute, Evil, Immoral, Low, Reprobate, Rotten, Sodom, Total, Turpitude, Ugly, Unholy, Vice, Vicious, Vile

Deprecate Censure, Deplore, Expostulate, Reproach

Depreciate Abase, Belittle, Derogate, Detract, Discount

Depredate, Depredation Pillage, Plunder, Rob

Depress(ed), Depressing, Depression Accablé, Agitated, Alamort, Alveolus, Amort, Astrobleme, Attrist, Black dog, Blight, Blue devils, Blues, Cafard, Caldron, Canada, Canyon, Chill, Col, Combe, Couch, Crab, Crush, Cyclone, Dampen, Deject, Dell, Demission, Dene, Dent, Despair, → **DIMPLE**, Dip, Dismal, Dispirit, Dolina, Doline, Doomy, Downlifting, Drear, Drere, Dumpish, Endogenous, Exanimate, Flatten, Fonticulus, Foss(ula), Fossa, Fovea, Frog, Geosyncline, Ghilgai, Gilgai, Gilgie, Glen, Gloom, Graben, Grinch, Ha-ha, Hammer, Heart-spoon, Hilar, Hilum, Hilus, Hollow, Howe, Hyp, Hypothymia, Indentation, Joes, Kettle, Kick(-up),

Lacuna, Leaden, Low(ness), Low-spirited, Megrims, Moping, Morose, Neck, Ocean basin, Pan, Pit, Polje, Postnatal, Prostrate, Punt, Qattara, Recession, Re-entrant, Retuse, Sad, Saddle, Sag, Salt-cellar, Salt-pan, Scrobicule, Sink, Sinkhole, Sinus, Sitzmark, Slot, → **SLUMP**, Slumpflation, Soakaway, Spiritless, Stomodaeum, Sump, Swag, Swale, Swallowhole, Trench, Trough, Umbilication, Vale, Vallecula, Valley, Wallow, Weigh down, Wet blanket

Deprivation, Deprive(d) Amerce, Bereft, Deny, Disenfranchise, Disfrock, Disseise, Disseize, Expropriate, Famine, Foreclose, Geld, Have-not, Hunger, Reduce, Remove, Rob, Sensory, Withhold

Depth Draught, Draw, F, Fathom, Gravity, Intensity, Isobath, Pit, Profundity

Deputise, Deputy Act, Agent, Aide, Assistant, Commis(sary), Delegate, Legate, Lieutenant, Locum, Loot, Mate, Number two, Prior, Pro-chancellor, Proxy, Represent, Secondary, Sidekick, Standby, Sub, Subchanter, Substitute, Succentor, Surrogate, Vicar, Vice, Viceregent, Vidame

Derange(d) Craze, Détraqué, Disturb, Insane, Loopy, Manic, Troppo, Unhinge, Unsettle

Derby Boot, Demolition, Donkey, Eponym, Hat, Kentucky, Kiplingcotes, Race, Roller

Derek Bo

Derelict Abandoned, → **DECREPIT**, Deserted, Negligent, Outcast, Ramshackle

Deride, Derision, Derisive Contempt, Gup, Guy, Hiss, Hoot, Jeer, Mock, Nominal, Pigs, Raspberry, → **RIDICULE**, Sardonic, Scoff, Scorn, Snifty, Snort, Yah, Ya(h)boo

Derive, Derivation, Derivative Amine, Ancestry, Creosote, Deduce, Descend, Extract, Get, Kinone, Of, Offshoot, Origin, Pedigree, Picoline, Secondary, Tyramine

▸ **Dermatitis** see **SKIN DISEASE**

Derogate, Derogatory Aspersion, Belittle, Decry, Defamatory, Demeaning, Detract, Discredit, Libellous, Pejorative, Personal, Slanderous, Slighting, Snide

Deronda Daniel

Derrick Crane, Davit, Hoist, Jib, Spar, Steeve

Dervish Calender, Doseh, Mawlawi, Mevlevi, Revolver, Santon, Whirling

Descant Comment, Discourse, Faburden, Melody, Song

Descartes René

Descend(ant), Descent Ancestry, Avail, Avale, Bathos, Blood, Cadency, Catabasis, Chute, Cion, Decline, Degenerate, Derive, Dismount, Dive, Drop, Epigon, Extraction, Heir, Heraclid, → **LINEAGE**, Offspring, Pedigree, Posterity, Progeny, Prone, Purler, Rappel, Said, Say(y)id, Scarp, Scion, Seed, Shelve, Sien(t), Sink, Spearside, Stock, Syen, Vest, Volplane

Describe, Describing, Description, Descriptive Blurb, Define, Delineate, Depict, Designate, Draw, Epithet, Exposition, Expound, Graphic, Job, Narrate, Outline, Paint, Portray, Rapportage, Recount, Relate, Report, Sea-letter, Semantic, Signalment, Sketch, Specification, Synopsis, Term, Trace, Vignette, Write-up

▷ **Describing** *may indicate* 'around'

Descry Behold, Discern, Get, Notice, Perceive

Desecrate, Desecration Abuse, Defile, Dishallow, Profane, Sacrilege, Unhallow

▷ **Desecrated** *may indicate* an anagram

Desert(er), Deserted, Deserts Abandon, Absquatulate, Apostasy, Arabian, Arid, Ar Rimal, Arunta, Atacama, AWOL, Badland, Barren, Bledowska, Bug, Bunk, Colorado, Come-uppance, D, Dahna, Defect, Desolate, Dissident, Due, Empty, Eremic, Etosha Pan, Factious, Fail, Fezzan, Foresay, Forhoo, Forhow, Forlorn, Forsake, Forsay, Frondeur, Garagum, Gibson, Gila, Gobi, Great Basin, Great Indian, Great Sandy, Great Victoria, Heterodox, Indian, Jump ship, Kalahari, Kara

Kum, Kavir, Kyzyl Kum, Libyan, Lurch, Meeds, Merit, Mohave, Mojave, Nafud, Namib, Negev, Nubian, Ogaden, Painted, Pategonian, Pindan, Rat, Refus(e)nik, Reg, → **RENEGADE**, Reward, Rub'al-Khali, Run, Runaway, Sahara, Sahel, Sands, Secede, Shamo, Simpson, Sinai, Sonoran, Sturt, Syrian, Tacna-Arica, Tergiversate, Thar, Turncoat, Ust(y)urt, Victoria, Void, Wadi, Waste, Western Sahara, Wild, Wilderness, Worthiness

Deserve(d) Condign, Earn, → **MERIT**, Rate, Well-earned, Worthy

Desiccate(d) Dry, Sere

Design(er) Adam, Aim, Amies, Arabesque, Architect, Armani, Ashley, Batik, Between-subjects, Broider, Calligram(me), Cardin, Cartoon, Castrametation, Chop, Cloisonné, Create, Cul de lampe, Damascene, Decal(comania), Decor, Deep, Depict, Devise, Dévoré, Dior, Draft, Embroidery, End, Engender, Engine(r), Engineer, Erté, Etch, Fashion, Feng-shui, Flanch, Former, Hepplewhite, Hitech, Iconic, Imagineer, Impresa, Imprese, Industrial, Inlay, Intend(ment), Intent(ion), Interior, Issigonis, Layout, Limit-state, Linocut, Logo, Marquetry, Mascle, Matched pairs, Mean, Meander, Mehndi, Millefleurs, Modiste, Monogram, Morris, Mosaic, Motif, Multifoil, Paisley, Pattern, → **PLAN**, Plot, Propose, Pyrography, Quant, Retro, Ruse, Schema, Scheme, Seal, Sheraton, Sketch, Sopwith, Spatterwork, Specification, Sprig, Stencil, Stubble, Stylist, Sunburst, Tatow, Tattoo, Tattow, Tatu, Think, Tooling, Trigram, Versace, Vignette, Watermark, Weiner, Werkstalte, Whittle, Within-subjects

Designate Earmark, Name, Note, Style, Title

Desirable, Desire, Desirous Ambition, Aphrodisia, Appetite, Aspire, Avid, Best, Cama, Conation, Concupiscence, Covet, Crave, Cupidity, Dreamboat, Earn, Eligible, Epithymetic, Fancy, Gasp, Greed, Hanker, Hope, Hots, Hunger, Itch, Kama(deva), Le(t)ch, Libido, List, Long, Luscious, Lust, Mania, Nymphomania, Orectic, Owlcar, Pica, Plum, Reak, Reck, Request, Residence, Salt, Slaver, Streetcar, Thirst, Velleity, Vote, Wanderlust, Want, Whim, Will, Wish, Yearn, Yen

Desist Abandon, Cease, Curb, Pretermit, Quit, Stop

Desk Almemar, Ambo, Bonheur-du-jour, Bureau, Carrel(l), Cash, Check-in, Cheveret, City, Copy, Davenport, Desse, Devonport, Enquiry, E(s)critoire, Faldstool, Lectern, Lettern, Litany, Pay, Pedestal, Prie-dieu, Pulpit, Reading, Roll-top, Scrutoire, Secretaire, Vargueno, Writing

Desman Pyrenean

Desolate, Desolation Bare, Barren, Desert, Devastate, Disconsolate, Forlorn, Gaunt, Godforsaken, Gousty, Moonscape, Waste, Woebegone

Despair, Desperate, Desperation Acharne, Anomy, De profundis, Despond, Dire, Dismay, Extreme, Frantic, Gagging, Giant, Gloom, Hairless, Headlong, Last-ditch, Last-gasp, Life and death, Reckless, Unhopeful, Urgent, Wanhope

▶ **Despatch** see **DISPATCH**

Desperado Bandit, Bravo, Ruffian, Terrorist

Despicable Abject, Base, Bleeder, Caitiff, Cheap, Churl, Contemptible, Heel, Heinous, Ignoble, Ignominious, Low-down, Mean, Moer, Poep(ol), Puke, Ratbag, Ratfink, Scumbag, Shabby, Toerag, Wretched

Despise Condemn, Conspire, Contemn, Forhow, Hate, Ignore, Scorn, Spurn, Vilify, Vilipend

Despite For, Malgré, Notwithstanding, Pace, Though, Venom

Despoil Mar, Ravage, Vandalise

Despondent Dejected, Downcast, Forlorn, Gloomy, Sad

Despot(ism) Autarchy, Autocrat, Bonaparte, Caesar, Darius, Dictator, Little Hitler, Napoleon, Nero, Satrap, Stratocrat, Tsar, Tyrant, Tzar

Dessert Afters, Baked Alaska, Baklava, Banana split, Bavarian cream, Bavarois, Bombe, Cannoli, Charlotte, Charlotte russe, Clafoutis, Cobbler, Compote, Coupe, Cranachan, Crème brulée, Crème caramel, Dulce de leche, Entremets, Flummery, Fool, Granita, Junket, Kissel, Knickerbocker glory, Kulfi, Marquise, Mousse, Mud pie, Nesselrode, Pannacotta, Parfait, Pashka, Pavlova, Peach Melba, → **PUDDING**, Rasmalai, Roulade, Sabayon, Sawine, Semifreddo, Shoofly pie, Split, Strudel, Sundae, Syllabub, Tart, Tartufo, Tiramisu, Tortoni, Trifle, Vacherin, Whip, Zabaglione

Destine(d), Destination Born, Design, End, Fate, Foredoom, Goal, Gole, Home, Intend, Joss, Meant, Port, Purpose, Vector, Weird

Destiny Doom, → **FATE**, Karma, Kismet, Lot, Manifest, Moira, Yang, Yin

Destitute Bankrupt, Bare, Broke, Devoid, Dirt-poor, Helpless, Impoverished, Indigent, Necessitous, Needy, Penniless, Poor, Sterile, Void

Destroy(er) Annihilate, Antineutrino, Antineutron, Antiparticle, Apollyon, Atomise, Blight, Can, D, Decimate, Deep-six, Deface, Delete, Demolish, Denature, Destruct, Dish, Dismember, Dissolve, Eat, Efface, End, Eradicate, Erase, Estrepe, Exterminate, Extirpate, Flivver, Fordo, Graunch, Harry, Iconoclast, Incinerate, → **KILL**, KO, Murder, Obliterate, Overkill, Perish, Predator, Q-ship, Ravage, Raze, Ruin, Saboteur, Sack, Scuttle, Slash, Smash, Spif(f)licate, Spoil, Sterilize, Stew-can, Stonker, Stultify, Subvert, Trash, Undo, Uproot, Vandal, Vitiate, Waste, Whelm, Wreck, Zap

Destruction, Destructive Adverse, Autolysis, Bane, Can, Catabolism, Collapse, Deathblow, Deleterious, Devastation, Doom, Downfall, Ecocide, End, Götterdämmerung, Grave, Havoc, Holocaust, Iconoclasm, Insidious, Internecine, Kali, Lethal, Loss, Maleficent, Pernicious, Pestilential, Pogrom, Quelea, Rack, Ragnarok, Ravage, Sabotage, Speciocide, Stroy, Wrack

Desultory Aimless, Cursory, Fitful, Idle

Detach(ed), Detachment Abstract, Alienate, Aloof, Body, Calve, Clinical, Cut, Detail, Discrete, Dispassionate, Insular, Isle, Isolate, Loose, Outlying, Outpost, Patrol, Picket, Picquet, Separate, Sever, Staccato, Stoic, Unfasten, Unhinge, Unit

Detached work Ravelin

Detail(s), Detailed Annotate, Dock, Elaborate, Embroider, Expatiate, Explicit, Expound, Instance, → **ITEM**, Itemise, Minutiae, Nicety, Particular(ise), Pedantry, Point, Recite, Relate, Respect, Send, Spec, Special, Specification, Technicality

▷ **Detailed** *may indicate* last letter missing

Detain(ee), Detention (centre) Arrest, Buttonhole, Collar, Custody, Delay, Detinue, Gate, Glasshouse, Hinder, Intern, Juvie, Keep, POW, Preventive, Retard, Sin bin, Stay, → **WITHHOLD**

Detect(or), Detective Agent, Arsène, Asdic, Bloodhound, Brown, Bucket, Busy, Catch, Chan, CID, Cuff, Dick, Discover, Divine, Doodlebug, Dupin, Espy, Eye, Fed, Find, Flambeau, Flic, Fortune, French, Geigercounter, Geophone, Gumshoe, Hanaud, Hercule, Holmes, Interpol, Investigator, Jack, Lecoq, Lupin, Maigret, Metal, Methanometer, Microwave, Mine, Minitrack®, Morse, Nail, Nose, Peeper, PI, Pinkerton, Plant, Poirot, Private, Private eye, Prodnose, Radar, Reagent, Rumble, Scent, Scerne, Sense, Sensor, Shadow, Shamus, Sherlock, → **SLEUTH**, Sleuth-hound, Sofar, Solver, Sonar, Sonobuoy, Spot, Tabaret, Take, Tec, Thorndyke, Toff, Trace, Trent, Vance, Wimsey, Yard

Detent Pawl, Trigger

Deter(rent) Block, Check, Daunt, Dehort, Delay, Disincentive, Dissuade, Prevent, Restrain, Turn-off, Ultimate

Detergent Cationic, Cleaner, Non-ionizing, Solvent, Surfactant, Syndet, Tepol, Whitener

Deteriorate, Deterioration Decadence, Degenerate, Derogate, Entropy, Pejoration, Relapse, Rust, Worsen

▷ **Deterioration** *may indicate* an anagram

▷ **Determination** *may indicate* 'last letter'

Determine(d), Determination Appoint, Arbitrament, Ardent, Ascertain, Assign, Assoil, Bent, Causal, Condition, Dead-set, → **DECIDE**, Define, Doctrinaire, Dogged, Do-or-die, Dour, Drive, Earnest, Fix, Govern, Granite, Grim, Grit(ty), Headstrong, Hell-bent, Indomitable, Influence, Intent, Judgement, Law, Liquidate, Orient, Out, Point, Pre-ordain, Purpose, Quantify, → **RESOLUTE**, Resolve, Rigwiddie, Rigwoodie, Self-will, Set, Settle, Set upon, Shape, Stalwart, Steely, Type, Weigh

Detest(able) Abhor, Despise, Execrable, Execrate, Hate, Loathsome, Pestful, Vile

Detonate, Detonator Blast, Explode, Fire, Fuse, Fuze, Ignite, Kindle, Plunger, Primer, Saucisse, Saucisson, Tetryl, Trip-wire

Detour Bypass, Deviate, Divert

Detract Belittle, Decry, Diminish, Discount, Disparage

Detriment(al) Adverse, Damage, Harm, Injury, Loss, Mischief

Deuce Dickens, Old Harry, Twoer

Deuteron Diplon

Devalue Debase, Impair, Reduce, Undermine

Devastate, Devastation Demolish, Destroy, Gut, Lay waste, Overwhelm, Ravage, Ruin, Sack, Traumatise, Waste, Wrack, Wreck

▷ **Develop** *may indicate* an anagram

Develop(er), Developed, Developing, Development Advance, Agile, Amidol®, Aplasia, Breakthrough, Breed, Bud, Build, Burgeon, Catechol, Creep, Cutting edge, Educe, Elaborate, Enlarge, Epigenetic, Escalate, Evolve, Expand, Expatriate, Foetus, Full-fledged, Fulminant, Genesis, Germinate, Gestate, Grow, Hatch, Hothouse, Hydroquinone, Hypo, Imago, Improve, Incipient, Incubate, Lamarckism, Larva, Mature, Metamorphose, Metol, Morphogenesis, Morphosis, Mushroom, Nascent, Nurture, Offshoot, Oidium, Ontogenesis, Pathogeny, Pullulate, Pupa, Pyro, Pyrogallol, Quinol, Ribbon, Ripe(n), Sarvodaya, Sensorimeter, Separate, Shape, Soup, Speciation, Sprawl, Subtopia, Technography, Teens, Tone, Unfold, Upgrow

Deviant, Deviate, Deviation Aberrance, Abnormal, Anomaly, Average, Brisure, Deflect, Deflexure, Depart, Derogate, Digress, Discrepant, Diverge, Divert, Drift, Error, Kinky, Kurtosis, List, Mean, Pervert, Quartile, Sheer, Solecism, Sport, Standard, Stray, Swerve, Transvestite, → **TURN**, Valgus, Varus, Veer, Wander, Wend

Device Allegory, → **APPARATUS**, Appliance, Artifice, Bush, Contraption, Contrivance, Deus ex machina, Dodge, Emblem, Expedient, Gadget, Gimmick, Gizmo, Gubbins, Instrument, Logo, Machine, Mnemonic, Motto, Pattern, Plan, Safeguard, → **STRATAGEM**, Subterfuge, Tactic, Tag, Thing, Tool, Trademark, Trick

---

DEVICES

3 letters:	Zip	Gobo	Skid
Bug		Grab	Spur
FET	*4 letters:*	Head	Stop
LED	Capo	Orle	Tram
Mux	Drag	Plug	Trap
Pad	Fret	Rest	
POP	Fuse	Shoe	

5 letters:
Audio
Balun
Chaff
Choke
Chuck
Clamp
Cleat
Combi
Conch
Cramp
Crank
Diode
E-nose
Frame
Gatso®
Gland
Input
Maser
Meter
Mixer
Modem
Mouli
Mouse
Optic®
Otter
Pager
Petar
Prism
Probe
Quipu
Relay
Rotor
Saser
Scale
Scart
Servo
Shear
Sieve
Siren
Snare
Sonde
Spool
Sprag
SQUID
Stent
Timer
Tromp
Truss
Turbo
Valve

V-chip
Waldo
Winch

6 letters:
Analog
Atlatl
Balise
Beeper
Biodot
Blower
Bungee
Buzzer
Charge
Chowri
Chowry
Cotter
Cursor
Cut-out
Dasher
Deckle
De-icer
Detent
Dimmer
Dongle
Elevon
Engine
Etalon
Faller
Feeder
Filter
Friend®
Imager
Jigger
Joypad
Keeper
Kludge
Logger
Masker
Nanite
Packer
Petard
Pick-up
Pinger®
Possum
Preset
Quippu
Rabble
Reverb
Rocker
Roller

Router
Selsyn
Sensor
Shaker
Shower
Socket
Stocks
Stoner
Switch
Swivel
Temple
Tipple
Tracer
Tremie
Triode
Trompe
Turtle
Tympan
Viewer
Wafter
Walker
Widget
Zapper

7 letters:
Air-trap
Bearing
Bendlet
Bleeper
Chopper
Clapper
Cleaver
Clicker
Coherer
Compass
Counter
Coupler
Dashpot
Denture
Digibox®
Divider
Doubler
Flip-top
Fuzzbox
Gas mask
Genlock
Gimbals
Grapnel
Hushkit
Imprese
Inhaler

Isotron
Jetpack
Krytron
Lighter
Limiter
Minicom
Monitor
Pelorus
Pessary
Pickoff
Plunger
Ratchet
Reactor
Roll-bar
Rotator
Rowlock
Scanner
Shut-off
Shutter
Shuttle
Slipper
Sniffer
Snorkel
Snubber
Snuffer
Sounder
Spoiler
Starter
Stinger
Storage
Sundial
Swatter
Synchro
Toaster
Tokamak
Tonepad
Vernier
Vocoder

8 letters:
Airscoop
Alcolock
Analogue
Anti-icer
Atomiser
Autodial
Ballcock
Barostat
Betatron
Bootjack
Calutron

Commutor
Conveyor
Coupling
Demister
Detector
Diagraph
Diestock
Ecraseur
Eggtimer
Enlarger
Episcope
Episemon
Expander
Firework
Geophone
Heat pump
Hotplate
Ignitron
Launcher
Light-pen
Monogram
Nailhead
Occluder
Odograph
Odometer
Orthosis
Paravane
Playback
Plectrum
Pulsator
Push-pull
Pyrostat
Radar gun
Radiator
Resister
Shoehorn
Shredder
Silencer
Slip ring
Snow-eyes
Snowshoe
Solenoid
Spray gun
Spreader
Squeegee
Sweatbox
Swellbox
Terminal
Thin-film
Trembler
Varactor

Varistor
Vibrator

9 letters:
Aspirator
Autometer
Autotimer
Capacitor
Compasses
Convector
Converter
Corkscrew
Decoherer
Deflector
Defroster
Delayline
Detonator
Dispenser
Dynamotor
Eccentric
Excelsior
Exerciser
Gear-lever
Gear-shift
Gearstick
Generator
Gyroscope
Headstock
Hendiadys
Hodoscope
Hydrofoil
Hydrostat
Hygrostat
Indicator
Insulator
Jack screw
Keylogger
Konimeter
Kymograph
Megaphone
Mekometer
Metronome
Milometer
Modulator
Nebuliser
Octophone
Optophone
Overdrive
Pacemaker
Parachute
Pedometer

Periscope
Photocell
Pitchbend
Polariser
Polygraph
Powerpack
Propeller
Rectifier
Regulator
Remontoir
Resonator
Responsor
Retractor
Rheotrope
Rotachute
Rotameter®
Satellite
Scrambler
Separator
Sequencer
Simulator
Smokejack
Sonograph
Spaceband
Spindryer
Sprinkler
Stairlift
Steadicam
Stretcher
Tabulator
Tape drive
Tape punch
Tasimeter
Telegraph
Telemeter
Telepoint
Thermette
Thyristor
Tonometer
Trackball
Tremulant
Well sweep

10 letters:
Acetometer
Anemoscope
Applicator
Attenuator
Autowinder
Blackberry®
Calculator

Ceilometer
Centrifuge
Chaingrate
Chronotron
Clapometer
Commutator
Comparator
Compressor
Copyholder
Cyclometer
Cyclostyle
Daisy-wheel
Databogger
Derailleur
Descendeur
Eprouvette
Groundprox
Humidistat
Hygroscope
Jawbreaker
Jaws of Life
Jellygraph
Kicksorter
Mason's mark
Metrostyle
Microphone
Microprobe
Microscope
Mileometer
Moulinette
Noisemaker
Otter-board
Peripheral
Phonoscope
Phonospore
Planometer
Remontoire
Respirator
Self-feeder
Siderostat
Snowplough
Spirograph
Stabiliser
Stimpmeter
Suppressor
Switchgear
Tachograph
Tachometer
Tape reader
Telewriter
Thermistor

10 letters – cont:
Thermopile
Thermostat
Tourniquet
Transducer
Transistor
Turbulator
Turnbuckle
Ventilator
Vertoscope®
Videophone
Viewfinder
Viscometer
Zener diode

11 letters:
Afterburner
Annunciator
Answerphone
Autochanger
Baffle-plate
Carburettor
Collet chuck
Compass rose
Distributor
Epidiascope
Floor turtle
Fluoroscope

Helping hand
Immobilizer
Insufflator
Intoximeter
Lie detector
Link trainer
Manipulator
Microfitter
Microreader
Microwriter
Multiplexer
Recuperator
Self-starter
Smokerlyzer
Snickometer
Solarimeter
Space heater
Spectograph
Speedometer
Stuffing-box
Swingometer
Telestrator
Thermoscope
Trackerball
Transceiver
Transformer
Transmitter
Transponder

12 letters:
Breathalyser
Concentrator
Desert cooler
Ebulliometer
Effusiometer
Electrometer
Evaporograph
Extinguisher
Intrauterine
Lithotripter
Make and break
Object finder
Oscillograph
Picturephone
Sensitometer
Snooperscope
Spectrometer
Spectroscope
Supercharger
Tape streamer
Telautograph
Teleprompter
Thermocouple
Turbidimeter
Viscosimeter

13 letters:
Baton-sinister
Contraceptive
Dead man's pedal
Electromagnet
Metal detector
Phonendoscope
Rack and pinion
Scintiscanner
Shock-absorber
Smoke detector

14 letters:
Anamorphoscope
Dead man's handle
Interferometer
Intervalometer
Peltier element
Plethysmograph
Retroreflector
Scintillometer
Spinthariscope

15 letters:
Radiogoniometer

Devil(ish), Demon Abaddon, Afreet, Afrit, Ahriman, Amaimon, Apollyon, Asmodeus, Atua, Auld Hornie, Azazel, Barbason, Beelzebub, Belial, Buckra, Cartesian, Clootie, Cloots, Dasyure, Davy Jones, Deev, Deil, Demogorgon, Demon, Deuce, Devling, Diable, Diabolic, Dickens, Div, Drudge, Dust, Eblis, Falin, Familiar, Fend, Fiend, Fient, Ghoul, Goodman, Goodyear, Grill, Hangie, Hornie, Iblis, Imp, Incubus, Infernal, Lamia, Legion, Lilith, Lord of the Flies, Lori, Lucifer, Mahoun(d), Man of Sin, Manta, Mara, Maxwell's, Mazikeen, Mephisto(pheles), Mischief, Nick, Nickie-ben, Old Bendy, Old Nick, Old One, Old Pandemonium, Old Poker, Old Roger, Old Split-foot, Old Toast, Printer's, Ragamuffin, Ragman, Rahu, Ralph, Satan, Sathanas, Satyr, Scour, Scratch, Screwtape, Season, Setebos, Shaitan, Shedeem, Snow, Sorra, Succubine, Succubus, Tailard, Tasmanian, Tempter, Titivil, Tutivillus, Wendigo, Wicked, Wicked One, Wirricow, Worricow, Worrycow, Zernebock

Devious Braide, Cunning, Deep, Eel(y), Erroneous, Evasive, Implex, Indirect, Scheming, Shifty, Stealthy, Subtle, Tortuous, Tricky

Devise(d) Arrange, Concoct, Contrive, Decoct, Hatch, Hit-on, Imagine, Invenit, Invent, Plot, Thermette

Devitrified Ambitty

Devoid Barren, Destitute, Empty, Vacant, Wanting

Devolve Occur, Result, Transmit

Devote(e), Devotion(al), Devoted Addiction, Aficionado, Âme damnée, Angelus, Attached, Bhakti, Buff, Bunny, Consecrate, Corban, Dedicate, Employ, Enthusiast,

Fan, Fervid, Fetishism, Fiend, Holy, Hound, Loyalty, Novena, Ophism, Passion, Pious, Puja, Religioso, Sacred, Saivite, Sea-green incorruptible, S(h)akta, Sivaite, Solemn, True, Voteen, Zealous

▷ **Devour** *may indicate* one word inside another

Devour(ing) Consume, Eat, Engorge, Engulf, Manducate, Moth-eat, Scarf, Scoff, Snarf, → SWALLOW, Vorant

Devout Holy, Pia, Pious, Reverent, Sant, Sincere, Solemn

Dew(y) Bloom, Gory, Moist, Mountain, Rime, Roral, Roric, Rorid, Roscid, Serein, Serene, Tranter

Dexterity, Dexterous Adept, Adroit, Aptitude, Cleverness, Craft, Deft, Feat(e)ous, Featuous, → HANDY, Knack, Shrewd, Sleight, Slick

Diabolic Cruel, → DEVILISH, Infernal

Diacritic (mark) Acute, Angstrom, Cedilla, Circumflex, Diaresis, Eth, Grave, Háček, Thorn, Tilde, Umlaut

Diadem Coronet, Fillet, Garland, Tiara

Diagnose, Diagnosis, Diagnostic Amniocentesis, Fetal, Findings, Identify, Iridology, Pulse, Radionics, Scan, Scintigraphy

Diagonal(ly) Bend(wise), Bias, Cater(-corner), Catty-cornered, Counter, Oblique, Slant, Solidus, Twill

Diagram Argand, Block, Butterfly, Chart, Chromaticity, Cladogram, Compass rose, Decision tree, Dendogram, Drawing, Fault-tree, Feynman, Figure, Flow, Graph, Graphics, Grid, Hertzsprung-Russell, Indicator, Logic, Map, Plan, Plat, Run-chart, Scatter, Schema, Schematic, Scintigram, Stem-and-leaf, Stemma, Stereogram, Tephigram, Topo, Tree, Venn, Wind rose

Dial(ling) Card, Face, Mug, Phiz, Phone, Pulse, Ring, STD, Visage

Dialect Acadian, Accent, Aeolic, Alemannic, Arcadic, Attic, Basuto, Burr, Castilian, Doric, Eldin, Eolic, Epic, Erse, Eye, Franconian, Friulian, Gallo-Romance, Gascon, Geechee, Geordie, Greenlander, Hassaniya, Hegelian, Idiom, Ionic, Isogloss, Jargon, Jockney, Joual, Khalka, Koine, Konkani, Ladin, Lallans, Landsmaal, Langobardic, Langue d'oc, Langue d'oil, Langue d'oui, Ledden, Lingo, Low German, Mackem, Min, Norman, Norn, Occitan, Old Icelandic, Old North French, Parsee, Patavinity, Patois, Pedi, Prakrit, Rhotic, Riffian, Rock English, Romans(c)h, Salish, Savoyard, Scouse, Sesotho, Syriac, Taal, Ta(d)jik, Tadzhik, Talkee-talkee, Talky-talky, Tongue, Tshi, Tuscan, Twi, Tyrolese, Vaudois, Vernacular, West Saxon, Wu, Yealdon, Yenglish, Yinglish

Dialogue Colloquy, Conversation, Critias, Discussion, Exchange, Interlocution, Lazzo, Pastourelle, Speech, Stichomythia, Talk, Upspeak

Dialysis Kidney, Peritoneal

Diameter Breadth, Calibre, Gauge, Systyle, Tactical, Width

Diamond(s), Diamond-shaped Adamant, Black, Boart, Brilliant, Bristol, Carbon, Carbonado, Cullinan, D, DE, Delaware, Eustace, False, Florentine, Hope, Ice, Industrial, Isomer, Jim, Koh-i-Noor, Lasque, Lattice, Lozenge, Paragon, Pick, Pitch, Pitt, Quarry, Rhinestone, Rhomb, Rock, Rose-cut, Rosser, Rough, Rustre, Sancy, Solitaire, Spark, Sparklers, Squarial, Suit

Diana Artemis, Di, Dors

Diapason Normal, Open, Ottava, Stopped

Diaphanous Clear, Sheer, Translucent

Diaphoretic Sweater

Diaphragm Cap, Iris, Mid-riff, Phrenic, Stop

Diaresis Trema

▶ **Diarist** *see* DIARY

Diarrhoea Collywobbles, Delhi belly, Gippy tummy, Lientery, Montezuma's revenge, Runs, Scours, Squitters, The shits, Trots, Verbal, Weaning-brash, Wood-evil

Diary, Diarist Blogger, Chronicle, Dale, Day-book, Evelyn, Hickey, Journal, Journal intime, Kilvert, Log, Nobody, Noctuary, Pepys, Planner, Pooter, Record, Video

Diaspora Exodus, Galuth

Diatribe Harangue, Invective, Philippic, Tirade

Dice(r), Dicey Aleatory, Astragals, Bale, Bones, Chop, Craps, Cube, Doctor, Dodgy, Fulham, Fullams, Fullans, Gourd(s), Highman, Jeff, Mandoline, Novum, Poker, Shoot, Snake-eyes, Tallmen

Dichotomy Split

▷ **Dick** *may indicate* a dictionary

Dick(y), Dickey Clever, Deadeye, Front, Ill, Moby, OED, Policeman, Rumble, Shaky, Shirt, Spotted, Tec, Tonneau, Tucker, Tumbledown, Unstable, Wankle, Weak, Whittington

Dickens Boz, Deuce, Devil, Mephistopheles

Dicker Bargain, Barter, Haggle, Trade

▷ **Dicky** *may indicate* an anagram

Dictate, Dictator(ial) Amin, Authoritarian, Autocrat, Big Brother, Caesar, Castro, Cham, Command, Czar, Decree, Demagogue, Despot, Duce, Franco, Fu(e)hrer, Gauleiter, Hitler, Impose, Lenin, Ordain, Overbearing, Peremptory, Peron, Pol Pot, Salazar, Shogun, Stalin, Tell, Tito, Totalitarian, Tsar, Tyrant, Tzar

Diction Language, Lexis, Palavinity, Speech, Style

Dictionary Alveary, Calepin, Chambers, Data, Etymologicon, Fowler, Gazetteer, Glossary, Gradus, Hobson-Jobson, Idioticon, Johnson's, Larousse, Lexicon, Lexis, OED, Onomasticon, Thesaurus, Vocabulary, Webster, Wordbook

Dictum Obiter, Say-so

Did Began, Couth, Fec(it), Gan

Didactic Sermonical

Diddle Cheat, Con, Hoax

Dido Antic, Caper, Carthaginian, Elissa

Die(d), Dying Ache, Buy the farm, Cark, Choke, Crater, Croak, Cube, D, Decadent, Desire, End, Evanish, Exit, Expire, Fade, Fail, Flatline, Forfair, Fulham, Fulhan, Fullam, Go, Go west, Hallmark, Highman, Hop, Kark, Long, Morendo, Moribund, Ob(iit), Orb, Pass, Peg out, Perdendosi, Perish, Peter, Pop off, Pop one's clogs, Slip the cable, Snuff, Snuff it, Solidum, Sphacelation, Stamp, Sterve, Succumb, Suffer, Swage, Swelt, Terminal, Tine, Touch, Wane

Diehard Blimp, Fanatic, Intransigent, Reactionary, Standpatter, Zealot

Diesel Red

Diet(er) Assembly, Atkins, Augsburg, Bant(ing), Cacotrophy, Council, Dail, Eat, Fare, Hay, Intake, Kashrut(h), Ketogenic, Landtag, Lent, Macrobiotic, Parliament, Pleading, Reduce, Regimen, Reichstag, Short commons, Slim, Solid, Sprat, Staple, Strict, Tynwald, Vegan, Vegetarian, Weightwatcher, Worms

Dietetics Sit(i)ology

Differ(ence), Differing, Different(ly) Allo, Barney, Change, Cline, Contrast, Contretemps, Deviant, Diesis, Disagree, Discord, Discrepant, Disparate, Dispute, Dissent, Dissimilitude, Distinct, Diverge, Diverse, Else, Elsewise, Epact, Heterodox, Nuance, Omnifarious, Other, Othergates, Otherguess, Otherness, Otherwise, Potential, Quantum, Separate, Several, Special, Symmetric, Tiff, Unlike, Variform, Various, Vary

Differential, Differentiate, Differentiation Calculus, Del, Distinguish, Nabla, Product, Secern, Taxeme, Wage

Difficult(y) Abstruseness, Ado, Aporia, Arduous, Augean, Badass, Balky, Ballbuster, Bitter, Block, Bolshie, Bother, Catch, Choosy, Complex, Complication, Corner, Crotchety, Deep, Depth, Dysphagia, Embarrassment, Extreme, Fiddly, Formidable, Gordian, → **HARD**, Hassle, Hazard, Hiccough, Hiccup, Hobble, Hole, Hoor, Hump, Ill, Impasse, Indocile, Intractable, Intransigent, Jam, Kink, Knot, Lob's pound, Lurch, Mulish, Net, Nodus, Obstacle, Parlous, Pig, Pitfall, Plight, Predicament, Quandary, Queer St, Recalcitrant, Rough, Rub, Scabrous, Scrape, Scrub, Setaceous, Shlep, Snag, Soup, Steep, Stey, Stick, Sticky, Stiff, Strait, Stubborn, Stymie, Tall order, Thorny, Ticklish, Tight spot, Trial, Tricky, Troublous, Une(a)th, Uphill, Via dolorosa

Diffident Bashful, Meek, Modest, Reserved, Shy

Diffuse, Diffusion Barophoresis, Disperse, Disseminate, Endosmosis, Exude, Osmosis, Pervade, Radiate, Run, Spread, Thermal

Dig(s), Digger, Digging, Dig up Antipodean, Australian, Backhoe, Beadle, Bed(e)ral, Bedsit, Billet, Bot, Burrow, Costean, Delve, Enjoy, Excavate, Flea-bag, Fossorial, Gaulter, Get, Gibe, Gird, Graft, Graip, Grub, Hoe, Howk, Jab, Kip, Lair, Like, Lodgings, Mine, Navvy, Nervy, Nudge, Pad, Pioneer, Probe, Prod, Raddleman, Resurrect, Root, Ruddleman, Sap, See, Spade, Spit, Spud, Star-nose, Taunt, Till, Tonnell, Trench, Tunnel, Undermine, Unearth

Digest(ible), Digestion, Digestive Abridgement, Absorb, Abstract, Aperçu, Archenteron, Assimilate, Codify, Concoct, Endue, Epitome, Eupepsia, Eupepsy, Fletcherism, Gastric, Indew, Indue, Light, Pandect, Pem(m)ican, Pepsin(e), Peptic, Précis, Salt-cat, Steatolysis, → **SUMMARY**

Digit(s) Binary, Bit, Byte, Check, Dactyl, Figure, Finger, Hallux, Mantissa, Number, Pollex, Prehallux, Thumb, Toe

Dignified, Dignify August, Elevate, Exalt, Grace, Handsome, Honour, Lordly, Majestic, Manly, Proud, Solemn, Stately, Statuesque

Dignitary Bigwig, Dean, Name, Personage, Provost, → **VIP**

Dignity Aplomb, Bearing, Cathedra, Decorum, Face, Glory, Grandeur, Gravitas, High horse, Maestoso, Majesty, Nobility, Poise, Pontificate, Presence, Scarf, Tiara

Digraph Ash, Eng, Ng

Digress(ion) Apostrophe, Deviate, Diverge, Ecbole, Episode, Excurse, Excursus, Maunder, Veer, Wander

Dike Bank, Channel, Cludgie, Dam, Ditch, → **DYKE**, Embank(ment), Estacade, Lav(atory), Levee, Wall

Dilapidated, Dilapidation Clapped out, Clunker, Decrepit, Desolate, Disrepair, Eroded, Rickle, Ruined, Rust bucket, Tumbledown

Dilate, Dilation, Dilatation Amplify, Develop, Diastole, Ecstasis, Enlarge, Expand, Increase, Mydriasis, Sinus, Swell, Telangiectasia, Tent, Varix

Dilatory Protracting, Slow, Sluggish, Tardy

Dilemma Casuistry, Choice, Cleft, Dulcarnon, Fix, Horn, Jam, Predicament, Quandary, Why-not

Dilettante Aesthete, Amateur, Butterfly, Dabbler, Playboy

Diligence, Diligent Active, Application, Assiduous, Coach, Conscience, Eident, Industry, Intent, Painstaking, Sedulous, Studious

Dill Anise, Pickle

Dilute, Dilution Adulterate, Allay, Deglaze, Delay, Diluent, Lavage, Qualify, Simpson, Thin, Water, Weaken

Dim(ness), Dimming, Dimwit(ted) Becloud, Blear, Blur, Brownout, Caligo, Clueless, Crepuscular, Dense, Dusk, Eclipse, Fade, Faint, Feint, Gormless, Ill-lit,

Indistinct, Mist, Nebulous, Ninny, Obscure, Overcast, Owl, Pale, Purblind, Shadow, Unsmart

Dimension(s) Area, Breadth, Extent, Fourth, Height, Length, Measure, New, Scantling, Size, Third, Volume, Width

Diminish(ed), Diminishing, Diminuendo, Diminution, Diminutive Abatement, Assuage, Baby, Bate, Calando, Contract, Cot(t)ise, Deactivate, Decline, Decrease, Détente, Detract, Disparage, Dissipate, Dwarf, Dwindle, Erode, Fourth, Hypocorism(a), Lessen, Lilliputian, Minify, Minus, Mitigate, Petite, Pigmy, Ritardando, Scarp, Small, Stultify, Subside, Toy, Trangle, Wane, Whittle

Dimple(d) Dent, Depression, Hollow, Orange-peel

Din Babel, Charivary, Chirm, Commotion, Deen, Discord, Gunga, Hubbub, → **NOISE**, Racket, Raird, Randan, Reel, Reird, Uproar, Utis

Dine(r), Dining Aristology, Café, Eat, Feast, Mess, Refect, Sup, Trat(toria)

Dingbat Doodad, Weirdo

Dinghy Pram, Shallop, Ship, Skiff

Dingo Warrigal

Dingy Crummy, Dark, Dirty, Drear, Dun, Fleapit, Fusc(ous), Grimy, Isabel(la), Isabelline, Lurid, Oorie, Ourie, Owrie, Shabby, Smoky

Dining-room Cafeteria, Cenacle, Commons, Frater, Hall, Langar, Mess hall, Refectory, Restaurant, Triclinium

Dinky Twee

Dinner Banquet, Collation, Feast, Hall, Kail, Kale, Meal, Prandial, Progressive, Repast, Spread

Dinosaur Aepyornus, Allosaurus, Ankylosaur, Apatosaurus, Atlantosaurus, Baryonyx, Brachiosaurus, Brontosaurus, Ceratopsian, Ceratosaurus, Ceteosaurus, Chalicothere, Coelurosaur, Compsognathus, Cotylosaur, Cynodont, Dinothere, Diplodocus, Dolichosaurus, Duck-billed, Elasmosaur, Galeopithecus, Glyptodon, Hadrosaur, Ichthyosaur(us), Iguanodon, Megalosaur, Microraptor, Mosasaur, Odontornithes, Ornithischian, Ornithopod, Ornithosaur, Oviraptor, Pelycosaur, Perissodactyl, Placoderm, Plesiosaur, Pliosaur, Prehistoric, Prosauropod, Pteranodon, Pterodactyl, Pterosaur, Pythonomorpha, Rhynchocephalian, Saurischian, Sauropod, Sauropterygian, Smilodon, Square, Stegodon(t), Stegosaur, Teleosaurus, Theropod, Titanosaurus, Titanothere, Triceratops, Tyrannosaurus, Uintothere, Velociraptor

Dint Brunt, Dent, Depression, Force, Means, Power

Diocese Bishopric, District, Eparchate, See

Diode Esaki, Tunnel, Zener

Diogenes Cynic

Dioxide Cassiterite, Needle-tin

Dip(per) Bagna cauda, Baptise, Basin, Bathe, Bob, Brantub, Dabble, Dap, Dean, Dib, Diver, Dop, Double, Duck, Dunk, Foveola, Geosyncline, Guacomole, H(o)ummus, Houmous, Hum(m)us, Immerge, Immerse, Intinction, Ladle, Lucky, Magnetic, Ousel, Ouzel, Paddle, Rinse, Rollercoaster, Sag, Salute, Sheep-wash, Star, Submerge, Tapenade, Taramasalata, Tzatziki, Ursa

Diphthong Synaeresis, Synaloepha, Synizesis

Diploma Bac, Charter, Parchment, Qualification, Scroll, Sheepskin

Diplomacy, Diplomat(ic) Alternat, Ambassador, Attaché, Career, CD, Chargé d'affaires, Chateaubriand, Cheque-book, Consul, DA, Dean, Discretion, Dollar, Doyen, El(t)chi, Envoy, Fanariot, Fetial, Finesse, Gunboat, Legation, Lei(d)ger, Megaphone, Phanariot, Plenipotentiary, Shuttle, Suave, → **TACT**

▷ **Dippy** *may indicate* a bather

Dipsomania Oenomania

Dire Dreadful, Fatal, Fell, Hateful, Ominous, Urgent

Direct(or), Directed, Directly Ad hominem, Administer, Advert, Aim, Airt, Auteur, Aventre, Board, Boss, Cann, Cast, Chairperson, Channel, Charge, Command, Compere, Con(n), Conduct, Control, Cox, Dead, Due, Dunstable road, Eisenstein, Enjoin, Executive, Explicit, Fast-track, Fellini, First-hand, Forthright, Frontal, Griffiths, Guide, Helm, Hitchcock, Huston, Immediate, Impresario, Instruct, Intendant, Kapellmeister, Korda, Lead, Lean, Losey, Manager, Mastermind, Navigate, Nonexecutive, Orson (Welles), Outright, Oversee, Pagnol, Pilot, Play, Point-blank, Ready, Reed, Refer, Régisseur, Rudder, Send, Set, Signpost, Slap-bang, Stear, → **STEER**, Straight, Tarantino, Tati, Teach, Tell, Truffaut, Unvarnished, Vector, Visconti, Welles

Direction Aim, Airt, Arrow, Astern, Bearings, Course, Cross-reference, E, End-on, Guidance, Guide, Heading, Keblah, L, Line, N, Orders, Orientation, Passim, Quarter, R, Route, Rubric, S, Sanction, Send, Sense, Side, Slap, Tack, Tenor, Thataway, Tre corde, Trend, W, Way, Wedelns

Direction-finder Asdic, Compass, Decca, Quadrant, Radar, Sextant, Sonar

Directory Crockford, Data, Debrett, Encyclop(a)edia, Folder, French, Kelly, List, Red book, Register, Root, Web, Yellow Pages®

Dirge Ballant, Coronach, Dirige, Epicedium, Knell, Monody, Requiem, Song, Threnody

Dirigible Airship, Balloon, Blimp, Zeppelin

Dirk Anelace, Dagger, Skean, Whinger, Whiniard, Whinyard

Dirt(y) Augean, Bed(r)aggled, Begrime, Bemoil, Cacky, Chatty, Clag, Clarty, Colly, Contaminate, Coom, Crock, Crud, Draggle, Dung, Dust, Earth, Festy, Filth, Foul, Gore, Grime, Grubby, Grufted, Grungy, Impure, Manky, Moit, Mote, Muck, Obscene, Ordure, Pay, Pick, Pollute, Ray, Scody, Sculdudd(e)ry, Scum, Scungy, Scuzzy, Skanky, Skulduddery, Smirch, Smut(ch), Soil, Sooty, Sordes, Sordor, Squalid, Squalor, Stain, Trash, Unclean, Unsatisfactory, Unwashed, Warb, Yucky, Yukky

Dis Hades, Hell

Disability, Disable(d) Cripple, Crock, Gimp, Handicapped, Hors de combat, Incapacitate, Kayo, Lame, Maim, Paralyse, Scissor-leg, Scotch, Wreck

Disadvantage Detriment, Disamenity, Downside, Drawback, Handicap, Mischief, Out, Penalise, Penalty, Prejudice, Supercherie, Upstage, Wrongfoot, Zugswang

Disagree(ing), Disagreeable, Disagreement Argue, Argy-bargy, Bad, Clash, Conflict, Contest, Debate, Differ, Discrepant, Dispute, Dissent, Dissonant, Evil, Fiddlesticks, Friction, Heterodoxy, Pace, Plagu(e)y, Rift, Troll, Unpleasing

Disallow Forbid, Overrule, Surcharge

Disappear(ing) Cook, Dispel, Evanesce, Evanish, Evaporate, Fade, Kook, Latescent, Melt, Occult, Pass, Skedaddle, Slope, → **VANISH**

Disappoint(ment), Disappointed, Disappointing Anticlimax, Balk, Baulk, Bombshell, Bummer, Chagrin, Comedown, Crestfallen, Delude, Disgruntle, Frustrate, Gutted, Heartsick, Lemon, Letdown, Mislippen, Off, Regret, Sell, Setback, Shucks, Sick, Suck-in, Sucks, Swiz(zle), Thwart, Underwhelm

Disapproval, Disapprove(d) Ach, Animadvert, Boo, Catcall, Censure, Condemn, Deplore, Deprecate, Discountenance, Expostulate, Fie, Frown, Harrumph, Hiss, Mal vu, Napoo, Object, Pejorative, Po-faced, Raspberry, Razz, Reject, Reproach, Reprobate, Squint, Tush, Tut, Tut-tut, Umph, Veto, Whiss

Disarm(ament), Disarming Bluff, Defuse, Demobilise, Nuclear, Winsome

Disarrange Disturb, Muddle, Ruffle, Tousle, Unsettle

Disarray Disorder, Mess, Rifle, Tash, Undress

Disaster, Disastrous Accident, Adversity, Apocalypse, Bale, Calamity, Cataclysm(ic), Catastrophe, Crisis, Debacle, Dire, Doom, Evil, Fatal, Fiasco, Flop, Impostor, Meltdown, Mishap, Pitfall, Rout, Ruin, Screw-up, Seism, Shipwreck, Titanic, Tragedy, Wipeout

Disavow Abjure, Deny, Disclaim, Recant, Retract

Disbelief, Disbelieve(r) Acosmism, Anythingarian, Atheism, Cor, Doubt, Gawp, Incredulity, Mistrust, Nothingarianism, Occamist, Phew, Phooey, Puh-lease, Puh-leeze, Question, Sceptic, Shoot, Stroll on, Voetsak

Disburse Distribute, Expend, Outlay, Spend

Disc, Disk Bursting, Button, CD, Cheese, Clay pigeon, Compact, Coulter, Counter, Diaphragm, Dogtag, EP, Epiphragm, Fla(w)n, Flexible, Floppy, Frisbee®, Gold, Gong, Granum, Hard, Hard card, Harrow, Impeller, Intervertebral, Laser, LP, Magnetic, Mono, O, Optic(al), Parking, Paten, Patin, Planchet, Plate, Platinum, Platter, Puck, RAM, Rayleigh, Record, Reflector, Rosette, Roundel, Roundlet, Rowel, Rundle, Sealed unit, Silver, Slipped, Slug, Stereo, Stylopodium, Sun, Swash plate, System, Tax, Token, Video, Wafer, Wharve, Whorl, Winchester, Wink, WORM, Zip®

Discard(ed) Abandon, Burn, Crib, Defy, Dele, Jettison, Kill, Leave, Obsolete, Off, Offload, Oust, Outtake, → **REJECT**, Scrap, Shed, Shuck, Slough, Sluff, Supersede, Throw over, Trash

Discern(ing), Discernment Acumen, Acute, Clear-eyed, Descry, Detect, Discrimination, Eagle-eyed, Flair, Insight, Perceive, Percipient, Perspicacity, Quick-sighted, Realise, Sapient, Scry, See, Skry, → **TASTE**, Tell, Wate

Discharge Absolve, Acquit, Arc, Assoil, Blennorrhoea, Blow off, Brush, Cashier, Catamenia, Catarrh, Conditional, Corona, Corposant, Dejecta, Deliver, Demob, Disembogue, Disgorge, Dishono(u)rable, Dismiss, Disruptive, Dump, Efflux, Effusion, Egest, Ejaculate, Eject, Embogue, Emission, Emit, Encopresis, Enfilade, Evacuate, Excrete, Execute, Exemption, Expulsion, Exude, Fire, Flashover, Flower, Flux, Frass, Free, Gleet, Glow, Lava, Lay off, Leak, Let off, Leucorrhoea, Lochia, Loose, Maturate, Menses, Mitimus, Muster out, Mute, Offload, Otorrhoea, Oust, Ozaena, Pass, Pay, Perform, Period, Planuria, Purulence, Pus, Pyorrhoea, Quietus, Rheum, Rhinorrhoeal, Run, Sack, Salvo, Sanies, Secretion, Seepage, Show, Shrive, Snarler, Spark, Suppurate, Teem, Unload, Unloose, Vent, Void, Water, Whites

Disciple(s) Adherent, Apostle, Babi, Baruch, Catechumen, Chela, Follower, John, Judas, Luke, Mark, Matthew, Peter, Simon, Son, Student, The Seventy, Thomist, Votary

Disciplinarian, Discipline Apollonian, Ascesis, Chasten, Chastise, Correct, Despot, Drill, Exercise, Feng shui, Inure, Judo, Martinet, Mathesis, Punish, Ramrod, Regimentation, Regulate, Sadhana, School, Science, Spartan, Stickler, Subject, Taskmaster, Train, Tutor

▶ **Disc jockey** *see* **DJ**

Disclaim(er) Deny, Disown, No(t)chel, Recant, Renounce, → **REPUDIATE**, Voetstoots

Disclose, Disclosure Apocalypse, Confess, Divulge, Expose, Impart, Leak, Manifest, Propale, → **PUBLISH**, Report, Reveal, Spill, Tell, Unheal, Unhele, Unrip, Unveil

Discoloration, Discolour(ed) Acrocyanosis, Bloodstain, Bruise, Cyanosis, Dyschroa, Ecchymosis, Fox, Livedo, Livid, Livor, Stain, Streak, Tarnish, Tinge, Weather

Discomfit(ure) Abash, Confuse, Disconcert, Disturb, Frustrate, Lurch, Shend

Discomfort(ed) Ache, All-overish, Angst, Dysphoria, Gyp, Heartburn, Pain, Unease

▷ **Disconcert(ed)** *may indicate* an anagram

Disconcert(ing) Abash, Astound, Confuse, Disturb, Embarrass, Faze, Feeze, Flurry, Fluster, Nonplus, Off-putting, Phase, Pheese, Pheeze, Phese, → **RATTLE**, Shatter, Tease, Throw, Upset, Wrong-foot

Disconnect(ed) Asynartete, Decouple, Detach, Disjointed, Off-line, Sever, Staccato, Trip, Uncouple, Undo, Ungear, Unplug

Disconsolate Desolate, Doleful, Downcast, → **GLOOMY**

Discontent(ed) Disquiet, Dissatisfied, Humph, Repined, Sour, Umph

Discontinue, Discontinuance, Discontinuity Abandon, Cease, Desist, Desuetude, Drop, Moho, Prorogue, Stop, Terminate

Discord(ant) Absonant, Ajar, Charivari, Conflict, Din, Dispute, Eris, Faction, Hoarse, Jangle, Jar, Raucous, Ruction, Strife

▷ **Discord(ant)** *may indicate* an anagram

Discount Agio, Cashback, Deduct, Disregard, Forfaiting, Invalidate, Quantity, → **REBATE**, Trade

Discountenance Disfavour, Efface, Embarrass

Discourage(ment) Caution, Chill, Dampen, Dash, Daunt, Deject, Demoralise, Deter, Dishearten, Disincentive, Dismay, Dissuade, Enervate, Frustrate, Intimidate, Opposition, Stifle, Unman

Discourse Address, Argument, Colloquy, Conversation, Descant, Diatribe, Dissertate, Eulogy, Expound, Homily, Lecture, Lucubrate, Orate, Philippic, Preach, Relate, Rigmarole, Sermon, Wash

Discourteous, Discourtesy Disrespect, Impolite, Insult, Rude, Slight, Uncivil, Unmannerly

Discover(y), Discoverer Amundsen, Anagnorisis, Ascertain, Betray, Breakthrough, Columbus, Cook, Descry, Detect, Discern, Discure, Esery, Eureka, → **FIND**, Heureka, Heuristic, Hit on, Learn, Locate, Manifest, Moresby, Protegé, Rumble, Serendip, Serendipity, Spy, Tasman, Trace, Treasure trove, Unearth, Unhale, Unmask, Unveil

▷ **Discovered in** *may indicate* an anagram or a hidden word

Discredit(able) Debunk, Decry, Disgrace, Explode, Infamy, Scandal, Smear, Unworthy

Discreet, Discretion Cautious, Circumspect, Finesse, Freedom, Judicious, Option, Polite, Politic, Prudence, Prudent, Trait, Unobtrusive, Wise

Discrepancy Difference, Gap, Lack, Shortfall, Variance

Discrete Distinct, Separate, Unrelated

Discriminate, Discriminating, Discrimination Ag(e)ism, Colour bar, Diacritic, Differentiate, Discern, Distinguish, Elitism, Fastidious, Handism, Invidious, Lookism, Nasute, Racism, Rankism, Reverse, Secern, Segregate, Select, Sexism, Siz(e)ism, Speciesism, Subtle, Taste

Discursive Roving

Discuss(ed), Discussion Agitate, Air, Canvass, Commune, Conf(erence), Consult, Corridor work, Debate, Dialectic, Dialogue, Dicker, Disquisition, En l'air, Examine, Excursus, Expatiate, Gabfest, Handle, Hob and nob, Interlocution, Issue, Korero, Moot, Negotiation, Over, Palaver, Parley, Pourparler, Prolegomenon, Quodlibet, Rap, Re, Symposium, Talk, Tapis, Treatment, Ventilate, Vex, Words

Disdain(ful) Belittle, Contempt, Coy, Deride, Despise, Geck, Poof, Pooh-pooh, Puh, Rats, Sassy, → **SCORN**, Scout, Sdei(g)n, Sniffy, Spurn, Supercilious, Ugh

Disease(d) Affection, Ailment, Communicable, Complaint, Deficiency, Defluxion, Epidemic, Fever, Functional, Industrial, Infection, Lurgi, Lurgy, Malady, Noso-,

Nosocomial, Nosography, Notifiable, Occupational, Organic, Pest(ilence), Rot, Scourge, Sickness

DISEASES

2 letters:
CD
MD
ME
MS
TB
VD

3 letters:
ALS
BSE
Flu
Haw
Pip
Pox
Sod
→ **STD**
TSE
Wog

4 letters:
Aids
Boba
Bunt
Clap
Conk
Gout
Keel
Kuru
Loco
Lues
Lyme
Roup
Wind
Yaws

5 letters:
Bang's
Black
Borna
Brand
Dread
Dutch
Ebola
Edema
Ergot

Favus
Fifth
Gapes
Hoove
Kwok's
Lupus
Mesel
Mumps
Ngana
Palsy
Pinta
Polio
Pott's
Rabid
Scall
Sprue
Surra
Tinea
Virus
Weil's
Worms

6 letters:
Anbury
Aphtha
Blight
Blotch
Border
Cancer
Canker
Chagas'
Chorea
Cowpox
Crohn's
Cruels
Dartre
Dengue
Eczema
Farcin
Graves'
Herpes
Income
Johne's
Mad cow
Marek's
Meazel

Mildew
Morbus
Mosaic
Nagana
Oedema
Paget's
Parrot
Rabies
Sapego
Scurvy
Social
Still's
Thrush
Tunnel
Typhus
Ulitis
Urosis
Yuppie
Zoster

7 letters:
Ascites
Batten's
Blue-ear
Bright's
British
Caisson
Cholera
Coeliac
Crewels
Crinkle
Dieback
Dourine
Endemic
English
Frounce
Gum rash
Hansen's
Hardpad
Hydatid
Icterus
Kissing
Leprosy
Lockjaw
Maidism
Malaria

Marburg
Miller's
Mimesis
Mooneye
Moor-ill
Murrain
Mycosis
Myiasis
Pébrine
Podagra
Purples
Redfoot
Rickets
Ring rot
Rosette
Scabies
Scrapie
Sequela
Serpigo
Tetanus
Tetters
Typhoid
Variola
Wilson's
Zymosis

8 letters:
Addison's
Alastrim
Aujesky's
Beri-beri
Blackleg
Black-rot
Bornholm
Club root
Crown rot
Cushing's
Cynanche
Diabetes
Dutch elm
Economo's
Fishskin
Fowl pest
Gape-worm
Gaucher's
Glanders

Glaucoma
Goujeers
Gummosis
Hodgkin's
Hookworm
Impetigo
Jaundice
Kala-azar
Kawasaki
Leaf-roll
Leaf-spot
Liver-rot
Loose-cut
Menière's
Minamata
Mycetoma
Myopathy
Myxedema
Nosology
Pandemic
Pathogen
Pellagra
Phthisis
Phytosis
Porrigro
Progeria
Pullorum
Rachitis
Raynaud's
Rose-rash
Scaly leg
Scrofula
Shingles
Smallpox
Soft sore
Suppeago
Swayback
Swinepox
Syphilis
Tay-Sachs
The bends
Time-zone
Trembles
Venereal
Vincent's
Zoonosis

9 letters:
Bilharzia
Blackhead
Black knot

Black-lung
Brown lung
Chancroid
Chlorosis
Christmas
Cirrhosis
Contagion
Diathesis
Distemper
Dysentery
Ear-cockle
Enteritis
Exanthema
Filanders
Gonorrhea
Idiopathy
Ixodiasis
Kawasaki's
Lathyrism
Leucaemia
Leukaemia
Loose smut
Myxoedema
Navicular
Nephritis
Nephrosis
Newcastle
New Forest
Pellagrin
Pemphigus
Phossy-jaw
Porphyria
Seborrhea
Siderosis
Silicosis
Toxicosis
Trichosis
Tularemia
Tulip root
Yuppie flu

10 letters:
Acromegaly
Alzheimer's
Amoebiasis
Asbestosis
Autoimmune
Babesiosis
Bagassosis
Bluetongue
Byssinosis

Chickenpox
Dandy-fever
Diphtheria
Erysipelas
Filariasis
Fire-blight
Fowl plague
Framboesia
Giardiasis
Gonorrhoea
Heartwater
Hemophilia
Iatrogenic
Ichthyosis
Impaludism
Leuchaemia
Limber-neck
Lou Gehrig's
Louping ill
Moniliasis
Muscardine
Neuropathy
Ornithosis
Parkinson's
Quarter-ill
Scarlatina
Seborrhoea
Topagnosia
Tularaemia

11 letters:
Anthracosis
Berylliosis
Brittle-bone
Cardiopathy
Consumption
Farmer's lung
Green monkey
Haemophilia
Hebephrenia
Huntington's
Isle of Wight
Kwashiorkor
Listeriosis
Myxomatosis
Parasitosis
Paratyphoid
Psittacosis
Rickettsial
Scleroderma
Septicaemia

Thalassemia
Trench mouth
Trichinosis
Woolsorter's
Yellow-fever

12 letters:
Avitaminosis
Black quarter
Ehrlichiosis
Enterobiasis
Fascioliasis
Finger and toe
Foot and mouth
Furunculosis
Hoof and mouth
Legionnaires'
Molybdenosis
Motor neurone
Osteomalacia
Osteoporosis
Scheuermann's
Shaking palsy
Slapped cheek
Thalassaemia
Tuberculosis
Uncinariasis

13 letters:
Elephantiasis
Leichmaniasis
Leptospirosis
Osteomyelitis
Poliomyelitis
Sclerodermata
Syringomyelia
Toxoplasmosis
Tsutsugamushi

14 letters:
Cystic fibrosis
Histoplasmosis
Leucodystrophy
Onchocerciasis
Pasteurellosis
Pneumoconiosis
Psillid yellows
River blindness
Sporotrichosis
Trichomoniasis
Trichophytosis

14 letters – cont:	15 letters:	16 letters:	17 letters:
Vincent's angina	Graft-versus-host	Pneumonoconiosis	Friedreich's ataxia
	Schistosomiasis	Sleeping sickness	Multiple sclerosis
	Trypanosomiasis	Sweating sickness	

▷ **Diseased** *may indicate* an anagram

Disembark Alight, Detrain, Land

Disembarrass Extricate, Rid, Unthread

Disembowel Eviscerate, Exenterate, Gralloch, Gut, Viscerate

Disenchant Disabuse, Disillusion, Dismay, Embitter

Disencumber Free, Rid, Unburden

Disengage(d), Disengagement Clear, Detach, Divorce, Liberate, Loosen, Release, Untie

Disentangle Debarrass, Extricate, Red(d), Solve, Unravel, Unsnarl

Disestablishmentarian Cosmist

Disfavour Doghouse, Maugre

Disfigure(ment), Disfigured Agrise, Agryze, Camsho, Club-foot, Deface, Deform, Goitre, Mutilate, Scar, Spoil, Tash, Ugly

▷ **Disfigured** *may indicate* an anagram

Disgorge Discharge, Spew, Spill, Vent, Void

Disgrace Atimy, Attaint, Baffle, Blot, Contempt, Contumely, Degrade, Discredit, Dishonour, Dog-house, Ignominy, Indignity, Infamy, Obloquy, Opprobrium, Pity, Scandal, Shame, Shend, Slur, Soil, Stain, Stigma, Yshend

Disgraceful Diabolical, Fie, Ignoble, Ignominious, Indign, Infamous, Mean, Notorious, Reprehensible, Scandalous, Shameful, Turpitude

Disgruntled Brassed off, Malcontent, Resentful, Sore

▷ **Disgruntled** *may indicate* an anagram

Disguise(d) Alias, Blessing, Camouflage, Cloak, Colour, Conceal, Cover, Covert, Dissemble, Hide, Hood, Incog(nito), Mantle, Mask, Masquerade, Obscure, Peruke, Pretence, Pseudonym, Ring, Shades, Travesty, Veil, Vele, Veneer, Visagiste, Visor, Vizard

▷ **Disguised** *may indicate* an anagram

Disgust(ing) Ach-y-fi, Ad nauseam, Aversion, Aw, Bah, Cloy, Discomfort, Execrable, Faugh, Fie, Foh, Fulsome, Grisly, Grody, Icky, Irk, Loathsome, Manky, Mawkish, Minging, Nauseous, Noisome, Obscene, Odium, Oughly, Ouglie, Pah, Pho(h), Pish, Pshaw, Pugh, Repel, Repugnant, Repulse, → **REVOLT**, Revulsion, Scomfish, Scumfish, Scunner, Scuzz, → **SICKEN**, Si(e)s, Sir-reverence, Slimeball, Slimy, Squalid, Tush, Ugh, Ugsome, Vile, Yech, Yu(c)k, Yucko, Yukky

Dish(y) Adonis, Allot, Apollo, Ashet, Basin, Belle, Bowl, Chafing, Charger, Cocotte, Concoction, Cook-up, Cutie, Dent, Diable, Dole, Dreamboat, Epergne, Flasket, Grail, Kitchen, Laggen, Laggin, Lanx, Luggie, Muffineer, Ovenware, Pan, Pannikin, Paten, Patera, Patin(e), Petri, Plat du jour, Plate, Platter, Porringer, Ramekin, Ramequin, Receptacle, Rechauffé, Remove, Sangraal, Sangrail, Sangreal, Satellite, Saucer, Scallop, Scorifier, Scupper, Serve, Service, Side, Smasher, Special, Squarial, Stunner, Toll, Watchglass

DISHES

3 letters:	4 letters:	Kiev	Milt
Poi	Flan	Melt	Olla
	Fool	Mess	Puri

Sate
Soss
Taco
Tian

5 letters:
Adobo
Balti
Bhaji
Bhuna
Bitok
Boxty
Brose
Champ
Curry
Dolma
Gomer
Kasha
Keema
Kibbe
Kofta
Korma
Laksa
Maror
Perog
Pilau
Pilow
Poori
Raita
Ramen
Rosti
Salad
Salmi
Satay
Sushi
Tamal
Tikka
Tripe

6 letters:
Bhagee
Bharta
Bhoona
Bridie
Chilli
Cou-cou
Cuscus
Entrée
Fondue
Haggis
Hotpot

Kimchi
Kishke
Kissel
Masale
Mornay
Mousse
Muesli
Nachos
Paella
Pakora
Panada
Pirogi
Quiche
Ragout
Regale
Roesti
Salmis
Sea-pie
Sowans
Sowens
Subgum
Surimi
Tamale
Tsamba

7 letters:
Biriani
Bobotie
Burrito
Calzone
Cannoli
Cassava
Ceviche
Chowder
Comport
Compote
Crowdie
Crubeen
Crumble
Custard
Cuvette
Dariole
Dhansak
Dopiaza
Egg roll
Fajitas
Fal-a-fel
Fel-a-fel
Foo yung
Friture
Grav lax

Marengo
Mousaka
Padella
Pierogi
Poutine
Rarebit
Ravioli
Sasatie
Sashimi
Seviche
Sosatie
Soufflé
Spag bol
Stir-fry
Stovies
Tartare
Tempura
Terrine
Timbale
Tostada

8 letters:
Bhelpuri
Brandade
Caponata
Chasseur
Chop suey
Chow mein
Coolamon
Coq au vin
Coquille
Couscous
Crostini
Dog's-body
Entremes
Feijoada
Flummery
Frittata
Gado-gado
Halloumi
Handroll
Jalfrezi
Kedgeree
Keftedes
Kickshaw
Kouskous
Kreplach
Linguini
Matelote
Mazarine
McCallum

Meat loaf
Meunière
Moussaka
Pandowdy
Pastrami
Porridge
Pot-au-feu
Pot-roast
Raclette
Shashlik
Sillabub
Souvlaki
Sukiyaki
Syllabub
Teriyaki
Tzatziki
Vindaloo
White-pot
Yakimono
Yakitori

9 letters:
Carbonara
Carpaccio
Cevapcici
Clafoutis
Compotier
Egg-fo-yang
Enchilada
Entremets
Escabeche
Fricassee
Galantine
Gravad lax
Guacamole
Howtowdie
Jambalaya
Lyonnaise
Manicotti
Marinière
Matelotte
Pastitsio
Pepper-pot
Reistafel
Rijstafel
Rogan josh
Shashlick
Souvlakia
Succotash
Surf n'turf
Turducken

10 letters:
Blanquette
Bombay duck
Cacciatore
Cottage pie
Coulibiaca
Couscousou
Doner kebab
Egg-foo-yung
Jugged hare
Koulibiaca
Mousseline
Nasi goreng
Parmigiana
Provençale
Quesadilla
Rijsttafel
Salmagundi

Sauerkraut
Scallopine
Shish kebab
Spitchcock
Spring roll
Steak diane
Stroganoff
Teppan-yaki
Zabaglione

11 letters:
Banana split
Buck-rarebit
Crappit-head
Fritto misto
Saltimbocca
Sauerbraten
Smorgasbord

Spanakopita
Surf and turf
Welsh rabbit

12 letters:
Buffalo wings
Eggs Benedict
Shepherd's pie
Solomon Gundy
Steak tartare
Sweet and sour
Taramasalata
Welsh rarebit

13 letters:
Fish and brewis
Rumbledethump
Salade nicoise

Skirl in the pan
Toad-in-the-hole

14 letters:
Beef stroganoff
Chilli con carne
Rumbledethumps
Scotch woodcock

15 letters:
Bubble and squeak
Eggs in moonshine

16 letters:
Potatoes and point

17 letters:
Cauliflower cheese

Dishabille Disarray, Négligé, Undress
Dishearten Appal, Core(r), Cow, Daunt, Depress, Discourage, Dispirit, Ettle
Dishevel(led) Blowsy, Blowzy, Daggy, Mess, Rumpled, Scraggly, Touse, Tousle, Touzle, Tumble, Uncombed, Unkempt, Untidy, Windswept
Dishonest(y) Bent, Crooked, Cross, Dodgy, False, Fraud, Graft, Hooky, Hot, Improbity, Jiggery-pokery, Knavery, Malpractice, Malversation, Maverick, Shonky, Snide, Stink, Twister, Underhand, Venal, Wrong'un
Dishonour Abatement, Defile, Disgrace, Disparage, Ignominy, Indignity, Seduce, → SHAME, Violate, Wrong
Disillusion Disenchant, Sour
Disincline(d), Disinclination Apathy, Averse, Loth, Off, Reluctant
Disinfect(ant) Acriflavin(e), Carbolic, Cineol(e), Cleanse, Dip, Eucalyptole, Formalin, Formol, Fuchsine, Fumigate, Lysol®, Phenol, Purify, Sheep-dip, Sheep-wash, TCP, Terebene
Disingenuous Insincere, Mask, Oblique, Two-faced
Disinherit Deprive, Dispossess
Disintegrate, Disintegration Break, Collapse, Crumble, Decay, Dialysis, Erode, Fragment, Lyse, Lysis, Osteoclasis, Rd, Rutherford
Disinter Exhume, Unearth
Disinterested Apathetic, Impartial, Incurious, Mugwump, Unbiased
Disjoint(ed) Bitty, Dismember, Incoherent, Rambling, Scrappy
Disjunction Exclusive, Inclusive
▶ **Disk** *see* DISC
Dislike Abhor, Allergy, Animosity, Animus, Antipathy, Aversion, Derry, Disesteem, Displeasure, Distaste, Gross out, Hate, Lump, Mind, Needle, Scunner, Warling
Dislocate, Dislocation Break, Diastasis, Displace, Fault, Luxate, Slip, Subluxate
Dislodge Budge, Displace, Expel, Luxate, Oust, Rear, Tuft, Unship, Uproot
Disloyal(ty) False, Treason, Unfaithful, Untrue
Dismal Black, Bleak, Cheerless, Dark, Dowie, Dowly, Drack, Dreary, Funereal, → GLOOMY, Grey, Long-faced, Morne, Obital, Sepulchral, Sombre, Sullen, Trist(e), Wae, Woebegone, Wormy

Dismantle(d), Dismantling Decommission, Derig, Divest, Get-out, Sheer-hulk, Strike, Strip, Unrig

Dismast Unstep

Dismay Amate, Appal, Confound, Consternation, Coo, Criv(v)ens, Daunt, Dread, Fie, Ha, Hah, Horrify, Lordy, Lumme, Qualms, Strewth

Dismember Quarter

Dismiss(al), Dismissive Airy, Annul, Ax, Boot, Bounce, Bowl(er), Brush off, Bum's rush, Cancel, Cashier, Catch, Chuck, Congé, Constructive, Daff, Discard, Discharge, Dooced, Expulsion, Fire, Forget, Golden bowler, Heave-ho, Kiss-off, Lay off, Marching orders, Mitten, Och, Prorogue, Push, Recall, Reform, Reject, Remove, R.O., Road, Sack, Scout, Send, Shoo, Shrug off, Skittle out, Spit, Spurn, Stump, Suka wena, Via, Voetsak, Walking papers, York

Dismount Alight, Hecht

Disobedience, Disobedient, Disobey Contumacy, Defy, Flout, Insubordination, Rebel, Sit-in, Wayward

▷ **Disorder(ed)** *may indicate* an anagram

Disorder(ly), Disordered Affective, Ague, Ailment, Anarchy, Ariot, Asthma, Ataxia, Catatonia, Chaos, Chlorosis, Clutter, Conduct, Confuse, Consumption, Contracture, Conversion, Defuse, Derange, Deray, Diabetes, Dishevel, Dissociative, DT's, Dyslexia, Dysthymic, Dystrophy, Echolalia, Entropy, Epilepsy, Farrago, Greensickness, Grippe, Haemophilia, Hallucinosis, Heartburn, Huntingdon's chorea, Hypallage, Inordinate, Irregular, Mange, Mare's nest, ME, Mental, Mess, Misrule, Mistemper, → **MUDDLE**, Muss(y), Neurosis, Oncus, Onkus, Pandemonium, Panic, Para-, Pell-mell, Personality, Phenylketonuria, Porphyria, Psychomatic, Psychoneurosis, Psychopathic, Psychosis, Ragmatical, Rile, Roughhouse, Rowdy, Rumple, SAD, St Vitus' Dance, Schizophrenia, Seborrh(o)ea, Shell-shock, Slovenly, Sydenham's chorea, Tarantism, Thalass(a)emia, Thought, Tousle, Turbulence, Unhinge, Unruly, Upheaval, Upset, Virilism

Disorganise(d) At sea, Deranged, Disorderly, Haphazard, Haywire, Ragtag, Scatterbrain, Scatty, Shambolic, Structureless

Disown Deny, Disclaim, Disinherit, Renig, Renounce, Repudiate, Unget

Disparage, Disparaging Abuse, Belittle, Decry, Defame, Denigrate, Depreciate, Detract, Discredit, Lessen, Pejorative, Poor mouth, Racist, Run down, → **SLANDER**, Slur, Snide, Traduce, Vilify

Dispassionate Calm, Clinical, Composed, Cool, Impartial, Objective, Serene

Dispatch Bowl, Celerity, Consign, Destroy, Dismiss, Expede, Expedite, Express, Gazette, Kibosh, Kill, Missive, Post, Pronto, Remit, Report, → **SEND**, Shank, Ship, Slaughter, Slay, Special

Dispel Disperse, Scatter

Dispensation, Dispense(r), Dispense with Absolve, Administer, Aerosol, Apothecary, Automat, Ax(e), Cashpoint, Chemist, Container, Distribute, Dose, Dropper, Exempt, Handout, Indult, Optic, Scrap, Spinneret, Vendor, Visitation

Dispersable, Disperse, Dispersion Deflocculate, Diaspora, Diffract, Diffuse, Disband, Dissolve, Evaporate, Lyophil(e), Mode, Scail, Scale, → **SCATTER**, Skail, Sow, Spread, Strew

Dispirit(ed), Dispiriting Chapfallen, Crestfallen, Dampen, Dash, Daunt, Discourage, Dishearten, Exorcism, Gloomy, Listless, Sackless

Displace(ment), Displaced Antevert, Blueshift, Chandler's wobble, Depose, Disturb, Ectopia, Ectopy, Fault, Heterotopia, Lateroversion, Load, Luxate, Move, Oust, Proptosis, Ptosis, Reffo, Shift, Stir, Subluxation, Unseat, Unsettle, Uproot, Upthrow, Valgus, Varus, Volumetric

Display, Display ground Air, Array, Blaze, Blazon, Brandish, Bravura, Depict, Eclat, Epideictic, Etalage, Evidence, Evince, Exhibition, Exposition, Express, Extend, Extravaganza, Exude, Fireworks, Flash, Flaunt, Float, Gala, Gondola, Hang, Head-down, Head-up, Heroics, Lay out, LCD, LED, Lek, Liquid crystal, Manifest, Mount, Muster, Ostentation, Outlay, Overdress, Pageant, Parade, Paraf(f)le, Peepshow, Pixel, Pomp, Present(ation), Propale, Pyrotechnics, Rode, Rodeo, Roll-out, Scene, Set piece, Shaw, → **SHOW**, Sight, Spectacle, Splash, Splurge, Sport, Spree, State, Stunt, Tableau, Tattoo, Tournament, Turn out, Up, Vaunt, Wear

Displease(d), Displeasure Anger, Dischuffed, Humph, Irritate, Provoke, Umbrage

Disport Amuse, Divert, Play

Dispose(d), Disposal, Disposition Affectation, Apt, Arrange, Attitude, Bent, Bestow, Bias, Bin, Cast, Despatch, Dump, Eighty-six, Humour, Inclination, Kibosh, Kidney, Kybosh, Lay(-out), Lie, Nature, Ordonnance, Penchant, Prone, Propensity, Sale, Sell, Service, Settle, Stagger, Talent, Temper(ament), Trim

▷ **Disposed, Disposition** *may indicate* an anagram

Dispossess(ed) Abate, Attaint, Bereft, Depose, Deprive, Evict, Oust

Disproportion(ate) Asymmetric, Extreme, Imbalance, Incommensurate, Unequal

Disprove, Disproof, Disproval Debunk, Discredit, Invalidate, Negate, Rebut, Rebuttal, Redargue, Reductio ad absurdum, Refel, Refute

Dispute(d), Disputant Argue, Barney, Brangle, Cangle, Case, Chaffer, Challenge, Chorizont(ist), Contend, Contest, Contravene, Contretemps, Controversy, Debate, Demarcation, Deny, Differ, Discept, Discuss, Eristic, Fracas, Fray, Haggle, Kilfud-yoking, Lock-out, Militate, Ob and soller, Odds, Oppugn, Plea, Polemic, Pro-and-con, Quarrel, → **QUESTION**, Quibble, Rag, Resist, Spar, Stickle, Threap(it), Threep(it), Tiff, Tissue, Tug-of-love, Variance, Wrangle

Disqualify Debar, Incapacitate, Recuse, Reject, Unfit

Disquiet(ed) Agitate, Concern, Discomboberate, Discombobulate, → **DISTURB**, Pain, Perturb(ation), Solicit, Turmoil, Uneasy, Unnerve, Unrest, Vex

Disraeli Dizzy, Tancred

Disregard(ed) Anomie, Anomy, Contempt, Defy, Disfavour, Flout, Forget, Ignore, Oblivion, Omit, Overlook, Oversee, Pass, Pretermit, Slight, Spare, Violate, Waive

Disrepair Dilapidation, Fritz, Ruin

Disreputable, Disrepute Base, Black sheep, Bowsie, Disgrace, Grubby, Louche, Low, Lowlife, Notorious, Raffish, Ragamuffin, Reprobate, Rip, Scuzz(ball), Seamy, Seamy side, Shady, Shameful, Shy, Shyster, Sleazy

Disrespect(ful) Contempt, Derogatory, Discourtesy, Flip(pant), Impiety, Impolite, Irreverent, Profane, Slight, Uncivil

Disrupt(ion) Breach, Cataclasm, Dislocate, Disorder, Distract, Hamper, Interrupt, Jetlag, Mayhem, Perturb, Quonk, Ruffle, Screw, Upheaval

▷ **Disruption** *may indicate* an anagram

Dissatisfaction Displeasure, Distaste, Humph, Umph

Dissect(ion) Analyse, Dismember, Examine, Necrotomy, Zootomy

Dissemble(r) Conceal, Feign, Fox, Hypocrite, Impostor, Misinform

Dissent(er), Dissension, Dissenting Contend, Differ, Disagree, Discord, Dissident, Faction, Flak, Heretic, Jain, Leveller, Lollard, Maverick, Noes, Non-CE, Non-con(formist), Occasional conformist, Old Believer, Pantile, Protest, Raskolnik, Recusant, Sectary, Separat(ion)ist, Splinter group, → **STRIFE**, Vary

Dissertation Essay, Excursus, Lecture, Thesis, Treatise

▶ **Dissident** *see* **DESERTER**

Dissimilar Different, Diverse, Heterogeneous, Unlike

Dissipate(d) Debauch, Diffuse, Disperse, Dissolute, Gay, Revel, Scatter, Shatter, Squander, Waste

▷ **Dissipated** *may indicate* an anagram

Dissociate Separate, Sever, Withdraw

Dissolute Degenerate, Demirep, Falstaffian, Hell, Lax, Libertine, Licentious, Loose, Rake-helly, Rakish, Rip, Roué, Wanton

▷ **Dissolute** *may indicate* an anagram

Dissolution Dismissal, Divorce, End, Repeal, Separation

Dissolve Deliquesce, Digest, Disband, Disunite, Lap, Liquesce, Melt, Repeal, Terminate, Thaw

Dissonance Wolf

Dissuade Dehort, Deter, Discourage

Distaff Clotho, Female, Lady, Rock, Stick

Distance Absciss(a), Afield, Apothem, Breadth, Coss, Declination, Eloi(g)n, Elongation, Farness, Focal, Foot, Headreach, Height, Hyperfocal, Intercalumniation, Interval, Klick, Kos(s), Latitude, League, Length, Maintenance, Mean, Mean free path, Middle, Mileage, Northing, Ordinate, Outland, Parasang, Parsec, Range, Reserve, Rod, Skip, Span, Spitting, Stade, Striking, Way, Yojan, Zenith

Distant Aloof, Cold, Far, Frosty, Hyperfocal, Icy, Long, Northing, Offish, Outland, Polar, Remote, Tele-, Timbuctoo, Timbuktu, Yonder

Distaste(ful) Dégoût, Gross-out, Repugnant, Ropy, Scunner, Unpalatable, Unpleasant, Unsavoury

Distemper Ailment, Colourwash, Equine, Hard-pad, Paint, Panleucopenia, Pip, Tempera

Distend(ed), Distension Bloat, Dilate, Ectasia, Emphysema, Expand, Hoove, Inflate, Meteorism, → **STRETCH**, Swell, Turgid, Tympanites, Varicocele, Varicose

Distil(late), Distillation, Distiller, Distilling Alcohol, Alembic, Anthracine, Azeotrope, Brew, Condense, Destructive, Drip, Fractional, Naphtha, Pelican, Pyrene, Pyroligneous, Rosin, Turps, Vacuum, Vapour

▷ **Distillation** *may indicate* an anagram

Distinct(ive) Apparent, Characteristic, Clear, Determinate, Different, Discrete, Evident, Grand, Individual, Peculiar, Plain, Separate, Several, Signal, → **SPECIAL**, Stylistic, Trenchant, Vivid

Distinction Beaut(y), Blue, Cachet, Credit, Diacritic, Difference, Dignity, Diorism, Disparity, Division, Eclat, Eminence, Honour, Lustre, Mark, Mystique, Nicety, Note, Nuance, OM, Prominence, Quiddity, Rank, Renown, Speciality, Style, Title

Distinguish(ed), Distinguishing Classify, Contrast, Demarcate, Denote, Diacritic, Different(iate), Discern, Discriminate, Divide, Elevate, Eximious, Mark, Nameworthy, Notable, Perceive, Pick out, Prestigious, Prominent, Rare, Renowned, Secern, Signal, Stamp, Tell

▷ **Distort(ed)** *may indicate* an anagram

Distort(ion), Distorted Anamorphosis, Bend, Bias, Colour, Contort, Deface, Deform, Dent, Fudge, Garble, Helium speech, Jaundiced, Mangle, Misshapen, Pervert, Rubato, Stretch, Thraw, Time-warp, Travesty, Twist, → **WARP**, Wow, Wrest, Wring, Wry

Distract(ed), Distraction Absent, Agitate, Amuse, Avocation, Bewilder, Divert, Embroil, Éperdu, Forhaile, Frenetic, Lost, Madden, Mental, Nepenthe, Perplex, Scatty, Sidetrack, Sledge, Upstage

▷ **Distract(ed)** *may indicate* an anagram

Distrain(t) Na(a)m, Poind, Sequestrate, Stress

Distraught Deranged, Elfish, Elvan, Frantic, Mad, Troubled

Distress(ed), Distressing Afflict, Ail, Alack, Alopecia, Anger, Anguish, Antique, Crise, Distraint, Dolour, Exigence, Extremity, Grieve, Harass, Harrow, Heartbreak, Hurt, Ill, → **IN DISTRESS**, Irk, Misease, Misfortune, Need, Oppress, Pain, Poignant, Prey, Sad, Shorn, Sore, SOS, Straiten, Straits, Tole, Tragic, Traumatic, Tribulation, → **TROUBLE**, Une(a)th, Unstrung

Distribute(d), Distribution, Distributor Allocate, Allot, Binomial, Busbar, Carve, Chi-square, Colportage, Deal, Deliver(y), Deploy, Dish, Dispense, Dispose, Exponential, F, Frequency, Gamma, Gaussian, Geographical, Geometric, Issue, Lie, Lot, Mete, Normal, Out, Pattern, Poisson, Prorate, Renter, Repartition, Send out, Serve, Share, Strew

▷ **Distributed** *may indicate* an anagram

District Alsatia, Amhara, Arcadia, Ards, Area, Arrondissement, Bail(l)iwick, Banat, Banate, Bannat, Barrio, Belt, Canton, Cantred, Circar, Classis, Community, Congressional, Diocese, Encomienda, End, Exurb, Falernian, Federal, Fitzrovia, Gau, Ghetto, Hundred, Land, Lathe, Liberty, Locality, Loin, Manor, Metropolitan, Nasik, → **NEIGHBOURHOOD**, Oblast, Pachalic, Pale, Pargana, Parish(en), Paroch, Pashalik, Patch, Peak, Pergunnah, Phocis, Precinct, Province, Quarter, Quartier, Rape, → **REGION**, Ride, Riding, Ruhr, Rural, Sanjak, Section, Sheading, Sircar, Sirkar, Soc, Soke(n), Stake, Stannary, Suburb, Sucken, Talooka, Taluk, Tenderloin, Township, Urban, Venue, Vicinage, Walk, Wapentake, Way, Wealden, Zila, Zillah, Zone

Distrust(ful) Caution, Doubt, Misanthropic, Misfaith, Suspect, Wariness

Disturb(ance), Disturbed, Disturbing Ado, Aerate, Affray, Agitate, Aggrieve, Atmospherics, Autism, Betoss, Brabble, Brainstorm, Brash, Brawl, Broil, Carfuffle, Collieshangie, Concuss, Delirium, Dementia, Derange, Desecrate, Disquiet, Dust, Dysfunction, Feeze, Firestorm, Fracas, Fray, Fret, Harass, Hoopla, Incident, Incommode, Infest, Interrupt, Intrude, Jee, Kerfuffle, Kick-up, Kurfuffle, Macabre, Muss, Outbreak, Perturb(ation), Prabble, Rammy, Ramp, Riot, Ripple, Romage, Rook, Roughhouse, Rouse, Ruckus, Ruction, Ruffle, Rumpus, Shake, Shellshock, Shindig, Shindy, Shook-up, Stashie, Static, Steer, Stir, Sturt, Tremor, Trouble, Turbulent, Unquiet, Unrest, Unsettle, Upheaval, Uproot, → **UPSET**, Vex

▷ **Disturb(ed)** *may indicate* an anagram

Disunite Alienate, Dissever, Divide, Divorce, Split

Disuse Abandon, Abeyance, Desuetude, Discard, Lapse

Ditch Abolish, Barathron, Barathrum, Channel, Chuck, Crash-land, Cunette, Delf, Delph, Dike, Discard, Donga, Drainage, Drop, Dyke, Euripus, Foss(e), Graft, Grip, Gully, Ha(w)-ha(w), Jettison, Khor, Level, Lode, Moat, Na(l)la(h), Nulla(h), Rean, Reen, Rhine, Rid, Sea, Sheuch, Sheugh, Sike, Sloot, Sluit, Spruit, Stank, Sunk-fence, Syke, Trench

Dither(ing) Agitato, Bother, Dicker, Faff, Hesitate, Indecisive, Pussyfoot, Twitter

Dittany Gas-plant

Ditty, Ditties Air, Arietta, Canzonet, Departmental, Jingle, Lay, Song

Diuretic Frusemide, Furosemide, Spironolactone

Diva Callas, Patti, Singer

Divan Compilement, Congress, Couch, Council, Settee, Sofa

Dive(r), Diving Armstand, Backflip, Belly-flop, Crash, Dart, Den, Duck, File, Full-gainer, Half-gainer, Header, Honkytonk, Jackknife, Joint, Ken, Nitery, Nose, Pass, Pickpocket, Pike, Plummet, Plunge, Plutocrat, Power, Saturation, Scoter, Skin, Sound, Stage, Steep-to, Stoop, Submerge, Swallow, Swan, Swoop, Tailspin, Urinant, Urinator

Diver(s) Didapper, Duck, Embergoose, Flop, Frogman, Gainer, Grebe, Guillemot, Loom, Loon, Lungie, Many, Merganser, Pearl, Pike, Plong(e), Pochard, Poker, Puffin, Sawbill, Scuba, Snake-bird, Speakeasy, Sundry, Urinator, Various, Zoom

Diverge(nce) Branch, Deviate, Divaricate, Spread, Swerve, Variant, Veer

Divers Miscellaneous, Some

Diverse, Diversify Alter, Branch out, Chequer, Dapple, Different, Eclectic, Interlard, Intersperse, Manifold, Motley, Multifarious, Separate, Variegate, Various, Vary

Diversion, Divert(ing) Amuse, Avocation, Beguile, Cone, Deflect, Detour, Disport, Dissuade, Distract, Entertain, Game, Hare, Hive off, Hobby, Interlude, Pastime, Pleasure, Prolepsis, Ramp, Red-herring, Refract, Reroute, Ruse, Shunt, Sideshow, Sidetrack, Siphon, Smokescreen, Sport, Stalking-horse, Steer, Stratagem, Sublimation, Sway, Switch, Syphon, Tickle, Upstage, Yaw

▷ **Diverting** *may indicate* an anagram

Divest Denude, Rid, Strip, Undeck, Undress

Divide(d), Divider, Divisible, Division Abkhazia, Adzharia, Amitosis, Angiosperm, Apportion, Arcana, Arm, Arrondissement, Bajocian, Balk, Banat(e), Band, Bannet, Bar, Bipartite, Bisect, Bizone, Branch, Brome, Caesura, Canto, Canton, Cantle, Cantred, Cantref, Cassini's, Caste, Category, Cell, Champart, Chancery, Chapter, Classification, Cleft, Cloison, Clove, Comitatus, Comminute, Commot(e), Commune, Compartment, Continental, Coralline Crag, Corps, County, Counter-pale, Crevasse, Curia, Cut, Deal, Demerge, Department, Dichotomy, Digital, Dimidiate, Disagreement, Dissever, Disunity, Duan, Estrange, Eyalet, Family, Farren, Fissile, Fork, Fragmentation, Great, Grisons, Guberniya, Gulf, Gulph, Hapu, Hedge, Hide, Hundred, Indent, Inning, Isogloss, Keuper, Kim(m)eridgian, Lathe, Leet, Legion, Lindsey, List, Lobe, Long, M(e)iosis, Mitosis, Mofussil, Nome, Pachytene, Parcel, Pargana, Part, Partition, Partitive, Party wall, Passus, Pentomic, Pergunnah, Period, Phatry, Phyle, Phylum, Pipe, Pitaka, Platoon, Plebs, Polarisation, Polarise, Potential, Presidency, Province, Queen's Bench, Quotation, Ramify, Rape, Red Crag, Reduction, Region, Rend, Reservation, Riding, Rift, Sanjak, Schism, Section, Sector, Sectionalise, Segment, Semeion, Separate, Sep(tate), Sever, Share, Sheading, Shed, Shire, Short, → SPLIT, Stage, Stake, Stanza, Subheading, Suborder, Sunder, Tahsil, Tanach, Taxis, Telophase, Tepal, Thanet, Trichotomy, Tribalism, Trio, Trisect, Trivium, Troop, Tuath, Unit, Utgard, Vilayet, Volost, Voltage, Wapentake, Ward, Watershed, Zone.

Dividend Bonus, Div, Interim, Into, Peace, Share

Divination, Diviner Anthroposcopy, Arithmancy, Augury, Auspices, Axinomancy, Belomancy, Bibliomancy, Botanomancy, Capnomancy, Cartomancy, Ceromancy, Chiromancy, Cleromancy, Coscinomancy, Crithomancy, Crystal-gazing, Crystallomancy, Doodlebug, Dowser, Empyromancy, Gastromancy, Geloscopy, Geomancy, Gyromancy, Hariolation, Haruspex, Hepatoscopy, Hieromancy, Hieroscopy, Hydromancy, I Ching, Intuition, Lampadomancy, Leconomancy, Lithomancy, Magic, Mantic, Myomancy, Omphalomancy, Oneiromancy, Onphalomancy, Onychomancy, Ornithomancy, Ornithoscopy, Osteomancy, Palmistry, Pegomancy, Pessomancy, Pyromancy, Radiesthesia, Rhabdomancy, Scapulimancy, Scapulomancy, Sciomancy, Seer, Sibyl, Sideromancy, Sortes, Sortilege, Spae(man), Spodomancy, Taghairm, Tais(c)h, Tephromancy, Theomancy, Tripudiary, Vaticanator, Xylomancy, Zoomancy

Divine, Divine presence, Divinity Acoemeti, Ambrose, Atman, Avatar, Beatific, Celestial, Clergyman, Conjecture, Curate, DD, Deduce, Deity, Douse, Dowse, Ecclesiastic, Forecast, Foretell, Fuller, → GOD, → GODDESS, Godhead, Guess, Hariolate, Heavenly, Holy, Hulse, Immortal, Inge, Isiac, Kami, Mantic, Numen,

Numinous, Olympian, Pontiff, Predestinate, Predict, Presage, Priest, Prophesy, RE, Rector, RI, Rimmon, Scry, Sense, Seraphic, Shechinah, Shekinah, Spae, Superhuman, Supernal, Theandric, Theanthropic, Theologise, Theology, Triune

Divisor Aliquant, Aliquot

Divorce(d) Alienate, Diffarreation, Disaffiliate, Dissolve, Disunion, Div, Estrange, Get(t), Part, Separate, Sequester, → **SUNDER**, Talak, Talaq

Divot Clod, Sod, Turf

Divulge Confess, Disclose, Expose, Publish, Reveal, Split, Tell, Unveil, Utter

DIY Flatpack

Dizziness, Dizzy Beaconsfield, Ben, Capricious, Dinic, Disraeli, Giddy, Giglot, Lightheaded, Mazey, Mirligoes, Scotodinia, Scotomania, Swimming, Vertiginous, → **VERTIGO**, Woozy

DJ Deejay, Mixmaster, Monkey-suit, Penguin suit, Presenter, Selecta, Shockjock, Tuxedo, Veejay

DNA Adenine, Antisense, Centromere, Chromatin, Cistron, Codon, Complementary, Cytosine, Exon, Gene, Heteroduplex, Homopolymer, Intron, Junk, Microsatellite, Mitochondrial, Muton, Nucleosome, Operator, Papovavirus, Plasmid, Polyoma, Poxvirus, Procaryote, Profiling, Prokaryote, Purine, Recombinant, Replication fork, Replicon, Retrotransposon, RNA, Satellite, Selfish, Southern blot, Synthetic, Telomere, Thymidine, Transcript(ion), Transfection, Transfer, Translation, Transposon, Vector, Watson-Crick model

▷ **Do** *may indicate* an anagram

Do(es), Doing Accomplish, Achieve, Act, Anent, Banquet, Beano, Begin, Blow-out, Char, Cheat, Chisel, Cod, Con, Cozen, Deed, Dich, Dish, Div, Doth, Dupe, Effectuate, Enact, Execute, Fare, Fleece, Function, Fuss, Gull, Handiwork, Hoax, Mill, Perform, Provide, Same, Serve, Settle, Shindig, Spif(f)licate, Suffice, Swindle, Thrash, Thrive, Tonic, Ut

Do away Abolish, Banish, Demolish, Kill

Dobbie Elf, Fairy

Docile Agreeable, Amenable, Biddable, Dutiful, Facile, Meek, Submissive, Tame, Tractable, Yielding

Dock(er), Docked, Docks Abridge, Barber, Basin, Bistort, Bob, Camber, Canaigre, Clip, Crop, Curta(i)l, Cut, Deduct, De-tail, Dry, Floating, Grapetree, Graving, Knotweed, Lay-up, Longshoreman, Lop, Lumper, Marina, Moor, Off-end, Pare, Patience, Pen, Pier, Quay, Rhubarb, Rumex, Rump, Scene, Seagull, Shorten, Snakeweed, Sorrel, Sourock, Stevedore, Tilbury, Watersider, Wet, Wharf, Wharfie, Yard

Docket Invoice, Label, Tag

Dockyard Arsenal, Rosyth

▷ **Doctor(ed)** *may indicate* an anagram

Doctor(s) Allopath, Alter, Arnold, Asclepiad, Barefoot, Barnardo, Bleeder, BMA, Bones, Breeze, Bright, Brighton, Brown, Caius, Castrate, Chapitalize, Clinician, Cook, Crocus, Cup(per), Cure(r), Dale, Diagnose, Dr, Dryasdust, Erasmus, Extern(e), Fake, Falsify, Family, Faustus, Feldsher, Fell, Fiddle, Finlay, Flying, Foster, Fundholder, Galen, Geriatrician, Geropiga, GP, Hakeem, Hakim, Healer, Homeopath, Houseman, Hyde, Imhotep, Intern, Internist, Jekyll, Jenner, Johnson, Kildare, Lace, Leach, Leech, Linacre, Load, Locum, Luke, Manette, Massage, MB, MD, Medicate, Medico, Mganga, Middleton, Mindererus, Minister, Misrepresent, MO, MOH, Molla(h), Moreau, Mulla(h), Neuter, No, Ollamh, Ollav, Paean, Paediatrician, Panel, Pangloss, Paracelsus, Paramedic, Pedro, PhD, Physician, Pill(s), Practitioner, Quack, Quacksalver, Rabbi, RAMC, Registrar, Resident, Rig,

Rorschach, Salk, Sangrado, Saw, Sawbones, School, Script, Seraphic, Seuss, Shaman, Slammer, Slop, Spay, Spin, Stum, Surgeon, Syn, Syntax, Thorne, Treat, Vaidya, Vet, Water, Watson, Who, Wind, Witch

Doctrine Adoptianism, Adoptionism, Antinomian, Apollinarian, Archology, Arianism, Averr(h)oism, Bonism, Brezhnev, Cab(b)ala, Cacodoxy, Calvanism, Catastrophism, Chiliasm, Consubstantiation, Credo, Creed, Determinism, Diabology, Ditheism, Ditheletism, Docetism, Dogma, Doxie, Doxy, Dualism, Dysteleology, Encratism, Eschatology, Esotery, Febronianism, Federalism, Fideism, Finalism, Functionalism, Gnosticism, Gospel, Henotheism, Holism, Idealism, Immaterialism, Immersionism, Indeterminism, Infralapsarianism, Islam, Ism, Jansenism, Krypsis, Laches, Lore, Machtpolitik, Malthusian, Manich(a)eism, Materialism, Metempsychosis, Modalism, Molinism, Monadism, Monergism, Monism, Monothel(et)ism, Monroe, Neomonianism, Nestorianism, Neutral monism, Nihilism, Panentheism, Pantheism, Pelagianism, Physiocracy, Pluralism, Pragmatism, Predestination, Premillennialism, Preterition, Probabilism, Psilanthropism, Pythagorean(ism), Quietism, Real presence, Reformism, Satyagrahi, Scotism, Secularism, Sharia, Sheria, Shibboleth, Solidism, Strong meat, Subjectivism, Sublapsarianism, Subpanation, Substantialism, Swedenborgianism, Syndicalism, Synergism, System, Teleology, → **TENET**, Terminism, Theory, Theravada, Thomism, Transubstantiation, Trialism, Tridentine, Tutiorism, Universalism, Utilitarianism, Voluntarism, Wasm, Weismannism, Whiteboyism, Zoism, Zwinglian

Document(s), Documentary Blog, Brevet, Bumf, Bumph, Carta, Certificate, Charge sheet, Charter, Chop, Contract, Conveyance, Covenant, Daftar, Deed, Diploma, Docket, Doco, Dompass, Dossier, Escrow, Fiat, Form, Grand Remonstrance, Holograph, Latitat, Logbook, Mandamus, Offer, Papers, Policy, Precept, Production, Pro forma, Public, Ragman, Ragment, Record, Resort, Roll, Roul(e), Screed, Sea brief, Source, Stamp note, Voucher, Warrant, Waybill, Weblog, Webpage, Writ, Write up

Dod Pet, Poll

Dodder(y) Old, Shake, Stagger, Strangleweed, Totter, Tremble

Doddle Easy

Dodge, Dodgy Artful, Avoid, Bell-ringing, Column, Elude, Evade, Evasion, Evite, Iffy, Jink, Jook, Jouk, Racket, Ruse, Shirk, Sidestep, Skip, Slalom, Slinter, Tip, Trick, Twist, Urchin, Weave, Welsh, Wheeze, Wire, Wrinkle

Doe(s) Deer, Faun, Hind

Doff Avail(e), Avale, Remove, Rouse, Shed, Tip

Dog(s), Doglike Assistance, Bowwow, Canes, Canidae, Canine, Cerberus, Cynic, Feet, Fire, Fog, Gelert, Guard, Guide, Hearing, Hot, Huntaway, Hunter, Kennel, Lassie, Leading, Mutt, Native, Nodding, Pluto, Police, Pooch, Pursue, Ratter, Rover, Sea, Search, Seeing-eye, Shadow, Shaggy, Shin-barker, Sirius, Sleeve, Sleuthhound, Sniffer, Spotted, Stalk, Strong-eye, Sun, Tag, Tail, Tike, Top, Toto, Touser, Towser, Tracker, Trail, Truffle, Tumbler, Turnspit, Tyke, Wammul, Water, Water dog, Whelp, Whiffet, Working, Yapper, Yapster, Yellow

---

DOGS

3 letters:	Pig	Yap	Bird
Cur	Pom		Brak
Eye	Pug	*4 letters:*	Bran
Gun	Rab	Barb	Bush

4 letters – cont:
Cant
Chow
Dane
Fido
Heel
Iron
Kuri
Kuta
Kuti
Leam
Lyam
Oath
Peke
Puli
Rach
Sled
Stag
Toby
Tosa
Tray
Wolf

5 letters:
Akita
Alans
Apsos
Argos
Boots
Boxer
Brach
Cairn
Coach
Dhole
Dingo
Haunt
Hound
Husky
Hyena
Kurre
Laika
Lorel
Luath
Merle
Moera
Pidog
Rache
Ratch
Shock
Spitz
Spoor

Zorro

6 letters:
Afghan
Bandog
Barbet
Barker
Basset
Beagle
Bitser
Blanch
Borzoi
Bounce
Bowler
Briard
Caesar
Canaan
Chenet
Cocker
Collie
Coyote
Dangle
Eskimo
Goorie
Heeler
Jackal
Katmir
Kelpie
Kennet
Ketmir
Kratim
Mauthe
Messan
Moppet
Pariah
Piedog
Poodle
Pye-dog
Ranger
Saluki
Setter
Shough
Sothic
Talbot
Teckel
Vizsla
Westie
Yorkie

7 letters:
Andiron

Basenji
Bobbery
Boerbul
Bouvier
Brachet
Bulldog
Coondog
Courser
Griffon
Harrier
Iceland
Lowchen
Lurcher
Maltese
Maremma
Mastiff
Mongrel
Orthrus
Pointer
Prairie
Raccoon
Reynard
Samoyed
Sapling
Sausage
Shar-Pei
Sheltie
Shih tzu
Showghe
Sloughi
Spaniel
Starter
→ **TERRIER**
Volpino
Whippet

8 letters:
Aardwolf
Aberdeen
Airedale
Alsatian
Blenheim
Bouvrier
Bratchet
Brittany
Carriage
Chow-chow
Doberman
Elkhound
Hovawart
Kangaroo

Keeshond
Komondor
Labrador
Landseer
Malamute
Malemute
Papillon
Pekinese
Pembroke
Pinscher
Samoyede
Sealyham
Sheepdog
Springer
Warragal
Warrigal

9 letters:
Buckhound
Chihuahua
Coonhound
Dachshund
Dalmatian
Deerhound
Dobermann
Draghound
Gazehound
Great Dane
Greyhound
Harlequin
Kerry blue
Lhasa apso
Molossian
Pekingese
Retriever
Schnauzer
Staghound
Wolfhound

10 letters:
Bedlington
Bloodhound
Blueheeler
Fox terrier
Otterhound
Pomeranian
Rottweiler
Schipperke
Tripehound
Weimaraner

11 letters:	Water spaniel	Brussels griffon	Dobermann-
Bichon frise	Welsh terrier	Estreia mountain	pinscher
Irish setter	West Highland	Hamilton stovare	
Jack Russell		Mexican hairless	*18 letters:*
Labradoodle	*13 letters:*	Norwegian buhund	Large
Montmorency	Affenpinscher	Portuguese water	Munsterlander
Skye terrier	Dandie Dinmont	Swedish vallhund	Old English
Tibetan apso	Scotch terrier		sheepdog
Trendle-tail	Sussex spaniel	*16 letters:*	Rhodesian
Trindle-tail		Australian cattle	ridgeback
Trundle-tail	*14 letters:*	Doberman-pinscher	
Wishtonwish	Italian spinone	Lancashire heeler	*20 letters:*
	Norwich terrier	Pyrenean mountain	Landseer
12 letters:	Tibetan mastiff	Russian wolfhound	Newfoundland
Border collie	Tibetan spaniel	Shetland sheepdog	
Gazelle hound	Tibetan terrier		*21 letters:*
Japanese chin		*17 letters:*	Polish Lowland
Newfoundland	*15 letters:*	Anatolian Shepherd	sheepdog
Saint Bernard	Bernese mountain		

Dog-bane Apocynum

Doge Dandolo

Dogfish Huss, Rigg, Rock salmon

Dogged Determined, Die-hard, Dour, Indefatigable, Pertinacious, Stubborn, Sullen, Tenacious

Doggerel Cramboclink, Crambo-jingle, Laisse, Rat-rhyme

Dog letter R

Dogma(tic) Assertive, Belief, Conviction, Creed, Doctrinal, En têté, Ideology, Ipse dixit, Opinionative, Pedagogic, Peremptory, Pontifical, Positive, → TENET

Do-gooder Piarist, Reformer, Salvationist, Samaritan, Scout

Dogsbody Bottle-washer, Gofer, Skivvy

Dog star Canicula, Lassie, Sirius, Sothic

Do it Dich

Dolce Stop, Sweet

Dole Alms, Batta, B(u)roo, Give, Grief, Maundy, Payment, Pittance, Pog(e)y, Ration, → SHARE, Tichborne, Vail, Vales

Doleful Sombre

Doll(y) Barbie®, Bobblehead, Bimbo, Common, Corn, Creeper, Crumpet, Dress, Dutch, Golliwog, Kachina, Kewpie®, Maiden, Marionette, Matryoshka, Maumet, Mommet, Moppet, Mummet, Ookpik®, Ornament, Paris, Parton, Pean, Peen, Peggy, Pein, Pene, Poppet, Puppet, Ragdoll, Russian, Sindy®, Sis(ter), Sitter, Tearsheet, Toy, Trolley, Varden, Washboard, Wax

Dollar(s) Balboa, Boliviano, Buck, Cob, Cob money, Euro, Fin, Greenback, Iron man, Peso, Petrol, Piastre, Pink, S, Sand, Sawbuck, Sawhorse, Scrip, Smacker, Spin, Sword, Top, Wheel

Dollop Glob, Helping, Share

▷ **Dolly** *may indicate* an anagram

Dolly-bird Dish

Dolly Varden Hat

Dolour Grief, Pain, Sorrow

Dolphin Amazon, Arion, Beluga, Bottlenose, Cetacean, Coryphene, Delphinus,

Grampus, Lampuka, Lampuki, Mahi-mahi, Meer-swine, Porpess(e), Risso's, River, Sea-pig

Dolt Ass, Blockhead, Clodhopper, Noodle, Oaf, Ouph(e), Owl, → **STUPID**

Domain Archaea, Bacteria, Bourn(e), Demain, Demesne, Eminent, Emirate, Empire, Estate, Eukarya, Manor, Predicant, Public, Rain, Realm, Region, Reign, Starosty

Dome(-shaped) Al-Aqsa, Bubble, Cap, Cupola, Cupula, Dagoba, Geodesic, Head, Imperial, Louvre, Millennium, Onion, Periclinal, Rotunda, Salt, Stupa, Tee, Tholos, Tholus, Tope, Vault, Xanadu

Domestic(ate) Char, Cleaner, Dom, Esne, Familiar, Home-keeping, Homely, House, Housetrain, Humanise, Interior, Internal, Intestine, Maid, Menial, → **SERVANT**, Swadeshi, Tame, Woman

Domicile Abode, Dwelling, Hearth, Home, Ménage

Dominate, Dominance, Dominant, Domination Ascendancy, Baasskap, Ballbreaker, Bethrall, Boss, Clou, Coerce, Control, Enslave, Hegemony, Henpeck, Maisterdome, Mesmerise, Momism, Monopolise, O(v)ergang, Overmaster, Override, Overshadow, Power, Preponderant, Preside, Rule, Soh, → **SUBDUE**, Subjugate, Top dog, Tower

Domineer(ing) Authoritarian, Boss, Henpeck, Lord, Ride, Swagger, Tyrannize

Dominica(n) Jacobite, Monk, OP, Preaching friar, Predicant, Savonarola, WD

Dominie Maister, Master, Pastor, Sampson, Schoolmaster

Dominion Dom, Empire, Khanate, NZ, Realm, Reame, Reign, → **RULE**, Supremacy, Sway, Territory

Domino(es) Card, Fats, Mask, Matador

Don Academic, Address, Assume, Caballero, Camorrist, Endue, Fellow, Garb, Giovanni, Indew, Juan, Lecturer, Mafia, Prof, Quixote, Reader, Señor, Spaniard, Tutor, Wear

Dona(h) Duckie, Love

Donate, Donation Aid, Bestow, Contribution, Gift, Give, Peter's pence, Present, Wakf, Waqf

Done Achieved, Complete, Crisp, Ended, Executed, Had, Over, Spitcher, Tired, Weary

Donjon Dungeon, Keep

Donkey Ass, Burro, Cardophagus, Cuddie, Cuddy, Dapple, Dick(e)y, Dunce, Eeyore, Funnel, Fussock, Genet(te), Jackass, Jennet, Jenny, Jerusalem pony, Kulan, Modestine, Moke, Mule, Neddy, Nodding, Onager, Stupid, Years

Donor Benefactor, Bestower, Settlor, Universal

Doo Dove

Doodle(r) Scribble, Yankee

Doodlebug Antlion, Larva, V1

Doofer Thingumabob

Doom(ed) Condemned, Damnation, Date, Destine, Destiny, → **FATE**, Fay, Fey, Fie, Goner, Ill-starred, Lot, Predestine, Preordain, Ragnarok, Ruined, Sentence, Spitcher, Star-crossed, Weird

Doone Carver, Lorna

Door(s), Doorstep, Doorway Aperture, Communicating, Damnation, Drecksill, Dutch, Elephant, Entry, Exit, Fire, Folding, Front, Gull-wing, Haik, Hake, Hatch, Heck, Ingress, Jib, Lintel, Louver, Louvre, Muntin, Oak, Open, Overhead, Patio, Portal, Postern, Revolving, Rory, Screen, Sliding, Stable, Stage, Storm, Street, Swing, Tailgate, Trap, Up and over, Vomitory, Wicket, Yett

Doorkeeper, Doorman Bouncer, Commissionaire, Concierge, Guardian, Janitor,

Nab, Ostiary, Porter, Tiler, Tyler, Usher

Doormat Subservient, Weakling

Doorpost Architrave, Dern, Durn, Jamb, Yate, Yett

Dope Acid, Amulet, Bang, Coke, Crack, → **DRUG**, Gen, Goose, Info, Lowdown, Narcotic, Nitwit, Nobble, Rutin, Sedate, Soup, → **STUPID PERSON**, Tea

Doppelganger Double, Ringer

Dorcas Gazelle, Needle, Shepherdess

Dorian, Doric Metope, Mutule

Doris Day, Lessing, Mollusc

Dormant Abed, Comatose, Hibernating, Inactive, Inert, Joist, Latent, Quiescent, Resting, → **SLEEPING**, Torpescent

Dormer Luthern

Dormitory Barrack, Bunkhouse, Dorter, Dortour, Hall, Hostel, Quarters

Dormouse Loir

Dorothy Bag, Dot, Sayers

Dorsal Back, Neural, Notal

Dory Fish, John

Dosage, Dose Absorbed, Acute, Administer, Aperient, Booster, Cascara, Cumulative, Drachm, Draught, Drench, Drug, Fix, Hit, Kilogray, Lethal, → **MEASURE**, Permissible, Physic, Posology, Potion, Powder, Rem, Standing off, Threshold, Tolerance

Doss (house) Dharmsala, Dharmshala, Kip, Padding-ken, Spike

Dossier File, Record

Dot(s), Dotted, Dotty Absurd, Bind(h)i, Bullet, Centred, Criblé, Dieresis, Dit, Dower, Dowry, Ellipsis, Engrailed, Leader, Lentiginous, Limp, Micro, Morse, Occult, Or, Particle, Pinpoint, Pixel, → **POINT**, Pointillé, Polka, Precise, Punctuate, Punctulate, Punctum, Schwa, Semé(e), Set, Speck, Spot, Sprinkle, Stigme, Stipple, Stud, Tap, Tittle, Trema, Umlaut

Dote, Dotage, Doting, Dotard Adore, Anile, Anility, Cocker, Dobbie, Idolise, Imbecile, Pet, Prize, Senile, Spoon(e)y, Tendre, Twichild

Double(s) Amphibious, Ancipital, Bi-, Bifold, Binate, Clone, Counterpart, Crease, Dimeric, Doppel-ganger, Doppio, Dual, Duo, Duple(x), Duplicate, Equivocal, Fetch, Fold, Foursome, Geminate, Gimp, Image, Ingeminate, Ka, Look-alike, Loop, Martingale, Pair, Parlay, Polyseme, Reflex, Replica, Ringer, Run, Similitude, Spit, Stuntman, Trot, Turnback, Twae, → **TWIN**, Two(fold)

Double-barrelled Tautonym

Double-cross, Double dealing Ambidext(e)rous, Two-time

Double-entendre Polyseme, Polysemy

Doublet Peascod, Pourpoint, TT

Doubt(s), Doubter, Doubtful Agnostic, Ambiguous, Aporia, Askance, But, Debatable, Discredit, Distrust, Dubiety, Dubitate, Hesitate, Hum, Iffy, Incertitude, Misgiving, Mistrust, → **NO DOUBT**, Or, Precarious, Qualm, Query, → **QUESTION**, Rack, Scepsis, Sceptic, Scruple, Second thoughts, Shady, Shy, Sic, Skepsis, Sus, Suspect, Suspicious, Suss, Thomas, Thos, Umph, Uncertain, Unsure, Waver

Doubtless Certain, Iwis, Probably, Sure, Truly, Ywis

Douceur Bonus, Sop, Sweetener

Douche Bath, Gush, Rinse, Shower, Wash

Dough(y) Boodle, Cake, Calzone, Cash, Duff, Gnocchi, Hush-puppy, Knish, Loot, Magma, Masa, Money, Paste, Pop(p)adum, Ready, Sad, Sour, Spondulicks, Strudel

Doughboy Dumpling, Soldier

Doughnut Bagel, Beavertail®, Cruller, Fried cake, Knish, Koeksister, Olycook,

Olykoek, Sinker, Torus

Doughty Brave, Intrepid, Resolute, Stalwart, Valiant

Dour Glum, Hard, Mirthless, Morose, Reest, Reist, Sinister, Sullen, Taciturn

Douse Dip, Drench, Extinguish, Snuff, Splash

Dove Collared, Columbine, Culver, Cushat, Diamond, Doo, Ground, Ice-bird, Mourning, Pacifist, → **PIGEON**, Queest, Quoist, Ring, Rock, Stock, Turtle

Dove-cot(e) Columbarium, Columbary, Louver, Louvre, Lover

Dovetail Fit, Interosculate, Lewis(son), Mortise, Tally, Tenon

Dowager Elder, Widow

Dowdy Frumpish, Mopsy, Mums(e)y, Plain Jane, Shabby, Sloppy, Slovenly

Dowel Peg, Pin

Down(s), Downbeat, Downsize, Downward, Downy A bas, Abase, Abattu, Alow, Amort, Bank, Below, Berkshire, Blue, Cast, Catabasis, Chapfallen, Comous, Cottony, Crouch, Darling, Dejected, Dowl(e), Drink, Epsom, Feather, Fledge, Floccus, Flue, Fluff, Fly, Fuzz, Goonhilly, Ground, Hair, Hill, Humble, Humiliate, Jeff, Kennet, Lanugo, Losing, Low, Lower, Miserable, Moxa, Nap, Neck, Oose, Ooze, Owing, Pappus, Pennae, Pile, Plumage, Powder, Quark, Quash, Repress, Scuttle, Sebum, Slim, Thesis, Thistle, Tomentum, Under, Unserviceable, Urinant, Vail, Wold, Wretched

Downcast Abject, Chapfallen, Despondent, Disconsolate, Dumpish, Hangdog, Hopeless, Melancholy, Woebegone

Downfall, Downpour Cataract, Collapse, Deluge, Fate, Flood, Hail, Onding, Overthrow, Rain, Ruin, Shower, Thunder-plump, Torrent, Undoing, Waterspout

Downgrade(d) Déclassé, Disrate

Downright Absolute, Arrant, Bluff, Candid, Clear, Complete, Flat, Plumb, Plump, Pure, Rank, Sheer, Stark, Utter

Downstairs Below

Downstream Tail

Downturn Slump

Downwind Leeward

Dowry Dot, Dower, Lobola, Lobolo, Merchet, Portion, Settlement, Tocher

Dowse(r), Dowsing Divine, Enew, Fireman, Radionics, Rhabdomancy, Water-witch

Doxology Gloria, Glory

Doxy Harlot, Loose woman, Wench

Doyen Dean, Senior

Doze Catnap, Ca(u)lk, Dove(r), Nap, Nod, Semi-coma, Sleep, Slip, Slumber

Dozen(s) Baker's, Daily, Long, Round, Thr(e)ave, Twal, Twelve

Dr Debtor, Doctor, Dram

Drab Ash-grey, Cloth, Dell, Dingy, Dull, Dun, Ecru, Hussy, Isabel(line), Lifeless, Livor, Mumsy, Olive, Prosaic, Pussel, Quaker-colour, Rig, Road, Scarlet woman, Slattern, Sloven, Strumpet, Subfusc, Tart, Taupe, Trull, Wanton, Whore

Drabble Bemoil, Draggle

Dracula Bat, Count, Vampire

Draft Cheque, Draw, Ebauche, Essay, Landsturm, Minute, MS, Outline, Plan, Press, Project, Rough, Scheme, Scroll, Scrowle, → **SKETCH**

Drag Car, Clothing, Drail, Dredge, Drogue, Elicit, Eonism, Epicene, Extort, Fiscal, Form, Gender-bender, Hale, Harl, → **HAUL**, Induced, Keelhaul, La Rue, Lug, Nuisance, Parasite, Pressure, Profile, Puff, Pull, Rash, Sag, Schlep, Shockstall, Shoe, Skidpan, Sled, Snake, Snig, Sweep, Toke, Tote, Tow, Trail, Trailing vortex, Train, Travail, Travois, Trawl, Treck, Trek, Tug, Tump, Vortex

Draggle Drail, Lag, Straggle

Dragon Aroid, Basilisk, Bel, Bellemère, Chaperon(e), Chindit, Draco, Drake, Fafnir, Fire-drake, Gargouille, Komodo, Kung-kung, Ladon, Lindworm, Opinicus, Peist, Puk, Python, Rouge, Safat, Shrew, Typhoeus, Wantley, Wivern, Worm, Wyvern

Dragonfly Aeschna, Demoiselle, Devil's darning needle, Nymph, Odonata

Dragon's teeth Cadmus, Spartae, Sparti

Dragoon Coerce, Force, Press, Trooper

Drain(ed), Drainage, Draining, Drainpipe Bleed, Brain, Buzz, Can(n)ula, Catchment, Catchwater, Channel, Cloaca, Condie, Cundy, Cunette, Delf, Delph, Dewater, Ditch, Dry, Ea(u), → **EMPTY**, Emulge(nt), Exhaust, Field, Fleet, Grating, Grip, Gully, Gutter, Ketavothron, Kotabothron, Lade, Leach, Leech, Limber, Lose, Lymphatic, Milk, Mole, Nala, Nalla(h), Nulla(h), Penrose, Pump, Rack, Rone, Sanitation, Sap, Scalpins, Scupper, Seton, Sew(er), Sheuch, Sheugh, Shore, Silver, Sink, Siver, Sluice, Sluse, Soakaway, Sough, Spend, Stank, Storm, Sump, Sure, Syver, Tile, Trench, Trocar, Unwater, Ureter, U-trap, Weary, Well

Dram Drink, Drop, Nipperkin, Nobbler, Portion, Snifter, Tickler, Tiff, Tot, Wet

Drama(tic), Drama school Auto, Azione, Catastasis, Charade, Closet, Comedy, Costume, Drastic, Epic, ER, Eumenides, Farce, Heroic, Histrionic, Kabuki, Kathakali, Kitchen sink, Legit, Legitimate, Mask, Masque, Mime, Moralities, No, Nogaku, Noh, Piece, Play, RADA, Sangeet, Scenic, Sensational, Singspiel, Stagy, Striking, Tetralogy, Theatric, The Birds, Thespian, Tragedy, Unities, Wagnerian, Wild

Dramatist Adamov, Aeschylus, Albee, Aristophanes, Beaumarchais, Beaumont, Brecht, Bridie, Calderon, Congreve, Corneille, Coward, Drinkwater, Euripides, Fletcher, Frisch, Fry, Gay, Genet, Gogol, Goldoni, Havel, Ibsen, Ionesco, Jarry, Kyd, Lyly, Mamet, Massinger, Menander, Middleton, Molière, Odets, O'Neill, Orton, Osborne, Otway, Pinero, Pirandello, Plautus, → **PLAYWRIGHT**, Racine, Rostand, Rowe, Rowley, Schiller, Seneca, Shadwell, Shaffer, Sherriff, Sophocles, Stoppard, Strindberg, Synge, Terence, Udall, Vanbrugh, Voltaire, Von Klinger, Webster, Wedekind, Wesker, Wilde, Wilder, Will, → **WRITER**, Yeats

Dram-shop Bar, Boozingken, Bousingken

Drape(ry) Adorn, Coverlet, Coverlid, Curtain, Festoon, Fold, Hang, Lambrequin, Mantling, Swathe, Valance, Veil, Vest

Draper Clothier, Gilpin, Haberdasher, Hosier, Mercer, Outfitter, Ruth, Scotch cuddy, Tailor

Drastic Dire, Dramatic, Extreme, Harsh, Purge, Senna, → **SEVERE**, Swingeing, Violent

Drat Bother, Dang, Darn

▷ **Draught** *may refer to* fishing

Draught(s), Draughtsman(ship) Aloetic, Aver, Breeze, Dam, Dams, Design, Drench, Drink, Fish, Gulp, Gust, Haal, Hippocrene, King, Line, Men, Nightcap, Outline, Plan, Potation, Potion, Pull, Quaff, Sketch, Sleeping, Slug, Swig, Tracer, Up-current, Veronal, Waucht, Waught, Williewaught

Draught-board Dam-board, Dambrod

Dravidian Tamil

▷ **Draw** *may indicate* something to smoke

Draw (off), Drawer(s), Drawing, Drawn Adduct, Allure, Attract, Bleed, Blueprint, Bottom, Cartoon, Charcoal, Cityscape, Cock, Crayon, Dead-heat, Delineate, Dentistry, Derivation, Describe, Detail, Diagram, Dis(em)bowel, Doodle, Dr, Draft, Drag, Dress, Educe, Elevation, Elongate, Entice, Equalise,

Evaginate, Extract, Fet(ch), Freehand, Fusain, Gather, Gaunt, Glorybox, Goalless, Graphics, Gut, Haggard, Hale, Halve, Haul, Indraft, Induce, Indue, Inhale, Isometric, Lead, Lengthen, Limn, Line, Longbow, Lottery, Mechanical, Monotint, No-score, Orthograph, Pantalet(te)s, Panty, Pastel, Pen and ink, Perpetual check, Petroglyph, Profile, Protract, Pull, RA, Rack, Raffle, Realize, Reel, Remark, Scenography, Scent, Score, Seductive, Sepia, Sesquipedalian, Shottle, Shuttle, Silverpoint, Siphon, Sketch, Slub, Snig, Spin, Stalemate, Stretch, Study, Stumps, Sweepstake, Syphon, Tap, Taut, Technical, Tempt, Tenniel, Tie, Till, Toke, Tole, Tombola, Top, Tose, Tow(age), Toze, Traction, Trice, Troll, Tug, Unsheathe, Uplift, Wash, Working

Drawback Catch, Downside, Ebb, Handicap, Impediment, → **OBSTACLE**, Rebate, Retraction, Shrink, Snag

Drawbridge Bascule, Pontlevis

Drawl Dra(u)nt, Haw, Slur, Twang

▷ **Drawn** *may indicate* an anagram

Drawn up Atrip, Drafted

Dray Cart, Lorry, Wagon

Dread(ed) Angst, Anxiety, Awe, Fear, → **HORROR**, Nosophobia, Rasta, Redoubt, Thing

Dreadful Awful, Chronic, Dearn, Dern, Dire, Formidable, Funk, Ghastly, Horrendous, Penny, Sorry, Terrible, Unholy, Willies

Dream(er), Dream home, Dream state, Dreamy Aisling, Alchera, Alcheringa, American, Aspire, Castle, Desire, Drowsy, Dwalm, Dwa(u)m, Fantast, Fantasy, Faraway, Gerontius, Idealise, Illusion, Imagine, Languor, Long, Mare, Mirth, Moon, Morpheus, Muse, Nightmare, On(e)iric, Pensive, Phantasmagoria, Phantom, Pipe, → **REVERIE**, Rêveur, Romantic, Somniate, Spac(e)y, Stargazer, Surreal, Sweven, Trance, Trauma, Vague, Vision, Walter Mitty, Wet, Wool-gathering

Dreary Bleak, Desolate, Dismal, Doleful, Dreich, Dull, Gloom, Gousty, Gray, Grey, Oorie, Ourie, Owrie, Sad

Dredge(r) Caster, Scoop, Unearth

Dreg(s) Bottom, Draff, Dunder, F(a)eces, Fecula, Gr(e)aves, Grounds, Lag(s), Lees, Legge, Mother, Mud, Residue, Riffraff, Scaff, Sediment, Settlings, Silt, Snuff, Ullage

Dreikanter Ventifact

Drench Dowse, Sluice, Sluse, Soak, Souse, Steep, Submerge

Dress(ing), Dressed Academic, Accoutre, Adjust, Adorn, Aguise, Align, Ao dai, Array, Attire, Attrap, Bandage, Bandoline, Bedizen, Black-tie, Bloomer, Blouson, Boast, Bodice, Boun, Bowne, Brilliantine, Busk, Caftan, Cataplasm, Charpie, Cheongsam, Chimer, Cimar, Clad, Clericals, → **CLOTHING**, Coat, Cocktail, Comb, Compost, Compress, Corsage, Corset, Costume, Court, Curry, Cymar, Dandify, Dashiki, Deck, Deshabille, Dight, Dink, Dirndl, Dizen, Doll, Dolly Varden, Dolman, Don, Drag, Dub, Dubbin, Elastoplast®, Empire, Endue, Enrobe, Evening, Fancy, Far(r)andine, Farthingale, Fatigues, Ferrandine, Fertiliser, Fig, Finery, Flamenco, French, Frock, Full, Gamgee tissue, Garb, Garnish, Gauze, Girt, Gown, Graith, Granny, Guise, Gymslip, → **HABIT**, Highland, Ihram, Italian, Jaconet, Kabuki, Ketchup, K(h)anga, Kimono, Kirtle, Kitenge, Line, Lint, Lounger, Marie Rose, Maxi, Mayonnaise, Merveilleuse, Midi, Mineral, Mob, Morning, Mother Hubbard, Mufti, Mulch, Muu-muu, National, Oil, Ore, Patch, Peplos, Pinafore, Plaster, Pledget, Plumage, Polonaise, Pomade, Potash, Poultice, Power, Prank, Preen, Prepare, Princess (line), Rag, Raiment, Rainbow, Ranch, Rational, Ray, Rehearsal, Rémoulade, Rig, Robe, Russet, Russian, Rybat, Sack, Sacque, Salad, Salad cream,

Samfoo, Samfu, Sari, Sarong, Sartorial, Sauce, Scutch, Seloso, Separates, Sheath, Shift, Shirt, Shirtwaist(er), Simar(re), Smock, Sterile, Stole, Stupe, Subfusc, Subfusk, Suit, Sundress, Symar, Tartan, Tartare, Tasar, Taw, Tent, Tenue, Tew, Thousand Island, Tiff, Tire, Tog, Toga, Toilet, Tonic, Top, Treat, Trick, Trim, Trollopee, Tunic, Tusser, Tussore, Tuxedo, Uniform, Vest, Vinaigrette, Wear, Wedding, Well, White-tie, Wig, Window, Yclad, Ycled

Dressage Demivolt(e), Manège, Passade, Passage, Pesade, Piaffe

▷ **Dressed up, Dressing** *may indicate* an anagram

Dresser Adze, Almery, Bureau, Chest, Couturier, Deuddarn, Dior, Lair, Lowboy, Sideboard, Transvestite, Tridarn, Welsh

Dressing-gown Bathrobe, Negligée, Peignoir

Dressing-room Apodyterium, Vestiary, Vestry

Dressmaker Costumier, Dorcas, Modiste, Seamstress, Tailor

Drew Steeld, Stelled

Dribble Drip, Drivel, Drop, Seep, Slaver, Slobber, Slop, Trickle

Dried fish Bum(m)alo, Bummaloti, Haberdine, Speld(r)in(g), Stockfish

▶ **Dried fruit** *see* **DRY FRUIT**

Drift(ing), Drifter Becalmed, Continental, Crab, Cruise, Current, Digress, Diluvium, Drumlin, Float, Flow, Genetic, Heap, Impulse, Longshore, Maunder, Natant, North Atlantic, Plankton, Purport, Rorke, Slide, Tendence, Tendency, → **TENOR**, Waft, Wander, Zooplankton

Drill(ing) Appraisal, Archimedean, Auger, Bore, Burr, Close order, Directional, Educate, Exercise, Fire, Form, Hammer, Jackhammer, Jerks, Kerb, Monkey, Pack, PE, Pierce, Pneumatic, Power, PT, Radial, Reamer, Ridge, Rimer, Rock, Seeder, Sow, Square-bashing, Teach, Train, Twill, Twist, Usage, Wildcat

Drink(er), Drunk(enness) AA, Absorb, Adrian Quist, Alkie, Alky, Babalas, Bacchian, Barfly, Bender, Beverage, Bev(v)y, Bezzle, Bib(ite), Bibber, Binge, Birl(e), Bladdered, Bland, Blatted, Blind, Blitzed, Bloat, Blootered, Blotto, Bombed, Boose, Booze, Borachio, Bosky, Bottled, Bouse, Bowl, Bowsey, Bowsie, Bracer, Brahms and Liszt, Bucket, Bumper, Burst, Capernoitie, Cap(p)ernoity, Carafe, Carousal, Cat-lap, Chaser, Chota peg, Compotation, → **CORDIAL**, Corked, Cot case, Crapulent, Crapulous, Cratur, Crocked, Cuppa, Cut, Demitasse, Digestif, Dipsomaniac, Double, Down, Drain, Draught, Drop, Ebriate, Ebriose, Elixir, Energy, Entire, Eye-opener, Febrifuge, Finger, Fleein', Flush, Flying, Fou, Fuddle-cap, Fuddled, Full, Glug, Gnat's piss, Grog, Half-cut, Half-seas-over, Happy, Heart-starter, Heavy wet, High, Hobnob, Hogshead, Honkers, Hooker, Hophead, Imbibe, In-cups, Indulge, Inhaust, Intemperate, Irrigate, Ivresse, Jag, Jakey, Jar, Juice, Juicehead, Kalied, Kaylied, Knock back, Lager lout, Langered, Lap, Legless, Lethean, Libation, → **LIQUOR**, Lit, Loaded, Lord, Lower, Lush(y), Maggoty, Maltworm, Maudlin, Mellow, Merry, Methomania, Methysis, Moon-eyed, Moony, Mops and brooms, Mortal, Mug, Mullered, Neck, Nipperkin, Nobbler, Nog(gin), Obfuscated, Oenomania, Oiled, One, Oppignorate, Overshot, Paid, Paint, Partake, Particular, Peg, Pickled, Pick-me-up, Pie-eyed, Pint(a), Piss-artist, Pissed, Pisshead, Pisspot, Piss-up, Pixil(l)ated, Pledge, Plonk(o), Potation, Poteen, Potion, Primed, Quaff, Quickie, Rat-arsed, Ratted, Refresher, Reviver, Roaring, Rolling, Rotten, Round, Rouse, Rumfustian, Rummer, St Martin's evil, Screamer, Screwed, Sea, Shebeen, Shicker, Short, Shotover, Silenus, Sip(ple), Skinned, Slake, Slewed, Sloshed, Slued, Slug, Slurp, Smashed, Snifter, Snort, Soak, Soused, Sozzled, Sponge, Spongy, Spunge, Squiffy, Steaming, Stewed, Stiffener, Stimulant, Stinko, Stocious, Stoned, Stonkered, Stotious, Stukkend, Stuporous, Sucker, Suiplap, Sundowner, Sup, Swacked, Swallow, Swig, Swill, Tank, Tanked up, Temulence, Tiddl(e)y, Tiff, Tift,

Tight, Tincture, Tipper, Tipple, Tipsy, Tope, Toss, Tossicated, Tost, Tot, Two-pot, Two-pot screamer, Under the weather, Up the pole, Usual, Wash, Wat, Wauch, Waught, Well-oiled, Wet, Whiffled, Williewaught, Winebag, Wine bibber, Wino, Wrecked, Zonked

DRINKS

2 letters:	Raki	Mixer	Coffee
It	Rosé	Mobby	Cognac
	Sack	Morat	Cooler
3 letters:	Sake	Mulse	Cooper
Ale	Saki	Nappy	Doctor
Ava	Soda	Negus	Eggnog
Bub	Soft	Pekoe	Enzian
Cha	Soma	Pepsi®	Geneva
Cup	Sour	Perry	Gimlet
Dop	Sura	Pimms	Grappa
Fap	Tape	Polly	Graves
Hom	Tass	Pombe	Gutrot
Kir	Tent	Punch	Hootch
Mum	Yill	Rakee	Keltie
Pop		Rumbo	Kephir
Red	**5 letters:**	Rummy	Kirsch
Rum	Assai	Sarsa	Kumiss
Rye	Bingo	Sarza	Kümmel
Sec	Bombo	Shake	Maotai
Tea	Bumbo	Shrub	Meathe
Vin	Cider	Skink	Mescal
	Cocoa	Sling	Mickey
4 letters:	Copus	Smile	Mobbie
Arak	Crush	Stout	Nectar
Asti	Doris	Toddy	Obarni
Beer	Float	Tonic	Old Tom
Bock	Glogg	Totty	Oolong
Bull	Haoma	Vodka	Orgeat
Cava	Hogan	White	Oulong
Coke®	Hooch	Xeres	Oxymel
Flip	Joram		Pastis
Hock	Jorum	**6 letters:**	Pernod®
Homa	Julep	Amrita	Plotty
Kava	Kefir	Apozem	Porter
Kola	Kelty	Arrack	Posset
Malt	Kvass	Bishop	Pulque
Marc	Lager	Brandy	Red-eye
Mead	Lassi	Burton	Rickey
Mild	Måcon	Busera	Rotgut
Nipa	Malwa	Cassis	Saloop
Ouzo	Mauby	Caudle	Samshu
Port	Meath	Cauker	Shandy
Purl	Medoc	Chasse	Sherry
Rack	Meths	Claret	Smiler

Squash
Stingo
Strega
Strunt
Taffia
Tisane
Waragi
Whisky
Yaqona
Zythum

7 letters:
Absinth
Akvavit
Alcopop
Amoroso
Aquavit
Bacardi®
Bitters
Campari®
Caribou
Chablis
Chianti
Cobbler
Curaçao
Curaçoa
Daquiri
Eggflip
Fairish
Fustian
G&T
Gin fizz
Guarana
Italian
Koumiss
L&P
Limeade
Madeira
Malmsey
Mineral
Oenomel
Oloroso
Persico
Philter
Philtre
Pilsner
Pink gin
Plottie
Ratafia
Rosiner
Rosolio

Sangria
Sazerac
Screech
Scrumpy
Sherbet
Sherris
Sloe gin
Soda pop
Stengah
Swizzle
Tequila
Tio Pepe®
Wassail
Whiskey

8 letters:
Absinthe
Aleberry
Ambrosia
Anisette
Aperitif
Armagnac
Babbelas
Bordeaux
Brown cow
Burgundy
Calvados
Champers
Charneco
Ciderkin
Coca-cola®
Cocktail
Cold duck
Daiquiri
Dog's nose
Dubonnet®
Eau de vie
Geropiga
Gin sling
Gluhwein
Highball
Hollands
Homebrew
Hydromel
Lemonade
Light ale
Mahogany
Nepenthe
Nightcap
Persicot
Pilsener

Ragmaker
Red biddy
Regmaker
Resinata
Resinate
Rice beer
Riesling
Root beer
Rosoglio
Sangaree
Schnapps
Skokiaan
Smoothie
Snowball
Spritzer
Switchel
Tequilla
Vermouth
Witblits

9 letters:
Applejack
Aqua libra®
Aqua vitae
Ayahuasca
Ayahuasco
Badminton
Buck's fizz
Burnt sack
Calabogus
Champagne
Chocolate
Claret cup
Cream soda
Cuba libre
Eccoccino
Firewater
Gingerade
Ginger pop
Grenadine
Hippocras
Lambswool
Manhattan
Metheglin
Milk punch
Milkshake
Mint julep
Moonshine
Moose milk
Orangeade
Rosa-solis

Sauternes
Slivocica
Slivovitz
Snakebite
Soda water
The cratur
Whisky mac

10 letters:
Blackstone
Bloody Mary
Buttermilk
Chartreuse®
Ginger beer
Ginger wine
Hippomanes
Hop bitters
Lolly water
Maraschino
Mickey Finn
Piña colada
Pousse-café
Shandygaff
Tom Collins

11 letters:
Aguardiente
Amontillado
Athole Brose
Benedictine
Bitter lemon
Black and tan
Black velvet
Boiler-maker
Doch-an-doris
Frappuccino
Half-and-half
Niersteiner
Screwdriver
Soapolallie
Tom and Jerry
Whiskey sour
Whisky toddy

12 letters:
Bloody Caesar
Brandy pawnee
Deoch-an-doris
Doch-an-dorach
Doch-an-doruis
Humpty-dumpty

12 letters – cont:	Sarsaparilla	Deoch-an-doruis	14 letters:
Jimmy Woodser		Ginger cordial	John Barleycorn
Marcobrunner	13 letters:	Mild and bitter	
Old-fashioned	Cobbler's punch	Prairie oyster	

Drink store Cellar

Drip Bore, Dew-drop, Dribble, Drop, Gloop, Gutter, IV, Leak, Post-nasal, Saline, Seep, Splatter, Stillicide, Trickle, Wimp

Dripstone Label, Larmier

Drive(r), Driving, Drive out AA, Acquired, Actuate, Amber gambler, Ambition, Automatic, Backseat, Banish, Beetle, Belt, Bullocky, Ca', Cabby, Campaign, Carman, Chain, Charioteer, Chauffeur, Coachee, Coact, Crankshaft, Crew, Crowd, Designated, Disk, Dislodge, Dr, Drover, Drum, Economy, Eject, Emboss, Energy, Enew, Enforce, Engine, Expatriate, Faze, Feeze, Ferret, Fire, Firk, Flash, Flexible, Fluid, Force, Four-stroke, Four-wheel, Front-wheel, Fuel, Gadsman, Goad, Hack, Hammer, Haste, Heard, Helmsman, Herd, Hie, Hish, Hiss, Hoon, Hoosh, Hot-rod, Hoy, Hunt, Hurl, Hydrostatic, Impact, Impel, Impetus, Impinge, Impulse, Jarvey, Jehu, Jockey, Juggernaut, Key(ring), Lash, Libido, Locoman, Lunge, M(a)cGuffin, Mahout, Make, Mall, Micro, Miz(z)en, Motor, Motorman, Offensive, Overland, Peg, Penetrate, Phase, Piston, Pocket, Power, Powertrain, Propel, Puncher, Push, Put, Quill, RAC, Rack, Rally(e), Ram, Rear-wheel, Rebut, Reinsman, Ride, Road, Roadhog, Run, Sales, Scorch, Screw, Scud, Senna, Sex, Shepherd, Shoo, Spank, Spin, Spur, Start, Steer, Stroke, Sumpter-horse, Sunday, Sweep, Swift, Tape, Task-master, Teamster, Tee, Test, Testosterone, Thrust, Thumb, Toad, Tool, Tootle, Torrential, Trot, Truckie, Truckman, Tup, Turn, Twoccer, Two-stroke, Urge, Urgence, USB, Vetturino, Wagoner, Warp, Whist, Wood, Wreak, Zest

Drivel Balderdash, Blether(skate), Drip, Drool, Humbug, Maunder, Nonsense, Pabulum, Pap, Rot, Salivate, Slabber, Slaver

Driving club AA, Iron, RAC

Drizzle Drow, Haze, Mist, Mizzle, Roke, Scotch mist, Scouther, Scowther, Serein, Skiffle, Smir(r), Smur, Spit

Droll Bizarre, Comic, Funny, Jocular, Queer, Waggish

Drone Bee, Buzz, Dog-bee, Doodle, Dor(r), Drant, Draunt, Drawl, Grind, Hanger-on, Hum, Idler, Parasite, Reedy, Tamboura, Thrum, Windbag

Drool Drivel, Gibber, Salivate, Slaver

Droop(y), Drooping Cernuous, Decline, Epinasty, Flaccid, Flag, Languish, Lill, Limp, Lob, Loll, Lop, Nutate, Oorie, Ourie, Owrie, Peak, Pendulous, Ptosis, → **SAG**, Slink, Slouch, Slump, Weeping, Welk(e), Wilt, Wither

Drop(s), Dropping Acid, Airlift, Apraxia, Bag, Bead, Beres, Blob, Cadence, Calve, Cascade, Cast, Chocolate, Cowpat, Dap, Decrease, Delayed, Descent, Deselect, Dink, Dip, Downturn, Drappie, Drib(let), Ean, Ease, Ebb, Escarp(ment), Fall, Floor, Flop, Fruit, Fumet, Gallows, Glob(ule), Gout(te), Guano, Gutta, Guttate, Instil, Knockout, Land, Lapse, Minim, Modicum, Muff, Mute, Omit, Pilot, Plap, Plonk, Plop, Plummet, Plump, Plunge, Plunk, Precepit, Precipice, (Prince) Rupert's, Rain, Scat, Scrap, Shed, Sip, Skat, Spill, Spraint, Stilliform, Tass, Taste, Tear, Thud, Turd, Virga, Wrist

Drop-out Beatnik, Hippie, Hippy

Drop-shot Dink

Dropsy Anasarca, Ascites, Edema, Oedema

Dross Chaff, Dregs, Recrement, Scoria, Scorious, Scum, Sinter, Slack, Slag, Waste

Drought Dearth, Drouth, Lack, Thirst

Drove(r) Band, Crowd, Flock, Herd, Host, Masses, Mob, Overlander, Puncher

Drown(ed), Drowning Drench, Drent, Drook, Drouk, Engulf, Inundate, Noyade, Overcome, Sorrows, Submerge

Drowse, Drowsiness, Drowsy Blet, Comatose, Doze, Hypnagogic, Hypnopompic, Lethargic, Nap, Narcolepsy, Narcosis, Nod, Snooze, Somnolent

Drub Anoint, Thrash

Drudge(ry) Devil, Dogsbody, Donkey-work, Fag, Grind, Hack, Jackal, Johnson, Plod, Scrub, Slave(y), Snake, Spadework, Stooge, Sweat, Swink, Thraldom, Toil, Trauchle, Treadmill

Drug(ged) Acaricide, ACE inhibitor, Anorectic, Antabuse®, Anti-depressant, Antimetabolite, Antipyrine, Bag, Barbiturate, Base, Blow, Bolus, Bomber, Boo, Botanical, Chalybeate, Cholagogue, Clofibrate, Clot buster, Contraceptive, Corrigent, Dadah, Deck, Depot, Depressant, Designer, DET, Diuretic, Dope, Downer, E, Ecbolic, Ecphractic, Elixir, Emmenagogue, Errhine, Euphoriant, Fantasy, Fertility, Fig, Galenical, Gateway, Gear, Generic, Hallucinogen, Hard, High, Hocus, Homeopathy, Immunosuppressant, Indinavir, Joint, Knockout drops, Largactic, Lifestyle, Line, Load, Mainline, Medicine, Mercurial, Mind-expanding, Miracle, Modified release, Monged, Nervine, Nobble, Nootropic, Obstruent, OD, Opiate, Orlistat, Painkiller, Paregoric, Parenteral, Peace, Pharmaceutics, Pharmacology, Pharmacopoeia, Poison, Popper, Prophylactic, Psychedelic, Psychoactive, Psychodelic, Recreational, Scag, Sedate, Sedative, Shit, Sialogogue, Smart, Snort, Soft, Soporific, Sorbefacient, Speedball, Spermicide, Spike, Stimulant, Stone(d), Stupefacient, Stupefy, Styptic, Substance, Sudorific, Synthetic, Tout, Tranquiliser, Truth, Upper, Vasoconstrictor, Vasodilator, Vermicide, Vermifuge, Weed, White stuff, Wonder, Wrap, Zeolitic

---

DRUGS

1 letter:
Q

3 letters:
AZT
Dex
Eve
GHB
Hop
Ice
INH
LSD
PCP®
STP
Tab
Tea

4 letters:
Acid
Adam
Aloe
Bang
Bute

Dopa
Hash
Hemp
Junk
Sida
Snow
Soma
SSRI
Toot
Trip
Whiz

5 letters:
Aloes
Benny
Bhang
Candy
Coxib
Crank
Dagga
Ganja
Grass
Hop-up

Intal®
L-dopa
Mummy
Opium
Picra
Quina
Rutin
Salep
Salop
Senna
Speed
Sugar
Sulfa
Taxol
Whizz
Zyban®

6 letters:
Amulet
Amytal®
Ativan®
Basuco
Bindle

Charas
Curare
Dragée
Heroin
Inulin
Joypop
Lariam®
Mescla
Mummia
Nubain®
Peyote
Pituri
Prozac®
Saloop
Statin
Sulpha
Valium®
Viagra®
Zantac®

7 letters:
Aricept®
Atabrin

7 letters – cont:
Atebrin®
Botanic
Cascara
Charlie
Churrus
Cocaine
Codeine
Damiana
Dapsone
Diconal®
Ecstasy
Eserine
Eucaine
Guarana
Hashish
Henbane
Hypnone
Insulin
Jellies
Librium®
Metopon
Miltown®
Mogadon®
Morphia
Nurofen®
Patulin
Quinine
Relenza®
Ritalin®
Seconal®
Septrin®
Seroxat®
Steroid
Suramin
Tacrine
Tamiflu
Trional
Triptan
Turpeth
Veronal®
Xenical®

8 letters:
Adjuvant
Ataraxic
Banthine
Benadryl®
Curarine
Diazepam
Doxapram

Fentanyl
Goofball
Hyoscine
Ketamine
Laetrile
Laudanum
Mersalyl
Mescalin
Methadon
Miticide
Moonrock
Morphine
Naloxone
Narcotic
Nembutal
Nepenthe
Nystatin
Oxytocic
Psilocin
Quaalude®
Retrovir®
Rifampin
Roborant
Rohypnol®
Scopolia
Serevent®
Snowball
Special K
Tetronal
Thiazide
Varidase®
Veratrin
Viricide
Zerumbet

9 letters:
Acyclovir
Analeptic
Angel-dust
Anovulant
Antrycide
Augmentin
Barbitone
Biguanide
Bupropion
Busulphan
Captopril
Carbachol
Celecoxib
Cisplatin
Clozapine

Compound Q
Corticoid
Cyclizine
Dexedrine®
Digitalis
Dramamine®
Electuary
Ephedrine
Foscarnet
Frusemide
Herceptin®
Ibuprofen
Iprindole
Isoniazid
Jaborandi
Largactil®
Lidocaine
Lorazepam
Marijuana
Meloxicam
Mepacrine
Methadone
Minoxidil
Modafinil
Mydriasis
Naltrexol
Novocaine
Nux vomica
Oxycodone
Oxycontin®
Paludrine®
Pethidine
Phenytoin
Practolol
Quinidine
Quinquina
Reserpine
Ritonavir
Synergist
Tamoxifen
Temazepam
Teniacide
Totaquine
Trinitrum
Verapamil
Veratrine
Wobbly egg
Zanamivir

10 letters:
Amantadine

Ampicillin
Antagonist
Anxiolytic
Atracurium
Belladonna
Benzedrine
Bufotenine
Cimetidine
Clomiphene
Clonazepam
Colestipol
Disulfiram
Endostatin®
Ergotamine
Ethambutol
Fluoxetine
Formestane
Furosemide
Gabapentim
Hicra-picra
Imipramine
Indapamide
Isoaminile
Isoniazide
Ivermectin
Lofexidine
Mefloquine
Methyldopa
Mickey Finn
Nalbuphine
Nifedipine
Nitrazepam
Omeprazole®
Papaverine
Paroxetine
Penicillin
Pentaquine
Phenacetin
Prednisone
Primaquine
Probenecid
Psilocybin
Quinacrine
Raloxifine
Rifampicin
Salbutamol
Saquinavir
Selegiline
Stramonium
Sucralfate
Tacrolimus

Taeniacide
Taeniafuge
Vancomycin
Worm-powder
Ziduvudine

11 letters:
Acamprosate
Alendronate
Allopurinol
Aminobutene
Amoxycillin
Amphetamine
Anastrozole
Beta-blocker
Butazolidin®
Carbimazole
Carminative
Chloroquine
Ciclosporin
Cinnarizine
Clenbuterol
Clindamycin
Clopidogrel
Cyclosporin
Deserpidine
Distalgesic
Finasteride
Fluconazole
Fluvoxamine
Galantamine
Ganciclovir
Gemcitabene
Gemfibrozil
Haloperidol

Idoxuridine
Indometacin
Ipratropium
Isoxsuprine
Magic bullet
Meprobamate
Neostigmine
Nikethamide
Ondansetron
Oseltamivir
Paracetamol
Pentamidine
Pentazocine
Phentermine
Pravastatin
Propranolol
Purple heart
Risperidone
Simvastatin
Succedaneum
Sulfadoxine
Terfenadine
Thalidomide
Theobromine
Tolbutamide
Tous-les-mois
Tropomyosin
Varicomycin
Vinblastine
Vincristine

12 letters:
Alpha-blocker
Anthelmintic
Antiperiodic

Arsphenamine
Atorvastatin
Azathioprine
Capecitabine
Chlorambucil
Clomipramine
Cyclandelate
Dipyridamole
Eflornithine
Fenfluramine
Fluphenazine
Glanciclover
Gonadotropin
Guanethidine
Indomethacin
Isoprenaline
Isotretinoin
Lansoprazole
Mecamylamine
Methaqualone
Methotrexate
Mifepristone
Noradrenalin
Perphenazine
Physotigmine
Promethazine
Revastigmine
Salicylamide
Streptomycin
Sulfadiazine
Temozolomide
Trimethoprim

13 letters:
Amitriptyline

Anthelminthic
Antihistamine
Carbamazepine
Depressometer
Flunitrazepam
Materia medica
Metronidazole
Nitroglycerin
Penicillamine
Phencyclidine
Pyrimethamine
Spectinomycin
Sulfadimidine
Sulfathiazole
Sulphadiazine
Thiabendazole
Triamcinolone

14 letters:
Bendrofluozide
Bisphosphonate
Butyrhophenone
Combretastatin
Cyclobarbitone
Cyclopentolate
Cyproheptadine
Discodermolide
Flucloxacillin
Norethisterone
Pentobarbitone
Phenacyclidine
Phenobarbitone
Phenylbutazone
Spironolactone
Sulphanilamide

Druid Gorsedd
Drum(mer), Drumming, Drumbeat Arête, Atabal, Barrel, Beatbox, Bodhran, Bongo, Brake, Carousel, Chamade, Conga, Cymograph, Daiko, Dash-wheel, Devil's tattoo, Dhol, Djembe, Dr, Drub, Ear, Flam, Gran cassa, Kettle, Kymograph, Lambeg, Mridamgam, Mridang(a), Mridangam, Myringa, Naker, Ngoma, Oil, Pan, Paradiddle, Percussion, Rappel, Rataplan, Reel, Rep, Ridge, Rigger, Ringo, Roll, Ruff, Ruffle, Salesman, Side, Skin, Snare, Steel, Tabla, Tabour, Tabret, Taiko, Tambour, Tambourine, Tam-tam, Tap, Tattoo, Thrum, Timbal, Timp(ano), Tom-tom, Touk, Traps, Traveller, Tuck, Tymbal, Tympanist, Tympano, Whim, Winding, Work
Drum-belly Hoven
Drumstick Attorney, Leg, Rute, Tampon
▶ **Drunk(ard)** *see* **DRINK**
▷ **Drunken** *may indicate* an anagram
Drupe(l) Etaerio, Tryma

Druse Crystal

Dry(ing), Drier, Dryness Air, Anhydrous, Arefaction, Arefy, Arid, Blot, Bone, Brut, Corpse, Crine, Dehydrate, Desiccate, Detox, Drain, Droll, Dull, Ensear, Evaporate, Exsiccator, Firlot, Fork, Harmattan, Hasky, Hi(r)stie, Humidor, Hydrate, Jejune, Jerk, Khor, Kiln, Mummify, Oast, → **PARCH**, Prosaic, Reast, Reist, Rizzar, Rizzer, Rizzor, Scarious, Sciroc, Scorch, Sear, Season, Sec(co), Seco, Sere, Shrivel, Siccative, Siroc(co), Sober, Sponge, Squeeze, Steme, Stove, Ted, Thirsty, Thristy, Toasted, Torrefy, Torrid, Towel, Tribble, Trocken, TT, Tumbler, Unwatery, Watertight, Welt, Wilt, Win(n), Windrow, Wipe, Wither, Wizened, Wry, Xeransis, Xerasia, Xero(sis), Xeroderma, Xerophthalmia, Xerostomia

Dryad Eurydice, Nymph

Dry fruit, Dried fruit Achene, Akene, Currant, Mebos, Prune, Raisin, Samara, Silicula, Siliqua, Silique, Sultana

Dry mouth Xerostoma

DT's Dingbats, Hallucinations, Zooscopic

Dual Double, Twin, Twofold

Dub Array, → **CALL**, Entitle, Hete, Knight, Name

Dubious Doubtful, Equivocal, Fishy, Fly-by-night, Hesitant, Iffy, Improbable, Left-handed, Questionable, Scepsis, Sceptical, Sesey, Sessa, → **SHADY**, Shonky, Suspect, Touch and go, Unlikely

▷ **Dubious** *may indicate* an anagram

Dubliner Jackeen

Duce Leader, Musso(lini)

Duchess Anastasia, Malfi, Peeress, Titled

Duchy Anhalt, Brabant, Brunswick, Cornwall, Dukedom, Franconia, Grand, Holstein, Limburg, Luxembourg, Nassu, Omnium, Realm, Savoy, Swabia, Valois, Westphalian

Duck(ling), Ducked Amphibian, Avoid, Aylesbury, Bald-pate, Bargander, Bergander, Blob, Blue, Bluebill, Bob, Bombay, Broadbill, Bufflehead, Bum(m)alo, Burrow, Butterball, Canard, Canvasback, → **COUPLE OF DUCKS**, Dead, Dearie, Decoy, Dip, Diving, Dodge, Dodo, Douse, Drook, Drouk, Dunk(er), Eider, Enew, Escape, Evade, Ferruginous, Flapper, Gadwall, Garganey, Garrot, Golden-eye, Goosander, Greenhead, Hareld, Harlequin, Heads, Herald, Immerse, Indian runner, Jook, Jouk, King-pair, Lame, Long-tailed, Mallard, Mandarin, Muscovy, Musk, Nil, Nodding, Nun, O, Oldsquaw, Old Tom, Orpington, Paddling, Pair of spectacles, Palmated, Paradise, Pekin(g), Pintail, Plunge, Pochard, Poker, Putangitangi, Redhead, Ruddy, Runner, Rush, St Cuthbert's, Scaup, Scoter, Sheld(d)uck, Shieldrake, Shovel(l)er, Shun, Sitting, Smeath, Smee(th), Smew, Sord, Souse, Sowse, Spatula, Spirit, Sprigtail, Steamer, Surf(scoter), Teal, Team, Tufted, Tunker, Ugly, Velvet scoter, Whio, Whistling, Widgeon, Wigeon, Wild, Wood, Zero

Duckbill Ornithorhynchus, Platypus

Duckwalk Waddle

Duckweed Lemna

Ducky Sweet, Twee

Duct Bile, Canal(iculus), Channel, Conduit, Diffuser, Diffusor, Emunctory, Epididymus, Fistula, Gland, Lachrymal, Lacrimal, Laticifer, Lumen, Mesonephric, Parotid, Passage, Pipe, Tear, Thoracic, Tube, Ureter, Vas deferens, Wolffian

Dud Bouncer, Failure, Flop, Shan(d), Stumer

Dude Cat, Coxcomb, Dandy, Fop, Lair, Macaroni, Popinjay, Roy

Dudgeon Anger, Hilt, Huff, Pique

Due(s) Adequate, Arrearage, Claim, Debt, Deserts, Forinsec, Geld, Heriot, Just,

Lot, Mature, Needful, Offerings, Owing, Reddendo, Rent, Right, → **SUITABLE**, Thereanent, Toll, Tribute, Worthy

Duel(list) Delope, Mensur, Monomachy, Principal, Tilt

Duenna Chaperone, Dragon

Duff Bungle, Dough, Nelly, NG, Plum, Pudding, Rustle

Duffer Bungler, Rabbit, Useless

Dug Ploughed, Teat, Titty, Udder

Dugong Halicore, Sea-cow, Sea-pig, Sirenian

Dug-out Abri, Canoe, Piragua, Pirogue, Shelter, Trench, Trough

Duke(dom) Albany, Alva, Chandos, Clarence, D, Duc, Ellington, Fist, Iron, Milan, Orsino, Peer, Prospero, Rohan, Wellington

Dulcimer Cembalo, Citole, Cymbalo, Santir, Sant(o)ur

Dull(ard), Dullness Anodyne, Anorak, Bald, Banal, Barren, Besot, Bland, Blear, Blockish, Blunt, Boeotian, Boring, Cloudy, Commonplace, Dead (and alive), Deadhead, Dense, Dim, Dinge, Dingy, Ditchwater, Doldrums, Dowf, Dowie, Drab, Drear, Dreich, Dry, Dunce, Faded, Flat, Fozy, Gray, Grey, Heavy, Hebetate, Ho-hum, Humdrum, Illustrious, Insipid, Jejune, Lacklustre, Lifeless, Log(y), Lowlight, Mat(t), Matte, Monotonous, Mopish, Mull, Mundane, Obtund, Obtuse, Opacity, Opiate, Ordinary, Overcast, Owlish, Pall, Pedestrian, Perstringe, Podunk, Prosaic, Prose, Prosy, Rebate, Rust, Slow, Solein, Sopite, Staid, Stick, Stodger, Stodgy, Stolid, Stuffy, Stultify, → **STUPID**, Sunless, Tame, Tarnish, Tedious, Ticky-tacky, Toneless, Torpor, Treadmill, Trite, Tubby, Unimaginative, Vapid, Wonk, Wooden, Zoid

Dumb(ness) Alalia, Aphonic, Crambo, Hobbididance, Inarticulate, Mute, Silent, Stupid, Thunderstruck

Dumbfound(ed) Amaze, Astound, Flabbergast, Stun, Stupefy, Stupent

Dumb ox Aquinas

Dummy Comforter, Copy, Effigy, Fathead, Flathead, Lummox, Mannequin, Mannikin, Mock-up, Model, Pacifier, Quintain, Soother, Table, Teat, Waxwork

Dump(ing), Dumps Abandon, Blue, Core, Dejection, Dispirited, Doldrums, Empty, Eyesore, Fly-tipping, Hole, Jettison, Jilt, Junk, Laystall, Mine, Scrap, Screen, Shoot, Store(house), Tip, Toom, Unlade, Unload

Dumpling Clootie, Dim sum, Dough(boy), Gnocchi, Gyoza, Knaidel, Knaidloch, Kneidlach, Knish, Kreplach, Matzoball, Norfolk, Perogi, Pi(e)rogi, Quenelle, Ribaude, Suet, Won ton

Dumpy Pudgy, Squat

Dun Annoy, Cow, Importune, Pester, → **SUE**, Tan

Duncan Isadora

Dunce Analphabet, Booby, Clod, Dolt, Donkey, Dullard, Fathead, Schmo, Schmuck, Schnook, Stupid

Dune Areg, Bar, Barchan(e), Bark(h)an, Erg, Sandbank, Seif, Star, Whaleback

Dung(hill) Argol, Buffalo chips, Buttons, Chip, Cock, Coprolite, Cowpat, Droppings, Fewmet, Fumet, Fumiculous, Guano, Hing, Manure, Midden, Mixen, Mute, Night soil, Ordure, Puer, Pure, Scat, Scumber, Shairn, Shard, Sharn, Siege, Skat, Skummer, Sombrerite, Sombrero, Spawn brick, Spraint, Stercoraceous, Tath

Dungarees Overalls

Dung-eating Merdiverous

Dungeon Bastille, Cell, Confine, Donjon, Durance, Oubliette, Souterrain

Dunk Immerse, Sop, Steep, Submerge

Dunnock Accentor

Duo Couple, Pair, Twosome

Dupe Catspaw, Chiaus, Chouse, Cony, Cull(y), Delude, Geck, Gull, Hoax, Hoodwink,

Mug, Pawn, Pigeon, Plover, Sitter, Soft mark, Sucker, Swindle, → **TRICK**, Victim

Duplex Twofold

Duplicate, Duplicator Clone, Copy, Counterpart, Cyclostyle, Double, Echo, Facsimile, Match, Ozalid®, Replica, Reproduce, Roneo®, Spare

Durable Enduring, Eternal, Eterne, Hardy, Lasting, Permanent, Stout, Tough

Duralumin® Y-alloy

Duration Extent, Period, Span

Duress Coercion, Pressure, Restraint

Durham Palatine

During Amid, Dia-, For, In, Live, Over, Throughout, While, Whilst

Dusk(y) Dark, Dewfall, Dun, Eve, Eventide, Gloaming, Gloom, Owl-light, Phaeic, Twilight, Umbrose

Dust(y) Arid, Ash, Bo(a)rt, Calima, Clean, Coom, Cosmic, Culm, Derris, Devil, Duff, Earth, Fuss, Gold, Khak(i), Lemel, Limail, Lo(e)ss, Miller, Nebula, Pellum, Pollen, Pother, Pouder, Poudre, Powder, Pozz(u)olana, Pudder, Rouge, Seed, Shaitan, Slack, Stour, Talc, Volcanic, Wipe

▷ **Dusted** *may indicate* an anagram

Duster Cloth, Feather, Red, Talcum, Torchon

Dustman Doolittle, Garbo(logist), Scaffie, Trashman

Dust measure Konimeter, Koniscope

Dutch(man), Dutchwoman Batavian, Boor, Butterbox, Cape, Courage, D(u), Double, Elm, Erasmus, Flying, Fri(e)sian, Frow, German, Kitchen, Knickerbocker, Middle, Missis, Missus, Mynheer, Parnell shout, Patron, Pennsylvania, Sooterkin, Taal, Wife

Dutiful, Duty Active, Ahimsa, Allegiance, Average, Blench, Bond, Charge, Corvee, Countervailing, Customs, Death, Debt, Deontology, Detail, Devoir, Docile, Drow, Due, Duplicand, End, Estate, Excise, Export, Fatigue, Feu, Function, Heriot, Homage, Import, Imposition, Impost, Incumbent, Lastage, Legacy, Likin, Mission, Mistery, Mystery, Obedient, Obligation, Octroi, Office, Onus, Pia, Picket, Pious, Point, Preferential, Prisage, Probate, Rota, Sentry-go, Shift, Stamp, Stillicide, Stint, Succession, Tariff, → **TASK**, Tax, Toll, Transit, Trow, Watch, Zabeta

Duvet Doona, Quilt

Dwarf(ism) Achondroplasia, Agate, Alberich, Andvari, Ateleiosis, Bashful, Belittle, Bes, Black, Bonsai, Brown, Doc, Dopey, Droich, Drow, Durgan, Elf, Gnome, Grumpy, Happy, Hobbit, Homuncule, Hop o' my thumb, Knurl, Laurin, Little man, Man(n)ikin, → **MIDGET**, Mime, Minikin, Minim, Nanism, Nectabanus, Ni(e)belung, Nurl, Overshadow, Pacolet, Pigmy, Pygmy, Red, Regin, Ront, Rumpelstiltskin, Runt, Skrimp, Sleepy, Sneezy, → **STUNT**, Tiddler, Titch, Tokoloshe, Tom Thumb, Toy, Troll, Trow, White

Dwell(er), Dwelling Abide, Aweto, Be, Bungalow, Cabin, Cell, Cot(tage), Descant, Discourse, Domicile, Habitation, Harp, Heteroscian, Hogan, House, Hut, Ice colours, Laura, Lavra, Live, Lodge, Longhouse, Maison(n)ette, Mansion, Messuage, Midgard, Midgarth, Mithgarthr, Palafitte, Pied-à-terre, Pueblo, Reside, Roof, Single-end, Sty, Tenement, Tepee, Terramara, Tipi, Two-by-four, Weem, Wigwam, Won(ing), Wonning, Woon

Dwindle Decline, Diminish, Fade, Lessen, Peter, Shrink, Wane

Dye(ing), Dyestuff, Dye-seller Acid, Alkanet, Amaranth, Anil, Anthracene, Anthraquinone, Archil, Azo(benzine), Azurine, Bat(t)ik, Benzidine, Brazil(e)in, Burnt umber, Camwood, Canthaxanthin, Carthamine, Catechin, Chay(a), Chica, Chicha, Chico, Choy, Cinnabar, Cobalt, Cochineal, Colour, Congo, Coomassie blue, Corkir, Crocein, Crotal, Crottle, Cudbear, Dinitrobenzene, Direct, Embrue,

Engrain, Envermeil, Eosin, Flavin(e), Fluoxene, Fuchsin(e), Fustic, Fustoc, Gambi(e)r, Gentian violet, Grain, Haematoxylin, Henna, Hue, Ikat, Imbrue, Imbue, Incarnadine, Indamine, Indican, Indigo, Indigocarmine, Indigotin, Indirubin, Indoxyl, Indulin(e), Ingrain, Kalamkari, Kamala, Kermes, Kohl, Korkir, Madder, Magenta, Mauvein(e), Mauvin(e), Methyl violet, Murex, Myrobalan, Nigrosin(e), Orcein, Orchel(la), Orchil, Para-red, Phenolphthalein, Phthalein, → **PIGMENT**, Ponceau, Primuline, Puccoon, Purple, Purpurin, Pyronine, Quercitron, Quinoline, Raddle, Resorcinol, Rhodamine, Rosanilin(e), Safranin(e), Salter, Shaya, → **STAIN**, Stone-rag, Stone-raw, Sumac(h), Sunfast, Tannin, Tartrazine, Tie-dye, Tinct, Tint, Tropaeolin, Turmeric, Turnsole, Valonia, Vat, Wald, Weld, Woad, Woald, Wold, Xanthium, Xylidine

▶ **Dying** *see* **DIE**

Dyke Aboideau, Aboiteau, Bund, Devil's, → **DIKE**, Ditch, Gall, Offa's, Ring

Dynamic(s) Ballistics, Ball of fire, Energetic, Forceful, Gogo, High-powered, Kinetics, Potent

Dynamite Blast, Explode, Gelignite, Giant powder, TNT, Trotyl

Dynamo Alternator, Armature, Tiger

Dynasty Abbasid(e), Angevin, Bourbon, Capetian, Carolingian, Chin(g), Ch'ing, Chou, Era, Fatimid, Frankish, Gupta, Habsburg, Han, Hapsburg, Holkar, Honan, House(hold), Hyksos, Khan, Manchu, Maurya, Merovingian, Ming, Omayyad, Osman, Pahlavi, Plantagenet, Ptolemy, Qajar, Q'ing, Rameses, Romanov, Rule, Safavid, Saga, Sassanid, Seleucid, Seljuk, Shang, Song, Sui, Sung, Tai-ping, Tang, Tudor, Umayyad, Wei, Yi, Yuan, Zhou

Dysentery Amoebic, Bloody flux, Slugellosis

Dysfunction Kernicterus

Dyslexia Strephosymbolia

Dyspeptic Cacogastric

Dysprosium Dy

Dystrophy Duchenne's, Muscular

Ee

E Boat, East, Echo, Energy, English, Spain

Each All, Apiece, Ea, → **EVERY**, Ilka, Per, Severally

Eager(ly) Agog, Antsy, Ardent, Avid, Beaver, Bore, Bright-eyed, Dying, Earnest, Enthusiastic, Fain, Fervent, Fervid, Fidge, Frack, Game, Greedy, Gung-ho, Hot, Intent, → **KEEN**, Perfervid, Prone, Race, Raring, Rath(e), Ready, Roost, Sharp-set, Sore, Spoiling, Thirsty, Toey, Wishing, Yare

Eagle Al(l)erion, Altair, American, Aquila, Bald, Bateleur, Berghaan, Bird, Double, Ensign, Erne, Ethon, Fish, Gier, Golden, Harpy, Hawk, Legal, Lettern, Nisus, Ossifrage, Sea, Spread, Tawny, Wedge-tailed

Ear(drum), Ear trouble Ant(i)helix, Attention, Audience, Auricle, Barotitis, Cauliflower, Cochlea, Concha, Conchitis, Deafness, Dionysius, Dolichotus, External, Glue, Hearing, Helix, Icker, Incus, Inner, Internal, Jenkins, Kieselguhr, Labyrinth, Labyrinthitis, Listen, Locusta, Lop, Lug, Malleus, Middle, Modiolus, Myringa, Myringitis, Nubbin, Otalgia, Otalgy, Otic, Paracusis, Paramastoid, Parotic, Pavilion, Periotic, Petrosal, Phonic, Pinna, Presby(a)c(o)usis, Prootic, Souse, Spike, Stapes, Thick, Tin, Tragus, Tympanitis, Utricle

Earl(dom) Belted, Mar, Peer, Sandwich

Earlier, Early Above, Ago, Ahead, Alsoon, AM, Antelucan, Auld, Betimes, Cockcrow, Daybreak, Ere-now, Ex, Germinal, Incipient, Or, Precocious, Precursor, Prehistoric, Premature, Prevernal, Previous, Primeur, Primeval, Primordial, Prior, Rath(e), Rath(e)ripe, Rear, Rough, Rudimentary, Soon, Timely, Tim(e)ous

▷ **Early** *may indicate* belonging to an earl

Early man Eoanthropus, Flat-earther

▷ **Early stages of** *may indicate* first one or two letters of the words following

Earmark Allocate, Bag, Book, Characteristic, Flag, → **RESERVE**, Tag, Target, Ticket

Earn(er), Earning(s) Achieve, Addle, Breadwinner, Curdle, Deserve, Digerati, Ern, Gain, Income, Invisible, Make, Merit, O.T.E., Rennet, Runnet, Win, Yearn

Earnest(ly) Ardent, Arle(s)(-penny), Deposit, Fervent, Imprest, Intent, Promise, Serious, Token, Wistly, Zealous

Earring Drop, Ear bob, Hoop, Keeper, Pendant, Sleeper, Snap, Stud

Earshot Hail, Hearing

Earth(y), Earthling Alkaline, Antichthon, Art, Asthenosphere, Barbados, Brown, Bury, Capricorn, Carnal, Clay, Cloam, Clod, Cologne, Craton, Den, Diatomite, Dirt, Drey, Dust, E, Eard, Edaphic, Epigene, Foxhole, Friable, Fuller's, Gaea, Gaia, Gault, Ge, Globe, Green, Ground, Heavy, Horst, Infusiorial, Kadi, Lair, Leaf-mould, Lemnian, Lithosphere, Loam, Malm, Mankind, Mantle, Mools, Mould, Mouls, Papa, Pise, Planet, Rabelaisian, Racy, Rare, Raunchy, Red, Samian, Seat, Sett, Sod, → **SOIL**, Subsoil, Taurus, Telluric, Tellus, Terra, Terrain, Terramara, Terran, Terrene, Topsoil, Tripoli, Virgo, Wad, Ye(a)rd, Yellow, Yird

Earth-bound Chthonian, Mundane

Earthenware Arretine, Biscuit, Ceramic, Creamware, Crock(ery), Delf(t),

Della-robbia, Delph, Faience, Figuline, Maiolica, Majolica, Pig, Pot, Queen's ware, Raku, Samian, Sanitary, Terracotta

Earthquake Aftershock, Aseismic, Bradyseism, Foreshock, Mercalli, Richter, Seism, Shake, Shock, Temblor, Trembler, Tremor

Earth's surface Sal, Sial

Earthwork Agger, Bank, Cursus, Gazon, Parados, Rampart, Remblai, Vallum

Earthworm Angledug, Angletwitch, Angleworm, Annelid, Bait, Night-crawler

Earwig Clipshear(s), Eavesdrop, Forkit-tail, Forky-tail

Ease, Easing, Easygoing Alleviate, Carefree, Clear, Clover, Comfort, Content, Defuse, Deregulate, Détente, Easy-osy, Facility, Genial, Hands down, Informal, Lax, Mellow, Mid(dy), Mitigate, Otiosity, Palliate, Peace, Pococurante, Quiet, Relieve, Reposal, Repose, Soothe

East(erly), Eastward Anglia, Asia, Chevet, E, Eassel, Eassil, Eothen, Eurus, Far, Levant, Middle, Morning-land, Near, Orient, Ost, Sunrise

Easter Festival, Island, Pace, Pasch, Pasque

Eastern(er), Eastern language Asian, Kolarian, Oriental, Ostman, Virginian

East European Lettic, Slovene

East German Ossi

Easy, Easily ABC, Breeze, Cakewalk, Carefree, Child's play, Cinch, Cushy, Degage, Doddle, Duck soup, Eath(e), Ethe, Facile, Free, Gift, Glib, Gravy train, Hands down, Independent, Jammy, Kid's stuff, Lax, Light, Midshipman, Natural, Nimps, No-brainer, Oldster, Picnic, Pie, Pushover, Romp, Scoosh, Simple, Sitter, Skoosh, Snotty, Soft, Tolerant, Turkey shoot, User-friendly, Walk-over, Well, Yare

▷ **Easy** *may indicate* an anagram

Easy-care Non-iron

Eat(able), Eater, Eating Bite, Bolt, Break bread, Champ, Chop, Commensal, Consume, Corrode, Devour, Dine, Edible, Edite, Endew, Endue, Erode, Esculent, Etch, Fare, Feast, → **FEED**, Fret, Gastronome, Gnaw, Go, Gobble, Gourman, Gourmet, Graze, Grub, Have, Hoe into, Hog, Hyperorexia, Hyperphagia, Ingest, Manducate, Mess, Muckamuck, Munch, Nosh, Nutritive, Omnivore, Partake, Phagomania, Phagophobia, Predate, Refect, Scoff, Snack, Stuff, Sup, Swallow, Syssitia, Take, Taste, Trencherman, Trophesy, Tuck away, Tuck into, Whale

Eavesdrop(per) Cowan, Detectophone, Earwig, Icicle, Listen, Overhear, Pry, Snoop, Stillicide, Tab-hang, Tap, Wiretap

Ebb(ing) Abate, Decline, Recede, Refluent, Sink, → **WANE**

Ebony Black, Cocus-wood, Coromandel, Hebenon, Jamaican

Ebullient Brash, Effervescent, Exuberant, Fervid

Eccentric Abnormal, Antic, Cam, Card, Character, Crank, Curious, Daffy, Dag, Deviant, Dingbat, Ditsy, Ditzy, E, Farouche, Fay, Fey, Fie, Freak, Fruitcake, Geek, Gonzo, Iffish, Irregular, Kinky, Kook(y), Mattoid, Monstre sacré, Nutcase, Nutter, Odd(ball), Offbeat, Off-centre, Off the wall, Original, Outré, → **PECULIAR**, Phantasime, Pixil(l)ated, Queer, Quirky, Quiz, Rake, Raky, Recondite, Rum, Scatty, Screwball, Screwy, Spa(e)y, Squirrelly, Wack(y), Way-out, Weirdie, Weird(o), W(h)acko

▷ **Eccentric** *may indicate* an anagram

Ecclesiastic(es), Ecclesiasticus Abbé, Clergyman, Clerical, Lector, Secular, Sir(ach), Theologian, The Preacher

Echelon Formation

Echinoderm Asteroidea, Basket-star, Brittle-star, Comatulid, Crinoid, Heart-urchin, Ophiurid, Sea-egg, Sea-lily, Sea-urchin, Starfish

Echo, Echoing, Echo-sounder Angel, Answer, Ditto, E, Fathometer®, Imitate,

Iterate, Phonocamptic, Rebound, Repeat, Repercussion, Reply, Resonant,
→ **RESOUND**, Respeak, Reverb(erate), Revoice, Ring, Rote, Tape

Eclat Flourish, Glory, Prestige, Renown

Eclectic Babist, Broad, Complex, Diverse, Liberal

Eclipse Annular, Block, Cloud, Deliquium, Excel, Hide, Lunar, Obscure, Occultation, Outmatch, Outshine, Outweigh, Overshadow, Partial, Penumbra, Rahu, Solar, Total, Transcend, Upstage

Eclogue Bucolic, Idyll, Pastoral

Eco-community Seral

Ecology Bionomics

Economist Angell, Bentham, Chrematist, Cole, Friedman, Giffen, Keynes, Malthus, Marginalist, Meade, Mill, Pareto, Physiocrat, Ricardo, Tinbergen, Tobin, Toynbee, Veblen, Webb

Economic(al), Economics, Economise, Economy Agronomy, Black, Budget, Careful, Cliometrics, Command, Conserve, Conversation, Dismal science, Eke, Entrench, Finance, Frugal, Hidden, Home, Husband, Intrench, Knowledge, Market, Mitumba, Mixed, Neat, New, Parsimony, Planned, Pinch, Political, Pusser's logic, Retrench, Retrenchment, Scimp, Shoestring, Siege, Spare, Sparing, Stagflation, Stakeholder, → **STINT**, Stumpflation, Supply-side, Thrift, Tiger, Token, Welfare.

Ecstasy, Ecstatic Bliss, Delight, Delirious, Dove, E, Exultant, Joy, Liquid, Lyrical, Nympholepsy, Pythic, Rapture, Rhapsodic, Sent, Trance, Transport

Ecumenical Catholic, Lateran

Eczema Pompholyx, Salt rheum, Tetter

Edda Elder, Prose, Younger

Eddy Backset, Curl, Duane, Gurge, Maelstrom, Nelson, Pirl, Purl, Rotor, Sousehole, Swelchie, Swirl, Vortex, Weel, Well, Whirlpool, Wiel

Eden Bliss, Fall, Heaven, Paradise, PM, Utopia

Edentate Ant-eater, Armadillo, Sloth, Tatou, Xenarthra

Edge, Edging, Edgy Advantage, Arris, Bleeding, Border, Bordure, Brim, Brink, Brittle, Brown, Burr, Chamfer, Chimb, Chime, Chine, Coaming, Costa, Cutting, Dag, Deckle, End, Flange, Flounce, Frill, Fringe, Frontier, Furbelow, Gunnel, Gunwale, Hem, Hone, Inch, Inside, Kerb, Knife, Leading, Leech, Limb(ate), Limbus, Limit, Lip, List, Lute, Marge(nt), Margin, Nosing, Orle, Outside, Parapet, Periphery, Picot, Pikadell, Piping, Rand, Rim, Rund, Rymme, Selvage, Selvedge, Sidle, Skirt, Strand, Tomium, Trailing, Trim, Tyre, Uptight, Verge, Wear, Whet

▶ **Edible** *see* **EATABLE**

Edict(s) Ban, Bull, Clementines, Decree, Decretal, Extravagantes, Fatwa, Firman, Interim, Irade, Nantes, Notice, Pragmatic, Proclamation, Pronouncement, Pronunciamento, Rescript, Sext, Ukase

Edifice Booth, Building, Structure, Stupa, Superstructure

Edify Instruct, Teach

Edinburgh Auld Reekie

Edit(or), Editorial Abridge, Amend, Article, City, Copy (read), Cut, Dele, Desk, Dramaturg(e), Ed, Emend, Expurgate, Footsteps, Garble, Leader, Manipulate, Nantes, Overseer, Prepare, Recense, Redact, Revise, Seaman

▷ **Edited** *may indicate* an anagram

Edith Sitwell

Edition Aldine, Bulldog, Bullpup, Ed, Extra, Facsimile, Ghost, Hexapla(r), Impression, Issue, Library, Limited, Number, Omnibus, Trade, Variorum, Version

Edmond, Edmund Burke, Gosse, Ironside(s), Rostand, Spenser

Educate(d) Baboo, Babu, Enlighten, Evolué, Informed, Instruct, Learned, Noursle, Nousell, Nousle, Nurture, Nuzzle, Polymath, Preppy, Scholarly, School, → **TEACH**, Train, Yuppie

Education(alist) Adult, Basic, B.Ed, Classical, Conductive, D.Ed, Didactics, Estyn, Further, Heurism, Learning, Literate, Mainstream, Montessori, Paedotrophy, Pedagogue, Pestalozzi, Physical, Piarist, Primary, Schooling, Special, Steiner, Teacher, Tertiary, Upbringing

Educe Elicit, Evoke, Extract, Infer

Edward Confessor, Ed, Elder, Lear, Martyr, Ned, Ted

Eel Conger, Congo, Electric, Elver, Glass, Grig, Gulper, Gunnel, Hagfish, Kingklip, Lamper, Lamprey, Lant, Launce, Leptocephalus, Moray, Murray, Murr(e)y, Olm, Paste, Salt, Sand(ling), Silver belly, Snake, Snig, Spitchcock, Tuna, Vinegar, Wheat, Wolf

Eerie Creepy, Spooky, Uncanny, Unked, Weird

Efface Cancel, Delete, Dislimn, → **ERASE**, Expunge, Obliterate

Effect(s), Effective(ness), Effectual Able, Achieve, Acting, Alienation, Auger, Babinski, Bags, Barkhausen, Belongings, Binaural, Bit, Bite, Bohr, Border, Border edge, Bricolage, Butterfly, Causal, C(h)erenkov, Chromakey, Coanda, Coastline, Competent, Compton, Consequence, Coriolis, Do, Domino, Doppler, Dr(y)ice, Eclat, Edge, Efficacious, Electro-optical, Enact, End, Estate, Execute, Experimenter, Fet, Foley, Fringe, Functional, Fungibles, Gear, General, Goods, Greenhouse, Ground, Gunn, Hall, Halo, Hangover, Hawthorne, Home, Horns and halo, Impact, Implement(al), Impression, Introgenic, Josephson, Joule(-Thomson), Kerr, Keystone, Knock-on, Magneto-optical, Magnus, Meissner, Militate, Moire, Mossbauer, Mutual, Neat, Nisi, Notch, Operant, Optical, Outcome, Ovshinsky, Oxygen, Parallax, Peltier, Perficient, Personal, Phi, Photoelectric, Photovoltaic, Piezoelectric, Piezomagnetic, Pinch, Placebo, Pogo, Position, Potent, Practical, Primary, Promulgate, Raman, Ratchet, Reaction, Recency, Redound, Repercussion, → **RESULT**, Ripple, Schottky, Seebeck, Shadow, Shore, Side, Skin, Slash-dot, Sound, Sovereign, Special, Spectrum, Spin-off, Stage, Stark, Striking, Stroop, Submarine, Subsidiary, Tableau, Teeth, Telling, Thermoelectric, Thomson, Toxic, Tunnel, Tyndall, Upshot, Valid, Viable, Virtual, Win, Withdrawal, Work, Zeeman

Effeminate Airtsy-mairtsy, Camp, Carpet-knight, Carpet-monger, Cissy, Coddle, Cookie-pusher, Dildo, Epicene, Female, Gussie, Jessie, Milksop, (Miss) Nancy, Molly(coddle), Nellie, Nelly, Panty-waist, Poovy, Pretty, Prissy, Punce, Queenie, Sissy, Swish, Tender, Tenderling, Tonk, Unman, Wuss(y)

Effervescence, Effervescent Bubbling, Ebullient, Fizz, Frizzante, Pétillant, Soda
▷ **Effervescent** *may indicate* an anagram

Effete Camp, Epigon(e)

Efficacious, Efficacy Effective, Operative, Potent, Sovereign, Value

Efficiency, Efficient Able, Businesslike, Capable, Competent, Current, Despatch, Ecological, Electrode, Ergonomics, High-powered, Luminous, Productivity, Quantum, Smart, Spectral luminous, Streamlined, Strong, Thermal, Volumetric

Effigy Figure, Guy, Idol, Image, Statua, Statue

Efflorescence Bloom, Blossom, Reh

Effluence, Effluent, Effluvia Air, Aura, Billabong, Discharge, Fume, Gas, Halitus, Miasma, Odour, Outflow, Outrush

Effort Achievement, Attempt, Best, Conatus, Concerted, Drive, Endeavour, Essay, Exertion, Fit, Frame, Hardscrabble, Herculean, Labour, Molimen, Nisus, Pains, Rally, Shy, Spurt, Stab, Strain, Struggle, Team, → **TRY**, Work, Yo

Effortless Lenis
Effrontery Audacity, Brass, Cheek, Face, Gall, Neck, Nerve, Temerity
Effulgent Bright, Radiant, Shining
Effuse, Effusion, Effusive Emanate, Exuberant, Exude, Gush, Lyric, Ode, Outburst, Prattle, Rhapsody, Sanies, Screed, Spill
Eft After
Eg As, Example
Egest Eliminate, Evacuate, Excrete, Void
Egg(s) Abet, Benedict, Berry, Blow, Bomb, Caviar(e), Cavier, Chalaza, Cheer, Cleidoic, Clutch, Cockney, Collop, Coral, Curate's, Darning, Easter, Edge, Fabergé, Fetus, Flyblow, Foetus, Free-range, Glair(e), Goad, Goog, Graine, Hoy, Incite, Instigate, Layings, Mine, Nest, Nidamentum, Nit, Oocyte, Oophoron, Ostrich, Ova, Ovum, Pace, Pasch, Plover's, Prairie oyster, Press, Raun, Roe, Rumble-tumble, Scotch, Scrambled, Seed, Setting, Spat, Spawn, Spur(ne), Tar(re), Thunder, Tooth, Tread(le), Urge, Whore's, Wind, Yelk, Yolk, Zygote
Egghead Brainbox, Don, Highbrow, Intellectual, Mensa, Pedant
Eggnog Flip
Egg-plant Aubergine, Brinjal
Egg-producer Gametophyte, Hen, Ovipositor
Egg-shaped Obovate, Oval, Ovate
Egg-white Albumen, Glair
Ego(ism), Egoist Che, Conceit, I, Narcissism, Not-I, Pride, Self, Solipsism, Ubu, Vanity
Egocentric Solipsistic
Egregious Eminent, Flagrant, Glaring, Shocking
Egypt(ian), Egyptologist Arab, Cairene, Carter, Cheops, Chephren, Cleopatra, Copt(ic), ET, Gippo, Goshen, Gyppo, Imhotep, Nasser, Nefertiti, Nilote, Nitrian, Old Kingdom, Osiris, Ptolemy, Rameses, Syene, UAR, Wafd, Wog
Eiderdown Bedspread, Duvet, Quilt
Eight(h), Eighth day Acht, Byte, Crew, Cube, Middle, Nundine, Oars, Octa, Octad, Octal, Octastrophic, Octave, Octet, Octonary, Ogdoad, Okta, Ottava, Ure, Utas
Eighteen Majority
Eighty Fourscore, R
Einsteinium Es
Either Also, Both, O(u)ther, Such
Ejaculate Blurt, Discharge, Emit, Exclaim
Eject Bounce, Disgorge, Dismiss, Emit, Erupt, Expel, Oust, Propel, Spew, Spit, Spue, Vent
Eke Augment, Eche, Enlarge, Husband, Supplement
Elaborate Creation, Detail, Develop, Dressy, Enlarge, Evolve, Flesh out, Florid, Imago, Improve, Intricate, Ornate, Rich, Spectacular, Stretch
Elan Dash, Drive, Esprit, → **FLAIR**, Gusto, Lotus, Panache, Spirit, Vigour
Elapse Glide, Intervene, Overpass, Pass
Elastic(ity) Adaptable, Bungee, Buoyant, Dopplerite, Elater, Flexible, Give, Resilient, Rubber, Scrunchie, Scrunchy, Spandex®, Springy, Stretchy, Tone, Tonus
Elastomer Adiprene®
Elate(d), Elation Cheer, Euphoric, Exalt, Exhilarate, Gladden, Hault, High, Ruff(e), Uplift
Elbow, Elbow tip Akimbo, Ancon, Angle, Bender, Cubital, Hustle, Joint, Jostle, Justle, Kimbo, Noop, Nudge, Olecranon, Tennis
El Cid Diaz

Elder(ly), Eldest Ainé(e), Ancestor, Ancient, Bourtree, Chief, Classis, Coffin dodger, Eigne, Geriatric, Greying, Guru, Kaumatua, Kuia, OAP, Presbyter, → **SENIOR**, Sire, Susanna, Wallwort
Eldorado Ophir
Eleanor(a) Bron, Duse, Nora(h)
Elect(ed), Election(eer), Electoral Ballot, Choice, Choose, Chosen, Co-opt, Eatanswill, Elite, General, Gerrymander, Hustings, In, Israelite, Khaki, Off-year, Opt, Pick, PR, Primary, Psephology, Rectorial, Return, Select, Stump
Electrical discharge Corposant, Ion, Zwitterion
Electrical instrument Battery, Charger, Galvaniser, Mains, Resistor, Rheostat, Shoe
Electrical unit Amp(ere), Coulomb, Farad, Kilowatt, Ohm, Volt, Watt
Electric eye Pec
Electrician Gaffer, Lineman, Ohm, Siemens, Sparks, Tesla
Electricity Galvanism, HT, Inductance, Juice, Mains, Negative, Positive, Power, Static, Utility, Vitreous
Electrify Astonish, Galvanise, Startle, Stir, Thrill
Electrode Anode, Cathode, Dynode, Element, Photocathode
Electrolyte Ampholyte
Electromagnet(ic) Abampere, Armature, Oersted, Solenoid, Weber
Electron(ic), Electronics, Electronic device Cooper pairs, Exciton, FET, Fly-by-wire, Linac, Lone pair, Martenot, Mole(cular), Polaron, Possum®, Quantum, Smart, Tetrode, Thermionics, Valence, Valency
Elegance, Elegant Artistic, Bijou, Chic, Classy, Dainty, Daynt, Debonair, Fancy, Feat, Finesse, Gainly, Galant, Grace, Jimp, Luxurious, Polished, Recherché, Refined, Ritzy, → **SMART**, Soigné(e), Suave, Svelte, Swish, Tall, Urbane
Elegy Dirge, Lament, Poem
Element(s), Elementary Abcee, Abecedarian, Absey, Air, Alloy, Atom, Barebones, → **COMPONENT**, Detail, Earth, → **ESSENCE**, Essential, Factor, Feature, Fire, Fuel, Heating, Hot-plate, Ideal, Identity, Inchoate, Insertion, Isotope, Logical, M(a)cGuffin, Milieu, Peltier, Pixel, Primary, Principle, Rare earth, Rudimental, Simple, Strand, Terra, Trace, Tramp, Transition, Water, Weather, Ylem

---

ELEMENTS

3 letters:	**6 letters:**	Silver (Ag)	Hassium (Hs)
Tin (Sn)	Barium (Ba)	Sodium (Na)	Holmium (Ho)
	Carbon (C)		Iridium (Ir)
4 letters:	Cerium (Ce)	**7 letters:**	Krypton (Kr)
Gold (Au)	Cesium	Arsenic (As)	Lithium (Li)
Iron (Fe)	Cobalt (Co)	Bismuth (Bi)	Mercury (Hg)
Lead (Pb)	Copper (Cu)	Bromine (Br)	Niobium (Nb)
Neon (Ne)	Curium (Cm)	Cadmium (Cd)	Rhenium (Re)
Zinc (Zn)	Erbium (Er)	Caesium (Cs)	Rhodium (Rh)
	Helium (He)	Calcium (Ca)	Silicon (Si)
5 letters:	Indium (In)	Dubnium (Db)	Sulphur (S)
Argon (Ar)	Iodine (I)	Fermium (Fm)	Terbium (Tb)
Boron (B)	Nickel (Ni)	Gallium (Ga)	Thorium (Th)
Niton	Osmium (Os)	Hafnium (Hf)	Thulium (Tm)
Radon (Rn)	Oxygen (O)	Hahnium (Hn)	Uranide
Xenon (Xe)	Radium (Ra)	Halogen	Uranium (U)

7 letters – cont:
Wolfram
Yttrium (Y)

8 letters:
Actinide
Actinium (Ac)
Antimony (Sb)
Astatine (At)
Chlorine (Cl)
Chromium (Cr)
Columbic
Didymium
Europium (Eu)
Fluorine (F)
Francium (Fr)
Hydrogen (H)
Illinium
Lutetium (Lu)
Masurium
Nebulium
Nitrogen (N)
Nobelium (No)
Platinum (Pt)
Polonium (Po)

Rubidium (Rb)
Samarium (Sm)
Scandium (Sc)
Selenium (Se)
Tantalum (Ta)
Thallium (Tl)
Titanium (Ti)
Tungsten (W)
Vanadium (V)

9 letters:
Alabamine
Aluminium (Al)
Americium (Am)
Berkelium (Bk)
Beryllium (Be)
Brimstone
Columbium
Germanium (Ge)
Jollotium
Lanthanum (La)
Magnesium (Mg)
Manganese (Mn)
Metalloid
Neodymium (Nd)

Neptunium (Np)
Palladium (Pd)
Plutonium (Pu)
Potassium (K)
Ruthenium (Ru)
Strontium (Sr)
Tellurium (Te)
Virginium
Ytterbium (Yb)
Zirconium (Zr)

10 letters:
Dysprosium (D)
Gadolinium (Gd)
Lanthanide
Lawrencium (Lr)
Meitnerium (Mt)
Molybdenum (Mo)
Phlogiston
Phosphorus (P)
Promethium (Pm)
Seaborgium (Sg)
Technetium (Tc)

11 letters:
Californium (Cf)
Einsteinium (Es)
Mendelevium (Md)
Transuranic
Unnilennium (Une)
Unnilhexium (Unh)
Unniloctium (Uno)
Ununquadium
(Uuq)

12 letters:
Darmstadtium
Kurchatovium
Nielsbohrium
Praseodymium (Pr)
Protactinium (Pa)
Unnilpentium (Unp)
Unnilseptium (Uns)

13 letters:
Rutherfordium
Transactinide
Unniliquadium
(Unq)

Elephant(ine) African, Babar, Hathi, Indian, Jumbo, Kheda, Mammoth, Mastodon, Oliphant, Pachyderm, Pad, Pink, Proboscidean, Rogue, Subungulata, Trumpeter, Tusker, White

Elephant-headed Ganesa

Elephant's ears Begonia

Elevate(d), Elevation, Elevator Agger, Attitude, Cheer, Colliculus, El, Eminence, Ennoble, Foothill, Glabella, Grain, Haute, Heighten, Hoist, Jack, Lift, Machan, Montic(u)le, Monticulus, Promote, → **RAISE**, Random, Relievo, Ridge, Rise, Steeve, Sublimate, Up(lift), Uplying, Upraise, Wallclimber

Eleven Elf, Hendeca-, Legs, O, Side, Tail-ender, Team, XI

Elf(in), Elves Alfar, Chiricaune, Dobbie, Dobby, Fairy, Fey, Fie, Goblin, Imp, Kobold, Ouph, Pigwiggen, Pixie, Ribhus, Sprite, Urchin

Elicit Evoke, Extract, Toase, Toaze, Tose, Toze

Eligible Available, Catch, Fit, Nubile, Parti, Qualified, Worthy

Eliminate, Elimination Cull, Deep-six, Delete, Discard, Exclude, Execute, Extirpate, Heat, Liquidate, Omit, Preclude, Purge, Red-line, Rid, Separate, Slay, Void, Zap

Elision Apocope, Synal(o)epha, Syncope

Elite Best, Choice, Crachach, Crack, → **CREAM**, Elect, Flower, Liberal, Meritocracy, Ton, Top drawer, Twelve pitch, U, Zaibatsu

Elixir Amrita, Arcanum, Bufo, Cordial, Daffy, Essence, Medicine, Panacea, Quintessence, Tinct

Elizabeth Bess(ie), Gloriana, Oriano

Elk Deer, Gang, Irish, Moose

Elkoshite Nahum

Ellipse, Elliptic Conic, Oblong, Oval

Elm Dutch, Rock, Slippery, Wahoo, Weeping, Wich, Winged, Wych

Elmer Gantry

Elongate Extend, Lengthen, Protract, Stretch

Elope Abscond, Decamp

Eloquence, Eloquent Articulate, Demosthenic, Facundity, Fluent, Honey-tongued, Oracy, Rhetoric, Speaking, Vocal

Else(where) Absent, Alibi, Aliunde, Et al, Other

Elucidate Explain, Expose, Interpret

Elude, Elusion, Elusive Avoid, Dodge, Eel, Escape, → **EVADE**, Evasive, Foil, Intangible, Jink, Slippy, Subt(i)le, Will o' the wisp

▶ **Elves** *see* **ELF**

Elysium Tir-nan-Og

Em Mut(ton), Pica

Emaciated, Emaciation Atrophy, Erasmus, Gaunt, Haggard, Lean, Skeleton, Skinny, Sweeny, Tabid, Thin, Wanthriven, Wasted

Email Flame, Spam

Emanate, Emanation Arise, Aura, Discharge, Exude, Issue, Miasma, Radiate, Spring

Emancipate(d), Emancipation Catholic, Deliver, Forisfamiliate, Free, → **LIBERATE**, Manumission, Uhuru

Emasculate Bobbitt, Castrate, Debilitate, Evirate, Geld, Unsex

Embalm Anoint, Mummify, Preserve

Embankment Berm, Bund, Causeway, Dam, Dyke, Earthwork, Levee, Mattress, Mound, Rampart, Remblai, Sconce, Staith(e), Stopbank, Terreplein

Embargo → **BAN**, Blockade, Edict, Restraint

Embark Begin, Board, Enter, Inship, Launch, Sail

Embarrass(ed), Embarrassing, Embarrassment Abash, Ablush, Awkward, Barro, Besti, Buttock-clenching, Chagrin, Cheap, Cringe-making, Cringe-worthy, Disconcert, Encumber, Gêne, Haw, Mess, Mortify, Pose, Predicament, Scundered, Scunnered, Shame, Sheepish, Squirming, Straitened, Toe-curling, Tongue-tied, Upset, Whoopsie, Writhing

▷ **Embarrassed** *may indicate* an anagram

Embassy Consulate, Embassade, Legation, Mission

Embed(ded) Fix, Immerse, Inlaid, Set

Embellish(ed), Embellishment Adorn, Beautify, Bedeck, Curlicue, Deck, Decorate, Dress, Embroider, Enrich, Fioritura, Frill, Garnish, Garniture, Mordent, → **ORNAMENT**, Ornate, Overwrought, Prettify, Rel(l)ish, Roulade, Story, Turn

Ember(s) Ash, Cinder, Clinker, Gleed

Embezzle(ment) Defalcate, Malversation, Peculate, Purloin, Shoulder, → **STEAL**

Embitter(ed) Acerbate, Aggravate, Enfested, Rankle, Sour

Emblem(atic) Badge, Bear, Colophon, Daffodil, Device, Figure, Ichthys, Impresa, Insignia, Kikumon, Leek, Lis, Maple leaf, Oak, Pip, Rose, Roundel, Shamrock, Sign, Spear-thistle, → **SYMBOL**, Tau-cross, Thistle, Token, Totem(ic), Triskelion, Wheel

Embody, Embodied, Embodiment Epitome, Fuse, Impanation, Incarnation, Incorporate, Personify, Quintessence, Version

Embolism Clot, Infarct

Emboss(ed) Adorn, Chase, Cloqué, Engrave, Matelassé, Pounce, Raise, Repoussé, Toreutic

Embrace(d) Abrazo, Accolade, Arm, Canoodle, Clasp, Clinch, Clip, Coll, Complect,

Comprise, Cuddle, Embosom, Encircle, Enclasp, Enclose, Enfold, Enlacement, Envelop, Espouse, Fold, Grab, Halse, Haulst, Hause, Hesp, Hug, Imbrast, Inarm, Inclasp, Inclip, Include, Inlace, Kiss, Lasso, Neck, Press, Snog, Snug(gle), Stemme, Twine, Welcome, Wrap

▷ **Embraces, Embracing** *may indicate* a hidden word

Embrocate, Embrocation Anoint, Arnica, Liniment

Embroider(y) Appliqué, Arrasene, Assisi, Battalia-pie, Braid, Brede, Couching, Crewellery, Crewel-work, Cross-stitch, Cutwork, Drawn threadwork, Embellish, Exaggerate, Eyelet, Fag(g)oting, Fancywork, Featherstitch, Filet, Framework, Gros point, Handiwork, Knotting, Lace(t), Laid work, Mola, Needlepoint, Needlework, Open-work, Opus anglicanum, Orfray, Ornament, Orphrey, Orris, Petit point, Pinwork, Pulled threadwork, Purl, Queen-stitch, Sampler, Sew, Smocking, Stitch, Stitchery, Stumpwork, Tambour, Tent, Wrap, Zari

Embroideress Mimi

Embroil Confuse, Entangle, Involve, Trouble

Embryo(nic), Embryologist Archenteron, Blastocyst, Blastospore, Blastula, Conceptus, Epicotyl, Fo(e)tus, Gastrula, Germ, Mesoblast, Morula, Nepionic, Neurula, Origin, Rudiment, Undeveloped, Wolff

Emend Adjust, Alter, Edit, Reform

Emerald Beryl, Gem, Green, Oriental, Smaragd, Uralian

Emerge(ncy), Emerging Anadyomene, Arise, Craunch, Crise, Crisis, Crunch, Debouch, Eclose, Emanate, Enation, Erupt, Exigency, Flashpoint, Hard-shoulder, Issue, Lash-up, Last-ditch, Loom, Need, Outcrop, Pinch, SOS, Spring, Stand-by, Stand-in, Strait, Surface

▷ **Emerge from** *may indicate* an anagram or a hidden word

Emerson Waldo

Emetic Apomorphine, Cacoon, Epicac, Evacuant, Ipecacuanha, Puke, Sanguinaria, Stavesacre, Tartar, Vomitory

Emigrant, Emigration Chozrim, Colonist, Italiot, Jordim, Redemptioner, Settler, When-we, Yordim

Emile Zola

Emily Ellis

Eminence, Eminent Alp, Altitude, Cardinal, Distinguished, Eximious, Grand, Height, Hill, Hywel, Inselberg, Knoll, Light, Lion, Lofty, Luminary, Noble, → **NOTABLE**, Note, Palatine, Prominence, Renown, Repute, Stature, Tor, Trochanter, → **VIP**, Wallah

Emirate Abu Dhabi, Dubai

Emissary Agent, Envoy, Legate, Marco Polo

Emission, Emit Discharge, Emanate, Field, Give, Issue, Spallation, Thermionic, Utter, Vent

Emmer Amelcorn, Wheat

Emollient Paregoric

Emolument Income, Perk, Remuneration, Salary, Stipend, Tip, Wages

Emotion(s), Emotional Affection, Anger, Anoesis, Atmosphere, Breast, Catharctic, Chord, Ecstasy, Empathy, Excitable, Feeling, Flare up, Freak-out, Gusty, Gut-wrenching, Hate, Heartstrings, Hoo, Hysteria, Intense, Joy, Limbic, Nympholepsy, Passion, Reins, Roar, Sensibility, Sensitive, Sentiment, Spirit, Theopathy, Torrid, Transport, Weepy

Emotionless Deadpan, Glassy

Empathy Identifying, Rapport, Rapprochement, Sympathy

Emperor Agramant(e), Akbar, Akihito, Antoninus, Augustus, Babur, Barbarossa,

Bonaparte, Caesar, Caligula, Caracalla, Charlemagne, Claudius, Commodus, Concerto, Constantine, Diocletian, Domitian, Ferdinand, Flavian, Gaius, Galba, Genghis Khan, Gratian, Great Mogul, Hadrian, Haile Selassie, Heraclius, Hirohito, HRE, Imp, Imperator, Inca, Jimmu, Justinian, Kaiser, Keasar, Kesar, King, Maximilian, Menelik, Mikado, Ming, Mogul, Montezuma, Mpret, Napoleon, Negus, Nero, Nerva, Otho, Otto, Penguin, Peter the Great, Purple, Pu-yi, Rex, Rosco, Ruler, Severus, Shah Jahan, Shang, Sovereign, Sultan, Tenno, Theodore, Theodosius, Tiberius, Titus, Trajan, Tsar, Valens, Valentinian, Valerian, Vespasian, Vitellius, Wenceslaus

Emphasis(e), Emphasize, Emphatic Accent, Birr, Bold, Dramatise, Ek se, Forcible, Foreground, Forzando, Hendiadys, Highlight, Italic, Marcato, Positive, Resounding, Risoluto, Sforzando, → **STRESS**, Underline, Underscore, Vehement

Empire Assyria, British, Byzantine, Celestial, Chain, Chinese, Domain, Empery, First, French, Georgia, Holy Roman, Indian, Kingdom, Latin, NY, Ottoman, Parthia, Persian, Principate, Realm, Reich, Roman, Russian, Second, Turkish, Western

Empiricism Positivism

Emplacement Battery, Platform

Employ(ment) Business, Calling, Designated, Engage, Exercitation, Hire, Occupy, Pay, Place, Portfolio, Practice, Pursuit, Service, Shiftwork, Trade, Use, Using, Utilise, Vocation

Employee(s) Barista, Casual, Clock-watcher, Factotum, Hand, Help, Hireling, Intrapreneur, Minion, Munchkin, Networker, Payroll, Pennyboy, Personnel, Rainmaker, Servant, Staff, Staffer, Valet, Walla(h), Worker, Workforce, Workpeople

Employer Baas, Boss, Malik, Master, Melik, Padrone, Taskmaster, User

▷ **Employs** *may indicate* an anagram

Emporium Bazaar, Shop, Store

Empower Authorise, Enable, Entitle, Permit

Empress Eugenie, Josephine, Messalina, Queen, Sultana, Tsarina, VIR

Empty Addle, Bare, Barren, Blank, Boss, Buzz, Claptrap, Clear, Deplete, Deserted, Devoid, Disembowel, Drain, Exhaust, Expel, Forsaken, Futile, Gousty, Gut, Hent, Hollow, Inane, Jejune, Lade, Lave, Meaningless, Null, Phrasy, Pump, Shallow, Teem, Toom, Tume, Unfurnished, Unoccupied, Unpeople, Vacant, Vacate, Vacuous, Vain, Viduous, → **VOID**

▷ **Empty** *may indicate* an 'o' in the word or an anagram

Empty-headed Vain

Emulate Ape, Copy, Envy, Equal, Imitate, Match

Emulsion Pseudosolution, Tempera

Enable Authorise, Capacitate, Empower, Permit, Potentiate, Qualify, Sanction

Enact Adopt, Effect, Ordain, Personate, Portray

Enamel(led), Enamel work Aumail, Champlevé, Cloisonné, Della-robbia, Dentine, Fabergé, Ganoin(e), Lacquer, Nail, Polish, Porcelain, Schwarzlot, Shippo, Smalto, Stoved, Vitreous

Encampment Bivouac, Douar, Dowar, Duar, Laager, Laer, Settlement

Encase(d), Encasement Box, Crate, Emboîtement, Encapsulate, Enclose, Obtect

Enchant(ing), Enchanted, Enchantment Bewitch, Captivate, Charm, Delight, Gramary(e), Incantation, Magic, Necromancy, Orphean, Rapt, Sirenize, Sorcery, Spellbind, Thrill

Enchanter, Enchantress Archimage, Archimago, Armida, Circe, Comus, Fairy, Lorelei, Magician, Medea, Mermaid, Prospero, Reim-kennar, Sorcerer, Vivien, Witch

Encircle(d) Belt, Enclose, Encompass, Enlace, Entrold, Gird, Hoop, Inorb, Introld,

Orbit, Pale, Ring, Stemme, → **SURROUND**, Wreathe

Enclave Cabinda, Ceuta, → **ENCLOSURE**, Melilla, Pocket, San Marino

Enclose(d), Enclosing, Enclosure Bawn, Beset, Boma, Box, Bullring, Cage, Carol, Carrel, Case, Circumscribe, Common, Compound, Corral, Court, Embale, Embowel, Embower, Enceinte, Enchase, Encircle, Enclave, Enhearse, Enlock, Enshrine, Fence, Fold, Forecourt, Garth, Haggard, Haining, Haw, Hem, Henge, Hope, Impound, In, Incapsulate, Inchase, Infibulate, Inlock, Insert, Interclude, Lairage, Obvolute, Paddock, Pale, Parrock, Peel, Pele, Pen(t), Petavius, Pightle, Pin, Pinfold, Pit, Playpen, Plenum, Rail, Rath, Recluse, Ree(d), Ring, Run, Saddling, Saleyard, Seal, Sekos, Sept, Seraglio, Serail, Several, Sin bin, Steeld, Stell, Stive, Stockade, Sty, → **SURROUND**, Tine, Unsaddling, Vibarium, Ward, Winner's, Wrap, Yard

Encode Cipher, Scramble

Encomium Eulogy, Praise, Sanction, Tribute

Encompass Bathe, Begird, Beset, Environ, Include, Surround

Encore Again, Agen, Ancora, Bis, Ditto, Do, Iterum, Leitmotiv, Recall, Repeat, Reprise

Encounter Battle, Brush, Close, Combat, Contend, Cope, Dogfight, Experience, Face, Hit, Incur, Intersect, Interview, → **MEET**, One-one, Rencontre, Ruffle, Skirmish, Tilt

Encourage(ment), Encouraging Abet, Acco(u)rage, Alley-oop, Animate, Attaboy, Bolster, Boost, Brighten, Buck, Cheer, Cohortative, Come-on, Comfort, Commend, Dangle, Egg, Elate, Embolden, Empatron, Exhort, Fillip, Fire, Fortify, Foster, Fuel, Gee, Hearten, Heigh, Help, Hope, Hortatory, Incite, Inspirit, Nourish, Nurture, Pat, Patronise, Proceleusmatic, Prod, Protreptic, Push, Reassure, Root, Stimulate, Support, Tally-ho, Train, Upcheer, Uplift, Urge, Wean, Yay, Yo

Encroach(ment) Eat out, Impinge, Infringe, Inroad, Intrude, Invade, Overlap, Overstep, Poach, Purpresture, Trespass, Usurp

Encrypt(ion) Coding, Public key

Encumber, Encumbrance Burden, Charge, Clog, Dead weight, Deadwood, Dependent, → **HANDICAP**, Impede, Load, Obstruct, Saddle

Encyclopaedic Comprehensive, Diderot, Extensive, Universal, Vast

End(ing) Abolish, Abut, Aim, Ambition, Amen, Anus, Arse, Big, Bitter, Bourn(e), Butt, Cease, Cessation, Cesser, Climax, Close, Closure, Cloture, Coda, Conclude, Crust, Culminate, Curtain, Curtains, Cut off, Dead, Death, Decease, Denouement, Desinence, Desistance, Destroy, Determine, Dissolve, Domino, Effect, Envoi, Envoy, Epilogue, Exigent, Expire, Explicit, Extremity, Fade, Fatal, Fattrels, Feminine, Fin, Final(e), Fine, Finis, → **FINISH**, Finite, Gable, Grave, Heel, Ice, Ish, Izzard, Izzet, Kill, Kybosh, Last, Let up, Little, Loose, Masculine, Mill, Nirvana, No side, Ort, Out, Outrance, Outro, Period, Peter, Pine, Point, Purpose, Quench, Receiving, Remnant, Rescind, Result, Roach, Round off, Runback, Scotch, Scrag, Shank, Slaughter, Sopite, Split, Sticky, Stub, Supernaculum, Surcease, Swansong, Tag, Tail, Tailpiece, Telesis, Telic, Telos, Term, Terminal, Terminate, Terminus, Thrum, Tip, Toe, Top, Ultimate, Up, Upshot, Utterance, West, Z

Endanger Hazard, Imperil, Periclitate, Risk, Threaten

Endear(ing), Endearment Adorable, Affection, Asthore, Bach, Caress, Cariad, Chuck, Darling, Dear, Ducks, Ducky, Enamour, Hinny, Honey(-bunch), Honey-chile, Ingratiate, Jarta, Lovey, Luv, Machree, Mavourneen, Peat, Pet, Pigsn(e)y, Sweet nothings

Endeavour Aim, Effort, Enterprise, Essay, Morse, Strain, Strive, Struggle, Try, Venture

Endemic Local, Prevalent

Endive Escarole

Endless Continuous, Ecaudate, Eternal, Eterne, Infinite, Interminable, Perpetual, Undated

▷ **Endlessly** *may indicate* a last letter missing

End of the world Doomsday, Ragnarok

Endorse(ment) Adopt, Affirm, Allonge, Approve, Assurance, Back, Certify, Confirmation, Docket, Initial, Okay, Oke, Ratify, Rubber stamp, Sanction, Second, Sign, Subscript, → **SUPPORT**, Underwrite, Visa

Endow(ment) Assign, Bequeath, Bestow, Bless, Cha(u)ntry, Dot, Dotation, Enrich, Foundation, Gift, Leave, Patrimony, State, Vest, Wakf, Waqf

Endurance, Endure(d), Enduring Abought, Aby(e), Bear, Bide, Brook, Dree, Dure, Face, Fortitude, Have, Hold, → **LAST**, Livelong, Lump, Marathon, Patience, Perseverance, Pluck, Ride, Stamina, Stand, Stay, Stomach, Stout, Substantial, Support, Sustain, Swallow, Tether, Thole, Timeless, Tolerance, Undergo, Wear, Weather

Endymion Bluebell

Enema Barium, Catharsis, Clyster, Purge

Enemy Adversary, Antagonist, Boer, Devil, Fifth column, Foe(n), Fone, Opponent, Public, Time

Energetic, Energise, Energy Active, Alternative, Amp, Animation, Arduous, Atomic, Binding, Bond, Cathexis, Chakra, Chi, Dash, Doer, Drive, Dynamic, Dynamo, E, Enthalpy, Entropy, EV, Fermi, Fireball, Firebrand, Firecracker, Force, Fossil, Free, Fructan, Fusion, Geothermal, Gism, Go, Go ahead, Graviton, Hartree, H.D.R., Horme, Input, Instress, Internal, → **JET**, Jism, Jissom, Joie de vivre, Joule, Kerma, Kinetic, Kundalini, Lattice, Libido, Life, Lossy, Luminous, Magnon, Moxie, Nuclear, Orgone, Pep, Phonon, Pithy, Potency, Potential, → **POWER**, Powerhouse, Prana, QI, Quantum, Quasar, Rad, Radiant, Radiatory, Renewable, Roton, Rydberg, Sappy, Second-wind, Solar, Stamina, Steam, Sthenic, Stingo, Tidal, Trans-uranic, Vehement, Verve, Vibrational, Vigour, Vim, Vital, Wave, Whammo, Whirlwind, Wind(-farm), Zappy, Zing, Zip

Enervate Exhaust

Enfold Clasp, Embrace, Envelop, Hug, Stemme, Swathe, Wrap

Enforce(ment) Administer, Coerce, Control, Exact, Implement, Impose

Eng Agma

Engage(d), Engagement, Engaging Absorb, Accept, Appointment, At, Attach, Bespoken, Betrothal, Bind, Book, Busy, Contract, Date, Embark, Employ, Engross, Enlist, Enmesh, Enter, Fascinate, Gear, Gig, Hire, Hold, Interest, Interlock, Lock, Mesh, Met, Occupy, Pledge, Promise, Prosecute, Reserve, Residency, Skirmish, Sponsal, Sponsion, Spousal, Sprocket, Trip, Wage, Winsome

▷ **Engagement** *may indicate* a battle

Engender Beget, Breed, Cause, Occasion, Produce

Engine, Engine part Air, Analytical, Athodyd, Atmospheric, Banker, Banking, Beam, Booster, Bricole, Bypass, Carburettor, Catapult, Compound, Diesel, Dividing, Donkey, Dynamo, Fan-jet, Fire, Four-cycle, Four-stroke, Gas, Gin, Heat, Humdinger, Internal combustion, Ion, Iron horse, Jet, Lean-burn, Light, Little-end, Locomotive, Machine, Mangonel, Mogul, → **MOTOR**, Nacelle, Oil, Onager, Orbital, Otto, Outboard, Overhead valve, Petard, Petrary, Petrol, Petter, Pilot, Plasma, Podded, Pony, Puffer, Pug, Pulp, Pulsejet, Push-pull, Put-put, Radial, Ramjet, Reaction, Reciprocating, Retrorocket, Rocket, Rose, Rotary, Scorpion, Scramjet, Search, Side-valve, Sleeve valve, Stationary, Steam, Stirling, Sustainer, Tank, Terebra, Testudo, Thermometer, Thruster, Top-end, Traction, Trompe, Turbine,

Turbofan, Turbojet, Turboprop, Two-handed, Two-stroke, V, Vernier, V-type, Wankel, Warwolf, Water, Wildcat, Winch, Winding

Engineer(ing), Engineers Aeronautical, AEU, Armstrong, Arrange, Austin, Badge, Baird, Barnes Wallis, Bazalgette, BE, Bessemer, Brindley, Brinell, Brunel, CE, Chartered, Concurrent, Contrive, De Lessops, Diesel, Eiffel, Fokker, Genetic, Greaser, Ground, Heinkel, Human, Interactive, Junkers, Kennelly, Knowledge, Liability, Manhattan District, Manoeuvre, Marconi, Marine, Mastermind, McAdam, Mechanical, Mechatronics, Military, Mime, Operator, Organise, Otto, Paper, Planner, Porsche, Process, RE, Repairman, Reverse, Rig, Rogallo, Royce, Sales, Samarski, Sanitary, Sapper, Savery, Scheme, Siemens, Sikorsky, Smeaton, Social, Software, Sound, Stage, Stephenson, Strauss, Systems, Telford, Tesla, Traffic, Trevithick, Wangle, Wankel, Watt, Whittle, Whitworth

England Albany, Albion, Blighty, Demi-paradise, Eden, John Bull, Merrie, Merry, Middle, The Old Dart

English(man) Angle, Anglican, Anglice, Baboo, Babu, Basic, Brit, Bro talk, Canajan, Choom, E, Ebonics, Eng, Estuary, Gringo, Hawaiian, Hong Kong, Indian, Irish, Jackeroo, John Bull, King's, Kipper, Limey, Middle, Mister, Modern, Newspeak, Norman, Officialese, Old, Oxford, Philippine, Pidgin, Plain, Pom(my), Pommie, Pongo, Pork-pudding, Queen's, Qui-hi, Qui-hye, Rock, Rooinek, Rosbif, Sassenach, Saxon, Scotic, Scottish, Seaspeak, Shopkeeper, Side, Singapore, Singlish, South African, South Asian, Southron, Southroun, Spanglish, Standard, Strine, Wardour Street, Woodbine, Yanqui, Yinglish

Engorge Devour, Glut, Swallow

Engraft Inset

Engrave(r), Engraving Aquatint, Blake, Carve, Cerography, Cerotype, Chalcography, Character, Chase, Cut, Die-sinker, Dry-point, Durer, Enchase, Eng, Etch, Glyptic, Glyptograph, Heliogravure, Hogarth, Impress, Inchase, Inciser, Inscribe, Insculp, Intagliate, Inter, Lapidary, Line, Mezzotint, Niello, Photoglyphic, Photogravure, Plate, Scalp, Scrimshander, Scrimshandy, Scrimshaw, Steel, Stillet, Stipple, Stylet, Stylography, Turn, Wood, Xylographer

Engross(ed) Absorb, Engage, Enwrap, Immerse, Inwrap, Monopolise, → **OCCUPY**, Preoccupy, Prepossess, Rapt, Sink, Writ large

Engulf Overwhelm, Swamp, Whelm

Enhance Add, Augment, Better, Elevate, Embellish, Exalt, Heighten, Improve, Intensify

Enigma(tic) Charade, Conundrum, Dilemma, Gioconda, Gnomic, Mystery, Oracle, Poser, Problem, → **PUZZLE**, Quandary, Question, Rebus, Recondite, Riddle, Secret, Sphinxlike, Teaser

Enjoin Command, Direct, Impose, Prohibit, Require

Enjoy(able), Enjoyment Apolaustic, Appreciate, Ball, Brook, Delectation, Fruition, Glee, Groove, Gusto, Have, High jinks, Lekker, Like, Own, Possess, Relish, Ripping, Savour, Taste, Wallow

Enlarge(ment), Enlarger Accrue, Acromegaly, Add, Aneurism, Aneurysm, Augment, Blow-up, Diagraph, Dilate, Exostosis, Expand, Expatiate, Explain, Increase, → **MAGNIFY**, Piece, Ream, Rebore, Sensationalize, Swell, Telescope, Tumefy, Upbuild, Varicosity

Enlighten(ed), Enlightenment Aufklarung, Awareness, Bodhisattva, Dewali, Disabuse, Divali, Edify, Educate, Explain, Haskalah, Illumine, Instruct, Liberal, Luce, Nirvana, Revelation, Satori, Verlig(te)

Enlist Attest, Conscript, Draft, Engage, Enrol, Induct, Join, Levy, Muster, Prest, Recruit, Rope in, Roster, Volunteer

Enliven(ed) Animate, Arouse, Brighten, Cheer, Comfort, Exhilarate, Ginger, Invigorate, Juice, Merry, Pep, Refresh, Warm

Enmity Animosity, Aversion, Bad blood, Hatred, Malice, Nee(d)le, Rancour, Spite

Ennoble(ment) Dub, Elevate, Ermine, Exalt, Honour, Raise

Ennui Boredom, Tedium

Enormous Colossal, Exorbitant, Gargantuan, Googol, Hellacious, Huge, Humongous, Humungous, → **IMMENSE**, Jumbo, Mammoth, Mega, Plonking, Vast, Walloper, Walloping

Enough Adequate, → **AMPLE**, Anow, Basta, Belay, Enow, Fill, Geyan, Nuff, Pax, Plenty, Qs, Sate, Satis, Sese, Sessa, Suffice, Sufficient, Via, When

Enounce Affirm, Declare, State

Enquire, Enquiring, Enquiry Ask, Case, Check, Curious, Eh, Examine, Inquest, Inquire, Organon, Public, Request, Research, Scan, See, Steward's, Trial

Enrage(d) Bemad, Emboss, Enfelon, Imboss, → **INCENSE**, Inflame, Infuriate, Livid, Madden, Wild

Enrapture(d) Enchant, Eprise, Ravish, Sent, Transport

Enrich Adorn, Endow, Enhance, Fortify, Fructify, Oxygenate

Enrol(ment) Attest, Conscribe, Conscript, Empanel, Enlist, Enter, Incept, → **JOIN**, List, Matriculate, Muster, Register

Ensconce(d) Establish, Niche, Settle, Shelter, Snug

Ensemble Band, Octet(te), Orchestra, Outfit, Ripieno, Set, Tout, Whole

Enshrine Cherish, Sanctify

Ensign Ancient, Badge, Banner, Duster, Ens, → **FLAG**, Gonfalon, Officer, Pennon, Red, White

Enslave(ment) Addiction, Bondage, Captivate, Chain, Enthral, Thrall, Yoke

Ensnare Illaqueate

Ensue, Ensuing Et sequens, Follow, Result, Succeed, Supervene, Transpire

Ensure Check

Entail Involve, Necessitate, Require

Entangle(ment) Ball, Cot, Elf, Embrangle, Embroil, Encumber, Ensnarl, Entrail, Fankle, Implicate, → **KNOT**, Mat, Ravel, Retiarius, Taigle, Trammel

Enter, Entry Admit, Board, Broach, Come, Enrol, Field, Infiltrate, Ingo, Inscribe, Insert, Intromit, Invade, Key in, Lodge, Log, Penetrate, Pierce, Post, Record, Run, Slate, Submit, Table, Wild card

Enterprise, Enterprising Adventure, Ambition, Aunter, Cash cow, Dash, Emprise, Forlorn hope, Free, Go ahead, Goey, Go-getter, Gumption, Industry, Minefield, Plan, Private, Project, Public, Push, Spirit, Starship, Stunt, Up and coming, Venture

Entertain(er), Entertaining, Entertainment Accourt, Acrobat, Afterpiece, All-dayer, All-nighter, Amphitryon, Amuse, Balladeer, Ballet, Beguile, Bread and circuses, Bright lights, Burlesque, Busk, Cabaret, Carnival, Cater, Charade, Cheer, Chout, Circus, Comedian, Comic, Concert, Conjure, Consider, Cottabus, Crack, Craic, Cuddy, Diseur, Diseuse, Distract, Divert, Divertissement, ENSA, Extravaganza, Fete, Fleshpots, Floorshow, Foy, Friendly lead, Fun, Gaff, Gala, Gas, Gaudy, Gig, Harbour, Harlequin, Have, Hospitality, Host(ess), Impressionist, Infotainment, Interest, Interlude, Intermezzo, Jester, Juggler, Karaoke, Kidult, Kursaal, Lap-dancer, Lauder, Leg-show, Levee, Light, Masque, Melodrama, Minstrel, Movieoke, Musical, Music hall, Olio, Opera, Palladium, Panto, Pap, Party, Peepshow, Performer, Piece, Pierrot, Play, Raree-show, Reception, Regale, Review, Revue, Rice, Ridotto, Rinky-dink, Roadshow, Rodeo, Rush, Serenade, Showbiz, Sideshow, Singer, Snake-charmer, Soirée, Son et lumière, Street theatre, Striptease,

Table, Tamasha, Tattoo, Treat, Variety, Vaudeville, Ventriloquist, Wattle

Enthral(l) Charm, Enchant, Enslave, Spellbind

Enthuse, Enthusiasm, Enthusiast(ic) Acclamatory, Amateur, Ardent, Ardour, Buff, Bug, Buzz, Cat, Cheerleader, Crazy, Crusader, Delirium, Demon, Devotee, Ebullience, Ecstatic, Empresse, Energy, Estro, Fandom, Fervid, Fiend, Fire, Flame, Freak, Furor(e), Geek, Get-up-and-go, Gung-ho, Gusto, Hacker, Hearty, Hype, Into, Keen, Lyrical, Mad, Mane, Mania, Motivated, Muso, Nethead, Nympholept, Oomph, Outpour, Overboard, Passion, Perfervid, Petrolhead, Preoccupation, Rah-rah, Raring, Rave, Relish, Rhapsodise, Schwärmerei, Sold, Spirit, Teeny-bopper, Verve, Warmth, Whacko, Whole-hearted, Wonk, Young gun, Zealot, Zest

Entice(ment), Enticing Allure, Angle, Cajole, Carrot, Dangle, Decoy, Draw, Lure, Persuade, Seductive, → **TEMPT**, Tole, Toll, Trepan

Entire(ly), Entirety Absolute, All, Bag and baggage, Clean, Complete, Full Monty, Genuine, Inly, Intact, Integral, In toto, Livelong, Lot, Purely, Root and branch, Systemic, Thorough, Total, Tout, → **WHOLE**

Entitle(ment) Birthright, Empower, Enable, Legitim, Name, Right

Entity Being, Body, Existence, Holon, Monad, Tao, Tensor, Thing, Virino

Entomologist Fabré

Entourage Cortège

Entrail(s) Bowels, Chawdron, Giblets, Gralloch, Guts, Ha(r)slet, Humbles, Lights, Numbles, Offal, Quarry, Tripe, Umbles, Viscera

Entrance(d), Entrant Access, Adit, Admission, Anteroom, Arch, Atrium, Attract, Avernus, Bewitch, Charm, Closehead, Contestant, Door, Doorstop, Double, Dromos, → **ENTER**, Eye, Fascinate, Foyer, Gate, Ghat, Hypnotise, In-door, Infare, Inflow, Ingate, Ingress, Inlet, Introitus, Jawhole, Jaws, Jib-door, Mesmerise, Mouth, Narthex, Pend, Porch, Porogamy, Portal, Porte-cochère, Postern, Propylaeum, Propylon, Ravish, Reception, Record, Regest, Registration, Single, Spellbound, Starter, Stem, Stoa, Stoma, Stulm, Throat, Torii

Entreat(y) Appeal, Ask, Beg, Beseech, Flagitate, Impetrate, → **IMPLORE**, Orison, Petition, Plead, Pray, Precatory, Prevail, Prig, Rogation, Solicit, Sue, Supplicate

Entrée Access, Dish, Entry, Ingate

Entrench(ment) Coupure, Encroach, Fortify, Trespass

Entrepreneur Businessman, E-tailer, Executor, Impresario, Wheeler-dealer

Entrust Aret(t), Charge, Confide, Consign, Delegate, Give

▶ **Entry** *see* **ENTRANCE**

Entwine Complect, Impleach, Intervolve, Lace, Twist, Weave

Enumerate, Enumeration Catalogue, Count, Detail, Fansi, List, Tell

Enunciate, Enunciation Articulate, Declare, Deliver, Diction, Elocution, Proclaim

Envelop(e) Arachnoid, Bangtail, Chorion, Corolla, Corona, Cover(ing), Cuma, Enclose, Entire, First day cover, Floral, Flown cover, Invest, Involucre, Jiffy(bag)®, Muffle, Mulready, Perianth, Sachet, Sae, Serosa, Shroud, Skin, Smother, Surround, Swathe, Window

Environment(s), Environmental(ist) ACRE, Ambience, Cyberspace, Ecofreak, Econut, Eco-warrior, Element, Entourage, Ergonomics, Green, Greenpeace, Habitat, Milieu, Realo, SEPA, Setting, Sphere, Surroundings, Umwelt, Vicinity

Envisage Contemplate, Imagine, Suppose

Envoi Farewell, RIP

Envoy Agent, Diplomat, Elchee, El(t)chi, Hermes, Legate, Plenipotentiary

Envy, Enviable, Envious Begrudge, Covet, Jaundiced, Jealousy, Penis, Plum

Enzyme ACE, Aldolase, Allosteric, Allozyme, Amylase, Amylopsin, Apyrase,

Arginase, Asparaginase, Autolysin, Bromel(a)in, Carbohydrase, Carbonic anhydrase, Carboxylase, Caspase, Catalase, Cathepsin, Cellulase, Cholinesterase, Chymopapain, Chymotrypsin, Coagulase, Collagenase, Constitutive, Cyclase, Cytase, Deaminase, Decarboxylase, Dehydrogenase, Diastase, Dipeptidase, Elastase, ELISA, Emulsin, Enolase, Enterokinase, Erepsin, Esterase, Fibrinolysin, Flavoprotein, Guanase, Histaminase, Hyaluronidase, Hydrase, Hydrolase, Inducible, Inulase, Invertase, Isomerase, Kallikrein, Kinase, Lactase, Lecithinase, Ligase, Lipase, Luciferase, Lyase, Lysin, Lysozyme, Maltase, Mutase, Neuraminidase, Nuclease, Oxdoreductase, Oxidase, Oxygenase, Papain, Pectase, Pectinesterase, Penicillinase, Pepsin(e), Peptidase, Permease, Peroxidase, Phosphatase, Phosphorylase, Plasmin, Polymerase, Protease, Proteinase, PSA, Ptyalin, Reductase, Ren(n)in, Restriction, Ribonuclease, Saccharase, Steapsin, Streptodornase, Streptokinase, Subtilisin, Sulfatase, Sulphatase, Synaptase, Telomerase, Thrombin, Thrombokinase, Thromboplastin, Transaminase, Transcriptase, Transferase, Transposase, Trehalase, Trypsin, Tyrosinase, Urease, Urokinase, Zymase

Eon Arch(a)ean, Epoch

Epaminondas Theban

Ephemera(l) Brief, Day, Drake, Fungous, Mayfly, Momentary, Passing, Transient, Transitory, Trappings

Epic Aeneid, Ben Hur, Beowulf, Calliope, Colossal, Dunciad, Edda, Epopee, Epyllion, Gilgamesh, Heroic, Homeric, Iliad, Kalevala, Lusiad(s), Mahabharata, Nibelungenlied, Odyssey, Ramayana, Rhapsody, Saga

Epicene Hermaphrodite

Epicure(an) Apicius, Apolaustic, Connoisseur, Friand, Gastronome, Gastrosopher, Glutton, → **GOURMAND**, Gourmet, Hedonist, Sybarite

Epidemic Pandemic, Pestilence, Plague, Prevalent, Rampant, Rash

Epigram Adage, Apophthegm, Gnomic, Mot, Proverb

Epigraph Citation, Inscription, RIP

Epilepsy, Epileptic Clonic, Eclampsia, Falling evil, Falling sickness, Fit, Grand mal, Petit mal, Turn

Epilogue Appendix, Coda, Postscript, Postlude

Epiphany Twelfthtide

Epiphenomenon ESP

Epiphyte Air-plant

Episcopalian PE, Prelatic

Episode(s), Episodic Bipolar, Chapter, Incident, Microsleep, Page, Picaresque, Scene, Serial

Epistle(s) Catholic, General, Lesson, Letter, Missive, Pastoral, Titus

Epitaph Ci-git, Hic jacet, Inscription, RIP

Epithet Adj(ective), Antonomasia, Apathaton, Byword, Curse, Expletive, Panomphaean, → **TERM**, Title

Epitome, Epitomise Abridge, Abstract, Digest, Image, Model, Summary, Typify

Epoch Age, Eocene, Era, Holocene, Magnetic, Miocene, Neogene, Oligocene, Palaeocene, Palaeolithic, Perigordian, Period, Pl(e)iocene, Pleistocene

Epsom salts Kieserite

Equable, Equably Calm, Just, Pari passu, Placid, Smooth, Tranquil

Equal(ly), Equality, Equal quantities Alike, All square, A(n)a, As, Balanced, Commensurate, Compeer, Egal(ity), Emulate, Equinox, Equiparate, Equity, Even, Even-steven, Ex aequo, Fe(a)re, Feer, Fiere, Fifty-fifty, For, Identical, Identity, Is, Iso-, Isocracy, Isonomy, Level, Level-pegging, Maik, Make, Match, Mate, Owelty,

Par, Parage, Parametric, Pari passu, → **PEER**, Peregal, Pheer(e), Rise, Rival, → **SO**, Square, Upsides, Wyoming, Ylike

Equanimity Aplomb, Balance, Poise, Serenity

Equate, Equation(s) Balance, Chemical, Cubic, Defective, Differential, Diophantine, Dirac, Exponential, Gas, Identity, Linear, Logistic, Maxwell, Parametric, Personal, Polar, Quadratic, Reduce, Relate, Rhizic, Schrödinger, Simultaneous, Van der Waals', Wave

Equator(ial) Celestial, Galactic, Line, Magnetic, Thermal, Tropical

Equerry Courtier, Officer, Page

Equilibrium Balance, Composure, Homeostasis, Isostasy, Poise, Punctuated, Stable, Stasis, Steady state, Tautomerism, Thermodynamic

Equinox Autumnal, Vernal

Equip(ment), Equipage Accoutrement, Adorn, Aguise, Aguize, Apparatus, Apparel, Appliance, Armament, Array, Attire, Carriage, Clobber, Codec, Deadstock, Deck, Dight, Expertise, → **FURNISH**, Gear, Gere, Get-up, Graith, Habilitate, Hand-me-up, Hardware, Headset, Kit, Material, Matériel, Mechanise, Muniments, Outfit, Paraphernalia, Plant, Receiver, Refit, Retinue, Rig, Sonar, Spikes, Stereo, Stock, Stuff, Tack(le), Tool, Trampet(te), Trampoline, Turn-out

Equity Actors, Equality, Justice, Law, Negative, Owner's, Union

Equivalence, Equivalent Akin, Amounting to, Correspondent, Dose, Equal, Equipollent, Ewe, Formal, In-kind, Same, Tantamount, Version

Equivocal Ambiguous, Dubious, Evasive, Fishy, Oracular, Vague

Equivocate Flannel, Lie, Palter, Prevaricate, Quibble, Tergiversate, Waffle, Weasel

Er Um

Era Age, Archaean, C(a)enozoic, Christian, Common, Cretaceous, Cryptozoic, Decade, Dynasty, Ediocaron, Eozoic, Epoch, Hadean, Hegira, Hej(i)ra, Hijra, Jurassic, Lias, Mesozoic, Palaeozoic, Period, Precambrian, Proterozoic, Republican, Torridonian, Vulgar

Eradicate, Erase Abolish, Delete, Demolish, Destroy, Dislimn, Efface, Expunge, Extirp, Obliterate, Purge, Root, Scrat, Scratch, Stamp-out, Strike off, Strike out, Uproot, Uptear

Erasmus Humanist

Eratosthenes Sieve

Erbium Er

Erect(ion), Erector Attolent, Boner, Build, Construct(ion), Elevate, Hard-on, Henge, Horn, Perpendicular, Priapism, Prick, Rear, Rigger, Stiffy, Straight-pight, Tentigo, Upright, Vertical

Ergo Argal, Hence, Therefore

Erica Heather, Ling

Ermine Fur, Minever, Miniver, Stoat

Ernie Bondsman

Erode, Erosion Abrade, Corrasion, Degrade, Denude, Destroy, Deteriorate, Detrition, Etch, Fret, Hush, Planation, Spark, Wash, Wear, Yardang

Eros, Erotic(a) Amatory, Amorino, Amorous, Aphrodisiac, Carnal, Cupid, Curiosa, Lascivious, Philtre, Prurient, Salacious, Steamy

Err(or) Aliasing, Anachronism, Bish, Blip, Blooper, Blunder, Boner, Boob(oo), Bug, Clanger, Comedy, Corrigendum, EE, Execution, Fat-finger, Fault, Fluff, Glaring, Heresy, Hickey, Human, Inaccuracy, Inherited, Jeofail, K'thibh, Lapse, Lapsus, Literal, Mackle, Mesprise, Mesprize, Misgo, Misprint, Misprise, Misprize, Misstep, → **MISTAKE**, Mumpsimus, Out, Parachronism, Probable, Rounding, Rove, Runtime, Sampling, Semantic, Sin, Slip, Slip-up, Solecism, Standard, Stray, Trip,

Truncation, Typo, Typographical, Unforced, Wander

Errand Ance, Chore, Commission, Fool's, Message, Mission, Once, Sleeveless, Task, Yince

Errand-boy Cad, Galopin, Page

Erratic Haywire, Spasmodic, Temperamental, Unstable, Vagary, Vagrant, Wayward

Erroneous False, Inaccurate, Mistaken, Non-sequitur

Ersatz Artificial, Synthetic

Erudite, Erudition Academic, Didactic, Learned, Savant, Scholar, Well-read, Wisdom

Erupt(ion), Erupture Belch, Brash, Burst, Ecthyma, Eject, Emit, Emphlysis, Exanthem(a), Exanthemata, → **EXPLODE**, Fissure, Flare, Fumarole, Hives, Hornito, Lichen, Mal(l)ander, Mallender, Morphew, Outbreak, Outburst, Papilla, Paroxysm, Plinian, Pompholyx, Pustule, Rash, Rose-drop, Scissure

Escalate, Escalator Accrescence, Expand, Granary, Grow, Lift, Snowball, Travolator

Escape(e), Escapade, Escapist Abscond, Atride, Avoid, Bale out, Bolt, Bolthole, Breakout, Caper, Close call, Eject, Elope, Elude, Elusion, Esc, Eschewal, Evade, Exit, Fire, Flee, Flight, Frolic, Fugacity, Gaolbreak, Hole, Hoot, Houdini, Houdini act, Hout, Lam, Lark, Leakage, Leg-it, Let-off, Levant, Loop(-hole), Meuse, Mews, Muse, Narrow, Near thing, Outlet, Prank, Refuge, Rollick, Runaway, Sauve qui peut, Scapa, Scarper, Seep(age), Shave, Slip, Splore, Vent, Walter Mitty, Wilding, Wriggle

Escapement Anchor, Dead-beat, Foliot, Recoil

Eschew Abandon, Avoid, For(e)go, Ignore, → **SHUN**

Escort Accompany, Attend, Beard, Bodyguard, Bring, Chaperone, Comitatus, Conduct, Convoy, Cortège, Corvette, Date, Destroyer, Entourage, Frigate, Gallant, Gigolo, Guide, Lead, Outrider, Protector, Retinue, See, Send, Set, Squire, Take, Tend, Usher, Walker

Escutcheon Achievement, Crest, Shield

Esker OS

Eskimo Aleut, Caribou, Husky, In(n)uit, Inuk, Inukitut, Thule, Yupik

Esoteric Abstruse, Acroamatic, Arcane, Inner, Mystic, Occult, Orphic, Private, Rarefied, Recondite, Secret

ESP Psi, Retrocognition

Especial(ly) Chiefly, Esp, Espec, Outstanding, Particular

Esperanto Ido, Zamenhof

Espionage Industrial, Spying, Surveillance

Esplanade Promenade, Walk

Esprit Insight, Spirit, Understanding, Wit

Esquire Armiger(o), Esq, Gent

Essay(s) Article, Attempt, Causerie, Critique, Dabble, Disquisition, Dissertation, Endeavour, Festschrift, Go, Paper, Prolusion, Sketch, Stab, Study, Theme, Thesis, Tractate, Treatise, Try

Essayist Addison, Bacon, Carlyle, Columnist, Elia, Ellis, Emerson, Hazlitt, Holmes, Hunt, Huxley, Lamb, Locke, Montaigne, Pater, Prolusion, Ruskin, Scribe, Steele, → **WRITER**

Essence Alma, Atman, Attar, Aura, Being, Core, Element, Entia, Esse, Extract, Fizzen, Flavouring, Flower, Foison, Gist, Heart, Hom(e)ousian, Inbeing, Inscape, Kernel, Marrow, Mauri, Mirbane, Myrbane, Nub, Nutshell, Oil, Ottar, Otto, Perfume, Per-se, Pith, Quiddity, Ratafia, Soul, Ylang-ylang

Essential(ly) Basic, Central, Crucial, Entia, Formal, Fundamental, Imperative, In, Indispensable, Inherent, Integral, Intrinsic, Kernel, Key, Lifeblood, Linch-pin,

Marrow, Material, Must, Necessary, Need, Nitty-gritty, Nuts and bolts, Part-parcel, Per-se, Prana, Prerequisite, Quintessence, Radical, Requisite, Sine qua non, Soul, Vital, Whatness

Essex Roseland

Establish(ed) Abide, Anchor, Ascertain, Base, Build, Chronic, Create, Deep-seated, Deploy, Embed, Enact, Endemic, Engrain, Ensconce, Entrench, Erect, Evince, Fix, → **FOUND**, Haft, Imbed, Ingrain, Instal(l), Instate, Instil, Institute, Inveterate, Ordain, Pitch, Pre-set, Prove, Raise, Redintegrate, Root(ed), Set, Stable, Standing, State, Stell, Substantiate, Trad, Trite, Valorise, Verify

Establishment Building, Business, CE, Church, Co, Concern, Creation, Hacienda, Household, Institution, Lodge, Proving ground, Salon, School, Seat, Succursal, System, Traditional

Estate, Estate-holder Allod(ium), Alod, Assets, Commons, Dais, Demesne, Domain, Dominant, Dowry, Est, Estancia, Fazenda, Fee-simple, Fee-tail, Fen, First, Fourth, General, Hacienda, Hagh, Haugh, Having, Hay, Housing, Industrial, Land-living, Latifundium, Legitim, Life, Manor, Messuage, Odal, Patrimony, Personal(ity), Plantation, Press, Princedom, → **PROPERTY**, Real, Runrig, Second, Situation, Spiritual, Standing, Talooka, Taluk(a), Temporal, Termer, Termor, Thanage, Third, Trading, Trust, Udal, Zamindari, Zemindari

Estate agent Realtor

Esteem(ed), Estimable Account, Admiration, Appreciation, Count, Have, Honour, Izzat, Los, Precious, Prestige, Price, Pride, Prize, Rate, → **REGARD**, Reputation, Respect, Store, Value, Venerate, Wonder, Worthy

Ester Benzocaine, C(o)umarin, Depside, Glyceride, Lactone, Olein, Palmitin, Phthalate, Psilocybin, Triglyceride, Urethan(e)

▶ **Estimable** *see* **ESTEEM**

Estimate, Estimation Appraise, Assess, Calculate, Carat, Conceit, Cost, Esteem, Extrapolation, Forecast, Gauge, Guess(timate), Inexact, Interval, Opinion, Point, Projection, Quotation, Rate, Rating, Reckon, Regard, Sight, Value, Weigh

Estrange Alienate, Disunite, Wean

Estuary Bay, Clyde, Creek, Dee, Delta, Firth, Gironde, Humber, Inlet, Mouth, Orwell, Ostial, Para, Rio de la Plata

Esurient Arid, Insatiable

Etc(etera) Et al(ia), So on

Etch(ing) Aquafortis, Aquatint(a), Bite, → **ENGRAVE**, Incise, Inscribe

Eternal(ly), Eternity Aeonian, Ageless, Endless, Everlasting, Evermore, Eviternal, Ewigkeit, Forever, Immortal, Infinity, Never-ending, Perdurable, Perpetual, Sempiternal, Tarnal, Timeless

Ether Atmosphere, Ch'i, Crown, Gas, Petroleum, Sky, Yang, Yin

Ethereal Airy, Delicate, Fragile, Heavenly, Nymph

Ethic(al), Ethics Deontics, Ideals, Marcionite, Moral, Principles, Situation, Work

Ethiopia(n) African, Amharic, Asmara, Cushitic, Falasha, Galla, Geez, Kabele, Kebele, Ogaden

Ethnic Racial, Roots

Ethyl ET

Etiquette Code, Conduct, Kawa, → **MANNERS**, Politesse, Propriety, Protocol, Ps and Qs, Punctilio

Etna Empedocles, Vessel, Volcano

Etonian Oppidan, Victim

Etruscan Tyrrhenian

Etymologist, Etymology Hobson-Jobson, Isodore

Eucalyptus Blackbutt, Bloodwood, Cadaga, Cadagi, Coolabah, Gum-tree, Ironbark, Jarrah, Mallee, Marri, Morrell, Red gum, Sallee, Sally, Stringybark, Sugar gum, Tallow wood, Tewart, Tooart, Tuart, Wandoo, Woolly butt, Yate

Eucharist Azymite, Communion, Housel, Mass, Prozymite, Supper, Viaticum

Euchre Jambone

Eugene Aram, Onegin

Eugenia Jambal, Jambolan(a), Jambu(l)

Eulogistic, Eulogy Encomium, Epaenetic, Epainetic, Laudatory, Panegyric, Praise, Tribute

Euphausia Krill, Shrimp

Euphemism Fib, Gosh, Gracious, Heck, Hypocorism

Euphoria, Euphoric Buzz, Cock-a-hoop, Ecstasy, Elation, High, Jubilation, Mindfuck, Nirvana, Rapture, Rush

Euphrasia Eyebright

Eurasian Chee-chee, Chi-chi

Europe(an) Balt, Bohunk, Bosnian, Catalan, Community, Continent, Croat, E, Esth, Estonian, Faringee, Faringhi, Feringhee, Fleming, Hungarian, Hunky, Japhetic, Lapp, Lett, Lithuanian, Magyar, Palagi, Polack, Ruthene, Ruthenian, Serb, Slavonian, Slovak, Slovene, Topi-wallah, Transleithan, Tyrolean, Vlach, Yugoslav

Europium Eu

Eustace Diamonds

Euthanasia Exit

Evacuate, Evacuation Excrete, Expel, Getter, Medevac, Movement, Planuria, Planury, Scramble, Stercorate, Stool, Vent, Void, Withdraw

Evade, Evasion, Evasive Ambages, Avoid, Circumvent, Cop-out, Coy, Dodge, Duck, Elude, Equivocate, Escape, Fence, Fudge, Hedge, Loophole, Mealymouthed, Parry, Prevaricate, Quibble, Quillet, Quirk, Salvo, Scrimshank, Shack, Shifty, Shirk, Shuffling, Sidestep, Skive, Skrimshank, Slippy, Stall, Subterfuge, Tergiversate, Waive, Weasel, Weasel out, Whiffler

Evaluate, Evaluation Appraise, Assess, Estimate, Gauge, Job, Ponder, Rate, Review, Waid(e), Weigh

Evanescent Cursory, Fleeting, Fugacious

Evangelical, Evangelist(ical) Buchman, Clappy-doo, Converter, Crusader, Fisher, Godsquad, Gospeller, Happy-clappy, Hot gospeller, Jansen, Jesus freak, John, Luke, Marist, Mark, Matthew, Missioner, Moody, Morisonian, Peculiar, Preacher, Revivalist, Salvationist, Salvo, Sankey, Sim(eonite), Stundist, Wild

Evaporate, Evaporation Condense, Dehydrate, Desorb, Disappear, Dry, Exhale, Steam, Steme, Ullage, Vaporise

Eve(ning) All Hallow's, Nightfall, Postmeridian, St Agnes's, Soirée, Subfusk, Sunset, Tib(b)s, Twilight, Vesperal, Vespertinal, Vigil, Yester

Evelyn Diarist, Hope

Even(ly), Evenness Aid, Albe(e), Albeit, All, Average, Balanced, Clean, Drawn, Dusk, Een, Ene, Equable, Equal, Erev, Fair, Fair play, Flush, Forenight, Iron, J'ouvert, Level, Level-pegging, Meet, Pair, Par, Plain, Plane, Plateau, Quits, Rib, Smooth, Square, Standardise, Temperate, Toss-up, Yet

Even-handed Ambidextrous

Evening flight Ro(a)ding

Evensong Vespers

Event Bash, Case, Circumstance, Contingency, Discus, Encaenia, Episode, Fest, Field, Fiesta, Gymkhana, Happening, Happy, Heat, Incident, Iron man, Landmark, Leg, Liquidity, Media, Meeting, Milestone, Occasion, Occurrence, Ongoing,

Outcome, Pass, Regatta, Result, Soirée, Stick-on, Three-day, Three-ring circus, Track, Triple

Even-toed Artiodactyl

Eventual(ity), Eventually Case, Contingent, Finally, Future, In time, Later, Nd, Sooner or later

Ever Always, Ay(e), Constantly, Eternal, Eviternity

Everglade Vlei

Evergreen Abies, Ageless, Arbutus, Cembra, Cypress, Gaultheria, Golden lie, Ivy, Myrtle, Olearia, Periwinkle, Pinaster, Privet, Thuja, Thuya, Washington, Winterberry, Yacca

Everlasting Cat's ear, Changeless, Enduring, Eternal, Immortal, Immortelle, Perdurable, Recurrent, Tarnal

Every(one), Everything All, A'thing, Complete, Each, Et al, Existence, Full Monty, Ilk(a), In toto, Monty, Sub chiz, Sum, The full monty, The works, To a man, Tout, Tout le monde, Universal, Varsal

Everyday Banal, Informal, Mundane, Natural, Ordinary, Plain, Routine

Everywhere Ambient, Omnipresent, Passim, Rife, Throughout, Ubique, Ubiquity

Evict(or) Disnest, Disseisor, Eject, Expel, Oust

Evidence, Evident Adminicle, Apparent, Argument, Axiomatic, Circumstantial, Clear, Compurgation, Confessed, Credentials, Direct, Distinct, DNA, Document, Empirical, Exemplar, Flagrant, Hearsay, Indicate, Internal, King's, Manifest, Marked, Material, Naked, Obvious, Overt, → **PATENT**, Plain, Premise, Prima facie, Probable, Proof, Queen's, Record, Sign, Smoking gun, State's, Surrebuttal, Testimony, Understandable

Evil Ahriman, Alastor, Amiss, Bad, Badmash, Bale, Beelzebub, Budmash, Corrupt, Depraved, Eale, Falling, Guilty, Harm, Heinous, Hydra, Ill, Immoral, Iniquity, King's, Malefic, Malign, Mare, Mischief, Monstrous, Necessary, Night, Perfidious, Rakshas(a), Shrewd, Sin, → **SINISTER**, Theodicy, Turpitude, Vice, Wicked

Evil eye Jettatura

Evince Disclose, Exhibit, Indicate, → **MANIFEST**, Show

Eviscerate(d) Debilitate, Disembowel, Drawn, Gralloch

Evoke Arouse, Awaken, Elicit, Move, Stir

▷ **Evolution** *may indicate* an anagram

Evolution(ary) Convergent, Countermarch, Development, Emergent, Growth, Holism, Lamarck, Lysenkoism, Moner(on), Neo-Lamarckism, Orthogenesis, Phylogeny, Social, Spencerman, Stellar, Transformism, Turning

Evolve Speciate

Ewe Crone, Gimmer, Keb, Rachel, Sheep, Teg, Theave

Ewer Aquamanale, Aquamanile, → **JUG**

Ex Former, Late, Quondam, Ten

Exacerbate Aggravate, Embitter, Exasperate, Irritate, Needle

Exact(ing), Exactitude, Exactly Accurate, Authentic, Careful, Dead, Definite, Due, Elicit, Estreat, Even, Exigent, Extort, Fine, Formal, It, Jump, Literal, Literatim, Mathematical, Meticulous, Nice(ty), Pat, Point-device, → **PRECISE**, Require, Slap-bang, Spang, Specific, Spot-on, Strict, Stringent, T, To a 't', Verbatim

Exaction Blackmail, Extortion, Impost, Montem, Sorelion, Tax

Exaggerate(d), Exaggeration Agonistic, Amplify, Ballyhoo, Boast, Brag, Camp, Colour, Distend, Dramatise, → **EMBROIDER**, Exalted, Goliathise, Hoke, Hyperbole, Inflate, Lie, Line-shoot, Magnify, Munch(h)ausen, Mythomania, Overdo, Overdraw, Overegg, Overpaint, Overpitch, Overplay, Overrate, Overstate, Overstretch, Over-the-top, Romance, Shoot a line, Steep, Stretch, Tall, Theatrical, Writ large

Exalt(ed), Exaltation Attitudes, Deify, Dignify, Elation, Enhance, Ennoble, Enthrone, Erect, Extol, Glorify, High, Jubilance, Larks, Lofty, Magnific, → **PRAISE**, Raise, Rapture, Ruff(e), Sama, Sublime, Supernal, Throne

Exam(ination), Examine, Examinee, Examiner Agrégé, A-level, Alnage, Analyse, Analyst, Appose, Assess, Audit, Auscultation, Autopsy, Baccalauréat, Biopsy, Case, Check-out, Check-up, Cognosce, Collate, Comb, Common Entrance, Consideration, Cross-question, CSE, Deposal, Depose, Disquisition, Dissect, Docimasy, Edexcel, Eleven plus, Endoscopy, Entrance, Expiscate, Explore, Eyeball, Finals, GCE, GCSE, Going-over, Grade(s), Great-go, Greats, Gulf, Haruspex, Hearing, Higher, Inspect, Inter, Interrogate, Interview, Introspection, Jerque, Jury, Laparoscopy, Little-go, Local, Mark, Matriculation, Medical, Mocks, Moderator, Mods, Mug, O-level, Once-over, Oral, Ordalian, Ordeal, Overhaul, Palp(ate), Paper, Peruse, Physical, Post-mortem, Prelims, Probe, Professional, Pry, Psychoanalyse, Pump, → **QUESTION**, Quiz, Ransack, Recce, Reconnaissance, Resit, Responsions, Review, Sayer, Scan, Schools, Scope, Scrutator, Scrutineer, Scrutinise, Search, Seek, Shroff, Sift, Sit, Smalls, Survey, Sus(s), Test, Trial, Tripos, Try, Unseen, Vet, Viva, Vivisection, Voir dire

Example Apotheosis, Assay-piece, Byword, Epitome, Erotema, Foretaste, → **FOR EXAMPLE**, Illustration, Instance, Lead, Lesson, Model, Paradigm, Paragon, → **PATTERN**, Praxis, Precedent, Prototype, Quintessence, Role model, Say, Shining, Showpiece, Specimen, Standard, Stormer, Such as, Touchstone, Type, Typify

Exasperate, Exasperating, Exasperation Anger, Embitter, Galling, Irk, Irritate, Nettle, Provoke

Excavate, Excavation, Excavator Armadillo, Burrow, Catacomb, Crater, Cutting, Delf, Delph, → **DIG**, Dike, Disinter, Ditch, Dragline, Dredge, Drift, Drive, Earthwork, Gaulter, Graft, Heuch, Heush, Hollow, JCB, Mine, Pichiciago, Pioneer, Pioner, Power shovel, Pyoner, Quarry, Shaft, Sink, Sondage, Steam-shovel, Stope, Well

Exceed, Exceeding(ly) Amain, Not half, Outdo, Outnumber, Overstep, Preponderate, Surpass, Transcend, Very

Excel(lence), Excellency, Excellent A1, Ace, Admirable, A-per-se, Assay-piece, Awesome, Bangin(g), Bang on, Beat, Beaut, Beezer, Better, Bitchin', Blinder, Bodacious, Boffo, Bonzer, Booshit, Boss, Bottler, Bravo, Brill, Bully, Capital, Castor, Champion, Cheese, Choice, Class(y), Classical, Cool, Copacetic, Copesettic, Copybook, Corking, Crack, Crackajack, Crackerjack, Crucial, Cushty, Daisy, Def, Dic(k)ty, Dilly, Dominate, Doozy, Dope, Elegant, Excelsior, Exemplary, Eximious, Exo, Extraordinaire, Fab, Fabulous, Fantastic, First rate, Five-star, Goodness, Great, Grit, Grouse, HE, High, Humdinger, Hunky(-dory), Inimitable, Jake, Jammy, Jim-dandy, Kiff, Knockout, La(l)la palooza, Laudable, Lollapalooza, Lummy, Matchless, Mean, Mega-, Merit, Neat, Noble, Olé, Out and outer, Outbrag, Outdo, Outstanding, Outtop, Overdo, Overpeer, Overtop, Paragon, Peachy, Peerless, Perfection, Phat, Prime, Pure, Quality, Rad, Rare, Rattling, Ring, Rinsin', Ripping, Ripsnorter, Say-piece, Shagtastic, → **SHINE**, Shit-hot, Sick-dog, Sik, Slammin(g), Socko, Spanking, Spiffing, Stellar, Stonking, Stupendous, Sublime, Superb, Super-duper, Superior, Supreme, Swell, Terrific, Tip-top, Top flight, Top-hole, Topnotch, Topping, Transcend, Transcendent, Triff, Virtue, Wal(l)y, War, Way-out, Wicked, Worth

Except(ion) Bar, But, Else, Exc, Nobbut, Omit, Save, Than, Then, Unless

Exceptional Abnormal, Anomaly, Cracker, Doozy, Egregious, Especial, Extraordinary, Gas, Rare, Ripsnorter, Select, Singular, Special, Uncommon, Zinger

Excerpt(s) Digest, Extract, Passage, Scrap

Excess(ive), Excessively All-fired, Basinful, Binge, Epact, Exaggeration,

Exorbitant, Extortionate, Extravagant, Flood, Fulsome, Glut, Hard, Inordinate,
→ **LAVISH**, Mountain, Needless, Nimiety, OD, Old, OTT, Outrage, Over, Overage,
Overblown, Overcome, Overdose, Overkill, Overmuch, Overspill, Over-the-top,
Owercome, Plethora, Preponderance, Profuse, Salt, Satiety, Spate, Spilth, Steep,
Superabundant, Superfluity, Surfeit, Surplus, Terrific, Thundering, Too, Troppo,
Ultra, Undue, Unequal, Woundily

Exchange Baltic, Bandy, Barter, Bourse, Cambist, Cash, Catallactic, Change, Chop,
Commodity, Commute, Confab, Contango, Convert, Cope, Corn, Ding-dong,
Employment, Enallage, Excambion, Foreign, Global, Inosculate, Interplay,
Ion, Labour, Logroll, → **MARKET**, Mart, Needle, Niffer, Paraphrase, PBX, Post,
Quid pro quo, Rally, Rate, Recourse, Redeem, Rialto, Royal, Scorse, Scourse,
Sister-chromated, Stock, Swap, Switch, Swop, Telephone, Tolsel, Tolsey, Tolzey,
→ **TRADE**, Traffic, Transfusion, Trophallaxis, Truck

Exchequer Remembrancer

Excise(man), Excise district Ablate, Bobbitt, Crop, Expunge, Gauger, Resect, Ride,
Tax

▷ **Excite(d)** *may indicate* an anagram

Excite(ment), Excitable, Excitability, Excited, Exciting Ablaze, Aboil, Abuzz,
Aerate, Aflutter, Agitate, Agog, Amove, Animate, Apeshit, Aphrodisiac, Arouse,
Athrill, Atwitter, Awaken, Brouhaha, Buck-fever, Climactic, Combustible,
Commotion, Delirium, Electrify, Emove, Enthuse, Erethism, Eventful, Feisty,
Fever, Fire, Flap, Flat spin, Frantic, Frenzy, Frisson, Furore, Fuss, Galvanise,
Gas, Grip, Headiness, Heat, Hectic, Het, Hey-go-mad, Highly-strung, Hilarity,
Hobson-Jobson, Hoopla, Hothead, Hyped, Hyper, Hypomania, Hysterical, Impel,
Incite, Inebriate, Inflame, Intoxicate, Jimjams, Kick, Kindle, Liven, Metastable,
Must, Neurotic, Oestrus, Orgasm, Overheat, Overwrought, Panic, Passion,
Pride, Prime, Provoke, Racy, Radge, Red-hot, Rile, Roil, → **ROUSE**, Rousement,
Ruff(e), Rut, Send, Sexy, Spin, Splash, Spur, Startle, Stimulate, Stir(e), Suscitate,
Swashbuckling, Temperamental, Tense, Tetanoid, Tetany, Tew, Thrill, Tickle,
Titillate, Turn-on, Twitter, Upraise, Va-va-voom, Waken, Whee, Whet, Whoopee,
Work up, Yahoo, Yerk, Yippee, Yoicks

Exclaim, Exclamation (mark) Ahem, Arrah, Aue, Begorra, Bliksem, Blurt,
Bo, Ceas(e), Crikey, Criv(v)ens, Dammit, Ecphonesis, Eina, Eish, Ejaculate,
Epiphonema, Eureka, Expletive, Fen(s), Good-now, Hadaway, Haith, Halleluiah,
Hallelujah, Heigh-ho, Hem, Hip, Hookey Walker, Hosanna, Inshallah, Interjection,
Moryah, Omigod, Oops, Phew, Pling, Pow, Protest, Pshaw, Sasa, Screamer, Sese(y),
Sessa, Unberufen, Vociferate, Walker, Whau, Whoops, Wirra, Wow, Yay, Yippee,
Yo-ho-ho, Yummy, Zounds

Exclave Cabinda

Exclude, Excluding, Exclusion Ban, Bar, Berufsverbot, Block, Competitive, Corner,
Debar, Deforcement, Disbar, Drop, Eliminate, Ex, Except, Excommunicate, Freeze
out, Omit, Ostracise, Outbar, Outwith, Pauli, Shut out, Social

Exclusive Cliquish, Closed-shop, Complete, Debarment, Elect, Esoteric, Monopoly,
Particular, Pure, Rare, Scoop, Select, Single, Sole

Excommunicate Curse

Excoriate Flay, Slam

Excrement, Excretion, Excretory Dirt, Doo-doo, Dung, Emunctory, Faeces,
Flyspeck, Frass, Jobbie, Keech, Meconium, Oliguria, Ordure, Poo(p), Poo-poo, Puer,
Pure, Refuse, Scatology, Shit(e), Sir-reverence, Stercoraceous, Strangury, Turd,
Urea, Waste, Whoopsie

Excrescence Aril, Carnosity, Caruncle, Enate, Gall, Growth, Knob, Knurl, Lump,

Nurl, Pimple, Pin, Spavin(e), Strophiole, Talpa, Twitter(-bone), Wart

Excruciate, Excruciating Agonising, Rack, Torment, Torture

Exculpate Acquit, Clear, Forgive

Excursion Airing, Cruise, Dart, Digression, Jaunt, Junket, Outing, Pleasure-trip, Road, Sally, Sashay, Sortie, Tour, Trip

Excuse, Excusable Absolve, Alibi, Amnesty, Bunbury, Condone, Essoin, Essoyne, Evasion, Exempt, Exonerate, Faik, Forgive, Let off, Mitigate, Occasion, Off come, Out, Overlook, Palliate, → **PARDON**, Plea, Pretext, Release, Salvo, Venial, Viable, Whitewash

Execrate Abhor, Ban, Boo, Curse

Execute(d), Executioner, Executive, Executor Abhorson, Accomplish, Account, Administrate, Behead, Carnifex, Deathsman, Despatch, Discharge, Dispatch, Exor, Finish, Fry, Gan, Gar(r)otte, Gin, Guardian, Hang, Headsman, Implement, Ketch, Kill, Koko, Literary, Lynch, Management, Martyr, Monsieur de Paris, Noyade, Official, Perform, Perpetrate, Pierrepoint, Politburo, Scamp, Top, Tower Hill, Trustee, Tyburn

Exemplar(y) Byword, Impeccable, Laudable, Model, Paragon, Perfect, St, Warning

Exemplify Cite, Epitomise, Illustrate, Instantiate, Satisfy

Exempt(ion) Dispensation, Exclude, Exeem, Fainites, Fains, Free, Immune, Impunity, Indemnity, Indulgence, Overslaugh, Quarter, Spare, Tyburn ticket, Vains

▷ **Exercise(d)** *may indicate* an anagram

Exercise(s) Aerobics, Air, Antic, Apply, Bench press, Burpee, Buteyko method, Cal(l)isthenics, Callanetics®, Chi kung, Cloze, Constitutional, Dancercise, Drill, Employ, Enure, Eurhythmics, Exert, Falun dafa, Falun gong, Five-finger, Floor, Gradus, Hatha yoga, Inure, Isometrics, Kata, Keepy-uppy, Kegel, Krav Maga, Lat spread, Lesson, Limber, Manual, Medau, Op, Operation, PE, Physical jerks, Pilates, Ply, Plyometrics, Popmobility, Practice, Practise, Preacher curl, Press-up, Prolusion, PT, Pull-up, Pump iron, Push-up, Qigong, Sadhana, Shintaido, Sit-up, Solfege, Solfeggi(o), Step (aerobics), Stretch, Tae-Bo®, Tai chi (ch'uan), Thema, Theme, Thesis, Train, Trampoline, Trunk curl, Use, Vocalise, Warm-down, Warm-up, Wield, Work, Work-out, Xyst(us), Yoglates, Yomp

Exert(ion) Conatus, → **EFFORT**, Exercise, Labour, Operate, Strain, Strive, Struggle, Trouble, Wield

Ex-European Japhetic

Exhalation, Exhale Breath, Fume, Miasma, Reek, Sigh, Steam, Transpire, Vapour

Exhaust(ed), Exhausting, Exhaustion, Exhaustive All-in, Backbreaking, Beaten, Beggar, Bugger(ed), Burn, Burn-out, Bushed, Clapped out, Consume, Deadbeat, Debility, Deplete, Detailed, Dissipate, Do, Done, Drain, Eduction, Effete, Emission, Empty, End, Enervate, Euchred, Fatigue, Flue, Fordo, Forfeuchen, Forfochen, Forfoughen, Forfoughten, Forjaskit, Forjeskit, Forspent, Forswink, Frazzle, Gruelling, Heat, Heatstroke, Inanition, Jet-lagged, Jet-stream, Jiggered, Knacker, Mate, Milk, Out, Outwear, Overtax, Peter, Play out, Poop, Powfagged, Puckerood, Puggled, Rag, Ramfeezle, Rundown, Sap, Shatter, Shot, Shotten, Spend, Spent, Stonkered, Tailpipe, Tire, Trauchled, Use, Used up, Wabbit, Wappend, Warby, Washed-up, Wasted, Waygone, → **WEARY**, Wind, Worn, Zonked

Exhibit(ing), Exhibition(ist), Exhibitioner Aquashow, Bench, Circus, Concours, Demo, Demonstrate, Demy, Diorama, Discover, Display, ENC, Endeictic, Evince, Expo, Expose, Fair, Hang, Indicate, Installation, Lady Godiva, → **MANIFEST**, Olympia, Pageant, Panopticon, Parade, Present, Retrospective, Rodeo, Salon, Scene, Set forth, Show(piece), Showcase, Show-off, Showplace, Sideshow, Stand, Viewing, Waxworks, Zoo

Exhilarate(d) Bubble, Cheer, Elate, Enliven

Exhort(ation) Admonish, Allocution, Caution, Counsel, Incite, Lecture, Par(a)
enesis, Persuade, Protreptic, Urge

Exhume Delve, Disinter, Resurrect, Unearth

Exigency, Exigent Demanding, Emergency, Pressing, Taxing, Urgent, Vital

Exile Adam, Babylon, Ban, Banish, Deport, Deportee, Emigré, Eve, Expatriate, Exul,
Galut(h), Ostracise, Outlaw, Relegate, Tax, Wretch

Exist(ence), Existing Be(ing), Corporeity, Dwell, Enhypostasia, Entelechy, Esse,
Extant, Haeccity, Identity, Inbeing, In esse, Inherent, Life, Lifespan, Live, Ontology,
Perseity, Solipsism, Status quo, Substantial, Ubiety

Existentialist Camus, Sartre

Exit Débouché, Door, Egress, Emergency, Gate, Leave, Log off, Log out, Outgate,
Outlet, Swansong, Vomitory

Exodus Book, Departure, Flight, Hegira, Hejira

Ex-official Outler

Exogamous Outbred

Exonerate(d) Absolve, Acquit, Clear, Excuse, Exempt, Shriven

Exorbitant Excessive, Expensive, Slug, Steep, Tall, Undue

Exorcise, Exorcist Benet, Lay

Exordium Opening, Preface, Prelude

Exotic Alien, Chinoiserie, Ethnic, Fancy, Foreign, Free, Outlandish, Strange

Expand(able), Expanse, Expansion Amplify, Boom, Branch out, Bulking, Develop,
Diastole, Dilate, Distend, Ectasis, Elaborate, → **ENLARGE**, Escalate, Flesh out,
Grow, Increase, Magnify, Ocean, Outspread, Outstretch, Snowball, Sprawl, Spread,
Stretch, Swell, Tensite, Vastitude, Wax, Wire-draw

Expatiate Amplify, Descant, Dwell, Enlarge, Perorate

Expatriate Banish, Colonial, Emigrate, Émigré, Exile, Outcast

Expect(ant), Expectation, Expected, Expecting Agog, Anticipate, Ask, Await,
Due, Foresee, Gravid, Hope, Imminent, Lippen, Look, Natural, On cue, Par, Pip,
Predict, Pregnant, Presume, Prim, Prospect, Require, → **SUPPOSE**, Tendance,
Think, Thought, Usual, Ween

Expectorant, Expectorate Expel, Guaiacol, Hawk, Spit

Expedient Advisable, Artifice, Contrivance, Fend, Make-do, Makeshift, Measure,
Politic, Resort, Resource, Shift, Stopgap, Suitable, Wise

Expedite, Expedition, Expeditious Advance, Alacrity, Anabasis, Celerity, Crusade,
Dispatch, Excursion, Fastness, Field trip, Hasten, Hurry, Kon-Tiki, Pilgrimage,
Post-haste, Quest, Safari, Short cut, Speed, Trek, Trip, Voyage

Expel Amove, Dispossess, Drum out, Egest, Evacuate, Evict, Excrete, Exile,
Exorcize, Hoof, Oust, Out(cast), Read out, Spit, Turn forth, Void

Expend(iture) Budget, Consume, Cost, Dues, Gavel, Goings-out, Mise, Occupy,
Oncost, Outgo(ing), Outlay, Poll, Squander, Tithe, Toll, Use, Waste

Expendable Cannon-fodder

Expense(s) Charge, Cost, Current, Exes, Fee, Housekeeping, Law, Oncost, Outgoing,
Outlay, Overhead, Price, Sumptuary

Expensive Chargeful, Costly, Dear, Executive, High, Salt, Steep, Upmarket,
Valuable

Experience(d) Accomplished, A posteriori, Assay, Blasé, Come up, Discovery,
Empiric, Encounter, Expert, → **FEEL**, Felt, Find, Foretaste, Freak-out, Gust,
Hands-on, Hard way, Have, Incur, Know, Learn, Live, Mature, Meet, Mneme,
Near-death, Old hand, Old-stager, Ordeal, Out-of-body, Pass, Plumb, Seasoned,
See, Senior, Sense, Sensory, Spin, Stager, Stand, Street-smart, Streetwise, Taste,

Transference, Trial, Trip, Trocinium, Try, Undergo, Versed, Veteran, Work, Worldly wise

Experiment(al) Attempt, Aufgabe, Avant-garde, Ballon d'assai, Control, Empirical, Essay, JET, Michelson-Morley, Peirastic, Pilot, Sample, Shy, Single-blind, Taste, Tentative, → **TRIAL**, Trial balloon, Try, Venture, Vivisection

Expert(ise) Accomplished, Ace, Adept, Adroit, Arch, Astacologist, Authority, Boffin, Buff, Cambist, Cocker, Cognoscente, Competent, Connoisseur, Crack, Craft, Dab(ster), Dabhand, Dan, Deft, Demon, Diagnostician, Digerati, Don, Egghead, Finesse, Fundi, Gourmet, Gun, Hotshot, Karateka, Know-all, Know-how, Luminary, Maestro, Masterly, Mastery, Maven, Mavin, Meister, Nark, Old hand, Oner, Oneyer, Oneyre, Peritus, Practised, Pro, Proficient, Pundit, Ringer, Savvy, Science, Shroff, Skill(y), Sly, Specialist, Technique, Technocrat, Troubleshooter, Ulema, Used, W(h)iz

Expiate, Expiation, Expiatory Amends, Atone, Penance, Piacular

Expire(d), Expiry Blow, Collapse, Croak, → **DIE**, End, Exhale, Invalid, Go, Ish, Lapse, Neese, Pant, Sneeze, Terminate

Explain(able), Explanation, Explanatory Account, Annotate, Apology, Appendix, Aread, Arede, Arreede, Clarify, Commentary, Conster, Construe, Decline, Define, Describe, Eclaircissement, Elucidate, Exegesis, Exegetic, Explicate, Exponible, Expose, Exposition, Expound, Extenuate, Farse, Gloss, Glossary, Gloze, Hypothesis, Justify, Key, Note, Parabolize, Preface, Reading, Rigmarole, Salve, Solve, Solution, Theory, Upknit.

Expletive Arrah, Darn, Exclamation, Oath, Ruddy, Sapperment

Explicit Clean-cut, Clear, Definite, Express, Frank, Full-on, Outspoken, → **PRECISE**, Specific, Unequivocal

Explode, Explosion, Explosive Agene, Airburst, Amatol, Ammonal, ANFO, Antimatter, Aquafortis, Backfire, Bang, Bangalore torpedo, Big bang, Blast, Booby-trap, Burst, C4, Cap, Cheddite, Chug, Controlled, Cordite, Cramp, Crump, Cyclonite, Debunk, Demolitions, Detonate, Dualin, Dunnite, Dust, Egg, Erupt, Euchloric, Euchlorine, Fireball, Firecracker, Firedamp, Firework, Flip, Fulminant, Fulminate, Gasohol, Gelatine, Gelignite, Grenade, Guncotton, Gunpaper, Gunpowder, HE, High, Initiator, Iracund, Jelly, Landmine, Low, Lyddite, Megaton, Melinite, Mine, Nail-bomb, Napalm, Nitre, Nitrobenzene, Nitrocotton, Nitro(glycerine), Outburst, Ozonide, Paravane, Payload, Petar(d), Petre, Phut, Plastic, Plastique, Pluff, Pop, Population, Pow, Priming, Propellant, Ptarmic, Pustular, Report, Roburite, SAM, Semtex®, Sheet, Shrapnel, Snake, Sneeze, Soup, Squib, Supernova, Tetryl, Thunderflash, Tinderbox, TNT, Tonite, Trinitrobenzene, Trotyl, Volatile, Volcanic, Warhead, Xyloidin(e)

Exploit(s), Exploiter, Exploitation Act, Adventure, Arbitage, Coup, Coyote, Deed, Develop, Escapade, Feat, Gest, Geste, Harness, Ill-use, Impose, Kulak, Manoeuvre, Milk, Mine, Mission, Parlay, Play on, Rachmanism, Ramp, Res gestae, Rip-off, Stunt, Sweat, Tap, Use, Utilise

Explore(r), Exploration Amerigo, Amundsen, Baffin, Balboa, Bandeirante, Banks, Barents, Bellingshausen, Bering, Boone, Burton, Byrd, Cabot, Cartier, Chart, Columbus, Cook, Cordoba, Cortes, Da Gama, Dampier, Darwin, De Soto, Dias, Diaz, Discover, Drake, Dredge, Eric, Eriksson, Examine, Feel, Field trip, Fiennes, Flinders, Frobisher, Fuchs, Humboldt, Investigate, Livingstone, Magellan, Map, Marco Polo, Mungo Park, Nansen, Navigator, Park, Pathfinder, Peary, Pioneer, Potholer, Probe, Przewalski, Rale(i)gh, Research, Rhodes, Ross, Scott, Scout, Search, Shackleton, Spaceship, Speke, Stanley, Sturt, Tasman, Vancouver, Vasco da Gama, Vespucci, Voyageur

▷ **Explosive** *may indicate* an anagram

Exponent Advocate, Example, Index, Interpreter, Logarithm

Export(s) Despatch, Frustrated, Invisible, Klondike, Klondyke, Ship, Visible

Expose(d), Exposure Air, Anagogic, Bare, Bleak, Blot, Blow, Burn, Crucify, Debag, Debunk, Denude, Desert, Disclose, Double, Endanger, En prisé, Exhibit, Flashing, Glareal, Indecent, Insolate, Moon, Nude, Object, Open, Out, Over, Paramo, Propale, Reveal, Showdown, Snapshot, Starkers, Streak, Strip, Subject, Sun, Time, Uncover, Unmask, Windburn, Windswept

Exposition Aperçu

Expostulate, Expostulation Argue, Arrah, Protest, Remonstrate

Expound(er) Discourse, Discuss, Exegete, Explain, Open, Prelict, Red, Scribe, Ulema

Express(ed), Expression, Expressionism, Expressive Abstract, Air, APT, Arrah, Aspect, Breathe, Cacophemism, Circumbendimus, Cliché, Colloquialism, Conceive, Concetto, Couch, Countenance, Declare, Denote, Eloquent, Embodiment, Epithet, Estafette, Explicit, Face, Fargo, Formulate, Godspeed, Good-luck, Gotcha, Gup, Hang-dog, Hell's bells, Idiom, Isit, Limited, Locution, Lyrical, Manifest, Metonym, Mien, Mot (juste), Neologism, Non-stop, Orient, Paraphrase, Phrase, Pleonasm, Pony, Precise, Pronouncement, Pronto, Put, Quep, Register, Say(ne), Shade, Show, Soulful, → **SPEAK**, State, Strain, Succus, Sumpsimus, Term, Token, Tone, Topos, Trope, Utterance, Vent, → **VOICE**

Expressionless Aphasia, Blank, Boot-faced, Deadpan, Impassive, Inscrutable, Po(ker)-faced, Vacant, Wooden

Expressman Fargo

Expropriate Dispossess, Pirate, Seize, Usurp

Expulsion Abjection, Discharge, Eccrisis, Ejection, Eviction, Exile, Pride's Purge, Sacking, Synaeresis

Expunge Cancel, Delete, Erase, Obliterate

Expurgate Bowdlerize, Castrate, Censor, Purge

Exquisite Beautiful, Choice, Ethereal, Fine, Intense, Lair, Macaroni, Pink, Princox, Refined, Soigné(e), Too-too

Ex-serviceman Vet

Extempore, Extemporise(d) Ad lib, Autoschediasm, Improvise, Pong

Extend(ed), Extension Add, Aspread, Augment, Conservative, Cremaster, Draw, Ecarté, Eke, Elapse, Ell, Elongate, Enlarge, Escalate, Expand, Exsert, Extrapolation, Fermata, Grow, Increase, Jumboise, Leaf, Length, Long, Long-range, Long-stay, Long-term, Offer, Outgrowth, Overbite, Overlap, Pong, Porrect, Proffer, Prolong, Propagate, Protract, Reach, Retrochoir, Span, Spread, Steso, → **STRETCH**, Substantial, Vert, Widen

Extensive, Extent Ambit, Area, Capacious, Catch-all, Compass, Comprehensive, Degree, Distance, Duration, Large, Latitude, Length, Limit, → **MAGNITUDE**, Panoramic, Range, Reach, Scale, Size, Spacious, Span, Spread-eagle, Sweeping, Wholesale, Wide, Widespread

Extenuate Diminish, Lessen, Mitigate, Palliate

Exterior Aspect, Crust, Derm, Exoteric, Facade, Outer, → **OUTSIDE**, Shell, Surface, Veneer

Exterminate, Extermination Abolish, Annihilate, Destroy, Ethnocide, Holocaust, The final solution, Uproot

External Exoteric, Exterior, Extraneous, Foreign, Outer

Extinct(ion) Archaeopteryx, Bucardo, Bygone, Chalicothere, Creodont, Dead, Death, Defunct, D(e)inothere, Dodo, Obsolete, Quagga, Quietus, Rasure, Rhytina, Saururae, Theodont

Extinguish Douse, Dout, Dowse, Dowt, Extirpate, Obscure, Quash, Quell, Quench, Slake, Slo(c)ken, Smother, Snuff, Stamp out, Stifle, Suppress

Extirpate End, Erase, Excise, Obliterate, Root, Uproot

Extol Commend, Enhance, Eulogise, Exalt, Laud, Puff

Extort(ion), Extortionate, Extortioner Barathrum, Blackmail, Bleed, Bloodsucker, Chantage, Chout, Churn, Compel, Exact, Force, Gombeen, Malversation, Montem, Outwrest, Rachman, Rack, Racketeer, Ransom, Rapacious, Screw, Shank, Sokaiya, Squeeze, Sweat, Urge, Vampire, Wrest, Wring

Extra Accessory, Additament, Addition(al), Additive, Adjunct, And, Annexe, Attachment, Bisque, Bonus, By(e), Debauchery, Encore, Etcetera, Frill, Further, Gash, Lagniappe, Left-over, Leg bye, Make-weight, More, Nimiety, No ball, Odd, Optional, Out, Over, Overtime, Perk, Plus, Plusage, Reserve, Ripieno, → **SPARE**, Spilth, Staffage, Sundry, Super, Supernumerary, Supplementary, Suppletive, Surplus, Trop, Undue, Walking-gentleman, Walking-lady, Wide, Woundy

Extract(ion), Extractor Apozem, Bleed, Breeding, Catechu, Clip, Corkscrew, Decoction, Descent, Distil, Draw, Educe, Elicit, Emulsin, Enucleate, Essence, Estreat, Excerpt, Exodontics, Extort, Gist, Gobbet, Insulin, Kino, Liver, Malta, Milk, Mine, Oust, Parentage, Passage, Pericope, Pick, Piece, Pituitary, Pry, Pyrene, Pyrethrin, Quintessence, Render, Retour, Smelt, Snippet, Soundbite, Squeeze, Stope, Suck, Summary, Tap, Tincture, Trie, Try, Vanilla, Vegemite®, Ventouse, Winkle, Worm, Wring, Yohimbine

Extradition Renvoi

Extraneous Extrinsic, Foreign, Irrelevant, Outlying, Spurious

Extraordinary Amazing, By-ordinar, Case, Curious, Egregious, Humdinger, Important, Nonesuch, Phenomenal, Preternatural, Rare, Singular, Startling, Strange, Unusual

Extrasensory Clairaudience, Clairvoyance, ESP

Extra time Lean

Extravagance, Extravagant, Extravaganza Bizarre, Bombastic, Dissipation, Enthusiasm, Excessive, Fancy, Feerie, Flamboyant, Glitzy, Heroic, High-flown, High roller, Hyperbole, Immoderate, Lavish, Luxury, Outré, Prodigal, Profligate, Profuse, Rampant, Reckless, Riotise, Romantic, Splash, Splurge, Squander, Sumptuous, Superfluous, Waste

▷ **Extreme** *may indicate* a first or last letter

Extreme(s), Extremely, Extremist, Extremity Acute, All-fired, Almighty, Butt, Deep-dyed, Desperate, Die-hard, Drastic, Edge, Exceptional, Farthermost, Gross, In spades, → **INTENSE**, Jacobin, Maximum, Mega-, Merveilleux, Militant, Minimum, Mondo, National Front, Nazi, Opposite, OTT, Over the top, Parlous, Pretty, Radical, Root and branch, Steep, Tendency, Terminal, The last cast, Thule, Too, Tremendous, Ultimate, Ultima thule, Ultra, Unco, Utmost, Utter, → **VERY**, Vitally, Wing

Extremity Bourn(e), Crisis, Digit, Ending, Finger(-tip), Limb, Limit, Outrance, Pole, Tip, Toe, Utterance

Extricate Liberate, Loose, Outwind, Rescue, Untangle

Extrinsic Aliunde, External, Irrelevant, Outward

Extrovert Lad, Outgoing

Extrude Debar, Eject, Project

Exuberance, Exuberant Brio, Copious, Ebullient, Effusive, Flamboyant, Gusto, Hearty, Joie de vivre, Lavish, Mad, Overflowing, Profuse, Rambunctious, Rumbustious, Skippy, Streamered

Exudation, Exude Bleed, Ectoplasm, Emit, Extravasate, Guttate, Ooze, Secrete,

Still, Sweat, Swelter, Ulmin, Weep

Exult(ant) Crow, Elated, → **GLOAT**, Glorify, Jubilant, Paeonic, Rejoice, Tripudiate, Triumphant, Whoop

Eye(s), Eye-ball, Eyeful, Eye movement, Eyepiece Aperture, Beady, Canthus, Compound, Cringle, Eagle, Ee, Eine, Electric, Emmetropia, Evil, Glad, Glass, Glim, Glom, Goggles, Hurricane, Huygen's, Iris, Jack, Keek, Klieg, Lamp, Lazy, Lens, London, Magic, Mincepie, Mind's, Mongoloid, Naked, → **OBSERVE**, Ocellar, Ocular, Ogle, Ommateum, Ommatidium, Optic, Orb, Pedicel, Peeper, PI, Pigsnie, Pigsn(e)y, Pineal, Private, Pupil, Regard, Retina, Rhabdom, Roving, Saccade, Saucer, Sclera, Screw, Seeing, Sheep's, Shufti, Shufty, Sight, Spy, Stemma, Storm-centre, Tec, Third, Uvea, Watch, Water-pump, Weather, Whally, Windows, Winker

Eyebright Euphrasy

Eyebrow Bree, Brent-hill, Glib, Penthouse, Superciliary

Eyeglass Loupe

Eyelash Cilium, Winker

Eyelet Cringle, Grommet, Hole

Eyelid Canthus, Ectropion, Haw, Palpebral, Winker

Eye-rod Rhabdom

Eye-shadow Kohl

Eyesore Blot, Disfigurement, Sty(e)

Eye-stalk Ommatophore, Stipes

Eye trouble Amblyopia, Ametropia, Aniridia, Aniseikonia, Anisomatropia, Aphakia, Asthenopia, Astigmatism, Caligo, Cataract, Ceratitis, Coloboma, Cycloplegia, Detached retina, Diplopia, Ectropion, Ectropium, Entropion, Erythropsia, Exophthalmus, Glaucoma, Gravel-blind, Hemeralopia, Hemi(an)op(s)ia, Hypermetropia, Hyperopia, Iritis, Keratitis, Leucoma, Lippitude, Micropsia, Miosis, Monoblepsis, Muscae volitantes, Mydriasis, Myosis, Nebula, Nyctalopia, Nystagmus, Ommateum, Palinop(s)ia, Photophobia, Photopsia, Pin and web, Pink-eye, Presbyopia, Proptosis, Ptosis, Retinitis, Retinoblastoma, Sandy blight, Scotoma(ta), Shiner, Stigmatism, Strabismus, Strephosymbolia, Strong, Stye, Synechia, Teichopsia, Thylose, Thylosis, Trachoma, Trichiasis, Tritanopia, Tylosis, Wall-eye, Xeroma, Xerophthalmia

Eye-wash Collyrium

Eyrie Nest

Ezra Pound

Ff

F Fahrenheit, Fellow, Feminine, Fluorine, Following, Force, Foxtrot
Fab Super
Fabian, Fabius Dilatory, Washington
Fable(s) Aesop, Allegory, Apologue, Exemplum, Fiction, Hitopadesa, La Fontaine, Legend, Lie, Marchen, Milesian, Myth, Panchatantra, Parable, Romance, Tale, Tarand
Fabric Acetate, → CLOTH, Contexture, Dévoré, Framework, Interfacing, Interlining, Orlon®, Plissé
Fabricate, Fabrication Artefact, Concoct, Construct, Contrive, Cook, Fake, Fangle, Figment, Forge, → INVENT, Lie, Make up, Porky, Trump, Weave, Web
Fabulous (beast), Fabulous place Apocryphal, Apologue, Chichevache, Chimera, Cockatrice, Eldorado, Fictitious, Fung, Gear, Griffin, Hippogriff, Hippogryph, Huma, Incredible, Jabberwock(y), Kylin, Legendary, Magic, Manticora, Manticore, Merman, Monoceros, Mythical, Opinicus, Orc, Phoenix, Roc, Romantic, Simorg, Simurg(h), Snark, Sphinx, Tarand, Tragelaph, Unicorn, Unreal, Utopia, Wivern, Wyvern, Yale
Facade Front(age), Frontal, Mask, Persona, Pretence
Face, Facing Abide, Affront, Ashlar, Ashler, Aspect, Audacity, Bold, Brave, Brazen, Caboched, Caboshed, Cheek, Chiv(v)y, Coal, Confront, Countenance, Culet, Dalle, Dare, Dartle, Deadpan, Dial, Eek, Elevation, Encounter, Facade, Fat, Favour, Features, Fineer, Fortune, → FRONT, Gardant, Girn, Gonium, Grid, Groof, Groue, Grouf, Grufe, Gurn, Hatchet, Head-on, Jib, Kisser, Light, Lining, Look, Lore, Mascaron, Meet, Metope, Moe, Mug, Mush, Obverse, Opposite, Outstare, Outward, Pan, Paper tiger, Pavilion, Phisnomy, Phiz(og), Physiognomy, Poker, Puss, Revet, Revetment, Roughcast, Rud, Rybat, Side, Snoot, Socle, Straight, Stucco, Tallow, Three-quarter, Type, Veneer, Vis(age), Visnomy, Withstand, Zocco(lo)
Face-ache Noli-me-tangere
Face-lift Rhytidectomy
Face-saving Redeeming, Salvo
Facet(ed) Angle, Aspect, Bezel, Culet, Face, Pavilion, Polyhedron
Facetious Frivolous, Jocular, Waggish, Witty
Facile Able, Adept, Complaisant, Ductile, Easy, Fluent, Glib
Facilitate, Facility Amenity, Assist, Benefit, Capability, Committed, → EASE, Expedite, Fluency, Gift, ISO, Knack, Provision, Skill
Facsimile Copy, Electrotype, Photostat®, Replica, Repro
Fact(s), Factual Actual, Brass tacks, Case, Corpus delicti, Correct, Data, Datum, Detail, Eo ipso, French, Gospel, Griff, In esse, Info, Literal, Mainor, Material, Nay, Poop, Really, Stat, Statistics, Truism, Truth, Veridical, Yes
Faction Bloc, Cabal, Camp, Caucus, Clique, Contingent, Ghibelline, Guelph, Junto, Red Army, Schism, Sect, Tendency, Wing
Factor(s) Agent, Aliquot, Broker, Cause, Chill, Clotting, Coagulation, Co-efficient,

Common, → **COMPONENT**, Divisor, Edaphic, Element, F, Feel-bad, Feel-good, Growth, House, Imponderabilia, Institorial, Intrinsic, Judicial, Load, Modulus, Multiple, Power, Q, Quality, Reflection, Representative, Rh, Rhesus, Risk, Safety, Steward, Unit, Utilization, Wind chill, X

Factory Brickworks, Cannery, Etruria, Gasworks, Glassworks, Hacienda, Maquiladora, Mill, Plant, Refinery, Sawmill, Shot tower, Steelworks, Sweatshop, Tanyard, Tinworks, Wireworks, Works, Workshop

Factotum Circar, Handyman, Servant, Sircar, Sirkar

Faculty Aptitude, Arts, Capacity, Department, Ear, Ease, Indult, Knack, Moral, Power, School, Sense, Speech, → **TALENT**, Teachers, Wits

Fad(dish) Crank, Craze, Cult, Fashion, Foible, Ismy, Thing, Vogue, Whim

Fade(d), Fading Blanch, Die, Diminuendo, Dinge, Elapsion, Etiolate, Evanescent, Fall, Filemot, Lessen, Mancando, Miffy, Pale, Passé, Perdendo(si), Peter, Smorzando, Smorzato, Stonewashed, Vade, Vanish, Wallow, Wilt, Wither

Faeces Cesspit, Dingleberry, Dung, Kak, Meconium, Motion, Mute, Number two, Scybalum, Skatole, Stercoraceous, Stools

Fag(g)ot(s) Bavin, Bundle, Fascine, Firewood, Homosexual, Kid, Knitch, Twigs

Fag(ging) Chore, Cigarette, Drag, Drudge, Fatigue, Gasper, Homosexual, Menial, Pennalism, Quean, Reefer, Snout, Tire, Toil, Weary

Fag-end Ash, Butt, Dout, Lag, Snipe, Stub

Fail(ing), Failure Achalasia, Ademption, Anile, Anuria, Awry, Backfire, Blemish, Blow, Bomb, Bummer, Burst-up, Cark, Chicken, → **COLLAPSE**, Conk, Crack up, Crash, Cropper, Debacle, Decline, Defalcation, Default, Defeat, Defect, Demerit, Demise, Die, Dog, Dry, Dud, Fault, Feal, Fiasco, Fink out, Flame out, Flivver, Flop, Flow, Flunk, Fold, Founder, Frost, Glitch, Gutser, Impotent, Infraction, Lapse, Lemon, Lose, Malfunction, Manqué, Meltdown, Mis-, Miscarry, Misfire, Misprision, Miss, Muff, Nerd, No-hoper, No-no, No-show, Omit, Outage, Oversight, Pip, Plough, Plow, Pluck, Pratfall, Reciprocity, Refer, Refusal, Respiratory, Shambles, Short(coming), Short circuit, Shortfall, Sink, Slippage, Smash, Spin, Stumer, Tank, Turkey, Vice, Wash-out, Waterloo, Weakness, White elephant, Wipeout

Fain Lief

Faineant Gallio

Faint(ness) Black-out, Conk, Darkle, Dim, Dizzy, Dwalm, Fade, Lassitude, Pale, Stanck, Swarf, Swarve, Swelt, Swerf, Swerve, Swoon, Swound, Syncope, Unclear, Wan, Whitish

Faint-heart Boneless, Coward, Craven, Eery, Timid, Wet

Fair Adequate, Aefauld, Aefwld, A(e)fald, Barnet, Bartholomew, Bazaar, Beauteous, Beautiful, Belle, Blond, Bon(n)ie, Bonny, Brigg, Decent, Dishy, Donnybrook, Equal, Equitable, Evenhanded, Exhibition, Expo(sition), Fancy, Feeing-market, → **FESTIVAL**, Fête, Fine, Fiona, Funfair, Gaff, Gala, Gey, Goose, Gwyn, Hiring, Honest, Hopping, Isle, Isold(e), → **JUST**, Kermess, Kermis, Kirmess, Market, Mart, Mediocre, Mela, Mop, Nundinal, Objective, OK, Paddington, Passable, Play, Pro rata, Rosamond, Sabrina, Sporting, Square, Statute, Steeple, Straight, Tavistock, Tidy, Tolerable, Tow-headed, Trade, Tryst, Unbias(s)ed, Vanity, Wake, Widdicombe, Xanthe

Fair-buttocked Callipygean

Fairing Ornament, Spat

Fairly Clearly, Enough, Evenly, Midway, Moderately, Pari passu, Pretty, Properly, Quite, Ratherish

Fairway Dog-leg, Pretty

Fairy, Fairies Banshee, Befana, Cobweb, Dobbie, Dobby, Elf(in), Fay, Gloriana, Good neighbour, Good people, Hob, Hop o' my thumb, Leprechaun, Lilian, Little people, Mab, Morgane(tta), Morgan le Fay, Moth, Nis, Oberon, Peri, Pigwidgin, Pigwiggen, Pisky, Pixie, Pouf, Puck, Punce, Queen Mab, Sandman, Seelie, Sidhe, Spirit, Sprite, Sugar-plum, Tink(erbell), Titania, Tooth, Unseelie, Urchin-shows

Faith(ful) Accurate, Achates, Belief, Constant, Creed, Cupboard, Devoted, Doctrine, Faix, Fay, Feal, Fegs, Fideism, Fiducial, Haith, Implicit, Islam, Lay, Loyal, Plerophory, Punic, Puritanism, Quaker, Religion, Shahada, Shema, Solifidian, Staunch, Strict, Troth, → **TRUE**, True-blue, Trust, Truth, Umma(h)

Faithless Atheist, Disloyal, False, Giaour, Hollow, Infidel, Nullifidian, Perfidious, Punic

Fake(d), Faker, Faking Bodgie, Bogus, Charlatan, Cod, Copy, Counterfeit, Duff(er), Ersatz, False, Fold, Forgery, Fraud, Fudge, Imitation, Imposter, Impostor, Paste, Phoney, Pirate(d), Postiche, Pretend, Pseudo, Sham, Spurious, Straw man, Toy, Trucage, Trumped up, Truquage, Truqueur, Unreal

Falcon Cast, Gentle, Hawk, Hobby, Iceland, Kestrel, Lanner(et), Merlin, Nyas, Peregrine, Prairie, Saker, Sakeret, Spar-hawk, Sparrow-hawk, Stallion, Staniel, Stannel, Stanyel, Stone, Tassel-gentle, Tassell-gent, Tercel-gentle, Tercel-jerkin

Falklander Kelper

Fall(s), Fallen, Falling, Fall out Abate, Accrue, Alopecia, Angel, Anticlimax, Arches, Astart, Autumn, Boyoma, Cadence, Caducous, Cascade, Cataract, Churchill, Chute, Collapse, Crash, Cropper, Cross press, Declension, Decrease, Degenerate, Descent, Dip, Domino effect, Douse, Downswing, Dowse, → **DROP**, Ebb, Firn, Flag, Flop, Flump, Folding press, Free, Grabble, Grand, Gutser, Gutzer, Horseshoe, Idaho, Iguaçu, Incidence, Kabalega, Kaieteur, Lag, Landslide, Lapse, Lin(n), Niagara, Oct(ober), Onding, Overbalance, Owen, Perish, Plonk, Plummet, Plump, Plunge, Precipitance, Prolapse, Ptosis, Purl(er), Rain, Reaction, Relapse, Ruin, Season, Sheet, Sin, Sleet, Snow, Soss, Spill, Stanley, Sutherland, Swallow, Tailor, Takakkau, Topple, Toss, Trip, Tugela, Tumble, Victoria, Voluntary, Wipeout, Yellowstone, Yosemite

Fallacious, Fallacy Elench(us), Error, Gamblers', Idolon, Idolum, Ignoratio elenchi, Illogical, Illusion, Material, Naturalistic, Pathetic, Sophism, Specious, Unsound

Fallible Human, Imperfect

▷ **Falling** *may indicate* an anagram or a word backwards

Fallow Barren, Lea, Tan, Uncared, Uncultivated, Untilled

False, Falsify, Falsification, Falsehood Adulterate, Assumed, Bastard, Bodgie, Bogus, Braide, Bricking, Calumny, Canard, Cavil, Charlatan, Cook, Counterfeit, Deceitful, Disloyal, Dissemble, Doctor, Fake, Feigned, Fiddle, Forge, Illusory, Knave, Lying, Meretricious, Mock, Obreption, Perjury, Pinchbeck, Postiche, Pretence, Pseudo, Rap, Refute, Roorback, Sham, Specious, Spoof, Spurious, Strumpet, Treacherous, Trumped-up, Two-faced, Untrue, Veneer

False notions Idola

Falter Hesitate, Limp, Stoiter, Totter, Waver

Fame, Famous Bruit, Cause célèbre, Celebrity, Distinguished, Eminent, Glitterati, Gloire, Glory, Greatness, History, Humour, Illustrious, Kudos, Legendary, Luminous, Megastar, Mononym, Name, Noted, Notorious, Prestige, Reclamé, Renown, Repute, Robert, Rumour, Splendent, Spotlight, Spur, Stardom, Word

Familiar(ise), Familiarity Accustom, Acquaint, Assuefaction, Au fait, Auld, Chummy, Comrade, Consuetude, Conversant, Couth, Crony, Dear, Demon, Easy, Free, Fresh, Friend, Habitual, Homely, Homey, Incubus, Intimate, Known, Liberty, Maty, Old, Old-hat, Privy, Python, Used, Versed, Warhorse

Family Ainga, Ancestry, Bairn-team, Blood, Breed, Brood, Clan, Class, Close-knit, Cognate, Consanguine, County, Descent, Dynasty, Extended, Eye, House(hold), Issue, Kin, Kind, Kindred, Line, Mafia, Medici, Name, Nuclear, One-parent, Orange, People, Phratry, Progeny, Quiverful, Race, Sept, Sib(b), Sibship, Single-parent, Stem, Stirps, Strain, Taffy, Talbot, Totem, Tribe, Whanau

Family tree Pedigree, Stemma

Famine Dearth, Lack, Scarcity

Famish(ed) Esurient, Hungry, Ravenous, Starving

▷ **Famished** *may indicate* an 'o' in the middle of a word

▷ **Fan** *may indicate* an anagram

Fan(s), Fan-like Adherent, Admirer, Aficionado, Alligator, Alluvial, Arouse, Bajada, Barmy-army, B-boy, Blow, Cat, Clapper, Claque, Colmar, Cone, Cool, Cuscus, Devotee, Diadrom, Dryer, Ducted, Enthusiast, Extractor, Fiend, Flabellum, Following, Goth, Grebo, Groupie, Headbanger, Hepcat, Khuskhus, Muso, Nut, Outspread, Partisan, Popette, Propellor, Punka(h), Rhipidate, Ringsider, Sail, Spectator, Spread, Supporter, Tail, Tifosi, Ventilate, Votary, Voteen, Washingtonia, Wind machine, Wing, Winnow, Zealot, Zelant

Fanatic(al) Bigot, Devotee, Energumen, Enthusiastic, Extremist, Fiend, Frenetic, Glutton, Mad, Maniac, Nut, Partisan, Phrenetic, Picard, Rabid, Santon, Ultra, Wowser, Zealot

Fancy, Fancies, Fanciful Caprice, Chim(a)era, Conceit, Concetto, Crotchet, Daydream, Dream, Dudish, Elaborate, Fangle, Fantasy, Fit, Flam, Florid, Frothy, Guess, Hallo, Idea(te), Idolon, → **IMAGINE**, Inclination, I say, Itch, Lacy, Liking, Maya, Mind, My, Nap, Notion, Opine, Ornamental, Ornate, Petit four, Picture, Pipe dream, Predilection, Reverie, Rococo, Suppose, Thought, Unreal, Urge, Vagary, Visionary, Ween, Whigmaleerie, Whigmaleery, Whim(sy), Woolgather

▷ **Fancy** *may indicate* an anagram

Fane Banner, Pronaos

Fanfare Flourish, Sennet, Show, Tantara, Trump, Tucket

Fang Tooth, Tusk

Fanny Adams, Bottom, Gas-lit, Price

Fantasist, Fantasy, Fantastic Absurd, Antic, Bizarre, Caprice, Centaur, Chimera, Cloud-cuckoo land, Cockaigne, Cockayne, Escapism, Fab, Fanciful, First class, Grotesque, Hallucination, Idol, Illusion, Kickshaw(s), Lucio, Mega, Myth, Outré, Phantasmagoria, Pipe-dream, Queer, Reverie, Romance, Schizoid, Unreal, Untrue, Walter Mitty, Wannabe(e), → **WHIM**, Whimsical, Wild, Wishful thinking

Far Apogean, Away, Distal, Distant, Eloi(g)n, Extreme, Outlying, Remote, Thether, Thither

Farce(ur), Farcical Burletta, Charade, Comedy, Exode, Feydeau, Lazzo, Mime, Mockery, Pantomime, Rex, Risible, Screaming, Sham, Travesty

Fare Apex, Charge, Cheer, Commons, Do, Eat, Excess, Excursion, → **FOOD**, Go, Passage, Passage money, Passenger, Rate, Table, Traveller

Farewell Adieu, Adios, Aloha, Apopemptic, Bye, Cheerio, Departure, Godspeed, → **GOODBYE**, Leave, Prosper, Sayonara, Send off, So long, Toodle-oo, Toodle-pip, Totsiens, Vale, Valediction

Far-fetched Fanciful, Improbable, Recherché

Farm(ing), Farmhouse Agronomy, Arable, Bender, Bocage, Bowery, City, Cold Comfort, Collective, Cooperative, Croft, Cultivate, Dairy, Deep-litter, Dry, Emmerdale, Estancia, Extensive, Factory, Fat, Fish(ery), Funny, Geoponical, Grange, Hacienda, Health, Home, Homestead, Husbandry, Intensive, Kibbutz, Kolkhoz, Land, Ley, Loaf, Location, Mailing, Mains, Mas, Mixed, No-tillage, Onstead, Orley,

Oyster, Pen, Plaas, Plough, Poultry, Ranch, Rent, Set-aside, Sewage, Shamba, Sheep station, Smallholding, Sovkhoz, Station, Stead(ing), Sted(d), Stedde, Steed, Stock, Store, Stump, Subsistence, Tank, Till, Toon, Toun, Town, Trash, Tree, Trout, Truck, Wick, Wind

Farmer Blockie, Boer, Campesino, Carl, Cockatoo, Cocklaird, Cocky, Collins Street, Colon, Cow cocky, Crofter, Estanciero, Gebur, Gentleman, George, Giles, Hick, Hobby, Husbandman, Macdonald, Metayer, Nester, NFU, Peasant, Pitt Street, Queen St, Ryot, Share-cropper, Smallholder, Sodbuster, Squatter, Stubble-jumper, Tax, Tenant, Tiller, Whiteboy, Yeoman, Zeminda(r)

Farmhand Cadet, Churl, Cottar, Cotter, Cottier, Cowman, Ditcher, Hand, He(a)rdsman, Hind, Land girl, Ploughman, Redneck, Rouseabout, Roustabout, Shearer, Stockman, Swineherd

▸ **Farmhouse** see FARM

Farmyard Barton, Homestall, Villatic

Faroe Islands FO

Farouche Awkward, Shy, Sullen

Farrago Hotch-potch, Jumble, Medley, Mélange

Farrier Marshal, Smith

Farrow Litter, Mia, Sow

Far-sighted Presbyte

Fart Poep, Trump

Farthing Brass, F, Fadge, Har(r)ington, Mite, Q, Quadragesimal, Rag

Fascia Band, Fillet, Platband

Fascinate(d), Fascinating, Fascinator Allure, Attract, Bewitch, → CHARM, Dare, Enchant, Engross, Enthral(l), Fetching, Inthral, Into, Intrigue, Jolie laide, Kill, Mesmeric, Rivet, Siren, Witch

Fascist Blackshirt, Blue shirt, Brownshirt, Dictator, Falange, Falangist, Iron Guard, Lictor, Nazi, Neo-Nazi, NF, Phalangist, Rexist, Sinarchist, Sinarquist

Fashion(able), Fashioned, Fashion house Aguise, À la (mode), Bristol, Build, Chic, Construct, Convention, Cool, Corinthian, Craze, Create, Cult, Custom, Cut, Dernier cri, Design, Directoire, Du jour, Elegant, Entail, Fad, Feat, Feign, Fly, Forge, Form, Genteel, Go, Hew, High, Hip, Hot, In, Invent, Kitsch, Look, → MAKE, Man-about-town, Manière, Manners, Method, Mode, Mondain(e), Mould, Newgate, Pink, Prada, Preppy, Rage, Rag trade, Rate, Roy, Sc, Shape, Smart, Smith, Snappy, Snazzy, Stile, Stylar, Style, Swish, Tailor, Ton, Ton(e)y, Tonish, → TREND(Y), Turn, Twig, Vogue, Way, Wear, With-it, Work, Wrought

Fast(ing), Faster Abstain, Apace, Ashura, Breakneck, Brisk, Citigrade, Clem, Clinging, Cracking, Daring, Dharna, Dhurna, Double-quick, Elaphine, Express, Fizzer, Fleet, Hypersonic, Immobile, Lent, Lightning, Loyal, Maigre, Meteoric, Moharram, Muharram, Muharrem, Pac(e)y, Posthaste, Presto, Pronto, Quadragesimal, Quick, Raffish, Raking, Ramadan, Ramadhan, Rash, Rathe, Relay, Siyam, Spanking, Speedy, Stretta, Stretto, Stuck, Supersonic, Sure, Swift, Tachyon, Thick, Tight, Tisha b'Av, TishaBov, Tishah-Baav, Tishah-b(e)Ab, Tishah-b(e)Av, Whistle-stop, Xerophagy, Yarer, Yom Kippur

Fast and loose Fickle, Prick-the-garter, Strap-game

Fasten(er), Fastening Anchor, Attach, Bar, Belay, Bind, Bolt, Buckle, Button, Chain, Clamp, Clasp, Click, Clinch, Clip, Cramp, Cufflink, Dead-eye, Diamond-hitch, Dome, Espagnolette, Eye-bolt, Frog, Gammon, Hasp, Hesp, Hitch, Hook, Infibulation, Lace, Latch, Lock, Moor, Morse, Nail, Netsuke, Nip, Nut, Padlock, Parral, Patent, Pectoral, Pin, Preen, Press stud, Reeve, Rivet, Rope, Rove, Screw, Seal, → SECURE, Sew up, Shut, Spar, Sprig, Staple, Steek, Stitch, Suspender,

Swift(er), Tach(e), Tag, Tape, Tassel, Tether, Thong, Tintack, Toggle, U-bolt, Velcro®, Wedge, Zip

Fastidious Chary, Critical, Dainty, Fusspot, Fussy, Neat, Nice, Overnice, Particular, Picky, Precieuse, Precious, Purism, Quaint, Queasy, Quiddler, Rosewater, Squeamish

Fat(s), Fatted, Fatten, Fatty Adipic, Adipocere, Adipose, Aldermanly, Aliphatic, Arcus, Atheroma, Bard, Batten, Battle, Blubber, Brown, Butter, Calf, Calipash, Calipee, Cellulite, Cholesterol, Chubbed, Chubby, Corpulent, Creesh, Degras, Deutoplasm, Dika-oil, Dosh, Dripping, Embonpoint, Enarm, Endomorph, Ester, Flab, Flesh, Flick, Fozy, Fubsy, Frank, Galam-butter, Grease, Gross, Keech, Kitchen-fee, Lanolin, Lard, Lard-ass, Leaf, Lipaemia, Lipid, Lipoma, Love handles, Margarine, Marge, Marrow, Mart, Moti, Motu, Obese, Oil, Oleomargarine, Olein, Olestra, OS, Palmitin, Pinguid, Plump, Poddy, Podgy, Polyunsaturated, Portly, Puppy, Pursy, Rich, Rolypoly, Rotund, Saddlebags, Saginate, Saim, Saturated, Schmal(t)z, Seam(e), Sebacic, Sebum, Shortening, Soil, Spare tyre, Spe(c)k, Squab, Stearic, Steatopygia, Steatorrhea, Suberin, Suet, Tallow, Tin, Tomalley, Triglyceride, Tub, Unsaturated, Vanaspati, Waller, Well-padded, Wool

Fatal(ism), Fate(s), Fated, Fateful Apnoea, Atropos, Cavel, Chance, Clotho, Deadly, Death, Decuma, Destiny, Doom, End, Fay, Fell, Joss, Karma, Kismet, Lachesis, Lethal, Lot, Meant, Moera, Moira, Morta, Mortal, Mortiferous, Nemesis, Nona, Norn(a), Parca, Pernicious, Portion, Predestination, Skuld, Urd, Verdande, Waterloo, Weird, Weird sisters

Father(s), Fatherly Abba, Abbot, Abuna, Adopt, Agnation, Apostolic, Bapu, Begetter, Breadwinner, Brown, City, Conscript, Curé, Da, Dad, Engender, Foster, Founding, Fr, Generator, Genitor, Getter, Gov, Governor, Guv, Male, NASCAR dad, Pa, Padre, Papa, Pappy, Parent, Pater(nal), Paterfamilias, Patriarch, Patroclinic, Père, Pilgrim, Pop(pa), Popper, Priest, Rev, Seraphic, Sire, Stud, Thames, Tiber, William

Father-lasher Sea-scorpion

Fathom Delve, Depth, Dig, F, Plumb, Plummet, Understand

Fatigue(d) Battle, Bonk, Combat, Compassion, Exhaust, Fag, Jade, Jet lag, ME, Metal, Neurasthenia, Overdo, Overwatch, Swinked, Time-zone, Tire, Weariness, Weary

Fatuous Gaga, Idiotic, Inane, Silly, Stupid

Faucet Cock, Spigot, Tap

Fault(y), Fault-finding Arraign, Bad, Beam, Blame(worthy), Blunder, Bug, Cacology, Captious, Carp, Compound, Culpa, Culpable, Defect, Demerit, Dip, Dip-slip, Drop-out, Duff, → **ERROR**, Failing, Flaw, Foot, Frailty, Gall, Glitch, Gravity, Henpeck, Hitch, Imperfect, Knock, Literal, Massif, → **MISTAKE**, Nag, Nibble, Niggle, Nit-pick, Oblique, Oblique-slip, Out, Outcrop, Overthrust, Pan, Para, Peccadillo, Pre-echo, Rate, Reprehend, Rift, Rupes Recta, San Andreas, Sclaff, Set-off, Short, Slip, Snag, Step, Strike, Strike-slip, Technical, Thrust, Trap, Trough, Underthrust, Upbraid, Vice

Faultless Immaculate, Impeccable, Lily-white, Perfect

Fauna Benthos, Mesobenthos, Wild life

Fauvist Matisse

Faux pas Blunder, Boner, Gaffe, Leglen-girth, Solecism

Favour(able), Favoured, Favourite Advance, Advantage(ous), Aggrace, Agraste, Alder-liefest, Approval, Auspicious, Back, Befriend, Behalf, Benign, Bless, Boon, Bribe, Cert, Chosen, Cockade, Condescend, Countenance, Curry, Darling, Ex gratia, Fancy, Favonian, Form horse, Good turn, Grace, Gracioso, Graste, Gratify, Gree, Hackle, Hot, In, Indulge, Kickback, Minion, Nod, Odour, Optimal, Particular, Peat,

Persona grata, Pet, Pettle, Popular, → **PREFER**, Promising, Propitious, Resemble, Rib(b)and, Roseate, Rose-knot, Rosette, Side, Smile, Toast, Token, Win-win

Fawn(er), Fawning Adulate, Bambi, Beige, Blandish, Brown-nose, Camel, Crawl, Creep, Cringe, Deer, Ecru, Flatter, Fleech, Footlick, Grovel, Ko(w)tow, Lickspittle, Obsequious, Servile, Slavish, Smarm, Smoo(d)ge, Subservient, Sycophant, Tasar, Toady, Truckle, Tussah, Tusseh, Tusser, Tussore

Fay Fairy, Korrigan, Peri

Faze Unnerve

FBI G-men

Fear Aichmophobia, Angst, Apprehension, Astra(po)phobia, Awe, Bathophobia, Bête noire, Bugbear, Claustrophobia, Cold sweat, Crap, Creeps, Cyberphobia, Dismay, Doubt, Drad, Dread, Dromophobia, Foreboding, → **FOR FEAR**, Fright, Funk, Genophobia, Hang-up, Horror, Kenophobia, Monophobia, Mysophobia, Nostopathy, Nyctophobia, Ochlophobia, Panic, → **PHOBIA**, Photophobia, Redoubt, Revere, Taphephobia, Taphophobia, Terror, Thalassophobia, Trepidation, Willies

Fearful Afraid, Cowardly, Dire, Horrific, Nervous, Pavid, Rad, Redoubtable, Timorous, Tremulous, Windy

Fearless Bold, Brave, Courageous, Daring, Gallant, Impavid, Intrepid

Fearsome Dire, Formidable

Feasible Goer, Likely, On, Possible, Practical, Probable, Viable

Feast(s) Adonia, Agape, Assumption, Banquet, Barmecide, Beano, Belshazzar's, Blow-out, Candlemas, Carousal, Celebration, Convive, Dine, Do, Double, Eat, Encaenia, Epiphany, Epulation, Festival, Fleshpots, Fool's, Gaudeamus, Gaudy, Hakari, Halloween, Hallowmas, Heortology, Hockey, Hogmanay, Holy Innocents, Id-al-Adha, Id-al-Fitr, Immaculate Conception, Ingathering, Isodia, Junket, Kai-kai, Lady Day, Lamb-ale, Lammas, Love, Luau, Lucullus, Martinmas, Michaelmas, Midnight, Movable, Noel, Passover, Pentecost, Pig, Potlatch, Purim, Regale, Revel, Roodmas, Seder, Shindig, Spread, Succoth, Sukkot(h), Tabernacles, Tuck-in, Wake, Wayzgoose, Weeks, Yule, Zagmuk

Feast-day Mass

Feat Achievement, Deed, Effort, Exploit, Gambado, Handspring, Stunt, Trick

Feather(s), Feathered, Feather-star Aigrette, Alula, Barbicel, Boa, Braccate, Cock, Contour, Covert, Crinoid, Crissum, Down, Duster, Egret, Filoplume, Flags, Fledged, Fletch, Flight, Gemmule, Hackle, Harl, Hatchel, Herl, Lei, Lure, Macaroni, Manual, Oar, Ostrich, Pen(na), Pin, Pinna, Pith, Plumage, Plume, Plumule, Prince's, Pteryla, Ptilosis, → **QUILL**, Rectrix, Remex, Remiges, Rocket-tail, Saddle-hackle, Scapular, Scapus, Secondary, Semiplume, Shaft, Shag, Sickle, Standard, Stipa, Swansdown, Tectrix, Tertial, Tippet, Vibrissa, White, Wing covert

Feather-worker Plumassier

Feature(s) Acoustic, Amenity, Appurtenance, Article, Aspect, Attribute, Brow, Character, Chin, Depict, Double, Eye, Eyebrow, Face, Facet, Figure, Hallmark, Highlight, Item, Jizz, Landmark, Lineament, Neotery, Nose, Nucleus, Overfold, Phiz(og), Physiognomy, Signature, Snoot, Spandrel, Star, Temple, Topography, Trait, Underlip

Featureless Flat

Febrifuge Atabrin, Atebrin®, Mepacrine, Quina

February Fill-dyke

Fecund(ity) Fertile, Fruitful, Prolific, Uberty

Fed Agent, G-man

Federal, Federation Alliance, Axis, Bund, Commonwealth, Interstate, League, Russian, Statal, Union

Fee(s) Base, Bench, Capitation, Charge, Chummage, Commitment, Common, Conditional, Contingency, Corkage, Corporation, Drop-dead, Dues, Duty, Emolument, Entrance, Entry, Faldage, Fine, Great, Groundage, Hire, Honorarium, Interchange, Mortuary, Mouter, Multure, Obvention, Pay, Pierage, Premium, Refresher, Retainer, Sub, Subscription, Transfer, Tribute

Feeble Banal, Characterless, Daidling, Debile, Decrepit, Droob, Effete, Feckless, Fizzenless, Flaccid, Foisonless, Footling, Fragile, Fus(h)ionless, Geld, Ineffective, Infirm, Jessie, Limp, Mimsy, Namby-pamby, Pale, Puny, Rickety, Sassy, Sickly, Slender, Slight, Soppy, Tailor, Tame, Thin, Tootle, Wallydrag, Wallydraigle, Washy, Wastrel, Weak, Weak-kneed, Weak-minded, Weed, Weedy, Wersh, Wet, Wimpish, Worn

Feed(er), Feeding Battle, Bib, Break, Browse, Cake, Cater, Cibation, Clover, Cowfeteria, Cram, Cue, Demand, Dine, Dressing, Drip, → **EAT**, Fatten, Filter, Fire, Fishmeal, Flushing, Fodder, Food, Force, Gavage, Graze, Hay, Input, Intravenous, Line, Lunch, Meal, Nourish, Nurse, Paid, Pecten, Provender, Refect, Repast, Sate, Soil, Stoke, Stooge, Stover, Suckle, Sustain, Tire, Tractor, Wean, Wet nurse

Feedback Negative, Positive

Feel, Feeling(s) Aesthesia, Affetuoso, Animus, Artificial, Atmosphere, Ballottement, Compassion, Darshan, Déja vu, → **EMOTION**, Empathy, Empfindung, Euphoria, → **EXPERIENCE**, Fellow, Finger, Flaw, Frisk, Grope, Groundswell, Handle, Hard, Heart, Heartstrings, Hunch, Intuit, Knock, Know, Palp, Passible, Passion, Phatic, Pity, Premonition, Presentiment, Probe, Realise, Sensate, Sensation, → **SENSE**, Sensitive, Sentiment, Somesthesis, Spirit, Sprachgefühl, Tactual, Tingle, Touch, Turn, Undercurrent, Vehemence, Vibes, Vibrations, Zeal

Feeler Antenna, Ballon d'essai, Barbel, Exploratory, Overture, Palp, Sensillum, Tentacle, Trial balloon

▶ **Feet** *see* **FOOT**

Feign Act, Affect, Colour, Fake, Malinger, Mime, Mock, → **PRETEND**, Sham, Simulate

Feint Deke, Disguise, Dodge, Faint, Fake, Spoof, Trick

Fel(d)spar Adularia, Albite, Anorthite, Bytownite, Gneiss, Hyalophane, Labradorite, Moonstone, Orthoclase, Peristerite, Petuntse, Petuntze, Plagioclase, Sanidine, Saussurite, Sun-stone

Felicity Bliss, Happiness, Joy, Relevance

▶ **Feline** *see* **CAT**

Fell Axe, Chop, Cruel, Deadly, Dire, Dread, Fierce, Heath, Hew, Hide, Hill, Inhuman, Knock-down, KO, Lit, Log, Malign, Moor, Pelt, Poleaxe, Ruthless, Sca, Shap, Skittle

Fellow(s), Fellowship Academic, Associate, Bawcock, Birkie, Bloke, Bo, Bro, Bucko, Buffer, Callan(t), Carlot, Cat, Chal, Chap, Chi, China, Chum, Co, Cock, Cod(ger), Collaborator, Co-mate, Communion, Companion, Comrade, Confrère, Cove, Cully, Cuss, Dandy, Dean, Dog, Don, Dude, Equal, F, Fogey, Fop, Gadgie, Gadje, Gaudgie, Gauje, Gink, Guy, Joe, Joker, Josser, Kerel, Lad, Like, M, Mall, Man, Mate, Member, Mister, Mun, Partner, Peer, Professor, Rival, Seniority, Sister, Skate, Sociate, Society, Sodality, Swab, Teaching, Twin, Waghalter, Wallah

Felon(y) Bandit, Convict, Crime, Gangster, Offence, Villain

Felt Bat(t), Drugget, Knew, Met, Numdah, Numnah, Pannose, Roofing, Sensed, Tactile, Underlay, Velour

▷ **Female, Feminine** *may indicate* an -ess ending

Female (bodies), Feminine, Feminist Anima, Bint, Bit, Dame, Distaff, Doe, F, Fair sex, Filly, Girl, Harem, Hen, Her, Kermes, Lady, Libber, Maiden, Muliebrity, Pen,

Petticoated, Pistillate, Riot girl, Sakti, Shakti, She, Sheila, Shidder, Soft, Spindle, Thelytoky, -trix, → **WOMAN**, Womens' libber, Yin

Fen Bog, Carr, Coin, Ea, Jiao, Marsh, Morass, Silicon, Wash, Yuan

Fence(r), Fencing (position) Appel, Balestra, Bar, Barrier, Botte, Carte, Croisé, Cyclone®, Deer, Derobement, Dogleg, Electric, Enclose, Épée, Feint, Flanconade, Flèche, Foils, Fraise, Froissement, Haha, Hay, Hedge, Hot, Hurdle, Iaido, Imbrocate, Inquartata, Kendo, Line, Link, Mensur, Molinello, Montant, Netting, Obstacle, Ox, Oxer, Pale, Paling, Palisade, Palisado, Parry, Passado, Pen, Picket, Post and rail, Quart(e), Quinte, Rabbit-fence, Rabbit-proof, Raddle, Rail, Rasper, Receiver, Reset, Ring, Scrimure, Seconde, Sepiment, Sept(um), Septime, Singlestick, Sixte, Snake, Snow, Stacket, Stockade, Stramac, Stramazon, Sunk, Swordplay, Tac-au-tac, Tierce, Touché, Trellis, Virginia, Wattle, Wear, Weir, Weldmesh®, Wire, Worm

Fend(er), Fend off Buffer, Bumper, Cowcatcher, Curb, Mudguard, Parry, Provide, Resist, Skid, Stiff-arm, Ward, Wing

Fennel Finnochio, Finoc(c)hio, Florence, Herb, Love-in-a-mist, Narthex, Ragged lady

Fent Offcut, Remnant, Slit

Feral Brutal, Fierce, Savage, Wild

Ferdinand Archduke, Bull

Ferment(ation) Barm, Enzym(e), Leaven, Mowburn, Protease, Ptyalin, Seethe, Solera, Storm, Stum, Trypsin, Turn, Vinify, Working, Ye(a)st, Zyme, Zymo-, Zymology, Zymosis, Zymotic, Zymurgy

Fermium Fm

Fern Acrogenous, Adder's-tongue, Adiantum, Archegonial, Asparagus, Aspidium, Asplenium, Azolla, Barometz, Beech, Bird's nest, Bladder, Bracken, Brake, Bristle, Buckler, Bungwall, Ceterach, Cinnamon, Coral, Cryptogam, Cyathea, Cycad, Dicksonia, Door, Elkhorn, Fairy moss, Filicales, Filices, Filmy, Fishbone, Grape, Hard, Hart's-tongue, Holly, Ice, Isoetes, Lady, Maidenhair, Male, Man, Mangemange, Marattia, Marsh, Marsilea, Marsilia, Meadow, Miha, Moonwort, Mosquito, Mulewort, Nardoo, Nephrolepis, Northern, Oak, Ophioglossum, Osmunda, Para, Parsley, Peppergrass, Pepperwort, Pig, Pillwort, Polypody, Polystichum, Ponga, Pteridology, Pteris, Punga, Rachilla, Rhizocarp, Rockbrake, Royal, Rusty-back, Salvinia, Scale, Schizaea, Scolopendrium, Seed, Shield, Silver, Snowbrake, Soft tree, Spleenwort, Staghorn, Sweet, Sword, Tara, Tree, Venus's hair, Walking, Wall rue, Water, Woodsia

Ferocious Brutal, Cruel, Fell, Predatory, Rambunctious, Savage, Tiger, Wild

Ferret Albin, Black-footed, Business, Fesnyng, Gill, Hob, Jill, Nose, Polecat, Ribbon, Rootle, Snoop, Trace, Unearth

Ferry(man) Charon, Convey, Flying bridge, Harper's, Hovercraft, Passage, Plier, Pont, Roll-on, RORO, Sealink, Shuttle, Soyuz, Train, Traject, Tranect

Fertile, Fertilisation, Fertilise(r), Fertility (symbol) Ammonia, Arable, Auxin, Ashtoreth, Battle, Bee, Bone-ash, Bone-earth, Bone-meal, Caliche, Caprify, Cleistogamy, Compost, Cross, Fat, Fecund, Fishmeal, Fruitful, Green, Guano, Heterosis, Humogen, Humus, In-vitro, IVF, Kainite, Linga, Manure, Marl, Nitrate, Nitre, Nitro-chalk, Pearl-ash, Phosphate, Pollen, Pollinator, Potash, Potassa, Priapus, Productive, Prolific, Rhiannon, Rich, Self, Sham, Stamen, Superphosphate, Uberous.

Fervent, Fervid, Fervour Ardent, Burning, Earnest, Heartfelt, Heat, Hwyl, Intense, Keen, Passionate, White-hot, Zeal, Zeloso

Fester Beal, Putrefy, Rankle, Rot, Suppurate

Festival, Festive, Festivity Adonia, Agon, Aldeburgh, Ale, Al Hijra(h), All Saints' Day, Ambarvalia, Anniversary, Anthesteria, Ashura, Assumption, Bairam, Baisak(h)i, Bayreuth, Beano, Beltane, Biennale, Bon, Candlemas, Carnival, Celebration, Cerealia, Chanuk(k)ah, Childermas, Church-ale, Circumcision, Commemoration, Convivial, Corpus Christi, Corroboree, Crouchmas, Dassehra, Day of awe, Dewali, Dionysia, Divali, Diwali, Doseh, Druid, Easter, Eisteddfod, Encaenia, En fête, Epiphany, → **FAIR**, Feast, Feast of weeks, Feis, Fête, Fête-champêtre, Fête-Dieu, Fête-galante, Fiesta, Fleadh, Fringe, Gaff, → **GALA**, Gaudy, Glastonbury, Glyndebourne, Gregory, Hallowmas, Hanukkah, Harvest, Harvest home, High day, Hock-tide, Hogmanay, Holi, → **HOLIDAY**, Holy-ale, Hosay, Hosein, Id-al-fitr, Imbolc, Imbolg, J'ouvert, Kermess, Kermiss, Kirmess, Kumbh Mela, Kwanzaa, Lady-Day, Lailat-ul-Qadr, Lammas, Laylat-al-Miraj, Lemural, Lemuria, Lesser Bairam, Let-off, Lughnasadh, Lupercalia, Martinmas, Matsuri, Mawlid, Mayday, Mela, Merry-night, Michaelmas, Miraj, Mod, Moomba, Navaratra, Navaratri, Noel, Obon, Palilia, Panathenaean, Panegyry, Pardon, Pasch, Passover, Pentecost, Pesa(c)h, Play, Plough Monday, Pongal, Pooja(h), Pop, Potlach, Puja, Purim, Quirinalia, Revel, Rosh Hashanah, Rush-bearing, Samhain, Saturnalia, Seder, Semi-double, Shabuath, Shavuath, Shemini Atseres, Shrove(tide), Simchas Torah, Simchat(h) Torah, Simchat Torah, Slugfest, Terminalia, Tet, Thargelia, Thesmophoria, Tide, Transfiguration, Up-Helly-Aa, Utas, Vesak, Vinalia, Visitation, Vulcanalia, Wake, Wesak, Woodstock, Yom Tob, Yomtov, Yuan Tan, Yule(tide)
Festoon Deck, Decorate, Encarpus, Garland, Swag, Wreathe
Fetch(ing) Arrive, Attract, Bring, Charming, Fet(t), Get, Gofer, Realise
Fête Bazaar, Champêtre, Entertain, → **FESTIVITY**, Gala, Honour, Tattoo
Fetish(ist) Charm, Compulsion, Gimp, Idol, Ju-ju, Obeah, Obi(a), Talisman, Totem, Voodoo
Fetter Basil, Bilboes, Chain, Gyve, Hamshackle, Hopple, Iron, Leg-iron, Manacle, Shackle
Fettle Arrange, Condition, Frig, Potter, Repair
Feu Tenure
Feud Affray, Blood, Clash, Feoff, Fief, Quarrel, Strife, → **VENDETTA**
Feudal (service), Feudalism Arriage, Auld-farrant, Fief, Forinsec, Old, Vassalage
Fever(ish) African coast, Ague, Beaver, Biliary, Blackwater, Brain, Breakbone, Buck, Cabin, Calenture, Camp, Cat-scratch, Cerebrospinal, Childbed, Dandy, Dengue, East coast, Enteric, Ferment, Fog, Frenetic, Gastric, Gate, Glandular, Haemorrhagic, Hay, Heatstroke, Hectic, Hyperpyretic, Insolation, Intense, Intermittent, Jail, Japanese river, Jungle, Kala-azar, Kissing disease, Lassa, Malaria, Malta, Marsh, Mediterranean, Miliary, Milk, Mono, Mud, Paratyphoid, Parrot, Parturient, Passion, Puerperal, Putrid, Pyretic, Pyrexia, Pyrogenic, Q, Quartan, Quintan, Quotidian, Rabbit, Ratbite, Recurrent, Relapsing, Remittent, Rheumatic, Rift Valley, Rock, Rocky Mountain spotted, Roseola, Sandfly, Scarlatina, Scarlet, Sextan, Ship, Splenic, Spotted, Spring, Stage, Sunstroke, Swamp, Swine, Tap, Temperature, Tertian, Texas, Tick, Trench, Typhoid, Typhus, Undulant, Valley, Verruga, Vomito, Weed, West Nile, Whot, Worm, Yellow(jack)
Few(er) Handful, Infrequent, → **LESS**, Limited, Scarce, Some, Wheen
Fey Clairvoyant, Eccentric, Elfin, Weird
Fez Tarboosh, Tarboush, Tarbush
Fiancé(e) Betrothed, Intended, Promised
Fiasco Bomb, Debacle, Disaster, Failure, Flask, Flop, Lash-up, Wash-out
Fiat Command, Decree, Edict, Order, Ukase

Fib Gag, → **LIE**, Prevaricate, Story, Taradiddle, Untruth

Fibre, Fibrous Abaca, Acrilan®, Acrylic, Aramid, Arghan, Backbone, Bass, Bast, Beta, Buaze, Bwazi, Cantala, Carbon, Coir, Constitution, Cotton, Courtelle®, Cuscus, Dietary, Dralon®, Elastane, Elastin, Filament, Filasse, Flax, Funicle, Giant, Glass, Gore-Tex®, Graded-index, Hair, Harl, Hemp, Henequen, Henequin, Herl, Hypha, Ispaghula, Istle, Ixtle, Jipyapa, Jute, Kapok, Kenaf, Kevlar®, Kittul, Lemniscus, Manilla, Monkey-grass, Monofil, Monomode, Moorva, Moral, Multimode, Mungo, Murva, Muscle, Myotube, Nap, Natural, Nerve, Noil(s), Nylon, Oakum, Olefin(e), Optic(al), Orlon®, Peduncle, Piassaba, Piassava, Pina, Pita, Polyarch, Pons, Pontine, Pulu, Raffia, Ramee, Rami, Ramie, Rayon, Rhea, Rock-cork, Roughage, Rove, Shoddy, Sida, Silk, Sisal, Slagwool, Sleave, Slub(b), Spandex, Splenium, Staple, Stepped-index, Sterculia, Strand, Strick, Sunn-hemp, Tampico, Tencel®, Toquilla, Tow, Uralite, Viver, Vulcanized, Wallboard, Watap, Whisker, Wood pulp

Fibula Bone, Brooch, Perone

Fickle(ness) Capricious, Change, False, Flibbertigibbet, Inconsistent, Inconstant, Kittle, Light, Mutable, Protean, Shifty, Varying, Volage, Volatile, Wind-changing

Fiction(al), Fictitious Airport, Bogus, Chick-lit, Cyberpunk, Fable, Fabrication, Legal, Myth, Pap, Phoney, Picaresque, Pulp, Romance, Science, Sex and shopping, Slash, Speculative, Splatterpunk, → **STORY**

Fiddle(r), Fiddling, Fiddlestring Amati, Bow, Calling-crab, Cello, Cheat, Crab, Cremona, Croud, Crouth, Crowd, Crwth, Do, Fidget, Fix, Gju, Ground, Gu(e), Gut-scraper, Jerrymander, Kit, Launder, Nero, Peculate, Petty, Potter, Racket, Rebec(k), Rig, Rote, Sarangi, Saw, Sawah, Scam, Scotch, Scrape, Scrapegut, Second, Spiel, Strad, Sultana, → **TAMPER**, Tinker, Toy, Trifle, Tweedle(-dee), Twiddle, Viola, → **VIOLIN**, Wangle

Fiddle-faddle Nipperty-tipperty

Fidelity Accuracy, Faith, Fealty, Loyalty, Troth

Fidget(y) Fantad, Fanteeg, Fantigue, Fantod, Fike, Fuss, Fyke, Hirsle, Hotch, Jimjams, Jittery, Niggle, Restive, Trifle, Twiddle, Twitch, Uneasy

Fiduciary Trustee

Fief Benefice, Fee

▷ **Field** *may indicate* cricket

Field(er), Fielding, Fields(man) Aalu, Aaru, Abroad, Aceldama, Aerodrome, Area, Arena, Arish, Arpent, Arrish, Campestral, Campestrian, Catch, Champ(s), Chief, Close, Coulomb, Cover, Cover-point, Diamond, Domain, Electric, Electromagnetic, Electrostatic, Elysian, Entry, Extra cover, Fid, Fine leg, Flodden, Flying, Force, Forte, Fylde, Glebe, Gracie, Gravitational, Grid(iron), Gull(e)y, Hop-yard, Ice, Keep wicket, Killing, Land, Landing, Lare, Lay, Lea(-rig), Leg slip, Ley, Line, Long leg, Long-off, Long-on, Longstop, Lords, Magnetic, Mead(ow), Mid-off, Mid-on, Mid-wicket, Mine, Oil, Padang, Paddock, Paddy, Parrock, Pasture, Peloton, Pitch, Playing, Point, Potter's, Province, Quintessence, Realm, Runners, Salting, Sawah, Scarecrow, Scope, Scout, Shamba, Short leg, Short stop, Silly, Slip, Sphere, Square leg, Stage, Stray, Stubble, Territory, Third man, Tract, Unified, Vector, Visual, W.C., World

Field marshal Allenby, Bulow, French, Haig, Ironside, Kesselring, Kitchener, Montgomery, Roberts, Robertson, Rommel, Slim, Wavell

Fieldwork Lunette, Ravelin, Redan, Redoubt, Tenaillon

Fiend Barbason, Demon, → **DEVIL**, Enthusiast, Flibbertigibbet, Frateretto, Hellhound, Hobbididance, Mahn, Modo, Obidicut, Smulkin, Succubus

Fierce(ly) Amain, Billyo, Breem, Breme, Cruel, Draconic, Dragon, Grim,

Hard-fought, Intense, Ogreish, Rampant, Renfierst, → **SAVAGE**, Severe, Tigerish, Tigrish, Violent, Wild, Wood, Wrathy, Wud

Fiery Ardent, Argand, Aries, Con fuoco, Dry, Fervent, Hot, Hotspur, Idris, Igneous, Impassioned, Leo, Mettlesome, Phlogiston, Sagittarius, Salamander, Zealous

Fiesta Festival, Fête, Gala, Holiday

Fife Piffero

Fifth Column, Diapente, Hemiol(i)a, Nones, Perfect, Quentin, Quint, Sesquialtera, Sextans

Fifty Bull, Demi-c, Jubilee, L

Fig Bania, Banyan, Benjamin-tree, Caprifig, Fico, Figo, Footra, Fouter, Foutra, Foutre, Hottentot, Indian, Moreton Bay, Mouldy, Sycamore, Sycomium, Sycomore, Trifle

Fight(er), Fighting Action, Affray, Agonistics, Aikido, Alpino, Altercate, Arms, Bandy, Bare-knuckle, Barney, → **BATTLE**, Bicker, Biffo, Blue, Bout, Box, Brave, Brawl, Bruiser, Bundeswehr, Bush-whack, Camp, Campaign, Chaud-mellé, Chetnik, Chindit, Combat, Compete, Conflict, Contest, Contra, Crusader, Cuirassier, Defender, Digladiation, Ding-dong, Dog, Donnybrook, Dreadnought, Duel, Encounter, Engagement, Extremes, Faction, Fecht, Fence, Fisticuffs, Flyting, Fray, Freedom, Free-for-all, Fund, Ghazi, Gladiator, Grap(p)le, Grudge, Gunslinger, Gurkha, Handicuffs, Hurricane, J(o)ust, Karate, Kite, Kumite, Lapith, Marine, Med(d)le, Medley, Mêlée, Mercenary, MIG, Militate, Mill, Mujahed(d) in, Mujahidin, Naumachy, Night, Partisan, Pellmell, Pillow, PLO, Prawle, Press, Pugilist, Pugnacity, Punch up, Rammy, Rapparee, Rejoneo, Repugn, Resist, Ring, Ruck, Ruction, Rumble, Run-in, Running, Savate, Sciamachy, Scold, Scrap, Scrape, Scrimmage, Scuffle, Shadow, Shine, Skiamachy, Skirmish, Slam, Soldier, Spar, Spat, Spitfire, Squabble, Stealth, Stoush, Straight, Strife, Struggle, Sumo, Swordsman, Tar, Tatar, Thersites, Toreador, Tuilyie, Tuilzie, Tussle, Ultimate, Umbrella, War(-dog), War-horse, War-man, Warplane, Warrior, Wraxle, Wrestle, Yike, Zero

Figment Delusion, Fiction, Invention

Figure(s), Figurine, Figurative Action, Arabic, Aumail, Bas-relief, Body, Build, Caganer, Canephorus, Cartouche, Caryatid, Cast, Chladni, Cinque, Cipher, Cone, Cube, Cypher, Decahedron, Digit, Ecorché, Effigy, Eight, Ellipse, Enneagon, Enneahedron, Epanadiplosis, Escher, → **FORM**, Fret, Fusil, Gammadion, Girth, Gnomon, Graph, Heptagon, Hexagon, Hour-glass, Icon, Icosahedron, Idol, Ikon, Image, Impossible, Insect, Intaglio, Integer, Interference, Lay, Lissajous, Magot, Manaia, Mandala, Matchstick, Moai, Monogram, Motif, Nonagon, Number, Numeral, Numeric, Octagon, Octahedron, Orant, Outline, Ovoid, Parallelepiped, Parallelogram, Pentacle, Pentalpha, Plane, Polygon, Polyhedron, Poussette, Prism, Puppet, Pyramid, Reckon, Repetend, Repoussoir, Rhomboid, See, → **SHAPE**, Sheela-na-gig, Significant, Simplex, Solid, Sonorous, Stat(istic)s, Statue(tte), String, Tanagra, Telamon, Tetragon, Tetrahedron, Torus, Triangle, Trigon, Trihedron, Triskele, Triskelion, Trisoctahedron, Tropology, Ushabti, Waxwork

Figure of speech Abscission, Allegory, Alliteration, Analogy, Antimask, Antimasque, Antimetabole, Antithesis, Asyndeton, Catachresis, Chiasmus, Deixis, Diallage, Ellipsis, Euphemism, Hendiadys, Hypallage, Hyperbaton, Hyperbole, Hysteron proteron, Irony, Litotes, Meiosis, Metalepsis, Metaphor, Metonymy, Onomatopoeia, Oxymoron, Paral(e)ipsis, Prolepsis, Prosopopoeia, Siddhuism, Simile, Solecism, Syllepsis, Synecdoche, Taxeme, Tmesis, Trope, Tropology, Zeugma

Figure study Arithmetic, Mathematics, Numeration

Figure-weaver Draw-boy

Filament Barbule, Byssus, Cirrus, Fibre, Fimbria, Floss, Gossamer, Hair, Hypha, Mycor(r)hiza, Myofibril, Paraphysis, Protonema, → **THREAD**, Whisker, Wreath

Filch Appropriate, Drib, Pilfer, Pinch, Prig, Purloin, Smouch, → **STEAL**

File, Filing(s) Abrade, Archive, Back up, Bastard, Batch, Binary, Box, Burr, Circular, Clyfaker, Coffle, Croc(odile), Crosscut, Database, Data set, Dead-smooth, Disc, Disk, Dossier, Enter, Floatcut, Folder, Generation, Half-round, In-box, Index, Indian, Lemel, Limail, Lever-arch, Limation, Line, Lodge, Nail, Out-box, Packed, Pickpocket, Pigeon-hole, Podcast, Pollute, Quannet, Rank, Rasp, Rat-tail, README, Riffler, Risp, Rolodex®, Row, Scalprum, Scratch, Single, Single-cut, String, Swap, Swarf, Text, Tickler, TIF(F)

Filial generation F1

Filibuster Freebooter, Hinder, Obstruct, Pirate, Run on, Stonewall

Filigree Delicate, Fretwork, Sheer

Filipino Igorot, Moro, → **PHILIPPINE(S)**

Fill(ing), Filler Anaplerosis, Balaam, Banoffee, Banoffi, Beaumontag(u)e, Beaumontique, Billow, Bishop, Bloat, Brick-nog, Brim, Bump, Centre, Charge, Cram, Fat-lute, Ganache, Gather, Gorge, Heart, Imbue, Implete, Impregn(ate), Inlay, Instill, Jampack, Line, Mastic, Occupy, Pabulous, Packing, Permeate, Plug, Replenish, Repletive, Salpicon, Sate, Satisfy, Sealant, Shim, Slush, Stack, Stock, Stocking, Stopping, → **STUFF**, Tales, Tank-up, Teem, Top up, Ullage

Fillet(s) Anadem, Annulet, Band, Bandeau, Bandelet, Bone, Cloisonné, Flaunching, Fret, Goujons, Grenadine, Headband, Infula, Label, Lemniscus, List(el), Mitre, Moulding, Reglet, Regula, Ribbon, Rollmop, Slice, Snood, Sphendone, Stria, Striga, Taeniate, Tape, Teniate, Tilting, Tournedos, Vitta

Fillip Boost, Kick, Snap, Stimulus, Tonic

Filly Colt, Foal, She

Film(s), Filmmaker, Filmy, Filming Acetate, Actioner, Amnion, Animatronics, Anime, Biopic, Blaxploitation, Blockbuster, Bollywood, Buddy, Carry On, Cartoon, Casablanca, Caul, Cel, Chick-flick, Chiller, Chopsocky, Cine, Cinema vérité, Cinerama®, Circlorama®, Cliffhanger, Cling, Clip, Coat, Colour, Compilation, Creature feature, Deepie, Dew, Diorama, Docudrama, Documentary, Dogme, Dramedy, Dust, Epic, ET, Exposure, Fantasia, Feature, Featurette, Fiche, Flick, Floaty, Footage, Gigi, Gossamer, Hammer, Haze, Hollywood, Horror, Horse opera, Infomercial, Jaws, Kell, Kidult, Lacquer, Lamella, Layer, Limelight, Loid, Machinima, Mask, Membrane, Microfiche, Mist, Molecular, Monochrome, Montage, Movie, Mylar®, Neo-noir, Newsreel, Noddy, Noir, Non-flam, Oater, Omnimax®, Outtake, Ozacling®, Panchromatic, Pathé, Patina, Pellicle, Photo, Pilot, Plaque, Prequel, Psycho, Quickie, Quota-quickie, Reel, Release, Reversal, Roll, Romcom, Rush, Safety, Scale, Scent-scale, Screen, Scum, Sepmag, Sheet, Shoot-'em-up, Short, Shot, Silent, Skin, Skin flick, Slasher-movie, Slashfest, Slick, Slo-mo, Snuff, Spaghetti western, Splatter, Star Wars, Studio, Super 8, Suspensor, Sword and sandal, Talkie, Tear-jerker, Technicolor, Titanic, Toon, Trailer, Travelogue, Trippy, Two-shot, Ultrafiche, Varnish, Vertigo, Vicenzi, Video, Videogram, Video-nasty, Vitaphone®, Web, Weepie, Weepy, Weft, Western, Wuxia

Filmgoer Cineaste

Film star Extra, Monroe, Vedette

Filter(ing) Band-pass, Clarify, Colour, Dialysis, Dichroic, High-pass, Leach, Low-pass, Percolate, Perk, Polarizing, Seep, Sieve, → **SIFT**, Sile, Skylight, Strain

Filth(y) Addle, Augean, Bilge, Bogging, Colluvies, Crock, Crud, Defile, Dirt, Dung, Feculent, Foul, Grime, Hard core, Litter, Lucre, Mire, Muck, Obscene, Pythogenic,

Refuse, Slime, Smut(ch), Soil, Squalor, Stercoral, Sullage, Yuck

Fin Adipose, Anal, Caudal, Crack, Ctene, Dollars, Dorsal, Fiver, Fluke, Pectoral, Pelvic, Pinna, Pinnule, Rib, Skeg, Skegg, Stabiliser, Ventral

Final(e), Finalise, Finally Absolute, At last, Closing, Coda, Conclusive, Cup, Decider, End, End-all, Epilogue, Eventual, Exam, Extreme, Grand, Last, Net(t), Peremptory, Sew up, Swansong, Terminal, Ultimate, Utter

Finance, Financial, Financier Ad crumenam, Angel, Back, Banian, Banker, Bankroll, Banyan, Bottomry, Cambism, Chrematistic, Equity, Exchequer, Fiscal, Forfaiting, Gnome, Grubstake, Mezzanine, Monetary, Moneyman, Revenue, Sponsor, Subsidise, Treasurer, Underwrite

Finch Bird, Brambling, Bunting, Canary, Charm, Chewink, Crossbill, Darwin's, Fringillid, Gouldian, Grosbeak, Linnet, Marsh-robin, Peter, Redpoll, Rosy, Serin, Siskin, Spink, Twite, Zebra

Find(er), Finding Ascertain, Come across, Detect, Dig up, Direction, Discover(y), Get, Hit, Inquest, → **LOCATE**, Meet, Provide, Rake up, Rarity, Rumble, Trace, Track down, Trouvaille, Unearth, Verdict

Fine, Fine words Admirable, A1, Amende, Amerce, Amerciament, Arts, Assess, Beau(t), Bender, Blood-wit(e), Bonny, Boshta, Boshter, Boss, Brandy, Brave, Braw, Bully, Buttock-mail, Champion, Dainty, Dandy, Dick, Dry, End, Eriach, Eric(k), Estreat, F, Fair, Famous, Forfeit, Gate, Godly, Good(ly), Gossamer, Gradely, Graithly, Grand, Grassum, Hair, Hairline, Handsome, Heriot, Hunkydory, Idle, Immense, Impalpable, Inconie, Incony, Infangthief, Issue, Keen, Leirwite, Log, Maritage, Merchet, Mooi, Mulct, Nice, Nifty, Niminy-piminy, Noble, OK, Oke, Okey-doke(y), Outfangthief, → **PENALTY**, Phat, Precise, Pretty, Pure, Relief, Righto, Safe, Sconce, Sheer, Sicker, Slender, Smart, Spanking, Subtle, Summery, Super, Sure, Tax, Thin, Ticket(t)y-boo, Tiptop, Topping, Transmission, Unlaw, Wally, Waly, Well, Wer(e) gild

Fine-collector Cheater

Finery Braws, Fallal, Frills, Frippery, Gaudery, Ornament, Trinket, Wally, Warpaint

Finesse Artifice, Artistry, Delicacy, Skill, Strategy

Fine-weather All-hallond, All-hallow(e)n, All-hollown

Finger(s), Fingernail Annular, Dactyl, Digit, Fork, Green, Handle, Idle worms, Index, Lunula, Medius, Name, Nip, Piggy, Pinky, Pointer, Potato, Prepollex, Pusher, Ring(man), Shop, Sponge, Talaunt, Talon, Tot, Trigger, White

Finger-hole Lill, Ring

Fingerprint(ing) Arch, Dabs, Dactylogram, DNA, Genetic, Loop, Whorl

Fingerstall Hutkin

Finial Bunch, Knob, Ornament, Tee

Finical, Finicky Faddy, Fastidious, Fussy, Particular, Pernickety, Precise

Finish, Finished, Finishing (touch) Arch, Blanket, Calendar, Close, Coating, Coda, Complete, → **CONCLUDE**, Crown, Die, Dish, Do, Dope, Dress, Egshell, → **END**, Epilog(ue), Epiphenomena, Exact, Full, Gloss, Grandstand, Kibosh, Lacquer, Log off, Mat(t), Mirror, Neat, Outgo, Outwork, Pebbledash, Peg out, Perfect, Photo, Picking, Polish off, Refine, Ripe, Round, Satin, Settle, Shot, Spitcher, Surface, Terminate, Through, Top out, Up (tie), Veneer, Wau(l)k, Wind-up

Finite Bounded, Limited

Finn(ish) Esth, Huck(leberry), Karelian, Lapp, Mickey, Mordvin, Suomic, Udmurt, Votyak

Fiord Bay, Hardanger, Inlet, Oslo, Randers, Trondheim

Fir Abies, Balsam, Douglas, Larch, Oregon, Scotch, Scots, Silver, Spruce, Umbrella

Fire(side) Accend, Agni, Aidan, Aiden, Animate, Anneal, Ardour, Arouse, Arson,

Atar, Axe, Bake, Bale, Barbecue, Barrage, Beacon, Behram, Blaze, Boot, Brand, Brazier, Brush, Burn, Bush, Cashier, Central, Chassé, Conflagration, Corposant, Covering, Delope, Discharge, Dismiss, Élan, Electric, Element, Embolden, Ena, Energy, Enfilade, Enkindle, Enthuse, Flak, Flame, Friendly, Furnace, Greek, Gun, Hearth, Hob, Ignite, Inferno, Ingle, Inspire, Kentish, Kiln, Kindle, Launch, Let off, Light, Liquid, Lowe, Oust, Pop, Prime, Prometheus, Pull, Pyre, Quick, Radiator, Rake, Rapid, Red, Red cock, Sack, St Anthony's, St Elmo's, Scorch, Shell, Shoot, Smudge, Spark, Spirit, Spunk, Stoke, Stove, Strafe, Torch, Tracer, Trial, Wake, Watch, Wisp, Zeal, Zip

▶ **Firearm** *see* **GUN**

Fireback Reredos

Fireball Bolide

Firebird Phoenix

Fire-break Epaulement, Greenstrip

Firedamp Blower

Fire-dog Andiron

Fire engine Green Goddess

Fire-extinguisher Halon, Hell-bender, Salamander

Firefly Glow-worm, Lightning-bug, Luciferin, Pyrophorus

Fire-guard Fender

Fireman Abednego, Brigade, Deputy, Prometheus, Stoker, Visiting

Fire-opal Girasol

Fireplace Camboose, Chiminea, Chimney, Grate, Hearth, Hob, Ingle, Loop-hole, Range

Fireplug H, Hydrant

Fireproof Abednego, Asbestos, Incombustible, Inflammable, Meshach, Salamander, Shadrach, Uralite

Firewalker Abednego, Salamander

Firewood Billet, Faggot, Knitch, Tinder

Firework(s) Banger, Bengal-light, Bunger, Catherine wheel, Cherry bomb, Cracker, Devil, Feu d'artifice, Firedrake, Fisgig, Fizgig, Flip-flop, Fountain, Gerbe, Girandole, Golden rain, Indian fire, Iron sand, Jumping jack, Maroon, Pastille, Peeoy, Petard, Pharaoh's serpent, Pinwheel, Pioy(e), Pyrotechnics, Realgar, Rocket, Roman candle, Serpent, Set piece, Skyrocket, Slap-bang, Sparkler, Squib, Tantrum, Throwdown, Tourbill(i)on, Volcano, Waterloo cracker, Wheel, Whizzbang

Fire-worshipper Parsee

Firing Baking, Fusillade, Mitten, Salvo, Touchpaper

Firm, Firmness Adamant, Agency, Al dente, Binding, Business, Collected, Compact, Company, Concern, Concrete, Conglomerate, Consistency, Constant, Crisp, Decided, Determined, Duro, Faithful, Fast, Fixed, Hard, Inc, Insistent, Loyal, Marginal, Oaky, Obdurate, Obstinate, → **RESOLUTE**, Sclerotal, Secure, Set, Siccar, Sicker, → **SOLID**, Sound, Stable, Stalwart, Staunch, Steady, Ste(a)dfast, Steely, Steeve, Stern, Stieve, Stiff, Strict, Sturdy, Sure, Tight, Tough, Unflinching, Unshakeable, Well-knit

Firmament Canopy, Empyrean, Heaven, Sky

First Ab initio, Alpha, Arch, Archetype, Best, Calends, Champion, Chief, Earliest, E(a)rst, Eldest, Foremost, Former, Front, Head, I, Ideal, Imprimis, Initial, 1st, Kalends, Led, Maiden, No 1, One, Opener, Or, Original, Pioneer, Pole, Pole position, Premier, Première, Prima, Primal, Prime, Primo, Principal, Prototype, Rudimentary, Senior, Starters, Top, Uppermost, Victor, Yama

First-aid(ers) Zambu(c)k

First born Ariki, Cain, Eigne, Eldest, Heir, Major, Primogeniture, Senior
First class, First rate A1, Crack, Plum, Prime, Pukka, Slap up, Supreme, Tiptop, Top(notch)
First day Calends
First fruits Annat, Arles, Primitiae, Windfalls
First man Adam, Ask, Gayomart, Premier, President, Yama, Ymer, Ymir
First offender Eve, Probationer
▶ **First rate** *see* **FIRST CLASS**
First woman Embla, Eve, Pandora, Premier
Firth Estuary, Forth, Inlet, Moray, Pentland, Solway, Tay
Fish(ing) Angle, Bob, Bottom, Cast, Catch, Chowder, Coarse, Cran, Creel, Deep-sea, Dib, Dredge, Dry, Dry-fly, Episcate, Fly, Flying, Frozen, Fry, Game, Gefilte, Gefulte, Goujons, Guddle, Halieutics, Haul, Hen, Inshore, Ledger, Mess, Net, Offshore, Oily, Otterboard, Overnet, Piscine, Queer, Roe, Rough, Runner, Sacred, Sashimi, Shoal, Skitter, Sleeper, Snigger, Sniggle, Spin, Spot, Surimi, Tiddler, Trawl, Troll, Tropical, Trotline, Tub, Walking, Wet, White

FISH

2 letters:	4 letters:	Jack	Scup
Ai	Barb	Kelt	Seer
Id	Bass	Keta	Seir
	Blay	Lant	Shad
3 letters:	Bley	Leaf	Sild
Aua	Brit	Ling	Slip
Ayu	Butt	Luce	Snig
Bar	Carp	Lump	Sole
Bib	Cero	Maid	Star
But	Chad	Maze	Tope
Cat	Char	Moki	Trot
Cod	Chub	Mola	Tuna
Cow	Chum	Mort	Tusk
Dab	Coho	Opah	Woof
Dap	Cray	Orfe	
Dog	Cusk	Parr	5 letters:
Eel	Dace	Peal	Ablet
Gar	Dare	Peel	Ahuru
Ged	Dart	Penk	Allis
Hag	Dory	Pike	Angel
Ide	Drum	Pink	Apode
Koi	Fugu	Poll	Aspro-
Lax	Gade	Pope	Basse
Lob	Goby	Pout	Belta
Par	Gump	Raun	Blain
Pod	Hake	Rawn	Bleak
Ray	Harl	Rigg	Bream
Rig	Hoka	Rudd	Brill
Sar	Hoki	Ruff	Bully
Tai	Huso	Scad	Capon
Top	Huss	Scar	Charr
	Ikan	Scat	Cisco

Clown	Scrod	Caribe	Lunker
Cobia	Sewen	Cheven	Mad Tom
Cohoe	Sewin	Clupea	Mahsir
Coley	Shark	Cockle	Maigre
Cuddy	Sheat	Comber	Marari
Danio	Skate	Conger	Marlin
Dorad	Slope	Conner	Meagre
Doras	Smelt	Cottus	Medaka
Doree	Snoek	Cudden	Medusa
Dorse	Snook	Cuddie	Megrim
Elops	Solen	Cuddin	Milter
Elver	Speck	Cunner	Minnow
Fluke	Sprat	Cuttle	Morgay
Gadus	Sprod	Darter	Mudcat
Gibel	Tench	Dentex	Mullet
Grunt	Tetra	Diodon	Murena
Jewie	Togue	Dipnoi	Nerite
Jurel	Torsk	Discus	Oyster
Koura	Trout	Doctor	Paddle
Laker	Tunny	Dorado	Paidle
Lance	Umber	Dun-cow	Pakoko
Loach	Wahoo	Ellops	Parore
Lythe	Whiff	Espada	Parrot
Maise	Wirra	Finnac	Patiki
Maize	Witch	Finnan	Pholas
Manta	Yabby	Fogash	Piraya
Masus	Zebra	Fumado	Plaice
Mease		Gadoid	Podley
Molly	*6 letters:*	Garvie	Pollan
Murre	Alevin	Gilgie	Porgie
Murry	Allice	Goboid	Puffer
Nerka	Anabas	Goramy	Redfin
Nurse	Angler	Grilse	Remora
Padle	Archer	Groper	Rewaru
Perai	Ballan	Gulper	Robalo
Perca	Barbel	Gunnel	Roughy
Perch	Belone	Gurami	Saithe
Pilot	Beluga	Gurnet	Salmon
Piper	Bichir	Haddie	Samlet
Pirai	Big-eye	Hapuka	Sander
Platy	Blenny	Hassar	Sardel
Pogge	Bonito	Inanga	Sargus
Powan	Bounce	Jerker	Sauger
Prawn	Bowfin	Jilgie	Saurel
Roach	Braise	Kipper	Scampi
Roker	Braize	Kokiri	Sea-bat
Royal	Bumalo	Labrus	Sea-owl
Ruffe	Burbot	Lancet	Seeder
Saith	Callop	Launce	Serran
Sargo	Caplin	Lizard	Shanny
Saury	Caranx	Louvar	Sheath

6 letters – cont:
Shiner
Skelly
Sparid
Splake
Sucker
Tailor
Tarpon
Tautog
Tinker
Toitoi
Tomcod
Trygon
Turbot
Twaite
Ulicon
Ulikon
Vendis
Weever
Wirrah
Wrasse
Yabbie
Zander
Zingel

7 letters:
Ale-wife
Anchovy
Anemone
Asterid
Azurine
Batfish
Bellows
Bergylt
Birchir
Bloater
Bluecap
Boxfish
Brassie
Buffalo
Bumallo
Bummalo
Cabezon
Candiru
Capelin
Cavalla
Cavally
Ceviche
Cichlid
Codfish
Copepod

Corvina
Cottoid
Crappie
Croaker
Crucian
Crusian
Cutlass
Dogfish
Eelfare
Eel-pout
Escolar
Fantail
Findram
Finnack
Finnock
Flattie
Garfish
Garoupa
Garpike
Garvock
Geelbek
Gemfish
Goldeye
Gourami
Grouper
Growler
Grunion
Gudgeon
Gurnard
Gwiniad
Gwyniad
Haddock
Hagdown
Hagfish
Halibut
Herling
Herring
Hirling
Hogfish
Homelyn
Houting
Ichthys
Inconnu
Jewfish
Kahawai
Keeling
Koi carp
Kokanee
Lampern
Lamprey
Lampuki

Lantern
Lingcod
Lobster
Lubfish
Lyomeri
Mahseer
Matelot
Medacca
Merling
Mojarra
Moon-eye
Morwong
Muraena
Oarfish
Old-wife
Oolakan
Opaleye
Osseter
Oulakan
Oulicon
Panchax
Pandora
Peacock
Pegasus
Pigfish
Pinfish
Piranha
Pollack
Pomfret
Pompano
Pupfish
Ragfish
Rasbora
Ratfish
Rat-tail
Redfish
Rorqual
Roughie
Sand dab
Sand-eel
Sardine
Scalare
Scallop
Sculpin
Sea-bass
Sea-cock
Sea-dace
Sea-moth
Sea-pike
Sea-star
Sea-wife

Sevruga
Sillock
Silurid
Skegger
Skipper
Snapper
Sock-eye
Sparoid
Speldin
Sterlet
Sunfish
Sunstar
Surgeon
Teleost
Tilapia
Titling
Torgoch
Torpedo
Tubfish
Ulichon
Vendace
Vendiss
Wall-eye
Whipray
Whistle
Whiting
Wide-gab

8 letters:
Albacore
Albicore
Anableps
Arapaima
Asteroid
Atherine
Billfish
Blennius
Bloodfin
Blowfish
Blueback
Bluefish
Bluegill
Boarfish
Brisling
Bullhead
Bullhorn
Bummallo
Cabezone
Cabrilla
Carangid
Cardinal

Cavefish
Characid
Characin
Chimaera
Coalfish
Corkwing
Cow-pilot
Cucumber
Cyprinid
Dealfish
Dragonet
Drumfish
Eagle-ray
Elephant
Escallop
Eulachon
Fallfish
Fighting
Filefish
Flathead
Flounder
Four-eyes
Frogfish
Gambusia
Ganoidei
Gillaroo
Gilthead
Goatfish
Gobiidae
Graining
Grayling
Greeneye
Hackbolt
Hair-tail
Half-beak
Hard-head
Holostei
Hornbeak
Hornpout
Kabeljou
Killfish
Kingfish
Kingklip
Kukukuma
Lionfish
Luderick
Lumpfish
Lungfish
Mackerel
Mahi-mahi
Mata Hari

Menhaden
Milkfish
Millions
Monkfish
Moonfish
Moray eel
Mosquito
Mulloway
Nannygai
Nennigai
Nine-eyes
Oulachon
Paradise
Patutuki
Pickerel
Pilchard
Pipefish
Pirarucu
Poor-john
Rascasse
Redbelly
Red roman
Reperepe
Rock-cook
Rockfish
Rockling
Roncador
Rosefish
Saibling
Sailfish
Saltfish
Sardelle
Scabbard
Scaridae
Sciaenid
Scorpion
Scuppaug
Sea-bream
Sea-devil
Seahorse
Sea-lemon
Sea-raven
Sea-robin
Sergeant
Serranus
Skipjack
Smear-dab
Snake-eel
Sparidae
Sparling
Spelding

Speldrin
Stenlock
Sting-ray
Stonecat
Sturgeon
Surffish
Tarakihi
Tarwhine
Teraglin
Terakihi
Tile-fish
Toadfish
Trevally
Tubenose
Tullibee
Weakfish
Whitling
Wolffish

9 letters:

Ahuruhuru
Amberjack
Anabantid
Anchoveta
Argentine
Barracuda
Blackfish
Butterfly
Carangoid
Cascadura
Ceratodus
Chaetodon
Chavender
Clingfish
Clupeidae
Coregonus
Coryphene
Cyprinoid
Devilfish
Gaspereau
Glassfish
Globefish
Goldfinny
Goldsinny
Golomynka
Goosefish
Greenbone
Greenling
Grenadier
Haberdine
Hornyhead

Hottentot
Houndfish
Ichthyoid
Jacksmelt
Jewelfish
Kabeljouw
Killifish
Labyrinth
Latimeria
Matelotte
Menominee
Mudhopper
Neon tetra
Pikeperch
Porbeagle
Porcupine
Queenfish
Quillback
Roussette
Scaldfish
Scalefish
Schnapper
Scorpaena
Selachian
Shubunkin
Siluridae
Slickhead
Snailfish
Snakehead
Snipefish
Solenette
Spadefish
Spearfish
Speldring
Stargazer
Steenbras
Stingaree
Stockfish
Stonefish
Surfperch
Surmullet
Sweetlips
Swellfish
Swinefish
Swordfish
Sword-tail
Thornback
Threadfin
Tittlebat
Topminnow
Trachinus

9 letters – cont:
Troutfish
Troutling
Trumpeter
Trunkfish
Whitebait
White-bass
Wreckfish
Yellowfin

10 letters:
Amblyopsis
Barracoota
Barracouta
Barramundi
Bitterling
Bombay duck
Bottlehead
Butterfish
Candlefish
Cockabully
Cofferfish
Cornetfish
Cyclostome
Damselfish
Demoiselle
Dollarfish
Etheostoma
Fingerling
Flutemouth

Groundling
Guitarfish
Horned pout
Lake-lawyer
Largemouth
Lumpsucker
Maskalonge
Maskanonge
Maskinonge
Midshipman
Mossbunker
Mudskipper
Needlefish
Nurse-hound
Paddlefish
Pakirikiri
Rabbitfish
Red emperor
Red-snapper
Ribbonfish
Rudderfish
Scopelidae
Sea-poacher
Sea-surgeon
Serrasalmo
Sheepshead
Ship-holder
Shovelnose
Silverside
Small mouth

Springfish
Squeteague
Teleostome
Titarakura
Tripletail
Yellowtail

11 letters:
Cephalis pie
Chondrostei
Cyprinodont
Dolly Varden
Istiophorus
Lapidosteus
Lepidosiren
Lophobranch
Maskallonge
Moorish idol
Muskellunge
Ostracoderm
Oxyrhynchus
Plagiostome
Plectognath
Pumpkinseed
Scolopendra
Seventy-four
Snail darter
Soldierfish
Stickleback
Stoneroller

Surgeonfish
Triggerfish
Trumpetfish
Water souchy
Yellowbelly

12 letters:
Ballan-wrasse
Elasmobranch
Father-lasher
Heterosomata
Histiophorus
Mangrove Jack
Miller's thumb
Mouthbreeder
Mouthbrooder
Orange roughy
Plectognathi
Rainbow-trout
Squirrelfish

13 letters:
Burnett salmon
Leatherjacket
Musselcracker
Sailor's choice
Sergeant Baker

15 letters:
Crossopterygian

Fish and chips Greasies
Fish-basket Creel, Hask, Kipe
Fish disease Argulus
Fisher(man) Ahab, Andrew, Angler, Black cat, Caper, Codder, Dragman, High-liner, Liner, Pedro, Peter, Piscator, Rodster, Sharesman, Walton
▶ **Fisherwoman** *see* FISHSELLER
Fish-hawk Osprey
Fishing-ground Haaf
Fishing-line G(u)imp, Gymp, Paternoster
Fishpond Ocean, Stew, Vivarium
Fishseller, Fisherwoman Fishwife, Molly Malone, Ripp(i)er, Shawley, Shawlie
Fishy Botargo, Suspicious, Vacant
Fission Multiple, Nuclear
Fissure Chasm, Cleft, Crack, Crevasse, Crevice, Gap, Grike, Gryke, Lode, Rent, Rift, Rolando, Sand-crack, Scam, Sylvian, Sylvius, Vallecula, Vein, Zygon
Fist Clench, Dukes, Hand, Iron, Join-hand, Mailed, Neaf(f)e, Neif, Neive, Nief, Nieve, Pud, Punch, Thump, Writing
Fit(s), Fitful, Fitter, Fitting(s), Fitness Able, Access, Adapt, Ague, Align, Aline, Apoplexy, Appointment, Appropriate, Apropos, Apt, A salti, Babbitt, Bayonet, Beseemly, Bout, Canto, Capable, Cat(a)leptic, Cataplexy, Click, Concinnous, Condign,

Congruous, Conniption, Convulsion, Culver-tail, Darwinian, Decent, Decorous, Desultory, Dod, Dove-tail, Due, Eclampsia, Egal, Eligible, Ensconce, Epilepsy, Equip, Exies, Expedient, Fairing, Fay, Fiddle, Form, Furniment, Furnishing, Fytte, Gee, Germane, Gusty, Habile, Hale, Hang, Health, Hinge, Huff, Hysterics, Ictus, Inclusive, In-form, Interference, Intermittent, In trim, Just, Kashrut(h), Like, Lune, Marry, Mate, Meet, Mood, Nest, Opportune, Paroxysm, Passus, Pertinent, Prepared, Press, → **PROPER**, Queme, Ready, Rig, Rind, Ripe, Rynd, Seemly, Seizure, Set, Shrink, Sit, Sliding, Slot, Snotter, Sort, Sound, Spasm, Spell, Start, Suit(able), Syncope, Tailor, Tantrum, Tenoner, Throe, To prepon, Tref(a), Treif, Turn, Up to, Well, Wobbler, Wobbly, Worthy, Wrath

▷ **Fit(ting)** *may indicate* a 't'

Fitment Adaptor, Unit

Fitzgerald Edward, Ella, Scott

Five(s), Fiver Cinque, Flim, Mashie, Pallone, Pedro, Pentad, Quinary, Quintet, Sextan, Towns, V

Five years Lustre, Lustrum

Fix(ed), Fixer, Fixative Affeer, Anchor, Appoint, Appraise, → **ARRANGE**, Assess, Assign, Attach, Bind, Brand, Cement, Clamp, Clew, Clue, Constant, Corking-pin, Cure, Decide, Destinate, Destine, Determine, Do, Embed, Empight, Encastré, Engrain, Establish, Fast, Fasten, Firm, Fit, Freeze, Gammon, Hold, Hypo(sulphite), Immutable, Impaction, Imprint, Inculcate, Ingrain, Jag, Jam, Locate, Lodge, Mend, Nail, Name, Narcotic, Nobble, Orientate, Peen, Peg, Persistent, Pin, Place, Point, Quantify, Repair, Resolute, Rig, Rigid, Rivet, Rove, Rut, Scrape, Screw, Seat, Seize, Set, Settle, Ship, Shoo, Skatole, Skewer, Splice, Stable, Stage, Staple, Static, Stell, Step, Stew, Stuck, Swing, Tie, Toe, Valorize, Weld

Fixture Attachment, Event, Match, Permanence, Rawlplug®, Unit

Fizz(ed), Fizzy Buck's, Effervesce, Gas, Hiss, Pop, Sherbet, Sod, Soda

Fizzle Failure, Flop, Hiss, Washout

▶ **Fjord** *see* **FIORD**

Flabbergast(ed) Amaze, Astound, Floor, Thunderstruck

Flabby Flaccid, Lank, Lax, Limp, Pendulous, Saggy

Flaccid Flabby, Lank, Limp, Soft

Flag(gy), Flags Acorus, Ancient, Ashlar, Banderol, Banner, Black, Blackjack, Blue (Ensign), Blue Peter, Bunting, Burgee, Calamus, Chequered, Colour(s), Dan(n) ebrog, Decline, Droop, Duster, Ensign, Fail, Faint, Falter, Fane, Fanion, Field colours, Gladden, Gonfalon, Green, Guidon, Hail, Hoist, House, Irideal, Iris, Jack, Jade, Jolly Roger, Kerbstone, Languish, Lis, Old Glory, Orris, Pave(ment), Pavilion, Pencel, Pennant, Pennon, Penoncel(le), Pensel, Pensil, Peter, Pilot, Pin, Prayer, Quarantine, Rag, Rainbow, Red, Red Duster, Red Ensign, Repeater, Sag, Sedge, Semaphore, Sett, Sick, Sink, Slab(stone), Slack, Stand, Standard, Stars and Bars, Stars and Stripes, Streamer, Substitute, Sweet, Tire, Tricolour, Union (Jack), Vane, Vexillology, Waft, Weaken, Whiff, Whift, White (ensign), Wilt, Wither, Yellow (Jack)

Flagday Tagday

Flagellate Beat, Euglena, Mastigophora, Scourge, Trypanosome, Whip

Flagon Bottle, Carafe, Ewer, Jug, Pitcher, Stoop, Stoup, Vessel

Flagpole Pin, Staff

Flagrant Egregious, Glaring, Heinous, Patent, Rank, Wanton

Flagship Admiral, Barge, Victory

Flag-waving Jingoism

Flail Beat, Drub, Swingle, Swip(p)le, Threshel

Flair Art, Bent, Élan, Gift, Knack, Nose, Panache, Style, → **TALENT**

Flak AA, Attack, Criticism

Flake Chip, Flame, Flaught, Flaw, Floccule, Flocculus, Fragment, Peel, Scale, Smut, Snow

Flam Impose

Flamboyant Baroque, Brilliant, Florid, Garish, Grandiose, Ornate, Ostentatious, Paz(z)azz, Piz(z)azz, Swash-buckler

Flame, Flaming Ardent, Blaze, Fire, Flake, Flambé, Flammule, Glow, Kindle, Leman, Lover, Lowe, Musical, Olympic, Oxyacetylene, Reducing, Sensitive, Sweetheart

Flan Pastry, Quiche, Tart

Flanders Mare, Moll

Flange Border, Collar, Collet, Lip, Rim

Flank(s) Accompany, Anta, Flange, Flitch, Ilia, Lisk, Loin, Side, Spur

Flannel Blather, Canton, Cloth, Cotton, Face, Flatter, Outing, Soft-soap, Waffle, Washrag, Zephyr

Flap(ped), Flapper, Flapping Ado, Agnail, Aileron, Alar, Alarm(ist), Aventaile(e), Bate, Beat, Bird, Bobbysoxer, Bustle, Chit, Dither, Earcap, Elevon, Epiglottis, Fipple, Flacker, Flaff, Flag, Flaught, Flutter, Fly, Fuss, Giglet, Giglot, Hover, → **IN A FLAP**, Labium, Labrum, Lapel, Loma, Louvre, Luff, Lug, Omentum, Operculum, Panic, Spin, Spoiler, State, Tab, Tag, Tailboard, Tailgate, Tiswas, To-do, Tongue, TRAM, Volucrine, Wave, Whisk

Flare(d), Flares, Flare up Bell, Bell-bottoms, Fishtail, Flame, Flanch, Flaunch, Godet, Magnesium, Scene, Signal, Skymarker, Solar, Spread, Spunk, Ver(e)y, Widen

Flash(y), Flasher, Flashpoint Bling, Brainstorm, Brash, Coruscate, Cursor, Electronic, Emicant, Essex Man, Exposure, Fire-flag, Flare, Flaught, Fulgid, Fulgural, Garish, Gaudy, Glaik, Gleam, Glint, Glisten, Glitzy, Green, Green ray, Helium, Indicate, Instant, Jay, Lairy, Levin, Lightning, Loud, Magnesium, Meretricious, Mo, Ostentatious, Photopsy, Raffish, Ribbon, Ring, Roary, Scintillation, Second, Sequin, Showy, Sluice, Snazzy, Spark, Sparkle, Sport, Streak, Strobe, Swank(e)y, Tick, Tigrish, Trice, Tulip, Twinkle, Vivid, Wire

▷ **Flashing** *may indicate* an anagram

Flask(-shaped) Ampulla, Aryballos, Bottle, Canteen, Carafe, Cask, Coffin, Conceptacle, Costrel, Cucurbit, Dewar, Erlenmeyer, Fiasco, Flacket, Flacon, Florence, Goatskin, Hip, Lekythos, Livery pot, Matrass, Mick(e)(y), Moon, Pocket-pistol, Powder, Reform, Retort, Thermos®, Vacuum, Vial

Flat(s), Flatten(ed), Flattener Adobe, Alkali, Amaze, Ancipital, Apartment, Bachelor, Bald, Banal, Beat, Bed-sit, Blow-out, Bulldoze, Callow, Cape, Complanate, Compress, Condominium, Corymb(ose), Cottage, Coulisse, Dead, Demolish, Dorsiventral, Double, Dress, Dry, Dull, Even, Feeble, Flew, Floor, Flue, Fool, Gaff, Garden, Granny, Guyot, Haugh, High-rise, Homaloid, Home-unit, Horizontal, Insipid, Ironed, Jacent, Key, KO, Law, Lay, Level, Lifeless, Llano, Lodge, Maderised, Marsh, Monotonous, Mud, Nitwit, Norfolk, Obcompressed, Oblate, Ownership, Pad, Pancake, Pedestrian, Peneplain, Peneplane, Penthouse, Pentice, Pied-à-terre, Plain, Planar, Plane, Planish, Plat, Plateau, Press, Prone, Prostrate, Recumbent, Rooms, Salt, Scenery, Service, Smooth, Splayfoot, Spread-edged, Squash, Studio, Tableland, Tabular, Tame, Tasteless, Tenement, True, Unsensational, Vapid, Walk-up

Flat-chested Cithara

Flat-faced Socle

Flat-foot(ed) Policeman, Splay

Flat-nosed Camus

Flatter(ing), Flatterer, Flattery Adulate, Becoming, Beslaver, Blandish, Blarney, Bootlick, Butter, Cajole, Candied, Carn(e)y, Claw(back), Complimentary, Comprabatio, Court-dresser, Earwiggy, En beau, Eyewash, Fawn, Fillibrush, Flannel, Flannen, Fleech, Flummery, Foot-licker, Fulsome, Gloze, Gnathonic(al), Honey, Imitation, Lip-salve, Moody, Palp, Phrase, Poodle-faker, Proneur, Puffery, Sawder, Smarm, Snow job, Soap, Soft soap, Soother, Souk, Spaniel, Stroke, Sugar, Sweet talk, Sycophant, Taffy, Toady, Treacle, Unction, Wheedle, Word

Flatulence, Flatulent Belch, Borborygmus, Burp, Carminative, Colic, Gas, Tympanites, Ventose, Wind, Wind dropsy

Flaunt Brandish, Flourish, Gibe, Parade, Skyre, Sport, Strout, Strut, Wave

Flavour(ed), Flavouring Absinth(e), Alecost, Anethole, Angostura, Anise, Aniseed, Aroma, Benne, Bergamot, Bold, Borage, Bouquet garni, Clove, Coriander, Cumin, Dill, Essence, Eucalyptol, Fenugreek, Flor, Garlic, Garni, Gingili, Marinate, Mint, Orgeat, Piperonal, Quark, Race, Ratafia, Relish, Rocambole, Sair, Sapor, Sassafras, Sesame, Tack, Tang, Tarragon, → **TASTE**, Til, Tincture, Twang, Umami, Vanilla

Flaw Blemish, Brack, Bug, Chip, Crack, Defect, Fallacy, → **FAULT**, Gall, Hamartia, Imperfection, Infirmity, Kink, Knothole, Lophole, Red-eye, Rima, Spot, Taint, Tear, Thief, Tragic, Windshake

Flawless Impeccable, Intact

Flax(en) Aleseed, Blonde, Codilla, Harakeke, Harden, Hards, Herden, Herl, Hurden, Line, Linseed, Lint, Lint-white, Linum, Mill-mountain, Poi, Tow

Flay Excoriate, Fleece, Flense, Scourge, Skin, Strip, Uncase, Whip

Flea Aphaniptera, Chigger, Chigoe, Chigre, Daphnid, Hopper, Itch-mite, Lop, Pulex, Sand, Turnip, Water

Flea-bane Erigeron

Fleabite Denier

Fleck Dash, Freak, Spot, Streak

Fledgling Aerie, Eyas, Sorage

Flee(ing) Abscond, Bolt, Decamp, Escape, Eschew, Fly, Fugacity, Lam, Loup, Run, Scapa, Scarper, Scram

Fleece, Fleecy Bleed, Coat, Despoil, Flocculent, Golden, Jib, Lambskin, Lanose, Pash(i)m, Pashmina, Plot, Pluck, Rifte, Ring, Rob, Rook, Shave, Shear, Sheepskin, Skin, Skirtings, → **SWINDLE**, Toison

Fleer Ogle

Fleet(ing) Armada, Brief, Camilla, Caravan, Convoy, Ephemeral, Evanescent, Fast, First, Flit, Flota, Flotilla, Fugacious, Fugitive, Glimpse, Hasty, Hollow, Lightfoot, Navy, Pacy, Passing, Prison, Spry, Street, Transient, Velocipede, Volatile

Flemish Flamingant

Flesh(y) Beefy, Body, Carneous, Carrion, Corporeal, Corpulent, Creatic, Dead-meat, Digastric, Finish, Goose, Gum, Hypersarcoma, Joint, Jowl, Ket, Longpig, Love handles, Lush, Meat, Mole, Mons, Muffin top, Mummy, Muscle, Mutton, Proud, Pulp, Quick, Sarcous, Spare tyre, Succulent, Tissue, Wattle

Flesh-eating Cannibalism, Carnassial, Creophagus, Omophagic

Fleshless Dry, Maigre, Pem(m)ican

Flex(ible), Flexibility Adaptable, Bend(y), Compliant, Double-jointed, Elastic, Genu, Leeway, Limber, Lissom(e), Lithe, Pliant, → **RESILIENT**, Rubato, Rubbery, Squeezy, Supple, Tensile, Tonus, Wieldy, Willing, Willowy, Wiry

▷ **Flexible, Flexuous** *may indicate* an anagram

Flick(er), Flicks Bioscope, Cinema, Fillip, Film, Flip, Flirt, Flutter, Glimmer, Gutter, Movie, Movy, Snap, Snow, Spang-cockle, Switch, Talkie, Twinkle, Waver, Wink, Zap

Flickertail ND

Flier Aerostat, Airman, Alcock, Amy, Aviator, → **BIRD**, Bleriot, Blimp, Brown, Crow, Daedalus, Erk, Fur, George, Gotha, Handout, Icarus, Leaflet, Lindbergh, Montgolfier, Pilot, RAF, Scotsman, Spec, Speedy

Flight(y) Backfisch, Birdbrain, Bolt, Bubble-headed, Capricious, Charter, Contact, Dart, Dash, Departure, Escalier, Escape, Exaltation, Exodus, Fast, Fickle, Flaught, Flibbertigibbet, Flip, Flock, Flyby, Fly-past, Free, Fugue, Giddy, Grece, Grese, Gris(e), Guy, Hegira, Hejira, Hejra, Hellicat, Hijra, Lam, Loup-the-dyke, Mercy, Milk-run, Mission, Open-jaw, Pair, Proving, R(a)iser, Redeye, Ro(a)ding, Rode, Rout, Runaway, Skein, Sortie, Stairs, → **STAMPEDE**, Stayre, Steps, Swarm, Test, Top, Tower, Trap, Vol(age), Volatile, Volley, Whisky-frisky, Wing

Flightless Kakapo, Nandoo, Ostrich, Rhea, Struthious

▷ **Flighty** *may indicate* an anagram

Flimsy Finespun, Gimcrack, Gossamer, Jimcrack, Lacy, Sleazy, Sleezy, Tenuous, Thin, Weak, Wispy

Flinch Blench, Cringe, Funk, Quail, Recoil, Shrink, Shudder, Start, Wince

Fling Dance, Flounce, Heave, Highland, Hurl, Lance, Pitch, Shy, Slat, Slug, Slump, Spanghew, Spree, Throw, → **TOSS**

Flint Chert, Firestone, Granite, Hag-stone, Hornstone, Microlith, Mischmetal, Optical, Pirate, Rock, Silex, Silica, Stone, Touchstone, Tranchet

Flip(pant), Flippancy, Flipping Airy, Bally, Brash, Cocky, Facetious, Flick, Frivolous, Impudent, Jerk, Nog, Persiflage, Pert, Purl, Sassy, Saucy, Toss, Turn

Flipper(s) Fin-toed, Paddle, Pinniped(e)

Flirt(ation), Flirting, Flirtatious Bill, Buaya, Carve, Chippy, Cockteaser, Come-hither, Come-on, Coquet(te), Dalliance, Demivierge, Footsie, Gallivant, Heart-breaker, Kittenish, Lumber, Mash, Minx, Neck, Philander(er), Pickeer, Prick-teaser, Rig, Toy, Trifle, Vamp, Wow

Flit Dart, Decamp, Flicker, Flutter, Moonlight, Scoot

Float(er), Floating, Flotation Balsa, Bob, Bubble, Buoy, Caisson, Camel, Carley, Clanger, Drift, Fleet, Flotsam, Flutterboard, Froth, Fucus, Jetsam, Jetson, Levitate, Lifebuoy, Milk, Natant, Neuston, Oropesa, Outrigger, Paddle, Planula, Pontoon, Pram, Quill, Raft, Ride, Sail, Skim, Sponson, Stick, Trimmer, Vacillate, Waft, Waggler, Waterwings

Floating garden Chinampa

Flock(s) Assemble, Bevy, Charm, Chirm, Company, Congregation, Dopping, Drove, Flight, Fold, Forgather, Gaggle, Gather, Gregatim, Herd, Mob, Paddling, Rally, Sedge, Sord, Spring, Trip, Troop, Tuft, Vulgar, Wing, Wisp, Wool

Flog(ger), Flogging Beat, Birch, Breech, Cane, Cat, Clobber, Exert, Flay, Hawk, Hide, Knout, Lace, Lambast, Larrup, Lash, Lather, Lick, Orbilius, Rope's end, Scourge, Sell, Strap, Tat, Taw, → **THRASH**, Thwack, Tout, Vapulate, Welt, Whip, Whipping-cheer

Flood(ed) Awash, Bore, Cataclysm, Deluge, Deucalion's, Diffuse, Diluvium, Drown, Dump, Eger, Flash, Freshet, Gush, Inundate, Irrigate, Noachic, Outpouring, Overflow, Overswell, Overwhelm, Pour, Rage, Smurf, Spate, Speat, Suffuse, Swamp, Tide, → **TORRENT**, Undam, Washland

Floodgate St(a)unch

Floodlight Ashcan, Blond(e), One-key

Floor(ing) Area, Astonish, Astound, Baffle, Barbecue, Beat, Bemuse, Benthos, Chess, Deck, Dev(v)el, Down, Entresol, Étage, Fell, Flags(tone), Flatten, Flight, Gravel, Ground, Kayo, KO, Mezzanine, Mould loft, Paralimnion, Parquet, Pelvic,

Piano nobile, Pit, Planch, Platform, Puncheon, Screed, Shop, Siege, Stage, Story, Stump, Terrazzo, Tessella, Tessera, Thill, Trading, Woodblock

Flop Belly-landing, Bomb, Collapse, Dud, Failure, Fizzer, Fosbury, Lollop, Mare's-nest, Misgo, Phut, Plump, Purler, Washout, Whap, Whitewash

Flora Benthos, Biota, Cybele, Flowers, Intestinal

Florence, Florentine Medici, Tuscan

Florid Coloratura, Cultism, Flamboyant, Fresh, Gongorism, High, Red, Rococo, Rubicund, Ruddy, Taffeta

Florida Fa

Florin Scotchman

Floss(y) Dental, Flashy, Florence, Ornate, Silk

▶ **Flotation** *see* **FLOAT**

Flotilla Armada, Escadrille

Flotsam Detritus, Driftwood, Flotage, Waift, Waveson, Weft

Flounce Falbala, Frill, Furbelow, Huff, Prance, Ruffle, Sashay, Toss

Flounder Blunder, Fluke, Reel, Slosh, Struggle, Stumble, Tolter, Toss, Wallop, Wallow

Flour Cassava, Couscous(ou), Cribble, Crible, Farina, Graham, Gram, Kouskous, Meal, Middlings, Pinole, Plain, Powder, Red-dog, Rice, Rock, Rye, Self-raising, Soy(a), Strong, Wheatmeal, White, Wholegrain, Wholemeal, Wholewheat, Wood

Flourish(ed), Flourishing Blague, Bless, Bloom, Blossom, Boast, Brandish, Bravura, Burgeon, Cadenza, Epiphonema, Fanfare, Fiorita, Fl, Flare, Floreat, Florescent, Grow, Kicking, Lick, Lush, Melisma, Mort, Omar, Palmy, Paraph, Prosper, Rubric, Scroll, Swash, Tantara, Thrive, Tucket, Veronica, Vigorous, Wampish, Wave, Welfare

Flout Disdain, Disobey, Insult, Malign, Mock, Profane, Scorn, Scout

Flow(ing) Abound, Afflux, Cantabile, Cash, Circumfluence, Current, Cursive, Cusec, Data, Distil, Ebb, Emanate, Estrang(h)elo, Fleet, Fluent, Fluid, Flush, Flux, Freeform, Gene, Gush, Knickpoint, Lahar, Laminar, Liquid, Loose-bodied, Nappe, Nickpoint, Obsequent, Onrush, Ooze, Popple, Pour, Purl, Rail(e), Rayle, Rill, Rin, Run, Scapa, Seamless, Seep, Seton, Setter, Slip, Slur, Spate, Spurt, Stream, Streamline, Teem, Tidal, Torrent, Trickle, Turbulent, Viscous

▷ **Flower** *may indicate* a river

Flower (part), Flowering, Flowers, Flower bed Best, Bloom, Bloosme, Blossom, Buttonhole, Composite, Cream, Develop, Efflorescence, Elite, Fiori, Inflorescence, Nosegay, Parterre, Plant, Pre-vernal, Prime, Quatrefeuille, Quatrefoil, Remontant, → **RIVER**, Rogation, Serotine, Spray, Square, Stalked, Stream, Trumpet, Verdoy, Vernal, Wreath

FLOWERS

3 *letters*:	Flag	Wald	Daisy
May	Gold	Weld	Enemy
Mum	Gool		Erica
Rue	Gule	**5 *letters*:**	Hosta
	Irid	Agave	Lotus
4 *letters*:	Iris	Aster	Lupin
Aloe	Knot	Brook	Orris
Arum	Lily	Bugle	Oxlip
Cyme	Pink	Camas	Padma
Disa	Rose	Canna	Pansy

5 letters – cont:
Phlox
Poppy
Spink
Stock
Tansy
Toran
Tulip
Umbel
Viola
Yulan

6 letters:
Adonis
Arabis
Camash
Camass
Corymb
Cosmos
Crants
Dahlia
Gollan
Henbit
Lupine
Madder
Maguey
Mallow
Mimosa
Nuphar
Onagra
Orchid
Oxslip
Paeony
Pompom
Pompon
Protea
Scilla
Sesame
Silene
Smilax
Spadix
Tassel
Thrift
Torana
Wasabi

Yarrow

7 letters:
Aconite
Alyssum
Amarant
Anemone
Astilbe
Bugloss
Campion
Cowslip
Freesia
Fumaria
Gentian
Gilt-cup
Glacier
Gladdon
Godetia
Golland
Gowland
Hawkbit
Ipomoea
Jonquil
Kikumon
Lobelia
Melilot
Mimulus
Passion
Petunia
Picotee
Primula
Quamash
Rampion
Statice
Sulphur
Tellima
Verbena

8 letters:
Abutilon
Amaranth
Argemone
Asphodel
Bindi-eye
Bluebell

Bullhoof
Carolina
Clematis
Cyclamen
Daffodil
Floscule
Foxglove
Gardenia
Geranium
Gillyvor
Gladioli
Glory-pea
Hepatica
Hesperis
Hibiscus
Kok-sagyz
Larkspur
Leucojum
Magnolia
Marigold
Myosotis
Oleander
Primrose
Scabious
Stapelia
Trollius
Tuberose
Turnsole
Valerian

9 letters:
Bald-money
Belamoure
Buttercup
Cineraria
Columbine
Edelweiss
Eglantine
Galingale
Gessamine
Hellebore
Hydrangea
Jessamine
Melampode
Pimpernel

Pyrethrum
Rudbeckia
Santonica
Saxifrage
Speedwell
Strobilus

10 letters:
Bellamoure
Coronation
Granadilla
Heliotrope
Immortelle
Nasturtium
Pentstemon
Poached egg
Poinsettia
Polyanthus
Pulsatilla
Quinsy-wort
Snapdragon
Stavesacre
Tibouchine
Touch-me-not

11 letters:
Boutonniere
Bur-marigold
Gillyflower
Loose-strife
Meadow-sweet
Saintpaulia

12 letters:
Hortus siccus
None-so-pretty
Pasqueflower
Pheasant's eye
Tradescantia

13 letters:
Flannelflower

14 letters:
Transvaal daisy

Flower arrangement, Flower work Barbola, Ikebana, Lei
Flowery Anthea, Anthemia, Damassin, Orchideous, → **ORNATE**, Pseudocarp, Verbose
Flu Fujian, → **INFLUENZA**, ME
Fluctuate(r), Fluctuation Ambivalence, Balance, Seiche, Trimmer, Unsteady,
   Vacillate, Vary, Waver

Flue Chimney, Duct, Funnel, Pipe, Recuperator, Tewel, Uptake, Vent

Fluent(ly) Eloquent, Facile, Flowing, Glib, Liquid, Oracy, Verbose, Voluble

Fluff(y) Bungle, Dowl(e), Down, Dust, Dust bunny, Feathery, Flocculent, Floss, Flue, Fug, Fuzz, Girl, Lint, Mess-up, Muff, Noil, Oose, Ooze, Plot, Thistledown

Fluid Aldehyde, Amniotic, Anasarca, Ascites, Broo, Chyle, Cisterna, Colostrum, Condy's, Coolant, Correcting, Dewdrop, Edema, Enema, Erf, Fixative, Fl, Humour, Joint-oil, Juice, Latex, → **LIQUID**, Lymph, Movable, Mucus, Oedema, Perfect, Perilymph, Plasma, Sap, Seminal, Serous, Serum, Shifting, Spermatic, Spittle, Succus, Synovia, Vitreum, Vril, Water

▷ **Fluid** *may indicate* an anagram

Fluke Accident, Anchor, Chance, Fan, Flounder, Ga(u)nch, Grapnel, Killock, Liver, Lobe, Redia, Schistosome, Scratch, Spud, Upcast

Flummery BS, Pudding

Flummox Baffle, Bamboozle, Floor, Nonplus

Flunk Fail

Flunkey Chasseur, Clawback, Haiduck, Heyduck, Jeames, Lackey, Servant, Toady

Fluorescence, Fluorescent Bloom, Day-glo, Epipolism, Glow, Phosphorescence, Uranin

Fluorine F

Flurry Bustle, Fluster, Haste, Hoo-ha, Shower

Flush(ed) Affluent, Beat, Busted, Even, Ferret, Florid, Flow, Gild, Hectic, Heyday, Hot, Level, Red, Rolling, Rose, Royal, Rud, Scour, Sluice, Spaniel, Start, Straight, Sypher, Thrill, Tierce, Vigour, Wash

Fluster(ed) Befuddle, Confuse, Disconcert, Faze, Flap, Jittery, Pother, Pudder, Rattle, Shake

Flute (player) Bellows-maker, Bohm, Channel, Claribel(la), Crimp, English, Fife, Fipple, Flageolet, German, Glass, Glyph, Groove, Marsyas, Nose, Ocarina, Piccolo, Pipe, Poogye(e), Quena, Shakuhachi, Sulcus, Thisbe, Tibia, Toot, Transverse, Whistle

Flutter Bat, Bet, Fan, Fibrillate, Flacker, Flaffer, Flaught, Flichter, Flicker, Flitter, Fly, → **GAMBLE**, Hover, Palpitate, Pitapat, Play, Pulse, Sensation, Twitter, Waft, Winnow

Flux D, Electric, Flow, Fusion, Luminous, Magnetic, Maxwell, Melt, Neutron, Panta rhei, Radiant, Tesla, Weber

Fly(ing), Flies Abscond, Agaric, Airborne, Alder, Alert, Antlion, Assassin, Astute, Aviation, Awake, Aware, A-wing, Baker, Bedstead, Bee, Black, Blister, Blowfly, Blue-arsed, Bluebottle, Bolt, Bot, Breese, Breeze, Brize, Brommer, Bulb, Bush, Cab, Caddis, Canny, Carriage, Carrot, Cecidomyia, Chalcid, Cheesehopper, Cheese skipper, Cleg, Cluster, Cock-a-bondy, Crane, Cuckoo, → **CUNNING**, Decamp, Deer, Diptera, Dobson, Doctor, Dolphin, Doodlebug, Dragon, Drake, Drone, Drosophila, Dry, Dung, Dutchman, Escape, Face, Fiacre, Flee, Flesh, Flit, Fox, Frit, Fruit, Gad, Glide, Glossina, Gnat, Goutfly, Grannom, Greenbottle, Greenhead, Hackle, Hairy Mary, Harl, Harvest, Hedge-hop, Herl, Hessian, Homoptera, Hop, Horn, Horse, Hover, Hurtle, Ichneumon, Instrument, Jenny-spinner, Jock Scott, Lace-wing, Lamp, Lantern, Laputan, March brown, Mosquito, Mossie, Moth, Motuca, Murragh, Musca, Mutuca, Namu, Needle, New Forest, Nymph, Onion, Opening, Ox-warble, Palmer, Para, Pilot, Pium, Plecopteran, Pomace, Rapid, Robber, Saucer, Sciaridae, Scorpion, Scotsman, Screwworm, Scud, Sedge, Silverhorn, Simulium, Smart, Smother, Snake, Snipe, Soar, Spanish, Speed, Spinner, Stable, Stream, Syrphidae, Tabanid, Tachina, Tail, Tear, Thrips, Tipula, Trichopteran, Tsetse, Tube, Turkey brown, Turnip, Vamoose, Vinegar, Volatic, Volitate, Warble, Watchet,

Water, Welshman's button, Wet, Wheat, Wide-awake, Willow, Wily, Wing, Yellow Sally, Yogic, Zebub, Zimb, Zipper

Fly-catcher Attercop, Clamatorial, Cobweb, Darlingtonia, Dionaea, King-bird, Phoebe, Spider, Tanrec, Tyrant, Yellowhead

Flying-fox Fruit-bat, Kalong

Flying saucer UFO

Fly-killer Chowri, Chowry, DDT, Swat

Flyover Overpass

Foam(ing) Aerogel, Barm, Bubble, Froth, Lather, Mousse, Oasis®, Polystyrene, Ream, Scum, Seethe, Spindrift, Spooming, Spume, Sud(s), Surf, Wake, Wild water, Yeast, Yest

Fob Chain, Defer, Fub, Pocket, Slang

Focal, Focus Centre, Centrepiece, Concentrate, Converge, Fix, Hinge, Hub, Narrow, Nub, Pinpoint, Point, Prime, Principal, Spotlight, Train

Fodder Alfalfa, Browsing, Buckwheat, Cannon, Clover, Eatage, Emmer, Ensilage, Foon, Forage, Gama-grass, Grama, Guar, Hay, Lucerne, Mangle, Oats, Oilcake, Pasture, Provender, Rye-grass, Sainfoin, Silage, Soilage, Stover, Straw, Vetch

Foe Arch, Contender, → **ENEMY**, Opponent, Rival

Foetus Embryo

Fog Aerosol, Brume, Cloud, Damp, Fret, Haar, (London) Particular, Miasm(a), Mist, Murk, Obscure, Pea-soup(er), Roke, Sea-fret, Sea-haar, Smog, Smoke, Soup, Thick, Vapour, Yorkshire

Fogey Die-hard

Fogg Phileas, Solicitor

Foible Failing, Flaw, Idiosyncrasy, Quirk, Weakness

Foil(ed) Ba(u)lk, Chaff, Cross, Dupe, Epée, Fleurette, Frustrate, Gold, Gold leaf, Lametta, Leaf, Offset, Paillon, Pip, Scotch, Scupper, Silver, Stooge, Stump, Sword, Tain, Thwart, Tinsel, Touché

Foist Fob, Insert, Insinuate, Suborn, Wish

Fold(er), Folding, Folded, Folds Anticline, Bend, Binder, Close, Collapse, Concertina, Convolution, Corrugate, Cote, Crash, Crease, Crimp, Crinkle, Crunkle, Diapir, Diptych, Dog-ear, Double, Duo-tang®, Epicanthus, Epiploon, Fake, Fan, File, Fourchette, Fr(a)enum, Frill, Furl, Gather, Geanticline, Groin, Gyrus, Inflexure, Intussuscept, Jacket, Jack-knife, Lap, Lapel, Lap(p)et, Lirk, Mantle, Mesentery, Mitre, Monocline, Nappe, Nympha, Obvolute, Octuple, Omentum, Origami, Pastigium, Pen, Pericline, Pintuck, Pleach, → **PLEAT**, Plica, Plunging, Ply, Prancke, Pran(c)k, Ptyxis, Recumbent, Ruck(le), Ruga, Sheep-pen, Syncline, Triptych, Tuck, Vocal, Wrap

Foliage Coma, Finial, Frond, Frondescence, Greenery, Leafage, Leaves

Folio(s) Crown, Elephant, F(f), File, Foolscap, Imperial, Percy, Royal

Folk(sy) Beaker, Homespun, Kin, People, Public

Follicle Graafian

Follow(er), Following Acolyte, Acolyth, Adhere, Admirer, After, Agree, Amoret, And, Anthony, Attend(ant), Believer, Clientele, Consequence, Copy, Dangle, Disciple, Dog, Echo, Ensew, Ensue, Entourage, Epigon(e), Equipage, F, Fan, Groupie, Heel(er), Henchman, Hereon, Hunt, Jacob, Man, Merry men, Minion, Muggletonian, Myrmidon, Neist, Next, Obey, Pan, Post, Pursue, Rake, Road, Run, Satellite, School, Secundum, Seewing, Segue, Sequel, Seriation, Servitor, Shadow, Sheep, S(h)ivaite, Sidekick, Stag, Stalk, Stear, Steer, Subsequent, Succeed, Sue, Suivez, Supervene, Tag, Tail, Tantony, Trace, Track, Trail, Train, Use, Vocation, Votary

▷ **Follower** 'a follower' *may indicate* B

Folly Absurd, Antic, Bêtise, Idiocy, Idiotcy, Imprudence, Lunacy, Madness, Mistake, Moria, Unwisdom, Vanity

Foment(ation) Arouse, Brew, Embrocation, Excite, Poultice, Stupe

Fond(ness) Amatory, Ardour, Dote, Keen, Loving, Partial, Penchant, Tender, Tendre

Fondant Ice, Sweet

Fondle Canoodle, Caress, Dandle, Grope, Hug, Nurse, Pet, Snuggle

Font Aspersorium, Bénitier, Bitmap, Delubrum, Ennage, Outline, Proportional, Source, True-type, Vector

Food Aliment, Ambrosia, Bakemeat, Balti, Batten, Battill, Battle, Bellytimber, Board, Bolus, Bord, Broth, Browse, Bully, Burger, Bush-tucker, Cate, Cereal, Chametz, Cheer, Cheese, Chop, Chow, Chuck, Chyme, Cocoyam, Collation, Comestible, Comfort, Commons, Convenience, Course, Curd, Deutoplasm, Dietetics, → **DISH**, Dodger, Dog's body, Dunderfunk, Eats, Esculents, Eutrophy, Falafel, Fare, Fast, Fast casual, Felafel, Fodder, Forage, Frankenstein, Freedom, Fuel, Functional, Giffengood, Grub, Gruel, Hangi, Hometz, Incaparina, Ingesta, Jootha, Jorts, Junk, Kai, Keep, Langar, Leben, Lerp, Long-pig, Maigre, Maki, Manna, Mato(o)ke, Matzoon, Meal, Meat, Muckamuck, Nacho, Nardoo, Nosebag, Nosh, Nourishment, Nourriture, Opsonium, Ort, Oven-ready, Pabulum, Pannage, Pap, Parev(e), Parve, Pasta, Pasture, Peck, Pemmican, Pizza, Prog, Provand, Provender, Provision, Pu(l)ture, Ration(s), Real, Risotto, Roughage, Rysttafel, Sambal, Samosa, Sap, Sashimi, Scaff, Schri, Scoff, Scran, Sitology, Sizings, Skin, Skran, Slow, Snack, Soil, Soul, Staple, Stodge, Sushi, Table, Tack, Takeaway, Tamale, Taro, Tempeh, Tempura, Teriyake, Tex-Mex, Tofu, Trimmings, Trophallaxis, Tuck(er), Vegeburger, Veggie-burger, Viand, Victuals, Vivers, Vivres, Waffle, Yantia, Yittles, Yog(h)urt

Food-plant Laser, Silphium

Foodstore Delicatessen, Grocery, Larder, Pantry, Silo

Fool(hardy), Foolish(ness) Air-head, Anserine, April, Asinico, Asinine, Assot, Berk, BF, Bob, Booby, Bottom, Brainless, Brash, Buffoon, Cake, Capocchia, Chump, Clot, Clown, Cockeyed, Coney, Coof, Coxcomb, Cuif, Cully, Daft, Dagonet, Daw, Delude, Dessert, Dilly, Divvy, Doat, Dote, Dummy, Dunce, Empty, Etourdi, Fatuous, Feste, Flannel(led), Folly, Fon, Fond, Fox, Gaby, Gaga, Galah, Git, Glaikit, Goat, Gobbo, Goon, Goose, Gooseberry, Groserts, Gubbins, Gull, Gullible, Halfwit, Hanky-panky, Hare-brained, Haverel, Highland, Huntiegowk, Hunt-the-gowk, Idiotic, Imbecile, Inane, Ineptitude, Injudicious, Insensate, Jest, Jester, Joke, Kid, Kissel, Lark, Loon, Madcap, Mamba, Misguide, Mislead, Mome, Moron, Muggins, Niaiserie, Nignog, Ni(n)compoop, Ninny, Nong, Noodle, Nose-led, Oanshagh, Omadhaun, Patch, Pea-brained, Poop, Poupe, Punk, Rash, Sawney, Scogan, Scoggin, Senseless, Shallow, Shmo, Simpleton, Snipe, Soft, Sot, Spoony, Stultify, → **STUPID**, Sucker, Tom (noddy), Trifle, Unwitty, Vice, Wantwit, Yap, Yorick, Yoyo, Zany

Foolproof Fail-safe

Foot(ing), Footwork, Feet Amphibrach, Amphimacer, Anap(a)est, Antibacchius, Antispast, Athlete's, Bacchius, Ball, Base, Board, Choliamb, Choree, Choriamb, Club, Cold, Cretic, Dactyl, Dance, Dipody, Dochmii, Dochmius, Epitrite, F, Ft, Hephthemimer, Hoof, Hoppus, Iamb(us), Immersion, Infantry, Ionic, Molossus, Ockodols, Pad, Paeon, Palama, Pastern, Paw, Pay, Pedate, Pedicure, Penthemimer, Pes, Plates, Podiatry, Podium, Proceleusmatic, Pyrrhic, Roothold, Scazon, Semeia, Serif, Shanks's mare, Shanks's pony, Spade, Splay, Spondee, Standing, Syzygy, Tarsus, Terms, Tootsie, Tootsy, Tootsy-wootsy, Tread, Trench, Tribrach, Trilbies,

Triseme, Trochee, Trotter, Tube, Ungula, Verse, Wrong

Football(er) Aerial pingpong, American, Association, Australian Rules, Back, Banyana-banyana, Barbarian, Ba'spiel, Best, Camp, Canadian, Centre, Fantasy, FIFA, Five-a-side, Flanker(back), Fly-half, Futsal, Gaelic, Goalie, Gridder, Half, Hooker, Keeper, Kicker, League, Libero, Lineman, Lock, Midfield, Moore, National code, Pack, Pele, Pigskin, RU, Rugby, Rugger, Rules, Safety, Seven-a-side, Sevens, Soccer(oos), Sport, Stand-off, Striker, Subbuteo®, Sweeper, Table, Tight-end, Togger, Total, Touch(back), Wallgame, Wing, Wingman

Footboard Stretcher

Foot-fault Bunion, Corn, Hammer-toe, Talipes, Verruca

Foothold Lodgement, Purchase, Stirrup

Footlights Floats

Footling Trivial

Footloose Peripatetic

Footman Attendant, Flunkey, Lackey, Pedestrian, Pompey, Valet de chambre, Yellowplush

Footnote Addendum, PS

Footpad Land-rat, Mugger, Robber

Footpath, Footway Banquette, Catwalk, Clapper, Track

Footplate Horseshoe

Footprint Ecological, Electronic, Ichnite, Ichnolite, Ornithichnite, Pad, Prick, Pug, Seal, Slot, Trace, Track, Tread, Vestige

Footrest, Footstool Coaster, Cricket, Hassock, Pouffe, Stirrup, Stool, Tramp

Footrot, Footsore Blister, Bunion, Corn, Halt, Surbate, Surbet, Weary, Wire-heel

Footslogger Infantryman

Footwashing Maundy, Nipter

Footwear Gumboot, Jackboot, → SHOE, Slipper, Sock, Spats, Stocking

Fop(pish) Apery, Barbermonger, Beau, Buck, Cat, Coxcomb, Dandy, Dude, Exquisite, Fallal, Fangled, Fantastico, Finical, La-di-da, Macaroni, Monarcho, Muscadin, Petit maître, Popinjay, Skipjack, Toff

For Ayes, Because, Concerning, Cos, Pro, Since, To

Forage Alfalfa, Fodder, Graze, Greenfeed, Ladino, Lucern(e), Pickeer, Prog, Raid, Rummage, Sainfoin, Search

Foray Attack, Creach, Creagh, Raid, Sortie, Spreagh

Forbear(ance), Forbearing Abstain, Clement, Endure, Indulgent, Lenience, Lineage, Longanimity, Mercy, Overgo, Pardon, Parent, Patient, Quarter, → REFRAIN, Suffer, Tolerant, Withhold

Forbid(den), Forbidding Ban, Bar, City, Denied, Don't, Dour, Enjoin, For(e)speak, Gaunt, Grim, Haram, Hostile, Loury, NL, Prohibit, Stern, Taboo, Tabu, Tapu, Tref(a), Verboten, Veto

Force(d), Forceful, Forces, Forcible, Forcing Activist, Agency, Air-arm, Army, Back emf, Bathmism, Bind, Birr, Bludgeon, Body, Bounce, Brigade, Bring, Brunt, Bulldoze, Cadre, Capillary, Cascade, Centrifugal, Centripetal, Chi, Coerce, Coercive, Cogency, Commando, Compel, Constrain, Coriolis, Cram, Delta, Detachment, Dint, Domineer, Downflow, Dragoon, Drive, Duress(e), Dynamic, Dyne, E, Edge, Electromotive, Emphatic, Energetic, Equilibrant, Erdgeist, Erg, Exchange, Expeditionary, Extort, Extrude, F, Farci, Fifth, Fire brigade, Foot-pound, Foot-ton, Foss, Frogmarch, Full-line, G, Gar, Gendarmerie, Gilbert, Gism, Gouge, Gravitational, Great Attractor, Hale, Host, Hurricane, Impetus, Impose, Impress, Inertial, Instress, Intense, Irgun, Irrupt, Jism, Juggernaut, Kinetic, Kundalini, Labour, Land, Lashkar, Legion, Leverage, Life, Lift, Linn, Lorentz, Magnetomotive,

Magnus, Make, Mana, Manpower, Market, Met, Militia, Moment, Momentum, Muscle, Nature-god, Navy, Newton, Numen, Oblige, Od, Odyl(e), OGPU, Old Contemptibles, Orgone, Orotund, Personnel, Phrenism, Physical, Pigs, Pion, Pithy, Plastic, Police, Posse, Potent, Pound, Poundal, Prana, Press(gang), Pressure, Prise, Procrustean, Psyche, Psychic, Pull, Pushy, Put, Qi, Railroad, Rape, Ravish, Reave, Red Army, Regular, Require, Restem, Route, Rush, SAS, Sforzando, Shear, Snorting, Spent, Spetsnaz, Squad, Squeeze, Squirt, Steam(roller), Stick, Stiction, Strained, Strength, → **STRESS**, Strong-arm, Subject, Sword, TA, Task, Teeth, Telergy, Telling, Territorial, The Bill, The Great Attractor, Thrust, Torque, Tractive, Troops, Upthrust, Van der Waals', Vehement, Vigorous, Vim, Violence, Vires, Vis, Vis visa, Vital, Vively, Vociferous, Vril, Weak, Wedge, Wrench, Wrest, Wring, Zap

▷ **Force(d)** *may indicate* an anagram

Forced labour Begar

Force-feeding Gavage

Forceps Bulldog, Capsule, Crow(s)bill, Hemostatic, Mosquito, Obstetrical, Pedicellaria, Pincers, Rongeur, Tenaculum, Thumb, Vulsella

Ford Anglia, Anna, Capri, Car, Crossing, Drift, Escort, Industrialist, Irish bridge, Sierra, Strid, Tin Lizzy, Wade

Forearm Cubital, Radius, Ulna

▶ **Forebear** *see* **FORBEAR**

Foreboding Anxiety, Augury, Cloudage, Croak, Feeling, Freet, Hoodoo, → **OMEN**, Ominous, Premonition, Presage, Presentiment, Sinister, Zoomantic

Forecast(er), Forecasting Augury, Auspice, Divine, Extrapolation, Horoscope, Long-range, Metcast, Metman, Numerical, Perm, Portend, Precurse, Predict, Presage, Prescience, Prevision, Prognosis, Prognosticate, Projection, Prophesy, Quant, Rainbird, Scry, Shipping, Skry, Soothsay, Spae, Tip, Weather

Foreclose Bar, Block, Obstruct, Preclude

Forefather(s) Ancestor, Elder, Forebear, Parent, Rude

Forefront Van, Vaward

Forehead Brow, Front(let), Frontal, Glabella(r), Sincipitum, Temple

▷ **Foreign** *may indicate* an anagram

Foreign(er) Adventitious, Alien, Amakwerekwere, Arab, Auslander, Barbarian, Easterling, Ecdemic, Eleanor, Ethnic, Étranger, Exclave, Exotic, External, Extraneous, Extrinsic, Forane, Forinsecal, Forren, Fraim, Fremit, Gaijin, German, Gringo, Gweilo, Malihini, Metic, Moit, Mote, Outlander, Outside, Oversea, Peregrine, Remote, → **STRANGE**, Stranger, Taipan, Tramontane, Uitlander, Unfamiliar, Wog

Foreign Office Quai d'orsay

Foreknowledge Prescience

Foreman Baas, Boss, Bosun, Chancellor, Clicker, Gaffer, Ganger, Manager, Overseer, Steward, Straw boss, Superintendent, Tool pusher, Topsman, Walla(h)

Foremost First, Front, Leading, Primary, Prime, Supreme, Upfront, Van

▷ **Foremost** *may indicate* first letters of words following

Forenoon Undern

Forepart Cutwater, Front

Forerunner Augury, Harbinger, Herald, Messenger, Omen, Pioneer, Precursor, Prequel, Trailer, Vaunt-courier

Foresee Anticipate, Divine, Preview, Prophesy, Scry

Foreshadow Adumbrate, Augur, Bode, Forebode, Hint, Portend, Pre-echo, Prefigure, Presage, Type

Foreshow Betoken, Bode, Signify

Foresight Ganesa, Prescience, Prophecy, Prospect, Providence, Prudence, Taish, Vision

Foreskin Prepuce

Forest(ry), Forested Arden, Ardennes, Ashdown, Black, Bohemian, Bracknell, Bush, Caatinga, Charnwood, Chase, Cloud, Dean, Deer, Elfin, Epping, Fontainebleau, Gallery, Gapo, Glade, Greenwood, Igapo, Jungle, Managed, Monte, Nandi, Nemoral, New, Petrified, Rain, Savernake, Selva, Sherwood, Silviculture, Taiga, Thuringian, Urman, Virgin, Waltham, Wealden, → **WOOD**, Woodcraft, Woodland

Forestall Anticipate, Head-off, Obviate, Pip, Pre-empt, Prevent, Queer, Scoop

Forester Foster, Kangaroo, Lumberjack, Verderer, Walker, Woodman, Woodward

Foretaste Antepast, Antipasto, Appetiser, Avant-goût, Pregustation, Prelibation, Preview, Sample, Trailer

Foretell(ing), Forewarn Augur, Bode, Caution, Divine, Fatidic, Forecast, Portend, Predict, Premonish, Presage, Previse, Prognosticate, Prophecy, Soothsay, Spae, Weird

Forethought Anticipation, Caution, Prometheus, Provision, Prudence

Forever Always, Amber, Ay(e), Constant, Eternal, Evermore, Keeps

▶ **Forewarn** *see* **FORETELL**

Foreword Introduction, Preamble, Preface, Proem, Prologue

For example Eg, Say, Vg, ZB

For fear Lest

Forfeit(ed) Confiscated, Deodand, Fine, Forgo, → **PENALTY**, Phillepina, Phillepine, Philop(o)ena, Relinquish, Rue-bargain, Sconce

Forge(d), Forger(y) Blacksmith, Copy, Counterfeit, Drop, Dud, Fabricate, Falsify, Fashion, Foundry, Hammer, Heater, Horseshoe, Ireland, Ironsmith, Lauder, Mint, Paper-hanger, Pigott, Progress, Rivet head, Rivet-hearth, Smith(y), Smithery, Spurious, Stiddie, Stiff, Stithy, Stumer, Tilt, Trucage, Truquage, Utter, Valley, Vermeer, Vulcan, Weld

Forget(ful), Forget-me-not Amnesia, Dry, Fluff, Lethe, Myosotis, Neglect, Oblivious, Omit, Overlook, Unlearn, Wipe

Forgive(ness), Forgiving Absolution, Amnesty, Clement, Condone, Divine, Excuse, Lenity, Merciful, Overlook, Pardon, Placable, Remission, Remittal, Tolerant

Forgo(ne) Abstain, Expected, Refrain, Renounce, Waive

Forgotten Bygone, Lost, Missed, Sad

Forjeskit Overscutched

Fork(ed), Fork out Bifurcate, Biramous, Branch, Caudine, Cleft, Crotch, Crutch, Divaricate, Forficate, Fourchette, Grain, Graip, Morton's, Osmeterium, Pay, Prong, Replication, Runcible, Slave, Sucket, Tine, Toaster, Toasting, Tormenter, Tormentor, Trident, Trifid, Tuner, Tuning, Y

Forlorn(ness) Abject, Aidless, Desolate, Destitute, Drearisome, Godforsaken, Lonely, Miserable, Nightingale, Sad, Woebegone

▷ **Form** *may indicate* a hare's bed

Form(s) Alumni, Bench, Bumf, Cast, Ceremonial, Charterparty, Class, Clipped, Constitute, Coupon, Create, Document, Draw up, Dress, Experience, Fashion, Feature, Fig, → **FIGURE**, Formula, Frame, Free, Game, Gestalt, Hare, Idea, Image, Inscape, Keto, Lexicalise, Life, Logical, Mode, Mood, Morph(ic), Morphology, Mould, Order, Originate, → **OUT OF FORM**, P45, Penitent, Physique, Protocol, Questionnaire, Redia, Remove, Rite, Ritual, Schedule, Shape, Shell, Sonata, Song, Stage, Stamp, State, Stem, Stereotype, Structure, Style, Symmetry, Talon, Ternary, Version

Formal Black tie, Ceremonious, Conventional, Dry, Exact, Fit, Literal, Methodic, Official, Pedantic, Perfunctory, Precise, Prim, Routine, Set, Solemn, Starched, Stiff, Stiff-necked, Stodgy, Stuffed shirt, Tails

Formality Amylum, Ceremony, Ice, Pedantry, Pomp, Protocol, Punctilio, Starch

Formation Battalion, Brown, Configuration, Diapyesis, Echelon, Eocene, Fours, Growth, Layout, Line, Manufacture, Origin, Pattern, Phalanx, Potence, Prophase, Reaction, Riss, Series, Serried, Wedge

▷ **Former** *may indicate* something that forms

Former(ly) Ance, Auld, Before, Ci-devant, Earlier, Ere-now, Erst(while), Ex, Late, Maker, Matrix, Old, Once, One-time, Past, Previous, Prior, Pristine, Quondam, Sometime, Then, Umquhile, Unwhile, Whilom, Yesterday

Formidable Alarming, Armipotent, Battleaxe, Fearful, Forbidding, Gorgon, Powerful, Redoubtable, Shrewd, Stoor, Stour, Stowre, Sture, Tiger

Formless Amorphous, Invertebrate, Nebulous, Shapeless

▷ **Form of, Forming** *may indicate* an anagram

Formosan Tai

Formula(te) Define, Devise, Doctrine, Empirical, Equation, Frame, Graphic, Incantation, Invent, Kekule, Lurry, Molecular, Paternoster, Prescription, Protocol, Prunes and prisms, → **RECIPE**, Reduction, Rite, Ritual, Stirling's, Structural

Forsake Abandon, Desert, Quit, Renounce

Forsooth Certes, Certy, Even, Marry, Quotha

For sure Pukka

Forswear Abandon, Abjure, Disavow, Renounce, Reny

Forsyte Fleur, Saga, Soames

Fort(ification), Fortress Abatis, Acropolis, Alamo, Alhambra, Balclutha, Bastel-house, Bastide, Bastille, Bastion, Battlement, Bawn, Blockhouse, Bonnet, Breastwork, Bridgehead, Burg, Casbah, Castellated, Castellum, Castle, Citadel, Contravallation, Counterscarp, Crémaillère, Demilune, Deva, Dun, Earthwork, Edinburgh, Enceinte, Epaule, Escarpment, Fastness, Fieldwork, Flanker, Flèche, Fortalice, Fortilage, Fortlet, Fraise, Ft, Gabion(ade), Garrison, Gatehouse, Golconda, Haven, Hedgehog, Hill, Hornwork, Kaim, Kame, Kasba(h), Keep, Knox, La(a)ger, Lauderdale, Legnaga, Line, Louisbourg, Maiden, Malakoff, Mantua, Martello tower, Masada, Merlon, Mile-castle, Moineau, Motte and bailey, Orillion, Pa(h), Peel, Pele, Pentagon, Peschiera, Place, Przernysl, Rampart, Rath, Ravelin, Redoubt, Reduit, Ring, Salient, Sallyport, Sangar, Sconce, Stavropol, Stronghold, Sumter, Talus, Tenaille, Terreplein, Tête-du-pont, Ticonderoga, Tower, Tower of London, Trench, Vallation, Verona, Vitrified, William, Worth

Forte F, Métier, Specialty, Strength

Forth Away, From, Hence, Out

Forthright(ness) Blunt, Candid, Direct, Four-square, Frank, Glasnost, Outspoken, Prompt

Forthwith Anon, Directly, Eft(soons), Immediately

Fortify Arm, Augment, Brace, Casemate, Embattle, Lace, Munify, Soup up, Steel, → **STRENGTHEN**

Fortitude Endurance, Grit, Mettle, Patience, Pluck, → **STAMINA**

Fortune, Fortunate, Fortuitous Auspicious, Blessed, Blest, Bomb, Coincident, Godsend, Happy, → **LUCKY**, Madoc, Opportune, Pile, Providential, Up, Well, Well off

Fortune teller, Fortune-telling Auspicious, Bonanza, Bumby, Cartomancy, Chaldee, Cha(u)nce, Destiny, Dukkeripen, Fame, Fate, Felicity, Genethliac, Geomancy, Hap, Hydromancy, I Ching, Lot, Luck, Mint, Motser, Motza, Oracle,

Packet, Palmist, Peripety, Pile, Prescience, Pyromancy, Sibyl, Soothsayer, Sortilege, Spaewife, Success, Taroc, Tarok, Tarot, Tyche, Wealth, Windfall

Forty, Forties Capot, F, Hungry, Kemple, Roaring

Forty-ninth Parallel

Forum Arena, Assembly, Debate, Platform, Tribunal

Forward(s) Accede, Advanced, Ahead, Along, Anterior, Arch, Assertive, Assuming, Bright, Cheeky, Early, Flanker, Forrad, Forrit, Forth, Fresh, Future, Hasten, Hooker, Immodest, Impudent, Insolent, Lock, Malapert, Number eight, On(wards), Pack, Pert, Petulant, Porrect, Precocious, → **PROGRESS**, Promote, Prop, Readdress, Redirect, Scrum, Send, Stem, Striker, To(ward), Van, Wing

Fossil(ised), Fossils Amber, Ammonite, Baculite, Belemnite, Blastoid(ea), Calamite, Ceratodus, Chondrite, Conodont, Corallian, Cordaites, Creodont, Crinite, Derived, Dolichosauria, Encrinite, Eohippus, Eozoon, Eurypterus, Exuviae, Fairy stone, Florula, Florule, Fogy, Goniatite, Graptolite, Hipparion, Hippurite, Hominid, Ichnite, Ichnolite, Ichnology, Ichthyodurolite, Ichthyolite, Index, Jew's stone, Kenyapithecus, Lepidostrobus, Lingulella, Living, Mosasauros, Nummulite, Odontolite, Olenellus, Olenus, Oligocene, Orthoceras, Osteolepis, Ostracoderm, Oxfordian, Pal(a)eo-, Pentacrinus, Petrifaction, Phytolite, Plesiosaur, Pliohippus, Pliosaur, Psilophyton, Pteridosperm, Pterodactyl(e), Pterygotus, Pythonomorph, Relics, Reliquiae, Remanié, Reworked, Sigillaria, Sinanthropus, Sivatherium, Snakestone, Stigmaria, Stromatolite, Taphonomy, Teleosaurus, Tentaculite, Thunderegg, Titanotherium, Trace, Trilobite, Uintatherium, Wood-opal, Zinganthropus, Zone, Zoolite

Foster (child, mother), Fostering Adopt, Cherish, Da(u)lt, Develop, Farm out, Feed, Fornent, Further, Harbour, Incubation, Metapelet, Metaplot, Nourish, Nourse(l), Noursle, Nousell, Nurse, Nurture, Nuzzle, → **REAR**

Foul, Foul-smelling Base, Bastardise, Beray, Besmirch, Besmutch, Bewray, Bungle, → **DEFILE**, Dreggy, Drevill, Enseam, Evil, Feculent, Funky, Gross, Hassle, Hing, Mephitic, Mud, Noisome, Olid, Osmeterium, Paw(paw), Professional, Putid, Putrid, → **RANK**, Reekie, Rotten, Sewage, Soiled, Squalid, Stagnant, Stain, Stapelia, Technical, Unclean, Unfair, Vilde, Vile, Violation, Virose

▷ **Foul** *may indicate* an anagram

Found (in) Among, Base, Bed, Bottom, Build, Cast, Caught, Emong, Endow, → **ESTABLISH**, Eureka, Institute, Introduce, Met, Occur, Plant, Recovered, Rest, Stablish, Start, Table

Foundation(s) Base, Bedrock, Corset, Cribwork, Establishment, Footing, Girdle, Grillage, Ground, Grounding, Groundwork, Hard-core, Hypostasis, Infrastructure, Institution, Matrix, Mattress, Panty girdle, Pile, Pitching, Roadbed, Rockefeller, Root, Scholarship, Stays, Stereobate, Subjacent, Substrata, Substructure, Trackbed, Underlie, Underlinen

▷ **Foundations** *may indicate* last letters

Founder Author, Bell, Collapse, Crumple, Fail, Inventor, Iron-master, Miscarry, Oecist, Oekist, Patriarch, Perish, Settle, Sink, Steelman, Stumble

Fount Aonian, Digital, Source, Springlet, Wrong

Fountain Acadine, Aganippe, Arethusa, Bubbler, Castalian, Cause, Conduit, Drinking, Fauwara, Forts, Gerbe, Head, Hippocrene, Jet, Pant, Pirene, Salmacis, Scuttlebutt, Soda, Spring, Trevi, Well-spring, Youth

Fountain basin Laver

Four(times), Foursome, Four-yearly Cater, Georges, Horsemen, IV, Mess, Mournival, Penteteric, Qid, Quartet, Quaternary, Quaternion, Reel, Tessara, Tessera, Tetrad, Tetralogy, Tiddy, Warp

Fourpence Groat
Fourteenth Bastille, Trecento, Valentine
Fourth Deltaic, Estate, Fardel, Farl(e), Firlot, Forpet, Forpit, July, Martlet, Perfect, Quarter, Quartet, Quaternary, Quintan, Sesquitertia, Tritone
Fowl Barnyard, Biddy, Boiler, Brahma, Brissle-cock, Burrow-duck, Capon, Chicken, Chittagong, Cob, Cock, Coot, Domestic, Dorking, Duck, Ember, Gallinaceous, Gallinule, Game, Gleenie, Guinea, Hamburg(h), Heather-bleat(er), → **HEN**, Houdan, Jungle, Knob, Kora, Leghorn, Mallee, Moorhen, Orpington, Papageno, Partridge, Pheasant, Pintado, Plymouth Rock, Poultry, Quail, Rooster, Rumkin, Rumpy, Scrub, Solan, Spanish, Spatchcock, Spitchcock, Sultan, Sussex, Teal, Turkey, Wyandotte
Fox(y) Alopecoid, Arctic, Baffle, Blue, Charley, Charlie, Corsac, Crafty, Cunning, Desert, Fennec, Floor, Flying, Fool, Friend, Fur, Grey, Kit, Lowrie(-tod), Outwit, Pug, Puzzle, Quaker, Red, Reynard, Rommel, Russel, Silver, Skulk, → **SLY**, Stump, Swift, Tod, Uffa, Uneatable, Vixen, White, Zerda, Zoril(le), Zorro
Foxglove Cowflop, Deadmen's bells, Digitalis, Witches'-thimble
Foxhole Earth
Foyer Hall, Lobby
Fracas Brawl, Dispute, Mêlée, Prawle, Riot, Rumpus, Scrum, Shindig, Uproar
Fraction Common, Complex, Compound, Continued, Decimal, Improper, Ligroin, Mantissa, Mixed, Packing, Part, Partial, Piece, Proper, Scrap, Simple, Some, Vulgar
Fracture Break, Colles, Comminuted, Complicated, Compound, Crack, Fatigue, Fault, Fissure, Greenstick, Hairline, Impacted, Oblique, Pathological, Platy, Pott's, Rupture, Shear, Simple, Spiral, Splintery, Split, Stress, Transverse
Fragile Brittle, Crisp, Delicate, Frail, Frangible, Nesh, Slender, Tender, Vulnerable, Weak
Fragment(s) Agglomerate, Atom, Bit, Bla(u)d, Brash, Breccia, Brockage, Brockram, Cantlet, Clastic, Crumb, Disjecta membra, End, Flinder, Fritter, Frust, Graile, Lapilli, Mammock, Mite, Morceau, Morsel, Ort, → **PARTICLE**, Piece, Piecemeal, Potshard, Potsherd, Relic, Restriction, Rubble, Scrap, Segment, Shard, Shatter, Sheave, Shiver, Shrapnel, Shred, Skerrick, Sliver, Smithereens, Smithers, Snatch, Splinter
▷ **Fragment of** *may indicate* a hidden word
Fragrance, Fragrant Aromatic, Attar, Balsam, Bouquet, Conima, Nosy, Odiferous, Odour, Olent, → **PERFUME**, Pot-pourri, Redolent, → **SCENT**, Sent, Spicy, Suaveolent
Frail Brittle, Creaky, Delicate, Feeble, Flimsy, → **FRAGILE**, Puny, Slight, Slimsy, Tottery, Weak
Framboesia Morula, Yaws
Frame(work) Adjust, Airer, Angle, Armature, Bail, Bayle, Body, Bow, Brickbat, Build, Cadge, Cadre, Cage, Case, Casement, Casing, Cent(e)ring, Centreing, Chase, Chassis, Clamper, Climbing, Coaming, Cold, Compages, Companion, Cowcatcher, Cradle, Cratch, Cribwork, Deckel, Deckle, Draw, Dutchwife, Entablature, Everest pack, Fabric, Falsework, Fender, Fiddley, Fit-up, Flake, Form, Frisket, Gallows, Gambrel, Gantry, Garden, Gate, Gauntry, Grid-iron, Haik, Hake, Heck, Horse, Hovel, Hull, Jungle gym, Lattice, Limit, Louvre, Mantel, Mixter, Monture, Mood, Mount, Mullion, Muntin(g), Newsreel, Ossature, Outrigger, Oxford, Pack, Pannier, Pantograph, Parameter, Partners, Passe-partout, Pergola, Physique, Pillory, Plant, Plot, Plummer-block, Poppet head, Portal, Pumphead, Punchboard, Puncheon, Quilting, Rack, Rave, Redact, Retable, Rib(bing), Rim, Sampling, Sash, Scaffold, Scuncheon, Sect(ion), Set, Setting, Skeleton, Spring-box, Stanchion, Stand, Stern,

Still(age), Stitch up, Stocking, Stocks, Straddle, Stretcher, Stretching, Stroma, → **STRUCTURE**, Studwork, Surround, Swift, Tabernacle, Taboret, Tambour, Tent(er), Tepee, Time, Timeline, Trave, Trellis, Tress, Tressel, Trestle, Tribble, Trussing, Vacuum, Victimize, Walking, Wattle, Ways, Window, Yoke, Zarf, Zimmer®

Framley Parsonage

Franc Fr, Leu, Lev, Lew

France Anatole, Marianne, RF, Thibault

Franchise Charter, Contract, Liberty, Pot-wall(op)er, Privilege, Right, Suffrage, Vote, Warrant

Franciscan Custos, Minorite, Observant, Salesian, Scotist, Tertiaries

Francium Fr

Franck Cesar

Frank(ish) Artless, Austrasia, Blunt, → **CANDID**, Direct, Easy, Four square, Free, Free-spoken, Honest, Ingenuous, Man-to-man, Merovingian, Natural, Open, Outspoken, Overt, Postage, Postmark, Raw, Ripuarian, Salian, Sincere, Squareshooter, Stamp, Straight, Straightforward, Sty, Upfront

Frankincense Laser, Olibanum, Thus

Frans, Franz Hals, Lehar

Frantic Demoniac, Deranged, Distraught, Frenzied, Hectic, Mad, Overwrought, Phrenetic, Rabid, Violent, Whirl(ing)

▷ **Frantic** *may indicate* an anagram

Frappé Iced

Fraternise, Fraternity Affiliate, Brotherhood, Burschenschaft, Consort, Elk, Fellowship, Lodge, Mingle, Moose, Order, Shrine, Sodality

Fratricide Cain

Fraud(ulent) Barratry, Bobol, Bubble, Chain-letter, Charlatan, Cheat, Chisel, Collusion, Covin, Cronk, Deceit, Diddle, Do, Fineer, Gyp, Humbug, Hypocrite, → **IMPOSTOR**, Imposture, Jiggery-pokery, Jobbery, Kite, Knavery, Liar, Peculator, Phishing, Piltdown, Pious, Pseud(o), Put-up, Quack, Ringer, Rip-off, Roguery, Rort, Salami technique, Scam, Shoulder surfing, South Sea Bubble, Stellionate, Sting, Supercherie, Swindle, Swiz(z), Swizzle, Tartuffe, Trick

Fraught Perilous

Fray(ed) Bagarre, Brawl, Contest, Feaze, Frazzle, Fret, Fridge, Ravel, Riot, Scrimmage, Wigs on the green

Freak(ish) Bizarre, Cantrip, Caprice, Chimera, Control, Deviant, Geek, Jesus, Lusus naturae, Mooncalf, Sport, Teras, Weirdo, Whim, Whimsy

Freckle Ephelis, Fern(i)tickle, Fern(i)ticle, Heatspot, Lentigines, Lentigo, Spot, Sunspot

Frederick Barbarossa, Carno, Great

▷ **Free** *may indicate* an anagram

Free(d), Freely Acquit, Assoil, At large, Buckshee, Candid, Canny, Church, Clear, Complimentary, Cuffo, Dead-head, Deliver, Deregulate, Devoid, Disburden, Disburthen, Disengage, Disentangle, Eleutherian, Emancipate, Enfranchise, Enlarge, Excuse, Exeem, Exeme, Exempt, Exonerate, Extricate, Familiar, Footloose, Frank, French, Gratis, House, Idle, Immune, Indemnify, Independent, Kick, Large, Lavish, Lax, Leisure, Let, Liberate, Loose, Manumit, Open, Parole, Pro bono, Quit(e), Range, Ransom, Redeem, → **RELEASE**, Relieve, Requiteless, Rescue, Reskew, Rick, Rid, Sciolto, Scot, Solute, Spare, Spring, Stald, Stall, Trade, Unbowed, Unlace, Unlock, Unloosen, Unmew, Unmuzzle, Unshackle, Unsnarl, Untangle, Untie, Untwist, Vacant, Verse, Voluntary

Freebooter Cateran, Corsair, Franklin, Marauder, Moss-trooper, Pad, Pindaree, Pindari, Pirate, Rapparee, Rider, Snapha(u)nce, Snaphaunch, Thief, Viking

Freedom Abandon, Autonomy, Breadth, Carte blanche, Eleutherian, Exemption, Fear, Fling, Four, Immunity, Impunity, Independence, Laisser aller, Laisser faire, Laissez aller, Laissez faire, Latitude, Liberty, Licence, Moksha, Play, Range, Releasement, Speech, Uhuru, UNITA, Want, Wiggle room, Worship

Free gift Bonus, Charism, Perk

Freehold(er) Enfeoff, Franklin, Frank tenement, Odal(l)er, Seisin, Udal(ler), Yeoman

Freelance Eclectic, Independent, Mercenary, Stringer

Freeloader Sponge

▷ **Freely** *may indicate* an anagram

Freeman Burgess, Ceorl, Churl, Franklin, Liveryman, Thegn, Thete, Villein

Freemason(ry), Freemason's son Craft, Lewis, Lodge, Moose, Templar

Free-range Eggs, Outler

Free State Orange

Freethinker Agnostic, Bradlaugh, Cynic, Libertine, Sceptic

Free-trade(r) Cobdenism, Wright

Free-wheel Coast, Idle

Freeze(s), Freezer, Freezing Alcarrazo, Arctic, Benumb, Congeal, Cool, Cryogenic, Cryonics, Eutectic, Freon®, Frost, Geal, Harden, Ice, Ice cold, Lyophilize, Moratoria, Nip, Numb, Paralyse, Regelate, Riss, Stiffen, Wage

Freight Cargo, Carriage, Fraught, Goods, Load

French(man), Frenchwoman Alain, Alsatian, Anton, Aristo, Basque, Breton, Cajun, Crapaud, Creole, Dawn, Dreyfus, Emil(e), Frog, Gallic(e), Gaston, Gaul, Gombo, Grisette, Gumbo, Homme, Huguenot, Joual, Jules, M, Mamselle, Marianne, Midi, Monsieur, Mounseer, Neo-Latin, Norman, Parleyvoo, Pierre, René, Rhemish, Savoyard, Yves

Frenetic Deranged, Frantic, Overwrought

Frenzied, Frenzy Amok, Berserk, Corybantic, Deliration, Delirium, Demoniac, Enrage, Enrapt, Euhoe, Euoi, Evoe, Feeding, Fit, Fury, Hectic, Hysteric, Lune, Maenad, Mania, Must, Nympholepsy, Oestrus, Phrenetic, Rage

Frequency, Frequent(er), Frequently Angular, Attend, Audio, Bandwidth, Channel, Common, Constant, Expected, Familiar, Forcing, Formant, FR, Fresnel, Gene, Habitué, Hang-out, Haunt, Hertz, High, Incidence, Intermediate, Low, Medium, Megahertz, Mode, Natural, Often, Passband, Penetrance, Pulsatance, Radio, Recurrent, Regular, Relative, Resort, Spatial, Spectrum, Superhigh, Thick, Ultrahigh, Video

Fresco Intonaco, Sinopia, Tempera

Fresh(en), Freshness Airy, Anew, Aurorean, Brash, Caller, Chilly, Clean, Crisp, Deodorise, Dewy, Entire, Evergreen, Forward, Green, Hot, Insolent, Live(ly), Maiden, Nas(s)eem, New, Novel, Quick, Rebite, Recent, Roral, Roric, Rorid, Smart, Span-new, Spick, Sweet, Tangy, Uncured, Verdure, Vernal, Virent, Virescent

Freshman, Fresher Bajan, Beginner, Bejan(t), Fresher, Frosh, Pennal, Plebe, Recruit, Student

Fret(ful) Chafe, Filigree, Fray, Grate, Grecque, Haze, Impatient, Irritate, Key, Ornament, Peevish, Repine, Rile, Ripple, Roil, Rub, Stop, Tetchy, Tracery, Whittle, Worry

Friable Crisp, Crumbling, Powdery

Friar(s) Augustinian, Austin, Bacon, Barefoot, Black, Brother, Bungay, Capuchin, Carmelite, Conventual, Cordelier, Crutched, Curtal, Dervish, Dominican, Fra(ter), Franciscan, Frate, Grey, Jacobin, Laurence, Limiter, Lymiter, Minim, Minor,

Minorite, → **MONK**, Observant, Observantine, Preaching, Predicant, Recollect, Recollet, Redemptionist, Rush, Tuck, White

Friction Attrition, Conflict, Dissent, Drag, Rift, Rub, Skin, Sliding, Stiction, Stridulation, Tribology, Tripsis, Wear, Xerotripsis

Friday Black, Casual, Girl, Golden, Good, Holy, Man, Person, Savage

Fridge Esky®, Freezer, Icebox, Rub

Fried cake Croquette, Cruller

Friend(ly), Friends Achates, Affable, Ally, Alter ego, Ami(cable), Amigo, Approachable, Associate, Avuncular, Belamy, Benign, Boet(ie), Bosom, Bra, Bro, Bru, Bud(dy), Buster, Butty, Cackermander, Cater-cousin, China, Choma, Chommie, Chum, Circle, Cobber, Cock, Cohort, Compadre, Companion, Companionable, Comrade, Confidant, Cordial, Couthie, Couthy, Crony, Cully, Damon, Downhome, Edwin, Ehoa, En ami, Fairweather, False, Familiar, Feare, Feathered, Feer, Fere, Fiere, Folksy, Gemütlich, Gossib, Gossip, Gregarious, Hail-fellow-well-met, Homeboy, Ingle, Intimate, Inward, Jong, Kith, Litigation, Lover, Marrow, Mate, McKenzie, Mentor, Mucker, Mutual, Near, Next, Oppo, Outgoing, Paisano, Pal, Paranymph, Pen, Penn, Pheere, Playmate, Privado, Prochain ami, Prochein ami, Pythias, Quaker, Sidekick, Sociable, Societal, Sport, Steady, Thawing, Thick, Tillicum, Tonga, Tosh, Wack(er), Warm, Well-disposed, Well-wisher, Wus(s), Yaar

Friendliness, Friendship Amity, Bonhomie, Camaraderie, Contesseration, Entente, Platonic, Rapprochement, Sodality

Frieze Dado, Metope, Penistone, Zoophorus

Fright(en), Frightened, Frightening, Frightful Afear, Affear(e), Agrise, Agrize, Agryze, Alarm, Aroint, Aroynt, Ashake, Chilling, Cow, Dare, Da(u)nt, Deter, Eek, Eerie, Eery, Faceache, Fear(some), Flay, Fleg, Fleme, Fley, Flush, Gallow, Gally, Ghast, Gliff, Glift, Grim, Grisly, Hairy, Horrid, Horrific, Intimidate, Ordeal, Panic, Scar, → **SCARE**, Scarre, Scaur, Schrecklich, Shocking, Sight, Skear, Skeer, Skrik, Spine-chilling, Spook, Stage, Startle, Terrible, Terrify, Terror, Tirrit, Unco, Unman, White-knuckle, Windy, Yitten

Frigid Bleak, Cold, Dry, Frory, Frosty, Ice, Indifferent, Serac, Stiff

Frill Armil, Armilla, Bavolet, Falbala, Flounce, Furbelow, Jabot, Newgate, Oriental, Ornament, Papillote, Ruche, Ruff(le), Tucker, Valance

▷ **Frilly** *may indicate* an anagram

Fringe(s), Fringed Bang, Border, Bullion, Celtic, Ciliated, Ciliolate, Edge, Fall, Fimbria, Frisette, Interference, Laciniate, Loma, Lunatic, Macramé, Macrami, Newgate, Pelmet, Peripheral, Robin, Ruff, Run, Thrum, Toupee, Toupit, Tsitsith, Tzitzit(h), Valance, Verge, Zizith

Frisian Holstein

Frisk(y) Caper, Cavort, Curvet, Fisk, Flimp, Frolic, Gambol, Search, Skip, Wanton

Fritillary Snake's-head

Fritter Batter, Beignet, Dribble, Dwindle, Fragment, Fribble, Pakora, Piddle, Potter, Puf(f)taloon, Squander, Waste, Wonder

Frivolous, Frivolity Butterfly, Empty(-headed), Etourdi(e), Facetious, Featherbrain, Flighty, Flippant, Frothy, Futile, Giddy, Idle, Inane, Levity, Light, Light-minded, Lightweight, Playboy, Skittish, Trifling, Trivial

Frizz(le), Frizzly Afro, Crape, Crimp, Crinkle, Curly, Fry, Fuzz, Hiss

Frock Dress, Gown, Ordain, Robe, Smock

Frog Anoura, Anura, Batrachia(n), Braid, Bullfrog, Cape nightingale, Crapaud, Depression, Flying, Fourchette, Frenchman, Frush, Goliath, Hairy, Hyla, Marsupial, Mounseer, Nic, Nototrema, Paddock, Paradoxical, Peeper, Pelobatid, Platanna, Puddock, Puttock, Rana, Ranidae, Tree, Wood, Xenopus

Frogman Diver

Frogmouth Mo(re)poke, Podargus

Frog spawn Redd, Tadpole

Frolic(some) Bender, Bust(er), Cabriole, Caper, Cavort, Curvet, Disport, Escapade,
→ FRISK(Y), Fun, Galravage, Galravitch, Gambol, Gammock, Gil(l)ravage, How's
your father, Jink, Kittenish, Lark, Play, Pollick, Prank, Rag, Rand, Rig, Romp,
Scamper, Skylark, Splore, Sport, Spree, Stooshie, Tittup, Wanton

From A, Against, Ex, For, Frae, Off, Thrae

Frond Fern, Leaf, Tendril

Front(al), Frontman Antependium, Anterior, Bow, Brass, Brow, Cold, Cover,
Dead, Dickey, Dicky, Esplanade, Facade, Face, Fore(head), Forecourt, Foreground,
Groof, Grouf, Grufe, Head, Home, Insolence, Metope, National, Newscaster, Nose,
Occluded, Paravant, People's, Plastron, Polar, Popular, Pose, Preface, Presenter,
Pro, Prom, Prow, Rhodesian, Sector, Sinciput, Stationary, Tabula, Temerity, Van,
Vaward, Ventral, Warm, Western

Frontier(sman) Afghan, Barrier, Border, Boundary, Checkpoint, Crockett, Limit,
Limitrophe, List, March, North-west, Outpost, Pathan, Wild West

Front page P1

Front-ranker Pawn

Frost(ing), Frosty, Frostbite Air, Alcorza, Black, Chill, Cranreuch, Cryo-, Freon®,
Frigid, Frore(n), Frorne, Glacé, Ground, Hoar, Hore, Ice, Icing, Jack, Mat, Nip, Rime,
Silver, Trench foot, White

Froth(y) Barm, Bubble, Cuckoospit, Cuckoospit(tle), Despumate, Foam, Frogspit,
Gas, Head, Lather, Mantle, Nappy, Off-scum, Ream, Saponin, Scum, Seethe,
Shallow, Spoom, Spoon, Spume, Sud, Yeasty, Yest, Zephir

Frown Glower, Knit, Lour, Lower, Scowl

Frozen Froren, Frorn(e), Frory, Gelid, Glacé, Graupel, Ice-bound, Spellbound, Static,
Tundra

Fructification, Fructify, Fructose Aeci(di)um, Basidium, Fertilise, Flower, Fruit,
Inulin

Frugal Meagre, Parsimonious, Provident, Prudent, Scant, Skimpy, Spare, Spartan,
Thrifty

Fruit(ing), Fruit tree, Fruity Accessory, Achene, Acinus, Akene, Allocarpy,
Apothecium, Autocarp, Bacciform, Catapult, Cedrate, Coccus, Compot(e), Confect,
Conserve, Cremocarp, Crop, Dessert, Drupe, Eater, Encarpus, Etaerio, First,
Follicle, Forbidden, Fritter, Harvest, Issue, Multiple, Orchard, Poof, Primeur,
Primitiae, Product(ion), Pseudocarp, Regma(ta), Replum, Result, Return, Rich,
Ripe, Schizocarp, Seed, Silicle, Siliqua, Silique, Soft, Sorosis, Stoneless, Succade,
Syconium, Syncarp, Utricle, Valve, Wall, Xylocarp, Yield

FRUIT

3 letters:	*4 letters:*	Jack	Sorb
Fig	Acai	Kaki	Star
Haw	Akee	Kiwi	Tuna
Hep	Bael	Lime	Ugli®
Hip	Bito	Pear	Yuzu
Hop	Cone	Pepo	
Jak	Date	Plum	*5 letters:*
Key	Gage	Pome	Ackee
Nut	Gean	Sloe	Anana

5 letters – cont:
Anona
Apple
Assai
Berry
Bread
Choko
Genip
Gourd
Grape
Guava
Jaffa
Lemon
Lotus
Mango
Melon
Nancy
Naras
Nashi
Nelis
Olive
Papaw
Prune
Rowan
Whort

6 letters:
Almond
Ananas
Babaco
Banana
Banian
Banyan
Carica
Cherry
Chocho
Citron
Citrus
Comice
Damson
Durian
Durion
Emblic
Feijoa
Lichee
Litchi
Longan
Lychee
Mammee
Medlar
Narras

Nelies
Oilnut
Orange
Papaya
Pawpaw
Pepino
Pomace
Pomelo
Pruine
Quince
Raisin
Rennet
Russet
Samara
Sapota
Sharon
Squash
Sweety
Tomato
Wampee

7 letters:
Apricot
Avocado
Bullace
Chayote
Crab-nut
Cypsela
Geebung
Genipap
Gherkin
Kumquat
Leechee
Litchee
Manjack
Morello
Passion
Pimento
Pinguin
Poperin
Pumpkin
Pupunha
Rosehip
Ruddock
Satsuma
Soursop
Sweetie
Tangelo
Winesap

8 letters:
Abricock
Apricock
Bergamot
Bilberry
Blimbing
Calabash
Caprifig
Dewberry
Fraughan
Goosegog
Hagberry
Hastings
Hedgehog
Kalumpit
Minneola
Mirliton
Mulberry
Physalis
Plantain
Prunello
Rambutan
Rathripe
Sebesten
Shaddock
Silicula
Sunberry
Tamarind
Tayberry
Teaberry
Waxberry

9 letters:
Algarroba
Apple-john
Aubergine
Bakeapple
Blueberry
Butternut
Canteloup
Carambola
Caryopsis
Cherimoya
Cranberry
Deerberry
Freestone
Haanepoot
Hackberry
Juneberry
Melon-pear
Mirabelle

Myrobalan
Naseberry
Nectarine
Neesberry
Ortanique
Persimmon
Plumdamas
Poppering
Ratheripe
Sapodilla
Saskatoon
Shadberry
Sorb-apple
Star-apple
Tangerine
Tomatillo
Victorine
Whimberry
Whinberry

10 letters:
Blackberry
Canteloupe
Cherimoyer
Chokeberry
Clementine
Clingstone
Elderberry
Granadilla
Grenadilla
Jargonelle
Mangosteen
Paddymelon
Pick-cheese
Punicaceae
Scaldberry
Watermelon
Youngberry

11 letters:
Boysenberry
Chokecherry
Hesperidium
Huckleberry
Lingonberry
Marionberry
Pampelmoose
Pampelmouse
Pomegranate
Pompelmoose
Pompelmouse

Salmonberry

Checkerberry
Custard-apple

13 letters:
Bullock's heart

14 letters:
Worcesterberry

12 letters:
Blackcurrant

Service-berry
Whortleberry

Sapodilla plum

Fruitcake Dundee, Madman
Fruitful(ness) Calathus, Ephraim, Fat, Fecund, Feracious, Fertile, Productive,
Prolific, Uberty, Worthwhile
Fruitless Bare, Fool's errand, Futile, Sisyphean, Sooterkin, Sterile, Useless, Vain
Frump(ish) Dowdy, Judy, Shabby, Unkempt
Frustrate(d) Baffle, Ba(u)lk, Beat, Blight, Bugger, Check, Cheesed off, Confound,
Countermine, Dash, Disappoint, Discomfit, Dish, Foil, Hogtie, Outwit, Scotch,
Spike, Stymie, Tantalise, Thwart
Fry, Fried Blot, Brit, Christopher, Elizabeth, Fricassee, Fritter, Frizzle, Parr, Sauté,
Sizzle, Small, Spawn, Whippersnapper, Whitebait
Fuddle(d) Drunk, Fluster, Fuzzle, Maudlin, Ta(i)vert, Tosticated, Woozy
▷ **Fuddle(d)** *may indicate* an anagram
Fudge Cook, Doctor, Dodge, Drivel, Evade, Fiddlesticks, Nonsense, Rot, Stop-press
Fuel Anthracite, Argol, Astatki, Atomic, Avgas, Benzine, Biodiesel, Biogas, Borane,
Briquet(te), Brown coal, Bunker, Butane, Candle-coal, Cannel, Carbonette, Charcoal,
Coal, Coalite®, Coke, Derv, Diesel, Eilding, Eldin(g), Ethane, Faggot, Feed,
Fire(wood), Fossil, Gasahol, Gasohol, Gasoline, Go-juice, Haxamine, Hydrazine,
Hydyne, Jud, Kerosene, Kerosine, Kindling, Knitch, Lignite, Mox, Napalm,
Naphtha, Nuclear, Orimulsion, Outage, Paraffin, Peat, Propane, Propellant,
Smokeless, Solid, Sterno®, Stoke, Tan balls, Triptane, Unleaded, Yealdon
Fug Frowst
Fugitive Absconder, Ephemeral, Escapee, Fleeting, Hideaway, Lot, Outlaw, Refugee,
Runagate, Runaway, Runner, Transient, Vagabond
Fugue Ricercar(e), Ricercata, Stretto
Fulcrum Key-pin, Pivot
Fulfil(ment) Accomplish, Complete, Consummate, Fruition, Honour,
Implementation, Meet, Pass, Realise, → **SATISFY**, Steed, Subrogation
Fulgent Bright, Shining
Full(ness), Fully Abrim, Ample, Arrant, Bouffant, Capacity, Chock-a-block,
Chocker, Complete, Copious, Embonpoint, Engorged, Entire, Fairly, Fat, Fed,
Flush, Fou, Frontal, German, High, Hoatching, Hotch, Mill, Orotund, Plein,
Plenary, Plenitude, Pleroma, Plethora, Plump, Replete, Rich, Rotund, Sated,
Satiated, Thorough, Torose, Torous, Toss, Turgid, Turgor, Ullage, Up, Wau(l)k,
Wholly
Full-faced Caboched, Caboshed
Full-throated Goitred
Fulminate, Fulmination Detonate, Explode, Levin, Lightning, Rail, Renounce,
Thunder
Fumarole Hornito, Mofette
Fumble Blunder, Faff, Grope, Misfield, Muff
Fume(s) Bluster, Gas, Halitus, Incense, Nidor, Rage, Reech, Reek, Settle, Smoke,
Stum, Vapours
Fumigate, Fumigator Disinfect, Pastil(le), Smoke, Smudge
Fun(ny), Funny bone Amusing, Antic, Boat, Buffo, Caper, Clownery, Comedy,
Comic(al), Crack, Craic, Delight, Droll, Frolic, Gammock, Gas, Gig, Giocoso, Glaik,
Guy, Hilarity, Humerus, Humorous, Hysterical, Ill, Jest, Jouisance, Jouysaunce,

Killing, Kinky, Lark, Music, Play, Pleasure, Priceless, Rag, Rib-tickling, Rich, Rummy, Scream, Sidesplitting, Skylark, Slap and tickle, Sport, Suspect, Uproarious, Weird(o), Wit, Yell

Funambulist Blondin, Equilibrist, Tight-rope

Function(s), Functional, Functioning Act, Algebraic, Antilog, Apparatchik, Arccos, Arcsine, Arctan, Assignment, Bodily, Bunfight, Business, Ceremony, Characteristic, Circular, Cosec, Cosh, Cot(h), Cotangent, Dance, Density, Discriminant, Distribution, Practicable, Dynamic, Exponential, Gamma, Gibbs, Hamilton(ian), Helmholtz, Hyperbolic, Integral, Integrand, Inverse, Jacobian, Job, Logarithm, Map(ping), → **OPERATE**, Periodic, Polymorphic, Probability, Propositional, Quadric, Quantical, Reception, Recursive, Role, Run, Secant, Sech, Sensation, Sentential, Service, Sine, Sinh, State, Ste(a)d, Step, Surjection, Tan(h), Tangent, Tick, Tool bar, Transcendental, Trigonometric, Truth, Use, Utensil, Utility, Versin, Vital, Wave, Wingding, → **WORK**

Functionary Official

Functionless Otiose

Fund(s), Funding, Fundraising Bank, Bankroll, Barrel, Capital, Chest, Consolidated, Emendals, Endow, Evergreen, Finance, Fisc, Fisk, Focus, Gap, Gild, Green, Hedge, Imprest, Index, Jackpot, Kitty, Maestro®, Managed, Mutual, Nest-egg, Pension, Pool, Pork-barrel, Prebend, Private, Public, Purse, Revolving, Roll-up, Sinking, Slush, Social, Sou-sou, Stabilisation, Stock, Store, Subsidise, Sustentation, Susu, Telethon, Tracker, Treasury, Trust, Vulture, Wage(s), War chest, Wherewithal

Fundamental(ist) Basic(s), Bedrock, Cardinal, Essence, Grass-roots, Hamas, Integral, Missing, Nitty-gritty, Organic, Prime, Principle, Radical, Rudimentary, Taleban, Taliba(a)n, Ultimate

Fund-holder Rentier

Funeral, Funereal Charnel, Cortege, Dismal, Exequy, Feral, Hearse, Obit, Obital, Obsequy, Sad-coloured, Solemn, Tangi

Fungicide Benomyl, Biphenyl, Bordeaux mixture, Burgundy mixture, Captan, Diphenyl, Ferbam, Menadione, PCP, Resveratrol, Thiram, Zineb

Fungoid, Fungus Agaric, Amadou, Amanita, Ambrosia, Anthersmut, Anthracnose, Apothecium, Armillaria, Asci(us), Ascomycete, Aspergillus, Barm, Basidium, Beefsteak, Bird's nest, Black, Blackknot, Blewits, Blue-mould, Blue-rot, Boletus, Bootlace, Botrytis, Bracket, Brand, Bread-mould, Bunt, Candida, Ceps, Chantarelle, Chanterelle, Chytrid, Cladosporium, Clubroot, Conk, Coral spot, Corn smut, Cramp-ball, Craterellus, Cryptococcus, Cup, Death angel, Death-cap, Death-cup, Dermatophytosis, Destroying angel, Discomycetes, Dutch elm, Earth-star, Elf-cup, Empusa, Endophyte, Ergot, Erumpent, Eumycetes, Fairy butter, Favus, Fission, Flowers of tan, Funnel-cap, Fusarium, Fuss-ball, Fuzz-ball, Gall, Gibberella, Gill, Honey, Horsehair, Hypersarcoma, Hypha, Imperfect, Ink-cap, Ithyphallus, Jelly, Jew's ear, Jupiter's beard, Lawyer's wig, Liberty cap, Lichen, Magic mushroom, Merulius, Mildew, Milk cap, Monilia, Morel, Mould, Mucor(ales), Mushroom, Mycelium, Mycetes, Mycology, Noble rot, Oak-leather, Oak-wilt, Oidium, Oomycete, Orange-peel, Penicillium, Pest, Peziza, Phallus, Phycomycete, Pileum, Plica Polonica, Polyporus, Porcino, Pore, Prototroph, Puccinia, Puckfist, Puffball, Pythium, Ray, Rhizomorph, Rhizopus, Rhytisma, Russula, Rust, Saccharomyces, Saprolegnia, Saprophyte, Sariodes, Scab, Shaggy cap, Shaggy ink cap, Shaggy mane, Shoestring, Slime, Smut, Sooty mould, Spunk, Stinkhorn, Stipe, Stromata, Sulphur tuft, Tarspot, Thalline, Thallophyte, Toadstool, Torula, Tremella, Trichophyton, Truffle, Tuber, Tuckahoe, Uredine, Ustilago, Velvet shank, Verticillium, Wax cap,

Wheat rust, Witches' meat, Wood hedgehog, Wood woollyfoot, Yeast, Yellow brain, Yellow rust, Yellows, Zygomycete, Zygospore

Fungus-eater Mycophagist

Funicular Cable-car

Funk(y) Blue, Dodge, Dread, Fear, Scared, Stylish

Funnel Buchner, Chimney, Choana, Drogue, Flue, Hopper, Infundibulum, Separating, Smokestack, Stack, Stovepipe, Tun-dish, Tunnel, Wine

Fur Astrakhan, Astrex, Beaver(skin), Boa, Broadtail, Budge, Calabre, Caracul, Castor, Chinchilla, Civet, Cony-wool, Coonskin, Crimmer, Ermelin, Ermine, Fitchew, Flix, Flue, Fun, Galyac, Galyak, Genet, Genette, Kolinsky, Krimmer, Lettice, Marten, Minever, Miniver, Mink, Mouton, Musquash, Ocelot, Otter, Palatine, Pane, Pashm, Pean, Pekan, Rac(c)oon, Roskyn, Sable, Sealskin, Sea-otter, Stole, Tincture, Tippet, Vair(e), Victorine, Wolverine, Zibeline, Zorino

Furbish Polish, Renovate, Spruce, Vamp

Furl Clew up, Fold, Roll, Stow, Wrap

Furlough Congé, Leave

Furnace Arc, Athanor, Blast, Bloomery, Bosh, Breeze, Calcar, Cockle, Cremator, Cupola, Destructor, Devil, Electric, Finery, Firebox, Forge, Gas, Glory-hole, Incinerator, Kiln, Lear, Lehr, Lime-kiln, Oast, Oon, Open-hearth, Oven, Pot, Producer, Reverberatory, Scaldino, Solar, Stokehold, Stokehole, Tank, Wind

Furnish(ing) Appoint, Array, Deck, Decorate, Endow, Endue, Equip, Feed, Fledge, Gird, Lend, Produce, Provision, Soft, Stock, Suit, Supply, Tabaret, Upholster

Furniture, Furniture designer Biedermeier, Chattels, Chippendale, Duncan Phyfe, Encoignure, Escritoire, Etagère, Flatpack, Fyfe, Hallstand, Hatstand, Hepplewhite, Highboy, Insight, Lowboy, Lumber, Moveable, Queen Anne, Screen, Sheraton, Sideboard, Sticks, Stoutherie, Street, Tire, Unit, Washstand, Whatnot

Furore Brouhaha, Commotion, Outburst, Outcry, Stink, Storm, Uproar

Furrier Trapper

Furrow(ed) Crease, Feer, Feerin(g), Furr, Groove, Gutter, Plough, Pucker, Rill(e), Rugose, Rut, Stria, Sulcus, Vallecula, Wrinkle

Fur-seal Seecatch(ie)

Further(more), Furthest Additional, Advance, Again, Aid, Also, Besides, Deeper, Else, Expedite, Extend, Extra, Extreme, Fresh, Infra, Longer, Mo(e), Mow, Other, Promote, Serve, Speed, Subserve, Then, To boot

Furtive(ly) Clandestine, Cunning, Hole and corner, Secret, Shifty, Sly, Sneaky, Stealthy, Stowlins, Stownlins

Fury, Furies, Furious Acharné, Agitato, Alecto, → **ANGER**, Apoplexy, Atropos, Avenger, Eriny(e)s, Eumenides, Exasperation, Frantic, Frenzied, Furor, Hectic, Incensed, → **IRE**, Livid, Maenad, Megaera, Paddy, Rabid, Rage, Red, Savage, Seething, Tisiphone, Virago, Wood, Wrath, Yond

Furze Gorse, Whin

Fuse(d), Fusion Anchylosis, Ankylosis, Blend, Coalesce, Cohere, Colliquate, Conflate, Encaustic, Endosmosis, Flow, Flux, Igniter, Knit, Match, Merge, Merit, Nuclear, Percussion, Portfire, Proximity, Rigelation, Run, Sacralization, Safety, Saucisse, Saucisson, Short, Slow-match, Solder, Symphytic, Syncretism, Syngamy, Time, Tokamak, Unite, Weld

Fuselage Body, Monocoque, Structure

Fuss(y) Ado, Agitation, Anile, Ballyho, Bobsie-die, Bother, Br(o)uhaha, Bustle, Carfuffle, Carry on, Chichi, Coil, Commotion, Complain, Cosset, Create, Cu(r)fuffle, Dust, Elaborate, Faff, Fantad, Fantod, Fiddle-faddle, Finical, Finikin, Futz, Hairsplitter, Hoohah, Hoopla, Mither, Mother, Niggle, Nit-pick, Noise,

Old-womanish, Overexact, Overnice, Overwrought, Palaver, Particular, Perjink, Pernickety, Picky, Pother, Precise, Prejink, Primp, Prissy, Pudder, Racket, Raise cain, Razzmatazz, Rout, Song, Song and dance, Spoffish, Spoffy, Spruce, Stashie, Stickler, Stink, → **STIR**, Stishie, Stooshie, Stushie, Tamasha, To-do, Tracasserie

Fustian Bombast, Gas, Pompous, Rant

Futile Empty, Feckless, Idle, Inept, No-go, Nugatory, Null, Otiose, Pointless, Sleeveless, Stultified, Trivial, Useless, → **VAIN**

Future(s), Futurist Again, Avenir, Be-all, By and by, Coming, Demain, Financial, Hence, Horoscope, Index, Interest-rate, Later, Long-range, Offing, Ovist, Paragogic, Posterity, Prospect, To-be, Tomorrow

Fuzz(y) Blur, Crepe, Down, Fluff, Foggy, Lint, Pig, Policeman

Gg

G George, Golf, Gravity

Gab(ble), Gabbler Chatter, Dovercourt, Jabber, Pie, Prattle, Talkative, Yabber

Gable Clark, Corbie, Jerkinhead, Pediment, Pine end

Gabriel Angel, Walter

Gad(about), Gadzooks Gallivant, Lud, Rover, Sbuddikins, Sdeath, Traipse, Trape(s), Viretot

Gadfly Breese, Breeze, Brize

Gadget Adaptor, Appliance, Artifice, Device, Dingbat, Dingus, Doodad, Doodah, Doofer, Doohickey, Gismo, Gizmo, Gubbins, Hickey, Jiggumbob, Jimjam, Notion, Possum, Tool, Toy, Utility, Waldo, Widget

Gadolinium Gd

Gadzooks Odsbobs

Gaekwar Baroda

Gael(ic) Celt, Erse, Goidel, Irish, Scottish, Teague

Gaff(e), Gaffer Bêtise, Blague, Bloomer, Error, Floater, Foreman, Gamble, Game, Solecism, Spar, Throat, Trysail, Yokel

Gag Brank, Choke, Estoppel, Joke, Pong, Prank, Retch, Silence(r), Smother, Wheeze

Gage Challenge, Pawn, Pledge, Plum

▶ **Gaiety** *see* **GAY**

Gain(s), Gained Acquire, Appreciate, Attain, Avail, Boodle, Boot, Bunce, Capital, Carry, Catch, Chevisance, Clean-up, Derive, Earn, Edge, Fruit, → **GET**, Good, Gravy, Land, Lucre, Obtain, Plus, Profit, Purchase, Rake-off, Reap, Thrift, Use, Velvet, Wan, Win, Windfall, Winnings

Gainsay Contradict, Deny

Gait Bearing, Canter, Pace, Piaffer, Rack, Trot

Gaiter(s) Cootikin, Cu(i)tikin, Gambado, Hogger, Legging(s), Puttee, Spat(s), Spattee, Spatterdash, Vamp

Gala Banquet, Festival

Galaxy, Galaxies Active, Andromeda, Blazar, Great Attractor, Heaven, Irregular, Local group, Magellanic cloud, Milky Way, Radio, Regular, Seyfert, Spiral, Stars

Galbanum Ferula

Gale(s) Backfielder, Equinoctial, Fresh, Moderate, Near, Peal, Ripsnorter, Sea turn, Snorter, Squall, Storm, Strong, Tempest, Whole, Winder

Gall, Gall bladder Aleppo, Bedeguar, Bile, Bitterness, Canker, Cholecyst, Crown, Ellagic, Enrage, Fell, Fungus, Irritate, Mad-apple, Maugre, Maulgre, Oak(nut), Oak apple, Saddle, Sage-apple, Sandiver, → **SAUCE**, Tacahout, Vine

Gallant(ry) Admirer, Amorist, Beau, Blade, Buck, Cavalier, Chevalier, Cicisbeo, Courtliness, Lover, Prow, Romeo, Sigisbeo, Spark, Valiance

Galleon Galloon, Ghostly, Ship

Gallery Accademia, Alure, Amphitheatre, Arcade, Assommoir, Belvedere, Brattice, Bretasche, Bretesse, Brettice, Brow, Burrell (Collection), Catacomb,

Celestials, Cupola, Dedans, Fly, Gods, Hayward, Hermitage, Jube, Ladies', Loft, Loggia, Louvre, Machicolation, Mine, Minstrel, National, Organ, Pawn, Picture, Pinacotheca, Pinakothek, Pitti, Prado, Press, Public, Rogues', Scaffolding, Serpentine, Shooting, Strangers', Tate, Terrace, Traverse, Tribune, Triforium, Uffizi, Veranda(h), Whispering, Whitechapel, Winning

Galley Bireme, Bucentaur, Caboose, Drake, Galliot, Kitchen, Lymphad, Penteconter, Proof

Gallimaufry Macedoine, Mishmash, Stew

Gallium Ga

Gallon(s) Bushel, Cong(ius), Cran, Hin, Imperial, Pottle, Tierce

Galloon Lace, Osiris

Gallop(er) Aide, Canter, Canterbury, Career, Lope, Trot, Wallop

Gallows Bough, Cheat, Drop, Dule-tree, Forks, Gibbet, Nub, Nubbing-cheat, Patibulary, Stifler, Three-legged mare, Tree, Tyburn, Tyburn-tree, Widow, Woodie

Gallows-bird Crack-halter, Crack-hemp, Crack-rope

Gall-stone Cholelith

Galore Abundance, À gogo, Plenty, Whisky

Galosh Overshoe, Rubber

Galvanise Activate, Buck up, Ginger, Rouse, Zinc

Galvanometer Tangent

Gam Pod

Gambia WAG

Gambit Manoeuvre, Ploy, Stratagem

Gamble(r), Gambling (place) Adventure, Amber, Ante, Back, Bet, Bouillote, Casino, Chance, Dice(-play), Flutter, Gaff, Hold, Jeff, Martingale, Mise, Pari-mutuel, Parlay, Partingale, Piker, Plunge, Policy, Punt(er), Raffle, Reno, Risk, Roulette, School, Spec, Speculate, Speculator, Sweep(stake), Throw(ster), Tinhorn, Tombola, Tontine, Treble chance, Two-up, → **WAGER**

Gambol Frisk, Frolic

Game, Game birds Bag, Fowl, Grouse, Guan, Hare, Meat, Partridge, Pheasant, Prairie chicken, Ptarmigan, Quail, → **QUARRY**, Rype(r), Snipe, Spatchcock, Woodcock

Game(s) Away, Circansian, Closed, Commonwealth, Computer, Console, Decider, Easy, Electronic, Elis, Fair, Frame, Gallant, Gammy, Ground, Gutsy, Highland, Home, Intrepid, Isthmian, Jeu, → **LAME**, Match, Middle, Mind, MUD, Nemean, Numbers, Olympic, On, Open, Panel, Paralympic, Parlour, Perfect, Platform, Play, Plaything, Preference, Pythian, Raffle, Ready, Road, Role-playing, Round, Rubber, Saving, Scholar's, Secular, Sport, Square, String, Table, Tie-break, Tournament, Vie, Waiting, Willing

GAMES

2 letters:	Loo	Tag	Dibs
Eo	Maw	Tig	Fa-fi
Go	Nap	War	Faro
PE	Nim		Goff
RU	Pam	*4 letters:*	Golf
	Pit	Base	Grab
3 letters:	Put	Brag	I-spy
Cat	Sim	Bull	Keno
Hob	Swy	Crap	Kino

Laik
Loto
Ludo
Main
Mora
Palm
Polo
Pool
Putt
Ruff
Scat
Skat
Slam
Snap
Solo
Taws
Vint
Wall
Word

5 letters:
Bingo
Bocce
Bowls
Cards
Catch
Chess
Cinch
Craps
Darts
Fives
Gleek
Goose
Halma
House
Jacks
Keeno
Lotto
Lurch
Merel
Meril
Monte
Morra
Noddy
Novum
Omber
Ombre
Pairs
Poker
Prime
Quino

Roque
Rummy
Shell
Shogi
Spoof
Stops
Tarok
Tarot
Touch
Trugo
Trump
Two-up
Ulama
Video
Whisk
Whist

6 letters:
Basset
Beetle
Boccia
Bo-peep
Boston
Boules
Bounce
Bridge
Casino
Chemmy
Clumps
Crambo
Ecarté
Euchre
Fantan
Footer
Gammon
Gobang
Gomoku
Hazard
Hearts
Hockey
Hoopla
Hurley
Kaluki
Kitcat
Merell
Peepbo
Pelota
Piquet
Quinze
Quoits
Shinny

Shinty
Soccer
Socker
Squail
Squash
Tenpin
Tipcat
Trunks
Uckers
Vigoro

7 letters:
Balloon
Ba'spiel
Bezique
Braemar
Camogie
Canasta
Cassino
Charade
Chicken
Codille
Conkers
Coon-can
Croquet
Curling
Diabolo
Doubles
Frisbee
Fusball
God game
Hangman
Hurling
Iceball
In-and-in
Jai alai
Jukskei
Kabaddi
Kalooki
Lottery
Mahjong
Mancala
Marbles
Matador
Muggins
Murphy's
Netball
Old maid
Pachisi
Pallone
Passage

Patball
Peekabo
Peevers
Pharaoh
Pinball
Plafond
Pontoon
Primero
Push-pin
Pyramid
Rackets
Reversi
Ring-taw
Seven-up
Singles
Snooker
Squails
Tag ends
Tenpins
Vingt-un
Zero-sum

8 letters:
All-fives
All-fours
Baccarat
Baseball
Bob-apple
Bumpball
Buzkashi
Canfield
Charades
Chequers
Chouette
Conquian
Cottabus
Cribbage
Dominoes
Draughts
Fivepins
Foosball
Football
Forfeits
Four-ball
Foursome
Fussball
Gin rummy
Goalball
Handball
Handicap
Hardball

8 letters – cont:
Kalookie
Kickball
Klondike
Klondyke
Korfball
Lacrosse
Leapfrog
Mahjongg
Michigan
Monopoly®
Napoleon
Ninepins
Nintendo®
Octopush
Pachinko
Pall-mall
Pastance
Patience
Peekaboo
Pegboard
Penneech
Penneeck
Penuchle
Petanque
Ping-pong
Pinochle
Pintable
Pope Joan
Push-ball
Pyramids
Reversis
Rolypoly
Roulette
Rounders
Sardines
Scrabble®
Scroller
Skittles
Slapjack
Softball
Sphairee
Subbuteo®
Teetotum
Trap-ball
Tray-trip
Tredille
Tric-trac
Verquere
Verquire

9 letters:
Acey-deucy
Aunt Sally
Badminton
Bagatelle
Billiards
Black-cock
Black-jack
Bob-cherry
Broomball
Crokinole
Cutthroat
Dodgeball
Duplicate
Fillipeen
Hacky Sack®
High-jinks
Hopscotch
Jingo-ring
Lanterloo
Level-coil
Matrimony
Mistigris
Mournival
Mumchance
Newmarket
Nineholes
Paintball
Parcheesi®
Pelmanism
Punchball
Quadrille
Quidditch®
Shell game
Shoot'em-up
Simon says
Solitaire
Solo whist
Spoilfive
Stoolball
Strap-game
Tip-and-run
Tredrille
Trick-trac
Tric-track
Twenty-one
Vingt-et-un
Water polo

10 letters:
Angel-beast

Backgammon
Basketball
Battledore
Bouillotte
Candlepins
Cat's cradle
Cup and ball
Deck tennis
Dumb crambo
Five-stones
Flapdragon
Geocaching
Handy-dandy
Horseshoes
Hot cockles
Jackstones
Jackstraws
Knurr-spell
Kriegspiel
Lansquenet
Paddleball
Paper chase
Phillipina
Phillipine
Philopoena
Pooh sticks
Punto-banco
Put and take
Shuffle-cap
Snapdragon
Spillikins
Strip poker
Tablanette
Tchoukball
Thimblerig
Trick-track
Troll-madam
Trou-madame
Volley-ball

11 letters:
Barley-brake
Barley-break
Bumble-puppy
Catch-the-ten
Chemin de fer
Family coach
Fox and geese
General post
Gerrymander
Hide and seek

Knucklebone
Kriegsspiel
Mumbletypeg
Post and pair
Puncto-banco
Racquetball
Rouge et noir
Sancho-pedro
Shovelboard
Speculation
Table-tennis
Tick-tack-toe
Tiddlywinks
Troll-my-dame

12 letters:
Bar billiards
Consequences
Fast and loose
Hoodman-blind
Housey-housey
Knucklebones
Minister's cat
One-and-thirty
Pitch and putt
Pitch and toss
Shuffleboard
Span-farthing
Squash-tennis
Troll-my-dames

13 letters:
Blind man's buff
Chicken-hazard
Chuck-farthing
Double or quits
French cricket
Jingling match
Kiss-in-the-ring
Musical chairs
Pitch-farthing
Postman's knock
Prisoner's base
Scavenger hunt
Space Invaders®
Spin-the-bottle
Squash rackets
Table football
Table-skittles
Tenpin bowling
Tickly-benders

14 letters:	Shove-halfpenny	Ninepenny morris	**17 letters:**
British bulldog	Snip-snap-snorum	Puss-in-the-corner	Noughts and
Crown and anchor	Tenpins bowling		crosses
Ducks and drakes	Three-card monte	**16 letters:**	Tom Tiddler's
Fives and threes		Piggy-in-the-	ground
Follow-my-leader	**15 letters:**	middle	
Hunt-the-slipper	Chinese whispers	Scotch and English	**20 letters:**
Nievie-nick-nack	Fivepenny morris	Snakes and ladders	Kiss-me-quick-in-
Nine men's morris	King-of-the-castle	Trente-et-quarante	the-ring
Pig-in-the-middle	Laugh and lay down		Nievie-nievie-nick-
Prick-the-garter	Laugh and lie down		nack

Gamekeeper Mellors, Velveteen, Venerer, Warrener

Gamete Ootid

Gaming place Bucket-shop, Casino, Saloon, Table

Gammerstang Taupie, Tawpie

Gammon Baloney, Bilge, Tosh

Gamut Compass, Range

Gander Airport, Look-see

Gandhi Mahatma

Gang Baader-Meinhof, Band(itti), Bevy, Bikers, Bing, Bunch, Canaille, Chain, Coffle, Core, Crew, Crue, Droog, Elk, Go, Group, Hell's Angels, Horde, Massive, Mob, Mods, Nest, Outfit, Pack, Posse, Press, Push, Ratpack, Rent-a-mob, Ring, Rockers, Shearing, Triad, Tribulation, Troop, Tsotsi, Yardie

Ganglia Basal

Gangrene Canker, Gas, Mortified, Necrose, Noma, Phaged(a)ena, Sphacelate, Thanatosis

Gangster Al, Bandit, Capone, Crook, Dacoit, Dakoit, Goodfella, Hatchet-man, Highbinder, Hood, Mafioso, Mobster, Ochlocrat, Scarface, Skollie, Skolly, Tsotsi, Yakuza, Yardie

Gangway Brow, Catwalk, Road

Gannet Alcatras, Booby, Guga, Solan(d)

Gantry Elmer

Ganymede Cupper

▶ **Gaol(er)** *see* JAILER

Gap Aperture, Belfort, Breach, Chasm, Chink, Credibility, Day, Deflationary, Diastema, Dollar, Embrasure, Energy, F-hole, Financing, Flaw, Fontanel(le), Gender, Generation, Gulf, Gulph, Hair-space, Hiatus, Hole, Inflationary, Interlude, Interstice, Kirkwood, Lacunae, Leaf, Lin(n), Loophole, M(e)use, Mews, Muset, Musit, Node of Ranvier, Opening, Ostiole, Pass, Rest, Rift, Rima, Shard, Sherd, Skills, Slap, → SPACE, Spark, Spread, Street, Synapse, Trade, Truth-value, Vacancy, Vent, Water, Wind, Window

Gape(r), Gaping Comber, Dehisce, Fatiscent, Gant, Ga(u)p, Gerne, Hiant, Mya, Outstare, Rictal, Rictus, Ringent, Rubberneck, Stare, Yawn, Yawp

Garage Barn, Carport, Chopshop, Hangar, Lock-up, Muffler shop

Garb Apparel, Costume, Gear, Gere, Guise, Ihram, Invest, Leotard, Raiment, Toilet

Garbage Bunkum, Junk, Refuse, Rubbish, Trash

Garble Edit, Jumble, Muddle

▷ **Garble** *may indicate* an anagram

Garden(ing), Gardens Arbour, Area, Babylon(ian), Bagh, Bear, Beer, Botanic, Chinampa, Colegarth, Container, Cottage, Covent, Cremorne, Dig, Eden,

Erf, Floriculture, Garth, Gethsemane, Hanging, Herb(ar), Hesperides, Hoe, Horticulture, Italian, Japanese, Kailyard, Kew, Kitchen, Knot, Landscape, Lyceum, Market, Monastery, NJ, Olitory, Paradise, Parterre, Physic, Plantie-cruive, Pleasance, Plot, Potager, Ranelagh, Rockery, Roji, Roof, Rosarium, Rosary, Rosery, Tea, Tilth, Topiary, Tuileries, Vauxhall, Walled, Welwyn, Window, Winter, Yard, Zoological

Gardener Adam, Capability Brown, Fuchs, Hoer, Hoy, Jekyll, Landscape, Mali, Mallee, Mary, Nurseryman, Topiarist, Tradescant, Trucker

Gargantuan Enormous, Huge, Pantagruel, Vast

Gargle Gargarism, Mouthwash

Gargoyle Waterspout

Garibaldi Biscuit, Red Shirt

Garish Criant, Flashy, Gaudy, Glitzy, Jazzy, Painty, Roary, Rorie, Rory, Technicolour

Garland Anadem, Anthology, Chaplet, Coronal, Crants, Festoon, Lei, Stemma, Toran(a), Vallar(y), Wreath

Garlic Cepaceous, Clove, Elephant, Hedge, Rams(on), Rocambole

Garment Aba(ya), Abba, Alb, Ao dai, Barrow, Blouse, Blouson, Bodice, Body suit, Body warmer, Bolero, B(o)ub(o)u, B(o)urk(h)a, Brassière, Breeks, Burnous, Burqa, Busuuti, Caftan, Catsuit, Cerements, Chador, Chasuble, Chausses, Chimer, Cilice, Cimar, Clout, Cote-hardie, Cothurnis, Cotta, Cover-slut, Crop top, Dalmatic, Dashiki, Dirndl, Dishdasha, Djibbah, Doublet, Dreadnought, → **DRESS**, Ephod, Exomion, Exomis, Fanon, Fleece, Foundation, Gambeson, Gilet, Gipon, Gown, G-suit, Habiliment, Habit, Hand-me-down, Himation, Housecoat, Hug-me-tight, Ihram, Izar, Jeistiecor, Jibbah, Jilabib, Jilbab, Jubbah, Jumpsuit, Jumper, Jupon, Kaftan, K(h)anga, Kanzu, Kaross, Kilt, Kittel, Leggings, Legwarmers, Leotard, Levis, Lingerie, Mandilion, Mandylion, Mantle, Mantua, Monokini, Nebris, Negligée, Nightdress, Nightgown, Nightie, Nightrobe, Nightwear, Nighty, One-piece, Outerwear, Pallium, Pannicle, Pantihose, Pantyhose, Partlet, Pelerine, Pelisse, Penitential, Peplos, Pilch, Polonaise, Polonce, Polony, Poncho, Popover, Rail, Ramée, Rami(e), Reach-me-down, Rochet, Rompers, Ruana, Sackcloth, Salopettes, Sanbenito, Sari, Sarong, Scapular, Shroud, Shug, Singlet, Skirt, Skivvy, Slipover, Slop, Smock, Soutane, Step-in, Sticharion, Stola, Stole, Sulu, Surcoat, Surplice, Sweatpants, Sweatshirt, Sweats(uit), Swimsuit, Tabard, Tanga, Tankini, Tank-top, Thong, Toga, Togs, Trunks, Tunic(le), Two-piece, Unitard, Vestment, Vesture, Waistcoat, Weed, Woollen, Woolly, Wrap(per), Yukata, Zephyr

Garnet Alabandine, Almandine, Andradite, Carbuncle, Demantoid, Essonite, Grossular(ite), Hessonite, Melanite, Pyrenite, Pyrope, Rhodolite, Spessartite, Topazine, Topazolite, Uvarovite

Garnish Adorn, Attach, Crouton, Decorate, Gremolata, Lard, Parsley, Sippet, Staffage

Garret Attic, Loft, Sol(l)ar, Sol(l)er

Garrison Fort, Man, Presidial

Garrulity, Garrulous Babbling, Gas, Gushy, Sweetiewife, Windbag

Garter Bowyang, Crewel, Flash, G(r)amash, Gramosh, Nicky-tam

Gary Glitter, Player

Gas(sy) Acetylene, Afterdamp, Air, Ammonia, Argon, Argonon, Arsine, Azote, Blah(-blah), Blather, Blether, Bloat, Blue water, Bottle(d), Butadiene, Butane, Butene, BZ, Calor®, Carbonic acid, Carburetted, Carrier, Chat, Chlorine, Chokedamp, Chrom(at)osphere, CN, Coal(-oil), Crab nebula, Crypton, CS, Cyanogen, Damp, Diphosgene, Dispersant, Electrolytic, Emanation, Ethane, Ethene, Ether(ion), Ethine, Ethylene, Euchlorine, Firedamp, Fizz, Flatulence,

Flatus, Flocculus, Flue, Fluorin(e), Formaldehyde, Fugacity, Gabnash, Greenhouse,
H, Halitus, He, Helium, Hot-air, Hydrogen, Ideal, Inert, Jaw, Ketene, Kr(ypton),
Laughing, Lewisite, Lurgi, Mace®, Marsh, Meteorism, Methane, Methylamine,
Mofette, Mustard, Napalm, Natural, Ne, Neon, Nerve, Nitric oxide, Nitrogen,
Nitrous oxide, Noble, Non-metallic, North Sea, Nox, O, Oil, Olefin(e), Orotund,
Oxyacetylene, Oxygen, Ozone, Perfect, Petrol, Phosgene, Phosphine, Plasma, Poep,
Poison, Prate, Producer, Propane, Propellant, Propene, Propylene, Protogalaxy,
Protostar, Radon, Rare, RN, Sarin, Semiwater, Sewage, Sewer, Silane, Solfatara,
Soman, Sour, Stibine, Sulphur dioxide, Swamp, Sweet, Synthesis, Tabun, → **TALK**,
Taraniki wind, Tear, Tetrafluoroethene, Tetrafluoroethylene, Therm, Thoron,
Town, Utility, V-agent, Vapour, VX, Waffle, War, Water, Whitedamp, → **WIND**,
Xenon, Yackety-yak

Gasbag Airship, Blimp, Envelope, Prattler

Gascon(ade) Boast, Braggart, Skite

Gash Incise, Rift, Score, Scotch, → **SLASH**

Gas-mask Inhaler

Gasp(ing) Anhelation, Apn(o)ea, Chink, Exhale, Kink, Oh, Pant, Puff, Singult, Sob

Gast(e)ropod Ataata, Conch, Cowrie, Cowry, Dog-whelk, Dorididae, Doris,
Euthyneura, Fusus, Glaucus, Haliotis, Harp-shell, Helmet-shell, Limpet, Mitre,
Mollusc, Money cowry, Murex, Nerita, Nerite, Nudibranch, Opisthobranch, Ormer,
Pelican's foot, Pennywinkle, Periwinkle, Pteropod, Purpura, Sea-ear, Sea-hare,
Slug, Snail, Spindle-shell, Streptoneura, Stromb, Top, Triton, Turbo, Turritella,
Unicorn, Wentletrap, Whelk, Winkle

Gate(s), Gateway Alley, Attendance, Bill, Brandenburg, Caisson, Cilician, Corpse,
Crowd, Decuman, Entry, Erpingham, Golden, Head, Iron, Ivory, Kissing, Lock,
Lych, Mallee, Menin, Moon, Moravian, Nor, Pearly, Port, Portal, Portcullis, Postern,
Praetorian, Propylaeum, Propylon, Pylon, Sallyport, Silver, Starting, Tail, Taranaki,
Toran(a), Torii, Traitor's, Turnout, Turnstile, Waste, Water, Wicket, Yate, Yet(t)

Gatecrash(er) Interloper, Intrude, Ligger, Sorn, Unasked

Gatepost Sconcheon, Scontion, Scuncheon

▷ **Gateshead** *may indicate* 'g'

Gather(ed), Gatherer, Gathering Accrue, AGM, Amass, Assemble, Bee,
Braemar, Cluster, Collate, → **COLLECT**, Colloquium, Concentration, Concourse,
Conglomerate, Congregate, Conventicle, Conversazione, Corral, Corroboree,
Crop, Crowd, Cull, Derive, Eve, Fest, Frill, Function, Gabfest, Galaxy, Get together,
Glean, Glomerate, Hangi, Harvest, Hear, Hootenanny, Hotchpot, Hui, Hunter,
Husking, In, Infer, Jamboree, Kommers, Learn, Lek, Lirk, Love-in, Meinie, Menyie,
Multitude, Pleat, Plica, Plissé, Pucker, Purse, Raft, Raising-bee, Rake, Rally, Rave,
Reef, Reunion, Round-up, Rout, Ruche, Ruck, Ruff(le), Salon, Scrump, Shindig,
Shir(r), Shoal, Shovel, Singsong, Social, Spree, Suppurate, Swapmeet, Take, Tuck,
Vindemiate, Vintage, Wappensc(h)aw, Witches' sabbath

Gauche Awkward, Clumsy, Farouche, Graceless

Gaudy Classy, Criant, Fantoosh, Flash, Garish, Glitz(y), Meretricious, Tacky, Tawdry,
Tinsel

Gauge Absolute, Alidad(e), Anemometer, → **ASSESS**, Block, Bourdon, Broad,
Calibre, Denier, Depth, Dial, Estimate, Etalon, Evaluate, Feeler, Judge, Lee,
Limit, Loading, Manometer, Marigraph, Measure, Meter, Narrow, Nilometer, Oil,
Ombrometer, Oncometer, Perforation, Plug, Pressure, Rain, Rate, Ring, Scantle,
Size, Slip, Standard, Steam, Strain, Tape, Template, Tonometer, Tram, Tread, Tyre,
Udometer, Vacuum, Water, Weather, Wind, Wire

Gauguin Paul

Gaul Asterix, Cisalpine, Transalpine, Vercingetorix

Gaunt Haggard, Lancaster, Lean, Randletree, Ranneltree, Rannletree, Rantletree, Rawbone, → **THIN**, Wasted

Gauntlet C(a)estus, Gantlope

Gauss G

Gautama Buddha

Gauze, Gauzy Dandy-roll, Gas mantle, Gossamer, Illusion, Muslin, Sheer, Tiffany, Wire

Gawky Clumsy, Cow, Gammerstang, Sloucher

Gawp Rubberneck

Gay, Gaiety Blithe, Bonny, Boon, Buxom, Camp, Canty, Daffing, Debonair, Festal, Frolic, Gallant, Gaudy, Gladsome, Glee, Gordon, Grisette, Inverted, Jolly, Lightsome, May, Merry, Nitid, Out, Rackety, Riant, Rorty, Tit(t)upy, Volatile

Gaze Moon, Pore, Regard, Stare

Gazelle Ariel, Gerenuk, Goa, Mhorr, Mohr, Tabitha, Thomson's

Gazette London, Paper

Gear(ing), Gearbox Alighting, Angel, Arrester, Attire, Bags, Bevel, Capital, Clobber, Dérailleur, Differential, Draw, Duds, Engrenage, Epicyclic, Fab, Finery, Granny, Harness, Helical, Herringbone, High, Hypoid, Idle wheel, Involute, Kit, Landing, Lay-shaft, Low, Mesh, Mess, Mitre, Neutral, Notchy, Overdrive, Planetary, Ratio, Reverse, Rig, Riot, Rudder, Running, Spur, Steering, Straight, Sun and planet, Switch, Synchromesh, → **TACKLE**, Timing, Tiptronic®, Top, Trim, Tumbler, Valve, Variable, Worm(-wheel)

Gecko Tokay

Gee Horse, Hump, My, Reist, Sulk, Tout, Towt, Urge

Geek Nerd, Nurd

Geiger-counter Scintillator

Geisha Maiko

Gel Hair, Pectin, Pectise, Silica

Gelatin(e), Gelatinous Blasting, Calipash, Coenchyma, Collagen, Glutinous, Isinglass, Size, Tunicin

Geld(ing) Castrate, Lib, Neuter, Sort, Spado

Gelignite Jelly

Geller Uri

Gem Abraxas, Agate, Alabandine, Alexandrite, Almandine, Amazonite, Amazon stone, Andradite, Asteria, Baguette, Birthstone, Bloodstone, Boule, Brilliant, Briolette, Cabochon, Cacholong, Cairngorm, Callais, Carbuncle, Carnelian, Cat's eye, Chalcedony, Chrysoberyl, Chrysolite, Chrysoprase, Cornelian, Cymophane, Demantoid, Diamante, Diamond, Draconites, Dumortierite, Emerald, Emeraude, Girasol(e), Girosol, Grossular(ite), Hawk's eye, Heliodor, Heliotrope, Hessonite, Hiddenite, Hyacinth, ID, Idaho, Indicolite, Iolite, Jacinth, Jargo(o)n, Jasper, Jaspis, → **JEWEL**, Kunzite, Lapis lazuli, Lherzolite, Ligure, Marcasite, Marquise, Melanite, Menilite, Mocha stone, Moonstone, Morganite, Morion, Moss agate, Onyx, Opal, Pear, Pearl, Peridot(e), Plasma, Pleonast(e), Prase, Pyrope, Rhinestone, Rhodolite, Rose-cut, Rose-diamond, Rubellite, Ruby, Sapphire, Sard, Sardius, Sardonyx, Scarab, Scarabaeoid, Smaragd, Solitaire, Sparkler, Spessartite, Starstone, Stone, Sunstone, Tiger's eye, Topazolite, Tourmaline, Turquoise, Uvarovite, Verd antique, Wood opal, Zircon

Gemination, Gemini Diplogenesis, Twins

Gemma Bud, Knosp

Gen Info

Gendarme Flic

Gender Form, Natural, Sex

Gene(tics) Allel(e), Allelomorph, Anticodon, Codon, Complementary, Creation, Designer, Disomic, Dysbindin, Episome, Exon, Factor, Gay, Genome, Hereditary, Heterogamy, Holandric, Hologynic, Intron, Jumping, Lysenkoism, Mendel, Michurinism, Molecular, Muton, Oncogene, Operon, Orthologue, Paralogue, Regulatory, Reporter, Reverse, Selfish, Structural, Synteny, Telegony, Terminator, Transposon, Weismannism

Genealogist, Genealogy Armory, Family, Heraldry, Line, Pedigree, Seannachie, Seannachy, Sennachie, Whakapapa

General Agamemnon, Agricola, Agrippa, Alcibiades, Allenby, Antigonus, Antipater, Antony, Ataman, At large, Banquo, Barca, Blucher, Booth, Botha, Boulanger, Broad, C in C, Clausewitz, Clive, Common, Communal, Conde, Coriolanus, Cornwallis, Crassus, Current, Custer, De Gaulle, De Wet, Diadochi, Eclectic, Ecumenical, Election, Fairfax, Franco, Gamelin, Gen, GOC, Gordon, Grant, Hadrian, Hannibal, Holofernes, Ike, Inspector, Joshua, Kitchener, Lafayette, Lee, Leslie, Macarthur, Main, Marius, Marshall, Massena, Montcalm, Montgomery, Monty, Napier, Napoleon, Omnify, Othello, Overall, Overhead, Patton, Pershing, Pompey, Prevailing, Public, Raglan, Regulus, Rife, Rommel, Scipio, Sherman, Shrapnel, Smuts, Stilwell, Strategist, Structural, Sulla, Sweeping, Tom Thumb, Turenne, → **UNIVERSAL**, Usual, Vague, Wide, Wolfe

Generate, Generation, Generator Abiogenetic, Age, Beat, Beget, Boomerang, Breeder, Charger, Cottonwool, Create, Dynamo, Electrostatic, Epigon, Father, Fuel-cell, House, Kipp, Loin, Lost, Magneto, Motor, Noise, Olds, Powerhouse, Signal, Sire, Spawn, Spontaneous, Stallion, Van de Graaff, Windmill, X, Yield

Generosity, Generous Bounty, Charitable, Free-handed, Free-hearted, Handsome, Kind, Largess(e), → **LAVISH**, Liberal, Magnanimous, Munificent, Noble(-minded), Open, Open-handed, Open-hearted, Philanthropic, Plump, Profuse, Selfless, Sporting, Unstinting

▶ **Genetic** *see* **GENE**

Geneva(n) Calvinist, Gin, Hollands

Genial(ity) Affable, Amiable, Benign, Bluff, Bonhomie, Chin, Convivial, Cordial, Human, Kindly, Mellow

Genie Djinn, Mazikeen, Shedeem

Genipap Lana

Genital(s) Ballocks, Bol(l)ix, Bollocks, Box, Cooze, Crack, Crotch, Cunt, Fanny, Fourchette, Front bottom, Labia, Lunchbox, Minge, Muff, Naff, Nympha, Private parts, Privates, Pubes, Pudendum, Pun(a)ani, Pun(a)any, Pussy, Quim, Secrets, Snatch, Tackle, Tail, Twat, Vagina, Vulva, Wedding tackle, Yoni

Genitive Ethical

Genius Agathodaimon, Brain, Daemon, Einstein, Engine, Flash, Ingine, Inspiration, Ka, Mastermind, Michaelangelo, Numen, Prodigy

Genome Prophage

Genre Splatterpunk, Tragedy

Gent(leman), Gentlemen, Gentlemanly Amateur, Baboo, Babu, Beau, Caballero, Cavalier, Dandy, Duni(e)wassal, Dunniewassal, Esq(uire), Gemman, Gemmen, Ja(u)nty, Knight, Messrs, Milord, Mister, Mr, Nob, Proteus, Ritter, Runner, Rye, Sahib, Senor, Signor, Sir, Sirra(h), Smuggler, Squire, Sri, Stalko, Stir(rah), Swell, Tea, Toff, Tuan, Von, Yeoman

Genteel Conish, Polite, Proper, Refined

Gentian European, Felwort, Violet, Yellow

Gentile(s) Aryan, Ethnic, Goy, Nations, Shi(c)ksa, Uncircumcised

Gentle(ness) Amenable, Amenage, Bland, Clement, Delicate, Gradual, Grub, Light, Maggot, Mansuete, Mansuetude, Mild, Soft, Sordamente, Tame, Tender

Gentry County, Landed, Quality, Squir(e)age

Gents Bog, John, Lav, Loo, WC

Genuflexion Bend, Curts(e)y, Kowtow, Salaam

Genuine Authentic, Bona-fide, Dinkum, Dinky-di, Echt, Frank, Heartfelt, Honest, Intrinsic, Jannock, Jonnock, Kosher, Legit(imate), McCoy, Nain, Proper, Pucka, Pukka, Pure, Pusser, → **REAL**, Real McCoy, Right, Simon-pure, Sincere, Square, Sterling, True, Unfeigned, Unsophisticated, Veritable

Genus Class, Form, -ia, Mustela

Geode Druse

Geographer, Geography Chorography, Dialect, Economic, Hakluyt, Linguistic, Mercator, Pausanias, Physical, Political, Strabo

Geology, Geologist Dynamic(al), Economic, Geodynamics, Hard-rock, Historical, Hutton, Isotope, Mineralogy, Phanerozoic, Seismology, Self-rock, Structural, Tectonics, Werner

Geometry, Geometrician, Geometer Affine, Analytical, Conics, Coordinate, Descriptive, Differential, Elliptic, Euclid(ean), Hyperbolic, Moth, Non-Euclidean, Parabolic, Plane, Porism, Projective, Riemannian, Solid, Spherics, Topologist

Geordie Guinea, Tynesider

George(s) Autopilot, Best, Borrow, Eliot, Farmer, Lloyd, Orwell, Pilot, Sand

Georgia(n) Abkhaz, Ga, Hanover, Iberian, Mingrel(ian)

Geraint Knight

Geranium Dove's foot, Rose, Stork's bill, Yellow

Gerbil Jird

Germ(s) Bacteria, Bug, Culture, Klebsiella, Seed, Spirilla, Staph(yllococcus), Strep, Virus, Wheat, Wog, Zyme

German(y) Al(e)main(e), Alemannic, Angle, Anglo-Saxon, Bavarian, Berliner, Blood-brother, Boche, Cimbri, Composer, Cousin, Denglish, Franconian, Frank, Fritz, G, Goth, Habsburg, Hans, Hapsburg, Herr, Hessian, High, Hun, Jerry, Jute, Kaiser, Kraut, Landgrave, Low, Ludwig, Lusatian, Neanderthal, Ossi, Ostrogoth, Otto, Palsgrave, Pennsylvania, Plattdeutsch, Pruce, Prussian, Salic, Saxon, Squarehead, Tedesco, Teuton(ic), Vandal, Visigoth, Volsungs, Wessi, Wolfgang

Germane Apt, → **PERTINENT**, Relevant

Germanium Ge

Germ-free Aseptic

Germinate Grow, Pullulate, Sprout

Gesticulate, Gesticulation, Gesture(s) Air quotes, Ameslan, Beck(on), Ch(e)ironomy, Fico, Fig, Gest(e), Harvey Smith, Mannerism, Mime, Motion, Mudra, Salaam, Salute, → **SIGN**, Signal, Snook, Token

Get(ting), Get back, Get off, Get(ting) by, Get(ting) on, Get out Acquire, Advance, Aggravate, Annoy, Attain, Bag, Become, Becoming, Brat, Bring, Capture, Cop, Cope, Debark, Derive, Draw, Escape, Fet(ch), Fette, Gain, Gee, Land, Learn, Make, Manage, Milk, Net, Noy, → **OBTAIN**, Pass, Peeve, Procure, Progress, Reach, Recure, Realise, Rile, Roil, Secure, See, Shift, Sire, Twig, Understand, Win

Getaway Disappearance, Escape, Vamoose

▷ **Getting** *may indicate* an anagram

Getting better Convalescing, Improving, Lysis

Get-up Tog(s)

Geum Avens

Gewgaw Bagatelle, Bauble, Doit, Tat, Trifle

Geyser Soffioni, Therm

Ghanaian Ashanti, Fantee, Fanti, Tshi, Twi

Ghastly Charnel, Gash, Grim, Hideous, Lurid, Macabre, Pallid, Spectral, Ugsome, Welladay, White

Gherkin Cornichon

Ghetto Barrio, Slum

Ghost(ly) Acheri, Apparition, Apport, Banquo, Caddy, Chthonic, Duende, Duppy, Eerie, Eery, Fantasm, Fetch, Gytrash, Haunt, Hint, Holy, Jumbie, Jumby, Larva(e), Lemur, Malmag, Masca, No'canny, Paraclete, Pepper's, Phantasm(agoria), Phantom, Poe, Revenant, Sampford, Shade, Shadow, Spectre, Spectrology, → **SPIRIT**, Spook, Trace, Truepenny, Umbra, Unearthly, Vision, Visitant, Waff, Wraith

Ghoul(ish) Fiend, Macabre

GI Joe, Yankee

Giant(ess) Alcyoneus, Alifanfaron, Anak, Antaeus, Archiloro, Argus, Ascapart, Atlas, Balan, Balor, Bellerus, Blunderbore, Bran, Briareus, Brobdingnagian, Cacus, Colbrand, Colbronde, Colossus, Coltys, Cormoran, Cottus, Cyclop(e)s, Despair, Drow, Enceladus, Ephialtes, Eten, Ettin, Ferragus, Gabbara, Galligantus, Gargantua, Géant, Gefion, Geirred, Gigantic, Gog, Goliath, Grim, Harapha, Hrungnir, Hymir, Idris, Irus, Jotun(n), Jumbo, Krasir, Lestrigon, Leviathan, Magog, Mammoth, Mimir, Monster, Oak, Og, Ogre, Orion, Otus, Pallas, Pantagruel, Patagonian, Polyphemus, Pope, Red, Rounceval, Skrymir, Slaygood, Talos, Talus, Thrym, Titan, Tityus, Tregeagle, Triton, Troll, Tryphoeus, Typhon, Urizen, Utgard, Ymir, Yowie

Gibberish Claptrap, Double Dutch, Greek, Jargon, Mumbo-jumbo

Gibbet Gallows, Patibulary, Potence, Ravenstone, Tree

Gibbon(s) Hoolock, Hylobate, Orlando, Siamang, Stanley, Wou-wou, Wow-wow

Gibe Barb, Brocard, Chaff, Fleer, Glike, Jeer, Jibe, Quip, Shy, Slant, Wisecrack

Gibraltar Calpe

Giddy (girl), Giddiness Capernoitie, Cap(p)ernoity, Dizzy, Fisgig, Fishgig, Fizgig, Giglot, Glaikit, Glaky, Haverel, Hellicat, Hoity-toity, Jillet, Light, Light-headed, Skipping, Staggers, Sturdy, Turn, Vertigo, Volage(ous), Wheel, Woozy

Gift(s), Gifted Ability, Alms, Aptitude, Bef(f)ana, Bequest, Blessing, Blest, Bonbon, Bonsel(l)a, Boon, Bounty, Charism(a), Congiary, Corban, Covermount, Cumshaw, Dash, Deodate, → **DONATION**, Etrenne, Fairing, Fidecommissum, Flair, Foy, Free, Freebie, Frumentation, Gab, Garnish, Godsend, Grant, Greek, Handout, Han(d)sel, Hogmanay, Indian, Knack, Koha, Kula, Lagniappe, Largesse, Legacy, Manna, Ne'erday, Nuzzer, Offering, Parting, Peace-offering, PET, Potlatch, → **PRESENT**, Presentation, Prezzie, Propine, Reward, Sop, Talent, Tongues, Treat, Tribute, Wakf, Waqf, Windfall, Xenium

Gig Cart, Dennet, Moze, Whisk(e)y

Gigantic Atlantean, Briarean, Colossal, Goliath, → **HUGE**, Immense, Mammoth, Monster, Patagonian, Rounceval, Titan, Vast

Giggle, Giggling Cackle, Fou rire, Ha, He-he, Keckle, Simper, Snicker, Snigger, Tehee, Titter

Gigolo Gallant, Ladykiller, Pimp, Romeo

Gilbert Bab, Gb, White, WS

Gild(ed), Gilding Checklaton, Embellish, Enhance, Inaurate, Ormolu, S(c)hecklaton, Vermeil

Gill(s) Beard, Branchia, Cart, Ctenidium, Jill, Noggin, Spiracle, Trematic

Gillman's Aqualung
Gilpin Draper, John, Renowned
Gilt Elt, Parcel, Sow
Gimcrack Gewgaw, Tawdry, Trangam
Gimmick Doodad, Doodah, Hype, Novelty, Ploy, Ruse, Stunt
Gin Bathtub, Blue ruin, Geneva, Genever, Hollands, Juniper, Lubra, Max, Mother's ruin, Noose, Old Tom, Pink, Ruin, Schiedam, Schnapp(s), Sloe, Snare, Springe, Square-face, Toil, Trap, Trepan, Twankay
Ginger, Ginger beer Activist, Amomum, Asarum, Californian bees, Cassumunar, Costus, Curcuma, Enliven, Galanga(l), Galengale, Galingale, Gari, Malaguetta, Nut, Pachak, Pep, Pop, Putchock, Putchuk, Race, Rase, Red(head), Root, Spice, Stem, Turmeric, Zedoary, Zingiber
Gingerbread D(o)um-palm, Lebkuchen, Parkin, Parliament(-cake), Pepper-cake
Gingivitis Ulitis
▶ **Gipsy** *see* **GYPSY**
Giraffe Camelopard, Okapi
Gird Accinge, Belt, Equip, Gibe, Jibe, Quip
Girder Beam, Binder, Box, H-beam, I-beam, Lattice, Loincloth, Spar
Girdle Baldric, Center, Cestus, Chastity, Cincture, Cingulum, Corset, Enzone, Equator, Hippolyte, Hoop, Mitre, Panty, Pectoral, Pelvic, Sash, Shoulder, Surcingle, Surround, Zona, Zone, Zonulet
▷ **Girl** *may indicate* a female name
Girl(s) Backfisch, Ball, Bimbo, Bint, Bird, Bit, Bobby-dazzler, Bobby-soxer, Bohemian, Bondmaid, Broad, Burd, Call, Charlie, Chit, Chorus, Coed, Colleen, Cover, Crumpet, Cummer, Cutey, Cutie, Cutty, Dam(o)sel, Deb, Dell, Demoiselle, Dish, Doll, Dollybird, Essex, Filly, Fisgig, Fizgig, Flapper, Flower, Fluff, Fraulein, Frippet, Gaiety, Gal, Gammerstang, Geisha, Gibson, Gill(et), Gilp(e)y, Giselle, Good-time, Gouge, Gretel, Grisette, Hen, Hoiden, Hoyden, Hussy, It, Italian, Judy, Kimmer, Kinchinmort, Ladette, Land, Lass(ock), Lorette, Maid(en), Mauther, Mawr, Mawther, May, Miss(y), Moppet, Mor, Mot, Mousmé, Mousmee, Mystery, Nautch, Number, Nymph(et), Nymphette, Oanshagh, Peach, Peacherino, Petticoat, Piece, Pigeon, Popsy, Poster, Principal, Puss, Quean, Queyn, Quin(i)e, Randy, Riot, Señorita, Sheila, Shi(c)ksa, Sis(s), Smock, Sweater, Tabby, Taupie, Tawpie, Teddy, Tiller, Tit, Tootsie, Totty, Trull, Vi, Weeny-bopper, Wench, Widgie, Wimp
Girl friend Baby, Chérie, Confidante, Date, Flame, Hinny, Leman, Moll, Peat
Girth Cinch, Compass, Exploitable, Size, Surcingle
Gist Drift, Essence, Kernel, → **NUB**, Pith, Substance
Give(r), Give up, Giving Abandon, Abstain, Accord, Administer, Afford, Award, Bend, Bestow, Buckle, Cede, Confiscate, Consign, Contribute, Dative, Dispense, Dole, → **DONATE**, Duck, Elasticity, Enable, Endow, Enfeoff, Forswear, Gie, Grant, Hand, Impart, Indian, Jack, Largition, Present, Provide, Render, Resign, Sacrifice, Sag, Spring, Stop, Tip, Vacate, Vouchsafe, Yeve, Yield
Give-away Freebie, Gift-horse
Given If
Give out Bestow, Dispense, Emit, Exude, Peter
Give over Cease, Lin
Glacial, Glaciation Gunz, Mindel, Riss, Wurm
Glacier Aletsch, Crevasse, Drumline, Fox, Franz-Josef, Hanging, Iceberg, Ice-cap, Icefall, Moraine, Moulin, Muir, Rhône, Riss, Serac, Stadial, Stoss, Tasman
Glad(ly), Gladden, Gladness Cheer, Fain, → **HAPPY**, Lettice, Lief, Willing
Glade La(u)nd

Gladiator Retiarius, Samnite, Spartacus

Glamour(ise), Glamorous Charm, Glitter(ati), Glitz, Halo, It, Prestige, SA, Sexy, Spell, Swanky

Glamour girl Cheesecake, Odalisk, Odalisque, Pin-up

Glance Allusion, Amoret, Argentite, Blink, Browse, Carom(bole), Copper-head, Coup d'oeil, Dekko, Draw, Eld, Eliad, Eye-beam, Galena, Glad eye, Glimpse, Illiad, Inwick, Lustre, Oeillade, Once-over, Peek, → **PEEP**, Ray, Redruthite, Ricochet, Scan, Sheep's eyes, Shufti, Shufty, Side, Silver, Skellie, Skelly, Slant, Snick, Squint, Squiz, Twire, Vision, Waff

Gland Acinus, Adenoid, Adenoma, Adrenal, Apocrine, Bartholin's, Bulbourethral, Colleterial, Conarium, Cowper's, Crypt, Dart-sac, Digestive, Ductless, Duodenal, Eccrine, Endocrine, Epiphysis, Exocrine, Goitre, Green, Holocrine, Hypophysis, Hypothalamus, Ink-sac, Lachrymal, Lacrimal, Liver, Lymph, Mammary, Melbomian, Musk-sac, Nectary, Oil, Osmeterium, Ovary, Pancreas, Paranephros, Parathyroid, Parotid, Parotis, Parotoid, Perineal, Pineal, Pituitary, Pope's eye, Preen, Prostate, Prothoracic, Salivary, Scent, Sebaceous, Sericterium, Shell, Silk, Sublingual, Submaxillary, Suprarenal, Sweat, Sweetbread, Tarsel, Tear, Testicle, Testis, Third eye, Thymus, Thyroid, Tonsil, Uropygial, Vesicle, Vulvovaginal, Zeiss

Glanders Farcy

Glandular (trouble) Adenitis

Glare, Glaring Astare, Blare, Dazzle, Flagrant, Garish, Gleam, Glower, Holophotal, Iceblink, Lour, Low(e), Naked, Shine, Vivid, Whally

Glass(es), Glassware, Glassy Amen, Ampul(la), Aneroid, Avanturine, Aventurine, Baccara(t), Barometer, Bell, Bifocals, Bins, Borosilicate, Bottle, Brimmer, Bumper, Burmese, Burning, Calcedonio, Case, Cheval, Claude Lorraine, Cloche, Cocktail, Cooler, Copita, Cordial, Coupe, Cover, Crookes, Crown, Crystal, Cullet, Cupping, Cut, Dark, Delmonico, Dildo, Diminishing, Eden, Euphon, Favrile, Fibre, Field, Flint, Float, Flute, Foam, Frigger, Frit, Fulgurite, Gauge, Glare, Goblet, Goggles, Granny, Green, Ground, Hand, Highball, Horn-rims, Humpen, Hyaline, Iceland agate, Jar, Jena, Jigger, Keltie, Kelty, Lace, Lalique, Laminated, Lanthanum, Larking, Latticinio, Lead, Lens, Liqueur, Liquid, Log, Lorgnette, Loupe, Lozen(ge), Lunette, Magma, Magnifying, Metal, Mica, Middy, Milk, Millefiori, Minimizing, Mirror, Moldavite, Monocle, Mousseline, Multiplying, Murr(h)ine, Muscovy, Musical, Nitreous, Object, Obsidian, One-way, Opal, Opal(ine), Opera, Optical, Pane, Parison, Paste, Pearlite, Pebble, Peeper, Pele, Pele's hair, Perlite, Perspective, Pier, Pince-nez, Pinhole, Pitchstone, Plate, Pocket, Pon(e)y, Pressed, Prospective, Prunt, Psyche, Pyrex®, Quarrel-pane, Quarry, Quartz, Reducing, Roemer, Ruby, Rummer, Safety, Schmelz, Schooner, Seam, Seidel, Shard, Sheet, Silex, Silica, Sleever, Slide, Smalt(o), Snifter, Soluble, Specs, → **SPECTACLES**, Spun, Stained, Stein, Stem, Stemware, Stone, Storm, Strass, Straw, Sun, Supernaculum, Tachilite, Tachylite, Tachylyte, Tektite, Telescope, Tiffany, Tiring, Toilet, Trifocals, Triplex®, Tumbler, Uranium, Varifocals, Venetian, Venice, Vernal, Vita, Vitrail, Vitreous, Vitrescent, Vitro-di-trina, Volcanic, Watch, Water, Waterford, Weather, Window (pane), Wine, Wire, Yard of ale

Glass-gall Sandiver

Glass-house Conservatory, Orangery

Glassite Sandemania

Glass-maker Annealer, Blower, Glazier, Lalique, Pontie, Pontil, Ponty, Puntee, Punty

Glaze(d), Glazing Aspic, Ciré, Coat, Double, Eggwash, Film, Flambé, Frit, Glost, Ice, Majolica, Peach-blow, Salt, Sancai, Slip, Tammy, Temmoku, Velatura, Vitreous

Gleam(ing) Blink, Flash, Glint, Glisten, Glitter, Gloss, Leme, Light, Lustre, Ray, Relucent, Sheen, Shimmer, → SHINE

Glean(er) Gather, Harvest, Lease, Stibbler

Glee Exuberance, Joy, Mirth, Song

Glen Affric, Ghyll, Gill, Rushy, Silicon, Vale

Glib Flip, Pat, Slick, Smooth

Glide(r), Glideaway, Gliding Aquaplane, Aviette, Chassé, Coast, Elapse, Float, Illapse, Lapse, Luge, Microlight, Monoplane, Off, On, Portamento, Rogallo, Sail, Sailplane, Sashay, Scorrendo, Scrieve, Skate, Ski, Skim, Skite, Skyte, Sleek, Slide, Slip, Slur, Swim, Volplane

Glimmer(ing) Gleam, Glent, Glint, Glow, Inkling, Light, Stime, Styme, Twinkle, Wink

Glimpse Aperçu, Flash, Glance, Gledge, Glisk, Stime, Styme, Waff, Whiff

Glint Flash, Shimmer, → SPARKLE, Trace, Twinkle

Glisten(ing) Ganoid, Glint, Sheen, Shimmer, → SHINE, Sparkle

Glitter(ing) Clinquant, Garish, Gemmeous, Glee, Paillon, Sequin, Spang(le), Sparkle, Tinsel

Gloat(ing) Crow, Drool, Enjoy, Exult, Schadenfreude

Globe, Globule Artichoke, Ball, Bead, Celestial, Drop, Earth, Orb, Pearl, Planet, Shot, Sphear, Sphere, Territorial, World

Globulin Legumin, Protein

Gloom(y) Atrabilious, Benight, Blues, Cheerless, Cimmerian, Cloud, Crepuscular, Damp, Dark, → DESPAIR, Dingy, Disconsolate, Dismal, Dool(e), Downbeat, Drab, Drear, Drumly, Dump(s), Dyspeptic, Feral, Funereal, Glum, Grey, Grim, Louring, Lowery, Mirk, Misery, Mopish, Morbid, Morne, Morose, Mumps, Murk, Obscurity, Overcast, Sable, Sad, Saturnine, Sepulchral, Shadow, Solein, Solemn, → SOMBRE, Sourpuss, Stygian, Sullen, Tenebrious, Tenebrose, Tenebrous, Unlit, Wan

Glorification, Glorify Aggrandise, Apotheosis, Avatar, Bless, → EXALT, Extol, Halo, Laud, Lionise, Praise, Radiance, Splendour

Glorious, Gloria, Glory Chorale, Grand, Halo, Hosanna, Ichabod, Knickerbocker, Kudos, Lustre, Magnificent, Nimbus, Strut, Sublime, Twelfth

Glory-pea Kaka-beak, Kaka-bill, Kowhai

Gloss(y) Ciré, Enamel, Gild, Glacé, Interpret, Japan, Lip, Lustre, Mag, Patina, → POLISH, Postillate, Sheen, Sleek, Slick, Slide, Slur, Supercalendered, Veneer, Wetlook, Whitewash

Glossary Catalogue, Clavis, Index, K'thibh

Gloucester Cheese

Glove Boxing, Cestus, Dannock, Gage, Gauntlet, Kid, Mermaid's, Mitten, Mousquetaire, Muffle, Oven, Rubber, Velvet

Glow(er), Glowing, Glowworm Aflame, Ashine, Aura, Bloom, Burn, Calescence, Candent, Candescence, Firefly, Flush, Foxfire, Gegenschein, Gleam, Glimmer, Halation, Iceblink, Incandescence, Lambent, Lamp-fly, Leam, Leme, Luculent, Luminesce, Lustre, Perspire, Phosphorescence, Radiant, Reflet, Rushlight, Shine, Snowblink, Translucent, → WARMTH

Glucin(i)um Gl

Glucose, Glucoside Aesculin, Amygdalin, Dextrose, Digitalin, Indican, Maltose, Salicin(e), Saponin, Solanine

Glue(y) Alkyd, Araldite®, Bee, Cement, Colloidal, Fish, Gelatin(e), Gunk, Hot-melt, Ichthyocolla, Isinglass, Marine, Paste, Propolis, Rice, Size, Solvent, Spetch

Glum Dour, Livery, Lugubrious, Moody, Morose, Ron, Sombre

Glut Choke, Gorge, Plethora, Sate, Satiate, Saturate, Surfeit

Gluten, Glutinous Goo, Ropy, Seiten, Sticky, Tar, Viscid, Zymome

Glutton(ous), Gluttony Bellygod, Carcajou, Cormorant, Edacity, Feaster, Free-liver, Gannet, Gorb, Gourmand, Greedyguts, Gulosity, Gutser, Gutsy, Gutzer, Hog, Lurcher, Pig, Ratel, Scoffer, Sin, Trencherman, Trimalchio, Wolverine

Glyceride, Glycerine Ester, Olein, Palmitin

Glycoside Hesperidin

Gnarl(ed) Knot, Knuckly, Knur, Nob

Gnash(ing) Bruxism, Champ, Grate

Gnat Culex, Culicidae, Midge, Mosquito

Gnaw(ing) Corrode, Erode, Fret, Lagomorph, Rodent

Gnome Adage, Bank-man, Chad, Cobalt, Epigram, Europe, Financier, Garden, Kobold, Maxim, Motto, Proverb, Saw, Sprite, Zurich

Gnostic(ism) (A)eon, Archontic, Cainite, Mand(a)ean, Marcionism, Ophite, Sabian, Tsabian, Zabian

Gnu Brindled, Horned horse, White-tailed, Wildebeest

Go, Going (after, back, for, off, on, through, up, etc) Advance, Afoot, Anabasis, Animation, Ascent, Assail, Attempt, Bash, Betake, Bing, Bout, Brio, Choof, Clamber, Comb, Continuance, Crack, Deal, Depart, Die, Do, Energy, Fare, Gae, Gang, Gee, Gonna, Green, Hamba, Hark, Heavy, Hence, Hie, Imshi, Imshy, Ish, Kick, → **LEAVE**, March, Match, Move, Off, Path, Pee, Pep, Perpetual, Ply, Quit, Raik, Repair, Resort, Resume, Run, Scat, Scram, Segue, Shoo, Shot, Skedaddle, Snick-up, Sour, Spank, Spell, Square, Stab, Success, Transitory, Trine, Try, Turn, Vam(o)ose, Vanish, Verve, Via, Viable, Vim, Wend, Work, Yead, Yede, Yeed, Zap, Zest, Zing, Zip

Goad Ankus, Brod, Gad, Impel, Incite, → **NEEDLE**, Prod, Rowel, Spur, Stimulate, Stimulus, Taunt

Goal(posts) Ambition, Basket, Bourn(e), Cage, Destination, Dool, Dream, Drop, Dule, End, Ettle, Field, Golden, Grail, Hail, Home, Horme, Hunk, Limit, Mark, Mission, Moksha, Net, Own, Score, Silver, Tap-in, Target, Touch-in, Ultima Thule, Uprights

Goalless Idle

Goat(-like) Alpine, Amalthea, Angora, Antelope, Antilope, Billy, Bok, Bucardo, Buck, Caprine, Cashmere, Cilician, Gait, Gate, Giddy, Goral, Hircine, Ibex, Izard, Kashmir, Kid, Libido, Markhor, Mountain, Nan(ny), Nubian, Rocky Mountain, Saanen, Sassaby, Serow, Serpent-eater, Steenbok, Steinbock, Tahr, Takin, Tehr, Thar, Toggenburg

Goatsucker Fern-owl, Nightjar

Gob(bet) Bespit, Clot, Dollop, Mouth, Sailor, Spit, Tar, Yap

Gobble Bolt, Devour, Gorge, Gulp, Slubber, Wolf

Gobelin Tapestry

Go-between Broker, Factor, Intermediate, Link, Mediate, Middleman, Pandarus, Pander, Shuttle

Goblet Chalice, Hanap

Goblin Banshee, Bargaist, Barg(h)est, Bodach, Bogey, Bogle, Bogy, Brownie, Bucca, Croquemitaine, Empusa, Erl-king, Esprit follet, Genie, Gnome, Gremlin, Knocker, Kobold, Lob-lie-by-the-fire, Lubberfiend, Lutin, Nis(se), Phooka, Phynnodderree, Pooka, Pouke, Puca, Pug, Red-cap, Red-cowl, Shellycoat, → **SPRITE**, Troll, Trow

Gobstopper Everlasting

Goby Dragonet

God(s) All-seer, Amen, Ancient of Days, → **DEITY**, Deus, Di, Divine, Gallery, Gracious, Holy One, Household, Immortals, Inner Light, Light, Maker, Od(d), Olympian, Prime Mover, Principle, Providence, Serpent, Supreme Being, The Creator, Tin, Trinity, Truth, Unknown, Vanir, War, Water

GODS

1 letter:
D

2 letters:
An
As
Ra
Re

3 letters:
Anu
Bel
Bes
Dis
Gad
Geb
Jah
Keb
Lar
Lir
Lug
Mot
Pan
Seb
Set
Sol
Tiu
Tiw
Tum
Tyr

4 letters:
Abba
Agni
Aitu
Amun
Apis
Ares
Asur
Aten
Atum
Baal
Brag
Bran
Cama
Deva
Dieu
Eros
Faun

Frey
Joss
Kama
Kami
Llyr
Loki
Lugh
Mars
Mors
Nebo
Odin
Ptah
Rama
Seth
Siva
Soma
Thor
Tyrr
Yama
Zeus

5 letters:
Aegir
Aesir
Allah
Ammon
Bragi
Comus
Cupid
Dagan
Dagon
Donar
Freyr
Haoma
Horus
Hymen
Indra
Janus
Khnum
Liber
Lludd
Mimir
Momus
Njord
Numen
Orcus
Orixa
Pales
Picus

Pluto
Rudra
Satyr
Sebek
Shiva
Sinis
Surya
Thoth
Titan
Wodan
Woden
Wotan
Yahve
Yahwe

6 letters:
Adonai
Aeolus
Amen-ra
Amon-ra
Anubis
Apollo
Ashtar
Asshur
Avatar
Balder
Boreas
Brahma
Cabiri
Chemos
Cronus
Delian
Elohim
Faunus
Ganesa
Ganesh
Garuda
HaShem
Helios
Hermes
Hughie
Hypnos
Kronos
Mahoun
Mammon
Marduk
Mexitl
Mextli
Mithra

Molech
Moloch
Nereus
Njorth
Oannes
Orisha
Ormazd
Ormuzd
Osiris
Panisc
Panisk
Plutus
Rimmon
Saturn
Somnus
Tammuz
Teraph
Teshup
Thamiz
Thunor
Triton
Uranus
Varuna
Vishnu
Vulcan
Yahweh
Zombie

7 letters:
Alastor
Alpheus
Angus Og
Anteros
Bacchus
Bhagwan
Chemosh
Daikoku
Ganesha
Hanuman
Heimdal
Jehovah
Jupiter
Krishna
Kuan Yin
Kwan Yin
Mahound
Mercury
Mithras
Neptune

Nisroch
Oceanus
Penates
Phoebus
Priapus
Proteus
Rameses
Sarapis
Sat Guru
Serapis
Setebos
Shamash
Silenus
Thammuz
Zagreus

8 letters:
Achelous

Dionysus
Heimdall
Hyperion
Kamadeva
Mahadeva
Morpheus
Mulciber
Nataraja
Pantheon
Poseidon
Quirinus
Silvanus
Sylvanus
Terminus
Trimurti
Wahiguru
Zephyrus

9 letters:
All-father
Asclepius
Fabulinus
Heimdallr
Jagganath
Promachos
Tetragram
Thunderer
Vertumnus
Zernebock

10 letters:
Ahura Mazda
Demogorgon
Elegabalus
Hephaestus
Hephaistos

Juggernaut
Karttikaya
Mumbo-jumbo
Prometheus
Trophonius

11 letters:
Adrammelech
Aesculapius
Bodhisattva

12 letters:
Quetzalcoati
Trismegistus

14 letters:
Tetragrammaton

God-bearing Deiparous
Goddess(es) Divine, Green, Muse, Sea nymph

GODDESSES

2 letters:
Ge

3 letters:
Ate
Eos
Hel
Mut
Nox
Nut
Nyx
Ops
Pax

4 letters:
Dian
Eris
Gaea
Gaia
Hera
Idun
Iris
Isis
Juno
Kali
Leda
Leto

Luna
Maat
Maut
Nike
Norn
Pele
Rhea
Sita
Thea

5 letters:
Aruru
Ceres
Diana
Dione
Durga
Erato
Flora
Freya
Grace
Horae
Houri
Hulda
Iduna
Irene
Kotys
Moera

Moira
Pales
Tanit
Terra
Tyche
Ushas
Venus
Vesta

6 letters:
Aglaia
Ashnan
Athene
Aurora
Bastet
Cybele
Cyrene
Eastre
Freyja
Frigga
Graeae
Graiae
Hathor
Hecate
Hertha
Hestia
Huldar

Hyaeia
Idalia
Ishtar
Ithunn
Lucina
Pallas
Parcae
Phoebe
Pomona
Satyra
Selene
Semele
Tellus
Tethys
Themis
Thetis

7 letters:
Artemis
Astarte
Astraea
Bellona
Cotytto
Cynthia
Demeter
Fortuna
Kotytto

7 letters – cont:
Lakshmi
Megaera
Minerva
Nemesis
Nepthys
Parvati
Sabrina

Strenia
Victory

8 letters:
Cloacina
Cytherea
Libitina
Rhiannon

Valkyrie
Victoria
Walkyrie

9 letters:
Aphrodite
Ashtaroth
Ashtoreth

Eumenides
Mnemosyne
Sarasvati

10 letters:
Amphitrite
Proserpina
Proserpine

Godfather, Godmother Capo, Cummer, Fairy, Gossip, Kimmer, Rama, Sponsor, Woden

Godless Agnostic, Atheistic, Atheous, Impious, Profane

Godly Deist, Devout, Holy, Pious

Godown Hong

God-willing Deo volente, DV, Inshallah, Mashallah

Go-getter Arriviste, Hustler

Goggle(s) Gaze, Snow-eyes, Stare

Going wrong Aglee, Agley, Misfiring

▷ **Going wrong** *may indicate* an anagram

Goitre Derbyshire neck, Exophthalmic, Graves' disease, Struma

Gold(en) Age, Amber, Apple, Ass, Au, Aureate, Auriferous, Bendigo, Bough, Bull, Bullion, California, Chryselephantine, Doubloon, Dutch, Eagle, Electron, Electrum, Emerods, Fairy, Filigree, Filled, Fleece, Fool's, Free, Fulminating, Gate, Gilden, Gule, Handshake, Hind, Horde, Horn, Ingot, Kolar, Leaf, Lingot, Moidore, Mosaic, Muck, Nugget, Oaker, Obang, Ochre, Ophir, Or, Oreide, Ormolu, Oroide, Pistole, Placer, Pyrites, Red, Reef, Rolled, Silence, Silver-gilt, Sol, Standard, Stream, Stubborn, Taelbar, Talmi, Thrimsa, Tolosa, Treasury, Venice, Virgin, Wash-up, White, Witwatersrand, Yellow

Gold-digger Forty-niner, Prospector

Golden fleece Phrixus

Goldfield Rand

Goldfinch Charm, Chirm, Redcap

Gold leaf Ormolu

Gold rush Kalgoorlie, Klondike

Goldsmith Cellini, Fabergé, Oliver

Golf (ball) Better-ball, Clock, Crazy, Foursome, Gutta, Matchplay, Medal play, Repaint, Round, Stableford

Golfer Alliss, Braid, Cotton, Els, Faldo, Hogan, Lyle, Pivoter, Rees, Roundsman, Seve, Snead, Teer, Texas scramble, Tiger Woods, Trevino, Wolstenholme, Yipper

Golly Cor, Crumbs, Gosh

Gondolier Balloonist, Bargee

Gone Ago, Dead, Defunct, Napoo, Out, Past, Ygo(e), Yod

▷ **Gone off** *may indicate* an anagram

Gone west Had it

Gong Bell, DSO, → **MEDAL**, Tam-tam, VC

Gonorrhoea Clap

Goo Gleet, Gloop, Gunge, Poise, Ulmin

Goober Monkey nut

Good(ness), Goody-goody Agatha, Agathodaimon, Altruism, Angelic, Ascertained, Bad, Bein, Benefit, Blesses, Bon, Bonzer, Bosker, Bounty, Brod, Budgeree, Canny, Castor, Civil, Clinker, Common, Coo, Cool, Crack(ing), Credit, Dab, Dandy, Def,

Divine, Dow, Enid, Estimable, Fantabulous, Finger lickin', First-class, G, Gear, Giffen, Glenda, Gosh, Guid, Humdinger, Lois, Lor, Ma foi, Neat, Nobility, → **NO GOOD**, Pi, Plum, Prime, Proper, Purler, Rattling, Rectitude, Riddance, Right, Rum, Sake, Salutary, Samaritan, Sanctity, Slap-up, Smashing, Spiffing, St, Suitable, Super, Taut, Tollol, Topping, Valid, Virtue, Virtuous, Weal, Welfare, Whacko, Wholesome, Worthy

Goodbye Addio, Adieu, Adios, Aloha, Apopemptic, Arrivederci, Cheerio, Ciao, Congé, Farewell, Haere ra, Hamba kahle, Hooray, Hooroo, Later, Sayonara, See-you, So long, Tata, Toodle-oo, Toodle-pip, Vale

Good evening Den

Goodfellow Brick, Puck, Robin, Samaritan, Worthy

Good-for-nothing Bum, Donnat, Donnot, Dud, Idler, Layabout, Lorel, Lorrell, Losel, Napoo, Naught, Sca(l)lawag, Scallywag, Scant o'grace, Sculpin, Shot-clog, Stiff, Useless, Vaurien, Waff, Waster, Wastrel

Good Friday Parasceve, Pasch of the Cross

Good-humour(ed), Good-natured Amiable, Bonhomie, Clever, Gruntled, Kind

Good-looking Bon(n)ie, Bonny, Bonwie, Comely, Fair, Handsome, Personable, Pretty, Wally

Good news Evangel

Good number Thr(e)ave

Good order Eutaxy, Shipshape

Goods Bona, Brown, Cargo, Commodities, Consumer, Disposable, Durable, Durables, Fancy, Flotsam, Freight, Futures, Gear, Hardware, Insight, Ironware, Lagan, Lay-away, Line, Luxury, Piece, Products, Property, Schlock, Soft, Sparterie, Truck, Wares, White

Goodwill Amity, Bonhom(m)ie, Favour, Gree

Goody Wrong'un

Goon Bentine, Eccles, Milligan, Secombe, Sellers

Goose, Geese Anserine, Barnacle, Bernicle, Blue, Brent, Canada, Cape Barren, Colonial, Daftie, Ember, Gaggle, Gander, Gannet, Golden, Greylag, Grope, Harvest, Hawaiian, Idiot, Juggins, MacFarlane's, Magpie, Michaelmas, Mother, Nana, Nene, Pink-footed, Quink, Roger, Saddleback, Silly, Simpleton, Skein, Snow, Solan, Strasbourg, Stubble, → **STUPID PERSON**, Swan, Team, Wav(e)y, Wawa, Wedge, Whitehead

Gooseberry Cape, Chaperon(e), Chinese, Coromandel, Detrop, Fool, Gog, Groser(t), Groset, Grossart, Grozer, Honey blob, Kiwi, Physalis, Tomato

Gooseflesh Horripilation

Goosefoot Allgood, Amarantaceae, Beet, Blite, Fat-hen, Mercury, Orache, Saltbush

Gooseherd Quill-driver

Gopher Camass-rat, Minnesota, Pocket

Gordian Knot

Gordon Chinese, Flash, Rioter

Gore, Gory Blood, Cloy, Danse macabre, Gair, Horn, Inset, Toss

Gorge(s) Abyss, Arroyo, Barranca, Barranco, Canyon, Chasm, Cheddar, Cleft, Couloir, Cram, Defile, Donga, Flume, Gap, Ghyll, Glut, Grand Canyon, Grand Coulee, Gulch, Ironbridge, Iron Gate, Khor, Kloof, Lin(n), Nala, Nalla(h), Nulla(h), Olduvai, Overeat, Overfeed, Pass, Pig, Ravine, Snarf, Staw, → **STUFF**, Throat, Tire, Tums, Valley, Yosemite

Gorgeous Delectable, Dreamboat, Grand, Splendid, Superb

Gorgon Euryale, Medusa, Ogress, Stheno

Gorilla Heavy, → **MONKEY**

Gorse Broom, Furze, Gosse, Ulex, Whin

Gosh Begad, Begorra, Blimey, Coo, Cor, Gadzooks, Gee, Gracious, Gum, Heavens, Lor, My, Och, Odsbobs, Odso, Shucks

Gospel(s), Gospeller Apocryphal, Creed, Diatessaron, Evangel, Fact, John, Kerygma, Luke, Mark, Matthew, Nicodemus, Prosperity, Protevangelium, Synoptic, Truth, Waldensian

Gossamer(y) Araneous, Byssoid, Cobwebby, Gauzy

Gossip Ana(s), Aunt, Backbite, Blether, Cackle, Cat, Causerie, Chat, Chin, Chitchat, Clash, Clash-me-clavers, Claver, Cleck, Clish-clash, Clishmaclaver, Confab, Coze, Crack, Cummer, Dirt, Flibbertigibbet, Gab(nash), Gabfest, Gas, Gash, Goster, Gup, Hearsay, Hen, Jaw, Loose-tongued, Maundrel, Nashgab, Natter, Newsmonger, Noise, On dit, Pal, Personalist, Prattle, Prose, Quidnunc, Reportage, Rumour, Scandal(monger), Schmooze, Scuttlebutt, Shmoose, Shmooze, Sweetie-wife, Tabby(cat), Talk(er), Tattle, Tattletale, Tibby, Tittle(-tattle), Twattle, Yatter, Yenta

Got Gat, Obtained

Goth(ic) Alaric, Lurid, Moesia

Gothamite Abderian, New Yorker

Gouge Chisel, Groove, Scoop

Gourd Bottle, Calabash, Courgette, Dishcloth, Guiro, Hercules' club, Loofa, Melon, Monkeybread, Pumpkin, Squash, Zucchini

Gourmand, Gourmet Aesthete, Apicius, → **EPICURE**, Gastronome, Gastrosopher, Lickerish, Table, Trencherman, Ventripotent

Gout Chiragra, Hamarthritis, Podagra, Taste, Tophus

Govern(or), Government Adelantado, Administer, Ag(h)a, Agricola, Alderman, Amban, Amman, Amtman, ANC, Andocracy, Archology, Aristocracy, Autarchy, Autocrat, Autonomy, Bahram, Ban, Bashaw, Beehive, Beg, Beglerbeg, Bencher, Bey, Bridler, Bureaucracy, Burgrave, Cabinet, Caciquism, Caretaker, Castellan, Catapan, Cham, Circar, Classis, Coalition, Command, Commonwealth, Condominium, Congress, Constable, Constitution, Consulate, Cybernetic, Darogha, Democracy, Dergue, Despotism, Despotocracy, Dey, Diarchy, Dictatorship, Dinarchy, Directoire, Directory, Domain, Dominate, Downing St, Duarchy, Dulocracy, Duumvirate, Dyarchy, Dynast, Earl, Ecclesiarchy, Empery, Eparch, Ergatocracy, Escapement, Ethnarch, Exarch, Fascism, Federal, G, Gauleiter, Gerontocracy, Gov, Grieve, Gubernator, Guv, Gynarchy, Hagiarchy, Hagiocracy, Hague, Hajjaz, Hakim, Haptarchy, Harmost, HE, Helm, Heptarchy, Hexarchy, Hierocracy, Honcho, Hospodar, Imperialism, Ins, Inspector, Isocracy, Junta, Kaimakam, Kakistocracy, Kawanatanga, Kebele, Kemalism, Khalifate, Khan, Kremlin, Legate, Local, Majlis, Majorism, Matriarchy, Monarchy, Monocracy, Mudir, Nabob, Naik, Nomarch, Nomocracy, Ochlocracy, Oireachtas, Oligarchy, Optic®, Pa, Pacha, Padishah, Pasha, Pater, Patriarchism, Pentarch, Père, Petticoat, Physiocracy, Pilate, Placemen, Plutocracy, Podesta, Polity, Polyarchy, Porte, Power, Priest-king, Proconsul, Propraetor, Proveditor, Provedor(e), Providor, Ptochocracy, Quadrumvirate, Quirinal, Raj, Realpolitik, Rection, Rector, Rectrix, Regency, Regié, Regime(n), Regulator, Reign, Rein, Ride, → **RULE**, Satrap, Senate, Serkali, Shogun, Signoria, Sircar, Sirkar, Stad(t)holder, Stakhanovism, Statecraft, Steer, Stratocracy, Subadar, Sway, Technocracy, Tetrarchy, Thalassocracy, Thalattocracy, Thatcherism, Thearchy, Theocracy, Theonomy, Timocracy, Totalitarianism, Triarchy, Triumvirate, Tuchun, Tyranny, Vali, Viceregal, Viceroy, Vichy, Wali, Warden, Wealsman, Whitehall, White House, Witan

Governess Duenna, Eyre, Fraulein, Griffin, Mademoiselle, Prism, Vicereine

Government revenue Jaghir(e), Jagir

Gown Banian, Banyan, Dressing, Empire, Geneva, Green, Johnny, Kirtle, Manteau, Manto, Mantua, Manty, Mazarine, Morning, Mother Hubbard, Peignoir, Polonaise, Robe, Sack, Silk, Slammakin, Slammerkin, Slop, Stola, Stuff, Tea, Wrap(per)

Grab Accost, Annexe, Areach, Bag, Clutch, Cly, Collar, Glaum, Grapnel, Hold, Holt, Rap, Reach, Seise, Seize, → SNATCH, Steal, Swipe

Gracchi Jewels

Grace(s), Graceful Aglaia, Airy, Amnesty, Anna, Bad, Beauty, Become, Benediction, Bethankit, Blessing, Charis(ma), Charites, Charity, Cooperating, Darling, Dr, Elegance, Euphrosyne, Fluent, Gainly, Genteel, Genty, Godliness, Grazioso, Handsome, Light, Mense, Mercy, Molinism, Mordent, Omnium, Ornament, Plastique, Polish, Pralltriller, Prayer, Sacrament, Saving, Spirituelle, Streamlined, Style, Thalia, Thanks, Thanksgiving, WG, Willowy

Grace note Nachschlag

Gracious Benign, By George, Charismatic, Generous, Good, Handsome, Hend, Merciful, Polite

Gradation Ablaut, Cline, Degree, Nuance, Stage

Grade, Gradient Alpha, Analyse, Angle, Assort, Beta, Bubs, Class(ify), Conservation, Dan, Degree, Delta, Echelon, Gamma, Geothermal, Gon, Gride, Hierarchy, Inclination, Kyu, Lapse, Measure, Order, Ordinary, Pressure, Rank, Reserve, Score, Seed, Slope, Stage, Standard, Status, Temperature, Thermocline

Gradual Gentle, Grail, Imperceptible, Inchmeal, Piecemeal, Slow

Graduate, Graduation Alumnus, BA, Bachelor, Calibrate, Capping, Classman, Incept, Laureateship, Licentiate, LlB, MA, Master, Nuance, Optime, Ovate

Graffiti Bomb, Doodle, Tag, Tagger

Graft Anaplasty, Autoplasty, Boodle, Bribery, Bud, Bypass, Cion, Cluster, Crown, Dishonesty, Dub, Enarch, Enrace, Flap, Hard, Heteroplasty, Imp, Implant, Inarch, Inoculate, Payola, Pomato, Racket, Scion, Shoot, Sien(t), Skin, Slip, Syen, Transplant, Whip, Ympe

Grail Chalice, Cup, Sangraal, Sangrail, Sangreal

Grain(y) Bajra, Bajree, Bajri, Barley, Bear, Bere, Boll, Bran, Cereal, Corn, Couscous, Crop, Curn, Curn(e)y, Cuscus, Distillers', D(o)urra, Extine, Floor, Frumentation, Gr, Graddan, Granule, Groats, Grumose, Intine, Kaoliang, Knaveship, Malt, Mashlam, Mashlin, Mashloch, Mashlum, Maslin, Mealie, Millet, Milo, Minim, Mongcorn, Oats, Panic(k), Pannick, Pickle, Pinole, Pollen, Polynology, Popcorn, Proso, Psyllium, Puckle, Quarter, Quinoa, Rabi, Raggee, Raggy, Ragi, Rhy, Rye, Sand, Scruple, Seed, Semsem, Sorghum, Thirlage, Tola, Touch, Wheat, Wholemeal

Gram Black, Chich, Chick-pea, Green, Teen, Tene, Urd

Grammar(ian), Grammatical Ablative absolute, Accidence, Amphibology, Anacoluthia, Anacoluthon, Anaphora, Anastrophe, Case, Cataphora, Categorical, Causative, Donat, Donet, Generative, Gr, Linguistics, Montague, Paradigm, Paucal, Pivot, Primer, Priscianist, Priscianus, Protasis, Scholiast, Stratificational, Syndetic, Syndeton, Synectics, Synesis, Syntax, Systemics, Tagmeme, Transformational, Trivium, Typto, Universal, Valency

Gramophone Record player, Victrolla®

Grampus Orc, Risso's dolphin, Thresher-whale, Whale

Granary Barn, Girnel, Silo

Grand(eur), Grandiose Big, Canyon, Epical, Flugel, G, Gorgeous, Guignol, High-faluting, Hotel, Imposing, La(h)-di-da(h), Long, Lordly, Magnificent, Majestic, Megalomania, Palatial, Piano(forte), Pompous, Regal, Splendid, Stately, Stoor, Stour, Stowre, Sture, Sublime, Swell, Tour

Grandchild Mokopuna, Niece, Oe, Oy(e)

Grandee Adelantado, Don, Magnifico

Grandfather Ancient, Avital, Clock, Goodsire, Gramps, Gudesire, Gutcher, Luckie-dad, Oldster, Old-timer, Oupa

Grandmother Babushka, Beldam, Gran(nie), Granny, Moses, Nan(a), Ouma

Grandparent(al) Aval, Avital

Grand Prix Race(-cup)

Grandsire Peal

Grange Moated

Granite Aberdeen, Chinastone, Graphic, Greisen, Luxul(l)ianite, Luxulyanite, NH, Pegmatite, Protogine

Grannie, Granny Cowl, Forebear, Knot, Nan(a)

Grant(ed) Accord, Aid, Allow, Award, Benefaction, Bestow, Beteem(e), Block, Bounty, Bursary, Carta, Cary, Cede, Charta, Charter, Concession, → **CONFER**, Cy, Datum, Endow, Enfranchise, Exhibition, Feoff, Give, Hugh, Land, Lend, Let, Munich, Obreption, Patent, President, Regium donum, Scholarship, Send, Sop, Subsidy, Subvention, Supply, Teene, Ulysses, Ure, Vouchsafe, Yeven, Yield

Granule, Granulate(d) Kern, Otolith, Pearl, Plastid, Pound, Prill, Volutin

Grape(s) Aligoté, Botros, Botryoid, Bullace, Cabernet, Cabernet Sauvignon, Carmerère, Catawba, Cépage, Chardonnay, Chenin blanc, Colombard, Concord, Delaware, Diamond, Fox, Gamay, Garnacha, Gewurztraminer, Grenache, Haanepoot, Hamburg(h), Hanepoot, Honeypot, Hyacinth, Lambrusco, Malbec, Malmsey, Malvasia, Malvesie, Malvoisie, Marsanne, Merlot, Muscadel, Muscadine, Muscat(el), Nebbiolo, Noble rot, Oregon, Petite Syrah, Pinot, Pinotage, Pinot blanc, Pinot Chardonnay, Primitivo, Ptisan, Racemose, Raisin, Rape, Riesling, Sangiovese, Sauvignon, Scuppernong, Sémillon, Sercial, Shiraz, Sour, Staphyline, Steen, Sultana, Sweet-water, Sylvaner, Syrah, Tokay, Uva, Verdelho, Véronique, Vino, Wineberry, Zinfandel

Grapefruit Pampelmoose, Pomelo, Pompelmouse, Pompelo, Pumple-nose, Shaddock, Ugli®

Grapeshot Mitraille

Grape-sugar Glucose

Grapevine Gossip, Hearsay, Mocassin telegraph, Moccasin telegraph

Graph, Graphic(s) Bar, Chart, Clip art, Computer, Contour, Diagram, Histogram, Learning curve, Nomograph, Ogive, Picturesque, Pie (chart), Plot, Profile, Sonogram, Table, Turtle, Vivid, Waveform, Waveshape

Graphite Kish, Plumbago

Grapple Clinch, Close, Hook, Lock, Struggle, Wrestle

Grasp(ing) Apprehend, Catch, Clat, Claut, Clinch, → **CLUTCH**, Compass, Comprehend, Fathom, Get, Go-getting, Grab, Grapple, Greedy, Grip(e), Hend, Hold, Hug, Knowledge, Prehend, Prehensile, Raptorial, Realise, Rumble, Sense, Snap, Snatch, Twig, Uptak(e)

Grass(land), Grass roots, Grassy Agrostology, Alang, Alfa(lfa), Arrow, Avena, Bahia, Bamboo, Bang, Barbed wire, Barley, Barnyard, Beard, Bennet, Bent, Bermuda, Bhang, Blade, Blady, Blue(-eyed), Blue moor, Bristle, Brome-grass, Bromus, Buffalo, Buffel, Bunch, Bush, Canary, Cane, Canna, Cannach, Carpet, Cat's tail, Cheat, Chess, China, Citronella, Cleavers, Clivers, Clover, Cochlearia, Cocksfoot, Cockspur, Cogon, Cord, Cortaderia, Cotton, Couch, Cow, Crab, Culm, Cuscus, Cutty, Dactylis, Danthonia, Dari, Darnel, Deergrass, Dhur(r) a, Diss, Divot, Dogstail, Dog's tooth, Dogwheat, Doob, Doura, Dura, Durra, Eddish, Eel, Eelwrack, Elephant, Emmer, Ers, Esparto, Feather, Fescue, Finger, Fiorin, Flinders, Floating, Flote, Fog, Foggage, Foxtail, Gage, Gama-grass, Ganja,

Gardener's garters, Glume, Glumella, Goose, Grama, Gramineae, Green(sward), Hair, Halfa, Harestail, Hashish, Hassock, Haulm, Hay, Haycock, Heath(er), Hemp, Herbage, High veld, Holy, Indian corn, → **INFORM**, Jawar(i), Job's tears, Johnson, Jowar(i), Kangaroo, Kans, Kentucky blue, Khuskhus, Kikuyu, Knoll, Knot, Lalang, Laund, Lawn, Lay, Lea, Lee, Lemon, Locusta, Lolium, Lop, Lucern(e), Lyme, Mabela, Machair, Maize, Manna, Marram, Marrum, Mary Jane, Mat, Materass, Matweed, Mead, Meadow(-fescue), Meadow foxtail, Mealies, Melic, Melick, Millet, Milo, Miscanthus, Monkey, Moor, Moss-crop, Nark, Nassella tussock, Nature strip, Negro-corn, Nose, Nut, Oat, Orange, Orchard, Oryza, Painted, Palet, Pamir, Pampas, Panic, Paspalum, Pasturage, Peach, Pennisetum, Pepper, Persicaria, Phleum, Plume, Poa, Porcupine, Pot, Purple moor, Puszta, Quack, Quaking, Quick, Quitch, Ramee, Rami(e), Rat, Rat on, Redtop, Reed, Rescue, Rhodes, Rib, Ribbon, Rice, Rips, Roosa, Rotgrass, Rough, Rumble(r), Rusa, Rush, Rye(-brome), Sacaton, Sago, Salt, Sand, Savanna(h), Saw, Scorpion, Scraw, Scurvy, Scutch, Sea-reed, Sedge, Seg, Sesame, Shave, Sheep's fescue, Shop, Sing, Sinsemilla, Sisal, Sneak(er), Snitch, Snout, Snow, Sorghum, Sour-gourd, Sourveld, Spanish, Spear, Spelt, Spike, Spinifex, Splay, Split, Squeal, Squirrel-tail, Squitch, Stag, Star(r), Stipa, Stool-pigeon, Storm, Sudan, Sugar, Sward, Swath(e), Sword, Tape, Taramea, Tath, Tea, Tef(f), Tell, Teosinte, Timothy, Toad, Toetoe, Toitoi, Triticale, Triticum, True-love, Tuffet, Turf, Tussac, Tussock, Twitch, Veld(t), Vernal, Vetiver, Viper's, Whangee, Wheat, Wheatgrass, Whitlow, Windlestraw, Wire, Witch, Wood melick, Worm, Yard, Yellow-eyed, Yorkshire fog, Zizania, Zostera, Zoysia

Grasshopper Cicada, Cricket, Grig, Katydid, Locust, Long-horned, Meadow, Tettix, Wart-biter, Weta

Grate(r), Grating Abrade, Burr, Cancelli, Chain, Chirk, Crepitus, Diffraction, → **FRET**, Graticule, Gravelly, Grid, Grill, Guichet, Guttural, Hack, Haik, Hake, Hearth, Heck, Hoarse, Ingle, Jar, Mort-safe, Nag, Portcullis, Rasp, Risp, Rub, Ruling, Scrannel, → **SCRAPE**, Scrat, Shred, Siver, Strident, Syver

Grateful Beholden, Cinders, Indebted, Obliged

Gratification, Gratify(ing) Aggrate, Indulge, Kick, Masochism, Narcissism, Oblige, Pleasure, Regale, Reward, Sadism, Sensuous, Yummy

Gratitude God 'a mercy, Ta, Thanks

Gratuitous, Gratuity Baksheesh, Beer-money, Bonsella, Bonus, Bounty, Cumshaw, Free, Glove-money, Gratis, Mag(g)s, Tip

Grave(yard) Accent, Arlington, Bass, Bier, Burial, Charnel, Chase, Critical, Darga, Demure, Dust, God's acre, Heavy, Heinous, Important, Ingroove, Kistvaen, Kurgan, Long home, Mool, Mould, Mound, Passage, Pit, Sad, Saturnine, Serious, Sober, Solemn, Sombre, Speos, Staid, Stern, Tomb, Watery

Grave-digger Bederal, Fossor, Sexton

Gravel(ly) Calculus, Channel, Chesil, Chisel, Eskar, Esker, Glareous, Grail(e), Grit, Hard, Hoggin(g), Murram, Nonplus, Pay, Pea, Pingo, Shingle

Gravity Barycentric, G, Geotaxis, Geotropism, Great Attraction, Magnitude, Mascon, Quantum, Specific, Weight, Zero

Gravy Baster, Bisto®, Browning, Coin, Jus, Milk, Sauce

Gravy-boat Argyle, Argyll

▶ **Gray** *see* **GREY**

Grayling Umber

Graze, Grazing, Grazier Abrade, Agist, Bark, Brush, Crease, Crop, Feed, Gride, Gryde, Heft, Herdwick, Leasow(e), Machair, Moorburn, Muirburn, Pascual, Pastoralist, Pasture, Rake, Rangeland, Scrape, Scrawn, Shave, Sheepwalk, Shieling, Zero

Grease, Greasy Bribe, Creesh, Dope, Dubbing, Elaeolite, Elbow, Enseam, Glit, Lanolin, Lard, Lubricate, Ointment, Pinguid, Saim, Seam(e), Shearer, Sheep-shearer, Smarm, Smear, Suint, Unctuous

Great(ly), Greater, Greatest, Greats Alfred, Ali, Astronomical, Brilliant, Bully, Capital, Classical, Colossus, Cosmic, Extreme, Fantastic, Gargantuan, Gatsby, Gay, Gey, Gran(d), Grit, Gt, Guns, Hellova, Helluva, Immortal, Important, Lion, Macro, Magnus, Main, Major, Massive, Mega, Mickle, Mochell, Modern, Much, Muchel(l), Muckle, No end, OS, Profound, Rousing, Splendiferous, Stoor, Stour, Stupendous, Sture, Sublime, Super, Superb, Swingeing, Synergy, Tall, Titan(ic), Top notch, Tremendous, Unco, Untold, Utmost, Vast, Voluminous, Wide, Zenith

Great deal Mort

Grebe Cargoose

Grecian Bend, Nose

Greed(y) Avarice, Avid, Bulimia, Bulimy, Cupidity, Edacious, Esurient, Gannet, Gare, Grabby, Grip(ple), Gulosity, Harpy, Insatiable, Killcrop, Lickerish, Liquorish, Mercenary, Money-grubbing, Piggery, Pleonexia, Rapacity, Selfish, Shark's manners, Solan, Voracity, Wolfish

Greek(s) Achaean, Achaian, Achilles, Aeolic, Agamemnon, Ajax, Ancient, Aonian, Arcadia, Archimedes, Argive, Aristides, Athenian, Attic, Boeotian, Byzantine, Cadmean, Cleruch, Corinthian, Cretan, Cumae, Cyzicus, Delphian, Demotic, Ding, Diomedes, Dorian, Doric, Elea, Eoka, Eolic, Epaminondas, Ephebe, Epirus, Euclid, Evzone, Fanariot, Gr, Helladic, Hellene, Hellenic, Hesychast, Homer, Hoplite, Ionian, Isocrates, Italiot(e), Javan, Katharev(o)usa, Klepht, Koine, Laconian, Lapith, Late, Leonidas, Linear B, Locrian, Lucian, Lysander, Macedonia, Medieval, Middle, Milesian, Modern, Molossian, Momus, Nestor, Nike, Nostos, Orestes, Paestum, Patroclus, Pelasgic, Pelopid, Perseus, Phanariot, Pythagoras, Romaic, Samiot, Seminole, Spartacus, Spartan, Stagirite, Strabo, Sybarite, Tean, Teian, Theban, Thersites, Theseus, Thessal(on)ian, Thracian, Timon, Typto, Uniat, Xenophon, Zorba

Green(ery) Almond, Apple, Avocado, Baggy, Bice, Biliverdin, Bleaching, Bottle, Bowling, Caesious, Callow, Celadon, Cerulein, Chard, Chartreuse, Chlorophyll, Chrome, Citron, Cole, Collard, Common, Copper, Corbeau, Crown, Cyan, Dioptase, Eau de nil, Eco-, Ecofriendly, Econut, Emerald, Emerande, Envious, Erin, Fingers, Foliage, Forest, Fundie, Fundy, Gaudy, Glaucous, Go, Goddess, Grass, Gretna, Gull, Immature, Inexpert, Jade, Jungle, Kendal, Kensal, Khaki, Lawn, Leafage, Lime, Lincoln, Loden, Lovat, Mead, Monastral®, Moss, Moulding, Naive, New, Nile, Oasis, Olive, Paris, Pea, Peridot, Pistachio, Porraceous, Putting, Raw, Realo, Reseda, Rifle, Rink, Sage, Sap, Scheele's, Sea, Sludge, Smaragdine, Sward, Teal, Tender, Terre-vert, Turacoverdin, Tyro, Unfledged, Uninitiated, Unripe, Untrained, Uranite, Verdant, Verd antique, Verdigris, Verdure, Vert, Virent, Virid, Vir(id)escent, Young

Greenheart Bebeeru

Greenhorn Baby, Dupe, Ingenue, Put(t), Rookie, Sucker

Greenhouse Conservatory, Cooohouse, Orangery, Phytotron, Polytunnel

Greens Broccoli, Cabbage, Calabrese, Cash, Money, Sprout, Vegetable(s)

Greet, Greeting(s) Abrazo, Accost, All hail, Aloha, Arvo, Banzai, Benedicite, Bid, Blubber, Bonsoir, Chimo, Ciao, Gorillagram, Hail, Hallo, Halse, Handclasp, Handshake, Haway, Heil, Heita, Hello, Herald, Hi, High-five, Hiya, Hongi, How, How d'ye do, Howsit, Jai Hind, Jambo, Kia ora, Kiss, Kissagram, Mihi, Namaskar, Namaste, Respects, Salaam, Salam alaikum, Salute, Salve, Save you, Sd, Shalom, Shalom aleichem, Sorry, Strippagram, Strippergram, Tena koe, Tena korua,

Tena koutou, Wave, → **WELCOME**, Wellmet, Wotcha, Wotcher, Yo

Gregarious Outgoing, Social

Gregorian Chant, NS, Plagal

▶ **Gremlin** *see* **GOBLIN**

Grenade, Grenadier Bomb, Egg, Fragmentation, Hand, Pineapple, Rat-tail, Rifle, Stun

Greta Garbo

Grey(ing), Gray, Greybeard Age, Agnes, Argent, Ashen, Ashy, Battleship, Beige, Bloncket, C(a)esius, Charcoal, Cinereous, Dapple, Dorian, Dove, Drab, Earl, Ecru, Feldgrau, Field, Glaucous, Gloomy, Gr, Gridelin, Griesie, Gries(l)y, Grise, Grisy, Grizzled, Gunmetal, Gy, Hoary, Hodden, Hore, Inn, Iron, Leaden, Liard, Livid, Lloyd, Lucia, Lyart, Mouse-coloured, Neutral, Oldster, Olive drab, Oyster, Pearl, Perse, Pewter, Poliosis, Putty, Sclate, Slaty, Steel, Taupe, Zane

Greyfriars Bunter, Magnet

Greyhound Grew, Italian, Lapdog, Longtail, Ocean, Persian, Saluki, Sapling, Whippet

Grey matter Cinerea

Grid(dle), Gridiron Bar, Barbecue, Brandreth, Cattle, Control, Dot matrix, Grate, Graticule, Grating, National, Network, Reseau, Reticle, Roo-bar, Screen, Starting, Suppressor, Tava(h), Tawa, Windscale

Gride Creak, Grate

Grief, Grievance, Grieve, Grievous Axe, Bemoan, Bitter, Complaint, Condole, Cry, Dear(e), Deere, Distress, Dole, Dolour, Gram(e), Gravamen, Grudge, Heartbreak, Hone, Illy, Io, → **MISERY**, Monody, Noyous, O(c)hone, Overset, Pain, Pathetic, Plaint, Rue, Score, Sore, Sorrow, Teen, Tene, Tragic, Wayment, Weeping, Woe, Wrong

Griffin Gripe, Grype, Novice, Pony

Grill(er), Grilling Braai, Brander, Broil, Carbonado, Crisp, Devil, Gridiron, Inquisition, Interrogate, Kebab, Mixed, Pump, Question, Rack, Radiator, Reja, Yakimona

Grim Austere, Dire, Dour, Forbidding, Gaunt, Glum, Gurly, Hard, Macabre, Stern

▷ **Grim** *may indicate* an anagram

Grimace Face, Girn, Moe, Mop, Moue, Mouth, Mow, Murgeon, Pout, Wince

Grime(s), Grimy Colly, Dirt, Grunge, Peter, Rechie, Reechie, Reechy, Soil, Sweep, Tash

Grin Fleer, Girn, Risus, Simper, Smirk, Sneer

Grind(ing), Grinder Bray, Bruxism, Chew, Crunch, → **CRUSH**, Droil, Drudgery, Gnash, Grate, Graunch, Grit, Home, Kern, Kibble, Labour, Levigate, Mano, Metate, Mill, Mince, Molar, Muller, Offhand, Pug, Pulpstone, Pulverise, Slog, Stamp, Triturate

Grip(ping), Gripper Absorb, Ascendeur, Bite, Chuck, Clam, Clamp, Cleat, Clip, Clutch, Craple, Dog, Embrace, Engrasp, Enthral, Get, Grapple, → **GRASP**, Haft, Hair, Hairpin, Hand(fast), Handhold, Headlock, Hend, Hold, Hug, Key, Kirby®, Lewis, Obsess, Pincer, Pinion, Pistol, Prehensile, Purchase, Raven, Rhine, Sally, Setscrew, Sipe, Strain, Streigne, Traction, Twist, Valise, Vice, Walise, Wrestle

Gripe(s) Colic, Complain, Ditch, Grasp, Griffin, Ileus, Pain, Tormina

Grisly Gory, Macabre

Grist Burden

Gristle, Gristly Cartilage, Chondroid, Lytta, Proteoglycan, Raven's bone

Grit(s), Gritty Blinding, Clench, Gnash, Granular, Grate, Guts, Hominy, Mattress, Millstone, Nerve, Pluck, Resolution, Sabulose, Sand, Shingle, Swarf, Valour, Yorkshire

Grizzle(d) Grey

Groan(er) Bewail, Bing, Moan, Titus

Grocer Grasshopper, Jorrocks, Pepperer, Symbol

Groggy Dazed, Shaky

Groin Gnarr, Inguinal, Lisk

▷ **Groom** *may indicate* an anagram

    Groom(ed) Brush, Coistrel, Coistril, Comb, Curry, Dress, Fettler, Kempt, Ostler, Palfrenier, Paranymph, Preen, Primp, Prink, S(a)ice, Smarten, Spouse, Strapper, Syce, Tiger, Tracer, Train, Wrangler

    Groove(s), Grooved, Groovy Bezel, Canal, Cannelure, Chamfer, Channel, Chase, Clevis, Cool, Coulisse, Croze, Dièdre, Exarate, Fissure, Flute, Fuller, Furr, Furrow, Glyph, Gouge, Hill and dale, Kerf, Key-seat, Keyway, Lead-in, Lead-out, Nock, Oche, Pod, Quirk, Rabbet, Race(way), Raggle, Raphe, Rare, Rebate, Rif(f)le, Rifling, Rigol(l), Rout, → **RUT**, Scrobe, Sipe, Slot, Sulcus, Throat, Track, Trough, Vallecula

    Grope(r) Feel, Fumble, Grabble, Hapuka, Ripe, Scrabble

    Gross All-up, Coarse, Coarse-grained, Complete, Crass, Dense, Earn, Earthy, Flagrant, Frankish, Fustilugs, Giant, Gr, Loathsome, Material, Obese, Outsize, Overweight, Pre-tax, Rank, Ribald, Rough, Stupid, Sum, Whole

▷ **Gross** *may indicate* an anagram

    Grotesque Antic, Bizarre, Fantastic, Fright, Gargoyle, Magot, Outlandish, Rabelaisian, Rococo, Teras

    Grotto Cave, Lupercal

▷ **Ground** *may indicate* an anagram

    Ground(s) Abthane, Arena, Astroturf, Basis, Bottom, Breeding, Campus, Cause, Common, Criterion, Crushed, Deck, Dregs, Eard, Earth, Edgbaston, Epig(a)eal, Epig(a)ean, Epig(a)eous, Epigene, Etching, Floor, Footing, Forbidden, Gathering, Grated, Grist, Grouts, Happy hunting, Headingley, High, Home, Hunting, Justification, Lees, Leeway, Lek, Lords, Lot, Marl, Meadow, Mealed, Middle, Motive, Occasion, Oval, Parade, Piste, Pitch, Plat, Pleasure, Plot, Policy, Proving, Quad, → **REASON**, Rec(reation), Réseau, Ring, Sandlot, Sediment, Slade, Soil, Solum, Sports, Stadium, Stamping, Strand, Terra, Terrain, Tom Tiddler's, Touch, Tract, Turf, Udal, Vantage, Venue, Waste(land), Yard, Yird

    Groundbait Chum

    Ground-breaker Pioneer

    Ground-crew Erk

    Ground-rent Crevasse

· **Groundsheet** Hutchie

    Groundsman Greenkeeper

    Group(ie), Grouping Abelian, Acyl, Affinity, 'A'list, Band, Batch, Battle, Beatles, Bee, Bevy, Bloc(k), Blood, Bloomsbury, Board, Body, Bracket, Bratpack, Break-out, Bruges, Bunch, Caboodle, Cadre, Camarilla, Camp, Cartel, Category, Caucus, Cave, Cell, Chain, Chordata, Circle, Clade, Clan, Class(is), Clique, Cluster, Clutch, Cohort, Colony, Combo, Commune, Community, Concertina, Confraternity, Conglomerate, Congregation, Consort(ium), Constellation, Contact, Contingent, Control, Convoy, Coterie, Covey, Crew, Decile, Dectet, Deme, Demi-monde, Denomination, Department, Detachment, Detail, Drove, Enclave, Encounter, Ensemble, Faction, Family, Fascio, Fauna, Flora, Focus, Fold, Follower, Fraternity, Front, Functional, Gaggle, Galère, Gang, Gemeinschaft, Gender, Generation, Genotype, Genus, Gesellschaft, Ginger, Globe, Guild, Hapu, Heading, Herd, Hexad, Hirsel, House, Income, In-crowd, Interest, Keiretsu, Ketone, Kit, Knob, Knot, League, Led

Zeppelin, Lichfield, Local, Lumpenproletariat, Marathon, Marshal, Minority, Minyan, Network, Nexus, Oasis, Order, Outfit, Oxford, Pack(et), Panel, Parti, Party, Passel, Peer, Phalange, Phratry, Phylum, Platoon, Pleiad, Plump, Pocket, Pod, Point, Pool, Pop, Posse, Pressure, Prosthetic, Push, Quincunx, Raceme, Racemose, Rap, Reading, Retinue, Ring, Rush, School, Sector, Seminar, Senate, Series, Set, Several, Sex, Shower, Society, Sort, Sorus, Splinter, Squad, Stick, Strain, Stream, String, Study, Subfamily, Sub-general, Sub-order, Subset, Support, Symbol, Syndicate, Synectics, T, Tales, Taxon, Team, Tetrad, Tithing, Topological, Trainband, T-Rex, Tribe, Tribune, Trilogy, Trio, Troika, Troop, Troupe, TU, Umbrella, Unit, User, Vertical, Vigilante, Workshop, Zaibatsu, Zupa

Grouse Black, Blackcock, Bleat, Blue, Caper(caillie), Capercailzie, Covey, Game, Gorcock, Greyhen, Gripe, Growl, Grumble, Hazel-hen, Heath-cock, Heathfowl, Heath-hen, Jeremiad, Moan, Moorcock, Moorfowl, Moor-pout, Muir-poot, Muir-pout, Mutter, Natter, Peeve, Pintail, Prairie-hen, Ptarmigan, Red, Red game, Resent, Ruffed, Rype(r), Sage, Sharp-tailed, Snarl, Spruce, Twelfth, Wheenge, W(h)inge, Willow

Grout Cement

Grove Academy, Arboretum, Bosk, Bosquet, Copse, Glade, Hurst, Lyceum, Motte, Nemoral, Orchard, Orchat, Silva, Tope

Grovel Cheese, Crawl, Creep, Fawn, Ko(w)tow, Worm

Grow(ing), Grow out, Growth Accrete, Accrue, Acromegaly, Adenoma, Aggrandisement, Angioma, Apophysis, Arborescence, Auxesis, Bedeguar, Boom, Braird, Breer, Burgeon, Car(b)uncle, Carcinoma, Chancre, Cholelith, Chondroma, Compensatory, Condyloma, Corn, Crescendo, Crop, Culture, Cyst, Down, Ectopia, Edema, Ellagic, Enate, Enchondroma, Enlarge, Epinasty, Epitaxy, Excrescence, Exostosis, Expansion, Fibroid, Flor, Flourish, Flush, Gain, Gall, Germinate, Get, Goitre, Hepatocele, Hummie, Hyperostosis, Hyponasty, Increase, Keloidal, Keratosis, Knur(r), Lichen, Lipoma, Mole, Monopodial, Moss, Mushroom, Myoma, Nur(r), Oedema, Oncology, Osselet, Osteoma, Osteophyte, Pharming, Polyp, Polypus, Proleg, Proliferate, Rampant, Rank, Scirrhus, Scopa, Septal, Snowball, Spavin, → **SPROUT**, Stalagmite, Stand, Stipule, Sympodial, Tariff, Thigmotropism, Thrive, Trichome, → **TUMOUR**, Tylosis, Vegetable, Wart, Wax, Weed, Wox

▷ **Grow(n)** *may indicate* an anagram

Growl(ing), Growler Fremescent, Gnar, Groin, Grr, Gurl, Iceberg, Roar(e), Roin, Royne, Snar(l)

Grown up Adult, Mature, Risen

Groyne Breakwater

Grub(by) Assart, Aweto, Bardie, Bardy, Bookworm, Caddis, Caterpillar, Cheer, Chow, Chrysalis, Deracinate, Dig, Eats, Fare, Fodder, → **FOOD**, Gentle, Groo-groo, Gru-gru, Larva, Leatherjacket, Mawk, Mess, Nosh, Palmerworm, Peck, Pupa, Root(le), Rout, Rowt, Sap, Slave, Stub, Tired, Wireworm, Witchetty, Wog, Worm

Grudge, Grudging Chip, Derry, Envy, Grievance, Grutch, Resent, Score, Sparse, Spite, Spleen

Gruel Brochan, Bross, Loblolly, Skilligalee, Skilligolee, Skilly

Gruesome Ghastly, Grisly, Grooly, Horror, Livid, Macaberesque, Macabre, → **MORBID**, Sick

Gruff Guttural, Hoarse, Surly

Grumble Beef, Bellyache, Bitch, Bleat, Chunter, Crab, Croak, Girn, Gripe, Grizzle, Groin, Growl, Moan, Murmur, Mutter, Nark, Natter, Repine, Rumble, Whinge, Yammer

Grump(y) Attercop, Bearish, Cross, Ettercap, Grouchy, Moody, Sore-headed, Surly

Grunt Groin, Grumph, Humph, Oink, Pigfish, Spanish, Ugh, Wheugh
Guano Dung, Sombrerite
Guanoco Llama
Guarantee Accredit, Assure, Avouch, Certify, Ensure, Gage, Hallmark, Insure,
  Mainprise, Money-back, Pignerate, Pignorate, → **PLEDGE**, Plight, Seal, Secure,
  Sponsion, Surety, Underwrite, → **VOUCHSAFE**, Warn, Warrandice, Warrant(y)
Guard(ed), Guards Acolouthos, Advance, Apron, Beefeaters, Blues, Bostangi,
  Bouncer, Bracer, Cabiri, Cage, Cag(e)y, Centry, Cerberus, Chamfrain, Chaperon(e),
  Chary, Cheesemongers, Cherry-pickers, Coast, Coldstream, Colour, Conductor,
  Cordon, Crinoline, Curator, Custodian, Custos, Diehards, Dragoons, Duenna,
  Equerry, Escort, Eunuch, Excubant, Exon, Fence, Fender, Gaoler, Gateman,
  Gauntlet, Grenadiers, Greys, Hedge, Home, Horse, INS, Insure, Iron, Irish, Jaga,
  Jailer, Keep, Lancers, Life, Lilywhites, Look out, Mask, Mort-safe, National,
  Nightwatch(man), Nutcrackers, Out-rider, Out-sentry, Pad, Palace, Patrol, Picket,
  Point, Praetorian, → **PROTECT**, Provost, Quillon, Rail, Red, Ride, Roof, Screw,
  Secure, Security, Sentinel, Sentry, Shadow, Shield, Shin, Shopping, Shotgun,
  Splashback, Splashboard, Splasher, SS, Strelitz, Streltzi, Swiss, Switzer, Tapadera,
  Tapadero, Tile, Toecap, Tsuba, Turnkey, Vambrace, Vamplate, Varangian,
  Vigilante, Visor, Wage, Wait(e), Ward, Warder, Wary, Watch (and ward),
  Watchdog, Watchman, Wear, Weir, Wire, Yeoman
Guardian Agathodaimon, Altair, Argus, Curator, Custodian, Custos, Dragon,
  Gemini, Granthi, Hafiz, Janus, Julius, Miminger, Patron, Protector, Templar,
  Trustee, Tutelar(y), Tutor, Warder, Watchdog, Xerxes
Guatemala(n) Mam
Gudgeon Fish, Pin, Trunnion
Gue(r)rilla Bushwhacker, Chetnik, Comitadji, Contra, ETA, Fedayee, Gook, Haiduk,
  Heyduck, Irregular, Khmer Rouge, Komitaji, Maquis, Mujahadeen, Mujahed(d)in,
  Mujahedeen, Mujahideen, Partisan, Phalanx, Red Brigade, Tamil Tiger, Terrorist,
  Tupamaro, Urban, Viet Cong, Zapata, Zapatista
Guenon Grivet, Vervet
Guess Aim, Aread, Arede, Arreede, Assume, Conjecture, Divine, Estimate, Harp,
  Hazard, Hunch, Imagine, Infer, Level, Mor(r)a, Mull, Psych out, Shot, Speculate,
  Stab, Suppose, Surmise, Theorise, Venture
Guessing game Handy-dandy, Mor(r)a, Quiz
Guest(s) Caller, Company, House-party, Inquiline, Invitee, Parasite, Paying, PG,
  Symbion(t), Symphile, Synoecete, Umbra, Visitant, → **VISITOR**, Xenial
Guesthouse B & B, Minshuku, Taverna, Xenodochium
Guff Bosh, Gas
Guianian S(a)ouari
Guidance, Guide, Guideline, Guiding Advice, Antibarbus, Aunt, Auspice,
  Baedeker, Bradshaw, Cicerone, Clue, Command, Concordance, Conduct, Counsel,
  Courier, Curb, Cursor, Director(y), Docent, Dragoman, Drive, Engineer, → **ESCORT**,
  Field, Gillie, Graticule, Helm, Heuristic, Homing, Index, Inertial, Inspire, Itinerary,
  Jig, Key, Lad, Landmark, Lead, Lodestar, Map, Mark, Marriage, Mentor, Michelin,
  Missile, Model, Navaid, Navigate, Nose, Pelorus, Pilot, Pointer, Postil(l)ion,
  Principle, Queen's, Rainbow, Range, Ranger, Reference, Rein, Relate, Rudder,
  Sabot, Shepherd, Sherpa, Shikaree, Shikari, Sight, Sign, Sixer, Stear, Steer, Stire,
  Template, Templet, Terminal, Terrestrial, Tiller, Train, Travelogue, Tutelage,
  Vocational, Voyageur, Waymark, Weise, Weize, Wise
Guild Artel, Basoche, Company, Freemason, Gyeld, Hanse, Hoastman, League,
  Mistery, Mystery, Society, Tong, Union

Guile Art, Cunning, Deceit, Dole, Malengine

Guillotine Closure, Decapitate, Louisiette, Maiden, Marianne

Guilt(y) Affluenza, Angst, Blame, Cognovit, Flagitious, Hangdog, Mea culpa, Nocent, Peccavi, Remorse, Wicked

Guinea(s) Canary, Geordie, Gns, Job, Ls, Meg, Spade

Guinea-fowl Pintado

Guinea-pig Abyssinian, Agoute, Agouti, Cavie, Cavy, Paca, Subject

Guinea-worm Dracunculus

Guise Form, Manner, Shape

Guitar(ist) Acoustic, Axe(man), Bass, Bottleneck, Cithern, Cittern, Dobro®, Electric, Fender®, Gittarone, Gittern, Hawaiian, Humbucker, Lute, Lyre, Pedal steel, Plankspanker, Samisen, Sancho, Sanko, Shamisen, Sitar, Slide, Spanish, Steel, Uke, Ukulele

Gulf Aden, Anadyr, Aqaba, Bay, Bothnia, California, Cambay, Campeche, Carpentaria, Chasm, Chihli, Corinth, Cutch, Darien, Dvina, Exmouth, Fonseca, Genoa, Gonaives, Hauraki, Honduras, Iskenderun, Isthmus, Izmit, Joseph Bonaparte, Kutch, Lepanto, Leyte, Lingayen, Lions, Mannar, Martaban, Maw, Mexico, Ob, Patras, Persian, Pozzuoli, Queen Maud, Rapallo, Riga, St Lawrence, St Vincent, Salerno, Salonika, Saronic, Saros, Siam, Sidra, Spencer, Taganrog, Taranto, Tongking, Tonkin, Trieste, Tunis, Van Diemen, Venice, Vorago

Gull(s) Black-backed, Bonxie, Cheat, Cob(b), Cod, Cony, Cozen, Cull(y), Dupe, Fool, Geck, Glaucous, Haglet, Have, Hoodwink, Hum, Ivory, Kittiwake, Laridae, Larus, Maw, Mew, Mollyhawk, Pickmaw, Pigeon, Queer, Rook, Sabine's, Saddleback, Scaury, Scourie, Scowrie, Sea-cob, Sea-mew, Sell, Simp, Skua, Sucker, Swart-back, Tern, Tystie, Xema

Gullet Crop, Enterate, Maw, Oesophagus, Throat, Weasand-pipe

Gullible Green, Mug punter, Naive, Starry-eyed, Sucker

Gulliver Lemuel

Gully Couloir, Donga, Fielder, Geo, Gio, Goe, Grough, Gulch, Infielder, Pit, Rake, Ravine, Sloot, Sluit, Wadi

Gulp Bolt, Draught, Gollop, Quaff, Slug, Sob, → SWALLOW, Swig, Swipe, Wolf

Gum (tree) Acacia, Acajou, Acaroid, Agar, Algin, Angico, Arabic, Arabin, Arar, Arctic, Asafoetida, Bablah, Balata, Balm, Bandoline, Bdellium, Benjamin, Benzoin, Bloodwood, Blue, Boot, Bubble, Cerasin, Chicle, Chuddy, Chutty, Coolabah, Courbaril, Cow®, Dextrin(e), Dragon's-blood, Ee-by, Eucalyptus, Euphorbium, Flooded, Frankincense, Galbanum, Gamboge, Ghost, Gingival, → GLUE, Goat's-thorn, Gosh, Grey, Guar, Ironbark, Juniper, Karri, Kauri, La(b)danum, Lac, Lentisk, Mastic(h), Mucilage, Myrrh, Nicotine, Olibanum, Opopanax, Oshac, Red, River red, Sagapenum, Sarcocolla, Scribbly, Size, Sleep, Snow, Spearmint, Spirit, Starch, Sterculia, Stringybark, Sugar, Sweet, Tacamahac, Tragacanth, Tupelo, Ulmin, Water, White, Xanthan

Gumbo Okra

Gumboil Parulis

Gumption Nous, Spirit

Gun(fire), Guns, Gunfight Amusette, Archibald, Archie, Arquebus, Automatic, Barker, Baton, Bazooka, Beanbag, Beretta, Big Bertha, Biscayan, Blunderbuss, Bofors, Bombard, Breech(-loader), Bren, Broadside, Brown Bess, Browning, Bulldog, Bullpup, Bundook, Burp, Caliver, Cannonade, Carbine, Carronade, Cement, Chokebore, Chopper, Coehorn, Colt®, Dag, Derringer, Electron, Elephant, Escopette, Falcon(et), Field, Fieldpiece, Firearm, Fire lock, Flame, Flash, Flintlock, Four-pounder, Fowler, Fowlingpiece, Full-bore, Garand, Gas, Gat(ling), Gingal(l),

Grease, HA, Hackbut, Half-cock, Harquebus, Heater, Hired, Howitzer, Jezail, Jingal, Kalashnikov, Lewis, Long Tom, Luger®, Machine, Magazine, Magnum, Maroon, Martini-Henry®, Matchlock, Mauser®, Maxim, Metal, Minnie, Minute, Mitrailleuse, Morris Meg, Mortar, Musket(oon), Muzzle-loader, Nail, Needle, Neutron, Noonday, Oerlikon, Ordnance, Over and under, Owen, Paderero, Paterero, Ped(e)rero, Pelican, Perrier, Petronel, Piece, Pistol(et), Pompom, Pump (action), Punt, Purdey®, Quaker, Radar, Ray, Repeater, Rev, Revolver, Riot, Rod, Roscoe, Saker, Sarbacane, Scatter, Self-cocker, Shooter, Shooting iron, Shoot-out, Sidearm, Siege, Smoothbore, Snapha(u)nce, Spear, Speed, Spray, Squirt, Staple, Starting, Sten, Sterculia, Sterling, Stern-cannon, Stern-chaser, Stun, Swivel, Taser®, Tea, Thirty eight, Thompson, Tier, Time, Tommy, Tool, Tupelo, Turret, Uzi, Walther, Wesson, Young, Zip

Gunge Gowl, Paste

Gunman Ace, Assassin, Bandit, Earp, Greaser, Pistoleer, Sniper, Starter

Gunner, Gunner's assistant Arquebusier, Arsenal, Artillerist, Cannoneer, Cannonier, Culverineer, Gr, Matross, RA

Gunpowder Charcoal, Pebble-powder, Saucisse, Saucisson

Gunwale Gunnel, Portland, Portlast, Portoise

Guppy Million

Gurgle Burble, Clunk, Glug, Gobble, Gollar, Goller, Guggle, Ruckle, Squelch

Gurnard Tubfish

Guru Lifestyle, Sadhu, Teacher

Gush(ing) Blether, Effusive, → **FLOOD**, Flow, Jet, Outpour, Rail, Raile, Regurgitate, Rhapsodize, Scaturient, Spirt, Spout, Spurt, Too-too

Gusset Godet, Gore, Insert, Inset, Mitre

Gust Blast, Blore, Flaught, Flaw, Flurry, Puff, Sar, Waff

Gusto Élan, Relish, Verve, Zest

Gut(s), Gutty Abdomen, Archenteron, Balls, Beer, Bowel(s), Chitterlings, Cloaca, Disembowel, Draw, Duodenum, Enteral, Enteron, Entrails, Fore, Gill, Hind, Ileum, Insides, Kyle, Mesenteron, Mid, Minikin, Omental, Omentum, Purtenance, Remake, Sack, Sand, Snell, Stamina, Staying-power, Strip, Thairm, Tripe, Ventriculus, Viscera

Gutta-percha Jelutong, Pontianac, Pontianak

Gutter(ing) Arris, Channel, Conduit, Coulisse, Cullis, Grip, Gully, Kennel, Rhone, Rigol(l), Roan, Rone, Sough, Spout, Strand, Swale, Swayl, Sweal, Sweel

Guttersnipe Arab, Gamin, Thief

Guttural Faucal, Throaty

Guy Backstay, Bo, Burgess, Cat, Chaff, Clewline, Decamp, Deride, Effigy, Fall, Fawkes, Fellow, Gink, Josh, Mainstay, Mannering, Parody, Rib, Rope, Scarecrow, Stay, Taunt, Tease, Vang, Wise

Guzzle(d) Gannet, Gorge, Go(u)rmandize, Overeat, Snarf

Gwyn Nell

Gym(nasium), Gymnast(ic) Acrobat, Akhara, Arena, Contortionist, Dojo, Exercise, Jungle, Lyceum, Palaestra, PE, PT, Rhythmic, Sokol, Tumbler, Turner

Gymnosophist , Yogi

Gypsum Alabaster, Gesso, Plaster, Satin-stone, Selenite, Terra alba

Gypsy, Gipsy Bohemian, Cagot, Caird, Caqueux, Chai, Chal, Chi, Collibert, Egyptian, Esmeralda, Faw, Gipsen, Gitano, Hayraddin, Lavengro, Meg, Pikey, Rom(any), Rye, Scholar, Tinker, Traveller, Travelling folk, Tsigane, Tzigane, Tzigany, Vagabond, Vlach, Walach, Wanderer, Zigan, Zigeuner, Zincala, Zincalo, Zingaro

Gyrate Revolve, Rotate, → **SPIN**, Twirl

Hh

H Ache, Aitch, Aspirate, Height, Hospital, Hotel, Hydrant, Hydrogen

Haberdasher(y) Clothier, Ferret, Hosier, Notions

Habit(s), Habitual, Habituate, Habitué Accustom, Addiction, Apparel, Assuefaction, Assuetude, Bent, Cacoethes, Chronic, Clothes, Coat, Consuetude, Crystal, Custom, Diathesis, Dress, Ephod, Frequenter, Garb, Hand-me-down, Inure, Inveterate, Motley, Mufti, Nature, Outfit, Pathological, Practice, Raiment, Regular, Riding, Robe, Rochet, Routine, Scapular, Schema, Season, Second nature, Set, Soutane, Suit, Surplice, Toge, Trait, Trick, Tway, Usual, Way, Won, Wont, Xerotes

Habitat(ion) Element, Environment, Haunt, Home, Locality, Station, Tel

Hacienda Ranch

Hack(er) Blackhat, Chip, Chop, Cough, Cut, Drudge, Garble, Gash, Ghost, Grub-Street, Hag, Hash, Hedge-writer, Heel, Hew, Horse, Journo, Mangle, Mutilate, Nag, Notch, Pad, Paper-strainer, Penny-a-liner, Phreak, Pick, Plater, Pot-boiler, Rosinante, Script kiddie, Spurn, Steed, Tadpole, Taper, Tap into, Tiger team, Tussis, Unseam, White hat

Hackle(s) Comb, Rough

Hackney(ed) Banal, Cab, Cliché, Corny, Percoct, Stale, Threadbare, Tired, Trite, Worn

Had (to) Moten, Must, Obliged, Threw

Haddock Arbroath smokie, Findram, Finnan, Fish, Norway, Rizzered, Smoky, Speldin(g), Speldrin(g), Whitefish

Hades Dis, Hell, Orcus, Pit, Tartarus

Haematite Oligist

Haemoglobin Chelate, Hb

Haemorrhoids Farmer Giles, Piles

Hafnium Hf

Hag(-like) Anile, Beldame, Besom, Carlin(e), Crone, Harpy, Harridan, Hell-cat, Hex, Moss, Nickneven, Occasion, Rudas, Runnion, Sibyl, Trot, Underwood, Witch

Haggard Drawn, → **GAUNT**, Pale, Rider

Haggis Kishke

Haggle Argue, Badger, → **BARGAIN**, Barter, Chaffer, Dicker, Horse-trade, Niffer, Palter, Prig

Ha-ha Dike, So there, Sunk-fence

Hahnium Hn

Hail(er) Acclaim, Ahoy, Ave, Bull-horn, Cheer, Fusillade, Graupel, Greet, Gunfire, Hi, Ho, Megaphone, Salue, Salute, Shower, Signal, Skoal, Skol, Sola, Stentor, Storm, Trumpet, What ho, Whoa-ho-ho

Hair(y), Haircut, Hairlike, Hair problem/condition, Hair style Afro, Ailes de pigeon, Ainu, Alopecia, Backcomb, Baldy, Bang, Barnet, Beard, Beehive, Bezoar, Bingle, Bob, Bouffant, Braid, Brede, Bristle, Brutus, Bumfluff, Bun, Bunches,

Bush, Butch, Cadogan, Camel, Capillary, Catogan, Chignon, Cilia, Cleopatra, Coat, Cockernony, Coif, Coiffure, Comal, Comate, Combings, Comb-over, Comose, Cornrow, Corymbus, Cowlick, Crepe, Crew-cut, Crinal, Cronet, Crop, Cue, Curlicue, DA, Dangerous, Dreadlocks, Dubbing, Duck's arse, Ducktail, Earmuffs, Elf locks, En brosse, Esau, Excrement, Eyelash, Feather, Feather-cut, Fetlock, Fibril, Filament, Flat-top, Floccus, Forelock, French pleat, French roll, Frenulum, Fringe, Fur, Garconne, Glib(s), Glochidium, Guard, Hackles, Heare, Heer(i)e, Hispid, Hog, Indumentum, Kemp, Kesh, Lanugo, Lash, List, Lock, Lovelock, Lowlights, Madarosis, Mane, Marcel, Mohawk, Mohican, Mop, Mullet, Muttonchops, Not(t), Number two, Pageboy, Pappus, Pashm, Peekabo(o), Pele(s), Pelt, Perm(anent), Pigtail, Pika, Pile, Pilus, Pincurl, Plait, Plica, Plica Polonica, Pompadour, Ponytail, Poodle cut, Porcupine, Pouf(fe), Pow, Prison crop, Psilosis, Puberulent, Pubescent, Pudding basin, Punk, Queue, Quiff, Radicle, Rat-tail, Red mullet, Rhizoid, Roach, Root, Rush, Scaldhead, Scalp lock, Scopate, Scopula, Sericeous, Set, Shag, Shingle, Shock, Sideburns, Sidelock, Snell, Spikes, Stinging, Strammel, Strand, Strigose, Strummel, Switch, Sycosis, Tête, Thatch, Tomentose, Tonsure, Toorie, Topknot, Tour(ie), Tragus, Tress, Trichoid, Trichology, Trichome, Trichosis, Trim, Velutinous, Vibrissi, Villi, Villosity, Villus, Wedge, Widow's peak, Wig, Wisp, → **WOOL**, Xerasia

Hair-cream, Hair-oil Conditioner, Pomade

Hairdresser Barber, Coiffeur, Comb, Crimper, Friseur, Marcel, Salon, Stylist, Trichologist

Hairless Bald, Callow, Glabrate, Glabrescent, Glabrous, Irate

Hairline Brow, Nape

Hairnet Kell, Snood

Hairpiece Frisette, Merkin, Postiche, Strand, Toupee, → **WIG**

Hairpin Barrette, Bodkin, Slide, U, U-turn

Hair-shirt Ab(b)a, Cilice

Haiti RH

Hal Prince

Halberd Spontoon

Halcyon Calm, Kingfisher, Mild

Hale(r) Drag, Healthy, Koruna, Raucle, Robust, Well

Half, Halved Bifid, Demi, Dimidiate, Dirempt, Divide, Hemi, Moiety, Semi, Share, Split, Stand-off, Term

Half-a-dozen Six, VI

Half-asleep, Half-conscious Dove, Dozy

Half-baked Foolish, Mediocre, Samel, Slack-bake

Half-breed, Half-caste Bastard, Baster, Creole, Eurasian, Mameluco, Mestee, Mestiza, Mestizo, Metif, Métis(se), Miscegen, Mongrel, Mulatto, Mustee, Octaroon, Quadroon, Quarteroon, Quintero, Quintroon, Sambo, Yellow-boy, Yellow-girl, Zambo

Half-guinea Smelt

Half-hearted Reluctant, Tepid

Half-hour Bell

Half-pence, Half-penny Mag, Magpie, Maik, Mail(e), Make, Obolus, Patrick, Portcullis, Posh, Rap, Wood's

Half-turn Caracol(e), Demivolt

Half-wit Changeling, Mome, Simpleton, → **STUPID**

Hall Anteroom, Apadana, Assembly, Atrium, Auditorium, Aula, Bachelor's, Basilica, Bingo, Carnegie, Casino, Chamber, Citadel, City, Concert, Concourse,

Corridor, Dance, Divinity, Dojo, Domdaniel, Dome, Dotheboys, Ex(h)edra, Festival, Foyer, Gallen, Guild, Hardwick, Holkham, Judgement, Kedleston, Liberty, Lobby, Locksley, Megaron, Mess, Moot, Music, Narthex, Newby, Odeon, Palais, Palais de danse, Passage, Prytaneum, Rathaus, Rideau, Salle, Saloon, Stationer's, Tammany, Tara, Tolsel, Town, Trullen, Valhalla, Vestibule, Walhall(a), Wildfell

Hallmark(ed) Brand, Contrôlé, Logo, Platemark, Seal, Stamp

Hallow Consecrate, Revere, Worship

Hallucinate, Hallucination, Hallucinogen Autoscopy, DT's, Fantasy, Formication, Freak, Freak out, Illusion, Image, Mirage, Negative, Photism, Psilocin, Psilocybin, Psychedelic, Trip

Halo Antheolion, Areola, Aura, Aureola, Corona, Galactic, Gloria, Gloriole, Mandorla, Nimbus, Rim, Vesica, Vesica piscis

Halogen Iodine

Halt(er) Abort, Arrest, Block, Brake, Bridle, Cavesson, Cease, Check, End, Full stop, Game, Hackamore, Heave-to, Hilch, Lame(d), Limp, Noose, Prorogue, Rope, Stall, Standstill, Staw, → **STOP**, Stopover, Toho, Tyburn-tippet, Whoa

Ham(s) Amateur, Barnstormer, Flitch, Gammon, Haunch, Hock, Hoke, Hough, Hunker, Jambon, Jay, Mutton, Nates, Overact, Overplay, Parma, Pigmeat, Prat, Prosciutto, Radio, Serrano, Tiro, Westphalian, York

Hamfisted Maladroit, Unheppen

Hamite Berber, Nilot(e)

Hamlet(s) Aldea, Auburn, Cigar, Clachan, Dane, Dorp, Hero, Kraal, Stead, Thorp(e), Tower, Vill(age), Wick

Hammer(ed), Hammerhead, Hammering About-sledge, Atmospheric, Ballpeen, Ballpein, Beetle, Bully, Bush, Celt, Claw, Dolly, Drop, Excudit, Flatten, Fore, Fuller, Gavel, Hack, Incuse, Jack, Kevel, Knap, Knapping, Kusarigama, Lump, Madge, Mall(et), Malleate, Martel, Maul, Mjol(l)nir, Monkey, Nevel, Oliver, Pane, Pean, Peen, Pein, Pene, Percussion, Percussor, Piledriver, Planish, Plessor, Plexor, Pneumatic, Rawhide, Repoussé, Rip, Rout, Sheep's-foot, Shingle, Sledge, Steam, Stone, Strike, Tack, Tenderizer, Tendon, Tilt, Trip, Umbre, Water, Wippen

▷ **Hammered** *may indicate* an anagram

Hammerthrower Thor

Hammock Cott

▷ **Hammy** *may indicate* an anagram

Hamper Basket, Cabin, Ceroon, Cramp, Cumber, Delay, Encumber, Entrammel, Hamstring, Handicap, Hobble, Hog-tie, Obstruct, Pad, Pannier, Ped, Pinch, Restrict, Rub, Sero(o)n, Shackle, Tangle, Trammel, Tuck

Hamster Cricetus, Idea

Hamstring Cramp, Hock, Hox, Lame, Popliteal, Thwart

Hand(s), Hand over, Hand down, Hand-like, Handwriting Assist(ance), Bananas, Bequeath, Cacography, Calligraphy, Charge, Chicane, Chirography, Clap(ping), Claque, Club, Clutch, Copperplate, Court, Crabbed, Crew, Cursive, Dab, Daddle, Danny, Dawk, Dead, Deal, Deck, Deliver, Devolve, Donny, Dukes, Dummy, Famble, Fin, Fist, Flipper, Flush, Free, Full, Glad, Graphology, Half-text, Help, Helping, Hidden, Hond, Hour, Impart, Iron, Israel, Italian, Jambone, Jamboree, Jemmy, Kana, L, Laydown, Lone, Loof, Man, Manual, Manus, Maulers, Medieval, Minute, Mitt(en), Mutton-fist, Nes(h)ki, Niggle, Operative, Orthography, Pad, Palaeography, Palm(atifid), Part, Pass, Paw, Podium, Post, Pud, R, Referral, Rein (arm), Round, Running, Script, Second, Secretary, Signature, Span, Spencerian, Stage, Station, Straight, Sweep, Text, Tiger, Uncial, Upper, Whip, Widow, Worker, Yarborough

Handbag Caba(s), Grip, Indispensable, Pochette, Purse, Reticule, Valise

Handbook Baedeker, Companion, Enchiridion, Guide, Manual, Vade-mecum

Handcuff(s) Bracelet, Darbies, Golden, Irons, Manacle, Mittens, Nippers, Snaps, Wristlet

Handful Few, Gowpen, Grip, Hank, Problem, Pugil, Rip(p), V

Handicap Bisque, Burden, Cambridgeshire, Ebor, Encumber, Half-one, Hamper, Impede, Impost, Lame, Liability, Lincolnshire, Mental, → **OBSTACLE**, Off, Physical, Restrict, Weigh(t), Welter-race

Handicraft Marquetry

Handkerchief, Hanky Bandan(n)a, Belcher, Billy, Buffon, Clout, Fogle, Foulard, Kleenex®, Madam, Madras, Monteith, Mouchoir, Muckender, Napkin, Nose-rag, Orarium, Romal, Rumal, Sudary, Tissue, Wipe(r)

Handle(d) Ansate, Bail, Bale, Behave, Bitstock, Brake, Broomstick, Cope, Crank, Dead man's, Deal, Doorknob, Dudgeon, Ear, Feel, Finger, Forename, Gaum, Gorm, Grab, Grip, Gunstock, Haft, Helve, Hilt, Hold, Knob, Knub, Lug, → **MANAGE**, Manipulate, Manubrium, Maul, Moniker, Name, Nib, Palp, Paw, Pistol-grip, Pommel, Process, Rounce, Shaft, Snath(e), Snead, Sneath, Sned, Staff, Staghorn, Stale, Starting, Steal(e), Steel, Steil, Stele, Stilt, Stock, Sweep, Tiller, Title, To-name, Touch, Transact, Treat, Use, Whipstock, Wield, Withe

Handmaid(en) Iras, Manicurist, Valkyrie

Hand-out Alms, Charity, Dole, Gift, Release, Sample

Handshake Golden

Hand-signal Beck(on), Point, Wave

Handsome Adonis, Apollo, Attractive, Bonny, Brave, Comely, Dashing, Dishy, Featuous, Fine, Gracious, Kenneth, Liberal, Seemly

Handspring, Handstand Cartwheel, Diamodov

Hand-warmer Muff, Pome

Hand-washer Pilate

▸ **Handwriting** *see* **HAND**

Handy(man) Accessible, Close, Convenient, Deft, Dext(e)rous, Digit, Factotum, Gemmy, Get-at-able, Jack(-of-all-trades), Jemmy, Near, Nigh, Palmate, Palmist, Ready, Skilful, Spartan, Useful

Hang, Hanger, Hanging(s) Append, Arras, Aweigh, Chick, Chik, Coat, Curtain, Dangle, Darn, Depend, Dewitt, Dossal, Dossel, Dosser, Drape, Droop, Execute, Frontal, Gobelin, Hinge, Hoove, Hove(r), Kakemono, Kilt, Lime, Lobed, Loll, Lop, Lynch, Mooch, Noose, Nub, Pend(ant), Sag, Scenery, Scrag, Set, Sit, Sling, String up, Suspend, Suspercollate, Swing, Tapestry, Tapet, Tapis, The rope, Toran(a)

Hanger-on Bur, Lackey, Leech, Limpet, Liripoop, Parasite, Satellite, Sycophant, Tassel, Toady

Hangman, Hangmen Bull, Calcraft, Dennis, Derrick, Gregory, Ketch, Lockman, Marwood, Nubbing-cove, Pierrepoint, Topsman

Hangnail Agnail

Hangover Canopy, Cornice, Crapulence, Drape, DT's, Head, Hot coppers, Katzenjammer, Mistletoe, Remnant, Tester, Valance

Hank Bobbin, Coil, Fake, Lock, Skein

Hanker(ing) Desire, Envy, Hunger, Itch, Long, Yearn, Yen

Hannibal Lecter, Punic

Hansard Minutes

Haphazard Casual, Chance, Helter-skelter, Higgledy-piggledy, Hit and miss, Hitty-missy, Promiscuous, → **RANDOM**, Rough and tumble, Scattershot, Slapdash, Willy-nilly

Happen(ing), Happen to Afoot, Are, Be, Befall, Befortune, Betide, Come, Crop up, Event(uate), Fall-out, Materialise, → **OCCUR**, Pan, Pass, Prove, Subvene, Thing, Tide, Transpire, Worth

Happiness, Happy Apposite, Ave, Beatific, Beatitude, Blessed, Bliss, Bluebird, Bonny, Carefree, Cheery, Chuffed, Cloud nine, Cock-a-hoop, Dwarf, Ecstatic, Elated, Eud(a)emony, Exhilarated, Felicity, Felix, Fool's paradise, Fortunate, Glad(some), Gleeful, Golden, Goshen, Gruntled, Halcyon, Half-cut, Hedonism, High-feather, Jovial, Joy, Kvell, Larry, Light-hearted, Merry, Opportune, Radiant, Rapture, Sandboy, Seal, Seel, Sele, Serene, Slap, Sunny, Tipsy, Trigger, Warrior

Hara-kiri Eventration, Seppuku, Suicide

Harangue Declaim, Diatribe, Earwigging, Lecture, Oration, Perorate, Philippic, Sermon, Speech, Spruik, Tirade

Harass(ed) Afflict, Annoy, Badger, Bait, Beleaguer, Beset, Bother, Chivvy, Distract, Dun, Gall, Grill, Grind, Grounden, Hassle, Haze, Heckle, Hector, Henpeck, Hound, Importune, Irritate, Needle, Persecute, Pester, Plague, Press, Tailgate, Thwart, Trash, Vex

Harbinger Herald, Omen, Precursor, Usher

Harbour(ed) Alee, Anchorage, Basin, Brest, Cherish, Dock, Entertain, Foster, Heard, Herd, Hide, Hythe, Incubate, Lodge, Manukau, Marina, Mulberry, Nurse, Pearl, PLA, Poole, Port, Quay, Reset, Scapa Flow, Seaport, → **SHELTER**, Watemata, Waterfront, Wellington

Hard(en), Hardness Abstruse, Adamant(ine), Adularia, Augean, Austere, Billy-o, Bony, Brindell, Brinell, Brittle, Bronze, Cake, Calcify, Callous, Caramel, Cast-iron, Chitin, Concrete, Cornute, Crusty, Dentin(e), Difficult, Dour, Draconian, Ebonite, Endure, Enure, Exacting, Firm, Flint(y), Geal, Granite, Gruelling, H, Hawkish, Hellish, Herculean, HH, Horny, Indurate, Inure, Iron(y), Jasper, Knotty, Liparite, Lithoid, Metallic, Metally, Moh, Moh's scale, Murder, Nails, Obdurate, Obdure, Osseous, Ossify, Permafrost, Permanent, Petrify, Picrite, Raw, Rugged, Ruthless, Scirrhus, Schist, Scleral, Set, Severe, Solid, Sore, Steel(y), Steep, Stereo, Stern, Sticky, Stiff, Stoic, Stony, Strongly, Teak, Temper, Temporary, Tough, Wooden

Hardback Case-bound

Hardboard Masonite®

Hard-core Riprap, Scalpins

Hard-headed Stegochepalian

Harding Warden

Hardliner Hawk

Hardly Borderline, Ill, Just, Scarcely, Uneath(es), Unnethes

Hard-pressed Strait, Taxed

Hardship Affliction, Austerity, Grief, Mill, Mishap, Penance, Privation, Rigour, Trial, Trouble

Hardware → **COMPUTER HARDWARE**, Gear, Ironmongery

Hardy Brave, Dour, Durable, Gritty, Manful, Oliver, Ollie, Rugged, Spartan, Sturdy, Thomas

Hare Arctic, Baud(rons), Bawd, Belgian, Doe, Dolicholis, Down, Electric, Husk, Jack-rabbit, Jugged, Jumping, Lam, Leporine, Malkin, Mara, March, Mawkin, Mountain, Mouse, Ochotona, Pika, Piping, Puss, Scut, Snowshoe, Spring, Wat

Hare-brained Giddy, Madcap, Scatty

Harem, Harem lady Gynaeceum, Gynoecium, Odalisque, Seraglio, Serai(l), Zenana

Hark(en) Ear, Hear, List(en)

Harlequin Chequered, Columbine, Pantaloon

Harlot Blue gown, Drab, Hussy, Loon, Loose, Paramour, Plover, Pusle, Pussel,

Quail, Rahab, Scrubber, Slut, Strumpet, Whore

Harm(ed), Harmful Aggrieve, Bane, Blight, Damage, Deleterious, Detriment, Endamage, Evil, Hurt, Inimical, Injury, Insidious, Maleficent, Malignant, Maltreat, Mischief, Nocuous, Noisome, Noxious, Pernicious, Sinister, Spoil, Wroken, Wrong

Harmless Benign, Canny, Drudge, Informidable, Innocent, Innocuous, Innoxious, Inoffensive

Harmonica Harp, Orpheus

Harmonious, Harmonise, Harmonist, Harmony Agree(ment), Alan, Allan, Allen, Alternation, Assort, Atone, Attune, Balanced, Barbershop, Blend, Chord, Close, Concent, Concentus, Concert, Concinnity, Concord, Congruous, Consonant, Consort, Coordinate, Correspondence, Counterpoint, Descant, Diapason, Diatessaron, Doo-wop, Euphony, Eur(h)ythmy, Faburden, Feng-shui, Go, Jibe, Keeping, Match, Melody, Mesh, Musical, Overblow, Overtone, Rappite, Salve, Solidarity, Symmetry, Sympathy, Symphonious, Sync, Thorough-bass, Tone, Tune, Unanimity, Unison, Unity

Harmotome Cross-stone

Harness(maker) Breeching, Bridle, Cinch, D-ring, Equipage, Frenum, Gear, Girth, Hitch, Inspan, Lorimer, Loriner, Pad-tree, Partnership, Swingletree, Tack(le), Throat-stop, Tie, Trace, Trappings, Whippletree, Yoke

Harp(sichord) Aeolian, Cembalo, Clairschach, Clarsach, Clavier, Drone, Dwell, Irish, Jew's, Kora, Lyre, Nebel, Trigon, Triple, Virginal, Welsh, Wind, Zither

Harpagon L'avare, Miser

Harpoon(er) Bart, Fis(h)gig, Fizgig, Grain, Iron, Lily iron, Peg, Spear, Specktioneer, Toggler, Tow-iron, Trident

Harpy Aello, Celeno, Eagle, Ocypete

Harridan Hag, Harpy, Shrew, Termagant, Xantippe, Zantippe, Zentippe

Harrier Hen, Montagu's

Harriet Hetty, Martineau

Harris Boatman, Cloth, Island, Isle, Rolf

Harrow(ing) Alas, Appal, Brake, Disc, Drag, Frighten, Herse, Lacerant, Pitch-pole, Plough, Rake, Rend, Shock, Welaway, Welladay, Wellanear, Wellaway

Harry Aggravate, Badger, Bother, Champion, Chase, Chivvy, Coppernose, Dragoon, Flash, Fret, Hal, Harass, Hassle, Hector, Herry, Houdini, Hound, Lauder, Lime, Maraud, Molest, Nag, Pester, Plague, Rag, Reave, Reive, Rieve, Rile, Tate, Tchick, Torment

▷ **Harry** *may indicate* an anagram

Harsh(ness) Abrasive, Acerbic, Austere, Barbaric, Brassy, Cacophonous, Coarse, Cruel, Desolate, Discordant, Draconian, Extreme, Glary, Grating, Gravelly, Grim, Gruff, Guttural, Hard, Inclement, Oppressive, Raucid, Raucle, Raucous, Raw, Rigour, Rude, Ruthless, Scabrid, Scrannel, Screechy, → **SEVERE**, Sharp, Spartan, Stark, Stern, Stoor, Stour, Stowre, Strict, Strident, Unkind

Hart Deer, Spade, Spay, Spay(a)d, Venison

Harte Bret

Hartebeest Bubal, Kaama, Kongoni, Sassaby, Tsessebe

Harum-scarum Bayard, Chaotic, Madcap, Rantipole

Harvest(er), Harvest home Combine, Crop, Cull, Fruit, → **GATHER**, Hairst, Hawkey, Hay(sel), Hockey, Horkey, In(ning), Ingather, Kirn, Lease, Nutting, Pick, Produce, Rabi, Random, Reap, Shock, Spatlese, Spider, Tattie-howking, Thresh, Vendage, Vendange

Has Habet, Hath, Owns, 's

Has-been Effete, Ex, Outmoded

Hash(ish) Benj, Bungle, Charas, Discuss, Garble, Garboil, Hachis, Lobscouse, Mince, Pi(e), Ragout

▷ **Hashed** *may indicate* an anagram

Hasn't Hant, Nas

Hassle Aggro, Bother, Moider, M(o)ither

Hassock Kneeler, Pouf(fe), Stool, Tuffet

Haste(n), Hastening, Hastily, Hasty Cursory, Despatch, Expedite, Express, Festinately, Fly, Hare, Headlong, Hie, Hotfoot, → **HURRY**, Hurry-scurry, Impetuous, Precipitant, Race, Ramstam, Rash, Rush, Scuttle, Speed, Spur, Stringendo, Subitaneous, Sudden, Tear, Tilt, Urge, Whistle-stop

Hastings Banda, Bustles, Senlac, Warren

Hat Akubra®, Ascot, Astrakhan, Balibuntal, Balmoral, Basher, Beanie, Beany, Bearskin, Beaver, Beret, Bicorn, Billycock, Biretta, Bluebonnet, Boater, Bobble, Bollinger, Bonnet, Bowler, Boxer, Brass, Breton, Broad-brim, Bronx, Busby, Cabbage tree, → **CAP**, Capotain, Cartwheel, Castor, Chaco, Chapeau, Cheese-cutter, Chimneypot, Christie, Christy, Claque, Cloche, Cocked, Cockle-hat, Coolie, Cossack, Cowboy, Crusher, Curch, Deerstalker, Derby, Dolly Varden, Dunstable, Envoy, Fedora, Fez, Flat-cap, Fore-and-after, Gaucho, Gibus, Gimme, Glengarry, Hard, Hattock, → **HEADDRESS**, Head-rig, Hennin, Homburg, Kamelaukion, Kepi, Lamington, Leghorn, Lid, Lum, Matador, Mitre, Mob-cap, Mountie's, Mushroom, Nab, Opera, Pagri, Panama, Petasus, Picture, Pilion, Pill-box, Pilleus, Pilos, Pith, Pixie, Planter's, Plateau, Plug, Poke(-bonnet), Pork-pie, Potae, Profile, Puggaree, Puritan, Ramil(l)ies, Red, Runcible, Safari, Sailor, Scarlet, Shacko, Shako, Shovel, Silk, Skimmer, Skull-cap, Slouch, Snap-brim, Snood, Sola(-helmet), Solah, Sola-topi, Sombrero, Songkok, Souwester, Steeple-crown, Stetson®, Stovepipe, Straw, Sugarloaf, Sunbonnet, Sundown, Sunhat, Tam (o'Shanter), Tarboosh, Tarb(o)ush, Tarpaulin, Ten-gallon, Terai, Thrummed, Tile, Tin, Tit(fer), Toorie, Top(per), Topee, Topi, Toque, Tricorn(e), Trilby, Turban, Tyrolean, Ugly, Wide-awake, Witch's

Hat-band Weeper

Hatch(ment), Hatching Achievement, Altricial, Booby, Breed, Brew, Brood, Cleck, Clutch, Companion, Concoct, Cover, Devise, Eclosion, Emerge, Escape, Incubate, Service, Set, Trap-door

Hatchet(-shaped) Axe, Bill, Chopper, Claw, Cleaver, Dolabriform, Tomahawk

▷ **Hatching** *may indicate* an anagram

Hatchway (surround) Companionway, Fiddley, Guichet, Porthole, Scuttle, Service

Hate(ful), Hatred Abhor, Abominable, Abominate, Anims, Antipathetic, Aversion, Bugbear, Detest, Enmity, Haterent, Loathe, Misogyny, Odium, Pet, Phobia, Racism, Resent, Spite, Ug(h), Vitriol

Hatless Bareheaded, Unbeavered

Hat-plant S(h)ola

Hatter Mad

Hatty Etta

Haughty, Haughtiness Aloof, Aristocratic, Arrogant, Bashaw, Cavalier, Disdainful, Dorty, Fastuous, High, Hogen-mogen, Hoity-toity, Hye, Imperious, Lofty, Morgue, Orgillous, Orgulous, Paughty, → **PROUD**, Scornful, Sdeignful, Sniffy, Stiff-necked, Toffee-nosed, Toplofty, Upstage

Haul(age), Haulier Bag, Bouse, Bowse, Brail, Carry, Cart, Catch, Drag, Heave, Hove, Kedge, Long, Loot, Plunder, Pull, Rug, Sally, Scoop, Snake, Snig, TIR, Touse, Touze, Tow(se), Towze, Transporter, Trice, Winch, Yank

Haunch Hance, Hip, Huckle, Hunkers, Quarter

Haunt(s) Catchy, Den, Dive, Frequent, Ghost, Hang-out, Honky-tonk, Houf(f), Howf(f), Infest, Obsess, Purlieu, Resort, Spot, Spright

Hauteur Bashawism, Height, Morgue, Vanity

Havana Cigar

Have, Having Bear, Ha(e), Han, Hoax, Hold, Know, Of, → **OWN**, Possess, Sell

Haven Asylum, Harbour, Hithe, Hythe, Oasis, Port, Refuge, Refugium, Retreat, Safe, Sekos, Shelter, Tax

Haver(s) Blether, Clanjamfray, Dither, Gibber, Nigel

▶ **Haversack** *see* **RUCKSACK**

Havoc Desolation, Devastation, Hell, Ravage, Waste

▷ **Havoc** *may indicate* an anagram

Haw Drawl, Hip, Sloe

Hawaiian Kanaka

Hawk(er), Hawkish Accipitrine, Auceps, Austringer, Badger, Bastard, Buzzard, Cadger, Camelot, Caracara, Cast, Cheapjack, Cooper's, Cry, Duck, Eagle, Elanet, Eyas, Falcon, Fish, Gerfalcon, Goshawk, Haggard, Hardliner, Harrier, Harrumph, Hobby, Honey-buzzard, Keelie, Kestrel, Kite, Lammergeier, Lanner(et), Marsh, Merlin, Molla(h), Monger, Moolah, Mosquito, Mullah, Musket, Night, Nyas, Osprey, Ossifrage, Passager, Pearlie, Pearly, Peddle, Pedlar, Peregrine, Pigeon, Privet, Ringtail, Sacre(t), Sell, Slab, Slanger, Soar(e), Sorage, Sore(-eagle), Sparrow, Spiv, Staniel, Stone, Sutler, Tallyman, Tarsal, Tarsel(l), Tassel, Tercel(et), Tiersel, Tout, Trant(er), Trucker, Warlike

Hawkeye IA, Iowa

Hawk-keeper Austringer, Ostreger

Hawser Line, Rope

Hawthorn Albespine, Albespyne, May(flower), Quickset, Quickthorn

Hay(cock), Hey, Haybox Antic, Cock, Contra-dance, Fodder, Goaf, Hi, Kemple, Math, Mow, Norwegian nest, Norwegian oven, Pleach, Pook, Salt, Stack, Straw, Truss, Windrow

Hayfever Pollenosis, Pollinosis

Haymaker Blow, Slog

Hayseed Chaw-bacon, Hodge, Joskin, Rustic

Hazard(ous) Bet, Breakneck, Bunker, Chance, Danger, Dare, Die, Dye, Game, Gremlin, Guess, Hero, Imperil, In-off, Jeopardy, Losing, Main, Minefield, Moral, Nice, Niffer, Occupational, Perdu(e), Peril, Pitfall, Play, Pothole, Queasy, → **RISK**, Stake, Trap, Venture, Vigia, Wage, Winning

Haze, Hazy Blear, Cloud, Filmy, Fog, → **MIST**, Mock, Muzzy, Nebulous, Smaze, Smog, Tease

▷ **Haze** *may indicate* an anagram

Hazel(wort) Amenta, Asarabacca, Catkin, Cob, Corylus, Filbert

HC Encomia, Encomium

He, HE A, Helium, Tag, Tig, → **TNT**, Tom

▷ **Head** *may indicate* the first letter of a word

Head(s), Heading, Headman, Head shaped, Heady Aim, Apex, Ard-ri(gh), Beachy, Bean, Behead, Bill, Block, Bonce, Boss, Bound, Brain, Brainpan, Bregma, Brow, But(t), Caboceer, Cape, Capitani, Capitate, Capitulum, Capo, Captain, Caption, Caput, Caudillo, Cephalic, Chaton, Chief, Chump, Coarb, Coconut, Coma, Comarb, Commander, Conk, Cop, Coppin, Costard, Cranium, Crest, Crisis, Crown, Crumpet, Crust, Cylinder, Dateline, Dean, Director, Dome, Dummy, Each, Ear, Exarch, Figure, Flamborough, Foam, Foreland, Froth, General, Glomerate, Grand Mufti, Hegumen(os), Herm(a), Hoe, Hogh, Huff-cap, Inion, Jowl, Karmapa,

Keyword, Knob, Knowledge-box, Lead(er), Lid, Lizard, Loaf, Loave, Loo, Lore, Malik, Manager, Mayor, Maz(z)ard, Melik, Mocuddum, Mogul, Mokaddam, Mr Big, Mull, Muqaddam, Nab, Nana, Napper, Nappy, Ness, Nob, Noddle, Noggin, Noll, Noup, Nowl, Nut, Obverse, Occiput, Onion, Panicle, Panorama, Parietal, Pash, Pate, Pater(familias), Patriarch, Pick-up, Point, Poll, Pow, Prefect, President, Pressure, Principal, Promontory, Provost, Ras, Read-write, Ream, Rector, Rubric, Sarpanch, Scalp, Scaup, Scaw, Scholarch, Scolex, Sconce, Short, Sinciput, Skaw, Skull, Sound, Source, Spume, Squeers, Stad(t)holder, Starosta, Strapline, Subject, Superior, Taipan, Talking, Tanadar, Tete, Thanadar, Throne, Tight, Tintagel, Tip, Title, Toilet, Top, Topic, Tsantsa, Twopenny, Upperworks, Vaivode, Velocity, Voivode, Yorick, Zupan

Headache Cephalalgia, Encephalalgia, Hangover, Hemicrania, Megrim, Migraine, Neuralgia, Red out, Scotodinia, Splitter

Headband Blindfold, Fillet, Garland, Infula, Sphendone, T(a)enia

Headbanger Nutcase

Headdress, Headcover Ampyx, Balaclava, Bandeau, Bas(i)net, Bonnet, Burnous(e), Busby, Calotte, Caul, Chaplet, Circlet, Comb, Commode, Cor(o)net, Cowl, Coxcomb, Crownet, Curch, Diadem, Doek, Dopatta, Dupatta, Fascinator, Feather bonnet, Fontange, Fool's cap, Frontlet, Hat(tock), Helm(et), Joncanoe, Juliet cap, Kaffiyeh, Kell, Kerchief, Kuffiyeh, Kufiah, Kufiya(h), Mantilla, Mitre, Mobcap, Modius, Mortarboard, Nubia, Periwig, Pill-box, Plug-hat, Porrenger, Porringer, Romal, Rumal, Sakkos, Ship-tire, Silly-how, Skullcap, Sphendone, Stephane, Taj, Tarbush, Tiara, Tire-vallant, Tower, Tulban, Turban, War bonnet, Wig, Wimple, Wreath

Header Bonder, Dive, Fall, Rowlock

Headhunter Naga

Headland Beachy Head, Bill, Cape, Cape Horn, Dungeness, Finisterre, Foreland, Head-rig, Hoe, Hogh, Land's End, Morro, Naze, Ness, Noup, Point, → **PROMONTORY**, Ras, Ross, St Vincent, Scaw, Skaw

Headless Acephalous

Headlight(s) Beam, Brights, Dip, Halo

Headline Banner, Caption, Drophead, Frown, Kicker, Ribbon, Scare-head, Screamer, Strapline, Streamer, Title

Headlock Chancery

Headlong Breakneck, Pell-mell, Precipitate, Ramstam, Reckless, Steep, Sudden, Tantivy, Tearaway

▶ **Headman** *see* HEAD

Headmaster Principal, Squeers

Headphone(s) Cans, Earpiece, Walkman®

Headquarters Base, Command, Command post, Depot, Guardhouse, Guildhall, Pentagon, Praetorium, SHAEF, SHAPE, Station

▷ **Heads** *may indicate* a lavatory

Headsman Executioner

Headstrong Obstinate, Rash, Stubborn, Unruly, Wayward, Wilful

Head-to-tail Tête-bêche

Headway Advancement, Headroom, Progress

Head-word Lemma

Heal(ing) Absent, Aesculapian, Ayurveda, Balsam, Chiropractic, Cicatrise, Cleanse, Curative, Cure, Distant, Esculapian, G(u)arish, Hele, Hippocratise, Intention, Knit, Mend, Mental, Naturopathy, New Thought, Olosis, Osteopathy, Restore, Sain, Salve, Sanative, Sanitary, Spiritual, Therapeutic, Vulnerary

Healer Althea, Asa, Doctor, Homeopath, Naturopath, Osteopath, Sangoma, Shaman, Time

Health(y) Bouncing, Bracing, Chin-chin, Constitution, Cosy, Doer, Fit, Flourishing, Gesundheit, Hail, Hale, Hartie-hale, Heart, Holism, Kia-ora, L'chaim, Lustique, Lusty, Medicaid, Medicare, Pink, Prosit, Public, Robust, Rosy, Ruddy, Salubrious, Sane, Slainte, Sound, Toast, Tope, Valentine, Valetudinarian, Vigour, Well, WHO, Wholesome

Heap(ed) Acervate, Agglomerate, Amass, Bing, Boneshaker, Bulk, Car, Clamp, Coacervate, Cock, Compost, Congeries, Cumulus, Drift, Hog, Jalopy, Lot, Pile, Raff, Raft, Rick(le), Ruck, Scrap, Shell, Slag, Stash, Tass, Toorie, Up-piled

Hear(ing) Acoustic, Attend, Audience, Audile, Avizandum, Captain's mast, Catch, Clairaudience, Dirdum, Ear, Harken, Learn, List(en), Oyer, Oyez, Panel, Paracusis, Pick up, Session, Subpoena, Try

▷ **Hear(say)** *may indicate* a word sounding like one given

Hearsay Account, Gossip, Report, Rumour, Surmise

Hearse Bier, Catafalco, Catafalque, Meat wagon, Shillibeer

Heart(en), Heartily, Hearty, Heart-shaped AB, Agood, Auricle, Backslapping, Beater, Bleeding, Bluff, Bosom, Bradycardia, Cant, Cardiac, Centre, Cheer, Cockles, Columella, Cordate, Cordial, Core, Courage, Crossed, Daddock, Embolden, Encourage, Essence, Fatty, Floating, Gist, H, Hale, Herz, Inmost, Jarta, Kernel, Lepid, Lonely, Memoriter, Mesial, Mid(st), Middle, Nub, Nucleus, Obcordate, Pericardium, Pith, Purple, Reassure, Robust, Root, Sacred, Sailor, Seafarer, Seaman, Sinoatrial, Staunch, Tachycardia, Tar, Ticker, Yarta, Yarto

Heart-break Crève-coeur, Grief, Sorrow

Heartfelt Deep, Genuine, Real, Sincere, Soulful, Triste

Hearth Cupel, Finery, Fireside, Home, Ingle, Killogie

Heartless Callous, Cored, Cruel, Three-suited

Heart's ease Pansy

Heart trouble, Heartburn Bradycardia, Brash, Cardialgia, Fallot's tetralogy, Fibrillation, Murmur, Pyrosis, Tachycardia

Heat(ed), Heater, Heating Anneal, Ardour, Arousal, Atomic, Background, Bainite, Barrage, Beath, Blood, Brazier, Calcine, Calescence, Califont, Caloric, Calorifier, Central, Chafe, Convector, Dead, Decay, Dielectric, Dudgeon, Eccaleobion, Element, Eliminator, Endothermic, Enthalpy, Estrus, Etna, Excite, Exothermic, Fan, Ferment, Fever, Fire, Fluster, Fug, Furnace, Het, Hibachi, Hyperthermia, Hypocaust, Immersion, Incalescence, Induction, J, Kindle, Latent, Liquate, Lust, Mowburn, Moxibustion, Normalise, Oestrus, Panel, Prelim, Prickly, Q, Radiant, Radiator, Rankine, Recalescence, Red, Render, Repechage, Rut, Salt, Scald, Sinter, Sizzle, Smelt, Solar, Space, Specific, Spice, Stew, Storage, Stove, Swelter, Teend, Temperature, Thermotics, Tind, Tine, Torrefy, Total, Tynd(e), Underfloor, Warming-pan, Warmth, White, Zip®

Heath(land) Bearberry, Bent, Briar, Brier, Egdon, Epacrid, Erica, Geest, Lande, Manoao, Manzanita, Moor, Muir, Stead, Ted

Heathen(s) Ethnic, Gentile, Infidel, Litholatrous, Nations, Pagan, Pa(i)nim, Paynim, Philistine, Primitive, Profane, Proselyte of the gate

Heather Bell, Broom, Calluna, Epacrid, Erica, Foxberry, Ling, Rhodora, Sprig

▷ **Heating** *may indicate* an anagram

▷ **Heave** *may indicate* 'discard'

Heave(d) Cast, Fling, Frost, Heeze, Hoise, Hoist, Hump, Hurl, Popple, Retch, Shy, Sigh, Vomit

Heaven(s), Heavenly Air, Aloft, Ama, Ambrosial, Arcady, Asgard, Bliss, Celestial,

Celia, Divine, Ecstasy, Elysian, Elysium, Empyrean, Ethereal, Fiddler's Green, Firmament, Hereafter, Himmel, Hog, Holy, Hookey Walker, Land o' the Leaf, Leal, Lift, Mackerel, New Jerusalem, Olympus, Paradise, Pole, Rapture, Seventh, Shangri-la, Sion, Sky, Supernal, Svarga, Swarga, Swerga, Tir na n'Og, Uranian, Welkin, Zion

Heavy(weight), Heavily, Heaviness Ali, Bodyguard, Clumpy, Dutch, Elephantine, Embonpoint, Endomorph, Grave, Hefty, Last, Leaden, Lumpish, Onerous, Osmium, Pesante, Ponderous, Roughneck, Sad, Scelerate, Stodgy, Stout, Top, Torrential, Upsee, Ups(e)y, Weighty, Wicked

Hebe Barmaid

Hebrew Aramaic, Eli, Heb, Jesse, Karaism, Levi, Mishnayoth, Modern, Rabbinical, Yid

Hebrides, Hebridean Harris, Western Isles

Heckle Badger, Gibe, Harass, Hatchel, Jeer, Needle, Spruik

Hectic Ding-dong, Feverish, Frenetic

Hector Badger, Bluster, Browbeat, Bully, → **HARASS**, Nag

Hedge, Hedging Box, Bullfinch, Enclosure, Equivocate, Evade, Haw, Hay, Lay off, Meuse, Mews, Muse, Pleach, Privet, Pussyfoot, Quickset, Raddle, Sepiment, Shield, Stonewall, Texas, Thicket, Waffle

Hedgehog Gymnure, Hérisson, Tenrec, Tiggywinkle, Urchin

Hedge-parson Bucklebeggar, Patercove

Hedge-sparrow Accentor

Hedonist Cyreniac, Epicurean, Playboy, Sybarite

Heed(ed), Heedful Attend, Cavendotutus, Listen, → **MIND**, Notice, Obey, Observe, Rear, Reck, Regard(ant), Reke, Respect, Rought, Tent, Tinker's cuss

Heedless Careless, Inattentive, Incautious, Rash, Scapegrace, Scatterbrain

Heel Achilles, Cad, Calcaneum, Cant, Careen, Cuban, Dogbolt, Foot, French, Kitten, List, Louse, Parliament, Rat, Rogue, Seel, Spike, Stacked, Stiletto, Tilt, Wedge

Heel-tap Snuff

Hefty Brawny, Heavy, Solid, Weighty

Heifer Io, Quey, Stirk

Height(en), Heights Abraham, Altitude, Cairngorm, Ceiling, Dimension, Elevation, Embroider, Eminence, Enhance, Golan, H, Hill, Hypsometry, Level, Might, Mount, Peak, Procerity, Roof, Spot, Stature, Stud, Sum, → **SUMMIT**, Tallness, Tor, X

Heinous Abominable, Atrocious, Flagrant

Heir Alienee, Claimant, Coparcener, Dauphin, Devisee, Distributee, Eigne, H(a)eres, Institute, Intitule, Legatee, Parcener, Scion, Sprig, Tanist

Heirless Escheat, Intestate

Held Captive, Hostage, Sostenuto, Ten(uto)

▷ **Held by** *may indicate* a hidden word

Helen Elaine, Nell(y)

Helicopter, Heliport Airstop, Chopper, Egg-beater, Gunship, Hover, Iroquois, Medevac, Rotodyne, Sea Cobra, Sea King, Sea Knight, Sea Sprite, Sea Stallion, Sikorsky, Sky-hook, Whirlybird

Helios Hyperion

Heliotrope Cherry-pie

Helium He

Helix Alpha, Double, Parastichy

Hell(ish) Abaddon, Abyss, Ades, Agony, Amenthes, Annw(yf)n, Avernus, Below, Blazes, Bottomless pit, Chthonic, Dis, Erebus, Furnace, Gehenna, Hades, Heck, Inferno, Jahannam, Lower regions, Malebolge, Naraka, Netherworld, Orcus,

Pandemonium, Perditious, Pit, Ruin, Sheol, Stygian, Tartar(ean), Tartarus, Tophet, Torment

Hellbender Menopome, Mud-puppy

Hellebore Itchweed, Setterwort, Melampode

Hellenic Dorian

Hellespont Dardanelles

Hello, Hallo, Hullo Aloha, Chin-chin, Ciao, Dumela, Golden, Hi, Ho(a), Hoh, Howdy, Howzit, Yoo-hoo

Helm(sman) Cox, Navigator, Pilot, Steer, Tiller, Timon(eer)

Helmet Armet, Balaclava, Basinet, Bearskin, Beaver, Burganet, Burgonet, Cask, Casque, Comb, Crash, Galea, Gas, Heaume, Knapscal, Knapscull, Knapskull, Montero, Mor(r)ion, Nasal, Pickelhaube, Pith, Plumed, Pot, Pressure, Salade, Sal(l)et, Shako, Skid-lid, Smoke, Tin hat, Topee, Topi

Helot Esne, Slave

Help(er), Helping, Helpful Abet, Accomplice, Adjuvant, Advantage, Aid(ance), Aidant, Aide, Alexis, Alleviate, Ally, Asset, → **ASSIST**, Avail, Back, Beet-master, Beet-mister, Befriend, Benefit, Bestead, Boon, Brownie, Char(woman), Coadjutor, Complice, Conducive, Daily, Dollop, Dose, Ezra, Forward, Further(some), Go, Hand, Handyman, Henchman, Hint, Home, Hyphen, Instrumental, Intercede, Kind, Leg-up, Life-saver, Maid, Mayday, Monitor, Obliging, Ophelia, Order, Patronage, Pitch in, Quantity, Ration, Recourse, Relieve, Servant, Serve, Slice, SOS, Stead, Sted, Subserve, Subvention, Succour, Taste, Therapeutic, Use

Helpless(ness) Adynamia, Anomie, Downa-do, Feeble, High and dry, Impotent, Incapable, Paralytic, Prostrate, Useless

Helpmate Consort

Hem Border, Fringe, Hoop, List

He-man Adonis, Hunk, Jock, Macho

Hemisphere, Hemispherical Antichthon, Cupular, Dominant, Magdeburg, Rose-cut, Western

Hemlock Conia, Cowbane, Insane root, Tsuga

Hemp Abaca, Bhang, Boneset, Bowstring, Carl(ot), Choke-weed, Codilla, Crotalaria, Dagga, Fimble, Ganja, Hards, Henequen, Hiniquin, Indian, K(a)if, Kef, Love-drug, Manil(l)a, Mauritius, Moorva, Murva, Neckweed, Pita, Sida, Sunn, Tat, Tow

Hen(s) Ancona, Andalusian, Australorp, Biddy, Buff Orpington, Chock, Clocker, Cochin, Deep litter, Dorking, Eirack, Fowl, Grig, Houdan, Langshan, Layer, Leghorn, Maori, Marsh, Mother, Mud, Orpington, Partlet, Pertelote, Plymouth Rock, Poulard, Poultry, Pullet, Ree(ve), Rhode Island red, Sitter, Spanish fowl, Speckled, Sultan, Tappit, Welsummer, Wyandotte

Hence Apage, Avaunt, Ergo, Go, Hinc, So, Therefore, Thus

Henchman Attendant, Follower, Myrmidon, Satellite

Hen-house Battery, Eggery

Henna Camphire

Hennery Run

Hen-pecked Pussy-whipped, Spineless, Woman-tired

Henry Eighth, H, Hal, Hank, Hooray, Hy, James, Navigator, O

Hep Bacca, Berry, Hip, Wise

Hepatic Scale-moss

Hepatitis Favism, Jaundice

Herald(ic), Heraldry Abatement, Albany, Al(l)erion, Argent, Armiger, Armory, Azure, Bagwyn, Bars, Baton sinister, Bearing, Bend, Bend sinister, Bendwise, Billet, Blazonry, Bloody Hand, Blue Mantle, Bordure, Caboched, Cabré, Calygreyhound,

Checky, Chevron, Chief, Cicerone, Cinquefoil, Clarenc(i)eux, Cleché, Cockatrice,
Compone, Compony, Couchant, Coue, Counter-passant, Coupee, Coward, Crest,
Crier, Debruised, Degraded, Difference, Dimidiate, Displayed, Dormant, Dragonné,
Eightfoil, Emblazon, Endorse, Enfiled, Erased, Fecial, Fess(e), Fetial, Fetterlock,
File, Flory, Forerunner, Fracted, Gardant, Garter, Gironny, Golp(e), Gules, Gyronny,
Hauriant, Herissé, Herisson, Hermes, Honour-point, Interfretted, Issuant,
King-of-arms, Lionel, Lis, Lodged, Lyon, Lyon King of Arms, Manchet, Martlet,
Messenger, Minocaine, Morne, Mullet, Naiant, Naissant, Nascent, Nebulé, Nebuly,
Nombril, Norroy, Nowed, Nowy, Opinicus, Or, Ordinary, Pale, Pallet, Paly, Passant,
Pheon, Pile, Portate, Portcullis, Portend, Posé, Potent, Precursor, Proclaim,
Purpure, Pursuivant, Quartering, Rampant, Red Hand, Regardant, Rouge Croix,
Rouge Dragon, Roundel, Roundle, Sable, Salient, Sans nombre, Scarp, Scrog, Sea
dog, Sea lion, Segreant, Sejant, Sejeant, Statant, Stentor, Subordinary, Supporter,
Tenné, Trangle, Tressure, Trick, Trippant, Trundle, Umbrated, Undifferenced,
Urinant, Usher, Vair(é), Vaunt-courier, Verdoy, Verrey, Vert, Voided, Vol(ant),
Vorant, Wivern, Woodhouse, Woodwose, Wyvern, Yale

Herb(s) Aconite, Agrimony, Ajowan, Alecost, Allspice, Aloe, Angelica, Anise,
Aniseed, Aristolochia, Arugula, Avens, Basil, Bay, Bennet, Bergamot, Borage,
Capers, Caraway, Cardamom, Catmint, Centaury, Chamomile, Chervil, C(h)ive,
Cilanto, Cohosh, Colic root, Comfrey, Coriander, Costmary, Cum(m)in, Dill, Dittany,
Echinacea, Eruca, Estragon, Exacum, Eyebright, Felicia, Fennel, Fenugreek,
Ferula, Feverfew, Fireweed, Fitch, Fluellin, Forb, Fuller's, Garlic, Garnish, Gentian,
Germander, Good-King-Henry, Gunnera, Haworthia, Hyssop, Inula, Kalanchoe,
Knapweed, Lamb's ears, Laserpicium, Laserwort, Lewisia, Lovage, Madder,
Madwort, Mandrake, Marjoram, Maror, Medic, Mint, Moly, Mountain flax,
Mustard, Oca, Oleraceous, Orache, Oregano, Origan(e), Origanum, Ornithogalum,
Orval, Paprika, Parakeelya, Parakelia, Parsley, Paterson's curse, Phlomis, Pia,
Pipsissewa, Plantain, Purpie, Purslane, Pussytoes, Reed-mace, Rest-harrow,
Rhizocarp, Rodgersia, Rosemary, Rue, Rupturewort, Saffron, Sage, Salad,
Saloop, Salsify, Savory, Senna, Sesame, Simple, Soapwort, Sorrel, Southernwood,
Spearmint, Staragen, Sweet cicely, Tacca, Tansy, Tarragon, Thyme, Tormentil,
Turmeric, Typha, Valerian, Veronica, Vervain, Vetch, Weed, Willow, Wormwood,
Wort, Yarrow, Yerba
Herbalist Simplist
Herbarium Hortus succus
Herbert Alan, AP(H), Lom, Spencer
Herbicide Agent Orange, Atrazine, Defoliant, Diquat, Glufosinate, Picloram, Simazine
Herbivore Iguanodon, Sauropod
Hercules Alcides, Huge, Rustam, Rustem
Herd(er), Herdsman Band, Corral, Drive, Drover, Flock, Gang, Marshal, Meinie,
Mein(e)y, Menyie, Mob, Pod, Raggle-taggle, Round-up, Shepherd, Tail, Tinchel,
Vaquero
Here Adsum, Hi, Hic, Hither, Local, Now, Oy, Present
Hereafter Other world
Hereditary, Heredity Ancestry, Blood, Breeding, Codon, Dynastic, Eugenics, Exon,
Genetics, Id(ant), Idioplasm, Inborn, Mendelism, Panagenesis
▷ **Herein** *may indicate* a hidden word
Here is laid HS
Heresiarch Nestor
Heresy, Heretic(al) Agnoitae, Albi, Albigensian, Apollinaris, Apostasy, Arian,
Arius, Bab, Bogomil, Bugger, Cathar, Cerinthus, Docete, Donatist, Dulcinist,

Encratite, Eudoxian, Giaour, Gnosticism, Heresearch, Heterodoxy, Lollard, Manichaean, Montanism, Nestorian, Nonconformist, Origen, Patarin(e), Pelagius, Phrygian, Racovian, Rebel, Unitarian, Zendik

Heritage Birthright, Due, NT, Odette, Ottilie, Patrimony

Hermaphrodite Androgynous, Gynandromorph, Monochinous, Monoecious, Prot(er)andry

Hermes (rod) Caduceus, Mercury

Hermetic Alchemist, Sealed

Hermit(age), Hermit-like Anchoret, Anchorite, Ascetic, Ashram(a), Augustinian, Austin, Cell, Cloister, Crab, Eremite, Grandmontine, Hieronymite, Loner, Marabout, Monk, Museum, Nitrian, Pagurid, Peter, Recluse, Retreat, Robber-crab, Sannyasi, Soldier-crab, Solitary, Troglodyte

Hernia Bubonocele, Cystocoele, Diverticulum, Enterocele, Eventration, Hiatus, Inguinal, Rectocele, Rupture

Hero(ic) Achilles, Aeneas, Agamemnon, Aitu, Ajax, Alcides, Amadis, Asterix, Bader, Balarama, Bellerophon, Beowulf, Brave, Bunyan, Champ(ion), Cid, Couplet, Crockett, Cuchulain, Cuchullain, Cyrano, Dambuster, Dan Dare, Demigod, Drake, El Cid, Epic, Eponym, Eric, Everyman, Faust, Fingal, Finn, Finn MacCool, Folk, Garibaldi, Glooscap, Gluscap, Gluskap, God, Goody, Great, Hector, Heracles, Hercules, Hiawatha, Howleglass, Hudibrastic, Icon, Ideal, Idol, Ivanhoe, Jason, Kaleva, Kami, Leonidas, Lion, Lochinvar, Lothair, Marmion, Meleager, Nestor, Noble, Odysseus, Oliver, Onegin, Orfeo, Orion, Owl(e)glass, Ow(l)spiegle, Paladin, Parashurama, Parsifal, Pericles, Perseus, Philoctetes, Priestess, Principal, Ramachandra, Rambo, Raven, Resolute, Revere, Rinaldo, Roderego, Roderick, Roland, Rustem, Rustum, Saladin, Shandy, Sheik, Siegfried, Sigurd, Superman, Tam o' Shanter, Tancred, Tarzan, Tell, Theseus, Tragic, Triptolemus, Tristan, Trist(r)am, Ulysses, Valiant, Vercingetorix, Virago, Volsung, Werther, White knight, Zorro

Herod Agrippa, Antipas

Heroin Chase-the-dragon, Dogfood, Doojie, Dynamite, Gumball, H, Harry, Henry, Horse, Jack, Junk, Scag, S(c)hmek, Shit, Skag, Smack, Snow, Snowball, Speedball, Sugar

Heroine Andromeda, Ariadne, Candida, Darling, Demigoddess, Hedda, Imogen, Isolde, Judith, Juliet, Leda, Leonora, Lulu, Manon, Mimi, Nana, Norma, Pamela, Star, Tess, Tosca, Una

Heron(s) Ardea, Bird, Bittern, Boat-billed, Butter-bump, Egret, Green, Handsaw, Kotuko, Screamer, Sedge, Siege, Squacco, Winnard

Herpes Cold sore, Dartre, Shingles, Shiver

Herring Bismarck, Bloater, Brisling, Brit, Buckling, Caller, Cisco, Clupea, Digby chick(en), Gaspereau, Glasgow magistrate, Kipper, Lake, Ma(a)tjes, Maise, Maize, Mattie, Maze, Mease, Menhaden, Norfolk capon, Ox eye, Rabbitfish, Red, Rollmop, Sea-stick, Shotten, Sild, Silt, Sparling, Teleost, Whitebait

Herringbone Sloping

Hesitant, Hesitate, Hesitation Balance, Boggle, Cunctation, Delay, Demur, Dicker, Dither, Doubtful, Dubitate, Er, Erm, Falter, Halting, Haver, Haw, Irresolute, Mammer, Mealy-mouthed, → **PAUSE**, Qualm, Scruple, Shillyshally, Shrink, Stagger, Stammer, Stutter, Swither, Tarrow, Teeter, Tentative, Think twice, Um, Um and ah, Ur, Vacillate, Wait, Waver

Hesperus Vesper

Hessian Burlap, Hireling

Heterodoxy Heresy

Heterogeneous Diverse, Motley, Piebald
Heterosexual Hasbian, Straight
Hew(er) Ax, Chop, Cut, Gideon, Hack, Sever
Hex Bewitch, Jinx, Voodoo
Hexameter Dolichurus, Miurus
▶ **Hey** *see* HAY
Heyday Prime, Summer
Hi Cooee, Hello, Howdie
Hiatus Caesura, Entr'acte, Gap, Hernia, Interact, Interregnum, Interval, Lacuna, Lull
Hibernal, Hibernate, Hibernating Estivate, Hiemal, Hole up, Latitant, Sleep, Winter
Hibernian Irish
Hibiscus Okra, Roselle, Rozelle
Hiccup Blip, Glitch, Hitch, Singultus, Snag, Spasm, Yex
Hick Jake, Oaf, Podunk, Rube, Yokel
Hickory Black, Jackson, Mockernut, Pecan, Scaly-bark, Shagbark
Hidden Buried, Cabalistic, Covert, De(a)rn, Doggo, Healed, Hooded, Latent, Obscure, Occult, Pentimento, Recondite, Screened, Secret, Shuttered, Sly, Ulterior, Unseen, Veiled, Wrapped
▷ **Hidden** *may indicate* a concealed word
Hide, Hiding (place) Abscond, Babiche, Basan, Befog, Bield(y), Blind, Box-calf, Burrow, Bury, Butt, Cache, Camouflage, Ceroon, Coat, → CONCEAL, Coonskin, Cootch, Cordwain, Couch, Cour, Crop, Curtain, Cwtch, Dearn, Deerskin, Doggo, Earth, Eclipse, Encave, Ensconce, Enshroud, Envelop, Epidermis, Fell, Flaught, Flay, Gloss over, Harbour, Heal, Heel, Hele, Hell, Hole-up, Hoodwink, Incave, Inter, Kip, Kipskin, Lair, Leather, Mai-mai, Mask, Mobble, Morocco, Nebris, → OBSCURE, Paper over, Parfleche, Pell, Pelt, Plank, Plant, Priest's hole, Repress, Robe, Saffian, Screen, Secrete, Shadow, Shellac(k), Shroud, Skin, Spetch, Stash, Strap-oil, Tappice, Thong, Thrashing, Trove, Veil, Wallop, Whang, Wrap
Hideous(ness) Deform(ed), Enormity, Gash, Grotesque, Horrible, Monstrous, Odious, Ugly, Ugsome
Hierarchic, Hierarchy Byzantine, Elite, Theocracy
Hieroglyph Cipher, Pictogram
Hi-fi, High-fidelity Ambisonics®, Ghetto blaster
Higgledy-piggledy Mixtie-maxtie
▷ **High** *may indicate* an anagram
High(er), Highly, Highness Alt(a), Altesse, Altissimo, Apogee, Atop, Brent, Climax, Doped, Drugged, E-la, Elation, Elevated, Eminent, Exalted, Excelsior, Frequency, Gamy, Haut(e), Intoxicated, Lofty, Maggotty, Mind-blowing, Orthian, Prime, Rancid, Ripe, School, Senior, Sent, Shrill, So, Steep, Stenchy, Stoned, String-out, Strong, Superior, Swollen, Tall, Tension, Tipsy, Top-lofty, Topmost, Treble, Ultrasonic, Up(per), Very, Wired, Zonked
High and mighty Haughty, Hogen-mogen
Highball Drink, Lob, Loft
Highbrow Brain, Egghead, Intelligentsia, Long-hair
High-class Best, Superior, U
High-crowned Copataine
Highest Best, Climax, Mostwhat, Ne plus ultra, Progressive, Supreme
Highest note E-la
High-flown Bombastic, Euphuism

Highland(er), Highlands Blue-bonnet, Blue-cap, Cameron, Cat(h)eran, Down, Duniwassal, Dun(n)iewassal, Gael, Irish Scot, Karoo, Kiltie, Masai, Nainsel(l), Plaid(man), Redshank, Riff, Scot, Seaforth, Shire, Teuchter

Highlight Accent, Feature, Focus, Heighten, Stress

▶ **High-pitched** *see* HIGH

High-spirited Extravert, Extrovert

High tension HT

Highway Alaska, Alcan, Autobahn, Autopista, Autostrada, Camino Real, Divided, Flyover, Freeway, Information, Interstate, King's, Motorway, Overpass, Pass, Queen's, Road, Rode, Tarseal, Thoroughfare, Tightrope, Tollway

Highwayman, Highway robber(y) Bandit, Bandolero, Duval, Footpad, Fraternity, Gilderoy, Jack Sheppard, Land-pirate, Land-rat, Latrocinium, MacHeath, Motorist, Rank-rider, Road-agent, Scamp, Skyjacker, Toby, Tobyman, Turpin, Twitcher, Wheel

Hijack(er) Abduct, Pirate

Hike(r) Backpack, Bushbash, Bushwalk, Raise, Rambler, Ramp, Rise, Traipse, Tramp, Trape(s), Upraise

Hilarious, Hilarity Hysterical, Jollity, Mirth, Riot

Hilary Term

Hill(s), Hillock, Hillside Ant, Antidine, Arafar, Areopagus, Aventine, Barrow, Beacon, Ben, Bent, Berg, Beverly, Black, Bluff, Bombay, Brae, Breed's, Brew, Broken, Bunker, Butte, Caelian, Calvan, Capitol(ine), Cheviots, Chiltern, Chin, Cleve, Coast, Cone, Coteau, Crag-and-tail, Crest, Damon, Djebel, Drumlin, Dun(e), Dunsinane, Eminence, Esquiline, Fell, Flodden, Gebel, Golan Heights, Golgotha, Gradient, Grampians, Hammock, Height, Helvellyn, Highgate, Holt, Horst, How, Howe, Hummock, Incline, Inselberg, Janiculum, Jebel, Kip(p), Knap, Knoll, Knot, Kop(je), Koppie, Lammermuir, Lavender, Law, Loma, Low, Ludgate, Malvern, Mamelon, Man, Marilyn, Matopo, Mendip, Merrick, Mesa, Monadnock, Monte Cassino, Monticule, Morro, Mound, Mount Lofty Ranges, Nab, Naga, Nanatak, Nilgiri(s), North Downs, Otway Ranges, Palatine, Pap, Pennines, Pike, Pingo, Pnyx, Quantocks, Quirinal, Rand, Range, Saddleback, Savoy, Scaur, Seven, Silbury, Sion, Stoss, Strawberry, Tara, Tel(l), Toft, Toot, Tor, Tump, Tweedsmuir, Valdai, Vatican, Viminal, Wolds, Wrekin, Zion

Hillbilly Yap

Hill-dweller Ant

Hillman Areopagite, Nepalese

Hilltop Crest, Knoll, Nab

Hilt Basket, Coquille, Haft, Handle, Hasp, Shaft

Him(self) He, Ipse, Un

Himalaya(n) Nepali, Panda, Sherpa, Tibetan

Hind(er), Hindering, Hindrance Back, Bar, Block, Check, Counteract, Cramp, Crimp, Cumber, Debar, → DELAY, Deter, Encumber, Estop, Hamper, Handicap, Harass, Holdback, Impeach, Impede, Inconvenience, Inhibit, Obstacle, Overslaugh, Porlock, Posterior, Preclusion, Pull-back, Rear, Rein, Remora, Retard, Rump, Rumple, Set back, Shackle, Slow, Stop, Stunt, Stymie, Taigle, Thwart, Trammel

Hind(most) Back, Deer, Lag, Rear, Starn, Stern

Hindi, Hindu(ism) Arya Samaj, Babu, Bania(n), Banyan, Brahman, Brahmin, Dalit, Gentoo, Gurkha, Harijan, Jaina, Kshatriya, Maharishi, Nagari, Pundit, Rajpoot, Rajput, Rama, Sad(d)hu, Saiva, S(h)akta, Saktas, Sanatana Dharma, Sankhya, Shaiva, Sheik(h), Shiv Sena, Shudra, Smriti, Sudra, Swami, Swinger, Trimurti, Untouchable, Urdu, Vaishnava, Vais(h)ya, Varna, Vedanta

Hindquarters Backside, Crupper, Haunches

Hinge(d) Butt, Cardinal, Cross-garnet, Drop-leaf, Garnet, Gemel, Gimmer, Ginglymus, Joint, Knee, Mount, Parliament, Pivot, Stamp, Strap

▷ **Hinge(s)** *may indicate* a word reversal

Hingeless Ecardinate

Hinny Ass, Donkey, Joe

Hint Allude, Clew, Clue, Cue, Echo, Element, Gleam, Hunch, Idea, Imply, Inkle, Inkling, Innuendo, Insinuate, Intimate, Key, Mint, Nuance, Office, Overtone, Pointer, Preview, Ray, Reminder, Scintilla, Shadow, Soupçon, → **SUGGEST**, Tang, Tip, Touch, Trace, Trick, Wind, Wink, Wisp, Word, Wrinkle

▷ **Hint** *may indicate* a first letter

Hip(pie), Hippy, Hips Cafard, Cheer, Coxa(l), Drop-out, Huck(le), Hucklebone, Hunkers, Ilium, Informed, Ischium, Pubis, Sciatic, Tonish

Hippopotamus Behemoth, River-horse, Sea-cow, Sea horse

Hire(d), Hiring Affreightment, Charter, Employ, Engage, Fee, Freightage, Job, Lease, Merc(enary), Never-never, Pensionary, Rent, Shape-up, Ticca, Wage

Hirsute Hairy, Pilose, Shaggy

▷ **His** *may indicate* greetings

Hispanic Latino

Hiss(ing) Boo, Fizzle, Goose, Hish, Sibilant, Siffle, Sizzle, Static, Swish

Historian Acton, Adams, Antiquary, Archivist, Arrian, Asellio, Bede, Biographer, Bryant, Buckle, Camden, Carlyle, Centuriator, Chronicler, Etain, Eusebius, Froude, Gibbon, Gildas, Green, Griot, Herodotus, Knickerbocker, Livy, Macaulay, Oman, Paris, Pliny, Plutarch, Ponsonby, Renan, Roper, Sallust, Spengler, Starkey, Strachey, Suetonius, Tacitus, Taylor, Thiers, Thucydides, Toynbee, Trevelyan, Wells, Xenophon

History, Historic(al) Account, Age, Anamnesis, Ancient, Annal, Bunk, Case, Chronicle, Clio, Diachronic, Epoch(a), Epoch-making, Ere-now, Ever, Heritage, Legend, Life, Living, Mesolithic, Modern, Natural, Ontogency, Oral, Past, Record, Renaissance, Story

Histrionic Operatic, Theatrical

Hit Bang, Bash, Baste, Bat, Bean, Belt, Bepat, Blip, Blockbuster, Bloop, Blow, Bludgeon, Boast, Bolo, Bonk, Bunt, Catch, Clobber, Clock, Clout, Club, Collide, Cuff, Dot, Flail, Flick, Flip, Foul, Fourpenny-one, Fungo, Fustigate, Get, Hay, Head-butt, Home(-thrust), Impact, Knock, Lam, Lob, Magpie, Mug, Pandy, Paste, Pepper, Pistol-whip, Polt, Prang, Punto dritto, Ram, Roundhouse, Sacrifice, Score, Sensation, Six, Skier, Sky, Slam, Slap, Slosh, Smash(eroo), Smit(e), Sock, Spank, Spike, Stoush, Straik, Stricken, Strike, Strook, Struck, → **SUCCESS**, Swat, Switch, Thwack, Tip, Tonk, Touché, Undercut, Venewe, Venue, Volley, Wallop, Wham, Wing, Ythundered, Zap, Zonk

Hitch(ed) Catch, Cat's paw, Contretemps, Edge, Espouse, Harness, Hike, Hirsle, Hoi(c)k, Hotch, Jerk, Lorry-hop, Rub, Setback, Sheepshank, Sheet bend, Shrug, Snag, Technical, Thumb, Wed

Hitherto Before, Yet

Hittite Uriah

Hive(s) Colony, Nettlerash, Skep, Spread, Swarm, Wheal

Hoar(y) Ashen(-grey), Canescent, Froren, Frost, Gaudy-day, Grizzled, Rime

Hoard(ing) Accumulate, Amass, Bill, Billboard, Cache, Coffer, Eke, Heap, Hoord, Husband, Hutch, Mucker, Plant, Pose, Salt away, Save, Sciurine, Snudge, Squirrel, Stash, Stock, Store, Stow, Treasure

Hoarse(ness) Croupy, Frog, Grating, Gruff, Husky, Raucous, Roar(er), Roopit, Roopy, Roup, Throaty

Hoax April-fish, Bam, Canard, Cod, Do, Doff, Fub, Fun, Gag, Gammon, Gowk, Gull, Have on, Hum, Huntie-gowk, Kid, Leg-pull, Piltdown, Put-on, Quiz, Sell, Sham, Skit, Spoof, String, Stuff, Supercherie, → **TRICK**

Hob Ceramic, Cooktop, Ferret, Goblin, Lout

Hobble, Hobbling Enfetter, Game, Hamshackle, Hilch, Hitch, Lame, Limp, Pastern, Picket, Spancel, Stagger, Tether

Hobby Avocation, Fad, Falcon, Interest, Pastance, → **PASTIME**, Predator, Pursuit, Recreation, Scrimshaw

Hobby-horse Dada, Obsession, Play-mare

Hobgoblin Bog(e)y, Bull-beggar, Puck, Worriecow

Hobnail Clinker, Tacket

Hobnob Chat, Mingle

Hobo Bum, Drifter, → **TRAMP**, Vagrant

Hock Cambrel, Dip, Gambrel, Gambril, Gammon, Ham, Heel, Hough, Hypothecate, Pawn, Pledge, Rhenish, Wine

Hockey Field, Grass, Hurling, Ice, Pond, Shinny, Shinty, Street

Hod Carrier, Tray

Hodge Peasant, Rustic, Yokel

Hoe Claut, Draw, Dutch, Grub, Grubbing, Jembe, Nab, Pecker, Prong, Rake, Scuffle, Thrust, Weed

Hog Babiroussa, Babirussa, Boar, Glutton, Guttle, Peccary, Pig, Porker, Puck, Road, Shoat, Shott, Whole

Hogmanay Ne'erday

Hog-rat Hutia

Hogshead Butt, Cask, Muid

Hogwash Bull, Nonsense, Swill, Twaddle

Hoi-polloi Prole(tariat), Rabble

Hoist Boom, Bouse, Bunk-up, Crane, Davit, Derrick, Garnet, Gin, Heft, Hills, Jack, Lewis, Lift, Raise, Shearlegs, Shears, Sheerlegs, Sheers, Sway, Teagle, Trice, Whip-and-derry, Wince, Winch, Windas, Windlass

Hold(er), Holding, Hold back, out, up, etc Absorb, Allege, Alow, Anchor, Apply, Backbreaker, Belay, Believe, Boston crab, Caesura, Canister, Cease, Cement, Cinch, Clamp, Clasp, Cling, Clip, Clutch, Contain, Cotland, Cresset, Defer, Delay, Detain, Display, Dog, Embrace, Engross, Er, Facebar, Farm, Fast, Fief, Fistful, Frog, Full nelson, Garter, → **GRASP**, Grip, Grovet, Half-nelson, Hammerlock, Handle, Haud, Have, Headlock, Heft, Heist, Hiccup, Hinder, Hitch, Ho(a), Hoh, Hoy, Hug, Impedance, Impede, Impediment, Impound, In chancery, Incumbent, Intern, Intray, Japanese stranglehold, Keep, Keepnet, Lease, Maintain, Manure, Nelson, Nurse, Occupant, Own, Port, Proffer, Purchase, Rack, Reach, Reluct, Reserve, Restrain, Retain, Rivet, Rob, Rundale, Runrig, Save, Scissors, Shelve, Shore, Sleeve, Sostenuto, Stand, Suplex, Suspend, Tenancy, Tenement, Tenure, Toehold, Toft, Tray, Tripod, → **WRESTLING**, Wristlock, Zarf, Zurf

Hole(s), Holed, Holey Ace, Agloo, Aglu, Albatross, Antrum, Aubrey, Beam, Birdie, Black, Bogey, Bolt, Burrow, Cat, Cave, Cavity, Cenote, Cissing, Coal, Coalsack, Collapsar, Crater, Cubby, Cup, Dell, Den, Dene, Dog-leg, Dolina, Doline, Dormie, Dormy, Dreamhole, Dry, Dugout, Eagle, Earth, Ethmoid, Eye(let), Faveolate, Finger, Foramen, Funk, Gap, Geat, Glory, Gnamma, Gutta, Hag(g), Hideout, Kettle, Knot, Lenticel, Lill, Limber, Loop, Loup, Lubber's, Lumina, Maar, Mortise, Moulin, Namma, Nineteenth, Oillet, → **OPENING**, Orifex, Orifice, Ozone, Perforate, Pierce, Pigeon, Pinprick, Pit, Pocket, Pore, Port, Pot, Potato, Priest's, Punctuate, Punctum, Puncture, Rabbet, Rivet, Rowport, Sallyport, Scupper, Scuttle, Scye,

Sinus, Situation, Slot, Snag, Snow, Soakaway, Socket, Sound, Spandrel, Spider, Spiraculum, Starting, Stead, Stew, Stop, Stove, Swallow, Tear, Thirl, Thumb, Tight spot, Touch, Trema, Vent, Ventage, Ventige, Voided, Vug, Watering, Well, White, Wookey

Holiday(s), Holiday maker Away, Bank, Benjo, Break, Busman's, Camper, Childermas, Days of Awe, Ferial, Festa, → **FESTIVAL**, Fête, Fiesta, Fly-drive, Furlough, Gala, Half(term), High, Honeymoon, Kwanzaa, Lag b'Omer, Laik, Leasure, Leave, Legal, Leisure, Long, Minibreak, Off-day, Off-time, Outing, Packaged, Pink-eye, Play-day, Playtime, Public, Purim, Recess, Repose, Rest, Roman, Schoolie, Seaside, Shabuoth, Shavuot, Sojourn, Statutory, Stay, Sunday, Tax, Trip, → **VACATION**, Villegiatura, Wake(s), Whitsun

Holinshed Chronicler

Holland(s) Batavia, Genevese, Gin, Hogen-mogen, Netherlands, NL

Hollow Acetabulum, Alveary, Antar, Antre, Antrum, Armpit, Axilla, Blastula, Boss, Bowl, Cave(rn), Cavity, Chasm, Chott, Cirque, Cleché, Comb(e), Concave, Coomb, Corrie, Crater, Cup(mark), Cwm, Deaf, Dean, Dell, Delve, Den(e), Dent, Dimple, Dingle, Dip, Dish(ing), Dolina, Doline, Empty, Fossette, Frost, Gilgai, Glenoid, Gnamma-hole, Gowpen, Groove, Grot(to), Hole, How, Howe, Igloo, Incavo, Insincere, Keck(sy), Kettle(hole), Kex, Khud, Lip-deep, Mortise, Namma-hole, Niche, Omphaloid, Orbita, Pan, Philtrum, Pit, Punt, Redd, Rout, Rut, Scoop, Shott, Sinus, Slade, Sleepy, Slot, Slough, Socket, Swire, Thank-you-ma'am, Trematic, Trough, Vlei, Vola, Wame, Wem

Holly Aquifoliaceae, Eryngo, Ilex, Mate, Winterberry, Yaupon

Hollyhock Althaea, Malva, Rose mallow

Hollywood Bowl, Tinseltown

Holm Isle

Holmes Sherlock, Wendell

Holmium Ho

Holocaust Churban, Shoah

Hologram, Holograph Laser, MS

Holothurian Trepang

Holster Sheath

Holy(man), Holiness Adytum, Alliance, Ariadne, Blessed, → **DIVINE**, Godly, Grail, Halidom, Hallowed, Helga, Hery, Khalif, Loch, Mountain, Olga, Orders, Pan(h)agia, Pious, Sacred, Sacrosanct, Sad(d)hu, Saintly, Sanctitude, Sannayasi(n), Santon, Sekos, Sepulchre, Shrine, Starets, Staretz, SV, Tirthankara, War

Holy books, Holy writing Adigranth, Atharvaveda, Bible, Gemara, Granth, Hadith, Hagiographa, Koran, Mishnah, NT, OT, Pia, Purana, Rigveda, Sama-Veda, → **SCRIPTURE**, Shaster, Shastra, Smriti, Sura(h), Tanach, Writ, Yajur-Veda

Holy building, Holy city, Holy place Chapel, Church, Kaaba, Mashhad, Mecca, Medina, Meshed, Najaf, Penetralia, Sanctum, Station, Synagogue, Temenos, Temple

Holy Ghost Paraclete

Holy water Amrit

Homage Bow, Cense, Honour, Kneel, Manred, Obeisance, Tribute, Vail

Home(land), Homeward Abode, Apartment, Base, Blighty, Bro, Broken, Burrow, Cheshire, Chez, Clinic, Community, Convalescent, Domal, Domicile, Earth, Eventide, Family, Fireside, Flat, Funeral, Gaff, Goal, Habitat, Harvest, Heame, Hearth, Heme, Hospice, House, In, Lair, Libken, Lockwood, Lodge, Maisonette, Mental, Mobile, Montacute, Nest, Nursing, Old sod, Pad, Penny-gaff, Pied à terre, Pile, Pit dwelling, Plas Newydd, Remand, Res(idence), Rest, Starter, Stately, Tepee, Turangawaewae, Up-along, Villa, Warren

Homecoming Nostos
Home counties SE
Homeless Bag lady, Gangrel, Outler, Rootless, Skell
Homer(ic) Comatose, Cor, Epic(ist), Maeonides, Nod, Pigeon, Somnolent
Home-rule Parnellism, Swaraj
Homesick(ness) Heimweh, Mal du pays
Homespun Cracker-barrel, Plain, Raploch, Russet, Simple
Homestead Ranch, Toft
Homework → DIY, Prep, Preparation
Homicidal, Homicide Chance-medley, Justifiable, Killing, Manslaughter
Homily Lecture, Midrash, Pi, Postil, Prone, Sermon, Tract
▷ **Homing** *may indicate* coming back
Hominid Oreopitheous
Homogeneous Indiscrete
Homogram, Homograph Abac, Heteronym
Homosexual(ity) Arse bandit, Auntie man, Bardash, Batty boy, Bender, Bent, Buftie, Bufty, Camp, Cat, Catamite, Closet queen, Cocksucker, Cottaging, Dike, Dyke, Fag(got), Fairy, Friend of Dorothy, Fruit, Gay, Gaydar, Ginger, Homophile, Invert, Lesbian, Meatrack, Moffie, Muscle Mary, Pederast, Ponce, Poof(tah), Poofter, Poove, Pouf(fe), Poufter, Puff, Punk, Quean, Queer, Quiff, Rough trade, Shirt-lifter, Slash, Swish(y), Tonk, Tribade, Uranism, Urning, Woofter
Hone Grind, → SHARPEN, Whet
Honest(y), Honestly Aboveboard, Afauld, Afawld, Amin, Candour, Clean, Fair dinkum, Genuine, Incorruptible, Injun, Jake, Jannock, Jonnock, Legitimate, Lunaria, Lunary, Mensch, Open-faced, Penny, Probity, Rectitude, Reputable, Righteous, Round, Sincere, Square, Squareshooter, Straight, Straight-arrow, Straight-out, Trojan, → TRUE, Truepenny, Upfront, Upright, Upstanding
Honey Comb, Flattery, Hybla(ean), Hymettus, Mel, Melliferous, Nectar, Oenomel, Oxymel, Palm, Peach, Popsy-wopsy, Sis, Sugar, Sweetheart, Sweetie, Virgin, Wild, Wood
Honeycomb(ed) Cellular, Faveolate, Favose, Favous, Smock, Waxwork
Honeydew Mildew
Honey-eater Bear, Blue-eye, Pooh
Honeypot Haanepoot
Honeysuckle Abelia, Anthemion, Caprifoil, Caprifole, Lonicera, Rewa rewa, Suckling, Woodbind, Woodbine
Honour(s), Honourable, Honoured, Honorary, Honorific A, Accolade, Ace, Adore, Birthday, Blue, Bow, CBE, Commemorate, Credit, Curtsey, Dan, Elate, Emeritus, Ennoble, → ESTEEM, Ethic, Face-card, Fame, Fête, Gloire, Glory, Grace, Greats, Homage, Insignia, Invest, Izzat, J, Jack, K, King, Knave, Knight, Kudos, Laudation, Laureate, Laurels, MBE, Mention, Military, OBE, Optime, Pundonor, Q, Queen, Remember, Repute, Respect, Revere, Reward, Ten, Tenace, Titular, Tripos, Venerate, White, Worship, Wranglers
Honourable companion CH
Honourless Yarborough
Hooch Hogan, Hogen, Moonshine
Hood(ed) Almuce, Amaut, Amice, Amowt, Apache, Balaclava, Bashlik, Biggin, Blindfold, Calash, Calèche, Calyptra, Capeline, Capuccio, Capuche, Chaperon(e), Coif, Cope, Cowl, Cucullate(d), Faldetta, Fume, Gangster, Jacobin, Kennel, Lens, Liripipe, Liripoop, Mantle, Mazarine, Nithsdale, Pixie, Robin, Rowdy, Snood, Trot-cosey, Trot-cozy, Visor

Hoodlum Gangster, Roughneck, Thug, Wanksta
Hoodoo Moz(z)
Hoodwink(ed) Blear, Bluff, Cheat, → DECEIVE, Gull, Nose-led, Seel
Hoof(ed) Artiodactyla, Cloot, Coffin, Frog, Trotter, Ungula
Hoohah Humdudgeon
Hook(er), Hooked, Hooks Addict, Adunc, Aduncous, Arrester, Barb(icel), Barbule, Becket, Butcher's, Cant(dog), Catch, Chape, Claw, Cleek, Clip, Clove, Cocotte, Corvus, Crampon, Cromb, Crome, Crook, Crotchet, Cup, Drail, Duck, Fifi, Fish, Floozy, Fluke, Fly, Gab, Gaff, Gig, Grapnel, Grappling, Gripple, Hamate, Hamose, Hamulus, Heel, Hitch, Inveigle, Kype, Meat, Pot, Prostitute, Pruning, Retinaculum, Sister, Snell, Sniggle, Swivel, Tala(u)nt, Tart, Tenaculum, Tenter, Tie, Trip, Uncus, Wanton, Welsh
Hookah Bong, Chillum, Hubble-bubble, Kalian, Narghil(l)y, Narg(h)ile, Nargileh, Nargil(l)y, Pipe
Hooligan Apache, Bogan, Casual, Desperado, Droog, Hobbledehoy, Hoon, Keelie, Larrikin, Lout, Ned, Rough(neck), Ruffian, Skollie, Skolly, Tearaway, Ted, Tityre-tu, Tough, Tsotsi, Vandal, Yahoo, Yob(bo)
Hoop(s) Bail, Band, Circle, Farthingale, Garth, Gird, Girr, Hula®, O, Pannier, → RING, Tire, Trochus, Trundle
Hooray Whoopee, Yippee
Hoot(er) Conk, Deride, Honk, Madge, Nose, Owl, Riot, Screech-owl, Siren, Ululate
Hoover Consume, Dam
Hop(per) An(o)ura, Ball, Bin, Cuscus, Dance, Flight, Jeté, Jump, Kangaroo, Leap, Lilt, Long, Opium, Pogo, Roo, Saltate, Scotch, Skip, Spring, Tremié, Vine
Hope(ful) Anticipate, Aspirant, Comer, Contender, Daydream, Desire, Dream, Esperance, Evelyn, Expectancy, Forlorn, Gleam, Good, Pipe-dream, Promising, Roseate, Rosy, Sanguine, Trust, Valley, Wannabe, White, Wish
Hopeless(ness), Hopeless quest Abattu, Anomie, Anomy, Black, Buckley's chance, Dead duck, Despair, Despondent, Forlorn, Goner, Non-starter, Perdu, Pessimist
Hopscotch Peevers
Horace Flaccus, Ode, Satirist
Horatio Nelson
Horatius Cocles
Horde Crowd, Golden, Many, Mass, Mob, Swarm
Horizon A, Apparent, Artificial, B, C, Celestial, Event, Gyro, Rational, Scope, Sea-line, Sensible, Skyline, Visible
Horizontal Advection, Flat, Level, Prone, Supine, Tabular
Hormone Abscision, ACTH, Adrenalin®, Adrenaline, Aldosterone, Androgen, Androsterone, Angiotensin, Antidiuretic, Autacoid, Auxin, Biosynthesis, Bursicon, Calcitonin, Catecholamine, Cholecystokinin, Corticoid, Corticosteroid, Corticosterone, Cortisone, Cytokinin, Ecdysone, Endocrine, Erythropoietin, Estrogen, Florigen, Folliculin, FSH, Gastrin, Ghrelin, Gibberellin, Glucagon, Gonadotrophic, Gonadotrop(h)in, Growth, Hydrocortisone, IAA, Inhibin, Insulin, Intermedin, Juvenile, Kinin, Leuteotropic, Levonorgestral, Lipotropin, Luteinizing, Lutetrophic, Melanotropine, Melatonin, Mineralocorticord, Noradrenalin(e), Norepinephrine, Oestradiol, Oestriol, Oestrogen, Oestrone, Oxytocin, Pancreozymin, Parathyroid, Pituitrin, Plant, Progesterone, Progestin, Progestogen, Prolactin, Prostaglandin, Relaxin, Secretagogue, Secretin, Secretion, Serotonin, Sex, Somatomedin, Somatostatin, Somatotrop(h)in, Steroid, Stilboestrol, Testosterone, Thymosin, Thyroid, Thyrotrop(h)in, Thyroxine, Trilodothyronine, TSH, Vasopressin

Horn(s), Horny Acoustic, Advancer, Amalthea, Antenna(e), Antler, Baleen, Basset, Beeper, Bez, Brass, Buck, Bugle, Bur(r), Cape, Ceratoid, Cor, Cornet, Cornett, Cornopean, Cornu(a), Cornucopia, Cromorna, Cromorne, Cusp, Dilemma, English, Exponential, Flugel-horn, French, Frog, Gemshorn, Golden, Gore, Hooter, → **HORNBLOWER**, Hunting, Ivory, Keratin, Klaxon, Lur, Morsing, Mot, Oliphant, Periostracum, Plenty, Post, Powder, Pryse, Ram's, Scur, Shofar, Shophor, Spongin, Tenderling, Trey, Trez, Trumpet, Tusk, Vulcan's badge, Waldhorn

Hornblende Syntagmatite

Hornblower Brain, Horatio, Peel, Triton, Trumpeter

Hornbook Battledoor, Battledore

Horned (sheep) Cabrié, Cabrit, Cornute, Hamate, Lunate, Mouflon, Muflon

Hornet Stinger

Hornless Doddy, Humbel, Humlie, Hummel, Mooly, Mul(l)ey, Poley, Polled

Hornpipe Matelote

Horoscope Figure, Future, Prophecy, Star-map

Horrible, Horror Aw(e)some, Beastly, Brat, Dire, Dread(ful), Execrable, Gashful, Ghastly, Grisly, Grooly, Gruesome, Grysie, Hideous, Loathsome, Minging, Nightmare, Odious, Panic, Shock, Terror, Ugh, Vile

Horrid, Horrific, Horrify(ing) Appal, Dire, Dismay, Dreadful, Frightful, Ghastly, Gothic, Grim, Grisly, H, Loathy, Odious, Spine chilling, Spiteful, Ugly

Hors d'oeuvres Antipasto, Canapé, Carpaccio, Ceviche, Hoummos, Houmus, Hummus, Mez(z)e, Pâté, Smorgasbord, Smor(re)brod, Smør(re)brød, Zak(o)uski

Horse Airer, Bidet, Bloodstock, Carriage, Cut, Cutting, Dark, Doer, Dray, Drier, Drug, Equine, Form, H, → **HEROIN**, High, Hobby, Iron, Knight, Kt, Light, Lot, Maiden, Malt, Non-starter, Outsider, Pack, Pantomime, Plug, Ride, Rocking, Sawbuck, Screen, Selling-plate, Sense, Stalking, Standard-bred, Starter, Stayer, Steeplechaser, Stiff, Stock, Teaser, Trestle, Vanner, Vaulting, Whistler, White, Willing, Wooden

HORSES

2 letters:	Colt	5 letters:	Shire
GG	Crib	Arion	Stage
	Dale	Arkle	Steed
3 letters:	Fell	Bevis	Tacky
Ass	Foal	Borer	Takhi
Bay	Hack	Caple	Trace
Cob	Jade	Capul	Troop
Dun	Mare	Favel	Waler
Gee	Pole	Filly	Wheel
Nag	Pony	Genet	
Pad	Post	Morel	6 letters:
Pot	Prad	Mount	Ambler
Rip	Roan	Neddy	Bayard
Tit	Scag	Pacer	Bronco
	Snow	Paint	Brumby
4 letters:	Span	Pinto	Calico
Arab	Stud	Poler	Canuck
Aver	Taki	Punch	Cayuse
Barb	Trot	Rogue	Chaser
Buck	Yale	Screw	Cooser
Cert	Yaud	Seian	Crollo

Curtal
Cusser
Dobbin
Entire
Exmoor
Favell
Ganger
Garran
Garron
Gennet
Hogget
Hunter
Jennet
Kanuck
Keffel
Lampos
Livery
Morgan
Mudder
Novice
Pad-nag
Plater
Pommel
Poster
Quagga
Randem
Remuda
Roarer
Rouncy
Runner
Sabino
Saddle
Shoo-in
Sorrel
String
Stumer
Summer
Tandem
Tarpan
Tracer
Trojan

7 letters:
Bobtail

Breaker
Cavalry
Centaur
Charger
Clipper
Coacher
Courser
Cuisser
Dappled
Draught
Eclipse
Eventer
Gelding
Hackney
Hobbler
Liberty
Marengo
Marocco
Morocco
Mustang
Palfrey
Pegasus
Piebald
Pointer
Quarter
Remount
Saddler
Sheltie
Spanker
Sumpter
Swallow
Swinger
Trigger
Trooper
Trotter
Walking
Wheeler
Xanthos
Xanthus

8 letters:
Aquiline
Bangtail
Bathorse

Boerperd
Buckskin
Camargue
Chestnut
Clay-bank
Cocktail
Dartmoor
Destrier
Eohippus
Friesian
Galloway
Highland
Holstein
Hyperion
Kochlani
Lusitano
Palomino
Schimmel
Shetland
Skewbald
Sleipnir
Springer
Stallion
Stibbler
Warragal
Warragle
Warragul
Warrigal
Welsh cob
Yarraman
Yearling

9 letters:
Appaloosa
Black Bess
Caballine
Clavileno
Coldblood
Connemara
Dapple bay
Gringolet
Houyhnhnm
Icelandic
Incitatus

Knabstrup
Percheron
Rosinante
Rozinante
Warmblood

10 letters:
Andalusian
Bucephalus
Buckjumper
Buttermilk
Clydesdale
Copenhagen
Dapple-grey
Lipizzaner
Lippizaner
Pliohippus
Przewalski
Showjumper
Stagecoach
Svadilfari
Wheelhorse

11 letters:
Daisy-cutter
High-stepper
Przewalski's

12 letters:
Cleveland Bay
Hambletonian
Suffolk Punch
Thoroughbred

13 letters:
Perissodactyl

16 letters:
Tennessee Walking

Horseback Croup
Horse-box Stable, Stall
Horse-chestnut Aesculus, Conker
Horse collar Brecham, Hame
Horse complaint, Horse disease, Horse problem, Horse trouble Blind
staggers, Blood spavin, Bogspavin, Bot(t)s, Broken wind, Capel(l)et, Canker, Cracked

heels, Cratches, Crepance, Curb, Dourine, Equinia, Eweneck, Farcin, Farcy, Fives, Founder, Frush, Glanders, Gourdy, Grape, Grass-sickness, Head staggers, Heaves, Hippiatric, Knee spavin, Laminitis, Lampas, Lampers, Malander, Mallander, Mallender, Megrims, Miller's disease, Mooneye, Mud fever, N(a)gana, Parrot mouth, Poll-evil, Quartercrack, Quitter, Quittor, Ringbone, Roaring, Sallenders, Sand crack, Scratches, Seedy-toe, Shaft, Spavie, Spavin, Springhalt, Staggers, Strangles, Stringhalt, Summer sores, Surra, Sway-back, Sween(e)y, Thorough-pin, Thrush, Toe-crack, Tread, Vives, Weed, Weid, Whistling, Windgall, Wind-sucking, Wire-heel, Yellows

Horse-dealer Buster, Coper

Horse-lover Philip

Horseman Ataman, Caballero, Cavalry, Centaur, Conquest, Cossack, Cowboy, Death, Dragman, Famine, Farrier, Hobbler, Hussar, Knight, Lancer, Nessus, Ostler, Parthian, Picador, Pricker, Quadrille, Revere, → **RIDER**, Slaughter, Spahi, Stradiot, Tracer, Wrangler

Horsemanship Manège

Horseplay Caper, Chukka, Knockabout, Polo, Rag, Rant, Romp

Horsepower Hp, Indicated, Ps

Horseradish Ben, Moringa

Horseshoe(-shaped) Henge, Hippocrepian, King-crab, Lunette, Manilla, Oxbow, Plate

Horsetail Equisetum

Horse thief Blanco, Rustler

Horticultural, Horticulture, Horticulturist Grower, Pomology, RHS

Hose Chausses, Fishnet, Galligaskins, Gaskins, Lisle, Netherstock(ing), Nylons, Panty, Sock, Stockings, Tabi, Tights, Trunk, Tube

Hospitable, Hospitality Cadgy, Convivial, Corporate, Entertainment, Euxine, Kidgie, Lucullan, Open house, Philoxenia, Social, Xenial

Hospital Ambulance, Asylum, Barts, Base, Bedlam, Booby hatch, Bughouse, Clinic, Cottage, Day, Dressing station, ENT, Field, Foundation, General, Guys, H, Home, Hospice, Hôtel dieu, Imaret, Infirmary, Isolation, Karitane, Lambarene, Lazaretto, Leprosarium, Leprosery, Lock, Loony bin, Lying-in, MASH, Mental, Nosocomial, Nuthouse, Nuttery, Ozzie, Pest-house, Polyclinic, Rathouse, San, Scutari, Sick bay, Snake-pit, Special, Spital, Spittle, Teaching, Trust, UCH

Host(s), Hostess Alternate, Amphitryon, Army, Barmecide, Bunny girl, Chatelaine, Compere, Crowd, Definitive, Emcee, Entertainer, Eucharist, Heavenly, Hirsel, Hotelier, Innkeeper, Intermediate, Inviter, Laban, Landlady, Landlord, Legend, Legion, Licensee, Lion-hunter, Lot, Mass, Mavin, MC, Number, Publican, Quickly, Sabaoth, Swarm, Taverner, Throng, Torrent, Trimalchio, Wafer

Hostage Gherao, Pawn, Pledge, POW

Hostel(ry) Asylum, Auberge, Dharms(h)ala, Dorm, Dormitory, Entry, Halfway house, Inn, YHA, Youth

Hostile, Hostility Adverse, Aggressive, Alien, Anger, Animus, Aversion, Bellicose, Bitter, Chilly, Currish, Diatribe, Feud, Forbidding, Hating, Icy, Ill, Ill-will, Inimical, Inveterate, Oppugnant, Unfriendly, Virulent, Vitriolic, War

Hot (tempered) Ardent, Big, Blistering, Breem, Breme, Cajun, Calid, Candent, Dog days, Enthusiastic, Facula, Fervid, Feverish, Fiery, Fuggy, Gospeller, Het, In, Incandescent, Irascible, Lewd, Live, Mafted, Mirchi, Mustard, Pepper, Piping, Potato, Quick, Randy, Red, Roaster, Scorcher, Sexpot, Sexy, Sizzling, Spicy, Spitfire, Stewy, Stifling, Stolen, Sultry, Sweaty, Sweltering, Sweltry, Tabasco®, Thermidor, Torrid, Toustie, Tropical, Zealful

Hotchpotch Bricolage, Farrago, Mish-mash, Powsowdy, Welter

Hotel, Hotelkeeper Bo(a)tel, Boutique, Commercial, Fleabag, Flophouse, Gasthaus, Gasthof, H, Hilton, Host, Hydro, Inn, Motel, Parador, Patron(ne), Posada, Private, Ritz, Roadhouse, Savoy, Tavern, Temperance, Trust, Waldorf, Watergate
Hothead(ed) Impetuous, Rash, Spitfire, Volcano
Hot-house Conservatory, Forcing-house, Nursery, Orangery, Vinery
Hot plate Salamander
Hot rod Dragster
Hotspur Harry, Hothead, Rantipole
Hottentot Griqua, Khoikhoi, Strandloper
Hot water Soup, Therm
Hound(s) Afghan, Basset, Beagle, Bellman, Brach, Cad, Canine, Cry, → **DOG**, Entry, Gabriel's, Gaze, Hamiltonstovare, Harass, Harrier, Hen-harrier, Ibizan, Javel, Kennet, Lyam, Lym(e), Mute, Otter, Pack, Pharaoh, Pursue, Rache, Ranter, Reporter, Saluki, Talbot, True, Tufter
Hound's bane Palay
Hour(s) Canonical, Complin(e), Elders', Eleventh, Flexitime, Golden, H, Happy, Holy, Hr, Literacy, Little, Lunch, None(s), Office, Orthros, Peak, Prime, Rush, Sext, Sidereal, Small, Staggered, Terce, Tide, Time, Undern, Unsocial, Vespers, Visiting, Witching, Working, Zero
Hourglass Meniscoid
House(s), Housing, Household(er) Abode, Accepting, Adobe, Aerie, Aery, Astrology, Audience, Auditorium, B, Bach, Bastide, Beehive, Beth, Bhavan, Bhawan, Biggin, Bingo, Black, Block, Boarding, Bondage, Brick veneer, Broadcasting, Broiler, Brownstone, Bundestag, Casa, Chalet, Chamber, Chapter, Charnel, Château, Chattel, Chez, Clapboard, Clearing, Coffee, Commercial, Concern, Convent, Cote, Cottage (orné), Council, Counting, Country, Crankcase, Crib, Custom(s), Dacha, Dail, Demain, Demesne, Derry, Des res, Discount, Disorderly, Domal, Domestic, Domicile, Donga, Door, Dower, Drostdy, Drum, Duplex, Dwelling, Dynasty, Edifice, Entertain, Establishment, Este, Eyrie, Familial, Fashion, Fibro(cement), Finance, Firm, Forcing, Frame, Fraternity, Free, Frontager, Full, Gaff, Gambling, Garage, Gite, Government, Grace and favour, Habitat, Habitation, Hacienda, Halfway, Hall, Harbour, Hearth, HK, Ho, Home, Homestead, Ice, Igloo, Infill, Inn, Insula, Issuing, Joss, Ken, Lodge, Lofted, Loose, Lot(t)o, Maison(ette), Malting, Manor, Manse, Mansion, Mas, Meeting, Meiney, Meinie, Meiny, Ménage, Menyie, Messuage, Mobility, Monastery, Montagne, Nacelle, Node, Open(-plan), Opera, Pad, Parliament, Pent, Picts, Picture, Pilot, Pleasure, Pole, Pondokkie, Post, Prefab, Printing, Public, Quinta, Radome, Ranch, Ratepayer, Register, Residence, Rooming, Root, Rough, Sacrament, Safe, Saltbox, Satis, Schloss, School, Seat, Semi, Shanty, Sheltered, Show, Sign, Social, Software, Spec-built, Sporting, Stable, State, Station, Steeple, Storey, Succession, Tavern, Tea, Tenement, Terrace, Theatre, Third, Tied, Toft, Tombola, Tower, Town, Tract, Treasure, Tree, Trust, Try, Upby, Vaulting, Vicarage, Villa, Villa(-home), Wash, Watch, Weather, Weatherboard, Weigh, Wendy, Whare, Wheel, White, Work, Zero, Zodiac

HOUSES

3 letters:	Keys	**5 letters:**	Usher
Leo	Syon	Lords	
	York	Scala	**6 letters:**
4 letters:		Tudor	Orange
Bush		Upper	Queen's

6 letters – cont:
Seanad
Stuart
Wilton

7 letters:
Althing
Althorp
Bourbon
Commons
Hanover
Kenwood
Knesset
Lodging

Osborne
Stewart
Trinity
Windsor

8 letters:
Burghley
Chequers
Harewood
Hatfield
Holyrood
Lagthing
Longleat
Petworth

Somerset

9 letters:
Admiralty
Chartwell
Knebworth
Lancaster
Odelsting

10 letters:
Chatsworth
Heartbreak
Kirribilli
Odelsthing

11 letters:
Plantagenet
Russborough
Sandringham

12 letters:
Lockwood Home

13 letters:
Seanad Eireann

15 letters:
Representatives

House-boat Wangun, Wan(i)gan
House-builder Jack
House-keeper Chatelaine, Go(u)vernante, Matron, Publican
House-leek Sengreen
Housemaid's knee Bursa
Houseman Betty, Doctor, Intern, Peer
Housemate Co-tenant
House-warming Infare
Housewife Etui, Needlecase, WI
Housework Chore, DIY
Housing Case, Crankcase, Shabrack, Shelter, Slum, Tenement
Hova Malagash
Hove Plim, Swell
Hovel Cru(i)ve, Den, Pigsty, Shack, Shanty
Hover Hang, Levitate, Lurk, Poise
Hovercraft Air-car
How Hill, Hollow
How'dyedo, How d'ye do Hallo, Pass, Salve
However Although, As, But, Even-so, Leastwise, Sed, Still, Though, Yet
Howitzer Gun
Howl(er) Banshee, Bawl, Bay, Bloop, Clanger, Hue, Mycetes, Slip up, Squawk,
  Ululate, War whoop, Wow, Yawl, Yowl
How much The
Hoy Bilander, Ship
HP Never-never
HQ Centre, Headquarters, SHAPE
Hub Boss, Boston, Centre, Focus, Hob, Nave, Pivot, Tee
Hubbub Charivari, Chirm, Coil, Din, Level-coil, Palaver, Racket, Row, Stir
Hubris Pride
Huckster Hawker, Kidd(i)er, Pedlar
Huddle Cringe, Gather, Hunch, Ruck, Shrink
Hudson River, Rock
Hue Colour, Dye, Outcry, Proscription, Steven, Tincture, Tinge, Utis
Huff Dudgeon, Hector, Pant, Pet, Pique, Snuff, Strunt, Umbrage, Vex
Hug Bear, Coll, Cuddle, → **EMBRACE**, Squeeze
Huge (number) Astronomical, Brobdingnag, Colossal, Enorm(ous), Gargantuan,

Giant, → **GIGANTIC**, Gillion, Ginormous, Humongous, Humungous, Immane, Immense, Leviathan, Lulu, Mega-, Milliard, Monolithic, Monster, Octillion, Prodigious, Socking, Stupendous, Tall, Titanian, Tremendous, Vast, Whacking

Hugo Victor

Huguenot Camisard

Hulk Lout, Ruin, Shale, Shell, Ship

Hull Bottom, Framework, Husk, Inboard, Monocoque, Pod, Sheal, Sheel, Shell, Shiel, Shill, Shiplap

Hullabaloo Outcry, Razzamatazz, Raz(z)mataz(z)

▶ **Hullo** *see* **HELLO**

Hum(ming) Bombilate, Bombinate, Bum, Chirm, Chirr, Drone, Lilt, Moan, Murmur, Nos(e)y, Odorate, Odorous, Pong, Ponk, Rank, Reek, Sowf(f), Sowth, Stench, Stink, Stir, Whir(r), Zing

Human(e), Humanist, Humanity Anthropoid, Bang, Colet, Earthling, Erasmus, Incarnate, Kindness, Mandom, Merciful, Mortal, Philanthropic, Species, Sympathy, Ubuntu, Virtual, Wight

Humble Abase, Abash, Afflict, Baseborn, Chasten, Cow, Degrade, Demean, Demiss(ly), Lower, Lowly, Mean, Mean-born, → **MEEK**, Modest, Morigerate, Obscure, Poor, Rude, Small, Truckle

Humbug Berley, Blague, Blarney, Buncombe, Bunk(um), Burley, Cant, Claptrap, Con, Delude, Eyewash, Flam, Flummery, Fraud, Fudge, Gaff, Gammon, Gas, Guff, Gum, Hoax, Hoodwink, Hookey-walker, Kibosh, Liar, Maw-worm, Nonsense, Prig, Shenanigan, Wind

Humdinger Cracker, Lulu

Humdrum Banal, Boredom, Bourgeois, Monotonous, Mundane, Ordinary, Prosaic, Tedious

Humid(ity) Clammy, Damp, Dank, Machie, Machy, Moch, Muggy, Saturation, Steam, Sticky, Sultry, Tropical

Humiliate(d), Humiliation, Humility Abase, Abash, Baseness, Degrade, Disbench, Eating crow, Fast, Indignity, Laughing stock, Lose face, Lowlihead, Mortify, Put-down, → **SHAME**, Skeleton, Take-down, Wither

Humming-bird Colibri, Hermit, Racket-tail, Rainbow, Sabre-wing, Sapphire-wing, Sappho, Sawbill, Sylph, Thornbill, Topaz, Trochilus

Hummock Tump

Humorist Cartoonist, Comedian, Jester, Leacock, Lear, Punster, Twain, Wodehouse

Humour, Humorous Aqueous, Bile, Blood, Caprice, Cardinal, Chaff, Choler, Coax, Cocker, Coddle, Cosher, Cuiter, Cuittle, Daut, Dawt, Dry, Facetious, Fun, Gallows, Ichor, Indulge, Irony, Jocose, Jocular, Juice, Kidney, Lavatorial, Levity, Light, Melancholy, → **MOOD**, Observe, One-liner, Pamper, Phlegm, Pun, Pythonesque, Ribaldry, Salt, Serum, Temper, Trim, Vein, Vitreous, Vitreum, Wetness, Whim, Whimsy, Wit

Humourless Dry, Po(-faced)

Hump(ed), Humping Boy, Bulge, Dorts, Dowager's, Gibbose, Gibbous, Hog, Huff, Hummock, Hunch, Middelmannetjie, Pip, Ramp, Road, Sex, Speed bump, Tussock

▶ **Humpback** *see* **HUNCHBACK**

Humphrey Bogart

Humus Compost, Leafmould, Moder, Mor, Mull

Hun Alaric, Atli, Attila, Fritz, German

Hunch(ed), Hunchback Camel, Chum, Crookback, Gobbo, Intuition, Kyphosis, Premonition, Quasimodo, Roundback, Sense, Squat, Urchin

Hundred(s), Hundredth Burnham, C, Cantred, Cantref, Cent, Centesimal, Centum,

Century, Chiltern, Commot, Days, Desborough, Great, Host, → **IN A HUNDRED**, Long, Northstead, Old, Shire, Stoke, Ton, Wapentake

Hundred and fifty CL, Y

Hundred and sixty T

Hundredweight Centner, Long, Metric, Quintal, Short

Hung Displayed, Executed, Framed, High

Hungarian, Hungary Bohunk, Cheremis(s), Csardas, Magyar, Nagy, Szekely, Tzigane, Ugric, Vogul

Hunger, Hungry Appestat, Appetite, Bulimia, Bulimy, Clem, → **CRAVE**, Desire, Edacity, Empty, Esurient, Famine, Famish, Fast, Hanker, Hunter, Pant, Peckish, Rapacious, Raven, Ravin, Sharp-set, Unfed, Unfuelled, Yaup, Yearn

▷ **Hungry** *may indicate* an 'o' in another word

Hunk(s) Beefcake, Chunk, Dry-fist, Miser(ly), Slab, Wedge

Hunker Squat

Hunt(er), Hunting, Huntress, Huntsman Actaeon, Alew, Archer, Artemis, Atalanta, Battue, Beagle, Bellman, Bounty, Calydon, Chace, Chase(r), Chasseur, Chevy, Cool, Coursing, Crockett, Cynegetic, Dog, Drag(net), Esau, Ferret, Fox, Free-shot, Gun, Halloo, Herne, Hound, Jager, Lamping, Leigh, Letterbox, Lurcher, Montero, National, Nimrod, Orion, Peel, Pig-sticking, Poacher, Poot, Pout, Predator, Pursue, Quest, Quorn, Rabbit, Rach(e), Rake, Ran, Rancel, Ranzel, Ride, Rummage, Run, Scavenge(r), Scorse, Scout, → **SEARCH**, Seek, Shikar(ee), Shikari, Skirter, Slipper, Stag, Stalk, Sticker, Still, Swiler, Terrier, Thimble, Ticker, Tinchel, Tower, Trail, Trap, Treasure, Venatic, Venator, Venerer, Venery, → **WATCH**, Whip, Whipper-in, Witch, Wolfer, Woodman, Woodsman, Yager

Hunting-call Rechate, Recheat, Tally-ho, View-halloo

Hunting-ground Forestation, Walk

Hurdle(r) Barrier, Doll, Fence, Flake, Gate, Hemery, Obstacle, Raddle, Sticks, Wattle

Hurdy (gurdy) Barrel-organ, Hainch, Haunch, Vielle

Hurl(ing) Camogie, Cast, Dash, → **FLING**, Heave, Put(t), Throw, → **TOSS**

Hurly-burly Furore, Noise

Hurrah Bravo, Cheers, Huzza, Io, Whee

Hurricane Baguio, Tornade, Tornado, Typhoon, → **WIND**

Hurry Belt, Bustle, Chivvy, Chop-chop, Dart, Dash, Drive, Festinate, Fisk, Frisk, Gad, Gallop, Giddap, Giddup, Giddy-up, Hadaway, Hare, Haste, Hie, Hightail, Induce, Mosey, Post-haste, Press, Push, Race, Railroad, → **RUSH**, Scamper, Scoot, Scramble, Scur(ry), Scutter, Scuttle, Skelter, Skurry, Spank, Speed, Streak, Tear, Whirr

Hurt(ful) Abuse, Ache, Aggrieve, Ake, Bruise, Cutting, Damage, De(a)re, Detriment, Disservice, Harm, Harrow, Hit, → **INJURE**, Lesion, Maim, Nocent, Nocuous, Noisome, Noxious, Noyous, Offend, Pain, Pang, Prick(le), Scaith, Wound, Wring

Hurtle Rush, Spin, Streak, Streek

Husband(ry), Husbands Add, Baron, Breadwinner, Consort, Darby, Ear, Eche, Economy, Eke, Ere, Farm, Gander-mooner, Georgic, Goodman, Groom, H, Hoddy-doddy, Hodmandod, Hubby, Ideal, Man, Manage, Mate, Partner, Polyandry, Retrench, Save, Scrape, Scrimp, Spouse, Squirrel, → **STORE**, Tillage

Hush(-hush) Bestill, Gag, Sh, Silent, Smug, St, Tace, Wheesh(t), Whisht

Husk(s), Husky Acerose, Bran, Draff, Eskimo, Hoarse, Hull, Malemute, Seed, Sheal, Shiel, Shuck

Hussar Cherry-picker, Cherubim

Hussite Calixtin(e), Taborite

Hussy Besom, Hen, Limmer, Loose, Minx, Vamp

Hustle(r) Fast talk, Frogmarch, Jostle, Pro, Push, Railroad, Shoulder, Shove, Skelp

Hut(s) Banda, Booth, Bothie, Bothy, Bustee, Cabin, Caboose, Chalet, Choltry, Gunyah, Hogan, Humpy, Igloo, Mia-mia, Nissen, Pondok(kie), Quonset®, Rancheria, Rancho, Rondavel, Shack, Shanty, Sheal(ing), Shebang, Shed, Shiel(ing), Skeo, Skio, Succah, Sukkah, Tilt, Tolsel, Tolsey, Tolzey, Tramping, Wan(n)igan, Whare, Wi(c)kiup, Wigwam, Wil(t)ja, Wurley, Wurlie

Hutch Buddle, Crate, Pen, Rabbit

Hyacinth Cape, Grape, Starch, Wild

Hybrid Bigener, Bois-brûlé, Cama, Catalo, Centaur, Chamois, Chichi, Chimera, Citrange, Cockatrice, Cross, Dso, Funnel, Geep, Graft, Hippogriff, Hircocervus, Incross, Interbred, Jersian, Jomo, Jumart, Lurcher, Mameluco, Mermaid, Merman, Metif, Métis, Mongrel, Mule, Mutation, Noisette, Opinicus, Ortanique, Ox(s)lip, Percolin, Plumcot, Pomato, Ringed, Single-cross, Tangelo, Tiglon, Tigon, Topaz, Ugli, Werewolf, Zho(mo)

▷ **Hybrid** *may indicate* an anagram

Hydra Polyp

Hydrant Fireplug, H

Hydrocarbon Acetylene, Aldrin, Alkane, Alkene, Alkyl, Alkyne, Amylene, Arene, Asphaltite, Benzene, Butadiene, Butane, Butene, Camphane, Camphene, Carotene, Cetane, Cubane, Cycloalkane, Cyclohexane, Cyclopropane, Cymogene, Decane, Diene, Dioxin, Diphenyl, Ethane, Gutta, Halon, Hatchettite, Heavy oil, Hemiterpene, Heptane, Hexane, Hexene, Hexyl(ene), Indene, Isobutane, Isoprene, Ligroin, Limonene, Mesitylene, Naphtha, Naphthalene, Naphthalin(e), Nonane, Octane, Olefin(e), Paraffin, Pentane, Pentene, Pentylene, Phenanthrene, Phene, Picene, Pinene, Polyene, Propane, Pyrene, Pyridine, Pyrimidine, Retene, Squalene, Stilbene, Styrene, Terpene, Toluene, Triptane, Wax, Xylene, Xylol

Hydrogen Deut(er)on, Diplon, Ethene, H, Heavy, Muonium, Protium, Replaceable, Tritium

Hydrolysis Saponification

Hydrometer Salinometer

Hydrophobia, Hydrophobic Rabid, St Hubert's disease

Hydroplane Skid

Hydroponic Soil

Hydrozoa(n) Campanularia, Millepore, Physalia, Portuguese man-of-war, Siphonophore

Hyena Aard-wolf, Earthwolf, Laughing, Nandi bear, Spotted, Strand-wolf, Tiger-wolf

Hygiene, Hygienic Aseptic, Dental, Oral, Sanitary, Sepsis, Sleep

Hymen Maidenhead

Hymn(s) Anthem, Benedictine, Bhajan, Canticle, Carol, Cathisma, Choral(e), Coronach, Dies Irae, Dithyramb, Doxology, Epithalamia, Gloria, Hallel, Introit(us), Ithyphallic, Lay, Magnificat, Mantra, Marseillaise, Nunc Dimittis, Ode, P(a)ean, Psalm, Recessional, Rigveda, Sanctus, Secular, Sequence, Stabat Mater, Sticheron, Tantum Ergo, Te Deum, Trisagion, Troparion, Veda

Hymnographer, Hymnologist David, Faber, Heber, Moody, Neale, Parry, Sankey, Watts

Hype(d) Aflutter

Hyperbola Rectangular

Hyperbole, Hyperbolic Auxesis, Exaggeration, Sech

Hypercritical Captious

Hyperion Titan

Hypersensitive, Hypersensitivity Allergic, Atopy, Idiosyncratic
Hypha(e) Conidiophore, Stroma
Hyphen(ated) Dash, Parasyntheton, Soft
Hypnosis, Hypnotise, Hypnotic, Hypnotism, Hypnotist Braidism, Chloral, Codeine, Enthral, Entrance, Hypotonia, Magnetic, Magnetise, Meprobamate, Mesmerism, Psychognosis, Svengali
Hypochondria(c) Atrabilious, Hyp, Nosophobia, Phrenesiac, Valetudinarian
Hypocrisy, Hypocrite, Hypocritical Archimago, Bigot, Byends, Cant, Carper, Chadband, Creeping Jesus, Deceit, Dissembler, Dissimulating, False-faced, Heep, Holy Willie, Humbug, Insincere, Janus-faced, Mucker, Nitouche, Pecksniff, Pharisaic, Pharisee, Piety, Prig, Sanctimony, Self-pious, Sepulchre, Tartuf(f)e, Two-faced, Whited sepulchre
Hypothesis, Hypothetical Avogadro, Biophor, Conditional, Continuum, Gluon, Graviton, Nebular, Notional, Null, Planetesimal, Sapir-Whorf, Suppositious, Virtual, Working
Hyrax Cony, Daman, Dassie, Klipdas, Rock rabbit
Hysteria, Hysteric(al) Achiria, Astasia, Conniption, Delirium, Frenzy, Meemie, Mother

Ii

I A, Ch, Cham, Che, Dotted, Ego, Ich, Indeed, India, Iodine, Italy, J, Je, Me, Muggins, Myself, One, Self, Yours truly
Iambus Scazon
Ian Scot
Iberian Celtiberean
Ibex Izard
Ibis Hadedah, Sacred, Waldrapp
Ice(d), Ice-cream, Icing, Icy A la mode, Alcorza, Anchor, Arctic, Ballicatter, Banana split, Berg, Black, Brash, Camphor, Cassata, Coconut, Cone, Cool, Cornet, Coupe, Cream, Crystal, Diamonds, Drift, Dry, Field, Floe, Frappé, Frazil, Freeze, Frigid, Frore, Frosting, Frosty, Gelato, Gelid, Gems, Glacé, Glacial, Glacier, Glare, Glaze, Glib, Granita, Graupel, Ground, Growler, Hailstone, Hok(e)y-pok(e)y, Hommock, Hummock, Kitty-benders, Knickerbocker glory, Kulfi, Lolly, Macallum, Marzipan, Neapolitan, Oaky, Pack, Pancake, Pingo, Polar, Popsicle®, Rime, Rink, Rivière, Ross, Royal, Sconce, Serac, Shelf, Sherbet, Slay, Slider, Slob, Sludge, Slush, Sorbet, Spumone, Spumoni, Stream, Sugar, Sundae, Tickly-benders, Topping, Tortoni, Tutti-frutti, Verglas, Virga, Wafer, Water, Wintry
Ice-axe Piolet
Iceberg Calf, Floe, Growler
Ice-box Cooler, Freezer, Fridge, Frig, Yakhdan
▶ **Ice-cream** *see* ICE
Iceland IS
Ice-skating Choctaw, Figure, Glide
Icicle Tangle
Icon Fashion, Idol, Image, Madonna, Sprite
Icterus Jaundice
ID PIN
Id(e) Ego, Fish, Orfe
Idea(s) Archetype, Brainchild, Brainwave, Clou, Clue, Conceit, Concept, Fancy, Figment, Fixed, Germ, Hunch, Idée fixe, Idolum, Image, Inkling, Inspiration, Interpretation, Keynote, Light, Meme, → NOTION, Obsession, Plan, Plank, Rationale, Recept, Theory, Thought, Whimsy, Zeitgeist
Ideal(ise) A1, Abstract, Apotheosis, Bee's knees, Cat's whiskers, Dream, Eden, Ego, Goal, Halo, Hero, Model, Monist, Mr Right, Nirvana, Notional, Paragon, Pattern, → PERFECT, Role-model, Romantic, Rose, Siddhi, Sidha, Sublimate, Transcendental, Utopian, Vision
Idealism, Idealist(ic) Dreamer, More, Perfectionist, Quixotic, Romantic, Transcendental, Utopian, Visionary
Identical Alike, Clone, Congruent, Equal, Indistinguishable, Menechmian, One, Same, Selfsame, Verbatim, Very
Identification, Identify Bertillonage, Codeword, Credentials, Designate, Diagnosis,

Differentiate, Discern, Document, Dog-tag, Earmark, Empathy, Espy, Finger(print), ID, Identikit®, Label, Mark, Monomark, Name, Name-tape, Password, Photofit®, Pin, Pinpoint, Place, Point up, Recognise, Reg(g)o, Secern, Spot, Swan-hopping, Swan-upping, Verify

Identikit® E-fit, Videokit

Identity Alias, Appearance, Corporate, Credentials, Equalness, Likeness, Mistaken, Numerical, Oneness, Personal, Qualitative, Seity, Self, Selfhood

Ideology, Ideologue Credo, Hard-liner, Ism

Idiom Americanism, Argot, Britishism, Cant, Expression, Idioticon, Jargon, Language, Pahlavi, Parlance, Pehlevi, Persism, Scotticism, Slavism, Syri(a)cism, Syrism

Idiosyncrasy, Idiosyncratic Foible, Mannerism, Nature, Quirk, Way, Zany

Idiot(ic), Idiocy Airhead, Congenital, Dingbat, Dipstick, Dolt, Eejit, Fatuity, Fool, Goose, Half-wit, Imbecile, Inane, Maniac, Moron, Nana, Natural, Nerk, Nidget, Noncom, Numpty, Oaf, Ouph(e), Stupe, → **STUPID**, Tony, Twit, Village, Whacko, Zany

Idle(ness), Idler Beachcomber, Bludger, Boondoggle, Bum, Bumble, Bummle, Cockaigne, Dally, Deadbeat, Diddle, Dilly-dally, Dole-bludger, Donnat, Donnot, Do-nothingism, Drone, Fainéant, Fallow, Farnarkel, Fester, Flaneur, Flim-flam, Footle, Frivolous, Gold brick, Groundless, Hawm, Inaction, Indolent, Inert, Lackadaisical, Laesie, Lallygag, Layabout, Laze, Lazy, Lead-swinger, Lie, Lig, Light, Limer, Loaf, Lollop, Lollygag, Lotophagus, Lounge, Lusk, Micawber, Mike, Mollusc, Mooch, Mouch, Otiose, Otium, Patagonian, Piddle, Ride, Scapegrace, Shiftless, Skive, Slob, Sloth, Sluggard, Spiv, Stalko, Stock-still, Stooge, Stroam, Tarry, Tick over, Transcendental, Trifle, Trock, Troke, Truant, Truck, Twiddle, Unbusy, Unoccupied, Vacuity, Vain, Vegetate, Veg out, Waste

Idol(ise) Adore, Adulate, Baal(im), Baphomet, Bel, Crush, Eikon, E(i)luned, Fetich(e), Fetish, God, Heartthrob, Hero, Icon, Image, Joss, Juggernaut, Lion, Mammet, Manito, Manitou, Matinee, Maumet, Mawmet, Molech, Moloch, Mommet, Moorish, Mumbo-jumbo, Stotter, Swami, Teraph(im), Termagant, Vision, Wood, Worship

Idyll(ic) Arcady, Eclogue, Eden, Paradise, Pastoral, Peneian

Ie Sc

If, If it All-be, An('t), Condition, Gif, Gin, In case, Pot, Provided, Sobeit, Whether

Igloo Snowden

Igneous Pyrogenic

Ignis-fatuus Elf-fire, Fire-dragon, Fire-drake, Friar's lanthorn, Wildfire

Ignite, Ignition Coil, Electronic, Flare, Kindle, Lightning, Spark, Starter

Ignoble Base, Inferior, Mean, Vile

Ignominious, Ignominy Base, Dishonour, Fiasco, Humiliation, Infamous, Scandal, → **SHAME**

Ignorance, Ignorant Agnoiology, Analphabet, Anan, Artless, Benighted, Blind, Clueless, Darkness, Green, Hick, Illiterate, Inerudite, Ingram, Ingrum, Inscient, Know-nothing, Lewd, Lumpen, Misken, Nescience, Night, Oblivious, Oik, Philistine, Purblind, Red-neck, Unaware, Uneducated, Unlettered, Unread, Unschooled, Untold, Unversed, Unwist

Ignore Alienate, Ba(u)lk, Blink, Bypass, Connive, Cut, Discount, Disregard, Forget, Neglect, Leave, Omit, Overlook, Override, Overslaugh, Pass, Pass up, Rump, Scrub round, Slight, Snub

Igor Prince

Iguana Chuckwalla

I know Iwis, Ywis

Iliad Homeric

Ill Adverse, All-overish, Bad, Bilious, Cronk, Crook, Evil, Grotty, Inauspicious, Income, Off-colour, Poorly, Queer, Sea-sick, → **SICK**, Strung out, Unweal, Unwell, Valetudinarian, Vomito, Wog, Wrong

▷ **Ill** *may indicate* an anagram

Ill-adjusted Sad sack

Ill-balanced Lop-sided

Ill-bred Churlish, Plebeian, Uncouth, Unmannerly

▷ **Ill-composed** *may indicate* an anagram

Ill-defined Diagnosis, Hazy, Unclear, Vague

Ill-dressed Frumpish

Illegal, Illicit Adulterine, Black, Bootleg, Breach, Contraband, Furtive, Ill-gotten, Malfeasance, Misbegotten, Pirated, Shonky, Unlawful

Illegitimate Baseborn, Bastard, By-blow, Come-o'-will, Fitz, Irregular, Love-child, Lucky-piece, Mamzer, Misbegotten, Misborn, Misfortunate, Momzer, Natural, Scarp, Slink, Spurious, Unlawful, Unlineal

Ill-favoured Lean, Offensive, Thin, Ugly

Ill-feeling, Ill-humour Bad blood, Bile, Complaint, Curt, Dudgeon, Glum, Hate, Miff, Peevish, Pique, Rheumatic

Illiberal Insular, Redneck, Skinflint, Strict

▶ **Illicit** *see* **ILLEGAL**

Illiterate Analphabet, Ignoramus, Letterless, Unlettered, Unread

Ill-looking Peaky, Poorly

Ill-luck Ambs-ace, Ames-ace, Bad trot, Deuce-ace, Misfortune

Ill-mannered, Ill-natured, Ill-tempered Attercop, Bitchy, Coarse, Crabby, Crotchety, Curst, Ethercap, Ettercap, Gnarly, Goop, Gurrier, Guttersnipe, Huffy, Stingy, Sullen, Ugly, Uncouth, Unkind

Illness Aids, Ailment, Attack, Autism, Brucellosis, Chill, Complaint, Croup, Death-bed, Diabetes, Disease, DS, Dwalm, Dwaum, Dyscrasia, Eale, Eclampsia, Grippe, Hangover, Hypochondria, Lockjaw, Malady, ME, SAD, Scarlatina, Sickness, Terminal, Toxaemia, Urosis, Weed, Weid, Wog

Ill-nourished Emaciated

Illogical Inconsequent, Non-sequitur

Ill-sighted Owl, Purblind

Ill-smelling F(o)etid, High, Hing, Miasmic, Stinking

▶ **Ill-tempered** *see* **ILL-MANNERED**

Ill-timed Inopportune, Unseasonable

Illuminate(d), Illumination, Illuminating Ambient, Aperçu, Brighten, Bright-field, Clarify, Cul-de-lampe, Decorate, Enlighten, Floodlit, Lamplight, Langley, Light, Limelight, Limn, Miniate, Nernst, Phot, Pixel, Radiate, Rushlight

Illusion(ary), Illusionist, Illusory, Illusive Air, Apparition, Barmecide, Chimera, Deception, Déjà vu, Eischer, Fallacy, Fancy, Fantasy, Hallucination, Ignis-fatuus, Mare's-nest, Maya, Mirage, Muller-Lyer, Optical, Phantasmal, Phantom, Phi-phenomenon, Size-weight, Specious, Transcendental, Trompe l'oeil, Unreality, Will o'the wisp

Illustrate(d), Illustration, Illustrator Artwork, Bleed, Case, Centrefold, Collotype, Demonstrate, Drawing, Eg, Elucidate, Epitomise, Exemplify, Explain, Figure, Frontispiece, Grangerize, Graphic, Half-tone, Hors texte, Illume, Illumin(at)e, Instance, Instantiate, Keyline, Limner, Lithograph, Pictorial, Plate, Show, Sidelight, Spotlight, Tenniel, Vignette, Visual

Illustrious Bright, Celebrated, Distinguished, Famous, Legendary, Renowned
Ill-will Animosity, Enmity, Grudge, Hostility, Malice, Maltalent, Mau(l)gre, Spite
I'm I'se
Image(s), Imaging Atman, Blip, Brand, Corporate, Discus, Effigy, Eidetic, Eidolon,
Eikon, Eiluned, Emotion, Enantiomorph, Favicon, Fine-grain, Graphic, Graven,
Hologram, Hypnagogic, Icon, Iconograph, Ident, Idol, Invultuation, Joss, Latent,
Likeness, Matte, Mirror, Morph, Murti, Paranthelium, Paraselene, Pentimento,
Persona, Phantasmagoria, Photogram, Photograph, Pic(ture), Pixel(l)ated,
Pixil(l)ated, Poetic, Profile, Public, Radionuclide, Real, Recept, Reflectogram,
Reflectograph, Representation, Scintigram, Search, Shadowgraph, Simulacrum,
Spectrum, Spitting, Split, Stereotype, Symbol, Teraph(im), Thumbnail, Tiki,
Tomogram, Totem, Venogram, Video, Virtual, Xoanon
Imagine(d), Imaginary (land), Imagination, Imaginative Assume,
Bandywallop, Believe, Boojum, Bullamakanka, Cloud-cuckoo-land, Cockaigne,
Cockayne, Conceive, Conjure, Cyborg, Dystopia, Erewhon, Esemplasy,
Faery, Faine, Fancy, Feign, Fictional, Fictitious, Fictor, Figment, Figure, Hallucinate,
Hobbit, Ideate, Invent, Mind's eye, Moral, Narnia, Otherworldly, Oz, Picture,
Poetical, Prefigure, Pretend, Propose, Recapture, Replicant, Scotch mist, Snark,
Straw, → **SUPPOSE**, Surmise, Think, Tulpa, Vicarious, Visualise, Whangam,
Wonderland
Imbecile Anile, Fool, Idiot, → **STUPID**
▷ **Imbecile** *may indicate* an anagram
Imbibe Absorb, Drink, Lap, Quaff, Suck, Swallow
Imbricate Overlie
Imbroglio Complication, Maze
Imbrue, Imbue Colour, Impregnate, Indoctrinate, Infuse, Inoculate, Permeate,
Soak, Steep
Imitate, Imitation, Imitator Act, Ape, Burlesque, Caricature, Copy(cat),
Counterfeit, Dud, Echo, Echopraxia, Emulate, Epigon(e), Ersatz, Fake, False, Faux,
Follow, Hit off, Marinist, Me-too, Mime, Mimesis, Mimetic, Mimic(ry), Mini-me,
Mockery, Monkey, Onomatopoeia, Parody, Parrot, Paste, Pastiche, Pinchbeck,
Potichomania, Repro, Rhinestone, Rip-off, Sham, Simulate, Stumer, Take-off,
Travesty
Immaculate Conception, Flawless, Lily-white, Perfect, Pristine, Spotless, Virgin
Immanentist Pantheist
Immaterial Insignificant, Spiritual, Trifling
▷ **Immature** *may indicate* a word incompleted
Immature(ly), Immaturity Beardless, Callow, Childish, Crude, Embryo, Ergate(s),
Green, Inchoate, Larval, Neotenic, Non-age, Puberal, Puberulent, Pupa, Raw,
Rudimentary, Sophomoric, Tender, Unbaked, Underage, Unformed, Unripe, Young
Immediate(ly) Alsoon, At once, B(e)live, Direct, Eftsoons, Ekdum, First-time,
Forthwith, Imminent, Incontinent, Instantaneous, Instanter, Lickety-split, Near,
Next, → **NOW**, Now-now, On the knocker, Outright, Present, Pronto, Right-off,
Short-term, Slapbang, Spontaneous, Stat, Statim, Straight, Straight off, Sudden,
Then, Tout de suite
Immense Astronomical, Brobdingnag, Cosmic, Enormous, → **GIGANTIC**, Huge,
Vast, Wide
Immerse Baptise, Demerge, Demerse, Drench, Embathe, Emplonge, Enew, Engage,
Imbathe, Plunge, Soak, Steep
Immigrant, Immigration, Immigrate Aliya(h), Aussiedler, Brain gain,
Carpet-bagger, Cayun, Chalutz, Freshie, Greener, Greenhorn, Halutz, Illegal,

Incomer, Issei, Jimmy Grant, Merino, Metic, New chum, Nisei, Non-quota, Olim, Outsider, Overstayer, Pilgrim, Pommy, Quota, Redemption(er), Reffo, Sanei, Sansei, Settler, Wetback, Whenwe

Imminent Approaching, Close, Immediate, Pending

Immobility, Immobile, Immobilise(r) Akinesia, Cataplexy, Catatonia, Hog-tie, Inertia, Pinion, Rigidity, Taser, Tether

Immoderate Excessive, Extreme, Inordinate, Intemperate, Lavish, Undue, Unreasonable

Immodest(y) Brash, Brazen, Forward, Impudicity, Indelicate, Unchaste

Immolation Sacrifice, Sati, Suttee

Immoral(ity) Corrupt, Degenerate, Dissolute, Evil, Lax, Libertine, Licentious, Loose, Nefarious, Peccable, Reprobate, Scarlet, Turpitude, Unholy, Unsavoury, Vice, Vicious, Wanton

Immortal(ity) Agelong, Amarant(h), Amarantin, Amritattva, Athanasy, Deathless, → **DIVINE**, Enoch, Eternal, Ever-living, Famous, Godlike, Memory, Sin, Struldbrug, Timeless, Undying

Immovable Fast, Firm, Gomphosis, Obdurate, Rigid, Stable, Stubborn

Immune, Immunisation, Immunise(r), Immunity Acquired, Active, Amboceptor, Anamnestic, Anergy, Bar, Cree, Diplomatic, Free, Humoral, Inoculate, Klendusic, Natural, Non-specific, Passive, Pasteurism, Pax, Premunition, Properdin, Serum, Tachyphylaxis, Vaccine

Immure Confine, Encloister, Imprison

Imp(ish) Devilet, Elf, Flibbertigibbet, Gamin(e), Gremlin, Hobgoblin, Limb, Lincoln, Litherly, Nickum, Nis(se), Puck, Ralph, Rascal, Spright, Sprite

Impact Bearing, Bump, Clash, Collision, Feeze, Glance, Head-on, High, Impinge, Jar, Jolt, Pack, Percuss, Pow, Slam, Souse, Strike home, Wham

Impair(ed), Impairment Appair, Cripple, Damage, Disease, Enfeeble, → **HARM**, Injure, Lame, Mar, Mental, Odd, Pair(e), Paralogia, Stale, Vitiate

Impala Pallah

Impale Elance, Ga(u)nch, Skewer, Spike, Transfix

Impart Bestow, Convey, Divulge, Impute, Infect, Shed, Tell

Impartial(ity) Candid, Detached, Dispassionate, Equitable, Equity, Even-handed, Fair, Just, Neutral, Unbiased

Impasse, Impassable Deadlock, Dilemma, Invious, Jam, Log jam, Mexican standoff, Snooker, Stalemate, Zugzwang

Impassioned Earnest, Emotional, Fervid, Fiery, Heated, Zealous

Impassive Apathetic, Deadpan, Stoical, Stolid, Unemotional

Impatience, Impatient Chafing, Chut, Dysphoria, Dysthesia, Fiddle-de-dee, Fiddlesticks, Fidgety, Fretful, Hasty, Hoot(s), Irritable, Och, Peevish, Peremptory, Petulant, Pish, Pshaw, Restless, Tilly-fally, Till(e)y-vall(e)y, Tut

Impeach Accuse, Challenge, Charge, Delate, Indict

Impeccable Faultless, Novice

Impecunious Penniless, Poor, Short

Impedance, Impede, Impediment Burr, Clog, Dam, Diriment, Encumber, Halt, Hamstring, Handicap, → **HINDER**, Hog-tie, Let, Log, Obstacle, Obstruct, Reactance, Rub, Shackle, Snag, Speed bump, Stammer, Stymie, Tongue-tie, Trammel, Veto, Z

Impel(led), Impelling Actuate, Coerce, Drave, Drive, Drove, Goad, Inspire, Projectile, → **URGE**

Impend(ing) Imminent, Looming, Toward

Impenetrable Adamantine, Air-tight, Dense, Hard, Impervious, Proof, Watertight

Imperative Categorical, Dire, Hypothetical, Jussive, Mood, Need-be, Pressing, Vital

Imperceptible, Imperceptive Blind Freddie, Intangible, Invisible, Latent, Minimal, Subtle

Imperfect(ion) Aplasia, Aplastic, Blotch, Defect, Deficient, Faulty, Feathering, Flawed, Half-pie, Kink, Kinkle, Lame, Poor, Rough, Second, Unideal

Imperial(ist), Imperious Beard, C(a)esarian, Commanding, Haughty, Lordly, Majestic, Masterful, Mint, Peremptory, Regal, Rhodes, Royal, Tuft

Imperil Endanger, Risk

Imperishable Eternal, Immortal, Indestructible

Impermeable Airtight, Athermanous, Proof, Resistant

Impersonal Abstract, Cold, Detached, Inhuman, Institutional

Impersonate(d), Impersonation, Impersonator Amphitryon, Ape, As, Double, Drag queen, Echo, Imitate, Imposter, Impostor, Impression, Mimic, Pose, Spoof

Impertinence, Impertinent Crust, Flip(pant), Fresh, Impudent, Irrelevant, Rude, Sass, Sauce

Imperturbable Cool, Placid, Stoic, Tranquil, Unruffable

Impervious(ness) Athermancy, Callous, Hardened, Obdurate, Proof, Tight

Impetigo Scrumpox

Impetuous, Impetuosity Birr, Brash, Bullheaded, Élan, Harum-scarum, → **HASTY**, Headstrong, Heady, Hothead, Impulsive, Rash, Rhys, Tearaway, Vehement, Violent, Young Turk

Impetus Birr, Drift, Incentive, MacGuffin, Momentum, Propulsion, Slancio, Steam, Swing

Impious Blasphemous, Godless, Irreverent, Unholy

Implacable Deadly

Implant(ation) AID, Cochlear, Embed, Engraft, Enrace, Enroot, Graft, Inset, Instil, Nidation, Silicone, Sow

Implausible Lame, Off-the-wall

Implement Agent, Apply, Backscratcher, Biffer, Celt, Cultivator, Disgorger, Do, Eolith, Execute, Flail, Follow out, Fork, Fulfil, Grater, Grubber, Hacksaw, Harrow, Hayfork, Mezzaluna, Mop, Muller, Pin, Pitchfork, Plectrum, Plough, Pusher, Rest, Ricker, Ripple, Scarifier, Scuffler, Scythe, Seed drill, Shoehorn, Sickle, Snuffer, Spatula, Splayd®, Squeegee, Strickle, Sucket fork, Sucket spoon, Tongs, → **TOOL**, Toothpick, Tribrach, Utensil

Implicate, Implication Accuse, Concern, Connotation, Embroil, Incriminate, Innuendo, → **INVOLVE**, Material, Overtone

Implore Beg, Beseech, Crave, → **ENTREAT**, Obsecrate, Petition, Plead, Pray

Imply, Implied Hint, Insinuate, Involve, Predicate, Signify, → **SUGGEST**, Tacit

Impolite Ill-bred, Rude, Uncivil

Import(s) Convey, Denote, Drift, Invisible, Mean, Moment, Parallel, Sense, Signify, Spell, Visible

Importance, Important (person) Big, Big cheese, Big pot, Big wheel, Billing, Calibre, Cardinal, Central, Cheese, Cob, Coming, Consequence, Considerable, Core, Cornerstone, Count, Critical, Crucial, Crux, Earth-shaking, Earth-shattering, Ego-trip, Eminent, Epochal, Grave, Gravitas, Gravity, Greatness, Heavy, High, High-muck-a-muck, His nibs, Historic, Honcho, Hotshot, Huzoor, Key, Keystone, Leading, Macher, Magnitude, Main, Major, Material, Matters, Megastar, Mighty, Milestone, Moment(ous), Nabob, Nawab, Nib, Note, Numero uno, Obbligato, Overriding, Personage, Pivotal, Pot, Preponderate, Prime, Principal, Red-carpet, Salient, Seminal, Serious, Signal, Significant, Something, Special, Stature, Status, Stress, Substantive, Tuft, Urgent, VIP, Weight, Weighty, Worth

Importune, Importunate Beg, Coax, Flagitate, Press(ing), Prig, Solicit, Urgent

Impose(r), Imposing, Imposition Allocate, Assess, August, Burden, Charge, Cheat, Diktat, Dread, Enforce, Enjoin, Epic, Fine, Flam, Foist, Fraud, Grand(iose), Hidage, Homeric, Hum, Impot, Inflict, Kid, Lay, Levy, Lumber, Majestic, Obtrude, Pensum, Pole, Scot, Sponge, Stately, Statuesque, Stonehand, Sublime, Try-on, Whillywhaw

Impossible Can't, Hopeless, Inconceivable, Incorrigible, Insoluble, Insurmountable, Irreparable, No-go, No-no, Unacceptable

Impost Excise, Levy, Tax, Toll

Imposter, Impostor Bunyip, Charlatan, Disaster, Faitor, Faitour, → FAKE, Fraud, Idol, Phantasm, Pretender, Ringer, Sham, Triumph, Warbeck

Impotent Barren, Helpless, Spado, Sterile, Weak

Impound(er) Appropriate, Bond, Confiscate, Intern, Pen, Pinder, Poind

Impoverish(ed) Bankrupt, Bare, Beggar, Exhaust, Indigent, Straiten

Impractical Absurd, Academic, Blue-sky, Chim(a)era, Idealist, Inoperable, Laputan, Non-starter, Not on, Other-worldly, Quixotic, Useless

Imprecation Drat, Oath, Pize, Rat(s), 'Slife

Imprecise Approximate, Inaccurate, Indeterminate, Intangible, Loose, Nebulous, Rough, Sloppy, Vague

Impregnable, impregnate Conceive, Embalm, Enwomb, Imbue, Inexpugnable, Inseminate, Milt, Permeate, Resinate

Impresario Maestro, Manager, Producer, Showman

Impress(ive), Impression(able) Air, Astonish, Awe, Blur, Blurb, Bowl over, Brand, Cliché, Commanding, Conscript, Crimp, Deboss, Dent, Dramatic, Edition, Effect, Engrain, Engram(ma), Engrave, Enstamp, Epic, Etch, Feel(ing), Fingerprint, Fossil, Frank, Gas, Glorious, Grab, Grandiose, Greeking, Heroic, Homeric, Idea, Idée, Imitation, Impinge, Imprint, Incuse, Intaglio, Kick ass, Knock, Let, Majestic, Name-drop, Niello, Noble, Note, Palimpsest, Plastic, Plate, Pliable, Powerful, Prent, Presence, Press(gang), Print, Proof, Recruit, Register, Repute, Resplendent, Responsive, Ripsnorter, Rotund, Seal, Seize, Sense, Shanghai, Slay, Smite, Soft, Spectacular, Stamp, Stereotype, Strike, Stunning, Susceptible, Sway, Tableau, Touch, Type, Vibrant, Watermark, Weal, Weighty, Woodcut, Wow

Impressionist Caxton, Cézanne, Impersonator, Liebermann, Lumin(ar)ist, Manet, Matisse, Monet, Morisot, Renoir

Imprint Edition, Engrave, Etch, Stamp

Imprison(ment) Cape, Committal, Confine, Constrain, Custody, Durance, False, Immure, Incarcerate, Intern, Jail, Penal servitude, Quad, Quod, Stretch, Time

Improbable Buckley's chance, Buckley's hope, Dubious, Far-fetched, Unlikely

Impromptu Ad lib(itum), Extempore, Improvised, Offhand, Pong, Spontaneous, Sudden, Unrehearsed

Improper, Impropriety Abnormal, Blue, Demirep, False, Illegitimate, Indecent, Indecorum, Naughty, Outré, Prurient, Solecism, Undue, Unmeet, Unseemly, Untoward

▷ **Improperly** *may indicate* an anagram

Improve(ment), Improver, Improving Advance, Ameliorate, Beat, Benefit, Bete, Break, Buck, Cap, Chasten, Conditioner, Convalesce, Cultivate, Détente, Didactic, Ease, Edify, Edutainment, Embellish, Emend, Enhance, Enrich, Eugenic, Euthenics, File, Gentrify, Kaizen, Meliorate, Mend, Potentiate, Promote, Rally, Refine, Reform, Resipiscence, Retouch, Revamp, Sarvodaya, Slim, Streamline, Surpass, Tart, Tatt, Titivate, Top, Touch-up, Turn round, Tweak, Uptrend, Upturn

Improvident Feckless, Micawber, Poor-white, Wasteful

Improvise(d), Improvisation Adlib, Break, Busk it, Devise, Drumhead, Extemporise, Gorgia, Invent, Knock-up, Lash-up, Noodle, On the fly, Ride, Scratch, Sodain, Sudden, Vamp, Wing it

Imprudent Foolhardy, Foolish, Impetuous, Impolitic, Indiscreet, Injudicious, Rash, Reckless, Unwary, Unwise

Impudence, Impudent Audacious, Backchat, Bardy, Bold, Brash, Brassy, Brazen, Cheeky, Cool, Crust, Effrontery, Forward, Gall, Gallus, Hussy, Impertinent, Insolent, Jackanapes, Jack-sauce, Lip, Malapert, Neck, → **NERVE**, Pert, Sass(y), Sauce, Saucebox, Saucy, Slack-jaw, Temerity, Whippersnapper, Yankie

Impugn Censure, Challenge, Defame, Impeach, Malign

Impulse, Impulsive Beat, Compelling, Conatus, Dictate, Drive, Efferent, Headlong, Horme, Ideopraxist, Impetus, Instigation, → **INSTINCT**, Libido, Madcap, Nerve, Nisus, Premature, Premotion, Send, Signal, Snap, Specific, Spontaneous, Tendency, Thrust, Tic, Urge, Whim

Impure, Impurity Adulterated, Contaminated, Donor, Faints, Feints, Indecent, Lees, Lewd, Regulus, Scum, Unclean

Imputation, Impute Ascribe, Attribute, Charge, Scandal, Slander, Slur

In A, Amid, Amidst, At, Batting, Chic, Current, Hip, Home, Hostel, I', Inn, Intil, Occupying, On, Pop(ular), Pub, Trendy, Within

Inability Agnosia, Anosmia, Aphagia, Aphasia, Apraxia, Ataxy, Prosopagnosia

Inaccessible Abaton, Eyrie, Impervious, Remote, Unattainable, Uncom(e)atable

Inaccurate Distorted, Erroneous, Faulty, Imprecise, Inexact, Out, Rough, Slipshod, Unfaithful

Inactive, Inaction, Inactivity Acedia, Anestrum, Anoestrus, Cabbage, Comatose, Dead, Dormant, Extinct, Fallow, Hibernate, Idle, Inert, Languor, Lotus-eater, Masterly, Moratorium, Passive, Quiescent, Racemic, Rusty, Sedentary, Sluggish, Stagnation, Stasis, Torpid, Vacancy, Veg(etate)

In addition Eke, Else, Further, Moreover, Plus, To boot, Too

Inadequate Derisory, Feeble, Inapt, Inferior, Joke, Pathetic, Poor, Ropy, Scanty, Slight, Thin, Unable, Unequal

Inadvertent(ly) Accidental, Careless, Chance, Unwitting

▷ **In a flap** *may indicate* an anagram

In a high degree So

In a hundred Percent

Inane Empty, Fatuous, Foolish, Imbecile, Silly, Vacant

Inanimate Abiotic, Lifeless

Inappropriate Amiss, Incongrous, Infelicitous, Malapropos, Off-key, Out of place, Pretentious, Unapt, Unbecoming, Undue, Unmeet, Unsuitable, Untoward

Inapt Maladroit, Unsuitable

Inarticulate(ness) Indistinct, Mumbling, Psellism

Inartistic Artless, Crude

Inattentive, Inattention Absent, Asleep, Deaf, Distrait, Dwaal, Dwa(l)m, Dwaum, Heedless, Loose, Slack, Unheeding, Unobservant

Inaudible Infrasonic, Silent, Superhet

Inaugurate Han(d)sel, Initiate, Install, Introduce

Inauspicious Adverse, Ominous, Sinister

▷ **In a whirl** *may indicate* an anagram

▷ **In a word** *may indicate* two clue words linked to form one

Inborn, Inbred Homogamy, Inherent, Innate, Native, Selfed, Sib

Inca Quechua, Quichua

Incalculable Endless, Unpredictable, Untold

Incandescent Alight, Bright, Brilliant, Excited, Radiant
Incantation Chant, Charm, Magic, Mantra, Spell
Incapable Can't, Downa-do, Powerless, Unable, Useless
Incarnation Advent, Avatar, Embodiment, Fleshing, Krishna, Rama,
Ramachandra
In case Lest, So
Incautious Foolhardy, Rash, Reckless, Unwary
Incendiary Arsonist, Combustible, Firebug, Fire-lighter, Fireship, Napalm,
Thermite
Incense(d), Incenser Anger, Aroma, Elemi, Enfelon, Enrage, Homage, Hot,
→ **INFLAME**, Joss-stick, Navicula, Onycha, Outrage, Pastil(le), Provoke, Thurible,
Thus, Vex, Wrathful
Incentive Carrot, Carrot and stick, Feather-bed, Fillip, Impetus, Inducement,
Motive, Premium, Spur, Stakhanovism, Stimulus, Wage
Incessant Constant, Endless, Unremitting
Incest Backcross, Spiritual
Inch(es) Ait, Column, Edge, Isle, Mil, Miner's, Sidle, Tenpenny, Uncial
Inchoate Formless, Immature, Incipient
Incident(al) Affair, Baur, Bawr, Carry-on, Case, Chance, Circumstance, Episode,
Event, Facultative, Handbags, Negligible, Occasion, Occurrent, Page, Peripheral,
Scene, Throwaway
Incinerate, Incinerator Burn, Combust, Cremate, Destructor
Incipient Beginning, Germinal, Inchoate, Nascent
Incise, Incision, Incisive(ness) Bite, Cut, Edge, Engrave, Episiotomy, Incavo,
Lobotomy, McBurney's, Mordant, Notch, Phlebotomy, Punchy, Rhizotamy, Scarf,
Scribe, Slit, Surgical, Thoracotomy, Tracheotomy, Trenchant
Incisor Foretooth
Incite(ment) Abet, Drive, Egg, Fillip, Good, Hortative, Hoy, Impassion, Inflame,
Instigate, Kindle, Motivate, Onsetting, Prod, Prompt, Provoke, Put, Rouse, Sa sa,
Sedition, Set, Sic(k), Sool, → **SPUR**, Stimulus, Sting, Suborn, Suggest, Tar, Urge
Incline(d), Inclination Acclivity, Angle, Aslant, Aslope, Atilt, Bank, Batter, Bent,
Bevel, Bias, Bow, Camber, Clinamen, Cock, Crossfall, Declivity, Dip, Disposed,
Drift, Enclitic, Glacis, → **GRADIENT**, Grain, Habitus, Hade, Heel, Hill, Italic, Kant,
Kip, Lean, Liable, Liking, List, Maw, Minded, Nod, On, Partial, Peck, Penchant,
Proclivity, Prone, Propensity, Rake, Ramp, Ready, Rollway, Set, Shelve, Slant,
→ **SLOPE**, Steep, Steeve, Stomach, Supine, Tend, Tilt, Tip, Trend, Upgrade, Velleity,
Verge, Weathering, Will
Include(d), Inclusion, Inclusive Add, All-told, Bracket, Compass, Comprise,
Connotate, Contain, Cover, Embody, Embrace, Enclose, Involve, Short-list, Social,
Subsume, Therein
Incognito Anonymous, Disguised, Faceless, Secret, Unnamed
Incoherent Confused, Disconnected, Disjointed, Gabbling, Garbled, Inarticulate,
Rambling, Spluttering
Incombustible Clinker
Income Annuity, Benefice, Discretionary, Disposable, Dividend, Earned, Entry,
Fixed, Franked, Livelihood, Living, Meal-ticket, Milch cow, National, Notional,
OTE, Penny-rent, Prebend, Primitiae, Private, Proceeds, Rent, Rente, Rent-roll,
Returns, Revenue, Salary, Stipend, Unearned, Unfranked, Wages
Incomeless E
Incommunicado Isolated, Silent
Incomparable Supreme, Unequalled, Unique, Unmatched

Incompatible, Incompatibility Clashing, Contradictory, Dyspathy, Incongruous, Inconsistent, Mismatched, Unsuited

Incompetent Bungler, Deadhead, Helpless, Hopeless, Ill, Inefficient, Inept, Palooka, Shower, Slouch, Unable, Unfit

Incomplete Broadbrush, Cagmag, Catalectic, Deficient, Inchoate, Lacking, Partial, Pendent, Rough, Sketchy, Unfinished

Incomprehensible, Incomprehension Acatalepsy, Acatamathesia, Double Dutch, Hard, Unbelievable

Inconceivable Impossible, Incredible

▷ **In confusion** *may indicate* an anagram

Incongruous, Incongruity Absurd, Discordant, Heterogenous, Irish, Ironic, Sharawadgi, Sharawaggi, Solecism

In connection with Re

Inconsiderable Light, Slight

Inconsiderate Asocial, High-handed, Hog, Light-minded, Petty, Presumptuous, Roughshod, Thoughtless, Unkind

Inconsistency, Inconsistent Alien, Anacoluthon, Anomaly, Contradictory, Discrepant, Oxymoronic, Paradoxical, Unequal, Unsteady, Variance

Inconsolable Heartbroken, Niobe

Inconspicuous Obscure, Small, Unobtrusive

Inconstant Chameleon, Desultory, Fickle, Light, Mutable, → **VARIABLE**

Inconvenience, Inconvenient Awkward, Bother, Discommode, Fleabite, Incommodious, Inopportune, Put out, → **TROUBLE**, Unseemly, Untoward

Incorporate(d), Incorporation Absorb, Embody, Inc, Inorb, Integrate, Introgression, Introject, Join, Merge, Subsume

Incorporeal Aery, Airy, Spiritual

Incorrect Catachresis, False, Improper, Invalid, Naughty, Wrong

Incorrigible Hopeless, Obstinate

Incorruptible Copper-bottomed, Honest, Immortal, Pure, Robespierre, Sea-green

Increase(s), Increasing Accelerando, Accelerate, Accession, Accrue, Add, Additur, Aggrandise, Amplify, Amp up, Appreciate, Approve, Augment, Auxetic, Bolster, Boost, Build up, Bulge, Crank up, Crescendo, Crescent, Crescive, Deepen, Dilate, Double, Ech(e), Eech, Eik, Eke, Enhance, Enlarge, Escalate, → **EXPAND**, Explosion, Gain, Greaten, → **GROW**, Heighten, Hike, Ich, Increment, Interbreed, Jack, Jack up, Joseph, Lift, Magnify, Mark up, Mount, Multiply, Plus, Proliferate, Propagate, Ramp up, Redshift, Reflation, Regrate, Rise, Snowball, Swell, Thrive, Up, Upsize, Upswell, Upswing, Wax, Write up

Incredible Amazing, Cockamamie, Extraordinary, Fantastic, Steep, Stey, Tall, Unreal

Incredulity, Incredulous Distrust, Infidel, Suspicion, Thunderstruck, Unbelief

Increment Accrual, Augment, Growth, Increase

Incriminate Accuse, Implicate, Inculpate, Stitch up

Incubate, Incubator Brooder, Develop, Eccaleobion, Hatch

Incubus Demon, Load, Nightmare

Inculcate Implant, Infuse

Incumbent Lying, Obligatory, Occupier, Official

Incur Assume, Earn, Involve

Incursion Foray, Inroad, Invasion, Raid, Razzia

Indecent Bare, Blue, Fescennine, Free, Immodest, Immoral, Improper, Lewd, Obscene, Rabelaisian, Racy, Scurril(e), Sotadic, Spicy, Sultry, Unnatural, Unproper, Unseem(ly), X-rated

Indecision, Indecisive Demur, Dithery, Doubt, Hamlet, Havering, Hesitation,

Hung jury, Inconclusive, Shilly-shally, Suspense, Swither, Weakkneed, Wishy-washy

Indeclinable Aptote

Indecorous Graceless, Immodest, Outré, Unbecoming

Indeed Absolutely, Atweel, Ay, Aye, Da, Een, Even, Faith, Haith, I, Insooth, Ja wohl, La, Marry, Quotha, Soothly, Truly, Verily, Yah, Yea

Indefensible Implausible, Inexcusable, Vincible

Indefinable Je ne sais quoi

Indefinite(ly) A, An, Any, Evermore, Hazy, Nth, Some, Undecided, Vague

Indelible Fast, Permanent

Indelicate Broad, Coarse, Improper, Sultry, Vulgar, Warm

Indemnify, Indemnification, Indemnity Assythement, Compensation, Double, Insurance

Indent(ed), Indentation Apprentice, Contract, Crenellate, Dancetty, Dimple, Impress, Niche, Notch, Order, Philtrum, Prophet's thumbmarks, Subentire

Independence, Independent Apart, Autocephalous, Autogenous, Autonomy, Crossbencher, Detached, Extraneous, Free(dom), Free-lance, Free spirit, Freethinker, I, Liberty, Mana motuhake, Maverick, Mugwump, Perseity, Self-contained, Self-sufficient, Separate, Separatist, Sui juris, Swaraj, Udal, UDI, Uhuru

Indescribable Incredible, Ineffable

Indestructible Enduring, Impenetrable, Inextirpable

Indeterminate Borderline, Formless, Incalculable, Open-ended, Unknown

Index Alidad(e), All-Ordinaries, Catalogue, Cephalic, Colour, Cranial, Dial, Dow Jones, Exponent, Facial, Finger, Fist, Fog, Footsie, Forefinger, Gazetteer, Glycaemic, Hang Seng, Kwic, Librorum Prohibitorum, Margin, Misery, Mitotic, Nasal, Nikkei, Opsonic, Power, Price, Refractive, → **REGISTER**, Rotary, Share, Stroke, Table, Thumb, TPI, UV, Verborum, Zonal

India(n) Adivisi, Asian, Assamese, Ayah, Baboo, Babu, Bharat(i), Bihari, Canarese, Carib, Chin, Dard, Dravidian, East, File, Gandhi, Goanese, Gond(wanaland), Gujarati, Harijan, Harsha, Hindu, Indic, Ink, Jain, Jat, Jemadar, Kafir, Kanarese, Kannada, Khalsa, Kisan, Kolarian, Kshatriyas, Lepcha, Ma(h)ratta, Maratha, Maya, Mazhbi, → **MEXICAN**, Mission, Mofussil, Mogul, Mulki, Munda, Munshi, Naga, Nagari, Nair, Nasik, Nation, Nayar, → **NORTH AMERICAN**, Nuri, Ocean, Oriya, Pali, Panjabi, Pargana, Parsee, Parsi, Pathan, Peshwa, Plains, Prakrit, Punja(u)bee, Punjabi, Red, Sanskrit, Sepoy, Shri, Sikh, Sind(h), → **SOUTH AMERICAN**, Sowar, Summer, Swadeshi, Taino, Tamil, Telegu, Vakeel, Vakil, West

Indiaman Clive

Indiana, Indianian Hoosier

Indicate, Indication, Indicative, Indicator Adumbrate, Allude, Argue, Bespeak, Blinker, Cite, Clue, Cursor, → **DENOTE**, Design, Designate, Desine, Dial, Dial gauge, Endeixis, Evidence, Evince, Fluorescein, Gesture, Gnomon, Hint, Litmus, Manifest, Mean, Mood, Nod, Notation, Performance, Pinpoint, Plan-position, Point, Portend, Proof, Ray, Register, Remarque, Representative, Reveal, Show, → **SIGN**, Signify, Specify, Symptom, Tip, Token, Trace, Trafficator, Trait, Winker

Indictment Accusation, Arraign, Caption, Charge, Dittay, Reproach, Trounce

Indifference, Indifferent Adiaphoron, Aloof, Apathetic, Apathy, Blasé, Blithe, Callous, Cavalier, Cold, Cool(th), Dead, Deaf, Detached, Disdain, Easy-osy, Empty, Incurious, Insouciant, Jack easy, Lax, Mediocre, Neutral, Nonchalant, Perfunctory, Phlegm, Pococurante, Sangfroid, So-so, Stoical, Supercilious, Supine, Tepid, Unconcerned

Indigence, Indigent Need, Pauper, Penury, Poverty, Want

Indigenous Aboriginal, Endemic, Native

▷ **Indi-gent** *may indicate* Baboo or Babu

Indigestion Apepsia, Apepsy, Dyspepsia, Heartburn

Indignant, Indignation Anger, Annoyed, Incensed, Irate, Outrage, Pique, Resentful, Steamed up, Wrathful

Indignity Affront, Outrage

Indigo Anil, Blue, Bunting, Carmine, Indole, Isatin(e), Wild

Indirect Aside, Back-handed, By(e), Devious, Implicit, Mediate, Oblique, Remote, Roundabout, Second-hand, Sidelong, Zig-zag

Indiscreet, Indiscretion Blabbermouth, Folly, Gaffe, Imprudence, Indelicate, Injudicious, Loose cannon, Rash, Unguarded, Wild oats

Indiscriminate Haphazard, Random, Scattershot, Sweeping, Wholesale

Indispensable Basic, Essential, King-pin, Linch-pin, Necessary, Requisite, Sine qua non, Vital

Indispose(d), Indisposition Adverse, Disincline, Ill, Incapacitate, Sick, Unwell

Indisputable Evident

Indistinct Ambiguous, Bleary, Blur, Bumble, Bummle, Faint, Fuzzy, Grainy, Hazy, Misty, Mush-mouthed, Nebulous, Neutral, Nondescript, Pale, S(c)hwa, Sfumato, Smudged, → **VAGUE**

Indistinguishable Nondescript

▷ **In distress** *may indicate* an anagram

Indite Compose, Pen, Write

Indium In

Individual(ist), Individuality Apiece, Being, Discrete, Exclusive, Free spirit, Gemma, Haecceity, Identity, Ka, Libertarian, Loner, Man, Man-jack, Morph, One-to-one, Own, Particular, Person, Poll, Respective, Seity, Separate, Single, Singular, Solo, Soul, Special, Unit, Zoon

Indoctrinate Brainwash, Discipline, Instruct

Indo-European Aryan, Jat(s)

Indolence, Indolent Bone idle, Fainéance, Inactive, Languid, Lazy, Otiose, Sloth, Sluggish, Supine

Indomitable Brave, Dauntless, Invincible

Indonesia(n) Batavian, Nesiot, RI

Indoor(s) Within

Indubitably Certainly, Certes, Manifestly, Surely

Induce(ment) Bribe, Carrot, Cause, Coax, Draw, Encourage, Get, Inveigle, Lead, Motivate, → **PERSUADE**, Prevail, Suasion, Suborn, Tempt

Induct(ion), Inductance Epagoge, Henry, Inaugurate, Initiate, Install, L, Logic, Mutual, Prelude, Remanence

Indulge(nce), Indulgent Absolution, Binge, Coddle, Drink, Favour, Gratify, Humour, Law, Luxuriate, Oblige, Orgy, Pamper, Pander, Pardon, Partake, Permissive, Pet, Pettle, Pig-out, Please, → **SATISFY**, Splurge, Spoil, Spoonfeed, Surfeit, Tolerant, Venery, Voluptuous, Wallow

Industrial, Industrious, Industry Appliance, Application, Basic, Business, Busy, Cottage, Deedy, Diligence, Eident, Energetic, Growth, Heavy, Labour, Millicent, Ocnus, Operose, Ruhr, Service, Smokestack, Sunrise, Technical, Technics, Tourism, Zaibatsu

▶ **Inebriate** *see* **INTOXICATE**

Inedible Inesculent, Noisome, Rotten

Ineffective, Ineffectual Chinless wonder, Clumsy, Deadhead, Drippy, Droob, Dud,

Empty, Fainéant, Fruitless, Futile, Idle, Ill, Impotent, Mickey Mouse, Neutralised, Null, Powerless, Resty, Sterile, Toothless, → **USELESS**, Void, Weak, Wet

Inefficient Clumsy, Incompetent, Lame, Shiftless, Slack

Inelegant Awkward, Inconcinnity, Stiff, Turgid, Unneat

Ineligible Unqualified

Inept Absurd, Anorak, Cack-handed, Farouche, Fumbler, Galoot, Maladjusted, Nerd, Otaku, Plonker, Sad sack, Schlimazel, Schmo, Unskilled, Wet

Inequality Anomaly, Chebyshev's, Disparity, Evection, Imparity, Injustice, Odds, Tchebyshev's

Inert(ia) Catatonia, Comatose, Dead, Dull, Excipient, Inactive, Languid, Leaden, Mollusc, Neon, Oblomovism, Potato, Rigor, Sluggish, Stagnant, Stagnation, Thowless, Torpid

Inestimable Incalculable, Invaluable, Priceless

Inevitable, Inevitably Automatic, Certain, Fateful, Inescapable, Inexorable, Infallible, Needs, Perforce, TINA, Unavoidable

Inexact(itude) Cretism, Incorrect, Terminological, Wrong

Inexorable Relentless

Inexpedient Impolitic, Imprudent, Unwise

Inexpensive Bargain, Cheap, Dirt-cheap, Economic

Inexperience(d), Inexpert Amateur, Callow, Colt, Crude, Fledgling, Fresh, → **GREEN**, Greenhorn, Ham, Ingénue, Jejune, Put(t), Raw, Rookie, Rude, Tender, Unconversant, Unseasoned, Unseen, Unversed, Waister, Yardbird, Youthful

Inexplicable Magical, Mysterious, Paranormal, Unaccountable

Infallible Foolproof, Right, Sure-fire, Unerring

Infamous, Infamy Base, Ignominious, Notorious, Opprobrium, Shameful, Villainy

Infant, Infancy Babe, Baby, Innocent, Lamb, Minor, Oral, Rug rat, The cradle

▷ **Infantry** *may refer to* babies

Infantry(man) Buff, Foot, Grunt, Jaeger, Phalanx, Pultan, Pulto(o)n, Pultun, → **SOLDIER**, Tercio, Turco, Twenty, Voetganger, Zouave

Infatuate(d), Infatuating, Infatuation Assot, Besot, Circean, Crush, Enamoured, Engou(e)ment, Entêté, Fanatic, Foolish, Lovesick, Mash, → **OBSESSION**, Pash, Rave, Turn

Infect(ed), Infecting, Infection, Infectious Angina, Anthrax, Babesiasis, Babesiosis, Candidiasis, Canker, Carrier, Catching, Catchy, Cholera, Communicable, Contagious, Contaminate, Corrupt, Cowpox, Cryptococcosis, Cryptospondiosis, Diseased, E-coli, Fascioliasis, Fester, Focal, Fomes, Giardiasis, Gonorrhoea, Herpes, Impetigo, Leishmaniasis, Listeria, Lockjaw, Mycetoma, NSU, Opportunistic, Orf, Overrun, Poison, Polio(myelitis), → **POLLUTE**, Py(a)emia, Pyoderma, Quittor, Ringworm, Roup, Salmonella, Sarcoid, SARS, Scabies, Septic, Shingles, Smit(tle), Strep throat, Strongylosis, Taint, Taking, Tetanus, Thrush, Tinea, Toxocariasis, Toxoplasmosis, Trichuriasis, Typhoid, Typhus, Varria, Virion, Virulent, Whitlow, Wog, Yersiniosis, Zoonosis, Zymosis

Infeftment Sasine, Seisin

▷ **Infer** *may indicate* 'fer' around another word

Infer(ence), Inferred Conclude, Conjecture, Deduce, Divine, Educe, Extrapolate, Generalise, Guess, Illation, Imply, Judge, Obversion, Putative, Surmise, Syllogism

Inferior Base, Bodgier, Cheap-jack, Cheesy, Coarse, Crummy, Degenerate, Dog, Ersatz, Gimcrack, Grody, Grub-Street, Impair, Indifferent, Infra, Jerkwater, Less, Lo-fi, Lower, Low-grade, Mediocre, Minor, Naff, Nether, One-horse, Ornery, Paravail, Petty, Poor, Rop(e)y, Schlock, Second, Second-best, Shilpit, Shlock, Shoddy, Sprew, Sprue, Subjacent, Subordinate, Substandard, Surat, Tatty, Tinpot,

Trashy, Under(man), Underneath, Understrapper, Untermensch, Waste, Worse

Infernal Cotton-picking, Demogorgon, Diabolic, Hellish, Phitonian, Tartarean, Unholy

Infertile Barren, Farrow, Sterile

Infest(ed), Infestation Acariasis, Acrawl, Beset, Blight, Dog, Hoatching, Overrun, Pediculosis, Phthiriasis, → **PLAGUE**, Stylopised, Swamp, Swarm, Torment, Trombiculiasis, Trombidiasis, Uncinariasis

Infidel Atheist, Caffre, Giaour, Heathen, Heretic, Kafir, Miscreant, Pagan, Paynim, Saracen

Infield Intown

Infiltrate(d), Infiltrator Encroach, Enter, Fifth columnist, Instil, Intrude, Pervade, Trojan horse

Infinite, Infinity Cosmic, Endless, Eternal, N

Infinitive Split

Infirm Decrepit, Doddery, Feeble, Frail, Lame, Shaky, Sick

▷ **Infirm** *may indicate* 'co' around another word

Infirmary Hospital, Sick bay

Inflame(d), Inflammable, Inflammation Afire, Anger, → **AROUSE**, Bloodshot, Enamoured, Enchafe, Enfire, Enkindle, Fever, Fire, Founder, Gleet, Ignite, Impassion, Incense, Infection, Ire, Methane, Napalm, Naphtha, → **RED**, Stimulate, Swelling, Touchwood

INFLAMMATIONS

3 letters:	7 letters:	Metritis	Cloacitis
Sty	Bubonic	Mycetoma	Dysentery
	Catarrh	Myelitis	Enteritis
4 letters:	Colitis	Myositis	Fasciitis
Acne	Ecthyma	Neuritis	Frostbite
Gout	Ignatis	Orchitis	Gastritis
Noma	Ileitis	Osteitis	Glossitis
Stye	Onychia	Ovaritis	Keratitis
	Pinkeye	Phlegmon	Laminitis
5 letters:	Prurigo	Pleurisy	Nephritis
Croup	Rosacea	Pyelitis	Onychitis
Felon	Sunburn	Rachitis	Parotitis
	Sycosis	Rectitis	Phlebitis
6 letters:	Tylosis	Rhinitis	Phrenitis
Ancome	Uveitis	Thylosis	Pneumonia
Angina	Whitlow	Uvulitis	Proctitis
Bunion		Vulvitis	Pyorrhoea
Canker	8 letters:	Windburn	Retinitis
Coryza	Adenitis		Scleritis
Eczema	Aortisis	9 letters:	Sinusitis
Garget	Bursitis	Arteritis	Splenitis
Iritis	Carditis	Arthritis	Strumitis
Otitis	Colpitis	Balanitis	Synovitis
Quinsy	Cystisis	Barotitis	Typhlitis
Thrush	Fibrosis	Carbuncle	Vaginitis
Ulitis	Hyalitis	Cheilitis	Vent gleet
	Mastitis	Chilblain	

10 letters:
Asbestosis
Bronchitis
Cellulitis
Cephalitis
Cerebritis
Cervicitis
Dermatitis
Duodenitis
Erysipelas
Fibrositis
Gingivitis
Hepatitis A
Hepatitis B
Intertrigo
Laryngitis
Meningitis
Oophoritis
Ophthalmia
Papillitis
Paronychia
Phlegmasia
Phlogistic
Stomatitis
Tendinitis
Thrombosis
Tracheitis
Tympanitis
Urethritis

Valvulitis
Vasculitis

11 letters:
Blepharitis
Farmer's lung
Mad staggers
Mastoiditis
Myocarditis
Parotiditis
Peritonitis
Pharyngitis
Pneumonitis
Prostatitis
Salpingitis
Sandy blight
Sclerotitis
Shin splints
Spondylitis
Staphylitis
Tennis elbow
Thoroughpin
Thyroiditis
Tonsillitis
Utriculitis
Woody-tongue

12 letters:
Appendicitis

Crystallitis
Encephalitis
Endocarditis
Endometritis
Folliculitis
Golfer's elbow
Lymphangitis
Lympodenitis
Mesenteritis
Osteoporosis
Panarthritis
Pancreatitis
Pericarditis
Perityphitis
Polymyositis
Polyneuritis
Sacroillitis
Swimmer's itch
Vestibulitis

13 letters:
Cholecystitis
Enterocolitis
Epicondylitis
Jogger's nipple
Labyrinthitis
Lymphadenitis
Osteomyelitis
Perihepatitis

Perinephritis
Periodontisis
Perityphlitis
Tenosynovitis
Tenovaginitis
Thrombophilia

14 letters:
Clergyman's knee
Conjunctivitis
Diverticulitis
Osteoarthritis
Pyelonephritis
Sleepy staggers
Trichomoniasis
Vincent's angina

15 letters:
Gastroenteritis
Pachymeningitis

16 letters:
Bronchopneumonia

17 letters:
Encephalomyelitis
Meningocephalitis

Inflate(d), Inflation Aerate, Aggrandise, Bloat, Bombastic, Bracket-creep, Cost-push, Dilate, Distend, Distent, Exaggerate, Grade, Increase, Pneumatic, Pump, Raise, Remonetise, RPI, Spiral, Stagflation, Stagnation, Swell, Wage-push
Inflect(ion) Accidence, Conjugation, Tone
Inflexible, Inflexibility Adamant(ine), Byzantine, Doctrinaire, Hard-ass, Hard-liner, Iron, Obstinate, Ossified, Relentless, Resolute, Rigid, Rigour, Set, Staid, Stubborn, Unbending
Inflict(ion) Deal, Force, Give, Impose, Subject, Trouble, Visit, Wreak
Inflorescence Bostryx, Catkin, Ci(n)cinnus, Drepanium, Glomerule, Panicle, Pleiochasium, Polychasium, Raceme, R(h)achis, Umbel, Verticillaster
Inflow Affluence, Influx
Influence(d), Influential Act, Affect, After, Backstairs, Charm, Clamour, Clout, Colour, Credit, Determine, Dominant, Drag, Earwig, Eclectic, Embracery, Éminence grise, Factor, Force, Get at, Govern, Hold, Hypnotise, Impact, Impinge, Impress, Incubus, Inspire, Interfere, Lead, Leverage, Lobby, Macher, Mastery, Militate, Mogul, Mould, Nobble, Octopus, Operation, Outreach, Power, Preponderant, Pressure, Prestige, → **PULL**, Push, Reach, Rust, Say, Seminal, Significant, Star, Star-blasting, Stimulus, Suggest, Svengali, Sway, Swing, Telegony, Undue, Weigh with, Will, Work, Wull
Influenza Asian, Equine, Flu, Gastric, Grippe, Lurgi, Spanish, Wog, Yuppie
Influx Inbreak

Inform(ation), Informant, Informed, Informer Acquaint, Advise, Agitprop, Apprise, Au fait, Aware, Beagle, Bit, Blow, Burst, Canary, Ceefax®, Clype, Contact, Cookie, Datum, Deep throat, Delate, Dicker, Dob(ber), Dobber-in, Dope, Education, Exposition, Facts, Fact sheet, Feedback, Fink, Fisgig, Fiz(z)gig, Gen, Genome, Good oil, Grapevine, Grass, Griff, Gunsel, Hep, Immersive, Input, Inside, Instruct, Izvesti(y)a, Light, Lowdown, Media, Metadata, Moiser, Nark, Nepit, Nit, Nose, Notify, Occasion, Oracle®, Peach, Pem(m)ican, Pentito, Pimp, Poop, Prestel®, Prime, Printout, Promoter, Propaganda, Prospectus, Rat, Read-out, Revelation, Rheme, Rumble, Shelf, Shop, Sidelight, Sing, Sneak, Snitch, Squeak, Squeal, Stag, Stoolie, Stool-pigeon, Supergrass, Sycophant, Teletext®, Tell, Throughput, Tidings, Tip-off, Up, Videotext®, Viewdata®, Whistle(-blower), Wire, Witting

Informal Casual, Intimate, Irregular, Outgoing, Rough and ready, Unofficial

Infra Under

Infra dig Ignominious

Infrequent Casual, Occasional, Rare, Scant, Seldom, Sparse

Infringe(ment) Contravene, Piracy, Violate

Infuriate Anger, Bemad, Bepester, Enrage, Exasperate, Incense, Madden, Pester, Provoke

Infuse(r), Infusion Brew, Distill, Gallise, Instil, Mash, Ooze, Saloop, Saturate, Steep, Tea, Tea-ball, Tea-egg, Tisane, Toddy, Uva-ursi

Ingenious, Ingenuity Adept, Adroit, Art, Artificial, Clever, Cunning, Cute, Inventive, Natty, Neat, Resourceful, Smart, Subtle, Trick(s)y, Wit

Ingenuous Artless, Candid, Green, Innocent, Naive, Open, Transparent

Ingest Eat, Endue, Incept, Indue, Swallow

Ingle Bardash, Hearth, Nook

In good condition Fit, Shipshape, Taut, Trim

Ingot Bar, Billet, Bullion, Lingot, Sycee, Wedge

Ingrain(ed) Deep-seated, Fix, Impregnate, Train

Ingrate Thankless, Viper

Ingratiate, Ingratiating Bootlick, Butter, Court, Flatter, Greasy, Pick-thank, Silken, Smarm(y)

Ingredient(s) Additive, Admixture, Basis, Content, Element, Factor, Formula, Makings, Staple

Ingrowing, Ingrowth Onychocryptosis, T(h)ylosis

Inhabit(ant), Inhabitants Affect, Children, Denizen, Dweller, Inholder, Inmate, Live, Native, Occupant, People, Resident, Towny

Inhale(r), Inhalation Aspirate, Breath(e), Draw, Gas, Inspire, Intal, Sniff, Snort, Snuff, Take, Toot, Tout

Inharmonious Out, Patchy

Inherent Characteristic, Essential, Immanent, Inbred, Innate, Native

Inherit(ance), Inherited, Inheritor Accede, Birthright, Borough-English, Congenital, Esnecy, Feoffee, Gene, Genom, Heirloom, Heritage, Inborn, Legacy, Legitim, Meek, Mendelism, Particulate, Patrimony, Portion, Reversion, Succeed, Tichborne, Ultimogenitive

Inhibit(ing), Inhibition, Inhibitor ACE, Anuria, Captopril, Chalone, Chalonic, Deter, Donepezil, Enalapril, Etanercept, Finasteride, Forbid, Hang-up, Protease, Restrain, Retard, Retroactive, Stunt, Suppress, Tightass

Inhuman Barbarous, Brutal, Merciless

Inimical Adverse, Harmful, Hostile

Iniquity, Iniquitous Diabolical, Evil, Offence, Sin, Vice

Initial Acronym, First, Letter, Monogram, Paraph, Prelim(inary), Primary, Rubric

▷ **Initially** *may indicate* first letters

Initiate(d), Initiating, Initiation, Initiative Baptism, Begin, Bejesuit, Blood, Bora, Bring, Ceremony, Debut, Démarche, Enter, Enterprise, Epopt, Esoteric, Gumption, Induct, Instigate, Instruct, → **LAUNCH**, Nous, Onset, Proactive, Spark, → **START**

Inject(or), Injection Antiserum, Bang, Blast, Booster, Collagen, Direct, Enema, Epidural, Epipen®, Fuel, Hypo, Immit, Implant, Innerve, Inoculation, Instil, Introduce, Jab, Jack up, Jag, Mainline, Pop, Reheat, Serum, Shoot, Shoot up, Skin-pop, Solid, Spike, Syringe, Transfuse, Venipuncture

Injunction Command, Embargo, Freezing, Mandate, Mareva, Quia timet, Swear, Writ

Injure(d), Injury, Injurious, Injustice ABH, Abuse, Accloy, Aggrieve, Bale, Barotrauma, Bled, Bruise, Casualty, Concuss, Contrecoup, Contuse, Damage, De(a)re, Disservice, Forslack, Frostbite, Gash, GBH, Harm, → **HURT**, Ill-turn, Impair, Industrial, Iniquity, Lesion, Malign, Mar, Mayhem, Mistreat, Mutilate, NAI, Needlestick, Nobble, Nocuous, Non-accidental, Noxal, Nuisance, Occupational, Oppression, Outrage, Packet, Paire, Prejudice, Rifle, RSI, Scaith, Scald, Scath(e), Scotch, Sore, Sprain, Teen(e), Tene, Tort, Trauma, Umbrage, Whiplash, Wound, Wrong

▶ **Injury** *see* **AFTER INJURY**

Ink(y) Atramental, Black, Bray, China, Chinese, Copying, Cyan, Gall, Gold, Indian, Invisible, Magnetic, Marking, Monk, Printer's, Printing, Sepia, Stained, Sympathetic, Tusche

Inkling Clue, Glimpse, Hint, Idea

Inkpot Standish

Inlaid, Inlay(er) Boulle, Buhl, Damascene, Emblemata, Empaestic, Enamel, Enchase, Incrust, Intarsia, Intarsio, Koftgar(i), Marquetrie, Marquetry, Pietra-dura, Piqué, Set, Tarsia, Veneer

Inland Hinterland, Interior, Up

Inlet Arm, Bay, Bohai, Cook, Cove, Creek, Entry, Estuary, Fiord, Firth, Fjord, Fleet, Flow, Geo, Gio, Golden Horn, Gulf, Gusset, Hope, Infall, Ingate, Jervis Bay, McMurdo Sound, Moray Firth, Pamlico Sound, Pearl Harbor, Plymouth Sound, Pohai, Port Jackson, Puget Sound, Solway Firth, Strait, Sullom Voe, Table Bay, The Wash, Tor Bay, Zuyder Zee

▷ **Inlet** *may indicate* 'let' around another word

Inmate Intern(e), Lodger, Patient, Prisoner, Resident

▷ **Inn** *may refer to* the law

Inn(s), Innkeeper Albergo, Alehouse, Auberge, Barnard's, Boniface, Caravanserai, Chancery, Change-house, Coaching, Court, Gray's, Halfway-house, Host, Hostelry, Hotel, House, Imaret, In, Inner Temple, Jamaica, Khan, Kneipe, Ladin(ity), Law, Licensee, Lincoln's, Lodging, Luckie, Lucky, Maypole, Middle Temple, Motel, Padrone, Parador, Patron, Porterhouse, Posada, Posthouse, Pothouse, Publican, Roadhouse, Ryokan, Serai, Stabler, Tabard, Taphouse, Tavern(er), Victualler

Innards Entrails, Giblets, Gizzard, Guts, Harigals, Harslet, Haslet, Omasa, Rein, Viscera

Innate Congenital, Essential, Inborn, Inbred, Inbuilt, Ingenerate, Instinctive, Natural

Inner(most) Bencher, Esoteric, Internal, Intima, Intimate, Lining, Man, Marrow, Medulla, Private, Red, Woman

Innings Chance, Knock, Turn

▶ **Innkeeper** *see* **INN**

Innocent Absolved, Angelic, Arcadian, Babe, Blameless, Canny, Chaste, Cherub,

Childlike, Clean, Dewy-eyed, Doddypoll, Dodipoll, Dove, Encyclical, Green, Guileless, Idyllic, Ingenue, Lamb, Lily-white, Maiden, Naive, Opsimath, Pope, → **PURE**, Sackless, Seely, Simple, St, Unwitting, White

Innocuous Harmless, Innocent

Innovate, Innovative, Innovation, Innovator Alteration, Cutting edge, Departure, Ground-breaking, Modernise, Newell, Novelty, Pioneer, Promethean, Radical

Inn-sign Bush

Innu Naskapi

Innumerable Countless, Infinite, Myriad, N

Inoculate, Inoculation Engraft, Immunise, Jab, Protect, Vaccine, Variolate

Inoffensive Anodyne, Mild, Neutral, Pleasant

Inoperative Futile, Nugatory, Silent, Void

Inopportune Disadvantageous, Inconvenient, Intempestive, Untimely

Inordinate Excessive, Irregular, Undue

▷ **Inordinately** *may indicate* an anagram

In place of For, Qua, Vice, With

Input Direct, OCR

Inquest Debriefing, Hearing, Inquiry, Investigation

Inquire, Inquiring, Inquiry Ask, Demand, Investigation, Maieutic, Nose, Organon, Probe, Public, Query, Question, See, Speer, Speir

Inquisition, Inquisitive, Inquisitor Curious, Interrogation, Meddlesome, Nosy, Prying, Rubberneck, Snooper, Spanish, Stickybeak, Torquemada

▷ **In revolt, In revolution** *may indicate* an anagram

Inroad(s) Breach, Encroachment, Honeycomb, Infall, Invasion

Insane, Insanity Absurd, Batty, Crack-brained, Crazy, Dementia, Deranged, Headcase, Hebephrenia, Loco, Lune, Mad, Manic, Mattoid, Nutso, Paranoia, Pellagra, Psycho, Schizo, Troppo, Yarra

Insatiable Greedy, Ravenous, Voracious

Insatiate child Killcrop

Inscribe(d), Inscription Chisel, Chronogram, Colophon, Dedicate, Emblazon, Endoss, Engrave, Enter, Epigraph, Epitaph, Exergue, Graffiti, Hic jacet, Hierograph, Lapidary, Legend, Lettering, Neum(e), Posy, Writ

Inscrutable Deadpan, Esoteric, Mysterious, Sphinx

Insect(s) Creepy-Crawly, Entomic, Nonentity, Non-person

INSECTS

3 *letters:*	4 *letters:*	5 *letters:*	
Ant	Flea	Aphis	Scale
Bee	Gnat	Borer	Stick
Bot	Grig	Brise	Zebub
Bug	Lice	Cimex	
Fly	Mite	Culex	6 *letters:*
Ked	Moth	Emmet	Acarid
Lac	Pium	Gogga	Breese
Nit	Pupa	Imago	Breeze
Wax	Tick	Louse	Capsid
Wog	Wasp	Midge	Chigoe
	Weta	Nymph	Cicada
	Zimb	Ox-bot	Cicala
			Coccid

Day-fly
Earwig
Elater
Gadfly
Hopper
Hornet
Instar
Locust
Maggot
Mantid
Mantis
Mayfly
Medfly
Noctua
Psocid
Psylla
Punkie
Redbug
Sawfly
Scarab
Slater
Spider
Tettix
Thrips
Vespid
Walker
Weevil

7 letters:
Antlion
Bee moth
Bristle
Buzzard
Carabid
Chalcid
Chigger
Corixid
Cornfly
Cricket
Culicid
Cutworm
Daphnid
Ergates
Firefly
Gallfly
Girdler
Gordius
Goutfly
Grayfly
Hexapod
Hive-bee

Humbuzz
Katydid
Ladybug
Ladycow
Ladyfly
Odonata
Oestrus
Oniscus
Phasmid
Pill-bug
Pyralis
Sandfly
Spectre
Spittle
Stylops
Tabanus
Termite

8 letters:
Alderfly
Bookworm
Cercopid
Circutio
Coccidae
Crane-fly
Dipteras
Firebrat
Fruit fly
Gall-wasp
Glossina
Goatmoth
Greenfly
Horntail
Horsefly
Isoptera
Itchmite
Lacewing
Ladybird
Lygus bug
Mealybug
Metabola
Milliped
Mosquito
Myriapod
Onion-fly
Pauropod
Pillworm
Puss-moth
Reduviid
Ruby-tail
Scarabee

Silkworm
Snowflea
Stinkbug
Stonefly
Symphile
Waterbug
Wheelbug
Whitefly
Wireworm
Woodworm

9 letters:
Ametabola
Booklouse
Butterfly
Caddis-fly
Campodeid
Centipede
Cochineal
Cockroach
Damselfly
Dobsonfly
Dor-beetle
Dragonfly
Ephemerid
Ergataner
Hemiptera
Homoptera
Leaf-miner
Mecoptera
Millepede
Millipede
Notonecta
Rearhorse
Robber-fly
Songololo
Squash bug
Synoekete
Tabanidae
Tiger-moth
Woodlouse
Xylophage

10 letters:
Apterygota
Bark mantis
Bluebottle
Casebearer
Cecidomyia
Chironomid
Cockchafer

Coleoptera
Collembola
Fan-cricket
Fen-cricket
Froghopper
Greendrake
Harvestman
Leaf-cutter
Leafhopper
Mallophaga
Orthoptera
Phylloxera
Plant-louse
Plecoptera
Pond-skater
Psocoptera
Rhipiptera
Silverfish
Spittlebug
Springtail
Thysanuran
Treehopper
Waterstick
Web spinner

11 letters:
Bristletail
Collembolan
Dermapteran
Grasshopper
Greenbottle
Heteroptera
Hymenoptera
Mole-cricket
Neuropteran
Plectoptera
Rhopalocera
Tiger-beetle
Trichoptera
Vine-fretter

12 letters:
Bishop's mitre
Dictyopteran
Groundhopper
Heteropteran
Neuropterous
Orthopterous
Rhipidoptera
San Jose scale
Strepsiptera

12 letters – cont:	13 letters:	Leatherjacket	14 letters:
Thousand-legs	Cotton stainer	Praying mantis	Strepsipterous
Thysanoptera	Daddy-long-legs	Staphylinidae	
Water boatman	Jenny-longlegs	Water scorpion	

Insecticide Aldrin, Allethrin, Aphicide, Carbaryl, Carbofuran, Chromene, Cube, DDT, Deet, Derris, Diazinon, Dieldrin, Endosulfan, Endrin, Flycatcher, Gammexane®, Ivermectin, Lindane®, Malathion®, Menazon, Methoxychlor, Miticide, Naphthalene, Parathion, Paris green, Piperazine, Pulicide, Pyrethrin, Pyrethrum, Rotenone, Spray, Systemic, Timbo, Toxaphene, Zineb

Insectivore Agoura, Desman, Donaea, Drongo, Drosera, Hedgehog, Jacamar, Nepenthaceae, Otter-shrew, Sarracenia, Tanrec, Tenrec(idae), Tupaia, Venus flytrap, Zalambdodont

Insecure Infirm, → LOOSE, Precarious, Shaky, Unsafe, Unstable, Unsteady, Vulnerable

Insensible Iron-witted

Insensitive, Insensitivity Analgesia, Blunt, Callous, Crass, Dead, Log, Numb, Obtuse, Pachyderm, Stolid, Tactless, Thick-skinned

Inseparable Indiscrete, One, United

Insert(ed), Insertion, Inset Anaptyxis, Cue, Empiecement, Enchase, Enter, Entry, Epenthesis, Foist, Fudge, Godet, Gore, Graft, Gusset, Immit, Imp, Implant, Inchase, Inject, Inlay, Input, Intercalar, Interject, Interpolate, Interpose, Intersperse, Introduce, Intromit, Intubate, Lexical, Mitre, Pin, Punctuate, Sandwich

Inside(r) Content, Core, Entrails, Gaol, Heart, Indoors, Interior, Internal, Interne, Inward, Inwith, Mole, Tum, → WITHIN

Insidious Artful, Crafty, Sly

Insight Acumen, Anagoge, Aperçu, Enlightenment, Hunch, Inkling, Intuition, → PERCEPTION, Profundity, Tais(c)h

Insignia Armour, Arms, Badger, Charge, Chevron, Mark, Order, Regalia, Ribbon, Roundel, Tab

Insignificant (person) Bobkes, Bubkis, Bupkes, Bupkis, Chickenfeed, Dandiprat, Fico, Fiddling, Flea-bite, Fractional, Gnat, Inconsiderable, Insect, Jerkwater, Mickey Mouse, Minimus, Miniscule, Minnow, Nebbich, Nobody, Nominal, Nondescript, Nonentity, Non-event, One-eyed, Peanuts, Petit, Petty, Pipsqueak, Pissant, Quat, Rabbit, Scoot, Scout, Scrub, Shrimp, Slight, Small potatoes, Small-time, Squirt, Squit, Tenuous, Trifling, Trivial, Two-bit, Unimportant, Venial, Warb, Whiffet, Whippersnapper, Wind

Insincere, Insincerity Affected, Artificial, Barmecide, Cant, Double, Double-faced, Duplicity, Empty, Factitious, Faithless, False, Forced, Glib, Greenwash, Hollow, Janus-faced, Lip service, Mealy-mouthed, Meretricious, Mouth-made, Pseudo, Shallow, Synthetic, Two-faced

Insinuate, Insinuating, Insinuation Allude, Foist, Hint, Imply, Innuendo, Intimate, Sleek, Slur, Sneck-draw

Insipid Banal, Blab, Bland, Drippy, Fade, Flat, Insulse, Jejune, Lash, Mawkish, Milk and water, Shilpit, Tame, Tasteless, Vapid, Weak, Wearish, Wersh

Insist(ent) Adamant, Assert, Demand, Dogmatic, Exact, Press, Stickler, → STIPULATE, Stress, Swear, Threap, Threep, Urge

Insolence, Insolent Audacity, Bardy, Brassy, Cheek, Contumely, Cub, Effrontery, Gum, Hectoring, Hubris, Hybris, Impudence, Lip, Rude, Snash, Stroppy, Wanton

Insoluble Cerasin, Hard, Irresolvable, Mysterious

Insolvent Bankrupt, Broke, Destitute, Penniless

Insomnia Agrypnotic, Sleeplessness, Wakefulness, White night

Insouciant Carefree, Careless, Cavalier

Inspect(ion), Inspector Alnage(r), Auditor, Case, Comb, Conner, Cook's tour, Darogha, Examine, Exarch, Go-over, Government, Investigator, Jerque, Keeker, Lestrade, Look-see, Morse, Muster, Once-over, Peep, Perlustrate, Proveditor, Rag-fair, Recce, Review, Sanitary, School, Scrutinise, Searcher, Spot check, Supervisor, Survey, Test, Vet, Vidimus, Visitation

Inspire(d), Inspiration, Inspiring Actuate, Aerate, Afflatus, Aganippe, Animate, Brainstorm, Brainwave, Breath(e), Castalian, Draw, Duende, Elate, Exalt, Fire, Flash, Geist, Hearten, Hunch, Hwyl, Idea, Illuminate, Imbue, Impress, Impulse, Induce, Inflatus, Infuse, Kindle, Motivate, Move, Muse, Pegasus, Plenary, Prompt, Prophetic, Satori, Sniff(le), Stimulus, Taghairm, Theopnautic, Theopneust(y), Uplift, Vatic, Verbal

In spite of Malgrado, Malgré, Maugre

Instability Anomie, Anomy

Install(ation) Elect, Enchase, Enthrone, Inaugurate, Induction, Infrastructure, Insert, Invest, Put (in)

Instalment Episode, Fascicle, Fascicule, Heft, Insert, Livraison, Never-never, Part, Serial, Tranche

Instance, Instant As, Case, Chronon, Example, Flash, Jiffy, Moment, Present, Say, Shake, Spur, Tick, Trice, Twinkling, Urgent

Instead (of) Deputy, For, Lieu, Locum, Vice

Instigate, Instigating Arouse, Foment, Impel, Incite, Proactive, Prompt, Spur

Instil(l) Implant, Inculcate, Infuse, Inspire, Teach, Transfuse

Instinct(ive) Automatic, Conation, Flair, Gut, Herd, Id, Impulse, Inbred, Innate, Intuition, Life, Nature, Nose, Pleasure principle, Prim(a)eval, Reflex, Talent, Tendency, Visceral

Institute, Institution Academy, Activate, Asylum, Bank, Begin, Bring, Broadmoor, Charity, College, Collegiate, Erect, Found(ation), I, Inaugurate, Mechanical, MORI, Orphanage, Poorhouse, Protectory, Raise, Redbrick, Retraict, Retrait(e), Retreat, Royal, Smithsonian, Start, Technical, University, Varsity, Women's, Workhouse

Instruct(ed), Instruction, Instructor ADI, Advice, Algorithm, Apprenticeship, Brief, CAI, Catechism, Chautauquan, Clinic, Coach, Course, Didactic, Direct(ive), Document, Edify, Educate, Enjoin, Ground(ing), Guide, How-to, Inform, Lesson, Loop, Macro, Manual, Mystagogue, Mystagogus, Notify, Order, Patch, Precept, Prescription, Program, RE, Recipe, RI, Rubric, Script, Sensei, Statement, Swami, → TEACH, Train, Tutelage, Tutorial, Up

Instrument(al) Ablative, Act, Agent, Dash(board), Helpful, Kit, Mean(s), Measure, Mechanical, → MUSICAL INSTRUMENT, Negotiable, → RESPONSIBLE, → TOOL, Transit, Transposing, → UTENSIL, Weapon

---

INSTRUMENTS

3 *letters:*	Fork	5 *letters:*	Meter
Fan	Mike	Brake	Miser
Gad	Prog	Curet	Organ
	Rasp	Fleam	Probe
4 *letters:*	Rote	Float	Sonde
Celt	Tram	Gadge	Wecht
Clam		Groma	
Dupe		Lance	

6 letters:
Bougie
Broach
Etalon
Megger®
Octant
Opener
Pallet
Peeler
Pestle
Scythe
Sector
Seeker
Speedo
Spline
Strobe
Trocar
Wimble
Xyster

7 letters:
Alidade
Cadrans
Caliper
Caltrop
Cautery
Compass
Curette
Dilator
Diopter
Flesher
Forceps
Grapple
Monitor
Organic
Pelican
Plogger
Plotter
Pointel
Pricker
Probang
Scalpel
Scriber
Scummer
Sextant
Shuttle
Sounder
Spatula
Stapler
Strigil
Swatter

Swazzle
Swingle
Swozzle
Syringe
Trammel
Vocoder

8 letters:
Barnacle
Boothook
Burdizzo
Calutron
Diagraph
Dividers
Ecraseur
Enlarger
Iriscope
Luxmeter
Myograph
Odometer
Ohmmeter
Otoscope
Oximeter
Picklock
Quadrant
Repeater
Rheostat
Scalprum
Scissors
Snuffler
Speculum
Stiletto
Strickle
Trephine
Tweezers
Vuvuzela
Waywiser

9 letters:
Algometer
Alphonsin
Arcograph
Areometer
Astrolabe
Atmometer
Auriscope
Auxometer
Barometer
Baryscope
Bolometer
Cauterant

Coelostat
Crows-bill
Cryoprobe
Cryoscope
Cymograph
Depressor
Dermatome
Dip-circle
Dosemeter
Dosimeter
Dropsonde
Eidograph
Endoscope
Ergograph
Eriometer
Extractor
Fadometer
Fetoscope
Flowmeter
Fluxmeter
Focimeter
Graduator
Haemostat
Heliostat
Hodometer
Hourglass
Konimeter
Kymograph
Lysimeter
Machmeter
Manometer
Marigraph
Megaphone
Megascope
Metronome
Microlith
Microtome
Milometer
Monochord
Nocturnal
Nut-wrench
Oedometer
Oncometer
Ondograph
Optometer
Optophone
Osmometer
Osteotome
Pedometer
Periscope
Pintadera

Polygraph
Potometer
Pyrometer
Pyroscope
Raspatory
Repositor
Retractor
Rheometer
Scalprium
Set square
Skiascope
Somascope
Sonograph
Tasimeter
Telemeter
Telescope
Tellurian
Tellurion
Tenaculum
Tonometer
Toothpick
Tripmeter
Voltmeter
Volumeter
Wavemeter
Xylometer
Zymometer

10 letters:
Acidimeter
Almacantar
Almucantar
Altazimuth
Anemograph
Anemometer
Araeometer
Buttonhook
Ceilometer
Clinometer
Colposcope
Comparator
Cross-staff
Cryophorus
Cyanometer
Cyclograph
Cystoscope
Declinator
Densimeter
Dictograph
Drosometer
Fibrescope

Gaussmeter
Geodimeter®
Goniometer
Gonioscope
Gradienter
Gravimeter
Heliograph
Heliometer
Hydrometer
Hydroscope
Hygrograph
Hygrometer
Hypsometer
Iconometer
Integrator
Lactoscope
Light organ
Lithoclast
Micrograph
Micrometer
Microphone
Microscope
Mileometer
Milliprobe
Multimeter
Nephograph
Nephoscope
Nitrometer
Opsiometer
Orthoscope
Oscillator
Osteoclast
Pachymeter
Pantograph
Photometer
Piezometer
Pilliwinks
Planigraph
Planimeter
Protractor
Pulsimeter
Pulsometer
Pycnometer
Radiometer
Radiophone
Radioscope
Radiosonde
Rhinoscope
Scotometer
Siderostat
Spirograph®

Spirometer
Tachograph
Tachometer
Telewriter
Tensimeter
Theodolite
Thermopile
Tribometer
Tromometer
Urinometer
Variometer
Voltameter

11 letters:

Actinometer
Auxanometer
Cardiograph
Chronograph
Chronometer
Chronoscope
Coercimeter
Colonoscope
Coronagraph
Craniometer
Crescograph
Dendrometer
Dilatometer
Fluorometer
Fugitometer
Gastroscope
Gradiometer
Helicograph
Intoximeter
Jacob's staff
Keratometer
Laparoscope
Nephroscope
Odontograph
Opeidoscope
Pinnywinkle
Pitchometer
Planetarium
Plastometer
Polarimeter
Polariscope
Proctoscope
Pstchograph
Psychograph
Pyranometer
Pyrgeometer
Quantometer

Ragman Rolls
Rangefinder
Rocketsonde
Sclerometer
Screwdriver
Seismograph
Seismometer
Seismoscope
Solarimeter
Spherometer
Stactometer
Stadiometer
Stauroscope
Stereometer
Stereoscope
Stethoscope
Stroboscope
Synthesizer
Tacheometer
Tensiometer
Thermometer
Thermoscope
Torsiograph
Vaporimeter
Vectorscope
Velocimeter
Voltammeter
Volumometer

12 letters:

Aethrioscope
Astrocompass
Bronchoscope
Camera lucide
Cathetometer
Cephalometer
Declinometer
Densitometer
Electrometer
Electroscope
Ellipsograph
Extensimeter
Extensometer
Galactometer
Galvanometer
Galvanoscope
Harmonograph
Harmonometer
Inclinometer
Isoteniscope
Kaleidoscope

Katharometer
Keraunograph
Laryngoscope
Magnetograph
Meteorograph
Methanometer
Myringoscope
Nephelometer
Oscilloscope
Penetrometer
Pinniewinkle
Psychrometer
Respirometer
Scarificator
Scintillator
Sensitometer
Snooperscope
Spectrometer
Spectroscope
Sphygmograph
Sphygmometer
Sphygmophone
Sphygmoscope
Synchroscope
Tellurometer
Thoracoscope
Turbidimeter
Urethroscope
Zenith-sector

13 letters:

Accelerometer
Alcoholometer
Dipleidoscope
Electrophorus
Inclinatorium
Opthalmometer
Perpendicular
Pharyngoscope
Phonendoscope
Pneumatograph
Pneumatometer
Potentiometer
Pyrheliometer
Reflectometer
Refractometer
Saccharometer
Sigmoidoscope
Stalagmometer
Tachistoscope
Weatherometer

14 letters:	Phosphoroscope	15 letters:	Sphygmomano-
Circumferentor	Pyrophotometer	Electromyograph	meter
Diffractometer	Scintillascope	Phenakestoscope	Telespectroscope
Dividing engine	Scintilloscope	Radiogoniometer	
Interferometer	Spinthariscope	Telestereoscope	17 letters:
Oesophagoscope	Synchronoscope		Spectrophotometer
Ophthalmometer		16 letters:	
Ophthalmoscope		Photopolarimeter	

Insubordinate Contumacious, Faction, Mutinous, Rebel, Refractory

Insubstantial Airy, Brief, Flimsy, Frothy, Illusory, Jackstraw, Slender, Slight, Syllabub, Thin, Wispy, Ye(a)sty

Insufferable Egregious

Insufficient Exiguous, Inadequate, Poor, Scant, Shortfall

Insular Isolated, Moated, Narrow, Xenophobe

Insulate, Insulation, Insulator Biotite, Corkboard, Dielectric, Electret, Enwind, Grommet, Haybox, Inwind, Lagging, Mica, Non-conductor, Padding, Pugging, Sleeving, Tog

Insult(ing) Abuse, Affront, Aspersion, Barb, Becall, Charientism, Contumely, Cut, Derogatory, Dyslogistic, Embarrass, Facer, Fig, Injurious, Lese-majesty, Mud, Mud-pie, Offend, Opprobrious, Rip on, Scurrilous, Skit, Slagging, Sledge, Slight, Slur, Snub, Trauma, Uncomplimentary, Verbal, Yenta, Yente

Insure(r), Insurance Abandonee, Accident, Comprehensive, Cover, Death futures, Endowment, Fidelity, Fire, Group, Guarantee, Hedge, Indemnity, Knock-for-knock, Life, Lloyds, Marine, Medibank, Medicare, Mutual, National, Participating, Pluvius, Policy, Public liability, Reversion, Safety net, Security, Social, Term, Underwrite, Whole-life

Insurgent, Insurrection Cade, Jacquerie, Mutiny, Outbreak, Pandy, Rebel, Revolt, Sedition, Terrorist, Uprising, Whisky

▷ **Insurgent** *may indicate* 'reversed'

Intact Complete, Entire, Inviolate, Unused, Whole

Intaglio, Intagliate Diaglyph, Incavo

Intake Absorption, Entry, Fuel

Integer, Integral Component, Definite, Entire, Improper, Inbuilt, Indefinite, Needful, Number, Organic, Unitary

Integrate(d), Integration Amalgamate, Assimilate, Combine, Coordinate, Fuse, Harmonious, Holistic, Large-scale, Mainstream, Merge, Postural, Tightknit

Integrity Honesty, Principle, Probity, Rectitude, Strength, Uprightness, Whole

Integument Coat, Primine, Secundine, Sheath, Skin, Velum

Intellect, Intellectual(s) Academic, Aptitude, Belligerati, Brain, Cerebral, Cultural, Dianoetic, Egghead, Eggmass, Far-out, Genius, Grey matter, Highbrow, Intelligent, Intelligentsia, -ist, Learned, Literati, Luminary, Mastermind, Mental(ity), Mind, Noesis, Noetic, Noology, Nous, Profound, Reason, Sublime, Titan

Intelligence, Intelligent Advice, Artificial, Boss, Brainiac, Brains, Bright, CIA, Discerning, Dope, Eggmass, Emotional, Esprit, G, Grey matter, GRU, Guile, Humint, Info, Ingenious, IQ, Knowledgeable, Machiavellian, Machine, MI, Mossad, Mother wit, News, Pate, Pointy-headed, Rational, Sconce, Sense, Sharp, Shrewd, Smart, Spetsnaz, Spetznaz, Tidings, Wit

Intelligible Exoteric

Intemperance Acrasia, Crapulent, Excess, Gluttony, Immoderation

Intend(ed), Intending Allot, Betrothed, Contemplate, Design, Destine, Ettle,

Fiancé(e), Going, → **MEAN**, Meditate, Planned, Propose, Purpose

Intense, Intensify, Intensity Acute, Aggravate, Ardent, Compound, Crash, Crescendo, Deep, Depth, Earnest, Earthquake, Emotional, Enhance, Escalate, Estro, Excess, Extreme, Fervent, Keen, Luminous, Might, Profound, Radiant, Redouble, Saturation, Sharpen, Vehement, Vivid, Warmth

Intent, Intention(al) À dessein, Aim, Animus, Deliberate, Design, Dole, Earmark, Earnest, Ettle, Hellbent, Manifesto, Mens rea, Mind, Paradoxical, Prepense, Purpose, Rapt, Resolute, Set, Studious, Systematic, Thought, Tire, Witting, Yrapt

Inter Bury, Entomb

Interaction Chemistry, Enantiodromia, Solvation

Interbreed(ing) Miscegenation

Intercalation Embolism

Intercede, Intercession Mediate, Negotiate, Plead, Prayer

Intercept Absciss(a), Abscisse, Check, Hack, Meet, Tackle, Waylay

Interchange(d) Altercation, Alternate, Clover-leaf, Crossing, Equivalent, Junction, Mutual, Permute, Reciprocate, Substitute, Transpose

Intercom Entryphone®

Intercourse Arse, Ball, Bang, Bed, Blow job, Boff, Bone, Bonk, Buggery, Bukkake, Bump, Coition, Coitus, Commerce, Commixture, Congress, Connection, Consummation, Converse, Copulation, Cottaging, Coupling, Cover, Cunnilingus, Deflowering, Enjoy, Fluff, Fornication, Gam, Gamahuche, Gamaruche, Gangbang, Greens, Hochmagandy, Houghmagandie, How's your father, Hump, Incest, Jass, Jazz, Jig(-a)-jig, Jiggy, Jiggy-jiggy, Jump, Knee-trembler, Knock, Know(ledge), Koap, Laying, Leg-over, Lie with, Make, Marriage bed, Mell, Mix, Nail, Naughty, Necrophilia, Nookie, Nooky, Nooner, Oats, On the job, One-night-stand, Poke, Poontang, Pussy, Quickie, Ride, Rim, Roger, Roll, Root, Rump, Rumpy(-pumpy), Satyriasis, Screw, Sexual, Shaft, Shag, Shtup, Sixty-nine, Sociality, Sodomy, Soixante-neuf, Stuff, Swive, Tail, Teledildonics, The other, Tie, Trade, Tribadism, Trock, Troilism, Truck, Tumble, Whoredom

Interdict Ban, Forbid, Prohibit, Taboo

Interest(ed), Interesting Amusive, APR, Attention, Behalf, Benefit, Care, Clou, Compound, Concern, Contango, Controlling, Coupon, Dividend, Double-bubble, Ear-grabbing, Engage, Engross, Enthusiasm, Fad, Fascinate, Fee-simple, Fee-tail, Grab, Hot, Human, Import, Income, Insurable, Int(o), Intrigue, Landed, Life, Line, Negative, Part, Partisan, Percentage, Readable, Rente, Respect, Revenue, Reversion, Riba, Riding, Scene, Sepid, Share, Side, Sideline, Simple, Spice, Stake, Tasty, Tickle, Topical, Usage, Usance, Use, Usure, Usury, Vested, Vig(orish), Warm

Interface Centronics, Spigot

Interfere(r), Interference Atmospherics, Busybody, Clutter, Disrupt, Hamper, Hinder, Hiss, Intrude, Mar, → **MEDDLE**, Molest, Nose, Officious, Pry, Radio, Shash, Shot noise, Static, Tamper, Teratogen

Interferometer Etalon

Intergrowth Perthite

Interim Break, Meantime, Meanwhile, Temporary

Interior Backblocks, Cyclorama, Domestic, Innards, Innate, Inner, Inside, Outback, Plain, Up-country, Vitals

Interject(ion) Ahem, Begorra(h), Chime-in, Doh, Duh, Gertcha, Haith, Hoo-oo, Interpolate, Lackaday, Lumme, Nation, Sese(y), Sessa, 'Sheart, 'Slid, Tarnation, Tush

Interlace Mingle, Pleach, Weave, Wreathe

Interlock Dovetail, Engage, Knit, Tangle

Interlocutor Elihu, MC, Questioner

Interloper Gate-crasher, Intruder, Trespasser

Interlude Antimask, Antimasque, Divertimento, Entr'acte, Interruption, Kyogen, Lunch-hour, Meantime, Pause, Verset

Intermediary, Intermediate, Intermediatory Agent, Bardo, Between, Bytownite, Comprador(e), Contact man, Go-between, In-between, Instar, Mean, Medial, Mesne, Mezzanine, Middleman, Middle-of-the-road, Negotiant, Thirdsman, Transitional

Interminable Endless, Infinite, Unending

Intermission Apyrexia, Break, Interval, Pause, Recess

Intermittent Broken, Fitful, Off-on, Periodic, Random, Spasmic, Spasmodic, Sporadic

Intermix, Intermingle Lace, Melting pot

Intern(e) Confine, Doctor, Impound, Restrict, Trainee

Internal Domestic, Inner, Internecine, Inward, Within

International Cap, Cosmopolitan, Fourth, Lion, Second, Test, Trotskyist, UN, Universal

Internet Dotcom, Infobahn, URL, Web, WWW

Interpolate(r), Interpolation Diaskeuast, Insert, Intercalate, Interrupt, Spatchcock, Tmesis

Interpose Butt in, Horn in, Interject, Interlay, Interprone, Intervene, Spatchcock, Stickle

Interpret(er) Aread, Ar(r)e(e)de, Conster, Construe, Decipher, Decode, Dobhash, Dragoman, Exegete, Explain, Exponent, Expositor, Expound, Glossator, Hermeneutist, Hierophant, Jehovist, Latiner, Lingster, Linguistic, Linkster, Medium, Moonshee, Moonshi, Moralise, Munshi, Oneirocritic, Oneiroscopist, Origenist, Prophet, Read, Rede, Reed(e), Render, Represent, Spokesman, Textualist, → **TRANSLATE**, Truchman, Ulema

Interpretation Anagoge, Anagogy, Analysis, Construction, Copenhagen, Dittology, Eisegesis, Euhemerism, Exegesis, Exegete, Gematria, Gloss(ary), Gospel, Halacha(h), Halakah, Hermeneutics, Midrash, Oneirocriticism, Portray, Reading, Rede, Rendition, Spin, Targum, Translation, Tropology

Interrogate, Interrogation Catechism, Debrief(ing), Enquire, Examine, Grill, Maieutic, Pump, → **QUESTION**, Quiz

Interrupt(ion), Interrupter Ahem, Aposiopesis, Blip, Break, Butt, Chequer, Chip in, Disturb, Entr'acte, Heckle, Hiatus, Intercept, Interfere, Interpellate, Interpolate, Interpose, Interregnum, Intrusion, Overtalk, Pause, Portage, Rheotome, Stop, Suspend, Tmesis, Time-out

Intersect(ion), Intersecting Carfax, Carfox, Carrefour, Chiasm(a), Clover-leaf, Compital, Cross, Crunode, Cut, Decussate, Divide, Groin, Metacentre, Node, Orthocentre, Quadrivium, Trace

Intersperse Dot, Interlard, Interpose, Scatter, Sprinkle

Interstice Areole, Interlude, Pore, Space

Intertwine Braid, Impleach, Knit, Lace, Plait, Splice, Twist, Writhe

Interval Between, Break, Breather, Class, Closed, Comma, Confidence, Contour, Diapente, Diastaltic, Diatesseron, Diesis, Distance, Ditone, Duodecimo, Entr'acte, Fifth, Gap, Half-time, Harmonic, Hiatus, Hourly, Imperfect, Interim, Interlude, Interregnum, Interruption, Interspace, Interstice, Leap, Limma, Lucid, Lunitidal, Meantime, Meantone, Meanwhile, Melodic, Microtone, Minor third, Ninth, Octave, Open, Ottava, Perfect, Pycnon, Respite, Rest, Schisma, Semitone, Seventh, Sixth, Space, Span, Spell, Third, Tritone, Twelfth, Unison, Wait

Intervene, Intervening, Intervention Agency, Arbitrate, Expromission, Hypothetical, Interfere, Interjacent, Interrupt, Mediate, Mesne, Theurgy, Up

Interview Audience, Audition, Beeper, Conference, Debriefing, Doorstep, Examine, Hearing, Oral, Press conference, See, Vox pop

Interweave, Interwoven, Interwove Entwine, Interlace, Monogram, Pirnit, Plait, Plash, Pleach, Raddle, Splice, Wreathed

Intestate Heirless, Unwilling

Intestinal, Intestine(s) Bowel, Chit(ter)lings, Derma, Duodenum, Enteric, Entrails, Guts, Harigals, Innards, Jejunum, Kishke, Large, Mesenteron, Omenta, Rectum, Small, Splanchnic, Thairm, Tripes, Viscera

Intimacy, Intimate(ly) Achates, À deux, Boon, Bosom, Close, Communion, Connote, Familiar, Far ben, Friend, Heart-to-heart, Inmost, Innuendo, Intrigue, Nearness, Opine, Pack, Private, Signal, Special, Thick, Throng, Warm, Well

Intimation Clue, Hint, Implication, Inkling, Innuendo, Si quis

Intimidate, Intimidating Awe, Browbeat, Bulldoze, Bully, Cow, Daunt, Dragon, Hector, Niramiai, Psych, Threaten, Tyrannise, Unnerve

Into At, Intil, Within

Intolerant, Intolerable Allergic, Bigotry, Egregious, Excessive, Illiberal, Impatient, Impossible, Insupportable, Ombrophobe, Self-righteous

Intone, Intonation Cadence, Just, Twang

In touch Au fait

Intoxicate(d), Intoxicant, Intoxicating, Intoxication Alcoholic, Areca-nut, Benj, Bhang, Coca, Corn, Crink, Cup, Disguise, Fuddle, Ganja, Half-cut, Heady, → **HIGH**, Hocus, Hou high, Inebriate, Jag, Krunk, La-la land, Merry, Mescal, Nitrogen narcosis, Peyote, Pixil(l)ated, Rapture of the deep, Rumbullion, Shroom, Slewed, Soma, Sozzle, Spirituous, Swacked, Temulent, The narks, Whiskeyfied, Whiskified, Zonked

Intractable Disobedient, Kittle, Mulish, Obdurate, Perverse, Surly, Unruly, Wilful

Intransigent Adamant, Inflexible, Rigid, Uncompromising

Intransitive Neuter, Objectless

Intravenous IV

Intrepid(ity) Aweless, Bold, Bottle, Brave, Dauntless, Doughty, Firm, Gallant, → **RESOLUTE**, Stout, Unafraid, Valiant

Intricate Complex, Daedal(ian), Daedale, Dedal, Gordian, Intrince, Involute, Knotty, Pernickety, Sinuous, Tirlie-wirlie, Tricky, Vitruvian

Intrigue(r), Intriguing Affaire, Artifice, Brigue, Cabal, Camarilla, Cloak and dagger, Collogue, Conspiracy, Fascinate, Hotbed, Ignatian, Interest, Jesuit, Jobbery, Liaison, Machinate, Plot, Politic, Rat, → **SCHEME**, Stairwork, Strategy, Traffic, Trinketer, Web

Intrinsic(ally) Basically, Genuine, Inherent, Innate, Inner, Per se

▷ **Intrinsically** *may indicate* something within a word

Introduce(r), Introduction, Introductory Acquaint, Anacrusis, Curtain-raiser, Debut, Emcee, Enseam, Exordial, Foreword, Immit, Import, Induct, Initiate, Inject, Insert, Instil(l), Institutes, Intercalate, Interpolate, Intrada, Introit, Isagogic, Lead-in, Lead up, Opening, Phase in, Plant, Preamble, Preface, Preliminary, Prelude, Prelusory, Preparatory, Present, Presentment, Proem, Prolegomena, Prolegomenon, Prologue, Proponent, Referral, Standfirst, Start, Usher

▷ **Introduction** *may indicate* a first letter

Intromission Vicious

Introspective Indrawn, Musing, Reflex, Ruminant

▷ **In trouble** *may indicate* an anagram

Introvert(ed) Cerebrotonic, Ingrow, In-toed, Invaginate, Reserved, Shy

Intrude(r), Intrusion, Intrusive Abate, Aggress, Annoy, Bother, Burglar, Derby dog, Disturb, → ENCROACH, Gatecrash, Hacker, Inroad, Interloper, Invade, Meddle, Nosey, Personal, Porlocking, Presume, Raid, Sorn, Trespass

Intuition, Intuitive Belief, ESP, Hunch, Insight, Instinct, Inwit, Noumenon, Premonition, Presentiment, Seat-of-the-pants, Telepathy, Theosophy, Visceral

▷ **In two words** *may indicate* a word to be split

Inuit Caribou, Eskimo, Inuk, Yupik

Inundate, Inundation Engulf, Flood, Overflow, Overwhelm, Submerge, Swamp

Inure Acclimatise, Accustom, Harden, Season, Steel

Invade(r), Invasion Angle, Attack, Attila, Dane, Descent, Encroach, Goth, Hacker, Hengist, Horsa, Hun, Incursion, Infest, Inroad, Intruder, Irrupt, Jute, Lombard, Martian, Norman, Norsemen, Occupation, Ostrogoth, Overlord, Overrun, Permeate, Raid, Trespass, Vandal, Viking, Visigoth

Invalid(ate), Invalidation Bad, Bogus, Bunbury, Cancel, Chronic, Clinic, Defunct, Diriment, Erroneous, Expired, False, Inauthentic, Inform, Inoperative, Irritate, Lapsed, Nugatory, Null, Nullify, Overturn, Quash, Refute, Shut-in, Terminate, Valetudinarian, Vitiate, Void

Invaluable Essential, Excellent, Precious, Useful

Invariable, Invariably Always, Constant, Eternal, Habitual, Perpetual, Steady, Uniform

Invective Abuse, Billingsgate, Diatribe, Philippic, Reproach, Ribaldry, Tirade

Inveigh Declaim, Denounce, Marprelate, Protest, Rail

Inveigle Charm, Coax, Entice, Persuade, Subtrude

Invent(ion), Inventive Adroit, Babe, Baby, Brainchild, Chimera, Coin, Contrive, Cook up, → CREATE, Creed, Daedal, Design, Device, Excogitate, Fabricate, Fain, Fantasia, Feign, Fiction, Figment, Imaginary, Improvise, Ingenuity, Make up, Mint, Myth, Originate, Patent, Plateau, Pretence, Resourceful, Synectics, Whittle, Wit

Inventor Archimedes, Arkwright, Artificer, Author, Babbage, Baird, Bell, Biro, Boys, Bramah, Brix, Cartwright, Celsius, Cockerell, Coiner, Creator, Crompton, Daedalus, Edison, Engineer, Galileo, Geiger, Hansom, Jubal, Marconi, Maxim, Mercator, Mills, Minié, Mint-master, Morse, Nernst, Newcomen, Nobel, Patentee, Savery, Sax, Schmidt, Siemens, Solvay, Tesla, Torricelli, Tull, Watt, Wheatstone, Whitney

Inventory Account, Index, Itemise, List, Perpetual, Personality, Register, Steelbow, Stock, Terrier

Inverse, Inversion, Invert(ed) Anastrophe, Antimetabole, Antimetathesis, Capsize, Chiasmus, Entropion, Entropium, First, Homosexuality, Lid, Opposite, Overset, Reciprocal, Resupinate, Reverse, Second, Tête-bêche, Turn, Upset

Invertebrate Acanthocephalan, Annelida, Anthozoan, Arrowworm, Arthropod, Brachiopod, Cnidarian, Coelenterate, Crinoid, Ctenophore, Decapod, Echinoderm, Echinoid, Entoprocta, Euripterid, Feather star, Gast(e)ropod, Globigerina, Hydrozoan, Mollusc, Onychophoran, Parazoan, Pauropod, Peritrich, Platyhelminth, Polyp, Poriferan, Protostome, Rotifer, Roundworm, Scyphozoan, Sea-cucumber, Sea-lily, → SHELLFISH, Slug, Spineless, Sponge, Spoonworm, Starfish, Tardigrade, Trepang, Trochelminth, Unio, Water bear, Worm, Zoophyte

▷ **Invest** *may indicate* one word surrounding another

Invest(or), Investment Agamemnon, Ambient, Angel, Bate, Beleaguer, Besiege, Bet, Blockade, Blue-chip, Bond, Bottom-fisher, Capitalist, Clothe, Collins Street farmer, Contrarian, Dignify, Dub, Embark, Empanoply, Enclothe, Endow, Enrobe, Ethical, Financier, Flutter, Gilt, Girt, Gross, Holding, Infeft, Install, Inward, On, Pannicle, Panniculus, Parlay, Place, Portfolio, Put, Ring, Robe, Saver, Share, Siege,

Sink, Spec, Speculation, Stag, Stake, Stock, Surround, Tessa, Tie up, Trust, Trustee, Venture, Zaitech

Investigate, Investigator, Investigation Canvass, Case, Chart, CID, Delve, Examine, Explore, Fed, Ferret, Fieldwork, Go into, Gumshoe, Hunt, Inquest, Inquirendo, Inquiry, Inquisition, McCarthyism, Nose, Organon, Organum, Probe, Pry, Quester, Rapporteur, Research, Scan, Scout, Screen, Scrutinise, Search, Sleuth, Snoop, Study, Suss, Tec, Test, T-man, Track, Try, Zetetic

Investiture Award, Inauguration

Inveterate Chronic, Double-dyed, Dyed-in-the-wool, Engrained, Habitual, Hardened

Invidious Harmful, Hostile, Malign

Invigilator Proctor

Invigorate, Invigorating, Invigoration Analeptic, Brace, Brisk, Cheer, Crispy, Elixir, Energise, Enliven, Fortify, Insinew, Pep, Refresh, Renew, Stimulate, Tonic, Vital

Invincible Almighty, Brave, Stalwart, Valiant

Inviolatable, Inviolate, Inviolable Intemerate, Sacred, Sacrosanct

Invisible Blind, Hidden, Imageless, Infra-red, Secret, Tusche, Unseen

Invite, Invitation, Inviting Ask, Attract, Bid, Call, Card, Overture, → **REQUEST**, Solicit, Stiffie, Summons, Tempt, Toothsome, Woo

Invocation, Invoke Appeal, Call, Conjure, Curse, Entreat, Epiclesis, Solicit, White rabbits

Invoice Account, Bill, Docket, Itemise, Manifest, Pro forma

Involuntary Automatic, Instinctive, Unwitting

Involve(d), Involvement Active, Commitment, Complicate, Complicit, Concern, Embroil, Engage, Enlace, Entail, Envelop, Imbroglio, Immerse, → **IMPLICATE**, Include, Intricate, Meet, Necessitate, Participate, Tangle, Tricksy

▷ **Involved** *may indicate* an anagram

Inward(s) Afferent, Centripuntal, Homefelt, Introrse, Mental, Private, Varus, Within

Iodine I, Kelp, Thyroxin(e)

Iolanthe Peri

Ion Ammonium, Anion, Carbanion, Carborium, Hydrogen, Hydronium, Hydroxyl, Isomer, Onium, Zwitterion

Ionian Iastic, Te(i)an

Iota Atom, Jot, Subscript, Whit

IOU Cedula, Market, PN, Shinplaster, Vowels

IOW Vectis

IRA Provisional, Provo

Iran(ian) Babist, Kurd, Mede, Osset, Pahlavi, Parsee, Pehlevi, Ta(d)jik, Tadzhik

Irascible Choleric, Crusty, Fiery, Peevish, Snappy, Tetchy, Toustie

Irate Angry, Cross, Infuriated, Wrathful

Ire Anger, Bait, Cholera, Fury, Rage, Wrath

Ireland Blarney-land, Composer, Deirdre, Gaeltacht, Hibernia, Innisfail, Irena, IRL, Iverna, Ould Sod, Twenty-six counties

Irenic Peaceful

Iridescence, Iridescent Chatoyant, Flambé, Opaline, Reflet, Shimmering, Shot, Water-gall

Iridium Ir

Iris Areola, Eye, Flag, Fleur-de-lis, Florence, Gladdon, Gladioli, Ixia, Lily, Lis, Orris, Rainbow, Roast-beef plant, Sedge, Seg, Stinking, Sunbow, Triandria, Uvea, Water flag

Irish(man) Bark, Bog-trotter, Boy, Celt(ic), Clan-na-gael, Declan, Defender, Dermot, Dubliner, Eamon(n), Eirann, Erse, Fenian, Gael, Gaeltacht, Goidel, Greek, Jackeen, Keltic, Kern(e), Mick(e)(y), Middle, Milesian, Mulligan, Ogamic, Orange(man), Ostmen, Paddy(-whack), Partholon, Pat(rick), Rapparee, Redshank, Reilly, Riley, Rory, Ryan, Sean, Shoneen, Teague, Temper, Ultonian, Whiteboy, Wildgeese

Irk(some) Annoy, Bother, Irritate, Needle, Tedious

Iron(s), Ironstone, Ironwork(s) Airn, Alpha, Angle, Beta, Bloom, Carron, Cast, Cautery, Chains, Chalybeate, Chancellor, Channel, Climbing, Coquimbite, Corrugated, Cramp(on), Crimp, Cross, Curling, Curtain, Delta, Derringer, Dogger, Dogs, Eagle-stone, Fayalite, Fe, Ferredoxin, Ferrite, Fetter, Fiddley, Flip-dog, Galvanised, Gamma, Gem, Golfclub, Goose, Grappling, Grim, Grozing, → **GUN**, Gyve, Horse, Ingot, Italian, Kamacite, Laterite, Lily, Lofty, Long, Maiden, Malleable, Marcasite, Mars, Martensite, Mashie, Mashy, Merchant, Meteoric, Mitis (metal), Pea, Pig, Pinking, → **PRESS**, Pro-metal, Rabble, Rations, Rod, Sad, Scrap, Shooting, Short, Smoother, Soft, Soldering, Spathic, Specular, Speeler, Spiegeleisen, Steam, Stirrup, Stretching, Strong, Taconite, Taggers, Terne, Tin terne, Toggle, Tow, Wafer, Waffle, Wear, Wedge, White, Wrought

Iron age Latene, Villanovan

Ironic, Irony Antiphrasis, Asteism, Dramatic, Meiosis, Metal, Ridicule, Sarcasm, Satire, Socratic, Tongue-in-cheek, Tragic, Trope, Wry

Ironside Edmund

Ironwood Pyengadu

▶ **Ironwork(s)** *see* **IRON**

Irrational Absurd, Brute, Delirious, Foolish, Illogical, Number, Superstitious, Surd, Wild, Zany

Irreconcilable Poles apart

Irrefutable Evident, Positive, Undeniable

▷ **Irregular** *may indicate* an anagram

Irregular(ity) Abnormal, Alloiostrophus, Anomaly, Aperiodic, A salti, Asymmetric, Atypical, Bashi-bazouk, Blotchy, Casual, Crazy, Episodic, Erratic, Evection, Fitful, Flawed, Formless, Free-form, Guerilla, Heteroclitic, Incondite, Inordinate, Jitter, Kink, Occasional, Orthotone, Para-military, Partisan, Patchy, Rambling, Random, Rough, Scalene, Scraggy, Scrawl, Sebundy, Sharawadgi, Sharawaggi, Snatchy, Solecism, Sporadic, TA, Uneven, Unsteady, Unwonted, Variable, Wayward, Zigzag

Irrelevant Academic, Digression, Extraneous, Gratuitous, Immaterial, Inapplicable, Inconsequent, Inept, Non sequitur, Pointless, Ungermane, Unrelated

Irreligious Heathen, Impious, Pagan, Profane

Irremedial Hopeless, Incurable, Laches

Irrepressible Resilient

Irreproachable Blameless, Spotless, Stainless

Irresistible Almighty, Endearing, Inevitable, Mesmeric, Overwhelming

Irresolute, Irresolution Aboulia, Doubtful, Hesitant, Timid, Unsure, Wavery, Weak-willed

Irresponsible Capricious, Feckless, Flighty, Fly-by-night, Gallio, Slap-happy, Strawen, Trigger-happy, Wanton, Wildcat

Irreverent Blasphemous, Disrespectful, Godless, Impious, Profane

Irrigate, Irrigation Canalise, Colonic, Douche, Drip, Enema, Flood, Get, Water

Irritable, Irritability, Irritant, Irritate(d), Irritation Acerbate, Anger, Annoy, Bête noire, Blister, Bother, Bug, Chafe, Chauff, Chippy, Chocker, Choleric, Crabbit, Crabby, Cross-grained, Crosspatch, Crotchety, Crusty, Dod, Dyspeptic, Eat,

Eczema, Edgy, Emboil, Enchafe, Erethism, Ewk, Exasperate, Eyestrain, Fantod, Feverish, Fiery, Fleabite, Frabbit, Fractious, Fraught, Fretful, Gall, Get, Goad, Grate, Gravel, Hasty, Heck, Hoots, Humpy, Impatience, Intertrigo, Irk, Itch, Jangle, Livery, Mardy, Narky, Needle, Nerk, Nettle, Niggly, Ornery, Peckish, Peevish, Peppery, Pesky, Pestilent(ial), Pet, Petulance, Pinprick, Pique, Prickly, Provoke, Rag'd, Ragde, Rankle, Rasp, Rattle, Ratty, Rile, Riley, Roil, Rub, Ruffle, Savin(e), Scratchy, Shirty, Snappy, Snit, Snitchy, Splenetic, Sting, Tease, Techy, Testy, Tetchy, Thorn, Tickle, Tiresome, Toey, Touchy, Uptight, → **vex**, Waxy, Windburn, Yuke
▷ **Irritated** *may indicate* an anagram
Irving Actor, Berlin
Is Est, Ist
Isaiah Is
Isinglass Carlock, Fish-glue, Mica, Sturgeon
Islam(ic) Al Queda, Crescent, Druse, Druz(e), Hamas, Kurd(ish), Pillars, Senus(si), Sheriat, Shia(h), Shiite, Sunni(te), Taleban, Taliban, Wah(h)abi
Island, Isle(t) Ait, Archipelago, Atoll, Cay, Char, Crannog, Desert, Eyot, Floating, Holm, I, Inch, Insula, Is, Key, Lagoon, Langerhans, Mainland, Motu, Refuge, Safety, Traffic, Volcano

ISLANDS

2 letters:	Dogs	Ross	Cocos
TT	Eigg	Saba	Coney
	Elba	Sark	Coral
3 letters:	Erin	Skye	Corfu
Aru	Fair	Spud	Crete
Cos	Fiji	Truk	Delos
Diu	Gozo	Uist	Disko
Fyn	Guam	Unst	Ellis
Hoy	Heat	Wake	Faial
Kos	Herm	Yell	Farne
Man	Holy		Faroe
May	Hova	5 letters:	Fayal
Rat	Idse	Aland	Funen
Rum	Iona	Apple	Haiti
Sea	Java	Arran	Hondo
Yap	Jolo	Aruba	Ibiza
	Jura	Banka	Islay
4 letters:	Keos	Banks	Isola
Amoy	King	Barra	Iviza
Aran	Line	Batan	Jerba
Arru	Long	Belle	Kiska
Attu	Mahe	Bioko	Kuril
Bali	Maui	Bohol	Lanai
Biak	Mazu	Bonin	Lewis
Bute	Mona	Canna	Leyte
Calf	Muck	Capri	Lundy
Cebu	Mull	Ceram	Luzon
Coll	Niue	Cheju	Maewo
Cook	Oahu	Chios	Malta
Cuba	Rona	Clare	Matsu

5 letters – cont:

Melos
Nauru
Naxos
Nevis
North
Oland
Ormuz
Palau
Panay
Papua
Paros
Pelew
Pemba
Pines
Qeshm
Qishm
Reil's
Rhode
Samar
Samoa
Samos
Saria
Seram
South
Spice
Sumba
Sunda
Thera
Thule
Timor
Tiree
Tonga
Upolu
Whale
White
Wight
Youth
Zante

6 letters:

Achill
Aegean
Aegina
Amager
Andros
Aurora
Avalon
Azores
Baffin
Banaba

Bangka
Barrow
Bedloe
Bikini
Borneo
Bounty
Butung
Caicos
Canvey
Cayman
Ceylon
Chiloe
Cyprus
Devil's
Diomed
Djerba
Easter
Eelpie
Ellice
Euboea
Flores
Fraser
Hainan
Harris
Hawaii
Hobart
Honshu
Hormuz
Icaria
Imbros
Indies
Ionian
Ischia
Ithaca
Jersey
Kodiak
Kurile
Kvaley
Kyushu
Labuan
Laputa
Laplos
Laptev
Lemnos
Lesbos
Leucas
Leukas
Levkas
Lipari
Lizard
Lombok
Madura
Majuro

Marajo
Mercer
Midway
Negros
Ogygia
Paphos
Patmos
Penang
Pharos
Philae
Phuket
Pladdy
Quemoy
Ramsey
Rhodes
Rialto
Robben
Royale
Ryukyu
Saipan
Savage
Savaii
Scilly
Sicily
Skerry
Skyros
Snares
Soemba
Soenda
Staffa
Staten
Tahiti
Taiwan
Thanet
Thasos
Tobago
Tresco
Tubuai
Tuvalu
Unimak
Ushant
Veneti
Virgin

7 letters:

Aeolian
Aldabra
Amboina
Andaman
Antigua
Austral

Bahamas
Baranof
Barbuda
Basilan
Batavia
Battery
Bedloe's
Bermuda
Bonaire
Cartier
Celebes
Channel
Chatham
Cipango
Corsica
Curacao
Cythera
Diomede
Elvissa
Emerald
Eriskay
Falster
Frisian
Fur Seal
Gambier
Gilbert
Gotland
Grenada
Hawaiki
Howland
Ireland
Iwo Jima
Jamaica
Keeling
Laaland
Ladrone
La Palma
Leeward
Liberty
Lofoten
Lolland
Madeira
Majorca
Mariana
Masbate
Mayotte
Mindoro
Minicoy
Minorca
Molokai
Moreton

Mykonos
Nicobar
Norfolk
Oceania
Okinawa
Orcades
Orkneys
Pacific
Palawan
Palmyra
Paracel
Phoenix
Purbeck
Rathlin
Reunion
Roanoke
Rockall
Salamis
San Juan
Sheppey
Shikoku
Society
Socotra
Sokotra
Solomon
Spratly
St Croix
Stewart
St Kilda
St Kitts
St Lucia
Sumatra
Sumbawa
Suqutra
Surtsey
Tenedos
Tokelau
Tortola
Tortuga
Tutuila
Visayan
Waihake
Watling
Western
Wrangel
Zealand
Zetland

8 letters:
Alcatraz
Alderney

Aleutian
Amindiva
Anglesey
Anguilla
Antilles
Atlantis
Auckland
Balearic
Barbados
Bathurst
Billiton
Blefuscu
Bora-Bora
Bornholm
Canaries
Caroline
Catalina
Choiseul
Colonsay
Cyclades
Dominica
Falkland
Farquhar
Flinders
Foulness
Friendly
Gothland
Gottland
Guernsey
Hamilton
Hatteras
Hebrides
Hokkaido
Hong Kong
Jan Mayen
Kangaroo
Kermadec
Kiribati
Ladrones
Lilliput
Lord Howe
Luggnagg
Mackinac
Maldives
Mallorca
Malvinas
Marianas
Marquesa
Marshall
Mauna Loa
Melville

Mindanao
Miquelon
Moluccas
Mustique
Njazidja
Northern
Pelagian
Pitcairn
Pleasant
Portland
Pribilof
Principe
Sakhalin
Sandwich
Sardinia
Schouten
Shetland
Soembala
Somerset
South Sea
Sporades
Sri Lanka
St Helena
St Helier
St Martin
St Thomas
Sulawesi
Svalbard
Sverdrup
Tasmania
Tenerife
Terceira
Thousand
Thursday
Trinidad
Tsushima
Unalaska
Venetian
Victoria
Viti Levu
Windward
Zanzibar

9 letters:
Admiralty
Alexander
Andreanof
Anticosti
Antipodes
Ascension
Barataria

Belle Isle
Benbecula
Chichagof
Christmas
Elephanta
Ellesmere
Falklands
Fortunate
Galapagos
Governors
Greenland
Hainan Tao
Halmahera
Innisfree
Jamestown
Kerguelen
Laccadive
Lampedusa
Lanzarote
Macquarie
Manhattan
Margarita
Marquesas
Mascarene
Mauritius
Melanesia
Nantucket
New Guinea
Polynesia
Rangitoto
Rarotonga
Runnymede
Saghalien
Santorini
Sao Miguel
Shetlands
Sjaelland
Stromboli
St Vincent
Teneriffe
Trobriand
Vancouver
Vanua Levu
Walcheren

10 letters:
Basse-Terre
Bermoothes
Campobello
Cape Barren
Cape Breton

10 letters – cont:
Cephalonia
Corregidor
Dodecanese
Formentera
Grand Manan
Grenadines
Guadeloupe
Heligoland
Hispaniola
Isle Royale
Kiritimati
Madagascar
Manitoulin
Marinduque
Martinique
Micronesia
Montserrat
New Britain
New Georgia
New Ireland
Pescadores
Poor Knight
Puerto Rico
Sahghalien
Samothrace

Sandalwood
Seychelles
Three Kings
Vesteralen
West Indies
Whitsunday

11 letters:
Austronesia
Dry Tortugas
Glubdubdrib
Grand Bahama
Grand Canary
Grande-Terre
Guadalcanal
Lakshadweep
Lesser Sunda
Lindisfarne
Mount Desert
New Siberian
Pantelleria
Philippines
San Salvador
Southampton
South Orkney
Spitsbergen

12 letters:
Bougainville
Cassiterides
Glubbdubdrib
Greater Sunda
Marie Galante
New Caledonia
Newfoundland
Nusa Tenggara
Prince Edward
San Cristobal
Santa Barbara
Seringapatam
South Georgia
Torres Strait

13 letters:
Espiritu Santo
Forneaux Group
Fuerteventura
Juan Fernandez
New Providence
Prince of Wales
Santa Catalina
South Shetland

14 letters:
Amboina oceanic
D'Entrecasteaux
Lesser Antilles
Papua New Guinea
Queen Charlotte
Queen Elizabeth
Tristan da Cunha
Turks and Caicos
Vestmannaeyjar

15 letters:
Greater Antilles
Mont-Saint-Michel
Wallis and Futuna

16 letters:
Heard and
  McDonald

17 letters:
Fernando de
  Noronha

Islander Bermudan, Chian, Cretan, D(a)yak, Filipino, Kanaka, Kelper, Laputan, Madeiran, Maltese, Mauritian, Native, Nesiot, Newfie, Orcadian, Parian, Rhodian, Samiot, Scillonian, Sican, Singalese, Taiwanese
Isle of Wight Vectis
Isn't Aint, Nis, Nys
Isolate(d) Alienate, Ancress, Apart, Backwater, Cleidoic, Cut off, Desolate, Enclave, Enisle, Exclude, Incommunicado, Inisle, In vacuo, Island, Lone, Lonely, Maroon, Pocket, Quarantine, Sea-girt, Seclude, Secret, Segregate, Separate, Sequester, Set apart, Six-finger country, Solitary, Sporadic, Stray
Isomer Carotene, Carotin, Carvacrol, Geranial, Neral, Pinene, Theophylline
Isopod Gribble
Isosceles Triangle
Isotope Actinon, Cobalt-60, Deuterium, Iodine-131, Muonium, Protium, Strontium-90, Thoron, Tritium
Israel(i) Beulah, IL, Meir, Sabra
Issue(s) Bonus, Capitalization, Children, Come, Crux, Debouch, Denouement, Derive, Disclose, Dispense, Edition, Effluence, Egress, → **EMANATE**, Emerge, Emit, Escape, Exit, Exodus, Family, Feigned, Fiduciary, Flotation, Fungible, General, Government, Gush, Handout, Immaterial, Ish, Litter, Material, Matter, Mise, Number, Offspring, Outflow, Part, Privatization, Proof, Publish, Result, Rights, Sally, Scrip, Seed, Side, Son, Spawn, Special, Spring, Stream, Subject, Topic, Turn, Utter
Istanbul Byzantium, Constantinople
Isthmus Darien, Karelian, Kra, Neck, Panama, San Blas, Suez, Tehuantepec

It A, Chic, Hep, Hip, Id, Italian, Oomph, SA, Sex appeal, 't, Vermouth

Italian, Italy Alpini, Ausonian, Bolognese, Calabrian, Chian, Dago, Ding, Este, Etnean, Etrurian, Etruscan, Eyeti(e), Eytie, Faliscan, Florentine, Genoese, Ghibelline, Guelf, Guelph, Hesperia, Irredentist, It, Latian, Latin, Lombard, Medici, Mezzogiorno, Moro, Oscan, Paduan, Patarin(e), Rocco, Roman, Sabine, Samnite, Sicel, Sienese, Signor(i), Sikel, Spag, Tuscan, Umbrian, Venetian, Vermouth, Volscian, Wop

Italic Swash

Itch(ing), Itchiness Acariasis, Annoy, Burn, Cacoethes, Dhobi, Euk, Ewk, Hanker, Heat rash, Hives, Jock, Miliaria, Photopsy, Prickle, Prickly heat, Prurience, Prurigo, Pruritis, Psora, Scabies, Scrapie, Seven-year, Tickle, → **URGE**, Urtication, Yeuk, Yen, Youk, Yuck, Yuke

Item(ise) Also, Article, Bulletin, Detail, Entry, Equipment, Flash, Line, List, Number, Pair, Piece, Point, Spot, Too, Topic, Unit

Iterate Repeat

Itinerant, Itinerary Ambulant, Didakai, Didakei, Did(d)icoy, Dusty Feet, Gipsy, Gypsy, Hobo, Journey, Log, Pedlar, Peripatetic, Pie-powder, Roadman, Roamer, Romany, Rootless, Route, Stroller, Traveller, Vagrom

Itself Per se, Sui

Ivan Russian, Terrible

Ivory (tower) Black, Bone, Chryselephantine, Dentine, Distant, Eburnean, Impractical, Incisor, Key, Solitude, Teeth, Tower, Tusk, Vegetable, Whale's bone

Ivy Ale-hoof, Angelica-tree, Aralia, Boston, Bush, Cat's-foot, Climber, Creeper, Evergreen, Gill, Grape, Ground, Hedera, Helix, Japanese, Panax, Poison, Rhoicissus, Shield, Sweetheart, Udo, Weeping

Izzard Z

Jj

J Curve, Juliet, Pen

Ja(c)ques Melancholy, Tati

Jab(ber) Chatter, Foin, Gabble, Immunise, Immunologist, Inject, Jaw, Jook, Nudge, One-two, Peck, Poke, Prattle, Prod, Proke, Punch, Puncture, Sook, Sputter, Stab, Stick, Venepuncture, Yak

Jack(s) AB, Apple, Artocarpus, Ass, Ball, Boot, Bower, Bowl(s), Boy, Card, Cheap, Coatcard, Crevalle, Deckhand, Dibs(tones), Five stones, Flag, Frost, Giant-killer, Hoist, Honour, Hopper, Horner, Hydraulic, Idle, J, Jock, Jumping, Ketch, Kitty, Knave, Knucklebones, Lazy, London, Loord, Lout, Lumber, Maker, Mark, Matlow, Mistress, Nob, Noddy, Pilot, Point, Pot, Pur, Rabbit, Raise, Rating, Ripper, Roasting, Robinson, Russell, Sailor, Salt, Screw, Seafarer, Seaman, Shaun, Sprat, Spring-heeled, Springtail, Steeple, Sticker, Straw, Tar, Tee, Tradesman, Turnspit, Union, Uplift, Wood, Yellow

Jackal Anubis, Dieb, Hack, Lion's provider, Stooge

Jackass Aliboron, Goburra, Kookaburra, Stupid

Jackdaw Bird, Chawk, Chough, Daw, Kae, Raven, Rheims, Thief

Jacket Acton, Afghanistan, Air, Amauti(k), Anorak, Atigi, Bainin, Baju, Bania(n), Banyan, Barbour®, Basque, Battle, Bawneen, Bed, Bellhop, Biker, Blazer, Blouse, Blouson, Body-warmer, Bolero, Bomber, Brigandine, Bumfreezer, Bush, Cagoul(e), Camisole, Can, Caraco, Cardigan, Carmagnole, Casing, → **COAT**, Combat, Cover, Dinner, Dolman, Donkey, Drape, Dressing, Dressing-sack, Duffel coat, Duffle coat, Dust-cover, Dustwrapper, Duvet, Fearnought, Flak, Fleece, Gambeson, Gendarme, Grego, Habergeon, Hacking, Ha(c)queton, Half-kirtle, Hug-me-tight, Jerkin, Jupon, Kagool, Kaross, Life, Life preserver, Lumber, Mackinaw, Mae West, Mandarin, Mandilion, Mao, Matinée, Mess, Monkey, Nehru, Newmarket, Norfolk, Parka, Pea, Petenlair, Pierrot, Pilot, Polka, Potato, Pyjama, Railly, Reefer, Roundabout, Sackcoat, Safari, Sayon, Shearling, Shell, Shooting, Shortgown, Simar(re), Sleeve, Slip-cover, Smoking, Spencer, Sports, Steam, Strait, Tabard, Tailcoat, Toreador, Tunic, Tux(edo), Tweed, Vareuse, Waistcoat, Wam(m)us, Wampus, Water, Windbreaker®, Windcheater, Windjammer, Wrapper, Zouave

Jackknife Dive, Fold, Jockteleg, Pike

Jackpot Cornucopia, Kitty, Pool

Jackson Stonewall

Jackstraw Spellican, Spil(l)ikin

Jacobite(s) Non-compounder, Non juror, Wild Geese

Jacquard Matelasse

Jade(d) Axe-stone, Bidet, Cloy, Crock, Disjaskit, Exhaust, Fatigue, Greenstone, Hack, Hag, Horse, Hussy, Limmer, Minx, Nag, Nephrite, Pounamu, Rip, Rosinante, Sate, Screw, Slut, Spleenstone, Stale, Tired, Trite, Weary, Yaud, Yu(-stone)

Jaeger Skua

Jag(ged) Barbed, Cart, Drinking, Erose, Gimp, Hackly, Injection, Laciniate, Ragde, Ragged, Serrate, Snag, Spree, Spur, Tooth

Jagger Mick, Pedlar

Jaguar American tiger, Car, Caracal, Cat, E-type, Ounce, Tiger

Jail(er) Adam, Alcaide, Alcatraz, Bastille, Bedford, Bin, Bridewell, Can, Clink, Commit, Cooler, Gaol, Hoosegow, Imprison, Incarcerate, Jug, Keeper, Kitty, Limbo, Lockup, Marshalsea, Newgate, Nick, Pen, Pokey, Porridge, → **PRISON**, Screw, Shop, Slammer, Spandau, Strangeways, Tronk, Turnkey, Warder

Jailbird Con, Lag, Lifer, Trusty

Jain(ism) Mahavira

Jakarta Batavia

Jake Honest, Hunkydory, OK, Rube

Jalopy Banger, Boneshaker, Buggy, Car, Crate, Heap, Shandry(dan), Stock-car

Jam(my) Apple butter, Block, Choke, Clog, Confiture, Crowd, Crush, Cushy, Dilemma, Extra, Fix, Gridlock, Hold-up, Hole, How d'ye do, Jeelie, Jeely, Lock, Log, Plight, → **PREDICAMENT**, Preserve, Press, Quince, Rush hour, Seize, Snarl-up, Spot, Squeeze, Stall, Standstill, Stick, Tailback, Tangle, Traffic, Vice, Vise, Wedge

Jamaica(n) Inn, Rasta(farian), Rastaman, Yardie

Jamb Doorpost, Durn, Sconcheon, Scontion, Scuncheon, Upright

James Agee, Bond, Bothwell, Henry, Jacobite, Jemmy, Jesse, Jim, Joyce, Screw, Seamus, Seumas, Sid, Watt

Jane Austen, Calamity, Eyre, Seymour, Shore, Sian

Jangle Clank, Clapperclaw, Clash, Rattle, Wrangle

Janitor Doorman, Porter, Servitor, Sweeper, Tiler

Jankers KP

Jansky Jy

Janus Two-faced

Japan(ese), Japanese drama Ainu, Burakumin, Daimio, Eta, Geisha, Genro, Gloss, Gook, Haiku, Heian, Hondo, Honshu, Issei, Kabuki, Kami, Kana, Kirimon, Lacquer, Mandarin, Meiji, Mikado, Mousmé, Mousmee, Nihon, Nip, Nippon, Nisei, No(h), Resin, Sansei, Satsuma, Shinto, Shogun, Taisho, Togo, Tycoon, Yamato, Yellow peril

Jape Jeer, Joke, Prank, Trick

Jar(ring) Albarello, Amphora, Bell, Canopus, Churr, Clash, Crock, Cruet, Din, Dissonant, Distune, Dolium, Enrough, Gallipot, Gas, Grate, Greybeard, Gride, Grind, Gryde, Humidor, Hydria, → **JOLT**, Kalpis, Kang, Kilner®, Leyden, Mason, Monkey, Off-key, Olla, Pint, Pithos, Pot(iche), Quarrel, Rasp, Rock, Screwtop, Shelta, Shock, Stamnos, Start, Stave, Stean, Steen, Stein, Tankard, Terrarium, Tinaja, Turn, Vessel, Water-monkey

Jargon Argot, Baragouin, Beach-la-mar, Buzzword, Cant, Chinese, Chinook, Cyberspeak, Eurobabble, Eurospeak, Geekspeak, Gobbledegook, Gobbledygook, Jive, Kennick, Legalese, Lingo, Lingoa geral, Lingua franca, Mumbo-jumbo, Netspeak, Newspeak, Officialese, Parlance, Patois, Patter, Patter-flash, Psychobabble, Shelta, Shoptalk, → **SLANG**, Sociologese, Technobabble, Technospeak, Vernacular

Jargoon Chinook

Jasmine Cape, Frangipani, Gelsemine, Gelsemium, Gessamine, Jessamy, Madagascar, Olea, Red

Jasper Basanite, Bloodstone, Egyptian, Porcelain, Touchstone

Jaundice(d) Cynical, Icterus, Prejudiced, Sallow, Yellow

Jaunt Journey, Outing, Sally, Stroll, Swan, Trip

Jaunty Airy, Akimbo, Chipper, Debonair, Perky, Rakish
▷ **Jaunty** *may indicate* an anagram
Java man Pithecanthropus
Javelin Dart, Gavelock, Harpoon, Jereed, Jerid, Pile, Pilum, Spear
Jaw(s), Jawbone Blab, Chaft, Chap, Chat, Chaw, Cheek, Chide, Chin, Entry, Glass, Gills, Gnathic, Gnathite, Gonion, Hypognathous, Jabber, Jobe, Kype, Lantern, Lumpy, Mandible, Masseter, Maxilla, Mesial, Muzzle, Mylohyoid, Natter, Opisthognathous, Overbite, Overshot, Phossy, Pi, Premaxillary, Prognathous, Ramus, Rubber, Shark, Stylet, Underhung, Undershot, Wapper-jaw, Ya(c)kety-Ya(c)k
Jay Bird, J, Sirgang, Whisky-jack, Whisky-john
Jazz(er), Jazzman Acid, Afro-Cuban, Barber, Barrelhouse, Basie, Bebop, Blues, Boogie, Boogie-woogie, Bop, Cat, Coleman, Cool, Dixieland, Enliven, Funky, Gig, Gutbucket, Hardbop, High life, Hipster, Jam, Jive, Latin, Lick, Mainstream, Modern, New Orleans, New Wave, Nouvelle Vague, Progressive, Ragtime, Riff, Scat, Skiffle, Slap base, Stomp, Swinger, Tailgate, Trad, Traditional, West Coast
Jealous(y) Envious, Green(-eyed), Green-eyed monster, Grudging, Zelotypia
Jean(s) Chinos, Denims, Levis®, Pants, Trousers, Wranglers®
Jeer(ing) Ballyrag, Barrack, Belittle, Birl, Boo, Burl, Digs, Fleer, Flout, Frump, Gird, Heckle, Hoot, Jape, Jibe, → **MOCK**, Rail, Razz, Ridicule, Scoff, Sling off, Sneer, Taunt, Twit, Yah
Jeeves Valet
Jehovah God, Lord, Yahve(h), Yahwe(h)
Jehovah's Witness Russellite
Jehu Charioteer, Driver
Jejune Arid, Barren, Dry, Insipid, Juvenile
Jelly Acaleph(a), Acalephe, Agar(-agar), Aspic, Brawn, Calf's foot, Chaudfroid, Comb, Cow-heel, Cranberry, → **EXPLOSIVE**, Flummery, Gel, Isinglass, Jam, Kanten, K-Y®, Liquid paraffin, Macedoine, Meat, Medusa, Mineral, Mould, Napalm, Neat's foot, Petrolatum, Petroleum, Quiddany, Royal, Shape, Sterno®, Tunicin, Vaseline®, Vitreous humour
▷ **Jelly** *may indicate* an anagram
Jellyfish Acaleph(a), Acalephe, Aurelia, Blubber, Box, Cnidaria, Discomedusae, Discophora, Hydromedusa, Hydrozoa, Irukandji, Medusa, Mesogloea, Nettlefish, Physalia, Planoblast, Portuguese man-of-war, Quarl, Scyphistoma, Scyphozoan, Sea-blubber, Sea-nettle, Sea-wasp, Strobila
Jemmy Betty, Crowbar, Lever
Jenkins Ear, Roy, Up
Jenny Ass, Lind, Long, Mule, Short, Spinner, Spinning, Spinster, Wren
Jeopardise, Jeopardy Danger, Double, Expose, Hazard, Peril, Risk
Jerboa Desert rat
Jeremiad Lament, Tragedy, Woe
Jeremy Fisher, Irons, Jerry
Jerk(y), Jerkily, Jerking, Jerks Aerobics, A salti, Bob, Braid, Cant, Diddle, Ebrillade, Flirt, Flounce, Gym(nastics), Hike, Hitch, Hoi(c)k, Idiot, Jigger, Jut, Kant, Knee, PE, Peck, Physical, Saccade, Shove, Shrug, Spasm, Start, Strobe, Surge, Switch, Sydenham's chorea, Tic, Toss(en), Tweak, → **TWITCH**, Wrench, Yank
Jerkin Body warmer, Jacket, Tabard
Jerome Kern, Vulgate
Jerry, Jerry-built Boche, Flimsy, Fritz, Hun, Kraut, Lego, Mouse, Po(t)
Jersey(s) Bailiwick, CI, Cow, Football, Frock, Gansey, Guernsey, Kine, Lily, Maillot, Polo, Roll-neck, Singlet, → **SWEATER**, Sweatshirt, V-neck, Yellow, Zephyr

Jerusalem Ariel, Hierosolymitan, Sion, Zion

Jess(e) James, Strap

Jest(er), Jesting Badinage, Barm, Baur, Bawr, Bourd(er), Buffoon, Clown, Cod, Comic, Droll, Gleek, Goliard, Inficete, Jape, Jig, Joculator, Joker, Josh, Merryman, Miller, Motley, Patch, Quip, Raillery, Ribaldry, Ribaudry, Rigoletto, Scogan, Scoggin, Sport, Toy, Trinculo, Wag, Waggery, Wit, Yorick

Jesuit Bollandist, Ignatius, Loyola, SJ

Jesus → CHRIST, Emmanuel, IHS, Immanuel, INRI, Isa, Jabers, Lord

Jet, Jet lag Airbus®, Aircraft, Beadblast, Black, Burner, Chirt, Douche, Fountain, Geat, Harrier, Ink, Jumbo, Plane, Pump, Sable, Soffione, Spirt, Spout, Spray, Spurt, Squirt, Stream, Time-zone disease, Time-zone fatigue, Turbine, Turbo, Vapour, Water

Jettison Discard, Dump, Flotsam, Jetsam, Lagan, Ligan

Jetty Groin, Mole, Pier, Wharf

Jew(ish), Jews Ashkenazi, Chas(s)id, Diaspora, Essene, Falasha, Grecian, Greek, Has(s)id, Hebrew, Hellenist, Hemerobaptist, Kahal, Karaite, Kike, Landsman, Levite, Lubavitch, Maccabee, Marrano, Misnaged, Mitnag(g)ed, Nazarite, Neturei Karta, Nicodemus, Peculiar People, Pharisee, Refusenik, Sabra, Sadducee, Semite, Sephardim, Sheeny, Shemite, Shtetl, Smouch, Smouse, Tobit, Wandering, Yid(dish), Zealot

Jewel(s), Jeweller(y) Agate, Aigrette, Almandine, Artwear, Beryl, Bijouterie, Bling(-bling), Brilliant, Cameo, Chrysoprase, Cloisonné, Cornelian, Costume, Crown, Diamond, Earbob, Ear-drop, Emerald, Ewe-lamb, Fabergé, Fashion, Ferron(n)ière, Finery, Garnet, → GEM, Girandole, Gracchi, Jade, Junk, Lherzolite, Marcasite, Navette, Olivine, Opal, Parure, Paste, Pavé, Pearl, Pendant, Peridot, Rivière, Rock, Rubin(e), Ruby, Sapphire, Sard, Scarab, Smaragd, Solitaire, Stone, Sunburst, Tiara, Tiffany, Tom, Tomfoolery, Topaz, Torc, Treasure, Trinket

Jezebel Harlot, Loose, Whore

Jib Ba(u)lk, Boggle, Boom, → DEMUR, Face, Flying, Foresail, Genoa, Milk, Reest, Reist, Stay-sail, Storm

Jibe Barb, Bob, Correspond, Crack, Dig, Fling, Gleek, → JEER, Mock, Quip, Sarcasm, Sideswipe, Slant, Taunt

Jiffy Mo, Pronto, Twinkling, Whiff

Jig(gle) Bob, Bounce, Dance, Fling, Frisk, Hornpipe, Jog, Juggle, Morris

Jigger(ed) Beat, Chigoe, Jolley, Ruin

Jill Ferret

Jilt(ed) Discard, Lorn, Reject, Shed, Throw-over

Jim(my) Diamond, Dismal, Jas, Lucky, Pee, Piddle, Riddle

Jingle(r) Clerihew, Clink, Ditty, Doggerel, Rhyme, Tambourine, Tinkle

Jingo(ism) Chauvin, Odzooks, Patriot, Sabre-rattling, War-rant

Jink Elude

Jinn(i) Afreet, Eblis, Genie, Jann, Marid, Spirit

Jinx Curse, Hex, Jonah, Kibosh, Moz(z), Spoil, Voodoo, Whammy

Jitter(s), Jittery Coggly, DT, Fidgets, Funk, Jumpy, Nervous, Willies

▷ **Jitter(s)** *may indicate* an anagram

Jo → LOVER, Sweetheart

▷ **Job** *may indicate* the biblical character

Job(bing) Agiotage, Appointment, Assignment, Berth, Career, Chore, Comforter, Crib, Darg, Errand, Gig, Hatchet, Homer, Inside, Métier, Mission, Nixer, Occupation, Oratorio, Paint, Patient, Pensum, Place(ment), Plum, Position, Post, Problem, Pursuit, Put-up, Sinecure, Snow, Spot, Steady, → TASK, Ticket, Trotter, Truck, Undertaking, Work

Jock Deejay, DJ, Mac, Sawn(e)y, Scot

Jockey Carr, Cheat, Diddle, Disc, Eddery, Jostle, Jump, Lester, Manoeuvre, Mouse, Piggott, Rider, Steve, Suicide, Swindle, Trick, Video, Winter

▷ **Jockey** *may indicate* an anagram

Jocose, Jocular, Jocund Cheerful, Debonair, Facete, Facetious, Jesting, Lepid, Scurril(e), Waggish

Joe(y), Joseph Addison, Dogsbody, GI, Kangaroo, Pal, Roo, Sloppy, Stalin, Surface, Trey

Jog(ger), Joggle, Jog-trot Arouse, Canter, Dog-trot, Dunch, Dunsh, Heich-how, Heigh-ho, Hod, Jiggle, Jolt, Jostle, Memo, Mosey, Nudge, Piaffe, Prompt, Ranke, Remind, Run, Shake, Shog, Tickle, Trot, Whig

Johannesburg Jozi

John(ny) Ajax, Augustus, Barleycorn, Beatle, Bog, Bright, Brown, Bull, Bunyan, Can, Cloaca, Collins, Dee, Doc, Doree, Dory, Elsan®, Elton, Evan, Gaunt, Gents, Gilpin, Groats, Halifax, Ia(i)n, Ivan, Lackland, Latecomer, Lat(rine), Lav, Lennon, Little, Loo, Peel, Po(t), Prester, Stage-door, Throne, Toot, Tout, WC

Johnny-come-lately Upstart

Johnson Cham, Doctor, Idler

Join(er), Joined, Joining Abut, Accede, Accompany, Add, Affix, Alligate, Ally, Amalgamate, And, Annex, Associate, Attach, Bond, Braze, Butt-end, Cement, Cleave, Combine, Conflate, Conglutinate, Conjugate, Conjunct, Connect, Cope, → **COUPLE**, Dovetail, Engraft, Enlist, Enrol, Enter, Federate, Fuse, Glue, Graft, Hasp, Hitch, Hyphen, Include, Inosculate, Interconnect, Jugate, Knit, Link, Marry, Meet, Member, Menuisier, Merge, Mix, Mortar, Mortise, Oop, Oup, Overlaunch, Piece, Piecen, Pin, Rebate, Regelation, Rivet, Scarf, Seam, Se-tenant, Sew, Siamize, Snug, Solder, Splice, Spot-weld, Squirrel, Staple, Stick, Stylolite, Tack-weld, Tenon, Unite, Wed, Weld, Yoke

Joint(ed) Ancon, Ankle, Arthrosis, Articular, Ball and socket, Bar, Baron, Butt, Capillary, Cardan, Carpus, Chine, Clip, Co, Cogging, Collar, Colonial goose, Commissure, Compression, Conjunction, Coursing, Cuit, Cup and ball, Cut, Dive, Dovetail, Drumstick, Elbow, Enarthrosis, Entrecôte, Expansion, False, First, Fish, Gambrel, Genu, Gimmal, Gimmer, Ginglymus, Hainch, Haunch, Heel, Hinge, Hip, Hough, Huck, Hunker, J, Joggle, Jolly, Junction, Knee, Knuckle, Lap(ped), Lith, Loin, Marijuana, Meat, Mitre, Mortise, Mouse (buttock), Mouse-piece, Mutton, Mutual, Phalange, Phalanx, Pin, Popliteal, Psoas, Push-fit, Rabbet, Rack, Raphe, Reducer, Reefer, Rhaphe, Ribroast, Roast, Saddle, Scarf, Schindylesis, Seam, Second, Shoulder, Silverside, Sirloin, Soaker, Splice, Spliff, Stifle, Straight, Strip, Symphysis, Syndesmosis, T, Tarsus, T-bone, Temporomandibular, Tenon, Together, Toggle, Tongue and groove, Topside, Trochanter, Trochite, Undercut, Universal, Vertebra, Water, Wedging, Weld, Wrist

Joist Accouplement, Bar, Beam, Dormant, Ground plate, Groundsill, H-beam, I-beam, Rib, Rolled-steel, Sleeper, Solive, String, Trimmer

Joke(r), Joke-book, Joking Banter, Bar, Baur, Bawr, Booby-trap, Bourdon, Card, Chaff, Chestnut, → **CLOWN**, Cod, Comedian, Comic, Crack, Cut-up, Farceur, Farceuse, Fool, Fun, Funster, Gab, Gag, Glike, Guy, Have-on, Hazer, Hoax, Hum, Humorist, In fun, Jape, Jest, Jig, Jocular, Josh, Knock-knock, Lark, Legpull, Merry-andrew, Merryman, Mistigris, One, One-liner, Pleasantry, Practical, Prank(ster), Pun, Punchline, Pundigrion, Quip, Rag, Rib-tickler, Rot, Sally, Scherzo, Scogan, Scoggin, Sick, Skylark, Sottisier, Squib, Standing, Wag, Wheeze, Wild, Wisecrack, Wit

Jollity, Jolly, Jollification 'Arryish, Bally, Beano, Bright, Cheerful, Convivial,

Cordial, Do, Festive, Galoot, Gaucie, Gaucy, Gawcy, Gawsy, Gay, Hilarious, Jocose, Jovial, Marine, Mirth, Rag, RM, Roger, Sandboy, Tar, Very

Jolt(ing) Bump, Jar, Jig-a jig, Jog(gle), Jostle, Jounce, Jumble, Shake, Shog, Start

Jonah Hoodoo, Jinx, Moz(z)

Jones Davy, Dow, Emperor, Inigo

Jordan(ian) Moabite, Pot, Urinal

Joris Horseman

▸ **Joseph** *see* **JOE**

Josh Chaff, Kid, Rib, Tease

Josiah Stamp, Wedgewood

Joss Incense, Luck, Stick

Jostle Barge, Bump, Compete, Elbow, Hog-shouther, Hustle, Jockey, Push, Shoulder, → **SHOVE**, Throng

Jot(ter), Jotting(s) Ace, Fig, Iota, Memo, Mite, Note, Pad, Stime, Styme, Tittle, Whit

Journal Band(e), Blog, Chronicle, Daily, Daybook, Diary, Ephemeris, E-zine, Gazette, Hansard, Lancet, Log, Noctuary, Organ, Paper, Periodical, Pictorial, Punch, Rag, Record, TES, TLS, Trade, Waste book, Weblog

Journalism, Journalist Cheque-book, Columnist, Commentariat, Contributor, Diarist, Diurnalist, Ed, Fleet St, Freelance, (GA) Sala, Gazetteer, Gonzo, Hack, Hackery, Hackette, Hatchetman, Inkslinger, Interviewer, Investigative, Keyhole, Lobby, Muckraker, Newshound, Northcliffe, NUJ, Penny-a-liner, Pepys, Press(man), Reporter, Reviewer, Scribe, Sob sister, Stead, Stringer, Wireman, → **WRITER**, Yellow

Journey Circuit, Cruise, Errand, Expedition, Eyre, Foray, Grand Tour, Hadj, Hop, Jaunce, Jaunse, Jaunt, Lift, Long haul, Mush, Odyssey, Passage, Periegesis, Ply, Raik, Rake, Red-eye, Ride, Round trip, Run, Sabbath-day's, Sentimental, Soup run, Step, Swag, Tour, Travel, Trek, Viatical, Walkabout

Journeyman Artisan, Commuter, Craftsman, Sterne, Yeoman

Joust Giust, Pas d'armes, Tilt, Tournament, Tourney

Jove Egad, Gad, Igad, Jupiter, Thunderbearer, Thunderer

Jovial Bacchic, Boon, Convivial, Cordial, Festive, Genial, Jolly

Jowl(s) Cheek, Chollers, Chops, Jaw

Joy(ful), Joyous Ah, Bliss, Blithe, Charmian, → **DELIGHT**, Dream, Ecstasy, Elation, Exulting, Fain, Felicity, Festal, Frabjous, Glad, Glee, Gloat, Groove, Hah, Hey, Jubilant, Nirvana, Rapture, Schadenfreude, Sele, Tra-la, Transport, Treat, Yay, Yippee

Joyce Haw Haw, Traitor

Joyrider Twoccer

JP Beak, Queer cuffin, Quorum

Jubilant, Jubilation, Jubilee Celebration, Cock-a-hoop, Diamond, Ecstatic, Elated, Exultant, Holiday, Joy, Triumphant

Judaism Semitism

Judas Double-crosser, Iscariot, Traitor, Tree

Judder Put-put, Shake, Vibrate

Jude Obscure

Judge(ment), Judges Absolute, Addoom, Adjudicator, Agonothetes, Alacus, Alcalde, Arbiter, Areopagite, Aret(t), Arrêt, Assess, Assize, Auto-da-fé, Avizandum, Banc, Brehon, Cadi, Calculate, Censure, Centumvirus, Chief Justice, Circuit(eer), Common Serjeant, Comparative, Connoisseur, Consider, Coroner, Court, Critic(ise), Daniel, Dayan, Daysman, Deborah, Decern(e), Decide, Decision, Decreet, Deem(ster), Dempster, Dicast, Dies irae, Dies non, Differential, Dikast,

Discern(ment), District, Ephor, Ermined, Estimate, Evaluate, Faisal, Faysal, Gauge, Gesse, Gideon, Good-sense, Guess, Hakeem, Hakim, Hearing, Hold, Honour, Inky-smudge, Interlocutor, J, Jeffreys, Jephthah, Justice, Justiciar, Last, Line, Lord Chief Justice, Lud, Lynch, Minos, Mufti, Non prosequitur, Nonsuit, Official Referee, Old Fury, Opine, Opinion, Ordinary, Outfangthief, Panel, Paris, Podesta, Providence, Provisional, Puisne, Puny, Ragnarok, Reckon(ing), Recorder, Ref(eree), Regard, Rhadamanthus, Ruler, Samson, Samuel, Sapience, Scan, Second guess, See, Sentence, Sentiment, Shallow, Sheriff, Sizer, Sober, Solomon, Sound, Suppose, Surrogate, Syndic, Tact, Think, Touch, Trior, Try, Umpire, Value, Verdict, Ween, Weigh up, Wig, Wik, Wisdom, Worship

Judicious Critical, Discreet, Politic, Rational, Sage, Sensible, Shrewd, Sound

Judo, Judo costume Dojo, Gi(e), Kyu, Shiai

Jug(s) Amphora, Aquamanale, Aquamanile, Bellarmine, Bird, Blackjack, Bombard, Breasts, Can, Cooler, Cream(er), Crock, Enghalskrug, Ewer, Flagon, Gaol, Gotch, Greybeard, Growler, John Roberts, Malling, Measuring, Olpe, Pitcher, Pound, Pourer, Pourie, → **PRISON**, Quad, Quod, Shop, Stir, Tits, Toby, Urceolus

Juggle(r) Conjuror, Cook, Escamotage, Fake, Fire-eater

Juice, Juicy Aloe vera, Bacca, Cassareep, Cassaripe, Cremor, Current, Fluid, Fruity, Gastric, Hypocist, Ichor, Jungle, La(b)danum, Laser, Latex, Lush, Moist, Must, Oil, Pancreatic, Perry, Petrol, Ptisan, Rare, Sap, Snake, Soma, Spanish, Succ(o)us, Succulent, Tarantula, Thridace, Vril, Walnut, Zest

Juju Charm, Fetish

Jujube Christ's thorn, Lotus, Nabk, Padma, Sweet

Jukebox Nickelodeon

Julian Apostate

July Dogdays

Jumble Cast offs, Chaos, Conglomeration, Farrago, Garble, Huddle, Jabble, Lumber, Mass, Medley, Mingle-mangle, Mish-mash, Mixter-maxter, Mixtie-maxtie, Mixture, Mix(t)y-max(t)y, Pastiche, Praiseach, Printer's pie, Raffle, Ragbag, Scramble, Shuffle, Wuzzle

▷ **Jumbled** *may indicate* an anagram

Jumbo Aircraft, Elephant, Jet, Large-scale, Mammoth, OS, Plane

Jump(er), Jumping, Jumpy Aran, Assemble, Axel, Base, Batterie, Boomer, Bound, Bungee, Bungy, Bunny-hop, Caper, Capriole, Cicada, Cicata, Crew-neck, Cricket, Croupade, Daffy, Desultory, Entrechat, Euro, Eventer, Flea, Fosbury flop, Frog, Gansey, Gazump, Gelande(sprung), Guernsey, Halma, Helicopter, High, Hurdle, Impala, Itchy, Jersey, Joey, Jolly, Kangaroo, Katydid, Kickflip, Knight, Lammie, Lammy, Leap(frog), Lep, Long, Lope, Lutz, Nervous, Nervy, Ollie, Para, Parachute, Pig, Pogo, Polo-neck, Pounce, Prance, Prank, Pronking, Puissance, Quantum, Quersprung, Rap, Salchow, Saltatory, Saltigrade, Saltus, Scissors, Scoup, Scowp, Shy, Skip, Skipjack, Skydiver, → **SPRING**, Star, Start, Straddle, Sweater, Toe(-loop), Trampoline, Triple, Turtle-neck, Vau(l)t, V-neck, Water, Western roll

Jumping jack Pantine

Junction Abutment, Alloyed, Angle, Box, Bregma, Carfax, Circus, Close, Clover-leaf, Connection, Crewe, Crossroads, Diffused, Gap, Intersection, Joint, Josephson, Knitting, Meeting, Node, P-n, Point, Raphe, Spaghetti, Stage, Suture, T, Tight, Union

Juneberry Saskatoon, Shadbush

Jungle Asphalt, Blackboard, Boondocks, Bush, Concrete, Forest, Shola, Tangle

Junior Cadet, Chota, Cion, Dogsbody, Filius, Fils, Minor, Name-son, Office, Petty, Puisne, Scion, Sub(ordinate), Underling, Understrapper, Younger

Juniper Cade, Pencil-cedar, Red-cedar, Savin(e)

▷ **Junk** *may indicate* an anagram

Junk(shop), Junkie Bric-à-brac, Chuck in, Jettison, Litter, Lorcha, Lumber, Refuse, Ship, Tagareen, Tatt, Trash, User

Junker Prussian

Junket(ing) Beano, Creel, Custard, Feast, Picnic, Rennet, Spree

Juno Lucina

Junta Cabal, Council

Jupiter Jove, Newspaper

Jurassic Bajocian, Lias, R(h)aetic

Jurisdiction Authority, Bailiwick, Domain, Province, Soke(n), Sucken, Verge

Juror(s), Jury Array, Assize, Blue-ribbon, Dicast, Grand, Hung, Inquest, Judges, Man, Mickleton, Old Fury, Pais, Panel, Party, Petit, Petty, Sail, Special, Strike, Tales, Talesman, Tribunal, Venire, Venireman, Venue

Just(ice) Adeel, Adil, Alcalde, All, Aristides, Astraea, Balanced, Barely, Condign, Cupar, Deserved, Equal, Equity, E(v)en, Fair, Fair-minded, Forensic, Honest, Impartial, J, Jasper, Jeddart, Jethart, Jurat, Kangaroo, Mere, Moral, Natural, Nemesis, Newly, Nice, Only, Palm-tree, Piso, Poetic, Provost, Puisne, Pure and simple, Quorum, Recent, Restorative, Right(ful), Righteous, Rightness, Rough, Shallow, Silence, Simply, Solely, Sommer, Street, Themis, Tilt, Upright

Justifiable, Justification, Justify Apology, Autotelic, Avenge, Aver, Avowry, Clear, Darraign(e), Darrain(e), Darrayn, Defend, Deraign, Excusable, Explain, Grounds, Pay off, Rationale, Reason, Vindicate, Warrant

Just so Exactly, Sic, Stories

Jut Beetle, Bulge, Overhang, Project, Protrude, Sail

Jute Burlap, China, Corchorus, Gunny, Hengist, Hessian, Horsa, Jew's mallow, Urena, Wool bale

Juvenile Childish, Teenage(r), Yonkers, Young, Younkers, Youth

Juxtaposition Parataxis

Kk

K Kelvin, Kilo, King, Kirkpatrick

K2 Dapsang, Godwin Austen

Kaffir Shares, Xosa

Kail, Kale Borecole, Cabbage, Cole, Curly-greens, Ninepins

Kaiser Doorn

Kaleidoscope Dappled, Motley, Myrioscope, Various

Kangaroo Bettong, Boodie-rat, Boomer, Boongary, Bounder, Brush, Cus-cus, Diprotodont, Euro, Forester, Joey, Macropodidae, Nototherium, Old man, Potoroo, Rat, Red, Steamer, Tree, Troop, Wallaby, Wallaroo

Kansas Sunflower

Kaolin Lithomarge

Karate Kung Fu, Shotokan, Wushu

Karma Destiny, Fate, Predestination

Kate Greenaway, Shrew

Kayak Bidarka

Kebab Cevapcici, Doner, Gyro, Satay, Sate, Shashli(c)k, Sosatie, Souvlakia

Keel Bilge, Bottom, Carina, Centreboard, Cheesecutter, Even, Faint, False, Fin, List, Overturn, Skeg(g), Sliding

Keen(ness), Keener Acid, Acute, Agog, Ardent, Argute, Aspiring, Astute, Athirst, Avid, Aygre, Bemoan, Bewail, Breem, Breme, Cheap, Coronach, Dash, Devotee, Dirge, Eager, Elegy, Enthusiastic, Fanatical, Fell, Game, Greet, Grieve, Hone, Hot, Howl, Into, Lament, Mourn, Mustard, Mute, Narrow, Ochone, Ohone, Overfond, Partial, Peachy, Perceant, Persant, Pie, Raring, Razor, Ready, Red-hot, Rhapsodic, Sharp, Shrewd, Shrill, Snell, Thirsting, Threnodic, Thrillant, Trenchant, Ululate, Wail, Whet, Zeal(ous)

Keep(er), Keeping Ames, Armature, Austringer, Castellan, Castle, Celebrate, Chatelain(e), Citadel, Conceal, Conserve, Curator, Custodian, Custody, Custos, Depositary, Depository, Detain, Donjon, Escot, Fastness, Finder, Fort, Gaoler, Goalie, Guardian, Harbour, Have, Hoard, → **HOLD**, Maintain, Nab, Net, Observe, Ostreger, Own, Park, Pickle, Preserve, Retain, Safe, Safeguard, Save, Stay, Stet, Stock, Store, Stow, Stumper, Support, Sustain, Tower, Warden, Withhold

Keep back Detain, Recoup, Reserve, Retard, Stave

Keepsake Memento, Souvenir, Token

Keep under Cow, Subdue, Submerge

Keg Barrel, Cask, Powder, Tub, Tun, Vat

Kelly('s) Eye, Gene, Ned

Kelvin Absolute, K

Ken Eyeshot, Know(ledge), Purview, Range

Kennel(s) Guard, Home, House, Shelter

Kent Lathe, SE, Superman

Kentuckian, Kentucky Chicken, Corn-cracker, Derby, KY

Kenya(n) Luo, Masai, Mau Mau
Kerala Nair, Nayar
Kerb Edge, Gutter, Roadside
Kerchief Babushka, Bandan(n)a, Headcloth, Romal, Scarf
Kernel Copra, Core, Corn, Grain, Nucleus, Pine, Praline, Prawlin
Kestrel Bird, Hawk, Keelie, Stallion, Staniel, Stannel, Stanyel, Windhover
Ket Carrion, Wool
Ketch Jack
Ketchup Relish, Sauce, Tomato
Kettle Boiler, Cauldron, Dixie, Dixy, Drum, Fanny, Pot, Tea, Turpin, War, Whistling
Key(s), Keyhole A, Ait, Allen, Alt, Ash, B, Backspace, Basic, C, Cay, Central, Chip, Church, Cipher, Claver, Clavis, Clew, Clink, Clue, Control, Crib, D, Del(ete), Dichotomous, Digital, Dital, Dominant, E, Enter, Esc(ape), Essential, F, Flat, Florida, Fruit, Function, G, Greek, Grecque, High, Holm, Hot, Ignition, Important, Inch, Index, INS, Instrumental, Islet, Ivory, Kaie, King-pin, Latch, Legend, Linchpin, Locker, Low, Main, Major, Master, Minor, Note, Nut, Octachord, Opener, Oustiti, Outsiders, Pass(word), Passe-partout, Piano, Pipe, Pivot, Pony, Prong, Reef, Return, Semibreve, Shift, Signature, Skeleton, Spanner, Spline, Stimulate, Subdominant, Supertonic, Swipecard, Tab, Table, Tipsy, Tonal, Turning, USB, Vital, Watch, Water, Wedge, Woodruff, Yale®
Keyboard, Keypad Azerty, Console, Digitorium, Dvorak, Electronic, Manual, Martenot, Numeric(al), Piano, Pianola®, Qwerty, Spinet
Keyholder Occupant, Resident, Tenant, Warder
Key man Islander, Kingpin
Keynote Line, Mese, Theme, Tonic
Keystone Cops, Crux, PA, Pennsylvania, Quoin, Sagitta, Voussoir
Keyword Kwic, Sesame
Khan Aga, Chagan, Cham, Serai, Shere
Kick(ing) Back-heel, Banana, Bicycle, Boot, Buzz, Corner, Dribble, Drop, Fling, Flutter, Fly, Free, Frog, Garryowen, Goal, Grub, Hack, Heel, High, Hitch, Hoof, Lash, Nutmeg, Pause, Penalty, Pile, Place, Punce, Punt, Recalcitrate, Recoil, Recoyle, Savate, Scissors, Sixpence, Speculator, Spot, Spur, Spurn, Squib, Stab, Tanner, Tap, Thrill, Toe, Up and under, Vigour, Volley, Wince, Yerk, Zip
Kid(s) Arab, Bamboozle, Befool, Billy, Brood, Cheverel, Chevrette, Child, Chit, Cisco, Con, Delude, Giles, Goat, Hircosity, Hoax, Hocus, Hoodwink, Hum, Joke, Josh, Leather, Mag, Minor, Misguide, Nipper, Offspring, Outwit, Pretend, Rag, Rib, Spoof, Suede, Sundance, → **TEASE**, Tot, Trick, Whiz(z), Wiz
Kidnap Abduct, Hijack, Plagium, Shanghai, Snatch, Spirit, Steal
Kidney(-shaped) Character, Mettle, Nature, Reins, Renal, Reniform, Sort, Type
Kildare Dr
Kill(ed), Killer, Killing Assassin, Asp, Attrit, Axeman, Battue, Behead, Biocidal, Boojum, Booth, Bump off, Butcher, Carnage, Carnifex, Category, Chance-medley, Choke, Comical, Coup de grâce, Croak, Crucify, Cull, Deep six, Despatch, Destroy, Electrocute, Euthanasia, Execute, Exhibition, Exterminate, Extirpate, For(e) do, Frag, Garotte, Germicide, Gun, Handsel, Hatchet man, Hilarious, Homicide, Honour, Humane, Ice, Immolate, Infanticide, Jugulate, K, Knacker, Knock off, Liquidate, Lynch, Mactation, Matador(e), Mercy, Misadventure, Mortify, Murder, Napoo, Necklace, Ninja, NK, Off, Orc(a), Penalty, Pesticide, -phage, Pick off, Pip, Predator, Prolicide, Quell, Quietus, Regrate, Sacrifice, Serial, Settle, Shochet, Shoot up, Slaughter, Slay(er), Slew, Smite, Snuff, Spike, Stifle, Stonker, Strangle, Swat,

Tailor, Take out, Thagi, Thug(gee), Top, Toreador, Total, Vaticide, Veto, Waste, Written off, Zap

Killjoy Crab, Puritan, Sourpuss, Spoilsport, Trouble-mirth, Wowser

Kiln Lime, Oast, Oven, Queen's tobacco pipe

Kilometre Km, Verst

Kilt Drape, Filabeg, Fil(l)ibeg, Fustanella, Phil(l)abeg, Phil(l)ibeg, Plaid, Tartan

Kimono Yukata

Kin(sman) Ally, Family, Kith, Like, Nearest, Relation, Sib(b), Sybbe

Kind(ly) Akin, Amiable, Avuncular, Benefic, Benevolent, Benign, Boon, Breed, Brood, Brotherly, Category, Class, Clement, Considerate, Favourable, Gender, Generic, Generous, Genre, Gentle, Genus, Good, Gracious, Humane, Ilk, Indulgent, Kidney, Kin, Lenient, Manner, Modal, Nature, Nice, Sisterly, → **SORT**, Species, Strain, Strene, Thoughtful, Trine, Type, Understanding, Variety, Well-disposed, Ylke

Kindle, Kindling Accend, Fire, Ignite, Incense, Incite, Inflame, Kitten, → **LIGHT**, Litter, Lunt, Stimulate, Teend, Tind, Tine, Touchwood, Tynd(e)

Kindness Aloha, Benevolence, Clemency, Favour, Humanity, Mitzvah, Ubuntu

Kindred Allied, Blood, Like, Related

King(s), Kingly Ard-ri(gh), Butcher, Coatcard, Cobra, Csar, Elvis, English, ER, Evil, Highness, Kong, Ksar, Majesty, Monarch, Negus, Pearly, Peishwa(h), Penguin, Peshwa, Pharaoh, Philosopher, Potentate, R, Raja, Ransom, Reigner, Rex, Rial, Roi, Royalet, Ruler, Ryal, Sailor, Seven, Shah, Shepherd, Shilling, Sophy, Sovereign, Stork, Tsar, Tzar

KINGS

2 letters:	Inca	Herod	Amasis
GR	Jehu	Hiram	Arthur
Og	Knut	Idris	Atreus
Re	Lear	Ixion	Attila
	Loki	James	Baliol
3 letters:	Nudd	Laius	Brutus
Asa	Numa	Lludd	Canute
Erl	Offa	Louis	Cheops
Ine	Olaf	Mesha	Clovis
Lir	Otto	Midas	Daneus
Log	Saul	Minos	Darius
Lud	Zeus	Mpret	Duncan
Zog		Ninus	Edmund
	5 letters:	Osric	Egbert
4 letters:	Apple	Penda	Farouk
Agag	Balak	Priam	Fergus
Agis	Basil	Rufus	Harold
Ahab	Brute	Uther	Hellen
Atli	Creon		Hyksos
Brut	Cyrus	**6 letters:**	Josiah
Ceyx	David	Acetes	Lucomo
Cnut	Edgar	Aegeus	Ludwig
Cole	Edwin	Alaric	Lycaon
Edwy	Etzel	Alfred	Memnon
Fahd	Gyges	Alonso	Miledh

Nestor
Oberon
Ogyges
Paphos
Peleus
Philip
Ramses
Rhesus
Utgard
Xerxes

7 letters:
Acestes
Admetus
Athamas
Baldwin
Balliol
Beowulf
Busiris
Caradoc
Cecrops
Cepheus
Croesus
Danaiis
Diomede
Elidure
Evander
Gentius
Gordius
Gunther
Jupiter
Kenneth
Macbeth
Malcolm

Oedipus
Porsena
Ptolemy
Pyrrhus
Rameses
Regulus
Servius
Sigmund
Solomon
Stephen
Tarquin
Umberto

8 letters:
Adrastus
Aegyptus
Alberich
Alcinous
Alphonso
Cambyses
Cophetua
Diomedes
Endymion
Ethelred
Hezekiah
Jereboam
Jonathan
Leonidas
Menander
Menelaus
Milesius
Nehemiah
Odysseus
Pentheus

Porsenna
Rehoboam
Sarpedon
Siegmund
Sisyphus
Tantalus
Thutmose
Thyestes
Tigranes
Zedekiah

9 letters:
Agamemnon
Ahasuerus
Alexander
Athelstan
Bretwalda
Brian Boru
Conchobar
Cunobelin
Cymbeline
Ethelbert
Florestan
Frederick
Gambrinus
Gargantua
Gilgamesh
Idomeneus
Lionheart
Lobengula
Nabonidus
Pygmalion
Ras Tafari
Rodomonte

Sigismund
Tarquinus
Tyndareus
Vortigern
Wenceslas

10 letters:
Belshazzar
Cadwaladar
Caractacus
Erechtheus
Ozymandias
Wenceslaus

11 letters:
Charlemagne
Hardicanute
Jehoshaphat
Melchizedek
Prester John
Sennacherib
Tutenkhamen

12 letters:
Wayland Smith

14 letters:
Harold Harefoot
Nebuchadnezzar
Sweyn
 Forkbeard
Uther Pendragon

Kingdom, Kingship Animal, An(n)am, Aragon, Arles, Armenia, Ashanti, Assyria, Austrasia, Babylonia, Barataria, Belgium, Bhutan, Bohemia, Brandenburg, Brunel, Burgundy, Castile, Cilicia, Connacht, Connaught, Dahomey, Dalriada, Darfur, Denmark, Dominion, Edom, Elam, Fes, Fez, Fife, Galicia, Granada, He(d)jaz, Heptarchy, Hijaz, Jordan, Latin, Leon, Lesotho, Lydia, Lyonesse, Macedon(ia), Media, Mercia, Meroe, Middle, Mineral, Moab, Morocco, Murcia, Naples, Navarre, Nepal, Netherlands, Neustria, Noricum, Northumbria, Norway, Parthia, Plant, Pontic, Realm, Reame, Reign, Royalty, Ruritania, Saba, Samaria, Sardinia, Saudi Arabia, Sennar, Sheba, Siam, Spain, Sphere, Swaziland, Sweden, Thailand, Throne, Tonga, Two Sicilies, Ulster, Vegetable, Wessex, Westphalia, World
Kingfisher Alcyone, Halcyon, Kookaburra, Laughing jackass
Kingmaker Neville, Warwick
King-of-arms Clarenc(i)eux, Garter, Lyon, Norroy (and Ulster)
King's evil Crewels, Cruels, Scrofula
Kingsley Amis, Charles
King's son Dauphin, Delphin, P, Prince

Kink(y) Bent, Buckle, Crapy, Curl, Enmeshed, Flaw, Gasp, Knurl, Null, Nurl, Odd, Perm, Perverted, Quirk, SM, Twist, Wavy

▷ **Kink(y)** *may indicate* an anagram

Kinkajou Honey-bear, Potto

Kip(per) At, Cure, Dosser, Doze, Limey, Nap, → **SLEEPER**, Smoke

Kipling Beetle

Kirkpatrick K

Kismet Destiny, Fate, Karma, Predestination

Kiss(er), Kissing Air, Baisemain, Buss, Butterfly, Caress, Contrecoup, Cross, Deep, French, Graze, Lip, Mouth, Mwah, Neck, Osculate, Pax(-board), Pax-brede, Peck, Pet, Plonker, Pree, Salue, Salute, Smack(er), Smooch, Smouch, Snog, Spoon, Suck face, Thimble, Trap, X, Yap

Kit Accoutrement, Amenity, Christopher, Clobber, Clothes, Dress, Housewife, Jack, Layette, Marlowe, Mess, → **OUTFIT**, Rig, Set, Slops, Sportswear, Strip, Tackle, Uniform

Kitchen Caboose, Chuck-wagon, Cookhouse, Cuisine, Galley, Scullery, Soup, Thieves

Kite Belly, Bird, Box, Chil, Crate, Dragon, Elanet, Forktail, Gled(e), Hawk, Milvus, Paunch, Puttock, Rokkaku

Kitten(ish) Cute, Kindle, Sexy

Kittiwake Bird, Gull, Hacklet, Haglet

Kitty Ante, Cat, Fisher, Float, Fund, Jackpot, Pool, Pot, Tronc

Kiwi Apteryx, Chinese gooseberry, Erk, NZ, Ratitae

Klu-Klux-Klan Nightrider

Knack Art, Faculty, Flair, Forte, Gift, Hang, Instinct, → **TALENT**, Technique, Trick

Knacker Castanet, Exhaust

Knapsack Musette

Knapweed Matfelon

Knave(ry) Bezonian, Bower, Boy, Cad, Card, Coatcard, Coistril, Coystril, Custrel, Dog, Drôle, Fripon, Jack(-a-napes), Jock, Loon, Makar, Maker, Nob, Noddy, One for his nob, Pam, Pur, Rapscallion, → **RASCAL**, Recreant, Ropery, Scoundrel, Skelm, Taroc, Tarot, Tom, Treachery, Two for his heels, Varlet, Villain

Knead Conche, Malax(ate), Massage, Mould, Pug, Pummel, Work

Knee(s), Knee-cap, Knee-pan Genicular, Genu, Hock, Housemaid's, Lap, Marrowbones, Patella, Poleyn, Popliteal, Punch, Rotula, Whirl bone

Kneel(er) Defer, Genuflect, Hassock, Kowtow, Prie-dieu, Truckle

Knell Bell, Curfew, Dirge, Peal, Ring, Toll

Knicker(bocker), Knickers Bloomers, Culottes, Directoire, Irving, Panties, Plus-fours, Shorts, Trousers

Knick-knack Bagatelle, Bibelot, Bric-à-brac, Gewgaw, Pretty(-pretty), Quip, Smytrie, Toy, Trangam, Trifle, Victoriana

Knife Anelace, Athame, Barlow, Barong, Bistoury, Blade, Boline, Bolo, Bolster, Bowie, Bush, Butterfly, Carver, Carving, Case, Catling, Chakra, Chiv, Clasp, Cleaver, Couteau, Cradle, Cuttle, Cutto(e), Da(h), Dagger, Dirk, Fleam, Flick, Fruit, Gamma, Gully, Hay, Hunting, Jockteleg, Kard, Keratome, Kukri, Lance(t), Machete, Matchet, Moon, Oyster, Palette, Panga, Paper, Parang, Peeler, Pen, Pigsticker, Pocket, Putty, Scalpel, Scalping, Sgian-dhu, Sgian-dubh, Sheath, Shiv, Simi, Skean-dhu, Slash, Snee, Snickersnee, Spade, Stab, Stanley, Steak, Sticker, Stiletto, Swiss army, Switchblade, Table, Toothpick, Tranchet, Trench

Knight(hood) Accolon, Aguecheek, Alphagus, Amfortas, Artegal, Balan, Banneret, Bayard, Bedivere, Black, Bliant, Bors, Britomart, Caballero, Calidore, Cambel, Caradoc, Carpet, Cavalier, Chevalier, Companion, Crusader, Douceper, Douzeper,

Dub, Equites, Errant, Galahad, Gallant, Gareth, Garter, Gawain, Geraint, Giltspurs, Grey, Guyon, Hospitaller, Jedi, Kay, KB, KBE, Kemper, KG, Lamorack, La(u)ncelot, Launfal, Lionel, Lochinvar, Lohengrin, Maecenas, Malta, Mark, Medjidie, Melius, Modred, Mordred, N, Noble, Orlando, Paladin, Palmerin, Palomides, Papal, Paper, Parsifal, Perceforest, Perceval, Percival, Pharamond, Pinel, Precaptory, Preux chevalier, Red Cross, Ritter, Round Table, St Columba, Samurai, Sir, Tannhauser, Templar, Teutonic, Tor, Trencher, Tristan, Tristram, Valvassor, Vavasour, White

Knit(ting), Knitter, Knitwear Aran, Cardigan, Contract, Crochet, Double, Entwine, Fair Isle, Hosiery, Intarsia, Interlock, Intertwine, Jersey, Jumper, K, Marry, Mesh, Porosis, Pullover, Purl, Seam, Set, Stockinet, Sweater, Tricoteuse, Weave, Woolly, Wrinkle

Knob(by) Berry, Boll, Boss, Botoné, Bottony, Bouton, Bur(r), Cam, Caput, Cascabel, Croche, Gear, Handle, Hill, Inion, Knub, Knur(r), Mouse, Mousing, Node, Noop, Pellet, Pommel, Protuberance, Pulvinar, Push-button, Snib, Snub, Snuff, Stud, Torose, Tuber, Tuner, Wildfowl

Knobless Enodal

Knock(er), Knocked, Knock(ed) down, (off, out), Knockout Bang, Beaut, Biff, Blow, Bonk, Bump, Ca(a), Chap, Clash, Clour, Collide, Con, Criticise, Dad, Daud, Dawd, Degrade, Denigrate, Deride, Dev(v)el, Ding, Dinnyhauser, Dod, Etherise, Eyeful, Floor, Grace-stroke, → **HIT**, Innings, KD, King-hit, KO, Lowse, Lowsit, Mickey Finn, Opportunity, Pan, Pink, Quietus, Rap, Rat-tat, Six, Skittle, Socko, Spat, Steal, Stop, Stoun, Strike, Stun(ner), Tap, Technical, Thump, Tonk, Wow

Knock-kneed Valgus

Knot(ted), Knotty Apollo, Baff, Bend, Bind, Blackwall hitch, Bow, Bowline, Bur(r), Burl, Carrick-bend, Cat's paw, Clinch, Clove hitch, Cluster, Crochet, Diamond hitch, Englishman's, Entangle, Figure of eight, Fisherman's (bend), Flat, French, Geniculate, Gnar, → **GNARL**, Gordian, Granny, Half-hitch, Harness hitch, Hawser-bend, Herculean, Hitch, Interlace, Knag, Knap, Knar, Knur(r), Loop, Love(r's), Macramé, Macrami, Magnus hitch, Marriage-favour, Matthew Walker, Mouse, Nirl, Node, Nowed, Nub, Nur(r), Overhand, Peppercorn, Picot, Porter's, Problem, Prusik, Quipu, Reef, Rolling hitch, Root, Rosette, Running, Seizing, Sheepshank, Sheetbend, Shoulder, Shroud, Sleave, Slip, Slub, Spurr(e)y, Square, Stevedore's, Surgeon's, Sword, Tangle, Tat, Thumb, Tie, Timberhitch, Torose, Truelove, True lover's, Tubercle, Turk's head, Virgin, Wale, Wall, Weaver's (hitch), Windsor, Witch

Know(how), Knowing(ly), Knowledge(able), Known Acquaintance, Au fait, Autodidactic, Aware, Carnal, Cognition, Common, Compleat, Comprehend, Cred, Epistemics, Erudite, Expertise, Famous, Fly, Gnosis, Gnostic, Have, Hep, Hip, Info, Information, Insight, Intentional, Intuition, Jnana, Ken, Kith, Kydst, Lare, Light, Lore, Mindful, Omniscience, On, On to, Pansophy, Paragnosis, Party, Polymath, Positivism, Privity, Realise, Recherché, → **RECOGNISE**, Sapient, Savvy, Science, Scienter, Scilicet, Sciolism, Sciosophy, Shrewd, Smattering, Suss, Technology, Telegnosis, Understand(ing), Up, Versed, Wat(e), Weet(e), Well-informed, Well-read, Wis, Wise, Wist, Wit, Wonk, Wost, Wot

Know-all Arrogant, Besserwisser, Bumptious, Cognoscenti, Pansophist, Polymath, Poseur, Smart alec(k), Smart-arse, Smart-ass, Wiseacre

Knuckle (bone) Apply, Dolos, Fist, Joint, Ossein, Submit

Koko List

Kookaburra Laughing jackass, Settler's clock

Kop Spion

Koran Scripture, Sura(h)

L1

L Latitude, League, Learner, Left, Length, Liberal, Lima, Litre, Long, Luxembourg, Pound

La Indeed, My

Label Badge, Band, Book-plate, Brand, Crowner, Designer, Docket, File, Identifier, Indie, Mark, Name tag, Own, Seal, Sticker, Style, Tab, Tag, Tally, Ticket, Trace

Labiate Catmint, Hoarhound, Horehound

Laboratory Lab, Language, Skylab, Space-lab, Studio, Workshop

Labour(er), Laboured, Laborious Aesthetic, Agonise, Arduous, Begar, Birth, Bohunk, Carl, Casual, Childbirth, Chore, Churl, Coolie, Cooly, Corvée, Cottager, Cottar, Culchie, Dataller, Day, Direct, Docker, Dwell, Emotional, Forced, Gandy-dancer, Ganger, Gibeonite, Grecian, Grind, Grunt, Hard, Hercules, Hod carrier, Hodge, Hodman, Ida, Indirect, Job, Journeyman, Kanaka, Katorga, Leaden, Manpower, Militant tendency, Moil, Navvy, New, Okie, Operose, Opposition, Pain, Peon, Pioneer, Prole, Redneck, Roll, Rouseabout, Roustabout, Rouster, Seagull, Serf, Sisyphean, Slave, Spalpeen, Statute, Stertorous, Stint, Strive, Sudra, Swagman, Sweated, Task, Tedious, The grip, The lump, → **TOIL(S)**, Toss, Travail, Uphill, Vineyard, Wetback, → **WORK(ER)**, Workmen, Yakka

Labrador Innu, Retriever, Tea

Laburnum Golden chain

Labyrinth Daedalus, Maze, Mizmaze, Warren, Web

▷ **Labyrinthine** *may indicate* an anagram

Lac Lacquer, Lakh, Resin, Shellac, Tomans

Lace, Lacy Alençon, Babiche, Beat, Blonde, Bobbin, Bone, Bourdon, Brussels, Chantilly, Cluny, Colbertine, Dash, Dentelle, Duchesse, Filet, Galloon, Guipure, Honiton, Inweave, Irish, Jabot, Lash, Macramé, Malines, Mechlin, Mignonette, Mode, Net, Orris, Pearlin, Picot, Pillow, Point, Queen Anne's, Reseau, Reticella, Ricrac, Rosaline, Seaming, Shoestring, Shoe-tie, Spiderwork, Spike, Stay, Tat(ting), Tawdry, Thrash, Thread, Yie, Torchon, Trim, Troll(e)y, Truss, Tucker, Valenciennes, Venise, Weave, Welt, Window-bar

Lacerate(d) Ganch, Gash, Gaunch, Maul, Rent, Rip, Slash, Tear

Lachrymose Maudlin, Niobe, Tearful, Water-standing, → **WEEPY**

Lack(ing), Lacks Ab(o)ulia, Absence, Aplasia, Bereft, Dearth, Decadent, Famine, Ha'n't, Insufficiency, Manqué, Minus, → **NEED**, Poverty, Privation, Remiss, Sans, Shortfall, Shy, Void, Want

Lackadaisical Languid, Listless, Torpid

Lackaday Haro

Lackey Boots, Flunkey, Moth, Page, Poodle, Satellite, Skip-kennel

Lacklustre Dull, Insipid, Matt

Lack of confidence Doubt, Scepsis

Laconic Blunt, Close-mouthed, Curt, Spartan, Succinct, Terse

Lacquer Coromandel, Enamel, Hair(spray), Japan, Shellac, → **VARNISH**

Lad Boy(o), Bucko, Callan(t), Chiel(d), Child, Geit, Gyte, Knight, Loonie, Master, Nipper, Shaver, Stableman, Stripling, Tad, Whipper-snapper

Ladder(y) Accommodation, Aerial, Bucket, Companion, Companionway, Etrier, Extension, Fish, Jack, Jacob's, Pompier, Potence, Rope, Run, Salmon, Scalado, Scalar, Scaling, Sea, Squash, Step, Stie, Sty, Stye, Trap, Turntable

▶ **Lade** *see* **LOAD**

Ladle Bail, Dipper, Divider, Punch, Scoop, Shank, Toddy

Lady, Ladies Baroness, Bevy, Bountiful, Burd, Dame, Dark, Dinner, Don(n)a, Duenna, Female, First, Frau, Frow, Gemma, Godiva, Hen, Khanum, Lavatory, Leading, Loo, Luck, Maam, Madam(e), Martha, Memsahib, Muck, Nicotine, Peeress, Señora, Shopping bag, Signora, Tea, WC, White, Windermere

▷ **Lady** *may indicate* an '-ess' ending

Ladybird Cushcow, Hen, Vedalia

▷ **Ladybird** *may indicate* a female of a bird family

Ladykiller, Ladies' man Bluebeard, Lothario, Masher, Poodle-faker, Wolf

Lady of the Lake Vivian

Lady's fingers Gumbo, Okra

Lady's maid Abigail

Lag(gard) Culture, Dawdle, Delay, Drag, Flag, Hysteresis, Inmate, Jailbird, Jet, Leng, → **LINGER**, Loiter, Prisoner, Retard, Slowcoach, Slowpoke, Time, Tortoise, Trail

Lager Pils(e)ner

Lagoon Aveiro, Barachois, Haff, Pontchartrain, Pool, Salina, Saline, Vistula

▶ **Laic, Laid** *see* **LAY**

Lair Couch, Den, Earth, Haunt, Hideaway, Kennel, Lodge, Warren

Lake(s) Alkali, Basin, Bayou, Carmine, Cirque, Cowal, Crater, Crimson, Cut off, Finger, L, Lacustrine, Lagoon, Lagune, Limnology, → **LOCH**, Lochan, Lough, Madder, Mead, Mere, Nyanza, Ox-bow, Playa, Poets, Pool, Red, Reservoir, Salina, Salt, Shott, Soda, Tank, Tarn, Turlough, Vlei, Wine

LAKES

2 letters:	Pink	Morar	Argyle
No	Taal	Mungo	Averno
	Tana	Mweru	Baikal
3 letters:	Thun	Myall	Barlee
Ewe		Nam Co	Bienne
Van	5 letters:	Neagh	Bitter
	Atlin	Nyasa	Broads
4 letters:	Chott	Onega	Cayuga
Amin	Cowan	Pitch	Corrib
Bala	Frome	Poopo	Edward
Biel	Garda	Pskov	Geneva
Bled	Gatun	Sevan	Kariba
Chad	Great	Tahoe	Kittle
Como	Huron	Taupo	Ladoga
Erie	Ilmen	Tsana	Lugano
Erne	Leman	Urmia	Malawi
Eyre	Leven	Volta	Miveru
Kivu	Lherz		Mobutu
Mead	Lower	6 letters:	Monona
Nyos	Malar	Albert	Nakuru

Nam Tso
Nyassa
Oneida
Peipus
Poyang
Rudolf
Saimaa
St John
Te Anau
Tekapo
Vanern
Varese
Zurich

7 letters:
Amadeus
Aral Sea
Avernus
Axolotl
Balaton
Bizerte
Dead Sea
Iliamna
Katrine
Koko Nor
Lucerne
Managua
Mendota
Nipigon
Ontario
Red Deer
Rotorua
Sempach
Shkoder
St Clair

Toronto
Torrens
Turkana
Vattern

8 letters:
Balkhash
Bodensee
Carnegie
Dongting
Gairdner
Grasmere
Issyk-kul
Kinneret
Maggiore
Manitoba
Masurian
Menindee
Michigan
Naumachy
Okanagan
Onondaga
Regillus
Reindeer
Schwerin
Superior
Tiberias
Titicaca
Tonle Sap
Tungting
Veronica
Victoria
Wakatipu
Wanawaka
Winnipeg

9 letters:
Athabasca
Bangweulu
Champlain
Constance
Ennerdale
Everglade
Genfersee
Great Bear
Great Salt
Innisfree
Killarney
Macquarie
Manapouri
Maracaibo
Naumachia
Neuchatel
Nicaragua
Nipissing
Serbonian
Thirlmere
Trasimene
Trasimono
Ullswater
Wairarapa
Wast Water
Winnebago
Ysselmeer

10 letters:
Buttermere
Chautawqua
Clearwater
Great Slave
Hawes Water

Ijsselmeer
Miraflores
Mistassini
Of the Woods
Okeechobee
Okefenokee
Serpentine
Tanganyika
Washington
Windermere

11 letters:
Lesser Slave
Paralimnion
Stanley Pool

12 letters:
Derwentwater
Memphremagog
Waikaremoana
Winnipegosis

13 letters:
Bassenthwaite
Coniston Water
Crummock Water
Pontchartrain

14 letters:
Chiputneticook
Disappointment
Ennerdale Water

Lake-dwelling Crannog

Lakeland Cumbria

Lam Flee, Scram

Lama Dalai, Karmapa, Panchen, Tashi

Lamb(skin) Baa, Barometz, Beaver, Budge, Bummer, Cade, Canterbury, Caracul, Cosset, Ean(ling), Elia, Fat, Fell, Grit, Innocent, Keb, Larry, Noisette, Paschal, Persian, Poddy, Rack, Shearling, Target, Yean(ling)

Lambent Flickering, Glowing, Licking

Lambert Constant, L

Lame(ness) Accloy, Claude, Cripple, Crock, Game, Gammy, Gimp(y), Halt, Hamstring, Hirple, Hors de combat, Maim, Main, Spavined, Springhalt, Stringhalt, Weak

Lament(able), Lamentation, Lamenter Bemoan, Bewail, Beweep, Boo-hoo, Complain, Croon, Cry, Deplore, Dirge, Dumka, Dump, Elegy, Funest, Jeremiad, Jeremiah, Keen, Meane, Mein, Mene, Moon, Mourn, Ochone, Paltry, Piteous, Plain,

Repine, Sigh, Sorry, Threne, Threnody, Ululate, → **WAIL**, Welladay, Wel(l)away, Yammer

Lamia Deadnettle

Lamina(te) Film, Flake, Folium, Formica®, Lamella, Layer, Plate, Scale, Table, Veneer

Lamp(s) Aladdin's, Aldis, Anglepoise, Arc, Argand, Blow, Bowat, Bowet, Buat, Cru(i)sie, Cru(i)zie, Crusy, Davy, Daylight, Discharge, Diya, Eye, Eyne, Flame, Fluorescent, Fog, Gas, Geordie, Glow, Head, Hurricane, Incandescent, Induction, Kudlik, Lampion, Lantern, Lava, Lucigen, Mercury vapour, Miner's, Moderator, Neon, Nernst, Nightlight, Padella, Pendant, Photoflood, Pilot, Platinum, Quartz, Reading, Riding, Safety, Sanctuary, Scamper, Searchlight, Signal, Sodium, Sodium-vapour, Spirit, Standard, Street, Stride, Stroboscope, Sun, Tail, Tantalum, Tiffany, Tilley, Torchier(e), Tungsten, Uplight(er), Veilleuse, Xenon

Lamplighter Leerie, Spill

Lampoon Caricature, Parody, Pasquil, Pasquin(ade), Satire, Skit, Squib

Lamprey Hag, Lampern, Sandpride

Lancaster Burt, Osbert

Lance Dart, Harpoon, Morne, Pesade, Pike, Prisade, Prisado, Rejôn, Spear, Speisade, Thermic, White arm

Lancelet Amphioxus

Lancer Bengal, Picador, Uhlan

Lancet Fleam

Land(s), Landed Acreage, Aina, Alight, Alluvion, Arpent, Bag, Beach, Bigha, Bovate, Byrd, Carse, Carucate, Cavel, Conacre, Corridor, Country, Croft, Crown, Curtilage, Debatable, Demain, Demesne, Disbark, Disembark, Ditch, Doab, Dock, Earth, Edom, Enderby, Estate, Fallow, Farren, Farthingland, Fee, Feod, Feoff, Feud, Fief, Freeboard, Gair, Glebe, Gondwanaland, Gore, Graham, Ground, Hide, Holding, Holm, Holy, Horst, Ind, Innings, Isthmus, Kingdom, La-la, Laurasia, Lea, Leal, Ley, Light, Link, Machair, Maidan, Manor, Marginal, Marie Byrd, Mesnalty, Métairie, Moose pasture, Morgen, Mortmain, Nation, Never-never, Nod, No man's, Odal, Onshore, Oxgang, Oxgate, Pakahi, Palmer, Pangaea, Panhandle, Parcel, Pasture, Peneplain, Peneplane, Peninsula, Piste, Plot, Ploughgate, Point, Polder, Pr(a)edial, Premises, Private, Promised, Property, Public, Purlieu, Queen Maud, Real estate, Realm, Realty, Reservation, Roman candle, Rundale, Runrig, Rupert's, Savanna(h), Set-aside, Settle, Several, Spit, Swidden, Tack, Taluk, Terra(e), Terra-firma, Terrain, Territory, Thwaite, Tie, Tir na n'Og, Touchdown, Turbary, Tye, Udal, Unship, Ure, Van Diemen's, Veld(t), Victoria, Wainage, Waste, Whenua, Wilkes, Yird

▶ **Landfall** *see* **LANDSLIDE**

Landing (craft, stair, system) Autoflare, Crash, Forced, Gallipoli, Gha(u)t, Half, Halfpace, Hard, Instrument, LEM, Module, Pancake, Pier, Quay, Quayside, Roman candle, Soft, Solar, Sollar, Sol(l)er, Splashdown, Three-point, Three-pricker, Touchdown, Undercarriage

Landlock Embay

Landlord, Land owner Absentee, Balt, Boniface, Bonnet laird, Copyholder, Eupatrid, Fiar, Franklin, Herself, Host, Innkeeper, Junker, Laird, Lessor, Letter, Licensee, Patron, Patroon, Proprietor, Publican, Rachman, Rentier, Squatter, Squattocracy, Squire, Squirearchy, Squireen, Thane, Zamindar(i), Zemindar

Landmark Meith, Watershed

Landmass Angaraland, Laurasia

Land right Emphyteusis

Landscape Karst, Paysage, Picture, Saikei, Scene, Stoss and lee, Vista

Landslide, Landfall Avalanche, Earthfall, Éboulement, Lahar, Scree, Slip
Landsman Lubber
Land tenure Frankalmoign, Raiyatwari, Rundale, Runrig, Ryotwari
Lane Bikeway, Boreen, Bus, Corridor, Crawler, Drangway, Drury, Express, Fast,
    Fetter, Gut, Inside, Loan, Lois, Loke, Lovers', Memory, Middle, Mincing, Nearside,
    Offside, Outside, Overtaking, Passage, Petticoat, Pudding, Ruelle, Sea-road, Slow,
    Twitten, Twitting, Vennel, Wynd
Langerhans Insulin, Islets
Language(s) Argot, Armoric, Artificial, Assembly, Auxiliary, Basic, Body, Cant,
    Centum, Clinic, Command, Community, Comparative, Computer, → **COMPUTER**
    LANGUAGE, Dead, Descriptive, Diachronic, Dialect, Estem, Formal, Georgian,
    Gothic, High-level, Hobson-Jobson, Humanities, Idioglossia, Idiolect, Idiom,
    Idiom neutral, Inclusive, Jargon, Langue, Ledden, Lingo, Lingua franca, Macaroni,
    Machine code, Median, Mellowspeak, Meta-, Mixed, Mobspeak, Modern, Mother
    tongue, Native, Natural, Neutral, Newspeak, Novelese, Object, Officialese, Page
    description, Parlance, Patois, Philology, Pidgin, Plain, Polysynthetic, Pragmatics,
    Private, Procedural, Programming, Prose, Query, Rabbinic, Register, Relay,
    Rhetoric, Sea-speak, Second, Sign, Sociolect, → **SPEECH**, Strong, Style, Symbolic,
    Synchronic, Synthetic, Target, Technobabble, Telegraphese, Tessaraglot, Tone,
    → **TONGUE**, Tropology, Tushery, Union, Verbiage, Vernacular, Vocabulary, Wawa,
    Words, World

LANGUAGES

3 letters:	Igbo	*5 letters:*	Koine
Ada	Inca	Aleut	Kriol
Bat	Innu	Aryan	Kuo-yu
Edo	Komi	Azeri	Ladin
Fur	Krio	Balti	Lamba
Giz	Lozi	Bantu	Lamut
Gur	Manx	Batak	Latin
Ibo	Mari	Cajun	Lubon
Ido	Maya	Carib	Lunda
Kwa	Motu	Chewa	Lyele
Luo	Naga	Cobol	Malay
Mam	Nuba	Dogon	Mande
Mon	Nupe	Doric	Maori
Neo	Pali	Dutch	Mayan
San	Pedi	Fanti	Munda
Tai	Pict	Farsi	Nguni
Tiv	Shan	Galla	Norse
Twi	Sulu	Ganda	Oriya
	Susu	Gondi	Oscan
4 letters:	Taal	Greek	Palau
Ainu	Thai	Hausa	Papua
Avar	Tshi	Hindi	P-Celt
Cham	Tupi	Hokan	Sakai
Dani	Urdu	Incan	Sango
Erse	Xosa	Indic	Satem
Geez	Zulu	Joual	Saxon
Hopi	Zuni	Kafri	Shona

5 letters – cont:
Shono
Shuar
Sindi
Sinha
Sioux
Sotho
Suomi
Swazi
Taino
Tajik
Tamil
Temne
Te reo
Tigre
Tonga
Turki
Ugric
Uzbeg
Uzbek
Vedic
Venda
Vogul
Welsh
Wolof
Xhosa
Yakut
Yuman
Yupik

6 letters:
Adyahe
Adygei
Adyghe
Altaic
Arabic
Aranda
Asante
Aymara
Bahasa
Baluch
Basque
Basutu
Berber
Bihari
Bokmal
Brahui
Breton
Celtic
Chadic
Coptic

Creole
Cymric
Danish
Dardic
Divehi
Eskimo
Evenki
Fantee
Fijian
Finnic
French
Fulani
Gaelic
Gagauz
German
Gullah
Hebrew
Herero
Italic
Ladino
Lahnda
Lakota
Lepcha
Lu-wian
Lycian
Lydian
Manchu
Micmac
Mishmi
Mixtec
Na-Dene
Nepali
Novial
Nubian
Nyanja
Ostyak
Pahari
Paiute
Pakhti
Papuan
Pashto
Pashtu
Polish
Pushto
Pushtu
Quapaw
Romany
Rwanda
Salish
Samoan
Shelta

Sindhi
Siouan
Slovak
Somali
Strine
Tanoan
Tartar
Telegu
Telugu
Tigray
Tongan
Tsonga
Tswana
Tuareg
Tungus
Turkic
Udmurt
Ugrian
Uralic
Yoruba
Zyrian

7 letters:
Adamawa
Amboina
Amerind
Amharic
Aramaic
Ashanti
Austric
Baluchi
Bengali
Bislama
Cabiric
Caddoan
Catalan
Chechen
Chaldee
Chinook
Chuvash
Cushite
Dhivehi
Dzongka
Elamite
Flemish
Frisian
Gagauzi
Gaulish
Guarani
Hamitic
Hittite

Italian
Janlish
Japlish
Judezmo
Kannada
Khoisan
Kirundi
Kurdish
Kushite
Lallans
Laotian
Lingala
Luganda
Malayan
Malinke
Marathi
Miao-Yao
Mingrel
Miskito
Mordvin
Nahuatl
Nauruan
Ndebele
Nilotic
Nyungar
Oceanic
Ossetic
Ottoman
Pahlavi
Pehlevi
Pictish
Prakrit
Punjabi
Pushtoo
Quechua
Romance
Romanes
Romansh
Saharan
Samnite
Samoyed
Semitic
Serbian
Servian
Sesotho
Sinhala
Sinitic
Slovene
Sogdian
Sorbian
Spanish

Sudanic
Swahili
Swedish
Tagalog
Tahitan
Tibetan
Tlingit
Turkish
Turkmen
Umbrian
Uralian
Venetic
Volapuk
Voltaic
Walloon
Wendish
Yerkish
Yiddish

8 letters:
Akkadian
Albanian
Arawakan
Assamese
Balinese
Bulgaric
Cheremis
Cherkess
Chibchan
Chichewa
Croatian
Cushitic
Dzongkha
Ethiopic
Etrurian
Etruscan
Faliscan
Fanagalo
Filipino
Frankish
Friesian
Goidelic
Gujarati
Gujerati
Gurkhali
Hiri-Motu
Illyrian
Japanese
Japhetic
Javanese
Judezono

Jugoslav
Kashmiri
Khoikhoi
Kingwana
Kolarian
Kwakiutl
Landsmal
Lusatian
Makyalam
Malagasy
Mandarin
Mongolic
Mon-Khmer
Mordvine
Netspeak
Nez Perce
Ossetian
Penutian
Phrygian
Pilipino
Polabian
Rhaetian
Romanian
Romansch
Rumansch
Rumonsch
Salishan
Sanscrit
Sanskrit
Scythian
Setswana
Shemitic
Shoshone
Slavonic
Sumatran
Sumerian
Tahitian
Teutonic
Thracian
Tigrinya
Tshiluba
Tungusic
Turanian
Turkoman
Tuvaluan
Ugaritic
Volscian
Wakashan
Warlpiri
Yanomani
Yugoslav

9 letters:
Abkhazian
Afrikaans
Algonkian
Algonquin
Anatolian
Brythonic
Cantonese
Chari-Nile
Cheremiss
Cingalese
Diglossia
Dravidian
Esperanto
Esthonian
Euskarian
Franglais
Goidhelic
Gujarathi
Gujerathi
Hottentot
Hungarian
Inuktitut
Iroquoian
Kamilaroi
Kiswahili
Landsmaal
Langue d'oc
Leizghian
Makyaalam
Malayalam
Marquesan
Messapian
Mongolian
Muskogean
Nostratic
Onondagan
Provençal
Putonghua
Roumanian
Roumansch
Sabellian
Sardinian
Semi-Bantu
Sinhalese
Tocharian
Tokharian
Tokharish
Tungurian
Ukrainian
Ursprache

Varangian
Winnebago

10 letters:
Algonquian
Araucanian
Athabascan
Azerbayani
Beach-la-Mar
Bêche-la-Mar
Caprolalia
Circassian
Eteocretan
Finno-Ugric
Gallo-Roman
Himyaritic
Hindustani
Indonesian
Langue d'oil
Langue d'oui
Lithuanian
Macedonian
Malayalaam
Melanesian
Mingrelian
Muskhogean
Niger-Congo
Papiamento
Phoenician
Police Motu
Portuguese
Proto-Norse
Rajasthani
Serbo-Croat
Singhalese
Ugro-Finnic
Union Shona
Ural-Altaic
Uto-Aztecan
Vietnamese

11 letters:
Azerbaijani
Belarussian
Celtiberean
Dagestanian
Finno-Ugrian
Interglossa
Interlingua
Kordofanian
Langobardic

11 letters – cont:	Sranantongo	Platt-deutsch	Serbo-Croatian
Micronesian	Tupi-Guarani	Tibeto-Burman	
Nilo-Saharan		Volga-Baltaic	14 letters:
Old Paissian	12 letters:		Thraco-Phrygian
Osco-Umbrian	Billingsgate	13 letters:	
Pama-Nyungan	Gallo-Romance	Neo-Melanesian	16 letters:
Sino-Tibetan	Indo-European	Semito-Hamitic	Malayo-Polynesian

Languid, Languish Die, Divine, Droop, Feeble, Flagging, Listless, Lukewarm, Lydia, Melancholy, Quail, Torpid, Wilt

Languor Lassitude

Langur Wanderoo

Lanky Beanpole, Gangly, Gawky, Spindleshanks, Windlestraw

Lanolin Woolfat, Wool oil, Yolk

Lantern Aristotle's, Bowat, Bowet, Buat, Bull's eye, Chinese, Dark(e)y, Epidiascope, Episcope, Friar's, Glim, Japanese, Jaw, Lanthorn, Magic, Sconce, Stereopticon, Storm, Turnip

Lanthanum La

Laodicean Lukewarm

Lap Circuit, Drink, Gremial, Leg, Lick, Lip, Luxury, Override, Pace, Sypher

Lapdog Messan, Shough, Showghe

▷ **Lapdog** *may indicate* 'greyhound'

Lapel Revers

Laplander, Lapp Saam(e), Sabme, Sabmi, Sami

Lappet Infula

Lapse Backslide, Drop, Error, Expire, Fa', Fall, Nod, Sliding, Trip

Lapwing Hornywink, Teru-tero

Larceny Compound, Grand, Petty, Simple

Larch Hackmatack, Tamarack

Lard Enarm, Leaf, Saim, Seam(e)

Larder Buttery, Pantry, Spence, Springhouse

Large(ness), Largest Ample, Astronomical, Big, Boomer, Bulky, Buster, Colossus, Commodious, Considerable, Decuman, Enormous, Epical, Extensive, Gargantuan, → **GIGANTIC**, Ginormous, Great, Grit, Gross, Handsome, Hefty, Helluva, Huge, Hulking, Humdinger, Humongous, Humungous, Kingsize, L, Lg, Lunker, Macrocephaly, Massive, Maximin, Maximum, Outsize, Plethora, Prodigious, Rounceval, Rouncival, Scrouger, Skookum, Slew, Slue, Sollicker, Spacious, Spanking, Stonker, Stout, Swingeing, Tidy, Titanic, Vast, Voluminous, Whopping

Large number Centillion, Fermi, Gazillion, Giga, Gillion, Googol, Googolplex, Grillion, Infinitude, Jillion, Lac, Lakh, Legion, Mille, Nation, Nonillion, Nth, Octillion, Quadrillion, Quintillion, Raft, Regiment, Ruck, Scads, Sea, Septillion, Sextillion, Shitload, Slather, Slew, Slue, Squillion, Toman, Trillion, Zillion

Largess Alms, Charity, Frumentation, Generosity

Lariat Lasso, Reata, Riata

Lark Adventure, Aunter, Caper, Dido, Dunstable, Exaltation, Fool, Gammock, Giggle, Guy, Laverock, Magpie, Mud, Pipit, Prank

Larkspur Stavesacre

Larva Ammacoete, Amphibiotic, Amphiblastule, Aphid lion, Army-worm, Augerworm, Axolotl, Bagworm, Bipinnaria, Bloodworm, Bookworm, Bot(t), Budworm, Cabbage worm, Caddice, Caddis(-worm), Cankerworm, Caterpillar, Cercaria, Chigger, Chigoe, Coenurus, Corn borer, Corn earworm, Cysticercoid,

Doodlebug, Grub, Glass-crab, Hellgram(m)ite, Hydatid, Indusium, Instar, Jigger, Jointworm, Leather-jacket, Leptocephalus, Maggot, Mealworm, Measle, Microfilaria, Miracidium, Muckworm, Mudeye, Naiad, Nauplius, Neoteny, Nigger, Nymph, Ox-bot, Planula, Pluteus, Porina, Redia, Screwworm, Shade, Silkworm, Strawworm, Tadpole, Trochophore, Trochosphere, Veliger, Water penny, Wireworm, Witchetty, Witchetty grub, Woodworm, Xylophage, Zoea

Larynx, Laryngitis Croup, Hives, Voice box

Lascar Seacunny, Tindal

Lascivious(ness) Crude, Drooling, Goaty, Horny, Lewd, Lubric, Paphian, Satyric, Sotadic, Tentigo, Wanton

Laser Argon

Lash(ed), Lashing(s) Cat, Cilium, Firk, Flagellum, Frap, Gammon, Knout, Mastigophora, Mousing, Oodles, Oup, Quirt, Riem, Rope's end, Scourge, Secure, Sjambok, Stripe, Swinge, Tether, Thong, Trice, Whang, → **WHIP**, Wire

Lass(ie) Damsel, Maid, Quean, Queyn, Quin(i)e

Lassitude Accidie, Acedie, Languor, Lethargy

Lasso Lariat, Reata, Rope

Last(ing) Abide, Abye, Aftermost, → **AT LAST**, Boot-tree, Bottom, Cargo, Chronic, Coda, Dernier, Dure, Eleventh, Endmost, Endurance, Endure, Extend, Extreme, → **FINAL**, Hinder, Hindmost, In extremis, Latest, Latter, Linger, Live, Load, Long-life, Model, Nightcap, Outstay, Perdure, Permanent, Perpetuate, Persist, Rearmost, Spin, Stable, Stamina, Stand, Stay, Supper, Survive, Swan-song, Thiller, Thule, Tree, Trump, Ult(imate), Ultimo, Utmost, Wear, Weight, Whipper-in, Yester, Z

Last drop Supernaculum

Last resort Pis aller

Last syllable Ultima

Last word(s) Amen, Envoi, Farewell, Ultimatum, Zythum

Latch Bar, Clicket, Clink, Espagnolette, Lock, Night, Sneck, Thumb, Tirling-pin

Late(r), Latest After(wards), Afterthought, Behindhand, Chit-chat, Dead, Deid, Ex, Former, Gen, Infra, Lag, Lamented, New(s), Overdue, Overrunning, Past, Recent, Serotine, Sine, Slow, State-of-the-art, Stop-press, Syne, Tardive, Tardy, Top shelf, Trendy, Umquhile

Late-learner Opsimath

Latent Concealed, Delitescent, Dormant, Maieutic, Potential

Lateral Askant, Edgeways, Sideways

Latex Antiar, Dental dam, Gutta-percha, Jelutong, Ule

Lath Lag, Splat

Lathe Capstan, Mandrel, Mandril, Turret

Lather Flap, Foam, Froth, Sapples, Suds, Tan

Latin(ist) Biblical, Classical, Criollo, Dago, Dog, Erasmus, Eyeti, Greaseball, High, Humanity, Italiot, L, Late, Law, Low, Medieval, Mexican, Middle, Modern, Neapolitan, New, Pig, Quarter, Rogues', Romanic, Romish, Scattermouch, Silver, Spic, Thieves', Vulgar, Wop

Latin-American Criollo, Tico

Latitude Breadth, Celestial, Ecliptic, Free hand, Horse, L, Leeway, Liberty, Licence, Meridian, Parallel, Play, Roaring forties, Scope, Tropic, Width

Latrine Ablutions, Benchhole, Bog, Cloaca, Furphy, Garderobe, Loo, Privy, Rear

Latter Last, Previous

Latter-day Recent, Saints, Young

Lattice Bravais, Cancelli, Clathrate, Espalier, Grille, Red, Space, Treillage, Trellis

Lattice-leaf Ouvirandra
Latvian Lett
Laud(able), Lauder Commend, Eulogist, Extol, Harry, Praise, Worthily
Lauderdale Caballer
Laugh(ing), Laughable, Laughter Belly, Boff, Cachinnate, Cackle, Chortle,
  Chuckle, Cod, Corpse, Democritus, Deride, Derision, Fit, Fou rire, Gelastic, Giggle,
  Goster, Guffaw, Ha, He-he, Ho-ho, Homeric, Hoot, Horse, Hout, Howl, Irrision,
  Isaac, Last, Lauch, Leuch, Levity, Ludicrous, → **MIRTH**, Mock, Nicker, Peal,
  Present, Riancy, Riant, Rich, Rident, Ridicule, Risus, Scream, Snigger, Snirt(le),
  Snort, Tehee, Titter, Yo(c)k
Laughing-stock Outspeckle, Sport
Launcelot Gobbo
Launch(ing), Launch pad Begin, Blast-off, Catapult, Chuck, Cosmodrome, ELV,
  Fire, Float, Hurl, Initiate, Lift-off, Moonshot, Motoscalp, Opening, Pioneer,
  Presentation, Release, Rolling, Roll out, Send, Shipway, Slipway, Start, Steam,
  → **TOSS**, Unstock, Upsend, VTO
Launder, Laund(e)rette, Laundress, Laundry Bagwash, Blanchisseuse, Clean,
  Coin-op, Lav, Linen, Steamie, Tramp, Transfer, Wash, Washhouse, Whites
Laurel(s) Aucuba, Bay, Camphor, Cherry, Daphne, Japan, Kalmia, Kudos, Mountain,
  Pichurim, Rose (bay), Sassafras, Spicebush, Spotted, Spurge, Stan, Sweet-bay, True
Laurence Sterne
Lava Aa, Block, Bomb, Coulée, Cysticercus, Dacite, Flood basalt, Lahar, Lapilli,
  Magma, Mud, Nuée ardente, Pahoehoe, Palagonite, Pillow, Pitchstone, Plug,
  Pumice, Pyroclast, Scoria, Tephra, Toadstone
Lavatory Ajax, Bogger, Brasco, Can, Carsey, Carzey, Cludgie, Comfort station,
  Convenience, Cottage, Dike, Draught, Dunnakin, Dunny, Dyke, Earth closet,
  Elsan®, Facilities, Forica, Furphey, Gents, Heads, Jakes, Jane, John, Kars(e)y,
  Karzy, K(h)azi, Kleinhuisie, Kybo, Ladies, Lat(rine), Loo, Necessary, Netty,
  Office, Outhouse, Portaloo®, Privy, Rear(s), Reredorter, Shithouse, Shouse,
  Siege, Smallest room, Superloo, Throne, Thunderbox, Toilet, Toot, Tout, Urinal,
  Washroom, WC
Lave Lip, Wash
Lavender Aspic, Sea, Spike
Lavengro Borrow
Laver Moabite, Nori, Ore-weed
Lavish Barmecidal, Copious, Excessive, Exuberant, Flush, Free, Fulsome, Generous,
  Liberal, Lucullan, Lush, Palatial, Prodigal, Shower, Slap-up, Sumptuous, Wanton,
  Waste
Law(s) Abingdon, Act, Agrarian, Anti-trust, Ass, Association, Avogadro's, Babo's,
  Bar, Barratry, Bernoulli's, → **BILL**, Biogenetic, Blue-sky, Bode's, Bonar, Bourlaw,
  Boyle's, Bragg's, Brehon, Brewster's, Brocard, Buys Ballot's, Byelaw, Byrlaw, Cain,
  Canon, Capitulary, Case, Chancery, Charles's, Civil, Code, Common, Constitution,
  Corn, Coulomb's, Criminal, Cupar, Curie's, Curie-Weiss, Cy pres, Dalton's,
  Dead-letter, Decree, Decretals, Decretum, De Morgan's, Deodand, Dharma,
  Dictate, Digest, Din, Distributive, Dry, Edict, Einstein's, Enact, Excise, Fiqh,
  Forensic, Forest, Fuero, Fundamental, Fuzz, Game, Gas, Gay-Lussac's, Graham's,
  Gresham's, Grimm's, Grotian, Haeckel's, Halifax, Hardy-Weinberg, Henry's,
  Homestead, Hooke's, Hubble's, Hudud, Hume's, International, Irade, Iure, Joule's,
  Jura, Jure, Jus, Kain, Kashrut(h), Kepler's, Kirchhoff's, Labour, Land, Lay, Leibniz's,
  Lemon, Lenz's, Lien, Liquor, Lor(d), Losh, Lydford, Lynch, Magdeburg, Mariotte's,
  Martial, May, Mendel's, Mercantile, Military, Mishna(h), Mishnic, Moral, Mosaic,

Murphy's, Natural, Newton's, Noahide, Nomistic, Nomothetic, Octave, Ohm's, Oral, Ordinance, Pandect, Parity, Parkinson's, Pass, Penal, Periodic, Planck's, Plebiscite, Poor, Principle, Private, Public, Regulation, Rhodian, Roman, Rubric, Rule, Salic, Salique, Scout, Sharia(h), Sheria(t), Shield, Shulchan Aruch, Snell's, Sod's, → **STATUTE**, Stefan's, Stokes, Sumptuary, Sunna, Sus(s), Sword, Table, Talmud, Tenet, The (long) robe, Thorah, Thorndike's, Torah, Tort, Tradition, Twelve Tables, Ulema, Unwritten, Use, Verner's, Vigilante, Written

Lawless(ness) Anarchy, Anomie, Anomy, Antinomian, Bushranger, Piratical, Rowdy

Lawmaker, Lawman, Lawyer Alfaqui, Ambulance chaser, Attorney, AV, Avocat, Barrack room, Barrister, Bencher, BL, Bluebottle, Bramble, Bush, Canon, Coke, Counsel, DA, Decemvir, Deemster, Defence, Dempster, Doge, Draco, Earp, Enactor, Fiscal, Greenbag, Grotius, Hammurabi, Jurisconsult, Jurist, Legal eagle, Legist, Mooktar, Moses, MP, Mufti, Mukhtar, Nomothete, Notary, Penang, Pettifoggers, Philadelphia, Proctor, Procurator fiscal, Prosecutor, Rabbi, Shirra, Shyster, Silk, Solicitor, Spenlow, Stratopause, Talmudist, Templar, Thesmothete, Vakil, WS

Lawn Cloth, Grass, Green, Linen, Sward, Turf

Lawrence DH, Ross, Shaw, TE

Lawrencium Lr

Lawsuit Case, Cause, Plea, Trover

▶ **Lawyer(s), Lawman** *see* **LAWMAKER**

▷ **Lax** *may indicate* an anagram

Lax(ity) Freedom, Inexact, Laissez-aller, Latitude, Lenience, Loose, Remiss, → **SLACK**, Wide, Wide-open

Laxative Aloin, Aperitive, Cascara, Cassia, Cathartic, Eccoprotic, Elaterin, Elaterium, Glauber's salt, Gregory (powder), Loosener, Magnesia, Physic, Purgative, → **PURGE**, Saline, Senna-pod, Taraxacum

Lay(ing), Layman, Laic, Laid, Laity Air, Amateur, Antepost, Aria, Ballad, Bed, Bet, Blow, Chant, Christian Brothers, Civil, Ditty, Drop, Earthly, Egg, Embed, Fit, Impose, Lied, Lodge, Man, Minstrel, Oat, Oblate, Ode, Ordinary, Outsider, Oviparous, Oviposit, Parabolanus, Pose, Secular, Set, Sirvente, → **SONG**, Sypher, Temporalty, Tertiary, Tribal, Untrained, Wager, Warp

Layabout Corner boy, Idler, Loafer, Lotophagus, Ne'er-do-well, Oaf, Slob

Lay-by Rest stop

Layer(s) Abscission, Aeuron(e), Ancona, Appleton, Battery, Bed, Boundary, Cake, Caliche, Cambium, Chromosphere, Cladding, Coating, Crust, D, Depletion, E, Ectoplasm, Ectosarc, Ekman, Epiblast, Epilimnion, Epitaxial, Epitheca, Epithelium, Erathem, E-region, Exine, Exocarp, F, Film, Flake, Friction, Ganoin, Germ, Gossan, Gozzan, Granum, Ground, Heaviside, → **HEN**, Herb, Hypotheca, Intima, Inversion, Kennelly(-Heaviside), Kerf, Lamella, Lamina, Lap, Leghorn, Lenticle, Lie, Malpighian, Media, Miocene, Ozone, Pan, Patina, Paviour, Photosphere, Ply, Retina, Reversing, Rind, Scale, Sclerite, Screed, Shrub, Skim, Skin, Skiver, Sliver, Spathic, Stratify, Stratopause, Stratum, Substratum, Tabular, Tapetum, Tier, Tremie, Trophoblast, Trophoderm, Uvea, Varve, Vein, Velamen, Veneer

Lay-off Dismiss, Hedge, Redundance

Lay-out Ante, Design, Fell, Format, Map, Mise, Pattern, Spend, Straucht, Straught, Streak, Streek, Stretch

Laze, Laziness, Lazy (person), Lazybones Bed-presser, Bone idle, Bummer, Cabbage, Couch potato, Faineant, Grunge, Hallian, Hallion, Hallyon, Indolent, Inert, Lackadaisical, Laesie, Languid, Layabout, Lie-abed, Lig(ger), Lime, Lither, Loaf, Lotus-eater, Lusk, Mollusc, Ne'er-do-well, Oblomovism, Resty, Sleepyhead,

Sloth, Slouch, Slug(-a-bed), Sluggard, Susan, Sweer, Sweir, Veg, Workshy
▷ **Lazily** *may indicate* an anagram
Lea Grass, Meadow
Leach(ing) Cheluviation, Lixivial, Ooze
Lead(er), Leading, Leadership Ag(h)a, Ahead, Akela, Amakosi, Anglesite, Article, Atabeg, Atabek, Ayatollah, Bab, Bellwether, Black, Bluey, Bonaparte, Brand, Cable, Cade, Calif, Caliph, Came, Capitano, Capo, Captain, Castro, Caudillo, Causal, Centre, Ceruse, Cheer, Chieftain, Chiliarch, Chin, China white, Choragus, Choregus, CO, Codder, Condottiere, Conducive, Conduct, Corporal, Coryphaeus, Coryphee, Dalai Lama, De Gaulle, Demagogue, Dictator, Drail, Duce, Dux, Editorial, Escort, Ethnarch, Extension, Figurehead, First, Flake-white, Floor, Foreman, Foremost, Frontrunner, Fu(e)hrer, Fugleman, Gaffer, Gandhi, Garibaldi, General, Gerent, Go, Graphite, Guide(r), Halter, Hand, Headman, Headmost, Headnote, Hegemony, Heresiarch, Hero, Hetman, Honcho, Idi, Imam, Imaum, Induna, Ink(h)osi, Inveigle, Jason, Jefe, Jeune premier(e), Jump, Juve(nile), Kabir, Kame, King, Ksar, Leam, Litharge, Livid, Loss, Lost, Lyam, Lyme, Mahatma, Mahdi, Main, Market, Marshal, Massicot, Masticot, Mayor, Meer, Mehdi, Minium, Mir, Nanak, No 1, Nomarch, Nose, Numero uno, Omrah, Open, Pacemaker, Pacesetter, Padishah, Panchen Lama, Pb, Pilot, Pioneer, Pit, Plumb(um), Plummet, PM, Precentor, Premier(e), President, Price, Rangitara, Ratoo, Rebbe, Rebecca, Red, Role, Ruler, Sachem, Sagamore, Saturn, Saturn's tree, Scotlandite, Scout, Scuddaler, Scudler, Shaper, Sharif, Sheik(h), Sixer, Skipper, Skudler, Soaker, Soul, Sounding, Spearhead, Staple, Star, Sultan, Supremo, Taoiseach, Tecumseh, Tetraethyl, Top banana, Top dog, Trail(blazer), Tribune, Tsaddik, Tsaddiq, Tzaddik, Up, Usher, Vaivode, Van(guard), Vanadinite, Va(u)nt, Vaunt-courier, Voivode, Vozhd, Waivode, Wali, Warlord, White, Whitechapel, Wulfenite, Youth, Zaddik, Zia
▷ **Lead(s), Leaders** *may indicate* first letters of words
Leaden Flat, Plumbeous, Saturnine
Lead-glance Galena
Leading to Pre
Leaf(y), Leaves Acanthus, Acrospire, Amphigastrium, Amplexicaul, Ascidia, At(t)ap, Baccy, Betel, Blade, Bract, Carpel, Cataphyll, Cladode, Coca, Compound, Consent, Corolla, Costate, Cotyledon, Dolma, Drop, Duff, Fig, Finial, Foil, Foliage, Foliar, Folio(se), Folium, Frond, Glume, Gold, Green, Holiday, Induviae, Jugum, K(h)at, Lattice, Lobe, Lobulus, Maple, Megaphyll, Microphyll, Needle, Nervate, Out, P, Pad, Page, Pan, Phyllid, Phyllome, Pot, Qat, Repair, Riffle, Rosula, Salad, Scale, Sclerophyll, Secede, Sepal, Sheet, Siri(h), Skip, Spathe, Sporophyll, Stipule, Tea, Title, Tobacco, TTL, Valve, Vert, Vine, Withdraw
Leafhopper Thrip
Leafless Ebracteate, Scape
Leaflet At(t)ap, Bill, Bracteole, Circular, Dodger, Fly-sheet, Foliolose, Handbill, Hand-out, Pinna, Pinnula, Prophyll, Stipel, → **TRACT**
League Achaean, Alliance, Amphictyony, Arab, Band, Bund, Compact, Decapolis, Delian, Denominal, Entente, Federation, Gueux, Guild, Hanse(atic), Holy, Ivy, Land, Major, Minor, Nations, Parasang, Primrose, Redheaded, Rugby, Solemn, Super, Union, Ypres, Zollverein, Zupa
Leak(y) Bilge, Drip, Escape, Extravasate, Gizzen, Holed, Holey, Ooze, Pee, Porous, Run, Seepage, Sype, Trickle, Wee, Weep, Wee-wee
Leak-proof Airtight
Leamington Spa

Lean(ing) Abut, Barren, Batter, Bend, Careen, Carneous, Carnose, Griskin, Heel, Hike out, → **INCLINE**, Lie, Lig(ge), Minceur, Prop, Propend, Rake, Rely, Rest, Scraggy, Scrawny, Skinny, Spare, Stoop, Taste, Tend, Thin, Tilt, Tip, Walty, Wiry

Leander Abydos

Lean-to Skillion

Leap(ing), Leapt Assemblé, Bound, Brisé, Cabriole, Caper, Capriole, Cavort, Clear, Croupade, Curvet, Echappé, Entrechat, Falcade, Fishdive, Frisk, Galumph, Gambade, Gambado, Gambol, Jeté, Jump, Loup, Luppen, Ollie, Over, Pigeon-wing, Pounce, Pronk, Quantum, Sally, Salto, Somersa(u)lt, Somerset, → **SPRING**, Stag, Transilient, Vault, Volte

Leap year Bissextile, Penteteric

Lear Edward, King, Nonsense

Learn(ed), Learner Beginner, Blue, Bluestocking, Chela, Classical, Con, Discover, Distance, Doctor, Don, Erudite, Gather, Get, Glean, Hear, Kond, L, Lear(e), Leir, Lere, Literate, Literati, Literato, Lucubrate, Master, Memorise, Mirza, Mug up, → **NOVICE**, Opsimath, Pandit, Polymath, Programmed, Pundit, Pupil, Rookie, Savant, Scan, Scholar, Scient, See, Starter, Student, → **STUDY**, Tiro, Trainee, Tutee, Tyro, Wise

Learning Associative, Blended, Culture, Discipline, Discrimination, Distance, Erudition, Index, Insight, Instrumental, Latent, Lifelong, Lore, Machine, New, Open, Opsimathy, Rep, Scholarship, Sleep, Visile, Wit

Lease(-holder) Charter, Farm, Feu, Gavel, Hire, Let, Long, Novated, → **RENT**, Set(t), Subtack, Tack, Tacksman

Leash Lead, Lune, Lyam, Lym(e), Slip, Three, Trash, Triplet

Least Minimum, Rap

Leather(s), Leathery Aqualeather, Artificial, Bouilli, Bouilly, Box-calf, Buckskin, Buff, Cabretta, Calf, Capeskin, Chammy, Chamois, Chaps, Checklaton, Cheverel, Chevrette, Chrome, Cordovan, Cordwain, Corium, Counter, Cowhide, Crispin, Cuir(-bouilli), Deacon, Deerskin, Diphthera, Doeskin, Dogskin, Durant, Fair, Foxing, Goatskin, Grain, Hide, Hog-skin, Horsehide, Japanned, Kid, Kip(-skin), Lacquered, Lamp, Levant, Marocain, Maroquin, Mocha, Morocco, Mountain, Nap(p)a, Neat, Nubuck®, Oak, Ooze, Oxhide, Paste-grain, Patent, Pigskin, Plate, Rand, Rawhide, Rexine®, Riem(pie), Roan, Rock, Rough-out, Russet, Russia, Saffian, Shagreen, Shammy, Sharkskin, Shecklaton, Sheepskin, Shoe, Skiver, Slinkskin, Snakeskin, Spetch, Split, Spur, Spur-whang, Stirrup, Strand, Strap, Suede, Tan, Taw, Thong, Upper, Wallop, Wash, Waxed, White, Whitleather, Yuft

Leatherneck Marine, RM

Leave(r), Leaving(s), Leave off Abandon, Abiturient, Abscond, Absit, Absquatulate, Acquittal, Adieu, Avoid, Bequeath, Blessing, Blow, Broken meats, Bug, Compassionate, Congé, Congee, Decamp, Depart, Desert, Desist, Devisal, Devise, Ditch, Evacuate, Except, Exeat, Exit, Exodus, Extrude, Forego, Forgo, Forsake, French, Furlough, Gardening, Garlandage, → **GO**, Inspan, Ish, Legate, Liberty, Licence, Maroon, Mass, Maternity, Mizzle, Omit, Orts, Pace, Parental, Park, Part, Paternity, → **PERMISSION**, Permit, → **QUIT**, Residue, Resign, Sabbatical, Scapa, Scat, Scram, Shore, Sick, Skedaddle, Skidoo®, Stick, Strand, Vacate, Vade, Vamo(o)se, Will, Withdraw

Leaven Barm, Ferment, Yeast

Lebanese, Lebanon Druse, RL

Lecher(ous), Lechery Gate, Goaty, Lascivious, Libertine, Lickerish, Lustful, Profligate, Rake, Roué, Salaciousness, Satirisk, Satyr, Silen, Whoremonger, Wolf

Lectern Ambo, Desk, Eagle, Oratory

Lecture(r), Lectures, Lecturing Address, Aristotelian, Chalktalk, Creed, Curtain, Dissert(ator), Docent, Don, Earful, Erasmus, Expound, Harangue, Homily, Hulsean, Jaw, Jawbation, Jobe, L, Lector, Pi-jaw, Prelect, Privatdocent, Prone, Rate, Read(er), Rede, Reith, Roasting, Rubber chicken circuit, Scold, Sententious, → **SERMON**, Spout, Talk, Teacher, Teach-in, Wigging, Yaff

Ledge Altar, Berm, Buttery-bar, Channel, Fillet, Gradin(e), Linch, Misericord(e), Nut, Rake, Scarcement, Settle, → **SHELF**, Window (sill)

Ledger Book, General, Purchase, Register

Lee(s) Dregs, Dunder, Grout, Heeltaps, Sediment, Shelter, Ullage

Leech Bleeder, Gnathobdellida, Horse, Medicinal, Parasite, Rhynchobdellida

Leek Allium, Fouat, Fouet, Porraceous, Rocambole, Sengreen

Leer Eliad, Fleer, Oeillade, Ogle, Perv

Leeway Drift

Left (hand), Left-handed, Left-hander, Left-winger Abandoned, Adrift, Balance, Bolshy, Corrie-fisted, Dolly-push, Gallock, Hie, High, Inherited, L, Laeotropic, Laevorotation, Larboard, Links, Loony, Lorn, Near, New, Other, Over, Pink, Pinko, Port, Portsider, Quit, Rad, Red, Relic, Residuum, Resigned, Secondo, Sinister, Soc(ialist), Southpaw, Thin, Titoism, Trot, Unused, Verso, Vo, Went, West, Wind, Yet

Left-over Astatki, Dregs, End, Gone, Lave, Oddment, Offcut, Orra, Remains, Remanet, → **REMNANT**, Residue, Rest, Waste

Leg(s), Leggings, Leggy, Leg-wear Antigropelo(e)s, Bandy, Barbados, Barley-sugar, Bow, Breeches, Cabriole, Cannon, Chaparajos, Chaparejos, Chaps, Crural, Crus, Dib, Drumstick, Fine, Fly-sail, Gaiter, Galligaskins, Gam(b), Gamash, Gambado, Garter, Gaskin, Giambeux, Gigot, Gramash, Gramosh, Ham, Haunch, Hest, Hock, Jamb, Jambeau, Jambeaux, Knock-knee(d), Limb, Long, Member, Milk, Myriapod, Oleo, On(side), Peg, Peraeopod, Periopod, Peroneal, Pestle, Pin, Podite, Proleg, Puttees, Pylon, Relay, Section, Shanks, Shanks's pony, Shaps, Shin, Short, Spats, Spatterdash, Spider, Spindleshanks, Square, Stage, Stump, Thigh, Tights, White

Legacy Bequest, Cumulative, Demonstrative, Dowry, Entail, General, Heirloom, Residuary, Specific, Substitutional

Legal(ism), Legally, Legitimate Bencher, Decriminalised, Forensic, Halacha, Halaka(h), Halakha, Lawful, Licit, Nomism, Scienter, Statutory

Legal book Halacha, Halaka(h), Halakha, Talmud

Leg-armour, Leg-covering Cootikin, Cu(i)tikin, Gambado, Jamb(e), Pad

Legate, Legator A latere, Ambassador, Consul, Devisor, Emissary, Envoy, Nuncio

▷ **Legend** *may indicate* leg-end e.g. foot, talus

Legend(ary) Arthurian, Caption, Edda, Fable, Folklore, Hadith, Motto, Myth, Saga, Story, Urban, Yowie

Leger Swindler

Leghorn Livorno

Legible Clear, Lucid, Plain

Legion(ary), Legionnaire Alauda, American, Army, British, Cohort, Countless, Deserter, Foreign, Geste, Honour, → **HOST**, Maniple, Many, Throng, Thundering, Zillions

Legislate, Legislation, Legislator, Legislature Assemblyman, Congress, Decemvir, Decree, Delegated, MP, Nomothete, Oireachtas, → **PARLIAMENT**, Persian, Senator, Solon, Supreme soviet, Zemstvo

Legitimate Kosher, Loyal, Proper, Valid

Legless Amelia, Blotto, Boozy, Caecilia, Drunk, Mermaid, Psyche

Leg-pull Chaff, Joke, Rise, Rot

Legume, Leguminous Bean, Guar, Lentil, Lomentum, Pea, Pipi, Pod, Pulse

Leibniz Monadism

Leigh Amyas

Leisure(ly) Adagio, Ease, Lento, Liberty, Moderato, Otium, Respite, Rest, Vacation

Lemming Morkin

Lemon Answer, Cedrate, Citron, Citrus, Smear-dab, Sole, Twist, Yellow

Lemur Angwantibo, Aye-aye, Babacoote, Bush-baby, Colugo, Cynocephalus, Galago, Half-ape, Indri(s), Loris, Macaco, Malmag, Mongoose, → **MONKEY**, Nagapie, Potto, Ringtail, Sifaka, Spectre, Tana, Tarsier

Lend(er) Advance, Library, Loan, Prest, Sub, Vaunce

Length(y), Lengthen(ing), Lengthwise Archine, Arsheen, Arshin(e), Aune, Barleycorn, Braccio, Cable, Chain, Cubit, Distance, Eke, Ell, → **ELONGATE**, Endways, Ennage, Epenthetic, Expand, Extensive, Focal, Foot, Footage, Furlong, Inch, Ley, Mile, Nail, Passus, Perch, Piece, Plethron, Pole, Prolate, Prolix, Prolong, Protract, Reach, Remen, Rod, Rope, Slow, Span, Stadium, Toise, Vara, Verbose, Yard

Lenient, Leniency Clement, Exurable, Lax, Mild, Permissive, Soft, Soft line, Tolerant

Lens Achromatic, Acoustic, Anamorphic, Anastigmat, Aplanatic, Apochromat(ic), Bifocal, Bull's eye, Compound, Contact, Corneal, Crookes, Crown, Crystalline, Dielectric, Diopter, Dioptre, Diverging, Electron, Electrostatic, Eye, Eyeglass, Eye-piece, Facet, Fish-eye, Fresnel, Gas-permeable, Gravitational, Hard, Immersion, Lentil, Macro, Magnetic, Metallic, Mirror, Object-glass, Optic, Pantoscope, Phacoid, Piano-concave, Piano-convex, Soft, Soft-focus, Stanhope, Sunglass, Telephoto, Toric, Trifocal, Varifocal, Water, Wide-angle, Zoom

Lent Carême, Fast, Laetare, Out, Quadragesimal, Term

Lentil(s) D(h)al, Dholl, Ervalenta, Lens, Phacoid, Pulse, Puy, Revalenta

Leonora Overture

Leopard Catamountain, Clouded, Hunting, Leap, Libbard, Oceloid, Ounce, Panther, Pard, Snow, Spots, Tiger

Leopold Bloom

Leotard Maillot

Leper, Leprosy, Leprous Gehazi, Hansen's disease, Lazar, Leontiasis, Lionism, Meazel, Mesel, Outcast, Pariah

Lepidopterist Aurelian, Moth-er, Pendleton, Treacler

Leprechaun Elf, Gremlin, Imp

Lepton Muon

Lesbian Boi, Bull dyke, Crunchie, Diesel, Dike, Dyke, Homophile, Lipstick, Sapphist, Tribade

Lese-majesty Treason

Lesion Cut, Gash, Pannus, Scar, Serpiginous, Sore, Wheal, Whelk

Less(en), Lesser, Lessening Abate, Alaiment, Bate, Comedown, Contract, Deaden, Decline, Deplete, Derogate, Dilute, → **DWINDLE**, Extenuate, Fewer, Junior, Littler, Meno, Minus, Play down, Reduce, Relax, Remission, Shrink, Subordinate, Subsidiary, Tail, Under

Lesson Class, Example, Lear(e), Lection, Leir, Lere, Life, Liripipe, Masterclass, Moral, Object, Parashah, Period, Sermon, Shiur, Tutorial

Let (go, off, out), Letting Allow, Cap, Charter, Conacre, Displode, Divulge, Enable, Entitle, Explode, Hire, Impediment, Indulge, Leak, Lease, Litten, Loot(en), Luit(en), Lutten, Net, Obstacle, Obstruct, → **PERMIT**, Rent, Reprieve, Sett, Tenancy, Unhand, Warrant

Let down Abseil, Betray, Lower, Sell, Vail

Let-down Disappointment, Non-event

Lethal Deadly, Fatal, Fell, Mortal

Lethargic, Lethargy Accidie, Apathy, Coma, Drowsy, Ennui, Hebetude, Inertia, Lassitude, Listless, Passive, Sleepy, Sluggish, Stagnant, Stupor, Supine, Torpid, Turgid

Letter(s) Ache, Aerogam, Aesc, Airgraph, Aleph, Alif, Alpha, Ascender, A(y)in, Bayer, Begging, Beta, Beth, Block, Breve, Cadmean, Canine, Caph, Capital, Capon, Casket, Chain, Cheth, Chi, Chitty, Circular, Col, Collins, Consonant, Covering, Cue, Cuneiform, Daled, Daleth, Dead, Dear John, Delta, Digamma, Digraph, Dominical, Edh, Ef(f), Emma, Encyclical, Ep(isemon), Epistle, Epsilon, Eta, Eth, Fan, Favour, Form, Fraktur, French, Gamma, Gimel, Grapheme, He, Heth, Hieratic, Initial, Iota, Izzard, Jerusalem, Kaph, Kappa, Koppa, Kufic, Labda, Lambda, Lamed(h), Landlady, Landlord, Lessee, Lessor, Literal, Love, Mail, Mail-shot, Majuscule, Mem, Memo, Miniscule, Minuscule, Missive, Monogram, Mu, Nasal, Night, Note, Notelet, Nu, Nun, Og(h)am, Omega, Omicron, Open, Ou, Pacifical, Pahlavi, Paston, Pastoral, Patent, Pe, Pehlevi, Phi, Pi, Plosive, Poison-pen, Polyphone, Postbag, Psi, Pythagorean, Qoph, Resh, Rho, Rhyme, Rom, Runestave, Sad(h)e, Samekh, Samian, Sampi, San, Scarlet, Screed, Screeve, Screwtape, Script, See, Shin, Ship, Siglum, Sigma, Sign, Signal, Sin, Sort, Stiff, Swash, Tau, Tav, Taw, Teth, Theta, Thorn, Toc, Tsade, Typo, Uncial, Upsilon, Vau, Vav, Versal, Vowel, Waw, Wen, Wyn, Wynn, Xi, Yod(h), Yogh, Ypsilon, Zayin, Zed, Zeta

Lettering Cufic, Kufic

Lettuce Batavia, Butterhead, Cabbage, Chicon, Corn-salad, Cos, Frog's, Iceberg, Lactuca, Lamb's, Lollo rosso, Mizuna, Romaine, Salad, Sea, Thridace

Leucoma Albugo

Levant(ine) Coptic, Go, Israelite, Jew, Ottamite, Ottomite

Levee Bank, Dyke, Embankment, Party

Level(ler) A, Abney, Abreast, Aclinic, Ad eundum, Aim, Awash, Bargaining, Base, Break even, Bulldoze, Champaign, Confidence, Countersink, Degree, Dumpy, Echelon, Energy, Equal, → **EVEN**, Extent, Eye, Flat, Flight, Flush, Fog, Grade, Horizontal, Impurity, Infill, Logic, Meet, O, Occupational, Ordinary, Par, Plane, Plat(eau), Point, Price, Race, Rank, Rase, Raze, Reduced, Savanna, Sea, Spirit, Split, Springing, → **SQUARE**, Status, Stratum, Street, Strew, Strickle, Subsistence, Summit, Support, Surveyor's, Tier, Top, Trophic, True, Water, Y

Lever(age) Backfall, Bell-crank, Brake, Cock, Crampon, Crowbar, Dues, Gear, Handspike, Jaw, Jemmy, Joystick, Key, Knee-stop, Landsturm, Pawl, Peav(e)y, Pedal, Prise, Prize, Pry, Purchase, Stick, Sweep, Swipe, Tappet, Throttle, Tiller, Treadle, Treddle, Tremolo arm, Trigger, Tumbler, Typebar, Whipstaff

Leviathan Whale

Levitate, Levitation Float, Hover, Rise, Yogic flying

Levity Flippancy, Glee, Humour, Jollity

Levy Capital, Estreat, Impose, Imposition, Leave, Militia, Octroi, Raise, Scutage, Stent, Talliate, Tax, Tithe, Toll

Lewd(ness) Bawdy, Blue, Debauchee, Impure, Libidinous, Lubricity, Obscene, Priapism, Prurient, Raunchy, Silen(us), Unclean

Lewis Carroll, Tenon

Lexicographer, Lexicon Compiler, Craigie, Drudge, Etymologist, Florio, Fowler, Glossarist, Grove, Johnson(ian), Larousse, Liddell, Mental, Murray, OED, Thesaurus, Vocabulist, Webster, Words-man

Liability, Liable Anme, Apt, Current, Debt, Employer's, Incur, Limited, Open, Product, Prone, Subject, Susceptible, White elephant

Liaison Affair, Amour, Contact, Link

Liana Guarana

Libel(lous) Blasphemous, Defamatory, Malign, Sclaunder, Slander, Smear, Sully, Vilify

Liberal(ity) Abundant, Adullamites, Ample, Besant, Bounteous, Bountiful, Breadth, Bright, Broad, Catholic, Enlightened, Free(hander), Free-hearted, → **GENEROUS**, Giver, Grey, Grimond, Grit, Handsome, Indulgent, L, Largesse, Latitudinarian, Lavish, Limousine, Octobrist, Open, → **PROFUSE**, Rad(ical), Samuelite, Simonite, Steel, Tolerant, Trivium, Unstinted, Verlig, Verligte, Whig

Liberate(d), Liberation, Liberator Bolivar, Deliver, Dissimure, Emancipate, Fatah, → **FREE**, Gay, Inkatha, Intolerant, Messiah, PLO, Release, Risorgimento, Save, Sucre, Unfetter, UNITA, Women's

Liberian Kroo, Kru

Libertarian, Libertine Chartered, Corinthian, Debauchee, Don Juan, Laxist, Lecher, Lothario, Lovelace, Playboy, Rake, Rip, Roué, Wencher, Wolf

Liberty Bail, Civil, Discretion, Franchise, Freedom, Hall, Latitude, Mill, Sauce

Library, Librarian Bibliothecary, BL, Bodleian, Bookmobile, British, Chartered, Circulating, Copyright, Cottonian, Film, Gene, Genomic, Harleian, Laurentian, Lending, Mazarin, Mobile, Morgue, PL, Public, Radcliffe, Reference, Rental, Subscription, Tauchnitz

Librettist Boito, Gilbert, Hammerstein, Lyricist

▶ **Lice** *see* **LOUSE**

Licence, License Abandon, Allow, Authorisation, Carnet, Charter, Dispensation, Driving, Enable, Exequatur, Fling, Franchise, Free(dom), Gale, Import, Imprimatur, Indult, → **LATITUDE**, Let, Marriage, Occasional, Passport, → **PERMIT**, Poetic, Pratique, Provisional, Road-fund, Rope, Slang, Special, Table, Ticket of leave

Licentious Artistic, Corinthian, Debauchee, Hot, Immoral, Large, Lax, Liberal, Loose, Prurient, Ribald, Sensual, Wanton

Lichen Apothecia, Archil, Corkir, Crotal, Crottle, Cup, Epiphyte, Epiphytic, Graphis, Korkir, Lecanora, Litmus, Moss, Orchel, Orchil(la), Orcine, Orseille, Parella, Parelle, Roccella, Rock tripe, Sea-ivory, Stone-rag, Stone-raw, Tree-moss, Usnea, Wartwort

Lick(ing) Bat, Beat, Deer, Felch, Lambent, Lap, Leather, Rate, Salt, Slake, Speed, Tongue, Whip

▶ **Licorice** *see* **LIQUORICE**

Lid Cover, Hat, Kid, Maximum, Opercula, Screwtop, Twist-off

Liddell Alice

Lido Beach, Pool

Lie(s), Liar, Lying Abed, Accubation, Accumbent, Ananias, Bam, Bare-faced, Bask, Billy, Bounce(r), Braide, Cau(l)ker, Cellier, Clipe, Clype, Concoction, Contour, Couchant, Cracker, Cram(mer), Cretism, Cumbent, Deception, Decubitous, Decumbent, Direct, Doggo, Fable, False(r), Falsehood, Falsify, Falsity, Fib, Fiction, Figment, Flam, Gag, Gonk, Hori, Incumbent, Invention, Inveracity, Kip, Lair, Leasing, Lee(ar), Lig(ge), Lurk, Mythomania, Nestle, Obreption, Oner, Perjury, Plumper, Porky (pie), Procumbent, Prone, Prostrate, Pseudologia, Recline, Recumbent, Repent, Repose, Reptant, Ride, Romance(r), Sham, Sleep, Strapper, Stretcher, Supine, Swinger, Tale, Tappice, Tar(r)adiddle, Thumper, Tissue, Try, Untruth, Whacker, Whid, White, Whopper, Yanker

Lied Art-song, Song

Lie-detector Polygraph

Lien Mortgage, Title

Lieu Locus, Place

Lieutenant Cassio, Flag, Loot, Lt, No 1, Sub(altern)

Life Age, Animation, Being, Bio, Biog(raphy), Brian, Brio, C'est la vie, Chaim, Clerihew, CV, Energy, Esse, Eva, Eve, Existence, Good, Heart, High, Mean, Memoir, Mortal coil, Nellie, Nelly, Night, Pep, Plasma, Private, Real, Riley, Shelf, Span, Spirit, Still, Subsistence, Time, True, Useful, Vita, Zoe

Life-blood Essence, Lethee

Lifeboat Ark

Life-cell Energid

Life-cycle Redia

Life-force, Life-style Chi, Mana, Port, Qi

Lifeguard Cheesemonger

Lifeless(ness) Abiosis, Algidity, Amort, Arid, Azoic, Barren, Catatonic, Cauldrife, → **DEAD**, Dull, Flat, Inanimate, Inert, Key-cold, Log, Mineral, Possum, Sterile, Stonen, Wooden

Lifelike Breathing, Speaking

Lifeline Umbilicus

Life-rent Usufruct

Life-saver Lineman, Mae West, Preserver, Raft, Reelman

Lift(ed), Lifter, Lifting Arayse, Arsis, Attollent, Bone, Cable-car, Camel, Chair, Cly, Copy, Crane, Davit, Dead, Dumb waiter, Elate, Elevator, Enhance, Extol, Filch, Fillip, Fireman's, Heave, Heeze, Heezie, Heft(e), Heist, Hitch, Hoise, Hoist, Hove, Jack, Jigger, Kleptomania, Leaven, Lefte, Lever, Lewis, Nab, Nap, Otis®, Paternoster, Pilfer, Press, Pulley, → **RAISE**, Ride, Scoop, Ski, Sky, Snatch, Spout, Stair, Steal, T-bar, Teagle, Theft, Thumb, Topping, Up, Winch, Windlass

Ligament Annular, Cruciate, Fr(a)enum, Paxwax, Peacock-stone, Spring, Suspensory, Tendon, Urachus

Ligation, Ligature Aesc, Ash, Bandage, Bind, Funicle, Tubal

▷ **Light** *may indicate an anagram*

Light(en), Lighting, Lighter, Lights Aerate, Afterglow, Airy, Albedo, Ale, Alow, Alpenglow, Amber, Ancient, Ans(wer), Arc, Aurora, Back-up, Barge, Batement, Batswing, Beacon, Beam, Bengal, Beshine, Bezel, Birlinn, Bleach, Brake, Breezy, Bude, Bulb, Calcium, Candle, Cannel, Casco, Casement, Chiaroscuro, Cierge, Clue, Courtesy, Day, Dewali, Diffused, Direct, Diwali, Dormer, Dream-hole, Drop, Drummond, Earth-shine, Eddystone, Electrolier, Ethereal, Fairy, Fall, Fan, Fantastic, Fastnet, Fetch-candle, Fidibus, Fill, Filter, Fire, First, Fixed, Flambeau, Flame, Flare, Flax(y), Flicker, Flippant, Flit(t), Floating, Flood, Fluorescent, Fog (lamp), Frothy, Fuffy, Gas-poker, Gegenschein, Gleam, Glim(mer), Glow, Gossamer, Green, Guiding, Gurney, Haggis, Hazard, Head, House, Idiot, Ignite, Illum(in) e, Incandescence, Indirect, Induction, Inner, Irradiate, Junior, Keel, Key, Kindle, Kiran, Klieg, Lamp, Lampion, Land, Lantern, Lanthorn, Laser, Leading, LED, Leerie, Leggiero, Levigate, Lime, Link, Linstock, Loadstar, Lobuli, Lodestar, Lozen, Lucarne, Lucigen, Luminaire, Lumine, Luminescence, Luminous, Lunt, Lustre, Lux, Mandorla, Match, Mercurial, Merry-dancers, Mithra(s), Moon, Naphtha, Navigate, Navigation, Neon, New, Nit, Northern, Obstruction, Od(yl), Offal, Optics, Pale, Pane, Parhelion, Pavement, Pennyweight, Phosphene, Phosphorescence, Phot, Photon, Photosphere, Pilot, Pipe, Polar, Pontoon, Portable, Pra(a)m, Producer-gas, Range, Rear, Red, Reflex, Relieve, Relume, Rembrandt, Reversing, Riding, Rocket, Running, Rush, Safe(ty), Satori, Scoop, Sea-dog, Search, Shine, Shy, Solid-state, Southern, Southern-vigil, Spill, Spot, Spry, Steaming, Strip, Strobe,

Stroboscope, Subtle, Sun, Sunshine, Suttle, Svelte, Tail, Tally, Taper, Taps, Tead, Threshold, Tind, Tine, Torch, Torchère, Touchpaper, Traffic, Trivial, Ultraviolet, Unchaste, Unoppressive, UV, Ver(e)y, Vesica, Vesta, Vigil, Watch, Wax, Welsbach burner, White, Windock, Window, Winnock, Zippo, Zodiacal

Light-hearted Gay

Lighthouse Beacon, Caisson, Eddystone, Fanal, Fastnet, Phare, Pharos, Sea-mark, Signal

Lightless Aphotic, Dark, Obscure, Unlit

Lightness Buoyancy, Galant, Levity, Pallor

Lightning Ball, Bolt, Catequil, Chain, Dry, Éclair, Enfouldered, Fireball, Fire flag, Forked, Fulmination, Heat, Levin, Sheet, Thunderbolt, Wildfire, Zigzag

Lightship Floating beacon, Nore

Lightweight Jack straw, Nobody, Oz, Trivial

Lignite Jet, Surtarbrand, Surturbrand

Like(ness), Liking À la, Analogon, As, Broo, Care, Corpse, Dig, Duplicate, Effigy, Eg, Egal, Enjoy, Equal, Fancy, Fellow, Guise, Lich, Palate, Parallel, Peas, Penchant, -philus, Please, Predilection, Semblant, Shine, Similar, Simile, Simulacrum, Smaak, Sort, Speaking, Taste, Tiki, Uniformity

Likely, Likelihood Apt, Fair, Maximum, Odds-on, Offchance, On, Plausible, Possible, Probable, Probit, Prone, Prospective

Likewise Also, Ditto, Do, Egally, Eke, Item, So, Too, Tu quoque

Lilac French, Laylock, Mauve, Pipe-tree, Syringa

Lilliputian Minute

Lilt Swing

Lily African, Agapanthus, Aloe, Amaryllis, Annunciation, Arum, Asphodel, Aspidistra, Belladonna, Blackberry, Calla, Camas(h), Camass, Canada, Candock, Chincherinchee, Colchicum, Colocasia, Convallaria, Corn, Crinum, Dale, Day, Easter, Elaine, Endogen, Fawn, Fleur de lys, Fritillary, Funkia, Galtonia, Guernsey, Haemanthus, Hellebore, Hemerocallis, Herb-Paris, Jacobean, Jacob's, Jersey, Kniphofia, Laguna, Lent, Leopard, Lote, Lotos, Lotus, Madonna, Mariposa, Martagon, Meadow, Moorva, Mount Cook, Nelumbo, Nenuphar, Nerine, Nuphar, Nymphaea, Orange, Padma, Phormium, Pig, Plantain, Pond, Quamash, Regal, Richardia, Sabadilla, Sansevieria, Sarsa, Scilla, Sego, Skunk cabbage, Smilax, Solomon's seal, Spider, Star of Bethlehem, Stone, Sword, Tiger, Trillium, Tritoma, Tuberose, Turk's cap, Vellozia, Victoria, Water, Water maize, Yucca, Zephyr

Lily-maid Elaine

Lima Sugar bean

Limb Arm, Bough, Branch, Crural, Exapod, Flipper, Hindleg, Imp, Leg, Leg-end, Member, Phantom, Proleg, Pterygium, Ramus, Scion, Shin, Spald, Spall, Spaul(d), Wing

Limbless Amelia

Limbo Bardo, Isolation

Lime Bass(wood), Beton, Calc, Calcicolous, Caustic, Lind(en), Malm, Mortar, Slaked, Soda, Teil, Tilia, Trap, Unslaked, Viscum, Whitewash

Limerick Doggerel, Twiner, Verse

Limestone Burren, Calc-sinter, Calm, Calp, Ca(u)m, Clint, Coquina, Coral Rag, Cornbrash, Cornstone, Forest Marble, Grike, Karst, Kentish rag, Kunkar, Kunkur, Landscape marble, Magnesian, Marble, Muschelkalk, Oolite, Pisolite, Rottenstone, Scaglia, Stalagma, Stinkstone, Travertin(e)

Limey Rooinek

▷ **Limit** *may indicate* 'surrounding'

Limit(ation), Limited, Limiting Ambit, Asymptote, Bind, Border, Borné, Bound,
Bourn(e), Brink, Cap, Cash, Ceiling, Chandrasekhar, Circumscribe, Climax,
Compass, Confine, Constrict, Curb, Deadline, Define, Demark, Determine, Earshot,
Eddington, Edge, End, Entail, Esoteric, → **EXTENT**, Extreme, Finite, Frontier, Gate,
Goal, Gole, Hourlong, Impound, Induciae, Insular, Limes, Line, Lite, Lynchet,
March, Maximum, Meare, Mete, Minimum, Nth, Outedge, Pale, Parameter,
Perimeter, Periphery, Predetermine, Qualify, Range, Rate-cap, Ration, Reservation,
Restrict, Rim, Roche, Roof, Scant, Shoestring, Sky, Speed, Stint, String, Sumptuary,
Tail(lie), Tailye, Tailzie, Term(inus), Tether, Three-mile, Threshold, Thule, Tie,
Time, Tropic, Twelve-mile, Utmost, Utter, Verge

Limner RA

Limousine Daimler, Rolls, Stretch, Zil

Limp Claudication, Dot, Droopy, Flabby, Flaccid, Flaggy, Flimsy, Floppy, Hamble,
Hilch, Hirple, Hitch, Hobble, Hop, Lank, Lifeless, Spancel, Tangle

Limpet Keyhole, Patella, Slipper, Streptoneura

Limpid Clear, Lucid, Pure

Linch Terrace

Lincoln(shire) Abe, Poacher, Yellow-belly

Linden Baucis, Lime, Tilia

Line(d), Lines, Lining Abreast, Aclinic, Agate, Agonic, Allan, Anacreontic,
→ **ANCESTRY**, Anent, Angle, Apothem, Arew, Asclepiadean, Assembly, Asymptote,
Attention, Axis, Babbitt, Bakerloo, Bar, Barcode, Baton, Battle, Baulk, Becket,
Bikini, Bluebell, Bob, Body, Bombast, Bottom, Boundary, BR, Brail, Branch,
Bread, Building, Bush, By, Canal, Carolingian, Carriage, Casing, Cathetus,
Cell, Cento, Ceriph, Chord, Ciel, Clew, Club, Coach, Coffle, Colour, Column,
Command, Contour, Cord(on), Coseismal, Course, Crease, Credit, Crib, Crocodile,
Crowfoot, Crow's feet, Cunard, Curve, Cushion, Dancette, Danger, Date, Datum,
Dead-ball, Delay, Descent, DEW, Diagonal, Diameter, Diffusion, Directrix, Distaff,
Dochmiachal, Dotted, Doublure, Downhaul, Downrigger, Dress, Dynasty, Earing,
El, E-la-mi, Encase, Equator, Equinoctial, Equinox, Faint, Fall(s), Fathom, Fault,
Feint, Fess(e), Fettle, File, Finishing, Firing, Firn, Flex, Flight, Frame, Fraunhofer,
Front, Frontier, Frost, Furr(ow), Geodesic, Geotherm, Germ, Gimp, Giron, Goal,
Graph, Grass, Green, Gridiron, Gymp, Gyron, Hachure, Halyard, Hard, Hatching,
Hawser, Header, Hemistich, Heptameter, Hexameter, Hexapody, High-watermark,
Hindenburg, Hockey, Hogscore, Hot, House, Impot, Inbounds, Inbred, Incase,
Inhaul(er), Insole, Interfluve, Intima, Isallobar, Isentrope, Isobar, Isobath,
Isobront, Isocheim, Isochime, Isochron(e), Isoclude, Isocryme, Isogloss, Isogonal,
Isogram, Isohel, Isohyet, Isolex, Isomagnetic, Isometric, Isonome, Isopach(yte),
Isophone, Isophote, Isopiestic, Isopleth, Isopyenal, Isotach, Isothere, Isotherm,
Kill, Knittle, L, Land, Lane, Lansker, Lap, Lariat, Lateral, Latitude, Lead, Leash,
Le(d)ger, Ley, Lie, Ling, LMS, Load, Log, Longitude, Lossy, Loxodrome, Lubber,
Lugger, Lye, Macron, Maginot, Main, Mainsheet, Mark, Marriage, Mason-Dixon,
Median, Meridian, Mesal, Metropolitan, Miurus, Monorail, Multiplet, Naman,
Nazca, Nidation, Noose, Norsel, Northern, Number, Oche, Octastichon, Ode,
Oder-Neisse, Og(h)am, Omentum, Onedin, Ordinate, Orphan, Orthostichy, Painter,
Panty, Parallel, Parameter, Parastichy, Party, Paternoster, Path, Penalty, Pencil,
Phalanx, Picket, Pinstripe, Plasterboard, Pleuron, Plimsoll, Plumb, Poetastery,
Police, Policy, Popping-crease, Poverty, Power, Princess, Product(ion), Profession,
Punch, Pure, Queue, Race, Radial, Radius, Rail, Rank, Raster, Ratlin(e), Ratling,
Rattlin, Ray, Receiving, Red, Reticle, Retinue, Rew, Rhumb, Ripcord, Rope, Route,
Row, Rugose, Rugous, Rule, Ry, Sarking, Scazon, Score, Scotch, Scrimmage, Script,

Secant, Seperatrix, Serif, Seriph, Service, Set, Shielded, Shore, Shout, Shroud,
Siding, Siegfried, Sield, Sight, Silver, Six-yard, Slur, Snood, Snow, Soft, Solidus,
Sounding, Spectral, Spider, Spilling, Spring, Spunyarn, Squall, SR, Staff, Stance,
Stanza, Starting, Static, Stave, Stean, Steen, Stein, Stem, Stich(os), Stock, Story,
Strap, Streak, Striate, String, Stripe, Stuff, Subtense, Swap, Swifter, Symphysis,
Syzygy, Tag, Tailback, Talweg, Tangent, Teagle, Tea lead, Terminator, Tetrameter,
Thalweg, Thin blue, Thin red, Thread, Throwaway, Tidemark, Tie, Tiercet, Timber,
Touch, Trade, Transmission, Transoceanic, Transversal, Tree, Trimeter, Tropic,
Trot, Trunk, Try, Tudor, Twenty-five, Twenty-two, Upstroke, Variety, Verse,
Vinculum, Virgule, Wad, Wallace's, Washing, Water(shed), White, Widow, Wire,
World, Wrinkle, Yellow, Zag, Zip, Zollner's

Lineage Ancestry, Descent, Extraction, Filiation, Parage, Pedigree

Linen Amice, Amis, Barb, Bed, Byssus, Cambric, Crash, Damask, Dornick, Dowlas,
Ecru, Flax, Harn, Huckaback, Inkle, Lawn, Line, Lint, Lockram, Moygashel, Napery,
Percale, Seersucker, Sendal, Silesia, Snow, Table, Toile, Undies

Liner Artist, Bin-bag, Eye, Ocean greyhound, RMS, Ship, Sleeve, Steamer, Steen,
Titanic

Linesman Parodist, → **POET**, Touch-judge

Linger(ing) Chronic, Dawdle, Dwell, Hang, Hove(r), Lag, Loaf, → **LOITER**, Straggle,
Tarry, Tie

Lingerie Bra, Drawers, Undies

Lingo Argot, Bat, Cant, Jargon, Polglish, Speech

Linguist(ic), Linguistics Clitic, Comparative, Descriptive, Glottic, Historical,
Philological, Phonemics, Polyglot, Pragmatics, Semantics, Structural, Stylistics,
Syntax, Tagmemics, Taxeme

Liniment Balm, Camphor, Carron-oil, Embrocation, Ointment, Opodeldoc, Salve

Link(ed), Linking, Links Associate, Between, Bond, Bridge, Chain, Cleek,
Colligate, Concatenation, Connect, Copula, Couple, Course, Cross-reference, Cuff,
Desmid, Drag, Ess, Flambeau, Golf, Hookup, Hot, Hotline, Incatenation, Index,
Interconnect, Interface, Internet, Interrelation, Intertwine, Karabiner, Krab, Liaise,
Machair, Missing, Modem, Nexus, On-line, Pons, Preposition, Relate, Tead(e),
→ **TIE**, Tie-in, Tie-line, Torch, Unite, Weakest, Yoke

Linkman Lamplighter, Mediator

Linnet Finch, Lintie, Lintwhite, Twite

Linoleum Waxcloth

Lint Charpie, Dossil

Lintel Summer, Transom

Lion(ess) Androcles, Aphid, Aslan, Chindit, Elsa, Glitterati, Hero, Leo, Maned,
Mountain, Nemean, Opinicus, Personage, Pride, Simba

Lionel Trilling

Lion-tamer Androcles, Dan(iel)

Lip(py), Lips Beestung, Cheek, Cupid's bow, Fat, Fipple, Flews, Hare, Helmet, Jib,
Labellum, Labiate, Labret, Labrum, Ligula, Muffle, Philtrum, → **RIM**, Rubies, Sass,
Sauce, Slack-jaw, Spout, Submentum

Lipase Steapsin

Lipid Inositol

Lipstick Chapstick

Liquefy Deliquesce, Dissolve, Fuse, Melt

Liqueur, Liquor Abisante, Absinthe, Advokaat, Aguardiente, Ale, Almondrado,
Amaretto, Anise, Anisette, Apry, Benedictine, Bree, Brew, Broo, Broth, Calvados,
Cassis, Cerise, Chartreuse, Chasse, Cherry brandy, Cherry Marnier®, Cher-suisse,

Chicha, Choclair, Chococo, Cocoribe, Cointreau®, Creature, Crème, Crème de cacao, Crème de menthe, Curaçao, Drambuie®, Eau des creoles, Elixir, Enzian, Feni, Fenny, Fraises, Framboise, Fumet, Fustian, Galliano, Geropiga, Grand Marnier®, Hogan, Hogan-mogen, Hogen, Hooch, John Barleycorn, Jungle juice, Kahlua®, Kaoliang, Kir, Kirschwasser, Kirsh(wasser), Kummel, Lager, Lap, Limoncello, Malt, Maraschino, Mastic, Metheglin, Mickey Finn, Midori®, Mirabelle, Mobbie, Mobby, Mother, Noyau, Oedema, Ooze, Ouzo, Parfait d'amour, Pasha, Pastis, Pernod®, Persico, Pot, Potation, Pousse-café, Prunelle, Rakee, Raki, Ratafia, Roiano, Roncoco, Rose, Rotgut, Rum, Rum shrub, Sabra, Sambuca, Samshoo, Schnapps, Sciarada, Shypoo, Skink, Stingo, Stock, Stout, Strega®, Strunt, Stuff, Supernaculum, Tape, Taplash, Tequila, Tia Maria®, Tickle-brain, Tiff, Triple sec, Van der Hum®, White lightning, Wine, Witblits, Wort

Liquid(ate), Liquidity, Liquids, Liquefaction Acetal, Amortise, Annihilate, Apprize, Aqua-regia, Azeotrope, Bittern, Bouillon, Bromine, Butanal, Butanol, Butyraldehide, Butyrin, Cacodyl, Cadaverine, Cash, Cash flow, Chloramine, Cinerin, Clyster, Court-bouillon, Creosol, Creosote, Decoction, Dispersant, Dope, Eluate, Erase, Ethanol, Ether, Eucalyptol, Eugenol, Flow, Fluid, Fural, Furfural, Furol, Halothene, Isoprene, Jaw, Kakodyl, Lewisite, Limonene, Linalool, Lye, Massacre, Mess, Minim, Mouillé, Nebula, Picamar, Pipe, Potion, Protoplasm, PSL, Ptisan, Pyrrole, Pyrrolidine, Quinoline, Raffinate, Rhigolene, Safrole, Semen, Serum, Solution, Solvent, Syrup, Terebene, Thixotropy, Titer, Titre, Tuberculin, Tusche, Ullage, Verjuice, Whey, Wind up, Wort

Liquorice Indian, Jequirity, Nail, Nail-rod, Pomfret, Pontefract-cake, Spanish juice, Sugarallie, Sugarally, Wild

Lis Iris, Lily

Lisa Mona

Lisp(er) Ephraimite, Sibilance

Lissom(e) Agile, Lithe, Nimble, Svelte

▷ **List** *may indicate* 'listen'

List(s), Listing A, Active, Agenda, Antibarbarus, Appendix, Army, Atilt, B, Barocco, Barrace, Bead-roll, Bibliography, British, Canon, Cant, Catalog(ue), Categorise, Catelog, Cause, Check, Choice, Civil, Class, Compile, Credits, Danger, Debrett, Docket, Empanel, Entry, Enumerate, Front, Glossary, Hark, Hearken, Heel, Hit, Hit-parade, Honours, Index, Indian, Interdiction, Inventory, Itemise, Laundry, Lean, Leet, Line-up, Linked, Litany, Lloyds, Mailing, Manifest, Menu, Navy, Notitia, Official, Panel, Paradigm, Party, Price, Prize, Register, Repertoire, Reserved, Retired, Roin, Roll, Roon, Roster, Rota, Rund, Schedule, Script, Short, Sick, Slate, Slope, Strip, Syllabus (of Errors), Table, Tariff, Tick, Ticket, Tilt, Timetable, Tip, Transfer, Union, Waiting, Waybill, White, Wine, Wish

Listen(er) Attend, Auditor, Auscultate, Bug, Ear, Eavesdropper, Gobemouche, Hark, → **HEED**, Lithe, Lug, Monitor, Oyez, Simon, Sithee, Wire-tap, Yo-ho(-ho)

▷ **Listen to** *may indicate* a word sounding like another

Lister Plough, Surgeon

Listless(ness) Abulia, Accidie, Acedia, Apathetic, Atony, Dawney, Draggy, Inanition, Indolent, Lackadaisical, Languor, Mooning, Mope, Mopus, Sloth, Thowless, Torpor, Upsitting, Waff

Lit Alight, Landed

▷ **Lit** *may indicate* an anagram

Litany Eirenicon, Lesser, Procession, Synapte

Literacy Emotional

Literal(ly), Literal sense Etymon, Misprint, Simply, Typo, Verbatim

Literary Academic, Bas bleu, Booksie, Erudite, Lettered
Literary girls Althea, Jenny, Maud, Pippa
Literature Belles lettres, Comparative, Corpus, Fiction, Gongorism, Hagiology, Midrash, Musar, Page, Picaresque, Polite, Prose, Responsa, Samizdat, Splatterpunk, Wisdom
Lithe Flexible, Limber, Pliant, Souple, → **SUPPLE**, Svelte, Willowy
Lithium Li
Litigant Barrator, John-a-Nokes, John-a-Stiles, John Doe, Party, Richard Roe, Suer, Suitor
Litmus Indicator, Lacmus, Lichen, Turnsole
Litre L
Litter Bed, Brancard, Brood, Cacolet, Cat, Cubs, Debris, Deep, Doolie, Duff, Emu-bob, Farrow, Jampan, Kago, Kajawah, Kindle, Mahmal, Mor, Nest, Norimon, Palankeen, Palanquin, Palkee, Palki, Pup, → **REFUSE**, Scrap, Sedan, Stretcher, Sweepings, Team
Little Bagatelle, Billee, Brief, Chota, Curn, Diddy, Dorrit, Drib, Drop, Fewtrils, Ickle, Insect, Iota, John, Jot, Leet, Lilliputian, Limited, Lite, Lyte, Means, Mini, Miniscule, Minnow, Minuscule, → **MINUTE**, Modicum, Morceau, Nell, Paltry, Paucity, Paul, Petite, Pink, Pittance, Ronte, Runt, Scant, Scut, Shade, Shoestring, Shred, Shrimp, Slight, Sma', → **SMALL**, Smattering, Smidge(o)n, Smidgin, Some, Soupçon, Spot, Tad, Teensy, Tich, Tiddly, Tine, Titch, Touch, Tyne, Vestige, Wee, Weedy, Whit, Women
Littoral Coast(al)
Liturgical, Liturgy Divine, Doxology, Hallel, Rite, Versicle
Live(d), Livelihood, Living, Liveliness, Lively, Lives Active, Alert, Allegretto, Allegro, Am, Animated, Animation, Animato, Are, AV, Awake, Be, Birkie, Bouncy, Breezy, Brio, Brisk, Cant(y), Capriccio(so), Cheery, Chipper, Chirpy, Cohabit, Con moto, Con spirito, Crouse, Durante vita, → **DWELL**, Dynamic, Ebullient, Entrain, Exist, Exuberant, Feisty, Frisky, Galliard, Gamy, Gay, Giocoso, Gracious, Grig, Hang-out, Hard, High jinks, Hijinks, Hot, Is, Jazz, Kedge, Lad, Lead, Mercurial, Merry, Mouvementé, Outgo, Pacey, Peart, Pep, Piert, Quicksilver, Rackety, Racy, Reside, Rousing, Salt, Saut, Scherzo, Skittish, Smacking, Spiritoso, Spirituel(le), Sprack, Spry, Spunky, Sustenance, Swinging, Vibrant, Vigoroso, Vital, Vitality, Vivace, Vive, Vivo, → **VOLATILE**, Vyvyan, Wick, Zappy, Zingy, Zippy, Zoe
▸ **Livelihood** see **LIVED**
Liver(ish) Foie gras, Hepar, Hepatic(al), Porta, Puce, Resident, Tomalley
Liverpool, Liverpudlian Scouse
Liverwort Gemma-cup, Hepatica, Riccia
Livery(man) Ermine, Flunkeydom, Goldsmith, Skinner, Tiger, Uniform
Livid Blae, Bruised, Cross, → **FURIOUS**, Pale
Living Advowson, Benefice, Biont, Bread, Canonry, Crust, Glebe, Inquiline, Lodging, Quick, Resident, Simony, Subsistence, Symbiotic, Vicarage, Vital
Livingstone Doctor, Ken
Liza, Lizzie Bess, Betty, Flivver, Hexam, Tin
Lizard Abas, Agama, American chameleon, Amphisbaena, Anguis, Anole, Basilisk, Bearded, Bearded-dragon, Blindworm, Blue-tongued, Brontosaurus, Chameleon, Chuckwalla, Dinosaur, Draco, Dragon, Eft, Evet, Fence, Flying, Frilled, Frill-necked, Galliwasp, Gecko(ne), Gila, Gila monster, Glass snake, Goanna, Gotcha, Guana, Hatteria, Hellbender, Horned, Iguana, Jew, Kabaragoya, Komodo (dragon), Lacerta, Legua(a)n, Lounge, Malayan monitor, Mastigure, Menopome, Mokomoko, Moloch, Monitor, Mosasaur(us), Mountain devil, Newt, Ngarara, Perentie, Perenty,

Reptile, Rock, Sand, Sauria, Scincoid, Seps, Skink, Slow-worm, Snake, Sphenodon, Stellio(n), Sungazer, Swift, Tegu(exin), Thorny devil, Tokay, Tuatara, Tuatera, Varan, Wall, Whiptail, Worm, Worral, Worrel, Zandoli, Zonure

Llama Alpaca, Alpaco, Cria, Guanaco, Huanaco, Paco, Vicuña

Load(ed), Loader, Loading, Loads Accommodation, Affluent, Back-end, Ballast, Base, Boot-strap, Boozy, Burden, Cargo, Charge, Cobblers, Dead weight, Disc, Dope, Drunk, Dummy, Fardel, Fother, Frau(gh)tage, Freight, Front-end, Fulham, Full, Gestant, Glyc(a)emic, Heap, Input, Jag, Lade, Lard, Last, Live, Onus, Pack, Packet, Pay, Peak, Power, Prime, Rich, Seam, Shipment, Shoal, Some, Span, Super, Surcharge, → **TIGHT**, Tipsy, Tod, Traction, Ultimate, Useful, Wealthy, Weight, Wharfinger, Wing

Loaf(er), Loaves Baguette, Barmbrack, Batch, Baton, Beachbum, Beachcomber, Bloomer, Bludge, Bonce, Boule, Brick, Bum, Bu(r)ster, Cad, Cob, Coburg, Cottage, Currant, Danish, Farmhouse, French stick, Hawm, Head, Hoe-cake, Idle, → **LAZE**, Long tin, Lusk, Manchet, Miche, Milk, Mouch, Pan, Pan(h)agia, Plait, Quartern, Roll, Roti, Shewbread, Showbread, Slosh, Split tin, Square tin, Stotty, Sugar, Tin, Vantage, Vienna, Yob

Loam Clay, Loess, Loss, Malm

Loan(s) Advance, Balloon, Benevolence, Bottomry, Bridging, Call, Consolidation, Debenture, Demand, Droplock, Imprest, Lane, Mutuum, Omnium, Out, Prest, Respondentia, Roll-over, Soft, Start-up, Sub, Time, Top-up, War

Loathe, Loathing, Loathsome Abhor(rent), Abominate, Carrion, Detest, Hate, Keck, Nauseate, Odious, Scunner, Ug(h)

Lob Loft, Sky, Underarm

Lobby Demo, Division, Entry, Foyer, Gun, Hall, Press, Urge

Lobe(d) Anisocercal, Fluke, Frontal, Glossa, Insula, Jugum, Lacinia, Lap, Occipital, Optic, Palmate, Parietal, Pinnule, Prostomium, Runcinate, Segment, Temporal, Uvula, Vermis

Lobster Cock, Crawfish, Crayfish, Crustacean, Decapoda, Langouste, Macrura, Newburg, Norway, Pot, Rock, Scampo, Spiny, Squat, Thermidor, Tomalley

▷ **Local** *may indicate* a dialect word

Local(ity) Area, Bro, Close, Des(h)i, Endemic, Home, Inn, Insider, Landlord, Native, Near, Nearby, Neighbourhood, Number, Parochial, Pub, Regional, Resident, Swadishi, Tavern, Topical, Vernacular, Vicinal

Locale Scene, Site

Locate(d), Location Address, Connect, Echo, Find, Fix, Lay, Milieu, Node, Pinpoint, Place, Placement, Plant, Put, Recess, Sat, Set-up, Site, Situate, Situation, Sofar, Spot, Theatre, Trace, Ubiety, Website, Where, Zone

Loch, Lough Allen, Ashie, Awe, Derg, Earn, Eil, Erne, Etive, Fine, Gare, Garten, Holy, Hourn, Katrine, → **LAKE**, Larne, Leven, Linnhe, Lomond, Long, Moidart, Morar, More, Nakeel, Neagh, Ness, Rannoch, Ryan, Shiel, Strangford, Tay, Torridon

Lock(ing), Locker, Locks, Lock up Bar, Barnet, Bolt, Canal, Central, Chain, Chubb®, Clinch, Combination, Cowlick, Curlicue, Davy Jones, Deadbolt, Detent, Drop, Fastener, Fermentation, Foretop, Gate, Haffet, Haffit, Handcuff, Hasp, Hold, Intern, Key, Latch, Lazaretto, Man, Mane, Mortise, Percussion, Prison, Quiff, Ragbolt, Rim, Ringlet, Safety, Sasse, Scalp, Scissors, → **SECURE**, Sluice, Snap, Spring, Sta(u)nch, Staircase, Stock, Strand, Tag, Talon, Tetanus, Time, Trap, Tress, Tuft, Tumbler, Vapour, Villus, Ward, Wheel, Wrestle, Yale®

Locket Lucy

Lockjaw Tetanus, Trismus

Locksmith Garret-master, Hairdresser

Locomotive Banker, Bogie, Bul(l)gine, Engine, Iron horse, Mobile, Mogul, Rocket, Steam, Steamer, Train

Locum Deputy, Relief, Stand-in, Stopgap

Locus Centrode, Horopter, Lemniscate, Place, Spot

Locust, Locust tree Anime, Carob, Cicada, Hopper, Nymph, Robinia, Seventeen-year, Voetganger

Lode Comstock, Lodge, Mother, Reef, Vein

Lodestone Magnes, Magnet

Lodge(r) Billet, Board(er), Box, Cosher, Deposit, Dig, Doss, Encamp, Entertain, Freemason, Grange, Grove, Guest, Harbour, Host, Inmate, Inquiline, Layer, Lie, Masonic, Nest, Orange, Parasite, PG, Porter's, Put up, Quarter, Rancho, Resident, Room(er), Roomie, Stay, Storehouse, Stow, Sweat, Tenant, Tepee, Wigwam

Lodging(s) Abode, B and B, Chummage, Dharms(h)ala, Diggings, Digs, Dosshouse, Ferm, Grange, Grove, Hospitium, Hostel, Inquiline, Kip, Minshuku, Pad, Padding-ken, Pension, Pied-à-terre, Quarters, Resiant, Rooms, Singleen, Sponging-house, Spunging-house, YHA

Loft(iness), Lofty Aerial, Airy, Arrogant, Attic, Celsitude, Chip, Choir, Exalted, Garret, Grand, Haymow, High, Jube, Lordly, Magniloquent, Noble, Olympian, Pulpitum, Rarefied, Rigging, Rood, Roost, Sky, Sublime, Tallat, Tallet, Tallot

Log(ging) Billet, Black box, Cabin, Chip, Chock, Deadhead, Diarise, Diary, Hack, Key(stroke), Ln, Mantissa, Nap(i)erian, Neper, Patent, Poling, → **RECORD**, Stock, Tachograph, Yule

Logarithm Common, Lod, Mantissa, Nap(i)erian, Natural

Logic(al) Alethic, Analytical, Aristotelian, Boolean, Chop, Cogent, Deontic, Dialectic(s), Distributed, Doxastic, Epistemics, Formal, Fuzzy, Heuristics, Iff, Mathematical, Modal, Organon, Philosophical, Premise, Pusser's, Ramism, Rational(e), Reason, Sane, Sequacious, Shared, Sorites, Syllogism, Symbolic, Tense, Trivium

Logo Brand, Colophon, Motif

Loin(s) Flank, Inguinal, Lisk, Lungie, Lunyie, Reins

Loincloth Dhoti, Lungi, Pareu, Waist-cloth

Loiter(ing) Dally, Dare, Dawdle, Dilatory, Dilly-dally, Idle, Lag, Lallygag, Leng, Lime, → **LINGER**, Lollygag, Mike, Mooch, Mouch, Potter, Saunter, Scamp, Suss, Taigle, Tarry

Lola Dolores

Loll Hawm, Lounge, Sprawl

Lollipop, Lolly Ice pole, Lulibub, Money, Popsicle®, Sucker, Sweetmeat

London(er) 'Arry, Big Smoke, Cockaigne, Cockney, Co(c)kayne, East-ender, Flat-cap, Jack, Port, Roseland, Smoke, Town, Troynovant, Wen

London pride None-so-pretty

Lone(r), Lonely Remote, Rogue, Saddo, Secluded, Sole, Solitary, Unked, Unket, Unkid

Long(er), Longing, Longs Ache, Aitch, Ake, Appetent, Aspire, Brame, Covet, Desire, Die, Earn, Erne, Eternal, Far, Greed, Green, Grein, → **HANKER**, Huey, Hunger, Inveterate, Island, Itch, L, Lanky, Large, Lengthy, Longa, Lust, Macron, Miss, More, → **NO LONGER**, Nostalgia, Option, Pant, Parsec, → **PINE**, Prolix, Sesquipedalian, Side, Sigh, Tall, Thirst, Trews, Weary, Wish, Wist, Yearn, Yen

Long-eared Spicate

Longitude Celestial, Ecliptic, Meridian

Long-lashed Mastigophora(n)

Long live(d) Banzai, Macrobian, Viva, Vive, Zindabad
Longshoreman Hobbler, Hoveller, Wharfinger
Long-sighted(ness) Hypermetropia
Long-suffering Job, Patient, Stoical
Long-tailed Macrural
Long-winded Prolix, Verbose, Wordy
Loo Ajax, Bog, Can, Chapel, Dike, Game, Gents, Jakes, John, Latrine, Privy, Toilet
Loofah Towel gourd
Look(s), Look at After-eye, Air, Aspect, Behold, Belgard, Bonne-mine, Browse, Busk, Butcher's, Butcher's hook, Case, Clock, Close-up, Crane, Daggers, Decko, Deek, Dekko, Ecce, Ecco, Expression, Eye, Eye-glance, Face, Facies, Gander, Gawp, Gaze, Geek, Glance, Glare, Gleam, Gledge, Glimpse, Glom, Glower, Goggle, Good, Grin, Hallo, Hangdog, Hey, Iliad, Inspect, Keek, La, Leer, Lo, Mien, New, Ogle, Old-fashioned, Peek, Peep, Prospect, Ray, Recce, Refer, → **REGARD**, Scan, Scrutinise, Search, See, Seek, Shade, Sheep's eyes, Shufti, Shufty, Spy, Squint, Squiz, Stare, Survey, Toot, V, Vista, Wet
Look-out (man) Cockatoo, Crow's nest, Dixie, Huer, Mirador, Nit, Sangar, Sentinel, Sentry, Spotter, Sungar, Tentie, Toot(er), Watch, Watchtower
▷ **Look silly** *may indicate* an anagram
Loom Beamer, Dobby, Emerge, Impend, Jacquard, Lathe, Menace, Picker, Temple, Threaten, Tower
Loon Diver
Loop(ed), Loophole, Loopy Articulatory, Becket, Bight, Billabong, Bouclé, Carriage, Chink, Closed, Coil, Eyelet, Eyesplice, Fake, Frog, Frontlet, Grom(m)et, Ground, Grummet, Hank, Henle's, Hysteresis, Infinite, Kink, Knop, Lasket, Lippes, Local, Lug, Noose, Oillet, Parral, Parrel, Pearl(-edge), Picot, Prusik, Purl, Scrunchie, Staple, Stirrup, Tab, Terry, Toe, Twist
Loos Anita
Loose(n), Loose woman Absolve, Abstrict, Afloat, Anonyma, Baggage, Bail, Besom, Bike, Bunter, Chippie, Chippy, Clatch, Cocotte, Cutty, Demi-mondaine, Demirep, Demivierge, Desultory, Dissolute, Dissolve, Doxy, Draggletail, Dratchell, Drazel, Ease, Emit, Flipperty-flopperty, Flirt-gill, Floosie, Floozie, Floozy, Floppy, Franion, Free, Gangling, Gay, Hussy, Insecure, Jade, Jay, Jezebel, Lax, Light-heeled, Limp, Loast, Loon, Mob, Mort, Naughty pack, Painted, Pinnace, Profligate, Promiscuous, Quail, Ramp, → **RELAX**, Sandy, Scrubber, Skanky-ho, Slag, Slapper, Slut, Streel, Strumpet, Tart, Tramp, Trull, Ungyve, Unhasp, Unhitch, Unknit, Unknot, Unlace, Unlash, Unleash, Unpin, Unreined, Unscrew, Unthread, Untie, Vague, Waistcoateer, Wappend, Whore
Loot Boodle, Booty, Cragh, Creach, Foray, Haul, Mainour, Peel, Pluck, → **PLUNDER**, Ransack, Rape, Reave, Rieve, Rob, Sack, Smug, Spoils, Spoliate, Swag, Treasure, Waif
Lop Behead, Clop, Curtail, Detruncate, Droop, Shroud, Sned, Trash
Lope Stride
Loquacious Chatty, Gabby, Garrulous, Rambling
Lord(s), Lordship, Lordly Adonai, Ahura Mazda, Anaxandron, Arrogant, Boss, Byron, Cripes, Cyril, Dieu, Domineer, Dominical, Duc, Earl, Elgin, Gad, Gilded Chamber, God, Haw-haw, Herr, Idris, Imperious, Jim, Justice, Kami, Kitchener, Landgrave, Law, Ld, Liege, Lonsdale, Losh, Lud, Mesne, Misrule, Mynheer, Naik, Oda Nobunaga, Omrah, Ordinary, Ormazd, Ormuzd, Palsgrave, Peer, Sea, Seigneur, Seignior, Shaftesbury, Sire, Spiritual, Taverner, Temporal, Tuan, Ullin
Lords and ladies Wake-robin

Lore Cab(b)ala, Edda, Lair, Lare, Riem, Upanis(h)ad

Lorelei Siren

Lorgnette Starers

Lorna Doone

Lorry Artic(ulated), Camion, Carrier, Crummy, Double-bottom, Drag, Drawbar outfit, Flatbed, Juggernaut, Low-loader, Rig, Tipper, Tonner, → **TRUCK**, Wagon

Lose(r) Also-ran, Decrease, Drop, Elude, Forfeit, Hesitater, Leese, Misère, Mislay, Misplace, Nowhere, Spread, Tank, Throw, Tine(r), Tyne, Underdog, Unsuccessful, Waste, Weeper

Loss, Lost Anosmia, Aphesis, Aphonia, Apocope, Apraxia, Astray, Attainder, Boohai, Chord, Cost, Dead, Decrease, Depreciation, Detriment, Disadvantage, Elision, Extinction, Foredamned, Forfeited, Forgotten, Forlorn, Gone, Hurtful, Lore, Lorn, Lurch, Missing, Omission, Outage, Pentimento, Perdition, Perdu, Perished, Preoccupied, Privation, Psilosis, Reliance, Tine, Tinsel, Tint, Toll, Traik, Tribes, Tyne(d), Ullage, Unredeemed, Wastage, Wasted, Will, Write-off, Wull

Loss of memory Amnesia, Black-out, Fugue, Infonesia, Paramnesia

▷ **Lost** *may indicate* an anagram or an obsolete word

Lot(s) Abundant, Amount, Aret(t), Badly, Batch, Boatload, Bomb, Caboodle, Cavel, Chance, Deal, Dole, Doom, Drove, Due, → **FATE**, Fortune, Group, Hantle, Hap, Heaps, Horde, Host, Item, Job, Kevel, Kismet, Lank, Lashings, Legion, Loads, Loadsa, Luck, Manifold, Many, Mass, Moh, Moira, Mony, Mort, Myriad, Oceans, Omnibus, Oodles, Oodlins, Pack, Parcel, Parking, Plenitude, Plenty, Portion, Power, Purim, Raft, Rich, Scads, Set, Sight, Slather, Slew, Slue, Sortilege, Sortition, Stack, Sum, Tall order, The works, Tons, Vole, Wagonload, Weird

Loth Averse, Circumspect, Sweer(t), Sweir(t), Unwilling

Lothario Lady-killer, Libertine, Poodle-faker, Rake, Womaniser

Lotion After-shave, Blackwash, Calamine, Collyrium, Cream, Emollient, Eye-wash, Humectant, Setting, Suntan, Unguent, Wash, Yellow wash

Lottery, Lotto Art union, Ballot, Bingo, Cavel, Draw, Gamble, National, Pakapoo, Pools, Postcode, Punchboard, Raffle, Rollover, Scratchcard, Sweepstake, Tattersall's, Tombola

Lotus (eater), Lotus land Asana, Djerba, Lotophagus, Padmasana, White

Louche Rip

Loud(ness), Loudly Bel, Big, Blaring, Booming, Brassy, Decibel, Ear-splitting, F, FF, Flashy, Forte, Fracas, Full-mouthed, Garish, Gaudy, Glaring, Hammerklavier, High, Lumpkin, Noisy, Orotund, Plangent, Raucous, Roarie, Siren, Sone, Stentor(ian), Strident, Tarty, Vocal, Vociferous, Vulgar

Loudspeaker Action, Boanerges, Bullhorn, Hailer, Megaphone, Squawk box, Stentor, Subwoofer, Tannoy®, Tweeter, Woofer

▶ **Lough** *see* **LOCH**

Louis Baker, Roi

Louisianian Cajun

Lounge(r) Cocktail, Da(c)ker, Daiker, Departure, Hawm, Idle, Laze, Lie, Lizard, Loll, Lollop, Parlour, Paul's man, Sitkamer, Slouch, Sun, Transit

Louse (up), Lousy, Lice Acrawl, Argulus, Bolix, Bollocks, Chat, Chicken, Cootie, Crab, Crummy, Fish, Head, Isopod(a), Kutu, Mallophaga, Nit, Oniscus, Pedicular, Phthiriasis, Plant, Psocoptera, Psylla, Slater, Snot, Sowbug, Sucking, Vermin, Whale

Lout Auf, Clod(hopper), Coof, Cuif, Hallian, Hallion, Hallyon, Hick, Hob, Hobbledehoy, Hooligan, Hoon, Jack, Jake, Keelie, Lager, Larrikin, Litter, Lob(lolly), Loord, Lubber, Lumpkin, Lycra, Oaf, Oik, Rube, Swad, Tout, Tripper, Yahoo, Yob(bo)

Louvre Shutter

Love(d), Lovable, Lover Abelard, Admire, Adore, Adulator, Affection, Agape, Alma, Amabel, Amanda, Amant, Amateur, Ami(e), Amoret, Amoroso, Amour, Angharad, Antony, Ardour, Ariadne, Aroha, Aucassin, Beau, Bidie-in, Blob, Calf, Care, Casanova, Chamberer, Cicisbeo, Concubine, Coquet, Court, Courtly, Cupboard, Cupid, Dear, Dona(h), Dotard, Dote, Doxy, Duck(s), Ducky, Dulcinea, Eloise, Eloper, Emotion, Enamorado, Eros, Esme, Fan, Fancy man, Flame, Frauendienst, Free, Galant, Goose-egg, Greek, Hon(ey), Idolise, Inamorata, Inamorato, Iseult, Isolde, Item, Jo, Kama, Lad, Lancelot, Leander, Leman, Like, Lochinvar, Loe, Loo, Lurve, Man, Nihility, Nil, Nothing, Nought, O, Pairs, Paramour, Pash, Passion, Pet, Philander, -phile, Platonic, Precious, Protestant, Psychodelic, Puppy, Revere, Rhanja, Romance, Romeo, Sapphism, Spooner, Stale, Storge, Suitor, Swain, Thisbe, Tough, Toyboy, Tristan, Troilus, True, Turtle(-dove), Valentine, Venus, Virtu, Woman, Worship, Zeal, Zero

Love-apple Tomato, Wolf's-peach

Love-bite Hickey

Love-child By-blow, Come-by-chance

Love-in-a-mist Nigella

Love letter Capon

Lovely Adorable, Belle, Dishy, Dreamy, Exquisite, Fair, Nasty

Love-making →INTERCOURSE, Kama Sutra, Sex, Snog

Love-sick Smit(ten), Strephon

Loving(ly) Amoroso, Amorous, Fond, Tender

Low(est), Low-born, Low-cut, Lower(ing), Low-key Abase, Abate, Abysmal, Amort, Area, Avail(e), Avale, B, Basal, Base(-born), Bass(o), Beneath, Blue, Caddish, Cartoonist, Cheap, Church, Condescend, Contralto, Cow, Croon, Crude, Darken, Debase, Décolleté, Deepmost, Degrade, Demean, Demit, Demote, Depress, Devalue, Dim, Dip, Dispirited, Doldrums, Drawdown, Drop, Early, Embase, Flat, Foot, Frown, Gazunder, Glare, Guernsey, Gurly, Gutterblood, Hedge, Humble, Ignoble, Imbase, Inferior, Jersey, Laigh, Lallan, Law, Light, Lite, Mass, Mean, Menial, Moo, Mopus, Morose, Nadir, Net, Nether, Nett, Non-U, Ostinato, Paravail, Plebeianise, Profound, Prole, Relegate, Ribald, Rock-bottom, Sad, Scoundrel, Scowl, Secondo, Settle, Shabby, Short, Soft, Stoop, Subordinate, Sudra, Undermost, Unnoble, Unobtrusive, Vail, Vulgar, Weak, Wretched

Lowbrow Philistine

Low country Flanders

Lowdown Gen, Info

▷ **Lower** *may refer to* cattle

Lowland(er) Carse, Gallovidian, Glen, Laigh, Lallans, Merse, Mudflat, Plain, Polder, Sassenach, Vlei

Low-lying Callow, Epigeous, Fens, Inferior, Sump

Low person Boor, Bunter, Cad, Caitiff, Cocktail, Demirep, Ratfink, Snot

Loyal(ty) Adherence, Allegiant, Brand, Brick, Dependable, Esprit de corps, Faithful, Fast, Fidelity, Gungho, Leal, Patriotic, Pia, Stalwart, Staunch, Troth, →**TRUE**, True blue, Trusty

Loyalist Hard core, Paisley, Patriot, Tory

Lozenge Cachou, Catechu, Fusil, Jujube, Mascle, Pastille, Pill, Rhomb, Rustre, Tablet, Troche, Voided

LSD Acid, Money

Lubber(ly), Lubbers Booby, Clod, Clumsy, Gawky, Hulk, Lob, Looby, Oaf, Slowback, Swab, Swads

Lubricant, Lubricate, Lubrication Carap-oil, Coolant, Derv, Fluid, Force-feed, Grease, Oil, Petrolatum, Sebum, Unguent, Vaseline®, Wool-oil

Luce Ged

Lucerne Alfalfa, Medick, Nonsuch

Lucia Mimi

Lucid Bright, Clear, Perspicuous, Sane

Lucifer Devil, Match, Proud, Satan

Luck(y) Amulet, Auspicious, Beginner's, Bonanza, Break, Caduac, Canny, Cess, Chance, Charmed, Chaunce, Daikoku, Dip, Fate, Fluke, → **FORTUNE**, Godsend, Hap, Heather, Hit, Jam(my), Joss, Lady, Lot, Mascot, Mercy, Mozzle, Pot, Prosit, Providential, Pudding-bag, Purple patch, Seal, Seel, Sele, Serendipity, Sess, Sonsie, Sonsy, Spawny, Star(s), Streak, Success, Talisman, Tinny, Tough, Turn-up, Windfall, Worse

Luckless Hapless, Wight

Lucre Money, Pelf, Tin

Lucy Locket

Lud Gad

Luddite Saboteur, Wrecker

Ludicrous Absurd, Bathetic, Bathos, Crackpot, Farcical, Fiasco, Inane, Irish, Jest, Laughable, Risible

Ludo Uckers

Luff Derrick

Lug Ear, Earflap, Sea-worm, Sowle, Tote, Tow

Luggage Bags, Carryon, Cases, Dunnage, Excess, Grip, Hand, Kit, Petara, Samsonite®, Suiter, Traps, Trunk

Luggage-carrier Grid

Lugubrious Dismal, Drear

Luke-warm Laodicean, Lew, Tepid

Lull, Lullaby Berceuse, Calm, Cradlesong, Hushaby, Respite, Rock, Sitzkreig, Soothe, Sopite

Lulu Stunner

Lumbar Hip

Lumber(ing) Clump, Galumph, Jumble, Pawn, Ponderous, Raffle, Saddle, Scamble, Timber

Lumberjack Bushwhacker, Feller, Logger, Logman

Luminance, Luminous, Luminosity, Luminescence Aglow, Arc, Dayglo, Foxfire, Glow, Ignis-fatuus, L, Light, Nit, Phosphorescent, Scintillon, Sea-dog, Wildfire, Will o' the wisp

Lumme Coo, Lor

Lump(y) Aggregate, Bubo, Bud, Bulge, Bur(r), Caruncle, Chuck, Chunk, Clat, Claut, Clod, Clot, Cob, Combine, Dallop, Da(u)d, Dollop, Enhydros, Epulis, Flocculate, Ganglion, Geode, Gnarl, Gob(bet), Goiter, Goitre, Grape, Grip, Hunch, Hunk, Inium, Knarl, Knob, Knub, Knur(r), Knurl, Lob, Lunch, Malleolus, Mass, Mote, Mott, Myxoma, Neuroma, Nibble, Nirl, Node, Nodule, Nodulus, Nub, Nubble, Nugget, Nur(r), Nurl, Osteophyte, Plook, Plouk, Quinsy, Raguly, Sarcoma, Scybalum, Sitfast, Slub, Strophiole, Tragus, Tuber(cle), Wart, Wodge

Lumpsucker Sea-owl

Lunacy, Lunatic Bedlam, Dementia, Demonomania, Folly, Insanity, Mad(ness), Psychosis

Lunar Evection, Mascon, Selenological

Lunatic Moonstruck

▷ **Lunatic** *may indicate* an anagram

Lunch(time) Bait, Crib, Dejeune, Déjeuner, Fork, L, Liquid, Nacket, Nocket, Nuncheon, Packed, Piece, Ploughman, Pm, Power, Tiff(in), Working

Lung(s) Alveoli, Bellows, Coalminer's, Farmer's, Green, Iron, Lights, Pulmo, Pulmonary, Soul

Lung disease Anthracosis, Atelectasis, Byssinosis, Emphysema, Farmer's lung, Pneumoconiosis, Siderosis, Silicosis, Tuberculosis

Lunge Breenge, Breinge, Dive, Soul, Stab, Thrust, Venue

Lungfish Dipnoi(an)

Lupin Arsene

Lurch Reel, Slew, Stoit, Stumble, Swee

Lure Bait, Bribe, Carrot, Decoy, Devon minnow, Entice, Horn, Inveigle, Jig, Judas, Plug, Roper, Spinner, Spoon, Spoonbait, Spoonhook, Squid, Stale, Temptation, Tice, Tole, Toll, Train, Trepan, Wormfly

Lurgi Illness

Lurid Gruesome, Purple

Lurk(ing) Dare, Latitant, Skulk, Slink, Snoke, Snook, Snowk

Lusatia(n) Wend(ic), Wendish

Luscious Succulent

Lush Alcoholic, Alkie, Alky, Dipso(maniac), Drunk, Fertile, Green, Juicy, Lydian, Sot, Succulent, Tosspot, Verdant

Lust(ful), Lusty Cama, Concupiscence, Corflambo, Desire, Eros, Frack, Greed, Kama, Lech(ery), Lewd, Megalomania, Obidicut, Prurience, Radge, Randy, Rank, Raunchy, Salacious, Venereous

Lustre, Lustrous Brilliance, Census, Chatoyant, Galena, Gaum, Gilt, Gloss, Gorm, Inaurate, Lead-glance, Lovelight, Pearly, Pentad, Reflet, Satiny, Schiller, → **SHEEN**, Water

Lute, Lutist Amphion, Chitarrone, Cither, Dichord, Orpharion, Pandora, Pandore, Pipa, Theorbo, Vielle

Lutetium Lu

Lutheran Adiaphorist, Calixtin(e), Pietist, Protestant, Ubiquitarian

Lux Lx

Luxemburg L

Luxuriant, Luxuriate, Luxurious, Luxury (lover) Apician, Bask, Clover, Cockaigne, Cockayne, Comfort, Copious, Delicate, Deluxe, Dolce vita, Extravagant, Exuberant, Fleshpots, Lavish, Lucullan, Lush, Mollitious, Ornate, Pie, Plush, Posh, Rank, → **RICH**, Ritzy, Sumptuous, Sybarite, Wallow

Lycanthropist Werewolf

Lydia Languish

Lye Buck

▶ **Lying** *see* **LIE**

Lymph Chyle

Lymphoma Burkett's

Lynch(ing), Lyncher Dewitt, Hang, Necktie party, Nightrider

Lynx Bay, Bobcat, Caracal, Desert, Rooikat

Lyre Cithern, Harp, Psaltery, Testudo, Trigon

Lyric(s), Lyrical, Lyricist, Lyrist Cavalier, Dit(t), Epode, Gilbert, Hammerstein, Melic, Ode, Orphean, Paean, Pean, Poem, Rhapsodic, Song, Spinto, Words

Mm

M Married, Member, Metre, Mike, Mile, Thousand
Mac Bo, Mino, Scot, Waterproof
Macabre Gothic, Grotesque, Sick
Macaroni Beau, Blood, Cat, Dandy, Elbow, Exquisite, Fop, Jack-a-dandy, Olio, Pasta, Petitmaitre
Macaroon Biscuit, Signal
Macaulay Layman
Mace Club, Nutmeg, Sceptre, Spice
Mace-bearer Beadle, Bedel, Poker
Macedonian Philip, Stagirite, Stagyrite
Machine(ry) Air-engine, Answering, Apparat(us), Appliance, Archimedean screw, Automaton, Bathing, Bulldozer, Burster, Calender, Centrifuge, Churn, Clobbering, Combine harvester, Cycle, Defibrillator, → **DEVICE**, Dialyser, Dredge(r), Drum, Dynamotor, Earth-mover, Emi-scanner®, Engine, Enginery, Excavator, Facsimile, Fax, Fourdrinier, Fruit, Gin, Grader, Haik, Hawk-Eye®, Heck, Hilatory, Hopper, Hot-press, Hummeller, Infernal, Instrument, Jawbreaker, Jukebox, Lathe, Life-support, Linotype®, Linter, Liquidiser, Lithotripter, Loom, Ludlow, Milling, Moulinet, Moviola®, Muckspreader, Mule, Nintendo®, Party, Passimeter, Perfector, Pile-driver, Planer, Plant, Poker, Pokie, Potcher, Press, Processor, Propaganda, Pulper, Pulsator, Robot, Rotavator®, Rototiller, Rowing, Sausage, Seeder, Separator, Sewing, Slasher, Slicer, Slipform paver, Slot, Spin, Spinning jenny, Stenotype®, Symatron, Tape, Teaching, Tedder, Throstle, Time, Transfer, Treadmill, Tumbler, Turbine, Turing, Twin tub, Typewriter, Vending, Virtual, War, Washing, Watersnail, Weighing, Willow, Wimshurst, Wind(mill), Wringer, Zamboni®
Macho Jock, Laddish
Mackerel Albacore, Amber-fish, Brack, Dory, Fish, Horse, Pacific, Pimp, Scad, Scomber, Sky, Spanish, Spotted, Trevally
Mackintosh Burberry®, Mac, Mino, Oilskin, Slicker, Waterproof
Macropus Euro, Wallaroo
Mad(den), Madman, Madness Angry, Balmy, Bananas, Barking, Barmy, Bedlam, Besotted, Bonkers, Crackbrained, Crackpot, Crazy, Cuckoo, Cupcake, Daffy, Delirious, Dement, Dêtraqué, Distract, Dotty, Enrage, Fay, Fey, Folie, Folly, Frantic, Frenetic(al), Fruitcake, Furioso, Fury, Gelt, Gyte, Harpic, Hatter, Idiotic, Incense, Insane, Insanie, Insanity, Into, Ireful, Irritate, Kook, Loco, Lunatic, Lycanthropy, Madbrained, Maenad, Mango, Mania, Mattoid, Mental, Meshug(g)a, Metric, Midsummer, Moonstruck, Motorway, Mullah, Nuts, Porangi, Psycho, Rabid, Rasputin, Raving, Redwood, Redwud, Scatty, Screwy, Short-witted, Starkers, Tonto, Touched, Troppo, Unhinged, Wacko, Wood, Wowf, Wrath, Wud, Xenomania, Yond, Zany
▷ **Mad(den)** *may indicate* an anagram

Madagascan, Madagascar Aye-aye, Hova, Indri, Lemur, Malagash, Malagasy, RM
Madam(e) Baggage, Bawd, Lady, M, Proprietress
Madcap Impulsive, Tearaway
Madder Alizari, Alyari, Chay(a), Gardenia, Genipap, Rose, Rubia, Shaya
Made (it) Built, Did, Fec(it), Ff, Gart, Invented
Madeira Cake
Madge Pie
▷ **Madly** *may indicate* an anagram
Madonna Lady, Lily, Mary, Pietà, Sistine, Virgin
Madras Chennai
Madrigal Ballet, Fala, Song
Maelstrom Voraginous, Vortex, Whirlpool
Maenad Devotee, Fan
Maestro Artist, Toscanini, Virtuoso
Mafia Camorra, Capo, Cosa nostra, Godfather, Goombah, Mob, Ndrangheta,
   Omerta, Padrone, The Mob
Mag Mail
Magazine Arsenal, Clip, Colliers, Contact, Cornhill, Cosmopolitan, Digizine,
   Economist, E-zine, Field, Girlie, Glossy, Granta, Jazz mag, Ladmag, Lady, Lancet,
   Life, Listener, Little, Magnet, New Yorker, Organ, Part work, Periodical, Pictorial,
   Playboy, Powder, Private Eye, Pulp, Punch, She, Skin, Slick, Spectator, Store,
   Strand, Tatler, Time, Vogue, Warehouse, Weekly, Yoof, Zine
Magdalene St Mary
Maggie Rita
Maggot Bot, Flyblow, Gentiles, Gentle, Grub, Larva, Mawk, Myiasis, Whim, Worm
Magi Balthazar, Gaspar, Melchior
Magic(al), Magician, Magic square Archimage, Art, Baetyl, Black, Black art,
   Charm, Circle, Conjury, Diablerie, Diablery, Druid, Enchanting, Faust, Faustus,
   Fetish, Genie, Goetic, Goety, Gramary(e), Grimoire, Hermetic, Houdini, Illusionist,
   Incantation, Makuto, Math, Medea, Merlin, Mojo, Moly, Morgan le Fay, Myal,
   Nasik, Natural, Necromancer, Obeah, Pawaw, Powwow, Prospero, Reim-kenner,
   Rhombus, Shamanism, Sorcery, Sortilege, Spell, Speller, Supernatural,
   Sympathetic, Talisman, Thaumaturgics, Theurgy, Voodoo, Warlock, White,
   Wizard, Zendik
Magistracy, Magistrate Aedile, Amman, Amtman, Archon, Avoyer, Bailie, Bailiff,
   Bailli(e), Beak, Bench, Burgess, Burgomaster, Cadi, Censor, Consul, Corregidor,
   Curule, Demiurge, Doge(ate), Draco, Edile, Effendi, Ephor, Field cornet, Finer,
   Foud, Gonfalonier, JP, Judiciary, Jurat, Justice, Kotwal, Landamman(n), Landdrost,
   Lord Provost, Maire, Mayor, Mittimus, Novus homo, Pilate, Podesta, Portreeve,
   Pr(a)efect, Pr(a)etor, Prior, Proconsul, Propraetor, Provost, Qadi, Quaestor,
   Recorder, Reeve, Shereef, Sherif, Stad(t)holder, Stipendiary, Syndic, Tribune,
   Worship
Magnanimity, Magnanimous Big, Charitable, → **GENEROUS**, Largeness, Lofty,
   Noble
Magnate Baron, Bigwig, Industrialist, Mogul, Onassis, Randlord, Tycoon,
   Vanderbilt, VIP
Magnesia, Magnesium Bitter-earth, Epsomite, Humite, Kainite, Mg, Periclase
Magnet(ic), Magnetism Animal, Artificial, Attraction, Bar, Charisma, Field,
   Gauss, Horseshoe, Induction, It, Loadstone, Lodestone, Maxwell, Od, Oersted,
   Oomph, Permanent, Personal, Polar, Pole, Pole piece, Poloidal, Pull, Remanence,
   Retentivity, Slug, Solenoid, Terrella, Terrestrial, Tesla, Tole, Weber

Magnificence, Magnificent Fine, Gorgeous, Grandeur, Imperial, Laurentian, Lordly, Noble, Pride, Regal, Royal, Splendid, Splendo(u)r, State, Sumptuous, Superb

Magnifier, Magnify(ing) Aggrandise, Augment, Binocle, → **ENLARGE**, Exaggerate, Increase, Loupe, Megaphone, Microscope, Teinoscope, Telescope

Magniloquent Bombastic, Orotund

Magnitude Absolute, Abundance, Amplitude, Apparent, Earthquake, Extent, First, Modulus, Muchness, Photoelectric, Scalar, Size, Visual

Magnolia An(n)ona, Beaver-tree, Champac, Champak, Mississippi, Sweet bay, Umbrella-tree, Yulan

Magpie Bell, Bird, Bishop, Chatterer, Madge, Mag, Margaret, Outer, Pica, Piet, Pyat, Pyet, Pyot

Magus Artist

Magyar Hungarian, Szekei, Szekel(y), Szekler, Ugrian, Ugric

Mahogany Acajou, African, Carapa, Cedrela, Philippine, Wood

Mahommedan Dervish, Shiah

Maid(en) Abigail, Aia, Amah, Biddy, Bonibell, Bonne, Bonnibell, Burd, Chamber, Chloe, Clothes-horse, Damosel, Dell, Dey, Dresser, Femme de chambre, First, Girl, Guillotine, Ignis-fatuus, Imago, Inaugural, Io, Iras, Iron, Lorelei, M, Marian, May, Miss, Nerissa, Nymph, Opening, Over, Parlour, Pucelle, Rhian, Rhine, Skivvy, Soubrette, Suivante, Table, Thestylis, Tirewoman, Tweeny, Valkyrie, Virgin, Walkyrie, Wench, Wicket

Maidenhair Fern, Ginkgo

Mail Air, → **ARMOUR**, Byrnie, Cataphract, Chain, Da(w)k, Direct, E(lectronic), Express, Fan, Gusset, Habergeon, Hate, Hauberk, Helm, Junk, Letter, Media, Metered, Panoply, Pony express, Post, Ring, Send, Snail, Spam, Surface, Tuille(tte), Voice

Mailbag Pouch

Mailboat Packet

Maim Cripple, Impair, Lame, Main, Mayhem, Mutilate, Vuln

Main(s) Atlantic, Brine, Briny, → **CENTRAL**, Chief, Cockfight, Conduit, Essential, Foremost, Gas, Generally, Grid, Gross, Head, → **KEY**, Lead(ing), Major, Pacific, Palmary, Predominant, Prime, Principal, Ring, → **SEA**, Sheer, Spanish, Staple, Water

Mainland Continent, Pomona

Mainstay Backbone, Bastion, Pillar, Support

Maintain(er), Maintenance Alimony, Allege, Ap(p)anage, Argue, Assert, Aver, Avouch, Avoure, Avow, Claim, Contend, Continue, Defend, Escot, Insist, Keep (up), Lengthman, Preserve, Run, Serve, Service, Sustain, Upbear, Uphold, Upkeep

Maize Corn, Hominy, Indian, Indian corn, Mealie, Milo, Popcorn, Samp, Silk, Stamp, Zea

Majestic, Majesty August, Britannic, Dignity, Eagle, Grandeur, Imperial, Maestoso, Olympian, Regal, SM, Sovereign, Stately, Sublime, Tuanku

Major (domo) Barbara, Drum, → **IMPORTANT**, Pipe, PM, Read, Seneschal, Senior, Sergeant, Star, Trumpet, Wig

Majority Absolute, Age, Body, Eighteen, Landslide, Latchkey, Maturity, Moral, Most, Preponderance, Relative, Silent, Working

▷ **Make** *may indicate* an anagram

Make(r), Make do, Making Amass, Brand, Build, Clear, Coerce, Coin, Compel, Compulse, Concoct, Creant, Create, Devise, Earn, Execute, Fabricate, Factive, Fashion, Faute de mieux, Fet(t), Forge, Form, Gar(re), God, Halfpenny, Mail(e),

Manage, Marque, Prepare, Production, Reach, Render, Shape, Sort, Temporise, Wright

Make believe Fantasy, Fictitious, Pretend, Pseudo

Make good Abet, Compensate, Remedy, Succeed, Ulling

Make hay Ted

Make off Bolt, Leg it, Mosey, Run, Scarper

Makeshift Bandaid, Crude, Cutcha, Expedient, Jury, Jury-rigged, Kacha, Kachcha, Kludge, Kutcha, Lash-up, Mackle, Pis-aller, Rude, Stopgap, Timenoguy

Make up Ad lib, Compensate, Compose, Concealer, Constitution, Cosmetics, Fucus, Gaud, Gawd, Gene, Greasepaint, Identikit®, Kohl, Liner, Lipstick, Maquillage, Mascara, Metabolism, Orchel, Paint, Pancake, Panstick, Powder, Reconcile, Rouge, Slap, Tidivate, Titivate, Toiletry, Visagiste, War paint, White-face

Maladroit Awkward, Clumsy, Graceless, Inelegant, Unperfect

Malady Disease, Illness

Malagas(e)y Hova, RM

Malaise Affluenza

Malapropism Catachresis, Slipslop

Malaria Ague, Falciparum, Marsh-fever, Paludism, Tap, Vivax

Malawi(an) Nyanja, Nyasa

Malay(an), Malaysian Austronesian, Bahasa, Bajou, Brunei, Datin, Datuk, D(a)yak, Jawi, Madurese, Moro, Sabahan, Sakai, Tokay, Tuan

Male Alpha, Arrhenotoky, Buck, Bull, Butch, Dog, Ephebe, Ephebus, Gent, Hob, John Doe, Macho, Mansize, Masculine, Ram, Rogue, Spear(side), Stag, Stamened, Telamon, Tom, Worthiest of the blood

Malediction Curse, Cuss, Oath, Slander

Malefactor Criminal, Felon, Villain

Malevolent, Malevolence Evil, Fell, Malign, Pernicious, Venomous

Malformation Teratogenesis

Malfunction Glitch, Hiccup

Mali RMM

Malice, Malicious Bitchy, Catty, Cruel, Despiteous, Envy, Hatchet job, Malevolent, Malign, Narquois, Prepense, Schadenfreude, Serpent, Snide, Spite, Spleen, Venom, Virulent, Vitriol

Malign(ant), Malignity Asperse, Backbite, Baleful, Bespatter, Defame, Denigrate, Evil, Gall, Harm, Hate-rent, Hatred, Libel, Poor-mouth, Sinister, Slander, Spiteful, Swart(h)y, Toxin, Traduce, Vicious, Vilify, Vilipend, Viperous, Virulent

Malinger(er) Dodge, Leadswinger, Scrimshank, Shirk, Skrimshank, Truant

Mall Parade

Mallard Duck, Sord

Malleable Clay, Ductile, Fictile, Pliable

▷ **Malleable** *may indicate* an anagram

Mallet Beetle, Club, Hammer, Mace, Maul, Serving, Stick

Mallow Abutilon, Dwarf, Musk, Sida, Urena

Malodorous Mephitic, Stenchy

Malpractice(s) Sculduggery, Skulduggery

Malt Brewer's grain, Diastase, Grains, Grist, Single, Straik, Wort

Maltese (cross) Falcon, GC

Maltreat Abuse, Harm, Maul, Mishandle, Misuse

Mammal Animal, Anta, Armadillo, Artiodactyl, Bear, Binturong, Bobcat, Cacomistle, Cacomixle, Caracal, Cervid, Cetacean, Chalicothere, Charronia, Chevrotain, Chiropteran, Ciscus, Colugo, Creodont, Dermoptera, Dhole, Dinothere,

Dolphin, Dugong, Echidna, Eutheria, Fisher, Giraffe, Glires, Glutton, Glyptodon, Grison, Guanaco, Hare, Hydrax, Hyrax, Indri, Jaguarondi, Jaguarundi, Kinkajou, Lagomorph, Leporid, Lemur, Linsang, Loris, Lynx, Manatee, Margay, Marten, Meerkat, Metatherian, Mongoose, Monodelphia, Monotreme, Musteline, Notocingulate, Numbat, Olungo, Otter, Pachyderm, Pangolin, Peba, Peccary, Pekan, Perissodactyl, Pika, Pine marten, Pinniped, Pipistrelle, Platypus, Polecat, Porpoise, Primate, Pronghorn, Prototherian, Pudu, Raccoon, Rasse, Ratel, Rhytina, Sable, Saola, Serval, Shrew, Sirenian, Skunk, Sloth, Solenodon, Springhaas, Stegodon(t), Taguan, Tahr, Takin, Tamandu(a), Tanrec, Tapir, Tayra, Teledu, Tenrec, Theria(n), Titanothere, Tylopod, Uintathere, Vicuña, Viverrid, Weasel, Whale, Wolverine, Zorilla

Mammon Money, Riches, Wealth

Mammoth Epic, Gigantic, Huge, Jumbo, Mastodon, Whopping, Woolly

Man(kind), Manly, Manliness Adam, Advance, Andrew, Ask(r), Belt, Best, Betty, Bimana(l), Biped, Bloke, Bo, Boxgrove, Boy, Boyo, Bozo, Cad, Cairn, Calf, Castle, Cat, Chal, Chap, Checker, Chequer, Chiel, Cockey, Cod, Contact, Continuity, Crew, Cro-Magnon, Cuffin, Cully, Dog, Don, Draught, Dude, Emmanuel, Essex, Everyman, Family, Fancy, Fella, Feller, Fellow, Folsom, Friday, Front, G, Gayomart, Geezer, Gent, Gingerbread, Grimaldi, Guy, He, Heidelberg, Himbo, Hombre, Hominid, Homme, Homo, Homo sapiens, Inner, IOM, Iron, Isle, It, Jack, Java, Joe (Bloggs), Joe Blow, Joe Sixpack, Joe Soap, John(nie), John Doe, Josser, Limit, Link, Lollipop, M, Mac, Male, Medicine, Microcosm, Mister, Mon, Mondeo, Mr, Muffin, Mun, Neanderthal, Numbers, Nutcracker, Oreopithecus, Organisation, Ou, Paleolithic, Party, Pawn, Peking, Person, Piece, Piltdown, Pin, Pithecanthropus, Property, Raff, Ray, Remittance, Renaissance, Resurrection, Rhodesian, Right-hand, Rook, Sandwich, Servant, Servitor, Ship, Sinanthropus, Sodor, Soldier, Solo, Spear, Staff, Stag, Standover, Straw, Third, Thursday, Trinil, Twelfth, Tyke, Type, Utility, Valet, Vir, Vitality, White van, Wight

Man-about-town Boulevardier

Manacle Fetter, Handcuff, Iron, Shackle

Manage(r), Manageable, Management, Managing Adhocracy, Administer, Agent, Amildar, Attain, Aumil, Behave, Boss, Chief, Come by, Conduct, Contrive, Control, Cope, Crisis, Darogha, Direct, Docile, Eke, Exec(utive), Fare, Fend, Find, Floor, Fund, Gerent, Get by, Govern, Grieve, Handle, Head bummer, Honcho, IC, Impresario, Intendant, Line, Logistical, MacReady, Maître d('hotel), Make do, Manipulate, Manoeuvre, Middle, Nomenklatura, Organise, Proctor, Procurator, Régisseur, Rig, Roadie, → **RUN**, Scrape, Shift, Steward, Strategy, Subsist, Succeed, Suit, Superintend, Supervisor, Swing, Sysop, Tawie, Top, Tractable, Transact, Treatment, Trustee, Wangle, Webmaster, Wield(y), Yare

Manatee Lamantum, Mermaid, Sea-ape

Manchu Fu

Mandarin Bureaucrat, Chinaman, Kuo-Yu, Nodding, Satsuma, Yamen

Mandate Authority, Decree, Fiat, Order

Mandela Madiba, Nelson

Mandrake Springwort

Mandrel Triblet

Mane(d), Manes Crest, Encolure, Jubate, Larva(e), Shades

Manège Horseplay, Train

Manganese Diagolite, Mn, Synadelphite, Wadd

Mange, Mangy Scabby

Manger Cratch, Crib, Hack, Stall

Mangle Agrise, Butcher, Distort, Garble, Hack, Hackle, Haggle, Mammock, Wring(er)

▷ **Mangle** *may indicate* an anagram

Mango Dika

Manhandle Frogmarch, Maul, Mousle, Rough

Manhater Misanthrope

Manhattan Bowery

Mania Cacoethes, Craze, Frenzy, Paranoia, Passion, Rage

Manichaean Albi

Manifest(ation), Manifestly Apparent, Attest, Avatar, Epiphany, Evident, Evince, Exhibit, Extravert, Extrovert, Feat, List, Marked, Mode, Notably, Obvious, Open, Show, Undisguised

Manifesto Communist, Plank, Platform, Policy, Pronunciamento

Manifold(ness) Many, Multeity, Multiple

Manila Abaca, Cheroot

Manioc Cassava

Maniple Fannel, Fanon

Manipulate, Manipulative, Manipulator, Manipulation Bend, Chiropractor, Cog, Control, Cook, Demagogic, Diddle, Fashion, Finagle, Finesse, Gerrymander, Handle, Hellerwork, Jerrymander, Juggle, Legerdemain, Logodaedalus, Masseuse, Master-slave, McTimoney chiropractic, Milk, Osteopath, Play off, Ply, Rig, Tong, Tweeze, Use, Wangle, → **WIELD**

▷ **Manipulate** *may indicate* an anagram

Manna Alhagi, Briancon, Food, Trehala, Turkish

Manner(ism), Mannerly, Manners Accent, Airs, À la, Appearance, Attitude, Bedside, Behaved, Behaviour, Bon ton, Breeding, Carriage, Conduct, Couth, Crew, Custom, Deportment, Ethos, Etiquette, Farand, Farrand, Farrant, Guise, Habit, How, Mien, Mister, Mode, Mood, Morality, Mores, Of, Ostent, Panache, Politesse, Presentation, P's & Q's, Quirk, Rate, Sort, Style, Table, Thew(s), Thewe(s), Trick, Upsee, Upsey, Upsy, Urbanity, Way, Wise

▷ **Manoeuvre** *may indicate* an anagram

Manoeuvre(s) Alley-oop, Campaign, Castle, Christie, Christy, Démarche, Engineer, Exercise, Faena, Fianchetto, Fork, Gambit, Half-board, Heimlich, Hot-dog, Jink(s), Jockey, Loop, Manipulate, Op(eration), Pendule, Pesade, Ploy, Pull out, Renversement, Ruse, Skewer, Stickhandle, Tactic, Takeover, Use, U-turn, Valsalva, Wear, Wheelie, Whipstall, Wile, Wingover, Zigzag

Man-of-war Armada, Bluebottle, Destroyer, Ironclad, Portuguese

Manor (house) Area, Demain, Demesne, Estate, Hall, Kelmscott, Schloss, Vill(a), Waddesdon

Mansion Broadlands, Burghley House, Casa, Castle Howard, Chatworth House, Cliveden, Knole, Luton Hoo, Mentmore, Penshurst Place, Queen's House, Seat, Stourhead, Stowe, Waddesdon Manor, Woburn Abbey

Mantle Asthenosphere, Authority, Burnous(e), Capote, Caracalla, Chlamydate, Dolman, Elijah, Gas, Lithosphere, Pall, Pallium, Paludament, Pelisse, Rochet, Sima, Toga, Tunic, Vakas, Veil

Mantuan Maro, Virgil

Manual Blue collar, Bradshaw, Cambist, Console, Enchiridion, Great (organ), Guide, Hand, Handbook, How-to, Portolan(o), Positif, Sign

Manufacture(r), Manufacturing Assemble, Fabricate, Industrial, Kanban, Make, Produce

Manure Compost, Dressing, Dung, → FERTILISER, Green, Guano, Hen-pen, Lime, Muck, Sha(i)rn, Tath

Manuscript(s) Book of Kells, Codex, Codicology, Folio, Hand, Holograph, Longhand, Miniscule, MS, Opisthograph, Palimpsest, Papyrus, Parchment, Script, Scroll, Scrowl(e), Slush-pile, Uncial, Vellum

▷ **Manx** *may indicate* a last letter missing

Manx(man) Cat, IOM, Kelly, Kelt

Many C, CD, Countless, Crew(e), D, Hantle, Herd, Horde, Host, L, Lot, M, Manifold, Mony, Multi(tude), Myriad, Power, Scad, Sight, Slew, Stacks, Tons, Umpteen, Untold

▷ **Many** *may indicate* the use of a Roman numeral letter

Maoist Naxalite, Red Guard

Maori (house) Hauhau, Hori, Jikanga, Mallowpuff, Moa hunter, Tangata whenua, Te reo, Wahine, Whare

Map(s), Mapping Atlas, A-Z, Bijection, Card, Cartogram, Chart, Chorography, Choropleth, Chromosome, Cognitive, Contour, Digital, Face, Genetic, Inset, Key, Loxodromic, Mappemond, Mental, Mosaic, Moving, Mud, OS, Perceptual, Plan, Plot, Portolano, Relief, Road, Sea-card, Sea-chart, Site, Star, Strip, Topography, Weather

Maple Acer, Bird's eyr, Flowering, Japanese, Manitoba, Mazer, Norway, Plane, Silver, Sugar, Sycamore, Syrup

Map-maker Cartographer, OS, Speed

Maquis Queach, Underground

Mar Blight, Denature, Dere, Impair, Poison, Soil, Spoil, Taint

Marabout Sofi, Sufi

Marathon Comrades, Huge, London, Long, Race, Two Oceans

Maraud(er) Amalekite, Attacker, Bandit, Hun, Pillager, Pirate, Predator, Prowler, Raid

Marble(s), Marbling Aeginetan, Agate, All(e)y, Arch, Arundelian, Bonce, Bonduc, Bool, Boondoggle, Bowl, Carrara, Chequer, Cipollino, Commoney, Devil's, Dump, Elgin, Forest, Humite, Hymettus, Knicker, Languedoc, Lucullite, Marl, Marmarosis, Marmoreal, Marver, Mosaic, Mottle, Nero-antico, Nickar, Nicker, Onychite, Onyx, Ophicalcite, Paragon, Parian, Pavonazzo, Pentelic(an), Petworth, Phigalian, Plonker, Plunker, Purbeck, Rance, Ringer, Ring-taw, Ruin, Sanity, Scagliola, Spangcockle, Taw, Variegate, Wits, Xanthian

Marcel Proust

▷ **March** *may indicate* 'Little Women' character, Amy, Beth, Jo, Meg

March(ing), Marcher Abut, Adjoin, Advance, Anabasis, Border(er), Borderland, Dead, Defile, Demo, Étape, File, Footslog, Forced, Freedom, Fringe, Galumph, Go, Goosestep, Grand, Hikoi, Hunger, Ides, Jarrow, Lide, Limes, Lockstep, Long, Meare, Music, → PARADE, Paso doble, Procession, Progress, Protest, Quick, Rogue's, Route, Saint, Slow time, Step, Strunt, Strut, Trio, Tromp, Troop, Wedding, Yomp

Marco Il Milione, Polo

Mare Dam, Flanders, Horse, M, MacCurdle's, Shanks's, Spanish, Yaud

Margaret Anjou, Meg, Peg, Rita

Margarine Oleo

Marge, Margin(al) Annotate, Bank, Border, Borderline, Brim, Brink, Curb, Edge, Fimbria, Gross, Hair's breadth, Kerb, Lean, Leeway, Limit, Lip, Littoral, Neck, Nose, Peristome, Profit, Rand, Repand, → RIM, Selvedge, Sideline, Spread, Tail, Term

Marginal note Apostil(le), K'ri, Postil

Margosa Melia, Nim
Maria(nne) France, Tia
Marie Dressler, Tempest
Marigold Calendula, Gool, Gule, Kingcup, Tagetes
Marijuana Alfalfa, Camberwell carrot, Dagga, Gage, Ganja, Grass, Greens, Gungeon, Ha-ha, Hay, Herb, J, Jive, Joint, Kaif, Kef, Kif, Leaf, Lid, Locoweed, Mary-Jane, Pot, Roach, Rope, Shit, Sinsemilla, Splay, Spliff, Tea, Toke, Weed
Marina Wharf
Marinade Chermoula, Escabeche
Marine (animal) Aquatic, Bootie, Bootneck, Cephalopod, Chaetognath, Cnidarian, Coelenterate, Comatulid, Ctenophora, Cunjevoi, Enteropneusta, Flustra, Foram(inifer), Galoot, Graptolite, Harumfrodite, Hemichorda, Holothurian, Horse, Hydrocoral, Hydroid, Hydromedusa, Jarhead, Jolly, Lancelet, Leatherneck, Lobster, Mercantile, Mere-swine, Mistress Roper, Oceanic, Otarine, Physalia, Pollywag, Pollywog, Salpa, Sea-soldier, Seston, Thalassian, Ultra
Mariner AB, Ancient, MN, Noah, RM, Sailor, Salt, Seafarer, Spacecraft, Tar
Marionette(s) Fantoccini, Puppet
Marjoram Amaracus, Origan, Pot, Sweet, Wild, Winter-sweet
Mark(ing), Marked, Marks, Marker Accent, Aesc, Antony, Apostrophe, Asterisk, Astrobleme, Badge, Banker, Bethumb, Biological, Birth, Blaze, Blot, Blotch, Bollard, Brand, Bruise, Buck, Bull, Buoy, Butt, Cachet, Cairn, Caract, Caret, Caste, CE, Cedilla, Chatter, Chequer, Cicatrix, Class, Clout, Colon, Comma, Coronis, Crease, Criss-cross, Cross(let), Cup (and ring), Dash, Denote, Dent, Diacritic, Diaeresis, Dieresis, Distinction, Ditto, DM, Duckfoot quote, Dupe, Emblem, Enseam, Ensign, Enstamp, Exclamation, Expression, Fanion, Feer, Flag, Fleck, Fox(ing), Freckle, Genetic, Glyph, Gnomon, Gospel, Grade, Guillemet, Gybe, Haček, Haemangioma, Hair-line, Hash, Hatch, Heed, High water, Hyphen, Impress(ion), Indicium, Infinitive, Ink, Inscribe, Insignia, Interrogation, Inukshuk, Keel, Kite, Kumkum, Label, Lentigo, Line, Ling, Livedo, Logo, Lovebite, Low water, M, Macron, Matchmark, MB, Medical, Merk, Mint, Minute, Mottle, NB, Nota bene, Notal, Note, Notice, Obelisk, Observe, Oche, Paginate, Paragraph, Paraph, Peg, Period, Pilcrow, Pit, Plage, Pling, Pock, Point, Popinjay, Port wine, Post, Presa, Printer's, Proof, Punctuation, Question, Quotation, Record, Reference, Register, Regulo, Remarque, Ripple, Roundel, Sanction, Scar, Score(r), Scratch, Section, See, Service, Shadow, Shilling, Shoal, Sigil, Sign, Smit, Smut, Smutch, Soft touch, Speck, Splodge, Splotch, Stain, Stencil, Stigma(ta), Strawberry, Stress, Stretch, Stroke, Sucker, Swan-upping, Symbol, Tag, Target, Tarnish, Tatow, Tattoo, Tee, Theta, Thread, Tick, Tide, Tie, Tika, Tikka, Tilak, Tilde, Tittle, Token, Touchmark, Trace, Track, Trout, Tug(h)ra, Twain, Umlaut, Ure, Victim, Wand, Warchalking, Watch, Weal, Welt
Market(ing), Market day, Market place Advergaming, Agora, Alcaiceria, Available, Baltic, Bazaar, Bear, Billingsgate, Black, Black stump, Borgo, Bull, Buyers', Capital, Captive, Cattle, Change, Chowk, Cinema, Circular, Cluster, Commodity, Common, Demo, Denet, Direct, Discount, Dragon, EC, Emerging, Emporium, Errand, Exchange, Exhibition, Fair, Farmers', Feeing, Flea, Forum, Forward, Free, Grey, Growth, Insert, Internal, Kerb, Lloyds, Main, Mandi, Mart, Mass, Meat, Mercat, Money, Niche, Nundine, Obigosony, Oligopoly, Open, Order-driven, Outlet, Overt, Pamphlet, Perfect, Piazza, Poster, Press, Publicity, Radio, Reach, Relationship, Sale, Sellers', Servqual, Share, Shop, Single, Social, Societal, Sook, Souk, Spot, Stance, Staple, Stock, Stock Exchange, Tattersall's, Terminal, Test, Third, Tiger, Trade, Tron, Tryst, USP, Vent, Viral, Wall Street

Market garden Truck-farm
Marksman Sharpshooter, Shootist, Shot, Sniper, Tell
Marlborough Blenheim
Marlene Lilli
Marmalade Cat, Mammee-sapota, Preserve, Squish
Marmoset Jacchus, Mico, Midas, Monkey, Wistiti
Marmot Bobac, Bobak, Dassie, Groundhog, Hoary, Hyrax, Rodent, Whistler,
Woodchuck
Maroon Brown, Castaway, Enisle, Firework, Inisle, Isolate, Strand
Marquee Pavilion, Tent, Top
Marquess, Marquis Granby, Lorne, Sade
Marquetry Boul(l)e, Buhl, Inlay
Marriage → ALLIANCE, Arranged, Bed, Beenah, Bigamy, Bridal, Buckle-beggar,
Civil, Coemption, Common law, Commuter, Companionate, Confarreation,
Conjugal, Connubial, Coverture, Digamy, Endogamy, Espousal, Exogamy,
Gandharva, Genial, Group, Hedge, Hetaerism, Hetairism, Hymen(eal), Jugal,
Ketubah, Knot, Lavender, Levirate, Match, Mating, Matrilocal, Matrimony,
Mésalliance, Mixed, Monandry, Monogamy, Morganatic, Noose, Nuptial, Open,
Pantagamy, Patrilocal, Polygamy, Punalua, Putative, Sacrament, Shidduch,
Shotgun, Tie, Trial, → UNION, Wedding, Wedlock
Marriageable Marrow, Nubile, Parti
Marriage-broker Shadchan
Marrow Courgette, Friend, Gist, Kamokamo, Medulla, Myeloid, Pith, Pumpkin,
Spinal, Squash, Vegetable
Marry, Married Ally, Amate, Buckle, Cleek(it), Confarreate, Couple, Coverture,
Espouse, Feme covert, Forsooth, Fuse, Goody, Hitch, Join, Knit, M, Mate, Matron,
Memsahib, Ming, Missis, Missus, Pair, Pardie, Quotha, Sannup, Splice, Tie, Tie the
knot, Troggs, Troth, Umfazi, Unite, W, Wed, Wive
Mars Areography, Ares, Red (planet)
Marsh(y) Bayou, Bog, Chott, Corcass, Emys, Everglades, Fen, Hackney, Maremma,
Merse, Mire, Morass, Ngaio, Paludal, Palustrine, Plashy, Pontine, Pripet,
Quagmire, Romney, Salina, Salt, Shott, Slade, Slough, Sog, Spew, Spue, Swale,
Swamp, Taiga, Terai, Vlei, Wetlands
Marshal Arrange, Array, Commander, Earp, Foch, French, Hickok, MacMahon,
Muster, Neil, Ney, Order, Pétain, Provost, Shepherd, Sky, Steward, Tedder, Usher,
Yardman
Marshmallow Althaea, Mallowpuff
Marsupial Bandicoot, Bilby, Cuscus, Dasyure, Dibbler, Didelphia, Diprotodon(t),
Dunnart, Honey mouse, Honey possum, Kangaroo, Koala, Macropod, Metatheria,
Notoryctes, Nototherium, Numbat, Opossum, Pademelon, Pad(d)ymelon,
Petaurist, Phalanger, Pig-rat, Polyprodont, Possum, Potoroo, Pouched mouse,
Pygmy glider, Quokka, Quoll, Roo, Tammar, Tasmanian devil, Theria, Thylacine,
Tuan, Wallaby, Wambenger, Wombat, Yapo(c)k
Marten Fisher, Mustela, Pekan, Pine, Sable, Woodshock
Martha Vineyard
Martial (arts) Bellicose, Budo, Capoeira, Capuera, Chopsocky, Dojo, Iai-do, Judo,
Ju-jitsu, Karate, Kendo, Kick boxing, Kumite, Kung fu, Militant, Muay thai,
Ninjitsu, Ninjutsu, Sensei, Shintaido, Tae Bo®, Tae kwon do, T'ai chi (chuan),
Warlike, Wushu
Martin Bird, Dean, Luther, Swallow
Martinet Captious, Ramrod, Stickler, Tyrant

Martini® Cocktail, Henry

Martyr(dom), Martyrs Alban, Alphege, Colosseum, Donatist, Justin, Lara, Latimer, Metric, MM, Passional, Persecute, Sebastian, Shaheed, Shahid, Stephen, Suffer, Tolpuddle, Wishart

Marvel(lous) Bodacious, Bully, Épatant, Fab, Fantabulous, Lulu, Magic, Marl, Miracle, Mirific, Phenomenon, Prodigious, Selcouth, Superb, Super-duper, Swell, Terrific, Wonder

Marx(ism), Marxist Aspheterism, Chico, Comintern, Commie, Groucho, Gummo, Harpo, Karl, Lenin, Mao, Menshevik, Revisionism, Tanky, Tipamaro, Zeppo

Mary Bloody, Celeste, Madonna, Moll, Morison, Our Lady, Tum(my), Typhoid, Virgin

Marylebone Station

Marzipan Marchpane

Mascara Eye-black

Mascot Charm, → **TALISMAN**, Telesm, Token

Masculine, Masculinity He, He-man, Linga(m), M, Machismo, Macho, Male, Manly, Virile, Yang

Maser Laser

Mash(er) Beat, Beau, Beetle, Brew, Lady-killer, Pap, Pestle, Pound, Sour, Squash

Mask(ed) Bird cage, Camouflage, Cloak, Cokuloris, Death, Disguise, Dissemble, Domino, Face pack, False face, Front, Gas, Hide, Larvated, Life, Loo, Loup, Mascaron, Matte, Oxygen, Persona, Respirator, Screen, Semblance, Shadow, Stalking-horse, Stocking, Stop out, Template, Visor, Vizard

Mason(ry) Ashlar, Ashler, Brother, Builder, Cowan, Emplecton, Isodoma, Isodomon, Isodomum, Jude, Lodge, Moellon, Monumental, Nogging, Opus, Perry, Random, Rubblework, Squinch, Stylobate

Masque(rade), Masquerader Comus, Domino, Guisard, Mum(m), Pose, Pretend

Mass(es) Aggregate, Agnus Dei, Anniversary, Atomic, Banket, Bezoar, Bike, Blob, Body, Bulk, Cake, Canon, Chaos, Clot, Compound, Congeries, Conglomeration, Consecration, Core, Crith, Critical, Crowd, Demos, Density, Flake, Flysch, Folk, Geepound, Gramme, Gravitational, Great, Herd, High, Horde, Hulk, Inertial, Jud, Kermesse, Kermis, Kilo(gram), Kirmess, Low, Lump, M, Majority, Missa, Missa solemnis, Mob, Month's mind, Mop, Nest, Phalanx, Pile, Plebs, Plumb, Pontifical, Populace, Proper, Raft, Requiem, Rest, Ruck, Salamon, Salmon, Scrum, Sea, Serac, Service, Shock, Sicilian, Size, Slub, Slug, Solar, Solemn, Solid, Stack, Stroma, Sursum Corda, Te Igitur, Tektite, Trental, Vesper, Vigil, Volume, Wad, Weight, Welter

Massacre Amritsar, Beziers, Blood-bath, Butcher, Carnage, Glencoe, Havock, Kanpur, Manchester, Peterloo, Pogrom, Purge, St Bartholomew's Day, Scullabogue, Scupper, September, Sicilian vespers, Slaughter, Slay, Wounded Knee

Massage, Masseur An mo, Cardiac, Chafer, Chavutti thirumal, Do-in, Effleurage, Hellerwork, → **KNEAD**, Malax, Palp, Petrissage, Physio, Rolf(ing), Rubber, Shampoo, Shiatsu, Stone, Stroke, Swedish, Tapotement, Thai, Tripsis, Tui na

Massif Makalu

Massive Big, Bull, Colossal, Gang, Gargantuan, Heavy, Herculean, Huge, Monumental, Ponderous, Strong, Titan

Mast(ed), Masthead Acorn, Banner, Captain's, Crosstree, Flag, Foretop, Foreyard, High top, Hounds, Jigger, Jury, M, Mizzen, Mooring, Pannage, Pole, Racahout, Royal, Ship-rigged, Spar, Top-gallant, Truck, Venetian

Master(ly), Mastery Artful, Baalebos, Baas, Beak, Beat, Boss, Buddha, Bwana, Careers, Checkmate, Choir, Chorus, Conquer, Control, Dan, Dominate, Dominie, Employer, Enslave, Exarch, Expert, Gov, Grand, Grip, Harbour, Herr, Himself,

International, Learn, Lord, MA, Maestro, Magistral, Mas(s), Massa, Mes(s), Nkosi, Old, Ollamh, Ollav, Oner, Oppress, Original, Overcome, Overlord, Overpower, Overseer, Passed, Past, Pedant, Question, Rabboni, Schoolman, Seigneur, Seignior, Signorino, Sir(e), Skipper, → **SUBDUE**, Subjugate, Superate, Surmount, Swami, Tame, Task, Thakin, Towkay, Tuan, Usher, Vanquish, Virtuoso

Mastermind Brain, Conceive, Direct

Masterpiece Chef d'oeuvre, Creation

Mastersinger Sachs

Master-stroke Coup, Triumph

Masturbate, Masturbation Abuse, Blow, Frig, Gratify, Jerk off, Jock, Onanism, Self-pollution, Toss off, Wank, Whack off

Mat(ted), Matting Bast, Capillary, Coaster, Doily, Dojo, Doyley, Dutch mattress, Felt, Inlace, Pad, Paunch, Place, Plat, Prayer, Rug, Surf, Table, Taggy, → **TANGLE**, Tat(ami), Tatty, Taut, Tautit, Tawt, Tomentose, Welcome, Zarf

Matador Card, Espada, Ordonez, Theseus, Torero

Match(ed) Agree, Alliance, Amate, Balance, Besort, Bonspiel, Bout, Carousel, Compare, Compeer, Congreve, Consolation, Contest, Cope, Correlate, Correspond, Counterpane, Doubles, Emulate, Engagement, Equal(ise), Equate, Even, Exhibition, Fellow, Fit, Fixture, Four-ball, Foursome, Friction, Friendly, Fusee, Fuzee, Game, Go, Greensome, Grudge, International, Joust, Light, Locofoco, Love, Lucifer, Main, Marrow, Marry, Meet, Mouse, Needle, Pair(s), Paragon, Parti, Pit, Play-off, Prizefight, Promethean, Replica, Reproduce, Return, Rival, Road game, Roland, Rubber, Safety, Semifinal, Sevens, Shield, Shoo-in, Shooting, Shouting, Singles, Slanging, Slow, Slugfest, Spunk, Striker, Suit, Sync, → **TALLY**, Team, Test, Texas scramble, Tie, Twin, Twosome, Union, Venue, Vesta, Vesuvian, Wedding

Matchbox label (collecting) Phillumeny

Match girl Bride

Match-holder Lin(t)stock

Matchless Non(e)such, Orinda

Matchmaker Blackfoot, Broker, Pairer, Promoter, Shadchan

Mate, Mating Achates, Adam, Amigo, Amplexus, Assortative, Bedfellow, Bo, Breed, Buddy, Buffer, Butty, Check, Chess, China, Chum, Cobber, Cock, Comrade, Consort, Crony, Cully, Digger, Eve, Feare, Feer, Fellow, Fere, Fiere, First, Fool's, Helper, Husband, Ilex, Maik, Make, Marrow, Marry, Match, Mister, Mucker, Nick, Nickar, Oldster, Oppo, → **PAIR**, Pal, Panmixia, Panmixis, Paragon, Partner, Pheer(e), Pirrauru, Running, Scholar's, Second, Serve, Sex, Skaines, Smothered, Soul, → **SPOUSE**, Tea, Tup, Wack, Wacker, Wife, Wus(s)

Material(ism) Agalmatolite, Aggregate, Agitprop, Appropriate, Apt, Armure, Austenite, Ballast, Blastema, Bole, Borsic, Byssus, Celluloid, Cellulose, Ceramic, Cermet, → **CLOTH**, Cob, Compo, Composite, Concrete, Copy, Corfam®, Corporeal, Data, Documentation, Earthy, Fablon®, → **FABRIC**, Factual, Fallout, Fertile, Fettling, Fibreboard, Fibrefill, Fibreglass, Fines, Flong, Fomes, Frit(t), Fuel, Gang(ue), Germane, Graphite, Gypsum, Historical, Hylic, Illusion, Illuvium, Interfacing, Lambskin, Leading, Macintosh, Matter, Metal, Moxa, Oasis®, Oilcloth, Oilskin, Papier-maché, Pertinent, Phantom, Physical, Pina-cloth, Plasterboard, Polystyrene, Polythene, Positive, Protoplasm, Protore, Pug(ging), Raw, Regolith, Relevant, Sackcloth, Sagathy, Samsonite®, Silicone, Skirting, Siporex®, Staff, Stuff, Substance, Swish, Tangible, Tape, Tartan®, Textile, Thermolite®, Thingy, Towelling, Tusser, Wattle and daub, Worldly, Ylem

Materialise Appear, Apport, Click, Reify

Materialist(ic) Banausian, Earthling, Hylist, Hyloist, Philistine, Somatist

Mathematician Agnesi, Apollonius, Archimedes, Archytas, Bernoulli, Bessel, Boole, Bourbaki, Briggs, Cantor, Cocker, De Morgan, Descartes, Diophantos, Dunstable, Eratosthenes, Euclid, Euler, Fermat, Fibonacci, Fourier, Friedmann, Gauss, Godel, Goldbach, Gunter, Hamilton, Hawking, Jacobi, Julia, Klein, Lagrange, Laplace, Leibniz, Lie, Mandelbrot, Mercator, Minkowski, Napier, Newton, Optime, Pascal, Penrose, Playfair, Poincare, Poisson, Ptolemy, Pythagoras, Pytheas, Riemann, Statistician, Torricelli, Turing, Von Leibnitz, Walker, Wrangler, Zeno

Mathematics, Mathematical, Maths Algebra, Applied, Arithmetic, Arsmetrick, Calculus, Combinatories, Exact science, Geometry, Higher, Logarithms, Mechanics, New, Numbers, Porism, Pure, Topology, Trig, Trigonometry

Matilda Liar, Swag, Untruthful, Waltzing

Matinee Coat, Idol, Show

Mating Pangamy

Matins Nocturn

Matricide Orestes

Matrimony Bed, Conjugal, Marriage, Sacrament, Spousal, Wedlock

Matrix Active, Array, Boston, Hermitian, Jacobian, Mould, Orthogonal, Pattern, Scattering, Square, Uterus

Matron Dame, Hausfrau, Lucretia, Nurse, Warden

Matt(e) Dense, Dingy, Dull

Matter Affair, Alluvium, Bioblast, Biogen, Body, Business, Concern, Condensed, Consequence, Dark, Degenerate, Empyema, Epithelium, Gear, Gluon, Go, Grey, Hyle, Impost(h)ume, Issue, Mass, Material, Molecule, Multiverse, Phlegm, Pith, Point, Positron, Premise, Protoplasm, Pulp, Pus, Quark, Reading, Reck, Reke, Scum, Shebang, Signify, Solid, Sputum, Stuff, Subject, → **SUBSTANCE**, Theme, Thing, Topic, Tousle, Touzle, White, Ylem

Matthew Arnold

Mattress Bed(ding), Biscuit, Dutch, Featherbed, Foam, Futon, Lilo®, Pa(i)lliasse, Pallet, Spring, Tick

Mature, Maturity Adult, Age, Blossom, Bold, Concoct, Develop, Grow (up), Mellow, Metaplasis, Old, Puberty, Ripe(n), Rounded, Seasoned, Upgrow(n)

Maudlin Fuddled, Mawkish, Sentimental, Slip-slop, Sloppy, Too-too

Maul Hammer, Manhandle, Paw, Rough, Savage

Maundy Money, Nipter, Thursday

Mauretanian, Mauritania(n) Moor, RIM

Mausoleum Helicarnassus, Mole, Sepulchre, Taj Mahal, Tomb

Mauve Lavender, Lilac, Mallow, Perkin's

Maverick Misfit, Nonconformist, Rogue

Mavis Throstle

Maw Crop, Gorge, Gull(et), Mouth, Oesophagus

Mawkish Sentimental, Sickly

Maxim Adage, Aphorism, Apo(ph)thegm, Axiom, Byword, Dictum, Gnome, Gorki, Gun, Hiram, Moral, Motto, Precept, Proverb, Restaurateur, → **RULE**, Saw, Saying, Sentence, Sentiment, Watchword

Maximum All-out, Full, Highest, Most, Peak, Utmost

May Blossom, Can, Hawthorn, Merry, Might, Month, Mote, Quickthorn, Shall, Whitethorn

Maybe Happen, Mebbe, Peradventure, Percase, Perchance, Perhaps, Possibly

▷ **May become** *may indicate* an anagram

May day Beltane, SOS

Mayfair WI
Mayfly Ephemera, Ephemeroptera, Green-drake, Sedge
Mayhem Chaos, Crime, Damage, Havoc, Pandemonium
Mayonnaise Aioli, Rémoulade
Mayor Alcaide, Burgomaster, Casterbridge, Charter, Councilman, Portreeve, Provost, Syndic, Whittington, Worship
Maze Honeycomb, Labyrinth, Meander, Network, Theseus, Warren, Wilderness
MC Compere, Host, Ringmaster
MD Doctor, Healer
ME Yuppie flu
Me I, Mi, One, Us
Mead(ow) Flood, Grass, Haugh, Hydromel, Inch, Ing, Lea(se), Ley, Meath(e), Metheglin, → **PASTURE**, Runnymede, Saeter, Salting, Water
Meadowsweet Dropwort
Meagre Arid, Bare, Exiguous, Measly, Paltry, Pittance, Scant, Scrannel, Scranny, Scrawny, Skimpy, Skinny, Spare, Sparse, Stingy, Thin
Meal(s), Mealie, Mealy Allseed, Banquet, Barbecue, Barium, Beanfeast, Blow-out, Board, Breakfast, Brunch, Buffet, Cassava, Cereal, Chilled, Cholent, Chota-hazri, Collation, Corn, Cornflour, Cottoncake, Cottonseed, Cou-cou, Cribble, Dejeune(r), Deskfast, Dinner, Drammock, Ear, Ervalenta, Fare, Farina, Feast, Flour, Food, Grits, Grout, Hangi, High tea, Iftar, Indian, Italian, Kai, Lock, Lunch, Mandioc, Mandioc(c)a, Mani(h)oc, Matzo, Melder, Meltith, Mensal, Mess, Morning, Mush, No-cake, Nosh, Nuncheon, Obento, Ordinary, Picnic, Piece, Plate, Poi, Polenta, Porridge, Prandial, Prix fixe, Rac(c)ahout, Refection, Repast, Revalenta, Rijst(t)afel, Salep, Scambling, Schri, Scoff, Seder, Smorgasbord, Snack, Sohur, Spread, Square, Suhur, Supper, Table d'hôte, Takeaway, Tea, Thali, Tiffin, Tightener, Twalhours, Undern
Meal-ticket LV
Mean(ing), Meant Aim, Arithmetic(al), Average, Base, Betoken, Bowsie, Caitiff, Cheap, Connotation, Curmudgeon, Definition, Denotate, Denote, Design, Dirty, Drift, Essence, Ettle, Feck, Footy, Foul, Geometric(al), Gist, Golden, Hang, Harmonic, Humble, Hunks, Ignoble, Illiberal, Imply, Import, Inferior, Insect, Intend, Intermediate, Kunjoos, Lexical, Low, Mang(e)y, Marrow, Medium, Mesquin, Method, Mid, Miserly, Narrow, Near, Norm, Nothing, One-horse, Ornery, Paltry, Par, Penny-pinching, Petty, Piker, Pinch-penny, Pith, Point, Purport, → **PURPOSE**, Quadratic, Ratfink, Revenue, Roinish, Roynish, Scall, Scrub, Scurvy, Semanteme, Semantic(s), Sememe, Sense, Shabby, Signify, Slight, Small, Sneaky, Snoep, Snot, Sordid, Sparing, Spell, Stingy, Stink(ard), Stinty, Substance, Symbol, Thin, Threepenny, Tight-lipped, Tightwad, Two-bit, Value, Vile, Whoreson
Meander Fret, Ring, Sinuate, Stray, Wander, Weave, Wind
Meaningless Ducdame, Empty, Hollow, Hot air, Insignificant, Nonny, Rumbelow
Means Agency, Dint, Income, Instrumental, Media, Method, Mode, Opulence, Organ, Private, Resources, Staple, Substance, Tactics, Visible, Ways, Wherewithal
Meantime, Meanwhile Among, Emong, Greenwich, Interim, Whilst
Measles Morbilli, Roseola, Rose-rash, Rubella, Rubeola, Sheep
Measure(d), Measuring, Measurement By(e)law, Calibre, Circular, Crackdown, → **DANCE**, Démarche, → **DIMENSION**, Distance, Dose, Drastic, Dry, → **GAUGE**, Gavotte, Gross, Imperial, Limit, Linear, Liter, Litre, Moratorium, Of, Offset, Precaution, Prophylactic, Quickstep, Ration, Remen, Share, Short, → **SIZE**, Standard, Statute, Step, Stichometry, Strike, Struck, Survey, Token, Triangulate, Wine

MEASUREMENTS

2 letters:
As
Em
En
Mu

3 letters:
Are
Bel
Cab
Cor
Ell
Erg
Fat
Hin
Lay
Lea
Ley
Log
Lug
Mil
Rod
Tot
Wey

4 letters:
Acre
Aune
Bath
Boll
Bolt
Comb
Cord
Coss
Cran
Culm
Dram
Epha
Foot
Gage
Gill
Hank
Hide
Inch
Koss
Last
Line
Link
Maze

Mete
Mile
Mole
Mott
Muid
Nail
Omer
Pace
Peck
Pint
Pipe
Pole
Pood
Ream
Reau
Rood
Rope
Shot
Span
Tape
Thou
Unit
Vara
Volt
Warp
Yard

5 letters:
Anker
Ardeb
Barye
Bekah
Bigha
Caneh
Carat
Chain
Clove
Combe
Coomb
Crore
Cubit
Cumec
Cusec
Depth
Ephah
Fermi
Float
Gauge
Grain

Groma
Hanap
Homer
Joule
Kaneh
Lento
Liang
Ligne
Lippy
Loure
Mease
Meter
Metre
Middy
Optic®
Perch
Plumb
Quart
Romer
Ruler
Scale
Skein
Sound
Stade
Stere
Tesla
Therm
Toise
Verst
Wecht
Yojan

6 letters:
Albedo
Alnage
Arpent
Arshin
Barrel
Barren
Beegah
Bovate
Bushel
Chenix
Chopin
Cicero
Cubage
Denier
Double
Etalon

Exergy
Fathom
Firkin
Firlot
Gallon
Height
Hemina
Jigger
Kelvin
Kilerg
League
Lippie
Liquid
Metage
Modius
Morgan
Mutton
Noggin
Oxgang
Parsec
Pascal
Pottle
Radius
Runlet
Sazhen
Stadia
Thread
Tierce
Yojana

7 letters:
Aneroid
Arshine
Braccio
Breadth
Burette
Caliper
Candela
Chalder
Choenix
Conguis
Coulomb
Cyathus
Decibel
Entropy
Furlong
Geodesy
Lambert
Leaguer

Pelorus
Quarter
Refract
Rundlet
Sleever
Spindle
Spondee
Venturi
Virgate

8 letters:
Angstrom
Calliper
Carucate
Chaldron
Crannock
Desyatin
Diameter
Exitance
Fistmele
Foot rule
Hogshead
Kilogray
Luxmeter
Mutchkin
Odometer
Oximeter
Parasang
Poulter's
Puncheon
Tape-line
Teraflop
Viameter

Waywiser

9 letters:
Astrolabe
Atmometer
Bolometer
Cryometer
Decalitre
Decastere
Dosimeter
Ergometer
Eriometer
Flowmeter
Hodometer
Kilometre
Konimeter
Lysimeter
Manometer
Mekometer
Nipperkin
Octameter
Oenometer
Pentapody
Potometer
Steradian
Tappet-hen
Telemeter
Titration
Tonometer
Yardstick

10 letters:
Acidometer

Amphimacer
Anemometer
Barleycorn
Bathometer
Centimetre
Chronotron
Coulometer
Cyclometer
Densimeter
Dessiatine
Dessyatine
Drosometer
Eudiometer
Geodimeter
Goniometer
Gravimeter
Humidistat
Hydrometer
Hygrometer
Lactometer
Micrometer
Millimetre
Opisometer
Photometer
Piezometer
Resistance
Touchstone
Tromometer
Winchester

11 letters:
Actinometer
Auxanometer

Calorimeter
Dioptometer
Dynamometer
Gradiometer
Intoximeter
Jacob's staff
Stereometer
Tacheometry
Venturi tube
Weighbridge

12 letters:
Cathetometer
Coulombmeter
Densitometer
Electrometer
Electronvolt
Extensimeter
Extensometer
Galactometer
Gravitometer
Katharometer
Nephelometer
Permittivity
Tellurometer
Viscosimeter

13 letters:
Saccharometer

15 letters:
Katathermometer

Meat(s) Aitchbone, Bacon, Bard, Beef, Beefsteak, Biltong, Brawn, Brisket, Brown, Burger, Cabob, Carbonado, Carrion, Charcuterie, Chop, Collop, Confit, Croquette, Cut, Dark, Devon, Dog-roll, Easy, Edgebone, Entrecôte, Escalope, Essence, Fanny Adams, Fleishig, Fleishik, Flesh, Flitch, Force, Galantine, Gigot, Gobbet, Gosht, Griskin, Ham, Haslet, Jerky, Joint, Junk, Kabab, Kabob, Kebab, Kebob, Lamb, Loin, Luncheon, Mart, Mince, Mutton, Noisette, Offal, Olive, Oyster, Pastrami, Paupiette, Pem(m)ican, Piccata, Pith, Pope's eye, Pork, Processed, Prosciutto, Rack, Red, Rillettes, Roast, Saddle, Sasatie, Satay, Scaloppino, Schnitzel, Scran, Scrapple, Sey, Shank, Shashlik, Shishkebab, Side, Sirloin, Sosatie, Spam®, Spare rib, Spatchcock, Spaul(d), Steak, Strong, Tenderloin, Tiring, Tongue, Variety, Veal, Venison, Vifda, Virgate, Vivda, White, Wiener schnitzel, Wurst

Meatball(s) Cecils, Croquette, Faggot, Falafel, Felafel, Fricadel, Frikkadell, Goujon, Knish, Kofta, Kromesky, Quenelle, Rissole

Meat extract Brawn, Gravy, Juice, Stock

Meatless Banian, Lent, Maigre, Vegetarian

Mecca Centre, Honeypot, Kaaba, Keblah, Kibla(h), Qibla

▷ **Mechanic(al)** *may indicate* characters from 'A Midsummer Night's Dream'

Mechanic(s) Apron-man, Artificer, Artisan, Banausic, Barodynamics, Bottom, Card, Celestial, Classical, Dynamics, Engineer, Fitter, Fluid, Fundi, Grease monkey, Greaser, Hand, Journeyman, Kinematics, Kinesiology, Kinetics, Newtonian, Operative, Quantum, Rock, Soil, Statics, Statistical, Technician, Wave

Mechanical, Mechanism Action, Apparatus, Auto, Autodestruct, Banausic, Clockwork, Defence, Dérailleur, Escape, Escapement, Foul-safe, Gimmal, Gust-lock, Instrument, Machinery, Movement, Organical, Pulley, Pushback, Rackwork, Regulator, Robotic, Servo, Synchroflash, Synchromesh, Traveller, Trippet, Works

Medal(lion)(s) Award, Bar, Bronze, Congressional, Croix de guerre, Decoration, Dickin, DSM, GC, George, Gold, Gong, Gorget, Military, MM, Numismatic, Pan(h)agia, Purple Heart, Putty, Roundel, Silver, Tony, Touchpiece, VC, Vernicle

Meddle(r), Meddlesome, Meddling Busybody, Dabble, Finger, Hen-hussy, → **INTERFERE**, Interloper, Marplot, Mell, Monkey, Officious, Pantopragmatic, Potter, Pragmatic, Pry, Snooper, Spoilsport, Tamper, Tinker, Trifle

Media Mass, Mixed, New, PR

Mediate, Mediator ACAS, Arbitrate, Intercede, Interpose, Intervene, Liaison, Muti, Referee, Stickler, Thirdsman, Trouble-shooter

Medic(k) Extern, Lucern(e), Nonesuch, Snail

Medical, Medicine (chest), Medicament, Medication Aesculapian, Algology, Allopathy, Aloetic, Alternative, Amulet, Andrology, Anodyne, Antacid, Antibiotic, Antidote, Antisepsis, Antiseptic, Arnica, Arrowroot, Asafetida, Aviation, Ayurveda, Bi, Bismuth, Blister, Brunonian, Buchu, Bucku, Calumba, Carminative, Charm, Chinese, Chiropody, Chlorodyne, Chrysarobin, Clinician, Complementary, Cordial, Corpsman, Cubeb, Curative, Defensive, Demulcent, Diapente, Diascordium, Diatessaron, Discutient, Doctor's stuff, Dose, Draught, Drops, → **DRUG**, Dutch drops, Eardrop, Electuary, Elixir, Emmenagogue, Empirics, Enema, Epulotic, Excipient, Expectorant, Fall-trank, Febrifuge, Feldsher, Folk, Forensic, Fringe, Galen, Galenism, Gelcap, Genitourinary, Gripe water®, Gutta, Haematinic, Herb, Herbal, Hesperidin, Holistic, Hom(o)eopathy, Horse-drench, Iatric(al), Imhotep, Indian, Industrial, Inhalant, Inro, Internal, Iodine, Ipecac(uanha), Iron, Ko cycle, Lariam®, Laxative, Leechcraft, Legal, Loblolly, Lotion, Magnesia, Menthol, Microbubbles, Mishmi, Mixture, Moxar, Muti, Nephritic, Nervine, Nosology, Nostrum, Nuclear, Nux vomica, Ob-gyn, Officinal, Oncology, Oporice, Orthopoedics, Osteopath, Palliative, Panacea, Paregoric, Patent, Pathology, Pectoral, Pharmacy, Phlegmagogue, Physic, Physical, Pill, Placebo, Polychrest, Polypill, Posology, Potion, Poultice, Preparation, Preventive, Proctology, Psionic, Psychiatry, Purgative, Quinacrine, Quinine, Quin(quin)a, Radiology, Red Crescent, Red Cross, Relaxative, → **REMEDY**, Salve, Sanative, Sanguinaria, Senna, Serology, Simple, Space, Specific, Sports, Steel, Stomachic, Stomatology, Stramonium, Stupe, Suppository, Synergast, Syrup, Tabasheer, Tabashir, Tablet, Tar-water, Tetracycline, Therapeutics, TIM, Tisane, Tocology, Tonic, Totaquine, Trade, Traditional Chinese, Traumatology, Treatment, Trichology, Troche, Valerian, Veronal, Veterinary, Virology

Medicine man, Medico Bone-setter, Koradji

Medieval Archaic, Feudal, Gothic, Med, Old, Trecento

Mediocre Fair, Indifferent, Middle-of-the-road, Middling, Ordinary, Pap, Respectable, Run-of-the-mill, So-So, Undistinguished

Meditate, Meditation, Meditator, Meditative Brood, Chew, Cogitate, Contemplate, Fifteen o's, Gymnosophy, Hesychast, Muse, Mystic, Pensive, Ponder,

Reflect, Reverie, Revery, Ruminate, Thanatopsis, Transcendental, Vipassana, Weigh, Yoga, Zazen

Mediterranean Great Sea, Levant, Med, Midi, Scattermouch

Medium (A)ether, Agency, Average, Channel, Clairvoyant, Contrast, Culture, Dispersive, Element, Ether, Even, Happy, Home, Intermediary, Interstellar, M, Magilp, Mean, Megilp, Midsize, Midway, Milieu, Oils, Organ, Ouija, Planchette, Press, Radio, Regular, Shaman, Spiritist, Spiritualist, Television, Telly, TV, Vehicle

Medley Charivari, Collection, Gallimaufry, Jumble, Macedoine, Melange, Mishmash, Mix, Pastiche, Patchwork, Pi(e), Pot-pourri, Quodlibet, Ragbag, Salad, Salmagundi, Series, Tat

▷ **Medley** *may indicate* an anagram

Medusa Jellyfish, Planoblast

Meek Docile, Griselda, Humble, Milquetoast, Patient, Sheepy, Tame

Meerkat Suricate

Meerschaum Sepiolite

Meet(ing), Meeting place Abide, Abutment, AGM, Appointment, Apropos, Assemble, Assembly, Assignation, Audience, Baraza, Bosberaad, Briefing, Camporee, Caucus, Chapterhouse, Chautauqua, Clash, Conclave, Concourse, Concur, Confluence, Confrontation, Congress, Connivance, Consistory, Consulta, Contact, Conterminous, Convene, Convent(icle), Convention, Converge, Conversazione, Convocation, Correspond, Cybercafé, Defray, Demo, EGM, Encounter, Ends, Experience, Face, Find, Fit, For(e)gather, Forum, Fulfil, Gemot, General, Giron, Gorsedd, Greeting, Guild, Gyeld, Gymkhana, Gyron, Howf(f), Hunt, Hustings, Imbizo, Indaba, Infall, Interface, Interview, Join, Junction, Kgotla, Korero, Lekgotla, Liaise, Marae, Moot, Mother's, Obviate, Occlusion, Occur, Oppose, Overflow, Partenariat, Pay, Plenary, Plenum, Pnyx, Pow-wow, Prayer, Prosper, Quadrivial, Quaker, Quorate, Quorum, Race, Races, Rally, Rencontre, Rencounter, Rendezvous, Reunion, Sabbat(h), Satisfy, Séance, See, Seminar, Session, Sit, Social, Sports, Suitable, Summit, Symposium, Synastry, Synaxis, Synod, Tackle, Talkfest, Talk-in, Talking-shop, Think-in, Town, Track, Tryst, Venery, Venue, Vestry, Wapinshaw, Wardmote, Wharenui, Wharepuni, Workshop

Megalith(ic) Sarsen, Skara Brae, Stonehenge

Megalomaniac Monarcho

Megaphone Bull-horn, Loudhailer

Megapode Mound-bird, Talegalla

Meiosis Understatement

Melancholy, Melancholic Adust, Allicholy, Allycholly, Anatomy, Atrabilious, Cafard, Despond(ency), Dreary, Dump(s), Gloom, Heart-sore, Hipped, Hump, Hyp, Hypochondria, Jaques, Lienal, Moper, Panophobia, Pensieroso, Pensive, Saturnine, Sombre, Spleen, Splenetic, Triste, Tristesse, Weltschmerz

Melanesian Kanak

Mêlée Brawl, Commotion, Fracas, Rally, Salmagundi, Scrum

Melia Margosa, Neem, Nim

Mellifluent, Mellifluous Cantabile, Melodic

Mellow Fruity, Genial, Mature, Ripe, Smooth

Melodrama(tic) Bathos, Histrionic, Sensation, Transpontine

Melody, Melodious Air, Arioso, Cabaletta, Canorous, Cantabile, Cantilena, Canto (fermo), Cantus, Cavatina, Chopsticks, Conductus, Counterpoint, Descant, Dulcet, Euphonic, Fading, Musical, Orphean, Part-song, Plainsong, Ranz-des-vaches, Refrain, Songful, Strain, Theme, Tunable, → **TUNE(S)**

Melon(like) Cantaloup(e), Cas(s)aba, Charentais, Galia, Gourd, Honeydew, Mango,

Musk, Nar(r)as, Ogen, Pepo, Persian, Rock, Spanspek, Winter

Melt(ed), Melting Ablate, Colliquate, → **DISSOLVE**, Eutectic, Eutexia, Flux, Found, Fuse, Fusil(e), Liquescent, Liquid, Run, Smectic, Syntexis, Thaw, Touch

Member Adherent, Arm, Branch, Bro(ther), Charter, Chin, Confrère, Cornice, Coulisse, Crossbeam, Crypto, Direction, Felibre, Fellow, Forearm, Forelimb, Founder, Gremial, Harpin(g)s, Insider, Keel, Leg, Limb, Lintel, Longeron, M, MBE, Montant, MP, Organ, Part, Partisan, Peer, Politicaster, Politician, Private, Rood-beam, Soroptomist, Stile, Stringer, Strut, Syndic, Tie, Toe

Membrane, Membranous Amnion, Arachnoid, Axilemma, Caul, Cell, Chorioallantois, Chorion, Choroid (plexus), Chromoplast, Conjunctiva, Cornea, Cyst, Decidua, Dissepiment, Dura (mater), Endocardium, Endometrium, Endosteum, Ependyma, Exine, Extine, Fell, Film, Frenulum, Fr(a)enum, Haw, Head, Hyaloid, Hymen, Indusium, Intima, Intine, Involucre, Mater, Mediastinum, Meninx, Mesentery, Mucosa, Mucous, Neurolemma, Nictitating, Parchment, Patagium, Pellicle, Pericardium, Pericarp, Perichondrium, Pericranium, Periost(eum), Periton(a)eum, Pia mater, Plasma, Plasmalemma, Pleura, Putamen, Retina, Rim, Sarcolemma, Scarious, Schneiderian, Sclera, Serosa, Serous, Skin, Synovial, Tectorial, Tela, Third eyelid, Tissue, Tonoplast, Trophoblast, Tunic, Tympan(ic), Vacuolar, Velamen, Velum, Vitelline, Web, Yolk-sac

Memento, Memoir Keepsake, Locket, Relic, Remembrancer, Souvenir, Token, Trophy

Memo(randum) Bordereau, Cahier, Chit, IOU, Jot, Jurat, Minute, Note, Notepad, → **REMINDER**, Slip

Memoirist Casanova

Memorable, Memorise, Memory Associative, ATLAS, Bubble, Cache, Catchy, Collective, → **COMPUTER MEMORY**, Con, Core, DRAM, Dynamic, Echoic, Engram(ma), Extended, Flash (bulb), Folk, Get, Highlight, Historic, Hypermnesia, Iconic, Immortal, Immunological, Learn, Living, Long-term, Main, Mainstore, Memoriter, Mind, Mneme, Mnemonic, Mnemosyne, Non-volatile, Noosphere, Notable, Pelmanism, Photographic, Race, Read-write, Recall, Recollection, Recovered, → **REMEMBER**, Retention, Retrospection, Ro(a)te, Samskara, Screen, Semantic, Short-term, Souvenir, Sovenance, Static, Video, Virtual, Volatile, Word, Working

Memorial Albert, Altar tomb, Cenotaph, Cromlech, Ebenezer, Gravestone, Hatchment, Headstone, Marker, Monument, Mount Rushmore, Obelisk, Plaque, Relic, Relique, Statue, Tomb, Trophy, War

▶ **Memory loss** *see* **LOSS OF MEMORY**

Men(folk) Amadoda, Chaps, Chess, Cuffins, Male, Messrs, Mortals, OR, People, Race, Troops

Menace, Menacing Danger, Dennis, Endanger, Foreboding, Jeopardise, Minatory, Ominous, Peril, Pest, Threat(en)

Menagerie Ark, Circus, Zoo

Mend Beet, Bete, Bushel, Cobble, Correct, Darn, Fix, Heal, Improved, Mackle, Patch, Piece, Recover, Remedy, → **REPAIR**, Set, Sew, Solder, Trouble-shoot

Mendelevium Md

Mendicant Beggar, Calender, Fakir, Franciscan, Servite

Menial Bottlewasher, Drudge, Drug, Eta, Fag, Flunkey, Lackey, Lowly, Scullion, Servile, Toady, Underling, Wood-and-water joey

Meninx (D)jerba

Menopause Andropause, Climacteric

Menstruation Menarche, Menses

▷ **Mental** *may indicate* the chin

Mental (condition), Mental disorder, Mentality Alienism, Bunker, Doolally, Eject, Hallucinosis, Insane, Noetic, Nut job, Nutty, Paranoia, Psychic

Mention(ed) Allusion, Bename, Benempt, Broach, Bynempt, Citation, Hint, Honourable, Name, Notice, Quote, Refer, Same, Speech, State, Suggest, Touch

Mentor Advisor, Guru, Rebbe, Tutor

Menu Agenda, Card, Carte, Carte du jour, Cascading, Drop-down, Fare, List, Option, Table d'hôte, Tariff

Mercantile Commercial, Trade

Mercator Cartographer

Mercenary Arnaout, Condottiere, Freelance, Greedy, Hack, Hessian, Hired gun, Hireling, Landsknecht, Legionnaire, Pindaree, Pindari, Rutter, Sordid, Spoilsman, Swiss Guard, Venal, Wildgeese

Merchandise Cargo, Goods, Line, Produce, Ware(s)

Merchant(man) Abudah, Antonio, Broker, Bun(n)ia, Burgher, Chandler, Chap, Commission, Crare, Crayer, Dealer, Factor, Flota, Gossip, Hoastman, Importer, Jobber, Law, Magnate, Marcantant, Mercer, Monger, Négociant, Pedlar, Polo, Provision, Retailer, Seller, Shipper, Speed, Squeegee, Stapler, Sutler, Trader, Vintner, Wholesaler

Mercia Offa

Merciful, Mercy Amnesty, Charity, Clement, Compassionate, Corporal, Grace, Humane, Kind, Kyrie, Lenient, Lenity, Miserere, Misericord(e), Pacable, Pity, Quarter, Ruth, Sparing, Spiritual

Merciless Cruel, Hard, Hard-hearted, Inclement, Pitiless

Mercurial, Mercuric sulphide, Mercury Azoth, Cyllenius, Dog's, Fulminating, Herald, Hermes, Hg, Horn, Hydrargyrum, Messenger, Quicksilver, Red, Red-man, Spurge, Tiemannite, Torr, Volatile

Mere(ly) Allenarly, Bare, Common, Lake, Pond, Pool, Pure, Sheer, Tarn, Ullswater, Very

Merge(r), Merging Amalgamate, Blend, Coalesce, Composite, Conflate, Consolidate, Die, Elide, Fusion, Incorporate, Interflow, Interpenetrate, Liquesce, Meld, Melt, Mingle, Syncretism, Synergy, Unify, Unite

Meridian Magnetic, Noonday, Prime

Meringue Pavlova

Merit(ed) CL, Condign, Deserve, Due, Earn, Found, Rate, Virtue, Worth(iness)

Mermaid Dugong, Halicore, Merrow, Siren, Tavern, Undine

Merriment, Merry Andrew, Blithe(some), Bonny, Boon, Cant, Cherry, Chirpy, Crank, Elated, Full, Gaudy, Gay, Gean, Gleesome, Greek, Jocose, Jocular, Jocund, Jolly, Joyous, L'allegro, Lively, Nitid, On, Page, Riant, Sportive, Sunny, Vogie, Waggery, Wassail

Merry-andrew Clown, Jack-pudding, Pickle-herring

Merry-go-round Carousel, Galloper, Whirligig

Merry-making Cakes and ale, Carnival, Festivity, Gaiety, Gaud, Gawd, Revel

Merrythought Clavicle, Collarbone, Wishbone

Mesh Cancellate, Chain, Entangle, Mantle, Net, Reseau, Screen

Mess(y), Mess up Balls-up, Bedraggled, Boss, Botch, Canteen, Caudle, Chaos, Clamper, Clutter, Cock-up, Dog's dinner, Failure, Farrago, Fiasco, Flub, Garboil, G(l)oop, Glop, Gory, Guddle, Gunge, Gunk, Gun-room, Hash, Horlicks, Hotch-potch, Hugger-mugger, Imbroglio, Lash-up, Louse, Mash, Meal, Mismanage, Mix, Mixter-maxter, Modge, Muck, Muff, Mullock, Muss, Mux, Pi(e), Piss-up, Plight, Pollute, Pottage, Screw-up, Scungy, Shambles, Shambolic,

Shemozzle, Sight, Slaister, Smudge, Snafu, Soss, Sty, Sully, Tousle, Trifle, Untidy, Wardroom, Whoopsie, Yuck(y)

Message(s) Aerogram, Bull, Bulletin, Cable, Contraplex, Dépêche, Despatch, Dispatch, Email, Errand, Error, Flame, Kissagram, Kissogram, Letter, Missive, News, Note, Pager, Ping, Posting, Postscript, Radiogram, Rumour, Signal, Slogan, SOS, Stripagram, Strippergram, Subtext, Telegram, Telephone, Teletype®, Telex, Text, Tidings, Toothing, Valentine, Wire, → **WORD**

Messenger Angel, Angela, Apostle, Azrael, Beadle, Caddie, Caddy, Chaprassi, Chuprassy, Corbie, Courier, Culver, Despatch-rider, Emissary, Envoy, Forerunner, Gaga, Gillie-wetfoot, Gillie whitefoot, Hatta, Herald, Hermes, Internuncio, Iris, Ladas, Mercury, Nuncio, Page, Peon, Post, Pursuivant, Runner, Send, Seraph, Shellycoat, Valet de place, Valkyrie

Messiah Christ, Emmanuel, Immanuel, Mahdi, Mashiach, Prince of peace, Saviour, Shiloh, Son of man, Southcott

Met Old Bill, Weather, Weatherman

Metabolism Basal, Cryptobiotic

Metal(s), Metallic, Metalware, Metalwork Ag, Aglet, Aiglet, Aiguillette, Al, Alkali, Aluminium, Antifriction, Antimony, Babbitt, Base, Bell, Billon, Brassy, Britannia, Cadmium, Chrome, Chromium, Cobalt, Copper, Death, Dutch, Dysprosium, Er(bium), Europium, Expanded, Filler, Fine, Foil, Fusible, Gallium, Germanium, Gib, Gold, Heavy, Hot, Ingot, Invar®, Iridium, Iron, Jangling, Kamacite, Leaf, Magnolia, Manganese, Mineral, Misch, Mitis, Monel(l), Muntz, Natrium, Nickel, Niello, Noble, Nonferrous, Ore, Ormolu, Osmium, Parent, Perfect, Planchet, Platinum, Precious, Prince's, Protore, Regulus, Rhenium, Road, Ruthenium, Samarium, Scrap, Sheet(-iron), Silver, Slug, Sm, Sn, Sodium, Speculum, Speiss, Sprue, Steel, Strontium, Taggers, Tantalum, Terbic, Terbium, Terne, Thallium, Thorium, Thrash, Tin, Titanium, Tole, Toreutics, Tramp, Transition, Tutania, Tutenag, Type, White, Wolfram, Yellow, Zinc

Metal-worker Founder, Lorimer, Smith, Spurrier, Tubal Cain

Metamorphose, Metamorphism Regional, Transmogrify

▷ **Metamorphosing** *may indicate* an anagram

Metaphor Conceit, Figure, Image, Kenning, Malonym, Mixed, Symbol, Trope, Tropical

Metaphysics Ontology, Scotism

Mete Inflict

Meteor(ic), Meteorite Achondrite, Aerolite, Aerosiderite, Bolide, Chondrite, Comet, Drake, Falling star, Fireball, Geminid, Iron, Leonid, Perseid, Quadrantid, Siderite, Siderolite, Star(dust), Stony, Tektite

Meter Alidad(e), Electric, Exposure, Flow, Gas, Light, Orifice, Parking, Postage, Postal, Torque, Torsion, Water, White

Methamphetamine Ice

Methane Alkane

Methedrine® Speed

Method(ology), Methodical Art, Billings, Buteyko, Direct, Feldenkrais, Formula, Gram's, Historical, Hi-tec(h), Kenny, Kumon, Line, Manner, Mode, Modus, Modus operandi, Monte Carlo, Montessori, Neat, Orderly, Organon, Organum, Ovulation, Painstaking, Plan, Ploy, Procedure, Process, Q, Rhythm, Schafer's, Scientific, Socratic, Stanislavski, Tactics, Technique, Way, Withdrawal

Methodism, Methodist Huntingdonian, Jumper, Methody, Primitive, Ranter, Scientism, Soper, Southcottian, Swaddler, Wesley

Meths White Lady

Methuselah Bottle, Macrobiote
Meticulous Careful, → **EXACT**, Finicky, Minute, Precise, Punctilious, Quiddler, Scrupulous, Thorough
Métier Line, Trade, Vocation
Metre, Metrical Alexandrine, Amphibrach, Amphimacer, Anapaest, Antispast, Arsis, Ballad, Cadence, Choliamb, Choree, Choriamb, Common, Dipody, Galliambic, Iambic, Ithyphallic, Long, M, Penthemimer, Prosody, Pyrrhic, Rhythm, Sapphic, Scansion, Scazon, Service, Short, Spondee, Strophe, Tripody, Trochee
Metric (system) MKS
Metroland Subtopia
Metropolitan Eparch
Metrosexual Epicene
Mettle Ardour, Bravery, Courage, Ginger, Guts, Pith, → **PLUCK**, Pride, Smeddum, Spirit, Spunk, Steel
Mew Caterwaul, Miaou, Miaow, Pen, Purr, Seagull, Waul, Wrawl
Mews Meuse, Muse(t), Musit, Stables
Mexican (Indian) Atlalt, Aztec, Carib, Chicano, Chichibec, Diaz, Greaser, Gringo, Hairless, Hispanic, Latino, Maya, Mixe-Zoque, Mixtec, Montezuma, Nahuatl, Norténo, Olmec, Otomi, Pachuco, Spic, Spik, Taino, Toltec, Wetback, Zapotec, Zuni
Mezzanine Entresol
Mezzo-soprano Tessa
Mica Biotite, Daze, Fuchsite, Glimmer, Isinglass, Lepidolite, Lepidomelane, Muscovite, Paragonite, Phlogopite, Rubellan, Sericite, Talc, Verdite, Vermiculite
Micawber Wilkins
Michael Mick(e)y
Mick(ey) Greek, Mouse
Micro Mu
Microbe, Microorganism Extremophile, Germ, Lactobacillus, Nanobe, Organism
Microphone Bug, Carbon, Crystal, Directional, Lavaliere, Lip, Mike, Phonic Ear®, Radio, Ribbon, Throat
Microscope Acoustic, Compound, Confocal, Darkfield, Dissecting, Electron, Engyscope, Field-ion, Lens, Optical, Phase-contrast, Phase-difference, Proton, Reading, Reflecting, SEM, Simple, Solar, TEM, Ultraviolet
Microwave Nuke
Mid(st) Amongst, Mongst
Midas Goldinger, Tamarin
Midday Meridian, N, Noon, Noon-tide, Noon-time
Middle, Middling Active, Ariston metron, Basion, Centre, Core, Crown, Enteron, Excluded, Eye, Girth, Heart, Innermost, Loins, Median, Mediocre, Meridian, Meseraic, Mesial, Mesne, Meso, Midriff, Moderate, Noon, Passive, Turn, Twixt, Undistributed, Via media, Wa(i)st
Middle age Menopause
Middle-Cambrian Menevian
Middle class Bourgeois, Hova, Mondeo Man
Middle Eastern Arab, Iraqi, Omani
Middleman Broker, Comprador(e), Diaphragm, Interlocutor, Intermediary, Jobber, Median, Navel, Regrater, Regrator
Middlesex Hermaphrodite
Midge Gall, Gnat
Midget Dwarf, Homunculus, Lilliputian, Pygmy, Shrimp
Midianite Prowler

Midlander Brummie
Midlands Mercia
Midnight G, O Am
▶ **Midnight** *see* **PAST MIDNIGHT**
Midriff Phrenic, Skirt, Waist
Midshipman Brass-bounder, Easy, Middy, Oldster, Reefer, Snottie, Snotty
▶ **Midst** *see* **MID**
Mid-Westerner Indianan
Midwife Accoucheur, Doula, Gran(nie), Granny, Howdie, Howdy, Lucina, Mab, Obstetric
Mien Air, Bearing, Demean, Manner
Might(iness), Mighty Force, Main, Maud, Mote, Nibs, Potence, → **POWER**, Prowess, Puissant, Should, Strength
Mignon(ette) Dyer's rocket, Fillet, Reseda, Weld
Migraine Megrim, Scotodinia, Teichopsia
Migrant Economic, Externe, Gastarbeiter, Lemming, Traveller
Migrate, Migration, Migratory Colonise, Diapedesis, Diaspora, Drift, Eelfare, Exodus, Fleet, Great Trek, Run, Tre(c)k, Volkwanderung
Mikado Emperor, Kami, Teno
Mike Bug, Stentorphone
Milanese Patarine
Mild(ly) Balmy, Benign, Bland, Clement, Euphemism, Genial, Gentle, Lenient, Litotes, Mansuete, Meek, → **MODERATE**, Pacific, Patient, Sarcenet, Sars(e)net, Temperate
Mildew Downy, Foxing, Fungus, Mould, Oidium, Powdery, Vine, Wheat
Mile(s) Admiralty, Coss, Coverdale, Food, Geographical, Irish, Knot, Kos, League, Li, Mi, Milliary, Nautical, Passenger, Roman, Royal, Scots, Sea, Soldier, Square, Standish, Statute, Swedish, Train
Milesian Teague
Milestone Milliary, MS
Milfoil Yarrow
Militant, Military Activist, Aggressive, Battailous, Black Panther, Black Power, Commando, Fortinbras, Hawkish, Hezbollah, Hizbollah, Hizbullah, Hostile, Ireton, Janjaweed, Janjawid, Kshatriya, Landsturm, Landwehr, Lumper, Mameluke, Martial, Presidio, Provisional, Provo, Soldatesque, Stratocracy, West Point
Militia(-man) Band, Fyrd, Guard, Haganah, Milice, Minuteman, Peshmerga, Reserve, Tanzim, Trainband, Yeomanry
Milk(er), Milky Acidophilus, Beestings, Bland, Bleed, Bonny-clabber, Bristol, Butter, Casein, Certified, Churn, Colostrum, Condensed, Creamer, Crud, Curd, Dairy, Emulge, Evaporated, Exploit, Galactic, Glacier, Goat's, Homogenised, Jib, Kefir, Kephir, K(o)umiss, Lactation, Lacteal, Latex, Maas, Madafu, Madzoon, Magnesia, Malted, Mamma, Matzoon, Mess, Moo-juice, Opaline, Pasteurised, Pigeon's, Pinta, Posset, Raw, Rice, Sap, Semi-skimmed, Shedder, Skim(med), Soya, Squeeze, Strippings, Stroke, Suckle, Town, UHT, Use, Whig, Whole, Yaourt, Yogh(o)urt
Milking-machine, Milking parlour Loan, Tapper
Milking-pail Leglan, Leglen, Leglin
Milkless Agalactic, Dry, Eild
Milkmaid, Milkman Chalker, Dey, Emulge, Kefir, Kephir, Radha, Rounder, Roundsman, Skimmed
Milksop Coward, Meacock, Namby-pamby, Nance, Pance, Weakling
Milk-vetch Loco
Milkweed Asclepias

Milkwort Senega
Milky Way Via Lactea
Mill(ing), Mills Aswarm, Ball, Barker's, Boxing, Coffee, Crazing, Economist, Flour,
Gang, Gastric, Gig, Grind(er), Hayley, Kibble, Knurl, Lumber, Malt, Mano, Melder,
Molar, Nurl, Oil, Paper, Pepper, Plunge-cut, Post, Powder, Press, Pug, Pulp,
Quartz, Quern, Reave, Rob, Rolling, Rumour, Satanic, Scutcher, Smock, Spinning,
Stamp, Stamping, Strip, Sucken, Sugar, Surge, Thou, Tide, Tower, Tuck, Water,
Wool(len), Works
Miller Dusty, Glen, Grinder, Jester, Joe, Molendinar, Multurer
Millet Bajra, Bajree, Bajrii, Couscous, Dari, Dhurra, Doura, Dur(r)a, Grain, Miliary,
Negro-corn, Pearl, Proso, Ragee, Raggee, Ragi, Whisk
Milliner Hatter, Modiste
Millionaire Astor, Carnegie, Rockefeller, Rothschild, Vanderbilt
Millions, Millionth Crore, Femto-, Milliard, Muckle, Pico-
Millipede Songololo
Millstone Ligger, Rind, Rynd
Mim Perjink
Mime, Mimic(ry) Ape, Batesian, Copycat, Farce, Imitate, Impersonate, Lipsync,
Marceau, Mina, Mock, Mullerian, Mummer, Parody, Sturnine, Take-off
Mimosa Cacoon, Raintree, Saman
Mince Cecils, Chop, Dice, Grate, Grind, Keema, Prance, Rice
Mind(er) Aide, Beware, Bodyguard, Brain, Gaum, Genius, Grasshopper, Handler,
Head, → **HEED**, Herd, Id, Intellect, Mentality, Month's, Noology, Noosphere, Nous,
One-track, Open, Phrenic, Psyche, Psychogenic, Resent, Sensorium, Tabula rasa,
Tend, Thinker, View, Wit, Woundwort, Year's
Mine, Mining Acoustic, Antenna, Biomining, Bomb, Bonanza, Bord and pillar,
Bottom, Bouquet, Burrow, Camouflet, Chemical, Claymore, Colliery, Contact,
Creeping, Dane-hole, Data, Dig(gings), Drifting, Egg, Eldorado, Excavate, Explosive,
Fiery, Floating, Flooder, Fougade, Fougasse, Gallery, Gob, Golconda, Gold, Gopher,
Grass, Homing, Land, Limpet, Magnetic, Microbiological, Naked-light, Nostromo,
Open-cast, Open-cut, Ophir, Pit, Placer, Pressure, Prospect, Rising, Sap, Set(t),
Show, Sonic, Stannary, Stope, Strike, Strip, Undercut, Wheal, Win, Workings
Mine-deflector Otter, Paravane
Mine-owner Operator
Miner, Mine-worker, Mine-working Bevin boy, Butty-gang, Collier, Continuous,
Corporal, Cutter, Digger, Faceworker, Forty-niner, Geordie, Leaf, Molly Maguire,
Noisy, NUM, Oncost(man), Pitman, Shot-firer, Stall, Tippler, Tributer, UDM
Mineral(s) Accessory, Essential, Index, Ore, Owre

MINERALS

3 letters:	Talc	Fluor	6 letters:
YAG	Trap	Macle	Acmite
	Urao	Mafic	Albite
4 letters:		Nitre	Augite
Clay	5 letters:	Prase	Blende
Foid	Balas	Topaz	Cerite
Gang	Borax	Trona	Galena
Mica	Chert	Umber	Gangue
Sard	Emery		Garnet
Spar	Flint		Glance

6 letters – cont:
Gypsum
Hauyne
Illite
Iolite
Jargon
Kermes
Lithia
Natron
Nosean
Pinite
Pyrite
Quartz
Rutile
Schorl
Silica
Sphene
Spinel
Tincal
Zircon

7 letters:
Alunite
Anatase
Apatite
Axinite
Azurite
Barytes
Biotite
Bornite
Brucite
Calcite
Calomel
Catseye
Cuprite
Cyanite
Diamond
Dysodil
Epidote
Euclase
Eucrite
Fahlore
Felspar
Gahnite
Göthite
Gummite
Hessite
Ice spar
Jadeite
Jargoon
Kainite

Kernite
Kyanite
Leucite
Mellite
Mullite
Nacrite
Niobite
Olivine
Pennine
Peridot
Pyrites
Realgar
Rosaker
Sylvine
Sylvite
Thorite
Thulite
Tripoli
Turgite
Ulexite
Uralite
Uranite
Uranium
Zeolite
Zeuxite
Zincite
Zoisite
Zorgite

8 letters:
Adularia
Allanite
Analcime
Analcite
Andesine
Ankerite
Antimony
Aphanite
Asbestos
Autunite
Blue john
Boehmite
Boracite
Braunite
Bronzite
Brookite
Calamine
Cerusite
Chlorite
Chromite
Cinnabar

Cleveite
Corundum
Crocoite
Cryolite
Datolite
Dendrite
Diallage
Diaspore
Disthene
Dolomite
Dysodile
Dysodyle
Epsomite
Erionite
Euxenite
Fayalite
Feldspar
Flinkite
Fluorite
Galenite
Gibbsite
Goethite
Gyrolite
Hematite
Idocrase
Ilmenite
Iodyrite
Jarosite
Lazulite
Lazurite
Lewisite
Limonite
Liparite
Massicot
Meionite
Melilite
Mimetite
Monazite
Nephrite
Noselite
Orpiment
Petuntse
Picotite
Prehnite
Pyroxene
Resalgar
Rock-salt
Sanidine
Saponite
Siderite
Smectite

Sodalite
Stannite
Stibnite
Stilbite
Sunstone
Taconite
Tenorite
Titanite
Troilite
Vesuvian
Xenotime
Zaratite

9 letters:
Alabaster
Allophane
Amazonite
Amphibole
Anglesite
Anhydrite
Anorthite
Aragonite
Argentite
Atacamite
Blackjack
Blacklead
Carnelian
Carnotite
Celestine
Celestite
Cerussite
Chabazite
Chalybite
Cheralite
Chondrule
Cobaltine
Cobaltite
Coccolite
Columbate
Columbite
Covellite
Cystolith
Dolomitic
Elaeolite
Endomorph
Enhydrite
Enstatite
Erythrite
Fibrolite®
Flowstone
Fluorspar

Gehlenite
Germanite
Geyserite
Gmelinite
Goslarite
Haematite
Harmotome
Hercynite
Hiddenite
Hornstone
Kaolinite
Kermesite
Kieserite
Magnesite
Magnetite
Malachite
Manganite
Marcasite
Margarite
Marialite
Microlite
Microlith
Millerite
Mispickel
Mizzonite
Moonstone
Muscovite
Natrolite
Nepheline
Nephelite
Niccolite
Nitratine
Olivenite
Ottrelite
Paramorph
Pargasite
Pectolite
Periclase
Pericline
Perimorph
Phenacite
Pleonaste
Polianite
Pollucite
Powellite
Proustite
Rhodonite
Rubellite
Scapolite
Scheelite
Scolecite

Septarium
Spodumene
Sylvanite
Tantalite
Tremolite
Troostite
Tungstite
Uraninite
Uvarovite
Variscite
Vulpinite
Wavellite
Wernerite
Willemite
Witherite
Wulfenite
Zinkenite

10 letters:
Actinolite
Alabandine
Alabandite
Andalusite
Bastnasite
Calaverite
Carnallite
Chalcocite
Chessylite
Chrysolite
Colemanite
Cordierite
Crocoisite
Dyscrasite
Forsterite
Gadolinite
Garnierite
Glauconite
Halloysite
Heulandite
Honey-stone
Hornblende
Indicolite
Indigolite
Jamesonite
Laurdalite
Meerschaum
Microcline
Mirabilite
Oligoclase
Orthoclase
Paragonite

Perovskite
Phosgenite
Piemontite
Polybasite
Polyhalite
Pyrolusite
Pyrrhotine
Pyrrhotite
Redruthite
Riebeckite
Ripidolite
Samarskite
Saphir d'eau
Sapphirine
Saussurite
Serpentine
Smaragdite
Sperrylite
Sphalerite
Staurolite
Tennantite
Thaumasite
Thenardite
Thorianite
Tiemannite
Torbernite
Tourmaline
Triphylite
Vanadinite
Wolframite

11 letters:
Alexandrite
Amblygonite
Annabergite
Apophyllite
Baddeleyite
Bastnaesite
Cassiterite
Chiastolite
Chrysoberyl
Clinochlore
Crocidolite
Dendrachate
Franklinite
Greenockite
Hypersthene
Idiomorphic
Josephinite
Labradorite
Molybdenite

Pentlandite
Phosphorite
Piedmontite
Pitchblende
Plagioclase
Pseudomorph
Psilomelane
Pyrargyrite
Pyrrhotiner
Sal ammoniac
Sillimanite
Smithsonite
Tabular spar
Tetradymite
Vermiculite
Vesuvianite
Ythro-cerite

12 letters:
Adularescent
Arfvedsonite
Arsenopyrite
Babingtonite
Chalcanthite
Chalcopyrite
Cristobalite
Dumortierite
Feldspathoid
Fluorapatite
Hemimorphite
Pyromorphite
Pyrophyllite
Senarmontite
Skutterudite
Strontianite
Synadelphite
Tetrahedrite
Wollastonite

13 letters:
Cummingtonite
Rhodochrosite

14 letters:
Yttro-tantalite

15 letters:
Gooseberry-stone
Montmorillonite

Mineralogy, Mineralogist Haüy, Heuland, Oryctology

Mineral water Apollinaris, Tonic

Minesweeper Oropesa, Unity

Mingle, Mingling Blend, Circulate, Consort, Interfuse, Mell, Merge, → **MIX**, Participate, Socialise, Theocrasy, Unite

Mini Cab, Car, Skirt, Teen(s)y, Teeny-weeny

Miniature, Miniaturist Cosway, Microcosm, Midget, Model, Toy, Young

Minimise, Minimum (range) Bare, Downplay, Fewest, Least, Neap, Shoestring, Stime, Styme, Threshold, Undervalue

▷ **Minimum of** *may indicate* the first letter

Minion Flunkey, Lackey, Pet, Subordinate, Tool, Vassal

Minister Ambassador, Attend, Buckle-beggar, Cabinet, Chancellor, Chaplain, Cleric, Coarb, Commissar, Deacon, Dewan, Diplomat, Divine, D(i)wan, Dominee, Dominie, Envoy, First, Foreign, Holy Joe, Mas(s)john, Mes(s)john, Moderator, Nurse, Officiant, Padre, Parson, Pastor, Peshwa, Preacher, Predikant, Presbyter, Priest, Prime, Rector, Richelieu, Secretary, Seraskier, → **SERVE**, Stick, Stickit, Subdeacon, Tend, Visier, Vizier, Wazir, Wizier

Ministry Defence, Department, Dept, DoE, MOD, MOT, Orders, Service

▷ **Ministry** *may indicate* some government department

Mink Kolinsky, Mutation, Vison

Minnow Devon, Penk, Pink, Tiddler

Minoan Knossus

Minor(ity) Child, Comprimario, Ethnic, Faction, Few, Incidental, Infant, Junior, Less, Minutia, Nonage, One-horse, Peripheral, Petty, Pupillage, Signed, Slight, Small-time, Sub, Trivial, Ward, Weeny

Minotaur Bull-headed, Cretan

Minstrel Allan-a-Dale, Bard, Blondel, Bones, Busker, Cantabank, Christy, Cornerman, Gleeman, Hamfatter, Joculator, Jongleur, Minnesinger, Nigger, Pierrot, Scop, Singer, Taillefer

Mint Aim, Bugle-weed, Catnip, Coin, Ettle, Fortune, Herb, Horse, Humbug, Labiate, Monarda, Monetise, Nep, New, Penny-royal, Pepper, Pile, Polo®, Poly, Royal, Selfheal, Spear, Stamp, Stone, Strike, Unused, Utter, Water

Minute(s), Minutiae Acta, Alto, Degree, Detailed, Diatom, Entry, Infinitesimal, Little, Micron, Mo, Mu, Nano-, New York, Pinpoint, Resume, Small, Teen(t)sy, Teeny, Tine, Tiny, Trivia, Tyne, Wee

Minx Hellion

Miracle(s), Miraculous, Miracle worker Cana, Marvel, Merel(l), Meril, Morris, Mystery, Phenomenon, Saluter, Supernatural, Thaumatology, Thaumaturgic, Theurgy, Wirtschaftswunder, Wonder, Wonderwork

Mirage Fata morgana, Illusion, Loom, Northern lights

Mire Bog, Glaur, Lair(y), Latch, Lerna, Lerne, Loblolly, Marsh, Mud, Quag, Sludge, Soil

Mirky Dark, Dirk(e)

Mirror(s), Mirrored Alasnam, Antidazzle, Busybody, Cambuscan, Catoptric, Cheval, Claude Lorraine glass, Coelostat, Conde, Conjugate, Dare, Driving, Enantiomorph, Glass, Image, Imitate, Keeking-glass, Lao, Magnetic, Merlin, One-way, Pierglass, Primary, Psyche, Rearview, → **REFLECT**, Reynard, Shisha, Siderostat, Sign, Specular, Speculum, Stone, Tiring-glass, Two-way, Vulcan, Wing

Mirror-image Perversion

Mirth(ful) Cheer, Dream, Festive, Hilarity, Joy, Laughter, Spleen

▷ **Misalliance** *may indicate* an anagram

Misanthrope Cynic, Timon
Misapplication Catachresis, Misuse
Misappropriate, Misappropriation Asport, Detinue, Purloin, Steal
Miscarry Abort, Backfire, Fail, Slink, Warp
Miscegenation Allocarpy
Miscellaneous, Miscellany Ana, Assortment, Chow, Collectanea, Diverse, Etceteras, Job lot, Misc, Odds and ends, Odds and sods, Olio, Omnium-gatherum, Potpourri, Raft, Ragbag, Sundry, Varia, Variety, Various
Mischance Misfare
Mischief(-maker), Mischievous Ate, Bale, Bane, Cantrip, Cloots, Devilment, Diablerie, Dido, Disservice, Gallus, Gremlin, Hanky-panky, Harm, Hellery, Hellion, Hob, Imp, Injury, Jinks, Larrikin, Limb, Litherly, Make-bate, Malicho, Mallecho, Monkey-tricks, Nickum, Owl-spiegle, Pestilent, Pickle, Prank, Puckish, Rascal, Scally(wag), Scamp, Scapegrace, Shenanigans, Spriteful, Tricksy, Wag, Wicked, Widgie
Misconception Delusion, Idol(on), Idolum, Misunderstanding
Misconduct Impropriety, Malfeasance, Malversation
Miscreant Reprobate, Sinner, Tortfeasor
Misdeed Offence, Peccadillo, Trespass, Wrong
▷ **Misdelivered** *may indicate* an anagram
Misdemeanour Delict, Offence, Peccadillo, Tort, Wrongdoing
Miser(ly) Carl, Cheapskate, Cheese-parer, Close, Curmudgeon, Flay-flint, Gare, Grasping, Harpagon, Hunks, Marner, Meanie, Mingy, Muckworm, Niggard, Nipcheese, Nipcurn, Nipfarthing, Pennyfather, Pinch-commons, Puckfist, Runt, Save-all, Scrape-good, Scrape-penny, Screw, Scrimping, Scrooge, Skinflint, Snudge, Storer, Tightwad, Timon
Miserable, Misery, Miserably Abject, Angashore, Bale, Cat-lap, Crummy, Distress, Dole, Face-ache, Forlorn, Gloom, Grief, Heartache, Hell, Joyless, Killjoy, Lousy, Perdition, Punk, Sad, Scungy, Sorry, Sourpuss, Tragic, Triste, → **UNHAPPY**, Woe(begone), Wretched
Misfire Dud
Misfit Drop-out, Geek, Loner, Maverick, Sad sack
Misfortune Accident, Affliction, Bale, Calamity, Curse, Disaster, Distress, Dole, Hex, Ill, Ill-luck, Reverse, Rewth, Ruth, Wroath
Misgiving(s) Anxiety, Doubt, Dubiety, Qualms, Scruples
Misguide(d) Impolitic, Off-beam
▷ **Misguided** *may indicate* an anagram
Mishandle Abuse
Mishap Accident, Contretemps, Drere, Misaunter, Misfortune, Pile-up, Wroath
Misheard Mondegreen
Mishit, Misstroke Crab, Draw, Edge, Fluff, Muff, Sclaff, Shank, Slice, Thin, Toe, Top
Misinterpret(ation) Mondegreen, Wrest
Mislay Leese, Lose
Mislead(ing) Blind, Bum steer, Cover-up, Deceive, Delude, Dupe, Equivocate, Fallacious, False, Gag, Red herring, Runaround, Smoke and mirrors
▷ **Misled** *may indicate* an anagram
Mismanage Blunder, Bungle, Muddle
Mismatch Kludge
Misplace(ment) Anachorism, Ectopia
Misplay Fluff, Whitechapel
Misprint Error, Literal, Literal error, Slip, Typo

Mispronunciation Cacoepy, Lallation, Lambdacism
Misrepresent(ation) Abuse, Belie, Calumny, Caricature, Colour, Distort, Falsify, Garble, Lie, Slander, Subreption, Traduce, Travesty
▷ **Miss** *may refer to* Missouri
Miss(ing) Abord, Air, Astray, Avoid, AWOL, Colleen, Desiderate, Dodge, Drib, Err(or), Fail, Forego, Gal, → **GIRL**, Kumari, Lack, Lass, Link, Lose, Mademoiselle, Maid, Maiden, Mile, Muff(et), Near, Neglect, Negligence, Omit, Otis, Overlook, Señorita, Shy, Skip, Spinster, Stoke, Unmeet, Wanting, Whiff
Missal Breviary, Te igitur, Triodion
Misshapen Crooked, Deformed, Dysmelia, Gnarled
Missile Air-to-air, ALCM, Ammo, Anti-ballistic, Arrow, Artillery, Atlas, Ball, Ballistic, Beam Rider, Blue streak, Bolas, Bolt, Bomb, Boomerang, Brickbat, Bullet, Condor, Cruise, Dart, Death star, Dingbat, Doodlebug, Dum-dum, Exocet®, Falcon, Fléchette, Genie, Grenade, Guided, HARM, Harpoon, Hawk, Hellfire, Hound Dog, ICBM, Interceptor, Jired, Kiley, Kyley, Kylie, Lance, Mace, MARV, Maverick, Minuteman, MIRV, Missive, Mx, Onion, Patriot, Pellet, Pershing, Phoenix, Polaris, Poseidon, Qual, Quarrel, Rocket, SAM, Scud, Sea Skimmer, Sergeant, Shell, Shillelagh, Shot, Shrike, Side-winder, Smart bomb, Snowball, Sparrow, Spartan, Spear, Sprint, SSM, Standard Arm, Standoff, Styx, Subroc, Surface to air, Surface to surface, Talos, Tartar, Terrier, Thor, Titan, Tomahawk, Torpedo, Tracer, Trident, UAM, Warhead
Mission(ary) Aidan, Alamo, Antioch, Apostle, Assignment, Augustine, Barnabas, Bethel, Caravan, Charge, Columba, Delegation, Embassage, Embassy, Errand, Evangelist, Foreign, Happy-clappy, Iona, Legation, Livingstone, LMS, Message, Missiology, NASA, Neurolab, Ninian, Op, Paul, Pr(a)efect, Quest, Reclaimer, Redemptorist, Schweitzer, Task, Vocation, Xavier
Missis, Missus, Mrs Devi, Maam, Mrs, Wife
Missive Letter, Message, Note
Missouri Mo
▶ **Misstroke** *see* **MISHIT**
Mist(y) Australian, Blur, Brume, Cloud, Dew, Drow, Dry-ice, Film, Fog, Fret, Haar, Haze, Hoar, Miasma, Moch, Nebular, Niflheim, Rack, Red, Roke, Scotch, Sea-fret, Sfumato, Smir(r), Smog, Smur, Spotted, Vapour
Mistake(n) Barry (Crocker), Bish, Bloomer, Blooper, Blue, Blunder, Boner, Boob, Booboo, Boss, Botch, Category, Clanger, Clinker, Confound, Deluded, Domino, Erratum, Error, Fault, Floater, Flub, Fluff, Folly, Gaffe, Goof, Hash, Horlicks, Howler, Identity, Incorrect, Lapse, Malapropism, Misprision, Miss, Muff, Mutual, Nod, Off-beam, Oops, Oversight, Plonker, Pratfall, Ricket, Screw-up, → **SLIP**, Slip-up, Solecism, Stumer, Trip, Typo
▷ **Mistake(n)** *may indicate* an anagram
Mister Babu, Effendi, Mr, Reb, Sahib, Señor, Shri, Sir, Sri
Mistletoe Album, Missel, Parasite, Sinker, Viscum
Mistreat Abuse, Attrite, Manhandle, Violate
Mistress Amie, Aspasia, Canary-bird, Chatelaine, Concubine, Courtesan, Demimondaine, Devi, Doxy, Goodwife, Herself, Hussif, Inamorata, Instructress, Kept woman, Lady, Leman, Maintenon, Martha, Montespan, Mrs, Natural, Paramour, Stepney, Teacher, Wardrobe, Wife
Mistrust(ful) Askant, Doubt, Gaingiving, Suspect, Suspicion
Misunderstand(ing) Disagreement, Discord, Mistake
Misuse Abuse, Catachresis, Defalcate, Malappropriate, Malapropism, Maltreat, Perversion, Torment

Mite Acaridian, Acarus, Berry bug, Bit, Bulb, Cheese, Child, Dust, Flour, Forage, Fowl, Gall, Harvest, Itch, Lepton, Little, (Red) spider, Rust, Sarcoptes, Speck, Sugar, Trombiculid, Tyroglyphid, Varroa, Widow's

Mitigate, Mitigating Abate, Allay, Allieve, Ameliorate, Assuage, Excuse, Extenuating, Lenitive, Lessen, Mease, Palliate, Quell, Relief, Relieve

Mitosis Anaphase

Mitre Hat, Tiar(a)

Mitt(en), Mittens Fist, Glove, Hand, Paw, Pockies

Mix(ed), Mixer, Mixture, Mix-up Alloy, Amalgam, Associate, Assortment, Attemper, Balderdash, Bigener, Bland, Blend, Blunge, Bombay, Bordeaux, Brew, Carburet, Card, Caudle, Chichi, Chow, Cocktail, Co-meddle, Compo, Compound, Conché, Conglomerate, Consort, Cross, Cut, Disperse, Diversity, Dolly, Drammock, Embroil, Emulsion, Eutectic, Farrago, Fold-in, Freezing, Garble, Grill, Griqua, Half-breed, Heather, Hobnob, Hotchpotch, Hybrid, Imbroglio, Interlace, Intermingle, Isomorphous, Jumble, Lace, Lard, Lignin, Linctus, Load, Macedoine, Marketing, Matissé, Meddle, Medley, Melange, Mell, Meng(e), Ment, Mess, Mestizo, Métis, Ming(le), Miscellaneous, Miscellany, Mishmash, Mong, Motley, Muddle, Muss(e), Neapolitan, Octaroon, Octoroon, Olio, Olla, Pi(e), Potin, Pousowdie, Powsowdy, Praiseach, Promiscuous, Raggle-taggle, Ragtag, Salad, Scramble, Shuffle, Soda, Spatula, Stew, Stir, Temper, Through-other, Trail, Vision, Witches' brew, Yblent

▷ **Mixed** *may indicate* an anagram

Mizzle Decamp, Scapa, Scarper

Mnemonic(s) Fleming's rules, Memoria technica, Quipo, Quipu, Reminder

Moab(ite) Balak, Ruth, Wash-pot

Moan(ing) Beef, Bewail, Bleat, Complain, Groan, Hone, Keen, → **LAMENT**, Meane, Plangent, Sigh, Snivel, Sough, Wail, W(h)inge

Moat Dike, Ditch, Foss(e)

Mob(ster) Army, Assail, Canaille, Crew, Crowd, Doggery, Faex populi, Flash, Gaggle, Gang, Herd, Hoi-polloi, Hoodlum, Horde, Lynch, Many-headed beast, Ochlocrat, Press, Rabble, Rabble rout, Raft, Ragtag, Ribble-rabble, Riff-raff, Rout, Scar-face

Mobile, Mobilise, Mobility Donna, Downward, Fluid, Horizontal, Intergenerational, Movable, Plastic, Rally, Thin, Upward(ly), Vagile, Vertical

Mob-rule Ochlocracy

Mocassin Larrigan, Shoe, Snake

Mock(ery), Mocking Ape, Banter, Chaff, Chyack, Cod, Cynical, Deride, Derisory, Dor, Ersatz, False, Farce, Fleer, Flout, Gab, Geck, Gibe, Gird, Guy, Imitation, Irony, Irrisory, Jape, → **JEER**, Jibe, Lampoon, Laugh, Mimic, Narquois, Parody, Paste, Pillorise, Rail(lery), Rally, Ridicule, Sacrilege, Sardonic, Satirise, Scorn, Scout, Serve, Sham, Simulate, Slag, Sneer, Sport, Travesty, Twit, Wry

Mocking-bird Mimus, Sage-thrasher

Mode Aeolian, Authentic, Church, Convention, Dorian, Ecclesiastical, Fashion, Form, Formal, Greek, Gregorian, Hyperdorian, Hypo(dorian), Hypolydian, Iastic, Insert, Ionian, Locrian, Lydian, Major, Manner, Material, Medieval, Minor, Mixolydian, Phrygian, Plagal, Rate, Real-time, Sleep, Step, Style, Ton

Model(ler), Modelling Archetype, Bozzetto, Cast, Copy, Demonstration, Diorama, Doll, Dress-form, Dummy, Ecorché, Effigy, Epitome, Example, Exemplar, Exemplary, Fictor, Figure, Figurine, Icon, Ideal, Image, Instar, Jig, Last, Lay-figure, Layman, Madame Tussaud, Manakin, Manikin, Mannequin, Maquette, Mark, Mirror, Mock-up, → **MOULD**, Norm, Original, Orrery, Papier-mâché, Parade, Paragon, Pattern, Phelloplastic, Pilot, Plasticine, Plastilina, Play-Doh®, Pose(r),

Posture-maker, Precedent, Prototype, Replica, Role, Scale, Schema, Sedulous, Sitter, Specimen, Standard, Superwaif, T, Template, Templet, Terrella, Toy, Trilby, Twiggy, Type, Typify, Waif, Waxwork, Working

▷ **Model(s)** *may indicate* an anagram

Modem Subset

Moderate(ly), Moderation Abate, Allay, Alleviate, Assuage, Attemper, Average, Ca'canny, Centre, Chasten, Continent, Decent, Diminish, Discretion, Ease, Gentle, Girondist, Ho, Lessen, Lukewarm, Measure, Mediocre, Medium, Menshevik, Mezzo, Middling, Mild, Mitigate, OK, Politique, Reason(able), Restraint, RR, Slake, So-so, Sumptuary, Temper(ate), Temperance, Tolerant, Tone, Via media, Wet

Modern(ise) AD, Aggiornamento, Contemporary, Fresh, Latter(-day), Milly, Neonomian, Neoterical, → **NEW**, New-fangled, Present-day, Progressive, Recent, Retrofit, Swinger, Trendy, Update, Up-to-date

Modest(y) Aidos, Blaise, Chaste, Coy, Decent, Demure, Discreet, Fair, Humble, Humility, Ladylike, Low-key, Lowly, Maidenly, Mim, Mussorgsky, Propriety, Prudish, Pudency, Pudicity, Pure, Reserved, Shame, Shamefaced, Shy, Unassuming, Unpretending, Unpretentious, Verecund

Modicum Dash

Modifiable, Modification, Modifier, Modify Adapt, Adjust, Adverb, Alter, Backpedal, Change, Enhance, Extenuate, H, Leaven, Misplaced, Plastic, Qualify, Retrofit, Sandhi, Scumble, Soup, Streamline, Temper, Top, Trim, Vary

Modulation, Module, Modulus Accent, Amplitude, Bulk, Cadence, Command, Distance, Excursion, Frequency, Habitat, Inflexion, Lem, Lunar, Mitigate, Phase, Pulse, Service, Tune, Unit, Vary, Velocity, Young's

Mogul Bigwig, Magnate, Nawab, Padishah, Plutocrat, Potentate, Taipan, VIP

Mohair Moire

Mohammed, Mohammedan (era) Hadith, Hegira, Hejira, Hejra, Hijra, Islamite, Mahdi, Mahoun(d), Moslem, Muezzin, Mussulman, Prophet, Said, Shiite, Sunna(h)

Moist(en), Moisture Baste, Bedew, Damp, Dank, De(a)w, Dewy, Humect, Latch, Love-in-a-mist, Madefy, Mesarch, Moil, Nigella, Oozy, Precipitation, Slake, Slocken, Soggy, Sponge, Wet

▷ **Moither** *may indicate* an anagram

Molar Cheek tooth, Grinder, Mill-tooth, Secodont, Tooth, Wang

Molasses Blackstrap, Sorghum, Treacle

Mole(hill) Beauty spot, Breakwater, Fen-cricket, Golden, Hydatidiform, Jetty, Marsupial, Miner, Mo(u)diewart, Moudi(e)wart, Mouldiwarp, Naeve, Notoryctes, Orology, Pier, Sea-wall, Shrew, Sleeper, Spot, Spy, Star-nose(d), Talpa, Want(hill), Want knap, Warp

Molecule, Molecular Acceptor, Aptamer, Atom, Buckyball, Carbene, Cavitand, Chiral, Chromophore, Closed chain, Cobalamin, Codon, Coenzyme, Cofactor, Dimer, DNA, Electrogen, Enantiomorph, Footballene, Fullerene, Gram, Hapten, Iota, Isomer, Kinin, Kisspeptin, Ligand, Long-chain, Metabolite, Metameric, Monomer, Nanotube, Peptide, Polymer, Polysaccharide, Quark, Replicon, Ribozyme, Semantide, Stereoisomer, Synthon, Trimer, Uridine, Vector

Molendinar Mill

Molest(er) Annoy, Bother, Disturb, Harass, Nonce, Scour

Moll(y), Mollie Bloom, Bonnie, Carousal, Cutpurse, Flanders, Girl, Maguire, Malone, May, Sissy

Mollify Appease, Fob, Mease, Mitigate, Pacify, Placate, Relax, Soften, Temper

Mollusc(s) Ammonite, Amphineura, Arca, Argonaut, Ark-shell, Auricula, Belemnite, Bivalve, Bulla, Capiz, Cephalopod, Chiton, Clam, Cockle, Conch,

Cone-shell, Cowrie, Cowry, Cuttle(fish), Dentalium, Doris, Gaper, Gast(e)ropod, Goniatite, Heart-cockler, Heart-shell, Helix, Horse mussel, Idler, Lamellibranch, Limpet, Malacology, Marine boxer, Money cowry, Monoplacophora, Murex, Mussel, Mya, Nautiloid, Nautilus, Neopilina, Octopod, Octopus, Olive, Opisthobranch, Oyster, Pandora, Paper nautilus, Paper-sailor, Pearly nautilus, Pecten, Pelecypoda, Pelican's-foot, Pholas, Piddock, Pinna, Polyp, Polyplacophora, Poulpe, Protostome, Pteropod, Quahaug, Quahog, Razor-clam, Razor-fish, Razorshell, Rock borer, Saxicava, Scallop, Scaphopoda, Sea-hare, Sea-lemon, Sea-slug, Sepia, → **SHELLFISH**, Shipworm, Slipper limpet, Slug, Snail, Solen, Spat, Spirula, Spoot, Squid, Strombus, Tectibranch, Tellen, Tellin, Teredo, Toheroa, Top-shell, Triton, Trochophore, Trochus, Trough-shell, Turbo, Tusk-shell, Unio, Univalve, Veliger, Venus, Venus shell, Vitrina, Wentletrap, Whelk, Wing-shell, Winkle, Wood-borer

Mollycoddle Indulge, Nanny, Pamper

Moloch Thorn-devil

Molten Dissolved, Fusil, Melted

Molybdenum Mo

Moment(s), Momentous Aha, Bending, Bit, Blonde, Dipole, Electromagnetic, Eureka, Eventful, Flash, Gliffing, Hogging, Import, Instant, Jiffy, Magnetic, → **MINUTE**, Mo, Nonce, Point, Psychological, Pun(c)to, Sagging, Sands, Sec, Senior, Shake, Stound, Stownd, Tick, Time, Trice, Twinkling, Weighty, Wink

Momentum Angular, Impetus, L, Speed, Thrust

Mona(s) I, IOM

Monaco Grimaldi

Mona Lisa La Gioconda

Monarch(y) Absolute, Autocrat, Butterfly, Caesar, Constitutional, Crown, Dual, Emperor, HM, K, Karling, King, Limited, Merry, Potentate, Q, Queen, R, Raine, Reign, Ruler, Tonga, Tsar

Monarchist Cavalier

Monastery, Monastic Abbey, Abthane, Celibate, Charterhouse, Chartreuse, Cloister, Community, Gompa, Holy, Hospice, Iona, Lamaserai, Lamasery, La Trappe, Laura, Monkish, Oblate, Priory, Secluded, Vihara, Wat

Monday Black, Collop, Handsel, J'ouvert, Meal, Oatmeal, Plough, Whit

Mondrian Piet

Money, Monetary Ackers, Akkas, Allowance, Annat, Ante, Appearance, Archer, Assignat, Banco, Batta, Blood, Blue, Blunt, Boodle, Bottle, Brass, Bread, Bread and honey, Broad, Bull's eye, Bunce, Cabbage, Capital, Cash, Caution, Century, Change, Chink, Circulating medium, Cob, Cock, → **COIN**, Collateral, Confetti, Conscience, Crackle, Cranborne, Crinkly, Crust, Currency, Danger, Dib(s), Dingbat, Dollar, Dosh, Dump, Dust, Earnest, Easy, Even, Fat, Fee, Fiat, Float, Folding, Fonds, Found, Fund, Funny, Gate, Gelt, Gilt, Godiva, Gold, Grand, Grant, Gravy, Greens, Hard, Head, Heavy sugar, Hello, Hoot, Hot, Housekeeping, Hush, Husk, Idle, Ingots, Investment, Jack, Kale, Kembla, Key, Knife, L, Legal tender, Lolly, Loot, Lucre, M, Mammon, Maundy, Mazuma, Means, Mint, Monkey, Monopoly, Moola(h), Narrow, Near, Necessary, Needful, Nest-egg, Note, Nugger, Numismatic, Nummary, Oaker, Ochre, Offertory, Oof, Option, Outlay, P, Packet, Paper, Passage, Pavarotti, Payroll, Peanuts, Pecuniary, Pelf, Pin, Pine-tree, Pittance, Plastic, Plum, Pocket, Pony, Posh, Press, Proceeds, Profit, Protection, Purse, Push, Quid, Ration, Ready, Reap silver, Rebate, Remuneration, Resources, Revenue, Rhino, Ring, Risk, Rogue, Rowdy, Salt(s), Score, Scratch, Scrip, Seed, Shekels, Shell, Shin-plaster, Ship, Short, Siller, Silly, Silver, Sinews of war, Slush, Smart, Soap, Soft, Spondulicks, Stake,

Sterling, Stipend, Stuff, Subsistence, Sugar, Sum, Surety, Table, Takings, Tender, Tin, Toea, Token, Tranche, Treaty, Tribute, Turnover, Viaticum, Wad, Wealth, Windfall, Wonga

Money-box Penny-pig, Piggy bank

Moneylender Gombeen, Scrivener, Shroff, Shylock, Usurer

Moneymaking Earner, Profitable, Quaestuary

Mongol(ian) Bashkir, Buriat, Buryat, Calmuck, Chuvash, Evenski, Golden Horde, Kalmuck, Kara-Kalpak, Kazak(h), Khalkha, Kubla(i) Khan, Kyrgyz, Lapp, Lepcha, Manchoo, Manchu, Mishmi, Mogul, Pareoean, Samoyed, Shan, Sherpa, Tamerlane, Tatar, Tungus(ic), Uig(h)ur, Ural-altaic, Uzbek

Mongoose Herpestes, Ichneumon, Mangouste, Meerkat, Suricate, Urva

Mongrel Bitser, Cross(bred), → **DOG**, Goorie, Goory, Hybrid, Kuri, Lurcher, Mutt, Quadroon, Tyke, Underbred, Zo

Monitor(ing) Dataveillance, Detect, Goanna, Iguana, Lizard, Observe, Offer, Ofgas, Ofgem, Oflot, Ofsted, Oftel, Ofwat, Prefect, Preview, Record, Regulator, Screen, Ship, Surveillance, Track, Warship, Watchdog, Whole-body, Worral, Worrel

Monk(s) Abbey-lubber, Abbot, Acoemeti, Angelico, Archimandrite, Arhat, Asser, Augustinian, Austin, Basilian, Bede, Beghard, Benedictine, Bernardine, Bethlehemite, Bhikhu, Black, Bonaventura, Bonze, Bro, Brother, Bruno, Caedmon, Caloyer, Camaldolite, Carthusian, Celestine, Cellarist, Cenobite, Cistercian, Cluniac, Coenobite, Cowl, Crutched Friar, Culdee, Dan, Dervish, Dom, Dominican, Félibre, Feuillant, Fra(ti), Fraticelli, Friar, General, Gyrovague, Hegumen, Hermit, Hesychast, Hildebrand, Ignorantine, Jacobin, Jacobite, Jerome, Lama, Maurist, Mechitharist, Mekhitarist, Mendel, Minor(ite), Norbertine, Obedientiary, Oblate, Olivetan, Order, Palmer, Pelagian, Possessionate, Prior, Rakehell, Rasputin, Recluse, Recollect, Religieux, Roshi, Salesian, Sangha, Savonarola, Simeon Stylites, Sub-prior, Talapoin, Theatine, Thelemite, Thelonious, Thomas à Kempis, Tironensian, Trappist, Votary

Monkey Anger, Ape, Aye-aye, Baboon, Bandar, Bobbejaan, Bonnet, Bushbaby, Capuchin, Catar(r)hine, Cebidae, Cebus, Chacma, Coaita, Colobus, Cynomolgus, Diana, Douc, Douroucouli, Drill, Durukuli, Entellus, Galago, Gelada, Gibbon, Gorilla, Grease, Green, Grison, Grivet, Guenon, Guereza, Hanuman, Hoolock, Howler, Hylobates, Indri, Jacchus, Jackey, Jocko, Kippage, Langur, Leaf, Lemur, Loris, Macaco, Macaque, Magot, Malmag, Mandrill, Mangabey, Marmoset, Meddle, Meerkat, Mico, Midas, Mona, Mycetes, Nala, Nasalis, New World, Old World, Orang-utang, Ouakari, Ouistiti, Phalanger, Platyrrhine, Powder, → **PRIMATE**, Proboscis, Pug, Puzzle, Rage, Ram, Rapscallion, Rascal, Rhesus, Sago(u)in, Saguin, Sai(miri), Sajou, Saki, Sapajou, Satan, Semnopithecus, Siamang, Sifaka, Silen(us), Silverback, Simian, Simpai, Slender loris, Spider, Squirrel, Talapoin, Tamarin, Tamper, Tana, Tarsier, Tee-tee, Titi, Toque, Trip-hammer, Troop, Tup, Uakari, Vervet, Wanderoo, White-eyelid, Wistiti, Wou-wou, Wow-wow, Wrath, Zati

Monkey-nut Earth-pea

Monkey-puzzle Araucaria, Bunya-bunya

Monkshood Aconite

Monocle Eye-glass, Gig-lamp, Lorgnon, Quiz(zing-glass)

Monocot(yledon) Araceae, Endogen, Tradescantia

Monodon Narwhal

Monogram, Monograph Chi-rho, Cipher, Study, Treatise, Tug(h)ra

Monolith Ayers Rock, Cenotaph, Chambers Pillar, Uluru

Monologue Interior, Patter, Rap, Recitation, Soliloquy, Speech

Monopolise, Monopoly Absolute, Appalto, Bloc, Bogart, Cartel, Coemption,

Corner, Engross, Octroi, Régie, Trust

Monorail Aerobus

Monosyllable Proclitic

Monotone, Monotonous, Monotony Boring, Dull, → FLAT, Grey, Humdrum, Same(y), Sing-song, Tedious, Thrum

Monsoon Dry, Hurricane, Typhoon, Wet, → WIND

▷ **Monsoon** *may indicate* weekend Mon soon

Monster, Monstrous Alecto, Apollyon, Asmodeus, Bandersnatch, Behemoth, Bunyip, Caliban, Cerberus, Cete, Charybdis, Chichevache, Chim(a)era, Cockatrice, Colossal, Cyclops, Dabbat, Deform, Dinoceras, Dismayd, Div, Dragon, Echidna, Enormous, Erebus, Erinys, Erl-king, Eten, Ettin, Evil-one, Fiend, Fire-drake, Frankenstein, Freak, Geryon, Ghost, Giant, Gila, Golem, Gorgon, Green-eyed, Grendel, Harpy, Hippocampus, Hippogriff, Hippogryph, Huge, Hydra, Jabberwock, Kraken, Lamia, Leviathan, Lilith, Lusus naturae, Mastodon, Medusa, Minotaur, Misbegotten, Moloch, Mooncalf, Mylodont, Nessie, Nicker, Nightmare, Ogopogo, Ogre, Ogr(e)ish, Opinicus, Orc, Outrageous, Pongo, Prodigy, Sasquatch, Satyral, Scylla, Serra, Shadow, Simorg, Simurg(h), Siren, Skull, Snark, Spectre, Sphinx, Spook, Stegodon, Stegosaur, Succubus, Taniwha, Teras, Teratism, Teratoid, Triceratops, Triffid, Troll, Typhoeus, Typhon, Unnatural, Vampire, Vast, Wasserman, Wendego, Wendigo, Wer(e)wolf, Wyvern, Xiphopagus, Yowie, Ziffius

Monstrance Ostensory

Month(ly) Ab, Abib, Adar, Anomalistic, April, Asadha, Asvina, August, Bhadrapada, Brumaire, Bul, Calendar, Cheshvan, Chislev, December, Dhu-al-Hijjah, Dhu-al-Qadah, Draconic, Elul, February, Floréal, Frimaire, Fructidor, Gander, Germinal, Hes(h)van, Iy(y)ar, January, July, Jumada, June, Jysaitha, Kartuka, Kisleu, Kislev, Lide, Lunar, Lunation, Magha, March, Margasirsa, May, Messidor, Mo, Moharram, Moon, Muharram, Muharrem, Nisan, Nivôse, Nodical, November, October, Periodical, Phalguna, Pluviôse, Prairial, Rabia, Rajab, Ramadan, Ramazon, Rhamadhan, Safar, Saphar, September, Sha(a)ban, Shawwal, S(h)ebat, Sidereal, Sivan, Solar, Stellar, Synodic, Tammuz, Tebeth, Thermidor, Tishri, Tisri, Tropical, Vaisakha, Veadar, Vendémiaire, Ventôse

Monument Ancient, Arch, Archive, Cairn, Cenotaph, Charminar, Column, Cromlech, Dolmen, Eugubine, Henge, Megalith, Memorial, Menhir, Monolith, National, Pantheon, Pyramid, Sacellum, Stele(ne), Stone, Stonehenge, Stupa, Talayot, Tombstone, Trilith, Trilithon, Urn

Mood(y) Active, Anger, Atmosphere, Attitude, Capricious, Conjunctive, Dudgeon, Emoticon, Enallage, Fettle, Fit, Foulie, Glum, Grammar, Humour, Hump, Imperative, Indicative, Infinitive, Mercurial, Miff, Morale, Optative, Passive, Peat, Pet, Revivalist, Sankey, Spleen, Subjunctive, Temper, Tid, Tone, Tune, Vein, Vinegar, Whim

Moon(light), Moony Aah, Alignak, Aningan, Apogee, Artemis, Astarte, Blue, Callisto, Calypso, Chandra, Cheese, Cynthia, Diana, Epact, Europa, Eye, Flit, Full, Gander, Ganymede, Gibbous, Glimmer, Grimaldi, Harvest, Hecate, Hunter's, Hyperion, Inconstant, Juliet, Leda, Lucina, Luna(r), Mani, Mascon, McFarlane's Buat, Midsummer, Mock, Month, Mooch, Mope, New, Nimbus, Nocturne, Octant, Oliver, Orb, Paddy's lantern, Paraselene, Paschal, Pasiphaë, Phobos, Phoebe, Plenilune, Proteus, Raker, Rear-view, Satellite, Selene, Set, Shepherd, Shot, Sickle, Sideline, Silvery, Sonata, Stargaze, Stone, Syzygy, Thebe, Thoth, Titan, Triton, Umbriel, Wander

Moonraker Astrogeologist, Gothamite

Moonshine(r) Balderdash, Hootch, Poteen, Rot, Shebeener

Moor(ing), Moorish, Moorland Berth, Bodmin, Culloden, Dock, Fen, Flow country, Grouse, Heath, Iago, Ilkley, Makefast, Marina, Marston, Moresque, Moroccan, Mudéjar, Othello, Otter, Palustrine, Roadstead, Ryepeck, Saracen, Sternfast, Tether, → **TIE**, Wharf, Wold

Mop(ping) Dwile, Flibbertigibbet, Girn, Glib, Malkin, Shag, Squeegee, Squilgee, Swab, Swob, Thatch, → **WIPE**

Mope Boody, Brood, Peak, Sulk

Mor Humus

Moral(ity), Morals Apologue, Austere, Deontic, Ethic(al), Ethos, Everyman, Fable, High-minded, Integrity, Message, Precept, Principled, Puritanic, Righteous, Sittlichkeit, Tag, Upright, Virtuous, Well-thewed

Morale Ego, Mood, Spirit, Zeal

Moralise, Moralising Preach, Sententious

Moralist Prig, Prude, Puritan, Whitecap

Morass Bog, Fen, Flow, Marsh, Moss, Quagmire, Slough

Morbid(ity) Anasarca, Ascites, Cachaemia, Dropsy, Ectopia, Ghoul(ish), Gruesome, Pathological, Plethora, Prurient, Religiose, Sick, Sombre, Unhealthy

Mordant Biting, Caustic, Critic(al), Sarcastic, Tooth

Mordent Inverted, Lower, Pralltriller, Upper

More Added, Additional, Else, Extra, Increase, Less, Mae, Merrier, Mo(e), → **NO MORE**, Over, Piu, Plus, Seconds, Stump, Utopia

Moreover Also, Besides, Eft, Either, Eke, Further, Too, Yet

Morgan Buccaneer, Pirate

Moribund Dying, Stagnant, Withered

Mormon Danite, Latter-day Saint, Salt Lake City, Utah, Young

Morning Ack-emma, Am, Antemeridian, Dawn, Daybreak, Early, Forenoon, Levée, Matin(al), Morrow, Sparrowfart

Morning-glory Bindweed, Ipomoea, Turbith, Turpeth

Morning-star Morgenstern, Phosphor(us), Threshel, Venus

Moroccan, Morocco Agadir, French, Leather, Levant, MA, Mo(o)r, Persian, Riff, Tangerine, Venus

Moron Fool, Idiot, Schmuck, → **STUPID**

Morose Acid, Boody, Churlish, Crabby, Cynical, Disgruntled, Gloomy, Glum, Grum, Moody, Sour-eyed, Sullen, Surly

Morph Phase

Morris Car, Dance, Fivepenny, Merel(l), Meril, Nine Men's, Ninepenny

Morrow Future

Morse Code, Endeavour, Iddy-umpty, Walrus

Morsel Bit, Bite, Bouche, Canape, Crumb, Dainty, Morceau, Ort, Scrap, Sippet, Sop, Tidbit, Titbit

Mortal(ity) Averr(h)oism, Being, Deathly, → **FATAL**, Grave, Human, Lethal, Yama

Mortar, Mortar-board Bowl, Cannon, Cement, Co(e)horn, Compo, Grout, Gunite, Hawk, Life, Metate, Mine-thrower, Minnie, Moaning (Minnie), Parget, Plaster, Pot gun, Screed, Square, Squid, Toc emma, Trench(er)

Mortgage(e) Balloon, Bond, Cap and collar, Cedula, Chattel, Debt, Dip, Encumbrance, Endowment, First, Hypothecator, Loan, Pension, Pledge, Repayment, Wadset(t)

Mortification, Mortified, Mortify Abash, Ashame, Chagrin, Crucify, Crush, Gangrene, Humble, Humiliate, Infarct, Necrose, Penance, Sick, Sphacelus, Wormwood

Mortuary Deadhouse

Mosaic Buhl, Cosmati, Impave, Inlay, Intarsia, Musive, Opus musivum, Pietra dura, Screen, Tarsia, Terrazzo, Tessella(te), Tessera, Tobacco, Venetian

Moscow Dynamo

Moses Grandma

▶ **Moslem** *see* MUSLIM

Mosque Dome of the Rock, El Aqsa, Jami, Masjid, Medina, Musjid

Mosquito Aedes, Anopheles, Culex, Culicine, Gnat, Parasite, Stegomyia

Moss(y) Acrogen, Agate, Bryology, Bur(r), Carrag(h)een, Ceylon, Club, Fairy, Fog, Fontinalis, Hag(g), Hypnum, Iceland, Irish, Lecanoram, Lichen, Litmus, Liverwort, Long, Lycopod, Marsh, Musci, Muscoid, Parella, Peat, Polytrichum, Reindeer, Rose, Scale, Selaginella, Spanish, Sphagnum, Staghorn, Tree, Usnea, Wall, Wolf's claw

Most Largest, Major, Maxi(mum), Optimum

Mot Quip, Saying

Mote Atom, Particle, Speck

Moth(s) Abraxas, Antler, Arch, Arctiidae, Atlas, Bag, Bee, Bell, Bobowler, Bogong, Bombycid, Brown-tail, Buff-tip, Bugong, Burnet, Cabbage, Cactoblastis, Carpenter, Carpet, Cecropia, Cinnabar, Clearwing, Clifden nonpareil, Clothes, Codlin(g), Corn (-borer), Dagger, Dart-moth, Death's head, Diamondback, Drepanid, Drinker, Eggar, Egger, Emerald, Emperor, Ermine, Flour, Fox, Geometer, Geometrid, Ghost, Giant peacock, Gipsy, Goat, Goldtail, Gooseberry, Grass, Gypsy, Hawk, Herald, Honeycomb, Hook-tip, House, Hummingbird, Imago, Io, Kentish glory, Kitten, Lackey, Lappet, Large emerald, Lasiocampidae, Leafroller, Leopard, Lepidoptera, Lichen, Lobster, Luna, Lymantriidae, Macrolepidoptera, Magpie, Meal, Microlepidoptera, Mother of pearl, Mother Shipton, Muslin, Night-fly, Noctua, Noctuid, Notodonta, Nun, Oak-egger, Old-lady, Owl, Owlet, Peach-bloom, Peppercorn, Peppered, Pine-beauty, Pine-carpet, Plane, Plume, Polyphemus, Privet hawk, Processionary, Prominent, Psyche, Pug-moth, Purple emperor, Puss, Pyralidae, Red underwing, Sallow-kitten, Saturnia, Saturniid, Scavenger, Silkworm, Silver-Y, Snout, Sphingid, Sphinx, Swift, Tapestry, Thorn, Tiger, Tinea, Tineidae, Tortrix, Turnip, Tussock, Umber, Underwing, Unicorn, Vapourer, Veneer, Wainscot, Wave, Wax, Wheat, Winter, Woodborer, Yellow underwing, Y-moth, Zygaena

Mothball(s) Abeyance, Camphor, Naphtha, Preserver

Mother Bearer, Church, Cognate, Cosset, Courage, Dam(e), Den, Dregs, Ean, Earth, Eve, Foster, Generatrix, Genetrix, Genitrix, Goose, Hubbard, Lees, Ma, Machree, Madre, Mam(a), Mamma, Mater, Matroclinic, Maya, Minnie, Mollycoddle, Mom, Multipara, Mum, Native, Nature, Nourish, Nursing, Parity, Pourer, Primipara, Reverend, Shipton, Slime, Superior, Surrogate, Theotokos, Wit

▷ **Mother** *may indicate* a lepidopterist moth-er

Motherless Adam, Orphan

Motif Anthemion, Design, Gist, Idée, Theme

Motion Angular, Blocking, Composite, Contrary, Direct, Diurnal, Early day, Fast, Free-fall, Gesture, Harmonic, Impulse, Kepler, Kinematics, Kinetic, Kipp, Link, Move, Oblique, Offer, Parallactic, Parallel, Peculiar, Perpetual, PL, Proper, Proposal, Rack and pinion, Rider, Similar, Slow, Spasm, Wave

Motionless Doggo, Frozen, Immobile, Quiescent, Stagnant, Stasis, Still, Stock-still

Motive, Motivate, Motivation Actuate, Cause, Drive, Ideal, Impel, Incentive, Intention, Mainspring, Mobile, Object, → PURPOSE, Spur, Ulterior

Motley Jaspé, Medley, Piebald, Pied

Motor(boat) Auto, Benz, Car, Dynamo, Electric, Engine, Hot rod, Hydroplane, Inboard, Induction, Jato, Linear, Mini, Outboard, Paint job, Rocket, Scooter,

Series-wound, Stator, Supermini, Sustainer, Synchronous, Thruster, Turbine, Universal, Water

Motorcycle, Motorcyclist Bambi, Bikie, Chookchaser, Chopper, Combination, Cyma recta, Farm-bike, Harley Davidson, Hell's Angel, Minimoto, Moped, Pipsqueak, Scooter, Scramble, Tourist Trophy, Trail bike, TT, Yamaha®

Motorist(s) AA, Driver, Petrolhead, RAC, Tripper

Motorman Austin, Benz, Ford, Morris

Motor race Rally, Scramble, TT

Motorway Autobahn, Autopista, Autoput, Autoroute, Autostrada, Expressway, M(1), Orbital, Superhighway, Throughway, Thruway

Mottle(d) Brindled, Chiné, Jaspé, Marbled, Marly, Mirly, Pinto, Poikilitic, Tabby

Motto Device, Epigraph, Excelsior, Gnome, Impresa, Imprese, Impress(e), Legend, Maxim, Mot, Poesy, Posy, Saw

Mou(e) Grimace, Mim

Mould(ed), Moulder, Mouldable, Moulding, Mouldy Accolade, Architrave, Archivolt, Astragal, Baguette, Balection, Bandelet, Beading, Bend, Black, Blow, Blue, Bolection, Bread, Briquet(te), Cabling, Casement, Cast(ing), Cavetto, Chain, Chessel, Chill, Cold, Cornice, Coving, Cyma, Cymatium, Dancette, Dariole, Die, Die-cast, Dogtooth, Doucine, Dripstone, Ductile, Echinus, Egg and dart, Emboss, Flong, → **FORM**, Foughty, Fousty, Fungose, Fungus, Fusarol(e), Fust, Gadroon, Geat, Godroon, Gorgerin, Green, Hood-mould, Hore, Humus, Injection, Iron, Jelly, Leaf, Machine, Matrix, Mildew, Model, Mool, Moulage, Mucedinous, Mucid, Mucor, Must, Mycetozoan, Myxomycete, Nebule, Necking, Noble rot, Ogee, Ovolo, Palmette, Papier-mâché, Penicillin, Phycomycete, Picture, Pig, Plasm(a), Plastic, Plastisol, Plat, Platband, Plate, Prototype, Prunt, Quarter-round, Reeding, Reglet, Rhizopus, Rib, Rot, Rust, Sandbox, Scotia, Shape, Slime, Smut, Soil, Soot(y), Spindle, Storiated, Stringcourse, Stucco, Surbase, Tailor, Talon, Template, Templet, Timbale, Tondino, Torus, Trochilus, Vinew, Water table

Moult(ing) Cast, Metecdysis, Mew, Shed

Mound Agger, Bank, Barp, Barrow, Berm, Cahokia, Cone, Dike, Dun, Embankment, Heap, Hog, Kurgan, Mogul, Molehill, Monticule, Mote, Motte, Orb, Pile, Pingo, Pome, Rampart, Rampire, Remblai, Tel(l), Teocalli, Teopan, Tuffet, Tumulus, Tussock

Mound-bird Leipoa, Megapode

Mount(ed), Mounting, Mountain (peak), Mountains Air, → **ALPINE**, Ascend, Aspiring, Back, Barp, Ben, Berg, Board, Breast, Butter, Chain, Charger, → **CLIMB**, Colt, Cordillera, Cradle, Dew, Display, Djebel, Dolly, Escalade, Frame, Hinge, Horse, Inselberg, Jebel, Massif, Monture, Mt, Nunatak, Orography, Orology, Passe-partout, Pike, Pile, Pin, Pownie, Quad, Ride, Saddlehorse, Saddle up, Scalado, Scale, Sclim, Set, Soar, Stage, → **STEED**, Stie, Strideways, Tel, Tier, Topo, Tor, Turret, Upgo, Volcano

MOUNTAINS

2 letters:	*4 letters:*	Hoss	Ubac
K2	Alai	Jaya	Zeil
	Blue	Jura	
3 letters:	Bona	Meru	*5 letters:*
Apo	Cook	Nebo	Abora
Ida	Etna	Oeta	Adams
Kaf	Fuji	Ossa	Aldan
Ore	Harz	Rigi	Altai

Amara
Andes
Aneto
Athos
Atlas
Badon
Black
Blanc
Coast
Djaja
Eiger
Ellis
Er Rif
Ghats
Green
Guyot
Hekla
Horeb
Idris
Kamet
Kenya
Logan
Munro
Ozark
Pelée
Rocky
Rydal
Sayan
Serra
Sinai
Siple
Smoky
Snowy
Table
Tabor
Tatra
Tirol
Tyree
Tyrol
Uinta
Urals
Welsh
White

6 letters:
Ala Dag
Alaska
Amhara
Anadyr
Arafat
Ararat

Averno
Balkan
Bogong
Carmel
Cho Oyu
Dragon
Egmont
Elbert
Elberz
Elbrus
Erebus
Gilead
Hermon
Hoggar
Hoosac
Katmai
Kazbek
Kunlun
Lhotse
Makalu
Mourne
Olives
Ortles
Pamirs
Pelion
Pindus
Pisgah
Pocono
Robson
Scopus
Sintra
Sorata
Steele
Tasman
Taunus
Taurus
Umbria
Vernon
Vosges
Zagros

7 letters:
Aetolia
Ala Dagh
Aorangi
Aragats
Arcadia
Bernina
Brocken
Buffalo
Calvary

Cariboo
Cascade
Chianti
Corbett
Dapsang
Estreia
Everest
Helicon
Kennedy
Khingan
Kuenlun
Lebanon
Lucania
Manaslu
Markham
Nan Shan
Olympic
Olympus
Palomar
Perdido
Pilatus
Rainier
Rhodope
San Juan
Scafell
Selkirk
Skiddaw
Snowdon
Sperrin
Stanley
St Elias
Sudeten
Tibesti
Travers
Troglav
Whitney
Wicklow

8 letters:
Anapurna
Ben Nevis
Cambrian
Carstenz
Catskill
Caucasus
Cevennes
Cumbrian
Demavend
Grampian
Guerrero
Hymettus

Illimani
Jungfrau
Kinabalu
King Peak
Leibnitz
McKinley
Mulhacen
Ngaliema
Ouachita
Pennines
Pyrenees
Rushmore
Seamount
St Helen's
Taraniki
Tian Shan
Tien Shan
Vesuvius
Victoria
Wrangell

9 letters:
Aconcagua
Allegheny
Annapurna
Apennines
Ben Lomond
Blackburn
Blue Ridge
Cairngorm
Carstensz
Catskills
Caucasian
Connemara
Demavrand
Dolomites
El Capitan
Grampians
Guadalupe
Helvellyn
Hercynian
Highlands
High Tatra
Himalayas
Hindu Kush
Jebel Musa
Karakoram
Lenin Peak
Longs Peak
Marmolada
Mont Blanc

9 letters – cont:
Monte Rosa
Nanda Devi
Parnassus
Pikes Peak
Ruwenzori
Shivering
Sugar Loaf
Tirich Mir
Trans Alai
Tupungato
Vancouver
Venusberg
Voralberg
Weisshorn
Woodroffe
Yablonovy
Zugspitze

10 letters:
Altazimuth
Arakan Yoma
Armageddon
Black Hills
Cantabrian
Carpathian
Delectable
Dhaulagiri
Equatorial
Erymanthus
Erzgebirge
Great Gable
Great Smoky
Harney Peak
Horselberg
Kongur Shan
Koscuiszko
Laurentian
Masharbrum
Masherbrum

Matterhorn
Monte Corno
Montserrat
Pentelicus
Pentelikon
Puncak Jaya
Puy de Sancy
Qomolangma
Sagarmatha
St Michael's
Tengri Khan
Teton Range
Vorarlberg
Washington
Waziristan
Wellington
Wetterhorn

11 letters:
Adirondacks
Alaska Range
Anti-Lebanon
Appalachian
Bartle Frere
Bimberi Peak
Brooks Range
Drakensberg
Fairweather
Gerlachovka
Kilimanjaro
Kirkpatrick
Kolyma Range
Nanga Parbat
Picode Anito
Salmon River
Scafell Pike
Sierra Madre

12 letters:
Albert Edward

Cascade Range
Eastern Ghats
Godwin Austen
Gran Paradiso
Ingleborough
Kanchenjunga
Monte Perdido
Ruahine Range
Sierra Morena
Sierra Nevada
Slieve Donard
Southern Alps
Tararua Range
Victoria Peak
Vindhya Range
Vinson Massif
Wasatch Range
Western Ghats

13 letters:
Carrantuohill
Croagh Patrick
Flinders Range
Great Dividing
Grossglockner
Humphrey's Peak
Kangchenjunga
Massif Central
Mount Klinovec
Petermann Peak
San Bernardino
Stanovoi Range
Tibesti Massif

14 letters:
Admiralty Range
Bohemian Forest
Carnarvon Range
Finsteraarhorn
Hamersley Range

Kaikoura Ranges
Kommunizma Peak
Liverpool Range
Musgrove Ranges
Queen Maud Range
Ruwenzori Range
Sangre de Cristo
Stirling Ranges
Thadentsonyane
Wind River Range

15 letters:
New England Range
Teutoburger Wald

16 letters:
Emperor
  Seamounts
Macdonnell Ranges
Owen Stanley
  Range
Thabana-Ntlenyana

17 letters:
Continental Divide
Transylvanian Alps

18 letters:
Great Dividing
  Range

19 letters:
Macgillicuddy's
  Reeks

20 letters:
Salmon River
  Mountains

Mountain-building Orogenesis

Mountaineer(ing) Aaron, Abseil, Alpinist, Arnaut, Climber, Hunt, Sherpa, Smythe, Upleader

Mountebank Antic(ke), Baladin(e), Charlatan, Jongleur, Quack, Saltimbanco

Mourn(er), Mournful, Mourning Adonia, Black, Dirge, Dole, Elegiac, Grieve, Grone, Half-mast, Hatchment, Jamie Duff, Keen, Lament, Mute, Niobe, Omer, Ovel, Plangent, Saulie, Shibah, Shivah, Shloshim, Sorrow, Tangi, Threnetic, Threnodial, Weeds, Weep, Willow

Mouse(like), Mousy Black eye, Church, Deer, Dun(nart), Fat, Field, Flitter, Harvest, Honey, House, Icon, Jerry, Jumping, Kangaroo, Marsupial, Meadow, Mickey,

Minnie, Muridae, Murine, Optical, Pocket, Pouched, Rodent, Shiner, Shrew, Vermin, Waltzer, White-footed

Mousetrap Samson's post

Mousse Styling

Moustache(d) Algernon, Boxcar, Burnside, Charley, Charlie, Chevron, Excrement, Fu Manchu, Handlebar, Hindenburg, Horseshoe, Kaiser, Mistletoe, Pencil, Pyramid, Regent, Roman T, Ronnie, Soupstrainer, Toothbrush, Walrus, Waxed, Wings, Zapata

Mouth(piece) Aboral, Bazoo, Bocca, Brag, Buccal, Cakehole, Chapper, Check, Crater, Debouchure, Delta, Embouchure, Estuary, Fauces, Fipple, Gab, Gam, Geggie, Gills, Gob, Gub, Gum, Hard, Horn, Kisser, Labret, Laughing gear, Lawyer, Lip, Manubrium, Maw, Neb, Orifex, Orifice, Os, Oscule, Ostium, Outfall, Outlet, Port, Potato trap, Rattle-trap, Speaker, Spokesman, Spout, Stoma, Swazzle, Swozzle, Teat, Trap, Trench, Uvula

Mouthful Bite, Gob, Gobbet, Morceau, Morsel, Sip, Sup, Taste

Mouthless Astomatous

Mouth-organ Harmonica, Harp, Palp, Sang

Mouth-watering Sialogogue

Move(d), Mover, Movable, Moving Act, Actuate, Affect, Andante, Astir, Aswarm, Budge, Career, Carry, Catapult, Chattel, Claw off, Coast, Counter-measure, Coup, Decant, Démarche, Displace, Disturb, Ease, Eddy, Edge, Evoke, Extrapose, False, Fidget, Flit, Flounce, Fluctuate, Forge, Fork, Frogmarch, Gambit, Gee, Go, Gravitate, Haulier, Hustle, Inch, Inspire, Instigate, Jee, Jink, Kedge, Kinetic, Knight's progress, Link, Lunge, March, Mill, Mobile, Mosey, Motivate, Nip, Opening, Overcome, Pan, People, Poignant, Prime, Proceed, Progress, Progressional, Prompt, Propel, Quicken, Qui(t)ch, Rearrange, Redeploy, Relocate, Remuage, Retrocede, Roll, Rollaway, Rouse, Roust, Sashay, Scoot, Scramble, Scroll, Scurry, Scuttle, Sealed, Sell, Shift, Shog, Shoo, Shunt, Sidle, Skelp, Slide, Soulful, Spank, Steal, Steer, Step, Stir, Styre, Surf, Swarm, Sway, Swish, Tack, Tactic, Taxi, Touch, Transfer, Translate, Translocate, Transplant, Transport, Travel, Troll, Trundle, Turn, Unstep, Up, Upsticks, Vacillate, Vagile, Veronica, Vire, Volt(e), Waft, Wag, Wapper, Whirry, Whish, Whisk, Whiz, Wuther, Yank, Zoom, Zwischenzug

Movement(s) Action, Advection, Aerotaxis, Akathisia, Al Fatah, Allegro, Allemande, Almain, Andantino, Antic, Antistrophe, Arts and crafts, Azapo, Badinerie, Bandwagon, Brownian, Buchmanism, Cadence, Capoeira, Cell, Charismatic, Chartism, Chemonasty, Constructivism, Course, Crusade, Dadaism, Diaspora, Diastole, Ecumenical, Enlightenment, Eoka, Eurhythmics, Expressionism, Faction, Feint, Fianchetto, Fris(ka), Gait, Gallicanism, Geneva, Gesture, Groundswell, Hip-hop, Honde, Imagism, Indraught, Inkatha, Intermezzo, Jhala, Jor, Kata, Keplarian, Kin(a)esthetic, Kinematics, Kinesis, Kinetic, Kipp, Larghetto, Largo, Lassu, Ligne, Logistics, Maltese cross, Manoeuvre, Men's, Motion, Mudra, Nastic, Naturalism, Naziism, Neofascism, Neorealism, New Urbanism, New Wave, Nihilism, Official, Operation, Orchesis, Oxford, Oxford Group, Pantalon, Parallax, Pase, Passade, Pedesis, Photokinesis, Photonasty, Piaffer, Pincer, Plastique, Play, Populist, Poule, Poulette, Procession, Progress, Provisional, Punk, Puseyism, Reformation, Regression, REM, Renaissance, Resistance, Revivalism, Ribbonism, Risorgimento, Romantic, Rondo, Saccade, Scherzo, Seiche, Seismic, Sinn Fein, Solifluction, Solifluxion, Spuddle, Stir(e), Sturm und Drang, Swadeshi, Swing, Symbolist, Tachism, Tamil Tigers, Tantrism, Taphrogenesis, Taxis, Tectonic, Telekinesis, Thermotaxis, Thigmotaxis, Tic, Tide, Tractarianism, Transhumance, Trend, Trenise, Ultramontanism, UNITA, Verismo, Veronica, Wave, Wheel,

Women's, Zionism

Movie Bioscope, Buddy, Cine(ma), Disaster, Film, Flick, Nudie, Popcorn, Road, Slasher, Snuff, Splatter, Star Wars, Talkie

Mow(er), Mowing Aftermath, Cut, Grimace, Lattermath, Lawn, Math, Rawing, Rawn, Reap, Rowan, Rowen, Rowing, Scytheman, Shear, Sickle, Strimmer®, Tass, Trim

MP Backbencher, Commoner, Gendarme, Knight of the Shire, Member, Oncer, Politico, Provost, Redcap, Retread, Snowdrop, Stannator, Statist, TD

▶ **Mr** *see* **MISTER**

▶ **Mrs** *see* **MISSIS**

Mrs Copperfield Agnes, Dora

Mrs Siddons Tragic muse

Muc(o)us Blennorrhoea, Catarrh, Phlegm, Pituate, Pituita, Salt rheum, Sleep, Snivel, Snot, Snotter, Sputum

Much Abundant, Far, Glut, Great, Lots, Mickle, Rotten, Scad, Sore, Viel

Mucilage Gum, → **MUCUS**, Putty, Resin

Muck (up), Mucky Bungle, Dirt, Dung, Island, Leep, Manure, Midden, Mire, Rot, Sludge, Soil, Sordid, Spoil, Stercoral

Mucker Fall, Pal, Purler

Mud(dy) Adobe, Clabber, Clart, Clay, Cutcha, Dirt, Drilling, Dubs, Fango, Glaur, Glob, Gutter, Kacha, Lahar, Lairy, Limous, Lumicolous, → **MIRE**, Moya, Ooze, Peloid, Pise, Red, Riley, Roily, Salse, Slab, Slake, Sleech, Slime, Slob, Slobland, Slough, Sludge, Slur(ry), Slush, Slutch, Tocky, Trouble, Turbid, Volcanic

Muddle(d) Befog, Bemuse, Botch, Cock up, Confuse, Disorder, Embrangle, Fluster, Gump, Higgledy-piggledy, Jumble, Mash, Mêlée, Mess, Mess up, Mix, Mull, Pickle, Puddle, Shemozzle, Snarl-up, Stupefy, Ta(i)vert, Tangle

▷ **Muddled** *may indicate* an anagram

Mudfish Lepidosiren

Mudguard Splashboard, Wing

Mudlark Ragamuffin, Urchin

Muesli Granola

Muff Boob, Botch, Bungle, Drop, Snoskyn

Muffin Bun, Mule, Popover

Muffle(d), Muffler Baffle, Damp, Deaden, Envelop, Hollow, Mob(b)le, Mute, Scarf, Silencer, Sourdine, Stifle

Mug(ger), Muggy Assault, Attack, Bash, Beaker, Bock, Can, Club, Con, Croc(odile), Cup, Dial, Dupe, Enghalskrug, Face, Fool, Footpad, Gob, Humid, Idiot, Latron, Learn, Mou, Noggin, Pan, Pot, Puss, Rob, Roll, Sandbag, Sap, Sconce, Simpleton, Steamer, Stein, Sucker, Swot, Tankard, Tax, Thief, Thug(gee), Tinnie, Tinny, Toby, Trap, Ugly, Visage, Yap

Mulatto Griff(e)

Mulberry Artocarpus, Breadfruit, Cecropia, Contrayerva, Cow-tree, Indian, Jack, Morat, Morus, Murrey, Osage orange, Overlord, Paper, Sycamine

Mulch Compost

Mulct Fine

Mule, Mulish Ass, Bab(o)uche, Barren, Donkey, Funnel, Hemionus, Hybrid, Mocassin, Moccasin, Moyl(e), Muffin, Muil, Obdurate, Pack, Rake, Shoe, Slipper, Spinning, Sumpter

Muleteer Arriero

Mull Brood, Chew, Kintyre, Ponder, Promontory, Study

Mullein Aaron's rod

Mullet Goatfish

Mullion Monial
Multi-coloured Scroddled
Multiform Allotropic, Diverse, Manifold
Multiple, Multiplication, Multiplied, Multiplier, Multiply Augment, Breed, Common, Double, Elixir, → INCREASE, Manifold, Modulus, Populate, Product, Proliferate, Propagate, Scalar, Severalfold
Multi-purpose Polychrest
Multitude Army, Crowd, Hirsel, Horde, Host, Legion, Populace, Shoal, Sight, Throng, Zillion
Mum(my) Boutonné, Carton(n)age, Corpse, Egyptian, Embalm, Mamma, Mine, Mute, Pharaoh, Quiet, Sh, Silent, Tacit, Whisht, Wordless
Mumble Grumble, Moop, Moup, Mouth, Mump, Mushmouth, Mutter, Royne, Slur
Mumbo jumbo Hocus pocus, Mammet, Maumet, Mawmet, Mommet
Mummer(y) Actor, Guising, Mime, Scuddaler, Scudler, Skudler
Mumps Parotitis
Munch Champ, Chew, Chomp, Expressionist, Moop, Moup, Scranch
Mundane Banal, Common, Earthly, Nondescript, Ordinary, Prosaic, Quotidian, Secular, Subcelestial, Trite, Workaday, Worldly
Mungo Park
Municipal Civic
Munificent Bounteous, Generous, Liberal, Profuse
Munition(s) Arms, Artillery, Matériel, Ordnance
Munro Saki
Mural(s) Fresco, Graffiti
Murder(er), Murderess, Murderous Aram, Assassin, Blue, Bluebeard, Bravo, Burke, Butcher, Butler, Cain, Cathedral, Crackhalter, Crippen, Crows, Cutthroat, Do in, Eliminate, End, Filicide, First degree, Fratricide, Genocide, Hare, Hatchet man, Hit, Hitman, Homicide, Hyde, Internecine, Judicial, → KILL, Liquidate, Locusta, Made man, Man-queller, Massacre, Matricide, Modo, Parricide, Patricide, Petty treason, Poison, Red, Regicide, Removal, Ripper, Ritual, Ritz, Rub out, Second degree, Sikes, Slaughter, Slay, Stiff, Strangle(r), Take out, Thagi, Throttle, Thug(gee), Ugly man, Vaticide, Whodun(n)it
Murk(y) Black, Dirk(e), Gloom, Obscure, Rookish, Stygian
Murmur(ing) Brool, Bruit, Bur(r), Burble, Coo, Croodle, Croon, Grudge, Heart, Hum, → MUTTER, Purr, Repine, Rhubarb, Rumble, Rumour, Souffle, Sowf(f), Sowth, Sturnoid, Syllable, Undertone, Whisper
Murphy Chat, Potato, Pratie, Spud, Tater
Muscle, Muscular Abductor, Abs, Accelerator, Accessorius, Adductor, Agonist, Anconeus, Aristotle's lantern, Aryepiglottic, Arytaenoid, Athletic, Attollens, Beef(y), Beefcake, Biceps, Bowr, Brachialus, Brawn, Buccinator, Buff, Cardiac, Ciliary, Clout, Complexus, Corrugator, Creature, Cremaster, Delt(oid), Depressor, Diaphragm, Digastric, Dilat(at)or, Duvaricator, Écorché, Effector, Elevator, Erecter, Erector, Evertor, Extensor, Eye-string, Flexor, Force, Gastrocnemius, Gemellus, Glut(a)eus, Gluteus maximus, Gracilis, Hamstring, Hiacus, Iliacus, Intrinsic, Involuntary, Kreatine, Lat, Latissimus dorsi, Laxator, Levator, Lumbricalis, Masseter, Mesomorph, Might, Motor, Mouse, Myalgia, Mylohyoid, Myology, Myotome, Nasalis, Oblique, Occlusor, Omohyoid, Opponent, Orbicularis, Pathos, Pec(s), Pectoral, Perforans, Perforatus, Peroneus, Plantaris, Platysma, Popliteus, → POWER, Pronator, Protractor, Psoas, Pylorus, Quad(riceps), Quadratus, Rambo, Rectus, Retractor, Rhomboid, Rhomboideus, Ripped, Risorius, Rotator, Sarcolemma, Sarcous, Sartorius, Scalene, Scalenus, Serratus, Sinew, Six-pack,

Smooth, Soleus, Sphincter, Spinalis, Splenial, Sthenic, Striated, Striped, Supinator, Suspensory, Temporal, Tenaculum, Tendon, Tensor, Teres, Thenar, Thew, Tibialis, Tonus, Trapezius, Triceps, Vastus, Voluntary, Xiphihumeralis, Zygomatic

Muscovite Mica, Talc

Muse(s), Muse's home, Musing Aglaia, Aonia(n), Attic, Calliope, Clio, Cogitate, Consider, Erato, Euphrosyne, Euterpe, Goddess, Helicon, Inspiration, IX, Laura, Melpomene, Mull, Nine, Nonet, Pensée, Pierides, Poly(hy)mnia, Ponder, → **REFLECT**, Ruminate, Study, Teian, Terpsichore, Thalia, Tragic, Urania, Wonder

Museum Alte-Pinakothek, Ashmolean, BM, British, Fitzwilliam, Gallery, Getty, Guggenheim, Heritage centre, Hermitage, Hunterian, Louvre, Metropolitan, Parnassus, Prado, Repository, Rijksmuseum, Science, Smithsonian, Tate, Uffizi, VA, V and A, Waxworks

Mush Cree, Glop, Goo, Mess, Pop, Porridge, Puree, Schmaltz, Slop

Mushroom Agaric, Blewits, Boletus, Burgeon, Button, Cep, Champignon, Chanterelle, Darning, Enoki, Escalate, Expand, Field, Fly agaric, → **FUNGUS**, Girolle, Grisette, Gyromitra, Honey fungus, Horse, Hypha(l), Ink-cap, Liberty cap, Magic, Matsutake, Meadow, Morel, Oyster, Parasol, Penny-bun, Pixy-stool, Porcino, Russula, Sacred, St George's, Scotch bonnet, Shaggymane, Shiitake, Sickener, Spread, Start-up, Straw, Truffle, Upstart, Velvet shank, Waxcap

Music A-side, B-side, Classical, Colour, Electro, Lesson, Melody, Minstrelsy, → **MUSICAL INSTRUMENTS**, Passage work, Phase, Piece, Pop(ular), Programme, Quotation, Score, Sheet, Sound, Strain, Table, Tremolando

---

MUSIC

2 letters:	Go-go	Bebop	Outro
Oi	Jazz	Benga	Piped
	Loco	Canon	Ragga
3 letters:	Meno	Chant	Rondo
Air	Mood	Cliff	Roots
AOR	Note	Crunk	Rough
Art	Opus	Cu-bop	Salon
Dub	Prom	Disco	Salsa
Emo	Raga	Dream	Salve
Gat	Rave	Dumka	Sokah
Jor	Riff	Early	Staff
Mas	Rock	Fugue	Suite
Pop	Romo	Funky	Swing
Rag	Roxy	Gabba	Thema
Rai	Soca	House	Tonal
Rap	Soul	Indie	Trash
Rug	Surf	Jhala	Truth
Ska	Tala	Krunk	Vocal
Son	Trad	Kwela	World
	Trio	Largo	
4 letters:	Tune	Light	*6 letters:*
Alap	Zouk	March	Arioso
Chin		Motet	Aubade
Duet	*5 letters:*	Muzak®	Bebung
Folk	Alaap	Neume	Bouree
Funk	Alapa	Nonet	Decani

Doo-wop
Enigma
Equali
Façade
Fugato
Fusion
Gagaku
Galant
Garage
Gospel
Gothic
Grunge
Hip-hop
Jungle
Khayal
Kirtan
Kwaito
Lounge
Lydian
Mantra
Marabi
Mashup
Motown®
New Age
Organa
Popera
Pycnon
Ragini
Redowa
Reggae
Rhythm
Rootsy
Sextet
Skronk
Sonata
Techno
Techno
Tenuto
Thrash
Trance
Verset
Zydeco

7 letters:
Allegro
Andante
Ars nova
Ballade
Baroque
Bhangra
Bluette
Bourree
Britpop
Cadenza
Calypso
Cantata
Ceilidh
Chamber
Chorale
Country
Dad rock
Europop
Euterpe
Fanfare
Gangsta
Hardbag
Introit
Klezmer
Landler
Marcato
Melisma
Messiah
Morceau
New Wave
Numbers
Nu-metal
Organum
Orphean
Partita
Passion
Pecking
Pibroch
Prelude
Qawwali
Quartet
Quintet
Ragtime
Rastrum
Requiem
Reverse
Romanza
Rondeau
Rondino
Rosalia
Roulade
Sanctus
Scherzo
Secondo
Setting
Skiffle
Soukous
Toccata

Trip hop
Ziganka

8 letters:
Absolute
Acid rock
Aleatory
Berceuse
Blue beat
Chaconne
Cock rock
Concerto
Concrete
Continuo
Coranach
Coronach
Entracte
Fantasia
Flamenco
Folk rock
Glam rock
Hard core
Hard rock
High life
In nomine
Janizary
Karnatak
Lollipop
Madrigal
Maggiore
Mariachi
Mbaqanga
Medieval
Modality
Nocturne
Notation
Old-skool
Oratorio
Parlando
Partitur
Pastiche
Postlude
Post-rock
Preludio
Psalmody
Punk rock
Rhapsody
Ricercar
Saraband
Serenade
Serenata

Symphony
Synth-pop
Waltzian
Warhorse

9 letters:
Acid-house
Allemande
Antiphony
Arabesque
Bagatelle
Bluegrass
Breakbeat
Cantilena
Capriccio
Dixieland
Drum'n'bass
Fioritura
Goa trance
Grandioso
Hillbilly
Honky-tonk
Interlude
Klezmorim
Obbligato
Partitura
Pastorale
Pastorali
Plainsong
Polyphony
Prick-song
Quodlibet
Reggaeton
Ricercare
Rock'n'roll
Septimole
Spiritual
Swingbeat
Tambourin
Technopop
Toccatina
Voluntary
Warehouse

10 letters:
Albumblatt
Anacrustic
Chopsticks
Coloratura
Death metal
Desert rock

10 letters – cont:
Electronic
Gangsta rap
Gothic rock
Heavy metal
Hindustani
Humoresque
Incidental
Intermezzo
Jam session
Lovers' rock
Martellato
Mersey beat
New Country
Percussion
Polyhymnia

Ragamuffin
Rare groove
Ritornello
Rockabilly
Rocksteady
Seguidilla
Toccatella
Twelve-tone
Urban blues

11 letters:
Motor rhythm
Passacaglia
Psychobilly
Raggamuffin
Renaissance

Rogues' march
Sinfonietta
Solmisation
Stadium rock
Third stream
Thrash metal

12 letters:
Blue-eyed soul
Boogie-woogie
Concertstück
Contrapuntal
Divertimento
Electroclash
Nunc Dimittis
Pralltriller

Western swing

13 letters:
Choral prelude
Detroit techno
Progressional

14 letters:
Durchkomponirt
Rhythm and blues

15 letters:
Durchkomponiert
Musique concrete
Progressive rock

Musical Arcadian, Azione, Brigadoon, Canorous, Carousel, Cats, Chess, Euphonic,
Evergreen, Evita, Gigi, Grease, Hair, Harmonious, Kabuki, Kismet, Lyric, Mame,
Melodic, Oliver, Opera, Operetta, Oratorio, Orphean, Revue, Showboat
Musical box Juke-box, Polyphon(e)
Musical chairs Level-coil

MUSICAL INSTRUMENTS

2 letters:
Ax
Gu

3 letters:
Axe
Gue
Kit
Oud
Saz
Uke
Zel

4 letters:
Buva
Chyn
Crwd
Drum
Erhu
Fife
Gong
Harp
Horn
Kora
Koto
Lure

Lute
Lyre
Moog®
Oboe
Pipa
Rate
Reed
Rote
Sang
Tuba
Vina
Viol
Zeze

5 letters:
Aulos
Banjo
Bugle
Cello
Clave
Cobza
Corno
Crowd
Crwth
Esraj
Flute

Gaita
Gazog
Guiro
Gusla
Gusle
Gusli
Kazoo
Mbira
Naker
Nebel
Organ
Piano
Quena
Rebec
Regal
Sanko
Sansa
Sarod
Shalm
Shawm
Sitar
Stick
Tabla
Tabor
Tenor
Tibia

Veena
Viola
Zanze
Zinke

6 letters:
Antara
Biniou
Bisser
Bongos
Citole
Cornet
Cymbal
Euphon
Flugel
Guitar
Kanoon
Maraca
Poogye
Racket
Rebeck
Ribibe
Sancho
Santir
Santur
Shalme

Shofar
Sittar
Spinet
Syrinx
Tom-tom
Trigon
Vielle
Violin
Yidaki
Zither
Zufolo

7 letters:
Alphorn
Anklong
Bagpipe
Bandore
Bandura
Baryton
Bassoon
Bazooka
Celesta
Celeste
Cembalo
Ceol mor
Chikara
Cithara
Cittern
Clarino
Clarion
Clavier
Clogbox
Console
Cornett
Dichord
Dulcian
Fagotto
Flutina
Gamelan
Gazogka
Gittern
Hautboy
Helicon
High-hat
Kalimba
Kantela
Kantele
Kithara
Klavier
Lyricon
Mandola

Marimba
Musette
Ocarina
Pandora
Pandore
Pandura
Pianola®
Piccolo
Poogyee
Posaune
Rackett
Ribible
Sackbut
Sambuca
Samisen
Santour
Sarangi
Saxhorn
Saxtuba
Serpent
Tambour
Tambura
Theorbo
Timbrel
Timpano
Trumpet
Tympany
Ukelele
Ukulele
Vihuela
Violone
Whistle
Zuffolo

8 letters:
Angklung
Archlute
Autoharp®
Barytone
Berimbau
Bombarde
Bouzouki
Calliope
Canorous
Carillon
Charango
Cimbalom
Clarinet
Clarsach
Clavecin
Cornetto

Cornpipe
Cromorna
Cromorne
Crumhorn
Dulcimer
Gemshorn
Guarneri
Guimbard
Handbell
Hautbois
Humstrum
Jew's harp
Key-bugle
Langspel
Lyra-viol
Mandolin
Manzello
Martenot
Melodeon
Melodica
Melodion
Mirliton
Oliphant
Ottavino
Pan pipes
Phorminx
Pianette
Polyphon
Psaltery
Recorder
Reco-reco
Slughorn
Spinette
Sticcado
Sticcato
Surbahar
Tamboura
Tamburin
Tenoroon
Theremin
Triangle
Trichord
Trombone
Virginal
Vocalion
Zambomba
Zampogna

9 letters:
Accordion
Aerophone

Alpenhorn
Balalaika
Bandoneon
Bandurria
Banjulele
Bombardon
Chalumeau
Clarionet
Cornemuse
Decachord
Dulcitone®
Euphonium
Flageolet
Flexatone
Flute-à-bec
Gittarone
Gutbucket
Harmonica
Harmonium
Idiophone
Kent-bugle
Krummhorn
Langspiel
Mandoline
Mellotron®
Monochord
Mouth-harp
Nose flute
Orpharion
Pantaleon
Pastorale
Polyphone
Saxophone
Seraphine
Slughorne
Snare-drum
Sonometer
Sopranino
Stockhorn
Trompette
Vibraharp
Washboard
Welsh harp
Xylophone
Xylorimba

10 letters:
Arpeggione
Bullroarer
Chitarrone
Clavichord

10 letters – cont:
Colascione
Concertina
Cor anglais
Cornettini
Didgeridoo
Flugelhorn
Fortepiano
French horn
Gramophone
Hurdy-gurdy
Kettledrum
Lagerphone
Light organ
Mellophone
Nun's fiddle
Ophicleide
Orpheoreon
Pentachord
Shakuhachi
Sousaphone
Squeeze-box

Stylophone®
Symphonium
Tambourine
Thumb piano
Tin whistle
Vibraphone
Wokka board

11 letters:
Chordophone
Clairschach
Contrabasso
Harmoniphon
Harpsichord
Heckelphone
Nickelodeon
Octave flute
Orchestrina
Orchestrion
Phonofiddle
Player piano
Stock-in-horn

Straduarius
Synthesizer
Trump-marine
Violoncello
Wobble-board

12 letters:
Chapman stick®
Chinese block
Clavicembalo
Glockenspiel
Harmonichord
Harmoniphone
Metallophone
Penny-whistle
Sarrusophone
Stock and horn
Stradivarius
Tromba-marina
Tubular bells

13 letters:
Contrabassoon
Contrafagotto
Ondes Martenot
Panharmonicon
Physharmonica

14 letters:
Clavicytherium
Glass harmonica
Jingling Johnny
Ondes musicales
Piano accordion
Swannee whistle

15 letters:
Moog synthesiser

18 letters:
Chinese temple
  block

Music-hall Alhambra, Disco, Empire, Odeon
Musician(s), Musicologist Accompanist, Arion, Arist, Armstrong, Beiderbecke, Boy band, Brain, Buononcini, Casals, Chanter, Clapton, Combo, → **COMPOSER**, Conductor, Crowder, Duet, Ensemble, Executant, Flautist, Gate, Grove, Guido d'Arezzo, Guslar, Handel, Jazzer, Jazzman, Joplin, Klezmer, Labelmate, Mahler, Mariachi, Menuhin, Minstrel, Muso, Noisenik, Nonet, Octet, Orphean, Pianist, Quartet, Quintet, Rapper, Reed(s)man, Répétiteur, Rubinstein, Septet, Session, Sextet, Sideman, Spohr, String, Techno, Tortelier, Troubador, Trouvère, Violinist, Waits
Musk Civet, Mimulus, Must
Musket Brown Bess, Caliver, Carabine, Eyas, Flintlock, Fusil, Hawk, Jezail, Nyas, Queen's-arm, Weapon
Musketeer Aramis, Athos, D'Artagnan, Fusilier, Ja(e)ger, Porthos, Rifleman, Sam
Muslim (ritual), Moslem Alaouite, Alawite, Ali, Almohad(e), Balochi, Baluchi, Berber, Black, Caliph, Dato, Dervish, Druse, Fatimid, Ghazi, Hadji, Hafiz, Hajji, Hezbollah, Iranian, Islamic, Ismaili, Karmathian, Khotbah, Khotbeh, Khutbah, Mahometan, Mawlawi, Meivievi, Mogul, Mohammedan, Moor, Morisco, Moro, Mufti, Mus(s)ulman, Mutazilite, Nawab, Panislam, Paynim, Pomak, Said, Saracen, Say(y)id, Senus(s)i, Shafiite, Shia(h), Shiite, Sofi, Sonnite, Sufi, Sulu, Sunna, Sunni(te), Tajik, Turk, Umma(h), Wahabee, Wahabi(te), Wahhabi
Muslin Butter, Cloth, Coteline, Gurrah, Jamdani, Leno, Mousseline, Mull, Nainsook, Organdie, Tarlatan, Tiffany
Musquash Ondatra
Mussel(s) Bearded, Bivalve, Clabby-doo, Clam, Clappy-doo, Deerhorn, Duck, Edible, Horse, Moules marinières, Mytilus, Naiad, Niggerhead, Pearl, Scalp, Swan, Unio, Unionidae, Zebra
Mussorgsky Modest
▷ **Must** *may indicate* an anagram
Must(y) Amok, Essential, Foughty, Fousty, Froughy, Frowsty, Frowy, Funky, Fust,

Gotta, Man, Maun(na), Mote, Mould, Mucid, Mun, Need(s)-be, Shall, Should, Stum, Vinew, Wine

Mustard Black, Brown, Charlock, Cress, English, Erysimum, French, Garlic, Gas, Nitrogen, Praiseach, Quinacrine, Runch, Sarepta, Sauce-alone, Senvy, Treacle, Wall, White, Wild, Wintercress

Mustard plaster Sinapism

Musteline Skunk

Muster Array, Assemble, Bangtail, Call up, Mass, Peacock, Raise, Rally, Really, Recruit, Round-up, Wappenshaw

Mutability Wheel

Mutate, Mutant, Mutation Auxotroph(ic), Change, Saltation, Somatic, Sport, Suppressor, Terata, Transform, Vowel

▷ **Mutation** *may indicate* an anagram

Mute(d) Deaden, Dumb, Harpo, Noiseless, Silent, Sordino, Sordo, Sourdine, Stifle

Mutilate(d), Mutilation Castrate, Concise, Deface, Dismember, Distort, Garble, Hamble, Injure, Maim, Mangle, Mayhem, Obtruncate, Riglin, Tear

▷ **Mutilate(d)** *may indicate* an anagram

Mutineer, Mutiny Bounty, Caine, Christian, Curragh, Indian, Insurrection, Jhansi, Meerut, Nore, Pandy, → **REVOLT**, Rising, Sepoy

Mutter(ing) Chunter, Fremescent, Grumble, Maunder, Mumble, Mump, Murmur, Mussitate, Rhubarb, Roin, Royne, Rumble, Whittie-whattie, Witter

Mutton Braxy, Colonial goose, Em, Ewes, Fanny Adams, Gigot, Macon, Rack, Saddle, Sheep, Theave, Traik

Mutual (aid) Common, Complementary, Interplay, Log-roll, Reciprocal, Symbiosis

Muzzle Decorticate, Gag, Jaw, Mouth, Restrain, Snout

My Christ, Coo, Gad, Gemini, Golly, Gorblimey, Gosh, Ha, Lor, Lumme, M, Musha, Odso, Oh, Our, Tush

Mynah Stare, Starling

Mynheer Stadholder

Myopia, Myopic Hidebound, Mouse-sight, Narrow, Short-sighted, Thick-eyed

Myriad Host, Zillion

Myristic Nutmeg

Myrrh Stacte

Myrtle Bog, Callistemon, Crape, Creeping, Crepe, Eucalyptus, Gale, Jambolana, Tasmanian, Tooart, Trailing, Tuart

Mysterious, Mystery Abdabs, Abdals, Acroamatic, Arcane, Arcanum, Cabbala, Closed book, Craft, Creepy, Cryptic, Dark, Deep, Delphic, Eleusinian, Enigma, Esoteric, Grocer, G(u)ild, Incarnation, Inscrutable, Miracle, Mystagogue, Numinous, Occult, Original sin, Orphic, Penetralia, Riddle, → **SECRET**, Telestic, Trinity, UFO, Uncanny, Unearthly, Whodunit

▷ **Mysterious(ly)** *may indicate* an anagram

Mystic (word), Mystical Abraxas, Agnostic, Cab(e)iri, Eckhart, Epopt, Fakir, Familist, Gnostic, Hesychast, Mahatma, Occultist, Quietism, Rasputin, Secret, Seer, Sofi, Sufi, Swami, Tantrist, Theosophy, Transcendental, Zohar

Mystify Baffle, Bamboozle, Bewilder, Metagrabolise, Metagrobolise, Perplex, Puzzle

Myth(ology), Mythological, Mythical (beast) Allegory, Atlantis, Behemoth, Bunyip, Centaur, Cockatrice, Dragon, Euhemerism, Fable, Fantasy, Fictitious, Folklore, Garuda, Geryon, Griffin, Hippocampus, Impundulu, Kelpie, Kylin, Legend, Leviathan, Lore, Lyonnesse, Otnit, Pantheon, Pegasus, Phoenix, Sea horse, Sea serpent, Selkie, Solar, Speewah, Sphinx, Sun, Tarand, Thunderbird, Tokoloshe, Tragelaph, Unicorn, Urban, Wivern, Wyvern, Yale, Yeti

Nn

N Name, Nitrogen, Noon, North, November

Nab Arrest, Capture, Collar, Confiscate, Grab, Seize

Nabob Deputy, Nawab, Wealthy

Nadir Bottom, Depths, Dregs, Minimum

Nag(ging) Badger, Bidet, Brimstone, Callet, Cap, Captious, Complain, Fret, Fuss, Harangue, Harp, Henpeck, Horse, Jade, Jaw, Keffel, Peck, Pester, Pick on, Plague, Rosinante, Rouncy, → **SCOLD**, Tit, Xant(h)ippe, Yaff

Nail(ed) Brad, Brod, Catch, Clinker, Clout, Coffin, Fasten, Frost, Hob, Horse, Keratin, Onyx, Pin, Rivet, Screw, Secure, Seize, Shoe, Sisera, Sixpenny, Sparable, Sparrow-bill, Spick, Spike, Sprig, Staple, Stub, Stud, Tack(et), Talon, Tenpenny, Tenterhook, Thumb, Tingle, Toe, Unguis, Wire

Naive(té) Artless, Green, Guileless, Gullible, Ingenuous, Innocence, Open, Pollyanna, Simpliste, Simplistic, Unsophisticated, Wide-eyed

Naked Adamical, Artless, Bare, Blunt, Buff, Clear, Cuerpo, Defenceless, Encuerpo, Exposed, Gymno-, Kaal gat, Nuddy, Nude, Querpo, Raw, Scud, Simple, Skyclad, Stark(ers), Uncovered

Namby-pamby Milksop, Nance, Sissy, Weak, Weakling, White-shoe

Name(d), Names Agnomen, Alias, Allonym, Anonym, Appellation, Appoint, Attribute, Baptise, Behight, Byline, Call, Celeb(rity), Christen, Cite, Cleep, Clepe, Cognomen, Day, Designate, Dinges, Dingus, Dit, Domain, Dub, Entitle, Epithet, Eponym, Exonym, Family, First, Font, Generic, Given, Handle, Hete, Hight, Hypocorism, Identify, Identity, Label, Maiden, Marque, Masthead, Mention, Metronymic, Middle, Moni(c)ker, Mud, N, Nap, Nemn, Nempt, Nom, Nomen(clature), Noun, Onomastics, Onymous, Patronymic, Pennant, Personage, Pet, Place, Praenomen, Proper, Proprietary, Pseudonym, Quote, Red(d), Repute, Scilicet, Sign, Signature, Sir, Specify, Stage, Street, Substantive, Tag, Teknonymy, Term, → **TITLE**, Titular, Titule, Toponymy, Trade, Trivial

Name-dropper Eponym

Nameless Anon, Unchrisom

Namely Ie, Sc, Scilicet, To-wit, Videlicet, Viz

Namesake Homonym

Name unknown Anon, A N Other, NU

Nancy Coddle, Effeminate, Milksop

Nanny Ayah, Foster, Goat, Nurse, Wet-nurse

Naos Cell(a)

Nap(py) Ale, Bonaparte, Diaper, Doze, Drowse, Fluff, Frieze(d), Fuzz, Happen, Hippin(g), Kip, Moze, Nod, Oose, Ooze, Oozy, Power, Put(t), Shag, Siesta, → **SLEEP**, Slumber, Snooze, Tease, Teasel, Teaze, Tipsy, Tuft

Nape Niddick, Noddle, Nucha, Scrag, Scruff, Scuff, Scuft

Napier Logarithm

Napkin Cloth, Diaper, Doily, Doyley, Linen, Muckender, Paper, Sanitary, Serviette, Table

Napless Threadbare

Napoleon Badinguet, Bonaparte, Boustrapa, Cognac, Coin, Consul, Corporal Violet, Corsican, December, Little Corporal, Nantz, Nap, Pig, Rantipole

▷ **Napoleon** *may indicate* a pig

Napper Bonce, Shearman

Narcissus Echo, Egocentric, Jonquil

Narcotic Ava, Benj, B(h)ang, Charas, Churrus, Coca, Codeine, Dagga, Datura, Dope, → **DRUG**, Heroin, Hop, Kava, Laudanum, Mandrake, Marijuana, Meconium, Methadone, Morphia, Narceen, Narceine, Nicotine, Opiate, Pituri, Sedative, Tea, Tobacco, Trional

Nark Grass, Inform, Irritate, Nose, Pique, Roil, Squealer, Stag

Narrate, Narration, Narrative, Narrator Allegory, Anecdote, Cantata, Describe, Diegesis, Fable, History, Oblique, Periplus, Plot, Raconteur, Récit, Recite, Recount, Saga, Sagaman, Scheherazade, Splatterpunk, Story, Tell, Thanatography, Voice-over

Narrow(ing), Narrow-minded Alf, Bigoted, Borné, Bottleneck, Constringe, Cramp, Ensiform, Grundy(ism), Hidebound, Illiberal, Insular, Kyle, Limited, Meagre, Nary, One-idead, Parochial, Phimosis, Pinch, Pinch-point, Provincial, Prudish, Puritan, Scant, Sectarian, Shrink, Slender, Slit, Specialise, Squeak, Stenosed, Strait, Straiten, Strait-laced, Strict, Suburban, Verkramp, Wafer-thin, Waist

Narwhal Monodon

Nasal Adenoidal, Rhinolalia, Sonorant, Twang

Nash Beau

Nashville Bath

Nastiness, Nasty Disagreeable, Drevill, Filth, Fink, Ghastly, Lemon, Lo(a)th, Malign(ant), Noisome, Noxious, Obscene, Odious, Offensive, Ogreish, Ribby, Scummy, Sif, Sordid, Vile

Nat(haniel) Hawthorne, Winkle

Natal Inborn, Native, Patrial

Natant Afloat, Swimming

Nation(s), National(ist), Nationalism Anthem, Baathist, Broederbond, Casement, Chetnik, Country, Cuban, Debt, Eta, Federal, Five, Folk, Grand, Hindutva, Indian, IRA, Israeli, Jingoist, Kuomintang, Land, Mexican, Oman, Pamyat, Parnell, Patriot, → **PEOPLE**, Plaid Cymru, Polonia, Race, Rainbow, Risorgimento, Scottish, Shivsena, Six, SNP, Subject, Swadeshi, Turk, United, Verkrampte, Vietminh, Wafd, Yemini, Young Ireland, Zionist

Native(s) Abo(rigin), Aborigine, African, Amerind, Annamese, Arab, Ascian, Australian, Autochthon, Aztec, Basuto, Belonging, Bengali, Boy, Bushman, Cairene, Carib, Carioca, Chaldean, Citizen, Colchester, Conch, Creole, Criollo, Domestic, Dyak, Edo, Enchorial, Eskimo, Fleming, Fuzzy-wuzzy, Genuine, Habitual, Home-bred, Inborn, Inca, Indigene, Indigenous, Inhabitant, Intuitive, John Chinaman, Kaffir, Libyan, Local, Malay, Maori, Mary, Micronesian, Moroccan, Norwegian, Oyster, Polack, Portuguese, Scythian, Son, Spaniard, Te(i)an, Thai, Tibetan, Uzbeg, Uzbek, Whitstable, Yugoslav

Nativity Birth, Jataka, Putz

Natron Urao

Natter Chat, Gossip, Jack, Prate

Natty Bumppo, Chic, Dapper, Leatherstocking, Smart, Spruce

Natural(ly), Naturalise(d), Naturalism Artless, Ass, Denizen, Easy, Endenizen, Genuine, Green, Homely, Idiot, Illegitimate, Inborn, Inbred, Indigenous,

Ingenerate, Inherent, Innate, Moron, Native, Nidget, Nitwit, Nude, Ordinary, Organic, Prat, Real, Simpleton, Simpliciter, Sincere, True, Undyed, Untaught, Verism

Naturalist Bates, Buffon, Darwin, De Lamarck, Durrell, Wallace, White

Nature Adam, Akin, Character, Disposition, Esse(nce), Ethos, Haecceity, Human, Hypostasis, Inbeing, Inscape, Manhood, Mould, Quiddity, Quintessence, Second, SN, Temperament

Naught Cypher, Failure, Nil, Nothing, Zero

Naughty Bad, Disobedient, Girly, Improper, Indecorous, Light, Marietta, Nonny, Rascal, Remiss, Spright, Sprite, Wayward

Nausea, Nauseous Disgust, Fulsome, Malaise, Queasy, Sickness, Squeamish, Wamble, Wambly

Nave Aisle, Apse, Centre, Hub, Modiolus, Nef

Navel Belly-button, Jaffa, Naff, Nave, Omphalos, Orange, Tummy button, Umbilicus

Navigate, Navigator Albuquerque, Bering, Bougainville, Cabot, Cartier, Columbus, Control, Da Gama, Dias, Direct, Franklin, Frobisher, Gilbert, Hartog, Haul, Henry, Hudson, Keel, Magellan, Navvy, Orienteer, Pilot, Raleigh, Sail, Star-read, → **STEER**, Tasman, Traverse, Vancouver, Vespucci, Weddell

Navigation (aid, system) Asdic, Cabotage, Celestial, Decca, Dectra, Echosounder, Fido, Gee, Inertial, Inland, Loran, Loxodromics, Navarho, Omnirange, Portolan(o), Portulan, Radar, Satnav, Seamark, Shoran, Tacan, Teleran®, Vor

Navvy Workhorse

Navy, Naval AB, Armada, Blue, Fleet, French, Maritime, Merchant, N, Red, RN, Senior Service, Wavy, Wren

Nawab Huzoor, Nabob, Viceroy

Nazi Brownshirt, Gauleiter, Hess, Hitler, Jackboot, SS, Stormtrooper, Wer(e)wolf

NB Niobium, Nota bene

NCO Bombardier, Corp(oral), Havildar, Noncom, Orderly, Sergeant, SM

Neanderthal Mousterian

Neap Low, Tide

Neapolitan Ice

Near(er), Nearest, Nearby, Nearly, Nearness About, Adjacent, All-but, Almost, Anigh, Approach, Approximate, Beside, By, Close, Cy pres, Degree, Even, Ewest, Feckly, Forby, Gain, Handy, Hither, Imminent, Inby(e), Mean, Miserly, Narre, Neist, Next, Nie, Niggardly, Nigh, Oncoming, Outby, Propinquity, Proximity, Short-range, Stingy, Thereabout(s), To, Upon, Warm, Well-nigh

Neat(ly) Bandbox, Cattle, Clean-cut, Clever, Dainty, Dapper, Deft, Dink(y), Doddy, Donsie, Elegant, Feat(e)ous, Featly, Featuous, Gayal, Genty, Gyal, Intact, Jemmy, Jimpy, Lower, Nett, Nifty, Ninepence, Orderly, Ox(en), Preppy, Pretty, Rother, Shipshape, Short, Smug, Snod, Spruce, Straight, → **TIDY**, Trig, Trim, Uncluttered, Unwatered, Well-groomed

Neb Beak, Bill, Nose, Snout

Nebula, Nebulous Aeriform, Celestial, Cloudy, Dark, Emission, Gum, Hazy, Horsehead, Obscure, Planetary, Reflection, Shadowy, Vague

Necessary, Necessarily Bog, Cash, De rigueur, → **ESSENTIAL**, Estovers, Imperative, Important, Indispensable, Intrinsic, Money, Moolah, Needful, Ought, Perforce, Prerequisite, Requisite, Vital, Wherewithal

Necessitate, Necessity Ananke, Compel, Constrain, Cost, Emergency, Entail, Exigent, Fate, Indigence, Logical, Mathematical, Moral, Must, Natural, Need, Need-be, Oblige, Perforce, Require, Requisite, Staple

Neck(ed) Bottle, Brass, Canoodle, Cervical, Cervix, Channel, Col, Crag, Craig, Crop,

Cuff, Embrace, Ewe, Gall, Gorgerin, Halse, Hause, Hawse, Inarm, Inclip, Isthmus, Kiss, Mash, Nape, Pet, Polo, Rack, Rubber, Scoop, Scrag, Scruff, Smooch, Snog, Stiff, Strait, Surgical, Swan, Swire, Theorbo, Torticollis, Trachelate, Vee

▷ **Necking** *may indicate* one word around another

Necklace Afro-chain, Anodyne, Brisingamen, Chain, Choker, Collar, Corals, Lava(l)lière, Lunula, Mangalsutra, Negligee, Pearls, Rope, Sautoir, String, Torc, Torque

Neckline Boat, Collar, Cowl, Crew, Décolletage, Lanyard, Palter, Plunging, Sweetheart, Turtle, Vee

Neckwear Ascot, Barcelona, Boa, Bow, Collar, Cravat, Fur, Rail, Steenkirk, Stock, Tie

Necromancer Goetic, Magician, Ormandine, Osmand, Witch, Wizard

Necrosis Infarct, Sphacelus

Nectar Ambrosia, Amrita, Honey, Mead

Ned(dy) Donkey, Kelly, Ludd

Need(ed), Needy Beggarly, Call, Demand, Desiderata, Egence, Egency, Exigency, Gap, Gerundive, Impecunious, Indigent, → **LACK**, Mister, Pressing, PRN, Require, Strait, Strapped, Want

Needle(s) Acerose, Acicular, Aciform, Between, Bodkin, Cleopatra's, Darner, Darning, Dip, Dipping, Dry-point, Electric, Etching, Goad, Gramophone, Hagedorn, Hype, Hypodermic, Ice, Icicle, Inoculate, Knitting, Leucotome, Magnetic, Miff, Monolith, Neeld, Neele, Netting, Obelisk, Packing, Pine, Pinnacle, Pique, Pointer, Prick, R(h)aphis, Sew, Sharp, Spanish, Spicule, Spike, Spine, Spud, Stylus, Tattoo, Tease, Thorn, Wire

Needlewoman Cleopatra, Seamstress

Needlework Baste, Crewel, Drawn(-thread), Embroidery, Fag(g)oting, Fancy work, Gros point, Mola, Patchwork, Petit point, Piqué, Plainwork, Rivière, Sampler, Smocking, Spanish, Tapestry, Tattoo, White-seam, Woolwork, Worsted-work

Ne'er-do-well Badmash, Budmash, Bum, Good-for-nothing, Scullion, Shiftless, Skellum, Waster, Wastrel

Negation, Negative Ambrotype, Anion, Apophatic, Cathode, Denial, Double, Enantiosis, False, Ne, No, Non, Nope, Nullify, Pejorative, Photograph, Refusal, Resinous, Unresponsive, Veto, Yin

Neglect(ed), Neglectful, Negligence, Negligent Careless, Casual, Cinderella, Contributory, Cuff, Default, Dereliction, Disregard, Disuse, Failure, For(e)slack, Forget, Forlorn, Heedless, Inadvertence, Inattention, Incivism, Laches, Malpractice, Misprision, Omission, Oversight, Pass, Pass-up, Rack and ruin, → **REMISS**, Scamp, Shirk, Slight, Slipshod, Undone, Unilateral, Waif, Wanton

▷ **Neglected** *may indicate* an anagram

Negligee Déshabillé, Manteau, Mob, Nightgown, Peignoir, Robe

Negligible Fig, Minimal

Negotiate, Negotiator Arbitrate, Arrange, Bargain, Clear, Confer, Deal, Diplomat, Haggle, Intercede, Interdeal, Intermediary, Liaise, Manoeuvre, Mediator, Parley, Petition, Trade, Transact, Treat(y), Tret, Weather

Negro(id) → **AFRICAN**, Baganda, Bambara, Barotse, Bemba, Bergdama, Bini, Black, Blackamoor, Buck, Chewa, Creole, Cuffee, Cuffy, Damara, Dinge, Duala, Dyula, Ebon(y), Edo, Efik, Ethiop, Ewe, Fang, Ga, Ganda, Gullah, Hausa, Hottentot, Hutu, Ibibio, Ibo, Igbo, Igorot, Jim Crow, Kikuyu, Kongo, Luba, Luganda, Malinke, Maninke, Mestee, Moke, Moor, Mossi, Mustee, Ndebele, Nilote, Nupe, Nyanja, Nyoro, Ovambo, Pondo, Quashee, Quashie, Sambo, Snowball, Sotho, Spade, Susu, Temne, Thick-lips, Tiv, Tonga, Tsonga, Tswana, Twi, Uncle Tom, Venda, Watu(t)si, Wolof, Xhosa, Yoruba, Zambo, Zulu

Negus Emperor, Rumfruction, Selassie

Nehru Pandit
Neigh Bray, Hinny, Nicker, Whicker, Whinny
Neighbour(ly), Neighbouring, Neighbours Abut(ter), Adjoin, Alongside, Amicable, Bor, Border, But, Friendly, Joneses, Nearby, Next-door, Vicinal
Neighbourhood(s) Acorn®, Area, Community, District, Environs, Locality, Precinct, Vicinage, Vicinity
Neither Nor
Nell(ie), Nelly Bly, Dean, Trent
Nelson Columnist, Eddy, Horatio
Nemesis Alastor, Avenger, Deserts, Downfall, Fate, Retribution, Revenge
Neodymium Nd
Neolithic Avebury, Halafian, Skara Brae, Stonehenge
Neon Ne
Nepalese Gurkha
Neper N
Nephrite Yu
Nepotism Kin, Partisan, Patronage
Neptune God, Planet, Poseidon
Neptunium Np
Nerd Anorak, Otaku
Nereid Cymodoce, Nymph, Panope
Nerve(s), Nervous(ness), Nervure, Nerve centre, Nervy Abdabs, Abducens, Accessory, Acoustic, Afferent, Aflutter, Afraid, Alveolar, Appestat, Auditory, Axon, Baroreceptor, Bottle, Bouton, Brass neck, Buccal, Butterflies, Chord, Chutzpah, Collywobbles, Column, Commissure, Cones, Courage, Cranial, Cyton, Depressor, Edgy, Effector, Efferent, Electrotonus, Epicritic, Excitor, Facial, Fearful, Fidgety, Gall, Ganglion, Glossopharyngeal, Grit, Guts, Habdabs, Heart-string, High, Highly-strung, Hyp, Hypoglossal, Impudence, Jitters, Jittery, Jumpy, Median, Mid-rib, Motor, Moxie, Myelon, Nappy, Neck, Neurological, Nidus, Oculomotor, Olfactory, On edge, Optic, Pavid, Perikaryon, Proprioceptor, Protopathic, Rad, Radial, Receptor, Restiform, Restless, Sacral, Sangfroid, Sauce, Sciatic, Screaming abdabs, Screaming meemies, Sensory, Shaky, Shpilkes, Solar plexus, Splanchnic, Spunk, Squirrel(l)y, Steel, Strung-up, Sympathetic, Synapse, Tense, Timorous, Tizzy, Toey, Tongue-tied, Trembler, Tremulous, Trigeminal, Trochlear, Twitchy, Ulnar, Uptight, Vagus, Vapours, Vasodilator, Vestibulocochlear, Wandering, Willies, Windy, Wired, Yips
Nervous disease, Nervous disorder Chorea, Epilepsy, Neuritis, Tetany
▷ **Nervously** *may indicate* an anagram
Ness Cape, Headland, Ras
Nessus Centaur
Nest Aerie, Aery, Aiery, Ayrie, Bike, Bink, Brood, Byke, Cabinet, Cage, Caliology, Clutch, Dray, Drey, Eyrie, Eyry, Hive, Lodge, Love, Nid, Nide, Nidify, Nidus, Norwegian, Sett, Termitarium, Turkey, Wurley
Nestle Burrow, Coorie, Cose, Courie, Cuddle, Nuzzle, Snug(gle)
Nestor Counsellor, Kea, King, Parrot, Sage
Net(ting), Nets, Network(ing), Networker Anastomosis, Bamboo, BR, Bunt, Butterfly, Cast, Casting, Catch, Caul, Clap, Clathrate, Clear, Co-ax(ial), Cobweb, → **COMPUTER NETWORK**, Crinoline, Criss-cross, Crossover, Diane, Drift, Earn, Eel-set, Enmesh, Equaliser, Fetch, File server, Filet, Final, Fish, Fisherman, Flew, Flue, Fret, Fyke, Gill, → **GRID**, Hammock, Heliscoop, Honeycomb, Hose, Insect, Kiddle, Lace, Land, Landing, Lattice, Leap, Line, Linin, Mains, Malines, Mattress,

Maze, → **MESH**, Mist, Mosquito, Nerve, Neuropil, Old boys', PCN, Plexus, Portal system, Pound, Pout, Purse-seine, Quadripole, Reseau, Rete, Retiary, Reticle, Reticulate, Reticulum, Ring, Safety, Sagene, Scoop, Screen, Sean, Seine, Senior, Set(t), Shark, Skype®, Snood, Speed, Stake, Sweep-seine, Symplast, System, Tangle, Tela, Telex, Toil, Torpedo, Trammel, Trap, Trawl, Trepan, Tulle, Tunnel, Wire

Netball Let

Nether Below, Inferior, Infernal, Lower, Under

Nettle(rash) Anger, Annoy, Day, Dead, Hemp, Hives, Horse, Irritate, Labiate, Nark, Ongaonga, Pellitory, Pique, Ramee, Rami, Ramie, Rhea, Rile, Roman, Ruffle, Sting, Urtica(ceae), Urticaria

Neuralgia, Neuritis Migraine, Pleurodynia, Sciatica, Tic

Neurosis Combat, Compulsion, Obsessive-compulsive, Shellshock

Neuter Castrate, Gib, Impartial, Neutral, Sexless, Spay

Neutral(ise) Alkalify, Angel gear, Buffer zone, Counteract, Degauss, Grey, Impartial, Inactive, Schwa, Sheva, Shiva, Unbiased

Neutron(s) Delayed, Fast, Nucleon, Prompt, Slow, Thermal, Virgin

Never(more) Nary, Nathemo(re), No more, Nowise, St Tibb's Eve

Never-ending Age-long

Never mind Nix my dolly

Nevertheless Algate, Anyhow, But, Even, Howbeit, However, Quand même, Still, Tout de même, Yet

▷ **New** *may indicate* an anagram

New(s), Newborn, News agency Bulletin, Copy, Coranto, Dope, Euphobia, Evangel, Flash, Forest, Fresh, Fudge, Gen, Green, Griff, Info, Innovation, Intelligence, Itar Tass, Item, Kerygma, Latest, Mint, Modern, N, Novel, Oil(s), Original, PA, Paragraph, Pastures, Pristine, Propaganda, Raw, Recent, Report, Reuter, Scoop, Span, Split, Stranger, Tass, Teletext®, Tidings, Ultramodern, Unco, Usenet, Wire service, Word

New boy Gyte

Newcomer Dog, Freshman, Griffin, Immigrant, Jackaroo, Jackeroo, Jillaroo, Johnny-come-lately, L, Learner, Newbie, Novice, Parvenu, Pilgrim, Settler, Tenderfoot, Upstart

Newfoundland Dog, Nana, Vinland

Newgate Calendar

Newly wed Benedick, Benedict, Bride, Groom, Honeymooner, Neogamist

Newman Cardinal, Noggs, Paul

New moon Rosh Chodesh

Newsman, News-reader Announcer, Editor, Journalist, Legman, Press, Reporter, Sub, Sysop

Newsmonger, News-vendor Butcher, Gossip, Quidnunc

Newspaper Blat(t), Broadsheet, Courier, Daily, Express, Fanzine, Feuilleton, Freesheet, Gazette, Guardian, Heavy, Herald, Intelligencer, Journal, Jupiter, Le Monde, Mercury, National, Organ, Patent inside, Patent outside, Post, Pravda, Press, Print, Rag, Red-top, Scandal sheet, Sheet, Spoiler, Squeak, Sun, Tabloid, Today

Newsreel Actualities

Newt(s) Ask(er), Eft, Evet, Swift, Triton, Urodela

Newton N

New World USA

New Year Hogmanay, Ne'er-day, Rosh Hashana(h), Tet

New York(er) Big Apple, Gotham, Knickerbocker

New Zealand(er) Aotearoa, Enzed, Jafa, Kiwi, Maori, Mooloo, Moriori, Pakeha, Pig Island, Ronz(er), Shagroon, Zelanian

Next Adjacent, Adjoining, After, Alongside, Beside, By, Following, Immediate, Later, Nearest, Neist, Proximate, Proximo, Sine, Subsequent, Syne, Thereafter

Nib(s) Cocoa, J, Pen, Point, Tip

Nibble Bite, Brouse, Browse, Byte, Canapé, Crop, Eat, Gnaw, Knap(ple), Moop, Moup, Munch, Nag, Nepit, Nosh, Peck, Pick, Snack

Niblick Wedge

Nice(ly), Nicety Accurate, Amene, Appealing, Cool, Dainty, Fastidious, Fine, Finical, Genteel, Lepid, Mooi, Ninepence, Pat, Pleasant, Precise, Quaint, Rare, Refined, Subtil(e), Subtle, Sweet, T, To a t

Niche Alcove, Almehrahb, Almery, Ambry, Apse, Aumbry, Awmrie, Awmry, Columbarium, Cranny, Exedra, Fenestella, Mihrab, Recess, Slot

Nicholas Santa

Nick(ed) Appropriate, Arrest, Bin, Blag, Can, Chip, Cly, Colin, Copshop, Crib, Cut, Denay, Dent, Deny, → **DEVIL**, Erose, Groove, Hoosegow, Kitty, Knock, Nab, Nap, Nim, Nock, Notch, Pinch, Pook, Pouk, Prison, Scratch, Sneak, → **STEAL**, Steek, Swan-upping, Swipe, Thieve, Whip, Wirricow, Worricow, Worrycow

Nickel (silver) Coin, Garnierite, Jitney, Millerite, Ni, Packfong, Paktong, Zaratite

Nicker Bonduc, Neigh, Whinny

Nickname Alias, Byname, Byword, Cognomen, So(u)briquet, To-name

Nicotine Tobacco, Weed

Nifty Smart, Stylish

Nigeria(n) Biafran, Cross River, Efik, Hausa, Ibibio, Ibo, Igbo, Nupe, Tiv, WAN, Yoruba

Niggard(ly) Dry-fist, Illiberal, Mean, Miser, Near-(be)gaun, Nippy, Nirlit, Parsimonious, Penny wise, Pinchcommons, Pinchgut, Pinchpenny, Scrunt, Skinflint, Tightwad

Niggle Carp, Gripe, Nag, Potter, Trifle

Night(s), Nightfall Acronical, Acronychal, Arabian, Burns, Darkling, Darkmans, First, Gaudy, Guest, Guy Fawkes, Hen, Leila, Nacht, Nicka-nan, Nutcrack, Nyx, School, Sleepover, Stag, Twelfth, Twilight, Walpurgis, Watch, White

Night-blindness Day-sight, Nyctalopia

Night-cap Biggin, Cocoa, Kilmarnock cowl, Nip, Pirnie, Sundowner

Nightclub Boite de nuit, Clip joint, Dive, Honkytonk, Hot spot

Night-dew Serein, Serene

Nightdress Wylie-coat

Nightingale Bulbul, Florence, Jugger, Lind, Philomel, Scutari, Swedish, Watch

Nightjar Chuck-will's-widow, Churn-owl, Evejar, Fern-owl, Goatsucker, Poorwill, Potoo

Night-light Moonbeam

Nightmare, Nightmarish Cacod(a)emon, Ephialtes, Incubus, Kafkaesque, Oneirodynia, Phantasmagoria

Night-rider Revere

Nightshade Atropin(e), Belladonna, Bittersweet, Black, Circaea, Deadly, Dwale, Enchanter's, Henbane, Morel, Solanum, Woody

Nightwatchman Charley, Charlie, Rug-gown

Nightwork Lucubrate

Nihilist Anarchist, Red, Sceptic

Nil Nothing, Nought, Zero

Nile Albert, Blue, Luvironza, Victoria, White

Nimble(ness), Nimbly Active, → AGILE, Alert, Deft, Deliver, Fleet, Legerity, Light, Light-footed, Lissom(e), Lithe, Quiver, Sciolto, Springe, Spry, Supple, Sure-footed, Swack, Wan(d)le, Wannel, Wight, Ya(u)ld

Nimbus Aura, Aureole, Cloud, Gloriole, Halo

Nimrod Hunter

Nincompoop Ass, Imbecile, Ninny, Stupid

Nine, Ninth Choral, Ennead, Muses, Nonary, Nonet, Novenary, Pins, Sancho, Skittles, Tailors, Worthies

Nine hundred Sampi

Nine of diamonds Curse of Scotland

Nineteen(th) Bar, Decennoval

Ninetieth, Ninety N, Nonagesimal

Ninevite Assyrian

Ninny (hammer) Fool, Goose, Idiot, Stupid, Tony

Ninon Nan

Niobium Nb

Nip(per), Nippers Bite, Brat, Check, Chela, Chill, Claw, Cutpurse, Dip, Dram, Fang, Foil, Gook, Jap, Lad, Lop, Nep, Nirl, Outsiders, Peck, Pickpocket, Pincers, Pinch, Pook, Pop, Scotch, Sneap, Susan, Tad, Taste, Tot, Tweak, Urchin, Vice, Vise

Nipa At(t)ap, Palm

Nipple Dug, Grease, Jogger's, Mastoid, Pap, Teat

Nis Brownie, Goblin, Kobold, Sprite

Nit Egg, Insect, Louse

Nit-picking Carping, Pedantry, Quibble

Nitre Saltpetre

Nitric, Nitrogen Azote, Azotic, Gas, N, Quinoline

Nitroglycerine Glonoin

Nitwit Ass, Flat, Fool, Simpleton, → STUPID

No Aikona, Denial, Na(e), Nah, Naw, Negative, Nix, Nope, Nyet, O, Refusal

Noah Arkite, Beery, Utnapishtim

Nob(by) Grandee, Parage, Prince, Swell, Toff

Nobble Dope, Hilch, Injure, Interfere

▷ **Nobbled** *may indicate* an anagram

Nobelium No

Noble(man), Noblewoman, Nobility, Nobly Adela, Adele, Adeline, Aneurin, Aristocrat, Atheling, Baron(et), Baronne, Bart, Blue blood, Boyar, Brave, Bt, Burgrave, Childe, Contessa, Count, County, Daimio, Dom, Don, Doucepere, Douzeper(s), Duc, Duke, Duniwassal, Earl, Empress, Eorl, Ethel, Eupatrid, Fine, Galahad, Gent, Glorious, Graf, Grandee, Grandeur, Great, Heroic, Hidalgo, Highborn, Illustrious, Infant, Jarl, Junker, King, Landgrave, Lord, Maestoso, Magnate, Magnificent, Magnifico, Manly, Margrave, Marquis, Mona, Nair, Nayar, Palatine, Patrician, Patrick, Peer, Rank, Ritter, Rose, Seigneur, Seignior, Sheik(h), Stately, Sublime, Thane, Thegn, Titled, Toiseach, Toisech, Vavasour, Vicomte, Vidame, Viscount

Noble gas(es) Argon, Helium, Krypton, Neon, Radon, Xenon

Nobody Diarist, Gnatling, Jack-straw, Nebbish, Nemo, None, Nonentity, Nyaff, Pipsqueak, Pooter, Quat, Schlepp, Scoot, Shlep, Zero

Nocturnal (creature) Bat, Galago, Moth, Night, Owl

Nod(ding) Agree, Assent, Beck(on), Bob, Browse, Catnap, Cernuous, Dip, Doze, Drowsy, Headbang, Mandarin, Nutant, Somnolent

Node, Nodular, Nodule Ascending, Boss, Descending, Enhydros, Geode, Knot, Lump, Lymph, Milium, Pea-iron, Ranvier, Root, Septarium, Swelling, Thorn, Tophus, Tubercle

No doubt Iwis, Ywis

Noel Christmas, Coward, Yule

Nog(gin) Ale, Cup, → **DRINK**, Peg

No go Anergia

No good Dud, NG, Ropy

No-hoper Gone goose, Goner

Noise, Noisy Ambient, Babel, Bedlam, Big, Blare, Bleep, Blip, Blue murder, Bobbery, Boing, Boink, Bray, Bruit, Cangle, Charm, Chellup, Clamant, Clamour, Clangour, Clash, Clatter, Clitter, Clutter, Coil, Crackle, Creak, Deen, Din, Dirdum, Euphonia, Euphony, F, Flicker, Fuss, Hewgh, Howlround, Hubbub, Hue, Hullabaloo, Hum, Hurly-burly, Knocking, Loud, Mush, Obstreperous, Ping, Pink, Plangent, Quonk, Racket, Raucous, Report, Risp, Roar, Robustious, Rorie, Rort, Rory, Row(dow-dow), Rowdedow, Rowdy(dow)(dy), Rucous, Rumble, Schottky, Schottky-Utis, Scream, Screech, Shindig, Shindy, Shot, Shreek, Shreik, Shriech, Shriek, Solar, Sone, Sonorous, Sound, Strepent, Strepitation, Strepitoso, Stridor, Surface, Thermal, Thunder, Tinnitus, Top, Tumult, → **UPROAR**, VIP, Visual, Vociferous, Whinny, White, Zoom

Noisome Fetid, Invidious, Noxious, Offensive, Rank

No longer Ex, Past

Nomad(ic) Amalekite, Ammonites, Bedawin, Bed(o)uin, Bedu, Berber, Chal, Edom(ite), Fula(h), Gypsy, Hottentot, Hun, Hunter-gatherer, Hyksos, Itinerant, Kurd, Kyrgyz, Lapp, Rom, Rootless, Rover, Saracen, Sarmatian, Strayer, Tsigane, Tsigany, Tuareg, Turk(o)man, Unsettled, Vagabond, Vagrant, Wanderer, Zigan

Noman Ta(r)tar

No man's land Tom Tiddler's ground

Nome Province

Nomenclature Term

Nominal Formal, Onomastic, Titular, Token, Trifling

Nominate, Nomination Appoint, Baptism, Designate, Elect, Postulate, Present, → **PROPOSE**, Slate, Specify, Term

Nomogram Abac

No more Gone, Napoo

Nomothete Enactor, Legislator

Non-Aboriginal Wudjula

Non-attender Absentee, Recusant

Non-attribute Ens

Non-believer Atheist, Cynic, Infidel, Sceptic

Non-catalyst Zymogen

Nonchalance, Nonchalant Blasé, Casual, Cool, Debonair, Insouciant, Jaunty, Poco

Non-Christian Saracen

Noncommittal Trimmer

Non-communist West

Non-conductor Insulator

Non-conformist, Non-conformity Beatnik, Bohemian, Chapel, Deviant, Dissent(er), Dissident, Drop-out, Ebenezer, Heresiarch, Heretic, Maverick, Odd-ball, Outlaw, Pantile, Patarine, Rebel, Recusant, Renegade, Renegate, Sectarian, Wesleyan

Nondescript Dull, Grey, Insipid, Neutral, Nyaff

Non-directional Scalar
Non-drip Thixotropic
None Nada, Nary, Nil, Nought, Zero
Nonentity Cipher, Nebbich, Nebbish(er), Nebish, Nobody, Pipsqueak, Quat
Non-essential Adiaphoron, Disposable, Extrinsic, Incidental
Nonesuch Model, Nonpareil, Paradigm, Paragon, Rarity
Nonetheless Mind you
▷ **Nonetheless** *may indicate* an 'o' to be omitted
Non-existent Unbeing, Virtual
Non-finite Verbid
Non-Gypsy Gajo, Gorgio
Non-interference Laissez faire
Non-Jewish Goy, Shi(c)ksa, Shkitzim, Sho(y)getz
Non-juror Usager
Non-Maori Tangata tiriti, Tauiwi
Non-Muslim Raia, Rayah
No-nonsense Hardball
Nonpareil Nonesuch, Pearl, Peerless, Type, Unequal, Unique
Nonplus(sed) Baffle, Bewilder, Blank, Perplex, Stump
Non-professional Amateur, Laic
Non-radiative Auger
Non-resident Extern, Outlier
Non-runner Scratched, Solid
Nonsense Absurdity, Amphigon, Amphigory, Balderdash, Baloney, Bilge, Bizzo,
    Blague, Blah, Blarney, Blat(her), Blatherskite, Blether, Bollocks, Boloney, Bora(c)k,
    Borax, Bosh, Bull, Bulldust, Bullshit, Bull's wool, Buncombe, Bunk, Bunkum,
    Clamjamfr(a)y, Clamjamphrie, Claptrap, Cobblers, Cock, Cockamamie, Cod,
    Codswallop, Crap, Crapola, Drivel, Dust, Eyewash, Faddle, Falderal, Fandangle,
    Fiddlededee, Fiddle-faddle, Fiddlesticks, Flannel, Flapdoodle, Flim-flam, Folderol,
    Footling, Fudge, Gaff, Galimatias, Gammon, Gas and gaiters, Get away, Gibberish,
    Gobbledygook, Guff, Gum, Hanky-panky, Haver, Hogwash, Hokum, Hooey,
    Hoop-la, Horsefeathers, Humbug, Jabberwocky, Jazz, Jive, Kibosh, Kidstakes,
    Malark(e)y, Moonshine, Mouthwash, My eye, Niaiserie, Phooey, Piffle, Pishogue,
    Pshaw, Pulp, Ratbaggery, Rats, Rawmaish, Rhubarb, Rigmarole, Rot, Rubbish,
    Scat, Shenanigans, Shit(e), Squit, Stuff, Tom(foolery), Tommy-rot, Tosh, Trash,
    Tripe, Tush, Twaddle, Unreason, Waffle
Non-sequitur Anacoluthia, Irrelevant
Non-starter No-no
Non-stick PTFE, Teflon®, Tusche
Non-stop Through
Non-U Naff
Non-violence Ahimsa, Pacificism, Satyagraha
Non-white Coloured, Yolk
Noodle(s) Capellini, Crispy, Daw, Fool, Head, Laksa, Lokshen, Manicotti, Mee,
    Moony, Ninny, Pasta, Sammy, Simpleton, Soba, Udon
Nook Alcove, Angle, Corner, Cranny, Niche, Recess, Rookery
Noon Am end, M, Midday, N, Narrowdale
No one Nemo, None
Noose Fank, Halter, Hempen caudle, Lanyard, Loop, Necktie, Rebecca, Rope, Rope's
    end, Snare, Twitch
▶ **Nor** *see* **NOT**

Nordic, Norse(man) Icelander, Norn, Scandinavian, Viking

▶ **Nordic** *see* **NORWAY, NORWEGIAN**

Norm Canon, Criterion, Rule, Standard

Normal Average, Conventional, Customary, Everyday, General, Natural, Norm, Ordinary, Orthodox, Par, Perpendicular, Regular, Standard, Unexceptional, Usu(al)

Normal eyes Emmetropia

Norman French, Rufus

▶ **Norse** *see* **NORWAY, NORWEGIAN**

North(ern), Northerner Arctic, Boreal, Cispontine, Copperhead, Dalesman, Doughface, Eskimo, Geographic, Hyperborean, Magnetic, N, Norland, Runic, Scotia, Septentrion, True, Up

North American (Indian) Ab(e)naki, Algonki(a)n, Algonqui(a)n, Angeleno, Apache, Arapaho, Assiniboine, Basket Maker, Blackfoot, Brave, Caddoan, Cajun, Cayuga, Cherokee, Cheyenne, Chibcha, Chickasaw, Chinook, Chipewyan, Choctaw, Comanche, Copperskin, Creek, Crow, Delaware, Dene, Erie, Five Nations, Fox, Galibi, Geronimo, Gwich'in, Haida, Hiawatha, Hopi, Huron, Injun, Innu, Iroquois, Kiowa Apache, Kloo(t)ch, Kootenai, Kootenay, Kutenai, Kwakiuti, Lakota, Mahican, Malecite, Mandan, Manhattan, Massachuset(ts), Melungeon, Menominee, Menomini, Mescalero, Micmac, Mikasuki, Miniconjou, Minneconjou, Miskito, Mission, Mixtec, Mogollon, Mohave, Mohawk, Mohegan, Mohican, Montagnais, Montagnard, Mound Builder, Mugwump, Musk(h)ogean, Muskogee, Narraganset, Natchez, Navaho, Nez Percé, Nootka, Norteno, Northern P(a)iute, Oglala, Ojibwa(y), Okanagon, Okinagan, Omaha, Oneida, Onondaga, Osage, P(a)iute, Palouse, Papago, Papoose, Pawnee, Pequot, Pima, Plains, Pocahontas, Pomo, Ponca, Pontiac, Potawatom, Pueblo, Quapaw, Red(skin), Sachem, Sagamore, Sahaptan, Sahapti(a)n, Salish, Sannup, Sauk, Scalper, Seminole, Senecan, Serrano, Shahaptin, Shawnee, Shoshone, Sioux, Sitting Bull, Siwash, Six Nations, Southern P(a)iute, Status, Suquamash, Susquehannock, Tahitan, Taino, Tarahumara, Teton, Tewa, Tiwa, Tlingit, Totemist, Tribe, Tsimshian, Tuscarora, Ute, Uto-Aztecan, Wampanoag, Wichita, Winnebago, Wyandot(te), Yalkama, Yanqui, Yuman, Zuni

Northern Ireland NI, Six Counties

North star Tyrian cynosure

Northwestern Aeolis

Norway, Norwegian Bokmal, Fortinbras, Landsma(a)l, N, Nordic, Norweyan, Nynorsk, Rollo, Scandinavian

Nose, Nosy A(d)jutage, Aquiline, Beak, Bergerac, Boko, Bouquet, Breather, Catarrhine, Conk, Copper, Cromwell, Curious, Desman, Droop, Fink, Flair, Gnomon, Grass, Grecian, Greek, Grog-blossom, Honker, Hooter, Index, Informer, Leptorrhine, Meddle, Muffle, Muzzle, Nark, Neb, Nozzle, Nuzzle, Parker, Platyrrhine, Proboscis, Prying, Pug, Red, Rhinal, Roman, Schnozzle, Shove, Smelly, Sneb, Sniff, Snoot, Snout, Snub, Squeal, Stag, Stickybeak, Toffee

Noseband Barnacle, Cavesson, Musrol

Nose-bleed Epistaxis

Nosh Eat, Food, Nibble, Snack

Nostalgia Longing, Memory lane, Retrophilia, Yearning

Nostril(s) Blowhole, Cere, Choana, Nare

Nostrum Elixir, Medicine, Remede, Remedy

Not, Nor Dis-, Na(e), Narrow A, Ne, Neither, Never, No, Pas, Polled, Taint

Notable, Notability Conspicuous, Distinguished, Eminent, Especial, Landmark, Large, Lion, Memorable, Personage, Signal, Striking, Unco, VIP, Worthy

Not allowed NL

▷ **Not allowed** *may indicate* a word to be omitted

Notary Apostolical, Ecclesiastical, Escribano, Scrivener

Notation(al) Benesh, Cantillation, Descriptive, Entry, Formalism, Hexadecimal, Infix, Memo, Octal, Polish, Positional, Postfix, Romic, Staff, Tablature

Notch(ed) Crena(l), Crenel, Cut, Dent, Erode, Erose, Gain, Gap, Gimp, Indent, Insection, Jag, Kerf, Mush, Nick, Nock, Raffle, Score, Serrate, Serrulation, Sinus, Snick, Tally, Vandyke

Not clear Blocked, NL, Obscure, Opaque, Pearl

Note(s), Notebook A, Acciaccatura, Accidental, Advance, Adversaria, Advice, Agogic, Apostil(le), Apparatus, Appoggiatura, Arpeggio, Auxiliary, B, Bill(et), Bradbury, Breve, C, Cedula, Chit(ty), Chord, Cob, Comment, Conceit, Continental, Cover, Credit, Crotchet, Currency, D, Debit, Delivery, Demand, Dig, Do(h), Dominant, Double-dotted, E, E-la, F, Fa(h), False, Fame, Fiver, Flat, Flim, G, Gamut, Gloss(ary), Gold, Grace, Greenback, Gruppetto, Heed, Hemiola, Hypate, Identic, Index rerum, IOU, Iron man, Item(ise), Jot(tings), Jug(-jug), Key, Kudos, La, Large, Leading, Lichanos, Line(r), Log, Long, Longa, Lower mordent, Marginalia, Masora(h), Masoretic, Me, Mediant, Melisma, Melody, Memo(randum), Mese, Mi, Minim, Minute, → **MONEY**, Mordent, Music, Nachschlag, Natural, NB, Nete, Neum(e), Oblong, Observe, Octave, Oncer, Open, Ostmark, Outline, Parhypate, Passing, Postal, Post-it®, Pound, Promissory, Prompt, Prosiambanomenos, Protocol, PS, Quarter, Quaver, Rag-money, Re, Record, Remark, Renown, Request, Right, Root, Scholion, Scholium, Scotch catch, Scotch snap, Semibreve, Semiquaver, Semitone, Sensible, Septimole, Sextolet, Sharp, Shinplaster, Shoulder, Si, Sick, Sixteenth, Sixty-fourth, Sleeve, Smacker, Snuff-paper, So(h), Sol, Stem, Strike, Subdominant, Submediant, Subtonic, Supertonic, Te, Ten(ner), Third, Thirty-second, Tierce, Tonic, Treasury, Treble, Undecimole, Ut, Variorum, Verbal, Wad, Warison, Whole, Wolf, Wood

Note-case Pochette, Purse, Wallet

▷ **Notes** *may indicate* the use of letters A-G

Noteworthy Eminent, Extraordinary, Memorable, Particular, Signal, Special

Nothing, Nought Buckshee, Bugger-all, Cipher, Damn-all, Devoid, Diddlysquat, Emptiness, FA, Gratis, Jack, Love, Nada, Napoo, Naught, Nihil, Niks-nie, Nil, Nix(-nie), Noumenon, Nowt, Nuffin, Nullity, O, Rap, Rien, Sweet FA, Void, Z, Zero, Zilch, Zip(po)

Notice(able) Ad(vertisement), Advance, Advice, Affiche, Apprise, Attention, Avis(o), Banns, Bill, Blurb, Bold, Caveat, Circular, Clock, Cognisance, Crit, D, DA, Descry, Detect, Discern, Dismissal, Enforcement, Gaum, Get, Gorm, Handbill, → **HEED**, Intimation, Marked, Mensh, Mention, NB, No(t)chel, Obit, Observe, Oyez, Perceptible, Placard, Plaque, Playbill, Poster, Press, Proclamation, Prominent, Pronounced, → **REMARK**, Review, See, Short, Si quis, Spot, Spy, Sticker, Tent, Whip

Notify, Notification Acquaint, Advise, Apprise, Aviso, Awarn, Inform, → **TELL**, Warn

Notion(al) Academic, Conceit, → **CONCEPT**, Crotchet, Fancy, Hunch, Idea, Idée, Idolum, Inkling, Opinion, Reverie, Vapour, Whim

Notoriety, Notorious Arrant, Byword, Crying, Egregious, Esclandre, Fame, Flagrant, Infamous, Infamy, Notour, Proverbial, Réclame, → **RENOWN**, Repute

No trump Laical, Lay, NT

Notwithstanding Although, Despite, Even, For, Howbeit, However, Mau(l)gre, Nath(e)less, Natheless(e), Naythles, Nevertheless, Spite

Nougat Montelimar, Sundae

▶ **Nought** *see* **NOTHING**

Noughts and crosses Tic(k)-tac(k)-to(e)
Noumenon Thing-in-itself
Noun Abstract, Agent, Agentive, Aptote, Collective, Common, Concrete, Count, Gerund, Mass, N, Proper, Seg(h)olate, Substantive, Tetraptote, Verbal, Vocative
Nourish(ing), Nourishment Aliment, Battill, Cherish, Cultivate, Feed, Ingesta, Meat, Nurse, Nurture, Nutrient, Promote, Replenish, Sustenance, Trophic
Nous Intellect, Intelligence, Reason
Nova Scotia(n) Acadia, Blue-nose
▷ **Novel** *may indicate* an anagram
Novel(ty) Aga-saga, Bildungsroman, Bonkbuster, Book, Campus, Change, Clarissa, Different, Dime, Dissimilar, Emma, Epistolary, Fad, Fiction, Fresh, Gimmick, Gothic, Graphic, Historical, Horror, Idiot, Innovation, Ivanhoe, Kenilworth, Kidnapped, Kim, Middlemarch, → **NEW**, Newfangled, Original, Outside, Page-turner, Pamela, Paperback, Pendennis, Penny dreadful, Persuasion, Picaresque, Pot-boiler, Primeur, Pulp, Rebecca, River, Roman-à-clef, Romance, Roman fleuve, Scoop, Sex and shopping, Shilling-dreadful, Shilling-shocker, Terror, Thesis, Ulysses, Unusual, Whodun(n)it, Yellowback
▶ **Novelist** *see* **WRITER**
Novice Acolyte, Apprentice, Beginner, Cadet, Chela, Colt, Cub, Greenhorn, Griffin, Jackaroo, Jillaroo, Johnny-raw, Kyu, L, Learner, Neophyte, New chum, Noob, Patzer, Postulant, Prentice, Rabbit, Rookie, Tenderfoot, Tyro(ne), Unweaned
Now(adays) AD, Alate, Anymore, Current, Here, Immediate, Instanter, Interim, Nonce, Nunc, Present, Pro tem, This
Nowhere Limbo
Nowt Cattle, Cows, Ky(e), Neat, Nothing
Noxious Harmful, Offensive, Poisonous, Toxic, Toxin, Venomous
Nozzle A(d)jutage, Aerospike, Fishtail, Nose, Nose-piece, Rose, Spout, Stroup, Syringe, Tewel, Tuyere, Tweer, Twier, Twire, Twyer(e)
Nuance Gradation, Nicety, Overtone, Shade
Nub Crux, Gist, Knob, Lump, Point
Nubile Beddable, Marriageable, Parti
Nuclear, Nucl(e)ide, Nucleus Cadre, Calandria, Centre, Core, Crux, Daughter, Deuteron, Eukaryon, Euratom, Even-even, Even-odd, Heartlet, Hub, Isomer, Isotone, Karyon, Kernel, Linin, Mushroom, Nuke, Pith, Prokaryon, Recoil, Synkaryon, Triton
▷ **Nucleus** *may indicate* the heart of a word
Nude, Nudism, Nudist, Nudity Adamite, Altogether, Aphylly, Bare, Buff, Eve, Exposed, Full-frontal, Gymnosophy, → **NAKED**, Nuddy, Scud, Stark, Stripped, Undress
Nudge Dunch, Dunsh, Elbow, Jostle, Poke, Prod
Nudibranch Sea-slug
Nugget Chunk, Cob, Gold, Lump
Nuisance Bore, Bot, Bugbear, Chiz(z), Drag, Impediment, Inconvenience, Mischief, Pest, Plague, Public, Terror, Trial
Null(ification), Nullify Abate, Cancel, Counteract, Defeasance, Destroy, Diriment, Disarm, Invalid(ate), Negate, Neutralise, Overturn, Recant, Terminate, Undo, Veto, Void
Numb(ness) Asleep, Blunt, Dead(en), Stun, Stupor, Torpefy, Torpescent, Torpid, Unfeeling
▷ **Number** *may indicate* a drug
Number(s) Abscissa, Abundant, Accession, Air, Aleph-null, Aleph-zero, Algebraic,

Algorithm, Aliquant, Aliquot, Amiable, Amicable, Anaesthetic, Analgesic, Antilog, Apocalyptic, Apostrophus, Army, Atomic, Augend, Avogadro, Babylonian, Binary, Box, Brinell, Calculate, Cardinal, Cetane, Chromosome, Class, Cocaine, Coefficient, Cofactor, Complex, Composite, Concrete, Constant, Coordination, Count, Cyclic, Decillion, Deficient, Deficit, Diapason, Digit, Drove, E, Edition, Epidural, Ether, Eucaine, Ex-directory, F, Feck, Figurate, Figure, Fraction, Friendly, Frost(bite), Froude, Gas, Gobar, Golden, Googol, Handful, Hantle, Hash(mark), Hemlock, Host, Hyperreal, Imaginary, Include, Incomposite, Index, Infimum, Integer, Irrational, Isospin, Isotopic, Item, Lac, Lakh, Legion(s), Lepton, Livraison, Local, Mach, Magazine, Magic, Mantissa, Mass, Melodic, Milliard, Minuend, Minyan, Mixed, Mort, Muckle, Multiple, Multiplex, Multiplicity, Multitude, Myriadth, Nasik, Natural, Neutron, No(s), Nonillion, Nth, Nuclear, Nucleon, Num, Numerator, Numerical, Octane, Octillion, Opiate, Opium, Opposite, Opus, Ordinal, OT, Paginate, Par, Paucal, Peck, Perfect, Pile, PIN, Plural, Polygonal, Prime, Procaine, Production, Proton, Quantum, Quarternion, Quorum, Quotient, Radix, Raft, Random, Rational, Real, Reckon, Registration, Regulo®, Repunit, Reynolds, Sampi, Scads, Serial, Show-stopper, Sight, Slew, Slue, Some, Square, Strangeness, Strength, Subtrahend, Summand, Surd, T, Tale, Telephone, Tell, Thr(e)ave, Totient, Totitive, Transcendental, Transfinite, Troop, Turn-out, Umpteen, Umpty, Urethan(e), Verse, Wave, Whole, Wrong, Zeroth

Numeral(s) Arabic, Chapter, Figure, Ghubar, Gobar, Integer, Number, Roman, Sheep-scoring

Numerous(ness) Divers, Galore, Legion, Lots, Many, Multeity, Myriad, Teeming

Numskull Blockhead, Booby, Dunce, Stupid

Nun Basilian, Beguine, Bhikkhuni, Clare, Cloistress, Cluniac, Conceptionist, Dame, Deaconess, Gilbertine, Minim, Minoress, Mother Superior, Outsister, Pigeon, Poor Clare, Prioress, Religeuse, Salesian, Sister, Sister of Mercy, Top, Trappistine, Ursuline, Vestal, Visitant, Vowess, Zelator, Zelatrice, Zelatrix

▷ **Nun** *may indicate* a biblical character, father of Joshua

Nuptial (chamber) Bridal, Marital, Marriage, Thalamus

Nurse, Nursery(man), Nursing Aia, Alice, Amah, Angel, Ayah, Barrier, Bonne, Caledonia, Candy-striper, Care(r), Cavell, Charge, Cherish, Conservatory, Consultant, Cradle, Crèche, Day, Deborah, District, Dry, EN, Flo(rence), Foster, Gamp, Garden, Glumdalclitch, Harbour, Health visitor, Hothouse, Karitane, Mammy, Midwife, Minister, Mother, Mrs Gamp, Nan(n)a, Nanny, Night, Nightingale, Nourice, Nourish, Parabolanus, Phytotron, Playroom, Playschool, Plunket, Probationer, Rhyme, RN, School, Seedsman, Seminary, SEN, Sister, Slope, Staff, Suckle, Tend, VAD, Visiting, Wet

▷ **Nursing** *may indicate* one word within another

Nurture Cradle, Cultivate, Educate, Feed, Foster, Suckle, Tend

Nut *may refer to* Egyptian god, father of Osiris

Nut(s), Nutcase, Nutshell, Nut tree, Nutty Acajou, Acorn, Almond, Amygdalus, Anacardium, Aphorism, Arachis, Areca, Arnut, Babassu, Barcelona, Barking, Barmy, Bats, Beech-mast, Bertholletia, Betel, Brazil, Briefly, Buffalo, Butterfly, Butternut, Cashew, Castle, Chock, Coal, Cob, Coco-de-mer, Coffee, Cohune, Coke, Cola, Conker, Coquilla, Coquina, Core, Cranium, Cream, Cuckoo, Dukka(h), En, Filberd, Filbert, Frog, Gelt, Gilbert, Gland, Glans, Goober, Gum, Hard, Hazel, Head, Hickory, Illipe, Ivory, Kachang puteh, Kernel, Kola, Lichee, Li(t)chi, Loaf, Lug, Lunatic, Lychee, Macadamia, Macahuba, Macaw-palm, Macoya, Manic, Marking, Mast, Mockernut, Monkey, Noisette, Noodle, Nucule, Oak, Oil, Pakan, Palmyra, Para, Pate, Pecan, Pekan, Philippina, Philippine, Philopoena, Physic, Pili, Pine,

Oo

O Blob, Duck, Nought, Omega, Omicron, Oscar, Oxygen, Spangle, Tan, Zero

Oaf Auf, Changeling, Dolt, Fool, Mou, Ocker, Ouph(e), Stupid, Twit, Yahoo

Oak(s) Bog, Bur, Cerris, Classic, Cork, Desert, Dumbarton, Durmast, Flittern, Fumed, Gabriel, Herne, Holly, Holm, Honour, Ilex, Jerusalem, Kermes, Live, Major, Native, Parliament, Pedunculate, Philemon, Poison, Quercus, Red, Roble, Royal, Sessile, Silky, Swamp, Swilcar, → **TREE**, Turkey, Valonia, Watch, White

Oakley Annie

Oar(s), Oarsmen Blade, Ctene, Eight, Leander, Organ, Paddle, Palm, Propel, Rower, Scull, Spoon, Stroke, Sweep

Oasis Biskra, Buraimi, Haven, Hotan, Hotien, Refuge, Spring, Tafilalet, Tafilelt

Oat(meal), Oats Ait, Athole brose, Avena, Brome-grass, Fodder, Grain, Grits, Groats, Gruel, Haver, Loblolly, Parritch, Pilcorn, Pipe, Porridge, Quaker®, Rolled, Wild

Oatcake Bannock, Clapbread, Farle, Flapjack, Jannock

Oath Affidavit, Begorrah, Blast, Bribery, Burgess, Curse, Dang, Demme, Doggone, Drat, Ecod, Egad, Expletive, God-so, Gospel, Halidom, Hippocratic, Igad, Imprecation, Jabers, Lumme, Lummy, Nouns, Oons, Promise, Sacrament, Sal(a)mon, Sapperment, Saucer, 'Sbodikins, Sbud(dikins), Sdeath, Sfoot, Sheart, Slid, 'Slife, 'Slight, Snails, Sonties, Strewth, Stygian, Swear, Tarnation, Tennis-court, Voir dire, Vow, Zbud, Zounds

Obdurate Adamant, Cruel, Flinty, Hard, Intransigent, Stony, Stubborn, Tenacious

Obedient, Obedience, Obey Bent, Bridlewise, Canonical, Comply, Dutiful, Follow, Hear, Mindful, Obsequious, Observe, Obtemper, Passive, Perform, Pliant, Servant, Yielding

Obeisance → **BOW**, Salaam

Obelisk, Obelus Aguilla, Column, Dagger, Monument, Needle, Pillar

Oberon King, Merle

Obese, Obesity Bariatrics, Corpulent, Fat, Stout

▷ **Object** *may indicate* a grammatical variant

Object(s), Objection(able), Objective(ness), Objector Ah, Aim, Ambition, Argue, Artefact, Article, Artifact, Bar, Beef, But, Case, Cavil, Challenge, Clinical, Cognate, Complain(t), Conchy, Conscientious, Cow, Demur, Detached, Direct, End, Exception, Found, Fuss, → **GOAL**, Her, Him, Impersonal, Improper, Indifferent, Indirect, Intensional, Intention, It, Item, Jib, Loathe, Mind, Moral, Near-earth, Niggle, Non-ego, Noumenon, Ob, Obnoxious, Offensive, Oppose, Outness, Percept, Perspective, Plan, Plot, Point, Protest, Proximate, Question, Quibble, Quasi-stellar, Quiddity, Rank, Rebarbative, Recuse, Refuse, Relation, Resist, Retained, Sake, Scruple, Sex, Subject, Sublime, Target, Thing, Transitive, Tut, Ultimate, Unbiased, Virtu, Wart

Objectless Intransitive

Oblate, Oblation Gift, Monk, Offering, Offertory, Prothesis, Sacrifice

Oblige, Obliging, Obligation, Obligatory Accommodate, Affable, Behold, Binding, Burden, Charge, Compel, Complaisant, Compliant, Contract, Corvée, Debt, De rigueur, Duty, Easy, Encumbent, Force, Giri, Gratify, Impel, Incumbent, IOU, Mandatory, Must, Necessitate, Novation, Obruk, Obstriction, Peremptory, Promise, Recognisance, Responsibility, Sonties, Synallagmatic, Tie, Wattle

▷ **Oblique** *may indicate* an anagram

Oblique(ly) Askance, Askew, Asklent, Asquint, Athwart, Awry, Cross, Diagonal, Indirect, Perverse, Plagio-, Separatrix, Sidelong, Skew, Skewwhiff, Slanting, Solidus, Squint, Virgule

Obliterate(d) Annul, Black out, Blot, Dele(te), Efface, Eradicate, Expunge, Exterminate, Rase, Rast, Raze, Wash away, Wipe, Zap

Oblivion, Oblivious Forgetful, Lethe, Limbo, Nirvana, Obscurity

Oblong Rectangular

Obloquy Opprobrium

Obnoxious Eyesore, Foul, Horrid, Offensive, Pestilent, Repugnant, Septic, Sod

Oboe Piffero

Obscene(ly), Obscenity Bawdy, Blue, Fescennine, Gross, Hard-core, Indecent, Lewd, Lubricious, Paw(paw), Porn(o), Profane, Ribald, Salacious, Scatology, Smut, Vulgar

Obscure, Obscurity Abstruse, Anheires, Becloud, Befog, Blend, Blot out, Break, Cloud, Cobweb, Conceal, Cover, Cryptic, Darken, Deep, Dim, Disguise, Eclipse, Encrypt, Engloom, Envelop, Esoteric, Filmy, Fog, Hermetic, Hide, Indistinct, Jude, Mantle, Mist, Murk, Nebular, Night, Nubecula, Obfuscate, Obnubilate, Opaque, Oracular, Overcloud, Overshade, Overshadow, Recherché, Recondite, Shadowy, Tenebrific, Twilit, Unclear, Unobvious, → **VAGUE**, Veil, Vele, Wrap

▷ **Obscure(d)** *may indicate* an anagram

Obsequious(ness) Bootlicker, Brown nose, Creeping Jesus, Fawn, Fulsome, Grovelling, Kowtowing, Menial, Parasitic, Pig, Servile, Slavish, Sleeveen, Slimy, Subservient, Suck-hole, Sycophantic, Tantony, Toady

Observance, Observant, Observation Adherence, Alert, Attention, Comment, Custom, Empirical, Espial, Experience, Eyeful, Holy, Honour, Lectisternium, Mass, → **NOTICE**, Obiter dicta, Perceptive, Percipient, Practice, Quip, Ready-eyed, Recce, Remark, Right, Rite, Ritual, Use, Vising

Observatory Arecibo, Atalaya, Greenwich, Herstmonceux, Hurstmonceux, Jodrell Bank, Lookout, Mount Palomar, Tower

Observe(d), Observer Behold, Bystander, Celebrate, Commentator, Detect, Espy, Eye, Fly-on-the-wall, Heed, Keep, Mark, NB, Note, Notice, Obey, Onlooker, Optic, Pharisee, Regard(er), Remark, Rite, Scry, See, Seer, Sight, Spectator, Spial, Spot, Spy, Study, Take, Twig, View, Voyeur, Watch, Witness

Obsess(ed), Obsession, Obsessive Anal, Besot, Bug, Bugbear, Craze, Dominate, Fetish, Fixation, Hang-up, Haunt, Hobbyhorse, Hooked, Idée fixe, Infatuation, Mania, Monomania, Necrophilia, Neurotic, One-track, Preoccupy, Smitten, Thing, Wonk

Obsidian Pe(a)rlite

Obsolete, Obsolescence, Obsolescent Abandoned, Antique, Archaic, Dated, Dead, Defunct, Disused, Extinct, Latescent, Obs, Outdated, Outworn, Passé, Planned

Obstacle Barrage, Barrier, Boyg, Cheval de frise, Chicane, Dam, Drag, Dragon's teeth, Drawback, Gate, Handicap, Hazard, Hindrance, Hitch, Hurdle, Node, Oxer, Remora, Rock, Sandbank, Snag, Stimie, Stumbling-block, Stymie, Tank-trap

Obstetrics Gynaecology, Midwifery, Tocology, Tokology

Obstinacy, Obstinate Asinine, Bigoted, Buckie, Bullish, Contrarian, Contumacious, Cussed, Die-hard, Dour, Entêté, Froward, Headstrong, High-stomached, Inflexible, Intractable, Intransigent, Mule, Persistent, Perverse, Pervicacious, Piggish, Pig-headed, Recalcitrant, Refractory, Restive, Rusty, Self-will, Stiff(-necked), Sture, Stubborn, Thraward, Thrawart, Wilful

Obstreperous Noisy, Stroppy, Truculent, Unruly

Obstruct(ion) Bar, Block, Bottleneck, Caltrop, Chicane, Clog, Crab, Cross, Cumber, Dam, Embolus, Fil(l)ibuster, Gridlock, Hamper, Hand-off, Hedge, Hinder, Hurdle, Ileus, Impede, Let, Obstacle, Occlude, Sab(otage), Sandbag, Snarl-up, Snooker, Stall, Stap, Stonewall, Stop, Stymie, Sudd, Thwart, Trammel, Trump

Obtain Achieve, Acquire, Cop, Exist, Gain, Get, Land, Pan, Prevail, Procure, Realise, Secure, Succeed, Wangle, Win

Obtrude, Obtrusive Expel, Impose, Loud, Prominent, Push, Sorn, Thrust

Obtuse Blunt, Dense, Dull, Purblind, Stupid, Thick

Obverse, Obversion Complement, Cross, Equipollence, Face, Front, Head, Permutation

Obviate Forestall, Preclude, Prevent

Obvious Apparent, Axiom, Blatant, Brobdingnag, Clear, Distinct, Evident, Flagrant, Frank, Inescapable, Kenspeck(le), Manifest, Marked, Open(ness), Open and shut, Overt, Palpable, Patent, Pikestaff, Plain, Pronounced, Salient, Self-evident, Stark, Transparent, Truism, Visible

Occasion Call, Cause, Ceremony, Encheason, Event, Fête, Field day, Nonce, → **OPPORTUNITY**, Reason, Ride, Sometime, Tide, Time

Occasional(ly) Casual, Chance, Daimen, Intermittent, Irregular, Motive, Orra, Periodic, Sometimes, Sporadic, While

Occident(al) West, Western(er)

Occlude, Occlusion Absorb, Clog, Coronary, Embolism, Obstruct

Occult(ist) Angekkok, Arcane, Art, Esoteric, I-Ching, Magic, Mysterious, Mystic, Supernatural

Occupant, Occupation, Occupy(ing) Absorb, Activity, Avocation, Beset, Business, Busy, Career, Denizen, Embusy, Employ, Engage, Engross, Fill, Hold, In, Incumbent, Indwell, Inhabitant, Inmate, Involve, Line, Métier, People, Profession, Pursuit, Reserved, Resident, Runrig, Sideline, Squat, Stay, Tenancy, Tenant, Tenure, Thrift, Trade, Upon, Use, Vocation, Walk of life

Occur(rence) Arise, Be, Betide, Betime, Case, Contingency, Crop up, Event, Fall, Happen, Incident, Instance, Outbreak, Outcrop, Pass, Phenomenon

Ocean(ic), Oceania Abundance, Abyssal, Antarctic, Arctic, Atlantic, Blue, Deep, German, Hadal, Herring-pond, High seas, Indian, Melanesia, Micronesia, Pacific, Panthalassa, Pelagic, Polynesia, Sea(way), Southern, Thalassic, Waves, Western

Och aye Troggs

Ochre Burnt, Keel, Lemnian ruddle, Rubric, Ruddle, Sienna

Octave Diapason, Diminished, Eight, Great, Ottava, Perfect, Small, Utas

Octopus Blue-ringed, Cephalopod, Cuero, Devilfish, Paper nautilus, Polyp, Poulp(e), Scuttle, Squid

Octoroon Mestee, Mestizo, Mustee

Od Energy, Force

Odd (person), Oddity Abnormal, Anomaly, Bizarre, Card, Cure, Curio, Droll, Eccentric, Eery, Erratic, Fishy, Gink, Impair, Imparity, Jimjam, Offbeat, Original, Orra, Outré, Paradox, Parity, Peculiar, Queer, Quiz, Random, Rare, Remote, Rum, Screwball, Singular, Spooky, → **STRANGE**, Unequal, Uneven, Unmatched, Unusual, Weird, Whims(e)y, Zany

▷ **Odd(s)** *may indicate* an anagram or the odd letters in words

Oddfellow OF

Odd job man Joey, Loppy, Orraman, Rouster, Smoot, Thronner

Odds, Oddments Bits, Carpet, Chance, Gubbins, Handicap, Line, Long, Price, Short, SP, Tails, Variance

Ode Awdl, Dit, Epicede, Epicedium, Epinicion, Epinikion, Genethliacon, Horatian, Hymn, Lay, Lyric, Monody, Paeon, Pindaric, Poem, Sapphic, Song, Stasimon, Strophe, Threne, Threnody, Verse

Odin One-eyed, Woden

Odium, Odious Comparison, Disestimation, Disgrace, Foul, Hatred, Heinous, Invidious, Ponce, Repugnant, Stigma

Odorous, Odour Air, Bad, BO, Flavour, Funk, Good, Hum, Opopanax, Perfume, Quality, Redolence, Sanctity, Scent, Smell, Waff, Waft, Whiff

Odourless Silent

Odyssey Epic, Journey, Wandering

Oedipus Complex, Parricide

Oeillade Glance, Leer, Ogle, Wink

Oesophagus Crop

Oestrogen, Oestrus Daidzein, Frenzy, Genistein®, Heat, Isoflavone, Mestranol, Must, Rut, Stilb(o)estrol

▷ **Of** *may indicate* an anagram

Of (me) About, Among, Aus, By, De, From, In, My, Re

Of course Certainly, Natch, Yes

Off Absent, Agee, Ajee, Away, Discount, Distance, Far, From, High, Inexact, Licence, Odd, Reasty, Reesty, Relâche, Start

▷ **Off** *may indicate* an anagram

Offal Cagmag, Carrion, Chidlings, Chitterling, Entrails, Fry, Giblets, Gralloch, Gurry, Haggis, Ha(r)slet, Heart, Innards, Kidney, Lamb's fry, Lights, Liver, Numbles, Pig's fry, Pluck, Sweetbread, Tripe, Variety meat

Off-beat Zoppo

Off-colour Pale, Seedy, Wan

▷ **Off-colour** *may indicate* an anagram

Offence Attack, Crime, Delict, Delinquency, Distaste, Fault, Huff, Hurt, Indictable, Lapse, Lese majesty, Miff, Misdemeanour, Misprision, Outrage, Peccadillo, Pip, Pique, Piracy, Regrate, Sedition, → **SIN**, Summary, Trespass, Umbrage, Violation

Offend(ed), Offender Affront, Anger, Annoy, Boobhead, Bridles, Culprit, Default, Delinquent, Disoblige, Displease, Distaste, Hip, Huff, Hurt, Hyp, Infringe, Inveigh, Miffy, Miscreant, Nettle, Nonce, Nuisance, Peeve, Perp, Provoke, Sin(ner), Sledge, Sting, Stray, Transgress, Twoccer, Umbrage, Violate, Wrongdoer

Offensive(ness) Affront, Aggressive, Alien, Attack, Bombardment, Campaign, Charm, Cruel, Derisatory, Dysphemism, Embracery, Euphemism, Execrable, Eyesore, Foul, Gobby, Hedgehog, Hedgepig, Indecent, Indelicate, Invidious, Inroad, Miasmic, Nasty, Noisome, Obnoxious, Obscene, Peccant, Personal, Push, Putrid, Rank, Repugnant, → **RUDE**, Scandalous, Scurrilous, Sortie, Storm, Ugly, Unbecoming, Unsavoury, War

Offer(ing) Alms, Altarage, Anaphora, Bargain, Bid, Bode, Bouchée, Cadeau, Corban, Deodate, Dolly, Epanophora, Extend, Ex voto, Gift, Godfather, Heave, Hold, Inferiae, Introduce, Invitation, Oblation, Overture, Peace, Peddle, Plead, Pose, Potla(t)ch, Present, Propine, → **PROPOSE**, Propound, Sacrifice, Shewbread, Shore, S(h)raddha, Special, Stamp, Stand, Submit, Suggestion, Tender, Utter, Volunteer, Votive, Wave, Xenium

Offhand Airy, Banana, Brevi manu, Brusque, Casual, Cavalier, Currente calamo, Curt, Extempore, Impromptu, Indifferent, Snappy

Office(s) Abbacy, Agency, Bedelship, Booking, Box, Branch, Broo, Bucket shop, Bureau, Buroo, Caliphate, Chair, Chancery, Circumlocution, Clerical, Colonial, Commonwealth, Complin(e), Consulate, Crown, Cube farm, Cutcher(r)y, Daftar, Dataria, Dead-letter, Deanery, Decemvirate, Den, Divine, Dogate, Drostdy, Employment, Evensong, Foreign, Front, Function, Holy, Home, Job, Land, Last, Left luggage, Lieutenancy, Little, Little hours, Loan, Lost property, Mayoralty, Met(eorological), Ministry, Missa, Mistery, Mudiria, Mutessarifat, Mystery, Nocturn, Nones, Obit, Oval, Palatinate, Papacy, Patent, Penitentiary, Personnel, Petty Bag, Pipe, Place, Plum, Portfolio, Position, Post, Prefecture, Prelacy, Press, Prime, Printing, Provosty, Record, Regency, Register, Registry, Rite, Satrapy, Scottish, Secretarial, Secretariat, See, Seraskierate, Shogunate, Sinecure, Situation, Sorting, Stamp, Stationery, Sultanate, Tariff, Tenebrae, Terce, Ticket, Tierce, Tol(l)booth, Tribunate, Vespers, War, Yamen

Officer(s) Acater, Adjutant, Admiral, Ag(h)a, Agistor, Aide, Air vice-marshal, Apparitor, Bailiff, Beatty, Bimbashi, Black Rod, Blimp, Blue Rod, Bombardier, Bos(u)n, Branch, Brass-hat, Brigadier, Bumbailiff, Capt(ain), Catchpole, Catchpoll, Cater, Cellarist, Centurion, CEO, Chamberlain, Chancellor, CIGS, Colonel, Commander, Commissioned, Commissioner, Commodore, Compliance, Constable, Cop(per), Co-pilot, Cornet, Coroner, Counter-round, Cursitor, Customs, Darogha, Datary, Deacon, Decurion, Dragoon, Drill-sergeant, Duty, Earl Marshal, Engineer, Ensign, Equerry, Exciseman, Executive, Exon, Familiar, Field Marshal, Filacer, Filazer, First, First mate, Flag, Flying, Gallant, Ga(u)ger, Gazetted, Gen(eral), GOC, Grand Vizier, Group, Group captain, Gunner, Havildar, Hayward, Hetman, Ima(u)m, Incumbent, Infirmarian, Intendant, Jamadar, Janty, Jauntie, Jaunty, Jemadar, Jemidar, Jonty, Jurat, Justiciar, Lance-sergeant, Liaison, Lictor, Lord High Steward, Lt, Major, Marshal, Mate, Messenger, Moderator, NCO, Non-commissioned, Number one, Nursing, Official Solicitor, Orderly, Oxon, Pacha, Pantler, Pasha, Peace, Petty, Pilot, Pipe major, PO, Police, Posse, Prefect, President, Presiding, Prison, Probation, Proctor, Procurator fiscal, Prorector, Provost, Provost-marshal, Purser, Pursuivant, Pusser, Quartermaster, Quartermaster-sergeant, Radio, Rector, Relieving, Remembrancer, Returning, Rodent, Rosser, Rupert, Safety, Samurai, Sbirro, Scene-of-crime, Schout, Sea Lord, Second mate, Securocrat, Select-man, Serang, Sergeant-major, Sewer, Sexton, Sheriff, Silver-stick, Skipper, SL, SM, Speaker, Staff, Striper, Sub(altern), Suba(h)dar, Subchanter, Sublieutenant, Supercargo, Superintendent, Tahsildar, Tidewaiter, Tindal, Tipstaff, Treasurer, Tribune, Usher, Varlet, Waldgrave, Warden, Warder, Wardroom, Warrant, Watch, Woodward, Yeoman

Office-worker Clerk, Peon, Temp, Typist

Official(s), Officiate, Officious Aga, Agent, Aleconner, Amban, Amtman, Apparatchik, Atabeg, Atabek, Attaché, Authorised, Beadle, Bossy, Bumble, Bureaucrat, Catchpole, Censor, Chamberlain, Chancellor, Chinovnik, Claviger, Commissar, Commissioner, Consul, Convenor, Coroner, Count, Count palatine, Dean, Dignatory, Diplomat, Dockmaster, Dogberry, Ealdorman, Ephor, Equerry, Escheater, Eurocrat, Executive, Fonctionnaire, → **FORMAL**, Fourth, Functionary, Gauleiter, Governor, Gymnasiarch, Handicapper, Hayward, Incumbent, Inspector, Intendant, Jack-in-office, Jobsworth, Keeper, Landdrost, Lictor, Line judge, Linesman, Macer, Mandarin, Marplot, Marshal, Mayor, MC, Meddlesome, Mirza, Mueddin, Mukhtar, Nazir, Notary, Notary public, Ombudsman, Omlah, Overbusy, Palatine, Paymaster, Placeman, Pleaseman, Plenipotentiary, Polemarch,

Pontificate, Poohbah, Postmaster, Praefect, Pragmatic, Prefect, Proctor, Procurator, Prog, Proveditor, Provedor(e), Providor, Reeve, Ref(eree), Régisseur, Registrar, Remembrancer, Scrutineer, Shammash, Shammes, Sherpa, Silentiary, Souldan, Spoffish, Staff, Steward, Subdean, Suffete, Suit, Syndic, Timekeeper, Tipstaff, Subdean, Touch judge, Tribune, Trier, Trior, Triumvir, Turncock, Valid, Valuer General, Veep, Verderer, Verger, Vicar-general, Vizier, Walla(h), Whiffler, Whip, Woodward, Yamen, Yeoman

Offprint Separate

Off-putting Dehortative, Discouraging, Mañana, Negative, Procrastination, Rebarbative, Repellent, Yips

Offset Balance, Cancel, Compensate, Counter(act), Counterbalance

Offshoot Bough, Branch, Cion, Limb, Lye, Member, Outgrowth, Plant, Scion, Sien, Sient, Swarm, Syen

Offspring Boy, Burd, Chick, Children, Daughter, Descendant, Family, Fry, Get, Girl, Heir, Litter, Procreation, Product, Progeny, Seed, Sient, Son, Spawn

Offstage Wings

Off-the-cuff Improv(isation)

Often Frequent, Habitual, Repeated

▷ **Often** *may indicate* 'of ten'

Ogee Cyma, Moulding, Talon

Ogle Drake, Eliad, Eye, Glad eye, Glance, Leer, Oeillade, Wodewose

Ogre(ss) Baba Yaga, Boyg, Brute, Eten, Etten, Fiend, Giant, Monster, Orc, Shrek

Ohio Buckeye

Oil(s), Oily, Oil producer Anele, Anoint, Balm, Black gold, Bribe, Crude, Derv, Diesel, Drying, Essence, Essential, Ethereal, Fatty, Fish, Fixed, Frying, Fuel, Good, Grease, Hair, Heavy, Joint, Lamp, Lipid, Long, Lube, Lubricant, Midnight, Mineral, Monounsaturated, Multigrade, Oint, Oleaginous, Pellitory, Polyunsaturated, Pomade, Seed, Short, Sleek, Slick, Smalmy, Smarmy, Smeary, Sweet, Topped crude, Unction

OILS

2 letters:		*5 letters:*	
BP®	Neem	Ajwan	Shale
	Nimb	Argan	Shark
	Oleo	Attar	Snake
3 letters:	Otto	Benne	Sperm
Ben	Palm	Benni	Spike
Emu	Poon	Clove	Stand
Gas	Rape	Colza	Thyme
Nim	Rock	Copra	Train
Nut	Rose	Fusel	Ulyie
	Rusa	Grass	Ulzie
4 letters:	Slum	Niger	Whale
Baby	Tall	Olive	
Bath	Tolu	Ottar	*6 letters:*
Bone	Tung	Poppy	Ajowan
Cade	Wood	Pulza	Almond
Coal	Wool	Rosin	Balsam
Corn	Yolk	Savin	Banana
Musk		Sebum	Butter
Nard			Canola

Carapa
Carron
Castor
Chrism
Cineol
Cohune
Croton
Elaeis
Illipe
Jojoba
Magilp
Megilp
Monola®
Neroli
Peanut
Ramtil
Savine
Semsem
Sesame
Shamoy
Tallow
Virgin
Walnut

7 letters:
Apiezon®
Bittern
Cajeput
Cajuput
Camphor
Cineole
Coconut
Dittany
Eugenol

Gingili
Linalol
Linseed
Lumbang
Menthol
Mirbane
Moringa
Mustard
Myrbane
Myrrhol
Naphtha
Picamar
Pyrrole
Retinol
Ricinus
Saffron
Safrole
Spindle
Verbena
Vitriol
Wallaba

8 letters:
Bergamot
Camphire
Cod-liver
Creasote
Creosote
Gingelli
Gingelly
Hazelnut
Kerosene
Kerosine
Lavender

Linalool
Macassar
North Sea
Oiticica
Pachouli
Paraffin
Photogen
Pristane
Rapeseed
Rosewood
Volatile

9 letters:
Aleuritis
Beech-mast
Candlenut
Carvacrol
Eleoptene
Golomynka
Grapeseed
Groundnut
Neat's-foot
Parathion
Patchouli
Patchouly
Petroleum
Photogene
Safflower
Sassafras
Spearmint
Spikenard
Star-anise
Sunflower
Vanaspati

Vegetable

10 letters:
Chaulmugra
Citronella
Cotton-seed
Elaeoptene
Eucalyptus
Guttiferae
Peppermint
Petit grain
Sandalwood
Turpentine
Ylang-ylang

11 letters:
Camphorated
Chaulmoogra
Chinese wood
Extra virgin
Stearoptene
Wintergreen

12 letters:
Benzaldehyde
Brilliantine

14 letters:
Glutaraldehyde
Parnassus grass

15 letters:
Evening primrose

Oilcake Poonac

Oilcan Pourie

Oilcloth American, Lino

Oilman Driller, Prospector, Rigger, Texan

Oil painting Master, Titian

Ointment Balm, Basilicon, Boracic, Boric, Cerate, Collyrium, Cream, Liniment, Lipsalve, Nard, Pomade, Pomatum, Salve, Spikenard, Theriac, Tiger balm®, Unction, Unguent, Vaseline®, Zinc

OK Agree(d), Approve, Authorise, Clearance, Copacetic, Copesettic, Go-head, Green light, Hunky-dory, Initial, Kosher, Mooi, No sweat, Respectable, Right(o), Sanction, Sound, U, Vet

Okra Bhindi, Gumbo, Lady's fingers

Old(er), Oldie Ae(t), Aged, Aine(e), Ancient, Antique, Auld, Bean, Decrepit, Dutch, Earlier, Fogram, Former, Gaffer, Geriatric, Glory, Golden, Gray, Grey, Hills, Hoary, Immemorial, Major, Mature, Methusaleh, Moore, Nestor, Nick, O, OAP, Obsolete, Off, Ogygian, One-time, Outworn, Palae-, Passé, Primeval, Ripe, Rugose,

Sen(escent), Senile, Senior, Shot, Signeur, Stager, Stale, Trite, Venerable, Veteran, Victorian(a), Worn

Old boy, Old girl Alumnae, Alumnus, Fossil, OB

Old days Once, Past, Yore

Old English OE

Old-fashioned Aging, Ancient, Antediluvian, Antwackie, Arch(aic), Arriéré, Bygone, Corn(y), Dated, Dodo, Dowdy, Fogey, Fuddy-duddy, Fusty, Medieval, Museum piece, Neanderthal, No tech, Obsolete, Ogygian, Oldfangled, Outdated, Outmoded, Outworn, Passé, Podunk, Primeval, Quaint, Relic, Retro, Rinky-dink, Schmaltzy, Shot, Square, Square-toes, Steam, Stick-in-the-mud, Traditional, Uncool, Vieux jeu, Worm-eaten

Old hat Clichéd

Old maid Biddy, Spinster

Old man, Old woman Anile, Aunty, Bodach, Buda, Budi, Burd, Cailleach, Carlin(e), Codger, Crinkly, Crow, Crumbly, Faggot, Fantad, Fantod, Fogey, Fogramite, Fogy, Fussy, Gammer, Geezer, Gramps, Grandam, Grannam, Greybeard, Greyhen, Husband, Kangaroo, Koro, Kuia, Luckie, Lucky, Matriarch, Methuselah, Mort, Mzee, OAP, Oom, Pantaloon, Patriarch, Presbyte, Rudas, Tripod, Trot, Trout, Whitebeard, Wife, Wight, Woopie, Wrinkly

Old-timer Hourglass, Sundial, Veteran

Oleander Nerium, Rhododaphne

Olid Fetid, Foul, High, Rancid, Rank

Olio Hash, Medley, Mess, Potpourri, Stew

Olive (grove), Olivine Calamata, Cerulein, Drupe, Dunite, Gethsemane, Kalamata, Lilac, Olea(ster), Peridot, Queen

Oliver Bath, Cromwell, Goldsmith, Hardy, Noll, Protector, Twist

Olympian, Olympics, Olympus Asgard, Athlete, Celestial, Coe, Elis, Pantheon, Quadrennium, Summer, Winter, Zeus

Omelette Crêpe, Foo yong, Foo yung, Frittata, Fu yung, Pancake, Spanish, Tortilla

Omen Abodement, Absit, Augury, Auspice, Foreboding, Forewarning, Freet, Freit, Portent, Presage, Prodrome, Sign, Token, Warning

Omentum Caul, Epiploon

Ominous Alarming, Baleful, Bodeful, Dire, Dour, Forbidding, Grim, Inauspicious, Oracular, Sinister, Threatening

Omission, Omit Aph(a)eresis, Apocope, Apospory, Apostrophe, Asyndeton, Caret, Disregard, Drop, Elide, Elision, Ellipse, Ellipsis, Failure, Haplography, Haplology, Lipography, Loophole, Miss, Neglect, Nonfeasance, Non-user, Oversight, Paral(e)ipomenon, Pass, Senza, Skip

Omnibus Anthology, Coach, Collection

Omniscient, Omniscience Encyclopedia, Pansophy

Omnivorous Pantophagous

▷ **On** *may indicate* an anagram

On (it) Aboard, About, Agreed, An, An't, At, Atop, By, Game, Half-cut, In, Leg, O', Of, Oiled, Over, Pon, Re, Tipsy, Up(on), Viable

On account of Over

▷ **On board** *may indicate* chess, draughts, or 'SS' around another word

Once(r) Ance, As was, → **AT ONCE**, Bradbury, Earst, Erst(while), Ever, Ex, Fore, Former, Jadis, Oner, Onst, Secular, Sole, Sometime, Whilom

One(self) A, Ace, Ae, Alike, An(e), Any, Body, Chosen, Eeny, Ego, Ein, Formula, I, Individual, Integer, Me, Monad, Per se, Single(ton), Singular, Solo, Tane, Un, Unify, Unit(y), Unitary, United, Us, We, Yin, You

One-act-er Playlet
One-eared Monaural
One-eyed Arimasp(ian), Cyclops
One-man band Moke
One o'clock 1 am, NNE
One-off Ad hoc
One-rayed Monact
Onerous Arduous, Exacting, Taxing, Tedious, Weighty
Ongoing Continual
Onion(s) Allium, Bengi, Bonce, Bulb, Chibol, Chive, Cibol, Cive, Eschalot, Green, Head, Ingan, Jibbons, Leek, Lyonnaise, Moly, Pate, Pearl, Ramp, Ramson, Rocambole, Ropes, Scallion, Scilla, Shal(l)ot, Soubise, Spanish, Spring, Squill, Sybo(e), Sybow, Tree, Welsh
Onlooker Bystander, Kibitzer, Observer, Rubberneck, Spectator, Witness
Only Allenarly, Anerly, But, Except, Just, Meer, Merely, Nobbut, Seul, Singly, Sole, Unique
Onset Affret, Attack, Beginning, Charge, Dash, Ending, Rush, → START, Thrust
Onslaught Attack, Dead-set, Onset, Raid, Spreagh, Storm, Swoop
On time Pat, Prompt, Punctual
Onus Burden, Charge, → DUTY, Responsibility
Onward Advance, Ahead, Away, Forth, Forward, Progress
Oodles Heaps, Lashings, Lots, Slather
Oolite Pisolite, Roestone
Oomph Energy, It, SA, Verve
Ooze, Oozy Drip, Exhale, Exude, Gleet, Ichorous, Mud, Percolate, Pteropod(a), Radiolarian, Seep, Sew, Sipe, Slime, Slob, Spew, Spue, Sweat, Sype, Transude
Opal(escent) Black, Cymophanous, Fire, Gem, Girasol, Girosol, Hyalite, Hydrophane, Liver, Menilite, Noble, Potch, Wood
Opaque, Opacity Dense, Dull, Intense, Leucoma, Obscure, Obtuse, Onycha, Onyx, Roil, Thick, Turbid
Open(er), Opening, Openness Adit, Aedicule, Ajar, Antithesis, Anus, Apert(ure), Apparent, Apse, Armhole, Autopsy, Bald, Bare, Bat, Bay, Begin, Bole, Breach, Break, Broach, Buttonhole, Candid, Cardia, Cavity, Champaign, Chance, Chasm, Chink, Circumscissile, Clear, Crevasse, Dehisce, Deploy, Dispark, Door, Dup, Embrasure, Exordium, Expansive, Eyelet, Fair, Fenestra, Fissure, Fistula, Flue, Fontanel(le), Foramen, Frank, Free, Free-for-all, Gambit, Gap, Gaping, Gat, Gate, Give, Glasnost, Glottis, Guichet, Gullwing, Hagioscope, Hatch, Hatchback, Hatchway, Hiatus, Hilus, → HOLE, Inaugural, Intake, Interstice, Intro, Key, Lacy, Lance, Lead, Loid, Loophole, Loose, Machicolation, Manhole, Meatus, Micropyle, Mofette, Moongate, Mouth, Nare, Oillet, Orifice, Os, Oscule, Osculum, Ostiole, Ostium, Overt, Overture, Patent, Peephole, Pert, Pervious, Pick(lock), Placket, Plughole, Pore, Port(age), Porta, Porthole, Preliminary, Premiere, Prise, Pro-am, Public, Pylorus, Receptive, Rent, Ring-pull, Riva, Room, Scuttle, Scye, Sesame, Sicilian, Sincere, Slit, Spare, Spirant, Squint, Start, Stenopaic, Stoma, Stulm, Syrinx, Thereout, Thirl, Touchhole, Transparent, Trapdoor, Trema, Trou, Truthful, Unbar, Unbolt, Unbutton, Uncork, Undo, Unfurl, Unhasp, Unlatch, Unscrew, Unstop, Unsubtle, Untie, Unzip, Upfront, Vent, Vulnerable, Wide, Window
Open air Alfresco, Sub divo, Sub Jove
Opera(tic), Opera house, Operetta Aida, Ariadne, Ballad, Bouffe, Buffo, Burletta, Carmen, Comic, Comique, Die Fledermaus, Don Carlos, Don Giovanni, Dramma giocoso, Electra, ENO, Ernani, Falstaff, Faust, Fedora, Fidelio, Glyndebourne,

Grand, Hansel and Gretel, Horse, Idomeneo, Iolanthe, I Puritani, Kirov, La Bohème, La Scala, Light, Lohengrin, Lulu, Macbeth, Magic Flute, Met, Musical, Nabucco, Norma, Oater, Oberon, Onegin, Open Wingrave, Orfeo, Otello, Parsifal, Pastorale, Patience, Peter Grimes, Pinafore, Rienzi, Rigoletto, Ring, Ruddigore, Rusalka, Salome, Savoy, Seria, Simon Boccanegra, Singspiel, Soap, Space, Tell, The Met, Threepenny, Tosca, Turandot, Verismo, Werther, Work, Zarzuela

Opera-glasses Jumelle

Opera-lover Wagnerite

Opera-singer Baritone, Bass, Contralto, Diva, Savoyard, Soprano

Operate, Operation(s), Operative Act(ion), Activate, Actuate, Agent, Artisan, Attuition, Barbarossa, Bypass, Caesarean, Campaign, Combined, Conduct, Couching, Current, Desert Storm, Detective, Doffer, Exercise, Function, Game, Hobday, Holding, Keystroke, Laparotomy, Leucotomy, Liposuction, Lithotomy, Lobotomy, Logical, Manipulate, Mechanic, Mules, Nip and tuck, Nose job, Oner, Overlord, Plastic, Practice, Run, Sealion, Shirodkar's, Sortie, Strabotomy, Surgery, Titration, Ure, Valid, Wertheim, Work

Operator Agent, Conductor, Dealer, Laplace, Manipulator, Nabla, Sawbones, Sparks, Surgeon

Opiate, Opium Buprenorphine, Dope, Drug, Hop, Laudanum, Meconin, Meconium, Morphine, Narcotic, Religion, Soporific, Thebaine

Opinion, Opinionative Attitude, Belief, Bet, Conjecture, Consensus, Cri, Deem, Dictum, Dogma, Doxy, Editorial, Entêté, Esteem, Feeling, Groundswell, Guess, Heresy, Impression, Judgement, Mind, Mumpsimus, Parti pris, Pious, Prejudice, Private, Public, Pulse, Say, Second, Sense, Sentence, Sentiment, SO, Stand, Take, Tenet, Utterance, View, Viewpoint, Voice, Vote, Vox pop, Vox populi

Opossum Lie, Marmose, Phalanger, Tarsipes, Vulpine, Water, Yapo(c)k

Oppidan Cit, Townsman, Urban

Opponent(s) Adversary, Antagonist, Anti, E-N, Enemy, E-S, Foe, Gainsayer, Mitnaged, N-E, N-W, S-E, Straw-man, S-W, W-N, W-S

Opportune, Opportunist, Opportunity Appropriate, Apropos, Break, Buccaneer, Carpetbagger, → **CHANCE**, Day, Equal, Facility, Favourable, Ganef, Ganev, Ganof, Godsend, Go-go, Golden, Gonif, Gonof, Heaven-sent, Occasion, Opening, Pat, Photo, Room, Seal, Seel, Sele, Snatcher, Tabula rasa, Tide, Timely, Timous, Vantage, Well-timed, Window

Oppose(d), Opposer, Opposing, Opposite, Opposition Against, Agin, Anti, Antipathy, Antipodes, Antiscian, Antithesis, Antithetic, Antitype, Antonym, Argue, At, Au contraire, Averse, Battle, Black, Breast, Colluctation, Combat, Confront, Contradict, Contrary, Converse, Counter, Diametric, Dis(en)courage, Disfavour, Dissent, Dissident, Distance, E contrario, Face, Foreanent, Fornen(s)t, Hinder, Hostile, Impugn, Inimical, Inverse, Meet, Militate, Mugwump, Noes, Object, Obscurant, Overthwart, Polar, Reactance, Reaction, Recalcitrate, Reluct, Repugn, Resist, Retroact, Reverse, Rival, Shadow, Subtend, Syzygy, Teeth, Terr, Thereagainst, Thwart, Toto caelo, Traverse, V, Versus, Vice versa, Vis-à-vis, Withstand

Oppress(ion), Oppressive Airless, Bind, Burden, Close, Crush, Dead hand, Despotic, Incubus, Jackboot, Laden, Onerous, Overpower, Persecute, Ride, Snool, Stifling, Sultry, Tyrannise

Opprobrium Disgrace, Envy, Odium, Scandal

Oppugn Attack, Criticise

Opt, Option(al) Alternative, Call, → **CHOICE**, Choose, Crown-jewel, Decide, Default, Double zero, Elect, Facultative, Fine, Leipzig, Local, Menu, Omissible, Pick, Plump,

Put, Select, Share, Soft, Swap, Trade(d), Traditional, Voluntary, Votive, Wale, Zero(-zero)

Optic(al), Optics Active, Adaptive, Electron, Fibre, Fire, Lens, Prism, Reticle, Visual

Optimism, Optimist(ic) Bull, Chiliast, Elated, Expectant, Feelgood, Hopeful, Micawber, Morale, Pangloss, Pollyanna, Rosy, Sanguine, Starry-eyed, Upbeat, Utopiast, Yea-sayer

Opulent Abundant, Affluent, Moneyed, Rich, Wealthy

Opus Piece, Study, Work

Or Au, Either, Ere, Gold, Ossia, Otherwise, Sol

Oracle(s), Oracular Delphi, Dodonian, Mirror, Prophet, Pythian, Pythoness, Sage, Seer, Sibyl(line), Thummim, Urim, Vatic

Oral Acroamatic, Sonant, Spoken, Unwritten, Verbal, Viva, Viva voce, Vocal

Orange Agent, An(n)atta, An(n)atto, Arnotto, Aurora, Bergamot, Bigarade, Bilirubin, Bitter, Blenheim, Blood, Blossom, Calamondin, Chica, Claybank, Clockwork, Croceate, Flame, Flamingo, Fulvous, Genip(ap), Jaffa, Kamala, Kamela, Kamila, Karaka, Kumquat, Mandarin, Mock, Naartje, Nacarat, Nartjie, Navel, Ochre, Osage, Petit grain, Pig, Roucou, Ruta, Satsuma, Seville, Shaddock, Sour, Sweet, Tangerine, Tenné, Ugli®, Ulsterman

Orang-utan Ape, Monkey, Satyr

Orate, Oration Address, Declaim, Eloge, Elogium, Elogy, Eulogy, Harangue, Panegyric, Philippics, Speech

Oratorio, Orator(y) Boanerges, Brompton, Brougham, Cantata, Cicero, Creation, Demosthenes, Diction, Elijah, Hwyl, Isocrates, Lectern, Morin, Nestor, Prevaricator, Proseucha, Proseuche, Rhetor, Samson, Spellbinder, Stump, Tub-thumper, Windbag, Yarra-banker

Orb Ball, Eyeball, Firmament, Globe, Mound, Ocellus, Pome, Sphere

Orbit Apse, Apsis, Circuit, Dump, Eccentric, Ellipse, Eye, Graveyard, Osculating, Parking, Path, Periastron, Perigee, Perihelion, Perilune, Periselenium, Polar, Revolution, Stationary, Synchronous

Orcadian Hoy

Orchard Arbour, Grove, Holt

Orchestra(te), Orchestration Chamber, Charanga, Concertgebouw, Concerto, ECO, Ensemble, Gamelan, Hallé, Instrumentation, LPO, LSO, Palm Court, Pit, Ripieno, Score, SNO, String, Symphony

Orchid Adam and Eve, Adder's mouth, Arethusa, Babe-in-a-cradle, Bee, Bee-orchis, Bird's nest, Bog, Burnt-tip, Butterfly, Calanthe, Calypso, Cattleya, Cooktown, Coralroot, Coral wort, Cymbidium, Cypripedium, Disa, Epidendrum, Fly, Fly orchis, Fragrant, Fringed orchis, Frog, Helleborine, Lady, Lady's slipper, Lady's tresses, Lizard, Man, Marsh, Military, Miltonia, Moccasin-flower, Monkey, Musk, Naked lady, Odontoglossum, Oncidium, Phalaenopsis, Pogonia, Purple-fringed, Puttyroot, Pyramidal, Rattlesnake plantain, Salep, Scented, Slipper, Snakemouth, Soldier, Spider, Spotted, Swamp pink, Swan, Twayblade, Vanda, Vanilla

Ord Beginning, Point

Ordain Arrange, Command, Decree, Destine, Enact, Induct, Japan, Priest

Ordeal Corsned, Disaster, Preeve, Test, → **TRIAL**, Via Dolorosa

Order(ed), Orderly, Orders Acoemeti, Adjust, Administration, Affiliation, Alphabetical, Anton Piller, Apollonian, Apple-pie, Arrange, Array, ASBO, Attachment, Attendant, Attention, Attic, Avast, Bade, Banker's, Bankruptcy, Bath, Batman, Battalia, Bed, Behest, Benedictine, Bernardine, Bespoke, Bid, Book, Call, Camaldolite, Canon, Category, Caveat, CB, Chaprassi, Charter, Cheque, Chit, Chuprassy, Class, Coherent, Command(ment), Committal, Compensation,

Composite, Corinthian, Cosmo, Cosmos, Court, Decorum, Decree, Demand, Dictate, Diktat, Direct(ion), Directive, Dispone, Distringas, Dominican, Doric, DSO, Edict, Embargo, Enclosed, Enjoin, En règle, Errand, Established, Establishment, Eutaxy, Eviction, Exclusion, Feldsher, Fiat, Fiaunt, Firing, Firman, Form(ation), Franciscan, Fraternity, Freemason, Full, Gagging, Garnishee, Garter, Gilbertine, Ginkgo, Good, Grade, Habeas corpus, Heast(e), Hecht, Hest, Holy, Indent, Injunction, Instruct, Interdict, Ionic, Irade, Khalsa, Kilter, Knights Hospitallers, Kosmos, Language, Large, Lexical, Loblolly boy, Loblolly man, Loose, Mail, Major, Mandamus, Mandate, Marching, Marist, Market, Marshal, Masonic, Medjidie, Merit, Methodical, Minor, Mittimus, Monastic, Money, Monitor, Moose, Natural, Neatness, Nunnery, OBE, Oddfellows, Official, OM, Open, Orange, Ord, Ordain, Organic, Pecking, Possession, Postal, Precedence, Precept, Premonstrant, Prescribe, Preservation, Proritise, Provisional, Pyragyrite, Rank, Receiving, Reception, Règle, Regular, Religious, Restraining, Return, Right, Rule, Ruly, Sailing, Sealed, Search, Seraphic, Series, Settle, Shipshape, Short, Side, Standing, Starter's, State, Statutory, Stop(-loss), Straight, Subpoena, Summons, Supersedere, Supervision, System, Tabulate, Tall, Taxis, Tell, Templar, Teutonic, Third, Thistle, Tidy, Trim, Tuscan, Ukase, Uniformity, Warison, Warrant, Word, Working, Writ

▷ **Ordering** *may indicate* an anagram

Ordinal Book, Number, Second, Sequence

Ordinance Byelaw, Capitulary, Decree, Edict, Law, Prescript, Rescript, Rite, Statute

Ordinary Average, Banal, Bog standard, Canton, Chevron, Comely, Common (or garden), Commonplace, Cot(t)ise, Everyday, Fess(e), Flanch, Flange, Folksy, Grassroots, Hackneyed, Mass, Mediocre, Middling, Mundane, → **NORMAL**, O, OR, Pedestrian, Plain, Prosy, Pub, Rank and file, Run-of-the-mill, Saltier, Saltire, Simple, So-so, Tressure, Trivial, Unexceptional, Uninspired, Usual, Vanilla, Workaday, Your

Ordnance Artillery, Cannon, Guns, Pelican, Supply

Ordure Cess, Dung, Fertiliser, Manure

Ore Alga, Babingtonite, Bauxite, Bornite, Braunite, Breunnerite, Calamine, Calaverite, Cerusite, Chalcocite, Chalcopyrite, Chloanthite, Coffinite, Coin, Coltan, Copper, Crocoite, Element, Enargite, Galenite, Glance, Haematite, Hedyphane, Horseflesh, Ilmenite, Iridosmine, Ironstone, Kidney, Limonite, Magnetite, Mat, Melaconite, Middlings, Millhead, Milling grade, Mineral, Minestone, Morass, Niobite, Oligist, Owre, Peacock, Pencil, Phacolite, Pipe, Pitchblende, Proustite, Psilomelane, Pyrargyrite, Pyromorphite, Realgar, Red-lead, Ruby silver, Schlich, Seaweed, Siderite, Sinoptite, Slime, Slug, Smaltite, Speiss, Sphalerite, Stephanite, Stilpnosiderite, Stockwork, Stream-tin, Taconite, Tailing, Tenorite, Tetrahedrite, Tin, Wad(d), White-lead, Yellow cake

Organ(s), Organic Adnexa, American, Anlage, Antimere, Apollonicon, Appendix, Archegonium, Barrel, Biogenic, Biotic, Calliope, Carpel, Carpogonium, Cercus, Chamber, Chemoreceptor, Choir, Chord, Claspers, Clave, Colour, Conch(a), Console, Corti's, Cribellum, Ctene, Ear, Echo, Electric, Electronic, Electroreceptor, End, Essential, Exteroceptor, Feeler, Fin, Flabellum, Fundus, Gametangium, Gill, Glairin, Gonad, Hammond®, Hand, Hapteron, Harmonica, Harmonium, Haustorium, House, Hydathode, Hydraulos, Imine, Isomere, Kerogen, Kidney, Lien, Light, Liver, Lung-book, Lyriform, Means, Mechanoreceptor, Media, Medulla, Melodion, Ministry, Modiolus, Nasal, Natural, Nectary, Nematocyst, Nephridium, Newspaper, Olfactory, Oogonia, Ovary, Ovipositor, Ovotestis, Palp, Pancreas, Parapodium, Part, Pedal, Photogen, Photophore, Photoreceptor, Physharmonics, Pipe, Pipeless, Placenta, Plastid, Portative, Positive, Procarp,

Prothallus, Pulmones, Purtenance, Pyrophone, Radula, Receptor, Recit, Reed, Regal, Relict, Rhizoid, Sang, Saprobe, Scent, Sense, Sensillum, Serinette, Serra, Siphon, Spinneret, Spleen, Sporangium, Sporophore, Stamen, Statocyst, Steam, Swell, Syrinx, Tentacle, Textual, Theatre, Theca, Thymus, Tongue, Tonsil, Tool, Tympanum, Uterus, Vegetative, Velum, Verset, Viscera, Viscus, Vitals, Voice, Voluntary, Womb, Wurlitzer®

Organelle Peroxisome

Organise(d), Organisation, Organiser Activate, Administer, Agency, Aggregator, Anatomy, Apparat, → **ARRANGE**, Association, Brigade, Caucus, Class(ify), Collect, Comecon, Company, Constitution, Coordinate, Design, Embody, Entrepreneur, Eoka, Fascio, Fatah, Firm, Guild, Impresario, Infrastructure, Jaycee, Ku Klux Klan, Logistics, Machine, Mafia, Marshal, Mobilise, Octopus, Opus Dei, Orchestrate, Outfit, Personal, PLO, Promotor, Quango, Rally, Regiment, Resistance, Rosicrucian, Run, Setup, Sharpbender, Social, Soroptimist, Sort, Stage, Stage manage, Stahlhelm, Steward, System, Tidy, Together, UN, Viet Minh

▷ **Organise(d)** *may indicate* an anagram

Organism(s) Aerobe, Agamic, Asymmetron, Auxotroph, Being, Biont, Biotic, Cell, Chimeric, Chlamydia, Ciliate, Clade, Coral, Diplont, Ecad, Endogenous, Entity, Eozoon, Epibenthos, Epizoite, Epizoon, Eucaryote, Euglena, Eukaryote, Eurytherm, Extremoplile, Germ, Halobiont, Halophile, Haplont, Hemiparasite, Holophyte, Holoplankton, Homeotherm, Incross, Infauna, Infusoria(n), Lichen, Macrobiote, Medusa, Meroplankton, Metamale, Microaerophile, Microbe, Moneron, Morphology, Nekton, Neuston, Paramecium, Pathogen, Periphyton, Ph(a)enology, Phenetics, Plankter, Plankton, Pleuston, Protist, Protista, Protozoan, Radiolarian, Saprobe, Saprotroph, Schizomycete, Streptococcus, Symbion(t), Teratogen, Thermophile, Torula, Virino, Volvox, Vorticella

Organ-part, Organ-stop Bourdon, Clarabella, Diapason, Gamba, Montre, Nasard, Principal, Pyramidon, Quint, Salicet, Stop

Organ-tuner Reed-knife

Orgasm Climax, Come

Orgy Bacchanalia(n), Binge, Blinder, Bust, Carousal, Dionysian, Feast, Revel, Saturnalia, Spree, Wassail

Orient(al) Adjust, Annamite, Chinoiserie, Dawn, Dayak, E, East(ern), Fu Manchu, Hindu, Laotian, Levant, Leyton, Malay, Mongol, Mongolian, Pareoean, Shan, Sunrise, Tatar, Thai, Tibetan, Turk(o)man

Orientation Tropism

Orifice Aperture, Blastosphere, Gap, Hole, Micropyle, Nare, Opening, Pore, Spiracle, Trema, Vent

Origen's work Tetrapla

Origin(al), Originate, Originating Abiogenesis, Abo, Adam, Arise, Beginning, Big bang, Birth, Come, Cradle, Creation, Derive, Editio princeps, Elemental, Emanate, Epicentre, Etymon, Extraction, First, Firsthand, Focus, Found, Generic, Genesis, Genetical, Germ, Grow, Hatch, Incunabula, Initial, Innovate, Invent, Master, Mother, Nascence, Natality, New, Novel, Ord, Precedent, Primal, Primary, Primigenial, Primordial, Pristine, Promethean, Prototype, Provenance, Provenience, Rise, Root, Seed, Seminal, Source, Spring, Start, Ur, Ylem, Zoism

Oriole Firebird, Hangbird

Orison Blessing, Prayer

Ormer Abalone, Haliotis

Ornament(al), Ornamentation Acroter(ia), Additament, Adorn, Aglet, Aiguillette, Anaglyph, Antefix, Anthemion, Aplustre, Arabesque, Bahuti, Ball-flower, Barbola,

Baroque, Barrette, Bead, Bedeck, Bez(z)ant, Billet, Blister, Boss, Bracelet, Breloque, Broider, Brooch, Bugle, Bulla, Cartouche, Charm, Chase, Clock, Cockade, Conceit, Corbeil(le), Cornice, Coromandel work, Crocket, Cross-quarters, Curin, Curlicue, Decor, Decorate, Decoration, Diamanté, Die-work, Diglyph, Dog's-tooth, Doodad, Dreamcatcher, Egg and anchor, Egg and dart, Egg and tongue, Embellish, Emblem(a), Enrich, Epaulet(te), Epergne, Fallal, Fandangle, Fiddlehead, Figuration, Figurine, Filagree, Filigrain, Filigree, Fillagree, Fleur de lis, Fleuret, Fleurette, Fleuron, Florid, Fret, Fretwork, Frill, Frounce, Furbelow, Furnish, Gadroon, Gaud, Gingerbread, Gorget, Griff(e), Guilloche, Gutta, Headwork, Hei-tiki, Helix, Hip-knob, Honeysuckle, Illustrate, Inlay, Knotwork, Labret, Lambrequin, Leglet, Lotus, Lunula, Macramé, Mantling, Mense, Millefleurs, Mordent, Moresque, Motif, Nail-head, Necklet, Netsuke, Nicknackery, Niello, O, Okimono, Ouch, Ovolo, Palmette, Parure, Patera, Paternoster, Paua, Pawa, Pectoral, Pendant, Picot, Pipe, Piping, Pompom, Pompo(o)n, Poppyhead, Pounce, Pralltriller, Prettify, Prunt, Purfle, Quatrefoil, Rel(l)ish, Rocaille, Rococo, Rosette, Scalework, Scrollwork, Shoulder-knot, Snowdome, Snowglobe, Spangle, Spar, Tassel, Tettix, Tiki, Tool, Torque, Torsade, Tracery, Trappings, Trill, Trimming, Trinket, Triquetra, Turn, Versal, Wally, Water-leaf, Whigmaleerie, Whigmaleery

Ornate Baroque, Churrigueresque, Dressy, Elaborate, Fancy, Florid, Flowery

▷ **Ornate** *may indicate* an anagram

Ornithologist Audubon, Birdman

Orotund Bombastic, Grandiose, Pompous, Rhetorical, Sonant

Orphan Annie, Foundling, Topsy, Ward

Orpiment Arsenic, Zarnich

Orpington Buff, Hen

Ort Bit, Crumb, Morsel, Remnant

Orthodox Bien-pensant, Cocker, Conventional, Hardshell, Proper, Sound, Standard

Orthorhombic Enstatite

Ortolan Bird, Bunting, Rail

Oscar Award, O, Wilde

Oscillate, Oscillation, Oscillator Dynatron, Excitor, Fluctuate, Librate, Local, Parasitic, Relaxation, Ripple, Rock, Seesaw, Seiche, Squeg, Surge, Swing, Vibrate, Waver

Osier Red, Reed, Sallow, Willow

Osmium Os

Osmosis Reverse

Osprey Fish-hawk, Lammergeier, Ossifrage, Pandion

Osseous Bony, Hard, Skeletal, Spiny

Ostensibly Apparent, External, Seeming

Ostentation, Ostentatious Camp, Display, Dog, Éclat, Epideictical, Extravagant, Fantoosh, Fastuous, Flamboyant, Flash(y), Flaunt, Florid, Flourish, Garish, Gaudy, Ghetto fabulous, Highfalutin(g), Large, Parade, Pomp, Ponc(e)y, Pretence, Puff, → **SHOW(ING)**, Side, Splash, Swank, Tacky, Tulip

Osteoporosis Sudeck's atrophy

Ostler Stabler

Ostracise, Ostracism Banish, Blackball, Blacklist, Boycott, Cut, Exclude, Exile, Petalism, Potsherd, Snub, Taboo, Tabu

Ostrich Em(e)u, Estrich, Estridge, Nandoo, Nandu, Ratite, Rhea, Struthio(nes), Titanis

Othello Moor, Morisco

Other(s), Otherwise Additional, Aka, Alia, Alias, Allo-, Alternative, Besides,

Different, Distinct, Else, Et al, Et alli, Etc, Excluding, Former, Further, It, Rest, Significant

Other things Alia

▷ **Otherwise** *may indicate* an anagram

Otiose Idle, Indolent, Ineffective, Lazy, Needless, Superfluous, Useless

Otis Bustard

Ottawa Bytown

Otter Edal, Paravane, Sea, Tarka, Waterdog

Otto Attar, Chypre, Mahratta

Ottoman Osmanli, Porte, Rumelia, Turk

Oubliette Dungeon, Pit, Prison

Ouch Brooch, Ornament, Ow

Ought All, Should

Ouida Ramée

Ounce Cat, Fluid, Liang, Oz, Panther, Snow leopard, Tael, Uncial

Our(selves) Us, We

▶ **Ousel** *see* **OUZEL**

Oust Depose, Dislodge, Eject, Evict, Expel, Fire, Supplant, Unnest, Unseat

Out Absent, Aglee, Agley, Al fresco, Asleep, Aus, Away, Begone, Bowl, Dated, En ville, Exposed, External, Forth, Furth, Haro, Harrow, Hence, Hors, Lent, Oust, Skittle, Striking, Stump, Taboo, Uit, Unfashionable, Up, York

▷ **Out** *may indicate* an anagram

Out and out Absolute, Arrant, Rank, Sheer, Stark, Teetotal, Thorough, Totally, Utter

Outback Backblocks, Bundu, The mulga

Outbreak Ebullition, Epidemic, Eruption, Explosion, Flare-up, Plague, Putsch, Rash, Recrudescence

Outburst Access, Blurt, Bluster, Boutade, Evoe, Explosion, Fit, Flaw, Furore, Fusillade, Gush, Gust, Paroxysm, Passion, Philippic, Salvo, Storm, Tantrum, Tumult, Volley

Outcast Cagot, Discard, Eta, Exile, Exul, Ishmael, Leper, Mesel, Pariah, Rogue

Outcome Aftermath, Consequence, Dénouement, Effect, Emergence, End, Event, Issue, → **RESULT**, Sequel, Upshot, Wash-up

Outcrop Basset, Blossom, Crag, Creston, Inlier, Mesa, Rognon, Spur, Tarpit

Outcry Alew, Blue murder, Bray, → **CLAMOUR**, Halloa, Halloo, Howl, Hue, Humdudgeon, Protest, Racket, Shright, Steven, Uproar, Utas

Outdated, Out of date Archaic, Dinosaur, Effete, Feudal, Fossil, Horse and buggy, Obsolete, Old hat, Outmoded, Passé, Square

Outdo Beat, Best, Cap, Picnic, Surpass, Top, Trump, Worst

Outdoor(s) Alfresco, External, Garden, Open air, Outbye, Plein-air

Outer External, Extrogenous, Magpie, Superficial, Top

Outfit(ter) Accoutrement, Catsuit, Drawbar, Ensemble, Equipage, Fitout, Furnish, Get-up, Haberdasher, Habit, Kit, Rig, Samfoo, Samfu, Strip, Suit, Team, Trousseau, Turnout, Weed(s), Whites

Outflank Overlap

Outflow Anticyclone, Discharge, Effluence, Eruption, Gorge, Issue, Surge

Outgoing Egression, Exiting, Extrovert, Open, Retiring

Outgrowth Ala(te), Aril, Bud, Caruncle, Enation, Epiphenomenon, Exostosis, Flagellum, Ligule, Offshoot, Osteophyte, Propagulum, Root-hair, Sequel, Strophiole, Trichome

Outhouse Lean to, Privy, Shed, Skilling, Skillion, Skipper, Stable

Outing Excursion, Jaunt, Junket, Picnic, Sortie, Spin, Spree, Treat, Trip, Wayzgoose

Outlandish Barbarous, Bizarre, Exotic, Foreign, Peregrine, Rum

Outlaw Allan-a-Dale, Attaint, Badman, Ban, Bandit(ti), Banish, Broken man, Bushranger, Exile, Fugitive, Hereward, Horn, Jesse James, Proscribe, Put to the horn, Robin Hood, Rob Roy, Ronin, Tory, Waive

Outlay Cost, Expense, Mise

Outlet Débouché, Egress, Escape, Estuary, Exit, Femerall, Market, Opening, Orifice, Outfall, Overflow, Sluice, Socket, Spout, Tuyere, Tweer, Twier, Twire, Twyer(e), Vent

Outline Adumbration, Aperçu, Circumscribe, Configuration, Contorno, Contour, Delineate, Digest, → **DRAFT**, Draught, Esquisse, Footprint, Layout, Note, Perimeter, Plan, Profile, Prospectus, Relief, Scenario, Schematic, Shape, Silhouette, Skeletal, Skeleton, Sketch, Summary, Syllabus, Synopsis, T(h)alweg, Trace

Outlook Casement, Perspective, Prospect, View, Vista, Weltanschauung

Outmoded Wasm

▷ **Out of** *may indicate* an anagram

Out of date Corny, Obs, Passé, Scrap, Square, Worn

Out of form Amorphous, Awry

Out of order Fritz

Out of sorts Cachectic, Nohow, Peevish, Poorly

▷ **Out of sorts** *may indicate* an anagram

Out of tune Discordant, Flat, Scordato, Scordatura

Outpost Colony, Picquet

Outpour(ing) Effuse, Flood, Flow, Gush, Libation, Stream, Torrent

Output Data, Emanation, Get, Gross, Produce, Production, Turnout, Yield

▷ **Output** *may indicate* an anagram

Outrage(ous) Affront, Appal, Atrocity, Desecrate, Disgust, Egregious, Enorm(ity), Flagitious, Flagrant, Insult, OTT, Rich, Sacrilege, Scandal, Shocking, Ungodly, Unholy, Violate

▷ **Outrageously** *may indicate* an anagram

Outright Clean, Complete, Entire, Point-blank, Utter

Outrun Spreadeagle

Outset Beginning, Start

Outshine Eclipse, Excel, Overshadow, Surpass, Upstage

Outside Ab extra, Crust, Exterior, External, Extramural, Front, Furth, Hors, Periphery, Plein-air, Rim, Rind, Rine, Surface

Outsider Alien, Bolter, Bounder, Cad, Extern, Extremist, Foreigner, Incomer, Oustiti, Palagi, Pariah, Ring-in, Roughie, Stranger, Stumer, Unseeded, Upstart

Outsize Capacious, Giant, Gigantic, Huge, OS

Outskirts Edge, Fringe, Periphery, Purlieu

Outspoken Bluff, Blunt, Broad, Candid, Explicit, Forthright, Frank, Plain, Rabelaisian, Round, Vocal, Vociferous

Outstand(ing) Ace, Beaut(y), Belter, Billowing, Bulge, Chief, Egregious, Eminent, Especial, Exceptional, Extant, Extraordinaire, First, Fugleman, Highlight, Humdinger, Impasto, Jut, Lulu, Marked, Matchless, Oner, Overdue, Owing, Paragon, Phenom(enal), Pièce de résistance, Prince, Prize, Prominent, Promontory, Prosilient, Protrude, Proud, Purler, Relief, Relievo, Salient, Signal, Special, Squarrose, Star, Stellar, Strout, Superb, Tour de force, Unpaid, Unsettled

Outstrip Best, Cap, Cote, Distance, Exceed, Overtake

Outward Efferent, Extern(e), External, Extrinsic, Extrorse, Extrovert, Posticous, Postliminary, Superficial

Outweigh Preponderate

Outwit Baffle, Best, Circumvent, Crossbite, Dish, Euchre, Fox, Outthink, Over-reach, → THWART, Trick

Outwork Demilune, Jetty, Moon, Tenail(le), Tenaillon

Outworn Decrepit, Obsolete, Used

Ouzel Ring, Water

Oval(s) Cartouche, Cassini, Ellipse, Henge, Navette, Obovate, Ooidal

Ovary Oophoron

Ovation Applause, Cheer, Standing

Oven(-like) Aga®, Calcar, Camp, Combination, Convection, Cul-de-four, Dutch, Electric, Fan, Furnace, Gas, Hangi, Haybox, Horn(it)o, Kiln, Lear, Leer, Lehr, Lime kiln, Maori, Microwave, Muffle, Norwegian, Oast, Oon, Stove, Umu

Over Above, Across, Again, Atop, C, Clear, Done, Finished, Hexad, Left, Maiden, Of, On, Ore, Ort, Owre, Past, Sopra, Spare, Superior, Surplus, Through, Uber, Wicket maiden, Yon

Overact Burlesque, Emote, Ham, Hell, Hoke

Overactive Hyper

Overall(s) Boiler suit, Chaps, Denims, Dungarees, Dust-coat, Fatigues, Jumper, Smicket, Smock, Tablier, Workwear

Overbearing Arrogant, Dogmatic, Domineering, High-muck-a-muck, Imperious, Insolent, Lordly, Macher, Supercilious

Overbid Gazump

Overcast Cloudy, Lowering, Sew, Sombre

Overcharge Clip, Extort, Fleece, Gyp, OC, Rack-rent, Rook, Rush, Soak, Sting

Overcoat Balmacaan, Benjamin, Benny, British warm, Chesterfield, → COAT, Crombie, Dolman, Grego, Inverness, Jemmy, Joseph, Paletot, Petersham, Pos(h)teen, Prince Albert, Raglan, Redingote, Spencer, Surtout, Tabard, Taglioni, Ulster, Warm, Wooden, Wrap-rascal

Overcome Beat, Bested, Conquer, Convince, Dead-beat, Defeat, Expugn, Hit for six, Kill, Master, Mither, Moider, Moither, Prevail, Quell, Speechless, Stun, Subdue, Subjugate, Superate, Surmount, Vanquish, Win

Overconfident, Overconfidence Besserwisser

Overcrowd Congest, Jam, Pack

Overdo(ne) Exceed, Ham, Hokey, Hokum, OTT, Percoct, Tire

Overdose OD

Overdraft Red

▷ **Overdrawn** *may indicate* 'red' outside another word

Overdress(ing) Dudism, Flossy, Overall

Overdue Behindhand, Belated, Excessive, Late

Overeat(ing) Binge, Gorge, Hypertrophy, Pig out, Satiate

Overemphasize Rub in, Stress

Overfeed(ing) Glut, Gorge, Sate, Stuff

Overflow(ing) Abrim, Lip, Nappe, Ooze, Ream, Redound, Spillage, Surfeit, Teem

Overfull Brimming, Hept

Overground Subaerial

Overgrow(n) Ivy'd, Jungle, Ramp(ant), Rank, Rhinophyma

Overhang(ing) Beetle, Bulge, Cornice, → JUT, Loom, Project, Shelvy

Overhaul Bump, Catch, Overtake, Recondition, Revision, Service, Strip

Overhead(s) Above, Aloft, Ceiling, Cost, Exes, Hair(s), Headgear, Oncost, Rafter, Upkeep, Zenith

Overhear Catch, Eavesdrop, Tap

Overheat Enrage

Overindulge(nt) Crapulent, Crass, Dissipated, Dissolute, Pig
Overjoy Elate, Thrill
Overland Portage
Overlap(ping) Correspond, Equitant, Imbricate, Incubous, Kern(e), Limbous, Obvolute, Stretto, Tace, Tasse
Overlay Ceil, Smother, Stucco, Superimpose, Veneer
Overlearned Pedantic
Overload Burden, Plaster, Strain, Surcharge, Tax
Overlook(ed) Condone, Disregard, Excuse, Forget, Miss, Omit, Pretermit, Superintend, Unnoticed, Waive
Overlord Edwin, Excess, Invasion
Overlying Incumbent, Jessant, Pressing
Overmuch Excessive, Surplus, Too, Undue
Overplay Ham, Hoke
Overpower(ing) Crush, Evince, Mighty, Onerous, Oppress, Overwhelm, Subdue, Surmount, Swelter, Whelm
Overpraise Adulate
Over-refined Dainty, Nice, Pernickety, Precious
Override, Overrule Abrogate, Disallow, Outweigh, Reverse, Talk down, Veto
Overrun Exceed, Extra, Infest, Inundate, Invade, Swarm, Teem
Overseas Abroad, Colonial, Outremer, Transmarine, Ultramarine
Oversee(r) Baas, Banksman, Boss, Captain, Care, Deputy, Direct, Eyebrow, Foreman, Forewoman, Grieve, Handle, Induna, Mediate, Moderator, Periscope, Steward, Supercargo, Survey(or)
Oversentimental Byronic, Slushy
Overshadow(ed) Cloud, Dominate, Eclipse, Obscure, Outclass, Umbraculate
Overshoe Arctic, Galosh, Sandal, Snowboot
Oversight Blunder, Care, Error, Gaffe, Lapse, Neglect, Parablepsis
Overstate(ment) Embroider, Exaggerate, Hyperbole
Overstrained Epitonic
Overt Manifest, Patent, Plain, Public
Overtake Catch, For(e)hent, Lap, Leapfrog, Overget, Overhaul, → **PASS**, Supersede, Usurp
Overthrow Dash, Defeat, Demolish, Depose, Down, Labefact(at)ion, Ruin, Smite, Stonker, Subvert, Supplant, Topple, Unhorse, Usurp, Vanquish, Whemmle, Whommle, Whummle, Worst
Overture Advance, Carnival, Concert, Egmont, French, Hebrides, Intro, Italian, Leonora, Offer, → **OPENING**, Prelude, Propose, Sinfonia, Toccata, Toccatella, Toccatina
Overturn(ing) Catastrophe, Coup, Cowp, Engulf, Quash, Reverse, Tip, Topple, Up(set), Upend, Whemmle
Overvalue Exaggerate, Salt
Overweening Bashaw, Cocky, Excessive, Imperious, Presumptuous
Overweight Sunk
Overwhelm(ed), Overwhelming Accablé, Assail, Banging, → **CRUSH**, Defeat, Deluge, Engulf, Flabbergast, Foudroyant, Inundate, KO, Mind-boggling, Oppress, Overcome, Scupper, Smother, Snow, Submerge, Swamp, Whup
Overwork(ed) Fag, Hackneyed, Ornament, Slog, Stale, Supererogation, Tax, Tire, Toil, Travail
Overwrought Frantic, Hysterical, Ore-rested, Ornate, Rococo
Ovid Naso

Ovum Egg, Oosphere, Seed

Owe(d), Owing Attribute, Due, OD

Owen Glendower

Owl(s) African, Barn, Barred, Blinker, Boobook, Brown, Bubo, Bunter, Chinese, Eagle, Elegant, English, Fish, Glimmergowk, Grey, Hawk, Hoo(ter), Horned, Howlet, Jenny, Little, Long-eared, Longhorn, Madge, Moper, Mopoke, Mopus, Night, Ogle, Parliament, Ruru, Saw-whet, Scops, Screech, Sea, Snowy, Strich, Striges, Strigiformes, Tawny, Wood

Own(er), Owning, Ownership Admit, Agnise, Confess, Domain, Dominium, Fess, Have, Hold, Mortmain, Nain, Of, Personal, Possess, Proper, Proprietor, Recognise, Reputed, Title, Use

Own way More suo

Ox(en) Anoa, Aquinas, Aurochs, Banteng, Banting, Bison, Bonas(s)us, Buffalo, Bugle, Bullock, Cat(t)alo, Fee, Gaur, Gayal, Gyal, Kouprey, Mart, Musk, Musk-sheep, Neat, Ovibos, Rother, Saola, Sapi-utan, S(e)ladang, Steare, Steer, Stirk, Taurus, Ure, Urus, Vu quang, Water, Water buffalo, Yak, Yoke, Zebu, Z(h)o

Oxford (group) Buchmanism, OU, Puseyism, Shoe

Oxhead Aleph

Oxidation, Oxide Alumina, Anatase, Ceria, Erbium, Eremacausis, Gothite, Gummite, Holmia, Kernite, Lithia, Magnesia, Nitrous, Psilomelane, Quicklime, Red lead, Rutile, Samarskite, Strontia, Thoria, Zaffer, Zaffre

▷ **Oxtail** *may indicate* 'x'

Oxygen (and lack of) Anoxia, Epoxy, Liquid, Lox, Loxygen, O, Vital air

Oyer Hearing, Trial

Oyster (bed), Oyster disease, Oyster-eater Avicula, Bivalve, Bonamia, Bush, Cul(t)ch, Kentish, Lay, Mollusc, Native, Ostrea, Ostreophage, Pandore, Pearl, Plant, Prairie, Salsify, Scallop, Scalp, Scaup, Seed(ling), Spat, Spondyl, Stew, Vegetable

Oyster-catcher Sea-pie

Oyster-plant Gromwell, Salsify

Oz Amos, Australia

Ozone Air, Atmosphere, Oxygen

Pp

P Papa, Parking, Penny, Piano, Prince
PA Aide, Tannoy
Pabulum Aliment, Cheer, Food, Fuel, Nourishment
Pace, Pacemaker Canter, Clip, Cracking, Dog-trot, Easter, Gait, Geometric, Heel and toe, Jog-trot, Lope, Measure, Military, Pari passu, Pioneer, → **RATE**, Roman, Scout's, Single-foot, Snail's, Spank, Speed, Step, Stride, Stroll, Tempo, Tramp, Tread, Trot
Pachyderm Armadillo, Elephant, Hippo, Mastodon, Rhino
Pacific, Pacify Appease, Bromide, Calm, Conciliate, Dove, Ease, Irenic, Lull, Mild, Moderate, Ocean, Placate, Placid, Quiet, Serene, Soothe, Subdue, Sweeten, Tranquil
Pacifist CO, Conciliator, D(o)ukhobor, Dove, Peacenik
Pack(age), Packed, Packing Back, Bale, Blister, Bobbery, Box, Bubble, Bundle, Cards, Cold, Compress, Congest, Cram, Crate, Crowd, Cry, Deck, Dense, Dunnage, Embox, Entity, Everest, Excelsior, Face, Fardel, Floe, Gasket, Gaskin, Glut, Hamper, Hunt, Ice, Jam, Kennel, Knapsack, Load, Matilda, Naughty, Pair, → **PARCEL**, Pikau, Power, Pun, Rout, Ruck, Rucksack, Set, Shiralee, Shrink-wrap, Steeve, Stow, Suits, Sumpter, Tamp, Team, Tread, Troop, Truss, Wad, Wet, Wolf, Wrap
Packet Boat, Bundle, Deck, Liner, Mailboat, Mint, Parcel, Pay, Red, Roll, Sachet, Steam, Steamboat, Wage
Pack-horse Sumpter
Packman Chapman, Hawker, Hiker, Pedlar, Tinker
Pact Agreement, Alliance, Bargain, Bilateral, Cartel, Contract, Covenant, Locarno, Munich, Stability, Suicide, → **TREATY**, Warsaw
Pad(ding) Batting, Bombast, Brake, Bustle, Compress, Condo, Crash, Cushion, Dabber, Damper, Dossil, Enswathe, Expand, Falsies, Filler, Flat, Frog, Gumshield, Hard, Hassock, Horse, Ink, Jotter, Launch, Leg-guard, Lily, Nag, Note, Numnah, Patch, Paw, Ped, Pillow, Pincushion, Plastron, Pledget, Plumper, Porters' knot, Pouf(fe), Protract, Pudding, Puff, Pulvillus, Pulvinar, Scratch, Shoulder, Stamp, Stuff, Sunk, Swab, Tablet, Thief, Touch, Tournure, Tylopod, Tympan, Velour(s), Velure, Wad, Wase, Writing
Paddington Bear, Station
Paddle, Paddle boat, Paddle-foot Canoe, Dabble, Doggy, Oar, Pinniped, Row, Seal, Side-wheel, Spank, Splash, Stern-wheeler, Wade
Paddock Field, Frog, Holding, Meadow, Park, Sacrifice
Paddy, Paddy field Fury, Ire, Irishman, Mick, Pat(rick), Pet, Rag, Rage, Sawah, Tantrum, Temper, Wax
Padre Chaplain, Cleric, Father, Monk, Priest
Paean Eulogy, Hymn, Ode, Praise, Psalm
Paediatrician Rett
Paedophile Nonce

Pagan(ism) Animist, Atheist, Gentile, Gentoo, Godless, Heathen, Idolater, Infidel, Odinist, Paynim, Saracen, Sun cult

Page(s), Pageboy Back, Bellboy, Bellhop, Bleep, Boy, Buttons, Callboy, Centrefold, Flyleaf, Fold out, Folio, Foolscap, Front, Gate-fold, Groom, Haircut, Hairdo, Home, Hornbook, Leaf, Master, Messenger, Moth, Octavo, Op-ed, P, Pane, PP, Problem, Quarto, Ream, Recto, Ro, Servant, Sheet, Side, Splash, Squire, Tear sheet, Tiger, Title, Varlet, Verso, Web, Yellow

Pageant Antique, Cavalcade, Pomp, Spectacle, Tattoo, Triumph

Pagoda Anking, Anqing, Temple, To

Pah Pish, Tush, Umph

▶ **Paid** *see* **PAY**

Pail Bucket, Kettle, Leglan, Leglen, Leglin, Piggin, Slop

▷ **Pain** *may indicate* bread French

Pain(ful), Pains A(a)rgh, Ache, Aggrieve, Agony, Ake, Algesis, Angina, Anguish, Arthralgia, Bad, Bale, Bedsore, Bitter, Bore, Bot(t), Bother, Burn, Causalgia, Colic, Cramp, Crick, Distress, Dole, Doleur, Dolour, Dool(e), Dysmenorhoea, Dysury, Eina, Excruciating, Fash, Fibrositis, Gastralgia, Gip, Grief, Gripe, Growing, Gyp, Harrow, Heartburn, Hemialgia, → **HURT**, Ill, Kink, Laborious, Lancination, Lumbago, Mal, Mastalgia, Mastodynia, Metralgia, Migraine, Misery, Mulligrubs, Myalgia, Neuralgia, Nociceptive, Pang, Persuant, Pest, Phantom, Pleurodynia, Prick, Pungent, Rack, Raw, Referred, Sair, Sciatica, Smart, Sore, Sorrow, Splitting, Sten(d), Sternalgia, Sting, Stitch, Strangury, Stung, Tarsalgia, Teen(e), Tene, Throe, Topalgia, Torment, Tormina, Torture, Travail, Twinge, Wo(e), Wrench, Wring

Painkiller Aminobutene, Analgesic, Bute, Cocaine, Distalgesic, Endorphin, Enkephalin, Jadeite, Meperidine, Metopon, Morphine, Number, Pethidine

Painless(ness) Analgesia, Easy

Painstaking Assiduous, Careful, Diligent, Elaborate, Exacting, Meticulous, Sedulous, Studious, Thorough

Paint(ed), Painting Abstract, Abstract expressionism, Acrylic, Action, Airbrush, Alla prima, Aquarelle, Arcimboldo, Art autre, Art deco, Artificial, Art nouveau, Ash Can School, Barbizon, Battlepiece, Bice, Blottesque, Camaieu, Canvas, Cellulose, Cerograph, Chiaroscuro, Clair-obscure, Clobber, Coat, Colour, Cubism, Dadaism, Daub, Dayglo, Decorate, Depict, Describe, Diptych, Distemper, Duco, Eggshell, Emulsion, Enamel, Encaustic, Fard, Fauvism, Finery, Finger, Flatting, Flemish, Fore-edge, Fresco, Fucus, Genre, Gild, Gloss, Gouache, Graining, Gravure, Grease, Grisaille, Guernica, Hard-edge, Historical, Icon, Impasto, Impressionism, Intimism(e), Intonaco, Intumescent, Lead, Limn, Lithochromy, Luminous, Magilp, Matt, Megilp, Mehndi, Miniate, Miniature, Modello, Mona Lisa, Monotint, Mural, Naive, Neo-Impressionism, Neo-Plasticism, Nightpiece, Nihonga, Nocturne, Non-drip, Oaker, Ochre, Oil, Old Master, Oleo(graph), Op art, Orphism, Paysage, Pentimento, Pict, Picture, Pigment, Pinxit, Plein air, Pointillism(e), Portray, Poster, Post-Impressionism, Predella, Primavera, Primitive, Quadratura, Raddle, Rag-rolling, Rosemaling, Roughstuff, Sand, Scenography, Scumble, Secco, Sfumato, Sien(n)ese, Skyscape, Spray, Stencil, Stereochrome, Still life, Stipple, Suprematism, Tablature, Tachism(e), Tag, Tall-oil, Tanka, Tempera, Tenebrism, Thangka, Tondo, Ukiyo-e, Umber, Umbrian, Undercoat, Underglaze, Vanitas, Veduta, Vorticism, War, Wax

Painted woman Courtesan, Harlot, Pict, Tart

Painter(s) Animalier, → **ARTIST**, Ash Can School, Colourist, Cubist, Decorator, Gilder, Illusionist, Impressionist, Limner, Little Master, Luminarist, Miniaturist, Old Master, Paysagist, Plein-airist, Primitive, Sien(n)ese, Soutine, Sunday

Pair(ing) Brace, Cooper, Couple(t), Doublet, Duad, Duo, Dyad(ic), Exciton, Fellows, Geminate, Item, Jugate, Jumelle, King, Link, Lone, Match, Mate, Minimal, Ocrea, Pigeon, Pr, Span, Spouses, Synapsis, Syndyasmian, Syzygy, Tandem, Thummim, Twa(e), Tway, Two, Urim, Yoke

Paisley Ian, Orange, Shawl

Pakistan(i) Pathan

Pal Ally, Amigo, Bud(dy), China, Chum, Comrade, Crony, Cully, Friend, Mate, Wus(s)

Pal(a)eolithic Acheulean, Acheulian, Azilian, Chellean, Clactonian, Gravettian, Levallois(ian), Lower, Madelenian, Magdalenian, Middle, Neanderthal, Perigordian, Solutrean, Strepyan, Upper

Palace Alcazar, Alhambra, Basilica, Blenheim, Buckingham, Court, Crystal, Edo, Élysée, Escorial, Escurial, Fontainebleau, Forbidden City, Fulham, Gin, Goslar, Holyrood, Holyroodhouse, Hotel, Istana, Lambeth, Lateran, Linlithgow, Louvre, Mansion, Nonsuch, Palatine, Picture, Pitti, Pushkin, Quirinal, St James's, Sans Souci, Schloss, Seraglio, Serail, Shushan, Topkapi, Trianon, Tuileries, Valhalla, Vatican, Versailles

Paladin Champion, Charlemagne, Defender, Douzeper, Fièrabras, Ganelon, → **KNIGHT**, Ogier, Oliver, Orlando, Rinaldo, Roland

Palanquin Doolie, Kago, Litter, Palkee, Palki, Sedan

Palatable, Palatalized, Palate Cleft, Dainty, Hard, Mouille, Relish, Roof, Sapid, Savoury, Soft, Taste, Toothsome, Uranic, Uraniscus, Uvula, Velum

Palatial Ornate, Splendid

Palatinate, Palatine Officer, Pfalz

Palaver Chatter, Debate, Parley, Powwow, → **TALK**

Pale, Paling Ashen, Blanch, Bleach, Cere, Dim, English, Etiolate(d), Fade, → **FAINT**, Fence, Ghostly, Haggard, Insipid, Jewish, Lily (white), Livid, Mealy, Ox-fence, Pallescent, Pastel, Peaky, Peelie-wally, Picket, Sallow, Shilpit, Stang, Verge, Wan, Whey-faced, White, Wishy-washy

Paleography Diplomatics

Paleozoic Permian, Silurian

Palestine, Palestinian Amorite, Fatah, Gadarene, Hamas, Intifada, Israel, Pal, Per(a)ea, Philistine, PLO, Samaria

Palette Board, Cokuloris

Palindrome, Palindromic Cancrine, Sotadic

Palisade Barrier, Fence, Fraise, Stacket, Stockade

Pall Bore, Cloy, Curtain, Damper, Glut, Hearse-cloth, Mantle, Mortcloth, Satiate, Shroud

Palladium Defence, Pd, Safeguard

Pallas Athene

Pallet Bed, Cot, Couch, Mattress, Tick

Palliate, Palliative Alleviate, Anetic, Ease, Extenuate, Lessen, Mitigate, Reduce, Relieve, Sedative

Pallid Anaemic, Ashen, Insipid, Pale, Wan, Waxy

Palm Accolade, Areca, Assai, Atap, Babassu, Bangalow, Betel, Buriti, Burrawang, Bussu, Cabbage, Calamus, Carna(h)uba, Carpenteria, Chamaerops, Chiqui-chiqui, Coco, Cohune, Conceal, Coquito, Corozo, Corypha, Cycad, Date (tree), Doom, Doum, Elaeis, Euterpe, Fan, Feather, Fob, Foist, Gomuti, Gomuto, Groo-groo, Gru-gru, Hand, Hemp, Ita, Itching, Ivory, Jip(p)i-Jap(p)a, Jipyapa, Jupati, Kentia, Kittul, Laurels, Loof, Looves, Macahuba, Macaw, Macoya, Moriche, Nikau, Nipa, Oil, Palmyra, Paxiuba, Peach, Pupunha, Raffia, Raphia, Rat(t)an, Royal, Sabal, Sago, Saw palmetto, Sugar, Talipat, Talipot, Thatch, Thenar, Toddy, Triumph,

Troelie, Troolie, Trooly, Trophy, Vola, Washingtonia, Wax, Wine, Zamia

Palmer Lilli, Pilgrim

Palmerston Pam

Palmistry Ch(e)irognomy

Palm-leaf Frond

Palpable Evident, Gross, Manifest, Patent, Plain, Tangible

Palpitate, Palpitation Flutter, Pitpat, Pulsate, Throb, Twitter, Vibrate

Palsy Bell's, Cerebral, Paralysis, Scrivener's, Shakes

Paltry Bald, Cheap, Exiguous, Mean, Measly, Peanuts, Pelting, Petty, Pimping, Poor, Puny, Scald, Scalled, Shabby, Shoestring, Sorry, Tin(-pot), Tinny, Trashy, Trifling, Two-bit, Vile, Waff, Whiffet

Pamper(ed) Cocker, Coddle, Cosher, Cosset, Cuiter, Feather-bed, Gratify, High-fed, → INDULGE, Mollycoddle, Overfeed, Pet, Pompey, Spoon-fed

Pamphlet Brochure, Catalogue, Chapbook, Leaflet, Notice, Sheet, Tract

Pan Agree, Auld Hornie, Bainmarie, Balit, Basin, Betel(-pepper), Braincase, Chafer, Dent, Dial, Drip, Dripping, Goat-god, Goblet, God, Hard, Ice-floe, Iron, Jelly, Karahi, Knee, Ladle, Lavatory, Muffin, Nature-god, Non-stick, Oil, Pancheon, Panchion, Patella, Patina, Peter, Poacher, Preserving, Prospect, Roast, Salt, Search, Skid, Skillet, Slag, Slate, Spider, Sweep, Vessel, Warming, Wo(c)k, Work

Panacea All-heal, Azoth, Catholicon, Cure(-all), Discatholicon, Elixir, Ginseng, Parkleaves, Remedy, Tutsan

Panache Bravura, Crest, Dash, Flair, Paz(z)azz, Piz(z)azz, Plume, Pzazz, Show, Talent

Pancake Blin(i), Blintz(e), Burrito, Crêpe (suzette), Crumpet, Drop(ped)-scone, Flam(m), Flapjack, Flaune, Flawn, Fraise, Fritter, Froise, Latke, Pikelet, Poppadum, Potato, Quesadilla, Scotch, Slapjack, Spring roll, Suzette, Taco, Tortilla, Tostada, Waffle

Pancreas Isles of Langerhans, Sweetbread

Panda Bear-cat, Car, Chi-chi, Chitwah, Common, Giant, Lesser, Red

Pandarus Go-between

Pandemonium Inferno, Uproar

Pander Broker, Indulge, Pimp, Procurer, Toady

Pane Glass, Light, Panel, Quarrel, Quarry, Sheet

Panegyric Encomium, Eulogy, Laudation, Praise, Tribute

Panel(ling) Adoption, Array, Board, Cartouche, Children's, Control, Dashboard, Fa(s)cia, Gore, Hatchment, Inset, Instrument, Jury, Lacunar, Mandorla, Mimic, Mola, Orb, Patch(board), People's, Reredorse, Reredos(se), Rocker, Screen, Skreen, Solar, Stile, Stomacher, Table, Tablet, Valance, Volet, Wainscot

Pang Achage, Ache, Crick, Qualm, Spasm, Stab, Stound, Twinge, Wrench

Pangloss Optimist

Pangolin Ant-eater, Manis

Panhandle(r) Beggar, W. Virginia

Panic Alar(u)m, Amaze, Consternation, Fear, Flap, Flat-spin, Flip, Fright, Funk, Guinea-grass, Lather, Millet, Raggee, Raggy, Ragi, Sauve qui peut, → SCARE, Scarre, Stampede, Stampedo, State, Stew, Tailspin, → TERROR

Panicle Thyrse

Panjandrum Bashaw

Pannier Basket, Cacolet, Corbeil, Dosser, Saddlebag, Skip, Whisket

Panoply Armour, Array, Pomp

Panorama, Panoramic Cyclorama, Range, Scenery, Veduta, View, Vista

Pansy Gay, Heart's-ease, Herb-trinity, Kiss-me-quick, Nance, Powder-puff, Queer, Viola

Pant(s) Bags, Breeches, Capri, Cargo, Chaps, Chinos, Culottes, Deck, Dhoti, Drawers, Fatigues, Flaff, Gasp, Gaucho, Harem, Hot, Long johns, Longs, Parachute, Pech, Pedal-pushers, Pegh, Puff, Ski, Slacks, Smalls, Stirrup, Stovepipe, Sweat, Throb, Toreador, Training, Trews, Trousers, Trunks, Wheeze, Yearn

Pantaloon Columbine, Dupe, Pants

Pantheism Idolatry, Immanency

Panther Bagheera, Black, Cat, Cougar, Grey, Jaguar, Leopard, Pink

Panties Briefs, Knickers, Scanties, Step-ins, Undies

Pantomime, Pantomime character Aladdin, Charade, Cheironomy, Dumb-show, Farce, Galanty, Harlequinade, Pierrot, Play

Pantry Buttery, Closet, Larder, Spence, Stillroom

Pap Dug, Mealie, Mush, Nipple, Teat, Udder

Papal, Papist, Papistry Catholic, Clementine, Concordat, Guelf, Guelph, Holy See, Legation, Pontifical, RC, Roman, Vatican

Paper(s), Paperwork, Papery Admin, Allonge, Antiquarian, Art, Atlas, Ballot, Baryta, Bible, Blotting, Bond, Brief, Broadsheet, Broadside, Bromide, Brown, Building, Bumf, Bumph, Butter, Cap, Carbon, Cartridge, Cellophane®, Chad, Chinese, Chiyogami, Cigarette, Colombier, Command, Commercial, Confetti, Corrugated, Cream-laid, Cream-wove, Credentials, Crêpe, Crown, Cutch, Daily, Decorate, Demy, Document, Dossier, Eggshell, Elephant, Emery, Emperor, Essay, Exam, File, Filter, Final, Flock, Folio, Foolscap, Fourdrinier, FT, Funny, Furnish, Galley, Garnet, Gazette, Gem, Glass(ine), Glumaceous, Government, Grand eagle, Grand Jesus, Graph, Greaseproof, Green, Guardian, Hieratica, Imperial, India, Japanese, Jesus, Journal, Kent cap, Kraft, Kutch, Lace, Laid, Lavatory, Legal cap, Linen, Litmus, Manifold, Manil(l)a, Marble, Mercantile, Mirror, MS, Munimenti, Music(-demy), Needle, News(print), Note, Notelet, Oil, Onion-skin, Order, Packing, Pad, Page, Papillote, Papyrus, Parchment, Pickwick, Plotting, Position, Post, Pot(t), Pravda, Press, Print, Printing, Quair, Quarto, Quire, Rag, Ramee, Rami(e), Ream, Red top, Retree, Rhea, Rice, Rolled, Rolling, Royal, Safety, Satin, Saxe, Scent, Scotsman, Scrip, Scroll, Scrowl, Sheaf, Sheet, Ship's, Silver, Skin, Slipsheet, Spoilt, Stamp, Starch, State, Sugar, Sun, Super-royal, Tabloid, Taffeta, Tap(p)a, Tar, Ternion, TES, Test, Thesis, Thread, Tiger, Tissue, Today, Toilet, Torchon, Touch, Tracing, Trade, Transfer, Treatise, Treeware, Turmeric, Two-name, Vellum, Velvet, Voucher, Walking, Wall, Waste, Watch, Wax(ed), Web, Whatman®, White, Willesden, Wirewove, Wood(chip), Woodfree, Worksheet, Wove, Wrapping, Writing, Zine

Paperback Limp(back)

Paper-cutting, Paper-folding Decoupage, Kirigami, Origami, Psaligraphy

Papier-mâché Carton-pierre, Flong

Paprika Spanish

Par Average, Equate, Equivalent, → **NORMAL**, Scratch

Parable Allegory, Fable, Proverb

Parabola Arc, Curve, Hyperbola

Parachute, Parachutist Aeroshell, Aigrette, Brake, Drag, Drogue, Extraction, Float, Freefall, Golden, Jump, Pack, Pappus, Para, Parabrake, Parapente, Red Devil, Ribbon, Silk, Sky-diving, Skyman, Thistledown, Umbrella

Parade (ground) Air, Arcade, Cavalcade, Church, Concours d'élégance, Display, Dress, Drill, Easter, Emu, Flaunt, Gala, Hit, Identification, Identity, Line-up, Maidan, March-past, Monkey-run, Pageantry, Passing-out, Pomp, Procession, Prom(enade), Sashay, Show, Sick, Stand-to, Ticker tape, Troop

Paradise Arcadia, Avalon, Bliss, Eden, Elysium, Fool's, Garden, Happy-hunting-ground, Heaven, Lost, Malaguetta, Nirvana, Park, Regained, Shangri-la, Svarga, Swarga, Swerga, → **UTOPIA**

Paradox(ical) Absurdity, Cantor's, Contradiction, Dilemma, Electra, Epimenedes, French, Gilbertian, Hydrostatic, Koan, Liar, Olber's, Puzzle, Russell's, Sorites, Twin, Zeno's

Paraffin Earthwax, Kerosene, Kerosine, Liquid, Ozocerite, Ozokerite, Photogen(e), Propane

Paragon Model, Non(e)such, Pattern, Pearl, Phoenix, Role model, Rose

Paragraph (mark) Balaam, Causerie, Note, Passage, Piece, Pilcrow

Parakeet Parrot, Popinjay, Rosella

Parallax Annual, Daily, Diurnal, Geocentric, Heliocentric

Parallel Analog, Collateral, Collimate, Corresponding, Equal, Even, Forty-ninth, Like

Parallelogram Rhomb

Paralysis, Paralyse Apoplexy, Cataplexy, Catatonia, Cramp, Curarise, Cycloplegia, Diplegia, Halt, Hemiplegia, Infantile, Lithyrism, Monoplegia, Numbness, Ophthalmoplegia, Palsy, Paraplegia, Paresis, Polio, Quadriplegia, Radial, Scram, Shock, Shut, Spastic, Spina bifida, Stun, Torpefy, Transfix

Paramedic Ambulance-man

Paramilitary Phalangist, SAS, Sena, UDA

Paramount Chief, Dominant, Greatest, Overall, Premier, → **SUPREME**, Topless, Utmost

Paramour Beau, Franion, Gallant, Leman, Lover, Mistress, Thais

Paranormal Clairvoyant, ESP, Spiritual, Telekinesis

Parapet (space) Barbette, Bartisan, Bartizan, Battlement, Breastwork, Brisure, Bulwark, Crenel, Flèche, Machicolation, Merlon, Rampart, Redan, Surtout, Terreplein, Top, Wall

Paraphernalia Belongings, Equipment, Gear, Trappings

Parasite, Parasitic Ascarid, Autoecious, Aweto, Babesiasis, Beech-drops, Bilharzia, Biogenous, Biotroph, Bladder-worm, Bloodsucker, Bonamia, Bot, Candida, Chalcid, Coccus, Conk, Copepod, Cosher, Crab-louse, Cryptosporidium, Cryptozoite, Dodder, Ectogenous, Ectophyte, Endamoeba, Endophyte, Entophyte, Entozoon, Epiphyte, Epizoon, Facultative, Filarium, Flatworm, Flea, Gapeworm, Giardia, Gregarinida, Haematozoon, Hair-eel, Heartworm, Heteroecious, Hook-worm, Ichneumon, Inquiline, Isopod, Kade, Ked, Lackey, Lamprey, Leech, Leishmania, Licktrencher, Liverfluke, Louse, Lungworm, Macdonald, Mallophagous, Measle, Mistletoe, Monogenean, Necrotroph, Nematode, Nit, Obligate, Orobanche, Pinworm, Plasmodium, Puccinia, Pulix, Quandong, Rafflesia, Redia, Rhipidoptera, Rickettsia, Root, Roundworm, Schistosoma, Scrounger, Shark, Smut-fungus, Sponge(r), Sporozoa(n), Strepsiptera, Strangleweed, Strongyle, Strongyloid, Stylops, Sucker, Symphile, Tachinid, Tapeworm, Tick, Toady, Toxoplasma, Trematode, Trencher-friend, Trencher-knight, Trichina, Trichomonad, Tryp(anosoma), Vampire, Viscum, Wheatworm, Whipworm, Worms

Parasol Awning, Brolly, En tout cas, Marquise, Sunshade, Umbrella

Paratrooper Skyman, Stick leader

Parcel Allocate, Allot, Aret, Bale, Bundle, Holding, Lot, Package, Packet, Sort, Wrap

Parch(ed) Arid, Bake, Dry, Graddan, Hot coppers, Roast, Scorched, Sere, Thirsty, Toast, Torrid

Parchment Diploma, Forel, Mezuzah, Panel, Papyrus, Pell, Pergameneous, Roll, Roule, Scroll, Scrow, Sheepskin, Vegetable, Vellum, Virgin

Pard Leopard, Pal, Partner

Pardon(able), Pardoner Absolve, Amnesty, Anan, Assoil, Clear, Condone, Eh, Excuse, → **FORGIVE**, Grace, Mercy, Quaestionary, Qu(a)estor, Quaestuary, Release, Remission, Remit, Reprieve, Venial, What

Pare Flaught, Flay, Peel, Shave, Skive, Sliver, Strip, Whittle

Parent(al) Ancestral, Father, Forebear, Generant, Genitor, Maternal, Mother, Paternal, Single, Solo, Storge

Parenthesis Aside, Brackets, Innuendo

Parhelion Sun-dog

Pariah Ishmael, Leper, Outcast, Pi(e)dog, Pyedog

Paris(ian), Parisienne Abductor, Athene, Elle, Gai, Gay, Grisette, Lutetia (Parisiorum), Lutetian, Maillotin, Midinette, Trojan

Parish Charge, District, Flock, Kirkto(w)n, Parischan(e), Parishen, Parochin(e), Peculiar, Province, Title

Parity Smithsonian

Park(ing) Algonquin, Alton Towers, Amusement, Banff National, Battery, Brecon Beacons, Business, Car, Caravan, Common, Country, Daintree, Dales, Dartmoor, Death Valley, Disneyland, Egmont National, Enclosure, Etosha, Everglades, Exmoor, Fiordland, Forest, Fun, Game, Garage, Gardens, Grand Canyon, Green, Green lung, Grounds, Hwange, Hyde, Industrial, Jasper, Jasper National, Jurassic, Kakadu, Kalahari Gemsbok, Katmai, Kejionkujik, Kobuk Valley, Kruger, Lake District, Lamington, Lassen Volcanic, Lung, Mammoth Cave, Mansfield, Mesa Verde, Motor, Mount Aspiring, Mount Kenya National, Mount McKinley, Mount Rainier, Mungo, Nahanni National, Nairobi, National, Northumberland, Osterley, Oyster, P, Paradise, Peak District, Phoenix, Pitch, Pittie-ward, Prater, Preserve, Rec, Regent's, Riding Mountain, Safari, Sanctuary, Sandown, Science, Sequoia, Sequoia National, Serengeti, Shenandoah National, Siding, Snowdonia, Stand, Stop, Technology, Theme, Trailer, Tsavo, Valet, Wildlife, Wind, Wood Buffalo, Yard, Yellowstone, Yosemite

Parka Atigi

Parker Dorothy, Nos(e)y

Parkleaves Tutsan

Parley Confer, Discourse, Palaver, Speak, Tret

Parliament Addled, Althing, Barebones, Black, Boule, Bundestag, Chamber, Commons, Congress, Cortes, Council, Cross-bench, Dail, Diet, D(o)uma, Drunken, Eduskunta, European, Folketing, House, Imperial, Knesset, Lack-learning, Lagt(h)ing, Landst(h)ing, Lawless, Legislature, Lok Sabha, Long, Lords, Majlis, Merciless, Mongrel, Odelst(h)ing, Political, Rajya Sabha, Reichsrat, Reichstag, Riksdag, Rump, St Stephens, Sanhedrin, Seanad, Seanad Éireann, Sejm, Short, Stannary, States-general, Stirthing, Stormont, Stort(h)ing, The Beehive, Thing, Tynwald, Tynwald (Court), Unicameral, Unlearned, Useless, Vidhan Sabha, Volkskammer, Volksraad, Westminster

Parliamentarian Cabinet, Fairfax, Ireton, Leveller, Member, MP, Roundhead, Whip

Parlour Beauty, Funeral, Ice-cream, Lounge, Massage, Milking, Salon, Snug, Spence

Parnassus Museum, Verse

Parochial Insular

Parody Burlesque, Cod, Lampoon, Mock, Piss-take, Satire, Send-up, Skit, Spoof, Travesty

Parole Pledge, Promise, Trust, Word

Paronychia Agnail, Felon, Whitlow

Paroxysm Fit, Frenzy, Rapture, Spasm, Subintrant, Throe

Parricide Cenci

Parrot Amazon, Cockatoo, Conure, Copy, Echo, Flint, Green leek, Grey, Imitate, Kaka(po), Kea, Lorikeet, Lory, Lovebird, Macaw, Mimic, Nestor, Owl, Parakeet, Paroquet, Poll(y), Popinjay, Psittacine, Quarrion, Repeat, Rosella, Rote, Shell, Stri(n)gops, T(o)uraco

Parrot-bill Glory-pea

Parry Block, Counter, Defend, Dodge, Forestall, Parade, Riposte, Sixte, Tac-au-tac, Thwart, Ward

Parsee Zoroastrian

Parsimonious, Parsimony Aberdonian, Cheese-paring, Mean, Narrow, Near(ness), Niggardly, Stingy, Tight

Parsley Apiol, Cicely, Dog, Kecks, Kex, Persillade, Pot-herb

Parsnip Buttered, Buttery, Dill, Masterwort, Sium, Skirret

Parson Clergyman, Cleric, Holy Joe, Minister, Non juror, Pastor, Priest, Rector, Rev, Sky-pilot, Soul-curer, Yorick

Parsonage Glebe, Manse, Rectory, Vicarage

Part(s), Parting Accession, Aliquot, Antimere, Area, Aught, Bad, Bulk, Bye, Cameo, Character, Chunk, Cog, Component, Constituent, Crack, Cue, Dislink, Diverge, Dole, Element, Episode, Escapement, Farewell, Fascicle, Fork, Fraction, Good, Goodbye, Great, Half, Ill, Imaginary, Instalment, Into, Lathe, Lead, Leave, Leg, Lill, Lilt, Lines, List, Livraison, Member, Meronym, Parcel, Passus, → PIECE, Portion, Primo, Principal, Private, Proportion, Pt, Quit, Quota, Rape, Ratio, Region, Rive, Role, Scena, Scene, Secondo, Section, Sector, Segment, Separate, Serial, Sever, Shade, Share, Shed, Sleave, Sle(i)ded, Small, → SOME, Spare, Split, Stator, Sunder, Synthon, Tithe, Tranche, Twin, Unit, Vaunt, Voice, Walking, Walk on, Wrench

Partake(r) Allottee, Eat, Participate, Share

Parthenogenesis Deuterotoky, Thelytoky

Partial(ity), Partially Biased, Ex-parte, Fan, Favour, Halflins, Imbalance, Incomplete, One-sided, Predilection, Slightly, Unequal, Weakness

Participate, Participant, Participation Audience, Engage, Join, Muck-in, Partake, Share, Traceur

Participle Dangling, Misrelated, Past, Perfect, Present

Particle(s) Alpha, Anion, Antineutron, Antiproton, Atom, Baryon, Beta, Bit, Boson, Charmonium, Corpuscle, Curn, Dander, Delta, Deuteron, Effluvium, Electron, Elementary, Episome, Fermion, Fleck, Fragment, Fundamental, Gauge boson, Gemmule, Globule, Gluon, Grain, Granule, Graviton, Hadron, Heavy, Higgs, Hyperon, Ion, J, Jot, J/psi, Kaon, Lambda, Lemail, Lemel, Lepton, Lipoplast, Liposome, Meson, Micelle, Microsome, Mite, Molecule, Monopole, Mote, Muon, Negatron, Neutralino, Neutrino, Neutron, Nibs, Nobiliary, Omega-minus, Parton, Pentaquark, Photon, Pion, Plasmagene, Platelet, Positon, Positron, Preon, Proton, Psi(on), Quark, Radioactivity, Shives, Shower, Sigma, Singlet, Sinter, Smithereen, Spark, Speck, Strange, Subatom, Submicron, Subnuclear, Tachyon, Tardyon, Tau neutrino, Tauon, Thermion, Tittle, Virion, W, Whit, WIMP, X-hyperon, Z

Parti-coloured Fancy, Motley, Piebald, Pied, Variegated

Particular Choosy, Dainty, → DETAIL, Endemic, Especial, Essential, Express, Fiky, Fog, Fussy, Item, Itself, London fog, Nice, Niffy-naffy, Own, Pea-souper, Peculiar, Pedant, Pernickety, Pet, Point, Prim, Proper, → RESPECT, Special, Specific, Stickler, Strict, Stripe

Partisan Adherent, Axe, Biased, Carlist, Champion, Devotee, Factional, Fan, Irregular, Partial, Provo, Queenite, Sider, Spear, Supporter, Yorkist

Partition(ed) Abjoint, Bail, Barrier, Brattice, Bretasche, Bulkhead, Cloison, Cubicle,

Diaphragm, Dissepiment, Divider, Division, Hallan, Mediastinum, Parpane, Parpen(d), Parpent, Parpoint, Perpend, Perpent, Replum, → **SCREEN**, Scriene, Septum, Skreen, Tabula, Wall, With

Partlet Hen, Overlaid

Partner(ship) Accomplice, Ally, Associate, Bidie-in, Butty, Cahoot(s), Coachfellow, Cohab(itee), Cohabitor, Colleague, Comrade, Confederate, Consort, Copemate, Couple, Dutch, Escort, E-W, Firm, Gigolo, Limited, Mate, N-S, Offsider, Oppo, Pair, Pal, Pard, Rival, Sidekick, Significant other, Silent, Sleeping, Sparring, Spouse, Stablemate, Stand, Symbiosis

▷ **Part of** *may indicate* a hidden word

Partridge Bird, Chik(h)or, Chukar, Chukor, Covey, Flapper, Quail, Red-legged, Tinamou, Ynambu

Party Acid house, Aftershow, Alliance, ANC, Apparat, Assembly, At-home, Ba'ath, Bake, Ball, Band, Barbecue, Bash, Beano, Bee, Bloc, Blowout, Body, Bottle, Buck's, Bunfight, Bust, Caboodle, Camp, Carousal, Carouse, Caucus, Celebration, Clambake, Coach, Cocktail, Colour, Commando, Communist, Concert, Congress, Conservative, Contingent, Cookie-shine, Cooperative, Coterie, Cult, Democratic, Detail, Ding, Discotheque, Do, Drum, Faction, Falange, Federalist, Fest, Fête champêtre, Fête Galante, Fianna Fáil, Fine Gael, Firing, Foy, Function, Funfest, Gala, Galravage, Gang, Garden, Ghibel(l)ine, Green, Greenback, Grumbletonian, Guelf, Guelph, Guilty, Hen, High heels, Hoedown, Hooley, Hootenannie, Hootenanny, Hoot(a)nannie, Hoot(a)nanny, House, Housewarming, Hurricane, Irredentist, Jana Sangh, Jol(lities), Junket, Junto, Kettledrum, Kitchen tea, Klat(s)ch, Knees-up, Kuomintang, L, Labour, Launch, Lawn, Lib, Liberal, Love-in, Low heels, Luau, Mallemaroking, Mollie, Movement, Musicale, National, Necking, Neck-tie, Octobrist, Opposition, Orgy, Peace, People's, Person, Petting, Plaid, Populist, Posse, Progressive, Prohibition, Pyjama, Radical, Rage, Rave, Rave-up, Razzle(-dazzle), Reception, Republican, Reunion, Revel, Ridotto, Roast, Rocking, Roister, Rort, Rout, SDP, Search, Sect, Set, Shindig, Shindy, Shine, Shivoo, Shower, Shower tea, Side, Sinn Fein, Slumber, Smoker, SNP, Soc(ialist), Social, Social Credit, Social Democratic, Socialise, Soirée, Spree, Squad(rone), Squadrone volante, Stag, Symposium, Tailgate, Tea, Teafight, Third, Thrash, Tory, Treat, Ultramontane, Unionist, United, Wafd, Wake, Warehouse, Whig, Whoop-de-do(o), Wine, Wingding, Working

Partygoer Raver, Reveller, Socialite

Party-piece Solo

Parvenu Arriviste, Upstart

Pascal Blaise, Pa, Pressure

Pash Crush, Devotion

Pasha Achmed, Dey, Emir, Ismet

Pass(ed), Passing, Pass on, Past Absit, Ago, Agon, Annie Oakley, Aorist, Approve, Arise, Arlberg, Before, Behind, Bernina, Beyond, Boarding, Bolan, Botte, Brenner, Brief, Burgess, By, Bygone, Caudine Forks, Centre, Cerro Gordo, Chal(l)an, Chilkoot, Chine, Chit(ty), Cicilian Gates, Clear, Col, Cote, Cross, Cursory, Death, Defile, Delate, Demise, Diadron, Die, Disappear, Double, Elapse, Emit, Enact, End, Ensue, Ephemeral, Exceed, Exeat, Faena, Flashback, Fleeting, Foist, Forby, Forgone, Former, Forward, Gap, Gate, Gha(u)t, Glencoe, Glide, Go, Go by, Gorge, Great St Bernard, Gulch, Halse, Hand, Happen, Hause, Hospital, Impart, Impermanent, Interrail, Interval, In transit, Jark, Khyber, Killiecrankie, Kloof, La Cumbre, Lap, Late, Lead, Live, Long syne, Mesmerism, Migrate, Mont Cenis, Moravian Gate, Nek, Nod through, Notch, Nutmeg, Nye, Occur, Oer, OK, Okay,

Oke, Omit, One-time, Overhaul, Overshoot, Overslaugh, Overtake, Pa, Palm, Parade, Participle, Perish, Permeate, Permit, Perpetuate, Poll, Poort, Predicament, Preterit(e), Pretty, Proceed, Propagate, Pun(c)to, Qualify, Railcard, Reach, Reeve, Refer, Relay, Retro, Retroactive, Retrospect, Reverse, Roncesvalles, Safe conduct, St Bernard, St Gotthard, San Bernardino, Sanitation, Scissors, Sea-letter, Senile, Serve, Shangri-la, Shipka, Simplon, Since, Skim, Skip, Skirt, Slap, Sling, Small and early, Snap, Spend, Stab, State, Thermopylae, Thread, Through, Ticket, Time immemorial, Tip, Transient, Transilient, Transitory, Transmit, Transude, Travel, Triptyque, Troop, Uspallata, Veronica, Vet, Visa, Visé, Wall, Wayleave, Weather, While, Wrynose, Yesterday, Yesteryear, Ygoe

Passable, Passible Adequate, Fair, Navigable, Patible, Tolerable

Passage Adit, Airway, Aisle, Alley(way), Alure, Apostrophe, Arcade, Archway, Areaway, Arterial, Atresia, Avenue, Bank, Breezeway, Bridge, Bylane, Cadenza, Caponier(e), Career, Channel, Chute, Citation, Clarino, Clause, Close, Coda, Condie, Conduit, Corridor, Creep, Crossing, Crush, Cundy, Dead-end, Deambulatory, Defile, Drake, Drift, Duct, Eel-fare, Episode, Excerpt, Extract, Fare, Fat, Fistula, Flat, Flight, Flue, Fogou, Gallery, Gangway, Gap, Gat, Gate, Ghat, Ginnel, Gut, Hall, Head, Inlet, Journey, Kyle, Labyrinth, Lane, Lapse, Larynx, Lick, Lientery, Loan, Lobby, Locus, Meatus, Melisma, Meridian, Middle, Mona, Moto perpetuo, Movement, Northeast, Northwest, Para(graph), Path, Pend, Pericope, Phrase, Pore, Portion, Prelude, Prose, Purple, Race, Retournelle, Ride, Ripieno, Rite, Ritornell(o), Road, Rough, Route, Sailing, Screed, Shaft, Shunt, Slap, Slype, Snicket, Solus, Sprue, Strait, Street, Stretta, Stretto, Subway, Sump, Text, Thirl, Thorough(fare), Throat, Tour, Trachea, Trance, Transe, Transit(ion), Travel, Tunnel, Tutti, Undercast, Unseen, Ureter, Voyage, Walkway, Way, Windpipe

▷ **Passage of arms** *may indicate* 'sleeve'

Passé Corny, Dated, Ex, Obsolete

Passenger(s) Cad, Commuter, Fare, Parasite, Payload, Pillion, Rider, Slacker, Steerage, Straphanger, Transit, Traveller, Voyager, Way, Wayfarer

▶ **Possible** *see* **PASSABLE**

Passion(ate), Passionately Anger, Appetite, Ardour, Con calore, Con fuoco, Duende, Fervour, Fire, Flame, Frampold, Fury, Gust, Gutsy, Hate, Heat, Hot, Hunger, Hwyl, Ileac, Iliac, Intense, Ire, Irish, Kama, Love, Lust, Mania, Obsession, Oestrus, Rage, Reverent, Sizzling, Stormy, Sultry, Torrid, Vehement, Violent, Warm, Wax, Wrath, Yen, Zeal

Passion-fruit Water-lemon

Passion play Oberammergau

Passive (stage) Apathetic, Dormant, Inert, Pathic, Patient, Pupa, Stolid, Supine, Yielding

Pass out Faint, Graduate, Swarf, Swarve, Swoon

Passover Agadah, Haggada, Omer, Pesach

Passport Access, Clearance, Congé(e), E, ID, Key, Laissez-passer, Nansen, Navicert, Sea-letter, Visa, Visitor's

Password Code, Countersign, Logon, Nayword, Parole, Sesame, Shibboleth, Sign, Tessera, Watchword

▶ **Past** *see* **PASS**

Pasta Agnolotti, Angel hair, Anelli, Bucatini, Cannelloni, Cappelletti, Cellentani, Conchiglie, Durum, Eliche, Farfal, Farfalle, Farfel, Fedelini, Fettuc(c)ine, Fusilli, Gnocch(ett)i, Lasagna, Lasagne, Linguini, Macaroni, Maccheroncini, Manicotti, Noodles, Orecchietti, Orzo, Penne, Perciatelli, Ravioli, Rigatoni, Ruote, Spaghetti, Spaghettina, Tagliarini, Tagliatelle, Tortelli(ni), Vermicelli, Ziti

Paste, Pasty Almond, Ashen, Batter, Beat, Berbere, Botargo, Boule, Bridie, Cerate, Clobber, Cornish, Dentifrice, Dough, E, Electuary, Fake, Filler, Fondant, Frangipane, Gentleman's Relish®, Glue, Guarana, Hard, Harissa, Knish, Lute, Magma, Marchpane, Marzipan, Masala, Mastic, Meat, Miso, Mountant, Pale, Pallid, Panada, Pâté, Patty, Pearl-essence, Pie, Piroshki, Pirozhki, Poonac, Pulp, Punch, Putty, Rhinestone, Rillettes, Rout, Samosa, Sham, Slip, Slurry, Soft, Spread, Strass, Tahina, Tahini, Tapenade, Taramasalata, Wan, Wasabi

Pastern Hobble, Knee, Tether

Pastiche Cento, Collage, Medley, Patchwork, Potpourri

Pastille Jujube, Lozenge

Pastime Diversion, Game, Hobby, Recreation, Seesaw, Sport

Past master Champion, Expert, Historian, Pro

Past midnight 1 am

Pastor(al) Arcadia, Bucolic, Curé, Eclogue, Endymion, Idyl(l), Minister, Priest, Rector, Rural, Shepherd, Simple

Pastry Apfelstrudel, Baclava, Bakemeat, Baklava, Beignet, Bouchée, Brik, Calzone, Cannoli, Chausson, Cheese straw, Choux, Clafoutis, Coquile, Creamhorn, Cream puff, Croustade, Cruller, Crust, Danish, Dariole, Dough, Eclair, Empanada, Feuilleté, Filo, Flaky, Flan, Frangipane, French, Gougère, Hamantasch, Millefeuille, Phyllo, Pie, Pie-crust, Pirog, Piroshki, Pirozhki, Profiterole, Puff, Quiche, Raised, Rough-puff, Rug(g)elach, Samosa, Shortcrust, Strudel, Tart, Turnover, Vol-au-vent

Pasture Alp, Eadish, Eddish, Feed, Fell, Fodder, Grassland, Graze, Herbage, Kar(r)oo, Lair, Lare, Lay, Lea, Lease, Leasow(e), Leaze, Lee, Ley, Machair, Mead(ow), Moose, Pannage, Pascual, Potrero, Raik, Rake, Soum, Sowm, Tie, Transhume, Tye

▶ **Pasty** *see* **PASTE**

Pat Apt, Bog-trotter, Butter, Chuck, Clap, Dab, Glib, Lump, On cue, Postman, Print, Prompt, Rap, Slap, Tap

Patch(work) Cento, Fleck, Miscellany, Mosaic, Motley, Piecing, Pocket, Sexton, Speculum, Turf

Patch(y) Bed, Bit, Cabbage, Chloasma, Clout, Coalsack, Cobble, Cooper, Court plaster, Cover, Friar, Fudge, → **MEND**, Mosaic, Nicotine, Pasty, Piebald, Piece, Plage, Plaque, Plaster, Pot, Purple, Shinplaster, Shoulder, Solder, Tingle, Tinker, Vamp, Variegated

Pate, Pâté Crown, Paste, Rillettes, Taramasalata, Terrine

Patent(ed) Brevet d'invention, Breveté, Clear, Copyright, Evident, Letters, Licence, License, Obvious, Overt, Plain, Rolls

Pater(nity) Father, Filiation, Walter

Paterfamilias Coarb, Master

Path(way) Aisle, Allée, Alley, Arc, Berm, Berme, Boreen, Borstal(l), Bridle, Bridleway, Byroad, Causeway, Causey, Clickstream, Corridor, Course, Eclipse, Embden-Meyerhof, Flare, Flight, Garden, Gate, Gennel, Ginnel, Glide, Lane, Ley, Lichwake, Lichway, Locus, Lykewake, Mean-free, Metabolic, Orbit, Packway, Pad, Parabola, Peritrack, Primrose, Ride, Ridgeway, Route, Run, Runway, Sidewalk, Slipway, Spurway, Stie, Sty(e), Swath(e), Taxiway, Tow, Track, Trail, Trajectory, Trod, Walkway, → **WAY**, Xystus

Pathan Pakhto, Pakhtu, Pashto, Pashtu, Pushto(o), Pushtu

Pathetic(ally) Abysmal, Doloroso, Drip, Forlorn, Piss-poor, Piteous, Poignant, Sad, Saddo, Schnook, Touching

Pathfinder Compass, Explorer, Guide, Pioneer, Scout

Pathogen Virus

Pathological Diseased, Gangrene, Morbid, Septic

Pathos Bathos, Pity, Sadness, Sob-stuff

Patience Calm, Endurance, Forbearance, Fortitude, Indulgence, Klondike, Klondyke, Longanimity, Monument, Operetta, Solitaire, Stoicism, Virtue

Patient(s) Calm, Case, Clinic, Forbearing, Grisel(da), Grisilda, Invalid, Job, Long-suffering, Passive, Private, Resigned, Stoic, Subject, Walking case, Ward

Patois Argot, Cant, Dialect, Gumbo, Jargon, Jive, Lingo, Scouse

Patriarch Aaron, Abraham, Abuna, Asher, Catholicos, Ecumenical, Elder, Enoch, Isaac, Job, Levi, Maron, Methuselah, Nestor, Noah, Pope, Simeon, Venerable

Patrician Aristocrat, Noble, Senator

Patrick Mick, Paddy, Pat, Spens

Patrimony Ancestry, Estate, Heritage

Patriot(ic), Patriotism Cavour, Chauvinist, DAR, Emmet, Flag-waving, Flamingant, Garibaldi, Hereward, Irredentist, Jingoism, Loyalist, Maquis, Nationalist, Revere, Tell, Zionist

Patrol Armilla, Guard, Outguard, Picket, Piquet, Prowl-car, Reconnaissance, Round, Scout, Sentinel, Sentry-go, Shark, Shore, Turm

Patron(age), Patroness, Patronise(d), Patronising Advowson, Aegis, Auspices, Benefactor, Business, Champion, Client, Customer, Donator, Egis, Fautor, Lady Bountiful, Maecenas, Nepotic, Protector, Protégé, Provider, Shopper, → **SPONSOR**, Stoop, Stoup

Patsy Dupe, Hendren, Scapegoat, Stooge

Patter Backchat, Cant, Jargon, Lingo, Mag, Pitch, Rap, S(c)htick, Schtik, Spiel

Pattern(ed) Agouti, Agouty, Aguti, Argyle, Bird's eye, Blueprint, Branchwork, Broché, Candy stripe, Check, Chequer, Chiné, Chladni figure, Clock, Design, Dévoré, Diaper, Diffraction, Dog's tooth, Draft, Egg and dart, Epitome, Example, Exemplar, Faconné, Fiddle, Figuration, Format, Fractal, Fret, Gestalt, Grain, Grammadion, Greek key, Greque, Herringbone, Holding, Hound's tooth, Intarsia, Intonation, Koru, Kowhaiwhai, Matel(l)asse, Matrix, Meander, → **MODEL**, Moire, Moko, Mosaic, Norm, Paisley, Paradigm, Paragon, Pinstripe, Plan, Polka-dot, Pompadour, Precedent, Prototype, Queenstitch, Quincunx, Radiation, Raster, Ribbing, Scansion, Shawl, Stencil, Symmetry, Syndrome, Tala, Talea, Tangram, Tarsia, Tattersall, Template, Tessella, Tessera, Tracery, Traffic, Tread, Type, Willow

Patty Bouchée, Fishcake, Pie

Paul Jones, Oom, Pry, Revere, Robeson, S, St

Pauline Day-boy, Perils

Paunch Belly, Corporation, Gut, Kite, Kyte, Pod, Rumen, Tripe, Tum

Pauper Bankrupt, Beggar, Have-not, Mendicant, Penniless

Pause Break, Breakpoint, Breather, Caesura, Cessation, Cesura, Comma, Desist, Er, Fermata, Hesitate, Hiatus, Interkinesis, Interregnum, Interval, Limma, Lull, Pitstop, Pregnant, → **RESPITE**, Rest, Selah, Stop, Tacet, Time out

Pave(d), Pavement, Paving Causeway, Causey, Clint, Cobble, Corsey, Crazy, Desert, Diaper, Flagging, Granolith, Limestone, Moving, Path, Plainstanes, Plainstones, Roadside, Set(t), Sidewalk, Tessellate, Travolator, Trottoir

Pavilion Chinese, Ear, Gazebo, Jingling Johnny, Kiosk, Marquee, Tent

Paw Kangaroo, Maul, Mitt, Pad, Pat, Pud, Pug, Pussyfoot

Pawky Dry, Humorous, Shrewd, Sly

Pawn(shop), Pawnbroker, Pawnee Agent, Betel, Chessman, Counter, Derby, Dip, Gage, Gallery, Hanging, Hock, Hockshop, Hostage, Isolated, Leaving-shop, Lumber, Lumberer, Moneylender, Monte-de-piété, Monti di pietà, Nunky, Pan, Passed, Peacock, Piece, Pignerate, Pignorate, Pledge, Pledgee, Pop, Security,

Sheeny, Siri, Spout, Stalking horse, Three balls, Tiddleywink, Tool, Tribulation, Uncle, Usurer, Wadset, Weed

Pax Peace, Truce

Pay(master), Payment, Paid, Pay off, Pay out Aby, Advertise, Agterskot, Amortise, Annat, Annuity, Ante, Arles, Atone, Balloon, Basic, Batta, Blench, Bonus, Bukshee, Bukshi, Cain, Cashier, Cens, Cheque, COD, Commute, Compensate, Consideration, Damage, Defray, Disburse, Discharge, Dividend, Down, Dub, E, Emolument, Endow, Equalisation, Eric, Escot, Farm, Fee, Feu-duty, Finance, Foot, Fork out, Fund, Gale, Gate, Give, Grassum, Grave, Greenmail, Guarantee, Han(d)sel, Hazard, Hire, Hoot(oo), HP, Imburse, Intown multure, Kain, Kickback, Leads and lags, Lobola, Lobolo, Mail, Meet, Merchet, Métayage, Mise, Modus, Mortuary, Overtime, Payola, Pension, Pittance, Pony, Posho, Prebendal, Premium, Primage, Pro, Pro forma, Progress, Purser, Quarterage, Quit(-rent), Ransom, Reap-silver, Redundancy, Refund, Remittance, Remuneration, Rent, Requite, Residual, Respects, Royalty, Salary, Satisfaction, Scot, Screw, Scutage, Settle, Severance, Shell, Shell out, Shot, Sick, Sink, Sold(e), Soul-scat, Soul-scot, Soul-shot, → **SPEND**, Square, Stipend, Strike, Stump, Sub, Subscribe, Sweetener, Table, Take-home, Tar, Tender, Token, Tommy, Transfer, Treasure, Treat, Tribute, Truck, Unpurse, Usance, Veer, Wage, Wardcorn, X-factor

PC Constable, Right on

PE Aerobics, Gym

Pea(s) Carling, Chaparral, Chickling, Desert, D(h)al, Dholl, Egyptian, Garbanzo, Goober, Hastings, Legume, Mangetout, Marrow, Marrowfat, Passiform, Petit pois, Pigeon, Pulse, Rounceval, Split, String, Sturt's desert, Sugar, Sugar snap

Peace(ful), Peaceable, Peace-keeper, Peace organisation, Peace symbol Ahimsa, Antiwar, Ataraxy, Calm, Ease, Frieda, Frith, Halcyon, Hush, Interceder, Irenic(on), King's, Lee, Lull, Nirvana, Olive, Order, Pacific, Pax, Pbuh, Queen's, Quiet, Repose, Rest, Roskilde, Salem, Serene, Sh, Shalom, Siegfried, Siesta, Silence, Solomon, Soothing, Still, Tranquil, Truce, UN

Peacemaker ACAS, Arbitrator, Conciliator, Mediator, Trouble-shooter, Wilfred

Peach Blab, Cling, Clingstone, Dish, Dob, Freestone, Humdinger, Inform, Laetrile, Malakatoone, Melba, Melocoto(o)n, Nectarine, Oner, Quandang, Shop, Sing, Sneak, Split, Squeak, Stunner, Tattle, Tell, Victorine

Peachum Polly

Peacock Coxcomb, Dandy, Fop, Junonian, Muster, Paiock(e), Pajock(e), Pavo(ne), Pawn, Payock(e), Pown, Sashay

Peak(y) Acme, Aiguille, Alp, Ancohuma, Apex, Ben, Cap, Climax, Comble, Communism, Cone, Crag, Crest, Darien, Drawn, Eiger, Flower, Gable, Gannett, Horn, Matterhorn, Meridian, Mons, → **MOUNTAIN**, Nevis, Nib, Nunatak, Optimum, Pale, Petermann, Pikes, Pin, Pinnacle, Piton, Pyramidal, Rainier, Sallow, Snowdon, Spire, Stalin, Sukarno, Top, Tor, Visor, Widow's, Zenith

Peal Carillon, Chime, Clap, Toll, Triple

Peanut(s) Arnut, Chickenfeed, Goober, Groundnut, Monkey-nut, Pittance

Pear Aguacate, Alligator, Anchovy, Anjou, Asian, Asparagus, Avocado, Bartlett, Bergamot, Beurré, Blanquet, Carmelite, Catherine, Choke, Colmar, Comice, Conference, Cuisse-madame, Dutch admiral, Jargonelle, Muscadel, Muscatel, Musk, Nashi, Neli(e)s, Nelis, Perry, Poperin, Poppering, Poprin, Prickly, Pyrus, Queez-maddam, Seckel, Seckle, Taylor's Gold, Warden, William

Pearl(s), Pearly Barocco, Barock, Baroque, Cultured, False, Gem, Imitated, Jewel, Mabe, Margaret, Margaric, Nacrous, Olivet, Onion, Orient, Prize, Rope, Seed, Simulated, String, Sulphur, Unio(n)

Pear-shaped Obconic, Pyriform

Peasant Bogtrotter, Bonhomme, Boor, Bumpkin, Chouan, Churl, Clodhopper, Contadino, Cossack, Cottar, Cott(i)er, Fellah(s), Fellahin, Hick, Jungli, Kern(e), Kisan, Kulak, M(o)ujik, Muzhik, Quashi(e), Raiyat, Roturier, Rustic, Ryot, Swain, Tyrolean, Volost, Whiteboy, Yokel

Pea-shaped Pisiform

Peat(y) Moss-litter, Sod, Turbary, Turbinacious, Turf, Yarfa, Yarpha

Pebble(s), Pebbly Banket, Bibble, Calculus, Cobblestone, Dornick, Dreikanter, Gallet, Gooley, Gravel, Psephism, Pumie, Pumy, Scotch, Scree, Shingle, Ventifact

Peccadillo Mischief, Misdemeanour, Offence

Peccary Mexican hog, Tayassuid

Peck Bill, Bushel, Dab, Forpet, Forpit, Gregory, Job, Kiss, Lip, Lippie, Nibble, Pickle, Tap

Pecksniff Charity

▷ **Peculiar** *may indicate* an anagram

Peculiar(ity) Appropriate, Characteristic, Distinct, Eccentric, Especial, Exclusive, Ferly, Funny, Idiosyncratic, Kink, Kooky, Odd, Own, Proper, Queer, Quirk, Royal, Singular, → **SPECIAL**, Specific, Strange, Unusual

Pedagogue Academic, B.Ed, Teacher

Pedal Accelerator, Bike, Brake, Chorus, Clutch, Cycle, Damper, Lever, P, Rat-trap, Soft, Sostenuto, Sustaining, Treadle, Treddle

Pedal-coupler Tirasse

Pedant(ic) Casaubon, Chop logic, Dogmatic, Don, Dryasdust, Elucubrate, Inkhorn, Intellectual, Jobsworth, Lucubrate, Nit-picking, Pedagogue, Pernickety, Pompous, Precisian, Quibbler, Scholastic, Sesquipedalian, Stickler

Peddle, Pedlar Bodger, Boxwallah, Camelot, Chapman, Cheapjack, Colporteur, Drummer, Duffer, Hawk, Huckster, Jagger, Packman, Pedder, Pether, Sell, Smouch, Smouse(r), Sutler, Tallyman, Tink(er), Yagger

▷ **Peddling** *may indicate* an anagram

Pedestal Acroter(ion), Axle guard, Dado, Footstool, Pillar, Support

Pedestrian Banal, Commonplace, Dull, Earth-bound, Ganger, Hack, Hike, Itinerant, Jaywalker, Laborious, Mediocre, Mundane, Trite, Voetganger, Walker

Pedigree(s) Ancestry, Blood, Breeding, Descent, Family tree, Genealogy, House, Lineage, Phylogeny, Stemma(ta), Stirp(s), Studbook, Thoroughbred, Whakapapa

Pediment Fronton

Peduncle Scape, Stalk

Peek Eye, Glance, Glimpse, Peep

Peel(er) Bark, Bobby, Candied, Decorticate, Desquamate, Exfoliate, Flype, Orange, Pare, PC, Pill, Rind, Rine, Rumbler, Scale, Shell, Skin, → **STRIP**, Tirr, Zest

▷ **Peeled** *may indicate* outside letters to be removed from a word

Peep(er), Peephole Cheep, Cook, Crow, Glance, Gledge, Judas, Keek, Kook, Lamp, Nose, Peek, Pink, Pry, Spy, Squeak, Squint, Stime, Styme, Voyeur

Peer(age), Peers Archduke, Aristocrat, Backwoodsman, Baron(et), Burke, Coeval, Daimio, Doucepere, Douzeper(s), Duke, Earl, Egal, Elevation, Equal, Eyeball, Gynt, Life, Lord, Match, Noble, Paladin, Peregal, Pink, Rank, Representative, Scry, Spiritual, Squint, Stare, Stime, Styme, Temporal, Toot, Tweer, Twire

Peerless Matchless, Nonpareil, Supreme

Peevish(ness) Capernoited, Captious, Crabby, Cross, Doddy, Frabbit, Frampal, Frampold, Franzy, Fretful, Girner, Hipped, Lienal, Meldrew, Moody, Nattered, Pet, Petulant, Pindling, Protervity, Querulous, Shirty, Sour, Spleen, Teachie, Testy, Te(t)chy

Peewit Lapwing, Peewee

Peg Cheville, Cleat, Clothespin, Cotter-pin, Crawling, Die, Drift-pin, Fix, Freeze, Knag, Leg, Margaret, Nail, Nog, Odontoid, Pin, Piton, Snort, Spigot, Spile, Square, Stengah, Stinger, Support, Tap, Tee, Thole, Tholepin, Thowel, Toggle, Tot, Tuning, Vent, Woffington

Pegboard Solitaire

Pelagic Deep-sea, Marine, Oceanic

Pelf Lucre, Mammon, Money, Notes, Riches

Pelican Alcatras, Bird, Crossing, Golden Hind, LA, Louisiana, Steganopode

Pellagra Maidism

Pellet Birdshot, Bolus, Buckshot, Bullet, Pill, Pithball, Prill, Slug

Pelmet Valance

Pelt Assail, Clod, Fleece, Fur, Hail, Hide, Hie, Lam, Pepper, Random, Sealskin, Shower, Skin, Squail, Stone

Peltast Soldier, Targeteer

Pelvis Ilium, Pubis, Renal

Pen Author, Ballpoint, Bamboo, Bic®, Biro®, Cage, Calamus, Can, Cartridge, Catching, Confine, Coop, Corral, Crawl, Crow-quill, Cru(i)ve, Cub, Cyclostyle, Dabber, Data, Enclosure, Fank, Farm, Felt(-tipped), Fold, Fountain, Gaol, Gladius, Hen, Highlighter, Hoosegow, J, → **JAIL**, Keddah, Kraal, Lair, Laser, Light, Marker, Mew, Mure, Music, Piggery, Poison, Pound, Quill(-nib), Ree, Reed, Ring, Rollerball, Scribe, Stell, Stie, Stir, Sty(e), Stylet, Stylo, Stylograph, Stylus, Submarine, Swan, Sweatbox, Tank, Weir, Write, → **WRITER**

▷ **Pen** *may indicate* a writer

Penal(ize) Cost, Fine, Gate, Handicap, Huff, Mulct, Punitive, Servitude

Penalty Abye, Amende, Card, Cost, Death, Eric, Fine, Fixed, Forfeit, Han(d)sel, Huff, Keltie, Kelty, Pain, Price, Punishment, Rubicon, Sanction, Ticket, Wide

Penance Atonement, Expiation, Shrift

Penates Lares

Pence D, P, Peter's

Penchant Predilection

Pencil Beam, Ca(l)m, Caum, Charcoal, Chinagraph®, Crayon, Draft, Draw, Eyebrow, Fusain, Grease, Harmonic, Ink, Keelivine, Keelyvine, Lead, Outline, Propelling, Slate, Stump, Styptic, Tortillon

Pendant Albert, Chandelier, Drop, Girandole, Laval(l)ière, Medallion, Necklace, Poffle, Sautoir, Stalactite

Pending Imminent, In fieri, Unresolved, Until

Pendragon Uther

Pendule Poffle

Pendulous, Pendulum Compensation, Dewlap, Foucault's, Metronome, Noddy, One-way, Seconds, Swing, Wavering

Penetrate, Penetrating, Penetration Acumen, Acuminate, Bite, Bore, Bridgehead, Cut, Enpierce, Enter, Imbue, Impale, Incisive, Indent, Indepth, Infiltrate, Insight, Into, Intrant, Lance, Permeate, Pierce, Probe, Sagacious, Shear, Strike, Thrust, Touch, X-ray

Penguin Adélie, Aeroplane, Anana, Auk, Blue, Emperor, Fairy, Gentoo, King, Korora, Little, Macaroni, Rock-hopper

Penicillin Cloxacillon, Fleming

Peninsula Alaska, Alte, Antarctic, Arabian, Ards, Arm, Avalon, Baja California, Balkan, Banks, Bataan, Black Isle, Boothia, Brittany, Cape, Cape Blanco, Cape Bon, Cape Cod, Cape Verde, Chalcidice, Chersonese, Chukchi, Coromandel,

Cowal, Crimea, Deccan, Delmarva, East Cape, Eyre, Florida, Freycinet, Furness, Fylde, Gallipoli, Galloway, Gaspé, Gower, Graham Land, Hispania, Iberia(n), Indo-China, Istria, Jutland, Kamchatka, Kathiawar, Kerch, Kintyre, Kola, Korea, Kowloon, Labrador, Leizhou, Liaodong, Liaotung, Lleyn, Luichow, Malay, Malaysia, Melville, Neck, Northland, Nova Scotia, Olympic, Otago, Palmer, Peloponnese, Portland, Promontory, Quiberon, Rhinns of Galloway, Scandinavian, Seward, Sinai, Spit, Spur, S.W. Malay, Taimyr, Tasman, Taymyr, The Lizard, Upper, Wilson's Promontory, Wirral, Yorke, Yucatan

Penis Archie, Chopper, Cock, Cor(e)y, Dick, Dildo(e), Dipstick, Dong, Ferret, Giggle(stick), Horn, Jack, John Thomas, Knob, Langer, Member, Membrum virile, Mojo, Organ, Pecker, Peezle, Percy, Peter, Phallus, Pillicock, Pintle, Pisser, Pizzle, Plonker, Prick, Putz, Rod, Roger, Schlong, Schmock, Shaft, Shmock, Shmuck, Stiffy, Tallywhacker, Tockley, Todger, Tonk, Tool, Weenie, Weeny, W(h)ang, Willie, Willy, Winkle, Yard, Zeppelin

Penitent(iary) Calaboose, Cilice, Clink, Contrite, Gaol, Jail, Jug, Prison, Repenter, Rosary, Stir

Pennant, Pennon Banner, Broad, Bunting, Fane, Flag, Guidon, Streamer

Penniless Bankrupt, Boracic, Broke, Bust, Impecunious, Poor, Skint, Strapped

Penny Bean, Cartwheel, Cent, Copper, D, Dreadful, Gild, Honest, New, P, Pretty, Sen, Sou, Sterling, Stiver, Win(n), Wing

Penny-farthing Bicycle, Ordinary

Pension(er) Allowance, Ann(at), Annuitant, Board, Chelsea, Cod, Cor(r)ody, Gasthaus, Gratuity, Guest-house, Half-board, Hotel, Non-contributory, Occupational, Old-age, Payment, Personal, Retire(e), Serps, SIPP, Stakeholder, Stipend, Superannuation

Pensive Dreamy, Moody, Musing, Thoughtful, Triste, Wistful

Pentameter Elegiac, Iambic

Pentateuch T(h)orah

Pentecost Whit(sun)

Penthouse Cat, Lean-to, Roof, Skyhome

Peon Peasant, Serf, Slave, Ticca

Peony Moutan

People Beings, Bods, Body, Chosen, Commonalty, Commons, Demos, Ecology, Enchorial, Flower, Folk, Fraim, Gens, Grass roots, Guild, Human, Inca, Inhabit, Janata, Kin, Land, Lapith, Lay, Man(kind), Men, Mob, Nair, Nation(s), Nayar, One, Peculiar, Personalities, Phalange, Populace, Proletariat(e), Public, Punters, Quorum, Race, September, Settle, Society, Souls, They, Tribe, Tuath, Volk

Pep Buck, Dash, Enliven, Gism, Go, Jism, Jissom, Stamina, Verve, Vim

Pepper Alligator, All-spice, Ancho, Ava, Betel, Bird, Black, Caper, Capsicum, Cayenne, Cherry, Chilli, Chipotle, Condiment, Cubeb, Devil, Dittander, Dittany, Ethiopian, Green, Guinea, Habanero, Jalapeno, Jamaica, Kava, Long, Malaguetta, Matico, Negro, Paprika, Pelt, Pim(i)ento, Piper, Piperine, Piquillo, Red, Riddle, Sambal, Scotch bonnet, Spice, Sprinkle, Sweet, Szechwan, Tabasco®, Wall, Water, White, Yaqona, Yellow

Peppercorn Nominal, → **PAYMENT**, → **RENT**

Peppermint Bull's Eye, Humbug, Pandrop

Peptide Cecropin, Substance P

Per By, Each, Through

Perambulate, Perambulator Buggy, Expatiate, Pedestrian, Pram, Stroller, Wagon, Walker

Perceive, Perception, Perceptive Acumen, Alert, Anschauung, Apprehend,

Astute, Clairvoyance, Clear-eyed, Cryptaesthetic, Descry, Dianoia, Discern, Divine, ESP, Extrasensory, Feel, Insight, Intelligence, Intuit(ion), Kinaesthesia, Noesis, Notice, Observe, Pan(a)esthesia, Remark, → **SEE**, Sense, Sensitive, Sentience, Shrewd, Sixth sense, Subliminal, Tact, Taste, Tel(a)esthesia, Telegnosis, Understanding

Percentage Agio, Commission, Contango, Cut, Mark-up, Proportion, Royalty, Scalage, Share, Vigorish

Perch(ing) Aerie, Alight, Anabis, Bass, Comber, Eyrie, Fish, Fogash, Gaper, Insessorial, Lug, Miserere, Ocean, Perca, Pole, Roost, Ruff(e), Seat, Serranid, → **SIT**, Wall-eye, Zingel

Percolate, Percolation Filter, Infiltrate, Leach, Lixiviate, Ooze, Osmosis, Permeate, Seep, Sipe, Soak, Strain, Sype

Percussion (cap) Amorce, Battery, Chinese temple block, Idiophone, Impact, Knee, Knock, Spoons, Thump, Timbrel, Traps

Percy Hotspur, Shelley

Perdition Ades, Hades

Peremptory Absolute, Decisive, Haughty, Imperative, Imperious

Perennial Continual, Enduring, Flower, Livelong, Perpetual, Recurrent

Perfect(ly), Perfection(ist) Absolute, Accomplish, Accurate, Acme, Apple-pie, Bloom, Complete, Consummation, Cross-question, Dead, Develop, Fare-thee-well, Finish, Flawless, Fulfil, Full, Holy, Ideal(ist), Impeccable, Intact, It, Mint, Par, Paradisal, Paragon, Past, Pat, Peace, Pedant, Point-device, Practice, Present, Pure, Quintessential, Refine, Salome, Siddha, Soma, Sound, Spot-on, Stainless, Sublime, The nines, Thorough, Three-pricker, To a t(ee), Unblemished, Unqualified, Utopian, Utter, Whole, Witeless

Perfidy Betrayal, Falsehood, Treachery, Treason

Perforate(d), Perforation, Perforator Cribrate, Cribrose, Drill, Eyelet, Hole, → **PIERCE**, Prick, Punch, Puncture, Riddle, Trephine, Trocar

Perforce Necessarily, Needs

Perform(ed), Performer, Performing Achieve, Act(or), Appear, Artist(e), Barnstorming, Basoche, Busk, Carry out, Chansonnier, Comedian, Contortionist, Discharge, Do, Duo, Enact, Entertainer, Execute, Exert, Exhibit, Fancy Dan, Fire-eater, Fulfil, Function, Geek, Hand, Headliner, Hersall, Hot dog, Houdini, Implement, Interlocutor, Majorette, Make, Moke, Nonet, Octet, Officiate, On, Perpetrate, Player, Praxis, Quartet(te), Quintet, Recite, Render, Ripieno, Septet, Sextet, Strongman, Supererogate, Sword-swallower, Throw, Trio, Vaudevillian, Virtuoso, Wire-dancer

Performance Accomplishment, Achievement, Act, Auto, Blinder, Bravura, Broadcast, Command, Concert, Dare, Deed, Demonstration, Discharge, Division, Double act, Floorshow, Entr'acte, Execution, Gas, Gig, Hierurgy, Holdover, Hootenanny, House, Master-class, Masterstroke, Matinee, Monodrama, One-night stand, Operation, Perpetration, Practice, Première, Production, Programme, Recital, Rehearsal, Rendering, Rendition, Repeat, Repertoire, Rigmarole, Scene, Show, Showing, Sneak preview, Solo, Specific, Spectacle, Stunt, Theatricals, Track record, Turn

Perfume (box) Abir, Ambergris, Angel water, Aroma, Attar, Bergamot, Cassolette, Chypre, Civet, Cologne, C(o)umarin, Eau de cologne, Eau de toilette, Enfleurage, Essence, Fragrance, Frangipani, Incense, Ionone, Lavender (water), Linalool, Millefleurs, Muscone, Muskone, Myrrh, Nose, Opopanax, Orris, Orrisroot, Otto, Patchouli, Patchouly, Pomander, Potpourri, Redolence, → **SCENT**, Smellies, Terpineol, Toilet water

Perfunctory Apathetic, Careless, Cursory, Indifferent, Token
Perhaps A(i)blins, Belike, Haply, Happen, May(be), Peradventure, Percase,
Perchance, Possibly, Relative, Say, Yibbles
▷ **Perhaps** *may indicate* an anagram
Perigee Apsis, Epigeum
Peril(ous) → **DANGER**, Hazard, Jeopardy, Precarious, Risk, Threat, Yellow
Perimeter Boundary, Circuit, Circumference, Limits
Period(ic), Periodical Abbevillian, Acheulian, AD, Age, Alcher(ing)a, Andropause,
Annual, Archaean, Aurignacian, Azilian, Base, Cal(l)ippic, Cambrian,
Carboniferous, Catamenia, Chalcolithic, Chukka, Chukker, Climacteric, Comic,
Cooling off, Cretaceous, Critical, Curse, Cycle, Day, Decad(e), Devonian, Diapause,
Digest, Dot, Down, Dreamtime, → **DURATION**, Economist, Eocene, Epoch, Etesian,
Excerpt, Floruit, Full-stop, Glacial, Grace, Haute époque, Hercynian, Holocene,
Horal, Incubation, Innings, Interregnum, Journal, Jurassic, Kalpa, Latency,
Latent, Lesson, Liassic, Limit, Listener, Mag, Meantime, Meanwhile, Menopause,
Menses, Mesolithic, Mesozoic, Middle Kingdom, Miocene, Monthly, Moratorium,
Neocomian, Neolithic, Neozoic, New Yorker, Octave, Olde-worlde, Oligocene,
Ordovician, Organ, Palaeogene, Paleolithic, Paper, Payback, Permian, Phanerozoic,
Phase, Phoenix, Pleistocene, Pliocene, Pre-Cambrian, Proterozoic, Protohistory,
Publication, Punch, Quarter, Quarternary, Rambler, Recurrent, Reformation,
Refractory, Regency, Rent, Review, Riss, Romantic, Safe, Saros, Season, Session,
Sidereal, Silurian, Solutrean, Solutrian, Span, Spasm, Spectator, Spell, Stage,
Stop, Strand, Stretch, Synodic, Tatter, Term, Tertiary, Tract, Trecento, Triassic,
Trimester, Usance, Window
Peripatetic Gadabout, Itinerant, Promenader, Travelling
Periphery Ambit, Bounds, Exurb, Fringe, Outskirts, Surface
Periscope Eye(-stalk)
Perish(able), Perished, Perishing Brittle, → **DIE**, End, Ephemeral, Expire, Fade,
Forfair, Fungibles, Icy, Tine, Tint, Transitory, Tyne, Vanish
Periwinkle Apocynum, Blue, Myrtle
Perjure(d) Forswear, Lie, Mansworn
Perk(s), Perky Brighten, Chipper, Freebie, Freshen, Jaunty, LV, Perquisite
Perm(anent) Abiding, Durable, Enduring, Eternal, Everlasting, Fixed, For keeps,
Full-time, Indelible, → **LASTING**, Marcel, Stable, Standing, Stative, Wave
Permeable, Permeability, Permeate Infiltrate, Leaven, Magnetic, Osmosis,
Penetrate, Pervade, Poromeric, Porous, Seep, Transfuse
Permission, Permit(ted) Allow, Authorise, By-your-leave, Carnet, Chop, Clearance,
Congé(e), Consent, Copyright, Enable, Give, Grant, Indult, Lacet, Laisser-passer,
Latitude, Leave, Legal, Let, Liberty, Licence, License, Lief, Luit, Nihil obstat, Ok(e),
Pace, Pass, Placet, Planning, Power, Pratique, Privilege, Remedy, Safe-conduct,
Sanction, Stamp-note, Suffer, Ticket, Triptyque, Visa, Vouchsafe, Way-leave, Wear
Pernicious Damnable, Evil, Harmful, Lethal, Noisome, Pestilent, Wicked
Pernickety Fikish, Niggly
Peroration Pirlicue, Purlicue
Peroxide Bleach, Blonde, Colcothar
Perpendicular Aplomb, Apothem, Atrip, Cathetus, Erect, Normal, Orthogonal,
Plumb, Sheer, Sine, → **UPRIGHT**, Vertical
Perpetrate Commit, Effect, Execute
Perpetual Constant, Eternal, Incessant, Sempiternal
Perplex(ed), Perplexity Anan, Baffle, Bamboozle, Beset, Bewilder, Bother, Buffalo,
Bumbaze, Cap, Confound, Confuse, Embarrass, Feague, Floor, Flummox, Knotty,

Meander, Mystify, Nonplus, Out, Pother, Pudder, Puzzle, Quizzical, Stump, Tangle, Tickle, Tostication

Perquisite Ap(p)anage, Emolument, Extra, Gratuity, → **PERK**, Tip

Perrier Stoner

Perry Mason

Persecute, Persecution Afflict, Annoy, Badger, Crucify, Dragon(n)ades, Harass, Haze, Intolerant, McCarthyism, Oppress, Pogrom, Ride, Torment, Torture, Witch hunt

Persevere, Perseverance Assiduity, Continue, Fortitude, Insist, Jusqu'auboutisme, Patience, Persist, Plug, Stamina, Steadfastness, Stick, Stickability, Tenacity

Persia(n) Achaemenid, Babee, Babi, Bahai, Cyrus, Dari, Farsi, Iran(ian), Mazdean, Mede, Middle, Pahlavi, Parasang, Parsee, Pehlevi, Pushtu, Samanid, Sassanid, Sohrab, Xerxes, Zoroaster

Persimmon Kaki, Sharon fruit

Persist(ence), Persistent Adhere, Assiduity, Chronic, Continual, Diligent, Doggedness, Endure, Importunate, Labour, Longeval, Lusting, Nag, Persevere, Press, Sedulous, Sneaking, Stick, Tenacity, Urgent

Person(s), Personal(ly) Alter, Artificial, Aymaran, Being, Bird, Bod(y), Chai, Chal, Character, Chav, Chi, Cookie, Displaced, Entity, Everyman, Figure, First, Fish, Flesh, Ga(u)dgie, Gadje, Gauje, Gut, Head, Human, Individual, In propria persona, Nabs, Natural, Nibs, One, Own, Party, Passer-by, Pod, Private, Quidam, Second, Selfhood, Skate, Sod, Soul, Specimen, Tales, Third, Walla(h), Wight

Personage, Personality Anima, Celeb(rity), Character, Charisma, Dignitary, Ego, Grandee, Identity, Jekyll and Hyde, Megastar, Multiple, Noble, Notability, Panjandrum, Presence, Psychopath, Sama, Schizoid, Seity, Sel, Self, Sell, Somatotonia, Split, Star, Tycoon, Viscerotonia

Personified, Personification, Personify Embody, Incarnate, Prosopop(o)eia, Represent

Personnel Employees, Hands, Liveware, Manpower, Staff

Perspective Aerial, Atmosphere, Attitude, Distance, Linear, Point of view, Proportion, Slant, Take, View, Vista

Perspicacious Astute, Clear-sighted, Discerning, Keen, Shrewd

Perspiration, Perspire, Perspiring Aglow, Forswatt, Glow, Hidrosis, Sudor, Suint, Sweat, Swelter

Persuade(d), Persuasion, Persuasive Cajole, Carrot and stick, Coax, Cogent, Conviction, Convince, Disarm, Eloquent, Faith, Feel, Forcible, Geed, Get, Induce, Inveigle, Lead on, Move, Plausible, → **PREVAIL**, Religion, Smooth-talking, Soft sell, Suborn, Sweet-talk, Truckled, Wheedle, Winning

Pert(ness) Bold, Brisk, Cocky, Dicacity, Flippant, Forward, Fresh, Impertinent, Insolent, Jackanapes, Minx, Quean, Saucy, Tossy

Pertain Apply, Belong, Concern, Effeir, Effere, Relate, Touch

Pertinacious Dogged, Obstinate, Persistent, Stickler, Stubborn

Pertinent Ad rem, Apropos, Apt, Fit, Germane, Relevant, Timely

Perturb(ation) Aerate, Confuse, Dismay, Disturb, Dither, State, Trouble, Upset, Worry

Peru(vian) Inca, PE, Quechua(n), Quichua(n)

Peruse, Perusal Examine, Inspect, Read, Scan, Scrutiny, → **STUDY**

Pervade, Pervasion, Pervasive(ness) Diffuse, Drench, Immanence, Permeate, Saturate

Perverse, Perversion, Pervert(ed), Perversity Aberrant, Abnormal, Algolagnia, Awkward, Awry, Balky, Cam(stairy), Camsteary, Camsteerie, Cantankerous, → **CONTRARY**, Corrupt, Crabbed, Cussed, Deviate, Distort, Donsie, False, Froward,

Gee, Kam(me), Kinky, Licentious, Misinterpret, Misuse, Nonce, Paraphilia, Protervity, Refractory, Sadist, Sicko, Stubborn, Thrawn, Traduce, Unnatural, Untoward, Uranism, Warp(ed), Wayward, Wilful, Wrest, Wry

▷ **Perverted** *may indicate* an anagram

Pessimism, Pessimist(ic) Alarmist, Bear, Cassandra, Crapehanger, Crepehanger, Cynic, Defeatist, Dismal Jimmy, Doom merchant, Doomwatch, Doomy, Doubter, Downbeat, Fatalist, Glumbum, Jeremiah, Killjoy, Negative

Pest(er) Aggravate, Badger, Bedbug, Blight, Bot, → **BOTHER**, Brat, Breese, Bug, Dim, Disagreeable, Earbash, Fly, Fowl, Pest, Greenfly, Harass, Irritate, Mither, Molest, Mouse, Nag, Nudnik, Nuisance, Nun, Pize, Plague, Rotter, Scourge, Tease, Terror, Thysanoptera, Vermin, Weevil

Pesticide Botanic(al), DDT, Derris, Dichlovvos, Endrin, Glucosinolate, Heptachlor, Mouser, Permethrin, Synergist, Warfarin

Pestilence, Pestilent Curse, Epidemic, Evil, Lues, Murrain, Murren, Noxious, Outbreak, Pernicious, Plague

Pet Aversion, Cade, Canoodle, Caress, Chou, Coax, Coddle, Cosset, Cuddle, Dandle, Daut(ie), Dawt(ie), Dod, Dort, Ducky, Favourite, Fondle, Glumps, Hamster, Huff, Hump, Ire, Jarta, Jo, Lallygag, Lapdog, Miff, Mouse, Neck, Pique, Rabbit, Smooch, Snog, Spat, Strum, Sulk(s), Tantrum, Teacher's, Tiff, Tout, Towt, Umbrage, Virtual, Yarta

Petal Ala, Keels, Labellum, Leaf, Standard, Vexillum

Petard Firework, Squib

Peter Aumbry, Bell, Dwindle, Grimes, Pan, Principle, Quince, Quint, Rabbit, Safe, Saint, Sellers, Simon, Simple, Wane, Weaken

Petite Dainty, Mignon, Small

Petition(er) Appeal, Beg, Boon, Crave, Entreaty, Litany, Millenary, Orison, Plaintiff, Postulant, Prayer, Representation, Request, Round robin, Solicit, Sue, Suit(or), Suppli(c)ant, Vesper

Pet-name Hypocorisma, Nickname, So(u)briquet

Petrel Bird, Mother Carey's chicken, Nelly, Prion, Procellaria, Stormbird, Stormy, Wilton's

Petrify(ing) Fossilise, Frighten, Lapidescent, Niobe, Numb, Ossify, Scare, Terrify

Petrol(eum) Cetane, Cutting, Diesel, Esso®, Ethyl, Fuel, Gas, High-octane, High-test, Ligroin, Maz(o)ut, Octane, Oilstone, Olein, Platforming, Refinery, Rock oil, Rock-tar, STP, Unleaded, Vaseline®

Petticoat Balmoral, Basquine, Crinoline, Female, Filabeg, Fil(l)ibeg, Jupon, Kilt, Kirtle, Phil(l)abeg, Phil(l)ibeg, Placket, Sarong, Shift, Underskirt, Wylie-coat

Pettifogger Lawmonger

Petty, Pettiness Baubling, Bumbledom, Childish, Little, Mean, Minor, Narrow, Niggling, Nyaff, One-horse, Parvanimity, Picayunish, Piffling, Pimping, Puisne, Shoestring, Small, Small-minded, Stingy, Tin, Trivial, Two-bit

Petulance, Petulant Fretful, Huff, Moody, Peevish, Perverse, Procacity, Querulous, Sullen, Toutie, Waspish

Pew Box, Carrel, Chair, Seat, Stall

Pewter Trifle, Tutenag

Phaeton Spider

Phalanger Cus-cus, Honey-mouse, Opossum, Petaurist, Phascogale, Possum, Sugar glider, Tait, Tarsipes, Tuan, Wambenger

Phalanx Cohort, Coterie, Legion

Phalarope Lobe-foot

Phallus Linga(m), Penis, Priapus

Phantasist, Phantasm Apparition, Chimera, Spectre, Werewolf

Phantom Apparition, Bogey, Bugbear, Eidolon, Feature, Idol, Incubus, Maya, Pepper's ghost, Shade, Spectre, Tut, Wild hunt, Wraith

Pharaoh Akhenaton, Amenhotep, Cheops, Egyptian, Rameses, River-dragon, Thutmose, Tut, Tutankhamen, Tutankhamun, Tyrant

Pharisee Formalist, Humbug, Hypocrite, Nicodemus

Pharmacist, Pharmacologist → CHEMIST, Dispenser, MPS, Officinal, Preparator

Phase Climacteric, Coacervate, Colour, Cycle, Form, Nematic, Period, Post-boost, Primary, Quarter, REM, Stage, State, Synchronise, Transition

Pheasant Argus, Bird, Fireback, Junglefowl, Mona(u)l, Nide, Nye, Peacock, Ring-necked, Tragopan

Phenol Orcine, Orcinol, Resorcinol, Xylenol

Phenomenon Autokinetic, Blip, Effect, Event, Figure ground, Flying saucer, Flysch, Heterography, Hormesis, Marvel, Miracle, Mirage, Paranormal, Parascience, Phenology, Phi, Psi, Rankshift, Reynaud's, Synergy

Phial Bologna, Bottle, Flask

Phil, Philip Fluter, Macedonia, Pip

Philander(er) Flirt, Keeper, Lothario, Playboy, Toyer, → TRIFLE, Wolf, Womaniser

Philanthropist, Philanthropy Altruist, Benefactor, Carnegie, Charity, Coram, Donor, Freemason, Humanist, Humanitarian, Nobel, Rockefeller, Samaritan, Shaftesbury, Tate, Wilberforce

Philately Timbromania

Phileas Fogg

▶ **Philip** *see* PHIL

Philippic Diatribe, Invective, Tirade

Philippine(s) Bisayan, Igorot, Moro, PI, RP, Tagalog, Visayan

Philistine, Philistinism Artless, Ashdod, Barbarian, Foe, Gath, Gaza, Gigman, Goliath, Goth, Lowbrow, Podsnappery, Vandal

Philology Linguistics, Semantics, Speechcraft

Philosopher, Philosophy Academist, Activism, Ahimsa, Analytical, Animism, Anthrosophy, Antinomianism, Antiochian, Atomic, Atomist, Attitude, Averr(h)oism, Cartesian, Casuist, Conceptualism, Conservatism, Cracker-barrel, Critical, Cynic, Deipnosophist, Deontology, Eclectic, Eleatic, Empiricism, Enlightenment, Epistemology, Ethics, Existentialism, Fatalism, Gnostic, Gymnosophist, Hedonism, Hobbism, Holist, Humanism, I Ching, Idealism, Ideology, Instrumentalism, -ism, Kaizen, Linguistic, Logical atomism, Logicism, Logos, Maieutic, Marxism, Materialism, Mechanism, Megarian, Metaphysician, Metaphysics, Metempiricism, Monism, Moral(ist), Natural, Neoplatonism, Neoteric, Nihilism, Nominalism, Occamist, Occam's razor, Ockhamist, Olbers, Opinion, Peripatetic, Phenomenology, Platonism, Populism, Positivism, Rationalism, Realism, Rosminian, Sage, Sankhya, Sceptic, Schoolman, Scientology, Sensist, Shankara(-charya), Sophist, Stoic, Synthetic, Taoism, Theism, Theosophy, Thomist, Transcendentalism, Ultraism, Utilitarianism, Utopianism, Voluntarism, Weltanschauung, Yoga, Yogi

PHILOSOPHERS

4 letters:			5 letters:
Ayer	Kant	Weil	Amiel
Hume	Mach	Wolf	Bacon
Jedi	Mill	Zeno	Comte
	Ryle		

Croce	Bentham	Foucault	Apemanthus
Dewey	Bergson	Hamilton	Apollonius
Hegel	Diderot	Harrison	Aristippus
Locke	Emerson	Menippus	Campanella
Paine	Erasmus	Old Moore	Chrysippus
Plato	Erigena	Plotinus	Democritus
Quine	Herbart	Plutarch	Empedocles
Renan	Hypatia	Rousseau	Heraclitus
Smith	Leibniz	Socrates	Hutchinson
Sorel	Malthus	Xenophon	Paracelsus
Taine	Marcion		Parmenides
	Marcuse	**9 letters:**	Protagoras
6 letters:	Mencius	Antiochus	Pythagoras
Agnesi	Meng-tse	Aristotle	Saint Simon
Cicero	Ptolemy	Bosanquet	Swedenborg
Engels	Rosmini	Cleanthes	Von Leibniz
Godwin	Russell	Confucius	Xenocrates
Herder	Schlick	Descartes	Xenophanes
Hobbes	Serbati	Euhemerus	
Ortega	Sheffer	Heidegger	**11 letters:**
Pascal	Spencer	Leucippus	Anaximander
Popper	Spinoza	Lucretius	Antisthenes
Pyrrho	Steiner	Nietzsche	Kierkegaard
Sartre	Vedanta	Santayana	Montesquieu
Scotus		Schelling	
Seneca	**8 letters:**	Whitehead	**12 letters:**
Tagore	Avicenna		Callisthenes
Thales	Berkeley	**10 letters:**	Schopenhauer
	Boethius	Anacharsis	Wittgenstein
7 letters:	Cyreniac	Anaxagoras	
Abelard	Diogenes	Anaximenes	
Aquinas	Epicurus	Antiochene	

Philosophic(al) Rational, Resigned, Thoughtful, Tranquil
Philtre Aphrodisiac, Charm, Drug, Hippomanes, Potion
Phlegm(atic) Calm, Composed, Pituita(ry), Pituite, Stolid, Unperturbed, Unruffled
Phloem Leptome, Liber
Phobia Aversion, Dread, Fear, Thing
Phoebe, Phoebus Apollo, Artemis, Day-star, Deaconess, Moon, Selene, Sol, Sun
Phoenician Tripolitania
Phoenix Bird-of-wonder, Fum, Fung, Paragon, Self-begotten
Phone Bell, Blower, Call, Cellular, Clamshell, Dial, Dual band, Flip, Intercom,
    Mob(i)e, Mobile, Moby, Pay, Picture, Ring, Smart, Talkback, → **TELEPHONE**, Text
Phonetic(s) Acoustic, Articulatory, Auditory, Interdental, Mouille, Oral, Palaeotype,
    Palatal, Palato-alveolar, Plosion, Spoken, Symbol, Synaeresis
▷ **Phonetically** *may indicate* a word sounding like another
Phon(e)y Bogus, Charlatan, Counterfeit, Fake, Hokey, Impostor, Poseur, Quack,
    → **SHAM**, Specious, Spurious
▷ **Phony** *may indicate* an anagram
Phosphate Monazite, Sphaerite, Torbernite, Vivianite, Wavellite, Xenotime
Phosphor(escent), Phosphorescence, Phosphorus Bologna, Briming, Cephalin,

Foxfire, Friar's lantern, Ignis fatuus, Jack o'lantern, Luminescent, Malathion®, Noctilucent, P, Pyrosome, Sarin, Sea-fire, Tabun, Will o' the wisp

Photo(copy), Photograph(y), Photographic, Photo finish Ambrotype, Anaglyph, Angiogram, Beefcake, Black and white, Blow-up, Cabinet, Calotype, Clog, Close-up, Composite, Contre-jour, Daguerrotype, Diazo, Duplicate, Enprint, Exposure, Ferroprint, Ferrotype, Film, Flash, Half-tone, Headshot, Heliochrome®, Heliotype, Hologram, Infra-red, Kallitype, Kirlian, Kodak®, Microdot, Microfilm, Microgram, Micrograph, Microprint, Monochrome, Montage, Mugshot, Negative, Nephogram, Opaline, Panel, Picture, Pinhole, Platinotype, Polaroid®, Positive, Print, Resorcin, Rotograph, Rotogravure, Schlieren, Sepia, Shoot, Shot, Shutterbug, Slide, Snap, Spirit , Stannotype, Still, Take, Talbotype, Time-lapse, Tintype, Tomography, Topo, Trimetrogon, Vignette, Wire, Woodburytype, Xerography, X-ray

Photographer Beaton, Brandt, Cameraman, Cameron, Cartier-Bresson, Daguerre, Fox Talbot, Paparazzo, Schlierin, Shutterbug, Snowdon, Stalkerazzi

Phrase Abject, Actant, Asyndeton, Buzzword, Catch(word), Catchcry, Cliché, Climacteric, Comma, Expression, Hapax legomenon, Heroic, Hook, Idiophone, Laconism, Leitmotiv, Locution, Mantra, Molto, Noun, Phr, Refrain, Riff, Slogan, Soundbite, Tag, Term, Trope

Phrygian Midas

Phthisis Decay, TB

Phylactery Amulet, Talisman, Tefillin, Tephillin

Phyllopod Brine-shrimp

Physic(s) Cluster, Cryogenics, Culver's, Cure, Dose, Electrostatics, Geostatics, Health, High-energy, Kinematics, Medicine, Nuclear, Nucleonics, Particle, Photometry, Purge, Remedy, Rheology, Science, Solid-state, Sonics, Spintronics, Thermodynamics, Ultrasonics

Physical Bodily, Carnal, Corpor(e)al, Material, Natural, Tangible

Physician Allopath, Buteyko, Chagus, Doctor, Erastus, Eustachio, Galen, Gilbert, Graves, Guillotin, Hakim, Hansen, Harvey, Hippocrates, Internist, Lamaze, Leech, Linacre, Lister, Medic(o), Menière, Mesmer, Mindererus, Paean, Paian, Paracelsus, Practitioner, Preceptor, Quack, Ranvier, Roget, Sézary, Stahl, Still, Therapist, Time

Physicist Alfren, Ampère, Angstrom, Appleton, Archimedes, Avogadro, Becquerel, Bernouilli, Bohr, Bondi, Born, Bose, Bragg, Brewster, Carnot, Cerenkov, Cockcroft, Coulomb, Crookes, Curie, Dalton, Davisson, Debye, Dicke, Dirac, Einstein, Faraday, Fermi, Friedmann, Galileo, Gamow, Gauss, Geiger, Gilbert, Giorgi, Gold, Hahn, Hawking, Heaviside, Heisenberg, Henry, Hertz, Hooke, Hoyle, Huygens, Joliot-Curie, Josephson, Joule, Kerv, Kirchhoff, Landau, Laplace, Lawe, Lodge, Lorentz, Mach, Marconi, Maxwell, Meitner, Michelson, Morley, Newton, Oersted, Ohm, Oppenheimer, Pauli, Peebles, Penzias, Pic(c)ard, Planck, Popov, Raman, Rankine, Rayleigh, Reaumur, Robertson, Ro(e)ntgen, Rutherford, Schottky, Schrödinger, Scientist, Sievert, Skyrme, Stark, Torricelli, Tyndall, Van Allen, Van der Waals, Volta, Watson-Watt, Weber, Wheeler, Wilson, Young

Physiognomist, Physiognomy Face, Features, Lavater

Physiology, Physiologist Malpighi, Pavlov, Wagner, Zoonomia

Physiotherapist Masseur

Physique Body, Build, Figure, Pyknic, Somatotype

Pi, Pious Breast-beater, Craw-thumper, Devotional, Devout, Fraud, Gallio, God-fearing, Godly, Holy, Holy Willie, Mid-Victorian, Religiose, Saintly, Sanctimonious, Savoury, Smug, Wise, Zaddik

Piaffe Spanish-walk

Pianist Anda, Arrau, Hambourg, Hess, Hofmann, Liszt, Mingus, Morton, Ogdon, Pachmann, Paderewski, Répétiteur, Schnabel, Tatum, Vamper, Virtuoso

Piano Baby grand, Bechstein, Boudoir grand, Celesta, Celeste, Concert grand, Cottage, Dumb, Flugel, Forte, Grand, Hammerklavier, Honkytonk, Keyboard, Mbira, Overstrung, P, Player, Prepared, Semi-grand, Softly, Steinway, Stride, Thumb, Upright

Piano-maker Erard

Picaresque Roman à tiroirs

Picaroon Brigand, Corsair, Pirate, Rogue

Piccadilly Whist

Piccolo Ottavino

Pick(er), Pickaxe, Picking, Pick up Break, Choice, → CHOOSE, Cream, Cull, Elite, Flower, Gather, Glean, Gurlet, Hack, Holing, Hopper, Mattock, Nap, Nibble, Oakum, Plectrum, Pluck, Plum, Select, Single, Sort, Steal, Strum, Tong, Wale

▷ **Picked** *may indicate* an anagram

Picket Demonstrate, Flying, Pale, Palisade, Protester, Stake, Tether, Tie

Pickings Harvest, Profits, Scrounging, Spoils

Pickle(r) Achar, Brine, Cabbage, Caper, Chow-chow, Chutney, Corn, Corner, Cucumber, Cure, Dilemma, Dill, Eisel, Esile, Gherkin, Girkin, Imp, Jam, Kimchi, Marinade, Marinate, Mess, Mull, Olive, Onion, Peculate, Peregrine, Piccalilli, → PLIGHT, Relish, Samp(h)ire, Scrape, Souse, Trouble, Vinegar, Wolly

Picklock Oustiti, Peterman

Pick-me-up Bracer, Drink, Restorer, Reviver, Tonic

Pickpocket(s) Adept, Bung, Cly-faker, Cutpurse, Dip, Diver, Fagin, File, Nipper, Swell mob, Swellmobsman, Wire

Pick-up Arrest, Light o'love, Truck, Ute

Picnic Alfresco, Braaivleis, Burgoo, Clambake, Fun, Outing, Push-over, Spread, Tailgate, Valium, Wase-goose, Wayzgoose

Picture(s) Anaglyph, Arpillera, Art, Bambocciades, Bitmap, Canvas, Cloudscape, Collage, Cutaway, Cyclorama, Decoupage, Depict, Describe, Diptych, Drawing, Drypoint, Emblem, Envisage, Epitome, Etching, Film, Flick, Fresco, Gouache, Graphic, Histogram, Icon, Identikit®, Imagery, Inset, Kakemono, Landscape, Lenticular, Likeness, Lithograph, Montage, Motion, Movie, Moving, Movy, Mugshot, Myriorama, Oil, Photo, Photofit®, Photogram, Photomontage, Photomosaic, Photomural, Pin-up, Pix, Plate, Polyptych, Portrait, Predella, Prent, Presentment, Print, Retraitt, Retrate, Rhyparography, Scene, Shadowgraph, Shot, Slide, Snapshot, Stereochrome, Stereogram, Stereograph, Stevengraph, Still-life, Table(au), Talkie, Thermogram, Tone, Topo, Transfer, Transparency, Vanitas, Vectograph, Vision, Votive, Vraisemblance, Word, Zincograph

Picturesque Idyllic, Scenic

Pidgin Chinook jargon, Creole, Fanagalo, Fanakalo, Hiri Motu, Japlish, New Guinea, Police Motu, Solomon Islands, Tok Pisin

▷ **Pie** *may indicate* an anagram

Pie(s) Anna, Banoffee, Battalia, Bridie, Camp, Chewet, Cobbler, Cottage, Coulibiac, Curry puff, Custard, Deep-dish, Easy, Flan, Floater, Florentine, Hash, Humble, Koulibiaca, Madge, Meat, Mess, Mince, Mud, Mystery bag, Pandowdy, Pastry, Pasty, Patty, Périgord, Pica, Piet, Pirog, Pizza, Printer's, Pyat, Pyet, Pyot, Quiche, Rappe, Resurrection, Shepherd's, Shoofly, Spoil, Squab, Stargaz(e)y, Star(ry)-gazy, Sugar, Tart, Tarte tatin, Torte, Tourtière, Turnover, Tyropitta, Umble, Vol-au-vent, Warden

Piebald Calico, Dappled, Motley, Paint, Pied, Pinto, Skewbald

Piece(s) Adagio, Add, Bishop, Bit, Blot, Cameo, Cannon, Cent, Charm,
→ **CHESSMAN**, Chip, Chunk, Coin, Companion, Component, Concerto,
Conversation, Crumb, Domino, End, Episode, Extract, Firearm, Fit, Flitters,
Fragment, Frust, Gat, Goring, → **GUN**, Haet, Hait, Hunk, Item, Join, Mammock,
Médaillons, Mite, Money, Morceau, Morsel, Museum, Nip, Novelette, Oddment,
Off-cut, Ort, Part, Party, Pastiche, Patch, Pawn, Period, Peso, Pin, Pistareen, Pole,
→ **PORTION**, Recital, Scliff, Scrap, Section, Set, Shard, Sherd, Skliff, Slice, Sliver,
Snatch, Sou, Spare part, Speck, String, Stub, Swatch, Tait, Tate, Tile, Toccata,
Truncheon, Wedge, Wodge

Pièce de résistance Star-turn

Piecemeal, Piecework Gradually, Intermittent, Jigsaw, Serial, Tut

Pie-crust Coffin, Lid, Pastry

Pied-à-terre Nest, Pad

Pieman Pastrycook, Shepherd

Pier(s) Anta, Chain, Groyne, Jetty, Jutty, Landing, Mole, Plowman, Quay, Slipway,
Swiss roll, Wharf

Pierce(d), Piercer, Piercing Accloy, Awl, Broach, Cleave, Cribrose, Dart, Drill,
Endart, Fenestrate(d), Fulminant, Gimlet, Gore, Gride, Gryde, Hull, Impale, Jag,
Keen, Lance, Lancinate, Lobe, Move, Needle, Penetrate, Perforate, Pike, Pink,
Poignant, Prince Albert, Punch, Puncture, Riddle, Rive, Shrill, Skewer, Slap,
Sleeper, Spear, Spike, Spit, Stab, Steek, Stiletto, Sting, Tap, Thirl, Thrill(ant)

Piety Devotion, Purity, Sanctity

Piffle Bilge, Codswallop, Hogwash, Poppycock, Tommy-rot, Twaddle

Pig(s), Piggy, Pigskin Anthony, Babe, Babirusa, Baconer, Barrow, Bartholomew,
Bessemer, Bland, Boar, Bonham, British Lop, Bush, Captain Cooker, Cutter, Doll,
Duroc, Elt, Farrow, Fastback, Football, Gadarene, Gilt, Gloucester, Gloucester
Old Spot, Glutton, Grice, Grumphie, Gryce, Guffie, Guinea, Gus, Gutzer, Ham,
Hog, Ingot, Iron, Javelina, Kentledge, Kintledge, Kunekune, Lacombe, Landrace,
Land-shark, Lard, Large Black, Large White, Lingot, Long, Middle White,
Napoleon, Old Spot, Peccary, Policeman, Pork(er), Raven, Razorback, Rosser,
Runt, Saddleback, Shoat, Shot(e), Shott, Slip, Snowball, Sounder, Sow, Squealer,
Sucking, Suid(ae), Tamworth, Tayassuid, Tithe, Toe, Tootsie, Truffle, Vietnamese
Pot-bellied, Warthog, Welsh, Yelt

Pig-disease Bullnose

Pigeon Archangel, Barb, Bird, Bronze-winged, Cape, Capuchin, Carrier, Clay,
Cropper, Culver, Cumulet, Danzig, Dove, Fairy Swallow, Fantail, Goura, Ground,
Gull, Homer, Homing, Horseman, Jacobin, Kereru, Kuku, Manumea, Mourning
dove, New Zealand, Nun, Owl, Passenger, Peristeronic, Piwakawaka, Pouter,
Ringdove, Rock(er), Roller, Ront(e), Ruff, Runt, Scandaroon, Solitaire, Spot, Squab,
Squealer, Stock-dove, Stool, Stork, Swift, Talkie-talkee, Tippler, Tooth-billed,
Trumpeter, Tumbler, Turbit, Wonga(-wonga), Zoozoo

Pigeonhole Classify, Compartment, File, Label, Postpone, Shelve, Slot, Stereotype

Pigeon-house Columbary, Cote, Dovecot(e)

Pig-food Mast, Swill

Pig-headed Self-willed

Pig-iron Kentledge, Kintledge

Pigment(s), Pigmentation Accessory, Anthoclore, Anthocyan(in), Argyria,
Betacyanin, Bilirubin, Biliverdin, Bister, Bistre, Bronzing, Cappagh-brown,
Carmine, Carotene, Carotenoid, Carotin, Carotinoid, Chloasma, Chlorophyll,
Chrome, Chromogen, Cobalt, Colcothar, Colour, Crocus, Curcumin, Dye, Etiolin,
Eumelanin, Flake-white, Flavin(e), Fucoxanthin, Gamboge, Gossypol, Green

earth, Haem, H(a)ematin, H(a)emocyanin, H(a)emoglobin, Hem(e), King's yellow, Lipochrome, Iodopsin, Lake, Lamp-black, Lithopone, Liverspot, Lutein, Luteolin, Lycopene, Madder, Madder lake, Melanin, Monastral®, Naevus, Naples yellow, Nigrosine, Ochre, Opsin, Orpiment, Paris-green, Phthalocyanine, Phycobilin, Phycocyan, Phycoerythrin, Phycophaein, Phycoxanthin, Phytochrome, Porphyrin, Porphyropsin, Pterin, Puccoon, Quercetin, Realgar, Red lead, Respiratory, Retinene, Rhiboflavin, Rhodophane, Rhodopsin, Saffron, Scheele's green, Sepia, Sienna, Sinopia, Sinopsis, Smalt, Tapetum, Tempera, Terre-verte, Tincture, Toner, Turacoverdin, Ultramarine, Umber, Urobilin, Urochrome, Verditer, Vermilion, Viridian, Whitewash, Xanthophyll, Xanthopterin(e), Zinc white

Pigtail Braid, Cue, Plait, Queue

Pi jaw Cant

Pike Assegai, Crag, Dory, Fogash, Gar(fish), Ged, Gisarme, Glaive, Hie, Holostei, Javelin, Lance, Luce, Partisan, Pickerel, Ravensbill, Scafell, Snoek, Spear, Speed, Spontoon, Vouge, Walleyed

▶ **Pilaster** *see* **PILLAR**

Pile(d), Piles, Piling Agger, Amass, Atomic, Bing, Bomb, Bubkes, Camp-sheathing, Camp-shedding, Camp-sheeting, Camp-shot, Clamp, Cock, Column, Crowd, Deal, Dolphin, Down, Emerods, Farmers, Fender, Fig, Floccus, Fortune, Galvanic, Hair, Haycock, Heap, Hept, Historic, Hoard, Load, Lot, Marleys, Mass, Moquette, Nap, Pier, Post, Pyre, Raft, Reactor, Ream(s), Rouleau, Screw, Shag, Sheet, Slush, → **STACK**, Starling, Stilt, Toorie, Trichome, Upheap, Velvet, Voltaic, Wealth, Windrow, Wodge

Pile-driver Tup

Pilfer(ing) Crib, Filch, Finger, Maraud, Miche, Nick, Peculate, Pickery, Pickle, Pinch, Plagiarise, Plunder, Purloin, Snitch, → **STEAL**

Pilgrim(age) Aske, Childe Harold, Expedition, Fatima, Gaya, Hadj(i), Haji, Hajj(i), Karbala, Kerbela, Kum, Loreto, Lourdes, Mathura, Mecca, Nasik, Nikko, Palmer, Pardoner, Qom, Qum, Umra(h), Reeve, Scallop-shell, Shrine, Voyage, Yatra

Pill(s) Abortion, Ball, Beverley, Bitter, Bolus, Caplet, Capsule, Chill, Dex, Doll, Dose, Globule, Golfball, Goofball, Lob, Medication, Medicine, Number nine, Peace, Peel, Pellet, Pep, Pilula, Pilule, Placebo, Poison, Protoplasmal, Radio, Sleeping, Spansule, Tablet, Troche, Trochisk, Upper

Pillage Booty, Devastate, Plunder, Ransack, Rapine, Ravage, Razzia, Robbery, Sack, Spoil

Pillar(ed), Pillars Anta, Apostle, Atlantes, Baluster, Balustrade, Boaz, Canton, Caryatides, Cippus, Columel, Column, Earth, Eustyle, Gendarme, Goal, Hercules, Herm, Impost, Islam, Jachin, Lat, Man, Modiolus, Monolith, Newel, Nilometer, Obelisk, Pedestal, Peristyle, Pier, Post, Respond, Saddle, Serac, Stack, Stalactite, Stalagmite, Stoop, Telamon, Tetrastyle, Trumeau

Pill-box Hat, Inro

Pillion Cushion, Pad, Rear

Pillory Cang(ue), Cippus, Crucify, Jougs, Little-ease, Pelt, Satirise, Slam

Pillow(case) Bear, Beer, Bere, Bolster, Cod, Cow, Cushion, Headrest, Hop, Lace, Pad, Pulvinar

Pilot Ace, Airman, Auto(matic), Aviator, Branch, Bush, Captain, → **CONDUCT**, Experimental, Flier, George, Govern, Guide, Hobbler, Lead, Lodesman, Lodestar, Palinure, Palinurus, Pitt, Prune, Shipman, Steer, Test, Tiphys, Trial, Usher, Wingman

Pimento Allspice

Pimp Apple-squire, Bludger, Fancyman, Fleshmonger, Hoon, Lecher, Mack,

Pandarus, Pander, Ponce, Procurer, Solicit, Souteneur

Pimpernel Bastard, Bog, Scarlet, Water, Wincopipe, Wink-a-peep, Yellow

Pimple, Pimply Blackhead, Botch, Bubukle, Button, Gooseflesh, Grog-blossom, Hickey, Horripilation, Milium, Papilla, Papula, Papule, Plook, Plouk, Pock, Pustule, Quat, Rumblossom, Rum-bud, Spot, Tetter, Uredinial, Wen, Whelk, Whitehead, Zit

Pin Bayonet, Belaying, Bolt, Brooch, Candle, Cask, Corking, Cotter, Curling, Dowel, Drawing, Drift, End, Fasten, Fid, Firing, Fix, Gam, Gudgeon, Hair, Hairgrip, Hob, Hook, Joggle, Kevel, King, Leg, Nail, Needle, Nog, Panel, Peg, Pintle, Pivot, Preen, Rivet, Rolling, Saddle, Safety, Scarf, SCART, Scatter, Shear, Shirt, Skewer, Skittle, Skiver, Spike, Spindle, Split, Staple, Stick, Stump, Swivel, Taper, Tertial, Thole, Thumbtack, Tie, Tre(e)nail, Trunnion, U-bolt, Woolder, Wrest, Wrist

Pinafore Apron, Brat, HMS, Overall, Pinny, Save-all, Tire

Pinball Pachinko

Pince-nez Nose-nippers

Pincers Chela, Claw, Forceps, Forfex, Nipper, Tweezers

Pinch(ed) Arrest, Bit, Bone, Chack, Constrict, Cramp, Crimp, Crisis, Emergency, Gaunt, Misappropriate, Nab, Nick, Nim, Nip, Nirlit, Peculate, Peel, Pilfer, Pocket, Pook(it), Pouk, Prig, Pugil, Raft, Rob, Save, Scrimp, Scrounge, Skimp, Smatch, Snabble, Snaffle, Sneak, Sneap, Sneeshing, Snuff, Squeeze, → STEAL, Swipe, Tate, Trace, Tweak, Twinge

Pine(s), Pining Arolla, Bristlecone, Celery, Cembra, Chile, Cluster, Cone, Conifer, Cypress, Droop, Dwine, Earn, Erne, Fret, Green, Ground, Hone, Hoop, Huon, Jack, Japanese umbrella, Jeffrey, Kauri, Languish, Languor, Loblolly, Lodgepole, Long, Longleaf, Monkey-puzzle, Moon, Norfolk Island, Norway, Nut, Oregon, Parana, Picea, Pinaster, Pitch, Radiata, Red, Scotch, Scots, Screw, Softwood, Spruce, Starve, Stone, Sugar, Tree, Umbrella, Urman, Waste, White, Yearn

Pineapple Anana, Bomb, Bromelia, Grenade, Piña, Poll, Sorosis, Tillandsia

Ping Knock, Whir(r)

Pinguin Anana(s)

Pinion Fetter, Penne, Pinnoed, Secure, Shackle, Wing

Pink Blush, Carnation, Carolina, Castory, Cheddar, Clove, Colour, Coral, Cyclamen, Dianthus, Dutch, Emperce, FT, Fuchsia, Gillyflower, Indian, Knock, Lake, Lily, Lychnis, Maiden, Moss, Mushroom, Old rose, Oyster, Peach-blow, Peak, Perce, Pierce, Pompadour, Pounce, Rose(ate), Ruddy, Salmon, Scallop, Sea, Shell, Shocking, Shrimp, Spigelia, Spit, Stab, Tiny

Pinnacle Acme, Apex, Crest, Crown, Gendarme, Height, Needle, Pinnet, Summit

Pinniped Seal

Pin-point Focus, Highlight, Identify, Isolate, Localise

Pint(s) Cab, Jar, Log, Reputed

Pintail Duck, Smeath, Smee(th)

Pin-up Cheesecake, Dish, Star, Sweater girl

Pioneer Baird, Bandeirante, Blaze, Boone, Colonist, Emigrant, Explore, Fargo, Fleming, Frontiersman, Harbinger, Innovator, Lead, Marconi, Oecist, Pathfinder, Planter, Rochdale, Sandgroper, Settler, Spearhead, Trail-blazer, Trekker, Voortrekker, Waymaker, Wells

▶ **Pious** *see* PI

Pip Ace, Acinus, Blackball, Bleep, Hip, Hump, Phil, Pyrene, Seed, Star

Pipe(s), Piper, Pipeline, Piping Antara, Aorta, Aulos, Balance, Barrel, Blub, Boatswain's, Bong, Briar, Briarroot, Broseley, Bubble, Calabash, Call, Calumet, Chanter, Cheep, Cherrywood, Chibouk, Chibouque, Chillum, Churchwarden,

Clay, Cob, Conduit, Corncob, Crane, Cutty, Dip, Division, Down, Downcomer, Drain, Drill, Drillstring, Drone, Dry riser, Duct, Dudeen, Dudheen, Ell, Escape, Exhaust, Faucet, Feed, Fistula, Flue, Flute, Gage, Gas main, Gedact, Gedeckt, Hawse, Hod, Hogger, Hooka(h), Hose, Hubble-bubble, Hydrant, Indian, Injection string, Irish, Jet, Kalian, Kelly, Mains, Manifold, Marsyas, Meerschaum, Mirliton, Montre, Narghile, Narg(h)il(l)y, Nargile(h), Oat(en), Oboe, Organ, Ottavino, Pan, Peace, Pepper, Pibroch, Piccolo, Pied, Pifferaro, Pitch, Poverty, Principal, Pule, Qanat, Quill, Rainwater, Recorder, Ree(d), Rise, Riser, Sack-doudling, Salicional, Sennit, Serpent, Service, Sewer, Shalm, Shawm, Shisha, Shoe, Shrike, Sing, Siphon, Skirl, Sluice, Soil, Squeak, Stack, Standpipe, Stopcock, Stummel, Sucker, Syrinx, Tail, Tee, Throttle, Tibia, Tootle, Trachea, Tremie, Tube, Tubule, Tweet, U-bend, Uillean(n), Union, Uptake, U-trap, U-tube, Vent, Ventiduct, Volcanic, Waste, Water(-spout), Watermain, Weasand, Whiss, Whistle, Woodcock's head, Woodnote, Worm

Pipefish Sea-adder

Pipe-laying Graft

Pipit Bird, Skylark, Titlark

Pippin Apple, Orange, Ribston

Pipsqueak Nobody

Piquancy, Piquant Pungent, Racy, Relish, Salt, Savoury, Sharp, Spicy, Tangy

Pique Dod, Huff, Resentment, Titillate

Piranha Caribe, Characinoid, Piraya

Pirate(s), Pirated, Piratical, Piracy Algerine, Barbarossa, Blackbeard, Boarder, Bootleg, Brigand, Buccaneer, Buccanier, Cateran, Condottier, Conrad, Corsair, Crib, Dampier, Fil(l)ibuster, Flint, Gunn, Hijack, Hook, Kidd, Lift, Loot, Morgan, Penzance, Picaro(on), Pickaroon, Plagiarise, Plunder, Rakish, Rover, Sallee-man, Sallee-rover, Sea-dog, Sea-king, Sea-rat, Sea-robber, Sea-wolf, Silver, Skull and crossbones, Smee, Steal, Teach, Thief, Unauthorised, Viking, Water-rat, Water-thief

Pistillate Female

Pistol Air, Ancient, Automatic, Barker, Barking-iron, Captive bolt, Colt®, Dag, Derringer, Gat, → **GUN**, Hackbut, Horse, Iron, Luger®, Pepperbox, Petronel, Pocket, Puffer, Revolver, Rod, Saloon, Shooter, Starter, Starting, Very, Water, Weapon

Piston Four-stroke, Plunger, Ram, Trunk

Pit(ted), Pitting Abyss, Alveolus, Antrum, Bottomless, Catch, Cave, Cesspool, Chasm, Cissing, Cloaca, Colliery, Crater, Den, Depression, Depth, Dungmere, Ensile, Fossa, Fougasse, Fovea, Foxhole, Gehenna, Hangi, Heapstead, Heartspoon, Hell, Hillhole, Hole, Hollow, Inferno, Inspection, Khud, Lacunose, Lime, Mark, Match, Measure, → **MINE**, Mosh, Orchestra, Parterre, Pip, Plague, Play, Pock-mark, Potato, Punctate, Putamen, Pyrene, Ravine, Rifle, Salt, Scrobicule, Silo, Slime, Soakaway, Solar plexus, Stone, Sump, Tar, Tear, Trap, Trous-de-loup, Underarm

Pitch(ed) Absolute, Asphalt, Atilt, Attune, Bitumen, Burgundy, Coal-tar, Concert, Crease, Diamond, Dive, Ela, Elect, Elevator, Encamp, Erect, Establish, Fever, Fling, Fork, Diesis, French, Ground, International, Intonation, Key, Knuckleball, Labour, Length, Level, Lurch, Maltha, Mineral, Nets, Neume, Patter, Peck, Perfect, Philharmonic, Philosophical, Piceous, Pight, Pin, Plong(e), Plunge, Pop, Purl, Resin, Rock, Ruff(e), Sales, Scend, Seel, Send, Shape, Sling, Slope, Soprarino, Spiel, Stoit, Tar, Tessitura, Tilt, Tone, Tonemic, Tonus, Tremolo, Tune, Unison, Vibrato, Wicket, Wood

Pitchblende Cleveite

Pitcher(-shaped) Aryt(a)enoid, Ascidium, Bowler, Cruse, Ewer, Jug, Steen, Urceolus

Pitchfork Hurl, Toss

Pitfall Ambush, Danger, Hazard, Snare, Trap

Pith(y) Ambatch, Aphorism, Apo(ph)thegm, Core, Down, Essence, Gnomic, Hat-plant, Heart, Marrow, Medulla, Moxa, Nucleus, Rag, Succinct, Terse

Pithead Broo, Brow, Minehead

Pithless Thowless

Pitiless Flint-hearted, Hard, Hard-headed, Ruthless

Piton Rurp

Pitt Chatham

Pity, Piteous, Pitiful, Pitiable Ah, Alack, Alas, Commiseration, → **COMPASSION**, Hapless, Mercy, Pathos, Pilgarlic, Poor, Red-leg, Rue, Ruth(ful), Seely, Shame, Sin, Sympathy

Pivot(al) Ax(i)le, Central, Focal, Fulcrum, Gooseneck, Gudgeon, Kingbolt, Marker, Revolve, Rotate, Slue, → **SWIVEL**, Trunnion, Turn, Wheel

Pixie Brownie, Elf, Fairy, Gremlin, Sprite

Pizza Calzone, Pepperoni

Placard Affiche, Bill, Playbill, Poster

Placate Appease, Conciliate, Pacify, Propitiate, Soothe

Place(ment) Ad loc, Aim, Allocate, Area, Arena, Assisted, Berth, Bro, Decimal, Deploy, Deposit, Fix, Habitat, Haunt, Hither, Howf, Identify, Impose, → **IN PLACE OF**, Install, Job, Joint, Juxtapose, Lay, Lieu, Locality, Locate, Locus, Parking, Pitch, Plat, Plaza, Point, Posit, → **POSITION**, Product, Put, Realm, Region, Repose, Resting, Room, Rowme, Scene, Second, Set, Site, Situate, Situation, Slot, Spot, Stead, Sted(e), Stedd(e), Stratify, Town, Vendôme

Placid Cool, Easy, Easy-osy, Even-tempered, Quiet, Tame, Tranquil

Plagiarise, Plagiarist Copy, Crib, Lift, Pirate, Steal

Plague (spot) Annoy, Bane, Bedevil, Black death, Boil, Bubonic, Burden, Cattle, Curse, Dog, Dun, Frogs, Gay, Goodyear, Goujeers, Harry, Infestation, Locusts, Lues, Molest, Murrain, Murran, Murrin, Murrion, Nag, Pest, Pester, Pox, Press, Scourge, Tease, Token, Torture, Try, Vex

Plaid Maud, Roon, Shepherd's, Tartan, Wales

Plain(s) Abraham, Archimedes, Artless, Ascetic, Au naturel, Bald, Banat, Bare, Blatant, Broad, Campagna, Campo, Campus Martius, Candid, Carse, Ceará, Chryse, Clavius, Clear, Cook, Dowdy, Downright, Dry, Esdraelon, Evident, Explicit, Flat, Flood, Girondist, Gran Chaco, Great, Homely, Homespun, Inornate, Jezreel, Kar(r)oo, Lande, Langrenus, Llano, Lombardy, Lowland, Maidan, Manifest, Marathon, Mare, Monochrome, Nullarbor, Obvious, Ocean of Storms, Oceanus Procellarum, Olympia, → **ORDINARY**, Outspoken, Overt, Packstaff, Pampa(s), Paramo, Patent, Pikestaff, Plateau, Playa, Polje, Prairie, Prose, Ptolemaeus, Purbach, Sabkha(h), Sabkha(t), Sailing, Salisbury, Savanna(h), Secco, Serengeti, Sharon, Simple, Sodom, Spoken, Staked, Steppe, Tableland, Thessaly, Tundra, Vanilla, Vega, Veldt, Visible, Walled

Plainchant Canto fermo

Plainsman Llanero

Plainsong Alternatim, Ambrosian, Chant

Plaint(ive) Complaint, Dirge, Lacrimoso, Lagrimoso, Lament, Melancholy, Sad, Whiny

Plaintiff Doe, Impeacher, Litigant, Suer

Plait Braid, Crimp, Cue, Frounce, Furbelow, Goffer, Intertwine, Pigtail, Plica, Plight, Queue, Ruche, Sennit, Sinnet, Splice

Plan(s), Planned, Planner, Planning Aim, American, Angle, Architect, Arrange,

Atlas, Axonometric, Blueprint, Brew, Budget, Care, Chart, Commission, Complot, Contingency, Contrive, Dalton, Dart, Deep-laid, Deliberate, Delors, Design, Desyne, Device, Devise, Diagram, Draft, Drawing, Elevation, Engineer, European, Family, Five-Year, Flight, Floor, Format, Galveston, Game, Ground, Hang, Ichnography, Idea, Idée, Instal(l)ment, Intent, Lay(out), Leicester, Leicestershire, Machinate, Map, Marshall, Master, Mastermind, Mean, Nominal, Open, Outline, Pattern, Pipe-dream, Plat, Plot, Ploy, Policy, Premeditate, Prepense, Procedure, Programme, Project, Projet, Proposal, Prospectus, Protraction, Rapacki, Road map, Scenario, Schedule, Scheme, Schlieffen, Shape, Spec(ification), Stratagem, Strategy, Subterfuge, System, Tactician, Town, Wheeze

Plane(s) Aero(dyne), Air, → **AIRCRAFT**, Airliner, Airship, Bandit, Basal, Block, Boeing, Bomber, Bus, Buttock, Camel, Canard, Cartesian, Chenar, Chinar, Comet, Concorde, Crate, Dakota, Datum, Delta-wing, Even, Facet, Fault, Fillister, Flat, Float, Focal, Galactic, Glider, Gliding, Gotha, Homaloid, Hurricane, Icosahedron, Icosohedra, Inclined, Jack, Jet, Jointer, Jumbo, Level, London, Main, MIG, Mirage, Mosquito, Moth, Octagon, Perspective, Platan(us), Polygon, Prop-jet, Pursuit, Rocket, Router, Shackleton, Shave, Smooth, Sole, Spitfire, Spokeshave, Spy, Stealth (bomber), STOL, Surface, Sycamore, Tail, Taube, Thrust, Tow, Trainer, Tree, Trident, Tropopause, Trying, Two-sater, Viscount

Plane figure Endecagon, Hendecagon

Planet(s), Planetary Alphonsine, Ariel, Asteroid, Body, Cabiri, Ceres, Chiron, Constellation, Dispositor, Earth, Eros, Extrasolar, Gas giant, Georgian, Giant, House, Hyleg, Inferior, Inner, Jovian, Jupiter, Lucifer, Major, Mars, Mercury, Minor, Moon, Neptune, Outer, Pallas, Pluto, Primary, Psyche, Quartile, Red, Satellitium, Saturn, Sedna, Significator, Sphere, Starry, Sun, Superior, Terrestrial, Uranus, Venus, Vista, Vulcan, World, Zog

Plangent Mournful

Plank Board, Chess, Deal, Duckboard, Garboard, Plonk, Sarking, Slab, Spirketting, Straik, Strake, Stringer, Weatherboard, Wood, Wrest

Plankton Nekton, Neuston, Pelagic, Red tide, Seston, Spatfall

Plant(s), Plant part Acrogen, Amphidiploid, Anemochore, Annual, Anther, Aphotoic, Autophyte, Bed, Biennial, Biota, Bloomer, Bonsai, Bryophyte, CAM, Chamaephyte, Chomophyte, Cotyledon, Cultigen, Cultivar, Dayflower, Dibble, Ecad, Eccremocarpus, Embed, Endogen, Enrace, Epilithic, Epiphyllous, Epiphyte, Establish, Factory, Fix, Forb, Geophyte, G(u)ild, Growth, Gymnosperm, Halophyte, Halosere, Herbage, Herbarium, House, Humicole, Hydrastus, Hydrophyte, Hygrophyte, Hylophyte, Incross, Insert, Instil, Inter, Labiate, Land, Lathe, Legume, Lithophyte, Livelong, Longday, Machinery, Mill, Monocotyledon, Ornamental, Perennial, Phanerogam, Phloem, Pilot, Pitcher, Power, Protophyte, Ramet, Resurrection, Root, Rosin, Saprophyte, Schizophyte, Sciophyte, Sclerophyll, Scrambler, Sensitive, Sere, Shortday, Shrub, Simple, Sow, Sponge, Steelworks, Stickseed, Sticktight, Strangler, Streptocarpus, Succulent, Superweed, Thallophyte, Therophyte, Thickleaf, Trailer, → **TREE**, Trifolium, Tropophyte, Twining, Vegetal, Vegetation, Washery, Wilding, Works, Zoophyte

---

PLANTS

3 letters:	Ivy	Pia	Til
Dal	Kex	Rue	Udo
Hom	Meu	Set	Urd
Hop	Nep	Soy	Yam

4 letters:
Alga
Aloe
Anil
Arum
Beet
Bixa
Chay
Cube
Daal
Dahl
Deme
Dhal
Dill
Fern
Flag
Flax
Geum
Grex
Guar
Hebe
Herb
Hioi
Homa
Hoya
Ixia
Kaki
Kali
Kava
Khat
Lily
Loco
Maté
Mint
More
Moss
Musk
Nard
Noni
Ombu
Pink
Pita
Rape
Reed
Rhus
Rose
Rush
Sage
Sego
Sida
Snow

Sola
Soma
Sunn
Tare
Taro
Thea
Vine
Weld
Woad
Wort
Yarr

5 letters:
Agave
Ajwan
Anise
Anona
Aroid
Aster
Basil
Benni
Betel
Blite
Bluet
Boree
Broom
Buchu
Bucku
Bugle
Calla
Camas
Canna
Carex
Chara
Chaya
Chufa
Clary
Clote
Cress
Cubeb
Cumin
Daisy
Erica
Ficus
Fitch
Fouat
Fouet
Fucus
Gemma
Glaux
Gorse

Guaco
Hosta
Hovea
Inula
Jalap
Kenaf
Kudzu
Laser
Ledum
Liana
Linum
Loofa
Lotus
Luffa
Lupin
Lurgi
Medic
Morel
Murva
Musci
Naiad
Orach
Orpin
Orris
Orval
Oshac
Oxeye
Oxlip
Panax
Pansy
Peony
Phlox
Pilea
Poppy
Sedge
Sedum
Senna
Shaya
Spink
Stock
Tansy
Tetra
Timbo
Tulip
Urali
Urari
Urena
Vetch
Vinca
Viola
Vitex

Vitis
Xyris
Yucca
Yulan
Zamia

6 letters:
Abelia
Acacia
Acorus
Ajowan
Alisma
Allium
Alpine
Althea
Ambari
Ambary
Amomum
Annona
Arabis
Aralia
Arnica
Aucuba
Azalea
Bablah
Balsam
Bamboo
Bauera
Betony
Borage
Briony
Bryony
Burnet
Cactus
Caltha
Camash
Camass
Cassia
Catnep
Catnip
Celery
Cicely
Cicuta
Cissus
Cistus
Cleome
Clivia
Clover
Clusia
Cnicus
Cockle

Cohage
Cohash
Coleus
Conium
Coonty
Cornel
Cosmea
Cosmos
Cotton
Cowpea
Crinum
Crocus
Croton
Cummin
Dahlia
Daphne
Darnel
Datura
Derris
Dodder
Echium
Endive
Erinus
Exacum
Exogen
Fat hen
Fennel
Ferula
Funkia
Garlic
Gnetum
Henbit
Hoodia
Hyssop
Iberis
Jojoba
Juncus
Kentia
Kerria
Kie-kie
Knawel
Kochia
Korari
Kumara
Kumera
Lentil
Lichen
Lolium
Loofah
Lovage
Lunary

Lupine
Luzula
Madder
Maguey
Mallow
Manioc
Medick
Mimosa
Monoao
Moorva
Nerine
Nerium
Nettle
Nuphar
Orache
Orchid
Orchis
Orpine
Ourali
Ourari
Oxalis
Oxslip
Oyster
Pachak
Paeony
Peanut
Pepino
Pepper
Pieris
Protea
Radish
Ramtil
Rattle
Reseda
Retama
Rubber
Ruscus
Salvia
Savory
Scilla
Senega
Sesame
Seseli
Silene
Smilax
Sorbus
Sorrel
Spider
Spirea
Spurge
Spurry

Squill
Styrax
Sundew
Teasel
Thrash
Thrift
Tomato
Tulipa
Turnip
Tutsan
Violet
Viscum
Wasabi
Yarrow
Yautia
Zinnia

7 letters:
Absinth
Aconite
Alkanet
All-good
Allheal
Allseed
Alyssum
Anchusa
Anemone
Arachis
Astilbe
Awlwort
Barilla
Bartsia
Bee-balm
Begonia
Bogbeam
Boneset
Brinjal
Bugbane
Bugloss
Burdock
Burweed
Calluna
Caltrap
Caltrop
Campion
Caraway
Cardoon
Carduus
Carline
Cassava
Catechu

Catmint
Cat's ear
Celosea
Century
Chayote
Chelone
Chervil
Chicory
Clarkia
Cocoyam
Comfrey
Compass
Coontie
Cowbane
Cowbird
Cowhage
Cowherb
Cowitch
Cowslip
Cudweed
Cumquat
Curcuma
Cushion
Dasheen
Deutzia
Diascia
Dioecia
Dittany
Dogbane
Dogwood
Drosera
Epacris
Ephedra
Erodium
Eugenia
Felicia
Felwort
Filaree
Fly-trap
Freesia
Frogbit
Fuchsia
Gazania
Genista
Gentian
Gerbera
Ginseng
Godetia
Gunnera
Haemony
Hawkbit

7 letters – cont:
Heather
Hemlock
Henbane
Hogweed
Ipomoea
Isoetes
Jasmine
Jonquil
Juniper
Kingcup
Kumquat
Lantana
Lettuce
Liatris
Lobelia
Logania
Lucerne
Lychnis
Lythrum
Madwort
Mahonia
Manihot
Maranta
Matweed
Mayweed
Melilot
Mercury
Milfoil
Mimulus
Monarda
Mudwort
Mugwort
Mullein
Mustard
Nelumbo
Nemesia
Nigella
Nonsuch
Olearia
Opuntia
Palmiet
Pareira
Parsley
Parsnip
Penthia
Petunia
Pigface
Pinguin
Potherb
Primula

Puccoon
Pumpkin
Ragwort
Rampion
Raoulia
Redroot
Rhatany
Rhodora
Rhubarb
Ricinus
Robinia
Romneya
Rosebay
Ruellia
Saffron
Salfern
Salsify
Salsola
Sampire
Sanicle
Sawwort
Scandix
Seakale
Sea pink
Senecio
Setwall
Skirret
Solanum
Spignel
Spinach
Spiraea
Spurrey
Squilla
Stachys
Stapela
Statice
Syringa
Tagetes
Thallus
Tobacco
Trefoil
Triffid
Tritoma
Turbith
Turpeth
Vanilla
Verbena
Vervain
Weigela
Woorali
Woorara

Wourali
Zebrina
Zedoary

8 letters:
Abelmosk
Absinthe
Abutilon
Acanthus
Achillea
Ageratum
Agrimony
Agueweed
Alocasia
Alumroot
Angelica
Apocynum
Arenaria
Argemone
Asphodel
Barometz
Bauhinia
Bear's ear
Bedstraw
Beetroot
Bellwort
Bergamot
Bergenia
Bignonia
Bindi-eye
Bindweed
Bird's eye
Bluebell
Bottonia
Boxberry
Brassica
Buckbean
Buddleia
Bull-hoof
Buplever
Caladium
Calamint
Calamite
Calathea
Calthrop
Camellia
Camomile
Canaigre
Cannabis
Capsicum
Cardamom

Cardamum
Carl-hemp
Catchfly
Cat's foot
Centaury
Charlock
Chayroot
Chenopod
Chickpea
Cilantro
Cleavers
Clematis
Clubrush
Coltwood
Costmary
Cow-wheat
Crowfoot
Crucifer
Cucurbit
Cumbungi
Cunjevoi
Cyclamen
Daffodil
Damewort
Dentaria
Diandria
Dianthus
Dicentra
Dielytra
Dogberry
Dog daisy
Dog's bone
Dracaena
Dropwort
Duckweed
Dumbcane
Earthnut
Eelgrass
Erigeron
Eucharis
Euonymus
Feverfew
Fireweed
Flax-lily
Fleabane
Fleawort
Fluellin
Foxglove
Fumitory
Furcraea
Galangol

Galtonia
Gardenia
Geranium
Gesneria
Gladioli
Gloriosa
Glory pea
Gloxinia
Glyceria
Gnetales
Goutweed
Grape ivy
Gromwell
Hag-taper
Harakeke
Hardhack
Harebell
Hawkweed
Helenium
Henequen
Hepatica
Hesperis
Heuchera
Hibiscus
Hippuris
Honewort
Hornwort
Horokaka
Hyacinth
Hydrilla
Hyperium
Japonica
Knapweed
Knotweed
Kohlrabi
Krameria
Larkspur
Lathyris
Lavatera
Lavender
Licorice
Lonicera
Lungwort
Macleaya
Mandrake
Marigold
Mariposa
Marjoram
Martagon
Milkweed
Milkwort

Miltonia
Monstera
Moonseed
Moonwort
Mosspink
Mouse-ear
Myosotis
Navicula
Nenuphar
Nepenthe
Nymphaea
Oleander
Oleaster
Oncidium
Opopanax
Origanum
Oxtongue
Pandanus
Paspalum
Phacelia
Phormium
Physalis
Pinkroot
Pipewort
Plantain
Plumbago
Pokeroot
Pokeweed
Polygata
Pondweed
Primrose
Prunella
Psilotum
Psoralea
Psyllium
Purslane
Putchock
Ratooner
Ratsbane
Redshank
Rock rose
Roly-poly
Rosemary
Sainfoin
Saltwort
Salvinia
Samphire
Sandwort
Scabious
Scammony
Sea-blite

Sea-holly
Self-heal
Sept-foil
Shamrock
Sidalcea
Silkweed
Silphium
Snowdrop
Soapwort
Solidago
Sowbread
Sparaxis
Spergula
Stapelia
Staragen
Starwort
Sweet pea
Tamarisk
Tarragon
Tayberry
Tigridia
Tree-lily
Trigynia
Trillium
Tritonia
Trollius
Tuberose
Tuckahoe
Turmeric
Turnsole
Valerian
Venidium
Veratrum
Veronica
Viburnum
Viscaria
Wait-a-bit
Wallwort
Water yam
Wistaria
Wisteria
Withwind
Woodroof
Woodruff
Woodrush
Wormseed
Wormwood
Xanthium

9 letters:
Aaron's rod

Achimenes
Adderwort
Alfilaria
Alfileria
Amaryllis
Anacharis
Andromeda
Anthurium
Aquilegia
Archangel
Arracacha
Arrowhead
Arrowroot
Artemisia
Artichoke
Artillery
Asclepias
Asparagus
Astrantia
Aubrietia
Ayabuasca
Bald-money
Baneberry
Beech fern
Bee-orchid
Birthroot
Birthwort
Bloodroot
Bog myrtle
Breadroot
Bromeliad
Brooklime
Brookweed
Broom-rape
Buckwheat
Buglewood
Burrawang
Butterbur
Buttercup
Calcicole
Calcifuge
Calendula
Calla lily
Campanula
Candytuft
Cardamine
Carnation
Catchweed
Celandine
Centaurea
Chamomile

9 letters – cont:

Cherry pie
Cineraria
Claytonia
Clianthus
Clintonia
Clove pink
Cocklebur
Cock's comb
Colchicum
Colicroot
Colicweed
Collinsia
Colocasia
Colocynth
Coltsfoot
Columbine
Cordaites
Coreopsis
Coriander
Corydalis
Creamcups
Crocosnia
Crowberry
Crowsfoot
Dandelion
Desert pea
Desmodium
Devil's bit
Didynanua
Digitalis
Dittander
Dock-cress
Dog fennel
Dog violet
Doronicum
Dulcamara
Dutch rush
Dyer's weed
Echeveria
Echinacea
Edelweiss
Eglantine
Equisetum
Erythrina
Euphorbia
Eyebright
Fenugreek
Feverwort
Flame tree
Forsythia

Fourcroya
Friar's cap
Galingale
Gelsemium
Germander
Gessamine
Gladiolus
Glasswort
Goldenrod
Goosefoot
Grass tree
Greenweed
Grindelia
Groundnut
Groundsel
Gypsywort
Hardheads
Heliconia
Hellebore
Helophyte
Herb-Paris
Herb Peter
Hieracium
Hoarhound
Hollyhock
Horehound
Horsemint
Horse-tail
House leek
Houstonia
Hydrangea
Hypericum
Impatiens
Jacaranda
Judas tree
Kalanchoe
Kniphofia
Lamb's ears
Laserwort
Liquorice
Lithodora
Liver-wort
Lousewort
Mare's-tail
Marijuana
Marshwort
Meadow-rue
Mistletoe
Mitrewort
Monandria
Moneywort

Monkshood
Monogynia
Monotropa
Moon daisy
Moschatel
Moss plant
Mousetail
Muscadine
Myristica
Naked lady
Narcissus
Navelwort
Nemophila
Nicotiana
Oenothera
Ouviranda
Parrot jaw
Patchouli
Pearlwort
Pellitory
Pennywort
Penstemon
Peperomia
Pimpernel
Pineapple
Pokeberry
Polygonum
Portulaca
Pyrethrum
Quillwort
Rafflesia
Rattlebox
Riverweed
Rocambole
Rosinweed
Rudbeckia
Sabadilla
Safflower
Sagebrush
Santoline
Santonica
Saponaria
Saxifrage
Screwpine
Sea-rocket
Shoreweed
Sinningia
Snakeroot
Snakeweed
Spearmint
Spearwort

Speedwell
Spikenard
Spikerush
Sprekalia
Stickweed
Stinkweed
Stone-crop
Strapwort
Sunflower
Sweet flag
Sweet-gale
Taraxacum
Telegraph
Thorow-wax
Tiger lily
Titan arum
Tomatillo
Toothwort
Tormentil
Twinberry
Vaccinium
Verbascum
Vetchling
Wake-robin
Waterleaf
Water vine
Wincopipe
Witchweed
Withywind
Wolf's bane
Wood avens
Woundwort
Xanthoxyl

10 letters:

Adder's wort
Agapanthus
Alexanders
Ampelopsis
Anacardium
Angiosperm
Artocarpus
Asarabacca
Aspidistra
Astralagus
Barrenwort
Beggarweed
Biddy-biddy
Bitter-king
Bitterweed
Bladder-nut

Bluebottle
Brugmansia
Busy Lizzie
Butterdock
Butterwort
Buttonbush
Calico-bush
Canada-lily
Candelilla
Catananche
Cat-cracker
China aster
Chionodoxa
Cinquefoil
Cloudberry
Commiphora
Coneflower
Coralberry
Corncockle
Cornflower
Cottonweed
Cow parsley
Cow parsnip
Crakeberry
Cranesbill
Crown vetch
Cuckoopint
Cupid's dart
Day-neutral
Deadnettle
Delphinium
Dog's-fennel
Dog's-tongue
Dragonhead
Dragonroot
Dyer's-broom
Earth-smoke
Easter lily
Elecampane
Escallonia
Eupatorium
Five-finger
Flamboyant
Fleur-de-lis
Foamflower
Four o'clock
Frangipani
Fraxinella
Friar's cowl
Fritillary
Frog's mouth

Gaillardia
Gaultheria
Glycophate
Gnaphalium
Goat-sallow
Goatsbeard
Goat's-thorn
Goat-willow
Goldenseal
Goldilocks
Goldthread
Goose grass
Gypsophila
Hawksbeard
Heart's-ease
Heathberry
Helianthus
Heliotrope
Herb-bennet
Herb-Robert
Hobble-bush
Hop-trefoil
Hyoscyamus
Icosandria
Illecebrum
Immortelle
Indian pink
Indian pipe
Indian poke
Indian shot
Jew's mallow
Jew's-myrtle
Jimsonweed
Joshua-tree
Lemon grass
Loganberry
Maidenhair
Marchantia
Marguerite
Masterwort
Meconopsis
Mexican-tea
Mignonette
Montbretia
Moonflower
Motherwort
Nasturtium
Nightshade
Nipplewort
Ouvirandra
Ox-eye daisy

Painted cup
Parkleaves
Parrot-beak
Parrot-bill
Passiflora
Pennycress
Pennyroyal
Pentagynia
Pentandria
Pentstemon
Peppermint
Pepperwort
Periwinkle
Pimpinella
Pipsissewa
Plume poppy
Poinsettia
Polemonium
Polianthes
Polyanthus
Potentilla
Puschkinia
Ragged lady
Ranunculus
Rest-harrow
Rhoicissus
Rock violet
Rose laurel
Rose mallow
Salicornia
Sarracenia
Sauce-alone
Scindapsus
Scorzonera
Setterwort
Silverweed
Sinsemilla
Snake's-head
Snapdragon
Sneezewort
Sparganium
Spiderwort
Stavesacre
Stitchwort
Stonebreak
Storksbill
Strelitzia
Sweetbriar
Thalictrum
Thunbergia
Tibouchina

Tillandsia
Touch-me-not
Tragacanth
Tree mallow
Tropaeolum
Tropaesium
Tumbleweed
Twinflower
Venus's comb
Wallflower
Watercress
Water lemon
Windflower
Woodsorrel
Yellowroot
Yellowweed
Yellowwort

11 *letters*:

Aaron's beard
Acidanthera
Adam's needle
Antirrhinum
Baby's breath
Bastard balm
Bear's-breech
Beggar's lice
Biscuit-root
Bishop's weed
Bittercress
Bittersweet
Bitter vetch
Bladderwort
Blazing star
Blood-flower
Bog asphodel
Bottlebrush
Bristle-fern
Bur-marigold
Burning bush
Calceolaria
Callitriche
Cheddar pink
Cheese plant
Convolvulus
Corn spurrey
Cotoneaster
Crape-myrtle
Crepe-myrtle
Dusty-miller
Dyer's rocket

11 letters – cont:
Erythronium
Fingergrass
Flamboyante
Forget-me-not
Fothergilla
Gentianella
Gillyflower
Globeflower
Gobe-mouches
Greendragon
Hart's tongue
Helichrysum
Herb of grace
Herb-trinity
Hippeastrum
Honeysuckle
Horseradish
Hurtleberry
Incarvillea
Kangaroo paw
Kiss-me-quick
Labrador tea
Lady's finger
Lady's mantle
Lamb's tongue
Lattice-leaf
Lithotripsy
London pride
Loosestrife
Love-in-a-mist
Madonna lily
Marsh mallow
Meadowsweet
Menispermum
Monadelphia
Mountain tea
Nancy-pretty
Oysterplant
Pachysandra
Paritaniwha
Parma violet
Parrot's bill
Pelargonium
Potamogeton
Proletarian
Ragged robin
Saintpaulia
Sansevieria
Schizanthus
Scurvy grass

Sea lavender
Sea milkwort
Selaginella
Slipperwort
Spanish moss
Sparaganium
Steeplebush
Stephanotis
St John's wort
Strawflower
Sweet cicely
Sweet sultan
Swiss cheese
Thimbleweed
Thoroughwax
Tiger flower
Tous-les-mois
Trumpetweed
Vallisneria
Water purple
Water violet
Welwitschia
Wild mustard
Wintercress
Wintergreen
Xeranthemum

12 letters:
Adam's flannel
Adder's tongue
Alstroemeria
American aloe
Aristolochia
Autumn crocus
Bacon and eggs
Brandy bottle
Branksursine
Cactus dahlia
Calico flower
Cape hyacinth
Cape primrose
Carolina pink
Checkerbloom
Cheese-rennet
Christophene
Christ's thorn
Cobblers' pegs
Corn marigold
Cuckoo flower
Cucumber tree
Darlingtonia

Devil-in-a-bush
Dragoon's head
Elephant's ear
Epacridaceae
Eschscholzia
Fennelflower
Flower delice
Flower deluce
Globe-thistle
Grapple-plant
Helianthemum
Hemp-agrimony
Hound's tongue
Iceland poppy
Indian turnip
Jacob's ladder
Lady's fingers
Lady's slipper
Lady's thistle
Lady's tresses
Lemon verbena
Leopard's bane
Lithospermum
Mariposa lily
Marvel of Peru
Midsummermen
Monkey flower
Morning glory
Mountain flax
None-so-pretty
Old man's beard
Ornithogalum
Parsley-piert
Pasqueflower
Philadelphus
Philodendron
Phytobenthos
Pickerelweed
Pitcher plant
Plantain lily
Pleurisy root
Prickly poppy
Pteridosperm
Pterydophyte
Rhododendron
Rose geranium
Rose of Sharon
Salpiglossis
Sarsaparilla
Scouring rush
Scrophularia

Sea buckthorn
Sempervivium
Shepherd's rod
Shirley poppy
Snow-in-summer
Solomon's seal
Southernwood
Stone parsley
Strophanthus
Sweet alyssum
Sweet William
Tradescantia
Venus flytrap
Virgin's bower
Wandering Jew
Water-soldier
Weatherglass
Wild hyacinth
Wild williams
Zantedeschia

13 letters:
African violet
Alligator pear
Asparagus fern
Barbados pride
Black bindweed
Bladder cherry
Bleeding heart
Bougainvillea
Butcher's broom
Butterfly bush
Carrion-flower
Christmas rose
Cranberry bush
Creeping jenny
Creosote plant
Crown imperial
Dieffenbachia
Dutchman's pipe
Elephant's ears
Elephant's foot
Eschscholtzia
Grape hyacinth
Greek valarian
Mariposa tulip
Marsh marigold
Marsh samphire
Meadow saffron
Mountain avens
Noli-me-tangere

Paschal flower
Passionflower
Rose of Jericho
Shepherd's club
Slipper orchid
Spathyphyllum
Summer cypress
Sweet woodruff
Swine's succory
Tortoise plant
Townhall clock
Traveller's joy
Venus's flytrap
Viper's bugloss
Virginia stock
Water chestnut
Water dropwort
Water hyacinth
Water plantain
Winter aconite

Bougainvillaea
Canterbury bell
Cape gooseberry
Cardinal flower
Castor-oil plane
Chincherinchee
Chinese cabbage
Chinese lantern
Gold-of-pleasure
Hen and chickens
Lords and ladies
Love-in-idleness
Partridgeberry
Prince's feather
Queen Anne's lace
Shepherd's glass
Shepherd's purse
Star-of-the-earth
Sweet horsemint
Treacle mustard
Witches' thimble

Evening primrose
Golden saxifrage
Jack-in-the-pulpit
Lily-of-the-valley
Meadow saxifrage
Michaelmas daisy
Shepherd's myrtle
Star of Bethlehem
Virginia creeper
Wandering sailor

16 letters:
Annunciation lily
Barren strawberry
Bird's foot trefoil
Carolina allspice
Clove gillyflower
Clowgillie-flower
Deadly nightshade
Herb of repentance
Livingstone daisy
Love-lies-bleeding
Mesembrianth-
emum
Poached-egg flower
Queen-of-the-
meadow
Swiss cheese plant

17 letters:
Devil's bit scabious
Dutchman's
breeches
Mother-of-
thousands
Sheep's bit scabious
Snow-on-the-
mountain
St Patrick's cabbage

18 letters:
Mother-in-law's
tongue
Venus's looking
glass

19 letters:
Ploughman's
spikenard

20 letters:
Chickweed
wintergreen

14 letters:
Alder-buckthorn
Barberton daisy
Belladonna lily
Bird of paradise
Black-eyed susan
Bladder campion

15 letters:
Bird's nest orchid
Burnet saxifrage
Christmas cactus
Creeping thistle
Dog's tooth violet

Plantagenet Angevin, Broom
Plantain Mato(o)ke, Ribwort, Waybread
Plantation Arboretum, Bosket, Bosquet, Estate, Grove, Hacienda, Pen, Pinetum, Ranch, Tara, Tope, Veticetum, Vineyard
Plant disease Anthracnose, Blight, Bunt, Club-root, Curlytop, Eyespot, Frogeye, Leaf curl, Leaf-roll, Leaf-spot, Psillid yellows, Rosette, Smut, Sooty mould
Planted In, Under
Planter Dibber, Farmer, Settler, Trowel
Plaque Calculus, Dental, Plateau, Scale
Plasm Germ
Plasma Dextran, Sigmond
Plaster(ed), Plaster board Artex®, Bandage, Blister, Blotto, Butterfly clip, Cake, Cataplasm, Clam, Clatch, Compo, Court, Daub, Diachylon, Diachylum, Drunk, Emplastrum, Fresco, Gesso, Grout, Gyprock®, Gypsum, Intonaco, Laying, Leep, Lit, Mud, Mustard, Oiled, Parge(t), Polyfilla®, Porous, Poultice, Render, Roughcast, Scratch-coat, Screed, Secco, Shellac, Sinapism, Smalm, Smarm, Smear, Sowsed, Staff, Sticking, Stookie, Stucco, Teer
Plastic Bakelite®, Cel(luloid), Cling film, Ductile, Fablon®, Fibreglass, Fictile, Fluon, Formica®, Ionomer, Laminate, Loid, Lucite®, Melamine, Mylar®, Perspex®, Plexiglass®, Pliant, Polyethylene, Polystyrene, Polythene, Polyvinyl, PVC, Reinforced, Styrene, Styrofoam®, Teflon®, Urea-formaldehyde, Vinyl, Wet-look, Yielding

▷ **Plastic** *may indicate* an anagram
Plastic surgeon McIndoe
Plastic surgery Neoplasty, Nose job, Otoplasty, Rhinoplasty
Plate(s), Plated, Platelet, Plating Acierage, Ailette, Anchor, Angle, Anode, Armadillo, Armour, Ashet, Baffle, Bakestone, Baleen, Base, Batten, Brass, Butt, Chamfrain, Chape, Charger, Chrome, Coat, Coccolith, Communion, Copper, Cramper, Cribellum, Ctene, Dasypus, Deadman, Denture, Diaphragm, Dinner, Disc, Dish, Echo, Electro, Electrotype, Elytron, Elytrum, Enamel, Entoplastron, Escutcheon, Face, Fashion, Feet, Fine, Fish, Flatware, Foil, Frog, Frons, Futtock, Glacis, Gold, Graal, Ground, Gula, Half, Hasp, Home, Horseshoe, Hot, Illustration, L, Lame, Lamella, Lamina, Lanx, Latten, Lead, Licence, Madreporic, Mascle, Mazarine, Nail, Nef, Neural, Nickel, Notum, Number, Ortho, Osteoderm, P, Paten, Patina, Patin(e), Pauldron, Peba, Petri, Phototype, Planometer, Plaque, Plastron, Platter, Pleximeter, Poitrel, Prescutum, Print, Pygal, Quarter, Race, Registration, Riza, Roof, Rove, Salamander, Scale, Screw, Scrim, Scutcheon, Scute, Scutum, Seg, Selling, Sheffield, Shield, Shoe, Side, Sieve, Silver, Slab, Soup, Spacer, Spoiler, Squama, Stall, Steel, Stencil, Stereo(type), Sternite, Strake, Surface, Swash, T, Tablet, Tace, Tasse(l), Tea, Tectonic, Tergite, Terne, Thali, Theoretical, Tin(ware), Torsel, Touch, Trade, Tramp, Trencher, Trivet, Trophy, Tsuba, Tuill(ett)e, Tymp, Urostegite, Vane, Vanity, Vassail, Vessail, Vessel, Wall, Water, Web, Wet, Whirtle, Whole, Wobble, Workload, Wortle, Wrap(a)round, Zincograph
Plateau Altiplano, Central Karoo, Chota Nagpur, Darling Downs, Dartmoor, Deccan, Durango, Eifel, Field, Fjeld, Had(h)ramaut, Highland, Highveld, Horst, Kalahari, Kar(r)oo, Kurdestan, Kurdistan, La Mancha, Langres, Laurentian, Mat(t)o Grosso, Mesa Verde, Meseta, Nilgiris, Ozark, Paramo, Piedmont, Puna, Shan, Shillong, Tableland, The Kimberleys, Ust Urt, Ustyurt
Platform Accommodation, Almemar, Bandstand, Barbette, Base, Bema, Bench, Bier, Bridge, Catafalque, Catwalk, Crane, Crow's nest, Dais, Deck, Dolly, Drilling, Emplacement, Entablement, Estrade, Exedra, Exhedra, Fighting top, Flake, Footpace, Footplate, Foretop, Gangplank, Gantry, Gauntree, Gauntry, Gravity, Hustings, Kang, Landing stage, Launch-pad, Machan, Oil, Oil-rig, Pad, Paint-bridge, Pallet, Perron, Plank, Podium, Predella, Production, Programme, Pulpit, Quay, Raft, Rig, Rostrum, Round-top, Scaffold, Shoe, Skidway, Soapbox, Space, Sponson, → **STAGE**, Stand, Stereobate, Stoep, Strandflat, Stylobate, Tee, Terminal, Thrall, Ticket, Top, Traverser, Tribunal, Tribune, Turntable, Wave-cut, Wharf
Platinum Pt, Ruthenium, Sperrylite
Platitude Bromide, Cliché, Commonplace, Truism
Platocephalus Flat-headed
Platonic, Platonist Academician, Ideal, Spiritual
Platoon Company, Squad, Team
Platter Dish, EP, Graal, Grail, Lanx, LP, Plate, Record, Salver, Trencher
Platypus Duckbill, Duck-mole, Water mole
Plausible, Plausibility Cogent, Credible, Fair, Glib, Logical, Oil, Probable, Proball, Sleek, Smooth, Specious
▷ **Play** *may indicate* an anagram
Play(s), Playing Accompany, Active, Amusement, Antic, Antigone, Assist, Brand, Busk, Candida, Caper, Charm, Chronicle, Clearance, Closet, Coriolanus, Crucible, Curtain-raiser, Daff, Dandle, Docudrama, Doodle, Drama, Echo, Endgame, Epitasis, Equus, Escapade, Everyman, Extended, Fair, Finesse, Foul, Freedom, Frisk, Frolic, Fun, Gamble, Gambol, Game, Ghosts, Grand Guignol, Hamlet, Harp, History, Holiday, Inside, Interlude, Jam, Jape, Jest, Jeu, Kinderspiel, Kitchen-sink,

Laik, Lake, Lark, Latitude, Lear, Leeway, Licence, Lilt, Long, Loot, Macbeth, Mask, Masque, Match, Medal, Melodrama, Miracle, Monodrama, Morality, Mousetrap, Mummers, Mysteries, Nativity, Nurse, Oberammergau, On, One-acter, Orestaia, Othello, Parallel, Passion, Pastorale, Perform, Personate, Peter, Portray, Prank, Pretend, Puppet, Recreation, Represent, Riff, Role, Rollick, Romp, Room, Rope, RUR, Satyr, Saw, Screen, Shadow, Shoot, Show, Shuffle, Sketch, Sport, Squeeze, Stage, Straight, Strain, Strike up, Stroke, Strum, Summerstock, Tolerance, Tonguing, Touchback, Toy, Tragedy, Tragicomedy, Trifle, Triple, Tweedle, Twiddle, Two-hander, Vamp, Vent, Whitechapel, Word

Playback Echo, Repeat, Replay

Playboy Casanova, Don Juan, Hedonist, Rake, Roué

Player(s) Actor, Athlete, Back, Backstop, Black, Brass, Bugler, Busker, Cast, CD, Centre, Centre forward, Centre-half, Colt, Contestant, Cornerback, Defenceman, Disc, DVD, E, East, ENSA, Equity, Fetcher, Fiddle, Flanker, Fly-half, Flying wing, Fly-slip, Franchise, Fullback, Gary, Ghetto-blaster, Goalie, Gramophone, Grand master, Half, Half-back, Half-forward, Harlequin, Hooker, Infielder, It, Juke-box, Keg(e)ler, Kest, Kicker, Linebacker, Lineman, Lion, Lock, Long-leg, Longstop, Lutanist, Lutenist, Man, Marquee, Midfield, Mid-on, Mime, Muffin, Musician(er), N, Nero, Nickelback, Nightwatchman, North, Nose tackle, Ombre, Onside, Orpheus, Outfielder, Out(side)-half, Pagliacci, Participant, Pianola®, Pitcher, Pocket, Pone, Pro, Prop, Quarterback, Receiver, Record, Red shirt, Reliever, Rover, S, Safetyman, Scrape, Scratch, Scrum half, Seagull, Secondo, Seed, Shamateur, Short-leg, Shortstop, Side, South, Split end, Stand-off, Stand-off half, Stereo, Striker, Strings, Strolling, Substitute, Super, Sweeper, Tabrere, Target man, Team, Thespian, Tight end, Troubador, Troupe, Upright, Utility, Virtuosi, W, Walker-on, Walkman®, West, White, Wing, Winger, Wingman

Playfair Code

Playfellow Actor, Chum, Companion

Playful Arch, Coy, Frisky, Humorous, Jocose, Kittenish, Ludic, Merry, Piacevole, Scherzo, Skittish, Sportive

Playgirl Actress, Electra

Playgoer Groundling

Playground Adventure, Close, Garden, Park, Rec(reational), Rectangle, Theatre, Tot lot, Yard

Playhouse Amphitheatre, Cinema, Theatre, Wendy

Playsuit Rompers

Playwright Aeschylus, Albee, Anouilh, Arden, Ayckbourn, Barrie, Barry, Beaumarchais, Beaumont, Beckett, Behan, Bellow, Bennett, Besier, Bolt, Brecht, Chekhov, Congreve, Corneille, Coward, Dekker, Delaney, → **DRAMATIST**, Dramaturge, Dramaturgist, Drinkwater, Dryden, Euripides, Feydeau, Fletcher, Frayn, Fry, Gems, Genet, Goldoni, Gorky, Hare, Harwood, Hay, Ibsen, Ionesco, Jonson, Marlowe, Massinger, Menander, Miller, Molière, Mortimer, Morton, O'Casey, Odets, O'Neill, Orton, Osborne, Pinero, Pinter, Pirandello, Plautus, Priestley, Racine, Rattigan, Rostard, Scriptwriter, Shaw, Sheridan, Sherry, Simpson, Sophocles, Stoppard, Storey, Strindberg, Synge, Tate, Terence, Thespis, Travers, Vanbrugh, Webster, Wesker, Wilde

Plea(s) Alford, Appeal, Claim, Common, Defence, Entreaty, Excuse, Exoration, Nolo contendere, Orison, Placit(um), Prayer, Rebuttal, Rebutter, Rogation, Suit

Plead(er), Pleading Answer, Argue, Beg, Entreat, → **IMPLORE**, Intercede, Litigate, Moot, Placitory, Special, Supplicant, Vakeel, Vakil

Please(d), Pleasant, Pleasing, Pleasure(-seeker), Pleasurable Aggrate,

Agreeable, Alcina, Algolagnia, Amenable, Amene, Amiable, Amuse, Apolaustic, Arride, Benign, Bitte, Braw, Cheerful, Chuffed, Comely, Comfort, Content, Cordial, Cute, Delectation, Delice, Delight, Do, Euphonic, Fair, Felicitous, Fit, Flatter, Fun, Genial, Glad, Gladness, Gratify, Harmonious, Hedonism, Jammy, Joy, Kama, Kindly, Lekker, Lepid, List, Naomi, Oblige, Piacevole, Primrose path, Prithee, Prythee, Purr, Queme, Sapid, Satisfy, Suit, Tasty, Thrill, Tickle, Tickle pink, Treat, Vanity, Voluptuary, Wally, Will, Winsome, Wrapped, Xanadu List

Pleasure-garden, Pleasure-ground Lung, Oasis, Park, Policy, Ranelagh, Tivoli

Pleat Accordion, Box, Crimp, Fold, French, Frill, Goffer, Gusset, Inverted, Kick, Knife, Plait, Pranck(e), Prank, Sunburst, Sunray

Pleb(eian) Common, Essex Man, Homely, Laic, Ordinary, Roturier

Pledge Affidavit, Arlene, Arles, Band, Betroth, Bond, Borrow, Bottomry, Dedicate, Deposit, Earnest(-penny), Engage, Fine, Frithborn, Gage, Gilbert, Giselle, Guarantee, Hand, Hock, Hypothecate, Impignorate, Mortgage, Oath, Pass, Pawn, Pignerate, Pignorate, Plight, Promise, Propine, Sacrament, Security, Sponsorship, Stake, Surety, Teetotal, Toast, Troth, Undertake, Vow, Wad, Wage(r), Wed

Pleiades Alcyone, Celaeno, Electra, Maia, Merope, Sterope, Taygete

Plenitude Stouth and routh

Plentiful, Plenty Abounding, Abundance, Abundant, Ample, Bags, Copious, Copy, Easy, Excess, Foison, Fouth, Ful(l)ness, Fushion, Galore, Goshen, Lashings, Loads, Lots, Oodles, Pleroma, Profusion, Quantity, Riches, Rife, Routh, Rowth, Scouth, Scowth, Slue, Sonce, Sonse, Teeming, Umpteen

Plenum Spaceless

Pliable, Pliant Amenable, Flexible, Limber, Limp, Lithe, Malleable, Plastic, Sequacious, Supple, Swack, Swank, Wanle

▶ **Pliers** see **PLY**

Plight Betrothal, Case, Misdight, Peril, Pickle, Pledge, State, Troth

Plimsoll(s) Dap, Gutty, Gym-shoe, Line, Mutton-dummies, Sandshoe, Tacky

Plinth Acroter, Base, Block, Socle, Stand, Zocco, Zoccolo

Plod(der) Drudge, Ploughman, Traipse, Tramp, Trog, Trudge

Plonk Rotgut, Wine

Plop Cloop, Drop, Fall, Plap, Plump

Plot(s) Allotment, Babington, Bed, Brew, Carpet, Chart, Cliché, Collude, Connive, Conspiracy, Conspire, Covin, Covyne, Engineer, Erf, Erven, Frame-up, Graden, Graph, Gunpowder, Imbroglio, Intrigue, Locus, Lot, Machination, Map, Meal-tub, Odograph, Pack, Parcel, Patch, Plan, Plat, Popish, Rye-house, Scenario, → **SCHEME**, Sect(ion), Seedbed, Shot, Site, Story, Storyline, Taluk, Terf, Turf, Web

Plotter Artist, Box (and whisker), Brutus, Cabal, Camarilla, Casca, Catesby, Conspirator, Digital, Engineer, Incremental, Microfilm, Oates, Schemer

Plough(man), Ploughed, Ploughing Arable, Ard, Arval, Big Dipper, Breaker, Bull tongue, Chamfer, Charles's Wain, Contour, Dipper, Disc, Drail, Drill, Ear, Earth-board, Ere, Fail, Fallow, Farmer, Feer, Flunk, Gadsman, Gang, Great bear, Harrow, Lister, Middlebreaker, Middlebuster, Mouldboard, Piers, Pip, Pleuch, Pleugh, Push, Rafter, Rib, Ridger, Rive, Rotary, Rove, Sand, Scooter, Septentrion(e)s, Sill, Sow, Stump-jump, Swing, The Wagon, Till(er), Tractor, Trench, Triones, Wheel

Plough-cleaner Pattle, Pettle

Ploughshare Co(u)lter, Sock

Ploughwise Boustrophedon

Plover Bud, Dott(e)rel, Lapwing, Pratincole, Prostitute, Stand, Tewit, Wing

Plowman Piers

Ploy Brinkmanship, Dodge, Gambit, Manoeuvre, M(a)cGuffin, Stratagem, Strike, Tactic, Wile

Pluck(ing), Plucky Avulse, Bare, Carphology, Cock, Courage, Deplume, Epilate, Evulse, Floccillation, Gallus, Game, → **GRIT**, Guts, Loot, Mettle, Pick, Pinch, Pip, Pizzicato, Plectron, Plectrum, Ploat, Plot, Plunk, Pook(it), Pouk(it), Pull, Race, Scrappy, Snatch, Spin, Spirit, Spunk, Summon, Tug, Twang, Tweak, Tweeze, Vellicate, Yank

Plug Access eye, Ad, Banana, Block, Bung, Caulk, Chaw, Chew, Commercial, Dam, DIN, Dook, Dossil, Dottle, Douk, Fipple, Fother, Gang, Glow, Go-devil, Heater, Hype, Jack, Lam, Operculum, Pessary, Phono, Prod, Promote, Publicity, Ram, Rawlplug®, Recommendation, Safety, Salt, Scart, Spark(ing), Spile, Spiling, Stop(per), Stopple, Strobili, Suppository, Tampion, Tap, Tent, Tompion, Vent, Volcanic, Wage, Wander, Wedge

Plum Beach, Bullace, Cherry, Choice, Damask, Damson, Gage, Greengage, Ground, Jamaica, Japanese, Java, Kaki, Mammee-sapota, Marmalade, Maroon, Mirabelle, Musk, Mussel, Myrobalan, Naseberry, Persimmon, Proin(e), Pruin(e), Prune, Quetsch, Raisin, Sapodilla, Sebesten, Victoria, Wodehouse

Plumage, Plume Aigrette, Crest, Eclipse, Egret, Feather, Hackle, Mantle, Panache, Preen, Ptilosis, Quill

Plumb(er), Plumbing Bullet, Dredge, Fathom, Lead(sman), Perpendicular, Plummet, Sheer, Sound, Test, True, U-trap, Vertical

Plumbago Graphite, Leadwort, Wad(d), Wadt

Plummet Dive, Drop, Lead, → **PLUNGE**

Plump(er) Bold, Bonnie, Bonny, Buxom, Choose, Chopping, Chubbed, Chubby, Cubby, Dumpy, Embonpoint, Endomorph, Fat, Fleshy, Flop, Fubsy, Full, Lie, Matronly, Opt, Plank, Plonk, Plop, Podgy, Portly, Pudgy, Roll-about, Rolypoly, Rotund, Round, Rubenesque, Sonsie, Sonsy, Soss, Souse, Squab, Squat, Stout, Swap, Swop, Tidy, Well-covered, Well-fed, Well-padded, Well-upholstered, Zaftig, Zoftig

Plunder(er) Berob, Booty, Depredate, Despoil, Devastate, Escheat, Fleece, Forage, Freebooter, Gut, Harry, Haul, Herriment, Herryment, Hership, Loot, Maraud, Peel, Pill(age), Prey, Privateer, → **RANSACK**, Rape, Rapparee, Raven, Ravin, Ravine, Reave, Reif, Reive, Rieve, Rifle, Rob, Sack, Scoff, Shave, Skoff, Spoil(s), Spoliate, Sprechery, Spuilzie, Spuly(i)e, Spulzie, Swag

Plunge(r) Dasher, Demerge, Dive, Douse, Dowse, Duck, Enew, Immerge, Immerse, La(u)nch, Nose-dive, Plummet, Plump, Raker, Send, Sink, Souse, Swoop, Thrust

Plural Multiply, Pl

Plus Addition, And, Gain, More, Positive

Plush(ed) Die, Luxurious, Rich, Smart, Tint, Velour, Velvet

Pluto(crat), Plutonic Abyssal, Dis, Dog, Hades, Hypogene, Magnate, Nob, Pipeline, Underground

Plutonium Pu

Ply, Plier(s) Bend, Birl, Cab, Exercise, Exert, Gondoliers, Importune, Layer, Practise, Run, Trade, Wield

▷ **Plying** *may indicate* an anagram

Plymouth Brethren Darbyite

PM Addington, Afternoon, Arvo, Asquith, Attlee, Autopsy, Bute, Cabinet-maker, Callaghan, Chamberlain, Chatham, De Valera, Disraeli, Gladstone, Major, Melbourne, Peel, Pitt, Portland, Premier, → **PRIME MINISTER**, Salisbury, Taoiseach

Pneumonia Lobar, Lobular, Visna

Poach Burn-the-water, Cook, Encroach, Filch, Lag, Steal, Trespass

Pochard Duck, Scaup

Pocket Air, Appropriate, Bag, Bin, Breast, Cavity, Cly, Cup, Enclave, Fob, Glom, Hideaway, Hip, Jenny, Misappropriate, Patch, Placket, Plaid-neuk, Pot, Pouch, Purloin, Purse, Sac, Sky, Slash, Sling, Slit, Steal, Take, Trouser, Vest, Watch, Whitechapel

Pocketbook Reader

Pod(s) Babul, Bean, Belly, Carob, Chilli, Dividivi, Engine, Gumbo, Lablab, Lomentum, Neb-neb, Okra, Pipi, Pregnant, Pudding-pipe, Siliqua, Tamarind, Vanilla, Vine

Podgy Roly-poly

Poem(s), Poetry Acmeism, Acrostic, Aeneid, Alcaic, Anthology, A Shropshire Lad, Awdl, Ballad(e), Beowulf, Bestiary, Bucolic, Byliny, Caccia, Canzone, Cargoes, Cento, Choliamb, Choriamb, Cicada, Cinquain, Complaint, Concrete, Decastich, Dit(t), Dithyramb, Divan, Dizain, Doggerel, Duan, Dub, Dunciad, Eclogue, Elegy, Elene, Epic(ede), Epigram, Epilogue, Epithalamium, Epode, Epopee, Epopoeia, Epos, Epyllion, Erotic, Fifteener, Finlandia, Gauchesco, Georgic, Ghazal, Graveyard, Haikai, Haiku, Heptastich, Heroic, Hexastich, Hokku, Hull, Hypermeter, Idyll, If, Iliad, Imagism, Inferno, Jazz, Kyrielle, Lay, Limerick, Logaoedic, London, Mahabharata(m), Mahabharatum, Meliboean, Melic, Metaphysical, Metre, Mock-heroic, Monostich, Monostrophe, Nostos, Ode, Odyssey, Palinode, Paracrostic, Parnassus, Pastoral, Penill(ion), Pentastich, Performance, Poesy, Prelude, Prose, Prothalamion, Punk, Purana, Qasida, Quatorzain, Quatrain, Quire, Ramayana, Rat-rhyme, Renga, Rhapsody, Rig-Veda, Rime, Rime riche, Rondeau, Rondel, Rubai(yat), Rune, Scazon (iambus), Senryu, Sestina, Sijo, Sirvente, Song, Sonnet, Sound, Spondee, Stanza, Stornello, Symphonic, Tanka, Telestich, Temora, Tercet, Tetrastich, Thebaid, Title, Tone, Triolet, Tristich, Vers(e), Versicle, Villanelle, Völuspá, Voluspe, Waka

Poet(s), Poetic Amorist, Bard(ling), Beatnik, Cavalier, Cumberland, Cyclic, Elegist, Georgian, Iambist, Idyllist, Imagist, Lake, Laureate, Layman, Lyrist, Makar, Maker, Meistersinger, Metaphysical, Metrist, Minnesinger, Minor, Minstrel, Mistral, Monodist, Odist, Parnassian, Performance, PL, Pleiad(e), Poetaster, Rhymer, Rhymester, Rhymist, Rymer, Scald, Scop, Skald, Smart, Sonneteer, Spasmodic, Spasmodic School, Thespis, Tragic, Trench, Troubadour, Trouvère, Trouveur, Verse-monger, Verse-smith, Versifier, Vers librist(e), Water

POETS

2 letters:	Gunn	Vega	Donne
AE	Hogg		Eliot
	Hood	5 letters:	Frost
3 letters:	Hugo	Arion	Gower
Gay	Hunt	Auden	Griot
Poe	Lang	Blair	Heine
	Lear	Blake	Hesse
4 letters:	Omar	Burns	Homer
Abse	Ovid	Byron	Horne
Baif	Owen	Cadou	Hulme
Blok	Pope	Carew	Iqbal
Cory	Rowe	Cinna	Keats
Dyer	Rumi	Clare	Keyes
Gray	Tate	Dante	Lewis

Logue
Lorca
Lucan
Marot
Meyer
Moore
Nashe
Noyes
Plath
Pound
Prior
Rilke
Rishi
Sachs
Tasso
Theon
Vazor
Wyatt
Yeats
Young

6 letters:
Alonso
Arnold
Austin
Barham
Barnes
Belloc
Borges
Brecht
Brooke
Butler
Clough
Cowper
Crabbe
Daurat
Dowson
Dryden
Dunbar
Ennius
George
Glycon
Goethe
Graves
Hesiod
Horace
Hughes
Landor
Larkin
Lawman
Lowell

Marini
Milton
Morris
Motion
Neruda
Ossian
Pindar
Racine
Sappho
Seaman
Shanks
Sidney
Tagore
Thomas
Villon
Virgil
Waller

7 letters:
Addison
Alcaeus
Aretino
Ariosto
Beddoes
Belleau
Bridges
Bunting
Caedmon
Campion
Chapman
Chaucer
Collins
Corinna
Cynwulf
Emerson
Flaccus
Flecker
Heredia
Herrick
Hopkins
Housman
Juvenal
Layamon
Martial
Marvell
Montale
Newbolt
Orpheus
Pushkin
Ronsard
Russell

Sassoon
Service
Shelley
Sitwell
Skelton
Sotades
Southey
Spender
Spenser
Statius
Terence
Thomson
Vaughan
Whitman

8 letters:
Anacreon
Betjeman
Brentano
Browning
Campbell
Catullus
Cummings
Cynewulf
Davenant
Day Lewis
De la Mare
Du Bellay
Ginsberg
Hamilton
Kynewulf
Laforgue
Langland
Leopardi
Lovelace
Macaulay
Mallarmé
Menander
Meredith
Petrarch
Rossetti
Schiller
Shadwell
Stephens
Suckling
Taliesin
Tennyson
Thompson
Traherne
Tyrtaeus
Verlaine

Whittier

9 letters:
Aeschylus
Bunthorne
Coleridge
Euripides
Goldsmith
Henderson
Lamartine
Lucretius
Marinetti
Masefield
Quasimodo
Shenstone
Simonides
Sophocles
Stevenson
Swinburne

10 letters:
Baudelaire
Chatterton
Drinkwater
Fitzgerald
Longfellow
McGonagall
Propertius
Tannhauser
Theocritus
Wordsworth

11 letters:
Apollinaire
Archilochus
Asclepiades
Bildermeier
Maeterlinck
Pherecrates

12 letters:
Archilochian
Aristophanes

14 letters:
Dante Alighieri

15 letters:
Ettrick Shepherd

Poetaster Della-Cruscan
Poetess Ingelow, Orinda
Poet laureate Motion, PL
▶ **Poetry** *see* **POEM**
Po-faced Stolid
Poignant Acute, Biting, Haunting, Keen, Moving, Pungent, Stirring, Touching
Point(ed), Pointer, Points Accumulation, Ace, Acerose, Acnode, Acro-, Aculeate, Aim, Antinode, Antler, Apex, Aphelion, Apogee, Appui, Apse, Apsis, Arrowhead, Ascendant, Bar, Barb, Barrow, Basis, Bisque, Boiling, Break(ing), Brownie, Burble, Burbling, Calk, Cape, Cardinal, Cash, Catch, Centre, Choke, Clou, Clovis, Clue, Colon, Comma, Compass, Compensation, Cone, Conic, Corner, Cover, Crag, Crisis, Critical, Crux, Culmination, Cultrate, Curie, Cursor, Cusp, Cuss, Cutting, Danger, Dead, Decimal, Degree, Descendant, Detail, Dew, Diamond, Direct, Dot, Dry, E, Ear, End, Entry, Epanodos, Épée, Equant, Equinoctial, Eutectic, Exclamation, Fang, Fastigiate, Feature, Fesse, Fielder, Firing, Fitch(e), Five, Fixed, Flash, Focal, Focus, Foreland, Fourteen, Freezing, Fulcrum, Gallinas, Game, Germane, Gist, Gnomon, Gold, Hastate, Head, High, Hinge, Hint, Home-thrust, Ideal, Index, Indicate, Indicator, Intercept, Ippon, Isoelectric, Jag, Jester, Jog, Juncture, Keblah, Kiblah, Kip(p), Knub, Lace, Lagrangian, Lance, Lead, Limit, Lizard, Locate, Locus, Low, Mandelbrot set, Mark, Match, Melting, Metacentre, Microdot, Moot, Mucro, Muricate, N, Nail, Nasion, Near, Neb, Needle, Neel, Ness, Nib, Nocking, Node, Nodus, Nombril, Now, Nub, Obconic, Obelion, Obelisk, Objective, Opinion, Ord, Organ, Oscillation, Particle, Peak, Pedal, Penalty, Perigee, Perihelion, Perilune, Pin, Pinch, Pinnacle, Place, Pour, Power, Pressure, Promontory, Prong, Prow, Punchline, Punctilio, Punctual, Punctum, Purpose, Radix, Rallying, Ras, Reef, Respect, Rhumb, Rhumbline, S, Sample, Saturation, Scribe, Seg(h)ol, Set, Setter, Shaft, Sheva, Show, Shy, Silly, Socket, Sore, Spearhead, Specie, Spicate, Spick, Spike, Spinode, Spinulose, Stage, Stagnation, Starting, Stationary, Steam, Sticking, Stigme, Stiletto, Sting, Stipule, Strong, Sum, Suspension, Synapse, Tacnode, Talking, Tang, Taper, Tax, Technicality, Tine, → **TIP**, Tongue, Trafficator, Train, Transition, Trig, Trigger, Triple, Turning, Urde(e), Urdy, Use, Vane, Vanishing, Vantage, Verge, Verse, Vertex, Vowel, Voxel, W, Weak, Yad, Yield, Yuko, Zenith
Pointless Blunt, Curtana, Flat, Futile, Idle, Inane, Inutile, Muticous, Otiose, Stupid, Vain
Point of honour Pundonor
Poise Aplomb, Balance, Composure, P, Serenity
Poison(er), Poisoning, Poisonous Abron, Aconite, Acrolein, Adamsite, Aflatoxin, Aldrin, Algae, Amanita, Antiar, Apocynum, Aqua-tofana, Arsenic, Aspic, Atropia, Atropin(e), Bane, Barbasco, Belladonna, Benzidine, Boletus, Borgia, Botulism, Brom(in)ism, Brucine, Bufotalin, Bufotenine, Cacodyl, Cadaverine, Calabar-bean, Cannabin, Cicuta, Ciguatera, Colchicine, Coniine, Contact, Cowbane, Coyotillo, Cube, Curara, Curare, Curari, Cyanide, Cyanuret, Datura, Daturine, Deadly nightshade, Deleterious, Digitalin, Dioxin, Dog's mercury, Dumbcane, Durban, Echidnine, Embolism, Emetin(e), Envenom, Ergotise, Exotoxin, Fluorosis, Flybane, Flypaper, Food, Fool's parsley, Formaldehyde, Fugu, Gelsemin(in)e, Gila, Gila monster, Gossypol, Hebenon, Hebona, Hemlock, Henbane, Hydrargyrism, Hydrastine, Hyoscyamine, Iodism, Jimson weed, Lead, Lewisite, Limberneck, Lindane, Listeriosis, Lobeline, Loco, Locoweed, Malevolent, Manchineal, Mandragora, Mephitic, Methanol, Mezereon, Miasma, Mineral, Miticide, Molybdosis, Monkshood, Muscarine, Mycotoxin, Nerve gas, Neurine, Neurotoxin, Neutron, Nicotine, Noogoora burr, Noxious, Obeism, Ouabain, Ourali, Ourari,

Oxalate, Paraquat®, Paris green, Phallin, Phalloidin, Phosphorism, Picrotoxin, Pilocarpine, Plumbism, Ptomaine, Py(a)emia, Raphania, Ratsbane, Ricin, Rot, Safrole, Salicylism, Salmonella, Samnitis, Santonin, Sapraemia, Sarin, Sassy wood, Saturnism, Saxitoxin, Septic(aemia), Sheele's green, Silver nitrate, Solanine, Solpuga, Soman, Stibine, Stibium, Stonefish, Strophanthus, Strychnine, Sugar of lead, Sulphur tuft, Surinam, Systemic, Tanghin, Tanghinin, Tetro(do)toxin, Thebaine, Thorn-apple, Timbo, Toxaphene, Toxic, Toxicology, Toxicosis, Toxin, Toxoid, Trembles, Tropine, Tutu, Upas, Urali, Urushiol, V-agent, Venefic, Venin, Venom(ous), Veratridine, Veratrin(e), Viperous, Virose, Virous, Virulent, Wabain, Warfarin, Wolfsbane, Woorali, Woorara, Wourali, Yohimbine

Poke, Poky Bonnet, Broddle, Chook, Dig, Garget, Itchweed, Jab, Jook, Meddle, Mock, Nousle, Nudge, Nuzzle, Ombu, Peg, Pick, Poach, Pote, Pouch, Powter, → PRISON, → PROD, Prog, Proke, Punch, Root(le), Rout, Rowt, Sporran, Stab, Thrust

Poker (work) Bugbear, Curate, Draw, Game, Gas, High-low, Lowball, Mistigris, Penny ante, Pyrography, Red-hot, Salamander, Strip, Stud(-horse), Texas hold'em, Tickler, Tine, Toe

Poland, Polish Cracovian, PL, Polack, Racovian, Sarmatia, Sejm, Slav, Stefan

Polaris Rhodanic, Rocket, Star

Polar, Pole(s), Poler Animal, Anode, Antarctic, Arctic, Boathook, Boom, Bowsprit, Bum(p)kin, Caber, Celestial, Clothes, Copernicus, Cowl-staff, Crossbar, Electret, Extremity, Fishgig, Fizgy, Flagstaff, Flagstick, Furlong, Galactic, Gas, Geomagnetic, Icy, Janker, Kent, Liberty, Lug, Magnetic, Mast, May, N, Nadir, Negative, Nib, North, Periscian, Po, Positive, Punt, Quant, Quarterstaff, Range, Ricker, Ripeck, Rood, Ry(e)peck, S, Shaft, South, Spar, Spindle, Sprit, Staff, Stake, Stanchion, Stang, Starosta, Stilt, Sting, Stobie, Telegraph, Terrestrial, Thyrsos, Thyrsus, Tongue, Topmast, Totem, Utility, Vegetal, Zenith

▷ **Polar** *may indicate* with a pole

Polecat Ferret, Fitch, Fitchet, Foulmart, Foumart, Quail, Weasel

Polemic(al) Argument, Controversy, Debate, Eristic(al)

Police(man), Policewoman Babylon, Bear, Beast, Beria, Bill, Bizzy, Black and Tans, Blue, Bluebottle, Bobby, Bog(e)y, Boss, Boys in blue, Bull, Busy, Carabinero, Carabiniere, Catchpole, Centenier, Cheka, Chekist, CID, Constable, Cop(per), Cotwal, Crusher, Detective, Dibble, Druzhinnik, Europol, Filth, Flatfoot, Flattie, Flic, Flying Squad, Force, Fuzz, Garda, Garda Siochana, Gendarme, Gestapo, Gill, G-man, Guard, Gumshoe, Harmanbeck, Heat, Hermandad, Inspector, Interpol, Jamadar, Jawan, Jemadar, John Hop, Keystone, KGB, Kitchen, Kotwal, Lawman, Limb, Mata-mata, Met(ropolitan), Military, Mobile, Morse, Mountie, MP, Mulligan, Nabman, Nark, Ochrana, Officer, OGPU, Ovra, Patrolman, PC, Peeler, Peon, Pig, Pointsman, Polis, Polizei, Porn squad, Posse (comitatus), Prefect, Provincial, Provost, Puppy-walker, Ranger, Redbreast, Redcap, Regulate, RIC, Riot, Robert, Rosser, Roundsman, Rozzer, RUC, Sbirro, SC, Secret, Securitate, Securocrat, Sepoy, Shamus, Sleeping, Slop, Smokey, Snatch squad, Sowar(ry), Special, Special Branch, Stasi, State Trooper, Super, Superintendent, Sureté, Sweeney, Texas Rangers, T(h)anadar, The Bill, The Law, Thirdborough, Thought, Traffic, Traps, Vice squad, Vigilante, Walloper, Wolly, Woodentop, Yardie squad, Zabtieh, Zaptiah, Zaptieh, Zomo

Police car Black Maria, Panda, Patrol, Prowl

Police station Copshop, Lock-up, Tana, Tanna(h), Thana(h), Thanna(h), Watchhouse

Policy Assurance, Ballon d'essai, CAP, Comprehensive, Course, Demesne,

Endowment, Expedience, First-loss, Floating, Good neighbour, Gradualism, Insurance, Knock for knock, Laisser-faire, Lend-lease, Line, Method, Open(-sky), Open door, Perestroika, Plank, Platform, Pork-barrel, Practice, Programme, Reaganism, Reaganomics, Revanchism, Scorched earth, Socred, Stop-go, Tack, Tactics, Ticket, Traditional, Valued, White Australia

Polish(ed), Polisher Beeswax, Black, Blacklead, Bob, Bruter, Buff, Bull, Burnish, Chamois, Complaisant, Edit, Elaborate, Elegant, Emery, Enamel, Finish, French, Furbish, Gentlemanly, Glass, Gloss, Heelball, Hone, Inland, Jeweller's rouge, Lap, Lustre, Nail, Perfect, Pewter-mill, Planish, Polite, Polverine, Pumice, Refinement, Refurbish, Rottenstone, Rub, Sand, Sandblast, Sandpaper, Sheen, Shellac, Shine, Sleekstone, Slick, Slickenside, Sophistication, Supercalender, Svelte, Tutty, Urbane, Veneer, Wax

Polite(ness) Cabinet, Civil, Courteous, Genteel, Grandisonian, Mannered, Suave, Urbane, Well-bred

Politic(al), Politics Apparat, Body, Chartism, Civic, Diplomacy, Discreet, Dog-whistle, Expedient, Falange, Fascism, Gesture, Leftism, Neoliberalism, Party, Poujadism, Power, Practical, Public, Radicalism, Rightism, State, Statecraft, Tactful, Wise, Yuppie, Yuppy

Politician(s) Bright, Carpet-bagger, Catiline, Chesterfield, Congressman, Coningsby, Demagogue, Demo(crat), Diehard, Disraeli, Eden, Euro-MP, Evita, Green, Incumbent, Independent, Ins, Isolationist, Laski, Left, Legislator, Liberal, Log-roller, MEP, Minister, Moderate, MP, Nazi, Obstructionist, Octobrist, Parliamentarian, Parnell, Politico, Polly, Poujade, Puppet, Rad, Rep, Richelieu, Senator, Socialist, Statesman, Statist, Tadpole, Taper, TD, Tory, Trotsky, Unionist, Veep, Warhorse, Whig, Wilberforce

▷ **Poll** *may indicate* a first letter

Poll(ing) Advance, Ballot, Bean, Canvass, Count, Cut, Deed, Dod, Election, Exit, Gallup, Head, Humlie, Hummel, Lory, MORI, Nestor, Not(t), Opinion, Parrot, Pineapple, Pow, Push, Referendum, Scrutiny, Straw, Votes

Pollack Fish, Lob, Lythe

Pollard Doddered

Pollen, Pollinate(d), Pollination Anemophilous, Beebread, Dust, Errhine, Farina, Fertilised, Geitonogamy, Intine, My(i)ophily, Palynology, Sternotribe, Witch-meal, Xenia

Pollenbrush Scopa

Pollex Thumb

Pollster Psephologist

Pollute(d), Pollutant, Pollution Acid rain, Adulterate, Atmosphere, Contaminate, Defile, Dirty, File, Foul, Impure, Infect, Light, Miasma, Noise, Nox, Oil slick, Rainout, Smog, Soil, Soilure, Stain, Sully, Taint, Violate, Waldsterben

Polly Flinders, Parrot, Peachum

Polo Bicycle, Chukka, Marco, Mint, Navigator, Rink, Water

Polonium Po

Poltergeist Apport, Ghost, Spirit, Trouble-house

Poltroon Coward, Craven, Dastard, Scald, Scaramouch

Polyandry Nair

Polygraph Lie-detector

Polymath Knowall, Toynbee

Polymer Elastomer, Fructans, Isotactic, Lignin, Oligomer, Paraldehyde, Resin, Seloxane, Silicone, Tetramer, Trimer

Polymorphic Multiform, Proteus, Variform

Polynesian Moriori, Tahitian, Tongan

Polyp(s) Alcyonaria, Cormidium, Gonophore, Hydra, Hydranth, Nematophore, Obelia, Sea-anemone, Tumour

Polyphemus Cyclops

Polyphony Counterpoint

Polystyrene Expanded

Polyzoan Sea-mat

Pom Choom

Pomander Pounce(t)-box

Pomegranate Punica, Punic apple

Pommel Beat, Knob, Pound, Pummel

Pomp(ous) Big, Bloviate, Bombastic, Budge, Ceremonial, Display, Dogberry, Euphuistic, Fustian, Grandiloquent, Grandiose, Heavy, Highfalutin(g), High-flown, High-muck-a-muck, High-sounding, Hogen-mogen, Inflated, Orotund, Ostentatious, Pageantry, Parade, Pretentious, Self-important, Sententious, Solemn, Splendour, Starchy, State, Stilted, Stuffed shirt, Stuffy, Turgid

Pom-pom Ball, Tassel

Ponce Pander, Solicit, Souteneur

Poncho Ruana

Pond(s) Curling, Dew, Dub, Flash, Hampstead, Lakelet, Lentic, Mill, Pool, Pound, Puddle, Settling, Shield(ing), Slough, Stank, Stew, Tank, Turlough, Vivarium, Viver

Ponder(ous) Brood, Cogitate, Contemplate, Deliberate, Heavy, Laboured, Mull, Muse, Perpend, Poise, Pore, Reflect, Ruminate, → **THINK**, Vise, Volve, Weight(y), Wonder

Poniard Bodkin, → **DAGGER**, Dirk, Stiletto

Pontiff, Pontifical, Pontificate Aaron, Aaronic, Antipope, Dogmatise, Papal

Pontoon Blackjack, Bridge, Caisson, Chess, Game, Twenty one, Vingt-et-un

Pony Bidet, Canuck, Cayuse, Cow, Dales, Dartmoor, Eriskay, Exmoor, Fell, Garran, Garron, Gen(n)et, GG, Griffin, Griffon, Gryfon, Gryphon, Jennet, Jerusalem, Mustang, New Forest, One-trick, Pit, Polo, Pownie, Sable Island, Shanks', Sheltie, Shetland, Show, Tangun, Tat(too), Timor, Welsh, Welsh Mountain, Western Isles

Ponytail Queue

Poodle Barbet, Swan

Pooh Bah, Bear, Pugh, Winnie, Yah

Pool Backwater, Bank, Bethesda, Billabong, Birthing, Bogey hole, Cenote, Cess, Collect, Combine, Dub, Dump, Flash, Flow, Gene, Hag, Hot, Jackpot, Jacuzzi®, Kitty, Lasher, Lido, Lin(n), Meer, Mere, Mickery, Mikvah, Mikveh, Millpond, Moon, Natatorium, Piscina, Piscine, Plash, Plesh, Plunge, → **POND**, Reserve, Share, Siloam, Snooker, Spa, Stank, Stanley, Sump, Tank, Tarn, Water(ing) hole, Wave

▷ **Poor** *may indicate* an anagram

Poor(ly) Bad, Bare, Base, Bijwoner, Breadline, Buckeen, Bywoner, Catchpenny, Cheapo, Churchmouse, Conch, Cronk, Destitute, Gritty, Half-pie, Hard-up, Have-nots, Hopeless, Humble, Hungry, Ill(-off), Impecunious, Indigent, Lazarus, Lean, Lo-fi, Lousy, Low, Low-downer, Low-fi, Low-paid, Lumpen, Meagre, Mean, Needy, Obolary, One-horse, Pauper, Peaky, Poxy, Redleg, Roinish, Rop(e)y, Roynish, Sad, Scrub, Shabby, Shitty, Sober, Sorry, Sub, Thin, Third-rate, Trashy, Undeserving, Unwell, Wattle, Wishy-washy

Poorhouse Union, Workhouse

Pooter Nobody, Nonentity

▷ **Pop** *may indicate* an anagram

Pop (off), Popper, Popping Bang, Brit, Burst, Cloop, Crease, Die, → **DRUG**, Father, Fr, Gingerbeer, Hip-hop, Hock, Insert, Lumber, Mineral, Nip, Party, Pater, Pawn, Pledge, Population, Press-stud, Punk, Sherbet, Soda, Splutter, Weasel

Pope(s) Adrian, Alexander, Atticus, Benedict, Black, Boniface, Borgia, Clement, Dunciad, Eminence, Fish, Great Schism, Gregory, Hildebrand, Holiness, Innocent, Joan, Leo, Papa, Pius, Pontiff, Ruff(e), Schism, Sixtius, Theocrat, Tiara, Urban, Vatican, Vicar-general of Christ, Vicar of Christ

Pop-gun Bourtree-gun

Popinjay Barbermonger, Coxcomb, Dandy, Fop, Macaroni, Parrot, Prig, Skipjack

Poplar Abele, Aspen, Balsam, Cottonwood, Lombardy, Trembling, Tulip, White, Yellow

Poppet Cutie pie, Valve

Poppy Argemone, Bloodroot, Blue, California, Chicalote, Coquelicot, Corn, Diacodin, Eschscholtzia, Field, Flanders, Horned, Iceland, Matilija, Mawseed, Opium, Papaver, Plume, Ponceau, Prickly, Puccoon, Rhoeadales, Shirley, Tall, Welsh

Poppycock Bosh, Nonsense, Rubbish

Popular(ity), Popularly Common, Crowd-pleaser, Cult, Democratic, Demotic, Enchorial, General, Grass roots, Heyday, Hit, In, Laic, Lay, Mass, Plebeian, Prevalent, Public, Street cred, Successful, Tipped, Trendy, Vogue, Vulgo

Population, Populace Catchment, Census, Closed, Demography, Inhabitants, Malthusian, Mass, Mob, Optimum, → **PEOPLE**, Public, Universe

Porcelain Arita, Artificial, Bamboo, Belleek®, Blanc-de-chine, Celadon, Chantilly, Chelsea, China, Coalport, Crackle(ware), Crouch-ware, Crown Derby, Derby, Dresden, Eggshell, Famille, Famille jaune, Famille noir, Famille rose, Famille verte, Frit, Goss, Hard-paste, Hizen, Imari, Ivory, Jasp(er), Jasper(ware), Kakiemon, Limoges, Lithophane, Meissen, Minton, Parian, Petuntse, Petuntze, Sèvres, Softpaste, Spode, Sung, Yuan

Porch Galilee, Lanai, Stoa, Stoep, Veranda(h)

Porcupine Hedgehog, Urson

Pore Browse, Hole, Hydrathode, Lenticel, Muse, Ostium, Outlet, Ponder, Stoma, Study

Porgy Braise, Scup(paug)

Pork(y) Bacon, Boar, Brawn, Chap, Char sui, Crackling, Flitch, Griskin, Ham, Lie, Pancetta, Salt, Scrapple, Scruncheon, Scrunchion, Spare-rib, Spek, Tenderloin

Porn(ography), Pornographic Curiosa, Erotica, Hard, Hard-core, Jazz mag, Rhyparography, Snuff-film, Soft, Soft-core

Porous Cellular, Permeable, Pumice, Sponge

Porpoise Bucker, Dolphin, Mereswine, Pellach, Pellack, Pellock, Phocaena, Sea pig, Sea swine

Porridge Berry, Bird, Brochan, Brose, Burgoo, Busera, Crowdie, Drammach, Drammock, Gaol, Grits, Grouts, Gruel, Hominy, Kasha, Mabela, Mahewu, Mealie pap, Mielie pap, Oaten, Oatmeal, Parritch, Pease-brose, Polenta, Pottage, Praiseach, Sadza, Samp, Sentence, Skilly, Stirabout, Stretch, Sup(p)awn, Time, Ugali

Porridge stick Thible, Thivel

Port(s) Beeswing, Carry, Cinque, Container (terminal), Entrepot, Free, Gate, Gateway, Geropiga, → **HARBOUR**, Haven, Hinterland, Hithe, Induction, Larboard, Left, Manner, Mien, Outport, Parallel, Ruby, Serial, Tawny, Treaty, USB, Wine

PORTS

3 letters:
Abo
Ayr
Gao
Hué
Rio
Rye
Tyr

4 letters:
Acre
Aden
Akko
Amoy
Apia
Baku
Bari
Boma
Cobh
Cork
Deal
Dill
Doha
Eisk
Elat
Faro
Gary
Hilo
Hull
Icel
I-pin
Kiel
Kiev
Kobe
Kure
Lima
Linz
Lomé
Luda
Naha
Oban
Omsk
Oran
Oslo
Oulu
Perm
Pori
Pula
Puri

Ruse
Safi
Said
Salé
Sfax
Suez
Susa
Suva
Tang
Tema
Tvev
Tyre
Vigo
Wick
Wuhu

5 letters:
Akaba
Anzio
Aqaba
Arhus
Arica
Aulis
Bahia
Bahru
Barry
Basra
Batum
Beira
Belem
Bharu
Blyth
Brest
Cadiz
Cairo
Canea
Colon
Dakar
Davao
Derry
Dilli
Dover
Duala
Dubai
Eilat
Elath
Emden
Gabes
Galle

Gavie
Genoa
Ghent
Gijon
Goole
Haifa
Hania
Horta
Hythe
Izmir
Jaffa
Jedda
Jembi
Jidda
Joppa
Kerch
Kochi
Larne
Leith
Lulea
Mainz
Malmo
Masan
Merca
Miami
Mocha
Mokpo
Narva
Newry
Omaha
Osaka
Ostia
Palos
Ponce
Poole
Pusan
Pylos
Rabat
Rouen
Saida
Sakai
Salto
Selby
Sidon
Skien
Split
Surat
Susah
Tajik

Tampa
Tanga
Tunis
Turku
Vaasa
Varna
Visby
Vlore
Volos
Yalta
Yeisk
Yeysk
Yibin

6 letters:
Aarhus
Abadan
Agadir
Albany
Alborg
Amalfi
Ancona
Andong
Annaba
Aveiro
Balboa
Bastia
Batumi
Bergen
Bilbao
Bissao
Bissau
Blanca
Bombay
Bootle
Boston
Braila
Bremen
Bukavu
Burgas
Cairns
Calais
Callao
Candia
Cannes
Canton
Cavite
Chania
Chi-lin

6 letters – cont:

Cochin	Mobile	Timaru	Corinth
Cuiaba	Mumbai	Tobruk	Corunna
Cuyaba	Muscat	Toledo	Cotonou
Da Nang	Namibe	Toulon	Derbent
Danzig	Nantes	Tromso	Detroit
Darwin	Napier	Tyumen	Drammen
Dieppe	Naples	Velsen	Dunedin
Djambi	Narvik	Venice	Dunkirk
Douala	Nassau	Vyborg	El Minya
Duluth	Nelson	Weihai	Ephesus
Dunbar	Newark	Whitby	Esbjerg
Dundee	Ningbo	Wismar	Foochow
Durban	Ningpo	Wonsan	Fukuoka
Durres	Nizhni	Yangon	Funchal
Elblag	Odense	Yantai	Geelong
Galata	Odessa		Grimsby
Galati	Oporto	**7 letters:**	Halifax
Gdansk	Ostend	Aalborg	Hamburg
Gdynia	Padang	Abidjan	Harwich
Harbin	Patras	Ajaccio	Heysham
Havana	Peoria	Alesund	Hodeida
Hobart	Pesaro	Almeria	Horsens
Ichang	Quebec	Antalya	Houston
Iligan	Quincy	Antibes	Hungnam
Iloilo	Rabaul	Antwerp	Incheon
Inchon	Ragusa	Aracaju	Iquique
Jaffna	Recife	Astoria	Iquitos
Jarrow	Rijeka	Augusta	Kaolack
Juneau	Rimini	Averiro	Karachi
Kalmar	Romney	Bangkok	Kavalla
Kisumu	Roseau	Bayonne	Kenitra
Lepaya	Rostov	Bengasi	Kherson
Lisbon	Samara	Berbera	Kinsale
Lobito	Samsun	Bizerta	Kolding
Lubeck	Santos	Bizerte	Konakri
Lushun	Sarnia	Bristol	Kowloon
Macelo	Sasebo	Buffalo	Kuching
Mackay	Savona	Bushire	La Plata
Madras	Skikda	Calabar	Latakia
Malabo	Smyrna	Cam Ranh	Legaspi
Malaga	Sousse	Canopus	Le Havre
Manado	Speyer	Cantala	Lepanto
Manama	Spires	Cardiff	Liepaja
Manaos	St John	Catania	Livorno
Manaus	St Malo	Changde	Lorient
Manila	St Paul	Changte	Makurdi
Maputo	Suakin	Chicago	Marsala
Matadi	Sydney	Chilung	Masbate
Menado	Syzran	Cologne	Massaua
Mersin	Tacoma	Colombo	Massawa
	Tajiki	Conakry	Maulman

Memphis
Messina
Milazzo
Mombasa
Moulman
Munster
Nanjing
Nanking
Nanning
Neusatz
Newport
Niigata
Niteroi
Novi Sad
Oakland
Okayama
Onitsha
Otranto
Pahsien
Palermo
Pelotas
Phocaea
Piraeus
Qingdao
Randers
Rangoon
Rapallo
Ravenna
Rosario
Rostock
Runcorn
Salerno
San Remo
Sao Luis
Seattle
Sekondi
Setubal
Seville
Shantou
Shantow
Sinuiju
Stettin
St John's
St Louis
Sukhumi
Swansea
Tadzhik
Tampico
Tangier
Taranto
Trabzon

Trapani
Trieste
Tripoli
Ushuaia
Vitebsk
Vitoria
Wanxian
Wenchou
Wenchow
Wenzhou
Whyalla
Yakutsk
Yichang
Yingkou
Yingkow

8 letters:
Aalesund
Aberdeen
Acapulco
Alicante
Alleppey
Arbroath
Auckland
Badalona
Barletta
Batangas
Bathurst
Benghazi
Benguela
Bobruisk
Bobryusk
Bordeaux
Boulogne
Brindisi
Brisbane
Bromberg
Caesarea
Cagliari
Calcutta
Castries
Changsha
Changteh
Chaochow
Cheribon
Chimbote
Chingtao
Chongjin
Cuxhaven
Drogheda
Duisburg

Dunleary
El Ferrol
Elsinore
Falmouth
Flushing
Freetown
Gisborne
Gonaives
Goteborg
Greenock
Haiphong
Hakodate
Halmstad
Hamilton
Hangchow
Hangzhou
Harfleur
Hartford
Hastings
Helsinki
Holyhead
Honolulu
Iraklion
Istanbul
Jayapura
Jinjiang
Kanazawa
Kawasaki
Keflavik
Kingston
Klaipeda
La Coruna
La Guaira
La Guyara
La Spezia
Lattakia
Les Cayes
Limassol
Limerick
Luderitz
Mariupol
Matanzas
Maulmain
Mayaguez
Mazatlan
Monrovia
Montreal
Moulmein
Murmansk
Mytilene
Nagasaki

Nan-ching
Newhaven
Nha Trang
Novgorod
Nykøbing
Pago Pago
Paramibo
Pavlodar
Paysandu
Peiraeus
Penzance
Pevensey
Plymouth
Pnom Penh
Port Said
Pozzuoli
Qui Nhong
Ramsgate
Rio Bravo
Salvador
Samarang
Sanarang
Sandakan
San Diego
Sandwich
Santarem
Santiago
Savannah
Schiedam
Selencia
Semarang
Shanghai
Sorrento
Stockton
Surabaja
Surabaya
Syracuse
Szczecin
Tadzhiki
Taganrog
Takoradi
Tangiers
Tarshish
Tauranga
Teresina
Tjirebon
Tsingtao
Valdivia
Valencia
Veracruz
Victoria

8 letters – cont:
Wanganui
Weymouth
Yarmouth
Yokohama
Yokosuka
Zaanstad

9 letters:
Anchorage
Angostura
Annapolis
Antserana
Archangel
Balaclava
Balaklava
Baltimore
Barcelona
Bass-Terre
Bhavnagar
Bujumbura
Bydgoszcz
Carnarvon
Cartagena
Cherbourg
Chisimaio
Chongqing
Chungking
Cleveland
Constanta
Dartmouth
Den Helder
Djajapura
Dordrecht
Dubrovnik
Ellesmere
Epidaurus
Esperance
Essaouira
Europoort
Famagusta
Fishguard
Fleetwood
Flensburg
Fortaleza
Fremantle
Gallipoli
Gateshead
Gravesend
Guayaquil
Hangchoio

Helsinger
Heraklion
Hiroshima
Immingham
Inhambane
Jasselton
Kagoshima
Kaohsiung
King's Lynn
Kingstown
Kirkcaldy
Kota Bahru
Kozhikode
Kronstadt
Las Palmas
Lowestoft
Magdeburg
Mahajanga
Mangalore
Maracaibo
Mariehamn
Marseille
Matamoros
Matsuyama
Melbourne
Milwaukee
Morecambe
Newcastle
Nuku'alofa
Palembang
Phnom Penh
Pontianak
Port Blair
Port Louis
Port Sudan
Reykjavik
Rotterdam
Santa Cruz
Santander
Schleswig
Sheerness
Singapore
Soerabaja
Stavanger
St George's
St Nazaire
Stornoway
Stralsund
Stranraer
Sundsvall
Takamatsu

Tarragona
Toamasina
Trebizond
Trondheim
Tynemouth
Volgograd
Walvis Bay
Waterford
Weihaiwei
Whangarei
Zamboanga
Zeebrugge

10 letters:
Alexandria
Belize City
Birkenhead
Bratislava
Bridgeport
Bridgetown
Caernarvon
Cap-Haitien
Casablanca
Charleston
Cheboksary
Chittagong
Cienfuegos
Copenhagen
Corrientes
Dzerzhinsk
East London
Felixstowe
Folkestone
Fray Bentos
Fredericia
Georgetown
Gothenburg
Hammerfest
Hartlepool
Herakleion
Iskenderun
Joao Pessoa
Karlskrona
Khabarovsk
Khota Bharu
Kitakyushu
La Rochelle
Launceston
Los Angelos
Louisville
Matozinhos

Montevideo
Mostaganem
New Bedford
New Orleans
Norrkoping
Paramaribo
Pittsburgh
Pontevedra
Port Gentil
Portobello
Portsmouth
Port Talbot
Providence
Queenstown
Sacramento
Santa Marta
Sebastopol
Sevastopol
Strasbourg
Sunderland
Talcahuano
Thunder Bay
Townsville
Valparaiso
Willemstad
Wilmington
Winchelsea

11 letters:
Antofagusta
Antseranana
Banjarmasin
Banjermasin
Baranquilla
Bremerhaven
Cheng-chiang
Dares Salaam
Fredrikstad
Grangemouth
Helsingborg
Hermoupolis
Kaliningrad
Makhachkala
New Plymouth
Newport News
Nuevo Laredo
Pointe-Noire
Port Moresby
Porto Alegre
Port of Spain
Punta Arenas

Rockhampton
San Fernando
Scarborough
Shimonoseki
Southampton
Telukbetong
Trincomalee
Vizagapatam
Vlaardingen
Vladivostok

12 letters:
Angtofagasta
Bandjarmasin
Bandjermasin
Barranquilla
Buenaventura
Chandemagore
Dun Laoghaire

Ho Chi Min City
Jacksonville
Kota Kinabalu
Kristiansand
Milford Haven
Philadelphia
Pointe-à-Pitre
Ponta Delgada
Port Adelaide
Port-au-Prince
Port Harcourt
Prince Rupert
Rio de Janeiro
San Francisco
San Sebastian
Santo Domingo
South Shields
St Petersburg
Tanjungpriok

Thessaloniki
Ujung Pandang
Usti nad Labem

13 letters:
Chandernagore
Charlottetown
Ciudad Bolivar
Corpus Christi
Florianopolis
Great Yarmouth
Ho Chi Minh City
Hook of Holland
Port Elizabeth
Tandjungpriok
Teloekbetoeng
Trois Rivières
Visakhapatnam
Wilhelmshaven

14 letters:
Mina Hassen Tani
Nizhni Novgorod
Santiago de Cuba
Vishakhapatnam

15 letters:
Alexandroupolis
Angra-de-Heroismo
Blagoveshchensk
Sault Saint Marie

16 letters:
Reggio di Calabria
Sault Sainte Marie

18 letters:
Castellon de la
Plana

Portable Lapheld, Laptop, Palmtop
Portend, Portent(ous) Augur, Awesome, Bode, Dire, Omen, Ostent, Phenomenon, Presage, → **WARN(ING)**
Porter Ale, Bearer, Bellboy, Bellhop, Bummaree, Caddie, Caddy, Cole, Concierge, Coolie, Door-keeper, Doorman, Dvornik, Entire, Gatekeeper, Hamaul, Ham(m)al, Humper, Janitor, October, Ostiary, Plain, Red-cap, Stout
Portfolio Holding
Portico Colonnade, Decastyle, Distyle, Dodecastyle, Exedra, Loggia, Narthex, Parvis(e), Porch, Propylaeum, Prostyle, Stoa, Veranda(h), Xyst(us)
Portion Aliquot, Ann(at), Bit, Deal, Distribute, Dole, Dose, Dotation, Fraction, Fragment, Helping, Heritage, Hunk, Instalment, Jointure, Lot, Measure, Meed, Mess, Modicum, Moiety, Nutlet, Ounce, Parcel, → **PART**, Piece, Ratio, Sample, Scantle, Scantling, Section, Segment, Serving, Share, Size, Slice, Something, Spoonful, Tait, Taste, Tate, Tittle, Tranche, Wodge
Portland Bill, Cement, Stone
Portly Ample, Corpulent, Gaucie, Gaucy, Gawcy, Gawsy, Stout
Portmanteau Bag, Combination, Holdall, Valise
Portrait(ist) Carte de visite, Composite, Depiction, Drawing, Eikon, Icon, Identikit®, Ikon, Image, Kit-cat, Lely, Likeness, Painting, Pin-up, Retraitt, Retrate, Sketch, Vignette
Portray(al) Caricature, Depict, Describe, Feature, Image, Limn, Paint, Personate, Render, Represent, → **SHOW**
Portsmouth Pompey
Portugal, Portuguese Lusitania(n), Luso-, Macanese, Senhor
Pose(r), Poseur Aesthete, Affect(ation), Arabesque, Asana, Ask, Contrapposto, Drape, Lotus, Mannequin, Man(n)ikin, Masquerade, Model, Place, Plastique, Posture, Pretend, Problem, Propound, Pseud, Puzzle, Sit, Stance, Sticker, Tableau vivant, Tickler
Poseidon Earthshaker
Posh Chic, Classy, Grand, Lah-di-dah, Ornate, Ritzy, Swanky, Swish, U
Position Asana, Attitude, Bearing(s), Case, Close, Codille, Delta, Emplacement,

Enfilade, False, Fixure, F(o)etal, Foothold, Fowler's, Grade, Instal, Lay, Lie, Location, Locus, Lodg(e)ment, Lotus, Missionary, Mudra, Office, Open, Pass, Peak, Place, Plant, Point, Pole, Possie, Post, Pozzy, Put, Recovery, Recumbent, Root, Seat, Set(ting), Sextile, Sims, Site, Situ, Situs, Stance, Standing, Standpoint, Station, Status, Strategic, Syzygy, Tagmeme, Thesis, Tierce, Trendelenburg's, Tuck, Viewpoint

Positive, Positivist Absolute, Anode, Assertive, Categorical, → **CERTAIN**, Comte, Definite, Emphatic, False, Plus, Print, Sure, Thetic, Upbeat, Veritable, Yang, Yes

Posse Band, Mob, Vigilantes

Possess(ed), Possession(s), Possessive Adverse, Apostrophe, Asset, Aver, Bedevil, Belonging(s), Demonic, Driven, Energumen, Estate, Have, Haveour, Haviour, Heirloom, His, Hogging, Know, Lares (et) penates, Mad, Obsessed, Occupation, → **OWN**, Proprietorial, Sasine, Seisin, Sprechery, Substance, Tenancy, Usucap(t)ion, Vacant, Worth

Possible, Possibility, Possibly Able, Contingency, Feasible, Likely, Maybe, Mayhap, Off-chance, On, Oyster, Peradventure, Perchance, Perhaps, Posse, Potential, Prospect, Resort, Viable, Well, Will

▷ **Possibly** *may indicate* an anagram

Possum Burramys, Cataplexy, Opossum, Pygmy, Ringtail, Sugar glider, Sugar squirrel, Tait

Post(s), Postage Affix, After, Assign, Bitt, Bollard, Carrick bitt, Command, Correspondence, Cossack, Dak, Dawk, Delivery, Dragon's teeth, Emily, Excess, Finger, First, Flagpole, Goal, Graded, Gradient, Guardhose, Heel, Hitching, Hovel, Hurter, Jamb, Joggle, King, Last, Listening, Log, Mail, Mast, Newel, Observation, Outstation, Pale, Paling, Parcel, Pendant, Penny, Picket, Pigeon, Pile, Piling, Piquet, Placard, Place, Plant, Plum, Pole, Position, Presidio, Puncheon, Pylon, Queen, Quintain, Quoin, Registered, Remit, Residency, RM, Rubbing, Samson's, Seat, Send, Sheriff's, Snubbing, Sound, Spile, Staff, Staging, Stake, Starting, Station, Stell, Stoop, Stoup, Stud, Studdle, Term(inal), Tom, Tool, Trading, Upright, Vacancy, Waymark, Winning

Postcard(s) Deltiology, Picture

Poster Advertisement, Affiche, Bill, Broadsheet, Pin-up, Placard, Playbill, Sender, Solus

Posterior Behind, Bottom, Jacksie, Jacksy, Later, Lumbar, Pygal, Rear, Tail

Post-free Franco

Postman, Postmaster, Postwoman Carrier, Courier, Emily, Hill, Messenger, Nasby, Pat, Portionist, Sorter

Postmark Frank

Post-modern Po-mo

Post mortem Autopsy, Enquiry, Necropsy

Postpone(ment), Postponed Adjourn, Backburner, Contango, Defer, Delay, Frist, Hold over, Lay over, Long-finger, Moratorium, Mothball, Pigeon-hole, Postdate, Prorogue, Put over, Remanet, Reprieve, Respite, Roll back, Shelve, Stay, Suspend, Withhold

Postulant Candidate, Noumenon, Novice

Postulate(s) Assert, Assume, Claim, Koch's, Propound

Posture(r), Posturing Affectation, Asana, Attitude, Birkie, Camp, Carriage, Counter-view, Decubitus, Deportment, Gesture, Mudra, Pose, Pretence, Site, Stance, Swank, Vorlage

Posy Bouquet, Buttonhole, Corsage, Nosegay, Tussiemussie, Tussle-mussle, Tuzzi-muzzy, Tuzzy-muzzy

Pot(s), Potting, Potty Abridge, Aludel, Ante, Bankroll, Basil, Belly, Billycan, Cafetière, Ca(u)ldron, Cannabis, Cannikin, Casserole, Ceramic, Chamber, Chanty, Chatti, Chatty, Chimney, Close-stool, Coal, Cocotte, Commode, Crewe, Crock(ery), Crucible, Cruse(t), Cupel, Delf(t), Dixie, Ewer, Flesh, Gage, Gallipot, Ganja, Gazunder, Grass, Hash(ish), Helmet, Hemp, Hooped, In off, Inurn, Jardinière, Jordan, Kaif, Kef, Kettle, Kitty, Livery, Lobster, Loco, Lota(h), Maiolica, Majolica, Marijuana, Marmite, Melting, Ming, Monkey, Olla, Olpe, Pan, Papper, Pat, Piñata, Pint, Pipkin, Planter, Po, Pocket, Poot, Posnet, → **POTTERY**, Pottle, Pounce, Pout, Prize, Quart, Samovar, Shoot, Skeet, Skillet, Smudge, Steamer, Stomach, Tajine, Tea, Test, Throw, Togine, Trivet, Tureen, Urn, Vial, Ware, Wash, Wok

Potash Kalinite, Polverine, Potassa, Sylvine, Sylvite

Potassium K, Kalium, Pearl ash, Saleratus, Saltpetre

Potation Dram, Drink

Potato(es) African, Aloo, Alu, Batata, Chat, Clean, Couch, Datura, Duchesse, Early, Fluke, Hashbrowns, Hog, Hole, Hot, Irish, Jacket, Jersey, Kidney, Kumara, Lyonnaise, Maris piper, Mash, Murphy, Parmentier, Peel-and-eat, Pratie, Praty, Roesti, Rumbledethump(s), Seed, Small, Solanum, Stovies, Sweet, Tatie, Tattie, Teddy, Tuber, Ware, White, Yam

Pot-bearer Trivet

Pot-bellied Kedge, Kedgy, Kidge, Paunchy, Portly, Stout

Potboiler Hob

Pot-boy Basil, Ganymede, Scullion

Potent(ate) Cogent, Dynamic, Emeer, Emir, Emperor, Huzoor, Influential, Kinglet, Mogul, Nawab, Panjandrum, Powerful, Ras, Ruler, Satrap, Squirearch, Sultan, Virile

Potential(ly) Action, Capacity, Chemical, Electric, Electrode, In posse, Ionization, Making(s), Manqué, Possible, Promise, Resting, Scope, Viable

▷ **Potentially** *may indicate* an anagram

Pothole(r) Chuckhole, Giant's kettle, Spelunker

Pot-house Shebeen, Tavern

Potion Dose, Draught, Drink, Dwale, Love, Mixture, Philtre, Tincture

Pot-pourri Hotchpotch, Medley, Miscellany, Pasticcio, Salmi

Potsherd Ostracon, Ostrakon

Pottage Berry

Potter Cue, Dabbity, Dabble, Dacker, Daidle, Daiker, Daker, Dibble, Dilly-dally, Dodder, Etruscan, Fettle, Fictor, Fiddle, Footer, Footle, Fouter, Gamesmanship, Harry, Idle, Mess, Minton, Muck, Niggle, One-upmanship, Plouter, Plowter, Poke, Spode, Thrower, Tiddle, Tink(er), Troke, Truck, Wedgewood, Wedgwood

▷ **Potter** *may indicate* a snooker-player

Pottery Agatewear, Bank, Basalt, Bisque, Cameo ware, Celadon, Ceramet, Ceramic, China, Creamware, Crock, Crouch-ware, Dabbity, Delf(t), Earthenware, Encaustic, Etruria(n), Faience, Flatback, Gombroon, Granitewear, Hollowware, Ironstone, Jomon, Lustreware, Maiolica, Majolica, Ming, Minton, Pebbleware, Raku, Red-figured, Satsuma, Scroddled, Sgraffito, Slab, Slipware, Smalto, Spode, Spongeware, Stoneware, Studio, Sung, Terra sigillata, Ware, Wedgwood®, Wemyss, Whieldon, Whiteware

Pouch(ed) Bag, Brood, Bum-bag, Bursa, Caecum, Cheek, Cisterna, Codpiece, Diverticulum, Fanny pack, Gill, Jockstrap, Marsupial, Marsupium, Poke, Posing, Purse, Sac, Scrip, Scrotum, Spleuchan, Sporran, Tobacco

Poultice Application, Cataplasm, Embrocation, Epithem(a), Lenient, Plaster

Poultry Dorking, Fowl, Gallinaceous, Plymouth Rock, Poot, Pout, Welsummer

Poultry disease Keel, Scaly-leg, Vent gleet

Pounce Claw, Jump, Lunge, Powder, Sere, Souse, Sprinkle, Swoop, Talon

Pound(er) Ache, As, Bar, Bash, Batter, Beat, Bombard, Bradbury, Bray, Broadpiece, Bruise, Catty, Clomp, Contund, Coop, Drub, Embale, Enclosure, Ezra, Fold, Green, Greenie, Greeny, Hammer, Hatter, Imagist, Intern, Iron man, Jail, Jimmy o'goblin, Kiddle, Kidel, Kin, Knevell, L, Lam, Lb, Lock, Mash, Nevel, Nicker, Oncer, One-er, Oner, Pale, Pen, Penfold, Pestle, Pin, Pindar, Pinfold, Powder, Pulverise, Pun, Quid, Quop, Rint, Scots, Smacker, Sov(ereign), Squid, Stamp, Sterling, Strum, Tenderise, Throb, Thump, Tower, Troy, Weight

Pour(ing) Affusion, Be mother, Birl(e), Bucket, Cascade, Circumfuse, Decant, Diffuse, Disgorge, Flood, Flow, Jaw, Jirble, Libate, Rain, Seil, Shed, Sile, Skink, Spew, Stream, Teem, Trill, Turn, Vent, Weep, Well

Pout Bib, Blain, Brassy, Eel, Fish, Horn(ed), Mope, Mou(e), Scowl, Sulk, Tout, Towt, Whiting

Poverty Beggary, Dearth, Deprivation, Illth, Indigence, → **LACK**, Locust years, Need, Paucity, Penury, Poortith, Puirtith, Squalor, Want

Powder(ed), Powdery Allantoin, Alumina, Amberite, Araroba, Baking, Ballistite, Bleaching, Boracic, Calamine, Chalk, Chilli, Colcothar, Cosmetic, Crocus, Culm, Curry, Custard, Cuttlefish, Dentifrice, Dover's, Dust, Dusting, Eupad, Explosive, Face, Flea, Floury, Fulminating, Giant, Glaucous, Goa, Gregory, Grind, Gun, Hair, Insect, Itching, Kohl, Levigate, Lithia, Litmus, Lupulin, Magnesia, Meal, Mepacrine, Mould-facing, Moust, Mu(i)st, Pearl, Pemoline, Percussion, Persian, Plaster of Paris, Plate, Polishing, Pollen, Pounce, Priming, Prismatic, Projecting, Pruinose, Pulver, Pulvil, Putty, Rachel, Rochelle, Rottenstone, Rouge, Saleratus, Seidlitz, Seme(e), Sherbet, Silver iodide, Sitosterol, Smeddum, Smokeless, Snuff, Soap, Spode, Spodium, Talc(um), Talcose, Thimerosal, Toner, Tooth, Triturate, Tutty, Washing, Zein

Power(ful), Powers Ability, Able, Aeon, Aggrandisement, Almighty, Alpha, Amandla, Arm, Arnold, Athletic, Atomic, Attorney, Audrey, Autarchy, Authority, Axis, Beef, Big, Capability, Chakra, Cham, Charisma, Clairvoyance, Clout, Cogency, Colossus, Command, Corridor, Cube, Danger, Despotic, Diadem, Dioptre, Dominion, Effective, Eminence, Éminence grise, Empathy, Empery, Energy, Eon, Exponent, Facility, Faculty, Fire, Flower, Force, Force majeure, Geothermal, Grey, Gutty, Hands, Hefty, Hegemony, High, Hildebrandic, Horse, Hot, Hp, Hydroelectric, Imperium, Influence, Kami, Kilowatt, Log, Logarithm, Lusty, Mana, Mastery, Megalomania, Might, Mogul, Motive, Motor, Movers and shakers, Muscle, Nature, Nth, Nuclear, Od-force, Omnificent, Omnipotent, Option, P, Panjandrum, People, Pester, Plenary, Plenipotency, Posse, Potency, Prepollence, Prepotent, Puissant, Punch, Purchasing, Regime, Resolving, Say-so, Siddhi, Sinew, Solar, Soup, Stamina, Staying, Steam, Steel, Stiff, Stopping, Stranglehold, Strength, → **STRONG**, Supercharge, Supreme, Suzerain, Teeth, Telling, Throne, Tidal, Tycoon, Tyranny, Tyrone, Ulric, Valency, Vertu(e), Vigour, Vis, Volt, Vroom, Water, Watt, Wattage, Wave, Weight, Welly, Wind, World, Yeast

Powerless Diriment, Downa-do, Failing, Freewheel, Hamstrung, Helpless, Impotent, Impuissant, Incapable, Inert, Unable, Unarmed, Weak

Powwow Confab, Conference, Council, Meeting

Pox Chicken, Cow, French, Great, Orf, Pize, Small, Spanish

Practical, Practicable, Practicalities Active, Applied, Brass tacks, Doable, Easy-care, Hands on, Hard-boiled, Joker, Logistics, No-nonsense, Nuts and bolts, On, Pragmatic, Realist(ic), Realpolitik, Rule of thumb, Sensible, Shrewd, Technical, Useful, Utilitarian, Viable, Virtual

Practice, Practise, Practitioner, Practised Abuse, Adept, Custom, Distributed, Do, Drill, Enure, Exercise, Fire, General, Graft, Group, Habit, Inure, Ism, Keep, Knock-up, Massed, Meme, Mock, Nets, Operate, Order, Ordinance, Ply, Policy, Praxis, Private, Prosecution, Pursuit, Rehearsal, Rehearse, Restrictive, Rite, Rule, Rut, Sadhana, Sharp, Sighter, Spanish, Target, Teaching, Test-run, Trade, Tradition, Train, Trial, Ure, Usage, Use, Wage

Pragmatic, Pragmatist Ad hoc, Busy, Dogmatic, Humanist, Meddling, Officious, Realist

Prairie IL, Illinois, Llano, Plain, Savanna, Steppe, Tundra, Veldt

Prairie dog Whippoorwill, Wishtonwish

Praise(worthy) Acclaim, Adulation, Alleluia, Allow, Anthem, Applause, Belaud, Bless, Blurb, Bouquet, Butter, Carol, Citation, CL, Commend(ation), Compliment, Congratulate, Cry up, Dulia, Ego boost, Encomium, Envy, Eulogise, Eulogium, Eulogy, Exalt, Exemplary, Extol, Gloria, Glory, Hero-worship, Herry, Hery(e), Hosanna, Hymn, Hype, Incense, Kudos, Laud, Lip service, Lo(o)s, Meritorious, Palmary, Panegyric, Puff(ery), Rap, Rave, Roose, Tribute

Pram Carriage, Cart, Dinghy, Scow

Prance Brank, Canary, Caper, Cavort, Galumph, Gambol, Jaunce, Jaunse, Prank(le), Swagger, Tittup, Trounce

Prang Accident, Crash, Smash, Whale

Prank(s) Attrap, Bedeck, Bedizen, Caper, Dido, Escapade, Fredaine, Frolic, Gaud, Jape, Lark, Mischief, Pliskie, Rag, Reak, Reik, Rex, Rig, Spoof, Trick, Vagary, Wedgie

Praseodymium Pr

Prat Bottom, → **STUPID PERSON**

Prate Babble, Boast, Haver, Talk

Prattle Babble, Blat(her), Chatter, Gab(nash), Gas, Gibber, Gossip, Gup, Lalage, Patter, Smatter, Yap

Prawn Banana, Crevette, Dublin Bay, King, Scampi, School, Shrimp

Pray(ing) Appeal, Bed, Beg, Beseech, Bid, Daven, → **ENTREAT**, Impetrate, Intone, Invoke, Kneel, Mantis, Solicit, Wrestle

▷ **Prayer** *may indicate* one who begs

Prayer(s), Prayer book Acoemeti, Act, Amidah, Angelus, Ardas, Ave (Maria), Bead, Beadswoman, Bede, Bene, Bidding, Breviary, Collect, Commination, Common, Confiteor, Cry, Cursus, Daven, Deus det, Devotion, Eleison, Embolism, Entreaty, Epiclesis, Euchologion, Evensong, Geullah, Grace, Habdalah, Hail Mary, Hallan-shaker, Imam, Intercession, Invocation, Kaddish, Khotbah, Khotbeh, Khutbah, Kol Nidre, Kyrie, Kyrie eleison, Lauds, Litany, Lord's, Loulat-ul-qadr, Lychnapsia, Ma(c)hzor, Mantis, Mat(t)ins, Mincha(h), Missal, Morning, Musaf, Novena, Orant, Orarium, Orison, Our Father, Paternoster, Patter, Petition, Phylactery, Placebo, Plea, Preces, Proseucha, Proseuche, Puja, Requiem, Requiescat, Responses, Rogation, Rosary, Salat, Secret, Shema, Siddur, State, Stations of the Cross, Suffrage, Te igitur, Tenebrae, Triduum, Venite, Vesper, Yajur-Veda, Yizkor

Preach(er) Ainger, Boanerges, Circuit rider, Dawah, Devil-dodger, Dominican, Donne, Ecclesiastes, Evangelist, Exhort, Gospeller, Graham, Holy Roller, Itinerant, Knox, Lecture, Local, Mar-text, Minister, Moody, → **MORALISE**, Patercove, Pontificate, Postillate, Predicant, Predicate, Predikant, Priest, Prophet, Pulpiteer, Rant, Revivalist, Sermonise, Soper, Spintext, Spurgeon, Teach, Televangelist

Preamble Introduction, Preface, Proem, Prologue

Prearrange(d) Stitch up

Pre-Cambrian Torridonian

Precarious Dangerous, Parlous, Perilous, Risky, Touch and go, Trickle, Uncertain, Unsteady, Unsure

Precaution Care, Fail-safe, Guard, In case, Prophylaxis, Safeguard

Precede(nce), Precedent Antedate, Example, Forego, Forerun, Head, Herald, Pas, Predate, Preface, Priority, Protocol

Precept(s) Adage, Canon, Commandment, Maxim, Mishna, Motto, Saw

Precession Larmor

Precinct(s) Ambit, Area, Banlieue, Close, Courtyard, District, Environs, Pedestrian, Peribolos, Region, Shopping, Temenos, Verge, Vihara

Precious Adored, Chary, Chichi, Costly, Dear, Dearbought, Ewe-lamb, La-di-da, Murr(h)a, Nice, Owre, Precise, Prissy, Rare, Valuable

Precipice Bluff, Cliff, Crag, Krans, Kran(t)z, Sheer

Precipitate, Precipitation, Precipitous, Precipitator Abrupt, Accelerate, Catalyst, Cause, Deposit, Hailstone, Headlong, Impetuous, Launch, Lees, Pellmell, Pitchfork, Rash, Sca(u)r, Sheer, Shoot, Sleet, Snowflake, Start, → **STEEP**, White

Précis Abstract, Aperçu, Epitome, Résumé, Summary

Precise(ly), Precisian, Precision Absolute, Accurate, Dry, Exact, Explicit, Fine-drawn, Literal, Minute, Nice(ty), Overnice, Particular, Perfect, Plumb, Point-device, Prig, Prim, Punctilious, Sharpness, Spang, Specific, Starchy, Stringent, Succinct, Surgical, Tight, Very

Preclude Bar, Debar, Estop, Foreclose, Hinder, Impede, Prevent

Precocious(ness) Advanced, Bratpack, Forward, Premature, Protogyny

Preconception Ideating

Precursor Avant-courier, Forerunner, Harbinger

Predator(y) Carnivore, Eagle, Fox, Glede, Harpy-eagle, Jackal, Kestrel, Kite, Lycosa, Mantis, Marauder, Predacious, Puma, Tanrec, Tarantula, Tenrec

Pre-dawn Antelucan, Ante lucem

Predecessor Ancestor, Forebear, Foregoer

Predestined Doomed, Fated, Tramway

Predicament Box, Dilemma, Embarrassment, Embroglio, Hobble, Hole, In chancery, Jam, Pass, Peril, Pickle, Plight, Quandary, Scrape, Spot

Predict(ion), Predictable, Predictor Astrologer, Augur, Belomancy, Bet, Damn, Divination, Far-seeing, Forecast, Foreordain, Foresay, Foresee, Foreshadow, Foreshow, Forespeak, Foretell, Formulaic, Forsay, Horoscope, Nap, Necromancy, Portend, Presage, Previse, Prognosis, Project, Prophecy, Prophesy, Regular, Second-guess, Soothsayer, Spae

Predilection Fancy, Liking, Prejudice, Taste, Tendency

Predisposition Aptitude, Inclination, Parti-pris, Tendency

Predominate Abound, Govern, Overshadow, Prevail, Reign

Pre-eminence, Pre-eminent Arch, Foremost, Palm, Paramount, Primacy, Supreme, Topnotch, Unique

Pre-empt Enter

Preen Perk, Primp, Prink, Prune, Titivate

Prefab(ricated) Quonset, Terrapin®

Preface Avant-propos, Foreword, Herald, Intro, Preamble, Precede, Proem, Prolegomenon, Usher

Prefect Pilate, Prepositor, Pr(a)eposter

Prefer(ence), Preferred Advance, Better, Choose, Discriminate, Druthers, Elect, Faard, Faurd, Favour, Imperial, Incline, Lean, Liquidity, Predilect(ion), Prefard,

Priority, Proclivity, Promote, Rather, Sooner, Stocks, Taste, Will

Prefix Eka, Introduce, Name

Pregnancy, Pregnant Big, Clucky, Cyesis, Ectopic, Enceinte, Fertile, F(o)etation, Gestation, Gravid(a), Great, Great-bellied, Heavy, Hysterical, In foal, In pig, In pup, Knocked-up, Phantom, Pseudocyesis, Pudding-club, Retirement, Stomack, Up the duff, Up the spout, Up the stick, With child

Prehistoric Ancient, Azilian, Beaker Folk, Boskop, Brontosaurus, Cambrian, Clovis, Cro-Magnon, Eocene, Folsom, Mound Builder, Ogygian, Primeval, Primitive, Pteranodon, Pterodactyl(e), Pterosaur, Saurian, Sinanthropus, Stonehenge, Titanis, Titanosaurus, Trilith(on)

Prejudice(d) Ageism, Bias, Bigotry, Derry, Discrimination, Down, Illiberal, Impede, Inequity, Injure, Insular, Intolerance, Partiality, Parti pris, Preoccupy, Prepossession, Racism, Sexism, Slant

Prelate Archiepiscopal, Cardinal, Churchman, Exarch, Monsignor, Odo, Priest

Preliminary Draft, Exploration, Heat, Initial, Introductory, Precursory, Preparatory, Previous, Prodrome, Prolusion, Propaedeutic, Rough, Title-sheet

Prelude Entrée, Forerunner, Intrada, Overture, Proem(ial), Ritornell(e), Ritornello

Premature Early, Precocious, Pre(e)mie, Premy, Pre term, Previous, Slink, Untimely, Untimeous

Premedication Atropia

Premeditate Anticipate, Foresee, Plan

Premier Chief, Leader, Main, PM, → **PRIME MINISTER**, Tojo

Premise(s) Assumption, Datum, Epicheirema, Ground, Hypothesis, Inference, Lemma, Major, Postulate, Property, Proposition, Reason

Premium Ap, Bond, Bonus, Discount, Grassum, Pm, Reward, Scarce, Share

Premonition Hunch, Omen, Presentiment, Prodromal, Warning

Preoccupation, Preoccupied, Preoccupy Absorb, Abstracted, Distrait, Engross, Hang-up, Intent, Obsess, Self-centred, Thing

Prepaid Pro-forma, Sae

Prepare(d), Preparation Address, À la, Arrange, Attire, Boun, Bowne, Busk, Calver, Cock, Concoct, Cooper, Countdown, Decoct, Did, Do, Dress, Edit, Forearm, Game, Groom, Ground, Groundwork, Inspan, Key, Lay, Legwork, Lotion, Measure, Mobilise, Parasceve, Pomade, Preliminary, Prime, Procinct, Prothesis, Provide, Psych, → **READY**, Rehearsal, Ripe, Rustle up, Set, Spadework, Stand-to, Suborn, Train, Trim, Truss, Type, Up to, Warm-up, Whip up, Yare

▷ **Prepare(d)** *may indicate* an anagram

Preponderance, Preponderant, Preponderate Important, Majority, Outweigh, Paramount, Prevalence, Sway

Preposition Premise

Prepossessing, Prepossession Attractive, Fetching, Predilection, Winsome

Preposterous Absurd, Chimeric, Foolish, Grotesque, Unreasonable

▷ **Preposterous** *may indicate* a word reversed

Pre-Raphaelite Rossetti, Waterhouse

Prerequisite Condition, Essential, Necessity, Sine qua non

Prerogative Faculty, Franchise, Liberty, Privilege, Right, Royal

Presage Abode, Foresight, Omen, Portend, Presentiment, Prophesy

Presbyter(ian) Berean, Blue, Cameronian, Classic, Classis, Covenanter, Elder, Knox, Macmillanite, Moderator, Sacrarium, Seceder, Secesher, Secession Church, Wee Free, Whig(gamore)

Prescient Clairvoyant, Fly

Prescribe, Prescription Appoint, Assign, Cipher, Decree, Direction, Dictate,

Enjoin, Formula, Impose, Medicine, Negative, Ordain, Positive, R, Rec, Receipt, Ritual, Rule, Scrip, Set, Specific.

Presence Aspect, Bearing, Closeness, Company, Debut, Face, Hereness, Real, Shechinah, Shekinah, Spirit

Present(ation), Presented, Presenter, Presently Ad sum, Advowson, Anchorman, Anon, Assists, Autocutie, Award, Befana, Bestow, Bonsela, Boon, Bounty, Box, Breech, By, By and by, Cadeau, Congiary, Coram, Current, Debut, Dee-jay, Demo, Deodate, DJ, Donate, Dotal, Douceur, Dower, Emcee, Endew, Endow, Endue, Enow, Étrenne, Exhibit, Existent, Exposition, Fairing, Feature, Format, Free-loader, Front-man, Gie, → **GIFT**, Give, Going, Grant, Gratuity, Hand, Here, Historical, Hodiernal, Inbuilt, Inst, Introduce, Jock(ey), Largess(e), Linkman, MC, Mod, Nonce, Now, Nuzzer, Offering, On hand, Porrect, Potlach, Pr, Prevailing, Produce, Proffer, Pro-tem, Put, Render, Serve-up, Show, Slice, Study, The now, Tip, Today, Vee-jay, Window dressing, Xenium, Yeven

Preserve(d), Preservative, Preserver Bottle, Burnettize, Can, Chill, Chow-chow, Confect, Confiture, Corn, Creosote, Cure, Dehydrate, Dry, Eisel, Embalm, Enshield, Fixative, Formaldehyde, Formalin, Freeze, Guard, Hain, Hesperides, Jam, Jerk, Keep, Kinin, Kipper, Konfyt, Kyanise, Lay up, Life, Lifebelt, → **MAINTAIN**, Marmalade, Mummify, On ice, Pectin, Peculiar, Piccalilli, Pickle, Pot, Powellise, Quinoline, Salt, Salve, Saut, Season, Souse, Store, Stratify, Stuff, Tanalith, Tanalized, Tar, Tin, Vinegar, Waterglass

Preshrunk Sanforized®

Preside(nt) Abe, Adams, Ataturk, Banda, Bush, Carter, Chair, Childers, Chief Barker, Cleveland, Coolidge, Coty, Dean, De Gaulle, Director, Eisenhower, Ford, Garfield, Grand Pensionary, Grant, Harding, Harrison, Hayes, Hoover, Ike, Jefferson, Johnson, Kennedy, Kruger, Lead, Lincoln, Madison, Mitterand, Moderator, Monroe, Nixon, Old Hickory, P, Peron, Polk, Pompidou, Pr(a)eses, Prexy, Reagan, Roosevelt, Sa(a)dat, Speaker, Superintendent, Supervisor, Taft, Tito, Truman, Tyler, Veep, Washington, Wilson

Press(ed), Pressing, Pressure Acute, Aldine, Armoire, Atmospheric, Bar, Bench, Blackmail, Blood, Bramah, Button, Cabinet, Chivvy, Cider, Clarendon, Closet, Clothes, Coerce, Compression, Copying, Cram, Crease, Crimp, Critical, Crowd, Crush, Cupboard, Cylinder, Dragoon, Drill, Dun, Durable, Duress, Duresse, Enforcement, Enslave, Exigent, Filter, Flat-bed, Fluid, Fly, Folding, Force, Fourth estate, Full-court, Goad, Greenmail, Gutter, Hasten, Head, Heat, Herd, Hie, High, Hug, Hurry, Hustle, Hydraulic, Hydrostatic, Impact, Important, Importune, Inarm, Intense, Iron, Isobar, Jam, Jostle, Knead, Leverage, Lie, Lobby, Low, Mangle, Megabar, Microbar, Mill, Minerva, Newspapers, Obligate, Oil, Onus, Osmotic, PA, Partial, Pascal, Peer, Permanent, Persist, Piezo-, Ply, Prease, Printing, Private, Psi, Pump, → **PUSH**, Racket, Ram, Ratpack, Record, Recruit, Reportage, Reporter, Ridge, Roll, Root, Rotary, Rounce, Rub, Rush, Samizdat, Screw, Scrooge, Scrouge, Scrowdge, Scrum, Serr(e), Sit, Speed, Spur, Squash, Squeeze, Stanhope, Static, Stop, Strain(t), Stress, Tension, Thlipsis, Threap, Three-line-whip, Threep, Throng, Throttle, Thrutch, Torr, Tourniquet, Turgor, → **URGE**, Urgence, Urgency, Vanity, Vapour, Vice, Waid(e), Wardrobe, Weight, Wine, Wring, Yellow

Press agent Flack, Spin doctor

Press-gang Crimp, Force, Impress, Shanghai

Pressman Ed, Journalist, Journo, PRO, Reporter, Twicer

Prestidigitate(r) Conjure, Juggle, Legerdemain, Magician, Palm

Prestige, Prestigious Asma, Cachet, Credit, Distinguished, Fame, Influence, Izzat, Kudos, Mana, Notable, Status

Presume, Presumably, Presumption, Presumptuous Allege, Arrogant, Audacity, Believe, Bold, Brass, Cocksure, Cocky, Doubtless, → **EXPECT**, Familiar, Forward, Gall, Impertinent, Insolent, Liberty, Outrecuidance, Overweaning, Pert, Probably, Put upon, Suppose, Uppish, Whipper-snapper

Pretence, Pretend(er), Pretext Act, Affect(ation), Afflict, Assume, Blind, Bluff, Charade, Charlatan, Claim, Claimant, Cover, Cram, Dauber(y), Dissemble, Dissimulate, Dive, Excuse, False, Feign, Feint, Gondolier, Guise, Hokum, Humbug, Hypocrisy, Impostor, Jactitation, Kid(stakes), Lambert Simnel, Let-on, Make-believe, Malinger, Masquerade, Obreption, Old, Parolles, Perkin Warbeck, Plea, Pose, Pretension, Profess, Pseud(o), Quack, Sham, Simulate, Stale, Stalking-horse, Subterfuge, Suppose, Swanking, Warbeck, Would-be, Young

Pretentious(ness), Pretension Arty, Bombast, Chi-chi, Fantoosh, Fustian, Gaudy, Grandiose, High-falutin(g), Kitsch, La-di-da, Orotund, Ostentatious, Overblown, Paraf(f)le, Pompous, Ponc(e)y, Pseud(o), Sciolism, Showy, Snob, Snobbish, Squirt, Tat, Tattie-peelin, Tinhorn, Toffee-nosed, Uppity, Wanky, Whippersnapper

Pretty Attractive, Becoming, Bobby-dazzler, Chocolate-box, Comely, Cute, Dear, Decorate, Dish, Elegant, Fair(ish), Fairway, Inconie, Incony, Keepsaky, Looker, Moderately, Pass, Peach, Picturesque, Primp, Pulchritudinous, Quite, Sweet, Twee, Winsome

Prevail(ing) Dominate, Endure, Go, Induce, Outweigh, Persist, Persuade, Predominant, Preponderate, Reign, Ring, Triumph, Victor, Win

Prevalent Catholic, Common, Dominant, Endemic, Epidemic, Obtaining, Rife, Set in, Widespread

Prevaricate, Prevarication Equivocate, Hedge, Lie, Runaround, Stall, Whiffle, Whittie-whattie

Prevent(ive) Avert, Bar, Debar, Deter, Disenable, Embar, Estop, Foreclose, Forfend, Help, Impound, Inhibit, Keep, Let, Obstruct, Obviate, Preclude, Prophylactic, Sideline, Stop, Theriac, Thwart, Trammel

Preview Sneak, Trailer, Vernissage

Previous(ly) Afore, Already, Before, Earlier, Ere(-now), Fore, Foreran, Former, Hitherto, Once, Prior

Prey Booty, Currie, Curry, Feed, Kill, Pelt, Plunder, Predate, Proul, Prowl, Quarry, Raven, Ravin(e), Soyle, Spreagh, Victim

Price(d), Pricing, Price-raising Appraise, Asking, Assess, Bride, Charge, Consequence, Contango, → **COST**, Cost-plus, Dearth, Due, Evens, Exercise, Expense, Factory-gate, Fee, Fiars, Hammer, Hire, Intervention, Issue, Limit, List, Loco, Market, Offer, Packet, Perverse, Predatory, Prestige, Quotation, Quote, Rack, Ransom, Rate, Regrate, Reserve, Sale, Selling, Shadow, Song, Spot, Starting, Street value, Striking, Subscription, Toll, Trade, Unit, Upset, Valorise, Value, Vincent, Weregild, Wergeld, Wergild, Worth, Yardage

Prick(ed), Prickle, Prickly Acanaceous, Accloy, Argemone, Arrect, Bearded, Brakier, Bramble, Brog, Bunya, Cactus, Cloy, Cnicus, Echinate, Goad, Gore, Hedgehog, Hedgepig, Impel, Inject, Jab, Jag, Jaggy, Jook, Juk, Kali, Penis, Perse, Pierce, Prod, Prog, Puncture, Rowel, Rubus, Ruellia, Seta, Setose, Smart, Spicula, Spinate, Stab, Star-thistle, Stimulus, Sting, Tattoo, Tatu, Teasel, Thistle, Thorn, Tingle, Urge

Prickly heat Miliaria

Prickly-pear Opuntia, Tuna

Pride Bombast, Brag, Conceit, Elation, Esprit de corps, Glory, Hauteur, Hubris, Inordinate, Lions, London, Machismo, Plume, Preen, Purge, Triumphalism, Vainglory, Vanity

Priest(ess), Priests Aaron, Abaris, Abbess, Abbot, Ananias, Annas, Archimandrite, Bacchae, Bacchantes, Baptes, Becket, Bonze, Brahmin, Caiaphas, Cardinal, Clergyman, Cleric, Cohen, Concelebrant, Corybant(es), Curé, Dalai Lama, Druid, Eli, Elisha, Father, Fetial, Flamen, Fr, Habacuc, Habakkuk, Hero, Hieratic, Hierophant, High, H(o)ungan, Io, Jethro, Kohen, Lack-Latin, Lama, Laocoon, Lazarist, Levite, Lucumo, Mage, Magus, Mallet, Mambo, Marabout, Metropolitan, Minister, Missionary, Monsignor, Mufti, Norma, Oratorian, P, Padre, Papa, Parish, Parson, Pastor, Patercove, Patrico, Pawaw, Père, Pontifex, Pontiff, Pope, Pope's knight, Powwow, Pr, Preacher, Prelate, Presbyter, Prior(ess), Pythia, Pythoness, Rabbi, Rebbe, Rector, Rev, Sacerdotal, Salian, Savonarola, Seminarian, Shaman, Shaveling, Sir John Lack-Latin, Sky pilot, Spoiled, Tohunga, Vicar, Vivaldi, Worker, Zadok

Prig(gish) Dandy, Fop, Humbug, Nimmer, Pilfer, Prim, Prude, Puritan

Prim Demure, Governessy, Mun, Neat, Old-maidish, Perjink, Preceese, Precise, Proper, Starchy

Prim(a)eval Ancient, Prehistoric, Primitive

Primacy, Primate Angwantibo, Ape, Aye-aye, Bandar, Bigfoot, Biped, Bishop, Bush baby, Cardinal, Catar(r)hine, Ebor, Gibbon, Hanuman, Hominid, Jackanapes, King Kong, Lemur, Loris, Macaque, Magot, Mammal, Marmoset, → **MONKEY**, Orang, Pongid, Potto, Prosimian, Protohuman, Quadruman, Ramapithecus, Rhesus, Sifaka, Tarsier, Zinjanthropus

Prima donna Diva, Patti, Star

Prime(r), Primary, Priming Arm, Basic, Bloom, Cardinal, Charging, Chief, Choice, Claircolle, Clearcole, Clerecole, Closed, Detonator, Direct, Donat, Donet, Election, Enarm, Fang, First, Flower, Heyday, Mature, Open, Original, Paramount, Peak, Radical, Remex, Sell-by-date, Supreme, Thirteen, Tip-top, Totient, Totitive, Valuable, Windac, Windas, Ylem

Prime Minister Asquith, Attlee, Baldwin, Balfour, Begin, Bute, Canning, Chamberlain, Chatham, Dewan, Diefenbaker, Disraeli, Diwan, Eden, Gladstone, Grafton, Grand Vizier, Grey, Home, Leaderene, Liverpool, Macmillan, Major, North, Number Ten, Palmerston, Peel, Perceval, Pitt, PM, Premier, Shastri, Tanaiste, Taoiseach, Thatcher, Trudeau, Walpole

Primitive Aborigine, Amoeba, Antediluvian, Arabic, Archaic, Atavistic, Barbaric, Caveman, Crude, Early, Evolué, Fundamental, Medi(a)eval, Naive, Neanderthal, Neolithic, Old, Persian, Prim(a)eval, Primordial, Pro, Prothyl(e), Protomorphic, Protyl(e), Radical, Rudimentary, Savage, Subman, Turkish, Uncivilised, Ur

Primordial Blastema, Fundamental, Original

Primrose, Primula Auricula, Bear's ear, Bird's eye, Cape, Evening, League, Oenothera, Onagra, Ox-lip, Pa(i)gle, Rosebery, Vicar, Yellow

Prince(ly) Ahmed, Albert, Ameer, Amir, Amphitryon, Anchises, Arjuna, Atheling, Barmecide, Black, Cadmus, Caliph, Chagan, Charming, Crown, Czarevich, Donalbain, Elector, Emir, Equerry, Eugene, Florizel, Fortinbras, Gaekwar, Gospodar, Guicowar, Hal, Highness, Hospodar, Huzoor, Igor, Inca, Infante, Khan, Ksar, Lavish, Lucumo, Maharaja, Margrave, Meleager, Merchant, Mir, Mirza, Nawab, Nizam, Noble, Orange, Otto, P, Pantagruel, Pendragon, Pirithous, Porphyrogenite, Potentate, Rainier, Rajah, Rana, Ras, Rasselas, Ratoo, Ratu, Regal, RH, Rudolph, Rupert, Serene, Sharif, Shereef, Sherif, Siegfried, Student, Tengku, Tereus, Tsar(evich), Tunku, Upper Roger

Princess Anastasia, Andromache, Andromeda, Anne, Ariadne, Begum, Creusa, Czarevna, Czarista, Danae, Di(ana), Electra, Electress, Eudocia, Europa, Grace, Helle, Hermione, Hesione, Ida, Imogen, Infanta, Iseult, Isolde, Jezebel, Maharanee,

Maharani, Medea, Palatine, Philomela, Pocahontas, Procne, Rani, Regan, Sadie, Sara(h), Tou Wan, Tsarevna, Tsarista, Turandot, Yseult

Principal Arch, Capital, Central, → **CHIEF**, Decuman, Especial, First, Foremost, Grand, Head, Leading, Main(stay), Major, Mass, Mistress, Protagonist, Ringleader, Staple, Star

Principality Andorra, Flanders, Liechtenstein, Moldavia, Moldova, Monaco, Muscovy, Orange, Wales, Wal(l)achia

Principle(s), Principled Accelerator, Animistic, Anthropic, Archimedes, Axiom, Basis, Bernouilli, Brocard, Canon, Carnot, Code, Contradiction, Correspondence, Cosmological, Criterion, Cui bono, Cy pres, D'Alembert's, Doctrine, Dogma, Element, Entelechy, Equivalence, Essential, Estoppel, Exclusion, Fermat's, First, Fourier, Gause's, Geist, Generale, Germ, Greatest happiness, Ground rule, Guideline, Hard line, Heisenberg uncertainty, Honourable, Huygen's, Ideal, Interdeterminacy, Key, Law, Least time, Le Chatelier's, Logos, Methodology, Modus, Object soul, Occam's razor, Organon, Ormazd, Ormuzd, Pauli-exclusion, Peter, Plank, Platform, Pleasure, Precautionary, Precept, Prescript, Psyche, Purseyism, Rationale, Reality, Reason, Reciprocity, Relativity, Remonstrance, Right-thinking, Rudiment, Rule, Sakti, Seed, Shakti, Spirit, Summum bonum, Tenet, Theorem, Ticket, Uncertainty, Verification, Vital, Yang, Yin

Prink Beautify, Bedeck, Dress

Print(er), Printing A la poupée, Baskerville, Batik, Benday, Bromide, Calotype, Caveman, Caxton, Chain, Chapel, Chromo, Cibachrome, Cicero, Collotype, Compositor, Contact, Copperplate, Counter, Creed, Cyclostyle, Dab, Dot matrix, Duotone, Electrothermal, Electrotint, Electrotype, Elzevir, Engrave, Etching, Ferrotype, Film set, Fine, Flexography, Font, Gravure, Gurmukhi, Gutenberg, Half-tone, Hectograph, Heliotype, HMSO, Image, Impact, Impress, Incunabula, India, Ink-jet, Intaglio, Italic, Jobbing, Laser, Letterpress, Letterset, Line, Line-engraving, Lino-cut, Lithograph, Logotype, Lower-case, Matrix, Metallographer, Mimeograph®, Monotype®, Moon, Non-impact, Off-line, Offset, Offset litho, Old-face, Oleo, Oleograph, Opaline, Perfect, Perfector, Phototype, Plate, Platinotype, Positive, Press, Process, Proof, Publish, Remarque, Report, Reproduction, Retroussage, Reverse, Rotogravure, Samizdat, Screen, Serigraph, Ship, Shout, Silk-screen, Small, Smoot, Splash, Spore, Stamp, Stenochrome, Stereotype, Stonehand, Strike, Thermal, Three-colour, Thumb, Trichromatic, Typesetter, Typography, Typewriter, Typothetae, Whorl, Woodburytype, Woodcut, Xerography, Xylograph, Zincograph

Printing-press Rounce

Prior(ity) Abbot, Afore, Antecedent, Anterior, Aperture, Earlier, Former, Grand, Hitherto, Monk, Overslaugh, Pre-, Precedence, Prefard, Preference, Previous, Privilege, Shutter, Triage, Until

▶ **Prise** *see* **PRIZE**

Prism(s), Prismatic Catadioptric, Iriscope, Nicol, Periaktos, Rhombohedron, Spectrum, Teinoscope, Wollaston

Prison Albany, Alcatraz, Bagnio, Barracoon, Bastille, Belmarsh, Big house, Bin, Bird, Boob, Bridewell, Brig, Brixton, Bullpen, Cage, Can, Cell, Chillon, Chok(e)y, Clink, Club, College, Confine, Cooler, Coop, Counter, Dartmoor, Dispersal, Dungeon, Durance, Encage, Fleet, Fotheringhay, Gaol, Glass-house, Guardhouse, Guardroom, Gulag, Hokey, Holloway, Hoos(e)gow, Hulk(s), Internment, → **JAIL**, Jug, Kitty, Labour camp, Limbo, Little-ease, Lob's pound, Lock-up, Logs, Lumber, Marshalsea, Massymore, Mattamore, Maze, Newgate, Nick, Oflag, Open, Panopticon, Pen, Penitentiary, Pentonville, Pit, Pok(e)y, Porridge, Pound,

Princetown, Quad, Quod, Rasp-house, Reformatory, Roundhouse, Scrubs, Shop, Sing-Sing, Slammer, Spandau, Stalag, State, Stir, Strangeways, The Leads, Tol(l)booth, Tower, Tronk, Wandsworth, Wormwood Scrubs

Prisoner Canary-bird, Captive, Collegian, Collegiate, Con(vict), Detainee, Detenu, Hostage, Inmate, Internee, Jailbird, Lag, Lifer, Parolee, Passman, Political, POW, Rule 43, Trustee, Trusty, Yardbird, Zek

Pristine Fire-new, Fresh, New, Original, Unmarked, Unspoiled

Private(ly) Ain, Aside, Atkins, Auricular, Buccaneer, Byroom, Clandestine, Close, Closet, Conclave, Confidential, Enisle(d), Esoteric, Homefelt, Hush-hush, In camera, Individual, Inner, Intimate, Non-com, Non-governmental, Own, Personal, Piou-piou, Poilu, Postern, Proprietary, Pte, Rank(er), Retired, Sanction, Sapper, Secret, Several, Single soldier, → **SOLDIER**, Squaddie, Sub rosa, Tommy, Under the rose

Privateer(s) Buccaneer, Corsair, Freebooter, Marque(s), Pirate

Privation Hardship, Penury, Want

Privilege(d) Birthright, Blest, Charter, Curule, Enviable, Exempt, Favour, Franchise, Freedom, Indulgence, Insider, Liberty, Mozarab, Nomenklatura, Octroi, Palatine, Parliamentary, Patent, Prerogative, Pryse, Regale, Regalia, Right, Sac

Privy Apprised, Can, Closet, Intimate, Jakes, John, Loo, Necessary, Reredorter, Secret, Sedge, Siege

Prize(s), Prizewinner, Prized Acquest, Apple, Archibald, Assess, Award, Best, Booby, Booker, Bravie, Capture, Champion, Consolation, Creach, Cup, Dux, Efforce, → **ESTEEM**, Force, Garland, Goncourt, Grice, Honour, Jackpot, Jemmy, Lever, Lot, Man Booker, Money, Nobel, Palm, Pearl, Pewter, Pie, Plum, Plunder, Pot, Premium, Prix Goncourt, Pulitzer, Purse, Ram, Reprisal, → **REWARD**, Rollover, Rosette, Scalp, Ship, Spreaghery, Sprechery, Stakes, Sweepstake, Taonga, Tern, Treasure, Trophy, Turner, Value, Wooden spoon

Pro Aye, Coach, For, Harlot, Moll, Paid, Tramp, Yea, Yes

▶ **Pro** *see* **PROSTITUTE**

Probable, Probability Apparent, Belike, Classical, Conditional, Ergodic, Feasible, Likely, Marginal, Mathematical, Possible, Posterior, Prior, Verisimilar

Probation(er) Cadet, Novice, Novitiate, Stibbler, Test, Trainee, Trial

Probe Antenna, Bore, Bougie, Canopus, Cassini, Corot, Delve, Dredge, Explore, Fathom, Feeler, Fossick, Galileo, Giotto, Inquire, Investigate, Magellan, Mariner, Mars Surveyor, Pelican, Pioneer, Poke, Pump, Ranger, → **SEARCH**, Seeker, Sonde, Sound, Space, Stardust, Stylet, Tent, Thrust, Tracer, Venera

Probity Honour, Integrity, Justice

Problem(s) Acrostic, BO, Boyg, Brainteaser, Business, Catch, Crisis, Crux, Dilemma, Egma, Enigma, Facer, Glitch, Handful, Hang-up, Headache, Hiccup, Hitch, Hurdle, Indaba, Issue, Knot(ty), Koan, Mind-body, Miniature, Musive, Net, Nuisance, Obstacle, Pons asinorum, Poser, Quandary, Question, Re, Rebus, Retractor, Riddle, Rider, Snag, Sorites, Sum, Teaser, Teething, Thing, Tickler, Toughie, Trouble, Tsuris, Yips

Problem-solving Synectics

Proboscis Haustellum, Promuscis, Snout, Trunk

Proceed(s), Proceeding, Procedure Acta, Afoot, Algorithm, Continue, Course, Derive, Do, Drill, Emanate, Fand, Flow, Fond, Goes, Haul, Issue, Machinery, March, Mechanics, Method, Mine, MO, Modal, Move, On, Pass, Practice, Praxis, Process, Profit, Protocol, Punctilio, Pursue, Put, Rake, Return, Rigmarole, Rite, Ritual, Routine, Sap, Steps, Subroutine, System, Take, Use, Yead(s), Yede, Yeed

Process(ing), Procession, Processor Acromion, Action, Additive, Ala,

Ambarvalia, Axon, Ben Day, Bessemer, Bosch, Calcination, Castner, Catalysis, Cavalcade, Cibation, Congelation, Conjunction, Cortège, Cyanide, Demo, Diagonal, Dissolution, Double, Exaltation, Fermentation, Frack(ing), Front-end, Haber, Handle, Managing, Markov, Method, Moharram, Mond, Motorcade, Muharram, Multiple pounding, Multiplication, Odontoid, Open hearth, -osis, Pageant, Parade, Parallel, Paseo, Photosynthesis, Pipeline, Planar, Pomp, Primary, Projection, Pterygoid, Puddling, Pultrusion, Purex, Putrefaction, Recycle, Ritual, Screen, Secondary, Separation, Series, Silkscreen, Single, Skimmington, Solvay, Speciation, Sterygoid, String, Sublimation, Subtractive, Thermite, Thought, Torchlight, Train, Transaction, Transverse, Treat, Trial, Turn(a)round, Unit, Vermiform, Xiphoid, Zygomatic

Proclaim, Proclamation Announce, Annunciate, Ban, Blaze, Blazon, Boast, Broadsheet, Cry, Edict, Enounce, Enunciate, Herald, Indiction, Kerygma, Oyez, Preconise, Predicate, Profess, Publish, Ring, Shout, Trumpet, Ukase

Proconsul Ape, Hominid

Procrastinate, Procrastinating, Procrastinator Cunctator, Defer, Delay, Dilatory, Dilly-dally, Linger, Pettifog, Postpone, Shelve, Temporise, Vacillate

Procreate Beget, Engender, Generate, Initiate

Procrustean Conformity

Proctor Agent, King's, Monitor, Prog, Proxy, Queen's

Procurator, Procure(r) Achieve, Aunt, Crimp, Earn, Get, Induce, Naunt, Obtain, Pander, Pilate, Pimp, Sort, Suborn

Prod Cattle, Egg, Goad, Impel, Jab, Job, Jog, Nudge, Poke, Pote

Prodigal Costly, Lavish, Profligate, Spendall, Unthrift, Wanton, Wasteful, Waster

Prodigious, Prodigy Abnormal, Amazing, Huge, Immense, Infant, Monster, Monument, Mozart, Phenomenal, Portentous, Tremendous, Wonder, Wonderwork, Wunderkind

Produce(r), Producing Afford, Bear, Beget, Breed, Cause, Create, Crop, Disney, Ean, Edit, Effect, Engender, Evoke, Exhibit, Extend, Fabricate, Fruit, Generate, Get, Grow, Home-grown, Impresario, Ingenerate, Issue, Kind, Make, Offspring, Onstream, Originate, Output, Propage, Propound, Raise, Son, Spawn, Stage, Supply, Teem, Throw, Tree, Trot out, Wares, Whelp, Yield

▷ **Produces** *may indicate* an anagram

Product(ion), Productive(ness), Productivity Actualities, Apport, Artefact, Ashtareth, Ashtaroth, Astarte, Autogeny, Bore, Cartesian, Coefficient, Commodity, Cross, Depside, Dot, Drama, End, Factorial, Fecund, Fertile, Fruit, Genesis, Global, Handiwork, Harvest, Net domestic, Net national, Output, Outturn, Pair, Partial, Primary, Profilic, Result, Rich, Scalar, Secondary, Set, Show, Speiss, Substitution, Uberous, Uberty, Vector, Waste, Work, Yield

▷ **Production** *may indicate* an anagram

Proem Foreword, Overture, Pre, Preface

Profane, Profanation, Profanity Blaspheming, Coarse, Coprolalia, Desecrate, Impious, Irreverent, Sacrilege, Unholy, Violate

Profess(ed), Professor Absent-minded, Academic, Adjoint, Admit, Artist, Aspro, Asset, Assistant, Associate, Avow, Challenger, Claim, Declare, Disney, Emeritus, Full, Higgins, Hodja, Kho(d)ja, Know-all, Ostensible, Own, Practise, Pundit, Regent, Regius, RP, STP, Visiting

Profession(al) Admission, Assurance, Avowal, Buppy, Business, Career, Creed, Expert, Métier, Practitioner, Pretence, Pursuit, Regular, Salaried, Skilled, Trade, Vocation, Yuppie

Proffer Give, Present, Proposition, Tender

Proficiency, Proficient Able, Adept, Alert, Dan, Expert, Forte, Past master, Practised, Skill, Technique

Profile Analysis, Contour, Cross, Half-cheek, Half-face, Long, Loral, Low, Market, Outline, Silhouette, Sketch, Statant, T(h)alweg, Vignette

Profit(able), Profiteer, Profits Advantage, Arbitrage, Asset, Avail, Benefit, Bestead, Boot, Bunce, Cash cow, Cere, Clear, Divi(dend), Earn, Economic, Edge, Emblements, Emoluments, Exploit, Extortionist, Fat, Gain, Gelt, Graft, Gravy, Grist, Gross, Income, Increment, Issue, Jobbery, Juicy, Landshark, Leech, Lucrative, Makings, Margin, Melon, Mesne, Milch cow, Mileage, Moneymaker, Negative, Net, Pay(ing), Perk, Pickings, Preacquisition, Productive, Rake-off, Return, Reward, Royalty, Scalp, Spoils, Tout, Use, Usufruct, Utile, Utility, Vail

Profligate Corinthian, Corrupt, Degenerate, Dissolute, Extravagant, Lech(er), Libertine, Lorel, Losel(l), Oatmeal, Rakehell, Reprobate, Roué, Spend-all, Unprincipled, Wastrel

Profound Altum, Bottomless, Complete, Deep, Intense, Recondite

Profuse, Profusion Abounding, Abundant, Copious, Excess, Free, Galore, Lavish, Liberal, Lush, Quantity, Rank, Rich, Two-a-penny

Progenitor, Progenitrix Ancestor, Ma, Predecessor, Sire, Stock

Progeny Burd, Children, Descendants, Fruit, Issue, Offspring, Seed

Prognosis Forecast, Prediction

Prognosticate, Prognostication Augur, Foretell, Omen, Predict, Presage, Prophesy

▶ **Program(ming), Programming language, Programmer** *see* COMPUTER PROGRAMS

Programme(s) Agenda, Broadcast, Card, Chat show, Code, Community, Countdown, Docudrama, Documentary, Docusoap, Double-header, Dramedy, Est, Event, Faction, Feature, Fly-on-the-wall, Infotainment, Linear, Mockumentary, Newscast, Newsreel, PDL, Phone-in, Pilot, Plan, Playbill, Prank, Radiothon, RECHAR, Regimen, Report, Schedule, Scheme, Sepmag, Serial, Shockumentary, Show, Simulcast, Sitcom, Sked, Soap, Software, Sustaining, Syllabus, System, Telecast, Teleplay, Telethon, Timetable, Webcast, YOP

Progress(ive), Progression → ADVANCE, Afoot, Arithmetic, Avant garde, Course, Fabian, Flow, Forge, Forward, Forward-looking, Gain, Geometric, Get along, Go, Growth, Harmonic, Headway, Incede, Knight's, Liberal, Move, Onwards, Paraphonia, Periegesis, Pilgrim's, Prosper, Rack, Radical, Rake's, Reformer, Roll, Run, Sequence, Series, Step, Stepping stone, Vaunce, Way, Yead, Yede, Yeed

Prohibit(ed), Prohibition(ist) Ban, Block, Debar, Dry, Embargo, Enjoin, Estop, Forbid, Hinder, Index, Injunct, Interdict, Noli-me-tangere, Off-limits, Prevent, Pussyfoot, Rahui, Suppress, Taboo, Tabu, Verboten, Veto

Project(ile), Projecting, Projection, Projector Aim, Ammo, Antitragus, Assignment, Astral, Astrut, Axonometric, Azimuthal, Ball, Ballistic, Beetle, Bullet, Butt, Buttress, Cam, Canopy, Cast, Catapult, Channel, Cinerama®, Cog, Conceive, Condyle, Conic, Conical, Console, Corbel, Coving, Crossette, Cutwater, Dendron, Denticle, Diascope, Discus, Eaves, Echinus, Elance, Enterprise, Episcope, Excrescence, Exsert, Extrapolate, Fet(ter)lock, Flange, Gair, Gore, Guess, Halter(e), Hangover, Helicity, Hoe, Homolosine, Housing, Hurtle, Inion, Jut, Kern, Kinetoscope, Knob, Ledge, Lobe, Lug, Magic lantern, Malleolus, Manhattan, Map, Mercator, Mitraille, Mohole, Mollweide, Mucro, Mutule, Nab, Nose, Nunatak(er), Olecranon, Opaque, Orillion, Orthogonal, Orthographic, Outcrop, Outjet, Outjut, Outrigger, Outshot, Overhang, Overhead, Oversail, Palmation, Peter's, Pitch, Planetarium, Planisphere, Polyconic, Pork barrel, Prickle, Promontory,

→ **PROTRUDE**, Proud(er), Pseudopod, Quillon, Raguly, Roach, Rocket, Sail, Salient, Sally, Sanson-Flamsteed, Scaw, Scheme, Screen, Shelf, Shrapnel, Sinusoidal, Skaw, Skeg, Slide, Snag, Snout, Spline, Sponson, Sprocket, Spur, Squarrose, Stand out, Stereopticon, Stick out, Stud, Tang, Tappet, Tenon, Throw, Toe, Tongue, Tracer, Trimetric, Trippet, Trunnion, Turnkey, Turtleback, Tusk, Umbo, Underhung, Undertaking, Villus, Vitascope, Whizzbang, Zenithal

Prolapse Procidence

Proletarian, Proletariat Jamahiriya, People, Plebeian, Popular

Proliferate Expand, Increase, Multiply, Propagate, Snowball, Teem

Prolific Abounding, Fecund, Fertile, Fruitful, Profuse, Teeming

Prolix(ity) Lengthy, Prosaic, Rambling, Rigmarole, Verbose, Wire-draw, Wordy

Prologue Introduce, Preface

Prolong(ed) Continue, Drag out, Extend, Lengthen, Protract, Sostenuto, Spin, Sustain

Prom(enade) Alameda, Boulevard, Cakewalk, Catwalk, Crush-room, Esplanade, Front, Mall, Parade, Paseo, Pier, Sea-front, Stroll, → **WALK**

Prometheus Fire

Promethium Pm

Prominence, Prominent Antitragus, Blatant, Bold, Colliculus, Condyle, Conspicuous, Egregious, Emphasis, Featured, Gonion, High profile, Important, Insistent, Luminary, Manifest, Marked, Mastoid, Obtrusive, Outstanding, Salient, Signal, Solar, Tall poppy, Teat, Toot, Tragus

Promiscuous, Promiscuity Casual, Chippie, Chippy, Demivierge, Fast, Free, Goer, Hornbag, Horny, Indiscriminate, Licentious, Light, Loslyf, Mixed, Motley, Pell-mell, Skanky(-ho), Slapper, Trollop, Whoredom

Promise, Promising Accept, Assure, Augur, Auspicious, Avoure, Behest, Behight, Behote, Bode, Coming, Compact, Covenant, Earnest, Engagement, Foretaste, Gratuitous, Guarantee, Hecht, Hest, Hete, Hight, IOU, Likely, Manifest, Oath, Parole, Pledge, Plight, Pollicitation, Potential, Pregnant, Recognisance, Recognizance, Rosy, Sign, Sponsor, Swear, Tile, Undertake, Upbeat, Vow, Warranty, Word

Promised land Beulah, Canaan, Israel

Promissory note IOU, PN

Promontory Bill, Cape Sable, Cliff, Flamborough Head, Foreland, Giant's Causeway, Hatteras, → **HEADLAND**, Hoe, Hogh, Land's End, Mull, Mull of Galloway, Naze, Ness, Nose, Peak, Pillars of Hercules, Ras, Spit, The Lizard, Tintagel Head

Promote(r), Promotion Adman, Advance, Advancement, → **ADVERTISE**, Advocate, Aggrandise, Aid, Assist, Blurb, Boost, Buggin's turn, Campaign, Churn, Dog and pony show, Elevate, Encourage, Eulogy, Exponent, Foment, Foster, Further, Help, Hype, Incite, Increase, Kick upstairs, Lord of Misrule, Mailshot, Make, Market, Pracharak, Prefer, Prelation, Promulgate, Provoke, Push, Queen, Raise, Rear, Remove, Roadshow, Run, Salutary, Sell, Sponsor, Spruik, Stage, Step, Subserve, Tendencious, Tendentious, Tout, Upgrade, Uplead, Uprate

Prompt(er), Promptly, Promptness Actuate, Alacrity, Autocue®, Believe, Celerity, Chop-chop, Cue, Egg, Expeditious, Feed, Frack, Idiot-board, Immediate, Incite, Inspire, Instigate, Move, On-the-nail, Opposite, Pernicious, Premove, Punctual, Quick, Ready, Sharp, Speed(y), Spur, Stage right, Stimulate, Sudden, Tight, Tit(e), Titely, Tyte, Urgent

Promulgate Preach, Proclaim, Publish, Spread

Prone Apt, Groof, Grouf, Grovel, Liable, Lying, Prostrate, Recumbent, Subject, Susceptible

Prong Fang, Fork, Grain, Peg, Tang, Tine

Pronghorn Cabrie, Cabrit

Pronoun Impersonal, Oneself, Personal, Reciprocal, Relative

Pronounce(d), Pronouncement Adjudicate, Affirm, Agrapha, Articulate, Assert, Asseveration, Clear, Conspicuous, Declare, Definite, Dictum, Emphatic, Enunciate, Fiat, Indefinite, Marked, Opinion, Palatalise, Pontificate, Predication, Recite, Utter, Velarise, Vocal, Voice, Vote

Pronto PDQ

Pronunciation Betacism, Cacoepy, Delivery, Diction, Etacism, Itacism, Lallation, Localism, Orthoepy, Phonetics, Plateasm, Proclitic, Received, Rhotacism, Sound, Tense

Proof(s) Apagoge, Argument, Artist's, Assay, Bona fides, Confirmation, Direct, Evidence, Firm, Foundry, Galley, Godel's, India, Indirect, Justification, Lemma, Positive, Preif(e), Probate, Pull, Quality, Refutation, Remarque, Reproduction, Resistant, Revision, Secure, Slip, Strength, Test, Tight, Token, Trial, Upmake, Validity

Prop Airscrew, Becket, Bolster, Buttress, Clothes, Crutch, Dog-shore, Fulcrum, Leg, Loosehead, Misericord(e), Pit, Point d'appui, Punch(eon), Rance, Rest, Scotch, Shore, Sprag, Spur, Staff, Stay, Stempel, Stemple, Stilt, Stoop, Stoup, Studdle, Stull, → **SUPPORT**, Tighthead, Trig, Underpin

Propaganda, Propagandist Agitprop, Ballyhoo, Black, Brainwashing, Chevalier, Doctrine, Exponent, Goebbels, Grey, Promotion, Psyop, Psywar, Publicity, Slogan, Spin doctor, White

Propagate, Propagator, Propagation Breed, Clone, Dispread, Generate, Graft, Hatch, Hotbed, Hothouse, Increase, Layering, Populate, Produce, Promulgate, Provine, Spread, Tan-bed

Propel(ler) Airscrew, Ca', Drive, Fin, Frogmarch, Launch, Leg, Lox, → **MOVE**, Oar, Paddle, Pedal, Pole, Project, Push, Rotor, Row, Screw, Send, Tail rotor, Throw, Thruster, Vane

Propensity Aptness, Bent, Inclination, Penchant, Tendency

Proper(ly) Ain, Convenance, Correct, Decent, Decorous, Due, Eigen, En règle, Ethical, → **FIT**, Genteel, Governessy, Kosher, Noun, Ought, Own, Pakka, Pathan, Prim, Pucka, Pukka, Puritanic, Real, Rightful, Seemly, Strait-laced, Suitable, Tao, Trew, True, Veritable, Well

Property, Properties Assets, Attribute, Aver, Belongings, Capacitance, Chattel, Chirality, Chose, Contenement, Dead-hand, Demesne, Des res, Dowry, Effects, Enclave, Escheat, Escrow, Estate, Fee, Feu, Flavour, Fonds, Freehold, Goods, Haecceity, Hereditament, Heritable, Hot, Hotchpot, Immoveable, Inertia, In rem, Intellectual, Jointure, Leasehold, Living, Means, Mortmain, Paraphernalia, Peculium, Personal, Personalty, Pertinent, Predicate, Premises, Private, Projective, Public, Quale, Quality, Real, Stock, Stolen, Theft, Thixotropy, Time-share, Timocracy, Trait, Usucapion, Usucaption

Prophesy, Prophecy, Prophet(s), Prophetess, Prophetic Amos, Augur, Bab, Balaam, Calchas, Cassandra, Daniel, Deborah, Divine, Druid, Elias, Elijah, Elisha, Ezekiel, Ezra, Fatal, Fatidical, Forecast, Foretell, Former, Geomancer, Habakkuk, Haggai, Hosea, Is, Isa, Is(a)iah, Jeremiah, Joel, Jonah, Latter, Mahdi, Mahound, Major, Malachi, Mani, Mantic, Micah, Minor, Mohammed, Mopsus, Mormon, Moses, Nahum, Nathan, Nostradamus, Obadiah, Old Mother Shipton, Ominous, Oracle, Portend, Predictor, Prognosticate, Pythoness, Samuel, Second sight, Seer, Sibyl, Tipster, Tiresias, Vatic, Vaticinate, Völuspá, Zachariah, Zarathustra, Zechariah, Zephaniah, Zoroaster, Zwickau

Prophylactic, Prophylaxis Inoculation, Preventive, Serum, Vaccine, Variolation

Propitiate Appease, Atone, Pacify, Reconcile, Sop

Propitious Benign, Favourable, Lucky

Proponent Advocate, Backer, Partisan

Proportion(ate) Commensurable, Cotangent, Dimension, Harmonic, Inverse, Portion, Pro rata, Quantity, Quota, Ratio, Reason, Regulate, Relation, Sine, Size, Soum, Sowm

Propose(r), Proposal Advance, Ask, Bid, Bill, Canvass, Eirenicon, Feeler, Fiancé, Irenicon, Mean, Motion, Move, Nominate, Offer, Overture, Plan, Pop, Premise, Proffer, Propound, Recommend, Resolution, Scheme, Slate, Submission, → **SUGGEST**, Table, Tender, Volunteer, Woot, Would

Proposition Asses' bridge, Axiom, Convertend, Corollary, Deal, Disjunction, Ergo, Hypothesis, Identical, Implicature, Lemma, Overture, Pons asinorum, Porism, Premise, Premiss, Rider, Sorites, Spec, Superaltern, Theorem, Thesis

Propound Advocate, Purpose, State

Proprietor, Propriety Bienséance, Convenance, Correctitude, Decorum, Etiquette, Grundy, Keeper, Lord, Master, Owner, Patron, Rectitude

Prosaic Common, Drab, Flat, Humdrum, Tedious, Workaday

Proscenium Forestage

Proscribe(d) Exile, Forbid, Outlaw, Prohibit, Tabu

Prose, Prosy Euphuism, Haikai, Polyphonic, Purple, Purple patch, Saga, Stich, Verbose, Version, Writing

Prosecute, Prosecutor, Prosecution Allege, Avvogadore, Charge, Crown, Fiscal, Furtherance, Impeach, Indict, Lord Advocate, Practise, Public, Sue, Wage

Proselytise(r), Proselytism Indoctrination, Propagandism, Souper

Prospect(or), Prospecting Bellevue, Costean, Dowser, Explore, Forty-niner, Fossick, Look-out, Mine, Opportunity, → **OUTLOOK**, Panorama, Perspective, Pleases, Possibility, Reefer, Scenery, Search, Sourdough, View, Vista, Visto, Wildcatter

Prospectus Menu, Pathfinder

Prosper(ity), Prospering, Prosperous Aisha, Ay(e)sha, Blessed, Blossom, Boom, Fair, Fat cat, Flourish, Get ahead, Heyday, Mérimée, Palmy, Sleek, → **SUCCEED**, Thee, Thrift, Thrive, Up, Warison, Wealth, Welfare, Well-heeled, Well-to-do

Prosthetic Fals(i)e

Prostitute, Prostitution Brass, Broad, Bulker, Callet, Catamite, Chippie, Cockatrice, Cocotte, Comfort woman, Convertite, Debase, Dell, Demi-mondaine, Dolly-mop, Doxy, Fancy woman, Fille de joie, Floozie, Floozy, Grande cocotte, Harlot, Hetaera, Hetaira, Hierodule, Ho, Hooker, Hustler, Jailbait, Laced mutton, Lady of the night, Loon, Loose-fish, Loose woman, Lowne, Madam, Magdalen(e), Moll, Mutton, Night-walker, Pict, Plover, Pole-cat, Pro, Public woman, Punk, Quail, Quiff, Rent-boy, Road, Rough trade, Scrubber, Shippie, Slap, Social evil, Stale, Stew, Streetwalker, Strumpet, Tart, Tramp, Trull, Venture, Wench, Whore, Working girl

Prostrate, Prostration Collapse, Exhausted, Fell, Flat, Flatling, Ko(w)tow, Laid, Obeisance, Overcome, Procumbent, Prone, Repent, Throw

Protactinium Pa

Protean Amoebic, Fusible, Variable

Protect(ed), Protection, Protector Adonise, Aegis, Aircover, Alexin, Amulet, Arm, Armour, Asylum, Auspice, Bastion, Bestride, Bield, Buckler, Bullet-proof, Cathodic, Chaffron, Chain mail, Chamfrain, Chamfron, Charm, Cherish, Cloche, Coat, Cocoon, Coleor(r)hiza, Conserve, Copyright, Cosset, Cover, Covert, Cromwell,

Cushion, Danegeld, Data, Defend, Defilade, Degauss, Egis, Enamel, Entrenchment, Escort, Estacade, Faun, Fence, Flank, Gobo, Groundsheet, Guard(ian), Gumshield, Hedge, House, Hurter, Immune, Inalienable, Indemnify, Indusium, Insure, Integument, Keckle, Keep, Kickback, Klendusic, Lee, Mac(k)intosh, Mail, Male, Mollycoddle, Mother, Mothproof, Mouthpiece, Mudguard, Muniment, Napkin, Noll, Nosey, Oliver, Ombrella, Orillion, Overall, Parados, Patent, Patron, Penthouse, Police, Polytunnel, Pomander, Preserve, Procrypsis, Rabbit's foot, Raymond, Redome, Revetment, Ride shotgun, Safeguard, Sandbag, Save, Schanse, Schan(t)ze, Screen, Scug, Shadow, Sheathing, Sheeting, Shelter, → **SHIELD**, Skug, Souteneur, Splashback, Splashboard, Splasher, Starling, Sunscreen, Talisman, Telomere, Testa, Tribute, Tutelar, Twilled, Umbrella, Underlay, Underseal, Vaccine, Ward(ship), Warhead, Warrant, Weatherboard, Weatherstrip, Windbreaker, Windshield, Wing, Write

Protectorate Qatar

Protégé Pupil, Tutee, Ward, Whiteheaded boy

Protein Abrin, Actin, Actomyosin, Adipsin, Alanine, Albumen, Albumin, Aleuron(e), Alexin, Allergen, Amandine, Analogon, Angiostatin, Angiotensin, Antibody, Apoenzyme, Aquaporin, Avidin, Bradykinin, Calmodulin, Capsid, Capsomere, Caseinogen, Ceruloplasmin, Collagen, Complement, Conchiolin, Conjugated, Copaxone®, CREB, Cyclin, Cytokine, Dystrophin, Elastin, Enzyme, Factor VIII, Ferritin, Ferrodoxin, Fibrillin, Fibrin, Fibrinogen, Fibroin, Fibronectina, Filalggrin, Flagellin, Gelatin, Gliadin(e), Glob(ul)in, Glutelin, Gluten, Haemoglobin, Haploglobin, Histone, Hordein, Huntingtin, Immunoglobulin, Incaparina, Integrin, Interferon, Interleukin, Lactalbumin, Lactoglobulin, Lectin, Legumin, Leptin, Leucin(e), Lewy bodies, Luciferin, Lymphokine, Lysin, Meat, Mucin, Myogen, Myoglobin, Myosin, Neurotrophin, Nuclein, Opsin, Opsonin, Ossein, Ovalbumin, Pepsin(e), Pellicle, Peptide, Phaseolin, Prion, Prolamin(e), Protamine, Proteose, Prothrombin, Pyrenoid, Quorn®, Renin, Repressor, Ribosome, Ricin, Sclerotin, Sericin, Serum albumin, Serum globulin, Single-cell, Soya, Spectrin, Spongin, Tempeh, Thrombogen, Toxalbumin, Transferrin, Tropomyosin, Troponin, TSP, Tubulin, TVP, Ubiquitin, Vitellin, Zein

Protest(er) Abhor, Andolan, Aver, Avouch, Black Bloc(k), Boycott, Clamour, Come, Complaint, Démarche, Demo, Demonstrate, Demur, Deprecate, Dharna, Dissent, Expostulate, Gherao, Go-slow, Hartal, Inveigh, Lock-out, Luddite, March, Moonlighter, Nimby, Object, Outcry, Picket, Plea, Refus(e)nik, Remonstrate, Sit-in, Squawk, Squeak, Squeal, Stand, Suffragette, Work-to-rule

Protestant Amish, Anabaptist, Anglo, Arminian, Calvin, Congregationalism, Covenanter, Cranmer, Dissenter, Evangelic, Gospeller, Huguenot, Independent, Lady, Loyalist, Lutheran, Mennonite, Methodist, Moravian, Neo-Orthodoxy, Nonconformist, Oak-boy, Orangeman, Peep o' day Boys, Pentecostal, Pietism, Prod, Puritan, Reformed, Religioner, Right-footer, Sacramentarian, Stundist, Swaddler, Wasp, Wesleyan

Protocol Agreement, Code, Convention, Etiquette, Geneva, Kyoto, Point-to-Point

Proton Nucleon, Quark

Protoplasm(ic) Coenocyte, Coenosarc, Cytode, Sarcode

Prototype Blueprint, Exemplar, Model, Original, Pattern

Protozoa(n) Am(o)eba, Foraminifer, Giardia, Globigerina, Gregarine, Heliozoan, Infusoria, Leishmania, Mastigophoran, Moner(a), Moneron, Paramecium, Peritricha, Phagocyte, Radiolaria, Rhizopod, Sea-mat, Thrichomonad, Trophozoite, Trypanosome, Volvox, Vorticella

Protract(ed) Delay, → **EXTEND**, Lengthen, Livelong, Long, Prolong

Protrude, Protrusion Bulge, Eventration, Exsert, Hernia, Jut, Pop, Pout, Project, Pseudopodium, Rectocele, Strout, Tel

Protuberance, Protuberant Apophysis, Bulge, Bump, Burl, Condyle, Crankle, Ergot, Gibbous, Hump, Knap, Knob, Malleolus, Node, Papillose, Papule, Spadix, Swelling, Tragus, Tuber, Tubersity, Venter

Proud Arrogant, Boaster, Cocky, Conceited, Dic(k)ty, Elated, Flush, Haughty, Haut, Level, Lordly, Orgulous, Protruding, Superb, Vain

Prove(d), Proving Apod(e)ictic, Argue, Ascertain, Assay, Attest, Authenticate, Aver, Confirm, Convince, Deictic, Establish, Evince, Justify, → **PROOF**, Quote, → **SHOW**, Substantiate, Test, Trie, Try

Proverb Adage, Axiom, Byword, Gnome, Maxim, Paroemia, Saw

▷ **Proverbial** *may refer to* the biblical Proverbs

Provide(d), Provident(ial) Afford, Allow, Arrange, Besee, Bring, Cater, Compare, Conditional, Endow, Equip, Far-seeing, Feed, Fend, Find, Furnish, Generate, Give, Grubstake, Heaven sent, If, Lay on, Maintain, Plenish, Proviso, Purvey, Quote, Serve, So, Sobeit, → **SUPPLY**, Suttle

Province, Provincial(ism) Area, Circar, District, Eparchy, Exclave, Eyalet, Forte, Insular, Land, Mofussil, Narrow, Nomarchy, Nome, Nomos, Oblast, Palatinate, Pale, Petrographic, Realm, Regional, Rural, Sircar, Sirkar, Subah, Suburban, Territory, Vilayet

PROVINCES

2 letters:	Natal	7 letters:	Rhaetia
NI	Otago	Alberta	Satrapy
	Tirol	Almeria	Shaanxi
4 letters:	Tyrol	Antwerp	Sichuan
Gaul		Brabant	Suiyuan
Ifni	6 letters:	Drenthe	Utrecht
Shoa	Acadia	Eritrea	Western
Sind	Artois	Gascony	Zeeland
	Basque	Gauteng	
5 letters:	Bengal	Granada	8 letters:
Anhui	Fujian	Guienne	Atlantic
Anjou	Fukien	Guizhou	Chekiang
Anwei	Hainan	Guyenne	Chinghai
Coorg	Kosovo	Hainaut	Connacht
Gansu	Marche	Jiangsu	Dauphine
Hebei	Poitou	Jiangxi	Hainault
Henan	Pontus	Jiazhou	Helvetia
Honan	Punjab	Kiangsi	Kiaochow
Hopeh	Quebec	Kiangsu	Leinster
Hopei	Raetia	Kwazulu	Liaoning
Hubei	Sanjak	Limpopo	Limousin
Hunan	Shansi	Livonia	Lorraine
Jehol	Shanxi	Munster	Lyonnais
Jilin	Shensi	Ningsia	Manitoba
Kansu	Sikang	Ontario	Maritime
Kirin	Ulster	Picardy	Ninghsia
Liege	Yunnan	Prairie	Normandy
Namur		Qinghai	Northern

8 letters – cont:
Pashalic
Pashalik
Provence
Shandong
Shantung
Szechuan
Szechwan
Touraine
Tsinghai
Zhejiang

9 letters:
Apeldoorn
Aquitaine
Connaught
Flevoland
Free State
Friesland
Groningen

Guangdong
Hainan Tao
Illyricum
Kurdistan
Languedoc
Lusitania
Nivernais
North West
Orleanais
Santa Cruz
Sungkiang
Transvaal

10 letters:
Gelderland
Mpumalanga
New Castile
Overijssel
Patavinity
Roussillon

Wellington

11 letters:
Balochistan
Baluchistan
Guelderland
Hesse-Nassau
Kaliningrad
Paphlagonia
West Prussia

12 letters:
Heilongjiang
New Brunswick
North Brabant
North Holland
Saskatchewan
South Holland

13 letters:
Syrophoenicia

14 letters:
Eastern Rumelia
Flemish Brabant
Walloon Brabant

15 letters:
British Columbia
Orange Free State

17 letters:
North West Frontier

23 letters:
Newfoundland and
Labrador

Proviso, Provision(al), Provisions Acates, A(p)panage, Board, Caution, Caveat, Clause, Condition, Fodder, Foresight, Insolvency, Interim, IRA, Joiture, Larder, Lend-lease, Makeshift, Nisi, On trial, Proggins, Reservation, Salvo, Scran, Skran, Stipulation, Stock, Supply, Suttle, Temporary, Tentative, Viands, Viaticum, Victuals

Provocation, Provocative, Provoke Agacant, Alluring, Egg, Elicit, Erotic, Exacerbate, Excite, Flirty, Gar, Harass, Incense, Induce, Inflame, Instigate, Irk, Irritate, Kindle, Needle, Nettle, Occasion, Pique, Prompt, Raise, Red rag, Sedition, Sound, Spark, Stimulate, Stir, Tar, Tarty, Tease, Urge, Vex, Wind up

Provost Dean, Keeper, Marshal, Warden

Prow Bow, Cutwater, Fore, Nose, Prore, Stem

Pro-war Hawk

Prowess Ability, Bravery, Forte, Fortitude

Prowl(er) Hunt, Lurch, Lurk, Mooch, Prog, Prole, Rache, Ramble, Ratch, Roam, Rove, Snoke, Snook, Snowk, Tenebrio, Tom

Proxime accessit Next best

Proximity Handiness

Proxy Agent, Attorn, Deputy, PP, Regent, Sub, Surrogate, Vicar, Vice

Prude(nce), Prudent, Prudery Bluenose, Canny, Caution, Circumspect, Comstocker, Conservative, Discreet, Discretion, Far-sighted, Foresight, Frugal, Grundyism, Judicious, Metis, Mrs Grundy, Politic, Prig, Prissy, Provident, Sage, Sensible, Sparing, Strait-laced, Strait-lacer, Thrifty, Tight-laced, Vice-nelly, Victorian, Ware, Wary, Well-advised, Wise

Prune(r) Bill-hook, Clip, Dehorn, Lop, Plum, Proign, Proin(e), Reduce, Reform, Secateur, Shred, Sned, Snip, Thin, Trim

Prunella Hedge-sparrow, Self-heal

Prurient Avaricious, Itchy, Lewd, Obscene

Prussia(n) Blue, Junker, Pruce, Spruce, Westphalian

Pry Ferret, Force, Lever, Meddle, Nose, Paul, Peep, Question, Search, Snoop, Stickyback, Toot

Psalm Anthem, Cantate, Chant, Chorale, Hallel, Hymn, Introit, Jubilate, Metrical,

Miserere, Neck-verse, Paean, Penitential, Proper, Ps, Song, Tone, Tract, Tractus, Venite

Pseud(o) Bogus, Mock, Posy, Sham, Spurious

Pseudonym Aka, Alias, Allonym, Anonym, Pen-name, Stage-name

Pshaw Chut, Pooh, Tilley-valley, Tilly-fally, Tilly-vally

Psyche Ego, Self, Soul, Spirit, Superego

Psychiatrist, Psychologist Adler, Alienist, Asperger, Clare, Coué, Ellis, Freud, Headshrinker, Jung, Laing, Müller-Lyer, Rat-tamer, Reich, Shrink, Skinner, Trick-cyclist

Psychic ESP, Lodge, Medium, Mind-reader, Seer, Telekinesis, Telepathic

Psychological, Psychology, Psychologist Analytical, Behaviourism, Clinical, Comparative, Constitutional, Depth, Development, Dynamic, Educational, Experimental, Eysenck, Gestalt, Hedonics, Humanistic, Industrial, James, Latah, Occupational, Organisational, Piaget, Social, Structural

Psychosis, Psychotic Korsakoff's, Manic-depressive, Organic, Schizophrenia

Psychotherapist, Psychotherapy Coué, Laing, Rebirthing

Ptarmigan Rype

Ptomaine Neurine

Pub Bar, Beerhall, Beverage room, Boozer, Chequers, Free-house, Gin-palace, Groggery, Houf(f), House, Howf(f), Inn, Jerry-shop, Joint, Local, Lush-house, Mughouse, Pothouse, Potshop, Rubbidy, Rubbity, Shanty, Tavern, Tiddlywink, Tied house

Puberty, Pubic Adolescence, Beaver, Bush, Hebetic, Teens

Pubescence Tomentum

Pubis Sharebone

Public Apert, Bar, Civil, Common, Demos, Estate, General, Great unwashed, Inn, Janata, Lay, Limelight, National, Open, Out, Overt, Populace, State, Vulgar, World

Publican Ale-keeper, Bung, Host, Landlord, Licensee, Tapster, Taverner

Publication Announcement, Bluebook, Book, Broadsheet, Edition, Ephemera, Exposé, Festschrift, Issue, → **JOURNAL**, Lady, Mag, Magazine, Organ, Pictorial, Samizdat, Tabloid, Tatler, Tract, Tribune, Yearbook

Publicise, Publicist, Publicity Ad(vert), Airing, Announce, Ballyhoo, Billing, Build up, Coverage, Exposure, Flack, Glare, Headline, Hype, Leakage, Limelight, Notoriety, Plug, PR(O), Promote, Promotion, Propaganda, Réclame, Spin-doctor, Splash

Publish(er), Published, Publishing, Publicise Air, Blaze, Cape, Delator, Desktop, Disclose, Edit, Electronic, Evulgate, Gollancz, Issue, Noise, OUP, Out, Pirate, Plug, Post, Print(er), Proclaim, Propagate, Put about, Release, Ren, Run, Stationer, Vanity, Vent, Ventilate

Puck Disc, Elf, Lob, Sprite, Squid

Pucker(ed) Bullate, Cockle, Contract, Gather, Plissé, Purse, Ruck, Shir(r), Wrinkle

Pud Fin, Paw

Pudding Afters, Baked Alaska, Bakewell, Black, Blancmange, Blood, Bread (and butter), Brown Betty, Cabinet, Charlotte, Christmas, Clootie dumpling, College, Crumble, Custard, → **DESSERT**, Dog's body, Drisheen, Duff, Dumpling, Eve's, Flummery, Fritter, Fromenty, Frumenty, Furme(n)ty, Furmity, Haggis, Hasty, Hodge, Hog's, Kugel, Lokshen, Mealie, Milk, Nesselrode, Panada, Pandowdy, Parfait, Pease, Plum, Plum-duff, Pockmanky, Pockmantic, Pock-pudding, Popover, Portmanteau, Queen's, Rice, Roly-poly, Sago, Savarin, Semolina, Sowens, Sponge, Spotted dick, Spotted dog, Stickjaw, Stodge, Suet, Summer, Sundae, Sweet, Tansy, Tapioca, Umbles, White, White hass, White hause, White hawse, Yorkshire, Zabaglione

Puddle Collect, Dub, Flush, Pant, Plash, Plouter, Plowter, Pool, Sop

Puff(ed), Puffer, Puffy Advertise, Blouse, Blow, Blowfish, Blurb, Bouffant, Breath, Chuff, Chug, Cream, Drag, Encomist, Eulogy, Exsufflicate, Fag, Flaff, Flatus, Fluffy, Fuff, Globe-fish, Grampus, Gust, Hype, Lunt, Pech, Pegh, Pluffy, Plug, Powder, Quilt, Recommend, Skiff, Slogan, Smoke, Steam, Swell, Toke, Twilt, Waff, Waft, Waif, Whiff, Whiffle

Puffin Fratercula, Rockbird, Sea-parrot, Tammie Norie, Tam Noddy

Pug(ilist), Pugilism Belcher, Boxer, Bruiser, Carlin, Fancy, Fistic, Monkey, Ring

Pugnacious Aggressive, Belligerent, Combative, Scrappy

Puke Retch, Sick, Vomit

Pukka Authentic, Genuine, Real, True, Valid

Pulchritude Beauty, Cheese-cake, Grace

Pull (up) Adduce, Attraction, Crane, Demand, Drag, Draw, Earn, Force, Haul, Heave, Heeze, Hook, → **INFLUENCE**, Lug, Mousle, Pluck, Rein, Ring, Rove, Rug, Saccade, Sally, Sole, Sool(e), Sowl(e), Stop, Tit, Touse, Touze, Tow, Towse, Towze, Trice, Tug, Undertow, Wrest, Yank

Pulley Block, Capstan, Idle(r), Jack-block, Swig, Trice, Trochlea, Truckle

Pullover Jersey, Jumper, Sweater, Sweatshirt, Tank-top, Windcheater

Pullulate Teem

▶ **Pull up** *see* **PULL**

Pulp Cellulose, Chyme, Chymify, Crush, Flong, Gloop, Kenaf, Marrow, Mash, Mush, Pap, Paste, Pomace, Pound, Puree, Rot, Rubbish, Squeeze, Squidge, Wood

Pulpit(e) Ambo(nes), Lectern, Mimbar, Minbar, Pew, Rostrum, Tent, Tub, Wood

Pulsar Geminga

Pulsate, Pulsatory Beat, Palpitate, Quiver, Systaltic, Throb, Vibrate

Pulse Adsuki, Adzuki, Alfalfa, → **BEAN**, Beat, Calavance, Caravance, Chickpea, D(h) al, Dholl, Dicrotic, Fava (bean), Flageolet, Garbanzo, Gram, Groundnut, Ictus, Lentil, Lucerne, Pea, Rhythm, Sain(t)foin, Soy beans, Sphygmic, Sync, Systaltic, Systole, Throb

Pulverise Calcine, Comminute, Contriturate, Demolish, Grind, → **POUND**, Powder

Puma Catamount, Cougar, Mountain lion, Panther

Pummel(ling) Beat, Drub, Fib, Knead, Nevel, Pound, Tapotement, Thump

▷ **Pummelled** *may indicate* an anagram

Pump(ing) Aerator, Air, Bellows, Bicycle, Bilge, Bowser, Breast, Centrifugal, Chain, Compressor, Cross-examine, Cross-question, Diaphragm, Donkey, Drive, Electromagnetic, Elicit, Feed, Filter, Foot, Force, Fork, Geissler, Grease-gun, Grill, Heart, Heat, Hydropult, Inflate, Interrogate, Knee-swell, Lift, Monkey, Mud, Nodding-donkey, Optical, Parish, Petrol, Piston, Pulsometer, Question, Rotary, Scavenge, Shoe, Sodium, Stirrup, Stomach, Suction, Turbine, Vacuum, Water, Wind

Pumpernickel Rye (bread)

Pumphandle Sweep

Pumpkin Butternut, Cashaw, Gourd, Pampoen, Quash, Queensland blue

Pun Calembour, Clinch, Equivoque, Jeu de mots, Paragram, Paronomasia, Quibble, Quip, Ram, Wordplay

Punch(ed) Antic, Bell, Biff, Blow, Boff, Bolo, Box, Bradawl, Bumbo, Card, Centre, Chad, Check, Chop, Clip, Cobbler's, Conk, Dry-beat, Fib, Fid, Fist(ic), Gang, Glogg, Haymaker, Hit, Hook, Horse, Jab, Key, Kidney, Knevell, Knobble, Knubble, KO, Lander, Mat, Milk, Nail set, Nevel, Nubble, One-er, One-two, Overhand, Perforate, Pertuse, Planter's, Plug, Poke, Polt, Pommel, Pounce, Prod, Pummel, Rabbit, Roundhouse, Rum, Rumbo, Slosh, Sock, Steed, Sting(o), Stoush, Sucker, Suffolk,

Sunday, Swop, Tape, Upper-cut, Wap, Wind, Zest

Punctilious Exact, Formal, Nice, Particular, Picked, Precise, Prim, Stickler

Punctual(ly), Punctual(iity) Politesse, Prompt, Regular, Sharp

Punctuate, Punctuation (mark) Apostrophe, Bracket, Close, Colon, Comma, Duckfoot quote, Emphasize, Guillemet, Interabang, Interrobang, Interrupt, Mark, Semicolon, Tittle

Puncture(d) Bore, Centesis, Criblé, Cribrate, Deflate, Drill, Flat, Hole, Lumbar, Perforate, Pierce, Pounce, Prick, Scarify, Thoracocentesis

Pundit Egghead, Expert, Guru, Maven, Oracle, Sage, Savant, Swami, Teacher

Pungency, Pungent Acid, Acrid, Acrolein, Alum, Ammonia, Bite, Bitter, Caustic, Hot, Mordant, Nidorous, Piquant, Poignant, Point, Racy, Sair, Salt, Spice, Sting, Tangy, Witty

▷ **Punish** *may indicate* an anagram

Punish(ment), Punished, Punishing Algates, Amerce, Attainder, Baffle, Bastinado, Beat, Birch, Brasero, Bum rap, Cane, Capital, Cart, Castigate, Chasten, Chastise, Come-uppance, Commination, Corporal, Correct, Cucking-stool, Dam(nation), Defrock, Desert(s), Detention, → **DISCIPLINE**, Fatigue, Fine, Flog, Gantlope, Gate, Gauntlet, Gruel, Hellfire, Hiding, High jump, Horsing, Hot seat, Imposition, Impot, Interdict, Jankers, Jougs, Keelhaul, Knee-capping, Knout, Laldie, Laldy, Lambast(e), Lines, Log, Marmalise, Necklace, Nemesis, Pack-drill, Padre Pio, Pandy, Pay out, Peine forte et dure, Penalise, Penance, Penology, Pensum, Perdition, Picket, Pillory, Pine, Rap, Reprisal, Retribution, Ruler, Scaffold, Scath, Scourge, Sentence, Serve out, Six of the best, Smack, Smite, Spank, Spif(f)licate, Stocks, Strafe, Straff, Strap, Strappado, Swinge(ing), Talion, Tar and feather, Toco, Toko, Tophet, Treadmill, Trim, Tron, Trounce, Tumbrel, Tumbril, Vice anglais, Visit, War(r)ison, What for, Whip, Wild mare, Ywrake, Ywroke

Punk Goop, Inferior, Ne'er-do-well, Nobody, Touchwood, Worthless

Punnet Basket, Pottle, Thug

Punt(er), Punting Antepost, Back, Bet, Gamble, Kent, Kick, Pound, Quant, Turfite, Wager

Puny Frail, Inferior, Petty, Reckling, Runtish, Scram, Shilpit, Sickly, Small, Weak

Pup(py) Cub, Whelp

Pupa Chrysalis, Exarate, Neanic, Nymph, Obtect

Pupil Abiturient, Apple, Apprentice, Boarder, Cadet, Catechumen, Dayboy, Daygirl, Disciple, Etonian, Exit, Eyeball, Fag, Follower, Greycoat, Gyte, Junior, L, Monitor, Prefect, Preppy, Protégé(e), Scholar, Senior, Student, Tutee, Ward

▷ **Pupil** *may refer to* an eye

Puppet(s), Puppeteer Bunraku, Creature, Doll, Dummy, Fainéant, Fantoccini, Galanty show, Glove, Guignol, Jack-a-lent, Judy, Mammet, Marionette, Mawmet, Mommet, Motion generative, Motion(-man), Pageant, Pawn, Pinocchio, Promotion, Punch(inello), Quisling, Rod, Tool

Purchase(r), Purchasing Acquisition, Bargain, Buy, Coff, Compulsory, Earn, Emption, Gadsden, Get, Grip, Halliard, Halyard, Hold, Layaway, → **LEVERAGE**, Louisiana, Money, Offshore, Oligopsony, Parbuckle, Perquisitor, Repeat, Secure, Shop, Toehold

Pure, Purity Absolute, Cando(u)r, Cathy, Chaste, Chiarezza, Clean(ly), Cleanness, Cosher, Fine, Glenys, Good, Holy, Immaculate, Incorrupt, Innocent, Intemerate, Inviolate, Kathy, Kosher, Lily, Lilywhite, Maidenhood, Me(a)re, Meer, Net(t), Pristine, Quintessence, Sanctity, Sheer, Simon, Simple, Sincere, Snow-white, Stainless, True, Unalloyed, Unapplied, Undrossy, Vertue, Virgin, Virtue, White

Puree Baba ghanoush, Coulis, Dahl, Dal, Dhal, Fool

Purgative, Purge Aloes, Aloetic, Araroba, Aryanise, Cacoon, Calomel, Cascara, Cassia, Castor-oil, Catharsis, Cholagogue, Colquintida, Croton, Delete, Diacatholicon, Diarrh(o)ea, Drastic, Elaterin, Elaterium, Eliminate, Eluant, Emetic, Enos®, Erase, Evacuant, Exonerate, Expiate, Flux, Gleichschaltung, Hiera-picra, Hydragogue, Ipecacuanha, Ipomoea, Jalap, Jalop, Laxative, McCarthyism, Number nine, Physic, Picra, Pride's, Relaxant, Scour, Scur, Senna, Soil, Turbith, Turpeth, Wahoo

Purgatory Cacatopia

Purification, Purifier, Purify(ing) Absolve, Bowdlerise, Catharsis, Clay, Clean(se), Depurate, Despumate, Dialysis, Distil, Edulcorate, Elution, Exalt, Expurgate, Filter, Fine, Gas-lime, Green vitriol, Lustre, Lustrum, Niyama, Refine, Retort, Samskara, Sanctify, Scorify, Scrub, Smudging, Sublime, Try

Puritan(ical) Bible belt, Bluenose, Browne, Digger(s), Ireton, Ironsides, Killjoy, Pi, Pilgrim, Plymouth Colony, Precisian, Prig, Prude, Prynne, Roundhead, Seeker, Strait-laced, Traskite, Waldenses, Wowser, Zealot

Purl(er) Cropper, Eddy, Fall, Knit, Ripple, Stream

Purloin Abstract, Annex, Appropriate, Lift, Nab, Pilfer, Snaffle, Sneak, Steal

Purple Amarantin(e), Amethyst, Assai, Aubergine, Burgundy, Cassius, Chlamys, Claret, Corkir, Cudbear, Dubonnet, Eminence, Fuchsia, Golp(e), Heather, Heliotrope, Hyacinthine, Imperial, Indigo, Korkir, Lavender, Lilac, Magenta, Mallow, Mauvin(e), Mulberry, Murrey, Orcein, Orcin(e), Orcinol, Pance, Pansy, Plum, Pompadour, Pontiff, Porporate, Proin(e), Prune, Puce, Puke, Punic, Purpure, Rhodopsin, Royal, Solferino, Tyrian, Violet, Visual

Purport Bear, Claim, Drift, Feck, Mean, Tenor

Purpose(ful) Advertent, Aim, Avail, Calculated, Cautel, Design, Errand, Ettle, Goal, Here-to, Idea, → **INTENT**, Marrow, Mean(ing), Meant, Mint, Mission, Motive, Object, Plan, Point, Raison d'être, → **REASON**, Resolution, Resolve, Sake, Telic, Telos, Tenor, Use, View

Purposeless Dysteleology, Futile, Indiscriminate, Otiose

Purr Curr, Rumble

Purse Ad crumenam, Bag, Bung, Caba, Clutch, Crease, Crumenal, Egg, Fisc, Fisk, Long Melford, Mermaid's, Pocket, Prim, Privy, Prize, Public, Pucker, Spleuchan, Sporran, Wallet, Whistle

▷ **Pursed** *may indicate* one word within another

Purser Mud-clerk

Purslane Sea, Water

Pursue(r), Pursuit Alecto, Business, Chase, Chivvy, Course, Dog, Follow, Follow up, Hobby, Hot-trod, Hound, Hunt, Line, Practice, Practise, Proceed, Prosecute, Quest, Scouring, Stalk, Trivial

Pursuivant Blue Mantle

Purulent Mattery

Purvey(or) Cater, Provide, Provisor, Sell, Supply

Pus Empyema, Matter, Purulence, Quitter, Quittor

Push(er), Push in Airscrew, Barge, Birr, Boost, Bunt, Butt, Detrude, Drive, Edge, Effort, Elbow, Fire, Horn, Hustle, Impulse, Invaginate, Jostle, Motivation, Nose, Nudge, Nurdle, Obtrude, Onrush, Pitchfork, Plod, Ply, Press, Promote, Propel, Railroad, Ram, Rush, Sell, Shoulder, → **SHOVE**, Snoozle, Subtrude, Thrust, Urge

Pushchair Baby Buggy®, Buggy, Stroller, Trundler

Pushover Doddle, Soda

Pusillanimous Coward, Timid, Weak, Weak-kneed, Wimp, Yellow

Puss(y) Amentum, → **CAT**, Catkins, Face, Feline, Galore, Hare, Malkin, Mouth,

Rabbit, Septic

Pussyfoot Dry, Equivocate, Inch, Paw, Steal, TT

Pustule Blotch, Pimple, Pock

Put (off; on; out; up) Accommodate, Add, Alienate, Bet, Cup, Daff, Defer, Dish, Do, Don, Douse, Implant, Impose, Incommode, Inn, Lade, Launch, Lay, Locate, Lodge, Lump, Oust, Pit, Place, Plonk, Set, Smore, Snuff, Station, Stow

Put away, Put by Distance, Save, Sheathe, Store, Stow

Put down Abase, Degrade, Demean, Disparage, Floor, Humiliate, Land, Repress, Reprime, Snuff, Write

▷ **Put off** *may indicate* an anagram

Putrefaction, Putrefy(ing), Putrid Addle, Bitter, Corrupt, Decay, Fester, Mephitic, Olid, Rot, Sepsis, Septic

Putsch Revolution

Putt(ing) Gimme, Gobble, Green, Hash, Pigeon, Sink, → **STUPID PERSON**

Putter Chug, Club

Put together Assemble, Compile, Synthesize

Putty Glaziers', Jewellers', Painters', Plasterers', Polishers'

Puzzle(r) Acrostic, Baffle, Bemuse, Bewilder, Brainteaser, Chinese, Confuse, Conundrum, Crossword, Crux, Crux medicorum, Egma, Elude, Enigma, Fox, Get, Glaik, Gravel, Intrigue, Jigsaw, Kakuro, Kittle, Logogriph, Magic pyramid, Mind-bender, Monkey, Mystify, Nonplus, Perplex, Ponder, Pose(r), Rebus, Riddle, Rubik's Cube®, Sorites, Sphinx, Stick(l)er, Stump, Sudoku, Tangram, Teaser, Thematic, Tickler, Wordsearch, Wordsquare

Pygmy Atomy, Dwarf, Hop o'my thumb, Negrillo, Negrito, Pyknic, Thumbling

Pyjamas Baby-doll, Churidars, Jimjams

Pyramid Cheops, Chephren, Frustum, Magic, Population, Stack, Teocalli

Pyre Bale(-fire), Bonfire, Brasero, Darga, Gha(u)t

Pyrenean Basque

Pyrites Arsenical, Cockscomb, Copper, Fool's gold, Iron, Magnetic, Mispickel, Mundic, Spear, White

Pyrotechnics Arson, Fireworks

Pyroxene Aegirine, Aegirite, Diopside

Pyrus Service-tree

Pythagoras Samian

Pythian (seat) Delphic, Tripod

Python Anaconda, Diamond, Kaa, Monty, → **SNAKE**, Zombi(e)

Qq

Q Koppa, Quebec, Question
Q-boat Mystery ship
QC Silk
Qua As
Quack Charlatan, Crocus, Dulcamara, Empiric, Fake, Homeopath, → **IMPOSTOR**, Katerfelto, Mountebank, Pretender, Saltimbanco
Quad(rangle) Close, Complete, Compluvium, Court, Em, En, Horse, Pane
Quadrilateral Lambeth, Tetragon, Trapezium, Trapezoid
Quadrille Dance, Lancers, Matador(e), Pantalon
Quaff Carouse, Drink, Imbibe
Quagmire Bog, Fen, Imbroglio, Marsh, Morass, Swamp, Wagmoire
Quahog Clam
Quail Asteria, Bevy, Bird, Blench, Bob-white, Button, Caille, Colin, Flinch, Harlot, Hen, Quake, Shrink, Tremble
Quaint Cute, Far(r)and, Farrant, Naive, Odd, Old-world, Picturesque, Strange, Twee, Wham, Whim(sy)
Quake(r), Quaking Aminadab, Broad-brim, Dither, Dodder, Fox, Friend, Fry, Hicksite, Obadiah, Penn, Quail, Seism, Shake(r), Shiver, → **TREMBLE**, Tremor, Trepid
Qualification, Qualified, Qualify Able, Adapt, Adverb, Capacitate, Caveat, Competent, Condition, Credential, Degree, Diplomatic, Entitle, Fit, Graduate, Habilitate, Higher Still, Meet, Modifier, Nisi, Parenthetical, Pass, Past-master, Proviso, Quantify, Restrict, Temper, Versed
Quality Aroma, Attribute, Body, Calibre, Cast, Charisma, Esse, Essence, Fabric, Fame, First water, Five-star, Flavour, Grade, Inscape, It, Kite-mark, Letter, Long suit, Mystique, Nature, Pitch, Plus, Premium, Primary, Property, Q, Quale, Reception, Savour, Sort, Standard, Stature, Style, Substance, Suchness, Terroir, Thew, Thisness, Timbre, Tone, Top notch, Total, Up-market, Vein, Vinosity, Virgin, Virtu(e), Water, Worth
Qualm Compunction, Misgiving, Scruple
Quandary Dilemma, Fix, Predicament, Trilemma
Quantity → **AMOUNT**, Analog(ue), Batch, Bundle, Capacity, Deal, Dose, Feck, Fother, Hank, Heaps, Hundredweight, Idempotent, Intake, Jag, Loads, Lock, Lot, Mass, Measure, Melder, Multitude, Myriad, Nonillion, Number, Ocean(s), Operand, Parameter, Parcel, Peck, Plenty, Posology, Pottle, Qs, Qt, Quire, Quota, Quotient, Ream, Scalar, Slather, Slew, Slue, Sum, Surd, Tret, Unknown, Vector, Wad, Warp, Whips
Quantum Graviton, Isospin, Magnon, Phonon, Photon, Roton
Quarantine Isolate, Lazarette
Quark Flavo(u)r, Strange
Quarrel(some) Affray, Aggress, Altercate, Arrow, Barney, Barratry, Barretry, Bate,

Bicker, Brabble, Brattle, Brawl, Breach, Breeze, Broil, Brulyie, Brulzie, Bust-up, Cagmag, Cantankerous, Carraptious, Cat and dog, Caterwaul, Chance-medley, Chide, Clash, Combative, Contretemps, Difference, Disagree, Dispute, Domestic, Dust-up, Eristic, Estrangement, Exchange, Fall out, Feisty, Fracas, Fractious, Fratch(et)y, Fray, Hassle, Issue, Jar, Loggerheads, Miff, Outcast, Outfall, Pugnacious, Ragbolt, Row, Spat, Squabble, Tangle, Tiff, Tile, Tink, Vendetta, Wap, Whid, Wrangle

Quarry, Quarry face Chalkpit, Chase, Currie, Curry, Game, Heuch, Mark, Mine, Pit, Prey, Scabble, Scent, Stone pit, Victim

Quart Winchester

Quarter(ing), Quarters Airt, Barrio, Billet, Canton(ment), Casbah, Casern(e), Chinatown, Chum, Clemency, Close, Coshery, District, Dorm, E, Empty, Enclave, Fardel, Farl, First, Fo'c'sle, Forecastle, Forpet, Forpit, Fourth, Ghetto, Ham(s), Harbour, Haunch, Last, Latin, Medina, → **MERCY**, N, Note, Oda, Pity, Point, Principium, Quadrant, Region, S, Season, Sector, Tail, Trimester, Two bits, W, Wardroom, Warp, Winter

Quarter-day LD

▷ **Quarterdeck** *may indicate* a suit of cards

Quartet Foursome, Mess, String, Tetrad

Quarto Crown, Demy, Foolscap, Imperial, Medium, Royal, Small

Quartz Agate, Amethyst, Bristol diamond, Buhrstone, Cacholong, Cairngorm, Chalcedony, Chert, Citrine, Flint, Granophyre, Granulite, Itacolumite, Jasp(er), Morion, Onyx, Plasma, Prase, Rainbow, Rose, Rubasse, Sapphire, Silex, Silica, Smoky, Spanish topaz, Stishovite, Tiger-eye, Tonalite, Whin Sill

Quash Abrogate, Annul, Nullify, Quell, Rebut, Recant, Scotch, Subdue, Suppress, Terminate, Void

Quaver(ing) Shake, Tremulous, Trill, Vibrate, Warble

Quay Bund, Landing, Levee, Wharf

Queasy Delicate, Nauseous, Squeamish

Quebec Q

Queen(ly) Adelaide, African, Alcestis, Alexandra, Anna, Anne, Artemesia, Atossa, Balkis, Beauty, Bee, Begum, Bess, Boadicea, Boudicca, Brunhild(e), Camilla, Candace, Card, Caroline, Cat, Christina, Cleopatra, Closet, Clytemnestra, Coatcard, Dido, Drag, Drama, Eleanor(a), Ellery, Ena, ER, Esther, FD, Gertrude, Guinevere, Hatshepset, Hatshepsut, Hecuba, Helen, Hera, Here, Hermione, Hippolyta, HM, Isabel, Isabella, Ishtar, Isolde, Jocasta, Juno, King, Leda, Maam, Mab, Maeve, Marie Antoinette, Mary, Matilda, May, Medb, Mobled, Monarch, Nance, Nefertiti, Omphale, Pance, Pansy, Parr, Paunce, Pawnce, Pearly, Penelope, Persephone, Phaedra, Prince, Prom, Proserpina, Qu, R, Ranee, Rani, Regal, Regina(l), Sara, Semiramis, Sheba, Sultana, Titania, Vashti, Victoria, Virgin, Warrior

Queen Anne Mrs Morley

Queer(ness) Abnormal, Berdash, Bizarre, Crazy, Cure, Curious, Fey, Fie, Fifish, Gay, Nance, Nancy, → **ODD**, Outlandish, Peculiar, Pervert, Poorly, Quaint, Rum, Spoil, Uranism, Vert

Quell Alegge, Allay, Calm, Quiet, Repress, Subdue, Suppress

Quench Assuage, Cool, Extinguish, Satisfy, Slake, Slo(c)ken, Sta(u)nch, Yslake

▶ **Query** *see* **QUESTION**

Quest Goal, Graal, Grail, Hunt, Pursuit, Search, Venture

Question(ing), Questionnaire Appose, Ask, Bi-lateral, Burning, Catechise, Chin, Contest, Conundrum, Cross-examine, Debrief, Dichotomous, Direct, Dispute, Dorothy Dixer, Doubt, Erotema, Eroteme, Erotesis, Examine, Fiscal, Good, Grill,

Heckle, Homeric, Impeach, Impugn, Indirect, Information, Innit, Interpellation, Interrogate, Interview, Koan, Leading, Loaded, Maieutic, Matter, Open, Oppugn, Peradventure, Pop, Pose, Previous, Probe, Problem, Pump, Q, Qu, Quaere, Quiz, Rapid-fire, Refute, Rhetorical, Riddle, Speer, Speir, Survey, Suspect, Tag, Teaser, Tickler, Vexed, West Lothian, WH, What, Worksheet

Questionable Ambiguous, Dubious, Fishy, Socratic

Question-master Interrogator, Socrates, Torquemada, Ximenes

Queue Braid, Breadline, Cercus, Crocodile, Cue, Dog, File, Kale, → **LINE**, Line up, Pigtail, Plait, Plat, Stack, Tail(back), Track

Quibble(r), Quibbling Balk, Carp, Carriwitchet, Casuist, Cavil, Chicaner, Dodge, Elenchus, Equivocate, Hairsplitting, Nitpick, Pedantry, Pettifoggery, Prevaricate, Pun, Quiddity, Quillet, Quirk, Sophist

Quiche Flan, Tart

Quick(en), Quickening, Quicker, Quickie, Quickly, Quickness Accelerate, Acumen, Adroit, Agile, Alive, Allegr(ett)o, Animate, Apace, Breakneck, Breathing, Bright, Brisk, Celerity, Chop-chop, Citigrade, Cito, Con moto, Core, Cracking, Cuticle, Dapper, Deft, Enliven, Existent, Expeditious, Express, Fastness, Festination, Foothot, Gleg, Hasten, Hie, High-speed, Hotfoot, Impulsive, Jiffy, Keen, Lickety-split, Living, Mercurial, Meteoric, Mistress, Mosso, Nailbed, Nimble, Nippy, Nooner, Pdq, Piercing, Piu mosso, Post-haste, Prestissimo, Presto, Prompt, Pronto, Rapid, Rath(e), Ready, Rough and ready, Schnell, Sharp, Skin, Slippy, Smart, Snappy, Snort, Sodain(e), Soon, Spry, Streamline, Stretta, Stretto, Sudden, Swift, Swith, Tout de suite, Trice, Up tempo, Veloce, Vital, Vite, Vivify, Wikiwiki, Yare

Quicksand Flow, Syrtis

Quicksilver Mercury

Quid Chaw, Chew, L, Nicker, Oner, Plug, Pound, Quo, Sov, Tertium, Tobacco

Quid pro quo Mutuum, Tit-for-tat

Quiescence, Quiescent Calm, Di(o)estrus, Inactive, Inert, Latent, Still

Quiet(en), Quieter, Quietly Accoy, Allay, Appease, Barnacle, Calm, Compose, Conticent, Decrescendo, Doggo, Ease, Easeful, Easy, Encalm, Entame, Gag, Grave, Kail, Laconic, Loun(d), Low, Lown(d), Low-profile, Lull, Meek, Mezzo voce, Mp, Muffle, Mute, P, Pacify, Pastel, Pauciloquent, Pause, Peace, Piano, Pipe down, Plateau, QT, Reserved, Reticent, Sedate, Settle, Sh, Shtoom, Shtum, Silence, Sitzkrieg, Sly, Sober, Soothe, Sotto voce, Still, Stum(m), Subact, Subdued, Tace, Taciturn, Tranquil, Wheesht, Whish, Whisht, Whist

Quill Calamus, Feather, Float, Plectre, Plectron, Plectrum, Plume, Remex

Quillwort Isoetes

Quilt(ed), Quilting Comfort(er), Continental, Counterpane, Cover, Crazy, Doona®, Duvet, Echo, Eiderdown, Futon, Kantha, Matel(l)asse, Patch(work), Puff, Trapunto

Quince Bael, Bel, Bengal, Bhel, Flowering, Japanese, Japonica

Quinine China, Crown-bark, Kina, Quina, Tonic

Quinsy Angina, Cynanche, Garget, Squinancy

Quintessence, Quintessential Classic, Heart, Pith

Quintet Pentad, Trout

Quip Carriwitchet, Crack, Epigram, Gibe, Jest, Jibe, Joke, Taunt, Zinger

Quirk Concert, Foible, Idiosyncrasy, Irony, Kink, Mannerism, Twist

Quisling Collaborator, Traitor

Quit(s) Abandon, Absolve, Ap(p)ay, Cease, Desert, Desist, Even(s), Go, Leave, Meet, Part, Resign, → **STOP**, Vacate, Yield

Quite Actually, All, Ap(p)ay, Clean, Dead, Enough, Enow, Fairly, Fully, Mezzo,

Precisely, Real, Right, Sheer, Very

Quiver(ing) Aspen, Quake, Shake, Sheaf, Sheath, The yips, Tremble, Tremolo, Tremor, Tremulate, Trepid, Vibrant, Vibrate, Wobble

Qui vive Go-go

Quixote, Quixotic Don, Errant, Impractical

Quiz Bandalore, Bee, Catechism, Examine, Interrogate, I-spy, Mastermind, Oddity, Probe, Pump, Question, Smoke, Trail, Yo-yo

Quizzical Askance, Curious, Derisive, Odd, Queer, Socratic

Quod Can, Clink, Jail, Prison

Quoit Disc(us), Disk, Ring

Quondam Once, Sometime, Whilom

Quorum Minyan

Quota Numerus clausus, Proportion, Ration, Share

Quotation, Quote(d), Quote Adduce, Citation, Cite, Co(a)te, Duckfoot, Epigraph, Evens, Extract, Forward, Instance, Name, Price, Recite, Reference, Say, Scare, Soundbite, Tag, Verbatim, Wordbite

Quoth Co, Said

Quotient Achievement, Intelligence, Kerma, Quaternion, Ratio, Respiratory

Rr

R Arithmetic, Canine letter, Dog letter, King, Queen, Reading, Recipe, Right, Romeo, Run, Writing

Rabbi Dayan, Mashgiah, Rav, Rebbe

Rabbit Angora, Astrex, Brer, British Lop, Buck, Bun(ny), Chat, Con(e)y, Cottontail, Daman, Dassie, Doe, Earbash, Harp, Haver, Hyrax, Jabber, Jack, Jaw, Klipdas, Long White, Lop-eared, Marmot, Muff, Nest, Novice, Oarlap, Palaver, Patzer, Prate, Rack, Rattle, Rex, Rock, Sage, Snowshoe, Tapeti, Terricole, Waffle, Welsh, White, Witter, Yak, Yap, Yatter

Rabble, Rabble-rousing Canaille, Clamjamphrie, Clanjamfray, Colluvies, Crowd, Demagoguery, Doggery, Galère, Herd, Hoi-polloi, Horde, Legge, Meinie, Mein(e)y, Menyie, Mob, Raffle, Rag-tag, Rascaille, Rascal, Riff-raff, Rout, Scaff-raff, Shower, Tag, Tagrag

Rabelaisian Pantagruel, Panurge

Rabid, Rabies Extreme, Frenzied, Hydrophobia, Lyssa, Mad, Raging, Virulent

Raccoon Coati(-mondi), Coati-mundi, Panda, Procyon

Race(course), Racing, Race meeting, Racetrack Aintree, Alpine, Ancestry, Arms, Ascot, Autocross, Autopoint, Bathtub, Belt, Boat, Boskop, Breed, Broose, Brouze, Bumping, Cambridgeshire, Career, Catadrome, Catterick, Caucus, Cesarewitch, Chantilly, Chase, Claiming, Classic, Comrades, Cone, Consolation, Contest, Corso, Country, Course, Criterium, Current, Cursus, Cyclo-cross, Dash, Derby, Doggett's Coat and Badge, Dogs, Doncaster, Drag, Dromos, Egg and spoon, Enduro, Epsom, Event, F1, Fastnet, Flapping, Flat, Flow, Formula One, Fun-run, Generation, Ginger, Goodwood, Grand National, Grand Prix, Guineas, Half-marathon, Handicap, Hare and hounds, Harness, Herrenvolk, Hialeah, High hurdles, Hippodrome, Human(kind), Hurdles, Hurry, Inca, Indy, Indy car, Kermesse, Kind, Lampadedromy, Lampadephoria, Leat, Leet, Leger, Le Mans, Lick, Lignage, Line(age), Longchamps, Madison, Man, Marathon, Master, Mediterranean, Meets, Mile, Monza, Motocross, Nascar, Nation, → **NATIONAL**, Newmarket, Nursery, Nursery stakes, Oaks, Obstacle, One-horse, Paceway, Palio, Paper chase, Pattern, Picnic, Plate, Pluck, Point-to-point, Potato, Pre-Dravidian, Prep, Pursuit, Rallycross, Rallying, Rapids, Rat, Redcar, Regatta, Relay, Rill, Rod, Ronne, Roost, Run-off, Sack, St Leger, Scramble, Scratch, Scud, Scurry, Seed, Selling, Shan, Sheep, Slalom, Slipstream, Sloot, Slot-car, Sluit, Smock, Speedway, Sprint, Stakes, Steeplechase, Stem, Stirp(s), Stirpes, Stock, Strain, Streak, Strene, Supermoto, Sweepstake, Tail, Taste, Tear, Thousand Guineas, Three-legged, Tide, Torch, Torpids, Towcester, Tribe, Trotting, TT, Turf, Two-horse, Two Thousand Guineas, Velodrome, Volsungs, Walking, Walk-over, Waterway, Welter, Wetherby, Whid, White, Wincanton

Racehorse, Racer Dragster, Eclipse, Filly, Go-kart, Hare, Maiden, Mudder, Neddy, Novice, Plater, Red Rum, Shergar, Snake, Steeplechaser, Trotter

Raceme Corymb, Panicle

Racial (area), Racialist Apartheid, Colour, Ethnic, Ghetto, National Front, Quarter
Rack Agonise, Bin, Cloud, Cratch, Drier, Flake, Frame, Hack, Hake, Heck, Pipe,
  Plate, Pulley, Roof, Stretcher, Toast, Torment, Torture, Touse, Towse
Racket(eer) Bassoon, → **BAT**, Battledore, Bloop, Blue murder, Brattle, Caterwaul,
  Chirm, Clamour, Con, Crime, Deen, Din, Discord, Earner, → **FIDDLE**, Gyp, Hubbub,
  Hustle, → **NOISE**, Noisiness, Protection, Ramp, Rort, Sokaiya, Stridor, Swindle,
  Tirrivee, Tumult, Uproar, Utis
Racy Ethnic, Piquant, Pungent, Ribald, Salty, Spicy, Spirited
Rad Rem
Radar Acronym, Angel, AWACS, Beacon, DEW line, Doppler, Gadget, Gee, Gull,
  Lidar, Loran, Monopulse, Navar, Rebecca-eureka, Shoran, Surveillance, Teleran®,
  Tracking
Raddle Hurdle, Ochre, Red
Radial Osteal, Quadrant, Rotula, Spoke, Tire, Tyre
Radiance, Radiant Actinic, Aglow, Aureola, Beamish, Brilliant, Gleam(y), Glory,
  Glow, Happy, Lustre, Refulgent, Shechina, Sheen, Shekinah
Radiate, Radiating, Radiation, Radiator Actinal, Adaptive, Air-colour,
  Annihilation, Beam, Black body, Bremsstrahlung, Cavity, Characteristic,
  C(h)erenkov, Disseminate, Dosimetry, Effulgence, Effuse, Emanate, Emit, Exitance,
  Fluorescence, Gamma, Glow, Hawking, Heater, Infrared, Insolation, Ionizing,
  Isohel, Laser, Millirem, Non-ionizing, Pentact, Photon, Pulsar, Quasar, Rem(s),
  Rep, Roentgen, → **SHINE**, Sievert, Soft, Spherics, Spoke, Stellate, Stray, SU, Sun,
  Synchrotron, Terrestrial, Ultra violet, UVA, UVB, Van Allen, Visible
Radical Acetyl, Allyl, Amide, Ammonium, Amyl, Aryl, Benzil, Benzoyl, Bolshevist,
  Bolshie, Butyl, Calumba, Carbene, Cetyl, Drastic, Dyad, Ester, Extreme, Free,
  Fundamental, Gauchist, Genre-busting, Glyceryl, Glycosyl, Hydroxy, Innate,
  Isopropyl, Jacobin, Leftist, Leveller, Ligand, Maximalist, Methyl, Montagnard,
  Nitryl, Oxonium, Parsnip, Phenyl, Phosphonium, Pink, Propyl, Red, Revolutionary,
  Rhizocaul, Root, Rudiment, Sulfone, Sulphone, Taproot, Trot(sky), Uranyl, Vinyl,
  Whig, Xylyl, Yippie, Yippy
Radio Beatbox, Blooper, Bluetooth, Boom-box, Cat's whisker, CB, Cellular, Citizen's
  band, Cognitive, Community, Crystal set, Digital, Ether, Gee, Ghetto-blaster,
  Local, Loudspeaker, Marconigraph, Receiver, Receiving-set, Rediffusion®, Reflex,
  Rig, Set, Simplex, Sound, Steam, Talk, Talkback, Tranny, Transceiver, Transistor,
  Transmitter, Transponder, Walkie-talkie, Walkman®, Walky-talky, Wireless
Radioactive, Radioactivity Actinide, Americium, Astatine, Autinite, Bohrium,
  Cobalt 60, Emanation, Fall-out, Hot, Niton, Nucleonics, Plutonium, Radon, Steam,
  Thorium, Torbernite, Uranite
Radiogram, Radiograph(y) Cable, Telegram, Venography, Ventriculography, Wire
Radiology Interventional
Radish Charlock, Mooli, Runch
Radium Ra
Radius Bone, Long, Schwarzschild, Short
Radon Rn
Raffia Rabanna
Raffle(s) Burglar, Draw, Lottery, Sweepstake
Raft(ing) Balsa, Carley float, Catamaran, Float, Kon-Tiki, Life, Mohiki, Pontoon,
  Slew, Whitewater
Rafter Barge-couple, Beam, Chevron, Jack, Joist, Principal, Ridge, Spar, Timber
Rag(ged), Rags Bait, Bate, Clout, Coral, Daily, Deckle, Dud(s), Duddery, Duddie,
  Duster, Fent, Figleaf, Glad, Gutter press, Guyed, Haze, Kid, Lap(pie), Lapje,

Mop, → **NEWSPAPER**, Nose, Paper, Red, Remnant, Revel, Rivlins, Roast, Rot, Scabrous, S(c)hmatte, Scold, Scrap, → **SHRED**, Slate, Slut, Splore, Tack, Tat(t), Tatter(demalion), Tatty, Taunt, → **TEASE**, Tiger, Tongue, Uneven

▷ **Rag(ged)** *may indicate* an anagram

Rage, Raging → **ANGER**, Ardour, Bait, Bate, Bayt, Boil, Chafe, Conniption, Explode, Fad, Fashion, Fierce, Fit, Fiz(z), Fume, Furibund, Furore, Fury, Gibber, Go, Ire, Mode, Monkey, Paddy(-whack), Passion, Pelt, Pet, Pique, Rabid, Rail, Ramp, Rant, Road, See red, Snit, Storm, Tear, Temper, Ton, Trolley, Utis, Wax, Wrath

Raglan Sleeve

Ragout Blanquette, Compot, Goulash, Haricot, Stew

Rag-picker Bunter

Raid(er) Assault, Attack, Baedeker, Bear, Bodrag, Bust, Camisado, Chappow, Commando, Corporate, Dawn, Do, For(r)ay, Imburst, Incursion, Inroad, Inrush, Invade, Jameson, Maraud, March-treason, Mosstrooper, Pict, Pillage, Plunder, Ram, Ransel, Razzia, Reive, Sack, Scrump, Skrimp, Skrump, Smash-and-grab, Sortie, Spreagh, Storm, Viking

Rail(er), Railing Abuse, Amtrack, Arm, Arris, Balustrade, Ban, Banister, → **BAR**, Barre, Barrier, Bird, Bullhead, Cloak, Communion, Conductor, Coot, Corncrake, Crake, Criticise, Dado, Fender, Fiddle, Fife, Flanged, Flat-bottomed, Flite, Flow, Grinding, Gush, Insult, Inveigh, Light, Limpkin, Live, Metal, Monkey, Neckerchief, Notornis, Parclose, Picture, Pin, Plate, Post, Pulpit, Pushpit, Rack, Rag, Rate, Rave, Rung, Scold, Slang-whang, Slate, Slip, Snash, Sneer, Sora, Soree, Spar, T, Taffrail, Takahe, Taunt, Thersites, Third, Towel, Train, Vituperation, Weka

Raillery Badinage, Banter, Chaff, Persiflage, Sport

Railroad, Railway Aerial, Amtrak, BR, Bulldoze, Cable, Cash, Coerce, Cog, Crémaillère, Dragoon, El, Elevated, Funicular, Gantlet, GWR, Inclined, L, Light, Lines, LMS, LNER, Loop-line, Maglev, Marine, Metro, Monorail, Mountain, Narrow-gauge, Rack, Rack and pinion, Rly, Road, Rollercoaster, Ropeway, ROSCO, Ry, Scenic, Ship, Siding, SR, Stockton-Darlington, Switchback, Telpher-line, Track, Train, Tramline, Tramway, Trans-Siberian, Tube, Underground

Railwayman Driver, Fettler, Gandy dancer, Guard, Length(s)man, Locoman, NUR, Stephenson, Stoker, Tracklayer

Raiment Apparel, Clothes, Garb, Ihram

Rain(y), Rainstorm Acid, Blash, Deluge, Downpour, Drizzle, Flood, Hyad(e)s, Hyetal, Mistle, Mizzle, Oncome, Onding, Onfall, Pelt, Pelter, Piss, Plump, Pluviose, Pluvious, Pour, Precipitation, Right, Roke, Scat, Seil, Serein, Serene, Shell, Shower, Sile, Silver thaw, Skiffle, Skit, Smir(r), Smur, Soft, Spat, Spet, Spit, Storm, Thunder-plump, Virga, Water, Weep, Wet, Yellow

Rainbow(-maker) Arc, Arc-en-ciel, Bifrost, Bruise, Dew-bow, Iridescence, Iris, Moon-bow, Spectroscope, Sunbow, Sundog, Torrent-bow, Water-gall, Weather-gall, White

Raincoat Burberry®, Cagoule, Gaberdine, Mac, Mino, Oils(kins), Slicker, Waterproof

Raingauge Ombrometer, Udometer

Rain-maker Indra

Rain tree Saman

Raise(d), Raising Advance, Aggrade, Attollent, Boost, Bouse, Bowse, Build, Buoy up, Cat, Coaming, Cock, Collect, Elate, → **ELEVATE**, Emboss, Enhance, Ennoble, Erect, Escalate, Exalt, Extol, Fledge, Grow, Heave, Heezie, Heft, High, Hike, Hoick, Hoist, Increase, Jack, Key, Leaven, Lift, Mention, Overcall, Perk, Rear, Regrate, Repoussé, Revie, Rouse, Saleratus, Siege, Sky, Snarl, Step-up, Sublimate, Upgrade,

Weigh

Rake, Raker, Rakish Buckrake, Casanova, Comb, Corinthian, Croupier, Dapper, Dissolute, Don Juan, Enfilade, Gay dog, Jaunty, Lecher, Libertine, Lothario, Raff, Reprobate, Rip, Roué, Scan, Scour, Scowerer, Scrape, Scratch, Strafe, Stubble, Swash-buckler, Swinge-buckler, Wagons

Rale Crepitus, Rattle

Rally, Rallying-point Autocross, Autopoint, Badinage, Banter, Demo, Gather, Jamboree, Meeting, Mobilise, Monte Carlo, Morcha, Muster, Oriflamme, Persiflage, Recover, Regroup, Rely, Rest, Revive, Risorgimento, Roast, Rouse, Scramble, Spirit

Ralph Imp, Nader, Rackstraw

Ram Aries, Battering, Buck, Bunt, Butt, Butter, Corvus, Crash, Drive, Hidder, Hydraulic, Mendes, Pun, Sheep, Stem, Tamp, Thrust, Tup, Wether

Ramble(r), Rambling Aberrant, Aimless, Digress, Incoherent, Liana, Liane, Maunder, Rabbit, Rigmarole, Roam, Rose, Rove, Skimble-skamble, Sprawl, Stray, Stroll, Vagabond, Wander

Rameses Pharaoh

Ramp Bank, Gradient, Helicline, Incline, Runway, Slipway, Slope, Speed

Rampage Fury, Spree, Storm, Warpath

Rampant Lionel, Predominant, Profuse, Rearing, Rife

▷ **Rampant** *may indicate* an anagram or a reversed word

Rampart Abat(t)is, Brisure, Butt, Defence, Fortification, Parapet, Terreplein, Vallum, Wall

Ramrod Gunstick

Ramshackle Decrepit, Heath Robinson, Rickety, Rickle

Ranch Bowery, Corral, Dude, Estancia, Farm, Fazenda, Hacienda, Spread, Stump

Rancid Frowy, Reast(y), Reest(y), Reist(y), Sour, Turned

Rancour Bad blood, Gall, Hate, Malgré, Malice, Resentment, Spite

Rand Border, R, Roon

Random Accidental, Aleatoric, Arbitrary, → **AT RANDOM**, Blind, Casual, Desultory, Fitful, → **HAPHAZARD**, Harvest, Hit-or-miss, Hobnob, Indiscriminate, Scattershot, Sporadic, Stochastic, Stray

▷ **Random(ly)** *may indicate* an anagram

Range(r), Rangy Admiralty, Align, Ambit, Andes, Atlas, AZ, Ballpark, Band, Bowshot, Bushwhack, Capsule, Carry, Cascade, Chain, Cheviot, Compass, Cotswolds, Course, Darling, Diapason, Dispace, Dolomites, Dynamic, Err, → **EXTENT**, Eye-shot, Flinders, Forest, Gamme, Gamut, Glasgow, Grade, Gunshot, Hamersley, Harmonic, Helicon, Himalayas, Home, Interquartile, Ken(ning), Kolyma, Ladakh, Leggy, Limit, Line, Long, Massif, Middleback, → **MOUNT**, Orbit, Oven, Owen Stanley, Palette, Point-blank, Prairie, Purview, Rake, Reach, Register, Repertoire, Rifle, Roam, Rocket, Rove, Run, Saga, Scale, Scope, Sc(o)ur, Selection, Serra, Shooting, Short, Sierra, Sloane, Spectrum, Sphere, Stanovoi, Stanovoy, Stove, Strzelecki, Tape, Tessitura, Teton, Texas, The Wolds, Tier, Urals, Waldgrave, Wasatch, Waveband, Woomera

Rank(s), Ranking Arrant, Assort, Ayatollah, Begum, Brevet, Caste, Category, Cense, Classify, Cornet, Curule, Degree, Dignity, Downright, Earldom, Echelon, Estate, État(s), Flight sergeant, Grade, Graveolent, Gree, Gross, High, Hojatoleslam, Hojatolislam, Majority, Olid, Parage, Percentile, Place, Rammish, Range, Rate, Rooty, Row, Seed, Seigniorage, Sergeant, Serried, Shoulder-strap, Sort, Stance, Stand(ing), → **STATION**, Status, Substantive, Table, Taxi, Tier, → **TITLE**, Titule, Utter, Viscount

Rankle Chafe, Fester, Gall, Irritate, Nag

Ransack Fish, Loot, Pillage, Plunder, Rifle, Ripe, Rob, Rummage

Ransom King's, Redeem, Release, Rescue

Rant(er), Ranting Bombast, Declaim, Fustian, Ham, Harangue, Rail, Rodomontade, Scold, Slang-whang, Spout, Spruik, Stump, Thunder, Tub-thump

Rap(ped) Blame, Censure, Chat, Clour, Gangsta, Halfpenny, Knock, Ratatat, Shand, Strike, Swapt, Tack, Tap

Rapacious Accipitrine, Esurient, Exorbitant, Greedy, Harpy, Kite, Predatory, Ravenous, Ravine

Rape Abuse, Assault, Belinda, Cole-seed, Colza, Creach, Creagh, Date, Deflower, Despoil, Gangbang, Grass(line), Hundred, Lock, Lucretia, Navew, Oilseed, Plunder, Ravish, Statutory, Stuprate, Thack, Tow, Violate, Vitiate

Rapid(ity), Rapidly Chute, Dalle, Double-quick, Express, Fast, Meteoric, Mosso, Presto, Pronto, Quick-fire, Riffle, Sault, Shoot, Skyrocket, Speedy, Stickle, Swift, Tantivy, Veloce, Vibrato, Whiz(zing), Wildfire

Rapier Sword, Tuck

Rappel Abseil

Rapport Accord, Affinity, Agreement, Harmony

Rapprochement Détente, Reconciliation

Rapt Riveted

Raptor Eagle, Kestrel, Osprey, Standgale, Staniel, Stannel, Stanyel, Stooper

Rapture, Rapturous Bliss, → **DELIGHT**, Ecstasy, Elation, Joy, Trance

Rare, Rarity Blue moon, Curio, Earth, Geason, Infrequent, Intemerate, One-off, Rear, Recherché, Scarce, Seeld, Seld(om), Singular, Thin, → **UNCOMMON**, Uncooked, Underdone, Unusual

Rare earth Lu(tetium)

Rarefied Thin

Rascal(ly) Arrant, Bad hat, Cad, Cullion, Cur, Deer, Devil, Gamin, Hallian, Hallion, Hallyon, → **KNAVE**, Limner, Loon, Losel, Low, Nointer, Rip, Rogue, Scallywag, Scamp, Scapegrace, Schelm, Skeesicks, Skellum, Skelm, Smaik, Spalpeen, Tinker, Toe-rag, Varlet, Varmint, Villain

Rash(ness), Rasher Acne, Bacon, Barber's, Brash, Collop, Daredevil, Eczema, Eruption, Erysipelas, Exanthem(a), Fast, Foolhardy, Gum, Harum-scarum, → **HASTY**, Headlong, Heat, Hives, Hotspur, Ill-advised, Impetigo, Impetuous, Imprudent, Impulsive, Indiscreet, Lardo(o)n, Lichen, Madbrain, Madcap, Miliaria, Morphew, Nappy, Nettle, Outbreak, Overhasty, Pox, Precipitate, Purpura, Reckless, Road, Roseola, Rubella, Sapego, Scarlatina, Serpigo, Spots, Temerity, Tetter, Thoughtless, Unheeding, Unthinking, Unwise, Urticaria

Rasp(er) File, Grate, Odontophore, Radula, Risp, Rub, Scrape, Scroop, Xyster

Raspberry Berate, Black(cap), Boo, Bronx-cheer, Etaerio, Hindberry, Razz, Wineberry

Rastafarian Dread

Rat(s), Ratty Agouta, Bandicoot, Blackleg, Blackneb, Boodie, Brown, Bug-out, Camass, Cane, Cur, Cutting grass, Defect, Desert, Fink, Footra, Foutra, Geomyoid, Gym, Heck, Hood, Hydromys, Informer, Kangaroo, Malabar, Mall, Maori, Mole, Moon, Norway, Pack, Pig, Poppycock, Potoroo, Pouched, Pshaw, Pup(py), Renegade, Renegate, Rice, Rink, Rodent, Roland, Rot(ten), Scab, Sewer, Shirty, Squeal, Stinker, Turncoat, Vole, Water, Wharf, Whiskers, White, Wood

Rat-catcher Cat, Ichneumon, Mongoose, Pied Piper

Rate(s), Rating A, Able, Able-bodied, Apgar, Appraise, Appreciate, Assess, Base, Basic, Birth, Bit, Carpet, Castigate, Cess, Classify, Conception, Cost, Count, Credit, Deserve, Effective, Erk, Estimate, Evaluate, Exchange, Grade, Headline, Hearty,

Hurdle, Incidence, Interest, ISO, Lapse, Leading, Mate's, Mortality, Mortgage, MPH, Mutation, Octane, Ordinary, OS, Pace, Penalty, Percentage, PG, Piece, Poor, Prime (lending), Rag, Rebuke, Red, Refresh, Reproof, Rocket, Row, Sailor, Scold, → **SET**, Slew, → **SPEED**, Standing, Starting, Surtax, Take-up, TAM, Tariff, Tax, Tempo, Tog, U, Upbraid, Value, Water, Wig, World-scale, X

Rather Assez, Degree, Fairly, Gey, Instead, Lief, Liever, Loor, More, Prefer, Pretty, Some(what), Sooner, Yes

Ratify Amen, Approve, Confirm, Homologate, Pass, Sanction, Validate

Ratio Advance, Albedo, Aspect, Bypass, Cash, Compound, Compression, Cosine, Distinctiveness, Duplicate, Focal, Fraction, Gear, Golden, Gyromagnetic, Inverse, Liquidity, Loss, Mark space, Mass, Neper, PE, Pi, Picture, Pogson, Poisson's, Position, Price-dividend, Prise-earnings, Proportion, Protection, Quotient, Reserve, Savings, Signal-to-noise, Sin(e), Slip, Space, Tensor, Trigonometric

Ration(s) Allocate, Apportion, Compo, Dole, Étape, Iron, K, Quota, Restrict, Scran, Share, Short commons, Size, Whack

Rational(ism), Rationalisation, Rationalize A posteriori, Descartes, Dianoetic, Dispassionate, Humanistic, Level-headed, Logical, Lucid, Matter-of-fact, Pragmative, Sane, Sapient, Sensible, Sine, Sober, Tenable, Wice

Rationale Motive

Rattle (box), Rattling Alarm, Chatter, Clack, Clank, Clap, Clatter, Clitter, Conductor, Crescelle, Crotalaria, Death, Demoralise, Discombobulate, Discomfort, Disconcert, Gas-bag, Hurtle, Jabber, Jangle, Jar, Maraca, Natter, Nonplus, Rale, Rap, Red, Reel, Rhonchus, Ruckle, Sabre, Shake, Sistrum, Sunn, Tirl, Upset, Yellow

Raucous Guttural, Hoarse, Loud, Strident

Ravage Depredation, Desecrate, Despoil, Havoc, Pillage, Prey, Ruin, Sack, Waste

Rave, Raving Adulate, Boil, Enthuse, Praise, Redwood, Redwud, Storm, Ta(i)ver, Tear

Ravel Disentangle, Entrammel, Explain, Fray, Involve, Snarl, Tangle

Raven(ous) Black, Corbel, Corbie, Corvine, Croaker, Daw, Grip, Hugin, Munin, Unkindness, Wolfish

Ravine Arroyo, Barranca, Barranco, Canada, Canyon, Chasm, Chine, Clough, Coulée, Couloir, Dip, Flume, Ghyll, Gorge, Goyle, Grike, Gulch, Gully, Kedron, Khor, Khud, Kidron, Kloof, Lin(n), Nal(l)a, Nallah, Nulla(h), Pit, Purgatory

Ravish Constuprate, Debauch, Defile, Devour, Outrage, Rape, Stuprate, Transport, Violate

Raw Brut, Chill, Coarse, Crude, Crudy, Damp, Fresh, Greenhorn, Natural, Recruit, Rude, Uncooked, Wersh

Raw-boned Gaunt, Lanky, Lean, Randle-tree

Ray(s), Rayed Actinic, Alpha, Beam, Beta, Canal, Cathode, Cosmic, Cramp-fish, Death, Delta, Devil, Devilfish, Diactine, Dun-cow, Eagle, Electric, Extraordinary, Fish, Gamma, Grenz, Guitarfish, Homelyn, Manta, Medullary, Monactine, Numbfish, Ordinary, Polyact, Positive, R, Radius, Re, Roentgen, Roker, Röntgen, Sawfish, Sea-devil, Sea-vampire, Sephen, Shaft, Skate, Starburst, Stick, Sting, Stingaree, Tetract, Thornback, Torpedo, Vascular

Rayon Acetate, Faille, Viscose

Raze Annihilate, Bulldoze, Demolish, Destroy, Level, Slight

Razor(-maker) Cut-throat, Occam, Safety, Straight

Razorbill Murre

Razor-fish Solen

Razz Raspberry

RE Sappers

Re About, Rhenium, Touching

Reach(ed) Ar(rive), Attain, Boak, Boke, Carry, Come, Get at, Get out, Grasp, Hent, Hit, Key-bugle, Lode, Octave, Peak, Raught, Rax, Retch, Ryke, Seize, Stretch, Touch, Win

Reach-me-downs Slop-clothing

React(or), Reaction(ary) Addition, Allergy, Anaphylaxis, Answer, Backlash, Backwash, Behave, Blimp, Blowback, Boiling water, Bourbon, Breeder, Bristle, Bummer, CANDU, Catalysis, Chain, Chemical, Converter, Convertor, Core, Counterblast, Dark, Dibasic, Diehard, Diels-Adler, Dinosaur, Double-take, Dounreay, Emotion, Exoergic, Falange, Fast(-breeder), Feedback, Fission, Flareback, Flehmen, Flinch, Furnace, Fusion, Gas-cooled, Graphite, Gut, Heavy-water, Hydrolysis, Imine, Incomplete, Insulin, Interplay, Inulase, Junker, Kickback, Knee-jerk, Light, Lightwater, Magnox, Molten salt, Neanderthal, Nuclear, Outcry, Oxidation, Pebble-bed, Photolysis, Pile, Poujade, Pressure-tube, Pressurized water, Reciprocate, Recoil, Redox, Repercussion, Respond, Reversible, Rigid, Sensitive, Solvolysis, Spallation, Sprocket, Stereotaxis, Swing-back, Thermal, Thermonuclear, Tokamak, Topochemistry, Ultraconservative, Vaccinia, Wassermann, Water

▷ **Reactionary** *may indicate* reversed or an anagram

Read(ing) Abomasum, Bearing, Browse, Decipher, Decode, Exegesis, First, Grind, Grounden, Haftarah, Haphtarah, Haphtorah, Interpret, Learn, Lection, Lesson, Lu, Maftir, Maw, Paired, Pericope, Peruse, Pore, Rad, Rennet-bag, Scan, Second, See, Skim, Solve, Speed, Stomach, → **STUDY**, Third, Uni(versity), Vell, Ycond

Reader(s) ABC, Academic, Alidad(e), Bookworm, Document, Editor, Epistoler, Gentle, Homeridae, Lay, Lector, Microfilm, Primer, Silas Wegg, Softa, Tape, Taster

Readiest, Readily, Readiness, Ready Alacrity, Alamain, Alert, Amber, Amenability, Apt, Atrip, Available, Boun, Bound, Braced, Brass, Cash, Conditional, Dough, Eager, Early, Eftest, Fettle, Fit, Forward, Game, Geared-up, Gelt, Go, Keyed, Latent, Lolly, Masterman, Money, On, Predy, Prepared, Present, Prest, Primed, Prompt, Promptitude, Reckoner, Ripe, Running costs, Set, Soon, Spot, Turnkey, Usable, Wherewithal, Willing, Yare, Yark

Readjust Mend, Regulate, Retrue

Readymade Bought, Precast, Prepared, Prêt-à-porter, Slops, Stock, Store

Reagent Analytical, Benedict's, Grignard, Ninhydrin, Reactor, Schiff's, Titrant

Real, Reality, Realities, Really Actual, Ah, Augmented, Bona-fide, Brass tacks, Coin, Deed, De facto, Dinkum, Dinky-di(e), Earnest, Echt, Ens, Entia, Entity, Essence, → **GENUINE**, Honest, Indeed, Mackay, McCoy, McKoy, Naive, Ontic, Positive, Quite, Royal, Simon Pure, Sooth, Sterling, Straight up, Substantial, Tangible, Tennis, The case, Thingliness, True, Verismo, Verity, Very, Virtual

Realgar Rosaker, Zarnec, Zarnich

Realise, Realisation, Realism, Realistic Achieve, Attain, Attuite, Cash, Dirty, Down-to-earth, Embody, Encash, Entelechy, Fetch, Fruition, Fulfil, Learn, Lifelike, Magic, Naive, Naturalism, Practical, Pragmatism, See, Sell, Sense, Socialist, Suss, Understand, Verismo, Verité

▶ **Realities, Reality** *see* **REAL**

Realm Domain, Dominion, Field, Kingdom, Land, Notogaea, Region, Special(i)ty, UK

Ream Bore, Foam, Froth, Paper, Printer's, Rime, Screed

Reap(er) Binder, Crop, Death, Earn, Gather, Glean, Harvest, Scythe, Shear, Sickleman, Solitary, Stibbler

Reappear(ance) Emersion, Materialise, Recrudesce

Rear(ing) Aft, Back(side), Background, Baft, Behind, Breeches, Bring-up, Bunt, Cabré, Catastrophe, Derrière, Empennage, Foster, Haunch, Hind, Hindquarters, Loo, Natch, Nousell, Nurture, Poop, Prat, → **RAISE**, Serafile, Serrefile, Stern, Sternward, Tonneau

Rearmament Moral

Rearrange(ment) Adjust, Anagram, Ectopia, Permute, Reorder, Shuffle

Reason(able), Reasoning A fortiori, Agenda, Analytical, Apagoge, A priori, Argue, Argument, Basis, Call, Casuistry, Cause, Colour, Consideration, Deduce, Economical, Expostulate, Fair, Ground(s), Hypophora, Ijtihad, Inductive, Intelligent, Ipso facto, Justification, Logic, Logical, Logistics, Logos, Metamathematics, Mind, Moderate, Motive, Noesis, Petitio principii, Plausible, Point, Practical, Pretext, Pro, Proof, Pure, Purpose, Ratiocinate, Rational(e), Sanity, Sense, Sensible, Settler, Somewhy, Sophism, Syllogism, Synthesis, Temperate, Think, Viable, What for, Why, Wit

Reave Despoil, Reif, Rob, Spoil

Rebate Diminish, Lessen, Refund, Repayment

Rebecca Sharp

Rebel(s), Rebellion, Rebellious Aginner, Apostate, Arian, Beatnik, Blouson noir, Bolshy, Boxer, Cade, Contra, Croppy, Danton, Defiance, Diehard, Disobedient, Emeute, Fifteen, Forty-five, Frondeur, Glendower, Green Mountain Boys, Hampden, Hereward the Wake, Hippy, Iconoclast, Insubordinate, Insurgent, Insurrection, IRA, Jacobite, Jacquerie, Kick, Luddite, Malignant, Mutine(er), Mutiny, Oates, Pilgrimage of Grace, Putsch, Rebecca, Recalcitrant, Recusant, Reluct, Resist, → **REVOLT**, Rise, Rum, Scofflaw, Sedition, Sepoy, Spartacus, Steelboy, Straw, Taiping, Ted, Titanism, Tyler, Venner, Warbeck, Wat Tyler, Whiteboy, Zealot

▷ **Rebellious** *may indicate* a word reversed

Rebirth Palingenesis, Reincarnation, Renaissance, Revival, Samsara

Rebound Backfire, Bounce, Cannon, Carom, Elastic, Recoil, Repercussion, Ricochet, Snapback

Rebuff Check, Cold-shoulder, Noser, Quelch, Repulse, Retort, Rubber, Setdown, Sneb, Snib, Snub

Rebuild Haussmannize

Rebuke Admonish, Berate, Check, Chide, Earful, Lecture, Neb, Objurgate, Rap, Rate, Razz, Reprimand, Reproof, Reprove, Rollick, Scold, Score, Slap, Slate, Snib, Snub, Strop, Threap, Threep, Tick off, Trim, Tut, Upbraid, Wig

Rebut Disprove, Elide, Refute, Repulse, Retreat

Recalcitrant Mulish, Obstinate, Renitent, Unruly, Wilful

Recall(ing) Annul, Echo, Eidetic, Encore, Evocative, Go over, Partial, Reclaim, Recollect, Redolent, Remember, Remind, Reminisce, Repeal, Retrace, Revoke, Total, Unsay, Withdraw

Recant(ation) Disclaim, Palinode, Retract, Revoke

Recap(itulate), Recapitulation Epanodos, Summarise

Recapture Rescue

▷ **Recast** *may indicate* an anagram

▶ **Recce** *see* **RECONNAISSANCE**

Recede Decline, Ebb, Lessen, Regress, Retrograde, Shrink, Withdraw

Receipt(s) Acknowledge, Chit, Docket, Quittance, Recipe, Revenue, Take, Voucher

Receive(d), Receiver Accept, Accoil, Acquire, Admit, Aerial, Antenna, Assignee, Bailee, Bleeper, Dipole, Dish, Donee, Ear, Earphone, Fence, Get, Grantee, Greet, Hydrophone, Inherit, Intercom, Official, Pernancy, Phone, Pocket, Radio,

Radiopager, Reset, Responser, Responsor, Roger, Set, Sounder, Take, Tap, Transistor, Transponder, Tuner, Wide

Recent(ly) Alate, Current, Fresh, Hot, Just, Late, Low, Modern, New, New-found, Yesterday, Yestereve, Yesterweek

Receptacle Ash-tray, Basket, Bin, Bowl, Box, Chrismatory, Ciborium, Container, Cyst, Hell-box, Locket, Loom, Monstrance, Muffle, Receiver, Reliquary, Relique, Reservatory, Sacculus, Spermatheca, Spittoon, Tank, Thalamus, Tidy, Tore, Torus, Trash can

Reception, Receptive Accoil, At home, Bel-accoyle, Couchée, Court, Durbar, Entertainment, First-class, Greeting, Helpdesk, Infare, Kursaal, Levée, Open, Ovation, Pervious, Ruelle, Saloon, Sensory, Soirée, Superheterodyne, Teleasthetic, Warm, Welcome

Receptor(s) Metabotropic, Steroid

▷ **Recess** *may indicate* 'reversed'

Recess(ion) Alcove, Antrum, Apse, Apsidal, Apsis, Bay, Bole, Bower, Break, Breaktime, Closet, Columbarium, Corner, Corrie, Cove, Croze, Dinette, Ebb, Embrasure, Exedra, Fireplace, Grotto, Hitch, Inglenook, Interval, Loculus, Mortise, → **NICHE**, Nook, Oriel, Outshot, Pigeonhole, Rabbet, Rebate, Respite, Rest, Slump, Withdrawal

Rechabite TT

Réchauffé Hachis, Hash, Salmi

Recidivist Relapser

▷ **Recidivist** *may indicate* 'reversed'

Recipe Dish, Formula, Prescription, R, Receipt, Take

Recipient Assignee, Beneficiary, Disponee, Donee, Grantee, Heir, Legatee, Receiver, Suscipient

Reciprocal, Reciprocate Corresponding, Elastance, Exchange, Inter(act), Mutual, Repay, Return

Recite(r), Recital, Recitation(ist) Ave, Concert, Declaim, Diseuse, Enumerate, Incantation, Litany, Monologue, Mystic, Parlando, Quote, Reading, Reel, Relate, Rhapsode, Say, Sing, Tell

▷ **Reckless** *may indicate* an anagram

Reckless(ness) Bayard, Blindfold, Careless, Catiline, Desperado, Desperate, Devil-may-care, Gadarene, Harum-scarum, Hasty, Headfirst, Headlong, Hell-bent, Irresponsible, Madcap, Perdu(e), Ramstam, Rantipole, → **RASH**, Slapdash, Temerity, Ton-up, Wanton, Wildcat

Reckon(ing) Assess, Bet, Calculate, Cast, Census, Computer, Consider, Count, Date, Doomsday, Estimate, Fancy, Figure, Guess, Number, Rate, Settlement, Shot, Tab

Reclaim(ed), Reclamation Assart, Empolder, Impolder, Innings, Novalia, Polder, Recover, Redeem, Restore, Swidden, Tame, Thwaite

Recline, Reclining Accubation, Accumbent, Lean, Lie, Lounge, Rest

Recluse, Reclusive Anchor(et), Anchorite, Ancress, Eremite, Hermit, Low-profile, Solitaire

Recognise(d), Recognition Accept, Acknow(ledge), Admit, Anagnorisis, Appreciate, Ascetic, Character, Cit(ation), Exequatur, Gaydar, Identify, Isolated, Ken, → **KNOW**, Nod, Notice, Oust, Own, Perception, Resipiscence, Reward, Salute, Scent, Standard, Sung, Voice, Weet, Wot

Recoil Backlash, Bounce, Kick(back), Quail, Rebound, Redound, Repercussion, Resile, Reverberate, Shrink, Shy, Spring, Start, Whiplash

Recollect(ion) Anamnesis, Memory, Pelmanism, Recall, → **REMEMBER**, Reminisce

▷ **Recollection** *may indicate* an anagram

Recommend(ation) Advise, Advocate, Counsel, Direct, Encourage, Endorse, Exhort, Nap, Praise, Precatory, Promote, Rider, Suggest, Testimonial, Tip, Tout, Urge

Recompense Cognisance, Deodand, Deserts, Expiate, Guerdon, Pay, Remunerate, Repayment, Requite, Restitution, Reward

Reconcile(d) Adapt, Adjust, Affrended, Atone, Harmonise, Henotic, Make up, Mend

Recondite Difficult, Esoteric, Mystic, Obscure, Occult, Profound

Reconnaissance, Reconnoitre Case, Investigate, Patrol, Recce, Scout, Survey

Reconstitute, Reconstitution Diagenesis

Reconstruction Perestroika, Telophase

Record(er), Recording (company) Acetate, Album, All-time, Ampex, Analogue, Annal(ist), Archive, Archivist, Audit trail, Aulos, Bench-mark, Black box, Blue Riband, Book, Campbell-Stokes, Can, Cardiograph, Cartulary, Casebook, CD, Chart, Chronicle, Clickstream, Clock, Clog-almanac, Coat(e), Congressional, Crash, Daybook, Decca, Diary, Dictaphone®, Dictograph®, Digital, Disc, Document, Dossier, Eloge, Elpee, EMI, Endorsement, English flute, Enter, Entry, EP, Ephemeris, Estreat, Ever, Filater, File, Film, Flight, Flute, Form, Forty-five, Ghetto blaster, Gram, Gramophone, Hansard, Helical scan, Herstory, Hierogrammat, Hill and dale, History, Hologram, Incremental, Indie, Journal, Lap-chart, Ledger, List, Log, Logbook, LP, Marigram, Mark, Maxi-single, Memento, Memo(randum), Memoir, Memorial, Memorise, Meter, Mind, Minute, Mono, Muniment, Noctuary, Notate, Notch, Note, Odometer, Open-seel, Oscillogram, Pass book, Platter, Playback, Practic(k), Pratique, Pressing, Previous, Protocol, Public, Quadrophonics, Quadruplex, Quipo, Quipu, Quote, Rapsheet, Rec, Reel-to-reel, Regest, Register, Release, Remembrancer, Roll, Score(board), Set down, Seven-inch, Seventy-eight, Shellac, Single, Spectogram, Sphygmogram, Spirogram, Stenotype®, Studbook, Sunshine, Tachograph, Tally, Tallyman, Tape, Thirty-three, Time sheet, TiVo®, Toast, Trace, Track, Transcript, Travelog, Trip, Twelve-inch, VERA, Vid(eo), Videotape, Vote, Wax, Wire, Wisden, Worksheet, Write

Record-holder Champion, Sleeve

Record-player DJ, Stereo

Recount Describe, Enumerate, → **NARRATE**, Relate, Tell

Recourse Access, Resort

Recover(y) Amend, Clawback, Comeback, Common, Convalescence, Cure, Dead cat bounce, Get over, Lysis, Over, Perk, Pull through, Rally, Rebound, Reclaim, Recoup, Redeem, Regain, Rehab, Repaint, Replevin, Replevy, Repo(ssess), Rescript, Rescue, Resile, → **RETRIEVE**, Revanche, Salvage, Salve, Second-wind, Spontaneous, Upswing, Upturn

Recreate, Recreation Diversion, Hobby, Palingenesia, Pastime, Play, Pleasure, Revive, Sport

Recriminate, Recrimination Ruction

Recruit(s) Attestor, Bezonian, Choco, Conscript, Crimp, Draft, Employ, Engage, Enlist, Enrol, Headhunt, Intake, Muster, Nignog, Nozzer, Press, Rookie, Sprog, Volunteer, Wart, Yardbird, Yobbo

Rectangle, Rectangular Dimetric, Golden, Matrix, Oblong, Quad, Quadrate, Square

Rectifier, Rectify Adjust, Amend, Dephlegmate, Redress, Regulate, → **REMEDY**, Right, Silicon

Recto Ro

Rector R

Rectum Tewel
Recuperate Convalesce, Rally, Recover
Recur(rent), Recurring Chronic, Quartan, Quintan, Recrudesce, Repeated, Repetend, Return
▷ **Recurrent** *may indicate* 'reversed'
Recycler, Recycling Freegan
▷ **Red** *may indicate* an anagram
Red(den), Redness Admiral, Alizarin, Anarch(ist), Angry, Archil, Arun, Ashamed, Auburn, Beet, Bilirubin, Bloodshot, Blush, Bolshevik, Brick, Burgundy, C, Cain-coloured, Carmine, Carroty, Castory, Cent, Cerise, Cherry, Chica, Chinese, Choy-root, Chrome, Cinnabar, Claret, Coccineous, Commo, Communist, Congo, Copper, Coquelicot, Coral, Coralline(e), Corkir, Cramesy, Cremosin, Crimson, Crocoite, Cuprite, Cyanin, Damask, Debit, Dubonnet, Duster, Embarrassed, Eosin, Eric, Erik, Erythema, Ffion, Flame, Flaming, Florid, Flush, Foxy, Garnet, Geranium, Ginger, Gory, Grog-blossom, Gule(s), Guly, Hat, Henna, Herring, Incarnadine, Indian, Indigo, Inflamed, Infra, Inner, Intertrigo, Iron, Jacqueminot, Judas-coloured, Keel, Kermes, Korkir, Lac-lake, Lake, Lateritious, Left(y), Lenin, Letter, Magenta, Maoist, Maroon, Marxist, McIntosh, Menshevik, Miniate, Minium, Modena, Mulberry, Murrey, Neaten, Orchel, Orchilla-weed, Orseille, Oxblood, Phenol, Pillar-box, Pinko, Plethoric, Plum, Pompeian, Ponceau, Poppy, Pyrrhous, Raddle, Radical, Raspberry, Raw, Realgar, Rhodamine, Rhodopsin, Ridinghood, Roan, Rosaker, Rose, Rot, Rouge, Roy, Rubefaction, Rubefy, Rubella, Rubescent, Rubicund, Rubric, Ruby, Ruddle, Ruddy, Rufescent, Rufus, Russ(e), Russet, Russian, Russky, Rust(y), Rutilant, Sang-de-boeuf, Sanguine, Santalin, Sard, Scarlet, Sericon, Setter, Solferino, Stammel, Tape, Tidy, Tile, Titian, Trot, Trotsky, Turacin, Turkey, Tyrian, Venetian, Vermeil, Vermilion, Vermily, Vinaceous, Wallflower, Wax, Wine
Redcoat Rust, Soldier
Redeem(er), Redemption Cross, Liberate, Lowse, Mathurin, Messiah, Ransom, Retrieve, Salvation, Save
Red-faced Coaita, Florid, Flushed
Red-handed Bang to rights
Red-head Auburn, Blue(y), Carroty, Commissar, Mao, Rufus
Red herring Norfolk capon, Soldier
▶ **Red Indian** *see* **NORTH AMERICAN INDIAN**
Redirect Sublimate
▷ **Rediscovered** *may indicate* an anagram
Redolent Aromatic, Fragrant, Reeking, Suggestive
Redoubtable Stalwart
Redress Amends, Offset, Recompense, Rectify, Regrate, Remedy, Right
Redshank Gambet, Totanus
Redskin Indian, Tomato
Red spot Tika
Reduce(r), Reduced, Reduction Abatement, Allay, Alleviate, Amortize, Attenuate, Bate, Beggar, Beneficiate, Calcine, Clip, Commute, Concession, Condense, Contract, Cull, Cut, Cutback, Damping, Debase, Decimate, Decrease, Decrement, Demote, Deoxidate, Deplete, Depreciation, Detract, Devalue, Diminish, Diminuendo, Discount, Downgrade, Downsize, Draw-down, Epitomise, Foreshorten, Grind, Hatchet job, Jeff, Kinone, → **LESSEN**, Lite, Markdown, Mitigate, Moderate, Palliate, Pot, Pulp, Put, Quinol, Razee, Remission, Retrench, Rundown, Scant, Shade, Shorten, Shrinkage, Slash, Strain, Supersaver, Taper,

Telescope, Thin, Weaken, Write-off
Redundancy, Redundant Frill, Futile, Needless, Otiose, Pink slip, Pleonasm, Retrenchment, Superfluous, Surplus
Redwood Amboyna, Mahogany, Sanders, Wellingtonia
Reed Arundinaceous, Broken, Calamus, Double, Free, Oboe, Papyrus, Pipe, Quill, Raupo, Rush, Sedge, Seg, Sley, Spear, Sudd, Syrinx, Thatch, Twill, Whistle
Reef Atoll, Barrier, Bioherm, Bombora, Bommie, Cay, Coral, Fringing, Great Barrier, Key, Knot, Lido, Motu, Saddle, Sca(u)r, Skerry, Witwatersrand
Reefer Cigarette, Jacket, Joint
Reek Emit, Exude, Stink
Reel Bobbin, Dance, Eightsome, Hoolachan, Hoolican, Lurch, Multiplier, News, Pirn, Spin, Spool, Stagger, Strathspey, Sway, Swift, Swim, Totter, Virginia, Wheel, Whirl, Wintle
Reestablish Redintegrate
Refectory Frater
Refer Advert, Allude, Assign, Cite, Direct, Mention, Pertain, Relate, Remit, Renvoi, Renvoy, See, Submit, Touch, Trade
Referee Arbiter, Commissaire, Linesman, Mediate, Oddsman, Official, Ref, Umpire, Voucher, Whistler, Zebra
Reference, Reference room Allusion, Apropos, Biaxal, Character, Coat, Grid, Guidebook, Index, Innuendo, Mention, Morgue, Passion, Quote, Regard, Renvoi, Respect, Retrospect, Testimonial, Vide
Referendum Mandate, Plebiscite, Vox populi
Refill Replenish
Refine(d), Refinement, Refiner(y) Alembicated, Attic, Catcracker, Couth, Cultivate, Culture, Cupellation, Cut-glass, Distil, Distinction, Elaborate, Elegance, Exility, Exquisite, Genteel, Grace, Nice, Nicety, Polish(ed), Polite, Précieuse, Pure, Rare(fy), Recherché, Saltern, Sieve, Sift, Smelt, Sophisticated, Spiritualize, Spirituel, Sublimate, Subtilise, Subtlety, Tasteful, Try, U, Urbane, Veneer
Reflect(ing), Reflection, Reflective, Reflector Albedo, Apotheosis, Blame, Catoptric, Cat's eye®, Chaff, Chew, Cogitate, → **CONSIDER**, Echo, Glass, Glint, Image, Meditate, Mirror, Muse, Nonspecular, Ponder, Redound, Repercuss, Ricochet, Ruminate, Spectacular, Speculum, Symmetrical, Tapetum, Thought
Reflex Achilles, Babinski, Bent, Cancrizans, In, Knee-jerk, Patellar, Pavlovian, Re-entrant, Single-lens, Tic, Twin-lens
▷ **Reform(ed)** *may indicate* an anagram
Reform(er), Reforming Amend, Apostle, Beveridge, Bloomer, Calvin, Chartism, Chastise, Convert, Correct, Enrage, Fourier, Fry, Gandhi, Gradualism, Howard, Hussite, Improve, Knox, Land, Lollard, Luther, Meiji, Melanchthon, Mend, Mucker, New Deal, Owenite, Pietism, PR, Progressionist, Protestant, Proudhon, Puritan, Rad(ical), Really, Recast, Reclaim, Reconstruction, Rectify, Regenerate, Resipiscence, Ruskin, Satyagraha, Savonarola, Syncretise, Tariff, Transmute, Tyndale, Wycliffe, Young Turk, Zwingli
Reformatory Borstal, Magdalen(e)
Refract(ion), Refractive, Refractor(y) Anaclastic, Double, Firestone, Obstinate, Perverse, Prism, Recalcitrant, Refringe, Restive, Stubborn, Sullen, Wayward
Refrain Abstain, Alay, Avoid, Bob, Burden, Chorus, Desist, Epistrophe, Faburden, Fa-la, Forbear, Hemistich, Mantra, O(v)erword, Owreword, Repetend, Ritornello, Rumbelow, Rum(p)ti-iddity, Rum-ti-tum, Spare, Tag, Tirra-lirra, Tirra-lyra, Turn again, Undersong, Waive, Wheel
Refresh(ment), Refresher Air, Bait, Be(a)vers, Buffet, Cheer, Elevenses, Enliven,

Exhilarate, Food, Four-hours, Nap, New, Nourishment, Purvey, Refection, Reflect, Refocillate, Reinvigorate, Renew, Repast, Restore, Revive, Seltzer, Shire, Slake, Water

Refrigerator Chill, Chiller, Cooler, Deep freeze, Esky®, Freezer, Freon, Fridge, Ice-box, Minibar, Reefer

Refuge Abri, Ark, Asylum, Bolthole, Bothie, Bothy, Burrow, Dive, Fastness, Funkhole, Girth, Grith, Harbour, Haven, Hideaway, Hole, Holt, Home, Hospice, Oasis, Port, Reefer, Resort, Retreat, Sanctuary, Sheet-anchor, → **SHELTER**, Soil, Stronghold, Women's

Refugee(s) Boat people, DP, Economic, Escapist, Fugitive, Grenzganger, Huguenot, Reffo

Refund Clawback, Repayment, Surcharge

Refurbish New, Renew

▷ **Refurbished** *may indicate* an anagram

Refusal, Refuse Attle, Bagasse, Ba(u)lk, Bilge, Bin, Black, Blackball, Boycott, Bran, Brash, Breeze, Brock, Bull, Bunkum, Cane-trash, Chaff, Clap-trap, Crane, Crap, Cul(t)ch, Debris, Decline, Denay, Deny, Disown, Draff, Drivel, Dross, Dunder, Dung, Eighty-six, Fag-end, Fenks, Fiddlesticks, Finks, First, Flock, Frass, Garbage, Gob, Guff, Hards, Hogwash, Hold-out, Hurds, Husk, Interdict, Jews' houses, Jews' leavings, Jib, Junk, Knickknackery, Knub, Lay-stall, Leavings, Litter, Lumber, Mahmal, Marc, Megass(e), Midden, Mullock, Mush, Nay(-say), Nill, No, Noser, Nould, Nub, Offal, Off-scum, Orts, Pellet, Pigwash, Potale, Punk, Radwaste, Rags, Raffle, Rape(cake), Rat(s), Rebuff, Recrement, Recusance, Red(d), Redargue, Redline, Reest, Regret, Reneg(u)e, Renig, Repudiate, Rot, → **RUBBISH**, Ruderal, Scaff, Scrap, Scree, Screenings, Scum, Sewage, Shant, Shell heap, Slag, Sordes, Spurn, Sullage, Sweepings, Swill, Tailings, Tinpot, Tip, Toom, Tosh, Trade, Trash, Tripe, Trock, Troke, Trumpery, Turndown, Twaddle, Unsay, Utter, Wash, Waste, Waste paper, Wastrel

▷ **Re-fused** *may indicate* an anagram

Refutation, Refute Deny, Disprove, Elench(us), Rebut, Redargue, Refel

Regain Recoup, Recover, Revanche

▶ **Regal** *see* **ROYAL**

Regalia → **CIGAR**, Mound, Orb, Sceptre

Regard(ing) Anent, As to, Attention, Care, Consider, → **ESTEEM**, Eye, Gaum, Look, Observe, Odour, Pace, Rate, Re, Repute, Respect, Revere, Sake, Steem, Value, Vis-à-vis

Regardless Despite, Heedless, In any event, Irrespective, Notwithstanding, Rash, Though, Uncaring, Unmindful, Willy-nilly

Regatta Head of the river, Henley

Regenerate Restore

Regent Interrex, Ruler, Viceroy

Regent's Park Zoo

Reggae Ska

Regicide Ireton, Macbeth

Regime(n) Administration, Control, Diet(etics), Method, Reich

Regiment Black Watch, Buffs, Colour(s), Discipline, Greys, Ironsides, Lifeguard, Marching, Monstrous, Nutcrackers, Organise, RA, RE, REME, Rifle, Royals, → **SAS**, Scots Greys, Tercio, Tertia

▷ **Regiment** *may indicate* an anagram

Region Aceh, Alsace, Alsatia, Amhara, Arctogaea, → **AREA**, Asir, Asturias, Bantustan, Belt, Bessarabia, Borders, Brie, Brittany, Bundu, Calabria, Camargue,

Cappadocia, Caria, Cariboo, Carniola, Carnnatic, Catalonia, Caucasia, Central, Chald(a)ea, Champagne-Ardenne, Chiasma, Cilicia, Circassia, Cleveland, Climate, Climature, Clime, Constantia, Critical, D, Dacia, District, Domain, Dust bowl, E, Ecosphere, End, Ethiopia, F, Guiana, Hinterland, Holarctic, Hundred, Illyria, Ionia, Kashmir, Katanga, Lacustrine, Lothian, Low Countries, Lusitania, Lycia, Lydia, Macao, Macedonia, Maghreb, Manchuria, Mascon, Masuria, Matabeleland, Mauretania, Mecklenburg, Mesopotamia, Midi, Molise, Moravia, Murcia, Mysia, Namaqualand, Negeb, Negev, Nejd, Neogaea, New Castile, New Quebec, Nubia, Nuristan, Offing, Ogaden, Old Castile, Opher, Oriental, Ossetia, Oudh, Pannonia, Pargana, Part, Pergunnah, Persis, Piedmont, Province, Quart(er), Realm, Refugium, Rhizosphere, Ruthenia, Sarmatia, Scythia, Sector, Slavonia, Sogdiana, Stannery, Strathclyde, Subtopia, Sumer, Tagma, Tayside, Territory, Tetrarchate, Thessaly, Thrace, Thule, Tibet, Tigray, Tigré, Tract, Transcaucasia, Transdniestria, Transylvania, Troas, Tundra, Turkestan, Turkistan, Tuscany, Ultima Thule, Umbria, Ungava, Val d'Aosta, Valois, Variable, Vaud, Veneto, Vojvodina, Vuelta Abajo, Weald, Zone, Zululand

Register(ing), Registration, Registry Actuarial, Almanac, Annal, Cadastral, Cadastre, Calendar, Cartulary, Cash, Census, Check-in, Child abuse, Dawn, Diptych, Docket, Enlist, Enrol, Enter, Flag out, Gross, Handicap, Index, Indicate, Inscribe, Inventory, Land, Ledger, List, Lloyd's, Log, Matricula, Menology, NAI, Net, Note, Notitia, Obituary, Parish, Park, Patent, Poll, Quotation, Read, Record, Reg(g)o, Rent-roll, Roll, Roule, Score, Shift(ing), Ship's, Sink in, Soprano, Terrier, Voice

Registrar Actuary, Greffier, Medical, Protocolist, Recorder, Specialist, Surgical

Regress(ion) Backslide, Recidivism, Revert

Regret(ful), Regrettable Alack, Alas, Apologise, Bemoan, Deplore, Deprecate, Ewhow, Forthwink, Ichabod, Lackaday, Lament, Mourn, Otis, Penitent, Pity, Remorse, Repentance, Repine, Resent, Rew, → **RUE**, Ruth, Sorrow, Tragic

Regular(ity), Regularly Clockwork, Constant, Custom, Episodic, Even, Giusto, Goer, Habitual, Habitué, Hourly, Insider, Methodic, Nine-to-five, Normal, Often, Orderly, Orthodox, Patron, Peloria, Periodic, Rhythmic, Routine, Set, Smooth, → **STANDARD**, Stated, Statutory, Steady, Strict, Symmetric, Uniform, Usual, Yearly

Regulate, Regulation, Regulator Adjust, Appestat, Ballcock, Bye-law, Code, Control, Correction, Curfew, Customary, Direct, Gibberellin, Governor, Guide, King's, Logistics, Metrostyle, Order, Ordinance, Police, Protocol, Queen's, Rule, Snail, Square, Standard, Statute, Stickle, Stopcock, Sumptuary, Thermostat, Valve

Regulus Matte

Regurgitation Trophallaxis

Rehab(ilitate), Rehabilitation AA, Cure, Orthotics, Physio(therapy), Repone

Rehearsal, Rehearse Band-call, Dress, Drill, Dry-block, Dry-run, Dummy-run, Practice, Practise, Preview, Recite, Repeat, Run through, Trial, Walk through

Reichenbach Falls, Od

Reign Era, Govern, Meiji, Prevail, Raine, Realm, Restoration, → **RULE**, Sway

Reimburse(ment) Indemnity, Recoup, Redress, Repay

Rein(s) Bearing, Caribou, Check, Control, Curb, Deer, Free, Gag, Leading strings, Long, Lumbar, Restrain, Ribbons, Safety, Stop, Tame, Tight, Walking

Reincarnation Palingenesis

Reindeer Blitzen, Caribou, Comet, Cupid, Dancer, Dasher, Donner, Moss, Prancer, Rudolf, Tarand, Vixen

Reinforce(ment) Aid, Augment, Beef up, Bolster, Boost, Brace, Buttress, Cleat, Counterfort, Line, Negative, Partial, Plash, Pleach, Positive, Re-bar, Recruit,

Reserve, Ripieno, → **STRENGTHEN**, Support, Tenaiile, Tenaillon, Tetrapod, Underline

Reinstate Repone

Reinvigorate Recruit

Reiterate(d), Reiteration Battology, Ding, Emphasize, Ostinato, Plug, → **REPEAT**

Reject(ion) Abhor, Abjure, Athetise, Bin, Blackball, Brush off, Cast, Cast off, Deny, Dice, Disallow, Discard, Disclaim, Discount, Disdain, Disown, Diss, Elbow, Eliminate, Export, Flout, Frass, Heave-ho, Iconoclasm, Jettison, Jilt, Kest, Kill, Knock-back, Ostracise, Oust, Outcast, Outtake, Pip, Plough, Rebuff, Recuse, Refuse, Reny, Repel, Reprobate, Repudiate, Repulse, Scout, Scrub, Spet, Spike, Spin, Spit, → **SPURN**, Sputum, Thumbs-down, Trash, Turndown, Veto

Rejoice, Rejoicing Celebrate, Exult, Festivity, Gaude, Glory, Joy, Maffick, Sing

Rejoin(der), Rejoined Answer, Counter, Relide, Reply, Response, Retort, Reunite

Rejuvenation Shunamitism

Relapse Backslide, Deteriorate, Hypostrophe, Recidivism, Regress, Revert, Sink

Relate(d), Relation(ship), Relations, Relative Account, Affair, Affine, Affinity, Agnate, Akin, Allied, Antibiosis, Appertain, Associate, Blood, Brer, Brisure, Causality, Cognate, Commensal, Concern, Connection, Connexion, Consanguinity, Coosen, Cousin, Coz, Deixis, Dependent, Dispersion, Eme, Enate, Equivalence, External, False, Formula, German(e), Granny, Guanxi, Heterogeneous, Homologous, Impart, Industrial, In-law, Internal, Item, Kin, Kinsman, Labour, Liaison, Link, Love-hate, Mater, Material, Matrix, Mutualism, Nan(n)a, Narrative, Naunt, Nooky, One-to-one, Osculant, Pertain, Phratry, Pi, Plutonic, Poor, Predation, Privity, → **PROPORTION**, Proxemics, Public, Race, Rapport, Rapprochement, Ratio, Reciprocity, Recite, Recount, Rede, Refer(ence), Relevant, Respect(s), Saga, Sib(b), Sibbe, Sibling, Sine, Sybbe, Symbiosis, Syntax, Tale, Tell, Truck, Who

Relating to Of

Relax(ation), Relaxant, Relaxed Abate, Atony, Autogenics, Calm, Chalone, Chill out, Com(m)odo, Contrapposto, Dégagé, Délassement, Détente, Diversion, Downbeat, Ease, Easy-going, Flaccid, Gallamine, Icebreaker, Informal, Laid-back, Laze, Leisured, Lesh states, Lighten, → **LOOSEN**, Mellow out, Mitigate, Outspan, Peace, Relent, Relief, Remit, Rest, Settle, Slacken, Sleep, Slump, Toneless, Unbend, Unknit, Unrein, Untie, Unwind, Veg out

▷ **Relaxed** *may indicate* an anagram

Relay(er) Convey, Medley, Race, Shift, Tell, Telstar, Torch-race, Webcast

▷ **Relay(ing)** *may indicate* an anagram

Release Abreact, Abrogation, Announcement, Bail, Block, Cable, Catharsis, Clear, Day, Death, Deliver(y), Desorb, Disburden, Discharge, Disclose, Disengage, Disimprison, Dismiss, Disorb, Emancipate, Enfree, Excuse, Exeem, Exeme, Exonerate, Extricate, Exude, Free, Handout, Happy, → **LIBERATE**, Manumit, Merciful, Moksa, Nirvana, Parole, Press, Quietus, Quitclaim, Quittance, Relinquish, Ripcord, Soft, Spring, Tre corde, Unconfine, Uncouple, Undo, Unhand, Unleash, Unloose, Unpen, Unshackle, Unsnap, Unteam, Untie

Relegate Banish, Consign, Demote, Exile, Marginalise, Sideline, Stellenbosch

Relent Bend, Mollify, Soften, Weaken, Yield

Relentless Cruel, Hard, Hardface, Indefatigable, Inexorable, Pitiless, Rigorous, Stern

Relevance, Relevant Ad rem, Applicable, Apposite, Apropos, Apt, Bearing, Germane, Material, Pertinent, Point, Valid

▶ **Reliable, Reliance** *see* **RELY**

Relic Antique, Ark, Artefact, Fly-in-amber, Fossil, Leftover, Memento, Neolith, Remains, Sangraal, Sangrail, Sangreal, Souvenir, Survival

Relict Survivor, Widow

Relief, Relieve(d) Aid, Air-lift, Allay, Allegeance, Alleviate, Alms, Anaglyph, Anastatic, Anodyne, Assistance, Assuage, Bas, Beet, Beste(a)d, Bete, Cameo, Catharsis, Cavo-relievo, Comfort, Cure, Détente, Ease(ment), Emboss, Emollient, Free, Grisaille, High, Indoor, Let-up, Lighten, Linocut, Low, Lucknow, Mafeking, MIRAS, On the parish, Outdoor, Palliate, Phew, Photo, Pog(e)y, Reassure, Redress, Remedy, Replacement, Repoussé, Reprieve, → **RESCUE**, Respite, Retirement, Rid, Spare, Spell, Stand-in, Stiacciato, Succour, Taper, Tax, Thermoform, Tondo, Toreutics, Wheugh, Whew, Woodcut

Religion, Religious (sect) Animism, Arya Samaj, Baha'i, Biblist, Bogomil, Brahmanism, Buddhism, Camaldolite, Candombie, Cargo cult, Carthusian, Celestine, Christadelphian, Christianity, Cistercian, Coenobite, Confucianism, Congregant, Creed, Culdee, Denomination, Devout, Din, Doctrine, Druse, Druz(e), Faith, Falun Gong, Familist, Gilbertine, Gnosticism, God-squad, Gueber, Guebre, Hadith, Hare Krishna, Has(s)id, Heathenism, Hieratic, Hospital(l)er, Ignorantine, Islam, Ismaili, Jain(a), Jansenism, Jehovah's Witness, Jesuit, Jewry, Judaism, Khalsa, Lamaism, Loyola, Lutheran, Macumba, Mahatma, MAM, Manichee, Maoism, Mathurin, Mazdaism, Mazdeism, Missionary, Missioner, Mithraism, Monastic, Moony, Mormonism, New Light, Nun, Oblate, Opium, Orphism, Pagan, Pantheist, Parseeism, Parsism, Pi, Piarist, Pietà, Postulant, Premonstratensian, Progressive, Rastafarian, Redemptionist, Reformation, Resurrectionist, Revealed, Revivalism, Russellite, Ryobu Shinto, Sabbatarian, Sabian, Sacramentarian, Salesian, Santeria, Scientology®, Serious, Shaker, Shamanism, Shango, Shiism, Shinto(ism), Sikhism, Sodality, Solifidian, Sons of Freedom, Spike, State, Sunna, Swedenborgian, Taoism, Theatine, Theology, The Way, Tractarianism, Trinitarian, Triphysite, Tsabian, Utraquist, Voodooism, Whore, Wicca, Zabian, Zarathustric, Zealous, Zend-Avesta, Zoroaster, Zwinglian

Religious book Bible, Koran, Missal, NT, OT, Sefer, Tantra, Targum, T(h)orah

Relinquish Abdicate, Cede, Demit, Discard, Drop, Forgo, Forlend, Remise, Surrender, Waive(r), Yield

Reliquary Chef, Encolpion, Encolpium, Simonious, Tope

Relish(ing) Aspic, Botargo, Caponata, Catsup, Chakalaka, Chow-chow, Condiment, Enjoy, Flavour, Gentleman's, Gout, Gust(o), Ketchup, Lap(-up), Lust, Opsonium, Palate, Pesto, Piccalilli, Pickle, Sapid, Sar, Sauce, Savour, Seasoning, Tang, Tooth, Worcester sauce, Zest

Reluctant Averse, Backward, Chary, Circumspect, Cockshy, Grudging, Half-hearted, Laith, Loath, Loth, Nolition, Renitent, Shy, Under protest, Unwilling

Rely, Reliance, Reliant, Reliable Addiction, Authentic, Bank, Brick, Confidence, Constant, Copper-bottomed, → **COUNT**, Dependent, Found, Honest, Hope, Inerrant, Jeeves, Leal, Lean, Loyal, Mensch, Presume, Pukka, Rest, Robin, Safe, Secure, Solid, Sound, Sponge, Stalwart, Stand-by, Staunch, Trade on, Trustworthy, Trusty, Unfailing

Remain(s), Remainder, Remaining Abide, Ash(es), Balance, Bide, Continue, Corse, Dreg(s), Dwell, Embers, Estate, Exuviae, Fag-end, Fossils, Kreng, Last, Late, Lave, Left, Lie, Locorestive, Manet, Nose, Oddment, Orts, Other, Outstand, Persist, Relic(ts), Reliquae, → **REMNANT**, Residue, Rest, Ruins, Scourings, Scraps, Stay, Stick, Stub, Surplus, Survive, Tag-end, Talon, Tarry, Wait, Wreck(age)

Remark Aside, Barb, Bromide, Comment(ary), Descry, Dig, Epigram, Generalise, Mention, Noise, → **NOTE**, Notice, Obiter dictum, Observe, Platitude, Pleasantry,

Reason, Sally, Shot, State

Remarkable, Remarkably Amazing, Arresting, Beauty, Bodacious, Come-on, Conspicuous, Dilly, Egregious, Extraordinary, Heliozoan, Legendary, Lulu, Mirable, Notable, Notendum, Noteworthy, Personal, Phenomenal, Rattling, → **SIGNAL**, Singular, Some, Striking, Tall, Unco, Uncommon, Visible

Remedial, Remedy Adaptogen, Aid, An mo, Antacid, Antibiotic, Antidote, Antiodontalgic, Antispasmodic, Arcanum, Arnica, Azoth, Bach®, Bach Flower®, Basilicon, Bicarb, Calomel, Catholicon, Corrective, Cortisone, → **CURE**, Decongestant, Dinic, Drug, Elixir, Febrifuge, Femiter, Feverfew, Fumitory, Ginseng, Heal, Ipecac, Leechdom, Medicate, Medicine, Moxa, Nosode, Nostrum, Palliative, Panacea, Panpharmacon, Paregoric, Poultice, Provisional, Rectify, Redress, Repair, Rescue®, Salutory, Salve, Simillimum, Simple, Specific, Taraxacum, Therapeutic, Tonga, Treatment, Tutsan

▷ **Remember** *may indicate* RE-member, viz. Sapper

Remember(ing), Remembrance Bethink, Commemorate, Con, Mem, Memorial, Memorise, Mention, Mneme, Poppy, Recall, Recollect, Remind, Reminisce, Retain, Rosemary, Souvenir

Remind(er) Aftertaste, Aide-memoire, Bethought, Bookmark, Evocatory, Evoke, Jog, Keepsake, Mark, Memento, Memo, Mnemonic, Mnemotechnic, Monition, Nudge, Phylactery, Prod, Prompt, Shades of, Souvenir, Token

Reminiscence(s), Reminiscent Ana, Evocative, Memory, Recall, Recollect, Remember, Retrospect

Remiss Careless, Derelict, Lax, Lazy, Negligent, Slack-handed, Tardy

Remission Abatement, Absolution, Acceptilation, Indulgence, Pardon, Pause, Spontaneous

Remit Excuse, Forward, Pardon, Postpone

Remnant Butt, End, Fent, Heeltap, Leavings, Left-over, Odd-come-short, Offcut, Relic, Relict, → **REMAINDER**, Rump, Trace, Vestige, Witness

Remonstrate Argue, Complain, Expostulate, Protest, Reproach

Remorse Angst, Ayenbite, Breast-beating, Compunction, Contrition, Had-i-wist, Pity, → **REGRET**, Repentance, Rue, Ruing, Ruth, Sorrow, Worm

Remote Aloof, Aphelion, Back blocks, Backveld, Backwater, Backwood, Boondocks, Bullamakanka, Bundu, → **DISTANT**, Far flung, Forane, Inapproachable, Insular, Irrelevant, Jericho, Long(inquity), Out(part), Outback, Remote, Scrub, Secluded, Shut-out, Slightest, Surrealistic, Unlikely, Withdrawn, Woop Woop, Wop-wops

Remount(s) Remuda

Removal, Remove(d) Abduct, Ablation, Abstract, Airbrush, Apocope, Asport, Banish, Blot, Circumcision, Clear, Couch, Deaccession, Declassify, Dele(te), Depilate, Depose, Deracinate, Detach, Dethrone, Detract, Dishelm, Dislodge, Disloign, Dismiss, Dispel, Doff, Efface, Eject, Eliminate, Eloi(g)n, Emend, Eradicate, Erase, Esloyne, Estrange, Evacuate, Evict, Exalt, Excise, Extirpate, Extradite, Extricate, Far, Flit, Huff, Nick, Raise, Raze, Razee, Recuse, Redline, Remble, Rid, Scratch, Sequester, Shift, Spirit, Strip, Sublate, Subtract, Supplant, Transfer, Transport, Unbelt, Unperson, Unseat, Uproot

Remuneration Pay, Return, Reward, Salary, Solde

Remus Uncle

Renaissance Awakening, Cinquecento, Early, High, Quattrocento, Revival

Rend Cleave, Harrow, Lacerate, Rip, Rive, Rupture, Tear

Render(ing) Construe, Deliver, Do, Gie, Give, Interpretation, Make, Melt, Pebble-dash, Plaster, Provide, Recite, Represent, Restore, Setting, Tallow, Try, Yeve, Yield

Rendezvous Date, Meeting, Philippi, Tryst, Venue

Rendition Account, Delivery, Interpretation, Translation, Version

René Descartes

Renegade, Renege, Renegue Apostate, Default, Defector, Deserter, Pipe, Rat(ton), Recreant, Traitor, Turncoat, Weasel out

▷ **Renegade** *may indicate* a word reversal

Renew(al) Instauration, Neogenesis, Palingenesis, Refresh, Replace, Resumption, Retrace, Revival, Urban

Rennet Steep, Vell

Renounce, Renunciation Abandon, Abdicate, Abjure, Abnegate, Disclaim, Disown, For(e)go, For(e)say, Forfeit, Forisfamiliate, Forsake, Forswear, Kenosis, Outclaim, Quitclaim, Recede, Relinquish, Renay, Retract, Sacrifice

Renovate(d), Renovation Duff, Face-lift, Instauration, Makeover, Refurbish, Renew, Repair, Restore, Revamp, Touch up, Translate

Renown(ed) Fame, Glory, Illustrious, Kudos, Lustre, Notoriety, Prestige, Stardom

Rent(er), Rented, Renting Broken, Charge, Cornage, Cost, Crack, Cranny, Cuddeehih, Cuddy, Division, Economic, Fair, Farm, Fee, Fissure, Gale, Gavel, Ground, → **HIRE**, Lease, Let, List, Mail, Market, Occupy, Pendicle, Penny(-mail), Peppercorn, Quit-rent, Rack, Rip, Rived, Riven, Screed, Seat, Slit, Split, Stallage, Subtenant, Tare, Tenant, Tithe, Tore, Torn, Tythe, White

Reorganise Rationalise

▷ **Reorganised** *may indicate* an anagram

Reorientate Rabat

Repair(s), Repairer, Reparation Amend(s), Anaplasty, Assythment, Botch, Cobble, Damages, Darn, Doctor, Excision, Expiation, Fettle, Fitter, Fix, Go, Haro, Harrow, Heel, Jury rig, → **MEND**, Overhaul, Patch, Piece, Recompense, Redress, Refit, Reheel, Remedy, Renew, Renovate, Repoint, Resort, Restore, Retouch, Revamp, Roadworks, Running, Satisfaction, Stitch, Tenorrhaphy, Ulling, Vamp, Volery

Repartee Backchat, Badinage, Banter, Persiflage, Rejoinder, Retort, Riposte, Wit, Wordplay

Repast Bever, Collection, Food, Meal, Tea, Treat

Repay(ment) Avenge, Compensate, Quit, Refund, Requite, Retaliate, Reward, Satisfaction

Repeal Abrogate, Annul, Cancel, Rescind, Revoke

Repeat(ed), Repeatedly, Repetition, Repetitive Again, Alliteration, Anadiplosis, Anaphora, Ancora, Battology, Belch, Bis, Burden, Burp, Copy, Cycle, Ditto(graphy), Do, Duplicate, → **ECHO**, Echolalia, Encore, Epanalepsis, Epistrophe, Epizeuxis, Eruct, Facsimile, Habitual, Harp, Image, Imitate, Ingeminate, Iterate, Iterum, Leit-motiv, Merism, Ostinato, Palillogy, Parrot, Parrot-fashion, Passion, Perpetuate, Playback, Polysyndeton, Recapitulate, Recite(r), Redo, Refrain, Regurgitate, Reiterate, Renew, Rep, Repetend, Reprise, Rerun, Retail, Rondo, Rosalia, Rote, Same(y), Screed, Segno, Symploce, Tautology, Tautophony, Thrum, Trite, Verbigerate

Repel(lent) Estrange, Harsh, Offensive, Rebarbative, Reject, Repulse, Revolt, Squalid, Turn-off, Ug(h), Ward

Repent(ant), Repentance Metanoia, Penitent, Regret, Rue, Sackcloth, Yamim Nora'im

Repercussion Backlash, Backwash, Echo, Effect, Impact, Recoil

Repertoire, Repertory Company, Depot, Rep, Store

▶ **Repetition** *see* **REPEAT**

Replace(ment), Replaceable, Replacing Change, Deputise, Diadochy, For,

Instead, Pre-empt, Prosthesis, Raincheck, Refill, Relief, Replenish, Restore, Stand-in, Substitute, Supersede, Supplant, Surrogate, Taxis, Transform, Transliterate, Understudy, Usurp

Replay Action, Instant, Iso(lated), Segno, Slo-mo

Replenish Refill, Refresh, Revictual, Stock, Supply, Top

Replete, Repletion Awash, Full, Gorged, Plenitude, Plethora, Sated, Satiation

Replica Clone, Copy, Duplicate, Facsimile, Image, Repetition, Spit

Reply Accept, Answer, Churlish, Duply, Echo, Over, Rejoinder, Replication, Repost, Rescript, Response, Retort, Roger, Surrebut, Surrebutter, Surrejoin, Triply

Report(s), Reporter Account, Announce, Annual, Auricular, Bang, Beveridge, Blacksmith, Bruit, Bulletin, Cahier, Clap, Columnist, Comment, Commentator, Compte rendu, Correspondent, Court, Cover, Crack, Crump, Cub, Debrief, Disclose, Dispatch, Dissertation, Explosion, Fame, Fireman, Grapevine, Hansard, Hearsay, Informant, Item, Jenkins, Journalist, Legman, Libel, News, Newsflash, Newshawk, Newshound, Newsman, Noise, Paper, Pop, Powwow, Pressman, Protocol, Rapporteur, Relate, Relay, Representation, Repute, Return, Roorback, Rumour, Sitrep, Sound(bite), Staffer, State(ment), Stringer, Tale, → **TELL**, Thesis, Transactions, Transcribe, Tripehound, Troop, Update, Weather, Whang, Wolfenden, Write up

▷ **Reported** *may indicate* the sound of a letter or word

Repose Ease, Kaif, Kef, Kif, Lie, Lig, Peace, Relax, → **REST**, Serenity

Repository Archive, Ark, Cabinet, Container, Genizah, Reservoir, Sepulchre, Vault

Reprehend, Reprehensible Base, Blame, Blameworthy, Censure, Criticise, Rebuke, Shameful, Warn

Represent(ation), Representative, Represented Agent, Ambassador, Anaconic, Caricature, Client, Commercial, Commissioner, Cross-section, Delegate, Depict, Deputation, Describe, Display, Drawing, Drummer, Effigy, Elchee, Eltchi, Emblem, Embody, Emissary, Epitomise, Example, Figurative, Histogram, Ikon, Image, Instantiate, John Bull, Legate, Lobby, Map, Mimesis, Mouthpiece, MP, Personate, Personify, Portray, Proportional, Quintessence, Rep, Resemble, Salesman, Senator, Shop steward, Simulacrum, Spokesman, Stand-in, Status, Steward, Symbolic, Syndic, Tableau, Tiki, Transcription, Traveller, Typical, Vakeel, Vakil, Vernicle, Vice-consul, Visitor-general

▷ **Represented** *may indicate* an anagram

Repress(ed) Check, Curb, Pent, Quell, Reprime, Sneap, Stifle, Stultify, Subjugate, Withhold

Reprieve Delay, Mercy, Postpone, Relief, Respite

Reprimand Admonish, Blast, Bounce, Carpet, → **CENSURE**, Chew out, Chide, Dressing-down, Earful, Jobe, Lace, Lambast, Lecture, Rark up, Rating, Rebuke, Reproof, Rocket, Rollicking, Slate, Strafe, Targe, Tick off, Tongue-lashing, Wig

Reprint Copy, Paperback, Replica

Reprisal(s) Marque, Recaption, Retaliation, Revenge

Reproach Besom, Bisom, Blame, Braid, Byword, Cataian, Catayan, Chide, Discredit, Dispraise, Exprobate, Gib, Mispraise, Odium, Opprobrium, Rebuke, Ronyon, Runnion, Scold, Shend, Sloan, Stigma, Taunt, Truant, Twat, Twit, Upbraid, Upcast, Yshend

Reprobate Cur, Lost soul, Outcast, Rascal, Scallywag, Scamp

Reprocess Re-make

▷ **Reproduce** *may indicate* an anagram

Reproduce(r), Reproduction, Reproductive (organ) Amphimixis, Ape, Apomixis, Archegonium, Arrhenotoky, Carpel, Clone, Copy, Counterfeit, Depict,

Ectype, Edition, Etch, Eugenics, Gamogenesis, Gemmate, Homogenesis, Isospory, Loins, Megaspore, Meristematic, Mono, Monogenesis, Monogony, Multiply, Oogamy, Ozalid®, Parthenogenesis, Phon(e)y, Pirate, Playback, Proliferate, Propagate, Pullulation, Refer, Replica, Roneo®, S(h)akti, Schizogony, Seminal, Simulate, Spermatia, Stereo, Strobilation, Syngamy, Syngenesis, Vegetative, Viviparism

Reproof, Reprove Admonish, Berate, Censure, Chide, Correction, Correption, Lecture, Rate, Rebuff, Rebuke, Scold, Sloan, Take to task, Tut, Upbraid

Reptile, Reptilian Agamid, Alligarta, Alligator, Base, Basilisk, Caiman, Cayman, Chameleon, Chelonian, Creeper, Crocodile, Cynodont, Diapsid, Dicynodont, Dinosaur, Galliwasp, Goanna, Herpetology, Lacertine, Lizard, Mamba, Pelycosaur, Pteranodon, Pterodactyl, Rhynchocephalian, Sauroid, → SNAKE, Sphenodon, Squamata, Synapsid, Tegu(exin), Thecodont, Therapsid, Theriodontia, Tortoise, Tuatara, Tuatera, Turtle, Worm

Republic(s) Banana, Federal, Fifth, First, Fourth, People's, Second, State, Third, Weimar

REPUBLICS

1 letter:
R

3 letters:
RMM
UAR
USA

4 letters:
Chad
Cuba
Eire
Fiji
Iran
Iraq
Komi
Laos
Mali
Peru
Togo
Tuva

5 letters:
Adhar
Altai
Belau
Benin
Chile
China
Congo
Czech
Egypt

Gabon
Ghana
Haiti
India
Italy
Kenya
Khmer
Libya
Malta
Nauru
Niger
Palau
Sakha
Sudan
Syria
Tatar
Yakut
Yemen
Zaire

6 letters:
Adygai
Adygei
Angola
Bharat
Biafra
Brazil
Bukavu
Buryat
France
Gambia
Greece

Guinea
Guyana
Ingush
Israel
Kalmyk
Latvia
Malawi
Mari-El
Mexico
Myanma
Panama
Poland
Rwanda
Serbia
Somali
Turkey
Udmurt
Uganda
Venice
Zambia

7 letters:
Adharca
Albania
Algeria
Andorra
Armenia
Austria
Bashkir
Belarus
Bolivia
Burkina

Burundi
Chechen
Chuvash
Comoros
Croatia
Ecuador
Estonia
Finland
Georgia
Germany
Hungary
Iceland
Ireland
Jibouti
Kalmuck
Kalmyck
Khakass
Lebanon
Liberia
Moldova
Myanmar
Namibia
Nigeria
Romania
Senegal
Somalia
Surinam
Tunisia
Ukraine
Uruguay
Vanuatu
Vietnam

7 letters – cont:
Yakutia

8 letters:
Botswana
Bulgaria
Buryatia
Cambodia
Cameroon
Chechnya
Colombia
Dagestan
Djibouti
Dominica
Esthonia
Honduras
Karelian
Kiribati
Malagasy
Maldives
Moldavia
Mongolia
Pakistan
Paraguay
Portugal
Roumania
Sinn Fein
Slovakia
Slovenia
Sri Lanka

Suriname
Tanzania
Zimbabwe

9 letters:
Argentina
Badakshan
Cape Verde
Costa Rica
Dominican
Guatemala
Indonesia
Kazakstan
Lithuania
Macedonia
Mauritius
Nicaragua
San Marino
Singapore
Venezuela

10 letters:
Azerbaijan
Bangladesh
Belarussia
El Salvador
Gorno-Altai
Kara-Kalpak
Kazakhstan
Kyrgyzstan

Madagascar
Mauritania
Montenegro
Mordvinian
Mozambique
North Korea
North Yemen
Seychelles
South Korea
South Yemen
Tajikistan
Ubang-Shari
Uzbekistan
Yugoslavia

11 letters:
Afghanistan
Burkina-Faso
Byelorussia
Cote d'Ivoire
Nakhichevan
Philippines
Sierra Leone
South Africa
Soviet Union
Switzerland
Tadjikistan
West Germany

12 letters:
Guinea-Bissau
South Vietnam
Turkmenistan

13 letters:
Bashkortostan
North Ossetian

14 letters:
Czechoslovakia

15 letters:
Gorno-Badakhshan
Kabardino-Balkar
Marshall Islands
United Provinces

16 letters:
Congo-Brazzaville
Equatorial Guinea
Karachai-Cherkess
São Tomé e Príncipe

17 letters:
Bosnia-Herzegovina
Mari
 El-Nakhichevan
Trinidad and
 Tobago

Republican Antimonarchist, Belarussian, Democrat, Fenian, Fianna Fáil, Girondist, GOP, International Brigade, IRA, Iraqi, Leveller, Montagnard, Mugwump, Plato, Red, Sansculotte, Sansculottic, Sinn Fein, Whig, Young Italy

Repudiate Abjure, Deny, Disaffirm, Discard, Disclaim, Disown, Ignore, Recant, Reject, Renounce, Repel, Retract

Repugnance, Repugnant Abhorrent, Alien, Disgust, Distaste, Fulsome, Horror, Loathing, Nastiness, Revulsion

Repulsive, Repulse Creepy, Grooly, Lo(a)th, Off-putting, Rebuff, Rebut, Refel, Refuse, Repel, Repugnant, Slimy, Squalid, Ugly, Vile

Reputable, Reputation, Repute(d) Bubble, Dit, Estimate, Fame, Good, Izzat, Loos, Los, Name, Note, Notoriety, Odour, Opinion, Prestige, Putative, Regard, Renown, Said, Sar, → **STANDING**, Status, Stink, Stock, Trustworthy

Request Adjure, Appeal, Apply, Ask, Beg, Desire, D-notice, Entreaty, Invite, Petition, Plea, Prayer, Precatory, Solicit, Supplication

Requiem Agnus Dei, Mass

Require(d), Requirement Charge, Crave, De rigueur, Desideratum, Desire, Enjoin, Entail, Exact, Expect, Incumbent, Lack, Necessity, Need, Prerequisite, Sine qua non, Stipulate, Then

Requisite, Requisition Commandeer, Due, Embargo, Essential, Indent, Necessary, Needful, Order, Press, Simplement

Rescind Abrogate, Annul, Recant, Remove, Repeal

Rescue(r) Aid, Air-sea, Deliver, Free, Liberate, Lifeline, Mountain, Ransom, Reclaim, Recover, Recower, Redeem, Regain, Relieve, Reprieve, Retrieve, Salvage, Salvation, → **SAVE**, White knight

Research(er) Audience, Boffin, Delve, Dig, Enquiry, Explore, Fieldwork, Indagator, Investigate, Legwork, Market, MORI, Motivation(al), Near-market, Operational, Pioneer, Psychical, Sus(s), Test, Think-tank

Resell Scalp

Resemblance, Resemble, Resembling Affinity, Apatetic, Approach, Assonant, Dead ringer, Homophyly, Likeness, -oid, -opsis, Replica, Similitude, Simulate

Resent(ful), Resentment Anger, Bridle, Chippy, Choler, Cross, Derry, Dudgeon, Grudge, Indignation, Ire, Jaundiced, Malign, Miff, Mind, Pique, Rankle, Smart, Snarling, Spite, Umbrage

Reservation, Reserve(d), Reservist(s) Aloof, Arrière-pensée, Backlog, Bashful, Book, By, Capital, Caveat, Central, Cold, Coy, Demiss, Detachment, Distant, Earmark, Engage, Ersatz, Except, Fall-back, Federal, Fort Knox, General, Gold, Hold, Husband, Ice, Indian, Introvert, Landwehr, Layby, Locum, Mental, Militiaman, Modesty, Nature, Nest-egg, Nineteenth man, Proviso, Qualification, Reddendum, Res, Rest, Restraint, Retain, Reticence, Retiring, Rez, Salvo, Sanctuary, Save, Scenic, Scruple, Set aside, Special, Spoken for, Stand-by, Stand-offishness, Starch, Stash, Stock(pile), Substitute, TA (men), Twelfth man, Uncommunicate, Understudy, Warren, Waves, Withhold

Reservoir Basin, Cistern, Font, G(h)ilgai, Gilgie, Header tank, Oilcup, Repository, Rybinsk, Service, Stock, Sump, Tank, Water tower, Well

Reset Taxis

Reside(nce), Resident(s), Residential Abode, Address, Amban, Chequers, Commorant, Consulate, Denizen, Domicile, Dwell, Embassy, Establishment, Expatriate, Exurb(anite), Gremial, Guest, Home, In, Indweller, Inholder, Inmate, Intern, Ledger, Lei(d)ger, Lieger, Liveyer(e), Lodger, Metic, Occupant, Pad, Parietal, Permanent, Resiant, Settle, Settlement, Sojourn, Squat, Stay, Tenant, Tenement, Up, Vicinage, Villager, Yamen

Residual, Residue Ash, Astatki, Boneblack, Calx, Caput, Chaff, Cinders, Coke, Crud, Dottle, Draff, Dregs, Expellers, Greaves, Heeltap, Leavings, Mazout, Mortuum, Prefecture, Remainder, Remanent, Remnant, Scourings, Slag, Slurry, Snuff, Vinasse

Resign(ed), Resignation Abandon, Abdicate, Demit, Fatalism, Heigh-ho, Leave, Meek, → **QUIT**, Reconcile, Stoic, Submit

Resilience, Resilient Bounce, Buoyant, Elastic, Flexible, Recoil, Springy

Resin Acaroid, Acrylic, Agila, Alkyd, Amber, Amine, Amino, Anime, Arar, Asaf(o)etida, Bakelite®, Bal(sa)m of Gilead, Balsam, Benjamin, Benzoin, Burgundy pitch, Bursera, Cachou, Cannabin, Cannabis, Caranna, Carauna, Catechu, Charas, Cholestyramine, Churrus, Colophony, Conima, Copai(ba), Copaiva, Copal(m), Coumarone, Courbaril, Cutch, Cymene, Dam(m)ar, Dammer, Dragon's blood, Elaterite, Elemi, Epoxy, Frankincense, Galbanum, Galipot, Gambi(e)r, Gamboge, Glyptal, Guaiacum, Gum, Hasheesh, Hashish, Hing, Jalapic, Jalapin, Kino, Labdanum, Lac, Ladanum, Lignaloes, Limonene, Lupulin, Mastic, Melamine, Methacrylate, Myrrh, Natural, Olibanum, Opopanax, Perspex®, Phenolic, Phenoxy, Plastisol, Podophyl(l)in, Polycarbonate, Polyester, Polymer, Polypropylene, Polysterene, Polyvinyl, Propolis, Retinite, Roset, Rosin, Rosit, Rozet, Rozit, Sagapenum, Sandarac(h), Saran®, Scammony, Shellac, Silicone, Storax, Styrene, Synthetic, Tacamahac, Tacmahack, Takamaka, Taxin, Thus, Urea, Vinyl, Xylenol

Resist Bristle, Buck, Combat, Contest, Defy, Face, Fend, Gainstrive, Impede, Oppose, Redound, Reluct, Stand (pat), Toughen, → **WITHSTAND**

Resistance, Resistant, Resistor Antibiotic, Barretter, Bleeder, Ceramal, Cermet, Chetnik, Coccidiostat, Combat, Consumer, Defiance, Drag, Element, Friction, Grapo, Hostile, Immunity, Impediment, Internal, Intifada, Invar, Klendusic, Klepht, Maquis, Maraging, Market, Megohm, Microhm, Negative, Obstacle, Ohm, Omega, Passive, Pat, Pull, R, Radiation, Reluctance, Renitent, Resilient, Rheostat, Sales, Satyagraha, Shockproof, Soul-force, Specific, Stability, Stand, Stonde, Stubborn, Tough

Resolute, Resolution Analysis, Bold, Cast-iron, Casuistry, Closure, Courage, Decided, Decision, Denouement, Determined, Doughty, → **FIRM**, Fortitude, Granite, Grim, Grit, Hardiness, Insist, Joint, Pertinacity, Promotion, Rede, Reed(e), Resolve, Stable, Stalwart, Staunch, Stout, Strength, Strong-willed, Sturdy, Telic, Tenacity, Unbending, Valiant, Willpower

Resolve(d), Resolver Analyse, Calculate, Decide, Declare, → **DETERMINE**, Deus ex machina, Factorise, Fix, Grit, Hellbent, Intent, Nerve, Pecker, → **PURPOSE**, Settle, Steadfast, Tenacity, Vow, Will

▷ **Resolved** *may indicate* an anagram

Resonance, Resonant, Resonator Canorous, Cavity, Electromer, Morphic, Orotund, Parallel, Rhumbatron, Ringing, Sonorous, Timbre, Vibrant

Resort Biarritz, Centre, Dive, Étaples, Expedient, Frame, Frequent, Haunt, Health, Hove, Hydro, Invoke, Klosters, Lair, Last, Las Vegas, Lowestoft, Malibu, Morecambe, Nassau, Paignton, Pau, Pis aller, Rapallo, Recourse, Repair, Riviera, Southend, Spa(w), Stand by, Use, Watering place, Worthing, Zermatt

▷ **Resort(ing)** *may indicate* an anagram

Resound(ing) Echo, Plangent, Reboant, Reboation, Reverberate, Ring

Resource(s), Resourceful Assets, Beans, Bottom, Chevisance, Clever, Enterprise, Faculty, Funds, Gumption, Human, Ingenious, Input, Inventive, Means, Natural, Renewable, Shared, Sharp, Stock-in-trade, → **VERSATILE**, Wealth

Respect(ed), Respectable, Respectful Admire, Ahimsa, Aspect, Behalf, Consecrate, Consider, Cred(it), Decent, Deference, Devoir, Duty, Eminent, Esteem, Gigman, Homage, → **HONOUR**, Intent, Kempt, Kowtowing, Latria, Obeisant, Officious, Pace, Particular, Preppy, Prestige, Proper, Reference, Regard, Relation, Reputable, Revere, Sir, S(t)irrah, U, Venerate, Wellborn, Well-thought-of, Wise, Worthy

Respirator, Respire, Respiration Artificial, Blow, Breathe, Exhale, External, Gasmask, Inhale, Iron lung, Mouth-to-mouth, Pant, Snorkel

Respite Break, Breather, Frist, Interval, Leisure, Let up, Pause, Reprieve, Rest, Stay, Truce

Respond, Response, Responsive Amenable, Answer, Antiphon, Autoreply, Backlash, Bi, Comeback, Conditioned, Counteroffer, Duh, Echo, Feedback, Flechman, Grunt, Immune, Kneejerk, Kyrie, Litany, Nastic, Pavlovian, Photonasty, Prebuttal, Psychogalvanic, React(ion), Reflex, Reply, Repost, Retort, Rheotaxis, Rheotropism, Rise, Sensitive, Stayman, Synapte, Syntonic, Tender, Thigmotropic, Tic, Tropism, Unconditioned, Voice, Warm, Wilco

Responsibility, Responsible Accountable, Anchor, Answerable, Baby, Blame, Buck, Charge, Collective, Culpable, Dependable, Diminished, Duty, Frankpledge, Guilty, Hot seat, Incumbent, Instrumental, Liable, Mea culpa, Onus, Pigeon, Sane, Solid, Stayman, Trust

Rest(ing), Rest day Alt, Anchor, Avocation, Balance, Bed, Beulah, Break, Breather, Calm, Catnap, Cetera, Comma, Depend, Dwell, Ease, Easel, Etc, Fermata, Feutre,

Fewter, Gallows, Gite, Half-time, Halt, Inaction, Jigger, Lance, Lave, Lean, Lie, Lie-in, Light, Lodge, Loll, Lound, Lull, Lyte, Minim, Nap, Noah, Nooning, Others, Outspan, Overlie, Pause, Quiescence, Quiet, Relâche, Relax, Rely, Remainder, Repose, Requiem, Reserve, Residue, Respite, Sabbath, Siesta, → **SLEEP**, Slide, Sloom, Slumber, Spell, Spider, Static, Stopover, Support, Surplus, Teabreak, Time out, Y-level

Re-start Da capo, Reboot

Restaurant, Restaurateur Automat, Beanery, Bistro, Brasserie, British, Cabaret, Café, Canteen, Carvery, Chew'n'spew, Chinkie, Chinky, Chip-shop, Chophouse, Commissary, Cook shop, Creperie, Diner, Eatery, Eating-house, Estaminet, Gastropub, Greasy spoon, Grill, Grillroom, Grub shop, Luncheonette, Maxim's, Noshery, Padrone, Porter-house, Rathskeller, Ratskeller, Raw bar, Roadhouse, Rotisserie, Slap-bang, Steakhouse, Takeaway, Taqueria, Taverna, Tea garden, Teahouse, Tearoom, Teashop, Trattoria

Rest-home Aggie, Hospice

Resting-place Bed, Couch, Dharmsala, Gite, Grave, Inn, Khan, Serai, She'ol, Stage

Restitute, Restitution Amends, Apocatastasis, Reparation, Restore, Return

Restive, Restless(ness) Chafing, Chorea, Fidgety, Fikish, Free-arm, Itchy, Jactitation, Spring fever, Toey, Unsettled

▷ **Restless** *may indicate* an anagram

Restoration, Restorative, Restore(d) Bring to, Cure, Descramble, Heal, Mend, Pentimento, Pick-me-up, Postliminy, Rally, Recondition, Redeem, Redintegrate, Redux, Refurbish, Regenerate, Rehabilitate, Reintegrate, Rejuvenate, Remedial, Renew, Renovate, Replenish, Replevy, Repone, Restitute, Resuscitate, Retouch, Revamp, Revive, Stet, Tonic, Whole

Restrain(ed), Restraint Abstinence, Ban, Bate, Bit, Bottle, Branks, Bridle, Cage, Chain, Chasten, → **CHECK**, Checks and balances, Coerce, Cohibit, Compesce, Confinement, Contain, Control, Cramp, Curb, Dam, Decorum, Detent, Dry, Duress, Embargo, Enfetter, Estoppel, Freeze, Gyve, Halt, Hamshackle, Handcuffs, Harness, Heft, Hinder, Hopple, Immanacle, Impound, Inhibit, Jess, Leg-iron, Lid, Low-key, Manacle, Measure, Mince, Moderation, Muzzle, Patient, Quiet, Rein, Repress, Restrict, Ritenuto, Shackle, Sober, Sobriety, Squeeze, Stay, Stent, Stint, Straitjacket, Strait-waistcoat, Temper, Tether, Tie, Trash, Underplay

Restrict(ed), Restriction Band, Bar, Bind, Bit, Burden, Cage, Catch, Censorship, Chain, Circumscribe, Closet, Condition, Cord, Corset, Cramp, Curb, Curfew, DORA, Fence, Fetter, Fold, Gate, Ground, Guard, Hamper, Hidebound, Hobble, Inhibit, Intern, Kennel, Let, → **LIMIT**, Localise, Lock, Mere, Narrow, Net, Nick, No-go, Pale, Parochial, Pen, Pent, Pier, Pin, Pot-bound, Private, Proscribed, Qualify, Regulate, Rein, Rent, Repression, Rope, Safety belt, Scant, Seal, Section, Selected, Shackle, Snare, Squeeze, Stenopaic, Stent, Stint, Stop, Straiten, Stunt, Swaddle, Tether, Tie

Restructure, Restructuring Perestroika

Result(s) After-effect, Aftermath, Ans(wer), Arise, Bring, Causal, Consequence, Effect, Emanate, End, Ensue, Entail, Event, Eventuate, Finding, Fruict, Fruits, Issue, Karmic, Knock-on, Lattermath, → **OUTCOME**, Outturn, Pan, Pay off, Proceeds, Quotient, Sequel, Side-effect, Sum, Upshot, Wale

Resume, Résumé Continue, Pirlicue, Purlicue, Summary

Resurrect(ion) Anabiosis, Anastasia, Rebirth, Revive, Zomb(ie)

Resuscitate(d), Resuscitation Mouth-to-mouth, Quicken, Redivivus, Restore, Revive

Retail(er) Category killer, Chandler, Dealer, → **NARRATE**, Regrate, Sell, Shopkeeper, Shopman, Stockist, Symbol, Tell

Retain(er), Retains Brief, Contain, Deposit, Fee, Hold, Hold-all, Keep, Panter, Pantler, Reserve, Retinue, Servant

Retaliate, Retaliation Avenge, Counter, Lex talionis, Quid pro quo, Quit(e), Redress, Repay, Reprisal, Requite, Retort, Talion

Retard(ed), Retardation Arrest, Belate, Brake, Cretin, Encumber, Hinder, Hysteresis, Slow, Stunt

Retch Boak, Bock, Boke, Cowk, Gap, Heave, Keck, Reach, Vomit

Reticence, Reticent Clam, Coy, Dark, Guarded, Reserve, Restraint, Secretive, Shy, Taciturn

Reticule, Reticulum Bag, Carryall, Dragnet, Lattice, Net

Retina Detached, Fovea, Macula lutea

Retinue Comitatus, Company, Cortège, Equipage, Following, Meiney, Meinie, Meiny, Menyie, Sowarry, Suite

Retire(d), Retiree, Retirement, Retiring Abed, Aloof, Asocial, Baccare, Backare, Backpedal, Blate, Bowler-hat, Bow out, Cede, Coy, Depart, Ebb, Emeritus, Essene, Former, Leave, Lonely, Modest, Mothball, Nun, Outgoing, Pension, Perfing, Private, Quit, Recede, Recluse, Reserved, Resign, Retract, Retread, Retreat, Retrocedent, Roost, Rusticate, Scratch, Sequester, Shy, Superannuate, Unassertive, Withdraw

▷ **Retirement** *may indicate* 'bed' around another word, or word reversed

Retort Alembic, Comeback, Courteous, Quip, Repartee, → **REPLY**, Retaliate, Riposte, Still, Tu quoque

Retract(ion) Backpedal, Backtrack, Disavow, Epanorthosis, Palinode, Recall, Recant, Renounce, Revoke

Retreat Abbey, Arbour, Ashram(a), Asylum, Backpedal, Backwater, Berchtesgaden, Bower, Bug, Camp David, Cell, Cloister, Convent, Crawfish, Dacha, Departure, Donjon, Funkhole, Girth, Grith, Hermitage, Hideaway, Hide-out, Hole, Interstadial, Ivory-tower, Katabasis, Lair, Lama(sery), Mew, Monastery, Nest, Neuk, Nook, Pullback, Recede, Recoil, Recu(i)le, Redoubt, Reduit, Refuge, Retire, Retraite, Right-about, Rout, Shangri-La, Shelter, Skedaddle, Stronghold, Withdraw

Retribution Come-uppance, Deserts, Nemesis, Revenge, Reward, Utu, Vengeance

Retrieve(r), Retrieval Access, Bird-dog, Chesapeake Bay, Field, Gundog, Labrador, Read-out, Recall, Recoup, Recover, Redeem, Rescue, Salvage

Retroflex Cacuminal

Retrograde Backward, Deasi(u)l, Deasoil, Decadent, Decline, Hindward, Rearward, Regrede

Retrospect(ive) Contemplative, Ex post facto, Hindsight, Regardant

Return(s) Agen, Answer, Bricole, Census, Comeback, Day, Diminishing, Dividend, Elect, Er, Extradite, Gain, Nil, Pay, Proceeds, Profit, Rebate, Rebound, Recur, Redound, Regress, Reject, Rejoin, Render, Rent, Repay, Replace, Reply, Requital, Respond, Rest, Restitution, Restore, Retour, Revenue, Reverse, Revert, Riposte, Takings, Tax, Traffic, → **YIELD**

Rev Gun, Minister

Reveal(ing), Revelation Acute, Advertise, Air, Apocalyptic, Bare, Betray, Bewray, Confess, Descry, Disclose, Discover, Discure, → **DIVULGE**, Epiphany, Exhibit, Explain, Expose, Eye-opener, Giveaway, Hierophantic, Impart, Indicate, Ingo, Kythe, Leak, Let on, Low-cut, Manifest, Open, Out, Pentimento, Satori, → **SHOW**, Spill, Tell-tale, Unclose, Uncover, Unfold, Unheal, Unmask, Unveil

Revel(ling), Revelry Ariot, Bacchanalia, Bend, Carnival, Carouse, Comus, Dionysian, Feast, Gloat, Glory, Joy, Maffick, Merriment, Orgy, Rant, Rejoice, Riot, Roister, Rollicks, Rout, Royst, Saturnalia, Splore, Swig, Upsee, Ups(e)y, Wallow,

Wassail, Whoopee

Reveller Bacchant, Birler, Corybant, Guisard, Guiser, Maenad, Merrymaker, Orgiast, Silenus

Revenant Fetch, Ghost, Spectre

Revenge(r), Revengeful Aftergame, Avenge, Commination, Goel, Grenville, Montezuma's, Nightrider, Payback, Reprise, Requite, Retaliation, Revanche, Ultion, Utu, Vindictive

Revenue Capital, Finance, Fisc(al), Fisk, Income, Inland, Internal, Jaghire, Jag(h)ir, Prebend, Primitiae, Rent, Taille, Tax, Turnover, Zamindar, Zemindar

Reverberate Echo, Recoil, Reflect, Repercuss, Resound

Revere(nce) Admire, Awe, Bostonian, Dread, Dulia, Esteem, Fear, Hallow, Hery, Homage, → **HONOUR**, Hyperdulia, Idolise, Latria, Obeisance, Paul, Respect, Venerate

Reverie Brown study, Daydream, Dream(iness), Fantasy, Memento

Revers Lap(p)el

Reversal, Reverse, Reversing, Reversion, Reversible Antithesis, Antonym, Arsy-versy, Atavism, Back(slide), B-side, Change-over, Chiasmus, Commutate, Counter(mand), Escheat, Evaginate, Exergue, Flip, Flip side, Inversion, Misfortune, → **OPPOSITE**, Overturn, Palindrome, Pile, Regress, Revoke, Rheotropic, Setback, Switchback, Tails, Throwback, Transit, Turn, Turnabout, Two-faced, Un-, Undo, U-turn, Verso, Vice versa, Volte-face, Woman

Revert Annul, Backslide, Regress, Relapse, Resort, Retrogress, Return

▷ **Review** *may indicate* an anagram or a reversed word

Review(er) Appeal, Censor, Credit, Critic, Critique, Editor, Encomium, Feuilleton, Footlights, Inspect, Judicial, Magazine, March-past, Notice, Pan, Peer, Recapitulate, Repeat, Revise, Rundown, Slate, Spithead, Summary, Summing-up, Survey, Write-up

Revile, Reviling Abuse, Execrate, Inveigh, Rail, Rayle, Vilify, Vituperate

▷ **Revise(d)** *may indicate* an anagram

Revise(r), Revision Alter, Amend, Change, Correct, Diaskeuast, Diorthosis, Edit, Peruse, Reappraise, Reassess, Recense, Reform, Rev, Update

Revive, Revival, Revivify, Reviving Araise, Classical, Enliven, Gothic, Greek, Rake up, Rally, Reanimate, Reawake(n), Rebirth, Redintegrate, Redux, Refresh, Rekindle, Relive, Renaissance, Renascent, Renew, Renovate, Restore, Resurrect, Resuscitate, Risorgimento, Romantic, Romo, Rouse, Wake

Revoke Abrogate, Cancel, Countermand, Negate, → **RECALL**, Repeal, Rescind

Revolt(ing), Revolution(ary) Agitator, Agitprop, American, Anarchist, Apostasy, Appal, Bloodless, Bolivar, Bolshevik, Bolshevist, Boxer, Bulldog, Cade, Castro, Chartist, Che, Chinese, Circle, Commune, Coup d'état, Cultural, Cycle, Danton, Defection, Dervish, Desmoulins, Disgust, Emeute, Emmet, Engels, Enragé, February, Fenian, Foul, French, Girondin, Girondist, Glorious, Green, Grody, Guevara, Gyration, Ho Chi Minh, Industrial, Inqilab, → **IN REVOLT**, Insurgent, Insurrection, Intifada, IRA, Jacobin, Jacquerie, Komitaji, Lap, Lenin, Leninist, Marat, Marx, Marxist, Maximalist, Maypole, Minimalist, Montagnard, Mutiny, Nauseating, Nihilist, October, Orbit, Outbreak, Paine, Palace, Paris Commune, Peasants, Poujadist, Putsch, Radical, → **REBEL**, Red, Red Guard, Red Shirt, Reformation, Riot, Rise, Robespierre, Roll, Rotation, Round, Run, Russian, Sandinista, Sansculotte(rie), Sedition, Sicilian Vespers, Spartacus, Syndicalism, The Mountain, Thermidor, Titanomachy, Trot(sky), Twist, Up(rise), → **UPRISING**, Upryst, Velvet, Villa, Wat Tyler, Weatherman, Whirl, Wolfe Tone, Young Turk, Zapata

▷ **Revolutionary** *may indicate* 'reversed'

Revolve(r), Revolving Carrier, Catherine wheel, Centrifuge, Colt®, Gat, Girandole, Grindstone, → **GUN**, Gyrate, Iron, Klinostat, Lathe, Maelstrom, Peristrephic, Pistol, Pivot, Planet, Roller, Rotate, Rotifer, Rotor, Roundabout, Run, Six-shooter, Spin, Tone, Turn(stile), Turntable, Turret, Wheel, Whirl(igig), Whirlpool

Revue Follies

Revulsion Abhorrence, Loathing, Repugnance, The creeps, Ugh

Reward(ing) Albricias, Bonus, Bounty, Compensate, Consideration, Desert, Emolument, Fee, Guerdon, Head money, Medal, Meed, Payment, Premium, Price, Prize, Profit, Purse, Reap, Recognise, Recompense, Reguerdon, Remuneration, Requital, Requite, S, Shilling, Tanti, Tribute, Wage, War(r)ison

Reword Edit, Paraphrase

Reworking Rifacimento

Rex Cornish, Devon, Priam, R

Reynolds Joshua, PRA

Rhapsodic, Rhapsody Ecstasy, Epic, Music, Unconnected

Rhea Em(e)u, Nandoo, Nandu, Nhandu, Ostrich, Rami

Rhenium Re

Rhesus Bandar, Macaque, Monkey

Rhetoric(al) Alliteration, Anaphora, Anastrophe, Antimetabole, Antithesis, Antostrophe, Apophasis, Aposiopesis, Assonance, Asyndeton, Aureate, Bombast, Brachylogia, Cacophony, Catachresis, Chiasmus, Ecbole, Eloquence, Enantiosis, Epanadiplosis, Epanados, Epanalepsis, Epanorthosis, Epexegesis, Epistrophe, Epizeuxis, Erotema, Eroteme, Erotesis, Euphemism, Hendiadys, Hypallage, Hyperbole, Litotes, Metonymy, Oratory, Oxymoron, Paradox, Paral(e)ipsis, Periphrasis, Peroration, Platform, Pleonasm, Scesisonomaton, Syllepsis, Synoeciosis, Trivial, Trivium, Zeugma

Rhino Blunt, Bread, Cash, Lolly, Loot, → **MONEY**, Tin

Rhinoceros Baluchitherium, Keitloa, Square-lipped, Sumatran, White

Rhodes, Rhodesia(n) Cecil, Colossus, Ridgeback, Scholar, Zimbabwe

Rhodium Rh

Rhomboid Fusil

Rhubarb Monk's, Pie-plant, Rhapontic, Rheum, Rot, Spat

Rhyme(s), Rhymer, Rhyming Assonance, Clerihew, Closed couplet, Counting out, Couplet, Crambo, Cynghanedd, Doggerel, Eye, Feminine, Head, Identical, Internal, Jingle, Male, Masculine, Measure, Near, Nursery, Pararhyme, Perfect, Poetry, Poulter's measure, Rich, Riding, Rime riche, Rondel, Royal, Runic, Sight, Slang, Slant, Tail(ed), Tercet, Terza-rima, Thomas, Triple, → **VERSE**, Virelay, Vowel

Rhythm(ic) Agoge, Alpha, Asynartete, Backbeat, Beat, Beta, Bo Diddley beat, Breakbeat, Cadence, Clave, Circadian, Dolichurus, Dotted, Duple, Euouae, Evovae, Hemiol(i)a, In-step, Meter, Movement, Oompah, Prosody, Pulse, Pyrrhic, Rove-over, Rubato, Scotch catch, Scotch snap, Sdrucciola, Sesquialtera, Singsong, Sprung, Stride piano, Swing, Syncopation, Tala, Talea, → **TEMPO**, Time, Voltinism

Rib(bed), Ribbing, Rib-joint Bar, Chaff, Chiack, Chip, Chyack, Cod, Cord, Costa, Cross-springer, Dutch, Eve, False, Fin, Floating, Futtock, Groin, Intercostal, Lierne, Nervate, Nervular, Nervure, Ogive, Persiflage, Rack, Rag, Rally, Short, Spare, Springer, Subcosta, Taunt, Tease, Tierceron, Tracery, True, Wife

Ribald(ry) Balderdash, Bawdy, Coarse, Scurrilous, Smut, Sotadic, Vulgar

Ribbon Band, Bandeau, Blue, Bow, Braid, Caddis, Caddyss, Cordon, Fattrels, Ferret, Fillet, Grosgrain, Hatband, Infula, Multistrike, Pad, Petersham, Radina, Red, Rein, Riband, Soutache, Taenia, Tape, Teniate, Tie, Torsade, Yellow

Ribless Ecostate

Rice Arborio, Basmati, Bir(i)yani, Brown, Canada, Carnaroli, Elmer, Entertainer, Golden, Indian, Kedgeree, Miracle, Paddy, Patna, Pilaf, Pilau, Pilaw, Pillau, Reis, Risotto, Spanish, Sushi, Twigs, Water, Wild, Zizania

Rich(es) Abounding, Abundant, Affluent, Amusing, Bonanza, Buttery, Comic, Copious, Croesus, Dives, Edmund, Edwin, Fat, Feast, Fertile, Filthy, Flamboyant, Flush, Fruity, Full, Golconda, Haves, Heeled, High, Larney, Loaded, Luscious, Lush, Luxurious, Mammon, Moneybags, Moneyed, Nabob, New, Oberous, Oofy, → **OPULENT**, Plenteous, Plush, Plutocrat, Resonant, Rolling, Silvertail, Sumptuous, Toff, Vulgarian, → **WEALTHY**, Well-heeled, Well off, Well-to-do

Richard Angevin, Burbage, Dick(y), Lionheart, Nixon, Rick, Roe

Richthofen Red Baron

Rick (burning) Goaf, Sprain, Swingism, Wrench

Rickets, Rickety Dilapidated, Rachitis, Ramshackle, Rattletrap, Shaky, Unsound

▷ **Rickety** *may indicate* an anagram

Rickshaw Pedicab, Tuktuk

Ricochet Boomerang, Glance, Rebound

Rid Clear, Deliver, Ditch, Eliminate, Eradicate, Expunge, Free, Obviate, Offload, Purge, Scrap, Scrub, Shot

Riddle Boulter, Charade, Colander, Dilemma, Enigma, Koan, Logogriph, Pepper, Perforate, Permeate, Puzzle, Screen, Searce, Search, Seil, Sieve, Sift, Sile, Siler, Sorites, Strain, Tems(e), Trommel

Ride, Riding Annoy, Aquaplane, Bareback, Bestride, Big dipper, Bruise, Burn, Canter, Coast, Crog(gy), Cycle, District, Division, Drive, Equitation, Field, Hack, Harass, Haute école, Hitchhike, Merry-go-round, Mount, Pick(-a-)back, Pickpack, Piggyback, Postil(l)ion, Rape, Revere's, Roadstead, Rollercoaster, Sit, Spin, Stang, Surf, Switchback, Third, Trot, Weather, Welter, Wheelie, Whip, White-knuckle

Rider(s) Addendum, Adjunct, Appendage, Attachment, Boundary, Bucket, Cavalier, Charioteer, Circuit, Clause, Codicil, Condition, Corollary, Dispatch, Equestrian, Eventer, Freedom, Gaucho, Godiva, Guidon, Haggard, Horseman, Jockey, Lochinvar, Messenger, Peloton, Postil(l)ion, Proviso, PS, Revere, Scrub, Spurrer, Transport, Walkyrie

Ridge(pole) Alveolar, Anthelix, Antihelix, Arête, Arris, As(ar), Balk, Bank, Baulk, Berm, Bur(r), Carina, Chine, Clint, Costa, Coteau, Crease, Crest, Crista, Cuesta, Culmen, Darling Range, Drill, Drum(lin), Dune, Eskar, Esker, Fret, Gonys, Gyrus, Hammock, Hoe, Hogback, Horst, Hummock, Interfluve, Kaim, Kame, Keel, Knur(l), Ledge, Linch, List(er), Lynchet, Mid-Atlantic, Mid-ocean, Missionary, Moraine, Nek, Nut, Oceanic, Offset, Pressure, Promontory, Ramp, Rand, Raphe, Razor-back, Reef, Rib, Riblet, Rig, Rim, Roof-tree, Sastruga, Screw-thread, Serac, Serpentine, Shoulder, Sowback, Torus, Varix, Verumontanum, Vimy, Wale, Weal, Whelp, Whorl, Windrow, Withers, Witwatersrand, Wrinkle, Yardang, Zastruga

Ridicule, Ridiculous Absurd, Badinage, Bathos, Chaff, Cockamamie, Deride, Derisory, Egregious, Foolish, Gibbet, Gibe, Gird, Guy, Haze, Jibe, Josh, Laughable, Ludicrous, Mimic, Mock, Paradox, Pasquin, Pillory, Pish, Pooh-pooh, Rag, Raillery, Rally, Rich, Risible, Roast, Satire, Scoff, Scout, Screwy, Send up, Sight, Silly, Skimmington, Taunt, Travesty

Ridinghood Nithsdale, Red, Trot-cos(e)y

Riding-master RM

Riding-school Manège

Rife Abundant, Manifest, Numerous, Prevalent

Riffle Rapid

Riff-raff Canaille, Hoi polloi, Mob, Populace, Rag-tag, Rag, tag and bobtail, Scaff, Scum, Trash

Rifle Air, Armalite®, Assault, Bone, Browning, Bundook, Burgle, Calic, Carbine, Chassepot, Enfield, Enfield musket, Escopette, Express, Garand, → **GUN**, Kalashnikov, Lee Enfield, Loot, Magazine, Martini®, Martini-Henry, Mauser®, MI, Minié, Pea, Petronel, Pick, Pilfer, Pillage, Ransack, Reave, Reive, Remington, Repeater, Rieve, Rob, Ruger, Saloon, Shiloh, Springfield, Winchester®

Rift Altercation, Canyon, Chasm, Chink, Cleft, Crevasse, Fault, Fissure, Gap, Gulf, Split

Rig(ging), Rigger Accoutre, Attire, Bermuda, Drilling, Equip, Feer, Frolic, Gaff, Get-up, Gunter, Hoax, Jack-up, Mainbrace, Manipulate, Marconi, Martingale, Oil, Outfit, Panoply, Ratline, Ropes, Roughneck, Schooner, Semisubmersible, Slant, Sport, Stack, Standing, Strip, Swindle, Tackle, Togs, Top hamper, Trull, Wanton

▷ **Rigged** *may indicate* an anagram

Right(s), Righten, Rightness Accurate, Advowson, Affirmative, Ancient lights, Angary, Animal, Appropriate, Appurtenance, Ay, Bang, Befit, Blue-pencil, BNP, Bote, Cabotage, Champart, Civil, Claim, Competence, Conjugal, Conservative, Copyhold, → **CORRECT**, Cor(r)ody, Coshery, Cuddy, Cure, Curtesy, Customer, Dead on, De jure, Dexter, Direct, Divine, Doctor, Droit, Due, Easement, Eminent domain, Emphyteusis, Equity, Esnecy, Estover, Ethical, Exactly, Faldage, Farren, Fascist, Feu, Fire-bote, Fitting, Forestage, Franchise, Free-bench, Freedom, Gay, Germane, Gunter, Haybote, Hedge-bote, Human, Infangthief, Interest, Isonomy, Iure, Junior, Jural, Jure, Jus (mariti), Leet, Legit, Letters patent, Liberty, Lien, Maritage, Maternity, Meet, Merit, Miner's, Miranda, Moral, Naam, New, Ninepence, Off, Offhand, Offside, OK, Okay, Oke, Okey-dokey, Option, Ortho-, Oughtness, Paine, Pannage, Passant, Pasturage, Pat, Patent, Paternity, Performing, Pit and gallows, Ploughbote, Pose, Postliminy, Pre-emption, Prerogative, Primogeniture, Priority, Prisage, Privilege, Proper, Property, Pukka, R, Rain, Reason, Recourse, Rectify, Rectitude, Redress, Remainder, Remedy, Repair, Rt, Sac, Sake, Side, Slap, So, Soc, Spot-on, Squatter's, Stage, Starboard, Stillicide, Suo jure, Suo loco, Tao, Tenants', Terce, Ticket, Tickety-boo, Title, Tory, Trivet, Trover, True, Turbary, User, Usucap(t)ion, Usufruct, Venville, Vert, Warren, Water, Women's

Right-angle(d) Orthogonal

Righteous(ness) Devout, Good, Just, Moral, Pharisee, Prig, Rectitude, Sanctimonious, Tzaddik, Virtuous

Right-hand Dexter, E, Far, Recto, RH, Ro

Right-winger Dry, Falangist, Neocon, Neo-fascist

Rigid(ity) Acierated, Catalepsy, Craton, Extreme, Fixed, Formal, Hard and fast, Hard-set, Hard-shell, Hidebound, Inflexible, Lignin, Renitent, Rigor, Set, Slavish, Starch(y), Stern, Stiff, Stretchless, Strict, Stringent, Tense, Turgor

Rigmarole Nonsense, Palaver, Paraphernalia, Protocol, Ragman, Ragment, Riddlemeree, Screed

Rigorous, Rigour Accurate, Austere, Cruel, Exact, Firm, Hard, Inclement, Iron-bound, Stern, Strait, Strict, Stringent

Rile Anger, Annoy, Harry, Irritate, → **NETTLE**, Vex

▷ **Rile(y)** *may indicate* an anagram

Rill Purl, Sike

Rim Atlantic, Border, Chimb, Chime, Edge, Felloe, Felly, Flange, Girdle, Kelyphitic, → **LIP**, Margin, Pacific, Strake, Verge

Rime Crust, Frost, Hoar, Rhyme, Rhythm

Rind Bark, Crackling, Peel, Skin

Ring(ed), Ringer, Ringing, Rings Anchor, Angelus, Annual, Annulus, Anthelion, Arcus, Arena, Band, Bangle, Bayreuth, Bell, Benzine, Betrothal, Boom-iron, Broch, Brogh, Call, Cambridge, Carabiner, Cartel, Cartouche, Change, Chime, Circinate, Circle, Circlet, Circlip, Circus, Claddagh, Clam, Clang, Clink, Coil, Collet, Cordon, Cornice, Corona, Corral, Corrida, Cramp, Crawl, Cricoid, Cringle, Cromlech, Cycle, Cyclic, Dead, Death's head, Dial, Dicyclic, Ding, Disc, Dohyo, Dong, D(o)uar, Draupnir, Echo, Encircle, Encompass, Engagement, Enhalo, Enlace, Environ, Enzone, Eternity, Extension, Eyelet, Fainne, Fairlead(er), Fairy, Ferrule, Fisherman, Fistic(uffs), Gas, Gimmal, Gimmer, Gird(le), Girr, Gloriole, Groin, Grom(m)et, Growth, Grummet, Guard, Gyges, Gymmal, Gyre, Halo, Hank, Hob, → **HOOP**, Hoop-la, Hula-hoop, Ideal, Inner, Inorb, Involucre, Jougs, Jow, Karabiner, Kartell, Keeper, Key, Knell, Knock-out, Kraal, Lactam, Lifebelt, Link, Loop, Luned, Lute, Magpie, Manacle, Manilla, Marquise, Mourning, Napkin, Newton's, Nibelung, Nimbus, Nose, O, Oil-control, Orb, Outer, Pappus, Parral, Parrel, Peal, Pele, Pen, Phone, Ping, Piston, Potato, Price, Prize, Puteal, Quoit, Resonant, Resound, Retaining, Round, Rove, Rowel, Rundle, Runner, Rush, Sale, Scarf, Scraper, Scrunchy, Seal, Signet, Slinger, Slip, Snap-link, Solomon, Sound, Spell, Split, Stemma, Stemme, Stonehenge, Surround, Swivel, Syndicate, Tang, Tattersall, Teething, Terret, Territ, Thimble, Thumb, Timbre, Ting, Tingle, Tink, Tinnitius, Tintinnabulate, Toe, Token, Toll, Toplady, Tore, Torquate, Torques, Torret, Torus, Travelling, Tree, Trochus, Troth, Turret, Tweed, Varvel, Vervel, Vice, Vortex, Wagnerian, Washer, Wedding, Welkin, Withe, Woggle, Zero
Ring-dance Carol
Ring-leader Bell-wether, Fugleman, Instigator
Ringlet Curl(icue), Lock, Tendril, Tress
Ringmaster Wagner
Ringworm Serpigo, Tinea
Rinse Bathe, Blue, Cleanse, Douche, Sind, Sine, Swill, Synd, Syne, Tint, Wash
Riot(er), Riotous(ly), Riots Anarchy, Brawl, Clamour, Demo, Deray, Gordon, Hilarious, Hubbub, Luddite, Medley, Mêlée, Nicker, Orgy, Pandemonium, Peterloo, Petroleur, Porteous, Profusion, Quorum, Race, Rag, Rebecca, Rebel, Roaring, Roister, Rout, Rowdy, Ruction, Ruffianly, Scream, Swing, Tumult
▷ **Rioters, Riotous** *may indicate* an anagram
Rip(per), Ripping, Rip off Avulse, Basket, Buller, Cur, Dilacerate, Grand, Handful, Horse, Jack, Lacerate, Rent, Rep, Roué, Splendid, Tear, Tide, Topnotch, To-rend, Unseam
Ripe, Ripen(ing) Auspicious, Full, Geocarpy, Mature, Mellow, Rathe, Ready
Riposte Repartee, Retaliate, Retort
Ripple Bradyseism, Fret, Overlap, Popple, Purl, Undulation, Wave, Wavelet, Wimple, Wrinkle
▷ **Rippling** *may indicate* an anagram
Rise(r), Rising Advance, Appreciate, Ascend, Aspire, Assurgent, Bull, Butte, Cause, Dry, Dutch, Easter, Eger, Elevation, Emerge, Émeute, Eminence, Erect, Escalate, Get up, Hance, Hauriant, Haurient, Heave, Heliacal, Hike, Hill, Hummock, Hunt's up, Improve, Increase, Incremental, Insurgent, Intifada, Intumesce, Jibe, Knap, Knoll, Lark, Levee, Levitate, Lift, Molehill, Mount, Mutiny, Orient, Origin, Peripety, Point, Prove, Putsch, Rear, Resurgent, Resurrection, → **REVOLT**, Saleratus, Scarp, Sklim, Soar, Stand, Stie, Sty, Stye, Surface, Surge, The Fifteen, Tor, Tower, Transcend, Up, Upbrast, Upburst, Upgo, Uprest, Upshoot, Upsurge, Upswarm, Upturn, Well
Risk(y) Actuarial, Adventure, Apperil, Back, Calculated, Chance, Compromise,

Counterparty, → **DANGER**, Daring, Dice, Dicy, Emprise, Endanger, Fear, Gamble, Game, Hairy, Hazard, Imperil, Impetuous, Jeopardy, Liability, Nap, Peril, Precarious, Security, Shoot the works, Spec, Throw, Touch and go, Touchy, Unsafe, Venture

Risorgimento Renaissance

Risqué Blue, Racy, Salty, Scabrous, Spicy

Rissole(s) Cecils, Chillada, Croquette, Faggot, Falafel, Felafel, Quennelle, Veggieburger

Rite(s) Asperges, Bora, Ceremony, Eastern, Exequies, Initiation, Last offices, Liturgy, Mystery, Nagmaal, Obsequies, Powwow, Ritual, Sacrament, Sarum use, Superstition, York

Ritual Agadah, Arti, Ceremony, Chanoyu, Cultus, Customary, Formality, Haggada, Lavabo, Liturgy, Mumbo-jumbo, Puja, Rite, Sacring, Seder, Social, Tantric, Use

Rival(ry), Rivals Absolute, Acres, Aemule, Binocular, Compete, Contender, Emulate, Emule, Envy, Fo(n)e, → **MATCH**, Needle, Opponent, Retinal, Touch, Vie

River Bayou, Dalles, Ea, Eau, Estuary, Flood, Flower, Fluvial, Potamic, Potamology, R, Riverain, Runner, Stream, Tide, Tributary, Waterway

---

RIVERS

2 letters:	Nar	Cher	Lahn
Ay	Oil	Culm	Lech
Ob	Oka	Dart	Lena
Po	Ord	Deva	Liao
Si	Red	Doon	Luan
Xi	San	Dove	Lune
	Tay	Drin	Maas
3 letters:	Tet	Earn	Main
Aar	Ure	East	Meta
Aln	Usk	Ebbw	Milk
Axe	Wye	Ebro	Mino
Ayr	Yeo	Eden	Mole
Bug		Eder	Nene
Cam	*4 letters:*	Elbe	Neva
Dee	Abus	Erne	Nile
Don	Abzu	Esla	Nith
Ems	Acis	Eure	Oder
Esk	Adda	Gila	Ohio
Exe	Adur	Gota	Oise
Fal	Aire	Huon	Ouse
Fly	Alma	Idle	Oxus
Fox	Alph	Isar	Prut
Han	Amur	Iser	Rock
Hsi	Aran	Isis	Ruhr
Hué	Aras	Isla	Saar
Inn	Arno	Jiul	Sava
Lee	Aude	Juba	Soar
Lot	Avon	Kama	Spey
Luo	Back	Kill	Styx
Lys	Beni	Kura	Swan
Mur	Bomu	Kwai	Swat

Taff	Drave	Rhône	Calder
Tana	Duero	Rogue	Canton
Tarn	Dvina	Saône	Chenab
Tees	Eblis	Seine	Clutha
Teme	Firth	Shari	Colima
Test	Fleet	Shire	Croton
Tone	Forth	Siang	Crouch
Tyne	Gogra	Siret	Cydnus
Uele	Green	Skien	Danube
Ural	Havel	Slave	Dawson
Uvod	Hotan	Snake	Donets
Vaal	Indre	Snowy	Duddon
Waal	Indus	Somme	Durack
Wear	Isere	Spree	Escaut
Xero	Ishim	Staff	Finlay
Yalu	James	Stour	Fraser
Yare	Jumna	Swale	Gambia
Yate	Juruá	Tagus	Ganges
Yser	Kasai	Tamar	Glomma
Yuan	Kaven	Tapti	Granta
Yuen	Kenga	Tarim	Harlem
	Kuban	Teign	Hodder
5 letters:	Lethe	Terek	Hsiang
Abana	Liard	Tiber	Hudson
Acton	Limay	Tisza	Humber
Adige	Loire	Tobol	Iguacu
Afton	Marne	Trent	Ijssel
Agate	Mbomu	Tweed	Irtish
Aisne	Meuse	Volga	Irtysh
Aldan	Minho	Volta	Irwell
Apure	Mosel	Warta	Isonzo
Argun	Mulla	Weser	Itchen
Avoca	Mures	Xiang	Japura
Benue	Namoi	Xingu	Javari
Boyne	Negro	Yaqui	Javary
Broad	Neman	Yarra	Jhelum
Cauca	Niger	Yonne	Jordan
Chari	Ogowe	Yssel	Kaduna
Clwyd	Onega	Yukon	Kagera
Clyde	Oreti		Kennet
Clyst	Peace	**6 letters:**	Kistna
Colne	Pearl	Allier	Kolyma
Congo	Pecos	Amazon	Komati
Conwy	Pelly	Anadyr	Liffey
Cross	Piave	Angara	Mamoré
Culbá	Pison	Arzina	Medway
Dasht	Plate	Atbara	Mekong
Desna	Purus	Barcoo	Mersey
Doubs	Rainy	Barrow	Mindel
Douro	Rance	Bio-Bio	Mohawk
Drava	Rhine	Broads	Molopo

6 letters – cont:
Morava
Moskva
Murray
Neckar
Neisse
Nelson
Nyeman
Ogooue
Orange
Orwell
Ottawa
Pahang
Parana
Peneus
Platte
Pripet
Prosna
Rakaia
Ribble
Riffle
Rother
Sabine
Salado
Sambre
Santee
Seneca
Severn
St John
Struma
Sutlej
Swanee
Tanana
Tarsus
Tevere
Teviot
Thames
Ticino
Tigris
Tugela
Tyburn
Ubangi
Ussuri
Vardar
Vienne
Vitava
Vyatka
Wabash
Wairau
Wensum
Wharfe

Wupper
Yarrow
Yellow

7 letters:
Acheron
Aruwimi
Bassein
Berbice
Berezua
Bermejo
Buffalo
Burnett
Caqueta
Cauvery
Chagres
Cocytus
Damodar
Darling
Derwent
Detroit
Dnieper
Dubglas
Durance
Ettrick
Fitzroy
Garonne
Genesee
Gironde
Guapore
Hari Rud
Helmand
Hooghly
Huang He
Hwangho
Iguassu
Irawadi
Kanawha
Krishna
Lachlan
Limpopo
Lualaba
Madeira
Manning
Maranon
Maritsa
Mataura
Meander
Moselle
Narbada
Narmada

Neuquén
Niagara
Nipigon
Oceanus
Orinoco
Orontes
Parrett
Pechora
Pharpar
Potomac
Red Deer
Rubicon
Sabrina
Salinas
Salween
Salzach
Sanders
Scheldt
Senegal
Shannon
Songhua
St Clair
St Croix
St Mary's
Swannee
Tapajos
Thomson
Tugaloo
Ucayali
Uruguay
Vistula
Waikato
Washita
Wateree
Welland
Yangtse
Yenisei
Yenisey
Zambese
Zambezi

8 letters:
Amu Darya
Anderson
Apurimac
Araguaia
Araguaya
Arkansas
Berezina
Blue Nile
Canadian

Charente
Cherwell
Chindwin
Chu Kiang
Clarence
Colorado
Columbia
Congaree
Daintree
Demerara
Dneister
Dordogne
Flinders
Franklin
Gascoyne
Godavari
Granicus
Guadiana
Hamilton
Illinois
Kentucky
Klondike
Kootenay
Maeander
Mahanadi
Manawatu
Menderes
Missouri
Mitchell
Ocmulgee
Okanagan
Okavango
Okovango
Ouachita
Pactolus
Paraguay
Parnaiba
Putumayo
Rio Negro
Safid Rud
Saguenay
Savannah
Suwannee
Syr Darya
Tonle Sap
Torridge
Toulouse
Tunguska
Van Hades
Veronezh
Victoria

Volturno	Pilcomayo	Kizil Irmak	Mississauga
Wanganui	Porcupine	Phlegethon	Mississippi
Windrush	Qu'Appelle	Rangitaiki	Monongahela
Zhu Jiang	Rangitata	Rangitikei	Shatt-al-Arab
	Richelieu	Sacramento	Susquehanna
9 letters:	Rio Branco	San Joaquin	Yellowstone
Allegheny	Rio Grande	Schuylkill	
Ashburton	Salambria	St Lawrence	**12 letters:**
Billabong	Santa Cruz	White Volta	Guadalquivir
Churchill	St George's	Yesil Irmak	Murrumbidgee
Crocodile	White Nile		Saõ Francisco
Des Moines	Wisconsin	**11 letters:**	Saskatchewan
Essequibo		Aegospotami	
Euphrates	**10 letters:**	Assiniboine	**13 letters:**
Irrawaddy	Black Volta	Brahmaputra	Little Bighorn
Kuskokwim	Blackwater	Connecticut	
Mackenzie	Chao Phraya	Cooper Creek	**17 letters:**
Magdalena	Courantyne	Delaguadero	North
Murchison	Cumberland	Guadalentin	Saskatchewan
Parnahiba	Great Slave	Lesser Slave	South
Perihonca	Housatonic	Madre de Dios	Saskatchewan

River-bank, Riverside Brim, Carse, Riparian

River-bed T(h)alweg

River-mouth Firth, Frith

Rivet(ing) Bolt, Clinch, Clink, Concentrate, Explosive, Fasten, Fix, Pean, Peen, Stud, Transfix, Unputdownable

Rivulet Beck, Brook, Burn, Gill, Rill, Runnel, Strand

RNA Antisense, → **DNA**, Initiator codon, Messenger, Molecule, M-RNA, Retrotransposon, Ribosomal, Ribosome, Ribozyme, Soluble, Transcribe, Transfer, Uracil, Viroid

Ro(u)manian, Rumanian Ro, R(o)uman, Vlach, Wal(l)achian

Roach Fish, Red-eye

Road(s), Roadside, Road surface A, A1, Access, Anchorage, Arterial, Asphalt, Autobahn, Autopista, Autostrada, Ave(nue), B, Beltway, Blacktop, Boulevard, Burma, Carriageway, Causeway, Clay, Clearway, Close, Cloverleaf, Coach, Concession, Corduroy, Corniche, Course, Crossover, Cul-de-sac, Dirt, Drift-way, Driveway, Drove, Dunstable, Escape, Exit, Expressway, Fairway, Feeder, Fly-over, Fly-under, Foss(e) Way, Freeway, Grid, Hampton, Highway, Horseway, Kerb, Lane, Loan, Loke, Mall, Metal, M1, Motorway, Off-ramp, Orbital, Overpass, Parkway, Path, Pike, Post, Private, Rat-run, Rd, Relief, Ride, Ridgeway, Ring, → **ROUTE**, Royal, Service, Shoulder, Shunpike, Side, Skid, Slip, Speedway, Spur(way), St(reet), Superhighway, Switchback, Tarmac, Tar-seal, Thoroughfare, Tobacco, Toby, Track(way), Trunk, Turning, Turnpike, Unadopted, Underpass, Unmade, Verge, Via, Viaduct, Way

Road-block Barrier, Cone, Jam, Toll

Road-keeper Way-warden

Road-maker Drunkard, Macadam, Navigator, Telford, Wade

Roadstead La Hogue

Roam Enrange, Extravagate, Peregrinate, Rake, Ramble, Rove, Stray, Wander, Wheel

Roan Barbary, Bay, Horse, Leather, Schimmel, Strawberry

Roar(ing) Bawl, Bell(ow), Bluster, Boom, Boys, Cry, Forties, Guffaw, Laugh, Roin, Rote, Rout, Royne, Thunder, Tumult, Vroom, Wuther, Zoom

Roast Bake, Barbecue, Baste, Birsle, Brent, Cabob, Cook, Crab, Crown, Decrepitate, Grill, Kabob, Pan, Pot, Ridicule, Scald, Scathe, Sear, Slate, Spit, Tan, Torrefy

Rob(bed), Robber(y) Abduct, Bandalero, Bandit, Barabbas, Bereave, Blag, Brigand, Burgle, Bust, Cabbage, Cacus, Cateran, Clyde, Dacoit, Dakoit, Daylight, Depredation, Despoil, Do, Drawlatch, Fake, Filch, Fleece, Flimp, Footpad, Gilderoy, Heist, Hership, Highjack, High toby, Highwayman, Hijack, Hold-up, Hustle, Job, Kondo, Ladrone, Land-pirate, Larceny, Latrocinium, Latron, Loot, Mill, Moskonfyt, Mosstrooper, Pad, Pandoor, Pandour, Pillage, Pinch, Piracy, Pluck, Plunder, Procrustes, Ramraid, Rapine, Reave, Reft, Reive, Rieve, Rifle, Roberdsman, Robertsman, Roll, Rover, Roy, Rubbet, Rustler, Sack, Sciron, Screw, Short change, Sinis, Skinner, Smash and grab, Snaphaunch, Spoiler, Spoliation, Spring-heeled Jack, → **STEAL**, Steaming, Stick-up, Sting, Swindle, Thief, Toby, Turn-over, Turpin

Robe(s) Alb, Amice, Amis, Attrap, Buffalo, Camis, Camus, Cassock, Chimer, Chrisom(-cloth), Christom, Dalmatic, Dolman, → **DRESS**, Gown, Ihram, Jilbab, Kanzu, Khalat, Khilat, Kill(a)ut, Kimono, Mantle, Night, Parament, Parliament, Pedro, Peplos, Pontificals, Purple, Regalia, Rochet, Saccos, Sanbenito, Soutane, Sticharion, Stola, Stole, Talar, Tire, Vestment, Yukata

Robert Bob(by), Bridges, Browning, Burns, Cop, Flic, Peel, Rab, Rob

Robin Adair, American, Bird, Cock, Day, Goodfellow, Hob, Hood, Puck(-hairy), Ragged, Redbreast, Reliant, Round, Ruddock, Starveling, Wake

Robot Android, Automaton, Cyborg, Dalek, Golem, Nanobot, Puppet, RUR, Telechir

Robust Hale, Hardy, Healthy, Hearty, Iron, Lusty, Muscular, Sound, Stalwart, Sthenic, Stout, Strapping, Sturdy, Vigorous

Roc Bird, Ruc, Rukh

Rock(s), Rocker, Rocking, Rocky Acid, Ages, Agitate, Ailsa Craig, Astound, Ayers, Boulder, Cap, Cock, Cockhorse, Country, Cradle, Destabilise, Edinburgh, Erratic, Fastnet, Garage, Gib(raltar), Heavy metal, Hybrid, Inchcape, Jow, Lorelei, Mantle, Marciano, Marlstone, Matrix, Native, Nunatak(kr), Permafrost, Peter, Petrology, Platform, Plymouth, Punk, Quake, Reel, Reggae, Reservoir, Rimrock, Rip-rap, Rudaceous, S. Peter, Sally, Scabland's, Scare, Scaur, Sclate, → **SHAKE**, Shoogle, Showd, Soft, Solid, Stone, Stonehenge, Stonen, Stun, Sway, Swee, Swing, Symplegades, Tarpeian, Ted, Teeter, The Olgas, Totter, Tremble, Uluru, Unstable, Unsteady, Weeping, Whin, Wind, Windsor

---

ROCKS

2 letters:	Crag	Tufa	Chert
Aa	Gang	Tuff	Cliff
	Glam	Wall	Craig
3 letters:	Jura	Zoic	Elvan
Gem	Lava		Emery
Ice	Lias	**5 letters:**	Flint
Tor	Noup	Arête	Geode
	Reef	Brash	Glass
4 letters:	Sill	Calpe	Krans
Bell	Sima	Chair	Loess
Coal	Trap	Chalk	Magma

Nappe
Scalp
Scrae
Scree
Shale
Slate
Trass
Wacke

6 letters:
Albite
Aplite
Arkose
Banket
Basalt
Dacite
Desert
Diapir
Dogger
Dunite
Flaser
Flysch
Fossil
Gabbro
Gangue
Garnet
Gibber
Gneiss
Gossan
Gozzan
Inlier
Kingle
Living
Marble
Masada
Norite
Oolite
Oolith
Ophite
Pelite
Pluton
Pumice
Rognon
Sarsen
Schist
Sinter
Skerry
Sklate
Synroc
Tephra

7 letters:
Aquifer
Archean
Arenite
Breccia
Clastic
Cuprite
Cyanean
Diamond
Diorite
Erathem
Eucrite
Felsite
Geofact
Granite
Greisen
Haplite
Igneous
Lignite
Marlite
Minette
Molasse
Moraine
Needles
Olivine
Ophites
Outcrop
Outlier
Peridot
Picrite
Remanie
Rhaetic
Sinking
Spilite
Stadium
Syenite
Terrane
Thulite
Tripoli
Wenlock

8 letters:
Adularia
Aegirine
Aiguille
Andesite
Aphanite
Archaean
Asbestos
Basanite
Brockram

Burstone
Calcrete
Calc-tufa
Calc-tuff
Ciminite
Diabasic
Dolerite
Dolomite
Eclogite
Eklogite
Elvanite
Eutaxite
Fahlband
Felstone
Footwall
Ganister
Hepatite
Hornfels
Idocrase
Isocline
Laterite
Lenticle
Lopolith
Mesolite
Mudstone
Mylonite
Obsidian
Peperino
Petuntse
Phyllite
Pisolite
Plutonic
Porphyry
Psammite
Psephite
Ragstone
Regolith
Rhyolite
Rocaille
Roe-stone
Saxatile
Saxonite
Scorpion
Sunstone
Taconite
Tephrite
Tonalite
Trachyte
Trappean
Volcanic
Xenolith

9 letters:
Anticline
Argillite
Batholite
Batholith
Bentonite
Bluestone
Buhrstone
Claystone
Colluvium
Cornstone
Dalradian
Diatomite
Dinantian
Dolostone
Eddystone
Evaporite
Firestone
Flagstone
Flowstone
Gannister
Goslarite
Granulite
Greensand
Greystone
Greywacke
Gritstone
Hornstone
Impactite
Intrusion
Ironstone
Laccolite
Laccolith
Lardalite
Larvikite
Limestone
Meteorite
Mica-slate
Migmatite
Monadnock
Monocline
Monzonite
Mortstone
Mugearite
Natrolite
Neocomian
Ophiolite
Ottrelite
Pegmatite
Phonolite
Phosphate

9 letters – cont:	**10 letters:**	Serpentine	**12 letters:**
Pleonaste	Amygdaloid	Sparagmite	Babingtonite
Propylite	Camptonite	Stinkstone	Baltic Shield
Protogine	Epidiorite	Stonebrash	Coal Measures
Quartzite	Foundation	Syntagmata	Granodiorite
Sandstone	Granophyre	Teschenite	Grossularite
Saprolite	Greenstone	Touchstone	Serpentinite
Schistose	Grey-wether	Travertine	Slickenslide
Siltstone	Hypabyssal	Troctolite	Straticulate
Soapstone	Ignimbrite		Stromatolite
Tachylyte	Kersantite	**11 letters:**	Syntagmatite
Theralite	Kimberlite	Agglomerate	Thunderstone
Tinguaite	Laurdalite	Amphibolite	
Toadstone	Laurvikite	Annabergite	**13 letters:**
Travertin	Lherzolite	Anorthosite	Hypersthenite
Underclay	Limburgite	Carbonatite	
Uriconian	Mica-schist	Geanticline	**14 letters:**
Variolite	Novaculite	Halleflinta	Knotenschiefer
Veinstone	Orthophyre	Lamprophyre	Roche moutonnée
Veinstuff	Palagonite	Metamorphic	
Ventifact	Peridotite	Monchiquite	**18 letters:**
Vulcanite	Phenocryst	Napoleonite	Scandinavian Shield
Whinstone	Pitchstone	Nephelinite	
White Lias	Pyroxenite	Phillipsite	
Whunstane	Rupestrian	Pyroclastic	
Zechstein	Schalstein	Sedimentary	

Rock-boring Pholas
Rock-cress Arabis
Rocket Arugula, Blue, Booster, Capsule, Carpet, Carrier, Congreve, Dame's, Delta, Drake, Dressing down, Dyer's, Earful, Engine, Eruca, Flare, Ion, Jato, Life, London, Missile, Multistage, Onion, Payload, Posigrade, Reprimand, Reproof, Retro, Rockoon, Rucola, Salad, SAM, Sea, Skylark, Soar, Sonde, Sounding, Step, Stephenson, Take-off, Thruster, Tourbillion, Ullage, Upshoot, V1, Vernier, Von Braun, Wall, Warhead, Weld, Yellow, Zero stage
Rock-living Rupicoline, Saxatile, Saxicoline, Saxicolous
Rock-pipit Sea-lark
▷ **Rocky** *may indicate* an anagram
Rococo Baroque, Fancy, Ornate, Quaint
Rod(-shaped), Rodlike, Rods Aaron's, Axle, Baculiform, Bar, Barbe(l)l, Barre, Birch, Caduceus, Caim, Came, Can, Cane, Centre, Connecting, Control, Cue, Cuisenaire®, Dipstick, Divining, Dopper, Dowser, Drain, Ellwand, Fasces, Filler, Fin-ray, Firearm, Fisher, Fishing, Fly, Fuel, Gauging, Gold stick, Gun, Handspike, Jacob's staff, Kame, King, Laver, Lightning, Linchpin, Lug, Mapstick, Mopstick, Moses, Napier's bones, Nervure, Newel, Notochord, Perch, Pin, Pistol, Piston, Pitman, Pointer, Poker, Poking-stick, Pole, Pontie, Pontil, Ponty, Probang, Puntee, Punty, Push, Raddle, Regulating, Rhabdoid, Rhabdus, Riding, Rood, Scollop, Shaft, Sounding, Spindle, Spit, Stadia, Stair, Stanchion, Staple, Stave, Stay-bolt, Stick, Sticker, Strickle, Switch, Tension, Tie, Track, Triblet, Tringle, Trocar, Twig, Urochord, Ventifact, Verge, Virgate, Virgulate, Wand, Welding, Withe

Rod-bearer Lictor
Rode Raid
Rodent Acouchi, Acouchy, Ag(o)uti, Agouty, Bandicoot, Bangsring, Banxring, Beaver, Biscacha, Bizcacha, Bobac, Bobak, Boomer, Capybara, Cavy, Chickaree, Chincha, Chinchilla, Chipmunk, Civet, Coypu, Cricetus, Dassie, Deer-mouse, Degu, Delundung, Dormouse, Fieldmouse, Gerbil(le), Glires, Glutton, Gnawer, Gopher, Groundhog, Guinea pig, Ham(p)ster, Hedgehog, Hog-rat, Hutia, Hyrax, Hystricomorph, Jerboa, Jird, Lemming, Mara, Marmot, Mole rat, Mouse, Murid, Mus, Musk-rat, Musquash, Nutria, Ochotona, Ondatra, Paca, Porcupine, Potoroo, Prairie dog, Rat, Ratel, Ratton, Renegade, Runagate, Sciurine, Sewellel, Shrew, Simplicidentate, S(o)uslik, Spermophile, Springhaas, Springhase, Squirrel, Taguan, Taira, Tuco-tuco, Tucu-tuco, Vermin, Viscacha, Vole, Woodchuck, Woodmouse
Roderick Random, Usher
Rodomontade Bluster, Boast, Bombast, Brag, Gas
Roe Avruga, Botargo, Bottarga, Caviar(e), Coral, Fry, Hard, Melt, Milt(z), Pea, Raun, Rawn, Soft
Roger Ascham, Bacon, Jolly, OK, Rights
Rogue, Roguish(ness) Arch, Bounder, Charlatan, Chiseller, Drole, Dummerer, Elephant, Espiègle(rie), Ganef, Ganev, Ganof, Gonif, Gonof, Greek, Gypsy, Hedge-creeper, Heel, Hempy, Herries, Imp, Knave, Latin, Limmer, Monkey, Palliard, Panurge, Picaresque, Picaroon, Pollard, Poniard, Rapparee, Ra(p)scal(l)ion, Riderhood, Savage, Scamp, Schellum, Schelm, Scoundrel, Skellum, Sleeveen, Slip-string, Sly, Swindler, Terror, Varlet, Villain, Wrong 'un
Roil Agitate, Annoy, Churn, Provoke, Vex
Roister(er) Blister, Carouse, Ephesian, Revel, Rollick, Scourer, Scowrer, Swashbuckler, Swinge-buckler
Role Bit, Cameo, Capacity, Function, Gender, Métier, → **PART**, Persona, Prima-donna, Stead, Title, Travesty
Roll(ed), Roller, Roll-call, Rolling, Rolls Absence, Bagel, Bap, Barrel, Beigel, Billow, Birmingham, Bolt, Bridge, Brioche, Butterie, Calender, Cambridge, Chamade, Comber, Convolv(ut)e, Cop, Couch, Court, Croissant, Cylinder, Dandy, Drum, Dutch, Electoral, Enswathe, Enwallow, Eskimo, Even, Fardel, Fardle, Flatten, Forward, Furl, Go, Goggle, Hotdog, Inker, Involute, Labour, List, Loaded, Lurch, Makimono, Mangle, Mano, Marver, Matricula, Motmot, Moving, Music, Muster, Notitia, Opulent, Pain au chocolat, Paradiddle, Patent, Paupiette, Pay, Petit-pain, Piano, Pigeon, Pipe, Platen, Porteous, Rafale, Ragman, Record, Reef, Reel, Register, Ren, Rent, Revolute, Revolve, Rhotacism, Ring, Road, Rob, Rolag, Roster, Rota, Rotate, Rotifer, Roul(e), Roulade, Rouleau, RR, Rub-a-dub, Rumble, Run, Sausage, Schnecke(n), Skin up, Snap, Somersault, Spool, Spring, Summer, Sway, Swell, Swiss, Table, Tandem, Taxi, Temple, Tent, Terrier, Thread, Toilet, Tommy, Trill, Trindle, Trundle, Valuation, Victory, Volume, Volutation, Wad, Wallow, Wamble, Waul, Wave, Wawl, Weather, Web, Welter, Western, Wince, Wrap, Yaw, Zorbing
Rollick(ing) Frolic, Gambol, Romp, Sport
▷ **Rollicking** *may indicate* an anagram
Roly-poly Chubby
Roman Agricola, Agrippa, Aurelius, Calpurnia, Candle, Catholic, Cato, Consul, CR, Crassus, Decemviri, Decurion, Empire, Flavian, Galba, Holiday, Italian, Jebusite, Latin, Maecenas, Papist, Patrician, PR, Quirites, Raetic, RC, Retarius, Rhaetia, Road, Scipio, Seneca, Sulla, Tarquin, Tiberius, Trebonius, Type, Uriconian, Veneti, Volsci

Romance, Romantic (talk) Affair, Amoroso, Amorous, Byronic, Casanova, Catalan, Dreamy, Fancy, Fantasise, Fib, Fiction, Gest(e), Gothic, Historical, Invention, Ladin(o), Ladinity, Langue d'oc(ian), Langue d'oil, Langue d'oui, Liaison, Lie, Neo-Latin, New, Novelette, Poetic, Quixotic, R(o)uman, Stardust, Tale

▶ **Romanian** *see* ROUMANIAN

Romanov Nicholas

▶ **Romany** *see* GYPSY

Rome Holy See, Imperial City

Romeo Casanova, Montagu, R, Swain

Romp(ing) Carouse, Escapade, Fisgig, Fizgig, Frisk, Frolic, Hoyden, Jaunce, Randy, Rig, Rollick, Skylark, Sport, Spree

Ron Glum, Moody

Rondo Rota

Ronnie Biggs

Röntgen R, X-ray

Roo Joey

Roof (edge), Roofing Belfast, Bell, Broach, Ceil, Cl(e)ithral, Cover, Curb, Divot, Dome, Drip, Eaves, French, Gable, Gambrel, Hardtop, Hip(ped), Home, Hypostyle, Imperial, Jerkin-head, Leads, M, Mansard, Monopitch, Onion dome, Palate, Pavilion, Pent, Pitched, Pop-top, Porte-cochère, Rag top, Rigging, Saddle, Saddleback, Shingle, Skillion, Skirt, Span, Sun(shine), Targa top, Tectiform, Tectum, Tegula, Thatch, Thetch, Tiling, Top, Uraniscus, Vaulting

Roof-climber Stegopholist

Roofless Hypaethral, Upaithric

Rook Bird, Castle, Cheat, Crow, Fleece, Fool, Overcharge, R, Swindle

Rookie Beginner, Colt, Galoot, Greenhorn, Learner, Nignog, Novice, Recruit, Tenderfoot, Tyro

Room(s), Roomy Antechamber, Anteroom, Apadana, Apartment, Assembly, Attic, Ben, Berth, Bibby, Boardroom, Boiler, Boudoir, Bower, But, Cabin(et), Calefactory, Camarilla, Camera, Capacity, Casemate, CC, Ceiling, Cell, Cellar, Cenacle, Chamber, Chancellery, Changing, Chat, Chaumer, Closet, Cockloft, Combination, Commercial, Commodious, Common, Compartment, Composing, Conclave, Consulting, Control, Cubicle, Cuddy, Cutting, Dark, Day, Delivery, Digs, Dinette, Dissecting, Divan, Dojo, Drawing, Dressing, Durbar, Elbow, End, Engine, Ex(h)edra, Extension, Foyer, Gap, Garret, Genizah, Green, Grill, Gun, Herbarium, Hostel, Incident, Kiva, Kursaal, Lab, Lamai, Latitude, Laura, Lavra, Lebensraum, Leeway, Leg, Library, Living, Locker, Lodge, Loft, Long, Loo, Lounge, Lumber, Margin, Megaron, Misericord(e), Mould-loft, Music, Oda, Operations, Oratory, Orderly, Oriel, Pad, Palm Court, Panic, Parlour, Parvis, Penetralia, Pentice, Pentise, Place, Powder, Press, Priesthole, Private, Projection, Property, Public, Pump, Rangy, Reading, Receiving, Reception, Recitation, Recovery, Recreation, Rest, Rm, Robing, Rubber, Rumpus, Sacristy, Sale(s), Salle, Salon, Sanctum, School, Scope, Scriptorium, Scullery, Serdab, Servery, Service, Shebang, Single, Single-end, Sitkamer, Sitting, Smoking, Snug, Solar, Solarium, → SPACE, Spacious, Spare, Spence, Spheristerion, Staff, Standing, Steam, Still, Stock, Stowage, Street, Strong, Studio, Study, Suite, Sun, Tap, Tea, Throne, Tiring, Tool, Twin, Two-pair, Ullage, Utility, Vestiary, Vestry, Voorkamer, Waiting, Ward, Wash, Wiggle, Work, Zeta

Roost(er) Cock, Perch, Siskin, Sit

Root(s), Rooted, Rooting Aruhe, Asarum, Beet, Buttress, Calamus, Calumba, Cassava, Cheer, Cocco, Contrayerva, Costus, Couscous, Cube, Culver's, Cuscus, Dasheen, Delve, Deracinate, Derivation, Derris, Dig, Eddo, Elecampane,

Eradicate, Eringo, Eryngo, Etymic, Etymon, Extirpate, Fern, Fibrous, Foundation, Gelseminine, Ginseng, Grass, Grout, Grub, Heritage, Horseradish, Hurrah, Immobile, Implant, Incorrigible, Insane, Irradicate, Jalap, Jicama, Khuskhus, Knee, Lateral, Licorice, Mallee, Mandrake, Mangold, Mishmee, Mishmi, Mooli, More, Myall, Navew, Nousle, Nuzzle, Origins, Orris, Pachak, Pleurisy, Pneumatophore, Poke, Prop, Pry, Putchock, Putchuk, Race, Radical, Radish, Radix, Repent, Rhatany, Rhizic, Rhizoid, Rhizome, Scorzonera, Senega, Sessile, Setwall, Snuzzle, Source, Square, Stilt, Stock, Strike, Tap, Taro, Tuber, Tuberous, Tulip, Turbith, Turnip, Turpeth, Vetiver, Yam, Zedoary

Rootless Psilotum

Rope(s) Abaca, Backstay, Ba(u)lk, Becket, Bind, Bobstay, Boltrope, Bracer, Brail, Breeching, Bunt-line, Cable, Cablet, Colt, Cord, Cordage, Cordon, Cringle, Downhaul, Drag, Earing, Fake, Fall, Flake, Flemish coil, Foot, Fore-brace, Foresheet, Forestay, Funicular, Futtock-shroud, Gantline, Garland, Grass line, Grist, Guest, Guide, Guy, Halliard, Halser, Halter, Halyard, Hawser, Hawser-laid, Headfast, Inhaul, Jack-stay, Jeff, Jib-sheet, Jump, Kernmantel, Kickling, Knittle, Ladder, Lanyard, Lasher, Lashing, Lasso, Lazo, Leg, Line, Longe, Lunge, Mainbrace, Mainsheet, Manil(l)a, Marlin(e), Match-cord, Messenger, Monkey, Mooring, Nettle, Nip, Noose, Oakum, Outhaul, Painter, Parbuckle, Pastern, Prolonge, Prusik, Pudding, Rawhide, Reef point, Riata, Ridge, Ringstopper, Roband, Robbin, Rode, Runner, St Johnston's ribbon, St Johnston's tippet, Sally, Salt-eel, Seal, Selvagee, Sennit, Sheet, Shroud, Sinnet, Span, Spancel, Spun-yarn, Stay, Sternfast, Stirrup, String, Strop, Sugan, Swifter, Tackle, Tail, Tether, Tie, Timenoguy, Tippet, Tow(line), Trace, Trail, Triatic, Triatic stay, Vang, Wanty, Warp, Widdy, Wire

Rosalind Ganymede

Rosary Beads, Mala, Paternoster

Rose(-red), Rosie, Rosy Albertine, Amelanchier, Aurorean, Avens, Bear's-foot, Blooming, Bourbon, Breare, Briar, Brier, Burnet, Cabbage, Canker, Ceiling, Cherokee, China, Christmas, Compass, Corn, Crampbark, Damask, Dog, Eglantine, Eglatère, England, English, Floribunda, Geum, Golden, G(u)elder, Hellebore, Hybrid, Jack, Jacque, Jacqueminot, Lal(age), Lancaster, Lee, Monthling, Moss, Multiflora, Musk, Noisette, Opulus, Peace, Petra, Pink, Potentilla, Promising, Provence, Province, Provincial, Provine, Pyrus, Quillaia, Quillaja, Rambler, Red(dish), Remontant, Rhoda, Rhodo-, Rock, Rugosa, Scotch, Snowball, Sprinkler, Standard, Sweetbrier, Tea, Tokyo, Tudor, White, Whitethorn, York

Rose-apple Jamboo, Jambu

Rose-bay Oleander

Rosemary Rosmarine

Rosette Buttonhole, Chou, Cockade, Favour, Patera, Rosula

Rosin Colophony, Resin, Roset, Rosit, Rozet, Rozit

Rosinante Jade

Roster List, Register, Scroll, Table

Rostrum Ambo, Bema, Lectern, Podium, Pulpit, Tribune

Rot(ten), Rotting Addle, Baloney, Boo, Bosh, Botrytis, Bull, Caries, Carious, Corrode, Corrupt, Crown, Daddock, Decadent, → **DECAY**, Decompose, Decrepitude, Degradable, Dotage, Dry, Eat, Erode, Fester, Foot, Foul, Gangrene, Kibosh, Manky, Mildew, Noble, Nonsense, Off, Poppycock, Poxy, Punk, Putid, Putrefy, Putrid, Rail, Rancid, Rank, Rat, Red, Ret, Rhubarb, Ring, Rust, Sapropel, Septic, Soft, Sour, Squish, Twaddle, Vrot, Wet

Rotate, Rotating, Rotation, Rotator Backspin, Crop, Feather, Gyrate,

Laevorotation, Lay-farming, Optical, Pivot, Pronate, Rabat(te), Reamer, Revolve, Roll, Selsyn, Succession, Teres, Trundle, Turn, Turntable, Twiddle, Vortex, Vorticose, Wheel, Windmill

Rote Heart, Memory, Recite, Routine

Rotor Auxiliary, Flywheel, Impeller, Tilt

▶ **Rotten** *see* **ROT**

▷ **Rotten** *may indicate* an anagram

Rotter Cad, Knave, Stinker, Swine

Rotund Chubby, Corpulent, Plump, Round, Stout, Tubby

Rotunda Pantheon

Roué Debauchee, Decadent, Libertine, Profligate, Rake(-shame), Rip

Rouge Blush, Gild, Jeweller's, Raddle, Redden, Reddle, Ruddle, Ruddy

Rough(en), Roughly, Roughness About, Abrasive, Approximate, Asper(ate), Broad, Burr, C, Ca, Choppy, Circa, Coarse, Craggy, Crude, Exasperate, Frampler, Grained, Gross, Gruff, Gurly, Gusty, Hard, Harsh, Hispid, Hoarse, Hoodlum, Hooligan, Impolite, Imprecise, Incondite, Inexact, Irregular, Jagged, Karst, Keelie, Kokobeh, Muricate, Obstreperous, Of sorts, Or so, Push, Ragged, Ramgunshoch, Raspy, Raucle, Rip, Risp, Robust, Row, Rude, Rugged, Rusticate, Rusty, Sandblast, Scabrid, Scabrous, Sea, Shaggy, Sketchy, Some, Spray, Spreathe, Squarrose, Stab, Strong-arm, Stubbly, Swab, Tartar, Tearaway, Ted, Textured, Tousy, Touzy, Towsy, Towzy, Uncut, Violent, Yahoo

Roughage Ballast, Bran, Fodder

Rough breathing Asper, Rale, Wheeze

Roughcast Harl

▷ **Roughly** *may indicate* an anagram

Roulette Russian

▷ **Round** *may indicate* a word reversed

Round(ness) About, Ammo, Ball, Beat, Bombe, Bout, Cartridge, Catch, Circle, Complete, Cycle, Dome, Doorstep, Fat, Figure, Full, Global, Globate, Hand, Heat, Jump-off, Lap, Leg, Milk, O, Oblate, Orb, Orbicular, Orbit, Orby, Ought, Patrol, Peri-, Pirouette, Plump, Pudsy, Qualifying, Quarter, Quarter-final, Rev, Ring, Robin, Roly-poly, Ronde, Rondure, Rota, Rotund, Route, Routine, Rundle, Rung, Salvo, Sandwich, Sarnie, Sellinger's, Semi-final, Shot, Skirt, Slice, Sphaer, Sphere, Spherical, Spiral, Step, Table, Tour, Tubby, U-turn, Walk

Roundabout Ambages, Approximately, Bypass, Carousel, Circle, Circuit, Circumambient, Circumbendibus, Circus, Devious, Eddy, → **INDIRECT**, Merry-go-round, Peripheral, Rotary, Tortuous, Traffic circle, Turntable, Waltzer, Whirligig, Windlass

Round building Tholos, Tholus

Rounders Patball

Round-mouth Hag

Round-up Bang-tail muster, Collate, Corner, Corral, Gather, Herd, Rodeo, Spiral

Roup Auction, Croak, Pip, Roop

Rouse(r), Rousing Abrade, Abraid, Abray, Amo(o)ve, Animate, Beat, Bestir, Cheerleader, Emotive, Enkindle, Firk, Flush, Hearten, Heat, Innate, Kindle, Knock up, Rear, Send, Stimulate, Suscitate, Unbed, Waken, Whip

Rousseau Émile

Rout Clamour, Debacle, Defeat, Drub, Fleme, Flight, Hubbub, Hurricane, Rabble, Retreat, Rhonchal, Snore, Thiasus, Upsee, Upsey, Upsy, Vanquish, Whoobub

Route Arterial, Autobahn, Avenue, Byroad, Camino real, Causeway, Course,

Direction, Itinerary, I-way, Line, Ling, M-way, Path, Red, Road, Stock, Track, Trade, Transit, Via, Walk, Way

Routine Automatic, Day-to-day, Drill, Everyday, Grind, Groove, Habitual, Heigh-ho, Helch-how, Ho-hum, Jogtrot, Journeywork, Monotony, Pattern, Perfunctory, Pipe-clay, Red tape, Rota, Rote, Round, Run-of-the-mill, Rut, S(c)htick, Schtik, Treadmill, Workaday

Rove(r), Roving Car, Discursive, Enrange, Errant, Freebooter, Gad, Globetrotter, Marauder, Nomad, Proler, Prowl, Ralph, Range, → **ROAM**, Slub(b), Stray, Vagabond, Varangarian, Viking, Wander

Row(er) Align, Altercation, Arew, Argue, Argument, Bank, Barney, Bedlam, Bobbery, Bow, Brattle, Cannery, Colonnade, Death, Debate, Deen, Din, Dispute, Dust-up, Feud, File, Fireworks, Food, Fyle, Hoo-ha, Hullabaloo, Leander, Line(-up), Noise, Note, Oar, Octastich, Orthostichy, Paddle, Parade, Peripteral, Pluriserial, Pull, Quarrel, Rammy, Range, Rank, Raunge, Remigate, Reproach, Rew, Rhubarb, Rotten, Ruction, Rumpus, Savile, Scene, Scrap, Scull, Series, Set, Shindig, Shindy, Shine, Skid, Spat, Splore, Stern, Stound, Street, Stridor, Stroke, Stushie, Sweep, Terrace, Tier, Tiff, Tone, Torpid, Wetbob, Wherryman

Rowan Ash, Quicken, Sorb

Rowdy, Rowdiness Cougan, Hoo, Hooligan, Loud, Noisy, Rorty, Rough, Roughhouse, Ruffian, Scourer, Scozza, Skinhead, Stroppy, Unruly, Uproarious

Roy Rob

Royal(ty), Royalist Academy, Angevin, Basilical, Battle, Bourbon, Emigré, Exchange, Fee, Hanoverian, HR(H), Imperial, Imposing, Inca, Kingly, King's man, Majestic, Malignant, Palatine, Payment, Pharaoh, Plantagenet, Prince, Princess, Purple, Queenly, Real, Regal, Regis, Regius, Regnal, Sail, Sceptred, Society

Rub(bing), Rubber(y), Rub out Abrade, Attrition, Balata, Buff, Buna®, Bungie, Bungy, Bunje(e), Bunjie, Bunjy, Butyl, Calk, Calque, Camelback, Caoutchouc, Chafe, Cold, Condom, Corrade, Corrode, Cow gum®, Crepe, Cul(t)ch, Destroy, Dunlop®, Ebonite, Efface, Elastic, Elastomer, Embrocate, Emery, Erase, Factice, Factis, Fawn, Foam, Fray, Fret, Friction, Fridge, Frottage, Frotteur, Fudge, Funtumia, Gall, Galoch, Goodyear®, Grate, Graze, Grind, Guayule, Gum elastic, Gutta-percha, Hale, Hard, Hevea, High-hysteresis, Hule, India, Inunction, Irritate, Isoprene, Jelutong, Lagos, Latex, Leather, Masseur, Negrohead, Neoprene, Nuzzle, Obstacle, Para, Polish, Pontianac, Pontianak, Root, Safe, Sandpaper, Scour, Scrub, Scuff, Seringa, Silastic®, Smoked, Sorbo®, Sponge, Stroke, Synthetic, Towel, Trace, Ule, Vulcanite, Wild, Wipe, Xerotripsis

▷ **Rubbed** *may indicate* an anagram

Rubbish Balls, Brash, Brock, Bull, Bunkum, Cack, Clap-trap, Cobblers, Codswallop, Culch, Debris, Detritus, Discredit, Dre(c)k, Drivel, Dross, Fiddlesticks, Garbage, Grot, Grunge, Hogwash, Kack, Kak, Landfill, Leavings, Litter, Mullock, Nonsense, Phooey, Piffle, Pish, Raff, Raffle, → **REFUSE**, Scrap, Sewage, Spam, Stuff, Tinpot, Tinware, Tip, Tom(fool), Tosh, Totting, Trade, Tripe, Trouch, Truck, Trumpery, Twaddle

Rubbish heap Dump, Lay-stall, Sweepings, Toom

Rubble Brash, Debris, Detritus, Hard-core, Moellon, Random, Remains, Riprap, Talus

Rubidium Rb

Ruby Agate, Balas, Brazilian, Colorado, Cuprite, Oriental, Pigeon's blood, Port, Red, Spinel, Star, Starstone

Ruck Furrow, Scrum, Wrinkle

Rucksack Backpack, Bergen, Pickapack, Pikau

Ruction Ado, Fuss, Quarrel
Rudder Budget, Helm, Steerer
Ruddle Lemnian
Ruddy Bally, Bloody, Flashy, Florid, Red, Roseate, Rubicund, Rufous, Sanguine
Rude Abusive, Barbaric, Bear, Bestial, Bumpkin, Callow, Churlish, Coarse,
  Discourteous, Elemental, Goustrous, Green, Ill-bred, Impolite, Indecorous,
  Inficete, Ingram, Ingrum, Insolent, Ocker, Offensive, Peasant, Profane, Raw,
  Risqué, Rough, Simple, Surly, Unbred, Uncomplimentary, Uncourtly, Unlettered,
  Unmannered, Vulgar, Yobbish
Rudiment(ary), Rudiments ABC, Absey, Anlage, Beginning, Element, Embryo,
  Foundation, Germ(en), Germinal, Inchoate, Primordial, Seminal, Vestige
Rudolph Hess, Reindeer
Rue(ful) Boulevard, Dittany, Goat's, Harmala, Harmel, Herb of grace, Meadow,
  Mourn, Poignant, Regret, Repent, Rew, Ruta, Sorry, Wall
Ruff Collar, Crest, Fraise, Frill, Mane, Partlet, Pope, Rabato, Rebato, Ree, Trump
Ruffian Apache, Bashi-bazouk, Brute, Bully, Cut-throat, Desperado, Goon(da),
  Highbinder, Hoodlum, Hooligan, Keelie, Larrikin, Lout, Miscreant, Mohock,
  Myrmidon, Phansigar, Plug-ugly, Raff, Rowdy, Skinhead, Sweater, Tearaway, Thug,
  Toe-ragger, Trailbaston, Tumbler
▷ **Ruffle** *may indicate* an anagram
Ruffle(d) Bait, Dishevel, Falbala, Flounce, Fluster, Fret, → **FRILL**, Gather, Irritate,
  Jabot, Peplum, Rouse, Ruche, Rumple, Shirty, Tousle
Rug Afghan, Bearskin, Bergama, Buffalo-robe, Carpet, Drugget, Ensi, Flokati,
  Gabbeh, Hearth, Herez, Heriz, Kelim, K(h)ilim, Kirman, Lap robe, Mat, Maud,
  Numdah, Oriental, Pilch, Prayer, Runner, Rya, Scatter, Tatami, Throw, Travelling
Rugby (player) Back, Fifteen, Forward, Harlequin, League, Lion, Pack, Quin, RU,
  Scrum, Sevens, Threequarter, Touch, Union, Wing
Rugged Craggy, Harsh, Knaggy, Rough, Strong
Ruin(ed), Ruins Annihilate, Banjax, Bankrupt, Blast, Blight, Blue, Carcase,
  Collapse, Corrupt, Crash, Crock, Damn, Decay, Defeat, Demolish, Despoil, Destroy,
  Devastate, Dilapidation, Disfigure, Dish, Disrepair, Dogs, Doom, Downcome,
  Downfall, End, Fini, Fordo, Hamstring, Heap, Hell, Insolvent, Inure, Kaput(t),
  Kibosh, Loss, Mar, Mocers, Mockers, Mother's, Overthrow, Perdition, Perish,
  Petra, Pigs and whistles, Pot, Puckerood, Ravage, Reck, Relic, Scotch, Scupper,
  Scuttle, Shatter, Sink, Smash, Spill, → **SPOIL**, Stramash, Subvert, Undo, Unmade,
  Ur, Violate, Vitiate, Whelm, Woe, Wrack
▷ **Ruined** *may indicate* an anagram
Rule(r), Rules, Ruling Advantage, Algorithm, Align, Aristocrat, Arrêt, Article,
  Bylaw, Caesar, Calliper, Canon, Chain, Club-law, Code, Condominium,
  Constitution, Control, Criterion, Decree, Domineer, Dominion, Em, Empire, En,
  Establishment, Estoppel, Etiquette, Fatwa, Feint, Fetwa, Fleming's, Formation,
  Formula, Gag, Global, Golden, Govern, Govern-all, Ground, Gynocracy, Home,
  In, Institutes, Jackboot, Law, Leibniz's, Lesbian, Lex, Lindley, Liner, Majority,
  Matriarchy, Maxim, McNa(u)ghten, Mede, Meteyard, Method, Ministrate, Mistress,
  Mobocracy, Motto, Naismith's, Netiquette, Norm(a), Oppress, Ordinal, Organon,
  Organum, Pantocrator, Parallel, Parallelogram, Phase, Phrase-structure, Pie,
  Placitum, Plumb, Precedent, Precept, Prescript, Prevail, Principle, Protocol,
  Ptochocracy, Pye, Rafferty's, Raine, Realm, Reciprocity, Rector, Regal, Regnant,
  Regula, Reign, Rewrite, Ring, Rubric, Scammozzi's, Setting, Slide, Standard,
  Statute, Stylebook, Sutra, Sway, Ten-minute, Ten-yard, Three, Thumb,
  Transformation(al), Trapezoid, T-square, Tycoon, Tyrant, Uti possidetis, Wield

RULERS

1 letter:
K
R

3 letters:
Ban
Bey
Dey
Mir
Oba
Raj
Rex

4 letters:
Amir
Cham
Czar
Doge
Duce
Emir
Imam
Inca
Khan
King
Nero
Pope
Rana
Shah
Tsar
Vali
Wali

5 letters:
Ameer
Ardri
Dewan
Diwan
Henry
Herod
Hoyle
Hyleg
Judge
Mogul
Mpret
Mudir
Nawab
Negus
Nizam
Pasha
Queen

Rajah
Shaka
Sheik
Sophi
Sophy
Tenno

6 letters:
Atabeg
Atabek
Bosman
Caliph
Castro
Chagan
Cheops
Dergue
Despot
Dynast
Exarch
Franco
Führer
Gerent
Harold
Hitler
Judges
Kabaka
Kaiser
Mamluk
Manchu
Mikado
Peshwa
Prince
Rajput
Regent
Ronald
Sachem
Satrap
Sherif
Shogun
Sirdar
Sovran
Squier
Squire
Stalin
Sultan
Swaraj
Walter

7 letters:
Abbasid

Ardrigh
Bajayet
Bajazet
Bodicea
Catapan
Chogyal
Elector
Emperor
Gaekwar
Gaikwar
Jamshid
Jamshyd
Khedive
Miranda
Monarch
Omayyad
Pharaoh
Podesta
Rajpoot
Richard
Saladin
Serkali
Souldan
Toparch
Umayyad
Viceroy
Zamorin

8 letters:
Archduke
Autocrat
Bismarck
Boudicca
Burgrave
Caligula
Caudillo
Cromwell
Dictator
Ethnarch
Frederic
Heptarch
Hespodar
Hierarch
Maharaja
Mamaluke
Mameluke
Napoleon
Oligarch
Overlord
Padishah

Pericles
Reginald
Roderick
Sagamore
Sassanid
Suleiman
Suzerain
Synarchy
Tetrarch
Thearchy

9 letters:
Alexander
Amenhotep
Bretwalda
Britannia
Cleopatra
Cosmocrat
Frederick
Montezuma
Ochlocrat
Pendragon
Plutocrat
Potentate
President
Sovereign
Tamerlane

10 letters:
Caractacus
Plantocrat
Principate
Rajpramukh
Stratocrat

11 letters:
Charlemagne
Genghis Khan
Prester John
Queensberry
Stadtholder
Tutankhamun

12 letters:
Chandragupta

13 letters:
Haile Selassie

Rule-book Code, Pie, Pye

Rum(mer) Abnormal, Bacardi, Bay, Cachaca, Curious, Daiquiri, Demerara, Eerie, Eery, Glass, Grog, Island, Jamaica, Odd(er), Peculiar, Quaint, Queer, Screech, Strange, Tafia, Weird

▶ **Rumanian** *see* **ROUMANIAN**

Rumble, Rumbling Borborygmus, Brool, Curmurring, Drum-roll, Groan, Growl, Guess, Lumber, Mutter, Roll, Rumour, Thunder, Tonneau, Twig

Ruminant, Ruminate Antelope, Cabrie, Camel, Cavicornia, Cervid, Champ, Chew, Contemplate, Cow, Gemsbok, Gnu, Goat, Ibex, Meditate, Merycism, Nilgai, Nyala, Okapi, Oorial, Palebuck, Pecora, Pronghorn

Rummage Delve, Ferret, Fish, Foray, Fossick, Jumble, Powter, Ransack, Rifle, Root, Rootle, Scavenge, Search, Tot

Rummy Canasta, Cooncan, Game, Gin, Queer

Rumour Breeze, Bruit, Buzz, Canard, Cry, Fame, Furphy, → **GOSSIP**, Grapevine, Hearsay, Kite, Kite-flying, Mail, Noise, On-dit, Pig's-whisper, Report, Repute, Say-so, Smear, Tale, Talk, Underbreath, Unfounded, Vine, Voice, Whisper, Word

Rump Arse, Bottom, Buttocks, Croup(e), Croupon, Crupper, Curpel, Derrière, Nates, Parliament, Podex, Pygal, Steak, Uropygium

Rumple Corrugate, Crease, Mess, Muss, Touse, Tousle, Touze, Towse, Towze, Wrinkle

Rumpus Bagarre, Commotion, Noise, Rhubarb, Riot, Row, Ruction, Shemozzle, Shindig, Shindy, Shine, Stushie, Tirrivee, Uproar

Run(ning), Run away, Run into, Run off, Runny, Runs Admin(ister), Arpeggio, Black, Bleed, Blue, Bolt, Break, Bunk, Bye, Career, Chase, Chicken, Coop, Corso, Course, Cresta, Cross-country, Current, Cursive, Cursorial, Cut, Dart, Dash, Decamp, Diarrhoea, Dinger, Direct, Double, Dribble, Drive, Dry, Dummy, Enter, Escape, Extra, Fartlek, Flee, Flit, Flow, Fly, Follow, Fun, Fuse, Gad, Gallop, Gauntlet, Go, Green, Ground, Hare, Haste(n), Hennery, Hie, Hightail, Home, Idle, Jog, Jump bail, Ladder, Lauf, Leg, Leg bye, Lienteric, Liquid, Lope, Manage, Marathon, Melt, Milk, Mizzle, Mole, Molt, Monkey, Neume, Now, On, On-line, Operate, Pace, Pacific, Paper chase, Parkour, Pelt, Ply, Pour, Print, Purulent, R, Race, Range, Rear end, Red, Renne, Rin, Roadwork, Romp, Roulade, Rounder, Ruck, Scamper, Scapa, Scarpa, Scarper, School, Schuss, Scud, Scuddle, Scutter, Scuttle, See, Sequence, Shoot, Single, Skate, Skedaddle, Ski, Skid, Skirr, Skitter, Slalom, Slide, Smuggle, Spew, Split, Spread, Sprint, Sprue, Squitters, Stampede, Straight, Streak, Stream, Taxi, Tear, Tenor, Tie-breaker, Tirade, Trial, Trickle, Trill, Trot

Runaway Drain, Easy, Escapee, Fugie, Fugitive, Refugee

Run down Asperse, Belie, Belittle, Calumniate, Denigrate, Derelict, Detract, Dilapidated, Infame, Knock, Low, Obsolesce(nt), Poorly, Rack, Résumé, Scud, Seedy, Tirade, Traduce

Rune, Runic Ash, Futhark, Futhorc, Futhork, Kri, Ogham, Spell, Thorn, Wen, Wyn(n)

Rung Crossbar, Roundel, Rundle, Stave, Step, Tolled, Tread

Runner(s) Atalanta, Bean, Blade, Bow Street, Carpet, Coe, Courser, Dak, Deserter, Emu, Field, Geat, Gentleman, Gillie-wetfoot, Harrier, Hatta, Hencourt, Internuncio, Lampadist, Leg bye, Legman, Messenger, Miler, Milk, Mohr, Mousetrap, Nurmi, Owler, → **RIVER**, Rug, → **RUN(NING)**, Sarmentum, Scarlet, Series, Slipe, Smuggler, Stolon, Series, Tailskid, Trial

▷ **Running, Runny** *may indicate* an anagram

Runt Dilling, Oobit, Oubit, Reckling, Scalawag, Scrog, Smallest, Titman, Woobut, Woubit

Run through Impale, Pierce, Rehearsal
Runway Airstrip, Drive, Slipway, Strip, Tarmac®
Run wild Lamp, Rampage
Rupee(s) Lac, Lakh, Re
Rupert Bear
Rupture Breach, Burst, Crack, Enterocele, Hernia, Rend, Rhexis, Rift, Scissure, Split
Rural Agrarian, Agrestic, Boo(h)ai, Booay, Boondocks, Bucolic, Country,
   Cracker-barrel, Forane, Georgic, Hick, Mofussil, Platteland, Praedial, Predial,
   Redneck, Rustic, Sticks, The Shires, Upland, Wop-wops
Ruse Artifice, Decoy, Dodge, Engine, Hoax, Pawk, Stratagem, → **TRICK**
Rush(ed) Accelerate, Barge, Bolt, Bustle, Career, Charge, Dart, Dash, Eriocaulon,
   Expedite, Faze, Feese, Feeze, Feze, Fly, Forty-nine, Frail, Friar, Gad, Gold, Gust,
   Hare, Hasten, High-tail, Horsetail, → **HURRY**, Hurtle, Jet, Juncus, Lance, Lash,
   Leap, Luzula, Moses, Odd-man, Onset, Palmiet, Pellmell, Phase, Pheese, Pheeze,
   Phese, Plunge, Pochard, Precipitate, Railroad, Rampa(u)ge, Rash, Rayle, Reed,
   Rip, Scamp(er), Scirpus, Scour, Scramble, Scud, Scurry, Sedge, Shave-grass, Spate,
   Speed, Stampede, Star(r), Streak, Streek, Surge, Swoop, Swoosh, Tear, Thrash,
   Thresh, Tilt, Torrent, Tule, Viretot, Whoosh, Zap, Zoom
Rusk Zwieback
Russell AE, Bertrand, Jack
Russet Rutile
Russia(n), Russian headman, Russian villagers Apparatchik, Ataman,
   Belorussian, Beria, Bolshevik, Boris, Boyar, Byelorussian, Cesarevitch, Chechen,
   Chukchee, Chukchi, Circassian, Cossack, Dressing, D(o)ukhobor, Esth, Igor,
   Ingush, Ivan, Kabardian, Kalmuk, Kalmyck, Leather, Lett, Mari, Menshevik,
   Mingrel(ian), Minimalist, Mir, Misha, Muscovy, Octobrist, Osset(e), Red, Romanov,
   Rus, Russ(niak), Russki, Ruthene, Salad, Serge, Sergei, Slav, Stakhanovite, SU,
   Thistle, Udmurt, Uzbeg, Uzbek, Vladimir, Vogul, White, Yakut, Yuri, Zyrian
Rust(y) Aeci(di)um, Blister, Brown, Corrode, Cor(ro)sive, Erode, Etch, Ferrugo,
   Iron oxide, Iron-stick, Maderise, Oxidise, Puccinia, Rubiginous, Soare, Stem,
   Teleutospore, Telium, Uredine, Uredo, Verdigris, Yellow
Rust-fungus Aecidiospore
Rustic Arcady, Bacon, Bor(r)el(l), Bucolic, Bumpkin, Carl, Chawbacon, Churl,
   Clodhopper, Clown, Corydon, Cracker-barrel, Culchie, Damon, Doric, Forest,
   Georgic, Hayseed, Hick, Hillbilly, Hind, Hob, Hobbinoll, Hodge, Homespun,
   Idyl(l), Pastorale, Peasant, Pr(a)edial, Put(t), Rube, Rural, Strephon, Swain, Sylvan,
   Uplandish, Villager, Villatic, Yokel
▷ **Rustic** *may indicate* an anagram
Rusticate Banish, Seclude
Rustle(r), Rustling Abactor, Crinkle, Duff, Fissle, Frou-frou, Gully-raker, Poach,
   Speagh(ery), Sprechery, Steal, Stir, Susurration, Swish, Thief, Whig
Rust-proof Zinced
Rut Channel, Furrow, Groove, Heat, Routine, Sulcus, Track
Ruth Babe, Compassion, Mercy, Pity, Remorse
Ruthenium Ru
Rutherfordium Rf
Ruthless Brutal, Cruel, Dog eat dog, Fell, Hard, Hardball, Hard-bitten
Rwanda(n) Tutsi
Rye Gentleman, Grain, Grass, Spelt, Whisky

Ss

S Ogee, Saint, Second, Sierra, Society, South, Square
SA It, Lure
Sabbatarian Wee Free
Sabbath Juma, Lord's Day, Rest-day, Shabbat, Sunday, Witches'
Sabbatical Leave
Sabine Horace, Women
Sable American, Black, Jet, Negro, Pean, Zibel(l)ine
Sabotage, Saboteur Cripple, Destroy, Frame-breaker, Hacktivism, Ratten, Spoil, Treachery, Undermine, Vandalise, Worm, Wrecker
Sabre, Sabre rattler Jingo, Sword, Tulwar
Sabrina Severn
Sac Air, Allantois, Amnion, Aneurism, Aneurysm, Bag, Bladder, Bursa, Caecum, Castoreum, Cisterna, Cyst, Diverticulum, Embryo, Follicle, Pericardium, Peritoneum, Pod, Scrotum, Spermatheca, Tylose, Tylosis, Vesica, Vocal, Yolk
Saccharine Dulcite, Dulcose
Sack(cloth), Sacking Bag, Bed, Boot, Bounce, Budget, Burlap, Can, Cashier, Chasse, Chop, Coal, Congé, Congee, Dash, Depose, Depredate, Despoil, Discharge, Doss, Fire, Gunny, Havoc, Hessian, Hop-pocket, Jute, Knap, Lay waste, Loot, Mailbag, Mat, Maraud, Mitten, Pillage, Plunder, Poke, Postbag, Push, Raid, Rapine, Reave, Replace, Rieve, Road, Rob, Sad, Sanbenito, Sherris, Sherry, Spoliate, Vandalise
▷ **Sacks** *may indicate* an anagram
Sacrament Baptism, Christening, Communion, Confirmation, Eucharist, Extreme unction, Housel, Lord's Supper, Matrimony, Nagmaal, Orders, Penance, Promise, Reconciliation, Ritual, Unction, Viaticum
Sacred (object), Sacred place Adytum, Churinga, Divine, Hallowed, Harem, Harim, Heart, Hierurgy, → **HOLY**, Ineffable, Manito(u), Nine, Omphalos, Padma, Pietà, Sacrosanct, Sanctum, Taboo, Tapu, Temenos
Sacrifice Alcestic, Cenote, Corban, Cost, Forego, Gambit, Gehenna, Hecatomb, Holocaust, Immolate, Iphigenia, Isaac, Lay down, Molech, Moloch, Molochize, Oblation, → **OFFERING**, Peace offering, Relinquish, Sati, Suovetaurilia, Supreme, Surrender, Suttee, Taurobolium, Tophet, Vicarious, Victim
Sacrilege, Sacrilegious Blaspheme, Impiety, Profane, Violation
Sacristan, Sacristy Diaconicon, Sceuophylax, Sexton
Sacrosanct Inviolable
Sad(den), Sadly, Sadness Alas, Attrist, Blue, Con dolore, Dejected, Depressed, Desolate, Disconsolate, Dismal, Doleful, Dolour, Downcast, Drear, Dull, Dumpy, Fadeur, Forlorn, Heartache, Lovelorn, Low, Lugubrious, Mesto, Mournful, Niobe, Oh, Plangent, Sorrowful, Sorry, Tabanca, Tearful, Tear-jerker, Threnody, Tragic, Triste, Tristesse, Unhappy, Wan, Weltschmerz, Wo(e)begone
Saddle (bag, cloth, flap, girth, pad) Alforja, Aparejo, Arson, Burden, Cantle, Cinch, Col, Crupper, Demipique, Kajawah, Lumber, Numnah, Oppress, Pack, Pad,

Panel, Pigskin, Pilch, Pillion, Seat, Sell(e), Shabrack, Shabracque, Side, Skirt, Stock, Tree, Western

Saddle-bow Arson

Saddler Whittaw(er)

Sadie Thompson

Sadism, Sadistic Algolagnia, Cruel

▷ **Sadly** *may indicate* an anagram

Safari Expedition, Hunt

Safe(ty) Active, Allright, Almery, Ambry, Awmrie, Coolgardie, Copper-bottomed, Delouse, Deposit, GRAS, Harmless, Hunk, Immunity, Impunity, Inviolate, Keister, Meat, Night, Passive, Peter, Reliable, Roadworthy, Sanctuary, Secure, Sound, Strong-box, Strongroom, Sure, Whole-skinned, Worthy

Safebreaker Yegg

Safeguard Bulwark, Caution, Ensure, Fail-safe, Frithborh, Fuse, Hedge, Palladium, Protection, Register, Ward

Saffron Bastard, Crocus, False, Meadow, Mock, Yellow

Sag(gy) Decline, Dip, Droop, Hang, Hogged, Lop, Slump, Swayback, Wilt

Saga Aga, Chronicle, Edda, Epic, Icelandic, Laxdale, Legend, Odyssey, Volsunga

Sagacity, Sagacious Astute, Commonsense, Depth, Elephant, Judgement, Sapience, Wisdom

Sage(s) Abaris, Aquinian, Bactrian, Bias, Carlyle, Cheronian, Chilo(n), Clary, Cleobulus, Confucius, Counsellor, Egghead, Greybeard, Hakam, Herb, Imhotep, Jerusalem, Maharishi, Mahatma, Malmesbury, Manu, Mirza, Orval, Pandit, Periander, Philosopher, Pittacus, Rishi, Salvia, Savant, Seer, Seven, Solon, Tagore, Thales, Wiseacre, Wood

Sage-brush Nevada

Sago Portland

Saharan Hassaniya, Sahrawi

Sahelian Chad, Mali, Mauritania, Niger

Sahib Burra, Pukka

Said Co, Emir, Port, Quo(th), Related, Reputed, Spoken, Stated

▷ **Said** *may indicate* 'sounding like'

Sail(s), Sailing Balloon, Bunt, Canvas, Circumnavigate, Cloth, Coast, Course, Cross-jack, Cruise, Drag, Drift, Fan, Fore(course), Fore-and-aft, Full, Gaff(-topsail), Gennaker, Genoa, Goose-wing, Head, Jib, Jigger, Jut, Land, Lateen, Leech, Luff, Lug, Moon, Moonraker, Muslin, Navigate, Orthodromy, Parachute spinnaker, Peak, Plain, Plane, Ply, Rag, Reef, Rig, Ring-tail, Royal, Sheet, Shoulder-of-mutton, Smoke, Solar, Spanker, Spencer, Spinnaker, Spritsail, Square, Staysail, Steer, Storm-jib, Studding, Stun, Suit, Top(-gallant), Top-hamper, Van, Vela, Wardrobe, Water, Yard

Sailor(s) AB, Admiral, Anson, Argonaut, Blue-jacket, Boatman, Boatswain, Bos'n, Bos(u)n, Budd, Canvas-climber, Commodore, Crew, Deckhand, Drake, Evans, Foremastman, Freshwater, Galiongee, Gob, Greenhand, Grommet, Hat, Hearties, Helmsman, Hornblower, Hydronaut, Jack, Janty, Jauntie, Jaunty, Jonty, Khalasi, Killick, Killock, Kroo(boy), Krooman, Kru(boy), Kruman, Lascar, Leadsman, Limey, Loblolly boy, Lt, Lubber, Mariner, Matelot, Matlo(w), Middy, MN, Nelson, Noah, NUS, Oceaner, Oldster, OS, Polliwog, Pollywog, Popeye, Powder monkey, Privateer, Rating, RN, Salt, Seabee, Seacunny, Sea-dog, Sea-lord, → **SEAMAN**, Serang, Shellback, Sin(d)bad, Stowaway, Submariner, Swabber, Tar, Tarp(aulin), Tarry-breeks, Tindal, Topman, Triton, Waister, Wandering, Water-dog, Wave, Wren, Yachtsman

Saint(ly), Saints Agatha, Agnes, Aidan, Alban, Alexis, Aloysius, Alvis, Ambrose, Andrew, Anselm, Anthony, Asaph, Audrey, Augustine, Barbara, Barnabas, Bartholomew, Basil, Bees, Benedict, Bernard, Bernardette, Boniface, Brandan, Brendan, Bridget, Brigid, Canonise, Canonize, Catharine, Cecilia, Chad, Christopher, Clement, Columba(n), Crispian, Crispin(ian), Cuthbert, Cyr, David, Denis, Denys, Diego, Dominic, Dorothea, Dunstan, Dymphna, Elmo, Eloi, Elvis, Eulalie, Francis, Genevieve, George, Gertrude, Giles, Hagiology, Hallowed, Helena, Hilary, Hilda, Holy, Hugh, Ignatius, Isidore, James, Jerome, John, Joseph, Jude, Just, Kentigern, Kevin, Kilda, Latterday, Lawrence, Leger, Leonard, Linus, Loyola, Lucy, Luke, Malo, Margaret, Mark, Martha, Martin, Matthew, Michael, Monica, Mungo, Nicholas, Ninian, Odyl, Olaf, Oswald, Pancras, Patrick, Patron, Paul(inus), Peter, Pi, Pillar, Plaster, Polycarp, Quentin, Regulus, Ride, Rishi, Roch, Ronan, Roque, Rosalie, Rule, S, Sebastian, Severus, Simeon, Simon, Simon Zelotes, SS, St, Stanislaus, Stephen, Sunday, Swithin, Templar, Teresa, Thaumaturgus, Thecia, Theresa, Thomas, Tobias, Ursula, Valentine, Veronica, Vincent, Vitus, Walstan, Wilfred, William, Winifred

Sake Account, Behalf, Cause, Drink

Sal Nitre, Salt, Volatile

Salacious, Salacity Fruity, Lewd, Lust, Obscene, Scabrous

Salad Beetroot, Burnet, Caesar, Calaloo, Calalu, Chef's, Chicon, Coleslaw, Corn, Cos, Cress, Cucumber, Days, Endive, Escarole, Fennel, Finnochio, Finoc(c)hio, Frisée, Fruit, Greek, Guacamole, Horiatiki, Lactuca, Lamb's lettuce, Lettuce, Lovage, Mesclum, Mesclun, Mixture, Niçoise, Purslane, Radicchio, Radish, Rampion, Rocket, Rojak, Roquette, Russian, Salmagundi, Salmagundy, Slaw, Tabbouleh, Tabbouli, Tomato, Waldorf, Word

▷ **Salad** *may indicate* an anagram

Salamander Axolotl, Congo eel, Ewt, Hellbender, Lizard, Menopome, Mole, Mudpuppy, Olm, Proteus, Siren, Snake, Spring-keeper

Salami, Salami technique Fraud, Peperoni

Salary Emolument, Fee, Hire, Pay, Prebend, Screw, Stipend, → **WAGE**

Sale(s) Auction, Breeze up, Cant, Car-boot, Clearance, Farm-gate, Fire, Garage, Jumble, Market, Outroop, Outrope, Pitch, Raffle, Retail, Roup, Rummage, Subhastation, Trade, Turnover, Upmarket, Venal, Vend, Vendue, Vent, Voetstoets, Voetstoots, Warrant, Wash, White, Wholesale, Yard

Saleroom Pantechnicon

Salesman, Saleswoman Agent, Assistant, Bagman, Broker, Buccaneer, Bummaree, Counterhand, Counter jumper, Drummer, Huckster, Loman, Pedlar, Rep, Retailer, Tallyman, Tout, Traveller, Vendeuse

Salient Coign, Jut, Projection, Prominent, Redan, Spur

Salisbury Cecil, Sarum

Saliva Drool, Parotid, Ptyalism, Sial(oid), Slobber, Spawl, Spit(tle), Sputum

Sallow Adust, Pallid, Pasty, Sale, Sauch, Saugh, Wan

Sally Aunt, Boutade, Charge, Dash, Escape, Excursion, Flight, Foray, Issue, Jest, Mot, Pleasantry, Quip, Ride, Sarah, Sortie, Wisecrack, Witticism

Salmagundi Mess

Salmon Alevin, Atlantic, Australian, Baggit, Blueback, Blue-cap, Boaz, Burnett, Chinook, Chum, Cock, Coho(e), Dog, Dorado, Grav(ad)lax, Grayling, Grilse, Humpback, Kelt, Keta, King, Kipper, Kokanee, Lax, Ligger, Lox, Masu, Mort, Nerka, Oncorhynchus, Ouananiche, Par(r), Peal, Pink, Quinnat, Red, Redfish, Rock, Samlet, Shedder, Silver, Skegger, Slat, Smelt, Smolt, Smout, Smowt, Sockeye, Sparling, Spirling, Springer, Sprod, Umber

Salon, Saloon Barrel-house, Car, Hall, Honkytonk, Last chance, Lounge, Nail bar, Pullman, Sedan, Shebang, Tavern

Salt(s), Salty AB, Acid, Alginate, Aluminate, Andalusite, Antimonite, Arsenite, Aspartite, Attic, Aurate, Azide, Base, Bath, Benzoate, Bicarbonate, Bichromate, Borate, Borax, Brackish, Brine, Bromate, Bromide, Capr(o)ate, Caprylate, Carbamate, Carbonate, Carboxylate, Celery, Cerusite, Chlorate, Chlorite, Chromate, Citrate, Complex, Corn, Cure(d), Cyanate, Cyclamate, Datolite, Deer lick, Diazonium, Dichromate, Dioptase, Dithionate, Double, Enos, Eosin, Epsom, Ferricyanide, Formate, Glauber, Glutamate, Halite, Halo-, Health, Hydrochloride, Hygroscopic, Iodide, Ioduret, Isocyanide, Kosher, Lactate, Lake-basin, Lithate, Liver, Magnesium, Malate, Malonate, Manganate, Mariner, Matelot, Microcosmic, Monohydrate, Mucate, Muriate, NaCl, Nitrate, Nitrite, Oleate, Orthoborate, Orthosilicate, Osm(i)ate, Oxalate, Palmitate, Pandermite, Perborate, Perchlorate, Periodate, Phosphate, Phosphite, Phthalate, Picrate, Piquancy, Plumbate, Plumbite, Potassium, Powder, Propionate, Pyruvate, Rating, Reh, Resinate, Rochelle, Rock, Rosinate, Sailor, Sal ammoniac, Salify, Sal volatile, Saut, Sea-dog, Seafarer, Seasoned, Sebate, Selenate, Smelling, Soap, Sodium, Solar, Sorrel, Stannate, Stearate, Suberate, Succinate, Sulfite, Sulphate, Sulphite, Sulphonate, Table, Tannate, Tantalate, Tartrate, Tellurate, Tellurite, Thiocyanate, Thiosulphate, Titanate, Tungstate, Uranin, Urao, Urate, Vanadate, Volatile, Water-dog, White, Wit(ty), Xanthate

Salt meat Mart

Saltpetre Caliche, Chile, Cubic, Nitre, Norway

Salt-water Sea

Salubrious Healthy, Sanitary, Wholesome

Salutary Beneficial, Good, Wholesome

Salutation, Salute Address, Asalam-wa-leikum, Australian, Ave, Banzai, Barcoo, Bid, Cap, Cheer, Command, Coupé(e), Curtsey, Embrace, Feu de joie, Fly-past, Genuflect, Greet, Hail, Hallo, Halse, Homage, Honour, Jambo, Kiss, Middle finger, Namas kar, Namaste, Present, Salaam, Salvo, Sieg Heil, Toast, Tribute, Wassail

Salvador Dali

Salvage Dredge, Lagan, Ligan, Reclaim, Recover, Recycle, Rescue, Retrieve, Tot

Salvation(ist) Booth, Redemption, Rescue, Socinian, Soterial, Yeo

Salve Anele, Anoint, Assuage, Ave, Lanolin(e), Lotion, Ointment, Remedy, Saw, Tolu, Unguent, Weapon

Salver Tray, Waiter

Salvo Fusillade, Salute, Volley

Sal volatile Hartshorn

Sam Browse, Soapy, Uncle, Weller

Samara Ash-key

Samaritan Good

Samarium Sm

Same(ness) Ae, Agnatic, Contemporaneous, Do, Egal, Ejusd(en), Equal, Ib(id), Ibidem, Id, Idem, Identical, Identity, Ilk, Iq, Like, One, Thick(y), Thilk, Uniform, Ylke

Samovar Urn

Samoyed Dog, Uralian, Uralic

Sample, Sampling Amniocentesis, Biopsy, Blad, Browse, Example, Fare, Foretaste, Handout, Matched, Muster, Pattern, Pree, Prospect, Quadrat, Quota, Scantling, Smear, Snip, Specimen, Spread, Stratified, Swatch, Switch, → **TASTE**, Taster, Transect, Try

Samuel Pepys, Smiles
Samurai Ronin
▷ **Sam Weller** *may indicate* the use of 'v' for 'w' or vice versa
Sanctify Consecrate, Purify, Saint
Sanctimonious Banbury, Creeping Jesus, Devout, Goody-goody, Holy, Pi, Religiose, Righteous, Saintly
Sanction(s), Sanctioned Allow, Appro, Approbate, Approof, Approve, Assent, Authorise, Bar, Countenance, Economic, Endorse, Fiat, Green light, Imprimatur, Legitimate, Mandate, OK, Pass, Pragmatic, Ratify, Smart, Sustain, Upstay, Warrant
Sanctities, Sanctity Halidom, Holiness, Hollidam, Sonties
Sanctuary, Sanctum Adytum, Asylum, By-room, Cella, Ch, Church, Delubrum, Frithsoken, Frithstool, Girth, Grith, Holy, Kaaba, Lair, Naos, Oracle, Penetralia, Preserve, Refuge, Sacellum, Sacrarium, → **SHELTER**, Shrine, Tabernacle, Temple
Sand(s), Sandbank, Sandbar, Sandy Alec, Alex, Alexander, Areg, Arena(ceous), Arenose, Arkose, As, Atoll, Bar, Barchan(e), Bark(h)an, Beach, Caliche, Dene, Desert, Dogger Bank, Down, Dudevant, Dune, Dupin, Eremic, Erg, Esker, Foundry, Gat, George, Ginger, Goodwin, Grain, Granulose, Hazard, Hurst, Light, Loess, Machair, Nore, Oil, Overslaugh, Podsol, Podzol, Portlandian, Psammite, Ridge, River, Sabulous, Sawney, Seif dune, Shelf, Shoal, Shore, Singing, Tar, Tee, Time, Tombolo
Sandal(s) Alpargata, Buskin, Calceamentum, Chappal, Espadrille, Flip-flop, Ganymede, Geta, Huarache, Jelly, Patten, Pump, Slip-slop, Talaria, Thong, Zori
Sandalwood Algum, Almug, Chypre, Pride, Santal
Sandarac Arar
Sander Pike-perch
Sandgroper Pioneer
Sandhopper Amphipod
Sandhurst RMA
Sand-loving Ammophilous, Psammophil
Sandpiper Bird, Dunlin, Knot, Oxbird, Ree, Ruff, Sandpeep, Stint, Terek
Sandstone Arkose, Calciferous, Cat's brains, Dogger, Fa(i)kes, Flysch, Grit, Hassock, Holystone, Itacolumite, Kingle, Molasse, New Red, Old Red, Psammite, Quartzite, Red, Sarsen, Silica
Sandstorm Haboob, Tebbad
Sandwich(es) Bruschetta, Butty, Club, Clubhouse, Croque-monsieur, Cuban, Doorstep, Earl, Hamburger, Hoagie, Island, Jeely piece, Open, Panini, Piece, Roti, Round, Sanger, Sango, Sarmie, Sarney, Sarnie, Smørbrød, Smörgåsbord, Smørrebrød, Stottie, Sub, Submarine, Tartine, Thumber, Toastie, Toebie, Triple-decker, Twitcher, Victoria, Wad, Zak(o)uski
▷ **Sandwich(es)** *may indicate* a hidden word
Sane, Sanity Compos mentis, Formal, Healthy, Judgement, Rational, Reason, Right-minded, Sensible, Wice
Sangfroid Aplomb, Cool, Poise
Sanguine Confident, Haemic, Hopeful, Optimistic, Roseate, Ruddy
Sanitary Hygienic, Salubrious, Sterile
Sanskrit Bhagavad-Gita, Panchatantra, Purana, Ramayana, Sutra, Upanishad, Vedic
Santa (Claus) Abonde, Kriss Kringle, Secret
Sap Benzoin, Bleed, Cremor, Drain, Enervate, Entrench, Ichor, Juice, Laser, Latex, Lymph, Mine, Mug, Pulque, Ratten, Resin, Roset, Rosin, Rozet, Rozit, Secretion, Soma, Sura, Swot, Undermine, Weaken
Sapid Flavoursome, Savoury, Tasty

Sapience, Sapient Discernment, Sage, Wisdom

Sapling Ash-plant, Flittern, Ground-ash, Plant, Tellar, Teller, Tiller, Youth

Sapper(s) Miner, RE

Sapphire Star, Water, White

Sappho Lesbian

Sapwood Alburnum

Sarah Battle, Gamp, Sal

Sarcasm, Sarcastic Acidity, Antiphrasis, Biting, Cutting, Cynical, Derision, Irony, Mordacious, Mordant, Pungent, Quip, Quotha, Sarky, Satire, Sharp, Sharp-tongued, Smartmouth, Snide, Sting, Wisecrack

Sardine Fish, Sard

Sardonic Cutting, Cynical, Ironical, Scornful, Wry

Sargasso Ore, Sea(weed)

Sark Chemise, CI, Shirt

Sarong Sulu

SAS Red Devils

Sash Baldric(k), Band, Belt, Burdash, Cummerbund, Fillister, Lungi, Obi, Scarf, Window

Sassaby Tsessebe

Sassenach English, Lowlander, Pock-pudding

Satan Adversary, Apollyon, Arch-enemy, Cram, → **DEVIL**, Eblis, Evil One, Lucifer, Prince of darkness, Shaitan, Tempter, The old serpent

Satchel Bag, Scrip

Sate(d), Satiate Cloy, Glut, Replete, Sad, Surfeit

Satellite Adrastea, Ananke, Ariel, Artificial, Astra, Atlas, Attendant, Aussat, Belinda, Bianca, Bird, Callisto, Calypso, Camenae, Carme, Charon, Communications, Comsat®, Cordelia, Cosmos, Cressida, Deimos, Desdemona, Despina, Dione, Disciple, Early bird, Earth, Echo, Elara, Enceladus, Europa, Explorer, Fixed, Follower, Galatea, Galilean, Ganymede, Geostationary, Helene, Henchman, Himalia, Hipparchus, Hyperion, Iapetus, Intelsat, Io, Janus, Lackey, Larissa, Leda, Lysithea, Meteorological, Metis, Mimas, Miranda, Moon, Mouse, Nereid, Oberon, Ophelia, Orbiter, Pan, Pandora, Pasiphae, Phobos, Phoebe, Planet, Portia, Prometheus, Puck, Rhea, Rosalind, Sinope, Space probe, SPOT, Sputnik, Syncom, Telesto, Telstar, Tethys, Thalassa, Thebe, Tiros, Titan, Titania, Triton, Umbriel, Weather

▸ **Satin** *see* **SILK**

Satire, Satirical, Satirist Arbuthnot, Archilochus, Burlesque, Butler, Candide, Chaldee, Dryden, Horace, Iambographer, Juvenal, Lampoon, Lash, Lucian, Mazarinade, Menippean, Mockery, Pantagruel, Parody, Pasquil, Pasquin(ade), Pope, Raillery, Sarky, Sotadic, Spoof, Squib, Swift, Travesty, Wasps

Satisfaction, Satisfactory, Satisfy(ing), Satisfied, Satisfactorily Adequate, Agree, Ah, Ap(p)ay, Appease, Assuage, Atone, Change, Compensation, Complacent, → **CONTENT**, Defrayment, Enough, Feed, Fill, Fulfil, Glut, Gratify, Happy camper, Indulge, Jake, Job, Liking, Meet, OK, Okey-dokey, Pacation, Palatable, Pay, Please, Pride, Propitiate, Qualify, Redress, Repay, Replete, Sate, Satiate, Serve, Settlement, Slake, Square, Suffice, Supply, Tickety-boo, Well

Saturate(d) Drench, Glut, Imbue, Impregnate, Infuse, Permeate, → **SOAK**, Sodden, Steep, Waterlog

Saturday Holy, Sabbatine

Saturn God, Kronos, Lead, Planet, Rocket

Satyr Faun, Leshy, Lesiy, Libertine, Marsyas, Pan, Silen(us), Woodhouse, Woodwose

Sauce, Saucy Agrodolce, Alfredo, Allemanse, Apple, Arch, Baggage, Barbecue, Béarnaise, Béchamel, Bigarade, Bold(-faced), Bolognese, Bordelaise, Bourguignonne, Bread, Brown, Caper, Carbonara, Catchup, Catsup, Chasseur, Chaudfroid, Cheek, Chilli, Chutney, Condiment, Coulis, Cranberry, Cream, Creme anglaise, Cumberland, Custard, Dapper, Dip, Dressing, Enchilada, Espagnole, Fenberry, Fondue, Fricasseé, Fudge, Fu yong, Fu yung, Gall, Garum, Gravy, Hard, Hoisin, Hollandaise, Horseradish, HP®, Impudence, Jus, Ketchup, Lip, Malapert, Marinade, Marinara, Matelote, Mayonnaise, Melba, Meunière, Mint, Mirepoix, Mole, Monkeygland, Mornay, Mousseline, Nam pla, Nerve, Newburg, Nuoc mam, Oxymal, Oyster, Panada, Parsley, Passata, Peart, Peking, Pert, Pesto, Piert, Piri-piri, Pistou, Pizzaiola, Ponzu, Portugaise, Ravigote, Relish, Remoulade, Rouille, Roux, Sabayon, Sal, Salad cream, Salpicon, Salsa, Salsa verde, Sambal, Sass, Satay, Shoyu, Soja, Soubise, Soy, Soya, Stroganoff, Sue, Supreme, Sweet and sour, Tabasco®, Tamari, Tartar(e), Tomato, Topping, Tossy, Velouté, Vinaigrette, White, Wine, Worcester, Worcestershire
Sauceboat-shaped Scaphocephalate
Saucepan Chafer, Goblet, Skillet, Steamer, Stockpot
Saucer Ashtray, Discobolus, Flying, Pannikin, UFO
Sauna Banya, Bath, Sudatorium, Sudorific
Saunter Amble, Dacker, Da(i)ker, Dander, Lag, Mosey, Promenade, Roam, Shool, Stroll, Toddle
Sausage(s) Andouille, Andouillette, Banger, Black pudding, Blood, Boerewors, Bologna, Boudin, Bratwurst, Cervelat, Cheerio, Chipolata, Chorizo, Corn dog, Cumberland, Devon, Drisheen, Frankfurter, Hot dog, Kielbasa, Kishke, Knackwurst, Knockwurst, Liver(wurst), Lorne, Mortadella, Mystery bag, Pep(p)eroni, Polony, Pudding, Salami, Sav(eloy), Snag(s), Snarler, Square, String, Weenie, Weeny, White pudding, Wiener(wurst), Wienie, Wurst, Zampone
Sausage-shaped Allantoid
Sauté Fry
Savage Ape, Barbarian, Boor, Brute, Cannibal, Cruel, Feral, Fierce, Frightful, Grim, Gubbins, Immane, Inhuman, Maul, Noble, Sadistic, Truculent, Vitriolic, Wild
Savanna Plain, Sahel
Savant Expert, Mahatma, Sage, Scholar
Save, Saving(s) Bank, Bar, Besides, But, Capital, Conserve, Cut-rate, Deposit, Economy, Except, Hain, Hoard, Husband, ISA, Keep, Layby, National, Nest egg, Nirlie, Nirly, Not, PEPS, Post office, Preserve, Put by, Reclaim, Redeem, Relieve, Reprieve, → **RESCUE**, Reskew, Sa', Salt, Salvage, Scrape, Scrimp, Shortcut, Slate club, Soak away, Sock away, Sou-sou, Spare, Stokvel, Succour, Susu, TESSA, Unless
Saviour Deliverer, Jesu(s), Messiah, Redeemer
Savour(ed), Savoury Aigrette, Bouchée, Canapé, Devils-on-horseback, Essence, Fag(g)ot, Flavour, Olent, Ramekin, Relish, Resent, Sair, Sapid, Sar, Smack, Starter, Tang, → **TASTE**, Umami, Vol au vent
Savoy Cabbage, Opera
Saw Adage, Aphorism, Apothegm, Azebiki, Back, Band, Beheld, Bucksaw, Buzz, Chain, Circular, Cliché, Compass, Coping, Cross-cut, Crown, Cut, Dictum, Dovetail, Dozuki, Flooring, Frame, Fret, Gang, Glimpsed, Gnome, Grooving, Hack, Hand, Jig, Keyhole, Legend, Log, Maxim, Met, Motto, Pad, Panel, Paroemia, Pitsaw, Proverb, Pruning, Quarter, Rabbeting, Rack, Ribbon, Rip, Ryoba, Sash, Saying, Scroll, Serra, Skil®, Skip-tooth, Slasher, Slogan, Span, Spied, Stadda, Stone, Sweep, Tenon, Trepan, Trephine, Whip, Witnessed
Sawbones Surgeon

Saw-toothed Runcinate

Sawyer Logger, Tom

Saxifrage Astilbe, Bishop's cap, Burnet, Golden, Heuchera, London pride, Mitre-wort, St Patrick's cabbage

Saxon Cedric, Hengist, Wend

Saxophone Axe

Say, Saying(s) Adage, Agrapha, Allege, Aphorism, Apophthegm, Apostrophise, Articulate, Axiom, Beatitude, Bon mot, Bromide, Byword, Cant, Catchphrase, Cliché, Declare, Dict(um), Eg, Enunciate, Epigram, Expatiate, Express, Fadaise, For instance, Gnome, Impute, Logia, Logion, → **MAXIM**, Mean, Mot, Mouth, Observe, Predicate, Pronounce, Proverb, Put, Quip, Recite, Rede, Relate, Remark, Report, Saine, Saw, Sc, Sententia, → **SPEAK**, Suppose, Sutra, Utter, Voice, Word

▷ **Say, Saying(s)** *may indicate* a word sounding like another

Scab(by) Blackleg, Crust, Eschar, Leggism, Leprose, Mangy, Rat, Scald, Scall, Sore, Strike-breaker

Scabbard Frog, Pitcher, Sheath, Tsuba

Scabies Itch, Psora, Scotch fiddle

Scabrous Harsh, Rough, Thersites

Scaffold(ing), Scaffolder Gallows, Gantry, Hoarding, Putlock, Putlog, Rig, Spiderman, Stage

Scald Blanch, Burn, Leep, Ploat, Plot

▷ **Scale(d)** *may indicate* a fish

Scale(s), Scaly Analemma, API gravity, Ascend, Balance, Baumé, Beaufort, Binet-Simon, Bismar, Brix, Bud, Burnham, Celsius, Centigrade, Ceterach, Chromatic, → **CLIMB**, Cottony-cushion, Dandruff, Desquamate, Diagonal, Diatonic, Douglas, Elo, Enharmonic(al), Escalade, Fahrenheit, Flake, Fujita, Full, Furfur, Gamme, Gamut, Ganoid, Gapped, Gauge, Gravity, Gunter's, Heptatonic, Hexachord, Humidex, Indusium, Interval, Kelvin, Ladder, Lamina, Layer, Leaf, Lepid, Lepidote, Leprose, Libra, Ligule, Likert, Lodicule, Loricate, Magnitude, Major, Mercalli, Mesel, Minor, Mohs, Munsell, Natural, Nominal, Octad, Ordinal, Palea, Palet, Patagium, Peel, Pentatonic, Pholidosis, Placoid, Plate, Platform, Ramentum, → **RANGE**, Rankine, Ratio, Réaumur, Regulo, Richter, San Jose, Scan, Scarious, Scent, Scincoid, Scurf, Scutellate, Shin, Skink, Sliding, Speel, Spring, Squama, Squame(lla), Submediant, Tegmentum, Tegula, Tonal, Tridymite, Tron(e), Unified, Vernier, Wage, Weighbridge, Wentworth, Whole-tone, Wind

Scallion Leek

Scallop(ed) Bivalve, Clam, Coquille, Crenate, Escalop, Frill, Gimp, Mush, Pecten, Queenie, Vandyke

Scallywag Rascal, Scamp, Skeesicks, Whippersnapper

Scalp Cut, Scrape, Skin, Trophy

Scalpel Bistoury, Knife

Scam Ramp

Scamp Fripon, Imp, Limb, Lorel, Lorrell, Losel, Lozell, Neglect, → **RASCAL**, Reprobate, Rip, Rogue, Scallywag, Skeesicks, Toerag

Scamper Gambol, Lamp, Run, Scurry, Skedaddle, Skelter, Skitter

Scan(ning), Scanner Barcode, CAT, CT, Examine, Flat-bed, Helical, Interlaced, OCR, Optical, Oversee, Peruse, PET, Rake, Raster, Scrutinise, Sector, SEM, Sequential, SPET, Survey, Tomography, Ultrasound, Vertical, Vet

Scandal(ous), Scandalise Belie, Canard, Commesse, Disgrace, Exposé, Gamy, Hearsay, Muck-raking, Opprobrium, Outrage, Shame, Slander, Stigma, Stink, Watergate

Scandinavian Dane, Finn, Laplander, Lapp, Nordic, Norman, Norseland, Northman, Olaf, Runic, Squarehead, Swede, Varangian, Viking

Scandium Sc

Scant(y), Scantness Bare, Brief, Exiguous, Ihram, Jejune, Jimp, Meagre, Oligotrophy, Poor, Scrimpy, Short, Shy, Skimpy, Slender, Spare, Sparse, Stingy

Scapegoat Butt, Fall-guy, Hazazel, Joe Soap, Patsy, Stooge, Target, Victim, Whipping-boy

Scapula Blade, Omoplate

Scar(face) Al, Blemish, Cheloid, Cicatrix, Cliff, Craig, Epulotic, Hilum, Keloid, Leucoma, Leukoma, Mark, Pockmark, Stigma, Ulosis, Wipe

Scarab Beetle, Gem

Scarce(ly), Scarcity Barely, Dear, Dearth, Famine, Few, Hardly, Ill, Lack, Paucity, Rare, Scanty, Seldom, Short, Strap, Uncommon, Want

Scare(mongering), Scaring, Scary Alarmist, Alert, Amaze, Fleg, Fright, Gally, Gliff, Glift, Hair-raising, Hairy, Panic, Petrify, Skeer, Spook, Startle, Tattie-bogle

Scarecrow Bogle, Bugaboo, Dudder, Dudsman, Gallibagger, Gallibeggar, Gallicrow, Gallybagger, Gallybeggar, Gallycrow, Malkin, Mawkin, Potato-bogle, Ragman, S(h)ewel, Tattie-bogle

Scarf Babushka, Belcher, Cataract, Comforter, Cravat, Curch, Doek, Dupatta, Fascinator, Fichu, Hai(c)k, Haique, Headsquare, Hyke, Lambrequin, Madras, Mantilla, Muffettee, Muffler, Neckatee, Neckcloth, Neckerchief, Neckgear, Neckpiece, Neckwear, Nightingale, Orarium, Pagri, Palatine, Pashmina, Pugg(a)ree, Rail, Rebozo, Sash, Screen, Stock, Stole, Tallith, Tippet, Trot-cosy, Trot-cozy, Vexillum

Scarifier Scuffler

Scarlet Cinnabar, Cochineal, Crimson, Pimpernel, Pink, Ponceau, Red, Vermilion

Scarper Abscond, Bunk, Hightail, Run, Shoo, Welsh

Scat Aroint, Dropping

Scathe, Scathing Caustic, Mordant, Sarcastic, Savage, Severe, Vitriolic

Scatter(ed), Scattering Bestrew, Broadcast, Diaspora, Disgregation, Disject, Dispel, → **DISPERSE**, Dissipate, Flurr, Inelastic, Interspace, Litter, Rayleigh, Rout, Scail, Skail, Sow, Sparge, Sparse, Splutter, Sporadic, Spread, Sprinkle, Squander, Straw, Strew, Strinkle

Scatterbrain(ed) Dippy, Ditsy, Ditz(y), Tête folie

Scavenge(r) Ant, Dieb, Forage, Hunt, Hy(a)ena, Jackal, Rake, Ratton, Rotten, Scaffie, Sweeper, Totter

Scenario Outline, Plot, Script, Worst case

Scene(ry) Arena, Boscage, Cameo, Coulisse, Decor, Flat(s), Landscape, Locale, Periaktos, Prop, Prospect, Set, Set piece, Sight, Site, Sketch, Stage, Tableau, Tormenter, Tormentor, Transformation, Venue, View, Wing

Scent Aroma, Attar, Chypre, Cologne, Eau de cologne, Essence, Fragrance, Frangipani, Fumet(te), Gale, Moschatel, Nose, Odour, Orris, Ottar, Otto, Perfume, Sachet, Smell, Spoor, Vent, Waft, Wind

Scentless Anosmia

Sceptic, Sceptical(ly), Scepticism Agnostic, Askant, Cynic, Doubter, Incredulous, Infidel, Jaundiced, Nihilistic, Nullifidian, Pyrrho(nic), Sadducee, Solipsism

Schedule Agenda, Calendar, Classification, Itinerary, Prioritise, Programme, Register, Slot, Table, Timescale, Timetable

Scheme(r), Scheming CATS, Colour, Concoct, Conspire, Crafty, Cunning, Dare, Darien, Dart, Decoct, Design, Devisal, Diagram, Dodge, Draft, Gin, Honeytrap,

Housing, Intrigue, Jezebel, Machiavellian, Machinate, Manoeuvre, Nostrum, Pilot, → **PLAN**, Plat, Plot, Project, Proposition, Purpose, Put-up job, Racket, Rhyme, Ruse, Scam, Set-aside, Stratagem, System, Table, Top-hat, Wangle, Wheeze

Schism(atic) Disunion, Division, Eastern, Great, Greek, Heterodox, Rent, Secession, Split, Western

Schizo(phrenia) Catatonic, Dementia praecox, Hebephrenia, LSD

Schmaltz(y) Goo, Slush, Tear-jerker

Schmieder S

Schmuck Gunsel

Schnapps Enzian

Scholar, Scholiast Abelard, Academic, Alcuin, Alumni, Atticus, BA, Bookman, Boursier, Catachumen, Clergy, Clerisy, Clerk, Commoner, Demy, Disciple, Erasmus, Erudite, Etonian, Exhibitioner, Extern(e), Externat, Goliard, Graduate, Grecian, Hafiz, Inkhorn, Jowett, Literate, Littérateur, MA, Mal(l)am, Masorete, Maulana, Noter, Occam Ulama, Ollamh, Ollav, Pauline, Plutarch, Polymath, Pupil, Rhodes, Sap, Savant, Saxonist, Schoolboy, Sizar, Soph, → **STUDENT**, Tabardar, Taberdar, Taberder, Tom Brown

Scholarship Bursary, Closed, Education, Erudition, Exhibition, Grant, Grant-in-aid, Learning, Lore, Mass, Rhodes

School Academy, Ampleforth, Approved, Ash Can, Barbizon, Bauhaus, Beacon, Benenden, Bluecoat, Board, Boarding, Charm, Charterhouse, Chartreux, Chautauqua, Cheder, Choir, Church, Classical, Cockney, Coed, Community, Composite, Comprehensive, Conservative, Conservatoire, Conservatory, Cool, Correspondence, Council, Crammer, Cult, Dada, Dame, Day, Direct grant, Dojo, Downside, Drama, Drill, Driving, Dual, Educate, Elementary, Essenes, Eton, Exercise, Externat, Faith, Fettes, Finishing, First, Flemish, Foundation, Frankfurt, Free, Gam, Giggleswick, Gordonstoun, Grade, Graduate, Grammar, Grant-aided, Grant-maintained, Greyfriars, Group, Gymnasien, Gymnasium, Harrow, Heder, Hedge, High, Historical, Home, Honour, Hospital, Hostel, Hypermodern, Independent, Industrial, Infant, Institute, Integrated, Intermediate, Ionic, Jim Crow, Junior, Kailyard, Kaleyard, Kant, Kindergarten, Lake, Lancing, Language, Life, List D, Loretto, Lower, LSE, Lycée, Lyceum, Madrassah, Magnet, Mahayana, Maintained, Maintaining, Manchester, Mannheim, Marlborough, Middle, National, Night, Normal, Nursery, Old, Oundle, Palaestra, Parnassian, Parochial, Pensionnat, Perse, Piano, Play, Pod, Poly, Porpoises, Prep, Preparatory, Primary, Private, Progymnasium, Provided, Public, RADA, Ragged, RAM, Ramean, Real, Reformatory, Repton, Residential, Rhodian, Roedean, Rossall, Rydal, Sabbath, Sadducee, St Trinian's, Satanic, Scandalous, Sciences, Scul, Scull(e), Secondary(-modern), Sect, Seminary, Separate, Shoal, Single-sex, Sink, Ski, Slade, Sole charge, Song, Spasmodic, Special, State, Stonyhurst, Stowe, Style, Summer, Sunday, Teach, Tech, Tenebrum, Tonbridge, Trade, → **TRAIN**, Tutor, Upper, Voluntary(-aided), Voluntary-controlled, Wellington, Whales, Winchester, Writing, Yeshiva

Schoolboy, Schoolgirl Carthusian, Coed, Colleger, East, Etonian, Fag, Gait, Geit, Gyte, Miss, Monitor, Oppidan, Petty, Stalky, Wykehamist

School-leaver Abiturient

Schoolma'am, Schoolman, Schoolmaster, Schoolmistress Aram, Beak, Dominie, Duns, Holofernes, Miss, Occam, Orbilius, Pedagogue, Pedant, Sir, Squeers, Teacher, Tutress, Ursuline

Schooner Glass, Hesperus, Prairie, Ship, Tern

Sciatica Hip-gout

Science Anatomy, Anthropology, Applied, Art, Astrodynamics, Astrophysics, Atmology, Avionics, Axiology, Behavioural, Biology, Biotech, Botany, Chemistry, Christian, Cognitive, Computer, Crystallography, Cybernetics, Dismal, Domestic, Earth, Ekistics, Electrodynamics, Entomology, Eth(n)ology, Euphenics, Exact, Forensic, Gay, Geodesy, Geology, Hard, Information, Life, Lithology, Macrobiotics, Materia medica, Mechanics, Metallurgy, Mineralogy, Natural, Noble, Nomology, Noology, Nosology, Occult, Ology, Ontology, Optics, Optometry, Pedagogy, Penology, Physical, Physics, Policy, Political, Pure, Rocket, Rural, Semiology, Serology, Skill, Social, Soft, Soil, Sonics, Stinks, Stylistics, Tactics, Technics, Technology, Telematics, Thremmatology, Toxicology, Typhlology, Zootechnics

Science fiction Cyberpunk

Scientist Alchemist, Anatomist, Archimedes, Aston, Astronomer, Atomist, Bacteriologist, Bell, → **BIOLOGIST**, Boffin, BSc, Cavendish, → **CHEMIST**, Climatologist, Copernicus, Curie, Dalton, Davy, Dopper, Egghead, Einstein, Experimenter, Expert, Faraday, Fourier, FRS, Galileo, Gay-Lussac, Geodesist, Harvey, Heaviside, Hooke, Kennelly, Lodge, Lovell, Mach, Magnetist, Mendeleev, Newton, Oersted, Pascal, Pasteur, Pauli, → **PHYSICIST**, Piccard, Potamologist, Réaumur, Researcher, Rocket, Theremin, Volta

Scimitar Acinaciform, Sword

Scintillate Dazzle, Emicate, Gleam, Glitter, → **SPARKLE**

Scion Cion, Graft, Imp, Offspring, Sien(t), Sprig, Sprout, Syen

Scissors Clippers, Criss-cross, Cutters, Forfex, Nail, Probe, Shears

Scoff Belittle, Boo, Chaff, Deride, Dor, Eat, Feast, Flout, Food, Gall, Geck, Gibe, Gird, Gobble, → **JEER**, Mock, Rail, Rib, Ridicule, Roast, Scaff, Scorn, Sneer, Taunt

Scold(ing) Admonish, Berate, Callet, Catamaran, Chastise, Chide, Clapperclaw, Cotquean, Do, Earful, Earwig, Flite, Flyte, Fuss, Jaw(bation), Jobation, Lecture, Nag, Objurgate, Philippic, Rant, Rate, → **REBUKE**, Reprimand, Reprove, Revile, Rouse on, Row, Sas(s)arara, Sis(s)erary, Slang, Slate, Termagant, Threap, Threep, Through-going, Tick-off, Tongue-lash, Trimmer, Upbraid, Virago, Wig, Xant(h)ippe, Yaff, Yankie, Yap

Sconce Candlestick, Crown, Forfeit, Head, Ice, Nole

Scone Drop, Girdle

Scoop Bale, Dipper, Exclusive, Gouge, Grab, Hollow, Ladle, Lap, Pale, Rout, Shovel, Trowel

Scooter Vespa®

Scope Ambit, Bargaining, Compass, Diapason, Domain, Elbow-room, Extent, Freedom, Gamut, Ken, Latitude, Leeway, Play, Purview, Range, Remit, Room, Rope, Scouth, Scowth, Size, Sphere

Scorch(er) Adust, Birsle, Blister, Brasero, → **BURN**, Char, Destroy, Frizzle, Fry, Parch, Scouther, Scowder, Scowther, Sear, Singe, Soar, Speed, Swale, Swayl, Sweal, Sweel, Torrefy, Torrid, Wither

Score(s), Scoring Apgar, Behind, Bill, Birdie, Bradford, Bye, Capot, Chalk up, Chase, Clock up, Conversion, Count, Crena, Debt, Dunk, Eagle, Etch, Full, Groove, Hail, Honours, Ingroove, Ippon, Koka, Law, Leaderboard, Lots, Magpie, Make, Music, Net, Nick, Notation, Notch, Nurdle, Open, Orchestrate, Partitur(a), Peg, Pique, Point, Record, Repique, Rit(t), Rouge, Run, Rut, Scotch, Scrat, Scratch, Scribe, Scrive, Set, Sheet music, Single, Spare, Stableford, Stria, String, Sum, Tablature, → **TALLY**, TE, Twenty, Vocal, Waza-ari, Win

Score-board, Score-sheet Card, Telegraph

▷ **Scorer** *may indicate* a composer

▷ **Scoring** *may indicate* an anagram

Scorn(ful) Arrogant, Bah, Contemn, Contempt, Contumely, Deride, Despise, Dis(s), Disdain, Dislike, Disparagement, Flout, Geck, Haughty, Insult, Meprise, Mock, Opprobrium, Phooey, Putdown, Rebuff, Ridicule, Sarcastic, Sardonic, Sarky, Scoff, Scout, Sdaine, Sdeigne, Sneer, Sniffy, Spurn, Wither

Scorpion Arachnid, Book, Chelifer, False, Father-lasher, Pedipalp(us), Vinegarroon, Water, Whip

Scot(sman), Scots(woman), Scottish Angus, Antenati, Berean, Blue-bonnet, Bluecap, Caledonian, Celt, Clansman, Covenanter, Duni(e)wassal, Dunniewassal, Erse, Fingal, Gael, Highland, Ian, Jock, Kelt, Kiltie, Kitty, Knox, Laird, Lallan(s), Lot, Lowland, Luckie, Lucky, Mac, Mon, Peght, Pict, Ross, Sandy, Sawn(e)y, Shetlander, Stuart, Tartan, Tax, Teuchter, Torridonian

Scotch(man) Censor, Dish, Distiller, Glenlivet®, Notch, Score, Scratch, Stop, Thwart, Usquebaugh, Whisky

Scot-free Wreakless

Scotland Alban(y), Albion, Caledonia, Gaeltacht, Gaidhealtachd, Lallans, Lothian, NB, Norland, Scotia

Scoundrel Cad, Cur, Dog, Fink, Heel, Hound, Knave, Miscreant, Rat, Reprobate, Scab, Smaik, Varlet, → **VILLAIN**

Scour Beat, Depurate, Full, Holystone, Purge, Quarter, Scrub

▷ **Scour** *may indicate* an anagram

Scourge Bible-thumper, Cat, Disciplinarium, Discipline, Flagellate, Flog, Knout, Lash, Pest, → **PLAGUE**, Scorpion, Whip, Wire

Scout Akela, Beaver, Bedmaker, Bird dog, Colony, Disdain, Explorer, Flout, Guide, King's, Outrider, Pathfinder, Pickeer, Pioneer, Queen's, Reconnoitre, Rover, Runner, Scoff, Scorn, Scourer, Scurrier, Scurriour, Sea, Sixer, Spial, Spyal, Talent, Tenderfoot, Tonto, Track, Vedette, Venture

Scowl(ing) Frown, Glower, Gnar, Lour, Lower, Sullen

Scrabble Paw

Scrag(gy) Bony, Dewitt, Ewe-necked, Neck, Scrawny

Scram Begone, Hence, Scat, Shoo

Scramble Addle, Clamber, Encode, Grubble, Hurry, Mêlée, Mix, Motocross, Muss(e), Scamble, Sprattle, Sprawl, Swerve, Texas

Scrap(s), Scrappy Abandon, Abrogate, → **BIT**, Cancel, Conflict, Cutting, Discard, Dump, → **FIGHT**, Fisticuffs, Fragment, Fray, Iota, Jot, Junk, Mêlée, Mellay, Morceau, Morsel, Odd, Off-cut, Ort, Ounce, Papier collé, Patch, Piece, Pig's-wash, Rag, Rase, Raze, Remnant, Scarmoge, Scissel, Scissil, Scroddled, Scrub, Set-to, Shard, Sherd, Shred, Skerrick, Skirmish, Snap, Snippet, Spall, Tait, Tate, Tatter, Titbit, Trash, Truculent, Whit

Scrap book Album, Grangerism

Scrap box Tidy

Scrape(r) Abrade, Agar, Bark, Clat, Claw, Comb, Curette, D and C, Erase, Escapade, Grate, Graze, Gride, Harl, Hoe, Hole, Jar, Kowtow, Lesion, Lute, Predicament, Racloir, Rake, Rasorial, Rasp, Rasure, Raze, Razure, Saw, Scalp, Scart, Scrat(ch), Scroop, Scuff, Shave, Skimp, Skive, Squeegee, Strake, Stridulate, Strigil, Xyster

Scraping noise Curr, Scroop

Scrap merchant Didakai, Didakei, Diddicoi, Diddicoy, Didicoi, Didicoy, Gold-end-man, Totter

▷ **Scratch(ed)** *may indicate* an anagram

Scratch(es), Scratched, Scratching Annul, Cancel, Cla(u)t, Claw, Cracked heels, Curry, Devil, Efface, Eradicate, Erase, Grabble, Graze, Key, Mar, Nick, Par, Periwig, Pork, Quit, Race, Rase, Rasp, Rast, Root, Satan, Scarify, Scart, Score, Scrab(ble),

Scram(b), Scrape, Scrattle, Scrawm, Scrawp, Scrooch, Scrorp, Scrub, Spag, Streak, Striation, Tease, Teaze, Wig, Withdraw

Scrawl Doodle, Scratch, Scribble, Squiggle

Scream(er) Bellow, Cariama, Caterwaul, Comedian, Comic, Cry, Eek, Headline, Hern, Hoot, Kamichi, Laugh, Priceless, Primal, Riot, Scare-line, Screech, Seriema, Shriek, Skirl, Squall, Sutch, Yell

Scree Bahada, Bajada, Eluvium, Talus

Screech(ing) Cry, Screak, Screich, Screigh, Scriech, Scritch, Skreigh, Skriech, Skriegh, Ululant, Whoot

Screed Megillah, Ms, Plastered, Rat-rhyme, Tirade

Screen(s), Screening Abat-jour, Air, Arras, Back projection, Backstop, Blind(age), Block, Blue, Boss, Brise-soleil, Camouflage, Cervical, Chancel, Check, Chick, Cinerama®, Cloak, Cornea, Coromandel, Cover, Cribble, Curtain, Divider, Dodger, Eyelid, Festoon-blind, Fight, Fire, Flat, Fluorescent, Glib, Gobo, Grid, Grille, Hallan, Help, Hide, Hoard, Hoarding, Iconostas(is), Intensifying, Jube, Lattice, Long-persistence, Mantelet, Mask, Monitor, Net, Nintendo®, Nonny, Obscure, Organ, Over-cover, Overhead, Parclose, Partition, Part-off, Pella, Plasma, Pulpitum, Purdah, Radar, Reardos, Reredorse, Reredos(se), Retable, Riddle, Rood, Scog, Sconce, Scope, → **SHADE**, Shelter, Shield, Shoji, Show, Sift, Sight, Silver, Skug, Small, Smoke, Split, Sunblock, Televise, Tems, Test, TFT, Touch, Transenna, Traverse, Umbrella, VDU, Vet, Wide, Windbreak, Window, Windshield, Winnow

Screw Adam, Allen, Archimedes, Butterfly, Cap, Coach, Countersunk, Double-threaded, Dungeoner, Extort, Female, Grub, Ice, Interrupted, Jailer, Jailor, Lag, Lead, Levelling, Lug, Machine, Male, Micrometer, Miser, Monkey-wrench, Niggard, Perpetual, Phillips®, Prop(ellor), Pucker, Robertson, Salary, Skinflint, Spiral, Swiz(zle), Thumb(i)kins, Twin, Twist, Vice, Wages, Whitworth, Worm

Screwdriver Pozidriv®, Ratchet, Stubby, Tweaker

Scribble Doodle, Pen, Scrawl

Scribe Clerk, Ezra, Mallam, Scrivener, Sopherim, Tabellion, Writer, WS

Scrimmage Bully, Maul, Mêlée, Rouge, Scrap, Skirmish, Struggle

Scrimp Economise, Pinch, Save, Scrape, Skrimp

Script Book, Calligraphy, Devanagari, Gurmukhi, Hand, Hiragana, Italic, Jawi, Kana, Kufic, Libretto, Linear A, Linear B, Lines, Lombardic, Longhand, Miniscule, Nagari, Nastalik, Nastaliq, Ogam, Prompt book, Ronde, Scenario, Screenplay, Shooting, Writing

Scripture(s), Scriptural version Adi Granth, Agadah, Alcoran, Antilegomena, Avesta, Bible, Gemara, Gematria, Gospel, Granth (Sahib), Guru Granth, Haggada(h), Hermeneutics, Hexapla, Holy book, Holy writ, Koran, K'thibh, Lesson, Lotus Sutra, Mishna(h), OT, Rig-veda, Smriti, Tantra, Targum, Testament, Upanishad, Veda, Vedic, Verse, Vulgate

Scrofula Crewels, Cruel(l)s, King's evil, Struma

Scroll(-work) Cartouche, Dead Sea, Gohonzon, Makimono, Megillah, Mezuza(h), Monkeytail, Parchment, Pell, Roll, Roul(e), Scrow, Sefer Torah, Stemma, Torah, Turbinate, Upcurl, Vitruvian, Volume, Volute

Scrooge Blagueur, Miser

Scrotum Oscheal

Scrounge(r) Blag, Bludge(r), Borrow, Bot, Cadge, Forage, Freeload, Layabout, Ligger, Scunge, Sponge

▷ **Scrub** *may indicate* 'delete'

Scrub(s), Scrubber Cancel, Chaparral, Cleanse, Dele(te), Exfoliate, Gar(r)igue, Hog,

Holystone, Horizontal, Loofa(h), Luffa, Mallee, Masseur, Negate, Pro, Rub, Scour, Sticks, Tart, Wormwood

Scruff(y) Dog-eared, Fleabag, Grubby, Nape, Raddled, Tatty, Uncombed, Untidy

Scrum(mage) Bajada, Maul, Melée, Mob, Pack, Rouge, Ruck

Scrummy, Scrumptious Delectable, Delicious, Toothy, Yum-yum

Scrunt Carl

Scruple(s), Scrupulous Compunction, Conscience, Doubt, Meticulous, Nicety, Precise, Punctilious, Qualm, Queasy, Righteous, Stickle

Scrutinize, Scrutiny Check, Docimasy, Examine, Inspect, Observe, Peruse, Pore, Pry, → SCAN, Size up, Study

Scud East, Scoot, Spark, Spindrift, Spoom, Spoon, Spray

Scuff Brush, Nape, Shuffle

Scuffle Bagarre, Brawl, Scarmage, Skirmish, Struggle, Tussle

▷ **Scuffle** *may indicate* an anagram

Scull Oar, Row

Sculpt(ure) Acrolith, Aeginetan, Bas-relief, Boast, Bronze, Bust, Calvary, Canephor(a), Canephore, Canephorus, Carve, Chryselephantine, Della-robbia, Figure, Glyptics, Kore, Kouros, Mezzo-relievo, Mezzo-rilievo, Mobile, Nude, Pergamene, Pietà, Relief, Relievo, Sc, Scabble, Scapple, Shape, Stabile, → STATUARY, Topiary

Sculptor Arp, Artist, Bartholdi, Bernini, Brancusi, Canova, Cellini, Daedalus, Della Robbia, Donatello, Giacometti, Gibbons, Gill, Hepworth, Klippel, Landseer, Michelangelo, Myron, Nollekens, Paclozzi, Phidias, Pisano, Praxiteles, Pygmalion, Rodin, Scopas, Stevens, Wheeler

Scum, Scumbag Confervoid, Dregs, Dross, Epistasis, Film, Glass-gall, Kish, Legge, Mantle, Mother, Pellicle, Pond, Rabble, Rat, Sandiver, Scorious, Scruff, Slag, Slime, Spume, Sullage, Vermin

Scupper Drain, Ruin, Scuttle, Sink

Scurf, Scurvy Dander, Dandriff, Dandruff, Furfur, Horson, Lepidote, Lepra, Leprose, Scabrous, Scall, Scorbutic, Whoreson, Yaw(e)y, Yaws

Scurrilous Cur, Fescennine, Profane, Ribald, Sotadic, Thersites, Vulgar

Scurry Beetle, Hurry, Scamper, Scutter, Skedaddle, Skelter

Scut Fud, Tail

Scute Plate

Scuttle Abandon, Dan, Dash, Hod, Purdonium, Scamper, Scoop, Scrattle, Scupper, Scurry, Sink, Wreck

Scythe Bushwhacker, Cut, Hook, Sickle, Sieth, Snath(e), Snead, Sneath, Sned

Sea(s) Adriatic, Aegean, Amundsen, Andaman, Arabian, Arafura, Aral, Azov, Baltic, Banda, Barents, Beam, Beaufort, Bellingshausen, Benthos, Bering, Billow, Biscay, Bismarck, Black, Blue, Bosp(h)orus, Brine, Briny, Caribbean, Caspian, Celebes, Celtic, Ceram, Channel, China, Chukchi, Coral, Cross, Dead, Ditch, Drink, East China, Euphotic, Euripus, Euxine, Flores, Foam, Four, Galilee, Great, Greenland, Head, Herring-pond, High, Hudson Bay, Icarian, Inland, Ionian, Irish, Japan, Java, Kara, Kattegat, Labrador, Laptev, Ler, Ligurian, Main, Mare, Mare clausum, Mare liberum, Marmara, Marmora, Med, Mediterranean, Molten, Narrow, Nordenskjold, North, Norwegian, → OCEAN, Offing, Offshore, Oggin, Okhotsk, Open, Pelagic, Philippine, Polynya, Quantity, Red, Ross, Sargasso, Seven, Short, Skagerrak, South, South China, Spanish Main, Strand, Sulu, Tasman, Tethys, Thalassic, Tiberias, Tide, Tide-rip, Timor, Tyrrhenian, Waddenzee, Water, Weddell, White, Yellow, Zee

Sea-anemone Actinia, Zoantharia

Sea-bear Fur-seal, Otary, Seal, Seecatchie

Sea-beast Ellops, Lamp-shell, Manatee

Sea-bream Carp, Fish, Porgie, Porgy, Tai

Sea-cow Dugong, Lamantin, Manatee, Rhytina, Sirenian

Sea-cucumber Bêche-de-mer, Trepang

Sea-dog Salt, Seal, Tar

Sea-ear Abalone, Paua

Sea-fight Naumachy

Seafood Crab, Crevette, → **FISH**, Lobster, Prawn, Shrimp, Whelk, Zooplankton

Sea-front, Seashore, Seaside Beach, Coast(line), Esplanade, Littoral, Orarian, Prom(enade), Seaboard

Sea-god Neptune, Nereus, Triton

Sea-green Glaucous, Incorruptible, Robespierre

Sea-horse Hippocampus, Hippodame, Lophobranchiate, Morse, Pipefish, Tangie

Seal(s), Sealed, Sealant, Seal box Airtight, Appose, Atlantic, Bachelor, Bladdernose, Block(ade), Bull(a), Cachet, Cap, Caulk, Chesterfield, Chop, Clinch, Close, Cocket, Common, Consign, Cork, Crab-eater, Cylinder, Eared, Earless, Elephant, Emblem, Fisherman's ring, Fob, Fur, Gasket, Great, Greenland, Grey, Hair, Harbour, Harp, Hermetic, Hooded, Hudson, Impress, Jark, Lemnian, Lute, Monk, Obsign, O-ring, Otary, Phoca, Pinnipedia, Pintadera, Pod, Privy, Proof, Putty, Quarter, Ribbon, Ringed, Ronan, Rookery, Saddleback, Sea-bear, Sealch, Sea-leopard, Sealgh, Seecatch(ie), Selkie, Sigil, Signet, Silkie, Silky, Size, Skippet, Solomon's, Sphragistics, Stamp, SWALK, Tar, Wafer, Washer, Water, Weddell, Whitecoat, Womb, Zalophus, Ziplock

Sea-legs Balance, Pleons

Sea-level Geoid

Sea-lily Crinoid, Palmatozoa

Seam Channel, Commissure, Dorsal suture, Fell, Felled, French, Furrow, Join, Layer, Middle-stitching, Monk's, Sew, Suture, Thread, Welt

Seaman, Seamen AB, Crew, Jack, Lascar, Lubber, Mariner, OD, Ordinary, PO, RN, → **SAILOR**, Salt, Swabby, Tar

Sea-mat Flustra, Hornwrack

Sea-matiness Gam

Sea-monster Kraken, Merman, Wasserman

Sea-mouse Bristle-worm

Séance Communication, Session, Sitting

Sea-parrot Puffin

Sear Brand, Burn, Catch, Cauterise, Frizzle, Parch, Scath(e), Scorch, Singe, Wither

Search(ing) Beat, Body, Comb, Dragnet, Examine, Ferret, Fingertip, → **FORAGE**, Fossick, Frisk, Global, Fish, Google(-whack), Grope, Home, Hunt, Indagate, Inquire, Jerk, Jerque, Kemb, Manhunt, Perquisition, Perscrutation, Probe, Proll, Prospect, Proul, Prowl, Quest, Rake, Rancel, Ransack, Ransel, Ranzel, Ravel, Ripe, Root, Rootle, Rummage, Scan, Scavenge, Scour, Scout, Scur, Sker, Skirr, Snoop, Strip, Thumb, Trace, Trawl, Zotetic

Sea-rover Norseman, Viking

Sea-serpent, Sea-snake Ellops, Hydrophidae, Phoca

▶ **Seaside** *see* **SEA-FRONT**

Sea-slug Bêche-de-mer, Trepang

Sea-snail Neritidae

Season(able), Seasonal, Seasoned, Seasoning Accustom, Age, Aggrace, Autumn, Betimes, Christmas, Close, Condiment, Devil, Dress, Duxelles, Easter, Enure, Etesian, Fall, Fennel, Festive, Fines herbes, Flavour, Garlic, G(h)omasco,

Growing, Hiems, High, In, Inure, Lent, Marjoram, Master, Mature, Noel, Nutmeg, Open, Paprika, Pepper, Powellise, Practised, Ripen, Salt, Sar, Seal, Seel, Seil, Sele, Silly, Solstice, Spice, Spring, Summer(y), Tahini, Ticket, Tide, Time, Whit, Winter, Xmas

Sea-squirt Ascidian, Cunjevoi

Seat Backside, Banc, Banquette, Barstool, Beanbag, Behind, Bench, Bleachers, Booster, Borne, Bosun's chair, Bottom, Box, Bucket, Bum, Bunker, Buttocks, Canapé, Catbird, Centre, Chair, Chaise longue, Coit, Couch, Country, Creepie, Croup(e), Croupon, Cushion, Davenport, Deckchair, Derrière, Dick(e)y, Dicky, Divan, Ejector, Epicentre, Faldistory, Faldstool, Foundation, Fud, Fundament, Gradin, Hall, Home, Hot, Houdah, Howdah, Humpty, Hurdies, Judgement, Jump, Knifeboard, Love, Marginal, Marquise, Mercy, Misericord, Natch, Nates, Ottoman, Palanquin, Palfrey, Perch, Pew, Pillion, Pit, Pouffe, Ringside, Rumble, Rumble-tumble, Rump, Saddle, Safe, Sagbag, Sedes, Sedile, Sedilium, See, Sell, Selle, Settee, Settle, Siege, Siege Perilous, Sliding, Sofa, Squab, Stool, Strapontin, Subsellium, Sunk(ie), Sunlounger, Synthronus, Throne, Tonneau, Window, Woolsack

Sea-urchin Asterias, Echinus, Pluteus, Whore's egg

Sea-vampire Manta

Sea-wall Bulwark, Dyke, Groyne

Sea-weed Agar, Alga(e), Arame, Badderlock, Bladderwort, Bladderwrack, Carrag(h)een, Ceylon moss, Chondrus, Conferva, Coralline, Cystocarp, Desmid, Diatom, Driftweed, Dulse, Enteromorpha, Florideae, Fucus, Gulfweed, Heterocontae, Hornwrack, Karengo, Kelp, Kilp, Kombu, Konbu, Laminaria, Laver, Lemon-weed, Maeri, Nori, Nullipore, Oarweed, Ore, Peacock's tail, Phyco-, Porphyra, Redware, Rockweed, Sargasso, Seabottle, Sea-furbelow, Sea-girdle, Sea-lace, Sea-lettuce, Sea-mat, Sea-moss, Sea-tangle, Seaware, Sea-whistle, Sea-wrack, Tang, Tetraspore, Ulva, Varec(h), Vraic, Wakame, Wakane, Ware, Wrack

Sea-wolf Pirate

Sea-worm Palolo, Spunculid

Sebastian Coe

Secede, Secession(ist) Adullamite, Antiburgher, Defy, Desert, Dissident, Flamingant, Separatist, Sever, Splinter

Seclude(d), Seclusion Cloister, Incommunicado, Isolate, Ivory tower, Maroon, Nook, Pleasance, Privacy, Purdah, Quarantine, Retiracy, Retreat, Secret, Sequester, Shyness, Solitude

Second(s), Secondary Abet, Alternative, Another (guess), Appurtenance, Assist, Atomic, Back(er), Beta, Collateral, Coming, Comprimario, Congener, Deuteragonist, Ephemeris, Flash, Friend, Handler, Imperfect, Indirect, Inferior, Instant, Jiffy, Latter, Leap, Lesser, Minor, Mo(ment), Nature, Other, Pig's-whisper, Redwood, Runner-up, Saybolt-Universal, Sec, Shake, Share, Side(r), Sight, Silver, Split, Subsidiary, Subtype, Support, Tick, Trice, Twinkling, Universal, Wind

Second-best Worsted

▶ **Second-class** *see* **SECOND-RATE**

Second coming Parousia

Second earth Antichthon

Second-hand Hand-me-down, Hearsay, Preloved, Reach-me-down, Re-paint, Tralactitious, Tralatitious, Used, Vicarious

Second-rate, Second-class B, Inferior, Mediocre

Second-sight Deuteroscopy, Divination, Tais(c)h

Second tine Bay, Bez

Second-year student Semi(e)(-bajan), Sophomore

Secrecy, Secret(s), Secretive Apocrypha, Arcana, Arcane, Arcanum, Backstairs,
Cabbalistic, Cagey, Clam, Clandestine, Closet, Code, Conference, Conventicle,
Couvert, Covert, Cranny, Cryptadia, Cryptic, Crypto, Dark, Dearn, Deep,
Deep-laid, Dern, Devious, Esoteric, Hidden, Hidling, Hidlin(g)s, Hole and
corner, Hugger-mugger, Hush-hush, Hushy, Inly, Inmost, In pectore, In petto,
Know-nothing, Latent, Mysterious, Mystical, Mystique, Open, Oyster, Password,
Penetralia, Petto, → **PRIVATE**, Privity, Privy, QT, Rune, Scytale, Shelta, Silent, Slee,
Sly, State, Stealth, Sub rosa, Tight-lipped, Top, Trade, Unbeknown, Underboard,
Undercover, Underhand, Undescried, Unknown, Unre(a)d, Unrevealed, Untold
Secretary Aide, Amanuensis, Chancellor, Chronicler, CIS, Desk, Desse, Famulus,
Home, Minuteman, Moonshee, Munshi, Notary, Parliamentary, Permanent,
Private, Prot(h)onotary, Scrive, Social, Steno(grapher), Stenotyper, Temp
Secretary-bird Messenger, Serpent-eater
Secrete, Secretion Aequorin, Aldosterone, Allomone, Apocrine, Autacoid,
Cache, Castor, Chalone, Colostrum, Cuckoo-spit, Discharge, Emanation, Exude,
Hide, Honeydew, Hormone, Juice, Lac, Lactate, Lerp, Melatonin, Mucus, Musk,
Osmidrosis, Pruina, Ptyalin, Recrement, Renin, Resin, Rheum, Saliva, Sebum,
Secern, Smegma, Spit(tle), Succus, Trypsin
Sect(arian), Secret society Abelite, Adamite, Ahmadiy(y)ah, Albigenses, Amish,
Anabaptist, Assassin, Babee, Babi, Bahai, Bigendian, Brahmin, Cabal, Cainite,
Calixtin(e), Camorra, Campbellite, Cathar, Clan, Clapham, Covenantes, Crypto,
Cult, Cynic, Danite, Darbyite, Disciples of Christ, Dissenter, Docate(s), Donatist,
Druse, Druze, Dunkard, Dunker, Ebionite, Encratite, Essene, Familist, Fifth
monarchy, Gabar, Gheber, Ghebre, Giaour, Glassite, Gnostic, Group, Gueber,
Guebre, Gymnosophist, Harmonist, Harmonite, Hassid, Hauhau, Hemerobaptist,
Hesychast, Hillmen, Holy Roller, Hutterite, Illuminati, Ismaili, Jacobite, Jansenist,
Jodo, Karaite, Karmathian, Little-endian, Lollard, Macedonian, Macmillanite,
Mandaean, Marcionite, Maronite, Mendaites, Monothelite, Montanist, Moonie,
Mormon, Mucker, Muggletonian, Nasorean, Nazarine, Noetian, Ophites,
Order, Partisan, Patripassian, Paulician, Perfectation, Perfectionist, Pharisee,
Philadelphian, Phrygian, Picard, Pietist, Plymouth Brethren, Plymouthite, Porch,
Pure Land, Rappist, Ribbonism, Sabbatian, Sabian, Sadducee, Saktas, Sandeman,
School, Schwenkfelder, Seekers, Senus(s)i, Seventh Day Adventist, Sex, Shafiite,
S(h)aiva, Shaker, Shembe, Shia(h), Soka Gakkai, Sons of Freedom, Taliban,
Therapeutae, Tunker, Unitarian, Utraquist, Vaishnava, Valdenses, Vaudois,
Wahabee, Wahabi(i)te, Waldenses, Yezdi, Yezidee, Yezidi, Zealot, Zen, Zezidee
Section, Sector Area, Balkanize, Caesarian, Chapter, Classify, Conic, Cross, Cut,
Division, Ellipse, Empennage, Eyalet, Gan, Golden, Gore, Hyperbola, Lith, Lune,
Meridian, Metamere, Mortice, Movement, Octant, Outlier, Panel, Passus, → **PIECE**,
Platoon, Private, Public, Pull-out, Quarter, Rhythm, Rib, S, Segment, Severy, Slice,
Stage, Ungula, Unit, Warm, Wing, Zenith, Zone
Secular(ise) Earthly, Laic, Non-CE, Profane, Temporal, Ungod, Worldly
Secure(d), Security Anchor, Assurance, Bag, Bail, Band, Bar, Basic, Batten, Belay,
Bellwether, Belt and braces, Bolt, Bond, Bottomry, Buck Rogers, Calm, Catch,
Cement, Chain, Cheka, Cinch, Clamp, Clasp, Clench, Clinch, Close, Cocoon,
Collateral, Collective, Come by, Consolidate, Consols, Cosy, Cushy, Debenture,
Disreputable, Dunnage, Engage, Enlock, Ensure, Equity, Establishment, Fasten,
Fastness, Fortify, Frap, Fungibles, Gain, Gilt, Gilt-edged, Grith, Guarantee, Guy,
Heritable, Hypothec, Immune, Impregnable, Indemnity, Inlock, Invest(ment),
Knot, Lace, Land, Lash, Latch, Lien, Listed, Lock, Lockaway, Lockdown, Lockfast,
Long-dated, Longs, Medium-dated, Mortgage, Nail, National, Obtain, Padlock,

Patte, Pin, Pledge, Pot, Pre-empt, Preference, Procure, Protect, Quad, Rope, Rug,
→ **SAFE**, Safety, Screw, Seal, Settle, Snell, Snug, Social, Sound, Stable, Stanchion,
Staple, Staylace, Stock, Strap, Sure(ty), Tack, Take, Tie, Tight, Trap, Trice, Tyde,
Warrant, Watertight, Wedge, Win

Sedan Battle, Brougham, Chair, Jampan(i), Jampanee, Litter, Palanquin, Palkee,
Palki, Saloon

Sedate Calm, Cool, Decorous, Demure, Dope, Douce, Drug, Sad, Serene,
Sober(sides), Staid, Stand

Sedative Amytal®, Anodyne, Aspirin, Barbitone, Bromal, Bromide, Chloral,
Depressant, Deserpidine, Hypnic, Laurel water, Lenitive, Lupulin, Meprobamate,
Metopryl, Miltown, Morphia, Narcotic, Nembutal®, Opiate, Paraldehyde,
Pethidine, Phenobarbitone, Premed(ication), Roofie, Scopolamine, Seconal®,
Soothing, Temazepam, Thridace, Valerian, Veronal®

Sedentary Inactive, Sessile, Stationary

Sedge Carex, Chufa, Cinnamon, Clubrush, Grey, Seg, Xyris

Sediment Alluvium, Chalk, Deposit, Dregs, F(a)eces, Fecula, Flysch, Foots, Grounds,
Grouts, Lees, Molasse, Placer, Residue, Salt, Sapropel, Silt, Sludge, Terrigenous,
Till, Turbidite, Varve, Warp

Sedition, Seditious Incitement, Insurrection, Revolt, Riot, Treason

▷ **Seduce** *may indicate* one word inside another

Seduce(r), Seductive Allure, Bed, Betray, Bewitch, Bribe, Cuckold-maker, Debauch,
Dishonour, Entice, Honeyed, Honied, Jape, Lothario, Luring, Mislead, Pull, Siren,
Slinky, Tempt, Trepan, Undo, Vamp, Wrong

See(ing) Acknow, Apostolic, Barchester, Behold, Bishopric, C, Carlisle, Consider,
Deek, Descry, Diocesan, Discern, Durham, Ebor, Ecce, Ely, Episcopal, Eye, Get,
Glimpse, Holy, La, Lo, Meet, Norwich, Notice, Observe, Papal, Perceive, Realise,
Remark, Ripon, Rochester, Rubberneck, Rumble, Since, Sodor and Man, Spae,
Spot, Spy, St David's, Truro, Twig, Understand, V, Vatican, Vid(e), View, Vision,
Visit, Voilà, Witness, York

Seed(s), Seedy Achene, Argan, Arilli, Arillode, Ash-key, Bean, Ben, Best, Blue,
Bonduc, Cacoon, Caraway, Cardamom, Carvy, Cebadilla, Cevadilla, Chickpea,
Cocoa, Colza, Coriander, Corn, Crabstone, Cum(m)in, Dragon's teeth, Embryo,
Endosperm, Ergot, Favourite, Fern, Germ, Grain, Gritty, Inseminate, Issue,
Ivory-nut, Kernel, Lima, Lomentum, Mangy, Mawseed, Miliary, Mote, Nickar,
Nicker, Niger, Nucellous, Nut, Offspring, Ovule, Pea, Pinon, Pip, Poorly, Poppy,
Sabadilla, Scuzz, Semen, Seminal, Senvy, Sesame, Shabby, Shea-nut, Silique,
Sorus, Sow, Sperm, Spore, Stane, Stone, Terminator, Thistledown, Zoosperm

Seed-case Aril, Bur(r), Endopleura, Husk, Pea(s)cod, Pod, Testa, Theca

Seed-leaf Cotyledon

Seedsman Driller, Nurseryman, Sower

Seek(er) Ask, Beg, Busk, Chase, Court, Endeavour, Ferret out, Gun for, Pursue,
Quest, Scur, Search, Skirr, Solicit, Suitor

Seem(ing), Seemingly Apparent, Appear, As if, Look, Ostensible, Purport, Quasi,
Think

Seemly Comely, Decent, Decorous, Fit, Suitable

Seep(age) Angel's share, Dribble, Exude, Leak, Ooze, Osmose, Percolate, Permeate

Seer Augur, Auspex, Eye, Melampus, Nahum, Observer, Oculiform, Onlooker,
Oracle, Prescience, Prophet, Sage, Sibyl, Soothsayer, T(e)iresias, Witness,
Zoroaster

Seesaw Bascule, Teeter(-totter), Teeter-board, Tilt, Vacillate, Wild mare

Seethe(d) Boil, Bubble, Churn, Ferment, Simmer, Smoulder, Sod

Segment Antimere, Arthromere, Cut, Division, Gironny, Gyronny, Intron, Lacinate, Lith, Lobe, Merome, Merosome, Metamere, Part, Piece, Pig, Proglottis, Propodeon, Prothorax, Scliff, Section, Share, Shie, Skliff, Somite, Split, Sternite, Syllable, Tagma, Telson, Trochanter, Urite, Uromere

Segregate, Segregation Apartheid, Exile, Insulate, Intern, → **ISOLATE**, Jim Crow, Seclude, Separate

Seidlitz Powder, Rochelle

Seismic, Seismography Richter, Terremotive

Seismograph Tromometer

Seize, Seizure Angary, Apprehend, Appropriate, Areach, Arrest, Assume, Attach(ment), Bag, Bone, Capture, Claw, Cleek, Cly, Collar, Commandeer, Confiscate, Distrain, Distress, Extent, For(e)hent, → **GRAB**, Grip, Hend, Impound, Impress, Maverick, Na(a)m, Nab, Nap, Nim, Poind, Possess, Pot, Raid, Replevy, Rifle, Sease, Sequestrate, Smug, Snag, Tackle, Trover, Usurp, Wingding

Seldom Infrequent, Rare, Unoften

Select(ion), Selecting, Selector Artificial, Assortment, Bla(u)d, Cap, Casting, Choice, Choose, Classy, Clonal, Cull, Darwinism, Discriminate, Draft, Draw, Eclectic, Edit, Elite, Excerpt, Exclusive, Extract, Favour, Garble, Inside, K, Kin, Nap, Natural, Pericope, → **PICK**, Pot-pourri, Prefer, Recherché, Sample, Seed, Sex, Single, Sort, Stream, Tipster, Triage, UCCA, Vote

Selenium Se, Zorgite

Self Atman, Auto, Character, Ego, Person, Psyche, Seity, Sel, Soul

Self-confident, Self-confidence, Self-willed Aplomb, Ego, Headstrong, Jaunty

Self-conscious Guilty

Self-contained Absolute, Reticent, SC, Taciturn

Self-contradictory Absurd, Irish

Self-control, Self-discipline Ascesis, Encraty, Modesty, Patience, Restraint, Temper(ance)

▶ **Self-defence** *see* **MARTIAL ARTS**

Self-esteem Amour-propre, Conceit, Confidence, Egoism, Pride, Vainglory

Self-evident Axiom, Manifest, Obvious, Patent, Truism, Truth

Self-existence Solipsism

Self-fertilisation, Self-origination Aseity, Autogamy

Self-governing Autonomy, Idior(r)hythmic, Kabele, Kebel, Puritanism, Swaraj

Self-help Smiles

Self-important, Self-indulgent, Self-interested Aristippus, Arrogant, Chesty, Cocky, Conceited, Egocentric, Immoderate, Jack-in-office, Licentious, Narcissistic, Pompous, Pragmatic, Primadonna, Profligate, Solipsist, Sybarite

Selfish(ness) Avaricious, Egocentric, Egoist, Grabby, Greedy, Hedonist, Mean, Solipsism

Selfless(ness) Non-ego, Tuism

Self-limiting Kenotic

▶ **Self-origination** *see* **SELF-FERTILISATION**

Self-pollinating Cl(e)istogamic

Self-possession Aplomb, Composure, Cool, Nonchalant, Phlegm

Self-satisfied, Self-satisfaction Complacent, Narcissism, Smug, Tranquil

Self-service Automat, Buffet, Cafeteria, Supermarket

Self-styled Soi-disant

Self-sufficient, Self-sufficiency Absolute, Autarky, Complete, Hunter-gatherer

Self-taught Autodidact

Sell(er), Selling Apprize, Auction, Barter, Bear, Betray, Blackmail, Blockbuster,

Cant, Catch, Chant, Chaunt, Cold-call, Cope, Costermonger, Direct, Dispose, Divest, Do, Fancier, Flog, Go, Hard, Have, Hawk, Huckster, Hustle, Inertia, Knock down, Market, Marketeer, Ménage, Merchant, Missionary, Oligopoly, Pardoner, Party, Peddle, Peddler, Pick-your-own, Purvey, Push, Pyramid, Rabbito(h), Realise, Rep, Retail, Ruse, Short, Simony, Soft, Stall-man, Sugging, Switch, → **TRADE**, Vend

Selvage Border, Edge, Roon, Rund

Semantics General, Generative, Interpretive, Notional, Onomasiology, Semasiology, Sematology

Semaphore Signal, Tic-tac, Wigwag

Semblance Aspect, Guise, Likeness, Sign, Verisimilitude

Semen Jis(so)m, Milt, Spoof, Spunk

Semi-circular D, Hemicycle

Semi-conductor Germanium, LED, Thryristor

Seminar(y) Class, → **COLLEGE**, Colloquium, Group, Theologate, Tutorial, Webinar, Yeshiva, Workshop

Semiotics Syntactics

Semi-paralysis Dyaesthesia

Semitic Accadian, Akkadian, Ammonite, Amorite, Arab, Aramaic, Canaanite, Chaldean, Geez, Jewish, Phoenician

Semitone Pycnon

Senate Council, Curia, Seanad (Eireann)

Senator Antiani, Cicero, Concept father, Elder, Legislator, Solon

Send, Sent Consign, → **DESPATCH**, Disperse, Emit, Entrance, Extradite, Issue, Launch, Mail, Order, Post, Rapt, Ship, Transmit, Transport

Send back Refer, Remand, Remit, Return

Send down Demit, Lower, Refer, Rusticate

Send up Chal(l)an, Lampoon, Promote

Senegal SN

Senescence Age

Senile, Senility Caducity, Dementia, Disoriented, Doddery, Doited, Doitit, Dotage, Eild, Eld, Gaga, Nostology, Twichild

Senior Aîné, Doyen, Elder, Father, Grecian, Mayor, Old(er), Oubaas, Père, Primus, Superior, Upper

Senna Bladder

Señor(a) Caballero, Don(a), Hidalga, Hidalgo

Sensation(al) Acolouthite, Anoesis, Aura, Blood, Commotion, Drop-dead, Emotion, Empfindung, Feeling, Gas, Impression, Lurid, Melodrama, Organic, Par(a)esthesia, Phosphene, Photism, Pyrotechnic, Shocker, Shock-horror, Showstopper, Splash, Stir, Styre, Synaesthesia, Thrill, Tingle, Vibes, Wow, Yellow

Sense, Sensual(ist), Sensing Acumen, Aura, Carnal, Coherence, Common, Dress, ESP, Faculty, Feel, Gaydar, Gross, Gumption, Gustation, Hearing, Horse, Idea, Import, Instinct, Intelligence, Intuition, Lewd, Marbles, Meaning, Moral, Nous, Olfactory, Palate, Perceptual, Rational, Receptor, Remote, Rumble-gumption, Rumgumption, Rum(m)el-gumption, Rum(m)le-gumption, Satyr, Sight, Sixth, Slinky, Smell, Spirituality, Sybarite, Synesis, Taste, Touch, Voluptuary, Voluptuous, Wisdom, Wit

Senseless Absurd, Anosmia, Illogical, Inane, Lean-witted, Mad, Numb, Stupid, Stupor, Unconscious, Unwise, Vegetal

Sensible Aware, Clear-headed, Dianoetic, Down to earth, No-nonsense, Prudent, Raisonné, Rational, Sane, Solid, Well-balanced

Sensitive, Sensitivity Algesia, Alive, Allergic, Atopy, Dainty, Delicate, Erethism,

Erogenous, Hypaesthesia, Keen, Nesh, Nociceptive, Orthochromatic, Passible, Radiesthesia, Sympathetic, Tactful, Tender, Thermaesthesia, Thin-skinned, Ticklish, Touchy(-feely), Vulnerable

Sensor(y) Cercus, Detector, Exteroceptor, Interoceptor, Palpi, Proprioceptor, Remote

Sentence(s) Antiphon, Assize, Bird, Carpet, Clause, Closed, Commit, Complex, Compound, Condemn, Custodial, Death, Decree(t), Deferred, Doom, Fatwah, Indeterminate, Judgement, Life, Matrix, Open, Pangram, Paragraph, Period(ic), Porridge, Predicate, Rap, Rheme, Rune, Simple, Stretch, Suspended, Swy, Tagmene, Time, Topic, Verdict, Versicle, Weigh off

Sententious Concise, Gnomic, Laconic, Pithy, Pompous, Terse

Sentiment(al), Sentimentality Byronism, Corn, Cornball, Drip, Feeling, Goo, Govey, Gucky, Gush, Hokey, Icky, Lovey-dovey, Maudlin, Mawkish, Mind, Mush, Namby-pamby, Nationalism, Nostalgia, Opinion, Posy, Romantic, Rose-pink, Rosewater, Saccharin, Schmaltzy, Sloppy, Slushy, Smoochy, Soppy, Spoony, Sugary, Syrupy, Tear-jerker, Too-too, Traveller, Treacly, Twee, View, Weepy, Wertherian, Yucky

Sentry Cordon sanitaire, Custodian, Guard, Jaga, Picket, Sentinel, Vedette, Vidette, Watch

Separate(d), Separation, Separately, Separatist Abscise, Abstract, Asunder, Atmolysis, Avulsion, Comma, Compartmentalise, Cull, Cut, Decollate, Decompose, Decouple, Deduct, Deglutinate, Demarcate, Demerge, Detach, Dialyse, Diastasis, Diazeuxis, Diremption, Disally, Discerp, Disconnect, Discrete, Disjunction, Dissociate, Distance, Distinct, Disunite, Divide, Division, Divorce, Eloi(g)n, Elute, Elutriate, Esloin, Estrange, ETA, Filter, Grade, Gulf, Heckle, Hive, Hyphenate, Insulate, Intervene, Isolate, Judicial, Laminate, Lease, Legal, Monosy, Part, Particle, Partition, Peel off, Piece, Prescind, Ramify, Red(d), Rift, Scatter, Schism, Screen, Scutch, Secern, Segregate, Sequester, Sever, Several, Shear, Shed, Shore, Shorn, Sift, Sleave, Sle(i)ded, Solitary, Sort, → **SPLIT**, Steam-trap, Stream, Sunder, Sundry, Tems(e), Tmesis, Try, Twin(e), Unclasp, Unhitch, Unravel, Winnow, Wrench, Yandy

Sepia Cuttle, Ink

Seppuku Hara-kiri, Hari-kari

Septic Festering, Poisonous, Rotting

Septimus Small

Septum Mediastinum

Sepulchral, Sepulchre Bier, Cenotaph, Charnel, Crypt, Easter, Funeral, Monument, Pyramid, Tomb, Vault, Whited

Sequel After-clap, Consequence, Effect, Offshoot, Outcome, Suite

Sequence, Sequential Agoge, Algorithm, Byte, Cadence, Chronological, Consecution, Consensus, Continuity, Continuum, Escape, Fibonacci, Intervening, Intron, Line, Linear, Main, Montage, Order, Peptide, Polar, Program(me), Routine, Run, Seriatim, Series, Shot, Signal, Succession, Suit, Suite, Train, Vector

Sequester, Sequestrate Confiscate, Esloin, Esloyne, Impound, Isolate, Retire, Seclude, Separate

Sequin Paillette, Zecchino

Sequoia Redwood

Seraph Abdiel, → **ANGEL**

Serb(ian) Chetnik

Sere Arid, → **DRY**, Scorch, Wither

Serenade(r) Aubade, Charivari, Horning, Love song, Minstrel, Nocturne, Shivaree, Sing-song, Wait, Wake

Serene, Serenity Calm, Composed, Impassive, Placid, Repose, Sangfroid, Sedate, Seraphic, Smooth, → **TRANQUIL**

Serf(dom) Adscript, Bondman, Ceorl, Churl, Helot, Manred, → **SLAVE**, Thete, Thrall, Vassal, Velle(i)nage, Villein

Serge Russian, Say

Sergeant Buzfuz, Chippy, Chips, Colour, Cuff, Drill, Flight, Havildar, Kite, Lance, Master, → **NCO**, Platoon, RSM, Sarge, SL, SM, Staff, Technical, Troy

Serial(ism) Episode, Feuilleton, Heft, Livraison, Total

Series Actinide, Actinium, Arithmetical, Balmer, Battery, Catena, Chain, Concatenation, Consecution, Continuum, Course, Cycle, Cyclus, Docusoap, Electromotive, Enfilade, Engrenage, En suite, Episode, Epos, Ethylene, Fibonacci, Fourier, Geometric, Gradation, Harmonic, Homologous, Lanthanide, Line, Links, Loop, Maclaurin's, Methane, Neptunium, Partwork, Pedigree, Power, Process, → **PROGRESSION**, Radioactive, Rest, Routine, Rubber, Run, Sequence, Ser, Set, Sitcom, String, Succession, Suit, Taylor's, Thorium, Time, Tone, Train, Uranium, World

Serious(ly) Critical, Earnest, Grave, Gravitas, Harsh, Heavy, Important, Intense, Major, Momentous, Pensive, Radical, Sad, Serpentine, Sober, Solemn, Sombre, Staid, Straight(-faced), Very

Sermon Address, Discourse, Gatha, Homily, Khutbah, Lecture, Preachment, Prone, Spital

Serow Goral, Thar

Serpent(ine) Adder, Amphisbaena, Anguine, Apepi, Apophis, Asp, Aspic(k), Basilisk, Boa, Caduceus, Cockatrice, Dipsas, Firedrake, Midgard, Nagas, Ophiolite, Ouroboros, Peridotite, Pharaoh's, Retinalite, Sea-snake, Shesha, → **SNAKE**, Traitor, Uraeus, Verd-antique, Verde-antico, Viper, Wyvern

Serrate(d) Diprionidian, Saw, Scallop, Serried

Serum Albumin, Antiglobulin, Antilymphocyte, Antitoxin, ATS, Fluid, Globulin, Humoral, Opsonin, Senega

Serval Bush-cat

Servant, Server Aid(e), Attendant, Ayah, Batman, Bearer, Bedder, Bedmaker, Between-maid, Boot-catcher, Boots, Boy, Butler, Caddie, Chaprassi, Chuprassy, Civil, Columbine, Cook, Daily, Domestic, Dromio, Drudge, Employee, Factotum, Famulus, File, Flunkey, Footboy, Footman, Friday, Gehazi, General, G(h)illie, Gip, Gully, Gyp, Haiduk, Handmaid, Helot, Henchman, Heyduck, Hind, Hireling, Iras, Jack, Jack-slave, Jeames, Khansama(h), Khidmutgar, Khitmutgar, Kitchen-knave, Kitchen-maid, Lackey, Lady's maid, Lazy Susan, Leroy, Maid, Major-domo, Man, Man Friday, Menial, Minion, Mixologist, Muchacha, Muchacho, Myrmidon, Nethinim, Obedient, Page, Pantler, Person, Pistol, Postman, Public, Pug, Retainer, Retinue, Scout, Scrub, Scullion, Servitor, Sewer, Skip, Slavey, Soldier, Soubrette, Steward, Tablespoon, Tapsman, Tendance, Theow, Thete, Tiger, Tweeny, Underling, Vails, Vales, Valet, Valkyrie, Varlet, Vassal, Waiter, Wash-rag, Weller

Serve, Service(s) Ace, Act, Active, All-up, Amenity, Answer, Arriage, Asperges, Assist, ATS, Attendance, Avail, Benediction, Breakfast, Campaign, Candlemas, Cannonball, Ceefax®, China, Christingle, Civil, Communion, Community, Complin(e), Conscription, Corvée, Credo, Devotional, Dien, Dinnerset, Diplomatic, Dish, Divine, Do, Dow, Drumhead, Dry, Duty, Ecosystem, Emergency, Employ, Evensong, Facility, Fault, Fee, Feudal, Fish, Foreign, Forensic, Forward, → **FUNCTION**, Further, Go, Help, Helpline, Hour, Ibadat, Jury, Ka(e), Kol Nidre, Let, Line, Ling, Lip, Litany, Liturgy, Ma'ariv, Mass, Mat(t)ins, Memorial, Mincha,

Minister, Ministry, Missa, National, Nocturn, Nones, Oblige, Office, Oracle, Overarm, Overhaul, Pass, Pay, Personal, Pit stop, Possum, Pottery, Prime, Proper, Public, Radio, RAF, Requiem, Rite, RN, Room, Sacrament, Secret, Selective, Senior, Sext, Shacharis, Shaharith, Shuttle, Silver, Social, Sorb, Stead, Sted, Sue, Tableware, Tea, Tenebrae, Tierce, Trental, Uncork, Under-arm, Use, Utility, Vespers, Wait, Waiterage, Watch-night, Wild, Worship, Yeoman('s)

Service-book Hymnal, Hymnary, Missal, Triodion

▷ **Serviceman** *may indicate* a churchman

Servile, Servility Abasement, Base, Crawling, Knee, Kowtowing, Lickspittle, Menial, Obsequious, Slavish, Slimy, Submissive, Suck-hole, Sycophantic, Tintookie, Truckle

Serving Helping, Heuristic, Portion

Servitude Bondage, Domination, Peonism, Slavery, Thirlage, Thrall, Vassalry, Yoke

Sesame Benne, Gingelly, Gingili, Grapple-plant, Jinjilli, Semsem, Tahini, Til

Session(s) All-nighter, Bout, Executive, Galah, Jam, Kirk, Meeting, Nightshift, Petty, Poster, Quarter, Rap, Round, Séance, Sederunt, Settle, Sitting, Term

Set(ting) (aside; down; in; off; out; up) Activate, Adjust, Appoint, Arrange, Batch, Bent, Bezel, Boun, Brooch, Cabal, Cake, Case, Cast, Chaton, Class, Claw, Clique, Cliveden, Closed, Coagulate, Cock, Cockshy, Codomain, Collection, Collet, Comp(ositor), Companion, Compose, Congeal, Context, Coterie, Couvert, Crew, Crystal, Cyclorama, Data, Dead, Decline, Decor, Detonate, Diorama, Dispose, Duchesse, Earmark, Earnest, Earth, Enchase, Ensky, Environment, Establish, Explode, Film, Fit, Flagstone, Flash, Flat(s), Found, Garniture, Geal, Gel, Genome, Group, Hairdo, Harden, Heliacal, Ilk, Inchase, Incrowd, Incut, Infinite, Inlay, Jee, Jeel, Jell(y), Jet, Julia, Kit, Laid, Land, Lay, Leg, Locale, Locate, Lot, Mandelbrot, Mental, Milieu, Mise en scène, Miserere, Monture, Mournival, Nail, Nest, Occident, Open, Ordered, Ordinate, Ouch, Pair, Parure, Pavé, Permanent, Physique, Pitch, Place(ment), Plant, Plaste, Ply, Point, Posed, Posit, Power, Put, Radio, Ready, Receiver, Relay, Rigid, Rooted, Rubber, Saw, Scenery, Series, Showcase, Sink, Smart, Solidify, Solution, Squad, Stand, Stationed, Stede, Stell, Stick, Stiffen, Still, Stream, Subscriber, Suit, Suite, Surround, Synchronize, Tar, Tea, Team, Teeth, Televisor, Telly, The four hundred, Theme, Tiffany, Till, Toilet, Trannie, Transistor, Trigger, Truth, Tube, TV, Union, Universal, Venn (diagram), Weather, Wide-screen, Yplast

Setback Bodyblow, Checkmate, Glitch, Hiccup, Hiccough, Jolt, Knock, Relapse, Retard, Retreat, Reversal, Scarcement, Sickener, Tes, Vicissitude, Whammy

Setter Cement, Comp, Dog, English, Gelatin(e), Gordon, Gundog, Hairspray, Irish, Pectin, Red, Smoot, Sphinx, Trend

Settle(d), Settler, Settlement Adjust, Agree, Alight, Appoint, Arrange, Ascertain, Ausgleich, Avenge, Balance, Bandobast, Bed, Bench, Boer, Borghetto, Botany Bay, Bundobust, Bustee, Camp, Clear, Clench, Clinch, Colonial, Colonise, Colony, Compose, Compound, Compromise, Crannog, Decide, Defray, Determine, Diktat, Discharge, Dispose, Dorp, Dowry, Ekistics, Encamp, Endow, Ensconce, Entail, Establish, Expat, Faze, Feeze, Finalise, Fix, Foot, Foreclose, Gravitate, Gridironer, Guilder, Habitant, Hama, Illegitimate, Informal, Jamestown, Jointure, Kibbutz, Land, Ledge, Light, Lull, Lyte, Manyat(t)a, Merino, Mise, Mission, Moreton Bay, Moshav, Nahal, Nest, Nestle, New Amsterdam, Oecist, Oikist, Opt, Outpost, Over, Pa(h), Pakka, Pale, Patroon, Pay, Peise, Penal, Perch, Pheazar, Pheese, Pheeze, Phese, Pilgrim, Pioneer, Placate, Planter, Populate, Port Arthur, Port Nicholson, Presidio, Pucka, Pueblo, Pukka, Rancheria, Rancherie, Readjust, Reduction, Reimburse, Remit, Reside, Resolve, Rest, Sate, Satisfaction, Seal, Seat, Secure,

Sedimentary, Set fair, Shagroon, Shtetl, Silt, Smoot, Sofa, Soldier, Solve, Soweto, Square, Square up, State, Still, Straits, Subside, Taurus, Township, Ujamaa, Utu, Vest(ed), Viatical, Voortrekker, Wrap up

▷ **Settlement** *may indicate* an anagram

▷ **Settler** *may indicate* a coin

Set upon Assail, Attack, Sick

Seven(th), Seven-sided Ages, Days, Dials, Great Bear, Hebdomad, Hepta-, Hills, Magnificent, Nones, Pleiad(es), S, Sages, Seas, Septenary, Septilateral, Septimal, Sins, Sisters, Sleepers, Stars, Wonders, Zeta

Seventy S

Seven-week Omer

Sever Amputate, Cut, Detach, Divide, Sunder

Several Divers, Many, Multiple, Some, Sundry

Severe(ly), Severity Acute, Austere, Bad, Caustic, Chronic, Cruel, Dour, Draconian, Drastic, Eager, Extreme, Grave, Grievous, Gruel(ling), Hard, → **HARSH**, Ill, Inclement, Morose, Penal, Rhadamanthine, Rigo(u)r, Roaming, Roundly, Ruthless, Serious, Sharp, Snell(y), Sore, Spartan, Stark, Stern, Strict, Swingeing

Sew(ing), Sew up Baste, Clinch, Cope, Embroider, Fell, Fine-draw, Machine, Mitre, Overcast, Overlock, Run, Seam, Seel, Stitch, Tack, Whip

Sewage, Sewer Cesspool, Cloaca, Culvert, Dorcas, → **DRAIN**, Effluence, Jaw-box, Jaw-hole, Mimi, Needle, Privy, Seamster, Shore, Soil, Sough, Soughing-tile, Sure, Waste

Sex(y), Sexist Bed-hopping, Carnal, Coupling, Cunnilingus, Erotic, Fair, Favours, Fellatio, Female, Foreplay, Fornication, French, Gam(ic), Gamahuche, Gamaruche, Gender, Greek love, Hanky-panky, Hump, Incest, Intercourse, Jailbait, Kind, Libidinous, Libido, Lingam, Lumber, Male, Mate, Non-penetrative, Nookie, Oomph, Opposite, Oral, Outercourse, Paedophilia, Pederasty, Phallocratic, Phat, Phone, Priapean, Race, Randy, Raunchy, Rut(ish), Safe, Salacious, Screw, Sect, Slinky, Steamy, Sultry, Tantric, Teledildonics, Troilism, Unprotected, Unsafe, Venereal, Venery, VI, Voluptuous, Weaker

Sex appeal It, Oomph, SA

Sexcentenarian Shem

Sexless Agamogenetic, Atoke, N, Neuter

Sextet Over, Six

Sexton Blake, Fossor, Sacristan, Shammes, Warden

Seychelles SY

Sh P, Quiet

Shabby Base, Buckeen, Dog-eared, Down-at-heel, Fusc(ous), Grotty, Mangy, Mean, Moth-eaten, Low-lived, Old hat, Oobit, Oorie, Oubit, Ourie, Outworn, Owrie, Raunch, Scaly, Scruffy, Seedy, Shoddy, Squalid, Tacky, Tatty, Unkempt, Worn, Woubit

Shack Fibro, Heap, Hideout, Hovel, Hut, Sheal

Shackle(s) Bilboes, Bind, Bracelet, Chain, Darbies, Entrammel, Fetter(lock), Gyve, Hamper, Irons, Manacle, Restrict, Tie, Trammel, Yoke

Shad Allice, Allis, Fish, Twait(e)

Shaddock Grapefruit, Pomelo

Shade(d), Shades, Shading, Shadow, Shady Adumbrate, Arbour, Arcade, Awning, Blend, Blind, Bongrace, Bowery, Brise-soleil, Brocken spectre, Buff, Cast, Chiaroscuro, Chroma, Cloche, Cloud, Cross-hatch, Degree, Dis, Dog, Dubious, Eclipse, Eye, Five o'clock, Galanty, Gamp, Ghost, Gnomon, Gradate, Gray, Hachure, Hell, Herbar, Hint, Hue, Inumbrate, Larva, Lee, Melt, Mezzotint, Nuance, Opaque,

Overtone, Parasol, Pastel, Phantom, Presence, Rain, Ray-Bans®, Satellite, Screen, Shroud, Sienna, Silhouette, Silvan, Skia-, Soften, Sound, Spectre, Spirit, Stag, Sunglasses, Swale, Swaly, Tail, Tenebrious, Tinge, Tint, Titian, Tone, Ugly, Umbra(tile), Umbrage(ous), Underhand, Velamen, Velar(ium), Velum, Visitant, Visor

Shadowless Ascian

Shaft(ed), Shafting Arbor, Arrow, Axle tree, Barb, Barrow-train, Beam, Capstan, Cardan, Chimney, Collet, Column, Crank, Cue, Diaphysis, Disselboom, Dolly, Downcast, Drive, Escape, Fil(l), Fust, Gleam, Idler, Incline, Journal, Lamphole, Lay, Limber, Loom, Mandrel, Mandril, Manhole, Moon pool, Moulin, Parthian, Passage, Pile, Pit, Pitbrow, Pitch, Pole, Propeller, Quill (drive), Ray, Rib, Rise, Scape, Scapus, Shank, Snead, Spindle, Staff, Stairwell, Stale, Steal(e), Steel, Steen, Stele, Stem, Stulm, Sunbeam, Telescopic, Thill, Tige, Tomo, Trave, Truncheon, Upcast, Well, Winning, Winze

Shag Cronet, Hair, Intercourse, Nap, Pile, Scart(h), Skart(h), Tire, Tobacco

Shaggy Ainu, Bushy, Comate, Hairy, Hearie, Hirsute, Horrid, Horror, Maned, Nappy, Rough, Rugged, Shock, Shough, Tatty, Tousy, Touzy, Towsy, Towzy, Untidy

Shah Ruler, Sophi, Sophy

▷ **Shake** *may indicate* an anagram

Shake(n), Shakes, Shake off, Shaky Agitate, Ague(-fit), Astonish, Bebung, Brandish, Coggle, Concuss, Dabble, Dick(e)y, Didder, Diddle, Disconcert, Dither, Dodder, → **DT'S**, Feeble, Groggy, Hod, Hotch, Jar, Jiggle, Joggle, Jolt, Jounce, Judder, Jumble, Lose, Milk, Mo, Nid-nod, Press flesh, Quake, Quiver, Quooke, Rattle, Rickety, Rickle, → **ROCK**, Rouse, Shimmer, Shiver, Shock, Shog, Shoogle, Shudder, Succuss(ation), Sweat, Tremble, Tremolo, Tremor, Tremulous, Trill(o), Tumbledown, Undulate, Vibrate, Vibrato, Wag, Waggle, Wind, Wobble, Wonky

Shakedown Blackmail, Chantage, Pallet

Shakespeare Bard, Will, WS

Shale Blaes, Fa(i)kes, Kerogen, Kupferschiefer, Oil, Rock, Till, Torbanite

Shall Sal

Shallot C(h)ibol, Onion, Scallion, Sybo(e), Sybow

Shallow(s) Ebb, Flat, Fleet, Flew, Flue, Justice, Neritic, Riffle, Sandbank, Sandbar, Shoal, Slight, Superficial

Sham Apocryphal, Bluff, Bogus, Braide, Charade, Counterfeit, Deceit, Fake, → **FALSE**, Hoax, Idol, Impostor, Mimic, Mock, Phony, Pinchbeck, Postiche, Potemkin, Pretence, Pseudo, Repro, Simulated, Snide, Spurious, Straw man

Shaman Angek(k)ok, Sorcerer

Shamble(s) Abattoir, Bauchle, Butchery, Mess, Shuffle, Totter, Tripple

Shame(ful), Shame-faced Abash, Aidos, Chagrin, Confusion, Contempt, Crying, Degrade, Discredit, Disgrace, Dishonour, Embarrass, Fi donc, Fie, Gross, Hangdog, Honi, Humiliate, Ignominy, Infamy, Inglorious, Modesty, Mortify, Ohone, Pity, Pudency, Pudor, Pugh, Shend, Sin, Slander, Stain, Stigma, Yshend

Shameless Audacious, Brash, Brazen, Flagrant, Immodest, Ithyphallic

Shampoo(ing) Massage, Tripsis, Wash

Shandy Drink, Sterne, Tristram

Shanghai Abduct, Kidnap, Trick

Shank Leg, Shaft, Steal(e), Steel, Steil, Stele, Strike

Shanty, Shanty town Bidonville, Boatsong, Bothy, Bustee, Cabin, Chant, Dog-hole, Favela, Forebitter, Hutment, Lean-to, Pondok, Sea, Shack, Shypoo, Song

Shape(d), Shapely, Shaping Blancmange, Boast, Bruting, Cast, Contour, Die-cast, Face, Fashion, Figure, Form, Format, Geoid, Gnomon, Headquarters, Hew, Holohedron, Jello, Model, Morph, Morphology, → **MOULD**, Net, Pendentive,

Polyomine, Ream, Rhomb(us), Roughcast, Scabble, Sculpt, Spile, Step-cut, Tromino, Turn, Voluptuous, Whittle, Wrought, Zaftig, Zoftig

Shapeless Amorphous, Chaos, Dumpy, Indigest, Vague

Shard Fragment, Sliver, Splinter

Share(d), Shares, Sharing Allocation, Allotment, Apportion, Blue-chip, Bovate, Cahoots, Chop, Co, Cohabit, Coho(e), Common, Communal, Contango, Co-portion, Culter, Cut, Deferred, Divi(dend), Divide, Divvy, Dole, Dutch, Equity, Finger, Founders, Golden, Grubstake, Impart, Interest, Job, Kaffer, Kaf(f)ir, Kangaroo, Lion's, Market, Moiety, Odd lot, Ordinary, Oxgang, Oxgate, Oxland, Parcener, → **PART**, Partake, Participate, Penny, PIBS, Plough, Plough-iron, Portion, Prebend, Pref(erred), Preference, Pro rata, Prorate, Quarter, Quota, Rake off, Ration, Rug, Rundale, Scrip, Security, Shr, Slice, Snack, Snap, Sock, Split, Stock, Taurus, Teene, Time, Tranche, Two-way, Whack

Shareholder Plough, Stag

Shark Angel, Basking, Beagle, Blue, Bluepointer, Bonnethead, Bronze-whaler, Bull, Carpet, Cestracion, Cow, Demoiselle, Dog(fish), Flake, Fox, Great white, Gummy, Hammerhead, Houndfish, Huss, Lemonfish, Leopard catshark, Loan, Mackerel, Mako, Miller's dog, Monkfish, Noah, Nurse, Penny-dog, Plagiostomi, Porbeagle, Requiem, Reremai, Rhin(e)odon, Rigg, Rook, Sail-fish, Saw, School, Sea-ape, Sea-fox, Sea-lawyer, Sevengill, Sharp, Shortfin mako, Shovelhead, Smoothhound, Soupfin, Spotted ragged-tooth, Squaloid, Swindler, Thrasher, Thresher, Tiger, Tope, Usurer, Whale, Whaler, Wobbegong, Zygaena

Sharkskin Shagreen

Sharp(er), Sharpen(er), Sharpness Abrupt, Accidental, Acerose, Acidulous, Acrid, Aculeus, Acumen, Acuminate, Acute, Alert, Angular, Arris, Astringent, Bateless, Becky, Benchstone, Bitter, Brisk, Cacuminous, Cheat, Clear, Coticular, Cutting, Dital, Edge(r), Fine, Fly, Gleg, Grind, Hone, Hot, Keen, Kurtosis, Massé, Oilstone, Penetrant, Peracute, Piquant, Poignant, Pronto, Pungent, Quick-witted, Razor, Rogue, Rook, Set, Shrewd, Snap, Snell, Sour, Spicate, Strop, Swindler, Tart, Testy, Tomium, Twenty-twenty, Varment, Vivid, Volable, Vorpal, Whet

Sharpshooter Bersaglier, Franc-tireur, Sniper, Tirailleur, Voltigeur

Shatter(ing) Astone, Astound, Break, Brisance, Bust, Craze, Dash, Explode, Shiver, Smash, Smithereen, Splinter, Unnerve

Shave(r), Shaving(s) Barb(er), Electric, Excelsior, Filings, Flake, Grain, Moslings, Pare, Plane, Pogonotomy, Poll, Raze, Scrape, Skive, Sliver, Splinter, Swarf, Todd, Tonsure, Whittle

Shaw Artie, Green, Spinn(e)y, Wood

Shawl Afghan, Buibui, Cashmere, Chuddah, Chuddar, Dopatta, Dupatta, Fichu, India, Kaffiyeh, Kashmir, Manta, Mantilla, Maud, Paisley, Partlet, Prayer, Serape, Sha(h)toosh, Stole, Tallis, Tallit(ot), Tallith, Tonnag, Tozie, Tribon, Whittle, Wrap(per), Zephyr

She A, Hoo

Sheaf, Sheave Aplustre, Bee, Bundle, Clevis, Dorlach, Folder, Gait, Garb(e), Gerbe, Mow, Shock, Thr(e)ave

Shear(s), Shearer Clip, Cut, Fleece, Greasy, Jaws of life, Pinking, Poll, Pruning, Ring(er), Shave, Snips, Trim, Wind

Sheath Axolemma, Capsule, Case, Cocoon, Coleoptile, Coleorhiza, Condom, Cover, Extine, Fingerstall, Glume, Medullary, Myelin, Neurilemma, Neurolemma, Oc(h)rea, Perineurium, Periosteum, Quiver, Rhinotheca, Root, Scabbard, Spathe, Thecal, Thumbstall, Urceolus, Vagina, Volva, Wing

Shed(ding), Shedder Autotomy, Barn, Byre, Cast, Cho(u)ltry, Coducity, Cootch,

Cwtch, Depot, Discard, Doff, Downsize, Drop, Ecdysis, Effuse, Emit, Exuviate,
Hangar, Hovel, Hut, Infuse, Lair, Lean-to, Linhay, Linn(e)y, Mew, Milking, Moult,
Outhouse, Pent, Potting, Salmon, Shearing, Shippen, Shippon, Shuck, Skeo,
Skillion, Skio, Slough, Sow, Spend, Spent, Spill, Tilt, Tool

Sheen Glaze, Gloss, Luminance, Lustre, Patina, Schiller, Shine

Sheep(ish) Ammon, Ancon(es), Aoudad, Argali, Barbary, Bell(wether), Bharal,
Bident, Bighorn, Black, Blackface, Blate, Border Leicester, Broadtail, Burhel,
Burrel(l), Caracul, Charollais, Cheviots, Coopworth, Corriedale, Cotswold,
Cotswold lion, Coy, Crone, Dinmont, Domestic, Dorset Down, Dorset Horn,
Down, Drysdale, Embarrassed, Ewe, Exmoor, Fank, Fat-tailed, Flock, Fold, Hair,
Hampshire, Hampshire Down, Hangdog, Herdwick, Hidder, Hirsel, Hog(g),
Hogget, Jacob, Jemmy, Jumbuck, Karakul, Kent, Kerry Hill, Lamb, Lanigerous,
Leicester, Lincoln, Lo(a)ghtan, Loghtyn, Long, Lonk, Marco Polo, Masham,
Merino, Mor(t)ling, Mouf(f)lon, Mountain, Muflon, Mug, Mus(i)mon, Mutton,
Oorial, Ovine, Oxford Down, Perendale, Portland, Ram, Rambouillet, Romeldale,
Romney Marsh, Rosella, Ryeland, Scottish Blackface, Shearling, Shetland, Shidder,
Short, Shorthorn, → **SHY**, Soay, Southdown, Spanish, Stone('s), Suffolk, Sumph,
Swaledale, Teeswater, Teg(g), Texel, Theave, Trip, Tup, Twinter, Two-tooth,
Udad, Urial, Vegetable, Welsh Mountain, Wensleydale, Wether, Wiltshire Horn,
Woollyback, Yow(e), Yowie

Sheep disease, Sheep problem Black, Blue tongue, Braxy, Dunt, Gid, Hoove,
Louping-ill, Orf, Ringwomb, Rubbers, Scabby mouth, Scrapie, Staggers, Sturdy,
Swayback, Variola, Water-brain, Wildfire, Wind

Sheepdog Collie, Huntaway, Maremma, Polish Lowland, Puli

Sheepfold Fank, Pen

Sheepskin Basan, Caracul, Karakul, Mouton, Roan, Wool

Sheeptrack Terracette

Sheer Absolute, Clear, Main, Mere, Peekaboo, Plumb, Precipitous, Pure, Simple,
Stark, Steep, Swerve, Thin, Utter

Sheet(s), Sheeting Balance, Cellophane, Cere-cloth, Cerement, Charge, Chart,
Clean, Crime, Cutch, Dope, Expanse, Film, Flow, Fly, Folio, Foolscap, Heft, Ice,
Inset, Intrusive, Lasagne, Leaf, Membrane, Nappe, Out-hauler, Page, Pane, Pot(t),
Pour, Proof, Prospectus, Rap, Ream, Rope, Sail, Scandal, Scratch, Shroud, Stern,
Stratus, Taggers, Tarpaulin(g), Tear, Tentorium, Terne, Thunder, Time, Title, Web,
White, Winding

Sheet-anchor Letter-weight, Paperweight

Sheet-iron Taggers, Terne(plate)

Sheik(dom) Abu Dhabi, Bahrein, Dubai

Shekel Mina, Sickle

Sheldrake Bergander

Shelf, Shelve(s) Bank, Bar, Bracket, Continental, Counter, Credence, Delay, Dresser,
Étagère, Gondola, Grand Banks, Hob, Ice, Ledge, Leeboard, Mantelpiece, Mantle,
Overmantel, Parcel, Postpone, Rack, Retable, Rick, Ross Ice, Shunt, Sidetrack, Sill,
Spinsterhood, Whatnot, Windowsill

Shell(ed), Shellfish, Shellwork Abalone, Acorn-shell, Admiral, Ambulacrum,
Ammo, Argonaut, Balamnite, Balanus, Balmain bug, Bivalve, Blitz, Boat, Bodywork,
Bombard, Buckie, Camera, Capiz, Capsid, Carapace, Cartridge, Casing, Chank,
Chelonia, Chitin, Clam, Cleidoic, Clio, Coat-of-mail, Cochlea, Cockle, Cohog,
Conch, Cone, Copepoda, Cover, Cowrie, Cowry, Crab, Cracked, Crustacea,
Cuttlebone, Dariole, Deerhorn, Dentalium, Dop, Drill, Electron, Escallop, Eugarie,
Foraminifer, Framework, Frustule, Gas, Geoduck, Globigerina, Haliotis, Hull,

Husk, Hyoplastron, Isopoda, Kernel, Lamp, Langouste, Limacel, Limpet, Live, Lobster, Lorica, Lyre, Malacostraca, Midas's ear, Mitre, Mollusc, Monocoque, Moreton Bay bug, Mother-of-pearl, Murex, Music, Mussel, Nacre, Nautilus, Olive, Ormer, Ostracod, Ostrea, Otter, Oyster, Paua, Pawa, Pea(s)cod, Peag, Peak, Pecten, Peel, Pereia, Periostracum, Periwinkle, Pilgrim's, Pipi, Pipsqueak, Plastron, Pod, Prawn, Projectile, Purple, Putamen, Quahaug, Quahog, Razor, Rocaille, Sal, Scalarium, Scallop, Scollop, Sea-ear, Sea-pen, Shale, Shard, Sheal, Sheel, Shiel, Shill, Shock, Shot, Shrapnel, Shrimp, Shuck, Sial, Smoke-ball, Spend, Spindle, Star, Stomatopod, Stonk, Straddle, Strafe, Stromb(us), Swan-mussel, Tear, Test(a), Thermidor, Toheroa, Tooth, Top, Torpedo, Tracer, Trivalve, Trough, Trumpet, Turbo, Turritella, Tusk, Univalve, Valency, Venus, Wakiki, Wampum, Whelk, Whiz(z)bang, Winkle, Xenophya, Yabbie, Yabby, Zimbi

▷ **Shelled** *may indicate* an anagram

Shell money Wakiki, Wampum, Zimbi

Shelter(ed) Abri, Anderson, Asylum, Awn, Awning, Bay, Belee, Bender, Bield, Billet, Blind, Blockhouse, Booth, Bunker, Burladero, Butt, Cab, Carport, Casemate, Cot(e), Cove, Covert, Coverture, Defence, Dodger, Donga, Dovecote, Dripstone, Dug-out, Fall-out, Garage, Gunhouse, Gunyah, Harbour, Haven, Hithe, Hospice, Hostel, House, Hovel, Humpy, Hut, Hutchie, Kipsie, Lee, Lee-gage, Loun, Lound, Lown, Lownd, Mai mai, Mission, Morrison, Nodehouse, Pilothouse, → **REFUGE**, Retreat, Roof, Sanctuary, Scog, Sconce, Scoog, Scoug, Screen, Scug, Shed, Shiel(ing), Shroud, Skug, Snowhole, Snowshed, Stell, Storm-cellar, Succah, Sukkah, Summerhouse, Suntrap, Tax, Tent, Testudo, Tortoise, Tupik, Twigloo, Umbrage, Weather, Wheelhouse, Wickyup, Wi(c)kiup, Wil(t)ja, Windbreak, Windscreen, Windshield

Shemozzle Debacle

Shenanigan Antic

Shepherd(ess) Abel, Acis, Amaryllis, Amos, Bergère, Bo-peep, Bucolic, Chloe, Clorin, Conduct, Corin, Corydon, Cuddy, Daphnis, Dorcas, Drover, Endymion, Escort, Ettrick, Flock-master, German, Good, Grubbinol, Gyges, Herdsman, Hobbinol, Lindor, Marshal, Menalcas, Padre, Pastor(al), Pastorella, Phebe, Sheepo, Strephon, Tar-box, Thenot, Thyrsis, Tityrus

Sheriff Bailiff, Deputy, Earp, Grieve, Land-dros(t), Lawman, Process-server, Shireman, Shire-reeve, Shirra, Shrievalty, Viscount

Sherry Amoroso, Bristol milk, Cobbler, Cream, Cyprus, Doctor, Dry, Fino, Gladstone, Jerez, Manzanilla, Oloroso, Palo cortado, Sack, Solera, Sweet, Whitewash, Xeres

Sherwood Anderson, Forest

Shiah Ismaili

Shibboleth Password

Shield(s), Shield-shaped Ablator, Achievement, Aegis, Ancile, Armour, Arms, Baltic, Biological, Bodyguard, Box, Buckler, Canadian, Cartouche, Clypeus, Defend, Dress, Escutcheon, Fence, Gobo, Guard, Gumshield, Gyron, Hatchment, Heat, Hielaman, Human, Inescutcheon, Insulate, Laurentian, Lozenge, Mant(e)let, Mask, Pavis(e), Pelta, Plastron, Protect, Randolph, Ranfurly, Riot, Rondache, Scandinavian, Screen, Scute, Scutum, Sheffield, Splashboard, Sternite, Targe(t), Thyroid, Vair, Visor, Water

Shift(er), Shifty Amove, Astatic, Back, Blue, Budge, Change, Chemise, Core, Cymar, Day, Devious, Displace, Dogwatch, Doppler, Dress, Dying, Einstein, Evasive, Expedient, Linen, Function, Graveyard, Great Vowel, Hedging, Lamb, Landslide, Lateral, Linen, Louche, Move, Night, Nighty, Paradigm, Red, Relay, Remove, Rota, Ruse, Scorch, Sell, Shirt, Shovel, Shunt, Simar(re), Slicker, Slip(pery), Sound, Spell, Split, Stagehand, Stick, Stint, Swing, Tour, Transfer, Tunic, Turn, Vary, Veer, Warp

▷ **Shift(ing)** *may indicate* an anagram

Shilling Bob, Deaner, Falkiner, Hog, King's, Queen's, S, Teston

Shilly-shally Whittie-whattie

Shimmer(ing) Avanturine, Aventurine, Chatoyant, Glint, Glitter, Iridescence, Mona(u)l, Shine

▷ **Shimmering** *may indicate* an anagram

Shin Clamber, Climb, Cnemial, Leg, Shank, Skink, Swarm

Shindig, Shindy Bobbery, Row, Rumpus, Shivoo, Uproar

Shine(r), Shining, Shiny Aglitter, Aglow, Beam, Bright, Buff, Burnish, Deneb, Effulge, Excel, Flash, Gleam, Glimmer, Glisten, Glitzy, Gloss, → **GLOW**, Irradiant, Japan, → **LAMP**, Leam, Leme, Lucent, Luminous, Lustre, Mouse, Nitid, Nugget, Phoebe, Phosphoresce, Polish, Radiator, Refulgent, Relucent, Resplend, Rutilant, Skyre, Sleek, Twinkle, Varnish

Shingle(s), Shingly Beach, Chesil, Cut, Dartre, Dartrous, Gravel, Herpes, Herpes Zoster, Herpetic, Loose metal, Shake, Shale, Stone, Zona, Zoster

Shinpad Greave

Shinty Caman, Camanachd

▷ **Shiny** *may indicate* a star

Ship(s), Shipping Boat, Convoy, Deepwaterman, → **DISPATCH**, Embark, Export, First-rate, Her, Hulk, Keel, Man, Marine, MV, Prize, Prow, Sail, She, SS, Transport, Tub, Vessel

SHIPS

1 letter:	Fire	Broke	Sabot
Q	Flat	Camel	Saick
	Grab	Canoe	Scoot
2 letters:	Isis	Cargo	Screw
PT	Koff	Coble	Scull
	Long	Coper	Shell
3 letters:	Nina	Crare	Skiff
Ark	Pink	Dandy	Slave
Cat	Pont	Dingy	Sloop
Cog	Post	Drake	Smack
Dow	Pram	Ferry	Tramp
Fly	Prau	Funny	Troop
Hoy	Proa	Jolly	U-boat
Kit	Raft	Ketch	Umiak
Ram	Ro-ro	Laker	Wager
Red	Saic	Liner	Whiff
	Scow	Moses	Xebec
4 letters:	Snow	Oiler	Yacht
Argo	Tall	Pinky	Zabra
Bark	Tern	Pinto	Zebec
Brig	Trow	Plate	
Buss	Yawl	Praam	*6 letters:*
Cock	Zulu	Prahu	Argosy
Cott		Prore	Banker
Dhow	*5 letters:*	Pucan	Barque
Dory	Aviso	Razee	Bateau
Duck	Barge	Rover	Bawley

Beagle
Bethel
Bireme
Borley
Bottom
Bounty
Caique
Carack
Carvel
Castle
Coaler
Cobble
Codder
Cooper
Crayer
Curagh
Cutter
Decker
Dingey
Dinghy
Dogger
Droger
Dromon
Drover
Dugout
Escort
Flying
Frigot
Galiot
Galley
Gay-you
Goldie
Hooker
Howker
Jigger
Launch
Lorcha
Lugger
Masula
Monkey
Mother
Nuggar
Packet
Pedalo
Pequod
Pinkie
Pirate
Pitpan
Pulwar
Puteli
Randan

Reefer
Saique
Sampan
Sandal
School
Schuit
Schuyt
Settee
Slaver
Tanker
Tartan
Tender
Tonner
Torpid
Trader
Trek-ox
Turret
Whaler
Wherry
Zebeck

7 letters:
Belfast
Bidarka
Bumboat
Capital
Caravel
Carrack
Carract
Carrect
Catboat
Clipper
Coaster
Collier
Consort
Coracle
Counter
Cruiser
Currach
Curragh
Dredger
Drifter
Drogher
Dromond
Factory
Felucca
Flattop
Flyboat
Frigate
Gabbard
Gabbart

Galleon
Galliot
Galloon
Geordie
Gondola
Gunboat
Jetfoil
Kontiki
Liberty
Lymphad
Masoola
Mistico
Monitor
Mudscow
Mystery
Oomiack
Patamar
Pelican
Pinnace
Piragua
Pirogue
Polacca
Polacre
Pontoon
Repulse
Revenge
Sculler
Shallop
Sharpie
Steamer
Stew-can
Tartane
Titanic
Trawler
Trireme
Tugboat
Vedette
Victory
Vidette
Weather

8 letters:
Acapulco
Bilander
Billyboy
Bylander
Cabotage
Corocore
Corocoro
Corvette
Dahabieh

Faldboat
Flagship
Flatboat
Foldboat
Galleass
Galliass
Gallivat
Hospital
Hoveller
Indiaman
Ironclad
Longboat
Longship
Mackinaw
Mary Rose
Masoolah
Merchant
Monohull
Mosquito
Pinafore
Sallyman
Savannah
Schooner
Shanghai
Showboat
Training

9 letters:
Bucentaur
Catamaran
Container
Cutty Sark
Dahabeeah
Dahabiyah
Dahabiyeh
Discovery
Dromedary
Freighter
Frigatoon
Hydrofoil
Klondiker
Klondyker
Lapstrake
Lapstreak
Leviathan
Lightship
Mayflower
Minelayer
Monoxylon
Multihull
Outrigger

9 letters – cont:
Peter-boat
Privateer
Sallee-man
Shear-hulk
Sheer-hulk
Steamboat
Submarine
Vaporetto
Whale-back
Whaleboat

10 letters:
Brigantine
Golden Hind

Hydroplane
Icebreaker
Knockabout
Mine-hunter
Paddleboat
Quadrireme
Santa Maria
Trekschuit
Triaconter
Windjammer

11 letters:
Barquentine
Bellerophon
Berthon-boat

Cockleshell
Dreadnought
Merchantman
Minesweeper
Penteconter
Quinquereme
Side-wheeler
Skidbladnir
Submersible
Supertanker
Three-decker
Three-master
Torpedo boat
Victualling

12 letters:
East Indiaman
Fore-and-after
Great Eastern
Marie Celeste
Stern-wheeler
Tangle-netter

13 letters:
Paddle steamer

14 letters:
Flying Dutchman
Ocean greyhound

Shipmate Crew, Hearty, Sailor
Shipping line P and O
Ship's biscuit Dandyfunk, Dunderfunk
Shipshape Apple-pie, Neat, Orderly, Tidy, Trim
Shipwreck Split
Shire Comitatus, County
Shirk(er) Cuthbert, Dodge, Embusqué, Evade, Funk, Gold brick, Malinger, Mike, Pike, Poler, Scrimshank, Skive, Skrimshank, Slack, Soldier
Shirt Aloha, Black, Boiled, Brown, Bush, Calypso, Camese, Camise, Chemise, Choli, Cilice, Dasheki, Dashiki, Dick(e)y, Dress, Fiesta, Garibaldi, Grandad, Hair, Hawaiian, Hoodie, Jacky Howe, Kaftan, Kaross, K(h)urta, Muscle, Nessus, Non-iron, Parka, Partlet, Polo, Rash, Red, Rugby, Safari, Sark, Serk, Set, Shift, Smock, Sports, Stuffed, Subucula, Swan(n)dri®, Sweat, T
Shiva Destroyer
▷ **Shiver(ed)** *may indicate* an anagram
Shiver(ing), Shivers, Shivery Aguish, Atingle, Break, Brrr, Chitter, Crumble, Dash, Dither, Fragile, Frisson, Grew, Grue, Malaria, Nither, Oorie, Ourie, Owrie, Quake, Quiver, → **SHAKE**, Shatter, Shrug, Shudder, Smash, Smither, Smithereens, Splinter, Timbers, Tremble
Shoal Bar, Fish, Quantity, Reef, Run, Sand-bar, School, Shallows, Shelf, Tail
Shock(ed), Shocker, Shocking Acoustic, Aghast, Agitate, Anaphylactic, Appal, Astound, Astun, Awhape, Bombshell, Brunt, Bunch, Consternate, Criminal, Culture, Defibrillate, Disgust, Dorlach, Dreadful, Drop, Earthquake, ECT, Egregious, Electric, Electrocute, EST, Epiphenomenon, Fleg, Floccus, Forelock, Gait, Galvanism, Gobsmack, Hair, Horrify, Impact, Infamous, Insulin, Jar, Jolt, Knock cold, Live, Mane, Mop, Numb, Obscene, Outrage, Poleaxe, Putrid, Recoil, Return, Revolt, Rick(er), Rigor, Scandal(ise), Seismic, Shaghaired, Shake, Sheaf, Shell, Shilling, Shog, Shook, Stagger, Start(le), Stitch, Stook, Stound, Stun, Surgical, Tangle, Thermal, Trauma, Turn
Shock-absorber Buffer, Oleo, Snubber
▷ **Shocked** *may indicate* an anagram
Shod Calced
Shoddy Cagmag, Catchpenny, Cheap, Cheapjack, Cheapo, Cloth, Cowboy, Drecky, Gimcrack, Imitation, Oorie, Ourie, Owrie, Poor, Rag-wool, Ropy, Schlock, → **SHABBY**, Slopwork, Tatty, Tawdry, Tinny

Shoe(s) Accessory, Arctic, Athletic, Ballet, Balmoral, Bauchle, Blocked, Boat, Boot, Bootee, Brake, Brogan, Brogue, Brothel creepers, Buskin, Calceate, Calk(er), Calkin, Carpet slipper, Casuals, Caulker, Cawker, Charlier, Chaussures, Chopin(e), Clodhopper, Clog, Co-respondent, Court, Creeper, Dap, Deck, Espadrille, Flattie, Galoche, Galosh, Gatty, Geta, Ghillie, Golosh, Gumboot, Gumshoe, Gym, High-low, High tops, Hot, Hush-puppies®, Jandal®, Jellies, Kletterschue, Kurdaitcha, Launch(ing), Loafer, Mary-Janes®, Mocassin, Moccasin, Muil, Mule, Open-toe, Oxford, Oxonian, Panton, Patten, Peeptoe, Pennyloafer, Pile, Plate, Plimsole, Plimsoll, Poulaine, Pump, Rivlin, Rope-soled, Rubbers, Rullion, Runner, Sabaton, Sabot, Saddle, Safety, Sandal, Sandshoe, Sannie, Scarpetto, Shauchle, Skid, Skimmer, Slingback, Slip-on, Slipper, Slip-slop, Sneaker, Snow, Sock, Soft, Solleret, Spike, Stoga, Stogy, Suede, Tackies, Takkies, Tennis, Tie, Topboot, Track, Trainer, Upper, Vamp(er), Veld-schoen, Veldskoen, Velskoen, Vibram®, Vibs, Wagon lock, Wedgie, Welt, Winkle-picker, Zori

Shoeless Barefoot, Discalced

Shoemaker Blacksmith, Clogger, Cobbler, Cordiner, Cordwainer, Cosier, Cozier, Crispi(a)n, Farrier, Gentle craft, Leprechaun, Sachs, Smith, Snob, Soutar, Souter, Sowter, Sutor

Shoe-string Cheap, Lace, Pittance

Shoe-toe Poulaine

Shoo Away, Begone, Hoosh, Off, Scat(ter), Voetsek

Shoot(er), Shooting Ack-ack, Airgun, Arrow, Bine, Bostryx, Braird, Breer, Bud, Bulbil, Catapult, Chit, Cion, Cyme, Dart(le), Delope, Discharge, Drib, Elance, Enate, Eradiate, Film, Fire, Flagellum, Germ, Germain(e), Germen, Germin(ate), Glorious twelfth, → **GUN**, Gunsel, Head-reach, Hurl, Imp, Jet, Layer, Limb, Loose, Offset, Photocall, Photograph, Pluff, Plug, Poot, Pop, Pot, Pout, Ramulus, Rapids, Ratoon, Riddle, Rod, Rove, Runner, Scion, Septembriser, Sien(t), Skeet, Snap, Snipe, Spire, Spirt, Spout, Spray, Sprout, Spurt, Spyre, Start, Stole, Stolon, Strafe, Sucker, Syen, Tellar, Teller, Tendril, Tiller, Trap, Turion, Twelfth, Twig, Udo, Vimen, Wand, Weapon, Whiz(z), Wildfowler, Zap

Shop(s), Shopper, Shopping Agency, Arcade, Assembly, Atelier, Betray, Body, Boutique, Bucket, Buy, Chain, Charity, Chippy, Closed, Coffee, Commissary, Cook, Co-op, Cop, Corner, Cut-price, Dairy, Delicatessen, Denounce, Dobbin, Dolly, Duddery, Duka, Duty-free, Emporium, Factory, Five and dime, Food court, Galleria, Gift, Grass, In bond, Inform, Junk, Luckenbooth, Machine, Mall, Mall-rat, Market, Megastore, Mercat, Messages, Muffler, Officinal, Off-licence, Off-sales, Open, Opportunity, Outlet, Parlour, Patisserie, Personal, Precinct, Print, PX, Rat on, Report, Retail, RMA, Salon, Sex, Shambles, Share, Shebang, Spaza, Squat, → **STORE**, Strip mall, Studio, Sundry, Superette, Supermarket, Superstore, Swap, Talking, Tally, Tea, Thrift, Tick, Tommy, Trade, Truck, Tuck, Union, Vintry, Warehouse, Whistle-blow, Works

Shopkeeper British, Butcher, Chemist, Clothier, Gombeen-man, Greengrocer, Grocer, Haberdasher, Hosier, Ironmonger, Merchant, Newsagent, Provisioner, Retailer, Stationer, Tradesman

Shoplift(er) Boost, Heist

Shore Bank, Beach, Buttress, Coast, Coastline, Coste, Eustatic, Foreside, Landfall, Lee, Littoral, Machair, Offing, Prop, Rance, Rivage, Saxon, Seaboard, Strand, Strandline, Support

Short(en), Shortly Abbreviate, Abridge, Abrupt, Anon, Apocope, Brief, Brusque, Close-in, Commons, Compendious, Concise, Contract, Crisp, Cross, Curt, Curtail, Curtal, Diminish, Drink, Eftsoons, Epitomise, Ere-long, Fubsy, Fuse, Impolite,

Inadequate, Lacking, Laconical, Light, Limited, Low, Mini, Near, Nip, Nutshell, Offing, Pudsey, Punch, Pyknic, Reduce, Reef, Retrench, Scanty, Scarce, Shrift, Shy, Soon, Sparse, Spirit, Squab, Squat, Squat(ty), Staccato, Stint, Stocky, Strapped, Stubby, Succinct, Syncopate, Systole, Taciturn, Teen(s)y, Telescope, Temporal, Temporaneous, Terse, Tight, Tot, Towards, Transient, Wee

Shortage Dearth, Deficiency, Deficit, Drought, Famine, Lack, Need, Paucity, Scarcity, Sparsity, Wantage

Short circuit Varistor

Shortcoming Sin, Weakness

Shorthand Diphone, Gregg, Outline, Phonographic, Phraseogram, Pitman, Speedwriting®, Stenography, Stenotypy, Tachygraphy, Tironian, Tironian notes, Triphone, Weblish

Short-headed Brachycephal

Short-lived Ephemeral, Fragile, Meson, Transitory

Shorts Bermuda, Board, Boxer, Briefs, Culottes, Cycling, Hot pants, Kaccha, Lederhosen, Plus-fours, Skort, Stubbies®, Trunks

Short-sight Myopia, Myosis

Short-winded Breathless, Concise, Puffed, Purfled, Pursy, Succinct

Shot(s) Aim, All-in, Ammo, Approach, Attempt, Backhand, Ball, Bank, Barrage, Bisque, Blank, Blast, Bricole, Bull, Bullet, Burl, Canna, Cannonball, Cartridge, Case, Chain, Chatoyant, Chip, Corner, Cover, Crab, Crack, Daisy cutter, Dink, Dolly, Dram, Draw, Drop, Duckhook, Dum dum, Dunk, Elt, Essay, Exhausted, Explosion, Forehand, Fusillade, Gesse, Get, Glance, Go, Grape, Guess, Gun-stone, Hook, In-off, Iridescent, Jump, Langrage, Langrel, Langridge, Lay-up, Longjenny, Magpie, Marksman, Massé, Matte, Mitraille, Money, Moon-ball, Mulligan, Multi-coloured, Musket, Noddy, Pack, Parthian, Parting, Passing, Pelican, Pellet, Penalty, Photo, Plant, Pluff, Pop, Pot, Puff, Push, Rake, Rid, Round, Safety, Salvo, Scratch, Shy, Sighter, Silk, Six, Slam-dunk, Slap, Slice, Slug, Slung, Sped, Spell, Spent, Square cut, Stab, Still, Streaked, Tap in, Tee, Throw, Tonic, Tracking, Trial, Try, Turn, Volley, Warning, Wrist

Should Ought

Shoulder(-blade) Carry, Cold, Crossette, Epaule, Frozen, Hard, Hump, Joggle, Omohyoid, Omoplate, Pick-a-back, Roadside, Scapula, Shouther, Soft, Spald, Spall, Spaul(d), Speal, Spule, Tote, Withers

Shout(er), Shouting Barrack, Bawl, Bellock, Bellow, Boanerges, Call, Claim, Clamour, Conclamation, Cry, Din, Exclaim, Geronimo, Heckle, Hey, Hoi(cks), Holla, Holla-ho(a), Holler, Hollo, Holloa, Hooch, Hosanna, Howzat, Hue, Oi, Oy, Parnell, Rah, Rant, Root, Round, Sa sa, Treat, Trumpet, Vociferate, Whoop, Yell(och), Yippee, Yoohoo, Yorp

Shove Barge, Birr, Elbow, Jostle, Push, Ram, Spoon, Thrust

Shovel Backhoe, Dustpan, Hat, Loy, Main, Peel, Power, Scoop, Shool, Spade, Steam, Trowel, Van

Show(ing), Shown, Showy Anonyma, Appearance, Aquacade, Bad, Bench, Betray, Branky, Broadcast, Brummagem, Burlesque, Cabaret, Cattle, Chat, Circus, Come, Con, Cruft's, Demo(nstrate), Depict, Dime museum, Diorama, Display, Do, Dramedy, Dressy, Dumb, Effeir, Effere, Endeictic, Entertainment, Epideictic, Establish, Evince, → **EXHIBIT**, Expo, Express, Extravaganza, Exude, Facade, Fair, Fangled, Farce, Flamboyant, Flash, Flaunt, Floor, Galanty, Game, Garish, Gaudy, Gay, Gig, Give, Glitter, Glitz(y), Gloss, Good, Horse, Indicate, Jazzy, Kismet, Light, Loud, Manifest, Matinée, Meretricious, Minstrel, Musical, Naumachy, One-man, Ostensible, Ostentatious, Pageant, Panel game, Pantomime, Parade, Patience,

Peacock, Performance, Phen(o), Phone-in, Point, Pomp, Portray, Presentation, Pretence, Pride, Procession, Prog(ramme), Project, Prominence, Prove, Pseudery, Puff, Puppet, Quiz, Raree, Razzmatazz, Reality, Register, Represent, Reveal, Revue, Road, Roll-out, Ruddigore, Rushes, Screen, Shaw, Sight, Sitcom, Slang, Soap, Son et lumière, Specious, Spectacle, Splash, Splay, Stage, Stunt, Talk, Tamasha, Tattoo, Tawdry, Telecast, Telethon, Theatrical, Three-man, Tinhorn, Tinsel(ly), Tulip, Unbare, Uncover, Usher, Vain, Variety, Vaudeville, Veneer, Viewy, Wear, Wild west, Zarzuela

Showdown Confrontation, Crunch

Shower Douche, Exhibitor, Flurry, Hail, Indicant, Indicator, Kitchen tea, Lavish, Meteor, Party, Pelt, Pepper, Precipitation, Rain, Scat, Scouther, Scowther, Skatt, Skit, Snow, Spat, Spet, Spit, Splatter, Spray, Sprinkle, Ticker tape

▷ **Showers** *may indicate* an anagram

Showgirl Evita, Nanette

▷ **Showing, Shown in** *may indicate* a hidden word

Showman Bailey, Barnum, Entertainer, Goon, Impresario, Lord Mayor, MC, Ringmaster

Show-off Coxcomb, Exhibitionist, Extrovert, Flash Harry, Jack the lad, Peacock, Piss artist, Poseur, Sport, Swagger, Swank

Showpiece Flagship

Show-place Exhibition, Olympia, Pavilion, Theatre

Shrapnel Fragment, Shell, Splinter

Shred Clout, Filament, Grate, Julienne, Mammock, Mince, Mummock, Rag, Screed, Swarf, Tag, Ta(i)ver, Tatter, Thread, To-tear, Wisp

Shrew Bangsring, Banxring, Callet, Catamaran, Elephant, Fury, Hellcat, Kate, Marabunta, Musk, Nag, Otter, Pygmy, Show, Solenodon, Sondeli, Sorex, Spitfire, Squirrel, Tana, Termagant, Tree, Trull, Tupaia, Virago, Vixen, Water, Xant(h)ippe, Yankie, Yenta

Shrewd Acute, Arch, Argute, Artful, Astucious, Astute, Callid, Canny, Clued-up, Cute, Far-sighted, File, Gnostic, Gumptious, Hard-nosed, Judicious, Knowing, Pawky, Politic, Prudent(ial), Sagacious, Sapient(al), Savvy, Wily, Wise

Shriek Cry, Scream, Scrike, Shright, Shrike, Shrill, Shritch, Skirl, Yell

Shrift Attention, Penance, Short

Shrike Bird, Butcher-bird

Shrill Argute, High, Keen, Piping, Reedy, Screech, Sharp, Skirl, Squeaky, Treble

Shrimp(s) Brine, Crevette, Fairy, Freshwater, Krill, Mantis, Midge, Opossum, Potted, Prawn, Runt, Sand, Skeleton, Small, Spectre, Squill(a), Stomatopod

Shrine Adytum, Altar, Dagaba, Dagoba, Dargah, Delphi, Fatima, Feretory, Harem, Holy, Joss house, Kaaba, Marabout, Martyry, Memorial, Naos, Pagoda, Reliquary, Scrine, Scryne, Stupa, Tabernacle, Temple, Tope, Vimana, Walsingham

Shrink(age), Shrinking, Shrunk Alienist, Analyst, Blanch, Blench, Boggle, Cling, Compress, Constringe, Contract, Cour, Cower, Creep, Crine, Cringe, Dare, Decrew, Depreciate, Dread, Dwindle, Flinch, Funk, Gizzen, Less, Nirl, → **PSYCHIATRIST**, Pycnosis, Quail, Recoil, Reduce, Retract, Sanforised, Shrivel, Shrug, Shy, Sphacelate, Timid, Violet, Wane, Waste, Wince, Wizened

Shrivel(led) Cling, Crine, Desiccate, Dry, Nirl, Parch, Scorch, Scrump, Sear, Shrink, Skrimp, Skrump, Tabid, Welk, Wither, Wizened, Writhled

Shropshire Salop

Shroud(s) Cerecloth, Chadri, Chuddah, Chuddar, Cloak, Cloud, Conceal, Cover, Futtock, Grave-cloth, Pall, Rigging, Screen, Sheet, Sindon, Turin, Veil, Winding-sheet, Wrap

Shrove Tuesday Fastens, J'ouvert, Pancake
Shrub(bery) Arboret, Brush, → **BUSH**, Dead-finish, Horizontal, Petty whin, Plant,
Undergrowth

SHRUBS

3 letters:	Senna	Savine	Weigela
Kat	Thyme	Smilax	
Qat	Toyon	Sorbus	*8 letters:*
Rue	Wahoo	Storax	Abutilon
	Yapon	Sumach	Allspice
4 letters:	Yupon	Tutsan	Barberry
Coca	Zamia	Yaupon	Bayberry
Cola			Berberis
Dita	*6 letters:*	*7 letters:*	Bignonia
Grex	Acacia	Acerola	Bilberry
Hebe	Alhagi	Akiharo	Bluebush
Kava	Ambach	Ambatch	Buddleia
Nabk	Aucuba	Arbutus	Camellia
Olea	Azalea	Bauhini	Caragana
Rhus	Bauera	Boronia	Coprosma
Ruta	Cobaea	Bullace	Cowberry
Sunn	Correa	Cascara	Danewort
Titi	Croton	Chamise	Euonymus
Tutu	Crowea	Cytisus	Gardenia
Ulex	Daphne	Deutzia	Hardhack
	Fatsia	Dogwood	Heketara
5 letters:	Feijoa	Emubush	Hibiscus
Aalii	Frutex	Epacris	Horopito
Bosky	Fustet	Ephedra	Inkberry
Brere	Fynbos	Filbert	Japonica
Buaze	Garrya	Fuchsia	Jetbread
Buazi	Jojoba	Guayule	Koromiko
Buchu	Kalmia	Hop-tree	Krameria
Caper	Laurel	Jasmine	Lavender
Gorse	Lignum	Juniper	Leadwort
Hakea	Manoao	Lantana	Magnolia
Hazel	Manuka	Mahonia	Mairehau
Henna	Maquis	Mesquit	Mezereon
Holly	Matico	Muntrie	Ninebark
Ledum	Mimosa	Oleacea	Ocotillo
Maqui	Myrica	Phlomis	Oleander
Monte	Myrtle	Rhatany	Oleaster
Mulga	Nebbuk	Romneya	Photinia
Nebek	Nebeck	Rosebay	Rangiora
Peony	Neinei	Savanna	Rock rose
Pyxie	Paeony	Shallon	Rosemary
Ramee	Pituri	Skimmia	Saltbush
Ramie	Privet	Syringa	Savannah
Salal	Protea	Tea-tree	Shadbush
Savin	Prunus	Waratah	Snowbush

Sorbaria
Spekboom
Sweetsop
Tamarisk
Viburnum
Waxplant

9 letters:
Andromeda
Bearberry
Buckthorn
Ceanothus
Clianthus
Cordyline
Coreopsis
Coyotillo
Croqberry
Eucryphia
Firethorn
Forsythia
Gelsemium
Grevillia
Hamamelis
Hydrangea
Jaborandi
Jessamine

Kumarahou
Manzanita
Melaleuca
Mistletoe
Patchouli
Pernettya
Perovskia
Phillyria
Rauwolfia
Snowberry
Spicebush
Sterculia
Tree peony
Widow wall
Wolfberry

10 letters:
Aphelandra
Callicarpa
Cascarilla
Crossandra
Embothrium
Eriostemon
Escallonia
Fatshedera
Frangipani

Fringe tree
Gaultheria
Goat's thorn
Gooseberry
Greasewood
Holodiscus
Joshua tree
Laurustine
Marcgravia
Mock orange
Mock privet
Parkleaves
Pilocarpus
Poinsettia
Potentilla
Pyracantha
Schefflera
Supplejack
Twinflower

11 letters:
Beautybrush
Bottlebrush
Carpenteria
Chaenomeles
Cotoneaster

Honeysuckle
Huckleberry
Japan laurel
Leatherwood
Mustard tree
Pittosporum
Postanthera
Staggerbush
Steeplebush
Stephanotis
Wintergreen
Wintersweet
Wortleberry

12 letters:
Phanerophyte
Philadelphus
Rhododendron
Serviceberry
Southernwood
Streptosolen
Strophanthus

13 letters:
Wayfaring tree
Winter jasmine

Shrug Discard, Toss
Shuck Peel
Shudder(ing) Abhor, Ashake, Frisson, Grew, Grise, Grue, Horror, Jerk, Quake, Shake, Spasm, Tremble, Tremor
Shuffle(d) Dodge, Drag, Hedge, Make, Mix, Palter, Permute, Randomise, Rearrange, Redeployment, Riffle, Scuff, Shamble, Shauchle, Soft-shoe, Stack
▷ **Shuffle(d)** *may indicate* an anagram
Shun Attention, Avoid, Eschew, Evade, Forbear, Ignore, Ostracise, Secede, → **SPURN**
Shunt Move, Shelve, Shuttle, Side-track
Shut(down; in; out; up), Shut(s) Bar, Cage, Close, Confined, Coop, Debar, Embar, Emure, Fasten, Fend, Impale, Impound, Latch, Lay-off, Lock, Occlude, Rid, Scram, Seal, Shet, Slam, Spar, Steek, Telescope, Tine, To
Shutter(s) Blind, B-setting, Damper, Dead-lights, Douser, Focal-plane, Jalousie, Louvre, Persiennes, Shade
Shuttle Alternate, Commute, Drawer, Flute, Go-between, Navette, Orbiter, Shoot, Shunt, Space, Tat(t), Weave
Shy Bashful, Blate, Blench, Cast, Catapult, Chary, Coy, Deficient, Demure, Farouche, Flinch, Funk, Heave, Introvert, Jerk, Jib, Laithfu', Leery, Lob, Mim, Mims(e)y, Mousy, Rear, Recoil, Reserved, Reticent, Retiring, Sheepish, Shrinking, Skeigh, Start, Thraw, Throw, Timid, Tongue-tied, Toss, Try, Verecund, Violet, Willyard, Willyart, Withdrawn
Shyster Ambulance chaser
Siamese, Siamese twins Chang, Eng, Parabiosis, Seal-point, T(h)ai
Siberia(n) Chukchi, Evenki, Ostiak, Ostyak, Samo(y)ed, Tungus, Vogul, Yakut, Yupik

Sibilant Hissing, Whistling
Sibling Brother, German, Kin, Sister
Sibyl Oracle, Prophetess, Seer, Soothsayer, Voluspa, Witch
Sicilian Sicanian, Trinacrian
Sick(en), Sickening, Sickliness, Sickly, Sickness Aegrotat, Affection, Ague, Ail, Altitude, Bad, Bends, Cat, Chalky, Chunder, Colic, Crapulence, Cringeworthy, Crook, Decompression, Delicate, Disorder, Donsie, Gag, Green, Hangover, Icky, Ill, Infection, Leisure, Maid-pale, Mal, Mawkish, Milk, Morbid, Morning, Motion, Mountain, Nauseous, Pale, Peaky, Peelie-wallie, Peely-wally, Pestilent, Pindling, Plague, Puly, Puna, Queachy, Queasy, Queechy, Radiation, Regorge, Repulsive, Retch, Serum, Shilpit, Sleeping, Sleepy, Soroche, Space, Spue, Squeamish, Sweating, Travel, Twee, Uncle Dick, Valetudinarian, Virus, Vomit, Wamble-cropped, Wan
Sick bay San
Sickle(-shaped) Badging-hook, Bagging-hook, Falcate, Falx, Grasshook, Hook, Scythe, Shear
Side Abeam, Airs, Ally, B, Beam, Blind, Border, Branch, Camp, Cis-, Distaff, Division, Edge, Effect, Eleven, English, Epistle, Ex intraque parte, Facet, Flank, Flip, Gospel, Gunnel, Hand, Heavy, Hypotenuse, Iliac, Lateral, Lee(ward), Left, Long, Obverse, Off, On, OP, Pane, Part, Partisan, Party, Port, Pretension, Profile, Prompt, Rave, Reveal, Reverse, Right, Rink, Short, Silver, Slip, Spear, Starboard, Swank, → **TEAM**, Tight, Weak, West, Wind, Windward, Wing, XI
Sideboard(s) Beauf(f)et, Buffet, Cellaret, Commode, Credence, Credenza, Dinner-wagon, Dresser, Whiskers
Side-effect, Side-issue Fall-out, Logograph, Logogriph, Offshoot, Secondary, Spin-off
Sidekick Right-hand man, Satellite
Side-line Hobby, Lye, Siding, Spur
Side-step Crab, Dodge, Evade, Hedge, Maori, Volt
Side-track Distract, Divert, Shunt
Sidewalk Crab, Footpath, Pavement
Sideways Askance, End-on, Indirect, Laterally, Laterigrade, Oblique
Siding Alliance, Byway, Lie, Lye, Spur, Turnout
Sidle Edge, Passage
Siege (work), Siege engine Alamo, Antioch, Antwerp, Beleaguer, Beset, Blockade, Bog, Charleston, Gherao, Investment, Khartoum, Ladysmith, Leaguer, Mafeking, Masada, Metz, Obsidional, Perilous, Pleven, Plevna, Poliorcetic, Ravelin, Sarajevo, Surround, Verdun, Vicksburg, Warsaw, Warwolf
Sienese Tuscan
Sienna Burnt, Raw
Siesta Nap, Noonday, Nooning
Sieve, Sift(ing) Analyse, Bolt(er), Boult(er), Bunting, Colander, Coliform, Cribble, Cribrate, Cribrose, Cullender, Eratosthenes, Ethmoid, Filter, Molecular, Rice, Riddle, Screen, Searce, Search, Separate, Siler, Strain, Sye, Tamis, Tammy, Tems(e), Trommel, Try, Winnow
Sigh Exhale, Heave, Lackaday, Long, Moan, Sithe, Sough, Suspire, Welladay
Sight(ed) Aim, Barleycorn, Bead, Conspectuity, Eye(ful), Eyesore, Glimpse, Ken, Long, Oculated, Panoramic, Peep, Prospect, Range, Rear, Riflescope, Scene, Scotopia, Second, See, Short, Spectacle, Taish, Telescopic, Vane, → **VIEW**, Visie, Vision, Vista, Vizy, Vizzie
Sight-screen Eyelid
Sightseer, Sightseeing Lionise, Observer, Rubberneck, Tourist, Tripper, Viewer

Sign(s), Signing, Signpost Accidental, Ache, Addition, Ale-stake, Ampassy, Ampersand, Aquarius, Archer, Aries, Arrow, Auspice, Autograph, Badge, Balance, Beck, Beckon, Birth, Board, Brand, Bull, Bush, Call, Cancer, Capricorn, Caract, Caret, Character, Chevron, Clue, Coronis, Crab, Cross, Cue, Dactylology, Dele, Denote, Diacritic, Di(a)eresis, Diphone, Division, Dollar, DS, Earmark, Emblem, Endeixis, Endorse, Endoss, Enlist, Evidence, Exit, Fascia, Fish, Gemini, Gesture, Goat, Grammalogue, Hallmark, Hamza(h), Harbinger, Harvey Smith, Hash, Hex, Hieroglyphic, Hint, Ideogram, Indian, Indicate, Indication, Indicium, Initial, INRI, Inscribe, Ivy-bush, Leo, Lexigram, Libra, Local, Logogram, Milepost, Milestone, Minus, Mudra, Multiplication, Negative, Neume, Nod, Notice, Obelisk, Obelus, Omen, Peace, Phraseogram, Pisces, Plus, Positive, Pound, Presa, Presage, Prodrome, Prodromus, Radical, Ram, Ratify, Rest, Rune, Sacrament, Sagittarius, Sain, Scorpio, Segno, Semeion, Semiotics, Shingle, Show, Sigil, Sigla, Signal, Star, Subscribe, Subtraction, Superscribe, Symbol, Symptom, Syndrome, Tag, Taurus, Tic(k)tac(k), Tilde, Titulus, Token, Trace, Triphone, Twins, Umlaut, V, Vestige, Virgo, Vital, Warning, Waymark, Word, Zodiac

Signal(ler) Alarm, Aldis lamp, Alert, Amber, Assemble, Baud, Beacon, Bell, Bleep, Bugle, Busy, Buzz, Call, Chamade, Code, Compander, Compandor, Cone, Cue, Detonator, Diaphone, Distant, Distress, Duplex, Earcon, Flag, Flagman, Flare, Flash, Fog, Gantry, Gesticulate, Gong, Griffin, Gun, Harmonic, Heliograph, Heliostat, Herald, Heterodyne, High sign, Hooter, Horse and hattock, Icon, Important, Interrupt, Interval, Luminance, Mark, Mase, Megafog, Message, Modem, Morse, Navar, NICAM, Notation, Noted, Output, Password, Peter, Pinger, Pip, Pollice verso, Prod, Pulsar, Radio, Renowned, Reveille, Robot, Salient, Semaphore, Semiology, Simplex, Singular, Smoke, Sonogram, SOS, Spoiler, Squawk, Taps, Target, Tattoo, Tchick, Telegraph, Teles(e)me, Thumb, Tic(k)-tac(k), Time, Traffic, Transmit, Troop, Vehicle-actuated, Very, Video, V-sign, Waff, Waft, Wave, Wave-off, Wigwag, Word

Signature Alla breve, Allograph, Autograph, By-line, Digital, Hand, John Hancock, John Henry, Key, Mark, Onomastic, Sheet, Specimen, Subscription, Time

Signet Ring, Seal, Sigil, Sphragistics

Significance, Significant Cardinal, Consequence, Cosmic, Emblem, Ethos, Great, Impact, Important, Indicative, Key, M(a)cGubbin, Magnitude, Major, Material, Matter, Meaningful, Milestone, Moment(ous), Noted, Noteworthy, Other, Paramount, Pith, Pregnant, Salient, Special, Telling

Signify Bemean, Denote, Imply, Indicate, Intimate, Matter, → **MEAN**, Represent

Sign language Ameslan, Semaphore, Tic(k)tac(k)

Sikh(ism) Granth, Kaccha, Kangha, Kara, Kesh, Khalsa, Kirpan, Mazhbi, Mechanised, Nanak, (Ranjit) Singh

Silas Uncle, Wegg

Silence(r), Silent Amyclaean, Choke-pear, Clam, Clamour, Conticent, Creepmouse, Dead air, Dumbstruck, Earplug, Gag, Hesychastic, Hist, Hush, Hushkit, Mim(budget), Muffler, Mum(p), Mumchance, Mute, Obmutescent, Omertà, Quench, Quiesce, → **QUIET**, Reticence, Shtoom, Shush, Speechless, Squelch, Still, Sulky, Tace(t), Tacit(urn), Throttle, Tight-lipped, Unvoiced, Wheesh(t), Whis(h)t

Silhouette Contour, Outline, Planform, Profile, Shadow figure, Shadowgraph, Shape, Skyline

Silica(te) Albite, Analcite, Andalusite, Chabazite, Chert, Cristobalite, Datolite, Diopside, Dioptase, Fayalite, Float-stone, Gadolinite, Garnierite, Harmotome, Heulandite, Hiddenite, Humite, Iolite, Kieselguhr, Kyanite, Monticellite, Montmorillonite, Olivine, Opal, Pectolite, Penninite, Phillipsite, Pinite, Rhodonite,

Riebeckite, Saponite, Scapolite, Silex, Spodumene, Staurolite, Stishovite, Tridymite, Tripoli, Ultrabasic, Vermiculite, Vitreosil®, Vitreous, Zeolite

Silicon Chip, Si

Silk(y), Silk screen Alamode, Artificial, Atlas, Barathea, Blonde-lace, Brocade, Bur(r), Charmeuse®, Chenille, Chiffon, Cocoon, Corn, Crape, Crepe, Duchesse, Dupion, Faille, Fibroin, Filature, Filoselle, Florence, Florentine, Flosh, Floss, Flox, Foulard, Gazar, Gazzatum, Georgette, Gimp, Glossy, Grosgrain, KC, Kincob, Lustrine, Lustring, Lutestring, Makimono, Malines, Marabou(t), Matelasse, Mercery, Moiré, Near, Ninon, Oiled, Organza, Ottoman, Paduasoy, Parachute, Peau de soie, Pongee, Prunella, Prunelle, Prunello, Pulu, QC, Raw, Samite, Sars(e)net, Satin, Schappe, Seal(ch), Sendal, Seric, Sericeous, Sericite, Serigraph, Shalli, Shantung, Sien-tsan, Sleave, Sleek, Sle(i)ded, Slipper satin, Smooth, Soft, Spun, Surah, Tabaret, Tabby, Taffeta, Tasar, Thistledown, Tiffany, Tram, Tulle, Tussah, Tusseh, Tusser, Tussore, Vegetable, Velvet, Wild

Silkworm (eggs), Silkworm disease Bombyx, Eria, Graine, Multivoltine, Muscardine, Sericulture, Tussore

Sill Ledge, Straining, Threshold, Whin

Silly, Silliness Absurd, Anserine, Apish, Brainless, Buffer, Crass, Cuckoo, Daft, Dandy, Ditsy, Divvy, Drippy, Dumb, Dunce, Fatuous, Fluffy, Folly, Fool, Foolery, Footling, Frivolous, Goopy, Goosey, Gormless, Hen-witted, Idiotic, Imbecile, Inane, Inept, Infield(er), Liminal, Mid-off, Mid-on, Mopoke, Puerile, Season, Simple, Soft(y), Spoony, → **STUPID**, Tomfoolery, Tripe, Wacky

▷ **Silly** *may indicate* relating to a sill

Silt Alluvium, Deposit, Dregs, Land, Lees, Loess, Residue, Sullage, Varve

▷ **Silver** *may indicate* a coin

Silver(skin) Ag, Albata, Alpac(c)a, Arg(ent), Argyria, British plate, Cardecue, Cat, Cerargyrite, Diana's tree, Electroplate, Free, Fulminating, German, Grey, Horn, Luna, Nickel, One-legged, Pakt(h)ong, Parcel-gilt, Pegleg, Piastre, Plate, Plateresque, Ruby, Stephanite, Sterling, Sycee, Thaler

Silversmith Demetrius, Lamerie, Plater

Simian Apelike, Catar(r)hine

Similar(ity) Analog(ue), Analogical, Corresponding, Equivalent, Etc, Homoeoneric, Homogeneous, Homoiousian, Homologous, Homonym, Isomorphism, Kindred, → **LIKE**, Parallel, Patristic, Resemblance, Samey, Suchlike

Simile Epic

Similitude Parable

Simmer Bubble, Poach, Seethe, Stew

Simon Bolivar, Cellarer, Magus, Peter, Pure, Simple

Simper Bridle, Giggle, Smirk

Simple(r), Simplicity, Simplify, Simply Aefa(u)ld, Afa(w)ld, Arcadian, Artless, Austere, Bald, Bare, Basic, Bog-standard, Breeze, Crude, Daw, Doddle, Doric, → **EASY**, Eath(e), Elegant, Elemental, ESN, Ethe, Facile, Fee, Folksy, Gomeral, Gotham, Green, Herb(alist), Herborist, Homespun, Idyllic, Incomposite, Inornate, Jaap, Japie, Mere, Moner(on), Naive(té), Naked, Niaiserie, Noddy, One-fold, Open and shut, Ordinary, Paraphrase, Pastoral, Peter, Plain, Pleon, Provincial, Pure, Reduce, Rustic, Saikless, Sapid, Semplice, Sheer, Silly, Simon, Spartan, Stupid, Tout court, Understated, Unsophisticated, Woollen

Simpleton Abderite, Airhead, Cokes, Cuckoo, Daw, Duffer, Flat, Fool, Gaby, Galah, Gomeral, Gomeril, Greenhorn, Juggins, Shot-clog, Spoon, → **STUPID PERSON**, Wiseacre, Zany

Simulate(d), Simulating Affect, Anti, Feign, Pretend, VR

Simultaneous Coinstantaneous, Contemporaneous, Synchronous, Together, Unison

Sin(ful) Aberrant, Accidie, Acedia, Actual, Anger, Avarice, Besetting, Bigamy, Capital, Cardinal, Covetousness, Crime, Deadly, Debt, Depravity, Envy, Err, Evil, Folly, Gluttony, Hamartiology, Harm, Hate, Impious, Lapse, Lust, Misdeed, Misdoing, Mortal, → **OFFENCE**, Original, Peccadillo, Piacular, Pride, Scape, Scarlet, Shirk, Sine, Sloth, Transgress, Trespass, Unrighteous, Venial, Vice, Wicked, Wrath, Wrong

Sinai Horeb, Mount

Since Ago, As, For, Meantime, Seeing, Sens, Sine, Sinsyne, Sith(en), Syne, Whereas, Ygo(e)

Sincere(ly), Sincerity Bona-fide, Candour, Earnest, Entire, Frank, Genuine, Heartfelt, Heartwhole, Honest, Open, Real(ly), Realtie, Simple-hearted, True, Verity, Whole-hearted

Sinclair Lewis, Upton

Sine Versed

Sinecure Bludge, Commendam

Sinew(y) Fibre, Ligament, Nerve, String, Tendinous, Tendon

▶ **Sinful** *see* **SIN**

Sing(ing) Antiphony, Barbershop, Bel canto, Belt out, Bhajan, Carol, Chant, Cheep, Chorus, Coloratura, Community, Cough, Croon, Crow, Diaphony, Diddle, Doo-wop, Glee club, Gorgia, Hum, Inform, Intone, Karaoke, Kirtan, La-la, Lilt, Lyricism, Melic, Parlando, Peach, Pen(n)illion, Pipe, Plainchant, Rand, Rant, Rap, Record, Render, Scat, Second(o), Serenade, Solmization, Sprechgesang, Sprechstimme, Squeal, Tell, Thrum, Trill, Troll, Vocalise, Warble, Woodshedding, Yodel

Singe Burn, Char, Scorch, Swale, Swayl, Sweal, Sweel

Singer(s) Alto, Balladeer, Bard, Baritone, Bass, Beatle, Bing, → **BIRD**, Blondel, Buffo, Callas, Canary, Cantabank, Cantatrice, Cantor, Car, Carreras, Caruso, Castrato, Chaliapin, Chanteuse, Chantor, Chauntress, Chazan, Cher, Chorister, Coloratura, Comprimario, Countertenor, Crooner, Dawson, Diva, Dylan, Ella, Falsetto, Folk, Gigli, Glee club, Gleemaiden, Gleeman, Grass, Griot, Haz(z)an, Heldentenor, Isaac, Kettle, Lark, Lauder, Lay clerk, Lead, Lind, Lorelei, Lulu, Mathis, Melba, Mezzo, Minstrel, Opera, Oscine, Patti, Piaf, Pitti, Precentor, Prima donna, Qawwal, Robeson, Semi-chorus, Session, Sinatra, Siren, Snitch, Songstress, Soprano, Soubrette, Stoolie, Succentor, Swan, Tatiana, Tenor, Tenure, Torch, Treble, Troubador, Vocalist, Voice, Wait, Warbler

Single, Singly Ace, Aefa(u)ld, Aefawld, Alone, Azygous, Bachelor, Celibate, Discriminate, EP, Exclusive, Feme sole, Haplo-, Individual, Matchless, Monact, Mono, Odd, One-off, Only, Pick, Run, Sole, Solitary, Spinster, Unary, Unattached, Uncoupled, Uniparous, Unique, Unwed, Versal, Yin

Single-cell Protista

Single-chambered Monothalamous

Singlestick Sword

Singlet Tunic, Vest

Singular(ity) Curious, Especial, Exceptional, Extraordinary, Ferly, Naked, Odd, Once, One, Peculiar, Queer(er), Rare, → **UNIQUE**, Unusual

Singultus Hiccup

Sinister Bend, Dark, Dirke, Evil, L, Left, Lh, Louche, → **OMINOUS**

Sink(ing), Sunken Abandon, Basin, Bog, Cadence, Carbon, Cower, Delapse, Depress, Descend, Devall, Dip, Down, Drain, Draught-house, Drink, Drop, Drown, Ebb, Flag, Founder, Gravitate, Heat, Hole, Immerse, Invest, Jawbox, Kitchen,

Lagan, Laigh, Lapse, Ligan, Merger, Pad, Poach, Pot, Prolapse, Put(t), Relapse, Sag, Scupper, Scuttle, Set, Settle, Shipwreck, Slump, Steep-to, Sty, Submerge, Subside, Swag, Swamp

Sinner Evildoer, Malefactor, Offender, Reprobate, Trespasser

Sinuous Curvy, Eely, Ogee, Slinky, Snaky, Wavy, Winding

Sinus Cavity, Recess

Sip(ping) Delibate, Hap'orth, Libant, Sample, Sowp, Sup, Taste, Tiff(ing)

Siphon Draw, Rack, Soda, Suck, Transfer

Sir Dan, Dom, K, Knight, Kt, Lord(ing), Sahib, Signor, Sirrah, Stir, Stirra(h), Towkay, Tuan

Sire Ancestor, Beget, Father, Get

Siren Alarm, Alert, Diaphone, Enchanter, Femme fatale, Hooter, Houri, Leucosia, Ligea, Lorelei, Mermaid, Oceanides, Parthenope, Salamander, Shark, Teaser, Temptress, Vamp

Sirenian Dugong, Lamantin, Manatee, Manati, Sea-cow

Sirloin Backsey

Sirree Bo

Sisal Agave

Siskin Aberdevine, Bird, Finch

Sister(s) Anne, Beguine, Carmelite, Fatal, Lay, Minim, → **NUN**, Nurse, Out, Religeuse, Sib, Sibling, Sis, Sob, Soul, Swallow, Theatre, Titty, Ugly, Ursuline, Verse, Ward, Weird

Sisyphean Uphill

Sit(ter), Sitting Bestride, Clutch, Dharna, Duck, Gaper, Lime, Lit de justice, Model, MP, Perch, Pose, Reign, Represent, Roost, Séance, Sederunt, Sejeant, Sesh, Session, Squat

Site, Siting Area, Arpa, Brownfield, Building, Camp, Caravan, Feng shui, Gap, Greenfield, Home-page, Location, Lot, Mirror, Pad, Place, Plot, Ramsar, Rogue, Sacred, Silo, Spot, Stance

Situation Affair, Ballpark, Berth, Cart, Case, Catch, Catch-22, Chicken and egg, Cliff-hanger, Contretemps, Cow, Dilemma, Drama, Galère, Hole, Hot seat, Job, Knife-edge, Lie, Location, Lurch, Matrix, Nail-biter, Niche, No-win, Office, Plight, Position, Post, Scenario, Scene, Schmear, Schmeer, Set-up, Shebang, Showdown, Status quo, Sticky wicket, Strait, Stringalong, Where, Worst case

Six(th) Digamma, French, German, Half(-a)dozen, Hexad, Italian, Neapolitan, Prime, Sax, Senary, Sestette, Sextet, Sice, Size, Vau, VI

Six counties NI

Six days Hexa(e)meron

Six feet, Six-footer Fathom, Insect, Miurus

Sixpence Bender, Kick, Slipper, Tanner, Tester(n), Testril(l), Tizzy, VID, VIP, Zack

Sixteen Sweet

Sixty Degree, Sexagesimal, Shock, Threescore

Size(able) Amplitude, Area, Bulk, Calibre, Clearcole, Countess, Demy, Displacement, → **EXTENT**, Format, Girth, Glair, Glue, Guar, Gum, Imperial, Measure, Particle, Party, Physique, Plus, Pot(t), Princess, Proportion, Tempera, Tidy, Trim

Sizzle Fry, Hiss, Scorch

Skate(r), Skateboard(er), Skateboarding, Skating Blade, Bob, Cheap, Choctaw, Cousins, Curry, Dean, Fakie, Figure, Fish, Free, Grommet, Half-pipe, Hot dog, In-line, Maid, Mohawk, Ollie, Rink, Rock(er), Roller, Rollerblade®, Runner, Short-track, Speed

Skedaddle Scarper, Shoo, Vamoose

Skein Hank, Hasp

Skeleton, Skeletal Anatomy, Atomy, Axial, Bones, Cadaverous, Cadre, Cage, Coenosteum, Coral, Corallite, Corallum, Family, Framework, Key, Ossify, Outline, Scenario, Sclere, Tentorium

Sketch(y) Bozzetto, Cameo, Character, Charade, Croquis, Delineate, Diagram, Doodle, Draft, → **DRAW**, Ébauche, Esquisse, Illustration, Limn, Line, Maquette, Modello, Outline, Pencilling, Playlet, Pochade, Précis, Profile, Skit, Summary, Tenuous, Thumbnail, Trick, Vignette, Visual

Skew Agee, Ajee, Oblique, Sheer, Squint, Swerve, Veer

Skewer Brochette, En brochette, Prong, Spit, Transfix

Ski(s), Skiing Aquaplane, Carving, Free ride, Glide, Glissade, Hot-dog, Langlauf, Mogul, Nordic, Schuss, Super G, Telemark, Vorlage, Wedeln

Skid Aquaplane, Drift, Jackknife, Side-slip, Slew, Slide, Slip, Slither, Spinout

▷ **Skidding** *may indicate* an anagram

Skiff Canoe, Dinghy, Outrigger

Skill(ed), Skilful Ability, Able, Ace, Address, Adept, Adroit, Art, Bravura, Canny, Chic, Competence, Craft, Deacon, Deft, Dextrous, Enoch, Expertise, Facility, Feat, Finesse, Flair, Gleg, Habile, Hand, Handicraft, Handy, Hend, Hot, Ingenious, Knack, Know-how, Knowing, Lear(e), Leir, Lere, Masterly, Masterpiece, Mastery, Mean, Métier, Mistery, Mystery, Mystique, Practised, Proficient, Prowess, Quant, Resource, Savvy, Science, Skeely, Sleight, Soft, Speciality, Tactics, Talent, Technic, Technique, Touch, Trade, Trick, Versed, Virtuoso

Skim Cream, Despumate, Flit, Glide, Graze, Plane, Ream, Scan, Scud, Scum, Skiff, Skitter

Skimp Restrict, Scamp, Scrimp, Stint

Skin(s) Ablate, Agnail, Armour, Bark, Basan, Basil, Bingo wing, Box-calf, Bronzed, Calf, Callus, Case, Cere, Chevrette, Coat, Corium, Cortex, Crackling, Cutaneous, Cuticle, Cutis, Deacon, Deer, Derm(a), Dermatome, Dermis, Dewlap, Disbark, Ectoderm, Enderon, Epicanthus, Epicarp, Epidermis, Eschar, Excoriate, Exterior, Fell, Film, Flaught, Flay, Flench, Flense, Flinch, Forel, Fourchette, Goldbeater's, Hangnail, Hide, Integra®, Jacket, Kip, Kirbeh, Leather, Membrane, Muktuk, Nebris, Pachyderm, Parfleche, Peau, Peel, Pell, Pellicle, Pelt, Perinychium, Plew, Plu(e), Prepuce, Pteryla, Rack, Rape, Rind, Scalp, Scarfskin, Serosa, Shell, Shoder, Spetch, Strip, Swindle, Tegument, Tulchan, Veneer, Water-bouget, Wattle, Woolfell

Skin disease, Skin problem, Skin trouble Boba, Boil, Buba, Causalgia, Chloasma, Chloracne, Cowpox, Cradle cap, Cyanosis, Dartre, Dermatitis, Dermatosis, Dyschroa, EB, Ecthyma, Eczema, Erysipelas, Exanthem(a), Favus, Flay, Framboesia, Gum rash, Herpes, Hives, Ichthyosis, Impetigo, Leishmaniasis, Leucodermia, Lichen, Livedo, Lupus vulgaris, Maidism, Mal del pinto, Mange, Miliaria, Morphew, Morula, Patagium, Pellagra, Pemphigus, Pinta, Pityriasis, Prurigo, Pseudofolliculitis, Psoriasis, Pyoderma, Rash, Red-gum, Ringworm, Rosacea, Rose-rash, St Anthony's fire, Sapego, Scabies, Sclerodermia, Scurvy, Seborrhoea, Serpigo, Strophulus, Telangiectasis, Tetter, Tinea, Vaccinia, Verruca, Verruga, Vitiligo, Xanthoma, Xerodermia, Yaws, Yawy

Skinflint Cheapo, Dryfist, Miser, Niggard, Pinch-gut, Scrooge, Tightwad

Skinful Drunk, Sausage

Skinhead Not, Punk, Scalp

Skink Seps

Skinless Ecorché

Skinny Barebone, Bony, Dermal, Emaciate, Lean, Scraggy, Thin, Weed
Skint Broke, Ghat, Penniless, Stony
Skip(ped), Skipper Boss, Caper, Captain, Cavort, Drakestone, Dumpster, Elater, Frisk, Hesperian, Jump, Jumping-mouse, Lamb, Luppen, Miss, Omit, Patroon, Ricochet, Saury, Scombresox, Spring, Tittup, Trip, Trounce(r)
Skirl Humdudgeon, Pibroch, Pipe, Screigh
Skirmish(er) Brawl, Brush, Dispute, Escarmouche, Fray, Pickeer, Spar, Tirailleur, Velitation, Voltigeur
Skirt(ing) Bases, Bell, Border, Bouffant, Bypass, Cheongsam, Circle, Coat, Crinoline, Culotte(s), Dado, Dirndl, Edge, Fil(l)ibeg, Fringe, Fustanella, Fustanelle, Girl, Gore, Grass, Harem, Hobble, Hoop, Hug, Hula, Kilt, Lamboys, Lava-lava, Marge, Mini, Mopboard, Pareo, Pareu, Pencil, Peplum, Petticoat, Philibeg, Pinafore, Piu-piu, Plinth, Puffball, Ra-ra, Rim, Sarong, Sidestep, Stringboard, Tace, Tail, Taslet, Tasse(t), Tonlet, Tube, Tutu, Washboard, Wrap(a)round, Wrapover
Skit Lampoon, Parody, Sketch
Skittish Coy, Curvetting, Frisky, Restless
Skittle(s) Bayle, Bowl, Kail(s), Kayle, Kingpin, Ninepin, Pin, Spare
Skive(r) Absentee, Scrimshank, Shirk
Skivvy Drudge, Slave
Skrimshank Bludge, Skive
Skulk Lurk, Mooch, Shool
Skull Brainpan, Bregma(ta), Calvaria, Cranium, Death's head, Fontanel, Harnpan, Head, Malar, Maz(z)ard, Obelion, Occiput, Pannikell, Phrenology, Scalp, Sinciput
Skullcap Ya(r)mulka, Yarmulke, Zucchetto
Skunk Atoc, Atok, Hognosed, Polecat, Pot, Teledu, Zoril(lo), Zorino
Sky(-high), Skywards Air, Azure, Blue, Canopy, Carry, El Al, E-layer, Element, Empyrean, Ether, Firmament, Heaven, Lift, Lob, Loft, Mackerel, Occident, Octa, Okta, Rangi, Uranus, Welkin
Sky-diver Para
Skylark Aerobatics, Bird
Skylight Abat-jour, Aurora, Comet, Companion, Lunette, Star
Skyline Horizon, Rooftops
Sky-pilot Chaplain, Vicar
Slab(s) Briquette, Bunk, Bunk(er), Cake, Cap(e)stone, Chunk, Dalle, Hawk, Ledger, Marver, Metope, Mihrab, Mud, Paving-stone, Planch, Plank, Sclate, Sheave, Slate, Slice, Stela, Stelene, Tab, Tile, Wood-wool
Slack(en), Slacker, Slackness Abate, Careless, Crank, Dilatory, Dross, Ease, Easy-going, Glen, Idle, Lax(ity), Lazybones, Let-up, Loose, Malinger, Nerveless, Relax, Release, Remiss, Shirk, Skive, Slatch, Slow, Surge, Unscrew, Unwind, Veer
Slag Basic, Calx, Cinder, Dross, Scoria, Scum, Sinter, Tap cinder, Tart
Slake Abate, Cool, Quench, Refresh, Satisfy
Slalom Super-G
Slam Crash, Criticise, Dad, Grand, Little, Pan(dy), Small, Sock, Swap, Swop, Vole, Wap
Slander(ous) Asperse, Backbite, Calumny, Defame, Derogatory, Detraction, Disparage, Libel, Malediction, Malign, Missay, Mud, Mudslinging, Obloquy, Sclaunder, Smear, Traduce, Vilify, Vilipend
Slang Abuse, Argot, Back, Berate, Blinglish, Cant, Colloquial, Ebonics, Flash, Jargon, Lingo, Nadsat, Parlyaree, Polari, Rhyming, Slate, Tsotsitaal, Verlan, Zowie
Slant(ed), Slanting Angle, Asklent, Atilt, Bevel, Bias, Brae, Cant, Careen, Chamfer, Clinamen, Diagonal, Escarp, Oblique, Prejudice, Slew, → **SLOPE**, Splay, Squint, Talus, Tilt, Virgule

Slap(ping) Clatch, Clout, Cuff, Happy, Make-up, Pandy, Piston, Sclaff, Scud, Skelp, Smack, Spat, Tape, Twank

Slapdash Careless, Hurried, Random

Slash(ed) Chive, Cut, Diagonal, Gash, Hack, Jag, Lacerate, Laciniate, Leak, Oblique, Rash, Rast, Reduce, Scorch, Scotch, Separatrix, Slice, Slit, Solidus, Stroke, Virgule, Wee

Slat(s) Fish, Jalousie, Louvre

Slate, Slaty, Slating Alum, Berate, Calm, Cam, Caum, Countess, Credit, Criticise, Decry, Diatribe, Double, Duchess, Duchy, Enter, Griseous, Imperial, Killas, Knotenschiefer, Lady, Log, Marchioness, Ottrelite, Pan, Peggy, Polishing, Princess, Queen, Rag(g), Roof, Schalstein, Shingle, Slat, Small, Small lady, Tabula, Tomahawk, Viscountess

Slater Hellier, Insect

Slattern Bag, Besom, Bisom, Drab, Drazel, Frump, Mopsy, Ragbag, Ragdoll, Slammakin, Slammerkin, Sloven, Slummock, Sozzle, Traipse, Trapes, Trollop

Slaughter(house), Slaughterer Abattoir, Behead, Bleed, Bloodshed, Butcher, Carnage, Decimate, Hal(l)al, Holocaust, Jhatka, Immolation, Kill, Mactation, → **MASSACRE**, S(c)hechita(h), Scupper, Shambles, Shochet, Smite

Slav Bohunk, Croat, Czech, Kulak, Lusatia, Polabian, Serb, Sorb, Wend(ic)

Slave(ry), Slaves, Slavish Addict, Aesop, Aida, Androcles, Barracoon, Blackbird, Bond, Bond(s)man, Bondwoman, Bordar, Boy, Caliban, Coffle, Contraband, Dogsbody, Drudge, Drug, Dulocracy, Dulosis, Esne, Galley, Gibeonite, Helot, Hierodule, Mameluke, Mamluk, Marmaluke, Maroon, Minion, Nativity, Odalisk, Odali(s)que, Peasant, Pr(a)edial, Rhodope, Serf, Servitude, Spartacus, Terence, Theow, Thersites, Thete, Thrall, Topsy, Vassal, Villein, Wage, Wendic, White, Yoke

Slave-driver, Slave-owner Assam, Sweater, Task-master

Slaver Bespit, Dribble, Drivel, Drool, Slabber, Slobber, Spawl, Spit

Slay(er), Slaying Destroy, Execute, Ghazi, → **KILL**, Mactation, Murder, Quell, Saul, Slaughter

Sleazy, Sleaze Flimsy, Red-light, Scuzzy, Seamy, Sordid, Squalid, Tack, Thin

Sled(ge), Sleigh(-ride) Bob, Dog train, Dray, Hurdle, Hurley-hacket, Kibitka, Komatic, Komatik, Lauf, Luge, Mud-boat, Mush, Polack, Pulk(h)(a), Pung, Skeleton bob(sleigh), Skidoo®, Slipe, Stoneboat, Tarboggin, Toboggan, Train, Travois

Sleek Bright, Shine, Silky, Smarm, Smooth, Smug

Sleep, Sleeper(s), Sleepiness, Sleeping, Sleepy Beauty, Bed, Bivouac, Blet, Bundle, Bye-byes, Car, Catnap, Coma, Couchette, Crash, Cross-sill, Cross-tie, Dormant, Dormient, Dormouse, Doss, Doze, Drop off, Drowse, Earring, Endymion, Epimenides, Flop, Gowl, Gum, Hibernate, Hypnology, Hypnos, Kip, Land of Nod, Lethargic, Lie, Morpheus, Nap, Narcolepsy, Narcosis, Nod, Oscitation, Over, Paradoxical, Petal, Pop off, Psychopannychism, REM, Repast, Repose, Rest, Rip Van Winkle, Rough, Sandman, Seven, Shuteye, Siesta, Skipper, Sloom, Slumber, Snooz(l)e, Somnolent, Sopor(ose), Sownd, Spine bashing, Swone, Tie, Torpid, Twilight, Wink, Zeds, Zizz

Sleeping place Bed, Cot, Dormitory, Kang, Roost

Sleeping sickness Trypanosomiasis

Sleepless Wake-rife, Wauk-rife

Sleep-walking Noctambulation, Somnambulism

Sleet Graupel, Hail, Virga

Sleeve (opening) Arm(hole), Balloon, Batwing, Bishop's, Bush, Cap, Collet, Cover, Dolman, Gatefold, Gigot, Gland, Kimono, Lawn, Leg-o'-mutton, Liner, Magyar,

Manche, Pagoda, Pudding, Querpo, Raglan, Record, Sabot, Scye, Slashed, Trunk, Turnbuckle, Wind

▶ **Sleigh** *see* **SLED**

Sleight Artifice, Conjury, Cunning, Dodge, Legerdemain, Trick

Slender(ness) Asthenic, Ectomorph, Elongate, Exiguity, Exility, Fine, Flagelliform, Flimsy, Gracile, Jimp, Leptosome, Loris, Narrow, Rangy, Skinny, Slight, Slim, Small, Spindly, Stalky, Styloid, Svelte, Swank, Sylph, Tenuous, Trim, Waif

Sleuth Bloodhound, Detective, Dick, Eye, Lime-hound, Lyam(-hound), Lyme(-hound)

Slew Number, Skid, Slide, Twist

Slice Cantle, Chip, Collop, Cut, Doorstep, Fade, Frustrum, Lop, Piece, Rasure, Round, Sector, Segment, Share, Sheave, Shive, Slab, Sliver, Spoon, Tranche, Wafer, Whang

▷ **Slice of** *may indicate* a hidden word

Slick Adroit, Glim, Mealy-mouthed, Oil, Sleeveen, Smooth, Suave

Slide Barrette, Chute, Cursor, Diapositive, Drift, Ease, Fader, Glissando, Hair, Helter-skelter, Hirsle, Hollow-ground, Ice-run, Illapse, Lantern, Mount, Pulka, Schuss, Scoop, Skid, Skite, Slip, Slippery dip, Slither, Snowboard, Transparency

Slight(ly) Affront, Belittle, Cold shoulder, Cut, Detract, Disparage, Disregard, Disrespect, Facer, Flimsy, Halfway, Insult, Minor, Misprise, Neglect, Nominal, Pet, Petty, Rebuff, Remote, → **SLENDER**, Slim, Slimsy, Slur, Small, Smattering, Sneaking, Snub, Sparse, Subtle, Superficial, Sylphine, Tenuous, Thin, Tiny, Wee, Wispy

Slim Bant, Jimp, Macerate, Reduce, Slender, Slight, Svelte, Sylph, Tenuous, Thin

Slime, Slimy Glair, Glareous, Glit, Gorydew, Guck, Gunk, Mother, Muc(o)us, Myxomycete, Oily, Ooze, Sapropel, Slake, Sludge, Uliginous

Sling Balista, Catapult, Drink, Fling, Hang, Parbuckle, Prusik, Shy, Support, Toss, Trebuchet

Slink Lurk, Skulk, Slope

Slip(ped), Slipping, Slips Boner, Come home, Cover, Cutting, Disc, Docket, Drift, EE, Elapse, Elt, Engobe, Error, Faux pas, Fielder, Form, Freudian, Glide, Glissade, Infielder, Label, Landslide, Lapse, Lapsus linguae, Lath, Lauwine, Lingual, Mistake, Muff, Nod, Oversight, Parapraxis, Petticoat, Pink, Prolapse, Ptosis, Quickset, Rejection, Relapse, Run, Scape, Sc(h)edule, Scoot, Set, Shim, Sin, Ski, Skid, Skin, Skite, Slade, Slidder, Slide, Slither, Slive, Spellican, Spillican, Stumble, Surge, Ticket, Trip, Tunicle, Underskirt, Unleash, Wage(s)

Slipper(s) Baboosh, Babouche, Babuche, Baffies, Calceolate, Carpet, Eel, Japanese, Mocassin, Moccasin, Moyl, Muil, Mule, Pabouche, Pampootie, Pantable, Pantof(f)le, Panton, Pantoufle, Pump, Rullion, Runner, Ski, Sledge, Sneaker, Sock

Slippery Eely, Foxy, Glid, Icy, Lubric, Shady, Shifty, Skidpan, Slick

Slipshod Careless, Hurried, Jerry, Lax, Slapdash, Slatternly, Sloppy, Slovenly, Toboggan

▷ **Slipshod** *may indicate* an anagram

Slit Buttonhole, Cranny, Cut, Fent, Fissure, Fitchet, Gash, Gill, Loop, Pertus(at)e, Placket, Placket-hole, Race, Rit, Scissure, Spare, Speld(er), Vent

Slithy Tove

Sliver Flake, Fragment, Moslings, Rove, Shaving, Slice, Splinter, Trace

Sloan Snib, Snub

Slob(ber) Drool, Lout, Slaver, Smarm, Wet

Sloe Blackthorn, Slae

Slog(ger) Drag, Logwork, Strike, Swink, Swot, Traipse, Tramp, Trape, Trauchle, Trudge, Yacker, Yakka, Yakker

Slogan Amandla, Byword, Catchword, Chant, Jai Hind, Masakhane, Mot(to), Murdabad, Phrase, Rallying-cry, Slughorn(e), Splash, Street cry, Tapline, Warcry, Watchword

Sloop Cutter, Hoy, Ship

Slop(s) Cop(per), Gardyloo, Jordeloo, Muck, Policeman, Rossers, Rozzers, Schmaltz, Shower, Sop, Spill, Swill

Slope(s), Sloping Acclivity, Angle, Anticline, Bahada, Bajada, Bank, Batter, Bevel, Borrow, Borstal(l), Brae, Breast, Camber, Chamfer, Cuesta, Declivity, Delve, Diagonal, Dip, Dry, Escarp, Escarpment, Fastigiate, Fla(u)nch, Foothill, Geanticline, Glacis, Grade, Gradient, Heel, Hill, Incline, Isoclinical, Kant, Lean, Natural, Nursery, Oblique, Pediment, Pent, Periclinal, Pitch, Rake, Ramp, Rollway, Scarp, Schuss, Scrae, Scree, Shelve, Sideling, Skewback, Slant, Slippery, Slipway, Splay, Steep, Stoss, Talus, Tilt, Verge, Versant, Weather

Sloppily, Sloppy Lagrimoso, Lowse, Madid, Mushy, Remiss, Schmaltzy, Slapdash, Slipshod, Sloven, Slushy, Sozzly, Untidy, Weepie

▷ **Sloppy** *may indicate* an anagram

Slosh(y) Dowse, Fist, Splash, Wet

Slot(ted) Expansion, Graveyard, Groove, Hasp, Hesp, Hole, Key, Keyway, Mortice, Mortise, Niche, Seat, Slit, Swanmark, Time

Sloth(ful) Accidie, Acedia, Ai, Bradypus, Edentate, Ground, Idle, Inaction, Indolent, Inertia, Lazy, Lie-abed, Megatherium, Mylodon, Slugabed, Sweer(t), Sweered, Sweir(t), Three-toed, Unau

Slot machine One-armed bandit, Pokey, Pokie

Slouch Lop, Mooch, Mope, Slump

Slough(ing) Cast, Despond, Ecdysis, Eschar, Exfoliate, Exuviae, Lerna, Marish, Marsh, Mire, Morass, Paludine, Shed, Shuck, Swamp

Sloven(ly) Careless, Dag(gy), Dishevelled, Down-at-heel, D(r)aggle-tail, Frowsy, Grobian, Jack-hasty, Mawkin, Rag-doll, Ratbag, Slaister, Slammakin, Slammerkin, Slattern, Sleazy, Slipshod, Slubberdegullion, Slubberingly, Slummock, Slut, Streel, Untidy

Slow(ing), Slower, Slowly Adagio, Allargando, Andante, Brady, Brake, Broad, Calando, Crawl, Dawdle, Decelerate, Deliberate, Dilatory, Dull, Dumka, ESN, Flag, Gradual, Inchmeal, Lag, Langram, Larghetto, Largo, Lash, Lassu, Late, Lean-witted, Leisurely, Lentando, Lento, Lifeless, Loiter, Losing, Meno mosso, Obtuse, Pedetentous, Rall(entando), Rein, Reluctant, Retard, Ribattuta, Rit, Ritardando, Ritenuto, Slack, Slug, Sluggish, Snaily, Solid, Stem, Tardigrade, Tardive, Tardy, Tardy-gaited

Slowcoach Slowpoke, Slug

Slow-match Portfire

Sludge Activated, Gunge, Mire, Muck, Sapropel, Slob

Slug(s) Ammo, Bêche-de-mer, Blow, Brain, Bullet, Cosh, Drink, Knuckle sandwich, Limaces, Limax, Linotype®, Mollusc, Nerita, Pellet, Shot, Snail, Trepang

Sluggard Drone, Lazy, Lie-abed, Lusk, Unau

Sluggish Dilatory, Drumble, Idler, Inactive, Inert, Jacent, Lacklustre, Laesie, Languid, Lazy, Lentor, Lethargic, Lug, Phlegmatic, Saturnine, Sleepy, → **SLOW**, Stagnant, Tardy, Torpid, Unalive

Sluice Aboideau, Aboiteau, Drain, Gutter, Koker, Penstock, Rinse, Sasse

Slum Basti, Bustee, Busti, Cabbagetown, Cardboard city, Ghetto, Pavela, Rookery, Shanty, Slurb, Warren

Slumber Doze, Drowse, Nap, Nod, Sleep, Sloom, Snooze

Slump Decrease, Depression, Deteriorate, Dip, Flop, Recession, Sag, Sink, Slouch, Sprawl

Slur(ring) Defame, Drawl, Innuendo, Libel, Opprobrium, Slight, Smear, Synaeresis, Tie

Slush(y) Bathos, Boodle, Bribe, Drip, Money, Mush, Pap, Slop, Sposh, Swash, Swashy

Slut Candle, Dollymop, Draggle-tail, Dratchell, Drazel, Floosie, Harlot, Slattern, Sow, Tart, Traipse, Trapes, Trollop

Sly Christopher, Clandestine, Coon, Covert, Cunning, Foxy, Furtive, Leery, Peery, Reynard, Secretive, Shifty, Slee, Sleekit, Sleeveen, Slicker, Sneaky, Stallone, Stealthy, Subtle, Surreptitious, Tinker, Tod, Tricky, Weasel, Wily

▷ **Slyly** *may indicate* an anagram

Smack(er) Aftertaste, Buss, Cuff, Flavour, Foretaste, Fragrance, Hooker, Kiss, Klap, Lander, Lips, Pra(h)u, Relish, Salt, Saut, Skelp, Slap, Slat, Smatch, Smell, Smouch, Soupçon, Spank, Spice, Splat, Tack, → **TANG**, Taste, Thwack, Tincture, Trace, Twang, X, Yawl

Small (thing), Smallest amount Ateleiosis, Atom, Bantam, Beer, Bijou, Bittie, Bitty, Centesimal, Chotta, Curn, Denier, Diminutive, Dinky, Dreg, Drib, Driblet, Elfin, Few, Fry, Grain, Haet, Ha'it, Half-pint, Handful, Hint, Hobbit, Holding, Hole-in-the-wall, Hyperosmia, Insect, Ion, Itsy-bitsy, Knurl, Leet, Leetle, Lilliputian, Limited, Lite, → **LITTLE**, Lock, Low, Meagre, Mean, Measly, Microscopic, Midget, Mignon, Miniature, Minikin, Minority, Minute, Mite, Modest, Modicum, Neap, Nurl, Peerie, Peewee, Petit(e), Petty, Pickle, Pigmean, Pigmy, Pink(ie), Pinky, Pint-size, Pittance, Pocket, Poky, Poujadist, Puckle, Rap, Reduction, Runt, S, Santilla, Scantling, Scattering, Scrump, Scrunt, Scut, Shortarse, Shrimp, Single, Skerrick, Slight, Slim, Smattering, Smidge(o)n, Smidgin, Smithereen, Smout, Snippet, Soupçon, Sprinkling, Spud, Squirt, Stim, Stunted, Tad, Teenty, Thin, Tidd(l)y, Tiny, Titch(y), Tittle, Tot(tie), Totty, Trace, Trivial, Unheroic, Wee, Weedy, Whit

Smallest Least, Minimal, Runt

Smallholder, Smallholding Croft, Nursery, Rundale, Share-cropper, Stead

Small-minded(ness) Parvanimity, Petty

Smallness Exiguity, Exility, Paucity

Smallpox Alastrim, Variola

Smarm(y) Oil, Smoothie, Unctuous

Smart(en), Smartest Ache, Acute, Alec, Astute, Best, Bite, Chic, Classy, Clever, Cute, Dandy, Dapper, Dressy, Elegant, Flash, Flip, Fly, Groom, Gussy up, Jemmy, Kookie, Kooky, Natty, Neat, Nifty, Nip, Nobby, Pac(e)y, Pacy, Posh, Preen, Primp, Prink, Pusser, Raffish, Rattling, Ritzy, Saucy, Slick, Sly, Smoke, Smug, Snappy, Snazzy, Soigné(e), Spiff, Sprauncy, Sprightly, Spruce, Sprush, Spry, Sting, Stylish, Swagger, Sweat, Swish, Tiddley, Tippy, Titivate, Toff, U, Well-groomed, Wiseacre

Smash(ed), Smasher, Smashing Atom, Bingle, Brain, Break, Corker, Crush, Demolish, Devastate, Dish, Forearm, High, Jarp, Jaup, Kaput, Kill, Lulu, Shatter, Shiver, Slam, Squabash, Stave, Super, Terrific, Tight, To-brake, → **WRECK**

▷ **Smash(ed)** *may indicate* an anagram

Smear Assoil, Bedaub, Besmirch, Blur, Borm, Cervical, Clam, Daub, Defile, Denigrate, Discredit, Drabble, Enarm, Gaum, Gild, Gorm, Lick, Oil, Pap(anicolaou), Pay, Plaster, Slairg, Slaister, Slake, Slander, Slather, Slime, Slubber, Slur, Smalm, Smarm, Smudge, Sully, Teer, Traduce, Wax

Smell(ing), Smelly Aroma, Asafoetida, BO, Caproate, Effluvium, Empyreuma, Fetor, F(o)etid, Fug, Gale, Gamy, Graveolent, Guff, Hing, Honk, Hum, Mephitis,

Miasm(a), Ming, Musk, Nidor, Niff, Nose, Odour, Olent, Olfact(ory), Osmatic, Osmic, Perfume, Pong, Ponk, Pooh, Rank, Redolent, Reech, Reek, Sar, Savour, → **SCENT**, Sensory, Sniff, Snifty, Snook, Snuff, Steam, Stench, Stifle, Stink, Tang, Whiff

Smelling salts Sal volatile

Smelt(ing) Atherinidae, Melt, Salmon, Scoria, Sparling, Speiss, Sperling, Spirling

Smile(s), Smiling Agrin, Beam, Cheese, Favour, Gioconda, Grin, Rictus, Samuel, Self-help, Simper, Smirk, Watch the birdie

Smirk Grimace, Simper

Smite, Smitten Assail, Enamoured, Epris(e), Hit, Strike, Strook

Smith Adam, Artisan, Farrier, FE, Forger, Hammerman, Mighty, Stan, Vulcan, Wayland

Smithy Forge, Smiddy, Stithy

Smock Blouse, Chemise, Drabbet, Gather, Shift, Slop, Smicket

Smoke(r), Smoking, Smoky Blast, Bloat, Censer, Chain, Chillum, → **CIGAR(ETTE)**, Cure, Drag, Fog, Fuliginous, Fume, Funk, Gasper, Hemp, Incense, Indian hemp, Inhale, Kipper, Latakia, London ivy, Lum, Lunt, Mainstream, Manil(l)a, Nicotian, Passive, Peat reek, Peaty, Pother, Pudder, Puff, Reech, Reek, Reest, Roke, Secondary, Sidestream, Smeech, Smeek, Smirting, Smoor, Smother, Smoulder, Smudge, Snout, Tear, Tobacconalian, Toke, Vapour, Viper, Water, Whiff, Wreath

Smoke-hating Misocapnic

Smoking-room Divan

Smollett Tobias

▶ **Smooch** *see* **SMOUCH**

Smooth(e), Smoother, Smoothly Alabaster, Bald, Bland, Brent, Buff, Chamfer, Clean, Clockwork, Dress, Dub, Easy, Even, Fettle, File, Flat, Fluent, Glabrous, Glare, Glassy, Glib, Goose, Iron, Legato, Level, Levigate, Linish, Mealy-mouthed, Mellifluous, Millpond, Oil, Plane, Plaster, Rake, Roll, Rub, Sand(er), Satiny, Scrape, Shiny, Sleek, Slick, Slickenslide, Slur, Smug, Snod, Sostenuto, Straighten, Streamlined, Suave, Swimmingly, Terete, Terse, Trim, Unwrinkled, Urbane

Smooth-haired Lissotrichous

Smother Burke, Choke, Dampen, Muffle, Oppress, Overlie, Smoor, Smore, Smoulder, Stifle, Suppress

Smouch Cheat, Kiss, Lallygag, Lollygag, Neck

Smoulder Burn, Seethe

Smudge Blur, Dab, Offset, Slur, Smear, Smooch, Stain

Smug Complacent, Conceited, Goody-goody, Goody-two-shoes, Neat, Oily, Pi, Sanctimonious, Self-satisfied, Trim

Smuggle(d), Smuggler, Smuggling Body-packer, Bootleg, Contraband, Contrabandist, Donkey, Fair trade, Free trader, Gunrunning, Moonshine, Mule, Owler, Rum-runner, Run, Secrete, Steal, Traffic

Smut(ty) Bawdy, Blight, Blue, Brand, Burnt-ear, Coom, Crock, Filth, Grime, Racy, Soot, Speck, Stinking

Smut-fungus Basidia, Ustilago

Snack Bever, Bhelpuri, Bite, Blintz, Bombay mix, Breadstick, Breakfast bar, Brunch, Butty, Canapé, Chack, Churro, Crisps, Crudités, Donar kebab, Elevenses, Entremets, Four-by-two, Gorp, Meze, Munchies, Nacho, Nacket, Nibble, Nigiri, Nocket, Nooning, Nuncheon, Padkos, Pie, Piece, Ploughman's lunch, Popcorn, Rarebit, Refreshment, Samo(o)sa, Sandwich, Sarnie, Savoury, Scroggin, Sloppy joe, Small chop, Tapa, Taste, Toast(y), Trail mix, Vada, Voidee, Wada, Wrap, Zakuska

Snaffle Bit, Bridoon, Grab, Purloin

Snag Catch, Contretemps, Drawback, Hindrance, Hitch, Impediment, Knob, Nog, Obstacle, Remora, Rub, Snubbe, Stub, Tear

Snail Brian, Cowrie, Cowry, Dew, Dodman, Escargot, Garden, Gasteropod, Giant African, Helix, Hodmandod, Limnaea, Lymnaea, Nautilus, Nerite, Planorbis, Pond, Ramshorn, Roman, Slow, Slug, Strombus, Unicorn-shell, Univalve, Wallfish, Whelk, Wing

Snake Adder, Aesculapian, Amphisbaena, Anaconda, Anguine, Anguis, Apod(e), Asp, Bandy-bandy, Berg-adder, Blacksnake, Blind, Blue-racer, Boa, Boma, Boomslang, Brown, Bull, Bush-master, Camoodi, Carpet, Cerastes, Clotho, Coachwhip, Cobra, Coluber, Congo, Constrictor, Copperhead, Coral, Corn, Cottonmouth, Cribo, Crotalidae, Daboia, Death-adder, Dendrophis, Diamond(-back), Dipsas, Drag, Dugite, Elaeis, Elaps, Ellops, Fer-de-lance, Flying, Garter, Glass, Gopher, Grass, Habu, Hamadryad, Hognose, Homorelaps, Hoop, Horned viper, Horsewhip, Hydra, Indigo, Jararaca, Jararaka, Joe Blake, Kaa, K(a)rait, King (cobra), Lachesis, Langaha, Mamba, Massasauga, Massasauger, Meander, Milk, Mocassin, Moccasin, Mulga, Naga, Naia, Naja, Ophidian, Pipe, Pit-viper, Plumber's, Puff-adder, Python, Racer, Rat, Ratbag, Rattler, Reptile, Ribbon, Ringhals, Ringneck, Rinkhals, River jack, Rock, Sand viper, Sea, Seps, → **SERPENT**, Sidewinder, Slither, Slowworm, Smooth, Spitting, Squamata, Sucurujú, Surucucu, Taipan, Takshaka, Thirst, Thread, Tiger, Timber rattlesnake, Tree, Uraeus, Vasuki, Viper, Water (moccasin), Whip, Wind, Worm

Snake-charmer Lamia

Snake-in-the-grass Peacher, Rat, Traitor

Snake-root Bistort, Senega, Snakeweed, Virginia, White

Snap(per), Snappy, Snap up Alligator, Autolycus, Bite, Break, Brittle, Camera, Click, Cold, Cold wave, Crack, Crocodile, Cross, Curt, Edgy, Fillip, Girnie, Glom, Gnash, Hanch, Knacker, Knap, Livery, Mugshot, Photo, Photogene, Scotch, Snack, Snatch, Spell, Still, Tetchy, Vigour

Snare Bait, Benet, Engine, Enmesh, Entrap, Gin, Grin, Honeytrap, Hook, Illaqueate, Inveigle, Net, Noose, Rat-trap, Springe, Springle, Toil, → **TRAP**, Trapen, Trepan, Web, Weel, Wire

Snarl(ing) Chide, Complicate, Cynic, Enmesh, Girn, Gnar(l), Gnarr, Growl, Grumble, Knar, Knot, Snap, Tangle, Yirr

Snatch Claucht, Claught, Excerpt, Fragment, Glom, Grab, Kidnap, Nip, Pluck, Race, Ramp, Rap, Rase, Raunch, Refrain, Snippet, Song, Spell, Steal, Strain, Take, Tweak, Whip up, Wrap, Wrest

▷ **Snatch** *may indicate* the first letter of a word

Snazzy Cat

Snead Snath

Sneak(y) Area, Carry-tale, Clipe, Clype, Furtive, Inform, Lurk, Mumblenews, Nim, Peak, Scunge, Skulk, Slink, Slip, Slyboots, Snitch, Snoop, Split, Steal, Stoolie, Surreptitious, Tell(-tale), Underhand

Sneer(ing) Barb, Critic, Cynical, Fleer, Gibe, Jeer, Scoff, Smirk, Snide, Twitch

Sneeze (at), Sneezing Atishoo, Errhine, Neese, Neeze, Ptarmic, Scorn, Sternutation

Snick Click, Cut, Edge, Glance

Snicker Snigger, Titter, Whinny

Snide Bitchy, Shand

Sniff Inhale, Nose, Nursle, Nuzzle, Scent, Smell, Snivel, Snort, Snuffle, Vent, Whiff

Snigger Giggle, Laugh, Snicker, Snirtle, Titter, Whicker

Snip(pet) Bargain, Cert, Clip, Cut, Doddle, Piece, Sartor, Snatch, Snick, Tailor

Snipe(r) Bird, Bushwhacker, Criticise, Franc-tireur, Dunlin, Gutter,

Heather-bleat(er), Heather-bluiter, Heather-blutter, Pick off, Potshot, Scape, Shoot, Walk, Wisp

Snitch Conk, Konk, Nose

Snivel Blubber, Snotter, Snuffle, Weep, Whine

Snob(bery), Snobbish Cobbler, Crachach, Crispin, Dic(k)ty, High-hat, Inverted, Scab, Side, Sloane, Snooty, Soutar, Souter, Sowter, Toffee-nose, Vain, Vamp

Snooker Crucible, Pool, Stimie, Stimy, Stym(i)e

Snoop(er) Curtain-twitcher, Meddle, Nose, Pry, Tec

Snooty Bashaw, Snob(bish)

Snooze Calk, Caulk, Dove, Dover, Doze, Nap, Nod, Siesta, Sleep

Snore, Snoring Rhonchus, Rout, Snort, Snuffle, Stertorous, Zz

Snort(er) Dram, Drink, Grunt, Nare, Nasal, Roncador, Snore, Toot

Snot(ty) Mucoid

Snout Bill, Boko, Cigar, Gasper, Gruntie, Informer, Muzzle, Nose, Nozzle, Proboscis, Schnozzle, Tinker, Tobacco, Wall

Snow(y), Snowdrift, Snowstorm Brig, Buran, Cocaine, Coke, Corn, Cornice, Crud, Firn, Flake, Flurry, Graupel, Half-pipe, Heroin, Marine, Mogul, Neve, Nival, Niveous, Nivose, Oncome, Onding, Powder, Red, Sastruga, Sleet, Spotless, Stall, Virga, White-out, Wintry, Wreath, Yellow, Zastruga

Snowball Accelerate, Cramp-bark, Cumulative, Guelder-rose, Increase, Magnify, Opulus, Pelt, Rose

Snowdrop Avalanche, Eirlys

Snowflake Leucojum, St Agnes' flower

Snow-goose Wav(e)y

Snowman Abominable, Eskimo, Junkie, Sherpa, Yeti

Snowmobile Sno-cat

Snowshoe Bear paw, Racket, Racquet

Snub Cut, Diss, Go-by, Lop, Pug, Put-down, Quelch, Rebuff, Reproof, Retroussé, Set-down, Short, Slap, Slight, Sloan, Sneap, Snool, Wither

Snuff(le) Asarabacca, Dout, Errhine, Extinguish, Maccabaw, Maccaboy, Maccoboy, Ptarmic, Pulvil, Rappee, Smother, Snaste, Sneesh(an), Sniff, Snift, Snush, Tobacco, Vent

Snuffbox Anatomical, Mill, Mull, Ram's horn

Snug(gle) Burrow, Comfy, Cose, → **cosy**, Couthie, Couthy, Croodle, Cubby, Cuddle, Embrace, Lion, Neat, Nestle, Nuzzle, Rug, Snod, Tight, Trim

So Argal, Ergo, Forthy, Hence, Sae, Sic(h), Sol, Such, Therefore, This, Thus, True, Very, Yes

Soak(ed) Bate, Bath(e), Beath, Bewet, Bloat, Blot, Buck, Cree, Deluge, Drench, Drink, Drook, Drouk, Drown, Drunk, Duck, Dunk, Embay, Embrue, Fleece, Grog, Imbrue, Impregnate, Infuse, Lush, Macerate, Marinate, Mop, Oncome, Permeate, Plastered, Rait, Rate, Ret(t), Rinse, Rob, Saturate, Seep, Sipe, Sog, Sop, Souce, Souse, Sows(s)e, Steep, Sype, Thwaite, Toper, Wet, Wino

Soap(y), Soap opera Cake, Carbolic, Castile, Coronation St, Eluate, Flake, Flannel, Flattery, Glass, Green, Hard, Joe, Lather, Lux®, Marine, Metallic, Moody, Mountain, Pears®, Pinguid, Saddle, Safrole, Saponaceous, Saponin, Sawder, Shaving, Slime, Soft, Spanish, Suds, Sudser, Sugar, Syndet, Tablet, Tall-oil, The Bill, Toheroa, Toilet, Washball, Windsor, Yellow

Soapstone French chalk, Spanish chalk, Steatite, Talc

Soar(ing) Ascend, Essorant, Fly, Glide, Hilum, Plane, Rise, Tower, Zoom

Sob (stuff) Blub(ber), Boohoo, Goo, Gulp, Lament, Singult, Singultus, Snotter, Wail, Weep, Yoop

Sober(sides) Abstemious, Calm, Demure, Pensive, Sedate, Staid, Steady, Steddy, TT
Sobriquet Byname, Cognomen, Nickname, To-name
So-called Alleged, Nominal, Soi-disant
Sociable, Sociability Affable, Cameraderie, Chummy, Clubby, Cosy, Extravert,
  Extrovert, Folksy, Friendly, Genial, Gregarious, Phatic
Social(ise) Barn dance, Convivial, Hobnob, Hui, Mingle, Mix, Musicale, Phatic,
  Tea-dance, Yancha
Socialism, Socialist Ba'(a)th, Champagne, Chartist, Dergue, Engels, Fabian,
  Fourierism, Guild, ILP, International, Karmathian, Lansbury, Left(y), Marxism,
  Menchevik, Menchevist, National, Nihilism, Owen(ist), Owenite, Parlour pink,
  Pasok, Pinko, Red, Revisionist, St Simonist, Sandinista, Spartacist, Utopian, Webb
Socialite Deb, Jet set, Sloane
Society Affluent, Alternative, Association, Band of Hope, Beau monde, Benefit,
  Blackhand, Body, Brahma, Brahmo, Broederbond, Building, Camorra, Carbonari,
  Choral, Class, Club, College, Company, Conger, Co-op, Cooperative, Culture,
  Danite, Defenders, Dorcas, Duddieweans, Eleuthri, Elite, Elks, Fabian, Fashion,
  Foresters, Freemans, Freemasons, Friendly, Friends, Glee club, Grand monde,
  Grotian, Group, Guarantee, Guilds, Haut monde, Hetairia, High, High life,
  Humane, Illuminati, Institute, Invincibles, John Birch, Ku-Klux-Klan, Kyrle, Law,
  Linnean, Lodge, Mafia, Malone, Masonic, Mau-Mau, Ménage, Molly Maguire,
  National, Oddfellows, Oral, Orangemen, Oratory, Order, Permissive, Phi Beta
  Kappa, Plunket, Plural, Pop, Provident, Repertory, Ribbonism, Rosicrucian, Rotary,
  Royal, S, Samaj, School, Secret, Soc, Somaj, Soroptomist, Sorority, Stakeholder,
  Surveillance, Tammany, Theosophical, Toc H, Ton, Tong, Triad, U, Whiteboy,
  World
Sociologist Weber
Sock(s) Argyle, Argyll, Biff, Bobby, Bootee, Digital, Hose(n), Lam, Leg warmer,
  Punch, Rock, Slipper, Slosh, Strike, Tabi, Trainer, Walk, Wind
Socket Acetabulum, Alveole, Budget, Eyepit, Gudgeon, Hollow, Hosel, Hot shoe,
  Jack, Keeper, Lampholder, Nave, Nozzle, Ouch, Outlet, Plug, Pod, Point, Port,
  Power-point, Shoe, Strike, Torulus, Whip
Sock-eye Nerka, Salmon
Socrates, Socratic Ironist, Maieutics, Sage
Sod Clump, Delf, Delph, Divot, Fail, Gazo(o)n, Mool, Mould, Mouls, Scraw, Sward,
  Turf
Soda, Sodium Acmite, Arfvedsonite, Baking, Barilla, Bicarb, Caustic, Club, Cream,
  La(u)rvikite, Na, Natrium, Natron, Reh, Saleratus, Splash, Thenardite, Trona,
  Washing
Sofa Canapé, Chaise longue, Chesterfield, Couch, Daybed, Divan, Dos-à-dos,
  Dosi-do, Lounge, Ottoman, Settee, Squab, Tête-à-tête
So far (as) As, As yet, Quoad, Until, Yonder
Soft(en), Softener, Softening, Softly Amalgam, Anneal, B, BB, Blet, Boodle,
  Calm, Casefy, Cedilla, Cottony, Cree, Cushion, Dim, Dolcemente, Doughy, Ease,
  Emolliate, Emollient, Flabby, Furry, Gentle, Hooly, Humanise, Intenerate, Lash,
  Lax, Lenient, Lenition, Limp, Low, Macerate, Malacia, Malax(ate), Malleable,
  Mardarse, Mardie, Mease, Mellow, Melt, Mild, Milksop, Mitigate, Modulate,
  Mollify, Mollities, Morendo, Mulch, Mush(y), Mute, Neale, Nesh, Option, P,
  Palliate, Pastel, Piano, Plushy, Porous, Propitiate, Rait, Rate, Relent, Scumble,
  Sentimental, Silly, Slack, Squashy, Squidgy, Squishy, Sumph, Talcose, Temper,
  → **TENDER**, Tone, Velvet, Weak
Softness Lenity

▶ **Software** *see* COMPUTER SOFTWARE

Sog(gy) Goop, Sodden

Soil(ed), Soily Acid, Adscript, Agrology, Agronomy, Alkali(ne), Alluvium, Azonal, Backfill, Bedraggle, Chernozem, Clay, Cohesive, Defile, Desecrate, Desert, Dinge, Dirt(y), Discolour, Earth, Edaphic, Edaphology, Frictional, Gault, Glebe, Grey, Grimy, Ground, Gumbo, Hotbed, Humus, Illuvium, Intrazonal, Lair, Land, Latosol, Lithosol, Loam, Loess, Lome, Loss, Mire, Mool, Mo(u)ld, Mud, Mulch, Mull, Night, Peat, Ped, Pedalfer, Pedocal, Pedology, Phreatic, Planosol, Podsol, Podzol, Prairie, Pure, Regar, Regolith, Regosol, Regur, Rendzina, Rhizosphere, Root-ball, Sal, Sedentary, Smudge, Smut, Solonchak, Solonetz, Solum, Soot, Stain, Stonebrash, Sub, Sully, Tarnish, Tash, Terrain, Terricolous, Tilth, Top, Tschernosem, Udal, Umber, Virgin, Yarfa, Yarpha, Zonal

Soirée Drum, Levee, Musicale

Sojourn Abide, Respite, Stay, Tabernacle, Tarry

Sol G, Soh, Sun

Solace Cheer, Comfort

Solar(ium) Heliacal, Tannery

Sold Had

Solder Braze, Join, Spelter, Tin, Weld

Soldier(s) Achilles, Alpini, Amazon, Ant, Anzac, Army, Arna(o)ut, Askari, Atkins, ATS, Banner, Bashi-Bazouk, Battalion, Bersaglier(e), Blue beret, Bluecoat, Bluff, Bod, Bombardier, Borderer, Botha, Brave, Brigade, Buff-coat, Buff-jerkin, Bullman, Butter-nut, Cadet, Caimac(am), Cameronian, Campaigner, Cannoneer, Cannon-fodder, Car(a)bineer, Car(a)binier, Cataphract, Centinel(l), Centonel(l), Centurion, Chasseur, Chindit, Chocko, Choco, Chocolate, Cohort, Colonel, Colours, Commando, Confederate, Continental, Contingent, Cornet, Corp(s), Cossack, Crusader, Cuirassier, Ded, Desert rat, Detail, Digger, Dog-face, Doughboy, Draftee, Dragoon, Dugout, Emmet, Engineer, Enomoty, Evzone, Fag(g)ot, Federal, Fencibles, Field-gray, Field-grey, Fighter, Flanker, Foederatus, Foot, Forlorn-hope, Fugleman, Fusilier, Fuzzy-wuzzy, Fyrd, Gallo(w)glass, Galoot, General, GI, GI Joe, Gippo, Goorkha, Grenadier, Greycoat, Grim dig, Grunt, Guardee, Guardsman, Guerilla, Gurkha, Gyppo, Hackbuteer, Hobbler, Hoplite, Hussar, Immortal, Imperialist, Impi, Inf(antry), Iron Duke, Ironside, Irregular, Jackman, Janissary, Janizary, Jawan, Jock, Joe, Johnny Reb(el), Kaimakam, Kern(e), Kitchener, Knight, Lancer, Landsknecht, Lansquenet, Lashkar, Leatherneck, Legionary, Legionnaire, Levy, Line, Linesman, Lobster, Maniple, Man o' war, Martinet, Men-at-arms, Miles (gloriosus), Militiaman, Miner, Minuteman, Missileer, Musketeer, Nahal, Naik, Nasute, Nizam, Non-com, Old Bill, Old Contemptibles, Old moustache, OR, Orderly, Palatine, Palikar, Pandoor, Pandour, Pandy, Paratroop, Partisan, Peltast, Peon, Perdu(e), Persevere, Phalanx, Pikeman, Piou-piou, Pistoleer, Platoon, Poilu, Point man, Pongo, Post, POW, Private, Rajput, Ranger, Rank(er), Rank and file, Rapparree, Rat-tail, Reb, Redcoat, Reformado, Regiment, Regular, Reiter, Reservist, Retread, Rifleman, Rutter, Sabre, Saddler, Sammy, Samurai, SAS, Sebundy, Sentinel, Sepoy, Serafile, Serviceman, Signaller, Silladar, Snarler, So(d)ger, Soldado, Sowar(ee), Sowarry, Spearman, Squaddie, Squaddy, Stalhelm(er), Stormtrooper, Strelitz, Subaltern, Swad(dy), Sweat, Targeteer, Tarheel, Templar, Terrier, Territorial, Timariot, Tin, Tommy, Toy, Train-band, Trencher, Trooper, Troops, Turco(pole), Uhlan, Unknown, Velites, Vet(eran), Voltigeur, Volunteer, Wagon, Warhorse, Warmonger, Warrior, Whitecoat, Wild Geese, Woodbind, Woodbine, Yardbird, Yeoman, Zouave

▷ **Soldiers** *may indicate* bread for boiled eggs

Sole, Solitaire, Solitary Alone, Anchoret, Anchorite, Clump, Convex, Corporation, Dover, Dropped, Fish, Incommunicado, Lemon, Lonesome, Megrim, Merl, Meunière, Monastical, Monkish, Only, Pad, Palm, Patience, Pelma, Planta(r), Plantigrade, Platform, Recluse, Sand, Scaldfish, Single(ton), Skate, Slip, Smear-dab, Tap, Thenar, Tread, Unique, Vibram®, Vola

Solemn Agelast, Austere, Devout, Earnest, Grave, Gravitas, Impressive, Majestic, Owlish, Po-faced, Sacred, Sedate, Serious, Sober, Sobersides, Sombre

Solent Lee

Solicit Accost, Approach, Ask, Attract, Bash, → **BEG**, Canvass, Commission, Cottage, Drum up, Importun(at)e, Plead, Ply, Proposition, Speer, Speir, Tout, Woo

Solicitor(s) Advocate, Attorney, Avoué, Beggar, Canvasser, Crown agent, Hallanshaker, Law-agent, Lawyer, Moll, Notary, Official, Side-bar, SL, Tout, Trull, Writer to the Signet, WS

Solid(arity), Solidify Cake, Chunky, Clot, Clunky, Compact, Comradeship, Concrete, Cone, Congeal, Consolidate, Cube, Cylinder, Dense, Enneahedron, Esprit de corps, Ethan, Firm, Foursquare, Freeze, Frustrum, Fuchsin(e), Gel, Hard, Holosteric, Impervious, Kotahitanga, Masakhane, Merbromin, Octahedron, Pakka, Parallelepiped, Petrarchan, Platonic, Polyhedron, Prism, Pucka, Pukka, Purin(e), Robust, Set, Skatole, Square, Stilbene, Sublimate, Substantial, Tetrahedron, Thick, Trusty, Unanimous

Solipsism Egotism, Panegoism

Solitary Antisocial, Friendless, On ice

▶ **Solitary** *see* **SOLE**

Solitude Privacy, Seclusion

Solo Aria, Cadenza, Cavatine, Concertante, Lone, Monodrama, Monody, Ombre, One-man, Scena, Unaided, Variation

Solon Sage

So long Cheerio, Ciao, Goodbye, Tata

Solstice Summer, Tropic, Winter

Soluble Alkaline, Consolute, Surfactant

Solution Acetone, Alkali, Ammonia, Amrit, → **ANSWER**, Austenite, Benedict's, Collodion, Colloidal, Dakin's, Dobell's, Éclaircissement, Electrolyte, Elixir, Emulsion, Eusol, Fehling's, Final, Hairspray, Key, Leachate, Limewater, Lixivium, Lye, Normal, Oleoresin, Rationale, Reducer, Ringer's, Rinse, Rubber, Saline, Solid, Solvent, Soup, Standard, Suspensoid, Tincture, Titrate, Viscose

▷ **Solution** *may indicate* an anagram

Solve(d), Solver Absolve, Assoil, Calculate, Casuist, Clear, Crack, Decode, Holmes, Loast, Loose, Read(er), Suss out, Troubleshoot, Unclew, Undo, Unriddle, Work

Solvent Above water, Acetaldehyde, Acetone, Afloat, Alcahest, Aldol, Alkahest, Anisole, Aqua-regia, Banana oil, Benzene, Chloroform, Cleanser, Cyclohexane, Cyclopentane, Cymene, Decalin, Diluent, Dioxan(e), Eleunt, Eluant, Ether, Funded, Furan, Hexane, Ligroin, Megilp, Menstruum, Methanol, Methylal, Naphtha, Paraldehyde, Picoline, Protomic, Pyridine, Sound, Stripper, Terebene, Terpineol, Tetrachloromethane, Thinner, Thiophen, Toluene, Toluol, Trike, Trilene, Turpentine

Sombre Dark, Drab, Drear, Dull, Funereal, Gloomy, Grave, Morne, Morose, Subfusc, Subfusk, Sullen, Triste

Some Any, Arrow, Ary, Certain, Divers, Few, One, Part, Portion, Quota, Sundry, These, They, Wheen

▷ **Some** *may indicate* a hidden word

Somebody Dignitary, Name, Notable, One, Person, Quidam, Someone, Tuft, → **VIP**

Somehow Somegate

▷ **Somehow** *may indicate* an anagram

Somersault Back-flip, Barani, Catherine wheel, Deltcher, Flip(-flap), Flip-flop, Handspring, Pitchpole, Pitchpoll

Something Aliquid, Chattel, Matter, Object, Summat, What, Whatnot

Sometime(s) Erstwhile, Ex, Former, Occasional, Off and on, Otherwhiles, Quondam

Somewhat Bit, -ish, Mite, Partly, Quasi, Quite, Rather, Relatively

Somewhere Somegate

Somnolence Drowsiness

Son Boy, Descendant, Disciple, Epigon(e), Fils, Fitz, Lad, Lewis, M(a)c, Native, Offspring, Prodigal, Progeny, Scion

Song Air, Amoret, Anthem, Antistrophe, Aria, Art, Aubade, Ayre, Ballad, Ballant, Ballata, Barcarol(l)e, Belter, Berceuse, Bhajan, Blues, Brindisi, Burden, Burthen, Cabaletta, Calypso, Cancionero, Cante hondo, Cante joudo, Canticle, Cantilena, Cantion, Canzona, Canzone, Canzonet(ta), Carmagnole, Carol, Catch, Cavatina, Chanson, Cha(u)nt, Come-all-ye, Conductus, Corn-kister, Corroboree, Cycle, Descant, Dirge, Dithyramb, Ditty, Elegy, Epithalamion, Epithalamium, Fado, Fit, Flamenco, Folk, Forebitter, Gaudeamus, Gita, Glee, Gorgia, Gradual, Hillbilly, Hum, Hymeneal, Hymn, Internationale, Jug(-jug), Lament, Lay, Lied(er), Lilt, Lullaby, Lyric, Madrigal, Magnificat, Marseillaise, Matin, Melic, Melisma, Melody, Mento, Minnesang, Negro spiritual, Noel, Number, Nunc dimittis, Oat, Paean, Pane, Part, Patter, Pennillion, Plain, Plaint, Plantation, Pop, Prick, Prothalamion, Prothalamium, Psalm, Qawwali, Rap, Recitativo, Red Flag, Relish, Rhapsody, Rispetto, Roulade, Roundelay, Rune, Scat, Scolion, Sea-shanty, Secular, Serenade, Shanty, Shosholoza, Siren, Sirvente, Skolion, Sososholoza, Spiritual, Stave, Stomper, Strain, Strophe, Swan, Taps, Tenebrae, Theme, Torch, Trill, Tune, Tyrolienne, Villanella, Volkslied, Waiata, War, Warble, Wassail, Waulking, Yodel, Yodle

Songbook Cancionero, Hymnal, Kommersbuch, Libretto, Psalter

Songsmith, Songwriter Carmichael, Dowland, Espla, Foster, Kern, Minot, Waitz, Zappa

Sonnet Amoret, Elizabethan, English, Italian, Miltonic, Petrarch(i)an, Shakespearean, Shakespearian, Spenserian

Sonometer Monochord

Soon(er) Anon, Directly, Enow, Erelong, Imminent, Lief, OK, Oklahoma, Presently, Shortly, Tight, Timely, Tit(ely), Tite, Tyte

Soot(y) Colly, Coom, Crock, Fuliginous, Gas black, Grime, Lampblack, Smut, Speck

Soothe, Soothing Accoy, Allay, Anetic, Anodyne, Appease, Assuage, Bucku, Calm, Compose, Demulcent, Dulcet, Emollient, Irenic, Lenitive, Lull, Mellifluous, Mollify, Pacific, Paregoric, Poultice, Quell, Rock

Soothsayer Astrologer, Augur, Calchas, Chaldee, Divine, Forecaster, Haruspex, Melampus, Oracle, Picus, Prophet, Pythoness, → **SEER**, Shipton, Tiresias

Sop Appease, Berry, Douceur, Rait, Ret, Sponge

Sophist(ic) Casuist, Elenchic, Quibbler

Sophisticate(d) Blasé, Boulevardier, City slicker, Civilised, Classy, Cosmopolitan, Couth, Doctor, High-end, Patrician, Polished, Sative, Slicker, Svelte, Urbane, Worldly

▷ **Sophoclean** *may indicate* Greek alphabet, etc

Sophomore Semie

Soporific Barbiturate, Bromide, Drowsy, Halothane, Hypnotic, Lullaby, Narcotic, Opiate, Sedative, Tedious

Soppiness, Soppy Maudlin, Schwärmerei, Sloppy, Slushy, Wet

Soprano Caballé, Castrato, Crespin, Descant, Lind, Patti, Treble

Sorb Wend

Sorbet Glacé, Water ice

Sorcerer, Sorceress, Sorcery Angakok, Ashipu, Circe, Conjury, Diablerie, Hoodoo, Kadaitcha, Kurdaitcha, Lamia, Mage, Magian, Magic(ian), Magus, Medea, Merlin, Morgan le Fay, Mother Shipton, Necromancer, Obi, Pishogue, Shaman, Sortilege, Venefic(ious), Voodoo, Warlock, Witch, Witch knot, Wizard

Sordid Base, Low-life, Miserable, Rhyparography, Scungy, Seamy, Sleazy, Squalid, Vile

Sore(ly), Sores Abrasion, Anthrax, Bitter, Blain, Boil, Canker, Chancre, Chap, Chilblain, Cold, Dearnly, Felon, Gall, Impost(h)ume, Ireful, Kibe, Nasty, Pressure, Quitter, Quittor, Raw, Running, Rupia(s), Saddle, Sair, Shiver, Sitfast, Surbate, Ulcer(s), Whitlow, Wound

Sore throat Garget, Prunella, Quinsy, Tonsillitis

Sorghum Kaoliang, Mabela, Milo

Sorrel Common, French, Hetty, Mountain, Oca, Roman, Sheep, Soar(e), Sore, Sourock

Sorrow(ful) Affliction, Distress, Dole, Dolente, Dolour, Emotion, Fee-grief, → **GRIEF**, Lament, Misery, Nepenthe, Ochone, Penance, Pietà, Remorse, Rue, Triste, Wae, Waugh, Wirra, Woe, Yoop

Sorry Ashamed, Contrite, Miserable, Oops, Penitent, Pitiful, Poor, Regretful, Relent, Simple, Wretched

▷ **Sorry** *may indicate* an anagram

Sort(ing) Arrange, Brand, Breed, Category, Character, Classify, Collate, Drive, Grade, → **KIND**, Nature, Pranck(e), Prank, Sift, Species, Stamp, Stripe, Tidy, Triage, Type, Variety

Sortie Attack, Foray, Mission, Outfall, Raid, Sally

▶ **Sorts** *see* **OUT OF SORTS**

So-so Average, Indifferent, Mediocre, Middling

So to speak Quasi

▷ **So to speak** *may indicate* 'sound of'

Sotto voce Murmur, Whisper

▶ **Soubriquet** *see* **SOBRIQUET**

Sough Rustle, Sigh

Soul(ful) Alma, Ame, Anima, Animist, Atman, Ba, Bardo, Brevity, Deep, Entelechy, Eschatology, Expressive, Heart, Inscape, Ka, Larvae, Lost, Manes, Object, Person, Pneuma, Psyche, Saul, Shade, Spirit, Traducian, Universal

Sound(ed), Sounding, Soundness, Sound system Accurate, Ach-laut, Acoustic, Affricate, Albemarle, Allophone, Allthere, Alveolar, Amphoric, Audio, Bay, Bleep, Blip, Bloop, Blow, Boing, Bong, Breathed, Cacophony, Chime, Chirl, Chirr(e), Chord, Chug, Clam, Clang, Clink, Cloop, Clop, Clunk, Consistent, Continuant, Copper-bottomed, Dah, Dental, Dit, Dive, Dolby®, Dream, Echo, Eek, Euphony, Fast, Fathom, Fere, Fettle, Fit, Foley, Glide, Good, Hale, Harmonics, Healthy, Hearty, Hi-fi, Ich-laut, Inlet, Islay, Jura, Kalmar, Knell, Kyle, Labiodental, Lo-fi, Long Island, Low, Lucid, Mach, Madrilene, McMurdo, Mersey, Milford, Mouillé, Monophthong, Musak, Music, Muzak®, Narrow, → **NOISE**, Onomatopaeia, Oompah, Optical, Orate, Orthodox, Palatal, Palato-alveolar, Pamlico, Paragog(u)e, Peal, Pectoriloquy, Phone(me), Phonetic, Phonic, Phonology, Pitter(-patter), Plap, Plink, Plonk, Plop, Plosion, Plumb, Plummet, Plunk, Plymouth, Probe, Puget, Put-put, Quadraphonic(s), Quadrophonic(s), Rale, Rational, Rat-tat, Real, Reliable,

Ring, Roach, Robust, Rong, Rumble, Rustle, Sabin, Safe, Sandhi, Sane, S(c)hwa, Scoresby, Sensurround®, Skirl, Solid, Sonance, Sone, Souffle, Sough, Sowne, Speech, Splat, Stereo, Stereophony, Strait, Surround, Swish, Tamber, Tannoy®, Tchick, Thorough, Timbre, Ting, Tone, Toneme, Trig, Triphthong, Trumpet, Twang, Ultrasonic(s), Unharmed, Uvular, Valid, Viable, Voice, Vowel, Wah-wah, Watertight, Well, Whine, Whistle, Whole(some), Whump, Wolf

Sounder Echo, Lead

Sounding board Abat-voix

Soundproof Deaden

Sound-track Dubbing, Movietone®, Stripe

Soup Alphabet, Avgolemono, Bird's nest, Bisk, Bisque, Borsch, Bouillabaisse, Bouillon, Brewis, Broth, Burgoo, Cal(l)aloo, Chowder, Cock-a-leekie, Cockieleekie, Cockyleeky, Consommé, Duck, Garbure, Gazpacho, Gomb(r)o, Gruel, Gumbo, Harira, Hoosh, Julienne, Kail, Kale, Lokshen, Madrilene, Marmite, Mess, Minestrone, Mock turtle, Mulligatawny, Oxtail, Palestine, Pea(se), Pho, Pot-au-feu, Pot(t)age, Primordial, Puree, Ramen, Rice, Rubaboo, Sancoche, Scotch broth, Shchi, Shtchi, Skilligalee, Skilligolee, Skilly, Skink, Stock, Tattie-claw, Toheroa, Turtle, Vichyssoise

▷ **Soup** *may indicate* an anagram

Soupçon Thought, Touch

Sour(puss) Acerb, Acescent, Acid, Acidulate, Aigre-doux, Alegar, Bitter, Citric, Crab, Eager, Esile, Ferment, Moody, Stingy, Subacid, → **TART**, Turn, Unamiable, Verjuice, Vinegarish

Source Authority, Basis, Bottom, Centre, Closed, Database, Derivation, Egg, Fons, Font, Fount, Fountain-head, Germ, Head-stream, Literary, Mine, Mother, Neutron, Origin, Parent, Pi, Pion, Point, Provenance, Quarry, Reference, Rise, Riverhead, Root, Seat, Seed, Spring, Springhead, Stock, Supply, Urn, Well, Wellhead, Wellspring, Widow's cruse, Ylem

Sour milk Curds, Smetana, Whey, Whig, Yogh(o)urt

Souse Beath, Duck, Immerse, Pickle, Plunge, Soak, Spree, Steep

South(ern), Southerner Austral, Confederacy, Dago, Decanal, Decani, Deep, Dixieland, Meridian, Meridional, S, Scallywag

South Africa(n) Azania, Bantu, Caper, Ciskei, Grikwa, Griqua, Hottentot, Kaf(f)ir, Qwaqwa, SA, Soutie, Soutpiel, Springbok, Swahili, Xhosa, ZA, Zulu

South American Araucanian, Arawak, Argentino, Aymara, Bolivian, Carib, Chibcha, Chilean, Galibi, Guarani, Inca, Jivaro, Kechua, Latin, Llanero, Mam, Mapuchi, Mayan, Mixe-Zogue, Mixtac, Mochica, Quechua, SA, Shuar, Tapuyan, Tupi

South-east Roseland, SE

Southwark Boro'

Souvenir Goss, Keepsake, Memento, Relic, Remembrance, Scalp, Token, Trophy

Sovereign(ty), Sovereign remedy Anne, Autocrat, Bar, Condominium, Couter, Dominant, Emperor, ER, Goblin, Haemony, Harlequin, Imperial, Imperium, James, King, L, Liege, Nizam, Pound, Quid, Rangatiratanga, Royalty, Ruler, Shiner, Supreme, Swaraj, Synarchy, Thick' un, Thin' un

Soviet Circassian, Council, Estonian, Russian, Stalin, Supreme, Volost

Sow(ing) Catchcrop, Elt, Foment, Gilt, Inseminate, Plant, Scatter, Seed, Sprue, Strew, Yelt

Soya Sitosterol, Tempe(h)

Spa Aachen, Baden, Baden-Baden, Bath, Buxton, Evian, Godesberg, Harrogate, Hydro, Kurhaus, Kursaal, Leamington, Malvern, Vichy

Space(d), Spacing, Spacious, Spaceman, Spatial Abyss, Acre, Area, Areola,

Bay, Bolthole, Bracket, Breathing, Bronchus, Cellule, Cislunar, Clearing, C(o)elom, Coelome, Compluvium, Concourse, Contline, Crookes, Cubbyhole, Daylight, Deducted, Deep, Diastema, Distal, Distance, Elbow-room, Elliptic, Esplanade, Ether, Exergue, Expanse, Extent, Flies, Footprint, Forecourt, Freeband, Gagarin, Gap, Glade, Glenn, Goaf, Gob, Gutter, Hair, Hash(mark), Headroom, Hell, Homaloid, Indention, Inner, Intergalactic, Interim, Interlinear, Interplanetary, Interstellar, Interstice, Invader, Kerning, Killogie, Kneehole, Lacuna, Lair, Leading, Lebensraum, Legroom, Life, Logie, Lumen, Lunar, Lung, Machicolation, Maidan, Manifold, Metope, Mihrab, Minkowski, Mosh pit, Muset, Musit, Orbit, Outer, Palatial, Parvis(e), Peridrome, Personal, Plenum, Polemics, Pomoerium, Priest hole, Proportional, Proxemics, Quad, Retrochoir, Riemannian, → **ROOM**, Ruelle, Sample, Sheets, Shelf room, Slot, Spandrel, Spandril, Step, Steric, Storage, Third, Topological, Tympanum, Ullage, Uncluttered, Vacua, Vacuole, Vacuum, Vast, Vector, Void, Volume

Spacecraft, Space agency, Space object, Spaceship, Space station Apollo, Capsule, Columbia, Columbus, Deep Space, Explorer, Galileo, Genesis, Giotto, Lander, LEM, Luna, Lunik, Mariner, MIR, Module, NASA, Orbiter, Pioneer, Probe, Quasar, Ranger, Salyut, Shuttle, Skylab, Soyuz, Sputnik, Starship, Tardis, Viking, Vostok, Voyager, Zond

Space walk EVA

Spade Breastplough, Caschrom, Cas crom, Castrato, Detective, Flaughter, Graft, Loy, Negro, Paddle, Paddle staff, Pattle, Peat, Pettle, Pick, S, Shovel, Slane, Spit, Suit, Turf, Tus(h)kar, Tus(h)ker, Twiscar

Spain E, Hesperia, Iberia, Wean

Spalpeen Sinner

Span Age, Arch, Attention, Bestride, Bridge, Chip, Ctesiphon, Extent, Life, Memory, Range, Timescale

Spangle(d) Avanturine, Aventurine, Glitter, Instar, O, Paillette, Sequin

Spaniard, Spanish Alguacil, Alguazil, Andalusian, Barrio, Basque, Cab, Caballero, Carlist, Castilian, Catalan, Chicano, Dago, Don, Fly, Grandee, Hidalgo, Hispanic, José, Main, Mestizo, Mozarab, Pablo, Papiamento, Señor, Spic(k), Spik

Spaniel Blenheim, Cavalier, Clumber, Cocker, Crawler, Creep, Dog, Fawner, Field, Irish water, King Charles, Maltese, Papillon, Placebo, Skip-kennel, Springer, Sussex, Tibetan, Toad-eater, Toady, Toy, Water, Welsh springer

Spank(ing) Cob, Paddywhack, Rapid, Scud, Slap, Slipper, Sprack

Spanner Arc, Box, Bridge, Clapper, Key, Ring, Shifter, Shifting, Socket, Spider, Torque, Wrench

Spar Barite, Barytes, Blue John, Boom, Bowsprit, Box, Cauk, Cawk, Derbyshire, Fight, Gaff, Heavy, Iceland, Icestone, Jib-boom, Mainyard, Manganese, Martingale, Mast, Nail-head, Outrigger, Rafter, Rail, Ricker, Satin, Schiller, Shearleg, Sheerleg, Snotter, Spathic, Sprit, Steeve, Stile, Tabular, Triatic, Whiskerboom, Whiskerpole, Yard

Spare, Sparing Angular, Cast-off, Dup(licate), Economical, Free, Frugal, Galore, Gash, Gaunt, Hain, Lean, Lenten, Narrow, Other, Pardon, Reserve, Rib, Save, Scant, Skimp, Slender, Stint, Subsecive, Thin

Spark Animate, Arc, Beau, Blade, Bluette, Dandy, Flash, Flaught, Flint, Funk, Ignescent, Kindle, Life, Muriel, Quenched, Scintilla, Smoulder, Spunk, Trigger, Vital, Zest

Sparkle(r), Sparkling Aerated, Aventurine, Bling, Burnish, Coruscate, Crémant, Diamanté, Effervesce, Élan, Emicate, Fire, Fizz, Flicker, Frizzante, Glamour, Glint, Glisten, Glitter, Life, Pétillant, Scintillate, Seltzer, Seltzogene, Spangle, Spritzig,

Spumante, Twinkle, Verve, Witty, Zap

Sparrow Bird, Cape, Chipping, Hedge, Isaac, Java, Junco, Mah-jong(g), Mossie, Passerine, Piaf, Prunella, Song, Spadger, Speug, Sprug(gy), Titling, Tree

Sparrow-grass Asparagus, Sprue

Sparse Meagre, Rare, Scant, Thin

Spartan(s) Ascetic, Austere, Basic, Enomoty, Hardy, Helot, Heraclid, Lacedaemonian, Laconian, Lysander, Menelaus, Severe, Valiant

Spasm(s), Spasmodic Ataxic, Blepharism, Chorea, Clonus, Convulsive, Cramp, Crick, Fit(ful), Hiccup, Hippus, Hyperkinesis, Intermittent, Irregular, → **JERK**, Kink, Laryngismus, Nystagmus, Paroxysm, Periodical, Start, Strangury, Tetany, Throe, Tonic, Tonus, Trismus, Twinge, Twitch, Vaginismus, Writer's cramp

▷ **Spasmodic** *may indicate* an anagram

Spastic Athetoid, Clonic, Jerky

Spat(s) Bicker, Brattle, Gaiters, Legging, Quarrel, Shower, Tiff

Spate Flood, Sluice, Torrent

▶ **Spatial** *see* SPACE(D)

Spatter Disject, Ja(u)p, Scatter, Splash, Splosh, Spot, Sprinkle

▷ **Spattered** *may indicate* an anagram

Spawn(ing), Spawning place Anadromous, Blot, Fry, Progeny, Propagate, Redd, Roud, Seed, Spat, Spet, Spit

Speak(er), Speaking Address, Articulate, Broach, Chat, Cicero, Collocuter, Communicate, Converse, Coo, Declaim, Dilate, Discourse, Diseur, Dwell, Effable, Elocution, Eloquent, Expatiate, Express, Extemporise, Filibuster, Intercom, Intone, Inveigh, Jabber, Jaw, Lip, Loq, Loquitur, Management, Mang, Mention, Mike, Mina, Mouth, Mouthpiece, Nark, Native, Open, Orate, Orator, Palaver, Parlance, Parley, Perorate, Pontificate, Prate, Preach, Prelector, Rhetor, → **SAY**, Sayne, Spout, Spruik, Squawk box, Stump, Talk, Tannoy®, Tongue, Trap, Tub-thumper, Tweeter, Utter, Voice, Waffle, Witter, Word

Speakeasy Fluent, Shebeen

Spear Ash, Asparagus, Assagai, Assegai, Barry, Dart, Demi-lance, Fishgig, Fizgig, Gad, Gavelock, Gig, Glaive, Gleave, Gum digger's, Gungnir, Hastate, Impale, Javelin, Lance(gay), Launcegaye, Leister, Morris-pike, Partisan, Pierce, Pike, Pilum, Prong, Skewer, Spike, Trident, Trisul(a), Waster

Spear-rest Feutre, Fewter

Special(ly) Ad hoc, Constable, Designer, Distinctive, Extra, Important, Notable, Notanda, Particular, Peculiar, Red-letter, S, Specific, Strong suit

Specialise, Specialist(s) Allergist, Authority, Concentrate, Connoisseur, Consultant, ENT, Expert, Illuminati, Maestro, Major, Quant, Recondite, Technician

Species Biotype, Class, Endangered, Genre, Genus, Indicator, Infima, Kind, Opportunistic, Pioneer, Strain, Taxa

Specific(ally), Specified, Specify, Specification Adduce, As, Ascribe, Assign, Concretize, Cure, Define, Detail, Explicit, Formula, Full-blown, Itemise, Medicine, Namely, Precise, Quantify, Remedy, Sp, Special, State, Stipulate, Stylesheet, The, Trivial

Specimen(s) Assay, Example, Exemplar, Imago, Model, Museum piece, Sample, Slide, Swab, Topotype, Type

Specious False, Glib, Hollow, Pageant, Plausible, Spurious

Speck, Speckle(d) Atom, Bit, Dot, Fleck, Floater, Freckle, Gay, Mealy, Muscae volitantes, Particle, Peep(e), Pip, Spot, Spreckle, Stud

Spectacle(s), Spectacled, Spectacular Arresting, Barnacles, Bifocals, Blazers, Blinks, Bossers, Cheaters, Colourful, Epic, Escolar, Giglamps, → **GLASSES**, Goggles,

Horn-rims, Lorgnette, Lorgnon, Nose-nippers, Oo, Optical, Outspeckle, Pageant, Pebble glasses, Pince-nez, Pomp, Preserves, Raree-show, Scene, Show, Sight, Son et lumière, Sunglasses, Tamasha, Tattoo, Trifocal, Varifocals

Spectate, Spectator(s) Audience, Bystander, Dedans, Etagère, Eyer, Gallery, Gate, Groundling, Kibitzer, Observer, Onlooker, Ringsider, Standerby, Witness

Spectograph, Spectometer Aston, Calutron

Spectral, Spectre Apparition, Boggle, Bogy, Brocken, Eidolon, Empusa, Ghost, Idola, Iridal, Larva, Malmag, Phantasm, Phantom, Phasma, Spirit, Spook, Tarsier, Walking-straw, Wraith

Spectrum Absorption, Band, Continuous, Emission, Fission, Iris, Optical, Radio, Rainbow, Sunbow, Sundog, Visible, X-ray

Speculate, Speculative, Speculator, Speculation Agiotage, Arbitrage, Bear, Better, Bull, Conjecture, Flier, Flyer, Gamble, Guess, Ideology, If, Imagine, Meditate, Notional, Operate, Pinhooker, Shark, Stag, Theoretical, Theorise, Theory, Thought, Trade, Wonder

Speech, Speech element Accents, Address, Argot, Articulation, Bunkum, Burr, Curtain, Delivery, Dialect, Diatribe, Diction, Direct, Discourse, Dithyramb, Drawl, Éloge, English, Epilogue, Eulogy, Filibuster, Free, Gab, Glossolalia, Grandiloquence, Harangue, Helium, Idiolect, Idiom, Inaugural, Indirect, Jargon, Keynote, King's, Lallation, → **LANGUAGE**, Lingua franca, Litany, Logopaedics, Maiden, Monologue, Morph(eme), Motherese, Musar, Oblique, Occlusive, Oral, Oration, Parabasis, Parle, Peroration, Phasis, Philippic, Phonetics, Prolocution, Prolog(ue), Queen's, Reported, Rhetoric, Sandhi, Scanning, Screed, Sermon, Set, Side, Slang, Soliloquy, Stemwinder, Stump, Tagmeme, Talk, Taxeme, Tirade, Tongue, Uptalk, Vach, Verbal, Visible, Voice, Wawa, Whaikorero, Whistle-stop, Xenoglossia

Speech defect, Speech disease Alalia, Alogia, Aposiopesis, Dysarthria, Dysphasia, Dysphoria, Echolalia, Idioglossia, Lallation, Lisp, Palilalia, Paralalia, Paraphasia, Pararthria, Psellism, Rhinolalia, Stammer, Stutter

Speechless Alogia, Dumb, Dumbstruck, Inarticulate, Mute, Silent, Tongue-tied

Speech-writer Logographer

Speed(ily), Speedy Accelerate, Alacrity, Amain, Amphetamine, Apace, Average, Bat, Belive, Belt, Breakneck, Burn, Cast, Celerity, Clip, Dart, Despatch, DIN, Dispatch, Expedite, Fang, Fast, Film, Fleet, Further, Gait, Gallop, Goer, Group, Gun, Hare, Haste, Hie, Hotfoot, Hypersonic, Induce, Instantaneous, Knot, Landing, Lick, Mach, Merchant, MPH, → **PACE**, Pelt, Phase, Pike, Post-haste, Pronto, Race, Rapidity, Rate, RPS, Rush, Scorch, Scud, Scurr, Skirr, Soon, Spank, Split, Stringendo, Supersonic, Swift, Tach, Tear, Tempo, Ton up, V, Velocity, Ventre à terre, Vroom, Whid, Wing, Zoom

Speedwell Brooklime, Fluellin, Germander, Veronica

Spelaean Troglodyte

Spelk Skelf, Splinter

Spell(ing) Abracadabra, Bewitch, Bout, Cantrip, Charm, Conjuration, Do, Elf-shoot, Enchantment, Entrance, Fit, Go, Gri(s)-gri(s), Hex, Incantation, Innings, Jettatura, Juju, Knock, Knur, → **MAGIC**, Mojo, Need-fire, Nomic, Open sesame, Orthography, Period, Philter, Philtre, Phonetic, Pinyin, Relieve, Ride, Romaji, Run, Rune, Scat, Shot, Signify, Sitting, Snap, Snatch, Sorcery, Sp, Span, Spasm, Splinter, Stint, Stretch, Tack, Tour, Trick, Turn, Weird, Whammy, Witchcraft

Spelling-book ABC, Grimoire

Spencer Bodice, Topcoat, Tracy, Vest

Spend(er), Spending Anticipate, Birl, Blow, Blue, Boondoggling, Consume, Deficit, Deplete, Disburse, Exhaust, Fritter, Lash out, Lay out, Live, Outlay, Pass, Pay,

Shopaholic, Splash, Splash out, Splurge, Squander, Squandermania, Ware

Spendthrift Essex Man, High-roller, Prodigal, Profligate, Profuser, Scattergood, Wastrel

Spent All-in, Consumed, Dead, Done, Expended, Stale, Tired, Used, Weak, Weary

Sperm Seed, Semen

Spew Eject, Emit, Gush, Spit, Vomit

Sphagnum Moss, Peat

Sphere, Spherical Armillary, Attraction, Ball, Benthoscope, Celestial, Discipline, Earth, Element, Field, Firmament, Globe, Magic, Mound, Orb(it), Planet, Primum mobile, Prolate, Province, Realm, Schwarzschild, Theatre, Wheel

Sphinx Criosphinx, Hawk-moth, Oracle, Riddler

Spice, Spicy Amomum, Anise, Aniseed, Aryl, Baltic, Caraway, Cardamom, Cardamon, Cardamum, Cassareep, Cassaripe, Chilli powder, Cinnamon, Clove, Clow, Coriander, Cubeb, Cum(m)in, Dash, Devil, Garam masala, Ginger, Mace, Malaguetta, Marjoram, Masala, Myrrh, Nutmeg, Oregano, Paprika, Peppercorn, Picante, Pimento, Piperic, Piquant, Root ginger, Saffron, Salsa verde, Season, Stacte, Staragen, Tamal(e), Tamara, Tansy, Tarragon, Taste, Turmeric, Vanilla, Variety

Spick Dink, Neat, Spike, Tidy

Spicule Sclere, Tetract

Spider(s) Anancy, Ananse, Arachnid, Aranea, Araneida, Arthrapodal, Attercop, Bird, Black widow, Bobbejaan, Bolas, Cardinal, Cheesemite, Chelicerate, Citigrade, Diadem, Epeira, Epeirid, Ethercap, Ettercap, Funnel-web, Harvester, Harvestman, House, Hunting, Huntsman, Jumping, Katipo, Lycosa, Mite, Money, Mygale, Orb-weaver, Pan, Phalangid, Podogona, Pycnogonid, Red, Redback, Rest, Ricinulei, Saltigrade, Scorpion, Solifugae, Solpuga, Spinner, Strap, Tarantula, Telary, Trapdoor, Violin, Water, Wolf, Zebra

Spiderwort Tradescantia

Spiel Pitch, Spruik

Spignel Baldmoney, Meu

Spigot Bung, Plug, Tap

Spike(d) Barb, Brod, Calk, Calt(h)rop, Chape, Cloy, Crampon, Ear, Fid, Foil, Gad, Gadling, Goad, Grama, Herissé, Icicle, Impale, Kebab, Lace, Locusta, Marlin(e), Nail, Needle, → PIERCE, Point, Pricket, Prong, Puseyite, Rod, Sharp, Shod, Skewer, Spadix, Spear, Spicate, Spicule, Spire, Strobiloid, Tang, Thorn, Tine

Spill(age) Divulge, Drop, Fidibus, Jackstraw, Lamplighter, Leakage, Let, Overflow, Overset, Reveal, Scail, Scale, Shed, Skail, Slart, Slop, Stillicide, Taper, Tumble

Spin(ner), Spinning (wheel) Aeroplane, Arabian, Arachne, Aswirl, Bielmann, Birl, Camel, Centrifuge, Chark(h)a, Cribellum, Cut, Day trip, Dextrorse, DJ, Flat, Flip, Gimp, Googly, Gymp, Gyrate, Gyre, Gyroscope, Hurl, Isobaric, Isotopic, Lachesis, Mole, Nun, Peg-top, Piecener, Piecer, Pirouette, Pivot, PR, Precess, Prolong, Purl, Reel, Rev(olve), Ride, Rotate, Royal, Screw, Side, Sinistrorse, Slide, Spider, Stator, Strobic, Swirl, Swivel, Throstle, Tirl, Toss, Trill, Trundle, Twirl, Twist, Wheel, Whirl, Whirligig, Work

Spinach Florentine, Orach(e), Popeye, Sa(a)g

Spinal (chord), Spine(d), Spiny Acanthoid, Acerose, Acromion, Aculeus, Areole, Arête, Backbone, Barb, Chine, Coccyx, Column, Doorn, Dorsal, Epidural, Muricate, Myelon, Notochord, Ocotillo, Prickle, Quill, Rachial, Ray, R(h)achis, Ridge bone, Thorn, Torso, Tragacanth

Spindle(-shanks), Spindly Arbor, Axle, Bobbin, Capstan, Fusee, Fusiform, Fusil, Mandrel, Mandril, Pin, Scrag, Staff, Triblet

▶ **Spine** *see* **SPINAL**

Spinel Balas, Picotite

Spineless Inerm, Muticous, Timid, Weak

Spinn(e)y Coppice, Shaw, Thicket

Spinning-wheel Chark(h)a

Spinster Discovert, Feme sole, Old maid, Tabby

Spiral Archimedes, Caracol, Chalaza, Cochlea, Coil, Curl, Dexiotropic, Dextrorse, Ekman, Genetic, Gyrate, Helical, Helix, Hyperbolic, Inflationary, Logarithmic, Loxodromical, Parastichy, Screw, Scroll, Sinistrorse, Spin, Tailspin, Turbinate, Turnpike, Vibrio, Volute, Whorl, Wind

Spire(-shaped) Broach, Flèche, Peak, Shaft, Steeple, Thyrsoid

Spirit(s), Spirited Ahriman, Akvavit, Alcohol, Ammonia, Angel, Animal, Animation, Apathodaimon, Applejack, Apsaral, Aquavit, Aqua vitae, Arak, Arch(a)eus, Ardent, Ariel, Arrack, Asmoday, Astral, Bitters, Blithe, Boggart, Bogie, Bogle, Bogy, Brandy, Bravura, Brio, Brollachan, Buggan(e), Buggin, Cant, Cherub, Cognac, Courage, Creature, Crême de menthe, Crouse, Daemon, Dash, Deev, Deva, Distillation, Div, Djinn(i), Domdaniel, → **DRINK**, Dryad, Duende, Duppy, Dybbuk, Eblis, Eidolon, Élan, Element(al), Emit, Empusa, Entrain, Erdgeist, Erl king, Esprit, Essence, Etheric, Ethos, Eudemon, Fachan, Faints, Familiar, Feints, Feisty, Feni, Fenny, Fetich(e), Fetish, Fettle, Fight, Firewater, Free, Fuath, Gamy, Geist, Geneva, Genie, Genius, → **GHOST**, Ghoul, Ginger, Ginn, Gism, Glastig, Glendoveer, Go, Grappa, Gremlin, Grit, Grog, Gumption, Gytrash, Hartshorn, Heart, Hollands, Holy, Huaca, Hugh, Imp, Incubus, Indwelt, Jann, Jinn(i), Jinnee, Jism, Jumbie, Jumby, Ka, Kachina, Kehua, Kelpie, Kindred, Kirsch, Kobold, Larva, Lemur(e), → **LIQUOR**, Lively, Loki, Manes, Manito(u), Manitu, Mare, Marid, Metal, Meths, Methyl(ated), Mettle, Mindererus, Mineral, Mobbie, Mobby, Morale, Mystique, Nain rouge, Neutral, Nis, Nix, Nobody, Numen, Numina, Ondine, Orenda, Panache, Paraclete, Party, Peart, Pecker, Pep, Peri, Pernod®, Petrol, Phantom, Pluck(y), Pneuma, Poltergeist, Pooka, Potato, Poteen, Presence, Pride, Proof, Psyche, Puck, Python, Racy, Rakee, Raki, Rakshas(a), Rectified, Rosicrucian, Ruin, Rum(bullion), Rye, Salt, Samshoo, Samshu, Saul, Schnapps, Scientology, Seraph, Shade, Shadow, Shaitan, She'ol, Short, Smeddum, Soul, Spectre, Spright, Sprite, Spunk, Steam, Strunt, Surgical, Sylph, Tafia, Tangie, Taniwha, Team, Tequila, Tokoloshe, Ton, Turpentine, Turps, Undine, Verve, Vigour, Vim, Vodka, Voodoo, Wairua, Water horse, Weltgeist, White, Wili, Wine, Witblits, Wood, Wraith, Zeitgeist, Zephon, Zing, Zombie

Spiritless Craven, Dowf, Insipid, Languid, Meek, Milksop, Poor, Tame, Vapid

Spirit-level Vial

Spiritual(ism), Spiritualist Aerie, Aery, Coon-song, Ecclesiastic, Ethereous, Eyrie, Eyry, Incorporeal, Negro, Planchette, Platonic, Psychic, Slate-writing, Swedenborg, Table-rapping, Table-turning

Spirt Gush, Jet, Rush

Spit(ting), Spittle Barbecue, Broach, Brochette, Chersonese, Dead ringer, Dribble, Drool, Emptysis, Eructate, Expectorate, Fuff, Gob, Golly, Gooby, Goss, Grill, Hawk, Hockle, Impale, Jack, Lookalike, Peninsula, Ras, Ringer, Rotisserie, Saliva, Skewer, Slag, Spade(ful), Spawl, Spear, Sputter, Sputum, Tombolo, Tongue, Yesk, Yex

Spite(ful) Backbite, Bitchy, Catty, Grimalkin, Harridan, Irrespective, Malevolent, Malgrado, Malgré, Malice, Mau(l)gre, Mean, Nasty, Petty, Pique, Rancour, Spleen, Venom, Viperish, Waspish

Spitfire Cacafogo, Cacafuego, Wildcat

Spittoon Cuspidor(e)

Spiv Lair, Rorter

Splash Blash, Blue, Dabble, Dash, Dog, Drip, Feature, Flouse, Fl(o)ush, Gardyloo, Jabble, Ja(u)p, Jirble, Paddle, Plap, Plop, Plowter, Sket, Slosh, Slush, Soda, Soss, Sozzle, Spairge, Spat(ter), Spectacle, Splat(ch), Splatter, Splodge, Splosh, Splotch, Spray, Spree, Squatter, Swash, Swatter, Water, Wet

Splay(ed) Curl, Flew, Flue, Patté(e), Spread

Spleen Acrimony, Bite, Lien, Melt, Milt(z), Pip, Stomach, Vitriol, Wrath

Splendid, Splendour Ah, Braw, Brilliant, Bully, Capital, Champion, Clinker, Dandy, Éclat, Effulgent, Excellent, Fine, Finery, Fulgor, Gallant, Garish, Glitterand, Glittering, Glorious, Glory, Gorgeous, Grand(eur), Grandiose, Ha, Heroic, Lustrous, Majestic, Mooi, Noble, Palatial, Panache, Pomp, Proud, Radiant, Rich, Ripping, Royal, Stunning, Super(b), Superduper, Wally, Zia

Splice(d) Braid, Eye, Join, Knit, Mainbrace, Wed

▷ **Spliced** *may indicate* an anagram

Splint Airplane, Banjo, Brace, Cal(l)iper, Splenial, Stent, T

Splinter(s) Bone-setter, Breakaway, Flinder, Fragment, Matchwood, Shatter, Shiver, Skelf, Sliver, Spale, Spall, Speel, Spelk, Spell, Spicula, Spill

Split(ting) Areolate, Axe, Banana, Bifid, Bifurcate, Bisect, Breach, Break, Broach, Burst, Chasm, Chine, Chop, Chorism, Clint, Clove(n), Crack, Crevasse, Cut, Decamp, Departmentalise, Disjoin, Distrix, → **DIVIDE**, Division, Divorce, End, Fissile, Fissure, Flake, Fork(ed), Fragment, Grass, Lacerate, Left, Partition, Red(d), Rift(e), Rip, Rive, Russian, Ryve, Schism, Scissor, Segregate, Separate, Septemfid, Sever, Share, Skive, Slit, Sliver, Spall, Spalt, Speld, Spring, Tattle, Tmesis, Told, To-rend, To-tear, Wedge

▷ **Split** *may indicate* a word to become two; one word inside another; or a connection with Yugoslavia

Splodge, Splotch Blot, Drop, Splash

Splurge Binge, Indulge, Lavish, Spend, Splash, Spree

Splutter Chug, Expectorate, Fizz, Gutter, Spray, Stammer

▷ **Spoil(ed), Spoilt** *may indicate* an anagram

Spoil(s), Spoiler, Spoilt Addle, Agrise, Agrize, Agryze, Air dam, Blight, Blunk, Booty, Botch, Bribe, Coddle, Corrupt, Crool, → **DAMAGE**, Dampen, Deface, Defect, Deform, Disfigure, Dish, Foul, Gum, Hames, Harm, Impair(ed), Impoverish, Indulge, Loot, Maderise, Maltreat, Mar, Mardy, Mollycoddle, Muck, Mutilate, Mux, Pamper, Pet, Pickings, Pie, Plunder, Prejudicate, Prize, Queer, Rait, Rate, Ravage, Ret, Rot, Ruin, Scupper, Spuly(i)e, Swag, Taint, Tarnish, Vitiate, Wanton, Winnings

Spoilsport Damper, Killjoy, Marsport, Meddler, Party pooper, Wet blanket, Wowser

Spoke(s) Concentric, Radius, Ray, Rung, Said, Sed, Strut

Spoken Dixi

▷ **Spoken** *may indicate* the sound of a word or letter

Spokesman Foreman, Mouthpiece, Orator, Prophet, Representative

Spoliation, Spoliative Devastation, Pillage, Plunder, Predatory, Reif

Sponge(r), Spongy Alcoholic, Ambatch, Argentine, Battenburg, Bum, Cadge, → **CAKE**, Cleanse, Diact, Diploe, Fozy, Free-loader, Glass-rope, Hexact, Hyalonema, Leech, Lig, Lithistid(a), Loofa(h), Madeira, Madeleine, Mermaid's glove, Mooch, Mop, Mouch, Mump, Parasite, Parazoa, Pentact, Poachy, Porifera(n), Quandong, Rhabdus, Sarcenchyme, Scambler, Schnorrer, Scrounge, Shark, Shool, Shule, Siphonophora, Smell-feast, Sooner, Sop, Sucker, Swab, Sweetbriar, Sycophant, Tectratine, Tetract, Tetraxon, Tiramisu, Tylote, Vegetable, Velamen, Venus's flowerbasket, Wangle, Wipe, Zimocca, Zoophyte

Spongewood Sola

Sponsor(ship) Aegis, Angel, Auspice, Backer, Egis, Finance, Godfather, Godparent, Gossip, Guarantor, Lyceum, Patron, Surety

Spontaneous Aleatoric, Autonomic, Exergonic, Gratuitous, Immediate, Impromptu, Improvised, Impulsive, Instant, Intuitive, Natural, Ultroneus, Unasked, Unpremeditated, Unprompted, Unrehearsed

Spoof Chouse, Cozenage, Deception, Delusion, Fallacy, → **HOAX**, Imposture, Ramp, Swindle, Trick

Spook(s), Spooky CIA, Eerie, Fantom, Frightening, Ghost, Phantom, Shade

Spool Bobbin, Capstan, Pirn, Reel, Spit, Trundle

Spoon(ful), Spoon-shaped Apostle, Canoodle, Cochlear, Deflagrating, Dollop, Dose, Eucharistic, Gibby, Greasy, Horn, Labis, Ladle, Mote, Neck, Rat-tail, Runcible, Salt, Scoop, Scud, Server, Snuff, Spatula, Sucket, Trolling, Trout, Woo, Wooden

Spoonerism Marrowsky, Metathesis

Spoor Trace, Track, Trail

Sporadic Fitful, Isolated, Occasional, Patchy

Spore(s), Spore case Asexual, Conidium, Ex(t)ine, Fungus, Glomerule, Lenticel, Palynology, Resting, Seed, Sexual, Sorus, Spreathed, Telium, Uredinium

Sporran Pock

Sport(s), Sporting, Sportive Amusement, Blood, Breakaway, Brick, By-form, Contact, Daff, Dalliance, Dally, Deviant, Extreme, Field, Freak, Frisky, Frolic, Fun, → **GAME**, Gent, In, Joke, Laik, Lake, Lark, Merimake, Merry, Morph, Mutagen, Pal, Recreate, Rogue, Rules, Spectator, Tournament, Tourney, Toy, Wear, Winter

SPORTS

2 letters:
RU

3 letters:
Gig

4 letters:
Polo
Sumo

5 letters:
Basho
Fives
Kendo

6 letters:
Aikido
Diving
Hockey
Karate
Shinny
Shinty
Squash
Tennis

7 letters:
Angling
Archery
Camogie
Curling
Fencing
Hurling
Netball
Parkour
Rafting
Skating
Snooker
Surfing
Tailing

8 letters:
Aquatics
Ballgame
Bonspiel
Eventing
Korfball
Lacrosse
Langlauf
Natation
Octopush

Softball
Speedway
Swoffing

9 letters:
Abseiling
Autocross
Autopoint
Canyoning
Potholing
Skijoring
Ski-kiting
Ski-towing
Skydiving
Speedball
Twitching
Wargaming
Water polo
Wrestling

10 letters:
Cyclo-cross
Drag-racing
Heli-skiing
Kickboxing

Monoskiing
Pancratium
Parakiting
Paraskiing
Rallycross
Skijorking
Sky-jumping
Sky-surfing
Street luge

11 letters:
Coasteering
Fell walking
Hang-gliding
Kite-surfing
Paragliding
Paralympics
Parapenting
Parasailing
Race-walking
Snorkelling
Table tennis
Truck racing
Water-skiing
Windsurfing

12 letters:
Bar billiards
Boardsailing
Cross country
Heli-boarding
Kite-boarding
Orienteering
Parascending

River bugging
Sailboarding
Snowboarding
Speed-skating
Steeplechase
Tag-wrestling
Trampolining
Trapshooting

Wakeboarding

13 letters:
Bungee-jumping
Prizefighting
Weightlifting

17 letters:
Whitewater rafting

18 letters:
White-water
 canoeing

▷ **Sport(s)** *may indicate* an anagram

Sportsground Rec

Sportsman, Sportsmen All-rounder, Athlete, Blue, Corinthian, Half-blue, Hunter, Nimrod, Pentathlete, Pitcher, Shamateur, Shikaree, Shikari, Showjumper

Sportswear Wet suit

Spot(s), Spotted, Spotting, Spotty Ace, Acne, Area, Areola, Areole, Baily's beads, Bausond, Bead, Beauty, Befoul, Bespatter, Blackhead, Blain, Blemish, Blind, Blip, Blister, Blob, Blot, Blotch(ed), Blur, Brind(l)ed, Café-au-lait, Carbuncle, Caruncle, Cash, Check, Cloud, Colon, Comedo, Corner, Curn, Cyst, Dance, Dapple(-bay), Defect, Dick, Dilemma, Discern, Discover, Dot, Drop, Eruption, Espy, Eye, Facula, Flat, Flaw, Fleck, Floater, Fogdog, Foxed, Freak, Freckle, Furuncle, G, Gay, Glimpse, Gout, Gräfenberg, Gricer, Guttate, High, Hot, Identify, Jam, Leaf, Lentago, Light, Little, Liver, Location, Loran, Mackle, Macle, Macul(at)e, Mail, Meal, Measly, Microdot, Milium, Moil, Mole, Morbilli, Mote, Motty, Muscae volitantes, Naevoid, Naevus, Note, Notice, Ocellar, Ocellus, Paca, Papule, Paraselene, Pardal, Parhelion, Patch, Peep(e), Penalty, Perceive, Performance, Petechia, Pied, Pimple, Pin, Pip, Place, Plague, Plight, Plook, Plot, Plouk, Pock, Point, Predicament, Punctuate, Pupil, Pustule, Quat, Radar, Rash, Recognise, Red, Rose-drop, Scene, Scotoma, Situation, Skewbald, Smut, Soft, Speck(le), Speculum, Splodge, Spoil, Spy, Stigma, Sully, Sun, Sweet, Taint, Tar, Tight, Touch, Trace, Trouble, Weak, Whelk, Whitehead, Witness, X, Yellow, Zit

Spotless Clean, Immaculate, Pristine, Virginal

Spotlight Ace, Baby, Bon-bon, Brute, Maxi-brute

Spot on To a t

Spouse Companion, Consort, Dutch, Feare, Feer, F(i)ere, Hubby, Husband, Mate, Oppo, Partner, Pheer, Pirrauru, Significant other, Wife, Xant(h)ippe

Spout(er) Adjutage, Erupt, Gargoyle, Geyser, Grampus, Gush, Impawn, Jet, Mouth, Nozzle, Orate, Pawn, Pourer, Raile, Rote, Spurt, Stream, Stroup, Talk, Tap, Vent

Sprain(ed) Crick, Rax, Reckan, Rick, Stave, Strain, Wrench, Wrick

Sprat Brit, Fish, Garvie, Garvock

Sprawl Grabble, Loll, Scramble, Sprangle, Spread, Stretch, Urban

Spray Aerosol, Aigrette, Antiperspirant, Atomiser, Bespatter, Blanket, Buttonhole, Corsage, Cyme, Egret, Fly, Hair, Mace®, Nasal, Nebuliser, Pesticide, Posy, Rose, Rosula, Shower, Sparge, Spindrift, Splash, Spoondrift, Sprent, Sprig, Sprinkle, Spritz, Strinkle, Syringe, Twig, Wet

▷ **Spray** *may indicate* an anagram

▷ **Spread** *may indicate* an anagram

Spread(ing), Spreader Air, Apply, Banquet, Bestrew, Beurre, Bid offer, Blow-out, Branch, Bush, Butter, Carpet, Centre, Circumfuse, Contagious, Couch, Coverlet, Coverlid, Deploy, Diffract, Diffuse, Dilate, Disperse, Dissemination, Distribute, Divulge, Double, Double-page, Drape, Dripping, Elongate, Emanate, Expand, Extend, Fan, Feast, Flare, Guac(h)amole, Honeycomb, Jam, Lay, Mantle, Marge,

Marmite®, Metastasis, Middle-age(d), Multiply, Mushroom, Nutter, Oleo, Open, Overgrow, Paste, Pâté, Patent, Patté, Patulous, Perfuse, Pervade, Picnic, Pour, Proliferate, Propagate, Radiate, Radiant, Rampant, Ran, Run, Scale, Scatter, Sea-floor, Set, Sheet, Slather, Smear, Smörgåsbord, Sow, Span, Speld, Spelder, Spillover, Splay, Sprawl, Spray, Straddle, Straw, Stretch, Strew, Strow, Suffuse, Systemic, Tath, Teer, Unfold, Unfurl, Unguent, Vegemite®, Widen, Wildfire

Spree Bat, Batter, Beano, Bender, Binge, Bum, Bust, Buster, Carousal, Frolic, Jag, Jamboree, Juncate, Junket, Lark, Loose, Randan, Rantan, Razzle(-dazzle), Revel, Rouse, Splore, Tear, Ups(e)y

Sprig Brad, Branch, Cion, Cyme, Nail, Scion, Sien, Sient, Spray, Syen, Twig, Youth

Sprightly, Sprightliness Agile, Airy, Chipper, Esprit, Jaunty, Mercurial

Spring(s), Springtime, Springy Aganippe, Air, Alice, Arise, Black smoker, Bolt, Bounce, Bound, Box, Bunt, Cabriole, Caper, Capriole, Castalian, Cavort, Cee, Coil, Dance, Elastic, Eye, Fount(ain), Gambado, Germinate, Geyser, Grass, Hair, Helix, Hippocrene, Hop, Hot, Jeté, Jump, Leaf, Leap, Lent, Lep, Litt, Low-water, May, Mineral, Originate, Persephone, Pierian, Pounce, Prance, Primavera, Prime, Resilient, Ribbon, Rise, Saddle, Season, Skip, Snap, Source, Spa, Spang, Spaw, Stem, Stot, Submarine, Sulphur, Summer, Suspension, Teal, Thermae, Thermal, Trampoline, Valve, Vault, Vaute, Vawte, Vernal, Voar, Ware, Watch, Waterhole, Weeping, Well(-head), Whip, Winterbourne

▷ **Spring(y)** *may indicate* an anagram

Springbok Amabokoboko

Springless Telega

Springtail Apterygota

Sprinkle(r), Sprinkling Asperge, Aspergill(um), Bedash, Bedrop, Bescatter, Caster, Disponge, Dispunge, Dredge, Dust, Hyssop, Lard, Pouncet, Powder, Rose, Scatter, Scouthering, Shower, Sow, Spa(i)rge, Spatter, Splash, Spray, Spritz, Strinkle

Sprint(er) Burst, Dash, Race, Rash, Run, Rush, Wells

Sprite Apsaras, Banshee, Croquemitaine, Dobbie, Dobby, Echo, Elf, Fairy, Fiend, Genie, Gnome, Goblin, Gremlin, Hobgoblin, Icon, Kelpie, Kelpy, Nickel, Ondine, Puck, Spirit, Troll, Trow, Umbriel, Undine

Sprout Braird, Breer, Brussels, Bud, Burgeon, Chit, Crop, Eye, Germ(inate), Grow, Pullulate, Shoot, Spire, Tendron, Vegetate

Spruce Balsam, Dapper, Engelmann, Hemlock, Natty, Neat, Norway, Picea, Pitch-tree, Prink, Shipshape, Sitka, Smart, Spiff, Tidy, Tree, Trim, Tsuga, White

Spry Active, Agile, Constance, Dapper, Nimble, Volable

Spud Murphy, Potato, Spade, Tater, Tatie

Spume Eject, Foam, Froth, Lather, Spet, Spit

Spunk Courage, Grit, Pluck, Tinder

Spur(s) Accourage, Activate, Aphrodisiac, Calcar(ate), Encourage, Fame, Fire, Galvanise, Gee, Gilded, Goad, Groyne, Heel, Incite, Limb, Lye, Needle, Offset, Prick, Rippon, Rowel, Shoot, Spica, Stimulus, Strut, Stud, Tar, Urge

Spurge (tree) Candelilla, Croton, Euphorbia, Kamala, Manihot, Poinsettia, Ricinus

Spurious Adulterine, Apocryphal, Bogus, Counterfeit, Dog, False, Phoney, Pseudo, Sciolism, Untrue

▷ **Spurious** *may indicate* an anagram

Spurn Despise, Disdain, Ignore, Jilt, Rebuff, Reject, → **SCORN**, Sdayn, Shun

Spurt Burst, Forge, Geyser, Jet, Outburst, Pump, Spout, Start

Sputter Fizzle, Spit, Splutter, Stutter

Spy(ing), Spies Agent, Beagle, Caleb, CIA, Cicero, Curtain-twitcher, Descry, Dicker, Double agent, Eavesdrop, Emissary, Espionage, Fink, Fuchs, Informer, Keeker,

Mata Hari, MI, Mole, Mouchard, Nark, Ninja, Nose, Operative, Pickeer, Pimp, Plant, Pry, Recce, Scout, See, Setter, Shadow, Sinon, Sleeper, Snoop, Spetsnaz, Spook, Tout, Wait

Spyhole Eyelet, Judas-hole, Oillet, Peephole

Squab Chubby, Cushion, Obese

Squabble Argue, Bicker, Brabble, Quarrel, Rhubarb, Row, Scrap

Squad(ron) Awkward, Band, Blue, Company, Crew, Death, Drugs, Escadrille, Fifteen, Firing, Flying, Force, Fraud, Hit, Nahal, Platoon, Porn, Red, Snatch, Vice, White, Wing

Squalid, Squalor Abject, Colluvies, Dickensian, Dinge, Dingy, Filth, Frowsy, Grungy, Mean, Poverty, Scuzzy, Seedy, Skid Row, Sleazy, Slum(my), Slurb, Sordid

Squall Blast, Blow, Chubasco, Commotion, Cry, Drow, Flaw, Flurry, Gust, Line, Sumatra, Wail, White, Yell, Yowl

Squander Blow, Blue, Dissipate, Fritter, Frivol, Lash, Mucker, Slather, Splash, Splurge, Ware, → **WASTE**

Square(d), Squares Agree, Anta, Arrière, Ashlar, Ashler, Bang, Barrack, Belgrave, Berkeley, Bevel, Block, Bribe, Chequer, Compone, Compony, Corny, Deal, Dinkum, Even(s), Fair, Fog(e)y, Forty-nine, Fossil, Four, Gobony, Grey, Grosvenor, Latin, Least, Leicester, Level, Magic, Market, Meal, Mitre, Nasik, Neandert(h)aler, Nine, Norma, Old-fashioned, Out, Palm, Passé, Pay, Perfect, Place, Platz, Plaza, Quad(rangle), Quadrate, Quarry, Quits, Red, Rood, S, Set(t), Sloane, Solid, Squier, Squire, Straight, T, Tee, Times, Traditionalist, Trafalgar, Try, Unhip

Squash(y) Adpress, Butternut, Conglomerate, Crush, Gourd, Kia-ora®, Knead, Marrow, Mash, Obcompress, Oblate, Pattypan, Press, Pulp, Shoehorn, Silence, Slay, Slew, Slue, Soft, Squeeze, Squidge, Squidgy, Suppress, Torpedo

Squat(ter), Squatting Bywoner, Caganer, Crouch, Croup(e), Cubby, Dumpy, Fubby, Fubsy, Hunker, Occupy, Pudsey, Pyknic, Rook, Ruck, Sit, Spud, Stubby, Stumpy, Swatter, Usucaption

Squaw Kloo(t)chman

Squawk Cackle, Complain, Cry, Scrauch, Scraugh

Squeak(er) Cheep, Creak, Narrow, Near, Peep, Pip, Scroop, Shoat, Squeal

Squeal(er) Blow, Creak, Eek, Howl, Inform, Pig, Screech, Sing, Sneak, Tell, Wee, Yelp

Squeamish(ness) Delicate, Disgust, Missish, Nervous, Prudish, Queasy, Reluctant

Squeeze(r) Bleed, Chirt, Coll, Compress, Concertina, Constrict, Cram, Cramp, Credit, Crowd, Crush, Dispunge, Exact, Express, Extort, Extrude, Hug, Jam, Mangle, Milk, Preace, Press, Sandwich, Sap, Scrooge, Scrouge, Scrowdge, Scruze, Shoehorn, Squash, Squish, Sweat, Thrutch, Thumbscrew, Vice, Wring

Squelch Gurgle, Squash, Squish, Subdue

Squib Banger, Damp, Firework, Lampoon

Squid Calamari, Calamary, Cephalopod, Cuttlefish, Ink-fish, Loligo, Mortar, Nautilus, Octopus, Sleeve fish

Squiffy Drunk, Tiddley

▷ **Squiggle** *may indicate* an anagram

Squill Sea, Spring

Squint(ing) Boss-eyed, Cast, Cock-eye, Cross-eye, Glance, Gledge, Glee, Gley, Hagioscope, Heterophoria, Louche, Opening, Proptosis, Skellie, Skelly, Sken, Squin(n)y, Strabism, Swivel-eye, Vergence, Wall-eye

Squire Armiger(o), Beau, Donzel, Escort, Hardcastle, Headlong, Land-owner, Scutiger, Swain, Western, White

Squirm(ing) Fidget, Reptation, Twist, Worm, Wriggle, Writhe

Squirrel, Squirrel's nest Aye-aye, Boomer, Bun, Cage, Chickaree, Chipmuck, Chipmunk, Dray, Drey, Flickertail, Flying (-fox), Gopher, Grey, Ground, Hackee, Hoard(er), Meerkat, Petaurist, Phalanger, Red, Sciuroid, Sewellel, Skug, S(o)uslik, Spermophile, Taguan, Vair, Zizel

Squirt(er) Chirt, Cockalorum, Douche, Jet, Scoosh, Scoot, Skoosh, Spirt, Spout, Spritz, Urochorda, Wet, Whiffet, Whippersnapper

Sri Lanka(n) Ceylon, Cingalese, CL, Serendip, Sinhalese, Tamil, Vedda

St Saint, Street

Stab Bayonet, Chib, Crease, Creese, Dag, Effort, Go, Gore, Guess, Jab, Knife, Kreese, Kris, Lancinate, Pang, Pierce, Pink, Poniard, Prick, Prong, Stick, Stiletto, Turk, Wound

Stabilise(r), Stability Aileron, Balance, Balloonet, Emulsifier, Even, Fin, Fixure, Gyroscope, Maintain, Pax Romana, Peg, Permanence, Plateau, Poise, Steady, Tail panel

Stable(s) Augean, Balanced, Barn, Byre, Certain, Constant, Durable, Equerry, Equilibrium, Firm, Livery, Loose box, Manger, Mews, Poise, Secure, Solid, Sound, Stall, Static(al), Steadfast, Steady, Stud, Sure, Together

Stableman Groom, Lad, Ostler

Stachys Betony

Stack(s) Accumulate, À gogo, Chimney, Clamp, Cock, End, Funnel, Heap, Lum, → **PILE**, Rick, Shock, Sight, Smoke, Staddle

Stadium Arena, Astrodome, Ballpark, Bowl, Circus, Circus Maximus, Coliseum, Hippodrome, Speedway, Velodrome

Staff Aesculapius, Alpenstock, Ash-plant, Bato(o)n, Bourdon, Burden, Caduceus, Cane, Crew, Crook, Crosier, Cross(e), Crozier, Crutch, Cudgel, Entourage, Equerry, État-major, Faculty, Ferula, Ferule, Flagpole, General, Ground, Jacob's, Jeddart, Linstock, Lituus, Mace, Man, Omlah, Pastoral, Personnel, Pike, Pole, Ragged, Rod, Rung, Runic, Sceptre, Seniority, Skeleton, Stave, Stick, Taiaha, Tapsmen, Tau, Thyrsus, Token, Truncheon, Verge, Wand, Workers, Workforce, Wring

Stag Actaeon, Brocket, Buck, Deer, For men, Hummel, Imperial, Knobber, Line, Male, Party, Royal, Rutter, Ten-pointer, Wapiti

Stage Act, Anaphase, Apron, Arena, Ashrama, Bandstand, Bardo, Bema, Boards, Catasta, Centre, Chrysalis, Committee, Diligence, Dog-leg, Estrade, Fare, Fargo, Fit-up, Grade, Hop, Imago, Juncture, Key, Landing, Leg, Level, Metaphase, Milestone, Moment, Mount, Oidium, Perform, Phase, Phasis, Pier, Pin, Platform, Podium, Point, Postscenium, Prophase, Proscenium, PS, Puberty, Report, Resting, Rostrum, Scene, Sensorimeter, Sound, Stadium, Step, Stor(e)y, Subimago, Theatre, Thrust, Transition, Wells Fargo, Trek, Yuga, Zoea

Stage-coach Diligence, Thoroughbrace

Stagecraft Pinafore

Stagehand Flyman, Grip

Stagger(ed) Alternate, Amaze, Astichous, Astonish, Awhape, Daidle, Falter, Floor, Lurch, Recoil, Reel, Rock, Shock, Stoiter, Stot(ter), Stumble, Sway, Teeter, Thunderstricken, Thunderstruck, Titubate, Tolter, Totter, Wamble, Wintle

▷ **Staggered** *may indicate* an anagram

Stagirite, Stagyrite Aristotle

Stagnant, Stagnation Cholestasis, Foul, Inert, Moribund, Scummy, Stasis, Static

Staid Decorous, Demure, Formal, Grave, Matronly, Prim, Prudish, Sad, Seemly, Sober, Stick-in-the-mud

Stain(er) Aniline, Bedye, Besmirch, Blemish, Blob, Blot, Blotch, Discolour, Dishonour, Dye, Embrue, Ensanguine, Eosin, Fox, Gram's, Grime, Imbrue, Inkspot,

Iodophile, Keel, Maculate, Mail, Meal, Mote, Portwine, Slur, Smirch, Smit, Soil, Splodge, Splotch, Stigma, Sully, Taint, Tarnish, Tinge, Tint, Vital, Woad

Stair(case), Stairs Apples, Apples and pears, Caracol(e), Cochlea, Companionway, Escalator, Flight, Moving, Perron, Rung, Scale (and platt), Spiral, Step, Tread, Turnpike, Vice, Wapping, Winding

Stake(s) Ante, Bet, Claim, Deposit, Extracade, Gage, Go, Holding, Impale, Impone, Interest, Lay, Loggat, Mark, Mise, Nursery, Paal, Pale, Paliform, Paling, Palisade, Peel, Peg, Pele, Picket, Pile, Play, Post, Pot, Punt, Put, Rest, Revie, Risk, Septleva, Set, Spike, Spile, Stang, Stob, Straddle, Sweep, Tether, Vie, Wager, Welter

Stalactite Dripstone, Dropstone, Helictite, Lansfordite, Soda straw

Stale Aged, Banal, Flat, Fozy, Frowsty, Fusty, Hackneyed, Handle, Hoary, Mouldy, Musty, Old, Pretext, Rancid, Urine, Worn

▷ **Stale** *may indicate* an obsolete word

Stalemate Deadlock, Dilemma, Draw, Hindrance, Impasse, Mexican standoff, Saw-off, Standoff, Tie, Zugswang

Stalk(s), Stalker Anthophore, Bennet, Bun, Cane, Caulicle, Follow, Funicle, Garb(e), Gynophore, Ha(u)lm, Keck(s), Kecksey, Keksye, Kex, Ommatophore, Pedicel, Pedicle, Peduncle, Petiole, Petiolule, Phyllode, Pursue, Reed, Rush, Scape, Seta, Shaw, Spear, Spire, Stem, Sterigma, Still-hunter, Stipe(s), Stride, Strig, Strut, Stubble, Stump, Trail, Yolk

Stalking-horse Stale

Stall(s) Arrest, Bay, Booth, Box, Bulk, Crib, → **DELAY**, Floor, Flypitch, Hedge, Horse-box, Kiosk, Loose-box, Orchestra, Pen, Pew, Prebendal, Seat, Shamble, Sideshow, Stand, Starting, Stasidion, Sty, Sutlery, Temporise, Trap, Traverse, Travis, Trevis(s), Whip, Whipstall

Stallion Cooser, Cuisser, Cusser, Entire, → **HORSE**, Stag, Staig, Stonehorse, Stud

Stalwart Anchor-man, Buirdly, Firm, Manful, Robust, Sturdy, Trusty, Valiant

Stamen(ed) Androecium, Octandria, Polyandria, Synandrium

Stamina Endurance, Fibre, Fortitude, Guts, Last, Stamen, Stay, Steel

Stammer(ing) Balbutient, Er, Hesitate, Hum, Psellism, Sputter, Stumble, → **STUTTER**, Waffle

Stamp(s), Stamped Albino, Appel, Cast, Character, Coin, Date(r), Die, Dry print, Enface, Fiscal, Frank, Gutter-pair, Health, Imperforate, Impress, Imprint, Incuse, Kind, Label, Matchmark, Mint, Pane, Penny black, Perfin, Philately, Pintadera, Postage, Press(ion), Rubber, Seal, Seebeck, Se-tenant, Signet, Spif, Strike, Swage, Tête-bêche, Touch, Touchmark, Trading, Trample, Tread, Tromp, Type

Stamp-collecting Philately, Timbrology, Timbrophily

Stampede Debacle, Flight, Panic, Rampage, → **RUSH**, Sauve qui peut

Stance Attitude, Ecarté, Pose, Position, Posture, Quinte

Stand(ing), Stand for, Stand up Apron, Arraign, Attitude, Base, Bay, Be, Bear, Bide, Bier, Binnacle, Bipod, Bristle, Brook, Canterbury, Caste, Confrontation, Cradle, Crease, Dais, Degree, Desk, Dock, Dree, Dumb-waiter, Easel, Epergne, Étagère, Face, Foothold, Freeze, Gantry, Gueridon, Hard, Hob, Importance, Insulator, Klinostat, Last, Lazy Susan, Lectern, Leg, Lime, Music, Nef, Odour, One-night, Ovation, Pedestal, Place, Plant, Podium, Pose, Position, Pou sto, Prestige, Promenade, Protest, Qua, Rack, Rank, Regent, Remain, Represent, Repute, Rise, Rouse, Stall, Statant, Station, → **STATUS**, Stay, Stillage, Stock, Stool, Straddle, Straphang, Stroddle, Strut, Table, Tantalus, Taxi, Teapoy, Terrace, Toe, → **TREAT**, Tree, Tripod, Trivet, Umbrella, Upright, Whatnot, Witness

Standard(s) Banner, Base, Baseline, Basic, Benchmark, Bog, Bogey, British, Canon, CAT, Classic(al), Cocker, Colour(s), Copybook, Criterion, Double, Eagle, English,

Ethics, Etiquette, Examplar, Example, Exemplar, Fiducial, Flag, Ga(u)ge, Gold, Gonfalon, Grade, Guidon, Ideal, Jolly Roger, Labarum, Level, Living, Model, Netiquette, Norm(a), Normal, Numeraire, Old Glory, Oriflamme, Par, Parker Morris, Pennon, Principle, Rate, Regular, Rod, Rose, Routine, Royal, → **RULE**, Silver, Spec(ification), Staple, Sterling, Stock, Time, Touchstone, Tricolour, Troy, Two-power, Usual, Valuta, Vexillum, Yardstick

Standard-bearer Alferez, Cornet, Ensign, Vexillary

Stand-by Adminicle, Reserve, Substitute, Support, Understudy

Stand-in Double, Locum, Stunt man, Sub(stitute), Surrogate, Temp, Understudy

Standish Miles

Stand-off(ish) Aloof, Remote, Reserved, Stalemate, Upstage

Standpoint Angle, Slant, View

Standstill Deadset, Halt, Jam

Stanley Baldwin, Knife, Rupert

Stannic Tin

St Anthony's fire Ergotism, Erysipelas

Stanza Ballad, Elegiac, Envoi, Envoy, Heroic, Matoke, Ottava, Ottava rima, Poem, Sixaine, Spenserian, Staff, Stave, Tetrastich, Verse

Staple Basic, Bread, Chief, Maize, Oats, Pin, Rice, Stock, Wool

Star(s) Aster(isk), Binary, Body, Celebrity, Companion, Constant, Constellation, Cushion, Cynosure, Dark, Death, Double, Esther, Exploding, Falling, Fate, Feather, Feature, Film, Fixed, Flare, Galaxy, Giant, Headline, Hero, Hester, Hexagram, Idol, Late type, Lead, Lion, Main sequence, Mogen David, Movie, Mullet, Multiple, Pentacle, Pentagram, Personality, Phad, Pip, Pointer, Principal, Pulsating, Sabaism, Seven, Shell, Shine, Shooting, Sidereal, Solomon's seal, Spangle, Starn(ie), Stellar, Stern, Swart, Top banana, Top-liner, Ultraviolet, Valentine, Variable, Vedette

STARS

3 letters:	Algol	Spica	Hyades
Dog	Alpha	Theta	Lizard
Sol	Ceres	Venus	Megrez
	Comet	Virgo	Merope
4 letters:	Delta	Wagon	Meteor
Argo	Deneb	Whale	Octans
Beta	Draco		Phecda
Grus	Dubhe	*6 letters:*	Plough
Lode	Dwarf	Alioth	Pollux
Lyra	Gamma	Alkaid	Psyche
Mira	Hyads	Altair	Pulsar
Nova	Indus	Aquila	Puppis
Pavo	Lupus	Auriga	Quasar
Pole	Mensa	Boötes	Saturn
Ursa	Merak	Carbon	Sirius
Vega	Mizar	Carina	Sothis
Vela	Norma	Castor	Uranus
Zeta	North	Cygnus	Vesper
	Polar	Dorado	Volans
5 letters:	Radio	Étoile	
Acrux	Rigel	Fornax	*7 letters:*
Agena	Rigil	Galaxy	Antares

Calaeno
Canopus
Capella
Cepheus
Chamber
Columba
Dolphin
Epsilon
Éstoile
Evening
Gemingo
Lucifer
Morning
Neutron
Perseus
Phoenix
Plerion
Polaris
Procyon
Proxima
Regulus
Sabaism
Serpens
Sterope

Triones
Wagoner

8 letters:
Achernar
Arcturus
Barnard's
Circinus
Denebola
Equuleus
Hesperus
Magnetar
Mira Ceti
Pegasean
Phosphor
Pleiades
Pointers
Praesepe
Red dwarf
Red giant
Scorpius
Synastry
Waggoner

9 letters:
Aldebaran
Andromeda
Bellatrix
Big Dipper
Black hole
Centaurus
Collapsar
Delphinus
Fire-drake
Fomalhaut
Meteorite
Ophiuchus
Pentagram
Rigil-Kent
Supernova
Wolf-Rayet

10 letters:
Betacrucis
Betelgeuse
Betelgeuze
Brown dwarf
Cassiopeia

Orion's Belt
Phosphorus
Supergiant
White dwarf

11 letters:
Circumpolar
The Pointers

12 letters:
Little Dipper
Septentrione

13 letters:
Grande vedette
Southern Cross

14 letters:
Camelopardalis

15 letters:
Proxima Centauri

Starboard Right

Starch(y), Starch producer Amyloid, Amylum, Animal, Arrowroot, Cassava, Ceremony, Congee, Conjee, Coontie, Coonty, Cycad, Farina, Fecula, Formal, Glycogen, Lichenin, Manioc, Maranta, Pentosan, Sago, Stamina, Statolith, Stiff, Tapioca, Tous-les-mois

Stare Eyeball, Fisheye, Gape, Gapeseed, Gawp, Gaze, Geek, Glare, Goggle, Gorp, Look, Ogle, Outface, Peer, Rubberneck, Scowl

Starfish Asterid, Asteroid(ea), Bipinnaria, Brittlestar, Ophiurid, Radiata

Star-gaze(r), Star-gazing Astrodome, Astronomy, Copernicus

Stark Apparent, Austere, Bald, Bare, Gaunt, Harsh, Naked, Nude, Sheer, Stiff, Utterly

Starling Bird, Gippy, Hill mynah, Murmuration, Pastor, Rosy pastor, Stare

Star of Bethlehem Chincherinchee, Chinkerinchee

▷ **Start** _may indicate_ an anagram or first letters

Start(ed), Starter Ab ovo, Abrade, Abraid, Abray, Activate, Actuate, Begin, Bhajee, Boggle, Boot-up, Bot, Broach, Bug, Bump, Chance, Commence, Course, Crank, Create, Crudités, Dart, Ean, Embryo, Face-off, False, Fire, Flinch, Float, Flush, Flying, Found, Gambit, Gan, Genesis, Getaway, Gun, Handicap, Head, Hot-wire, Impetus, Imprimis, Incept(ion), Initiate, Instigate, Institute, Intro, Jar, Jerk, Judder, Jump, Jump lead, Jump-off, Kick-off, L, Lag, Launch, Lead, Novice, Off, Offset, Onset, Ope(n), Ord, Origin, Outset, Potage, Preliminary, Prelude, Proband, Push, Put-up, Reboot, Resume, Roll, Roul, Rouse, Scare, Set off, Shy, Slip, Snail, Soup, Spring, Springboard, Spud, String, Tee-off, Wince

Startle(d), Startling Agape, Alarm, Bewilder, Disturb, Eye-opener, Flush, Frighten, Magical, Rock, Scare

Starvation, Starve(d), Starving Anorexia, Anoxic, Bant, Clem, Cold, Deprive, Diet, Famish, Inanition, Macerate, Perish, Pine, Undernourished

▷ **Starving** *may indicate* an 'o' in the middle of a word
Stash Secrete
State(s), Stateside Affirm, Alle(d)ge, Aread, Arrede, Assert, Assever, Attest, Aver,
Avow, Buffer, Case, Circar, Cite, Client, Commonwealth, Condition, Confederate,
Construct, Country, Critical, Cutch, Declare, Dependency, Dirigisme, Emirate,
Empire, État, Federal, Fettle, Flap, Free, Habitus, Humour, Kingdom, Land,
Lesh, Mess, Metastable, Mode, Name, Nanny, Nation, Native, Palatinate, Papal,
Para, Plateau, Plight, Police, Posit, Predicament, Predicate, Premise, Pronounce,
Protectorate, Puppet, Quantum, Realm, Republic, Rogue, Samadhi, Satellite, Say,
Sircar, Sirkar, Slave, Sorry, Standing, Steady, Succession, Threeness, Uncle Sam,
Union, United, Welfare

STATES

2 letters:	Osun	**6 letters:**	Sokoto
Ga	Shan	Alaska	Sonora
Ia	Swat	Balkan	Sparta
Md	Togo	Baltic	Styria
Me	Utah	Baroda	Tassie
Mi		Bauchi	Tonkin
NC	**5 letters:**	Belize	
NY	Amapa	Bremen	**7 letters:**
Pa	Assam	Brunei	Alabama
RI	Bahar	Cochin	Alagoas
UK	Benin	Colima	Anambra
US	Benue	Dakota	Andorra
Ut	Ceará	Hawaii	Arizona
Va	Dixie	Jigawa	Barbary
	Dubai	Johore	Bavaria
3 letters:	Gabon	Kaduna	Belerus
Ark	Ghana	Kansas	Buffalo
Del	Hesse	Kerala	Chiapos
Fla	Idaho	Khelat	Croatia
Goa	Kalat	Kuwait	Durango
Oyo	Kedah	Madras	Florida
Wis	Kutch	Malawi	Georgia
	Kwara	Mysore	Grenada
4 letters:	Lippe	Nevada	Gujarat
Abia	Maine	Oaxaca	Gujerat
Acre	Malay	Oregon	Haryana
Chad	Mewar	Orissa	Hidalgo
Conn	Nepal	Pahang	Indiana
Gulf	Oshun	Parana	Ireland
Iowa	Perak	Penang	Jalisco
Kano	Piaui	Perlis	Jamaica
Kogi	Qatar	Puebla	Jodhpur
Mass	Reich	Punjab	Kashmir
Ogun	Sabah	Rivers	Malacca
Ohio	Samoa	Saxony	Manipur
Oman	Texas	Serbia	Mizoram
Ondo	Tyrol	Sikkim	Montana

Morelos
Nayarit
New York
Nirvana
Paraiba
Pradesh
Prussia
Roraima
Sarawak
Sergipe
Sinaloa
Tabasco
Tongkin
Tonking
Tripura
Trucial
Udaipur
Vermont
Vietnam
Wyoming
Yucatan

8 letters:
Abu Dhabi
Amazonas
Arkansas
Campeche
Carolina
Coahuila
Colorado
Delaware
Ethiopia
Honduras
Illinois
Jharkand
Kelantan
Kentucky
Maranhao
Maryland

Michigan
Missouri
Nagaland
Nebraska
Oklahoma
Rondonia
Saarland
Sao Paulo
Selangor
Tanzania
Tasmania
Tiaxcala
Tongking
Veracruz
Victoria
Virginia

9 letters:
Chihuahua
Costa rica
Dixieland
Guatemala
Karnataka
Louisiana
Manchukuo
Meghalaya
Michoacán
Minnesota
Nassarawa
New Jersey
New Mexico
Nuevo Léon
Queretaro
Rajasthan
Rajputana
St Vincent
Tamil Nadu
Tennessee
Thuringia

Tocantins
Trengganu
Venezuela
Wisconsin
Zacatecas

10 letters:
California
Guanajuato
Jamahiriya
Jumhouriya
Manchoukuo
Orange Free
Pernambuco
Queensland
Tamaulipas
Tanganyika
Terengganu
Travancore
Washington

11 letters:
Brandenberg
Connecticut
Jamahouriya
Maharashtra
Mecklenburg
Minas Gerais
Mississippi
North Dakota
Quintana Roo
South Dakota
Uttaranchal
Vatican City

12 letters:
Chhattisgarh
Madhya Bharat
New Hampshire

Pennsylvania
Saxony-Anholt
Uttar Pradesh
West Virginia

13 letters:
Andhra Pradesh
Madhya Pradesh
Massachusetts
Negri Sembilan
New South Wales
San Luis Potosi
Santa Catarina
South Carolina

14 letters:
Rio Grande do Sul
South Australia
Vindhya Pradesh

15 letters:
Himachal Pradesh
Schaumburg-Lippe
St Kitts and Nevis

16 letters:
Rio Grande do
   Norte

17 letters:
Schleswig-Holstein

19 letters:
Rhineland-
   Palatinate

20 letters:
North Rhine-
   Westphalia

▷ **Stated** *may indicate* a similar sounding word
Stately, Stately home August, Dome, Grand, Imposing, Junoesque, Majestic,
   Mansion, Noble, Regal, Solemn
Statement Accompt, Account, Affidavit, Aphorism, Assertion, Asseveration,
   Attestation, Avowal, Axiom, Bill, Bulletin, Case, Communiqué, Deposition, Dictum,
   Diktat, Encyclical, Evidence, Expose, Factoid, Generalisation, Grand Remonstrance,
   Indictment, Invoice, Jurat, Manifesto, Mission, Outline, Paraphrase, Pleading,
   Press release, Profession, Pronouncement, Proposition, Protocol, Quotation,
   Release, Report, Sentence, Shema, Soundbite, Sweeping, Testimony,
   Theologoumenon, Truism, Utterance, Verb
Stateroom Bibby, Cabin

Statesman American, Attlee, Augustus, Botha, Briand, Bright, Canning, Cato, Clarendon, Diplomat, Disraeli, Draco, Elder, Flaminius, Franklin, Gandhi, Genro, Georgian, Gladstone, Gracchi, Grotius, Guy, Kissinger, Kruger, Lafayette, Lie, Mitterand, Nasser, North, Politician, Politico, Seneca, Smuts, Stein, Talleyrand, Tasmanian, Thiers, Tito, Walpole, Walsingham, Wealsman, Yankee

Static Atmospherics, Becalmed, Electricity, Inert, Maginot-minded, Motionless, Sferics, Stagnant, Stationary

Station(s) Action, Base, Berth, Birth, Camp, Caste, CCS, Coaling, Comfort, Crewe, Deploy, Depot, Docking, Dressing, Euston, Filling, Fire, Garrison, Gas, Generation, Halt, Head, Hill, Hilversum, Ice, Lay, Location, Marylebone, Nick, Outpost, Paddington, Panic, Pay, Petrol, Pitch, Place, Plant, Point, Police, Polling, Post, Power, Powerhouse, Quarter, Radio, Rank, Relay, Rowme, Seat, Service, Sheep, Sit, Space, Stance, Stand, Status, Stond, Subscriber, Tana, Tanna(h), Terminus, Testing, Thana(h), Thanna(h), Tracking, Transfer, Triangulation, Victoria, Waterloo, Waverley, Way, Weather, Whistlestop, Wind farm, Wireless, Work

Stationary At rest, Fasten, Fixed, Immobile, Parked, Sessile, Stable, Static

Stationer(y), Stationery-case Continuous, Multi-part, Papeterie

Statistic(ian), Statistics Actuary, Bose-Einstein, Descriptive, Fermi-Dirac, Figure, Gradgrind, Graph, Inferential, Isotype, Lod, Nonparametric, Number, Parametric, Percentage, Quant(um), Sampling, Student's t, Vital

Statuary, Statue(tte) Acrolith, Bronze, Bust, Colossus (of Rhodes), Discobolus, Effigy, Figure, Figurine, Galatea, Idol, Image, Kore, Kouros, Liberty, Memnon, Monolith, Monument, Oscar, Palladium, Pietà, Sculpture, Sphinx, Stonework, Stookie, Tanagra, Torso, Xoanon

Stature Growth, Height, Inches, Rank

Status Beacon, Caste, Class, Political, → **POSITION**, Prestige, Quo, Rank, Standing

Statute Act, Capitular, Chapter 11, Chapter 7, Decree, Edict, Law, Limitations, Novels, Westminster

Staunch Amadou, Leal, Resolute, Steady, Stem, Stout, Styptic, Watertight

Stave Break, Dali, Forestall, Lag, Slat, Stanza, Ward

Stay(s) Alt, Avast, Bide, Board, Bolster, Cohab(it), Corselet, Corset, Embar, Endure, Fulcrum, Gest, Guy, Hawser, Hold, Indwell, Jump, Lie, Lig, Linger, Lodge, Manet, Moratorium, Piers, Postpone, Prop, → **REMAIN**, Reprieve, Restrain, Settle, Sist, Sleepover, Sojourn, Stem, Stop off, Stop-over, Strut, Sustain, Tarry, Triatic, Villeggiatura

Stay-at-home Indoor, Tortoise

STD Aids, Herpes, Telephone, VD

Steadfast Changeless, Constance, Constant, Dilwyn, Firm, Implacable, Perseverant, Resolute, Sad, Stable

Steady Andantino, Ballast, Beau, Boyfriend, Changeless, Composer, Consistent, Constant, Even, Faithful, Firm, Girlfriend, Measured, Regular, Rock, Rock-solid, Stabilise, Stable, Unswerving

Steak Carpet-bag, Chateaubriand, Chuck, Diane, Entrecote, Fillet, Flitch, Garni, Mignon, Minute, Pope's eye, Porterhouse, Rump, Slice, Tartare, T-bone, Tenderloin, Tournedos, Vienna

Steal(ing), Steal away Abstract, Bag, Bandicoot, Bone, Boost, Cabbage, Cly, Condiddle, Convey, Creep, Crib, Duff, Edge, Elope, Embezzle, Filch, Glom, Grab, Half-inch, Heist, Hotting, Joyride, Kidnap, Knap, Knock down, Knock off, Lag, Liberate, Lift, Loot, Mag(g), Mahu, Mill, Misappropriate, Naam, Nam, Nap, Nick, Nim, Nip, Nobble, Nym, Peculate, Phone-jack, Pilfer, Pillage, Pinch, Piracy, Plagiarise, Plunder, Poach, Pocket, Prig, Proll, Purloin, Ram-raid, Remove, Rifle,

Rip-off, Rob, Rustle, Scrump, Skrimp, Smug, Snaffle, Snatch, Sneak, Snitch, Souvenir, Swipe, Take, Theft, Thieve, Tiptoe, TWOC, Whip

Stealth(y) Art, Catlike, Covert, Cunning, Furtive, Obreption, Stolenwise, Surreptitious, Tiptoe

Steam(ed), Steaming, Steamy Boil, Condensation, Cushion, Dry, Fume, Gaseous, Het, Humid, Live, Livid, Mist, Porn, Radio, Roke, Sauna, Spout, Vapor, Vapour, Wet

Steamer, Steamboat Hummum, Kettle, Showboat, Side-wheeler, SS, Str, Tramp, Turbine

Steam-hammer, Steamroller Crush, Ram

Steed Charger, Horse, Mount

Steel(y) Acierate, Adamant, Bethlehem, Blade, Blister, Bloom, Brace, Carbon, Cast, Chrome, Chromium, Cold, Concrete, Crucible, Damascus, Damask, High-carbon, High-speed, Low-carbon, Magnet, Manganese, Maraging, Martensite, Metal, Mild, Nickel, Pearlite, Ripon, Rolled, Shear, Silver, Sorbite, Spray, Stainless, Structural, Sword, Terne plate, Toledo, Tool, Tungsten, Vanadium, Wootz

Steelyard Bismar

Steep(ening) Abrupt, Arduous, Bold, Brent, Cliff-face, Costly, Embay, Expensive, High-pitched, Hilly, Krans, Krantz, Kranz, Macerate, Marinade, Marinate, Mask, Monocline, Precipice, Precipitous, Rait, Rapid, Rate, Ret, Saturate, Scarp, → **SHEER**, Soak, Sog, Sop, Souse, Stey, Stickle, Tan

Steeple(jack) Spiderman, Spire, Turret

Steer(er), Steering Ackerman, Airt, Buffalo, Bullock, Bum, Cann, Castor, Con(n), Cox, Direct, → **GUIDE**, Helm, Navaid, Navigate, Ox, Pilot, Ply, Power, Rudder, Stot, Whipstaff, Zebu

St Elmo's fire Corona discharge, Corposant

Stem Alexanders, Arrow, Axial, Biller, Bine, Bole, Caudex, Caulicle, Caulome, Check, Cladode, Cladophyll, Confront, Corm, Culm, Dam, Epicotyl, Floricane, Ha(u)lm, Kex, Pedicle, Peduncle, Pin, Pseudaxis, Rachis, R(h)achilla, Rhachis, Rhizome, Rise, Rod, Sarment, Scapus, Seta, Shaft, Shank, Sobole(s), Spring, Stalk, Staunch, Stipe, Stolon, Stopple, Straw, Sympodium, Tail

Stench F(o)etor, Funk, Miasma, Odour, Smell, Stink, Whiff

Stencil Copy, Duplicate, Mimeograph®, Pochoir

Stenographer, Stenography Amanuensis, Secretary, Shorthand, Typist

Step(s) Act, Apples and pears, Balancé, Chassé, Choctaw, Corbel, Corbie, Curtail, Dance, Degree, Démarche, Echelon, Escalate, False, Flight, Fouetté, Gain, Gait, Glissade, Goose, Grade, Grapevine, Grecian, Greece, Grees(e), Greesing, Grese, Gressing, Grice, Griece, Grise, Grize, Halfpace, Lavolt, Lock, Measure, Move, Notch, Pace, Pas, Pas de souris, Phase, Pigeon('s) wing, Quantal, Raiser, Ratlin(e), Rattlin(e), Rattling, Roundel, Roundle, Rung, Sashay, Shuffle, Slip, Stage, Stair, Stalk, Stile, Stope, Stride, Sugarfoot, Toddle, Trap, Tread, Trip, Unison, Waddle, Walk, Whole, Winder

Stephen Martyr, Stainless

Stepmother Novercal

Stepney Spare

Steppe Kyrgyz, Llano, Plain

Stereo IPod®, Personal

Stereotype(d) Hackney, Ritual

Sterile, Sterilise(r), Sterilisation, Sterility Acarpous, Aseptic, Atocia, Autoclave, Barren, Clean, Dead, Fruitless, Impotent, Infertile, Neuter, Pasteurise, Spay, Tubal ligation, Vasectomy

Sterling Excellent, Genuine, Pound, Silver, Sound

Stern Aft, Austere, Back, Counter, Dour, Flinty, Grim, Hard, Implacable, Iron, Isaac, Nates, Poop, Rear, Relentless, Rugged, Stark, Strict, Tailpiece, Transom

Steroid Anabolic, Androsterone, Calciferol, Cortisone, Dexamethasone, Ergosterol, Fusidic, Lipid, Lumisterol, Mifepristone, Nandrolone, Predniso(lo)ne, Spironolactone, Stanozolol, Testosterone, Tetrahydrogestrinone

Sterol Stigmasterol

Stertorous Snore

Stet Restore

Stevedore Docker, Dockhand, Longshoreman, Stower, Wharfinger

Stevenson RLS, Tusitala

Stew(ed), Stews Bagnio, Bath, Blanquette, Boil, Bordel(lo), Bouillabaisse, Bouilli, Bourguignon, Braise, Bredie, Brothel, Burgoo, Carbonade, Carbonnade, Casserole, Cassoulet, Cholent, Chowder, Coddle, Colcannon, Compot(e), Daube, Flap, Fuss, Goulash, Haricot, Hash, Hell, Hot(ch)pot(ch), Irish, Jug, Lather, Lobscouse, Maconochie, Matapan, Matelote, Mulligan, Navarin, Olla podrida, Osso bucco, Oyster, Paddy, Paella, Pepperpot, Pot-au-feu, Pot-pourri, Ragout, Ratatouille, Rubaboo, Salmi, Sass, Scouse, Seethe, Simmer, Slumgullion, Squiffy, Stie, Stove, Stovies, Sty, Succotash, Sweat, Swelter, Tajine, Tatahash, Tzimmes, Zamzawed, Zarzuela

Steward Butler, Cellarer, Chamberlain, Chiltern Hundreds, Dewan, Factor, Hind, Keeper, Malvolio, Manciple, Maormor, Mormaor, Official, Oswald, Panter, Purser, Reeve, Seneschal, Sewer, Shop, Smallboy, Sommelier, Waiter

▷ **Stewed** *may indicate* an anagram

St Francis Seraphic Father

Stibnite Antimony, Kohl

Stick(ing) (out), Sticks, Sticky, Stuck Adhere, Affix, Agglutinant, Aground, Ash, Ashplant, Atlatl, Attach, Bamboo, Bastinado, Bat, Baton, Bauble, Bayonet, Beanpole, Blackthorn, Bludgeon, Bond, Boondocks, Caman, Cambrel, Cammock, Cane, Celery, Cement, Chalk, Chapman, Clag, Clam(my), Clarty, Clave, Cleave, Cleft, Cling, Clog, Club, Cocktail, Cohere, Coinhere, Composing, Control, Crab, Crayon, Crosier, Cross(e), Crotch, Crozier, Crummack, Crummock, Cue, Distaff, Divining-rod, Dog, Dure, Endure, Fag(g)ot, Firewood, Fix, Flak, Founder, Fuse, Gad(e), Gaid, Gambrel, Gelatine, Glair, Gliadin, Glit, Glue, Goad, Gold, Goo, Gore, Ground-ash, Gum, Gunge, Gunk, Harpoon, Hob, Hold on, Hurley, Immobile, Impale, Inhere, Isinglass, Jab, Jam, Joss, Jut, Kebbie, Kid, Kierie, Kindling, Kip, Kiri, Knife, Knitch, Knobkerrie, Ko, Lance, Lath(i), Lathee, Lentisk, Limy, Lug, Message, Minder, Molinet, Needle, Orange, Parasitic, Paste, Penang-lawyer, Persist, Phasmid, Piceous, Pierce, Piolet, Plaster, Pogo, Pole, Posser, Pot, Protrude, Protuberant, Pugol, Q-tip, Quarterstaff, Rash, Ratten, Rhubarb, Rhythm, Rod, Ropy, Scouring, Seat, Shillela(g)h, Shooting, Size, Ski, Smudge, Spanish windlass, Spear, Spillikin, Spurtle, Squail(er), Stab, Staff, Stand, Stang, Stob, Stodgy, Stubborn, Supplejack, Swagger, Switch, Swizzle, Swordstick, Tacamahac, Tack(y), Tally, Tar, Thick, Throwing, Toddy, Tokotoko, Truncheon, Trunnion, Twig, Vare, Viscid, Viscous, Waddy, Wait, Walking, Wand, Wedge, White, Woolder, Woomera(ng), Yardwand

Sticker Araldite®, Barnacle, Bumper, Bur, Burr, Flash, Gaum, Glue, Pin, Label, Limpet, Partisan, Poster, Slogan, Viscose

Stickler Pedant, Poser, Problem, Purist, Rigid, Rigorist, Tapist

Stiff, Stiffen(er), Stiffening, Stiffness Anchylosis, Angular, Ankylosis, Baleen, Bandoline, Brace, Buckram, Budge, Corpse, Corpus, Dear, Defunct, Expensive,

Formal, Frore(n), Frorn(e), Gammy, Goner, Gromet, Grommet, Grummet, Gut, Hard, Lignin, Mort, Myotonia, Petrify, Pokerish, Prim, Ramrod, Rigid, Rigor, Rigor mortis, Sad, Set, Shank-iron, Size, Solid, Starch, Stark, Stay, Steeve, Stieve, Stilted, Stoor, Stour, Stowre, Sture, Trubenize®, Unbending, Unyielding, Whalebone, Wigan, Wooden

Stifle Crush, Dampen, Depress, Funk, Muffle, Scomfish, Smore, Smother, Stive, Strangle

Stigma(tise) Blemish, Brand, Carpel, Discredit, Note, Slur, Smear, Spot, → **STAIN**, Wound

Stile Gate, Slamming, Steps, Sty

Stiletto Bodkin, Heel, Knife

Still Accoy, Airless, Alembic, Assuage, At rest, Becalm, Calm, Check, Current, Doggo, Ene, Even(ness), Freeze-frame, Higher, Howbe, However, Hush, Illicit, Inactive, Inanimate, Inert, Kill, Languid, Limbec(k), Lull, Motionless, Nevertheless, Nonetheless, Patent, Peaceful, Photograph, Placate, Placid, Posé, Pot, Quiescent, Quiet, Resting, Silent, Snapshot, Soothe, Stagnant, Static, Stationary, Though, Windless, Yet

Stilt Avocet, Bird, Poaka, Prop, Scatch

Stilted Formal, Pedantic, Stiff, Unruffled, Wooden

Stimulate, Stimulus, Stimulant, Stimulation Activate, Adrenaline, Anilingus, Ankus, Antigen, Aperitif, Aphrodisiac, Arak, Arouse, Auxin, Benny, Caffeine, Cinder, Clomiphene, Coca, Conditioned, Coramine, Cue, Dart, Dex(edrine)®, Digitalin, Digoxin, Doxapram, Egg, Energise, Erotogenic, Evoke, Excitant, Fillip, Foreplay, Fuel, Galvanize, Ginger, Goad, Grains of Paradise, G-spot, Guinea grains, Hormone, Incentive, Incite, Innerve, Inspire, Irritate, Jog, Key, K(h)at, Kick, L-dopa, Mneme, Motivate, Nikethamide, Oestrus, Oxytocin, Paraphilia, Paratonic, Pemoline, Pep, Pep pill, Peyote, Philtre, Pick-me-up, Piquant, Pituitrin, Potentiate, Prod, Promote, Provoke, Psych, Qat, Rim, Roborant, → **ROUSE**, Rowel, Rub, Sassafras, Sensuous, Spark, Spur, Sting, Stir, Suggestive, Tannin, Tar, Theine, Tickle, Tik-tik, Titillate, Tone, Tonic, Tropism, Unconditioned, Upper, Whet(stone), Wintergreen, Winter's bark

Sting(ing) Aculeate, Barb, Bite, Cheat, Cnida, Goad, Nematocyst, Nettle(tree), Overcharge, Perceant, Piercer, Poignant, Prick, Provoke, Pungent, Rile, Scorcher, Scorpion, Sephen, Smart, Spice, Stang, Stimulus, Surcharge, Tang, Tingle, Trichocyst, Urent, Urtica, Venom

Sting-ray Sephen, Trygon

Stingy Cheeseparing, Chintzy, Close, Costive, Hard, Illiberal, Mean, Miserly, Narrow, Near, Niggardly, Nippy, Parsimonious, Save-all, Skimpy, Snippy, Snudge, Tight(wad), Tight-arse

▷ **Stingy** *may indicate* something that stings

Stink(er), Stinking, Stinks Abroma, Atoc, Atok, Brock, Cacodyl, Crepitate, Desman, Fetor, Foumart, Guff, Heel, Hellebore, Malodour, Mephitis, Miasma, Ming, Niff, Noisome, Pong, Ponk, Rasse, Reek, Rich, Science, → **SMELL**, Sondeli, Stench, Teledu

Stinkbird Hoa(c)tzin

Stint Chore, Economise, Limit, Scamp, Scantle, Scrimp, Session, Share, Skimp, Spell

Stipend Ann(at), Annexure, Pay, Prebend, Remuneration, Salary, Wages

Stipulate, Stipulation Clause, Condition, Covenant, Insist, Provision, Proviso, Rider, Specify

Stipule Ocrea

Stir(red), Stirrer, Stirring Accite, Admix, Ado, Afoot, Agitate, Amo(o)ve, Animate,

Annoy, Arouse, Awaken, Bird, Bother, Bustle, Buzz, Can, Churn, Cooler, Excite, Foment, Furore, Fuss, Gaol, Hectic, Impassion, Incense, Incite, Inflame, Instigate, Insurrection, Intermix, Jee, Jog, Kitty, Limbo, Live, → **MIX**, Molinet, Move, Noy, Paddle, Penitentiary, Poach, Poss, Pother, → **PRISON**, Prod, Provoke, Quad, Quatch, Quetch, Quinche, Qui(t)ch, Quod, Rabble, Rear, Roil, Rouse, Roust, Rummage, Rustle, Sod, Steer, Styre, Swizzle, To-do, Upstart, Wake

▷ **Stir(red), Stirring** *may indicate* an anagram

Stirrup (guard) Bone, Footrest, Footstall, Gambado, Iron, Stapes, Tapadera, Tapadero

Stitch(ing), Stitch up Bargello, Bar tack, Basket, Baste, Blanket, Blind, Box, Buttonhole, Cable, Chain, Couching, Crewel, Crochet, Cross, Daisy, Embroider, Fancy, Feather, Fell, Flemish, Florentine, Garter, Gathering, Grospoint, Hem, Herringbone, Honeycomb, Insertion, Kettle, Knit, Lazy daisy, Lock, Middle, Monk's seam, Moss, Needle, Open, Overcast, Overlock, Pearl, Petit point, Pinwork, Plain, Purl, Queen, Rag, Railway, Rib, Rope, Running, Saddle, Satin, Screw, Sew, Slip, Smocking, Spider, Stab, Stay, Steek, Stem, Stockinette, Stocking, Straight, Sutile, Suture, Tack, Tailor's tack, Tent, Topstitch, Vandyke, Wheat-ear, Whip, Whole, Zigzag

St James Scallop-shell

St Jerome Hieronymic

St John's bread Carob

St Lucia WL

Stock(ed), Stocks, Stocky Aerie, Aery, Alpha, Ambulance, Amplosome, Barometer, Blue-chip, Bouillon, Bree, Breech, Brompton, Buffer, But(t), Capital, Cards, Carry, Cattle, Choker, Cippus, Common, Congee, Conjee, Court-bouillon, Cravat, Dashi, Debenture, Delta, Die, Endomorph, Equip, Evening, Fumet, Fund, Gamma, Gear(e), Government, Graft, Growth, Gun, Handpiece, He(a)rd, Hilt, Hoosh, Industrial, Intervention, Inventory, Joint, Just-in-time, Kin, Larder, Laughing, Line, Little-ease, Locuplete, Night-scented, Omnium, Pigeonhole, Preferred, Pycnic, Race, Ranch, Recovery, Rep(ertory), Replenish, Reserve, Rolling, Root, Scrip, Seed, Shorts, Soup, Squat, Staple, Steale, Steelbow, Stirp(e)s, → **STORE**, Strain, Stubby, Supply, Surplus, Talon, Tap, Taurus, Team, Tie, Trite, Trust(ee), Utility, Virginian, Water

Stockade Barrier, Eureka, Zare(e)ba, Zereba, Zeriba

Stocking(s) Bas, Body, Boot-hose, Fishnet, Hogger, Hose, Leather, Legwarmer, Moggan, Netherlings, Netherstocking, Nylons, Popsock, Seamless, Sheer, Silk, Sock, Spattee, Support, Surgical, Tights

Stockman, Stockbroker Broker, Jobber, Neatherd

Stodge, Stodgy Dull, Filling, Heavy

Stoic(al) Impassive, Job, Logos, Patient, Philosophical, Plato, Porch, Seneca(n), Spartan, Stolid, Zeno

Stoke(r), Stokes Bram, Chain grate, Coal-trimmer, Fire(man), Fuel, S, Shovel

Stole(n) Bent, Epitrachelion, Hot, Maino(u)r, Manner, Manor, Nam, Orarion, Orarium, Reft, Scarf, Soup, Staw, Tippet, Tweedle, Waif, Wrap

Stolid Beefy, Deadpan, Dull, Impassive, Phlegmatic, Po(-faced), Thickset, Wooden

Stomach(ic) Abdomen, Abomasum, Accept, Appetite, Belly, Bible, Bingy, Bonnet, Bread-basket, Brook, C(o)eliac, Corporation, Epigastrium, Epiploon, Fardel-bag, Gaster, Gizzard, Gut, Heart, Inner man, Jejunum, King's-hood, Kite, Kyte, Little Mary, Manyplies, Mary, Maw, Mesaraic, Midriff, Omasum, Opisthosoma, Paunch, Potbelly, Propodon, Proventriculus, Psalterium, Puku, Pylorus, Read, Rennet, Reticulum, Rumen, Stand, Stick, Swagbelly, → **SWALLOW**, Tripe, Tum, Tun-belly, Urite, Vell, Venter, Wame, Washboard, Wem, Zingiber

Stomach-ache Colic, Colitis, Collywobbles, Gastralgia, Giardiasis, Gripe, Gutrot, Mulligrubs

Stone(s), Stone age, Stoned, Stony Blotto, Boulder, Cast, Cromlech, Curling, Door, Flag, Foundation, Gem, Gooley, Goolie, Gooly, Henge, Imposing, Ink, Inukshuk, Kerb, Lucky, Lydian, Masonry, Megalith, Menhir, Monolith, Mort, Niobe(an), Omphalos, Parpane, Parpend, Parpent, Paste, Paving, Pebble, Pelt, Perpend, Perpent, Philosopher's, Precious, Putting, Quern, Quoin, Quoit, Rocking, Rolling, Rubbing, Scone, Seeing, Sermon, Shingle, Slab, Staddle, Standing, Step(ping), Through, Tile, Touch, Trilith, Trilithon, Tusking

STONES

2 letters:
St

3 letters:
Gem
Hog
Pit
Rag
Tin

4 letters:
Bath
Blue
Celt
Hone
Horn
Iron
Jasp
Lias
Lime
Lode
Onyx
Opal
Plum
Ragg
Sard
Skew
Soap
Trap

5 letters:
Agate
Amber
Balas
Beryl
Black
Chalk
Chert
Coade

Culch
Drupe
Flint
Grape
Jewel
Kenne
Lapis
Logan
Menah
Metal
Mocha
Penny
Prase
Pumie
Rubin
Rufus
Rybat
Satin
Scree
Slate
Slick
Sneck
Stela
Stele
Topaz
Wacke
Wyman

6 letters:
Amazon
Arthur
Ashlar
Ashler
Baetyl
Bezoar
Brinny
Chesil
Chisel
Cobble

Coping
Cultch
Dolmen
Flusch
Fossil
Gibber
Gravel
Humite
Iolite
Jargon
Jasper
Kidney
Kingle
Ligure
Lithic
Metate
Mihrab
Mosaic
Muller
Nutlet
Oamaru
Pencil
Pot-lid
Pumice
Pyrene
Rip-rap
Samian
Sarsen
Scarab
Summer
Tanist
Yonnie

7 letters:
Asteria
Avebury
Blarney
Bologna
Breccia

Callais
Cat's eye
Chuckie
Clinker
Girasol
Granite
Hyacine
Hyalite
Jargoon
Lia-fail
Lithoid
Moabite
Olivine
Peacock
Pennant
Peridot
Petrous
Pudding
Purbeck
Putamen
Rosetta
Sardine
Sardius
Sarsden
Scaglia
Schanse
Schanze
Smaragd
Tektite
Telamon
Thunder
Tripoli
Urolith

8 letters:
Aerolite
Aerolith
Amethyst
Asteroid

8 letters – cont:
Baguette
Cabochon
Calculus
Cinnamon
Cryolite
Ebenezer
Elf-arrow
Endocarp
Essonite
Ganister
Girasole
Lapidate
Menamber
Nephrite
Onychite
Parpoint
Peastone
Petrosal
Phengite
Pisolite

Portland
Potstone
Rollrich
Sapphire
Sardonyx
Scalpins
Schantze
Specular
Tonalite
Traprock
Voussoir

9 letters:
Alabaster
Asparagus
Cairngorm
Carnelian
Cholelith
Chondrite
Cornelian
Crossette

Dichroite
Firestone
Gannister
Greensand
Hessonite
Hoarstone
Lithiasis
Meteorite
Paleolith
Pipestone
Rubicelle
Scagliola
Turquoise
Ventifact

10 letters:
Adamantine
Alectorian
Aragonites
Chalcedony
Draconites

Enhydritic
Gastrolith
Grey-wether
Kimberlite
Lherzolite
Lithophyte
Pearlstone
Penny-stone
Rhinestone
Sleekstone
Slickstone

11 letters:
Meteorolite
Pencil-stone
Peristalith

12 letters:
Carton-pierre

Stone-crop Orpin(e), Sedum, Succulent
Stone-pusher Sisyphus
Stone-thrower Bal(lista), Catapult, David, Mangonel, Onager, Perrier, Sling, Trebuchet
Stone-wall(er) Block, Jackson, Mule, Revet
Stoneware Crouch-ware
Stone-worker Jeweller, Knapper, Sculptor
Stooge Butt, Cat's-paw, Feed, Joe Soap, Straight man
Stook(s) Sheaf, Stack, Thr(e)ave
Stool Bar, Buffet, Coppy, Cracket, Creepie, Cricket, Cucking, Curule, Cutty, Ducking, Faeces, Foot, Hassock, Litany, Milking, Music, Piano, Pouf(fe), Repentance, Ruckseat, Seat, Sir-reverence, Step, Stercoral, Sunkie, Taboret, Tripod, Tripos, Turd
Stoop Bend, Condescend, C(o)urb, Crouch, Daine, Deign, Incline, Lout, Lowt, Porch, Slouch
Stop(page), Stopcock, Stopper, Stopping Abort, Adeem, An(n)icut, Arrest, Aspirate, Avast, Bait, Ba(u)lk, Belay, Bide, Blin, Block, Brake, Buffer, Bung, Canting-coin, → CEASE, Cessation, Chapter, Check, Checkpoint, Cheese, Cholestasis, Clarabella, Clarino, Clarion, Clog, Close, Colon, Comfort, Comma, Conclude, Conversation, Cork, Coupler, Cremo(r)na, Cremorne, Cromorna, Cut, Cut out, Deactivate, Debar, Demurral, Desist, Deter, Devall, Diapason, Diaphone, Discontinue, Discourage, Dit, Dolce, Dot, Dulciana, Echo, Embargo, End, Expression, Extinguish, Fare stage, Field, Fifteenth, Flag, Flue, Flute, Forbid, Foreclose, Forestall, Foundation, Fr(a)enum, Freeze, Frustrate, Full, Full point, Gag, Gamba, Gemshorn, Glottal, Gong, Halt, Hamza(h), Hartal, Heave to, Hinder, Hitch, Ho, Hoa, Hoh, Hold, Hoy, Inhibit, Intermit, Ischuria, Jam, Kibosh, Let-up, Lill, Lin, Lute, Media, Mutation, Nasard, Oboe, Obstruent, Obturate, Occlude, Oppilate, Organ, Outage, Outspan, Pause, Period, Piccolo, Pit, Plug, Point, Poop, Preclude, Prevent, Principal, Prop, Prorogue, Pull-in, Pull over, Pull-up, Punctuate, Pyramidon, Quash, Quint, Quit, Racket, Red, Reed, Refrain, Register, Rein,

Remain, Request, Rest, Salicet, Salicional, Scotch, Screw-top, Semi-colon, Sese, Sesquialtera, Sext, Sist, Sneb, Snub, Sojour, Solo, Spigot, Stall, Stanch, Standstill, Stash, Stasis, Station, Staunch, Stay, Stent, Stive, Strike, Subbase, Subbass, Suction, Supersede, Suppress, Suspend, T, Tab, Tamp(ion), Tap, Tenuis, Terminate, Toby, Toho, Truck, Twelfth, Voix celeste, Vox angelica, Vox humana, Waldflute, Waldhorn, Waypoint, When, Whistle, Whoa

Stopgap Caretaker, Gasket, Gaskin, Interim, Makeshift, Pis aller, Temporary

Stopwatch Chronograph

Storage, Store(house) Accumulate, Archive, Armoury, Arsenal, Associative, Backing, Barn, Bin, Bottle, Bottom drawer, Boxroom, Buffer, Bunker, Buttery, Cache, Capacitance, Catacomb, Cell, Cellar, Chain, Clamp, Clipboard, Convenience, Co-op(erative), Co-operative, Cootch, Core, Cupboard, Cutch, Database, Deep freeze, Deli, Dene-hole, Dépanneur, Department(al), Depository, Depot, Dime, Discount, Dolia, Dolly-shop, Elevator, Emporium, Ensile, Entrepot, Étape, External, Fund, Galleria, Garner, Gasholder, Genizah, Girnal, Glory hole, Go-down, Granary, Groceteria, Hive, → **HOARD**, Hog, Hold, Hope chest, House, Houseroom, Humidor, Husband, Hypermarket, Imbarn, Larder, Lastage, Lazaretto, Liquor, Locker, Lumber room, Magazine, Main, Mart, Mattamore, Memory, Mine, Minimart, Morgue, Mothball, Mow, Multiple, Nest-egg, Off-licence, One-step, Package, Pantechnicon, Pantry, Pithos, Provision, Pumped, Rack(ing), RAM, Reel, Repertory, Reposit, ROM, Root house, Save, Sector, Shed, → **SHOP**, Silage, Silo, Spence, Spooling, Springhouse, Squirrel, Stack, Stash, Stock, Stockpile, Stockroom, Stow, Superbaza(a)r, Superette, Supermarket, Supply, Tack-room, Tank, Thesaurus, Tithe-barn, Tommy-shop, Virtual, Volutin, Warehouse, Woodshed, Woodyard, Wool (shed)

▶ **Storey** *see* **STORY**

Stork Adjutant, Antigone, Argala, Bird, Jabiru, Marabou(t), Marg, Saddlebill, Shoebill, Wader, Whale-headed, Wood, Wood ibis

Stork's bill Erodium

Storm(y) Ablow, Adad, Assail, Attack, Baguio, Blizzard, Bluster, Bourasque, Brouhaha, Buran, Calima, Charge, Cockeye(d) bob, Cyclone, Devil, Dirty, Dust, Electric, Enlil, Expugn, Furore, Gale, Gusty, Haboob, Hurricane, Ice, Line, Magnetic, Monsoon, Onset, Oragious, Pelter, Rage(ful), Raid, Rain, Rampage, Rant, Rave, Red spot, Rugged, Rush, Shaitan, Snorter, Squall, Sumatra, Tea-cup, Tebbad, Tempest, Tornade, Tornado, Tropical, Unruly, Violent, Weather, Willy-willy, Wroth, Zu

▷ **Stormy** *may indicate* an anagram

Story, Storyline, Storey, Stories Account, Allegory, Anecdote, Apocrypha, Arthuriana, Attic, Bar, Basement, Baur, Bawr, Biog, Blood and thunder, Chestnut, Clearstory, Clerestory, Cock and bull, Conte, Cover, Decameron, Edda, Epic, Episode, Étage, Exclusive, Exemplum, Fable, Fabliau, Feature, Fib, Fiction, Flat, Floor, Folk-lore, Folk-tale, Gag, Geste, Ghost, Glurge, Hair-raiser, Hard-luck, Heptameron, Hitopadesa, Horror, Idyll, Iliad, Jataka, Lee, Legend, Lie, Mabinogion, Märchen, Mezzanine, Myth(os), Mythus, Narrative, Nouvelle, Novel(la), Oratorio, Parable, Passus, Pentameron, Photo, Plot, Rede, Report, Romance, Rumour, Saga, Scoop, Script, Serial, SF, Shaggy dog, Shocker, Short, Smoke-room, Sob, Spiel, Spine-chiller, Splash, Stage, Success, Tale, Tall, Thread, Thriller, Tier, Triforium, Upper, Version, Yarn

Story-teller Aesop, Fibber, Griot, Liar, Munchausen, Narrator, Raconteur, Shannachie, Tusitala, Uncle Remus

Stoup Benitier, Bucket, Vessel

Stout(ness) Ale, Beer, Black velvet, Burly, Chopping, Chubby, Cobby, Corpulent, Embonpoint, Endomorph, Entire, Fat, Fubsy, Hardy, Humpty-dumpty, Lusty, Manful, Milk, Obese, Overweight, Porter, Portly, Potbelly, Robust, Stalwart, Stalworth, Sta(u)nch, Strong, Stuggy, Sturdy, Substantial, Tall, Velvet

Stove Baseburner, Break, Calefactor, Chauf(f)er, Cockle, Cooker, Cooktop, Furnace, Gasfire, Oven, Potbelly, Primus®, Range, Salamander

Stow Cram, Flemish (down), Load, Pack, Rummage, Stack, Stash, Steeve

St Paul's Wren-ch

Strabismus Squint

Straddle, Straddling Bestride, Enjamb(e)ment, Strodle

Strafe Bombard, Shell, Shoot

Straggle(r), Straggly Estray, Gad, Meander, Ramble, Rat-tail, Spidery, Sprawl, Stray, Wander

Straight(en), Straightness Align, Bald, Beeline, Boning, Correct, Die, Direct, Downright, Dress, Frank, Gain, Het(ero), Home, Honest, Lank, Legit, Level, Line, Neat, Normal, Ortho-, Orthotropous, Rectilineal, Rectitude, Righten, Sheer, Slap, Tidy, True, Unbowed, Uncurl, Unlay, Upright, Veracious, Virgate

Straight edge Lute, Ruler

Straightfaced Agelast

Straightforward Candid, Direct, Downright, Easy, Even, Forthright, Honest, Jannock, Level, Plain sailing, Pointblank, Simple, Uncomplicated

Straight-haired Leiotrichous

Strain(ed), Strainer, Straining Agonistic, Ancestry, Aria, Breed, Bulk, Carol, Charleyhorse, Clarify, Colander, Distend, Drawn, Effort, Exert, Filter, Filtrate, Fit, Fitt(e), Force, Fray, Fytt(e), Intense, Kind, Melody, Milsey, Minus, Molimen, Music, Nervy, Note, Overtask, Passus, Percolate, Plus, Pressure, Pull, Purebred, Rack, Raring, Reck(an), Repetitive, Retch, Rick, Seep, Seil(e), Set, Shear, Sieve, Sift, Sile, Stape, Start, Stirps, Stock, Streak, Stress, Stretch, Sye, Tamis, Tammy, Tax, Tems(e), Tenesmus, Tense, Tension, Threnody, Try, Tune, Unease, Vein, Vice, Work, Wrick

Strait(s) Bab el Mandeb, Basilan, Bass, Bering, Bosp(h)orus, Canso, Channel, Condition, Cook, Crisis, Cut, Dardanelles, Davis, Denmark, Desperate, Dover, Drake Passage, Euripus, Florida, Formosa, Foveaux, Gat, Gibraltar, Golden Gate, Great Belt, Gut, Hainan, Hormuz, Hudson, Johore, Juan de Fuca, Kattegat, Kerch, Korea, Kyle, Little Belt, Lombok, Mackinac, Magellan, Malacca, Menai, Messina, Mona Passage, Narrow, North Channel, Otranto, Palk, Predicament, Soenda, Solent, Sound, St, Sumba, Sunda, Taiwan, Tatar, Tiran, Torres, Tsugaru, Windward Passage

Straiten(ed) Impecunious, Impoverish, Poor, Restrict

Strait-laced Blue-nosed, Narrow, Prig, Primsie, Prudish, Puritan, Stuffy

Strand(ed) Abandon, Aground, Bank, Beach, Desert, Fibre, Haugh, Hexarch, Isolate, Lock, Maroon, Neaped, Ply, Rice, Rope, Shore, Sliver, Thread, Three-ply, Tress, Twist, Wisp

▷ **Strange** *may indicate* an anagram

Strange(ness), Stranger Alien, Aloof, Amphitryon, Curious, Dougal, Eerie, Exotic, Ferly, Foreign, Fraim, Frem(d), Fremit, Frenne, Funny, Guest, Jimmy, Malihini, New, Novel, Odd(ball), Outlandish, Outsider, Quare, Quark, Queer, Rum, S, Screwy, Selcouth, Singular, Surreal, Tea-leaf, Uncanny, Unco, Uncommon, Unfamiliar, Unked, Unket, Unkid, Unused, Unusual, Wacky, Weird, Weyard, Wondrous

Strangle(r) Bindweed, Choke, Garotte, Jugulate, Suffocate, Suppress, Throttle, Thug(gee)

Strap(ping) Able-bodied, Band, Barber, Beat, Bowyangs, Braces, Brail, Braw, Breeching, Browband, Cheekpiece, Crownpiece, Crupper, Cuir-bouilli, Curb, Deckle, Girth, Halter, Harness, Holdback, Jess, Jock(ey), Kicking, Larrup, Lash, Ligule, Lorate, Lore, Manly, Martingale, Nicky-tam, Octopus, Overcheck, Palmie, Pandy, Rand, Rein, Robust, Shoulder, Sling, Spaghetti, Spider, Strop, Surcingle, Suspender, T, Tab, Taws(e), T-bar, Thong, Throatlash, Throatlatch, Trace, Tump-line, Wallop, Watch, Watchband

Stratagem, Strategist, Strategy Artifice, Clausewitz, Contrivance, Coup, Deceit, Device, Dodge, Exit, Fetch, Finesse, Fraud, Heresthetic, Kaupapa, Lady Macbeth, Maskirovka, Masterstroke, Maximum, Minimax, Plan, Rope-a-dope, → **RUSE**, Salami, Scheme, Scorched earth, Sleight, Subterfuge, Tack, Tactic(s), Tactician, Trick, Wile

Stratum, Strata Bed, Coal Measures, Kar(r)oo, Layer, Neogene, Permian, Schlieren, Seam, Syncline

Straw(s), Strawy Balibuntal, Boater, Buntal, Chaff, Cheese, Crosswort, Halm, Hat, Haulm, Hay, Insubstantial, Kemple, Last, Leghorn, Monkey-pump, Nugae, Oaten, Panama, Parabuntal, Pea(se), Pedal, Rush, Short, Sipper, Stalk, Stramineous, Strammel, Strummel, Stubble, Trifles, Truss, Wisp, Ye(a)lm

Strawberry Alpine, Barren, Birthmark, Fragaria, Fraise, Garden, Hautbois, Hautboy, Potentilla, Wild

Stray(ing) Abandoned, Aberrant, Alleycat, Chance, Depart, Deviate, Digress, Err, Forwander, Foundling, Gamin, Maverick, Meander, Misgo, Pye-dog, Ramble, Roam, Sin, Straggle, Streel, Traik, Unowned, Waff, Waif, Wander

Streak(ed), Streaker, Streaky Archimedes, Bended, Blue, Brindle, Comet, Flambé, Flaser, Flash, Fleck, Freak, Hawked, Highlights, Lace, Layer, Leonid, Lowlight, Marble, Mark, Merle, Mottle, Primitive, Race, Run, Schlieren, Seam, Shot, Striate, Striga, Strip(e), Vein, Venose, Vibex, Waif, Wake, Wale, Yellow

Stream Acheron, Anabranch, Arroyo, Beam, Beck, Bogan, Bourne, Brook, Burn, Consequent, Course, Current, Driblet, Fast, Flow, Flower, Freshet, Gulf, Gush, Headwater, Influent, Jet, Kill, Lade, Lane, Leet, Logan, Meteor, Nala, Nalla(h), Nulla(h), Obsequent, Pokelogan, Pour, Pow, Riffle, Rill, River, Rivulet, Rubicon, Run, Runnel, Sike, Slough, Spill, Spruit, Star, Strand, Streel, Subsequent, Syke, The Fleet, Third, Thrutch, Tide-race, Torrent, Tributary, Trickle, Trout, Watercourse, Water-splash, Winterbourne

Streamer Banderol(e), Bandrol, Banner(all), Bannerol, Pennon, Pinnet, Ribbon, Tape, Tippet, Vane

Streamline(d), Streamliner Clean, Fair, Fairing, Simplify, Sleek, Slim

Street Alley, Ave(nue), Bay, Boulevard, Bowery, Broad, Carey, Carnaby, Cato, Causey, Champs Elysées, Cheapside, Civvy, Close, Corso, Court, Crescent, Downing, Drive, Easy, Fleet, Gate, Grub, Harley, High(way), Kármán vortex, Lane, Lombard, Main, Meuse, Mews, One-way, Parade, Paseo, Poultry, Queer, Road, Sesame, Side, Sinister, St, Strand, Terrace, Thoroughfare, Threadneedle, Throgmorton, Two-way, Vortex, Wall, Wardour, Watling, Way, Whitehall

Street arab Mudlark

Streetcar Desire, Tram

Strength(en), Strengthened, Strengthening Afforce, Anneal, Arm, Asset, Augment, Ausforming, Bant, Beef, Brace, Brawn, Build, Confirm, Consolidate, Edify, Embattle, Enable, Energy, Field, Fish, Foison, Force, Forte, Fortify, Fortitude, Freshen, Fus(h)ion, Grit, Heart, Herculean, Horn, Intensity, Invigorate, Iron, Line, Main, Man, Might, Munite, Muscle, Nerve, → **POWER**, Prepotence, Pre-stress, Proof, Reinforce, Roborant, Shear, Sinew, Spike, Spine, Stamina, Steel,

Sthenia, Stoutness, → **STRONG**, Tensile, Thews, Titration, Ultimate, Unity, Vim, Yield

Strenuous Arduous, Effort, Exhausting, Hard, Laborious, Vehement

Strephon Rustic, Wooer

Stress(ed), Stressful Accent, Arsis, Birr, Brunt, Careworn, Drive home, Emphasis, Ictus, Impress, Italicise, Marcato, Orthotonesis, Oxidative, Oxytone, Paroxytone, Post-traumatic, Primary, Proclitic, Proof, PTSD, Rack, Ram, Rhythm, RSI, Secondary, Sentence, Sforzando, Shear, Strain, Taut, Tense, → **TENSION**, Testing, Try, Underline, Underscore, Urge, Wind shear, Word, Yield (point)

Stretch(able), Stretched, Stretcher, Stretching Belt, Brick, Crane, Distend, Doolie, Draw, Ectasis, Eke, Elastic, Elongate, Exaggerate, Expanse, Extend, Extensile, Farthingale, Fib, Frame, Give, Gurney, Home, Lengthen, Lie, Litter, Narrows, Outreach, Pallet, Pandiculation, Porrect, Procrustes, Prolong, Protend, Pull, Rack, Rax, → **REACH**, Sentence, Shiner, Span, Spell, Spread, Spreadeagle, Strain, Streak, Taut, Tend, Tense, Tensile, Tenter, Term, Time, Tract, Tractile, Traction, Tree, Trolley

Stretcher-bearer Fuzzy-wuzzy angel

Striate Lineolate, Vein

Stricken Beset, Hurt, Overcome, Shattered

Strict Dour, Exacting, Harsh, Literal, Medic, Narrow, Orthodox, Penal, Proper, Puritanical, Rigid, Rigorous, Severe, Spartan, Stern, Strait(-laced), Stringent

Stride Gal(l)umph, Leg, Lope, March, Pace, Piano, Stalk, Sten, Stend, Straddle, Stroam, Strut, Stump

Strident Brassy, Grinding, Harsh, Raucous, Screech

Strife Bargain, Barrat, Bate(-breeding), Brigue, Colluctation, Conflict, Conteck, Contest, Discord, Disharmony, Dissension, Feud, Food, Friction, Ignoble, Scrap(ping), Sturt

Strike(s), Striker, Striking, Strike out Affrap, Air, Alight, Annul, Appulse, Arresting, Attitude, Backhander, Baff, Band, Bandh, Bang, Bash, Bat, Baton, Batsman, Batter, Beat, Belabour, Better, Biff, Black, Bla(u)d, Bonanza, Bop, British disease, Buff, Buffet, Bund(h), Butt, Cane, Catch, Chime, Chip, Clap, Clash, Clatch, Clip, Clock, Clout, Club, Cob, Collide, Conk, Constitutional, Coup, Cue, Cuff, Dad, Dent, Dev(v)el, Ding, Dint, Dismantle, Distingué, Douse, Dowse, Dramatic, Drive, Dush, Éclat, Événement, Fat, Fet(ch), Fillip, Firk, Fist, Flail, Flog, Frap, General, Get, Gnash, Go-slow, Gowf, Hail, Handsome, Hartal, Head-butt, → **HIT**, Horn, Hour, Hunger, Ictus, Illision, Impact, Impinge, Impress, Jarp, Jaup, Jole, Joll, Joule, Jowl, Knock, Lam, Lambast, Laser, Lay(-off), Lightning, Match, Middle, Mint, Notable, Noticeable, Official, Out, Pash, Pat(ter), Pat, Pean, Peen, Pein, Pene, Percuss, Picket, Pize, Plectrum, Pronounced, Pummel, Punch, Quarter-jack, Ram, Rap, Remarkable, Rolling, Roquet, Salient, Scrub, Scutch, Shank, Sick out, Sideswipe, Signal, Sitdown, Sit-in, Sizzling, Slam, Slap, Slat, Slog, Slosh, Smack, Smash, Smite, Sock, Souse, Sowce, Sowse, Spank, Stayaway, Stop(page), Stub, Swap, Swat, Swinge, Swipe, Swop, Sympathy, Tan, Tangent, Tapotement, Tat, Thump, Thwack, Tip, Token, Tonk, Tripper, Twat, Unconstitutional, Unofficial, Walk-out, Wallop, Wap, Whack, Whale, Whang, Whap, Wherret, Who does what, Whomp, Whop, Wick, Wildcat, Wipe, Wondrous, Zap

Strike-breaker Blackleg, Fink, Rat, Scab

String(s), Stringy Anchor, Band, Bant, Beads, Bootlace, Bow, Bowyang, Cello, Chalaza, Chanterelle, Cord, Cosmic, Creance, Cremaster, Drill, Enfilade, Fiddle, Fillis, First, G, Glass, Gut, Henequin, Heniquin, Hypate, Idiot, Injection, Keyed, Kill, Lace, Lag, Leading, Lichanos, Macramé, Mese, Necklace, Nete, Nicky-tam,

Oil, Paramese, Pledget, Production, Proviso, Purse, Quint, Ripcord, Rope, Rosary, Rough, Second, Series, Shoe(-tie), Silly®, Sinewy, Snare, Spit, Stable, Straggle, Strand, Sultana, Sympathetic, Team, Tendon, Thairm, Tie, Tough, Train, Trite, Twiddling-line, Viola, Violin, Worry-beads, Wreathed

String-course Moulding, Table

Stringent Extreme, Rigid, Severe, Strict, Urgent

Strip(ped), Stripper, Striptease Airfield, Armband, Band, Bare, Bark, Batten, Belt, Bereave, Bimetallic, Blowtorch, Casparian, Chippendale, Comic, Cote, Defoliate, Denude, Deprive, Derobe, Despoil, Devest, Disbark, Dismantle, Dismask, Disrobe, Divest, Doab, Dosing, Drag, Ecdysiast, Ecdysis, Écorché, Fannel(l), Fiche, Film, Flashing, Flaught, Flay, Fleece, Flench, Flense, Flight, Flinch, Flounce, Flype, Furring, Gaza, Goujon, Hatband, Infula, Jib, Label, Landing, Lap-dancer, Lardon, Lath, Ledge, Linter, List, Littoral, Loading, Locust, Nail-rod, Maniple, Median, Möbius, Panhandle, Parting, Peel, Pillage, Pluck, Pull, Puttee, Puttie, Rand, Raunch, Raw, Reservation, Ribbon, Ring-bark, Roon, Royne, Rumble, Rund, Runway, Screed, Scrow, Shear, Shed, Shim, Shred, Shuck, Skin, Slat, Slit, Sliver, Spellican, Spilikin, Spill(ikin), Splat, Splent, Spline, Splint, Splinter, Spoil, Straik, Strake, Strap, Streak, Strop, Sugar soap, Swath, Sweatband, Tack, Tear, Tear-off, Tee, Thong, Tirl, Tirr, Tongue, Unbark, Uncase, Unclothe, Undeck, Undress, Unfrock, Unrig, Unrip, Unrobe, Unvaile, Valance, Weather, Widow, Zona, Zone

Stripe(d) Band, Bausond, Candy, Chevron, Cingulum, Cove, Endorse, Go-faster, Lance-jack, Laticlave, Line, List, Magnetic, → **NCO**, Ombré, Pale, Paly, Pin, Pirnie, Pirnit, Slash, Snip, Straik, Strake, Streak, Stroke, Tabaret, Tabby, Tiger, Tragelaph(us), Vitta, Weal

Strive, Striving Aim, Aspire, → **ATTEMPT**, Contend, Endeavour, Enter, Kemp, Labour, Nisus, Pingle, Press, Strain, Struggle, Toil, Try, Vie

Stroke Apoplex(y), Backhander, Bat, Bisque, Blow, Boast, Breast, Butterfly, Caress, Carom, Chip, Chop, Counterbuff, Coup, Coy, Crawl, Dash, Dint, Dog(gy)-paddle, Down-bow, Drear(e), Drere, Dropshot, Effleurage, Estrarnazone, Exhaust, Feat, Flick, Fondle, Foozle, Forehand, Glance, Ground, Hairline, Hand(er), Ictus, Inwick, Jenny, Jole, Joll, Joule, Jowl, Knell, Knock, Lash, Lightning, Like, Line, Loft, Long jenny, Loser, Massé, Oarsman, Oblique, Odd, Off-drive, Outlash, Palp, Paw, Pot-hook, Pull, Punto reverso, Put(t), Reverso, Ridding straik, Roquet, Rub, Scart, Scavenge, Sclaff, Scoop, Seizure, Sheffer's, Short jenny, Sider, Sixte, Slash, Smooth, Solidus, Spot, Strike, Stripe, Sweep, Swipe, Tact, Tittle, Touch, Touk, Trait, Trudgen, Trudgeon, Tuck, Upbow, Virgule, Wale, Whang, Wrist shot

Stroll(er), Strolling Ambulate, Bummel, Dander, Daun(d)er, Dawner, Flânerie, Flâneur, Frescade, Idle, Lounge, Perambulate, Ramble, Saunter, Stravaig, Stray, Toddle, Walk, Walkabout, Wander

Strong(est) Able, Boofy, Brawny, Cast-iron, Doughty, Durable, F, Firm, Fit, Forceful, Forcible, Forte, Full-blown, Hale, Heady, Hercules, High-powered, Humming, Husky, Intense, Mighty, Nappy, Pithy, Pollent, Potent, Powerful, Pungent, Racy, Rank, Robust, Samson, Solid, Sour, Stale, Stalwart, Stark, Steely, Sthenic, Stiff, Stout, Str, Strapping, → **STRENGTH**, Sturdy, Substantial, Suit, Tarzan, Tenable, Thesis, Thickset, Trusty, Vegete, Vehement, Vigorous, Violent, Virile, Well-built, Well-set, Wight, Ya(u)ld

Stronghold Acropolis, Aerie, Bastion, Castle, Citadel, Eyrie, Eyry, Fastness, Fortalice, Fortress, Keep, Kremlin, Redoubt, Tower

Strongroom Genizah, Safe

Strontium Sr

Strop(py) Cantankerous, Leather, Sharpen, Strap

Struck Aghast, Raught, Smitten

Structural, Structure Acrosome, Allotrope, Analysis, Anatomy, Armature, Atomic, Building, Catafalque, Cold frame, Compage(s), Conus, Data, Deep, Edifice, Erection, Fabric, Fairing, Flaser, Format(ion), Formwork, Frame, Galea, Gantry, Heterarchy, Hyperbolic, Hyperfine, Ice-apron, Idant, Kekulé, Lantern, Lattice, Macrocosm, Malpighian, Manubrium, Mole, Organic, Palmation, Parawalker, Pediment, Pergola, Phloem, Physique, Pod, Power, Protein, Retinaculum, Set-up, Shape, Shell, Skeleton, Sponson, Sporocarp, Squinch, Staging, Stand, Starling, Stylobate, Surface, Syntax, System, Tectonic, Telomere, Texas, Texture, Trabecula, Trochlea, Undercarriage

Struggle, Struggling Agon(ise), Agonistes, Amelia, Buckle, Camp, Chore, Class, Conflict, Contend, Contest, Cope, Debatement, Duel, Effort, Encounter, Endeavour, Fight, Flounder, Grabble, Grapple, Jockey, Kampf, Labour, Luctation, Mill, Pingle, Rat-race, Reluct, Resist, Scrabble, Scramble, Scrape, Scrimmage, Scrum, Scrummage, Scuffle, Slugfest, Sprangle, → **STRIVE**, Toil, Tug, Tussle, Uphill, Vie, War(sle), Wrestle

▷ **Struggle** *may indicate* an anagram

Strum Thrum, Twang, Tweedle, Vamp

Strumpet Cocotte, Harlot, Hiren, Lorette, Paramour, Succubus, Waistcoateer, Wench

Strut(ter), Strutting Bracket, Brank, Bridging, Cock, Dolphin striker, Flounce, Haught(y), Jet, Kingrod, Longeron, Martingale boom, Member, Nervure, Peacock, Pown, Prance, Pronk, Prop, Scotch, Shore, Spur, Stalk, Stretcher, Strunt, Swagger, Swank, Tail-boom, Tie-beam

Stuart Anne, James, Pretender

Stub(by) Butt, Counterfoil, Dout, Dowt, Dumpy, Squat, Stob, Stocky

Stubble Ar(r)ish, Bristle, Designer, Hair, Ill-shaven, Stump

Stubborn(ness) Adamant, Bigoted, Bull-headed, Contumacious, Cross-grained, Cussed, Diehard, Dogged, Entêté, Hard(-nosed), Hidebound, Intransigent, Inveterate, Moyl(e), Mulish, Mumpsimus, Obdurate, Obstinate, Opinionated, Ornery, Ortus, Pertinacious, Perverse, Recalcitrant, Reesty, Refractory, Rigwiddie, Rigwoodie, Self-willed, Stiff, Stout, Tenacious, Thrawn, Wrong-headed

Stuck Fast, Glued, Jammed, Set, Stopped, Wedged

Stuck-up Chesty, Highty-tighty, Hoity-toity, La(h)-di-da(h), Proud, Sealed, Toffee-nosed, Vain

Stud(ded) Boss, Cooser, Cripple, Cu(i)sser, Doornail, Farm, Frost, He-man, Knob, Nail, Press, Race, Rivet, Seg, Set, Shear, Sire, Stop

Student(s) Abiturient, Alphabetarian, Alumnus, Apprentice, Bajan, Bejant, Bursar, Bursch(en), Cadet, Candle-waiter, Catechumen, Class, Coed, Commoner, Dan, Dig, Disciple, Dresser, Dux, Exchange, Exhibitioner, Extensionist, External, Form, Fresher, Freshman, Gownsman, Graduand, Green welly, Gyte, Ikey, Internal, Junior, Kommers, Kyu, → **LEARNER**, Magistrand, Matie, Mature, Medical, Nomologist, NUS, Opsimath, Ordinand, Oxonian, Peking duck, Pennal, Plebe, Poll, Postgraduate, Preppy, Pupil, Reader, Rushee, Sap, → **SCHOLAR**, Self-taught, Semi, Seminar, Seminarian, Senior, Shark, Sizar, Sizer, Smug, Softa, Soph(omore), Sophister, Spod, Subsizar, Swot, Templar, Tiro, Tosher, Trainee, Tuft, Tukkie, Tutee, Undergraduate, Wedge, Welly, Witsie, Wonk, Wooden wedge, Wrangler, Year

Studio(s) Atelier, Bottega, Elstree, Gallery, Lot, Pinewood, Workshop

Study, Studies, Studied, Studious, Studying Analyse, Bone, Brown, Carol, Case, Classics, Comparability, Con(ne), Conscious, Consider, Course, Cram, Den, Dig,

Étude, Eye, Feasibility, Field, Gen up, Isagogics, Learn, Liberal, Lucubrate, Media, Motion, Mug up, Mull, Muse, Nature, Perusal, Peruse, Pilot, Pore, Post-doctoral, Prep(aration), Probe, Read, Recce, Reconnoitre, Research, Reverie, Revise, Sanctum, Sap, Scan, Scrutinise, Shiur, Specialize, Stew, Swat, Swot, Take, Time and motion, Trade-off, Tutorial, Typto, Voulu, Work

Stuff(iness), Stuffing, Stuffy Airless, Bombast, Canvas, Close, Cloth, Codswallop, Cram, Crap, Dimity, Farce, Feast, Fiddlesticks, Fill, Force, Forcemeat, Frows(t)y, Frowzy, Fug, Gear, Glut, Gobble, Gorge, Guff, Havers, Hooey, Horsehair, Hot, Lard, Line, Linen, → **MATERIAL**, Matter, Musty, No-meaning, Nonsense, Overeat, Pad, Pang, Panne, Pompous, Ram, Replete, Rot, Salpicon, Sate, Satiate, Scrap, Sob, Stap, Steeve, Stew, Stifling, Taxidermy, Trig, Upholster, Wad, Youth

Stultify Repress, Ridicule, Smother

Stumble Blunder, Bobble, Daddle, Err, Falter, Flounder, Founder, Lurch, Peck, Snapper, Stoit, Titubate, Trip

Stump(ed), Stumps, Stumpy At sea, Black, Butt, Clump, Fag-end, Floor, More, Nog, Nonplus, Orate, Runt, Scrag, Snag, Snooker, Squab, St, Staddle, Stob, Stock, Stool, Stub(ble), Stud, Tortillon, Tramp, Truncate, Wicket

Stun(ning), Stunned Astonish, Astound, Awhape, Bludgeon, Concuss, Cosh, Daze, Dazzle, Deafen, Donnard, Donnert, Dove(r), Drop-dead, Glam, KO, Numb, Poleaxe, Shell-shocked, Shock, Stoun, Stupefy, Taser®

Stunner Belle, Bobby-dazzler, Cheese, Cosh, Doozy, KO, Peach, Taser®

Stunt(ed) Aerobatics, Confine, Droichy, Dwarf, Escapade, Feat, Gimmick, Hot-dog, Hype, Jehad, Jihad, Loop, Nirl, Puny, Ront(e), Runt, Ruse, Scroggy, Scrub(by), Scrunt(y), Stub, Trick, Wanthriven, Wheelie

Stupefaction, Stupefy(ing), Stupefied Amaze(ment), Assot, Benumb, Catatonic, Dozen, Dumbfound, Etherise, Fuddle, Hocus, Moider, Moither, Mull, Narcoses, Numb, Stonne, Stun

Stupid, Stupid person Anserine, Asinine, Besotted, Blithering, Blockish, Braindead, Clay-brained, Crass, Daft, Datal, Dense, Desipient, Dim(wit), Donner(e)d, Dozy, Dull(ard), Fatuous, Flat, Foolish, Gross, Half-arsed, Half-baked, Hammerheaded, Hare-brained, Hen-witted, Inane, Insensate, Insipient, Lamming, Mindless, Natural, Obtuse, Senseless, Silly, Thick, Thick-witted, Torpid, Vacuous, Wooden(head)

STUPID PERSON

3 letters:	Owl	Clod	Fool
Ass	Put	Clot	Fozy
Auf	Sap	Cony	Gaby
Bev	Sot	Coof	Gaga
Bob	Wof	Coot	Geck
Cod	Yap	Dill	Gelt
Daw		Ditz	Goat
Div	4 letters:	Doat	Goof
Fon	Berk	Dodo	Goon
Git	Bete	Does	Goop
Jay	Bobb	Dolt	Gorm
Lob	Bozo	Dorb	Gouk
Log	Burk	Dork	Gowk
Nit	Cake	Dote	Gull
Oaf	Calf	Fogy	Gump

4 letters – cont:
Hash
Jaap
Jerk
Lown
Lunk
Meff
Mome
Mong
Mook
Mutt
Nana
Nerd
Nerk
Nong
Nurd
Ouph
Poon
Poop
Prat
Putt
Putz
Rook
Simp
Slow
Stot
Tony
Tube
Twit
Warb
Yo-yo
Zany

5 letters:
Bevan
Blent
Bobby
Booby
Brute
Bumbo
Chick
Chump
Clunk
Cokes
Cuddy
Cully
Dicky
Diddy
Divvy
Dorba
Dubbo

Dumbo
Dummy
Dunce
Dweeb
Eejit
Fogey
Galah
Golem
Goofy
Goose
Hoser
Idiot
Kerky
Klutz
Looby
Loony
Lowne
Moron
Neddy
Ninny
Nitty
Noddy
Ocker
Ouphe
Patch
Plank
Prune
Quo-he
Schmo
Simon
Snipe
Spoon
Stock
Stupe
Sumph
Twerp
Twerp
Waldo
Wally
Yampy

6 letters:
Bampot
Bauble
Boodle
Buffer
Cretin
Cuckoo
Cuddie
Dawney
Dickey

Dodkin
Donkey
Doofus
Dottle
Drongo
Gander
Gaupus
Gunsel
Ignaro
Ingram
Ingrum
Johnny
Josser
Loonie
Lummox
Lurdan
Lurden
Nidget
Nig-nog
Nincum
Nitwit
Noodle
Nudnik
Numpty
Oxhead
Schlep
Schmoe
Scogan
Shmock
Shmuck
Sucker
Tavert
Thicko
Tosser
Tumphy
Turkey
Turnip
Wigeon
Wommit
Zombie

7 letters:
Airhead
Asinico
Barmpot
Becasse
Buffoon
Charlie
Cupcake
Damfool
Dawbake

Dawcock
Dim bulb
Dizzard
Donnard
Donnart
Donnert
Fuckwit
Gomeral
Gomeril
Gubbins
Half-wit
Haverel
Insulse
Jackass
Johnnie
Juggins
Jughead
Lurdane
Mafflin
Mampara
Muggins
Palooka
Pampven
Pillock
Pinhead
Plonker
Pot-head
Saphead
Schmock
Schmuck
Schnook
Scoggin
Taivert
Thickie
Tosspot
Twinkle
Want-wit
Wazzock

8 letters:
Abderian
Abderite
Baeotian
Boeotian
Bonehead
Boofhead
Bullhead
Clodpate
Clodpole
Clodpoll
Crackpot

Deadhead
Dickhead
Dipstick
Dodipoll
Dotterel
Dottrell
Dumbbell
Flathead
Gobshite
Goofball
Goose-cap
Gormless
Imbecile
Knobhead
Liripipe
Liripoop
Lunkhead
Maffling
Meathead
Moon-calf
Numskull
Omadhaun

Pea-brain
Shithead
Shot-clog
Softhead
Tom-noddy
Wiseacre
Woodcock

9 letters:
Beccaccia
Birdbrain
Blockhead
Capocchia
Chipochia
Clarthead
Cornflake
Doddipoll
Doddypoll
Dottipoll
Dumb-cluck
Gothamite
Ignoramus

Jobernowl
Lamebrain
Malt-horse
Nicompoop
Numbskull
Pigsconce
Schlemiel
Schlemihl
Simpleton
Thickhead
Woodentop

10 letters:
Analphabet
Changeling
Dummelhead
Dunderhead
Dunderpate
Headbanger
Hoddy-doddy
Loggerhead
Muttonhead

Nickumpoop
Nincompoop
Sheepshead
Thickskull
Thimblewit
Touchstone

11 letters:
Chowderhead
Featherhead
Knucklehead
Leather-head
Ninny-hammer
Simple Simon
Van der Merwe

12 letters:
Featherbrain
Shatterbrain

Stupidity Goosery, Hebetude, Oscitancy, Thickness, Torpor
Stupor Catatony, Coma, Daze, Dwa(u)m, Fog, Lethargy, Narcosis, Trance
Sturdy Burly, Dunt, Gid, Hardy, Hefty, Lubbard, Lubber, Lusty, Robust, Solid, Stalwart, Staunch, Steeve, Stieve, Strapping, Strong, Stuffy, Thickset, Turnsick, Vigorous
Sturgeon Beluga, Ellops, Fish, Huso, Osseter, Sevruga, Sterlet
Stutter(ing) Blaise, Hesitate, Stammer
St Vincent WV
Sty Frank, Hogpen, Hovel, Pen
Stye Eyesore, Hordeolum
Style(s), Stylish, Stylist Adam, À la, A-line, Anime, Band, Barocco, Barock, Baroque, Biedermeier, Blocked, Blow-dry, Brachylogy, Burin, Call, Cantilena, Carry-on, Chic, Chinoiserie, Chippendale, Class, Cultism, Cut, Dapper, Dash, Decor, Decorated, Demotic, Diction, Directoire, Dub, Élan, Elegance, Empire, Entitle, Euphuism, Execution, Face, Farand, → **FASHION**, Finesse, Flamboyant, Flava, Flossy, Fly, Form(at), Free, Genre, Ghetto fabulous, Gnomon, Gongorism, Gothic, Grace, Gr(a)ecism, Grand, Groovy, Hair-do, Hand, Hepplewhite, Heuristic, Hip, Homeric, House, International (Gothic), Intitule, Katharev(o)usa, Lapidary, Locution, Manner, Marivaudage, Mod(e), Modernism, Modish, Natty, New, Nib, Nifty, Old, Panache, Pattern, Pen, Perm, Perpendicular, Personal, Phrase, Picturesque, Pistil, Pointel, Port, Post-modernism, Preponderant, Probe, Queen Anne, Rakish, Rank, Regency, Retro, Ritzy, Rococo, Romanesque, Sheraton, Silk, Snazzy, Spiffy, Sporty, Street, Swish, Taste, Term, Title, Ton, Tone, Touch, Traditional, Tuscan, Uncial, Vein, Verismo, Vogue, Way
Stymie Baulk, Frustrate, Thwart
Styptic Alum, Amadou, Matico, Sta(u)nch
Suave Bland, Debonair, Oily, Smooth, Unctuous, Urbane
Sub Advance, Due, Fee, Submarine, Subordinate, U-boat, Under

Subarea Talooka
Sub-atomic Mesic
Subconscious Inner, Instinctive, Not-I, Subliminal, Suppressed
Sub-continent India(n)
Subcontract Outsource
Subdivision Arm, Branch, Commot(e), Cotyledon, Oblast, Sanjak, Senonian, Sheading, Tepal, Wapentake
Subdominant Fah
Subdue(d) Abate, Adaw, Allay, Chasten, Conquer, Cow, Crush, Dant(on), Daunt(on), Dominate, Entame, Lick, Low-key, Master, Mate, Mute, Overbear, Overpower, Quail, → **QUELL**, Quieten, Reduce, Refrain, Repress, Slow, Sober, Soft pedal, Subact, Suppress, Tame, Under
Subfusc, Subfusk Dim, Dressy, Dusky, Evening, Sombre
Subhuman Apeman, Bestial
Subject(s), Subjection, Subject to Amenable, Art, Bethrall, Caitive, Case, Citizen, Contingent, Core, Cow, Dhimmi, Donné(e), Enthrall, Foundation, Gist, Hobby, Hobby-horse, Inflict, Liable, Liege(man), Matter, Metic, National, On, Oppress, Overpower, PE, People, Poser, Rayah, RE, RI, Serf, Servient, Servitude, Sitter, Slavery, Snool, Submit, Suit, Syllabus, → **THEME**, Thirl, Thrall, Topic, Under, Vassal, Villein
Subjugate Enslave, Master, Oppress, Overcome, Reduce, Repress, Suppress
Sublieutenant Cornet
Sub-lieutenant Cornet
Sublimate(r) Aludel, Cleanse, Suppress, Transfer
Sublime Ali, Alice, August, Empyreal, Grand, Great, Holy, Lofty, Majestic, Outstanding, Perfect, Porte, Splendid
▷ **Submarine** *may indicate* a fish
Submarine Diver, Innerspace, Nautilus, Pig-boat, Polaris, Sub, U-boat, Undersea, X-craft
Submerge(d) Dip, Dive, Drown, Embathe, Engulf, Imbathe, Impinge, Lemuria, Overwhelm, Ria, Sink, Take, Whelm
Submissive, Submission, Submit Acquiesce, Bow, Capitulate, Comply, Defer, Docile, File, Folio, Knuckle, Meek, Obedient, Obtemperate, Passive, Pathetic, Refer, Render, Resign, Snool, Stepford, Stoop, Succumb, Truckle, → **YIELD**
Subordinate Adjunct, Dependent, Flunky, Inferior, Junior, Minion, Myrmidon, Offsider, Postpone, Secondary, Second banana, Servient, Stooge, Subject, Subservient, Subsidiary, Surrender, Under(ling), Underman, Under-strapper, Vassal
Subscribe(r), Subscription Abonnement, Approve, Assent, Conform, Due, Pay, Sign(atory), Signature, Undersign, Underwrite
Subsequent(ly) Anon, Consequential, Future, Later, Next, Postliminary, Since, Then, Ulterior
Subservient Kneel, Obedient, Obsequious
Subside, Subsidence, Subsidy Abate, Adaw, Aid, Assuage, Bonus, Cauldron, Diminish, Ebb, Grant, Headage, Sink, Sit, Swag
Subsidiary, Subsidise Auxiliar(y), By(e), By-end, Feather-bed, Junior, Secondary, Second banana, Side, Sideline, Spin-off, Succursal
Subsist(ence) Batta, Bread-line, Dole, Keep, Live, Maintain, Rely, Survive
Substance, Substantial Ambergris, Anethole, Antithrombin, Antitoxin, Apiol, Blanco, Blocky, Body, Calyx, Castoreum, Cermet, Chalone, Chemzyne, Chitin, Chromatin, Colloid, Considerable, Content, Cosmin(e), Creatine, Ectocrine,

Ectoplasm, Elemi, Enzyme, Essential, Excipient, Extender, Exudate, Fabric, Fixative, Getter, Gist, Gluten, Gossypol, Gravamen, Growth, Guanazolo, Hearty, Hefty, Hirudin, Imine, Indol, Inhibitor, Iodoform, Iodophor, Isatin(e), Isomer, Kryptonite, Lase, Lecithin, Lectin, Leucotriene, Linin, Luciferin, Material, Matter, Meaning, Meat(y), Metabolite, Metol, Mineral, Misoprostol, Mitogen, Mole, Morphogen, Mucigen, Murr(h)ine, Mutagen, Myelin, Naloxone, Neotoxin, Neurotoxin, Orgone, Papier mâché, Particulate, Phlogiston, Pith, Polymer, Proinsulin, Promoter, Prostaglandin, Protyl(e), Purin(e), Queen (bee), Quid, Reality, Resin, Secretagogue, Sense, Sequestrant, Smeclic, Solid, Sorbitol, Stramonium, Stuff, Suint, Sum, Surfactant, Sympathin, Synergist, Syntonin, Tabasheer, Tabashir, Taeniafuge, Tangible, Thiouracil, Thiourea, Tusche, Viricide, Volutin, Weighty, Ylem

Substandard Infra dig, Off, Poor, Schlo(c)k, Second, Small

▸ **Substantial** *see* **SUBSTANCE**

Substantiate Confirm, Flesh, Prove, Strengthen, Support

Substantive Direct, Noun

Substitute, Substitution Acting, Carborundum®, Change, Changeling, Commute, Creamer, Deputy, Dextran, Double, Dub, Emergency, Ersatz, -ette, Euphemism, Eusystolism, Exchange, Fill-in, Imitation, Improvise, Instead, Lieu(tenant), Locum, Makeshift, Metonymy, Novation, Pinch-hit, Proxy, Regent, Relieve, Replace, Represent, Reserve, Resolution, Ringer, Sentence, Seth, Simulacrum, Stalking-horse, Stand-in, Stead, Stopgap, Subrogate, Succedaneum, Supernumerary, Supply, Surrogate, Switch, Swop, Synthetic, Understudy, Vicar(ial), Vicarious

Substructure Base, Foundation, Keelson, Platform, Podium

Subterfuge Artifice, Chicane, Evasion, Hole, Manoeuvre, Off-come, Ruse, Strategy, Trick

Subterranean Concealed, Mattamore, Sunken, Underground, Weem

Subtle(ty) Abstruse, Alchemist, Crafty, Fine(spun), Finesse, Ingenious, Nice(ty), Overtone, Refinement, Sly, Suttle, Thin, Wily

Subtle difference Nuance

Subtract(ion) Commission, Deduct, Discount, Sum, Take, Tithe, Withdraw

Suburb(s) Banlieue, Dormitory, Environs, Exurbia, Faubourg, Garden, Metroland, Outskirts, Purlieu, Subtopia

Subversion, Subvert Fifth column, Overthrow, Reverse, Sabotage, Sedition, Treasonous, Undermine, Upset

Subway Dive, Metro, Passage, Tube, Underground

Succeed, Success(ful) Accomplish, Achieve, Arrive, Blockbuster, Boffo, Breakthrough, Chartbuster, Contrive, Coup, Do well, Éclat, Effective, Efficacious, Fadge, Felicity, Flourish, Follow, Fortune, Gangbuster, Get, Go, Hit, Hotshot, Inherit, Killing, Landslide, Luck, Made, Make it, Manage, Masterstroke, Mega, Midas touch, Offcome, Parlay, Pass, Prevail, Procure, Prosper, Purple patch, Reach, Replace, Result, Riot, Score, Seal, Seel, Sele, Sell out, Soaraway, Socko, Speed, Stardom, Superstar, Sure thing, Take, Tanistry, The bitch goddess, Triumph, Up, Up and coming, Upstart, Vault, Weather, W(h)iz(z)kid, Win, Wow, Wunderkind

Succession Apostolic, Chain, Cognate, Dead men's shoes, Ecological, Line, Mesarch, Neum(e), Order, Reversion, Sequence, Seriatim, Series, String, Suite

Successor Co(m)arb, Deluge, Descendant, Ensuite, Epigon(e), Heir, Incomer, Inheritor, Khalifa, Next, Syen

Succinct Brief, Cereus, Compact, Concise, Houseleek, Laconic, Pithy, Short

Succour Aid, Assist, Help, Minister, Relieve, Rescue, Sustain

Succulent Agave, Aloe, Cactus, Echeveria, Juicy, Lush, Rich, Saguaro, Sappy, Spekboom, Tender, Toothy

Succumb Capitulate, Fall, Go under, Surrender, Yield

Such Like, Sae, Sike, Similar, So, That

Suck(er), Sucking Absorb, Acetabular, Acetabulum, Amphistomous, Antlia, Aphis, Aspirator, Ass, Bull's eye, Culicidae, Dracula, Drink, Dupe, Fawn, Felch, Fellatio, Gnat, Graff, Graft, Gull, Haustellum, Haustorium, Hoove, Lamia, Lamprey, Leech, Liquorice, Lollipop, Mammal, Monotremata, Mouth, Mug, Muggins, Osculum, Patsy, Plunger, Remora, Rook, Shoot, Siphon, Slurp, Smarm, Spire, Spyre, Straw, Surculus, Swig, Sycophant, Tellar, Teller, Tick, Tiller, Toad-eater, Turion, Vampire

Suckle Feed, Mother, Nourish, Nurse, Nurture

Suction Adhere, Pump, Siphon

Sud(s) Foam, Lather, Sapples

Sudanese Dinka, Mahdi, Nuba

Sudden(ly) Abrupt, Astart, Astert, Extempore, Ferly, Flash, Fleeting, Foudroyant, Fulminant, Hasty, Headlong, Impulsive, Overnight, Precipitate, Rapid, Slap, Sodain, Subitaneous, Subito, Swap, Swop, Unexpected

Sue Apply, Ask, Beseech, Dun, Entreat, Implead, Implore, Litigate, Petition, Pray, Process, Prosecute, Woo

Suede Split

Suffer(er), Suffering Abide, Aby(e), Ache, Affliction, Agonise, Auto, Be, → **BEAR**, Brook, Calvary, Cop, Die, Distress, Dree, Dukkha, Endurance, Endure, Feel, Gethsemane, Golgotha, Grief, Hardship, Have, Hell, Incur, Languish, Let, Luit, Mafted, Martyr, Pain, Passible, Passion, Passive, Patible, Patience, Pellagrin, Permit, Pine, Plague, Purgatory, Stand, Stomach, Sustain, Thole, Tolerate, Toll, Torment, Trial, Tribulation, Undergo, Use, Victim

Suffering remnant Macmillanite

Suffice, Sufficient Adequate, Ample, Basta, Do, Due, Enough, Enow, Experimental, Nuff, Run to, Satisfy, Serve

Suffix Enclitic

Suffocate Asphyxiate, Choke, Smoor, Smore, Smother, Stifle, Stive, Strangle, Throttle

Suffrage(tte) Ballot, Feminist, Franchise, Manhood, Vote

Suffuse Colour, Glow, Imbue, Saturate, Spread

Sugar(y), Sugar cane Aldohexose, Aldose, Amygdalin, Arabinose, Barley, Beet, Blood, Brown, Candy, Cane, Caramel, Carn(e), Cassonade, Caster, Cellobiose, Cellose, Chaptalise, Confectioner's, Daddy, Demerara, Deoxyribose, Dextrose, Disaccharide, Flattery, Fructose, Fucose, Furanose, Galactose, Gallise, Glucose, Glucosoric, Glycosuria, Goo(r), Granulated, Grape, Gur, Heroin, Hexose, Honeydew, Hundreds and thousands, Iced, Icing, Inulin, Invert, Jaggary, Jaggery, Jagghery, Ketose, Lactose, Laevulose, Loaf, Lump, Maltose, Manna, Mannose, Maple, Milk, Money, Monosaccharide, Muscovado, Nectar, Nucleoside, Palm, Panocha, Pentose, Penuche, Raffinose, Rhamnose, Ribose, Saccharine, Saccharoid, Simple, Sis, Sorbose, Sorg(h)o, Sorghum, Sparrow, Spun, Sweet, Trehalose, Triose, White, Wood, Xylose

Sugar-daddy Lyle, Tate

Suggest(ion), Suggestive Advance, Advice, Advise, Connote, Counter-proposal, Cue, Hint, Hypnotic, Idea, Imply, Innuendo, Insinuate, Intimate, Mention, Modicum, Moot, Posit, Posthypnotic, Prompt, Proposal, Propound, Provocative, Racy, Raise, Recommend, Redolent, Reminiscent, Risqué, Savour, Smacks, Soft core, Suspicion, Touch, Trace, Twang, Undertone, Vote, Wind, Wrinkle

Suicide Felo-de-se, Hara-kiri, Hari-kari, Kamikaze, Lemming, Lethal, Sati, Seppuku, Shinju, Suttee

Suit Action, Adapt, Adjust, Agree, Answer, Anti-G, Apply, Appropriate, Become, Befit, Beho(o)ve, Bequest, Beseem, Besit, Birthday, Boiler, Cards, Case, Cat, Clubs, Conform, Courtship, Demob, Diamonds, Dittos, Diving, Do, Drapes, Dress, Dry, Effeir, Effere, Etons, Fadge, Fashion, Fit, G, Garb, Gee, Gree, Hearts, Hit, Jump, Lis pendens, Long, Lounge, Major, Mao, Match, Minor, Monkey, NBC, Noddy, Orison, Outcome, Paternity, Petition, Plaint, Play, Plea, Please, Point, Prayer, Pressure, Process, Pyjama, Quarterdeck, Queme, Romper(s), Safari, Sailor, Salopettes, Samfoo, Samfu, Satisfy, Serve, Shell, Siren, Skeleton, Slack, Space, Spades, Strong, Sun, Sunday, Supplicat, Sweat, Swim, Swords, Tailleur, Three-piece, Track, Trouser, Trumps, Tsotsi, Tweeds, Twin, Two-piece, Uniform, Union, Wet, Wingsuit, Zoot

Suitable Apposite, Appropriate, Apropos, Apt, Becoming, Capable, Competent, Congenial, Consonant, Convenance, Convenient, Due, Expedient, → **FIT**, Giusto, Habile, Keeping, Meet, Opportune, Relevant, Seasonal, Seemly, Sittlichkeit, Very, Worthy

Suite Allemande, Apartment, Chambers, Court, Edit, Ensemble, Entourage, Hospitality, Lounge, Nutcracker, Partita, Retinue, Rooms, Serenade, Set, Skybox, Tail, Three-piece, Train, Two-piece

Suitor Beau, Gallant, John Doe, Lover, Petitioner, Pretendant, Pretender, Suppli(c)ant, Swain, Wooer

Sulk(y), Sulkiness B(r)oody, Disgruntled, Dod, Dort, Gee, Glout(s), Glower, Glum, Grouchy, Grouty, Grumps, Gumple-foisted, Huff, Hump, Jinker, Mardy, Maungy, Mope, Mulligrubs, Mump, Pet, Petulant, Pique, Pout, Snit, Spider, Strunt, Stuffy, Stunkard, Sullen, Tout(ie), Towt, Umbrage

Sullen Dorty, Dour, Farouche, Glum(pish), Grim, Moody, Mumpish, Peevish, Stunkard, Sulky, Sumph, Surly, Truculent

Sully Assoil, Bedye, Besmirch, Blot, Defile, Glaur(y), Smear, Smirch, Smutch, Soil(ure), Tarnish, Tar-wash

Sulphate, Sulphide Alum, Alunite, Blende, Bluestone, Bornite, Copperas, Coquimbite, Glance, Melanterite, Pyrites, Zarnec, Zarnich

Sulphur Baregine, Brimstone, Cysteine, Hepar, Oleum, S, Stannite, Thionic

Sultan(a), Sultanate Brunei, Caliph, Emir, Grand Seignoir, Grand Turk, Hen, Kalif, Nejd, Oman, Osman, Padishah, Roxane, Saladin, Soldan, Suleiman, Tippoo, Tipu, Wadai

Sultry Humid, Sexy, Smouldering, Steamy, Tropical

Sum(s), Sum up Add(end), Aggregate, All, Amount, Arsmetric, Bomb, Connumerate, Encapsulate, Foot, Logical, Lump, Number, Perorate, Plumule, → **QUANTITY**, Re-cap, Refund, Remittance, Reversion, Solidum, Total, Vector

Summarize, Summary Abridge, Abstract, Aperçu, Bird's eye, Brief, Compendium, Condense, Conspectus, Digest, Docket, Epanodos, Epitome, Gist, Instant, Memo, Minute, Offhand, Outline, Overview, Pirlicue, Précis, Purlicue, Recap, Resume, Résumé, Round-up, Rundown, Short (shrift), Syllabus, Synopsis, Tabloid, Tabulate, Tabulation, Wrap-up

Summer(time) Aestival, August, BST, Computer, Estival, Heyday, Indian, Lintel, Luke, Prime, St Luke's, St Martin's, Season, Solstice, Totter

Summerhouse Belvedere, Chalet, Conservatory, Folly, Gazebo, Pavilion

Summit Acme, Acro-, Apex, Braeheid, Brow, Climax, Conference, → **CREST**, Crown, Height, Hillcrest, Jole, Mont Blanc, Peak, Pike, Pinnacle, Spire, Vertex, Vertical, Yalta

Summon(s) Accite, Arraign, Arrière-ban, Azan, Beck(on), Call, Call in, Cist, Cital, Citation, Command, Conjure, Convene, Convent, Drum, Evoke, Garnishment, Gong, Hail, Invocation, Muster, Order, Originating, Page, Post, Preconise, Rechate, Recheat, Reveille, Signal, Sist, Ticket, Warn, Warrant, Whoop, Writ

Sumo (wrestling) Makunouchi, Niramial, → **WRESTLING**, Yokozuna

Sump Bilge, Drain, Pool, Sink

Sumpter Led horse, Pack-horse

Sumptuous Expensive, Lavish, Luxurious, Palatial, Rich(ly), Superb

Sun(-god), Sunlight, Sunny, Sunshine Albedo, Amen-Ra, Amon-Ra, Apollo, Ashine, Aten, Bright, Cheer, Combust, Daily, Day(star), Dry, Earthshine, Eye of the day, Glory, Heater, Helio(s), Helius, Horus, Mean, Midnight, Mock, New Mexico, Nova, Orb, Paranthelion, Parhelion, Pet-day, Phoebean, Photosphere, Ra, Radiant, Rays, Re, Rising, Shamash, Sol(ar), Soleil, Sonne, Surya, Svastika, Swastika, Tabloid, Tan, Titan, UV

Sunbathe Apricate, Bask, Brown, Tan

Sunbeam Car, Ray

Sunblock Parasol

Sunburn Bronze, Combust, Peeling, Tan

Sunday Advent, Best, Cantate, Care, Carle, Carling, Dominical, Easter, Fig, Jubilate, Judica, Laetare, Lord's Day, Lost, Low, Mid-Lent, Mothering, Orthodox, Palm, Passion, Quadragesima, Quasimodo, Quinquagesima, Refection, Refreshment, Remembrance, Rogation, Rose, Rush-bearing, S, Septuagesima, Sexagesima, Stir-up, Tap-up, Trinity, Whit

Sunday school SS

Sunder Divide, Divorce, Part, Separate, Sever, Split

Sundew Drosera, Eyebright

Sundial Analemma, Gnomon, Solarium

Sundry Divers, Several, Various

Sunflower Kansas, KS

Sunglasses Ray-Bans®, Shades

▶ **Sun-god** *see* **SUN**

▶ **Sunken** *see* **SINK**

Sunrise, Sun-up Aurora, Cosmical, Dawn, East

Sunset Acronical, Evening

Sunshade Awning, Brise-soleil, Canopy, Chi(c)k, Cloud, Parasol, Umbrella

Sunspot Facula, Freckle, Macula

Sunstroke Heliosis, Siriasis

Sunwise Deasi(u)l, Deasoil, Deis(h)eal, Eutropic

Sun-worshipper Heliolater

Sup Dine, Eat, Feast, Sample, Sip, Swallow

Super A1, Actor, Arch, Extra, Fab(ulous), Great, Grouse, Ideal, Lulu, Paramount, Superb, Terrific, Tip-top, Tops, Walker-on, Wizard

Superadded Advene

Superb A1, Concours, Fine, Grand, Great, Majestic, Peerless, Phat, Splendid, Top-notch

Supercilious Aloof, Arrogant, Bashaw, Cavalier, Haughty, Lordly, Snide, Sniffy, Snooty, Snotty, Snouty, Superior, Toffee-nosed, Upstage

Superficial Cosmetic, Cursenary, Cursory, Dilettante, Exterior, Facile, Glib, Outside, Outward, Overlying, Perfunctory, Shallow, Sketchy, Skindeep, Smattering, Veneer

▷ **Superficial(ly)** *may indicate* a word outside another

Superfluous, Superfluity Cheville, De trop, Extra, Lake, Mountain, Needless,

Otiose, Pleonastic, Plethora, Redundant, Spare, Unnecessary

Superhuman Bionic, Herculean, Heroic, Supernatural

Superintend(ent) Boss, Curator, Director, Foreman, Guide, Janitor, Oversee(r), Preside, Provost, Sewer, Supercargo, Surveillant, Warden, Zanjero

Superior(ity) Abbess, Abeigh, Above, Advantage, Aloof, Atop, Better, Brahmin, Choice, Condescending, Custos, De luxe, Dinger, Elite, Eminent, Excellent, Exceptional, Finer, Forinsec, Gree, Herrenvolk, High-class, High-grade, Jethro, Lake, Liege, Master race, Mastery, Morgue, Mother, Nob, Outstanding, Over, Overlord, Paramount, Pooh-Bah, Posh, Predominance, Prestige, Pretentious, Prior, Smug, Superordinate, Supremacy, Swell, Top(-loftical), Transcendent(al), U, Udal, Upper(most), Uppish, Upstage

Superlative Best, Exaggerated, Peerless, Smasheroo, Supreme, Utmost

Superman Batman, Bionic, Titan, Übermensch

Supermarket Co-op, Fund, GUM, Self service, Store

Supernatural Divine, Eerie, Fay, Fey, Fie, Fly, Gothic, Kachina, Mana, Metaphysical, Paranormal, Sharp, Siddhi, Uncanny, Unearthly, Wight

Supernova Plerion

Supernumerary Additional, Corollary, Extra, Mute, Orra

Supersede Replace, Stellenbosch, Supplant

Superstition Aberglaube, Abessa, Fable, Folk-lore, Freet, Myth, Pisheog, Pishogue, Uncertainty

Superstructure Mastaba(h)

Supertonic Ray

Supervise(d), Supervision, Supervisor Administer, Chaperone, Check, Direct, Engineer, Floorwalker, Foreman, Grieve, Handle, Honcho, Invigilate, Manager, Monitor, Officiate, Overman, Oversee(r), Probation, Proctor, Seneschal, Shopwalker, Stage-manage, Steward, Targe, Under, Walla(h)

Supine Inactive, Inert, Lying, Passive, Protract

Supper Bar, Burns, Dinner, → **DRINK(ER)**, Fork, Hawkey, Hockey, Horkey, Last, Meal, Nagmaal, Repast, Soirée

Supplant Displace, Exchange, Oust, Overthrow, Pre-empt, Replace, Substitute, Supersede

Supple Compliant, Leish, Limber, Lissom(e), → **LITHE**, Loose, Loose-limbed, Lythe, Pliable, Sinuous, Souple, Wan(d)le, Wannel, Whippy

Supplement(ary) Addend(um), Addition, Adjunct, And, Annex(e), Appendix, Augment, Auxiliary, Bolt-on, Codicil, Colour, Eche, Eik, Eke, Extra, Incaparina, Paralipomena, Postscript, Practicum, PS, Relay, Ripienist, Ripieno, Rutin, Weighting

Supplicant, Supplicate Beg, Entreat, Importune, Invoke, Petition, Plead, Request, Schnorr, Sue

Supply, Supplies, Supplier Accommodate, Advance, Afford, Cache, Cater, Commissariat, Contribute, Crop, Endue, Equip, Excess, Exempt, Feed, Fill, Find, Fit, Foison, Fund, Furnish, Give, Grist, Grubstake, Heel, Holp(en), Indue, Issue, Lay on, Lend, Lithely, Mains, Matériel, Pipeline, Plenish, Ply, → **PROVIDE**, Provision, Purvey, Push, RASC, Replenishment, Reservoir, Resource, Retailer, Serve, Source, Stake, Stock, → **STORE**, Viands, Vintner, Water, Widow's cruse, Yield

Support(er), Supporting Abacus, Abet, Abutment, Adherent, Adminicle, Advocate, Aegis, Affirm, Aficionado, Aftercare, Aid, Aidance, Aliment(ative), Ally, Ammunition, Anchor, Ancillary, Andiron, Anta, Appui, Arch, Arm, Assistant, Athletic, Axle, Back(bone), Back-up, Baculum, Baluster, Banister, Bankroll, Barrack, Barre, Base, Batten, Beam, Bear, Befriend, Behind, Belt, Bibb, Bier, Bolster, Boom,

Bouclée, Bra, Brace, Bracket, Brassiere, Breadwinner, Breast-summer, Bridge, Bridgeboard, Buttress, C(ee)-spring, Chair, Champion, Chaptrel, Circumstantiate, Clientele, Column, Confirm, Console, Corbel, Corbel-table, Cornerstone, Countenance, Cradle, Cross-beam, Cruck, Crutch, Dado, Diagrid, Dog-shore, Doula, Easel, Encourage, Endorse, Endow, Engager, Enthusiast, Espouse, Family, Fan, Favour, Fid, Finance, Flying buttress, Fly-rail, Footrest, Footstool, For, Friend, Gamb, Gantry, Garter, Girder, Glia, Grass roots, Groundswell, Handrail, Hanger, Harpin(g)s, Headrest, Help, Henchman, Hold with, Home help, Horse, Hound, I-beam, Idealogue, Impost, Income, Instantiate, Ite, Jack, Jackstay, Jockstrap, Joist, Keep, Kingpost, Knee, Knife rest, Knighthead, Learning, Lectern, Leg, Lierne, Lifebelt, Lifebuoy, Lobby, Loper, Loyalist, Mahlstick, Mainbrace, Mainstay, Maintain, Makefast, Mill-rind, Miserere, Misericord(e), Monial, Moral, Mortsafe, Mount, Nervure, Neuroglia, -nik, Nourish, Pack, Pack-frame, Packstaff, Paranymph, Parawalker, Partisan, Partizan, Partners, Patronage, Pedestal, Pessary, Phalanx, Pier, Pillar, Pin, Plinth, Poppet, Post, Potent, Price, Prop, Proponent, Prop-root, PTA, Pull-for, Purlin(e), Purlins, Pylon, Raft, Rally round, Regular, Reinforce, Relieve, Respond, Rest, Rind, Rod, Roof-plate, Root, Royalist, Rynd, Samaritan, Sanction, Sawhorse, Scaffolding, Second, Shoetree, Shore, Skeg, Skeleton, Skewput, Skid, Sleeper, Sling, Snotter, Socle, Solidarity, Spectator, Splat, Splint, Sponson, Sprag, Spud, Staddle, Staddlestone, Staff, Staging, Stake, Stalwart, Stanchion, Stand(-by), Stay, Steady, Stem(pel), Step, Stick, Stirrup, Stool, Stringer, Strut, Stylobate, Subscribe, Subsidy, Succour, Suffragist, Summer, Suppedaneum, Suspender, Sustain, Sustentacular, Sustentaculum, Tailskid, Tartan army, Technical, Tee, Telamon, Tendril, Third, Tie, Tige, Torsel, Trabecula, Tress(el), Trestle, Tripod, Trivet, Truss, Underlay, Underpin, Understand, Unipod, Uphold, Upkeep, Verify, Viva, Walker, Waterwings, Welfare, Well-wisher, Y-level, Yorkist, Zealot

Suppose(d), Supposition An, Assume, Believe, Daresay, Expect, Guess, Hypothetical, Idea, If, Imagine, Imply, Infer, Opine, Presume, Putative, Said, Sepad, Theory, What if

Suppository Pessary

Suppress(ion), Suppressed Abolish, Adaw, Burke, Cancel, Censor, Check, Clampdown, Conditioned, Crush, Cushion, Ecthlipsis, Elide, Elision, Gag, Gleichschaltung, Hush-up, Mob(b)le, Quash, Quell, Quench, Restrain, Silence, Sit on, Smother, Squash, Squelch, Stifle, Submerge, Subreption, Throttle, Under

Suppurate, Suppuration Diapyesis, Discharge, Exude, Fester, Maturate, Ooze, Pus, Pyorrhoea, Rankle

Supreme, Supremacy, Supremo Apical, Baaskap, Caudillo, Consummate, Kronos, Leader, Napoleon, Overlord, Paramount, Peerless, Pre-eminent, Regnant, Sovereign, Sublime, Sudder, Superlative, Top, Utmost, White

Surcharge Addition, Extra, Tax

Surd Voiceless

Sure(ly) Assured, Ay, Bound, Cert(ain), Confident, Definite, Doubtless, Firm, Indeed, Infallible, Know, Pardi(e), Pardy, Perdie, Positive, Poz, Safe, Secure, Shoo-in, Sicker, Syker, Uh-huh, Unerring, Yeah, Yep, Yes

Surety Bail, Frithborth, Guarantee, Mainprise, Security, Sponsional

Surf(er), Surfing Breach, Breaker, Browse, Grommet, Internet, Lurk, Rollers, Rote, Sea, Waxhead

Surface Aerofoil, Appear, Area, Arise, Astroturf®, Camber, Carpet, Caustic, Control, Crust, Cutis, Day, Dermal, Dermis, Emerge, Epigene, Exterior, External, Face, Facet, Finish, Flock, Interface, Linish, Macadam, Meniscus, Nanograss, Notaeum,

Out, Outcrop, Outward, Overglaze, Paintwork, Patina, Pave, Plane, Reveal, Rise, Salband, Side, Skin, Soffit, Spandrel, Superficial, Superficies, Tarmac®, Tar-seal, Texture, Top, Topping, Toroid, Wearing course, Worktop

Surf-boat, Surfboard(ing) Goofy-footer, Masoola(h), Masula

Surfeit(ed) Blasé, Cloy, Excess, Glut, Overcloy, Plethora, Satiate, Stall, Staw

▷ **Surfer** *may indicate* programming

Surge Billow, Boom, Drive, Gush, Onrush, Seethe, S(c)end, Storm, Sway, Swell, Wind

Surgeon Abernethy, Barber, BCh, BS, CHB, CM, Doctor, Dupuytren, House, Hunter, Lister, Medic, Operator, Orthopod, Plastic, Sawbones, Staff, Tang, Vet(erinary)

Surgery Anaplasty, Bypass, Cosmetic, Facelift, Hobday, Keyhole, Knife, Laparotomy, Laser, LASIK, Mammoplasty, Medicine, Nip and tuck, Nose job, Op, Open-heart, Orthop(a)edics, Osteoplasty, Plastic, Prosthetics, Reconstructive, Repair, Spare-part, Ta(g)liacotian, Thoracoplasty, Tuboplasty, Zolatrics

Surly Bluff, Cantankerous, Chough, Chuffy, Churl(ish), Crabby, Crusty, Cynic, Glum, Gruff, Grum, Grumpy, Rough, Snarling, Sullen, Truculent

Surmise Extrapolate, Guess, Imagine, Infer, Presume, Suppose

Surmount Beat, Climb, Conquer, Crest, Master, Overcome, Scan, Superate, Tide, Transcend

Surname Cognomen, Patronymic

Surpass(ing) Bang, Beat, Best, Cap, Cote, Ding, Eclipse, Efface, Exceed, Excel, Frabjous, Outdo, Outgo, Outgun, Out-Herod, Outman, Outreach, Outshine, Outstrip, Overshadow, Overtop, Transcend, Trump

Surplice Cotta, Ephod, Rochet, Sark, Serk, Vakass

Surplus De trop, Excess, Extra, Glut, Lake, Mountain, Out-over, Over, Overabundance, Overage, Overcome, Remainder, Rest, Spare, Surfeit

Surprise(d), Surprising Ag, Alert, Amaze, Ambush, Arrah, Astonish, Aykhona wena, Bewilder, Blimey, Boilover, Bombshell, By Jove, Caramba, Catch, Confound, Coo, Cor, Crick(e)y, Crikey, Criminé, Cripes, Criv(v)ens, Crumbs, Dear, Eye-opener, Gadso, Gee, Geewhiz, Gemini, Geminy, Gemony, Gobsmacked, Godsend, Golly, Good-lack, Gorblimey, Gordon Bennett, Gosh, Great Scott, Ha, Hah, Hallo, Heavens, Hech, Heck, Heh, Hello, Hey, Ho, Jeepers, Jeepers creepers, Jeez(e), Jinne, Jirre, Law, Lawks, Lor, Lordy, Lumme, Lummy, Man alive, Marry, Musha, My, Nooit, Obreption, Och, Odso, Omigod, Oops, Open-mouthed, Overtake, Phew, Pop-eyed, Really, Sheesh, Shock, Singular, Sjoe, Spot, Stagger, Startle, Strewth, Struth, Stun, Sudden, Treat, Turn-up, Uh, Whew, Whoops, Wide-eyed, Wonderment, Wow, Wrongfoot, Yikes, Yipes, Yow, Zinger, Zowie

Surrealist Bizarre, Dali, Ernst, Grotesque, Magritte, Man Ray, Miró

Surrender Capitulate, Cave-in, Cessio honorum, Cession, Enfeoff, Extradite, Fall, Forego, Forfeit, Handover, Hulled, Kamerad, Naam, Recreant, Release, Relinquish, Remise, Rendition, Roll over, Strike, Submit, Succumb, Waive, → **YIELD**, Yorktown

Surreptitious Clandestine, Covert, Fly, Furtive, Secret, Slee, Sly, Stealthy, Underhand

Surrey Carriage, Sy

Surrogate Agent, Depute, Deputy, Locum, Proxy

Surround(ed), Surrounding(s) Ambient, Amongst, Architrave, Background, Bathe, Bego, Beset, Bundwall, Circumvallate, Circumvent, Compass, Doughnutting, Ecology, Embail, Encase, → **ENCIRCLE**, Enclave, Enclose, Encompass, Enfold, Entomb, Envelop, Environ, Enwrap, Fence, Gherao, Gird, Girt, Hedge, Hem in, Impale, Inorb, Invest, Mid, Orb, Orle, Outflank, Outside, Perimeter, Setting, Wall

Surtees Jorrocks, Sponge

Surveillance, Survey(ing), Surveyor Behold, Cadastre, Case, Census, Chartered, Conspectus, Dialler, Domesday, Doomwatch, Espial, Examination, Eye, Geodesy, Geological, Groma, Look-see, Once-over, Ordnance, Overeye, Patrol, Poll, Prospect, Quantity, Recce, Reconnaissance, Regard, Review, Scan, Scrutiny, Stakeout, Straw poll, Supervision, Terrier, Theodolite, Triangulate, Trilateration, Vigil, Watch

Survival, Survive, Surviving, Survivor Cope, Die hard, Endure, Extant, Finalist, Hibakushka, Last, Leftover, Live, Outdure, Outlast, Outlive, Outwear, Overlive, Persist, Pull through, Relic(t), Ride, Street-wise, Viability, Warhorse, Weather

Susan Lazy

Susceptible, Susceptibility Anaphylaxis, Electrical, Impressionable, Liable, Receptive, Vulnerable

Suspect, Suspicion, Suspicious Askance, Assume, Breath, Cagey, Dodgy, Doubt, Dubious, Equivocal, Fishy, Grain, Grey list, Guess, Hinky, Hint, Hunch, Hunky, Jalouse, Jealous, Leery, Misdeem, Misdoubt, Misgiving, Mislippen, Mistrust, Modicum, Notion, Paranoia, Queer, Scent, Sense, Smatch, Soupçon, Thought, Tinge, Whiff

▷ **Suspect, Suspicious** *may indicate* an anagram

Suspend(ed), Suspense, Suspension Abate, Abeyance, Adjourn, Anabiosis, Anti-shock, Cliffhanger, Colloid, Dangle, Defer, Delay, Dormant, Freeze, Ground, → **HANG**, Hydraulic, Independent, Intermit, Lay off, Mist, Moratorium, Nailbiter, Pensile, Poise, Prorogue, Put on ice, Reprieve, Respite, Rub out, Rusticate, Sideline, Sol, Stand off, Stay, Swing, Tension, Tenterhooks, Truce, Withhold

▷ **Suspended** *may indicate* 'ice' on ice at the end of a down light

Sussex Rape

Sustain(ed), Sustaining, Sustenance Abide, Afford, Aliment, Bear, Constant, Depend, Endure, Food, Keep, Last, Maintain, Nutrient, Nutriment, Nutrition, Pedal, Prolong, Sostenuto, Succour, Support, Ten(uto), Upbear

Sutler Vivandière

Suture Button, Catgut, Cobbler, Coronal, Lambda, Pterion, Purse-string, Sagittal, Stitch

Suzanne, Suzie Lenglen, Wong

Svelte Lithe, Slender, Slim

Swab Dossil, Dry, Mop, Pledget, Scour, Sponge, Squeegee, Stupe, Tampon, Tompon, Wipe

Swaddle, Swaddling Bind, Envelop, Incunabula, Swathe, Wrap

Swag Booty, Encarpus, Festoon, Haul, Loot, Maino(u)r, Manner, Matilda, Shiralee, Toran(a)

Swagger(er), Swaggering Birkie, Bluster, Boast, Brag, Bragadisme, Bravado, Bucko, Cock, Cockiness, Crow, Jaunty, Matamore, Nounce, Panache, Pra(u)nce, Roist, Roll, Rollick, Roul, Royster, Ruffle, Sashay, Side, Strive, Swagman, Swank, Swash(-buckler), Tigerism

Swain Amoretti, Beau, Churl, Corin, Damon, Hind, Lover, Rustic, Shepherd, Strephon, Wooer

Swallow(able), Swallowing Accept, Aerophagia, Ariel, Barn, Bird, Bolt, Cliff, Consume, Deglutition, Devour, Down, Drink, Eat, Endue, Englut, Engulf, Engulph, Esculent, Glug, Gobble, Gula, Gulp, Hirundine, Incept, Ingest, Ingulf, Ingurgitate, Itys, Lap, Martin, Martlet, Neck, Progne, Quaff, Shift, Sister, Slug, Stomach, Swig, Take, Take off

Swamp(y) Bog, Bunyip, Cowal, Cypress, Deluge, Dismal, Drown, Engulf, Everglade, Flood, Great Dismal, Inundate, Lentic, Lerna, Lerne, Loblolly, Mar(i)sh, Morass, Muskeg, Okavango, Okefenokee, Overrun, Overwhelm, Pakihi, Paludal, Purgatory,

Quagmire, Slash, Slough, Sudd, Uliginous, Urman, Vlei, Vly, Wetland

Swan(s) Avon, Bewick's, Bird, Black, Cob, Cygnet, Cygnus, Game, Leda, Lindor, Mute, Pen, Seven, Seward, Song, Stroll, Trumpeter, Whistling, Whooper, Whooping

Swank(y) Boast, Lugs, Pretentious, Side, Style

Swan-song Finale, Last air

Swap, Swop → BARTER, Chop, Commute, Exchange, Scorse, Switch, Trade, Truck

▷ **Swap(ped)** *may indicate* an anagram

Sward Grass, Green, Lawn, Sod, Turf

Swarm(ing) Abound, Alive, Bike, Bink, Byke, Cast, Clamber, Cloud, Crowd, Flood, Geminid, Hoatching, Host, Hotter, Infest, Meteor, Overrun, Pullulate, Rife, Shin, Shoal, Throng

Swarthy Black-à-vised, Dark, Dusky, Melanotic

Swash Send, Swig, Swill

Swash-buckler Adventurer, Boaster, Braggart, Gascon, Swordsman

Swastika Filfot, Fylfot, Gamma(dion), Hakenkreuz

▶ **Swat** *see* SWOT

Swathe Bind, Enfold, Enroll, Swaddle, Wrap

Sway(ing) Careen, Carry, Command, Diadrom, Domain, Dominion, Flap, Fluctuate, Govern, Hegemony, Influence, Lilt, Oscillate, Prevail, Reel, Reign, Rock, Roll, Rule, Sally, Shog, Shoogie, Shoogle, Swag, Swale, Swee, Swing(e), Teeter, Titter, Totter, Vacillate

Swear(ing), Swear word Attest, Avow, Billingsgate, Coprolalia, Curse, Cuss, Depose, Execrate, Expletive, Invective, Jurant, Juratory, Oath, Pledge, Plight, Rail, Sessa, Tarnal, Tarnation, Verify, Vow

Sweat(ing), Sweaty Apocrine, Beads, Clammy, Cold, Dank, Diaphoresis, English, Excrete, Exude, Flop, Forswatt, Glow, Hidrosis, Lather, Ooze, Osmidrosis, → PERSPIRE, Secretion, Slave, Stew, Sudament, Sudamina, Sudate, Swelter

Sweater Aran, Argyle, Circassian, Circassienne, Cowichan, Fair Isle, Gansey, Guernsey, Indian, Jersey, Polo, Pullover, Roll-neck, Siwash, Skinny-rib, Skivvy, Slip-on, Slop-pouch, Sloppy Joe, Turtleneck, Woolly

Swede Inga, Nordic, Olaf, Rutabaga, Scandinavian, Sven, Turnip

Sweeney Police, Todd

Sweep(er), Sweeping(s) Besom, Broad, Broom, Brush, Chimney, Chummy, Clean, Curve, Debris, Detritus, Expanse, Extensive, Lash, Libero, Lottery, Net, Oars, Pan, Phasing, Police-manure, Range, Scavenger, Scud, Sling, Snowball, Soop, Sooterkin, Street, Stroke, Surge, Swathe, Sway, Vacuum, Waft, Well, Wide

Sweepstake Draw, Gamble, Lottery, Raffle, Tattersall's, Tombola

Sweet(s), Sweeten(er), Sweetmeat, Sweetness Acesulflame-K, Acid drop, Adeline, Afters, Alcorza, Aldose, Amabile, Aspartame, Barley sugar, Bombe, Bonbon, Bonus, Brandyball, Bribe, Bubble gum, Bull's eye, Burnt-almonds, Butterscotch, Candy, Candyfloss, Caramel, Chaptalise, Charity, Charming, Cherubic, Choc(olate), Choccy, Cloying, Coconut ice, Comfit, Confect(ion), Confetti, Confiserie, Confit, Conserve, Cracknel, Crème, Cute, Cyclamate, → DESSERT, Dolce, Dolly, Dolly mixture, Douce(t), Dowset, Dragée, Dulcet, Dulcie, Dulcitude, Elecampane, Eringo, Eryngo, Fairy floss, Flummery, Fondant, Fool, Fragrant, Fresh, Fudge, Glucose, Glycerin, Gob-stopper, Goody, Gum(drop), Gundy, Hal(a) vah, Halva, Honey(ed), Humbug, Hundreds and thousands, Ice, Icky, Indican, Jelly baby, Jelly bean, Jube, Jujube, Kiss, Lavender, Lemon drop, Licorice, Liqueur, Liquorice, Lollipop, Lolly, Lozenge, Luscious, Marchpane, Marshmallow, Marzipan, Melodious, Mint, Mousse, Muscavado, Nanaimo Bar, Nectared, Noisette,

Nonpareil, Nothing, Nougat, Pandrop, Pastille, Pea, Peardrop, Peppermint cream, Peppermint drop, Pet, Pick'n'mix, Pie, Praline, Pud(ding), Redolent, Rock, Romic, Saccharin(e), Scroggin, Seventeen, Sillabub, Sixteen, Solanine, Soot(e), Sop, Sorbet, Spice, Split, Stickjaw, Sucker, Sucrose, Sugar, Sugarplum, Sugary, Swedger, Syllabub, Syrupy, Tablet, Taffy, Tart, Thaumatin, Toffee, Torte, Trifle, Truffle, Turkish delight, Twee, Uses, William, Wine-gum, Winsome, Xylitol, Zabaglione

Sweetbread Bur(r), Inchpin, Pancreas, Thymus

Sweetheart Amoret, Amour, Beau, Darling, Dona(h), Dowsabel(l), Doxy, Dulcinea, Flame, Follower, Honey(bunch), Honeybun, Jarta, Jo(e), Lass, Leman, Lover, Masher, Neaera, Peat, Romeo, Steady, Toots(y), True-love, Valentine, Yarta, Yarto

Sweet-seller Butcher, Confectioner

Sweet talk Taffy

Swell(ing) Adenomata, Ague-cake, Anasarca, Aneurysm, Apophysis, Bag, Balloon, Bellying, Berry, Billow, Blab, Blister, Bloat, Blow, Boil, Boll, Bolster, Botch, Braw, Bubo, Bulb, Bulge, Bump, Bunion, Burgeon, Capellet, Carnosity, Cat, Chancre, Chilblain, Clour, Cratches, Curb, Cyst, Dandy, Desmoid, Diapason, Dilate, → **DISTEND**, Dom, Don, Eche, Ectasia, Eger, Elephantiasis, Encanthis, Enhance, Entasis, Epulis, Excellent, Farcy-bud, Frog, Gall, Gathering, Gent, Goiter, Goitre, Gout, Grandee, Ground, H(a)ematoma, Heave, Heighten, Hove, Hydrocele, Hydroma, Hygroma, Increase, Inflate, Intumesce, Kibe, L, Lampas(se), Lampers, Louden, Lump, Macaroni, Mouse, Nodule, Odontoma, Oedema, OK, Onco-, Ox-warble, Parotitis, Plim, Plump, Protrude, Protuberance, Proud, Pulvinus, Rise, Roil, Scirrhus, Scleriasis, Sea, Shinsplints, Splenomegaly, Strout, Struma, Stye, Stylopodium, Surge, Teratoma, Toff, Torose, Torulose, Tragus, Tuber(cle), Tumefaction, Tumescence, Tumour, Tympany, Upsurge, Varicocele, Venter, Wallow, Warble, Wen, Whelk, Windgall, Xanthoma

▷ **Swelling** *may indicate* a word reversed

Swelter(ing) Perspire, Stew, Sweat, Tropical

Swerve, Swerving Bias, Broach, Careen, Deflect, Deviate, Lean, Sheer, Shy, Stray, Sway, Swee, Swing, Warp, Wheel

Swift(ly) Apace, Bird, Dean, Dromond, Fleet, Flock, Hasty, Martlet, Newt, Nimble, Presto, Prompt, Pronto, Quick, → **RAPID**, Reel, Slick, Spanking, Velocipede, Wight

Swig Drink, Gulp, Nip, Scour, Swill, Tighten

Swill Guzzle, Leavings, Rubbish, Slosh, Swash

▷ **Swilling** *may indicate* an anagram

▷ **Swim** *may indicate* an anagram

Swim(ming) Bathe, Bogey, Bogie, Crawl, Dip, Float, Freestyle, Naiant, Natant, Natatorial, Paddle, Reel, Run, Skinny-dip, Soom, Synchro(nized), Trudgen, Whim, Whirl

Swimmer Bather, Cichlid, Copepod(a), Duckbill, Duckmole, Dugong, Frogman, Leander, Pad(d)le, Paidle, Planula, Pleopod, Pobble, Terrapin, Trudgen, Webb

▷ **Swimmer** *may indicate* a fish

Swimming costume Bathers, Bikini, Cossie, Maillot, Monokini, One-piece, Tanga, Tankini, Tog, Trunks

Swindle(r) Beat, Bite, Bucket-shop, Bunco, Bunkosteerer, Cajole, Champerty, → **CHEAT**, Chouse, Con, Concoct, Crimp, Defraud, Diddle, Do, Escroc, Fake, Fiddle, Finagle, Fineer, Fleece, Fraud, Gazump, Gip, Gold brick, Goose-trap, Graft, Grifter, Gyp, Hocus, Hoser, Hustler, Leg, Leger, Long-firm, Magsman, Mountebank, Mulct, Nobble, Peter Funk, Plant, Racket, Ramp, Rig, Rogue, Scam, Sell, Shaft, Shakedown, Shark, Sharper, Shicer, Shyster, Skelder, Skin, Skin game, Slicker, Sting, Stitch-up, Stumer, Suck, Swiz(z), Take, Trick, Tweedle, Twist, Two-time

Swine(herd) Boar, Brute, Cad, Eumaeus, Gadarene, Heel, Hog, Peccary, Pig, Porcine, Pork, Rotter, Sounder, Sow, Sybotic

Swing(er), Swinging Colt, Dangle, Flail, Hang, Hep, Hip, Kip(p), Lilt, Metronome, Mod, Music, Oscillate, Pendulate, Pendulum, Reverse, Rock, Rope, Shog, Shoogie, Shuggy, Slew, Swale, Sway, Swee, Swerve, Swey, Swipe, Trapeze, Vibratile, Voop, Wave, Western, Wheel, Whirl, Yaw

Swipe(s) Backhander, Beer, Haymaker, Seize, Steal, Strike, Tap-lash

Swirl Eddy, Purl, Swoosh, Tourbill(i)on, Twist, Whirl

▷ **Swirling** *may indicate* an anagram

Swish Cane, Frou-frou, Rustle, Smart, Whir, Whisper

Swiss Genevese, Ladin, Roll, Tell, Vaudois

Switch(ed), Switches, Switching Birch, Change, Churn, Convert, Crossbar, Cryotron, Dimmer, Dip, Dolly, Exchange, Gang, Hairpiece, Knife, Legerdemain, Master, Mercury, Mercury tilt, Message, Pear, Point, Replace, Retama, Rocker, Rod, Scutch, Thyristor, Time, Toggle, Tress, Trip, Tumbler, Twig, Wave, Zap

Switchback Rollercoaster

▷ **Switched** *may indicate* an anagram

Switzerland CH, Helvetia

Swivel Caster, Pivot, Root, Rotate, Spin, Terret, Territ, Torret, Turret, Wedein

Swiz Chiz(z)

Swollen Blown, Bollen, Bombe, Bulbous, Full, Gourdy, Gouty, Incrassate, Nodose, Puffy, Tumid, Turgescent, Turgid, Varicose, Ventricose, Vesiculate

Swoon Blackout, Collapse, Deliquium, Dover, Dwa(l)m, Dwaum, Faint, Swarf, Swerf

Swoop Descend, Dive, Glide, Plummet, Souse

▶ **Swop** *see* **SWAP**

Sword(-like), Swordplay Andrew Ferrara, Anelace, Angurvadel, Anlace, Arondight, Assegai, Balisarda, Balmunc, Balmung, Bilbo, Blade, Brand, Brandiron, Broad(sword), Brondyron, Caliburn, Cemitare, Claymore, Colada, Court, Curtal-ax, Curtana, Curtax, Cutlass, Daisho, Damascene, Damaskin, Damocles, Dance, Dirk, Duranda(l), Durindana, Ensate, Ensiform, Epée, Espada, Estoc, Excalibur, Falchion, Faulchi(o)n, Firangi, Foil, Forte, Fox, Gladius, Glaive, Gleave, Glorious, Hanger, Iai-do, Jacob's staff, Joyeuse, Katana, Kendo, Khanda, Kirpan, Kreese, Kris, Kukri, Kusanagi, Machete, Mandau, Merveilleuse, Mimming, Montano, Morglay, Nothung, Parang, Philippan, Rapier, Reverso, Rosse, Sabre, Samurai, Schiavone, Schläger, Scimitar, Semita(u)r, Shabble, Shamshir, Sharp, Sigh, Simi, Skene-dhu, Smallsword, Spadroon, Spirtle, Spit, Spurtle(blade), Steel, Toasting-iron, Toledo, Tuck, Tulwar, Two-edged, Waster, Whinger, Whiniard, Whinyard, White-arm, Xiphoid, Yatag(h)an

Sword-bearer, Swordsman(ship), Swordswoman Aramis, Athos, Blade, Brenda(n), D'Artagnan, Fencer, Frog, Gladiator, Matador, Porthos, Sai-do, Selictar, Spadassin, Spadroon, Spartacus, Swashbuckler, Zorro

Sword-dancer Matachin

Swordfish Espada, Istiophorus, Xiphias

Sword-swallower Samite

Swot Dig, Grind, Kill, Mug, Read up, Smug, Stew, Strike, Swat

Sybarite Aristippus, Epicure, Hedonist, Voluptuary

Sycamore Acer, Maple, Plane, Tree

Sycophant(ic) Apple polisher, Brown-nose, Claqueur, Crawler, Creeper, Damocles, Fawner, Gnathonic, Groveller, Hanger-on, Lickspittle, Parasite, Pickthank, Placebo, Toad-eater, Toady, Yesman

Syllabary Hiragana, Kana, Katakana

Syllable(s) Acatalectic, Anacrusis, Aretinian, Nonsense, Om, Outride, Tonic

Syllabus Program(me), Prospectus, Résumé, Summary, Table, Timetable

Syllogism Argument, Conclusion, Deduction, Enthymeme, Epicheirema, Sorites

Sylph Ariel, Nymph

Symbol(s), Symbolic, Symbolism, Symbolist Acrophony, Agma, Algebra, Allegory, Ampersand, Aniconic, Ankh, Apostrophus, Aramanth, Asterisk, Badge, Cachet, Caduceus, Caret, Cedilla, Character, Charactery, Chord, Choropleth, Christogram, Cipher, Clef, Colon, Crest, Daffodil, Decadent, Del, Descriptor, Diesis, Dingbat, Double-axe, Eagle, Emblem, Emoticon, Eng, Equal, Fertility, Filfot, Fylfot, Grammalogue, Grapheme, Hash, Hashmark, Heitiki, Hieroglyph, Hierogram, Hiragana, Ichthus, Icon, Iconography, Ideogram, Index, Kalachakra, Kanji, Length mark, Lexigram, Logo(gram), Logograph, Mandala, Mark, Menorah, Metalanguage, Metaphor, Mezuzah, Minus, Mogen David, Moral, Motif, Mystical, Nabla, Neum(e), Nominal, Notation, Obelus, Om, Omega, One, Operator, Ouroborus, Paragraph, Pentacle, Phonetic, Phonogram, Phraseogram, Pi, Pictogram, Pictograph, Placeholder, Plus, Presa, Punctuation, Quantifier, Redon, Rose, Rune, Sacrament, Segno, Semicolon, Semiotic, Sex, Shadowy, Shamrock, Sigla, Sign, Slur, Smiley, Star of David, Status, Svastika, Swastika, Syllabary, Syllabogram, Synthetism, Tag, Talisman, Tetragrammaton, Thistle, Tiki, Tilde, Token, Totem, Trademark, Triskele, Triskelion, Type, Uraeus, Waymark, Weather, Wild card, Yoni

Symmetric(al), Symmetry Balance, Bilateral, Digonal, Diphycercal, Even, Harmony, Isobilateral, Mirror, Pseudocubic, Radial, Regular, Skew

Sympathetic, Sympathise(r), Sympathy Approval, Commiserate, Commiseration, Compassion, Condole(nce), Condone, Congenial, Crypto, Dear-dear, Empathy, Fellow-traveller, Humane, Mediagenic, Par, Pathos, Pity, Rapport, Ruth, Side, Understanding, Vicarious, Well-disposed

Symphony Clock, Concert, Drum-roll, Echo, Eroica, Farewell, Fifth, Horn-signal, Hunt, Jupiter, London, Manfred, Matin, Midi, Music, New World, Opus, Oxford, Pastoral, Queen, Sinfonia, Sinfonietta, Surprise, Unfinished

Symposium Assembly, Conference, Synod

Symptom(s) Epiphenomenon, Feature, Indicia, Merycism, Mimesis, Prodrome, Semiotic, Sign, Syndrome, Token, Trait, Withdrawal

Synagogue Beit Knesset, Beth Knesseth, Shul, Temple

Synchronise(r) Coincide, Genlock, Tune

Synclinal Basin

Syncopated, Syncopation, Syncope Abridged, Breakbeat, Revamp, Vasovagal, Zoppa, Zoppo

Syndicate Associate, Cartel, Combine, Mafioso, Pool, Ring, Stokvel

Syndrome Adams-Stokes, Asperger's, Carpal tunnel, Cerebellar, Characteristic, China, Chinese restaurant, Chronic fatigue, Compartment, Couvade, Cri du chat, Crush, Cushing's, De Clerambault's, Down's, Economy-class, Empty nest, Erotomania, False memory, Fetal alcohol, Fragile X, Goldenhar's, Gorlin, Guillain-Barré, Gulf War, Hughes, Hutchinson-Gilford, Irritable-bowel, Jerusalem, Klinefelter's, Korsakoff's, Locked-in, Long QT, Marfan, ME, Menières, Metabolic, Munch(h)ausen's, Nonne's, Overuse, Parkinson's, Pattern, POS, Postviral, Prader-Willi, Premenstrual, Proteus, Reiter's, Rett's, Reye's, SADS, SARS, Savant, Sezary, Sick building, SIDS, Sjogren's, Stevens-Johnson, Stockholm, Stokes-Adams, Sturge-Weber, Tall-poppy, Temperomandibular, TMJ, Total allergy, Tourette's, Toxic shock, Turner's, Wag the dog, Wernicke-Korsakoff, Williams, Wobbler, XYY

Synod Assembly, Conference, Convocation, General, Robber, Whitby

Synonym(ous) Comparison, Reciprocal
Synopsis Abstract, Blurb, Conspectus, Digest, Outline, Résumé, Schema,
→ **SUMMARY**
Syntax Grammar
Synthesis Amalgam, Aperture, Fusion, Merger
Synthesizer Moog®, Vocoder, Wind
Synthetic Empirical, Ersatz, Fake, False, Mock, Neoprene, Plastic, Polyamide,
Silicone, Spencerian
Syphilis Chancre, French pox, Lues, Pip, Pox
Syrian Aramaean, Aramaic, Druse, Druz(e), Hittite, Hurrian, Levantine, Phoenician
Syringe(s) Douche, Flutes, Harpoon, Hypo, Hypodermic, Needle, Reeds, Spray,
Squirt, Wash, Works
Syrphid Hoverfly
Syrup Capillaire, Cassareep, Cassis, Cocky's joy, Coquito, Corn, Diacodion,
Diacodium, Flattery, Glycerol, Golden, Goo, Grenadine, Linctus, Maple, Molasses,
Moskonfyt, Orgeat, Quiddany, Rob, Sorghum, Sugar, Treacle
System(s), Systematic ABO, Alpha, An mo, BACS, Beam, Bertillon, Binary, Black,
Bordereau, Braille, Carboniferous, Centauri, Circulatory, Code, Colloidal, Colonial,
Compander, Continental, Copernican, Cosmos, Course, Crystal, Cybernetics,
Decimal, Delsarte, Dewey (Decimal), Dianetics, Distributed, Dolby®, Early
warning, Economy, Eocene, Ergodic, Establishment, Expert, Feng Shui, Feudal,
Fixed, Folksonomy, Formal, Fourierism, Froebel, Front-end, Giorgi, Grading,
Harvard, Hexagonal, HLA, Honour, Hub and spoke, Iastic, I Ching, Immune,
Imprest, Imperial, Imputation, Induction loop, Inertial, ISA, Ism, Kalamazoo,
Kanban, Life-support, Limbic, Lobby, Long wall, Loop, Lymphatic, Madras,
Mercantile, Mereology, Merit, → **METHOD**, Metric, Microcosm, Midi, Minitel,
Miocene, MKSA, Movable, Muschelkalk, Natural, Navigational, Nervous, Network,
Nicam, Notation, Number, Octal, Operating, Order, Organon, Orphism, Orrery,
Panel, Periodic, Permian, Pleiocene, Plenum, Points, Process, Ptolemaic, Public
address, Purchase, Quota, Quote-driven, Raisonné, Regime, Regular, Respiratory,
Root, Run-time, Scheme, Scientific, Servo, Sexual, SI, Sofar, Solar, Solmisation,
Sonar, Sound, Spoils, Sprinkler, Squish lip, Stack(ing), Staff, Stand-alone,
Stanislavski, Star, Stakhanovism, Tactic,
Talk-down, Tally, Ternary, Theory, Third-rail, Tommy, Touch, Trias(sic), Truck,
Turnkey, Tutorial, Two-party, Universe, Unix, Urogenital, Vestibular, VOIP,
Warehousing, Water, Water vascular, Weapon

Tt

T Bone, Junction, Potence, Tango, Tau-cross, Tee, Time, Toc(k)

Tab Bill, Check, Decimal, → **LABEL**, Ring-pull, Slate, Stay-on, Tally, Trim, Trimming

Tabby Blabbermouth, Brindled, → **CAT**, Gossip, Mottled, Spinster, Striped, Trout

Tabitha Gazelle

Table(-like) Alphonsine, Altar, Board, Bradshaw, Breakfast, Calendar, Capstan, → **CHART**, Coffee, Communion, Console, Contingency, Corbel, Counter, Credence, Credenza, Cricket, Decision, Desk, Diagram, Dinner, Dissecting, Dolmen, Draw-leaf, Draw-top, Dressing, Drop-leaf, Drum, Ephemeris, Experience, Food, Gateleg, Gate-legged, Glacier, Graph, Green-cloth, Gueridon, High, Imposing, Index, Key, Ladder, League, Life, Light, → **LIST**, Log, Lord's, Lowboy, Mahogany, Matrix, Mensa(l), Mesa, Monopode, Mortality, Multiplication, Occasional, Operating, Orientation, Pembroke, Periodic, Piecrust, Pier, Plane, Platen, Pool, Prothesis, Pythagoras, Ready-reckoner, Reckoner, Refectory, Roll, Round, Rudolphine, Sand, Schedule, Scheme, Slab, Sofa, Spoon, Stall, Statistical, Stone, Taboret, Tabular, Tea, Te(a)poy, Throwing, Tide, Times, Toilet, Toning, Top, Traymobile, Trestle, Trolley, Truth, Twelve, Washstand, Water, Whirling, Wool, Workbench, Writing

Tableau Semantic

Tablecloth Damask, Linen

Table-land Barkly, Kar(r)oo, Mesa, Plateau, Puna

Table-list Memo, Menu

Tablet Abacus, Album, Aspirin, Caplet, Eugebine, Graphics, Hatch, Medallion, Opisthograph, Osculatory, Ostracon, Ostrakon, → **PAD**, → **PILL**, Pilule, Plaque, Slate, Stele, Stone, Tabula, Tombstone, Torah, Triglyph, Triptych, Troche, Trochisk, Ugarit, Votive

Table-talker Deipnosophist

Table-turner Tartar

Table-ware China, Cutlery, Silver

Taboo, Tabu Ban(ned), Bar, Blackball, Forbidden, Incest, Non dit, No-no, Unclean

Tachograph Spy-in-the-cab

Tacit, Taciturn(ity) Implicit, Laconic, Mumps, Oyster, Reticent, Silent, Understood

Tack(y) Bar, Baste, Beat, Boxhaul, Brass, Cheesy, Cinch, Clubhaul, Cobble, Gybe, Leg, Martingale, Nail, Saddlery, Salt-horse, → **SEW**, Sprig, Stirrup, Tailor's, Tasteless, Veer, Wear, White-seam, Yaw, Zigzag

Tackle Accost, Approach, Attempt, Beard, Bobstay, Burton, Cat, Chin, Claucht, Claught, Clevis, Clew-garnet, Collar, Dead-eye, Fishing, Garnet, Gear, Haliard, Halyard, Harness, Jury-rig, Nose, Rig, Rigging, Sack, Scrag, Spear, Straight-arm, Topping-lift, Undertake

Tact, Tactful Delicacy, Diplomacy, Diplomatic, Discreet, Discretion, Politic, Savoir-faire

Tactic(s) Audible, Finesse, Hardball, Manoeuvre, Masterstroke, Plan, Ploy, Ruse,

Salami, Scare, Shock, Smear, → **STRATEGY**, Strong-arm, Zwischenzug

Tactless(ness) Blundering, Brash, Crass, Gaffe, Gauche, Indelicate, Indiscreet, Loud mouth, Maladroit

Tadpole Ascidian, Polliwig, Polliwog, Pollywig, Pollywog, Porwiggle

Taffy Thief, Toffee, Welshman

Tag Aglet, Aiguillette, Cliché, Dog, Electronic, End, Epithet, → **FOLLOW**, Kabaddi, Kimball, Label, Meta, Price, Question, Quote, Remnant, Tab, Tail end, → **TICKET**, Treasury

Tail, Tailpiece, Tailboard All-flying, Amentum, Apocopate, → **APPENDAGE**, Bob, Brush, Caudal, Cercal, Cercus, Coda, Codetta, Colophon, Cue, Dock, Empennage, Endgate, Fan, Fee, Flag, Floccus, → **FOLLOW**, Fud, Liripoop, Parson's nose, Point, Pole, Pope's nose, PS, Queue, Rumple-bane, Scut, Seat, Shirt, Stag, Stern, Telson, → **TIP**, Train, Uro(some), Uropod, Uropygium, Women

Tailless Acaudal, An(o)urous, Fee-simple

Tail-lobes Anisocercal

▷ **Tailor** *may indicate* an anagram

Tailor(ed) Adapt, Bespoke, Bushel, Cabbager, Couturier, Cutter, Darzi, Draper, Durzi, Epicene, Feeble, Flint, Form, Merchant, Nine, Outfitter, Pick-the-louse, Pricklouse, Sartor, Seamster, Snip, Starveling, Style, Whipcat, Whipstitch

Taint(ed) Besmirch, Blemish, Fly-blown, Foughty, High, Infect, Leper, Off, Poison, → **SPOIL**, Stain, Stale, Stigma, Tinge, Trace, Unwholesome

Taiwan RC

Take(n), Take in, Taking(s), Take over, Takeover Absorb, → **ACCEPT**, Adopt, Assume, Attract, Bag, Beg, Bewitch, Bite, Bone, Borrow, Bottle, → **CAPTURE**, Catch, Charming, Claim, Cop, Coup, Detract, Dishy, Distrain, Entr(y)ism, Eat, Epris, Exact, Expropriate, Film, Get, Grab, Greenmail, Handle, Haul, Hent, House, Howe, Huff, Incept, Ingest, Leveraged buy out, Mess, Misappropriate, Nick, Occupy, On, Pocket, Quote, R, Rec, Receipt, Receive, Recipe, Reverse, Rob, Seise, Sequester, Ship, Smitten, Snatch, Sneak, → **STEAL**, Stomach, Subsume, Swallow, Sweet, Swipe, Toll, Trump, Turnover, Usher, Usurp, Wan, Winsome, Wrest

Take away, Take-away, Take off Aph(a)eresis, Asport, Carry-out, Deduct, Dock, Doff, Esloin, Exenterate, Expropriate, Indian, Jato, Minus, Parody, Parrot, Press-gang, Shanghai, Skit, Subtract, Vertical, VTO(L)

Take care Guard, See, Tend, Watch

▷ **Taken up** *may indicate* reversed

Take part Act, Engage, Side

Talbot House Toc H

Talc Potstone, Rensselaerite, Soapstone, Steatite, Venice

Tale(s) Aga-saga, Allegory, Anecdote, Blood, Boccaccio, Conte, Decameron, Edda, Fable, Fabliau, Fairy, Fairy story, Fiction, Folk, Gag, Geste, Hadith, Iliad, Jataka, Jeremiad, Legend, Lie, Mabinogion, Maise, Ma(i)ze, Märchen, Mease, Milesian, Narrative, Odyssey, Old wives', Pentameron, Rede, Saga, Sandabar, Score, Sinbad, Sind(a)bad, Sob-story, Spiel, → **STORY**, Tradition, Traveller's, Weird

Tale-bearer, Tale-teller Gossip, Grass, Informer, Sneak, Tattler, Tusitala

Talent(ed) Ability, Accomplishment, Aptitude, Bent, Budding, Dower, Faculty, Flair, Forte, Genius, Gift, Idiot savant, Ingenium, Knack, Long suit, Nous, Prodigy, Schtick, Strong point, Versatile, Virtuoso, W(h)iz(z), Whiz-kid

Talion Reprisal

Talisman Amulet, Charm, Mascot, Saladin, Sampo, Scarab, Telesm

Talk(ing), Talking point, Talker, Talks Address, Ana, Articulate, Babble, Bibble-babble, Blab, Blague, Blat, Blather, Blether-skate, Cant, Chalk, Chat,

Chinwag, Chirp, Circumlocution, Colloquy, Commune, Confabulate, Confer, Converse, Coo, Cross, Descant, Dialog(ue), Diatribe, Dilate, Discourse, Diseur, Dissert, Double, Earbash, Earful, Express, Fast, Filibuster, Froth, Gab, Gabble, Gabnash, Gas, Gibber, Gossip, Grandiloquence, Guff, Harp, High-level, Hobnob, Imparl, Jabber, Jargon, Jaw, Jazz, Korero, Lalage, Lalla, Lip, Logorrhoea, Macrology, Mang, Maunder, Mince, Monologue, Motormouth, Nashgab, Natter, Noise, Omniana, Palabra, Palaver, Parlance, Parley, Patter, Pawaw, Pep, Perorate, Phraser, Pidgin, Pillow, Pitch, Potter, Powwow, Prate, Prattle, Presentation, Prose, Proximity, Ramble, Rap, Rigmarole, Rote, Sales, SALT, Shop, Slang(-whang), Small, Soliloquy, → **SPEAK**, Spiel, Spout, Straight, Sweet, Table, Tachylogia, Topic, Turkey, Twaddle, Twitter, Unbosom, Up(s), Utter, Vocal, Waffle, Wibble, Witter, Wongi, Wrangle, Yabber, Yack, Yad(d)a-yad(d)a-yad(d)a, Yak, Yalta, Yammer, Yap, Yatter

Talkative Chatty, Fluent, Gabby, Garrulous, Gash, Glib, Loquacious, Vocular, Voluble

Tall Etiolated, Exaggerated, Far-fetched, Hie, High, Hye, Lanky, Lathy, Leggy, Lofty, Long, Order, Procerity, Randle-tree, Rantle-tree, Tangle, Taunt, Tower, Towery

Tallboy Chest, Dresser

Tallow Greaves, Hatchettite, Lead-arming, Mineral, Vegetable, Wax

Tally Accord, → **AGREE**, Census, Correspond, Count, Match, Nickstick, Notch, Record, → **SCORE**, Stick, Stock, Tab, Tag

Talmud Gemara, Mishna(h)

Talon Claw, Ogee, Single

Talus Scree

Tamarind Assam

Tamasha Fuss, To-do

Tame Amenage, Break, Docile, Domesticate, Lapdog, Mail, Mansuete, Meek, Mild, Safe, Snool, Subdue

Tammany Hall, Sachem

Tamp, Tampon Plug

Tamper(ing) Bishop, Cook, Doctor, Fake, Fiddle, Meddle, Medicate, Monkey, Nobble, Phreaking

Tam-tam Gong

Tan(ned), Tanned skin, Tanning Adust, Bablah, Babul, Bark, Basil, Beige, Bisque, Boarding, Bronze, → **BROWN**, Canaigre, Catechu, Furan, Furfuran(e), Insolate, Lambast, Leather, Neb-neb, Paste, Pipi, Puer, Pure, Spank, Sun, Sunbathe, Tenné, Umber, Val(l)onia, Ybet

Tandem Duo, Random

Tang Relish, Smack, Taste

Tangent Ratio, Slope, Touching

Tangible Concrete, Palpable, Plain, Solid, Tactual

Tangle Alga, Badderlock, Burble, Driftweed, Dulse, Embroil, Entwine, Fank, Fankle, Heap, Hole, Implication, Ket, → **KNOT**, Labyrinth, Laminaria, Lutin, Mat, Mess, Mix, Nest, Oarweed, Ore, Perplex, Pleach, Raffle, → **RAVEL**, Sea-girdle, Seaweed, Skean, Skein, Snarl, Taigle, Taut(it), Tawt, Thicket, Tousle, Varec

▷ **Tangled** *may indicate* an anagram

Tank(ed) Abrams, Alligator, Amphibian, Aquarium, Back boiler, Belly, Bosh, Casspir, Centurion, Cesspool, Challenger, Chieftain, Cistern, Crusader, Drop, Drunk, Feedhead, Fail, Float, Flotation, Fuel, Gasholder, Gasometer, Header, Keir, Kier, Mouse, Panzer, Pod, Quiescent, → **RESERVOIR**, Ripple, Sedimentation, Septic, Sherman, Shield pond, Sponson, Sump, Surge, Think, Tiger, Valentine, Vat, Venter, Ventral, Vivarium, Whippet

Tankard Blackjack, Peg, Pewter, Pot, Stein, Tappit-hen

Tanker Bowser, Lorry, Oiler

Tanner(y) Bender, Currier, Kick, Solarium, Sunbather, Sunshine, Tawery, Tester(n), 'Vld', Zack

Tannin Catechu

Tantalise Entice, Tease, Tempt, Torture

Tantalum Ta

Tantivy Alew, Halloo

Tantrum Hissyfit, Paddy, Pet, Rage, Scene, Snit, Tirrivee, Tirrivie

Tanzania EAT

Tap(ping), Taps Accolade, Bibcock, Blip, Bob, Broach, Bug, Cock, Col legno, Drum, Eavesdrop, Faucet, Fillip, Flick, Hack, Listen, Mag, Milk, Mixer, Monitor, Paracentesis, Pat, Patter, Percuss, Petcock, → **RAP**, Screw, Spigot, Spinal, Stopcock, Stroup, Tack, Tat, Tit, Touk, Tuck, Water

Tape Chrome, DAT, → **DRINK**, Duct, Ferret, Finish, Friction, Gaffer, Grip, Idiot, Incle, Inkle, Insulating, Magnetic, Masking, Measure, Metal, Narrowcast, Paper, Passe-partout, Perforated, Punched, Record, Red, Scotch, Sellotape®, Shape, Stay, Sticky, Ticker, Tit, Video, Welding

Taper(ed), Tapering Diminish, Fastigiate, Featheredge, Flagelliform, Fusiform, Lanceolate, Morse, Narrow, Nose, Subulate, Tail

Tapestry Alentous, Arras(ene), Aubusson, Bayeux, Bergamot, Crewel-work, Dosser, Gobelin, Hanging, Oudenarde, Petit point, Tapet, Weaving

Tapeworm Coenurus, Echinococcus, Hydatid, Measle, Scolex, Strobila, Taenia, Teniasis

Tapioca Cassava, Pearl, Yuca, Yucca

Tapir Anta, S(e)ladang

Tar, Tar product AB, Aniline, Bitumen, Carbazole, Coal, Creosote, Egg, Furan, Gas, Gladwellise, Gob, Indene, Maltha, Matelot, Matlo, Mineral, Naphtha, Needle, OS, Parcel, Pay, Picamar, Picene, Pine, Pitch, Rating, Retene, Sailor, Salt, Uintahite, Uintaite, Wood, Wood pitch, Wren, Xylol

Tardy Behindhand, Dilatory, Late, → **SLOW**

Tare Tine, Vetch

Target → **AIM**, Attainment, Blank, Butt, Clout, Cockshy, Dart, Drogue, End, Hit, Home, Hub, Inner, Magpie, Mark, Mark-white, Motty, → **OBJECT**, Outer, Peg, Pelta, Pin, Prey, Popinjay, Prick, Quintain, Sitter, Sitting, Tee, Victim, Wand, Zero in, Zero on

Tariff List, Menu, Preferential, Protective, Rate, Revenue, Zabeta

Tarnish Defile, Discolour, Soil, Stain, Sully, Taint

Taro Arum, Coc(c)o, Dasheen, Eddo

Tarot Arcana

Tarpaulin Weathercloth

Tarragon Staragen

Tarry Bide, Dally, Leng, → **LINGER**, Stay, Sticky

Tarsier Malmag

Tarsus Saul

Tart Acetic, Acid, Bakewell, Broad, Charlotte, Cheesecake, Cocotte, Croquante, Cupid, Custard, Dariole, Doxy, Duff, Flam(m), Flan, Flawn, Frock, Harlot, Hussy, Jade, Lemony, Mirliton, Moll, Mort, Nana, Painted woman, → **PIE**, Pinnace, Piquant, Pro, Quean, Quiche, Quine, → **SHARP**, Slag, Slapper, Slut, Snappy, Sour, Stew, Strumpet, Tatin, Tramp, Treacle, Trollop, Trull, Unsweet

Tartan Argyle, Argyll, Maud, Plaid, Set(t), Trews

Tartar Argal, Argol, Beeswing, Calculus, Crust, Hell, Plaque, Rough, Scale, Tam(b) erlane, Zenocrate

Tarzan Greystoke

Tashkent Uzbek

Task Assignment, Aufgabe, → **CHORE**, Clat, Duty, Errand, Exercise, Fag, Imposition, Legwork, Mission, Onus, Ordeal, Pensum, Stint, Thankless, Vulgus

Tasmania Apple Isle, Van Diemen's Land

Tassel Pompom, Toorie, Tourie, Tsutsith, Tuft

Taste(ful), Taster, Tasty Acquired, Aesthetic, Appetite, Degust, Delibate, Delicious, Discrimination, → **EAT**, Elegant, Fashion, Flavour, Form, Gout, Gust, Gustatory, Hint, Lekker, Lick, Palate, Penchant, Pica, Pree, Refinement, Relish, → **SAMPLE**, Sapor, Sar, Savour, S(c)hme(c)k, Sensation, Sip, Smack, Smatch, Smattering, Snack, Soupçon, Stomach, Succulent, Tang, Titbit, Toothsome, → **TRY**, Umami, Vertu, Virtu, Waft, Wine

Tasteless Appal, Brassy, Fade, Flat, Insipid, Insulse, Kitsch, Stale, Tacky, Vapid, Vulgar, Watery, Wearish, Wersh

Tat, Tatter, Tatty Flitter, Grot, Rag, Ribbon, Roon, Scrap, Shred, Tag, Ta(i)ver, Tan, Untidy

Tattie-bogle Scarecrow

Tattle(r) Blab, Chatter, Gash, → **GOSSIP**, Prate, Rumour, Sneak, Snitch, Totanus, Willet

Tattoo Devil's, Drum, Edinburgh, Moko, Rataplan, Row-dow, Tat

Tatum Art

Taught Up

Taunt Dig, Fling, Gibe, Gird, → **JEER**, Jest, Rag, Ridicule, Twight, Twit

Taut Stiff, Tense

Tavern Bar, Bodega, Bousing-ken, Bush, Fonda, → **INN**, Kiddleywink, Kneipe, Mermaid, Mitre, Mughouse, Night-house, Pothouse, Shebeen, Taphouse

Taw Alley, Ally, Marble

Tawdry Brash, Catchpenny, → **CHEAP**, Flashy, Gaudy, Gingerbread, Raffish, Sleazy, Tatty, Tinsey

Tawny Brindle, Dusky, Fawn, Fulvous, Mulatto, Port, Tan

Tawse Cat, Lash, Thong, Whip

Tax(ing), Taxation ACT, Agist, Aid, Alms-fee, Assess, Capitation, Carbon, Carucage, Cense, Cess, → **CHARGE**, Corporation, Council, Custom, Danegeld, Death duty, Deferred, Direct, Duty, Energy, EPT, Escot, Escuage, Eurotax, Exact, Excise, Exercise, EZT, Fat, Gabelle, Geld, Gift, Head, Head money, Hearth money, Hidage, Impose, Imposition, Impost, Impute, Indirect, Inheritance, IR, Jaghir(e), Jagir, Land, Levy, Likin, Lot, Murage, Negative, Octroi, Operose, Overwork, Pavage, PAYE, Peter-pence, Poll, Poundage, Precept, Primage, Property, Proportional, PT, Punish, Purchase, Rate, Regressive, Road, Rome-pence, Sales, Scat(t), Scot (and lot), Scutage, Sess, SET, Sin, Single, Skat, Stealth, Stent, Streetage, Stumpage, Super, Taille, Tallage, Talliate, Tariff, Tartan, Task, Teind, Tithe, Tobin, Toilsome, Toll, Tonnage, Tribute, Try, Turnover, Unitary, Value-added, VAT, Wattle, Wealth, Weary, White rent, Windfall, Window, Withholding, Zakat

Tax area Tahsil, Talooka, Taluk(a)

Tax-collector, Taxman Amildar, Cheater, Exciseman, Farmer, Gabeller, Ghostbuster, Inspector, IR(S), Publican, Stento(u)r, Tithe-proctor, Tollman, Undertaker, Vatman, Zemindar

Taxi(s) Cab, Gharri, Gharry, Hackney, Joe baxi, Minicab, Samlor, System, Zola Budd

Taxidermist Venus

Taxiway Peritrack
▶ **Taxman** *see* **TAX-COLLECTOR**
TB Scrofula
TE Lawrence, Ross, Shaw
Tea Afternoon, Assam, Beef, Black, Bohea, Brew, Brew-up, Brick, Bubble, Bush, Cambric, Camomile, Caper, Ceylon, Cha, Chai, Chamomile, Chanoyu, China, Chirping-cup, Congo(u), Cream, Cuppa, Darjeeling, Earl Grey, Grass, Green, Gunfire, Gunpowder, Herb(al), High, Hyson, Ice(d), Indian, Jasmine, K(h)at, Kitchen, Labrador, Lapsang, Lapsang Souchong, Leaves, Ledum, Lemon, Malt, Manuka, Marijuana, Maté, Mexican, Mint, Morning, Mountain, New Jersey, Oolong, Orange pekoe, Oulong, Paraguay, Pekoe, Post and rail, Pot, Qat, Red-root, Rooibos, Rosie Lee, Russian, Sage, Senna, Souchong, Stroupach, Stroupan, Switchel, Tay, Thea, Theophylline, Tousy, Twankay, Yerba (de Maté)
Teach(er), Teaching (material), Teachings Acharya, Adjoint, Advisory, Agrege, AMMA, Anthroposophy, Apostle, Aristotle, AUT, Barbe, Beale, BEd, Bhagwan, Buss, Catechist, Chalk and talk, Chalkface, → **COACH**, Con(ne), Didactic, Didascalic, Docent, Doctrine, Dogma, Dominie, Dressage, Edify, → **EDUCATE**, Educationalist, Edutainment, EIS, ELT, Explain, Faculty, Froebel, Gerund-grinder, Gooroo, Gospel, Governess, Guru, Head, Heuristic, Hodja, Inculcate, Indoctrinate, Inform, Instil, Instruct, Ism, Kho(d)ja, Kindergart(e)ner, Kumon (Method), Lair, Lancasterian, Larn, Lear(e), Lecturer, Leir, Lere, Maam, Maggid, Magister, Maharishi, Mahavira, Mallam, Marker, Marm, Master, Maulvi, Mentor, Message, Miss, Mistress, Molla(h), Monitor, Montessorian, Moola(h), Moolvi(e), Mufti, Mullah, Munshi, Mwalimu, Mystagogue, Nuffield, Paedotribe, Pedagogue, Pedant, Peripatetic, Phonic method, Posture-master, Pr(a)efect, Preceptor, Privat-docent, Proctor, Prof, Prog, PT, Pupil, Rabbetzin, Rabbi, Rav, Realia, Rebbe, Remedial, Rhetor, Scholastic, Schoolie, Schoolman, Scribe, Sensei, Show, Sir, Smriti, Socrates, Sophist, Staff, Starets, Staretz, Sunna, Supply, Swami, Tantra, Team, Tonic sol-fa, Train(er), Tutelage, Tutor, Tutress, Tutrix, Usher
Teach-in Seminar
Teahouse Sukiya
Teak African, Bastard, White
Teal Spring
Team Argyll, Bafana Bafana, Colts, Crew, Dream, Écurie, Eleven, Équipe, Farm, Fifteen, Outfit, Oxen, Panel, Possibles, Probables, Proto, Relay, Scrub, → **SIDE**, Span, Special, Spurs, Squad, Squadron, Staff, Syndicate, Tiger, Troupe, Turnout, Unicorn, United, XI
Tea-party Boston, Bunfight, Cookie-shine, Drum, Kettledrum, Shine
Teapot Billycan, Cadogan, Samovar
Tear(s), Tearable, Tearful, Tearing Beano, Claw, Crocodile, Divulsion, Drop, Eye-drop, Eye-water, Greeting, Hurry, Lacerate, Lachrymose, Laniary, Mammock, Pelt, Ranch, Rash, Reave, → **REND**, Rheum, Rip, Rive, Rume, Scag, Screed, Shred, Snag, Split, Spree, Tire, Waterworks, Wet, Worry, Wrench, Wrest
Tearaway Get, Hothead, Ned
Tear-jerker Melodrama, Onion
Tear-pit Crumen, Larmier
Tease, Teaser, Teasing Arch, Backcomb, Badinage, Bait, Banter, Card, Chaff, Chap, Chiack, Chip, Chyack, Cod, Coquet, Enigma, Grig, Guy, Hank, Imp, Ironic, Itch, Josh, Kemb, Kid, Mag, Mamaguy, Nark, Persiflage, → **RAG**, Raillery, Rally, Razz, Rib, Rip on, Rot, Strip, → **TANTALISE**, Toaze, Torment(or), Touse, Touze, Towse, Towze, Twilly, Twit, Worrit

Teasel Dipsacus, Valerian

Teat Dug, Dummy, Mamilla, Mastoid, Nipple, Pap, Soother, Tit

Tea-time Chat

Teaze Gig, Moze

Technetium Tc

Technical, Technician, Technique Adept, Alexander, Artisan, Brushwork, Campimetry, College, Cusum, Delphi, Execution, Foley artist, Footsteps editor, Harmolodics, Honey-trap, Junior, Kiwi, Know-how, Layback, Manner, Metamorphic, → **METHOD**, Operative, Phasing, Pixil(l)ation, Reflectography, Salami, Sandwich, Science, Senior, Serial, Split-screen, Stop-motion, Toe and heel

Technology, Technological High, Information, Intermediate, IT, Pull, Push, State of the art, Stealth

Ted(dy) Bodgie, Dexter, Ducktail, Moult, Widgie, Yob

Tedium, Tedious Boring, Chore, Deadly, Doldrums, Drag, Dreich, Dull, Ennui, Foozle, Heaviness, Langueur, Long, Longspun, Longueur, Monotony, Operose, Prosy, Soul-destroying, Tiresome, → **TIRING**, Twaddle, Wearisome, Yawn

Tee Hub, Umbrella, Wind

Teem(ing) Abound, Bustling, Empty, Great, Pullulate, Swarm

Teenager Adolescent, Bobbysoxer, Junior, Juvenile, Minor, Mod, Rocker, Sharpie, Skinhead, Youth

▶ **Teeth** *see* **TOOTH**

Teething ring Coral

Teetotal(ler) Abdar, Blue Ribbon, Nephalist, Rechabite, Temperate, TT, Water-drinker, Wowser

Tegument Seed coat

Telecommunications Cellnet®, Vodafone®

Telegram, Telegraph Bush, Cable, Ems, Facsimile, Fax, Grapevine, Greetings, International, Message, Moccasin, Mulga wire, Overseas, Quadruplex, Radiogram, Singing, Telautograph®, Telex, Wire

Telepathy, Telepathic Clairvoyance, ESP, Psychic, Seer

Telephone Ameche, ATLAS, Bell, Blower, BT, Call, Cellphone, Centrex, Cordless, Detectophone, Dial, Dog and bone, Freephone®, GRACE, Handset, Horn, Hotline, Intercom, Line, Lo-call®, Mercury, Mobile, Noki, Patchboard, Payphone, Pay-station, Pdq, → **PHONE**, POTS, Ring, Snitch line, Speakerphone, Squawk box, STD, Textphone, Tie line, Touch-tone, Utility, Vodafone®, Wire

Teleprinter Creed

Telescope Altazimuth, Astronomical, Binocle, Cassegrain(ian), Collimator, Comet finder, Coronagraph, Coronograph, Coudé, Electron, Equatorial, Finder, Galilean, Gemini, Glass, Gregorian, Heliometer, Hubble, Interferometer, Intussuscept, Meniscus, Newtonian, Night-glass, Optical, Palomar, Perspective, Radio, Reading, Reflecting, Reflector, Refractor, Schmidt, Shorten, Sniperscope, Snooperscope, Spyglass, Stadia, Terrestrial, Tube, X-ray, Zenith

Teletext® Ceefax®, Oracle®

Television, Telly Appointment, Box, Breakfast, Cable, Closed-circuit, Confessional, Digibox®, Digital, Diorama, Docu-soap, Event, Flatscreen, Goggle box, Image orthicon, Interactive, ITV, MAC, Narrowcast, PAL, Pay, Plumbicon®, Projection, RTE, Satellite, SECAM, Set, Small screen, Subscription, Tree and branch, Tube, → **TV**, Video

Tell(ing), Telltale Acquaint, Announce, Apprise, Archer, Beads, Blab, Break, Clipe, Clype, Compt, Direct, → **DISCLOSE**, Divulge, Effective, Grass, Impart, Influential, Inform, → **NARRATE**, Noise, Notify, Number, Recite, Recount, Relate, Report,

Retail, Rumour, Scunge, Sneak, Snitch, Spin, Teach, Unbosom, William

Tellurium Te

Temerity Cheek, Gall, Impertinence, Imprudence, Impudence, Incaution, Rashness, Recklessness

Temper, Temperate Abstemious, Abstinent, Allay, Anneal, Assuage, Attune, Balmy, Bate, Bile, Blood, Calm, Cantankerous, Choler, Comeddle, Continent, Dander, Delay, Ease, Fireworks, Flaky, Inure, Irish, Leaven, → **MILD**, Mitigate, Moderate, Modify, → **MOOD**, Neal, Paddy, Paddywhack, Pet, Radge, Rage, Season, Short fuse, Snit, Sober, Soften, Spitfire, Spleen, Strop, Swage, Tantrum, Techy, Teen, Teetotal, Tetchy, Tiff, Tone, Trim, Tune

Temperament(al) Bent, Blood, Choleric, Crasis, Cyclothymia, Disposition, Equal, Just, Kidney, Mean-tone, Melancholy, Mettle, Moody, → **NATURE**, Neel, Over-sensitive, Phlegmatic, Prima donna, Sanguine, Unstable, Viscerotonia

Temperance Good Templar, Moderation, Pledge, Rechabite

Temperature Absolute, Black body, Celsius, Centigrade, Chambré, Colour, Core, Critical, Curie, Dew point, Eutectic, Fahrenheit, Fever, Flashpoint, Heat, Heterothermal, Hyperthermia, Ignition, Kelvin, Melting, Néel, Permissive, Regulo, Restrictive, Room, Supercritical, T, Thermodynamic, Transition, Weed, Weid

Tempest(uous) Bourasque, Euraquilo, Euroclydon, Gale, High, Marie, → **STORM(Y)**, Wrathy

Temple, Temple gate Abu Simbal, Abydos, Adytum, Amphiprostyle, Artemis, Capitol, Cella, Chapel, Church, Delphi, Delubrum, Ephesus, Erechtheum, Erechthion, Fane, Gompa, Gurdwara, Haffet, Haffit, Heroon, Inner, Josshouse, Mandir(a), Masjid, Middle, Monopteron, Monopteros, Mosque, Museum, Naos, Nymphaeum, Pagod(a), Pantheon, Parthenon, Sacellum, Serapeum, → **SHRINE**, Shul(n), Teocalli, Teopan, Torii, Vihara, Wat

Tempo Agoge, Lento, Rate, → **RHYTHM**, Rubato

Temporal Petrosal, Petrous

Temporary Acting, Caretaker, Cutcha, Ephemeral, Fleeting, Hobjob, Impermanent, Interim, Jury-rigged, Kutcha, Lash-up, Locum, Makeshift, Pro tem, Provisional, Quick-fix, Short-term, Stopgap, Temp, Transient, Transitional

Temporise(r) Politique

Tempt(ation), Tempting, Tempter, Temptress Allure, Apple, Bait, Beguile, Beset, Circe, Dalilah, Dangle, Decoy, Delilah, → **ENTICE**, Eve, Groundbait, Impulse, Lure, Peccable, Providence, Satan, Seduce, Serpent, Siren, Snare, Tantalise, Test, Tice, Trial

Ten Commandments, Decad, Dectet, Decury, Denary, Googol, 10, Iota, Long, Tera-, Tribes, X

Tenacious, Tenacity Clayey, Determined, Dogged, Fast, Guts, Hold, Intransigent, Persevering, Persistent, Resolute, Retentive, Sticky

Tenancy, Tenant(s) Bordar, Censuarius, Cosherer, Cottar, Cottager, Cotter, Cottier, Dreng, Feuar, Feudatory, Gavelman, Homage, Ingo, Inhabit, Kindly, Leaseholder, Lessee, Liege, → **LODGER**, Metayer, Occupier, Pendicler, Periodic, Regulated, Rentaller, Renter, Secure, Shorthold, Sitting, Socager, Socman, Sokeman, Suckener, Tacksman, Valvassor, Vassal, Vavasour, Villein, Visit

Tend(ing) Apt, Care, Dress, Herd, Incline, Lean, Liable, Mind, Nurse, Prone, Run, Shepherd, Verge

Tendency Apt, Bent, Bias, Central, Conatus, Disposition, Drift, Genius, Idiosyncrasy, Import, Militant, Orientation, Penchant, Proclivity, Propensity, Trend

Tender(iser), Tenderly, Tenderness Affettuoso, Amoroso, Bid, Bill, Coin, Con amore, Crank, Dingey, Ding(h)y, Fond, Frail, Gentle, Green, Humane, Jolly-boat,

Legal, Nesh, Nurse, → **OFFER**, Painful, Papain, Pinnace, Pra(a)m, Prefer, Present, Proffer, Proposal, Quotation, Red Cross, Sair, Shepherd, → **SOFT**, Sore, SRN, Submit, Sweet, Sympathy, Tendre

Tenderfoot Babe, Chechacho, Chechako, Cub, Greenhorn, Innocent

Tenderloin Psoas, Undercut

Tendon Achilles, Aponeurosis, Hamstring, Kangaroo, Leader, Paxwax, Sinew, String, Vinculum, Whitleather

Tendril(led) Capreolate, Cirrose, Cirrus, Tentacle

Tenement(s) Dominant, Land, Rook, Rookery, Tack

Tenet Adiaphoron, Creed, → **DOCTRINE**, Dogma

Tenfold Decuple

Tennis Close, Court, Deck, Jeu de paume, Lawn, LTA, Real, Royal, Set, Short, Sphairistike, Squash, Table, Wimbledon

Tenon Cog, Dovetail, Lewis, Lewisson, Tusk

Tenor Caruso, Course, Domingo, → **DRIFT**, Effect, Ferreras, Gigli, Gist, Heroic, Pavarotti, Purport, Sense, Singer, T, Tide, Timbre, Trial, Vein

Tense Aor, Aorist, Case, Clench, Conditional, Drawn, Edgy, Electric, Essive, Flex, Fraught, Imperfect, Keyed up, Knife-edge, Mood(y), Nervy, Overstrung, Past, Perfect, Pluperfect, Preterit, Preterite, Rigid, Simple, Stiff, Strained, Stressed(-out), Strict, T, → **TAUT**, Tighten, Uptight

Tensing Sherpa

Tension Creative, High, Isometrics, Isotonic, Meniscus, Nerviness, Premenstrual, → **STRAIN**, Stress, Stretch, Surface, Tone, Tonicity, Tonus, Yips

Tent Bell, Bivvy, Cabana, Douar, Dowar, Duar, Ger, Gur, Kedar, Kibitka, Marquee, Oxygen, Pavilion, Probe, Pup, Red wine, Ridge, Shamiana(h), Shamiyanah, Shelter, Tabernacle, Teepee, Tepee, Tilt, Tipi, Top, Topek, Trailer, Tupek, Tupik, Wigwam, Wine, Y(o)urt

Tentacle Actinal, Cirrate, Feeler, Hectocotylus, Horn, Limb, Lophophore

Tentative Empirical, Experimental, Gingerly, Peirastic

Tent-dweller, Tent-maker Camper, Indian, Kedar, Omar, St Paul

Tenth Disme, Teind, Tithe

Ten Thousand Toman

Tenuous Frail, Slender, Slight, Thin, Vague

Tenure Blench, Burgage, Copyhold, Cottier(ism), Drengage, Fee, Fee-farm, Feu, Frankalmoi(g)n(e), Frank-fee, Gavelkind, Leasehold, Manorial, Occupation, Raiyatwari, Rundale, Runrig, Ryotwari, Socage, → **TERM**, Vavasory, Venville, Zemindar

Tepid Laodicean, Lew, Lukewarm

Terbium Tb

Terete Centric(al)

Term(s), Terminal, Termly Air, Anode, Buffer, Buzzword, Cathode, Coast, Container, Coste, Designate, Desinent(ial), Distal, Distributed, Dub, Dumb, Easy, → **EPITHET**, Euphemism, Expression, Final, Gnomon, Goal, Half, Hilary, Inkhorn, Intelligent, Law, Lent, Major, Michaelmas, Middle, Minor, → **PERIOD**, Point-of-sale, Rail(head), Real, Removal, Sabbatical, School, Semester, Session, Stint, Stretch, Trimester, Trimestrial, Trinity, Ultimatum, Waterloo, → **WORD**, Work station, Zeroth

Termagant Jade, Shrew, Shrow, Spitfire, Virago, Vixen

Terminate, Termination, Terminus Abolish, Abort, Axe, Cease, Conclude, Depot, Desinent, Earth, → **END**, Expiry, → **FINISH**, Goal, Liquidate, Naricorn, Railhead, Suffix

Termite Duck-ant
Tern Egg-bird, Scray, Three, Trio
Terpene Squalene
Terrace Barbette, Beach, Bench, Kop, Linch, Lynchet, Offset, Patio, Perron, River, Row house, Shelf, Stoep, Tarras, Undercliff, Veranda(h)
Terra-cotta Della-Robbia, Tanagra
Terrain Area, Landscape, Scablands, Tract
Terrapin Diamondback, Emydes, Emys, Slider, Turtle
Terrible, Terribly Appalling, Awful, Deadly, Dire, Fell, Fiendish, Frightful, Ghastly, Hellacious, Horrible, Humgruffi(a)n, Ivan, Much, Odious, Very
Terrible person Humgruffi(a)n, Ivan, Ogre
Terrier Aberdeen, Airedale, Apsos, Australian, Australian silky, Bedlington, Black and tan, Border, Boston, Bull, Catalogue, Cesky, Dandie Dinmont, Fox, Glen of Imaal, Griffon, Irish, Jack Russell, Kerry blue, Lakeland, Maltese, Manchester, Norfolk, Norwich, Pinscher, Pit bull, Ratter, Register, Schauzer, Scotch, Scottie, Scottish, Sealyham, Silky, Skye, Soft-coated wheaten, Staffordshire bull, Sydney silky, TA, Tibetan, Welsh, West Highland, West Highland white, Westie, Wire-haired, Yorkshire
Terrific, Terrified, Terrify(ing) Affright, Aghast, Agrise, Agrize, Agryze, Appal, Awe, Blood-curdling, Enorm, Fear, Fine, Fley, Gast, Helluva, Huge, Overawe, → PETRIFY, Scare, Superb, Unman, Yippee
Territory Abthane, Ap(p)anage, Colony, Domain, Dominion, Duchy, Emirate, Enclave, Exclave, Goa, Indian, Latium, Lebensraum, Mandated, Manor, Margravate, No-man's-land, Northern, Northwest, Nunavut, Palatinate, Panhandle, Papua, Petsamo, Principate, Protectorate, Province, Realm, → REGION, Rupert's Land, Scheduled, Sphere, Sultanate, Swazi, Ter(r), Trieste, Trust, Tuath, Union, Yukon
Terror(s) Blue funk, Bugaboo, Bugbear, Eek, → FEAR, Fright, Holy, Imp, Night, Panic, Skrik
Terrorism, Terrorist Alarmist, Al Fatah, Anarchist, Black Hand, Bogeyman, Bomber, Bully, Cagoulard, Consumer, Death squad, Desperado, Dynamitard, Eta, Grapo, Hijacker, Ku Klux Klan, Mau-mau, Maximalist, Mountain, Nightrider, Nihilist, OAS, Pirate, Player, PLO, Provo, Red Brigade, Robespierre, Ustashi
Terry Ellen, Towel
Terse Abrupt, Brusque, Curt, Laconic, Pithy, Precise, Succinct
Tertiary Cainozoic, Eocene, Miocene, Oligocene, Palaeogene, Pliocene
Tessellation Mosaic
Test(er), Testing Achievement, Acid, Alpha, Ames, Amniocentesis, Analyse, Apgar, Appro, Aptitude, Assay, Audition, Barany, Bench, Bender, Benedict, Beta, Bioassay, Blood, Breath, Breathalyser®, Brinell, Burn-in, Candle, Canopy, Check, Chi-square, Cis-trans, Cloze, Conn(er), Coomb's, Crash, Criterion, Crucial, Crucible, Crunch, Dick, Docimastic, Driving, Drop, Dummy-run, Éprouvette, Esda, Examine, Exercise, Experiment, Field, Flame, Frog, Hagberg, Ink-blot, Intelligence, International, Litmus, Mann-Whitney, Mantoux, Match, Mazzin, Means, Medical, Mom, MOT, Mug, Neckverse, Needs, Objective, Oral, Ordalian, → ORDEAL, Pale, Pap, Papanicolaou, Paraffin, Patch, Paternity, Performance, Personality, PH, Pilot, Pons asinorum, Pree, Preeve, Preif, Preve, Probative, Probe, Projective, Proof, Prove, Proving-ground, Pyx, Q-sort, Qualification, Quiz, Rally, Reagent, Reliability, Road, Rorschach, SAT, Scalogram, Scan, Schick's, Schilling, Schutz-Charlton, Scientise, Scratch, Screen, Shadow, Shibboleth, Showdown, Shroff, Sign, Signed-ranks, Significance, Sixpence, Skin, Slump, Smear, Smoke,

Snellen, Soap, Sound, Sounding, Spinal, Stanford-Binet, Stress, Tempt, Tensile, Tongue-twister, Touch, Touchstone, Trial, Trier, Trior, Try, Turing, Ultrasonic, Viva, Wassermann's, Weigh, Wilcoxon, Zack, Zohar

Testament Bible, Covenant, Hagographa, Heptateuch, Hexateuch, Hornolog(o)umena, Midrash, New, Old, Pentateuch, Scripture, Septuagint, Tanach, Targum, Will

Testicle(s) Ballocks, Balls, Bollix, Bollocks, Bush oyster, Cobblers, Cojones, Cruet, Doucets, Dowsets, Family jewels, Gool(e)y, Goolie, Knackers, Monkey-gland, Monorchid, Nads, Nuts, Orchis, Pills, Prairie oyster, Ridgel, Ridgil, Rig(gald), Rocks, Stone

Testify, Testimonial, Testimony Character, Chit, Declare, Depone, Deposition, → EVIDENCE, Rap, Scroll, Tribute, Viva voce, Vouch, Witness

Testy, Tetchy Cross, Narky, Peevish, Ratty

Tetanus Lockjaw

Tête-à-tête A quattr' occhi, Collogue, Confab, Hobnob, Twosome

Tether Cord, Endurance, Hitch, Knot, Lariat, Noose, Picket, Seal, Stringhalt, → TIE

Tetrahedrite Fahlerz, Fahlore

Tetrarchy Iturea

Tetrasyllabic Paeon

Tetrode Resnatron

Teuton(ic) Erl-king, German, Goth, Herren, Vandal

Texas Ranger

Text(s), Textbook, Texting ABC, Apocrypha, Body, Brahmana, Church, Codex, Donat, Ennage, Greeked, Harmony, Libretto, Mandaean, Mantra, Mezuzah, Minitel, Octapla, Op-cit, Philology, Plain, Proof, Pyramid, Quran, Responsa, Rubric, Script, S(h)astra, Shema, SMS, → SUBJECT, Sura, Sutra, Tefillin, Tephillin, Tetrapla, Thesis, Topic, Tripitaka, Typography, Upanis(h)ad, Urtext, Variorum, Viewdata, Vulgate, Zohar

Textile Cloth, Fabric, Mercy

Texture Constitution, Feel, Fiber, Fibre, Grain, Open, Set(t), Wale, Weave, Woof

Thai(land) Karen, Lao(s), Mon, Shan, Siam

Thalamus Optic

Thallium Tl

Thames Father, Tamesis

Than And

Thane Banquo, Ross

Thank(s), Thankful, Thanksgiving Appreciate, Collins, Deo gratias, Gloria, Grace, Gramercy, Grateful, Gratitude, Kaddish, Mercy, Roofer

Thankless Ingrate, Vain

That (is), That one As, Cestui, Das heisst, Dh, Exists, How, Id est, Ie, Ille, Namely, Que, Sc, Such, Thence, Thon(der), What, Which, Yon, Yonder, Yt

Thatch(er), Thatching At(t)ap, Daych, Hair, Heard, Hear(i)e, Hele, Hell, Lath, Mane, PM, Reed, Straw, Sway, Thack, Theek, Wig

Thaw Debacle, Defreeze, Defrost, Detente, Freeze, → MELT, Melt-water, Relax

▷ **Thaw** *may indicate* 'ice' to be removed from a word

The Der, Die, El, Il, La, Le, Los, T', That, Ye, Ze

Theatre(s), Theatrical(ity) Abbey, Absurd, Adelphi, Aldwych, Arena, Balcony, Broadway, Camp, Cinema, Circle, Coliseum, Criterion, Crucible, Drama, Drury Lane, Epic, Event, Everyman, Field, Fourth-wall, Fringe, Gaff, Gaiety, Globe, Grand Guignol, Great White Way, Hall, Haymarket, Hippodrome, Histrionic, House, Kabuki, La Scala, Legitimate, Little, Living, Lyceum, Melodramatic, Mermaid,

Music-hall, National, News, Nickelodeon, Noh, Odeon, Odeum, Off-Broadway, Off-off-Broadway, Old Vic, Operating, OUDS, Palladium, Panache, Pennygaff, Pit, Playhouse, Political, Rep(ertory), Sadler's Wells, Shaftesbury, Sheldonian, Shop, Stage, Stalls, Stoll, Straw-hat, Street, Summer stock, Total, Touring, Vic, Windmill, Zarzuela

Theatregoer Circle, Gallery, Gods, Pit, Pittite, Stalls

Theft, Thieving Appropriation, Bluesnarfing, Burglary, Heist, Identity, Kinchinlay, Larceny, Maino(u)r, Manner, Petty larceny, Pilfery, Plagiarism, Plunder, Pugging, Ram-raid, Rip off, Robbery, Stealth, Stouth(rief), → **THIEF**, Touch, TWOC, Walk-in

Their Her

Theist Believer, Unitarian

Them 'Em, Hem, Tho

Theme Burden, Crab canon, Donnée, Fugue, Idea, Leitmotiv, Lemma, Lemmata, → **MELODY**, Motif, Mythos, Mythus, Peg, Question, → **SUBJECT**, Subtext, Text, Topic, Topos

Then(ce) Already, Away, Next, Since, Sine, So, Syne, Thereupon, Tho

▷ **The northern** *may indicate* t'

Theodolite Diopter, Dioptre, Groma, Tacheometer, Tachymeter, Transit

Theologian, Theologist, Theology Abelard, Aquinas, Arminius, Barth, Calvin, Christology, Colet, DD, Divine, Eckhart, Erastus, Eschatology, Eusebius, Exegetics, Fideism, Genevan, Hase, Infralapsarian, Irenics, Jansen, Kierkegaard, Knox, Liberation, Luther, Moral, Mullah, Natural, Newman, Niebuhr, Origen, Paley, Pastoral, Pectoral, Pelagius, Peritus, Pusey, Rabbi, Religious, Sacramentarian, Schoolman, Schwenkfeld, Scotus, Softa, STP, Supralapsarian, Swedenborg, Tertullian, Thomas à Kempis, Ulema, Universalist

Theory, Theorem, Theoretical, Theorist Academic, Atomic, Attachment, Attribution, Automata, Band, Bayes(ian), Bernouilli's, Big bang, Binomial, Bohr, Boo-hurrah, Calorific, Catastrophe, Chaos, Communications, Complexity, Connectionism, Conspiracy, Corpuscular, Creationism, Darwinian, Decision, Deduction, Dependency, Dictum, Doctrinaire, Domino, Double aspect, Dow, Einstein, Emboîtement, Empiricism, Epigenesist, Euhemerism, Exponential, Fermat's (last), Fortuitism, Gaia, Galois, Game, Gauge, Germ, Gödel's, Grand Unified, Grotian, Group, Guess, Holism, Hormic, Hypothesis, Ideal, Identity, Ideology, Information, Ism(y), James-Lange, Kinetic, Koch's, Laingian, Lamarckism, Lemma, Lunar, MAD, Milankovitch, Model, Monism, Mythical, Neovitalism, Nernst heat, Notion, Number, Object relations, Perturbation, Petrinism, Pluralism, Poynting, Probability, Proof, Pure, Pythagoras, Quantity, Quantum, Queueing, Random walk, Reception, Relativism, Relativity, Satisfaction, Set, Solipsism, Speculative, Steady state, String, Superdense, Superstring, Supersymmetry, System, Tachyon, TOE, Traducianism, Twistor, Tychism, Utilitarianism, Voluntarism, Vortex, Vulcanist, Wages fund, Wasm, Wave, Wholism, Wolfian

Therapy, Therapeutic, Therapist Acupressure, Acupuncture, Analyst, Art, Aura-Soma, Auricular, Aversion, Behaviour, Bowen, Brachytherapy, Cellular, Chavuttithirumal, Chelation, Chemotherapy, Client-centred, Cognitive, Cognitive-behavioural, Colour, Combination, Craniosacral, Crystal (healing), CST, Curative, Curietherapy, Deep, Dianetics, Drama, ECT, Electric shock, Electroconvulsive, Electroshock, Electrotherapy, Family, Faradism, Fever, Flotation, Gate control, Gemstone, Gene, Germ(-line), Gerson, Gestalt, Group, Heliotherapy, Hellerwork, HRT, Hypnosis, Immunotherapy, Implosive, Insight, Larval, Light, Live cell, Logop(a)edics, Looyenwork, Magnetic, Metamorphic technique, Minimal

invasive, MLD, Movement, Music, Narco, Narcotherapy, Natal, Natural, Non
directive, Occupational, ORT, Osteopathy, Past life, Pattern, Physical,
Phytotherapy, Polarity, Pressure, Primal, Primal (scream), Psychodrama,
Psychosynthesis, Radiation, Radio, Radium, Rainbow, Reflexology, Regression,
Reichian, Reiki, Relaxation, Retail, Rogerian, Rolfing, Röntgenotherapy,
Root-canal, Sanatory, Scientology®, Scream, Serum, Sex, SHEN, Shiatsu,
Shiatzu, Shock, Sitz-bath, Sound, Speech, Speleotherapy, Supportive, TENS,
Thalassotherapy, Theriacal, Thermotherapy, Touch, → **TREATMENT**, Water cure,
X-ray, Zone

There(after), Thereby, Thereupon Attending, Holla, Ipso facto, Present, Thither,
Thon, Upon, With that, Y, Yonder

Therefore Argal, Ergo, Forthy, Hence, So, Why

Thermodynamic Enthalpy, Entropy

Thermometer Aethrioscope, Centesimal, Clinical, Cryometer, Gas, Glass,
Katathermometer, Maximum and minimum, Psychrometer, Pyrometer,
Resistance, Thermograph, Water, Wet and dry bulb, Wet bulb

Thermoplastic Cel(luloid), Resin

Thesaurus Dictionary, Lexicon, Roget, Treasury, Word-finder

These Thir

Theseus Champion

Thesis Argument, Dissertation, Doctorial, Theme

Thespian → **ACTOR**, Ham, Performer

Thessalonian Lapith

They A

Thick(en), Thickening, Thickener, Thickness, Thickset Abundant, Algin,
Burly, Bushy, Callosity, Callus, Clavate, Cloddy, Cruddle, Curdle, Dense, Dextrin(e),
Dumose, Engross, Grist, Grouty, Grume, Guar, Gum, Hyperostosis, Incrassate,
Inspissate, Kuzu, Liaison, Lush, Nuggety, Pally, Panada, Reduce, Roux, Sclerosis,
→ **SOLID**, Soupy, Squat, Stumpy, → **STUPID**, Thieves, This, Thixotropic, Waulk,
Wooden, Xantham

Thick-coated Atheromatous

Thicket Bosk, Brake, Brush, Cane-brake, Chamisal, Chapparal, Coppice, Copse,
Dead-finish, Fernshaw, Greve, Grove, Macchia, Maquis, Queach, Reedrand,
Reedrond, Salicetum, Shola

Thick-lipped Labrose

Thick-skinned Armadillo, Callous, Pachyderm, Tough

Thief, Thieves, Thievish Abactor, Area sneak, Autolycus, Blood, Bulker, Chummy,
Coon, Corsair, Cutpurse, Dismas, Dysmas, Filcher, Flood, Footpad, Freebooter,
Furacious, Ganef, Gestas, Gully-raker, Heist, Hotter, Huaquero, Ice-man, Jackdaw,
Kiddy, Kondo, Larcener, Lifter, Light-fingered, Limmer, Looter, Mag, Montith,
Nip(per), Nuthook, Pad, Peculator, Pickpocket, Pilferer, Pirate, Plagiarist, Poacher,
Poddy-dodger, Prig, Raffles, River-rat, → **ROBBER**, Rustler, St Nicholas's clerks,
Shark, Shop-lifter, Sneak, Snowdropper, Sticky fingers, Taffy, Tarry-fingered, Taker,
Tea-leaf, Thick, Twoccer

Thigh Femoral, Gaskin, Ham, Haunch, Hock, Meros

Thin(ner), Thinness Acetone, Atomy, Attenuate, Bald, Beanpole, Bony, Cornstalk,
Cull, Diluent, Dilute, Ectomorph, Emaciated, Enseam, Fine, Fine-drawn, Flimsy,
Gaunt, Hairline, Hair('s-)breadth, Inseam, Lanky, Lean, Matchstick, Mawger, Puny,
Rackabones, Rangy, Rare, Rarefied, Reedy, Scant, Scraggy, Scrannel, Scrawny,
Sheer, Sieve, Skeletal, Skimpy, Skinking, Slender, Slim, Slimline, Slink, → **SPARE**,
Sparse, Spindly, Stilty, Stringy, Subtle, Taper, Tenuous, Threadbare, Turps, Wafer,

Washy, Waste, Watch, Water(y), → **WEAK**, Weedy, Whirtle, Wiry, Wispy, Wortle, Wraith

Thing(s) Alia, Article, Chattel, Chose, Craze, Doodah, Doofer, Entia, Fetish, First, Fixation, It, Item, Jingbang, Job, Last, Material, Matter, Near, Noumenon, → **OBJECT**, Obsession, Paraphernalia, Phobia, Res, Tool, Vision, Whatnot

Thingumabob, Thingummy Dingbat, Dinges, Doodad, Doodah, Doofer, Doohickey, Gubbins, Hoot(a)nanny, Hootenanny, Jigamaree, Oojamaflip, Whatsit, Yoke

Think(er), Thinking Associate, Believe, Brain, Brood, Casuistry, Cogitate, Cognition, Conjecture, Consider, Contemplant, → **CONTEMPLATE**, Deem, Deliberate, Descartes, Dianoetic, Divergent, Esteem, Fancy, Fear, Feel, Fogramite, Ghesse, Gnostic, Guess, Hegel, Hold, → **IMAGINE**, Judge, Lateral, Meditate, Mentation, Mindset, Mull, Muse, Opine, Pensive, Philosopher, Phrontistery, Ponder, Pore, Presume, Ratiocinate, Rational, Reckon, Reflect, Reminisce, Ruminate, Synectics, Trow, Vertical, Ween, Wishful

Thin-skinned Sensitive

Third, Third rate Bronze, C, Eroica, Gamma, Gooseberry, Interval, Major, Mediant, Minor, Picardy, Quartan, Tertiary, Tertius, Tierce, Trisect

Third man Abel, Lime

Thirst(y) Adry, → **CRAVE**, Dives, Drought, Drouth, Dry, Hydropic, Nadors, Pant, Polydipsia, Thrist

Thirteen Baker's dozen, Devil's dozen, Long dozen, Riddle, Triskaidekaphobia, Unlucky

Thirty Lambda

Thirty nine books All-OT, OT

This Hic, Hoc, The, Thick, Thilk, Thir

Thistle Canada, Carduus, Carline, Cnicus, Creeping, Dayshell, Echinops, Milk, Musk, Rauriki, Russian, Safflower, Scotch, Sow, Spear, Star, Thrissel, Thristle

This year Ha

Thomas Aquinas, Arnold, Christadelphian, De Quincey, Didymus, Doubting, Dylan, Erastus, Hardy, Loco, Parr, Rhymer, Tompion, True, Turbulent

Thomas Aquinas Angelic Doctor

Thong Babiche, Jandal®, Lash, Latchet, Leather, Lore, Riem, Riempie, Shoe-latchet, → **STRAP**, Strop, Taws(e), Whang, Whip

Thor Thunderer

Thorax Chest, Peraeon, Pereion, Scutellum, Throat

Thorium Th

Thorn(y) Acantha, Aculeus, Bael, Bel, Bhel, Bramble, Briar, Coyotillo, Doom, Edh, Eth, Irritation, Jerusalem, Jew's, Mahonia, Mayflower, Nabk, Nebbuk, Nebe(c)k, → **NEEDLE**, Paloverde, Pricker, Prickle, Slae, Spine, Spinescent, Spinulate, Trial, Wagn'bietjie, Y, Ye, Zare(e)ba, Zariba, Zeriba

Thorn-apple Jimpson-weed

Thornless Inerm

Thorough(ly) À fond, Complete, Deep, Even-down, Firm, Fully, Ingrained, Inly, Out, Out and out, Painstaking, Pakka, Pucka, Pukka, Radical, Ripe, Root and branch, Searching, Sound, Strict, Total, Tout à fait, Up

Thoroughbred Arab, Bloodstock, Pedigree, Post-vintage

Thoroughfare Avenue, Broadway, Causeway, Freeway, Highway, Parkway, → **ROAD**, Street

Those Thae, Thaim, Them, Tho, Yon

Thou M, Mil

Though Albe, Albeit, All-be, Ever, Tho, Whenas

Thought(s), Thoughtful(ness) Avisandum, Broody, Censed, Cerebration, Cogitation, Concept, Considerate, Contemplation, Dianoetic, Felt, Idea, Indrawn, Innate, Kind, Maieutic, Mind, Musing, Notion, Opinion, Pansy, Pensée, Pensive, Philosophy, Reason, Reflection, Rumination, Second

Thoughtless Blindfold, Careless, Heedless, Improvident, Incogitant, Inconsiderate, Pillock, → **RASH**, Reckless, Reflexive, Remiss, Scatter-brained, Vacant, Vain

Thousand(s) Chiliad, Gorilla, K, Lac, Lakh, M, Millenary, Millennium, Myriad, Octillion, Plum, Sextillion, Toman

Thracian Spartacus

Thrall Captive, Esne, Serf, Slave

Thrash(ing) → **BEAT**, Belabour, Belt, Bepelt, Binge, Bless, Cane, Dress, Drub, Flail, Flog, Jole, Joll, Joule, Jowl, Lace, Laidie, Laidy, Lambast, Larrup, Lather, Leather, Lick, Marmelise, Onceover, Paste, Ploat, Quilt, Slog, Smoke, Strap-oil, Swaddle, Swat, Tank, Targe, Thraiping, Towel, Trim, Trounce, Wallop, Whale, Whap, Writhe, Work over

Thread, Threadlike Acme screw, Ariadne, Bar, Bottom, Bride, Buttress, Chalaza, Chromatid, Chromatin, Chromosome, Clew, Clue, Cop(pin), Cord, Coventry blue, Eel-worm, End, Female, Fibre, Filament, File, Filiform, Filose, Filoselle, Float, Flourishing, Gist, Gold, Gossamer, Heddle, Ixtle, Lace, Lap, Lingel, Lingle, Link, Lisle, Lurex®, Male, Meander, Mycellum, Nematode, Nematoid, Organzine, Pack, Pearlin(g), Pick, Plasmodesm, Ravel, Reeve, Sacred, Screw, Sellers screw, Seton, Shoot, Silver, Single, Spider line, Spireme, Stamen, → **STRAND**, Stroma, Suture, Tassel, Tendril, Theme, Thrid, Thrum, Trace, Tram, Trundle, Tussore, Twine, Two-start, Warp, Watap, Wax(ed), Weft, Whitworth, Whitworth screw, Wick, → **WIND**, Wisp, Worm

Threadbare Hackneyed, Motheaten, Napless, Shabby, Worn

Threadworm Nemathelminth, Strongyl, Vinegar-eel

Threat(en), Threatened, Threatening Baleful, Black(en), Blackmail, Bluster, Brew, Brutum fulmen, Coerce, Comminate, Face, Fatwa, Fraught, Greenmail, Greymail, Hazard, Impend, Imperil, Loom, → **MENACE**, Minacious, Minatory, Mint, Omen, Ominous, Overcast, Overhang, Parlous, Peril, Portent, Ramp, Sabre-rattling, Shore, Strongarm, Ugly, Veiled, Warning

Three, Threefold, Three-wheeler, Thrice Graces, Har, Harpies, Jafenhar, Leash, Muses, Musketeers, Pairial, Pair-royal, Parial, Prial, Ter, Tern, Terzetta, Thrice, Thridi, Tid, T.i.d, Tierce, Tray, Trey, Triad, Trial, Tricar, Triennial, Trifid, Trigon, Trilogy, Trinal, Trine, Trinity, Trio, Triple, Triptote, Troika

Three-D(imensional) Cinerama, Lenticular, Stereopsis

Three-day Triduan, Triduum

Threehalfpence Dandiprat, Dandyprat

Three-handed Cutthroat

Three-headed Cerberus, Geryon

Three hundred B, Carpet

Three-legged IOM, Triskele, Triskelion

Threepence, Threepenny bit Tickey, Tray, Trey, Treybit

Three-quarter Wing

Three-year old Staggard

Threnody Dirge, Epicede, → **LAMENT**

Thresh Beat, Flail, Separate

Threshold Absolute, Brink, Cill, Difference, Doorstep, Limen, Liminal, Nuclear, Sill, Tax, Verge

▶ **Thrice** *see* **THREE**

Thrift(y) Economy, Frugal, Husbandry, Oeconomy, Sea-grass, Sea-pink, Virtue, Wary

Thrill(er), Thrilling Atingle, Buzz, Delight, Dindle, Dinnle, Dirl, Dread, Dynamite, Emotive, → **ENCHANT**, Enliven, Excite, Film noir, Frisson, Gas, Jag, Kick, Page-turner, Perceant, Plangent, Pulsate, Pulse, Quiver, Sensation, Thirl, Tinglish, Tremor, Vibrant, Whodunit, Wow

Thrive Batten, Blossom, Boom, Do, Fl, → **FLOURISH**, Flower, Grow, Mushroom, → **PROSPER**, Succeed, Thee

Throat(y) Craw, Crop, Deep, Dewlap, Fauces, Gorge, Gular, Gullet, Guttural, Hot coppers, Jugular, Laryngeal, Maw, Pereion, Pharynx, Prunella, Quailpipe, Red lane, Roopit, Roopy, Strep, Swallet, Thrapple, Thropple, Throttle, Weasand, Wesand, Whistle, Windpipe

Throb(bing) Beat, Palpitate, Pant, Pit-a-pat, Pound, Pulsate, Quop, Stang, Tingle, Vibrato

▷ **Throbbing** *may indicate* an anagram

Throe(s) Agony, Pang, Paroxysm

Thrombosis Deep-vein

Throne Bed-of-justice, Cathedra, Episcopal, Gadi, → **LAVATORY**, Mercy-seat, Peacock, Rule, Seat, See, Siege, Tribune

Throng(ing) Crowd, Flock, Host, Press, Resort, Swarm

Throttle → **CHOKE**, Gar(r)otte, Gun, Mug, Regulator, Scrag, Silence, Stifle, Strangle, Strangulate, Thrapple, We(a)sand

Through, Throughout Along, Ana, By, Dia-, During, Everywhere, Over, Passim, Per, Pr, Sempre, Sic passim, To, Trans, Via, Yont

▶ **Throw(n)** *see* TOSS

Throw (up), Thrower, Throw-out Bin, Cast-off, Chunder, Discobolus, Egesta, Emesis, Estrapade, Flying mare, Go, Jettison, Pash, Puke, Spew, Squirt, Squit, → **TOSS**

Throwback Atavism, Echo

Thrush Ant, Aphtha, Bird, Chat, Fieldfare, Hermit, Homescreetch, Mavis, Missel, Mistle, Olive-back, Pitta, Prunella, Redwing, Sprue, Turdine, Veery

Thrust, Thruster Abdominal, Aventre, Bear, Boost, Botte, Burn, Burpee, Detrude, Dig, Drive, Elbow, Exert, Extrude, Flanconade, Foin, → **FORCE**, Gist, Hay, Imbroc(c)ata, Impulse, Job, Lunge, Montant(o), Muscle, Obtrude, Oust, Pass, Passado, Peg, Perk, Pitchfork, Poach, Poke, Potch(e), Pote, Probe, Prog, Propel, Pun, Punto, → **PUSH**, Put, Ram, Remise, Repost, Run, Shoulder, Shove, Single-stock, Sock, Sorn, Squat, Stap, Stick, Stoccado, Stoccata, Stock, Stuck, Thrutch, Tilt, Tuck, Venue

Thud Drum, Dump, Flump, Phut, Plod, Thump, Whump

Thug(s) Brute, Gangster, Goon(da), Gorilla, Gurrier, Hoodlum, Keelie, Loord, Ninja, Ockers, Phansigar, Plug-ugly, Roughneck, SS, Strangler, Ted, Tityre-tu, Tsotsi, Yahoo

Thule Ultima

Thulium Tm

Thumb Bally, Green, Hitch, Midget, Ovolo, Pollex, Scan, Sore, Tom

Thump(ing) Blow, Bonk, Clobber, Cob, Crump, Da(u)d, Dawd, Ding, Dod, Drub, Dub, Hammer, Knevell, Knock, Lamp, Nevel, Oner, Paik, → **POUND**, Pummel, Slam, Slosh, Souse, Swat, Swingeing, Thud, Trounce, Tund, Whud

Thunder(ing), Thunderstorm Astrophobia, Bolt, Boom, Clap, Coup de foudre, Donnerwetter, Foudroyant, Foulder, Fulminate, Intonate, Lei-king, Pil(l)an, Raiden, → **ROAR**, Rumble, Summanus, Tempest, Thor, Tonant

Thursday Chare, Holy, Maundy, Sheer, Shere

Thus Ergo, Sic, So, Therefore

Thwart Baffle, Balk, → **CROSS**, Dash, Dish, Foil, Frustrate, Hamstring, Hogtie, Obstruct, Outwit, Pip, Prevent, Scotch, Snooker, Spike, Spite, Stonker, Stymie, Transverse

Thy Yourn

Thyme Basil, Lemon, Water

Thyroid Goitre, Myxodema

Tiara Cidaris, Crownet, Triple crown

Tiberius Gracchus

Tibetan Lamaist, Naga, Sherpa, Sitsang

Tic Vocal

Tick, Tick off Acarida, Acarus, Beat, Bloodsucker, Check, → **CHIDE**, Click, Cr, → **CREDIT**, Deer, HP, Idle, Instant, Jar, Ked, Mattress, Mile, Mo, Moment, Ricinulei, Second, Sheep, Soft, Strap, Worm

Ticket(s) Billet, Bone, Brief, Carnet, Commutation, Complimentary, Coupon, Day, Docket, Dream, E(lectronic), Excursion, Hot, Kangaroo, Label, Meal, One-day, One-way, Open-jaw, Parking, Pass, Pass-out, Pasteboard, Pawn, Platform, Raffle, Raincheck, Return, Round-trip, Rover, Saver, Scratchcard, Season, Single, Soup, Split, Straight, Stub, Supersaver, → **TAG**, Tempest, Tessera(l), Through, Tix, Transfer, Tyburn, Unity, Voucher, Walking, Zone

Ticket-seller Scalper

Tickle, Ticklish Amuse, Delicate, Divert, Excite, Gratify, Gump, → **ITCH**, Kittle, Queasy, Thrill, Titillate

Tiddler Brit, Tom

Tide, Tidal Current, Drift, Eagre, Easter, Eger, Estuary, Flood, High, High water, Lee, Low, Marigram, Neap, Red, Rising, River, Roost, Sea, Seiche, Slack water, Spring, Surge, Trend, Wave

Tide-gate Aboideau, Aboiteau, Weir

Tidings Gospel, → **NEWS**, Rumour, Word

Tidy Big, Comb, Considerable, Curry, Do, Fair, Fettle, Groom, Kempt, Large, Neat, Neaten, → **ORDER**, Pachyderm, Predy, Preen, Primp, Red(d), Slick, Snug, Sort, Spruce, Trim, Valet

Tie, Tied, Tying Ascot, Attach, Barcelona, Berth, Bind, Black, Bolo, → **BOND**, Bootlace, Bow, Bowyang, Cable, Cope, Cravat, Cup, Dead-heat, Drag, Draw, Fetter, Four-in-hand, Frap, Halter, Handicap, Harness, Hitch, Holdfast, Kipper, → **KNOT**, Lace, Lash, Level, Ligament, Ligate, Ligature, Link, Marry, Match, Moor, Neck and neck, Oblige, Obstriction, Old School, Oop, Oup, Overlay, Raffia, Restrain, Rod, Scarf, School, Score draw, Scrunchie, Semifinal, Shackle, Sheave, Shoelace, Shoestring, Sleeper, Slur, Solitaire, Soubise, Splice, Stake, Strap, String, Tawdry-lace, Tether, Together, Trice, Truss, Unite, White, Windsor

Tier Apron, Bank, Gradin(e), Knotter, Layer, Range, Rank, Stage, Storey

Tierce Leash, Tc

Tiff Bicker, Contretemps, Difference, Dispute, Exchange, Feed, Feud, Huff, Miff, Skirmish, Spat, Squabble

Tiffany Gauze

Tiger Bengal, → **CAT**, Clemenceau, Demoiselle, Lily, Machairodont, Machairodus, Man-eater, Margay, Paper, Sabre-tooth, Smilodon, Stripes, Tamil, Tasmanian, Woods

Tight(en), Tightness, Tights Boozy, Bosky, Brace, Cinch, Close(-hauled), Constriction, Cote-hardie, → **DRUNK**, Fishnet, Fleshings, High, Hose, Jam,

Leggings, Leotards, Lit, Loaded, Maillot, Mean, Merry, Niggardly, Oiled, Pang, Pantihose, Phimosis, Pickled, Pinch(penny), Plastered, Prompt, Proof, Rigour, Snug, Squiffy, Stenosis, → **STINGY**, Stinko, Strict, Stringent, Swift, Swig, Taut, Tense, Tipsy, Trig, Woozy

Tight-lipped Shtum

Tightrope(-walker) Aerialist, Blondin, Equilibrist, Funambulist, Petauriste

Tightwad Cheapskate, → **MISER**, Scrooge

Tile(s), Tiled Antefix, Arris, Azulejo, Carpet, Chapeau, Dalle, Derby, Dutch, Encaustic, Field, → **HAT**, Imbrex, Imbricate, Lid, Lino, Mahjong(g), Ostracon, Ostrakon, Peever, Quarrel, Quarry, Rag(g), Ridge, Rooftop, Sclate, Shingle, Slat, → **SLATE**, Tegular, Tessella, Tessera, Titfer, Topper, Wall, Wally

Till Cashbox, Checkout, Coffer, Ear, Eulenspiegel, Farm, Hasta, Hoe, Husband, Lob, Peter, → **PLOUGH**, Set, Unto

Tiller Gardener, Helm, Ploughman, Rotavator, Wheel

Tilt Awning, Bank, Camber, Cant, Cock, Dip, Heel, Hut, Joust, Just, → **LIST**, Quintain, Rock, Tip, Trip, Unbalance

Timber Apron, Ashlaring, Balk, Batten, Beam, Bolster, Bond, Bridging, Cant-rail, Carapa, Cedarwood, Chess, Clapboard, Compass, Coulisse, Cross-tree, Cruck, Dogshores, Driftwood, Druxy, Dwang, Elmwood, Flitch, Float, Four-by-two, Futchel, Futtock, Greenheart, Groundsell, Hardwood, Harewood, Intertie, Iroko, Ironwood, Joist, Knee, Knighthead, Lauan, Ligger, Lintel, Log, Lumber, Nogging, Nothofagus, Plank-sheer, Purlin(e), Putlock, Putlog, Pyengadu, Radiata, Ramin, Rib, Ridgepole, Roundwood, Rung, Sandalwood, Sapele, Sapodilla, Satinwood, Scantling, Shook, Shorts, Sissoo, Skeg, Sneezewood, Softwood, Souari, Stemson, Stere, Sternpost, Sternson, Straddle, Stud, Stull, Stumpage, Summer, Swing-stock, Tilting fillet, Towing-bitts, Transom, Trestletree, Two-by-four, Wale, Wall plate, Weatherboard, Whitewood, → **WOOD**, Yang

Timbre Clang, Klang(farbe), Register, → **TENOR**, Tone

Time(s), Timer Access, African, Agoge, Apparent, Assymetric, Astronomical, Atlantic, Atomic, Autumn, Awhile, Bird, BST, Central, Chronaxy, Chronic, Chronometer, Chronon, Clock, Closing, Common, Compound, Connect, Core, Counter, Cryptozoic, Date, Day, Dead, Decade, Dimension, Double, Duple, Duration, Early, Eastern, Eastern Standard, Egg-glass, Enemy, Eon, Ephemeris, Epoch, Equinox, Era, European, Eve(ning), Extra, Father, Flexitime, Fold, Forelock, Four-four, Free, Full, Geological, Gest, Glide, Half, Healer, High, Horologe, Hour, Hourglass, Hr, Idle, Imprisonment, Injury, Innings, Instant, Interim, Interlude, Jiff, Juncture, Kalpa, Killing, Latent, Lay-day, Lead, Lean, Leisure, Life, Lighting-up, Lilac, Local, Lowsing, Mean, Menopause, Metronome, Mountain standard, Multiple, Needle, Nonce, Nones, Normal, Occasion, Oft, → **ON TIME**, Opening, Pacific, Paralysis, Part, Peak, Period, Phanerozoic, Pinger, Porridge, Post, Prelapsarian, Prime, Proper, Quadruple, Quality, Question, Quick, Reaction, Real, Reaper, Recovery, Response, Responsum, Reverberation, Rhythm, Run(ning), Sandglass, Seal, → **SEASON**, Seel, Seil, Semeion, Serial, Session, Shelf-life, Sidereal, Sight, Simple, Sith(e), Slow, Solar, Solstice, Space, Span, Spare, Spell, Spin, Split, Spring, Squeaky-bum, Standard, Stoppage, Stopwatch, Stound, Stownd, Stretch, Summer, Sundial, Sundown, Sythe, T, Tem, Tempo, Tempore, Tense, Thief, Three-four, Thunderer, Tick, Tid, Tide, Trice, Triple, True, Turnaround, Two-four, Universal, Usance, What, While, Winter, X, Yonks, Zero

Timebomb Demographic

Time-keeper, Timepiece Ben, Chronometer, Clock, Hourglass, Ref, Sand-glass, Sundial, Ticker, Tompion, Watch

Timeless Eternal, Nd, Undying
Timely Appropriate, Apropos, Happy, Heaven-sent, Opportune, Pat, Prompt, Punctual
Timescale Geological
Time-server Prisoner, Trimmer
Timeshare Box and cox
Timetable ABC(ee), Absee, Bradshaw, → **CHART**, Schedule
Timid, Timorous Afraid, Aspen, Bashful, Blate, Chicken, Cowardly, Eerie, Eery, Faint-hearted, Fearful, Hare, Hen-hearted, Milquetoast, Mouse, Mous(e)y, Pavid, Pigeon-hearted, Pusillanimous, Pussy, Quaking, Schnok, Shrinking, → **SHY**, Skeary, Sook, Tremulous, Wuss, Yellow
Timothy Cat's-tail, Grass, Phleum
Tin(ned), Tinfoil, Tinny Argentine, Block, Britannia metal, Can, Cash, Debe, Dixie, Maconochie, Mess, → **MONEY**, Moola(h), Ochre, Plate, Rhino, Sn, Stannary, Stannic, Stream, Tain, Tole
Tincture Arnica, Bufo, Chroma, Elixir, Fur, Infusion, Laudanum, Metal, Or, Sericon, Sol, Spice, Taint, Tenné, Vert
Tinder Amadou, Faggot, Fuel, Funk, Punk, Spark, Spunk, Touchwood
Tine Antler, Bay, Cusp, Grain, Prong, Snag, Spire, Surroyal, Trey
Tinge(d) Dye, Eye, Flavour, Gild, → **HUE**, Infuscate, Taint, Tincture, Tone, Touch
Tingle, Tingling Dinnle, Dirl, Paraesthesia, Pins and needles, Prickle, Thrill, Throb, Tinkle
Tinker Bell, Caird, Coster, Didakai, Didakei, Diddicoy, Didicoy, Didikoi, → **FIDDLE**, Gypsy, Mender, Pedlar, Potter, Prig, Putter, Repair, Sly, Snout, Tamper, Tramp, Traveller, Tweak
Tinkle, Tinkling Pink, Thin
Tinsel(ly) Clinquant, Gaudy, Glitter, O, Spangle, Turkey
Tint Colour, Henna, Hue, Pigment, → **STAIN**, Tinct, Tinge, Tone, Woad
Tiny Atto-, Baby, Diddy, Dwarf, Ha'it, Infinitesimal, Itsy-bitsy, Lilliputian, Midget, Minikin, Minim, Mite, Negligible, Petite, Pittance, Small, Smidgeon, Stime, Teeny, Tiddl(e)y, Tiddy, Tim, Tine, Tottie, Totty, Toy, Wee
Tip (off), Tipping Apex, Arrowhead, Ash-heap, Asparagus, Backshish, Baksheesh, Batta, Beer-money, Bonsel(l)a, Bonus, B(u)onamono, Cant, Cert, Chape, Counsel, Coup, Cowp, Crown, Cue, Cumshaw, Douceur, Dump, Extremity, Fee, Felt, Ferrule, Filter, Forecast, Glans, Gratillity, Gratuity, Heel, → **HINT**, Hunch, Inkle, Iridise, Lagniappe, Largess(e), List, Mess, Middenstead, Nap, Nib, Noop, Ord, Perk, Perquisite, Point, Pointer, Pour, Pourboire, Previse, Prong, Straight, Suggestion, Summit, Tag, Tail, Tilt, Toom, Touch, Tronc, Upset, Vail, Vales, Warn, Whisper, Wink, Wrinkle
Tippet Cape, Fur, Scarf
Tipple Bib, Booze, → **DRINK**, Paint, Pot, Poteen
Tipster Prophet, Tout
Tipsy Bleary, Boozy, Bosky, → **DRUNK**, Elevated, Moony, Nappy, Oiled, On, Rocky, Screwed, Slewed, Slued, Squiffy, Tight, Wet
▷ **Tipsy** *may indicate* an anagram
Tiptoe Digitigrade, Spanish, Walk
Tirade Diatribe, Invective, Jobation, Laisse, Philippic, Rand, Rant, Screed, Slang
Tire(d), Tiredness, Tiring All-in, Aweary, Beat, Bore, Bushed, Caparison, Deadbeat, Dress, Drowsy, → **EXHAUST**, Fag, Fagged out, Fatigue, Flag, Fordid, Fordod, Forjeskit, Frazzle, Gruel, Irk, Jack, Jade, Lassitude, Limp, ME, Overspent, Pall, Poop, Puggled, → **ROBE**, Rubber, Sap, Shagged, Sicken, Sleepry, Sleepy, Spent,

Swinkt, Tax, Tedious, Tucker, Wabbit, Wappend, Weary, Wrecked

Tiresome Boring, Exhausting, Humdrum, Pill, Tedious, Vexing

Tirl Rattle, Risp, Strip, Turn

▶ **Tiro** *see* **TYRO**

Tissue Adenoid, Adhesion, Adipose, Aerenchyma, Aponeurosis, Archesporium, Bast, Callus, Carbon, Cartilage, Cementum, Chalaza, Cheloid, Chlorenchyma, Coenosarc, Collagen, Collenchyma, Commissure, Conducting, Connective, Cortex, Dentine, Diploe, Elastic, Elastin, Epimysium, Epineurium, Epithelium, Eschar, Evocator, Fabric, Fascia, Filament, Flesh, Gamgee, Gauze, Gleba, Glia, Granulation, Granuloma, Gum, Heteroplasia, Histogen, Histoid, Infarct, Interlay, Junk, Keloid, Kleenex®, Lamina, Liber, Lies, Ligament, Luteal, Lymphate, Lymphoid, Macroglia, Marrow, Matrix, Mechanical, Medulla, → **MEMBRANE**, Meristem, Mesenchyme, Mesophyll, Mestom(e), Mole, Muscle, Myelin(e), Myocardium, Neoplasm, Neuroglia, Nucellus, Olivary, Pack, Palisade, Pannus, Paper, Papilla, Parenchyma, Periblem, Perichylous, Pericycle, Peridesmium, Perimysium, Perinephrium, Perineurium, Perisperm, Phellogen, Phloem, Pith, Placenta, Plerome, Polyarch, Pons, Primordium, Procambium, Prosenchyma, Prothallis, Pterygium, Pulp, Radula, Sarcenet, Sars(e)net, Scar, Sclerenchyma, Scleroma, Sequestrum, Sinew, Soft, Somatopleure, Stereome, Stroma, Submucosa, Suet, Tarsus, Tela, Tendon, Tonsil, Trace, Tunica, Vascular, Velum, Web, Wound, Xylem, Zoograft

Tit, Tit-bit(s) Analecta, Canapé, Crested, Currie, Curry, Delicacy, Dug, Nag, Nipple, Nun, Pap, Quarry, Sample, Scrap, Snack, Teat, Tug, Twitch, Willow, Wren, Zakuska

Titan(ic), Titaness Atlas, Colossus, Cronos, Cronus, Drone, Enormous, Giant, Huge, Hyperion, Kronos, Large, Leviathan, Liner, Oceanus, Phoebe, Prometheus, Rhea, Themis, Vast

Titanium, Titanite Rutin, Sagenite, Sphene, Ti

Tit for tat Deserts, Revenge, Talion

Tithe Disme, Dyzemas, Frankpledge, Teind, Tenth

Titian Abram, Auburn

Titillate(r), Titillating Delight, Excite, Fluffer, Naughty, Tickle

Titivate Preen, Primp

Title Abbé, → **ADDRESS**, Ag(h)a, Agname, Antonomasia, Appellative, Bahadur, Baroness, Baronet, Bart, Bastard, Bhai, Bretwalda, Burra sahib, Calif, Caliph, Caption, Charta, Chogyal, Claim, Conveyance, Count(ess), Courtesy, Credit, Dan, Datin, Datuk, Dauphin, Dayan, Deeds, Devi, Dom, Don, Don(n)a, Dowager, Dub, Duchess, Duke, Earl, Effendi, Eminence, Epithet, Esquire, Excellency, Fra, Frau(lein), Ghazi, Gospodin, Grand Master, Great Mogul, Gyani, Hafiz, Handle, Header, Heading, Headline, Highness, Hojatoleslam, Hon, Honour, Imperator, Interest, Kabaka, Kalif, Kaliph, Kaur, King, Kumari, Lady, Lala, Lemma, → **LIEN**, Lord, Mal(l)am, Marchesa, Marchese, Marquess, Marquis, Master, Masthead, Maulana, Memsahib, Meneer, Mevrou, Miladi, Milady, Milord, Mirza, Mr(s), Name, Native, Negus, Nemn, Nizam, Nomen, Padishah, Pasha, Peerage, Pir, Polemarch, Prefix, Prince(ss), Queen, → **RANK**, Reb, Reverence, Reverend, → **RIGHT**, Rubric, Running, Sahib, Sama, San, Sardar, Sayid, Senhor(a), Señor(a), Shri, Singh, Sir, Sirdar, Son, Sowbhagyawati, Sri, Stratum, Tannie, Tenno, Titule, Torrens, Tuanka, Tycoon, U, Worship

Title-holder Cartouche, Champion, Landlord, Noble

Titmouse Bird, Hickymal, Mag, Reedling, Tit

Titter Giggle, Snigger, Tehee

Tittle Jot

Titus Oates

Tizz(y) Pother, Spin, Tanner, Testril, VId

TNT Explosive, Trotyl

To(wards) At, Beside, Inby, Intil, Onto, Prone, Shet, Shut, Till, Until

Toad(y) Bootlicker, Bufo, Bumsucker, Cane, Clawback, Cocksucker, Crapaud, Crawler, Fawn, Frog, Horned, Jackal, Jenkins, Knot, Lackey, Lick-platter, Lickspittle, Midwife, Minion, Natterjack, Nototrema, Paddock, Parasite, Pick-thank, Pipa, Placebo, Platanna, Poodle, Puddock, Queensland cane, Sook, Spade-foot, Surinam, Sycophant, Tree, Tuft-hunter, Walking, Warty, Xenopus, Yesman

Toadstool Amanita, Death-cap, Death-cup, Destroying angel, Fly agaric, → **FUNGUS**, Grisette, Horsehair, Marasmus, Paddock-stool, Parrot, Saffron milk cap, Sickener, Sulphur tuft, Verdigris, Wax cap

Toast(er) Bacchus, Bell, Birsle, Brindisi, → **BROWN**, Bruschetta, Bumper, Cheers, Chin-chin, Crostini, Crouton, Drink-hail, French, Gesundheit, Grace-cup, Grill, Health, Iechyd da, Immortal memory, Kia-ora, L'chaim, Lechayim, Loyal, Melba, Pledge, Pop up, Propose, Prosit, Round, Scouther, Scowder, Scowther, Sentiment, Sippet, Skoal, Slainte, Slainte mha(i)th, Soldier, Sunbathe, Wassail, Zwieback

Toastmaster MC, Symposiarch

Tobacco, Tobacco-field Alfalfa, Bacchi, Baccy, Bird's eye, Broadleaf, Burley, Canaster, Capa, Caporal, Cavendish, Chew, Dottle, Filler, Honeydew, Indian, Killikinnick, Kinnikinick, Latakia, Mundungus, Nailrod, Navy-cut, Negro-head, Nicotian, Nicotine, Niggerhead, Perique, Pigtail, Plug, Quid, Rapper, Régie, Returns, Shag, Sneesh, Snout, Snuff, Straight cut, Stripleaf, Turkish, Twist, Vega, Virginia, Weed, Wrapper

To be arranged TBA

Toboggan Sled(ge), Sleigh

To boot Furthermore

Toby Dog, High, Highwayman, Jug, Low

Tocsin Alarm, Siren

Today Hodiernal, Now, Present

Toddle(r) Baim, Gangrel, Mite, Tot, Totter, Trot, Waddle

Toddy Arrack, → **DRINK**, Sura, Whisky

To-do Sensation, Stir

Toe(s) Dactyl, Digit, Fissiped, Hallux, Hammer, Piggy, Pinky, Pointe, Poulaine, Prehallux, Tootsie

Toff Nob, Nut, Snob, Swell

Toffee Banket, Butterscotch, Caramel, Cracknel, Gundy, Hard-bake, Hokey-pokey, Humbug, Tom-trot

Toga Palla

Together Among, At-one, Atone, Attone, En bloc, En masse, Gathered, Hand-in-glove, Hand-in-hand, Infere, → **JOINT**, Pari-passu, Sam, Unison, Wed, Y, Yfere, Ysame

Toggle Fastener, Netsuke

Togs Clothes, Gear, Rig, Strip

Toil(s) Drudge, Fag, Industry, → **LABOUR**, Mesh, Net, Seine, Sisyphus, Slog, Sweat, Swink, Tela, Tew, Trap, Trauchle, Travail, Tug, Web, → **WORK**, Wrest, Yacker, Yakka, Yakker

Toilet Can, Chemical, Coiffure, John, Lat(rine), Lavabo, → **LAVATORY**, Loo, Necessary house, Necessary place, Pot, Powder room, Toot, WC

Token Abbey-piece, Buck, Check, Chip, Counter, Coupon, Disc, Double-axe, Emblem, Gift, Indication, Mark, → **MEMENTO**, Monument, Nominal, Portend,

Seal, Sign, Signal, Slug, Symbol, Symptom, Tessella, Tessera, Valentine

Tolerable Acceptable, Bearable, Mediocre, Passable, So-so

Tolerance, Tolerant, Tolerate(d) Abear, Abide, → **ALLOW**, Bear, Broadminded, Brook, Endure, Enlightened, Good-natured, Hack, Had, Immunological, Latitude, → **LENIENT**, Lump, Mercy, Permit, Stand, Stick, Stomach, Studden, Suffer, Support, Thole, Wear, Zero

Toll Chime, Chok(e)y, Customs, Due, Duty, Excise, Jole, Joll, Joule, Jowl, Light-dues, Octroi, Pierage, Pike, Pontage, Rates, → **RING**, Scavage, Streetage, Tariff, Tax

Tom(my) Atkins, Bell, Bowling, Bread, Brown, → **CAT**, Collins, Edgar, Gib, Grub, Gun, He-cat, Jerry, Jones, Mog(gy), Nosh, Peeping, Private, Pro(stitute), Pte, Puss, Ram-cat, Sawyer, Snout, Soldier, Stout, Thos, Thumb, Tiddler, Tucker

Tomato Beef(steak), Cherry, Gooseberry, Husk, Love-apple, Plum, Portuguese, Strawberry, Tamarillo, Tree, Wolf's peach

Tomb(stone) Burial, Catacomb, Catafalque, Cenotaph, Cist, Coffin, Dargah, Durgah, Grave, Hypogeum, Inurn, Kistvaen, Marmoreal, Mastaba, Mausoleum, Megalithic, Monument, Pyramid, Repository, → **SEPULCHRE**, Sepulture, Serdab, Shrine, Speos, Tell el Amarna, Tholos, Tholus, Through-stane, Through-stone, Treasury, Vault

Tombola Draw, Lottery, Raffle

Tomboy Gamine, Gilpey, Gilpy, Hoyden, Ladette, Ramp, Romp

Tome → **BOOK**, Volume

Tomfoolery Caper, Fandangle, Shenanigan

Tomorrow Future, Manana, Morrow

Tompion Watchman

Tom Snout Tinker

Ton(nage) C, Chic, Displacement, Freight, Gross, Hundred, Long, Measurement, Metric, Net register, Register, Shipping, Short, T

Tone, Tonality Aeolian, Brace, Combination, Compound, Dialling, Difference, Differential, Engaged, Fifth, Gregorian, Harmonic, Hum, Inflection, Key, Klang, Minor, Ninth, Partial, Passing, Pure, Qualify, Quarter, Real, Resultant, Ring, Ringing, Side, → **SOUND**, Strain, Summational, Temper, Tenor, Timbre, Touch, Trite, Whole

Tong(s) Curling, Lazy, Sugar, Wafer

Tongue, Tonguing Brogue, Burr, Chape, Clack, Clapper, Doab, Double, Final, Flutter, Forked, Glossa, Glossolalia, Glottal, Jinglet, → **LANGUAGE**, Languet(te), Lap, Ligula, Lill, Lingo, Lingual, Lingulate, Mother, Organ, Radula, Ranine, Rasp, Red rag, Single, Spit, Tab, Triple, Voice, Vulgar

Tongue-tied Mush-mouthed

Tongue-twister Jaw-breaker, Shibboleth

Tonic Booster, Bracer, Cascara, C(h)amomile, Doh, Key, Keynote, Mease, Medicinal, Mishmee, Mishmi, Myrica, Oporice, Pareira brava, Pick-me-up, Quassia, Refresher, Roborant, Sage tea, Sarsaparilla, Solfa

▷ **Tonic** *may indicate* a musical note

Tonsil, Tonsillitis Amygdala, Antiaditis, Pharyngeal, Quinsy

Tonsure(d) Epilate, Haircut, Peel, Pield

Tony Bête, Chic, Classy, Fool, Smart, U

Too Als(o), As well, Besides, Eke, Excessive, Item, Likewise, Moreover, Oer, Over, Overly, Plus, Troppo

Took Naam, Nam, Set, Stole, Wan, Won

Tool(s) Adze, Aiguille, Airbrush, Auger, Awl, Ax(e), Beetle, Bevel, Billhook, Bit, Bodkin, Broach, Brog, Bur(r), Burin, Calipers, Carbide, Catspaw, Chaser, Chisel,

Chopper, Clippers, Come-along, Croze, Dibber, Dibble, Die, Dolly, Drawknife, Drawshave, Drift(pin), Drill, Drove, Eatche, Edger, Elsin, Eolith, Facer, Fid, File, Findings, Firmer, Flatter, Float, Float-stone, Fore-hammer, Former, Fraise, Fretsaw, Froe, Frow, Fuller, Gad, Gimlet, Glass-cutter, Gnomon, Go-devil, Gouger, Grapnel, Grattoir, Graver, Hammer, Hardware, Hardy, Hedge-trimmer, Hob, Hoe, Hopdog, Husker, Icepick, → IMPLEMENT, Insculp, → INSTRUMENT, Iron, Jackal, Jackhammer, Jemmy, Jim Crow, Jointer, Jumper, Laster, Lewis, Loggerhead, Loom, Lute, Machine, Maker, Mallet, Marlin(e)spike, Microkeratome, Microlith, Mitre square, Moon-knife, Muller, Nail gun, Nail set, Nippers, Oustiti, Outsiders, Palaeolith, Pattle, Pawn, Penis, Percussion, Pestle, Pick, Pickaxe, Picklock, Pitchfork, Pitching, Piton, Plane, Pliers, Plough-staff, Plunger, Pointer, Power, Pricker, Property, Prunt, Punch, Puncheon, Rabble, Rasp, Reamer, Ripple, Rirp, Rocking, Roll(er), Rounder, Router, Sander, Saw, Saw set, Scalpel, Scauper, Scissors, Scorper, Scraper, Screwdriver, Scriber, Scutch, Scythe, Seamset, Secateurs, Set, Shoder, Shooting stick, Sickle, Slasher, Slater, Sledge-hammer, Sleeker, Snake, Snap, Spade, Spanner, Spirit-level, Spitsticker, Spokeshave, Spudder, Strickle, Strike, Strimmer®, Swage, Swingle, Swipple, Switch, Tint, Tjanting, Toothpick, Tranchet, Triblet, Trowel, Try square, Tweezers, Twibill, Upright, Vibrator, Vice, Wimble, Wire-stripper, Wrench
Toot(er) Blow, Horn, Parp, Trumpet
Tooth(ed), Toothy, Teeth Baby, Bicuspid, Bit, Buck, Bunodont, Cadmean, Canine, Carnassial, Chactodon, Cheek tooth, Chisel, Choppers, Cog, Comb, Comer, Cott's, Crena(te), Ctenoid, Cusp, Denticle, Dentin(e), Dentures, Egg, Eye, False, Fang, Gam, Gap, Gat, Gnashers, Grinder, Heterodont, Impacted, Incisor, Ivory, Joggle, Laniary, Milk, Mill, Molar, Nipper, Odontoid, Orthodontics, Overbite, Pawl, Pearly gates, Pectinate, Periodontics, Peristome, Permanent, Phang, Plate, Poison-fang, Pre-molar, Prong, Ratch, Ratchet, Scissor, Secodont, Sectorial, Selenodont, Serration, Set, Snaggle, Sprocket, Store, Sweet, Trophi, Tush, Tusk, Uncinus, Upper, Wallies, Wang, Wiper, Wisdom, Wolf, Zalambdodont
Toothache, Tooth troubles Caries, Odontalgia
Toothless(ness) Anodontia, Edentate, Gummy, Pangolin
Toothpaste Dentifrice
▷ **Top** *may indicate* first letter
Top (drawer; hole; line; notcher), Topmost, Topper Ace, Acme, Altissimo, A1, Apex, Apical, Behead, Best, Better, Big, Blouse, Blouson, Boob tube, Brow, Bustier, Cacumen, Cap, Capstone, Ceiling, Coma, Cop, Coping, Corking, Cream, → CREST, Crista, Crop, Crown, Culmen, De capo, Decollate, Diabolo, Dog, Dome, Double, Drawer, Dreid(e)l, Dux, Elite, Execute, Fighting, Finial, Flip, Gentry, Gyroscope, Halterneck, Hard, Hat, → HEAD, Height, Hummer, Humming, Imperial, Jumper, Lid, Maillot, Nun, One-er, Optimate, Orb, Parish, → PEAK, Peerie, Peery, Peg, Peplos, Peplus, Pinnacle, Pitch, Quark, Replenish, Ridge, Roof, Sawyer, Screw, Secret, Shaw, Shirt, Skim, Sky, Slay, Soft, Spinning, Star, Summit, Superate, Superb, Supernal, Supreme, Supremo, Surface, Sweater, Table, Tambour, Targa, Teetotum, Texas, Tile, Trash, T-shirt, Turbinate, Up(most), Uppermost, V, Vertex, Whipping, Whirligig
Topaz Citrine, Colorado, Occidental, Oriental, Pycnite, Rose, Scottish, Spanish
Topcoat Finish, Overcoat, Ulster
Tope(r) Boozer, Bouser, Dagaba, Dagoba, → DRUNK, Sot, Tosspot
Topic(al) Head, Hobbyhorse, Item, Local, Motion, Place, Shop, Subject, Text, → THEME

Top-knot Tuft
Topping Grand, Icing, Meringue, Pepperoni, Piecrust, Streusel
Topple Oust, Overbalance, Overturn, Tip, Upend, → UPSET
Topsy Parentless
Topsy-turvy Careen, Cockeyed, Inverted, Summerset, Tapsalteerie, Tapsleteerie
Torah Maftir
Torch Blow, Brand, Cresset, Fire, Flambeau, Hards, Hurds, Lamp, Lampad, Link, Olympic, Plasma, Roughie, Tead(e), Weld, Wisp
Torch-bearer Usherette
Toreador Escamillo, Matador, Picador, Torero
Torment(ed), Tormentor Agony, Anguish, Bait, Ballyrag, Bedevil, Butt, Cruciate, Crucify, Curse, Distress, Excruciate, Frab, Gehenna, Grill, Hag-ridden, Harass, Harry, Hell, Martyrdom, Molest, Nag, Nettle, Pang, Pine, Plague, → RACK, Sadist, Tantalise, Tease, Wrack
Tornado Cyclone, Twister, Waterspout
Toronto Hogtown
Torpedo Bangalore, Bomb, Fish, Missile, Ray, Subroc, Tin fish, Weapon
Torpedo-guard Crinoline
Torpid, Torpor Accidie, Acedia, Comatose, Dormant, Gouch, Inertia, Languid, Lethargic, Sluggish, Slumbering
Torrent Flood, Spate
Torrid Amphiscian, Fiery, Hot, Sultry, Tropical
Torsk Cusk
Torso Body, Midriff, Trunk
Tortilla Pancake, Taco, Tostada
Tortoise Chelonia, Emydes, Emys, Galapagos, Giant, Hic(c)atee, Kurma, Pancake, Snapping-turtle, Terrapin, Testudo, Timothy, Turtle, Water
Tortoiseshell Epiplastra, Hawksbill, Testudo
Tortuous Ambagious, Twisty, Winding
▷ **Tortuous** *may indicate* an anagram
Torture, Torture chamber, Torture instrument Agonise, Auto-da-fé, Bastinade, Bastinado, Boot, Bootikin, Catasta, Chinese burn, Chinese water, Crucify, Devil-on-the-neck, Engine, Excruciate, Flageolet, Fry, Gadge, Gauntlet, Gyp, Hell, Iron maiden, Knee-cap, Naraka, Peine forte et dure, Persecute, Pilliwinks, Pine, Pinniewinkle, Pinnywinkle, → RACK, Sadism, Scaphism, Scarpines, Scavenger, Scavenger's daughter, Scourge, Skeffington's daughter, Skevington's daughter, Strappado, Tantalise, Third degree, Thumb(i)kins, Thumbscrew, Torment, Tumbrel, Tumbril, Water, Wheel, Wrack
▷ **Tortured** *may indicate* an anagram
Torturer Torquemada
Torus Disc, Stellarator
Tory Abhorrer, Blimp, Blue, C, Catholic, Opposition, Right, Tantivy, Taig, Unionist, Young England
Toss(ing), Throw(n) Abject, Bandy, Bounce, Buck, Bung, Buttock, Cant, Canvass, Cast, Catapult, → CHUCK, Cottabus, Crabs, Crap, Cross-buttock, Dad, Daud, Dawd, Deal, Discomfit, Dink, Disconcert, Dod, Elance, Estrapade, Falcade, Faze, → FLING, Flip, Floor, Flump, Flutter, Flying (head)-mare, Free, Full, Gollum, Hanch, Haunch, Heave, Hipt, Hoy, → HURL, Jack, Jact(it)ation, Jaculation, Jeff, Juggle, Jump, Lance, Lob, Loft, Nick, Pash, Pick, Pitch, Purl, Put(t), Round-arm, Salad, Seamer, Shy, Slat, Sling, Squail, Unhorse, Unseat, Upcast, Wheech, Yuko
Toss-up Cross and pile, Heads or tails

Tot Add, Babe, Bairn, → CHILD, Dop, Dram, Infant, Mite, Nightcap, Nip(per), Nipperkin, Slug, Snifter, Snort, Tad

Tota(ity), Toto Absolute, Aggregate, All(-out), All told, Amount, Balance, Be-all, → COMPLETE, Entire, Gross, Lot, Mass, Ouroborus, Overall, Sum, Tale, Tally, Unqualified, Uroborus, Utter, Whole

Totalitarian Autocrat, Despot, Étatiste, Fascist

Tote Bear, → CARRY, Yomp

Totem Fetish, Icon, Image, Pole

Tottenham Hotspur

Totter Abacus, Daddle, Daidle, Didakai, Didakei, Did(d)icoy, Didicoi, Halt, Ragman, Reel, Rock, → STAGGER, Swag, Sway, Topple, Waver

Toucan Ariel, Ramphastos

Touch(ed), Touching, Touchy Accolade, Adjoin, Affect, Anent, Badass, Barmy, Cadge, Captious, Carambole, Caress, Carom, Common, Concern, Connivent, Contact, Contiguous, Dash, Easy, Emove, → FEEL, Feisty, Finger, Finishing, Flick, Fondle, Haptic, Heart-warming, Huffish, Huffy, → IN TOUCH, Iracund, Irascible, J'adoube, Liaison, Libant, Loan, Loco, Meet, Midas, Miffy, Near, Nie, Nigh, Nudge, Palp, Pathetic, Paw, Potty, Re, Sense, Shade, Skiff, Soft, Sore, Spice, → SPOT, Tactile, Tactual, Tag, Tangible, Tap, Taste, Tat, Tetchy, Tickle, Tig, Tinderbox, Tinge, Titivate, Trace, Trait, Trifle, Tuck, Vestige

Touchdown Rouge

Touchline Tangent

Touchstone Basanite, Criterion, Norm, Standard

Touch wood Unberufen

Touchwood Absit omen, Monk, Punk, Spunk, Tinder

Tough(en) Adamantine, Anneal, Apache, Arduous, Ballsy, Burly, Chewy, → HARD, Hardball, Hard-boiled, Hard-nosed, Hard nut, Hardy, Heavy duty, He-man, Hood, Hoodlum, Husky, Indurate, Keelie, Knotty, Leathern, Leathery, Nut, Pesky, Rambo, Rigwiddie, Rigwoodie, Roughneck, Sinewy, Skinhead, Spartan, Steely, Stiff, Strict, String, Sturdy, Teuch, Thewed, Tityre-tu, Virile

Toupee Hairpiece, Rug, Tour, → WIG

Tour(er), Tourism, Tourist Adventure, Barnstorm, Benefit, Circuit, Conducted, Cook's, Emmet, Excursion, Gig, Grand, Grockle, GT, Holiday-maker, Itinerate, → JOURNEY, Lionise, Mystery, Outing, Parra, Posting, Pub crawl, Roadie, Road show, Rubberneck, Safari, Sightsee, Swing, Tiki, → TRAVEL, Trip(per), Viator, Whistle-stop

Tourmaline Indicolite, Indigolite, Schorl, Zeuxite

Tournament American, Basho, Bonspiel, Bridge drive, Carousel, Drive, Event, Jereed, Jerid, Joust, Just, Ladder, Plate, Pro-am, Pro-celebrity, Round robin, Royal, Super Twelve, Swiss, Tilt, Tourney, Whist drive, Wimbledon

Tourniquet Garrot, Throttle, Torcular

Tousle Dishevel, Rumple

Tout Barker, Laud, Ply, Praise, Runner, Solicit, Toot, Work-watcher

Tow(ing) Aquaplane, Button, Fibre, → HAUL, Pull, → ROPE, Ski, Skijoring, Stupe, Track

▶ **Towards** *see* TO

Towel Dry, Jack, Nappy, Roller, Rub, Sanitary, Tea, Tea-cloth, Terry, Turkish

Tower AA, Aspire, Atalaya, Babel, Barbican, Bastille, Bastion, Belfry, Bell, Bloody, Brattice, Brettice, Brogh, Campanile, Clock, Conning, Control, Cooling, Donjon, Dungeon, Edifice, Eiffel, Fly, Fortress, Gantry, Garret, Gate, Giralda, Gopura(m), Guérite, Hawser, Horologium, Husky, Ivory, Keep, Leaning, Loom, Maiden,

Martello, Minar(et), Monument, Mooring, Mouse, Nuraghe, Nurhag, Overtop, Peel, Pinnacle, Pisa, Pound, Pylon, Rear, Rise, Rolandseck, Rood, Round, Sail, Sears, Shot, Sikhara, Silo, Ski-lift, Space Needle, Specula, Spire, Stealth, Steeple, Swiss Re, Tête-de-pont, Texas, Tractor, Tugboat, → **TURRET**, Victoria, Watch, Water, Yagura, Ziggurat, Zikkurat

Town, Township Boom, Borgo, Borough, Bourg, Burg(h), City, Conurbation, County, Deme, Dormitory, Dorp, Favella, Garrison, Ghost, Ham(let), Intraurban, Market, Municipal, Nasik, One-horse, Open, Place, Podunk, Pueblo, Satellite, Shanty, Soweto, Staple, Tinsel, Tp, Twin, Urban, Whistle stop, Wick

Townee, Townsman Cad, Cit(izen), Dude, Freeman, Oppidan, Philister, Resident, Snob

Town hall Prytaneum

Toxaemia Eclampsia

Toxic(ity), Toxin Abrin, Aflatoxin, Antigen, Botox®, Botulin, Cadaverine, Cadmium, Chlorin(e), Coumarin, Curare, Deadly, Dioxan, Dioxin, Eclampsia, Fluorin(e), Lethal, Melittin, Muscarine, Phalloidin, Phenol, Phenothiazine, Pre-eclampsia, Psoralen, Ricin, Sepsis, Serology, Venin, Venomous, Virulence, Zootoxin

Toy Bauble, Bottle-imp, Bull-roarer, Cartesian devil, Cockhorse, Coral, Cyberpet, Dally, Dandle, Dinky®, Doll, Executive, Faddle, Finger, Flirt, Frisbee®, Gewgaw, Golly, Gonk, Jack-in-the-box, Jumping-jack, Kaleidoscope, Kickshaw, Knack, Lego®, Meccano®, Newton's cradle, Noah's ark, Novelty, Paddle, Pantine, Peashooter, Pinwheel, Plaything, Pogo stick, Praxinoscope, Quiz, Rattle, Russian doll, Scooter, Shoofly, Skipjack, Stroboscope, Tantalus-cup, Taste, Teddy, Thaumatrope, Top, → **TRIFLE**, Trinket, Tu(r)ndun, Wheel of life, Whirligig, Windmill, Yoyo, Zoetrope

Trace Atom, Cast, Derive, Describe, Draft, Draw, Dreg, Echo, Footprint, Ghost, → **HINT**, Leaf, Limn, Mark, Memory, Outline, Relic, Relict, Remnant, Scintilla, Semblance, Sign, Smack, Soupçon, Strap, Tinge, → **TOUCH**, Track, Vestige, Whiff, Whit

Tracery Filigree, Frostwork

Track(s), Tracker, Tracking, Trackman Aintree, Aisle, Band, B-road, Caterpillar®, Cinder, Circuit, Course, Crawler, Cycleway, Dirt, Dog, DOVAP, Drift, Ecliptic, El, Fast, Fettler, Flap(ping), Footing, Gandy dancer, Green road, Greenway, Hunt, Ichnite, Ichnolite, Icknield Way, Inside, Lane, Ley, Line, Loipe, Loopline, Mommy, Monitor, Monza, Pad, → **PATH**, Persue, Piste, Pug, Pursue, Race, Raceway, Rail, Railway, Rake, Ridgeway, Riding, Route, Run, Rut, Siding, Sign, Skidway, Sleuth, Slot, Sonar, Speedway, Spoor, Tan, Tan-ride, Taxi, Tenure, Tideway, Title, → **TRAIL**, Trajectory, Tram, Tramline, Tramroad, Tramway, Tread, Trode, Tug(boat), Twin, Wake, Wallaby, Way, Y

Tract(able), Tracts Area, Belt, Bench, Clime, Colporteur, Common, Dene, Digestive, Enclave, Flysheet, Lande, Leaflet, Monte, Moor, Olfactory, → **PAMPHLET**, Park, Prairie, Province, Purlieu, Pusey, Region, Screed, Taluk, Tawie, Terrain, Wold

Tractarian(ism) Newman, Oxford movement, Pusey(ism)

Tractor Back hoe, Bombardier®, Bulldozer, Cat, Caterpillar®, Chelsea, Fendalton, Pedrail, Remuera, Skidder, Tower

Tracy Dick, Spencer

Trade(r), Tradesman, Trading Arb(itrageur), Art, Banian, Banyan, Bargain, Barter, Bilateral, Bricks and clicks, Bun(n)ia, Burgher, Business, Cabotage, Calling, Carriage, Chaffer, Chandler, Chapman, Cheapjack, Clicks and mortar, Coaster, Comanchero, → **COMMERCE**, Coster, Costermonger, Crare, Crayer, Deal(er), Dicker,

Easterling, Errand, Exchange, Exporter, Factor, Fair, Floor, Free, Galleon, Handle, Horse, Hosier, Hot, Importer, Indiaman, Industry, Insider, Ironmonger, Jobber, Logrolling, Line, Mercantile, Merchant, Mercosur, Métier, Middleman, Mister, Monger, Mystery, Occupy, Outfitter, Paralleling, Pitchman, Ply, Program(me), Rag, Retailer, Roaring, Rough, Roundtripping, Scalp, Screen, Sell, Simony, Slave, Stallenger, Stallholder, Stallinger, Stationer, Sutler, Suttle, → **SWAP**, Traffic, Transit, Trant, Truck, Union, Vaisya, Vend, Wholesaler, Wind

Trademark, Trade name Brand, Chop, Idiograph, Label, Logo, Tm, TN

Trade union Amicus, ASLEF, COHSE, Local, Samiti, Solidarity, Syndicalism, UNISON, USDAW

Trading money, Trading post Cabotage, Fort, Wampum

Tradition(s), Traditional(ist) Ancestral, Classical, Convention, Custom(ary), Eastern, Folksy, Folkway, Hadith, Heritage, Legend, Lore, Mahayana, Misoneist, Old guard, Old-line, Old-school, Orthodox, Pharisee, Pompier, Practice, Purist, Square, Suburban, Time-honoured, Trad, Tralaticious, Tralatitious, Unwritten

Traduce Abuse, Asperse, Defame, Impugn, Malign, Smear, Vilify

Traffic, Traffic pattern Air, Barter, Broke, Cabotage, Clover-leaf, Commerce, Contraflow, Deal, Export, Negotiate, Passage, Run, Slave trade, Smuggle, Tailback, Through, Trade, Truck, Vehicular

Tragedian, Tragedy, Tragic Aeschylus, Buskin, Calamity, Cenci, Corneille, Dire, → **DRAMA**, Euripides, Lear, Macready, Melpomene, Oedipean, Oresteia, Otway, Pathetic, Seneca, Sophoclean, Thespian, Thespis

Trail(er), Trailing Abature, Advert, Audit, Bedraggle, Caravan, Condensation, Creep, Dissipation, Drag, Draggle, Follow, Horsebox, Ipomaea, Ivy, Lag, Liana, Liane, Nature, Oregon, Paper, Path, Persue, Preview, Promo(tion), Pursue, Repent, Runway, Santa Fe, Scent, Shadow, Sickle-cell, Sign, Sleuth, Slot, Spoor, Straggle, Stream, Streel, Tag, Trace, → **TRACK**, Trade, Traipse, Trape, Trauchle, Trayne, Troad, Vapour, Vine, Virga, Wake

▷ **Train(ed)** *may indicate* an anagram

Train(er), Training Accommodation, Advanced, APT, Autogenic, Baggage, BR, Breed, Brighton Belle, Bullet, Caravan, Cat, Cavalcade, Choo-choo, Circuit, Coach, Commuter, Condition, Cortège, Diesel, Direct, Discipline, Dog, Double-header, Dressage, Drill, Drive, Educate, Entourage, Enure, Epicyclic, Eurostar®, Excursion, Exercise, Express, Fartlek, Field, Flier, Flight simulator, Freightliner®, Fuse, Gear, Ghan, Ghost, Gravy, Grounding, GWR, Handle(r), → **INSET**, Instruct, Intercity®, Interval, Jerkwater, Journey, Liner, Link, LMS, LNER, Loco, Longe, Lunge, Maglev, Mailcar, Manège, Manrider, Meinie, Mein(e)y, Mentor, Milk, Mixed, Nopo, Nurture, Nuzzle, Omnibus, Orient Express, Outward Bound®, Owl, Pack, Paddy, Parliamentary, PE, Pendolino, Personal, Potty, Practise, → **PREPARE**, Procession, PT, Puffer, Puff-puff, Push-pull, Q, Queue, Rattler, Rehearse, Retinue, Road, Roadwork, Rocket, Ry, Sack, Sacque, → **SCHOOL**, Series, Shoe, Shuttle service, Siege, Sinkansen, Skill centre, Sloid, Sloyd, Sowarree, Sowarry, Special, SR, Steer, String, Suite, Tail, Tame, → **TEACH**, Through, Tire, Tirocinium, Track shoe, Trail, Trellis, Tube, Twin bill, Wage, Wagon, Wave, Way

Trainee → **APPRENTICE**, AT, Cadet, Cub, Intern, Jackaroo, Jackeroo, Learner, Ordinand, Rookie, Rooky, T

Train-spotter Gricer

Trait Characteristic, Feature, Knack, Ph(a)enotype, Sickle-cell, Strain, Thew, Trick, Vein

Traitor Benedict Arnold, Betrayer, Casement, Dobber-in, Fifth column, Joyce, Judas, Judas Maccabaeus, Nid(d)ering, Nid(d)erling, Nithing, Proditor, Quisling,

Renegade, Reptile, Tarpeian, Traditor, Treachetour, Turncoat, Viper, Wallydraigle, Weasel

Trajectory Parabola, Track

Tram Tip

▷ **Trammel** *may indicate* an anagram

Tramp, Trample Bog-trotter, Bum, Caird, Clochard, Clump, Crush, Deadbeat, Derelict, Derro, Dingbat, Dosser, Down and out, Estragon, Footslog, Freighter, Gadling, Gangrel, Gook, Hike, Hobo, Knight of the road, Meff, Override, Overrun, Pad, Piker, Plod, Poach, Potch(e), Prostitute, Rover, Scorn, Ship, Splodge, Sundowner, Swagman, → **TINKER**, Toe-rag(ger), Tom, Track, Traipse, Tread, Trek, Trog, Tromp, Truant, Trudge, Tub, Vagabond, Vagrant, Weary Willie

Trampoline Trampet(te)

Trance Catalepsy, Cataplexy, Goa, Narcolepsy, Somnambulism

Tranche Gold, Reserve

Tranquil(lity) Ataraxy, Calm, Composure, Easy, Halcyon, Lee, Peaceful, Placid, Quietude, Restful, Sedate, → **SERENE**

Tranquillise(r) Appease, Ataractic, Ataraxic, → **CALM**, Diazepam, Downer, Hypnone, Hypnotic, Largactil®, Librium®, Nervine, Nitrazepam, Oxazepam, Placate, Satisfy, Soothe, Still, Valium®

Transact, Transaction(s) Affair, Agio, Brokerage, Deal, Escrow, Fasti, Leaseback, Passage, Put through, Tr

Transcend(ent), Transcendental(ist), Transcendentalism Emerson, Excel, Mystic, Overtop, Surpass, Thoreau

Transcribe, Transcript(ion) Copy, Inclusive, Rescore, Tenor, → **TRANSLATE**, Transume

Transfer(ence), Transferance Alien, Alienate, → **ASSIGN**, Attorn, Bosman, Calk, Calque, Cede, Chargeable, Communize, Consign, Convey(ance), Credit, Crosstalk, Dabbity, Decal, Deed, Demise, Devolve, Download, Embryo, Exchange, Explant, Flit, Hive off, Make over, Mancipation, Metathesis, Mortmain, Nuclear, On-lend, Pass, Photomechanical, Print through, Provection, Reassign, Redeploy, Remit, Remove, Render, Repot, Second, Settlement, Slam, Thought, Transduction, Transfection, Transhume, Translocation, Uproot, Vire, Virement

▷ **Transferred** *may indicate* an anagram

Transfix Impale, Rivet, → **SKEWER**, Spear, Spit

Transform(ation), Transformer Affine, Alchemist, Alter, Apotheosis, Balun, Change, Fourier, Lorentz, Metamorphism, Metamorphose, Metamorphosis, Metaplasia, Metastasis, Morphallaxis, Morphing, Permute, Rectifier, Sea change, Sepalody, Tinct, Toroid, Toupee, Transmogrify, Variation, Wig

▷ **Transform(ed)** *may indicate* an anagram

Transfusion Apheresis

Transgress(ion) Encroach, Err, Infraction, Infringe, Offend, Overstep, Peccancy, → **SIN**, Violate

Transient, Transit(ion), Transitory Brief, Caducity, Ephemeral, Evanescent, Fleeting, Fly-by-night, Forbidden, Fugacious, Hobo, Metabasis, Passage, Passing, Provisional, Seque, Sfumato, T, Temporary

Transistor Drift, Emitter, Epitaxial, Field-effect, Junction

Translate, Translation, Translator Calque, Construe, Convert, Coverdale, Crib, Decode, Explain, Free, Horse, Interpret, In vitro, Jerome, Key, Linguist, Loan, Machine, Metaphrase, Nick, Paraphrase, Pinyin, Polyglot, Pony, Reduce, Render, Rendition, Rhemist, Septuagint, Simultaneous, Targum, Tr, Transcribe, Transform, Trot, Unseen, Version(al), Vulgate, Wycliffe

▷ **Translate(d)** *may indicate* an anagram

Transmigrate, Transmigration Exodus, Metempsychosis, Passage, Trek

Transmit(ter), Transmitted, Transmission Air, Allele, Analogue, Automatic, Band, Baseband, Beacon, Broadband, → **BROADCAST**, Cable, Carry, CB, Communicate, Compander, Compandor, Conduct, Consign, Contagion, Convection, Convey, Digital, Diplex, Facsimile, Filler, Forward, Gearbox, Gene, Heredity, Impart, Intelsat, Localizer, Manual, Mast, Microphone, Modem, Nicol, Permittivity, Pipe, Propagate, Racon, Radiate, Radio, Receiver, Responser, Simplex, Simulcast, Sonabuoy, Spark, Synchronous, Tappet, Telautograph®, Telecast, Telegony, Telematics, Telemetry, Teleprinter, Teletex, Televise, Telex, Tiptronic®, Tiros, Traduce, Traject, Tralaticious, Tralatitious, UART, Ultrawideband, Uplink, Upload, Walkie-talkie, Webcam, Wi-Fi®

Transom Reverse, Traverse

Transparent, Transparency Adularia, Clarity, Clear, Crystal(line), Diaphanous, Dioptric, Glassy, Glazed, Hyaloid, Iolite, Leno, Limpid, Lucid, Luminous, Patent, Pellucid, Sheer, Slide, Tiffany

Transpire Happen, Occur

Transplant Allograft, Anaplasty, Graft, Repot, Reset, Shift

Transport(ed), Transporter, Transportation Active, Aerotrain, Ar(a)ba, Argo, Bear, Bike, Broomstick, BRS, Buggy, Bus, Cargo, Carract, → **CARRY**, Cart, Casevac, Cat-train, Charabanc, Charm, Convey, Cycle, Delight, Ecstasy, Elation, Electron, Eloin, Enrapt, Enravish, Entrain, Esloin, Estro, Fishyback, Freight, Haul(age), Hearse, Helicopter, Jerrican, Joy, Kurvey, Lift, Lug, Maglev, Mambrane, Matatu, Medevac, Monorail, Overjoy, Pack animal, Palanquin, Pantechnicon, Park and ride, Public, Put, Rape, Rapine, Rapture, Roadster, Ship, Shorthaul, Shuttle, Sidecar, Sledge, Snowmobile, Supersonic, Tandem, Tanker, Tape, Tote, Train, Tramway, Trap, Troopship, Tuktuk, Waft, Wheels, Wireway

Transpose, Transposition Anagram, Commute, Convert, Invert, Metathesis, Shift, Spoonerism, Switch, Tr

▷ **Transposed** *may indicate* an anagram

Transsexual Invert

Transubstantiate, Transubstantiation Capernaite

Transverse Across, Crosscut, Diagonal, Obliquid, Thwart

Transvest(it)ism, Transvestite Berdache, Berdash, Cross-dressing, Eonist

Tranter Dolly

Trap(s), Trapdoor, Trapped, Trappings Ambush, → **BAGGAGE**, Bags, Belongings, Booby, Buckboard, Bunker, Carriage, Catch, Catch-pit, Clapnet, Corner, Cru(i)ve, Deadfall, Death, Decoy, Dip, Dogcart, Downfall, Drain, Eelset, Emergent, Ensnare, Entrain, Fall, Fit-up, Fly, Flypaper, Frame-up, Fyke, Gig, Gin, Gob, Grin, Hatch, Housings, Ice-bound, Jinri(c)ksha(w), Keddah, Kettle, Kheda, Kiddle, Kidel, Kipe, Kisser, Knur(r), Light, Lime, Live, → **LUGGAGE**, Lure, Mesh, Mouth, Net, Nur(r), Paraphernalia, Pitfall, Plant, Polaron, Police, Pot, Poverty, Putcheon, Putcher, Quicksand, Radar, Regalia, Sand, Scruto, Scuttle, → **SNARE**, Speed, Spell, Spider, Springe, Stake-net, Star, Steam, Stench, Sting, Stink, Sun, Tangle, Tank, Teagle, Toil, Tonga, Trapfall, Trojan horse, Trou-de-loup, Two-wheeler, U, U-bend, Vampire, Web, Weel, Weir, Wire

Trapezist Leotard

Trapper Carson, Voyageur

Trash(y) Bosh, Deface, Desecrate, Dre(c)k, Garbage, Junk, Kitsch, Pulp, → **RUBBISH**, Schlock, Scum, Tinpot, Trailer, Vandalise, White, Worthless

Trauma Insult, Shell-shock, Shock

Travel(ler), Travelling Aeneas, Backpack, Bagman, Bushwhacker, Columbus, Commercial, Commute, Crustie, Crusty, Drive, Drummer, Explorer, Fare, Fellow, Fly, Fogg, Geoffrey, Gipsen, Gipsy, Gitano, Globe-trotter, Go, Gulliver, Gypsy, Hike, Hitchhiker, Interrail, Itinerant, Journey, Long-haul, Marco Polo, Meve, Migrant, Motor, Move, Mush, New Age, Nomad, Odysseus, Passenger, Passepartout, Peregrination, Peripatetic, Pilgrim, Ply, Polo, Pootle, Range, Rep, Ride, Road, Rom(any), Rove, Safari, Sail, Salesman, Samaritan, Space, Teleport, Tool, → **TOUR**, Trek, Tripper, Tsigane, Viator, Voyage, Wanderjahr, Wayfarer, Wend, Wildfire, Zigan

Traverse Cross, Girdle, Measure, Quest, Trace

Travesty Burlesque, Charade, Distortion, Parody, Show, Skit

Trawl Beam, Drag-net, Hose-net, Net

Tray Antler, Bottle-slide, Carrier, Case, Charger, Coaster, Gallery, Joe, Lazy Susan, Mould, Plateau, → **SALVER**, Shower, Tea, Trencher, Typecase, Voider, Waiter

Treacherous, Treachery Bad faith, Deceit, Delilah, Fickle, Ganelon, Guile, Insidious, Judas-kiss, Knife, Mala fide, Medism, Perfidious, Punic, Punic faith, Quicksands, Serpentine, Sleeky, Snaky, Sneaky, Trahison, Traitor, → **TREASON**, Two-faced, Viper, Weasel

Treacle Black(jack), Butter, Molasses, Venice

Tread Clamp, Clump, Dance, Pad, Step, Stramp, Track, Trample

Treadle Footboard

Treason Betrayal, Constructive, High, Insurrection, Lèse-majesté, Lese-majesty, Perduellion, Petty, Sedition, → **TREACHERY**

Treasure(r), Treasury Banker, Bursar, Cache, Camera, Camerlengo, Camerlingo, Cherish, Chest, Cimelia, Coffer, Ewe-lamb, Exchequer, Fisc(al), Fisk, Godolphin, Golden, Heritage, Hoard, Montana, Palgrave, Pork barrel, → **PRIZE**, Procurator, Purser, Quaestor, Relic, Riches, Steward, Taonga, Thesaurus, Trove

Treat, Treatment Actinotherapy, Action, Acupuncture, Allopathy, Antidote, Apitherapy, Archilowe, Arenation, Aromatherapy, Balneotherapy, Beano, Beneficiate, Besee, Body wrap, Botox®, Capitulate, Care, Chemotherapy, Chiropractic, Condition, Course, Crymotherapy, Cryotherapy, Cupping, Cure, Deal, Detox(ification), Dialysis, Do, → **DOCTOR**, Dose, Dress, Dutch, Enantiopathy, Entertain, Est, Facial, Faith-healing, Fango, Faradism, Figuration, Foment, Frawzey, Handle, Holistic, Homeopathy, HRT, Hydrotherapy, Hypnotherapy, Immunotherapy, Intermediate, Jin shin do, Kenny, Laser, Manage, Massotherapy, Mechanotherapy, Medicate, Mesotherapy, Moxibustion, Narcotherapy, Naturopathy, Negotiate, Opotherapy, Organotherapy, Orthoptics, Osteopathy, → **OUTING**, Pasteur, Pedicure, Pelotherapy, Phototherapy, Physiatrics, Physic, Physiotherapy, Pie, Poultice, Probiotics, Process, Prophylaxis, Psychoanalysis, Psychodrama, Psychotherapy, Radiotherapy, Regale, Rehab(ilitation), Rest cure, Root, Secretage, Serotherapy, Setter, Shout, Shrift, Sironise, Smile, Speleotherapy, → **STAND**, Tablet, Tebilise®, Thalassotherapy, Themotherapy, Therapy, Titbit, Traction, Twelve-step, UHT, Usance, Use, Vet

▷ **Treated** *may indicate* an anagram

Treatise Almagest, Bestiary, Commentary, Cybele, Didache, Discourse, Dissertation, Essay, Monograph, Pandect, Prodrome, Profound, Summa, Tract(ate), Upanishad, Vedanta

Treaty Agreement, Alliance, Assiento, Concordat, Covenant, Entente, Jay's, Lateran, Locarno, Lunéville, Maastricht, Nijmegen, North Atlantic, → **PACT**, Paris, Private, Protocol, Rapallo, Rijswijk, Ryswick, San Stefano, Sovetsk, Test-ban, Utrecht, Verdun, Versailles, Yorktown

Treble Castrato, Choirboy, Chorist(er), Pairial, Soprano, → **TRIPLE**, Triune, Voice

Tree(s) Actor, → **ANCESTRY**, Axe-breaker, Axle, Beam, Bluff, Bonsai, Boom, Bosk, Clump, Conifer, Coppice, Corner, Cross, Daddock, Deciduous, Decision, Dendrology, Descent, Evergreen, Family, Fault, Fringe, Gallows, Genealogical, Grove, Hang, Hardwood, Igdrasil, Jesse, Nurse, Pedigree, Pole, Rood, Roof, Sawyer, Shoe, Softwood, Staddle, Stemma, Summer, Timber, Tyburn, Vista, Wicopy, → **WOOD**, Ygdrasil, Yggdrasil

TREES

2 letters:
Bo
Ti

3 letters:
Ake
Ash
Asp
Bay
Bel
Ben
Box
Cow
Elm
Fig
Fir
Gum
Ita
Jak
Koa
Mot
Nim
Oak
Oil
Sal
Tea
Til
Ule
Wax
Yew

4 letters:
Acer
Akee
Aloe
Amla
Arar
Atap
Bael
Bhel
Bito
Cade
Coco
Cola
Dali
Dhak
Dika
Dita
Eugh
Gean
Hule
Jack
Kaki
Karo
Kiri
Kola
Lead
Lime
Lote
Mako
Meal
Milk
Ming
Mira
Mott
Mowa
Neem
Nipa
Noni
Olea
Ombu
Palm
Pine
Pipe
Pith
Plum
Poon
Puka
Rain
Rata
Rhus
Rimu

Sack
Shea
Silk
Sloe
Soap
Sorb
Tawa
Teak
Teil
Titi
Toon
Tung
Tutu
Upas
Wych
Yang
Yuzu

5 letters:
Abele
Abies
Ackee
Afara
Agila
Alamo
Alder
Alnus
Anona
Areca
Argan
Aspen
Babul
Banak
Beech
Belah
Birch
Bodhi
Boree
Bunya
Butea
Cacao

Carap
Cedar
Ceiba
China
Cocoa
Cocus
Coral
Ebony
Elder
Fagus
Fever
Flame
Fruit
Gauze
Genip
Grass
Guava
Hakea
Hazel
Hevea
Holly
Iroko
Ivory
Jambu
Jarul
Judas
Kapok
Karri
Kauri
Khaya
Klaat
Kokum
Larch
Lemon
Lichi
Lilac
Lotus
Mahoe
Mahua
Mahwa
Maire

Mamey
Mango
Mapau
Maple
Marri
Matai
Melia
Motte
Mowra
Mugga
Mulga
Mvule
Myall
Ngaio
Nikau
Nyssa
Olive
Opepe
Osier
Palas
Palay
Panax
Peach
Pecan
Pinon
Pipal
Pipul
Pitch
Plane
Quina
Ramin
Roble
Rowan
Sabal
Saman
Sassy
Scrog
Silva
Smoke
Sumac
Tawai
Taxus
Thorn
Thuja
Thuya
Tilia
Tsuga
Tuart
Tulip
Vitex
Wahoo

Wenge
Wilga
Withy
Xylem
Yacca
Yulan
Zaman
Zamia

6 letters:
Abroma
Acacia
Akeake
Alerce
Angico
Annona
Antiar
Arbute
Arolla
Babaco
Bablah
Balsam
Banyan
Baobab
Bilian
Bombax
Bo-tree
Bottle
Buriti
Cadaga
Cadagi
Carapa
Carica
Cashew
Cembra
Cercis
Cerris
Chaste
Chenar
Cherry
Chinar
Citron
Coffee
Cordon
Cornel
Cornus
Damson
Deodar
Diana's
Dragon
Durian

Durion
Emblic
Eumong
Eumung
Feijoa
Fustet
Fustic
Gallus
Garjan
Gidgee
Gidjee
Gingko
Ginkgo
Glinap
Gnetum
Gopher
Guango
Gurjun
Gympie
Hupiro
Illipe
Illipi
Illupi
Jarool
Jarrah
Joshua
Jujube
Kamahi
Kamala
Kamela
Kapuka
Karaka
Karamu
Karite
Kowhai
Laurel
Lebbek
Linden
Locust
Longan
Loquat
Lucuma
Lungah
Macoya
Mallee
Manuka
Mastic
Mazard
Medlar
Mimosa
Missel

Mopane
Mopani
Myrtle
Nutmeg
Obeche
Orange
Orihou
Padauk
Padouk
Pagoda
Papaya
Pawpaw
Peepul
Pepper
Platan
Pomelo
Poplar
Popple
Protea
Puriri
Quince
Red-bud
Red gum
Ricker
Roucou
Rubber
Sabicu
Sallow
Samaan
Sapele
Sapium
Sapota
Saxaul
She-oak
Sinder
Sorrel
Souari
Spruce
Styrax
Sumach
Sunder
Sundra
Sundri
Tallow
Tamanu
Tawhai
Tewart
Thyine
Titoki
Tooart
Totara

6 letters – cont:
Tupelo
Waboom
Wandoo
Wicken
Willow
Witgat
Yarran
Zamang

7 letters:
Ailanto
Amboina
Apricot
Arbutus
Avodire
Bebeeru
Bilimbi
Bilsted
Bubinga
Buck-eye
Bursera
Cajeput
Cajuput
Calamus
Camphor
Camwood
Canella
Carbeen
Cascara
Cassava
Catalpa
Champac
Champak
Chayote
Coquito
Corylus
Corypha
Cumquat
Dagwood
Dogwood
Dryades
Durmast
Geebung
Genipap
Gluinap
Gumtree
Hickory
Hog-plum
Holm-oak
Houhere

Jipyapa
Kumquat
Lacquer
Lagetto
Lentisk
Logwood
Lumbang
Madrono
Mahaleb
Manjack
Marasca
Margosa
Mazzard
Mesquit
Moringa
Morrell
Mustard
Papauma
Pereira
Pilinut
Pimento
Platane
Pollard
Populus
Pukatea
Quassia
Quicken
Quillai
Quinain
Radiata
Rampick
Rampike
Redwood
Rock elm
Saksaul
Sandbox
Saouari
Sapling
Saturn's
Sausage
Sequoia
Seringa
Service
Shittah
Sourgum
Soursop
Spindle
Sundari
Talipat
Talipot
Taraire

Taupata
Tawhiri
Trumpet
Varnish
Wallaba
Wirilda
Witchen
Wych-elm
Xylopia
Zelkova

8 letters:
Aguacate
Algaroba
Aquillia
Bangalay
Bangalow
Basswood
Benjamin
Bergamot
Berrigan
Blackboy
Blimbing
Bountree
Bourtree
Breadnut
Brigalow
Calabash
Cinchona
Cinnamon
Cocoplum
Coolabah
Coolibah
Corkwood
Crabwood
Cucumber
Cudgerie
Dendroid
Dracaena
Espalier
Flittern
Fraxinus
Garcinia
Ghost-gum
Gnetales
Guaiacum
Hagberry
Hawthorn
Hinahina
Hornbeam
Huon-pine

Inkberry
Ironbark
Ironwood
Jelutong
Kawakawa
Kingwood
Laburnum
Lacebark
Lecythis
Loblolly
Magnolia
Mahogany
Makomako
Mangrove
Manna-ash
Mesquite
Mulberry
Ocotillo
Oiticica
Oleaceae
Oleaster
Pachouli
Palmetto
Pandanus
Parapara
Pichurim
Pinaster
Pithtree
Pyinkado
Quandang
Quandong
Quantong
Quillaia
Quillaja
Raintree
Rambutan
Rangiora
Rewa-rewa
Sago-palm
Sandarac
Santalum
Sapindus
Sapucaia
Sasswood
Sea grape
Shagbark
Simaruba
Snowball
Snowdrop
Soapbark
Sourwood

Standard
Stinging
Sweet gum
Sweetsop
Sycamine
Sycamore
Sycomore
Tamarack
Tamarind
Tamarisk
Taxodium
Umbrella
Whitegum
Wine-palm

9 letters:
Agila-wood
Ailantous
Albespine
Angophora
Araucaria
Azedarach
Bilimbing
Bitternut
Blackbutt
Blackjack
Blackwood
Bloodwood
Bolletrie
Boobialla
Broadleaf
Bully-tree
Bulwaddee
Burrawary
Butternut
Caliatour
Caliature
Candlenut
Canoewood
Carambola
Casuarina
Chempaduk
Cherimoya
Chincapin
Chinkapin
Coachwood
Cordyline
Courbaril
Cupressus
Eaglewood
Firewheel

Flame-leaf
Greenwood
Grevillea
Hackberry
Ivory palm
Jacaranda
Kahikatea
Krummholz
Kurrajong
Lancewood
Lemonwood
Leylandii
Macadamia
Marmalade
Mirabelle
Mockernut
Monkeypot
Naseberry
Nectarine
Nux vomica
Paloverde
Paperbark
Patchouli
Patchouly
Paulownia
Persimmon
Pistachio
Pitch-pine
Poinciana
Ponderosa
Pontianac
Prickwood
Pricky ash
Quebracho
Rauwolfia
Rose-apple
Sapodilla
Saskatoon
Sassafras
Satinwood
Shellbark
Simarouba
Soapberry
Star-anise
Star-apple
Stinkwood
Sweetwood
Tacamahac
Tamarillo
Terebinth
Toothache

Torchwood
Wagenboom
Wayfaring
Whitebeam
Whitewood
Wineberry
Wych-hazel
Zebrawood

10 letters:
Arbor Vitae
Bitterbark
Blackbully
Breadfruit
Bulletwood
Bunya-bunya
Buttonball
Buttonwood
Calamondin
Calliature
Candle-wood
Cannonball
Chamaerops
Chaulmugra
Cheesewood
Chinaberry
Chinquapin
Cottonwood
Cowrie-pine
Eucalyptus
Fiddlewood
Flamboyant
Flindersia
Frangipani
Ginkgoales
Green-heart
Hackmatack
Ilang-ilang
Jaboticaba
Jippi-jappa
Kaffirboom
Kotokutuku
Letter-wood
Lilly-pilly
Macrocarpa
Manchineel
Mangabeira
Mangosteen
Marblewood
Nithofagus
Palisander

Paper birch
Pepperidge
Pohutukawa
Quercitron
Ribbonwood
Sandalwood
Sappanwood
Silk-cotton
Silverbell
Sneezewood
Spotted gum
Strawberry
Tawheowheo
Traveller's
Turpentine
Witch-hazel
Witgatboom
Woollybutt
Yellowwood
Ylang-ylang

11 letters:
Anchovy-pear
Appleringie
Bladderwort
Cabbage-palm
Chaulmoogra
Chokecherry
Copperbeech
Cryptomeria
Dipterocarp
Eriodendron
Flamboyante
Fothergilla
Gingerbread
Honey locust
Horseradish
Jesuit's bark
Leatherwood
Lignum vitae
Liquidambar
Maceranduba
Metasequoia
Pomegranate
Purpleheart
Shittimwood
Sitka spruce
Stringybark

12 letters:
African tulip

Haemotoxylon	Masseranduba	Wellingtonia	**14 letters:**
Hercules' club	Monkey-puzzle		Western hemlock
Liriodendron	Raspberry jam	**13 letters:**	
Mammee-sapota	Washingtonia	Paper-mulberry	

Tree-climber, Tree-dweller Monkey, Opossum, Sciurus, Squirrel, Unau
Tree disease Dutch elm, Waldsterben
Tree-man Ent
Tree-moss Usnea
Tree-paeony Moutan
Tree-pecker Picus
Tree-shrew Tana
Trefoil Bird's foot, Clover, Hop, Lotos, Lotus
Trek Hike, Journey, Leg, Odyssey, Safari, Yomp
Trellis Espalier, Lattice, Pergola, Treillage, Treille
Tremble, Trembling, Tremor Aftershock, Ashake, Butterfly, Dither, Dodder, Foreshock, Hotter, Intention, Judder, Marsquake, Milk sickness, Moonquake, Palpitate, Quail, Quake, Quaver, Quiver, Seismal, → **SHAKE**, Shiver, Shock, Shudder, Stound, Temblor, Titubation, Trepid, Twitchy, Vibrant, Vibrate, Vibration, Vibratiuncle, Vibrato, Wobble, Wuther, Yips
Tremendous Big, Enormous, Howling, Immense, Marvellous, Thundering
Tremolo Bebung, Quaver, Trill(o)
▶ **Tremor** *see* **TREMBLE**
Tremulous Dithering, Hirrient, Quaking, Shaky, Timorous
Trench(er) Boyau, Cunette, Cuvette, Delf, Delph, Dike(r), → **DITCH**, Dyke(r), Encroach, Fleet, Foss(e), Foxhole, Fur(r), Furrow, Grip, Gullet, Gutter, Leat, Line, Mariana, Moat, Oceanic, Outwork, Rill, Rille, Ring-dyke, Robber, Salient, Sap, Shott, Slidder, Slit, Sod, Sondage
Trenchant Acid, Cutting
Trend(y), Trendsetter Bellwether, Bent, Bias, Chic, Climate, Drift, Fashion, Hep, Hip, In, Mainstream, New Age(r), Newfangled, Pacemaker, Pop, Poserish, Posey, Rage, Right-on, Smart, Style, Swim, Tendency, Tendenz, Tenor, Tide, Tonnish
Trespass(ing) Aggravated, Encroach, Errant, Hack, Impinge, Infringe, Offend, Peccancy, Sin, Trench, Wrong
Tress(es) Curl, Lock, Ringlet, Switch, Tallent
Trestle Sawhorse
Triad Chord, Ternion, Trimurti
Trial Acid test, Adversity, Affliction, Appro, Approbation, Approval, Assize, Attempt, Bane, Bernoulli, Bout, Burden, Clinical, Compurgation, Corsned, Court-martial, Cow, Cross, Dock, Drumhead, Empirical, Essay, → **EXPERIMENT**, Field, Fitting, Go, Hearing, Jeddart justice, Jethart justice, Lydford law, Nuremberg, Ordeal, Pilot, Pree, Probation, Proof, Race, Rehearsal, Salem, Scramble, Sheepdog, Show, State, Taste, Test, Time
Triangle(d), Triangular Acute, Bermuda, Circular, Cosec, Deltoid, Equilateral, Eternal, Gair, Golden, Gore, Gyronny, Isosceles, Obtuse, Pascal's, Pedimental, Pendentive, Pyramid, Rack, Right-angled, Scalene, Similar, Spherical, Trigon, Triquetral, Tromino, Warning
Trias(sic) Bunter, Keuper, Muschelkalk, Rhaetic
Tribe(s), Tribal, Tribesmen Amalekite, Ammonites, Ashanti, Asher, Benjamin, Celt, Cherokee, Cimmerii, Clan(nish), Cree, Creek, Dan, D(a)yak, Dinka, Dynasty, Edomites, Ephraim, Family, Gad, Gens, Gentes, Gentilic, Gond, Goth, Guarani,

Hapu, Helvetii, Hittite, Horde, Hottentot, Ibo, Iceni, Israelite, Issachar, Iwi, Jat, Judah, Kaffir, Kenite, Kurd, Lashkar, Levi, Levite, Longobardi, Lost, Manasseh, Masai, Moabite, Mongol, Moro, Naga, Naphtali, Nation, Nervii, Ngati, Ordovices, Ostrogoths, Pathan, Phyle, Picts, → **RACE**, Reuben, Riff, Rod, Sakai, Salian, Schedule, Senones, Senussi, Sept, Shawnee, Silures, Simeon, Strandloper, Tasaday, Teuton, Trinobantes, Ute, Vandals, Wolof, Wyandot(te), X(h)osa, Zebulun

Tribune, Tribunal Aeropagus, Bema, Bench, → **COURT**, Divan, Employment, Forum, Hague, Industrial, Leader, Platform, Rienzi, Rota, Star-chamber, Waitangi

Tributary Affluent, Bogan, Branch, Creek, Fork

Tribute Cain, Capelline, Citation, Commemoration, Compliment, Crants, Dedication, Deodate, → **DUE**, Encomium, Epitaph, Festschrift, Gavel, Heriot, Homage, Kain, Memento, Ode, Panegyric, Peter's pence, → **PRAISE**, Rome-penny, Rome-scot, Scat(t), Tax, Testimonial, Toast, Wreath, Wroth

Trice Flash, Instant

Trichosanthin Q

▷ **Trick** *may indicate* an anagram

Trick(ed), Trickery, Tricks(ter), Tricky Antic, Art, Artifice, Attrap, Awkward, Bamboozle, Begunk, Book, Bunco, Bunko, Cantrip, Capot, Catch, Charley pitcher, Cheat, Chicane(ry), Chouse, Claptrap, Cod(-act), Cog, Con(fidence), Coyote, Crook, Davenport, Deception, Deck, Delicate, Delude, Device, Dirty, → **DO**, → **DODGE**, Double, Dupe, Elf, Elfin, Elvan, Fard, Feat, Fetch, Fiddle, Finesse, Finicky, Flam, Flim-flam, Fob, Fox, Fraud, Fun, Gambit, Game, Gaud, Gleek, Glike, Gowk, Guile, Had, Hanky-panky, Hey presto, Hoax, Hocus(-pocus), Hoodwink, Hornswoggle, Hot potato, Hum, Illude, Illusion, Illywhacker, Jadery, Jape, Jockey, John, Kittle, Knack, Lark, Magsman, Mislead, Monkey, Monkey-shine, Murphy's game, Nap, Nasruddin, Palter, Parlour, Pass, Pawk, Pleasantry, Pliskie, Prank, Prestige, Put-on, Quick, Ramp, Raven, Reak, Reik, Rex, Rig, Rope, Ropery, Roughie, Ruse, Scam, Sell, Set-up, Shanghai, Shavie, Shenanigan, Shifty, Shill, Skin-game, Skite, Skul(l)duggery, Skylark, Slam, Sleight, Slight, Slinter, Sophism, Spoof, Stall, Stint, Subterfuge, Sug, Swiftie, Thimble-rig, Three-card, Ticklish, Tip, Trap, Tregetour, Trump, Turn, Tweedler, Undercraft, Underplot, Vole, Wangle, Wheeze, Wile, Wrinkle

Trickle Drib(ble), Driblet, Dropple, Gutter, Leak, Rill, Seep

Trickless Misère

Triclinic Anorthic

Trident Fork, Plane, Trisul(a)

Trifle(s), Trifling Bagatelle, Banal, Baubee, Bauble, Bibelot, Birdseed, Bit, Bubkas, Cent, Chickenfeed, Coquette, Dabble, Dalliance, → **DALLY**, Denier, Desipient, Dessert, Do, Doit, Faddle, Falderal, Falderol, Fallal, Fattrell, Feather, Fewtril, Fiddle, Fiddle-faddle, Fig, Fingle-fangle, Fizgig, Flamfew, Fleabite, Flirt, Folderol, Fool, Footle, Fribble, Frippery, Fritter, Frivol, Gewgaw, Idle, Insignificant, Iota, Kickshaw, Knick-knack, Luck-penny, Mess, Mite, Nick-nacket, Niff-naff, Nothing, Nugae, Nugatory, Nyaff, Old song, Palter, Paltry, Peanuts, Peddle, Peppercorn, Petty, Philander, Picayune, Piddle, Piffle, Pin, Pingle, Pittance, Play, Potty, Quelquechose, Quiddity, Quiddle, Slight, Small beer, Smatter, Song, Sport, Stiver, Strae, Straw, Sundry, Sweet Fanny Adams, Tiddle, Tom, Toy, Trinket, Trivia, Whifflery, Whim-wham, Whit

Trig(onometry) Neat, Sech, Spherical, Tosh, Trim

Trigger Activate, Detent, Hair, Instigate, Krytron, Pawl, Precipitate, Schmitt, Start, Switch on, Touch off

Trill(ed), Triller, Trilling Burr, Churr, Hirrient, Quaver, Ribattuta, Roll, Staphyle, Trim, Twitter, Warble

Trilobite Olenellus, Olenus, Paradoxide

Trim(med), Trimmer, Trimming Ballast, Barb, Bleed, Braid, Bray, Chipper, Clip, Dapper, Dinky, Dress, Ermine, Face, Falbala, Fettle, File, Froufrou, Garni, Garnish, Garniture, Gimp, Guimpe, Macramé, Macrami, Marabou, Neat, Net(t), Ornament, Pare, Passament, Passement(erie), Pipe, Plight, Posh, Preen, Proign, Proyn(e), Pruin(e), Prune, Roach, Robin, Ruche, Sax, Sett, Shipshape, Smirk, Smug, Sned, Snod, → **SPRUCE**, Straddle, Stroddle, Strodle, Stylist, Svelte, Tiddley, → **TIDY**, Time-server, Top, Torsade, Trick, Whippersnipper, Wig

Trinidadian Carib

Trinity, Trinitarian Mathurin(e), Prosopon, Triad, Trimurti, Triune, Word

Trinket(s) Bauble, Bibelot, Bijou(terie), Charm, Fallal, Nicknack, Toy, Trankum, Trumpery

Trio Catch, Graces, Randan, Randem, Skat, Terzetto, Threesome

▷ **Trip** *may indicate* an anagram

Trip(per) Awayday, Cruise, Dance, Day, Ego, Errand, → **FALL**, Field, Flight, Flip, Guilt, Head, High, Joint, Jolly, Journey, Junket, Kilt, Link, Outing, Passage, Pleasure, Ply, Power, Ride, Round, Run, Sail, Sashay, Spin, Spurn, → **STUMBLE**, Tootle, Tour, Trek, Trial, Voyage

Tripe Abracadabra, Bosh, Caen, Entrails, Honeycomb, Offal, Plain, Rot

Triple, Triplet Codon, Hemiol(i)a, Perfect, Sdrucciola, Ternal, Tiercet, Treble, Trifecta, Trilling, Trin(e), Tripling

Tripod Cat, Cortina, Highhat, Oracle, Triangle, Trippet, Trivet

Triptych Volet

Trishaw Cycle

Trite Banal, Boilerplate, Cornball, Corny, Hackneyed, Hoary, Laughable, Mickey Mouse, Novelettish, Platitude, Rinky-dink, Stale, Stock, Time-worn, Worn

Triton Eft, Evet, Ewt, Newt, Trumpet-shell

Triumph(ant) Cock-a-hoop, Codille, Cowabunga, Crow, Eureka, Exult, Glory, Impostor, Killing, Oho, Olé, Ovation, Palm, Prevail, Victorious, → **WIN**

Triumvir Caesar, Crassus, Pompey

Trivet Brandise, Tripod, Trippet

Trivia(l), Triviality Adiaphoron, Bagatelle, Balaam, Bald, → **BANAL**, Footling, Frippery, Frothy, Futile, Idle, Inconsequential, Light, Minutiae, Nitpicking, No-brainer, Nothingism, Paltry, Pap, Peppercorn, Pettifoggery, Petty, Picayune, Piddling, Piffling, Puerile, Shallow, Small, Small beer, Small fry, Snippety, Squirt, Squit, Toy(s), Twaddle, Vegie

Trochee Choree

Troglodyte Ape, Caveman, Hermit, Spelean, Wren

Trojan Aeneas, Agamemnon, Dardan(ian), Iliac, Paris, Priam, Teucrian, Troic

Troll → **FISH**, Gnome, Rove, Spoon, Trawl, Warble

Trolley Brute, Cart, Crane, Dinner-wagon, Dolly, Gurney, Hostess, Shopping, Tea, Teacart, Traymobile, Truck, Trundler

▶ **Trollop** *see* **LOOSE WOMAN**

Trombone Bass, Posaune, Sackbut, Tenor

Trompe l'oeil Quadratura, Quadrature

Troop(s), Trooper Alpini, Band, BEF, Brigade, Company, Depot, Detachment, Guard, Horde, Household, Logistics, Midianite, Militia, Monkeys, Pultan, Pulton, Pultoon, Pultun, SAS, School, Shock, → **SOLDIER**, Sowar, State, Storm, Subsidiary, Tp, Turm(e), Velites

Troopship Transport

Trophy Adward, Ashes, → **AWARD**, Bag, Belt, Cup, Emmy, Memento, Palm, Plate, → **PRIZE**, Scalp, Schneider, Spoils, Tourist, TT

Tropic(al) Cancer, Capricorn, Derris, Jungle, Neogaea, Sultry

Trot(ter), Trot out Air, Clip, Crib, Crubeen, Hag, Job, Jog, Passage, Pettitoes, Piaffe, Pony, Ranke, Red(-shirt), Rising, Tootsie, Trotskyist

Troth Perfay, Troggs

Trotsky(ist) Entr(y)ism, Leon, Militant Tendency

Troubador Blondel, Griot, Manrico, Minstrel, Singer, Sordello

Trouble(s), Troublemaker, Troublesome Ache, Ado, Affliction, Aggro, Agitate, Ail, Alarm, Annoy, Bale, Barrat, Bedevil, Beset, → **BOTHER**, Bovver, Brickle, Burden, Care, Coil, Concern, Debate, Disaster, Disquiet, Distress, Disturb, Dog, Dolour, Eat, Esclandre, Exercise, Fash, Fashious, Finger, Firebrand, Fossick, Frondeur, Gram(e), Grief, Hag-ride, Harass, Harry, Hassle, Hatter, Heat, Heist, Hellion, Hot water, Howdyedo, Hydra, Inconvenience, Infest, → **IN TROUBLE**, Jam, Kaugh, Kiaugh, Mess, Mixer, Moil, Molest, Noy, Perturb, Pester, Pestiferous, Picnic, Plague, Play up, Poke, Reck, Rub, Scamp, Scrape, Shake, Shtook, Shtuck, Soup, Spiny, Stir, Stirrer, Storm, Sturt, Tartar, Teen, Teething, Thorny, Tine, Toil, Trial, Tsouris, Tsuris, Turn-up, Tyne, Unpleasant, Unsettle, Vex, → **WORRY**

Trouble-free Gallio

Trouble-shooter Ombudsman

▷ **Troublesome** *may indicate* an anagram

Trough Back, Bed, Bucket, Buddle, Channel, Chute, Culvert, Graben, Hod, Hutch, Langmuir, Launder, Leachtub, Manger, Pneumatic, Puerto Rico, Stock, Straik, Strake, Syncline, Troffer, Tundish, Tye, Watering

Trounce → **BEAT**, Hammer, Thump

Trouser(s) Bags, Bell-bottoms, Bloomers, Breeches, Bumsters, Capri pants, Cargo pants, Chinos, Churidars, Clam-diggers, Combat, Continuations, Cords, Corduroys, Cossacks, Culottes, Daks, Denims, Drainpipe, Drawers, Ducks, Dungarees, Eel-skins, Flannels, Flares, Galligaskins, Gaskins, Gauchos, Hip-huggers, Hipsters, Inexpressibles, Innominables, Jazzpants, Jeans, Jodhpurs, Jog-pants, Kaccha, Ke(c)ks, Knee cords, Lederhosen, Levis, Longs, Loon-pants, Loons, Moleskins, Overalls, Oxford bags, Palazzo (pants), Palazzos, Pantalet(te)s, Pantaloons, Pants, Pedal pushers, Pegtops, Plus-fours, Plus-twos, Pyjamas, Reach-me-downs, Salopettes, Shalwar, Ski pants, Slacks, Stirrup pants, Stovepipes, Strides, Strossers, Sweatpants, Thornproofs, Trews, Trouse, Unmentionables, Unutterables, Utterless

Trout Aurora, Brook, Brown, Bull, Coral, Finnac(k), Finnock, Fish, Gillaroo, Hag(fish), Herling, Hirling, Kamloops, Peal, Peel, Phinnock, Pogies, Quintet, Rainbow, Salmon, Sewen, Sewin, Speckled, Splake, Steelhead, Togue, Whitling

Trow Faith, Meseems

Trowel Float, Slicker

Troy Ilium, Laomedon, Sergeant, T, Weight

Truant Absentee, AWOL, Bunk off, Dodge, Hooky, Kip, Mich(e), Mitch, Mooch, Mouch, Wag

Truce Armistice, Barley, Ceasefire, Fainites, Fains, Hudna, Interlude, Keys, Pax, Stillstand, Treague, Treaty

Truck Bakkie, Bogie, Breakdown, Business, Cabover, Cattle, Cocopan, Dealings, Dolly, Dumper, Flatbed, Forklift, Haul, Hopper, Journey, → **LORRY**, Low-loader, Monster, Pallet, Panel, Pick-up, Road-train, Semi, Sound, Stacking, Tipper, Tommy, Tow(ie), Traffic, Tram, Trolley, Trundle, Ute, Utility, Van, Wrecker

Trudge Footslog, Jog, Lumber, Pad, Plod, Stodge, Stramp, Taigle, Traipse, Trash, Trauchle, Trog, Vamp

True Accurate, Actual, Apodictic, Axiomatic, Candid, Constant, Correct, Exact, Factual, Faithful, Genuine, Honest, Indubitable, Leal, Literal, Loyal, Platitude, Plumb, Pure, Real, Realistic, Richt, Right, Sooth, Vera, Very

Truffle Tartuffe, Tuber, Tuberaceae

Trug Basket, Wisket

Truly Certainly, Certes, Fegs, Forsooth, Honestly, Indeed, Insooth, Surely, Verily, Yea

Trump(s), Trumpet(er) Agami, Alchemy, Alchymy, Armstrong, Bach, Blare, Blast, Bray, Buccina, Bugle(r), Call, Card, Clang, Clarion, Conch, Cornet, Corona, Crossruff, Crow, Daffodil, Ear, Elephant, Extol, Fanfare, Hallali, Honours, → **HORN**, Invent, Jew's, Last, Lituus, Long ten, Lur(e), Lurist, Manille, Marine, Megaphone, → **NO TRUMP**, Overruff, Pedro, Proclaim, Ram's-horn, Rant, Resurrect, Ruff, Salpingian, Salpinx, Sancho, Satchmo, Sennet, Shell, Shofar, Shophar, Slug-horn, Speaking, Splash, Surpass, Tantara, Tantarara, Tar(at)antara, Theodomas, Tiddy, Triton, Triumph

Trumpery Fattrels, Jimcrack, Paltry, Trashy

Truncate(d) Abrupt, Cut, Dock, Shorten, Snub

Truncheon Billie, Billy, Blackjack, Cosh, Night-stick, Warder

Trundle Hump, Roll, Trill, Troll, Wheel

Trunk(s) Aorta(l), A-road, Body, Bole, Box, Bulk, Bus, But(t), Caber, Cabin, Carcase, Chest, Coffer, Hose, Imperial, Log, Peduncle, Pollard, Portmanteau, Portmantle, Proboscis, Ricker, Road, Saratoga, Shorts, STD, Stock, Stud, Synangium, Torso, Valise, Wardrobe

Truss → **BIND**, Ligate, Oop, Oup, Sheaf, Tie, Upbind

Trust(y), Trusting, Trustworthy Active, Affy, Apex, Authentic, Belief, Blind, Box, Camaraderie, Care, Cartel, Charge, Charitable, Combine, Confide, Count on, Credit, Dependable, Discretionary, → **FAITH**, Fidelity, Fiduciary, Foundation, Gullible, Honest, Hope, Hospital, Investment, Leal, Lippen, Loyal, National, NT, Reliable, Reliance, Rely, Repose, Reputable, Sound, Special, Split, Staunch, Tick, Trojan, Trow, True, Trump, Unit

Trustee Agent, Executor, Fiduciary, Judicial, Pensioneer, Public, Tr

Truth(ful), Truism Accuracy, Alethic, Axiom, Bromide, Cliché, Cold turkey, Dharma, Dialectic, → **FACT**, Facticity, Forsooth, Gospel, Griff, Home, Honesty, Idea(l), Logical, Maxim, Naked, Necessary, Pravda, Principle, Reality, Sooth, Soothfast, Troggs, Veracity, Veridical, Verisimilitude, Verity, Vraisemblance

Try(ing) Aim, Approof, Assay, Attempt, Audition, Bash, Bate, Bid, Birl, Burden, Burl, Conative, Contend, Crack, Effort, Empiric(utic), → **ENDEAVOUR**, Essay, Examine, Experiment, Fand, Fish, Fling, Foretaste, Go, Gun for, Harass, Hard, Hear, Impeach, Importunate, Irk, Noy, Offer, Ordalium, Penalty, Pop, Practise, Pree, Prieve, Prove, Push-over, → **SAMPLE**, Seek, Shot, Sip, Stab, Strain, Strive, Taste, Tax, Tempt, Test, Touchdown, Whirl

Tryst Date, Rendezvous

Tsar(ist) Alexis, Emperor, Godunov, Octobrist, Romanov, Ruler

TT Dry, Race, Rechabite

Tub(by), Tubbiness, Tub-thumper Ash-leach, Back, Bath, Boanerges, Bran, Bucket, Corf, Cowl, Dan, Diogenes, Dolly, Endomorph, Firkin, Keeve, Kid, Kieve, Kit, Luckydip, Mashing, Meat, Pin, Podge, Pot-bellied, Powdering, Pudge, Pulpit, Seasoning, Stand, Swill, Tun, Twin, Vat, Wash, Whey

Tuba Bombardon, Euphonium, Helicon

Tube, Tubing, Tubular Acorn, Arteriole, Artery, Barrel, Blowpipe, Bronchus,

Buckyball, Buckytube, Burette, Calamus, Camera, Canaliculus, Can(n)ula, Capillary, Casing, Catheter, Cathode-ray, Cave, Conduit, Crookes, Digitron, Diode, Discharge, Drain, Draw, Drift, Dropper, Duct, Electron, Endiometer, Epididymis, Eustachian, Extension, Fallopian, Fistula, Flash, Fluorescent, Fulgurite, Geissler, Germ, Glowstick, Grommet, Hawsepipe, Hose, Iconoscope, Image (orthicon), Inner, Kinescope, Klystron, Macaroni, Malpighian, Matrass, Metro, Morris, Nasogastric, Neural, Nixie, Optic, Orthicon, Oval, Oviduct, Pastille, Peashooter, Pentode, Picture, Pilot-static, → **PIPE**, Pipette, Piping, Pitot, Pitot(-static), Pneumatic, Pollen, Postal, Promethean, Salpinx, Saticon®, Saucisse, Saucisson, Schnorkel, Shadow-mask, Shock, Sieve, Siphon, Siphonet, Siphonostele, Siphuncle, Skelp, Skiatron, Sleeve, Slide, Snorkel, Spaghetti, Speaking, Spout, Staple, Static, Stent, Stone canal, Storage, Strae, Straw, Strobotron, Subway, Sucker, Swallet, Telescope, Teletron, Television, Terete, Test, Tetrode, Thermionic, Thyratron, Tile, Torpedo, Torricellian, Trachea, Travelling-wave, Triniscope, Trocar, Trochotron, Trunk, Tunnel, Tuppenny, U, Underground, Ureter, Urethra, Vacuum, Vas, VDU, Vein, Vena, Venturi, Video, Vidicon®, Worm, X-ray

Tuber(s) Arnut, Arracacha, Bulb, Chufa, Coc(c)o, Dahlia, Dasheen, Earth-nut, Eddoes, Ginseng, Jicama, Mashua, Oca, Potato, Salep, Taproot, Taro, Tuckahoe, Yam

Tuberculosis Consumption, Crewels, Cruel(l)s, Decline, King's evil, Lupus, Lupus vulgaris, Phthisis, Scrofula, White plague

Tuck Dart, Friar, Gather, Grub, Hospital corner, Kilt, Pin, Pleat, Scran, Truss, Tummy

Tudor Stockbrokers'

Tuesday Hock, Pancake, Shrove, Super

Tuff Schalstein

Tuft(ed) Aigrette, Amentum, Beard, Candlewick, Catkin, C(a)espitose, Cluster, Coma, Comb, Cowlick, Crest, Dollop, Flaught, Floccus, Flock, Goatee, Hassock, Knop, Lock, Pappus, Penicillate, Quiff, Scopate, Shola, Tait, Tassel, Tate, Toorie, Topknot, Toupee, Tourie, Tussock, Tuzz, Whisk

Tug Chain, Drag, Haul, Jerk, Lug, Pug, → **PULL**, Rive, Saccade, Ship, Sole, Soole, Sowl(e), Tit, Tow, Towboat, Yank

Tui Poebird

Tuition Grind, Masterclass, Seminal

Tully Cicero

Tumble, Tumbler Acrobat, Cartwheel, Drier, Fall, → **GLASS**, Header, Jack, Jill, Pitch, Popple, Purl, Realise, Spill, Stumble, Tailer, Topple, Touser, Towser, Trip, Twig, Voltigeur, Welter

▷ **Tumble** *may indicate* an anagram

Tumbledown Decrepit, Dilapidated, Ramshackle, Rickle, Ruinous

Tumbril Caisson

Tummy Belly, Colon, Mary, Paunch, Pod

Tummy-ache Colic, Gripe, Tormina

Tumour Adenoma, Anbury, Angioma, Angiosarcoma, Astroblastoma, Astrocytoma, Burkitt('s) lymphoma, Cancer, Carcinoid, Carcinoma, Carcinosarcoma, Chondroma, Condyloma, Crab(-yaws), Craniopharyngioma, Dermoid, Encanthis, Encephaloma, Enchondroma, Endothelioma, Epulis, Exostosis, Fibroid, Fibroma, Ganglion, Germinoma, Gioblastoma, Glioma, Granuloma, Grape, → **GROWTH**, Gumma, Haemangioma, Haematoma, Hepatoma, Lipoma, Lymphoma, Medullablastoma, Melanoma, Meningioma, Mesothelioma, Metastasis, Mole, Myeloma, Myoma, Myxoma, Neoplasm, Nephroblastoma, Neuroblastoma, Neuroma, Odontoma,

-oma, Oncology, Osteoclastoma, Osteoma, Osteosarcoma, Papilloma, Polypus, Retinoblastoma, Rhabdomyoma, Sarcoma, Scirrhous, Secondary, Seminoma, Steatoma, Struma, Syphiloma, Talpa, Teratoma, Thymoma, Wart, Warthin's, Wen, Wilm's, Windgall, Wolf, Xanthoma, Yaw

Tumult Brattle, Brawl, Coil, Deray, Ferment, Fracas, Hirdy-girdy, Hubbub, Hurly-burly, Reird, Riot, → **ROAR**, Romage, Rore, Stoor, Stour, Stowre, Stramash, Tew, Tristan, Tristram, → **UPROAR**

Tumulus Barrow, How(e), Mote, Motte

Tun Cask, Keg

Tuna Pear, Skipjack, Yellowfin

Tundra Barren Grounds, Barren Lands

Tune(s), Tuneful, Tuner, Tuning Adjust, Air, Aria, Canorous, Carillon, Catch, Choral, Dump, Earworm, Étude, Fine, Fork, Harmony, Hornpipe, Hunt's up, Jingle, Key, Maggot, Measure, Melisma, → **MELODY**, Morrice, Morris, Old Hundred, → **OUT OF TUNE**, Peg, Planxty, Port, Potpourri, Raga, Rant, Ranz-des-vaches, Reel, Signature, Snatch, Song, Spring, Strain, Sweet, Syntonise, Syntony, Temper, Temperament, Theme, Tone, Toy, Tweak

Tungstate, Tungsten Scheelite, W, Wolfram

Tunic Ao dai, Caftan, Chiton, Choroid, Cote-hardie, Dalmatic, Dashiki, Gymslip, Hauberk, Kabaya, Kaftan, Kameez, K(h)urta, Salwar kameez, → **SINGLET**, Surcoat, Tabard, Toga

Tunicate Pyrosoma, Salpa

Tunnel(ler) Blackwall, Bore, Channel, Chunnel, Condie, Countermine, Culvert, Cundy, Earthworm, Euro, Gallery, Head, Mine, Mole, Qanat, Rotherhithe, Simplon, Smoke, Stope, Subway, Syrinx, Tube, Transmanche, Underpass, Water, Wind, Wormhole

Tunny Bonito, Tuna

Turban Bandanna, Hat, Mitral, Pagri, Puggaree, Puggery, Puggree, Sash, Scarf, Tulipant

Turbid Cloudy, Dense, Drumly, Roily

Turbine Francis, Gas, Impulse, Ram air, Reaction, Steam, Water, Wind

Turbulence, Turbulent Atmospheric, Becket, Bellicose, Buller, Factious, Fierce, Overfall, Rapids, Roil, Stormy, Unruly

▷ **Turbulent, Turbulence** *may indicate* an anagram

Turf Caespitose, Clod, Divot, Earth, Fail, Feal, Flaught, Gazo(o)n, → **GRASS**, Greensward, Kerf, Peat, Screw, → **SOD**, Sward

Turk(ish) Anatolian, Bashaw, Bashkir, Bey, Bimbashi, Bostangi, Byzantine, Caimac(am), Crescent, Effendi, Golden Horde, Grand, Gregory, Horse(tail), Irade, Kaimakam, Kazak(h), Kurd, Mameluke, Mutessarif(at), Omar, Osman(li), Ottamite, Ottoman, Ottomite, Rayah, Scanderbeg, Selim, Seljuk(ian), Seraskier, Spahi, Tartar, Tatar, Timariot, Usak, Uzbeg, Uzbek, Yakut, Young

Turkey, Turkey-like Anatolia, Antioch, Brush, Bubbly(-jock), Cold, Curassow, Eyalet, Flop, Gobbler, Norfolk, Plain, Scrub, Sultanate, Talegalla, Talk, TR, Trabzon, Vulturn

Turkish delight Rahat lacoum, Trehala

Turmeric Curcumine

Turmoil Ariot, Chaos, Din, Ferment, Mess, Pother, Pudder, Stoor, Stour, Tornado, Tracasserie, Tumult, → **UPROAR**, Welter

▷ **Turn(ing)** *may indicate* an anagram

Turn(ing), Turned away, Turned up, Turns Acescent, Act, Adapt, Addle, Advert, Antrorse, Apostrophe, Apotropaic, Avert, Bad, Bank, Become, Bend,

Buggins, Bump, Canceleer, Cancelier, Caracol(e), Careen, Cartwheel, Cast, Chainé, Chandelle, Change, Char(e), Chore, Christiana, Christie, Christy, Churn, Cock, Coil, Crank(le), Cuff, Curd(le), Curve, Defect, Deflect, Demi-volt(e), Detour, Deviate, Dig, Digress, Divert, Ear, Earn, Elbow, Evert, Fadge, Flip, Forfend, Go, Good, Gruppetto, Hairpin, Handbrake, Head-off, Hie, High, Hinge, Hup, Immelmann, Influence, Innings, Intussuscept, Invert, Jar, Jink, Jump, Keel, Kick, Laeotropic, Lodging, Lot, Luff, Mohawk, Nip, Number, Obvert, Parallel, Parry, Penchant, Pivot, Plough, Pronate, Prove, PTO, Quarter, Quersprung, Rebut, Refer, Refract, Remuage, Retroflex, Retroussé, Retrovert, Rev, Revolt, Ride, Riffle, Rocker, Roll, Root, → **ROTATE**, Rote, Roulade, Rout, Routine, Screw, Secund, Sheer, → **SHOT**, Shout, Sicken, Skit, Slew, Slue, Solstice, Sour, → **SPELL**, Spin, Spot, Sprain, Star, Start, Stem, Step, Swash, Swing, Swivel, Telemark, Thigmotropism, Three-point, Throw, Tiptilt, Tirl, Torque, Transpose, Trend, Trick, Trie, Trochilic, Turtle, Twiddle, Twist, U, Uey, Up, Veer, Versed, Version, Vertigo, Volta, Volte-face, Volutation, Wap, Warp, Wedeln, Wend, Went, → **WHEEL**, Whelm, Whirl, Whorl, Wimple, Wind, Wrast, Wrest, Wriggle, Zigzag

Turn-coat Apostate, Cato, Defector, Quisling, Rat, Renegade, Tergiversate, Traitor

Turner Axle, Lana, Lathe, Painter, Pivot, Rose-engine, Spanner, Tina, Worm, Wrench

Turning point Crisis, Crossroads, Landmark, Watershed

Turnip(-shaped) Baggy, Bagie, Hunter, Indian, Jicama, Napiform, Navew, Neep, Prairie, Rutabaga, Shaw, → **STUPID PERSON**, Swede, Tumshie

Turnkey Gaoler, Jailer, Locksman

Turn-out Eventuate, Gathering, Product, Rig, Splay, Style, Team

Turn over Capsize, Careen, Flip, Inversion, Production, PTO, Somersault, TO, Up-end

Turnpike Highway, Toll

Turnstile Tourniquet

Turntable Racer, Rota, Rotator

Turpentine Galipot, Rosin, Thinner, Turps, Venice

Turquoise Bone, Fossil, Ligure, Occidental, Odontolite, Oriental, Turkey stone

Turret(ed) Barmkin, Bartisan, Garret, Louver, Louvre, Mirador, Pepperbox, Sponson, → **TOWER**, Turriculate

Turtle, Turtle head Bale, Calipash, Calipee, Chelone, Diamondback, Emys, Floor, Green, Hawk(s)bill, Inverted, Leatherback, Loggerhead, Matamata, Mossback, Mud, Musk, Ridley, Screen, Snapper, Snapping, Soft-shelled, Stinkpot, Terrapin, Thalassian

Tuscany Chiantishire

Tusk Gam, Horn, Ivory, Tooth, Tush

Tusker Dicynodont, Elephant, Mastodon

Tussle Giust, Joust, Mêlée, Scrimmage, Scrum, Scuffle, Skirmish, Touse, Touze, Towse, Towze, Tuilyie, Wrestle

Tussock Hassock, Niggerhead, Tuft

Tut(-tut) Och, Pooh

Tutelary Guardian, Protector

Tutor Abbé, Aristotle, Ascham, Bear, → **COACH**, Crammer, Don, Instruct, Leader, Mentor, Preceptor, Répétiteur, Supervisor, Teacher

Tuxedo DJ

TV Baird, Box, Cable, Digibox®, Digital, Docudrama, Docusoap, Idiot-box, Lime Grove, Monitor, NICAM, PAL, Pay, Reality, SECAM, Sitcom, Sky, Tele, → **TELEVISION**, Telly, Tie-in, Tube, Video

Twaddle Blether, Drivel, Fadaise, Rot, Slipslop, Tripe
Twang Nasal, Pluck, Plunk, Rhinolalia
Tweak Pluck, Primp, Twiddle, Twist, Twitch
Tweed(y) Donegal, Harris®, Homespun, Lovat, Raploch
Tweet Chirrup
Twelfth, Twelve Apostles, Dozen, Epiphany, Glorious, Grouse, Midday, Midnight,
N, Night, Noon, Ternion, Twal
Twenty, Twenty-sided Icosahedron, Score, Vicenary, Vicennial, Vicesimal,
Vigesimal
Twenty-five, Twentyfifth Pony, Quartern, Semi-jubilee
Twenty-four Thr(e)ave
Twerp Pipsqueak
▸ **Twice** *see* **TWO**
Twice-yearly Biennial, Equinox
Twiddle Fidget, Twirl
Twig(s) Besom, Birch, Cotton, Cow, Dig, Grasp, Kow, Osier, Realise, Reis, Rice,
Rod, Rumble, Sarment, See, Sprig, Sticklac, Switch, Understand, Walking, Wand,
Wattle, Whip, Wicker, Withe
Twilight Astronomical, Civil, Cockshut, Crepuscular, Demi-jour, Dimpsy, Dusk,
Gloam(ing), Götterdämmerung, Nautical, Ragnarok, Summerdim
Twill Cavalry, Chino, Serge
Twin(s) Asvins, Castor, Coetaneous, Conjoined, Didymous, Dioscuri, Ditokous,
Dizygotic, Double, Fraternal, Gemel, Hemitrope, Identical, Isogeny, Juxtaposition,
Kindred, Kray, Look-alike, Macle, Monozygotic, Parabiotic, Pigeon-pair, Pollux,
Siamese, Thomas, Tweedledee, Tweedledum
Twine Binder, Braid, Coil, Cord, Inosculate, Packthread, Sisal, Snake, String, Twist,
Wreathe
Twinge Pang, Scruple, Stab, Twang
Twinkle, Twinkling Glimmer, Glint, Mo(ment), → **SPARKLE**, Starnie, Trice
Twirl Spin, Swivel, Tirl, Tirlie-wirlie, Trill, Trundle, Twiddle, Twizzle, Whirl
▹ **Twirling** *may indicate* an anagram
Twist(ed), Twister, Twisting, Twisty Anfractuous, Askant, Askew, Baccy, Becurl,
Bought, Braid, Buckle, Card-sharper, Chisel, Coil, Contort, Convolution, Crinkle,
Crinkum-crankum, Crisp, Cue, Curl(icue), Curliewurlie, Cyclone, Deform, Detort,
Dishonest, Distort, → **DODGE**, Entrail, Entwine, Garrot, Helix, Imposture, Kink,
Lemon peel, Loop, Mangulate, Mat, Möbius strip, Oliver, Pandanaceous, Plait,
Quirk, Raddle, Ravel, Rick, Rogue, Rotate, Rove, Serpent, Skew, Slew, Slub(b), Slue,
Snake, Snarl, Spin, Spiral, Sprain, Squiggle, Squirm, Swivel, Tendril, Thrawn, Torc,
Tornado, Torque, Torsade, Torsion, Torticollis, Tortile, Turn, Tweak, Twiddle,
Twine, Twirl, Twizzle, Typhoon, Valgus, Volvulus, Wamble, Warp, Welkt, Wigwag,
Wind, Wound-wrap, Wrast, Wreathe, Wrench, Wrest, Wrethe, Wrick, Wriggle,
Wring, Writhe, Wry, Zigzag
▹ **Twisted, Twisting** *may indicate* an anagram
Twit, Twitter Chaff, Cherup, Chirrup, Dotterel, Gear(e), Giber, → **JEER**, Stupid,
Taunt, Tweet, Warble
Twitch(ing), Twitchy Athetosis, Clonic, Fibrillation, Grass, Jerk, Life-blood,
Saccadic, Start, Subsultive, Tic, Tig, Tit, Tweak, Twinge, Vellicate, Yips
Two(some), Twofold, Twice Bice, Bis, Bisp, Both, Brace, Couple(t), Deuce,
Double, Duad, Dual, Duet, Duo, Duple, Dyad, Item, → **PAIR**, Swy, Tête-à-tête,
Twain, Twins, Twister
Two-edged Ancipitous

Two-faced Dihedral, Dorsiventral, Hypocritical, Janus, Redan
Two-gallon Peck
Two-headed Amphisbaenic, Dicephalous, Orthos
Two hundred H
Two hundred and fifty E, K
Two-master Brig
Two-pronged Bidental
Two-rayed Diactinal
Two-sided Bilateral, Equivocatory
Two thousand Z
Two-up Kip, Swy
Two-wheeler Bicycle, Scooter
Tycoon Baron, Empire-builder, Magnate, Mogul, Nabob, Onassis, Plutocrat, Shogun
Tympany Castanets, Cymbal, Drum, Kitchen, Triangle, Xylophone
Type(s), Typing A, Agate, Aldine, Antimony, Antique, B, Balaam, Baskerville, Bastard, Batter, Beard, Bembo, Black-letter, Block, Blood, Bodoni, Body, Bold face, Bourgeois, Braille, Brand, Brevier, Brilliant, Canon, Caslon, Category, Character, Chase, Cicero, Clarendon, Class, Columbian, Condensed, Cut, Egyptian, Elite, Elzevir, Em, Emblem, Emerald, En(nage), English, Face, Font, Footer, Form(e), Founder's, Fount, Fraktur, Fudge, Garamond, Gem, Genre, Gent, Gothic, Great primer, Gutenberg, Hair, Ilk, Image, Kern(e), Key, Keyboard, Kidney, Kind, Late-star, Ligature, Light-faced, Logotype, Longprimer, Ludlow, Mating, Melanochroi, Minion, Modern, Monospaced, Moon, Mould, Non-pareil, Norm, Old English, Old-face, Old Style, Paragon, Pattern, Pearl, Peculiar, Personality, Pi, Pica, Pie, Plantin, Point, Primer, Print, Quad(rat), Roman, Ronde, Ruby, Sanserif, Secretary, Semibold, Serif, Serological, Slug, → **SORT**, Sp, Species, Spectral, Stanhope, Style, Times, Tissue, Touch, Version
▷ **Type of** *may indicate* an anagram
Typesetting Hot metal
Typewriter Golfball, Portable, Stenograph, Stenotype®, Varityper®
Typhoid, Typhus Camp-fever, Scrub, Tick-borne
Typhoon Cyclone, Hurricane, Monsoon, Tornado, Wind
Typical Average, Characteristic, Classic, Echt, Everyman, Normal, Representative, Standard, Symbolic, True-bred, Usual
Typist Audio, Copy, Printer, Steno(grapher), Temp
Tyrannise(d) Domineer, Lord, Under
Tyrant, Tyranny, Tyrannical Absolutism, Autocrat, Caligula, Czar, Despot, Dictator, Drawcansir, Gelon, Herod, Lordly, Nero, Oppressor, Pharaoh, Sardanapalus, Satrap, Stalin, Totalitarian, Tsar, Yoke
Tyre(s) Balloon, Cross-ply, Cushion, Earthing, Michelin®, Pericles, Pneumatic, Radial, Radial(-ply), Recap, Remould, Retread, Shoe, Sidewall, Slick, Snow, Spare, Stepney, Tread, Tubeless, Whitewall
Tyro Beginner, Ham, → **NOVICE**, Rabbit, Rookie, Rooky, Starter
Tyrolese R(h)aetian

Uu

U, U-type Gent, Unicorn, Universal, Uranium
Ubiquitous Everywhere, Inescapable, Omnipresent
Udder Bag, Dug
UFO Roswell
Ugandan Obote
Ugly Butters, Cow, Crow, Customer, Eyesore, Faceache, Foul, Gorgon, Gruesome, Hideous, Homely, Huckery, Jolie laide, Loath, Loth, Mean, Ominous, Plain, Sight
Ugrian Ostiak, Ostyak, Samo(y)ed, Vogul
UK GB
Ukase Decree
Ukraine Ruthene, UA
Ulcer(ous) Abscess, Aphtha, Bedsore, Canker, Chancre, Chancroid, Decubitus, Duodenal, Enanthema, Gastric, Helcoid, Noli-me-tangere, Noma, Peptic, Phagedaena, Plague-sore, Rodent, Rupia, Sore, Varicose, Wolf
Ulster NI, Overcoat, Raincoat, Ulad
Ulterior External, Hidden
Ultimate(ly) Absolute, Basic, Deterrent, Eventual, Final, Furthest, Last, Maximum, Mostest, Omega, So, Supreme, Thule, Ult
Ultra Drastic, Extreme, Radical
Ultra-modern Space age
Ultra-republican Leveller
Ultrasound Lithotripsy
Ulysses Bloom, Grant, Odysseus
Umbellifer(ous) Angelica, Arnut, Car(r)away, Dill, Honewort, Narthex, Pig-nut, Seseli
Umber Burnt, Mottled, Raw, Waved
Umbrage Offence, Pique, Resentment, Shade
Umbrella(-shaped) Bubble, Bumbershoot, Chatta, Gamp, Gingham, Gloria, Mush(room), Nuclear, Parasol, Sunshade, Tee
Umbria Eugubine, Iguvine
Umpire Arb(iter), Byrlawman, Daysman, Decider, Judge, Oddjobman, Odd(s)man, Overseer, Oversman, Referee, Rule, Stickler, Thirdsman
Unabashed Bare-faced, Brazen, Shameless
Unable Can't, Downa-do, Incapable
Unaccented Atonic, Proclitic
Unacceptable Non-U, Not on, Out, Repugnant, Stigmatic
Unaccompanied A cappella, Alone, High-lone, Secco, Single, Solo, Solus
Unaccustomed Desuetude, New, Unwonted
Unadorned Au naturel, Bald, Plain, Stark
Unadulterated Sincere
Unaffected Artless, Genuine, Homely, Insusceptible, Natural, Plain, Sincere, Unattached

Unaided Single-handed, Solo
Unaltered Constant, Same
Unambiguous Categorical, Univocal
Unanimous Accord, Nem con
Unanswerable Erotema, Irrefragable, Irrefutable
Unappealing Distasteful, Grim, Offensive, Rank
Unappreciated, Unappreciative Ingrate, Thankless
Unarguable Erotema
Unarmed Inerm, Naked, Vulnerable
Unashamed Blatant, Brazen, Open
Unassigned Adespota, Anonymous, Vacant
Unassisted Naked eye
Unassuming Lowly, Modest
Unattached Freelance, Loose
Unattractive Drac(k), Lemon, Minger, Munter, Plain, Plug-ugly, Rebarbative,
   Seamy, Skanky, Ugly
Unattributable Anon
Unauthentic Plagal
▷ **Unauthentic** *may indicate* an anagram
Unavail(able), Unavailing Bootless, Futile, Ineluctable, Lost, NA, No use, Off,
   Useless, Vain
Unavoidable Ineluctable, Inevitable, Necessary, Perforce
Unaware(ness) Coma, Heedless, Ignorant, Incognisant, Innocent, Oblivious,
   Stupor
Unbalanced Asymmetric, Deranged, Doolalli, Doolally, Loco, Lopsided, Nutty, Out
   to lunch, Uneven
Unbearable Bassington, Intolerable
Unbeaten, Unbeatable All-time, Perfect
Unbecoming, Unbefitting Improper, Infra dig, Shabby, Unfitting, Unseemly,
   Unsuitable, Unworthy
Unbelievable, Unbeliever Agnostic, Atheist, Cassandra, Doubter, Giaour,
   Heathen, Incredible, Infidel, Pagan, Painim, Paynim, Sceptic, Tall, Zendik
Unbend Relent
Unbent Relaxed
Unbiased Fair, Impartial, Just, Neutral, Objective, Unattainted
Unblemished Spotless, Vestal
Unblinking Alert, Astare, Fearless
Unborn Future, Unbred
Unbowed In-kneed, Resolute
Unbranded Cleanskin
Unbreakable Infrangible, Inviolate
Unbridled Fancy free, Footloose, Lawless, Uncurbed, Unrestricted, Unshackled,
   Untramelled
Unburden Confide, Offload, Relieve, Unload
Uncanny Eerie, Eldritch, Extraordinary, Geason, Rum, Spooky, Wanchancie,
   Wanchancy, Weird
Uncastrated Stone
Unceasing Continuous
▷ **Uncertain** *may indicate* an anagram
Uncertain(ty) Acatalepsy, Agnostic, Blate, Broken, Chancy, Chary, Contingent,
   Delicate, Dicey, Dither, Dodgy, Doubtful, Dubiety, Grey, Heisenberg, Hesitant, Iffy,

Indeterminate, Indistinct, Irresolute, Peradventure, Precarious, Queasy, Risky, Slippery, Tentative, Vor, Wide open

Unchallengeable, Unchallenge(d) Irrecusable, Sackless

Unchangeable, Unchanged, Unchanging As is, Enduring, Eternal, Idempotent, Immutable, Monotonous, Pristine, Stable, Standpat

Uncharacteristic Atypical

Uncharged Neutral, Neutron

Unchaste Corrupt, Immodest, Immoral, Impure, Lewd, Light-heeled, Wanton

Unchecked Rampant

Uncivil(ised) Barbaric, Benighted, Boondocks, Discourteous, Disrespectful, Giant-rude, Goth, Heathen, Impolite, Liberty, Military, Rude, Rudesby, Unmannerly

Uncle Abbas, Afrikaner, Arly, Bob, Dutch, Eme, Nunky, Oom, Pawnbroker, Pledgee, Pop-shop, Remus, Sam, Tio, Tom, Usurer, Vanya

Unclean Defiled, Dirty, Impure, Obscene, Ordure, Squalid, Tabu, T(e)refa(h)

Unclear Ambitty, Cloudy, Hazy, Nebulous, Obscure, Opaque

Unclothed Bald, Nude

Uncloven Soliped

Uncomfortable Mean, Uneasy

Uncommitted Evasive, Free-floating, Laodicean

Uncommon Rara avis, Rare, Sparse, Strange, Unusual

▷ **Uncommon(ly)** *may indicate* an anagram

Uncommunicative Reserved, Tight-lipped

Uncompanionable Threesome

Uncomplimentary Blunt

Uncomprehending Anan, Ignorant

Uncompromising Cutthroat, Hardline, Hardshell, Intransigent, Relentless, Rigid, Strict, Ultra

Unconcealed Open, Pert

Unconcerned Bland, Careless, Casual, Cold, Indifferent, Insouciant, Nonchalant, Strange

Unconditional Absolute, Free, Pure

Unconnected Asyndetic, Detached, Disjointed, Off-line

Unconscious(ness) Asleep, Catalepsy, Cold, Comatose, Instinctive, Non-ego, Not-I, Subliminal, Syncope, Trance, Unaware, Under

Unconsidered Impetuous, Rash

Unconsummated Mariage blanc

Uncontrolled Adrift, Atactic, Free, Incontinent, Loose, Loose cannon, Wild

Unconventional Avant garde, Beatnik, Bohemian, Drop-out, Eccentric, Far-out, Gonzo, Heretic, Heterodox, Hippy, Informal, Irregular, Offbeat, Off-the-wall, Original, Outlandish, Outré, Out there, Raffish, Rebel, Spac(e)y, Unorthodox, Way-out

▷ **Unconventional** *may indicate* an anagram

Unconverted Neat

Unconvincing Farfet(ched), Lame, Thin, Wafer-thin

Uncooperative Recalcitrant

Uncoordinated Asynergia, Ataxic, Awkward, Clumsy

Uncorrect Stet

Uncouth(ness) Backwoodsman, Bear, Boorish, Churlish, Crude, Gothic, Inelegant, Rough, Rube, Rude, Rugged, Uncivil

Uncover(ed) Bare, Disclose, Dismask, Expose, Inoperculate, Open, Overt, Peel,

Reveal, Shave, Shill, Shuck, Uncap, Unveil

Unction, Unctuous(ness) Anele, Balm, Chrism, Extreme, Oil(y), Ointment, Oleaginous, Ooze, Smarm, Soapy

Uncultivated, Uncultured Artless, Bundu, Fallow, Ignorant, Incult, Philistine, Rude, Tramontane, Wild

Undamaged Intact, Sound, Whole

Undated Sine die

Undecided Doubtful, Moot, Non-committal, Open-ended, Pending, Pendulous, Uncertain, Wavering

Undefiled Chaste, Clean, Pure, Virgin

Undeniable Fact, Incontestable, Irrefutable

Under Aneath, Below, Beneath, Hypnotized, Hypo-, Sotto, Sub-, Unconscious, Unneath

Underarm Axilla, Lob

Underburnt Samel

Under-butler Bread-chipper

Undercarriage Bogie, Chassis

Undercoat Base, Primer

Undercooked Rare, Raw, Samel

Undercover Espionage, Secret, Veiled

Undercurrent Acheron, Undertone, Undertow

Underdeveloped, Underdevelopment Ateleiosis, Retarded

Underdog Cerberus, Loser, Victim

▶ **Undergarment** *see* **UNDERWEAR**

Undergo Bear, Dree, Endure, Solvate, Sustain

Undergraduate Commoner, Fresher, L, Pup, Questionist, Sizar, Sophomore, Student, Subsizar, Tuft

Underground (group) Basement, Catacomb, Cellar, Fogou, Hell, Hypogaeous, Irgun, Kiva, Macchie, Maquis, Mattamore, Metro, Phreatic, Pict, Plutonia, Pothole, Secret, Souterrain, Subsoil, Subterranean, Subway, Tube

Undergrowth Brush, Chaparral, Firth, Frith, Scrub

Underhand Backstair, Dirty, Haunch, Insidious, Lob, Oblique, Scullduggery, Secret, Shady, Sinister, Sly, Sneaky, Surreptitious

Underlease Subtack

Underlie, Underlying Subjacent, Subtend

Underline Emphasise, Insist, Sublineation

Underling Bottle-washer, Cog, Inferior, Jack, Menial, Minion, Munchkin, Subordinate

Undermine Erode, Fossick, Handbag, Sap, Subvert, Tunnel, Weaken

Undernourished Puny, Starveling

Underpaid Rat

Underpass Simplon, Subway

Underside Bed, Soffit

Understand(able), Understanding Accept, Acumen, Agreement, Apprehend, Capeesh, Clear, Cognisable, Comprehend, Conceive, Concept, Connivance, Cotton-on, Deal, Dig, Enlighten, Entente, Exoteric, Fathom, Follow, Gather, Gauge, Gaum, Geddit, Gorm, Grasp, Grok, Have, Head, Heels, Hindsight, Insight, Intuit, Ken, Kind, Knowhow, Learn, Light(s), Omniscient, Pact, Plumb, Prajna, Rapport, Rapprochement, Realise, Savey, Savvy, See, Sense, Sole, Substance, Tolerance, Treaty, Tumble, Twig, Uptak(e), Wisdom, Wit

Understate(d), Understatement Litotes, M(e)iosis, Subtle

Understood Implicit, Lucid, OK, Perspicuous, Roger, Tacit, Unspoken

Understudy Deputy, Double, Stand-in, Sub

Undertake, Undertaking Attempt, Contract, Covenant, Emprise, Enterprise, Essay, Feat, Guarantee, Pledge, Promise, Scheme, Shoulder, Task, Venture, Warranty

Undertaker Editor, Entrepreneur, Mortician, Obligor, Sponsor, Upholder

Under-ten Unit, Yarborough

Undertone Murmur, Rhubarb, Sotto voce

Underwater Demersal

Underwear Balbriggan, Balconette, Bloomers, Bodice, Body, Body stocking, Body suit, Bra(ssiere), Briefs, Broekies, Butt bra, Camiknickers, Camisole, Chemise, Chemisette, Chuddies, Combinations, Combs, Corset, Dainties, Drawers, (French) knickers, Frillies, Girdle, Grundies, Innerwear, Jump, Linen, Lingerie, Linings, Long johns, Pantalets, Pantaloons, Panties, Pantihose, Panty girdle, Petticoat, Scanties, Semmit, Shift, Shimmy, Shorts, Singlet, Skivvy, Slip, Smalls, Stays, Step-ins, Subucula, Suspender-belt, Suspenders, Tanga, Teddy, Thermal, Trunks, Underdaks, Undergarments, Underlinen, Underpants, Underset, Undershirt, Underthings, Undies, Unmentionables, Vest, Wyliecoat, Y-fronts®

Underworld Chthonic, Criminal, Hades, Hell, Lowlife, Mafia, Pluto, Shades, Tartar(e), Tartarus, Tartary

Underwrite, Underwritten Assure, Endorse, Guarantee, Insure, Lloyds, PS

Undeserving Immeritous

Undesirable Kibitzer, Riff-raff

Undeveloped Ament, Backward, Depauperate, Green, Inchoate, Latent, Nubbin, Ridgel, Ridgil, Ridgling, Rig, Riggald, Riglin(g), Rudimentary, Seminal

Undifferentiated Thalliform, Thallus

Undigested Crude

Undignified (end) Disaster, Foot, Improper, Infra dig, Unseemly

Undiluted Neat, Pure, Sheer, Straight

Undiminished Entire, Intact, Whole

Undiplomatic Brusque, Tactless

Undisciplined Hothead, Rule-less, Rulesse, Sloppy, Unruly, Wanton

Undisclosed Hidden, In petto

Undisguised Apert, Clear, Plain

Undistinguished Nameless, Plebeian

Undisturbed Halcyon

Undivided Aseptate, Complete, Entire, Indiscrete, One

Undo(ing) Annul, Defeat, Destroy, Disconnect, Downfall, Dup, Poop, Poupe, Release, Rescind, Ruin, Unravel

Undoctored Neat

Undone Arrears, Left, Postponed, Ran, Ruined, Unlast

Undoubtedly Certes, Ipso facto, Positively, Sure

Undress(ed) Bare, Disarray, Disrobe, En cuerpo, Expose, Négligé, Nude, Nue, Peel, Querpo, Raw, Rough, Self-faced, Spar, Strip, Unapparelled

Undulate, Undulating Billow, Nebule, Ripple, Roll, Wave

▷ **Unduly** *may indicate* an anagram

Undyed Greige

Undying Amaranthine, Eternal

Unearth(ly) Astral, Dig, Discover, Disentomb, Exhumate, Indagate

Unease, Uneasiness, Uneasy Angst, Anxious, Creeps, Disquiet, Inquietude, Itchy, Malaise, Queasy, Restive, Shy, Tense, The willies, Uptight, Windy, Womble-cropped

Unedifying Idle

Unembarrassed Blasé, Dégagé

Unemotional Bland, Clinical, Cool, Iceberg, Matter-of-fact, Sober, Stolid

Unemployed, Unemployment Drone, Idle, Laik, Lake, Latent, Lay-off, Redundant, Residual, Stalko, Surfie

Unending Chronic, Eternal, Lasting, Sempiternal

Unenlightened Ignorant, Nighted

Unenthusiastic Cool, Damp, Tepid

Unenveloped Achlamydeous

Unequal(led) Aniso-, Disparate, Non(e)such, Scalene, Unjust

Unerring Dead, Exact, Precise

Unestablished Free

Unethical Amoral, Corrupt, Immoral, Shyster

Uneven(ness) Accident, Blotchy, Bumpy, Erose, Irregular, Jaggy, Patchy, Ragged, Scratchy

▷ **Unevenly** *may indicate* an anagram

Unexceptional Ordinary, Workaday

Unexciting Flat, Staid, Tame

Unexpected(ly) Abrupt, Accidental, Adventitious, Fortuitous, Inopinate, Ironic, Snap, Sodain(e), Sudden, Turn-up, Unawares, Unforeseen, Untoward, Unware, Unwary

Unexperienced Strange

Unexplained Obscure

Unexploded Live

Unfading Evergreen, Immarcescible

Unfailing Sure

Unfair Bias(s)ed, Crook, Dirty, Inclement, Iniquitous, Invidious, Mean, Partial, Unsportsmanlike

Unfaithful Disloyal, Godless, Infidel, Traitor, Two-timing

Unfamiliar Alien, Disinure, New, Quaint, Strange

Unfashionable Cube, Daggy, Dowdy, Lame, Out(moded), Out-of-date, Passé, Square

▷ **Unfashionable** *may indicate* 'in' to be removed

Unfasten Undo, Untie, Untruss

Unfathomable Bottomless

Unfavourable Adverse, Ill, Inimical, Poor, Untoward

Unfeeling Adamant, Callous, Cold, Cruel, Dead, Hard, Inhuman(e), Insensate, Iron-witted, Robotic

Unfinished, Unfinishable Crude, Inchoate, Incondite, Raw, Scabble, Scapple, Sisyphean, Stickit

▷ **Unfit** *may indicate* an anagram

Unfit(ting) Cronk, Disabled, Faulty, Ill, Impair, Inept, Outré, Trefa, Tre(i)f, Unable

Unfixed Isotropic, Loose

Unfledged Gull

Unflinching Fast, Staunch

Unfold Deploy, Display, Divulge, Evolve, Interpret, Open, Relate, Spread

Unforced Voluntary

Unforeseen Accident, Sudden

Unfortunate(ly) Accursed, Alack, Alas, Devil, Hapless, Ill-starred, Indecorous, Luckless, Shameless, Sorry, Star-crossed, Unlucky, Worse luck

Unfounded Groundless

Unfriendly Aloof, Antagonistic, Asocial, Chill(y), Cold, Fraim, Fremd, Fremit, Hostile, Icy, Remote, Surly, Wintry

Unfruitful Abortive, Barren, Sterile

Unfulfilled Frustrated, Manqué

Ungainly Awkward, Gawkish, Uncouth, Weedy

Ungenerous Small

Ungodliness, Ungodly Impiety, Pagan, Perfidious, Profane, World

Ungracious Cold, Mesquin(e), Offhand, Rough, Rude

Ungrammatical Anacoluthia

Ungrateful Ingrate, Snaky

Unguent Nard, Pomade, Salve

Ungulate Anta, Antelope, Dinoceras, Eland, Equidae, Hoofed, Moose, Pachydermata, Rhino, Ruminantia, Takin, Tapir, Tylopoda

Unhappily, Unhappy, Unhappiness Blue, Depressed, Disconsolate, Dismal, Distress, Doleful, Downcast, Down-hearted, Dysphoria, Glumpish, Love-lorn, Lovesick, Miserable, Sad, Sore, Tearful, Unlief, Upset

▷ **Unhappily** *may indicate* an anagram

Unharmed Safe, Scatheless, Spared

Unharness Outspan

Unhealthy Bad, Clinic, Diseased, Epinosic, Insalubrious, Morbid, Noxious, Peaky, Poxy, Prurient, Sickly

Unholy Profane, Wicked

Unhurried Gradual, Patient

Unhurt Whole-skinned

Unhygienic Grubby

Uniat Maronite, Melchite

Unicorn Ch'i-lin, Coin, Monoceros, Moth, Myth, Narwhal

Unidentified Anon, Anonym(ous), Incognito, Ligure

Unification, Unify(ing) Esemplastic, Henotic, Integrate, Risorgimento, Unite

Uniform Abolla, Alike, Battledress, Consistent, Doublet, Dress, Equable, Equal, Even, Flat, Forage-cap, Homogeneous, Homomorphic, Identical, Khaki, Kit, Livery, Regimentals, Regular, Rig, Robe, Same, Sole, Standard, Steady, Strip, Unvaried

Unimaginative Banausic, Literalistic, Pedestrian, Pooter, Slavish

Unimpaired Entire, Intact, Sound

Unimportant Academic, Cog, Down-the-line, Expendable, Fiddling, Footling, Frivolous, Idle, Immaterial, Inconsequent, Inconsiderable, Insignificant, MacGuffin, Makeweight, Minnow, Minutiae, Negligible, Nugatory, Peddling, Peripheral, Petty, Piddling, Small-time, Trifling, Trivia(l)

Unimpressible Cynical

Uninformed Ingram

Uninhabited Bundu, Deserted, Lonely

Uninhibited Bold, Raunchy

Uninjured Inviolate

Uninspired Bored, Humdrum, Pedestrian, Pompier, Tame

Unintelligent Dumb, Obtuse, Stupid, Witless

Unintelligible Arcane, Code, Greek, Inarticulate

Unintentional Inadvertent, Unwitting

Uninterested, Uninteresting Apathetic, Bland, Dreary, Dry, Dull, Grey, Incurious, Nondescript

Uninterrupted Constant, Continuous, Incessant, Running, Steady

Uninvited Gatecrasher, Interloper, Intruder, Sorner, Trespasser, Umbra

Union(ist) Affiance, African, Agreement, Allegiance, Alliance, Anschluss, Art, Association, Bed, Benelux, Bond, Brotherhood, Civil, Close, Combination, Company, Concert, Confederacy, Covalency, Craft, Credit, Customs, Diphthong, Economic, Enosis, Ensemble, Equity, EU, European, Fasciation, Federal, Federation, French, Frithgild, Fusion, Group, Guild, Heterogamy, Horizontal, Impanation, Industrial, Integration, Knight of labour, Latin, Liaison, Liberal, Link-up, Management, Marriage, Match, Merger, NUM, Nuptials, NUR, NUS, NUT, OILC, Pan-American, Parabiosis, Pearl, Postal, Print, RU, Rugby, Samiti, Sex, Sherman, Solidarity, Soviet, Splice, Sponsal, Student, Symphysis, Syngamy, Synizesis, Synostosis, Synthesis, Syssarcosis, Teamsters, Tenorrhaphy, → **TRADE UNION**, TU, U, UNISON, USDAW, Uxorial, Verein, Vertical, Vienna, Wedding, Wedlock, Wield, ZANU, Zollverein, Zygosis

Unique(ness) Alone, A-per-se, Farid, Hacceity, Inimitable, Irreplaceable, Lone, Matchless, Nonesuch, Nonpareil, Nonsuch, One-off, One(-to)-one, Only, Peerless, Rare, Singular, Sole, Sui generis

Unisex(ual) Epicene, Hermaphrodite

Unison Chorus, Harmony, One, Sync

Unit Abampere, Absolute, Ace, Acre(-foot), Amp, Angstrom, Archine, Archiphoneme, Astronomical, Bar, Bargaining, Barn, Base, Baud, Becquerel, Bioblast, Biogen, Biophor(e), Bit, Board of Trade, Bohr magneton, Brigade, BTU, Bushel, Byte, Cadre, Calory, Candela, Cell, Cent(i)are, Centimorgan, Centipoise, Chaldron, Chronon, Codon, Cohort, Commune, Congius, Control, Corps, Coulomb, Crith, Cusec, Dalton, DALY, Daraf, Darcy, Debye, Degree, Denier, Derived, Dessiatine, Detachment, DIN, Dioptre, Division, Dobson, Dol, Dyne, Echelon, Ecosystem, Electromagnetic, Electron, Electrostatic, Element, Em, EMU, En, Energid, Ensuite, Episome, Erg, Erlang, Farad, Feedlot, Fermi, Field, Flight, Foot-candle, Foot-lambert, Foot-pound, Foot-ton, Fps, Fresnel, Fundamental, Gal, Gauss, Gestalt, GeV, Gigabit, Gigaflop, Gigahertz, Gigawatt, Gilbert, Glosseme, Gram, Grav, Gray, Hank, Hapu, Hartree, Henry, Hertz, Hide, Hogshead, Holon, Home, Hoppus foot, Hub, Income, Ion, Item, Jansky, Joule, K, Katal, Kelvin, Kilderkin, Kilerg, Kilowatt, Lambert, Langley, Last, League, Lexeme, Lumen, Lux, Maceral, Magneton, Man-hour, Maxwell, Measure, Megabyte, Megahertz, Megaton, Megawatt, Megohm, Message, Metre, Mho, Micella, Micelle, Microcurie, Microinch, Micron, Mil, Module, Mole, Monad, Monetary, Mongo(e), Morgen, Morpheme, Mutchkin, Neper, Nepit, Nest, Newton, Nit, Octa, Oersted, Ohm, Okta, Organelle, Panzer, Parasang, Pascal, Patrol, Ped, Peninsular, Pennyweight, Period, Peripheral, Petaflop, Phoneme, Phot, Phyton, Pica, Pixel, Ploughgate, Point, Poise, Pond, Poundal, Power, Practical, Probit, Protoplast, Qubit, RA, Radian, Rem, Remen, Rep, Reverb, Ro(e)ntgen, Rood, Rutherford, Sabin, Sealed, Second, Secure, Segment, Semeion, Sememe, Shed, SI, Siemens, Sievert, Singleton, Sink, Slug, Sone, Steradian, Stere, Stilb, Stock, Stoke(s), Strontium, Syllable, Syntagm(a), TA, Tagmeme, Terabyte, Teraflop, Terminal, Tesla, Tetrapody, Tex, Theme, Therblig, Therm, Timocracy, Tog, Token, Torr, Tower, Tripody, Vanitory, Vanity, Var, Vara, Volt, Wall, Watt, Watt-hour, Weber, Wing, X, Yrneh

Unitarian Arian, Paulian, Racovian, Socinian

Unite(d), Uniting, Unity Accrete, Bind, Coalesce, Combine, Concordant, Connate, Connect, Consolidate, Consubstantiate, Covalent, Ecumenical, Fay, Federal, Federalise, Federate, Fuse, Gene, Graft, Injoint, Inosculate, Join, Joinder, Kingdom, Knit, Lap, Link, Marry, Meint, Meng, Ment, Merge, Meynt, Ming, Nations, Oop, Oup, Piece, Siamese, Solid, States, Tie, Unify, → **WED**, Weld, Yoke

United Ireland Fine Gael
United Kingdom Old Dart, UK
Unity Harmony, One, Solidarity, Sympathy, Togetherness
Univalent Monatomic
Universal, Universe All, Catholic, Cosmos, Creation, Ecumenic(al), Emma,
Expanding, General, Global, Infinite, Inflationary, Island, Macrocosm, Mandala,
Microcosm, Oscillating, Sphere, U, Via Lactea, World(wide)
University Academe, Academy, Alma mater, Aston, Bath, Berkeley, Bonn, Brown,
Campus, Civic, College, Columbia, Cornell, Dartmouth, Exeter, Gown, Harvard,
Heidelberg, Ivy League, Keele, Open, OU, Oxbridge, Pennsylvania, Princeton,
Reading, Redbrick, St Andrews, Sorbonne, Stamford, Varsity, Whare wanaga,
Wittenberg, Yale
Unjust(ified) Groundless, Inequitable, Inequity, Iniquitous, Invalid, Tyrannical
Unkempt Dishevelled, Bushy, Greebo, Mal soigné, Raddled, Ragged, Raggle-taggle,
Scody, Scraggy, Scuzzy, Shaggy, Tousy, Touzy, Towsy, Towzy
Unknot Burl
Unknown, Unknowable Acamprosate, Agnostic, Anon, A.N. Other, Hidden, Ign,
Incog(nito), Inconnu, N, Nobody, Noumenon, Occult, Quantity, Secret, Soldier,
Strange, Symbolic, Tertium quid, Unchartered, Untold, Warrior, X, Y
Unleavened Azymous
Unless Nisi, Save, Without
Unliable Exempt
Unlicensed Illicit
Unlike(ly) As if, Difform, Disparate, Dubious, Far-fetched, Improbable,
Inauspicious, Last, Long shot, Outsider, Remote, Tall, Unlich
Unlimited Almighty, Boundless, Indefinite, Measureless, Nth, Open-ended, Pure,
Universal, Vast
Unlisted Ex-directory
Unload Disburden, Discharge, Drop, Dump, Jettison, Land, Strip
Unlock(ed) Bald
Unlucky Donsie, Hapless, Ill(-starred), Inauspicious, Infaust, Jonah, Misadventure,
Misfallen, S(c)hlimazel, Sinister, Stiff, Thirteen, Untoward, Wanchancie,
Wanchancy, Wanion
Unman Castrate
Unmannerly Crude, Discourteous, Impolite, Low bred, Rude, Solecism
Unmarried Bachelor, Common-law, Single, Spinster
Unmask Expose, Rumble
Unmatched Bye, Champion, Orra, Unique
Unmentionable(s) Bra, Foul, No-no, Secret, → **UNDERWEAR**, Undies
Unmindful Heedless, Oblivious
Unmistakable Clear, Manifest, Plain
Unmitigated Absolute, Arrant, Sheer, Ultra
Unmixed Me(a)re, Meer, Neat, Nett, Pure, Raw, Straight
Unmoved, Unmoving Adamant, Doggo, Firm, Serene, Static, Stolid
Unnamed Anon
Unnatural Abnormal, Absonant, Affected, Cataphysical, Contrived, Eerie, Flat,
Geep, Irregular, Strange, Transuranian
▷ **Unnaturally** *may indicate* an anagram
Unnecessary De trop, Extra, Gash, Gratuitous, Needless, Otiose, Redundant,
Superfluous
Unnerve, Unnerving Discouraging, Eerie, Faze, Rattle

Unobserved Backstage, Sly, Unseen
Unobtainable Nemesis
Unobtrusive Low profile, Stealthy
Unoccupied Désouvré, Empty, Idle, Otiose, Vacant, Void
Unofficial Disestablish, Fringe, Wildcat
Unoriginal Banal, Copy, Derivative, Imitation, Plagiarised, Slavish
Unorthodox Heretic, Heterodox, Maverick, Off-beat, Off-the-wall, Outré, Unconventional
▷ **Unorthodox** *may indicate* an anagram
Unpaid Amateur, Brevet, Hon(orary), Outstanding, Voluntary
Unpaired Azygous, Bye
Unpalatable Acid, Bitter, Unsavoury
Unparalleled Supreme, Unique
Unpartitioned Aseptate
Unperturbed Bland, Calm, Serene
Unplanned Impromptu, Improvised, Spontaneous
Unpleasant, Unpleasant person Cow, Creep, Fink, God-awful, Grim, Grotty, Gruesome, Harsh, Hoor, Horrible, Icky, Insalubrious, Invidious, Nasty, Obnoxious, Odious, Offensive, Painful, Pejorative, Poxy, Rank, Rebarbative, Shady, Shitty, Shocker, Snarky, Sour, Sticky, Thorny, Toerag, Wart
Unploughed Lea-rig
Unpolluted Sterile
Unpopular Detested, Hat(e)able
Unpractical Futile, Orra
Unpredictable Aleatory, Dicy, Erratic, Maverick, Wild card
Unprepared Ad lib, Extempore, Impromptu, Last minute, Raw, Unready
Unpretentious Quiet
Unprincipled Amoral, Dishonest, Irregular, Opportunist, Reprobate, Unscrupulous
Unproductive Arid, Atokal, Atokous, Barren, Dead-head, Eild, Fallow, Futile, Lean, Poor, Shy, Sterile, Yeld, Yell
Unprofessional Laic, Malpractice
Unprofitable Bootless, Fruitless, Lean, Thankless, Wasted
Unprogressive Inert, Square
Unprotected Exposed, Nude, Vulnerable
Unpublished Inedited
Unpunctual Tardy
Unqualified Absolute, Entire, Outright, Perfect, Profound, Pure, Quack, Sheer, Straight, Thorough, Total, Utter
Unquestionably, Unquestioning Absolute, Certain, Doubtless, Implicit
Unravel(ling) Construe, Denouement, Disentangle, Feaze, Fray, Solve
Unreadable Poker-faced
Unready Unripe
Unreal(istic) Alice-in-Wonderland, Eidetic, En l'air, Escapist, Fake, Fancied, Illusory, Insubstantial, Mirage, Oneiric, Phantom, Phon(e)y, Planet Zog, Pseudo, Romantic, Sham, Spurious
Unreasonable, Unreasoning Absurd, Bigot, Exorbitant, Extreme, Illogical, Irrational, Misguided, Perverse, Rabid, Steep, Tall order
Unrecognised Incognito, Inconnu, Invalid, Thankless, Unsung
Unrefined Coarse, Common, Crude, Earthy, Gur, Impure, Rude, Vul(g), Vulgar
Unregistered Flapping
Unrehearsed Extempore, Impromptu

Unrelenting Implacable, Remorseless, Severe, Stern

Unreliable Broken reed, Dodgy, Dubious, Erratic, Fair-weather, Fickle, Flibbertigibbet, Flighty, Fly-by-night, Kludge, Shonky, Unstable, Wankle, Weak sister, Wonky

Unremarkable Nondescript

Unremitting Dogged, Intensive

Unresponsive Aloof, Blank, Cold, Frigid, Nastic, Rigor

Unrest Discontent, Ferment, The Troubles

Unrestrained Ariot, Effusive, Extravagant, Free, Freewheeling, Hearty, Homeric, Immoderate, Incontinent, Lax, Lowsit, Rampant, Wanton, Wild

Unreturnable Ace

Unrighteousness Adharma

Unrivalled Nonesuch

Unromantic Classic(al), Mundane, Prosaic

Unruffled Calm, Placid, Serene, Smooth, Tranquil

Unruly Anarchic, Bodgie, Buckie, Camstairy, Camsteary, Camsteerie, Coltish, Exception, Fractious, Lawless, Obstreperous, Obstropalous, Ragd(e), Raged, Ragged, Rambunctious, Rampageous, Rattlebag, Riotous, Tartar, Turbulent, Turk, Wanton, Wayward, Zoo

▷ **Unruly** *may indicate* an anagram

Unsafe Deathtrap, Fishy, Insecure, Perilous, Precarious, Unsound, Vulnerable

Unsatisfactory, Unsatisfying Bad, Lame, Lousy, Meagre, Rocky, Thin, Wanting

Unsavoury Epinosic, On the nose

Unscramble Decode, Decrypt

Unscripted Ad lib

Unscrupulous Chancer, Rascally, Shyster, Slippery

Unseasonable, Unseasoned Green, Murken, Raw, Untimely

Unseat Depose, Dethrone, Oust, Overset, Overthrow, Throw

Unseemly Coarse, Improper, Incivil, Indecent, Indecorous, Indign, Seedy, Untoward

Unselfish Altruist, Generous

Unsent Square

Unsettle(d) Faze, Homeless, Hunky, Indecisive, Nervous, Outstanding, Queasy, Restive, Restless, Troublous

▷ **Unsettled** *may indicate* an anagram

Unsexy N, Neuter

Unsheltered Bleak, Exposed, Homeless

Unsight(ed), Unsightly Eyeless, Hideous, Repulsive, Ugly

Unsinning Impeccable, Pure

Unskilled Awkward, Dilutee, Gauche, Green, Hunky, Inexpert, Raw, Rude

Unsmiling Agelastic

Unsociable Anchoretic, Grouchy, Solitary, Stay-at-home

Unsolicited Sponte sua

Unsophisticated Alf, Boondocks, Boonies, Bushie, Cornball, Corny, Cracker-barrel, Direct, Down-home, Faux-naïf, Hillbilly, Homebred, Homespun, Inurbane, Jaap, Jay, Naive, Natural, Primitive, Provincial, Rube, Rustic, Verdant

Unsound Barmy, Infirm, Invalid, Shaky, Wildcat, Wonky

▷ **Unsound** *may indicate* an anagram

Unsparing Severe

Unspeakable Dreadful, Ineffable, Nefandous

Unspecific, Unspecified Broad, General, Generic, Somehow, Such, Vague

Unspoiled, Unspoilt Innocent, Natural, Perfect, Pristine, Pure, Virgin

Unspoken Silent, Tacit

Unspotted Innocent

Unstable, Unsteady Anomic, Astatic, Bockedy, Casual, Crank, Crank(y), Dicky, Erratic, Fitful, Flexuose, Flexuous, Fluidal, Giddy, Groggy, Infirm, Insecure, Labile, Minute-jack, Rickety, Shaky, Shifty, Skittish, Slippy, Tickle, Top-heavy, Tottery, Totty, Variable, Volatile, Walty, Wambling, Wankle, Warby, Wobbly

Unstated Concordat, Tacit, Unknown

▶ **Unsteady** *see* **UNSTABLE**

Unstressed Enclitic

▷ **Unstuck** *may indicate* an anagram

Unsubstantial Aeriform, Airy, Flimsy, Paltry, Shadowy, Slight, Thin, Yeasty

Unsubtle Overt

Unsuccessful Abortive, Duff, Futile, Joyless, Manqué, Vain

Unsuitable Amiss, Ill-timed, Impair, Improper, Inapt, Incongruous, Inexpedient, Malapropos, Misbecoming, Unbecoming, Unfit

Unsupported, Unsupportable Astylar, Floating, Stroppy, Unfounded

Unsure Hesitant, Tentative

Unsurpassed All-time, Best, Supreme

Unsuspecting Credulous, Innocent, Naive

Unsweetened Brut, Natural

Unsymmetrical Heterauxesis(m), Irregular, Lopsided

Unsympathetic Short shrift

Unthinking Inadvertent, Mechanical

Untidy Daggy, Dishevelled, Dog's breakfast, Dog's dinner, Dowd(y), Frowzy, Litterbug, Ragged, Raunchy, Scruff(y), Slipshod, Slovenly, Tatty

▷ **Untidy** *may indicate* an anagram

Untie Free, Undo, Unlace

Until Hasta

Untilled Fallow

Untiring Assiduous

Untold Secret, Umpteen, Unread, Unred, Vast

Untouchable Burakumin, Dalit, Harijan, Immune, Sacrosanct, Sealed

Untouched Intact, Inviolate, Pristine, Virgin

▷ **Untrained** *may indicate* 'BR' to be removed

Untried New, Virgin

Untroubled Insouciant

Untrue, Untruth Apocryphal, Eccentric, Fabrication, Faithless, False(hood), Lie, Prefabrication, Unleal

Untrustworthy Dishonest, Fickle, Fly-by-night, Mamzer, Momzer, Shifty, Sleeky, Tricky

Untypical Anomalous, Etypic(al), Isolated, Unusual

Unused, Unusable Impracticable, New, Over, Wasted

▷ **Unusual** *may indicate* an anagram

Unusual(ly) Abnormal, Atypical, Exceptional, Extra(ordinary), Freak, Kinky, New, Novel, Odd, Offbeat, Out-of-the-way, Outré, Particular, Queer, Rare, Remarkable, Singular, Special, → **STRANGE**, Unco, Unique, Untypical, Unwonted

Unutterable Ineffable

Unvarying Constant, Eternal, Monotonous, Stable, Static, Uniform

Unveil Expose, Honour

Unvoiced Surd

Unwanted De trop, Exile, Gooseberry, Nimby, Outcast, Sorn

Unwashed Grubby

Unwavering Steadfast

Unwed Celibate, Single

Unwelcome, Unwelcoming Frosty, Hostile, Icy, Lulu, Obtrusive, (Persona) Non grata

Unwell Ailing, Crook, Dicky, Ill, Impure, Poorly, Quazzy, Queasy, Rop(e)y, Seedy, Shouse, Toxic

Unwholesome Insalutary, Miasmous, Morbid, Noxious, Stinkpot

Unwieldy Cumbersome, Elephantine

Unwilling(ness) Averse, Disinclined, Intestate, Loath, Loth, Nolition, Nolo, Obdurate, Perforce, Reluctant, Tarrow

Unwind Relax, Straighten, Unclew, Undo, Unreave, Unreeve

▷ **Unwind** *may indicate* an anagram

Unwinnable Catch 22

Unwise Foolish, Ill-advised, Ill-judged, Impolitic, Imprudent, Inexpedient, Injudicious, Rash

Unwitting Accidental, Nescient

Unwonted Inusitate

Unworkable Impossible, Inoperable

Unworldly Naif, Naive

Unworried Carefree

Unworthy Below, Beneath, Indign, Inferior, Infra dig

Unwritten Verbal

Unyielding Adamant, Eild, Firm, Granite, Hardline, Inexorable, Inextensible, Intransigent, Obdurate, Rigid, Steely, Stubborn, Tough, Unalterable

Unyoke Outspan

Up(on), Upturned, Upper, Uppish A, Acockbill, Afoot, Antidepressant, Arrogant, Astir, Astray, Astride, Cloud-kissing, Erect, Euphoric, Heavenward, Hep, Horsed, Incitant, Off, On, Overhead, Primo, Quark, Range, Ride, Riding, Risen, Skyward, Speed, → UPPER CLASS, Vamp, Ventral

Up-anchor Atrip, Weigh

Upbeat Anacrusis, Arsis

Upbraid Abuse, Rebuke, Reproach, Reprove, Scold, Storm, Twit

Upcountry Anabasis, Inland

Update Brief, Refresh, Renew, Report, Sitrep

Upfront Open

Upheaval Cataclysm, Chaos, Eruption, Rummage, Seismic, Shake out, Stir

▷ **Upheld** *may indicate* 'up' in another word

Uphill Arduous, Borstal, Sisyphean

Uphold Assert, Defend, Maintain, Sustain

Upholstery Lampas, Moquette, Trim

Upkeep Support

Upland(s) Alps, Downs, Hilly, Wold

Uplift Boost, Edify, Elate, Elevation, Exalt, Hoist, Levitation, Sky

Upper class, Upper crust Aristocrat, County, Crachach, Nobility, Patrician, Posh, Sial, Top-hat, Tweedy, U

Upright(s), Uprightness Aclinic, Anend, Apeak, Apeek, Aplomb, Arrect, Atrip, Erect, Goalpost, Honest, Incorrupt, Jamb, Joanna, Merlon, Moral, Mullion, Orthograde, Perpendicular, Piano, Pilaster(s), Post, Probity, Rectitude, Roman, Splat, Stanchion, Stares, Stile, Stud, Vertical, Virtuous, White

Uprising Incline, Insurrection, Intifada, Meerut, Rebellion, Revolt, Tumulus

Uproar(ious) Ballyhoo, Bedlam, Blatancy, Brouhaha, Charivari, Clamour, Clangour, Collieshangie, Commotion, Cry, Din, Dirdam, Dirdum, Durdum, Emeute, Ferment, Flaw, Fracas, Furore, Garboil, Hell, Hoopla, Hubbub(oo), Hullabaloo, Hurly(-burly), Imbroglio, Katzenjammer, Madhouse, Noise, Noyes, Outcry, Pandemonium, Racket, Raird, Randan, Reird, Riotous, Roister, Romage, Rough music, Rowdedow, Rowdydow(dy), Ruckus, Ruction, Rumpus, Shemozzle, Stramash, Turmoil, Utis, Whoobub

Uproot Deracinate, Eradicate, Evict, Outweed, Supplant, Weed

▷ **Upset** *may indicate* an anagram; a word upside down; or 'tes'

Upset(ting) Aerate, Aggrieve, Alarm, Applecart, Bother, Capsize, Catastrophe, Choked, Coup, Cowp, Crank, Derail, Derange, Dip, Discomboberate, Discombobulate, Discomfit, Discomfort, Discommode, Disconcert, Dismay, Disquiet, Distraught, Disturb, Dod, Eat, Fuss, Gutted, Heart-rending, Inversion, Keel, Miff, Nauseative, Offend, Overthrow, Overtip, Overturn, Peeve, Perturb, Pip, Pother, Purl, Rattle, Renverse, Rile, Ruffle, Rumple, Sad, Seel, Shake, Sore, Spill, Tapsalteerie, Tip, Topple, Trauma, Undo, Unsettled

Upshot Outcome, Result, Sequel

Upside down Inverted, Resupinate, Tapsie-teerie, Topsy-turvy

Upstart Buckeen, Jumped-up, Mushroom, Parvenu, Vulgarian

▷ **Upstart** *may indicate* 'u'

Upstream Thermal

Upsurge Thrust, Waste

Uptake Shrewdness, Understanding, Wit

Up to Till, Until

Up-to-date Abreast, Advanced, Contemporary, Current, Mod, New-fashioned, Right-on, State-of-the-art, Swinging, Topical, Trendy

Upwards Acclivious, Aloft, Antrorse, Cabré

Uranium Depleted, Pitchblende, U, Yellowcake

Urban Civic, Megalopolis, Municipal, Town

Urbane, Urbanity Civil, Debonair, Eutrapelia, Refined, Townly

Urchin Arab, Asterias, Brat, Crinoid, Crossfish, Cystoid, Echinoderm, Echinoidea, Echinus, Gamin, Guttersnipe, Gutty, Heart, Mudlark, Nipper, Pluteus, Ragamuffin, Sand-dollar, Sea, Sea-egg, Spatangoidea, Spatangus, Street-arab, Townskip

Urge, Urgency, Urgent Admonish, Acute, Ca, Coax, Constrain, Crying, Dire, Drive, Egg, Enjoin, Exhort, Exigent, Goad, Hard, Haste, Hie, Hoick, Hunger, Hurry, Id, Immediate, Impel, Impulse, Incense, Incite, Insist(ent), Instance, Instigate, Itch, Kick, Libido, Nag, Orexis, Peremptory, Persuade, Press(ing), Prod, Push, Scrub, Set on, Spur, Strenuous, Strident, Strong, Threapit, Threepit, Wanderlust, Whig, Yen

▷ **Urgent** *may indicate* 'Ur-gent', viz. Iraqi

Uriah Hittite, Humble, Umble

Urinal Bog, John, Jordan, → **LAVATORY**, Loo, Pissoir

Urinate(d), Urine Chamber-lye, Emiction, Enuresis, Lant, Leak, Micturition, Number one, Oliguria, Pee, Piddle, Piss, Planuria, Relieve, Slash, Stale, Strangury, Tiddle, Uresis, Werris (Creek), Whiz(z), Widdle

Urn(s), Urn-shaped Canopic, Cinerarium, Ewer, Grecian, Lachrymal, Olla, Ossuary, Samovar, Storied, Tea, Urceolate, Vase

Us 's, UK, Uns, We

Usage, Use(r), Used, Utilise Application, Apply, Avail, Boot, Consume, Custom, Deploy, Dow, → **EMPLOY**, End, Ex, Exercise, Exert, Expend, Exploit, Flesh, Function, Habit, Hand-me-down, Inured, Manner, Ply, Practice, Sarum, Spare, Spent, Sport, Take, Tradition, Treat, Try, Ure, Utilisation, Wield, With, Wont

Useful Asset, Availing, Commodity, Dow, Expedient, Invaluable, Practical

Useless Appendix, Base, Bung, Cumber, Cumber-ground, Dead-wood, Dud, Empty, Futile, Gewgaw, Grotty, Ground, Idle, Inane, Ineffective, Lame, Lemon, Nonstarter, Nugatory, Otiose, Plug, Sculpin, Sterile, Swap, US, Vain, Void, Wet

Usher Black Rod, Blue Rod, Chobdar, Commissionaire, Conduct(or), Doorman, Escort, Gentleman, Guide, Herald, Huissier, Macer, Rod, Show, Steward

Usual Common, Customary, Habit(ual), Most, Natural, Normal, Ordinary, Routine, Rule, Solito, Standard, Stock, Typical, Vanilla, Wont

Usurer, Usury Gombeen, Gripe, Lender, Loanshark, Moneylender, Note-shaver, Shark, Uncle

Usurp(er) Abator, Arrogate, Encroach, Invade

Ut As, Doh, Utah

Utah Ut

Utensil(s) Batterie, Battery, Canteen, Ca(u)ldron, Chopsticks, Colander, Cookware, Corer, Double boiler, Fish-kettle, Fork, Funnel, Gadget, Grater, Gridiron, Holloware, Implement, Instrument, Jagger, Knife, Mandolin(e), Ricer, Scoop, Skillet, Spatula, Spoon, Things, Tool, Whisk, Zester

▶ **Utilise** *see* USE

Utilitarian Benthamite, Mill, Practical, Useful

Utility Elec(tricity), Expected, Gas, Public, Water

Utmost Best, Extreme, Farthest, Maximum, Nth

Utopia(n) Adland, Cloud-cuckoo-land, Ideal, Pantisocracy, Paradise, Perfect, Shangri-la

Utter(ance), Uttered, Utterly Absolute, Accent, Agrapha, Agraphon, Aread, Arrant, Cry, Dead, Deliver, Dictum, Dog, Downright, Ejaculate, Emit, Enunciate, Express, Extreme, Glossolalia, Issue, Judgement, Lenes, Lenis, Locution, Mint, Most, Oracle, Pass, Phonate, Pronounce, Pure, Quo(th), Rank, Rap, Rattle, Remark, Saw, → SAY, Sheer, Speak, Spout, Stark, State, Syllable, Tell, Thorough, Tongue, Vend, Vent, Very, Voice

Uvula Staphyle

Vv

V Anti, Bomb, Del, Five, Nabla, See, Sign, Verb, Verse, Versus, Victor(y), Volt, Volume

Vacancy, Vacant Blank, Empty, Glassy, Hole, Hollow, Inane, Place, Space, Vacuum

Vacation Holiday, Leave, Long, Non-term, Outing, Recess, Trip, Voidance

Vaccination, Vaccine Antigen, Antiserum, Attenuated, Bacterin, Cure, HIB, Jenner, MMR, Sabin, Salk, Serum, Subunit

Vacillate, Vacillating Chop, Dither, Feeble, Hesitate, Shilly-shally, Trimmer, Wabble, Wave(r), Whiffle

Vacuous Blank, Empty, Toom, Vacant

Vacuum Blank, Cleaner, Dewar, Emptiness, Magnetron, Nothing, Plenum, Thermos®, Torricellian, Ultra-high, Void

Vade-mecum Ench(e)iridion, Notebook

Vagabond Bergie, Gadling, → **GYPSY**, Hobo, Landlo(u)per, Outcast, Picaresque, Rapparee, Romany, Rover, Runabout, Runagate, Tramp

Vagina Box, Crack

Vagrant Beachcomber, Bum, Bummer, Caird, Crusty, Derro, Dosser, Drifter, Gangrel, Gang-there-out, Goliard, Gypsy, Hobo, Landlo(u)per, Lazzarone, Nomad, Patercove, Pikey, Rinthereout, Rogue, Romany, Scattering, Strag, Straggle, Stroller, Swagman, Tinker, Tinkler, → **TRAMP**, Truant, Walker

Vague(ness) Amorphous, Bleary, Blur, Confused, Dim, Equivocal, Hazy, Ill-defined, Ill-headed, Indeterminate, Indistinct, Loose, Mist, Nebulous, Obscure, Shadowy, Woolly-minded

▷ **Vaguely** *may indicate* an anagram

Vain Bootless, Conceited, Coxcomb, Coxcomical, Dandyish, Egoistic, Empty, Fruitless, → **FUTILE**, Hollow, Idle, Peacock, Pompous, Profitless, Proud, Strutting, Unuseful, Useless, Vogie

Vainglory Panache

Valance Pand, Pelmet

Vale Addio, Adieu, Cheerio, Coomb, Dean, Dedham, Dene, Ebbw, Enna, Evesham, Glamorgan, Glen, Tara, Ta-ta, Tempé, Valley

Valediction, Valedictory Apopemptic, Cheerio, Farewell

Valentine Card, Sweetheart

Valerian All-heal, Cetywall, Greek, Red, Setuale, Setwale, Setwall, Spur

Valet Aid, Andrew, Gentleman's gentleman, Jeames, Jeeves, Man, Passepartout, Quint, Servant, Skip-kennel

Valetudinarian Hypochondriac, Invalid

Valiant Brave, Doughty, Heroic, Redoubtable, Resolute, Stalwart, Stouthearted, Wight

Valid(ity), Validate Confirm, Establish, Just, Legal, Probate, Rational, Right, Sound

Valise Bag, Case, Dorlach, Satchel

Valkyrie Brynhild

Valley Ajalon, Aosta, Argolis, Baca, Barossa, Bekaa, Beqaa, Bolson, Cleavage, Cleugh, Clough, Comb(e), Coomb, Cwm, Dale, Dargle, Dean, Death, Defile, Dell, Den, Dene, Dingle, Dip, Drowned, Dry, Gehenna, Ghyll, Glen, Glencoe, Glyn, Gorge, Graben, Great Glen, Great Rift, Grindelwald, Hanging, Haugh, Heuch, Hollow, Hope, Humiliation, Hutt, Ladin, Lagan, Lallan, Nemea, Olympia, Ravine, Rhondda, Ria, Rift, Ruhr, San Fernando, Seaton, Silicon, Slack, Slade, Strath(spey), Tempe, Tophet, Trossachs, Umbria, U-shaped, Valdarno, Vale, Vallambrosa, Water, Water gap, Yosemite

Valour Bravery, Courage, Heroism, Merit, Prowess

Valuable, Valuation, Value(s) Absolute, Acid, Appraise, Appreciate, Apprize, Assess(ment), Asset, Attention, Bargain, Book, Break up, Calibrate, Calorific, Carbon, Checksum, Cherish, CIF, Cop, Cost, Crossover, Datum, Denomination, Entry, Equity, Esteem, Estimate, Exit, Expected, Face, Feck, Hagberg, Intrinsic, Jew's eye, Limit, Market, Merit, Modulus, Net present, Net realizable, Nominal, Nuisance, Omnium, Par, PH, Place, Prairie, Precious, Premium, Present, Price, Prize, Prys, Q, Quartile, Rarity, Rate, Rateable, Rating, Regard, Residual, Respect, Rogue, Salt, Sentimental, Set, Snob, Steem, Stent, Store, Street, Surrender, Taonga, Time, Treasure, Tristimulus, Truth, Valuta, → **WORTH**

Valueless Bum, Fig, Mare's nest, Orra, Useless, Worthless

Valve Acorn, Air, Aortic, Ball, Bicuspid, Bleed, Blow, Butterfly, Check, Clack, Cock, Diode, Drawgate, Dynatron, Escape, Eustachian, Exhaust, Flip-flop, Foot, Gate, Induction, Magnetron, Mitral, Mixing, Needle, Non-return, Pallet, Pentode, Petcock, Piston, Poppet, Pulmonary, Puppet, Radio, Resnatron, Safety, Seacock, Semilunar, Shut-off, Side, Sleeve, Slide, Sluice, Sluicegate, Snifter, Snifting, Stopcock, Suction, Tap, Tetrode, Thermionic, Throttle, Thyratron, Triode, Turncock, Vacuum, Ventil, Vibroton

Vamoose Abscond, Decamp, Scat, Scram

Vamp Adlib, Charm, Maneater, Rehash, Seduce, Siren, Strum, Twiddle

Vampire Bat, Dracula, False, Ghoul, Lamia, Lilith, Pontianak, Stringes

Van(guard) Advance, Box-car, Brake, Breakdown, Camper, Cart, Cube, Delivery, Dormobile®, Forefront, Foremost, Freight-car, Front, Furniture, Guard's, Head, Kombi®, Lead, Leader(s), Lorry, Loudspeaker, Luggage, Meat wagon, Panel, Panel-truck, Pantechnicon, Patrol-wagon, Prison, Removal, Spearhead, Truck, Ute, Wagon

Vanadium V

Vandal(ise), Vandalism Desecrate, Hooligan, Hun, Loot, Pillage, Ravage, Rough, Sab(oteur), Sack, Saracen, Skinhead, Slash, Smash, Trash, Wrecker

Vandyke Beard, Painter

Vane(s) Dog, Fan, Guide, Rudder, Swirl, Telltale, Vexillum, Weather(cock), Web, Wind (tee), Wing

Vanessa Butterfly

Vanilla Pinole

Vanish(ed), Vanishing Cease, Disappear, Disperse, Dissolve, Evanesce(nt), Evaporate, Extinct, Faint(ed), Mizzle, Slope, Transitory, Unbe

Vanity Amour-propre, Arrogance, Ego, Esteem, Futility, Pomp, Pretension, Pride, Self-conceit, Self-esteem

Vanquish Beat, Conquer, Floor, Master, Overcome, Rout

Vantage (point) Ascendancy, Coign(e), Height

Vaporise, Vapour Boil, Cloud, Contrail, Effluent, Fog, Fume, Halitus, Inhalant, Iodine, Miasma, Mist, Reek, Roke, Skywriting, → **STEAM**, Steme, Water

▶ **Variable, Variance, Variant, Variation** see **VARY**

Varicose Haemorrhoids

▶ **Varied, Variety** *see* **VARY**

▷ **Varied** *may indicate* an anagram

Variegate(d) Calico, Dappled, Flecked, Fretted, Harlequin, Motley, Mottle, Pied, Rainbow, Skewbald, Tissue

▷ **Variety of** *may indicate* an anagram

Various Divers(e), Manifold, Multifarious, Separate, Several, Sundry

Various years Vy

Varlet Cad, Knave, Rascal, Rogue

Varnish(ing) Arar, Bee-glue, Copal, Cowdie-gum, Dam(m)ar, Desert, Dope, Dragon's-blood, French polish, Glair, Japan, Lacquer, Lentisk, Nail, Nibs, Oil, Resin, Sandarac, Shellac, Spirit, Tung-oil, Tung-tree, Vernis martin, Vernissage

Vary(ing), Variable, Variance, Variant, Variation, Varied, Variety Ablaut, Aelotropy, Alter, Amphoteric, Assortment, Breed, Brew, Cepheid, Change, Chequered, Colour, Contrapuntal, Counterpoint, Daedal(e), Dedal, Dependent, Differ, Discrepancy, Diverse, Diversity, Dummy, Eclectic, Eclipsing, Enigma, Farraginous, Fickle, Fluctuating, Form, Grid, Iid, Inconsistent, Inconstant, Independent, Intervening, Isochor, Isopleth, Isotopy, Line, Local, Medley, Mix, Morph, Morphosis, Multifarious, Multiplicity, Music hall, Mutable, Nimrod, Nuance, Nutation, Olio, Omniform, Orthogenesis, Parametric, Partita, Protean, Random, Remedy, Response, Smörgåsbord, Sort, Species, Spice, Sport, Stirps, Stochastic, Strain, String, Timeserver, Tolerance, Twistor, Var, Versatile, Versiform, Version, Vicissitude, Vl, Wane, Wax, X, Y, Z

Vase Bronteum, Canopus, Cornucopia, Diota, Hydria, Jardinière, Kalpis, Lachrymal, Lecythus, Lekythos, Lustre, Moon flask, Murr(h)a, Portland, Pot, Potiche, Stamnos, Urn, Vessel

Vasectomy Desexing

Vassal Client, Daimio, Feoffee, Lackey, Liege, Liegeman, Man, Manred, Servant, Vavaso(u)r

Vast(ness) Big, Cosmic, Cyclopic, Enormous, Epic, Extensive, Googol, Huge(ous), Immense, Mighty, Monumental, Ocean, Prodigious

Vat Back, Barrel, Blunger, Chessel, Copper, Cowl, Cuvée, Fat, Girnel, Keir, Kier, Pressfat, Stand, Tank, Tan-pit, Tub, Tun, Winefat

Vatican Rome, V

Vaudeville Zarzuela

Vaughan Silurist

▷ **Vault** *may indicate* an anagram

Vault(ed), Vaulting Arch, Barrel, Cavern, Cellar, Chamber, Charnel house, Clear, Cross, Crypt, Cul-de-four, Cupola, Dome, Dungeon, Fan, Firmament, Fornicate, Groin, Hypogeum, Jump, Kiva, Leap(frog), Lierne, Mausoleum, Ossuary, Palm, Pend, Pendentive, Pole, Rib, Safe, Sepulchre, Serdab, Severy, Shade, Souterrain, Tholus, Tomb, Tunnel, Underpitch, Vaut, Wagon, Weem, Wine

Vaunt Boast, Brag, Crow

Veal Escalope, Fricandeau, Galantine, Scallop, Schnitzel, Vituline, Wiener schnitzel

Vector, Vector operator Del, Dyad, Expression, Nabla, Phasor, Polar, Radius

Veda Yajurveda

Veer Bag, Boxhaul, Broach, Deviate, Draw, Gybe, Splay, Swerve, Tack, Turn, Wear, Yaw

Vegan Parev(e), Parve

Vegetable(s) Alexanders, Allium, Aloo, Alu, Artichoke, Asparagus, Aubergine, Bamboo shoot, Beans, Beet(root), Borecole, Brassica, Broccoli, Cabbage, Calabrese,

Calaloo, Calalu, Camote, Cardoon, Carrot, Castock, Cataloo, Catalu, Cauliflower, Cavalo nero, Celeriac, Celery, Chana, Chard, Chayote, Chicory, Chiffonade, Chive, Choko, Chufa, Cocoyam, Colcannon, Cole, Collard, Corn-on-the-cob, Coulis, Courgette, Crout, Cucumber, Custock, Daikon, Endive, Escarole, Eschalot, Fennel, Filasse, Finocchio, Flora, Frisée, Garlic, Gherkin, Greens, Guar, Hastings, Inert, Ingan, Jardinière, Jerusalem artichoke, Jicama, Kale, Kohlrabi, Kumara, Lablab, Leek, Legume(n), Lettuce, Macedoine, Mangel(-wurzel), Mangetout, Mangold, Marrow(-squash), Mato(o)ke, Mibuna, Mirepoix, Mooli, Navew, Neep, Oca, Okra, Okro, Olitory, Onion, Orach(e), Parsnip, Pea(se), Pepper, Pimento, Plant, Pomato, Potato, Pot herb, Pottage, Pratie, Primavera, Pulse, Pumpkin, Quinoa, Radicchio, Radish, Rapini, Ratatouille, Rocambole, Romanesco, Root, Runner bean, Rutabaga, Sabji, Salad, Salsify, Samphire, Sauce, Sauerkraut, Savoy, Scorzonera, Shallot, Sibol, Sium, Skirret, Sorrel, Spinach(-beet), Spinage, Spring onion, Sprouts, Spud, Squash, String bean, Succotash, Swede, Sweet corn, Sweet potato, Taro, Tomato, Tonka-bean, Triffid, Truck, Turnip, Tuskan kale, Udo, Wakame, Witloof, Wort, Yam, Zucchini
Vegetable extract Solanine
Vegetarian Herbivore, Lactarian, Maigre, Meatless, Parev(e), Parve, Pythagorean, Vegan, Veggie
Vegetate, Vegetator, Vegetation Alga, Brush, Cover, Flora, Fynbos, Gar(r)igue, Greenery, Herb, Lemna, Maquis, Quadrat, Scrub, Stagnate, Sudd, Transect
Vehemence, Vehement(ly) Amain, Ardent, Fervid, Forcible, Frenzy, Heat, Hot, Intense, Violent
Vehicle Ambulance, Amtrack, Artic, Articulated, ATV, Autocycle, Autorickshaw, Biga, Blokart, Brake, Brancard, Buckboard, Buggy, Bus, Cab, Cable car, Camper, Capsule, Car, Caravan, Carry-all, Cart, Casspir, Channel, Chariot, Chelsea tractor, Commercial, Conveyance, Crate, Crew cab, Curricle, Cycle, Delta, Dennet, Dog-cart, Dormobile®, Double-decker, Dragster, Dray, Duck, Dune buggy, Estate car, Fiacre, Float, Fly, Four-by-four, Four-seater, Gharri, Gharry, Gladstone, Go-cart, Go-kart, Go-Ped®, Gritter, Growler, Half-track, Hansom, Hatchback, Hearse, High occupancy, Hovercraft, Hummer, Humvee®, Hybrid, Jeep®, Jeepney, Jet-Ski, Jingle, Jinker, Jitney, Juggernaut, Kago, Kart, Koneke, Landau, Land Rover®, Launch, LEM, Limber, Litter, Load-lugger, Lorry, Machine, Mammy wagon, Matatu, Means, Medium, Micro-scooter, Minibus, Minicab, Minivan, Motor, Motorhome, Multipurpose, Norimon, Offroad, Paddock-basher, Pantechnicon, Pedicab, Penny-farthing, People carrier, People-mover, Perambulator, Personnel carrier, Phaeton, Pick-up, Quad, Rail bus, Recreational, Recovery, Re-entry, Ricksha(w), Roadroller, Rover, Runabout, Rust-bucket, Samlor, Sand-yacht, Scow, Shay, Shebang, Shuttle, Sidecar, Single-decker, Skibob, Skidoo®, Sled(ge), Sleigh, Sno-Cat®, Snowmobile, Snowplough, Soyuz, Space, Spider, Stanhope, Station wagon, Steam-car, Sulky, Surrey, Tarantas(s), Tardis, Taxi, Taxi cab, Tempera, Three-wheeler, Tipcart, Tip-up, Tonga, Tracked, Tractor, Trailer, Tram, Transporter, Trap, Tricar, Tricycle, Trishaw, Troika, Trolley, Trolleybus, Truck, Tuk tuk, Tumble-car(t), Tumbril, Turbo, Two-seater, Two-wheeler, Unicycle, Ute, Utility, Vahana, Velocipede, Vespa®, Volante, Wagon, Wagonette, Weasel, Wheelbarrow, Wheels, Wrecker
Veil Burk(h)a, Calyptra, Chad(d)ar, Chador, Chuddah, Chuddar, Cloud, Cover, Curtain, Envelop, Eucharistic, Hejab, Hijab, Humeral, Kalyptra, Kiss-me, Lambrequin, Mantilla, Mist, Niqab, Obscure, Purdah, Sacramental, Scene, Veale, Volet, Weeper, Wimple, Yashmak
Vein Artery, Azygas, Basilic, Brachiocephalic, Coronary, Costa, Diploic, Epithermal,

Fahlband, Gate, H(a)emorrhoid, Hemiazygous, Innominate, Jugular, Ledge, Lode, Mainline, Media, Midrib, Mood, Nervure, Organic, Outcrop, Percurrent, Pipe, Portal, Postcava, Precava, Pulmonary, Radius, Rake, Rib, Saphena, Sectorial, Spur, Stockwork, Stringer, Style, Thread, Varicose, Varix, Vena, Venule, Vorticose

Vellum Cutch, Japanese, Kutch, Parchment

Velocity Angular, Circular, Escape, Mustard, Muzzle, Orbital, Parabolic, Radial, Rate, Speed, Terminal, V

Velvet(y) Bagheera, Chenille, National, Panné, Pile, Three-pile, Velour, Velure, Villose, Villous

Venal Corruptible, Mercenary, Sale

Vend(or) Hawk, Peddle, Pedlar, Rep, Sammy, Sell, Sutler

Vendetta Feud

Veneer Facade, Gloss, Varnish

Venerable Aged, August, Augustus, Bede, Guru, Hoary, Iconic, Sacred, Sage, Vintage

Venerate, Veneration Adore, Awe, Douleia, Dulia, Filiopietistic, Hallow, Homage, Honour, Hyperdulia, Idolise, Latria, Revere, Worship

Venereal NSU, VD

Venery Chase

Venetian Aldine, Blind, Doge, Gobbo, Polo

Vengeance, Vengeful Commination, Erinyes, Reprisal, Ultion, Vindictive, Wannion, Wrack, Wreak

Venice La Serenissima

Venison Cervena, Deer

Venom(ous) Gall, Gila, Jamestown-weed, Jim(p)son-weed, Poison, Rancour, Solpuga, Spite, Toxic, Virus, Zootoxin

Vent Airway, Aperture, Belch, Chimney, Emit, Express, Fumarole, Hornito, Issue, Louver, Louvre, Ostiole, Outlet, Smoker, Solfatara, Spiracle, Undercast, Wreak

Venter Uterus

Ventilate, Ventilator Air, Air-brick, Air-hole, Discuss, Express, Louvre, Plenum, Shaft, Voice, Windsail, Windway, Winze

Venture(d) Ante, Callet, Chance, Dare, Daur, Durst, Enterprise, Flutter, Foray, Handsel, Hazard, Jump, Opine, Presume, Promotion, Prostitute, Risk, Spec, Throw

Venue Bout, Locale, Place, Showground, Stadium, Stateroom, Tryst, Visne

Venus Clam, Cohog, Cytherean, Hesper(us), Love, Lucifer, Morning-star, Phosphorus, Primavera, Quahaug, Quahog, Rokeby, Vesper

Venus fly-trap Dionaea

Veracity, Veracious Accurate, Factual, Sincere, Truth(ful)

Veranda(h) Balcony, Gallery, Lanai, Patio, Piazza, Porch, Sleep-out, Stoep, Stoop, Terrace

Verb(al), Verbs Active, Argy-bargy, Auxiliary, Causative, Conative, Copula, Ergative, Factitive, Finite, Infinitive, Intransitive, Irregular, Modal, Passive, Perfective, Performative, Phrasal, Preterite, Stative, Transitive, Vb, Word-of-mouth

Verbascum Mullein

Verbatim Literally

Verbena Vervain

Verbose, Verbosity Padding, Prolix, Talkative, Wordy

Verdant Lush

Verdict Decision, Fatwah, Formal, Judg(e)ment, Majority, Open, Opinion, Pronouncement, Resolution, Ruling, Special

Verdigris Aeruginous, Patina

Verge Border, Brink, → **EDGE**, Hard shoulder, Incline, Long paddock, Rim, Threshold
Verger Beadle, Pew-opener
Verify, Verification Affirm, Ascertain, Check, Confirm, Constatation, Control, Crosscheck, Prove, Validate
Verily Yea
Verisimilitude Artistic, Authenticity, Credibility
Verity Fact, Sooth, Truth
Vermifuge Cow(h)age, Cowitch
Vermilion Cinnabar, Minium, Red
Vermin(ous) Carrion, Catawampus, Lice, Mice, Pest, Ratty, → **RODENT**, Scum
Vermouth Absinthiated, French, It(alian), Martini®
Vernacular Common, Dialect, Idiom, Jargon, Lingo, Native, Patois, Vulgate
Veronica Hebe, Hen-bit, Speedwell
Verruca Wart
Versatile Adaptable, All-rounder, Flexible, Handy, Many-sided, Protean, Resourceful
Verse(s), Versed Free, Linked, Logaoedic, Passus, Poetry, Political, Reported, → **RHYME**, System

VERSES

1 letter:
V

3 letters:
Fit

4 letters:
Awdl
Blad
Duan
Epic
Epos
Fitt
Hymn
Neck
Poem
Rime
Sijo
Song
Vers

5 letters:
Blank
Blaud
Canto
Comus
Epode
Fitte
Fytte
Gazal

Haiku
Hokku
Ionic
Lyric
Meter
Poesy
Renga
Rubai
Spasm
Stave
Tanka
Tract
Triad

6 letters:
Adonic
Ballad
Burden
Dactyl
Ghazal
Ghazel
Gnomic
Haikai
Heroic
Jingle
Laisse
Miurus
Octave
Pantun
Rondel

Scazon
Stanza
Strain
Tercet
Vulgus

7 letters:
Alcaics
Couplet
Dimeter
Elegiac
Epigram
Fabliau
Huitain
Leonine
Pantoum
Pennill
Prosody
Pythian
Rondeau
Sapphic
Sestina
Sestine
Sixaine
Stiches
Strophe
Tiercet
Triolet
Tripody

8 letters:
Cinquain
Clerihew
Doggerel
Glyconic
Hexapody
Kyrielle
Madrigal
Nonsense
Pindaric
Quatrain
Rhopalic
Rove-over
Rubaiyat
Scansion
Senarius
Sing-song
Sirvente
Syllable
Terzetta
Trimeter
Tristich
Versicle

9 letters:
Amphigory
Asclepiad
Beatitude
Dithyramb
Ditrochee

Goliardic	**10 letters:**	Tetrameter	**12 letters:**
Hexameter	Asynartete	Tetrastich	Archilochian
Macaronic	Catalectic	Villanelle	Asclepiadean
Monometer	Cynghanedd		Hudibrastics
Monorhyme	Fescennine	**11 letters:**	Octosyllabic
Monostich	Hypermeter	Acatalectic	
Octameter	Mock-heroic	Alexandrine	**14 letters:**
Octastich	Ottava rima	Hudibrastic	Longs and shorts
Saturnian	Pennillion	Octastichon	
Stornello	Pentameter	Riding-rhyme	
Terza rima	Rhyme-royal	Septenarius	
Vers libre	Serpentine		

▷ **Versed** *may indicate* reversed

Versed sine Sagitta

Versifier, Versification Lyricist, Poetaster, Prosody, Rhymer, Rhymester

Version Account, Adaptation, Authorised, Cephalic, Cover, Edition, Form, Paraphrase, Rede, Remake, Rendering, Rendition, Revised, Revision, Rhemish, Standard, Translation

Vertebra(e), Vertebrate Agnathan, Amniote, Amphioxus, Ascidian, Atlas, Axis, Bone, Centrum, Cervical, Chordae, Coccyx, Cyclostome, Dorsal, Gnathostome, Ichthyopsida, Lamprey, Lumbar, Placoderm, Reptile, Sacral, Sauropsida, Spondyl, Tetrapod, Tunicata, Vermis

Vertex Apex, Crest, Crown, Summit, Zenith

Vertical Apeak, Apeek, Atrip, Erect, Lapse, Montant, Ordinate, Perpendicular, Plumb, Prime, Sheer, Standing, Stemmed, Stile, Upright

Vertigo Dinic, Dizziness, Fainting, Giddiness, Megrim, Nausea, Staggers, Whirling

Verve Dash, Energy, Go, Gusto, Panache, Vigour

Very (good, well) A1, Ae, Assai, Awfully, Boffo, Bonzer, Boshta, Boshter, Dashed, Dead, Def, Ever, Extreme(ly), Fell, Frightfully, Gey, Grouse, Heap, Hellova, Helluva, Highly, Jolly, Keen, Light, Mighty, Molto, Much, OK, Opt, Precious, Precise, Purler, Real, Right, Self same, So, Sore, Stinking, Très, Unco, Utter, V, VG, Way

Vesicle Ampul, Bladder

Vespers Evensong, Lychnic, Placebo, Sicilian

Vessel → **BOAT**, Capillary, Container, Craft, Dish, Logistics, Motor, Pressure, Receptacle, Seed, → **SHIP**, Utensil, Vascular, Weaker

VESSELS

3 letters:	Vas	Grab	**5 letters:**
Bin	Vat	Horn	Aorta
Cog		Lota	Blood
Cup	**4 letters:**	Olpe	Cogue
Dow	Back	Raft	Crare
Fat	Bowl	Skin	Crewe
Obo	Buss	Snow	Crock
Pan	Cask	Vase	Cruet
Pig	Cowl	Vein	Cruse
Pyx	Dhow	Vena	Cupel
Tub	Etna	Vial	Dandy
Urn	Font	Zulu	Dixie

5 letters – cont:
Gourd
Ketch
Laver
Lotah
Mazer
Oiler
Phial
Pokal
Quart
Round
Scoop
Shell
Sloop
Stean
Steen
Stoop
Stoup
Tazza
Varix
Xebec
Zabra

6 letters:
Aludel
Argyle
Argyll
Artery
Banker
Beaker
Bicker
Bouget
Bucket
Carafe
Carboy
Chatty
Copper
Crayer
Dinghy
Dogger

Dolium
Elutor
Flagon
Frigot
Galiot
Galley
Goblet
Goglet
Guglet
Humpen
Jet-ski
Kettle
Lorcha
Mortar
Noggin
Retort
Rumkin
Sailer
Sampan
Sconce
Settee
Shippo
Situla
Steane
Tassie
Trough
Tureen
Venule
Wherry

7 letters:
Amphora
Ampulla
Canteen
Chalice
Cistern
Coaster
Costrel
Creamer
Cresset

Cuvette
Cyathus
Dredger
Drifter
Felucca
Four oar
Frigate
Galleon
Galliot
Gunship
Gurglet
Jugular
Mudscow
Patamar
Pinnace
Pitcher
Polacca
Precava
Sharpie
Steamer
Tankard
Terreen
Vedette
Washpot

8 letters:
Billycan
Calabash
Cauldron
Ciborium
Colander
Coolamon
Crucible
Cucurbit
Decanter
Figuline
Flatboat
Galleass
Galliass
Gallipot

Gallivat
Hoveller
Hydroski
Jerrican
Longboat
Monteith
Pancheon
Panchion
Pannikin
Sinusoid
Workboat

9 letters:
Alcarraza
Autoclave
Bucentaur
Calandria
Casserole
Cullender
Destroyer
Hydrofoil
Privateer
Tappit-hen

10 letters:
Bathyscaph
Deep-sinker
Jardinière
Triaconter

11 letters:
Aspersorium
Bathyscaphe
Side-wheeler

12 letters:
Fore-and-after
Lachrymatory
Stern-wheeler
Sternwheeler

Vest Beset, Confer, Crop top, Gilet, Modesty, Rash, Semmit, Singlet, Skivvy, Spencer, Sticharion, String, Undercoat, Undershirt, Waistcoat

Vestibule Anteroom, Atrium, Entry, Exedra, Foyer, Hall, Lobby, Narthex, Oeil-de-boeuf, Porch, Portico, Pronaos, Tambour

Vestige Hint, Mark, Mention, Shadow, Sign, Trace

Vestment Alb, Breastplate, Canonicals, Chasuble, Chimar, Chimer(e), Cotta, Dalmatic, Ephod, Fannel, Fanon, Garb, → **GARMENT**, Maniple, Mantelletta, Omophorion, Pallium, Parament, Ph(a)elonian, Pontificals, Raiment, Rational, Rochet, Rocquet, Sakkos, Sticharion, Stole, Superhumeral, Surplice, Tunic(le)

Vestry Common, Sacristy, Select

Vet(ting), Veterinary, Vets Check, Doc(tor), Examine, Ex-serviceman, Horse-doctor, Inspect, OK, Positive, Screen, Veteran, Zoiatria, Zootherapy

Vetch Bitter, Ers, Fitch, Kidney, Locoweed, Milk, Tare, Tine

Veteran BL, Expert, GAR, Master, Oldster, Old sweat, Old-timer, Old 'un, Retread, Seasoned, Soldier, Stager, Stalwart, Stalworth, Vet, War-horse, Warrior

▷ **Veteran** *may indicate* 'obsolete'

Veto Ban, Bar, Blackball, Debar, Item, Line-item, Local, Negative, Pocket, Reject, Taboo, Tabu

Vex(ing), Vexed Ail, Anger, Annoy, Bepester, Bother, Chagrin, Debate, Fret, Gall, Grieve, Harass, Haze, Irritate, Madden, Mortify, Noy, Pester, Rankle, Rile, Sore, Spite, Tease, Torment, Trouble, Worrisome

Vexation(s) Barrator, Chagrin, Drat, Grief, Nuisance, Pique, Spite, Trouble

Vexatious Trying

Vexillum Web

Via By, Per, Through

Viable Economic, Going, Healthy, Possible

Vial Spirit-level

Viand Cate

Vibrate, Vibration(s), Vibrant Atmosphere, Chatter, Diadrom, Dinnle, Dirl, Energetic, Flutter, Free, Fremitus, Harmonogram, Hotter, Jar, Judder, Oscillate, Plangent, Pulse, Quake, Resonance, Resonant, Rumble, Seiche, Shimmy, Shudder, Thrill, Throb, Tingle, Tremble, Tremor, Trill, Trillo, Twinkle, Uvular, Wag, Whir(r)

Viburnum Opulus

Vicar Apostolic, Bray, Choral, Elton, Forane, General, Incumbent, Lay, Pastoral, Plenarty, Primrose, Rector, Rev(erend), Trimmer

Vice Clamp, Cramp, Crime, Deputy, Eale, Evil, Foible, Greed, Iniquity, Instead, Jaws, Regent, Second (in command), → **SIN**, Stair

Vice-president Croupier, Veep

Viceroy Khedive, Nawab, Provost, Satrap, Willingdon

Vichy water Eau

Vicinity Area, Environs, Hereabouts, Locality, Neighbourhood, Region

Vicious Cruel, Flagitious, Hotbed

Victim(s) Abel, Angel, Butt, Casualty, Currie, Curry, Dupe, Easy meat, Fall guy, Fashion, Frame, Hitlist, Host, Lay-down, Mark, Martyr, Nebbich, Neb(b)ish, Pathic, Patsy, Pigeon, Prey, Quarry, Sacrifice, Scapegoat, Target

Victor(y) Bangster, Banzai, Beater, Cadmean, Cannae, Captor, Champ(ion), Conqueror, Conquest, Epinicion, Epinikion, Eunice, Flagship, Fool's mate, Gree, Gris, Hallelujah, Hugo, Jai, Jai Hind, Kobe, Landslide, Lepanto, Ludorum, Mature, Moral, Nike, Palm, Philippi, Pyrrhic, Romper, Runaway, Scalp, Shut-out, Signal, Squeaker, Triumph, VE (day), Vee, Vic, Walk-away, Walkover, Win(ner)

Victoria(n) Aussie, Empress, Plum, Prig, Station

Victualler Caterer, Grocer, Licensed, Purveyor, Supplier, Vivandière

Video(-tape) Betacam®, Cassette, Digital, Full-motion, Interactive, Laser vision, Minitel, Pixelation, Promo, Quadruplex, Reverse, Scratch, Still, Vera

Vie Compete, Contend, Emulate, Strive

Vienna Wien

Vietcong Charley, Charlie

Vietnam(ese) Cham, VN

View(er) Aim, Angle, Aspect, Belief, Bird's eye, Cineaste, Consensus, Consider, Cosmorama, Dekko, Dogma, Doxy, Endoscope, Exploded, Eye, Facet, Gander, Glimpse, Grandstand, Helicopter, Idea, Introspect, Kaleidoscope, Landscape,

Line, Notion, Opinion, Optic®, Outlook, Pan, Panorama, Point, Private, Profile,
→ **PROSPECT**, Scan, Scape, Scene(ry), Scope, See, Sight, Skyscape, Slant, Specular,
Spyglass, Standpoint, Stereoscope, Strain, Synop(sis), Tenet, Terrain, Thanatopsis,
Theory, Vantage-point, Veduta, Vista, Visto, Watch, Witness, Worm's eye

Viewpoint Angle, Attitude, Belvedere, Conspectus, Eyeshot, Grandstand, Instance,
Observatory, Perspective, Sight, Sightline, Tendentious, Voxpop, Watch tower

Vigil, Vigilant(e) Awake, Aware, Baseej, Basij, Deathwatch, Eve, Guardian angel,
Hawk-eyed, Lyke-wake, Pernoctate, Wake, Wake-rife, Wary, Watch, Waukrife,
Whitecap

Vignette Print, Profile, Sketch

Vigorous(ly), Vigour Athletic, Bant, Billy-o, Billy-oh, Birr, Blooming, Brio,
Brisk, Con brio, Cracking, Drastic, Élan, Emphatic, Energetic, Flame, Forceful,
Full-blooded, Furioso, Go, Green, Heart(y), Heterosis, Hybrid, Lush, Lustihood,
Lustique, Lusty, P, Pep, Pith, Potency, Punchy, Pzazz, Racy, Rank, Raucle, Robust,
Round, Rude, Smeddum, Spirit, Sprack, Sprag, Steam, Sthenic, Stingo, Strength,
Strenuous, Strong, Thews, Tireless, Tone, Tooth and nail, Trenchant, Up, Vegete,
Vim, Vitality, Vivid, Vivo, Voema, Zip

▷ **Vigorously** *may indicate* an anagram

Viking Dane, Norseman, Rollo, R(y)urik, Sea king, Sea wolf, Varangian

Vile(ness) Base, Corrupt, Depraved, Dregs, Durance, Earthly, Infamy, Mean,
Offensive, Scurvy, Vicious

Vilify Smear

Villa Bastide, Chalet, Dacha, House

Village Aldea, Auburn, Borghetto, Burg, Clachan, Corporate, Dorp, Endship, Global,
Gram, Greenwich, Hamlet, Kaik, Kainga, Kampong, Kirkton, Kraal, Legoland,
Manyat(t)a, Mir, Outlet, Outport, Pit, Pueblo, Rancheria, Rancherie, Shtetl, Skara
Brae, Thorp(e), Ujamaa, Vill, Wick

Villain(y) Baddy, Bluebeard, Bravo, Crim(inal), Crime, Dastard, Dog, Heavy, Iago,
Knave, Lawbreaker, Macaire, Miscreant, Mohock, Nefarious, Ogre, Reprobate,
Rogue, Scab, Scelerat, Scoundrel, Skelm, Tearaway, Traitor

Villein Bordar, Churl, Serf

Vim Go, Vigour, Vitality, Zing

Vincent Van Gogh

Vindicate, Vindication Absolve, Acquit, Apologia, Avenge, Clear, Compurgation,
Darraign(e), Darrain(e), Darrayn, Defend, Deraign, Exculpate, Justify

Vindictive Bunny-boiler, Hostile, Malevolent, Repay(ing), Spiteful, Vengeful

Vine(yard) Akatea, Ampelopsis, Ayahuasco, Balloon, Balsam apple, Bine, Bush
rope, Château, Clinging, Clos, Colocynth, Cross, Cru, Cubeb, Cypress, Dodder,
Domaine, Grapery, Hop, Idaean, Kangaroo, Kudzu, Lawyer, Liana, Martha's,
Matrimony, Muskmelon, Naboth's, Potato, Puncture, Quinta, Russian,
Sarsaparilla, Stephanotis, Supplejack, Swallowwort, Trumpet, Turpeth, Vitis,
Winery, Wonga-wonga, Yam, Yquem

Vinegar Acetic, Acetum, Alegar, Balsam, Balsamic, Eisel(l), Esile, Malt, Oxymel,
Tarragon, Wine, Wood

Vintage Classic, Crack, Cru, Old, Quality

Viol(a), Violet African, Alto, Amethyst, Archil, Crystal, Dame's, Dog, Dog's tooth,
Gamba, Garden, Gentian, Gridelin, Heart's ease, Hesperis, Ianthine, Indole,
Ionone, Kiss-me, Lyra, Mauve, Methyl, Neapolitan, Orchil, Pansy, Parma, Prater,
Quint(e), Rock, Saintpaulia, Shrinking, Sweet, Tenor, Visual, Water

Violate, Violating, Violation Abuse, Breach, Contravene, Defile, Desecrate,
Fract, Infraction, → **INFRINGE**, March-treason, Outrage, Peccant, Rape, Ravish,

Solecism, Stuprate, Transgress, Trespass

Violence, Violent(ly) Acquaintance, Amain, Attentat, Bangster, Berserk, Bloody, Brutal, Brute force, Drastic, Droog, Extreme, Fierce, Flagrant, Force, Frenzied, Furious, Heady, Het, High, Hot, Inbreak, Mighty, Onset, Rage, Rampage, Rampant, Riot, Rough, Rough stuff, Rude, Severe, Slap, Stormy, Strongarm, Ta(r)tar, Tearaway, Terrorism, Thuggery, Tinderbox, Tub-thumping, Vehement, Vie, Wrath

Violet Iodine, Lilac, → **VIOLA**

Violin(ist), Violin-maker, Violin-shaped Alto, Amati, Cremona, Fiddle, Griddle, Gu(e), Guarneri(us), Guarnieri, Kennedy, Kit, Kubelik, Leader, Luthier, Menuhin, Nero, Oistrakh, Paganini, Pandurate, Rebeck, Rote, Stradivarius

VIP Bashaw, Bigshot, Bigwig, Brass, Cheese, Cob, Effendi, Envoy, Grandee, Imago, Kingpin, Magnate, Magnifico, Mugwump, Nabob, Nib, Nob, Pot, Snob, Someone, Swell, Tuft, Tycoon, Worthy

Viper Asp, Cerastes, Gaboon, Horned, Judas, Pit, Rattlesnake, River-jack, Russell's, Sand, Saw-scaled, → **SNAKE**, Traitor, Villain

Virago Amazon, Battle-axe, Beldam(e), Harpy, Randy, Shrew, Termagant

Virgil Maro

Virgin(al), Virginity, Virgin Mary Airline, Blessed, Celibate, Chaste, Cherry, Extra, Intact, Maiden, Maidenhead, Maidenhood, May, New, Pan(h)agia, Parthenos, Pietà, Pucel(l)age, Pucelle, Pure, Queen, Snood, Tarpeia, Theotokos, Untainted, Vestal, Zodiacal

Virginia(n) Creeper, Old Dominion, Tuckahoe, Va, Wade

Virile, Virility Energetic, Machismo, Macho, Manly, Red-blooded

Virtu Curio

Virtue(s), Virtuous, Virtual Angelic, Aret(h)a, Assay-piece, Attribute, Cardinal, Caritas, Charity, Chastity, Continent, Dharma, Efficacy, Ethical, Excellent, Faith, Foison, Fortitude, Fus(h)ion, Good, Goody-goody, Grace, Hope, Justice, Moral(ity), Natural, Patience, Plaster-saint, Practical, Principal, Prudence, Qua, Say-piece, Squeaky-clean, Straight and narrow, Temperance, Theological, Upright, Worth

Virtuosity, Virtuoso Artist, Bravura, Brilliance, Excellence, Executant, Maestro, Paganini, Savant

Virulent Acrimonious, Deadly, Hostile, Malign, Noxious, Toxic, Vitriolic, Waspish

Virus AIDS, Antigen, Arbovirus, Bacteriophage, Boot, Capsid, Computer, Contagium, Coxsackie, Defective, DNA, EB, Ebola, Echo, Enterovirus, Epstein-Barr, Filovirus, Filterable, Fowlpest, Germ, Granulosis, Hantavirus, Hendra, Herpes, HIV negative, HIV positive, Lassa, Latent, Leaf-mosaic, Lentivirus, Michelangelo, Microorganism, Norwalk, Oncogen, Parainfluenza, Parvo(virus), Pathogen, Peach-yellow, Picornavirus, Polyoma, Prophage, Reovirus, Retrovirus, Rhabdovirus, Rhinovirus, Ross River, Rotavirus, SARS, Shingles, Slow, Street, SV40, Tobacco mosaic, Varicella, Virino, Virion, West Nile, Zoster

Visa Transit

Viscera Bowels, Entrails, Giblets, Guts, Harigal(d)s, Haslet, Innards, Omentum, Splanchnic, Umbles, Vitals

Viscount Vis

Viscous (liquid), Viscosity Absolute, Glaireous, Gluey, Gummy, Kinematic, Slab, Specific, Sticky, Stoke, Tacky, Tar, Thick, Thixotropic

Visible Clear, Conspicuous, Evident, Explicit, In sight, Obvious

Visigoth Asaric

Vision(ary) Aery, Aisling, Apparition, Awareness, Beatific, Binocular, Bourignian, Day-dreamer, Double, Dream(er), Emmetropia, Fancy, Fantast, Fey, Idealist, Ideologist, Illusionist, Image, Kef, Moonshine, Mouse-sight, Mystic, Ocular,

Phantasm(a), Phantom, Pholism, Photism, Photopia, Rainbow-chaser, Romantic, Seeing, Seer, Sight, Stereo, Sweven, Tunnel, Twenty-twenty, Viewy

Visit(or) Affliction, Alien, Caller, Domiciliary, ET, Event, First-foot, Frequent, Gam, Guest, Habitué, Haunt, Health, Hit, Kursaal, Look up, Manuhiri, Pop in, Prison, See, Sightseer, Stay, Stranger, Take, Wait upon

Visor, Vizor Eyeshade, Face-saver, Mesail, Mezail, Umbrel, Umbr(i)ere, Umbril, Vent(ayle)

Vista Enfilade, Outlook, Scene, View

Visual(ise) Envisage, Ocular, Optical, Visible

Vital(ity) Alive, Bounce, Central, Critical, Crucial, Energy, Esprit, Essential, Existent, Foison, Gusto, Indispensable, Key, Kick, Life-blood, Linchpin, Lung, Mites, Momentous, Necessary, Oomph, Organ, Pizzazz, Pulse, Salvation, Sap, Viable, Vigour, Zing, Zoetic

Vitals Numbles, Umbles, Viscera

Vitamin(s) A, Aneurin, Axerophthol, B, Bioflavonoid, Biotin, C, Calciferol, Calcitriol, Citrin, Cobalamin, D, E, Ergocalciferol, Folacin, H, Inositol, K, Linoleic, Menadione, Menaquinone, Niacin, P, Pan(to)thenol, Phylloquinone, Phytonadione, Pyridoxine, Retinene, Retinol, Riboflavin, Ribose, Thiamin(e), Tocopherol, Torulin, Tretinoin

Vitiate(d) Flaw(ed)

Vitreous Glassy, Hyaline

Vitriol(ic) Acid, Acrimonious, Biting, Blue, Caustic, Green, Mordant, White

Vituperate Abuse, Berate, Castigate, Censure, Defame, Inveigh, Lash, Rail, Scold

Viva Oral

Vivacity, Vivacious Animation, Brio, Esprit, Exuberant, Sparkle, Spirit, Sprightly, Verve

Vivid Bright, Brilliant, Dramatic, Eidetic, Fresh, Graphic, Keen, Live, Pictorial, Picturesque, Sharp, Violent

Vivien Leigh

Vixen Catamaran, Harridan, Shrew, Virago

Viz Sc, Videlicet

Vizier Pheazar, Wazir

▶ **Vizor** *see* **VISOR**

Vocabulary Active, Glottochronology, Idiolect, Idioticon, Jargon, (Kata)kana, Lexicon, Lexis, Meta-language, Nomenclator, Passive, Wordbook

Vocal(isation), Vocalist Articulate, Doo-wop, Eloquent, Minstrel, Oral, Singer, Songster, Sprechgesang

Vocation Call, Career, Métier, Mission, Priesthood, Profession, Pursuit, Shop

Vociferous(ly) Clamant, Loud, Ore rotundo, Strident

Vogue Chic, Day, → **FASHION**, Groovy, It, Mode, Rage, Style, Ton

Vogul Ugrian, Ugric

Voice(d) Active, Air, Alto, Ancestral, Bass, Chest, Contralto, Countertenor, Descant, Edh, Emit, Eth, Express, Falsetto, Glottis, Harp, Head, Inner, Intonate, Lyric, Mezzo-soprano, Middle, Mouth, Opinion, Passive, Phonic, Pipe, Presa, Quill, Say, Sonant, Soprano, Speak, Spinto, Sprechstimme, Steven, Syrinx, Tais(c)h, Tenor, Throat, Tone, → **TONGUE**, Treble, Utter, White

Voiceless Aphonia, Aphony, Dumb, Edh, Eth, Mute, Silent, Tacit

Void Abyss, Annul, Belch, Blank, Chasm, Counter, Defeasance, Defecate, Diriment, Empty, Evacuate, Gap, Hollow, Inane, Invalid, Irritate, Lapse, Negate, Nullify, Quash, Space, Vacuum

Volatile Excitable, Explosive, Inconsistent, Latin, Live(ly), Mercurial, Skittish, Temperamental, Terpene

Volcano(es), Volcanic Agglomerate, Amygdale, Andesite, Black smoker, Burning mountain, Cone, Conic, Fumarole, Hornito, Ice, Idocrase, Igneous, Ignimbrite, Monticule, Mud, Obsidian, Pele, Pelée, Plinian, Pozz(u)olana, Pumice, Puzzolana, Sandblow, Shield, Soffioni, Solfatara, Stratovolcano, Tephra, Trass, Tuff

VOLCANOES

2 letters:
Aa

3 letters:
Aso
Puy

4 letters:
Etna
Fuji
Maui
Taal

5 letters:
Askja
Hekla
Kauai
Mayon
Misti
Okmok
Salse
Thera

6 letters:
Ararat
Asosan
Azores
Egmont
Erebus
Ischia
Katmai

Kazbek
Lipari
Semeru
Tolima

7 letters:
Aragats
Comoros
El Misti
Huascan
Iliamna
Iwo Jima
Mofette
Rotorua
Ruapehu
Semeroe
St Kilda
Tambora

8 letters:
Antisana
Cameroon
Cotopaxi
Jan Mayan
Krakatoa
Mauna Kea
Mauna Loa
St Helena
St Helens
Taraniki
Unalaska

Vesuvius

9 letters:
Aniakchak
Corcovado
Haleakala
Helgafell
Huascaran
Mount Fuji
Nevis Peak
Paricutin
Scablands
Stromboli
Tangariro

10 letters:
Chimborazo
Lassen Peak
Montserrat
Mount Eigon
Mount Kenya
Mount Pelée
Nyiragongo

11 letters:
Erciyas Dagi
Kilimanjaro
Mount Erebus
Mount Katmai
Mount Kazbek
Nyamuragira

Olympus Mons
Pico de Teide
Pico de Teyde

12 letters:
Citlaltépetl
Ixtaccahuatl
Iztaccahuatl
National Park
Popocatepetl

13 letters:
Mount Demavend
Mount St Helens

14 letters:
Mount Suribachi
Nevada de Colima
Nevada de Toluca
Soufrière Hills

17 letters:
Fernando de
  Noronha
Warrumbungle
  Range

20 letters:
D'Entrecasteau
  Islands

Vole Arvicola, Meadow mouse, Muskrat, Musquash, Ondatra
Volition Velleity, Will
Volley Barrage, Boom, Broadside, Platoon, Salvo, Tirade, Tire
Volt(age) BeV, Bias, Grid bias, HT
Voltaire Arouet
Volte face U-turn
Voluble Fluent, Glib
Volume Atomic, Band, Bande, Barrel, Book, Bushel, Capacity, CC, Code(x), Content, Critical, Cubage, Gallon, Hin, Loudness, Mass, Ml, Molecular, Omnibus, Peck, Pint, Quart, Quart(o), Roll, Roul(e), Size, Space, Specific, Stere, Swept, Tidal, Tom, Tome, Ullage, Vol
Voluntary, Volunteer Docent, Enlist, Fencible, Free, Free-will, Honorary, Offer,

Postlude, Reformado, Spontaneous, Tender, Tennessee, Terrier, TN, Ultroneous, Yeoman

Voluptuary, Voluptuous Carnal, Hedonist, Houri, Luscious, Sensuist, Sensuous, Sybarite

Volute Helix, Roll

Vomit(ing) Anacatharsis, Barf, Black, Boak, Boke, Cascade, Cat, Chuck up, Chunder, Disgorge, Egist, Egurgitate, Emesis, Fetch-up, Haematemesis, Honk, Keck, Kotch, Parbreak, Posset, Puke, Ralph, Regorge, Regurgitate, Retch, Rolf, Spew, Technicolour yawn, Throw up, Upchuck

Voodoo Charm, Jettatura, Kurdaitcha, Macumba, Mambo, Obeah, Sorcery, Zombi(e)

Voracious, Voracity Bulimia, Edacity, Gluttony, Greed, Ravenous, Serrasalmo

Vortex Charybdis, Eddy, Gyre, Trailing, Whirlpool

Votary Adherent, Cenobite, Devotee, Disciple, Fan, Nun, Swinger, Zealot

Vote(r), Votes, Voting Alternative, Assentor, Aye, Ballot, Ballotee, Block, Card, Casting, Choose, Colonist, Coopt, Cross, Crossover, Cumulative, Division, Donkey, Fag(g)ot, Floating, Franchise, Free, Grey, Informal, Mandate, Nay, Negative, No, Opt, People, Placet, Plebiscite, Plump, Plural, Poll, Postal, Pot-wabbler, Pot-waller, Pot-walloner, Pot-walloper, Pot-wobbler, PR, Preferential, Proportional representation, Qualified majority, Referendum, Return, Scrutin de liste, Scrutiny, Show of hands, Side, Single transferable, Straw(-poll), Suffrage, Swinging, Tactical, Ten-pounder, The stump, Theta, Ticket, Token, Transferable, Voice, X, Yea, Yes

Vote-catcher Pork

Vouch(er), Vouchsafe Accredit, Assure, Attest, Beteem(e), Book token, Chit, Coupon, Endorse, Gift, Guarantee, Luncheon, Meal-ticket, Receipt, Ticket, Token, Warrant

Voussoir Quoin, Wedge

Vow Affirm, Baptismal, Behight, Behot(e), Earnest, Ex voto, Hecht, Hest, I do, Nuncupate, → **OATH**, Pledge, Plight, Promise, Simple, Solemn, Swear, Troth, Vum

Vowel(s) Ablaut, Anaptyxis, Aphesis, Breve, Cardinal, Diphthong, Gradation, Indeterminate, Monophthong, Murmur, Mutation, Point, Rhyme, S(c)hwa, Seg(h)ol, Svarabhakti, Triphthong

Voyage(r) Anson, Columbus, Course, Cruise, Launch, Maiden, Passage, Peregrinate, Sinbad, Travel

Voyeur Peeping Tom, Scopophiliac

VTOL Convertiplane

Vulcan(ite) Blacksmith, Ebonite, Fire, Mulciber, Spock, Wayland

Vulgar(ian) Banausic, Barbaric, Base, Blatant, Blue, Brassy, Buffoon, Canaille, Cheap, Cit, Coarse, Common, Crude, Demotic, Flash, Forward, Gaudy, General, Gent, Gorblim(e)y, Gross, Heel, Hussy, Ignorant, Indecent, Laddish, Lavatorial, Lewd, Low(-life), Naff, Obscene, Ostentatious, Pandemian, Plebby, Plebeian, Popular, Proletarian, Raffish, Ribald, Riff-raff, Rude, Scaff, Scurrilous, Snob, Tacky, Tawdry, Threepenny, Tiger, Tink, Upstart, Vulg

Vulnerable Defenceless, Exposed, Open, Susceptible, Unguarded, Wide-open

Vulture Aasvogel, Bearded, Bird, Buzzard, California (condor), Condor, Culture, Falcon, Gallinazo, Gier, Griffon, Gripe, Grype, King, Lammergeier, Lammergeyer, Ossifrage, Predator, Turkey, Urubu, Zopilote

Ww

W Watt, West, Whisky, Women

Wad(ding) Batt(ing), Lump, Pad, Pledget, Roll, Swab, Wodge

Waddle Toddle, Waggle

Waddy Club, Cowboy, Stick

Wade(r), Wading Antigropelo(e)s, Crane, Curlew, Dikkop, Egret, Flamingo, Gallae, Godwit, Grallatorial, Greenshank, Gumboot, Heron, Ibis, Jacksnipe, Limpkin, Oyster-catcher, Paddle, Phalarope, Plodge, Sarus, Seriema, Shoebill, Snipe, Splodge, Stilt(bird), Terek, Virginia

Waesucks Ewhow, O(c)hone

Wafer Biscuit, Cracker, Crisp, Gaufer, Gaufre, Gofer, Gopher, Host, Papad, Seal

Waff Flap, Flutter, Wave

Waffle Adlib, Blather, Equivocate, Gas, Gaufer, Gaufre, Gofer, Gopher, Hedge, Poppycock, Prate, Rabbit, Wibble

Waft(ing) Airborne, Aura, Blow, Drift, Float

Wag(gish), Waggle Arch, Card, Comedian, Facetious, Joker, Lick, Niddle-noddle, Nod, Rogue, Shake, Sway, Wit(snapper), Wobble

Wage(s) Ante, Award, Fee, Hire, Income, Living, Meed, Minimum, Nominal, Pay, Portage, Practise, Prosecute, Rate, Salary, Screw, Subsistence

Wage-earner Breadwinner, Employee, Proletariat(e)

Wager Ante, Back, → BET, Gamble, Lay, Pascal's, Stake, Wed

Wagon(er) Ar(a)ba, Aroba, Boötes, Boxcar, Brake, Break, Buck, Buckboard, Buggy, Caisson, Carriage, Cart, Cattle truck, Chuck, Coachman, Cocopan, Conestoga, Corf, Covered, Democrat, Drag, Dray, Flatcar, Fourgon, Freight-car, Gambo, Go-cart, Hopper, Hutch, Low-loader, Mammy, Paddy, Palabra, Patrol, Plaustral, Police, Prairie schooner, Rave, Reefer, Rubberneck, Shandry, Station, Tank, Tartana, Telega, Tender, Trap, Trekker, Truck, Van, Victoria, Wain, Water

Waif Arab, Foundling, Jetsam, Stray, Urchin, Victoria, Wastrel, Water, Weft

Wail(er) Banshee, Bawl, Blubber, Howl, Keen, Lament, Moan, Skirl, Threnody, Threnos, Ululate, Vagitus, Wah-wah, Yammer

Wain Cart, Dray, Wagon

Waist(band) Belt, Cummerbund, Girdlestead, Girth, Hour-glass, Middle, Midship, Obi, Sash, Shash, Wasp, Zoster

Waistcoat Gilet, Jerkin, Lorica, MB, Pressure, Sayon, Shawl, Sleeve(d), Vest, Weskit

Wait(er), Waiting Abid(e), Ambush, Barista, Bide, Busboy, Butler, Buttle, Carhop, Commis, Cupbearer, Dally, Delay, Estragon, Expect, Flunkey, Frist, Garçon, Hang on, Hesitate, Hover, Interval, Khidmutgar, Lead time, Lime, Linger, Lurch, Maître d', Maître d'hôtel, Minority, Omnibus, Pannier, Pause, Penelope, Pozzo, Queue, Remain, Serve(r), Sommelier, Stacking, Stay, Steward, Suspense, Taihoa, Tarry, Tend(ance), Tray, Vladimir, Wine, Won

Waitress Hebe, Miss, Mousme(e), Nippy, Server

Waive Abandon, Defer, Forgo, Overlook, Postpone, Relinquish, Renounce

Wake(n) Abrade, Abraid, Abray, Aftermath, Alert, American, Animate, Arouse, Astern, Deathwatch, Excite, Hereward, Keen, Knock-up, Like, Lyke, Prod, Rear, → ROUSE, Surface, Train, Wash

Waldo Emerson

Wale(r) Prop, Ridge, Weal

Wales Cambria, Cymru, Dyfed, Principality

Walk(er), Walking, Walkabout, Walkway Alameda, Alley, Alure, Amble, Ambulate, Arcade, Berceau, Birdcage, Charity, Cloister, Clump, Constitutional, Daddle, Dander, Dauner, Emu, Esplanade, EVA, Expatiate, Flânerie, Frescade, Gait, Gallery, Ghost, Go, Gradient, Gressorial, Heel and toe, Hike, Hookey, Hump, Lambeth, Leg, Lumber, Mainstreeting, Mall, March, Mince, Mosey, Nordic, Pace, Pad, Pasear, Paseo, Passage, Path, Ped, Perambulate, Pergola, Perp, Pipe-opener, Pole, Pound, Power, Prance, Prom(enade), Rack, Ramble, Rampart, Random, Ring, Routemarch, Sashay, Shamble, Sidle, Slommock, Space, Spanish, Sponsored, Stalk, Step, Stoa, Striddle, Stroll, Strut, Stump, Terrace, Toddle, Tramp, Trash, Travolator, Tread, Trog, Truck, Trudge, Turn, Wade, Wander, Wayfare, Wend, Widow's, Xyst

Walk-over Doddle, Pie, Scratch

Wall Antonine, Bail, Bailey, Barrier, Berlin, Berm, Cavity, Cell, Chinese, Climbing, Countermure, Crib, Curtain, Dado, Dam, Dike, Dry-stone, Enceinte, Epispore, Exine, Fail-dike, Fourth, Fronton, Frustule, Gable, Great, Hadrian's, Hanging, Hangman, Head, Immure, Intine, Mahjongg, Mani, Merlon, Mutual, Myocardium, Non-bearing, Parapet, Parietal, Parie(te)s, Parpane, Parpen(d), Parpent, Parpoint, Partition, Party, Peribolos, Pericarp, Perpend, Perpent, Pleuron, Podium, Puteal, Qibla, Retaining, Revet(ment), Ring, River, Roman, Roughcast, Screen, Sea, Septum, Severus, Side, Somatopleure, Spandrel, Spandril, Street, Studding, Tambour, Tariff, Trumeau, Vallation, Vallum, Video, Wa', Wailing, Western, Withe, Zooecia

Wallaby Brusher, Dama, Kangaroo, Pad(d)ymelon, Pademelon, Quokka, Tammar, Whiptail

Wallah Competition

Wallaroo Euro

Wall-covering, Wallpaper Anaglypta®, Arras, Burlap, Flock, Lincrusta, Paper, Tapestry, Tapet, Woodchip

Waller Fats, Mason

Wallet Billfold, Case, Flybook, Folder, Notecase, Pochette, Pocket-book, Purse, Scrip

Wallflower Crucifer, Dowd(y), Pariah

Wall-game Eton, Mahjongg

Wallop Bash, Baste, Batter, Beat, Biff, Clout, Cob, → HIT, Lam, Lounder, Oner, Polt, Pound, Slog, Strap, Swinge, Tan, Tat, Trounce

Wallow(ing) Bask, Flounder, Luxuriate, Revel, Roll, Slubber, Splash, Swelter, Tolter, Volutation, Welter

Wall-painting Fresco, Graffiti, Grisaille

▸ **Wallpaper** see WALL-COVERING

Wall-plate Tassel, Torsel

Wall-support Beam, Foundation, Pier, Rear-arch, Rere-arch

Wally Dipstick, Nincompoop, Prat

Walnut Black, Butternut, Hickory, Juglans, Satin, White

Walrus Morse, Moustache, Pinniped, Rosmarine, Sea-horse, Tash

Walter Bruno, Mitty, Pater, Scott

Waltz Anniversary, Blue Danube, Boston, Concert, Dance, Hesitation, Rotate, Valse

Wampum Peag(e), Shell-money

Wan Lurid, Pale, Pallid, Pasty, Sanguine, Sorry

Wanchancy Unlucky

Wand Baton, Caduceus, Rod, Runic, Stick, Thyrse, Thyrsus, Vara, Vare

Wander(er), Wandering Aberrance, Amble, Bedouin, Berber, Bum, Caird, Daiker, Delirious, Desultory, Deviate, Digress, Divagate, Drift, Errant, Estray, Evagation, Excursive, Expatiate, Extravagate, Gad(about), Grope, Hobo, Jew, Landloper, Maunder, Meander, Meandrian, Mill, Mither, Moider, Moither, Moon, Nomad(e), Odysseus, Pedder, Peregrine, Peripatetic, Polar, Prodigal, Rache, Ramble, Range, Ratch, Roamer, Romany, Room, Rove, Solivagant, Stooge, Straggle, Stravaig, Stray, Strayve, Streel, Stroam, Stroll, Swan, Ta(i)ver, Tramp, Troll, Truant, Tuareg, Vagabond, Vagile, Vagrant, Vague, Waif, Wend, Wheel, Wilder, Wolves

▷ **Wandering** *may indicate* an anagram

Wane Decline, Decrease, Diminish, Ebb

Wangle Arrange, Finagle, Trick

Want(ing), Wants Absence, Conative, Covet, Crave, Dearth, Defect, Deficient, Derth, Desiderata, → **DESIRE**, Destitution, Envy, For, Hardship, Indigent, Itch, Lack, Long, Mental, Moldwarp, Mole, Need, Penury, Require, Scarceness, Scarcity, Shortfall, Shy, Void, Wish, Yen

Wanton(ness) Bona-roba, Cadgy, Chamber, Cocotte, Colt's tooth, Deliberate, Demirep, Filly, Flirt-gill, Gammerstang, Giglet, Giglot, Gillflirt, Hussy, Jay, Jezebel, Jillflirt, Lewd, Licentious, Light o' love, Loose, Nice, Protervity, Rig, Roué, Slut, Smicker, Sportive, Sybarite, Toyish, Twigger, Unchaste, Wayward

Wap Blow, Knock, Strike

War(fare), Wars American Civil, American Independence, Ares, Armageddon, Arms, Asymmetrical, Attrition, Bacteriological, Barons', Bate, Battle, Biological, Bishop, Chemical, Civil, Clash, Class, Cod, Cold, Combat, Conflict, Crescentade, Crimean, Crusade, Electronic, Emergency, Feud, → **FIGHT**, Flagrante bello, Flame, Food, Franco-Prussian, Fray, Germ, Gigantomachy, Great, Guer(r)illa, Gulf, Holy, Hostilities, Hot, Hundred Years', Information, Internecine, Jehad, Jenkins' ear, Jihad, Jugurthine, Korean, Krieg, Limited, Mars, Mexican, Napoleonic, Nuclear, Opium, Peasants', Peloponnesian, Peninsular, Phony, Price, Private, Propaganda, Psychological, Punic, Push-button, Queen Anne's, Rebellion, Revolutionary, Roses, Russo-Japanese, Secession, Seven against Thebes, Seven Years', Shooting, Six Day, Social, Spam, Spanish-American, Spanish Civil, Star, Stoush, Sword, Terrapin, Theomachy, Thirty Years', Total, Trench, Trojan, Turf, Vietnam, Winter, World, Yom Kippur

Warble(r) Carol, Cetti's, Chiff-chaff, Chirl, Fauvette, Peggy, Record, Rel(l)ish, Trill, Vibrate, Yodel, Yodle

War-chant, War-cry Alalagmos, Haka, Slogan

Ward (off) Artemus, Averruncate, Avert, Care, Casual, Casualty, Charge, Defend, District, Fend, Guard, Hand-off, Inner, Marginal, Maternity, Nightingale, Oppose, Outer, Parry, Protégé, Pupil, Soc, Soken, Vintry, Wear, Weir

Warden Caretaker, Church, Concierge, Constable, Crossing, Curator, Custodian, Game, Guardian, Keeper, Maori, Meter maid, Pear, Provost, Ranger, Septimus, Sidesman, Spooner, Steward, Traffic, Way

Warder Beefeater, Gaoler, Guardian, Keeper, Provost, Screw, Turnkey, Twirl

Wardrobe Almirah, Armoire, Breakfront, Capsule, Closet, Clothes, Garderobe, Outfit, Vestuary

Ware(s) Arretine, Basalt, Beware, Biscuit, Cameo, Canton, Chelsea, China, Etruria, Fabergé, Faience, Goods, Hollo(w)ware, Jasper, Lapis lazuli, Lustre, Merchandise,

Palissy, Plate(d), Queen's, Samian, Sanitary, Satsuma, Shippo, Truck, Wemyss
Warehouse Bonded, Data, Depository, Entrepôt, Freight-shed, Go-down, Hong, Store
▸ **Warfare** *see* **WAR**
War-game Kriegs(s)piel
War-god Ares, Mars, Tiu, Tiw, Tyr
Warhead Atomic, Supremo
Warhorse Charger, Destrier, Fighter
Wariness, Wary Ca'canny, Cagey, Careful, Cautel, Caution, Chary, Discreet, Distrust, Gingerly, Guarded, Leery, Mealy-mouthed, Prudent, Sceptical, Suspicious, Tentie, Tenty, Vigilant
Warlike Battailous, Bellicose, Gung-ho, Lachlan, Martial, Militant
Warlord Haw-haw, Kitchener, Shogun
Warm(er), Warming, Warmth Abask, Admonish, Air, Ardour, Balmy, British, Calefacient, Calid(ity), Cardigan, Chambré, Cordial, Empressement, Enchafe, Fervour, Flame, Foment, Gemütlich, Genial, Global, Glow, → **HEAT**, Hot, Incalescent, Kang, Lew, Logic, Loving, Muff, Muggy, Mull, Radiator, Tepid, Thermal, Toast, Toasty
Warm-blooded Homothermal, Homothermic, Homothermous, Idiothermous
Warmonger Hawk
Warn(ing) Admonish, Alarum, Alert, Amber, Aposematic, Apprise, Beacon, Beware, Bleep, Buoy, Caution, Caveat, Caveat emptor, Commination, Cone, Counsel, Cowbell, Detector, DEW, Document, Early, En garde, Example, Foghorn, Fore, Foretoken, Gardyloo, Garnishment, Griffin, Harbinger, Hazchem, Heads up, Hoot, Horn, Klaxon, Knell, Larum, Lesson, Light, Maroon, Monition, Nix, Noli-me-tangere, Nota bene, Notice, Omen, Pi-jaw, Portent, Premonish, Premonitory, Presage, Prodromal, Profit, Protevangelium, Riot Act, Rumble strip, Scaldings, Scarborough, Sematic, Shore, Signal, Storm, Tattler, Threat, Timber, Tip-off, Token, Vigia, Vor, Yellow card
Warner Alarm, Fore, Plum, Siren
Warp(ed) Bias, Buckle, Cast, Contort, Distort, Kam, Kedge, Pandation, Spring, Time, Twist, Weft, Zag
Warpath Rampage
▹ **Warped** *may indicate* an anagram
Warrant(y) Able, Authorise, Behight, Behote, Bench, Caption, Certificate, Death, Deserve, Detainer, Distress, Dividend, Fiat, Fiaunt, Fugle, General, Guarantee, Justify, Mittimus, Peace, Permit, Precept, Reprieve, Royal, Search, Sepad, Special, Swear, Transire, Vouch, Warn, Writ
Warren Burrow, Colony, Hastings, Rabbit
Warrior Achilles, Agamemnon, Ajax, Amazon, Anzac, Attila, Berserk(er), Brave, Cold, Cossack, Crusader, Eorl, Fianna, Fighter, Finlay, Finley, Geronimo, Ghazi, Haiduk, Heimdall, Heyduck, Housecarl, Impi, Lewis, Louis, Myrmidon, Nestor, Rainbow, Rajpoot, Rajput, Roger, Samurai, Soldier, Tatar, Unknown, Warhorse, Warwolf, Zulu
Warship Battleship, Blockship, Castle, Cog, Corvette, Cruiser, Destroyer, Drake, Dromon(d), Frigate, Invincible, Man-o-war, Mine-layer, Monitor, Privateer, Ram, Repulse, Wooden Walls
Wart(y) Anbury, Angleberry, Blemish, Keratose, Lump, Muricate, Plantar, Tuberous, Verruca, Wen
Warwick Kingmaker
▸ **Wary** *see* **WARINESS**

Was Erat, Existed, Lived, Past

Wash(ed), Washer, Washing (up), Wash out Ablution, Affusion, Alluvion, Bath, Bay(e), Bidet, Bubble-dancing, Bur(r), Calcimine, Circlip, Clean(se), Cradle, D, Dashwheel, Dele(te), Dip, Edulcorate, Elute, Elutriate, Enema, Erode, Fen, Flush, Freshen, Gargle, Grommet, Grummet, Hush, Irrigate, Kalsomine, Lap, → **LAUNDER**, Lavabo, Lave, Leather, Lip, Lotion, Marsh, Maundy, Mop, Nipter, Pan, Pigswill, Poss, Purify, Rinse, Sapple, Scrub, Shampoo, Shim, Sind, Sloosh, Sluice, Soogee, Soojee, Soojey, Squeegie, Stream, Sujee, Swab, Synd, Syne, Tie, Toilette, Top and tail, Twin tub, Tye, Wake, Wudu, Yellow

Washbasin, Washing machine, Washtub, Washhouse Copper, Dash-wheel, Lavabo, Steamie

Washerman, Washerwoman Dhobi, Laundress

Washington Wa

Wasn't Nas, Wasna

▷ **Wasp** *may indicate* a rugby player

Wasp(ish) Appledrain, Bembex, Bink, Bite, Chalcid, Cuckoo-fly, Cynipidae, Cynips, Digger, European, Fig, Fretful, Gall(-fly), Gold, Hornet, Horntail, Hoverfly, Irritable, Marabunta, Mason, Miffy, Muddauber, Paper, Peevish, Pompilid, Potter, Ruby-tail, Sand, Seed, Solitary, Spider, Syrphus, Velvet ant, Vespa, Wood, Yellow jacket

Wasp's nest Bike, Bink, Byke

Wassail Carouse, Pledge, Toast

Wast Wert

Wastage, Waste(d), Wasting, Wasteful, Wasteland, Waster, Wastrel Amyotrophy, Atrophy, Blow, Blue, Bluer, Boondoggle(r), Cesspit, Cirrhosis, Colliquative, Consume, Contabescent, Coom(b), Cotton, Crud, Culm, Decay, Dejecta, Desert, Detritus, Devastate, Dilapidate, Dissipate, Dross, Dung, Dwindle, Dwine, Dystrophy, Effluent, Egesta, Emaciate, Erode, Estrepe, Excrement, Exhaust, Expend, Exudate, Faeces, Flue, Forpine, Fribble, Fritter, Garbage, Gash, Gob, Gunge, Haggard, Havoc, Hazardous, High-level, Husk, Idler, Knub, Lavish, Loose, Lose, Loss, Low-level, Marasmus, Merino, Misspent, Moor, Moulder, Muir, Mullock, Mungo, Natural, Novalia, Nub, Nuclear, Offal, Oller, Ordure, Pellagra, Perish, Phthisis, Pigswill, Pine, Prodigalise, Profligate, Radioactive, Rammel, Rank and manger, Ravage, Recrement, Red mud, Red tape, → **REFUSE**, Reif, Rubble, Ruderal, Scant o' grace, Scattergood, Schappe, Scissel, Scoria, Scrap, Sewage, Slag, Slurry, Spend, Spend-all, Spendthrift, Spill, Spoil(age), Squander, Stalko, Sullage, Syntexis, Tabes, Tailing, Thin, Thwaite, Ureal, Urine, Uropoiesis, Vagabond, Vast, Wanze, Wear, Wilderness, Yearn

▷ **Wasted** *may indicate* an anagram

Watch(er) Accutron®, Analog(ue), Analogon, Argus, Await, Bark, Behold, Bird-dog, Black, Clock, Coastguard, Cock-crow, Digital, Dog, Eryl, Espy, Eyeball, Fob, Glom, Gregory, Guard, Half-hunter, Huer, Hunter, Kettle, Latewake, Lever, Lo, Look, Look-out, Middle, Monitor, Morning, Nark, Neighbourhood, Night, Nit, Note, Nuremberg egg, Observe, Overeye, Patrol, Pernoctation, Posse, Quartz, Regard, Repeater, Rolex®, Scout, Sentinel, Sentry, Shadow, Snoop, Spectate, Spie, Spotter, Spy, Stemwinder, Suicide, Surveillance, Tend, Ticker, Timekeeper, Timepiece, Timer, Tompion, Tout, Turnip, Vedette, → **VIGIL**, Voyeur, Wait, Wake, Weather eye, Wrist(let)

Watch-chain Albert, Slang

Watch-control Escapement

Watchful(ness) Alert, Aware, Care, Dragon, Ira, Jealous, Vigilant, Wakerife, Wary, Waukrife, Weather eye

Watchman Argus, Bellman, Charley, Charlie, Chok(e)y, Cho(w)kidar, Guard, Sentinel, Sentry, Speculator, Tompion, Viewer
Watch-tower Atalaya, Barbican, Beacon, Garret, Mirador, Sentry-go, Turret
Watchword Cry, Password, Shibboleth, Slogan
Water(ed), Waters, Watery Adam's ale, Adam's wine, Aerated, Amrit, Apollinaris, Aq(ua), Aquatic, Aqueous, Ascites, Barley, Bayou, Bedabble, Bilge, Bound, Branch, Brine, Broads, Brook, Burn, Canal, Cancer, Chresard, Chuck, Cold, Cologne, Compensation, Conductivity, Connate, Dead, Deaw, Deg, Demersal, Dew, Dill, Dilute, Dribble, Drinking, Eau, Ebb, Echard, Element, Ennerdale, Epilimnion, Euphotic, Evian®, First, Flood, Ford, Fossil, Functional, Gallise, Gallize, Ganga jal, Grey, Gripe, Ground, Hard, Heavy, Hectum, Hellespont, High, Holy, Hot, Hungary, Hydatoid, Irrigate, Javel(le), Kuroshio, Kyle, Lagoon, Lagune, Lake, Lant, Laurel, Lavender, Leachate, Lentic, Light, Limnology, Lithia, Loch(an), Lode, Lotic, Lough, Low, Lubricated, Lymph, Melt, Meteoric, Mineral, Miner's inch, Moiré, Mother, Nappe, North, Oasis®, Oedema, Orange-flower, Overfall, Pani, Pawnee, Pee, Perrier®, Phreatic, Pisces, Polly, Polynia, Polynya, Poppy, Potash, Potass, Pump, Purest, Quarry, Quick, Quinine, Rain, Rapids, Rate, Reach, Rheumy, Rice, Rip, Riverine, Rose, Running, Runny, Rydal, Saltchuck, Scorpio, Sea, Seltzer, Sera, Serous, Serum, Shoal, Shower, Simpson, Skinkling, Slack, Slick, Sluice, Soda, Sodden, Soft, Solent, Sound, Souse, Southampton, Stream, Surface, Tabby, Table, Tam, Tap, Tar, Territorial, Thin, Tide, Toilet, Tonic, Urine, Utility, Vadose, Vichy, Viscous, Vlei, Vly, Wai, Wash(y), Weak, Wee, Whey, White, White coal, Wild, Wishy-washy
Waterbaby Moses, Tom
Water-boa Anaconda
Water-boatman Notonecta
Water-brash Pyrosis
Water-buckets Noria
Water-carrier Aqueduct, Bheestie, Bheesty, Bhistee, Bhisti, Bucket, Carafe, Chatty, Drain, Furphy, Hose, Hydra, Hydria, Kirbeh, Pail, Pitcher, Rigol
Water-chestnut Saligot
Water-colour Aquarelle, Painting, Pastel, RI
Water-course Arroyo, Billabong, Canal, Ditch, Dyke, Falaj, Furrow, Gutter, Khor, Lead, Leat, Nala, Nalla(h), Nulla, Nullah, Rean, Rhine, River(et), Riverway, Shott, Spruit, Wadi, Whelm
Watercress Nasturtium
Water-device Shadoof, Shaduf
Water-diviner Dowser, Hydrostat
Waterfall Angel (Falls), Cataract, Churchill, Chute, Cuquenan, Espelands, Force, Foss, Iguaçú, Kabiwa, Kaieteur, Kile, Lasher, Lin(n), Lower Mar Valley, Mardel, Mtarazi, Niagara, Overfall, Rapid, Salmon leap, Sault, Sutherland, Takakkaw, Tugela, Tyssestrengene, Utigord, Victoria, Yellowstone, Yosemite
Water-fern Marsilea, Salvinia
Water-gate Penstock, Sluice, Sluse
Water-god Aleion, Aleyin, Alpheus
Water-hen Gallinule
Water-hole Bore, Gilgai, Mickery, Oasis
Water-lily Candock, Lotus, Nenuphar, Nuphar, Spatterdock, Victoria
Waterloo Rout
Waterman Aquarius, Bargee, Ferryman, Oarsman
Water-monster Nicker

Water-nymph Kelpie, Kelpy, Naiad, Ondine, Rusalka

Water-parsnip Sium, Skirret

Water-plant Alisma, Aquatic, Cress, Crowfoot, Elodea, Gulfweed, Lace-leaf, Lattice-leaf, Nelumbo, Nenuphar, Nuphar, Ouvirandra, Pontederia, Quillwort, Reate, Sea-mat, Sedge, Seg, Stratiotes, Urtricularia, Vallisneria

Waterproof, Water-tight Caisson, Camlet, Caulk, Cerecloth, Cofferdam, Corfam®, Dampcourse, Dubbin(g), Groundsheet, Loden, Mac, Mino, Oilers, Oilskin, Pay, Seaworthy, Stank, Sta(u)nch, Tarp, Tar-paper, Tarpaulin, Waders

Water-rat Arvicola, Musk-rat, Ratty, Vole

Watershed Divide, Hilltop

Water-spout Gargoyle, Geyser, Hurricano

Water-sprite Kelpie, Kelpy, Nix(ie), Nixy, Tangie, Undine, Water-nymph

Water supply Dewpond, H, Hydrant, Spring, Tank, Tap

Waterway Aqueduct, Billabong, Canal, Channel, Creek, Culvert, Ditch, Igarapé, Illinois, Intracoastal, Lode, River, St Lawrence Seaway, Sny(e), Sound, Straight, Suez

Water-wheel Noria, Pelton, Sakia, Saki(y)eh, Tympanum

Wattle(s) Acacia, Boobialla, Boree, Dewlap, Gills, Golden, Mimosa, Mulga, Sallow, Savanna, Snot, Snotter

Wave(s), Waved, Waveform, Wavelength, Wavy Alfven, Alpha, Band, Beachcomber, Beam, Beck, Beta, Billow, Bore, Bow, Brain, Brandish, Breaker, Carrier, Circular polarisation, Clapotis, Cold, Comber, Complementary, Complex, Continuous, Crenulate, Crest, Crime, Crimp, Crispate, Cymotrichous, De Broglie, Decuman, Delta, Dominant, Dumper, Electromagnetic, Feather, Finger, Flap, Flaunt, Float, Flote, Flourish, Fourier series, Gesticulate, Gravitational, Gravity, Graybeard, Ground, Groundswell, Gyrose, Harmonic, Haystack, Head sea, Heat, Hertzian, Internal, Ionospheric, Lee, Long, Longitudinal, Marcel, Matter, Medium, Mexican, Nebule, New, Oundy, Peristalsis, Perm(anent), Plunger, Primary, Pulse, Radar, Radiation, Radio, Rayleigh, Repand, Rip, Ripple, Roller, Rooster, Sastrugi, Scrub, Sea, Secondary, Seiche, Seismic, Shake, Shock, Short, Sine, Sinuate, Skipper's daughter, Sky, Skyrmion, Snaky, Soliton, Sound, Spiller, Square, Squiggle, Standing, Stationary, Stern, Stream, Supplementary, Surf, Surge, Sway, Tabby, Theta, Third, Thought, Tidal, Tidal bore, Tide, Train, Transverse, Travelling, Tsunami, Ultrashort , Ultrasonic, Undate, Unde, Undulate, Vermicular, Waffle, Waft, Wag, Waive, Wash, Waw, Wawe, Whelm, Whitecap, White-horse, Wigwag

▷ **Wave(s)** *may indicate* an anagram

Wave-band Channel

Wave-detector Coherer

▶ **Wavelength** *see* WAVE

Waver(ing), Waverer Dither, Double-minded, Falter, Flag, Gutter, Halt, Hesitate, Indecision, Oscillate, Reel, Stagger, Sway, Swither, Teeter, Trimmer, Vacillate, Waffle, Wet, Wow

Wax(ed), Waxing, Waxy Adipocere, Ambergris, Appal, Bate, Bees, Bone, Brazilian, Candelilla, Carna(h)uba, Cere, Ceresin, Cerumen, Chinese, Cobbler's, Cutin, Earth, Effuse, Enseam, Ethal, Geraldton, Grave, Greaves, Grow, Heelball, Honeycomb, Increase, Increscent, Inseam, Ire, Japan, Kiss, Lecithin, Lipide, Livid, Lost, Lyrical, Mineral, Montan, Mummy, Myrtle, Ozocerite, Ozokerite, Paraffin, Parmacitie, Pela, Petroleum, Propolis, Pruina, Rage, Seal, Sealing, Spermaceti, Suberin, Tallow, Tantrum, Temper, Toxaphene, Vegetable, White, Yielding

Waxwing Cedar-bird, Icarus

Way(s), Wayside Access, Agate, Appian, Autobahn, Avenue, Borstal(l), Budo,

Bypass, Companion, Course, Crescent, Defile, Direction, Door, Draw, E, Each, Entrance, Family, Fashion, Flaminian, Four-foot, Foss(e), Gate, Habit, Hatch, Hedge, High, Hither, How, Icknield, Lane, Manner, Means, Method, Milky, MO, Mode, Modus, N, Pass, Path, Pennine, Permanent, Pilgrim's, Procedure, Railroad, Regimen, Ridge, → **ROAD**, Route, S, Sallyport, St(reet), Style, System, Taoism, Technique, Third, Thoroughfare, Thus, Trace, Trail, Troade, Turnpike, Underpass, Untrodden, Via, W, Wise

Wayfarer Commuter, Piepowder, Pilgrim, Traveller, Voyager

Waylay Accost, Ambuscade, Ambush, Beset, Bushwhack, Buttonhole, Molest, Obstruct, Stick up

Way-out Advanced, Bizarre, Egress, Esoteric, Exit, Exotic, Extreme, Offbeat, Trendy

Wayward Capricious, Disobedient, Errant, Erratic, Loup-the-dyke, Obstreperous, Perverse, Stray, Unruly, Wilful

WC Gents, Ladies, Lav, Loo

We I and I, Oo, Royal, Us

Weak(er), Weaken(ing), Weakest, Weakness Achilles' heel, Acrasia, Adynamia, Antimnemonic, Aphesis, Appair, Appal, Arsis, Asthenia, Attenuate, Blot, Brickle, Brittle, Cachexia, Cataplexy, Chink, Cissy, Cripple(d), Debile, Debilitate, Decrease, Delay, Delicate, Deplete, Dilling, Dilute, Disable, Effete, Emasculate, Embrittle, Enervate, Enfeeble, Entender, Fade, Faible, Failing, Faint, Fatigue, Feeble, Fissile, Flag, Flaw, Flimsy, Foible, Fragile, Frail(tee), Frailty, Give, Glass chin, Gone, Groggy, Ham, Hamartia, Helpless, Honeycomb, Impair, Impotence, Infirm, Knock-kneed, Labefaction, Lame, Lassitude, Leptosomatic, Loophole, Low, Low ebb, Meagre, Mild, Milk and water, Myasthenia, Namby-pamby, Pale, Pall, Paraparesis, Paresis, Penchant, Puny, Push-over, Pusillanimous, Reckling, Reduce, Simp, Slack, Soft spot, Tenuous, Thesis, Thin, Thready, Tottery, Unable, Underdog, Undermine, Unman, Unnerve, Unstable, Vapid, Velleity, Vessel, Vulnerability, W, Washy, Water(y), Wish(y)-wash(y), Wuss(y)

Weakling Dilling, Drip, Milksop, Nerd, Nisgul, Reed, Softie, Wuss

Weal Ridge, Stripe, Urticant, Wealth, Welfare, Welt, Whelk

Wealth(y) Abundance, Affluence, Bullion, Croesus, Digerati, Ease, Fat-cat, Fortune, Golconda, Jet-set, Klondike, Klondyke, Load(sa), Loaded, Loadsamoney, Lolly, Mammon, Means, Mine, Mint, Moneyed, Nabob, Opulence, Ore, Pelf, Plutocrat, Reich, Rich, Ritzy, Solid, Substance, Treasure, Trustafarian, Untold, Well-heeled, Well-off, Well-to-do

Wean Ablactation, Bairn, Spain, Spane, Spean

Weapon(s) Ammo, Arm, Arsenal, Assault, Binary, Deterrent, Greek fire, → **GUN**, Hoplology, Long-range, Missile, Munition, Nuclear, Nuke, Piece, → **PISTOL**, → **SWORD**, Theatre, Tool, Traditional

WEAPONS

2 letters:	Gat	Club	Spat
Da	Rod	Cosh	Sten
V1	SAM	Dart	Tank
		Gade	Tuck
3 letters:	*4 letters:*	Gaid	
Axe	Beam	Kris	*5 letters:*
Bow	Bill	Mere	Arrow
Dag	Bolo	Mine	Baton
Gad	Bomb	Pike	Blade

Brand
Estoc
Flail
Knife
Kukri
Lance
Lathi
Maxim
Orgue
Panga
Pilum
Rifle
Sabre
Saker
Spear
Staff
Stick
Sting
Taser®
Vouge

6 letters:
Airgun
Archie
Cestus
Cohorn
Creese
Cudgel
Dagger
Dragon
Duster
Gingal
Glaive
Jingal
Katana
Lathee
Mauser®
Mortar
Musket
Onager
Rapier
Sparke

Sparth
Taiaha
Tomboc
Voulge

7 letters:
Arblast
Assegai
Ataghan
Bayonet
Bazooka
Blowgun
Bondook
Caliver
Caltrap
Caltrop
Carbine
Chopper
Coehorn
Cutlass
Dragoon
Enfield
Fougade
Gingall
Gisarme
Grenade
Halberd
Halbert
Harpoon
Hatchet
Javelin
Longbow
Machete
Matchet
Petrary
Poleaxe
Poniard
Sandbag
Shotgun
Sidearm
Torpedo
Trident

Warhead

8 letters:
Alderman
Arbalest
Armalite®
Arquebus
Ballista
Blowpipe
Bludgeon
Calthrop
Catapult
Culverin
Elf-arrow
Fougasse
Howitzer
Mangonel
Nunchaku
Partisan
Petronel
Revolver
Scimitar
Scorpion
Shuriken
Skean-dhu
Skene-dhu
Spontoon
Stiletto
Stinkpot
Tomahawk
Whirl-bat
Whorl-bat
Yataghan

9 letters:
Arquebuse
Backsword
Battleaxe
Boomerang
Catchpole
Chainshot
Derringer

Doodlebug
Escopette
Excalibur
Flintlock
Forty-five
Harquebus
Sarbacane
Slingshot
Sword cane
Tormentum
Trebuchet
Truncheon
Welsh hook

10 letters:
Broadsword
Knobkerrie
Pea-shooter
Shillelagh
Smallsword
Swordstick
Throw-stick

11 letters:
Morgenstern
Morning star
Snickersnee

12 letters:
Dagger of lath
Flamethrower
Jeddart staff
Quarterstaff

13 letters:
Knuckleduster
Life-preserver
Manrikigusari

14 letters:
Nunchaku sticks

▷ **Wear** *may indicate* the NE eg Sunderland

Wear(ing), Wear Out Abate, Ablative, Abrade, Air, Attrition, Chafe, Corrade,
Corrode, Deteriorate, Detrition, Efface, Erode, Erosion, Fashion, For(e)spend, Fray,
Frazzle, Fret, Garb, Impair, In, Mush, Pack, Sap, Scuff, Sport, Stand, Tedy, Tolerate,
Utility

Weariness, Wearisome, Weary(ing) Beat, Bejade, Blethered, Bore, Cloy,
Dog-tired, Ennui, Ennuyé, Exhaust, Fag, Fatigate, Fatigue, Harass, Hech,
Heigh-ho, Irk, Jade, Lacklustre, Lassitude, Pall, Puny, Ramfeezle, Sick, Sleepy,

Spent, Tire, Tiresome, Trash, Try, Tucker, Wabbit, Worn

Weasel Beech-marten, Cane, Delundung, Ermine, Ferret, Glutton, Grison, Kolinsky, Marten, Mink, Mustela, Pekan, Pine-marten, Polecat, Stoat, Taira, Tayra, Vermin, Whitterick, Whit(t)ret, Whittrick, Wolverine, Woodshock

Weather, Weather forecast Atmosphere, Climate, Cyclone, Discolour, Ecoclimate, Elements, El Niño, Endure, Hail, La Nina, Met, Monkey's wedding, Rain, Sky, Snow, Stand, Survive, Tiros, Undergo, Withstand

Weatherboard Rusticating

Weathercock Barometer, Fane, Vane

Weave(r), Weaves, Weaving Arachne, Basket, Broché, Cane, Complect, Contexture, Entwine, Finch, Fishnet, Folk, Heald, Heddle, Interlace, Jacquard, Lace, Lease, Leno, Lion, Loom, Marner, Osiery, Penelope, Pick, Plain, Plait, Raddle, Ripstop, Rya, Shuttle, Sparrow, Spider, Splice, Stevengraph, Taha, Textorial, Texture, Throstle, Throwster, Tissue, Tweel, Twill, Twine, Wabster, Waggle, Webster, Zigzag

Weaver-bird Amadavat, Avadavat, Quelea, Rice-bird, Taha

Web(bed), Webbing, Web-footed, Web-site Aranea, Fissipalmate, Food, Fourchette, Hit, Infomediary, Internet, Mat, Maze, Mesh(work), Offset, Palama, Palmate, Palmiped, Patagium, Pinnatiped, Portal, Retiary, Skein, Snare, Spider, Tear, Tela, Tissue, Toil, Totipalmate, World Wide

Webster Spider, Weaver

Wed(ding), Wedlock Alliance, Bet, Diamond, Espousal, Golden, Hymen, Join, Knobstick, Liaison, Link, Marriage, Marry, Mate, Matrimony, Meng(e), Me(i)nt, Meynt, Ming, Monkey's, Nuptials, Pair, Penny, Ruby, Shotgun, Silver, Spousal, → **UNION**, Unite, White, Y

Wedge(d) Accretionary, Canting-coin, Chock, Chunk, Cleat, Cotter, Cuneal, Doorstop, Feather, Forelock, Gagger, Gib, Impacted, Jack, Jam, Key, Niblick, Pitching, Prop, Quoin, Sand, Scotch, Shim, Spaceband, Sphenic, Stick, Texas, Trig, Vomerine, Voussoir, Whipstock

Wedgwood Benn, China

Wednesday Ash, Midweek, Pulver, Spy

Wee Leak, Little, Pee, Slash, Sma(ll), Tinkle, Tiny, → **URINATE**, Widdle

▷ **Weed** *may indicate* 'urinated'

Weed(y) Adderwort, Agrestal, Alga, Allseed, Anacharis, Arenaria, Bedstraw, Bell-bind, Blinks, Burdock, Buttercup, Carpetweed, Catch, Charlock, Chickweed, Chlorella, Cigar(ette), Cissy, Clotbur, Clover, Cobbler's pegs, Cockle, Cocklebur, Colonist, Coltsfoot, Corncockle, Couch, Daisy, Dallop, Dandelion, Darnel, Dock, Dollop, Dulse, Elder, Elodea, Ers, Fag, Fat hen, Femitar, Fenitar, Fluellen, Fluellin, Fork, Fucoid, Fumitory, Gangly, Goutweed, Goutwort, Ground elder, Groundsel, Helodea, Hoe, Indian, Joe-pye, Knapweed, Knawel, Knot-grass, Lanky, Lemna, Mare's-tail, Marijuana, Matfelon, Mayweed, Nard, Nettle, Nipplewort, Nostoc, Onion, Oxygen, Paterson's curse, Pearlwort, Pilewort, Pineapple, Piri-piri, Plantain, Potamogeton, Purslane, Ragi, Ragwort, Reate, Rest-harrow, Ribbon, Ribwort, Ruderal, Runch, Sagittaria, Sargasso, Scal(l)awag, Scallywag, Senecio, Softy, Sorrel, Speedwell, Spurge, Spurrey, Sudd, Sun-spurge, Swine's-cress, Tab, Tansy, Tare, Thistle, Tine, Tobacco, Tormentil, Twitch, Ulotrichale, Ulva, Vetch, Viper's bugloss, Wartcress, Widow's, Winnow, Yarr

Weedkiller Arsenic, Atrazine, Dalapon, Diquat, Diuron, Herbicide, Paraquat®, Selective, Simazine

Week(s), Weekly Ember, Expectation, Great, Hebdomadary, Holy, Omer, Orientation, Ouk, Oulk, Passion, Periodical, Prophetic, Rag, Rogation, Schoolies, Sennight, Working

Weekday Feria

Weekend K, Sat, Sun

Weep(er), Weeping, Weepy, Wept Bawl, Blubber, Cry, Grat, Greet, Lachrymose, Lament, Loser, Maudlin, Niobe, Ooze, Pipe, Screet, Seep, Sob, Wail, Waterworks

Weevil Anthonomous, Bean, Boll, Bug, Cornworm, Curculio, Diamond-beetle, Grain, Insect, Nut, Pea, Rice, Seed, Snout beetle

Weft Roon, Shot, Texture, Warp, Woof

Weigh(ing), Weigh down, Weight(s), Weighty All-up, Apothecaries', Arroba, Artal, As, Atomic, Avoirdupois, Balance, Bantam, Baric, Bob, Bow, Bulk, Burden, Candie, Candy, Cantar, Carat, Catty, Cental, Centner, Clout, Clove, Consider, Count, Counterpoise, Cruiser, Ct, Dead, Decagram(me), Deliberate, Derham, Dirham, Dirhem, Drachm(a), Drail, Dram, Dumbbell, Emphasis, Equivalent, Feather, Firkin, Fother, G, Gerah, Grain, Gram, Grammage, Great, Gross, Heft, Importance, Impost, Incumbent, Journey, Kandy, Kantar, Kat(i), Katti, Kerb, Khat, Kin, Kip, Last, Liang, Libra, Lisp(o)und, Live, Load, Mark, Massive, Maund, Metage, Metrology, Mina, Minimum, Mna, Molecular, Moment, Mouse, Nail, Nett, Obol, Oke, Onerous, Oppress, Ounce, Overpoise, Oz, Pease, Peaze, Peck, Peise, Peize, Perpend, Pesante, Peyse, Pikul, Plumb-bob, Plummet, Poise, Ponderal, Pood, Pound, Pregnant, Preponderance, Prey, Pud, Pudge, Quintal, Rate, Recul, Rod, Rotl, Rotolo, Sash, Scruple, Seer, Semuncia, Ser, Sinker, Sit, Slang, Slung-shot, Stone, Stress, Talent, Tare, Throw, Tical, Tod, Tola, Ton(nage), Tonne, Tophamper, Tron(e), Troy, Truss, Trutinate, Unce, Unmoor, Welter, Wey, Wt

Weighing machine Bismar, Scales, Steelyard, Tron(e)

Weightless Agravic

Weight-lifter Crane, Lewis, Windlass

Weir Cauld, Dam, Garth, Kiddle, Kidel, Lasher, Pen, Watergate

Weird Bizarre, Curious, Dree, Eerie, Eery, Eldritch, Far out, Kookie, Offbeat, Spectral, Strange, Supernatural, Taisch, Uncanny, Zany

Welch, Welsh Abscond, Cheat, Default, Embezzle, Levant, Rat, Reneg(u)e, Renig, Skedaddle, Weasel

Welcome, Welcoming Aloha, Ave, Bel-accoyle, Ciao, Embrace, Entertain, Glad-hand, Greet, Haeremai, Hallo, Halse, Hello, Hi, Hospitable, How, Hullo, Karanga, Open house, Powhiri, Receive, Reception, Salute, Ticker-tape, Yellow-ribbon

Weld(ing) Arc, Butt, Cold, Explosion, Fillet, Friction, Fuse, Gas, Join, Merge, MIG, Resistance, Seam, Sinter, Stud, Tack, TIG, Ultrasonic, Unite

Welfare Advantage, Alms, Benison, Common weal, Ha(y)le, Heal, Health, Sarvodaya, Social, Weal

Welkin Firmament, Sky

Well (done) Artesian, Atweel, Aweel, Bien, Bore(hole), Bravo, Carbon, Casinghead, Cenote, Chipper, Development, Discovery, Dropping, Dry hole, Easily, Euge, Famously, Fine, Fit, Foot, Gas, Gasser, Good, Gosh, Gusher, Hale, → **HEALTHY**, Hot, Inkpot, Ka pai, Law, Mickery, My, Namma hole, Odso, Oh, Oil, Phreatic, Potential, Pump, So, Source, Spa, Spouter, Spring, Sump, Surge, Teek, Um, Upflow, Wildcat, Worthily, Zemzem

Wellbeing Atweel, Bien-être, Comfort, Euphoria, Euphory, Good, Health, Oomph, Welfare

Well-born Eugene

Well-bred Genteel

Well-built Sturdy, Tight

Well-covered Chubby, Padded
Well-curb Puteal
Welles Orson
Wellington, Welly Accelerate, Boot, Green, Gumboot, Iron Duke, Nosey
Well-known Famous, Illustrious, Notorious, Notour, Prominent
Well-off Affluent, Far, Rich, Wealthy
Well part Bucket, Shadoof, Shaduf
Wells Bombardier, Fargo, Sadler's
Well-wisher Friend
▶ **Welsh** *see* **WELCH**
Welsh(man), Welshwoman Aled, Briton, Brittonic, Brython, Cake, Cambrian,
    Celtic, Cog, Crachach, Cym(ric), Cymry, Dafydd, Dai, Ebbw, Emlyn, Evan, Fluellen,
    Gareth, Harp, Idris, Ifor, Ivor, Keltic, Megan, P-Celtic, P-Keltic, Rabbit, Rarebit,
    Rees, Rhys, Sion, Taff(y), Tudor, W, Walian
Wen Cyst, Talpa, Tumour, Wart
Wench Blowze, Court, Girl, Gouge, Hussy, Maid, Ramp, Rig, Smock, Strumpet
Wend Meander, Sorb, Steer
Wendy Darling, House
Went Left, Sold, Yode
Werewolf Loup-garou, Lycanthrope, Nazi, Turnskin, Vampire
Wesleyan Epworth, Methodist
West(ern), Westerly Ang mo, Far, Favonian, Hesperian, Mae, Middle, Movie,
    Oater, Occidental, Ponent, Spaghetti, Sunset, W, Westlin, Wild
West African Fantee, Fanti, Kroo, Mandingo, Wolof
▷ **West end** *may indicate* 't' or 'W1'
West Indian Carib, Creole, Jamaican, Quashee, Quashie, Taino
Westminster SW1
Wet(ting), Wetland Bedabble, Bedraggled, Clammy, Daggle, Damp, Dank, Dew,
    Dip, Douse, Dowse, Drench, Drip(ping), Drook, Drouk, Embrue, Enuresis, Feeble,
    Humect, Humid, Hyetal, Imbrue, Imbue, Irrigate, Irriguous, Madefy, Madid,
    Marshy, Moil, Moist(en), Molly, Namby-pamby, Pee, Piddle, Pouring, Rainy,
    Ramsar site, Ret(t), Rheumy, Roral, Roric, Runny, Saturate, Shower, Simp(leton),
    Sipe, Sissy, Sluice, → **SOAK**, Sodden, Sopping, Sour, Steep, Tiddle, Tipsy, Urinate,
    Wat, Wee, Widdle, Wimpy, Wringing
Wetsuit Steamer
Whack(ed), Whacking Astronomic, Belt, Bemaul, Biff, Deadbeat, Joll, Joule, Jowl,
    Lambast, Lounder, Share, Swat, Swish, Thump
▷ **Whale** *may indicate* an anagram
Whale(meat), Whaling Baleen, Beaked, Beluga, Black, Blower, Blubber, Blue,
    Bottlehead, Bottlenose, Bowhead, Bull, Cachalot, Calf, Cetacea(n), Cete, Cow,
    Cowfish, Dolphin, Dorado, Fall, Fin(back), Finner, Gam, Glutton, Grampus,
    Greenland (right), Grey, Greyback, Humpback, Killer, Kreng, Leviathan, Manatee,
    Minke, Monodon, Mysticeti, Narwhal, Odontoceti, Paste, Physeter, Pilot, Pod,
    Porpoise, Right, River dolphin, Rorqual, School, Scrag, Sea-canary, Sea-unicorn,
    Sei, Social, Sperm, Spouter, Sulphur-bottom, Thrasher, Toothed, Toothless, White,
    Zeuglodon(t)
Whalebone Busk
Whaler Ahab, Harpooner, Ship, Specksioneer, Specktioneer, Waister
Whales' meat Clio
Wham Bang, Collide
Whang Blow, Flog, Thrash, Whack

Wharf(inger) Dock(er), Jetty, Key, Landing, Pier, Quay, Roustabout, Rouster, Staith(e)

What, Whatever Anan, Eh, How, Pardon, Que, Regardless, Siccan, That, Which

Whatnot, What's-its-name Dinges, Dingus, Doings, Doobrey, Doobrie, Étagère, Gismo, Jiggamaree, Jiggumbob, Thingamy, Thingumajig, Thingumbob, Thingummy, Timenoguy

Wheat Amber, Amelcorn, Bald, Beard(ed), Beardless, Blé, Bulg(h)ur, Cone, Couscous, Cracked, Durum, Einkorn, Emmer, Federation, Fromenty, Frumenty, Furme(n)ty, Furmity, Grain, Hard, Mummy, Red, Rivet, Sarrasin, Sarrazin, Seiten, Semolina, Sharps, Soft, Spelt, Spring, Summer, Triticum, White, Winter

Wheatsheaf Bale, Gerbe, Stook

Wheedle Banter, Barney, Blandish, Butter up, Cajole, Coax, Cog, Cuiter, Cuittle, Flatter, Inveigle, Tweedle, Whilly(whaw)

Wheel(er) Balance, Bedel, Bevel, Bicycle, Big, Bogy, Breast, Bucket, Buff(ing), Caracol(e), Cart's tail, Caster, Castor, Catherine, Chain, Chark(h)a, Circle, Cistern, Count, Crown, Cycle, Daisy, Diamond, Disc, Driving, Emery, Epicycloidal, Escape, Fan, Felloe, Felly, Ferris, Fifth, Fortune, Gear, Grinding, Gyrate, Helm, Hurl, Idle(r), Jagger, Jigger, Jolley, Joy, Kick, Lantern, Magnate, Master, Medicine, Mitre, Monkey, Mortimer, Nabob, Nose, Paddle, Pattern, Pedal, Pelton, Perambulator, Persian, Pin, Pinion, Pitch, Pivot, Planet, Potter's, Prayer, Pulley, Rag, Ratchet, Rhomb, Roll, Roller, Rotate, Roulette, Rowel, Sheave, Snail, Spare, Spider, Spinning, Sprocket, Spur, Star, Steering, Stepney, Stitch, Swing, Tail, Throwing-table, Tread, Treadmill, Trindle, Trochus, Trolley, Truckle, Trundle, → **TURN**, Tympan(um), Water, Web, Wharve, Wire, Worm, Zoetrope

Wheelbarrow Hurlbarrow, Monotroch

Wheelhouse Caravan, Paddle-box

Wheel-hub Axle, Nave

Wheelman Cyclist, Ixion

Wheelwright Spokesman

Wheeze Asthma, Jape, Joke, Pant, Ploy, Rale, Reak, Reik, Rhonchus, Ruse, Stridor, Trick, Whaisle, Whaizle

Whelk Buckie, Limpet, Shellfish, Stromb, Triton

Whelm Nalla(h), Nulla(h)

Whelp Bear, Bra(t)chet, Pup

When(ever) Although, As, If, Once, Though, Time

Where(abouts) Location, Neighbourhood, Place, Site, Vicinity, Whaur, Whither

Wherefore Cause, Reason, Why

Whereupon So, When

Wherewithal Finance, Means, Money, Needful, Resources

Wherry Barge, Rowboat

Whet(stone) Coticular, Excite, Hone, Oilstone, Rubstone, Sharpen, Stimulate

Whether Conditional, If

Whey Plasma, Serum, Whig

Which(ever), Which is Anyway, As, QE, Whatna, Whilk, Who

Whiff Breath, Cigarette, Gust, Hum, Puff, Redolence, Smatch, Sniff, Trace, Waft

Whig Adullamite, Jig, Rascal, Tory, Whey

While Although, As, Interim, Since, Space, Span, Spell, Though, Throw, Time, When, Whenas, Whereas, Yet

Whim(s), Whimsical, Whimsy Bizarre, Caprice, Conceit, Crotchet, Fad, Fancy, Fantastic, Fay, Fey, Fie, Flisk, Impulse, Kicksy-wicksy, Kink, Notion, Quaint, Quirk, Tick, Toy, Vagary

Whimper Cry, Grizzle, Mewl, Pule, Snivel, Whine
Whin Furze, Gorse, Ulex
Whine, Whinge Cant, Carp, Complain, Cry, Grumble, Kvetch, Mewl, Moan, Peenge, Pule, Snivel, Whimper, Yammer
Whinny Neigh, Nicker, Whicker
Whip(ped), Whip out, Whipping Beat, Braid, Brede, Bullwhack, Bullwhip, Cat, Cat o' nine tails, Chabouk, Chantilly, Chastise, Chief, Cilium, Colt, Crop, Drive, Feague, Firk, Five-line, Flagellate, Flagellum, Flay, Gad, Hide, Jambok, Knout, K(o)urbash, Larrup, → **LASH**, Leather, Limber, Limber, Lunge, Quirt, Rawhide, Riem, Scourge, Sjambok, Slash, Steal, Stock, Strap-oil, Swinge, Swish, Switch, Taw, Thong, Three-line, Thresh, Trounce, Welt, West Country, Whap, Whop
Whippersnapper Dandiprat, Dandyprat, Pup, Squirt
Whippoorwill Wishtonwish
Whirl(er), Whirling Bullroarer, Circumgyrate, Dervish, Eddy, Gyrate, → **IN A WHIRL**, Pivot, Reel, Spin, Swing, Swirl, Vortex, Vortical, Vorticose, Vortiginous, Whirry
Whirlpool Eddy, Gulf, Gurge, Maelstrom, Moulin, Sea purse, Swelchie, Vorago, Vortex, Weel, Wiel
Whirlwind Cyclone, Dust devil, Eddy, Sand-devil, Tornado, Tourbillion, Typho(o)n, Vortex, Willy-willy
Whirr Birr
Whisk Balloon, Chowri, Chowry, Fly, Swish, Switch, Whid, Whip
Whisk(e)y Alcohol, Barley-bree, Barley-broo, Barley-broth, Bond, Bourbon, Canadian, Cape smoke, Chain lighting, Corn, Cratur, Crayther, Creature, Fife, Fire-water, Hard stuff, Hard tack, Highball, Hokonui, Hoo(t)ch, Irish, Malt, Monongahela, Moonshine, Morning, Mountain dew, Nip, Peat-reek, Pot(h)een, Ragwater, Red eye, Rye, Scotch, Sourmash, Southern Comfort®, Spunkie, Tanglefoot, Tarantula juice, Usquebaugh, Wheech, Whiss
Whisker(s) Beard, Beater, Burnsides, Cat's, Dundreary, Excrement, Face fungus, Hackle, Hair, Moustache, Mutton-chop, Samuel, Satyric tuft, Side(-boards), Side-burns, Stibble, Stubble, Vibrissa
▷ **Whisky** *may indicate* an anagram
Whisper Breath(e), Bur(r), Hark, Hint, Innuendo, Murmur, Pig's, Round, Rumour, Rustle, Sigh, Stage, Susurrus, Tittle, Undertone, Whittie-whattie
Whist Dummy, Hush, Long, Progressive, Quiet, Sh, Short, Solo, Whisk and swabbers
Whistle(r) Blow, Boatswain's, Calliope, Catcall, Feedback, Flageolet, Hewgh, Hiss, Marmot, Pedro, Penny, Phew, Ping, Pipe, Quail-pipe, Ref, Siffle(ur), Sowf(f), Sowth, Steam, Stop, Stridor, Swab(ber), Swanee, Tin, Toot, Tweedle, Tweet, Warbler, Wheeple, Wheugh, Whew, Whiffle, Wolf
Whit Atom, Doit, Figo, Haet, Hait, Hate, Iota, Jot, Particle, Pentecost, Point, Red cent, Straw
White(n), Whitener, Whiteness, White-faced Agene, Agenise, Alabaster, Albedo, Albescent, Albino, Albugineous, Albumen, Argent, Ashen, Au lit, Bakra, Blameless, Blanch, Blanche, Blanco, Bleach, Buckra, Cabbage, Calm, Cam, Camstone, Candid, Candida, Candour, Canescent, Canities, Caucasian, Caum, Chardonnay, China, Chinese, Christmas, Cliffs, Collar, Company, Cream, Dealbate, Egg, Elephant, Ermine, European, Fang, Fard, Feather, Flag, Flake, French, Glair, Gwen(da), Gwendolen, Gwyn, Hawked, Hock, Honorary, Hore, House, Innocent, Ivory, Large, Leucoma, Lie, Lily, Livid, Man, Marbled, Mealy, Niveous, Opal, Oyster, Pakeha, Pale(face), Pallor, Paper, Paris, Pearl, Poor, Pure, Redleg, Russian,

Sclerotic, Selborne, Sheep, Silver, Small, Snow(y), Spanish, Taw, Vitiligo, Wan, Wedding, Wyn, Zinc

Whitefish Menominee

Whitefriars Alsatia

Whitehall Ministry

Whitehead Milium

White horse(s) Skipper's daughters, Wave

White man Anglo, Ba(c)kra, Buckra, Caucasian, Corn-cracker, Cracka, Gora, Gub(bah), Haole, Honkie, Honky, Kabloona, Larney, Mzungu, Occidental, Ofay, Pakeha, Paleface, Redleg, Redneck, Umlungu, WASP, Wigga, Wigger

Whitewash Calcimine, Excuse, Kalsomine, Lime, Skunk, Trounce

Whitlow Ancome, Felon, Panaritium, Paronychia

Whitsun Pentecost, Pinkster, Pinxter

Whittle Carve, Pare, Sharpen

Whizz Wheech

Who As, Doctor

Whodunit Mystery

Whole, Wholehearted, Wholeness, Wholly All, Cosmos, Eager, Entire(ty), Entity, Every inch, Fully, Hale, Indiscrete, Intact, Integer, Integrity, Largely, Lot, Sum, Systemic, Thoroughly, Total, Tout à fait, Unbroken, Uncut

Wholesale(r) Cutprice, En bloc, Engrosser, Ingross, Jobber, Root and branch, Stockjobber, Supplier, Sweeping

Wholesome Clean, Good, Healthy, Physical, Salutary, Sound

Whoop(er), Whooping cough Alew, Celebrate, Chincough, Crane, Cry, Excite, Kink(cough), Kink-host, Pertussis, Swan, War

Whoopee Carouse, Evoe, Hey-go-mad, Roister

Whoosh Birr, Swish

Whopper, Whopping Barn, Crammer, Huge, Immense, Jumbo, Lie, Lig, Oner, Out and outer, Scrouger, Slapper, Slockdolager, Soc(k)dalager, Soc(k)dolager, Soc(k)doliger, Soc(k)dologer, Sogdolager, Sogdoliger, Sogdologer, Stonker, Tale, Taradiddle

Whore Drab, Harlot, Loose woman, Pinnace, Pro, Prostitute, Quail, Road, Strumpet, Tart

Whorl Corolla, Eucyclic, Spiral, Swirl, Verticil, Volute, Volution

Why Raison d'être, Reason, Yogh

Wick Farm, Rush, Snaste, Snuff, Vill(age)

▷ **Wicked** *may indicate* containing a wick

Wicked(ness) Adharma, Atrocity, → **BAD**, Candle, Criminal, Cru(i)sie, Crusy, Depravity, Devilish, Evil, Facinorous, Flagitious, Goaty, Godless, Heinous, High-viced, Immoral, Impious, Improbity, Iniquity, Lantern, Miscreant, Nefarious, Night-light, Perverse, Ponerology, Pravity, Rush, Satanic, Scelerate, Sin(ful), Taper, Turpitude, Unholy, Vile

Wicker(work) Basketry, Sale, Seal

Wicket Gate, Hatch, Infield, Pitch, Square, Sticky, Stool, Stump, Yate

Wicket-keeper Stumper

Wide, Widen(ing), Width Abroad, Ample, Bay, Braid, Broad, Comprehensive, Dilate, Drib, Eclectic, Expand, Extend, Far, Flanch, Flange, Flare, Flaunch, Ga(u)ge, General, Latitude, Miss, Prevalent, Roomy, Set, Spacious, Span, Spread, Sundry, Sweeping, Vast

Wide-awake Alert, Fly, Hat, Wary, Watchful

Widespread Catholic, Diffuse, Epidemic, Extensive, General, Pandemic,

Panoramic, Pervasive, Prevalent, Prolate, Rife, Routh(ie), Sweeping, Universal

Widow(ed) Bereft, Black, Dame, Discovert, Dowager, Golf, Grass, Hempen, Jointress, Relict, Sati, Sneerwell, Suttee, Vidual, Viduous, Whydah-bird, Widdy

Wield Brandish, Control, Exercise, Handle, → MANIPULATE, Ply, Sound

Wife, Wives Bride, Concubine, Consort, Devi, Dutch, Enid, Evadne, Feme, Feme covert, Fiere, Frau, Goody, Haram, Harem, Harim, Helpmate, Helpmeet, Hen, Her indoors, Kali, Kickie-wickie, Kicksy-wicksy, Kloo(t)chman, Lakshmi, Little woman, Mate, Memsahib, Missis, Missus, Mrs, Mummer's, Partner, Penelope, Pirrauru, Potiphar's, Rib, Seraglio, Spouse, Squaw, Stepford, Trophy, Trouble and strife, Umfazi, Ux(or), Vrou, W

Wig Adonis, Bagwig, Bob(wig), Brigadier, Brutus, Buzz-wig, Cadogan, Campaign, Carpet, Cauliflower, Caxon, Chevelure, Chide, Cockernony, Dalmahoy, Fright, Full-bottomed, Gizz, Gooseberry, Gorgone, Gregorian, Hair(piece), Heare, Jas(e)y, Jazy, Jiz, Macaroni, Major, Periwig, Peruke, Postiche, Ramil(l)ie(s), Rate, Reprimand, Rug, Scold, Scratch, Sheitel, Spencer, Targe, Tie, Toupee, Toupet, Tour

Wiggle, Wiggly Jiggle, Scoleciform, Wobble, Wriggle

Wight Man, Vectis

Wigwam Te(e)pee

Wild Aberrant, Agrestal, Angry, Barbarous, Berserk, Bundu, Bush, Chimeric, Crazy, Dionysian, Earl, Errant, Erratic, Extravagant, Farouche, Feral, Frantic, Frenetic, Haggard, Hectic, Lawless, Mad(cap), Manic, Meshugge, Myall, Natural, Outlaw, Rampant, Raver, Riotous, Romantic, → SAVAGE, Skimble-skamble, Unmanageable, Unruly, Violent, Warrigal, West, Woolly

▷ **Wild(ly)** *may indicate* an anagram

Wild beast Eyra, Sapi-utan, Scrubber

Wildcat Lion, Manul, Ocelot, Strike, Tiger

Wilde Marty, Oscar

Wilderness Bush, Desert, Negev, Ruderal, Sinai, Solitude, Waste

Wild goose Chase, Greylag

Wild oats Haver

Wile, Wily Art, Artful, Artifice, Astute, Braide, → CUNNING, Deceit, Foxy, Peery, Ruse, Shifty, Shrewd, Slee, → SLY, Spider, Stratagem, Streetwise, Subtle, Trick, Versute, Wide

Wilful Deliberate, Headstrong, Heady, Obstinate, Recalcitrant, Wayward

Will, Willing(ly) Alsoon, Amenable, Bard, Bequeath, Bewildered, Biddable, Bill(y), Complaisant, Compliant, Conation, Content, Desire, Devise, Fain, Force, Free, Game, General, Hay, Holographic, Leave, Legator, Leve, Lief, Lieve, Living, Noncupative, Obedient, On, Please, Prone, Purpose, Raring, Rather, Ready, Receptive, Scarlet, Soon, Spirit, Swan, Testament, Testate, Thelma, Volens, Volition, Voluntary, Volunteer, Way, Wimble, Woot

▷ **Will** *may indicate* an anagram

William(s) Bill(y), Conqueror, Occam, Orange, Pear, Rufus, Silent, Sweet, Tell, Tennessee

Will o' the wisp Fatuous fire, Fen-fire, Friar's lantern, Ignis-fatuus, Jack o'lantern, Min min, Nightfire, Rush, Spunkie

Willow(ing), Willowy Arctic, Crack, Diamond, Lissom(e), Lithe, Osier, Poplar, Port Jackson, Pussy, Salix, Sallow, Sauch, Saugh, Supple, Twilly, Weeping, Withy

Willpower Ab(o)uha, Determination, Resolve, Strength

Willy-nilly Nolens volens, Perforce

Wilt Decline, Droop, Fade, Flag, Sap, Shalt, Wither

Wiltshireman Moonraker

▶ **Wily** *see* **WILE**

Wimp(ish) Drip, Mouse, Namby-pamby, Pantywaist, Saddo, Weed

Wimple Gorget, Meander, Ripple, Turn

▷ **Wimple** *may indicate* an anagram

Win(ner), Winning Achieve, Acquire, Ahead, Appealing, Backgammon, Bangster, Banker, → **BEAT**, Capot, Carry off, Cert, Champion, Conciliate, Conquer, Cup, Cute, Decider, Disarming, Dormie, Dormy, Earn, Effect, Endearing, Engaging, First, Gain, Gammon, Hit, Jackpot, Land, Laureate, Lead, Medallist, Motser, Motza, Nap hand, Nice, Pile, Pot, Prevail, Profit, Purler, Repique, Result, Rubicon, Scoop, Shoo-in, Slam, Snip, Success, Sweet, Take, Top dog, → **TRIUMPH**, Up, Vellet, Velvet, Victor(y), Vole, Walk over, Wrest, Yokozuna

Wince Blench, Cringe, Flinch, Recoil

Winch Crab, Crane, Jack, Windlass

Winchester® Rifle, Wykehamist

Wind(er), Winding(s), Windy Aeolian, Air, Airstream, Ambages, Anabatic, Anfractuous, Anti-trade, Aquilo(n), Argestes, Auster, Backing, Baguio, Bend, Berg, Bise, Blore, Blow, Bluster, Bora, Boreas, Bottom, Bourasque, Brass, Breeze, Brickfielder, Buran, Burp, Buster, Cape doctor, Capstan, Carminative, Caurus, Chili, Chill, Chinook, Coil, Colic, Cordonazo, Corus, Crank, Creeky, Curl, Curve, Cyclone, Downwash, Draught, Draw, Dust devil, Easterly, Etesian, Euraquilo, Euroclydon, Eurus, Evagation, Favonian, Favonius, Fearful, Firn, Flatulence, Flatus, Flaw, Fo(e)hn, Gale, Gas, G(h)ibli, Greco, Gregale, Gust, Haboob, Harmattan, Heaves, Hurricane, Hurricano, Jet stream, Kamseen, K(h)amsin, Katabatic, Knee-swell, Levant(er), Libecc(h)io, Libs, Link, Maestro, Meander, Meltemi, Mistral, Monsoon, Muzzler, Nervous, Noreast, Norther, Nor(th)wester(ly), Noser, Notus, Ostro, Pampero, Periodic, Ponent, Poop, Prevailing, Puna, Purl, Quarter, Quill, Reeds, Reel, Rip-snorter, Roll, Samiel, Sciroc, Scirocco, Screw, Sea, Second, Series, Serpentine, Serpentize, Shamal, Shimaal, Simoom, Simoon, Sinuous, Sirocco, Slant, Snake, Snifter, Snorter, Solano, Solar, Sough, Souther, Southerly buster, Spiral, Spool, Squall, Stellar, Sumatra, Surface, Swirl, Tail, Taranaki, Tehuantepecer, Thread, Throw, Tornado, Tortuous, Tourbillon, Trade, Tramontana, Trend, Turn, Twaddle, Twine, Twister, Twisty, Typhon, Typhoon, Vayu, Veer, Veering, Ventose, Volturnus, Waffle, Weave, Wester, Westerly, Whirlblast, White squall, Williwaw, Willy-willy, Winch, Windle, Winnle, Woold, Wrap, Wreathe, Wrest, Wuthering, Zephyr(us), Zonda

Windbag Balloon, Bore, Drogue, Prattler, Whoopee cushion, Zeppelin

Windfall Bonanza, Buckshee, Caduac, Fortune, Godsend, Manna

Windflower Anemone

Windlass Differential, Spanish, Whim, Winch

Windmill Pinwheel, Post, Smock, Whirligig

Window(s) Atmosphere, Bay, Bow, Casement, Catherine-wheel, Companion, Compass, Day, Deadlight, Dormer, Dream-hole, Eye, Eyelids, Fanlight, Fenestella, Fenestra, French, Gable, Garret, Glaze, Guichet, Jalousie, Jesse, Judas, Jut, Lancet, Lattice, Launch, Loop-light, Louver, Louvre, Lozen, Lucarne, Lunette, Luthern, Lychnoscope, Marigold, Mezzanine, Mirador, Monial, Mullion, Oculus, Oeil-de-boeuf, Ogive, Opportunity, Orb, Oriel, Ox-eye, Pane, Pede, Picture, Pop-under, Pop-up, Porthole, Quarterlight, Radio, Re-entry, Rosace, Rose, Round, Sash, Sexfoil, Shop, Shot, Spyhole, Storm, Transom, Trellis, Ventana, Weather, Wheel, Wicket, Windock, Winnock

Window-bar, Window-fastening Astragal, Espagnolette

Windpipe Bronchus, Gular, Throat, Trachea, Weasand

Windscale Beaufort
Windsock Drogue, Sleeve
Windsor Castle, Knot
Windswept Scud
Wind-up End, Fright, Liquidate, Miff, Span
Windward Ahold, Aloof, Laveer, Luff, Up
Wine Bin, Blanc, Blush, Cabinet, Case, Château, Château cardboard, Cup, Cuvée, Doc, En primeur, Espumoso, Essence, Fortified, Grand cru, Low, Must, Oenology, Ordinaire, Piece, Pigment, Plonk, Premier cru, Prisage, Red, Rosé, Rosy, Rotgut, Rouge, Sparkling, Steen, Table, Tafelwein, Tannin, Terroir, The grape, Tirage, Varietal, Vat, Vin, Vin Ordinaire, Vintage, White, Zymurgy

WINES

2 letters:
It

3 letters:
Dao
Sec
Tun

4 letters:
Asti
Brut
Cava
Hock
Mull
Palm
Pipe
Port
Race
Sack
Sekt
Stum
Tent
Tutu
Vino

5 letters:
Anjou
Anker
Biddy
Bombo
Comet
Gallo
Gamay
Macon
Médoc
Mirin
Mosel

Negus
Pinot
Rhine
Rioja
Soave
Straw
Syrah
Tavel
Toddy
Tokay
Xeres

6 letters:
Alsace
Barley
Barolo
Barsac
Beaune
Bishop
Bubbly
Canary
Claret
Ginger
Graves
Lisbon
Malaga
Merlot
Muscat
Piment
Plotty
Red Ned
Sherry
Shiraz
Solera

7 letters:
Alicant

Amoroso
Auslese
Bastard
Catawba
Chablis
Chianti
Cowslip
Currant
Demi-sec
Dessert
Eiswein
Fendant
Icewine
Madeira
Malmsey
Margaux
Marsala
Moselle
Oenomel
Orvieto
Pomerol
Pommard
Retsina
Rhenish
Sangria
Sherris
Vouvray

8 letters:
Bordeaux
Bucellas
Buckfast®
Burgundy
Cabernet
Champers
Charneco
Dubonnet®

Essencia
Frascati
Gluhwein
Jerepigo
Kabinett
Log-juice
Malvasia
Malvesie
Montilla
Mountain
Muscadel
Muscadet
Muscatel
Nebbiolo
Pinotage
Pradikat
Red biddy
Resinata
Rheingau
Riesling
Sancerre
Sangaree
Sauterne
Sémillon
Spätlese
Spumante
St Julien
Sylvaner
Verdelho
Vermouth

9 letters:
Bacharach
Bardolino
Carmenère
Champagne
Falernian

Gladstone	Bull's blood	Petite Sirah	Johannisberger
Hermitage	Chambertin	Pouilly-Fumé	
Hippocras	Chardonnay	Rudesheimer	*15 letters:*
Hoccamore	Constantia	Scuppernong	Lachryma Christi
Inglenook	Elderberry	Steinberger	Liebfrauenmilch
Lambrusco	Genevrette		
Languedoc	Hochheimer	*12 letters:*	*16 letters:*
Loll-shrob	Loll-shraub	Johannisberg	London particular
Malvoisie	Manzanilla	Marcobrunner	
Meersault	Montrachet	Supernaculum	*17 letters:*
Minervois	Muscadelle	Valpolicella	Cabernet Sauvignon
Muscadine	Napa Valley		Nuits Saint Georges
Pinot noir	Peter-see-me	*13 letters:*	
Sauvignon	Piesporter	Beerenauslese	*20 letters:*
Sauvignon	Sangiovese	Entre-Deux-Mers	Trockenbeeren-
St Emilion	Vinho verde	Liebfraumilch	auslese
Tarragona		Montepulciano	
Zinfandel	*11 letters:*	Pouilly-Fuissé	
	Amontillado		
10 letters:	Dom Perignon	*14 letters:*	
Beaujolais	Niersteiner	Gewürztraminer	

Wine-cellar, Wine-shop Bistro, Bodega, Vault, Vaut(e)
Wine-glass Flute
Wine-making Gallising, Remuage
Wing(s), Winged, Winger, Wing-like Aerofoil, Ala(r), Alula, Annexe, Appendage, Arm, Bastard, → **BIRD**, Branch, Buffalo, Canard, Cellar, Corium, Coulisse, Delta, Dipteral, El(l), Elevon, Elytral, Elytriform, Elytron, Elytrum, Fender, Flap, Flew, Flex, Flipper, Flying, Forward, Gull, Halteres, Hurt, Left, Limb, Offstage, Parascenia, Parascenium, Patagium, Pennate, Pennon, Pinero, Pinion, Pip, Pterygoid, Putto, Right, Rogallo, Sail, Samariform, Scent-scale, Segreant, Seraphim, Split, Standard, Sweepback, Sweptback, Sweptwing, Swift, Swingwing, Tailplane, Tectrix, Tegmen, Tormentor, Transept, Van, Vol(et), Water, Wound(ed)
Winged sandals Talaria
▷ **Winger** *may indicate* a bird
Wing-footed Aliped, Fleet, Swift
Wingless Apteral
Wink (at) Atone, Bat, Condone, Connive, Eyelid, Flicker, Ignore, Instant, Nap, Nictitate, Pink, Twinkle
Winnie Pooh
Winnow Fan, Riddle, Separate, Sift, Van, Wecht
Winsome Bonny, Engaging, Gay, Pleasant
Winter, Wintry Blackthorn, Bleak, Brumal, Cold, Dec, Fimbul, Frigid, Frore, Hibernate, Hiemal, Hiems, Hodiernal, Jack Frost, Jasmine, Nuclear, Shrovetide, Snowy, W
Winter cherry Chinese lantern
Wintergreen Chickweed, Pyrola, Sarcodes
Winter pear Nelis
Winter-sport Ski
Wipe (out), Wiping Abolish, Abrogate, Absterge, Amortise, Cancel, Cleanse, Demolish, Destroy, Deterge, Dicht, Dight, Efface, Eradicate, Erase, Expunge,

Forget, Hanky, Mop, Nose-rag, Null, Purge, Raze, Retroussage, Slorm, Sponge, Tersion, Tissue

Wire(s), Wiry Aerial, Barb(ed), Cable, Cat's whiskers, Chicken, Coil, Earth, Element, Fencing, Filament, Filar, File, Heald, Heddle, High, Kirschner, Lean, Lecher, Live, Marconigram, Messenger, Mil, Nichrome®, Nipper, Number eight, Piano, Pickpocket, Razor, Sevice, Shroud, Sinewy, Snake, Solenoid, Spit, Staple, Stilet, Strand, String, Stylet, Telegram, Telegraph, Thoth, Thread, Trace, Trip

Wireless (operator), Wireless part Baffle, Set, Sparks, Valve

Wise(acre), Wisdom Advisedly, Ancient, Astute, Athena, Athene, Canny, Depth, Ernie, Ganesa, Gothamite, Gudrun, Hep, Hindsight, Judgement, Judicious, Learned, Long-headed, Lore, Manner, Mimir, Minerva, Norman, Oracle, Owl, Penny, Philosopher, Philosophy, Politic, Polymath, Prajna, Profound, Prudence, Sagacity, Sage, Salomonic, Sapience, Savvy, Shrewd, Smartie, Solomon, Solon, Sophia, Tooth, Wice

Wisecrack Dig, One-liner, Quip

Wise man Balthazar, Caspar, Gaspar, Heptad, Melchior, Nestor, Sage, Sapient, Seer, Solomon, Swami, Thales, Tohunga, Worldly

Wish(es), Wishing Ache, Ake, Covet, Crave, Death, Desiderate, → **DESIRE**, For, Hope, Itch, List, Long, Pant, Pleasure, Pray, Precatory, Regards, RIP, Velleity, Want, Yearn

Wishbone Furcula, Marriage-bone, Merrythought, Skipjack

Wishy-washy Bland, Feeble, Insipid, Irresolute, Milksop, Weak, Wheyey

Wisp(y) Cirrate, Frail, Scrap, Shred, Virga, Wase

Wit(s), Witticism, Witty Acumen, Attic, Badinage, Banter, Brevity, Commonsense, Concetto, Cunning, Dry, Epigram, Esprit, Estimation, Eutrapelia, Eutrapely, Facetious, Fantasy, Gnome, Hartford, Humour, Imagination, Intelligence, Irony, Jest, Jeu d'esprit, Joke, Marbles, Marinism, Memory, Mind, Mot, Mother, Native, Nous, Pawky, Pun, Quipster, Repartee, Rogue, Sally, Salt, Saut, Sconce, → **SENSE**, Shaft, Smart, Videlicet, Viz, Wag, Weet, Wisecrack, Word-play

Witch(craft) Besom-rider, Broomstick, Cantrip, Carline, Circe, Coven, Craigfluke, Crone, Cutty Sark, Diabolism, Enchantress, Ensorcell, Galdragon, Glamour, Goety, Gramary(e), Gyre-carlin, Hag, Hecat(e), Hex, Invultuation, Lamia, Magic, Medea, Myal(ism), Necromancy, Night-hag, Obeahism, Obia, Obiism, Pishogue, Pythoness, Salem, Selim, Sibyl, Sieve, Sorceress, Speller, Sycorax, Trout, Valkyrie, Vaudoo, Vilia, Voodoo, Water, Weird, Wicca, Wise woman

Witch-doctor Animist, Boyla, Medicine man, Mganga, Obi, Pawaw, Powwow, Sangoma, Shaman

Witch-hazel Fothergilla, Platan(e), Winter-bloom

Witch-hunter McCarthy

With And, By, Con, Cum, Hereby, In, Mit, Of, Plus, W

Withdraw(al), Withdrawn Abdicate, Alienate, Aloof, Back out, Breakaway, Cold turkey, Cry off, Detach, Disengage, Distrait, Enshell, Evacuate, Hive off, Inshell, Introvert, Leave, Offish, Palinode, Phantom, Precede, Preserve, Recant, Recoil, Repair, Resile, Reticent, Retire, Retract(ion), Retreat, Revoke, Revulsion, Scratch, Secede, Secesh, Sequester, Shrink, Shy, Stand down, Subduce, Subduct, Unreeve, Unsay

Wither(ed), Withering, Withers Arefy, Atrophy, Blight, Burn, Corky, Die, Droop, Dry, Evanish, Fade, Forpine, Gizzen, Googie, Languish, Marcescent, Miff, Nose, Scram, Sere, Shrink, Shrivel, Welk, Welt

Withershins Eastlin(g)s

▷ **With gaucherie** *may indicate* an anagram

Withhold(ing), Withheld Abstain, Conceal, Curt, Deny, Detain, Detinue, Hide, Keep, → RESERVE, Ritenuto, Trover

Within Enclosed, Endo-, Immanent, Indoors, Inside, Interior, Intra

With it Hep, Hip, Syn, Trendy, W

Without Bar, Beyond, Ex, Lack(ing), Less, Minus, Orb, Outdoors, Outside, Sans, Save, Sen, Senza, Sine, X

▷ **Without** *may indicate* one word surrounding another

▷ **Without restraint** *may indicate* an anagram

Without stimulus Nastic

Withstand Blight, Brave, Contest, Defy, Endure, Oppose, Resist, Weather

Witless Crass, → STUPID PERSON

Witness Attend, Attest, Bystander, Catch, Character, Compurgator, Confirm, Crown, Deponent, Depose, Endorse, Evidence, Experience, Expert, Eye, Glimpse, Hostile, Jehovah's, Mark, Martyr, Material, Muggletonian, Note, Notice, Observe, Obtest, Onlooker, Perceive, Proof, → SEE, Show, Sight, Sign, Spy, Stander-by, Survey, Testament, Teste, Testify, Testimony, View, Vouchee, Watch

Witness-box Peter, Stand

▶ **Witticism** *see* WIT

Wizard (priest) Archimage, Carpathian, Conjuror, Demon, Expert, Gandalf, Hex, Magician, Merlin, Obiman, Oz, Prospero, Shaman, Sorcerer, Super, Warlock, → WITCH-DOCTOR

Wizen(ed) Dehydrate, Dry, Sere, Shrivel, Sphacelate, Wither

Woad Anil, Dye, Indigo, Isatis, Pastel, Pastil

Wobble, Wobbling, Wobbly Chandler's, Coggle, Precess, Quaver, Reel, Rock, Shimmy, Shoggle, Shoogle, Teeter, Totter, Tremble, Trillo, Unstable, Wag, Waggle, Walty, Waver, Wibble

Wodehouse Plum

Woe(ful) Alack, Alas, Bale, Bane, Distress, Doole, Dule, Ewhow, Execrable, Gram, Grief, Hurt, Jeremiad, Lack-a-day, Misery, Pain, Plague, → SORROW, Torment, Tribulation, Unhappy

Wolds Lincoln(shire), Yorkshire

Wolf(ish), Wolf-like Akela, Assyrian, Bolt, Cancer, Carcajou, Casanova, Coyote, Cram, Dangler, Dire, Earth, Engorge, Fenrir, Fenris, Gorge, Grey, Ise(n)grim, Lobo, Lone, Lothario, Lupine, Luster, Lycanthrope, MI, Michigan, Pack, Prairie, Rake, Ravenous, Red, Rip, Roué, Rout, Rudolph, Rye, Scoff, Sea, Seducer, Strand, Tasmanian, Thylacine, Tiger, Timber, Wanderer, Were, Whistler

Wolfram Tungsten

Wolf's bane Aconite, Friar's-cap

Wolseley Sir Garnet

Woman(hood), Women Anile, Bellibone, Besom, Biddy, Bimbo, Bint, Bit, Boiler, Broad, Cailleach, Callet, Chai, Chapess, Chook, Citess, Cotquean, Crone, Crumpet, Cummer, Dame, Daughter, Distaff, Doe, Dona(h), Dorcas, Doris, Drab, Duenna, Eve, F, Fair, Fair sex, → FEMALE, Feme, Femme fatale, Flapper, Floozy, Frail, Frow, Gammer, Gimmer, Gin, Girl, Gyno-, -gyny, Harpy, Harridan, Hen, Her, Ho, Inner, It, Jade, Jane, Kloo(t)chman, Lady, Liberated, Lilith, Lorette, Madam(e), Mademoiselle, Maenad, Mary, Miladi, Milady, Millie, Minge, Mob, Mort, Ms, Muliebrity, Painted, Pandora, Peat, Pict, Piece, Piece of goods, Placket, Popsy, Puna(a)ni, Puna(a)ny, Quean, Queen, Ramp, Rib, Ribibe, Ronyon, Rudas, Runnion, Sabine, Sakti, Scarlet, Shakti, Shawlay, Shawlie, She, Skirt, Sloane Ranger, Sort, Squaw, Tail, Tedesca, Tib, Tiring, Tit, Tottie, Totty, Trot, Umfazi, Vahine, Wahine, Weaker sex, Wifie, Zena

Womaniser Casanova, Lady-killer, Poodle-faker, Wolf

Womb Belly, Matrix, Metritis, Side, Uterus, Ventricle
Women's club, Women's lib S(h)akti, Soroptimist
Won Chon, W
Wonder(s) Admire, Agape, Amazement, AR, Arkansas, Arrah, Awe, Chinless, Colossus, Ferly, Grape-seed, Marle, → **MARVEL**, Meteor, Mirabilia, Miracle, Muse, Nine-day, Phenomenon, Prodigy, Seven, Speculate, Stupor, Suppose, Surprise, Thaumatrope, Wheugh, Whew, Wow
Wonderful(ly) Amazing, Bees' knees, Bitchin(g), Chinless, Divine, Épatant, Fantastic, Far-out, Ferly, Geason, Gee-whiz, Glorious, Gramercy, Great, Heavenly, Keen, Lal(l)apalooza, Magic, Mirable, Old, Purely, Ripping, Smashing, Sublime, Superb
Wonder-worker Fakir, Thaumaturgist, Thaumaturgus
Wonky Cockeyed
Wont(ed) Accustomed, Apt, Custom, Habit, Shan't, Used, Winna
Woo(er) Address, Beau, Carve, Court, Seduce, Suitor, Swain
▷ **Wood** *may indicate* an anagram in sense of mad
Wood(s), Wooden, Woodland, Woody Arboretum, Batten, Beam, Board, Boord(e), Brake, Cask, Channel, Chipboard, Chuck, Chump, Clapboard, Conductor, Dead, Deadpan, Expressionless, Fardage, Fathom, Fire, Fish, Funk, Furious, Gantry, Gauntree, Guthrie, Hanger, Hard, Hyle, Kindling, Knee, Krummholz, Late, Lath, Lumber, Mad, Magnetic, Miombo, Nemoral, Nemorous, Offcut, Pallet, Plastic, Pulp, Pulpwood, Punk, Silvan, Slat, Spinney, Splat, Spline, Splint, Stolid, Sylvan, Tenon, Three-ply, Timber, Tinder, Touch, Treen, Trees, Twiggy, Vert, Xylem, Xyloid

WOODS

3 letters:	Pine	Green	Tulip
Ash	Rata	Grove	Zante
Box	Rock	Heben	Zebra
Cam	Shaw	Hurst	
Elm	Soft	Igapó	**6 letters:**
Log	Spar	Iroko	Alerce
Red	Wild	Jarul	Bamboo
	Yang	Joist	Beaver
4 letters:		Kokra	Birnam
Beef	**5 letters:**	Lance	Bocage
Bent	Afara	Maple	Brazil
Bowl	Agila	Mazer	Calico
Carr	Algum	Myall	Canary
Cord	Almug	Opepe	Carapa
Cork	Balsa	Peach	Cheese
Deal	Bavin	Plane	Citron
Eugh	Beech	Ramin	Citrus
Gapó	Cedar	Rowan	Dingle
Holt	Copse	Sapan	Forest
Iron	Drive	Spoon	Fustet
King	Ebony	Stink	Fustic
Lana	Elfin	Taiga	Fustoc
Lima	Firth	Thorn	Gaboon
Lime	Frith	Tiger	Gopher

Herman
Jarool
Jarrah
Letter
Lignum
Loggat
Manuka
Obeche
Orache
Orange
Paddle
Poplar
Raddle
Sabele
Sabicu
Sandal
Sapele
Sappan
Sissoo
Sponge
Tallow
Violet
Waboom
Walnut
Wandoo
Yellow

7 letters:
Amboina
Barwood
Boscage

Brassie
Cambium
Cerrado®
Coppice
Dudgeon
Dunnage
Duramen
Gambrel
Gumwood
Hadrome
Hickory
Leopard
Meranti
Nutwood
Palmyra
Paranym
Pimento
Sanders
Sapwood
Shawnee
Shittim
Trumpet
Wallaba

8 letters:
Agalloch
Alburnum
Basswood
Bushveld
Caatinga
Coulisse

Harewood
Hornbeam
Kingwood
Laburnum
Ligneous
Mahogany
Masonite®
Mountain
Ovenwood
Pyengadu
Pyinkado
Rosewood
Sapucaia
Shagbark
Southern
Tamarack

9 letters:
Briarwood
Butternut
Caliature
Campeachy
Coachwood
Cocuswood
Driftwood
Eaglewood
Fruitwood
Heartwood
Ivorywood
Matchwood
Partridge

Porcupine
Quebracho
Satinwood
Snakewood
Torchwood

10 letters:
Afrormosia
Blockboard
Bulletwood
Calamander
Candlewood
Cheesewood
Chittagong
Coromandel
Fiddlewood
Greenheart
Hackmatack
Nettle-tree
Palisander
Sneezewood
Springwood
Summerwood

11 letters:
Lignum-vitae
Sanderswood
Slippery elm

Wood-carver Bodger, Gibbons, Whittler

Woodchuck Bobac, Marmot

Woodcock Becasse, Beccaccia, Snipe

Woodlouse Isopod, Oniscus, Slater

Woodman Ali (Baba), Coureur de bois, Feller, Forester, Hewer, Logger, Lumberjack, Sawyer

Woodpecker Bird, Flicker, Hickwall, Picarian, Rainbird, Sapsucker, Saurognathae, Witwall, Woodspite, Woodwale, Yaffle

Wood-pigeon Bird, Cushat, Que(e)st, Qu(o)ist, Torquate

Wood-sorrel Oca

Wood-tar Furan, Furfuran

Woodwind Bassoon, Clarinet, Cornet, Flute, Oboe, Piccolo, Pipe, Recorder, Reed

Woodwork(er) Ebonist, Forestry, Intarsia, Marquetrie, Marquetry, Sloid, Sloyd, Tarsia, Termite

Woodworm Gribble, Termes

Wookey Stalactite

Wool(len), Woolly (haired) Alpaca, Angora, Aran, Ardil, Bainin, Barège, Beige, Berlin, Botany, Bouclé, Calamanco, Cardi(gan), Cashmere, Cas(s)imere, Clean, Clip, Combings, Cotton, Crutchings, Daglock, Delaine, Doeskin, Dog, Doily,

Down, Doyley, Drugget, Duffel, Fadge, Fingering, Fleece, Flock, Frib, Frieze, Fuzz, Glass, Greasy, Guernsey, Hank, Hause-lock, Hogget, Indumentum, Jaeger, Jersey, Kashmir, Ket, Lanate, Laniferous, Lanigerous, Lanose, Lock, Loden, Merino, Mineral, Mortling, Moul, Mullein, New, Noil(s), Nun's-veiling, Offsorts, Oo, Pashm, Pelage, Persian, Pine, Qiviut, Rock, Rolag, Sagathy, Saxon, Say, Shahtoosh, Shalloon, Shamina, Shetland, Shoddy, Skein, Skin, Slag, Slipe, Slip-on, Slub, Smart, Spencer, Staple, Steel, Strouding, Stuff, Swansdown, Tamise, Tammy, Telltale, Thibet, Three-ply, Tod, Tricot, Tweed, Twin set, Ultrichous, Vicuña, Virgin, Wire, Wood, Worcester, Yarn, Zephyr, Zibel(l)ine

Wool-gather(er), Woolgathering Argo, Dreamer, Reverie

Wool-holder, Woolsack Bale, Distaff

Woolly-bear Tiger-moth, Woubit

Wool-oil Yolk

Wooster Bertie

Woozy Drunk, Faint, Vague, Woolly

Worcester Wigorn

Word(s), Wording, Wordy Al(l)-to, Appellative, Bahuvrihi, Buzz, Cataphor(a), Catch, Cheville, Claptrap, Clipped, Clitic, Code, Comment, Content, Dick, Dit(t), Echoic, Embolalia, Enclitic, Epos, Etymon, Faith, Four-letter, Function, Functor, Ghost, Grace, Hapax legomenon, Hard, Heteronym, Hint, Homograph, Homonym, Horseman's, Household, Hyponym, → **IN A WORD**, → **IN TWO WORDS**, Janus, Jonah, Key, Last, Lexeme, Lexicon, Lexis, Loan, Logia, Logos, Long-winded, Lyrics, Mantra, Meronym, Message, Morpheme, Mot, Neologism, News, Nonce, Nonsense, Noun, Om, Operative, Oracle, Order, Palabra, Paragram, Paranym, Parenthesis, Parlance, Parole, Paronym, Paroxytone, Particle, Perissology, Peristomenon, Phrase, Piano, Pledge, Pleonasm, Polysemen, Portmanteau, Preposition, Prolix, Promise, Pronoun, Reserved, Rhematic, Rhyme, Rumbelow, Rumour, Saying, Selah, Semantics, Signal, Subtitle, Surtitle, Syntagma, Tatpurusha, Term, Tetragram, Text, Trigger, Trope, Typewriter, Verb, Verbiage, Verbose, Vocab(ulary), Vogue, Warcry, Weasel, Winged, Wort, Written

Word-blindness Alexia, Dyslexia

Word-play Charade, Paronomasia, Pun

Workable Feasible, Practical

Workaholic, Work(er), Working(-class), Workmen, Works, Workman(ship) Act(ivate), Aga saga, Ant, Appliqué, Apronman, Artefact, Artel, Artifact, Artificer, Artisan, At it, At task, Barmaid, Beamer, Beaver, Bee, Blue-collar, Blue-singlet, Bohunk, Boondoggle, Boon(er), Bull, Business, Busy, Careerist, Casual, Char, Chare, Chargehand, Chigga, Chippy, Chore, Claim, Clock, Colon, Community, Coolie, Corvée, Craftsman, Crew, Darg, Do, Dog, Dogsbody, Draft-mule, Droil, Drudge, Drug, Dung, Earn, Effect, Effort, Em, Erg(ataner), Ergatoid, Erg-nine, Ergon, Ergonomics, Erg-ten, Eta, Everything, Evince, Exercise, Exergy, Exploit, Factotum, Facture, Fast, Fat, Fettler, Field, Flex(i)time, Floruit, Fret, Fuller, → **FUNCTION**, Gastarbeiter, Gel, Go, Graft, Grass, Grind, Grisette, Guest, Hand, Harness, Hat, Hobo, Horse, Hot-desking, Hunky, Industry, Innards, Job, Journeyman, Key, Knead, Knowledge, Kolhoznik, Labour, Laid, Luddite, Lump, Machinist, Maid, Man, Manipulate, Manpower, McJob, Mechanic, Meng, Menge, Menial, Midinette, Mine, Ming, MO, Moider, Moil, Moonlight, Movement, Navvy, Neuter, Number, Oeuvre, On, Op, Opera(tion), Operative, Operator, Opus, Opusc(u)le, Outreach, Outside, Ouvrier, Ox, Parergon, Part, Passage, Peasant, Peg, Pensum, Peon, Pink-collar, Plasterer, Ply, Poker, Portfolio, Potboiler, Practise, Production, Prole(tariat), Prud'homme, Public, Pursuit, Red-neck, Reduction,

Rep, Ride, Robot, Roughneck, Rouseabout, Roustabout, Run, Salaryman, Samiti, Sandhog, Satisfactory, Scabble, Scapple, Serve, Service, Servile, Seven, Sewage, Shift, Shop, Situation, Skanger, Slogger, Smithy, Social, Soldier, Spide, Staff, Stakhanovite, Stevedore, Stint, Strap, Straw, Strive, Support, Surface, Swaggie, Swagman, Sweat, Swink, Take, Tamper, Task, Team, Technician, Telecommuter, Temp, Tenail(le), Tenaillon, Termite, Tew, Tick, Till, Toccata, Toil, Toreutic, Travail, Treatise, Trojan, TU, TUC, Turk, Tut, Typto, Uphill, Wage plug, Walla(h), Wark, Welfare, White-collar, Wobblies, Yacker, Yakka, Yakker, Yarco

Work-basket, Workbox Caba(s), Nécessaire

Workbench Banker, Siege

Workhouse Casual ward, Spike, Union

▷ **Working** *may indicate* an anagram

Working-party Bee, Quilting-bee, Sewing-bee, Squad

Workmate Yokefellow

Work out Deduce

Works, Workplace, Workshop Atelier, Engine, Factory, Forge, Foundry, Garage, Hacienda, Hangar, Innards, Lab, Mill, Passage, Plant, Public, Shed, Shipyard, Shop, Skylab, Smithy, Studio, Study, Sweatshop, Telecottage, Time, Tin, Turnery, Upper

Workshy Indolent, Lazy, Sweer(ed), Sweert, Sweir(t)

World(ly), Worldwide Adland, Carnal, Chthonic, Cosmopolitan, Cosmos, Cyberspace, Dream, Earth, First, Fleshly, Fourth, Free, Ge, Globe, Kingdom, Lay, Lower, Mappemond, Meatspace, Microcosm, Mondaine, Mondial, Mould, Mundane, Nether, New, Old, Orb, Other, Oyster, Planet, Possible, Second, Secular, Sensual, Small, Society, Sphere, Spirit, Temporal, Terra, Terrene, Terrestrial, Third, Universe, Vale, Web, Welt, Whole

Worm(-like), Worms, Wormy Acorn, Anguillula, Annelid, Annulata, Apod(e), Apodous, Army, Arrow, Articulata, Ascarid, Bilharzia, Bladder, Blind, Blood, Bob, Bootlace, Brandling, Bristle, Caddis, Capeworm, Caseworm, Catworm, Cercaria, Cestode, Cestoid, Chaetopod, Clamworm, Copper, Dew, Diet, Diplozoon, Dracunculus, Edge, Enteropneust, Fan, Filander, Filaria, Flag, Flat, Flesh, Fluke, Galley, Gape, Gilt-tail, Gordius, Gourd, Gru-gru, Guinea, Hair, Hair-eel, Hairworm, Heartworm, Helminth, Hemichordata, Hookworm, Horsehair, Idle, Inchworm, Leech, Liver-fluke, Lob, Lumbricus, Lytta, Maw, Measuring, Merosome, Miner's, Mopani, Muck, Nemathelminthes, Nematoda, Nematode, Nematodirus, Nematomorpha, Nemertea, Nemertina, Nereid, Night-crawler, Oligochaete, Onychophoran, Paddle, Palmer, Palolo, Paste-eel, Peripatus, Pile, Pin, Piper, Planarian, Platyhelminth, Polychaete, Ragworm, Redia, Ribbon, Roundworm, Sabella, Sand-mason, Schistosome, Scoleciform, Scolex, Screw, Seamouse, Serpula, Servile, Ship, Sipunculacea, Sipunculoidea, Stomach, Strawworm, Strongyl(e), Taenia, Tag-tail, Taint, Tapeworm, Tenioid, Teredo, Termite, Threadworm, Tiger, Tiger tail, Tongue, Toxocara, Trematode, Trichin(ell)a, Trichinosed, Triclad, Tube, Tubifex, Turbellaria, Vermiform, Vinegar, Vinegar eel, Wheat-eel, Wheatworm, Whipworm

Wormkiller Anthelmintic, Santonin

Wormwood Absinth, Appleringie, Artemisia, Moxa, Mugwort, Santonica, Southernwood

Worn (out) Attrite, Bare, Decrepit, Detrition, Effete, Épuisé, Exhausted, Forfairn, Forfoughten, Forjaskit, Forjeskit, Frazzled, Knackered, Old, On, Passé, Raddled, Rag, Seedy, Shabby, Shopsoiled, Shot, Spent, Stale, Threadbare, Tired, Traikit, Trite, Used, Weathered, Whacked

Worried, Worrier, Worry Agonise, Angst, Annoy, Anxiety, Badger, Bait, Beset,

Bother, Brood, Burden, Care(worn), Cark, Chafe, Concern, Deave, Deeve, Distress, Disturb, Dog, Eat, Exercise, Faze, Feeze, Frab, Fret, Fuss, Gnaw, Harass, Harry, Headache, Hyp, Inquietude, Knag, Nag, Perturb, Pester, Pheese, Pheeze, Phese, Pingle, Pium, Preoccupy, Rile, Sool, Stew, Tew, Touse, Towse, Trouble, Unease, Unnerve, Vex, Wherrit, Worn

▷ **Worried** *may indicate* an anagram

Worse(n) Adversely, Degenerate, Deteriorate, Exacerbate, Impair, Inflame, Pejorate, Regress, Relapse, War(re), Waur, Well away

Worship(per) Adore, Adulation, Ancestor, Angelolatry, Aniconism, Autolatry, Bless, Churchgoer, Cosmolatry, Cult, Deify, Devotion, Dote, Douleia, Dulia, Epeolatry, Exercise, Fetish, Glorify, Gurdwara, Happy-clappy, Henotheism, Hero, Ibadah, Idolatry, Idolise, Latria, Lauds, Lionise, Liturgics, Lordolatry, Mariolatry, Meeting-house, Monolatry, Oncer, Orant, Praise, Puja, Revere, Sabaism, Sakta, Service, Shacharis, Shakta, Sun, Synaxis, Thiasus, Vaishnava, Venerate, Votary, Wodenism

Worst Beat, Best, Defeat, Get, Less, Nadir, Outdo, Overpower, Pessimum, Rock-bottom, Scum, Severest, The pits, Throw, Trounce

Worsted Caddis, Caddyss, Challis, Coburg, Genappe, Lea, Ley, Serge, Shalli, Tamin(e), Whipcord

▷ **Worsted** *may indicate* an anagram

Wort Hopped, Laser, Parkleaves, Plant, Sweet, Tutsan

Worth(while), Worthy, Worthies Admirable, Asset, Be, Cop, Cost, Cost effective, Deserving, Eligible, Estimable, Face value, Feck, → **MERIT**, Nine, Notable, Substance, Tanti, Use, Value, Venerable, Vertu, Virtuous, Wealth

Worthless (person) Average, Base, Beggarly, Bilge, Blown, Bodger, Bootless, Bum, Catchpenny, Cheapjack, Crumb, Cypher, Damn, Despicable, Docken, Dodkin, Doit, Doitkin, Draffish, Draffy, Dreck, Dross, Duff, Fallal, Footra, Fouter, Foutre, Frippery, Gimcrack, Gingerbread, Glop, Gubbins, Hilding, Javel, Jimcrack, Knick-knack, Left, Light, Lorel, Lorrell, Losel, Lozell, Manky, Mare's nest, Mauvais sujet, Mud, Nugatory, Nyaff, Obol, Orra, Otiose, Paltry, Pin, Poxy, Punk, Raca, Rag, Rap, Razoo, Riffraff, Rubbishy, Scabby, Scrote, Scum, Shinkin, Shotten, Siwash, Sorry, Straw, Tinhorn, Tinpot, Tinsel, Tittle, Toerag, Trangam, Trashy, Trumpery, Tuppenny, Twat, Two-bit, Twopenny, Useless, Vain, Vile, Waff, Wanworthy, Wauff, Zero

Wotchermean Anan

Would be Assumed, Pseudo, Soi-disant

Wouldn't Nould(e)

Wound(ed) Battery, Bite, Bless, Blighty, Bruise, Chagrin, Coiled, Crepance, Cut, Dere, Dunt, Engore, Entry, Exit, Flesh, Ganch, Gash, Gaunch, Gore, Harm, Hurt, Injury, Lacerate, Lesion, Maim, Maul, Molest, Mortify, Offend, Pip, Sabre-cut, Scab, Scar, Scath, Scotch, Scratch, Shoot, Snaked, Snub, Sore, Stab, Sting, Trauma, Twined, Umbrage, Vuln, Vulnerary, Walking, Wing, Wint

Woundwort Clown's, Marsh

Woven Faconne, Inwrought, Knitted, Pirnit, Textile, Wattle

Wow Amaze, Howl, Impress, My, Success

Wrack Destroy, Downfall, Kelp, Ore, Torment, Varec(h), Vengeance

Wraith Apparition, Fetch, Ghost, Phantom, Shadow, Spectre

Wrangle(r), Wrangling Altercate, Argie-bargie, → **ARGUE**, Bandy, Bicker, Brangle, Broil, Cample, Controvert, Dispute, Haggle, Horse, Mathematical, Rag, Second, Senior, Vitilitigation

Wrap(per), Wrapped, Wrapping, Wraparound, Wrap up Amice, Amis, Bag, Bathrobe, Bind, Body, Bubble, Bundle, Cellophane®, Cere, Clingfilm, Cloak, Clothe,

Cocoon, Conclude, Drape, Emboss, Enfold, Enrol(l), Ensheath(e), Envelop(e),
Enwind, Foil, Folio, Furl, Gladwrap®, Hap, Hem, Infold, Kimono, Kraft, Lag, Lap,
Mail, Mob, Muffle, Negligee, Nori, Outsert, Package, Parcel, Plastic, Roll, Rug,
Shawl, Sheath(e), Sheet, Shrink, Shroud, Stole, Swaddle, Swathe, Throw, Tinfoil,
Tsutsumu, Velamen, Wap, Wimple

Wrasse Conner, Cunner, Parrot-fish, Scar

Wrath Anger, Cape, Fury, Ire, Passion, Vengeance

Wreak Avenge, Indulge, Inflict

Wreath(e) Adorn, Anadem, Bridal, Chaplet, Civic crown, Coronal, Crown, Entwine,
Festoon, Garland, Laurel, Lei, Steven, Torse, Tortile, Twist

Wreathe(d) Hederated

Wreck(age), Wrecked, Wrecker Ban-jax, Blotto, Crab, Debris, Demolish,
Devastate, Flotsam, Founder, Goner, Hesperus, Hulk, Lagan, Ligan, Loss, Luddite,
Mutilate, Nervous, Ruin(ate), Sabotage, Shambles, Shatter, Sink, Smash, Subvert,
Torpedo, Trash, Vandalise, Wrack

▷ **Wrecked** *may indicate* an anagram

Wren Architect, Bird, Fairy, Fire-crested, Golden-crested, Hannah, Heath, Jenny,
Kinglet, Rifleman-bird, Sailor, Superb blue, Willow

Wrench Allen, Bobbejaan, Box, Fit, Jerk, Lug, Mole, Monkey, Nut, Pin, Pipe, Pull,
Screw, Socket, Spanner, Spider, Sprain, Stillson®, Strain, Strap, T-bar, Tear,
Torque, Twist, Windlass, Wrest

Wrestle(r), Wrestling All-in, Antaeus, Arm, Backbreaker, Basho, Bearhug,
Bodycheck, Boston crab, Catch-as-catch-can, Catchweight, Clinch, Clothes line,
Cross press, Featherweight, Flying mare, Folding-press, Freestyle, Full-nelson,
Gr(a)eco-Roman, Grapple, Grovet, Half-nelson, Hammerlock, Haystacks,
Headlock, Hip-lock, → **HOLD**, Indian, Judo, Knee-drop, Makunouchi, Milo, Monkey
climb, Mud, Nelson, Niramiai, Ozeki, Palaestral, Pancratium, Pinfall, Posting,
Rikishi, Sambo, Stable, Straight arm lift, Stranglehold, Struggle, Sumo, Sumotori,
Suplex, Tag (team), Tussle, Whip, Wraxle, Wristlock, Writhe, Yokozuna

Wretch(ed) Abject, Bally, Blackguard, Blue, Caitiff, Chap-fallen, Crumb, Cullion,
Darned, Donder, Forlorn, Git, Hapless, Lorn, Low, Measly, Miser, Miserable,
Peelgarlic, Pilgarlick, Pipsqueak, Pitiable, Poltroon, Poor, Punk, Rakeshame,
Rascal, Rat, Scoundrel, Scroyle, Seely, Snake, Sorry, Unblest, Wo(e), Woeful

▷ **Wretched** *may indicate* an anagram

Wriggle Hirsle, Shimmy, Squirm, Twine, Wiggle, Writhe

Wring(er) Drain, Extort, Mangle, Screw, Squeeze, Twist

Wrinkle(d), Wrinkly Clue, Cockle, Corrugate, Crankle, Crease, Crepy, Crimple,
Crimpy, Crinkle, Crow's-foot, Crumple, Fold, Frounce, Frown, Frumple, Furrow,
Gen, Groove, Headline, Hint, Idea, Knit, Line, Lirk, Plissé, Plough, Pucker, Purse,
Ridge, Rimple, Rivel, Rop(e)y, Ruck(le), Rugose, Rumple, Runkle, Seamy, Shrivel,
Sulcus, Time-worn, Tip, Whelk, Wizened, Wrizled

Wrist Carpus, Radialia, Shackle-bone

Writ(s) Attachment, Audita querela, Capias, Certiorari, Cursitor, Dedimus,
Devastavit, Distringas, Elegit, Fieri facias, Filacer, Habeas corpus, Holy, Injunction,
Jury process, Latitat, Law-burrows, Mandamus, Mise, Mittimus, Noverint,
Praemunire, Process, Quare impedit, Quo warranto, Replevin, Scirefacias,
Significat, Subpoena, Summons, Supersedeas, Supplicavit, Tolt, Venire, Venire
facias, Warrant

Write(r), Writing Allograph, Amphigory, Annotator, Apocrypha, → **AUTHOR**,
Automatic, Ballpoint, Bellet(t)rist, BIC®, Biographer, Biro®, Bloomsbury Group,
Book-hand, Boustrophedon, Calligraphy, Causerie, Cento, Charactery, Clerk,

Clinquant, Collectanea, Columnist, Continuity, Copperplate, Creative, Cuneiform, Cursive, Diarist, Dissertation, Dite, Draft, → **DRAMATIST**, Elohist, Endorse, Endoss, Engross, Enrol, Epigrammatise, Epistle, → **ESSAYIST**, Expatiate, Farceur, Festschrift, Feudist, Fist, Form, Formulary, Freelance, Ghost, Gongorism, Graffiti, Grammatology, Graphite, Hack, Hairline, Hand, Haplography, Hieratic, Hieroglyphics, Hierology, Hiragana, Indite, Ink, Inkhorn-mate, Ink-jerker, Inkslinger, Inscribe, Join-hand, Jot(tings), Journalese, Journalist, Journo, Kalakana, Kaleyard School, Kana, Kanji, Katakana, Keelivine, Keelyvine, Leader, Lexigraphy, Lexis, Linear A, Lipogram, Littérateur, Longhand, Lucubrate, Marivaudage, Memoirist, Mimographer, Minoan, Mirror, Miscellany, Ms(s), Nesk(h), Nib, Notary, Notate, Novelese, → **NOVELIST**, Palaeography, Paragraphia, Pasigraphy, Pen, Pencil, Penmanship, Penne, Penny-a-liner, Pentel®, Phrasemonger, Picture, Pinyin, Planchette, → **POET**, Polemic, Polygraphy, Pot-hook, Prosaist, Proser, Pseudepigrapha, Psychogram, Psychography, Purana, Purple patch, Quill, Rhymer, Roundhand, Samizdat, Sanskrit, Sci-fi, Scissorer, Scratch, Screed, Screeve, Scribe, Scrip(t), Scripture, Scrivener, Scrow, Scytale, Secretary, Shaster, Shastra, Sign, Sling-ink, Small-hand, Space, Spirit, Stichometry, Style, Stylography, Subscript, Superscribe, Sutra, Syllabary, Syllabic, Syllabism, Syngraph, Tantra, Text, Tractarian, Transcribe, Treatise, Tushery, Uncial, Varityper®, Wordsmith, Zend-Avesta

WRITERS

3 letters:
APH
Eco
Lee
Paz
Poe
RLS

4 letters:
Amis
Asch
Aymé
Bede
Behn
Bolt
Cary
Dahl
Elia
Gide
Hope
Hugo
Hunt
King
Lamb
Lang
Loos
Loti
Lyly

Mann
More
Nash
Opie
Ovid
Pope
Roth
Saki
Sand
Shaw
Snow
Ward
West
Zola

5 letters:
Acton
Adams
Albee
Auden
Ayres
Bates
Blair
Blake
Caine
Camus
Corvo
Crane

Defoe
Doyle
Dumas
Eliot
Ellis
Genet
Gogol
Gorki
Gorky
Gosse
Greer
Grimm
Hardy
Harte
Henty
Hesse
Heyer
Homer
Hoyle
Ibsen
Innes
James
Joyce
Kafka
Lewis
Lodge
Lorca
Mason

Milne
Munro
Musil
Nashe
Orczy
Ouida
Pater
Paton
Pliny
Pound
Powys
Reade
Renan
Rilke
Sagan
Scott
Seuss
Shute
Spark
Stark
Stein
Swift
Synge
Twain
Verne
Vidal
Waugh
Wells

White
Wilde
Woolf
Yates
Yonge

6 letters:
Ambler
Arnold
Artaud
Asimov
Atwood
Austen
Balzac
Baring
Barrie
Belloc
Bellow
Borges
Borrow
Braine
Bronte
Buchan
Bunyan
Butler
Capote
Cicero
Clarke
Conrad
Cowper
Cronin
Daudet
Dryden
Engels
Fowles
France
Gibbon
Goethe
Graves
Greene
Heller
Hobbes
Hughes
Huxley
Jerome
Jonson
Le Fanu
London
Lucian
Lytton
Mailer

Malory
Mannin
Masoch
Miller
Milton
Morgan
Nerval
Nesbit
O'Brien
Onions
Orwell
Proust
Racine
Romaji
Runyon
Ruskin
Sapper
Sappho
Sayers
Sendac
Sewell
Smiles
Steele
Sterne
Stoker
Storey
Thomas
Updike
Virgil
Walton
Wilder

7 letters:
Addison
Aldrich
Aretino
Bagehot
Bagnold
Ballard
Beckett
Bennett
Bentley
Boileau
Boswell
Burgess
Carlyle
Chaucer
Chekhov
Cobbett
Cocteau
Colette

Collins
Cookson
Coppard
Corelli
Cranmer
Deeping
Dickens
Dodgson
Drabble
Dreiser
Durrell
Emerson
Fenelon
Feydeau
Forster
Fuentes
Gissing
Golding
Haggard
Herbert
Hichens
Johnson
Kipling
Lardner
Marryat
Maugham
Mauriac
Mérimée
Mitford
Moravia
Murdoch
Nabokov
Naipaul
Peacock
Pushkin
Pynchon
Ransome
Robbins
Rostand
Rushdie
Saroyan
Sassoon
Shelley
Simenon
Sitwell
Surtees
Terence
Thoreau
Tolkien
Tolstoy
Travers

Wallace
Walpole
Wharton
Whitman
Wyndham

8 letters:
Anacreon
Andersen
Beaumont
Bradbury
Browning
Caldwell
Cartland
Chandler
Childers
Christie
Constant
De la Mare
Disraeli
Faulkner
Fielding
Flaubert
Forester
Goncourt
Ishiguro
Kingsley
Langland
Lawrence
Mannheim
Meredith
Perrault
Plutarch
Proudhon
Rabelais
Rattigan
Remarque
Rousseau
Salinger
Schiller
Sillitoe
Smollett
Stendhal
Taffrail
Traherne
Trollope
Turgenev
Voltaire
Williams

9 letters:	Lermontov	10 letters:	12 letters:
Aeschylus	Linklater	Ballantyne	Aristophanes
Ainsworth	Lovecraft	Chesterton	Quiller-Couch
Blackmore	Mackenzie	Dostoevsky	Solzhenitsyn
Boccaccio	Madariaga	Fitzgerald	
Burroughs	Mansfield	Galsworthy	13 letters:
Cervantes	Martineau	Mandeville	Chateaubriand
Corneille	Oppenheim	Maupassant	Sackville-West
Dos Passos	Pasternak	Richardson	
Du Maurier	Priestley	Williamson	15 letters:
Edgeworth	Santayana		Somerset Maugham
Goldsmith	Sholokhov	11 letters:	
Hawthorne	Steinbeck	Machiavelli	
Hemingway	Stevenson	Maeterlinck	
Isherwood	Thackeray	Shakespeare	
La Bruyère	Wodehouse		

Write-off Amortise, Annul, Cancel, Scrap

Writhe, Writhing Athetosis, Contort, Curl, Scriggle, Squirm, Thraw, Twist, Wriggle

▷ **Writhing** *may indicate* an anagram

Writing-case Kalamdan

Writing-room Scriptorium

▷ **Wrong** *may indicate* an anagram

Wrong(ful), Wrongdoer Aggrieve, Agley, Amiss, Astray, Awry, Bad, Bum, Chout, Delict, Disservice, Err, Fallacious, False, Falsism, Harm, Ill, Immoral, Improper, Incorrect, Injury, Mischief, Misfaring, Misintelligence, Misled, Mistake(n), Misuse, Nocent, Offbase, Offend, Pear-shaped, Peccadillo, Perpetrator, Perverse, Private, Public, Sin(ful), Sinner, Tort, Tortious, Transgress, Unethical, Unright, Unsuitable, Withershins, Wryly, X

Wrong opinion Cacodoxy

Wrought (up) Agitated, Beaten, Carved, Created, Excited, Filigree, Freestone, Shaped

Wrung Twisted, Withers

Wry Askew, Contrary, Devious, Distort, Droll, Grimace, Ironic

Wryneck Iynx, Jynx, Torticollis, Yunx

Wycliffian Lollard

Wyoming Wy

X(-shaped) Buss, By, Chi, Christ, Cross, Decussate, Drawn, Kiss, Ten, Times, Unknown, X-ray

Xant(h)ippe Battle-axe, Dragon

Xenon Xe

Xenophobia Insularism

Xerophyte, Xerophytic Cactus, Cereus, Mesquite, Tamaricaceae, Tamarisk

Xhosan Caffre, Kaf(f)ir

Ximenes Cardinal

▸ **Xmas** *see* CHRISTMAS

X-ray Angiogram, Anticathode, C(A)T-scanner, Characteristic, Cholangiography, Emi-Scanner, Encephalogram, Encephalograph, Fermi, Grenz, Mammogram, Plate, Pyelogram, Radiogram, Radioscopy, Rem, Roentgen, Sciagram, Screening, Skiagram, Tomography, Venogram, Xeroradiography

Xylophone Marimba, Sticcado, Sticcato

Yy

Y Samian, Unknown, Yankee, Yard, Year, Yen, Yttrium

Yacht Britannia, Dragon, Ice, Keelboat, Ketch, Knockabout, Land, Maxi, Sailboat, Sand, Yngling

Yachtsman, Yachtsmen Chichester, RYS

Yak Gup, Talk

Yale® Key, Lock

Yam Adjigo, Batata, Breadroot, Camote, Dioscorea, Diosgenin, Kumara

▷ **Yank** *may indicate* an anagram

Yank(ee) Bet, Carpetbagger, Hitch, Jerk, Jonathan, Lug, Northerner, Pluck, Pull, Rug, Schlep(p), So(o)le, Sowl(e), → **TUG**, Tweak, Twitch, Wrench, Wrest

Yap Bark, Yelp

Yard(s) Area, CID, Close, Court, Farm-toun, Garden, Hard, Haw, Hof, Junk, Kail, Knacker's, Main, Marshalling, Mast, Measure, Navy, Patio, Poultry, Prison, Ree(d), Sail, Scotland, Show, Spar, Sprit, Steel, Stick, Stride, Switch, Tilt, Timber, Victualling, Y, Yd

Yarn(s) Abb, Berlin, Bouclé, Caddice, Caddis, Chenille, Clew, Clue, Cop, Cord, Crewel, Fib, Fibroline, Fingering, Genappe, Gimp, Gingham, Guimp(e), Gymp, Homespun, Jaw, Knittle, Knot, Lay, Lea, Ley, Line, Lisle, Lurex®, Marl, Merino, Mohair, Nylon, Organzine, Orlon®, Ply, Rigmarole, Ripping, Rogue's, Rope, Saxony, Schappe, Sennit, Sinnet, Skein, Spun, Story, Strand, Tale, Taradiddle, Thread, Thrid, Thrum(my), Tram, Twice-laid, Warp, Water twist, Weft, Woof, Wool, Worsted, Zephyr

Yarrow Milfoil

Yashmak Veil

Yaw(s) Boba, Buba, Deviate, Framboesia, Lean, Morula, Tack, Veer

Yawn(ing) Boredom, Chasmy, Fissure, Gant, Gape, Gaunt, Greys, Hiant, Oscitation, Pandiculation, Rictus

Yea Certainly, Truly, Verily, Yes

Year(ly), Years A, Age, Anno, Annual, Anomalistic, Astronomical, Calendar, Canicular, Civil, Common, Cosmic, Decennium, Donkey's, Dot, Ecclesiastical, Egyptian, Embolismic, Equinoctial, Financial, Fiscal, Gap, Great, Hebrew, Holy, Indiction, Julian, Leap, Legal, Light, Locust, Lunar, Lunisolar, Natural, PA, Perfect, Platonic, Riper, Sabbatical, School, Sidereal, Solar, Sothic, Summer, Sun, Tax, Theban, Time, Towmon(d), Towmont, Tropical, Twelvemonth, Vintage, Wander(jahr), Zodiac

Yearbook Annual

Yearling Colt, Hogget, Stirk, Teg

Yearn(ing) Ache, Ake, Aspire, Brame, Burn, Covet, Crave, Curdle, Desire, Erne, Greed, Green, Grein, Hanker, Hone, → **LONG**, Lust, Nostalgia, Pant, Pine, Sigh

▷ **Yearning** *may indicate* an anagram

Year's end Dec

Yeast Barm, Bees, Brewer's, Ferment, Flor, Leaven, Saccharomycete, Torula, Vegemite®

Yell Cry, Hue, Shout, Skelloch, Squall, Thunder, Tiger, Waul, Yoick

Yellow(ish) Abram, Amber, Anthoclore, Auburn, Back, Beige, Bisque, Bistre, Buff, Butternut, Cadmium, Canary, Chartreuse, Chicken, Chrome, Citrine, Clay-bank, Cowardly, Craven, Curcumin(e), Daffadowndilly, Daffodil, Eggshell, Etiolin, Fallow, Fever, Filemot, Flavescent, Flavin(e), Flavon, Flaxen, Fulvous, Gamboge, Gold, Icteric, Isabel(le), Isabella, Jack, Jaundiced, King's, Lammer, Lemon(y), Lupulin, Lurid, Lutein, Luteous, Lutescent, Mustard, Nankeen, Naples, Oaker, Ochery, Ochre(y), Ochroid, Or(eide), Oroide, Pages, Peach, Peril, Pink, Primrose, Queen's, River, Saffron, Sallow, Sand, Sear, Sherry, Spineless, Strae, Straw, Sulphur, Tawny, Topaz, Tow, Vitelline, Weld, Xanthous, Yolk

Yellowhammer Bunting, Yeldring, Yeldrock, Yite, Yoldring

Yellow-wood Gopher

Yelp Cry, Squeal, Whee, Ya(w)p

Yemeni Adeni, Saba, Sabean, Sheba

Yen Desire, Itch, Longing, Urge, Y, Yearn

Yeoman Beefeater, Exon, Goodman, Goodwife, Salvation

Yep OK, Yes

Yes Ay(e), Da, Indeed, Ja, Jokol, Nod, OK, Oke, Quite, Sure, Truly, Uh-huh, Wilco, Yea, Yokul, Yup

Yesterday Démodé, Eve, Hesternal, Pridian

Yet But, Even, How-be, Moreover, Nay, Nevertheless, Now, Still, Though

Yeti Abominable snowman, Sasquatch

Yew Podocarp(us), Taxus, Yvonne

Yibbles A(i)blins

Yield(ing), Yielded Abandon, Afford, Bend, Bow, Breed, Capitulate, Catch, Cede, Come, Comply, Concede, Crack, Crop, Defer, Dividend, Docile, Ductile, Easy, Elastic, Exert, Facile, Flaccid, Flexible, Give, Harvest, Interest, Knock under, Knuckle, Knuckle under, Meek, Meltith, Mess, Output, Pan, Pay, Pliant, Produce, Quantum, Redemption, Relent, Render, Return, Sag, Soft, Squashy, → **SUBMIT**, Succumb, Surrender, Susceptible, Sustained, Temporise, Truckle, Weak-kneed, Yold

Yob Lout

Yodel Song, Warble

Yog(h)urt Dahi, Madzoon, Matzoon, Tzatziki

Yoga, Yogi As(h)tanga (vinyasa), Bear, Bhakti, Bikram, Fakir, Hatha, Hot, Maha, Power, Raja, Sid(d)ha, Sivananda

Yoke Bow, Cang(ue), Collar, Couple, Harness, Inspan, Jugal, Oxbow, Pair, Span, Square, Tucker

Yokel Boor, Bumpkin, Chaw(-bacon), Clumperton, Culchie, Hayseed, Hick, Jake, Jock, Peasant, Rustic

Yolk Parablast, Vitellicle, Vitellus, Yelk, Yellow

Yon(der) Distant, Further, O'erby, Thae, There, Thether, Thither

Yore Agone, Olden, Past

Yorick Sterne

York(shire), Yorkshireman Batter, Bowl, Ebor, Pudding, Ridings, See, Tyke

Yorker Tice

You One, Sie, Thee, Thou, Usted, Wena, Ye

Young (person), Youngster, Youth(ful) Adolescent, Ageless, Amorino, Bairn, Bev(an), Bodgie, Boy, Boyhood, Brigham, Bub, Buckie, Buppie, Calf-time, Ch,

Charver, Chick, Chicken, Chiel, Child, Chile, Cion, Cockerel, Cockle, Colt, Comsomol, Cornstalk, Cub, Day-old, Dell, Dilling, DJ, Early, Ephebe, Ephebus, Esquire, Flapper, Fledgling, Foetus, Fox, Fry, Gigolo, Gilded, Gillet, Girl, Gunsel, Halfling, Hebe, Hobbledehoy, Immature, Imp, Infant, Issue, Jeunesse d'orée, Junior, Juvenal, Juvenesce, Juvenile, Keral, Kid, Kiddo, Kiddy, Kipper, Knave-bairn, Komsomol, Lad, Lamb, Latter-day, Leaping-time, Less, Litter, Little, Loretta, Middle, Minor, Misspent, Mod, Mormon, Mot, Muchacha, Nance, Narcissus, Neanic, Ned(ette), Neophyte, Nestling, New, New Romantic, Nipper, Nurs(e)ling, Nymph, Plant, Popsy, (Pre-)pubescent, Progeny, Protégé(e), Punk, Pup, Salad days, Sapling, Scent, Scion, Shaveling, Shaver, Sien(t), Skinhead, Slip, Small, Son, Spawn, Sprig, Springal(d), Stripling, Subteen, Swain, Syen, Ted, Teenager, Teens, Teenybopper, Tit, Toyboy, Vernal, Waif, Well-preserved, Whelp, Whippersnapper, Widge, Wigga, Wigger, Wimp, Yippy, Yoof, Yopper, Younker, Yumpie, Yuppie

Younger, Youngest Baby, Benjamin, Cadet, Last born, Less, Minimus, Seneca, Wallydrag, Wallydraigle, Yr

Your(s) Thee, Thine, Thy

▶ **Youth** *see* **YOUNG PERSON**

Yo-yo Bandalore

Ytterbium Yb

Yttrium Y

Yucatan Maya

Yucca Adam's needle

Yucky Gooey, Grooly, Sickly, Sticky

Yugoslav Croat(ian), Serb, Slovene, Ustashi

Yukon YT

Yuletide Advent, Dec, Noel, Xmas

Zz

Z Izzard, Izzet, Zambia, Zebra

Zamenhof Esperanto

Zander Fogash, Sander

Zany Bor(r)el, Comic, Cuckoo, Idiotic, Mad, Offbeat

Zanzibar Swahili

Zeal(ous) Ardour, Bigotry, Devotion, Eager, Earnest, Enthusiasm, Evangelic, Fanatical, Fanaticism, Fervour, Fire, Hamas, Perfervid, Rabid, Study, Zest

Zealot Bigot, Crusader, Devotee, Fan(atic), St Simon, Votary

Zebra Convict, Quagga

Zebu Brahmin bull, Brahmin cow

Zenith Acme, Apogee, Height, Pole, Summit, Vertex

Zeno Colonnade, Elea, Stoic

Zeolite Analcime, Analcite, Gmelinite

Zephyr Breeze, Wind

Zeppelin Airship, Balloon, Dirigible

Zero Absolute, Blob, Cipher, Circle, Donut, Double, Ground, Nil, None, Nothing, Nought, O, Status, Year, Z

Zest Condiment, Crave, Élan, Enthusiasm, Gusto, Pep, Piquancy, Relish, Spark, Spice, Tang, Zap, Zing

Ziegfeld Flo

Zigzag Crémaillère, Crinkle-crankle, Dancette, Feather-stitch, Indent, Major Mitchell, Ric-rac, Slalom, Stagger, Switchback, Tack, Traverse, Vandyke, Yaw

Zinc Blende, Gahnite, Mossy, Sherardise, Spelter, Sphalerite, Tutenag, Tutty, Willemite, Wurtzite, Zn

Zip(per) Dash, Energy, Fastener, Fly, Go, Nada, O, Oomph, Presto, Side fastener, Stingo, Verve, Vim, Vivacity, Whirry, Zero

Zircon Hyacinth, Jacinth, Jargo(o)n

Zirconium Baddeleyite, Zr

Zither Autoharp, Cithara, Kantela, Kantele, Koto

Zodiac(al) Aquarius, Archer, Aries, Bull, Cancer, Capricorn, Counter-glow, Crab, Fish, Gegenschein, Gemini, Goat, Horoscope, Leo, Libra, Lion, Ophiuchus, Pisces, Ram, Sagittarius, Scales, Scorpio(n), Taurus, Twins, Virgin, Virgo, Watercarrier

Zola Budd, Emile, Nana, Realism

Zombie Catatonic, Dolt, Robot, Undead

Zone(s) Abyssal, Anacoustic, Area, Arid, Auroral, Band, Bathyal, Belt, Benioff, Buffer, Canal, Climate, Collision, Comfort, Convergence, Crumple, Demilitarized, Drop, Economic, Ecotone, End, Enterprise, Erogenous, Euro, Exclusion, Exclusive, F layer, Fracture, Free, Fresnel, Frigid, Hadal, Home, Hot, Impact, Ionopause, Krumhole, Low velocity, Mix, Neutral, No-fly, Nuclear-free, Precinct, → **REGION**, Rift, Ring, Russian, Sahel, Sector, Shear, Skip, Smokeless, Soviet, Stratopause, Strike, Subduction, T, Temperate, Time, Tolerance, Torrid, Tundra, Twilight, Z

Zoo Bedlam, Circus, Menagerie, Vivarium, Whipsnade

Zoologist, Zoology Biologist, Botanist, Cetology, Naturalist, Primatology, Schneider

Zoom Close-up, Speed

Zoroastrian Gabar, Gheber, Ghebre, Gueber, Guebre, Magus, Mazdaist, Mazdean, Ormazd, Ormuzd, Parsee, Parsi

Zulu Chaka, Impi, Inkatha, Matabele, Niger, Shaka, Warrior

Zut Crimini

Zygote Oospore